WEBSTER'S
NEW WRLD®
CROSSWORD PUZZLE
DICTIONARY

SECOND EDITION

Compiled by
Jane Shaw Whitfield

HOUGHTON MIFFLIN HARCOURT

BOSTON   NEW YORK

ISBN: 978-1-328-71031-4

Visit our website: hmhco.com

Library of Congress Cataloging-in-Publication Data
Whitfield, Jane Shaw
Webster's new world crossword puzzle dictionary /compiled by Jane Shaw Whitfield.—2nd ed.
p. cm.
ISBN 978-0-02-861212-6 (pbk.)
1. Crossword puzzles—Glossaries, vocabularies, etc. I. Title.
GV1507.C7W485 1997
793.73'2'0321—dc20
96-2077

Manufactured in the United States of America
28 29 30 31 – DOC – 22 21 20 19 18
4500698747

CONTENTS

STAFF

FOREWORD

This new edition of *Webster's New World Crossword Puzzle Dictionary* represents a thorough revision and updating of the highly successful work originally compiled by Jane Shaw Whitfield. Thousands of new clue words and answer terms have been added from crossword puzzles published since the last revision. Biographical and geographical entries are now completely up to date. Tables have been introduced to provide a particularly effective and convenient way to locate large blocks of related terms in one place. In addition, a user's guide created especially for this edition will assist readers in finding precisely the words they want quickly and easily.

Crossword puzzle dictionaries and crossword puzzle solvers share, predictably, some special characteristics. Both are distinguished by their breadth of vocabulary and by their unique intellectual focus on the relationship between clues and answers. The editors of Webster's New World dictionaries wish to acknowledge the contributions to this edition of one very gifted crossword puzzle enthusiast, Mr. Joe Forest of Sharonville, Ohio, whose insightful suggestions have been invaluable.

This all-new second edition remains in one respect unchanged, namely, it is, as Jane Shaw Whitfield wrote in her foreword to the first edition, dedicated "to all enthusiasts of crossword puzzles and to their creators."

1. *The Arrangement of Entries*—Each entry block has a clue word set in boldface type as its headword. All clue words, including single words, hyphenated and unhyphenated compounds, idioms, phrases, and proper names, are listed in strict alphabetical order:

> **A** . . .
> **aa** (Haw) . . .
> **aal** . . .
> **Aani** (Egypt) . . .
> **abdominal limb** (crustacean) . . .
> **Abel's brother** . . .
> **aberration** . . .

2. *Clue Words and Answer Terms*—Answer terms for each clue word are arranged by the count of letters in each word or phrase. Answer terms of varying parts of speech may be gathered together in a single entry block. Words in each group of answers with the same letter count are arranged in alphabetical order:

> **abandon** . . . **4.** quit **5.** cease, leave, remit, waive, yield **6.** abjure, depart, desert, disuse, give up, maroon, reject, resign, vacate
> **7.** cast off, discard, forsake, freedom, neglect
> **8.** abdicate, forswear, renounce
> **9.** surrender, turpitude **10.** relinquish
> **11.** abandonment, discontinue, unrestraint
> **12.** carelessness, heedlessness

3. *Variant Spellings and Forms*—When variants are some distance apart alphabetically, the full entry appears at the spelling or spellings most frequently used, and the other spellings are cross-referred to this entry:

> **align, aline** . . . **4.** true **5.** level, match **6.** equate, line up . . .
>
> . . .
>
> **aline** . . . see *align*

Variants not alphabetically distant are given together in boldface type:

> **harbor, harbour** . . . **3.** bay **4.** cave, port
> **5.** haven **6.** covert, foster, . . .

narghile, nargile, nargileh . . . **4.** pipe
6. hookah

Variant spellings of answer words are given
immediately after the answer word in parentheses:

monument . . . **4.** tomb **5.** cairn, stele (stela),
tower, vault **6.** . . .

4. *Labels, Abbreviations, and Explanatory Notes—*
Additional information for either clue words or answer
terms may appear abbreviated in parentheses. A list of
abbreviations used in this book appears below, p. x.

Aaru (Egypt Relig) . . . **12.** fields of Aaru
14. abode of the dead

monopoly . . . **5.** grant, right, trust . . .
10. possession (exclusive)

oomancy (divination by) . . . **4.** eggs

5. *Cross-references—*Cross-references to related terms are
introduced by "see" or "see also" and given in italics:

absence of . . . (see also *without*)

6. *Subcategories—*Answer terms may be divided into
informational subcategories related to the clue word.
They are introduced by the label "(pert to)":

cardinal (pert to) . . .
astrology . . **5.** nadir **6.** zenith
astronomy . . **10.** solstitial **11.** equinoctial . . .
compass point . . **4.** east, west **5.** north, south . . .
virtues (Theol) . . **4.** hope **5.** faith **7.** charity

7. *Variety Lists—*When the clue word is a general term
covering a variety of things, a list of those is supplied,
introduced by the label "(types of)":

flower (types of) . . . **3.** gul (rose) **4.** iris, ixia, lily,
pink, rose **5.** aster, calla, canna, . . .

8. *Tables—*Tables at the end of this book provide lists of
persons, things, or events in a particular category along
with a letter count for each item.

ABBREVIATIONS USED IN THIS WORK

Abbr	Abbreviation	Eccl	Ecclesiastical	Maced	Macedonia
abdom	abdominal	Educ	Education	Malay	Malayan
aborig	aboriginal	Egypt	Egyptian	Math	Mathematics
Acad	Academy	Elec	Electricity	MD	Doctor of Medicine
adj	adjective	Eng	England, English	Med	Medical
adm	admitted	Episcop	Episcopal	Mex	Mexican
Afr	African	equiv	equivalent	Mil	Military
Agric	Agriculture	Esk	Eskimo	Mohamm	Mohammedan
Alex	Alexander	est	established	Mt(s)	Mountain(s)
Am Ind	American Indian	Eur	Europe(an)	Mus	Music
Anat	Anatomy	exclam	exclamation	Myth	Mythology
anc	ancient	ext	extinct		
Anglo-Ir	Anglo-Irish			Nat'l	National
Anthrop	Anthropology	FDR	Franklin D. Roosevelt	Naut	Nautical
Antiq	Antiquity	Fem	Feminine	Nav	Naval, Navy
Arab	Arabian	Finan	Finance, Financial	neg	negative
Arch	Architecture	Flem	Flemish	New Test	New Testament
Archaeol	Archaeology	Fr	France, French	NZ	New Zealand
Astrol	Astrology			No	North
Astron	Astronomy	Gen	General	No Am	North American
Austral	Australia(n)	Geog	Geography		
		Geol	Geology	obs	obsolete
Babyl	Babylonia(n)	Geom	Geometry	Old Test	Old Testament
Belg	Belgium	Ger	German	opp	opposite
Bib	Bible, Biblical	Gov	Governor	Orient	Oriental
Biol	Biology	Govt	Government	Oxf Univ	
Bot	Botany	Gr	Greek		Oxford University
Braz	Brazil(ian)	Gram	Grammar		
Brit	Britain, British	Gr Brit	Great Britain	Penol	Penology
Brit Col	British Columbia			Pers	Persian
Buddh	Buddhism	Haw	Hawaiian	pert	pertaining
Bus	Business	Heb	Hebrew	Petrol	Petrology
		Hem	Hemisphere	Pg	Portuguese
Can	Canada, Canadian	Her	Heraldry	Pharm	Pharmaceutical
Capt	Captain	Hind	Hinduism	Philat	Philately
Caucas	Caucasian	Hindu	Hindustani	Phil I	Philippine Islands
Celt	Celtic	Hist	Historical	Philol	Philology
Cent	Central, Century	Holl	Holland	Philos	Philosophy
Cent Am	Central America	Horol	Horology	Phonet	Phonetics
Chem	Chemistry	Hung	Hungarian	Phys	Physical
Chin	Chinese			pl	plural
Chr	Christian	illeg	illegal	PO	Post Office
coll	colloquialism	Ind	India, Indian	poet	poetic
comb form		Indo-Chin	Indo-China	Polit	Politics, Political
	combining form	Ins	Insurance	Polyn	Polynesian
Confed	Confederation	Internat	International	ppty	property
Constell	Constellation	Ir	Irish	pref	prefix
contemp	contemporary	irreg	irregular	P Rico	Puerto Rico
Criminol	Criminology	Isl(s)	Island(s)	Pros	Prosody
		It	Italian	pseud	pseudonym
Dan	Danish				
Dept	Department	Jap	Japanese	R	Roman
derog	derogatory	Jew	Jewish	RCCh	
dial	dialectal				Roman Catholic Church
div	division	L	Latin	Rd	Road
Du	Dutch	Legislat	Legislature	ref	referring
		Lit	Literature	Relig	Religion
E	East	Log	Logic	R Estate	Real Estate
East Ch	Eastern Church			Rev War	Revolutionary War

Rhet   Rhetoric
Riv   River
Rom   Roman
rr   railroad
Rum   Rumania
Russ   Russian

S   South
Scot   Scotland, Scottish
Scand   Scandinavian
Shaksp   Shakespeare
sing   singular
sl   slang
Slav   Slavonic
So Afr   South Africa
So Am   South America
Sp   Spanish
Surg   Surgical
sym   symbol

Tag   Tagalog
Tahit   Tahiti
Terat   Teratology
terr   territory
Teut   Teutonic
Theat   Theatrical
Theol   Theology
Theos   Theosophy
triang   triangular
TID   Ter in die
Trop   Tropical
Turk   Turkish
TV   Television

U   Union
Univ   University
USS   United States Ship
USSR   Union of Soviet
    Socialist Republics

Vet   Veterinary

W   West
WAC
    Women's Army Corps
W Indies   West Indies
WWI   World War I
WWII   World War II

Yidd   Yiddish
YMCA   Young Men's
    Christian Association
yr   year

Zool   Zoology

WEBSTER'S NEW WORLD®

CROSSWORD PUZZLE DICTIONARY

SECOND EDITION

A

A ... **5.** alpha, first **7.** article
A 1 ... **5.** prime **6.** symbol **8.** superior **10.** first-class
aa (Haw) ... **4.** lava
aal ... **8.** morindin (dye), mulberry
aam (Du) ... **7.** measure (liquid) **11.** water bucket
Aani (Egypt) ... **3.** ape (sacred) **6.** baboon **12.** cynocephalus
aardvark ... **3.** pig **6.** farrow **8.** anteater
aardwolf ... **5.** hyena **8.** Proteles
Aaron (pert to) ...
  ally (Bib) .. **3.** Hur
  brother .. **5.** Moses
  burial place .. **3.** Hor
  leader (Jew) .. **9.** Levitical **10.** High Priest
  rod .. **4.** wand (magic) **7.** molding, mullein
  sister .. **6.** Miriam
  son .. **5.** Abihu, Nadab
Aaru (Egypt Relig) ... **12.** fields of Aaru **14.** abode of the dead
aasvogel ... **7.** vulture
abaca ... **4.** hemp **5.** lupis **6.** linaga
abacus ... **4.** slab **8.** cupboard **10.** calculator **11.** compartment
Abaddon ... **3.** pit (bottomless) **4.** Hell **5.** Sheol **8.** Apollyon (angel) **11.** destruction
abaft ... **3.** aft **5.** after **6.** astern, behind
abalone ... **5.** awabi, ormer, uhllo (ullo) **6.** sea ear **8.** ear shell
abandon ... **4.** quit **5.** cease, leave, remit, waive, yield **6.** abjure, depart, desert, disuse, give up, maroon, reject, resign, vacate **7.** cast off, discard, forsake, freedom, neglect **8.** abdicate, forswear, renounce **9.** surrender, turpitude **10.** relinquish **11.** abandonment, discontinue, unrestraint **12.** carelessness, heedlessness
abandoned ... **4.** left, lost **7.** disused, forlorn, given up **8.** derelict, deserted, forsaken **9.** desolated, discarded, neglected **11.** surrendered **12.** relinquished, unredeemable, unrestrained
abase ... **5.** lower, shame **6.** bemean, depose, humble, reduce **7.** degrade, mortify **8.** cast down, disgrace **9.** humiliate **10.** depreciate
abash ... **5.** shame **6.** appall, dismay **7.** astound, confuse, disturb, mortify **8.** bewilder, confound **9.** discomfit, embarrass, humiliate **10.** disconcert, put to shame
abate ... **3.** ebb **4.** lull, wane **5.** let up, relax, remit **6.** deduct, lessen, reduce **7.** abolish, nullify, qualify, slacken, subside **8.** decrease, diminish, discount, moderate
abatement ... **5.** letup **6.** myosis (miosis), rebate **8.** decrease **9.** lessening, reduction **10.** diminution, mitigation, moderation
abb ... **4.** wool, yarn **6.** fleece (pert to)
Abba ... **5.** abbot, title **6.** Father
abbe ... **4.** monk **6.** cleric, curate, priest
abbess ... **4.** amma **15.** spiritual mother
abbreviate ... **7.** abridge, curtail, shorten **8.** compress, condense, contract, simplify **9.** epitomize **11.** make briefer
abbreviation ... **5.** brief, lapse **6.** digest **8.** abstract **9.** reduction **10.** abridgment, compendium, shortening **11.** contraction **12.** condensation
abdicate ... **4.** cede, quit **5.** demit, leave **6.** depose, disown, resign, retire **7.** lay down **8.** disclaim, renounce, withdraw **9.** surrender **10.** disinherit, relinquish
Abdiel (Heb) ... **5.** angel **12.** servant of God
abdomen ... **3.** gut, pot (sl) **4.** wame **5.** belly, tharm (obs) **6.** paunch, venter **7.** stomach **8.** potbelly **12.** pelvic cavity
abdominal ... **7.** coeliac, gastric, ventral **11.** ventricular
abdominal limb (crustacean) ... **7.** pleopod
Abel's brother ... **4.** Cain, Seth
aberration ... **5.** mania, wrong **6.** lunacy, oddity **7.** errancy, madness **8.** dementia, insanity **9.** departure, deviation, variation, wandering **10.** alienation, digression, divergence **11.** abnormality, derangement, distraction, peculiarity **12.** eccentricity, irregularity **14.** disorientation
abet ... **3.** aid, egg **4.** back, help **5.** egg on **6.** assist, foment, incite, second, succor, uphold **7.** connive, endorse, support, sustain **8.** advocate **9.** encourage, instigate **11.** countenance
abeyance ... **4.** rest, stay **5.** lapse, pause **7.** waiting **9.** inertness **10.** expectancy, suspension
abhor ... **2.** ug **4.** hate, shun **6.** detest, loathe **7.** despise, dislike **8.** execrate **9.** abominate
abhorrence ... **5.** odium **6.** hatred, horror **7.** dislike **8.** aversion, loathing **9.** antipathy, disliking, repulsion **10.** repugnance
abide ... **4.** bide, live, stay, wait **5.** await, dwell, pause, tarry **6.** endure, remain, reside **7.** sojourn **8.** continue, submit to, tolerate **9.** acquiesce, withstand
abide by ... **3.** own **4.** avow, heed **5.** admit, allow, yield **6.** accept, follow, regard **7.** concede, respect **8.** adhere to **9.** conform to **11.** acknowledge
abiding ... **7.** durable, lasting **8.** constant, enduring **9.** permanent, steadfast **10.** continuing, indwelling, persisting
Abies ... **4.** firs **5.** pines **8.** conifers **10.** evergreens
abigail ... **4.** ayah, maid **5.** bonne **7.** servant **9.** soubrette
Abijah's son (Bib) ... **3.** Asa

ability . . . **4.** gift **5.** force, might, power, skill **6.** genius, talent **7.** caliber, faculty, fitness, potency **8.** aptitude, capacity, strength **10.** capability, competence, efficiency **11.** proficiency, sufficiency **13.** qualification

abiosis . . . **11.** without life

abject . . . **3.** low **4.** base, mean, meek, vile **6.** humble, menial, supine **7.** hangdog, ignoble, servile, slavish **8.** beggarly, contrite, cringing, degraded, wretched **9.** groveling, miserable **10.** despicable, obsequious

abjuration . . . **6.** denial **8.** palinode (song), yielding **9.** disavowal, rejection, surrender **10.** abjurement, retraction, withdrawal **11.** abandonment, forswearing, recantation, repudiation **12.** disclamation **14.** relinquishment

abjure . . . **4.** deny, wave **6.** disown, recant, reject, revoke **7.** abandon, disavow **8.** disclaim, forswear, renounce **9.** disaffirm, repudiate

able . . . **3.** can, fit **5.** adept, smart **6.** clever, fitted, suited **7.** adapted, capable, learned, solvent **8.** adjusted, literate, powerful, skillful (skilful), vigorous **9.** competent, effective, efficient, qualified **10.** omnipotent, proficient

able (pert to) . . .
  suffix . . **7.** capable, fitness
  to pay . . **7.** moneyed, solvent **8.** affluent **10.** prosperous
  to read and write . . **8.** lettered, literate **10.** book taught

ablepsia . . . **9.** blindness

ably . . . **7.** capably **11.** competently, effectively, efficiently

abnormal . . . **6.** albino **7.** erratic, unusual **8.** aberrant **9.** deviative, eccentric, irregular, unnatural **11.** exceptional **13.** extraordinary

aboard . . . **4.** onto **6.** across **7.** athwart **9.** alongside

abode . . . **3.** dar, hut **4.** cell, cote, Eden, home **5.** delay, house, lodge **7.** habitat, Olympus, sojourn **8.** dwelling, tenement **9.** apartment, residence **10.** habitation

abode of the dead . . . **3.** Dar **4.** Aalu, Aaru, Hell **5.** Aralu, Hades, limbo, Orcus, Sheol **6.** Asgard, heaven, Naraka **7.** Abaddon, Elysium, Nirvana **8.** paradise, Valhalla **9.** perdition, purgatory **11.** Pandemonium

abolish . . . **4.** undo **5.** annul, quash **6.** cancel, recall, repeal, revoke, vacate **7.** destroy, nullify, rescind, retract, reverse **8.** abrogate, withdraw **10.** annihilate, invalidate **11.** countermand

abominable . . . **4.** base, dire, foul, vile **5.** awful, gross **6.** odious, wicked, woeful **7.** beastly, hateful **8.** dreadful, grievous, infamous, shocking, terrible, wretched **9.** execrable, loathsome, obnoxious **10.** despicable, detestable, outrageous, unpleasant **12.** disagreeable, disreputable

Abominable Snowman . . . **4.** Yeti

abominate . . . **4.** hate **5.** abhor **6.** detest, loathe **8.** execrate

abomination . . . **3.** woe **4.** evil **5.** odium, wrong **6.** hatred, horror, plague **7.** disgust, outrage **8.** aversion, loathing, vexation **9.** grievance **10.** abhorrence, defilement, odiousness, repugnance

aboriginal . . . **5.** first, natal **6.** binghi, native **7.** ancient **8.** original **9.** beginning, primitive **10.** autochthon, indigenous

aborigines . . . **4.** Ainu (Aino), Toda **5.** lubra, Sakai, Vedda **7.** cave men, Indians, natives, savages **9.** indigenes, old-timers **10.** Dravidians **11.** preadamites

abortion . . . **6.** arrest **7.** failure **11.** embryoctomy, miscarriage, miscreation **13.** misconception

abound . . . **4.** flow, teem **5.** swarm **8.** overflow **9.** exuberate, plentiful

abounding . . . **4.** rife **5.** ample, flush **7.** copious, teeming **8.** abundant **9.** exuberant, luxuriant, plentiful

abounding in . . .
  blossoms . . **7.** flowery
  forests . . **6.** sylvan
  grass . . **6.** cressy
  snow . . **5.** nival

about . . . **2.** of, on, re **3.** amb (pref) **5.** anent, astir, circa **6.** almost, around, nearly **8.** circiter **10.** concerning **13.** approximately

about to happen . . . **8.** imminent

above . . . **2.** on, up **3.** o'er, sur (pref) **4.** atop, over, upon **5.** aloft, super, supra (pref)

abrade . . . **3.** rub **4.** file, fret, gall **5.** chafe, grate **6.** scrape **9.** excoriate

Abraham (pert to) . . .
  birthplace . . **2.** Ur
  concubine . . **5.** Hagar
  father . . **5.** Terah
  grandfather . . **5.** Nahor
  grandson . . **4.** Esau
  nephew . . **3.** Lot
  son . . **4.** Shua (Shuah) **5.** Isaac, Medan **7.** Ishmael
  wife . . **5.** Sarah (Sara, Sarai) **7.** Keturah

abrasion . . . **4.** flaw, gall, hurt **5.** scuff **6.** lesion, scrape **8.** limation **9.** attrition

abrasive . . . **4.** file, sand **5.** emery **6.** garnet, polish, pumice **7.** erodent **8.** abradant, corundum **9.** attritive, sandpaper

abraxas . . . **3.** gem **5.** charm, stone

Abraxas (pert to) . . .
  god (anc Gnostic) . . **12.** Supreme Deity
  source of mind . . **4.** Nous
  the Word . . **5.** Logos

abreast . . . **4.** even (with) **6.** beside **8.** opposite **9.** alongside

abrege . . . **7.** epitome **10.** abridgment

abri . . . **4.** shed **6.** cavity, dugout **7.** shelter

abridge . . . **5.** brief, razee (rasee) **7.** curtail, shorten **8.** abstract, condense, diminish, retrench **9.** epitomize **10.** abbreviate

abridgment . . . **6.** digest **7.** compend, epitome, summary **8.** abstract, syllabus, synopsis **9.** lessening, reduction **10.** compendium, diminution **11.** deprivation

abroad . . . **4.** away **5.** forth **6.** astray,

widely **7.** at large, broadly, distant
8. away from **9.** spread out **11.** widely
apart

abrogate . . . **5.** annul, quash **6.** cancel,
repeal, revoke **7.** abolish, rescind **8.** set
aside **10.** put an end to

abrogation . . . **8.** quashing **9.** annulling,
cessation **10.** rescinding, rescission
11. dissolution

abrupt . . . **4.** curt, rude **5.** blunt,
hasty, quick, sharp, sheer, steep,
terse **6.** broken, craggy, sudden
7. brusque **8.** headlong, vertical
9. broken off, impetuous **10.** unexpected
11. precipitous **12.** disconnected
13. perpendicular, unceremonious

abruptly . . . **7.** briefly, in brief **8.** suddenly

Absalom (pert to) . . .
father . . **5.** David (King)
host's captain . . **5.** Amasa
sister . . **5.** Tamar
slayer . . **4.** Joab

abscond . . . **3.** run **4.** bolt, flee, hide
5. elope **6.** decamp, desert, eloine,
levant **8.** steal off

absence . . . **4.** AWOL, lack, void, want
5. exeat, leave **6.** vacuum **7.** silence
10. deficiency, withdrawal
13. nonappearance, nonattendance

absence of . . . (see also *without*)
animal, plant . . **8.** lipotype
hair . . **6.** acomia
pain . . **8.** anodynia
pigment . . **8.** alphosis
self-worth . . **7.** modesty
taste . . **7.** ageusia

absent . . . **3.** off, out **4.** away, gone, lost
6. dreamy, musing, truant **7.** lacking
8. absorbed **9.** engrossed **10.** abstracted
11. preoccupied **12.** nonattendant

absinthe . . . **5.** green **6.** ajenjo, liquor
8. wormwood

absolute . . . **4.** alod, dead, pure, real, true,
very **5.** freed, sheer, total, utter, whole
6. empery, simple **7.** certain, elative,
perfect, plenary **8.** absolved, complete,
positive **9.** arbitrary, downright,
unlimited **10.** autocratic, disengaged,
peremptory **11.** categorical,
independent **13.** unconditional
15. plenipotentiary

absolute (pert to) . . .
dominion . . **6.** empery
property . . **4.** alod **7.** alodium
sovereign . . **8.** autocrat
superlative . . **7.** elative
time . . **9.** Greenwich, universal

absolutely . . . **3.** yea, yes **5.** stark
6. wholly **7.** utterly **8.** entirely
10. altogether, positively, thoroughly
13. unequivocally **15.** unconditionally

absolution . . . **6.** pardon, shrive
7. penance **9.** acquittal, remission
11. exculpation, forgiveness

absolve . . . **4.** free **5.** remit **6.** acquit,
finish, pardon **9.** discharge, exonerate
10. accomplish

absonant . . . **8.** contrary **10.** discordant
12. unreasonable

absorb . . . **3.** eat **4.** soak, suck **5.** drink,
eat up, learn, use up **6.** corner,

digest, engulf, imbibe, soak up, sponge
7. consume, swallow **10.** assimilate,
monopolize, understand **11.** incorporate

absorbed . . . **4.** deep, lost, rapt, sunk
6. buried, intent, lost in **7.** bemused,
devoted, engaged **8.** occupied
9. engrossed **11.** monopolized,
preoccupied

absorbent . . . **5.** fomes **6.** spongy
7. blotter **9.** adsorbent **10.** imbibitory

absorption . . . **10.** imbibition

abstain . . . **4.** deny, fast, hold, shun
5. avoid, cease, forgo, waive **6.** eschew
7. forbear, refrain **8.** restrain, teetotal,
withhold

abstemious . . . **5.** sober **7.** sparing
8. moderate **9.** abstinent, temperate
11. abstentious

abstinence . . . **6.** disuse **7.** encraty
8. sobriety **9.** restraint, sacrifice
10. abstention, continence, desistance,
moderation, self-denial, temperance
11. abandonment, forbearance, self-
control **13.** self-restraint
14. abstemiousness, discontinuance

abstract . . . **4.** deed, part, take **5.** brief,
steal **6.** deduct, noetic (purely), remove
7. abridge, epitome, shorten, summary
8. argument, condense, syllabus,
withdraw **9.** capsulize, statement
10. abridgment, compendium
12. nonobjective

abstract being . . . **3.** ens **6.** entity

abstruse . . . **4.** deep **6.** hidden **7.** obscure
8. esoteric, profound **9.** concealed,
recondite **10.** acroamatic (acroatic)
16. incomprehensible

absurd . . . **4.** wild **5.** droll, inept, silly
6. stupid **7.** asinine, foolish **8.** fabulous,
farcical **9.** ludicrous **10.** impossible,
irrational, ridiculous **11.** incongruous,
nonsensical **12.** inconsistent,
unbelievable, unreasonable

absurdity . . . **5.** farce **7.** twaddle
8. nonsense **10.** absurdness
11. foolishness **13.** contradiction,
impossibility **14.** ridiculousness
16. inconceivability

abundance . . . **4.** mass, much, rife
5. ample **6.** galore, plenty, riches,
volume **8.** fullness (fulness), opulence,
overflow, quantity **9.** affluence
10. exuberance **11.** copiousness,
superfluity **12.** extravagance,
generousness **13.** plenteousness

abundant . . . **4.** lush, much, rich, rife,
teem **5.** ample **6.** galore, plenty
7. copious, profuse **9.** abounding,
exuberant, luxuriant, plentiful
10. sufficient

abundant, not . . . **5.** spare **6.** lenten,
meager (meagre)

abuse . . . **4.** gali, harm, hurt, maul, rail,
rape **5.** crime, curse, scold, snash
6. berate, ill use, injure, insult, malign,
misuse, ravish, revile **7.** calumny,
deceive, obloquy, offense, pervert,
traduce, upbraid **8.** dishonor, maltreat,
misapply, reproach **9.** contumely,
disparage, invective, violation
10. opprobrium, revilement, scurrility

11. debauchment, malediction, objurgation 12. mistreatment, vituperation

abusive . . . 3. mud (throw) 10. scurrilous 12. catachrestic

abut . . . 4. butt, join 5. touch 6. adjoin, appose, border, rest on 7. conjoin, connect 8. adjacent, neighbor

abutment . . . 4. arch, pier, wall 6. alette 7. abuttal, sea wall 8. buttress, shoulder 13. fortification

abysmal . . . 4. deep 7. yawning 8. profound, unending 9. plumbless 10. bottomless, fathomless

abyss . . . 3. pit 4. Absu, gulf, hell, hole, void, well 5. abysm, chaos, chasm, cleft, shaft 6. cavity, vorago 15. infernal regions

Abyssinia, Ethiopia . . .
capital . . 10. Addis Ababa
city . . 5. Aduwa, Aksum (Axum) 6. Gondar 7. Ankober, Gambela, Magdala
dialect . . 4. Geez
Empire (old) . . 7. Axumite
Hamite . . 4. Afar
King . . 13. Haile Selassie
kingdom (former) . . 4. Shoa 5. Tigre 6. Amhara
river (famed) . . 5. Abdai (Blue Nile)
sea . . 3. Red
title (anc) . . 12. Negusa Nagast

Abyssinian (pert to) . . .
fly . . 4. zimb
gold (artificial) . . 5. talmi
lyre . . 6. kissar
tea leaves . . 3. kat
wolf . . 6. kaberu

academic . . . 4. moot 5. ideal, rigid 6. formal 7. classic, elegant 8. abstract, pedantic, Platonic 9. scholarly 10. Ciceronian, scholastic 11. educational, impractical, speculative, theoretical 12. conventional, hypothetical 13. institutional

academy . . . 5. école , lycée 6. lyceum, manège, school, Schule 7. college, escuela, society 8. academie, seminary 9. accademia, Gymnasium, institute 10. university 11. institution

Academy of Plato . . . 7. Academe

Acadia . . . 6. Acadie 10. Nova Scotia

acarpous . . . 7. sterile 9. fruitless

acaudal . . . 7. anurous 8. tailless

accede . . . 5. agree, enter, grant, yield 6. assent, attain, comply, concur, relent, submit 7. conform, consent 9. acquiesce 11. acknowledge

accelerate . . . 4. rush 6. hasten, step up 7. advance, forward, further, quicken, speed up 8. activate, dispatch, expedite

acceleration . . . 5. haste 6. pickup 8. velocity 9. catalysis, hastening 10. expedition, quickening 11. advancement

accelerator . . . 6. muscle 7. speeder 8. betatron, throttle 9. cyclotron, quickener 11. atom smasher, synchrotron

accent . . . 4. beat, mark, tone 5. breve, ictus, pitch, twang 6. brogue, stress 7. cadence, dialect 8. emphasis 9. emphasize 10. accentuate, expression, inflection, modulation 12. accentuation

accent (pert to) . . .
Irish . . 4. blas 6. brogue
on last syllable . . 7. oxytone
Scot . . 4. birr
unaccented syllable . . 5. arsis

accept . . . 2. OK 3. buy, own 4. avow, fang, take 5. admit, adopt, agree, allow, grant, trust, yield 6. assent, comply, credit, expect, ratify 7. approve, believe, certify, condone, confess, consent, embrace, receive, swallow (coll) 8. accredit, tolerate, validate 9. undertake 11. countenance

accept (as one's own) . . . 12. nostrificate (of foreign degrees)

acceptable . . . 2. OK 6. worthy 7. welcome 8. eligible, passable, pleasant, pleasing, suitable 9. agreeable, allowable, desirable, expedient, qualified, tolerable 10. admissible 11. comfortable 12. satisfactory

accepted . . . 6. chosen, deemed 7. adopted, assumed, popular, reputed, trusted 8. admitted, approved, believed, credited, embraced, espoused, inferred, orthodox, received, standard, supposed 9. customary, prevalent 10. accredited, understood, undertaken 11. traditional 12. conventional, unquestioned 13. authoritative

access . . . 3. way 4. adit, door, gain 5. entry 6. avenue, entree, ingate, tunnel 7. ingress 8. approach, entrance, entryway, increase 9. accession, accretion, admission 10. admittance 11. entranceway 13. accessibility, attainability 15. approachability

accessible . . . 4. open 5. handy 6. open to, public 7. getable 8. amenable, pervious 9. admissive, available, permeable, reachable, receptive 10. attainable, obtainable, open-minded, penetrable, procurable 11. persuasible 12. approachable 13. communicative

accession . . . 6. access, assent, attack, growth 7. adjunct, consent, joining, uniting 8. addition, increase 9. accretion, agreement, increment 10. acceptance, affixation, annexation, attainment, compliance, concession, coronation 12. acquiescence 13. reinforcement 14. aggrandizement

accessory, accessary . . . 5. extra, party 7. abettor 8. addition, litigant 9. adjective, appendage, assistant, attendant, auxiliary, obbligato 10. accomplish, additional, collateral, subsidiary 11. appurtenant, concomitant, participant 12. accompanying, appurtenance, contributory, nonessential, participator 13. accompaniment, supplementary

accident . . . 3. hap 4. luck 6. chance, hazard, mishap 8. calamity, casualty, disaster 9. adventure, befalling,

mischance 10. misfortune
11. catastrophe
accidental . . . 6. casual, chance
9. unwitting 10. contingent, unforeseen,
unintended
acclaim . . . 4. hail, laud 6. praise
7. applaud 8. applause 11. acclamation,
approbation
acclamation . . . 3. cry, joy 5. shout
7. acclaim, ovation, plaudit 8. applause,
approval 9. unanimity
acclimate . . . 5. adapt, inure 6. adjust,
season 8. accustom 9. condition,
habituate 10. naturalize 11. acclimatize,
familiarize
acclivity . . . 4. bank, brow, hill, rise
5. climb, slope, talus 6. ascent
7. upgrade 9. ascendant (ascendent)
11. inclination
accolade . . . 4. fold, rite 5. award,
brace, clasp, Oscar 6. praise, reward
7. embrace, tribute 8. encomium
9. panegyric 10. enfoldment
accommodate . . . 3. fit 4. help, lend,
meet, suit 5. adapt, favor, lodge, shape,
yield 6. adjust, afford, comply, invest,
oblige, orient, settle, supply 7. conform,
furnish 9. reconcile 10. correspond
accommodation . . . 3. aid 4. loan,
room 5. limit, space, terms 6. giving,
volume 7. advance, lodging, service
8. capacity 9. advantage, provision
10. adaptation, adjustment, attunement,
conformity, settlement 11. convenience,
integration, orientation, subsistence
12. coordination 13. harmonization
14. reconciliation
accompaniment . . . 7. adjunct, descant,
support 8. ornament 9. attendant,
obbligato 11. concurrence
12. concomitance
accompany . . . 4. join 6. attend, convoy,
escort, follow, squire 7. conduct
11. synchronize 12. contemporize
accomplice . . . 3. pal 4. aide, ally, chum
6. stooge 7. abettor 9. accessory,
assistant, associate 11. confederate,
conspirator
accomplish . . . 2. do 3. win 4. make,
work 5. enact, equip 6. attain,
effect 7. achieve, compass, execute,
furnish, operate, perfect, produce,
realize, succeed 8. contrive, engineer
9. negotiate 10. consummate, effectuate
accomplishment . . . 4. deed, feat
5. skill 8. dispatch 9. discharge,
execution 10. attainment, completion
11. achievement, acquirement,
fulfillment, performance, proficiency,
transaction 12. effectuation
accord . . . 5. award, grant, unity 6. accede,
unison 7. comport, concede, concert,
concord, harmony, rapport 8. diapason,
symphony 9. agreement, harmonize,
reconcile, unanimity 10. accordance,
conformity, uniformity 11. concurrence
accordant . . . 7. attuned 8. agreeing,
suitable 9. agreeable, assenting,
consonant 10. concordant, concurrent,
consenting, consilient, consistent
11. conformable, homogeneous

13. corresponding
accordingly . . . 2. so 4. then, thus
9. therefore 12. consequently
according to . . . 3. a la, aux 4. alla, fact,
true 5. datal 7. a la mode 8. pursuant
accost . . . 4. hail, meet 5. greet, speak
6. halloo, salute 7. address 8. approach
accoucheuse . . . 7. midwife
account . . . 3. sum, tab 4. bill, cast, sake,
tale, word 5. debit, honor, score, tally
6. assign, credit, esteem, profit, reckon,
regard, report 7. compute, memoirs,
recital 9. narration, reckoning, rehearsal,
statement, summation 10. numeration,
recitation 11. description, explanation,
information 13. communication
accountable . . . 6. liable 8. amenable,
knowable 9. divinable, traceable
10. answerable, ascribable, assignable,
calculable, explicable, fathomable
11. explainable, predictable, responsible
12. attributable, intelligible
13. apprehensible 14. comprehensible
accountant . . . 5. clerk 7. actuary, auditor
8. reckoner 9. defendant, registrar
10. bookkeeper, calculator
accouter, accoutre . . . 3. fit, rig 4. deck,
gird, suit 5. array, dress, equip, habit
6. attire, fettle, outfit 7. appoint,
costume, furnish, provide
accouterment, accoutrement . . .
5. dress, sword 6. attire 8. trapping
9. equipment, haversack
accoy . . . 4. tame 5. daunt 6. soothe,
subdue
accredit . . . 5. trust 6. accept, affirm,
credit, depute, ratify 7. approve, ascribe,
believe, certify, confirm, empower,
endorse 8. deputize, sanction, validate
9. authorize 10. commission
accrete . . . 3. add 6. attach
accretion . . . 4. gain 6. growth 8. addition,
adhesion, increase 9. coherence,
increment 10. concretion
11. coagulation, enlargement
12. accumulation, augmentation
13. amplification
accrue . . . 4. grow 5. arise, ensue, issue
6. mature, result 7. acquire, collect,
redound 8. accresce 10. accumulate
accumulate . . . 4. grow, heap, mass,
save 5. amass, hoard, store 6. accrue,
garner, gather, muster 7. advance,
collect, store up 8. increase 9. aggregate
accumulation . . . 4. fund, gain, mass
5. hoard, store 7. accrual 8. gleaning,
increase, treasure 9. accession,
accretion, extension, gathering
10. acervation, assemblage, collection
11. acquisition, serendipity
12. augmentation 13. amplification
14. aggrandizement
accuracy . . . 6. nicety 9. exactness,
fussiness, precision, rightness
11. correctness 14. meticulousness,
scrupulousness
accurate . . . 4. just, nice, prim 5. close,
exact, right 6. proper, strict 7. correct,
perfect, precise 8. faithful 9. syntactic
10. meticulous, particular
11. grammatical

accursed . . . **6.** cursed, damned, doomed
9. execrable, execrated **10.** detestable
13. anathematized

accusation . . . **5.** blame **6.** attack,
charge, taxing **7.** calumny **8.** reproach
9. complaint **10.** imputation, indictment
11. impeachment **12.** denunciation

accuse . . . **3.** tax **5.** blame **6.** attack,
charge, delate, indict **7.** arraign,
censure, impeach **8.** denounce
9. criminate **11.** incriminate, recriminate

accuser . . . **7.** delator **8.** accusant, libelant
(libellant) **9.** plaintiff **10.** prosecutor
11. complainant **12.** incriminator

accustom . . . **3.** use **4.** wont **5.** enure,
habit, inure, train **6.** addict **7.** educate,
toughen **9.** habituate **11.** familiarize

accustomed . . . **4.** used, wont **5.** usual
6. enured, inured **8.** familiar
9. customary, sedentary (to sit)

ace . . . **3.** jot, one, pip, tib **4.** atom, card,
dole, dram, unit, whit **5.** monad, pilot,
point, shark (sl) **7.** aviator **8.** particle,
pittance, superior **10.** crackajack (sl),
proficient **11.** crackerjack (sl)

ace (pert to) . . .
ace-queen . . **6.** tenace
of clubs . . **5.** basto

acedia (Gr) . . . **5.** sloth **6.** torpor

acedia (Sp) . . . **8.** flatfish

Aceldama, Akeldama (Bib) . . . **12.** Field
of Blood, potter's field

acemila . . . **8.** pack mule

acephalous . . . **8.** headless **10.** leaderless

acephalus . . . **15.** headless monster

acerb . . . **4.** sour **5.** harsh, sharp **6.** bitter,
unripe **7.** acerbic, austere, pungent

acerbity . . . **7.** acidity **8.** acridity,
acrimony, asperity, mordancy,
pungency, severity **9.** harshness
10. bitterness, causticity **11.** astringency

acetic acid . . . **7.** vinegar **8.** vesicant
9. corrosive

Achaean, Achaian . . . **5.** Greek (a)
6. Greece

ache . . . **4.** burn, long, pain, pang
5. throb, yearn **6.** grieve, sorrow,
twinge **7.** agonize, longing **10.** suffer
pain

achieve . . . **2.** do **3.** get, win **4.** gain,
kill **6.** arrive, attain, effect, finish
7. compass, execute, fulfill, perform,
produce, realize, succeed **8.** complete,
conclude, contrive **10.** accomplish,
consummate, effectuate

achievement . . . **3.** act **4.** deed, feat
5. doing, stunt **6.** action, record
7. arrival, exploit **8.** dispatch
9. adventure **10.** attainment, escutcheon
(Her) **11.** fulfillment, performance,
transaction **12.** effectuation
14. accomplishment, implementation

Achilles (pert to) . . .
advisor . . **6.** Nestor
dipped into . . **9.** River Styx
father . . **6.** Peleus
friend . . **9.** Patroclus
horse . . **7.** Xanthus
mother . . **6.** Thetis
slayer . . **5.** Paris
slayer of . . **6.** Hector

son . . **7.** Pyrrhus **11.** Neoptolemus
vulnerable spot . . **4.** heel

achromatic . . . **4.** gray **8.** achromic
9. achromous, colorless, uncolored
13. free from color

achropsia . . . **14.** color blindness

acid . . . **4.** keen, sour, tart **5.** acrid, amino,
boric, malic, mucic, pyrol **6.** acetic,
arabic, biting, bromic, nitric, oxalic,
tannic **7.** acetose, caustic, chloric,
racemic, stearic, terebic, vinegar
8. carbolic, lysergic, sulfuric **9.** corrosive
11. acrimonious **12.** hydrochloric

acid, removing . . . **12.** edulcoration

acidity . . . **4.** acor, sour **8.** acrimony,
mordancy, sourness, tartness, verjuice
9. sharpness **10.** bitterness
13. acidulousness

acknowledge . . . **3.** nod, own, pay, say
4. avow, sign **5.** admit, allow, grant,
own up, reply, swear, thank, vouch,
yield **6.** accede, accept, answer, assent,
attest, redeem **7.** certify, concede,
confess, testify **8.** disclose **9.** recognize

acknowledgment . . . **5.** favor, reply
6. answer, avowal, avowry, shrift,
thanks **7.** apology, epistle, receipt,
voucher, warrant **8.** rescript
9. admission **10.** acceptance,
concession, confession, disclosure,
owning up to **11.** recognition
12. thanksgiving

acme . . . **3.** top **4.** apex **5.** limit **6.** apogee,
climax, crisis, heyday, summit, tip-top,
vertex, zenith **7.** ceiling, maximum
11. culmination **12.** consummation

acology, science of . . . **8.** remedies

acolyte . . . **7.** patener **8.** altar boy
9. assistant

acomia . . . **8.** alopecia, baldness
12. hairlessness

aconite . . . **8.** Cammarum, Eranthis
9. monkshood

acorn . . . **3.** nut **4.** duck **6.** camata
10. meadowlark (color)

acosmic . . . **11.** unorganized

acquaint . . . **4.** tell **6.** advise, impart,
inform **7.** apprise **9.** enlighten, introduce
11. familiarize

acquaintance . . . **3.** ken **5.** amigo **6.** friend
7. privity **8.** familiar, intimacy, intimate
9. companion, knowledge **10.** fellowship
11. familiarity, information, sympathizer
15. familiarization

acquainted . . . **6.** au fait **7.** versant
8. familiar **9.** cognizant **10.** conversant

acquiesce . . . **3.** bow **5.** abide, agree,
chime, yield **6.** accede, assent,
comply, concur, relent, resign, submit
7. conform, consent, succumb

acquire . . . **3.** buy, get, win **4.** earn,
gain, reap **5.** adopt, catch, incur,
learn, steal **6.** attain, effect, obtain,
secure **7.** procure, receive **8.** contract
9. cultivate

acquire (pert to) . . .
beforehand . . **7.** pre-empt
feathers . . **6.** fledge
immunity . . **14.** serum injection
knowledge . . **5.** clear, study **9.** ascertain

acquit . . . **4.** free **5.** clear **6.** excuse,

pardon, pay off **7.** absolve, fulfill, release, requite **9.** exculpate, exonerate
acquittal . . . **7.** freeing, payment, release **8.** clearing, requital **9.** clearance, discharge **10.** observance **11.** exculpation, fulfillment **12.** satisfaction
acquittance . . . **7.** payment, quietus, receipt **9.** discharge, quittance
acre . . . **5.** field **6.** arpent **7.** measure **8.** farmhold
acre (pert to) . . .
half . . **3.** erf (So Afr)
hundred . . **7.** hectare (metric)
quarter . . **4.** rood (Brit)
acres . . . **5.** lands **6.** estate, ground
acrid . . . **4.** acid, bask (dial), keen, sour, tart **5.** harsh, rough, sharp **6.** acetic, biting, bitter **7.** acetose, caustic, mordant, pungent, reeking **8.** unsavory, virulent **9.** acidulous, corrosive **10.** escharotic, irritating **11.** acrimonious
acrimonious . . . **4.** acid, keen **5.** acrid, angry, gruff, harsh, irate, sharp **6.** bitter **7.** caustic **8.** stinging **9.** rancorous, resentful
acrimony . . . **5.** venom **6.** rancor **7.** ill will, vitriol **8.** acerbity, acridity, asperity, mordancy, pungency, rudeness, severity, sourness, tartness **9.** animosity, virulence **10.** bitterness, causticity, resentment **11.** astringency, crabbedness
acroamatic . . . **4.** oral **5.** parol **6.** arcane, occult, secret, verbal **8.** abstract, abstruse, anagogic, esoteric, profound **9.** recondite, unwritten **11.** nuncupative
acrobat . . . **7.** gymnast, tumbler **8.** balancer **10.** ropedancer, ropewalker **11.** funambulist **13.** contortionist, schoenobatist
acrochordon . . . **4.** wart (small)
Acrocorinth, Acrocorinthus . . . **9.** acropolis (Corinth) **12.** Pirene Spring (site)
acromegaly . . . **7.** disease **11.** enlargement (head, hands, feet)
acronical, acronichal (opp of cosmical) . . . **10.** rising star **11.** setting star
acronyx . . . **13.** ingrowing nail
acrophobia . . . fear of **7.** heights
acropolis . . . **6.** refuge **7.** citadel
Acropolis (pert to) . . .
Argos . . **7.** Larissa
Corinth . . **11.** Acrocorinth
Thebes . . **6.** Cadmea
across . . . **4.** over, span **5.** cross **6.** thwart **7.** athwart **8.** crossway, traverse **9.** crossways, crosswise **10.** crisscross, transverse
across (pref) . . . **3.** dia **4.** tran **5.** trans
acrostic . . . **4.** agla, game, poem **6.** puzzle **7.** erratic **8.** wordplay **9.** crosswise, jeu de mots, telestich
act . . . **2.** do **3.** jus, law, lex **4.** deed, feat, play, skit, turn, work **5.** actus, emote, favor, of God, stunt **6.** action, behave, demean, motion **7.** comport, measure, perform, pretend, process **8.** function,

kindness, simulate **9.** enactment, represent **10.** enterprise, exert power, theatrical **11.** impersonate, legislation, performance, transaction
act (pert to) . . .
a part . . **8.** simulate **9.** dissemble
causing ruin . . **11.** Kiss of Death
criminal . . **8.** villainy
detestable . . **11.** abomination
formal . . **10.** instrument
game . . **7.** charade
illegal . . **4.** tort **5.** crime **6.** delict
nonsense . . **10.** tomfoolery
planned . . **12.** premeditated
pompously . . **11.** pontificate
suffix . . **3.** ure
acting . . . **5.** doing **6.** action, posing **7.** playing, serving **8.** pretense **9.** dramatics, execution, operating **10.** masquerade, performing, simulating **11.** make-believe **13.** impersonating, impersonation
acting with force . . . **8.** vehement
action . . . **2.** re **3.** act, res **4.** deed, feat, play, stir, suit, work **5.** award, doing, order, works **6.** battle, decree, motion, praxis, ruling **7.** conduct, contest, lawsuit, verdict, working **8.** activity, behavior, demeanor, exercise, movement, sentence **9.** mechanism, operation **10.** automation, enterprise **11.** performance **13.** pronouncement
active . . . **4.** spry **5.** acute, agile, alert, brisk, quick, ready, smart, yauld **6.** breezy, dapper, lively, nimble, prompt, strong **7.** dynamic, intense, kinetic, vibrant **8.** animated, forceful, spirited, vigorous **9.** assiduous, effective, effectual, energetic, energized, operating, pragmatic, sprightly, vivacious **11.** industrious
active, not . . . **6.** static **7.** dormant **11.** inoperative
activity . . . **3.** ado, gog, pep, vir **4.** stir, work **5.** vigor **6.** action, energy **7.** agility, bristle **8.** business, movement **9.** athletics, briskness, operation, quickness **10.** activeness, employment, nimbleness, occupation
act of . . .
cutting . . **4.** kerf **8.** shearing
endearment . . **4.** kiss **6.** caress
God . . **8.** accident, disaster
kindness . . **5.** favor
leaving . . **6.** congee, egress
respect . . **6.** curtsy, homage
ruling . . **5.** regle
self-examination . . **13.** introspection
sharing . . **13.** participation
witnessing . . **11.** attestation
working together . . **13.** collaboration
worship . . **6.** prayer **8.** devotion
actor . . . **3.** ham **4.** doer, hero, mime, star, supe **5.** agent **6.** mummer, player, worker **7.** Roscius, trooper **8.** aisteoir, comedian, histrion, Thespian **9.** performer, portrayer, pretender, tragedian **10.** comedienne, dramatizer, pantomimic, personator **11.** barnstormer, entertainer, pantomimist, protagonist, tragedienne

12. impersonator
actor (personage) . . . **4.** Lunt, Ward
5. Booth **7.** Skinner **8.** Warfield
9. Faversham
actors' group . . . **4.** cast **6.** troupe
actor's hint . . . **3.** cue **12.** teleprompter
actress (personage) . . . **5.** Adams, Bates,
Hayes, Terry **6.** Robson, Scheff
7. Marlowe, Russell **8.** Fontanne,
Modjeska **9.** Bernhardt
actual . . . **4.** real, true **5.** posit **7.** factual,
genuine, present **8.** absolute, positive,
tangible **9.** practical, veritable
11. substantial
actual being . . . **4.** esse
actuality . . . **4.** fact **6.** verity **7.** reality
8. realness **9.** existence **10.** factuality
14. substantiality
actually . . . **5.** quite, truly **6.** indeed,
really, verily **8.** actively **9.** assuredly,
certainly
actuary . . . **5.** clerk **9.** registrar
10. accountant, bookkeeper, calculator
13. arithmetician, mathematician
actuate . . . **3.** egg **4.** move **5.** force, impel,
rouse **6.** arouse, induce, prompt, propel
7. animate **8.** motivate **9.** stimulate
acuate . . . **7.** sharpen **12.** needle-shaped,
sharp-pointed
acumen . . . **7.** insight **8.** gumption,
keenness, sagacity **9.** acuteness,
sharpness **10.** astuteness, perception,
shrewdness **11.** discernment
12. perspicacity **14.** discrimination
acute . . . **4.** high, keen, tart, thin
5. canny, sharp, smart, vivid **6.** accent,
biting, crafty, fierce, severe, shrewd,
shrill, subtle **7.** crucial, cutting,
dynamic, intense, knowing, painful,
pointed, violent **8.** critical, deep-felt,
forceful, incisive, piercing, poignant,
rigorous, stabbing, stinging, vigorous
9. energetic, ingenious, sensitive
11. sharp-witted **13.** perspicacious
14. discriminating
acuteness of . . .
sight . . **7.** oxyopia **10.** oxyblepsia
taste . . **9.** oxygeusia
touch . . **8.** oxyaphia
A.D. . . . **10.** Anno Domini
Adam (pert to) . . .
grandson . . **4.** Enos
son . . **4.** Abel, Cain, Seth
wife . . **3.** Eve **6.** Lilith (legend)
adage . . . **3.** saw **5.** maxim **6.** saying
7. proverb
adamant . . . **4.** hard **8.** stubborn
10. unyielding
Adam's . . .
ale . . **5.** water
apple . . **6.** larynx **10.** pomum Adami
herb . . **7.** mullein
needle . . **5.** yucca
adapt . . . **3.** fit, set **4.** suit **6.** adjust,
attune, comply, modify, orient, season
7. arrange, conform, prepare, qualify
8. accustom, regulate **9.** acclimate,
condition, habituate, harmonize,
reconcile **11.** accommodate
adaptable . . . **7.** elastic, pliable
9. tractable, versatile **10.** adjustable,

responsive **11.** conformable
13. accommodative
adaptation . . . **7.** fitting **10.** adjustment,
attunement, conformity, regulation
11. arrangement, habituation,
orientation **12.** conditioning,
coordination, modification
13. accommodation, harmonization,
orchestration, qualification
15. familiarization
add . . . **3.** eke, tot **4.** foot, give, join,
plus, tote **5.** affix, annex, sum up,
total, unite **6.** append, attach, reckon
7. accrete, augment, compile, compute,
put with, subjoin **8.** increase **9.** calculate
10. supplement
adda . . . **5.** skink (scink) **6.** lizard **7.** reptile
addax . . . **6.** pygarg (Bib) **8.** antelope
added . . . **3.** and **4.** plus **5.** extra
6. joined, united **7.** affixed, annexed
8. appended, attached **9.** appendant
13. supplementary
adder . . . **3.** asp **5.** Bitis, krait, snake,
viper **6.** nedder **7.** machine, serpent
13. mathematician
addict . . . **4.** buff **5.** fiend **7.** adjudge,
devotee, hophead **9.** habituate **15.** apply
habitually
addicted . . . **4.** wont **5.** prone **8.** attached,
disposed, inclined **9.** devoted to
10. accustomed, habituated **11.** given
over to
addiction . . . **5.** habit **9.** surrender
10. attachment **11.** enslavement
Addison, name for . . . **4.** Clio (The
Spectator) **7.** Atticus (by Pope)
addition . . . **3.** and, ell, too **4.** also,
gain, plus, wing **5.** farse (Relig),
rider **6.** addend, augend, lean-to
7. additum, adjunct, joining, uniting
8. addendum, additory, increase
9. accession, accretion, amendment,
appendage, extension, reckoning
10. annexation **11.** calculation,
computation, enlargement
12. augmentation
additional . . . **3.** new **4.** else, more
5. added, extra, fresh, spare **7.** another,
besides, further **9.** auxiliary, extrinsic
12. supervenient, supplemental
13. supplementary
additional (pert to) . . .
explanation . . **10.** epexegesis
11. elucidation
grant . . **3.** ann **5.** bonus
specimen . . **6.** cotype
address . . . **3.** air, wit, woo **4.** call, hail,
mien, pray, tact, talk **5.** abode, court,
grace, greet, guise, place, skill, speak
6. accost, direct, eulogy, salute, sermon,
speech **7.** arrange, conduct, consign,
declaim, finesse, lecture, manners,
oration, prepare, prowess, request
8. behavior, demeanor, greeting,
harangue, inscribe, perorate, petition,
presence **9.** dexterity, diplomacy,
direction, discourse, ingenuity,
readiness **11.** comportment, destination,
inscription, savoir-faire
14. sophistication, superscription
addressee . . . **8.** occupant **10.** inhabitant

12. communicator **13.** correspondent
adduce . . . **4.** cite, name **5.** argue, infer, offer, plead, quote **6.** allege, assign **7.** advance, mention, present, produce
Adelphi . . . **7.** theater (Strand, London) **13.** London Quarter
adeps . . . **4.** lard **9.** animal fat
adept . . . **3.** ace, apt **4.** deft, whiz (coll) **6.** adroit, artist, expert, versed **7.** capable, dabster, mahatma, skilled **8.** skillful (skilful) **9.** alchemist (formerly), occultist **10.** conversant, proficient **11.** crackerjack
adequate . . . **3.** due, fit **4.** able, full **5.** ample, digne, equal **6.** enough **7.** capable **8.** all right, equalize, suitable **9.** competent, effective, effectual, sufficing, tolerable **10.** sufficient **12.** commensurate, satisfactory **13.** proportionate
adhere . . . **4.** cleg, glue, hold **5.** cling, stick **6.** cleave, cohere **7.** accrete, observe, persist
adherent . . . **4.** ally **6.** adnate, sticky, votary **7.** dangler, sequela **8.** adhesive, clinging, disciple, faithful, follower, hanger-on, partisan, sticking, upholder **9.** appendage, dependent, supporter
adherent to the Crown . . . **4.** Tory
adhesive . . . **3.** gum, wax **4.** glue **5.** paste **6.** cement, mastic, sticky **8.** adherent, mucilage **9.** tenacious
adhesiveness . . . **4.** stay **8.** tenacity **12.** cohesiveness **13.** tenaciousness **16.** stick-to-itiveness
adhibit . . . **3.** use **5.** admit, affix, apply **6.** attach, devote **7.** bring in **10.** administer
adieu . . . **4.** vale **5.** adios, aloha **6.** good-by, so long (sl) **7.** cheerio, good-bye, good day **8.** au revoir, farewell **11.** leave-taking
adipose . . . **3.** fat **4.** oily **5.** fatty, plump, pursy, squab **9.** sebaceous
adit . . . **3.** way **4.** duct **5.** entry, stulm **6.** access, ingate, intake, tunnel **7.** channel, conduit, haulage, ingress, passage **8.** approach, drainage, entrance **9.** admission **11.** entranceway, ventilation
adjacent . . . **4.** abut, near, nigh **5.** close, handy **6.** next to **7.** meeting, nearest **8.** abutting, touching **9.** adjoining, bordering **10.** contiguous, juxtaposed **11.** neighboring **12.** conterminous
adject . . . **3.** add **4.** join **5.** annex
adjective . . . **3.** the **6.** adnoun **7.** epithet (significant) **8.** modifier **9.** accessory, dependent
adjective (pert to) . . .
demonstrative . . **4.** that, this **5.** these, those
suffix . . **2.** ic, il **3.** ent, ial, ian, ile, ish, ist, ite, ive, ous
verbal . . **9.** gerundive
adjoin . . . **3.** add **4.** abut, butt, join **5.** unite **6.** attach, border **7.** conjoin **8.** neighbor
adjourn . . . **3.** end **5.** close, defer, delay **6.** recess **7.** suspend **8.** dissolve, postpone, prorogue **11.** discontinue

adjudge, adjudicate . . . **3.** try **4.** deem, doom, find, hold, pass **5.** award, judge, order **6.** assign, decree, esteem, ordain, reckon, regard, settle **7.** condemn **8.** consider, sentence **9.** determine
adjunct . . . **4.** ally, word **5.** added **6.** device **7.** additum, annexed, consort **8.** addition, appanage (apanage) **9.** appendant, associate, auxiliary, colleague, companion, component, qualifier **11.** confederate **12.** appurtenance, nonessential
adjuration . . . **4.** oath, plea **6.** appeal, avowal, charge **8.** entreaty, swearing, vouching **10.** deposition **11.** beseechment, obsecration, obtestation
adjure . . . **3.** ask, beg, bid **4.** bind, pray **5.** plead **6.** appeal, charge **7.** beseech, command, entreat, implore, swear in
adjust . . . **3.** fit, fix, set **4.** meet, size, suit, trim, true **5.** adapt, align, amend, frame, group, match, right, shape **6.** accord, attune, orient, remedy, settle, square **7.** arrange, conform, correct, justify, mediate, rectify, redress **8.** accustom, organize, regulate **9.** condition, habituate, harmonize, reconcile **10.** compromise, coordinate, straighten **11.** accommodate, systematize
adjuster, adjustor . . . **6.** fitter **8.** arranger **11.** coordinator
adjustment . . . **4.** gear **5.** means, terms **7.** fitting, suiting **8.** bearings, disposal **9.** bundobust **10.** adaptation, attunement, compromise, concession, conclusion, conformity, regulation, settlement **11.** arrangement, disposition, habituation, orientation **12.** assimilation, coordination, organization **13.** harmonization, methodization, rectification **14.** naturalization, reconciliation
adjutant . . . **4.** aide, ally **6.** helper **7.** officer **9.** assistant, auxiliary
adjutant bird . . . **5.** stork **6.** argala **7.** hurgila, marabou
ad lib, ad libit, ad libitum . . . **6.** make up **7.** cadenza **9.** extempore, impromptu, improvise **10.** at pleasure **11.** play it by ear **13.** accompaniment
administer . . . **4.** give **5.** apply, issue **6.** bestow, direct, govern, manage, supply, tender **7.** adhibit, conduct, dispose, execute, fulfill, furnish, give out, husband, perform **8.** dispatch, dispense, transact **9.** discharge **10.** distribute **12.** administrate
administer extreme unction . . . **5.** anele **6.** anoint
administration . . . **3.** use **4.** rule **6.** employ, giving, policy **7.** conduct, regimen **8.** bestowal, disposal, issuance, ministry **9.** direction, execution **10.** employment, government, management, regulation **11.** application, directorate, disposition **12.** dispensation, ministration **13.** apportionment
administration of justice . . .

10. judicatory, judicature
administrator . . . **2.** fu **5.** dewan
   7. alcalde, manager, provost, trustee
   8. director, executor **9.** dispenser,
   executive **12.** entrepreneur
admirable . . . **5.** sweet **6.** worthy
   7. likable (likeable), winning, winsome
   8. adorable, laudable **9.** estimable,
   excellent, marvelous, wonderful
   10. creditable **11.** commendable,
   meritorious **12.** praiseworthy
admiration . . . **6.** esteem, liking, regard,
   wonder **7.** respect **8.** surprise
   9. adoration, amazement, reverence
   10. wonderment **11.** astoundment,
   idolization **12.** appreciation,
   confoundment
admire . . . **4.** like, love **5.** adore, honor
   6. esteem, regard, revere **7.** approve,
   idolize, respect **8.** venerate
admissible . . . **3.** fit **4.** just, sane **5.** sound
   6. worthy **7.** apropos, germane, logical
   8. apposite, eligible, rational, relevant,
   suitable **9.** admissory, agreeable,
   allowable, desirable, pertinent,
   qualified, receptive, tolerable
   10. acceptable, applicable, legitimate,
   reasonable **11.** justifiable, permissible,
   warrantable **12.** satisfactory
admission . . . **4.** adit **5.** entry **6.** access,
   assent, avowal, entree, shrift
   8. entrance **9.** agreement, allowance,
   inclusion, letting in, receiving,
   reception, testimony **10.** accordance,
   admittance, allegation, avouchment,
   compliance, concession, confession,
   initiation, permission **11.** affiliation,
   affirmation, declaration
   12. acquiescence, assimilation
   14. acknowledgment, naturalization
   15. enfranchisement
Admission Day holiday . . . **6.** Nevada
   (Oct 31) **7.** Arizona (Feb 14)
   10. California (Sept 9)
admit . . . **3.** own **4.** avow **5.** adopt, allow,
   enter, grant, let in, own up, trust,
   yield **6.** accept, credit, embody, permit
   7. adhibit, believe, concede, confess,
   embrace, include, profess, receive
   8. initiate **9.** affiliate **10.** naturalize
   11. acknowledge, incorporate
admittance . . . **6.** access **8.** entrance,
   sanction **9.** admission, letting in
   10. initiation
admitted . . . **6.** indeed **8.** believed,
   conceded **12.** acknowledged
admixture . . . **5.** alloy, blend **6.** fusion
   7. mixture **8.** compound, infusion
   7. mixture **8.** compound, infusion
   10. minglement **11.** combination,
   composition
admonish . . . **4.** warn **5.** chide, scold
   6. advise, enjoin, exhort, preach,
   rebuke, remind **7.** caution, monitor,
   reprove, upbraid **8.** dissuade
   9. reprimand **11.** expostulate,
   remonstrate, give warning
admonition . . . **6.** advice **7.** caution,
   censure, reproof, warning **8.** reminder
   10. counseling (counselling), dissuasion
   11. exhortation **12.** remonstrance,

reprehension
ado . . . **4.** fuss, stir **5.** doing, hurry
   6. bustle, flurry, hubbub, pother,
   rumpus, tumult **7.** trouble, turmoil
   9. commotion **10.** excitement
   11. disturbance
adobe . . . **4.** clay, silt **5.** brick, house
   (clay)
adolescent . . . **3.** lad **5.** minor, youth
   6. nonage **9.** pubescent, youngster
   10. developing
Adonis (pert to) . . .
   beloved by . . **9.** Aphrodite
   festival . . **6.** Adonia
   modern youth . . **6.** a dandy
   mother . . **5.** Myrrh
   slain by . . **8.** wild boar
adopt . . . **4.** take **5.** admit, usurp
   6. accept, assume, borrow, choose,
   father, mother, select **7.** embrace,
   espouse, receive, welcome **9.** affiliate
   10. assimilate, naturalize **11.** appropriate
adoption . . . **6.** choice **8.** espousal
   9. admission, borrowing, reception
   10. acceptance, assumption, conversion,
   redemption, usurpation
   11. embracement **13.** appropriation
   14. naturalization
adore . . . **4.** love **5.** enjoy, honor **6.** esteem,
   regard, revere **7.** idolize, worship
   8. venerate
adorn . . . **4.** clad, deck, trim **5.** array,
   begem, drape, grace, primp, prink
   6. attire, bedeck, clothe, enrich
   7. bedight, bejewel, dignify, festoon,
   garnish **8.** beautify, decorate
   9. embellish
adorn (with) . . .
   color . . **4.** gild **5.** paint **7.** emblaze
   feathers . . **7.** implume
   needlework . . **9.** embroider
   ornaments . . **6.** tinsel **7.** imagery
adorned . . . **4.** clad **6.** ornate **7.** clothed,
   prinked **9.** decorated
   16. chryselephantine
adornment . . . **5.** decor, frill **6.** frills,
   tinsel **10.** decoration, embroidery
   13. embellishment **14.** beautification
ad patres . . . **4.** dead **12.** to his Fathers
Adriatic (pert to) . . .
   city . . **5.** Fiume **6.** Venice **7.** Lagosta,
   Trieste **8.** Brandisi
   island . . **7.** Lagosta
   peninsula . . **6.** Istria
   wind (cold) . . **4.** bora
adrift . . . **4.** asea, free, lost **5.** at sea,
   loose **6.** afloat, astray, aweigh, undone
   7. aimless, unfixed **8.** aberrant, derelict,
   floating, insecure, straying, unmoored,
   unstable **9.** erroneous **10.** bewildered,
   unanchored, unfastened, without aim
adroit . . . **4.** neat **5.** quick, ready,
   smart **6.** clever, expert, habile,
   nimble **7.** cunning **8.** skillful (skilful)
   9. dexterous, ingenious
adroitness . . . **4.** tact **5.** knack, skill
   7. address **9.** dexterity, ingenuity,
   readiness, smartness
adsorbent, absorbent . . . **6.** spongy
   7. osmotic, soaking **8.** blotting
   12. assimilative

adulation . . . 6. praise 8. flattery
9. adoration 10. compliment
adult . . . 6. mature, X-rated 7. grown up
adulterate . . . 3. mix 5. alter, taint
6. debase, defile 7. corrupt 8. denature
11. contaminate
adulterated . . . 6. impure 7. debased
8. spurious 9. denatured 11. counterfeit
12. contaminated
adust . . . 3. tan (color) 4. burn 5. burnt,
dried, fiery 6. singed 7. parched
8. scorched 9. blistered
advance . . . 2. go 3. aid 4. gain,
inch, loan, move, near, nose, pass,
push, rise (in price) 5. ahead, boost,
creep, march, raise 6. better, stride
7. elevate, process, promote, propose
8. approach, heighten, increase,
progress 9. aforehand, elevation,
promotion, upgrading 10. accelerate,
beforehand, preferment
11. advancement, development,
furtherance, improvement, progression
advanced . . . 3. old 4. aged 6. modern
7. elderly, forward 8. bettered,
enhanced, enriched, foremost,
unproved 9. venerable 10. in the front,
precocious, senectuous 11. enlightened,
progressive
advanced (pert to) . . .
equally . . 7. abreast
study . . 7. seminar
time . . 6. modern 8. up-to-date
12. contemporary
advantage . . . 3. use 4. boot, bote (bot),
edge, gain, good, hold, odds 5. avail,
favor, start, stead 6. behalf, behoof,
profit 7. benefit, further, promote,
service, vantage 8. facility, interest,
purchase 9. appliance 10. expedience
11. convenience, superiority
13. accommodation, vantage ground
advantageous . . . 5. handy 6. aidful,
useful 7. helpful 8. edifying, salutary
9. expedient, favorable 10. auspicious,
beneficial, convenient, profitable,
propitious, worthwhile 11. encouraging
advent . . . 6. coming 7. arrival 8. approach
11. forthcoming
Advent (Eccl) . . . 14. Coming of Christ
adventitious . . . 4. rale 6. casual
8. acquired 9. extrinsic 10. accidental,
incidental 12. nonessential
adventure . . . 3. act (heroic), hap 4. bout,
dare, deed, feat, gest, risk 5. event,
quest, stunt 6. action, hazard 7. episode,
exploit, fortune, venture 8. escapade,
incident (novel), maneuver, occasion
9. happening 10. enterprise, experience,
occurrence 11. performance, undertaking
12. happenstance 13. striking event
14. accomplishment
adventurer . . . 4. goer 5. sport 7. bounder,
gambler, Hessian, parvenu, soldier,
upstart 8. gamester, hazarder,
merchant, traveler 9. sportsman
10. speculator 16. soldier of fortune
adventuress . . . 7. demirep 10. gold
digger
adventurous . . . 4. rash 5. risky 6. daring
8. reckless 9. dangerous, foolhardy,

hazardous, venturous 11. venturesome
12. enterprising, presumptuous
adversary . . . 3. foe 5. enemy, Satan
6. foeman 8. opponent 9. archfiend,
assailant 10. antagonist, competitor,
Philistine
adverse . . . 3. ill 4. anti 5. loath 7. opposed
8. contrary, converse, opposing,
sinister, untoward 9. reluctant, unwilling
10. afflictive, calamitous, indisposed
11. conflicting, disinclined, unfavorable
12. antagonistic, unpropitious
adversity . . . 6. misery 7. trouble
8. calamity, distress, hardship
9. suffering 10. affliction, misfortune,
opposition 11. destitution
advert . . . 5. recur, refer 6. allude, return
advertent . . . 7. heedful 9. attentive
advertise . . . 4. plug, warn 5. boast,
boost 6. notify 7. promote, publish
8. announce, ballyhoo, proclaim
9. publicize 10. promulgate
advertisement . . . 2. ad 4. bill, copy,
Neon, plug, sign 6. notice, poster,
spread 7. placard 10. commercial (TV)
advice . . . 4. rede 5. aviso 6. caveat,
wisdom 7. counsel, opinion, warning
8. prudence, reminder 9. knowledge
10. admonition, suggestion
11. exhortation, information, instruction
12. consultation, deliberation,
intelligence 13. consideration
14. recommendation
advice, containing . . . 9. mentorial
advisable . . . 6. proper 7. prudent
9. befitting, desirable, expedient
11. commendable 13. recommendable
advise . . . 4. rede, tell, warn 5. coach
6. exhort, impart, inform, remind
7. apprise, bethink, caution, counsel,
suggest 8. acquaint, admonish, advocate
9. enlighten, recommend 11. communicate, familiarize, take counsel
adviser, advisor . . . 5. guide 6. Egeria,
nestor 7. monitor 8. appriser, kibitzer
(sl) 9. counselor (counsellor), informant
10. admonisher
advisers, advisors . . . 7. Cabinet, Council
10. councilors, counselors, informants
advocate . . . 3. pro 4. urge 6. advise,
backer, defend, deputy, lawyer
7. endorse, espouse, pleader, support
8. attorney, champion, defender,
exponent, plead for 9. barrister,
counselor, justifier, paraclete,
proponent, recommend, solicitor,
supporter 11. protagonist
advocate of the simple life . . .
14. simplicitarian
adytum . . . 6. shrine 7. chamber (inner),
sanctum 9. sanctuary
Aeetes (pert to) . . .
daughter . . 5. Medea
keeper of . . 12. Golden Fleece
king of . . 7. Colchis
Aegean Islands . . . 5. Chios, Samos
6. Lesbos 8. Cyclades 10. Dodecanese
aegis, egis . . . 4. care 5. guard 6. screen,
shield, symbol (anc) 7. backing, defense
8. guidance 9. fosterage, patronage
10. protection

Aello (Gr) ... 5. Harpy 7. monster
Aeneid ... 4. poem (Vergil)
aerage ... 11. ventilation
aerate ... 6. aerify 7. freshen, inflate,
refresh 9. ventilate
aerial ... 3. ear 4. aery, airy, mast
5. aeric, lofty 6. unreal 7. airlike,
antenna 8. ethereal, fanciful, vaporous
9. pneumatic 10. chimerical
12. aeronautical 13. unsubstantial
aerie, eyrie ... 4. nest 5. brood (birds)
6. family 9. penthouse
aeriform ... 6. unreal 7. gaseous
aeroplane ... 8. airplane
Aesir, Norse Gods ... 3. Tyr (Tiu), Ull
4. Odin (Woden), Thor (Donar), Vali
5. Bragi 6. Balder, Hoenir 7. Forseti
8. Heimdall
Aeson's son ... 5. Jason (Gr Myth)
Aesop (Gr) ... 5. fable, moral
affability ... 6. comity 8. civility, courtesy,
urbanity 9. geniality 10. amiability,
cordiality, politeness 11. sociability
12. conviviality 14. gregariousness
16. companionability
17. communicativeness
affable ... 4. mild 5. civil, suave
6. benign, fluent, social 7. amiable
8. gracious, sociable 9. convivial,
courteous 10. accessible, gregarious
11. complaisant 13. communicative
affair ... 4. duel, love 5. fight, issue,
thing, topic 6. action, gadget, matter,
object, soiree 7. concern, problem
8. business, interest, question, sociable
9. gathering, reception, something
10. proceeding 11. get-together,
transaction 12. circumstance
affect ... 4. melt, move, stir 5. feign,
grate, haunt, touch 6. assume,
excite, regale, relate, soften, thrill
7. concern, involve, operate, pretend,
qualify 8. frequent, interest, simulate
9. influence 11. counterfeit, hypothecate
affectation ... 3. air 4. pose, sham
7. display, foppery, pietism 8. elegance,
pretense 9. mannerism 12. affectedness
13. artificiality 14. grandiloquence
15. pretentiousness
affected ... 4. airy, sham 5. faked,
moved, posey, put-on 6. fal-lal, formal
7. assumed, beloved, elegant, feigned,
gushing, stilted 8. disposed, mannered
9. impressed, pretended, unnatural
10. artificial, euphuistic 11. pretentious
12. ostentatious 13. counterfeited,
grandiloquent
affected by ...
  age .. 6. senile
  love .. 4. smit 7. smitten
  pain .. 4. pang 6. twinge
  paralysis .. 7. paretic
  wonder .. 6. marvel 9. convulsed
affectedly languid ... 13. lackadaisical
affectedly shy ... 3. coy, mim 4. prim
6. demure 10. coquettish
affection ... 4. amor, love 6. animus,
defect, storge (animal) 7. disease,
emotion, feeling, illness, leaning,
passion 8. devotion, fondness, tendency
9. attribute, infirmity, sentiment

10. affliction, attachment, disability,
proclivity, propensity, tenderness
11. disposition, inclination,
temperament
affectionate ... 4. fond, soft, warm
6. ardent, loving, tender 7. adoring,
devoted, earnest, zealous 8. attached,
friendly, parental, romantic
10. headstrong 13. demonstrative
afferent ... 6. esodic (nerves), inward
7. sensory 11. centripetal
affiance ... 5. faith, troth, trust 6. belief,
pledge, plight 7. betroth, promise
8. credence, reliance 9. assurance,
betrothal 10. confidence, engagement
affiche ... 6. poster 7. placard
affidavit ... 4. oath 9. statement
10. deposition 11. affirmation,
certificate, declaration
affiliation ... 4. body, sect 5. group,
union 6. church, fusion, hookup, league
7. faction, lineage 8. adoption, alliance,
espousal, relation 9. admission,
alignment, coalition 10. connection,
federation, fellowship, persuasion
11. association, cooperation
12. denomination, organization
13. confederation, consanguinity
14. naturalization
affinity ... 3. kin 6. accord, family, liking
7. kinship, rapport 8. relation, soul mate
9. agreement 10. attraction, connection,
similarity 11. propinquity, resemblance
12. congeniality, relationship
13. compatibility, rapprochement
affirm ... 3. say 4. aver, avow 5. posit,
state, swear, vouch 6. allege, assert,
attest, avouch, ratify 7. assever, certify,
confirm, declare, endorse, profess,
testify, warrant 8. sanction, validate
9. predicate, pronounce 10. asseverate
12. authenticate, substantiate
affirmation ... 3. vow 4. amen, oath,
word 5. basis 6. ground 7. premise
8. averment 9. admission, assertion,
statement, testimony 10. affirmance,
allegation, avouchment, deposition,
foundation, profession 11. declaration,
proposition 12. confirmation, ratification
affirmative ... 3. aye (ay), nod, yea, yes
8. dogmatic, positive, thumbs up (coll)
10. cataphatic (rare) 11. affirmation,
declarative, predicative
affirmatory ... 9. assertive 11. affirmative,
assertional
affix ... 3. add, fix, pen, tag 4. seal
5. annex, stamp 6. anchor, append,
attach, fasten, impose 7. connect,
subjoin 9. increment 11. superimpose
afflict ... 3. ail, try, vex 4. hurt,
pain 5. upset, wound 6. grieve,
harass, sicken 7. agitate, chasten,
derange, disturb, oppress, torment,
trouble 8. disorder, distress, lacerate
9. overthrow, persecute
afflicted ... 3. sad 5. ailed 6. pained
7. smitten, wounded 8. troubled
9. depressed, suffering 10. distressed
affliction ... 3. woe 4. airs, bane, evil,
pain, pest 5. curse, grief 6. misery,
plague 7. illness, scourge, torment,

trouble 8. calamity, distress, hardship
9. adversity 10. misfortune, visitation
12. wretchedness
afflictive ... 6. severe 11. causing pain,
distressing
affluence ... 4. ease, flow 6. afflux, influx,
plenty, riches, wealth 8. opulence,
richness 9. abundance, concourse,
plenitude, profusion 10. prosperity
affluent ... 4. rich 5. flush 6. fluent
7. copious, moneyed, opulent, wealthy
8. abundant, well-to-do 9. luxuriant,
pecunious, plenteous 10. prosperous
afford ... 4. bear, cost, give, lend
5. allow, endow, grant, spare, stand,
yield 6. accord, confer, invest, supply
7. furnish, provide, support, undergo
affray ... 3. war 4. feud, fray, riot 5. brawl,
fight, melee, scrap (sl), set-to (coll)
6. battle, combat, tumult 7. assault,
contest, quarrel, scuffle 9. encounter
11. disturbance
affright ... 5. alarm, scare 6. appall
(appal), dismay 7. confuse, startle,
terrify 8. frighten
affront ... 4. defy, face, meet, slap
5. abuse 6. harass, insult, offend,
oppose 7. offense, outrage, provoke
8. confront, dishonor, envisage, ill-
treat, irritate 9. encounter, humiliate,
indignity 11. provocation
afghan (pert to) ...
fox .. 6. corsac
language .. 11. Afghanistan
prince .. 4. amir (ameer), emir (emeer)
rug .. 5. Herat 6. carpet
stitch .. 7. crochet
wrap .. 7. blanket (woolen)
Afghanistan ...
capital .. 5. Kabul
city .. 5. Herat 8. Kandahar
language .. 6. Pushtu 7. Persian
mountain .. 9. Hindu Kush
Pass (famed) .. 6. Khyber
pony .. 4. yabu (yaboo)
religion .. 5. Islam
river .. 5. Indus
Africa ... see also *African*
desert .. 6. Libyan, Sahara 8. Kalahari
gulf .. 4. Aden 5. Gabes, Sidra
island (largest) .. 10. Madagascar
lake .. 6. Nyassa 8. Victoria
10. Tanganyika
Mt. .. 5. Atlas, Kenya, Natal 7. Stanley
8. Cameroon 9. Ruwenzori
11. Kilimanjaro
river .. 4. Nile 5. Congo, Niger 7. Senegal,
Zambezi
size (in world) .. 6. second
African (pert to) ...
charm, fetish .. 4. juju 6. grigri
drum .. 8. bamboula
enclosure .. 4. boma 5. kraal
garment .. 4. haik, tobe 6. kaross
grass .. 7. esparto
grassland .. 4. veld (veldt) 8. bushveld
harp (Nubian) .. 5. nanga
hemp .. 3. ife
herb .. 4. ocra
instrument .. 4. gora (gorah) 5. nanga,
rebab 6. balafo

language .. 3. Ibo 4. Zulu 5. Bantu, Sotho,
Tonga 6. Somali, Yoruba 7. Ashanti
(Ashantee)
palm .. 6. ronier 7. palmyra
secret society .. 4. Egbo 6. Mau Mau
8. Bachichi (cannibal)
soldier .. 5. spahi 6. askari
sorcery .. 5. obeah
spiritual power .. 4. ngai
thong (rawhide) .. 4. riem
tree .. 3. oak 4. akee, baku, cola
(kola), etua, shea 5. artar, sassy, siris
6. baobab
African people (pert to) ...
Islamitic sect .. 9. Almohades
Natal .. 4. Zulu 6. kaffir 7. Amazulu
people .. 3. Ibo 4. Arab, Boer, Copt,
Hutu, Kafa (Kaffa), Zulu 5. Bantu,
Fulah, Negro, Pygmy, Tutsi 6. Berber,
Kabyle, Nubian, Semite, Somali, Yoruba
7. Ashanti (Ashantee), Bushman,
Swahili 8. Bechuana 9. Hottentot
African wildlife (pert to) ...
antelope .. 3. gnu 4. oryx 5. addax,
eland, oribi 6. dik-dik, impala, rhebok
7. blaubok (small), blesbok, gemsbok
10. duikerbuck, hartebeest
bird .. 4. lory, taha 6. weaver 8. umbretti
9. beefeater, hammerkop
fly .. 4. kivu 6. tsetse
goat .. 5. Capra
horse disease .. 5. surra
mammal .. 8. anteater, pangolin
monkey .. 4. mona, waag 6. baboon,
grivet, guenon 7. guereza 8. talapoin
peacock .. 5. paauw
rhinoceros .. 6. borele 7. keitloa
rodent .. 4. jird 5. ratel
sheep .. 4. zenu 5. oudad (udad)
squirrel .. 5. xerus
stork .. 6. simbil 7. marabou
toad .. 7. Xenopus
worm .. 3. loa
aft, after ... 4. anon, past, rear 5. abaft,
later, since 6. astern, behind 9. posterior
10. subsequent, succeeding
after (pert to) ...
all .. 11. considering 12. nevertheless
awhile .. 4. anon 5. later
breast (Zool) .. 10. metathorax
date .. 8. postdate
dinner .. 12. postprandial
dinner coffee .. 9. demitasse
prefix .. 4. meta, post
aftermath ... 4. crop 5. rowen
9. afterglow 12. consequences
aftermost ... 4. last 7. aftmost
8. hindmost, rearmost
afterpiece ... 3. act 4. heel 5. epode,
exode 8. postlude 9. aftercome,
afterpart, tailpiece
after song ... 5. epode
afterthought ... 6. regret, sequel
10. reflection 13. arrière-pensée, second
thought
afterward, afterwards ... 4. next 5. after,
later, since 6. ensues 7. by and by
9. afterhand 10. thereafter 11. in the
future 12. subsequently
aga, agha ... 5. chief, title 9. commander
agacant, agacante ... 8. exciting

11. provocative
agacella (Her) . . . 8. antelope
again . . . 2. re (pref) 3. yet 4. anew,
anon, back, over, then 5. ditto, newly,
often, recur 6. afresh, de novo, encore,
rather 7. freshly 8. eftsoons (eftsoon),
likewise, moreover, once more 9. twice
over 10. repeatedly, second time
11. furthermore
against . . . 2. on, to, vs 3. con, non
4. agin (dial), anti, upon 6. contra,
versus 7. counter, opposed, towards
8. averse to, converse, opposite
against the . . .
 clock . . 4. race, time 7. in haste
 current . . 8. upstream
 grain . . 6. across 7. oblique 9. backwards
 10. contrarily 11. unwillingly
 law . . 7. illegal, illicit 8. wrongful
 12. illegitimate
 sun . . 16. counterclockwise
agal . . . 4. cord (Bedouin head wrap)
agalloch . . . 4. agar 5. aloes 7. linalon
8. calambac 9. eaglewood, lignaloes
agama, agamoid . . . 6. iguana, lizard
Agamemnon (pert to) . . .
 brother . . 8. Menelaus
 daughter . . 7. Electra 9. Iphigenia
 father . . 6. Atreus
 king of . . 7. Mycenae
 rival . . 9. Aegisthus
 son . . 7. Orestes
 wife . . 12. Clytemnestra
 wife's paramour . . 9. Aegisthus
agape . . . 4. agog, ajar 6. aghast,
gaping 7. curious, yawning 8. open-
eyed 9. expectant, love feast (Chr)
10. astonished, bewildered, breathless
agate . . . 3. taw 4. onyx, ruby, type 5. color
6. achate, marble (game), pebble,
quartz 10. birthstone, chalcedony
agave . . . 4. aloe 5. datil, istle 6. maguey,
mescal, pulque 8. henequen
age . . . 3. eon, era, old 4. aeon, date,
eral, eval, time 5. cycle, epoch, major,
minor, older, ripen 6. junior, mature,
mellow, modern, period, remote, senior
7. century, grow old 8. eternity, lifetime,
maturity 9. antiquate, senectude
10. generation
Age . . . 3. Air, Ice, Jet 4. Iron, Jazz,
Yuga 5. Azoic, Kalpa, Space, Steel,
Stone 6. Atomic, Bronze, Copper,
Eocene, Gilded, Golden, Heroic,
Silver 7. Glacial, Homeric, Miocene
8. Cambrian, Cenozoic, Mesozoic
10. Geological, Supersonic
11. Elizabethan
aged . . . 3. eld, old 5. anile, hoary, olden
6. feeble, infirm, senile 7. ancient,
elderly, Ogygian 8. gerontic
9. Nestorian 10. senectuous
agency . . . 5. means 6. action, medium,
office 8. function 9. operation
10. collection, commission, efficiency,
management 14. intermediation
15. instrumentality
agenda . . . 5. slate 6. docket 7. agendum
(sing), program 9. memoranda
14. memorandum book, things to be
done

agent . . . 3. spy 4. doer, test, tool 5. actor,
buyer, envoy, proxy 6. author, broker,
deputy, factor, medium 7. creator,
proctor, reagent, scalper 8. aumildar,
emissary, operator, salesman
9. canvasser, comprador, consignee,
go-between, operative 10. instrument,
originator 11. facilitator 12. intermediary
14. representative
Age of Reason . . . 7. Diderot 8. Voltaire
9. d'Alembert 10. philosophe
12. Encyclopedia 13. Enlightenment
Ages . . . 4. Dark 6. Middle
aggrandize . . . 5. add to, exalt 6. extend
7. advance, enhance, enlarge, glorify,
magnify, promote 8. increase
10. exaggerate
aggravate . . . 3. irk, nag, vex 4. miff,
rile, twit 5. anger, annoy, chafe, pique,
sting, taunt, tease, worry 6. nettle,
pester, ruffle, worsen 7. bedevil, disturb,
incense, magnify, provoke 8. heighten,
increase, irritate 9. infuriate, intensify
10. exasperate
aggravation . . . 6. bother 7. anguish,
torment, trouble 8. vexation
9. annoyance, worsening 10. affliction,
excitement, irritation, resentment
11. displeasure, provocation
12. exasperation 15. intensification
aggregate . . . 3. all, sum 4. mass 5. total,
whole 6. amount, volume 8. compound,
ensemble 9. accretion 10. collection
11. combination 12. accumulation
aggregate (pert to) . . .
 definable member . . 4. unit
 fruit . . 7. etaerio
 in the . . 7. en masse, totally 8. together
 12. collectively
 of plants . . 5. flock, flora 7. cluster
aggregation . . . 4. heap 5. group, union
9. congeries 10. assemblage, collection
11. combination 12. accumulation,
amalgamation 13. consolidation
aggression . . . 6. attack, injury 7. assault,
offense 8. invasion 9. hostility,
intrusion, offensive 10. enterprise,
initiative 11. provocation
12. encroachment 14. aggressiveness
aggressive . . . 7. hostile, pushing
9. assertive, attacking, bellicose,
combative, offensive 10. assaulting,
pugnacious 11. belligerent, contentious,
provocative 12. enterprising
aggrieve . . . 4. pain 6. grieve 7. afflict,
oppress, trouble 9. displease, persecute,
tyrannize
aggrieved . . . 6. pained, woeful 7. doleful
8. mournful 9. sorrowful 10. displeased
aghast . . . 4. agog 5. agape 6. afraid
8. appalled, dismayed 9. astounded,
horrified, terrified 10. astonished
agile . . . 4. fast, spry 5. alert, brisk, quick,
ready, swift 6. active, lively, nimble,
prompt, supple 7. lissome, springe
11. expeditious
aging . . . 6. doting, fading 8. maturing,
ripening 9. mellowing, senescent
10. senescence
agio . . . 7. premium 8. discount, exchange
9. brokerage 13. money changing

agitate . . . 3. fan, jar, wey 4. fret, move,
plot, rile, stir 5. alarm, churn, rouse,
shake, upset 6. debate, devise, excite,
foment, incite, ruffle 7. canvass, perturb,
revolve, trouble 8. disquiet, distract,
distress 10. discompose
agitated . . . 7. anxious, excited, ruffled
8. alarming, troubled 9. disturbed,
perturbed, turbulent 10. distressed
11. discomposed, overwrought
agitation . . . 4. fury, rage, stir 5. alarm,
storm 6. debate, dither, foment, frenzy,
furore, hubbub, tumult, unrest, uproar
7. anxiety, flutter, shaking, turmoil
8. disorder, distress, upheaval, vexation
9. commotion, trepidity 10. discussion,
excitement, incitement, turbulence
11. disturbance, fomentation,
trepidation 12. deliberation,
perturbation, restlessness
agnate . . . 3. sib 4. akin 6. allied
7. connate, kindred, related (father's
side) 10. equiparent 11. correlative
14. consanguineous
agnomen . . . 4. name 5. alias, nomen
7. epithet, surname 8. nickname
agnus castus (Eccl) . . . 4. lamb 6. chaste
14. tree of chastity
Agnus Dei, Lamb of God . . . 4. disk
6. anthem, prayer 7. the Mass (part)
ago, agone . . . 2. by 4. erst, gone, over,
past, yore 5. since 6. bygone, passed
7. extinct
agog . . . 4. avid, keen 5. agape, astir, eager
6. lively, wonder 7. all eyes, curious,
excited, zestful 8. open-eyed, vigilant
9. expectant, impatient 10. astonished,
breathless
agonize . . . 4. pain, rack 6. grieve, harrow,
strive 7. crucify, torture 8. struggle
10. excruciate
agony . . . 4. pain, pang, rack 5. grief,
gripe, panic, throe 7. anguish, torment,
torture 8. distress 9. suffering
11. crucifixion
agrarian . . . 5. rural 6. rustic, sylvan
(silvan) 7. bucolic, hoosier 8. agrestic,
Arcadian, frontier, pastoral
10. campestral, hinterland, provincial
11. countrified 12. agricultural
agree . . . 3. fit 4. give, jive, make, rime,
side 5. chime, ditto, grant, match,
rhyme, tally 6. accede, accord, assent,
commit, comply, concur, engage,
submit 7. bargain, comport, concede,
conform, consent, promise 8. coincide,
contract 9. acquiesce, harmonize,
stipulate 10. coordinate, correspond
agreeable . . . 4. nice 5. amene, sapid,
suave 6. comely, dulcet, savory
7. amiable, likable, welcome, willing
8. charming, friendly, obliging, pleasant,
pleasing 9. accordant, compliant,
desirable, indulgent 10. acceptable,
compatible, concordant, consenting,
euphonious, harmonious
11. conformable, considerate
12. reconcilable, satisfactory
agreement . . . 4. mise, pact 5. terms
6. accord, assent, cartel, parity,
treaty, unison 7. bargain, compact,

concord, consent, entente, promise,
rapport 8. contract, covenant, identity
9. accession, consensus
10. accordment, comparison,
compliance, conformity, similarity
11. coincidence, concurrence,
parallelism, stipulation
agrestic . . . 5. rural 6. rustic 7. bucolic
8. pastoral 10. provincial
agriculture . . . 7. culture, farming, tillage
8. agrology, agronomy 9. husbandry
10. agrotechny 11. cultivation
13. sharecropping
agriculture (pert to) . . .
goddess of . . 3. Ops 4. Gaea (Gaia)
5. Ceres, Flora 6. Pomona, Vacuna
7. Demeter
god of . . 4. Nabu, Nebo 6. Faunus
8. Dionysus
means of . . 3. hoe 4. plow (plough)
6. harrow, header, reaper, seeder
7. combine, planter, tractor 8. thrasher
10. cultivator 11. caterpillar
ref to . . 7. georgic
science, crop growing . . 11. arviculture
terms . . 5. arado, grove, ranch, thorp
6. garden, hamlet 7. cropper, orchard
8. haymaker, vineyard 9. homestead
agriculturist . . . 6. farmer 7. planter
10. agricolist, husbandman
Agrippina's son . . . 4. Nero
agrise . . . 5. abhor, dread 6. loathe
7. shudder, terrify, tremble 8. affright
agronomy, study of . . . 11. agriculture
aground . . . 5. stuck 6. ashore
7. swamped, wrecked 8. grounded,
stranded 10. high and dry
agrypnia . . . 5. vigil 8. insomnia
13. sleeplessness
agua . . . 4. toad 5. water
aguacate . . . 7. avocado
ague . . . 5. chill, fever 7. disease, malaria,
shaking, shivers 9. shivering
ague tree . . . 9. sassafras
agueweed . . . 7. boneset, gentian
Ahab (pert to) . . .
daughter . . 7. Athalie
king of . . 6. Israel
wife . . 7. Jezebel
ahead . . . 2. on 3. pre (pref) 4. fore
5. afore, early 6. before, onward
7. advance, forward, leading
10. successful, surpassing
ahoy . . . 4. hail, yo-ho 5. hello 8. ship
ahoy 9. attention
ahu . . . 5. mound 7. gazelle 8. memorial
ai . . . 5. sloth 11. exclamation
aid . . . 4. abet, aide, help, pony 5. allay,
devil (printer's), favor, serve 6. assist,
helper, incite, relief, remedy, succor
7. benefit, service, stipend, subsidy,
support 8. befriend, ministry
9. alleviate, allowance, assistant
10. assistance, benefactor
11. countenance 13. accommodation
aim . . . 3. end, fix, way 4. bent,
goal, plan 5. point, scope 6. aspire,
direct, intend, intent, object, strive
7. bearing, current, meaning, purpose
8. endeavor 9. direction, intention,
objective 11. destination

aimful ... 8. aspiring 10. purposeful
aimless ... 4. idle 5. blind, loose
6. chance, random 8. drifting
9. desultory, orderless, senseless
10. designless, unarranged, undirected
11. meaningless, purposeless,
unorganized
aine ... 5. elder 6. senior
air ... 3. gas, oam, sky 4. aria, aura,
mien, tune, wind 5. draft, ether, ozone,
vapor 6. aerate, aerial, aspect, breath,
breeze, bubble, manner, melody,
oxygen 7. aerator, bearing, climate,
display, hyaline, posture, publish,
refresh 8. attitude, aviation, behavior,
buoyance, demeanor, hydrogen,
presence 9. lightness, publicize,
ventilate 10. appearance, atmosphere,
deportment, navigation 11. haughtiness
12. stratosphere
air (pert to) ...
  disease.. 5. bends 7. caisson
  12. aeroembolism
  music.. 4. aria, lilt, solo, tune 6. melody
  7. arietta, sortita
  passage.. 4. duct, flue, vent 7. pharynx
  9. ventiduct
  pressure unit.. 8. millebar
  stone.. 8. aerolite 9. meteorite
  term.. 5. aural 6. flight, flying 9. jet
  stream, katabatic 11. aeronautics
  tight.. 5. close, proof 6. sealed
  7. compact 8. hermetic 9. resistant
  11. impermeable
  travel.. 6. jet lag 7. skyjack
aircraft ... 3. jet 4. kite, link 5. avion,
blimp 6. bomber, glider 7. airship,
aviette, balloon, biplane, chopper
8. airplane, jetliner, triplane, turbojet,
zeppelin 9. amphibian, dirigible, fixed-
wing, monoplane, orthopter, simulator,
spaceship, transport, turboprop
10. helicopter, hydroplane, whirlybird
aircraft (pert to) ...
  carrier.. 7. flattop
  designer.. 8. Sikorsky
  formation.. 5. fleet 7. echelon
  inventor.. 6. Wright (Brothers)
  motorless.. 6. glider
  part.. 3. fin, pod 4. keel, tail, wing
  5. rotor 6. cabane 7. aileron, cockpit,
  nacelle 8. fusilage 9. empennage (tail)
airily ... 5. gaily 6. thinly 7. lightly, loftily
8. jauntily 10. delicately
13. pretentiously 14. ostentatiously
airiness ... 6. rarity 7. tenuity 8. delicacy
9. gauziness, gustiness, lightness,
loftiness, unreality, windiness
10. breeziness, jauntiness
16. lightheartedness, unsubstantiality
airing ... 4. walk 8. exposure
air mail ... 8. par avion
airport (pert to) ... 4. beam, dock, gate,
shed, taxi 5. apron, pylon, tower
6. hangar, runway, skycap 7. airpost,
fairway, jetport, taxiway 8. airfield,
airstrip, heliport 9. aerodrome
(airdrome), helidrome
airy ... 3. gay 4. aery, cool, rare,
thin 5. foamy, light, lofty, merry,
windy 6. aerial, breezy, drafty, frothy,

jaunty, lively 7. gaseous, haughty,
soaring 8. animated, aspiring, delicate,
ethereal, fanciful, feathery, flippant,
towering, volatile 9. gossamery,
vivacious 10. chimerical, phantasmal
11. atmospheric 12. lighthearted,
ostentatious
aiseweed ... 8. goutweed
aisle ... 4. lane, nave 5. alley 6. artery,
avenue 7. passage 8. corridor
10. passageway
ait, eyot ... 3. oat 4. holm, isle, reef
5. atoll, islet 6. island
aitu ... 3. god 5. demon 6. spirit
Aix ... 4. duck
aizle ... 4. soot 5. ember, spark
Ajax (pert to) ...
  called.. 11. Ajax the Less (next swiftest
  to Achilles)
  father.. 7. Telamen
  hero of.. 8. The Iliad (Homer)
ajonjoli ... 6. sesame
a k a ... 5. alias
akimbo ... 4. bent 6. angled, hooked
7. angular, crooked
akin ... 3. sib 4. like, near 5. close
6. agnate, allied 7. cognate, germane,
kindred, related, similar 9. connected
10. correlated 14. consanguineous
ala ... 4. wing 8. winglike
a la ... 2. so 4. thus 11. identically 13. in
the manner of
Alabama ...
  capital.. 10. Montgomery
  Capitol, Confederate (2 months)..
  10. White House (1st 1861)
  carnival.. 11. Azalea Trail
  city.. 6. Mobile 7. Gadsden
  10. Birmingham
  monument.. 11. Russell Cave
  museum.. 22. George Washington
  Carver
  native woman (famed).. 11. Helen Keller
  President Confederate.. 5. Davis
  (Jefferson)
  State admission.. 12. Twenty-second
  State bird.. 12. yellowhammer
  State flower.. 8. camellia
  State motto.. 21. We Dare Defend Our
  Rights
  State nickname.. 12. Heart of Dixie
  statue (huge).. 6. Vulcan
alabaster ... 6. gypsum, marble
7. mineral
alacrity ... 4. zest 7. avidity 9. briskness,
eagerness, immediacy, quickness,
readiness, swiftness 10. promptness
11. promptitude, punctuality,
willingness 13. sprightliness
Aladdin (pert to) ...
  possessor of (magic).. 4. lamp, ring
  spirit (of Magic).. 4. jinn
  window.. 4. task (impossible)
  youth (character).. 13. Arabian Nights
á la diable ... 7. deviled (devilled)
8. seasoned
alameda ... 4. mall, walk 5. prado
9. esplanade, promenade
Alamo ... 6. poplar (tree) 7. Mission
(San Antonio, Tex)
a la mode ... 4. mode 5. smart 6. modish,

spruce **7.** fashion, stylish, voguish
8. up-to-date **9.** stylishly **11.** fashionably
12. with ice cream
alan . . . **3.** dog (Her)
alar (pert to) . . . **4.** wing **6.** pteric
8. axillary, shoulder
alarm . . . **3.** din **4.** call, fear, flap
5. alert, broil, clock, daunt, panic,
scare **6.** alarum, arouse, dismay, fright,
terror, tocsin **7.** startle, terrify, warning
8. affright, frighten **11.** trepidation
12. apprehension **13.** consternation
alarmist . . . **6.** scarer **9.** pessimist, terrorist
10. frightener **11.** scaremonger
alas . . . **2.** ah, ay, oh **3.** ach, heu, och
4. oime **5.** alack, ohone **6.** dear me
7. woe is me **8.** lackaday
Alaska . . . see also *Alaskan*
capital . . **6.** Juneau
city . . **4.** Nome **5.** Sitka **7.** Skagway
9. Anchorage, Fairbanks, Ketchikan
discoverer . . **11.** Vitus Bering
fish . . **6.** salmon, wachna **7.** inconnu
glacier . . **4.** Muir
highway . . **5.** Alcan **6.** Alaska
island . . **6.** Kodiak, Unimak **7.** Diomede
(Little), Nunivak **9.** Aleutians, Probilofs
mountain . . **3.** Ada **7.** Foraker **8.** McKinley
(highest in N Am), Wrangell
northernmost point . . **11.** Point Barrow
oil region . . **10.** Prudhoe Bay
peninsula . . **5.** Kenai **6.** Seward
port (oil) . . **6.** Valdez
rapids . . **10.** Whitehorse
river . . **5.** Yukon **9.** Kuskokwim
State admission . . **10.** Forty-ninth
State bird . . **9.** (willow) ptarmigan
State flower . . **11.** forget-me-not
State symbol . . **9.** bald eagle
strait . . **6.** Bering
volcano . . **6.** Katmai **8.** Wrangell
Alaskan (pert to) . . .
boat . . **5.** kayak, umiak **7.** bidarka
(bidarkee)
codfish . . **6.** wachna
liquor . . **9.** hoochinoo
people . . **3.** Aht **5.** Aleut, Haida, Tinna
6. Ahtena, Eskimo **7.** Tlingit **8.** Aleutian
9. Tsimpsean **10.** Athapascan
albacore . . . **4.** tuna **5.** tunny **6.** bonito,
germon
Albania . . .
capital . . **6.** Tirana
city . . **5.** Berat **6.** Durres, Valona **7.** Scutari
8. Elbasani
dialect . . **4.** Gheg, Tosk
lake . . **6.** Prespa **7.** Scutari
mountain . . **5.** Koreb **6.** Pindus
river . . **4.** Drin **6.** Bojana
soldier . . **7.** palikar
triba . . **4.** Cham
albatross . . . **5.** nelly (sooty) **6.** burden
7. pelican **9.** mallemuck
albatross around the neck . . . **6.** burden
8. distress (cause of)
albe (anc) . . . **5.** album
albert (pert to) . . .
jewelry . . **10.** watch chain
medal . . **4.** gold (for bravery)
Albion . . . **7.** England (Poet)
albumin . . . **5.** glair **7.** protein

9. endosperm
alcazar . . . **6.** palace **8.** fortress
alchemy . . . **5.** magic **6.** change **7.** sorcery
10. changeover, conversion
alcohol . . . **5.** drink **6.** liquor **7.** ethanol,
spirits, talitol, terpene **8.** beverage
9. aqua vitae, firewater **10.** intoxicant
alcoholic beverage . . . **3.** gin, rum
4. beer, brew, grog, malt, mead,
wine **5.** booze, hooch, negus, punch,
vodka **6.** arrack (arrak), brandy, mao-
tai, whisky (whiskey) **7.** bourbon,
cordial, liqueur, tequila **8.** champers
(Brit sl), cocktail, highball **9.** applejack,
champagne, moonshine
alcoholism . . . **9.** addiction, oenomania
10. dipsomania **11.** drunkenness
12. intoxication
Alcott character . . . **2.** Jo **3.** Amy, Meg
4. Beth
alcove . . . **3.** bay **4.** cove, nook **5.** arbor,
bower, kiosk, niche, oriel **6.** carrel,
recess **7.** cubicle, dinette, pergola
8. alhacena
alder (pert to) . . .
chief . . **5.** ruler **6.** prince
fishing . . **3.** fly (artificial)
tree . . **8.** sagerose (yellow)
ale . . . **3.** mum **4.** beer, flip **5.** stout
6. alegar, liquor (malt) **8.** festival
alee . . . **7.** leeward (opp of windward)
Aleppo (pert to) . . .
city . . **5.** Syria
grass . . **7.** Johnson
stone . . **3.** gem **5.** agate **8.** eye agate
alert . . . **4.** keen, warn, wary **5.** agile,
alarm, alive, aware, brisk, peart (pert),
quick, ready, sharp **6.** active, bright,
lively, nimble, prompt **7.** guarded
8. vigilant, watchful **9.** attentive,
observant, sprightly, wide-awake
11. circumspect
Aleut . . . **4.** Atka **6.** Eskimo **7.** Unungun
8. Unalaska
Aleutians . . .
islands (chain) . . **8.** volcanic
native of . . **5.** Aleut
site . . **6.** Alaska **9.** Bering Sea
alewife . . . **4.** fish **7.** herring, pompano,
walleye **9.** gaspereau
Alexander the Great (pert to) . . .
birthplace . . **5.** Pella (Macedonia)
conqueror of . . **6.** Persia
expedition . . **10.** Hellespont
horse . . **10.** Bucephalus
Alexandria, Egypt . . .
bishop . . **5.** Arius **10.** Athanasius
12. Eratosthenes
island . . **6.** Pharos
obelisks . . **17.** Cleopatra's Needles (now
in NY City & London)
ruler . . **7.** Ptolemy
world wonder . . **10.** Lighthouse (Pharos)
alfa . . . **5.** grass **7.** esparto
alfalfa . . . **3.** hay **5.** medic **6.** clover,
fodder **7.** lucerne (lucern)
alforja . . . **3.** bag **5.** pouch **6.** wallet
9. saddlebag
alfresco . . . **4.** airy **7.** open-air, outside
alga, algae . . . **4.** cell, moss, nori
5. Dasya, fungi **6.** Alaria, diatom, fungus

7. seaweed 8. plankton 9. spirulina, stonewort

Algeria . . .
capital . . **7.** Algiers
Mohammedan saint . . **8.** Marabout
monastery . . **5.** ribat
mountain . . **5.** Atlas (Range)
native . . **5.** Arabs **7.** Berbers, Kabyles
ruler . . **3.** bey, dey
ship . . **5.** xebec
soldier . . **5.** spahi (spahee) **6.** Zouave

algid . . . **3.** icy **4.** cold **5.** brisk, crisp, nippy **6.** frigid, frosty, wintry **7.** ice-cold

algodon . . . **6.** cotton

algology, study of . . . **5.** algae **8.** seaweeds

Algonquian spirit . . . **6.** manito (manitou)

Algonquian people . . . **4.** Cree, Sauk **5.** Miami **6.** Ottawa **7.** Arapaho, Ojibway, Shawnee **8.** Cheyenne, Delaware **9.** Blackfoot

Alhambra (pert to) . . .
architecture . . **7.** Moorish
palace, alcazar of . . **12.** Moorish Kings
site . . **7.** Granada (Spain)

alias . . . **6.** anonym **7.** epithet **8.** cognomen, nickname **9.** otherwise, pseudonym, sobriquet

Ali Baba (pert to) . . .
adventurer . . **4.** cave (Forty Thieves)
password to cave . . **6.** Sesame
tale . . **13.** Arabian Nights

alien . . . **3.** ger **5.** fremd **6.** exotic, remote **7.** adverse, foreign, hostile, opposed, strange **8.** outsider, stranger **9.** foreigner, peregrine, unrelated **10.** extraneous, unfriendly **11.** incongruous

alienate . . . **4.** part, wean **6.** demise, detach, devest, divest, divide **8.** disunite, estrange, separate

alienation . . . **4.** outs **5.** split **6.** breach **8.** disfavor **10.** conveyance, falling-out, withdrawal **12.** amortization, disaffection, estrangement

alienist . . . **12.** psychiatrist

aliform . . . **8.** winglike **10.** wing-shaped

alight . . . **4.** land, rest, stop **5.** ditch, lodge, perch **6.** settle **7.** burning, descend, lighted **8.** dismount

align, aline . . . **4.** true **5.** level, match **6.** equate, line up **7.** arrange, marshal **10.** collineate, straighten **11.** parallelize

alike . . . **3.** iso (comb form) **4.** akin, like, same, twin **7.** similar, uniform **8.** selfsame **9.** duplicate, identical **10.** homonymous **17.** indistinguishable

aliment . . . **4.** food, keep **5.** broma, manna **7.** nurture, pabulum, support **9.** nutriment, nutrition, refection **10.** sustenance **11.** nourishment, refreshment

alimentary canal, part . . . **5.** mouth **7.** pharynx, stomach **9.** esophagus, intestine

alimony . . . **7.** stipend **8.** estovers **9.** allotment

aline . . . see *align*

alipin . . . **5.** slave (Phil)

alipod . . . **3.** bat **10.** wing-footed

aliquid . . . **8.** somewhat **9.** something

aliquot . . . **4.** part **5.** prime **7.** decimal, digital, divisor, partial **10.** fractional, reciprocal **11.** submultiple (opp of aliquant)

alive . . . **3.** vif **4.** keen **5.** alert, awake, brisk, vital **6.** extant, lively, loving, zoetic **7.** animate, current, topical **8.** animated, existent **9.** breathing, conscious, sensitive, sprightly **11.** clear-witted, unforgotten

alkali . . . **3.** lye **4.** salt, soda **8.** saltwort

alkaline . . . **3.** reh **4.** usar **6.** alkali **7.** antacid, nonacid

alkaline forming . . . **10.** kaligenous

alkaloid . . . **6.** codein, conine, eserin **7.** aricine, caffein, cocaine, codeine **8.** atropine, morphine **10.** strychnine **13.** physostigmine

alkaloid (pert to) . . .
bark . . **7.** aricine
bean . . **13.** physostigmine
beverage . . **8.** caffeine (caffein)
drug . . **7.** cocaine, codeine, eucaine **8.** morphine **10.** strychnine
extract . . **6.** curare (curari) **11.** arrow poison
hemlock . . **7.** coniine
ipecac . . **7.** emetine
lupine . . **8.** lupinine
mustard seed . . **7.** sinapin

all . . . **3.** pan (pref), sum **4.** omni (pref), only, toto **5.** alone, every, sum of, total, tutti, whole **6.** entire, wholly **7.** perfect **8.** ensemble, entirely, totality **9.** aggregate, everybody **10.** altogether, completely, everything, thoroughly **11.** exclusively

all (pert to) . . .
absorbing . . **4.** main **5.** chief, prime **6.** ruling **7.** capital, leading, primary **8.** foremost **9.** paramount, principal **11.** controlling
around . . **5.** handy **9.** versatile
devouring . . **6.** greedy **9.** rapacious **10.** gluttonous
in all . . **9.** generally **10.** on the whole
inclusive . . **6.** global **7.** omneity **8.** catholic, ecumenic, pandemic **9.** universal **12.** cosmopolitan
knowing . . **4.** wise **6.** divine **10.** omniscient
powerful . . **6.** divine **7.** all-wise, supreme **8.** absolute, almighty **9.** all-seeing **10.** all-knowing, omnipotent, omniscient, ubiquitous
the same . . **9.** identical **10.** equivalent **12.** nevertheless
together . . **7.** en masse

Allah . . . **3.** God **5.** deity **12.** Supreme Being

allay . . . **4.** cool, ease **5.** abate, check, slake **6.** pacify, soothe, subdue **7.** appease, assuage, compose, relieve, repress, satisfy **8.** moderate **9.** alleviate

allée . . . **4.** mall, walk **5.** aisle **6.** avenue **7.** passage

allege . . . **4.** aver, cite **5.** offer, plead, quote, state **6.** adduce, affirm, assert, assign **7.** advance, ascribe, declare, present, pretend, profess, propose **8.** maintain **9.** attribute

allegiance . . . **3.** tie **4.** bond **5.** faith, liege **6.** fealty, homage **7.** loyalty **8.** devotion, fidelity, firmness **9.** adherence, constancy **12.** faithfulness **13.** steadfastness

allegory . . . **5.** fable, story **6.** emblem **7.** parable **8.** apologue

alleviate . . . **4.** ease **5.** abate, allay, erase, quiet, salve, slake **6.** lessen, pacify, reduce, soften, solace, soothe **7.** assuage, compose, lighten, relieve **8.** mitigate, moderate, palliate **9.** extenuate **11.** tranquilize

alley . . . **3.** mig (marble), way **4.** lane, mall, path, slum **5.** aisle, byway, tewer **6.** arcade, artery, byroad **8.** cul-de-sac

alliance . . . **4.** pact **5.** union **6.** fusion, league, treaty **7.** compact, entente **8.** affinity, agnation, covenant **9.** coalition **10.** federation **11.** association, combination, confederacy **13.** confederation

allied . . . **4.** akin **6.** agnate, linked, united **7.** cognate, germane, kindred, leagued, related, similar **10.** associated, correlated

alligator . . . **5.** gator, niger **6.** Caiman, cayman, jacare (yacare) **7.** lagarto **9.** crocodile

alligator pear . . . **7.** avocado **8.** aguacate

alliteration . . . **4.** rime **5.** rhyme **6.** jingle **9.** assonance **10.** repetition

allocate . . . **4.** deal, mete **5.** allot **6.** assign, locate, ordain **7.** appoint, arrange, consign, reserve **9.** apportion **10.** distribute

allocation . . . **8.** disposal **9.** billeting **11.** collocation, disposition **12.** distribution

allot . . . **3.** fix **4.** cast, dole, mete **5.** grant **6.** assign, billet, design, intend, ordain, ration, select **7.** appoint, destine, specify **9.** apportion, attribute, prescribe **11.** appropriate

allotment . . . **5.** cavel, share **6.** ration **7.** subsidy **10.** allocation, assignment, ordainment **13.** apportionment

allow . . . **3.** let **4.** bear, give **5.** admit, think **6.** endure, permit, rebate, suffer **7.** approve, concede, suppose **8.** consider, discount, tolerate **9.** authorize **11.** acknowledge

allowance . . . **3.** fee **4.** tare, tret **5.** arras, grant **6.** ration **7.** pension, scalage, stipend **8.** appenage (prince's), discount, granting, sanction **9.** admitting, allotment, conceding, tolerance **10.** permission **11.** scholarship **13.** authorization

allowing for . . . **2.** if **8.** provided

allow to pass . . . **5.** lapse **6.** expire, revert

alloy . . . **3.** mix **4.** asem **5.** blend, mokum **6.** billon, fusion, oroide **7.** amalgam, bullion, corrupt, mixture **8.** compound **9.** composite **10.** adulterate, amalgamate

alloys . . .
copper, aluminum . . **9.** duralumin
copper, sulphur . . **6.** niello
copper, tin . . **6.** bronze

copper, white metal . . **6.** oroide
copper, zinc . . **5.** brass **6.** tombac
copper, zinc, iron . . **4.** Aich (Chin)
copper, zinc, nickel . . **4.** iron **7.** paktong (packtong)
copper, zinc, nickel, iron . . **7.** rheotan
German silver . . **6.** albata
gold, silver . . **4.** asem
iron, carbon . . **5.** steel
iron, nickel . . **6.** Calite (trademark)
lead, tin . . **6.** pewter, solder
nickel, steel . . **5.** Invar

All Saints' Day . . . **4.** Nov 1 **10.** Allhallows

allspice tree . . . **7.** pimento

alltud . . . **5.** alien, slave **9.** foreigner

allude . . . **4.** hint **5.** get at, imply, point, refer **6.** relate **7.** mention, suggest **8.** indicate, intimate **9.** insinuate

allure . . . **3.** win **4.** bait, draw, lead, lure, tice, tole **5.** charm, decoy, snare, tempt **6.** entice, entrap, invite, seduce **7.** attract, prevail **8.** inveigle, persuade **9.** captivate, fascinate, influence

allurement . . . **4.** bait, lure **5.** bride **7.** glamour (glamor) **8.** agacerie, coquetry **10.** attraction, enticement, inducement, temptation **12.** inveiglement

allusion . . . **4.** clue, hint **7.** inkling **8.** innuendo, instance **9.** reference **11.** implication

alluvial deposit . . . **3.** mud **4.** silt **5.** delta, geest **6.** placer

ally . . . **3.** pal **4.** aide, join **5.** union **6.** fellow, friend, league **7.** comrade, consort, kinsman, partner **8.** adherent, relative **9.** associate, attendant, colleague **10.** accomplice **11.** confederate **12.** collaborator

Alma (It) . . . **4.** soul **6.** spirit **10.** cherishing, nourishing

alma . . . **6.** fabric (silk)

almacen . . . **4.** shop **8.** magazine **9.** warehouse

Alma Mater . . . **6.** school **7.** college **9.** goddesses **10.** university

almanac . . . **5.** fasti **6.** record **7.** calends (kalends) **8.** calendar, register **9.** ephemeris (obs)

almighty . . . **5.** great **6.** divine **10.** omnipotent **11.** all-powerful **12.** irresistible

almond (pert to) . . .
confection . . **8.** marzipan
dish with . . **8.** amandine
liqueur . . **8.** amaretto

almost . . . **4.** most, nigh **5.** anear, close **6.** all but, nearly **8.** well-nigh **9.** nearabout **13.** approximately

alms . . . **4.** dole, mite **6.** aumous, bounty, corban, relief **7.** charity, handout **8.** donation, gratuity, pittance **12.** contribution, philanthropy

alms (pert to) . . .
box . . **4.** arca **5.** chest
giver . . **5.** donor **7.** almoner **11.** contributor **14.** philanthropist
man . . **5.** donee **6.** pauper **7.** feoffee **9.** pensioner

alodium . . . **4.** land **6.** tenure **8.** freehold **10.** real estate

aloe, aloes . . . 4. drug 5. agave, plant
  6. tambac 7. incense 8. agalloch
aloft . . . 2. up 4. high, over 5. aloof
  7. skyward 8. overhead
aloha . . . 4. hail, love 7. good-bye
  9. affection, greetings 11. salutations
Aloha State . . . 6. Hawaii
aloin . . . 4. drug 5. aloes 8. nataloin
  9. barbaloin (Barbados) 12. isobarbaloin
alone . . . 4. solo 5. apart, solus 6. single,
  singly, solely, unique 8. desolate,
  homeless, isolated, separate, solitary
  9. exclusive, matchless 10. unassisted
  12. single-handed 13. companionless,
  independently, unaccompanied
along . . . 2. on 3. via 4. with 6. beside,
  onward 7. forward 8. together
alongside . . . 2. by 4. near 6. beside
  7. abreast 8. parallel
aloof . . . 6. offish, remote 7. distant,
  haughty 8. reserved 10. unsociable
  11. indifferent, standoffish
  15. uncommunicative
aloofness . . . 7. reserve 10. offishness,
  remoteness 11. haughtiness
  12. indifference 13. unsociability
alopecia . . . 6. acomia 8. baldness
  12. hairlessness
aloud . . . 4. oral 6. loudly 7. audibly,
  plainly
alp . . . 3. tor 4. peak, pico, pike 6. summit
  8. mountain 9. bullfinch
alp (Teut Folklore) . . . 5. demon, witch
  9. nightmare
alpaca . . . 4. coat, paco 5. llama
  7. garment
Alph . . . 11. sacred river (Kubla Khan)
alpha . . . 4. star 5. prime 6. letter 7. initial,
  numeral 9. beginning
alphabet . . . 4. ABC's 6. Sarada (Kashmir)
  9. abecedary 10. Davanagari (Sanskrit)
alphabet characters (Teut) . . . 4. ogam,
  rune
alphabetize . . . 4. file 5. group, index
  6. codify, letter 8. classify, tabulate
  9. catalogue (catalog) 10. categorize
alpha test (Army) . . . 12. intelligence
alpine . . . 5. alpen, hilly 6. knobby
  10. alpestrine 11. mountainous
Alpine (pert to) . . .
  climber . . 10. alpestrian
  dance . . 7. gavotte (gavot)
  dress . . 6. dirndl
  dwelling . . 6. chalet
  goat . . 4. ibex
  herdsman . . 4. senn
  peak . . 5. Blanc 9. Monte Rosa
    10. Matterhorn
  plant . . 9. edelweiss
  province . . 5. Tyrol
  shelter . . 7. hospice
  snowfield . . 4. firn, neve
  tunnel . . 7. Simplon 10. St Gotthard
  wind . . 4. bise 5. foehn
Alps . . . 5. Blanc, Tirol (Tyrol) 6. Julian
  7. Dinaric 8. Jungfrau 9. Dolomites,
  Monte Rosa (peak) 10. Matterhorn
already . . . 3. ere, yet 5. afore 6. before
  7. earlier 8. hitherto 10. heretofore
  11. theretofore
also . . . 2. as, et, so 3. and, too, yet

4. more, plus 7. besides, further
  8. likewise, moreover 9. similarly
  11. furthermore
altar (pert to) . . .
  boy . . 7. acolyte
  cloth . . 6. dossal (dossel) 7. haploma
    9. ependytes
  constellation . . 3. Ara
  curtain . . 6. riddel
  end of church . . 4. apse 7. chancel
  Greek . . 5. bomos 6. hestia 7. eschara
  Latin . . 7. scrobis
  ledge . . 7. retable
  platform . . 8. predella
  screen . . 7. reredos
  shelf, table . . 6. gradin 7. retable
    8. credence
  step . . 8. predella
  top slab . . 5. mensa
alter . . . 4. geld, vary, veer 5. amend,
  emend, reset, shift 6. adjust, change,
  immute, modify, mutate, revise 7. falsify
  8. castrate 9. transform
alteration . . . 6. change 9. diversity,
  variation 10. castration, correction
  12. modification 13. interpolation
  15. diversification
altercation . . . 3. row 4. feud, spat,
  tiff 5. fight, snarl 6. fracas, strife
  7. dispute, quarrel, wrangle 8. squabble,
  vendetta 9. imbroglio 10. contention
  11. controversy
alter ego . . . 4. mate, self, twin 7. oneself
  10. complement 11. counterpart
alternate . . . 4. vary 5. proxy 6. change,
  deputy, rotate, seesaw 7. reverse,
  stand-in 8. delegate 9. oscillate
  10. substitute 11. alternative,
  interchange, reciprocate
alternate writing mode (anc) . . .
  13. boustrophedon
alternative . . . 2. or 3. nor 5. other
  6. choice, either, option, switch
  7. dilemma 8. election, loophole
  9. secondary 10. nip-and-tuck,
  preference, substitute 11. replacement
although, altho . . . 4. even, when 5. while
  6. albeit, though 7. despite, whereas
  15. notwithstanding
altimetry . . . 6. height 10. hypsometry
  11. measurement
altitude . . . 6. height (highth) 7. heroics,
  stature 8. eminence, highness, tallness
  9. elevation, loftiness
altogether . . . 5. fully, quite 6. bodily,
  wholly 7. utterly 8. entirely, outright
  9. generally 10. completely, thoroughly
  12. collectively
alto horn . . . 7. althorn, saxhorn
  10. mellophone
altruism . . . 7. charity, concern 8. kindness
  11. beneficence, benevolence
  12. philanthropy
aluminum ore . . . 7. bauxite
alumnus (alumni) . . . 4. grad 5. pupil
  6. alumna (alumnae) 8. graduate,
  postgrad 12. postgraduate
alveary . . . 4. hive 6. apiary 7. beehive
alveola . . . 3. dip, pit 4. pore, sink 6. crater,
  pocket
alveolar . . . 6. pitted, pocked 7. notched

8. indented 9. depressed
always . . . 2. ay 3. aye, e'er 4. ever
6. anyway, semper 7. forever
8. evermore 9. eternally, uniformly
10. constantly, invariably
11. continually, everlasting, perpetually,
universally
ama . . . 4. tree 5. amula (Bib) 6. vessel
amabile . . . 6. gentle, tender 9. agreeable
Amadis de Gaul (Arthurian) . . . 4. hero
5. lover
amadou . . . 4. punk 6. tinder 7. styptic
amah . . . 5. nurse 7. servant 9. nursemaid
11. maidservant
amain . . . 5. apace 7. hastily, quickly,
swiftly 9. posthaste
amalgamate . . . 3. mix 4. fuse, join,
weld 5. blend, merge, unite 6. commix
7. combine 8. coalesce, compound,
intermix 11. consolidate
amalgamation . . . 6. fusion, merger
7. mixture 11. combination
Amalkite . . . 4. Agag (King) 5. nomad
7. Bedouin
amant . . . 5. lover 6. amante
amaryllis . . . 4. bulb, lily 5. agave, plant
6. flower 8. mistress 10. sweetheart
11. shepherdess
amass . . . 4. save 5. hoard, stack, store
6. gather 7. collect 8. assemble
10. accumulate
amate . . . 5. daunt 6. subdue
10. dishearten
amateur . . . 3. ham 4. tyro 6. novice
7. dabbler, fancier 8. beginner, virtuoso
10. aficionado, apprentice, dilettante
15. nonprofessional
amateurish . . . 5. inapt 9. unskilled,
untrained, untutored 10. unfinished
15. nonprofessional
Amati . . . 6. family, violin
amatory . . . 4. fond 6. ardent, erotic,
loving, tender 7. amorous, philter
9. loverlike 10. passionate
amaze . . . 3. awe 4. stun 7. astound,
perplex, stagger, startle, stupefy
8. astonish, bewilder, confound,
surprise 9. dumbfound, overwhelm
amazement . . . 3. awe 5. alarm 6. wonder
8. surprise 10. perplexity
12. bewilderment 13. consternation
Amazon . . . 5. Queen (Myth), river
6. virago 9. androgyne 10. warrioress
11. Penthesilea
Amazon river (pert to) . . .
  cetacean . . 4. Inia
  discoverer . . 6. Pinzon (1500)
  mouth . . 4. Para
  rain forest . . 5. selva
  tributary . . 3. Apa 4. Napo
ambary . . . 2. da 4. hemp 5. fiber 6. Nolita
ambassador . . . 5. envoy 6. legate,
nuncio 8. diplomat, emissary, minister
9. messenger 12. intermediary
14. representative 15. plenipotentiary
amber . . . 6. yellow 8. electrum
ambidextrous . . . 7. capable 8. two-faced
9. two-handed, versatile
11. ambidextral, treacherous 13. double-
dealing
ambiguous . . . 6. double 7. Delphic,

dubious 9. equivocal, uncertain,
unsettled 10. indefinite, indistinct,
mistakable 12. questionable
13. indeterminate
ambit . . . 5. orbit, scope 6. extent, sphere
7. circuit 8. precinct
ambition . . . 4. goal, spur 6. desire
10. aspiration
amble . . . 4. pace, rack, trot 7. piaffer
ambrosia . . . 4. food 5. honey, manna
6. nectar 7. perfume 8. delicacy, libation
ambulate . . . 4. hike, move, walk
ambush . . . 4. trap 5. snare 6. hiding,
waylay 7. mantrap 9. ambuscade
10. subterfuge 11. concealment
ameliorate . . . 4. ease, mend 5. emend
6. better 7. improve 8. progress
9. meliorate
amelioration . . . 10. betterment
11. improvement, restoration
amenable . . . 6. liable, pliant 7. movable
9. receptive 10. answerable, open-
minded, responsive 11. accountable,
persuadable, responsible
amend . . . 4. beat (dial), beet (beete)
5. alter, atone, emend 6. reform, repeal
7. convert, correct, improve, rectify,
redress, restore
amendment . . . 5. rider 8. addition
10. conversion, correction
11. improvement, reformation
amends . . . 7. redress 8. reprisal
9. atonement 10. recompense,
reparation 11. restitution
amenities . . . 5. mores 7. decorum,
manners 9. etiquette 10. civilities,
courtesies 11. formalities, gentilities,
proprieties
ament . . . 6. catkin 7. cattail
American (pert to) . . .
  bear . . 7. musquaw (black)
  buffalo . . 5. bison
  cactus . . 4. bleo 7. saguaro
  carnivore . . 4. puma
  cataract . . 7. Niagara (Falls)
  cedar (red) . . 5. savin
  elk . . 6. wapiti
  Japanese . . 5. Nisei 6. Kibbei
  leopard . . 6. ocelot
  marsupial . . 7. opossum
  merganser . . 4. duck (fish-eating)
  Mexican . . 6. gringo
  mink . . 5. vison
  moth . . 2. io
  nickname . . 6. Yankee (Yank)
  ostrich . . 4. rhea
  palm . . 5. Sabal 8. palmetto
  quail . . 5. colin
  rail . . 4. sora
  squirrel . . 9. chickaree (red)
  vulture . . 5. urubu 6. condor
American, famed . . .
  architect . . 3. Pei 6. Wright 7. Johnson,
  Venturi 8. Sullivan
  artist . . 4. Cole, West 5. Homer, Marsh,
  Mount, Peale, Wyeth 6. Benton,
  Demuth, Hopper, O'Keefe, Rivers,
  Stuart, Warhol 7. Bellows, Bingham,
  Gropper, Pollock, Sargent 8. Rockwell
  9. Remington 10. Burchfield
  chemist . . 6. Carver (G Washington)

composer.. **4.** Ives, Kern **5.** Grofé, Sousa
  6. Barber, Foster **7.** Copland, Rodgers
  (Richard) **8.** Gershwin **9.** Bernstein,
  Ellington
crusader (Temperance).. **12.** Carrie
  Nation
doctor, surgeon.. **4.** Mayo **6.** Schick
  7. Cushing
dramatist.. **4.** Rice **5.** Albee, Odets
  6. Miller, O'Neill, Wilder **8.** Williams
  (Tennessee)
educator.. **4.** Hume, Mann **5.** Eliot
  10. Washington (Booker T)
explorer.. **4.** Byrd **5.** Boone, Clark, Lewis,
  Peary **6.** Carson (Kit) **9.** Ellsworth
naturalist.. **4.** Muir **5.** Beebe **7.** Audubon,
  Burbank
patriot.. **4.** Clay, Hale, Otis **5.** Dawes,
  Henry (Patrick), Paine (Thomas)
  6. Revere
physicist.. **6.** Teller (H-bomb)
pianist.. **5.** Blake (Eubie), Tatum
  6. Duchin, Levant, Morton (Jelly Roll)
  7. Cliburn (Van) **8.** Horowitz, Liberace
  10. Gottschalk
poet.. **5.** Auden, Eliot, Frost, Pound
  6. Kilmer, Lowell, Millay **7.** Whitman
  8. Cummings, Ginsberg, Sandburg,
  Teasdale **9.** Dickinson **10.** Longfellow
Red Cross organizer.. **6.** Barton (Clara)
Scouts (Girl) organizer.. **3.** Low (Juliette)
sculptor.. **6.** Calder **7.** Borglum
singer.. **4.** Cole (Nat), Pons **5.** Lanza,
  Sills, Torme **6.** Callas, Crosby, Jolson
  7. Garland, Holiday (Billie), Merrill,
  Presley, Robeson, Sinatra **9.** Streisand
  10. Fitzgerald (Ella)
writer.. **3.** Poe **5.** Crane, James
  (Henry), Lewis (Sinclair), Stowe, Twain
  (Clemens) **6.** Cather, Cooper, Ferber,
  Irving, Mailer **7.** Dreiser, Emerson,
  Thoreau, Wharton **8.** Faulkner, Melville
  9. Hawthorne, Hemingway, Steinbeck
  10. Fitzgerald
American Indian (pert to) . . .
chief.. **5.** brave **6.** sachem
child.. **7.** papoose
conference.. **6.** powwow
girl.. **7.** Nokomis (Myth) **9.** Minnehaha,
  Sacagawea (Sakajawea) **10.** Pocahontas
hero (Myth).. **8.** Hiawatha
magician.. **6.** shaman, wabeno (Ojibway)
shelter.. **4.** tent **5.** hogan, tepee (teepee)
  6. wigwam **7.** wickiup (wikiup)
American Indian people . . . see also
  Indian **3.** Fox, Oto (Otoe), Ree, Sac,
  Ute **4.** Cree, Crow, Erie, Hopi, Iowa,
  Pima **5.** Creek, Kansa, Osage, Piute,
  Sioux **6.** Cayuga, Dakota, Mohawk,
  Oneida, Pueblo, Seneca **7.** Arapaho,
  Choctaw, Mohican, Ojibway, Siksika
  8. Cherokee, Chippewa, Iroquois,
  Onondaga, Seminole **9.** Algonquin,
  Blackfoot, Chickasaw **10.** Athapascan,
  Muskhogean
ami . . . **5.** lover **6.** friend (law)
amiable . . . **6.** kindly **7.** lovable
  8. charming, friendly, pleasant, pleasing
  9. agreeable, indulgent **10.** hospitable
amicable . . . **4.** kind **8.** friendly, sociable
  9. congenial, peaceable **10.** harmonious

amicus curiae . . . **5.** judge **6.** deputy,
  lawyer **16.** friend of the court
amid, amidst . . . **2.** in **5.** among
  7. amongst, between
amigo . . . **6.** friend **8.** neighbor
amiss . . . **3.** ill **5.** badly, fault, wrong
  6. astray, sinful **8.** faultily, improper
  10. disorderly **11.** erroneously
amity . . . **4.** love **5.** peace **7.** harmony
  10. friendship **11.** sociability
  12. congeniality, friendliness
amma . . . **6.** abbess, mother (spiritual)
ammonia . . . **9.** hartshorn **10.** fertilizer
  11. refrigerant
ammoniac plant . . . **5.** oshac
ammunition (pert to) . . .
box.. **9.** bandoleer
chest.. **7.** caisson
type.. **4.** arms, bomb, shot **7.** bullets
  8. grenades, missiles, munition,
  shrapnel **10.** explosives
wagon.. **7.** caisson
amnesty . . . **6.** pardon **8.** oblivion
  9. acquittal **13.** forgetfulness
amoeba, ameba . . . **3.** olm **4.** cell
  7. proteus **10.** protoplasm
  13. microorganism
among, amongst . . . **2.** in **3.** mid
  4. amid, with **5.** midst **6.** amidst, imelle
  7. between
among nations . . . **13.** international
amontillado . . . **6.** sherry
Amor . . . **4.** Eros **5.** Cupid
AMORC . . . **11.** Rosicrucian
amorous . . . **4.** fond **6.** ardent, erotic,
  loving, tender **7.** adoring, devoted
  8. enamored **10.** passionate
  12. affectionate
amorous looks . . . **4.** ogle **5.** stare
  8. coquetry **10.** come-hither, flirtation
amorphous . . . **8.** abnormal, formless
  9. deviative, shapeless, subnormal
  14. uncrystallized
amorphous mineral . . . **4.** opal
amort . . . **8.** dejected, lifeless **9.** inanimate
  10. spiritless
amortize . . . **5.** clear **6.** convey, payoff,
  settle **9.** discharge, negotiate
amount . . . **3.** lot, sum **4.** cost, rate, rise,
  unit **5.** chunk, price, ratal, store, total
  6. ascend, degree **7.** quantum, signify
  8. quantity
amount (pert to) . . .
due.. **5.** price **6.** arrear **7.** default, deficit
mean.. **7.** average
realized.. **4.** take **6.** intake **8.** proceeds
small.. **6.** morsel **7.** modicum
smallest.. **5.** least
to.. **3.** all **4.** even **5.** equal, match, total
  10. correspond
amour . . . **6.** affair **7.** liaison, romance
  8. intrigue, triangle **10.** flirtation
ampere . . . **3.** amp **4.** unit **6.** ohmage
  7. current, voltage
ampersand . . . **3.** and **4.** also
Amphibia . . . **5.** Anura, frogs, toads
  7. Aglossa **8.** tadpoles **9.** Salientia
  11. salamanders
amphibious . . . **5.** mixed **9.** adaptable
  10. fifty-fifty **11.** half-and-half, mixed
  nature (land and water)

amphibole . . . **7.** edenite, mineral, uralite **8.** aluminum, nephrite
amphigory, amphigouri . . . **5.** rhyme **6.** jingle, poetry **8.** doggerel **9.** rigmarole
amphilogism, amphilogy . . . **9.** ambiguity, duplexity (meaning) **10.** equivocacy
Amphion (pert to) . . . *capturer of* . . **6.** Thebes *husband of* . . **5.** Niobe *son of* . . **4.** Zeus *twin of* . . **6.** Zethus
amphitheater . . . **4.** bowl **5.** arena, cavea, scene, stage **6.** circus, cirque **7.** stadium **8.** coliseum, platform **10.** hippodrome
amphora . . . **3.** jar, urn **4.** vase **5.** diota, prize **7.** measure **8.** ornament
ample . . . **4.** full, rich, wide **5.** broad, large, roomy **6.** enough, plenty **7.** liberal **8.** abundant **9.** bountiful, capacious, extensive, plenteous, plentiful, unstinted **10.** munificent **12.** satisfactory
ampliation . . . **5.** flare **9.** expansion, extension **11.** enlargement **12.** postponement **13.** amplification **14.** aggrandizement
amplify . . . **3.** pad **5.** widen **6.** dilate, extend **7.** develop, enlarge **8.** increase **9.** aggravate, expatiate **10.** exaggerate, overstress
amplitude . . . **4.** size **6.** amount **7.** breadth **8.** fullness **9.** greatness, plenitude **12.** spaciousness
amputate . . . **4.** trim **5.** prune, sever **6.** cut off **8.** mutilate, retrench, truncate
amuck, amok . . . **3.** fit **4.** rage **6.** attack, frenzy, malady **12.** corybantiasm
amulet . . . **3.** gem **5.** charm **6.** fetish, scarab, voodoo **7.** periapt **8.** ornament, talisman **10.** protection
amuse . . . **3.** wow **6.** divert, please, regale, tickle **7.** beguile, gratify **8.** recreate **9.** entertain, titillate **10.** exhilarate
amusement . . . **3.** fun **4.** play **5.** farce, mirth, sport **7.** pastime **9.** avocation, diversion **10.** recreation, relaxation **13.** divertisement, entertainment
amusement place . . . **4.** club, park **6.** casino, midway **7.** cabaret, theater
ana . . . **5.** books **6.** events **8.** analecta, excerpts **9.** Americana **10.** collection **11.** collectanea, compilation, memorabilia
anachronous . . . **8.** misdated, mistimed **10.** beforehand, behindhand
anaglyph . . . **5.** cameo, carve **6.** chisel, plaque, relief **10.** embossment
Anak (Eccl) . . . **5.** giant (Canaan) **6.** Anakim
analogous . . . **4.** like **7.** similar **8.** parallel **10.** comparable, equivalent **11.** correlative
analogue . . . **8.** parallel **11.** resemblance **13.** correspondent **14.** correspondence
analogy . . . **8.** likeness, sameness **9.** agreement **10.** accordance, comparison, similarity **14.** correspondence
analysis . . . **5.** assay, logic **6.** biopsy, theory **9.** breakdown, diagnosis **10.** compendium, discussion, dissection **11.** examination **14.** classification

analyze . . . **5.** assay, parse, study **7.** discuss, dissect, examine **8.** classify, describe, diagnose, separate
Ananias (Bib) . . . **4.** liar **8.** disciple (Damascus), Shadrack (Sidrack) **10.** high priest **12.** prevaricator
anarch, anarchist . . . **3.** red **7.** radical **8.** nihilist **9.** socialist, terrorist **13.** revolutionist
anarchy . . . **4.** riot **5.** chaos **6.** acracy **7.** license, misrule **8.** disorder **9.** confusion, mobocracy, rebellion **10.** ochlocracy
anathema . . . **3.** ban **5.** curse **9.** damnation **11.** abomination, imprecation, malediction
Anatolian rug . . . **4.** Kurd **5.** Tuzla
anatomy . . . **4.** body **5.** build, frame **7.** carcass **8.** analysis, skeleton **9.** formation, structure **11.** arrangement
anatomy of animals . . . **7.** zootomy
ancestor . . . **4.** Adam, sire **5.** elder, stock **6.** atavus, family, parent **8.** forebear **9.** patriarch, precursor **10.** antecedent, forefather, forerunner, progenitor **11.** grandfather, predecessor
ancestral . . . **4.** aval **6.** avital, lineal **7.** atavism **8.** maternal, paternal **9.** atavistic, primitive **10.** hereditary **11.** patrimonial
ancestral spirits . . . **5.** lares, manes **7.** lemures, penates
ancestry . . . **4.** race, rank **5.** birth, blood **7.** descent, lineage **11.** antecedents **14.** progenitorship
anchor . . . **3.** fix, tie **4.** hook, moor, rest, stop **5.** affix, clamp, kedge **6.** attach, batten, fasten, secure **7.** grapnel, killick
anchor (pert to) . . . **3.** arm, cat, pee **4.** cast, palm, tore (ring) **5.** fluke **7.** capstan
anchorite, anchoret . . . **6.** hermit, shut-in **7.** ascetic, eremite, recluse, stylite **8.** homebody
anchor-shaped . . . **8.** ankyroid **10.** hook-shaped
anchovy . . . **4.** alec **5.** sauce, sprat **7.** herring
ancienne noblesse . . . **5.** elect, elite **7.** royalty **8.** nobility **11.** aristocracy
ancient . . . **3.** eld, old **4.** aged, auld, wise **5.** adept, early, hoary, olden **7.** antique **8.** historic, obsolete, outdated, primeval, pristine **9.** grandeval, primitive, venerable **10.** aboriginal, antiquated, preadamite **12.** antediluvian
ancient (pert to) . . . *chariot* . . **5.** essed *city* . . **4.** Elis, Tyre **5.** Argos, Sedon **6.** Athens, Sparta, Thebes *drink* . . **5.** morat *empire* . . **4.** Gaul **5.** Roman **6.** Lydian **7.** Persian **8.** Assyrian, Athenian, Chaldean, Hellenic **10.** Babylonian, Phoenician *god* . . **4.** Esus (Gaulish) *isles* . . **5.** Chios, Crete, Samos **6.** Aegina, Ionian, Ithaca, Lemnos, Lesbos, Rhodes **7.** Salamis **8.** Cyclades *language* . . **4.** Pali **5.** Latin **6.** Celtic, Gaelic **7.** Cornish, Gaulish *mariner* . . **4.** Rime (of) **5.** rover **6.** roamer,

sailor, seaman **8.** seafarer, wanderer
9. navigator
soldier . . **7.** peltast
theater . . **5.** odeum
and . . . **2.** et **4.** also, plus **8.** et cetera
9. ampersand, including **12.** additionally
andante . . . **5.** largo, tempo **6.** slowly
Andean (pert to) . . .
beast . . **5.** llama **6.** alpaca, vicuña
7. guanaco
deer . . **4.** pudu
region, wind . . **4.** puna
term . . **5.** grand, lofty
andiron . . . **3.** dog **7.** firedog, Hessian
and others . . . **4.** et al
andrenid . . . **3.** bee **10.** Andrenidae
androgyny . . . **9.** sissiness **10.** effeminacy
11. unmanliness **15.** hermaphroditism
android . . . **5.** robot **9.** automaton
anecdote . . . **4.** tale, yarn **5.** story
7. account **9.** chronicle, narrative
anecdotes . . . **3.** ana **7.** sayings, stories
anemone . . . **7.** actinia **10.** windflower
anent . . . **2.** of, on, re **4.** upon, with
5. about **8.** opposite **10.** concerning
anesthesia, anaesthesia . . . **8.** deadness,
numbness **13.** insensibility
anesthetic . . . **3.** gas **5.** ether **8.** freezing,
Novocain, procaine **9.** pentothal
10. chloroform **13.** refrigeration
anesthetize . . . **4.** dull, numb, stun
6. benumb, deaden, freeze **7.** stupefy
8. etherize, paralyze **9.** narcotize
10. chloroform **11.** desensitize
anew . . . **5.** again, newly **6.** afresh, de
novo **8.** recently
angel . . . **6.** cherub, genius, seraph (seraf)
7. Madonna, prophet
angel (pert to) . . .
Arab (apostate) . . **5.** Eblis
archangel . . **5.** Uriel **7.** Gabriel, Michael,
Raphael
Biblical . . **6.** bishop, pastor
Fallen . . **6.** Belial, Mammon
financial . . **6.** backer, patron **7.** sponsor
8. promoter
fish . . **5.** shark **9.** spadefish
Hebrew . . **6.** Abdiel **8.** cherubim,
seraphim
Jewish . . **6.** Azrael (of death) **7.** Zadkiel
(of planet Jupiter) **8.** Metatron
Mohammedan (Mus) . . **7.** Israfil (Israfeel)
Moslem . . **5.** Nakir (Repudiating)
6. Munkar (Unknown)
angelic . . . **5.** godly **7.** lovable, saintly
8. cherubic, heavenly, seraphic, virtuous
9. celestial **10.** beneficent
angelica . . . **4.** herb **6.** lovely **7.** liqueur
Angelus . . . **4.** bell, call **6.** prayer
8. devotion
anger . . . **3.** ire, vex **4.** fume, rage,
rile **5.** annoy, chafe, wrath **6.** choler,
dander, enrage, nettle, offend, temper
7. dudgeon, emotion, inflame, madness,
passion, trouble **8.** vexation **9.** infuriate
10. affliction, enragement, irritation,
resentment **11.** displeasure, indignation
12. exasperation
angered . . . **3.** mad **5.** irate, wroth
8. incensed, wrathful **9.** indignant,
irascible

angle . . . **3.** ell, tee, zig **4.** axil, coin, fish,
fork, hade, nook **5.** acute, ancon, arris,
right, slant, story **6.** akimbo, distal,
epaule, obtuse, octant **7.** bastion,
outlook, ravelin, salient **8.** attitude
9. incidence, rectangle, viewpoint
angler . . . **6.** fisher **7.** dibbler, trawler,
troller **8.** piscator **9.** fisherman,
Waltonian
angler's basket . . . **5.** creel
Anglican . . . **7.** English
Anglo-Celtic . . . **7.** British **10.** Anglo-
Saxon
Anglo-Indian (pert to) . . .
Empire founder . . **5.** Clive
measure . . **3.** ser **4.** tola
pageant . . **7.** tamasha
peasant . . **4.** ryot
princess . . **5.** begum
wealthy . . **5.** nabob
Anglo-Saxon (pert to) . . .
armor . . **7.** hauberk
assembly . . **4.** moot **5.** gemot (gemote)
attendant . . **5.** thane
consonant . . **3.** edh, eth
council . . **9.** heptarchy
councilman . . **5.** witan
epic (heroic) . . **7.** Beowulf
native . . **7.** English **11.** Anglo-Celtic
prince (heir apparent) . . **8.** atheling
slave . . **4.** esne
tenant . . **6.** geneat
warrior . . **5.** thane
Angora . . .
capital of . . **6.** Turkey
garment . . **5.** shawl
goat . . **6.** chamal
wool fabric . . **6.** mohair
angry . . . **3.** hot, mad **4.** sore **5.** cross,
grame, irate, irked, vexed **6.** ireful,
stormy **7.** enraged, painful, steamed
8. inflamed, wrathful **9.** indignant,
irascible, resentful, ticked off, turbulent
10. passionate
anguish . . . **3.** woe **4.** bale, pain, pang
5. agony, dolor, grief, throe **6.** misery
7. remorse, sadness, torment, torture
8. distress **9.** heartache **10.** desolation
11. lamentation
angular . . . **4.** bent, bony, edgy **5.** gaunt,
sharp **6.** abrupt, akimbo, forked
7. crooked, pointed, scrawny
8. cornered, crotched
ani . . . **8.** keelbill (keelbird) **9.** blackbird
animadversion . . . **7.** censure, comment,
obloquy **8.** judgment, reproach
9. aspersion, criticism **10.** imputation,
reflection **12.** condemnation
animadvert . . . **4.** note **5.** watch **6.** notice,
regard, remark **7.** censure, comment,
observe **9.** criticize (criticise)
anima humana . . . **4.** mind, self, soul
5. heart, human **6.** psyche, spirit
animal (pert to) . . .
anatomy . . **7.** zootomy
back, spine . . **4.** nota **5.** chine
Biblical . . **8.** Behemoth
body . . **4.** soma
castrated . . **3.** seg (segg)
coat . . **6.** pelage
cud . . **5.** rumen

disease . . **8.** enzootic
enclosure . . **3.** pen, sty **4.** cage, coop,
   cote, reem, yard **5.** hutch, kraal, stall
   6. corral **7.** pasture
fabulous . . **7.** griffin
group . . **3.** gam, pod **4.** herd **5.** drove,
   flock, pride **9.** menagerie
hairless . . **5.** pelon
hindleg part . . **4.** crus
hornless . . **7.** pollard
hybrid . . **4.** mule **5.** hinny
hypnosis . . **9.** cataplexy
male . . **3.** tom **4.** bull, jack, stag **5.** steer
   8. stallion
many-egged . . **5.** zooid
many-footed . . **7.** polyped
molt . . **8.** exuviate
mother . . **3.** dam
no feet . . **4.** apod
nose . . **5.** snout
oar-footed . . **7.** remiped
one-egged . . **4.** zoon
one-footed . . **6.** uniped
pet . . **4.** cade
reference to . . **4.** wild **6.** carnal **7.** bestial,
   fleshly, kingdom **8.** domestic **12.** ferae
   naturae **14.** domitae naturae
regional . . **5.** fauna
small . . **10.** animalcule
symbolic . . **5.** totem
track, trail . . **4.** rack **5.** piste, spoor
web-footed . . **8.** pinniped
wing-footed . . **6.** aliped
worship . . **8.** zoolatry
young . . **3.** cub, kid, pup **4.** calf, colt,
   fawn, foal, lamb **5.** filly, puppy **6.** kitten
animal family . . .
   bear . . **6.** ursine
   cat . . **6.** feline
   cow . . **6.** bovine
   deer . . **7.** cervine
   dog . . **6.** canine
   fox . . **7.** vulpine
   horse . . **6.** equine
   pig . . **7.** porcine
   sheep . . **5.** ovine
   wolf . . **6.** lupine
animal stomach . . .
   1st . . **5.** rumen **6.** paunch
   2nd . . **5.** tripe **9.** honeycomb, reticulum
   3rd . . **6.** omasum **9.** manyplies
   4th . . **3.** maw **4.** read (reed) **8.** abomasum
animate . . . **3.** act **4.** fire, live, move
   5. alive, cheer, imbue, impel, liven
   6. arouse, ensoul, spirit, vivify
   7. enliven, inspire, organic, refresh
   8. energize, vitalize **9.** stimulate
   10. exhilarate
animated . . . **3.** gay **5.** alive, brisk
   6. active, lively, living, minded
   8. disposed (in mind), prompted
   9. energetic, refreshed
animated spirit . . . **6.** animus
animation . . . **3.** pep **4.** brio, dash,
   life **5.** ardor **6.** energy, gaiety,
   spirit **8.** airiness, buoyancy, vivacity
   10. excitement, liveliness, motivation
   11. earnestness, inspiration
   12. invigoration, vivification
   13. sprightliness
animation suspended . . . **6.** apathy,

torpor **8.** dormancy, lethargy
animé . . . **6.** bright **8.** animated
animosity . . . **5.** clash, spite **6.** enmity,
   hatred, rancor **7.** ill will **8.** conflict
   9. antipathy, hostility **10.** antagonism,
   opposition, repugnance
animoso . . . **6.** lively **8.** animated
   9. energetic
animous . . . **3.** hot **8.** resolute, vehement
animus . . . **4.** mind, will **6.** desire,
   hatred, spirit, temper **8.** attitude,
   volition **9.** intention **10.** discretion
   11. disposition, inclination
anise-flavored liqueur . . . **4.** anis, ouzo
   6. pastis **8.** anisette
ankh (Egypt) . . . **3.** tau **4.** life **5.** cross
   6. emblem, symbol
ankle . . . **4.** tali (pl) **5.** joint, pivot, talus
   6. tarsus **8.** astragal **9.** ginglymus
   10. astragalus **11.** diarthrosis
ankle cover . . . **4.** spat **6.** gaiter
ankylostoma . . . **7.** lockjaw
annalist . . . **6.** writer **8.** recorder
   9. historian **10.** chronicler
   11. memorialist **12.** chronologist
annals . . . **5.** diary **6.** record **7.** history,
   journal **8.** register **9.** chronicle
   11. publication
Annam . . . **5.** Hanoi **6.** Tonkin (Tongking)
Annamese . . . **7.** Chinese **8.** Buddhist
   9. Mongolian
anneal . . . **4.** fuse, heat **6.** harden, temper
   7. inflame, toughen **8.** indurate
Anne Hathaway's home . . . **8.** Shattery
annelid . . . **3.** lug **4.** lurg, naid, worm
   6. phylum **7.** lugworm
annex . . . **3.** add, ell **4.** join, wing **5.** affix
   6. append, attach, fasten **7.** acquire,
   subjoin **8.** addition **9.** extension
annexation . . . **7.** adjunct **8.** addition
   9. accession **10.** affixation
   13. appropriation
Annie Oakley . . . **4.** pass **6.** ticket (free)
annihilate . . . **4.** undo, void **5.** erase,
   wreck **6.** quench, reduce, stifle
   7. abolish, destroy, expunge, nullify,
   smother **8.** decimate **9.** extirpate
   10. extinguish, obliterate
   11. exterminate
annihilation . . . **5.** death **6.** demise
   7. passing **10.** extinction **11.** destruction,
   dissolution **13.** extermination
   14. extinguishment
anniversary . . . **5.** cycle **6.** course
   7. jubilee, wedding **8.** birthday
   10. centennial, regularity
   13. commemoration
annotation . . . **4.** note **5.** gloss **7.** apostil,
   comment **8.** exegesis, notation, rescript,
   scholium **9.** reference **10.** commentary
annotator . . . **6.** critic **7.** analyst
   9. expositor, expounder, publicist,
   scholiast **10.** glossarist **11.** commentator
announce . . . **3.** bid **4.** call, tell **5.** bruit
   6. affirm, assert, herald, notify
   7. declare, forerun, gazette, presage
   8. proclaim **9.** advertise, broadcast,
   pronounce **10.** annunciate, promulgate
announcement . . . **4.** fiat **5.** blurb, edict
   6. decree, notice **8.** bulletin **9.** manifesto
   10. commercial **11.** affirmation,

declaration **12.** notification,
proclamation **13.** advertisement
announcer ... **4.** page **5.** crier, emcee
6. nuncio **9.** harbinger, informant
10. newscaster, proclaimer
11. broadcaster
annoy ... **3.** irk, nag, try, vex **4.** bore,
rile **5.** anger, devil, harry, peeve,
spite, tease **6.** bother, harass, molest,
offend, pester, ruffle **7.** disturb, trouble
8. irritate **9.** displease **13.** inconvenience
annoyance ... **4.** bore, pest **8.** nuisance,
vexation **10.** resentment **11.** molestation
13. inconvenience
annoying ... **4.** sore **7.** galling **9.** vexatious
11. distressing
annual ... **4.** book **5.** plant **6.** yearly
7. etesian **10.** periodical **11.** publication
annuity ... **5.** rente, trust **6.** income (life)
7. pension, subsidy, tontine **9.** allotment
10. investment, life income
annul ... **4.** cass, undo, void **5.** avoid,
blank, quash **6.** cancel, repeal, revoke
7. abolish, nullify, rescind **8.** abrogate,
derogate, overrule, withdraw
9. disaffirm **10.** invalidate, neutralize,
obliterate **11.** countermand
annular ... **6.** banded, cyclic, ringed
8. cingular, circular
annulet ... **4.** ring (Her) **6.** fillet **7.** circlet,
ringlet
annulment ... **6.** repeal **7.** erasure,
vacatur **9.** abolition **10.** abrogation,
defeasance, revocation **12.** invalidation
14. neutralization
annunciate ... **6.** affirm, assert
8. announce, proclaim
annunciation ... **11.** affirmation
12. announcement, proclamation
13. pronouncement
anoa ... **2.** ox (wild) **8.** sapiutan
anode ... **8.** terminal (positive)
9. electrode (opp of cathode)
anodic ... **12.** turned toward
anodyne ... **4.** balm **6.** opiate **7.** soother
8. antalgic, narcotic, pacifier, sedative
9. analgesic **10.** depressant, palliative
anoesia ... **6.** idiocy
anoint ... **3.** oil **4.** balm, cere, nard
5. anele, bribe, smear **6.** chrism,
grease, spread **7.** moisten **8.** medicate
9. embrocate, lubricate **10.** consecrate
Anointing of the Sick ... **9.** last rites,
sacrament **14.** Extreme Unction
anoli, anole ... **6.** lizard
anomalous ... **3.** odd **7.** erratic, strange,
unusual **8.** aberrant, abnormal, peculiar
9. eccentric, irregular **10.** dissimilar
11. exceptional **13.** unconformable
anomaly ... **6.** oddity, rarity
11. abnormality, nondescript
12. irregularity
anomy ... **7.** miracle
anon ... **4.** soon **5.** again, later **6.** mañana,
thence **7.** by-and-by **8.** tomorrow
10. eventually **11.** straightway
anonymous (opp of onomatous) ...
7. unknown **8.** nameless, unavowed
9. undefined
anoöpsia ... **10.** strabismus (upward)
Anopheles ... **10.** mosquitoes

anophthalmia ... **13.** absence of eyes
(congenital)
anopia ... **15.** defective vision
anorak ... **5.** parka **12.** hooded jacket
(Arctic)
anorexia ... **10.** no appetite
anorthopia ... **15.** distorted vision
anosmia ... **11.** loss of smell
another ... **3.** new **4.** more **5.** alias, extra,
other **6.** second **7.** further **10.** additional
another time ... **5.** again **10.** otherwhile
ansa ... **4.** loop **6.** ansate, handle
anserine ... **6.** stupid **9.** gooselike
answer ... **2.** do **3.** say **4.** echo
5. avail, reply, sauce, serve **6.** oracle,
retort **7.** defense, epistle, respond,
riposte **8.** conclude, reaction, repartee,
response, solution **9.** rejoinder
10. correspond, responsory
11. acknowledge **16.** counterstatement
answerable ... **6.** liable **8.** amenable,
solvable **11.** responsible
12. commensurate **13.** proportionate
answer the purpose ... **2.** so **3.** fit **4.** suit
5. avail, serve **6.** become **7.** benefit,
satisfy, suffice
ant (pert to) ...
family .. **10.** Formicidae, Myrmicidae
11. Formicoidea (super), Hymenoptera
feeding on .. **13.** formicivorous
genus .. **6.** Eciton, Termes **7.** Formica
killer .. **9.** formicide
male .. **8.** macraner (large), micraner
(small)
nest .. **9.** formicary
ref to .. **6.** formic
type .. **5.** emmet **7.** formica, pismire
white .. **4.** anay (anai) **7.** termite
wingless .. **8.** ergatoid
worker .. **6.** ergate **9.** harvester
antacid ... **6.** alkali, remedy **8.** medicine
9. absorbent **11.** neutralizer
12. counteragent **13.** counteractant
Antaeus, Antaios (Gr) ... **5.** giant
6. Libyan **8.** wrestler
antagonism ... **3.** war **5.** clash **8.** conflict
9. antipathy, hostility **10.** opposition,
repugnance **11.** contrariety
12. disagreement **13.** counteraction
antagonist ... **3.** foe **5.** enemy, rival
6. foeman **8.** opponent **9.** adversary
antagonistic ... **7.** hostile, opposed
8. contrary, converse, inimical, opposite
9. repugnant **10.** unfriendly
11. belligerent, disagreeing
13. counteractive
Antarctic ...
Circle .. **4.** Pole **6.** region
Coast .. **6.** Adélie
continent .. **10.** Antarctica
explorer .. **4.** Byrd, Ross
islands .. **11.** Archipelago
rel to .. **8.** subpolar **9.** antipodal, South
Pole
sea .. **4.** Ross **7.** Weddell
seal (brown) discoverer .. **7.** Weddell
volcano .. **6.** Erebus
ante ... **3.** pay, pot **4.** bank, fund, pool
5. kitty, stake **7.** jackpot
anteater ... **5.** Manis **7.** echidna
8. aardvark, edentate, pangolin,

tamandua
antebellum ... **6.** prewar
antecede ... **4.** head **5.** front **6.** prefix
7. outrank, precede, preface
antecedent ... **4.** fore **5.** prior, scout
6. former **7.** pioneer **8.** ancestor,
previous **9.** foregoing, precedent,
preceding, precursor **10.** forerunner,
precedence **11.** voortrekker (Dutch)
12. avant-courier
antecedents ... **7.** fathers **9.** ancestors,
forebears **10.** ascendants (ascendents)
11. forefathers **12.** predecessors
13. prerequisites
antechamber ... **4.** hall **5.** lobby **6.** lounge
7. chamber **8.** anteroom **9.** vestibule
antedate ... **7.** precede, predate
8. datemark, pre-exist **10.** anticipate
antelope ... **3.** gau, gnu, goa, kob, nil
4. guib, koba, oryx, roan **5.** addax,
bovid, eland, goral, oribi, peele, saiga,
serow **6.** cabree, dik-dik, dzeren,
impala, nilgai, pygarg **7.** blaubok,
blesbok, bubalia, chamois, gazella,
gazelle, gemsbok, sassaby **8.** agacella,
bontebok, steinbok **9.** duikerbok,
pronghorn **10.** hartebeest
antenna ... **4.** horn, mast, palp **5.** clava
(Zool), tower **6.** aerial, feeler **7.** scanner
antepast ... **6.** canape, repast **8.** aperitif
9. antipasto, appetizer, foretaste
11. hors d'oeuvre, prelibation
anteroom ... **4.** hall **5.** lobby **6.** lounge
7. chamber **9.** vestibule
11. antechamber
anthem ... **3.** lay **4.** hymn, song **5.** motet,
music, psalm **7.** chorale **8.** doxology
9. antiphony, offertory **10.** responsory
anthill ... **5.** mound **9.** formicary
anthology ... **3.** ana **5.** album **6.** corpus
7. omnibus, prayers **8.** analects
9. potpourri **10.** collection
11. collectanea, compilation
Anthozoa ... **6.** corals, polyps
8. anemones
anthropoid ... **3.** ape, lar, man **6.** gibbon
7. gorilla, primate, siamang
9. orangutan (orangoutang)
10. chimpanzee, troglodyte
12. Anthropoidea (suborder)
anthropophagi ... **9.** cannibals, man-
eaters
anti ... **6.** contra **7.** adverse, counter,
opposed **8.** contrary, converse
13. contradictory
antibiotics ... **5.** drugs **7.** vaccine
10. penicillin **12.** streptomycin
antic ... **4.** dido **5.** caper, prank, stunt
6. frolic, gambol **7.** bizarre, buffoon,
gambado **9.** grotesque **11.** merry-
andrew, monkeyshine
anticipate ... **4.** hope **5.** await, dread
6. expect **7.** foresee, obviate, portend,
prevent **8.** preclude **9.** forestall,
foretaste, forethink **11.** contemplate
anticipation ... **4.** hope **9.** foresight,
foretaste, intuition, prolepsis
10. foreboding **11.** expectation,
forethought **12.** presentiment
13. preoccupation
anticlimax ... **6.** bathos **8.** comedown,

decrease
antidote ... **6.** remedy **10.** corrective,
preventive **11.** neutralizer
12. counteragent, prophylactic
13. counteractant
Antilles ...
Greater .. **4.** Cuba **7.** Jamaica
10. Hispaniola, Puerto Rico
Lesser .. **7.** Leeward (Islands)
8. Windward (Islands)
Antioch ... **7.** capital (Syria)
antipathy ... **6.** hatred, nausea **7.** dislike
8. aversion, loathing **9.** disrelish,
hostility **10.** abhorrence, antagonism,
opposition, reluctance, repugnance
11. contrariety, detestation, inimicality
13. counteraction **14.** disinclination
antipodal ... **5.** polar **7.** counter (global)
8. contrary, opposite **14.** contrapositive
antiquated ... **4.** aged **5.** passé **6.** bygone,
voided **7.** antique, archaic, elderly
8. absolute, medieval **9.** Victorian
10. fossilized **12.** antediluvian, old-
fashioned **13.** superannuated
antique ... **3.** old **5.** hoary, relic
7. ageless, ancient **8.** dateless,
outmoded **9.** venerable **12.** old-
fashioned
antiquities ... **5.** codex, ruins **6.** relics
7. fossils, papyrus, remains, tablets
9. archaisms, artifacts, monuments
11. manuscripts, palimpsests
antiquity ... **3.** ago, eld **4.** past, yore
7. oldness **9.** paleology **11.** ancientness,
elderliness **13.** aboriginality,
primitiveness
antisepsis ... **7.** asepsis **11.** prophylaxis
12. disinfection, immunization
13. sterilization
antiseptic ... **5.** Salol **6.** cresol, iodine
(iodin), phenol **7.** alcohol, aristol,
aseptic **8.** creosote, peroxide
9. germicide **12.** disinfectant,
formaldehyde, prophylactic
antispasmodic ... **7.** anodyne **8.** sedative
9. asadulcis (deadly carrot), asafetida
(asafoetida) **10.** depressant
12. tranquilizer
antithesis (opp of thesis) ... **8.** contrast,
opposite **9.** antipodes **10.** opposition
11. contrariety **14.** contraposition
antitoxin ... **5.** serum **7.** vaccine
8. antibody **9.** antivenin (antivenene)
10. antibiotic **11.** antipyretic,
immunotoxin
antler ... **3.** dag **4.** horn, snag, tine
5. dague, point, prong, spike **6.** bosset,
rights **8.** advancer **10.** caducicorn
Antony & Cleopatra characters ...
4. Eris, Iras **6.** Caesar **7.** Octavia
9. Demetrius
antonym (opp of synonym) ... **7.** reverse
8. contrary, opposite
antrum ... **3.** pit **5.** sinus **6.** cavern,
cavity, hollow **10.** depression
Anu ... **3.** god (sky, heavens)
Anubis ... **3.** god (Necropolis) **6.** Hermes
Anura ... **4.** Rana **5.** frogs, toads
9. Salientia **10.** amphibians
anvil ... **5.** block, incus, teest **6.** stithy
7. bickern, incudes (pl) **8.** beakiron

(horned)

anxiety . . . **4.** care, fear **5.** angst, dread, worry **7.** concern, trouble **8.** disquiet, distress, neurosis, suspense **9.** eagerness, misgiving **10.** foreboding, perplexity, solicitude, uneasiness **12.** apprehension, restlessness

anxious . . . **4.** cark **5.** antsy, eager **6.** uneasy **7.** fearful, unquiet **8.** watchful **9.** concerned, disturbed, expectant, impatient **10.** disquieted

any . . . **3.** all, ary (dial), one, oni (dial) **4.** some, that, this **5.** aught, every **8.** quantity **9.** unlimited **10.** unmeasured **12.** undetermined

anybody . . . **3.** any, one **5.** aught **6.** anyone **7.** someone, whoever **15.** no-account person

anything . . . **3.** any **4.** some **5.** at all, aught **7.** anywise **8.** no choice, whatever **9.** something **14.** choicelessness

anything (pert to) . . .
existing . . **6.** entity **8.** quiddity
of value . . **5.** asset
of value, least . . **5.** plack
puzzling . . **4.** crux **11.** mind-boggler
remote . . **6.** forane
small . . **3.** tot **5.** minim
spiral . . **4.** gyre **5.** helix
terrifying . . **5.** ghost **9.** scarecrow
true . . **4.** fact **7.** certitude
worthless . . **4.** mean **7.** useless **9.** valueless

aoudad . . . **5.** sheep **7.** chamois

apa . . . **7.** wallaba

Apache (pert to) . . .
French . . **4.** thug **5.** dance **8.** assassin
Indian . . **5.** nomad
Indian Chief (famed) . . **8.** Geronimo
Indian jacket (deerskin) . . **6.** bietle
State . . **7.** Arizona

apart . . . **3.** dis (pref) **4.** away **5.** alone, aloof, aside, solus, split **6.** singly **7.** asunder, distant **8.** secluded, separate, unjoined **9.** severally, unrelated **10.** separately

apartheid . . . **4.** bias **5.** twist **7.** bigotry **9.** prejudice **11.** segregation **13.** provincialism **14.** discrimination

apartment . . . **3.** pad (sl) **4.** flat **5.** condo, suite **6.** studio **7.** chamber **8.** tenement **11.** compartment, condominium

apathetic . . . **4.** dull **5.** inert **6.** torpid **7.** passive **8.** listless, sluggish **10.** insouciant, phlegmatic **11.** indifferent, unconcerned

apathy . . . **6.** acedia (in a monastery), torpor **7.** languor **8.** neurosis **9.** lassitude, unconcern **12.** indifference, sluggishness **13.** insensibility, unfeelingness

ape . . . **4.** copy, dupe, fool, mine **5.** mimic **6.** alalus, mocker, monkey, parrot **7.** barbary, copycat, emulate, imitate, portray **8.** imitator, mimicker, simulate **10.** anthropoid **11.** impersonate

ape (pert to) . . .
anthropoid . . **6.** pongid **10.** chimpanzee, troglodyte
Egypt Relig . . **4.** Aani
genus . . **5.** Cebus, Simia
India . . **3.** kra
kind . . **6.** simian **7.** macaque
largest . . **6.** baboon **7.** gorilla
Malay . . **3.** lar **5.** orang **6.** gibbon **9.** orangutan (orangoutang)
nocturnal . . **5.** lemur

aperitif . . . **5.** drink **6.** canape **8.** antepast **9.** antipasto, appetizer **11.** hors d'oeuvre

aperture . . . **3.** gap, vue **4.** hole, leak, pore, rift, rima, slit, slot, vent **5.** chasm, chink, cleft, inlet, mouth, stoma **6.** hiatus, window **7.** fissure, foramen, opening, orifice, osteole **8.** fenestra **10.** passageway

apex . . . **3.** tip, top **4.** acme, cone, cusp, noon **5.** point, spire **6.** apogee, height, macron, summit, tittle, vertex, zenith **7.** cacumen **8.** pinnacle **11.** culmination

apex ornament . . . **6.** finial

aphid . . . **5.** Aphis, louse **6.** insect **7.** puceron

aphorism . . . **3.** saw **5.** adage, axiom, gnome, maxim, moral **6.** dictum, saying **7.** proverb **8.** apothegm

Aphrodite (pert to) . . .
consort . . **4.** Ares **10.** Hephaestus
father . . **4.** Zeus
goddess of . . **4.** love **6.** beauty
Roman equivalent . . **5.** Venus
sacred birds . . **5.** doves **8.** sparrows
statue . . **17.** Aphrodite of Cnidus (by Praxiteles)
zoology . . **9.** butterfly

apiarist . . . **9.** beekeeper

apiary . . . **7.** beehive

Apis . . . **4.** bull (sacred)

aplomb . . . **5.** poise **6.** surety **7.** balance **8.** fastness, firmness, security, solidity **9.** assurance, erectness, plumbness, restraint, soundness, stability **10.** confidence, equanimity **11.** equilibrium

apocalypse . . . **8.** prophecy, teaching **9.** discovery, scripture **10.** revealment, revelation

a poco . . . **6.** little, slowly **9.** gradually

apocryphal . . . **4.** mock, sham **5.** bogus, false **6.** mythic, unreal **8.** doubtful, mythical, spurious **9.** imitative **10.** fictitious, unorthodox **11.** counterfeit **15.** unauthoritative

apod . . . **8.** footless

Apodes . . . **4.** eels **6.** morays

apogee (opp of perigee) . . . **4.** acme, apex, peak **6.** climax, summit, zenith **11.** culmination

apograph . . . **4.** copy **5.** tenor **7.** tracing **8.** transfer **9.** recording **10.** transcript **13.** transcription

Apoidea . . . **4.** Apis, bees **9.** honeybees **11.** Hymenoptera

Apollo (pert to) . . .
birthplace . . **5.** Delos
father . . **4.** Zeus
festival . . **5.** Delia
god . . **3.** sun (personified)
mother . . **4.** Leto **6.** Larona
oracle . . **6.** Delphi
sage follower . . **6.** Abaris
sister (twin) . . **5.** Diana (Rom) **7.** Artemis
son . . **3.** Ion **5.** Hymen, Linos

apologetic . . . **5.** sorry **7.** apology
   8. excusing **10.** excusatory, justifying,
   remorseful **11.** vindicative
   12. propitiatory **13.** justification
apologue . . . **4.** myth **5.** fable, story
   6. legend **7.** fantasy, parable **8.** allegory
apology . . . **4.** plea **5.** excuse **7.** pretext,
   regrets **9.** makeshift **11.** explanation,
   vindication **13.** justification
   14. acknowledgment
aport . . . **8.** larboard, leftward **9.** sinistrad
apostasy . . . **5.** lapse **9.** desertion,
   recreancy **11.** backsliding
apostate . . . **6.** bolter **7.** pervert, runaway,
   seceder **8.** deserter, recreant, renegade,
   turncoat, turntail **10.** unfaithful
apostle . . . **5.** saint **8.** disciple, follower
   10. evangelist
Apostle (Bib) . . . **4.** John, Jude **5.** James,
   Judas (Iscariot), Peter (Simon Peter),
   Simon **6.** Andrew, Philip, Thomas
   7. Matthew **8.** Matthias
   11. Bartholomew (Nathanael)
Apostle of . . .
   France (Gauls) . . **5.** Denis
   Franks . . **4.** Remi
   Gentiles . . **4.** Paul
   Germany . . **8.** Boniface
   Goths . . **7.** Ulfilas
   Indies . . **6.** Xavier
   Ireland . . **7.** Patrick
   Rome . . **4.** Neri
Apostle to the Indians . . . **5.** Eliot
apostolic . . . **5.** faith, papal **6.** gospel
   8. Biblical **9.** evangelic **10.** pontifical,
   scriptural
apostrophe . . . **8.** squiggle **9.** soliloquy
apothecary . . . **8.** druggist, gallipot
   9. dispenser **10.** pharmacist, posologist
   13. pharmaceutist **14.** pharmacologist
apothecary measure . . . **4.** dram, pint
   5. minim, ounce
apothecary weight . . . **4.** dram **5.** grain,
   ounce, pound **7.** scruple
apothegm . . . **3.** saw **4.** dict **5.** adage,
   axiom, gnome, maxim **6.** dictum,
   saying **7.** precept **8.** aphorism
apotheosis . . . **5.** ideal **10.** exaltation
   11. deification, ennoblement, idolization
   12. resurrection **13.** dignification,
   glorification, magnification
   14. aggrandizement
apotheosize . . . **5.** deify, exalt **7.** ennoble,
   glorify, idolize **8.** enshrine
   11. immortalize
appall, appal . . . **3.** awe **5.** shock
   6. dismay
appalling . . . **4.** grim **5.** awful **7.** awesome,
   fearful **8.** dreadful, shocking, terrible,
   terrific **9.** frightful **10.** remarkable
appalto . . . **8.** monopoly
appanage . . . **7.** adjunct, pendant
   8. property **9.** appendage, endowment
   10. perquisite **11.** prerogative
   12. appurtenance
apparatus . . . **4.** gear, tool **6.** outfit
   7. machine, rigging, trapeze **8.** recorder
   9. appliance, equipment, mechanism,
   trappings **10.** instrument
   13. paraphernalia
apparatus (pert to) . . .

distillation . . **7.** alembic
dyeing . . **4.** ager
heating . . **4.** etna **5.** stove **6.** boiler
   7. furnace **8.** radiator
hoisting . . **3.** pry **4.** jack **5.** davit, lever,
   lewis **7.** capstan, derrick
planetarium . . **6.** orrery
steering . . **4.** helm **5.** wheel **6.** rudder,
   tiller
water . . **4.** pump **5.** noria **6.** faucet,
   siphon, tremie
apparel . . . **3.** alb **4.** deck, duds, garb,
   gear, togs, wear **5.** dress, equip, habit
   6. attire **7.** clothes, costume, garment,
   raiment, toggery, vesture **8.** clothing,
   fatigues **10.** garmenture **11.** habiliments
apparent . . . **4.** open **5.** clear, overt, plain
   6. patent, visual **7.** certain, evident,
   obvious, seeable, seeming, visible
   8. distinct, illusory, manifest, specious
   9. notorious, plausible **10.** ostensible
   11. discernible, indubitable, perceivable,
   superficial **12.** recognizable
apparently . . . **7.** visibly **9.** evidently,
   obviously, seemingly **10.** manifestly,
   presumably, speciously **11.** perceptibly
apparition . . . **4.** bogy, form **5.** ghost,
   shade, spook **6.** shadow, spirit, sprite,
   vision, wraith **7.** eidolon, fantasy,
   phantom, specter (spectre) **8.** illusion,
   phantasm, revenant **9.** hobgoblin
   10. appearance, phenomenon,
   revelation
appassionato . . . **9.** emotional
   11. impassioned
appeal . . . **3.** beg, cry **4.** call, cite,
   plea, pray, suit **5.** charm, plead
   6. avouch, invoke, prayer **7.** address,
   beseech, entreat, implore, request,
   solicit **8.** entreaty, petition **9.** importune
   10. lovability, loveliness, supplicate
   11. winsomeness **12.** supplication
appealing . . . **4.** nice **7.** winsome
   8. alluring, charming, engaging,
   pleasant **9.** agreeable, glamorous,
   imploring **10.** attractive, beseeching,
   bewitching, delightful, enchanting,
   entreating **11.** fascinating, interesting
appear . . . **4.** loom, seem **5.** occur
   6. arrive, attend, emerge **11.** materialize
appearance . . . **3.** air **4.** form, look, mien
   5. front, guise, looks, phase **6.** aspect,
   format, manner, ostent **7.** arrival,
   feature, specter (spectre) **8.** illusion,
   presence, pretense **9.** emergence,
   semblance **10.** apparition, disclosure,
   revelation **11.** resemblance
   13. manifestation
appearance (pert to) . . .
   book . . **6.** format
   brief . . **5.** cameo
   false . . **8.** disguise
   first . . **4.** dawn **5.** debut **8.** premiere
   frontal . . **6.** facade
   surface . . **6.** patina
   truth (appearance of) . . **14.** verisimilitude
   white . . **6.** pallid
appease . . . **4.** calm **5.** allay, atone,
   mease, quiet, salve **6.** pacify, soothe
   7. content, placate, relieve, satisfy
   8. mitigate **10.** conciliate **11.** tranquilize

appeasement . . . 6. relief 7. salving
8. easement 10. compromise,
mitigation, palliation 12. pacification
appellation . . . 3. tag 4. name 5. label,
style, title 7. calling, epithet
8. cognomen, nickname 9. sobriquet
11. designation 12. denomination,
nomenclature 14. identification
append . . . 3. add 4. hang 5. affix,
annex 6. adjoin, attach 7. subjoin
11. superimpose
appendage . . . 3. arm, awn, cue, tab,
tag 4. barb, flap, lobe, tail 5. cauda,
queue 6. ligule (Bot), palpus 7. adjunct,
pigtail 8. addition, hanger-on, pendicle
9. accessory, tailpiece 10. dependency
12. appurtenance 13. accompaniment
appendix . . . 6. sequel 7. codicil, process
8. addendum, addition 9. accessory,
appendage 10. dependency
12. augmentation
appertain . . . 4. bear 5. apply 6. affect,
belong, regard, relate 7. involve, pertain
appetite . . . 4. zest 5. taste 6. desire,
hunger, orexis, thirst 7. longing, passion
8. cupidity 9. appetency 10. hungriness,
propensity
appetizer . . . 4. fish (sauce) 6. canape
8. antepast, aperitif 9. antipasto,
foretaste 11. hors d'oeuvre
appetizing . . . 6. savory 7. piquant
8. tempting 9. appealing, desirable
10. attractive 11. captivating,
provocative, tantalizing
applaud . . . 4. clap, hail, laud, root,
yell 5. cheer, extol, shout 6. hurrah,
praise 7. acclaim, approve, commend,
endorse 10. compliment
applauders (paid) . . . 6. claque 8. clappers
9. claqueurs
applause . . . 4. clap, hand 5. bravo, éclat,
huzza 6. encore, praise 7. acclaim,
ovation 8. plaudits 11. acclamation
12. commendation
apple . . . 3. May, Spy 4. crab, pome
6. annona, pippin, rennet, russet
7. Baldwin, codling (codlin), costard,
Newtown, Roxbury, winesap
8. Greening, Jonathan, Mandrake,
McIntosh, queening 9. astrachan,
Delicious 10. bellflower, Rome Beauty
11. Granny Smith, Gravenstein,
Northern Spy
apple (pert to) . . .
acid . . 5. malic
brandy . . 8. Calvados
crushed . . 6. pomace
dessert . . 10. brown betty
disease . . 7. stippen
genus . . 5. Malus
juice . . 5. cider 9. applejack
love . . 6. tomato
seed . . 3. pip
shaped . . 8. pomiform
Apple of Discord (Gr Myth) . . . 4. Eris
apple of one's eye . . . 3. pet 4. idol
5. jewel, pupil 7. darling, desired
8. favorite 10. preference
applesauce . . . 4. bunk, pooh 5. tripe
6. phooey 7. baloney, hogwash
8. malarkey, nonsense, tommyrot

appliance . . . 3. dam (dental) 4. tool
6. device, gadget 7. utensil 8. facility
9. commodity, implement
10. instrument 11. application,
contraption, convenience
applicable . . . 3. apt, fit 6. usable
7. pliable 8. apposite, relative, relevant
9. compliant, pertinent 11. appropriate
application . . . 3. use 6. appeal, effort
7. bearing, concern, request 8. petition,
recourse 9. attention, constancy,
diligence, relevance, relevancy
10. connection, employment, pertinence
11. attribution, disposition,
engrossment, persistence, requisition
12. perseverance 14. administration
application (body) . . . 4. balm 5. salve,
stupe (hot) 7. plaster 8. cosmetic,
poultice
apply . . . 3. use 4. suit 6. appose,
bestow, comply, devote, employ, relate
7. solicit, utilize 9. associate, attribute
10. administer 11. appropriate
appoggiature . . . 9. grace note
13. embellishment
appoint . . . 3. fix 4. name 5. equip
6. assign, decree, depute, detail, ordain
7. destine, prepare 8. delegate, deputize
9. designate, establish, prescribe
10. constitute
appointment . . . 4. date 5. order, tryst
7. command 8. position 9. direction,
equipment, ordinance 10. engagement
11. designation 13. establishment
appointments . . . 6. things 8. fittings,
fixtures 9. equipment, furniture
10. belongings, upholstery
11. acquirement, furnishings
12. accumulation, conveniences
13. accouterments, paraphernalia
apportion . . . 3. fix, lot 4. deal, dele,
mete, part 5. allot, carve, share
6. assign, budget, divide 7. arrange,
dispose 8. allocate 9. collocate, partition
10. distribute
appose . . . 4. abut 5. audit, liken,
place 6. adjoin 7. compare, examine
9. juxtapose
apposite . . . 3. apt 4. like 5. close, match
6. timely 7. fitting, germane 8. position,
relative, relevant 9. pertinent
11. appropriate
appraise . . . 4. mark, rank, rate 5. assay,
gauge, judge, price, value 6. assess,
evalue, praise 7. apprise, commend,
measure 8. consider, estimate, evaluate
10. adjudicate, appreciate
appraiser (tax) . . . 5. rater 6. lister
8. assessor
appreciable . . . 3. any 8. tangible
9. estimable 11. perceptible
appreciate . . . 4. feel, grow, know
5. enjoy, prize, savor, value 6. admire,
esteem 7. advance, amplify, approve,
augment, realize, respect 8. estimate,
increase, treasure
appreciation . . . 7. respect 9. appraisal,
awareness, gratitude 10. estimation
11. realization, recognition, sensibility
12. gratefulness, thankfulness

apprehend . . . **3.** ken, see **4.** know, take
5. dread, grasp, pinch (sl), savvy,
seize, sense **6.** arrest **7.** capture,
imagine, realize **8.** conceive, perceive
10. anticipate, comprehend, understand

apprehensible . . . **8.** knowable
9. scrutable **10.** explicable, fathomable
11. accountable **12.** discoverable,
intelligible **14.** comprehensible,
understandable

apprehension . . . **4.** fear, idea **5.** alarm,
doubt, dread, qualm **6.** arrest **7.** anxiety,
capture, concern, opinion, seizure
8. distress, distrust, suspense
9. misgiving, suspicion **10.** foreboding,
solicitude, uneasiness **11.** fearfulness,
premonition **12.** intelligence
13. understanding

apprehensive . . . **5.** smart **6.** uneasy
7. alarmed, fearful, knowing, nervous,
worried **8.** troubled **9.** cognizant,
concerned, conscious, perturbed
10. perceptive, solicitous

apprentice . . . **4.** tyro **6.** novice
7. amateur, trainee **8.** beginner

apprize, apprise . . . **4.** rate, tell **5.** price,
value **6.** advise, assess, impart, inform,
reckon **8.** acquaint, appraise **9.** enlighten
11. communicate

apprized . . . **5.** aware **8.** informed
9. cognizant

approach . . . **3.** way **4.** adit, come, near,
road **5.** stalk, verge **6.** access, accost,
advent, impend **7.** arrival, nearing, sea
gate **8.** entryway, likeness, nearness,
overture, resemble **11.** approximate,
entranceway

approachable . . . **4.** open **8.** gettable,
passable **9.** reachable **10.** accessible,
attainable **13.** communicative

approbation . . . **5.** favor, proof **6.** praise
7. plaudit **8.** applause, approval,
sanction **10.** acceptance, admiration
12. commendation, confirmation

appropriate . . . **3.** apt, fit **4.** akin,
meet, take **5.** allot, steal, usurp
6. borrow, pirate, proper, timely,
worthy **7.** condign, germane, related,
special **8.** deserved, relevant, suitable
9. befitting, expedient, favorable,
opportune, pertinent **10.** assimilate,
monopolize, plagiarize **11.** conformable

appropriately . . . **4.** duly **5.** aptly **6.** timely

appropriation . . . **5.** theft **6.** corner,
taking **8.** monopoly **9.** allotment
10. assignment, possession, usurpation

approval . . . **6.** assent **7.** consent,
support **8.** sanction **10.** admiration
11. approbation, endorsement
12. ratification

approve . . . **2.** OK **4.** like, okay, pass, sign,
test **6.** attest, ratify **7.** applaud, betoken,
certify, confirm, endorse (indorse),
signify **8.** accredit, sanction, validate
9. authorize, undersign **10.** appreciate
11. countenance **12.** authenticate

approve of . . . **5.** favor **6.** accept
7. endorse (indorse) **8.** sanction
11. countenance

approximate . . . **4.** near **5.** about, circa,
match **8.** approach, draw near, parallel,

resemble **10.** correspond

approximately . . . **4.** or so **5.** about, circa
6. around, nearly **11.** thereabouts

appui . . . **4.** prop, stay **6.** bridle (manège)
7. support

appulse . . . **6.** syzygy **7.** impinge
8. approach **9.** collision **11.** conjunction
(Astron)

appurtenance . . . **4.** gear **7.** adjunct
8. addition **9.** accessory, apparatus,
appendage, belonging, component

appurtenant . . . **7.** annexed **8.** incident,
relevant **9.** appendant, belonging
11. appropriate

après . . . **5.** after **10.** afterwards

apricot (pert to) . . .
  African . . **6.** meebos (dried)
  beverage . . **7.** cordial, liqueur, persico
  color . . **9.** red-yellow
  confection . . **6.** meebos (mebos)
  Japanese . . **3.** ume **4.** ansu
  vine . . **6.** maypop

a priori (opp of posteriori) . . . **9.** deductive
11. conditional, presumptive
12. hypothetical **13.** presumptively

apron . . . **3.** bib **4.** boot, brat, tier **5.** smock
6. barvel (barvell), runway **7.** garment,
tablier **8.** airstrip, lambskin (Masonic),
pinafore **9.** appendage

apropos, a propos . . . **3.** apt, pat
7. germane, purpose **8.** by the
way, relevant, suitably **9.** pertinent
10. applicable, seasonable
11. appurtenant, opportunely
12. incidentally

apt . . . **3.** fit, pat **4.** deft **5.** adept,
prone, ready, smart **6.** clever, expert,
likely, prompt, suited **7.** capable,
elegant, subject **8.** apposite, disposed,
inclined, skillful, suitable **9.** competent,
dexterous, ingenious, masterful,
pertinent, qualified, teachable
10. proficient **11.** appropriate

apteral . . . **8.** apterous, wingless

Apteryx . . . **3.** moa (extinct) **4.** kiwi

aptitude . . . **3.** art **4.** bent, gift, turn **5.** flair,
skill **6.** genius, talent **7.** ability, aptness,
fitness, leaning **8.** penchant, tendency
9. liability **10.** likelihood, proclivity
11. inclination **12.** suitableness
15. appropriateness

aptly . . . **7.** exactly, readily **8.** suitably
11. pertinently

aptness . . . **5.** skill **7.** fitness **8.** tendency
9. smartness **11.** suitability
12. teachability

aqua . . . **3.** eau **4.** agua **5.** water

aquatic . . . **6.** natant, wading, watery
8. natatory, swimming **12.** grallatorial
13. water-dwelling

Aquila . . . **6.** eagles **13.** constellation
(Milky Way)

aquiline . . . **6.** hanate, hooked **7.** curving
8. aduncous, unciform **10.** Roman-
nosed

ara . . . **5.** macaw **7.** goddess (vengeance)
8. aracanga **9.** screw pine
13. constellation

Arab . . . **4.** waif **5.** gamin, horse,
nomad **6.** Semite **7.** Bedouin, Saracen
8. wanderer, Yemenite **9.** Caucasian

araba . . . **3.** cab **5.** coach **6.** monkey (howling)

Arabia . . . see *Saudi-Arabia*

Arabian (pert to) . . .
antelope . . **5.** addax
beverage . . **4.** boza (bosa) **5.** leban (lebban)
bird . . **7.** phoenix
chief . . **5.** sheik
cloth (shoulder) . . **6.** cabaan (caban)
demon . . **5.** Eblis, jinni (jinnee) **6.** afreet
father . . **3.** Abu (Ab, Abou) **4.** Abba
garment . . **3.** aba **4.** haik **8.** burnoose
gazelle . . **4.** cora, oryx **5.** ariel
horse . . **4.** Kohl **8.** kadischi, palomino
jasmine . . **4.** bela
judge . . **4.** cadi
juniper (Bib) . . **5.** retem
nomad . . **7.** Saracen
peasant . . **6.** fellah
people (anc) . . **3.** Aus
physician . . **8.** Avicenna
poet . . **5.** Antar
prince . . **4.** emir (amir) **5.** emeer (ameer), sheik **6.** sherif, sultan
ravine . . **4.** wadi
romance . . **5.** Antar (Antara)
ruler . . **6.** caliph (calif)
Satan . . **5.** Eblis **6.** Azazel
scripture . . **7.** Alcoran
seaport . . **4.** Aden **5.** Mocha
state of bliss . . **3.** kef (kaif)
street urchin . . **5.** gamin
tambourine . . **4.** taar
vessel . . **4.** dhow **6.** boutre, sambuk
winds (hot) . . **6.** simoom (simoon)

Arabic letter . . . **4.** alif

arable land . . . **4.** farm **5.** arada, arado **6.** plowed, tilled **10.** cultivated

arachnid . . . **4.** mite, tick **6.** spider **8.** scorpion **9.** Arachnida

Aralu . . . **5.** Hades

Aram (Bib) . . . **6.** Rimmon (deity) **7.** Aramaic, Semitic **8.** language

araneous . . . **4.** thin **7.** weblike **8.** delicate **10.** cobweblike

arapunga . . . **8.** bellbird **9.** campanero

Arawak . . . **5.** Guana **6.** Indian

arbeit . . . **4.** work **8.** research

arbiter . . . **3.** ump **5.** judge **6.** umpire **7.** arbiter, referee **8.** mediator **9.** moderator **10.** arbitrator

arbitrary . . . **6.** thetic **8.** absolute, despotic, dogmatic **9.** imperious, unlimited **10.** autocratic, capricious, high-handed, peremptory, tyrannical **11.** determinate, dictatorial **13.** discretionary

arbitrate . . . **6.** decide **7.** bargain, mediate **9.** determine, intervene, negotiate **12.** intermediate

arbitrator . . . **5.** judge **6.** umpire **7.** arbiter, referee **8.** mediator **9.** moderator **11.** conciliator

arbor, arbour . . . **5.** bower, kiosk **6.** alcove, garden, pandal **7.** pergola, retreat, trellis **11.** latticework, summerhouse

arboreal . . . **6.** ramous **8.** branched, treelike **10.** arboriform

arboreal mammal . . . **2.** ai **4.** unau **5.** lemur, sloth **6.** aye-aye, monkey

arc . . . **3.** bow **5.** curve **6.** radian **7.** azimuth, rainbow

arca . . . **3.** box **5.** chest, paten **9.** reliquary

arcade . . . **3.** orb **4.** arch, hall **6.** arches, avenue **7.** gallery, portico **8.** arcature, corridor **9.** colonnade, peristyle **10.** passageway

Arcadia . . .
composition . . **4.** poem **5.** prose **7.** romance
district . . **6.** Greece
huntress . . **8.** Atalanta
pert to . . **5.** rural **6.** rustic **8.** pastoral
poetic . . **6.** Arcady
priestess . . **4.** Auge
woodland spirit . . **3.** Pan

arcanum . . . **6.** elixir, enigma, remedy, secret **7.** mystery

arch . . . **3.** arc, sly **4.** ogee **5.** chief, hance (part), ogive, vault **6.** fornix, instep **7.** cunning, eminent, roguish **8.** greatest, memorial, monument **9.** principal **11.** mischievous

arch (pert to) . . .
enemy . . **5.** devil, Satan **9.** adversary
inner curve . . **8.** intrados
memorial . . **6.** pailou (pailoo)
stone . . **8.** keystone
title . . **4.** duke **6.** bishop, deacon **7.** duchess

archaic . . . **3.** old **8.** obsolete, old-world **10.** antiquated **12.** old-fashioned

archangel (celestial) . . . **5.** Uriel **7.** Gabriel, Michael, Raphael

archangel plant . . . **4.** mint **8.** angelica

archbishop . . . **6.** bishop (chief), exarch **9.** patriarch

arched . . . **6.** curved **7.** embowed

Archer (Astron) . . . **11.** Sagittarius

archery . . . **3.** bow **4.** vane **5.** arrow, clout **6.** quiver **8.** fistmele, shooting **10.** ballistics

archetype . . . **4.** idea **5.** model **7.** pattern **8.** standard **9.** prototype

Archie (sl) . . . **3.** gun **12.** antiaircraft

Archipelago (pert to) . . .
Alaska . . **9.** Alexander
Australia . . **8.** Bismarck
Indonesia (largest) . . **5.** Malay
Italy . . **6.** Aegean

architect . . . **6.** artist, author **7.** builder, planner **8.** designer **9.** artificer, draftsman **11.** constructor, enterpriser

architectural (pert to) . . .
arch . . **8.** keystone, voussoir
base . . **5.** socle **6.** plinth
construction . . **8.** tectonic
ornament (part) . . **5.** gutta **6.** bezant, finial, frieze **8.** acanthus, dosseret, fretwork **10.** chambranle
pier . . **4.** anta
space (triang) . . **8.** pediment
style . . **5.** Doric, Greek, Ionic, Tudor **6.** Gothic **7.** Baroque, Cape Cod, Moorish, Spanish **8.** Colonial, Etruscan, Georgian **9.** Byzantine, Palladian **10.** Corinthian, Romanesque **11.** Renaissance **13.** Mediterranean

archives . . . **6.** annals **7.** records **8.** chancery, registry **9.** documents, registers **10.** chronicles

arch traitor . . . **6.** Arnold (Benedict), Brutus **8.** Quisling **13.** Judas Iscariot
archway . . . **6.** pailou (pailoo)
arctic . . . **5.** polar **6.** boreal, frigid, galosh **7.** Alaskan **8.** hibernal, Northern, Siberian **11.** hyperborean
Arctic (pert to) . . .
 base . . **4.** Etah (Greenland)
 bird . . **3.** auk **4.** skua, xema **6.** falcon
 cetacean . . **7.** narwhal
 current . . **8.** Labrador
 dog . . **5.** Husky (Siberian) **8.** Malemute
 food . . **8.** pemmican (pemican)
 jacket (hooded) . . **5.** parka (parkee) **6.** anorak
 native . . **5.** Aleut **6.** Eskimo, Indian
 polar . . **6.** Circle
 sea . . **7.** Barents **8.** Beaufort
arctoid . . . **6.** ursine **8.** bearlike
Arctoidea . . . **4.** bear **6.** weasel **7.** raccoon
ardent . . . **3.** hot **4.** avid, keen, warm **5.** eager, fiery, rethe **6.** fervid, fierce **7.** amorous, cordial, fervent, flaming, glowing, intense, shining, violent, zealous **8.** eloquent, vehement **10.** passionate **12.** affectionate, enthusiastic
ardilla . . . **8.** squirrel
ardor . . . **4.** élan, fire, heat, love, zeal **5.** estro, flame, gusto, verve **6.** fervor, fougue, spirit, warmth **8.** fervency **9.** affection, eagerness, eloquence, intensity **10.** enthusiasm **11.** impetuosity
arduous . . . **4.** hard **5.** steep **6.** trying **7.** onerous **8.** toilsome **9.** difficult, laborious, strenuous, wearisome **10.** burdensome, exhausting
area . . . **4.** belt, loci (pl), size, zone **5.** areal, basin, field, locus, range, scope, space, tract **6.** extent, locale, region, sector, sphere **7.** circuit, compass, environ, expanse **8.** province, vicinity **9.** bailiwick, territory **12.** neighborhood
Areca . . . **4.** palm
arena . . . **4.** bowl, oval, ring, rink **5.** court, field **6.** campus, circus **7.** cockpit, stadium, theater **8.** coliseum, platform **9.** gymnasium **10.** hippodrome **12.** amphitheater
arenose . . . **5.** sandy **6.** grainy, gritty **8.** sabulous
areola . . . **4.** halo, ring **5.** space **6.** armlet, wreath **7.** aureole, garland **10.** interstice
Ares (pert to) . . .
 consort . . **9.** Aphrodite
 father . . **4.** Zeus
 god . . **3.** war
 Roman name . . **4.** Mars
argala . . . **7.** marabou **8.** adjutant (bird)
argent . . . **5.** white **6.** silver **7.** shining, silvery **9.** whiteness
Argentina . . .
 capital . . **11.** Buenos Aires (1535)
 city . . **5.** Lanus **6.** Paraná **7.** Cordoba, Mendoza, Rosario
 Indian . . **4.** Lule
 mountain . . **5.** Andes **9.** Aconcagua (peak) **10.** Cordillera (Range)
 native . . **7.** Mestizo
 Plains . . **6.** Pampas **9.** Gran Chaco
 plateau . . **9.** Patagonia

 poet . . **7.** Andrade **10.** Echeverria
 river . . **5.** Plata **6.** Chubut, Paraná
Argentine (pert to) . . .
 color . . **7.** silvery **8.** art brown
 cowboy . . **6.** gaucho
 dance . . **5.** tango
Argonauts (pert to) . . .
 destination . . **7.** Colchis (anc)
 leader . . **5.** Jason
 objective . . **12.** Golden Fleece
 of '49 . . **6.** miners (gold)
 ship . . **5.** Argos
 sorceress . . **5.** Medea
Argos . . . **3.** dog (of Odysseus)
argosy . . . **4.** ship **5.** fleet **6.** armada, vessel **8.** flotilla
argot . . . **4.** cant, jive **5.** lingo, slang **6.** jargon, patois **7.** dialect **10.** vernacular
argue . . . **3.** rap **4.** moot, spar **5.** plead, prove **6.** bicker, debate, evince, reason **7.** contend, contest, discuss, dispute, wrangle **8.** indicate, maintain, persuade **10.** controvert **11.** expostulate, ratiocinate, remonstrate
argument . . . **4.** case, plea, spar **5.** cavil, lemma, proof, theme **6.** debate, hassle **7.** defense, dispute, fallacy, polemic, premise, sophism **8.** brouhaha, squabble **9.** dialectic, discourse, enthymeme, pro and con **10.** discussion **11.** altercation, disputation **13.** consideration, ratiocination
argumentative . . . **7.** eristic **8.** forensic **10.** indicative, rhetorical **11.** belligerent, contentious, presumptive, quarrelsome **12.** disputatious **13.** controversial
Argus (Gr Myth) . . . **7.** monster (founder of Argos)
Argus-eyed . . . **8.** vigilant **9.** observant **11.** hundred-eyed **12.** sharpsighted
argute . . . **5.** acute, sharp **6.** astute, shrewd, shrill, subtle **9.** sagacious
aria . . . **3.** air, lay **4.** solo, song, tune **5.** canto **6.** cantus, melody, strain **7.** ariette, sortita
arid . . . **3.** dry **4.** dull **6.** barren, jejune, vacant **7.** parched, sterile, thirsty **9.** anhydrous, waterless **13.** unimaginative
Arid Austral zone . . . **7.** Sonoran
Ariel . . . **5.** angel, sylph **6.** spirit **7.** lioness **9.** Jerusalem
ariel . . . **7.** gazelle
Aries (Astron) . . . **3.** ram **4.** sign **6.** meteor **13.** constellation
aries . . . **12.** battering-ram (anc)
aright . . . **4.** fine, well **7.** exactly **8.** directly, straight **11.** straightway
aril . . . **3.** pod **7.** arillus, coating **8.** arillode (false), covering
Arion . . . **4.** poet (of Lesbos) **5.** horse (talking)
arioso . . . **7.** melodic, tuneful **9.** melodious
arise . . . **4.** lift, rise, soar, stem, zoom **5.** begin, issue, mount, occur, rebel, surge, tower, waken **6.** appear, ascend, emerge, revolt, spring **7.** emanate **9.** originate
Aristarch . . . **6.** critic **10.** grammarian
Aristides . . . **7.** The Just **9.** statesman

(Athens)

aristocracy . . . **5.** elite **7.** peerage, royalty **8.** nobility **10.** government, patriciate, upper class

aristocrat . . . **4.** lord, peer **5.** noble **7.** aristos, Brahman, Brahmin, grandee, parvenu **8.** cavalier, eupatrid (Athens), nobleman **9.** blueblood, patrician **12.** silk-stocking

aristology, science of . . . **6.** dining

Aristole (pert to) . . .
birthplace . . **6.** Thrace **7.** Stagira (Macedonia)
famed as . . **9.** scientist **11.** philosopher **12.** The Stagirite
school . . **6.** Athens
teacher . . **5.** Plato
wife . . **7.** Pythias

arithmetic . . . **4.** sums **7.** numbers **11.** computation, enumeration, mathematics

arithmetic terms . . . **5.** prime **6.** result **7.** divisor, product **8.** dividend, multiple, quotient **9.** remainder **10.** multiplier **12.** multiplicand

Arizona . . .
capital . . **7.** Phoenix
city . . **4.** Yuma **5.** Tempe **6.** Bisbee, Tucson
famed site . . **9.** Hoover Dam **11.** Grand Canyon **13.** Painted Desert **15.** Petrified Forest
Indian . . **4.** Hano, Hopi, Pima **6.** Apache, Navaho (Navajo)
river . . **4.** Gila **8.** Colorado
State admission . . **11.** Forty-eighth
State bird . . **10.** cactus wren
State flower . . **6.** cactus **7.** saguaro
State motto . . **9.** Ditat Deus **11.** God Enriches
State nickname . . **11.** Grand Canyon

ark . . . **3.** vat **4.** boat, ship **5.** chest, haven **6.** asylum, refuge, vessel **8.** flatboat **9.** broadhorn, sanctuary (Ararat)

Arkansas . . .
capital . . **10.** Little Rock
city . . **8.** El Dorado **9.** Fort Smith
famed for . . **8.** diamonds (found in Murfreesboro)
famed newspaper . . **7.** Gazette (1819)
mountain . . **6.** Ozarks **9.** Ouachitas
Park (Nat) . . **10.** Hot Springs
river . . **5.** White **11.** Mississippi
State admission . . **11.** Twenty-fifth
State bird . . **11.** mockingbird
State flower . . **12.** apple blossom
State motto . . **13.** Regnat Populus **16.** Let the People Rule
State nickname . . **17.** Land of Opportunity

arm . . . **4.** limb **5.** equip, saber, sword **6.** branch, member, pistol, tappet, weapon **7.** forearm, fortify, protect, quillon (of sword), support **8.** revolver **9.** appendage **10.** projection **12.** ramification

arm (pert to) . . .
armpit . . **5.** oxter **6.** axilla
bone . . **4.** ulna **6.** radius **7.** humerus
hole . . **4.** scye (of sleeve)
muscle . . **6.** biceps **7.** triceps **8.** pronator

9. supinator

projection . . **6.** tappet
sea . . **4.** gulf, mere **5.** bayou, firth, inlet **7.** estuary
sundial . . **6.** gnomon
walk arm in arm . . **5.** oxter

armada . . . **5.** fleet **6.** argosy **8.** armament, flotilla, squadron, warships **10.** escadrille

Armada (famed) . . . **7.** Spanish (1588) **10.** Invincible

armadillo . . . **4.** apar, peba (peva) **5.** apara, poyou, tatou (tatu) **6.** mulita, peludo (giant) **7.** tatouay **10.** pichiciago, Tolypeutes **11.** quirquincho (hairy)

Armageddon . . . **3.** war **7.** Megiddo (Bib) **8.** conflict, world war

armed . . . **6.** fitted, rigged **7.** clothed, endowed **8.** equipped, invested, prepared, provided, supplied **9.** furnished, outfitted **10.** laquearian (with noose)

armed (pert to) . . .
conflict . . **3.** war **6.** combat **7.** warfare **11.** hostilities
forces . . **4.** army, host **5.** ranks **6.** troops **8.** military **9.** besiegers
vessel . . **3.** HMS, sub, USS **5.** U-boat **9.** destroyer, submarine **10.** battleship **11.** battlewagon

Armenia . . .
anc name . . **9.** Armenenak
capital . . **6.** Erivan
founder . . **4.** Haik
herb . . **5.** cumin **7.** caraway
highlanders . . **5.** Gomer
mountain . . **6.** Ararat, Taurus
river . . **3.** Kur **5.** Cyrus **6.** Araxes, Tigris **9.** Euphrates
worshiper . . **7.** Yesidio (Yesdi) **9.** Gregorian

armistice . . . **5.** peace, truce **9.** cessation **12.** pacification

armoire . . . **5.** ambry **8.** cupboard, wardrobe **10.** repository

armor . . . **4.** arms, bard (barde), egis, jamb, mail, tace **5.** acton, aegis, plate, seton, tasse **6.** cuisse, gorget, graith, greave, helmet, lorica, sconce, shield, tasset, tuille **7.** ailette, cuirass, hauberk, jambeau, panoply **8.** aventail, brassort, ordnance, pallette, solleret **9.** cubitiere, epauliere, gardebras, mainferre, rerebrace **10.** cataphract

armor-bearer . . . **6.** squire **7.** armiger, esquire

armored . . . **6.** mailed **8.** equipped, ironclad, mailclad **9.** cuirassed, loricated, panoplied

armpit . . . **5.** oxter **6.** axilla

arms . . . **7.** weapons **8.** armament, ordnance **9.** munitions

arms depository . . . **5.** depot **6.** armory **7.** arsenal

army . . . **3.** mob **4.** host, unit **5.** array, crowd, horde, posse **6.** forces, galaxy, legion, rabble, throng, troops **9.** multitude, Salvation

army (pert to) . . .
brown . . **7.** rosario
commission (special) . . **6.** brevet

trader.. **6.** sutler
army unit ... **4.** ROTC **5.** corps, guard
(Nat), squad **7.** brigade, cavalry,
company, militia, platoon, Sabaoth
(Bib) **8.** division, infantry, Landwehr,
regiment, reserves **9.** artillery, battalion,
minutemen **10.** volunteers
Arnold's co-conspirator ... **5.** Andre
(Maj)
aroma ... **4.** musk, odor, tang **5.** attar,
balmy, nidor, savor, scent, smell, spice
6. flavor **7.** bouquet, feature, incense,
perfume **9.** fragrance, muskiness,
redolence **11.** peculiarity, singularity
aromatic ... **5.** spicy **6.** savory **7.** odorous,
pungent **8.** fragrant, redolent
11. fluorescent
aromatic (pert to) ...
gum.. **5.** myrrh **12.** frankincense
herb.. **4.** mint **5.** clary, nondo
oil.. **4.** balm **6.** balsam **9.** sassafras
seed.. **4.** anis **6.** nutmeg **7.** aniseed,
caraway
tree.. **5.** aromo **6.** balsam **7.** champac
8. huisache
around ... **4.** near, peri (pref) **5.** about,
circa **9.** bordering, somewhere
11. thereabouts **13.** approximately
arouse ... **4.** fire, stir, wake **5.** alarm,
anger, evoke, pique, raise, rally, roust
6. awaken, elicit, excite, incite, kindle,
summon **7.** animate
arpa ... **4.** harp
arpeggio ... **5.** chord **7.** roulade
8. division, flourish
arraign ... **4.** cite **6.** accuse, charge, indict
7. impeach **8.** denounce, reproach
9. prosecute
arrange ... **3.** fix **4.** cast, cite, file,
plan, plot, sort **5.** adapt, aline, besee,
drape, ettle, frame, grade, preen,
range, stack **6.** adjust, deploy, design,
devise **7.** dispose, mediate, prepare,
provide, seriate **8.** classify, contract,
contrive, laminate, organize, tabulate
9. catalogue (catalog), negotiate
10. distribute, paniculate
11. alphabetize, systematize
arranged ... **5.** fixed, timed **6.** ranked,
sorted **7.** aligned, grouped, ordered,
orderly, planned, settled, uniform
9. regulated **10.** contracted
arranged in ...
fives.. **7.** quinate
fours.. **11.** tetramerous
hours.. **9.** staggered
rays.. **6.** radial
threes.. **7.** ternate
arrangement ... **3.** art, rig (sails)
4. plan, rank **5.** order, setup **6.** series,
syntax, system **7.** echelon (troops),
musical **8.** disposal, neatness, trimness
9. agreement, condition, structure
10. adaptation, engagement, settlement
11. collocation, combination,
permutation, preparation
12. distribution
arrant ... **3.** bad **6.** wicked **8.** rascally
9. confirmed, shameless
11. unmitigated **12.** disreputable
array ... **3.** don **4.** deci, robe **5.** adorn,

align, dress, order **6.** clothe, muster,
series, throng **7.** arrange, dispose,
envelop, marshal **8.** clothing, garments
9. adornment **11.** arrangement
arrears ... **3.** due **4.** debt **5.** short
7. wanting **9.** arrearage, deficient
10. behindhand, defaulting
arrest ... **4.** halt, hold, stop **5.** check,
delay, seize **6.** detain, hinder, impede,
retard **7.** custody, seizure **8.** obstruct,
restrain, stoppage **9.** apprehend,
hindrance, intercept, restraint
11. retardation
arrested ... **6.** behind **7.** checked, delayed,
impeded, stopped **8.** detained, retarded
10. restrained **11.** intercepted
arrested development ... **6.** simple
7. dwarfed, idiotic, moronic
8. backward, retarded **10.** half-witted
13. unintelligent
arrival ... **5.** comer (anc) **6.** advent,
coming **7.** landing **8.** approach,
reaching **10.** attainment, homecoming
11. achievement
arrive ... **4.** come **5.** debus, reach **6.** alight,
debark, happen **7.** detrain **9.** disembark
arrogance ... **5.** pride **7.** conceit,
disdain, hauteur **8.** audacity, rudeness,
snobbery **9.** brashness, insolence,
loftiness **10.** effrontery **11.** haughtiness
12. impertinence
arrogant ... **4.** bold, pert **5.** cocky, lofty,
proud **6.** lordly, uppish **7.** forward
8. impudent, insolent **9.** audacious,
insulting, masterful, presuming
10. disdainful **11.** domineering, highfalutin, impertinent, overbearing
12. contemptuous, contumelious,
presumptuous, supercilious
arrogate ... **5.** seize, usurp, wrest
6. assume **11.** appropriate
arrow ... **4.** barb, dart, reed, vire
(feathered) **5.** guide, shaft **6.** finger
7. missile, pointer **10.** guideboard
arrow (pert to) ...
astronomy.. **7.** Sagitta
bows.. **6.** bowyer (maker, seller)
case.. **6.** quiver
end.. **4.** nock **9.** arrowhead
feather (to).. **6.** fletch
handle.. **5.** stele
head.. **4.** dart
poison.. **4.** inee, upas **5.** urali **6.** curare,
uzarin
poisoned.. **6.** sumpit **8.** sumpitan
propeller.. **3.** bow
shape.. **6.** beloid **9.** cuneiform, sagittate
stone.. **9.** belemnite
variety.. **4.** self **6.** footed **7.** chested
9. bobtailed
arrowroot ... **3.** pia **5.** araru **6.** ararao,
starch **7.** Maranta
arroyo ... **5.** brook, creek **6.** ravine,
stream **11.** watercourse
arroz ... **4.** rice
arse ... **4.** butt, rump (vulgar) **8.** buttocks
9. posterior
arsenal ... **4.** dump **5.** depot, plant
6. armory **7.** factory **8.** magazine
10. depository, storehouse
arsis ... **5.** ictus **6.** accent, stress (opp

of thesis), upbeat
arson . . . **7.** burning, cautery **9.** pyromania **12.** incendiarism
art . . . **4.** wile **5.** cameo, craft, knack, skill, taste, trade **6.** design **7.** calling, cartoon, cunning, drawing, science **8.** aptitude, artifice, artistry, business, ceramics, drafting, intaglio, painting, vocation **9.** dexterity, duplicate, engraving, ingenuity, readiness, sculpture, sketching **10.** adroitness, decoration, profession **11.** contrivance, photography, portraiture **12.** architecture
art (pert to) . . .
  addict . . **8.** aesthete (esthete)
  decoration . . **9.** sgraffito
  design . . **7.** graphic
  fancier . . **10.** dilettante
  gallery . . **5.** salon
  grotesque . . **11.** incongruous
  mystic . . **6.** cabala
  of assaying . . **8.** docimasy
  of discourse . . **8.** rhetoric
  of embossing . . **9.** toreutics
  of government . . **8.** politics
  of horsemanship . . **6.** manège
  of imitation . . **7.** mimicry
  of manual craft . . **5.** sloyd
  of memory . . **10.** mneumonics
  of metal inlay . . **6.** niello
  primitive . . **9.** artifacts
  realistic . . **5.** genre
  rhyming . . **5.** poesy **6.** poetry
  self-defense . . **6.** boxing **7.** fencing, jujitsu (jiujitsu)
  style, movement . . **3.** pop **6.** cubism, rococo **7.** baroque, Bauhaus, Dadaism, Fauvism **8.** futurism **9.** modernism **10.** surrealism **11.** romanticism **13.** expressionism, impressionism
  theme . . **5.** motif
  tooling . . **10.** diesinking
  transmutation . . **7.** alchemy
Artemis (pert to) . . .
  brother (twin) . . **6.** Apollo
  epithet (Homeric) . . **6.** Phoebe
  father . . **4.** Zeus
  goddess of . . **4.** moon **6.** nature **7.** the Hunt **8.** Olympian
  Mother . . **4.** Leto
  religion . . **4.** Upis
  Roman equivalent . . **5.** Diana
artery . . . **4.** tube, vein **6.** avenue, street, vessel **7.** channel, highway, passage **8.** ligament **10.** passageway
artery (Anat) . . . **4.** tube, vein **5.** aorta **6.** vessel **7.** anonyma, carotid, trachea **9.** capillary, pulmonary **10.** innominate
artery pulsation . . . **4.** beat **5.** ictus
artful . . . **3.** sly **4.** foxy, wily **5.** cagey **6.** adroit, clever, crafty, shrewd, subtle, tricky **7.** crooked, cunning, knowing, politic **8.** skillful, stealthy **9.** deceitful, deceptive, designing, dexterous, imitative **10.** artificial
Artful Dodger . . . **3.** fox **6.** rascal **7.** slicker **8.** deceiver **11.** John Dawkins (Dickens tale) **12.** crafty person
artfulness . . . **5.** skill **7.** finesse **8.** artifice, subtlety, wiliness **9.** stratagem

10. cleverness, refinement, shrewdness
arthron . . . **5.** hinge, joint, pivot **12.** articulation
Arthurian abode . . . **6.** Avalon **9.** Lyonnesse (Leonnoys)
Arthurian character . . . **6.** Arthur (King), Elaine, Merlin **7.** Geraint **8.** Lancelot **9.** Percivale
artichoke . . . **6.** canada, Cynara **7.** chorogi, thistle **9.** Jerusalem
article . . . **3.** mat **4.** item, news, term **5.** scoop, story, thing **6.** belief, clause, detail, gadget, object, treaty **7.** camelot, feature (news), grammar, integer **8.** treatise **9.** commodity, editorial **10.** particular **11.** composition, stipulation
article (Gram) . . .
  English . . **1.** a **2.** an **3.** the
  French . . **2.** la, le, un **3.** les, une
  Spanish . . **2.** el, un **3.** las, los, una
article (of) . . .
  agreement . . **8.** contract
  apparel . . **5.** smock, tunic **6.** duster, gaiter, mantle **8.** pinafore
  faith . . **5.** canon, creed, dogma, tenet **6.** belief **7.** precept
  property . . **7.** chattel
  virtu . . **5.** curio, relic **6.** rarity **7.** antique
articulation . . . **4.** tone **5.** hinge, joint, sound, voice **7.** voicing **8.** locution, sonation **9.** phonation, utterance **11.** enunciation **12.** vocalization **13.** pronunciation
artifact . . . **5.** curio, relic, virtu **6.** fossil **7.** antique, remains **8.** archaism
artifice . . . **4.** plot, ruse, wile **5.** blind, chest, craft, dodge, fraud, guile, shift, trick **6.** deceit **7.** cunning, evasion, finesse, knavery, sleight **8.** intrigue, maneuver, trickery **9.** chicanery, collusion, deception, expedient, imposture, stratagem **10.** connivance, imposition, subterfuge **11.** contrivance, machination, skulduggery
artificer . . . **5.** smith **6.** artist, framer **7.** artisan, creator, deviser, workman **8.** Daedalus, inventor, mechanic **9.** architect, carpenter, craftsman, goldsmith **11.** coppersmith, silversmith
artificial . . . **4.** fake, faux, mock, sham **5.** bogus, dummy, false, phony **6.** ersatz, forged, unreal **7.** assumed, bastard, elegant, feigned **8.** affected, fabulous, spurious **9.** imaginary, imitation, pretended, unnatural **11.** adulterated, counterfeit, unauthentic **12.** supposititious
artificial (pert to) . . .
  butter . . **4.** oleo **13.** oleomargarine
  channel . . **3.** gat **4.** leat **5.** canal, flume **6.** sluice
  gum . . **7.** dextrin
  language . . **2.** ro **3.** Ido **5.** Arulo **7.** Volapuk **9.** Esperanto **10.** Occidental
  silk . . **5.** nylon, rayon
  surface . . **4.** rink
  voice . . **8.** falsetto
artillery . . . **4.** army, guns **5.** bombs **6.** cannon, slings **7.** cavalry, gunners, gunnery, mortars **8.** ordnance

9. arbalests, catapults 10. ballistics
artillery (pert to) . . .
emplacement . . 7. battery
fire . . 5. salvo 6. rafale
man . . 6. gunner 8. rifleman, topechee
9. cannoneer, musketeer 11. artillarist
wagon . . 7. battery
artiodactyl . . . (opp of perissodactyl) 2. ox
3. pig 4. deer, goat 5. camel, sheep
6. artiad 7. giraffe 12. hippopotamus
artisan . . . 6. artist, limner 7. painter,
workman 8. mechanic, virtuoso
9. artificer, craftsman
artist . . . 5. rapin (Fr pupil) 6. etcher,
limner, potter 7. artisan, painter
8. designer, sculptor 9. architect,
decorator 10. cartoonist, ceramacist
11. illustrator 12. photographer
artist (pert to) . . .
equipment . . 5. easel 7. palette
8. maquette
sleight of hand . . 4. mage 5. Magus
8. magician 9. alchemist
artiste . . . 5. actor, adept 6. dancer, singer
7. artisan 8. musician 9. performer
artistic . . . 4. pure 6. ornate 7. classic
8. graceful, skillful, tasteful 9. aesthetic
(esthetic), art-minded, beautiful,
exquisite
artistic (pert to) . . .
ardor . . 5. verve 6. spirit
dance . . 6. ballet
quality . . 6. virtue
symbol of the dead . . 5. orant
temperament . . 7. caprice, emotion
artless . . . 4. naif, open, rude 5. frank,
naive 6. candid, simple 7. natural,
sincere 8. ignorant 9. guileness,
ingenuous, unskilled 10. inartistic,
unaffected, uncultured 11. undesigning
15. unsophisticated
artlessness . . . 6. candor 7. naiveté
9. frankness, innocence 11. naturalness
13. ungenuousness
arts (pert to) . . .
liberal . . 7. trivium 10. quadrivium
quadrivium . . 5. music 8. geometry
9. astronomy 10. arithmetic
trivium . . 5. logic 7. grammar 8. rhetoric
aru . . . 6. indeed, really
arui . . . 5. oudad, sheep 7. chamois (Bib)
arum . . . 4. taro 5. calla (lily) 6. starch
9. arrowroot
arx . . . 7. citadel
Aryan (pert to) . . .
God of Fire . . 4. Agni
invader . . 4. Pict
people . . 4. Mede 5. Hindu 9. Caucasian
11. Indo-Iranian
as . . . 3. qua 4. como, than, thus 5. since,
while 7. because, equally, similar
9. similarly
Asa . . . 11. King of Judah
asafetida . . . 8. medicine
13. antispasmodic
Asa's son . . . 11. Jehoshaphat
ascend . . . 3. fly 4. rise, soar, upgo
5. arise, climb, mount, scale, tower
6. aspire, uprise 7. clamber, upsurge
ascendancy . . . 4. sway 7. control,
mastery 8. dominion, prestige, priority

9. authority, influence, supremacy
10. domination 11. sovereignty,
superiority 12. predominance
13. preponderance
ascendant, ascendent . . . 5. elder
6. father 7. supreme 8. ancestor,
forebear, superior 9. governing,
patriarch 10. antecedent, decoration
(Arch)
ascended . . . 4. rose 5. arose, risen
6. uprose
ascending . . . 6. anodic, rising 7. scaling,
sloping 8. mounting, racemose
9. emanating
ascending signs . . . 5. Aries 6. Gemini,
Pisces, Taurus 8. Aquarius 9. Capricorn
ascenseur . . . 8. elevator
Ascension Day . . . 8. Thursday (Holy)
(40 days after Easter)
Ascension lily . . . 7. Madonna
ascertain . . . 4. find 5. learn, prove, solve
6. decide 7. certify 9. determine
ascetic . . . 4. yati, yoga, yogi 5. fakir,
stoic 6. Essene, hermit, strict 7. austere,
eremite, puritan, recluse 8. anchoret,
Diogenes, solitary 9. abstainer,
anchorite, mendicant 10. abstemious
asceticism . . . 4. Yoga 9. austerity,
nephalism 10. abstention, abstinence,
puritanism 11. anchoritism, teetotalism
ascribable . . . 3. due 9. traceable
10. assignable 11. attributive
12. attributable
ascribe . . . 5. count, refer 6. assign,
attach, credit, impute, reckon 7. ascribe
8. accredit 9. attribute
ascus fruit . . . 8. truffles
asepsis . . . 6. purity 7. clarity 9. sterility
13. taintlessness
ash . . . 4. sorb, tree 5. rowan 6. samara
(fruit) 8. Fraxinus
ashes . . . 4. dust, lava, lees, slag 5. dregs,
ruins 6. embers 7. cinders, residue
ash tree symbol (Norse Myth) . . .
10. Yggdrasill (horse of Yggr)
Asia . . . 4. East 6. Orient, region 7. Far
East 8. Old World 9. continent
Asia Minor . . .
city (anc) . . 4. Myra, Teos, Troy
5. Ilium, Issus, Lydia 6. Nicaea, Sardes
7. Ephesus
district . . 4. Aria 5. Ionia, Troad (The
Troad) 6. Aeolis
island . . 6. Lesbos
language (anc) . . 6. Lycian, Lydian
8. Etruscan
mountain . . 3. Ida
old name . . 8. Anatolia
sea . . 5. Black 6. Aegean 7. Marmosa
13. Mediterranean
Asiatic (pert to) . . .
barbarian (anc) . . 3. Hun 6. Vandal
cyclone . . 7. typhoon
desert . . 4. Gobi
gulf . . 4. Aden, Oman, Siam 6. Tonkin
7. Persian
island . . 4. Java 5. Luzon, Malay
7. Celebes, Diomede (Big), Formosa,
Sumatra 8. Japanese, Mindanao,
Sakhalin 11. Philippines
mountain . . 4. Ural 5. Altai, Sayan

7. Everest **8.** Caucasus, Himalaya
9. Hindu Kush
native . . **4.** Arab, Turk, Yuit **5.** Tatar
   6. Indian, Innuit (Esk), Syrian **7.** Chinese,
   Malayan **8.** Annamese, Japanese
   9. Mongolian
nomad . . **4.** Arab
river . . **2.** Ob **4.** Amur, Lena, Yalu
   5. Huang (Hwang), Indus **6.** Ganges,
   Tigris **7.** Yangtze, Yenisei **9.** Euphrates,
   Irrawaddy **11.** Brahmaputra
sea . . **4.** Azov (Azof) **5.** Black, China,
   Japan **6.** Bering, Yellow **7.** Caspian,
   Okhotsk
wind . . **7.** monsoon
Asiatic animal . . .
   antelope . . **5.** goral
   ass . . **6.** onager
   camel . . **8.** Bactrian **9.** dromedary
   carnivore . . **5.** panda, tiger
   cattle . . **4.** zobo
   deer . . **4.** axis **10.** chevrotain
   elephant . . **7.** Elephas
   fox . . **6.** corsac
   gazelle . . **3.** ahu
   goat . . **5.** serow
   lemur . . **5.** loris **6.** macaco
   lynx . . **7.** caracal
   mongoose . . **4.** urva
   monkey . . **6.** langur (long-tailed)
   ox . . **3.** yak
   rodent . . **4.** pika
   sheep . . **3.** sha **5.** uriel **6.** argali
   squirrel . . **8.** jelerang **10.** polatouche
Asiatic bird . . .
   finch . . **9.** brambling
   jay . . **7.** sirgang
   owl . . **4.** utum
   partridge . . **6.** seesee
   plover . . **8.** dotterel
   songless . . **7.** Pitta
   talking . . **4.** myna (mynah)
Asiatic snake . . . **3.** asp **5.** cobra
   8. ringhals
Asiatic storm (pert to) . . .
   sand . . **6.** simoom (simoon) **7.** tebbard
   snow . . **5.** buran
   wind . . **5.** buran **7.** monsoon
aside . . . **4.** away **5.** apart, hence **6.** aslant,
   astray, beside **7.** whisper **8.** sidewise
   9. alongside, privately, sotto voce
   12. interjection
asinine . . . **4.** dumb **5.** inane, inept, silly
   6. mulish, stupid **7.** doltish, foolish,
   idiotic **9.** obstinate
ask . . . **3.** beg **4.** quiz **5.** claim, exact,
   query, speer **6.** assess, demand, invite
   7. beseech, entreat, implore, inquire,
   request, require, solicit **8.** petition,
   question **9.** catechize, obsecrate (Relig)
   11. interrogate
askance . . . **4.** awry **5.** askew **7.** asquint,
   crooked **8.** sideways **9.** obliquely
askew . . . **4.** agee, alop, awry **5.** agley,
   amiss **6.** faulty **7.** askance, asquint,
   crooked **8.** deranged **9.** distorted,
   obliquely **10.** catawampus, disorderly
aslant . . . **5.** atilt **6.** tilted, tipped
   7. athwart, leaning, listing, pitched,
   sloping **8.** inclined **9.** careening,
   obliquely

asleep . . . **4.** dead, dull, numb **7.** dormant,
   unaware **8.** deadened, sleeping,
   unarisen **9.** oblivious, senseless,
   unruffled **10.** motionless **11.** inattentive,
   insensitive, unconscious
Asoka's Empire (anc Ind) . . . **5.** Patna
asp . . . **5.** cobra, snake, viper **6.** uraeus
   (sacred sym)
aspect . . . **3.** air **4.** look, mien, pose,
   side, view **5.** angle, decil, facet, guise,
   phase, shape, sight, state **6.** decile,
   facies, status, visage **7.** bearing,
   posture, scenery **8.** attitude **9.** astrology,
   component, influence, seaminess,
   situation **10.** appearance
   11. countenance
aspen . . . **4.** tree, wood **6.** poplar
   7. quaking **9.** quivering, shivering,
   trembling, tremulous, vibrating
asperge . . . **3.** wet **4.** damp **5.** spray,
   water **7.** baptize **8.** humidify, sprinkle
asperge . . . **9.** asparagus
Asperges . . . **4.** rite **6.** anthem
   10. sprinkling (altar)
aspergillum . . . **5.** brush **7.** sprayer
   8. baptizer **9.** sprinkler
asperity . . . **5.** rigor **7.** raucity **8.** acerbity,
   acrimony, hardship, severity, tartness
   9. bleakness, roughness **10.** causticity,
   difficulty, inclemency, moroseness,
   resentment
asperse . . . **4.** slur **5.** abuse, decry,
   libel **6.** defame, malign, revile, vilify
   7. blacken, slander, traduce **8.** besmirch
   9. bespatter, discredit **10.** calumniate
aspersion . . . **4.** rite, slur **6.** insult
   7. affront, baptism, calumny, outrage,
   wetting **8.** innuendo **9.** indignity
   10. defamation, sprinkling
   12. calumniating, calumniation
   13. disparagement
asphalt . . . **4.** pave **5.** pitch **7.** bitumen,
   mineral **8.** blacktop, pavement, uintaite
   9. gilsonite **10.** macadamize
asphyxia . . . **5.** apnea (apnoea) **7.** choking
   11. suffocation **12.** smotheration
aspic . . . **3.** asp (poet) **5.** jelly **6.** cannon
   8. lavender **9.** galantine
aspiration . . . **3.** aim **4.** hope, wish
   5. ideal **6.** breath, desire **7.** pumping,
   sucking, suction **8.** ambition, staccato
   9. breathing **10.** exhalation
   11. inspiration
aspire . . . **4.** long, plan, rise, soar
   5. tower **6.** attain, desire, expect, intend
   7. breathe, propose
ass . . . **3.** ono (comb form) **4.** dolt, dope,
   fool, jack **5.** burro, jenny
assail . . . **4.** pelt **5.** beset, stone **6.** attack
   7. assault **9.** implicate **11.** incriminate
assailant . . . **3.** foe **5.** enemy **7.** invader
   8. assailer, attacker, opponent
   9. adversary, aggressor **10.** antagonist,
   challenger
Assam . . .
   capital . . **8.** Shillong
   native . . **4.** Ahom **8.** Assamite **11.** Indo-
   Chinese
   people . . **3.** Aka **4.** Garo, Naga
   province of . . **5.** India
   river . . **11.** Brahmaputra

tribe . . **2.** Ao **3.** Aka **4.** Garo, Naga
assassin . . . **4.** Cain, thug **5.** bravo
  6. apache, cuttle, gunman, killer, slayer
  7. gorilla, ruffian **8.** murderer, sicarian
  9. manslayer **11.** slaughterer
assassination . . . **5.** purge **6.** murder
  7. killing **8.** regicide **11.** liquidation
  12. manslaughter
Assassin Order . . . **8.** Ismalian
  10. Mohammedan
assault . . . **5.** onset, storm **6.** assail, attack,
  charge **7.** descent, seizure **8.** invasion
  9. incursion **13.** incrimination
assay . . . **3.** try **4.** test **5.** prove, trial
  6. accost **7.** attempt **8.** analysis,
  docimasy (art), endeavor
  10. experiment **12.** verification
assay cup . . . **5.** cupel
assemblage . . . **3.** all **4.** herd **6.** throng
  8. assembly, entirety **9.** gathering
  12. congregation
assemblage (pert to) . . .
  cattle . . **5.** drove, rodeo **7.** roundup
  fashionable . . **5.** salon
  mob . . **4.** rout **6.** rabble
  splendid . . **6.** galaxy
  tents . . **4.** camp **10.** encampment
assemble . . . **3.** pod **4.** mass, meet
  5. amass, piece, rally, unite **6.** couple,
  gather, muster **7.** cluster, collect,
  convene, convoke, recruit
  10. congregate
assembly . . . **4.** bevy, diet, moot **5.** agora,
  gemot, group, synod, troop **6.** assize,
  sabbat **7.** company, council, landtag,
  meeting **8.** auditory, conclave (secret),
  folkmoot (Hist) **9.** concourse, gathering
  10. collection, convention
  11. convocation **12.** congregation
assent . . . **3.** aye, nod, yea, yes **4.** amen
  5. admit, agree, grant **6.** accede,
  accord, concur **7.** consent **8.** sanction
  9. acquiesce, agreement **10.** compliance
  12. acquiescence
assert . . . **3.** say **4.** aver, pose **5.** claim,
  plead, posit, state, voice **6.** affirm,
  allege, avouch, relate, uphold
  7. contend, declare, profess, protest,
  support **8.** advocate **9.** pronounce,
  vindicate **10.** asseverate
assertion . . . **5.** claim **6.** remark, thesis
  7. premise **8.** averment **9.** statement
  10. assumption, hypothesis
  11. affirmation, declaration,
  maintenance, proposition, vindication
assertiveness . . . **10.** pragmatism
  14. aggressiveness
assertor . . . **8.** affirmer, defender
  9. supporter **10.** vindicator
assess . . . **3.** ask, tax **4.** cess, levy, mise,
  rate **5.** price, value **6.** charge **7.** measure
  8. appraise, estimate
assessment . . . **3.** fee, tax **4.** levy,
  rate, scot **5.** ratal, stock, value
  6. surtax **7.** pricing, scutage **8.** estimate
  9. appraisal, valuation **10.** evaluation
  11. measurement
assets . . . **5.** funds, means **6.** wealth
  7. capital **8.** accounts, property
  9. resources
asseverate . . . **3.** say, vow **4.** aver

5. state, swear **6.** affirm, allege, assert
  7. contend, declare, profess, protest
  8. maintain **9.** pronounce
asseveration . . . **3.** vow **4.** oath (solemn)
  8. averment **9.** assertion **11.** affirmation,
  declaration **13.** pronouncement
assiduity . . . **8.** industry **9.** diligence
  11. painstaking, persistence
  12. perseverance
assiduous . . . **4.** busy **6.** active **7.** intense,
  zealous **8.** diligent, sedulous
  9. energetic, laborious, unwearied
  11. industrious, perseverant
  13. indefatigable, unintermitted
assign . . . **3.** fix, set **4.** cast, cede, seal
  5. allot, refer **6.** allege, commit, detail
  7. address, adjudge, appoint, ascribe,
  consign, empower **8.** accredit, allocate,
  delegate, nominate, transfer **9.** attribute
  10. commission **11.** appropriate
assignment . . . **3.** job **4.** task **5.** chore,
  stint **6.** lesson **7.** mission **8.** exercise,
  transfer **9.** allotment **10.** allocation,
  commission, commitment
  11. attribution **13.** specification
assimilate . . . **5.** adapt, learn, liken
  6. absorb, digest, imbibe **7.** convert
  10. understand **11.** approximate
assimilation . . . **8.** imbibing, learning
  9. anabolism, digestion, ingestion,
  reduction **10.** absorption, adaptation,
  comparison, conversion
  14. naturalization
assist . . . **3.** aid **4.** abet, back, help **5.** avail,
  boost, favor **6.** attend, prompt, second,
  succor **7.** benefit, relieve, support,
  sustain **8.** befriend **9.** accompany,
  subsidize
assistance . . . **3.** aid **4.** help **5.** grant
  6. relief, succor **7.** service, subsidy,
  support **10.** logrolling (Polit)
  11. furtherance
assistant . . . **4.** aide, ally **5.** tutor
  6. deputy, helper **7.** abettor, famulus,
  servant, teacher **9.** associate, attendant,
  auxiliary **11.** subordinate **12.** right-hand
  man
assize . . . **3.** fix **4.** rate **5.** edict, trial,
  value **6.** assess, decree **9.** ordinance
  10. regulation **11.** instruction,
  measurement
associate . . . **3.** mix, pal **4.** ally, chum,
  mate **5.** buddy, crony **6.** fellow,
  friend, hobnob, mingle **7.** combine,
  comrade, consort, partner **9.** colleague,
  companion **10.** accomplice
  11. concomitant, confederate
associated . . . **6.** allied, banded, joined,
  united **7.** coupled, leagued, related
  9. connected **10.** affiliated, concurrent
associates . . . **4.** crew **5.** force, staff
  7. retinue **9.** personnel **12.** constituency
association . . . **4.** body, club **5.** artel,
  cabal, guild, hanse (Hist), union
  6. league, lyceum, symbol **7.** company,
  society **8.** alliance, relation, sodality,
  sorority **9.** syndicate **10.** fellowship,
  fraternity **11.** affiliation, combination,
  comradeship, concurrence, corporation
  13. communication, interrelation
assonance . . . **3.** pun **4.** rime **5.** rhyme

8. paragram 9. agreement
11. paronomasia, resemblance
12. alliteration
as soon as possible ... 4. ASAP
assort ... 4. sort, suit 5. adapt, class, grade, group 7. consort (with) 8. classify, separate 9. associate (with) 10. categorize, distribute
assortment ... 3. mix, set 4. hash, mess, olio 5. class, group 6. jumble, medley 7. mélange, mixture, sorting 9. potpourri 10. collection, hodgepodge, miscellany 11. arrangement 14. conglomeration
assuage ... 4. calm, ease 5. allay, slake 6. lessen, mellow, pacify, quench, soften, solace, soothe 7. appease, comfort, gratify, qualify, relieve, satisfy 8. mitigate, palliate 9. alleviate
assuasive ... 5. balmy 6. easing 8. remedial, soothing 9. relieving, softening 10. mitigating, palliative 11. alleviative 13. tranquilizing
assume ... 3. don 4. deem, sham, take 5. adopt, feign, guess, imply, infer, judge, think, usurp 6. affect, allege, betake, borrow, deduce 7. believe, imagine, premise, presume, pretend, suppose, surmise 8. arrogate, conclude, simulate 9. undertake 11. appropriate, counterfeit
assume (pert to) ...
  character .. 11. impersonate
  different forms .. 7. protean
  unduly .. 5. usurp 8. arrogate
  without proof .. 11. theoretical 12. hypothetical
assumed ... 6. deemed 7. alleged, implied, thought 8. affected, inferred, presumed, supposed 9. fictional, pretended 10. fictitious, understood, undertaken 11. conjectured, make-believe, presumptive, presupposed, theoretical 12. appropriated, hypothetical, suppositious
assuming ... 5. lofty 8. arrogant, superior 9. presuming 10. assumptive 11. overweening, pretentious 12. presumptuous
assumption ... 8. adoption 9. arrogance, postulate, reception 10. usurpation 11. implication, proposition, supposition 13. appropriation, incorporation 14. presupposition
assurance ... 4. hope, oath 5. poise, trust 6. aplomb, belief, pledge, surety 7. comfort, courage, promise 8. security, sureness 9. certainty, guarantee, impudence, insurance 10. confidence, steadiness 11. assuredness, intrepidity 12. cocksureness 14. self-confidence
assure ... 4. aver 5. vouch 6. assert, avouch, depose, ensure, insure, secure 7. confirm, declare, protest, satisfy 8. convince, embolden, persuade, reassure 9. encourage, guarantee 10. asseverate
Assyria ...
  capital .. 7. Nineveh
  city .. 5. Calab (Bib) 9. Khorsabad (ruins)
  empire (anc) .. 5. Assur (Ashur)

  language .. 6. Semite 9. cuneiform (written)
  people .. 6. Semite 7. Amorite (Bib)
Assyrian god ...
  atmosphere .. 5. Hadad
  fire .. 5. Nusku
  hunt .. 7. Ninurta
  moon .. 3. Sin
  storm .. 2. Zu
  sun .. 7. Shamash
  war .. 6. Nergal 7. Ninurta
  winds .. 4. Adad 5. Hadad
Assyrian goddess ... 5. Nanai 6. Allatu, Ishtar 9. Sarpanitu (Zirbanit)
Assyriology, science of ... 8. language 11. antiquities
aster ... 4. star 9. asterwort, karyaster 10. Carduaceae
asterisk ... 4. mark (reference), star 6. accent, figure (star) 9. highlight 10. asteriskos (Eccl)
astern ... 3. aft 4. baft, rear 5. abaft, after 6. behind 8. hindward, rearward, tailward
asteroid ... 5. Ceres (largest) 6. planet 8. starlike 9. planetoid
Asteroidea ... 8. starfish
astir ... 2. up 5. about, afoot, eager 6. active, moving 8. stirring 11. forthcoming
as to ... 7. apropos, suppose 9. regarding 10. concerning, respecting
astonish ... 4. stun 5. amaze, appal 7. astound, stagger, startle 8. bewilder, confound, surprise 9. overwhelm
astonishing ... 7. amazing 8. fabulous 9. appalling, marvelous, wonderful 10. incredible, remarkable
astound ... 4. stun 5. abash, amaze, shock 6. appall (appal), dismay 7. stagger, stupefy 8. astonish, surprise 10. disconcert
astounding ... 8. horrible, shocking 9. appalling, frightful 10. horrendous, horrifying 11. astonishing
astraddle ... 7. astride 9. horseback, pickaback (piggyback) 10. straddling
astral ... 6. spirit, starry 7. stellar 8. sidereal, starlike 9. celestial 11. star-studded
astray ... 4. lost 5. amiss, wrong 6. adrift, afield, erring 8. aberrate, mistaken 9. erroneous 10. bewildered
astray, to go ... 3. err, sin 4. mang, rove 5. drift, lapse, stray 6. wander 7. deviate, digress 8. miscarry 9. backslide 10. misbelieve
astriction ... 4. bond 7. binding 8. thirlage 9. fastening 10. litigation 11. confinement, contraction 12. constipation
astride ... 8. straddle 9. astraddle, horseback, pickaback (piggyback)
astringent ... 4. acid, alum, sloe, sour 5. acerb, acrid, harsh, sapan, stern 6. tannin 7. austere, bitters, caustic, pungent, rhatany (root), styptic 9. vitriolic 10. antiseptic 11. acrimonious, argentamine 12. constrictive
astrologer ... 8. Chaldean 9. stargazer

11. astrologian, astromancer,
Nostradamus
astrology (pert to) . . . **5.** house, signs
6. aspect, zodiac **7.** mansion, mundane
8. siderism **9.** horoscope, planetary
11. horoscopist
astronaut . . . **7.** Martian **8.** spaceman
9. cosmonaut, rocketeer
astronomer . . . **9.** stargazer
11. uranologist **12.** uranographer
13. meteorologist, uranographist
astronomer, famed . . . **6.** Kepler
7. Galileo **12.** Eratosthenes
astronomical . . . **4.** huge, vast **5.** large
6. cosmic, uranic **7.** immense,
mammoth, Uranian **8.** colossal,
empyreal, heavenly **9.** celestial
10. prodigious, stupendous,
tremendous
astronomy (pert to) . . . **4.** coma (the)
5. apsis, saros (Bab) **6.** syzygy
7. almanac, apsides, azimuth, gibbous
8. sidereal **9.** idiometer, insulated
11. debilissima
astute . . . **3.** sly **4.** keen, wily **5.** acute,
canny, smart **6.** artful, clever, crafty,
shrewd **7.** cunning, skilled **9.** insidious,
sagacious **10.** discerning
14. discriminating
asunder . . . **5.** apart, cleft, rived (riven),
split **6.** atwain, halved **7.** divided
9. disjoined, separated
as yet . . . **8.** hitherto
asylum . . . **3.** ark **4.** home, jail, port
5. haven **6.** harbor, refuge **7.** retreat,
shelter **9.** hospitium, infirmary,
sanctuary **10.** stronghold **11.** institution
asymmetrical . . . **6.** uneven, warped
7. twisted, unequal **9.** contorted,
distorted **11.** zygomorphic
16. disproportionate
at . . . **2.** by, in **4.** near, nigh **5.** there
8. location, position **9.** direction,
situation
at (pert to) . . .
great length . . **7.** on and on **9.** tediously
home . . **2.** in **4.** here **9.** en famille
last . . **3.** end **7.** finally **9.** extremely
10. ultimately
once . . **3.** now **7.** readily
the same . .
time . . **6.** coeval **10.** coetaneous
12. contemporary
atabal . . . **4.** drum **5.** tabor **10.** kettledrum
atabeg . . . **5.** title **6.** vizier
Atalanta (pert to) . . .
defeated in romantic race by . .
10. Hippomenes **17.** three golden
apples (Gr Myth)
famed . . **8.** huntress
foe . . **9.** Aphrodite
husband . . **8.** Milanion
legend . . **8.** Arcadian, Boeotian
atalaya . . . **10.** watchtower
atap . . . **4.** nipa, palm
atavism . . . **8.** heredity **9.** reversion
10. regression
ate . . . **5.** dined, fared **6.** dieted, gnawed,
supped
Ate . . . **7.** goddess (of infatuation)
atelier . . . **5.** easel **6.** studio **8.** workshop

a tempo . . . **4.** time
Aten (Egypt) . . . **9.** solar disk
ates . . . **8.** sweetsop
athanasia . . . **8.** athanasy **11.** immortality
13. deathlessness **15.** imperishability
athanor (Fr) . . . **7.** furnace (alchemist's)
Athapascan Indian . . . **5.** Tinne
6. Apache, Navaho (Navajo)
atheist . . . **5.** pagan **7.** heathen, infidel,
nastika **8.** agnostic **10.** unbeliever
11. disbeliever, unchristian
13. antichristian
Athena (pert to) . . .
attributes . . **3.** owl **5.** aegis **7.** serpent
festival . . **11.** Panathenaea
Rom equivalent . . **7.** Minerva
shrine . . **9.** Parthenon (Athens)
Athena, goddess of . . .
arts, crafts . . **6.** Ergane
health . . **6.** Hygeia
horses, tamer of . . **6.** Hippia
light . . **4.** Alea
maid of Athens . . **12.** Pallas Athene
poetry . . **6.** Pallas
victory . . **4.** Nike
wisdom . . **8.** Palladis
Athenian (pert to) . . .
assembly . . **4.** Pnyx
Bee . . **5.** Plato
general . . **8.** Xenophon
lawgiver . . **5.** Draco, Solon
sculptor . . **7.** Phidias
statesman . . **8.** Pericles **9.** Aristides
(The Just) **10.** Alcibiades
temple . . **11.** Nike Apteros
Athens . . .
capital of . . **6.** Attica (anc), Greece
citadel . . **9.** Acropolis
magistrate . . **5.** Draco, Solon
rival . . **6.** Sparta (anc)
senate . . **5.** boule
temple . . **9.** Parthenon
Athens of . . .
America . . **6.** Boston **9.** Nashville (The
South)
Ireland . . **4.** Cork **7.** Belfast
North . . **9.** Edinburgh **10.** Copenhagen
Switzerland . . **6.** Zurich
West . . **7.** Cordoba
athlete . . . **7.** acrobat, gymnast, tumbler
11. funambulist, palaestrian, pancratiast
13. contortionist
athlete (pert to) . . .
foot disease . . **15.** dermatophytosis
of Christendom . . **10.** Scanderbeg
portico (Gr, Rom) . . **6.** xystus (xyst)
athletic . . . **5.** lusty, thewy, yauld
6. brawny, robust, sinewy, strong
8. muscular, stalwart, vigorous
9. acrobatic, agonistic, gymnastic
10. palaestral (palestral) **15.** broad-
shouldered
athwart . . . **6.** across, aslant **8.** sideways,
sidewise, traverse **9.** crosswise,
obliquely **10.** crisscross, perversely
atimon . . . **9.** muskmelon
Atlantean . . . **6.** strong **7.** titanic
8. gigantic **9.** Atlaslike **10.** Gargantuan
atlantes (opp of caryatids) . . . **7.** columns
(carved men) **9.** telamones
Atlantic Sisters (Gr) . . . **8.** Pleiades (stars)

Atlas (pert to) . . .
converted into . . **7.** Mt Atlas
daughter . . **7.** Calypso **8.** Pleiades
famed as a . . **5.** giant, Titan
king of . . **10.** Mauretania
mother . . **4.** Asia **7.** Clymene
supporter of . . **5.** earth **10.** the heavens
Atman (Hind) . . . **3.** ego **4.** Self, Soul
6. Brahma
atmosphere . . . **3.** air **4.** aura, mood
5. ether, ozone **7.** climate
10. aerosphere, background
11. environment, hydrosphere
atmosphere (pert to) . . .
condition . . **9.** epedaphic
density . . **8.** isostere, isoteric
disturbance . . **5.** storm **6.** static
9. tornadoes, whirlwind
pressure . . **10.** barometric
shooting star . . **6.** meteor
spectrum . . **7.** rainbow
atole . . . **5.** gruel **8.** porridge
atoll . . . **4.** belt, reef (coral) **6.** island
atom . . . **3.** ace, bit, ion, jot **4.** gram,
iota, mite, whit **5.** monad **8.** particle
9. corpuscle
atom (pert to) . . .
central part . . **7.** nucleus
charged . . **3.** ion
energy . . **5.** gluon **6.** photon **7.** quantum
particle . . **4.** muon **5.** boson, meson,
quark **6.** baryon, lepton **7.** fermion,
neutron **8.** electron, neutrino
atomic . . . **3.** Age, ray **4.** beam, bomb, tiny
5. power **6.** energy, minute, number,
radius, weight **7.** nuclear **9.** atomistic,
molecular, radiation **10.** intangible
11. microscopic **13.** infinitesimal
atomize . . . **4.** fume **5.** smash, spray
6. aerate, gasify **7.** fission, perfume,
shatter **8.** dissolve, fumigate, nucleize
9. carbonate, decompose, evaporate,
micronize, pulverize **11.** disorganize
12. disintegrate
atom smasher . . . **11.** accelerator
atomy . . . **4.** atom, mote **5.** dwarf,
pygmy **6.** droich, midget **8.** skeleton
10. micromorph
atonement . . . **6.** amends **7.** apology,
penance, redress **8.** requital
10. recompense, redemption, reparation
11. reclamation, restitution
12. propitiation **15.** indemnification
Atreus (pert to) . . .
brother . . **8.** Thyestes
father . . **6.** Pelops
king of . . **7.** Mycenae
mother . . **10.** Hippodamia
slayer of . . **12.** Thyestes' sons
son . . **8.** Menelaus **9.** Agamemnon
wife . . **6.** Aerope
atrium . . . **4.** hall, room **5.** court (inner)
6. cavity (Anat) **7.** chamber **9.** peristyle
atrocious . . . **4.** rank, vile **5.** awful,
cruel, grave **6.** brutal, savage, sinful,
wicked **7.** heinous, vicious, violent
8. dreadful, flagrant, horrible, infamous,
ruthless, shocking, terrible, wretched
9. monstrous, nefarious **10.** abominable,
deplorable, detestable, outrageous
atrociousness . . . **8.** baseness, vileness

12. dreadfulness, shamefulness
13. nefariousness **15.** Schrecklichkeit
atrocity . . . **4.** evil, harm **5.** abuse, havoc,
wrong **7.** misdeed, outrage **8.** enormity
9. indignity **12.** mistreatment
atrophy . . . **5.** tabes **7.** disease
8. marasmus **10.** emaciation
11. attenuation
Atropos (Gr) . . . **7.** goddess (Fate)
attach . . . **3.** add, fix, pin, put, tag, tie
4. bind, glue, join, vest **5.** affix, annex,
hitch, paste, seize, unite **6.** append,
assign, fasten **7.** ascribe, connect,
postfix, subjoin **9.** associate, attribute
11. superimpose
attached . . . **4.** fond **6.** adnate, welded
7. annexed, devoted, engaged, sessile
(Bot), smitten **8.** cemented, enamored
attachment . . . **4.** bond, love **5.** fancy
6. liking, regard **7.** adjunct, fixture
8. addition, devotion, fidelity, fondness
9. accession, adherence, affection,
fastening, increment **10.** annexation
11. attribution **12.** augmentation
attack . . . **3.** fit **4.** pang, raid **5.** beset, blitz,
drive, feint, foray, ictus, onset, sally,
siege, spasm **6.** affret, assail, charge,
onrush, oppugn, sortie **7.** aggress,
assault, bowling, descent, offense,
seizure **8.** camisado (anc), paroxysm,
sickness **9.** offensive, onslaught
10. aggression **11.** enunciation
13. incrimination
attain . . . **2.** do **3.** get, win **4.** earn, gain
5. enact, reach **6.** accede, arrive, effect,
obtain **7.** achieve, acquire, compass,
fulfill, perform, realize **9.** discharge
10. accomplish, consummate
attainable . . . **8.** gettable **9.** available
10. achievable
attainment . . . **5.** skill **7.** arrival **8.** learning
9. accession **11.** acquirement,
acquisition, cultivation, edification,
realization **14.** accomplishment
attar . . . **4.** otto **5.** scent **6.** parfum
7. essence, perfume, rose oil
attempt . . . **3.** aim, jab (sl), try **4.** dare,
seek, stab **5.** assay, ensue, essay,
fling, offer, onset, siege, trial **6.** attack,
effort, result **7.** venture **8.** endeavor
9. undertake
attend . . . **4.** hark, heed, help, mind,
note, tend, wait **5.** ensue, nurse, serve,
treat, visit **6.** doctor, escort, follow,
foster, listen, result **7.** conduct, hearken,
nurture, observe **9.** accompany
attendance . . . **4.** draw **5.** court **7.** service,
turnout **8.** presence, tendance
9. following **13.** accompaniment
attendant . . . **4.** maid, page **5.** nurse, staff,
usher **6.** caddie, escort, gillie, porter,
waiter **7.** bellboy, orderly **8.** follower
9. associate, attending, companion
10. subsequent **11.** concomitant,
ministering
attendants, train of . . . **5.** suite
7. cortege, retinue **9.** entourage
attention . . . **3.** ear **4.** care, heed, hist,
note **6.** notice, regard **7.** concern,
hearing, respect, thought **8.** courtesy
11. mindfulness **13.** concentration,

consideration

attentive ... **5.** alert, awake, eared
6. intent **7.** careful, heedful, mindful
8. obedient, vigilant, watchful
9. courteous, listening, observant,
wide-awake **10.** meticulous, respectful
11. circumspect, considerate, surveillant

attenuated ... **3.** cut **4.** fine, rare, slim,
thin **6.** svelte, wasted **7.** diluted,
gracile, reduced, slender, thinned,
watered **8.** lessened, rarefied, weakened
9. decreased, emaciated

attest ... **4.** seal **5.** vouch **6.** adjure,
affirm, avouch, depose **7.** certify,
testify, witness **8.** evidence, indicate,
manifest **9.** testimony **10.** deposition
12. authenticate

attestation ... **4.** oath (solemn) **5.** proof
6. avowal **8.** swearing **9.** assertion
10. allegation **11.** affirmation, certificate,
declaration, testimonial **13.** testification
14. authentication

attic ... **3.** top **4.** dome, head, loft, wall
6. belfry, garret **8.** cockloft

Attic ... **5.** salty, witty **6.** simple **7.** elegant,
refined **8.** academic, Athenian, tasteful
9. classical **10.** Ciceronian

Attic (pert to) ...
Bee .. **9.** Sophocles (poet)
bird .. **11.** nightingale (Milton)
Muse .. **8.** Xenophon
native .. **8.** Athenian
school .. **9.** sculpture

Attica (pert to) ...
capital of .. **6.** Athens
state of .. **6.** Greece (anc)
famed as .. **15.** world's first city

Attila ... **3.** Hun (leader) **5.** Etzel (fabled)
12. Scourge of God

attired ... **7.** arrayed, clothed, dressed

attitude ... **3.** air, set **4.** pose, view
5. angle, slant, stand **7.** bearing, feeling,
opinion, outlook, posture, thought
8. position, reaction **9.** arabesque
(dance), sentiment, viewpoint
10. estimation, impression

attitude (reverent) ... **6.** salaam
8. kneeling **9.** obeisance
12. genuflection (genuflexion)

attorney ... **6.** lawyer **7.** counsel, pleader
9. barrister, counselor (counsellor)
11. intercessor

attract ... **4.** bait, draw, lure, pull
5. charm, tempt **6.** appeal, beckon,
enamor, engage, entice, invite
8. interest **9.** captivate, fascinate,
influence, magnetize

attraction ... **4.** lure, pull, star **6.** appeal
7. gravity **8.** affinity, headline, interest,
penchant **9.** magnetism, seduction
10. allurement **11.** fascination

attractive ... **4.** cute **5.** lovely, pretty,
taking **7.** winsome **8.** alluring, engaging,
fetching, graceful, magnetic **9.** allicient,
appealing, beauteous, beautiful,
desirable **10.** attracting, delightful
11. captivating, interesting

attractive and repellent ...
10. ambivalent

attrahent ... **6.** magnet **7.** drawing
8. sinapism (Med) **10.** attracting

attribute ... **3.** owe **5.** refer, trait
6. impute, nature, symbol **7.** ascribe,
feature, quality **8.** property **9.** adjective,
qualifier, specialty

attrition ... **4.** wear **5.** grief (Theol)
7. massage **8.** abrasion, friction,
limation **9.** detrition **10.** contrition

attune ... **4.** tune **5.** chime **6.** accord,
adjust **7.** concord, harmony, syntony
9. melodious **10.** symphonize
11. concordance

atwain ... **7.** asunder

atweel ... **5.** truly **6.** surely

aubade (Fr) ... **3.** lay **4.** poem, song
6. ballad **7.** concert (morning)
8. serenade

auberge ... **3.** inn

aubergiste ... **9.** innkeeper

auction ... **3.** bid **4.** cant, roup, sale
5. block **6.** vendue **7.** bidding

auction (game) ... **4.** pool **5.** pitch
6. bridge, euchre, hearts **8.** pinochle

audacious ... **4.** bold **5.** saucy **6.** brazen,
daring **7.** defiant **8.** impudent, insolent,
intrepid, spirited **9.** barefaced,
foolhardy, insulting **11.** adventurous,
challenging, impertinent, presumptive,
venturesome

audacity ... **5.** cheek, crust, nerve
6. daring **7.** courage **8.** defiance,
temerity **9.** assurance, hardihood,
impudence, insolence, sauciness
10. effrontery, enterprise
11. presumption **12.** impertinence
13. audaciousness, foolhardiness,
shamelessness

audible ... **5.** aloud, clear **8.** distinct,
hearable **10.** articulate

audible respiration ... **4.** sigh

audience ... **3.** ear **5.** house, trial
6. parley, tryout **7.** hearing, theater
8. audition, auditory, congress
9. interview, listeners **10.** conference
12. congregation

audit ... **5.** check **6.** reckon, verify
7. certify, collate **10.** accounting
11. examination

audition ... **6.** try out

auditor ... **5.** clerk **6.** censor, hearer
7. actuary, apposer **8.** examiner,
listener **10.** accountant, bookkeeper
11. comptroller

auditorium ... **4.** hall, nave (anc)
5. house **7.** theater **8.** auditory, building
9. Guildhall

auditory ... **4.** otic **5.** audio, aural
6. phonic **7.** hearers **8.** audience
9. accoustic, auricular **12.** congregation

au fait ... **4.** able **6.** expert **7.** equal
to **8.** informed, skillful **9.** qualified
10. conversant (with)

au fond ... **9.** basically, primarily
11. essentially **13.** fundamentally

auger ... **3.** bit **4.** bore, tool **5.** borer,
drill **6.** gimlet, wimble **10.** perforator

aught ... **3.** any **4.** none, some, zero
5. ought **6.** cipher **7.** nothing **8.** anything

augment ... **3.** add, eke **5.** affix,
annex, exalt, swell **6.** expand, extend
7. amplify, broaden, develop, enhance,
enlarge **8.** increase **9.** reinforce

Augsburg Church ... 8. Lutheran
augur ... 4. bode, omen, seer 5. sibyl, vates (Gauls) 6. oracle 7. betoken, presage 8. forebode, forecast, foretell, forewarn, haruspex (Rom), indicate, prophesy 10. anticipate, astrologer, conjecture, soothsayer 13. prognosticate 14. prognosticator
augury ... 4. omen, rite 7. auspice, portent 8. ceremony
august ... 5. awful, grand, novel, regal 6. sedate, solemn 7. courtly, eminent, stately 8. imposing, majestic 9. dignified, honorable, important, venerable 11. magnificent, ritualistic 12. aristocratic
August ... 6. Lammas 8. Sextilis 10. First month (Rom year)
August meteor (11th of month) ... 7. Perseid
auk ... 4. Alca, Alle, bird (sea), falk 5. murre, noddy 6. auklet, rotche (rotch) 7. Alcidae, dovekie 9. guillemot, razorbill
Auk ... 6. Indian 7. Alaskan, Tlingit 9. Koluschan
aula ... 4. hall, room 5. court 6. emblic (E Ind tree) 9. ventricle
aulos ... 5. flute 8. woodwind 9. woodwinds (collectively)
au naturel ... 4. nude 5. naked
aura ... 3. air 4. glow, halo, ring 6. astral, circle, fringe (Psychol), nimbus 7. aureola 9. effluvium, emanation 10. atmosphere, exhalation
aureole ... 4. halo 5. glory 6. circle, nimbus
auricle ... 3. ear 4. lobe 5. pinna 6. atrium (heart) 9. appendage
auricular ... 4. otic 5. aural, eared 6. phonic 8. acoustic, auditory
aurifex ... 9. goldsmith
aurochs ... 3. tur 4. goat, urus 5. bison
aurora ... 3. eos 4. dawn 5. sunup 7. sunrise 8. borealis, daybreak, daylight 9. australis 11. polar lights
aurora borealis ... 14. northern lights
auroral ... 4. dawn, eoan, rosy 7. eastern, radiant, roseate
auspices ... 3. aid 4. care, sign, wing 5. aegis (egis) 6. charge 7. backing, custody 8. guidance 9. patronage 10. management, protection 11. sponsorship, supervision
auspicious ... 4. good 6. timely 9. favorable, fortunate, opportune 10. convenient, propitious, prosperous, seasonable 12. advantageous
Aussie ... 6. digger 10. Australian
Auster ... 9. southland, south wind
austere ... 4. dour, hard 5. acrid, harsh, rigid, rough, stern 6. bitter, severe, strict 7. ascetic, pungent 8. exacting 10. astringent
Australasia ... 7. Oceania 15. South Sea Islands
Australasian bird ... 8. lorikeet 9. pardalote
Australia ... see also *Australian*
capital .. 8. Canberra
city .. 5. Perth 6. Sidney (largest)

8. Adelaide, Brisbane 9. Melbourne
desert .. 10. Great Sandy 13. Great Victoria
explorer .. 4. Cook
First Englishman (1688) .. 14. William Dampier
holiday .. 13. Foundation Day (Jan 26)
inlet .. 9. Botany Bay
island .. 8. Tasmania
mountain peak .. 9. Kosciusko
ocean .. 6. Indian
river .. 6. Murray
sea .. 5. Coral 6. Tasman
state .. 8. Victoria 10. Queensland 13. New South Wales
Tropic (southern) .. 9. Capricorn
Australian (pert to) ...
bee .. 5. karbi
bedroll .. 6. bindle 7. matilda
candy .. 5. lolly
feast .. 10. corroboree
fish .. 4. mako (shark) 5. yabby
flag .. 13. Southern Cross
flower .. 7. waratah (tulip) 9. rhodanthe
hut .. 6. miamia
native .. 5. myall 6. Aussie, binghi 8. kangaroo, warragal 9. aborigine, Dravidian
reptile .. 6. elapid, goanna, lizard (barking, frilled)
soldier .. 5. Anzac 6. digger
Australian animal ...
dog (wild) .. 5. dingo
horse (wild) .. 6. brumby
sheep dog .. 6. kelpie
mammal .. 7. daysure 8. duckbill, platypus 9. blind mole
marsupial .. 4. tait 5. koala 6. wombat 7. echidna 8. anteater, kangaroo 9. phalanger, teddy bear 10. kookaburra 14. Tasmanian Devil
Australian bird ... 3. emu, owl 4. lory, titi 5. arara, ariel, galah 6. leipoa, petrel 7. boobook, bustard, corella (parrot), grinder, rosella (parakeet) 8. ganggang, lorikeet, lyrebird, morepork, nightjar, paradise 9. bowerbird, cassowary, pardalote 10. flycatcher, goatsucker 11. budgereegah (parakeet)
Australian tree ... 4. teak, toon 5. belah, penda 6. jarrah, mallee, marara, she-oak, wattle 7. gunnung (mahogany) 8. Alstonia (dogbane), ironbark (eucalypt) 9. boobyalla (willow)
Austria ...
alpine lake .. 8. Bodensee (Ger) 9. Constance
capital .. 4. Wien (Ger) 6. Vienna
city .. 4. Graz, Linz 8. Salzburg 9. Innsbruck
forest belt .. 10. Wiener Wald
monarchy .. 14. Austria-Hungary
mountain .. 4. Alps 6. Otztal 9. Dolomites
mountain peak .. 10. Wildspitze 13. Gross-Glockner
Pass (famed) .. 7. Brenner
river .. 3. Inn, Mur 6. Danube
Austrian (pert to) ...
artist .. 5. Klimt
author .. 10. Schnitzler
botanist .. 6. Mendel

chemist, inventor.. **8.** Welsbach
composer.. **4.** Berg **5.** Haydn **6.** Mozart, Webern **7.** Strauss (Johann) **8.** Bruckner, Schubert
physicist.. **7.** Doppler **11.** Schrödinger
psychiatrist.. **5.** Adler, Freud
ruler (former).. **6.** kaiser
soldier.. **5.** jäger
theaterman.. **9.** Reinhardt (Max)
violinist.. **8.** Kreisler
autarch ... **6.** despot, tyrant **8.** autocrat
authentic ... **4.** pure, real, true **5.** valid **6.** native **7.** certain, correct, genuine, natural **8.** bona fide, credible, official, original, orthodox, reliable **9.** firsthand **11.** trustworthy **13.** authoritative
authenticate ... **6.** affirm, attest, ratify **7.** certify, confirm, warrant **8.** validate **12.** substantiate
authenticity ... **11.** genuineness, reliability **13.** dependability **15.** trustworthiness
author ... **4.** doer, poet **5.** ghost, maker **6.** parent, penman, writer **7.** creator, inditer **8.** annalist, begetter, compiler, composer, essayist, inventor, novelist, producer **9.** dramatist, scribbler **10.** originator **13.** encyclopedist (encyclopaedist)
authoritative ... **4.** wise **5.** valid **6.** potent, ruling, strong **7.** weighty **8.** approved, forceful, official, oracular, orthodox, positive, powerful **9.** authentic, imperious **10.** commanding, peremptory **11.** dictatorial, influential **13.** determinative
authoritative (pert to) ...
command.. **4.** fiat **5.** usage **6.** decree, dictum **7.** mandate
example.. **9.** precedent **10.** antecedent
letter.. **4.** writ **5.** breve
authority ... **5.** judge, power, right **6.** critic, expert, oracle, regent **7.** command, warrant, witness **8.** dominion, validity **9.** influence, testimony **10.** commission, competency **11.** connoisseur, prerogative **12.** carte blanche, jurisdiction **13.** authorization
authorize ... **6.** accept, permit, ratify **7.** certify, charter, empower, endorse, entitle, justify, license, warrant **8.** accredit, delegate, sanction, validate **10.** commission **11.** enfranchise **12.** legitimatize
authorless ... **8.** nameless **9.** anonymous
autobiography ... **7.** journal, letters, memoirs **11.** memorabilia
autochton ... **6.** binghi, native **8.** indigene **9.** primitive **10.** aboriginal
autocracy ... **8.** monarchy **9.** despotism **10.** absolutism **15.** totalitarianism
autocrat ... **4.** czar (tsar) **5.** mogul **6.** despot **7.** arbiter, monarch **8.** dictator **9.** sovereign **10.** taskmaster
autodidactic ... **8.** self-made **10.** self-taught **12.** self-educated
autograph ... **4.** seal, sign **5.** cross **9.** signature **11.** John Hancock
automatic ... **7.** machine **10.** mechanical, self-acting **11.** instinctive, involuntary, spontaneous

automatic device ... **3.** gun **4.** gear **5.** drill, pilot, rifle, robot **6.** pistol, switch **8.** computer, revolver **10.** six-shooter
automaton ... **5.** golem, robot **6.** puppet **7.** android, machine
automobile ... **3.** cab, car **4.** auto, taxi **5.** coupe **6.** jalopy **7.** autocar, flivver, machine, taxicab, vehicle **8.** motorcar
autosuggestion ... **7.** therapy **8.** hypnosis **9.** hypnology, mesmerism **10.** psychology **14.** self-suggestion
autumn ... **4.** fall **6.** mature, old age, season (yearly) **7.** equinox, harvest, October **8.** maturity, November **9.** September
auxiliary ... **4.** ally, plus **5.** extra **6.** aiding, helper **7.** adjunct, helping **9.** accessory, ancillary, assistant, attendant, coadjutor, colleague, companion, secondary **10.** additional, subsidiary, supporting **11.** confederate, cooperating, subordinate, subservient **12.** nonessential, supplemental **13.** supplementary
auxiliary army ... **6.** relief **7.** support **8.** Landwehr, recruits, reserves **11.** contingents **14.** reinforcements
auxiliary verb ... **3.** can, had, has, may **4.** hast, have, will **5.** could, shall, would **6.** should
avail ... **3.** use **4.** good, help **5.** value **6.** inform, profit **7.** benefit, service, utility **9.** advantage, expedient
availability ... **7.** utility **9.** usability **10.** usefulness **13.** acquirability, attainability **14.** serviceability
available ... **4.** free, open **5.** handy, ready, valid **6.** on hand, usable, vacant **8.** unfilled **9.** securable **10.** accessible, attainable, convenient, obtainable, unoccupied
avalanche ... **5.** slide **7.** descent (sudden) **8.** slippage
avant-garde ... **3.** van **8.** vanguard
avant-propos ... **7.** preface **12.** introduction (remarks)
avarice ... **4.** lust **5.** greed **7.** avidity **8.** avidness, cupidity, grasping, rapacity, voracity **10.** greediness **12.** covetousness
avarice demon ... **6.** Mammon
avaricious ... **5.** close **6.** grabby, greedy **7.** miserly **8.** covetous, grasping **9.** niggardly, penurious, rapacious, voracious **12.** parsimonious
avatar ... **8.** epiphany **10.** embodiment **11.** incarnation **14.** transmigration
avatars of Vishnu (Hind Relig) ... **11.** incarnation (deity to man)
avaunt ... **4.** away **5.** allez, boast, scram, vaunt **6.** begone, depart **7.** advance, vamoose
ave ... **4.** hail, viva, vive **8.** farewell
avec (Fr) ... **4.** with
Ave Maria ... **4.** bead (rosary), song **6.** prayer **10.** devotional
Avena ... **4.** oats **7.** grasses
avenge ... **7.** requite **9.** retaliate, vindicate
Avenging Angels ... **8.** nickname (Polit 1858) **10.** Danite Band (Mormons)
Avenging Spirit ... **4.** Fate, Fury **6.** Erinys

7. Alastor, Atropos

avenue . . . 3. rue 4. land, pike, road, vent 5. alley 6. arcade, artery, defile, egress, outlet, street 7. channel, freeway, highway, opening 8. corridor, turnpike 9. boulevard, concourse 10. passageway 12. thoroughfare

aver . . . 3. say 5. state 6. affirm, allege, assert 7. declare, profess, protect 10. asseverate

average . . . 2. go 3. par, run 4. mean, rule 6. common, medial, medium, normal 7. balance 8. mediocre 10. generality

averment . . . 6. dictum, remark 7. witness 9. assertion, statement, testimony, utterance 10. allegation 11. affirmation, attestation 12. verification 13. pronouncement

Avernus . . . 4. lake (poison vapors) 5. Hades

averse . . . 5. loath 7. adverse 9. reluctant, unwilling 11. disinclined

aversion . . . 4. hate 5. odium 6. hatred, horror 7. disgust, dislike 9. antipathy, repulsion 10. abhorrence, repugnance 11. abomination 12. estrangement 13. indisposition, unwillingness

aversion to . . . see also *fear of*
novelty . . 9. neophobia
society . . 14. anthropophobia
strangers . . 10. xenophobia
wine . . 10. oenophobia

avert . . . 4. fend, save 5. check, deter, evade, repel 6. forbid, retard, switch, thwart 7. deflect, prevent 8. alienate, prohibit 9. forestall, sidetrack

aviary . . . 4. cage 5. house 7. dovecot (dovecote) 8. ornithon 9. birdhouse, columbary, enclosure 11. columbarium

aviation . . . 6. flight, flying 7. winging 9. skyriding 10. airplaning 11. aeronautics

aviation maneuver . . . 9. Immelmann (Ger)

aviator . . . 3. Ace 5. flier (flyer), pilot 6. airman, Icarus (fabled first) 7. wingman 8. aeronaut, aviatrix, operator 9. astronaut, birdwoman, Immelmann

avichi (Buddh) . . . 4. Hell 5. Hades 9. depravity, perdition 10. underworld

avid . . . 4. agog, keen 5. eager 6. grabby, greedy 7. anxious, craving, zestful 8. grasping 9. rapacious, voracious 10. avaricious

avidity . . . 4. lust 5. greed 7. avarice 8. cupidity, grasping 9. eagerness 10. greediness 12. covetousness

avion . . . 5. plane 8. airplane

avis . . . see *rara avis*

avisa . . . 4. news 6. advice, caveat 7. tidings, warning 11. information

Avis Indica (Astron) . . . 4. Apus 13. constellation

avital . . . 9. ancestral

avoid . . . 4. shun, snub 5. annul, dodge, elude, evade 6. escape, eschew, repeal, revoke, vacate 7. abstain, forbear 10. invalidate

avoidance . . . 6. outlet 7. evasion, removal 8. emptying, shunning,

vacating 9. annulment 10. withdrawal

avoirdupois . . . 4. beef 6. weight 7. gravity, tonnage 8. poundage 9. heaviness

avoirdupois weight . . . 3. ton 4. dram 5. grain, ounce, pound 13. hundred-weight

avow . . . 3. own, vow 5. admit, swear, vouch 6. allege, assert, pledge 7. confess, declare, profess, promise 10. avouchment 11. acknowledge

avulsion . . . 7. removal 9. severance 10. extraction, separation (ppty), withdrawal

awabi . . . 7. abalone

awaft . . . 6. adrift, afloat, wafted

await . . . 4. bide, come, heed, loom, pend, wait 5. abide, tarry, watch 6. ambush, attend, expect, impend, waylay 8. approach 9. forthcome

awake . . . 5. alert, alive, astir, rouse 6. arouse, excite, waking 8. open-eyed 9. attentive, conscious, sleepless, wide-awake

awaken . . . 5. awake 6. arouse, excite, stir up 8. roust out

award . . . 4. gift, give, meed, mete 5. allot, grant, medal, prize 6. reward, trophy 7. adjudge, present, verdict 8. accolade 9. medallion

award (pert to) . . .
book . . 4. Hugo 5. Edgar 6. Nebula
film . . 5. Oscar
television . . 4. Emmy
theater . . 4. Tony

aware . . . 3. hep 4. know 5. sense 7. mindful 8. apprized, sensible 9. cognizant, conscious 11. intelligent

awareness . . . 5. sense 7. feeling 9. sensation 10. impression, perception 11. mindfulness, sensibility 13. consciousness

away . . . 2. on 3. awa, far, fro, off, out 4. gone 5. aside, hence 6. abroad, absent, begone, onward, thence 7. escaped 8. vanished 9. elsewhere

away from . . .
body center . . 5. ectad 6. distal
mouth . . 6. aborad, aboral
wind . . 4. alee

awe . . . 3. cow 4. fear 5. dread 6. regard, terror, wonder 7. emotion, respect 8. astonish, frighten, surprise 9. reverence 10. admiration, veneration, wonderment 13. consideration

aweather (opp of alee) . . . 8. windward 11. weatherward

awe-inspiring . . . 5. eerie (eery) 7. awesome, ghostly 8. glorious, imposing, splendid, terrific 9. wonderful 10. impressive 11. magnificent

awe-struck . . . 4. awed 9. terrified 10. astonished, fear-struck, spellbound 12. wonder-struck 13. thunderstruck

awful . . . 4. awed, ugly 5. dread, great, gross 6. sacred, silent, solemn, woeful 7. awesome, fearful, hideous 8. dreadful, infamous, reverent, shocking, terrible 9. appalling, atrocious, deathlike, ludicrous, venerable, wonderful 10. deplorable,

impressive, outrageous, unpleasant
11. exceedingly
awkward ... **5.** gawky, inapt, inept
6. clumsy, gauche **7.** froward, loutish,
unhandy **8.** bungling, clownish,
lubberly, perverse, ungainly, unwieldy
9. graceless, inelegant, lumbering,
maladroit, ponderous **10.** backhanded,
blundering, ungraceful
12. embarrassing, incommodious,
inconvenient
awkward age ... **4.** teen **5.** teens
awkward fellow ... **6.** galoot
11. hobbledehoy
awless, aweless ... **4.** bald **6.** brazen
8. fearless, unafraid **9.** bold-faced,
dauntless **10.** irreverent **11.** unsurprised
12. unastonished
awn ... **4.** barb **5.** beard (plant) **6.** arista,
papous **7.** bristle
awning ... **6.** canopy, screen, shield
7. shelter **8.** velarium (anc)
AWOL ... **5.** hooky **7.** truancy **9.** truantism
11. absenteeism
awry ... **4.** agee **5.** agley, amiss, askew
6. faulty **7.** askance, asquint, crooked,
oblique **9.** distorted **10.** disorderly
11. disarranged **12.** disorganized
ax, axe ... **3.** adz (adze), ask (dial) **4.** tool
6. hammer, poleax (poleaxe) **7.** hatchet
(small) **8.** axhammer **9.** discharge,
dismissal
ax (pert to) ...
ancient .. **4.** celt **6.** chisel
blade .. **3.** bit
execution .. **10.** guillotine
handle .. **4.** haft **5.** helve
axial ... **7.** central, midmost, pivotal
axilla ... **3.** ala **4.** axil **5.** oxter **6.** armpit
8. shoulder
axiom ... **3.** law, saw **4.** rule **5.** adage,
maxim, motto, truth **6.** byword,
dictum, saying, truism **7.** dictate,
precept, proverb, theorem
8. aphorism, apothegm **9.** principle
11. proposition
axiomatic ... **10.** aphoristic, proverbial
11. self-evident, sententious

12. epigrammatic
axis ... **3.** hub **4.** axle, bloc, nave,
stem **5.** pivot, stalk **6.** caulis, center,
league **7.** fulcrum **8.** alliance, vertebra
9. coalition
axle ... **3.** pin **4.** axis **5.** pivot, shaft
6. swivel **7.** spindle **8.** axletree
axle tooth ... **5.** molar
ayal ... **4.** amah, maid **5.** mammy
9. governess, nursemaid
11. maidservant
aye ... **2.** ay **3.** pro, yea, yes **4.** ever, vote
5. voice **6.** always, assent **8.** thumbs
up, viva-voce
aye-aye ... **5.** lemur (Madagascar)
ayes ... **10.** all in favor
Azazel ... **5.** Eblis, Satan **9.** scapegoat
Azerbaijanian ... **4.** Turk
14. Transcaucasian
azimuth ... **3.** arc **4.** dial **6.** circle
7. compass, horizon **8.** distance,
magnetic **10.** North point
Azores ...
capital .. **5.** Angra
city .. **5.** Horta
group (islands) .. **6.** St Mary **8.** St
George **9.** St Michael
locale .. **8.** Atlantic (Ocean)
owner .. **8.** Portugal
Aztec (pert to) ...
calendar .. **7.** Mexican
capital (anc) .. **12.** Tenochtitlan
emperor .. **9.** Montezuma
god .. **4.** Xipe (sowing) **12.** Quetzalcoatl
(peace)
hero .. **4.** Nata (Myth) **6.** Cortez
language .. **7.** Nahuatl
locale (anc) .. **6.** Aztlan
Noah (Mex) .. **6.** Coxcox
people .. **7.** Nahuatl (Nahuatlan)
stone .. **12.** chalchiuitl
temple .. **8.** teocalli
azure ... **4.** blue **7.** celeste, sky-blue
8. bice blue, cerulean **9.** blue vault,
cloudless **11.** lapis lazuli
azygous ... **3.** odd **4.** only, sole **6.** single,
unique **8.** singular **10.** unrepeated
azymous ... **10.** unleavened

B

B ... **4.** beta **6.** letter (2nd)
ba (Egypt) ... **3.** khu **4.** soul
baa ... **5.** bleet
baahling ... **4.** lamb
Baal ... **4.** idol **5.** deity **6.** Baalim (pl)
7. Baalath **8.** false god **9.** fertility
baba (pert to) ...
India .. **4.** baby **5.** child
Malaya .. **4.** male
Slavic .. **5.** nurse **7.** midwife **8.** old
woman
Turkey .. **5.** title (of respect)
babacoote ... **5.** lemur (Madagascar)
Babbar ... **3.** Utu (Utug) **6.** sun god
babbo ... **5.** daddy **6.** father

babel ... **5.** clang **6.** jargon, tumult
7. discord **9.** confusion
11. pandemonium
Babel (pert to) ...
Bible .. **5.** Tower **8.** ziggurat
presently .. **14.** Temple of Marduk
site (ancient) .. **6.** Shinar (land of)
site (present) .. **7.** Babylon
babirusa, babiroussa ... **9.** quadruped
(hoglike)
Babism (Persia) ... **4.** sect
baboon ... **3.** ape **5.** Papio **6.** chacma
7. babuina, monster **8.** mandrill
babushka ... **11.** grandmother
baby ... **4.** babe, doll **6.** coward, infant,

puppet, weanie **7.** bambino, chicken
8. juvenile, weakling **9.** miniature,
youngling, youngster **10.** diminutive
baby carriage ... **4.** pram **5.** wagon
6. go-cart **8.** stroller **12.** perambulator
babyish ... **6.** simple **7.** dollish, puerile
8. childish **9.** childlike, infantile
Babylon ... see also *Babylonian*
capital of .. **9.** Babylonia
kingdom .. **4.** Elam **5.** Akkad (Accad)
meaning .. **9.** Gate of God
mountain .. **6.** Ararat
river .. **6.** Tigris **9.** Euphrates
World Wonder .. **14.** Hanging Gardens
Babylonian (pert to) ...
abode of the dead .. **5.** Aralu
chaos .. **4.** Apsu
deity .. **5.** Alalu (Alala), Siris
earth mother .. **6.** Ishtar
god .. **2.** Ea, Zu **3.** Anu, Bel **4.** Adad,
Apsu, Irra **5.** Dagan, Enlil **6.** Nergal
7. Shamash
goddess .. **3.** Aya **4.** Nina **5.** Belit (Beltis)
hero (Myth) .. **5.** Adapa, Etana
9. Tilgamesh
king .. **6.** Sargon **9.** Habonidus,
Hammurabi **10.** Nabonassar
14. Nebuchadnezzar (Nebuchadrezzar)
temple, tower .. **8.** ziggurat
bacach ... **6.** beggar **7.** cripple
bacalao ... **7.** codfish, grouper
bacalao bird ... **3.** auk **5.** murre
9. guillemot
Bacardi ... **3.** rum
bacca ... **5.** berry
baccalaureate ... **6.** degree (college),
sermon **8.** bachelor
baccate ... **5.** pulpy **9.** berrylike
bacchanal ... **7.** reveler **8.** carouser
Bacchanalia ... **4.** orgy **5.** feast
7. debauch **8.** festival (Bacchus)
bacchante ... **6.** maenad **7.** bacchae
Bacchus ... **4.** wine **9.** god of wine
baccivorous ... **11.** berry-eating
bachelor ... **4.** male **6.** degree (Acad),
garçon **8.** benedict, celibate
10. misogamist
bacillus ... **9.** bacterium
Bacis ... **2.** Ra **4.** bull (sacred)
back ... **3.** aft, aid, fro **4.** abet, hind,
past, rear **5.** stern **6.** behind, second,
uphold **7.** finance, sponsor, support,
sustain **8.** extrados, intrados, resource
9. encourage, posterior **10.** background
back (Anat) ... **4.** loin, nape **5.** notum
6. dorsal, dorsum, lumbar, tergal,
tergum **7.** occiput **8.** backbone, notalgia
10. opisthenar (hand)
backbone ... **4.** grit, guts **5.** nerve, pluck,
spunk **6.** mettle, spirit **7.** courage,
stamina, support **8.** firmness,
gameness, mainstay **10.** dependence
backbone (Anat) ... **4.** axis **5.** brace,
chine, spine **6.** column, spinal
7. spinule, support **8.** ossicles
9. vertebrae
backer ... **5.** angel **6.** patron **7.** abettor,
sponsor **8.** financer, promoter, upholder
9. supporter, sustainer **10.** maintainer
background (opp of foreground) ...
4. rear **5.** stage **6.** offing **7.** horizon,

setting **8.** backdrop, distance, practice,
training **9.** education **10.** experience
11. savoir-faire
backhanded ... **6.** clumsy **7.** awkward,
devious **9.** insincere, insulting, sarcastic
10. circuitous
backslider ... **8.** apostate, deserter,
recreant **10.** unfaithful
back-to-back ... **7.** dos-à-dos
backward ... **4.** back, dull, late **5.** arear,
loath, tardy **6.** averse, modest,
stupid **7.** bashful, belated, reverse
8. arrested, dilatory, perverse, rearward,
retarded, reticent, retrorse, reversed
9. hindwards, recessive, reluctant,
subnormal, unwilling **10.** behindhand,
hesitating, regressive, retrograde
11. unfavorable **13.** retrogressive,
retrospective
bacon ... **4.** lard, pork, side **5.** prize
6. flitch, gammon, rasher **8.** Canadian,
sowbelly
Bacon's Rebellion ... **6.** revolt (Va 1676)
bacteria ... **5.** cocci, germs **7.** aerobes,
aerobia, bacilli **8.** microbes, spirilla
9. organisms
bacteriologist culture ... **4.** agar
Bactrian camel ... **9.** two-humped
bad ... **3.** ill, mal (pref) **4.** evil, fell,
foul, poor, vile **5.** drole, fetid,
nasty, wrong **6.** arrant, in pain,
putrid, rotten, sinful, wanton, wicked
7. corrupt, hurtful, naughty, noxious,
spoiled, tainted, unlucky, unmoral,
unsound, vicious **8.** annoying, criminal,
improper, inferior, iniquity, sinister
9. dangerous, defective, offensive,
perverted, worthless **10.** iniquitous,
malodorous, unsuitable **11.** inexpedient,
inopportune **12.** disagreeable,
inauspicious
bad (pert to) ...
blood .. **4.** feud **6.** enmity, rancor **7.** ill
will **10.** bitterness, resentment
custom .. **9.** cacoethes
film .. **4.** bomb
legislation .. **7.** dysnomy
luck .. **5.** deuce **7.** ambsace
man's oatmeal .. **7.** hemlock (poison)
11. wild chervil
writer .. **4.** hack
Baden ... **3.** spa
badge ... **3.** pin **4.** mark, sign, star
5. index, token **6.** emblem, ensign,
plaque, shield, symbol **7.** earmark
8. insignia **14.** identification
badger ... **3.** nag, rag **4.** bait **5.** harry,
tease, worry **6.** bother, extort, harass,
hawker, heckle, hector, pester
8. huckster
badger (animal) ... **5.** Meles (anc), pahmi,
ratel **6.** bauson, mammal, teledu,
wombat **9.** bandicoot, mistonusk
Badger State ... **9.** Wisconsin
badinage ... **4.** fool **5.** joker, sport
6. banter **8.** raillery **9.** badinerie,
simpleton **10.** persiflage, pleasantry
badly ... **3.** bad, ill **4.** sick **5.** amiss,
wrong **6.** poorly, unwell **8.** faultily,
wickedly **9.** viciously **11.** exceedingly,
imperfectly **12.** disagreeably, unskillfully

13. unfortunately
badly off... 3. sad 7. hapless, unblest,
  unhappy, unlucky 8. luckless
  11. impecunious, unfortunate
  12. unprosperous 14. unprovidential
baff... 4. beat, blow, thud 6. strike,
  stroke (golf)
baffle... 4. balk, foil 5. cheat, elude,
  evade, spike 6. defeat, delude,
  muffle, puzzle, thwart 7. mystify,
  nonplus, perplex 8. bewilder, confound
  9. bamboozle, frustrate 10. disconcert
baffling... 7. elusive, evasive 8. puzzling
  9. bothering, confusing, dismaying
  10. mystifying, perplexing, perturbing
  11. frustrating 13. disconcerting
baft... 3. aft 4. baff 5. abaff, cloth, shaft
  6. astern
bag... 3. net, pac, pot, sac, sag 4. etui,
  grip, load, poke, sack, trap 5. ascus,
  belly, catch, droop, pouch, purse, seize,
  snare, steal 6. entrap, sachet, valise
  7. bladder, capture, distend, handbag,
  pannier, satchel 8. reticule, suitcase
  9. Gladstone, haversack, sac de nuit
  10. pocketbook 11. portmanteau
bag and baggage... 10. completely
  11. impedimenta
bagatelle... 3. toy 4. game 6. bauble,
  geegaw, trifle 7. trinket 10. knickknack,
  triviality 12. fiddle-faddle
Bagdad, Baghdad...
  capital of.. 4. Iraq
  character.. 6. Sinbad (The Sailor)
  founder (762).. 8. Almanzor
  kingdom (anc).. 11. Mesopotamia
  Oriental term.. 8. lambskin (raw)
  river.. 6. Tigris
  transportation (famed).. 7. Railway
bagpipe, bagpipes... 5. drone, pipes
  7. musette 9. Dudelsack 10. doodlesack,
  sordellina
bagpipe (pert to)...
  music variations.. 7. pibroch
  parts.. 4. lill, oboe 5. drone 7. chanter
  9. chalumeau
  player.. 5. piper
  tube.. 6. drones 7. chanter
  tune.. 4. port
Bahamas, Bahama Islands...
  capital.. 6. Nassau
  discoverer.. 8. Columbus
  native.. 5. conch
  naval base (US).. 9. Mayaguana
  San Salvador (now).. 14. Watlings
  Island (Watling Island)
bahan... 6. poplar, willow (Bib)
bahay... 5. house
bahi... 7. fortune (gypsy)
bail... 3. dip 4. bond, hoop, lade,
  lave, ring, rynd 5. court, ladle, throw
  6. bucket, dipper, handle, pledge,
  secure, surety 8. replevin, security
  9. guarantee
bailiff... 5. agent, bobby, reeve, staff
  6. deputy, staves (pl) 7. marshal, officer,
  sheriff, shrieve, steward 8. bluecoat,
  gendarme, overseer 9. constable
  12. understeward
bailiwick... 6. canton, county, domain
  7. commune, diocese 8. precinct,

province 12. municipality
bain... 4. near 5. lithe, ready, short
  6. direct, limber, supple 7. forward,
  willing
bairn... 3. kid, tot 4. mite 5. child
  6. urchin
bait... 3. fly 4. feed, hook, lure, trap
  5. bribe, decoy, snare 6. badger,
  harass, hockle 7. fulcrum, torment
  8. inveigle 9. persecute 10. enticement,
  exasperate, temptation
bait... 3. dap, dib 4. fish, hook 6. dibble
bakal (Orient)... 9. tradesman
  10. shopkeeper
bake... 3. dry 4. cake, cook, fire, kiln
  5. roast 6. anneal, harden 8. clambake
  9. dehydrate
bakehead... 4. rail 5. guard, shack
  6. stoker 7. fireman 8. trainman
baken... 4. buoy 6. beacon 8. landmark
baker's dozen... 4. long 6. devil's
  7. inbread 8. thirteen
baksheesh... 3. sop, tip 5. bribe
  7. largess (largesse) 8. gratuity
  12. compensation
bal... 4. ball, mine, prom
balance... 4. even, rest, rule 5. poise,
  ratio, scale, weigh 6. adjust, aplomb,
  normal, offset, reason, rhythm, sanity
  7. average, ballast, compare, euphony,
  measure, remains, surplus 8. equality,
  equalize, leftover, residual, saneness,
  serenity, symmetry 9. composure,
  equipoise, remainder, stability
  10. equanimity, neutralize, proportion,
  symmetrize 11. equilibrium
  12. counterpoise
balanced... 4. even, just 6. poised
  7. equable 8. measured 9. equitable
  10. euphonious 11. symmetrical
  13. self-possessed
balancer... 7. acrobat, gymnast
  10. ropedancer 11. equilibrist
balcony... 4. dais 5. stage 6. podium
  7. estrade, gallery, rostrum 8. brattice,
  platform
bald... 4. bare, dull, mere, open 5. crude,
  naked, plain 6. simple 7. epilose
  8. depilous, hairless 9. bald-pated
  11. unconcealed
baldachin, baldaquin... 6. canopy (St
  Peter's, Rome), fabric
Balder (pert to)...
  father.. 4. Odin
  god of.. 5. light, peace
  mother.. 5. Frigg
  slain by.. 9. mistletoe (dart)
  wife.. 5. Nanna
balderdash... 3. rot 4. bosh 5. trash
  6. bunkum, jargon 7. bombast
  8. buncombe, falderal, nonsense,
  tommyrot 9. poppycock
baldness... 6. acomia 8. alopecia
  11. phalacrosis 12. hairlessness
baldric... 4. belt (ornament) 6. zodiac
  7. support (sword)
bale... 3. woe 4. bind, load, pack 5. truss
  6. ballot, bundle, burden, misery,
  packet, seroon 7. anguish, package
  11. encumbrance
Balearic Islands... 5. Ibiza (Iviza), Palma

(capital) **7.** Majorca (Mallorca), Minorca **10.** Formentera

baleful . . . **3.** bad, sad **4.** dire **6.** woeful **7.** baneful, harmful, malific, noisome, noxious **8.** damaging **9.** ill-omened, malignant **10.** pernicious **12.** inauspicious

balk . . . **4.** foil **5.** check, ridge **6.** baffle, defeat, fallow, rafter, signal (fishing), thwart **7.** blunder, faux pas, stickle **9.** frustrate, hindrance **10.** bafflement, disappoint **14.** disappointment

Balkan Peninsula . . .
native . . **4.** Serb
river . . **3.** Une **4.** Sava **6.** Danube
sea . . **5.** Black **6.** Aegean **7.** Marmosa **8.** Adriatic **13.** Mediterranean
State . . **6.** Bosnia, Greece, Serbia, Turkey (Eur) **7.** Albania, Rumania **8.** Bulgaria **10.** Yugoslavia

balky . . . **7.** restive **9.** faltering, obstinate, shrinking, stickling

ball . . . **3.** bal, fly, hop, lob, orb **4.** bead, clew (yarn), pill, shot **5.** dance, globe, pearl, pinda (rice) **6.** pellet, pelota, sphere **7.** rissole **8.** conglobe, snowball **9.** eight ball **10.** cannonball **12.** medicine ball

ball (of games) . . . **4.** golf, hand, polo, soft **6.** basket, tennis, volley **7.** bowling, cricket, croquet, jai alai **8.** baseball, billiard, ping-pong

ballad . . . **3.** lay **4.** lied, poem, song **5.** derry, rhyme, verse **6.** sonnet **7.** ballade, canzone

ballast . . . **5.** poise **6.** aplomb, steady, weight **7.** balance **9.** kentledge, saburrate, stabilize **10.** equanimity, equivalent **14.** counterbalance

balled up . . . **7.** complex, mixed up, muddled **8.** confused, fouled up **9.** befuddled, entangled, snarled up **10.** disordered **11.** complicated

ballet (pert to) . . .
arrangement . . **12.** choreography
dance . . **6.** adagio **9.** pantomime
dancer . . **8.** coryphee, danseuse **9.** ballerina
jump . . **4.** jeté **5.** coupé
lover . . **11.** balletomane
music . . **5.** opera **6.** comedy **7.** d'action **14.** divertissement
painter of . . **5.** Degas
skirt . . **4.** tutu

balloon . . . **3.** bag **4.** ball, tire **5.** barge (Siam), blimp, swell **6.** aviate, ballon, dilate, expand, gasbag **7.** distend, nacelle **8.** aerostat, aircraft **9.** dirigible

balloon (type) . . . **4.** free, kite **5.** pilot **7.** captive **8.** sounding **11.** montgolfier, observation

ballot . . . **4.** bale, poll, vote **5.** elect, slate, voice **6.** select, ticket **8.** suffrage

ballyhoo . . . **4.** plug **5.** boost, noise **6.** fracas, hoopla, hubbub, ruckus, rumpus **7.** promote **9.** advertise, publicity **10.** hullabaloo

balm . . . **3.** oil **4.** bito, calm **5.** cream, salve **6.** balsam, elixir, lotion, pacify **7.** anodyne, cushion, Melissa, perfume, relieve, unction, unguent **8.** liniment,

mitigate, ointment **9.** calmative, fragrance, mitigator **10.** palliative

balm (pert to) . . . **5.** Vicks **6.** arnica, zachun **7.** camphor, lanolin, menthol **8.** glycerin, ointment, vaseline **10.** petrolatum

Balm of . . . **6.** Gilead

balmy . . . **4.** mild **5.** batty, daffy, dippy, drunk, goofy, moony, spicy, sweet **6.** dreamy, insane, savory **7.** healing **8.** aromatic, fragrant, lenitive, redolent, soothing **9.** ambrosial, assuaging, emollient **10.** palliative, refreshing **11.** odoriferous **12.** sweet-scented

balsam . . . **3.** fir **4.** riga, tolu **5.** resin **6.** embalm, poplar, storax **7.** benzoin, perfume **8.** bdellium (Bib), medicine **9.** oleoresin **12.** Balsam of Peru, Balsam of Tolu

Baltic States . . . **6.** Latvia **7.** Estonia **9.** Lithuania

Baltimore . . .
Belle . . **4.** rose
bird . . **6.** oriole
butterfly . . **7.** phaeton
city of . . **8.** Maryland
hemp . . **4.** flax
history of . . **18.** Star Spangled Banner (1814)

baluster . . . **4.** post **7.** support, upright **8.** banister

bam . . . **4.** fake, hoax, mock, sham **5.** cheat, spoof, trick **6.** deceit **7.** wheedle **8.** flimflam **9.** deception, imitation

bambino . . . **4.** babe, baby, icon **5.** child, Pietà **6.** infant (Christ)

bamboo (pert to) . . .
curtain . . **8.** frontier
English . . **10.** Philippine
genus . . **7.** Bambuss
sacred . . **6.** nandin
sprouts (pickled) . . **5.** achar
stems . . **4.** cane
sugar . . **6.** silica **9.** tabasheer

bamboozle . . . **4.** dupe, hoax **5.** trick **6.** baffle, cajole, humbug **7.** beguile, deceive, mystify, perplex **9.** victimize

ban . . . **4.** coin, tabu, veto **5.** curse, edict, taboo, title (anc) **6.** muslin, outlaw **7.** embargo, exclude, kokumin **8.** anathema **9.** interdict, ostracism, ostracize **10.** injunction, kokumingun **11.** malediction, prohibition **12.** proscription **15.** excommunication

banal . . . **4.** flat **5.** corny, stale, trite **6.** cliché, common, old hat **11.** commonplace, stereotyped **13.** platitudinous

banana . . . **4.** Musa, saba **6.** ensete **8.** Musaceae, plantain

banana (pert to) . . .
Bananaland . . **10.** Queensland
bananalike . . **8.** plantain
bird . . **4.** quit **6.** oriole
boa . . **5.** snake
color . . **7.** sunbeam
fish . . **8.** ladyfish
freckle . . **7.** disease
leaf . . **5.** frond
oil . . **7.** lacquer
Philippine . . **7.** saguing

shrub . . 9. evergreen
bananas . . . 5. crazy 7. excited
band . . . 3. bar, tie 4. belt, body, crew,
  hoop, line, pack, ring, sash, zone
  5. bunch, corps, group, patte, strap,
  stria, strip, tribe, unite 6. cohort,
  collar, fascia, fillet, girdle, ligula,
  outfit, pledge, radula (Zool), tether
  7. bandage, company 8. cincture,
  encircle, ensemble, neckband, striping
  9. frequency (radio), orchestra, striation
bandage . . . 3. gag 4. bind, tape
  5. sling, spica, truss 6. ligate,
  swathe 7. wrapper 8. compress,
  dressing, ligature 9. accipiter, blindfold
  10. tourniquet
bandicoot . . . 3. rat 9. Perameles
bandit . . . 4. thug 5. thief 6. dacoit,
  outlaw, robber 7. bandido, brigand,
  footpad, ladrone 8. marauder, picaroon
  9. bandolero 10. highwayman
bandmaster . . . 5. Sousa 6. leader
  7. maestro 8. choragus, director
  9. conductor 13. Kapellmeister
bandolero . . . 5. thief 6. robber
  10. highwayman
bandy . . . 4. beat, cart, game 5. bowed
  6. curved, strive, stroke (tennis)
  7. contend, embowed 8. carriage (Ind),
  exchange, to and fro 9. bowlegged
  11. bandy-legged, reciprocate
bandy words . . . 5. argue 6. bicker, parley
  7. contend, wrangle 8. converse
bane . . . 3. woe 4. evil, harm, kill,
  pest, ruin 5. curse, venom 6. injury,
  plague, poison, slayer 7. disease
  (sheep), scourge 8. murderer, vexation
  9. grievance 10. affliction, pestilence,
  visitation
baneful . . . 3. ill 4. vile 7. harmful,
  noxious 9. injurious 10. pernicious
  11. detrimental
bang . . . 3. hit, rap 4. beat, blow, dash,
  drub, kick, lift, shut, slam 5. crack,
  knock, pound, punch, smack, thump,
  verve, whack 6. energy, report, strike,
  thrash, thrill 7. collide 8. coiffure
bangle . . . 5. charm 7. circlet 8. bracelet
banish . . . 3. ban 4. oust 5. exile,
  expel 6. deport, dispel, outlaw,
  punish 7. condemn, dismiss, exclude
  8. relegate 9. ostracize, proscribe
  10. expatriate 13. excommunicate
banister . . . 4. post, rail 8. baluster
  10. balustrade
banjo . . . 7. samisen
bank . . . 3. row 4. brae, edge, heap,
  quay, ripa 5. brink, flock, hurst
  (sandy), marge, shoal, shore, slope,
  table 6. aviate, margin, quarry, rivage,
  series, stakes, strand 7. anthill, barrier,
  deposit, incline 8. buttress, treasury
  9. acclivity, riverside 13. fortification
bank account . . . 5. funds, means
  6. assets, moneys 8. finances
  9. exchequer
banker . . . 4. game 6. broker, lender
  9. financier 11. moneylender 12. money-
  changer
bankrupt . . . 4. bust, ruin 5. broke,
  smash 6. failed, quisby (sl) 7. failure

9. destiture, insolvent, moneyless,
  penniless 12. impoverished
banner . . . 4. fane, flag 6. ensign,
  poster 7. leading, pennant, placard
  8. foremost, headline, standard,
  streamer 9. exemplary 10. surpassing
banns, marriage . . . 6. notice 7. sibrede
  12. proclamation
banquet . . . 4. fete 5. diffa, feast, festa
  6. fiesta, junket, regale, repast, spread
  8. festival, jamboree 10. regalement
Banquo . . . 9. character (Macbeth)
banshee, banshie . . . 4. shee 5. fairy,
  Geist, sidhe 6. spirit, sprite
banshee, banshie (pert to) . . . 3. cry
  4. keen, wail 5. death
bantam (pert to) . . .
cock . . 3. fop 5. dandy, sport 7. peacock
  8. strutter 9. swaggerer
  12. swashbuckler
Java . . 4. duck, fowl 5. breed 6. Brahma,
  Cochin
slang . . 4. runt 6. peewee, shrimp
sports . . 6. weight
bantamweight . . . 5. boxer (118 lbs)
  7. fighter 8. pugilist 9. contender
  10. contestant
banter . . . 4. jest, josh, mock, twit
  5. borak, chaff, sport, tease, trick
  6. delude, deride, satire 7. asteism,
  wheedle 8. badinage, raillery, ridicule
  10. persiflage, pleasantry
Bantu, South Africa . . .
language . . 3. Ila 8. Kongoese
people . . 4. Vili, Zulu 5. Duala,
  Xhosa 6. Basuto, Damara 7. Swahili
  8. Bechuana
banzai . . . 4. hail 5. hello, hullo 6. attack,
  charge 9. greetings 11. salutations
baobab tree (pert to) . . .
bark . . 4. rope 5. cloth, paper
fruit . . 11. monkey bread
genus . . 9. Adansonia
pulp . . 8. beverage
baptism . . . 4. rite 6. naming 7. wetting
  8. ablution 9. aspersion, immersion,
  sacrament 10. initiation, sprinkling
  11. christening 12. consecration,
  purification, regeneration (spiritual)
baptism (pert to) . . .
cloth . . 7. chrisom
dead (RCCh) . . 5. Blood 6. Desire
fire . . 9. fuertaufe
place . . 4. font 10. baptistery (anc)
receptacle . . 5. basin 7. piscina
water . . 5. laver
bar . . . 3. ban, dam, fid, pry, pub, rod
  4. bolt, deny, fess, joke, line, rack, rail,
  sess, type 5. betty (thieves' slang),
  block, court, deter, easer, estop, ingot,
  lever, shoal, space, staff 6. except,
  forbid, hinder, lounge, ripper, saloon,
  stitch, stripe, tavern 7. barrier, barroom,
  bass-bar, chevron, counter, crowbar,
  exclude, gin mill, prevent, railing,
  sandbar, trapeze 8. blockade, disallow,
  obstacle, obstruct, preclude, prohibit
  9. barricade, hindrance, roadhouse
  10. impediment, profession, singletree
  11. obstruction, rathskeller, whippletree
  12. underscoring, watering hole

barb ... **3.** jag **4.** clip, flue, harl, herl, seta
   5. horse, point, ramus, scarf (nun's),
   speed **6.** setula, striga **7.** bristle,
   feather, pinnula **8.** kingfish **9.** arrowhead
   10. projection

Barbados Island ...
   capital .. **10.** Bridgetown
   drink .. **3.** rum
   government .. **7.** British
   location .. **8.** Antilles (Lesser) **10.** West
   Indies
   native .. **3.** Bim (nickname)

barbarian ... **3.** hun **4.** Goth, rude
   5. beast, brute **6.** savage, vandal
   8. cannibal, man-eater **9.** untutored,
   vulgarian **10.** extraneous, Philistine,
   unlettered **11.** uncivilized
   15. anthropophagite

barbaric ... **5.** cruel **6.** brutal, Gothic,
   savage **7.** foreign, inhuman, vicious
   8. non-Greek, non-Latin, ruthless
   9. barbarous, primitive **10.** extraneous
   11. uncivilized **12.** non-Christian

barbarism ... **6.** ferity **8.** rudeness,
   solecism **9.** barbarity, crudeness,
   Gothicism, ignorance, vulgarism
   10. coarseness, corruption, foreignism
   11. impropriety

Barbarossa ... **7.** emperor (Rom) **8.** red
   beard

Barbary ape ... **5.** magot

Barbary State (former) ... **5.** Tunis
   7. Algiers, Morocco **12.** Tripolitania

barbate ... **7.** bearded, stubbly
   9. whiskered **11.** barbigerous

barbecue ... **5.** feast, roast **6.** animal
   (whole), picnic **7.** brazier, hibachi
   9. Dutch oven **10.** shish kebab
   13. entertainment (out-of-doors)

barber ... **5.** shave **6.** figaro, shaver,
   tonsor **7.** tonsure **10.** haircutter
   12. tonsorialist

Barber of Seville character ... **6.** Figaro,
   Rosina

Barcelona, Spain ...
   building (famed) .. **6.** palace (Kings of
   Aragon) **9.** Cathedral (Gothic)
   port .. **13.** Mediterranean
   street (famed) .. **6.** Rambla

bard ... **4.** muse, poet, scop (Hist) **5.** druid,
   runer, vates **8.** minstrel, musician
   (wandering) **10.** Parnassian

Bard of ...
   Avon .. **11.** Shakespeare
   Ayrshire .. **5.** Burns
   Rydal Mount .. **10.** Wordsworth

bare ... **3.** raw **4.** bald, mere, nude,
   open **5.** alone, empty, naked, plain,
   shear, sheer, stark, strip **6.** barren,
   denude, divest, expose, reveal, simple,
   vacant **7.** exposed, unarmed, uncover
   8. desolate, disclose, stripped
   9. destitute, unadorned, uncovered
   10. stark-naked, threadbare
   11. defenseless, unconcealed

barefaced ... **4.** bare, bold **6.** brassy,
   brazen **8.** impudent **9.** audacious,
   shameless **11.** undisguised

barely ... **4.** jimp, only **5.** faint **6.** hardly,
   merely, nudely, poorly, simply
   7. nakedly **8.** narrowly, scantily, scarcely

14. insufficiently

bargain ... **3.** buy **4.** deal, pact, prig, sell
   5. trade **6.** barter, chisel, dicker, haggle
   7. chaffer, compact, mediate **8.** contract,
   covenant, purchase **9.** agreement,
   Bon Marché, cheapness, negotiate
   10. engagement **11.** stipulation,
   transaction

barge ... **3.** ark, hoy **4.** raft, scow, ship
   5. ferry, float, praam, scold **6.** berate,
   lumber, rebuke, tender **7.** birlinn
   (birling), lighter **9.** transport

barge in ... **5.** enter **6.** bungle, butt in,
   invade, push in **7.** blunder, intrude

barghest ... **6.** goblin

bargoose ... **4.** duck **9.** merganser,
   sheldrake

bark ... **3.** bay, yap, yip **4.** bang, bast,
   husk, peel, rind, ross, ship, skin, tapa,
   yelp **5.** cough, niepa, shout, strip, youff
   6. bowwow, clamor, cortex, outcry,
   packet, scrape **7.** canella **8.** ballyhoo,
   periderm **9.** sassafras

barker ... **4.** tout **6.** pistol **7.** spieler
   9. solicitor **10.** ballyhooer, theaterman

barking ... **7.** latrant **8.** hylactic

Barlaam and Josaphet (Joasaph) ...
   11. Buddha story (Christian version)

barley ... **4.** bigg, food, seed **5.** grain
   6. ptisan, tsamba **7.** Hordeum

barley (pert to) ...
   bird .. **6.** siskin **7.** wagtail (yellow),
   wryneck **11.** nightingale
   bree .. **3.** ale **6.** liquor
   shaped .. **10.** hordeiform

barlow ... **9.** jackknife (one-bladed)

barm ... **5.** froth, yeast **6.** leaven
   7. ferment

barn ... **3.** bay, mow **4.** loft

barnacle ... **4.** bray (Her) **5.** acorn, goose,
   leech **6.** animal, sucker **8.** adherent,
   parasite **9.** sycophant **10.** Cirripedia,
   crustacean

barnstormer ... **5.** actor **7.** aviator
   11. entertainer

baron ... **4.** peer **5.** mogul, noble
   6. daimio, tycoon **7.** freeman
   8. nobleman, somebody **9.** financier,
   personage **10.** capitalist **13.** industrialist

baroque ... **6.** ornate, quaint, rococo
   7. bizarre **9.** irregular **11.** extravagant

barracks ... **4.** camp, huts **6.** casern,
   laager **9.** barracoon **10.** encampment

barraclade ... **7.** blanket (homemade)

barracuda ... **4.** fish, spet **5.** barry
   (Bahamas) **6.** sennet

barrage ... **3.** dam **4.** weir **5.** blitz
   6. strafe **7.** barrier, gunfire, milldaw
   9. cannonade, roadblock **11.** obstruction

barrage (military) ... **3.** box **5.** mines
   6. normal **7.** balloon **8.** creeping,
   standing **9.** emergency **12.** anti-aircraft

barranca ... **4.** bank **5.** bluff **6.** ravine

barratry ... **6.** breach, simony **8.** bad faith,
   mala fide **10.** infidelity **11.** dereliction

barred ... **6.** cooped, fenced, grated,
   ribbed **7.** striped **8.** confined, debarred,
   excluded, streaked

barrel ... **3.** box, keg, tun **4.** cade, cask,
   drum, knag **5.** quill, speed **6.** runlet,
   tierce **7.** calamus (Zool), rundlet

8. cylinder, hogshead 9. kilderkin
barrel (pert to) . . .
maker . . 6. cooper
miscellaneous . . 3. gun, pen 4. pipe
6. pencil
sling . . 9. parbuckle
stopper . . 4. bung
barren . . . 3. dry 4. arid, bare, dull 5. blank,
empty, heath, inane 6. desert, effete,
jejune, karroo, meager, Sahara, stupid
7. sterile 8. desolate, impotent, unpoetic
9. infertile 10. unfruitful, unprolific
12. unproductive, unprofitable
barricade . . . 3. bar 4. bolt, rail, seal, stop
5. block, close, fence 6. abatis 7. barrier,
padlock 8. blockade, obstacle, obstruct
11. obstruction 13. fortification
barrico . . . 3. keg 4. cask
barrier . . . 3. Alp, bar, dam 4. clog,
door, gate, wall, weir 5. block, fence,
hedge, panel 6. screen 7. parapet,
railing 8. blockade, boundary, fortress,
obstacle, stockade, stoppage
9. partition, restraint 10. impediment,
portcullis 11. obstruction
Barrie's boy . . . 8. Peter Pan
barrikin (Eng sl) . . . 6. jargon 9. gibberish
barrister . . . 6. lawyer 7. adviser, pleader
8. advocate, attorney 9. counselor
(counsellor), solicitor
barroom . . . 3. bar, pub, tap 6. lounge,
saloon, tavern 7. cantina, gin mill,
taproom 8. alehouse 9. roadhouse
11. rathskeller 12. watering hole
barrow . . . 3. hod, hog (male) 4. brae,
fell, hill, knap, moor 5. grave (anc),
mound 7. tumulus 8. mountain
11. wheelbarrow 12. Reihengräber
bartender . . . 5. mixer 6. barman, bistro
7. barkeep, tapster 8. publican
barter . . . 4. deal, sell, swap 5. trade,
truck 7. bargain, permute, traffic
8. commerce, exchange
Bartholomew (pert to) . . . 4. Fair, Play
(Shaksp) 5. Saint 6. martyr 7. Apostle
(one of 12) 8. Massacre
Bartimeus (Bib) . . . 6. beggar (blind)
barton . . . 4. farm 5. abode, manor
6. grange 7. demesne 8. farmyard,
hacienda 9. homestead
baru . . . 4. tree (fiber) 7. majagua
base . . . 3. bed, low 4. dado, evil, foot,
foul, mean, root, seat, site, sole
5. basis, basso, cause, petty, radix,
socle, voice 6. abject, bottom, center,
factor, patten, plinth, podium, singer,
sordid, vulgar, wicked 7. servile, station
8. basement, cosmetic, degraded,
infamous, inferior, pedestal, shameful,
standard 9. principle, worthless
10. despicable, foundation, villainous
12. contemptible, dishonorable,
headquarters
baseball (terms) . . . 3. bag, bat, box,
fan, fly, hit, lob, out, RBI, run 4. ball,
base, bunt, deck, foul, home, nine, pill,
sack, save, walk, wild 5. bench, clout,
coach, count, curve, drive, error, field,
first, force, glove, homer, liner, mound,
pitch, plate, pop-up, score, slide, sport,
swing, third 6. assist, batter, bungle,

double, dugout, fumble, ground, putout,
rubber, runner, screen, second, series,
single, sinker, stance, strike, string,
target, triple, windup 7. battery, bullpen,
diamond, fielder, floater, rhubarb (sl),
squeeze, stretch 8. backstop, grounder,
keystone, knuckler, outfield, pinch-
hit, powdered, spit ball 9. sacrifice,
strikeout 10. ballplayer
baseborn . . . 3. low 4. mean 5. lowly,
plain 6. common, humble 7. bastard,
ignoble, lowborn 8. plebeian, spurious
11. commonplace 12. illegitimate
based on . . .
evidence . . 7. damning 8. decisive
10. conclusive
experience . . 7. empiric 9. empirical
numbers . . 5. hexad 6. nonary, senary
7. tertial
baseness . . . 6. infamy 7. badness
9. servility, vulgarity 10. wickedness
11. inferiority 13. dastardliness,
subordination
bash . . . 3. bat, jab, lam 4. beat, belt, biff,
blow, conk, mash, slug, sock 5. clout,
paste, punch, smack, whack 6. bruise,
strike, wallop 7. clobber
Basham's King . . . 2. Og
bashful . . . 3. coy, shy 5. heloe, mousy,
timid 6. demure, modest 8. blushing,
retiring, sheepish, timorous, verecund
9. diffident 13. self-conscious
basic . . . 4. root 5. basal, basis 7. essence,
primary 8. alkaline, original 9. essential
10. underlying 11. fundamental
Basilian . . . 3. art 4. monk, rule 6. bishop
7. liturgy, St Basil (The Great)
8. precepts 10. Cappadocia
basilica . . . 5. major, minor, title
6. canopy, church, shrine, temple
11. patriarchal
Basilican (pert to) . . .
books . . 5. sixty 6. Digest
century . . 5. Tenth
empire . . 9. Byzantine
laws . . 9. Justinian
basin . . . 3. bed (water), cup, pit, tub
4. bowl, cock, font, hole, sink, tank
5. laver, plain, playa, stoup 6. cavity,
chafer, coulee, ground, lavabo, marine,
valley, vessel 7. lowland, piscina
8. curvette 9. washbasin 10. depression
basis . . . 4. base, fond, root 5. cause,
start 6. bottom, factor, motive, reason,
thesis 7. premise, warrant 9. assertion,
principle 10. foundation, groundwork
13. justification
bask . . . 3. sin, tub 4. warm 5. bathe,
revel 7. suffuse 8. apricate 9. luxuriate
basket . . . 3. bin, box, car (balloon), net,
ped, pod 4. caba, cage, kish, skep,
trug 5. cabas 6. dosser, gabion, vessel,
wisket 7. corbeil, hanaper, pannier,
scuttle, wattage 9. container
basket (pert to) . . .
coal mine . . 3. tub 4. corf
fig . . 5. frail 6. tapnet
fire . . 5. grate 7. cresset
fishing . . 3. pot 4. buck (eel), caul, weel
5. crail, crate, creel 6. hamper
making . . 5. slath 6. slarth

wicker .. **3.** cob **5.** cesta, osier **6.** hamper **7.** hanaper **8.** bassinet
Basque (pert to) ...
ancestors .. **8.** Iberians
cap .. **5.** beret
home .. **5.** Spain **8.** Pyrenees
bas-relief ... **7.** carving, relievo **12.** basso-relievo (basso-rilievo)
bass ... **4.** fish **5.** fiber, voice (low) **6.** singer **8.** weakfish **13.** basso profundo
bassoon ... **4.** oboe **6.** fagott **7.** fagotto
bast ... **4.** bass **5.** fiber
Bast (Egypt) ... **4.** Ptah **7.** goddess **10.** lady of life
bastard ... **3.** odd **4.** heel (sl), sham **5.** false, louse (sl) **7.** bâtarde (Fr) **8.** abnormal, bantling, spurious **9.** scoundrel **10.** adulterate **12.** illegitimate **13.** nullius filius
baste ... **3.** hit, sew **4.** cook, lard, lash, tack, whip **6.** stitch, thrash **7.** trounce **8.** lambaste
bastion ... **5.** redan **8.** fastness **10.** stronghold **13.** fortification
bat ... **3.** hit, jag, lam, rap **4.** belt, blow, clip, club, slug, sock, swat, wink **5.** binge, clout, paste, smack, spree, stick, whack **6.** bender, cudgel, racket, wallop **7.** clobber
bat (mammal) ... **6.** aliped, fox bat, kalong **7.** noctule, vampire **8.** serotine **9.** flying fox, pipistrel (pipistrelle), reremouse **10.** Chiroptera
batch ... **3.** lot **4.** heap, lump, mess, slew **5.** bunch, group, stack **6.** amount, baking **7.** mixture **8.** quantity **10.** collection
bath ... **3.** dip, tub **4.** sitz **5.** steam, sweat, vapor **6.** plunge, shower, sponge **7.** Finnish, mineral, sulphur
bath (pert to) ...
Eccl .. **8.** ablution
house .. **6.** bagnic, cabana **8.** balneary **10.** natatorium
photography .. **5.** toner **9.** developer
Roman .. **7.** balneum **11.** Warm Springs
sitz .. **5.** bidet
warm .. **5.** therm
bathe ... **3.** tub, wet **4.** bask, lave, swim, wash **5.** flush **6.** drench **7.** immerse, moisten, pervade, suffuse **8.** medicate, permeate
baton ... **3.** rod **4.** mace, wand **5.** staff, stick **6.** baston, cudgel, fasces **7.** scepter, support **9.** truncheon
Batrachia ... **5.** Anura, frogs, toads **7.** Surinam **8.** Salienta
Battalion of Death (Russ) ... **13.** legion of women
batten ... **5.** close, gloat **6.** fasten, fatten, secure, thrive, timber
battered ... **6.** beaten, pasted **7.** bruised **8.** impaired **9.** shattered, weathered
battery ... **3.** set **4.** guns, pack **6.** cohort, series **7.** assault, platoon **8.** baseball (term) **9.** artillery
battery (Elec) ... **4.** cell, grid, pole **5.** anode, plate **6.** Leyden **7.** storage, voltaic **9.** electrode
battle ... **3.** war **4.** fray, meet, tilt **5.** brush, fight, joust, scrap **6.** action, affray,

barney, combat, tussle **7.** contest, scuffle, warfare **8.** conflict, skirmish, struggle **9.** challenge, encounter **10.** engagement
Battle (pert to) ...
Bib .. **8.** Aceldama **12.** potter's field
Civil War .. **7.** Bull Run **15.** Lookout Mountain
formation .. **4.** line **5.** herse, order
Great .. **10.** Armageddon
Hundred Years (1346) .. **5.** Crecy
Revolution .. **10.** Bunker Hill
slogan .. **8.** aux-armes **9.** battle cry
World War I .. **6.** Verdun (1916)
World War II .. **11.** Pearl Harbor (1941)
battologize ... **6.** repeat **7.** iterate, recount, restate **9.** reiterate **12.** recapitulate
bauble ... **3.** toy **4.** gaud **6.** doodad, geegaw, trifle, trivia **7.** bibelot, trinket **8.** falderal (folderol) **9.** bagatelle, plaything **10.** knickknack
bauxite product ... **8.** aluminum
Bavaria ...
capital .. **6.** Munich
city .. **8.** Augsburg, Wurzburg **9.** Nuremburg **12.** Ludwigshafen
freeway .. **8.** autobahn
king (former) .. **10.** Maximilian
prince .. **6.** Rupert
river .. **4.** Eger, Isar
bawdy ... **3.** lewd **6.** coarse, ribald, risqué
bawl ... **3.** cry, say, sob **4.** bark, howl, roar, wail, weep, yell **5.** blare, shout **6.** bellow, boohoo, plaint **8.** proclaim **10.** vociferate
bay ... **3.** ria **4.** cove, howl, roan, wail **5.** bight, horse, inlet, oriel, sinus **6.** recess, window **7.** ululate
bay (pert to) ...
antler .. **9.** stag's tine (2nd)
bird .. **5.** snipe **6.** curlew, godwit, plover
color .. **4.** roan
tree .. **6.** laurel
Bayard ... **5.** horse, steed (Rinaldo's)
bayonet ... **5.** lance, saber, spear, sword **6.** dagger, weapon **7.** poniard
bayou ... **5.** creek, marsh **6.** slough, stream **7.** channel **11.** watercourse
Bayou State ... **11.** Mississippi
Bay State ... **13.** Massachusetts
bazaar ... **4.** fair, shop **6.** market **7.** canteen (army) **10.** exposition
be ... **2.** am **3.** are **4.** live **5.** exist **7.** prevail
beach ... **5.** coast, plage, playa, praya, sands, shore **6.** shilla, strand **9.** waterside
beachcomber ... **4.** wave **6.** loafer **8.** vagabond
beach shelter ... **6.** cabana
beacon ... **4.** beam, flag, sign, vane **5.** fanal, light, radar, radio **6.** marker, pharos, signal **7.** cresset, lantern, seamark **10.** lighthouse, watchtower
bead ... **4.** ball, drop **5.** bugle, pearl, sight (firearm) **6.** rondel **8.** ornament
beads ... **5.** grain, sewan **6.** rosary **7.** chaplet, granose (antennae), jewelry, prayers
beak ... **3.** neb, nib **4.** bill, lora, nose, peck, prow **5.** judge, mouth, spout,

tutel **10.** magistrate **11.** stipendiary
beaker ... **3.** cup **6.** vessel (Chem)
beakless ... **9.** erostrate
beam ... **3.** ray **4.** emit, grin, sile, sill, stud **5.** caber, gleam, joist, shaft, shine, smile, tonka, trave **6.** girder, mantel, rafter, timber **7.** radiate, support, trimmer **8.** trabeate
bean ... **4.** buck, faba, gram, lima, mung, navy, seed, snap, soya **5.** black, coral, pinto, Sieva **6.** adzuki, castor, frijol (frijole), kidney, legume, lentil, string **7.** calabar **9.** Phaseolus
bean (pert to) ...
eye of.. **5.** hilum
game.. **7.** beanbag
licorice seed.. **9.** jequirity
lima.. **4.** haba
seed (string bean).. **7.** haricot
shaped.. **8.** fabiform
slang.. **4.** buck, head **5.** brain **6.** dollar, noodle, trifle
bear ... **3.** aim, cub, lug **4.** dubb, tote, turn, ursa **5.** bring, brown, bruin, carry, clack, crank, koala, polar, press, short, sloth, stand, ursus, yield **6.** animal, endure, grouch, harbor, Kodiak, stress, suffer, Syrian, uphold **7.** Ephraim (nickname), furnish, grizzly, incline, musquaw, produce, support **8.** cinnamon, fructify, maintain, Melursus, sorehead, tolerate **10.** speculator **11.** short seller (Finan)
bear (pert to) ...
cat.. **5.** panda **9.** binturong
class.. **6.** ursine **7.** Ursidaw
color.. **6.** yellow
constellation.. **9.** Ursa Major, Ursa Minor
flag.. **10.** California (State)
head.. **4.** hure
The.. **6.** Russia
beard ... **3.** awn **6.** arista, goatee **7.** stubble, Vandyke **8.** whiskers
bearded ... **5.** awned **7.** barbate, pappose **8.** aristate **9.** whiskered
beards, science of ... **10.** pogonology
bearer ... **3.** boy **5.** macer, usher **6.** porter, tender **7.** carrier **8.** cargador, conveyor, escudero **9.** attendant **10.** khidmatgar, pallbearer
bearing ... **3.** air **4.** mien, port **5.** poise **6.** bel air, regard **7.** concern, conduct, dignity, meaning, posture **8.** behavior, carriage, demeanor, relation, tendency **9.** direction, influence, relevance **10.** connection, deportment, supporting **12.** significance
bearing (Her) ... **4.** enté, orle **5.** bevel, pheon **6.** billet
bear witness ... **6.** attest **7.** testify
beast ... **4.** bête, game, lion, pard **5.** brute, camel, demon, fiend, horse, spado, tiger **6.** animal, cattle, dragon, savage **7.** carrier, critter, leopard, monster **8.** behemoth, creature **9.** dromedary
beastly ... **5.** gross **6.** animal, bloody, carnal, odious **7.** bestial, brutish, hideous, inhuman, leonine, theroid, ungodly **8.** dreadful **9.** execrable **10.** abominable, disgusting
beat ... **3.** hit, lam, tan, taw, wap **4.** bang,

bash, best, cane, drub, drum, flog, lace, lash, maul, pelt, tund **5.** baste, excel, pound, pulse, route, scoop, throb, thump **6.** bruise, cudgel, defeat, larrup, pommel, punish, rhythm, strike, stroke, swinge, thrash, thresh **7.** baffled, belabor, cadence, clobber, conquer, flutter, musical, pulsate, routine, surpass, trounce **8.** chastise, fatigued, lambskin, overcome, vanquish **9.** exhausted, pulsation
beat (pert to) ...
back.. **7.** repulse
black and blue.. **9.** suggilate
down.. **6.** haggle **7.** cheapen
into plate.. **8.** malleate
slang.. **4.** blow **5.** scoot, scram **6.** beat it, skidoo **7.** vamoose
traverse.. **6.** patrol
beatify ... **5.** bless, cheer, saint **6.** hallow **7.** gladden, glorify **8.** enshrine, sanctify
beatnik ... **8.** Bohemian, maverick, sulphite **13.** nonconformist
beau ... **3.** fop **5.** blade, dandy, flame, lover, spark, swain **6.** escort, squire **7.** admirer, courter **9.** caballero, inamorato **10.** beau-garçon
Beau Brummell ... **3.** fop **5.** dandy
beaucoup (Fr) ... **4.** many, much
Beaumarchais comedy ... **15.** Barber of Seville **16.** Marriage of Figaro
beautiful ... **4.** fair, fine **5.** bonny, kalon (Gr) **6.** comely, lovely, poetic, pretty **7.** elegant, Tempean **8.** graceful, handsome, stunning **9.** aesthetic (esthetic), exquisite **15.** pulchritudinous
beautify ... **4.** deck, trim **5.** adorn, grace **6.** bedeck, doll up, enrich **8.** decorate, prettify **9.** embellish, glamorize
beauty ... **5.** belle, charm, glory, grace **8.** elegance **10.** loveliness, prettiness **11.** pulchritude
beauty, famed ...
Egypt.. **9.** Cleopatra
Greek.. **4.** Hebe **6.** Graces **9.** Aphrodite **11.** Helen of Troy
Historical.. **4.** Lais
Persian.. **4.** peri **5.** houri
Norse.. **5.** Freya
Roman.. **5.** Venus
Becken ... **7.** cymbals
beckon ... **4.** beck **5.** court **6.** invite, summon **7.** gesture **11.** gesticulate
becloud ... **5.** bedim, cloud, shade, smoke **6.** bemist, darken, opaque **7.** conceal, encloud, obscure **8.** nubilate, overcast **9.** adumbrate
become ... **2.** go **3.** fit, get, wax **4.** grow, rise, suit **5.** befit, grace **6.** befall, beseem, mature, mellow **7.** behoove, benefit **8.** befuddle **9.** originate
becoming ... **3.** fit **6.** comely, decent, fitted, likely, proper, seemly, suited **7.** decorum, suiting **8.** decorous, pleasing, suitable, tasteful **9.** befitting, expedient **11.** appropriate
Becquerel rays ... **9.** gamma rays
bec-scie ... **4.** duck **9.** merganser
becuna ... **9.** barracuda
bed ... **3.** cot, kip, tye (feather) **4.** bunk, crib, doss, lair, nest **5.** basin, berth,

couch, futon **6.** billet, bottom, flower, litter, pallet **7.** channel, feather, stratum **8.** bassinet **9.** stretcher **10.** foundation
bed (pert to) . . .
canopy . . **4.** ceil **6.** tester
coverlet . . **5.** quilt **6.** spread **7.** blanket **9.** comforter **11.** counterpane
famed . . **15.** bed of Procrustes
bedaub . . . **3.** dab **4.** blur, daub, soil **5.** paint, smear, stain **6.** belaud, smudge **7.** bedizen, besmear **8.** besmudge, ornament
bedazzle . . . **4.** daze, stun **5.** blind, shine **6.** dazzle **7.** astound, confuse **8.** astonish, bewilder
bedeck . . . **3.** gem **4.** trim **5.** adorn, array, grace, prink **6.** clothe, rag out **7.** bedrape **8.** ornament
bedevil . . . **3.** hex **4.** foul, ride **5.** abuse, tease **6.** befoul, muddle, needle, pester, plague **7.** bewitch, confuse, torment **8.** demonize **9.** diabolize, tantalize **10.** complicate
bedight . . . **5.** adorn, array, equip
bedikah . . . **6.** ritual
bedim . . . **3.** dim, fog **4.** blur, fade **5.** blear, cloud **6.** bemist, darken **8.** bedarken
bedlam . . . **3.** din **6.** clamor, tumult, uproar **8.** madhouse **9.** charivari **11.** pandemonium
Bedlam (London) . . . **6.** priory (1247) **8.** Hospital (St Mary of Bethlehem)
Bedouin . . . **4.** Arab, Moor **5.** gypsy, nomad **7.** Saracen, vagrant
Bedouin head cord . . . **4.** agal
bedroll . . . **6.** bindle **7.** matilda
bee . . . **3.** dor **4.** apis **5.** drone, karbi, queen **6.** insect, worker **8.** andrenid, angelito, honeybee **9.** bumblebee **12.** carpenter bee
bee (pert to) . . .
fear of . . **9.** apiphobia
glue . . **8.** propolis
hive . . **4.** butt, scap, skep (straw) **6.** apiary **7.** alveary **8.** workshop
keeper . . **8.** apiarist, skeppist
sociable . . **7.** husking, raising **8.** quilting, spelling
study . . **10.** apiculture **11.** melittology
wax . . **7.** beeswax, ceresin, cerotic **9.** cera flava
Beebe, William . . . **13.** ichthyologist
beef . . . **4.** heft, kine, thew **5.** brawn, sinew, steer **6.** buccan (dried), cattle, muscle **8.** poundage **10.** brawniness **11.** muscularity
Beelzebub (pert to) . . .
Bible . . **5.** deity **6.** oracle **14.** prince of demons
literature . . **5.** demon (Prince), devil **11.** fallen angel
zoology . . **6.** monkey
beer . . . **3.** ale **4.** bock, flip, suds **5.** lager, stout, weiss **6.** liquor, porter, swipes **8.** Pilsener (Pilsner)
beer (pert to) . . .
cask . . **4.** butt
inventor . . **9.** Gambrinus (Myth king)
making . . **4.** hops, malt, wort
mug . . **4.** toby **5.** stein **8.** schooner
vessel . . **6.** tanker **9.** blackjack

beet . . . **4.** Beta **5.** chard **6.** mangel **8.** beet root **9.** sugar beet
Beethoven, Ludwig Van (pert to) . . .
birthplace . . **4.** Bonn (Ger)
composed . . **6.** Eroica **7.** Fidelio **10.** symphonies
famed as . . **7.** pianist **8.** composer
beetle . . . **3.** bat, bug, dor, jut, ram **4.** June, rose **5.** Amara, gogga, Hispa, meloe, snout **6.** chafer, elater, golach, goloch, hammer, masher, sawyer, scarab, weevil **7.** ladybug, prionid **8.** circulio, sharnbud, skipjack **9.** cockroach, dorbeetle **10.** cockchafer, Elateridae
beetlehead . . . **5.** stupe **6.** plover (bird), stupid **8.** bonehead **9.** blockhead **10.** loggerhead
befall . . . **3.** hap **4.** come **5.** occur **6.** betide, chance, happen **9.** eventuate, transpire
befit . . . **4.** suit **5.** serve **6.** become, beseem, please
befitting . . . **3.** fit **4.** meet **6.** filial, proper, seemly, timely **7.** ethical, fitting, suiting **8.** becoming, decorous, suitable **9.** expedient **10.** seasonable **11.** appropriate
befog . . . **3.** dim, fog **5.** blind, cloud **6.** bemist **7.** becloud, conceal, confuse, mystify, obscure
before . . . **3.** ere **5.** afore, ahead, avant, early, prior **6.** anteal, facing, openly, sooner **7.** already, earlier, forward, yestern **8.** anterior, foremost, formerly, hitherto **9.** foregoing, preceding **10.** beforehand, face to face, heretofore, previously **11.** theretofore
before (pert to) . . .
birth . . **8.** prenatal
long . . **4.** soon
mentioned . . **4.** said, same, such **5.** named **6.** former **10.** aforenamed
others . . **5.** first
this . . **3.** ere **5.** prior **6.** erenow
before (pref) . . . **3.** pre, pro **4.** ante, prae
befoul . . . **4.** soil **5.** taint **6.** bemire, defile, muddle **7.** bedevil **8.** entangle **10.** complicate **11.** contaminate
befriend . . . **3.** aid **4.** abet, help **5.** favor **6.** assist, foster, succor **7.** benefit, support, sustain **11.** countenance
befuddle . . . **3.** fog **5.** addle, besot **6.** fuddle, muddle **7.** becloud, confuse **9.** inebriate **10.** intoxicate
beg . . . **3.** ask, sue, woo **4.** pray, sorn **5.** cadge, crave, mooch, plead, touch (sl) **6.** appeal **7.** beseech, entreat, implore, solicit **8.** petition **9.** importune **10.** supplicate
beget . . . **3.** ean **4.** sire **5.** breed, hatch, spawn **6.** father **7.** develop **8.** engender, generate **9.** procreate, reproduce
begetter . . . **4.** sire **5.** pater **6.** author, father, mother, parent **7.** creator **10.** procreator, progenitor
beggar . . . **3.** bum **4.** hobo, waif **5.** fakir (Muslim), gamin, lazar, rogue **6.** loafer, pauper, wretch **7.** almsman, dervish, vagrant, wastral **8.** indigent, vagabond **9.** mendicant, suppliant **10.** panhandler, ragamuffin **14.** tatterdemalion

beggarly . . . **3.** low **4.** base, mean, poor, rank **5.** petty **6.** abject, meanly, paltry, vulgar **7.** hangdog, ignoble **8.** bankrupt, indigent, infamous, wretched **9.** miserable, niggardly **10.** despicably, obsequious **12.** contemptible

Beggars, King of (Eng) . . . **5.** Carew

beggary . . . **4.** want **6.** penury **9.** indigence, mendicity, pauperism **10.** mendicancy **11.** destitution, panhandling

begin . . . **4.** open **5.** enter, start **6.** attack **8.** commence, initiate, take rise **9.** institute, introduce, originate **10.** inaugurate

begin again . . . **5.** renew **6.** resume **10.** recommence

beginner . . . **3.** dub **4.** tyro (tiro) **5.** chela **6.** infant, novice **7.** amateur, entrant, recruit **8.** begetter, freshman, neophyte **9.** debutante, fledgling, initiator, novitiate **10.** catechumen, originator, tenderfoot **11.** inaugurator

beginning . . . **4.** head, rise, root **5.** alpha, birth, debut, onset, start **6.** origin, outset, source **7.** genesis, infancy, opening **8.** entrance, inchoate, nascency, outstart, starting **9.** inception, threshold **10.** derivation, foundation, incomplete, initiation **12.** commencement, introduction

begone . . . **3.** out **4.** away, scat, shoo **5.** allez, scram **6.** aroint, avaunt, depart **7.** vamoose

begrudge . . . **4.** envy **5.** covey, stint **6.** grudge, refuse **7.** grumble

beguile . . . **4.** dupe, lure, vamp **5.** amuse, charm, cozen, elude, spend, trick **6.** delude, divert, regale **7.** bewitch, deceive, ensnare, mislead **8.** enthrall, intrigue **9.** bamboozle, captivate, deception, entertain, fascinate, victimize **11.** double-cross **14.** disappointment

begum (Hind) . . . **5.** queen **7.** heiress **8.** princess

begunk . . . **4.** jilt **5.** trick

behalf . . . **4.** gain, good, part, sake, side **5.** avail, stead **6.** affair, matter, profit **7.** benefit, defense, service, support, welfare **8.** interest **9.** advantage

behalf of . . . **3.** for **6.** lieu of, rather **7.** defense (of), instead

Behan Boy . . . **7.** Borstal

behave . . . **2.** do **3.** act **4.** bear **5.** carry **6.** demean, deport, manage **7.** conduct **8.** regulate, restrain

behavior, behaviour . . . **3.** air **4.** mien **6.** action, manner **7.** actions, address, bearing, conduct, decorum, manners **8.** carriage, demeanor, maintien **10.** deportment **11.** comportment

behavior (pert to) . . .
good . . **7.** decorum, P's and Q's
riotous . . **7.** rampage
wicked . . **10.** wrongdoing

behead . . . **7.** execute **9.** decollate **10.** decapitate, guillotine

Behemoth (Bib) . . . **5.** beast **12.** hippopotamus

behest . . . **3.** vow **5.** order **7.** bidding, command, mandate, promise **10.** injunction **11.** commandment

behind . . . **3.** aft **4.** late, past, rear, rump (vulgar), slow, tail **5.** abaff, abaft, after, ahind, arear, later, tardy **6.** astern **7.** delayed, impeded **8.** arrested, backward, retarded **9.** in the past, posterior, remaining

behindhand . . . **4.** late **5.** tardy **7.** arrears, belated, overdue **8.** backward, dilatory, misdated, mistimed **10.** defaulting, delinquent

behind the times . . . **5.** passé

behold . . . **2.** lo **3.** see **4.** ahoy, ecce, ecco, espy, look, scan, view **5.** voilà **6.** descry, regard, retain **7.** discern, observe, witness **8.** maintain, perceive

beholden . . . **5.** bound **7.** bounden, obliged **8.** grateful, indebted, thankful **9.** obligated

beholder . . . **5.** gazer **7.** watcher, witness **8.** looker-on, observer, onlooker **9.** spectator

beige . . . **4.** ecru, hopi **5.** grège **6.** dorado **13.** reddish-yellow

being . . . **3.** ego, ens, man, one **4.** bion, body, esse, home, life, self **5.** entia, gnome, human, thing, wight **6.** actual, animal, entity, extant, mortal, person **7.** Adamite, essence, present, reality **8.** creature, existent, existing, organism, presence **9.** actuality, existence, personage, something **10.** individual **11.** subsistence

being (pert to) . . .
celestial . . **4.** deva **5.** angel **6.** cherub, seraph
imaginary . . **4.** pixy (pixie) **5.** fairy, sylph
science of . . **8.** ontology
supernatural . . **6.** Garuda (Hind)
Supreme . . **3.** God **7.** Creator

Belarus (pert to) . . .
capital . . **5.** Minsk
name, former . . **10.** Belorussia **11.** Byelorussia, White Russia

belaud . . . **4.** laud **5.** extol **6.** praise **7.** glorify

belay . . . **4.** halt, quit, stop **5.** beset, cease, cover, halte **6.** fasten, invest, waylay **7.** besiege, silence **8.** encircle

belch . . . **4.** burp, emit, vent **5.** eject, eruct, erupt, spout, vomit **7.** gush out **8.** disgorge, eructate **9.** small beer (vulgar) **10.** eructation

beldam, beldame . . . **3.** cat, hag **4.** fury **5.** crone, frump, shrew, vixen, witch **6.** virago **7.** she-wolf, tigress **8.** ancestor (fem), harridan **9.** termagant **11.** grandmother

Belgian (pert to) . . . see also *Belgium*
anthem . . **13.** La Brabanconne
artist . . **8.** Magritte
hare . . **8.** leporide
horse . . **9.** Brabancon
marble . . **5.** rance
resort . . **6.** Ostend
sheep dog . . **8.** Malinois **11.** Groenendael
violinist . . **5.** Ysaye

Belgian Congo . . . see *Zaire*

Belgium . . .
capital . . **8.** Brussels

city . . **5.** Ghent, Liege **6.** Bruges
7. Antwerp, Louvain **9.** Charleroi
commune . . **3.** Ath
forest . . **8.** Ardennes
king . . **6.** Albert **7.** Leopold **8.** Baudouin
native . . **7.** Fleming (of Flanders),
Flemish, Walloon
nickname . . **15.** cockpit of Europe
World War I Battles of . . **5.** Ypres
World War II Battle of . . **8.** The Bulge
Belgravia (London) . . . **8.** district (fashion)
Belial . . . **5.** devil, Satan (New Test)
10. wickedness (Old Test) **11.** Fallen
Angel
belie . . . **4.** deny **6.** belong, defame,
oppose, oppugn **7.** besiege, falsify,
gainsay, pertain, slander **8.** disclaim,
disprove, surround **9.** encompass
10. calumniate **12.** misrepresent
belief . . . **3.** fay (anc), ism **4.** cult, rule,
sect, view **5.** credo, creed, dogma,
faith, maxim, tenet **7.** opinion, precept
8. credence, doctrine, reliance, religion,
teaching **9.** assurance, certainty,
principle **10.** confidence, conviction,
persuasion **13.** Apostles' Creed
believe . . . **3.** buy **4.** deem, feel, trow,
ween **5.** think, trust **6.** accept, credit,
reckon **7.** suppose, swallow **8.** conceive,
consider
believer (pert to) . . .
all religions . . **6.** omnist
facts . . **7.** realist
religion . . **5.** deist **6.** theist **9.** Adventist,
Calvinist **13.** particularist
Belit (Bab) . . . **7.** goddess (wife of Bel)
belittle . . . **4.** slur **5.** decry, dwarf,
scoff, scorn **6.** debase, demean,
deride, impugn **7.** detract, run down
8. minimize **9.** discredit, disparage,
underrate **10.** depreciate
13. underestimate
bell . . . **4.** gong **5.** codon, knell **6.** curfew,
tocsin **7.** campana, cowbell **8.** carillon,
doorbell **9.** ship's bell **10.** dinnerbell,
schoolbell **12.** glockenspiel
13. tintinnabulum
bell, bells (pert to) . . .
bird . . **9.** campanero **10.** wood thrush
botany . . **7.** corolla
evening . . **6.** curfew **7.** Angelus
flat . . **4.** gong **6.** tam-tam (Chin), tom-tom
funeral . . **5.** knell
nautical . . **8.** half hour
ringer . . **6.** toller
ringing . . **7.** peeling **14.** tintinnabulism
science of . . **11.** campanology
set of . . **6.** chimes **8.** carillon
shaped . . **11.** campaniform
specialist . . **9.** campanist
13. campanologist
tongue . . **7.** clapper
tower . . **6.** belfry **9.** campanile
warning . . **6.** tocsin
belle . . . **4.** lady (fine) **5.** toast **6.** beauty
7. charmer **8.** handsome **10.** grande
dame
belles-lettres . . . **8.** classics
10. humanities (The), literature
bellflower . . . **8.** daffodil
belligerent . . . **7.** hostile, scrappy, warlike

8. choleric, militant **9.** bellicose,
irascible, litigious, offensive, wrangling
10. aggressive, pugnacious
11. contentious, quarrelsome
12. disputatious
belligerent's right (Internat law) . . .
6. angary
bellow . . . **3.** cry, low, moo, say **4.** bawl,
roar, wail, yawp **5.** blare, shout
6. clamor **7.** thunder **10.** vociferate
bellows . . . **4.** fish **5.** gills, lungs **6.** blower,
lights (Zool), rotary **8.** ctenidia (Zool)
bellwether . . . **5.** sheep **6.** leader, wether
(with bell)
belly . . . **3.** bag, pot **4.** crap, wame
5. bulge, front, tummy **6.** bottom,
paunch, venter **7.** abdomen, stomach
8. potbelly, swell out **9.** ingluvies
bellyache . . . **5.** gripe **7.** grumble
8. complain
belong (to) . . . **6.** answer, inhere **7.** pertain,
related **9.** appendant, ingrained,
possessed (by) **10.** correspond
belonging (to) . . .
collector, hobbyist . . **10.** collection
11. collectible (collectable)
dean . . **7.** decanal
era . . **7.** epochal
Fall . . **8.** autumnal
pencil, a . . **6.** desmic
people . . **7.** endemic
present, the . . **7.** current
Spring . . **6.** vernal
Summer . . **7.** estival
Winter . . **6.** hiemal
belongings . . . **4.** duds, gear **5.** goods,
traps **6.** family, things **7.** baggage,
effects, kinsmen **8.** chattels, property
9. homefolks, relations, trappings
11. connections, perquisites,
possessions **13.** accouterments,
appurtenances
beloved . . . **3.** pet **4.** dear **6.** prized
7. darling **8.** precious, truelove
9. cherished, inamorata
beloved physician . . . **6.** St Luke
below . . . **4.** alow, here, less **5.** Hades,
neath, sotto, under **6.** aneath, in hell
7. beneath, short of **10.** downstairs
11. belowstairs
Belshazzar (Bib) . . . **11.** crown prince
Bel's wife . . . **5.** Belit (Beltis)
belt . . . **3.** bar, bat, hit **4.** area, band,
beat, blow, cest, mark, pelt, ring,
sash, sock, whip, zone **5.** apron,
Libya, strap, whack, zonar **6.** cestus,
cingle, cordon, fascia, fasten, fillet,
girdle, region, strait, streak, stripe
7. baldric, kurbash, sjambok, stratum,
terrain **8.** cincture, encircle, surround
9. encompass **10.** cummerbund
Belteshazzar (Bib) . . . **6.** Daniel
belt of heaven . . . **6.** zodiac **7.** circuit
beluga . . . **5.** whale (white)
Belus (pert to) . . .
father of . . **4.** Dido
king of . . **4.** Tyre **7.** Assyria
son of . . **5.** Libya
sons . . **7.** Cepheus, Phineus **8.** Aegyptus
belvedere . . . **5.** cigar **7.** cypress (mock)
10. watchtower **11.** summerhouse

bema . . . **8.** platform **9.** sanctuary
bemoan . . . **4.** pity, wail **5.** mourn
  6. bewail, grieve, lament, regret, repine
  7. deplore **10.** sympathize
bemuse . . . **4.** daze **5.** addle, besot
  6. absorb, muddle **7.** stupefy
  8. befuddle, distract **10.** intoxicate
ben . . . **2.** in **3.** oil, son **4.** tree (Moringa)
  6. within
bench . . . **3.** pew **4.** banc (judge's), seat
  5. chair, court, siege, staff, stand, stool,
  table **6.** exedra, settee, settle **7.** terrace
  8. platform, woolsack **9.** committee
bend . . . **3.** bow, nod, ply, sag, sny
  4. bias, flex, genu, kink, knot, sway,
  turn, warp **5.** crimp, crook, curve,
  drink, kneel, prone, squat, stoop,
  twist, yield **6.** buckle, crouch, curtsy,
  direct, divert, humble, inflex, kowtow,
  pleach, relent, salaam, strain, swerve
  7. bendlet (Her), chevron (Her), incline,
  refract, retract **9.** genuflect, introvert,
  sinuosity **10.** inflection
bend (pert to) . . .
  an ear . . **4.** hear, heed **6.** listen
  one's will . . **4.** bias, move, sway
  the elbow . . **5.** drink
  the knee . . **5.** kneel **6.** kowtow, salaam
  9. genuflect
  the mind . . **5.** think
bends . . . **7.** caisson, disease **8.** blackout
  (aeronaut)
beneath . . . **4.** alow **5.** below, lower
  (than), neath, under **6.** aneath, nether
  7. in Hades **11.** underground
beneath one's dignity . . . **8.** infradig
  15. infra dignitatem
benedict . . . **7.** husband **10.** bridegroom,
  married man (newly)
benediction . . . **4.** rite **6.** praise, prayer,
  thanks **7.** benison **8.** blessing
  10. invocation **12.** thanksgiving
benefaction . . . **4.** alms, boon, gift, good
  5. favor **7.** benefit, present **8.** courtesy,
  donation, gratuity, kindness **9.** beau
  geste **11.** beneficence, benevolence
benefactor . . . **5.** angel, donor **6.** backer,
  helper, patron **8.** promoter
  10. befriender
beneficence . . . **7.** charity **8.** goodness,
  kindness **11.** benefaction, benevolence
  12. philanthropy
beneficial . . . **4.** good **6.** benign, useful
  7. helpful **8.** edifying, salutary
  9. favorable, healthful, lucrative,
  wholesome **10.** profitable, salubrious
  11. serviceable **12.** advantageous,
  remunerative
beneficiary . . . **4.** heir **5.** donee **6.** vassal
  7. devisee, feoffee, grantee, legatee
  8. assignee **9.** annuitant
benefit . . . **3.** aid, use **4.** boon, gift, good,
  help, vail **5.** avail, favor, trust **6.** profit,
  relief, succor **7.** advance, concert,
  improve, service, welfare **8.** blessing,
  kindness **9.** advantage **11.** benefaction,
  convenience, performance
benevolence . . . **3.** tax **4.** gift, good
  6. bounty, giving **7.** charity **8.** altruism,
  bestowal, blessing, donation, kindness
  10. generosity, liberality **11.** munificence

  12. contribution, philanthropy
  14. charitableness
benevolent . . . **4.** free, good, king
  6. benign **7.** liberal **8.** generous, princely
  9. benignant, bountiful **10.** altruistic,
  charitable, munificent **11.** magnanimous
  13. philanthropic
Bengal, Indian State . . .
  capital . . **8.** Calcutta
  gentleman . . **5.** baboo (babu)
  language . . **7.** Bengali
  native . . **3.** Kol (Kohl) **6.** banian **7.** Bengali
  river . . **6.** Ganges **11.** Brahmaputra
  river boat . . **7.** bauleah
benign . . . **4.** mild **5.** bland **6.** genial,
  humane, kindly **7.** benefic (Astrol),
  liberal **8.** gracious, salutary
  9. benignant, favorable, healthful,
  wholesome **10.** propitious, salubrious
benignity . . . **5.** favor **7.** benefit
  8. blessing, goodness, mildness
  9. salubrity **10.** kindliness
  11. benevolence **12.** graciousness
benison . . . **8.** blessing **9.** beatitude
  10. invocation **11.** benediction
benjamin . . . **6.** jacket **7.** benzoin
  8. overcoat **9.** spicebush
Benjamin (Bib), (pert to) . . .
  father . . **5.** Jacob
  history . . **5.** tribe
  mother . . **6.** Rachel
Benjamin's mess . . . **6.** big end **10.** lion's
  share
benjy (Brit sl) . . . **3.** hat (straw) **9.** waistcoat
benne . . . **6.** sesame
bennet . . . **4.** herb **5.** daisy **7.** hemlock
bent . . . **3.** aim, way, wry **4.** bias, turn,
  warp **5.** drift, grass, slant, tenor,
  trend, twist **6.** course, curved, desire,
  minded, nature, swayed **7.** angular,
  aptness, crooked, heather, leaning,
  stooped **8.** aptitude, penchant, tendency
  9. obliquity, prejudice, proneness
  10. propensity **11.** disposition,
  inclination **12.** idiosyncrasy, predilection
  13. prepossession **14.** predisposition
Benthamism . . . **9.** welfarism
  14. utilitarianism
benthonic . . . **7.** benthal, deep sea
benthonic plant . . . **6.** enalid
benthos . . . **5.** deeps **6.** depths **8.** ocean
  bed **16.** Davy Jones's locker
benumb . . . **3.** nip **4.** drug, numb, stun
  5. chill **6.** deaden, freeze **7.** stupefy
  8. paralyze **11.** anesthetize, desensitize
Beowulf . . . **4.** epic, poem (oldest in
  Teutonic language)
bequeath . . . **4.** give, will **5.** endow, leave
  6. bestow, demise, devise, invest, will
  to **7.** bequest **8.** transmit
bequest . . . **4.** will **6.** devise, legacy
  8. heritage **9.** patrimony, testament
  10. birthright **11.** inheritance
berate . . . **3.** jaw, nag **4.** lash, rail **5.** chide,
  scold, slate **7.** censure, reprove, upbraid
Berber . . . **4.** Riff **6.** Hamite, Kabyle,
  Taureg
berceau . . . **4.** walk (leaf-covered) **5.** arbor,
  bower **6.** cradle
berceuse . . . **10.** cradlesong
  11. composition

bereave . . . **3.** die, rob **5.** leave, strip **6.** divest, orphan, sadden **7.** deprive, despoil **10.** disentitle, dispossess
bereavement . . . **4.** loss **5.** death **9.** privation **10.** divestment
bereft . . . **4.** lorn **7.** denuded, fleeced, shorn of, witless **8.** bereaved, divested, orphaned, stripped **9.** senseless **10.** parentless, pauperized
Bereshith (Jew) . . . **7.** Genesis **9.** Beginning
beret . . . **3.** cap, tam **7.** biretta
bergamot . . . **4.** pear **5.** snuff **6.** orange **7.** essence **9.** fragrance
beriberi . . . **5.** kakke **7.** disease
Berkeleianism (pert to) . . .
  founder . . **8.** Berkeley (Bishop)
  science . . **10.** philosophy
  system . . **8.** idealism **13.** immaterialism
Berlin, Germany . . .
  avenue . . **14.** Unter den Linden
  capital . . **7.** Germany
  garden (Zool) . . **10.** Tiergarten
  gate . . **11.** Brandenburg
  government . . **9.** Reichstag
berm, berme . . . **4.** mall, path **5.** prado **6.** runway **7.** terrace **8.** shoulder (road)
Bermuda . . .
  capital . . **8.** Hamilton
  color . . **12.** geranium pink
  discoverer . . **8.** Bermudez
  government . . **7.** British
  grass . . **5.** decil
  ocean site . . **8.** Atlantic
Bernardine Order . . . **11.** Cistercians
Berne, Bern (Switz) . . . **7.** capital
Bernstein musical . . . **13.** West Side Story
Bernoulli forte . . . **8.** calculus
berry . . . **3.** haw **4.** buck, seed **5.** bacca, cubeb, fruit, grain, money **6.** acinus, kernel
berry, fruit . . . **5.** grape, salal **6.** banana, tomato **7.** currant **8.** bilberry, dewberry, hagberry, mulberry **9.** bearberry, blueberry, cranberry, raspberry **10.** blackberry, elderberry, gooseberry, loganberry, strawberry **11.** boysenberry, huckleberry **12.** checkerberry, whortleberry
berserk . . . **4.** amok, bunk, dock, post, room **5.** house, roost **6.** billet, marina, office, reside **8.** quarters **9.** situation **11.** appointment
bertha . . . **4.** cape **6.** cannon, collar **7.** Perchta (goddess) **9.** Big Bertha (Ger gun)
Besant belief . . . **9.** theosophy
beseech . . . **3.** beg, sue **4.** pray **5.** crave, plead **6.** obtest **7.** entreat, implore, solicit **9.** obsecrate **10.** supplicate
beset . . . **3.** dun, ply, vex **4.** stud **5.** harry, haunt, hem in, siege, worry **6.** attack, harass, infest, invade, obsess, plague, ravage **7.** besiege **8.** blockade, surround **9.** beleaguer, importune, infatuate
beset with danger . . . **5.** risky **6.** chancy **8.** perilous **9.** dangerous **10.** jeopardous
beset with hairs . . . **7.** barbate, bearded
beside, besides . . . **2.** by **3.** too, yet **4.** also, else, near, nigh, para (pref)

5. about, along **6.** nearby **8.** likewise, moreover **9.** other than **11.** furthermore **12.** over and above
beside oneself . . . **3.** mad **4.** wild **5.** crazy, rabid **6.** beserk, raging, raving **7.** frantic, ranting **8.** frenzied **9.** desperate, overjoyed **10.** distracted, distraught **11.** overwrought
besiege . . . **5.** beset **6.** attack, harass, obsess, plague **7.** torment **8.** blockade, surround **9.** beleaguer
besmear . . . **3.** dab **4.** coat, daub, mark, soil, spot **5.** paint, smear, stain, taint **6.** bedaub **7.** tarnish **8.** besmudge
besmirch . . . **4.** blot, soil **5.** smear, sully **6.** defile, smirch, smudge, vilify **7.** besmear, blacken, tarnish **8.** discolor
besom . . . **5.** broom, hussy
besotted . . . **4.** dull **5.** drunk **7.** muddled, sottish **8.** obsessed **9.** senseless, stupefied **10.** infatuated **11.** intoxicated
bespangled . . . **5.** aglow **7.** lighted, studded, trimmed **8.** spangled **9.** decorated, garnished **10.** glittering, ornamented **11.** embellished, illuminated
bespatter . . . **3.** wet **4.** blot, spot **5.** dirty, slosh, smear, stain, sully **6.** splash, vilify **7.** asperse, scatter, spatter, tarnish **8.** besmirch, splatter, sprinkle **9.** denigrate **10.** stigmatize
bespeak . . . **4.** mean, show **5.** imply **6.** ask for, attest, engage, evince **7.** address, betoken, connote, exhibit, suggest, testify **8.** foretell, indicate, manifest **11.** demonstrate
Bessemer product . . . **5.** steel
best . . . **4.** aces, beat, most, tops **5.** cream, elite, queen **6.** choice, finest **7.** largest **8.** champion, outstrip **9.** nonpareil, overmatch **11.** superlative
bestial . . . **3.** low **4.** vile **5.** cruel **6.** brutal, filthy, savage **7.** beastly, brutish, inhuman, sensual **8.** depraved, ruthless **9.** barbarous
bestow . . . **4.** deal, give **5.** allot, apply, award, grant, spend **6.** accord, confer, convey, demise, devote, donate, impart, render, tender **7.** deposit, present **8.** transmit **10.** administer
bestow honor upon . . . **5.** adorn, exalt, grace **6.** dignify, ennoble, glorify **10.** aggrandize **11.** distinguish
bestride . . . **4.** pass **5.** mount **7.** climb on, protect, support **8.** straddle **10.** bestraddle
bet . . . **3.** bas (roulette), pot **4.** play **5.** stake, wager **6.** gamble, hazard, pledge
beta test (army) . . . **12.** intelligence
bête . . . **5.** beast, silly **6.** stupid **7.** foolish
betel (pert to) . . .
  leaf . . **3.** pan **4.** buyo, paun (pan)
  palm . . **5.** areca
  pepper . . **4.** itmo (ikmo)
bête noire . . . **4.** ogre **7.** bugbear **10.** black beast, frightener, mumbo jumbo
bethel . . . **4.** kirk **6.** chapel, church **8.** Bethesda (Jerusalem) **12.** meetinghouse
bethink . . . **5.** think **6.** recall **7.** reflect

8. cogitate, remember 9. cerebrate, recollect
betide . . . 3. hap 4. fall 5. occur 6. befall, happen 7. betoken, presage 9. come about, eventuate, transpire
betimes . . . 4. anon, soon 5. early 7. ere long, shortly 8. directly, speedily 9. forthwith, presently 10. beforehand, seasonably 12. occasionally
betise . . . 5. folly 9. asininity, silliness, stupidity 11. foolishness
betoken . . . 4. mark, mean, note 5. augur 6. denote, typify 7. bespeak, connote, express, portend, presage, purport, signify 8. evidence, indicate 9. foretoken, symbolize
betray . . . 4. blab, dupe, hoax, sell 5. bluff, peach, trick 6. reveal, seduce, tattle 7. beguile, deceive, divulge, mislead, sell out 8. disclose, inform on 9. bamboozle, victimize 11. double-cross
betrayal . . . 4. ruse 5. trick 7. sellout, treason 8. giveaway 9. Judas kiss, seduction, treachery 10. disclosure
betrayer . . . 5. Judas 6. Arnold, Brutus 7. seducer, traitor 8. derelict, informer, Quisling, turncoat 10. treasonist 13. double-crosser, Judas Iscariot
betroth . . . 4. affy, earl 5. tryst 6. engage, pledge, plight 7. espouse, promise 8. affiance, contract, espousal 10. engagement
better . . . 3. top 4. more 5. amend, emend, excel, raise (poker), safer, wiser 6. bigger, exceed, outwit, reform 7. advance, choicer, greater, improve, promote, surpass, victory 8. improved, superior 9. advantage, meliorate 10. ameliorate, preferable 11. superiority
betting term . . . 4. ante, odds, tout 6. exacta, parlay 7. pyramid 8. perfecta, quinella, trifecta 10. parimutuel 11. sweepstakes
between . . . 5. among, mesne 6. atween 7. average, betwixt
bevel . . . 4. edge, ream 5. angle, bezel, slant, slope, snape, splay 6. square 7. incline, oblique 8. obliquity
beverage . . . 3. ade, opo (comb form), pop, tea 4. coke, malt, maté, mead, milk, soda 5. cider, cocoa, drink, leban, morat (anc), punch, water 6. coffee, eggnog, frappé, nectar 7. Seltzer 8. Adam's ale, Coca-Cola, lemonade, root beer, sourdook 9. ginger ale, orangeade, phosphate 10. buttermilk, grape juice 12. sarsaparilla
beverage (alcoholic) . . . 3. ale, gin, rum 4. beer, brew, grog, kava, port, raki 5. booze, cider, hooch, julep, lager, negus, punch, smash, vodka 6. arrack, bishop, brandy, cognac, eggnog, kumiss, kummel, likker, porter, posset, sherry, tiswin, whisky (whiskey), zythum (anc) 7. Bacardi, bootleg, bourbon, cordial, liqueur, martini, tequila 8. absinthe, aleberry, Burgundy, cocktail, highball, muscatel, sauterne, vermouth 9. applejack, aqua vitae,

firewater, Manhattan 10. shandygaff, Tom Collins 11. Benedictine, boilermaker, grasshopper, mountain dew
bevy . . . 4. bund, gang, herd, host 5. covey, flock, group, party, troop 6. galaxy, throng 7. company 8. assembly 10. collection
bewail . . . 3. rue 4. keen, mean 5. mourn 6. bemoan, grieve, lament, regret, repine, sorrow 7. deplore
bewilder . . . 3. fog 4. daze 5. addle, amaze 6. baffle, dazzle, puzzle 7. buffalo, confuse, fluster, mystify, nonplus, perplex 8. astonish, confound, distract 9. bamboozle, embarrass
bewilderment . . . 3. awe, fog 4. maze 6. wonder 9. confusion 10. perplexity 11. distraction 12. perturbation 13. disconcertion, embarrassment
bewitch . . . 3. hex 5. charm, witch 6. enamor, entice, hoodoo, voodoo 7. beguile, delight, enchant 8. enthrall 9. captivate, enrapture, ensorcell, fascinate, infatuate
bewitching . . . 5. siren 6. hexing, lovely 7. magical 8. alluring, charming, enticing 10. enchanting 11. captivating, fascinating
bey (Turk) . . . 5. title 8. governor
Beyle's pseud . . . 8. Stendahl
beyond . . . 2. by 3. too, yet 4. meta (pref), past, plus, well 5. above, extra, ultra 6. yonder 7. besides, farther, further, yonside 8. moreover 9. exceeding, Hereafter (The) 11. furthermore 12. additionally, ultraliminal
beyond hope . . . 9. desperate
bezant (pert to) . . .
  architecture . . 4. disc 8. ornament
  coin (anc) . . 7. solidus (gold)
  heraldry . . 4. disc (gold)
  offering (Eng king) . . 4. gold
bezel . . . 4. edge 5. crown (gem), facet 6. chaton, flange 8. pavilion, template (templet) 9. obliquity
bezonian . . . 6. mucker, wretch 7. budmash, caitiff, recruit 8. blighter 9. pilgarlic, scoundrel
bhikshu . . . 6. gelong 7. ascetic 8. sannyasi 9. mendicant
bhut (Dravidian) . . . 5. demon, ghost 6. goblin
bias . . . 3. ply 4. awry, bent, turn, warp 5. amiss, slant, twist 6. desire 7. leaning, oblique 8. diagonal, slanting, tendency 9. obliquity, prejudice 10. favoritism, partiality, prepossess, transverse 11. disposition
biased . . . 4. bent 6. narrow, swayed 7. bigoted, partial 8. diagonal, partisan, slanting 10. prejudiced
bib . . . 3. sip, sup 4. swig 5. apron, drink, quaff 6. guzzle, imbibe, tipple, tucker 7. tablier 8. pinafore
bibacious . . . 6. toping 7. drunken, sottish 8. bibulous, drinking, tippling
Bible . . . 7. The Book, The Word, Vulgate 10. Scriptures, Testaments (Old, New) 11. The Good Book
Bible (pert to) . . .

battle site .. **10**. Armageddon
city .. **2**. Ur **5**. Joppa, Sidon, Sodom
   6. Hebron **9**. Bethlehem, Jerusalem
coin .. **6**. talent
Commandments .. **9**. Decalogue
Holy Land .. **9**. Palestine
interpretation .. **7**. anagoge
introduction .. **9**. Isagogics
kingdom .. **4**. Elam **6**. Basham, Canaan
   7. Chaldea
land of plenty .. **6**. Goshen
language .. **7**. Aramaic
mountain .. **4**. Ebol, Zion **5**. Horeb,
   Sinai **6**. Ararat, Gilead, Moriah, Olives
   (Olivet), Pisgah
pause .. **5**. selah
pool .. **6**. Siloam
precious stone .. **6**. ligure (jacinth)
Promised Land .. **6**. Canaan
sea .. **3**. Red **4**. Dead **7**. Galilee
Sermon on the Mount .. **10**. Beatitudes
sheep .. **7**. chamois
town .. **4**. Edar **5**. Babel
Wells of .. **5**. Hagar, Jacob
Bible character ...
archangel .. **7**. Raphael
giant .. **4**. Anak **7**. Goliath
High Priest .. **3**. Eli
hunter .. **6**. Nimrod
liar .. **7**. Ananias
patriarch .. **5**. Jacob **6**. Israel
prophet .. **4**. Amos, Joel **5**. Hosea,
   Jonah, Micah, Nahum **6**. Daniel,
   Haggai, Isaiah, Joseph, Joshua,
   Samuel **7**. Ezekiel, Malachi, Obadiah
   8. Habakkuk, Jeremiah **9**. Zachariah,
   Zephaniah
Bible version ... **5**. Douay, Reims
   6. Geneva **7**. Bishop's, Luther's,
   Revised, Targums, Vulgate
   8. Cranmer's, Matthew's, Peshitta,
   Tyndale's, Wartburg, Wycliffe
   9. Jerusalem, King James, Maccabees
   10. Great Bible, Septuagint
   15. American Revised
bicker ... **5**. argue, cavil **6**. hassle,
   quiver, strife **7**. dispute, flicker, flutter,
   quarrel, quibble, rhubarb (sl), wrangle
   8. argument, pettifog **9**. scrimmage,
   tremulous **10**. contention **11**. altercation
bicuspid ... **5**. bifid, tooth, valve
   6. cuspid **8**. premolar **10**. two-pointed
   13. double-pointed
bid ... **3**. beg **4**. pray **5**. offer, order,
   utter **6**. charge, direct, enjoin, invite,
   reveal, tender **7**. command, declare,
   entreat, offered, summons **8**. overture,
   proclaim **9**. quotation **12**. presentation
biddy ... **3**. hen **4**. dame **5**. skirt
   6. female **7**. chicken, Partlet **8**. bedmaker
   11. maidservant
bide ... **4**. bear, stay, wait **5**. abide,
   await, tarry **6**. endure, remain, suffer
   8. continue, tolerate **9**. encounter,
   withstand
bield ... **3**. den **4**. cozy **7**. comfort,
   courage, hearten, shelter **8**. boldness,
   embolden **9**. sheltered **10**. confidence,
   habitation
bien ... **4**. fine, good, snug
bienseance ... **7**. decorum, manners

9. propriety **11**. correctness, proprieties
   (the) **12**. mannerliness
   17. conventionalities
bier ... **6**. coffin, litter **10**. catafalque
Bier ... **4**. beer
biff ... **4**. bash, blow, slug, sock **5**. paste,
   punch
bifold ... **4**. dual **5**. duple **6**. binary,
   binate, double **7**. twofold
bifurcate ... **3**. wye (letter) **4**. fork
   7. forking, furcate **8**. biforked, branched,
   forklike **9**. two-forked
big ... **4**. huge **5**. bulky, grand, great,
   grown, jumbo, large **6**. august,
   famous, mighty **7**. massive, pompous,
   teeming **8**. boastful, powerful, pregnant,
   swelling **9**. momentous **10**. tremendous
   11. magnanimous, pretentious
big (pert to) ...
shot .. **3**. VIP
stick .. **5**. power (T Roosevelt)
toe .. **6**. hallux
top .. **6**. circus
wig .. **3**. VIP (humorous)
Big (pert to) ...
Ben .. **5**. clock **13**. Tower of London
Bend State .. **9**. Tennessee
Bertha .. **3**. gun **5**. Krupp (factory)
Blue .. **3**. IBM
Board .. **4**. NYSE **13**. stock exchange
Easy .. **10**. New Orleans
House .. **3**. pen **6**. prison (State)
   12. penitentiary
Push (WWI) .. **5**. Somme
Bigfoot ... **9**. Sasquatch
bight ... **3**. bay **4**. bend, gulf, loop
   5. angle, noose, point **6**. corner, hollow
   7. estuary
bigot ... **3**. bug, nut **6**. zealot **7**. fanatic
   9. dogmatist, hypocrite, illiberal
   10. enthusiast, opinionist, positivist
bigoted ... **5**. petty **6**. little, narrow
   10. intolerant, prejudiced **12**. narrow-
   minded
bijou ... **5**. jewel **7**. trinket
bilbi, bilby ... **8**. kangaroo
bilbo ... **5**. sword **6**. rapier
bilingual ... **6**. diglot **12**. linguistical
bilious ... **3**. ill **8**. choleric, liverish
   9. dyspeptic, jaundiced **11**. ill-tempered
bilk ... **2**. do **3**. gyp **4**. balk, hoax, sell
   5. cheat, cozen, trick **6**. delude, fleece,
   illude **7**. decaive, defraud, swindle
   8. flimflam **11**. hornswoggle
bill ... **3**. dun, nab, nib, pee, tab, Vee
   ($5) **4**. beak, deed, list, menu, sign
   5. carte, money **6**. docket, pickax,
   poster, ticket **7**. account, invoice,
   mattock, placard, program, receipt,
   statute, voucher **8**. billhook, schedule
   9. publicize, statement **10**. prospectus
   11. legislative **13**. advertisement
billet ... **3**. bar, log **4**. note, pass
   5. berth, stick, strap **6**. assign, docket,
   letter, notice, ticket **7**. bearing (Her),
   epistle, missive, molding **8**. dispatch,
   document, insignia, position, quarters
   11. appointment
billiard shot ... **5**. carom, masse
   6. cannon
Billingsgate ... **4**. Gate (London) **10**. fish

market **12.** vituperation
billow . . . **3.** sea **4.** roll, toss, wave
5. eagre, heave, surge, swell **6.** dilate
7. distend **10.** undulation
billowy . . . **4.** wavy **5.** surgy **7.** surging
8. swelling **10.** undulating
bin . . . **3.** box **4.** crib, loft, vina **5.** frame,
kench, pungi (Hind flute) **6.** manger
8. elevator
binary . . . **4.** dual **6.** bifold, binate, double,
duplex **9.** duplicate
bind . . . **3.** jam, tie **4.** ally, frap, gird,
gyve, hold, lace, lash, rope, tape
5. chain, leash, stick, truss, withe
6. engage, fasten, fetter, pinion, pledge,
secure **7.** confine, shackle **8.** obligate
10. constipate
binding . . . **4.** tape **5.** valid **6.** binder,
edging **7.** girding, joining, liaison
8. trimming, trussing, wrapping
9. bordering, fastening, stringent
10. astringent, compulsory, obligatory
11. restraining, restrictive
binding (agreement) . . . **4.** bond, pact
7. bargain, promise **8.** contract
binding (book) . . . **4.** yapp **5.** cover
6. jacket **10.** bibliopegy
binge . . . **4.** bout **5.** spree **6.** bender
8. carousal **11.** celebration
bingo . . . **3.** pop **4.** bang, keno **5.** lotto,
socko **6.** brandy **7.** tombola
biographer . . . **8.** annalist **9.** historian
10. chronicler **11.** biographist,
memorialist
biography . . . **4.** life **6.** memoir **7.** history,
memoire, recount **8.** memorial
11. hagiography
biological . . . **4.** gene **5.** class, genus,
order, vital **6.** biotic, family **7.** animate,
organic, paracme, species
biology, science of . . . **6.** botany
7. ecology, zoology **8.** eugenics,
genetics **9.** bionomics, organisms
10. embryology, morphology,
physiology
biopsy (Med) . . . **8.** analysis (tissue)
9. diagnosis **11.** examination
(microscopic)
biped . . . **3.** man **9.** two-legged
birch . . . **4.** flog **5.** stick **6.** switch
birch tree (pert to) . . .
family . . **10.** Betulaceae
genera . . **5.** alder, birch, hazel
order . . **7.** Fagales
product . . **16.** oil of wintergreen
variety . . **5.** paper, river, sweet, white
6. cherry, yellow
bird (pert to) . . .
best swimmer . . **4.** loon **6.** gannet
cage . . **6.** aviary **7.** paddock **8.** dovecote
Class . . **4.** Aves
crested . . **7.** hoatzin **9.** stinkbird
extinct . . **3.** moa **4.** dodo
fabled, sacred . . **3.** roc **4.** ibis
fastest flyer . . **4.** hawk **5.** eagle, swift
6. falcon
fastest runner . . **7.** ostrich
feathers . . **5.** remix (sing) **7.** remiges
first . . **13.** archaeopteryx
footless . . **4.** apod
greatest traveler . . **4.** tern

greatest wingspread . . **9.** albatross
halcyon . . **10.** kingfisher
highest flyer . . **5.** goose
immortal . . **7.** phoenix
killing . . **7.** avicide
largest . . **6.** condor **7.** ostrich
13. whooping crane
Latin . . **4.** avis
life . . **5.** ornis
longest-lived . . **5.** macaw
lover . . **12.** ornithophile
most dangerous . . **9.** cassowary
naked hatched . . **11.** gymnogenous
of prey (prized) . . **6.** falcon
oldest known . . **13.** archaeopteryx
one year old . . **8.** annotine
Order . . **7.** Rasores **8.** Raptores
smallest . . **14.** bee hummingbird
smartest . . **4.** crow
study . . **6.** oology
young . . **4.** eyas **8.** birdikin, nestling
9. fledgling
bird, anatomy (pert to) . . .
beak . . **3.** neb, nib **4.** bill, lora **5.** ceral
7. rostrum
eye process . . **6.** pecten
head . . **4.** lore **6.** pileum
jaw . . **4.** mala
leg (featherless) . . **9.** cnemidium
wing part . . **5.** alula
bird, Arctic . . . **3.** auk **4.** gull, skua **5.** brant
6. dunlin, fulmar, jaeger **7.** penguin
9. ptarmigan
bird, colorful . . . **3.** kea **5.** egret, macaw
6. magpie, parrot, trogon **7.** peacock,
quetzal (quezal) **8.** lyrebird **10.** kingfisher
14. bird of paradise
bird, common . . . **3.** ani, daw, owl
4. chat, dove, lark, pisk, wren **5.** finch,
pipit, robin, vireo **6.** dunlin, linnet,
martin, oriole, phoebe, pigeon, shrike,
siskin, thrush, towhee **7.** blue jay,
bunting, catbird, cowbird, flicker,
grackle, kinglet, sparrow, swallow,
tanager, warbler, waxwing **8.** blackcap,
bluebird, bobolink, cardinal, grosbeak,
kingbird, redstart, starling, titmouse
9. chickadee, goldfinch, nighthawk,
sandpiper **10.** flycatcher, meadowlark,
turtledove, woodpecker
11. hummingbird, mockingbird,
nightingale, pyrrhuloxia
12. whippoorwill, yellowhammer
14. scarlet tanager
bird, crow family . . . **4.** crow, rook
5. crake, raven **6.** chough, magpie
7. corvine, jackdaw
bird, duck family . . . **4.** clee, coot, lory,
smew, teal, wood **5.** eider, goose
6. scoter **7.** gadwall, mallard, Muscovy,
pintail, pochard **8.** baldpate, redshank,
shoveler **9.** merganser **10.** bufflehead,
canvasback
bird, flightless . . . **3.** emu, moa **4.** dodo
(ext), kiwi, rhea, weka **7.** apteryx,
ostrich, peacock, penguin **8.** Notornis
9. cassowary
bird, foreign . . .
Africa . . **4.** taha **5.** crane **6.** cuckoo
7. ostrich **8.** umbrette **10.** weaverbird
Arctic . . **3.** auk **4.** gull, skua **5.** brant

6. dunlin, falcon, jaeger 7. penguin
8. grayling 9. gyrfalcon, ptarmigan
Asia . . 4. myna 5. pitta 6. bulbul,
linnet 7. boobook, peacock, sirgang
8. dotterel, leaf bird 9. brambling,
muted swan
Australia . . 3. emu 4. kiwi, lory
5. lowan 6. leipoa 7. boobook,
grinder 8. ganggang, lorikeet, lyrebird,
morepork, parakeet, platypus
9. bowerbird, cassowary, pardalote
Central America . . 6. barbet, toucan
7. quetzal (quezal) 8. puffbird
Cuba . . 6. trogon 8. tocororo 14. bee
hummingbird
England . . 4. kite, rook 9. cormorant
11. carrion crow
Europe . . 4. merl 5. pipit, stilt (3-
toed), stork (white), swift, tarin
6. godwit, hoopoe, merlin, roller, siskin
7. bittern, ortolan, skylark, starnel 8. bee
eater, dotterel, garganey, nuthatch,
redstart 9. brambling, chaffinch,
gallinule, sheldrake 10. lammergeir,
turtledove 11. nightingale, wallcreeper
12. capercaillie (grouse)
Hawaii . . 2. io, o-o 3. ava, iwa, poe
4. iiwi, mamo 6. parson 7. frigate
India . . 5. shama 8. amadavat, pheasant
11. red hornbill
Java . . 7. sparrow 8. rice bird 9. fruit
dove
New Guinea . . 9. cassowary 14. bird
of paradise
New Zealand . . 3. ihi, kea, moa, tui
4. kuku, weka
So America . . 4. guan 5. macaw
6. barbet, motmot, toucan 7. jacamar,
tinamou, warrior 8. boatbill, caracara
9. trumpeter 11. scarlet ibis
bird, game . . . 4. teal 5. brant, goose,
quail, snipe 6. grouse, pigeon,
plover, turkey (wild) 7. bustard,
gadwall, mallard 8. bobwhite, pheasant,
woodcock 9. partridge, ptarmigan
10. canvasback 14. prairie chicken
bird, group . . .
partridge . . 5. covey
pheasant . . 3. nye 4. nide
quail . . 4. bevy
bird, long-legged . . . 4. ibis, rail, sora
5. crane, egret, heron, stilt, stork
6. avocet, curlew, jacana 7. seriema
8. flamingo 9. sandpiper 10. demoiselle
Bird of . . .
Freedom . . 9. bald eagle
Jove . . 5. eagle
June . . 7. peacock
Minerva . . 3. owl
Wonder . . 7. phoenix
bird, pet . . . 4. myna (mynah) 6. canary,
parrot 8. cockatoo, lovebird, parakeet
bird, poultry . . . 4. duck 5. goose
6. pigeon, turkey 7. chicken 8. pheasant
bird, shore . . . 4. swan 5. egret, heron,
stork 6. avocet, curlew, plover, willet
7. frigate, pelican 8. dotterel, killdeer
10. demoiselle
bird, sky . . . 4. erne (ern), gier (Bib),
hawk, kite 5. Buteo, eagle, saker
6. condor, falcon, gannet, jaeger,

merlin, osprey 7. buzzard, harrier,
kestral, vulture 8. caracara, ringtail
9. Accipiter 10. lammergeir
bird, water . . . 3. auk 4. coot, gull,
ibis, loon, rail, shag, skua, swan
5. cahow, crane, grebe, heron, stork
6. curlew, cygnet, gannet, jabiru,
jacana, petrel, plover 7. bittern, bustard,
dovekie, pelican, seriema, skimmer
8. dabchick, flamingo, umbrette
9. albatross, cormorant, gallinule,
guillemot, phalarope, spoonbill
10. kingfisher, yellowlegs
biretta . . . 8. skullcap 9. headdress
birl . . . 4. spin 6. rattle 7. resolve
birler . . . 10. lumberjack
Biro . . . 9. ballpoint
birth . . . 3. nee 4. line 5. blood,
breed 6. origin 7. descent, genesis,
lineage 8. heritage, nativity, nobility
9. beginning 10. derivation, extraction,
renascence 11. inheritance, Renaissance
birthday (pert to) . . .
astrology . . 7. casting, lineage (the gods)
nativities . . 9. genethlic 10. genethliac
poems . . 12. genethliacon
birth flower (by months) . . .
Jan . . 9. carnation
Feb . . 8. primrose
Mar . . 6. violet
Apr . . 5. daisy
May . . 15. lily of the valley
June . . 4. rose
July . . 8. sweet pea
Aug . . 9. gladiolus
Sept . . 5. aster
Oct . . 6. dahlia
Nov . . 13. chrysanthemum
Dec . . 5. holly 10. poinsettia
birthmark . . . 4. mole 5. nevus (naevus)
birthright . . . 6. rights 8. heritage
9. privilege 10. possession
11. inheritance
birth seniority . . . 9. first-born
13. primogeniture
birthstone (by days) . . .
Sun . . 5. topaz 7. diamond
Mon . . 5. pearl 7. crystal
Tues . . 4. ruby 7. emerald
Wed . . 8. amethyst 9. loadstone
Thurs . . 8. sapphire 9. carnelian
Fri . . 7. cat's eye, emerald
Sat . . 7. diamond 9. turquoise
birthstone (by months) . . .
Jan . . 6. garnet
Feb . . 8. amethyst
Mar . . 10. aquamarine, bloodstone
Apr . . 7. diamond
May . . 7. emerald
June . . 5. pearl 11. alexandrite
July . . 4. ruby
Aug . . 7. peridot 8. sardonyx
Sept . . 8. sapphire
Oct . . 4. opal 10. tourmaline
Nov . . 5. topaz 7. citrine
Dec . . 6. zircon 9. turquoise
bis . . . 5. again, ditto, twice 6. encore,
repeat 7. replica 8. repetend 9. duplicate
10. repetition
biscuit . . . 3. bun, doe 4. rusk 5. bread,
cooky, scone, wafer 6. pommel

7. cracker 8. biscotin, zwieback
bise . . . 4. wind (cold) 6. winter 7. Norther
bisect . . . 4. fork 5. cross, halve, split
   6. cleave, divide
bishop . . . 4. Abba 7. pontiff, prelate
   8. chessman, director, overseer
   9. churchman, clergyman, inspector
   14. superintendent
bishop (pert to) . . .
   Bible . . 10. Great Bible
   cap . . 4. hura 5. miter
   revenue . . 7. annates
   staff . . 7. baculus, crosier (crozier)
   throne . . 3. see 4. apse
   vestment . . 4. cope 5. stole 6. rochet
      7. gremial, pallium 8. dalmatic
      10. omophorion
bishopric . . . 3. see 4. seat 7. diocese
   10. episcopacy, episcopate
Bismark . . . 14. Iron Chancellor
bison . . . 2. ox 4. gaur, urus 6. catalo
   (hybrid) 7. aurochs, buffalo
   9. quadruped
bisque (pert to) . . .
   ceramics (unglazed) . . 7. biscuit
   color . . 9. red-yellow
   food . . 4. soup 8. ice cream
   term (sports) . . 4. turn 5. point 6. stroke
bissext (pert to) . . .
   calendar . . 6. Julian (Rom)
   day . . 5. sixth (intercalary)
   year . . 8. Leap Year
bistro . . . 4. cafe 6. tavern 7. barroom
   8. wine shop 10. restaurant
bit . . . 3. ace, jot, ort 4. atom, bite, coin,
   iota, mite, mote, part (acting), role, snip,
   tool, tube, whit 5. check, crumb, hitch,
   money, piece, scrap, speck 6. morsel,
   smidge, tittle 7. portion, smidgen,
   traneen 8. somewhat 9. something
bit (harness) . . . 4. curb 6. bridle, Pelham
   7. snaffle 9. Liverpool
bit (money) . . .
   two bits . . 7. quarter 9. ninepence
   (Bahamas)
   four bits . . 10. half dollar
bitch . . . 6. female (animal) 8. slattern,
   strumpet 9. complaint
bite . . . 3. cut, eat, nip, zip 4. food, gnaw,
   grip, hold, knap, pang, tang, zest
   5. champ, smart, snack, sting, taste
   6. morsel, nibble, pierce 8. pungency
biting . . . 4. acid, tart 5. acerb, acrid, sharp
   6. bitter, rodent 7. caustic, cutting,
   mordant, nipping, painful, piquant,
   pungent 8. piercing, poignant, scathing,
   stinging 9. sarcastic, trenchant, vitriolic,
   withering 10. astringent, irritating
   11. acrimonious, penetrating
biting nails . . . 12. phaneromania
bito (pert to) . . .
   bark . . 10. fish poison
   seeds . . 6. zachun (oil)
   tree . . 7. hajilij
bitter . . . 4. acid, cold, keen, sore, sour
   5. acerb, acrid, irate, sharp 6. severe
   7. cutting, hostile, pungent 8. grievous,
   stinging, virulent 9. rancorous, resentful
   10. embittered, unpleasant
   11. acrimonious, distressful, reproachful
bitter (pert to) . . .

apple (herb) . . 9. colocynth
chemical . . 4. alum
earth . . 8. magnesia
gentian . . 9. baldmoney
grass . . 9. colicroot
herb . . 3. rue 4. aloe 5. aloin 8. centaury
plant . . 10. bitterroot 11. bittersweet
   (poisonous)
prefix . . 5. picro
salts . . 5. Epsom
suffix . . 6. picrin
vetch . . 3. ers
waters (Bib) . . 5. Marah
wintergreen . . 10. pipsissewa
wormwood . . 8. de Gaulle (said of)
bitterness . . . 3. rue 5. venom 6. rancor
   7. remorse 8. acerbity, acrimony,
   tartness, wormwood 9. animosity,
   poignancy, virulence 10. causticity,
   resentment
bivalve . . . 4. clam, spat, Unio 5. pinna
   6. Anomia, mussel, oyster, Teredo
   7. mollusk, pandora, scallop
   10. brachiopod (fossil form)
bivocal . . . 9. diphthong (dipthong)
bivouac . . . 4. camp 6. encamp, laager
   7. camping, leaguer (Hist)
   10. encampment
biwa . . . 6. loquat
bizarre . . . 3. odd 5. dedal, outré, queer
   6. absurd, exotic, quaint, rococo
   7. baroque 8. fanciful 9. eccentric,
   fantastic, grotesque, highflown
   11. extravagant, sensational
Bizen . . . 7. pottery (unglazed)
Bizet opera . . . 6. Carmen
bizzarro (Mus) . . . 7. bizarre 9. whimsical
blab . . . 6. gossip, reveal, snitch, tattle,
   tell on 7. blabber, chatter 8. informer,
   squealer, telltale 10. taleteller, tattletale
   11. taletelling
blabber . . . 4. blab 6. babble, gabber,
   gossip, tattle 7. chatter, twaddle
   8. informer, nonsense
black . . . 3. ink, jet 4. ebon, evil, foul,
   inky, noir 5. color, cruel, ebony, murky,
   niger (L), raven, sable, tarry 6. dismal,
   filthy, gloomy, pitchy, somber, sullen,
   wicked 7. hateful, melanic, nigrine,
   nigrous, ominous, unclean 8. atrament,
   menacing, mournful, sinister
   9. atrocious, lightless, nigricant
   10. calamitous, disastrous, forbidding
black (pert to) . . . see also *Black*
   African . . 10. blackamoor
   alloy . . 6. niello
   and blue . . 5. livid 7. bruised
      10. discolored, ecchymosed,
      ecchymosis 11. bluish-black, lead-
      colored
   art . . 5. magic 7. alchemy 8. wizardry
      10. black magic
   ball . . 7. exclude 9. ostracize
   bird . . 2. Zu (Myth) 3. ani, daw, pie
      4. crow, merl, rook 5. amsel, ouzel,
      raven 6. thrush 7. grackle, jackdaw
      10. Melanesian, Polynesian
   bottom . . 9. clog dance
   coffee . . 8. café noir
   diamond . . 4. coal
   duck . . 6. Cayuga

earth .. **4.** mold **9.** chernozem (Russ)
face .. **4.** type **5.** sheep **8.** minstrel
fish .. **6.** tautog
garnet .. **8.** melanite
gibbon .. **7.** siamang
guard .. **5.** drole, gamin, knave, rogue, scamp **6.** rascal **7.** vagrant, villain **8.** criminal, scalawag, scullion, vagabond **9.** scoundrel **11.** rapscallion
Harry .. **7.** sea bass
jack .. **4.** flag (pirate) **6.** coerce, cudgel, hijack **9.** strong-arm **10.** Jolly Roger
partridge .. **9.** francolin
rhinoceros .. **7.** borelle
sheep .. **10.** scapegrace
smith .. **5.** smith **6.** forger, smithy **7.** farrier
spruce .. **7.** yewpine
strap .. **8.** molasses
widow spider .. **6.** pokomo
Black (pert to) ...
Bess .. **4.** mare (Dick Turpin's)
Current .. **5.** Japan
Death .. **6.** Plague (bubonic)
Foot .. **6.** Indian (Siksika) **10.** Algonquian
Friar .. **4.** monk **9.** Dominican (mendicant Order)
Friday .. **4.** Fisk **5.** Gould, panic **10.** Good Friday
Hand .. **7.** anarchy, Camorra, Society (secret) **9.** blackmail
Hawk .. **3.** War (1831) **11.** Indian Chief
Hole .. **8.** Calcutta
Jack (General) .. **5.** Logan (Civil War) **8.** Pershing (WWI)
Maria .. **7.** vehicle (prisoner's) **14.** explosive shell
Monday .. **12.** Easter Monday (1630)
Monk .. **11.** Benedictine
Plague .. **7.** bubonic
Prince .. **6.** Edward
Republic .. **5.** Haiti
Rood .. **8.** crucifix, Holy Rood (anc)
Sea .. **6.** Euxine (anc), Odessa (port) **8.** Bosporus (Bosphorus) (strait)
Shirt .. **7.** Fascist **9.** Mussolini
Watch .. **16.** Royal Highlanders
Water State (nickname) .. **8.** Nebraska
blacken ... **5.** sully **6.** defame **9.** denigrate
bladder ... **3.** bag, sac **4.** sack **5.** pouch **6.** bubble, pocket **7.** blister, globule
blade ... **3.** arm, bit, fop **4.** beau, dude, edge, epee, foil, leaf, vane **5.** blood, dandy, frond, knife, spark, spear, spire, sport, sword **6.** cutter, rafter (roof), runner, Toledo (sword) **7.** gallant, sabreur, scapula, traneen **9.** swordsman
blague ... **6.** humbug **8.** claptrap
blah ... **4.** bunk **8.** contempt, nonsense
blain ... **4.** bleb, sore **6.** bulla **7.** blister, inflame, pustule **8.** swelling **9.** chilblain
blame ... **5.** chide, curse, shend **6.** accuse, charge, revile **7.** accusal, censure, obloquy, reproof, reprove **8.** denounce, reproach **9.** criticism, damnation, reprehend **10.** accusation, imputation **11.** attribution, reprobation **12.** condemnation, denunciation, reprehension **14.** responsibility
blameless ... **7.** sinless **8.** innocent **9.** faultless, guiltless **12.** sans reproche

blame taker ... **4.** goat **9.** scapegoat
blameworthy ... **8.** culpable **10.** censurable, reprovable **11.** impeachable **13.** reprehensible
blanch ... **4.** fade, pale **5.** gloss, scald **6.** whiten **8.** etiolate **9.** whitewash
blanc mange ... **7.** dessert, pudding
bland ... **4.** glib, mild, oily, smug, soft, tame **5.** suave **6.** gentle, smooth **7.** affable **8.** soothing (manner), unctuous **9.** temperate **10.** flattering **12.** hypocritical, ingratiating, mealy-mouthed, smooth-spoken
blandishment ... **7.** amenity, coaxing, palaver **8.** cajolery, flattery **9.** wheedling **10.** allurement, inducement
blank ... **4.** arid, bare, dash, dull, form, nude, null, void **5.** empty, naked, verse **6.** closed, hollow, jejune, poetry, stupid, vacant, vacuum **8.** bull's-eye, document, spotless (domino) **9.** fruitless, unadorned, untrimmed **10.** instrument (law), tabula rasa **11.** empty-headed, thoughtless **13.** unembellished, unintelligent **14.** expressionless
blank book ... **5.** album **6.** tablet **8.** memo book, notebook **10.** memorandum, pocketbook
blanket ... **3.** rug **4.** robe **5.** bluey, cloak, cotta, cover, manta, quilt, throw **6.** afghan, shroud, spread **7.** lap robe **8.** covering, coverlet **10.** barraclade (homespun)
blankness ... **7.** vacancy, vacuity **8.** negation **9.** emptiness
blare ... **4.** bawl, blow, bray, honk, peal, toot **5.** blast, blaze, glare **6.** bellow **7.** fanfare, tantara **9.** tantarara
blarney ... **6.** bunkum **7.** wheedle **8.** buncombe, cajolery, flattery, soft-soap **9.** adulation
Blarney Stone site ... **13.** Blarney Castle (Cork, Ir)
blart ... **4.** blab, roar **5.** bleat **6.** bellow
blasé ... **5.** bored, sated **6.** casual **9.** easygoing, sans souci, surfeited **10.** hard-boiled, nonchalant **11.** indifferent, self-assured, unconcerned, worldly-wise **12.** disenchanted **13.** disillusioned, disinterested, lackadaisical
blaspheme ... **4.** damn **5.** abuse, curse, swear **6.** revile, vilify **10.** calumniate
blasphemy ... **7.** cursing, impiety **8.** anathema, swearing **9.** profanity, sacrilege **10.** execration **11.** desecration, imprecation, irreverence, malediction
blast ... **3.** jet, pop **4.** bang, blow, gust, ruin, shot, toot **5.** curse, stunt **6.** blight, flurry, onrush, wither **7.** blowout, explode **9.** discharge, explosion, explosive, frustrate **10.** detonation, propulsion **11.** fulmination
blasted ... **5.** blown **6.** blamed, cursed, danged (sl), darned, ruined **7.** wrecked **8.** blighted **10.** confounded
blatant ... **5.** crude, noisy **6.** garish, puling, vulgar **7.** flaring, glaring, howling, ululant, wailing **8.** brawling **9.** clamorous, turbulent **10.** blustering,

uproarious, vociferous 12. obstreperous

blate ... 4. blab, dull, slow 5. bleat, blunt, prate, timid 7. bashful 8. sheepish 9. diffident 10. spiritless

blaw ... 4. blow, brag 5. boast

blaze ... 4. fire, gash, mark (trail), sign 5. flame, flare 6. luster 7. bonfire, flare-up 8. eruption, outburst, radiance, splendor 9. explosion, firebrand 10. effulgence 11. resplendent

blazer ... 6. jacket

blazon ... 4. deck, show 5. adorn, blaze, grace, paint 6. enrich, shield 7. display, étalage, exhibit, furbish 8. proclaim 9. embellish 10. coat of arms, exhibition 11. publication

blazoning arms ... 8. bearings, heraldry

bleach ... 3. lye, sun 4. lime 6. blanch, purify, whiten 7. decolor, lighten 8. chemical, chlorine, etiolate, peroxide 9. whiteness 10. dealbation, decolorant 11. decolorizer

bleaching vat ... 4. kier 5. kieve

bleak ... 3. dry, raw 4. arid, bare, cold, pale 5. gaunt, sharp 6. bitter, desert, dismal, dreary, frigid, pallid, severe 7. cutting, exposed 8. desolate, rigorous 9. cheerless, wind-blown, wind-swept 10. depressing

blear ... 3. dim, fog 4. blur, dull, film 6. bleary 7. blurred 10. indistinct

bleat ... 3. baa 4. blat 5. blate, whine 7. blather

bleb ... 5. bulge, bulla 6. bubble 7. bladder, blister, globule, pustule, vesicle

bleed ... 3. cup, tap 4. milk, soak 5. drain 6. fleece, grieve, let out, suffer 7. agonize, despoil, exploit, overtax 8. let blood, transude 9. surcharge 10. hemorrhage, overcharge

bleeding ... 7. cupping 9. hemorrhea 10. hemorrhage, phlebotomy 11. venesection 12. bloodletting

blemish ... 3. mar 4. blot, blue, dent, flaw, mole, mote, pock, rift, scar, spot, wart 5. crack, fault, nevus, sully, taint 6. breach, macula, macule, stigma 7. failing, fissure, freckle, lentigo 8. cicatrice, pockmark 9. birthmark, cicatrix, deformity, disfigure 10. defacement, deficiency 12. imperfection 13. disfigurement

blench ... 4. duck, pale, wile 5. blink, dodge, quail, trick, wince 6. bleach, cringe, flinch, recoil, shrink, whiten 9. stratagem 10. disconcert

blend ... 3. mix 4. fuse, melt 5. merge, shift, unite 6. fusion, mingle 7. combine, mixture, scumble 8. coalesce, compound, tincture 9. commingle, composite, harmonize 10. amalgamate 11. combination, incorporate

blended ... 5. fondu, mixed 6. merged 7. mingled 9. confluent

blending ... 6. crasis 11. inheritance

blessing ... 4. boon, gift, good, luck, rite 5. favor, grace 7. benefit, benison, fortune, godsend, service, welfare 8. good turn, kindness 9. advantage 10. benedicite, good

wishes 11. benediction, benevolence 12. felicitation 13. beatification

Bligh's ship ... 6. Bounty

blight ... 3. mar, nip 4. dash (hope), ruin, rust, seer, smut 5. blast, crush, spoil 6. freeze, mildew, wither 7. destroy, shatter 9. frustrate 10. disappoint

blighter ... 4. chap 6. beggar (anc), fellow

blimp ... 6. ballon 7. airship, balloon 8. potbelly, zeppelin 9. dirigible 10. bureaucrat 12. Graf Zeppelin, stuffed shirt

blind ... 3. dim 4. ante (poker), mask, peed, ruse, seel, slat, veil, wile 5. ciego, guise, trick 6. ambush, scheme, screen 7. benight, conceal, dim-eyed, eyeless, gimmick, obscure, pretext, shutter 8. artifice, hoodwink, jalousie, purblind, unseeing 9. dead-drunk, senseless, sightless 10. ableptical, dim-sighted, subterfuge 11. inattentive 12. undiscerning 13. stalking-horse

blind (pert to) ...
alley .. 7. impasse 8. cul-de-sac
fear .. 5. panic
girl (of Pompeii) .. 5. Nydia
gut .. 6. caecum, window 10. persiennes
one eye .. 4. peed
printing for .. 7. braille

blindness ... 7. anopsia, meropia (part) 8. ablepsia 9. achropsia, amaurosis 10. bleariness, nyctalopia 11. gutta serena, hemeralopia 13. achromatopsia

blink ... 4. wink 5. light, quail, wince 6. cringe, flinch 7. flicker, glimmer, glimpse, glitter, nictate, shimmer, twinkle 9. nictitate 10. bat the eyes

blink at ... 6. accept, ignore 7. condone 8. overlook, tolerate 9. be blind to, disregard

bliss ... 3. joy 4. Eden 6. heaven 7. delight, harmony, rapture 8. felicity, gladness 9. beatitude, happiness 11. blessedness 12. spirituality 14. blithesomeness

blissful ... 4. holy 5. seely 6. Edenic 7. blessed, Elysian, Utopian 8. ecstatic 9. beatified, glorified

blister ... 4. bleb, blob, burn, flay 5. blain, bulge, bulla, roast 6. beat up, bubble, oyster, scorch (with words), thrash 7. bladder, blemish, pustule, trounce, vesicle 9. criticize 10. vesicatory

blistered ... 6. seared, singed 7. parched 8. scorched 9. vesicated

blithe ... 4. airy, glad 5. merry 6. cheery, joyous 7. jocular 8. cheerful 10. blithesome

blitz ... 5. shell 6. strafe 7. bombard 10. blitzkrieg

blizzard ... 4. blow, wind 5. purga 7. tornado 9. snowstorm 10. snow squall 11. white squall

Blizzard State ... 11. South Dakota

bloated ... 5. cured (herring), proud, tumid 6. sodden, turgid 7. dilated, pompous, swollen 8. inflated, puffed up, tumefied 9. distended, flatulent, plethoric 10. incrassate 13. emphysematous

bloated plutocrat ... 9. bourgeois

10. capitalist
blob . . . **3.** wen **4.** bleb, blot, daub, drop, lump, mark **5.** bulge **6.** bubble, pimple **7.** blister, globule, pustule, splotch
bloc (political) . . . **4.** axis **5.** cabal, union **6.** league **7.** faction **8.** alliance **9.** coalition **11.** combination
block . . . **3.** bar, dam, set **4.** cake, clog, cube, mass, peck, plot, stop **5.** check, parry, shape, solid **6.** hamper, hinder, impede, oppose, shares, stymie **7.** auction, barrier, outline **8.** blockage, obstacle, obstruct **9.** barricade **10.** impediment **11.** obstruction
block (pert to) . . .
architecture . . **5.** socle **6.** dentil, mutule, plinth **7.** tessera
blacksmith's . . **5.** anvil
coal (Eng) . . **3.** jud
executioner's . . **10.** guillotine
falconry . . **5.** perch
finance . . **6.** shares
football . . **4.** clip
glacier . . **5.** serac
insulating . . **6.** taplet
land . . **4.** city **5.** tract **7.** section
medicine . . **10.** anesthesia
railroad . . **6.** signal
sandstone (Eng) . . **6.** sarsen
blockade . . . **3.** bar, dam **5.** hem in, siege **6.** shut in **7.** closure, exclude, fortify **8.** obstacle, obstruct **9.** exclusion **11.** obstruction
blockhead . . . **3.** oaf **4.** dolt, fool, mome (anc) **5.** dunce, idiot **7.** half-wit, tomfool **8.** bonehead, lunkhead **11.** knucklehead
blockhouse . . . **4.** fort **7.** shelter **8.** log cabin **10.** stronghold
bloke . . . **3.** man **4.** bird, chap, tuff **6.** fellow **9.** personage
blond, blonde . . . **4.** fair **5.** color, light **6.** flaxen **10.** goldilocks
blood . . . **4.** cell, clot, type, vein **5.** aorta, fluid, group, grume, hemad (haemad), hemal, hemic, ichor (gods'), lymph, serum **6.** artery, factor, fibrin, haemal, plasma, Rhesus (type) **7.** blister, carotid **8.** platelet **9.** corpuscle, hemamoeba, leucocyte **10.** hemachrome, hemoglobin, hemorrhage, phlebotomy **11.** erythrocyte, transfusion **12.** bloodletting
blood (pert to) . . .
classification . . **3.** ABO
clotted . . **4.** gore **5.** cruor **8.** thrombus
color . . **7.** crimson, para red **8.** blood red, sanguine **11.** sanguineous **13.** sanguinaceous
disease . . **6.** anemia **8.** leukemia (leukaemia, leucemia)
feud . . **8.** vendetta
flower . . **5.** hippo **9.** blood lily
horse . . **7.** blooded **12.** thoroughbred
hound . . **4.** lyam (lyme)
money (anc) . . **3.** cro **4.** eric **7.** galanas, wergild **9.** bloodwite
particle (foreign) . . **7.** embolus
poisoning 6. pyemia (pyaemia)
pressure . . **12.** hypertension
pudding . . **7.** sausage
relationship . . **3.** sib **6.** agnate **7.** cognate,

kinship, kinsman, progeny, sibship
shed . . **6.** murder **7.** killing, slaying **9.** slaughter
stone . . **10.** chalcedony
sucker . . **5.** leech **8.** parasite **10.** sanguisuge
thirsty . . **5.** cruel **8.** sanguine **9.** ferocious, murderous **10.** sanguinary **11.** ensanguined
vessel . . **3.** vas **4.** vein **6.** artery **9.** capillary
blood, kinship . . . **4.** race, ties **5.** birth, breed, stock **6.** strain **7.** descent, kinsman, lineage, royalty, sibship **8.** heredity, nobility, relation **9.** blue blood, lifeblood, life force **10.** extraction **13.** consanguinity
bloodless . . . **4.** pale **5.** ashen, faint **6.** anemic (aenemic) **7.** ghastly, inhuman **8.** lifeless, peaceful **9.** unfeeling **11.** cold of heart
bloody . . . **4.** gory **5.** cruel, wound **6.** cruent (obs), cursed **7.** smeared **8.** infamous **9.** murderous **10.** sanguinary **11.** ensanguined **12.** bloodstained, bloodthirsty
Bloody (pert to) . . .
Angle . . **11.** battlefield (Spotsylvania, 1860)
Mary . . **5.** Queen (Eng) **8.** cocktail
bloom . . . **3.** dew **4.** glow, posy **5.** blush, flush, youth **6.** beauty, flower, health, heyday, thrive **7.** blossom **11.** healthiness
bloomer . . . **5.** boner, error **6.** bobble, boo-boo **7.** blooper, blunder, failure, faux pas, mistake, trouser
blossom . . . **4.** bell, blow, grow, posy **5.** bloom, ripen **6.** floret, flower, mature, thrive **7.** develop, prosper **8.** flourish, floweret, progress **10.** effloresce **13.** efflorescence
blossoming . . . **4.** rise **6.** growth **8.** anthesis, blooming **9.** flowerage, flowering **10.** florescent, unfoldment **11.** development, florescence, flourishing, progressing **13.** efflorescence, inflorescence
blot . . . **3.** dry, mar **4.** blur, soil, spot **5.** erase, error, fleck, smear, speck, stain, sully **6.** absorb, blotch, damage, impair, smutch, soak up, sponge, stigma **7.** blacken, blemish, erasure, expunge **9.** bespatter **10.** obliterate, stigmatize **12.** obliteration
blot out . . . **3.** fix **4.** dele, kill **5.** purge **6.** absorb, cancel, delete, efface, excise, rub out **7.** bump off, destroy, expunge, obscure, wipe out **8.** black out **10.** obliterate
blotch . . . **4.** bleb, mark, soil, spot **5.** patch, stain **6.** macula, mottle, stigma **7.** blemish
blotched . . . **4.** pied **5.** pinto **6.** spotty **7.** mottled **8.** speckled
blouse . . . **4.** blou, sark **5.** bluey, middy, shift, shirt, smock, tunic, waist **6.** basque **7.** casaque **10.** shirtwaist
blow . . . **3.** dab, hit, rap, tap **4.** brag, bump, coup, gust, pant, puff, slap, toot, waft, wind **5.** bloom, devel,

feint, impel, knock, shock, sound, utter
6. expand, puff up **7.** beating, bluster,
whiffle **8.** calamity, disaster, disclose,
lambskin (obs) **14.** disappointment
blow . . . **4.** flee, over, rant, slog **5.** boast,
clout, scram **6.** beat it, betray, buffet,
depart, wallop **8.** squander **10.** blow
me down
blow (pert to) . . .
hard . . **6.** blower **7.** windbag **8.** braggart
11. braggadocio
hot and cold . . **4.** vary **5.** shift, waver
6. seesaw **7.** quibble **9.** fluctuate,
vacillate **12.** shilly-shally
out . . **5.** douse, snuff **10.** extinguish
blower . . . **4.** blow, gale, wind **5.** whale
6. puffer (fish), squall **7.** bellows,
bloomer, blowgun, boaster, monsoon,
tornado **8.** braggart **9.** hurricane,
whirlwind, windstorm **11.** braggadocio
blow up . . . **4.** fail, rage **5.** blast, bloat,
burst, fluff **6.** berate, dilate, excite,
expand, forget, praise **7.** blow out,
enlarge, explode, inflate **8.** demolish,
detonate, disprove **9.** fulminate
10. exaggerate
blowzy . . . **5.** dowdy, ruddy, tacky
6. coarse, frowzy, sloppy, untidy
7. unkempt **8.** careless, frumpish,
slovenly **10.** disheveled, slatternly
blubber . . . **3.** fat **4.** weep **6.** bubble
7. whimper **8.** whale fat
blubbery . . . **3.** fat **7.** swollen **9.** quivering
10. gelatinous
bludgeon . . . **3.** bat, hit **4.** beat, club,
mace **5.** billy, bully, stick **6.** coerce,
cudgel, menace **8.** browbeat, bulldoze,
threaten **9.** truncheon **10.** intimidate,
shillelagh (shillalah)
blue . . . **4.** anil, baby, bice, bleu,
navy **5.** azure, beryl, Ching, email,
king's, merle, perse, royal, smalt
6. cobalt, cyanic, French, indigo, powder
7. aniline, azarite, cesious, Dresden,
Dumont's, gobelin, lobelia, mesange,
peacock, Persian **8.** caesious, calamine,
cerulean, Coventry, electric, lavender,
midnight, pavonine, sapphire, wisteria
9. turquoise **10.** aquamarine, cornflower
blue (pert to) . . . see also *Blue*
baby . . **8.** cyanotic
bonnet . . **3.** cap **4.** Scot **6.** flower (Texas
State) **8.** Scotsman, titmouse
china . . **7.** Nanking
circle (archery) . . **6.** target
day . . **6.** Monday
emblem of . . **6.** Oxford **9.** Cambridge
grass . . **3.** poa
ground . . **10.** kimberlite
hero . . **9.** Bluebeard
melancholy . . **3.** sad **6.** gloomy
7. pensive, wistful **8.** tristful
9. cheerless, depressed, penseroso
10. atrabiliar **11.** atrabilious,
melancholic **13.** hypochondriac
nose . . **4.** snob **5.** prude **7.** Puritan
10. goody-goody **11.** Nova Scotian
pencil . . **4.** dele, edit **6.** delete, excise,
revise
print . . **4.** plan, plot **5.** graph **6.** layout
7. diagram, program **8.** schedule

9. cyanotype **10.** master plan,
photograph, photoprint
ribbon . . **5.** award, badge **10.** cordon
bleu, decoration
skin . . **5.** livid
sky . . **5.** ether, vault **6.** caelum, heaven,
welkin **7.** the blue **8.** empyrean
9. firmament **10.** blue yonder, the
heavens
stocking . . **4.** blue **6.** pedant **7.** bas
bleu **8.** Gamaliel (Bib) **9.** formalist,
pedagogue **10.** Parliament
Blue (pert to) . . .
Boy . . **8.** painting (Gainsborough)
Grass State . . **8.** Kentucky
Grotto site . . **5.** Capri
Law State . . **11.** Connecticut
Bluebeard's wife . . . **6.** Fatima
blue-gray . . . **7.** cesious (caesious)
blue-green . . . **8.** calamine
bluff . . . **4.** bank (steep), crag, curt,
dupe, fool, rude, wall **5.** brash,
cliff, frank, gruff, krans, sheer, short
6. abrupt, crusty **7.** beguile, blinder,
blinker, bluffer, bluster, brusque,
deceive, pretend, uncivil **8.** impolite
9. bamboozle, blusterer, charlatan,
falseness, four-flush, precipice **11.** four-
flusher **13.** unceremonious
bluffer . . . **5.** quack **9.** blusterer, charlatan
10. mountebank **11.** four-flusher
bluffness . . . **6.** candor **9.** bluntness
10. abruptness **11.** brusqueness
blunder . . . **3.** err, mix **4.** bull, goof, slip
5. boner, botch, error, misdo **6.** boo-
boo, bungle, fumble **7.** faux pas,
mistake, stumble **8.** flounder, solecism
(speech) **9.** mismanage
blunt . . . **4.** curt, dull, open **5.** bluff, frank,
gruff, plain **6.** benumb, candid, deaden,
obtund, obtuse, snippy, stupid, weaken
7. artless, brusque, sincere **8.** hebetate
9. ingenuous **13.** unceremonious
blur . . . **3.** bog, dim, hum **4.** blob, blot,
film, mist, soil, spot **5.** blear, cloud,
smear, stain **6.** blotch, darken, mackle
7. blemish, dimness, obscure, splotch
9. disfigure
blurb . . . **2.** ad **4.** plug **5.** boost, brief
6. notice **7.** write-up **8.** ballyhoo
9. publicity **12.** announcement,
commendation **13.** advertisement
blurt out . . . **4.** blab, bolt **7.** blunder
9. ejaculate
blush . . . **4.** glow, look **5.** bloom,
color, flush **6.** glance, mantle, redden
7. modesty, redness **9.** suffusion
blushing . . . **4.** meek **5.** ruddy **6.** modest
7. roseate **8.** flushing, sheepish
9. reddening, rubescent **10.** erubescent
bluster . . . **4.** blow, bray, fume, rage,
rant, roar **5.** broil, bully, furor,
noise **6.** flurry, hoopla, hubbub,
squall, tumult **7.** roister, swagger,
turmoil **8.** boasting, bullying, threaten
9. agitation, confusion **10.** swaggering,
turbulence **11.** rodomontade
blusterer . . . **5.** bully **7.** boaster
8. blowhard, braggart **9.** roisterer,
swaggerer **11.** braggadocio
12. swashbuckler

bo . . . **4.** hobo **5.** buddy, tramp
9. sundowner **10.** landlouper **11.** bindle
stiff
bo, boh (Burma) . . . **5.** chief **6.** leader
7. captain
boa . . . **5.** aboma, scarf (feather), snake
8. anaconda
boar . . . **3.** hog, sus **4.** apex, hure (head)
5. swine **6.** barrow, hogget (2-year)
9. hoggaster (3-year)
board . . . **4.** deal, doll, feed, lath,
side, slat, wood **5.** curia (anc),
enter, forum, meals, plank, table
6. border, lumber, timber **7.** binding
(book), council, lodging **8.** approach,
exchange (Finan), tribunal **9.** committee,
provision **11.** accommodate, bed
and board, directorate, refreshment
14. accommodations
boast . . . **4.** brag, crow **5.** extol, exult,
glory, pride, vapor, vaunt **6.** menace
7. bluster, swagger **8.** braggart, flourish
9. gasconade
boastful . . . **4.** vain **8.** bragging
9. conceited, overproud, presuming
11. thrasonical **12.** vainglorious **13.** self-
important
boat . . . **3.** ark, bac, gig, tub, tug **4.** brig,
dhow, dory, junk, punt, saic, scow, ship,
trow, yawl **5.** aviso, balsa, barge, canoe,
craft, dandy, dhoni, dingy, ferry, kayak,
ketch, liner, oolak, praam, scull, skiff,
U-boat, umiak, xebec, yacht **6.** argosy,
baidak, bateau, convoy, cutter, dinghy,
dogger, launch, mistic, oomiac, packet,
randan, sampan, settee, tanker, vessel,
· whaler **7.** bidarka, caravel, coracle
(anc), cruiser, gondola, masoola,
piragua, pirogue, rowboat, scooter,
shallop, trawler, tugboat, warship
8. dahabeah, man-of-war, palander,
sailboat, seaplane **9.** catamaran,
destroyer, steamship, submarine
10. brigantine, windjammer **11.** side-
wheeler, treckschuyt
boat (pert to) . . .
boatswain . . **5.** bosun **6.** serang
captain . . **4.** rais (reis) **6.** master
7. skipper
deck . . **4.** poop **6.** flight **9.** promenade
man . . **5.** rower **6.** bargee **7.** ferrier,
oarsman **9.** gondolier, yachtsman
sail . . **3.** jib **4.** main, reef **6.** lateen,
mizzen
shaped . . **9.** navicella, navicular
side . . **7.** gunwale
song . . **7.** chantey **9.** barcarole
bob . . . **3.** bow, cut, nod, rap, tap **4.** bend,
jeer, jerk, jest **5.** cheat, filch, float, flout,
plumb, shake, taunt, trick **6.** bobble,
curtsy, delude, hairdo, kowtow, sinker,
weight **7.** haircut **8.** coiffure, greeting,
shilling **9.** obeisance, oscillate
bobac . . . **5.** pahmi **6.** marmot
bobber . . . **4.** duck (ruddy) **5.** float
6. bobfly **7.** dropper **8.** deadhead
bobbin . . . **3.** pin **4.** coil, cord, pirn, reel
5. braid, spool **7.** spindle
bobble . . . **3.** bob, dib (angling) **4.** muff
5. shake **6.** boggle, bungle, fumble
7. blunder **9.** oscillate

bobby . . . **6.** peeler **9.** policeman
Boccaccio's tales . . . **9.** Decameron
Boche . . . **6.** German (a)
bodach . . . **5.** churl, clown **7.** bugaboo
bodacious . . . **4.** bold **8.** insolent, reckless
9. audacious, bumptious, insulting
12. contumelious
bode . . . **5.** augur **6.** divine **7.** portend,
presage **8.** forebode, foreshow, foretell
13. prognosticate
bodhisattva . . . **8.** Buddhism
13. Enlightenment
bodice . . . **4.** belt **5.** stays, waist **6.** basque,
girdle **7.** corsage, garment
bodily . . . **6.** carnal **7.** fleshly, somatic
8. corporal, material, physical
9. corporeal **10.** completely
boding . . . **7.** ominous **10.** foreboding,
portentous, prediction, prognostic
12. apprehension
bodkin . . . **3.** awl **6.** dagger, needle
7. hairpin, poniard **8.** stiletto **9.** eyeleteer
body . . . **3.** man **4.** deha (Theos), homo,
soma **5.** being, human, trunk **6.** corpse,
entity, licham, mortal, person **7.** carcass
8. creature, organism **9.** substance
10. individual **13.** corpus delicti
14. substantiality
body (pert to) . . .
armed . . **5.** corps, posse
business . . **7.** company **11.** cooperation
12. organization
celestial . . **3.** sun **4.** luna, star **5.** comet
6. meteor, planet
church . . **4.** nave
dead . . **6.** corpse **7.** cadaver
division (mollusk) . . **7.** prosoma
injury . . **6.** mayhem, trauma
petrified . . **6.** fossil
political . . **4.** weal **6.** senate **7.** cabinet
11. legislature
small . . **6.** nanoid **8.** dwarfish
body of . . .
people . . **3.** mob **4.** band, bevy, gang,
host **5.** bunch, crowd, flock, group,
horde **6.** rabble, throng **9.** multitude
singers . . **5.** choir **6.** chorus
soldiers . . **4.** file **5.** corps, squad, troop
7. brigade, company, platoon **8.** division
water . . **3.** bay, sea **4.** lake, pond, pool
5. fiord (fjord), inlet, ocean **6.** lagoon
9. reservoir
Boeotian (pert to) . . .
city . . **5.** Ionia (Dist) **6.** Thebes
figurine . . **7.** Tanagra
king (Myth) . . **6.** Ogyges
Boer (pert to) . . .
General, statesman . . **5.** Botha
language . . **4.** Taal **9.** Afrikaans
War site . . **9.** Ladysmith (So Afr)
bog . . . **3.** bug, fen **4.** blei, bold,
holm, mire, moor, moss, ooze, quag,
sink **5.** jheel, marsh, saucy, swamp
6. morass, slough **8.** quagmire
9. everglade
bogey, bogie, bogy . . . **3.** par **5.** Devil
6. goblin **7.** bugaboo, bugbear
boggle . . . **3.** shy **4.** foil, quip **5.** botch,
cavil, demur, parry, pause, start
6. bicker, bungle, falter, object, shrink
7. dispute, quibble, scruple **8.** hesitate,

sidestep **9.** dissemble, objection
10. difficulty, equivocate
bogglebo . . . **5.** bogle **7.** bugaboo, specter
9. hobgoblin, scarecrow
bogus . . . **4.** fake, mock, sham **5.** phony,
queer **8.** spurious **10.** apocryphal,
factitious, fictitious **11.** counterfeit
bohawn . . . **3.** hut **5.** cabin **7.** cottage
Bohemia . . .
capital . . **6.** Prague
city . . **5.** Praha **6.** Aussig, Pilsen
7. Budweis, Teplitz **11.** Reichenberg
dance . . **6.** redowa
measure . . **5.** stopa **6.** merice
mineral . . **6.** egeran
reformer . . **4.** Huss
river . . **4.** Elbe, Iser **6.** Moldau
vagabond . . **5.** gypsy (gipsy)
bohunk . . . **6.** Slovak **7.** laborer
8. Bohemian, Croatian (formerly)
boil . . . **3.** sty (styr) **4.** buck, cook, fume,
stew **5.** churn, steam **6.** bubble, pimple,
seethe **7.** bristle **8.** furuncle
boiling . . . **5.** angry **7.** cooking, flushed,
stewing **8.** seething, sizzling **9.** agitating,
ebullient **10.** smoldering
bois (Fr) . . . **4.** wood
boisterous . . . **4.** loud **5.** noisy, rough,
rowdy **6.** stormy **7.** blatant, excited,
furious, roaring, violent **8.** brawling
9. clamorous, turbulent **10.** blustering,
roisterous, tumultuous, unyielding
12. obstreperous
Bokhara (pert to) . . .
fur . . **9.** astrakhan, broadtail
rug . . **8.** Turkoman
sheep . . **7.** karakul (caracul)
site . . **4.** Asia (Russ)
bola . . . **4.** tree (fiber) **6.** weapon
bold . . . **4.** deep, pert, rash, rude, snug
5. steep, stout **6.** abrupt, brazen, daring,
heroic, raised **7.** dashing, defiant,
eminent, forward, salient, valiant
8. fearless, immodest, impudent, in
relief, intrepid, powerful, repoussé,
stalwart **9.** audacious, confident,
dauntless, shameless, unabashed
10. courageous **11.** lionhearted,
outstanding, precipitous, venturesome
12. presumptuous, stouthearted
boldness . . . **5.** valor **6.** defial, virtue
7. bravery, courage **8.** audacity,
defiance, salience, temerity
9. assurance, gallantry, hardihood,
immodesty, impudence **10.** brazenness,
confidence, effrontery, prominence,
resolution **11.** forwardness, intrepidity,
obviousness **12.** protuberance
13. dauntlessness **14.** courageousness
bolero . . . **5.** dance, music, waist **6.** jacket
boliche . . . **3.** inn **5.** bowls
Bolivia . . .
capital . . **5.** La Paz (Polit), Oruro (anc),
Sucre (law)
hero . . **5.** Sucre **7.** Bolivar, Pizarro
Indian . . **3.** Uro **4.** Iten, Moxo
lake . . **8.** Titicaca (world's highest)
mountain . . **5.** Andes **6.** Sorata **8.** Illimani
product . . **3.** tin **8.** tungsten
river . . **4.** Beni **6.** Blanco
bolo . . . **5.** knife **7.** machete **8.** pacifist

(Bolo Pasha, traitor) **9.** defeatist
Bolshevik, bolshevik . . . **5.** Lenin
7. Marxian, radical (Bolsheviki)
9. Communist (1918), Socialist
13. revolutionist **14.** Social Democrat
18. Third International
bolster . . . **3.** pad **4.** bear, hold **5.** boost
6. pillow **7.** cushion, support, sustain
8. maintain
bolt . . . **3.** bar **4.** dart, flee, lock, roll,
sift **5.** arrow, rivet, scram, screw,
shaft, speed **6.** decamp, devour,
faster, flight, pintle, secede, staple,
toggle **7.** missile, padlock **8.** firebolt,
separate **10.** projectile **11.** eat greedily,
fulguration, thunderbolt
bolus . . . **4.** bite, clay, clod, food (chewed),
mass, pill **6.** tablet, troche **8.** mouthful
bomb . . . **3.** dud, egg **5.** shell **6.** petard
7. grenade, missile **8.** divebomb,
fireball, surprise **9.** bombshell,
pineapple **10.** projectile
bomb (type of) . . . **4.** time **5.** stink **6.** aerial,
atomic, rocket **7.** nuclear, tear gas
8. hydrogen **10.** demolition
bombard . . . **3.** zap **5.** blitz, shell **6.** assail,
attack, strafe **7.** atomize, barrage
9. cannonade
bombardier . . . **5.** jager **6.** bomber,
gunner **9.** cannoneer, musketeer
12. artilleryman
bombast . . . **4.** blow, brag, rage, rant, rave
5. boast **7.** fustian **8.** boasting, inflated,
stuffing (hist) **9.** bombastic, turgidity
11. rodomontade **12.** magniloquent
13. grandiloquent
bombastic . . . **5.** tumid **7.** orotund,
pompous, stilted **8.** boastful, inflated
12. high-sounding **13.** grandiloquent
Bombay . . .
capital of . . **11.** Maharashtra (state)
college . . **11.** Elphinstone
duck . . **10.** lizard fish
hemp . . **4.** sunn **6.** ambary
merchant . . **4.** Arab
seaport of . . **5.** India
bombed . . . **5.** drunk
bomber . . . **5.** stuka **10.** bombardier
Bombyx . . . **4.** eria, moth **8.** silkworm
bona fide . . . **4.** real **7.** genuine
9. authentic **10.** constantly, faithfully,
legitimate
bona mano . . . **3.** tip **8.** gratuity
bon ami . . . **5.** lover **6.** friend **10.** good
friend, sweetheart
bonanza . . . **6.** riches **8.** El Dorado (Myth),
gold mine (US)
Bonanza State . . . **7.** Montana
Bonaparte . . . see *Napoleon I*
bond . . . **3.** tie, vow **4.** duty, gyve, link,
mise, pact, yoke **5.** chain, nexus,
rente **6.** fetter, league **7.** entente,
manacle, shackle **8.** contract, covenant,
relation, security (Finan) **9.** agreement,
captivity **10.** allegiance, connection
11. association, certificate
bondage . . . **4.** yoke **6.** chains **7.** serfdom,
slavery **9.** captivity, restraint, servitude,
thralldom **11.** enslavement, subjugation
bondman, bondsman . . . **4.** esne, serf
5. churl, helot, slave **6.** thrall, vassal

7. servant 8. bailsman 9. guarantor
bone . . . 2. os 4. chip 5. boner 6. dollar, osteon 7. blunder, counter (game), ossicle 8. skeleton, wishbone 9. funny bone (humerus), pygostyle (bird's), whalebone
bone (Anat) . . . 3. rib 4. ulna 5. femur, ilium, incus (ear), malar, skull, spine, talus, tibia 6. carpus, coccyx, fibula, tarsus 7. humerus, maxilla, patella, scapula, sternum 8. astragal, clavicle, mandible, phalange, vertebra 9. calcaneus, occipital 10. metacarpus, metatarsus
bone (pert to) . . .
bonelike . . 6. osteal 7. osteoid
cell . . 10. osteoblast
china . . 7. English
curvature . . 8. lordosis
divination . . 10. osteomancy
fish . . 9. operculum
marrow . . 7. medulla
process . . 7. mastoid 8. alveolar 9. apophysis
science . . 9. osteology
surgery . . 9. osteotomy 11. osteoclasis 12. osteoplastic
tissue . . 6. ossein
tumor . . 7. osteoma
bones . . . 4. body, dice, form, ossa 5. cubes, frame, money, torso, trunk 6. end man, refuse 7. carcass, ivories 8. skeleton 11. rattlebones
boneyard . . . 4. bank (game) 8. golgotha 9. graveyard 10. necropolis 11. polyandrium
Bonheur subject . . . 6. animal
bonhomie . . . 8. pleasant 9. good humor 10. affability, amiability
Bonhomme Richard . . . 4. ship 8. man-of-war (1779) (opponent of Serapis)
bonito, bonita . . . 4. nice 6. pretty 8. mackerel, skipjack
bon mot . . . 9. witticism 10. jeu d'esprit 11. smart saying
bonne . . . 5. mammy 9. nursemaid 10. baby sitter 11. maidservant
bonnet . . . 3. cap, hat 4. coif, hood, poke 5. toque 7. chapeau 9. headdress
bonnetman . . . 10. Highlander
bonny, bonnie . . . 3. bon 4. good 5. plump 6. comely, lively, pretty 7. healthy, très bon 8. handsome 9. beautiful
Bontok . . . 7. Malayan (Luzon) 10. Indonesian
bonus . . . 3. tip 4. cash, gift 5. batta, bribe, extra, share, stock (Finan) 7. cumshaw, douceur, premium, rake-off, subsidy 8. dividend, gratuity 9. Trinkgeld 10. honorarium
bon vivant . . . 7. epicure, gourmet 8. gourmand, hedonist, sybarite 10. boonfellow, good fellow, voluptuary 12. Heliogabalus (anc)
bony . . . 4. hard, thin 6. osteal, skinny 7. osseous 8. rawboned, skeletal
bonze (Far East) . . . 2. bo 4. monk
boo . . . 4. hoot, jeer, razz 7. catcall, feather (ostrich) 9. raspberry 10. Bronx cheer
boob . . . 4. dupe, fool, goon, jerk

5. chump, dunce 6. nitwit 7. fathead 9. schlemiel, simpleton
boobook . . . 3. owl 8. morepork
booby hatch . . . 3. can, jug 4. jail 6. asylum, cooler, prison 8. hoosegow, madhouse 11. institution (mental)
boodle . . . 3. sop 4. loot, swag 5. booty, bribe, bunch, crowd, graft, money (hush) 6. spoils 8. caboodle 10. pork barrel 11. counterfeit
boohoo . . . 3. rob 4. bawl, hoot, weep 5. shout 8. sailfish
book . . . 2. mo (abbr) 3. day 4. hire, opus, tome 5. album, atlas, Bible, canto, diary, folio, liber, novel 6. agenda, engage, ledger, manual, missal, primer, record, sign up, volume 7. diurnal, journal, mystery 8. brochure, libretto, register, schedule, songbook, whodunit 9. paperback, storybook 10. literature, memorandum 11. publication
book (pert to) . . .
announcement . . 5. blurb
back . . 5. spine
binder . . 12. bibliopegist
binding devise . . 7. trindle
collector . . 10. bibliothec 12. bibliomaniac 14. bibliothecaire
cover . . 5. recto 6. jacket
destroyer . . 11. biblioclast
division . . 7. chapter
lore . . 10. bibliology
lover . . 11. bibliophile
one versed in . . 11. bibliognost
page . . 5. folio
seller . . 10. bibliopole (rare books)
sheath . . 5. forel
size . . 6. quarto
stealer . . 11. biblioklept
style . . 6. Aldine 8. Etruscan 9. Arabesque
treatise . . 8. isagogue
worshiper . . 11. bibliolater
writer . . 13. bibliographer
book (religious) . . . 4. Ordo 5. Bible, Kells, Tobit 6. Esdras, Mormon 7. Psalter 8. Holy Writ 9. Apocrypha, Catechism, Testament 10. Pentateuch, Scriptures
Book of . . .
award (Harvard) . . 5. detur
Concord . . 8. Lutheran
Discipline . . 12. Presbyterian
Hours . . 5. Horae
Moses (Laws) . . 10. Pentateuch
Psalms . . 7. Psalter
the Dead . . 12. Pyramid Texts
boom . . . 3. hum 4. gain, peal, raft, roar, spar, zoom 5. boost, cable, speed, sprit, withe 6. thrive, upturn 7. pontoon, resound, thunder 8. bowsprit, flourish, increase 9. cannonade, Golden Age, outrigger 10. navigation, prosperity
boomerang . . . 6. resile 7. rebound 8. backfire, ricochet
Boomer State . . . 8. Oklahoma
boon . . . 3. gay 4. bene, gift, good, nice 5. favor, jolly 6. jovial, kindly 7. benefit, gleeful, godsend, present 8. blessing 9. convivial 11. benefaction
boor . . . 3. cad, oaf 4. hick, lout 5. churl, clown, yokel 6. rustic 7. bumpkin, cauboge, peasant, ruffian 9. roughneck,

vulgarian **10.** clodhopper; husbandman
boorish . . . **4.** rude **5.** gawky, surly
6. clumsy, rustic, sullen **7.** awkward,
crabbed, loutish, uncouth **8.** churlish,
inurbane, lubberly, ungainly
9. farmerish, unrefined **11.** countrified
boost . . . **4.** help, hike, lift, plug, push
5. heist, raise, shove **6.** assist,
thrust **7.** commend, hearten, inspire,
promote, upswing **8.** advocate, increase
9. promotion, publicize **10.** assistance
11. advancement **12.** commendation
boot . . . **3.** pac **4.** kick, pack, sack, shoe
5. armor, bonus, jemmy, kamik, wader
6. buskin, fumble, rookie, sheath
7. dismiss, recruit, trainee **8.** balmoral,
enlistee, inductee, napoleon
9. discharge
booth . . . **3.** hut, pew **4.** crib, loge **5.** stall,
stand, store **6.** manger **11.** compartment
booty . . . **4.** gain, loot, pelf, swag **5.** graft,
prize, spoil **6.** spoils **7.** pillage, plunder
booze . . . **4.** bout **5.** drink, spree **6.** liquor
8. potation
boozer . . . **3.** pub, sot **5.** toper **6.** barfly,
bibber, saloon **7.** guzzler, reveler, tippler
8. drunkard **9.** alcoholic, inebriate
11. dipsomaniac
borax . . . **4.** salt **5.** cheap
Bordeaux, France . . .
  capital . . **7.** Gironde
  entrance gate . . **16.** Porte de Bourgogne
  Roman name . . **9.** Burdigala
  wine . . **5.** Cotes, Medoc, Palus **6.** claret
  (best-known), Graves
border . . . **3.** hem, rim, tip **4.** abut,
brow, dado, edge, line, rand, rund
5. bound, brink, flank, limit, marge,
shore, skirt, touch, verge, wings
6. adjoin, fringe, margin, ruffle
7. bordure, confine, flounce, selvage,
valance **8.** boundary, frontier, neighbor
9. periphery **10.** borderland, sidepieces
border (pert to) . . .
  heraldry . . **4.** orle **7.** bordure
  lace . . **5.** picot **9.** hemstitch
  picture . . **3.** mat **4.** orle
  stamps (PO) . . **8.** tressure
  wall . . **4.** dado
Border Country (Russ) . . . **6.** Latvia,
Poland **7.** Estonia, Finland, Romania
9. Lithuania
bordering . . . **4.** near **6.** edging **7.** binding
8. abutting, adjacent, marginal, skirting,
trimming **9.** adjoining, immediate
10. contiguous
Border State (Civil War Era) . . .
8. Arkansas, Delaware, Kentucky,
Maryland, Missouri, Virginia
9. Tennessee **10.** North Carolina
bore . . . **3.** irk, tap **4.** drip, hole, pest,
pill, ream **5.** auger, drill, eagre (tidal
wave), weary **6.** bother, cavity, pierce
7. caliber, carried **8.** diameter, nuisance,
ordnance (anc), puncture, terebate
9. penetrate, perforate, tidal wave,
worriment **10.** capability **11.** perforation
boreal . . . **8.** northern
boredom . . . **5.** ennui **6.** tedium
Borglum work . . . **8.** Rushmore
boring . . . **3.** dry **5.** yawny **6.** tiring

7. irksome, tedious **8.** piercing,
tiresome, wearying **11.** penetrating
boring tool . . . **3.** awl, bit **4.** rime (Eng)
5. auger, drill **6.** gimlet, reamer, wimble
born . . . **3.** ean, nee **4.** bred, foal, lamb
5. calve, hatch, issue **7.** hatched,
quicken **9.** originate
born (pert to) . . .
  after father's death . . **10.** posthumous
  again (Theos) . . **7.** renewed
  high . . **8.** imperial **11.** to the purple
  14. porphyrogenite
  in the country . . **10.** rurigenous
  well . . **7.** eugenic
  yesterday . . **5.** naive **6.** simple **8.** gullible
borne . . . **4.** held **6.** eolian, upheld
7. aeolian, carried, endured **8.** produced
9. cherished, supported **10.** maintained
borné . . . **6.** narrow **7.** limited **12.** narrow-
minded
Borneo . . .
  aborigine . . **4.** Dyak (Dayak), Iban
  5. Dusun, Malay
  ape . . **9.** orangutan (orangoutang)
  island of . . **11.** Archipelago (Malay)
  mountain . . **8.** Kinibalu
  pirate people (anc) . . **5.** Bajau **9.** Samal
  Laut
  protectorate . . **6.** Brunei **7.** Sarawak
  river . . **6.** Rejang
  rubber . . **9.** gutta susu
  sea . . **4.** Java, Sulu **10.** South China
  tree (antproof) . . **7.** billian
borough . . . **4.** burg, town, ward **5.** burgh,
manor **6.** suffix **8.** precinct, township
10. municipium **11.** corporation
12. municipality
borrow . . . **4.** copy, take **5.** adopt,
steal, touch **8.** simulate **10.** plagiarize,
substitute **11.** appropriate
borscht, borsch . . . **4.** soup (beet juice)
6. ragout
borscht belt . . . **6.** resort **9.** Catskills
borzoi . . . **9.** wolfhound
Bos . . . **2.** ox **3.** cow **4.** beef, calf, neat
6. cattle **8.** ruminant **9.** quadruped
bosh . . . **4.** bull, bunk **5.** trash **6.** humbug,
piffle **7.** baloney **8.** buncombe, falderal,
nonsense **9.** poppycock **10.** balderdash
bosky . . . **5.** braky, bushy, shady, tipsy,
woody **6.** woodsy **7.** fuddled, shadowy
11. intoxicated (Eng)
Bosnia . . .
  capital . . **8.** Sarajevo
  site . . **10.** Yugoslavia (formerly)
  15. Balkan Peninsula
bosom . . . **4.** bust **5.** chest **6.** breast,
dickey, spirit **7.** cherish, embrace
8. inner man, interior **9.** enclosure
(loving), innermost **10.** affections
12. heartstrings
boss . . . **4.** dean **6.** manage, master
7. foreman **8.** director **9.** supervise
14. superintendent
boss (pert to) . . .
  architecture . . **4.** knob, stud
  12. protuberance
  politics . . **4.** whip **6.** leader **7.** cacique
  (W Indies) **8.** dictator
  sculpture . . **5.** chase, raise **6.** emboss,
  relief **7.** relievo **8.** ornament

shield . . **4**. umbo
bosthoon (Anglo-Ir) . . . **4**. boor, dolt
 5. clout
Boston . . .
 building (Hist) . . **11**. Faneuil Hall **14**. Old
  North Church
 capital of . . **13**. Massachusetts
 famed names . . **6**. Holmes, Lowell
  7. Emerson **8**. Whittier **9**. Hawthorne
  10. Longfellow
 hero . . **10**. Paul Revere
 history . . **8**. Massacre (1770), Tea Party
  (1773)
 Puritan leader . . **8**. Winthrop (Gov)
 river . . **7**. Charles
botany (pert to) . . .
 development (plant) . . **7**. peloria
  10. craticular
 research terms . . **7**. ecology **8**. cytology,
  taxonomy **9**. pathology **10**. morphology
 science . . **7**. biology **9**. plant life
Botany Bay . . .
 colony (original) . . **5**. penal
 discoverer . . **4**. Cook (1770)
 settlers . . **8**. convicts (Eng)
 site . . **9**. Australia
botch . . . **3**. fix, mar **4**. hash, mend, mess,
 mull **5**. patch, spoil **6**. boggle, bungle,
 fiasco, goof up, muddle **7**. blunder,
 failure
both . . . **3**. two **4**. duad, pair **5**. twain
 6. as well **7**. equally
bother . . . **3**. ado, ail, nag **4**. fuss,
 to-do **5**. annoy, tease **6**. badger,
 bustle, harass, molest, pester, pother
 7. concern, confuse, fluster, torment,
 trouble **8**. bewilder, distress, irritate,
 nuisance **9**. commotion
 10. discommode, excitement, perplexity
 11. botheration, disturbance
 13. inconvenience
bothersome . . . **6**. trying **7**. galling,
 irksome, onerous **8**. annoying
 9. difficult, worrisome **10**. disturbing
 11. troublesome
both sexes . . . **7**. epicene, sexless
 10. effeminate
bo tree (Buddh) . . . **5**. pipal **6**. sacred
 (at Buddh Gaya)
Botticelli masterpiece . . . **12**. Birth of
 Venus
bottle . . . **3**. pig **4**. lota, vial **5**. cruet,
 flask, gourd, phial **6**. carafe, carboy,
 flagon, lagena, matara, vacuum
 7. ampoule (ampule), ampulla (anc),
 costrel, enclose **8**. borachio, calabash,
 decanter, preserve **9**. aryballus (anc)
bottom . . . **3**. bed (water) **4**. base, glen,
 hulk, less, root, rump, vale, vlei
 5. basin, fanny, floor, marsh, nadir
 6. coulee, hopper (RR) **7**. bedrock,
 channel **9**. underside **10**. nethermost
bottomless . . . **7**. abysmal, abyssal
 8. baseless, plumbless, soundless
 10. fathomless **12**. unfathomable
boudoir . . . **7**. bedroom, cabinet, chamber
 10. bedchamber
bouffant . . . **4**. full **7**. bulging **9**. puffed
 out
bough . . . **4**. fork, limb, spur, twig **5**. shoot,
 spray, sprig **6**. branch **8**. offshoot

bought . . . **8**. boughten (dial) **9**. purchased
 (see also *buy*)
bouillabaisse . . . **7**. chowder (fish)
boulangerie (Fr) . . . **6**. bakery
boulevard . . . **4**. pike **7**. highway
 8. highroad, turnpike **12**. thoroughfare
bounce . . . **3**. hop **4**. bang, brag, bump,
 jump, kick, leap, snap **5**. bound, burst,
 carom, eject, shake, thump, verve
 6. levity, recoil, spring **7**. bluster,
 bravado, rebound **8**. buoyancy,
 outburst, ricochet **9**. discharge,
 lightness **10**. resilience **11**. fanfaronade,
 ostentation, springiness
 16. lightheartedness
bouncer . . . **4**. liar **5**. bully **6**. fibber,
 ouster **7**. boaster, chucker, whopper
 8. braggart, fanfaron **9**. falsehood
bound . . . **3**. hop, run **4**. jump, leap,
 skip, tied **5**. ambit, limit, speed,
 taped, tiled (secrecy), vault, verge
 6. border, bounce, bourne, domain,
 hurdle, spring, sprint **7**. barrier, certain,
 confine, cramped, limited, obliged,
 pledged, rebound, secured, trussed
 8. beholden, boundary, confined,
 enclosed, frontier, precinct, promised,
 resolved, surround **9**. committed,
 duty-bound, encompass (incompass)
 10. borderland, determined, restrained,
 restricted **11**. termination
 12. circumscribe
boundary . . . **3**. end, rim **4**. edge, mere
 (obs), mete, term, wall **5**. ambit,
 bourn, fence, limit, march, verge
 7. barrier **8**. terminus **9**. perimeter
 11. conterminal, termination
 13. circumference
bounder . . . **3**. cad **4**. snob **6**. rotter
 7. epicier, parvenu, upstart
bounding (Mus) . . . **8**. saltando
boundless . . . **4**. vast **7**. endless **8**. infinite,
 termless **9**. limitless, unlimited
 10. unconfined **11**. illimitable
 12. interminable, unfathomable
bounds . . . **4**. pale **6**. frames, limits,
 skirts **7**. borders, margins **8**. confines,
 outlines **9**. outskirts **10**. delineated
 11. limitations
bounteous . . . **5**. ample **6**. freely, lavish
 7. liberal **8**. generous, prodigal
 9. bountiful, plentiful **10**. munificent
 11. extravagant
bountiful . . . **4**. rich **7**. copious, fertile,
 liberal, teeming, uberous **8**. abundant,
 fruitful, generous, prolific **9**. bounteous,
 exuberant, luxuriant, plentiful
bounty . . . **3**. fee **4**. gift **5**. bonus
 6. reward **7**. largess, premium,
 subsidy **8**. gratuity, solatium, sportula
 9. pourboire **10**. generosity, liberality
 11. beneficence **12**. compensation
bouquet . . . **4**. odor, posy **5**. aroma,
 cigar, spray **7**. corsage, flowers,
 incense, nosegay, perfume **9**. fragrance,
 redolence **10**. compliment
Bourbon, bourbon . . .
 ancient . . **7**. Reunion (Isl)
 dynasty . . **5**. Spain **6**. France, Naples
 famed personage . . **4**. Duke **13**. French
  General

famed ruins .. **7.** castles (Dukes')
liquor .. **6.** whisky (whiskey)
rose .. **9.** Le Phoenix
bourd ... **3.** fun **4.** jest **7.** mockery
bourdon ... **4.** stop (organ) **5.** baton,
music (bagpipe), spear, staff **6.** burden
(Fr), cudgel
bourgeois ... **4.** type (size) **8.** commoner
9. common man, plutocrat **10.** capitalist
11. middle-class, proletarian
bourn, bourne ... **3.** aim **4.** goal,
port **5.** bound, brook, limit, realm
6. arroyo, stream **7.** rivulet **8.** boundary
11. destination
bourock ... **3.** hut **4.** heap (stone)
5. crowd, mound **7.** cluster
Bourse ... **5.** Board **8.** Exchange **13.** Stock
Exchange
bouse ... **3.** cup **4.** haul (Naut), swig,
tope **5.** booze, drink, heave **6.** beaker
7. carouse
bouser ... **5.** toper **6.** boozer, bursar
7. fuddler, swigger
bout ... **2.** go **3.** act, war **4.** coup,
fray, game, spar, turn **5.** cycle, fight,
match, revel, round, scrap, set-to,
spree, trial **6.** fracas, inning, series,
stroke **7.** attempt, circuit, contest,
exploit **8.** conflict, maneuver, rotation
9. encounter **10.** enterprise, prize fight
11. celebration
boutade ... **4.** whim **5.** dance, prank
7. caprice **8.** outbreak **11.** composition
(Mus)
boutonniere ... **6.** flower **7.** bouquet,
nosegay **8.** incision **10.** buttonhole
bovine ... **2.** ox **3.** Bos, cow, yak **4.** bull,
dull, goat, kine, zebu **5.** bison, dogie,
steer, stirk, zebus **6.** catalo, cattle,
oxlike, stolid, stupid **7.** bullock, cattalo,
taurine, vaccine **8.** maverick, sluggish
10. complacent **11.** beef-brained
bow ... **3.** arc, bob, nod **4.** arch, beak,
bend, knot, node, prow **5.** bulge,
curve, debut, embow, kneel, stoop,
yield **6.** assent, convex, curtsy, encore,
kowtow, salaam, submit, weapon
7. curtain (Theat), incline, rainbow
8. crossbow, greeting **9.** obeisance
11. fiddlestick **12.** bow and scrape
bow (out) ... **4.** exit **6.** depart **7.** concede,
dismiss
Bow Bells (pert to) ...
area .. **10.** cockneydom
bells of .. **9.** Bow Church (St Mary le
Bow)
city .. **6.** London
bowels ... **3.** pit **4.** guts **5.** abyss,
chasm, depth **7.** innards, insides,
viscera **8.** entrails, interior (earth)
10. compassion (Shaksp), tenderness
bower ... **5.** abode, arbor, cards (game),
kiosk **6.** alcove, pandal **7.** retreat,
shelter **11.** summerhouse
Bowery denizen ... **4.** wino
bowfin ... **4.** Amia **7.** mudfish
bowhead (Arctic) ... **10.** Right whale
Bowie, bowie (pert to) ...
instrument .. **5.** knife
knife inventor .. **5.** Bowie (James)
Scottish .. **3.** tub **4.** cask **8.** milk pail

State nickname .. **8.** Arkansas
bowkail ... **4.** kale (kail) **7.** cabbage
bowl ... **3.** cup, jug **4.** ball, roll, vase
5. arena, basin, kitty (poker), mazer,
rogan **6.** cavity, crater, hollow, patina
(anc), vessel **7.** stadium **8.** washbowl
9. washbasin **10.** hippodrome,
receptacle **12.** amphitheater
Bowl (sports) ...
Abilene .. **5.** Pecan
Atlanta .. **5.** Peach
Dallas .. **6.** Cotton
El Paso .. **3.** Sun
Honolulu .. **4.** Hula
Houston .. **10.** Bluebonnet
Jacksonville .. **5.** Gator
Memphis .. **7.** Liberty
Miami .. **6.** Orange
Mobile .. **6.** Senior
New Orleans .. **5.** Sugar
Orlando .. **9.** Tangerine
Pasadena .. **4.** Rose
Sacramento .. **8.** Camellia
bowlegged ... **6.** valgus
bowler ... **3.** hat **5.** derby **6.** kegler
7. trundle
bowling ... **4.** ball, rink **5.** alley, green,
spare **6.** strike **7.** rolling, tenpins
8. ninepins **10.** greensward, playground
Bowling Green ... **4.** Park (Ky, NY)
bowsprit ... **3.** jib **4.** boom **6.** steeve
box ... **2.** ro (Jap) **3.** bin, pew, pyx **4.** arca
(alms), cage, case, cist (anc), cuff, kist,
kite, loge, safe, spar, tray **5.** brace
(faro), caddy (tea), cheat, crate, stall,
vault **6.** buffet, carton, casket, coffin,
encase **7.** confine, enclose **8.** bungalow
9. fisticuff **11.** compartment
box (pert to) ...
alms .. **4.** arca
bed .. **7.** springs
cosmetic .. **4.** inro
floating .. **3.** car (for fish)
lifesaving .. **9.** faking box
railroad .. **6.** boxcar **8.** box wagon
resistance .. **8.** rheostat
sewing .. **5.** plait, pleat
sleigh .. **4.** pung
sports .. **5.** score
tea .. **5.** caddy **8.** canister
theater .. **4.** loge, seat
tree .. **8.** Buxaceae
boxer ... **3.** dog, pug **5.** champ **6.** miller
7. bruiser, fighter, sparrer **8.** derby hat,
pugilist **11.** fisticuffer **12.** prizefighter
13. militia member (Chin)
boxer weight ... **3.** fly **5.** heavy, light
6. bantam, middle, welter **7.** feather
10. light heavy
boxing ... **4.** bout **5.** match, set-
to **7.** contest, crating **8.** pugilism,
sparring **10.** encasement, fisticuffs
12. shadowboxing
boy ... **2.** bo **3.** bat, bus, lad, tad, tot
4. nino, page, puer **5.** child, gamin,
knave, rogue, water, youth **6.** garcon,
laddie, master, rascal, shaver, urchin,
varlet **7.** callant, gossoon **8.** muchacho
boy (pert to) ...
book author .. **5.** Alger, Henty
errand .. **4.** page **9.** messenger

friend.. **4.** beau **10.** sweetheart
interjection.. **5.** Oh boy
organization.. **6.** Scouts
Scout founder.. **11.** Baden-Powell
street.. **4.** Arab **6.** urchin
boycott... **3.** ban **6.** oppose, strike
9. blackball, ostracize
Boz (pseud)... **7.** Dickens
brace... **3.** leg, tie, two **4.** bind, cord,
gird, pair, prop, span, stay, yoke
5. spale, staff, stave, strut **6.** couple
7. bandage, bracket, fulcrum, refresh,
rigging, support **8.** encircle **9.** reinforce,
stimulate **10.** invigorate, recuperate,
strengthen
bracelet... **5.** armil, armor, chain
6. sankha **7.** armilla **8.** handcuff,
vambrace **10.** calombigas
bracer... **4.** prop **5.** tonic **7.** reviver,
support **8.** pick-me-up, roborant
9. stimulant
bracing... **5.** crisp, tonic **10.** salubrious
11. stimulating **12.** invigorating
bracken... **4.** fern **5.** brake, plaid
bracket... **4.** mark **5.** ancon, angle,
group, strut **6.** corbel, sconce **7.** fixture
11. electrolier
brackish... **4.** foul **5.** salty **7.** saltish
8. nauseous **11.** distasteful
bract... **4.** leaf **5.** glume, palea, palet
6. spathe **8.** bractlet **9.** bracteole
brad... **3.** pin **4.** nail **5.** sprig
brae... **4.** bank, down, hill, moor **5.** slope
6. valley **8.** hillside
brag... **4.** crow **5.** bluff, boast, vaunt
6. flaunt **7.** blow off, bluster, deceive,
roister, swagger **8.** braggart
9. gasconade **11.** braggadocio
braggart... **4.** brag **6.** crower **7.** boaster
8. boastful, fanfaron **9.** blusterer,
swaggerer **11.** braggadocio
12. swashbuckler
bragging... **11.** thrasonical
Brahma... **3.** God **4.** fowl **5.** Hindu
Brahman (pert to)...
learned.. **6.** pundit
precept.. **5.** sutra **8.** netineti
sacred book.. **4.** Veda
Sanskrit scholar.. **6.** pundit
Supreme soul.. **6.** Brahma
title.. **3.** Aya
Trinity.. **4.** Siva **6.** Brahma, Vishnu
woman created by.. **6.** Alalya
Brahmin... **4.** prig, snob **7.** egghead
8. highbrow **10.** high-hatter
12. intellectual
braid... **3.** cue **4.** cord, gimp, hair, plat,
trim **5.** lacet, orris, plait, pleat, queue,
tress, twist, weave **6.** oxreim, sennit
7. entwine, outline, pigtail, topknot
8. ornament, soutache **9.** interlace
10. interweave
brain... **4.** head, mind, nous **6.** psyche,
reason **9.** intellect, mentality
10. encephalon, vital organ
brain (pert to)...
canal.. **4.** iter
case.. **3.** pan **5.** skull **7.** cranium
child.. **4.** idea **5.** storm
division.. **8.** cerebrum **10.** cerebellum
11. pons Varolii **16.** medulla oblongata

matter.. **4.** alba, dura, tela
operation.. **6.** trepan **8.** trephine
term.. **4.** lobe, lura
6. sulcus **7.** fissure **9.** ventricle
11. convolution
tumor.. **6.** glioma
X-ray.. **14.** encephalograph
brainless... **4.** dumb **5.** dizzy, giddy,
silly **6.** unwise **7.** asinine, foolish,
witless **9.** senseless **10.** unthinking
11. thoughtless **14.** scatterbrained
brainy... **5.** smart **6.** bright, clever
9. brilliant
brake... **4.** cage, curb, drag, fern,
reef, skid, trap **5.** check, delay, snare
6. bridle, retard **7.** dilemma, thicket
9. canebrake **10.** decelerate
bramble... **4.** burr **5.** berry, brier, shrub
(prickly), thorn **6.** nettle **7.** prickle,
thicket **9.** brierbush **10.** blackberry
12. brambleberry
branch... **3.** arm, set **4.** axil, fork, limb,
rame, stem, twig, wing **5.** bough,
class, frond, ramus, shoot, spray,
sprig, vimen, withe **6.** divide, member,
ramify, sprout, stolon, stream, switch
7. descent, diverge, lineage **8.** category,
division, offshoot **9.** affiliate, bloodline,
filiation **10.** department, descendant,
triskelion (three branches)
Branchiata (Group)... **6.** fishes
9. Crustacea **10.** Amphibians
brand... **4.** burn, iron, kind, mark, sear,
smit **5.** label, stamp, sword, torch
6. smirch, stigma **7.** earmark, feature,
hot iron, quality **8.** gridiron (Hist),
hallmark **9.** trademark **10.** stigmatize
brandish... **5.** shake, swing, wield
6. flaunt **7.** flutter, glitter **8.** flourish
brandy... **4.** marc **6.** cognac, grappa,
kirsch **8.** Armagnac, eau de vie (Fr)
9. applejack, slivovitz
brash... **4.** dash, rain, rash **5.** gruff,
saucy, storm **6.** scurry **7.** brittle (lumber)
8. impudent, tactless **9.** impetuous
brass... **4.** cash, gall **5.** alloy, braze,
cheek, money, nerve, plate **6.** latten,
ormolu, platen **8.** brass hat, officers,
sisterce (anc coin) **9.** impudence
10. instrument (wind)
brass (wind instrument)... **5.** bugle
6. cornet, lituus (anc) **7.** althorn,
brasses, clarion, saxhorn, trumpet
8. trombone **9.** saxophone
10. flügelhorn, French horn
brasserie... **6.** saloon **7.** brewery **8.** beer
shop
brassy... **4.** bold **6.** aerose, brazen
8. impudent
brat... **3.** bib, elf, imp **4.** film, minx,
scum **5.** apron, bairn, child, cloak,
minor **6.** mantle **7.** garment **8.** clothing
9. offspring **14.** enfant terrible,
whippersnapper
brattice... **7.** support **9.** partition (mining)
10. breastwork
bravado... **6.** bounce, daring, defial
7. bluster, bombast, bravery, bravura
8. defiance **11.** braggadocio
brave... **4.** bold, buck, dare, game,
hero, meet **5.** boast, bravo, bully,

front, manly, showy, stout **6.** daring,
endure, heroic, Indian **7.** Amerind,
gallant, soldier, spartan, valiant,
warrior **8.** confront, fearless, intrepid,
valorous **10.** courageous, untimorous
12. stouthearted
bravery ... **5.** valor **7.** bravado, bravura,
courage
bravo ... **3.** mug **4.** good, thug **5.** rough,
tough **6.** bandit **7.** gorilla, ruffian
8. assassin **9.** blusterer, cutthroat,
roisterer, roughneck, swaggerer
11. exclamation
bravura ... **4.** dash **5.** macho **6.** daring
7. bravado, bravery **10.** brilliance (Mus)
confidence
brawl ... **3.** row **4.** fray, fury, rage, riot
5. broil, fight, furor, melee, scold
6. affray, clamor, fracas, hubbub,
rumpus, shindy, tumult, uproar
7. dispute, quarrel, rampage, turmoil,
wrangle **10.** hullabaloo, turbulence
11. altercation, embroilment
brawny ... **5.** beefy, burly, lusty, thewy
6. fleshy, robust, sinewy, strong,
sturdy **7.** callous **8.** muscular, powerful,
stalwart **9.** corpulent
bray ... **4.** beat **5.** blare, bleat, grind, neigh
6. heehaw, powder, thrash, whinny
9. pulverize, triturate **12.** disintegrate
braze ... **4.** weld **5.** plate (with metal)
6. solder
brazen ... **4.** bold, pert **5.** brass, brave,
harsh **6.** brassy, cheeky, harden
7. aweless, callous **8.** immodest,
impudent, indurate, insolent, metallic
9. bold-faced, shameless, unabashed
10. unblushing **13.** bronze-colored,
harsh-sounding
brazier ... **5.** grill **6.** brazer **7.** hibachi
8. barbecue, gridiron **10.** money chest
(anc)
brazil ... **3.** red **4.** wood (hard) **8.** dyestuff
Brazil ... see also *Brazilian*
capital .. **8.** Brasilia **12.** Rio de Janeiro
(old)
city .. **5.** Bahia, Belem **6.** Recife, Santos
8. Sao Paulo **9.** Horizonte **11.** Porto
Alegre, Sao Salvador
discoverer .. **6.** Cabral (1500)
Falls (world wonder) .. **6.** Iguacu
lake .. **12.** Lago dos Patos
product .. **6.** coffee
river .. **5.** Negro **6.** Amazon, Branco,
Paraná **7.** Madeira, Orinoco **8.** Paraguay
9. Tocantins
Brazilian (pert to) ...
aborigine .. **5.** Carib
ant (powerful) .. **9.** tucandera
bird .. **3.** ani, ara **5.** arara, macaw
6. cuckoo, darter, tiribo **7.** maracan,
sierema
crab (land) .. **8.** horseman
dance .. **5.** samba **6.** maxixe
drink .. **5.** assai
flycatcher .. **6.** yetapa
Indian .. **4.** Anta **5.** Arara, Araua, Guana
6. Tupian **8.** Araquayu, Arawakan
mammal .. **5.** tapir
parrot .. **3.** ara **5.** macaw **6.** tiriba
plant .. **4.** yaje **5.** caroa **7.** ayapana

(Med)
tree .. **3.** apa **4.** anda (oil), jara **5.** assai
(palm) **6.** embuia, satiné **7.** araroba,
gomavel, seringa (rubber), wallaba
8. bakupari **10.** barbatimao
weight .. **4.** onza **5.** libra **6.** arroba
7. quintal
breach ... **3.** gap **4.** rent, rift **5.** break,
burst, chasm, cleft, split **6.** schism
7. caesura, dispute, quarrel, rupture
8. fracture, solecism **9.** violation
10. disruption, falling-out, infraction,
separation **12.** infringement,
interruption **16.** misunderstanding
bread ... **3.** rye **4.** naan, pita, rusk
5. matzo, quick **6.** simnel **7.** anadama
challah, chapati, hoecake **8.** baguette,
hardtack, tortilla, zwieback **9.** sourdough
12. pumpernickel
bread (pert to) ...
basket .. **7.** stomach
bread and butter .. **5.** plate **6.** letter
(of thanks), pickle, staple **7.** prosaic
8. juvenile
fruit .. **3.** nut **4.** tree **6.** simnel **7.** castana
8. chestnut
winner .. **6.** earner, toiler, worker
7. workman **8.** provider **10.** wage
earner
break ... **3.** gap **4.** dash, knap, luck,
lull, rent, rift, ruin, rush, slip, snap,
stop **5.** blank, burst, cleft, lapse,
letup, pause, smash, train **6.** breach,
chance, change, depose, escape,
hiatus, injury, lacuna, market (Finan),
recess, subdue, weaken **7.** blunder,
caesura (cesura), disrupt, getaway,
respite, rupture, shatter, violate **8.** bad
break, bankrupt, breakage, breather,
fracture, interval **9.** interlude, jail break,
violation **10.** depreciate, falling-out,
infraction, suspension **11.** fragmentize
12. intermission, interruption
13. discontinuity
break down ... **3.** cry, sob **4.** bawl,
raze, weep **5.** crush **6.** boohoo,
divide, master, reduce, revolt, subdue
7. analyze, crack up, dissect, resolve,
unnerve **8.** classify, collapse, separate
9. decompose, overwhelm, subdivide
breakdown ... **7.** debacle, failure
8. analysis **9.** cataclysm **10.** dissection,
impairment, revolution
breakfast ... **6.** brunch (late) **8.** dejeuner
10. chota hazri
break in ... **4.** open, tame **5.** enter,
force, train **6.** butt in, subdue **7.** barge
in, intrude, prepare **9.** interrupt
10. housebreak
break up ... **4.** cure, rift, ruin **5.** decay,
leave, smash, spall, split, upset
7. adjourn, atomize, crumble, disband,
relieve, scatter, shatter **8.** disperse,
dissolve, separate, unsettle
9. decompose **10.** demobilize,
dispersion, disruption **11.** disorganize,
dissolution **12.** disintegrate
breakwater ... **4.** dike, mole, pier
5. jetty, jutty **6.** refuge, riprap **7.** sea
wall **8.** buttress **10.** embankment
11. obstruction

bream . . . **4.** fish, scup **5.** clean (Naut)
breast . . . **4.** bust, soul, teat **5.** bosom,
cheat, gland (mammary), heart **6.** spirit,
thorax **8.** inner man **9.** encounter
breast (pert to) . . .
absence of . . **7.** amastia
bone . . **6.** ratite **7.** sternum
breastlike . . **7.** mastoid
plate . . **4.** Urim **5.** armor, ephod
6. gorget, lorica **7.** poitrel
12. breastsummer
works . . **7.** defense, parapet, railing
(Naut), ravelin **8.** mantelet **9.** banquette
breath . . . **3.** air **4.** fume, life, odor,
pant, puff, wind **5.** draft, pause,
prana, scent, smell, touch, vapor, whiff
6. breeze, caress, flatus, pneuma, spirit
7. halitus, respite, whisper **8.** breather
9. emanation, ozostomia, utterance
10. exhalation **11.** respiration
breathe . . . **3.** say, tip **4.** gulp, live, mean,
pneo (comb form), rest, sigh, tell
5. exist, imbue, imply, scent, smell,
snuff **6.** evince, exhale, infuse, inhale,
let out, reveal **7.** bespeak, divulge,
emanate, instill (instil), pervade, respire,
suspire, whisper **8.** aspirate, indicate
breathe (pert to) . . .
comb form . . **4.** pnea, pneo
convulsively . . **4.** sigh
hard . . **4.** pant
one's last . . **3.** die **6.** expire, perish
7. decease, succumb
vengeance . . **9.** retaliate
breather . . . **4.** lull, rest **5.** break, pause,
truce **6.** recess **7.** interim, respite
9. interlude **12.** intermission
breathing . . . **5.** alive, vital **6.** living,
zoetic **7.** animate, panting, respite
8. animated **9.** conscious, phonation,
utterance **10.** aspiration **11.** respiration,
respiratory, ventilation **12.** articulation
breathing (pert to) . . .
apertures . . **5.** stoma **8.** spiracle
morbid . . **4.** rale **7.** stridor **8.** rhonchus
painful . . **8.** dyspnoea
pause . . **7.** caesura
smooth . . **4.** lene
breathless . . . **4.** awed, dead, gone, keen
5. eager **6.** ardent, fervid, winded
7. airless, demised, fervent **8.** deceased,
lifeless, windless, wordless **9.** impatient
10. astonished, speechless, spellbound
bred . . . **6.** hybrid, inbred, reared, tablet
(compressed) **7.** lowbred, mongrel
8. exogamic, purebred **9.** autogamic,
crossbred, endogamic, half-caste,
interbred **11.** half-blooded,
impregnated, inseminated
12. thoroughbred
bree . . . **4.** brow **5.** broth, scare **6.** liquor
7. eyebrow **9.** commotion
11. disturbance
breech . . . **4.** doup, rump, tall **5.** fanny,
stern **6.** bottom **8.** buttocks **9.** posterior,
underside
breeches . . . **5.** chaps, jeans, pants,
trews **8.** britches, jodhpurs, trousers
10. pantaloons **12.** galligaskins (jocular)
breed . . . **3.** ilk **4.** kind, race, rear, sort
5. beget, brood, caste, class, mixed,

raise, stock, train, tribe **6.** family
7. descent, educate, lineage, mongrel,
produce **8.** engender, generate, instruct
9. originate, posterity, procreate,
propagate **10.** crossbreed
breeding . . . **6.** polish **7.** culture, decorum,
exogamy, manners, raising, rearing
8. autogamy, endogamy, hatching,
training **9.** education, fostering, gentility
10. deportment, upbringing
11. instruction, procreation, propagation
breeding place . . . **4.** nest **5.** nidus
7. brooder **8.** hatchery **9.** incubator
10. birthplace
breeze . . . **3.** air, row **4.** aura, pirr, snap,
stir, wind **5.** cinch, rumor **6.** squall,
zephyr **7.** ill wind, whisper **8.** duck soup,
pushover **9.** commotion **11.** disturbance
breezy . . . **4.** airy, spry **5.** blowy, brisk,
gusty, windy **6.** drafty, jaunty, lively
7. squally **8.** animated, blustery, spirited
9. vivaceous **12.** lighthearted
Brehon Law . . . **4.** eric (anc) **10.** Senchus
Mor **12.** Book of Aicill
breve . . . **4.** note (Mus), writ **5.** brief,
order **7.** compose
brevet . . . **4.** fiat **5.** ukase **6.** decree
7. warrant **10.** commission **11.** certificate
(teaching)
breveté . . . **8.** patented
breviary . . . **6.** manual, ritual **7.** compend,
epitome
brevity . . . **9.** briefness, shortness,
terseness **11.** conciseness, transcience
12. succinctness
brew . . . **3.** ale, mix **4.** grog, plot **5.** hatch,
steep **6.** cook up, foment, gather,
menace, scheme **7.** concoct, distill
(distil) **8.** contrive, threaten **9.** aqua
vitae
brewer's grain . . . **4.** corn, malt **6.** barley
brewer's yeast . . . **4.** barm **6.** leaven
bribe . . . **3.** oil, sop **5.** bonus **6.** boodle,
buy off, grease, suborn **9.** hush money
bric-a-brac . . . **6.** curios **7.** artware
8. antiques, trinkets **9.** artifacts, objet
d'art **11.** knickknacks
bric-a-brac cabinet . . . **7.** étagère,
whatnot
brick . . . **3.** bat **4.** dobe, tile **5.** adobe,
stone **6.** pament (pamment) **7.** clinker
8. hardness
brick (pert to) . . .
color . . **3.** red **7.** Saravan
kiln . . **5.** clamp
layer . . **3.** cad (helper) **5.** mason
laying . . **8.** toothing
slang . . **3.** pip **4.** lulu **5.** dilly, peach
6. corker, winner **8.** jim-dandy
10. sweetheart **11.** crackerjack
12. lollapaloosa
unburned . . **5.** samel
brickbat . . . **4.** rock **5.** stone **7.** affront,
missile, offense **9.** indignity
bridal (pert to) . . .
chest . . **9.** trousseau
flower . . **13.** orange blossom
ode, song . . **9.** Brautlied **11.** Epithalamon
(anc)
portion . . **3.** dot **5.** dower, dowry
(dowery)

rite . . **7.** wedding **8.** marriage, nuptials

bridge . . . **3.** tie **4.** arch, bond, link, pons, pont, span **5.** unite **7.** connect, passage (Mus), ponteon, viaduct **9.** structure **13.** steppingstone

bridge (pert to) . . . **4.** deck, game, nose **5.** magas, truss **6.** phoebe (bird) **7.** bascule, trestle **9.** dentistry **10.** ponticello (Mus)

bridge, historic . . .
Bridge of Boats . . **10.** Hellespont
Bridge of Sighs . . **6.** Venice (Doge's Palace) **7.** Al Sirat (Muslim, over infernal fire)
Norse Myth . . **7.** Bifrost (rainbow)
Old Bridge . . **12.** Ponte Vecchio (Florence It, 1345)

Bridge game . . . **3.** bid **4.** pass, ruff, slam **5.** Goren (expert) **6.** honors, points, renege, tenace **7.** finesse **9.** part-score

bridle . . . **3.** bit **4.** cord (kite), curb, rein **5.** check, guide, smirk **6.** fetter, govern, halter, master, simper, subdue **7.** harness, manacle, repress, shackle, snaffle **8.** cavesson, headgear, noseband, restrain, suppress **9.** hackamore, headstall, restraint

brief . . . **4.** curt, plan, writ **5.** breve, charm, pithy, short, terse **6.** report **7.** compact, concise, laconic, summary **8.** fleeting, instruct, succinct **9.** condensed, ephemeral, summarize, transient **10.** compendium, short-lived, transitory **11.** compendious **14.** inconsiderable

brier, briar . . . **4.** burr, pipe **5.** heath, shrub, spine, thorn **7.** bramble, bruyère, clotbur, prickle, sticker, thistle **8.** adherent **11.** French brier

brig . . . **4.** boat **6.** vessel **10.** guardhouse

brigade . . . **4.** unit **6.** troops **7.** company **8.** regiment

brigand . . . **5.** rover, thief **6.** bandit, dacoit, pirate, robber **7.** bedouin, cateran, ladrone **8.** picaroon **10.** highwayman

bright . . . **3.** apt, gay **4.** naif, rosy **5.** alert, beamy, fresh, lucid, nitid, palmy, sleek, smart, sunny, vivid, witty **6.** brainy, clever, florid, garish, golden **7.** halcyon, radiant, shining, unfaded **8.** cheerful, colorful, flashing, gleaming, luminous, lustrous, splendid **9.** brilliant, effulgent, refulgent, sparkling **10.** auspicious, epiphanous, glistening, glittering, optimistic **11.** intelligent, resplendent

brightness . . . **5.** sheen **6.** luster **7.** sparkle **8.** radiance, splendor **9.** alertness, clearness, smartness **10.** brilliance **12.** cheerfulness, colorfulness, pleasantness

brilliance, brilliancy . . . **5.** éclat, glory **6.** luster **7.** glitter, oriency, success **8.** radiance, splendor **9.** smartness, vividness **10.** brightness, cleverness

brilliant . . . **5.** smart, vivid, witty **6.** bright **7.** eminent, radiant, shining **8.** gorgeous, meteoric, splendid **9.** refulgent, sparkling **10.** glittering **11.** illustrious

brilliant group . . . **6.** galaxy

brim . . . **3.** hem, lip, rim **4.** edge **5.** brink, marge, verge **6.** border, margin

7. selvage

brine . . . **3.** sea **4.** main, salt **5.** brack, ocean, tears **6.** pickle **7.** the deep **12.** preservative

bring . . . **3.** get **4.** bear, cost, haul, lead **5.** carry, fetch, go get, yield **6.** convey, entail, induce, obtain **7.** contain, involve, require **8.** comprise **9.** transport

bring about . . . **2.** do **4.** make **5.** cause **6.** create, effect **7.** achieve, produce **8.** generate **9.** instigate **10.** accomplish, consummate, effectuate

bring around . . . **4.** cure, heal, ween **5.** renew, sober **6.** revive **7.** convert, restore, win over **8.** persuade **10.** rejuvenate

bring back . . . **5.** fetch **6.** recall, return, revive **7.** restore **8.** rekindle, remember, retrieve **9.** recollect, resurrect

bring forth . . . **3.** ean **4.** bear, rise **5.** beget, breed, cause, educe, hatch, spawn, yield **6.** adduce, elicit, reveal **7.** develop, produce **8.** disclose, fructify, generate, manifest

bring forward . . . **4.** cite **5.** offer **6.** adduce, broach, submit **7.** advance, improve, promote, propose **8.** manifest **9.** introduce

bring into . . .
bondage . . **7.** enslave
court . . **7.** arraign
harmony . . **6.** attune
position . . **5.** align, aline
union . . **9.** correlate

bring together . . . **5.** amass, group **6.** gather **7.** cluster, compile, reunite **8.** assemble **9.** harmonize, reconcile **10.** accumulate

bring to light . . . **4.** find **5.** trace **6.** elicit, expose, reveal **7.** uncover, unearth **8.** disclose, discover

bring to mind . . . **6.** recall, remind **8.** look like, remember, resemble

bring to pass . . . **2.** do **5.** cause **6.** author, father **9.** originate **10.** accomplish, effectuate

bring up . . . **4.** rear, spew **5.** drill, raise, train, vomit **6.** foster, muster **7.** advance, educate, nurture, propose **9.** challenge, condition, cultivate **10.** discipline **11.** regurgitate

bring up to date . . . **4.** post **6.** update **9.** modernize **10.** streamline

brink . . . **3.** lip, rim **4.** bank, brow, edge, near **5.** ditch, marge, skirt, verge **6.** border, margin

briny . . . **3.** sea **4.** salt **5.** salty **6.** saline **8.** brackish

Brisbane, capital of . . . **10.** Queensland (Austral)

Brisbane tree . . . **3.** box **8.** quandong

brisk . . . **3.** gay **4.** cold, fast, keen, racy, spry, yern **5.** agile, alert, alive, crisp, fresh, peart, quick, sharp, tangy, zippy **6.** breezy, lively, nimble, snappy **7.** caustic, pungent **8.** animated, forceful, spirited, vigorous **9.** energetic, sprightly, vivacious **11.** stimulating

bristle . . . **4.** barb, hair, seta **5.** anger, seton **6.** chaeta, palpus, ruffle, rumple, see red, setula, setule **7.** acicula, prickle,

stubble
bristling . . . **5.** angry **6.** horrid (anc)
7. horrent **9.** offensive
bristly . . . **5.** rough, setal **6.** hispid, setose,
thorny **7.** prickly, scopate, unshorn
8. acicular, echinate **9.** setaceous
11. bristlelike
Bristol . . .
church (England's finest) . . **15.** St Mary
Redcliffe
fashion . . **6.** ataunt **9.** shipshape
library . . **6.** oldest (British Isles)
milk . . **6.** sherry
Britain . . .
name, ancient . . **6.** Albion
name, modern . . **12.** British Isles,
Commonwealth, Great Britain
13. United Kingdom
name, Roman . . **9.** Brittania
native . . **5.** Iceni, Jutes, Picts, Scots
6. Angles **7.** Britons, Silures
native (sl) . . **5.** limey (limy), tommy
7. Blighty
sea . . **5.** Irish, North **8.** Atlantic, Hebrides
British (pert to) . . . see also *English*
battle . . **8.** Hastings
boat (anc) . . **7.** coracle
cavalry . . **8.** yeomanry
emblem . . **4.** lion
fish . . **8.** dragonet (gobylike)
oak . . **5.** robur
Order of . . **9.** The Garter
prison . . **4.** gaol
pudding . . **4.** suet **9.** Yorkshire
tavern . . **3.** pub **9.** beerhouse, jerry shop
thief (wharf) . . **6.** tosher
Z (letter) . . **3.** Zed
British people . . .
buccaneer . . **4.** Kidd **5.** Drake **6.** Morgan
explorer . . **4.** Cook, Ross **6.** Baffin
7. Stanley **11.** Livingstone
hero (sea) . . **6.** Nelson
king (legend, Myth) . . **3.** Lud **4.** Beli,
Bran, Brut **7.** Belenus
soldier . . **7.** Redcoat (Hist)
Brittany . . . **7.** Armoric **8.** Bretagne
brittle . . . **4.** weak **5.** brash, candy, crisp,
frail **6.** feeble, infirm, slight **7.** fragile,
friable **8.** delicate, insecure **9.** breakable,
frangible **11.** shatterable
broad . . . **4.** free, girl, lake (Eng), wide
5. ample, large, roomy, thick, wench
7. breadth, diffuse, general, liberal
8. spacious, strumpet, sweeping,
tabulate, tolerant **9.** expansive,
extensive **10.** collective, commodious,
indefinite, voluminous
13. comprehensive
broad (pert to) . . .
arrow . . **5.** pheon (Her) **6.** stigma
8. insignia
footed . . **8.** platypod
hearted . . **8.** generous **11.** magnanimous
minded . . **7.** liberal **8.** tolerant
9. receptive
broaden . . . **5.** swell, widen **6.** dilate,
expand, extend, spread **7.** augment,
enlarge, ennoble **8.** increase
broadly . . . **3.** far **6.** widely **10.** far and
wide **11.** extensively **12.** indefinitely,
right and left

broadside . . . **4.** guns, side **6.** folder
7. gunfire, quarter, surface **8.** enfilade,
sideways **10.** broadsheet, floodlight
11. breadthwise
broadsword . . . **7.** cutlass, Ferrara
8. claymore, scimitar
Brobdingnagian . . . **5.** giant, titan
8. colossal, gigantic **10.** gargantuan
brocade . . . **6.** broché, fabric **8.** baudekin
9. baldachin
brochan . . . **7.** oatmeal **8.** porridge
brochure . . . **5.** tract **6.** folder **7.** booklet,
leaflet **8.** chapbook, pamphlet
brod . . . **3.** awl **4.** goad, pike, urge **5.** thorn
6. sprout **9.** incentive
brode, brodee . . . **11.** embroidered
brodyaga . . . **7.** vagrant **8.** vagabond
brogan, brogue . . . **4.** shoe
brogue . . . **4.** burr **5.** twang **6.** accent
7. dialect
broil . . . **4.** cook, fray, fume **5.** brawl,
grill, melee **6.** affray, braise (braize),
scorch **7.** contest, discord, dispute,
quarrel **8.** conflict, grillade, scramble
10. contention, dissension, turbulence
11. altercation, embroilment
broke . . . **4.** flat **6.** busted, ruined
8. bankrupt, strapped **9.** destitute,
insolvent, penniless
broken . . . **4.** tame **5.** broke, bumpy,
burst, rough, tamed **6.** chined, ruined,
shaken, uneven, zigzag **7.** crushed,
décousu, severed, subdued **8.** bankrupt,
detached, impaired, ruptured, sporadic,
weakened **9.** conquered, dispersed,
irregular, shattered, unsettled
10. incoherent, incomplete
11. fragmentary, housebroken,
interrupted **12.** disconnected,
domesticated, intermittent
13. discontinuous
broken pottery (anc) . . . **5.** shard (sherd)
8. potsherd
broker . . . **5.** agent **6.** dealer, jobber
7. cambist, scalper (ticket) **8.** marriage
9. go-between, insurance, middleman,
schatchen **10.** pawnbroker, real estate
11. internuncio, stockbroker
12. intermediary
brokerage . . . **3.** fee **4.** agio **6.** charge
8. agiotage, business **9.** exactment
10. commission
brolly . . . **5.** chute **8.** umbrella **9.** brollyhop,
parachute
bromide . . . **4.** corn **5.** trite **6.** Babbit,
cliché, halide, old hat **8.** banality,
sedative **9.** conformer, criticism,
platitude **10.** conformist, Philistine
15. conventionalist
bronco, broncho . . . **4.** pony **5.** horse
6. cayuse **7.** mustang **10.** broomstick
bronc, bucking . . . **9.** estrapade
broncobuster, bronchobuster . . .
6. cowboy **7.** trainer, vaquero
Brontë (pert to) . . .
Charlotte . . **7.** Shirley **8.** Jane Eyre,
Villette **10.** Currer Bell (pseud)
Emily . . **16.** Wuthering Heights
Bronx cheer . . . **3.** boo **4.** hiss, razz
9. raspberry
bronze . . . **3.** aes (anc), tan **5.** alloy, color

6. ormolu, patina, suntan **9.** sculpture
Bronze Age . . . **6.** Aegean **9.** Neolithic
11. Aeneolithic
Bronze Plaques (pert to) . . .
called . . **14.** Eugubine Tables (Iguvine
Tables, 1444)
number . . **5.** Seven
site . . **6.** Gubbio (It)
brooch . . . **3.** bar, pin **4.** boss, ouch
5. cameo, clasp **6.** fibula (anc), shield
8. pectoral **9.** breastpin
brood . . . **3.** fry, nye, set **4.** kind, mope,
mull, muse, nide, race **5.** breed,
covey, folks, hatch, pride (lions),
young **6.** clutch, family, farrow
(pigs), litter, ménage, people, strain
7. lineage, progeny, reflect **8.** cogitate,
incubate, meditate, ruminate, soredium
9. household, offspring **11.** contemplate
brood over . . . **4.** fret, mope **5.** hover
6. grieve, ponder **7.** agonize
8. remember
brook . . . **3.** run **4.** bear, beck, burn,
rill, sike **5.** abide, bourn, creek,
crick **6.** arroyo, endure, rillet, runlet,
suffer **7.** freshet, rivulet **8.** brooklet
9. arroyuelo, streamlet
broom . . . **5.** besom, shrub, spart, sweep,
whisk
broth . . . **4.** soup **5.** stock **6.** brewis
8. bouillon, consommé
brother . . . **3.** fra **4.** mate, monk **5.** friar,
title **6.** frater, friend, member, oblate
8. alter ego, relative **9.** associate
11. counterpart
brotherhood . . . **5.** lodge **7.** kinship,
society **8.** sodality **10.** fellowship,
fraternity **11.** association
12. fraternalism **13.** confraternity
brotherly . . . **4.** kind **6.** tender **8.** friendly
9. fraternal **11.** sympathetic
12. affectionate
Brothers . . . **7.** Danites (Mormon)
9. Christian (RCCh)
brothers and sisters (same family) . . .
8. siblings
brow . . . **3.** cap, rim, tip, top **4.** brae
5. brink, crest, crown **6.** border, summit,
tiptop, visage **7.** eyebrow, feature
8. boldness, forehead **9.** gangplank
10. effrontery **11.** countenance
browbeat . . . **3.** cow **5.** bully **6.** hector
7. buffalo, henpeck **8.** bulldoze,
domineer **10.** intimidate
brown . . . **4.** dark **5.** cheat, dusky
6. august, braise, tanned **9.** red-yellow
(class)
brown . . . **3.** bay, dun, nut, tan **4.** ecru,
faon, fawn, roan, rust, seal **5.** acorn,
cocoa, hazel, henna, khaki, mocha,
olive, otter, sepia, snuff, sumac, tawny,
tenné, toast, topaz **6.** auburn, bister,
bronze, burnet, coffee, copper, loutre,
oriole, russet, sienna, sorrel, titian,
walnut **7.** asphalt (smoke), gazelle,
perique, rosario (army) **8.** chestnut,
cinnamon, mahogany **9.** buckthorn,
chocolate **10.** café au lait, terra cotta
brown (pert to) . . .
Bess . . **6.** musket
betty . . **5.** daisy **7.** pudding

10. coneflower
earth . . **5.** umber
ebony . . **6.** wamara **10.** coffeewood
browned in deep fat . . . **7.** rissole
Brownian movement (Bot) . . . **7.** pedesis
brownie . . . **3.** elf **4.** cake **5.** dwarf, gnome,
nisse, pixie, Scout, urisk **6.** camera,
goblin **9.** sandpiper
Brownism (Eng) . . .
17. Congregationalism
browze . . . **4.** brut (obs), read, scan
5. graze **6.** nibble
bruckle . . . **5.** frail **7.** brittle **9.** breakable
10. changeable, inconstant
bruin . . . **4.** bear
bruise . . . **4.** bash, beat, hurt, maul
5. abuse, crush, dinge, pound, wound
6. batter, buffet, injury **7.** contuse
8. abrasion, black eye **9.** contusion,
pulverize, triturate
bruiser . . . **3.** mug, pug **5.** boxer, bravo,
tough **7.** fighter, ruffian, sparrer
8. pugilist **11.** fisticuffer
bruit, bruit about . . . **3.** din **4.** fame,
hawk, tell **5.** bandy, noise, rumor
6. clamor, report **9.** advertise
brujo . . . **8.** magician, sorcerer **11.** witch
doctor
brumal . . . **4.** cold **6.** hiemal, wintry
8. hibernal **10.** winterlike
brune . . . **6.** brunet (brunette)
11. Melanochroi
Brunhild . . . **5.** Queen (wife of Siegfried)
8. Valkyrie (Myth)
brunt . . . **3.** rub **4.** crux **5.** pinch, shock
6. stress **7.** squeeze
brush . . . **3.** art **4.** bush, comb, tail
(fox), tuft **5.** besom, briar, broom,
clash, graze, groom, sweep, touch
6. artist, forest, pappus, stroke, teazel
7. painter, scuffle, thicket **8.** conflict
9. brushwood, encounter **10.** paintbrush
11. undergrowth
brush aside . . . **5.** spurn **6.** reject
7. dismiss **8.** shrug off **9.** disregard
brush wolf . . . **6.** coyote
brusque . . . **4.** curt **5.** bluff, blunt, brash,
brusk, frank, gruff, rough, sharp, short
6. abrupt, candid, snippy
brutal . . . **5.** cruel, gross **6.** animal, carnal,
coarse, savage **7.** bestial, inhuman
8. ruthless **9.** barbarous
brutality . . . **7.** cruelty **9.** barbarian,
carnality **12.** ruthlessness
brute . . . **5.** beast, gross, harsh, rough
6. animal **7.** beastly, bestial, sensual,
varment **8.** soulless **9.** barbarian,
inanimate **10.** unpolished **11.** uncivilized
brutish . . . **4.** rude **5.** cruel, gross
6. brutal, carnal, fierce, savage, stupid
7. bestial, inhuman, sensual, vicious
9. barbarous, ferocious, insensate,
unfeeling **10.** insensible, irrational
Brutus . . . **3.** wig **6.** hairdo, peruke
7. traitor (Julius Caesar)
13. chrysanthemum
Bryan's speech (1896) . . . **11.** Cross of
Gold **13.** Crown of Thorns
bryology, science of . . . **6.** mosses
10. bryophytes, liverworts
Brython . . . **4.** Celt **6.** Briton **8.** Welshman

Brythonic god . . . **3.** Ler **4.** Bran
Brythonic goddess . . . **9.** Arianrhod
bubble . . . **4.** bead, bleb, blob, boil, foam
   5. bulge, empty, fancy, tumor **6.** burble,
   gurgle, murmur, ripple, scheme,
   trifle **7.** chimera (chimaera), globule,
   trickle **8.** bubbling, delusive, illusion
   9. ephemeron, intumesce, lightness
   10. effervesce **16.** unsubstantiality
buccal . . . **4.** oral **5.** cheek, mouth
buccaneer . . . **4.** Kidd (Capt) **5.** rover
   6. Morgan, pirate, rifler, viking
   7. corsair, Lafitte, spoiler **8.** marooner,
   picaroon **9.** privateer **10.** Blackbeard
   (Capt Teach), freebooter
Bucephalus . . . **5.** horse, steed **7.** charger
   8. war horse (Alex the Great)
buck . . . **3.** man, ram, rat **4.** bunt, butt,
   deer, goat, hare, jump, male, sore (4-yr
   deer) **5.** fight, sasin **6.** animal, combat,
   dollar, Indian, oppose **7.** contest,
   launder, pricket **8.** antelope, sawhorse
   10. fallow deer
buckaroo . . . **6.** cowboy **7.** trainer,
   vaquero **8.** horseman **12.** broncobuster
   (bronchobuster)
bucket . . . **3.** tub **4.** bail, bowk, pail, ship
   5. chest, cozen, scoop, skeel **6.** bailer,
   bushel, drench, sityla **10.** bucket shop
Buckeye State . . . **4.** Ohio
Buckingham Palace . . . **9.** residence
   11. St James Park (London)
buckle . . . **3.** bow **4.** bend, curl, kink,
   warp **5.** tache **6.** fasten **8.** marriage
   9. fastening
buckthorn . . . **4.** tree **5.** brown, shrub
   7. cascara, Rhamnus
buckwheat . . . **4.** cake, coal, herb, seed,
   titi **5.** flour
bucolic . . . **4.** idyl, poem, poet **5.** idyll,
   local, rural **6.** farmer, poetic, rustic
   7. eclogue, georgic **8.** agrestic, pastoral
   9. bucoliast
bud . . . **3.** deb **4.** bulb, cion, germ, grow,
   knop, stem **5.** brier, buddy, gemma,
   graft, plant, shoat, youth **6.** embryo,
   sprout **7.** blossom, brother, burgeon,
   develop **8.** rudiment, soredium
   9. debutante, germinate
Buddha (Gautama) . . . **2.** Fo **4.** sage
   (Shakya) **5.** amita, deity **7.** ascetic,
   teacher **8.** Daibutsu **10.** Blessed One
Buddhism (pert to) . . .
   church . . **4.** tera
   city (sacred) . . **5.** Lassa (Lhasa)
   evil spirit . . **4.** Mara
   fate . . **5.** Karma
   festival . . **3.** Bon
   friar, monk . . **2.** Bo **5.** arbat, bonze
      6. bhikku, gelong **7.** Mahatma
      8. poonghia **9.** Dalai Lama
   goal . . **13.** Enlightenment
   hell . . **6.** Naraka
   language (sacred) . . **4.** Pali **5.** sutra
      9. Tripitaka
   liberation . . **7.** Nirvana
   monk . . **4.** lama (Tibet)
   mountain (sacred) . . **4.** Omei (Chin)
   paradise . . **4.** Jodo **8.** gokuraku
   sect . . **3.** Zen
   shrine (Ind) . . **4.** tope **5.** stupa **6.** dagoba

   temple . . **4.** rath, Tera **6.** vihara
   temple column . . **3.** lat
   term . . **6.** nidana
buddy . . . **3.** pal **4.** chum, mate **5.** crony
   7. brother, comrade **8.** tentmate
   9. bedfellow, companion
budge . . . **3.** fur (lambskin) **4.** grog, move,
   stir **5.** booze, brisk, stiff **6.** guzzle,
   jocund, liquor, solemn, tipple **7.** austere,
   pompous **8.** movement **11.** nervousness
budget . . . **3.** bag **4.** bulk, plan, sack
   5. funds, pouch, purse, store **6.** agenda,
   assets, bundle, moneys, packet,
   parcel, ration, wallet **7.** program,
   stipend **8.** finances, quantity, schedule
   9. allowance, statement
   12. accumulation
Buenos Aires (pert to) . . .
   avenue (famed) . . **13.** Avenida de Mayo
   bourse . . **5.** Bolsa
   capital . . **9.** Argentina
   river . . **7.** La Plata
buff . . . **3.** rub **4.** hide (animal) **5.** color,
   scour **6.** polish **7.** burnish, leather
buffalo (animal) . . .
   American . . **5.** bison
   Asian, African . . **2.** ox **4.** arna, Cape,
      gaur **8.** seladang
   European . . **7.** aurochs
   hybrid . . **7.** cattalo (catalo)
   Indian . . **4.** arna
   Philippines . . **7.** carabao, timarau
buffalo (pert to) . . .
   grass . . **5.** grama **6.** guinea **11.** St
      Augustine
   pea . . **4.** plum **5.** vetch **10.** bluebonnet
   slang . . **3.** cow **5.** bully **7.** perplex
      8. bulldoze, confound
Buffalo Bill . . . **11.** William Cody
buffer . . . **4.** buff **5.** guard, wheel
   6. bumper **7.** bulwark, cushion
   8. backstop, polisher
buffet . . . **3.** bar, box, hit **4.** beat,
   blow, cuff, slap, toss, whip **5.** abuse,
   smite, stool **6.** bruise, oppose, strike
   12. chastisement **14.** disappointment
buffet . . . **6.** supper **7.** counter, hassock
   8. cupboard **9.** sideboard
buffo . . . **7.** buffoon **10.** bass singer
   (comic opera), buffo-basso
buffoon . . . **4.** fool, mima (fem), mime,
   zany **5.** actor, clown, droll, mimer
   6. jester, mummer **8.** humorist,
   ridicule **9.** Hanswurst, harlequin
   12. Eulenspiegel (Tyll) **13.** pickel-herring
   (pickle-herring)
buffoonery . . . **6.** japery, pranks **7.** fooling
   8. clownery, drollery, trickery
   9. slapstick **10.** buffoonism
   12. harlequinade
bug (insect) . . . **3.** fly, sow **4.** flea,
   gnat, moth, pill, tick **5.** Anasa,
   aphid, Aphis, cimex, louse **6.** beetle,
   cicada, earwig, locust, mantis, needle,
   scarab, slater, spider, weevil **7.** firefly,
   hexapod, katydid, ladybug, Ranatra,
   termite **8.** chilipod, diplopod, mosquito,
   myriapod **9.** arthropod (jointed),
   centipede, cockroach, lightning,
   millipede, tarantula **10.** silverfish
   11. grasshopper

bug (slang) . . . **3.** nut **4.** bogy, flaw, rage **5.** craze, fault, manis **6.** defect, zealot **7.** bugaboo, bugbear, fanatic, passion **9.** energumen

bugaboo . . . **4.** bogy, ogre, trap (golf)

bugan . . . **5.** ghost **6.** spirit (evil) **9.** hobgoblin

bugger . . . **3.** guy, rat **4.** chap, heel **6.** booger, jasper, wretch

buggy . . . **3.** bus **4.** ga-ga, shay **5.** wagon **6.** cuckoo **7.** caboose, foolish, haywire, vehicle **8.** carriage, demented, infested, stanhope **9.** insectile **10.** insectlike

bug juice . . . **6.** liquor (strong), whisky (inferior)

bugle . . . **3.** iva (ragweed) **4.** bead, call (mating), honk, horn, nose, toot **7.** clarion, trumpet **9.** schnozzle **10.** instrument

bugle call . . . **4.** taps **6.** alerte, sennet (Hist) **7.** retreat, tantara **8.** last post, reveille

build . . . **4.** form, rear **5.** edify, erect, found, frame, raise, shape **6.** create, evolve, figure, nidify **7.** fashion, stature **8.** increase, physique **9.** construct, establish

building . . . **4.** barn, casa, crib, shed, wing **5.** annex, tower **6.** casino, castle, lean-to, making, museum **7.** edifice, factory, forming, rookery, rotunda, theater **8.** creation, dwelling, erecting, erection, tenement **9.** apartment, structure **10.** fashioning, production, skyscraper, storehouse **11.** fabrication

build-up . . . **5.** boost **9.** promotion **11.** advertising **12.** commendation

built . . . **4.** made **6.** formed, shaped **7.** crested, erected **9.** fashioned **10.** fabricated **11.** constructed

bulb . . . **3.** bud **4.** corm, lily, root, sego, stem **5.** onion, swell, tuber, tulip **6.** bulbil, camass, crocus, dahlia **7.** bulblet, globule, rhizome **8.** earthnut

bulbous . . . **5.** round **7.** bulbose, bulging **8.** swelling, tuberous

Bulgaria . . .
capital . . **5.** Sofia
city . . **5.** Varna **6.** Plevna, Sliven **7.** Ruschuk
native . . **6.** Bulgar
origin . . **4.** Slav **9.** Mongolian
river . . **6.** Danube, Marica (Maritsa), Struma

bulge . . . **3.** bow **4.** bump, edge, hump, jump, knob, odds **5.** bilge, bloat, flash, pouch, swell **6.** convex, wallet **7.** vantage **9.** advantage **10.** projection **12.** protuberance

bulk . . . **3.** sum **4.** loom, mass, most, size **6.** extent, staple, volume **7.** bigness, quantum **8.** majority, quantity **9.** dimension, largeness, substance, thickness **11.** massiveness **12.** accumulation **13.** preponderance

bulky . . . **5.** heavy, hulky, stout, thick **6.** clumsy **7.** awkward, lumpish, massive **8.** unwieldy **9.** corpulent, policemen (Eng sl), ponderous **10.** cumbersome, unwielding **11.** substantial

bull . . . **4.** fiat, seal **5.** edict, error, large, ukase **6.** brevet, decree, firman, humbug, letter (papal), market (Finan), rising, Taurus **7.** blunder **8.** nonsense, solecism **9.** Irish bull, policeman **10.** speculator

bull (male animal) . . . **2.** ox **3.** cow **4.** Apis (sacred), stot, toro, zebu **5.** moose, steer, whale **6.** walrus **7.** bullock **8.** elephant, Minotaur, terrapin

bull (slang) . . . **4.** blah, bosh, bunk **5.** hokum **6.** hot air **7.** baloney **8.** buncombe, flimflam

bulla . . . **4.** bleb, boss, case (leather), knob, seal (papal), stud **6.** button **7.** blister, globule, pendant, vesicle **8.** ornament

bulldog . . . **3.** ant **4.** pipe **5.** leech **7.** courage, forceps **8.** barnacle, stubborn, tenacity **9.** newspaper (early), tenacious

bulldoze . . . **3.** cow **5.** bully, grade, level **6.** coerce, harass **7.** buffalo **8.** browbeat **10.** intimidate

bullet . . . **4.** ball (cannon), shot, slug **6.** dumdum, pellet, sinker (angling), tracer **7.** missile

bulletin . . . **5.** brief, flash **6.** notice, record **7.** account, message **8.** newsbill **9.** statement **10.** newsletter, periodical **11.** publication **12.** announcement

bullfighting (pert to) . . .
assistant . . **9.** cuadrilla
bullfighter . . **6.** torero **7.** matador, picador **8.** toreador
dart . . **10.** banderilla
final thrust . . **8.** estocada **13.** moment of truth
maneuver . . **4.** pase **5.** faena **8.** veronica
matador, famed . . **8.** Belmonte, Manolete **10.** El Cordobés
matador's tool . . **4.** capa **6.** muleta
music . . **9.** pasodoble
parade . . **5.** paseo
program, series . . **7.** corrida
shout . . **3.** olé

bullfinch . . . **3.** alp **4.** nope **5.** hedge **11.** pyrrhuloxia **12.** gray grosbeak

Bull Moose . . . **16.** Progressive Party

bullpen (pert to) . . .
camp . . **8.** barracks **9.** enclosure
ice hockey . . **5.** bench (penalty)
ring cell . . **5.** toril
Western US . . **6.** corral

Bull Run (battle) . . . **8.** Manassas

bully . . . **4.** beef **6.** hector, jovial **7.** gleeful, ruffian **8.** browbeat, bulldoze **9.** bulldozer, tormentor **10.** browbeater, intimidate

bulwark . . . **4.** bank **6.** buffer, sconce **7.** barrier, parapet, rampart **8.** abutment, buttress **10.** protection **13.** fortification

bum . . . **3.** beg **5.** idler, revel, rummy, souse, spree **6.** beggar, loafer, tipple, wretch **7.** budmash, moocher, wastrel **8.** blighter, drunkard, vagabond **9.** lazzarone, schnorrer **10.** panhandler

bump . . . **3.** hit, jog **4.** bang, clop, jolt, lump, meet, push, thud **5.** bulge, cahot, crash, crump, knock, lower, plunk, tumor **6.** demote, impact, reduce, strike **7.** collide **8.** demotion, dilation, swelling **9.** air pocket, collision, downgrade

bumpkin . . . **4.** boor, clod, gawk, hick, lout, rube, tike **5.** yokel **6.** farmer, rustic **7.** cauboge, hayseed, hoosier, lumpkin **9.** chawbacon **10.** clodhopper

bumptious . . . **8.** insolent **9.** audacious, insulting **12.** contumelious

bunch . . . **3.** bob, lot, mop, set **4.** pack, tuft, wisp **5.** batch, clump, covey, crowd, flock, grist, group **6.** bundle **7.** cluster, company **8.** assemble, quantity **9.** multitude **10.** congregate

bundle . . . **3.** lot, wad **4.** bale, bolt, hank, pack, send **5.** bluey, bunch, fagot, sheaf, shook **6.** bindle, fardel, fascis, packet, parcel, seroon **7.** fascine, package, rouleau **10.** collection

bung . . . **3.** tap **4.** cork, plug, stop **5.** spile **6.** bruise **7.** contuse, stopper, stopple, tampeon, tampoon **8.** bankrupt, bunghole **9.** falsehood

bungle . . . **3.** err **4.** muff **5.** botch, fudge **6.** bobble, foozle, fumble, tailor (hunting) **7.** blunder

bungling . . . **5.** fudgy **6.** clumsy **7.** awkward, unhandy **8.** botchery **9.** unskilled **10.** blundering, unskillful

bunion . . . **12.** hallux valgus

bunk . . . **3.** bed, kip, rot **4.** blah, brag **5.** abide, berth, couch, dwell, hokum, hooey, sleep **6.** humbug, kibosh **7.** baloney, hogwash **8.** nonsense, tommyrot **9.** cross-beam (logging)

Bunker Hill (Mass) . . . **6.** battle (1775)

bunkum . . . see *buncombe*

Bunsen . . . **4.** cell, disk **5.** flame, valve **6.** burner **9.** Professor (Ger)

bunt . . . **3.** bat, dig, jab, jog, tap **4.** blow, bump, butt, pike, push, tail (Scot) **5.** knock, shove **7.** bunting **10.** propulsion

bunting . . . **4.** flag, hood **5.** flags **6.** banner, pennon **7.** pennant **8.** streamer

bunting (bird) . . . **3.** red **4.** cirl, corn, crow, lark, pape (Creole) **5.** finch **6.** indigo, towhee **7.** cowbird, ortolan **8.** bobolink **12.** yellowhammer

Bunyan (John) **work** . . . **16.** Pilgrim's Progress

Bunyan (Paul) **ox** . . . **4.** Babe, blue

buoy . . . **3.** dan **4.** bell **5.** float **6.** marker **7.** can buoy, nunbuoy **8.** bell buoy, deadhead, life buoy, spar buoy **11.** mooring buoy **12.** breeches buoy **13.** whistling buoy

buoyance, buoyancy . . . **4.** hope, snap **5.** verve **6.** bounce **7.** flotage **9.** lightness **10.** levitation, resilience **12.** floatability **16.** lightheartedness

buoyant . . . **5.** light **7.** elastic **8.** cheerful, floating, levitate, volatile **11.** supernatant **12.** lighthearted, recuperative

bur, burr . . . **3.** nut **5.** thorn **8.** adherent (see also *burr*)

burble . . . **6.** muddle **7.** confuse, trouble **8.** disorder

burbot . . . **4.** ling, Lota **7.** eelpout

burden . . . **3.** key, tax **4.** birn, care, cark, clog, lade, load, note, onus, task, tone **5.** cargo, cross, music, tenor, voice

6. charge, cumber, hamper, saddle, weight **7.** bourdon, freight, oppress, payload, refrain **8.** capacity, overload, pressure **10.** impediment, imposition **11.** encumbrance

burdensome . . . **5.** heavy **7.** arduous, massive, onerous, weighty **8.** unwieldy **9.** difficult, laborious, ponderous **10.** cumbersome, oppressive **11.** troublesome **12.** impedimental

bureau . . . **4.** desk, shop **6.** office **7.** dresser **8.** chambers **10.** chiffonier, department

bureaucracy . . . **10.** government **11.** directorate, officialdom, officialism

burgeon . . . **3.** bud **4.** grow **5.** gemma, shoot, sprit **6.** sprout

burglar . . . **4.** yegg **5.** thief **9.** cracksman **11.** safecracker **12.** housebreaker

burglary . . . **5.** theft **6.** burgle **7.** larceny, robbery **8.** stealage **13.** housebreaking

burgle . . . **3.** rob **8.** burglary **10.** burglarize

burgomaster . . . **5.** mayor **7.** alcalde **10.** magistrate **11.** burghmaster

burgoo, burgout . . . **4.** stew **5.** gruel **7.** pudding (oatmeal) **8.** porridge

burial . . . **5.** inurn **7.** funeral **9.** interment, sepulture **10.** engulfment, inhumation, submersion **11.** concealment, submergence

burial ground . . . **4.** pyre **5.** grave **6.** barrow **7.** tumulus **8.** bone yard, catacomb, cemetery, golgotha **9.** graveyard **10.** churchyard, necropolis **11.** polyandrium **12.** potter's field

burlesque . . . **3.** fun **4.** jest **5.** farce, comic **6.** parody, review, satire **7.** mimicry, mockery, overact, take-off **8.** burletta, doggerel, ridicule, travesty **9.** charivari, imitation, travestie **10.** caricatura, caricature **13.** entertainment

Burlingame Treaty . . . **11.** Immigration (Chin 1868)

burly . . . **3.** fat **5.** bulky, large, noble, obese, stout **6.** brawny **7.** stately **8.** imposing, stalwart **9.** corpulent, excellent

Burma, Burmese . . .
alphabet . . **4.** Pali
capital (anc) . . **3.** Ava **4.** Pegu
capital, modern . . **6.** Yangon **7.** Rangoon
city . . **8.** Mandalay
dagger . . **3.** dah (dhao)
gibbon . . **3.** lar
girl . . **4.** mima
monk . . **2.** bo
native . . **3.** Lai
people . . **3.** Mon, Tai **4.** Laos, Shan **7.** Siamese
relation . . **5.** Thais (Tais) **6.** Malays **7.** Chinese **8.** Tibetans **10.** Mongolians
religion . . **8.** Buddhism
robber . . **6.** dacoit
shed (public) . . **5.** zayat
viol . . **4.** turr (3-stringed)

Burma Road . . . **6.** Lashio (to China, 1938--1942, replaced by Ledo Rd)

burn . . . **3.** dry, tan **4.** char, fire, glow, hurt, pain, sear, sere **5.** blaze, brand, brook, cense, flame, scald, singe **6.** ignite, injury, scorch **7.** cremate, encauma,

flicker, sunburn, swelter, torrefy
9. cauterize, sacrifice **10.** incandesce, incinerate
burner . . . **3.** jet **4.** lamp **5.** torch
6. Bunsen, candle, censer (incense)
7. cresset **9.** blowtorch **10.** lucubrator
11. incinerator
burning . . . **3.** hot **4.** fire, pain, sore
5. afire, angry, ardor, arson, blaze, fiery, flame **6.** ablaze, ardent, fervid **7.** blazing, cautery, excited, fervent, flaming, glowing, shining, zealous **8.** eloquent, feverish, inustion **9.** cremating, cremation, execution **10.** combustion, ustulation **13.** conflagration
burning place . . . **4.** ghat **9.** crematory
10. cinerarium
burnish . . . **3.** rub **4.** buff **5.** glaze, gloss, shine **6.** patina, polish
burnt . . . **3.** red **5.** dried **6.** burned, seared, singed **7.** charred **8.** hardened, scorched, sunburnt **9.** blistered, sunburned
burnt (pert to) . . .
art . . **11.** pygrography, pyrogravure
color . . **4.** rose **5.** ocher, topaz **6.** almond, orange, russet, sienna **8.** amethyst
sugar . . **7.** caramel
burn with anger, excitement . . . **4.** fume
5. smoke **6.** seethe, simmer, sizzle
7. smolder
burp . . . **5.** belch, eruct **8.** eructate
burr . . . **3.** cut, hem **4.** buzz, whir
5. brier, drone, gnarl, knurl, thorn
6. brogue, corona (moon), meatus (ear)
7. bramble, clotbur, prickle, silique, sticker **8.** excavate, follicle **9.** cocklebur, whetstone
burro . . . **3.** ass **4.** jack **5.** cuddy, neddy
6. dickey, donkey **7.** jackass
burrow . . . **3.** dig **4.** abri, hide, hole, lair, mine **5.** couch (otter's), lodge (beaver's) **6.** search, tunnel **7.** shelter
burrowing . . . **9.** effodient, fossorial
11. lithodomous (in rock)
burrowing animal . . . **4.** mole, peba
5. poyou **6.** peludo **8.** suricate
9. armadillo
burst . . . **3.** pop **4.** bang, rend **5.** blast, blaze, break, broke, erupt, flare, flash, shots, spurt **6.** volley **7.** explode, flare-up, gunfire, implode **8.** outbreak, outburst, ruptured **9.** discharge, explosion, fractured **10.** detonation
11. dissiliency
burst (forth) . . . **4.** grow **5.** erupt, sally
6. sprout
burst (pert to) . . .
applause . . **5.** éclat, hands **7.** ovation, plaudit **8.** clapping
cheers . . **5.** salvo
gunfire . . **6.** rafale
laughter . . **3.** fit **4.** peal, roar
10. convulsion
temper . . **4.** rage **5.** scene, storm
7. passion **9.** explosion
bursting . . . **4.** full **7.** brimful, crammed, excited, replete **8.** overfull, thrilled, volcanic **9.** explosive, surfeited
10. detonating **11.** impassioned, overflowing, overwhelmed

bury . . . **4.** hide, sink **5.** cache, cover, inter, inurn, plant, stash **6.** engulf, entomb, inhume **7.** conceal, embosom, repress, secrete **8.** submerge **9.** overwhelm, sepulture
bus . . . **6.** jitney **7.** omnibus **10.** motor coach
bush . . . **3.** tod **4.** shag (hair) **5.** brush, plain, shrub, wahoo, wilds **6.** branch, lining **7.** boscage, bushing **8.** bushveld, woodland **10.** hinterland
bushed . . . **4.** beat **5.** all in **6.** pooped
7. baffled **8.** dog-tired **9.** exhausted, nonplused, perplexed, played out
10. nonplussed
bushel . . . **3.** foo **4.** full **6.** basket, vessel
7. measure (dry) **8.** imperial, standard
10. Winchester
Bushido (Jap) . . . **11.** code of honor
bushing . . . **4.** bush **6.** lining, sleeve (mach) **7.** bearing, padding (piano)
Bushman . . . **3.** San **4.** Saan **5.** nomad, pygmy **6.** Abatua, rustic **8.** woodsman
9. aborigine
bushmaster . . . **5.** snake
bushwhacker . . . **7.** pioneer **8.** guerilla
10. forerunner **11.** bushfighter, voortrekker **12.** frontiersman
bushy . . . **5.** hairy, thick, woody
6. dumose, shaggy, woodsy **7.** hirsute, scrubby, shrubby
business . . . **3.** job **4.** firm, game, line, work **5.** craft, house, trade **6.** affair, career, matter, racket **7.** calling, company, concern, pursuit
8. commerce, industry, interest, practice, vocation **10.** enterprise, occupation, proceeding, profession
11. transaction **13.** establishment
business (pert to) . . .
agreement . . **6.** cartel
businesslike . . **11.** pragmatical
customer . . **6.** patron
cycle . . **9.** recession **10.** depression, prosperity **11.** liquidation
deal . . **4.** turn **9.** operation
11. negotiation, transaction
Exchange . . **4.** bank **5.** Bolsa **6.** Bourse
11. stock market
man . . **6.** tycoon **8.** salesman **9.** solicitor
place . . **4.** mart, shop **5.** store **6.** office, shoppe **8.** Exchange
bust . . . **4.** bang, fail, hand (Bridge), tame (bronco) **5.** burst, chest, crash, flunk, spree **6.** breast, figure **7.** degrade, explode, failure **8.** collapse, demotion, fracture **9.** sculpture **10.** bankruptcy
bustard . . . **4.** bird (Old World), kori, Otis
5. goose, paauw **6.** curlew **8.** Otididae
busted . . . **4.** flat **5.** broke **6.** broken, failed, ruined **7.** severed **8.** bankrupt, ruptured, strapped **9.** insolvent, penniless
10. stone-broke
bustle . . . **3.** ado **4.** fuss, stir, to-do
5. haste, whirl **6.** flurry, hubbub, hustle, pother, scurry, tumult **7.** bluster, ferment, fluster, scamper, turmoil
8. activity **9.** agitation, commotion
10. excitement, hurly-burly
11. disturbance
bustling . . . **6.** active **7.** hurried, rushing

8. eventful, stirring

busy . . . 4. nosy, work 5. drive 6. active, devote, employ, engage, occupy 7. engaged, on the go, operose 8. diligent, employed, meddling, occupied, on the run, sedulous 9. assiduous, attentive, laborious, officious 10. meddlesome 11. industrious, inquisitive, persevering

busy . . . 4. dick 6. gossip 7. gumshoe, meddler 8. busybody, flatfoot 9. detective

busybody . . . 6. gossip 8. quidnunc 9. pragmatic

but . . . 2. ma 3. yet 4. even, just, mere, save 5. hence, outer, still 6. except 7. however, without 10. regardless 12. nevertheless 15. notwithstanding

butcher . . . 3. fly (angling), mar 4. kill, slay 5. botch, spoil 6. killer, vendor 7. croaker, meatman 8. merchant, train-boy 9. slaughter 11. slaughterer 12. bloodshedder

butchery . . . 6. murder 7. carnage 8. business, massacre, shambles 9. slaughter 14. slaughterhouse

butt . . . 3. aim, end, jut, pit, ram, tun, tup 4. buck, bunt, cart, cask, goat, rump, stub 5. cigar, hinge, joint, mound, piece, stump 6. target (archery), thrust (fencing) 7. buttock, parapet, project 8. flatfish 9. cigarette 13. laughingstock

butter . . . 3. pat 4. coat, ghee (ghi), oleo 5. smear 6. bedaub, spread 7. butyric 8. flattery 9. margarine, suaveness 10. semiliquid 13. oleomargarine

butter-and-eggs . . . 8. flaxweed, ranstead, toadflax

buttercup fruit . . . 6. achene 7. crowtoe

butterfingered . . . 6. clumsy 7. awkward, unhandy 8. bungling, careless 9. all thumbs 10. blundering

butterflies (slang) . . . 6. nerves 7. fidgets, jitters

butterfly (pert to) . . .
American . . 7. viceroy
family . . 10. Agapetidae 11. Rhopalocera
genus . . 7. Lycaena 11. Lepidoptera
large . . 7. monarch
larva . . 11. caterpillar
lily . . 4. sego 8. mariposa
peacock . . 2. io 7. buckeye
swallowtail . . 5. black, tiger, zebra
type . . 4. moth 5. satyr 10. fritillary, silverspot

buttocks . . . 4. butt (vulgar), hips, rear, rump, seat 5. fanny, podex 6. bottom 8. haunches, maneuver (wrestling) 9. backsides, posterior

buttress . . . 4. pier, pile, prop, stay 5. brace, tower 7. shelter, support 8. abutment 10. projection, strengthen 11. counterfort 13. fortification

buttress (Arch) . . . 4. pier 6. flying 7. hanging

buxom . . . 3. gay 4. boon, rosy 5. jolly, plump 6. blithe, jocund, jovial 7. gleeful

buy . . . 5. bribe 6. accept, redeem 7. bargain, expiate 8. purchase

buy back . . . 6. redeem

Buyer Beware . . . 12. Caveat Emptor

buzz . . . 3. hum, saw 5. rumor, snore 6. bustle, murmur, rumble 7. ferment, whisper 9. fricative, murmuring 10. sibilation

buzzard . . . 4. aura (turkey), hawk, pern 5. buteo 6. osprey, stupid 7. harrier 9. dorbeetle, senseless 10. cockchafer

buzz bomb . . . 9. doodlebug 10. bumblebomb 14. Chase-Me-Charlie

bwana (Afr) . . . 4. boss 6. master

by . . . 2. at, in, on 3. ago, bei, par, per, via 4. away, gone, near, over, pass (bridge), past, with 5. after, aside 6. beside, beyond, nearby, toward 7. abreast, close by, through 9. in reserve

by-and-by . . . 4. anon, soon 5. later, sweet 6. mañana 7. betimes, bientôt, ere long, shortly 8. directly 9. presently 11. tout à l'heure

by birth . . . 3. nee

bygone . . . 3. ago 4. lost, over, past 6. buried, bypast, gone by, passed 7. elapsed, extinct 8. departed, preterit (preterite)

byname . . . 6. eponym 7. babyism, epithet, surname 8. cognomen, monicker, nickname 9. sobriquet 10. patronymic 11. appellation

bypass . . . 4. go by, miss 5. byway, elude 6. byroad, detour, escape 7. deviate, digress 8. side path 10. circumvent, roundabout

By the Grace of God . . . 9. Dei Gratia

byword . . . 3. mot, saw 5. adage, maxim 6. byname, phrase, saying, slogan 7. adagium, parable, proverb 8. aphorism, nickname, reproach 9. catchword, sobriquet 10. shibboleth

by word of mouth . . . 4. oral 5. parol (parole)

Byzantine Empire . . .
architecture . . 7. St Marks (Venice) 9. elaborate
bookbinding . . 9. unadorned (earlier) 10. bejewelled (later)
church . . 7. Eastern
city . . 14. Constantinople (Istanbul)
creator . . 11. Constantine (the Great)
historian . . 9. Procopius 11. Anna Comnena
poetry . . 5. hymns
scepter . . 6. ferula
writer . . 6. Prazes 7. Priscus, Romanus

Byzantium . . . 14. Constantinople (Istanbul)

C

C . . . **4.** clef **7.** cedilla, century, hundred, keynote
caama . . . **3.** fox **4.** asse **10.** hartebeest
cab . . . **4.** pony, taxi **7.** measure, purloin, shelter, taxicab, vehicle **8.** carriage (anc) **9.** cabriolet **10.** locomotive (part) **11.** translation
cabal . . . **4.** clan, plot **5.** group, junta, party **7.** chatter, complot, coterie, dispute, faction **8.** intrigue **9.** camarilla, collusion, Committee **10.** complicity, conspiracy
cabala . . . **7.** mystery **9.** mystic art, occultism
cabalessou . . . **9.** armadillo (giant)
cabalistic . . . **6.** occult **7.** cabalic **8.** abstract, anagogic, esoteric, mystical **10.** mysterious
caballeria . . . **7.** measure (land) **8.** chivalry **10.** knighthood
caballero . . . **5.** lover, rider **6.** knight **8.** cavalier, horseman **9.** chevalier, gentleman **10.** equestrian
caballo . . . **5.** horse
cabaret . . . **3.** inn **4.** cafe **6.** hostel, posado, tavern **7.** barroom **9.** night club, roadhouse **11.** café dansant **13.** entertainment
cabbage . . . **3.** kos (cos) **4.** cole, kale, palm **5.** colza, savoy **7.** collard **8.** colewort, kohlrabi **11.** cauliflower **15.** Brussels sprouts
cabbage (pert to) . . .
  curly leaf . . **5.** savoy
  daisy . . **11.** globeflower
  fermented . . **5.** kraut
  headless . . **4.** kale
  salad . . **4.** slaw
  seed . . **5.** colza
  slang . . **4.** crib, fool **6.** pilfer **7.** fathead, purloin **9.** numbskull **11.** cabbagehead, knucklehead
  species . . **8.** Brassica
  tree . . **4.** palm **7.** angelin **8.** palmetto
  white . . **9.** butterfly
  yellows . . **7.** disease (destructive)
caber . . . **4.** apar, beam, pole **6.** rafter, timber
cabin . . . **3.** hut **4.** shed **5.** booth, coach (Naut), house, hovel, lodge, shack **6.** cabana, saloon **7.** caboose **10.** blockhouse
cabinet . . . **3.** box, den **4.** Body, buhl, case **6.** bureau, closet, office **7.** almirah, boudoir, council, étagère, whatnot **8.** cellaret, cupboard, ministry **9.** committee
cable . . . **4.** boom, cord, rope, wire **5.** chain, twine **6.** fasten, hawser **7.** coaxial, measure, molding, ropeway **8.** telegram **9.** cablegram
cable (pert to) . . .
  car . . **7.** telpher
  holder (Naut) . . **7.** wildcat **10.** cable wheel

  post . . **4.** bitt
cabling . . . **9.** rudenture
cabochon . . . **5.** jewel, stone (uncut), style (convex cut) **8.** ornament
caboodle . . . **3.** all, kit, lot **5.** bunch, whole **10.** collection **14.** kit and caboodle
caboose . . . **3.** car (RR) **5.** buggy **6.** galley **7.** kitchen **9.** deckhouse
cabotin . . . **5.** actor (strolling) **9.** charlatan
cachaca . . . **3.** rum (white)
cache . . . **4.** hide, hole **5.** stash, store **7.** conceal, hide-out, retreat **8.** hideaway **10.** storehouse
cachet . . . **4.** seal **5.** sigil, stamp, wafer **6.** signet **7.** capsule
cachilla . . . **8.** white man
cachot . . . **7.** dungeon
cackle . . . **3.** gab **4.** cank, chat, crow, talk **5.** clack, laugh, prate **6.** babble, gabble, giggle, gossip, jabber **7.** chatter, prattle **8.** laughter
cacodemon . . . **4.** deva **5.** devil, fiend, Indra **10.** evil spirit
cacology . . . **10.** bad diction, corruption (speech) **16.** mispronunciation
cacophonous . . . **7.** raucous **8.** jangling, strident **9.** diaphonic, dissonant **10.** discordant **11.** unmelodious
cacophony . . . **5.** clash **6.** jangle **7.** discord **8.** diaphony (Mus) **9.** harshness **10.** dissodence
cactus . . . **4.** bleo **5.** agave **6.** chaute, cholla, mescal **7.** Opuntia, saguaro **8.** fishhook **9.** Turk's-head **11.** prickly pear **12.** Echinocactus
cad . . . **4.** boor, chum, heel, hick **5.** yokel **6.** mucker **7.** bounder, servant **8.** townsman **9.** scoundrel, vulgarian
cadaver . . . **4.** body (dead) **5.** stiff **6.** corpse **7.** carcass **8.** skeleton
cadaverous . . . **4.** pale **5.** gaunt, lurid **6.** sickly, wasted **7.** ghastly, haggard **9.** emaciated **10.** attenuated, corpselike
caddis (pert to) . . .
  bait . . **3.** fly **4.** worm **5.** cadew
  material . . **4.** yarn **5.** twill **6.** crewel **7.** worsted
  worm . . **5.** larva (aquatic)
caddle . . . **4.** fuss **5.** annoy, worry **6.** gossip **7.** confuse, trouble **8.** disarray **9.** confusion
cade . . . **3.** keg, oil (Med), pet **4.** cask, lamb (orphan) **6.** barrel, coddle, petted
cadeau . . . **4.** gift
cadence . . . **4.** beat, lilt, tone **5.** meter **6.** rhythm **7.** balance **9.** free verse, vers libre **10.** modulation
cadence . . . **4.** half **5.** trill **6.** plagal **7.** perfect **9.** authentic, deceptive, imperfect, suspended **11.** interrupted
cadency (Her) . . . **4.** rose **5.** label **6.** mullet **7.** annulet, martlet **8.** crescent **10.** fleur-de-lis **11.** cross moline
cadenza . . . **7.** cadence **8.** flourish
cadet . . . **3.** son **4.** pleb **5.** color (blue),

youth **6.** junior **10.** midshipman

cadge . . . **3.** beg **4.** hawk **5.** fakir, mooch **6.** beggar, hawker, mumper, peddle, sponge, vendor **7.** carrier, moocher, sponger **8.** huckster, sannyasi

cadgy . . . **6.** wanton **7.** lustful **8.** cheerful, mirthful

Cadmus (pert to) . . .
daughter . . **3.** Ino **6.** Semele
father . . **6.** Agenor
founder of . . **6.** Thebes (Boetia)
sister . . **6.** Europa
wife . . **8.** Harmonia

cadre . . . **4.** list, unit **5.** frame, panel **6.** line-up, roster, scheme **8.** cadastre, register, schedule, skeleton **9.** framework

caduceus (Gr Antiq) . . . **4.** wand (Hermes') **5.** staff **6.** symbol **8.** insignia (Med Corps)

Caesar (pert to) . . .
betrayer . . **6.** Brutus
colleague . . **7.** Bibulus
death site . . **4.** Nola
Emperor, Dictator of . . **4.** Rome
fatal day . . **4.** Ides (of March) **11.** Ides of March
language . . **5.** Latin
rival . . **6.** Pompey
river . . **7.** Rubicon
sister . . **4.** Atia
uncle . . **11.** Caius Marius
wife . . **8.** Cornelia

caesura, cesura . . . **4.** rest **5.** break, colon, comma, pause **8.** interval **12.** interruption

cafard . . . **5.** bigot, blues **6.** humbug **9.** hypocrite **10.** depression

café . . . **5.** coffe **6.** coffee **10.** restaurant **11.** coffeehouse

café (pert to) . . .
au lait . . **5.** brown **6.** alesan **10.** French nude
creme . . **5.** suede (color)
noir . . **4.** musk (color) **11.** black coffee
parfait . . **8.** beverage

cafetière . . . **9.** coffeepot **10.** percolator

caffeine . . . **6.** coffee, theine (in tea) **8.** alkaloid **9.** stimulant

cafila . . . **7.** caravan (camel)

cage . . . **3.** mew, pen **4.** coop **6.** corral **7.** confine, goal net, impound **8.** goal post

cagey . . . **3.** sly **4.** foxy, wary, wily **5.** canny, leery **6.** artful, crafty, shifty, shrews **7.** cunning, evasive, knowing

Cain (pert to) . . .
brother . . **4.** Abel
founder of . . **5.** Enoch (1st city)
Land of . . **3.** Nod
slayer of . . **4.** Abel
son . . **5.** Enoch

cairn . . . **4.** heap (stones) **6.** menhir **8.** catstone (catstane), landmark, memorial, monument

Cairo . . .
capital . . **5.** Egypt
city gate (famed) . . **9.** Bab-el-Nasr
mosque . . **12.** Sultan Hassan
resident . . **7.** Cairene
river . . **4.** Nile
seaport . . **10.** Alexandria

tomb . . **10.** Mehemet Ali
warrior . . **9.** Rameses II

caisson . . . **3.** box **4.** case **5.** chest, wagon **7.** chamber

caitiff . . . **4.** base, mean, vile **6.** coward, wicked, wretch **7.** budmash, captive **10.** despicable

cajole . . . **4.** coax, urge **5.** cheat, jolly **6.** delude **7.** flatter, palaver, sweeten, wheedle **8.** blandish **9.** importune **10.** honeyfogle

Cajun (pert to) . . .
descent . . **6.** French (Canadian)
dialect . . **5.** Cajun
home (present) . . **9.** Louisiana
native of . . **6.** Acadia (Nova Scotia)

cake . . . **3.** bun, wig **4.** bake, food, lump, mass, wigg **5.** batty, block, crust, solid, torte, wafer **6.** gateau, harden **7.** bannock, congeal, oatcake, pancake **8.** corn pone, solidify **9.** charlotte, simpleton **11.** griddle-cake

cake (pert to) . . .
almond paste . . **7.** ratafia
corn . . **4.** pone
flat . . **7.** placent
fried . . **7.** cruller **8.** doughnut
Lenten . . **6.** cimbal, simnel
Scotch . . **4.** farl (farle) **5.** scone
unleavened . . **8.** tortilla

Cake Day (Scot) . . . **8.** hogmanay (New Year's)

calabar bean . . . **6.** myotic, ordeal **7.** eserine **8.** alkaloid **13.** physostigmine

calabash . . . **5.** gourd **6.** baobab, bronze (color)

calaboose . . . **4.** gaol, jail **5.** choky, clink **6.** bagnio, lockup, prison **8.** bastille, calabozo **9.** Bridewell

calamitous . . . **3.** sad **4.** dire, evil **5.** black **6.** tragic, woeful **7.** adverse, baleful, ruinous, unhappy **8.** grievous, tragical, wretched **10.** afflictive, deplorable, disastrous **11.** cataclysmic, destructive, distressful, unfortunate **12.** catastrophic

calamity . . . **4.** blow, evil, ruin **5.** wrack **6.** mishap **7.** tragedy **8.** casualty, disaster, distress, fatality **9.** adversity **10.** affliction, misfortune **11.** catastrophe, direfulness, unhappiness **12.** wretchedness

calathiform . . . **9.** cup-shaped

calcarea . . . **5.** coral **7.** sponges

calceiform . . . **10.** orchidlike **13.** clipper-shaped

calcitrant . . . **8.** stubborn **12.** recalcitrant

calcitrate . . . **4.** boot, kick **6.** oppose

calculate . . . **3.** aim **4.** deem, rate, tell **5.** allow, count, frame, judge, score, tally, think **6.** cipher, deduce, figure, gather, number, reckon **7.** average, compute, suppose **8.** conclude, estimate **9.** determine, enumerate

calculated . . . **7.** advised, studied, weighed **8.** measured **10.** considered, deliberate **11.** intentional **12.** contemplated

calculating . . . **8.** plotting, scheming **9.** computing, designing, judicious **10.** estimating, numerative, reflecting, thoughtful **11.** circumspect, considerate

14. discriminative
calculator . . . **5.** table **6.** abacus **7.** suan
pan (swan pan, Chin) **8.** computer
9. estimator, tabulator **10.** parimutuel
11. Comptometer, totalizator
caldron, cauldron . . . **3.** pot, red (color),
vat **6.** boiler, kettle, mortar, retort
7. alembic **8.** crucible
Caleb (pert to) . . .
daughter . . **7.** Achsaph
literally . . **3.** dog
son . . **3.** Hur, Iru
spy of . . **6.** Canaan
calèche . . . **7.** vehicle (Quebec)
Caledonia (anc) . . . **8.** Scotland
Caledonia bird . . . **4.** kagu
Caledonian . . . **5.** brown **6.** Scotch
8. Scotsman, Scottish
calefacient . . . **4.** warm **6.** remedy
7. heating **11.** calefactory
calendar . . . **4.** list, Ordo **5.** index, slate
6. docket, line-up, record **7.** almanac,
calends (kalends), program **8.** register,
schedule **9.** catalogue, ephemeris
10. chronology, prospectus
calendar (type) . . . **5.** Roman, Swiss
6. Jewish, Julian **7.** Chinese
9. Cotsworth, Gregorian, perpetual
13. International (fixed)
calenture . . . **4.** glow **5.** ardor, fever
7. passion, pyrexia **9.** febrility, sunstroke
calepin . . . **4.** book (ref) **7.** lexicon
10. dictionary
calf . . . **3.** leg (part) **4.** dolt, fool, skin
6. bovine, island, weaner **7.** iceberg,
leather **9.** youngling
calf (pert to) . . .
flesh . . **4.** veal
hide . . **3.** kip
leg (part) . . **5.** sural
motherless . . **5.** dogie **8.** maverick
sweetbread . . **9.** ris de veau
time . . **5.** youth
Caliban (pert to) . . .
character . . **5.** brute, slave (The Tempest)
deity . . **7.** Setebos
mother . . **7.** Sycorax (witch)
caliber, calibre . . . **4.** bore **7.** ability
calico . . . **4.** dame **5.** cloth **6.** salloo
8. goldfish **12.** multicolored
calico (pert to) . . .
bird . . **9.** turnstone
bush . . **6.** laurel
horse, pony . . **5.** pinto **7.** piebald
printing . . **4.** teer **7.** topical
calid . . . **3.** hot **4.** mild, warm **6.** genial
7. burning, thermal
California . . .
bay . . **8.** Monterey
capital . . **10.** Sacramento
city . . **6.** Fresno **7.** Oakland **8.** San Diego,
Stockton **9.** Long Beach **10.** Los Angeles
12. San Francisco, Santa Barbara
desert . . **6.** Mojave **8.** Colorado
discoverer . . **6.** Cortez (1535)
fault . . **10.** San Andreas
flower . . **5.** poppy
history . . **8.** Gold Rush (1848), Missions
11. Sutter's Mill
lake . . **5.** Tahoe **8.** Elsinore **9.** Salton
Sea

lowest point . . **11.** Death Valley
missionary . . **5.** Serra
mountain . . **6.** Lassen, Shasta **7.** Whitney
river . . **4.** Kern **7.** Feather, Russian
10. Sacramento
pageant . . **10.** Rose Parade
17. Tournament of Roses
State admission . . **11.** thirty-first
State motto . . **6.** Eureka
State nickname . . **6.** Golden
State tree . . **7.** redwood
wine region . . **4.** Napa
caliph, calif . . . **3.** Ali (4th) **4.** Imam
(Imaum), Omar **6.** Othman **7.** Abu Bekr
8. Islamite
Caliph Ali's descendants . . . **5.** Alids
(Alides)
caliphate . . . **7.** Omniads, Shiites
(Sectaries) **8.** Idrisids **9.** Fatimites
calk, caulk . . . **4.** copy, plug, stop **5.** close,
sleep (Naut sl) **6.** calque, catnap,
chinse, plug up, stop up **7.** occlude
call . . . **3.** bid, cry, dub, hip, nod **4.** ahoy,
beck, dial, name, plea, ring, soho,
sook (hog), taps, term, yell **5.** alarm,
basis, cause, clepe, rally, rouse,
shout, style, visit, waken **6.** appeal,
beckon, demand, ground, invoke,
motive, muster, option, reason, sennet,
signal, slogan, summon **7.** appoint,
bidding, collect, convoke, fanfare,
summons, trumpet **8.** assemble,
nominate, occasion, reveille **9.** battle
cry, challenge, designate, induction,
telephone, watchword **10.** denominate,
invitation **11.** recruitment, requisition
12. conscription **13.** justification
call (pert to) . . .
attention . . **6.** direct, remind **8.** point
out
back . . **6.** recall, recant, repeal, revive,
revoke **7.** retract **8.** remember
9. recollect
down . . **6.** invoke **7.** bawl out, reprove,
tell off
evil upon . . **8.** execrate
forth . . **5.** evoke, rouse **6.** elicit, excite,
induce, prompt, summon
names . . **4.** cite **5.** abuse, curse **6.** insult,
revile, vilify **8.** besmirch **10.** vituperate
together . . **6.** muster, summon
7. convoke
to mind . . **4.** cite **8.** remember **9.** visualize
callant, callan . . . **3.** boy, lad **4.** chap
5. youth **6.** fellow, garcon, laddie
8. customer, muchacho
11. hobbledehoy
calle . . . **6.** street
called . . . **5.** named **6.** dubbed, y-clept,
yermed **7.** y-cleped
calling . . . **3.** art, nod **4.** beck, lure,
name, work **5.** trade **6.** career, metier,
naming, outcry **7.** bidding, mission,
pursuit, styling, summons **8.** biddance,
business, labeling (labelling), practice,
vocation **9.** condition, evocation
10. employment, invitation, occupation,
profession **13.** circumstances
calling crab . . . **7.** fiddler
calling hare . . . **4.** pika
Calliope . . . **4.** Muse (poet) **5.** organ

8. asteroid
Calliope's son . . . 7. Orpheus
callous, calloused . . . 4. horn, sear
   5. horny, inure 6. harden, seared
   8. hardened 9. heartless, indurated,
   unfeeling 10. impervious
   11. hardhearted 12. thick-skinned
   14. pachydermatous
callow . . . 5. crude, green 6. tender,
   unripe, vernal 7. budding 8. immature,
   unformed 9. unfledged 10. unseasoned
   11. undeveloped 15. unsophisticated
callus . . . 6. tyloma
calm . . . 3. lay 4. cool, dill, fair, lull, mild
   5. allay, balmy, peace, quiet, sober,
   still 6. becalm, hushed, pacify, placid,
   sedate, serene, smooth, soothe, steady
   7. appease, compose, halcyon, orderly,
   pacific, placate, restful, unmoved
   8. peaceful, tranquil 9. quiescent,
   unruffled 10. phlegmatic 11. tranquilize,
   undisturbed 13. dispassionate,
   imperturbable
calmant, calmative . . . 7. anodyne,
   soother 8. lenitive, pacifier, sedative,
   soothing 10. depressant, palliative
   11. alleviative 12. tranquilizer
calmato (Mus) . . . 4. calm 8. tranquil
calmness . . . 4. calm, lull 5. peace, poise,
   quiet 6. repose 8. quietude, serenity
   9. composure, placidity 10. equanimity,
   quiescence 11. restfulness, self-control
calor . . . 4. heat 5. therm 7. thermal
calorifics . . . 4. heat 7. heating
calumet . . . 9. peace pipe
calumniate . . . 4. slur 5. belie, libel
   6. accuse, malign, revile 7. asperse,
   slander, traduce 9. blaspheme
calumnious . . . 7. abusive 8. derisive,
   insolent, libelous 9. insulting
   10. defamatory, derogatory, slanderous
   11. maledictory, opprobrious
calumny . . . 5. abuse 7. lampoon, slander
   9. contumely 10. detraction, scurrility
   11. malediction 12. vilification
calvary . . . 8. crucifix
Calvary (Bib) . . . 8. Damascus, Golgotha
   9. Jerusalem
Calvinism (pert to) . . .
   author . . 6. Calvin
   doctrine . . 5. Grace 9. Atonement,
   Depravity (total) 12. Perseverance (of
   Saints) 14. Predestination
   site . . 6. Geneva
Calvinistic Methodist . . . 5. Welsh
   10. Whitefield 14. Lady Huntingdon
Calypso . . . 6. Ogygia (home) 8. Cytherea,
   sea nymph (The Odyssey)
calyx . . . 3. cup 4. husk 5. galea, sepal
   6. corona 7. corolla 8. epicalyx, perianth
camarada . . . 7. comrade, partner
   9. companion
camaraderie . . . 8. good will
   11. familiarity 14. good-fellowship
camarilla . . . 5. cabal 6. clique 7. council
camata . . . 6. acorns 8. oak fruit
cambist . . . 6. banker, broker 9. financier
   11. moneylender 12. money-changer
Cambodia . . .
   capital . . 6. Angkor 8. Pnom-Penh
   king . . 8. Sihanouk

language . . 5. Khmer 9. Cambodian
name, former . . 9. Kampuchea
religion . . 8. Buddhism
Cambria . . . 5. Wales
Cambridge University (pert to) . . .
   English examination . . 6. tripos
   English student . . 5. sizar 6. optime
   (honor)
   Massachusetts . . 3. MIT 7. Harvard
camel . . . 4. oont 5. llama 6. deloul,
   mammal, vicuna 7. Camelus 8. Bactrian
   (2-humped) 9. Camelidae, dromedary
camel hair shawl . . . 8. cashmere
camelopard . . . 7. giraffe 13. constellation
Camelot . . . 6. legend 10. King Arthur,
   palace site, Round Table
cameo . . . 4. onyx 7. relievo 8. anaglyph
camera type . . . 5. Kodak 7. Brownie
   10. Rollieflex
Cameroon . . .
   capital . . 7. Yaounde (Afr)
   native . . 4. Sara
   people . . 3. Abo 5. Bantu
   river . . 5. Shari
   seaport . . 6. Douala
Camino Real (Calif) . . . 9. Royal Road
   12. El Camino Real, King's Highway
Camorra (It) . . . 12. organization (secret)
camouflage . . . 7. falsify 8. disguise
   9. dissemble 10. false front
   12. misrepresent
camp . . . 4. clan, tent 5. abode, etape,
   junto, tabor 6. campoo, clique, laager
   7. bivouac, faction 10. encampment
campaign . . . 5. serve 7. crusade
   9. operation
camphorated tincture of opium . . .
   9. paregoric
campus . . . 4. quad 5. field (academic)
can . . . 3. jar, may, tin 6. hopper,
   vessel 7. capable 8. canister, conserve
   9. competent 10. receptacle
can . . . 5. skill 7. ability 9. competent
   10. receptacle
can (sl) . . . 3. jug, tin 4. boot, bump,
   fire, jail, john, kick 6. bounce, cooler,
   toilet 7. dismiss 9. discharge 11. give
   the gate
Canaan . . . 9. Palestine 12. Promised
   Land
Canada . . . see also *Canadian*
   capital (Federal) . . 6. Ottawa
   city . . 7. Toronto 8. Hamilton, Montreal,
   Winnipeg 9. Vancouver
   discoverer . . 9. John Cabot (1497)
   Hudson's Bay Co. . . 8. fur trade
   native . . 6. French 7. English
   nickname . . 6. Canuck
   park . . 6. Jasper
   peninsula . . 5. Gaspé
   police . . 8. Mounties 12. Royal Mounted
   (7,000)
   river . . 5. Peace, Slave 6. Fraser, Nelson,
   Ottawa 8. Gatineau 9. Athabasca,
   Churchill, Mackenzie 10. St Lawrence
Canadian (pert to) . . .
   flour . . 6. Shorts (milling) 8. canaille
   jay . . 9. moose bird 10. whisky jack
   lynx . . 5. pishu
   plum . . 6. cheney
   porcupine . . 5. urson 7. cawquaw

squaw . . **6.** mahala
canaille . . . **3.** mob **4.** ruck **6.** rabble,
ragtag, Shorts **8.** riffraff **10.** roughscuff
canal . . **4.** duct, iter (brain), pipe, tube
5. drain **6.** meatus **7.** acequia, channel
10. waterspout **11.** watercourse
Canal . . . **4.** Erie, Kiel, Suez **6.** Panama
13. Sault Ste Marie (Soo)
Canal Zone Lock . . . **5.** Gatun
10. Miraflores
canard . . . **4.** duck, hoax **5.** rumor
6. humbug **9.** falsehood
canary . . . **6.** yellow **8.** song-bird, songster,
weakling
Canary Islands . . .
capital . . **9.** Santa Cruz (Teneriffe)
city . . **9.** Las Palmas (Grand Canary)
commune . . **4.** Icod
owner . . **5.** Spain
cancel . . . **4.** blot, dele, kill, omit, undo
5. annul, erase **6.** delete, excise, recall,
repeal, revoke **7.** abolish, destroy,
nullify, rescind, retract **8.** write off
10. invalidate, neutralize, obliterate
11. countermand
cancellation . . . **6.** repeal **7.** erasure
8. deletion, write-off **10.** moratorium
12. obliteration
cancer . . . **4.** evil **5.** tumor **6.** canker,
growth **7.** sarcoma **8.** neoplasm
9. carcinoma
Cancer . . . **4.** crab **7.** mansion (moon)
10. zodiac sign **13.** constellation
cancion . . . **4.** song **5.** lyric
Candia . . . **5.** Crete (Isl)
candid . . . **4.** fair, just, open, pure **5.** frank
6. direct, honest **7.** sincere **9.** guileless,
impartial, ingenuous **10.** impersonal
13. dispassionate **15.** straightforward
candidate . . . **6.** seeker **7.** aspirer,
electee, nominee **8.** aspirant, selectee
9. applicant, appointee, postulant
10. solicitant
candidate list . . . **4.** leet **5.** slate **6.** roster
Candide (pert to) . . .
hero, title . . **5.** novel
novel, author . . **8.** Voltaire
philosophy . . **8.** optimism
candied . . . **5.** sweet **7.** honeyed
9. congealed, incrusted, preserved
10. flattering, granulated **12.** crystallized
candied sea holly . . . **6.** eryngo (eringo)
candle . . . **3.** dip, wax **5.** light, power,
taper **6.** bougie, cierge, tallow, votive
7. paschal **8.** bayberry **9.** chandelle
candlestick (pert to) . . .
Bib . . **6.** lampad
branched . . **9.** girandole
ornamental . . **10.** candelabra
Scot . . **6.** crusie
spike . . **7.** pricket
three-branched . . **9.** tricerion
torch type . . **8.** flambeau
wall . . **6.** sconce
candlewood . . . **6.** flower **8.** ocotillo
candor . . . **8.** fairness, openness
9. frankness, sincerity, unreserve
10. directness **11.** artlessness,
unrestraint **13.** outspokenness
candy . . . **5.** sweet **6.** penide (pulled),
sweets **7.** sweeten **8.** crystals

9. granulate, sweetmeat **10.** confection
11. crystallize **13.** confectionary
candy (type) . . . **4.** mint **5.** fudge, taffy
6. bonbon, nougat, toffee **7.** brittle,
caramel, fondant, panocha, penuche,
praline **8.** licorice, lollipop **9.** chocolate
11. marshmallow
candytuft . . . **6.** iberis
cane . . . **3.** rod **4.** beat, club, reed, stem,
whip **5.** crook, sorgo, staff, stick, sugar
6. bamboo, rattan **7.** bagasse, bourdon,
sorghum, sucrose **9.** handstaff,
truncheon **12.** swagger stick
canescent . . . **5.** hoary, white **7.** grizzly,
silvery, whitish **9.** snow-white
Canfield . . . **9.** solitaire
canine . . . **3.** cur, dog, fox, pug, pup
4. lobo, mutt, tike **5.** dingo, pooch,
puppy, whelp **6.** animal, coyote
7. Canidae, doggish, laniary, mastiff,
mongrel, reynard **8.** dogtooth, eyetooth
canis . . . **3.** dog
Canis Majoris . . . **13.** Constellation (with
Dog Star, Sirius)
cannibalism . . . **9.** barbarity, endophagy
10. perversion **11.** blood thirst
13. anthropophagy
cannon . . . **3.** gun **5.** crash **6.** mortar
7. firearm, robinet **8.** dog of war,
howitzer, ordnance **9.** artillery, collision
cannon (pert to) . . .
ball . . **6.** pellet **7.** missile
bore . . **6.** breech
fire . . **7.** barrage
handle . . **4.** anse
nautical . . **5.** chase
part . . **8.** cascabel
pivot . . **8.** trunnion
platform . . **10.** terreplein
plug . . **7.** tampion
shot . . **5.** grape
shoulder part . . **7.** rimbase
cannonade . . . **4.** boom, peal, roar **5.** blitz,
shell **6.** rumble, strafe **11.** bombardment
canny . . . **3.** sly **4.** foxy, wary, wily **6.** artful,
frugal, shrewd, subtle **7.** cunning,
knowing, prudent, thrifty **8.** cautious
9. sagacious
canoe . . . **4.** kiak, pahi, proa, waka
5. bongo, bungo, kayak, umiak, waapa
6. corial, dugout, oomiak, pitpan
7. almadia, buckeye (bugeye), coracle,
piragua, pirogue **12.** pambanmanche
canon . . . **3.** law **4.** code, list, rule,
type **5.** model, nodus (Mus) **6.** belief,
clergy, decree, ritual **7.** measure,
precept **8.** decision **9.** catalogue,
criterion **10.** regulation **11.** composition
12. constitution
canonical . . . **4.** None (hour), Sext
(hour) **5.** Lauds, Prime **6.** Matins
7. creedal **8.** dogmatic, orthodox
9. doctrinal **10.** scriptural **11.** theological
14. ecclesiastical
canonization . . . **8.** sainting
10. ordainment, ordination
12. consecration, enshrinement
canopy . . . **3.** sky **4.** ceil, cope, dais,
tent **5.** cover, shade, vault **6.** awning,
tester **7.** blanket, marquee, shelter
8. caponier (caponiere), ciborium,

pavilion 9. baldachin, firmament
canorous ... 5. clear 8. sonorous
9. melodious 10. euphonious
cant ... 3. tip 4. lean, list, sing, song,
sway, tack, tilt 5. angle, argot, chant,
lingo, pitch, slang, slope, whine
6. careen, intone, jargon, patois,
snivel 7. auction, incline, mummery
8. pretense 9. hypocrisy 10. intonation,
sanctimony 17. sanctimoniousness
cantabank ... 6. singer (ballad)
cantador ... 6. singer (folk songs)
cantankerous ... 8. perverse 9. malicious
10. contention, ill-natured 12. cross-
grained
cantata ... 5. motet 8. serenata
9. pastorale
canter ... 4. gait, lope 6. gallop
(Canterbury) 8. vagabond
Canterbury ...
archbishop .. 7. Cranmer, Primate
13. Thomas à Becket (murdered)
capital (Eng) .. 14. ecclesiastical
famed building .. 9. Cathedral
gallop .. 5. aubin 6. canter
Tales, author .. 7. Chaucer
canticle ... 3. lay, ode 4. hymn, lied,
song 5. carol, ditty 6. Te Deum
Canticle of Canticles (Bib) ... 11. Song
of Songs 13. Song of Solomon
cantilena ... 6. legato, melody 8. graceful
cantina ... 3. bag 6. pocket, saloon
7. canteen
cantle ... 4. nook, part 5. crown, slice
6. corner, saddle (part) 7. segment
11. cornerpiece
canto ... 4. book, song 5. poems (div
of), tenor, verse 6. cantus, melody,
poetry 7. descort
canton ... 3. Uri (Switz) 6. county
7. commune, quarter 8. district, insignia
(Her), mofussil (Ind) 9. bailiwick,
partition
cantor ... 6. leader, singer 7. soloist
8. melodist, vocalist 9. precentor
cantoria ... 7. balcony, gallery (choir)
cantrip ... 5. charm, magic, spell, trick
canty ... 6. lively 7. chipper 8. cheerful
9. sprightly
Canuck ... 8. Canadian
canvas ... 4. sail, tent, tuke (tewke)
5. cloth 6. circus 7. picture, tentage
8. covering, likeness, pavilion
9. tarpaulin 14. representation
canvasback ... 4. duck
canvass ... 4. poll 5. study 6. survey
7. examine, inquiry, solicit 8. campaign,
consider 10. scrutinize 11. electioneer
12. solicitation 13. questionnaire
canyon, cañon ... 4. abra (mouth)
5. chasm, dalle (wall), gorge, gulch
6. arroyo, coulee, ravine, violet
7. couloir
canzone, canzonetta ... 4. poem, song
6. ballad, melody 8. canzonet, madrigal
caoba ... 8. mahogany, muskwood
caoutchouc ... 3. ule 6. caucho, rubber
cap ... 3. fez, hat, lid, taj, tam 4. atef,
coif, hood, kepi 5. beret, boina, busby,
shako, toque 6. barret, biggin, bonnet,
calpac, cloche, pileus, turban 7. biretta

(beretta), calotte, calpack, chapeau
8. Balmoral, havelock 9. headdress,
headpiece, shtreimal, sou'wester,
zucchetto 10. cervelière
11. mortarboard, tam-ó-shanter
cap (outer part) ... 3. lid, tip, top 4. dome,
fuze, peak, type 5. cover, crown, excel,
match, spire, trump 6. summit, top
off 7. capital (Arch), overlie, patella
8. complete 9. copestone, detonator
capa ... 5. cloak 6. mantle 7. tobacco
capability ... 5. power, skill 6. genius
7. ability, caliber, faculty, potency
8. ableness, adequacy, capacity
10. competence 13. qualification
capable ... 3. apt, can, fit 4. able 5. adept
6. expert 7. equal to, skilled 8. adequate
9. competent, effective, efficient,
qualified 10. proficient 12. accomplished
capable of ...
boring .. 10. zylotomous
carrying .. 9. portative
flying .. 6. volant
growing .. 6. viable
living in harmony .. 10. compatible
penetration .. 8. pervious
suffering .. 8. passible 9. sensitive
capable of being ...
ascertained .. 12. determinable
cultivated .. 6. arable
cut .. 7. sectile
defended .. 7. tenable
done .. 10. effectible
heard .. 7. audible
prevented .. 9. avertible
proved .. 8. testable 12. demonstrable
regulated .. 12. controllable
separated .. 9. divisible
spread .. 10. infectious 12. communicable
thrown .. 7. missile
uttered .. 7. effable
capacious ... 4. full, much, wide 5. ample,
broad, large, roomy 8. generous,
spacious 9. expansive, extensive
10. commodious, voluminous
12. considerable 13. comprehensive
capacitance unit ... 5. farad
capacity ... 4. role, room, size 5. limit,
power, skill, space 6. extent, spread,
status, talent, volume 7. caliber,
content, faculty, fitness, measure
8. adequacy, aptitude, function,
position, relation, strength 9. character
10. capability, efficiency 11. capacitance
(Elec) 12. intelligence
13. accommodation
capacity for knowing ... 9. intellect
cap and bells ... 6. bauble, comedy
(symbol), motley 7. costume, marotti
9. headdress
caparison ... 3. rig 4. tack 5. armor, dress,
get-up 6. livery 7. harness, housing,
panoply 10. horsecloth 12. horse
blanket
cape ... 3. ras 4. hood, mino, naze, ness,
spur 5. amice, cappa, cloak, fichu, orale,
point, sagum, talma 6. mantle, sontag,
tippet 8. pelerine (fur) 9. Inverness
cape (pert to) ...
gooseberry .. 4. poha
hen .. 4. skua 6. petrel

pigeon .. **7.** pintado
polecat .. **5.** zoril
ruby .. **6.** garnet, pyrope
sheep .. **9.** albatross (Naut term)
Cape Cod turkey ... **7.** codfish (humor)
Cape Dutch ... **9.** Afrikaans (language)
Cape of Good Hope discoverer ...
    4. Diaz (1488)
Capek play ... **3.** RUR
caper ... **3.** tea **4.** dido, leap, romp,
    skip **5.** antic, berry, dance, frisk,
    prank **6.** cavort, frolic, gambol, prance
    8. capriole, marigold **9.** privateer (Hist)
capercaille ... **6.** grouse **13.** cock of the
    wood
caper herb family ... **6.** Cleome
    8. Capparis **9.** Polanisia
    10. clammyweed **13.** Capparidaceae
capias ... **4.** writ **6.** caveat **7.** process,
    warrant **8.** mandamus **9.** nisi prius
capillary ... **4.** fine, tube **6.** minute,
    vessel **7.** slender **8.** hairlike, trichoid
capilliform ... **7.** thready **8.** hairlike
capillus ... **4.** hair
capistrate ... **6.** cowled, hooded
capital ... **3.** top **4.** city, main, rare,
    seat, type **5.** chief, crest, crown, funds,
    major, means, prime, vital **6.** assets,
    letter, ruling, supply **7.** leading, primary,
    serious, weighty **8.** cardinal, dominant,
    foremost, splendid **9.** excellent,
    financial, important, paramount,
    principal, prominent **10.** commanding,
    preeminent, shoestring
capitalism ... **8.** politics **10.** government
    11. bourgeoisie **14.** free enterprise
capitalist ... **5.** baron **6.** tycoon **7.** rich
    man **8.** investor **9.** bourgeois, financier,
    plutocrat
capital letter ... **6.** uncial **9.** majuscule
capital punishment ... **5.** noose
    7. gallows, hanging **8.** shooting,
    the chair **9.** beheading, execution,
    fusillade **10.** guillotine **12.** decapitation
    13. electrocution
capitano ... **3.** don **4.** capo **5.** chief
    7. captain, headman
capitate ... **7.** globose **8.** enlarged,
    headlike
Capitol (pert to) ...
    Federal .. **10.** Washington (DC)
    State .. **10.** Statehouse
capitulate ... **4.** cede, fall **9.** surrender
capitulation ... **6.** resumé, review, treaty
    7. recount, summary **9.** agreement,
    reckoning, rehearsal, statement,
    summation, surrender **10.** compendium
    11. enumeration, stipulation
    14. relinquishment
capon ... **3.** hen **4.** cock, fowl **6.** pullet,
    rabbit (castrated) **7.** chicken, poulard,
    poultry, rooster
caporal ... **4.** boss **7.** foreman, tobacco
    8. overseer
capote ... **4.** hood **5.** cloak **6.** bonnet,
    mantle, piquet **8.** overcoat
capped ... **7.** crested, pileata, pileate
Capri ...
    beverage .. **4.** wine (white)
    color .. **4.** blue **9.** blue-green
    island site .. **11.** Bay of Naples

ruins (famed) .. **7.** palaces (Tiberius)
    8. grottoes **10.** Blue Grotto
caprice ... **3.** fad, toy **4.** kink, mood,
    whim **5.** fancy, freak, humor, prank,
    quirk **6.** vagary **7.** whimsey (whimsy)
    8. crotchet, escapade, flimflam
capricious ... **5.** moody **6.** fickle, fitful
    7. erratic, wayward **8.** fanciful, freakish,
    humorous, notional, sporadic, unsteady
    9. arbitrary, crotchety, eccentric,
    fantastic, whimsical **10.** inconstant
    12. inconsistent **13.** temperamental
Capricorn ... **4.** goat **7.** mansion (of
    Saturn) **10.** zodiac sign **13.** constellation
capriole ... **4.** leap **5.** caper **6.** cavort,
    curvet, gambol
capsicum ... **4.** herb **5.** chili **6.** pepper
capsize ... **5.** spill, upset **7.** subvert, tip
    over **8.** overturn **9.** overthrow **10.** turn
    turtle
capsule ... **3.** sac **4.** pill **5.** ascus, brief,
    theca, wafer **6.** précis, sheath **7.** enclose,
    epitome **8.** abstract, envelope, pericarp,
    seedcase, synopsis **10.** compendium
capsulize ... **5.** brief **7.** abridge, outline
    8. abstract, condense **9.** epitomize,
    summarize
captain ... **4.** skip **5.** chief, ruler
    6. leader, master, patron, police
    7. headman, officer, skipper **8.** overlord
    9. commander **10.** shipmaster
Captain Kidd ... **6.** pirate
Captains Courageous (pert to) ...
    author .. **7.** Kipling
    setting .. **9.** Grand Bank (Newfoundland)
    tale of .. **7.** romance
caption ... **5.** title **6.** legend, rubric
    7. capture, seizure **8.** headline, subtitle
captious ... **6.** severe **7.** carping, cynical,
    peevish **8.** caviling, critical **9.** bickering,
    paltering, quibbling **12.** equivocatory,
    faultfinding **13.** hypercritical
captivate ... **4.** lure, vamp **5.** charm,
    snare **6.** allure, enamor, ravish, seduce
    7. attract, becharm, beguile, bewitch,
    capture, delight, enchant **8.** enthrall
    9. enrapture, fascinate, infatuate,
    transport
captive ... **4.** bond, serf **5.** helot
    6. détenu, thrall, unfree, vassal
    7. hostage **8.** conquest, enslaved,
    prisoner **10.** subjugated
captivity ... **6.** duress **7.** bondage,
    durance, serfdom, slavery **9.** detention,
    servitude, thralldom **10.** internment,
    subjection **11.** confinement,
    impoundment **12.** imprisonment
    13. incarceration
captor ... **5.** taker **7.** catcher **8.** capturer
capture ... **3.** beg, nab, net, win **4.** gain,
    haul, take **5.** catch, pinch, raven, snare
    6. arrest, collar **7.** caption, seizure
    9. apprehend, detention
    12. apprehension
capuche (Eccl) ... **4.** cowl, hood
capuchin ... **3.** sai **5.** Cebus **6.** monkey,
    pigeon
caput ... **3.** cap, top **4.** head **5.** crest,
    crown **7.** chapter, section **9.** paragraph
car ... **4.** auto, cart, jeep, tram **5.** coupe,
    motor, sedan, truck, wagon **6.** hot rod,

jalopy, wheels (sl) **7.** caboose, chariot, clunker (sl), compact, flivver, machine, Pullman, vehicle **8.** carriage **9.** dune buggy, hatchback **10.** automobile, subcompact

carabao . . . **5.** mango **7.** buffalo

carabinieri . . . **9.** policeman **10.** carabineer

caracal . . . **3.** fur **4.** lynx, pelt

caracara . . . **4.** hawk **8.** carancha

caracole . . . **5.** caper (manège) **9.** staircase

caract . . . **5.** charm **6.** symbol (magic)

carafe . . . **6.** bottle

carafon . . . **8.** decanter

carapace . . . **5.** plate, shell (turtle) **6.** chitin, lorica, shield **7.** carapax

caravan . . . **3.** van **5.** wagon **6.** cafila (camel) **9.** cavalcade, motorcade **10.** expedition, procession

caravansary . . . **3.** inn **4.** khan (chan) **5.** hotel, serai **6.** hostel, imaret, posado **8.** hostelry **9.** resthouse, roadhouse

carbine . . . **5.** rifle **6.** musket **7.** escopet

carbohydrate . . . **5.** sugar **6.** starch **7.** dextrin, glucose, lactose, maltose, sucrose **8.** dextrose, glycogen, nutrient **9.** cellulose **10.** saccharide, saccharose

carbon . . . **4.** coke, copy, fuel, lead, soot **7.** diamond, residue **8.** graphite

carbonate . . . **3.** ore **5.** trona **6.** aerate, natron **9.** carbonize **11.** chemicalize

carbon dioxide . . . **3.** gas **6.** dry ice **7.** seeding (cloud) **11.** refrigerant

Carborundum . . . **5.** emery **8.** abrasive **14.** silicon carbide

carcass . . . **4.** body **5.** bones, kreng (whale) **6.** corpse **7.** cadaver, remains **8.** skeleton

carcer . . . **5.** stall (Rom circus) **6.** prison

card . . . **3.** map, tum **4.** comb, menu, post, rove **6.** docket, domino, oddity, postal, record, ticket **7.** calling, program **8.** calendar, schedule **9.** character **13.** communication

card game . . . **3.** gin, hoc, loo, pan **4.** bank, faro, keno, skat **5.** cinch, comet, monte, pitch, poker, rummy, stuss, tarot, whist **6.** bridge, casino, écarté, hearts, piquet, rounce **7.** auction, bezique, canasta, cassino, cayenne **8.** baccarat, contract, cribbage, pinochle **9.** solitaire, panguingui

card game term . . . **3.** ace **4.** meld, pass, pone, slam, trey, vole **5.** joker, pedro, tarot **6.** cathop, misère, tenace, tricon **7.** declare **9.** mistigris

cardinal . . . **3.** red **4.** bird, fish, main **5.** chief **6.** bishop, deacon, number, priest, ruling **8.** crowning, dominant, foremost **9.** paramount, principal **10.** preeminent

cardinal (pert to) . . .
astrology . . **5.** nadir **6.** zenith
astronomy . . **10.** solstitial **11.** equinoctial
biology . . **7.** maximum, minimum, optimum
compass point . . **4.** east, west **5.** north, south
number . . **7.** primary (one, two, three)
office . . **6.** datary **7.** dataria
virtues . . **7.** justice **8.** prudence **9.** fortitude **10.** temperance
virtues (Theol) . . **4.** hope **5.** faith **7.** charity

cardinal's hat . . . **3.** red **4.** rank **6.** office

care . . . **4.** duty, fret, heed, reck, task, tend, wish **5.** aegis, worry **6.** desire, regard **7.** anxiety, caution, cherish, concern, custody, keeping **9.** attention, patronage **10.** affliction, protection, solicitude **11.** carefulness, heedfulness, supervision, thriftiness **12.** jurisdiction **13.** consideration

careen . . . **3.** tip **4.** cant, heel, keel, lean, list, tilt **5.** slant, slope

career . . . **3.** set **4.** flow, flux, line, work **6.** course, stream **7.** calling, mission, passage, pursuit **8.** business, practice, progress, vocation **10.** occupation, profession

care for . . . **4.** help, like, love, mind, reck, tend **5.** fancy, guard, nurse, prize, watch **6.** attend, dote on, foster, mother, relish, wait on **7.** nurture **10.** appreciate

carefree . . . **5.** happy **6.** jaunty **8.** debonair **10.** insouciant **12.** lighthearted

careful . . . **4.** wary **5.** canny, chary, exact **7.** anxious, guarded, heedful, mindful, prudent, thrifty **8.** cautious, discreet, gingerly, vigilant **9.** advertent, attentive **10.** meticulous, scrupulous, solicitous, thoughtful **11.** circumspect, considerate, painstaking, punctilious

careless . . . **3.** lax **5.** loose **6.** rakish, remiss, sloppy **8.** heedless, mindless, reckless, slipshod, slovenly **9.** impulsive, negligent, unheeding, unmindful **10.** nonchalant, regardless, unthinking **11.** inadvertent, thoughtless, unconcerned **13.** inconsiderate

carelessness . . . **8.** bungling, disorder **9.** disregard, unconcern **10.** blundering, negligence **11.** nonchalance **12.** heedlessness, indifference, recklessness **13.** impulsiveness **15.** inconsideration, thoughtlessness

caress . . . **3.** pat, pet **4.** bill, kiss **5.** touch **6.** coddle, cosset, dandle, fondle, pamper, stroke **10.** endearment

caressing . . . **7.** hugging, kissing **8.** fondling **9.** endearing

cargo . . . **4.** load **5.** goods **6.** burden, charge, lading **7.** carload, freight **8.** boatload, shipload **9.** truckload

cargo (pert to) . . .
afloat . . **7.** flotsam
cast overboard . . **6.** jetsam
loader, unloader . . **9.** stevedore

Carib . . . **6.** Indian

caribou . . . **4.** deer **8.** reindeer

caricature . . . **5.** comic **6.** overdo, parody **7.** cartoon, lampoon, picture **8.** satirize, travesty **9.** burlesque **10.** caricatura, distortion **12.** exaggeration

caricaturist . . . **6.** artist **8.** humorist, parodist **10.** burlesquer

caries . . . **5.** decay (Dent) **10.** ulceration

carillon . . . **4.** lyra **5.** bells (fixed) **6.** chimes **12.** glockenspiel

cark . . . **3.** vex **4.** care, heed, load **5.** pains, worry **6.** burden, charge, harass **7.** trouble **8.** distress

carl, carlot . . . **4.** boor **5.** churl **6.** rustic
  7. peasant, villein **8.** bondsman
  10. husbandman, pinchpenny
Carmelite . . . **3.** nun **4.** monk **5.** friar
  8. White Nun **10.** White Friar
carmen . . . **4.** poem, song **11.** incantation
Carmen . . . **5.** gypsy, opera (1875)
  7. heroine, romance
carmine . . . **3.** red **5.** color, stain
  7. crimson, scarlet
carnage . . . **8.** butchery, massacre
  9. bloodshed, slaughter **10.** decimation
carnal . . . **4.** lewd **6.** bodily, fleshy
  7. earthly, mundane, sensual, worldly
  9. corporeal **11.** unspiritual
  12. bloodthirsty
carnation . . . **3.** red **4.** pink, self **7.** bizarre,
  picotee **8.** Dianthus
carnelian . . . **4.** sard **9.** copper red
  10. chalcedony
carnival . . . **4.** fair, show **6.** circus
  7. revelry **8.** feasting, festival
  9. amusement, Mardi Gras
  11. merrymaking **12.** masquerading
carnivore . . . **3.** cat, dog **4.** bear, lion,
  puma, seal **5.** civet, coati, genet, hyena,
  otter, panda, ratel, sable, tiger, ursus
  6. badger, mammal, marten, weasel
  7. meerkat, raccoon **8.** mongoose
  9. ichneumon **10.** cacomistle
carnivorous . . . **10.** meat-eating,
  predaceous **11.** omophageous
carol . . . **3.** lay **4.** lied, lilt, noel, sing,
  song **5.** dance (anc) **6.** ballad, warble
  7. rejoice
Caroline Islands (coral) . . . **3.** Yap
  5. Parao **6.** Ponape
carom . . . **4.** bump **6.** bounce, cannon,
  strike **8.** ricochet
carousal . . . **4.** lark, orgy, romp **5.** binge,
  feast, fling, revel, spree **6.** frolic
  7. banquet, carouse, revelry, wassail
carouse . . . **4.** birl **5.** bouse, drink, spree,
  toast **9.** dissipate
carpet . . . **3.** mat, rug **4.** Agra, Kali,
  Kuba **5.** Herat (Herati), namda,
  tapis **6.** nammad, Wilton **7.** drugget
  8. Brussels, flooring, moquette
  9. Axminster, broadloom
  11. Baluchistan
carpetbagger . . . **8.** swindler **10.** politician
carriage . . . **3.** air **4.** mien, pose **7.** bearing,
  posture **8.** attitude, demeanor, presence
  10. deportment
carriage (pert to) . . .
  English . . **6.** waggon **7.** growler
    8. dormeuse, stanhope
  French . . **6.** fiacre **7.** caliche, voiture
  general . . **3.** bus, cab, car, gig, rig,
    van **4.** baby, hack, pram, shay, trap
    5. buggy, coach, wagon **6.** calssh,
    chaise, cisium, dennet, go-cart, hansom,
    landau, surrey, tandem **7.** cariole,
    chariot, omnibus, phaeton, tallyho,
    vehicle **8.** carryall, clarence, dearborn,
    rockaway, victoria **9.** kittereen, landaulet
    10. conveyance, shandrydan
    12. perambulator
  history . . **7.** tumbrel, vis-à-vis, whiskey
    8. curricle
  Indian . . **4.** okka **5.** tonga **6.** gharry

  7. hackery
  Italian . . **7.** vettura
  one-horse . . **3.** gig **4.** shay **5.** sulky
  Orient . . **4.** sado **10.** jinrikisha
  Philippines . . **9.** carromata
  Russia . . **5.** araba **6.** troika **7.** droshky
    9. tarantass
carried . . . **5.** borne, giddy, toted
  6. carted, lugged **8.** conveyed, ravished
  11. transported
carrier . . . **3.** boy **4.** mail, mule, rail,
  ship, wave **5.** crate **6.** bearer,
  coolie, pigeon, porter, redcap, runner,
  vessel **7.** courier, drayman, express
  8. cargador, conveyor, teamster
  9. messenger, stevedore
carrier (pert to) . . .
  disease . . **3.** fly, rat **7.** typhoid
    8. mosquito
  Indian . . **5.** Tinne (Brit)
  staff . . **5.** macer
carrion . . . **4.** vile **6.** corpse, rotten
  7. carcass, corrupt **9.** loathsome
carrion (pert to) . . .
  bug . . **6.** beetle
  buzzard . . **4.** hawk **7.** vulture **8.** caracara
  flower . . **5.** morel
  fungus . . **9.** stinkhorn
carrot . . . **5.** drias (deadly) **6.** Daucus (Old
  World) **9.** Ammiaceae **10.** nivernaise
  (glazed), umbellifer
carrousel . . . **9.** whirligig **10.** roundabout,
  tournament **12.** merry-go-round
carry . . . **3.** lug **4.** bear, cart, hold, take,
  tote, wart **5.** ferry **6.** convey **7.** conduct,
  publish **8.** transfer, transmit **9.** transport
carry away, off . . . **3.** win **6.** abduct,
  eloign, enamor, remove **7.** succeed
  9. fascinate **10.** accomplish
carry on . . . **4.** rage, wage **6.** endure,
  frolic, manage **7.** conduct, operate
  8. continue **9.** misbehave, persevere
carry out, through . . . **2.** do **5.** apply
  6. ravish **7.** execute, perform, sustain
  8. complete, continue, transact
  10. accomplish
cart . . . **4.** dray, wain **5.** carry, sulky,
  wagon **6.** convey, reckla, telega
  7. morfrey (morphrey), tumbrel (anc),
  vehicle (2-wheeled)
carta, Charta . . . **4.** deed **5.** Magna (Eng)
  7. charter **9.** parchment
cartage . . . **7.** drayage, portage **8.** carriage,
  teamster, truckage **10.** expressage
  14. transportation
carte . . . **3.** map **4.** card, list, menu
  5. chart **7.** diagram **10.** bill of fare
cartel . . . **4.** bloc (Polit), defy, pact,
  pool **5.** paper, truce, trust **6.** letter
  7. compact, entente **8.** covenant
  9. agreement, challenge, syndicate
  10. convention **11.** arrangement
Carthage . . . see also *Carthaginian*
  capital . . **13.** Vandal Kingdom
  destroyer . . **6.** Romans
  queen . . **4.** Dido
  rebuilt by . . **8.** Augustus
Carthaginian (pert to) . . .
  apple . . **11.** pomegranate
  foe . . **4.** Cato
  general . . **6.** Xerxes **8.** Hannibal

god.. **6.** Moloch **8.** Melkarth
language.. **5.** Punic
Lion.. **8.** Hannibal
magistrate.. **7.** suffete
name (later).. **15.** Justinianopolis
wars (three).. **5.** Punic
Carthusian Order (pert to)...
founder.. **7.** St Bruno
monastery.. **7.** Certosa (It, 1396)
site.. **8.** Grenoble (Fr)
cartilage ... **4.** bone (ossified) **6.** tissue
  7. gristle
cartload ... **6.** fother
cartograph ... **3.** map **4.** plat **5.** chart
cartoon ... **6.** design, sketch **7.** pattern,
  picture **10.** caricature
cartoonist ... **4.** Arno, Capp, Ding, Nast
  6. Disney
cartouche ... **5.** shell **6.** corbel, design,
  shield (Her), tablet **7.** console
  9. cartridge **10.** cantilever (Arch)
cartwheel ... **4.** coin **6.** dollar **8.** somerset
  10. handspring, somersault
carve ... **3.** cut, hew **4.** form, make
  5. chase, grave, sever, shape **6.** chisel,
  cleave, furrow, incise **7.** engrave,
  fashion **9.** apportion, fabricate,
  sculpture
carving ... **5.** cameo **8.** diaglyph, intaglio
  9. anaglyphy, embossing, sculpture
  11. anaglyptics
caryatid ... **6.** column, figure (fem)
  8. pilaster **11.** priestesses (temple)
casa ... **5.** adobe, cabin, house **8.** building
cascade ... **4.** fall, linn **5.** Falls, Sault
  7. Niagara **8.** cataract **9.** waterfall
case ... **3.** box **4.** etui, file **5.** cover,
  crate, crush (sl), event, folio **6.** carton,
  coffer, pillow, sheath, victim **7.** attaché,
  cabinet, example, holster, lawsuit
  8. argument, covering, cupboard,
  instance **9.** condition, portfolio
  10. receptacle **12.** circumstance
case (in any) ... **3.** yet **4.** even
  6. anyhow, anyway **7.** anywise,
  however **8.** possibly, provided
  10. regardless **15.** notwithstanding
case (pert to) ...
arrow.. **6.** quiver
book.. **5.** forel
bottle (liquor).. **8.** cellaret
cigar.. **7.** humidor
conscience (Sci).. **9.** casuistry
grammar.. **6.** dative **8.** ablative, genitive,
  vocative **10.** nominative
history (disease).. **6.** record **9.** anamnesis
image (Bib).. **5.** ephod
jewel, relics.. **3.** tye **4.** apse
spore.. **5.** ascus
surgeon's.. **7.** trousse
cash ... **4.** coin, dust (gold) **5.** darby,
  funds, money **6.** silver, specie **7.** capital,
  coinage, mintage **8.** currency
  9. spondulix
cashmere ... **4.** goat, wool **5.** shawl
  6. fabric
casino ... **6.** tavern **7.** cabaret, cassino
  (game) **8.** ballroom, gambling
  9. roadhouse **11.** summerhouse
cask ... **3.** tun **4.** butt, case, drum, pipe
  5. terce **6.** bareca, barrel, casket, firkin,

tierce **8.** puncheon **9.** kilderkin
cask (pert to) ...
amt when not filled.. **6.** ullage
bulge.. **5.** bilge
oil.. **4.** rier
part.. **3.** lag **4.** hoop **5.** stave
rim.. **5.** chime (chimb)
support.. **8.** stillage
casket ... **3.** box, pyx, tye (jewel)
  4. cist, kist, tomb **5.** chest **8.** cassette
  11. sarcophagus
casserole ... **4.** dish, mold **5.** brown
  (color) **6.** vessel **8.** saucepan
cassine ... **4.** game (card)
cast ... **3.** hue **4.** form, hurl, kind,
  look, mold, role, shed, tone, toss,
  type **5.** eject, fling, heave, model,
  pitch, sling, throw **6.** glance, matrix,
  squint, troupe **7.** pattern **8.** template
  9. facsimile **10.** impression, strabismus
  16. dramatis personae
cast (pert to) ...
aside.. **4.** jilt, junk, shed **5.** scrap **6.** reject
  7. discard
away.. **5.** eject, wreck **6.** unmoor
  9. shipwreck
blame.. **6.** accuse **7.** censure **8.** reproach
  9. reprehend
off.. **4.** doff, knit, molt, shed **5.** untie
  6. unmoor **7.** discard **9.** eliminate
castaway ... **6.** pariah **7.** outcast
  8. derelict **9.** reprobate
caste ... **4.** race, rank **5.** breed, class,
  stock **6.** status **7.** lineage, society
  8. standing
caste (Ind) ... **3.** Dom, Meo **4.** Ahir, Jati,
  Koli, Magi, Mali, Pasi, Teli **5.** Gaddi,
  Sudra, Varna **6.** banian, pariah, Vaisya
  7. Brahman **9.** Kshatriya
caster, castor ... **4.** vial **5.** cruet, horse
  (old), wheel **6.** roller, vessel (condiment)
castigate ... **5.** emend **6.** punish, revise,
  strafe **7.** chasten, correct, reprove
  8. chastise, penalize **9.** criticize
  10. discipline
Castile ... **4.** soap **7.** kingdom
Castilian ... **7.** Iberian, Spanish
castle ... **4.** fort, keep, rook (chess)
  5. house, tower, villa **6.** donjon
  7. chateau, citadel **8.** fortress
  10. stronghold **13.** fortification
Castor (pert to) ...
brother (twin).. **6.** Pollux
constellation.. **6.** Gemini
mother.. **4.** Leda
stars.. **6.** Castor, Pollux
castrate ... **4.** geld, spay **5.** alter, prune
  10. emasculate
castrated (pert to) ...
bull.. **5.** steer
cat.. **3.** gib
horse.. **7.** gelding
man.. **6.** eunoch
rooster.. **5.** capon
casual ... **5.** stray **6.** chance, random
  9. offhanded **10.** contingent, fortuitous,
  incidental, occasional, unforeseen
  11. indifferent **14.** unpremeditated
casual observation ... **6.** remark
casualty ... **6.** chance, hazard, injury,
  mishap **7.** payment, tragedy **8.** accident,

calamity, disaster, fatality 9. mischance
10. misfortune 11. contingency,
contretemps 12. misadventure
casus (pert to) . . .
act of God . . 14. casus fortuitus
common law . . 12. casus omissus
conscience . . 17. casus conscientiae
Latin . . 4. case 5. event 8. occasion
treaty . . 13. casus foederis
war . . 10. casus belli
cat . . . 3. gib 4. balu, eyra, lynx, pard,
puma 5. alley, civet, Felid, Felis,
genet, hyena, manul, ounce, tabby,
tiger 6. caffre, cougar, feline, jaguar,
margay, ocelot, pajero, rasset, serval
7. cheetah, dasyure, leopard, panther,
wildcat 9. catamount, grimalkin
cat (pert to) . . .
cartoon . . 5. Felix 8. Krazy Kat
fear of . . 12. ailurophobia
fictional . . 8. Cheshire 9. Mehitabel
fish . . 4. pout, raad 6. hassar, tandan
7. eelpout
game . . 6. tipcat
gut . . 5. tharm 6. string (violin)
slang . . 6. hepcat
term . . 3. tom 5. kitty, pussy, tabby
6. feline, kitten, mouser 9. grimalkin
wild . . 4. lion, lynx, puma 5. tiger
6. bobcat, cougar, jaguar, ocelot, tiglon
7. cheetah, leopard, panther, wildcat
cat (breed) . . . 3. Rex 4. Manx 5. korat
6. Angora, Birman, Bombay 7. Burmese,
Maltese, Persian, Siamese, Turkish
(Van) 8. Egyptian (Mau) 9. shorthair
10. Abyssinian
cataclysm . . . 4. ruin 6. deluge 7. debacle
8. calamity, disaster, The Flood,
upheaval 10. convulsion, inundation,
revolution 11. catastrophe
catacomb . . . 4. tomb 5. crypt, vault
6. grotto, locule 8. cemetery
(underground) 9. Appian Way
catalepsy . . . 6. trance 8. hypnosis
9. cataplexy 10. thanatosis
catalogue . . . 4. book, file, list 5. index,
tally 6. codify, digest, record
8. calendar, classify, pamphlet, register,
schedule, tabulate 11. enumeration
catamaran . . . 4. boat, raft 5. balsa, float
6. vessel 7. jangada
catamount . . . 3. cat 6. cougar
12. catamountain
catapult . . . 4. hurl 5. shoot, sling
6. engine, onager 7. robinet 8. arbalest,
ballista, scorpion 9. slingshot
cataract . . . 4. fall, linn 5. Falls, flood,
sault (soo) 6. deluge 7. cascade,
disease, Niagara, opacity (eye), torrent
8. downpour, Victoria 9. cachoeira,
waterfall
cataria . . . 6. catnip
catasta . . . 5. stage (slave traffic) 6. stocks
8. scaffold
catastrophe . . . 4. doom, ruin 6. finale,
mishap, payoff 7. tragedy 8. calamity,
disaster 9. cataclysm 10. denouement,
misfortune, revolution 11. termination
catastrophic . . . 4. dire 5. black 7. ruinous
10. calamitous, deplorable, disastrous
catawba . . . 4. wine 5. color (red), grape

6. Indian
catch . . . 3. get, nab 4. draw, hear, hold,
hook, take, trap 5. fault, ketch, prize,
reach, rondo, seize, snare, trick, troll
6. detent (clock), engage, entrap, ignite
7. attract, capture, seizure 8. overtake
9. intercept
catch (pert to) . . .
a likeness . . 4. draw 6. depict 7. portray
a ride . . 4. hook 5. hitch, thumb
9. hitchhike
sight of . . 3. see 4. espy 6. behold,
descry 7. discern, glimpse
catchword . . . 3. cry, cue 6. byword,
phrase, slogan 7. formula 10. shibboleth
cate . . . 4. food 6. viands 8. dainties
10. delicacies, provisions (bought)
catechism . . . 5. guide 6. belief, manual
9. questions (set of) 11. instruction
(oral)
catechumen . . . 5. chela, pupil 6. layman,
novice 7. convert 8. disciple, neophyte
categoric, categorical . . . 6. direct
7. crucial, logical 8. absolute, explicit,
positive 9. arbitrary, pragmatic
10. convincing 11. dictatorial,
unequivocal, unqualified
category . . . 4. head 5. class, genre,
genus, group, order, state 6. branch,
family, specie 7. bracket, species
8. division 12. denomination
14. classification
catena . . . 5. chain 6. series 8. sequence
10. continuity
catenary . . . 5. curve (Math) 9. chainlike
cater, cater to . . . 4. feed 5. favor, humor,
serve, toady 6. oblige, pander, please,
purvey 7. indulge, procure, provide,
satisfy 10. minister to 11. diagonalize
13. cater-cornered
caterpillar . . . 4. grub, weri 5. aweto,
eruca, larva 7. tractor
caterwaul . . . 3. woo (derog) 4. meow,
wail 5. court, miaow 7. screech
cathedral . . . 3. dom 4. fane (anc)
5. duomo 6. church 8. official 10. ex
cathedra 13. authoritative
Cathedral . . .
England . . 6. Durham 9. Salisbury
10. Canterbury
France . . 5. Reims (Rheims) 6. Amiens
8. Chartres 9. Notre Dame
Istanbul (Constantinople) . . 8. St Sophia
Italy . . 7. Lateran, St Mark's 8. St Peter's
Scotland . . 7. St Giles
cathedral (pert to) . . .
chair (Bishop's) . . 8. cathedra
chapter member . . 10. capitulary
part . . 4. apse, nave 5. choir 6. chapel
7. chancel, narthex 8. sacristy, transept
10. baptistery (baptistry)
style . . 6. Gothic
catholic . . . 4. wide 5. broad 6. church,
global 7. general, liberal 8. orthodox,
pandemic 9. Christian, universal
10. ecumenical 12. cosmopolitan
Catholic Church (Roman) . . .
Bible books . . 16. deuterocanonical
calendar . . 4. ordo
clergy . . 4. monk 5. friar 6. bishop,
Jesuit, priest 8. cardinal 9. monsignor

head.. **4.** pope **7.** pontiff
papal residence, state.. **7.** Vatican
rite.. **4.** Mass **7.** baptism, penance
  9. Communion, Eucharist, matrimony,
  sacrament **10.** Holy Orders
  12. confirmation
seat of authority.. **7.** Holy See
catkin ... **5.** ament, spike **7.** cattail
catlike ... **5.** catty **6.** feline **8.** stealthy
  9. noiseless
catling ... **3.** cat (little) **6.** kitten, string
  (violin)
Cato (pert to) ...
  author of.. **13.** De Agri Cultura
  famed as.. **7.** General **9.** statesman
  10. ambassador (to Carthage)
  nickname.. **8.** The Elder **11.** Cato of
  Utica
Catoism ... **9.** austerity, harshness
cats ... **8.** Kilkenny
cat's cradle ... **3.** hei **4.** game **7.** ribwort
cat's-paw ... **4.** dupe, gull, loof, pawn,
  tool **5.** cully, hitch (knot) **6.** breeze
  (Naut), puppet, stooge **10.** instrument
cattail ... **4.** musk, reed, tule **5.** ament,
  raupo, teree **6.** catkin, totora **7.** matreed
  9. Typhaceae
cattle ... **3.** Bos **4.** cows, kine, neat,
  oxen, stot, yaks **5.** asses, goats, mules,
  sheep, stock, swine **6.** bovine, camels,
  horses, llamas, niatas, rabble , Taurus
  7. banteng, chattel **8.** bullocks, property
  9. livestock
cattle (breed) ... **4.** Zebu **5.** Angus,
  Devon, Kerry, Niata, Welsh **6.** Brahma,
  Durham, Jersey, Sussex **7.** Dishley
  8. Guernsey, Hereford, Holstein,
  Longhorn **9.** Charolais, Leicester,
  Shorthorn **14.** Santa Gertrudis
cattle (pert to) ...
  collection.. **4.** herd **5.** drove
  disease.. **7.** murrain **10.** rinderpest
  driver.. **6.** drover
  food.. **6.** fodder, forage, silage
  herder.. **6.** cowboy, drover
  hybrid.. **4.** Zobo **7.** cattalo **9.** cattleyak
  motherless.. **6.** dogies
  pen.. **4.** crew **5.** barth, reeve
  shed.. **6.** hemmel
  stealer.. **7.** abactor, abigeus, rustler
  unbranded.. **9.** mavericks
catty ... **6.** feline, weight **7.** catlike, cattish
  8. spiteful, stealthy **11.** treacherous
cauboge ... **4.** boor **7.** bumpkin
Caucasian ... **4.** race, Slav, Svan,
  Turk **5.** gypsy, Latin, Norse, Osset,
  Pshav, white **6.** Hebrew, Semite,
  Teuton, Viking **8.** Armenian, Bohemian,
  Georgian, White Man **10.** Anglo-Saxon
  11. Xanthochroi
Caucasian (pert to) ...
  blond.. **6.** Teuton **8.** Estonian
  11. Xanthochroi
  brunette.. **7.** Iberian **8.** Armenian
  11. Melanochroi
  Chinese.. **4.** Lolo, Nosu
  dialect.. **4.** Andi, Avar, Svan
  European.. **8.** Japhetic
  goat (wild).. **3.** tur
  liquor.. **5.** kefir
  Moslem.. **3.** Laz (Laze, Lazi) **7.** Sunnite

mountain.. **8.** Caucasus
peak.. **6.** Elbrus (Elbruz), Kazbek
cauchemar ... **9.** nightmare
caucus ... **7.** meeting (Polit), primary
  8. assembly
cauda ... **4.** scut, tail **9.** appendage
caudata ... **5.** newts **8.** Amphibia
  11. salamanders
caught ... see also *catch* **5.** treed
  7. latched **8.** cornered
caught (pert to) ...
  napping.. **7.** unready **8.** unprimed
  10. unprepared
  sight of.. **3.** saw **6.** espied **8.** descried
  up in.. **4.** tied **7.** engaged, tangled
  8. absorbed, intent on, involved
  10. implicated
caul ... **3.** net **6.** basket **7.** netting,
  network, omentum **8.** membrane
cause ... **5.** aetio (comb form), agent,
  basis, drive, greed **6.** create, factor,
  ground, induce, motive, reason,
  source **7.** crusade, produce, provoke
  8. campaign, etiology, movement,
  occasion **9.** originate **10.** mainspring
  13. justification
cause (pert to) ...
  approach.. **7.** attract
  be done.. **4.** writ **11.** fieri facias
  bring about.. **6.** effect
  buy and sell.. **7.** whipsaw
  coagulate.. **4.** curd **6.** curdle **7.** congeal,
  thicken
  contract unevenly.. **6.** pucker
  face East.. **6.** orient
  harm.. **4.** bane
  irritate.. **6.** rankle
  raise in relief.. **6.** emboss
  remember.. **6.** remind
  roll.. **7.** trundle
  speed up.. **10.** accelerate
  take root.. **8.** radicate
causerie ... **4.** chat, talk **6.** parley **7.** article
  8. converse, treatise **9.** paragraph
  10. discussion **12.** conversation
causes, science of ... **8.** etiology
causeuse ... **4.** sofa **9.** tête-à-tête
causeway ... **4.** dike **7.** highway
  10. embankment
causing ...
  destiny.. **5.** fatal
  emotion.. **7.** emotive
  forgetfulness.. **8.** nepenthe
  laughter.. **8.** risorial
  motion.. **6.** motile
caustic ... **4.** acid, tart **5.** acrid, curve
  (optic), sharp **6.** biting, bitter, severe
  7. acerbic, burning, cutting, erodent,
  mordant, pungent, pyrotic **8.** snappish,
  stinging, virulent **9.** corrosive, satirical,
  vitriolic **10.** astringent, escharotic
  11. acrimonious, penetrating
caustic agent ... **3.** lye **4.** alum, lime
  7. erodent **9.** quicklime
cautel ... **5.** trick **7.** caution **8.** prudence
  9. direction (Eccl) **10.** precaution
cauterize ... **4.** burn, char, sear **5.** brand,
  singe **7.** torrefy
cautery ... **7.** burning, searing **8.** inustion
  10. instrument **13.** cauterization
caution ... **4.** card (coll), care, heed, warn

5. aviso 6. advice, caveat, notice, oddity 7. anxiety, counsel, precept, proviso, warning 8. forecast, prudence, wariness 9. chariness, vigilance 10. admonition, providence, solicitude 11. exhortation, forethought, mindfulness 12. cautiousness, notification, watchfulness 14. circumspection

cautious . . . 4. wary 5. canny, chary 6. Fabian 7. careful, guarded, heedful, mindful, prudent 11. circumspect

cautiously . . . 6. cagily, warily 7. cannily, charily 8. gingerly 9. carefully, guardedly, heedfully, mindfully, prudently 10. discreetly 13. circumspectly

cavalcade . . . 4. raid, ride 5. march 6. parade, review 7. caravan, pageant 9. motorcade 10. procession

cavalier . . . 3. gay 4. coin (Fr), curt 5. brave, frank, lover, rider 6. escort, knight, squire 7. admirer, brusque, esquire, gallant, haughty, soldier 8. horseman, Royalist 9. caballero, cavaliere, chevalier, Roundhead 10. disdainful, equestrian 12. high-spirited, supercilious

cavalry . . . 4. army 6. horses, yellow (color) 8. horsemen 10. knighthood

cavalry (pert to) . . .
  horse . . 6. lancer
  man . . 5. spahy, uhlan 6. Hussar, lancer 7. dragoon, trooper
  unit . . 5. troop
  weapon . . 5. lance, saber 9. demilance

cave . . . 3. den, mew 4. abri, cove, grot, hole, lair 5. antre, cover, lodge (beaver), speos 6. antrum, cavern, cellar, covert, dugout, grotto, subway, tunnel 7. chamber, shelter, spelunk 10. subterrane

cave (pert to) . . .
  fish . . 9. blindfish
  man . . 11. Paleolithic
  nature of . . 9. speluncar
  study of . . 10. speleology

cave canem . . . 11. Beware of Dog

cave dweller . . . 10. troglodyte

Cave of Adullam . . . 9. Seceeders (1866)

caviar, caviare . . . 3. roe 5. garum 6. relish 8. delicacy, fish eggs

cavil . . . 4. cark, carp, marl, quip 5. dodge, evade, parry, shift 6. bicker, boggle, haggle, palter 7. quibble, shuffle 9. criticize, pussyfoot 10. equivocate

caviler . . . 5. momus 6. critic, hedger 8. frondeur, quibbler 10. criticizer 11. equivocator, faultfinder

cavity . . . 3. dip, pit, sac, vug (voog) 4. aula, bore (gun), cava, hole, sink, well 5. abyss, antra, atria, bursa, chasm, fossa, fosse, geode, lumen, shaft, sinus 6. antrum, areole, atrium, caries, coelom, crater, hollow 7. cochlea, loculus 10. depression 11. compartment

cavort . . . 4. dido, romp, skip 5. antic, caper, cut up, frisk, prank 6. curvet, gambol, prance 7. flounce, gambade, gambado

cavy . . . 3. pig 4. paca 5. stray 6. agouti, rodent 8. capybara (capibara) 9. guinea pig

caw . . . 3. cry 5. croak, quark, quawk 11. exclamation

cay . . . 3. kay 5. islet

cease . . . 3. end 4. quit, rest (law), stop 5. avast, pause, stint 6. desist, perish 7. abandon, fade out, refrain 8. intermit, leave off, shutdown 9. disappear, pretermit 11. discontinue

ceaseless . . . 7. endless, nonstop 8. constant, unbroken, unending 9. continued, incessant, perennial, perpetual, unceasing 10. continuous 12. interminable 13. round the clock, uninterrupted

ceaselessness . . . 9. constancy 10. continuity, incessancy, perpetuity 11. endlessness 14. successiveness

cease to be . . . 3. die 6. expire, perish 8. dissolve 9. disappear

cease to please . . . 4. pall

Cebus . . . 3. sai 6. monkey 8. capuchin

cecils . . . 10. croquettes

cecity . . . 9. blindness

Cecrops (pert to) . . .
  daughter . . 5. Herse 8. Aglauros
  founder of (tradition) . . 6. Athens
  king of . . 6. Attica
  symbol . . 7. half man 10. half dragon

cedar (pert to) . . .
  bird . . 7. waxwing
  class . . 7. conifer
  fruit . . 6. cedron
  genus . . 5. Thuja, Toona 6. Cedrus 9. Juniperus
  green . . 5. cedre
  moss . . 8. hornwort
  type . . 5. savin 6. deodar, sabine 7. incense, juniper, Lebanon (Bib), Spanish 10. arborvitae 11. cryptomeria

cede . . . 5. grant, waive, yield 6. assign, confer 7. abandon 8. renounce 9. surrender 10. capitulate, relinquish

cedula . . . 3. tax 6. permit 8. schedule, security (Finan) 10. obligation 11. certificate

ceil . . . 4. line 5. cover 7. overlay 8. wainscot

ceiling . . . 4. acme, roof 5. astel, limit, price, trave 6. apogee, lining, screen, utmost 7. curtain, lacunar, maximum, plafond 8. covering 9. lacunaria 10. planchment, visibility 12. consummation

celebrant . . . 6. priest (Eucharist) 9. worshiper (worshipper) 11. communicant

celebrate . . . 4. keep, laud, sing 5. extol, honor, revel 6. herald, praise 7. glorify, maffick, observe, roister 8. emblazon, proclaim 9. solemnize 11. commemorate, memorialize

celebrated . . . 5. famed, noted 6. famous 7. feasted, honored, popular 8. far-famed, observed, renowned 9. distingué, well-known 11. illustrious 13. distinguished

celebration . . . 4. bout, fete, rite 5. fling, revel, spree 6. bender 7. fanfare, jubilee 8. ceremony, function 9. epinicion, festivity, rejoicing 10. observance

13. commemoration
celebrity . . . 3. VIP 4. fame 5. éclat, glory 6. notary 7. notable 8. luminary, somebody 10. famousness, popularity 11. recognition
celerity . . . 5. haste, speed 8. dispatch, rapidity, velocity 9. swiftness 10. speediness
celery . . . 4. ache 8. smallage (wild) 9. Ammiacaea
celestial . . . 6. astral, divine, uranic 7. angelic, sky blue 8. ethereal, heavenly 12. paradisaical
Celestial (pert to) . . .
being . . 5. angel 6. cherub, seraph
body . . 4. star 5. comet 6. nebula
city . . 6. heaven, utopia 9. Jerusalem
empire . . 7. Chinese, Tien Chu
equator . . 8. meridian
mind elevation . . 7. anagoge
teacher . . 6. Taoist
celibate . . . 4. monk 6. single 8. bachelor, monastic, Platonic, spinster 9. abstinent, continent, unmarried
cell . . . 3. egg, kil 4. cyst, germ, ovum 5. cnida, crypt 6. cytode, prison 7. alveola, cellule, dungeon 11. compartment
cell (pert to) . . .
animal . . 6. amoeba (ameba) 7. rotifer 8. protozoa
biology . . 7. energid, meiosis, mitosis, nucleus, spireme
cell-like . . 9. celliform
division . . 5. linin 7. spireme 8. amitosis
eating . . 9. cytophagy
Egyptian (tomb) . . 6. serdab
honeycomb . . 8. alveolus
Irish . . 3. kil (kill)
locomotive . . 5. sperm, zooid
Roman . . 4. alla, naos
study . . 8. cytology
substance . . 5. linin
walls . . 9. cellulose
cellaret . . . 4. case 8. tantalus 9. sideboard
Celt . . . 4. Erse, Gael, Manx, Scot 5. Welsh 6. Breton 7. Cornish
Celtic (pert to) . . .
abbot . . 5. coarb
bard . . 6. Ossian
cattle . . 2. ox
church . . 9. Christian
deity . . 7. Taranis
foot soldier . . 4. kern
horse . . 4. pony (Shetland)
island . . 4. Manx
king . . 4. Bran
language . . 4. Erse
minstrel . . 4. bard
Mother of Gods . . 3. Ana (Anu)
mountain . . 3. ben
Neptune . . 3. Ler
nickname . . 10. Turtleback
Order . . 5. Druid
people . . 5. Gauls, Irish, Scots, Welsh 7. Bretons, Britons
perfume . . 4. nard 9. spikenard
sun god . . 3. Lug (Lugh)
cembalo . . . 8. dulcimer 11. harpsichord 12. clavicembalo
cement . . . 4. bind, fuse, glue, join,

paar, pave 5. putty, stick, unite 6. cohere, fasten, mastic, mortar, solder 8. adhesive, concrete, pavement, solidify
cemetery . . . 6. litten 7. Calvary 8. boneyard, catacomb, Golgotha, lich gate (entrance); mortuary 9. graveyard, mausoleum 10. churchyard, necropolis 11. polyandrium 12. potter's field
cenobite . . . 4. Monk 5. Order (anc) 6. Essene 7. recluse
cenotaph . . . 4. tomb (empty) 7. memento 8. memorial, monument
censer bearer . . . 7. acolyte 8. altar boy, thurifer
censor . . . 5. judge 6. critic 7. monitor 8. censurer, reviewer, superego 11. faultfinder
censure . . . 4. flay 5. blame, chide, slate, targe 6. accuse 7. chasten, condemn, impeach, inveigh, reprove, slating 8. reproach 9. damnation, expurgate, reprimand 11. reprobation 12. condemnation, denunciation, reprehension
cent . . . 4. coin, game (old) 5. penny 6. copper, trifle 7. hundred, red cent
centaur (Myth) . . . 4. race (Thessaly) 6. Nessus 8. Lapithae, man-horse (half man) 9. bucentaur, Centaurus (Astron)
centennial . . . 4. game (dice) 9. hundredth, red-yellow 11. anniversary
Centennial State . . . 8. Colorado
center . . . 3. cor, hub 4. base, core, nave 5. axial, focus, heart, midst 6. kernel, marrow, middle 7. midmost, nucleus, pivotal, seaport 8. emporium
center (pert to) . . .
away from . . 6. distal
bull's-eye . . 5. clout 6. target
line . . 6. axiate, cesura
center of . . .
attention . . 8. cynosure
earth . . 9. epicenter
gravity . . 6. kernel 7. centrum
nervous system . . 5. brain
sail . . 4. bunt
target . . 3. eye 8. bull's-eye
centerpiece . . . 4. bowl 7. epergne
centipede . . . 4. rope (Naut) 6. earwig, insect 8. chilipod, myriapod
central . . . 3. mid 4. arch, main 5. axial, basic, chief, focal, prime 6. master, middle 7. capital, centric, leading, midmost, pivotal, primary 8. cardinal, dominant, foremost 9. principal 11. equidistant
Central America . . .
bird . . 7. jacamar 8. puffbird
boat . . 6. cayuco, pitpan
country . . 6. Panama 8. Honduras 9. Costa Rica, Guatemala, Nicaragua 10. El Salvador
Indian . . 4. Maya 5. Carib
monkey . . 4. mono
rodent . . 4. paca
snake . . 10. bushmaster
tree . . 3. ebo, ule 5. amate 9. sapodilla
Central Asia (pert to) . . .
gazelle . . 3. ahu

wild horse.. **6.** tarpan
wind storm.. **5.** buran
Central State... **6.** Kansas
centuries (ten)... **7.** chiliad
century... **3.** Age **4.** aeon (eon) **7.** centred
(anc), hundred **8.** eternity **9.** centenary
10. centennial
century plant... **4.** aloe **5.** agave
6. maguey
ceorl (Eng Hist)... **5.** churl, thane
7. freeman, villein
cepa... **5.** onion
cephalon... **4.** head (Zool)
cephalopod... **3.** ink (secretion) **5.** sepia
6. cuttle **7.** octopus **10.** cuttlefish
ceramics... **4.** tile **5.** china, delft,
spode **6.** mosaic **7.** pottery, Satsuma
8. crockery, majolica, Wedgwood
9. porcelain
ceramics term... **4.** clay, kiln, laun
5. adobe, stove, wheel **6.** sleeve (silk)
7. furnace **8.** ceramist **10.** ceramicist
12. ceramography
ceratoid... **5.** horny **8.** hornlike **10.** horn-
shaped
cere... **3.** wax **4.** wrap (dead body)
6. anoint **12.** protuberance (bird's)
cereal... **4.** bran, mush, rice **5.** grits,
gruel, maize, wheat **6.** farina, hominy
7. granola, oatmeal **8.** porridge **10.** corn
flakes
cereal grass... **3.** oat, rye **4.** ragi **5.** grain,
maize, wheat **6.** barley, millet, raggee
cereal spike... **3.** ear
cerebellum... **5.** brain (part)
cerebral (pert to)... **4.** lobe **5.** brain
6. speech **8.** arteries, peduncle
9. consonant (Phonet) **11.** crus cerebri,
hemispheres
cerebrum... **5.** brain **10.** encephalon
cere cloth... **7.** wrapper (corpse)
8. cerement, chrismal **12.** grave clothes
ceremonial... **4.** prim **5.** stiff **6.** custom,
formal, ritual **7.** precise, service,
studied **8.** ceremony, function, liturgic
9. formality **11.** punctilious
12. conventional
ceremonial (pert to)...
chamber.. **4.** kiva
departure.. **6.** congee
splendor.. **9.** pageantry
ceremonious... **6.** formal, polite
7. precise **8.** gracious **9.** attentive,
courteous **10.** ceremonial, respectful
11. deferential, ritualistic
ceremony... **4.** form, pomp, rite, show
6. parade, review, ritual **8.** function
9. formality, solemnity **10.** observance
11. performance
ceremony, without... **6.** humbly,
meekly, simply **7.** quietly **8.** casually,
modestly **9.** sans façon **10.** informally
15. unceremoniously
Ceres, Rom (pert to)...
astronomy.. **8.** asteroid (1st found)
father.. **6.** Saturn
Feast.. **8.** Cerialia (Apr 19)
Goddess of.. **4.** Corn **5.** Grain **9.** Fertility
11. Agriculture
Greek name.. **7.** Demeter
mother.. **3.** Ops

Cereus... **6.** cactus **7.** saguaro **13.** night-
blooming
cerise... **5.** color **7.** blue-red, fuchsia
10. cherrylike
ceroplastics... **8.** modeling, waxworks
certain... **3.** one **4.** sure **5.** clear, exact,
fixed, plain **7.** assured, decided, insured,
precise **8.** absolute, definite, positive
9. certified, confident, exclusive,
indubious, undoubted, warranted
10. guaranteed, inevitable, undeniable,
undoubting **11.** determinate,
trustworthy **14.** unquestionable
16. incontrovertible
certainly... **3.** yea, yes **4.** amen **5.** truly
6. indeed, really, surely, verily **7.** clearly,
in truth, utterly **8.** actually, of course
9. assuredly, precisely **10.** absolutely,
by all means, definitely, inevitably,
positively
certainty... **5.** cinch **6.** pledge, shoo-
in, surety **8.** sureness **9.** assurance,
certitude **13.** inevitability, infallibility
certificate... **5.** check, money **6.** ticket
7. diploma, voucher **10.** credential
11. testimonial
certificate (pert to)...
financial.. **3.** IOU **5.** draft, scrip
9. debenture
India.. **5.** hundi
medical (Eng college).. **8.** aegrotat
certification... **2.** OK **3.** fix **5.** proof
8. sanction **10.** validation
11. affirmation, attestation, certificate,
endorsement **12.** confirmation,
ratification **13.** ascertainment,
authorization **14.** substantiation
certify... **5.** prove, swear, vouch
6. assure, attest, avouch, ratify, verify
7. approve, confirm, endorse, witness
8. accredit, validate **9.** ascertain,
determine, establish, guarantee
11. acknowledge, corroborate
cerulean... **4.** blue **5.** azure **7.** sky-blue
cerumen... **6.** earwax
cervine... **8.** deerlike
cess... **3.** bag, tax **4.** cede, duty, levy,
toll **5.** yield **6.** assess, impost, tariff
7. revenue **9.** surrender **10.** assessment
cessation... **3.** end **4.** lull, stay
5. letup, truce **7.** respite **8.** abeyance,
desition **9.** interlude **10.** suspension
12. intermission, interruption
14. discontinuance
cetacea, cetacean... **3.** orc **4.** apod,
orca, susu (blind) **5.** whale **6.** whales
7. cowfish, finback, grampus, narwhal
(narwal), rorqual
Cete... **5.** whale **10.** The Cetacea
Cetus... **8.** The Whale **13.** constellation
(Equator)
Ceylon...
capital.. **7.** Colombo
city.. **5.** Galle, Kandy (famed Buddhist
Temple) **6.** Jaffna
mountain peak.. **14.** Pidurutalagala
new name.. **8.** Sri Lanka
ocean.. **6.** Indian
old name.. **9.** Taprobane
people.. **5.** Tamil **6.** Malays, Veddas
8. Malabars **10.** Singhalese

Ceylon (pert to) . . .
boat . . **5.** dhoni (doni)
canoe . . **5.** balsa
Festival . . **8.** Perahera
garment . . **6.** sarong
hill dweller . . **4.** Toda
monkey . . **4.** maha **6.** langur, rillow
moss . . **4.** alga **6.** Jaffna **7.** gulaman
8. agar-agar
palm . . **7.** talipot
rat . . **9.** bandicoot
sand (sea bottom) . . **4.** paar
tree . . **4.** doon
chabouk, chabuk (Ind) . . . **4.** whip
9. horsewhip
chacma . . . **6.** baboon
chafe . . . **3.** cut, irk, rub, vex **4.** fret,
fume, fuss, gall, heat, rage, skin, warm
5. anger, annoy, grate, grind, pique,
scuff, worry, wound **6.** abrade, banter,
excite, harass, injure, nettle, rankle
7. inflame **8.** irritate
chaff . . . **3.** hay **4.** bran, husk, quiz, twit
5. dregs, fluff, husks, palea, straw,
trash, waste **6.** banter, cobweb, glumes,
refuse, scraps **7.** remains, residue,
tailing **8.** raillery, ridicule, riffraff
chaffer . . . **5.** trade, wares **6.** buying,
dicker, haggle, higgle, market
7. bargain, chaffer, chatter, selling
9. negotiate **11.** merchandise
chafing dish . . . **7.** cresset
chagrin . . . **7.** anxiety, mortify **8.** distress,
troubles, vexation **13.** mortification
chain . . . **4.** bind, bond, boom, gyve, reef,
torc **5.** cable, range **6.** catena, fasten,
fetter, secure, series, tether, torque
7. creeper, sorites **15.** contravallation
(fort series)
chair . . . **4.** seat, sill **5.** bench, sedan
6. rocker, throne **7.** enchair, speaker
chair (pert to) . . .
back . . **5.** splat **7.** upright
collegiate . . **10.** fellowship
13. professorship
cover . . **4.** tidy **12.** antimacassar
India . . **6.** musnud
Japan . . **4.** kago
maker . . **5.** caner **6.** reeder
chair (type of) . . . **4.** camp, deck, easy,
high, lawn, wing **6.** lounge, Morris,
swivel **7.** contour, folding, steamer,
Windsor **8.** armchair, captain's, electric,
fauteuil, straight **10.** ladder-back
11. overstuffed
chairman . . . **7.** officer, speaker **8.** director
9. moderator
chalcedony . . . **4.** onyx, opal, sard
5. agate **6.** jasper, quartz **7.** opaline
9. carnelian **11.** chrysoprase
Chaldean (pert to) . . . **2.** Ur **4.** seer
6. Semite **10.** astrologer, soothsayer
13. Neo-Babylonian (language)
chalice . . . **3.** ama, cup **5.** amula (anc),
calix, grail **6.** goblet **8.** daffodil
chalice pall . . . **4.** veil **8.** animetta
chalk . . . **4.** draw, mark, pale, tick **5.** score
6. blanch, bleach, crayon, credit,
pastel, whiten **7.** account, drawing
9. limestone, reckoning
chalker . . . **7.** milkman (Eng sl)

chalklike . . . **10.** calcareous
chalky . . . **5.** white **7.** crumbly, friable,
powdery **10.** cretaceous
challenge . . . **4.** dare, defy, gage **5.** claim,
doubt, query **6.** accost, cartel, defial,
demand, impugn **7.** dispute, protest
8. question, reproach **10.** accusation,
controvert **11.** questioning
chamal . . . **4.** goat (Angora)
chamber . . . **4.** cave, hall, kiva, room
5. court **6.** camera, cavity **7.** bedroom,
boudoir, cabinet, chambre, cubicle
10. bedchamber **11.** compartment
chamber (pert to) . . .
harem . . **3.** oda
heart . . **7.** auricle **9.** ventricle
King's . . **9.** camarilla
music . . **14.** sonata da camera
chambers . . . **4.** flat **5.** suite **6.** office
9. apartment, bicameral (Legis) **14.** Inns
of Chancery (Eng)
chameleon . . . **6.** lizard **10.** vacillator
13. changeability, constellation
chamfer (to) . . . **5.** bevel, carve, flute,
score **6.** chisel, groove
chamois . . . **5.** Gemse, izard **8.** antelope
champ . . . **4.** bite, chew, mash **5.** gnash
6. victor **7.** trample **11.** battlefield
champagne . . . **4.** wine **9.** red-yellow
13. chrysanthemum
champaign . . . **5.** field, plain **7.** expanse
11. battlefield
champion . . . **3.** Ace **4.** best, hero
5. champ **6.** defend, expert, victor,
winner **7.** espouse, fighter, titlist
8. advocate, defender **9.** combatant,
conqueror **10.** unexcelled
champion (pert to) . . .
Christian (anc) . . **3.** Cid
constellation . . **7.** Perseus
knight (legend) . . **7.** Paladin
Spanish . . **12.** conquistador
chance . . . **3.** die, hap, lot **4.** fate, luck,
odds, risk, turn **6.** casual, gamble,
happen, mishap, tossup **7.** fortune,
lottery, tychism **8.** fortuity, Lady Luck,
occasion **9.** happening, mischance
10. likelihood **11.** opportunity,
possibility, probability **12.** happenstance
chancel (pert to) . . .
part . . **4.** bema
screen . . **4.** jube
seats . . **7.** sedilia
change . . . **4.** flux, move, turn, vary,
veer **5.** alter, amend, break, coins,
money, shift **6.** modify, mutate, switch
7. caprice, convert, deviate, variety
8. transfer **9.** diversity, transform,
transmute, variation **10.** alteration,
fickleness, modulation **11.** inconstancy,
vicissitude **12.** substitution
13. metamorphosis **14.** transformation
15. diversification
change (pert to) . . .
color . . **3.** dye, wan **4.** fade, pale **5.** blush
6. blanch, redden
medicine . . **11.** heterotopia
mind . . **6.** repent **12.** tergiversate
music . . **4.** muta
order of . . **9.** metabolic, rearrange,
transpose

changeable . . . **6.** fickle, fitful, mobile **7.** erratic, flighty, mutable, protean **8.** freakish, notional, unstable, variable, volatile, weathery **9.** alterable, chameleon, metabolic, uncertain, unsettled, whimsical **10.** capricious, inconstant **15.** interchangeable

changeling . . . **3.** oaf **4.** dolt **5.** idiot **7.** waverer **8.** imbecile, renegade, turncoat **9.** simpleton **10.** substitute (child)

channel . . . **3.** bed, cut, gat, way **4.** dike, duct, gate, gurt, lane, leat, pass, vein **5.** basin, canal, ditch, drain, flume, flute, fosse, radio, river, sinus, stria **6.** alveus, avenue, coulee, groove, gutter, outlet, sluice, trench, trough **7.** conduit, tideway **8.** aqueduct, tailrace **9.** broadcast **10.** passageway

Channel Islands . . . **4.** Sark (Sercq) **6.** Jersey **8.** Alderney

chanson . . . **4.** song **5.** lyric **6.** ballad

chant . . . **3.** say **4.** sing **6.** intone, melody, warble **7.** introit, singing **8.** canticle **10.** intonation **11.** composition

chanter . . . **6.** cantor, singer **7.** bagpipe (part), intoner, sparrow (hedge) **8.** songster, vocalist **9.** chanteuse, chorister

chanticleer . . . **4.** cock **7.** rooster **11.** cock-a-doodle **14.** cock-a-doodle-doo

chaos . . . **2.** Nu (Egypt) **3.** pie (type) **4.** gulf, mess **5.** abyss, babel, chasm **7.** anarchy **8.** disorder **9.** confusion, imbroglio **10.** unruliness **13.** orderlessness

Chaos (pert to) . . .
daughter . . **3.** Nox, Nyx
parent of . . **5.** earth **6.** heaven **8.** Creation
son . . **6.** Erebus

chaotic . . . **6.** muddle **8.** confused, formless **12.** disorganized

chap . . . **3.** boy, buy, guy, lad, man **4.** kibe (sore) **5.** buyer, chink, cleft, crack, scout, split, youth **6.** barter, choose (Scot), fellow, galoot **7.** chapman **8.** customer

chapeau . . . **3.** cap, hat, lid **5.** beret

chapel . . . **4.** cape, cope, cowl, hood **5.** altar, choir **6.** bethel **7.** chantry, galilee, oratory, service, Sistine **8.** sacellum (anc) **9.** reliquary

chaperon . . . **4.** hood **6.** attend, duenna, escort **8.** guardian **9.** attendant **10.** gooseberry

chaplet . . . **4.** band **5.** beads **6.** anadem, wreath **7.** garland, prayers **8.** beadroll, insignia, necklace

chappaul . . . **9.** squawfish

chaps . . . **8.** overalls **10.** chaparajos

chapter . . . **4.** Sura **5.** topic **6.** clause **7.** council, meeting, passage, section, Society **8.** division **9.** capitular **10.** fraternity **12.** organization

chaptrel . . . **6.** impost

char . . . **4.** burn **5.** trout **6.** scorch **8.** charcoal, sandbank

character . . . **4.** hero, kind, mark, role, sign, star **5.** trait **6.** cipher, letter, nature, repute, status, symbol **7.** quality **8.** function **9.** reference **10.** reputation **11.** temperament **14.** characteristic

character (pert to) . . .

giver . . **5.** toner
Hebrew . . **3.** Tav, Taw
Irish . . **5.** Ogham
musical . . **3.** bar **4.** clef, rest **5.** neume
of people . . **5.** ethos
real . . **7.** essence
science of . . **8.** ethology
Teutonic . . **4.** rune

characteristic . . . **4.** mark **5.** habit, trait **7.** feature, impress, quality, typical **8.** peculiar, symbolic **9.** attribute, character, idiopathy, lineament, specialty **11.** distinctive, peculiarity, singularity, symptomatic **13.** individualism

characteristic (pert to) . . .
descent . . **6.** racial
peculiar . . **9.** idiopathy
spirit . . **5.** ethos
tone (Mus) . . **7.** seventh

characterization . . . **4.** role **5.** drama **9.** depiction, portrayal **11.** description, distinction **13.** impersonation **14.** identification, representation

characterize . . . **4.** mark, name **5.** enact **7.** engrave, imprint, portray **8.** describe, inscribe **9.** delineate, designate, epitomize, represent **11.** distinguish

characterized by . . .
abstinence . . **7.** ascetic
bacteria exclusion . . **7.** asepsis
cruelty . . **7.** Neronic
exact thinking . . **13.** ratiocinative
melody . . **6.** ariose
poison (bloodstream) . . **6.** sepsis
pomposity . . **13.** grandiloquent

characterless . . . **5.** inane **9.** colorless, pointless

charcoal . . . **4.** coke, fuel, lave, peat **5.** black, chark **6.** carbon, fusain **7.** drawing, residue **9.** boneblack, briquette

charge . . . **4.** bill, cost, dues, fill, load, onus, rate, task, toll, ward **5.** blame, chore, debit, onset, order, price, trust **6.** accuse, advice, advise, allege, amount, attack, client, commit, credit, demand, dictum, impute, indict **7.** assault, command, concern, custody, expense, impeach, keeping, mandate, precept, primage, protége **8.** guidance, insignia, instruct, tutelage **9.** dependent, electrify, exactment **10.** accusation, commission, imposition, impregnate, injunction, management **11.** arrangement, attribution, instruction, supervision **13.** incrimination **14.** responsibility

charged atom . . . **3.** ion

charge of affairs . . . **8.** diplomat **15.** chargé d'affaires

charge off . . . **5.** debit **6.** forget **7.** dismiss, forgive **8.** discount

charges (law) . . . **4.** dues, fees **5.** costs **9.** retainers

charge with . . .
crime . . **6.** indict **7.** impeach **11.** incriminate
debt . . **5.** debit
gas . . **6.** aerate
offense . . **6.** accuse

to .. 5. blame 7. ascribe 9. attribute
charily ... 6. cagily, warily 8. frugally
9. carefully, thriftily 10. cautiously
12. economically, suspiciously
chariness ... 7. caution 8. caginess,
distrust, wariness 9. frugality
11. heedfulness, thriftiness
chariot ... 3. car 4. biga, cart, rath (ratha),
wain 5. essed (anc), wagon 7. vehicle
8. quadriga
charioteer ... 6. Auriga (Astron), Ben
Hur
charitable ... 3. big 4. kind 6. kindly
7. lenient, liberal 8. generous, tolerant
9. forgiving, indulgent 10. altruistic,
benevolent, bighearted 11. beneficient
12. eleemosynary, humanitarian
13. compassionate, philanthropic
charity ... 4. alms, dole 6. bounty, virtue
7. handout, largess 8. lenience, pittance
9. tolerance 10. almsgiving, liberality
11. benevolence 12. philanthropy
charity dispenser ... 7. almoner
charivari ... 5. babel 6. medley, uproar
8. serenade (mock) 10. callithump
charlatan ... 5. faker, fraud, phony, quack
6. humbug 7. empiric 8. impostor
9. pretender 10. medicaster,
mountebank
Charlemagne, Emperor (pert to) ...
brother .. 8. Carloman
emperor of .. 7. The West
father .. 5. Pepin (the Short)
name also .. 15. Charles The Great
nephew .. 7. Orlando
charm ... 3. obi 4. lure, mojo, play,
song 5. grace, magic, oomph, spell
6. allure, amulet, appeal, beauty,
enamor, entice, fetish, glamor, scarab
7. beguile, bewitch, cantrip, delight,
enchant, glamour, periapt 8. breloque,
elegance, entrance, ornament, talisman
9. captivate, fascinate, sex appeal,
sweetness 10. allurement, attraction,
brimborion (brimborium), lovability
11. captivation, conjuration, incantation,
pulchritude, winsomeness
12. antinganting 14. attractiveness,
delightfulness
charmer ... 5. siren 6. beauty 7. enticer
8. exorcist, magician, sorcerer
9. bewitcher
charming ... 7. winsome 8. alluring,
pleasing 10. bewitching, delightful
11. captivating, fascinating
Charon's river ... 4. Styx
chart ... 3. map 4. list, plat, plot
7. diagram
charter ... 4. hire 5. carta, grant 6. charta,
firman, treaty 7. license 9. privilege
(special), purwannah
chartreuse ... 4. mold (cookery) 5. color
7. liqueur
Chartreuse ... 9. monastery 18. La
Grande Chartreuse (Grenoble)
chary ... 4. wary 5. cagey 6. frugal,
skimpy 7. thrifty 8. cautious
10. suspicious 12. parsimonious
Charybdis ... 6. Scylla 8. Galofaro
9. whirlpool (Messina)
chase ... 3. gun (Naut), set (gem) 4. hunt,

park, race 5. chevy (chivy), raise,
sport, track 6. emboss, follow, furrow,
groove, hasten, pursue, shikar, stroke
(tennis) 7. engrave, pursuit, repulse
8. ornament 12. steeplechase
Chase (The)**, goddess of** ... 5. Diana
chasm ... 3. gap, pit 4. gulf, hole, rift,
well 5. abyss, cleft, shaft 6. breach,
canyon, cavity, hiatus 7. fissure,
opening 8. crevasse
chasma ... 7. yawning
chasse ... 4. step (dance) 6. shrine
9. reliquary
chaste ... 4. pure 6. modest, simple
8. innocent, virtuous 9. continent,
uncorrupt, undefiled, unmarried
10. immaculate
chasten ... 4. rate 5. smote 6. punish,
refine 7. correct 8. chastise, penalize,
restrain 9. castigate 10. discipline
chastened ... 4. meek 5. smote
7. subdued 8. punished, purified,
tempered 10. restrained
chastise ... 4. beat, slap, whip 5. amend,
blame, scold, spank, taunt 6. punish,
rebate, rebuke, swinge 7. correct,
reprove 9. castigate 10. discipline
chastity ... 6. purity, virtue 9. cleanness
10. chasteness 12. virtuousness
chat ... 3. gab, rap, yak 4. chin, coze, jist,
talk, tove 5. prate 6. babble, confab,
gabble, gibber, gossip, jabber 7. chatter,
prattle 8. causerie, chitchat, converse
12. conversation 14. chitter-chatter
chatelaine ... 3. pin 4. etui, hook 5. clasp,
purse, watch 6. brooch, torque
chattels ... 4. naam 5. goods, money,
wares 6. estate 7. effects 8. holdings,
property 9. livestock, principal
11. possessions
chatter ... 3. gab, yap 5. clack, prate
7. clatter, prattle
chatterer ... 3. jay, mag 4. bird, piet
6. magpie 10. chatterbox
chatty ... 3. pot (earthen) 4. glib 5. gabby
7. affable 8. sociable 9. garrulous,
prattling, talkative 14. conversational
Chaucer (pert to) ...
author of .. 15. Canterbury Tales
Inn .. 6. (The) Tabard
pilgrimage city .. 10. Canterbury
style of work .. 7. novella
chauvinist ... 5. jingo 6. Rajput
7. chauvin, patriot 8. jingoist
9. warmonger 10. militarist
cheap ... 5. small, tacky, tinny, trade,
value 6. cheesy, paltry, plenty, sleazy
7. abashed, bargain, chintzy, cut-
rate, reduced, schlock 9. niggardly
11. inexpensive
cheapen ... 3. cut 4. trim 5. lower, slash
6. debase, reduce 7. degrade 8. mark
down
cheat ... 2. do 3. ban, con, fob, gyp
4. bilk, fake, flam, hoax, liar, rook,
scam, sell, sham 5. cozen, elude, guile,
phony, scalp 6. deceit, fleece, humbug,
hustle, illude, rip-off 7. deceive,
finesse, sharpen, swindle 8. artifice,
impostor 9. bamboozle, overreach,
stratagem, victimize 10. thimblerig

13. bait-and-switch
check . . . 3. nip, tab 4. balk, curb, damp,
mark, rein, stem, stop, test 5. agree,
brake, count, delay, limit, money,
plaid, repel, stunt, tally 6. bridle,
cheque, detain, detent, impede, oppose,
rebuff, retard, ticket, verify 7. counter,
examine, inhibit, measure, monitor,
pattern, repress 9. hindrance, restraint
12. verification
check (pert to) . . .
in . . 3. die 6. arrive 8. register
out . . 3. die 5. croak, leave 6. assess
8. withdraw
pattern . . 11. houndstooth
game, term . . 5. chess 8. gambling
checkered . . . 4. vair 5. diced, plaid
6. mosaic, tartan, varied 7. checked
10. changeable, tesserated, variegated
11. diversified
checkers, chequers . . . 4. game
8. draughts (Brit)
cheek . . . 4. gall, gena, jowl 5. brass,
bucca, crust, malar, nerve 8. audacity,
chutzpah 9. impudence 10. buccinator
cheer . . . 3. rah 4. yell 5. bravo,
elate, huzza, liven, mirth, salvo
6. gaiety, hurrah, regale, repast, salute,
solace 7. animate, applaud, console,
gladden, hearten, jollity, refresh, rejoice
8. applause, inspirit, pleasure, vivacity
9. encourage, merriment 10. exhilarate
12. conviviality
cheerful . . . 3. gay 4. gleg (Scot), rosy
5. happy, peart, sunny 6. blithe,
cheery, genial, hearty, jocund, joyful
8. gladsome, homelike 9. contented,
lightsome 12. lighthearted
cheerfulness . . . 3. joy 4. glee 5. cheer,
mirth 6. gaiety 7. jollity 8. gladness,
hilarity 9. happiness, merriment
12. exhilaration
cheerio . . . 5. adios, aloha, skoal, toast
6. hurrah, prosit 8. au revoir, farewell,
Godspeed 9. greetings
cheerless . . . 3. sad 4. cold, drab
5. drear 6. dismal, dreary, gloomy
7. forlorn, joyless, unhappy 8. dejected
9. unsmiling 10. depressing, melancholy
11. dispiriting 12. disconsolate
cheese . . . 4. blue (bleu), brie, Edam,
feta, jack 5. cream, Gouda, Swiss
6. chevre, Romano 7. Cheddar,
cottage, fromage (Fr), Gruyère, havarti,
ricotta, sapsago, Stilton 8. American,
Monterey (jack), Muenster, Parmesan
9. Camembert, Jarlsberg, Limburger,
Roquefort 10. Gorgonzola, Neufchâtel
cheese dish . . . 6. fondue, omelet, quiche,
strata 7. rarebit, soufflé
cheesy . . . 3. bad 6. paltry 8. inferior
9. worthless 12. disreputable
cheetah . . . 3. cat 5. youse (youze)
7. guepard (gueparde)
cheilos . . . 3. lip
chela . . . 4. claw 6. novice 8. disciple
Chelonia . . . 7. reptile, turtles 9. tortoises
chemical (pert to) . . .
analysis . . 5. assay
cleanser . . 6. kryton
etching . . 11. chemigraphy

strength . . 5. titer (titre)
term . . 3. gas 4. acid, atom, base, salt
5. imine 6. alkali, eluate 7. hormone,
nonacid, organic, radical, valence
8. catalyst, compound 10. bathoflore
11. bathochrome
vessel . . 4. etna 6. aludel, retort
7. alembic 8. crucible, reductor
chemical suffix . . . 2. ac, el, yl 3. ane,
ene, ile, ine, ole, ose 4. enol, olic,
osan
chemin de fer . . . 7. railway 8. baccarat,
railroad
chemise . . . 4. slip 5. shift
chemist . . . 7. analyst 8. druggist
9. alchemist 10. apothecary, biochemist
12. iatrochemist (anc)
cherish . . . 3. aid, hug, pet, woo 4. love
5. adore, cheer, nurse, prize 6. caress,
faddle, fondle, foster 7. care for,
comfort, nourish, nurture, protect,
support 8. enshrine, remember,
treasure 9. cultivate, encourage,
entertain
cheroot . . . 5. cigar
cherry . . . 3. pin 4. Bing, bird, gean,
ming 5. black 6. egriot, Prunus
7. capulin, marasca, mazzard, Morello,
oxheart 8. Napoleon 9. amarelles,
bigarreau, Queen Anne 11. chokecherry,
Montmorency
cherub . . . 5. angel, child, saint 6. seraph,
spirit 7. darling, eudemon 8. cherubim,
seraphim
chess (pert to) . . .
chessman . . 4. king, pawn, rook 5. piece,
queen 6. bishop, castle, knight
Italian . . 7. scacchi
term . . 4. dual, move 5. debut 6. chassé,
fidate, gambit 7. endgame, opening,
problem 9. checkmate, en passant,
roo k's tour, stalemate 10. fianchetto
chesslike . . . 8. scacchic
chest . . . 3. ark, box 4. arca, cist, kist
5. bahut 6. breast, cajeta, coffer, coffin,
locker 7. highboy, wanigan (wangan)
10. chiffonier 11. gardeviance
chest (pert to) . . .
ammunition . . 7. caisson
animal . . 7. brisket
human . . 6. thorax 7. midriff
sound . . 4. rale
sepulchral . . 6. larnax
Chester (Eng), **inhabitant** . . . 8. Cestrian
chesterfield . . . 4. sofa 5. divan
8. overcoat 9. cigarette, davenport
chestnut . . . 4. ling, rata 5. horse, water
6. marron 7. buckeye 8. Aesculus,
Castanea 10. breadfruit, chinquapin
chestnut . . . 4. joke 6. cliché 7. bromide
8. banality
chestnut color . . . 4. roan 5. brown
6. sorrel 12. reddish-brown
chevalier . . . 5. cadet (nobility), noble
6. knight 7. gallant 8. cavalier,
horseman 10. greenshank (bird)
chevron . . . 4. beam 5. glove 6. rafter,
stripe, zigzag 8. insignia
chevrotain . . . 4. napu 7. deerlet, kenchil,
meminna 9. Tragulina
chevy . . . 3. cry (hunting) 4. game, hunt

5. chase 6. flight, harass, pursue
7. torment
chew . . . 3. cud 4. bite, chaw, gnaw,
quid 5. champ, chomp, grind, munch
6. chavel, ponder 8. meditate, ruminate
9. masticate
chiasma . . . 11. decussation
12. intersection
chiasmus . . . 9. inversion (of words)
chib (Gypsy) . . . 6. tongue 8. language
chic . . . 4. trig, trim 5. natty, smart
6. modish, spruce 7. stylish
Chicago's nickname . . . 9. Windy City
chicanery . . . 4. ruse, wile 5. feint, trick
6. deceit 7. knavery 8. artifice, trickery
9. stratagem 11. skulduggery
chickadee . . . 8. titmouse 10. Pebthestes
chicken . . . 3. hen 4. cock, fowl,
girl 5. biddy, capon, chick, deedy,
fryer, poult, young 6. coward, pullet
7. broiler, rooster 8. cockerel, weakling
9. youngling 11. chanticleer,
milquetoast
chickenhearted . . . 5. timid 8. cowardly
12. fainthearted
chicory . . . 6. endive 7. succory
12. Cichoriaceae
chickpea . . . 8. garbanzo
chide . . . 4. rate 5. blame, scold 6. berate,
rebuke 7. censure, reprove, wrangle
8. admonish, reproach 9. reprimand
chief . . . 3. dux, top 4. arch, head,
main, rais (reis) 5. first, forte, major,
mogul 6. leader, primal, staple, syndic
7. kingpin, supreme 9. directing,
governing, paramount, potentate,
principal, prominent 11. predominant
chief (pert to) . . .
African . . 3. dey 4. kaid 5. negus
6. induna
Am Indian . . 6. sachem 7. Osceola
8. sagamore
Arab . . 5. sheik
Chinook . . 4. tyee
Cossack . . 6. ataman, hetman
Egypt . . 3. Min (Panopolis)
Europe . . 6. syndic
Germany . . 6. Führer (Fuehrer), Kaiser
Iran . . 9. ayatollah
Italy . . 4. doge, duce
Japan . . 6. mikado, shogun
Mexico . . 7. cacique
Nepal . . 4. Rais
Oriental . . 4. kahn 6. sirdar
Persia . . 4. shah
Russia . . 4. czar (tsar)
Spain . . 7. alcalde
Tibet . . 9. Dalai Lama
Turkey . . 3. aga (agha) 6. vizier
chilblain . . . 6. pernio
child . . . 3. imp, kid, tad, tot 4. babe,
baby, bata, brat, teen, tike, waif
5. bairn, cupid, elfin, fetus 6. cherub,
childe (anc), infant, urchin 7. adoptee,
nestler, preteen, progeny 9. offspring,
youngster 10. descendant
childish . . . 4. weak 5. naive, petty,
young 6. senile, simple 7. babyish,
kiddish, puerile, unmanly 8. immature
9. infantile, kittenish
children (pert to) . . .

doctor . . 12. pediatrician
mythology . . 6. Titans
Patron Saint . . 5. Santa
slain by Herod . . 12. The Innocents
study of . . 8. pedology 10. pediatrics
Chile . . . see also *Chilean*
cape . . 4. Horn
capital . . 8. Santiago (1541)
city . . 4. Lota 5. Arica 8. Valdivia
10. Concepcion, Valparaiso (1543)
conqueror . . 7. Pizarro 8. Valdivia
desert . . 7. Atacama
explorer . . 8. Magellan (1520)
mountain . . 5. Andes
poet . . 6. Neruda
river . . 3. Loa 6. Biobio
settlement (southernmost) . . 8. Navarino
(Isl) 14. Puerto Williams
Chilean (pert to) . . .
coconut . . 7. coquito
evergreen . . 6. pepino 10. arborvitae
shrub (poison) . . 5. lithi
wind . . 5. sures 11. sures pardos
workman . . 4. rote
chiliad . . . 8. thousand 9. millenium
13. thousand years
chill . . . 3. ice, raw 4. ague, cold, damp
5. algor, frost, rigor 6. damper, formal,
shiver 7. malaria 8. coldness, coolness,
dispirit 10. depressing 11. refrigerate
chilly . . . 3. raw 4. ague, cold 5. gelid
6. aguish, freeze, frosty 12. refrigerated
chiloplasty . . . 10. lip surgery 12. mouth
surgery
chime . . . 4. bell, peal, ring, suit 5. agreé,
bells, prate, rhyme 6. accord, concur,
cymbal, jingle 7. harmony
chimera . . . 5. dream, fancy, vapor
6. bubble, utopia 7. monster 8. illusion,
paradise (fool's)
chimerical . . . 4. vain 7. utopian
8. delusive, fanciful, romantic
9. fantastic, imaginary, unfounded
chimney . . . 3. lum 4. flue 5. cleft, stack,
tewel 10. smokestack
chimpanzee . . . 6. gibbon, nohega
7. gorilla
chin . . . 4. talk 5. genio (comb form)
6. mentum, weight (Chin) 8. converse
10. chew the rag 11. genioplasty (Surg),
mentoplasty (Surg)
china . . . 7. Dresden, pottery 8. crockery
9. porcelain 11. earthenware
China . . . see also *Chinese*
Buddha . . 2. Fo
capital . . 7. Beijing
capital, old name . . 7. Peiping (Peking)
city . . 4. Amoy, Tsin, Wuhu 6. Canton,
Hankow, Ningpo 7. Foochow, Nanking,
Soochow 8. Hangchow, Shanghai,
Tientsin
Communist leader . . 3. Mao 4. Deng
dynasty . . 3. Han, Kin, Sui 4. Chou,
Hsia (BC), Ming, Tsin, Yuan 5. Ching
6. Manchu, Mongol (Kublai Khan's)
island . . 5. Matsu 6. Quemoy, Taiwan
(Formosa)
magistrate . . 5. tupan 6. tuchun
8. mandarin
Mainland . . 15. People's Republic
Military Academy . . 7. Whompoa

Mongol . . **3.** Hun
mountain . . **7.** Kuen-lun **9.** Himalayas
Nationalist leader . . **13.** Chiang Kai-shek
nickname . . **14.** Flowery Kingdom
philosopher . . **6.** Laotse **9.** Confucius
poet . . **4.** Li Po **7.** Li Tai Po
race . . **9.** Mongoloid
religion . . **6.** Taoism **8.** Buddhism
　9. Confucian **12.** Confucianism
revolutionary leader . . **9.** Sun Yat-sen
river . . **5.** Chang (formerly Yangtze)
　7. Huang He (formerly Hwang Ho)
sea . . **5.** China **6.** Yellow
treaty port . . **4.** Amoy
Chinese (pert to) . . .
antelope . . **6.** dzeren
boat . . **4.** junk **5.** tanka **6.** sampan
cabbage . . **7.** pakchoi
card game . . **6.** fantan
carpet . . **6.** Khotan **7.** Kashgar, Yarkand
　9. Samarkand, Turkestan
Catholic Church . . **11.** Tien Chu T'ang
　12. Tien Chu Chiao
chestnut . . **4.** ling
confection . . **8.** chowchow
deer . . **8.** elaphure
defense . . **4.** Wall (2,000 mi long)
desert . . **4.** Gobi **5.** Shamo
dragon . . **6.** chi-lin
fabric . . **3.** sha **7.** nankeen
festival (Spring) . . **9.** Ch'ing Ming
flute . . **4.** tche (che)
fruit . . **6.** litchi (nut)
game . . **6.** fantan
ginger . . **9.** galingale
God . . **4.** Shen (Chr) **7.** Shangti, Tien
　Chu (RCCh)
gong . . **6.** tam-tam, tom-tom
grass . . **5.** ramee
idol . . **4.** joss **6.** pagoda (pagod)
instrument . . **3.** che, kin **4.** tche **5.** sheng
　(cheng)
jade . . **2.** yu
jute . . **7.** chingma
laborer . . **6.** coolie
lily . . **9.** narcissus
liquor . . **6.** samshu (rice)
literary degree . . **8.** hsiu tsai
monkey . . **4.** douc
nurse . . **4.** amah
officer . . **4.** kwan
oil . . **4.** tung
ox . . **4.** zebu
pagoda . . **3.** taa
paradise (Buddh) . . **4.** Jodo **7.** Ching-tu
　8. Gekuraku
philosophy . . **10.** Yang and Yin
religion . . **6.** Taoism **8.** Buddhism
　12. Confucianism
residence (official) . . **5.** yamen
screen (folding) . . **10.** Coromandel
silkworm . . **4.** sina **9.** ailanthus
silver ingot . . **5.** sycee
sky . . **4.** tien
society (secret) . . **3.** hui (hoey) **4.** tong
vessel . . **4.** junk **6.** lorcha
chink . . . **4.** rent, rift, rima, rime, ring
　5. cleft, crack **6.** cranny, furrow
　7. bunting (bird), fissure **10.** interstice
chinook . . . **4.** herb, wind **6.** salmon
　7. quinnat

Chinook (pert to) . . .
chief . . **4.** tyee
people . . **8.** Flathead
State (nickname of) . . **10.** Washington
chinquapin . . . **3.** oak **6.** bonnet (water)
　8. chestnut
chip . . . **3.** cut, hew **4.** coin **5.** break, carve,
　flake, piece, scrap, token **6.** chisel,
　gallet (stone) **7.** counter
chipmunk . . . **6.** hackee
chipped stone (instrument) . . .
　9. paleolith
chipper . . . **5.** chirp **6.** babble, chisel,
　hammer, lively **7.** chirrup, twitter
　8. cheerful
chirognomy . . . **9.** palmistry
　10. chiromancy
chironomy . . . **7.** gesture (hands)
　9. pantomime
chiropter . . . **3.** bat **6.** aliped
chirp . . . **3.** pew (pue) **4.** peep **5.** cheep,
　chirl, tweet **7.** chirrup, twitter
chisel . . . **3.** cut, gad, hew **4.** celt (anc),
　form, pare **5.** bruzz, burin, carve, cheat,
　drove, gouge, grave **6.** furrow, jagger,
　mallet, peeker, pommel **7.** engrave,
　swindle **9.** sculpture
chit . . . **4.** note, runt, wisp **5.** child,
　shoot **6.** sprout **10.** memorandum
　14. recommendation
chitarra, chitarrine . . . **6.** guitar
chiton . . . **7.** garment (anc), mollusk
chivalrous . . . **5.** brave **6.** gentle,
　heroic **7.** gallant, valiant **8.** knightly
　9. courteous **11.** magnanimous
chive . . . **4.** stab **5.** onion, plant **6.** garlic
chloride . . . **3.** ore **4.** salt **5.** ester
　7. calomel
chlorine . . . **2.** Cl **7.** bromine, halogen,
　radical **8.** cyanogen, fluorine
chloroform . . . **4.** dope, kill **6.** poison
　7. stupefy **9.** narcotize **11.** anesthetize
chlorophyll . . . **5.** ester, green **7.** etiolin
　9. deodorant
chocolate . . . **5.** brown, cacao, candy,
　cocoa, color **6.** pinole **8.** beverage
　13. Sterculiaceae
choice . . . **4.** beat, rare, will **5.** prime
　6. dainty, option, select, tidbit
　8. election, free will, uncommon
　9. recherché, selection **10.** preference,
　well-chosen **11.** alternative
choir . . . **6.** chorus **7.** singers
choir leader . . . **6.** cantor **9.** precentor
choke . . . **3.** gag, jam, ram **4.** clog **5.** burke,
　check **6.** hinder, impede, muffle, stifle
　7. garrote, repress, smother **8.** obstruct,
　strangle, throttle **9.** constrict, suffocate
choler . . . **3.** ire **4.** bile, foam, gall, rage
　5. anger, wrath **6.** spleen **10.** resentment
　11. biliousness **12.** irascibility
choleric . . . **5.** angry, testy **7.** bilious,
　enraged, iracund **8.** wrathful
　9. dyspeptic, irascible **10.** passionate
chololith . . . **9.** gallstone
choose . . . **3.** opt **4.** cull, like, list, pick,
　want **5.** elect **6.** desire, optate, prefer,
　select
choosing . . . **6.** optant **8.** eclectic, elective
　9. selecting
chop . . . **3.** axe, cut, hew, jaw, lop

4. dice, fell, hack, jowl, meat, raze,
seal 5. cheek, mince, prune, sever,
stamp 7. griskin 8. noisette (eye of)
choppy ... 5. bumpy, rough 6. uneven
7. jolting 8. unstable, variable
9. irregular 10. changeable, incoherent
13. discontinuous
chord ... 4. rope 6. radius, secant,
string, tendon 7. concord, harmony
8. arpeggio, concento, filament
chord (terms) ... 5. major, minor, tonic,
triad 6. broken, common, tetrad
7. seventh 8. dominant, unbroken
10. enharmonic
chords ... 4. tune 7. cadence, cantata
chore ... 3. job (odd) 4. task, work 5. stint
10. assignment
chorography ... 5. chart 7. diagram
10. topography 11. cartography,
description (region), ichnography
chortle ... 5. laugh, snort 7. chuckle,
snortle
chorus ... 4. echo 5. choir 6. accord,
outcry, unison 7. refrain, singers
8. chanters 9. unanimity
chorus (pert to) ...
girl .. 7. chorine, chorist
leader .. 8. choragus 9. conductor
small .. 7. octette
Chosen (Jap) ... 5. Korea
Chosen People ... 10. Israelites
chrism ... 7. unction, unguent
10. anointment 12. confirmation
christen ... 4. name 6. launch 7. baptize
10. denominate, inaugurate
12. Christianize
Christian (pert to) ...
Eastern .. 5. Uniat
feast .. 5. agape (anc) 8. Epiphany
9. Christmas
martyr (first) .. 7. Stephen
philosopher (anc) .. 6. Jesuit
9. Schoolman 10. Scholastic
sect .. 7. Docetae
symbol .. 5. orant (fem)
Christie detective ... 10. Jane Marple
13. Hercule Poirot
Christmas (pert to) ...
bag .. 6. piñata
carol .. 4. Noel
decoration .. 6. crèche
feast .. 4. Yule
hymn .. 13. Adeste Fideles
mummer .. 6. guiser
plant .. 5. holly 9. evergreen, mistletoe
term .. 4. Noel, Xmas 8. Nativity, Yuletide
11. Weihnachten
time before .. 6. Advent
Christ's-thorn ... 4. nabk
chromosome ... 2. id 5. idant 8. biophore,
germ cell
chronic ... 7. abiding 8. constant,
enduring, habitual 9. confirmed
10. continuous, inveterate, persistent
14. valetudinarian
chronicle ... 4. sard 5. annal, diary
6. record 7. account, archive, history
8. register 9. narrative 10. chronology
chronicler ... 6. writer 8. annalist,
compiler, recorder 9. historian
12. chronologist

chronology error ... 9. prolepsis
chronometer ... 5. clock, timer, watch
6. ghurry 7. sundial 9. hourglass,
metronome, timepiece
chrysolite ... 5. green (color) 7. olivine,
peridot
chthonian ... 4. gods (underworld)
7. hellish, worship 9. diabolist
11. demonolater
chub ... 4. bass, dace, dolt, fool, lout
6. shiner, tautog 8. fallfish 9. hornyhead,
squawfish
chubby ... 3. fat 5. plump, pudgy, round
6. stocky, stubby 9. corpulent
chuck ... 4. beef, cast, food, hurl, jerk,
toss 5. fling, heave, pitch, throw
9. eliminate
chuckle ... 5. cluck, laugh 6. cackle,
wabble 7. chortle
chuff ... 3. fat 4. boor 5. churl,
clown, cross, proud, sulky, surly
6. chubby, elated, rustic 9. conceited
11. ill-tempered
chum ... 3. pal 4. bait, pard 5. buddy,
crony 6. fellow, hobnob 7. company,
comrade, consort, partner 8. playmate,
roommate 9. associate, classmate,
colleague, companion
chump ... 3. ass 4. dolt, dupe, fool, head
5. block, booby 8. endpiece
chunk ... 3. dab, gob, pat, wad 4. hunk,
junt, lump, slug (metal) 5. stick, stump,
throw 8. fragment
chunky ... 3. fat 4. game (Am Ind), junt
5. lumpy, stout, tubby 6. chubby, portly,
stocky, stodgy, stubby 8. thickset
church ... 3. dom 4. fane (anc), kirk,
sect 5. abbey 6. bethel, temple
7. Lateran, minster, templet 8. basilica,
conclave 9. cathedral 10. House of
God, worshipers 11. Christendom
12. denomination
church (pert to) ...
assistant .. 5. Elder
attendant .. 5. usher 6. sexton, verger
calendar .. 4. ordo
Court .. 10. Consistory
dignitary .. 4. dean 6. bishop, priest
7. prelate, primate 8. benefice, cardinal,
minister 9. monsignor
dissenter .. 7. sectary 10. anti-Nicean,
anti-Nicene
doctrine (State, church) .. 8. Erastian
dominion .. 10. sacerdotum
doorkeeper .. 7. ostiary
Elder .. 9. Presbyter
feast .. 4. utas (octave of) 6. Easter
governing body .. 7. classis
law .. 5. canon, synod 7. council
part .. 4. apse, bema, nave 5. altar,
canon 7. chancel, narthex 8. transept
10. clerestory
peace device .. 8. irenicon
property .. 5. glebe
receptacle .. 10. monstrance
Roman .. 7. Lateran 8. basilica
screen .. 4. rood
seats .. 4. pews 7. sedilla
service (part) .. 3. pax 4. Mass 5. crede
7. epistle, introit, sanctus 8. Agnus
Dei, blessing 9. communion

stipend . . **7.** prebend
traffic (preferments) . . **6.** simony
vessel . . **3.** ama, pyx (pix) **6.** lavabo
   7. chalice **8.** ciborium
vestry . . **8.** sacristy
churl . . . **3.** cad, oaf **4.** boor, carl, hind,
   lout, serf **5.** ceorl, knave **6.** rustic
   7. bondman, freeman, peasant, villain
   9. vulgarian **10.** countryman
churlish . . . **4.** mean **5.** gruff, rough,
   surly **6.** rustic, sordid, sullen, vulgar
   7. boorish, crabbed, knavish
   9. gruffness, niggardly **10.** ill-humored
   11. countrified
churn . . . **4.** beat, kirn, stir, whip **5.** mixer,
   shake **6.** beater, seethe, vessel **7.** agitate
   8. agitator, emulsify
chute . . . **4.** tube **5.** flume, scarp, slide
   6. trough **7.** channel, incline, passage
   9. parachute
cibel . . . **5.** chive, onion **7.** shallot
ciborium . . . **3.** pyx **6.** canopy, coffer,
   vessel
cicada . . . **6.** dog-day, locust **9.** Cicadidae
cicatrix . . . **4.** mark, scar **7.** blemish
Cid . . . **3.** Ruy **4.** hero, poem **5.** Chief
   6. leader (Christian) **7.** Rodrigo
cider (weak) . . . **6.** perkin
Cid's sword . . . **6.** colada
cienaga . . . **5.** marsh, swamp
cigar . . . **4.** rope, toby **5.** claro **6.** corona,
   Havana, maduro, stogie **7.** cheroot
   8. panatela **9.** cigarillo
cigarette . . . **3.** fag **4.** pill **5.** cubeb, smoke
   6. gasper, reefer **9.** cigarillo **10.** coffin
   nail
cilium . . . **4.** hair, lash **7.** eyelash
   8. barbicel, ciliolum, filament
   9. eyewinker
cimarron . . . **6.** marron **7.** bighorn, wild
   dog **8.** district (Okla)
cimex . . . **6.** bedbug
Cimmerian, Homer Myth . . . **4.** dark
   5. Nomad (anc) **6.** gloomy (abode)
   8. Cimmeria
cinch . . . **4.** game (cards), grip, sure
   5. girth **6.** fasten **7.** harness (part)
   9. certainty, sure thing
cinders . . . **3.** ash **4.** lava, slag **5.** ashes,
   dross **6.** embers **7.** residue **8.** clinkers
cinerarium . . . **8.** mortuary
cinerator . . . **7.** furnace **9.** crematory
   11. crematorium, incinerator
cingular . . . **7.** annular **8.** circular
cinnamon . . . **5.** brown, spice **6.** cassia
   8. ishpingo (So Am) **10.** Cinnamomum
cinque . . . **4.** dice, five
cipher . . . **3.** nil **4.** code, zero **5.** aught
   6. figure, nobody, number, symbol
   7. compute **9.** calculate, character,
   nonentity
circa . . . **5.** about **6.** around
   13. approximately
Circe (pert to) . . .
   brother . . **6.** Aeetes
   father . . **6.** Helios
   Island abode . . **5.** Aeaea
   role, Odyssey . . **5.** siren **7.** charmer
   9. sorceress, temptress
   sister . . **5.** Medea
circle . . . **3.** orb **4.** halo, hoop, loop, ring

5. ambit, orbit, rhomb, rigol, round,
   wheel **6.** clique, cordon, girdle, rotate,
   sphere **7.** annulus, aureole, circuit,
   compass, enclose, revolve **9.** circulate,
   encompass **13.** circumference
circle (pert to) . . .
   astronomy . . **6.** tropic
   celestial . . **6.** colure **10.** almucantar
   Japan . . **4.** maru
   luminous . . **6.** corona
   of hell (8th) . . **9.** Malebolge
   of monoliths . . **8.** cromlech **9.** cyclolith
   part . . **3.** arc **6.** areola, octant, radius,
   sector **7.** sextant **8.** diameter
circuit . . . **3.** lap, orb **4.** bout, gyre,
   loop, tour, zone **5.** ambit, cycle, orbit,
   relay, round, route **6.** circle, detour
   7. compass **9.** round trip **10.** revolution
circuit court . . . **4.** eyre
circuitous . . . **4.** mazy **6.** curved
   7. crooked, devious, sinuous, twisted,
   vagrant, winding **8.** circular, flexuous,
   indirect, tortuous **9.** deceitful, deviating,
   underhand, wandering **10.** roundabout,
   serpentine **12.** disingenuous,
   labyrinthine **14.** circumlocutory
circular . . . **5.** round **6.** ringed **7.** annular,
   discoid, program **8.** cingular, coronary,
   ringlike **9.** crownlike, orbicular
   10. circuitous, roundabout
   13. advertisement
circular (pert to) . . .
   enclosure . . **3.** lis (liss)
   indicator . . **4.** dial
   letter . . **10.** encyclical
   ornament . . **6.** patera
circulate . . . **4.** pass **5.** issue **6.** circle,
   rotate, spread **7.** diffuse, publish
   8. monetize **9.** propagate
   11. disseminate
circumference . . . **4.** girt **5.** ambit, bound,
   girth **6.** bounds **7.** circuit, compass
   8. encircle, surround **9.** outskirts,
   perimeter, periphery
circumscribe . . . **5.** bound, fence, limit
   6. define **7.** enclose, environ **8.** encircle,
   restrict **9.** encompass
circumscribed . . . **6.** finite, narrow
   9. definable **10.** restricted
circumspect . . . **4.** wary **5.** chary
   7. careful, politic, prudent **8.** cautious,
   discreet **9.** judicious **10.** thoughtful
   11. considerate
circumstance . . . **4.** fact, item, pomp
   5. event, state **7.** proviso **8.** incident,
   occasion, position **9.** condition,
   provision, situation **10.** occurrence,
   particular **11.** arrangement, opportunity,
   stipulation
circumstantial . . . **5.** exact **6.** minute
   7. precise **8.** detailed **10.** evidential,
   incidental, particular **11.** conditional
   12. nonessential
circumvent . . . **5.** cheat, evade **6.** delude,
   entrap, outwit, thwart **7.** capture, circuit,
   deceive **8.** surround **9.** encompass,
   frustrate
circus . . . **4.** hawk, ring, show **5.** arena
   6. big top, circle, cirque **7.** harrier,
   theater **8.** carnival, side show
   12. amphitheater

circus (pert to) . . .
concessionaire . . **7.** grifter
hawk . . **15.** circus assimilis
rider . . **8.** desultor
Roman . . **13.** Circus Maximus
sideshow . . **6.** freaks
superintendent . . **10.** ringmaster
cirque . . . **6.** circle, corrie **7.** circlet
cis (pref) . . . **8.** this side
cist . . . **3.** box, pit **5.** chest **7.** chamber
8. cistvaen (kistvaen)
Cistercian . . . **4.** monk, Rule (Benedictine)
5. Order **8.** Trappist
cistern . . . **3.** bac, sac, tub, vat **4.** back,
tank, well **7.** cuvette, raintub
9. impluvium, reservoir
citadel . . . **3.** arx **4.** fort **5.** Alamo, tower
6. castle **7.** bastion, bulwark **8.** fastness,
fortress **9.** acropolis **10.** stronghold
13. fortification **14.** propungnaculum
citation . . . **5.** honor **6.** eulogy, notice
7. mention, summons **8.** subpoena
9. quotation **11.** enumeration
12. verification
cite . . . **5.** quote **6.** adduce, allege, repeat,
summon **7.** extract **8.** indicate
citizen . . . **3.** cit **6.** native **7.** citoyen,
denizen (of beasts), dweller **8.** civilian,
townsman **10.** inhabitant
citizenship . . . **10.** citizenism
15. enfranchisement
citron . . . **5.** melon **6.** cedrat (cedrate),
citrus, yellow
citrus fruit . . . **4.** lime **5.** lemon **6.** orange
7. kumquat **8.** citrange, shaddock
10. grapefruit
cittern, cithern . . . **4.** lute (anc) **6.** zither
7. cithara, gittern
city . . . **4.** town **8.** township **10.** metropolis
12. municipality
city (parts) . . . **4.** ward **5.** civic, urban
8. district, precinct
City of . . .
Bells . . **10.** Strasbourg
Bridges . . **6.** Bruges
Brotherly Love . . **12.** Philadelphia
Churches . . **8.** Brooklyn
David . . **9.** Jerusalem
Dead (The) . . **8.** cemetery **10.** Necropolis
Elms . . **8.** New Haven
Gods . . **6.** Asgard (Asgarth)
Golden Gate (The) . . **12.** San Francisco
Great King . . **9.** Jerusalem
Hundred Towers . . **5.** Pavia
Kings . . **4.** Lira
Lilies . . **8.** Florence
Magnificent Distances . . **10.** Washington
(DC)
Masts . . **6.** London
Palms (Bib) . . **7.** Jericho
Prophet (The) . . **6.** Medina
Rams . . **6.** Canton
Saints . . **8.** Montreal
Seven Hills . . **4.** Rome
Straits . . **7.** Detroit
Sun (the) . . **7.** Baalbek **10.** Heliopolis
Victory . . **5.** Cairo
Violated Treaty . . **8.** Limerick
Violet Crown . . **6.** Athens
civet . . . **5.** fossa, genet, rasse **6.** foussa,
musang **7.** nandine **10.** paradoxure

civic . . . **5.** civil, urban **6.** public **7.** burghal,
oppidan **9.** municipal **12.** metropolitan
civil . . . **4.** hend (hende) **5.** suave **6.** decent,
polite, public, urbane **7.** affable,
courtly, elegant, secular **8.** discreet,
gracious, obliging, polished, well-bred
9. courteous, political **10.** respectful
11. complaisant **13.** condescending
civil (pert to) . . .
dress . . **5.** mufti **7.** civvies
fraud (Rom) . . **11.** stellionate
process . . **4.** writ
strife . . **6.** stasis
wrong . . **4.** tort
civility . . . **6.** comity **7.** amenity
8. courtesy, urbanity **9.** attention,
etiquette, gentility **10.** affability,
politeness
civilization . . . **6.** kultur, polish **7.** culture
10. refinement **11.** cultivation
civilize . . . **4.** tame **6.** polish **8.** humanize,
urbanize **9.** cultivate **11.** domesticate
clad . . . **5.** robed **6.** decked, garbed
7. arrayed, attired, clothed, dressed
9. appareled, garmented
claim . . . **3.** hak (hakh) **4.** case, lien,
name **5.** right, title **6.** assert, demand
7. preempt, profess, require **8.** arrogate,
maintain, pretense (pretence), proclaim
9. postulate **10.** pretension
claimant . . . **7.** claimer **9.** applicant,
plaintiff, pretender **10.** solicitant
clairvoyance . . . **3.** ESP **7.** insight
8. lucidity, sagacity **9.** intuition
10. divination **11.** penetration
clairvoyant . . . **4.** seer **7.** prophet, seeress
9. sagacious **12.** clearsighted
clam . . . **3.** Mya **5.** Chama, razor, Solen
6. gweduc, Mactra, quahog **7.** mollusk
10. veneriform (shape)
clam destroyer . . . **6.** winkle
10. periwinkle
clammy . . . **4.** cool, damp, dank, soft
5. moist, mucid **6.** sticky, sweaty
clamor . . . **3.** cry, din, hue **4.** roar, wail
5. decry, noise, vocal **6.** hubbub, outcry,
racket, uproar **10.** hullabaloo
clamorous . . . **4.** loud **5.** noisy **7.** blatant,
clamant, excited **8.** brawling
9. demanding, insistent, turbulent
10. blustering, uproarious, vociferous
clamp . . . **4.** vise **6.** fasten **9.** appliance
clan . . . **3.** set **4.** camp, club, cult, gens,
race, sept **5.** group, party, tribe **6.** circle,
clique, family **7.** coterie, society
clan (quarrel) . . . **4.** feud **8.** vendetta
clandestine . . . **3.** sly **5.** privy **6.** covert,
secret **7.** furtive, illicit **8.** stealthy
9. concealed, underhand **10.** frandulent,
undercover **11.** unobtrusive
13. surreptitious
clang . . . **4.** ding, ring **5.** clank, sound
6. jangle **7.** ringing
clang color . . . **6.** timbre **8.** tonality
clangor . . . **3.** din **4.** ring **5.** clang, noise
6. fracas, hubbub, jangle, racket, ruckus,
rumpus, tumult, uproar **7.** discord,
ringing
clank . . . **4.** ring **5.** clang **7.** ringing
clapper . . . **4.** bell, clap **5.** bones (minstrel)
claque . . . **8.** chaqueur, opera hat

9. applauder

clarify ... **5.** clear **6.** filter, purify, refine, render, strain **7.** cleanse, explain, rectify

clash ... **3.** jar **4.** bang, bump **5.** crash **6.** impact, jangle, tussle **7.** collide, scuffle **8.** conflict, disagree, skirmish **9.** collision, encounter, hostility **10.** dissonance

clasp ... **3.** hug **4.** belt, grip, hasp, hold, ouch (anc), tach **5.** grasp, morse (priest's), seize, stick, tache (anc) **6.** buckle, enwrap, fasten, secure **7.** agraffe (agrafe), embrace, tendril **8.** fastener **10.** chatelaine

class ... **3.** ilk **4.** rank, sect **5.** caste, genus (pl genera), grade, order, tribe **6.** brevet (mil), status **7.** station **8.** category, classify, division **9.** catalogue **14.** classification

class (learned) ... **8.** literate, literati **14.** intelligentsia

classical ... **4.** pure **5.** Attic **6.** chaste **7.** classis, elegant **8.** academic, literary, tasteful **10.** Ciceronian

classification ... **4.** rank, sort **5.** genus, grade **6.** rating, system **7.** species **8.** analysis, category, grouping **12.** distribution

classify ... **4.** list, rank, rate, sort, type **5.** grade, label, range **6.** assort, digest, ticket **7.** aggroup, arrange **8.** register **9.** catalogue

clatter ... **3.** din, jar **5.** noise, rumor **6.** babble, gabble, hubbub, racket, rattle, rumpus, tattle, uproar **7.** chatter, prattle **9.** commotion **11.** disturbance

clause ... **5.** rider **6.** phrase **7.** passage, proviso, section

claustral ... **9.** cloistral **10.** cloistered

claw ... **4.** hand, nail, unce **5.** chela, cloof, clufe, talon **6.** nipper, unguis

claw ... **3.** dig **4.** grab, grip, pull, tear **5.** grasp, seize **6.** clutch, scrape, snatch **7.** grapple, scratch

clay ... **3.** mud **4.** marl, mire, soil **5.** argil, earth **6.** corpse, kaolin

clay (pert to) ...
baked .. **4.** tile **5.** brick
box .. **6.** sagger
covered .. **6.** lutose
mix .. **3.** pug
mold .. **3.** dod
molded .. **7.** fictile
nodule .. **10.** eaglestone
pipe .. **2.** TD **10.** meerschaum
plug .. **4.** bott
polish .. **5.** rabat
softening .. **8.** malaxage
variety .. **4.** bole, loam, marl **5.** gault, ocher, tasco **8.** petuntse

clayey ... **4.** soft **5.** adobe, bolar **6.** earthy **12.** argillaceous

clean, cleanse ... **4.** dust, swab, wash, wipe **5.** brush, purge, rinse, scrub **6.** kosher, purify, refine **7.** cleanse, deterge, launder **8.** absterge, depurate, renovate **9.** disinfect, elutriate, expurgate

cleanness ... **6.** purity (of life) **7.** clarity **8.** chastity, elegance, neatness, pureness, tidiness **10.** immaculacy

13. impeccability

clear ... **3.** net, rid **4.** free, gain, over, pure **5.** clean, lucid, plain **6.** acquit, excuse, exempt, hurdle, limpid, pardon, purify **7.** absolve, concise, crystal, evident, explain, graphic, lighten, release **8.** apparent, distinct, incisive, luculent **9.** cloudless, exonerate, extricate, vindicate

clear land ... **7.** thwaite (Eng)

clearsighted ... **4.** keen **10.** discerning **13.** perspicacious

cleat ... **4.** bitt **5.** level, strip, wedge **7.** joinery

cleave ... **3.** cut **4.** part, rend, rive, tear **5.** clave, cling, clove, crack, sever, shear, split **6.** adhere, bisect, cohere, divide, pierce **7.** dispart **8.** separate

cleek ... **5.** marry, pluck, seize **6.** clutch, snatch

clef ... **1.** C, F, G **4.** alto, bass **6.** treble **7.** descant, soprano **9.** character

cleft ... **3.** gap **4.** reft, rent, rift, rima **5.** chasm, chink, crack, notch, riven, split **6.** chappy, cranny, gaping, recess **7.** crevice, fissure **8.** scissure

cleft palate operation ...
13. staphyloraphy (staphylorrhaphy)

clemency ... **5.** favor, grace, mercy **6.** lenity **7.** quarter **8.** kindness, leniency, mildness **10.** compassion, indulgence **11.** forbearance

Clemens (Samuel) **pen name** ... **9.** Mark Twain

clench ... **4.** fist, grip, grit, hold **5.** grasp **6.** clinch, clutch **8.** purchase **9.** interlock

Cleopatra (pert to) ...
attendant .. **4.** Iras
downfall .. **3.** asp
lover .. **6.** Antony (Marc), Caesar
obelisk (two) .. **6.** Needle
queen of .. **5.** Egypt
river .. **4.** Nile

clepe ... **3.** bid **4.** call, name **6.** invite, invoke **7.** address **8.** christen

clergy ... **5.** cloth **6.** pulpit **9.** clergymen, clericals **10.** priesthood

clergyman ... **4.** abbé, dean **5.** canon, vicar **6.** cleric, curate, divine, parson, pastor, priest, rector **7.** dominie, prelate **8.** minister, preacher, sky pilot **9.** presbyter **12.** ecclesiastic

clergywoman ... **3.** nun **8.** minister **9.** parsoness, priestess **10.** religieuse

cleric, non ... **4.** laic

clerical ... **7.** scribal **11.** ministerial

clerical (pert to) ...
attire .. **3.** alb **5.** amice, cloth, fanon, orale, stole
collar .. **5.** rabat
hat .. **7.** biretta

clerk ... **3.** nun **4.** monk **5.** write **6.** cleric, hermit, layman, scribe **7.** scholar (anc) **8.** salesman **9.** assistant, clergyman **12.** ecclesiastic

cleronomy ... **8.** heritage **11.** inheritancy

clever ... **3.** apt **4.** able, cute, deft **5.** handy, slick, smart, witty **6.** adroit, astute, brainy, bright, expert, habile, nimble **7.** amiable, cunning, parlous **8.** pleasing, skillful, talented **9.** brilliant, dexterous, ingenious 11. good-natured

cleverness ... 4. tact, wits 5. skill 6. esprit 7. cunning 9. ingenuity, smartness, wittiness 10. adroitness, astuteness, shrewdness

clew, clue ... 3. key 4. ball, loop (Naut), rope 5. globe 6. cocoon, tackle (see also *clue)*

cliché ... 4. joke 5. banal, trite 6. old saw 7. bromide 8. banality, chestnut 9. Joe Miller, platitude

click ... 3. rap 4. snap 5. clack 6. go over 7. prosper, succeed

click beatle ... 3. dor (dorr) 6. elater

cliff ... 3. gat 4. crag, klip, rock, wall 5. bluff, cleve, crest, scarp, slope 6. rocher 7. clogwyn 8. palisade 9. precipice 10. escarpment

climax ... 3. cap, epi (Arch) 4. acme, near, peak, shut 5. tight 6. apogee, result, summit 7. heights 11. culmination 12. consummation

climb ... 3. fly, gad 4. shin 5. grimp, scale, speel 6. ascend, ascent 7. clamber, upgrade 9. acclivity

climbing ... 7. scaling 8. scandent 10. scansorial

climbing plant ... 3. hop, ivy 4. bine, nito, vine 5. betel, liana 6. bryony

clime ... 4. zone 5. realm, tract 6. region 7. climate

clinch ... 4. bind, grip, hold, seal 5. grasp, prove, seize 6. clutch, fasten, secure 7. confirm, grapple 8. conclude, purchase 9. establish

cling ... 4. hold 5. stick 6. adhere, cohere

clingfish ... 6. testar

clink ... 4. rime, slap 5. rhyme 6. jingle, lockup, prison, strike 9. assonance

clinquant ... 4. gold, sham 6. tinsel 8. frippery, tinseled 10. glittering

clip ... 3. bob, lop, mow 4. barb, blow, dock, gaff, snip, trim 5. clasp, prune, shear 6. clutch, fasten 7. curtail, scissor, shorten 8. ornament 10. instrument

clique ... 3. set 4. cell, clan, club, ring 5. group, Junta, junto 6. circle (people) 7. coterie

Cloaca Maxima (anc Rome) ... 5. sewer 10. repository

cloak ... 3. aba 4. cape, mask, pall, wrap 5. cover, grego, jelab, manta, sagum 6. abolla, capote, dolman, mantle, mantua, screen, serape, shield 7. chlamys (anc), conceal, galabia, manteau, paenula (anc), paletot, pelisse, pretext, protect 8. disguise 9. dissemble, new-market 10. witzchoura

clobber ... 3. hit 4. beat, conk, poke, swat 5. clout, punch, whack 6. defeat, strike, wallop

clock ... 3. nef (ship's) 4. dial, time 5. knock 6. record 7. digital 8. recorder, sidereal 9. clepsydra, metronome, timepiece 10. isochronon 11. chronometer

clockwise ... 6. deasil (dessil) 11. withershins 14. dextrorotation, dextrorotatory

clog ... 4. stop 5. choke, dance 6. daggle, hamper, impede 8. encumber, obstruct, restrain

clog shoe ... 4. geta 5. sabot 6. chopin, cobcab (Orient), patten 7. chopine

cloister ... 4. stoa 5. abbey 6. arcade, friary, immure, priory 7. confine, convent, nunnery, retreat 9. anchorage, hermitage, monastery, peristyle 10. passageway

cloistered ... 7. recluse 8. enclosed, monastic 11. sequestered

clone ... 4. copy, twin 7. replica

close ... 2. at, by 3. end 4. near, nigh, seal, shut, slam 5. dense, finis, stingy 6. finale, finish, period, secret, stingy, sultry 7. airless, extreme, occlude, related 8. complete, conclude, familiar, imminent, intimate, stifling 9. extremity, secretive, terminate 11. approximate, termination 13. juxtaposition

close (pert to) ...

eyes (the) .. 4. seel 5. blink

fasten .. 6. batten

of day .. 8. eventide 9. nightfall

poetic .. 4. nigh 5. anear

tightly .. 3. bar 4. bung, seal 6. clench, enseal 8. obturate

closely ... 4. just 6. almost, barely, nearly 8. narrowly

closely allied ... 6. chummy 7. germane 8. intimate

closeness ... 7. density, secrecy 8. fidelity, intimacy, likeness, nearness, sameness 9. tightness 10. chumminess, narrowness, similarity, stinginess, strictness, sultriness 11. airlessness, compactness, conciseness, familiarity, resemblance 14. oppressiveness

closet ... 5. ambry, cuddy, emery 6. locker, pantry 7. cabinet 8. cupboard, wardrobe 9. cloakroom, storeroom

closing device ... 3. key 4. lock, snap 5. clasp, hinge, latch 6. Velcro (tm), zipper

closing measure (Mus) ... 4. coda

clot ... 4. lump, mass 5. grume 7. thicken 8. coagulum, concrete 9. coagulate 12. crassamentum

cloth ... 3. net, tat 4. brin, crea, drap, felt, lamé, silk, tapa, wool 5. adati, baize, bezan, bluet, carda, crash, crepe, denim, khaki, linen, manta, nylon, orlon, rayon, satin, scrim, surat, tamis, terry, tulle, twill, voile 6. alpaca, burlap, calico, canvas, chintz, cotton, damask, dimity, dowlas, duffel, faille, jersey, madras, mohair, muslin, nankin, pongee, poplin, samite (gold), sateen, velour 7. acetate, baracan, brocade, bunting, cambric, challis, chiffon, drap d'or, flannel, foulard, gingham, nankeen, organdy, organza, percale, sacking, spandex, taffeta, ticking, worsted 8. cashmere, chambray, corduroy, cretonne, drilling, nainsook, Shantung 9. crinoline, gabardine, polyester, sailcloth, tarpaulin, tricotine 10. broadcloth, seersucker 11. cheesecloth, drap d'argent (silver), marquisette

cloth (pert to) ...

checkered .. 5. plaid

dealer.. **6.** draper
finisher.. **7.** beetler
measure.. **4.** nail
piece.. **4.** bolt **5.** scrap
ridge.. **4.** wale
selvage.. **4.** roon **6.** border **7.** listing
twilled.. **5.** denim, serge
weaving.. **4.** warp, weft, woof
clothe ... **3.** tog **4.** deck, garb, gird, robe,
   vest **5.** array, drape, dress, endue, indue
   6. afford, enrobe, invest **7.** empower,
   provide, sheathe **8.** accouter
clothes ... **3.** rig **4.** duds, garb, togs
   5. guise, habit, jeans, Levis **6.** attire,
   bikini, briefs **7.** apparel, costume,
   raiment, regalia, threads (sl) **8.** clothing,
   garments, leotards, swimsuit
   9. dungarees **10.** bedclothes,
   garmenture **11.** habiliments, investiture
cloud ... **3.** fog, low **4.** dust, film, haze,
   mist, rack, scud **5.** nepho (comb
   form), nubia, stain, sully, taint, vapor
   6. cirrus, damage, darken, defame,
   defect, nebule, nimbus, shadow, stigma
   7. blacken, blemish, cumulus, nubilus,
   obscure, pea-soup, stratus, tarnish,
   tornado **8.** cat's-tail, cocktail, overcast
   10. horizontal
clouds (pert to) ...
astronomy.. **4.** coma **9.** nubeculae
kind.. **6.** cirrus, nimbus **7.** cumulus,
   fractus, stratus **9.** mare's-tail
luminous.. **5.** nimbi
Magellanic.. **5.** Major, Minor
photography.. **9.** nephogram
science of.. **9.** nephology
seeding.. **10.** nucleation
vapory.. **4.** rack
cloudy ... **4.** dark, hazy **5.** filmy, foggy,
   misty, murky, shady, vague **6.** gloomy,
   lowery, opaque **7.** nebular, obscure
   8. confused, overcast, vaporous
   9. cloudlike **10.** indistinct, lackluster
clout ... **3.** hit, jab, rag **4.** blow, bump,
   clod, mend, nail, swat **5.** patch,
   power, shred, smack **9.** influence
   12. handkerchief
clove ... see also *cleave* **5.** spice
clover ... **3.** red **4.** bush **5.** lotus, snail,
   white **6.** alsike **7.** crimson, melilot,
   prairie, spotted **9.** Melilotus
clown ... **3.** oaf **4.** boor, fool, lout,
   mime, mome, zany **5.** comic, Kelly
   (Emmet), mimer, yahoo **6.** jester, rustic
   7. buffoon **9.** harlequin **10.** countryman
   11. merry-andrew
clownish ... **4.** rude **5.** gawky, rough
   6. clumsy, coarse, rustic **7.** awkward,
   boorish, ill-bred, loutish, uncivil
   8. churlish, ungainly **9.** untutored
   10. buffoonish **11.** countrified
cloy ... **4.** clog, glut, pall, sate **5.** gorge,
   stuff **6.** accloy **7.** satiate, satisfy, surfeit
club ... **3.** bat, hit **4.** beat, join, mace
   5. billy, clout, staff, unite, yokel
   6. cudgel, league, weapon **7.** society
   8. bludgeon, spontoon **9.** boomerang,
   espantoon **10.** nulla-nulla, pogamoggan
   11. association
club (pert to) ...
actors.. **6.** Friars

historic.. **5.** Whigs **8.** Jacobins
   10. Cordeliers
Service.. **7.** Kiwanis
Women's (first).. **7.** Sorosis
clubfoot ... **7.** talipes **9.** deformity, pes
   valgus **13.** talipes valgus
club-shaped ... **7.** clavate
clue, clew ... **3.** key, tip **4.** data, hint
   5. scent **6.** thread **7.** inkling **8.** evidence
   9. suspicion **11.** fingerprint
clump ... **3.** tod **4.** heap, lump, thud,
   tuft **5.** bunch, chunk, group, motte
   (mott), patch, stamp **6.** growth, trudge
   7. cluster, thicket
clumsy ... **4.** ugly **5.** bulky, gawky,
   inapt, inept, unfit **6.** gauche, oafish
   7. awkward, uncouth, unhandy
   8. slipshod, ungainly, unwieldy
   9. inelegant, lumbering, maladroit,
   misshapen **10.** blundering,
   cumbersome, left-handed
   13. inappropriate
clumsy person ... **4.** gawk **5.** jumbo,
   staup **7.** bungler
clupeoid fish ... **7.** herring
cluster ... **4.** crop, cyme, gang, tuft
   5. bunch, clump, group **6.** huddle
   8. fascicle **9.** glomerule
cluster (pert to) ...
bean.. **4.** guar **6.** legume
fibers.. **3.** nep
flowers.. **6.** raceme **7.** rosette
   8. anthemia, panticle
fruit.. **6.** grapes
spores.. **5.** sorus
stars.. **8.** Globular, Pleiades (The)
clustery ... **8.** racemose
clutch ... **3.** nab **4.** claw, grip, hold, nest
   5. brood, catch, clasp, grasp, seize
   6. clench, cletch, crisis
clyster ... **5.** enema **6.** lavage **9.** injection
Clytemnestra's mother ... **4.** Leda
cnemis ... **4.** shin **5.** tibia
coach ... **3.** car, rig **5.** prime, stage,
   train, tutor **6.** direct, fiacre, jarvey
   7. adviser, prepare, tallyho, teacher
   8. carriage, equipage, instruct, preparer
   9. charabanc **10.** instructor
coach dog ... **9.** Dalmatian
coachman ... **3.** fly (angling) **4.** fish,
   jehu, whip **6.** driver
coagulate ... **3.** gel, jel, set **4.** cake, clot,
   curd, lump **6.** curdle, posset **7.** congeal
   8. solidify
coagulator ... **6.** enzyme, rennet
coagulum ... **4.** clot, curd **5.** grume
   7. clabber
coal ... **4.** fuel **5.** black, ember **6.** carbon,
   cinder **7.** lignite, residue
coal (pert to) ...
bin.. **6.** bunker
car.. **3.** dan **4.** corf, tram **6.** hopper
dust.. **4.** coom (coomb), culm, smut
gas.. **7.** Pintsch **9.** acetylene
miner.. **7.** collier
miner's disease.. **11.** anthracosis
oil.. **8.** kerosene
residue.. **4.** coke
tar.. **5.** lysol, pitch **6.** cresol, decane,
   phenol **7.** toluene
tunnel.. **4.** adit

type.. **3.** egg, nut, pea **4.** dant, hard, peat, soft **6.** broken, cannel **8.** charcoal, chestnut **9.** buckwheat **10.** anthracite, bituminous

coalition... **4.** bloc **5.** trust, union **6.** fusion, hookup, league, merger **7.** society **8.** alliance **10.** federation **11.** affiliation, combination, confederacy, conjunction

coalition advocate... **9.** fusionist

coals... **5.** gleed **6.** embers **7.** cinders

coarse... **3.** fat, low **4.** dank, lewd, rude, vile **5.** broad, crass, gross, thick **6.** carnal, earthy, impure, ribald, rustic, vulgar **7.** goatish, obscene, sensual **8.** granular, immodest, indecent, inferior, unchaste **9.** inelegant, offensive, unrefined **10.** unfinished, unpolished

coarse (pert to)...
grain.. **4.** meal
grass.. **4.** reed **5.** sedge **6.** quitch
hominy.. **4.** corn, samp

coast... **4.** sail **5.** beach, glide, shore, slide **6.** rivage **7.** seaside **8.** seaboard, seashore

coast (pert to)...
dweller.. **7.** orarian
live oak.. **6.** encina
projection.. **4.** cape, ness

coat... **4.** jupe **5.** cloak, frock, parka, tunic **6.** blazer, capote, duster, jacket, raglan, reefer, trench, tuxedo, ulster **7.** cassock, cutaway, paletot, slicker **8.** gossamer, Mackinaw, tegument **9.** newmarket, redingote

coat (pert to)...
fastener.. **4.** frog **6.** zipper
of animal.. **3.** fur **4.** pelt, wool **6.** pelage **8.** feathers
of arms.. **5.** crest **8.** blazonry **10.** escutcheon
of mail.. **6.** byrnia **7.** hauberk
of the eye (inner).. **6.** retina

coati... **5.** Nasua **6.** narica **7.** raccoon

coating (pert to)...
cake.. **5.** glacé, icing **8.** frosting
copper, bronze.. **6.** patina
grain.. **4.** bran
medical.. **9.** collodion
metal.. **4.** plate
seed.. **5.** testa **6.** tegmen **10.** endopleura
tin, lead.. **5.** terne
vitreous.. **6.** enamel

coax... **3.** beg, ply **4.** lure, urge **5.** press, tease **6.** cajole, entice, exhort **7.** beguile, flatter, implore, wheedle **8.** blandish, inveigle, persuade **9.** importune **10.** manipulate

cob... **4.** axis, blow, gull, loaf, mole, pier, swan **5.** block, chief, horse **6.** basket, leader, muffin, spider **7.** beating, corncob **8.** dumpling **10.** breakwater

cobbler... **3.** pie **5.** coler, sutor **6.** bungle, repair, souter **7.** botcher, crispin **9.** fortescue (fortesque), shoemaker

cobbra... **4.** head **5.** skull

cobby... **5.** stout **6.** hearty, lively, stocky **10.** headstrong

cobra... **3.** asp **4.** Naga (Myth), Naja **5.** mamba, snake, viper **8.** ringhals

cobweb... **3.** net **4.** trap **5.** snare, wevet **7.** fiction, network **8.** filament, gossamer **9.** intricacy

cobweblike... **8.** araneous **9.** arachnoid

cocaine... **4.** coca, snow (sl) **8.** narcotic **9.** mydriatic **10.** anesthetic

coccus... **4.** cell **5.** spore **9.** bacterium, cochineal

cochleate... **6.** spiral **11.** shell-shaped

cock... **3.** nab, tap **4.** bird, heap, kora, pile, vane (weather) **5.** strut, valve **6.** faucet, grouse, leader, muckna **7.** rooster, swagger

cockade... **4.** knot **7.** rosette

Cockade State... **8.** Maryland

cockatoo... **3.** ara **5.** arara (palm), galah **6.** parrot **8.** ganggang

cockle... **4.** boat, gith, kiln, oast **5.** shell, stove **6.** pucker **7.** mollusk, wrinkle

cockpit... **3.** pit **4.** well **5.** arena, cabin (airplane) **7.** gallera

cockscomb (coxcomb)... **5.** crest, plant

cocktail... **5.** cloud, drink, horse **6.** beetle **9.** appetizer

cocky... **4.** pert **5.** saucy **6.** jaunty **7.** stuck-up **9.** conceited

cocoa... **5.** broma, cacao **8.** beverage **9.** chocolate **11.** theobromine

coconut (pert to)...
fiber.. **4.** coir, kyar
India.. **6.** nargil (narghile)
meat.. **5.** copra
tree.. **4.** palm

cocoon... **3.** pod **4.** bave (silk), clew, kell, pupa **9.** chrysalis

cod... **3.** bib, cor **4.** fish, ling **5.** scrod, sprag **6.** burbot, cultus, gadoid **7.** bacalao

coddle... **3.** pet **4.** baby, cock **5.** humor, spoil **6.** caress, fondle, pamper **11.** mollycoddle

code... **3.** law **5.** canon, codex, Morse, salic **6.** digest, equity, signal, symbol **7.** pandect, precept **12.** Commandments

codfish (pert to)...
Alaska.. **6.** wachna
genus.. **5.** Gadus
ready for cooking.. **5.** scrod
type.. **3.** cod, red **4.** cusk, rock **6.** Murray, tomcod **7.** buffalo

codger... **5.** crank, miser **6.** oddity

codicil... **4.** will **5.** rider **6.** sequel **8.** addition, appendix **10.** instrument

Cody (William)... **11.** Buffalo Bill

coerce... **4.** curb **5.** force **6.** compel **7.** dragoon, enforce, repress **9.** blackjack, strong-arm, terrorize **10.** intimidate

coercion... **5.** force **6.** duress **8.** violence **10.** compulsion, constraint

coffee (pert to)...
bean.. **3.** nib
container.. **8.** canister
cup holder.. **4.** zarf
drink.. **8.** espresso **10.** café au lait, cappuccino
extract.. **8.** caffeine
kind.. **3.** Rio **4.** Java, Kona **5.** Kenya, Milds, Mocha **6.** Bogota, Brazil, Santos **7.** Sumatra, Turkish **8.** Medellin **9.** Maracaibo

mix . . **7.** chicory
pot . . **6.** biggin **10.** percolator
coffin . . . **3.** box, urn **4.** bier, case, kist,
mold **5.** chest, crust **6.** basket, casing,
casket **11.** sarcophagus
coffin (pert to) . . .
cloth . . **4.** pall **5.** cloak
litter . . **4.** bier
nail . . **9.** cigarette
prehistoric . . **4.** cist **5.** chest
structure . . **10.** catafalque
cog . . . **3.** cam **4.** boat (fishing), gear
5. catch, cheat, cozen, tenon, tooth
7. ratchet, wheedle **8.** sprocket
9. deception
cogent . . . **5.** valid **6.** potent, strong
7. telling **8.** powerful **9.** effective
10. compelling, conclusive, convincing,
persuasive
cogitate . . . **4.** mull, muse, plan **5.** think
6. ponder **8.** meditate **9.** cerebrate
cognizance . . . **3.** ken **4.** heed, plea
5. badge (knight's) **9.** knowledge
11. recognition **12.** apprehension
cognizant . . . **5.** aware **7.** knowing
8. sensible **9.** conscious **10.** perceptive
11. intelligent
cognomen . . . **4.** name **5.** title **6.** y-clept
7. surname **8.** nickname **10.** patronymic
11. appellation
coheir . . . **5.** joint **8.** parcener
cohere . . . **5.** agree, cling, serry, stick,
unite **6.** adhere, cleave **9.** glutinate
coherence . . . **5.** cling **8.** adhesion,
cohesion, sticking **9.** adherence,
connected **11.** consistency
coil . . . **4.** ansa, clew, curl, loop, mesh,
wind **5.** querl, twine, twist **6.** spiral
7. haycock **8.** encircle **11.** convolution
coiled . . . **7.** tortile, twirled
coin . . . **3.** rin, sou, yen **4.** cash, cent
5. money, penny, stamp **6.** specie
coin (pert to) . . .
Bib . . **6.** talent
brass . . **13.** Rosa Americana (1722)
gold . . **3.** lev **4.** ryal (rial) **5.** daric, eagle
6. guinea
minor . . **4.** doit
parts of . . **4.** flan **5.** field, tails, verso
6. legend **7.** exergue, obverse (front),
reverse
silver . . **4.** batz, obol, ryal (rial) **5.** crown,
ducat, sceat **6.** tester
tester . . **6.** shroff (saraf)
coincide . . . **5.** agree, check, chime,
match, tally **6.** concur **7.** consent
10. correspond **11.** synchronize
coincident . . . **9.** consonant **10.** concurrent
12. contemporary
coiner . . . **8.** inventor **9.** neologist (words)
10. fabricator **13.** counterfeiter
coins (pert to) . . .
roll of . . **7.** rouleau
science of . . **11.** numismatics
specialist . . **11.** numismatist
colander . . . **5.** sieve **6.** filter, sorter
8. strainer
Colchis King . . . **6.** Aeetes
cold . . . **3.** icy, nip, raw **4.** dank, dead,
drow, dull, frio, sure **5.** algid, bland,
bleak, frore (anc), gelid **6.** chilly, frigid,

frosty **7.** chilled, cinched **8.** chilling,
reserved, unheated **9.** heartless
10. lackluster **11.** indifferent,
passionless, unconscious
cold (pert to) . . .
blooded . . **9.** heartless, unfeeling
13. dispassionate, heterothermal
14. poikilothermal
feet . . **9.** cowardice
infection . . **4.** post **5.** rheum **6.** coryza
7. catarrh
sore . . **6.** herpes **7.** simplex, vesicle
14. herpes labialis
steel . . **5.** sword **7.** bayonet, weapons
term . . **8.** frigoric
wind . . **4.** bise
Coleoptera . . . **7.** beetles, insects
Coleridge (Samuel Taylor) (pert to) . . .
place . . **6.** Xanadu
poem . . **9.** Kubla Khan
Rime of the . . **14.** Ancient Mariner
river . . **4.** Alph
colewort . . . **4.** kale **7.** cabbage
colic . . . **4.** pain **5.** gripe, spasm **7.** tormina
10. enteralgia **11.** stomachache
coliseum . . . **4.** bowl **5.** arena **6.** circus
7. stadium, theater **9.** Colosseum
10. hippodrome **12.** amphitheater
collaborate . . . **3.** aid **6.** co-work
8. coauthor **9.** cooperate **10.** fraternize
collage . . . **6.** gluing **7.** montage
8. abstract, adhesive **9.** cyclorama
collapse . . . **4.** cave, fail, fall **5.** crash,
slump **6.** cave-in, defeat **7.** crack-up,
debacle, deflate, failure **8.** downfall
9. breakdown, shrinking **10.** bankruptcy,
exhaustion **11.** prostration
collar . . . **4.** band, grab, ruff **5.** chain,
rabat, ruche **6.** arrest, bertha, rabato,
tackle, torque **7.** barghan, capture,
harness (part), shackle **8.** carcanet,
neckband **10.** pickadilly
collard . . . **4.** kale
collate . . . **5.** audit, check **6.** verify
7. certify, compare, examine
collateral . . . **5.** extra **6.** margin **7.** related
8. indirect, relation (folks), security
9. accessory, secondary **10.** contingent,
obligation, subsidiary **11.** subordinate
12. nonessential
collation . . . **3.** tea **4.** meal **5.** lunch
6. repast, sermon **7.** address, reading
8. luncheon, treatise **10.** collection,
comparison, conference
12. consultation, contribution
colleague . . . **6.** fellow **7.** compeer,
comrade, consort, partner **8.** camarada,
confrere **9.** associate, companion
11. confederate
collect . . . **3.** bag, tax **4.** levy, mass
5. amass, glean, raise, rally **6.** deduce,
forage, garner, gather, muster, prayer,
sheave **7.** compile, procure **8.** assemble,
mobilize **9.** aggregate **10.** accumulate,
congregate
collection . . . **3.** ana, bag, set **4.** book,
olio **5.** group, hoard, store **6.** rosary,
sorite **8.** assembly, donation, offering
9. aggregate, congeries, gathering,
repertory **10.** assemblage, repertoire
11. acquisition

collection (pert to) . . .
anecdotes . . **3.** ana **4.** data **8.** analecta
animals (wild) . . **3.** zoo **9.** menagerie
bubbles . . **4.** foam
curiosities . . **6.** museum
documents . . **4.** Veda **6.** corpus **7.** dossier
fruit . . **7.** syncarp
implements (Surg) . . **7.** trousse
of four . . **6.** tetrad
of twenty-four . . **5.** quire
poems . . **5.** sylva **9.** anthology
proper names . . **11.** onomasticon
type . . **4.** font
writing . . **10.** literature
collector (pert to) . . .
bird eggs . . **8.** oologist
books . . **10.** bibliothec **11.** bibliophile
12. bibliomaniac
coins . . **11.** numismatist
rent . . **8.** landlord
stamps . . **11.** philatelist
colleen . . . **4.** girl, lass, maid **6.** damsel,
maiden **7.** girleen
college . . . **6.** school **7.** academy, society
9. Alma Mater, institute **10.** université,
university **11.** corporation, institution
college (pert to) . . .
campus . . **4.** lawn, quad **7.** grounds
graduate . . **6.** alumna **7.** alumnus
license for absence . . **5.** exeat
official . . **4.** dean **5.** prexy **6.** beadle,
bursar, regent **7.** proctor
collegiate . . . **8.** academic **9.** collegian,
scholarly **11.** college-bred
collide with . . . **3.** hit, ram **5.** clash, crash
6. hurtle, strike **7.** contend **8.** conflict,
disagree
collier . . . **5.** miner **6.** plover
collieshangie . . . **3.** row **7.** quarrel
8. squabble **11.** disturbance (noisy)
collision . . . **4.** bump **5.** clash, crash
6. impact **7.** smashup **8.** accident
9. hostility **11.** composition,
impingement **12.** interference
colloquial . . . **6.** common **8.** everyday,
familiar, informal **9.** unstudied
10. vernacular **11.** undignified
14. conversational
colloquy . . . **4.** chat, talk **6.** parley
9. discourse **10.** conference
12. conversation
Cologne Kings (legend) . . . **4.** Magi
6. Gaspar **8.** Melchior **9.** Balthasar
Colombia . . .
capital . . **6.** Bogota (1538)
city . . **4.** Cali **5.** Pasto **8.** Medellin
9. Cartagena **10.** Santa Marta
Falls . . **10.** Tequendama
Liberator . . **7.** Bolivar (Simon)
mountain . . **5.** Andes **11.** Cordilleras
river . . **9.** Magdalena
colonize . . . **6.** gather, people, settle
8. populate **9.** establish
colonizer . . . **3.** ant **6.** oecist **7.** planter,
settler
colonnade . . . **3.** row (columns) **4.** stoa
6. arcade **7.** columns, pillars, portico
8. cloister **9.** peristyle
colony . . . **4.** body **5.** group, swarm
8. dominion **9.** community
10. dependency, settlement

colophon . . . **4.** logo **6.** emblem
9. bookplate **11.** inscription (book)
color . . . **3.** dun, dye, hue **4.** tint, tone
5. blush, paint, shade, stain, terne,
tinge **6.** flaxen, nuance, pastel, sallow,
timbre **7.** piebald, pigment **8.** tincture
(Her) **10.** complexion
color (pert to) . . .
application (paste) . . **7.** impasto
blending . . **4.** teer **5.** fondu **9.** scumbling
blind . . **13.** achromatopsia
clouded . . **9.** nebulated
colorful . . **9.** chromatic
colorless . . **4.** drab, dull, pale **6.** pallid
7. whitish **8.** blanched **10.** achromatic
irregularity . . **5.** fleck **6.** streak
10. rivulation
material . . **5.** eosin, morin, smalt
7. pigment **11.** chlorophyll
off color . . **6.** risqué **8.** improper
organ . . **8.** clavilux
paint, rouge . . **6.** ruddle **7.** blusher
science of . . **10.** chromatics
11. spectrology
variegated . . **7.** rainbow, The Flag,
vibgyor **8.** spectrum **11.** iridescence
Colorado . . .
canyon . . **5.** Black **10.** Royal Gorge
capital . . **6.** Denver
city . . **5.** Aspen, Lamar **6.** Pueblo
7. Boulder, Manassa, Manitou
Indian . . **7.** Arapaho
lake (highest) . . **10.** Frozen Lake
Mt peak . . **6.** Elbert **9.** Pike's Peak
park . . **5.** Estes **15.** Garden of the Gods
river . . **4.** Gila **6.** Platte **8.** Arkansas
State admission . . **12.** Thirty-eighth
State bird . . **11.** lark bunting
State flower . . **9.** columbine
State motto . . **13.** Nil Sine Numine
(Nothing Without God)
State nickname . . **10.** Centennial
colossal . . . **4.** huge **5.** great, large
6. absurd, superb **7.** mammoth
8. gigantic **9.** monstrous
colossal beast . . . **8.** behemoth (Bib)
colt . . . **3.** gun **4.** foal **5.** filly, horse
8. yearling
Columbus (pert to) . . .
birthplace . . **5.** Genoa (It)
companion . . **5.** Ojeda
discoverer . . **7.** America (1492)
landing site . . **11.** San Salvador
sailing site . . **5.** Palos (Sp)
vessel . . **4.** Nina **5.** Pinta **10.** Santa
Maria
column . . . **3.** lat (Buddh) **4.** anta **5.** pylon,
shaft, stele (stela) **6.** pillar **7.** telamon
8. baluster, caryatid, pilaster
column (pert to) . . .
base . . **5.** socle **6.** plinth **9.** stylobate
military . . **4.** unit **9.** formation
Order (Arch) . . **5.** Doric, Ionic **6.** Tuscan
9. Composite **10.** Corinthian
ref to . . **5.** train **7.** cortege **8.** cylinder,
memorial, monument **10.** procession
shaft . . **4.** fust **5.** scape **8.** apophyge
term . . **5.** bague, galbe, shank **7.** capital,
entasis
coma . . . **4.** daze, tuft **5.** carus, sleep,
sopor **6.** stupor, trance **9.** catalepsy

12. sluggishness **13.** insensibility
15. unconsciousness
comatose . . . **6.** drowsy, torpid
  9. apathetic, lethargic **10.** cataleptic,
  insensible **11.** unconscious
comb . . . **4.** card, wave **5.** cock's, crest,
  curry, groom, scour, tease **6.** search
  7. rummage **8.** caruncle
combat . . . **3.** war **4.** cope, duel, fray, tilt
  5. fight, joust (anc), repel **6.** action,
  battle, karate, kung fu, oppose, strife
  7. contest, jujitsu, scuffle **8.** argument,
  conflict **9.** withstand **10.** antagonize,
  contention, engagement
combat (pert to) . . .
  challenge . . **6.** cartel **8.** gauntlet
  code . . **6.** duello
  scene . . **5.** arena **8.** coliseum
combatant . . . **6.** dueler **7.** battler, fighter
  8. disputer **9.** contender **10.** competitor,
  contestant
combative . . . **8.** militant **9.** agonistic,
  bellicose **10.** aggressive, pugnacious
  11. belligerent, contentious
combination . . . **4.** gang, pact, pool
  5. blend, combo, party, trust, union
  6. clique, fusion, hookup, league,
  merger **7.** amalgam, combine, faction,
  mixture **8.** alliance, coalesce, ensemble,
  junction **9.** camarilla, coalition,
  synthesis **10.** embodiment
  11. aggregation, association,
  confederacy, unification
  12. undergarment **13.** incorporation
combine . . . **3.** add, mix **4.** join, pool
  5. merge, unite **6.** concur, mingle
  7. machine **10.** synthesize
combining form . . .
  above, beyond . . **3.** sur **5.** ultra
  across . . **4.** tran **5.** trans
  bad . . **3.** dys, mal
  black . . **4.** mela
  earth . . **3.** geo **5.** terra
  equal . . **3.** iso **4.** homo, pari
  far . . **3.** tel **4.** tele
  good . . **2.** eu
  hundred . . **4.** cent
  inner, within . . **4.** ento (ent)
  kidney . . **4.** reni
  middle . . **4.** medi **5.** medio
  mountain . . **3.** oro
  needle . . **3.** acu
  new . . **3.** neo
  not . . **2.** un **3.** non
  old, ancient . . **5.** paleo
  one . . **3.** uni **4.** mono
  outside, without . . **3.** ect, ext **4.** ecto
  personal . . **4.** idio
  soft . . **4.** leni
  stone . . **4.** lith
  thought . . **4.** ideo
  thrice . . **3.** ter
  tooth . . **6.** odonto
  touch . . **3.** tac
  up, upward . . **3.** ano
  watery . . **4.** sero
comblike . . . **7.** ctenoid **8.** pectinal
combustible . . . **5.** fiery, quick **7.** piceous
  8. volcanic **9.** flammable, irascible
  10. accendible **11.** hot-tempered,
  inflammable

combustion . . . **4.** fire **6.** tumult **7.** blazing,
  flaming **8.** ignition **9.** agitation,
  confusion, cremation **12.** inflammation
  13. conflagration
come . . . **3.** hop **4.** near **5.** issue, occur
  6. appear, arrive, happen **8.** approach
  9. transpire
come (pert to) . . .
  across . . **3.** pay **4.** meet **7.** confess
  10. contribute
  back . . **6.** answer, retort, return
  7. rebound, recover **8.** remember,
  repartee
  before . . **4.** lead **7.** precede, prevene
  8. antecede, antedate
  between . . **6.** divide **8.** estrange, interlie
  9. interpose, intervene
  by . . **3.** get **4.** gain **6.** obtain **7.** acquire,
  inherit, receive
  forth . . **3.** jet **4.** gush, spew **5.** hatch,
  issue, occur **6.** appear, emerge, spring
  7. emanate **9.** originate
  together . . **4.** join, knit, meet **5.** clash,
  merge **7.** collide, convene **8.** assemble,
  converge
come (to) . . .
  light . . **7.** develop
  maturity . . **5.** ripen
  pass . . **5.** occur **6.** befall, betide, happen
  9. eventuate
  rest . . **3.** sit **5.** light **6.** settle
comedian, comedienne . . . **3.** wit **4.** buff
  5. actor, comic **6.** player **7.** farcist
  8. funnyman **9.** dramatist
comedy . . . **5.** drama, farce, revue
  7. comedie, stand-up **8.** travesty
  9. burlesque, slapstick
comestibles . . . **4.** food **5.** manna
  8. eatables, victuals
comet (pert to) . . .
  cloud . . **4.** Oort
  famous . . **7.** Halley's **8.** Kohoutek
  part . . **4.** coma, tail **7.** nucleus
comfort . . . **4.** ease **5.** cheer, quilt **6.** relief,
  solace, soothe, succor **7.** confirm,
  console, enliven, fortify, refresh, relieve,
  support, sustain **8.** inspirit, nepenthe
  (drug) **9.** enjoyment **10.** invigorate,
  strengthen **11.** consolation
  12. satisfaction
comfortable . . . **4.** cozy, easy, snug
  5. scarf **8.** adequate, cheerful, homelike,
  wristlet **9.** contented, endemonic
  10. complacent, prosperous
  11. consolatory, encouraging
comforter . . . **5.** quilt **6.** tippet **7.** solacer
  8. pacifier **9.** Paraclete
comfortless . . . **7.** forlorn **8.** desolate
  9. cheerless, heartsick **10.** despairing
  11. distressing **12.** disconsolate,
  inconsolable
comic, comical . . . **3.** odd **5.** cutup, droll,
  funny, queer, witty **6.** absurd, quaint
  7. cartoon, risible **8.** comedian, farcical,
  humorous **9.** burlesque, laughable,
  ludicrous, quizzical, whimsical
  10. capricious, outlandish
coming . . . **3.** due **6.** access, advent, future
  7. arrival, forward, looming **8.** eventual,
  expected, imminent **9.** imminence
  11. approaching, forthcoming

coming into being . . . 7. genesis, nascent

comity . . . 7. amenity, suavity 8. civility, courtesy, urbanity 10. affability

command . . . 3. bid, gee, haw, hup 4. bade, beck, fiat, hest, rule, sway 5. avast, check, edict, exact, grasp, order, power, ukase 6. behest, charge, compel, decree, direct, enjoin, govern 7. control, dictate, mandate, mastery 8. dominion, restrain 9. authority, prescribe 10. domination 11. commandment 12. jurisdiction

commander . . . 3. cid 5. chief, ruler 6. leader 7. admiral, captain, skipper 8. dictator, governor, myriarch, overlord

commander, Eastern . . . 3. ras 4. amir, emir, Imam, khan, rani 5. ameer, begum, dewan, emeer, nawab, Nizam 6. caliph, regent, Sultan

commanding . . . 8. dominant 9. imperious 10. imperative 13. authoritative

commandments . . . 4. laws 6. orders, tables 8. mandates, precepts 9. Decalogue (Ten)

comme il faut . . . 8. properly 9. correctly 10. decorously 12. as it should be

commemoration . . . 7. service 8. Encaenia (Oxford Univ) 10. observance 11. anniversary, celebration, remembrance 13. solemnization

commence . . . 4. open 5. arise, begin, start 6. spring 8. initiate 9. originate

commencement . . . 4. rite 6. source 8. ceremony, nascency 9. beginning, formality, inception, novitiate 10. initiation

commend . . . 4. plug 5. boost, extol, offer 6. assign, commit, praise, remand, resign 8. approve, deliver, entrust 8. advocate, delegate 9. recommend 10. compliment

commendation . . . 4. hype, plug, puff 5. boost, kudos 8. approval 10. assignment, commitment, compliment, delegation 11. approbation, consignment, entrustment

comment . . . 4. note, talk 6. gossip, postil, remark, report 7. descant, discuss, explain, mention 8. annotate, critique 9. criticism, discourse

commentary . . . 5. gloss 6. memoir 7. remarks 8. treatise 9. memoranda 10. annotation 11. explanation

commerce . . . 5. trade 7. traffic 8. dealings 9. communion 11. interchange 13. communication

commis . . . 5. agent, clerk 6. deputy

commiserate . . . 4. pity 7. condole, console 10. sympathize

commiseration . . . 4. pity, ruth 5. mercy 6. sorrow 7. empathy, feeling 8. sympathy 10. compassion, condolence

commission . . . 4. duty, task 5. allot, board, share, trust 6. brevet, depute, office, ordain 7. empower, mandate, mission, payment, rake-off, warrant 8. delegate 9. authority 10. assignment, constitute, delegation, deputation

11. performance 12. perpetration

commissioned . . . 8. allotted, assigned, breveted 9. delegated 10. accredited, authorized

commissioner . . . 5. envoy 6. dubash, legate 7. steward 8. delegate, emissary, official 9. commissar

commissure . . . 4. seam 5. cleft, joint, mitre, raphe 6. stitch, suture 7. closure 8. juncture 10. interstice

commit . . . 2. do 3. con 4. game (cards) 5. refer 6. remand 7. confide, consign, entrust, promise 8. memorize, relegate 10. commission, perpetrate

commode . . . 3. cap 5. chest 8. fontange 9. washstand 10. chiffonier

commodious . . . 3. fit 5. ample, roomy 6. proper 8. suitable 9. capacious, expansive, opportune 10. convenient 11. comfortable, serviceable 13. accommodating

commodity, commodities . . . 5. goods, wares 6. profit 7. staples

common . . . 4. park 5. cheap, plain, stale, trite, usual 6. mutual, paltry, vulgar 7. average 8. familiar, frequent, mediocre, ordinary, plebeian 9. customary, household, universal 11. commonplace

common (pert to) . . .

ancestor . . 4. Adam 10. progenitor

funds . . 4. pool 7. tontine

gender . . 6. unisex 7. epicene

informer . . 7. delator

people . . 3. mob 5. demos, gente 6. vulgus 7. demotic 8. populace

commonly accepted . . . 7. vulgate

commonly thought . . . 8. putative

commonplace . . . 5. banal, daily, stale, theme, trite, usual 6. truism 7. humdrum, prosaic 8. ordinary, workaday 9. platitude

commonwealth . . . 5. group, State 7. society 8. Kentucky, Virginia 9. Australia, community 12. Pennsylvania 13. Massachusetts

commotion . . . 3. ado 4. fray, riot, stir, to-do, whir 5. flare, tizzy 6. flurry, fracas, hubbub, rumpus, tumult, unrest 7. turmoil 8. foofaraw, uprising 9. agitation, confusion 10. concussion (med), excitement, turbulence 12. perturbation

commune . . . 4. area, soil 5. realm, share 6. confer, impart 7. kibbutz 8. converse 9. communion 10. commonalty 11. intercourse (spiritual) 12. conversation

Commune of Paris (1871) . . . 10. government

communicate . . . 3. say 4. give, join 5. share 6. bestow, impart, inform 7. apprize 8. converse, transmit 9. communion

communication . . . 4. word 5. radio 6. letter, report 7. account, contact, epistle, message 8. buzzword, feedback 9. statement 10. communique, connection 11. computerese, impartation, information, intercourse 12. body language 14. word processing

communion . . . 5. share 6. church
7. concord, rapport 8. converse
9. agreement 11. intercourse
12. denomination 13. participation
Communion . . . 4. host 9. Eucharist,
Sacrament 10. intinction, Last Supper
communion (pert to) . . .
bread (blessed) . . 4. host 5. wafer
7. eulogia 9. antidoron
cloth . . 8. corporal, corporas
plate . . 5. paten 12. processional
table . . 5. altar
vessel . . 3. ama, pyx
communique . . . 4. word 7. message
8. dispatch 13. communication
comose . . . 5. hairy 6. tufted
compact . . . 4. etui, firm, pact, plot, snug,
trim 5. brief, close, dense, pithy, press,
solid, terse, tight 6. treaty, united, vanity
7. concise, crowded, entente, leagued,
serried 8. alliance, compress, contract,
covenant, succinct 9. agreement,
condensed 10. compressed, conspiracy
11. compendious, sententious,
stipulation
companion . . . 3. pal 4. ally, fare, mate,
twin 5. amigo, crony 6. fellow, shadow
7. Achates, compeer, comrade, consort
8. alter ego, co-worker 9. associate
11. confederate, counterpart
companionship . . . 5. amity 7. society
10. fellowship, fraternity
11. comradeship, sociability
13. accompaniment
company . . . 3. set 4. band, bevy, body,
crew, gang, ging, host 5. crowd, flock,
group, party, troop 6. circle, cohort,
throng, troupe 9. concourse, gathering
company (pert to) . . .
detachment . . 5. posse
people, players . . 4. bevy, crew, gang,
team 5. troop 6. galaxy, guests, troupe
9. cavalcade
ships . . 5. fleet 6. armada 8. squadron
soldiers . . 5. corps, squad 7. brigade,
phalanx, platoon 9. battalion
travelers . . 7. caravan 8. pilgrims, tourists
9. merchants
comparative . . . 5. equal, rival 8. relative
10. comparable, relational
compare . . . 4. even 5. liken 6. confer,
semble 7. collate, examine 8. contrast
comparison . . . 6. simile 7. analogy,
parable 8. likening, metaphor
10. accordance, similarity
11. parallelism
compartment . . . 3. bin 4. cell, part 5. stall
6. alcove 7. cellule, chamber, quarter
8. district, division 10. department
compass . . . 3. arc 4. area, plot, ring
5. guide, range (Mus), reach, solar,
sweep 6. attain, bounds, circle, curved,
degree, extent 7. circuit, divider,
enclose, imagine 8. circular, distance,
surround
compass (pert to) . . .
housing . . 8. binnacle
part . . 3. pen 6. needle
point . . 4. airt 5. rhumb 7. azimuth
sight . . 4. vane
suspender . . 6. gimbal

compassion . . . 4. pity, ruth (anc) 5. mercy
8. humanity, sympathy 10. condolence
13. commiseration
compassionate . . . 6. gentle, humane
7. clement, pitiful 8. merciful
11. sympathetic, warmhearted
12. sympathizing
compatible . . . 8. affinity, suitable
9. accordant, agreeable, congruous
10. consistent, harmonious
12. congeniality
compeer . . . 4. mate, peer 5. equal,
match, rival 7. comrade 9. companion
compel . . . 4. urge 5. drive, force,
impel, press 6. coerce, incite, oblige,
obsess 7. actuate, dragoon, require
9. constrain, influence, instigate
compelling . . . 6. urgent 7. driving
8. pressing 9. insistent, necessary,
obsessing 10. compulsory, motivating,
obligatory, persuasive
compelling assent . . . 6. cogent
compelling attention . . . 9. insistent
compendious . . . 5. brief, short, terse
7. compact, concise 8. abridged,
succinct 9. condensed 10. summarized
compendium . . . 5. brief 6. abrégé,
digest 7. capsule, epitome, medulla,
pandect, summary 8. abstract, syllabus,
synopsis 9. comprisal 10. abridgment
11. compilation, contraction
12. abbreviation
compensate . . . 3. pay 5. atone, repay
6. reward 7. redress, requite
9. indemnity 10. recompense,
remunerate 14. counterbalance
compensation . . . 3. pay 4. hire 5. bonus,
wages 6. manbot (manbote), reward,
salary 7. penalty, stipend 8. gratuity,
pittance, requital, solatium
9. atonement, indemnity 10. reparation
12. remuneration, satisfaction
15. indemnification
compete . . . 3. vie 4. cope 5. match
6. outvie, strive 7. contend, contest,
emulate
competence . . . 5. means, skill 7. ability,
fitness 8. adequacy, capacity, property
10. capability, efficiency 11. proficiency,
sufficiency, suitability 13. effectiveness,
qualification
competent . . . 3. apt, can, fit 4. able
5. capax, smart 7. capable 8. adequate,
suitable 9. effective, effectual, efficient,
qualified 10. catechumen, sufficient
12. appertaining (to)
competition . . . 5. match, trial 6. strife
7. contest, rivalry 8. ambition, concours
9. emulation 10. corrivalry
compilation . . . 5. cento 6. digest
9. Americana 10. collection
compile . . . 3. add 4. edit 5. amass
6. gather 8. assemble
complacent . . . 4. smug 6. bovine
7. fatuous 9. contented, satisfied
11. considerate 13. self-satisfied
complain . . . 4. beef, carp, fret, kick,
pule, wail 5. gripe, growl, whine
6. accuse, bewail, grieve, grouse,
lament, murmur, mutter, repine,
squawk, yammer 7. deplore, grumble,

protest 9. bellyache
complaint... 4. beef 6. charge, lament,
malady 7. ailment, disease, illness,
protest 8. disorder, repining, reproach
9. grievance, murmuring 10. accusation,
imputation 11. declaration, lamentation
complaisance... 6. regard 7. amenity,
concern, suavity 8. civility, courtesy,
urbanity 10. indulgence, solicitude,
submission, toleration 13. consideration
complaisant... 4. easy, kind 5. civil
6. polite 7. lenient 8. gracious, obliging
9. compliant, courteous
complement... 4. crew 7. adjunct
8. addition, complete 10. correspond,
supplement 11. counterpart
complete... 3. all, end 4. dead, fill, full,
sole 5. stark, total, utter, whole 6. effect,
entire, finish, intact, mature 7. achieve,
execute, germane, perfect, plenary,
realize 8. absolute, conclude, detailed,
outright 9. terminate 10. accomplish,
complement, consummate
11. unqualified
completely... 3. all 5. fully, quite, stark
6. in toto 7. solidly, totally, utterly
8. entirely
completeness... 9. entelechy, integrity
complex... 4. mazy 5. mixed 6. knotty
7. twisted 8. involute, involved
9. entangled, intricate, perplexed
10. interlaced 11. complicated
complexion... 4. blee, mode, tone
5. color, guise, tinge 10. appearance
compliance... 6. assent 7. consent
9. accession, obedience 10. concession,
conformity, observance, submission
11. willingness 12. acquiescence
compliant... 6. docile 7. duteous, dutiful,
willing 8. obedient 10. submissive
11. acquiescent, complaisant,
conformable
complicated... 6. daedal 7. complex,
Gordian, snarled, tangled 8. involved
9. difficult, embroiled, intricate
11. embarrassed 12. labyrinthine
complication... 4. node (drama)
5. nodus 7. illness 9. complexus
10. complexity 11. combination
compliment... 6. praise 7. adulate,
commend, flatter 8. encomium, flattery
12. blandishment, commendation
14. congratulation
comply... 4. obey 5. agree, yield
6. accede, accord, assent, submit
7. conform, observe 9. acquiesce
compone... 6. settle 7. arrange, compose
8. compound
component... 3. ion 4. part 5. basis
6. factor 7. element 8. integral
10. ingredient 11. constituent
comport... 3. act 6. accord, behave
7. conduct 10. correspond
comfortable... 8. suitable 10. consistent
compose... 3. pen 4. calm, form, make
5. order, score, write 7. arrange,
fashion, prepare 8. compound, melodize
9. reconcile 10. constitute
11. orchestrate, tranquilize
composed... 4. calm, cool 5. quiet,
sober, wrote 6. sedate, serene 7. consist

8. arranged, tranquil 9. collected
11. unflappable
composed of...
flat plates.. 9. lamellate
lobes.. 6. lobate
composer... 6. author 7. idylist (idyllist)
10. compositor, typesetter
composer of...
Aida.. 5. Verdi
Carmen.. 5. Bizet
Faust.. 6. Gounod
La Boheme.. 7. Puccini
Merry widow.. 5. Lehar
Mikado.. 8. Sullivan
Naughty Marietta.. 7. Herbert
Stars and Stripes Forever.. 5. Sousa
composition... 4. opus 5. piece, theme
6. make-up 7. melange 9. formation,
synthesis 12. constitution, construction
composition (pert to)...
literature.. 5. cento, essay, poesy, prose
6. poetry, satire, thesis 8. treatise
10. brainchild
music.. 2. op 4. aria, glee, hymn, opus
5. drama, étude, motet, nonet, opera,
rondo, suite 6. anthem, septet (septuor),
sextet (sestet), sonata 7. duetino,
quartet 8. concerto, oratorio, postlude,
symphony
composure... 6. repose 8. calmness,
coolness, serenity 9. placidity
10. equanimity, quiescence, sedateness
11. tranquility
compound... 3. mix 4. olio 5. agree,
amide, ester, oxide, pyran, unite
6. anisil, elixir, iodide, ketone
7. ammonia, combine, farrago,
metamer 8. tincture 9. composite
comprehend... 3. see 4. know 5. grasp,
sense 6. embody, fathom 7. enclose,
imagine, include, involve, realize
8. comprise, conceive 10. understand
comprehensible... 8. exoteric, included,
knowable 9. comprised 11. conceivable,
discernible, perceptible 12. intelligible
comprehensive... 4. full, wide 5. large
7. generic, knowing 8. thorough
9. extensive, inclusive, universal
11. compendious
compress... 4. firm 5. cling, crowd,
pinch, press, stupe 7. compact,
densify, embrace, squeeze 8. astringe,
condense, contract, decrease
comprise, comprize... 5. imply
6. number 7. contain, embrace,
enclose, include, involve 8. perceive
10. comprehend, constitute
compromise... 4. bind 6. adjust
8. compound, trade-off 9. agreement
10. adjustment, concession, settlement
11. appeasement, arbitration
compulsion... 5. drive, force 6. duress,
urging 7. impulse 8. coaction, coercion
9. necessity, obsession 10. compelling
compulsory... 7. driving 9. mandatory,
necessary 10. compelling, imperative,
obligatory 11. involuntary
compunction... 3. rue 5. guilt, pangs,
qualm 6. regret 7. remorse 8. pricking
9. penitence 11. impenitence
13. regretfulness

compute ... **5.** count, score, tally **6.** cipher, figure, number, reckon **8.** estimate **9.** calculate, enumerate

computer terms ... **3.** bit, LAN, RAM, ROM **4.** byte, GIGO **5.** BASIC, COBOL, coder, e-mail, input, modem **6.** access, analog, glitch, laptop, Pascal, server **7.** digital, FORTRAN, monitor **8.** database, download, gigabyte, Internet, megabyte, printout, software, terminal **9.** mainframe, videodisc **10.** cyberspace, floppy disc **11.** computerese **12.** minicomputer **13.** microcomputer, word processor

comrade ... **3.** pal **4.** ally, chum, mate, peer **5.** buddy, crony **6.** fellow, frater **7.** compeer **8.** camarada, sidekick **9.** associate, colleague, companion

con ... **2.** no **3.** nay **4.** know, read, scam **5.** cheat, learn, steer, study **6.** peruse **7.** convict, deceive, swindle **8.** memorize, negative **10.** understand **13.** confidence man

conceal ... **4.** dern, hide, mask, palm, veil **5.** cloak, cover, derne, eloin, feign **6.** eloign, pocket, screen **7.** secrete **8.** bescreen, disguise, enshield

concealed ... **5.** doggo **6.** covert, hidden, latent, perdue, secret, veiled, velate **7.** covered, larvate, obscure, unknown, velated **9.** disguised, incognito, insidious **11.** clandestine

concede ... **3.** own **5.** admit, agree, allow, grant, yield **6.** accord **7.** confess, consent **8.** consider **9.** surrender **11.** acknowledge

conceit ... **3.** ego **4.** idea **5.** fancy, pride **6.** vagary, vanity **7.** caprice, egotism, foppery, tympany **8.** priggery **12.** boastfulness

conceited ... **4.** smug, vain **5.** proud **7.** foppish **8.** arrogant, boastful, priggish **9.** egotistic, pragmatic **11.** egotistical, opinionated **12.** stuffed shirt

conceivable ... **7.** tenable **8.** credible **9.** plausible **10.** believable, imaginable **12.** intelligible

conceive ... **5.** dream, fancy, think **6.** create, devise, ideate **7.** imagine, produce, realize, suppose, suspect **9.** originate **10.** understand

concentrate ... **4.** mass **5.** focus **6.** center **7.** compact, densify, extract **8.** condense, converge **9.** intensify **10.** centralize **11.** consolidate

concept ... **4.** idea **5.** image **7.** opinion, thought **8.** category

conception ... **4.** idea **5.** image, savvy **6.** notion **7.** conceit, opinion **9.** pregnancy **12.** apprehension **13.** comprehension, understanding

concern ... **4.** care, firm, sake **5.** event, grief **6.** affair, affect, import, matter **7.** anxiety, pertain **8.** business, interest, salience **9.** relevance **10.** importance **11.** consequence **12.** significance **13.** consideration

concerning ... **3.** for **4.** as to, over, upon **5.** about, anent **9.** regarding **10.** respecting

concert ... **6.** aubade **7.** recital

9. agreement, unanimity **11.** co-operation, performance

concert hall ... **5.** odeum (odeon) **6.** lyceum **7.** theater **9.** music hall, playhouse

concession ... **5.** grant **6.** market **7.** consent **8.** discount **10.** compromise, confession **13.** qualification

concierge ... **6.** porter, warden **7.** ostiary **8.** chokidar **10.** doorkeeper

conciliate ... **4.** ease **6.** pacify **7.** appease, mollify, placate **9.** reconcile **10.** propitiate

conciliatory ... **6.** assent, irenic **8.** irenical **9.** appeasing, forgiving **10.** mollifying

concise ... **4.** curt, neat **5.** brief, crisp, pithy, terse **6.** précis **7.** laconic, pointed, serried, summary **8.** succinct **11.** compendious, sententious **13.** comprehensive

conclude ... **3.** end **4.** rest **5.** close, infer **6.** deduce, endeth, finish, settle **7.** arrange, presume, resolve, suppose **8.** complete **9.** determine, terminate

conclusion ... **3.** end **4.** last **5.** close, finis **6.** finale, finish, result **8.** decision, epilogue **9.** deduction, diagnosis, inference **10.** completion **13.** determination

conclusive ... **5.** final, valid **8.** decisive, ultimate **9.** mandatory **10.** convincing, evidential **11.** irrefutable, sockdologer (answer) **12.** unanswerable

concoct ... **3.** mix **4.** brew, cook, make **6.** devise, digest, invent, scheme **7.** perfect, prepare **9.** fabricate

concoction ... **4.** dish, plan, plot **6.** device **7.** mixture **8.** compound **9.** falsehood, invention **11.** combination, fabrication, preparation

concomitant ... **9.** accessory, attendant, co-operant **10.** coincident, concurrent **11.** synchronous **12.** accompanying, simultaneous

concord ... **4.** tune **5.** chord, peace **6.** accord, treaty, unison **7.** concert, harmony, rapport **8.** symphony **9.** agreement, unanimity

Concorde ... **3.** SST

concordant ... **8.** agreeing, harmonic, unisonal **9.** consonant, unanimous **10.** harmonious **11.** conformable **13.** correspondent

concrete ... **4.** hard, pave **5.** béton, solid **6.** cement **7.** congeal, plaster **8.** hardness, pavement, solidify **11.** substantial

concur ... **5.** agree, chime, unite **6.** accede, assent **7.** approve, combine, consent **9.** acquiesce, co-operate **11.** synchronize

concurrence ... **6.** united **7.** joining **9.** adherence, concourse, unanimity **11.** coincidence, conjunction, convergence, co-operation, parallelism

concurrent ... **5.** joint **6.** united **7.** meeting, uniting **8.** parallel, syndrome **9.** unanimous **10.** associated, coincident, synergetic **11.** co-operative, synchronous **12.** accompanying, simultaneous

concussion . . . 5. clash, shock, smash, wound 6. injury, trauma 9. collision
condemn . . . 3. ban 4. doom 5. blame, decry 7. adjudge, censure, convict 8. penalize, sentence
condense . . . 3. mix 5. unite 6. absorb, decoct, deepen, harden, lessen, narrow, reduce 7. abridge, combine, compact, densify, enhance, shorten, squeeze, thicken 8. compress, contract, diminish, heighten, solidify 9. constrict, intensify 11. concentrate, consolidate
condensed . . . 7. compact, concise, cramped, tabloid 9. shortened 10. compressed, contracted 12. concentrated
condenser (anc) . . . 9. Leyden jar
condescend . . . 5. deign, stoop 6. submit, unbend 7. concede, descend 9. patronize, vouchsafe
condign . . . 3. fit 4. just 6. severe, worthy 7. fitting 8. adequate, deserved, suitable
condiment . . . 3. soy 4. dill, mace, mint, sage, salt 5. chili, clove, curry, sauce, spice 6. catsup, garlic, ginger, nutmeg, pepper, relish 7. cayenne, ketchup, mustard, paprika, vinegar 9. seasoning 10. peppermint
condition . . . 2. if 4. case, haze, rank, term 5. covin, limit, stage, state 6. estate, fettle, health, plight, status 7. posture, proviso, quality, station 8. capacity, position, standing 9. requisite, situation 10. limitation 11. predicament 12. circumstance
condition (pert to) . . .
  favorable . . 4. odds
  flushed . . 4. rosy
  habitual . . 5. tenor
  hypnotic . . 4. daze 6. stupor, trance 7. narcose
  made . . 7. premise
  murk . . 3. fog 4. haze, mist 5. gloom
  proper . . 6. kilter
  stipulation . . 7. proviso
conditionally . . . 2. if 8. provided 11. tentatively 13. provisionally
condone . . . 5. remit 6. accept, excuse, pardon 7. absolve, forgive 8. tolerate 11. countenance
condor . . . 6. falcon 7. vulture
conduce . . . 4. lend, tend 5. serve 6. effect 7. advance, dispose, incline, redound 10. contribute
conducive . . . 6. useful 7. helpful 11. implemental, serviceable 12. instrumental
conduct . . . 3. act, run 4. lead, mien, rule 5. guide, usage, usher 6. action, convey, convoy, direct, escort, govern, manage 7. bearing, comport, control, manners 8. behavior, demeanor, regulate 9. operation, supervise 10. deportment, management 11. comportment, superintend
conduct (pert to) . . .
  a cause . . 5. plead
  breach . . 6. guilty
  doctrine of . . 6. morals
  one's self . . 6. behave, demean 7. comport

conducting inward . . . 9. afference
conductor . . . 5. guide 6. escort, leader 7. cathode, maestro, manager 8. cicerone, director, operator, trainman
conduit . . . 3. way 4. adit, duct, pain, pipe, tube 5. canal, sewer 6. course 7. channel 8. aqueduct
cone (pert to) . . .
  conelike . . 5. conic 6. pineal 7. conical
  pine . . 8. strobile
  silver . . 4. pina
  tree . . 5. larch 7. conifer
confab, confabulation . . . 4. chat, talk 7. palaver, prattle 8. chinfest, talkfest 12. conversation
confection . . . 3. jam 5. candy, dulce, icing, jelly 6. cimbal, comfit, nougat, sweets 7. caramel, fondant, praline, succade 8. preserve 9. sweetmeat 11. bittersweet, marshmallow
confederacy . . . 5. cabal, hanse, union 6. fusion, league 8. alliance, covenant 9. coalition 10. complicity, conspiracy, federation 11. affiliation, association, combination 13. consolidation
confederate . . . 3. pal, reb 4. ally 5. stall 7. abettor 9. accessory, assistant, associate, auxiliary 10. accomplice
confer . . . 4. give 6. advise, bestow, invest, parley 7. collate, commune, consign, consult, counsel 8. ordinate (knighthood) 10. deliberate
conference . . . 5. trust 6. huddle, parley, powwow 7. council, palaver 9. interview 10. discussion 12. consultation
conferring respect . . . 9. honorific
conferring title . . . 9. ennobling
confess . . . 3. own, rue 4. avow 5. admit, own up 6. regret, repent, reveal, shrive 7. concede 11. acknowledge
confession . . . 5. credo (of faith), creed 6. avowal, shrift 9. admission, communion 10. profession 14. acknowledgment (acknowledgement)
confetti . . . 5. paper 6. ribbon 7. bonbons 9. cascarons (in eggshells) 10. sweetmeats 11. confections
confidant . . . 6. friend 8. intimate
confide . . . 4. hope, rely 5. trust 6. commit, depend, repose
confidence . . . 5. faith, poise 6. aplomb, belief, morals, secret 7. courage 8. credence, sureness 9. assurance, impudence 10. effrontery 12. impertinence
confident . . . 4. smug, sure 6. secure 7. assured, certain, hopeful, reliant 8. cocksure, positive, sanguine, unafraid 9. convinced 10. determined
confidential . . . 5. privy 6. secret 7. private 8. esoteric, intimate 9. auricular 10. unquotable 11. trustworthy
confidentially . . . 7. sub rosa
configuration . . . 4. form 5. shape 6. figure 7. contour, Gestalt, pattern 8. asterism 13. constellation
confine . . . 3. dam, hem, mew, pen, sty, tie 4. bind, cage, coop, jail, lock 5. bound, limit, stint 6. border, immure,

intern, secure, strain **7**. compass
8. imprison, restrain **9**. enclosure
11. incarcerate, restriction
12. circumscribe
confined . . . **4**. pent **5**. bound, caged
6. shut-in **7**. cribbed, endemic,
limited **8**. esoteric, impended, interned
9. bedridden, impounded, invalided,
parochial
confinement . . . **5**. limbo **7**. durance,
lying-in **9**. detention, isolation, restraint
10. cabin fever, childbirth
12. accouchement, imprisonment
13. incomm unicado **15**. circumscription
confirm . . . **4**. seal **5**. prove **6**. assure,
attest, ratify, settle, verify **7**. approve,
fortify, sustain **8**. convince, sanction,
validate **9**. establish **11**. corroborate
12. substantiate
confirmed . . . **6**. proved **7**. chronic
8. habitual, ratified **10**. encouraged,
inveterate **11**. established
confiscate . . . **5**. seize, usurp **7**. impound
11. appropriate
conflagrant . . . **5**. afire **6**. ablaze, aflame
7. blazing, burning
conflagration . . . **4**. fire **5**. blaze, fever
8. wildfire **9**. holocaust **12**. inflammation
conflict . . . **3**. war **4**. bout, duel, fray
5. clash, fight, run-in **6**. action,
battle, combat, oppose, strife, tussle
7. contend, contest, discord **8**. clashing,
struggle **9**. antipathy, collision,
encounter, hostility **10**. contention,
donnybrook, opposition **11**. competition
confluence . . . **4**. flow **5**. crowd **6**. stream
7. flowing (together), meeting
8. junction **10**. assemblage
11. concurrence, convergence
12. assimilation
conform . . . **2**. go **3**. fit **4**. lean, obey,
suit **5**. adapt, agree **6**. adjust, concur,
settle **7**. compose, consent, observe
8. coincide, fine-tune **9**. reconcile
11. accommodate
conformity . . . **6**. dharma **7**. harmony
8. legality, symmetry **9**. agreement,
congruity **10**. compliance
15. conventionality
confound . . . **3**. mix **5**. abash, amaze
6. baffle, dismay, puzzle, thwart
7. astound, buffalo, mystify, nonplus,
perplex **8**. astonish, bewilder
9. dumbfound, embarrass, frustrate
10. complicate, contradict, disconcert
11. intermingle
confront . . . **4**. face, meet **5**. front
6. oppose **7**. compare **9**. encounter
confrontation . . . **6**. crisis **7**. face-off
8. showdown **9**. encounter
10. opposition
confuse . . . **3**. mix **4**. maze **5**. abash,
addle, upset **6**. baffle, flurry, garble,
jumble, muddle **7**. derange, fluster
8. befuddle, bewilder, disorder, distract,
entangle **9**. embrangle **10**. complicate,
disarrange, discompose, disconcert
confused . . . **4**. asea **6**. addled **7**. chaotic,
jumbled, rattled **8**. deranged
9. chagrined, flustered, perplexed,
uncertain **10**. indistinct

confusion . . . **3**. ado, din **4**. mess, moil
5. babel, chaos **6**. jumble, pother, welter
7. anarchy, clutter, turmoil **8**. disarray,
disorder **9**. abashment, agitation
10. perplexity **11**. derangement
12. bewilderment **13**. embarrassment
confute . . . **4**. deny **5**. rebut **6**. answer,
expose, refute **7**. dismiss **8**. confound,
overcome, redargue **9**. overwhelm (by
argument)
congeal . . . **3**. gel, ice, set **4**. rime **6**. freeze
7. pectize, thicken
congenial . . . **4**. boon **7**. kindred **8**. friendly
9. accordant, agreeable **10**. affinitive,
compatible **11**. sympathetic
congenital . . . **6**. inborn, innate
7. connate, genetic, natural
14. constitutional
conger . . . **3**. eel **8**. cucumber
13. Leptocephalus
congeries . . . **4**. heap **9**. amassment
10. collection **11**. aggregation
congestion . . . **3**. jam **4**. heap **8**. fullness,
stoppage **9**. gathering **11**. obstruction
12. accumulation
Congo . . .
capital . . **11**. Brazzaville
city . . **6**. Makoua **7**. Louboma
port . . **11**. Pointe Noire
river . . **5**. Congo (Zaire) **6**. Sangha
congratulate . . . **4**. laud **5**. bless **6**. salute
7. rejoice **8**. macarize **10**. compliment,
felicitate
congregate . . . **4**. herd, mass, meet
5. group, troop **6**. gather, muster
7. collect **8**. assemble **9**. forgather
congregation . . . **4**. mass **5**. house,
laity **7**. council **8**. assembly, audience
9. gathering **10**. collection
11. churchgoers
congress . . . **4**. diet **5**. synod **6**. durbar,
indaba, soviet **7**. council, meeting
8. assembly, conclave **9**. Sanhedrin
10. convention, parliament
11. convergence, convocation
legislature **12**. congregation
congruous . . . **3**. fit **4**. meet **6**. proper
7. fitting **8**. agreeing, becoming, suitable
9. consonant
conic, conical . . . **8**. parabola
9. pyramidal **10**. cone-shaped, funnellike
conifers . . . **4**. yews **5**. pines **6**. cedars
7. larches, Pinales, Sabines, spruces,
Torreys **8**. hemlocks, Soledads
9. Coniferae, Corsicans **10**. evergreens
conjecture . . . **3**. aim **5**. ettle, guess,
opine, think **6**. divine **7**. conjoin,
imagine, presume, suppose, surmise,
suspect **8**. supposal **9**. inference
10. assumption, hypothesis
11. supposition
conjoin . . . **4**. join, link, yoke **5**. hitch,
unite **6**. adjoin, concur **7**. combine,
connect **8**. corelate **9**. correlate
conjoined parts . . . **6**. adnexa
conjointly . . . **10**. hand-in-hand
conjugal . . . **7**. marital, nuptial
9. connubial **11**. matrimonial
conjugate . . . **4**. join **5**. yoked **6**. couple,
united **7**. coupled, related **8**. bijugate,
combined **10**. paronymous

12. etymological
conjugation ... **5.** union **6.** fusion
7. duality, joining, uniting
10. assemblage **11.** combination
13. juxtaposition
conjunct ... **6.** united **8.** combined
9. conjoined, corporate
conjunction ... **2.** as, et, if, or **3.** and,
but, nor **4.** than, that **5.** since,
union **6.** casual, though **7.** whether
10. connection **11.** adversative,
association, combination, concurrence,
correlative
conjure ... **4.** pray **5.** charm **6.** adjure,
enjoin, invoke, juggle, summon (magic)
7. beseech, enchant, entreat, implore
10. supplicate
conjure (up) ... **5.** raise **6.** call up
8. exorcise (exorcize), remember
9. visualize
conjurer, conjuror ... **4.** mage **6.** voodoo,
wizard **7.** juggler **8.** exorcist, magician
conk ... **4.** head, nose **5.** decay (tree)
conk out ... **4.** fade, fail **5.** stall **6.** fizzle,
perish, weaken
connate ... **4.** akin **6.** allied **7.** cognate,
related, similar **9.** congenial
10. congenital
connect ... **3.** tie **4.** ally, join, link, meet
5. unite **6.** adjoin, attach, couple,
enlink, fasten, relate **7.** bracket, succeed
9. associate, hyphenate
connected ... **3.** met **5.** telic **6.** adnate,
joined **7.** serried, similar **8.** coherent,
inlinked, syndetic **10.** continuous,
correlated
Connecticut ...
capital .. **8.** Hartford
city .. **6.** Darien, Mystic **7.** Meriden
8. Hartford, New Haven **9.** Waterbury
10. Bridgeport
college (famed) .. **4.** Yale (1701)
historic site .. **10.** Charter Oak (1687,
Hartford)
museum .. **6.** Barnum (P T)
river .. **6.** Thames **9.** Naugatuck
10. Hoosatonic **11.** Connecticut
State admission .. **5.** Fifth
State Motto .. **21.** Qui Transtulit Sustinet
(He Who Transplants Sustains)
State nickname .. **6.** Nutmeg
12. Constitution
connecting link ... **3.** tie **4.** bond
6. connex **7.** kiaison **8.** ligament,
vinculum **11.** intermedium
12. intermediary
connection ... **4.** bond **5.** nexus, union
6. clevis, family, series **7.** kinship,
passage **8.** alliance, commerce,
junction, relation **9.** coherence, go-
between, relevance **10.** continuity
11. association, intercourse
12. intermediary, relationship
13. communication, juxtaposition
conner ... **5.** pilot **6.** balker, tester
7. peruser **8.** examiner **9.** inspector
connive ... **4.** plot, wink **5.** blink **6.** scheme
7. collude, complot, finagle **8.** conspire,
contrive, maneuver, overlook
conniving ... **8.** scheming **9.** collusive,
deceitful **10.** conspiring **11.** calculating

connoisseur ... **5.** judge, maven **6.** expert
7. epicure, gourmet **8.** gourmand
11. cognoscente, connaisseur
connotation ... **5.** sense **6.** import,
intent **7.** meaning, purport **8.** overtone
10. denotation **11.** implication
12. significance **13.** comprehension
connubial ... **7.** martial, nuptial
8. conjugal **11.** matrimonial
12. epithalamium (song)
conquer ... **3.** win **4.** beat, best **5.** crush
6. defeat, humble, master, reduce,
subdue **7.** subject **8.** overcome,
overturn, surmount, vanquish
9. discomfit, overpower, overthrow,
subjugate
conqueror ... **4.** hero **6.** captor, Cortez,
victor, winner **7.** subduer **10.** subjugator
12. conquistador
conquest ... **6.** Norman (1066) **7.** mastery,
triumph, victory
consanguinity ... **5.** nabob **7.** kinship,
sibship **8.** affinity, relation (blood)
12. relationship
conscience ... **4.** mind, self **6.** psyche
8. superego **9.** casuistry
conscientious ... **7.** dutiful, servile
8. faithful **10.** fastidious, meticulous,
scrupulous **11.** punctilious
conscientious objection ... **7.** scruple
conscious ... **4.** keen **5.** alive, awake,
aware, vital **7.** animate, feeling
8. sensible, sentient **9.** breathing,
cognizant **13.** self-conscious
consecrate ... **4.** sain **5.** bless, exalt
6. anoint, devote, hallow, ordain
7. glorify **8.** dedicate, sanctify
consecrated (pert to) ...
bread .. **4.** host **5.** wafer
oil .. **6.** chrism
thing .. **6.** sacrum
consent ... **4.** give **5.** agree, grant, yield
6. accede, accord, assent, concur,
permit **8.** approval **9.** acquiesce
10. compliance, permission
11. concurrence **13.** understanding
consequence ... **3.** end **5.** event **6.** course,
effect, result, weight **7.** dignity,
outcome **8.** pursuant (in), sequence
9. aftermath, inference, influence,
loftiness, outgrowth **10.** importance,
notability **11.** distinction
consequential ... **7.** pompous **8.** eventual
9. important **13.** self-important
consequently ... **2.** do **4.** ergo, then
5. hence **9.** as a result, therefore,
wherefore **12.** subsequently
13. consecutively
conservative ... **4.** Tory **5.** staid **7.** die-
hard, fogyish, old-line **8.** moderate
10. long-haired **11.** reactionary
12. preservative **13.** unprogressive
conserve ... **3.** jam **4.** save **5.** guard,
uvate **6.** defend, secure, shield,
uphold **7.** protect, sustain **8.** maintain
9. preserves, sweetmeat
consider ... **3.** ain, see **4.** care, deem,
heed, muse, rate **5.** judge, think, treat,
weigh **6.** esteem, intend, ponder,
regard **7.** discuss, examine, reflect,
revolve **8.** cogitate, meditate, ruminate

10. deliberate 11. contemplate

considerable . . . 5. great, large 7. notable, several 8. numerous 9. important 10. noteworthy, remarkable 13. authoritative

considerate . . . 4. kind 6. gentle 7. careful, heedful, prudent, serious 8. obliging 9. attentive, judicious 10. deliberate, reflective, solicitous, thoughtful

consideration . . . 4. self 5. study 6. esteem, regard 7. respect, thought 9. attention, deference, incentive, influence 10. cogitation, importance, meditation, reflection, reputation, rumination 11. examination 12. compensation, deliberation

considering . . . 2. if 5. since 8. after all, inasmuch, in view of

consign . . . 5. allot 6. assign, commit, devote, remand, resign 7. deliver, entrust 8. transfer 11. subscribe to

consignee . . . 6. factor 7. awardee 8. assignee 9. committee

consign to . . .
a place . . 8. allocate
prison . . 6. commit, send up
ruin . . 4. doom
unimportance . . 8. relegate

consistent . . . 5. equal, solid, stiff 7. equable, logical, uniform 8. coherent 9. agreement, consonant, steadfast 10. persisting

consisting of . . .
cavities . . 9. cellulose
layers (thin) . . 8. laminate
names . . 8. onomatic
one word . . 7. monepic
pages . . 7. paginal
three measures . . 8. trimeter
three spots . . 4. trey
three styles (Bot) . . 10. tristylous
two parts . . 6. binary

consist of . . . 5. imply 6. embody 7. contain, embrace, enclose, involve 8. comprise (comprize)

consolation . . . 6. solace 7. comfort 10. condolence

console . . . 4. desk 5. cheer, organ, table 6. solace, soothe 7. bracket, cabinet, comfort, support, sustain 9. alleviate, encourage

consolidate . . . 4. knit, mass 5. merge, unify, unite 7. combine, densify 8. coalesce, compress, organize, solidify 9. intensify 10. strengthen

consonant . . . 4. lene, surd 5. lenis, nasal, velar 6. dental, labial 7. lingual, palatal, spirate 8. gutteral 9. accordant, congruous 10. compatible, concordant, consistent

consonant (pert to) . . .
hissing . . 8. sibilant
rustling . . 9. fricative
voiceless (breathed) . . 6. atonic 7. spirate

consort . . . 4. Devi (of Siva), mate, wife 5. group, Sakti 6. mingle, spouse 7. husband, partner 9. associate, colleague, companion, harmonize 11. combination, confederate, conjunction

conspicuous . . . 6. famous, signal

7. eminent, glaring, obvious, salient, visible 8. distinct, lionized, manifest, striking 9. important, prominent 10. celebrated, noticeable, remarkable 11. illustrious, outstanding 13. distinguished

conspiracy . . . 4. plot 5. cabal, unite 6. scheme 8. intrigue 9. collusion 10. connivance 11. confederacy, machination

conspire . . . 4. plot 5. unite 6. concur, scheme 7. collude, complot, finagle 9. fainaigue 11. confederate

constable . . . 3. cop 5. staff 6. beadle, keeper, warden 7. bailiff 8. tipstaff 9. policeman

constabulary . . . 6. bureau (police) 10. constables

constancy . . . 4. zeal 5. ardor, faith, truth 6. fealty, garnet (symbol) 7. honesty, loyalty 8. devotion, fidelity 9. adherence, continual, eagerness, integrity, stability 10. allegiance, attachment, permanence, perpetuity, uniformity 11. devotedness, earnestness 12. faithfulness

constant . . . 4. firm, true 5. fixed 7. regular, uniform 8. faithful, resolute 9. continual, invariant, parameter (Math), perpetual, steadfast 10. continuous, invariable, persistent 12. unchangeable

constant desire . . . 4. itch 9. hankering

Constantine (pert to) . . .
birthplace . . 4. Nish (Nis) 7. Naissus (now Yugoslavia)
known as . . 8. The Great
title . . 7. Emperor (Rome)

Constantinople . . .
official name . . 8. Istanbul
patriarch . . 9. Nestorius
site . . 6. Turkey (Eur)

constellation . . . 5. stars 6. galaxy 8. asterism 10. luminaries 13. configuration (stars)

Constellations (partial list) . . .
arrow . . 7. Sagitta
bears (Dipper) . . 9. Ursa Major, Ursa Minor
Bird of Paradise (S Pole) . . 4. Apus
bull . . 6. Taurus
crab . . 6. Cancer
crane . . 4. Grus
crow . . 6. Corvus
dog . . 5. Canis
dragon . . 5. Draco
eagle . . 6. Aquila
fishes . . 6. Pisces
goat . . 9. Capricorn
goldfish . . 6. Dorado
hunter . . 5. Orion (most conspicuous)
lion . . 3. Leo
Noah's Ark . . 4. Argo
Northern Crown . . 14. Corona Borealis, Northern Lights
peacock . . 4. Pavo
scorpion . . 7. Scorpio
serpent (sea) . . 5. Hydra
Southern Cross . . 4. Crux
swan . . 6. Cygnus
Twins . . 6. Gemini

virgin .. **5.** Virgo
water bearer .. **8.** Aquarius
whale .. **6.** Cestus
winged horse .. **7.** Pegasus
wolf .. **5.** Lupus
Constellations' brightest star ... **3.** Cor
Constellations of the Zodiac ... **3.** Leo
5. Aries, Libra, Virgo **6.** Cancer, Gemini,
Pisces, Taurus **7.** Scorpio **8.** Aquarius
11. Capricornus, Sagittarius
constituent ... **5.** voter **6.** factor,
matter **7.** elector, element, essence
8. elective **9.** component **10.** ingredient
11. determinant (Math)
constituent of ...
blood serum .. **7.** opsonin
coal .. **6.** carbon
coffee, tea .. **8.** caffeine
hair, nails .. **7.** keratin
oil of cloves .. **7.** eugenol
constitute ... **4.** form **5.** enact, found
6. create, depute **7.** appoint, compose
8. legalize **9.** determine, establish
constitution ... **3.** law **6.** crasis, custom
7. passage **8.** creation **9.** enactment,
essential, ordinance, structure
11. composition, institution
12. organization
Constitution (ship) ... **12.** Old Ironsides
constitutional ... **5.** legal, valid **6.** innate
9. essential, healthful **12.** governmental
13. dispositional
constitutional (pert to) ...
health .. **4.** walk **6.** stroll **8.** exercise
right .. **9.** franchise
temperament .. **6.** crasis
vigor .. **5.** nerve
Constitution State ... **11.** Connecticut
constrain ... **4.** curb, urge **5.** chain, check,
drive, force, impel, press **6.** compel,
oblige **7.** confine, repress **8.** restrain
11. necessitate
constrained ... **6.** forced, modest
7. cramped **8.** moderate, reserved
9. obligated
constraint ... **4.** bond, urge **5.** force
6. duress, stress **7.** modesty, reserve
8. coercion, pressure **9.** restraint,
stiffness **10.** compulsion, moderation
11. confinement
constrict ... **3.** tie **4.** bind **5.** cramp
6. narrow, shrink **7.** squeeze, tighten
8. astringe, condense, contract
10. constringe
constriction ... **9.** narrowing, stricture,
tightness **11.** contraction
13. strangulation
constrictor ... **3.** boa **5.** snake **7.** serpent,
styptic **9.** sphincter **10.** compressor
construct ... **4.** make, rear **5.** build,
erect, frame **6.** create **7.** compose
9. establish, fabricate, originate
constructive ... **7.** virtual **8.** creative,
implicit **9.** anabolism **10.** suggestive
14. interpretation, interpretative
construe ... **5.** parse **6.** deduce, render
7. explain **9.** interpret, translate
consuetude ... **5.** habit, usage **6.** custom
consuetudinary ... **6.** manual (customs),
ritual **9.** customary
consult (with) ... **6.** advise, confer, take

up **7.** discuss **10.** deliberate
consultation ... **7.** counsel **8.** audition,
congress **9.** interview **10.** conference,
discussion **12.** deliberation
consume ... **3.** eat, use **4.** burn **5.** spend,
waste **6.** absorb, devour, expend
7. destroy (fire) **8.** squander **9.** dissipate
12. disintegrate
consumed ... **3.** pau
consummate ... **3.** end, top **4.** ripe
5. ideal **6.** finish, utmost **7.** achieve,
perfect **8.** complete **10.** accomplish
consumption ... **3.** use **4.** loss **5.** decay,
waste **6.** eating **7.** disease, using up
8. phthisis **9.** decrement **11.** destruction
12. tuberculosis **13.** deterioration
contact ... **4.** meet **5.** touch, union
6. impact, syzygy (Astron) **7.** meeting,
oscnode (Math) **8.** junction, tangency,
touching **10.** contiguity
13. communication
contain ... **4.** have, hold, keep **5.** cover
6. embody, number, retain **7.** embrace,
enclose, include, involve, subsume
8. comprise, restrain **9.** divisible (by)
10. comprehend
container ... **3.** bag, bin, box, can, cup,
jar, jug, lug, pan, pod, pot, tin, tub,
urn, vat **4.** case, crib, ewer, pail, sack,
vase **5.** crate, cruet, pouch **6.** basket,
bottle, carboy, carton, hamper, hatbox
7. capsule, hanaper **8.** canister, decanter
containing ...
air .. **9.** pneumatic
antimony .. **8.** stibiate
boron .. **5.** boric **7.** boracic
carbon .. **7.** organic **13.** carboniferous
copper .. **6.** cupric
fire .. **7.** igneous
gold .. **4.** doré **5.** auric
iron .. **6.** ferric
silver .. **5.** lunar
slag .. **6.** drossy
ten .. **6.** denary
tin .. **7.** stannic
containing maxims ... **6.** gnomic
contaminate ... **4.** slur, soil **5.** stain,
sully, taint **6.** befoul, defile, infect,
poison **7.** corrupt, debauch, degrade,
pollute, vitiate **8.** dishonor **9.** desecrate
10. adulterate
contemn ... **4.** defy, hate **5.** scorn, spurn
6. reject **7.** despise, disdain
contemplate ... **4.** muse, plan, scan,
view **5.** study **6.** design, expect, intend,
ponder **7.** examine, foresee, propose
8. consider, envision, meditate
contemplation ... **5.** study **6.** musing
7. theoria, thought **8.** scrutiny
9. foresight, intuition **10.** expectancy,
reflection **11.** examination, expectation,
speculation
contemplative ... **6.** sedate **7.** pensive
10. meditative, reflective, ruminative,
thoughtful **11.** speculative
13. retrospective
contemporary ... **6.** coeval **7.** present
10. coetaneous, coexistent, coincident
11. concomitant, synchronous
12. simultaneous **15.** contemporaneous
contempt ... **4.** fico, geck **5.** scorn, shame,

sneer **7.** despect, disdain **8.** defiance, derision, ridicule **9.** arrogance, contumely **10.** disrespect **12.** disobedience

contemptible ... **3.** low **4.** base **5.** cheap, petty, sorry **6.** abject, paltry, sordid **7.** pitiful **8.** beggarly, inferior, unworthy **9.** groveling, worthless **10.** despicable **13.** insignificant

contemptuous ... **6.** sneery **7.** haughty **8.** insolent, scornful **10.** disdainful **12.** contumelious, supercilious

contemptuous action ... **9.** indignity **10.** incivility

contend ... **3.** vie, war **4.** cope, deal, race **5.** argue, fight **6.** assert, bicker, insist, strive **7.** compete, contest, grapple, quarrel, wrangle **8.** contrive, maintain, militate

content, contents ... **4.** list, room **5.** index, space **6.** amount, please, volume **7.** filling, gratify, makings, satisfy, suffice **8.** capacity **9.** contented, happiness, satisfied **10.** components, dimensions **11.** ingredients

contention ... **3.** war **4.** feud **6.** combat, debate, strife **7.** quarrel, rivalry **8.** argument, conflict, struggle, variance **9.** emulation **10.** dissension, litigation **11.** altercation, competition, controversy **12.** disagreement

contentious ... **7.** peevish **8.** perverse **9.** combative, litigious, wrangling **10.** pugnacious **11.** belligerent, dissentious, quarrelsome **13.** argumentative

contentment ... **4.** ease **5.** bliss **8.** pleasure **11.** peace of mind **12.** satisfaction **13.** contentedness, gratification

conterminous ... **4.** next **8.** abutting, adjacent, proximal **9.** adjoining

contest ... **3.** sue, vie **4.** agon, bout, cope, deny, game, race, tilt **5.** argue, set-to, trial **6.** debate, oppose, strife, strive, tryout **7.** contend, dispute, tourney, wrangle **8.** argument, disclaim, litigate, skirmish, struggle **9.** emulation **10.** engagement **11.** altercation, competition

contest (pert to) ...
art of .. **10.** agonistics
draw .. **9.** stalemate
log hurling .. **5.** roleo
prize .. **5.** stake
undecided .. **4.** draw

contestant ... **5.** rival **6.** player **7.** athlete, entrant **8.** opponent **9.** candidate, combatant, contender **10.** competitor

contiguous ... **4.** near, next **8.** adjacent, touching **9.** adjoining, immediate, proximate **11.** neighboring

continent ... **4.** Asia **6.** Africa, Europe **7.** Eurasia, Lemuria **8.** Atlantis (lost), Cascadia, landmass **9.** Australia, Greenland **10.** Antarctica **12.** North America, South America

contingency ... **4.** case **5.** event **6.** chance **8.** accident, casualty, exigency, juncture **9.** emergency, liability **11.** eventuality, possibility, uncertainty

contingent ... **6.** casual **8.** eventual **9.** dependent (law), provisory **10.** accidental, fortuitous, incidental **11.** conditional, provisional

continual ... **7.** endless, eternal, regular, undying, uniform **8.** constant, enduring, frequent, unbroken **9.** ceaseless, connected, continued, incessant, perennial, permanent, perpetual, unceasing **10.** continuous, invariable **11.** everlasting, intermitted, unremitting **12.** imperishable **13.** uninterrupted

continually ... **3.** aye **4.** ever **5.** often **7.** eternal **9.** eternally **10.** constantly **11.** perpetually, unceasingly **12.** continuously

continuation ... **6.** sequel **8.** addition, sequence **10.** continuity **11.** continuance, propagation, protraction **12.** postponement, prolongation

continue ... **3.** run **4.** go on, last, stay **5.** abide **6.** endure, extend, remain, resume **7.** perdure, persist, proceed, sustain **8.** protract **9.** persevere, steadfast (be)

continuing ... **5.** still **7.** chronic, durable, lasting **9.** permanent **10.** continuous **11.** persevering

continuous ... **7.** chronic, endless, uniform **8.** unbroken **9.** continued, perpetual **13.** uninterrupted

contorted ... **3.** wry **4.** bent **6.** coiled, warped **7.** garbled, gnarled, twisted, wristed **8.** deformed **9.** perverted

contour ... **4.** form, line **5.** curve, graph **6.** figure **7.** isobase, outline, profile **9.** lineament, periphery **13.** configuration

contra ... **6.** offset **7.** against, counter, reverse **8.** contrary, opposite **9.** vice versa **10.** conversely **12.** contrariwise

contraband ... **7.** bootleg, illegal, illicit **8.** unlawful **9.** moonshine **10.** prohibited

contract ... **4.** hale, knit, pact **5.** incur, lease **6.** cartel, engage, pledge, reduce, shrink **7.** bargain, compact, promise, shorten, shrivel **8.** covenant **9.** agreement, constrict, indenture **10.** convention, obligation, straighten **11.** arrangement **13.** understanding

contraction ... **3.** tic **4.** coup, fist **5.** spasm **7.** elision, systole **8.** decrease **9.** reduction, short-hand, stricture **11.** compression

contrada ... **3.** way **4.** ward **6.** street **7.** quarter

contradict ... **4.** deny **5.** belie, rebut **6.** impugn, negate, oppose, refute **7.** gainsay **10.** counteract

contradiction ... **6.** denial **7.** paradox **10.** opposition, refutation **11.** contrariety **13.** counteraction

contradictory ... **7.** denying **8.** contrary, opposite **10.** refutatory **12.** inconsistent

contrary ... **7.** adverse, counter, froward, opposed, reverse **8.** captious, inimical, opposite, perverse, refutive **9.** different, repugnant **10.** discordant, unorthodox **12.** antagonistic

contrast ... **7.** compare **8.** opposite

11. contrariety

contravene . . . **4.** defy **6.** hinder, oppose, refute, thwart **7.** violate **8.** infringe **9.** disregard

contravention . . . **6.** denial **9.** violation **10.** opposition, refutation

contribute . . . **3.** aid **4.** give **6.** donate **7.** benefit, conduce, provide **9.** subscribe

contribution . . . **3.** tax, tip **4.** boon, gift, scot **6.** tariff **7.** payment, tribute **8.** donation **12.** subscription **13.** participation

contrite . . . **6.** abject, humble **8.** penitent **9.** repentant, sorrowful **10.** remorseful **11.** penitential

contrition . . . **7.** remorse **9.** attrition, penitence **11.** compunction

contrivance . . . **3.** art **5.** means, shift **6.** design, devise **7.** coinage, machine, measure, project **8.** artifice, intrigue **9.** expedient, invention, makeshift **11.** contraption

contrive . . . **4.** plan, plot **5.** frame, hatch, weave **6.** design, devise, invent, manage, scheme **7.** fashion, project **9.** fabricate

control . . . **4.** hold, rein, rule, sway, test **5.** check, gripe, guide, leash, power, wield **6.** direct, govern, manage, subdue **7.** conduct, mastery, preside, regimen **8.** dominate, dominion, ironhand, regulate, restrain **9.** direction, influence, regulator, restraint **10.** management, regulation **11.** self-control, superintend

controller, comptroller . . . **7.** auditor **8.** governor **9.** dominator, regulator

controversial . . . **7.** eristic, polemic **9.** eristical, polemical, pro and con **11.** contentious **12.** disputatious, questionable **13.** argumentative

controversy . . . **6.** debate **7.** dispute, quarrel, wrangle **8.** argument **10.** contention **11.** altercation **12.** disagreement, disputatious

controvert . . . **4.** deny, moot **5.** argue **6.** debate, oppose, refute **7.** discuss, dispute **10.** contradict

contumacious . . . **6.** unruly **7.** riotous **8.** mutinous, perverse **9.** seditious **10.** headstrong, rebellious, refractory, unyielding **11.** disobedient, intractable **12.** ungovernable **13.** insubordinate

contumelious . . . **7.** haughty **8.** insolent **9.** insulting **10.** derogatory, despiteful, disdainful **12.** contemptuous

contumely . . . **5.** scorn **8.** contempt **9.** indignity, insolence **10.** revilement **11.** humiliation, malediction

contusion . . . **4.** blow **6.** bruise, injury **8.** black eye **13.** discoloration

conundrum . . . **5.** rebus **6.** enigma, puzzle, riddle **7.** charade

convalesce . . . **5.** rally **7.** recover, recruit **10.** recuperate

convene . . . **3.** sit **4.** come, meet **5.** unite **6.** summon **8.** assemble **10.** congregate, foregather

convenient . . . **5.** handy, ready **6.** fitted, nearby, suited, timely **7.** adapted **8.** suitable **9.** agreeable, available, opportune **10.** accessible, commodious,
seasonable **11.** comfortable

convent . . . **4.** meet **6.** concur, friary, priory **7.** convene, nunnery **8.** cloister, lamasery **9.** monastery, sanctuary

convention . . . **4.** rule **5.** usage **6.** accord, custom **7.** meeting **8.** assembly **9.** gathering, tradition **10.** assemblage, compliance, conformity

conventional . . . **5.** fixed, nomic, usual **6.** formal, modish **7.** correct **8.** accepted, orthodox **9.** customary **10.** ceremonial **11.** established, traditional

converge . . . **4.** meet **5.** focus, unite

conversant (with) . . . **5.** adept **6.** expert, versed (in) **7.** skilled **8.** familiar **9.** practiced **10.** acquainted, proficient

conversation . . . **4.** chat, talk **7.** trialog **8.** causerie, converse, dialogue **9.** communion, discourse **10.** conference **11.** association **13.** conversazione, interlocution

conversationalist . . . **6.** talker **9.** converser **10.** discourser **12.** confabulator

converse . . . **4.** chat, talk **8.** contrary, opposite

convey . . . **4.** cede, deed, pass, send **5.** bring, carry, eloin, grant **6.** assign, convoy, demise, devise, impart, import **7.** dispone **8.** transfer, transmit **9.** transport **10.** commission **11.** communicate

conveyance . . . **3.** bus, car, van **4.** auto, sled, taxi, tram **5.** plane, train **6.** demise, litter **7.** cession, norimon, trailer, vehicle **8.** airplane, carriage **10.** automobile

conveyer, conveyor . . . **6.** bearer, coolie, pigeon (homing), porter **7.** bheesty, carrier **8.** cargador **9.** stevedore

convict . . . **4.** damn **5.** felon, lifer **6.** refute, termer, trusty **7.** condemn, culprit **8.** refute **8.** criminal, prisoner **10.** malefactor

conviction . . . **4.** hope **6.** belief **7.** opinion **9.** certainty **10.** persuasion **12.** condemnation

convince . . . **6.** assure, subdue **7.** confute, jawbone **8.** overcome, persuade **9.** overpower

convincing . . . **5.** proof **6.** cogent, potent **7.** telling **8.** assuring **10.** conclusive, persuasive, satisfying

convivial . . . **3.** gay **4.** gala **5.** jolly, merry **6.** festal, jovial, joyful, joyous, social **7.** festive, jocular **9.** hilarious

convocation . . . **4.** diet **5.** synod **7.** bidding, council, meeting, summons **8.** assembly, congress **10.** convention **12.** congregation

convoke . . . **4.** call **6.** summon **7.** convene **8.** assemble

convoy . . . **5.** guard, guide **6.** attend, escort **7.** conduct **8.** navigate **9.** accompany, conductor

convulse . . . **5.** amuse, shake **6.** regale **7.** agitate, disturb, torture **9.** entertain **10.** discompose

convulsion . . . **5.** cramp, spasm, throe **6.** tumult, uproar **8.** laughter, paroxysm **9.** agitation, commotion **10.** revolution **11.** disturbance

cony, coney . . . 3. das, fur 4. dupe, hare, pika 5. daman, hyrax 6. burbot, rabbit
cony catcher . . . 5. cheat 7. sharper 8. swindler
coo . . . 4. bill (and), curr 5. chirr 6. murmur, mutter
cook . . . 4. bake, boil, chef, stew 5. broil, roast, sauté, spoil (chess), steam, trill 6. braise, seethe 7. parboil, stir-fry 8. barbecue, magirist 9. charbroil, cuisinier
cookie . . . 5. scone 7. biscuit, brownie 8. macaroon 10. gingersnap, ladyfinger, shortbread
cooking (pert to) . . .
art . . 8. magirics
device . . 3. wok 4. etna, olla 5. grill, plate, stove 6. spider 7. griddle 9. autoclave, microwave (oven)
room . . 6. galley 7. cuisine, kitchen 8. scullery 11. kitchenette
scent . . 4. reek 5. nidor
cool . . . 3. fan, ice 4. calm 5. chill, fresh, nervy, sober, tepid 6. chilly, freeze, sedate, serene, temper 7. unmoved 8. careless, composed, impudent, mitigate, reserved, tranquil 9. apathetic, collected, unruffled 10. nonchalant, unfriendly, unsociable 11. indifferent, levelheaded, unconcerned 13. dispassionate, imperturbable, self-possessed
cooler . . . 4. icer, jail 6. icebox, lockup, prison 7. chiller 10. ventilator 11. refrigerant 12. refrigerator
coolness . . . 4. cold 5. nerve 6. aplomb 7. reserve 12. indifference 14. unfriendliness
coop . . . 3. mew, pen 4. cage, cote, yard 5. court, hutch 7. confine 9. enclosure
cooper . . . 5. drink 6. vessel 8. grogshop (floating) 11. barrel maker 12. wine retailer
Cooper, (James Fenimore) (pert to) . . .
hero . . 10. Deerslayer, Natty Bumpo, Pathfinder
tales . . 15. Leatherstocking
cooperate . . . 4. join, tend 5. agree, coact 6. concur 7. combine, conduce, connive 8. conspire 9. interface, synergize 10. contribute 11. collaborate
coordinate . . . 5. talky 6. adjust 7. syntony (radio) 8. classify, equalize, organize, regulate 9. harmonize, integrate 10. proportion 11. systematize
copious . . . 4. full, rich 5. ample 7. diffuse, profuse 8. abundant, numerous 9. exuberant, plenteous, plentiful 11. overflowing
copper . . . 2. Cu 3. aes 4. cent, coin 5. metal, penny 6. cuprum 9. policeman 12. reddish-brown
copper (pert to) . . .
alloy . . 5. brass 6. bronze, oroide
brass . . 6. chalco
cup . . 3. dop
engraving . . 9. mezzotint
film . . 6. patina
kettle (anc) . . 5. lebes
pewter . . 7. rheotan

Copperfield characters . . . 4. Dora 6. Dartle 8. Micawber 9. Uriah Heep 11. Little Emily
coppice . . . 4. bosk, holt 5. copse, grove 6. growth 7. boscage, thicket 9. brushwood, underwood
Coptic (pert to) . . .
church . . 8. Egyptian
color . . 7. oxblood
title . . 4. anba
copy . . . 3. ape 4. news 5. clone, model, Xerox (tm) 6. ectype, follow 7. edition, estreat, imitate, pattern, replica, reprint, tracing 8. protocol, revision 9. duplicate, imitation 10. transcribe, transcript 11. counterfeit 12. reproduction
coquet, coquette . . . 4. vamp 5. flirt 7. amorous 11. hummingbird
coquille . . . 5. shell 7. ruching
Coquille . . . 6. Indian 10. Athapascan
coquin . . . 5. knave, rogue 6. rascal
coral . . . 3. red 6. polyps, porite 8. Anthozoa 9. madrepore, millepore
coral (pert to) . . .
branch . . 7. ramicle
division . . 7. Aporosa
formation . . 5. palus
island . . 3. key 5. atoll
ridge . . 4. reef 5. shoal
snake . . 5. Elaps 6. garter 7. Micurus
worm . . 6. palolo
corbie (Scot) . . . 4. crow. 5. raven
cord . . . 3. guy, rib 4. lace, line, rope, welt, wood 5. sinew, twine 6. lariat, sennet, spinal, string, tendon 7. measure (cubic), skirreh 8. corduroy, shoelace 9. hamstring 11. clothesline
cordage . . . 5. ropes 7. rigging 8. ropework
Corday's victim . . . 5. Marat
cordelle . . . 6. hauler 7. towline, towrope
cordial . . . 4. real, warm 6. ardent, elixir, genial, hearty, liquor 7. fervent, liqueur, sincere, zealous 8. friendly, vigorous 9. unfeigned 10. hospitable
cordial (liqueur) . . . 5. shrub 6. kummel 8. anisette, periscot 9. Cointreau 11. Benedictine, crème de moka 13. crème de menthe
cordiality . . . 4. zeal 5. ardor 6. fervor 7. ardency 8. kindness, warmness 9. geniality 11. hospitality 12. empressement, friendliness
corduroy feature . . . 4. wale
core . . . 3. ame, hub, nub, nut 4. gist, nave, pith 5. heart, nowel 6. center, kernel, matrix 7. nucleus 9. substance
Corinthian (pert to) . . .
Age . . 5. plush 11. extravagant
color . . 3. red 4. pink 6. purple
Epistles (Bib) . . 12. New Testament
General (Rom) . . 9. Flaminius
King . . 8. Polybius
Spring . . 14. Pirene Fountain
Temple . . 5. Doric 7. Minerva
cork . . . 3. ork 4. bark, bung, plug 5. float, shive, suber (oak) 7. blacken, stopgap, stopper, stopple
corm . . . 4. bulb (flower)
cormorant . . . 4. bird, shag 5. norie, scart, urile 8. ravenous 9. snakebird,

voracious **13.** Phalacrocorax
corn... 4. joke **5.** grain, grist **6.** cliché, kaffir, kernel, liquor
corn (pert to)...
bread.. **4.** pone **8.** dumpling **10.** corndodger
goddess.. **5.** Ceres
hulled.. **4.** samp **6.** hominy
Indian.. **3.** Zea **5.** maize
lily.. **4.** Ixia **8.** bindweed **10.** wandflower
liquor.. **6.** whisky (whiskey)
meal.. **4.** masa **7.** hoecake
porridge.. **5.** atole
salad.. **8.** fetticus
Corn Belt... 4. Iowa, Ohio **6.** Dakota, Kansas **7.** Indiana **8.** Illinois, Missouri, Nebraska **9.** Minnesota
Corncracker State... 8. Kentucky
corner... 2. in **4.** nook, pose, trap, tree **5.** angle, coign (coigne), herne, ingle, niche, quoin
cornered... 5. cater (diagonal), sharp, treed **7.** angular, up a tree **10.** cornerwise
cornerstone... 4. coin **5.** quoin **8.** keystone **10.** foundation
Cornhusker State... 8. Nebraska
cornice... 4. drip, eave **7.** antefix **8.** astragal
Cornish... 3. elm **4.** fowl **5.** heath **7.** dialect, diamond (Cornwall)
Cornwallis surrender site... 4. York (Va)
corolla... 5. galea (Her), petal **8.** perianth
corollary... 6. effect, porism, result **7.** adjunct **8.** addition **9.** deduction **11.** proposition
corona... 4. coin, halo **5.** cigar, crown **6.** circle **7.** aureole, circlet, garland, scyphus **8.** Borealis **11.** corona lucis
Corona Australis... 13. Southern Crown
Corona Borealis... 13. Northern Crown
coronet... 5. crown, tiara **6.** anadem, circle, diadem, wreath **8.** insignia, ornament
Corot subject... 9. landscape
corporate... 5. joint **6.** united **7.** leagued **8.** conjoint **10.** associated
corporeal... 5. hylic, somal **6.** bodily **7.** fleshly, somatic **8.** corporal, material, physical, tangible
corpse... 4. body **7.** cadaver, carcass **9.** endowment (Eccl)
corpulent... 3. fat **5.** bulky, obese, stout **6.** fleshy
corpus... 4. body, mass **9.** principal **10.** collection
corpuscle... 11. poikilocyte, schistocyte **12.** erythroblast
corral... 3. mew, pen, sty **4.** coop, herd **5.** atajo, pound, tambo **7.** impound **8.** stockade **9.** enclosure, inclosure
correct... 2. OK **4.** edit, okay, true **5.** amend, emend, right **6.** better, proper, punish, reform, remedy, revise, strict **7.** chasten, improve, perfect, rectify, regular, retouch **8.** accurate, definite, orthodox, rigorous **9.** faultless **10.** particular, scrupulous **11.** grammatical, punctilious **12.** conventional

correlative... 2. or **3.** nor **6.** mutual **7.** similar **8.** conjoint **10.** reciprocal **11.** conjunction, counterpart **13.** corresponding
correspond... 3. fit **4.** suit **5.** agree, equal, match, tally **6.** accord **7.** comport **8.** assonate (sound), coincide, parallel **9.** analogous, harmonize **11.** parallelize
correspondence... 4. mail **8.** homology (Biol), identity, symmetry **10.** conformity, epistolary, similarity **11.** equivalence, intercourse
corresponding... 8. balanced **9.** analogous, homologic, isometric **10.** coinciding **11.** paralleling
corrida sound... 3. olé
corridor... 4. hall **5.** aisle **6.** airway, arcade **7.** gallery **10.** passageway
corrige (obs)... **6.** punish **7.** correct
corrigible... 8. amenable **10.** submissive **11.** rectifiable
corroborate... 5. prove **7.** certify, confirm, support **8.** calidate, roborate **9.** establish **12.** adminiculate, substantiate
corroborative... 11. adminicular
corrode... 3. eat **4.** bite, etch, gnaw, rust **5.** erode, waste **11.** deteriorate **12.** disintegrate
corrosive... 4. acid **7.** caustic, erodent, erodine, mordant **9.** corroding **10.** escharotic **14.** disintegrative
corrugate... 5. crimp **6.** rugate **7.** crumble, wrinkle **8.** crumpled, furrowed, wrinkled
corrupt... 3. rot **5.** bribe, taint, venal **6.** Augean, debase, putrid, rotten **7.** attaint, crooked, defiled, deprave, putrefy, vitiate **8.** polluted **9.** dishonest **11.** adulterated **12.** contaminated
corruption... 5. taint **6.** pidgin (language) **8.** impurity **9.** chicanery, pollution **10.** debasement, defilement, distortion **11.** depravation, putrescence **12.** adulteration **13.** contamination
corsage... 5. waist **6.** bodice **7.** bouquet (boquet), flowers
corsair... 5. rover **6.** pirate **7.** Saracen **8.** picaroon, rockfish **9.** buccaneer, privateer **10.** freebooter
Corsica...
capital.. **7.** Ajaccio
birthplace of.. **8.** Napoleon
feud (blood).. **8.** vendetta
seaport.. **6.** Bastia
cortege... 5. train **6.** parade **7.** funeral, retinue **10.** procession
Cortes palace site... 8. Coyoacan (Mexico)
cortex... 4. bark, peel, rind
corundum... 3. gem **5.** emery **7.** mineral **8.** abrasive
corundum colors...
blue.. **5.** white **8.** sapphire
brown.. **14.** adamantine spar
green.. **7.** emerald
purple.. **8.** amethyst
red.. **4.** ruby
topaz.. **6.** yellow
coruscate... 5. gleam, shine **7.** glitter, radiate, sparkle **11.** scintillate

cosmetic . . . **5.** cream, henna, paint, rouge **6.** enamel, lotion, make-up **7.** blusher, mascara **8.** lipstick, toiletry **11.** beautifying

cosmic . . . **4.** vast **5.** great **7.** orderly **8.** catholic, infinite **9.** grandiose, universal **10.** harmonious

Cosmic Order . . . **4.** Rita (Vedic law)

Cossack (pert to) . . .
chief . . **6.** ataman, hetman
district . . **6.** Voisko
native . . **5.** Tatar **7.** Russian
squadron . . **6.** sotnia
village . . **8.** stanitsa (stanitza)
whip (knotted) . . **5.** knout

cosset . . . **3.** pet **4.** lamb **6.** caress, coddle, cuddle, fondle, pamper

cost . . . **4.** loss, rate **5.** price **6.** amount, charge, figure, outlay, rental **7.** expense **9.** detriment, suffering **11.** deprivation, expenditure

costa . . . **3.** rib **4.** vein (Bot) **5.** ridge **6.** border, midrib

Costa Rica . . .
capital . . **7.** San José
crater (world's greatest) . . **4.** Poas
discovered . . **8.** Columbus (4th visit)
export . . **6.** coffee **7.** bananas
port . . **5.** Limon **10.** Puntarenas

costate . . . **6.** ribbed (Bot)

costermonger . . . **6.** coster, hawker **7.** peddler **9.** costerman **11.** apple seller

costly . . . **4.** dear, rich **8.** gorgeous, splendid **9.** expensive, sumptuous **10.** high-priced **11.** extravagant

costume . . . **3.** rig **4.** garb, suit **5.** dress, habit **6.** attire, tights **7.** apparel, raiment **8.** clothing

cot . . . **3.** bed, hut, pen, set **4.** boat (Ir), coop, cote **5.** cabin, cover, house **6.** cabana **7.** charpoy, cottage, shelter **8.** bedstead

cote . . . **3.** hut, pen **4.** coop **5.** house **7.** cottage, shelter **9.** sheepfold

Côte d'Azur . . . **7.** Riviera

coterie . . . **3.** set **4.** clan, club, ring **5.** cabal, group, junto **6.** circle, clique **9.** camarilla (secret)

cotillion . . . **4.** ball **5.** belle, dance **9.** debutante, petticoat, quadrille

cottage . . . **3.** cot, hut **4.** shed **5.** cabin, house, villa **6.** cabana **7.** shelter **8.** bungalow

cottager . . . **6.** cottar (cotter) **7.** cottier, laborer, peasant

cotton (pert to) . . .
cloth . . **4.** jean, lawn **5.** denim, khaki, scrim, surat, terry **6.** calico, dimity, madras, nettle **7.** batiste, percale
fiber . . **4.** lint **6.** staple **7.** viscose
gin inventor . . **7.** Whitney (Eli)
knot . . **3.** nep
layer . . **7.** batting
medical . . **5.** gauze **6.** sponge
raw . . **5.** bayal
roll . . **4.** slub
seed . . **4.** bole, boll
seed sugar . . **9.** raffinose
staple . . **6.** upland (short) **8.** Egyptian (long) **9.** Sea Island (long)

thread . . **5.** lisle

Cotton State . . . **7.** Alabama

couch . . . **3.** bed, cot **4.** lair, sofa **5.** divan **6.** canapé, canopy, litter, lounge, pallet, phrase **8.** loveseat **9.** embroider (with gold), stretcher

cougar . . . **3.** cat **4.** lion, puma **7.** panther **9.** catamount

cough . . . **4.** bark (sl), hack **6.** tussis

council . . . **4.** diet, rede **5.** cabal, synod **6.** senate **7.** cabinet **8.** assembly, conclave, tribunal **10.** conference, parliament **12.** consultation **15.** League of Nations

council table cover . . . **5.** tapis

counsel . . . **4.** rede **6.** advice, advise, confer, lawyer **8.** guidance **9.** recommend **10.** suggestion **11.** instruction **12.** deliberation

counselor, counsellor . . . **4.** sage **6.** lawyer, mentor, nestor **7.** adviser, advisor, counsel **8.** attorney **9.** barrister, solicitor

count . . . **3.** sum, tot **4.** tale, tell **5.** check, judge, relay, tally **6.** number, reckon, rely on **7.** compute, summary **8.** nobleman, quantify **9.** calculate, enumerate, reckoning, summation **12.** capitulation

Count (pert to) . . .
Mayence . . **3.** Gan **7.** Ganelon
Monte Cristo . . **6.** Dantes
Rousillon . . **7.** Bertram

countenance . . . **3.** aid **4.** abet, brow, face, mien **6.** aspect, permit, visage **7.** approve, endorse, support **8.** approval, sanction, tolerate **9.** composure, encourage **10.** appearance, permission

counter . . . **4.** chip **5.** table, token **7.** adverse **8.** computer, contrary, opposite **9.** retaliate **10.** calculator

counteract . . . **6.** offset, oppose, thwart **7.** nullify **8.** antidote **10.** neutralize **11.** countermand

counter current . . . **4.** eddy **5.** swirl **6.** vortex **9.** whirlpool **12.** counterforce

counterfeit . . . **4.** base, fake, mock, sham **5.** bogus, false, feign, forge, phony, queer **6.** assume, forged, unreal **7.** falsify, forgery, imitate **8.** simulant, spurious **10.** artificial, fictitious **11.** unauthentic

counterirritant . . . **4.** moxa **5.** seton **6.** arnica, iodine, pepper **7.** mustard

countermand . . . **5.** annul **6.** cancel, forbid, recall, revoke **7.** abolish, reverse **8.** prohibit **9.** frustrate **10.** counteract **12.** counterorder

counterpane . . . **5.** quilt **8.** bedcover, coverlet **9.** comforter **10.** counterpin **11.** comfortable

counterpart . . . **4.** copy, like, twin **5.** image **6.** double, eponym (name) **8.** parallel **9.** duplicate **10.** complement, equivalent

counterpoise . . . **6.** offset **8.** equalize **10.** compensate, counteract **12.** counterforce **14.** counterbalance

countersign . . . **4.** sign **6.** signal **7.** tessera **8.** password **9.** signature, watchword

10. mot de passé, open sesame
12. counterstamp
countersink ... 4. ream 5. bevel
6. deepen 7. chamfer
countertenor ... 4. alto (male) 8. falsetto
counterthrust (fencing) ... 7. riposte
(ripost) 12. return thrust
countless ... 8. infinite 10. numberless,
unnumbered 11. innumerable
12. incalculable
countrified ... 5. rural 7. boorish, hickish,
uncouth 8. inurbane 10. unpolished
country ... 4. land, pais (law), vale
5. rural, state, weald 6. nation,
region 9. territory 10. fatherland
12. commonwealth
country (pert to) ...
alien.. 7. enclave, exclave
ancient.. 4. Aram, Elis, Gaul
bumpkin.. 4. clod, jake, rube 5. churl,
yokel 9. greenhorn
gallant.. 5. swain
mythical.. 2. Oz
native (earliest).. 9. aborigine
Roman.. 8. campagna
term.. 5. rural, urban 6. rustic 8. agrestic,
pastoral, praedial (predial)
countryman ... 4. rube 5. yokel 6. rustic
7. hayseed, patriot, peasant
10. compatriot, home towner
county ... 4. seat 5. shire 6. domain,
parish 8. district
coup ... 3. buy 4. blow, move (games)
5. scoop, upset 6. barter, strike,
stroke (master) 8. overturn, strategy
9. overthrow, trump card
coup de grâce ... 9. deathblow
coup de main ... 6. attack (sudden)
8. strategy 9. stratagem
coup d'état ... 6. stroke (political)
8. strategy 9. overthrow
couple ... 3. duo, tie, two 4. bond, dyad,
join, link, mate, pair, span, team, twin,
yoke 5. brace, marry, twain, unite
6. Gemini 8. bracket
coupled ... 5. gemel, mated 6. braced,
joined, linked, paired, teamed, united
7. leagued, married
couplet ... 3. two 4. pair 5. brace, verse
7. distich, doublet
coupon ... 5. scrip, stock, token 6. ticket
11. certificate (Finan)
courage ... 4. grit, sand, will 5. heart,
metal, moxie, nerve, pluck, spine,
valor 7. bravery, heroism, prowess
8. audacity, backbone, boldness,
firmness 9. fortitude, gallantry,
hardihood 11. intrepidity
12. fearlessness 13. dauntlessness
courageous ... 4. bold, game 5. brave,
hardy, manly, stout 6. daring, heroic,
spunky 7. gallant, spartan, valiant
8. fearless, intrepid, knightly, resolute,
stalwart, valorous 11. adventurous
12. enterprising, stouthearted
courant ... 4. romp 5. caper 6. letter
7. gazette, running (Her) 9. messenger,
newspaper
courier ... 5. guide 8. dragoman,
horseman 9. attendant, messenger
course ... 3. run 4. flow, line, mode, path,

road, rote, tack 5. route, study, trend
6. career, manner, method, policy,
series, stream 8. progress 9. direction,
procedure 10. succession
course (pert to) ...
college.. 7. seminar
direct.. 7. beeline
golf.. 5. links
regular.. 4. rote 6. regime 7. routine
roundabout.. 6. detour 11. indirection
course of ...
action.. 5. habit 7. routine 9. procedure
eating.. 4. diet
instruction.. 6. lesson
procedure.. 4. rule
thought.. 5. tenor
courser ... 5. horse, steed 6. hunter,
plover 7. charger 8. war horse
court ... 3. see (papal), woo 4. area, eyre,
fawn (upon), rota 5. atria, curia, dairi,
gemot, patio, spark 6. palace, parvis,
street 7. council, tribune 8. tribunal
10. attendance, curry favor, quadrangle
court (Eng) ... 3. soc 4. eyre, leet
8. woodmate 10. court-baron
court (pert to) ...
assistant.. 5. staff 6. elisor
crier, cry.. 4. hear, oyez (oyes) 6. beadle
criminal.. 6. assize
exemption, excuse.. 6. essoin
game.. 6. tennis 9. badminton
hearing.. 4. oyer
minutes.. 4. acta
order.. 4. writ 5. arret 6. capias
7. summons 8. subpoena
public.. 5. forum 8. forensic
sitting.. 7. session
courteous ... 5. civil 6. gentle, polite,
urbane 7. affable, gallant 8. debonair,
gracious 9. attentive 10. respectful
courtly ... 4. hend (hende) 5. aulic, civil
7. elegant, gallant, stately 9. dignified
10. obsequious 11. ceremonious
courtship ... 4. suit 6. plight, wooing
7. romance 8. courting
covenant ... 4. bond, pact 6. engage
7. bargain, compact, entente, promise
8. contract 9. agreement, stipulate,
testament 11. undertaking
Covenant of God to Noah ... 7. rainbow
Coventry equestrienne ... 6. Godiva
cover ... 3. cap, lap, lid 4. coat, cozy,
hide, mask, pale, pave, roof, span, veil
5. blind, crust, drape, tapis 6. canopy,
mantle, purdah, screen, shield, thatch
7. elytron, overlay, shelter 8. chrismal,
coverlet 9. tarpaulin 10. overspread
cover (pert to) ...
alloy.. 5. terne
cork.. 9. corticate
crumbs.. 5. bread
dots.. 7. stipple
figures (Her).. 4. seme
straw.. 6. thatch
turf.. 3. sod
up.. 4. bury 5. inter 7. conceal
8. submerge 10. camouflage
with wax.. 4. cere
covering ... 3. mat, rug 4. caul, film,
hull, tile 5. apron, armor, shell, testa
6. awning, carpet, cestus, lorica,

pelage, screen, shroud 7. epeiric, shelter, tegumen, wrapper 8. lineolum, pericarp 9. caparison 10. integument, protection 11. smoke screen
covering (head) . . . 3. cap, hat, wig 4. hood 5. beret, scarf, snood 6. bonnet, peruke, toupee 7. chapeau 10. fascinator
coverlet . . . 5. quilt 6. afghan, spread 7. blanket, lap robe 11. counterpane
covert . . . 3. den, lie 4. abri, lair 6. hidden, refuge, secret 7. covered, private, thicket 9. concealed, disguised, insidious, sheltered
covet . . . 4. envy 5. crave, yisse (obs) 6. aspire, desire, grudge, hanker 7. long for 8. begrudge
covetousness . . . 5. greed 7. avarice
covey . . . 4. bevy, pack 5. brood, flock, hatch 6. flight 7. company 9. multitude
cow . . . 3. awe 5. abash, daunt 7. overawe, terrify 8. browbeat, frighten 10. intimidate
cow (animal) . . . 3. Bos 4. calf, kine, moil 5. Angus, bossy, brock (obs), Kerry, vache 6. bovine, heifer 7. pollard 8. Ayrshire, maverick, moulleen
cow (pert to) . . .
barn . . 4. byre, shed 5. reeve, stall 6. stable 7. vaccary, vachery
food (chewed) . . 3. cud 5. rumen
hornless . . 6. mulley 7. pollard 8. moulleen
sea . . 6. dugong, walrus 7. manatee, Sirenia 12. hippopotamus
tether . . 4. rope 6. baikie
unbranded . . 8. maverick
young . . 4. calf 6. heifer
coward, cowardly . . . 3. shy 5. sneak 6. afraid, craven, scared, yellow 7. caitiff, chicken, dastard, milksop 8. poltroon, recreant, weakling 9. dastardly, fraidy-cat, jellyfish 12. uncourageous 13. pusillanimous
cowboy . . . 5. roper, waddy 6. herder 7. llamero, puncher, vaquero 8. jackaroo, neatherd 12. broncobuster (sl)
cowboy garb . . . 5. chaps 7. Stetson 8. jodhpurs
cower . . . 4. fawn 5. crawl, quail, stoop 6. cringe, crouch, grovel
cowfish . . . 3. ray 4. toto 7. dolphin, grampus, manatee 8. porpoise
cowled . . . 9. cucullate
coxcomb . . . 3. fop 4. dude, fool 5. cleat (Naut), dandy 8. popinjay
coy . . . 3. shy 4. arch 5. timid 6. demure, modest 7. bashful 10. coquettish 13. self-conscious
coyote . . . 4. wolf (prairie)
Coyote State . . . 11. South Dakota
coypu . . . 6. nutria, rodent
cozen . . . 5. cheat, trick 7. beguile, deceive, defraud
cozy . . . 4. easy, snug 6. chatty 8. cheerful, familiar, homelike, sociable 9. contented, talkative 11. comfortable
crab . . . 3. Uca 4. king, Maia (genus) 5. ayuyu (Guam) 6. nebula, partan, spider 7. fiddler, limulus, mollusk,

Ocypode 8. Lithodes 9. horseshoe 10. crustacean
crabbed . . . 5. cross 6. bitter, crusty, morose, trying 7. bilious, peevish 8. abstruse, liverish 9. difficult, fractious, irascible, irregular 10. perplexing
crab claw . . . 5. chela 6. metope, nipper
crab walk . . . 5. sidle
crachoir . . . 8. cuspidor, spittoon
crack . . . 4. blow, chap, clap, flaw, kibe, leak, quip, rift, rime, snap 5. brack, break, chink, craze, spang, split 6. breach, cleave, cranny 7. crackle, crevice, fissure, rupture 8. fracture
Cracker State . . . 7. Georgia
crackle . . . 4. snap 5. craze (art), crink 9. crepitate
crackman . . . 4. yegg 7. burglar
cradle . . . 4. slee (ship's) 7. infancy, nursery 8. bassinet, cunabula 10. beginnings, incunabula
cradle book . . . 11. incunabulum
Cradle of Liberty . . . 11. Faneuil Hall (Boston)
cradle song . . . 7. lullaby 8. berceuse 13. Schlummerleid
craft . . . 3. art 4. boat 5. skill, trade 6. device, tender 7. cunning, finesse, know-how, prowess 8. aptitude, vocation 9. dexterity 10. employment, handicraft, occupation, watercraft 12. skillfulness
craftsman . . . 6. artist, writer 7. artisan, workman 9. artificer
crafty . . . 3. sly 4. foxy, slim, wily, wise 6. artful, astute, shifty, shrewd, subtle, tricky 7. cunning 8. skillful (skilful) 9. deceitful, ingenious, underhand 10. fraudulent 13. Machiavellian 15. Mephistophelean
crag . . . 3. tor 4. spur 5. arête, cliff 7. nunatak 9. precipice
craggy . . . 5. rough 6. cliffy, clifty, jagged, knotty, rugged
cram . . . 4. fill 5. choke, crowd, drive, force, gorge, press, study, stuff 9. overstuff 10. gluttonize
cramp . . . 4. pain 5. stunt 6. hamper 7. confine, seizure 8. compress, restrict 9. hindrance, paralysis (muscle) 11. restriction
cranberry . . . 3. red 9. sourberry
cranberry center of trade . . . 10. Barnstable (Mass)
crane . . . 3. gib, jib 5. davit, jenny, titan 7. derrick, machine
crane . . . 4. Grus 5. heron, sarus 7. Gruidae 9. cormorant 10. Gruiformes 13. constellation
cranial nerve . . . 5. radix, vagus
cranium . . . 5. skull 8. cerebrum
crank . . . 3. wit 4. bear, crab 5. crook, winch 6. griper, grouch, handle 7. fanatic, growler, hothead 8. frondeur, grumbler, sorehead 9. eccentric 10. bellyacher, crosspatch, monomaniac
cranny . . . 4. hole, nook 5. chink, cleft, crack 6. corner, furrow 7. crevice, fissure 8. crevasse
crash . . . 4. bank, fail 5. smash 7. debacle, failure, intrude, shatter 8. accident

9. collision 10. bankruptcy
crate . . . 3. box 4. case 6. basket, cradle, encase, hamper 8. airplane 9. container 10. automobile
crater . . . 3. pit 6. cavity 7. caldera 13. constellation (The Cup)
cravat . . . 3. tie 4. teck 5. ascot, stock 7. bandage, bolo tie, necktie 9. neckcloth 10. four-in-hand
crave . . . 3. ask, beg 4. long, seek 5. covet, yearn 6. desire, hanker 7. beseech, entreat, implore, request, solicit 10. supplicate
craven . . . 6. afraid, coward 7. caitiff, dastard 8. cowardly, poltroon, recreant 12. fainthearted 13. pusillanimous
craving . . . 4. pica 6. desire, thirst 7. longing 8. appetite, yearning
craw . . . 3. maw 4. crop 6. gebbie 7. gizzard, stomach 9. ingluvies
crawfish . . . 5. yabby (yabbie) 7. back out, crawdad, lobster, retreat 8. crayfish
crawl . . . 4. fawn, inch, shug 5. creep 6. cringe, grovel, recant
crayon . . . 5. chalk 6. pastel, pencil 8. charcoal
craze . . . 3. fad 4. flaw, maze 5. crack (ceramics), crush, furor, mania, vogue 6. defect, whimsy 7. crackle, fashion 9. infirmity 11. infatuation
craze (for) . . . see also *madness, mania*
foreign customs . . 9. xenomania
freedom . . 14. eleutheromania
love (erotic) . . 10. erotomania
music . . 9. melomania
setting fires . . 9. pyromania
shopping . . 9. oniomania
single subject . . 9. monomania
stamps (postage) . . 11. timbromania
stealing . . 11. kleptomania
wandering . . 10. dromomania
wealth . . 10. plutomania
crazed . . . 4. amok 6. insane, marked (with crazes) 7. severed 8. deranged 10. distraught
crazy . . . 3. mad 4. amok, daft, loco 5. batty, loony, nutty, silly 6. dottle, insane 7. damaged, foolish, unsound 9. deficient
cream . . . 4. best, ream 5. elite 6. lotion 8. sillabub (with wine)
cream of tartar . . . 5. argol
crease . . . 4. fold, ruck 5. crimp, pleat 7. wrinkle 9. plication
create . . . 4. make 5. build, cause, clone, hatch 6. invent 7. fashion, produce 8. generate 9. originate
creation . . . 3. art 5. virtu, world 6. cosmos, making 7. classic, fantasy, forming, product 8. artifact, universe 9. objet d'art 10. providence 11. composition, fabrication, manufacture, masterpiece
creator . . . 5. maker 6. author 8. designer, inventor, producer 10. originator
Creator . . . 3. God 5. Maker 7. Jehovah 8. Almighty, Demiurge 11. King of Kings
creature (pert to) . . .
civetlike . . 3. cat
duplicate . . 5. clone

elflike . . 4. peri 6. hobbit
evil . . 7. helicat 8. hellicat
fire . . 10. salamander
folklore . . 3. elf 4. Yeti 5. dwarf, fairy, pixie 9. sasquatch
ghost . . 11. poltergeist
minute . . 10. animalcule
outer space . . 5. alien
sentient . . 6. animal
timid . . 4. deer 5. sheep
underground . . 5. gnome
water . . 5. sylph 6. undine
winged (Myth) . . 6. wivern 10. cockatrice
crèche figure . . . 4. Magi 6. Infant 8. shepherd
credence . . . 5. trust 6. belief, credit 8. affiance, reliance 10. acceptance, confidence, dependence 15. trustworthiness
credential . . . 7. voucher 11. certificate, testimonial 14. recommendation
credible . . . 6. likely 7. tenable 8. probable 9. plausible 10. believable 11. well-founded
credit . . . 5. faith, honor, trust 6. belief, esteem, impute 7. account, believe 8. accredit, credence 10. estimation, regulation 15. trustworthiness
creditor . . . 5. agent (collection) 6. debtee, dunner, usurer 7. Shylock (greedy)
creed . . . 5. credo, dogma, tenet 6. belief, Nicene 8. Apostles' 9. Catechism 10. Athanasian, confession
creek . . . 3. rio 4. burn, slue, wick 6. arroyo, estero, slough, spruit, stream
creel . . . 4. rack, trap 6. basket (fish)
creep . . . 5. crawl, prowl, skulk, slink, sneak, steal (away) 6. grovel 8. scramble 9. pussyfoot
creeping . . . 4. slow 7. reptant 8. crawling 10. slithering 11. reptatorial
Cremona, famed name . . . 5. Amati 8. Guarneri 10. Stradivari
crena . . . 4. gash, kerf, nick 5. cleft, notch 7. scallop 10. depression 11. indentation
creole . . . 6. French 7. mestizo 9. half-breed, janissary
Creole State . . . 9. Louisiana
crepitate . . . 4. snap 7. crackly
crescent . . . 4. cusp, horn, lune 5. curve 8. meniscus
crescent-shaped . . . 4. horn, lune 6. bicorn, lunate 7. lunular 8. lunulate 9. horseshoe, meniscate, semilunar
crest . . . 3. top 4. comb, peak, tuft 5. arête, crown, ridge 6. copple, crista, height, summit 7. panache, topknot, wave top 8. feathers, insignia, pinnacle 9. cockscomb 11. mountaintop
crested . . . 6. capped, topped, tufted 7. coppled, cristed, crowned, pileate
creta . . . 5. chalk
Crete . . .
capital . . 5. Canea
city . . 6. Candia, Khanis
civilization (anc) . . 6. Aegean, Minoan
king (anc) . . 5. Minos (Gr)
monster . . 8. Minotaur (man, bull)
mountain . . 3. Ida 9. Theodoros
priests . . 7. Curetes
cretin . . . 5. idiot 8. imbecile

crevice ... **3.** gap **4.** rift **5.** chink,
cleft **6.** cranny **7.** fissure, opening
8. peephole **10.** interstice
crew ... **3.** men **4.** band, body, gang, pack
5. force, staff **7.** company **9.** employees,
personnel
crib ... **3.** bed, bin, den (gambling)
5. cheat, stall, steal **6.** Cratch (stars),
manger, pilfer **7.** brothel **8.** Praesepe
cricket ... **4.** game, grig **6.** acheta,
cicada, locust **7.** katydid **9.** footstool
10. Orthoptera **11.** grasshopper
cricket (pert to) ...
  game term .. **3.** bye, run **6.** yorker
  noise .. **5.** chirp **7.** stridor
  symbol (Myth) .. **4.** tice **5.** ashes
cried ... **4.** wept **6.** bawled, called, wailed,
yelled **7.** shouted, uttered **8.** lamented,
screamed, shrieked **9.** exclaimed
10. proclaimed
crime ... **3.** sin **4.** evil **5.** guilt, wrong
6. delict, felony, mayhem **7.** offense
8. delictum, iniquity **9.** violation
10. illegality, wickedness, wrongdoing
11. malfeasance
crime (pert to) ...
  benefice (Eccl) .. **6.** simony
  goddess (Myth) .. **3.** Ate
  of 1873 .. **12.** Silver Dollar
  scene .. **5.** venue
Crimea ...
  city .. **5.** Kerch, Yalta **6.** Odessa
  10. Sevastopol
  isthmus site .. **8.** Black Sea
  Russian .. **4.** Krim
  sea (Russ) .. **4.** Azof
criminal ... **4.** thug, yegg **5.** crook,
felon, thief **6.** nocent **7.** convict,
yeggman **8.** swindler **9.** desperado,
dishonest, felonious **10.** malefactor,
recidivist **11.** blameworthy, disgraceful
13. reprehensible
criminal refuge ... **7.** Alsatia
11. Whitefriars (London)
criminology ... **8.** penology
crimp ... **4.** curl, fold **5.** frizz, notch, plait
6. ruffle, thwart **7.** crinkle, wrinkle
8. Shanghai
cringe ... **4.** fawn **5.** cower, quail, sneak,
wince **6.** flinch, grovel, shrink, submit
7. truckle
crinkle ... **4.** curl, kink, turn, wind **5.** twist
6. rustle **7.** wrinkle
crinose ... **5.** hairy **7.** hirsute
11. barbigerous
cripple ... **4.** halt, hock, lame, maim
6. injure, weaken **7.** amputee, disable
8. handicap **9.** hamstring
12. incapacitate
crisis ... **5.** cycle, peril **8.** exigency,
juncture **9.** criterion, emergency
11. climacteric
crisp ... **4.** cold **5.** curly, flaky, sharp,
short, spalt **7.** brittle, concise, crackle,
crinkle, friable **8.** clear-cut **9.** frangible
criterion ... **4.** norm, rule, test, type
5. canon, model **7.** measure **8.** standard
9. yardstick
critic ... **5.** judge, Momus (Myth)
6. censor, slater, Zoilus **8.** collator,
reviewer **9.** literator **11.** connoisseur,

criticaster, faultfinder
critical ... **4.** edgy **7.** carping, crucial,
cynical, Zoilean **8.** captious, caviling,
exacting **10.** censorious, particular
12. faultfinding **13.** hairsplitting
14. discriminating
Critical system of philosophy ...
10. Kantianism
criticism ... **3.** rap **5.** cavil, roast **6.** report,
review **7.** censure, Zoilism **8.** critique,
judgment **9.** aspersion **10.** commentary
criticize, criticise ... **3.** pan **4.** carp, flay
5. cavil, judge, knock, slate **6.** review
7. censure, comment **9.** castigate
10. animadvert
Croatian capital ... **6.** Zagreb
crock ... **3.** ewe (old), jug, pot, urn
4. smut, soil, soot **5.** horse (old)
7. ceramic **8.** potsherd **11.** earthenware
crocodile ... **3.** goa **5.** nakoo **6.** gavial,
mugger **7.** reptile, sophism **9.** Niloticus
10. Crocodilia, Crocodilus
crocus ... **4.** bulb, herb, iris **6.** flower,
yellow **7.** saffron
croft ... **5.** crypt, field, vault **6.** carafe,
cavern **7.** hillock
cromlech ... **6.** dolmen **8.** monument
crone ... **3.** ewe (old), hag **5.** witch
6. beldam (beldame)
Cronus (pert to) ...
  god of .. **8.** Harvests
  father .. **6.** Uranus
  son .. **4.** Zeus
  wife .. **4.** Rhea
crony ... **3.** pal **4.** chum **5.** buddy **6.** friend
9. companion **10.** playfellow
crook ... **4.** bend, warp **5.** angle, curve,
staff, thief **6.** akimbo **7.** crosier
8. criminal, insignia **10.** camshachle
crooked ... **3.** wry, zag **4.** agee, awry,
bent **5.** agley, askew, false **6.** aslant,
curved, hooked, zigzag **7.** angular,
askance, asquint, oblique **8.** deformed
9. dishonest, distorted **10.** circuitous,
fraudulent **12.** dishonorable
crooked legs ... **8.** rhebosis (rhaebosis)
10. tortuosity
croon ... **3.** hum **4.** boom, sing, wail
5. whine **6.** bellow, lament, murmur
8. complain
crop ... **3.** lop, maw **4.** clip, craw,
dick, reap, whip **5.** belly, shear,
yield **6.** gebbie, growth, sheave
7. harvest, produce, soilage, stomach
11. cultivation
cross ... **2.** go **3.** tau **4.** crux, ford,
rood **5.** bless, corse, croix (Fr),
irate, staff **6.** oppose, thwart, touchy
7. athwart, fretful, oblique, peevish,
pettish **8.** crucifix, insignia, monument,
obstruct, petulant, snappish, swastika,
traverse **9.** hybridize, intersect, irritable
10. disappoint, transverse **11.** crucifixion
cross (pert to) ...
  archaeology .. **4.** ankh
  astronomy .. **13.** Southern Cross
  barred .. **11.** trabeculate
  beam .. **5.** spale, trave **6.** girder
  bow .. **8.** arbalest
  breed .. **5.** Husky (dog) **6.** hybrid
  British .. **6.** Celtic

Egypt . . **10.** life symbol
eye . . **9.** esotropia **10.** strabismus
heraldry . . **6.** pattée **7.** erminee, patonce
Latin . . **12.** crux commissa
palm . . **5.** bribe (gypsy)
St Anthony's . . **3.** tau
stroke . . **5.** serif
tau-shaped . . **10.** crux ansata
crossing . . . **6.** voyage **7.** chiasma,
fording, passage **8.** cheating, opposing
9. hybridism **10.** traversing
13. crossbreeding
crossing (famed) . . .
Alps . . **8.** Hannibal, Napoleon
Hellespont . . **6.** Xerxes
Pyrenees . . **8.** Hannibal
Rubicon . . **6.** Caesar
crouch . . . **4.** bend, fawn **5.** cower, squat,
stoop **6.** cringe, grovel, hunker
crow . . . **3.** daw **4.** brag, rook **5.** aylet,
boast, crake, raven, vaunt **6.** chough,
Corvus, Indian (Sioux) **7.** corvine,
jackdaw **8.** laughter **13.** constellation
crowbar . . . **5.** jimmy, lever **7.** gablock
crowberry . . . **5.** shrub **8.** bilberry
9. cranberry
crowd . . . **3.** jam, mob **4.** bike (Scot), cram,
host, pack, push, ruck, urge **5.** crush,
drive, drove, horde, press, serry,
swarm, three, wedge **6.** galaxy, hasten,
legion, masses, throng **7.** squeeze
8. compress **9.** multitude
10. assemblage
crowded . . . **6.** packed **7.** compact,
crammed, serried, teeming
8. numerous, populous **9.** congested,
jampacked
crown . . . **3.** cap, top **4.** atef, coin, pate,
peak, poll, tiar **5.** crest, miter (mitre),
tiara **6.** anadem, circle, corona, diadem,
fillet, reward, summit, trophy, wreath
7. chaplet, coronet, garland, glorify,
install **8.** coronate, enthrone, ornament,
pinnacle, surmount
crowning glory . . . **8.** last word
crucial . . . **5.** final **6.** severe, trying,
urgent **7.** crossed **8.** critical, decisive
9. cruciform **13.** demonstrative
crucible . . . **3.** pot **4.** etna, test **6.** retort,
vessel **10.** conversion
crucifix . . . **3.** pax **4.** rood **5.** cross
6. emblem
crucifixion . . . **5.** death (on a cross)
7. torture **9.** execution, suffering
11. persecution
crude . . . **3.** raw **4.** rude **5.** crass, green,
rough **6.** callow, coarse, common,
garish, savage, vulgar **8.** unseemly
9. inelegant, rough-hewn, tasteless,
uncourtly, unrefined **10.** outlandish,
unpolished **13.** inexperienced
crudity . . . **7.** rawness **9.** crassness,
harshness, roughness, vulgarity
10. immaturity
cruel . . . **4.** fell, hard **5.** harsh **6.** brutal,
savage, severe, unkind **7.** inhuman,
painful, unhuman **8.** dreadful, fiendish,
pitiless, ruthless, sadistic, tyrannic
9. ferocious, heartless, merciless,
murderous, truculent **11.** remorseless
cruelty . . . **9.** brutality **10.** inclemency,

inhumanity **12.** ruthlessness
13. heartlessness **15.** remorselessness
cruelty, lover of . . . **6.** sadist **9.** masochist
cruet . . . **3.** ama **4.** vial **6.** bottle, caster
(castor), vessel **7.** ampulla, urceole
crulier . . . **7.** olycook (olykoek)
8. doughnut **9.** friedcake
crumb . . . **3.** bit **5.** break, piece **6.** little
8. fragment
crumble . . . **5.** decay **6.** molder, powder
7. friable **9.** pulverize **12.** disintegrate
crumple . . . **4.** ruck **6.** crease, raffle,
rumple **7.** wrinkle **9.** corrugate
cruor . . . **4.** gore **5.** blood, ichor
crusade . . . **5.** cause, drive, issue,
jihad (jehad) **7.** crusado **8.** campaign
10. expedition
Crusades . . . **8.** Holy Land **9.** Children's
(1212)
crush . . . **3.** jam **4.** bray, mash, sink
5. crash, crowd, grind, press, smash
6. bruise, crunch **7.** conquer, mortify,
oppress, shatter, squeeze **8.** compress,
suppress **9.** humiliate, pulverize
11. infatuation
crushed sugar cane . . . **7.** bagasse
Crusoe's creator . . . **5.** Defoe
crust . . . **4.** rind **5.** shell **8.** dumpling,
exterior **9.** impudence **11.** lithosphere
14. aggressiveness
crustacean . . . **4.** crab **5.** prawn **6.** huitre,
isopod, limpet, mussel, oyster, shrimp
7. limulus, lobster, scallop **8.** barnacle,
crawfish, starfish **9.** shellfish, trunkfish
10. coquillage, periwinkle
crustacean (pert to) . . .
extinct . . **5.** Eryon
footless . . **4.** apod, apus
fossil . . **9.** trilobite
genus . . **5.** Hippa **6.** Triops **7.** Caridea
(Carida) **8.** Copepoda, Decapoda
10. Notostraca
larva . . **5.** alima
limb . . **6.** endite, podite
crutch . . . **5.** brace, staff, stave **6.** crotch
7. support
cry . . . **3.** baa, caw, cri, hue, mew, olé,
sob **4.** alas, barr, call, evoe, home,
hoot, mewl, pish, pule, wail, weep,
yell, yelp **5.** alack, avast, bleat, crook,
miaou, yoick **6.** bellow, boohoo, clamor,
outcry, scream, shriek, slogan, snivel,
squawk **7.** tantivy (hunting), trumpet,
weeping **8.** entreaty, jeremiad, lackaday,
proclaim **10.** shibboleth **11.** lamentation
cry (out) . . . **5.** crake, decry, shout
6. accuse, clamor, object, scream,
suffer **7.** censure, exclaim **8.** complain,
denounce **10.** vociferate
crying . . . **6.** puling, urgent **7.** clamant,
heinous, howling, sobbing, weeping
9. insistent, notorious
crying bird . . . **6.** Aramus **7.** courlan,
limpkin **8.** raillike
crypt . . . **4.** tomb **5.** vault **6.** cavity, recess
7. chamber
cryptic . . . **4.** Rite (Freemasonry)
6. hidden, occult, secret **8.** puzzling
9. concealed, enigmatic **10.** mysterious
11. problematic **12.** hieroglyphic
cryptogram . . . **4.** code **5.** agama

7. writing (secret) 8. symbolic
crystal ... 4. dial 5. clear, glass, lucid
6. argent (Her), quartz 7. diamond
8. pellucid 9. glassware, snowflake
11. crystalline, transparent
crystal (pert to) ...
diamond .. 7. glassie
gazer .. 4. seer 7. diviner 8. presager
10. soothsayer 13. fortuneteller
gazing .. 4. scry
twin .. 5. macle
crystalline ... 4. pure 8. pellucid
11. transparent 12. crystal-clear
crystalline (pert to) ...
colorless .. 7. orcinol
compound .. 5. oscin 6. anisil, dulcin
mineral .. 4. spar 7. apatite 8. elaterin,
feldspar
rock .. 7. diorite, greisen
salt .. 5. borax 8. analgene (analgen)
cub ... 3. bin, boy, fox, pen, pup 4. bear,
coop, crib, lion, shed 5. shark, stall,
tiger, whale, whelp 8. boy scout,
cupboard 9. youngling
Cuba ...
capital .. 6. Havana
castle .. 5. Morro
city .. 8. Santiago 10. Bahia Honda,
Guantánamo
discoverer .. 8. Columbus (1492)
island .. 11. Isle of Pines (Isla de Pinos)
mountain .. 8. Camaguey 9. Las Villas
12. Pico Turquino
nickname .. 18. Pearl of the Antilles
province .. 7. Oriente
Cuban (pert to) ...
asphalt .. 9. chapapote
bird .. 6. trogan 8. tocororo
dance .. 5. rumba
fish .. 4. bobo
rodent .. 5. hutia (jutia) 6. pilori
rum .. 7. Bacardi
cube ... 3. die 4. dice 5. solid 6. triple
7. tessera (marble) 10. third power
cubic (pert to) ...
body .. 3. die 4. dice
decimeter .. 5. litre
math .. 9. isometric
measure .. 4. cord
meter .. 5. stere
shape .. 6. cuboid 8. cubiform
cubicle ... 4. cell, room, tomb
7. bedroom, chamber, roomlet
9. cubiculum
cuckoo ... 5. mimic 8. imitator, songbird
cuckoo (pert to) ...
ally .. 3. ani
American .. 8. Coccyzus
bees .. 9. Nomadidae
bird (Orient) .. 4. coel (koel)
cap .. 9. monkshood
family .. 9. Cuculidae
fool .. 7. wryneck
pint .. 4. arum 10. cuckoo spit
cucullate (Bot) ... 6. cowled, hooded
cucumber ... 4. cuke, pepo 6. pedata
(sea), pepino
cucurbit ... 5. flask, gourd 7. matrass
cud ... 4. bite, quid 5. rumen 8. merycism
cuddle ... 3. hug, pet 6. fondle, nestle
7. snuggle

cudgel ... 3. bat, hit 4. beat, club, drub
5. baste, staff, stave, stick 6. alpeen
7. belabor 9. fustigate, shillalah
(shillelagh)
cue ... 3. nod, rod, tip 4. ball, clue,
hint, role, tail 5. braid, queue, twist
6. prompt 8. billiard (term), function
9. catchword 10. intimation
cuerpo ... 4. body, hulk 5. naked, torso
10. dishabille (in)
cuff ... 3. hit 4. band, blow, slap 5. clout
6. strike 8. chastise, gauntlet, handcuff
12. chastisement
cuirass ... 4. mail 5. armor 6. lorica
11. breastplate
cul-de-sac ... 5. alley (blind) 7. impasse
14. pouch of Douglas
cull ... 4. pick 6. assort, choose, gather,
select 8. separate
culmination ... 3. end 4. acme, apex,
auge, noon 6. ascent, climax, result,
vertex, zenith 10. perfection
12. consummation
culpability ... 5. blame, fault, guilt
11. criminality 15. blameworthiness
culpable ... 6. faulty, guilty 7. immoral
8. criminal 9. accusable, imputable
10. censurable, indictable
11. blameworthy 12. reproachable
13. reprehensible
cult ... 4. sect 9. following
cultivate ... 3. ear (dial), hoe 4. farm,
grow, plow, teel, till 5. court, train
6. excite, foster, harrow, plough, refine
7. educate, improve 8. approach, civilize
cultivated ... 4. grew, hoed 6. seeded,
tilled, urbane 7. genteel, refined
8. cultured, polished, well-bred
cultivation ... 5. tilth 7. culture, farming,
tillage 9. husbandry 10. refinement
12. civilization
culver ... 4. dove 6. pigeon 10. wood
pigeon
cumbersome ... 5. bulky 6. clumsy
8. cumbrous, unwieldy 10. burdensome
cummer ... 4. lass 5. witch 6. friend (girl)
7. midwife 9. companion, godmother
cummerbund ... 4. band, belt, sash
6. cestus, girdle
cumshaw ... 3. tip 5. bonus 6. thanks
7. present 8. gratuity
cunning ... 3. sly 4. cute, foxy, wile,
wily 5. sharp, skill 6. artful, clever,
crafty, dainty, shrewd, subtle, tricky
7. politic, shyness 8. dextrous,
foxiness, skillful, stealthy, trickery
9. designing, dexterity, ingenious,
ingenuity, insidious 13. Machiavellian
cunningly formed ... 6. daedal (dedal)
cup ... 3. ama, can, dop, mug, tyg
4. tass, teet, Toby 5. calyx, chark,
cruse, cupel, cylix, grail, jorum, ladle,
stein 6. beaker, goblet, noggin, trophy
7. chalice, tumbler
cupbearer ... 4. Hebe, saki 8. Ganymede
cupboard ... 3. kas 5. ambry (anc)
6. buffet, closet, larder, pantry
7. armoire, dresser 8. aparador
9. sideboard
Cupid ... 3. boy, Dan 4. amor, Eros, Kama,
love 5. Freya 7. Amorino, cupidon

Cupid (pert to) . . .
  mother . . **5.** Venus
  sweetheart . . **6.** Psyche
  title . . **3.** Dan
cupidity . . . **4.** lust **5.** greed **6.** desire
  7. avarice, avidity, longing **8.** appetite,
  avidness, rapacity
cuplike (pert to) . . .
  calyx . . **9.** calicular
  stone . . **5.** geode
  vessel . . **4.** zarf
cupola . . . **4.** dome, kiln **5.** tower **6.** concha
  (Arch) **7.** ceiling, furnace (foundry)
cur . . . **3.** dog **4.** mutt **7.** gurnard (fish),
  mongrel **9.** goldeneye
curare, curari . . . **5.** urali **7.** extract
  9. Strychnos **11.** arrow poison
curate . . . **4.** abbé **6.** cleric, parson, pastor,
  priest **7.** dominie **9.** clergyman
curator . . . **6.** keeper **7.** manager, steward
  8. guardian **9.** custodian, librarian,
  treasurer
curb . . . **3.** bit **4.** rein **5.** check, limit
  6. arrest, border, bridle, market (Finan)
  7. control, inhibit, repress **8.** restrict
  9. hindrance, restraint
curd . . . **4.** crud **6.** casein
curds and whey . . . **7.** clabber
cure . . . **4.** balm, heal, salt **5.** smoke
  6. elixir, remedy, rizzor **7.** nostrum,
  panacea, restore, therapy **8.** preserve
  10. corrective
curio . . . **8.** artifact **9.** bric-a-brac, curiosity
curiosity . . . **5.** curio **6.** gabion (rare),
  oddity, prying, wonder **8.** interest
  9. exception, spectacle
  14. meddlesomeness **15.** inquisitiveness
curious . . . **3.** odd **4.** rare **5.** nosey (nosy),
  outre, queer **6.** prying, quaint **7.** careful,
  strange, unusual **8.** cautious, meddling,
  singular **9.** inquiring, intrusive
  10. meticulous **11.** inquisitive
curl . . . **4.** coil, kink, lock, roll **5.** crimp,
  crisp, frizz, tress, twirl, twist **6.** marcel,
  spiral **7.** crinkle, frizzle, ringlet
  8. curlicue **9.** corkscrew **11.** convolution
curled . . . **5.** curly, spiry **6.** coiled
  7. crimped, savoyed, twisted **8.** wrinkled
  (Bot)
curlew . . . **4.** bird, fute **5.** kioea, snipe,
  whaup **6.** marlin **7.** bustard **8.** whimbrel
curlewlike . . . **6.** godwit **9.** sandpiper
curly . . . **4.** wavy **5.** kinky, oundy (obs)
  6. crispy, frizzy, kinked **8.** crinkled
curmudgeon . . . **4.** crab **5.** churl, miser
  7. niggard **8.** tightwad **9.** skinflint
currant . . . **3.** red **5.** berry, Ribes **6.** raisin,
  rizzar (rizzart)
currency . . . **5.** money, scrip **6.** dinero
  9. publicity **10.** greenbacks, popularity,
  prevalence **15.** fashionableness
current . . . **4.** eddy, flow, race (water),
  rife, tide **5.** draft, going, rapid, trend,
  usual **6.** course, stream **7.** present,
  topical **8.** existent **9.** direction, prevalent
  11. fashionable
current regulator . . .
  electric . . **9.** rheometer **12.** galvanometer
  physiology . . **11.** hematometer
curriculum . . . **7.** courses, studies, Three
  R's **8.** curricle

curry . . . **4.** comb, cook, drub **5.** dress,
  groom **6.** cajole **9.** condiment
curry favor . . . **6.** cajole **7.** flatter,
  smoodge (smooge), wheedle
curse . . . **3.** ban **4.** bane, damn, oath
  5. swear **7.** bewitch, malison
  8. anathema, execrate **9.** blaspheme
  10. affliction **11.** imprecation,
  malediction **13.** excommunicate
cursed . . . **6.** damned, odious, wicked
  7. hateful **8.** damnable, shrewish
  9. execrable **12.** cantankerous
Cursores . . . **5.** birds (long-legged)
  7. spiders (wolf)
Cursoria . . . **6.** mantes (mantis)
  10. Orthoptera **11.** cockroaches
cursory . . . **5.** hasty **6.** fitful, roving,
  slight **7.** passing **8.** careless, rambling
  9. desultory, irregular **10.** evanescent
  12. disconnected, unmethodical
curt . . . **4.** buff **5.** bluff, brief, brusk,
  gruff, short, terse **6.** abrupt **7.** brusque,
  concise, curtate, laconic **9.** condensed
curtail . . . **3.** lop **4.** crop, dock, pare,
  slip **5.** short **6.** lessen, reduce
  7. abridge, shorten **8.** compress,
  decrease, diminish, retrench
curtain . . . **4.** mask, veil **5.** drape, shade
  6. coster (altar), encore, purdah, riddel,
  screen, shadow, shield **7.** drapery,
  secrecy, shelter, vitrage **8.** portiere
curtsy, curtsey . . . **3.** bow, nod **4.** bend
  6. kowtow, salaam **12.** genuflection
curvature . . . **3.** arc, bow **4.** arch,
  bend **5.** plane, sinus **6.** camber
  7. arching, curving, evolute **8.** aduncity,
  cyrtosis, lordosis, vaulting **9.** curvation
  11. convolution
curve . . . **3.** arc, bow, ess **4.** arch,
  bend, ogee, turn **5.** crook, polar
  6. spiral, toroid **7.** cissoid, evolute,
  flexure **8.** extrados, parabola, sinusoid
  9. curvature, sinuosity
curved (pert to) . . .
  arch . . **8.** arciform, arcuated
  glass . . **4.** lens
  inward . . **5.** adunc **8.** aduncous
  molding . . **4.** ogee
  planking (ship's) . . **3.** sny
  process . . **5.** hamus (Zool)
  roundabout . . **10.** circuitous
  staircase . . **8.** caracole
  wedge . . **3.** cam
curvet . . . **4.** leap **5.** bound, caper, frisk,
  prank **6.** frolic, gambol
cush . . . **3.** cow **5.** money **7.** cookery,
  sorghum
Cush (pert to) . . .
  father . . **3.** Ham
  land of . . **8.** Ethiopia **10.** land of Cush
  son . . **4.** Seba **6.** Nimrod
cushion . . . **3.** pad **4.** mute, seat **6.** ignore,
  pillow, sachet **7.** brioche, conceal,
  dashpot, muffler **8.** plantula, pulvinus,
  suppress, swelling (Queen Mary's)
  9. pulvillus **10.** pincushion
cusk . . . **4.** fish (codlike), tusk **5.** torsk
  6. burbot
cusp . . . **3.** end, tip **4.** apex, peak **5.** crown,
  point **6.** cantle, corner **8.** paracone
custard . . . **4.** flan **7.** charlet, pudding

custard apple . . . 4. tree 5. papaw
   8. sweetsop
custodian . . . 5. guard 6. bailee, jailer,
   keeper, warden, warder 7. curator,
   janitor 8. curatrix, guardian
custody . . . 4. care, keep 5. trust
   6. charge 8. guidance 10. protection
   12. guardianship, jurisdiction
custom . . . 3. fad, law, mos, use 4. mode,
   wont 5. habit, mores, usage, vogue
   7. fashion 8. practice 9. patronage,
   tradition 10. consuetude, consuetudo
customary . . . 5. usual 6. wonted
   7. general, usitate 8. habitual, orthodox
   11. traditional 12. conventional
customs . . . 4. duty 5. mores, taxes
cut . . . 3. bob, lob, lop, mow, nip,
   rip 4. blow, chop, crop, dock, edit,
   fell, gash, hack, make, mode, nick,
   open, pain, pare, reap, slit, snee,
   snip, snub, trim 5. canal, carve,
   cleft, lance, notch, piece, plate, scarp,
   sever, share, shear, shorn, slash, slice,
   slish (Shaksp), snick, split, vogue
   6. dilute, furrow, injury, mangle, reduce,
   trench 7. affront, curtail, engrave,
   offense, sectile, serrate, truancy,
   whittle 8. discount, excision, incision
   9. engraving, indignity, reduction
   10. adulterate
cut (pert to) . . .
   and furrow . . 7. chamfer
   and polish . . 8. lapidate
   and weave . . 5. plash
   back . . 6. polled 7. shorten
   capable of being . . 7. sectile
   down . . 5. razee
   fine . . 5. mince
   in . . 7. intrude 9. interpose, interrupt,
   introduce
   in half . . 9. dimidiate
   in squares . . 4. dice
   into . . 6. incise
   jaggedly . . 4. snag
   out . . 6. excide, excise
   up . . 6. frolic, grieve 9. apportion,
   misbehave
   vertically . . 5. scarp, slice
   with shears . . 4. snip 5. shirl
cutaneous . . . 4. skin 6. dermal, dermic
cute . . . 4. keen 5. peart, sharp 6. brainy,
   clever, dainty, pretty, shrewd 7. cunning
   10. attractive 11. picturesque
cuticle . . . 4. skin 5. cutin, cutis
   8. membrane, pellicle 9. epidermis,
   scarfskin 10. integument
cut of beef . . . 4. loin, ribs, rump 5. chine,
   roast, steak 6. corned, cutlet, rosbif,
   saddle 7. brisket, icebone 8. shoulder
   9. aitchbone, roundbone
cut off . . . 3. bob 4. crop, dock, drib,
   snip 5. elide, pared, roach (Naut)
   6. bereft, bobbed, divest, lopped, screen
   7. abscind, abscise, clipped, deprive,
   severed 8. amputate 9. amputated,
   apocopate, intercept 10. disinherit
cut off (pert to) . . .
   by bits . . 4. drib
   edges (coins) . . 3. nig
   on slant . . 4. bias 5. bevel, miter
   short . . 3. bob 4. crop

syllable . . 5. elide
with die . . 4. dink
wool . . 3. dod (dodd)
cut short . . . 3. bob, lop 4. crop, dock,
   halt, stop 5. check 6. arrest 7. clipped,
   cropped, curtail, shorten 9. terminate
cutter . . . 4. boat 5. knife, sloop, tooth
   6. sleigh, vessel 7. incisor
cutting . . . 4. cold, slip, tart 5. piece,
   scion, sharp 6. biting, secant, severe
   7. caustic, incisal, satiric, sectile
   8. chilling, piercing 9. sarcastic,
   severance, trenchant 10. separating
   11. penetrating 12. adulteration
cutting (pert to) . . .
   diamonds (imperfect) . . 4. bort
   edge . . 5. blade
   in two . . 6. secant
   last letter of word . . 7. apocope
   off . . 7. apocope 10. abscission,
   amputation
   tool . . 3. axe (ax), bit 4. adze 5. razor
   6. chisel
   wit . . 6. satire
cuttle . . . 4. thug 5. knife 7. ruffian
   8. assassin 9. swaggerer
cuttlebone . . . 7. osselet
cuttlefish . . . 5. Sepia, squid 7. mollusk,
   octopus
cuttlefish secretion . . . 3. ink (black)
cuttyhunk . . . 11. fishing line
Cuzco native . . . 4. Inca
Cyclades Islands (Gr) . . . (200 in all)
   3. Ios 5. Delos (smallest), Melos,
   Naros, Paros, Tenos, Thera 6. Andros
   7. Amorgos, Myconus
cycle . . . 3. Age, eon, era 4. aeon
   5. orbit, recur, saros (Astron), wheel
   6. course, period, series 7. bicycle,
   circuit 8. electric, tricycle 9. Arthurian
   10. revolution 12. Carlovingian
   (Charlemagne)
cyclone . . . 5. storm 6. baguio 7. tornado,
   twister, typhoon 9. hurricane
cyclopean . . . 4. huge, vast 7. massive,
   one-eyed 8. gigantic
Cyclops (pert to) . . .
   assistant to . . 6. Vulcan (Fire God)
   father . . 6. Uranus
   forger of . . 12. thunderbolts
   home . . 6. Sicily (Mt Etna)
   oddity . . 7. one-eyed
   race (Myth) . . 6. giants
cygneous . . . 8. swanlike
cygnet . . . 4. swan
cylinder . . . 4. drum, pipe, roll, tube
   5. inker, stele 6. barrel, gabion,
   platen, record, roller, rounce, terete
   10. cylindroid
cylindrical . . . 5. conic 6. terete 7. tubular
cymbal, cymbals . . . 3. tal, zel 6. Becken,
   piatti 7. potlids 8. doughnut
Cymric . . . 5. Welsh 9. Brythonic
Cymric (pert to) . . .
   bard . . 6. Merlin 7. Aneurin
   god of the dead . . 5. Pwyll
   god of the sky . . 7. Gwydion
   god of the sun . . 4. Lleu
   god of the waves . . 5. Dylan
cynic . . . 5. Timon 7. ascetic, doglike,
   egotist, snarler 9. pessimist

11. misanthrope
Cynic (pert to) . . .
pupil . . **8.** Socrates
school . . **10.** Philosophy
teacher . . **8.** Diogenes
teaching . . **6.** virtue
cynical . . . **7.** currish **8.** captious,
snarling **9.** sarcastic **11.** pessimistic
12. misanthropic
cynosure . . . **5.** guide **8.** lodestar
(loadstar), polestar **9.** celebrity, North
Star **13.** constellation
cyprinoid (fish) . . . **2.** id **3.** ide, orf
(orfe) **4.** bass (black), carp, chub,
dace **6.** chevin, shiner **7.** herring
(lake) **8.** fallfish **9.** hornyhead,
squawfish
Cyprus . . .
capital . . **7.** Nicosia (Sicily)
colonizer (anc) . . **11.** Phoenicians
history . . **11.** New Stone Age
mountain . . **7.** Troodos
port . . **7.** Lorcana **8.** Limassol
9. Famagusto
Cyrenaic (pert to) . . .
city . . **6.** Cyrene
country . . **9.** Cyrenaica (Afr)
division of . . **5.** Libya

harbor . . **6.** Tobruk **7.** Bengazi
philosophy . . **8.** hedonism, pleasure
Cyrene . . . **4.** city (anc) **5.** nymph
7. goddess
cyrus . . . **5.** crane, sarus
Cyrus the Elder (pert to) . . .
conqueror of . . **7.** Babylon
founder of . . **6.** Persia (Empire)
king of . . **5.** Lydia, Media
subduer of . . **9.** Palestine
cyst . . . **3.** box, sac, wen **5.** chest, pouch
7. vesicle
Czar . . . **4.** Ivan, tsar, tzar **5.** Peter
8. Nicholas
Czechoslovakia . . .
capital . . **6.** Prague (Praha)
city . . **6.** Pilsen **7.** Ostrava **10.** Bratislava
divided (1993) . . **8.** Slovakia **13.** Czech
Republic
empire (anc) . . **7.** Bohemia, Moravia
8. Slovakia
forest . . **12.** Great Bohemia
mountain, peak . . **3.** Ore **6.** Tatras
11. Carpathians
people . . **6.** Czechs **7.** Slovaks
river . . **4.** Elbe (Labe), Iser, Oder **6.** Vltava
statesman . . **7.** Masaryk
czigany . . . **5.** gypsy

D

D . . . **3.** 500 **6.** letter (4th)
dab . . . **3.** hit, tap **4.** blow **5.** paint, smear
6. expert, lizard, smooth **7.** dabster
8. flatfish
dabble . . . **4.** mass **5.** dally **6.** befoul,
meddle, paddle, potter, splash, tamper,
trifle **7.** spatter **8.** sprinkle
dabbler . . . **7.** trifler **8.** sciolist
10. dilettante
dabchick . . . **5.** grebe **9.** gallinule
dab hand . . . **6.** expert
dacha (Russ) . . . **5.** villa **12.** country house
dacoit . . . **6.** bandit, robber
dacry, dacryo (comb form) . . . **5.** tears
dactyl . . . **3.** toe **4.** foot **6.** finger
8. dactylus
dactyliomancy . . . **17.** divination by rings
(finger)
dactylogram . . . **11.** fingerprint
dactylology . . . **12.** sign language
Dadaism . . . **4.** cult **8.** negation
daddy longlegs . . . **5.** stilt **6.** curlew,
spider, Tipula **7.** spinner **10.** harvestman
daedal, dedal . . . **4.** rich **6.** varied
8. artistic, skillful (skilful) **9.** ingenious,
intricate **10.** variegated
Daedalus (Gr Myth) . . . **9.** artificer
daemon (Gr Myth) . . . **6.** spirit **8.** guardian
daffodil . . . **6.** yellow **9.** narcissus
10. bellflower
daffy, daft . . . **3.** gay, mad **4.** wild **5.** batty,
crazy, giddy, goofy, loony **6.** insane
7. foolish, idiotic
Dagda (pert to) . . .
children . . **6.** Aengus (Angus), Brigit

famed as . . **7.** harpist
Gaelic name . . **7.** Jupiter
god of . . **10.** pagan Irish
dagger . . . **4.** dirk, kris, snee **5.** kalar
6. anlace, bodkin, creese **7.** bayonet,
poniard **10.** misericord
Dahomey . . . **5.** Benin
Daibutsu (pert to) . . .
famed image . . **6.** Buddha
Japanese Bronze . . **11.** Great Buddha
site . . **8.** Kamakura (near Tokyo)
daikon . . . **6.** radish
daily . . . **4.** a day **7.** diurnal, journal
9. hodiurnal, newspaper, quotidian
11. day in day out
daily food . . . **4.** fare **5.** bread
10. livelihood **11.** subsistence,
substenance
dainties . . . **5.** cates, estes **7.** titbits
(tidbits)
dainty . . . **4.** fair, fine, rare **5.** frail, small
6. choice, pretty, select **8.** elegance
9. exquisite, toothsome **10.** fastidious
dairy . . . **4.** farm **8.** creamery **9.** lactarium
dairymen caste (Ind) . . . **4.** Ahir
dais . . . **5.** stage, table **6.** podium
7. estrade **8.** platform
daisy . . . **5.** gowan, oxeye **6.** morgan,
Shasta **7.** Gerbera **9.** Whiteweed
dale . . . **4.** dell, dene, vale **5.** spout
6. dingle, ravine, trough, valley
dalles . . . **5.** dells **11.** canyon walls
dalliance . . . **4.** chat **5.** delay **6.** gossip,
trifle **8.** fondling, trifling **10.** flirtation
dally . . . **3.** toy **5.** tarry **6.** dawdle, linger

13. procrastinate
Dalmatia . . .
capital . . **7.** Spalato (Yugoslavia)
cherry . . **7.** marasca
coast . . **8.** Adriatic
dog . . **5.** coach **8.** carriage
home of . . **10.** Diocletian
people . . **5.** Serbs **8.** Adriatic **9.** Yugoslavs
product . . **4.** lace
dam . . . **4.** stay, stem, stop, weir **5.** Aswan, block, check, choke, Gatun (CZ) **6.** Hoover (Boulder), mother, Norris, parent **7.** barrier **8.** millpond, obstruct, Oroville, restrain **9.** Roosevelt **10.** Bull Shoals, Glen Canyon **11.** Grand Coulee
damage . . . **3.** mar **4.** harm, hurt, loss, maim, noxa **6.** impair, injury, mayhem, scathe, strafe **8.** disserve, sabotage **9.** detriment, vandalism **10.** impairment
daman . . . **4.** cony (Bib) **5.** Hyrax **6.** mammal **8.** Procavia
Damascus, Syria (pert to) . . .
Bib scene . . **20.** Street Called Straight
division . . **6.** Jewish, Moslem **9.** Christian
history . . **16.** world's oldest city (inhabited)
mosque (renowned) . . **7.** Ommiade
river . . **5.** Abana **6.** Barada
damask . . . **3.** red (color) **5.** cloth, steel (Damascus) **8.** to deface (the Great Seal, Eng)
dame . . . **4.** lady, Miss **5.** Madam, title **6.** matron, Nature, parent
damn . . . **4.** cuss, ruin **5.** abuse, curse **6.** revile, shucks **7.** accurse, condemn, swear at
damp . . . **3.** wet **5.** moist
dampen . . . **3.** wet **6.** dismay **7.** depress, moisten
damsel . . . **4.** girl, lass **5.** Rhoda (Bib), wench **7.** colleen **10.** damoiselle
dance . . . **4.** jazz, prom, skip, trip **5.** frisk, glide **6.** cavort, frolic, gambol **7.** flicker, flutter, rejoice, saltate **10.** tripudiate
dance (pert to) . . .
art . . **12.** choreography
clumsily . . **6.** balter
mimetic (Rom) . . **5.** Salii **7.** Luperci **8.** Curetics
movement . . **6.** chassé, gestic **7.** saltant **9.** pirouette
step . . **3.** pas **5.** coupe **6.** chassé **7.** gambado (gambade), shuffle **8.** glissade **9.** arabesque, grapevine **10.** pigeonwing
dance (type) . . . **3.** bal, hop, jig, tap, toe **4.** ball, clog, haka, kolo, polo, reel, shag **5.** gavot (gavotte), gigue, pavan, polka, tango, twist, waltz **6.** althea, apache, ballet, bolero, cancan, cha-cha, corant, maxixe, minuet, morris, redowa, rhumba (rumba), shimmy, square, watusi **7.** beguine, coranto (old), courant, foxtrot, gavotte, hoedown, mazurka, one-step, ridotto, tempete, two-step **8.** bunny hug, cakewalk, courante, fandango, flamenco, halliard (anc), hornpipe, lanciers, rigadoon, saraband **9.** allemande (anc), butterfly, farandole, polonaise, quadrille **10.** Charleston,

tarantella **11.** schottische (schottish)
dancer . . . **6.** hoofer **7.** danseur **8.** coryphee, danseuse, stripper **9.** ballerina, ecdysiast, jitterbug **11.** terpsichore **13.** choreographer
dancer (pert to) . . .
Bib . . **6.** Salome
Egyptian . . **4.** alme (almeh) **7.** ghawazi **8.** Baramika
Japanese . . **6.** geisha (girl)
Oriental . . **4.** hula **6.** nautch **8.** bayadere
dancing (pert to) . . .
arrangement . . **12.** choreography
Muse of . . **11.** Terpsichore
term . . **6.** ballet, chassé, gestic **7.** hoofing, saltant
dandelion . . . **4.** herb **5.** plant **6.** yellow **9.** Taraxacum
dander . . . **3.** ire **5.** anger **6.** temper
dandified . . . **7.** foppish
dandify . . . **6.** spruce **7.** adonize, smarten **8.** titivate (tittivate)
dandy . . . **3.** fop **4.** beau, dude, good, toff **5.** daisy **6.** Adonis **7.** coxcomb **9.** exquisite **11.** Beau Brummel
dangerous . . . **3.** bad **4.** dire **5.** feral, risky **6.** chancy **7.** ominous, parlous **8.** alarming, critical, insecure, menacing, perilous **9.** hazardous **10.** jeopardous, precarious
dangle . . . **3.** lop **4.** hang, loll, yawl **5.** droop, swing **6.** flaunt, mizzen
Daniel (pert to) . . .
Bib . . **4.** Book (Old Test) **7.** prophet (Heb)
form of verse . . **7.** lyrical, sestina
verse adopted by . . **5.** Dante **8.** Petrarch
Danish . . see also *Denmark*
capital . . **10.** Copenhagen
council (anc) . . **8.** Rigsraad
country . . **7.** Denmark
doctor . . **6.** Finsen
export . . **8.** cryolite
fiord . . **3.** Ise
flag . . **9.** Dannebrog
island . . **3.** Als (Alsen) **5.** Faroe **9.** Greenland
King (anc) . . **6.** Canute
native . . **4.** Dane **12.** Scandinavian
parliament . . **7.** Rigsdag
prince (legend) . . **6.** Hamlet
settlers in Ireland . . **6.** Ostmen
storyteller . . **8.** Andersen (Hans Christian)
dank . . . **3.** wet **4.** damp **5.** humid, moist, muggy
Dan McGrew . . . **11.** Hound of Hell
danseuse . . . **7.** danseur **8.** coryphee **9.** ballerina
Dante (pert to) . . .
birthplace . . **8.** Florence
famed as . . **4.** poet **6.** lyrist
famed poem . . **12.** Divine Comedy
poem's companion . . **6.** Vergil (Virgil)
poem's division . . **4.** Hell **6.** Heaven **9.** Purgatory
poem's love . . **8.** Beatrice
Danube River (pert to) . . .
end . . **8.** Black Sea
source . . **11.** Black Forest
tributary . . **4.** Isar, Raab **5.** Drava **6.** Morava

Danubian (pert to) . . .
color . . **5.** green
fish . . **6.** huchen (huch)
goose . . **10.** Sevastopol
Danzig . . .
Polish name . . **6.** Gdansk
river site . . **7.** Vistula
Sea . . **6.** Baltic
territory of (now) . . **6.** Poland
dap . . . **3.** bob, dab, dib, dip **6.** bounce,
dibble, guddle **7.** rebound
Daphne (pert to) . . .
Bib . . **4.** Park (Antioch, Syria)
father . . **5.** Ladon **6.** Peneus
lover . . **6.** Apollo
transformation . . **10.** laurel tree
dapper . . . **4.** braw, neat, pert, trim
5. natty, sleek **6.** jaunty, little, lively,
spruce **7.** dashing, finical
dappled . . . **6.** dotted **7.** flecked, piebald,
spotted
dare . . . **4.** daze, defy, face, osse,
risk **5.** brave **6.** assume, dazzle
7. venture **8.** confront, defiance,
paralyze **9.** challenge, undertake
daring . . . **4.** bold, rash **5.** brave, manly
8. boldness, defiance **9.** audacious,
foolhardy **11.** adventurous,
venturesome **12.** enterprising
dark . . . **3.** dim, mum, sad **4.** ebon
5. black, blind, dense, faint, mirky,
murky, night, unlit, vague **6.** closed,
gloomy, occult, opaque, secret, wicked
7. joyless, melanic, obscure, stygian
8. abstruse, darkling (poet), ignorant,
moonless **9.** ambiguous, atrocious,
Cimmerian (realm), lightless, nightfall,
tenebrous, uncertain **10.** foreboding,
indistinct
dark (pert to) . . .
Ages . . **6.** Middle **8.** Medieval **9.** Neolithic
Continent . . **6.** Africa (formerly)
10. unexplored
horse . . **7.** unknown **9.** candidate
hue . . **5.** dusky, swart **6.** somber
7. swarthy
moon area . . **4.** mare
darken . . . **3.** dim **4.** dull **5.** blind, umber
6. darkle, sadden, shadow **7.** becloud,
blacken, confuse, eclipse, enshade
8. bewilder **9.** obfuscate
darkness . . . **4.** dark, dusk, mirk, murk
5. shade **6.** Erebus, shadow **7.** dimness,
tenebra **9.** blackness, blindness,
ignorance, obscurity **10.** opaqueness
darling . . . **2.** jo **3.** pet **4.** dear, idol, lief
5. cheri, sweet **6.** minion **7.** acushla,
beloved **8.** favorite **9.** mavournin
10. mavourneen, sweetheart
13. cushlamochree (cushlamachree)
darnel . . . **4.** tare, weed **5.** grass **6.** Lolium
dart . . . **4.** barb, bolt, flit, leap, vire
5. arrow, bound, lance, scoot, shoot,
start, throw **6.** dartle, elance, glance,
spring, weapon **7.** javelin, missile,
stinger **8.** jaculate
Darwinism . . . **9.** Evolution (theory, 1858)
12. Evolutionism
das, dasse . . . **6.** badger
dash . . . **4.** code, élan, gift, race, ruin,
rush, slam **5.** ardor, crash, haste, onset,

plash, smash, speed, swash **6.** energy,
obelus (anc), spirit, sprint, strike, stroke
7. bravura, spatter, splurge **8.** confound,
gratuity **9.** animation **11.** punctuation
dashing . . . **3.** gay **4.** fast **5.** showy
6. dapper, jaunty, sporty **7.** stylish
dastardly . . . **4.** base, foul **6.** craven
8. cowardly
data . . . **5.** facts, logic **7.** grounds (for
facts) **11.** information
date . . . **3.** age **4.** line (newspaper), time
5. fruit, tryst **6.** person **10.** engagement
11. appointment
date (pert to) . . .
birth . . **5.** natal
coin line . . **7.** exergue
error . . **11.** anachronism
fruit of . . **4.** palm
plum . . **6.** sapote
dated . . . **8.** outmoded **10.** antiquated
12. old-fashioned
daub . . . **3.** dab **4.** blob, gaum, soil, teer
5. paint, smear, stain, sully **6.** bedaub
7. besmear, picture (art), plaster
8. scribble
daughter . . . **5.** child **7.** cadette **9.** offspring
10. descendant
daughter of . . .
Inachus (river god) . . **2.** Io
Night . . **7.** Nemesis
the moon . . **7.** Nokomis
the Spanish king . . **7.** infanta
daunt . . . **3.** awe, cow **4.** faze **5.** amate
(anc) **6.** dismay, subdue **7.** overawe,
repress **10.** discourage, dishearten,
intimidate
dauntless . . . **4.** bold **7.** aweless (awless)
8. fearless, intrepid, resolute
9. dreadless **11.** unfaltering
davenport . . . **3.** bed **4.** desk, sofa **5.** divan
12. Chesterfield
David (Bib) . . .
daughter . . **5.** Tamar
father . . **5.** Jesse
helpers . . **4.** Igal **5.** Abner **7.** Shammah
king of . . **6.** Israel (40 years)
slayer of . . **7.** Goliath
son . . **7.** Solomon
wife . . **7.** Abigail
davit . . . **4.** spar **5.** crane
dawdle . . . **3.** lag **4.** idle, poke, toit **5.** dally
6. linger, loiter, potter, trifle **9.** vacillate
10. dillydally **13.** procrastinate
dawn . . . **2.** eo (comb form) **3.** Eos
(goddess), red **4.** morn **5.** sunup
6. appear, aurora, sink in **7.** sunrise
8. daybreak **9.** beginning, penetrate
day (pert to) . . .
Athenians, Jews . . **6.** sunset
Babylonians . . **7.** sunrise
blindness . . **10.** nyctalopia
11. hemeralopia
divisions . . **5.** lunar, solar **8.** sidereal
dream . . **4.** muse **5.** fancy **7.** fantasy,
reverie **8.** phantasy
Egyptians, Romans . . **8.** midnight
god . . **5.** Horus
nursery . . **6.** crèche
scholar . . **7.** externe
Day of . . .
Atonement . . **9.** Yom Kippur

Brahma . . **9.** Maha Yugas
doom . . **8.** Judgment
day's march . . . **5.** étape
day's work . . . **4.** darg (dargue)
daze . . . **3.** fog **4.** asea, maze, stun
  5. sopor, swoon **6.** benumb, dazzle,
  stupid, trance **7.** confuse, stupefy
  8. bewilder **9.** dumbfound **12.** razzle-
  dazzle
dazzling . . . **6.** bright, garish **7.** glaring
  8. blinding, gorgeous **9.** beautiful,
  brilliant **11.** bewildering
dead . . . **3.** fey **4.** flat, numb, obit
  5. amort, blind, inert, napoo, passé
  6. active, barren, lapsed **7.** defunct,
  expired, insipid, tedious **8.** ad patres,
  complete, deceased, inactive, lifeless,
  obsolete **9.** apathetic, inanimate
  10. lusterless, motionless, spiritless,
  unexciting **11.** nonexistent
dead (pert to) . . .
  Dead Sea apple . . **12.** Apple of Sodom
  Dead Sea country . . **4.** Moab **5.** Sodom
  8. Gomorrah
  language . . **5.** Latin
  rise from the . . **7.** resurge **9.** reanimate,
  resurrect
  set (slang) . . **8.** full tilt, hell-bent
  tree . . **7.** rampike (rampick)
deaden . . . **4.** damp, dull, mute, numb
  6. muffle, obtund, opiate, weaken
  7. relieve, repress **8.** enfeeble
  10. devitalize
deadly . . . **4.** dire, mort **5.** fatal **6.** lethal,
  mortal **7.** deathly **8.** venomous
  10. implacable, lifelessly **11.** destructive,
  internecine
dead ringer . . . **9.** look-alike
deaf . . . **4.** surd **7.** earless **10.** intolerant
  11. inattentive, preoccupied
deaf alphabet . . . **11.** dactylology **12.** sign
  language
deaf and dumb . . . **9.** surdomute
  10. deaf-mutism **11.** surdimutism
deafness . . . **6.** amusia (tone) **7.** surdity
  13. insensibility
deafness operation . . . **8.** fenestra
deal . . . **3.** lot **4.** dole, give, mede,
  mete, sale, sell **5.** allot, share, trade,
  treat **6.** parcel **7.** dispose, portion,
  wrestle **8.** business, dispense, quantity
  9. apportion, entertain **10.** administer,
  distribute
dealer (pert to) . . .
  cattle . . **6.** drover, herder
  cloth . . **6.** draper, mercer
  drug . . **8.** druggist **10.** apothecary,
  pharmacist **14.** pharmacopolist
  retail . . **6.** grocer, monger **8.** merchant
  9. tradesman
  stock exchange . . **6.** broker, jobber,
  trader **11.** stockbroker
dean, dene . . . **4.** dell **6.** valley
dean . . . **4.** head, Inge **5.** decan, doyen
  6. fellow (Educ) master, senior, verger
  7. officer **9.** churchman, principal
dear . . . **5.** chere, cheri, deary, lover, sugar,
  sweet **7.** beloved, darling **8.** precious
  9. expensive **10.** sweetheart
dearth . . . **4.** want **6.** famine, rarity
  7. paucity, poverty **8.** rareness, scarcity,

sparsity
death . . . **4.** doom, mort, obit **5.** sleep
  (eternal) **6.** demise **7.** decease, passing,
  quietus, release **10.** euthanasia (mercy),
  expiration **11.** evanishment
death (pert to) . . .
  after . . **10.** posthumous
  eternal . . **9.** perdition
  foreboding . . **6.** funest **7.** doleful
  lawless . . **8.** lynching
  notice . . **4.** obit **5.** orbit **8.** obituary
  of a deity . . **4.** Mors
  rattle . . **4.** rale
  stoning (by) . . **8.** lapidate
deathlessness . . . **9.** athanasis
  11. immortality **15.** everlastingness
debacle . . . **4.** rout **5.** crash, flood
  7. washout **8.** collapse, stampede
  9. breakdown, cataclysm
  11. catastrophe, destruction
debar . . . **3.** bar **4.** deny **5.** estop **6.** forbid,
  hinder, refuse **7.** exclude **8.** obstruct,
  preclude, prohibit
debark . . . **4.** land **8.** go ashore
  9. disembark
debase . . . **5.** abase, alloy, lower
  6. demean, demote, reduce **7.** corrupt,
  degrade, deprave **8.** disgrace
  10. adulterate, depreciate **11.** deteriorate
debasement . . . **8.** demotion
  9. abasement, abjection, reduction,
  vitiation **11.** degradation
  13. deterioration
debatable . . . **4.** moot **9.** refutable
  10. disputable **11.** contestable
  13. controversial
debate . . . **4.** agon (anc) moot **5.** argue,
  forum, plead, weigh **6.** reason
  7. analyze, closure, cloture, dispute,
  wrangle **8.** argument, consider, forensic,
  militate **9.** quodlibet **10.** deliberate,
  discussion **11.** controversy
  12. deliberation, dissertation
  13. argumentation
debauch . . . **4.** bout, orgy **5.** broil, spree,
  taint **6.** defile, seduce, splore **7.** mislead
  8. carousal, escapade **9.** disaffect,
  dissipate **11.** contaminate
debauchee . . . **4.** rake, roué **5.** satyr
  7. rounder **9.** libertine **10.** profligate
debenture (Finan) . . . **4.** bond **5.** claim
  6. pledge **7.** voucher **10.** instrument
  11. certificate
debilitated . . . **4.** weak **5.** seedy **6.** feeble,
  infirm, sapped, sickly **7.** languid
  8. asthenic, impaired, weakened
  9. enfeebled, langorous **11.** devitalized
debility . . . **5.** atony **7.** languor
  8. adynamia, asthenia, cachexia,
  weakness **9.** infirmity, lassitude
  10. feebleness, sickliness
debit . . . **4.** debt **5.** entry **6.** charge
debonair, debonaire . . . **4.** airy **5.** suave
  6. breezy, jaunty, urbane **7.** affable,
  buoyant **8.** carefree
debris . . . **4.** junk **5.** attle, ruins, scrap,
  talus, trash **6.** litter, refuse, rubble
  7. deposit, remains, rubbish **8.** detritus
  10. clamjamfry
debt . . . **3.** due, IOU, sin (Bib) **7.** arrears,
  default **8.** trespass **9.** arrearage, liability

10. obligation
debut ... 3. bow 8. entrance (formal)
9. coming out 12. introduction,
presentation
debutante ... 3. bud, deb 6. subdeb
9. socialite
decade ... 3. ten 9. decennium
decadence ... 5. decay 7. decline
13. deterioration, retrogression
Decalogue ... 15. Ten Commandments
Decameron author ... 9. Boccaccio
decamp ... 4. flee 6. depart 7. abscond,
vamoose 12. absquatulate
decanter ... 4. ewer 5. croft 6. bottle,
carafe, vessel (liquors)
decapitate ... 6. behead 10. guillotine
decapod ... 4. crab 5. prawn 6. shrimp
7. Homarus, lobster 8. Decapoda
10. crustacean
decay ... 3. rot 4. blet, doty 5. spoil, waste
6. caries, wither 7. crumble, mortify,
putrefy 8. spoilage 9. decadence,
decompose 11. deteriorate, dissolution
13. decomposition, deterioration
deceased ... 4. dead, gone, late 6. at
rest 7. defunct, demised 8. decedent,
departed
deceit ... 5. covin, craft, fraud, guile,
guise 7. cunning 8. artifice, cozenage,
intrigue, subtlety, trickery, wiliness
9. chicanery, deception, duplicity,
imposture, mendacity, sophistry,
treachery 10. craftiness, sneakiness
13. deceitfulness, dissimulation
14. tergiversation 15. treacherousness
deceitful ... 4. wily 5. false 6. artful,
crafty, sneaky, tricky 8. guileful,
scheming, trickish 9. deceptive,
gnathonic, insincere 10. fraudulent
11. treacherous 13. Machiavellian
deceive ... 3. cog, lie 4. bilk, dupe, flam,
fool, gull, hoax, sile 5. cheat, cozen,
elude, hocus, trick, troil 6. baffle,
delude, illude, seduce 7. beguile,
mislead 8. hoodwink
deceiver ... 3. gay 5. cheat 6. hoaxer,
trepan (trapan) 8. betrayer, impostor
9. trickster
decency ... 7. decorum, fitness, modesty
8. chastity, niceness 9. propriety
10. seemliness 12. tastefulness
decent ... 4. kind 6. comely, kindly,
proper, seemly 7. clothed 8. adequate,
gracious, suitable, tasteful 9. tolerable
deception ... 3. lie 4. hoax, wile 5. cheat,
fraud, guile 6. deceit, misled 7. fallacy
8. artifice, deceived, flimflam, illusion
9. duplicity, imposture
deceptive ... 5. vague 8. illusive,
illusory 9. deceiving, sirenical (sirenic)
10. fallacious
decide (upon) ... 3. opt 4. vote 5. adapt,
elect, judge 6. choose, settle 7. referee,
resolve 9. arbitrate, ascertain,
determine, influence
decided ... 8. clear-cut, definite
10. determined
decima ... 4. stop (organ) 5. tenth, tithe
8. interval
decimal ... 3. ten 5. tenth 7. tenfold
8. repetend

decimate ... 3. few 4. kill, slay 5. burke,
tenth 6. divide 7. destroy 8. subtract
9. devastate, slaughter
decipher ... 4. read 5. crack 6. decode,
detect 7. unravel 8. discover 9. translate
decision ... 4. grit 5. arret, nerve, pluck
6. mettle, report 7. verdict 8. firmness
10. conclusion, resolution, settlement
12. announcement 13. determination
decisive ... 3. end 5. final 7. certain,
crucial 8. critical, resolute 9. mandatory
10. conclusive, convincing
decisive moment ... 6. crisis
deck (ship's) ... 3. gun 4. main,
poop 5. orlop, upper 6. bridge
7. scupper (gutter) 8. hatchway,
platform 9. promenade 10. forecastle
deck ... 4. gild 5. adorn, array, cards
(playing), equip, floor 6. blazon, clothe,
enrich 7. bedizen, dress up 8. emblazon
9. knock down
declaim ... 4. rant, rave 5. orate, spiel,
spout 6. herald, recite 8. denounce,
harangue, perorate 9. discourse
11. declamation
declamation ... 7. lecture 9. elocution
10. recitation
declaration ... 3. vow 4. oath 6. avowal,
decree, oracle 8. pleading (law)
9. assertion, manifesto, testimony
10. confession (of faith) 11. affirmation
12. proclamation 13. pronouncement
declare ... 3. say 4. aver, avow, meld
5. bruit, state 6. affirm, allege, assert,
blazon, herald, spread 7. publish
8. announce, indicate, maintain
9. advertise
declare (pert to) ...
against .. 6. indict
as fact .. 5. posit
innocent .. 6. acquit
declension ... 4. drop, fall 5. slope
7. decline, descent, refusal 10. inflection
13. deterioration
decline ... 3. dip, ebb, set 4. fade, fail, fall,
flag, sink, wane 5. droop, repel, slope,
slump, stoop 6. refuse, reject, weaken
7. dwindle 8. decrease, downhill
9. decadence, declivity, repudiate
10. retrograde 12. depreciation
declivity ... 3. dip 4. drop, hill 5. scarp,
slope 7. descent 8. downgate
9. downgrade
decoction ... 4. sapa (sape) 6. apozem,
cremor, tisane 7. boiling 10. extraction
11. preparation
décolleté ... 6. low-cut 8. plunging
9. revealing
decompose ... 3. rot 4. frit 5. decay
7. resolve 10. photolysis 12. disintegrate
decorate ... 4. deck, trim 5. adorn, honor
6. emboss 7. bedizen, brocade, miniate
8. beautify, ornament 9. scrimshaw
decorated ... 5. fancy 6. ornate
7. adorned 8. nielloed 9. sigillate
(pottery) 11. embellished
decoration ... 4. buhl 5. gutta (anc),
medal 6. plaque, purfle, ribbon
7. epergne, festoon, garnish 8. gold
star, ornament, trimming 9. adornment,
garniture, sgraffito 10. cordon bleu,

emblazonry, embroidery

decorous . . . **4.** calm, prim **5.** grave, quiet, staid **6.** decent, demure, modest, proper, sedate, seemly, serene **7.** fitting, regular, settled **8.** becoming, composed, suitable, tasteful **9.** unruffled **12.** conventional

decorticate . . . **4.** bark, flay, husk, pare, peel, skin **5.** strip **9.** excoriate

decoy . . . **4.** bait, lure, tole **6.** capper, entrap **8.** by-bidder **9.** come-on man **11.** stool pigeon

decrease . . . **3.** ebb **4.** drop, sink, wane **5.** abate, waste **6.** decess, lessen, reduce, shrink **7.** decline, dwindle, shorten, slacken, subside **8.** compress, diminish, moderate **9.** abatement, deduction, deflation, lessening **10.** diminution **11.** contraction **12.** depreciation

decree . . . **3.** act, law **4.** bull, fiat, rede (anc), will **5.** arret, canon, edict, enact, irade, order, ukase **6.** dictum, ordain **7.** command, mandate, verdict **8.** decision, rescript **9.** ordinance

decree beforehand . . . **7.** destine

decree nisi . . . **7.** divorce

decrepit . . . **3.** old **4.** aged, lame, weak **6.** infirm, senile, wasted (with age) **7.** worn out **8.** unstable, unsturdy

decry . . . **3.** boo **4.** slur **5.** lower **7.** condemn, degrade, detract **8.** belittle, denounce, derogate **9.** discredit, disparage, underrate **10.** depreciate, undervalue

dedal . . . see *daedal*

dedicate . . . **6.** devote, hallow **7.** address **8.** inscribe **10.** consecrate

deduce . . . **5.** infer **6.** deduct, derive, elicit, evolve **7.** suppose

deduct . . . **4.** bate, faik, take **6.** remove **8.** discount, retrench, separate, subtract

deduction . . . **6.** rebate **7.** reprise **8.** discount, illation **9.** allowance, corollary, induction, inference, reasoning, syllogism

deed . . . **3.** act, ado **4.** feat, fiat, gest (geste) **5.** actum, actus, stunt, title **6.** action, doings **7.** exploit **8.** contract, tenendum **11.** achievement, malefaction, performance

deem . . . **5.** judge, opine, think **6.** esteem, regard **7.** believe, presume, suppose **8.** conclude, consider **10.** adjudicate

deemed . . . **7.** assumed, reputed **8.** adjudged, inferred, presumed, supposed **10.** considered

deep . . . **3.** low, pit **4.** rich, wide, wise **5.** great **6.** hidden, remote, solemn **7.** learned, obscure, serious **8.** immersed, involved, powerful, profound **9.** engrossed, entangled, sagacious **10.** deep-seated, mysterious

deep (pert to) . . .
dish pie . . **7.** cobbler
sea . . **6.** depths
seated . . **8.** habitual **9.** ingrained **11.** established
sleep . . **5.** sopor
sound . . **4.** bell, gong

deepen . . . **5.** lower **6.** dredge **7.** broaden,

enhance **9.** aggravate, intensify **10.** strengthen

deer . . . **3.** elk, red, roe **4.** buck, fawn, hart, hind, maha, stag **5.** eland, moose, ratwa **6.** fallow, sambar, wapiti **7.** caribou, deerlet, roebuck **8.** reindeer, ruminant

deer (pert to) . . .
antler . . **3.** dag **4.** snag **8.** tres-tine (royal)
Asiatic . . **6.** sambar
barking . . **7.** muntjac (muntjak)
deerlike . . **10.** chevrotain
female . . **3.** doe, roe **4.** hind
genus . . **4.** Dama **6.** Cervus **8.** Cervidae
Japanese . . **4.** sika
Java . . **4.** napu **7.** muntjac (muntjak)
Lapland . . **8.** reindeer
male . . **4.** buck, hart, stag **6.** havier **7.** brocket (brok), pricket
meat . . **7.** venison
mouse . . **7.** plandok
Oriental . . **4.** axis, Rusa **5.** kakar **6.** chital, rativa, sambar **7.** kanchil, muntjac (muntjak)
Russian . . **4.** olen
S American . . **4.** pita **6.** guemal (guemul) **7.** brocket, spitter
Tibet . . **4.** shou
tiger . . **6.** cougar
tracks . . **3.** run **4.** slot **5.** spoor
type . . **3.** red, roe **4.** mule **6.** fallow **11.** black-tailed, white-tailed

deface . . . **3.** mar **4.** ruin, scar **5.** spoil **6.** damage, injure **7.** blemish, distort **9.** discredit, disfigure

defalcate . . . **8.** embezzle

defamation . . . **5.** libel **7.** calumny, slander, spatter **8.** disgrace, dishonor **9.** aspersion **10.** defilement, detraction

defame . . . **5.** libel **6.** accuse, charge, infamy, malign, vilify **7.** asperse, blacken, detract, slander, traduce **8.** dishonor **10.** calumniate

default . . . **4.** fail, lack, loss, mora **7.** deficit, failure, neglect **9.** deficient, denigrate, oversight **10.** nonpayment **11.** delinquency **14.** nonfulfillment

defeat . . . **4.** beat, best, lose, rout **5.** worst **6.** baffle, derout, master, refute **7.** beating, clobber, confute, conquer, failure, mastery, repulse, triumph (over), undoing **8.** Waterloo **9.** frustrate, overthrow **10.** disappoint **11.** subjugation **12.** discomfiture **14.** disappointment

defeating . . . **7.** beating, routing **10.** anatreptic, conquering **11.** vanquishing

defeatism . . . **6.** malism **7.** Boloism **10.** retreatism

defect . . . **4.** flaw, lisp, lock, quit, want **5.** fault **7.** blemish, forsake **8.** discredit **10.** deficiency, inadequacy **12.** imperfection, irregularity

defection . . . **4.** loss **7.** failing, failure **9.** desertion **10.** abjurement **11.** abandonment

defective . . . **3.** bad **4.** lame **5.** idiot **6.** cretin, faulty **7.** half-wit, lacking **8.** crippled **9.** deficient, imperfect, subnormal **10.** incomplete

defective vision ... 6. anopia, myopia

defend ... 4. save, ward 5. guard, plead, shend, watch 6. screen, secure, shield, uphold 7. contest, justify, protect, shelter, support, sustain 8. enshield, preserve 10. controvert

defendant ... 4. reus 7. accused, libelee, suspect 8. appellee 10. respondent

defender ... 8. advocate, champion 9. justifier, protector 10. vindicator

defense ... 4. boma, fort, plea 5. alibi, guard 6. abatis (abattis), glacis (slope) 7. bastion, bulwark, rampart, ravelin 8. estacade (dike), sepiment, stockade 10. protection 12. counterscarp 13. justification, machicolation

defenseless ... 7. aidless, forlorn, unarmed 8. helpless 9. unarmored, unguarded 10. undefended, unshielded 11. unfortified, unprotected

defer ... 3. bow 4. wait 5. delay 6. retard 7. adjourn, suspend 8. postpone, protract, stave off 13. procrastinate

defer (to) ... 5. yield 6. admire, regard, submit 7. concede, respect 9. recognize 11. acknowledge

deference ... 5. honor 6. esteem, fealty, homage, regard 7. respect 8. courtesy 9. reverence 10. politeness, submission 12. complaisance 13. consideration

deferential ... 8. obeisant 9. attentive, courteous 10. respectful, submissive 11. ceremonious

defiance ... 6. defial 8. audacity, boldness 9. challenge, disregard, insolence

deficiency ... 4. lack, want 6. dearth, ullage 7. aneuria, deficit 8. scarcity, shortage 10. inadequacy 13. insufficiency 14. incompleteness

deficient ... 5. minus, short 6. faulty, meager (meagre), scarce 7. lacking, missing, wanting 8. inferior 9. defective, imperfect 10. inadequate, incomplete 12. insufficient

defile ... 4. file, pass (Mt), soil 5. dirty, gorge, notch, sully, taint 6. befoul, debase, ravine, vilify 7. corrupt, debauch, deprave, pollute, tarnish 8. dishonor 10. passageway

define ... 3. fix 4. name 5. bound, limit 6. decide 7. delimit, explain, outline 8. boundary 9. delineate, determine, stipulate 11. distinguish 12. characterize, circumscribe

defined (sharply) ... 8. clear-cut 9. trenchant

defined track ... 3. rut 4. slot

definite ... 4. sure 7. certain, limited, precise 8. absolute, distinct, explicit, manifest, positive 10. undeniable 11. determining, unqualified 12. unmistakable 14. unquestionable

definitely ... 10. explicitly, positively 12. conclusively, unmistakably

definition ... 6. naming 7. clarity, meaning 9. sharpness 11. description, explanation 12. delimitation, distinctness 14. interpretation

deflation ... 7. decline 8. collapse 9. reduction 10. cheapening 11. devaluation, humiliation

12. depreciation

deflect ... 4. bend, warp 5. avert 6. divert 7. deviate

Defoe character ... 6. Crusoe, Friday, Roxana 12. Moll Flanders

deformed ... 5. varus 7. taliped 8. formless 9. amorphous, distorted, grotesque, loathsome, malformed, misshapen, monstrous 10. clubfooted

defraud ... 3. gyp, rob 4. bilk, gull 5. cheat, cozen 6. fleece 7. swindle

deft ... 3. apt, fit, pat 4. meet, trim 5. adept, handy, quick 6. adroit, clever, expert 8. skillful (skilful) 9. dexterous, masterful

defunct ... 3. die 4. dead, gone 6. depart, finish 7. extinct 8. deceased 11. nonexistent

defy ... 4. dare 5. beard, brave, stump 6. cartel 7. disdain, disobey 9. challenge

degenerate ... 6. debase, wicked, worsen 7. atrophy, corrupt, degrade, deprave 8. decadent 10. retrogress 11. deteriorate

degeneration ... 7. decline 9. decadence, turpitude 10. degeneracy 11. degradation 13. deterioration, retrogression

degradation ... 5. shame 7. censure, decline 8. demotion, disgrace, ignominy 9. reduction, turpitude 10. debasement, punishment 11. humiliation 13. deterioration

degrade ... 5. abase, lower 6. debase, demean, demote, depose, humble 7. corrupt 8. disgrace, dishonor 9. humiliate 10. depreciate

degrade (socially) ... 8. déclassé

degree ... 4. rank, step, tate 5. class, grade, order, point, scope, shade, stage, stair 6. extent 7. station 8. capacity, relation 9. intensity

degree (pert to) ...
academic .. 8. bachelor 9. doctorate, masterate 11. engineering 13. baccalaureate
slight .. 5. shade 9. gradation
to what .. 9. howsoever 10. howsomever
with honors .. 8. cum laude

dehydrate ... 3. dry 5. dry up 6. wither 8. preserve 9. anhydrate, dessicate, evaporate, exsiccate

deify ... 5. exalt 7. ennoble, glorify, idolize 8. enshrine 11. apotheosize, immortalize

deign ... 7. consent 9. vouchsafe 10. condescend

deity ... 2. El 3. Dea, God 4. Deus, deva 5. numen 6. Elohim 7. goddess, godhead, godhood 8. Almighty, Divinity, Immortal 12. Supreme Being

deity (aboriginal) ... 4. mana, Zemi 5. huaca, wakan 6. manito (manitou), nagual, orenda, pokunt 8. tamanoas

deity (pert to) ...
avenging .. 6. Erinys 7. Alastor, Anteros
destroying .. 4. Siva (Shiva)
evil .. 5. Sebek (crocodile-headed)
hearth .. 5. Vesta
household .. 3. Lar 7. Penates
human sacrifice .. 6. Moloch

judge of the dead .. **4.** Yama
love .. **4.** Amor, Eros **5.** Cupid
mockery .. **5.** Momus
music .. **6.** Apollo
solar .. **5.** Mentu (Ment, falcon-headed)
sun .. **2.** Ra
supreme .. **6.** Ormazd
two-faced .. **5.** Janus
underworld .. **3.** Dis **4.** Gwyn **5.** Pluto
   6. Osiris
war .. **4.** Ares
woodland .. **3.** Pan **4.** faun **5.** satyr
   7. silenus
dejected ... **3.** sad **5.** amort **6.** abased,
   droopy **7.** à la mort, lowered
   8. downcast **9.** depressed, prostrate
   10. despondent **11.** downhearted,
   low-spirited
dejection ... **7.** lowness, sadness
   10. depression, melancholy
   11. despondency
déjeuner ... **5.** lunch
Delaware ...
beach .. **8.** Rehoboth
capital .. **5.** Dover
church (oldest Prot) .. **9.** Old Swedes
city .. **5.** Lewes **9.** New Castle
   10. Wilmington (Fort Christina, 1638)
corporation .. **6.** DuPont
product .. **9.** chemicals **13.** Blue Hen
   chicks
river .. **8.** Delaware **10.** Brandywine
State admission .. **5.** first
State motto .. **22.** Liberty and
   Independence
State nickname .. **5.** First **7.** Diamond
delay ... **3.** lag **4.** halt, mora, stay, wait
   5. block, check, daily, defer, demur,
   pause, tarry **6.** arrest, detain, hinder,
   impede, loiter, retard **7.** confine,
   setback **8.** lateness, obstruct, postpone,
   reprieve, slow-down **9.** detention,
   hindrance **10.** cunctation, moratorium
   13. procrastinate **15.** procrastination
delayed ... **4.** late, slow **5.** tardy
   7. belayed, overdue **10.** behindhand
delectable ... **6.** savory **8.** luscious,
   pleasing **9.** ambrosial, delicious
   10. delightful **11.** scrumptious
delegate ... **4.** name, send **6.** assign,
   commit, depute, deputy, legate
   7. appoint, consign, entrust **8.** deputize
   9. authorize **10.** commission
   12. commissioner **14.** representative
delete ... **4.** dele **5.** erase **6.** cut out,
   excise, remove **7.** edit out, expunge
   9. eradicate **10.** obliterate
deleterious ... **7.** harmful, hurtful,
   noxious **9.** injurious **10.** pernicious,
   prejudiced **11.** destructive, detrimental,
   prejudicial
deletion ... **4.** stet **7.** apocope **8.** excision
   9. expunging
delf, delft ... **3.** pit **4.** mine **6.** quarry
Delhi ... **7.** capital (Ind)
deliberate ... **4.** cool, muse, pore, slow
   5. study, think, weigh **6.** ponder
   7. discuss, reflect, studied **8.** consider,
   measured, prepense **9.** calculate,
   leisurely, speculate, unhurried,
   voluntary **11.** contemplate, intentional,

premeditate **12.** premeditated
   13. dispassionate
deliberately ... **6.** slowly **7.** tardily **8.** by
   design **9.** expressly, purposely, willfully
   13. intentionally
delicacy ... **4.** cate, tact **5.** snack, taste
   6. caviar, luxury, nicety, tidbit **7.** finesse,
   frailty, tenuity **8.** fineness, niceness,
   softness, subtlety **9.** exactness, fragility,
   precision **10.** daintiness, refinement,
   slightness **11.** sensitivity
delicate ... **3.** sly **4.** fine, lacy, nice, soft
   5. frail, light **6.** dainty, mignon, petite,
   pretty, queasy, subtle, tender **7.** elegant,
   fragile, minikin, refined, tenuous
   8. araneous, graceful, luscious, tasteful
   9. exquisite, sensitive **10.** fastidious,
   meticulous, scrupulous **11.** considerate
delicious ... **5.** tasty **8.** luscious
   9. ambrosial, nectarean **10.** delightful,
   nectareous
delight ... **3.** joy **4.** glee **5.** amuse,
   bliss, charm, exult, mirth **6.** divert,
   please, ravish, regale, relish **7.** enchant,
   gratify, overjoy **8.** pleasure **9.** delectate,
   enrapture, happiness **13.** gratification
delightful ... **6.** lovely, savory **7.** amusing,
   winsome **8.** charming, engaging,
   pleasant **9.** appealing, delicious,
   enjoyable **10.** enchanting **11.** fascinating
delineate ... **3.** map **4.** draw, limn, line
   5. trace **6.** define, depict **7.** outline,
   picture, portray **8.** describe **9.** represent
delinquency ... **7.** default, failure
   8. omission **9.** violation **10.** nonpayment
   11. malfeasance, misdemeanor,
   misfeasance **13.** nonobservance
deliquesce ... **4.** give, melt **6.** ramify
   7. liquefy **8.** diminish, dissolve
delirious ... **6.** insane, raving **8.** frenzied
   9. wandering (mental) **14.** disorientation
delirium ... **4.** fury, rage **6.** frenzy,
   lunacy **7.** madness, passion **8.** insanity
   9. phrenitis **10.** aberration, excitement,
   unsaneness **11.** derangement
   13. hallucination
deliver ... **4.** free, give, save **5.** speak
   6. commit, impart, ransom, redeem,
   render, resign **7.** consign, release,
   relieve **8.** transfer **9.** discharge,
   enunciate, extradite, surrender
deliver of evil spirits ... **8.** exorcise
deliver oration ... **7.** declaim
dell ... **4.** dale, dene, vale **5.** slade **6.** dalles
   (pl), dingle, ravine, valley
Delos ...
famed for .. **5.** ruins **10.** Stone Lions
island group .. **8.** Cyclades
sea .. **6.** Aegean
Delphi, Delphoi (Gr) ...
god .. **6.** Apollo
modern name .. **6.** Kastri
mount .. **9.** Parnassus
oracle .. **7.** Delphic **8.** Delphian
priestess .. **6.** Pythia
delude ... **3.** jig **4.** dupe, flam, fool, hoax
   5. elude, trick **6.** befool **7.** beguile,
   deceive, mislead **9.** bamboozle,
   frustrate, victimize **11.** double-cross
deluge ... **5.** flood **6.** drench **7.** freshet,
   Niagara, torrent **8.** cataract, flooding,

inundate, overflow, submerge, The
Flood 9. cataclysm, overwhelm
10. oversupply 14. superabundance

delusion . . . 4. ruse 6. mirage 7. fallacy,
fantasm 8. illusion, phantasm
9. deception 10. misleading
13. hallucination

delve . . . 3. dig 4. mine, till 5. gouge,
scoop, spade 6. exhume 8. excavate

demand . . . 3. ask, COD, cry, dun, fee
4. call, need 5. claim, query 6. elicit
7. require 8. exaction, question
9. requisite, ultimatum 11. requirement,
requisition

demandant . . . 9. plaintiff

demeanor, demeanour . . . 4. mien
7. bearing, conduct, posture 8. behavior,
carriage 11. comportment

demented . . . 3. mad 4. daft, loco,
luny 5. crazy, loony 6. crazed, insane
7. cracked 8. deranged 10. unbalanced
11. disoriented

demesne . . . 4. land 6. estate
10. possession

Demeter . . . 7. goddess (Agric)

demigod . . . 4. hero 5. satyr (sylvan)
6. Triton 7. godling, half-god
10. semidivine

demise . . . 5. death, lease 6. convey
7. decease 8. bequeath 10. alienation,
conveyance

demit . . . 4. quit 5. leave 6. resign,
vacate 8. abdicate 10. relinquish
11. resignation

demiurgic . . . 8. creative 9. formative

demivolt . . . 4. jump 5. vault (half)
6. curvet 8. capriole

Democrat (Polit slang) . . . 6. Hunker

demoded . . . 5. passe 6. passed 10. out
of style

demolish . . . 4. rase, raze, ruin, undo
5. level, wreck 7. destroy, shatter
9. devastate, dismantle, overthrow
11. disassemble

demon, daemon . . . 3. hag, imp, nat
4. atua, jinn, Mara, ogre, Rahu 5. asura,
devil, Eolis, fiend, genie, jinni (jinnee),
lamia, Satan 6. afreet 7. Amaimon,
villain 8. Asmodeus 9. cacodemon
(cacodaemon)

demoniac . . . 8. devilish, fiendish

demons (pert to) . . .
adjurers . . 9. exorcists
assembly of . . 6. sabbat
charm against . . 10. demonifuge
possessed of . . 8. demoniac
theory of . . 10. demonology
worship of . . 11. demonolatry

demonstrate . . . 4. show 5. prove
6. evince, typify 7. display, explain,
portray 8. manifest 9. exemplify

demonstrative . . . 7. gushing 8. effusive
9. emotional 10. indicative
11. explanatory 12. affectionate,
illustrative

Demosthenes (Gr) . . . 6. orator (greatest)

demotic . . . 6. common 7. popular
8. everyday 10. vernacular

demur . . . 4. stay 5. delay, pause,
tarry 6. linger, object (to) 7. scruple
8. demurrer, hesitate 9. objection

12. irresolution

demure . . . 3. coy, mim, shy 4. prim,
smug 5. grave, staid, timid 6. sedate,
solemn, stuffy 7. bashful, prudish,
serious 8. decorous

den . . . 4. cave, cell, lair, nest, room
5. cavea (anc), group (scouts), haunt,
study 6. cavern, grotto, hollow, ravine
7. retreat 8. hideaway

denial . . . 5. cross 7. refusal 8. demurrer,
negation 9. disavowal, disowning,
rejection 10. refutation 11. deprivation
12. disallowance 13. disaffirmance

denizen . . . 3. cit 6. native 7. citizen,
dweller, hellion (of hell) 9. indweller
10. inhabitant 11. cosmopolite

Denmark . . . see also *Danish*
anc name . . 5. Thule
capital . . 10. Copenhagen
city . . 6. Nyborg (Fyn Isl), Odense
7. Aalborg 8. Elsinore
founder . . 7. Absalon (Axel)
Hamlet's grave . . 8. Elsinore
island possession . . 6. Faroes
9. Greenland
peninsula . . 7. Jutland
river . . 5. Guden
ruler (anc) . . 6. Canute (Kanute)

denomination . . . 3. ism 4. cult, name,
sect 5. class, party, value 6. church,
number, school 7. society 8. category
10. persuasion 11. appellation,
designation, stipulation

denote . . . 4. mark, mean, note, show
5. imply 6. convey 7. bespeak, betoken,
connote, express, purport, signify
8. indicate 10. denominate

denoting (pert to) . . .
equal pressure . . 8. isobaric
final end (Gram) . . 5. telic
usual action . . 9. usitative

denouement . . . 3. end 5. issue 6. result
7. outcome (plot) 8. solution
10. revelation

denounce . . . 4. damn, rail (at, against)
6. accuse, assail, scathe 7. arraign,
censure, condemn, upbraid 9. reprobate
10. denunciate, stigmatize

de novo . . . 3. new 4. anew 5. fresh,
newly 6. afresh

dense . . . 4. dewy, firm 5. close,
crass, gross, heavy, solid, thick
6. opaque, stupid 7. compact, crowded
8. populous, thickset 11. thickheaded

density . . . 4. dord (Chem) 8. dumbness
9. stupidity 11. compactness

dent . . . 3. pit 4. dint 5. dinge, notch, tooth
6. batter, hollow, indent 7. imprint
10. depression, impression
11. indentation

dentagra . . . 7. forceps 9. dentalgia,
toothache

dental (pert to) . . .
appliance . . 3. dam 6. scaler 7. forceps
drill . . 8. cavitron
filling . . 5. inlay
measure . . 10. dentimeter
toothache . . 8. dentagra 9. dentalgia

dentate . . . 7. serried, toothed

dentine . . . 5. ivory

dentist . . . 10. exodontist 12. orthodontist

14. prosthodontist

denude . . . 4. bate 5. scalp, strip 6. divest, expose, unrobe 7. uncover

denunciation . . . 6. menace, threat 7. inveigh 8. reproach 10. accusation 11. arraignment

deny . . . 4. nego 5. debar 6. abjure, impugn, negate, recant, refuse, renege 7. confute, disavow, dispute, gainsay 8. disclaim, forswear, traverse 9. repudiate 10. contradict, contravene, controvert

deodar (species) . . . 5. cedar

depart . . . 2. go 3. die 4. exit, quit 5. leave, mosey 6. decamp, demise, egress, perish 7. abscond, vamoose 8. separate (Chem), withdraw

depend . . . 4. rely 5. hinge

depraved . . . 4. evil, vile 6. shrewd, wicked 7. corrupt, immoral, vicious 8. vitiated 9. debauched, dissolute, perverted 10. degenerate

depravity . . . 8. depraved 9. turpitude 10. corruption, wickedness 15. incorrigibility

depreciate . . . 4. fall 5. lower, slump 6. debase, lessen, reduce, shrink 7. cheapen, deflate 8. belittle, discount, pejorate, vilipend 9. disparage 10. undervalue

depreciation . . . 8. decrease, discount 9. deflation 10. cheapening, pejoration 12. belittlement 13. disparagement 14. undervaluation

depredator . . . 5. thief 6. looter, robber 7. spoiler 8. marauder, ravisher 9. despoiler, plunderer

depress . . . 4. dent, sink 5. lower 6. dampen, deepen, deject, indent, reduce, sadden 7. flatten, imprint, oppress 8. dispirit, enfeeble 10. discourage

depressed . . . 3. low, sad 4. dire, sunk 6. dismal, oblate 8. dejected, downcast 9. debruised (Her), flattened (vertically) 10. dispirited 11. downhearted 12. disheartened

depressing . . . 5. chill 6. dismal, dreary, gloomy, somber 7. joyless 9. saddening 10. melancholy

depression . . . 3. col, dip, pit 4. dent, fall 5. blues, fossa (Anat), gloom, gully 6. cavity, crater, ravine, trough, vapors 10. melancholy 11. despondency, humiliation

deprivation . . . 4. loss, want 7. deposal, ousting, removal 9. privation, unseating 10. divestment 11. bereavement

deprive . . . 3. rob 4. take 5. debar, mulct, strip 6. divest, remove 7. bereave, despoil 10. dispossess

deprived of . . .
authority . . 9. dethroned
life . . 5. slain 6. killed 12. exterminated
limb . . 6. maimed
natural qualities . . 9. denatured
possessions . . 12. expropriated
professional standing . . 8. laicized
rank . . 7. deposed
reason . . 8. demented
vigor . . 6. sapped 8. deadened, unnerved

9. enervated, enfeebled

depth . . . 5. abyss, midst 6. extent 9. intensity 10. profundity

depths . . . 3. sea 5. adyta (spiritual), ocean 16. Davy Jones's locker

depute . . . 6. assign, devote 7. appoint 8. delegate, deputize

deputy . . . 5. agent, envoy, proxy, vicar 6. legate 8. alter ego 9. alternate 10. substitute

deracinate . . . 6. evulse, unroot, uproot 7. extract (forcibly)

deride . . . 3. pan 4. dupe, geck, gibe, jeer, mock, razz 5. cheat, fleer, flout, scoff, scorn, trick 6. insult 8. ridicule

derision . . . 5. fleer, scorn 7. asteism, mockery 8. contempt, ridicule

derivation . . . 6. effect, origin, source 7. descent, lineage 9. deduction, education, evolution 10. derivative 12. transmission

derivation of . . .
descent . . 7. lineage 8. pedigree 9. genealogy
name (race, tribe) . . 7. eponymy
word . . 9. etymology

derivative of . . .
bauxite . . 8. aluminum
benzine . . 6. phenol
coal tar . . 8. creosote
flax . . 5. linen
mercury . . 11. quicksilver
milk . . 6. lactic
morphine . . 6. heroin
pitchblende . . 6. radium 7. uranium
sorrel . . 10. oxalic acid

derogate . . . 5. annul, decry 6. repeal 7. detract 8. restrict, withdraw 9. disparage

derogatory . . . 10. detracting, detractory, pejorative 11. deprecatory, disparaging 12. depreciatory

derrick . . . 3. rig 4. spar 5. crave, hoist, tower 6. lifter, steeve, tackle 7. hangman, staging

dervish . . . 4. monk 5. fakir, friar 6. beggar, fakeer 7. ascetic 11. religionist

dervish cap . . . 3. taj 4. atef

dervishes . . .
howling . . 8. Rufaiyah
wandering . . 12. Kalandariyah
whirling, dancing . . 10. Maulawiyah

Descartes (pert to) . . .
geometry . . 8. analytic 10. coordinate
system . . 9. Cartesian
tenet . . 13. cogito ergo sum

descend . . . 4. fall, sink 5. deign, stoop 6. alight, unbend 7. decline 9. gravitate 10. condescend

descendant . . . 3. son 5. child, scion 8. daughter, offshoot 9. offspring

descendants . . . 5. breed 7. progeny 9. posterity

descent . . . 4. drop, fall, root 5. birth, issue, scarp, slope, stock 7. assault, decline, lineage 8. ancestry, downfall, invasion (sea), pedigree 9. declivity, incursion, posterity 10. extraction 11. degradation

describe . . . 4. name 5. paint, parse, state 6. define, depict, relate 7. explain, express, narrate, outline **9.** delineate, designate, represent **12.** characterize

description . . . **4.** idyl, kind, sort **5.** idyll **7.** account, version **8.** features, relation **9.** discourse, narration, narrative, portrayal **10.** definition **11.** delineation, explanation **14.** representation **18.** descriptio personae

descry . . . **3.** see **4.** espy, view **6.** behold, detect, reveal **7.** discern, observe, witness **8.** discover **9.** determine **11.** distinguish

Desdemona's husband . . . **7.** Othello

desecrate . . . **5.** abuse **6.** misuse **7.** profane, violate **8.** misapply

Deseret . . . **4.** Utah (1849)

desert . . . **3.** due **4.** bolt, fail **5.** merit, oasis **6.** defect, renege, reward **7.** abandon, forsake **8.** desolate **10.** apostatize, relinquish, wilderness

desert (pert to) . . .
Africa . . **5.** El Erg **6.** Karroo, Sahara **8.** Kalahari
Algeria . . **3.** Erg
Australia . . **10.** Great Sandy **13.** Great Victoria
beast . . **5.** camel
dweller . . **4.** Arab
Mongolia (Asia) . . **4.** Gobi
phenomenon . . **6.** mirage
prospector . . **3.** rat
ship . . **5.** camel
shrub . . **5.** ratem **6.** Alhagi **7.** juniper (Bib)
train, travelers . . **7.** caravan
US . . **6.** Mojave (Mohave) **7.** Painted **11.** Death Valley
wind (hot) . . **6.** simoom (simoon) **7.** sirocco

deserter . . . **3.** rat **6.** bolter **8.** apostate, recreant, renegade, turncoat, turntail

deserved . . . **3.** due **4.** fair, just **5.** rated **6.** earned, worthy **7.** condign, merited **8.** rightful **9.** justified, warranted **11.** appropriate

deserving . . . **6.** worthy **8.** laudable **10.** creditable, entitled to **11.** commendable, meritorious **12.** praiseworthy

desiccated . . . **3.** dry **4.** arid, sere **5.** dried **6.** seared **7.** parched **9.** preserved **10.** dehydrated, exsiccated

design . . . **3.** aim, art, end **4.** draw, form, idea, mean, plan, plot **5.** ettle **6.** intent, layout, motive, object, scheme, sketch **7.** destine, drawing, meaning, outline, pattern, propose **8.** artifice, artistry, contrive **11.** arrangement

design (pert to) . . .
carved . . **4.** seme **5.** cameo **8.** intaglio
metal glass . . **4.** etch **6.** niello
ornamental . . **9.** medallion **10.** needlework
pattern . . **5.** batik **6.** mosaic
skin . . **6.** tattoo

designate . . . **3.** fix, set **4.** call, mark, name, show **5.** state, style, title **6.** select **7.** appoint, entitle, specify **8.** describe, indicate, nominate **9.** determine, stipulate **10.** denominate **11.** distinguish **12.** characterize

designation . . . **4.** name **7.** meaning **9.** selection **10.** indication **12.** denomination **13.** signification

desire . . . **3.** yen **4.** care, urge, want, wish **5.** covet, crave, yearn **6.** aspire, hunger, prefer, thirst **7.** craving, longing, passion, request **8.** appetite **9.** appetency, eagerness **10.** desiderium **11.** inclination

desire (pert to) . . .
expectant . . **4.** hope
greatly . . **6.** aspire
liquid . . **6.** thirst
ungovernable . . **5.** mania

desirous . . . **4.** avid **5.** eager **6.** ardent **7.** envious, lustful, willing **8.** covetous, spirited **9.** ambitious **10.** solicitous

desist . . . **2.** ho **3.** end **4.** don't, halt, quit, stay, stop **5.** cease **6.** lay off **7.** forbear, refrain **8.** cut it out **11.** discontinue

desk . . . **4.** ambo, dais **5.** board, table **6.** pulpit **7.** lectern, rostrum **8.** kneehole **9.** monocleid (monocleide), secretary **10.** escritoire

desolate . . . **3.** sad **4.** arid, lorn, ruin **5.** alone, bleak, drear, gaunt **6.** barren, dismal, gloomy, lonely, ravage **7.** forlorn **8.** deserted, forsaken, solitary, wretched **9.** destitute **10.** depopulate **11.** comfortless, uninhabited

desolation . . . **3.** woe **4.** ruin **5.** gloom, grief, havoc, waste **6.** ravage **7.** sadness **10.** gloominess, loneliness, melancholy **11.** destitution, destruction, devastation, forlornness **12.** depopulation, solitariness, wretchedness

despair . . . **11.** desperation, despondency, forlornness **12.** hopelessness

desperado . . . **5.** brave **6.** outlaw **7.** ruffian **8.** criminal **10.** lawbreaker

desperate . . . **3.** mad **4.** rash, wild **7.** frantic, furious **8.** headlong, heedless, hopeless, reckless **10.** despairing, desponding, distraught, infuriated **11.** extravagant, precipitate **13.** irretrievable

despicable . . . **4.** base, vile **6.** odious, shabby **8.** terrible, unworthy, wretched **9.** miserable **12.** contemptible, contemptuous, disreputable, vilipendious

despise . . . **4.** defy, hate **5.** scorn, scout, spurn **6.** detest, slight **7.** contemn, disdain **8.** vilipend **9.** disregard

despised being . . . **6.** pariah **7.** outcast

despoil . . . **3.** rip, rob **4.** riot **5.** reave, rifle, strip **6.** divest, fleece, injure, ravage, ravish **7.** bereave, debauch, deprive, disrobe, pillage, plunder **9.** depredate

despondency . . . **7.** despair **10.** depression **11.** desperation **13.** heartlessness

despot . . . **4.** czar (tsar), lord **6.** master, satrap, tyrant **8.** autocrat, dictator **9.** patriarch

despotic . . . **8.** arrogant **9.** arbitrary, tyrannous **10.** autocratic, tyrannical **11.** dictatorial, patriarchal **12.** governmental

dessert . . . **3.** ice, pie **4.** cake **5.** fruit,

glacé, sweet **6.** mousse, pastry, sweets **7.** parfait, pudding, sherbet, strudel **8.** ice cream **10.** shoofly pie

destination ... **3.** end **4.** goal, port **5.** bourn (bourne) **7.** address, destiny **9.** objective

destine ... **4.** doom, fate **5.** allot **6.** design, devote, intend, ordain **7.** appoint **8.** set apart **9.** designate **10.** foreordain, predestine **12.** predetermine

destiny ... **3.** end, lot, ure (anc) **4.** bahi, doom, eure, fate, goal **5.** karma, stars **6.** Kismet **7.** fortune **11.** destination

destitute ... **4.** void **5.** needy **6.** bereft, devoid **7.** forlorn, lacking **8.** bankrupt, forsaken, homeless **9.** abandoned, penniless **10.** down-and-out

destitution ... **6.** penury **7.** poverty **11.** deprivation **12.** helplessness

destroy ... **3.** end **4.** kill, rase, raze, root, ruin, sack, slay, undo **5.** abash, annul, erase **6.** ravage **7.** abolish, consume, nullify, unbuild **8.** decimate, demolish, overturn **9.** dismantle, eradicate **10.** annihilate, neutralize **11.** exterminate

destroyer ... **3.** hun **6.** ruiner, vandal **7.** marplot, wrecker **8.** nihilist, saboteur **9.** iconclast (of images) **11.** torpedo boat

destroying angel ... **6.** Danite **7.** Abaddon, Amanita (fungus) **8.** Apollyon

destruction ... **4.** loss, ruin **5.** havoc, waste **7.** killing **8.** downfall, genocide, ravaging, sabotage, shambles **9.** holocaust, overthrow, perdition, ruination **10.** decimation, demolition, desolation, extinction, subversion **11.** devastation, dissolution, extirpation **13.** extermination

destructive ... **5.** fatal **6.** deadly, mortal **7.** baleful, fateful, ruinous **8.** aneretic (anaeretic), ravaging **10.** calamitous, catawampus, pernicious, subversive

desuetude ... **6.** disuse, nonuse **9.** cessation **12.** obsolescence **13.** nonemployment **14.** discontinuance

desultory ... **4.** idle **5.** hasty **6.** roving, wanton **7.** aimless, cursory, wayward **8.** rambling, unsteady, wavering **9.** deviative, orderless, unsettled **10.** discursive, inconstant

detach ... **4.** part, wean **5.** sever **7.** disjoin, isolate **8.** disunite, separate, withdraw **9.** disengage

detached ... **4.** free **5.** alone, aloof, scarp **7.** detaché, retired, severed **8.** isolated, secluded, separate, solitary **9.** unrelated, withdrawn **11.** unconnected **12.** disconnected

detachment ... **8.** disunion **9.** aloneness, aloofness, isolation, seclusion, unconcern **10.** separation **11.** disjunction **14.** demobilization

detail ... **4.** item, unit **6.** assign **7.** appoint, itemize, minutia, narrate, specify **9.** enumerate, narrative **10.** particular **12.** technicality

details ... **6.** trivia **8.** minutiae **10.** ins and outs **11.** particulars

detain ... **4.** hold, keep, stop **5.** check, delay **6.** arrest, hinder, intern, retard **8.** imprison, restrain, withhold

detect ... **3.** see, spy **4.** show, spot, tail **6.** accuse, descry, reveal **7.** discern, find out, uncover **8.** discover, perceive **9.** recognize

detective ... **4.** dick **6.** beagle, sleuth, tailer, tracer **7.** gumshoe, spotter **8.** exposing, flatfoot, Hawkshaw, mouchard **9.** operative **12.** investigator

detent ... **3.** dog **4.** pawl **5.** catch, click, fence **6.** tongue **7.** ratchet

detention ... **5.** delay **6.** duress **7.** detinue **9.** captivity, hindrance **10.** detainment, internment **11.** restraining, retardation, withholding **12.** imprisonment

deter ... **5.** daunt, delay, repel **6.** divert, hinder **7.** prevent **8.** restrain **10.** discourage, disincline

deterge ... **5.** purge **6.** purify **7.** cleanse **8.** depurate **9.** elutriate

detergent ... **4.** soap **7.** cleaner, purging, saponin (saponine), smectic, solvent **8.** cleanser, medicine, purifier **9.** cleansing **10.** abstergent, lixiviator

deteriorate ... **4.** wear **6.** impair, weaken, worsen **10.** degenerate, retrogress

deterioration ... **5.** decay **7.** decline **9.** decadence **10.** debasement, declension, impairment, perversion **11.** degradation **12.** degeneration **13.** retrogression

determinate ... **5.** fixed **6.** cymose **7.** certain, special **8.** definite, resolute, resolved, specific **9.** arbitrary **10.** definitive, invariable **11.** established, unqualified

determination ... **4.** will **5.** limit, proof **6.** choice **7.** purpose, resolve, verdict **8.** decision, firmness, judgment **9.** impulsion **10.** conclusion, definition, discussion, resolution, settlement **11.** disputation, measurement, termination **12.** decisiveness, dijudication, resoluteness **13.** specification

determine ... **3.** end **5.** impel, learn, prove, state **6.** assess, choose, decide, define, direct, ordain, settle **7.** delimit, resolve, specify **8.** conclude, discover **9.** arbitrate, ascertain, stipulate, terminate, variously **10.** dijudicate, foreordain

determined ... **3.** set **4.** sure **5.** fixed **6.** mulish **7.** assured, cinched, decided, settled **8.** foregone, perverse, resolute, stubborn **9.** obstinate, pigheaded

detest ... **4.** hate **5.** abhor **6.** loathe **8.** execrate **9.** abominate

detestable ... **6.** odious **7.** hateful **8.** accursed, terrible **9.** abhorrent, execrable, loathsome, obnoxious **10.** abominable **12.** contemptible

dethrone ... **6.** depose, disbar, divest **7.** uncrown **8.** disbench

detonation ... **4.** bang, boom **5.** blast **7.** blowout **8.** backfire **9.** discharge, explosion **10.** combustion

detract ... **6.** deduce, deduct, vilify **7.** asperse, traduce **8.** belittle, derogate, distract, subtract, withdraw 9. disparage 10. depreciate

detraction . . . 5. delay 7. calumny, slander 9. aspersion 10. belittling 11. distraction, subtraction

detriment . . . 4. hurt, loss 6. damage, injury 8. mischief, weakness 10. impairment, impediment 12. disadvantage

detrimental . . . 7. baleful, baneful, harmful, hurtful, noxious 9. injurious 10. pernicious 11. deleterious, mischievous, prejudicial 15. disadvantageous

Deus Fidius . . . 7. Jupiter

Deus vobiscum . . . 12. God be with you

Deus vult . . . 8. God wills (anc cry)

deuterogamy . . . 6. digamy

Deuteronomy (pert to) . . .
comprising . . 10. law of Moses
Fifth Book of . . 10. Pentateuch
meaning . . 11. repeated law (of Moses)

devastate . . . 4. rape, ruin, sack 5. havoc, strip, waste 6. ravage 7. destroy, pillage, plunder, scourge 8. demolish, desolate 10. depopulate

devastation . . . 4. ruin 5. havoc, waste 6. ravage 7. scourge

develop . . . 4. grow 5. arise, ripen, train 6. appear, detect, evolve, expand, mature, reveal 7. advance, convert, enlarge, expound, further, improve, perfect, promote 8. discover, generate 9. elaborate (details)

developed . . . 4. ripe, zoon 5. adult 6. mature, mellow 7. grownup 8. improved 9. perfected 10. precocious

development . . . 6. growth 7. changes, endysis 8. increase, maturity 9. evolution, expansion, formation, unfolding 10. maturation 11. elaboration, improvement, ontogenesis 12. phylogenesis

devest . . . 5. strip 6. denude, divest 7. deprive, undress 8. alienate

Devi (Hind) . . . 3. Uma 4. Kali 5. Durga, Gauri 6. Chandi, Shakti 7. heroine, Parvati 8. divinity 9. Haimavati

deviate . . . 3. err, yaw 4. hade, miss, slew, vary, veer 5. sheer, stray 6. change, depart, swerve, wander 7. deflect, digress, diverge

deviation . . . 3. yaw 5. lapse 6. change 7. circuit, synesis 8. aberrant 9. aberrance, deformity, departure, diverging, obliquity, variation 10. deflection, difference, digressing, digression, distortion, divergence 11. abnormality 12. eccentricity

device . . . 4. plan, tool 5. motto, shift, trick 6. design, desire, dingus, gadget, scheme 7. adjunct, compass, project, purpose 8. artifice, insignia 9. appliance, expedient, implement, invention, stratagem 10. instrument 11. contrivance

device (pert to) . . .
bark peeling . . 8. stripper
clamping . . 4. vise 7. pincers
distilling . . 7. alembic
fabric stretching . . 7. stenter

heating . . 4. etna 5. stove
hoisting . . 5. crane, davit, lewis 6. garnet 7. derrick 8. elevator 9. parbuckle
leveling . . 6. gimbal
measuring . . 4. gage, tape 5. chain, gauge, meter, ruler 9. ergometer, yardstick 10. micrometer
nautical . . 4. bitt 5. cleat, otter 6. becket 8. paravane
regulating . . 5. valve 9. remontoir
spraying . . 8. atomizer 9. sprinkler
steering . . 4. helm 5. wheel 6. rudder, tiller
stopping . . 5. brake, sprag

devil . . . 3. imp 4. deil, deva, evil, haze 5. annoy, demon, error, fiend, grill, ruler (of Hell), Satan, tease 7. hellion, serpent, tempter, torment 8. printer's 9. archenemy, daredevil, dust devil

devil (pert to) . . .
dog . . 6. marine
bird . . 3. owl 5. swift 10. goatsucker
fish . . 3. ray 5. manta, whale (gray) 7. octopus
grass . . 7. Bermuda
lore . . 10. demonology
tree . . 4. dita

Devil, the . . . 5. Deuce, Eblis, Satan 6. Azazel, Belial, Diablo, Teufel 7. Ahriman, Amaimon (Amammion), diavolo, Evil One, Lucifer, Old Nick, Sammael, Shaitan (Sheitan) 8. Apollyon, Asmodeus, Diabolos 9. Archenemy, Archfiend, Beelzebub 11. Auld Clootie 14. Mephistopheles

devilish . . . 5. cruel 6. daring, rakish, wicked 7. extreme, hellish, satanic 8. fiendish, infernal 9. chthonian 10. demoniacal 11. mischievous

deviltry . . . 6. malice 7. cruelty, devilry 8. mischief 9. diablerie, diabolism 10. black magic, wickedness 12. fiendishness

devious . . . 6. errant, erring, roving, sinful 7. oblique, vagrant, winding 8. rambling, tortuous 9. deviative, eccentric 10. circuitous 11. out-of-the-way 14. unconventional

devise . . . 3. aim 4. form, plan 5. array, build, frame 6. create, divide, evolve, invent, scheme, will to 7. appoint, arrange, bequest, concoct, fashion 8. bequeath, contrive 9. fabricate 10. distribute, excogitate 11. distinguish

deviser of IQ test . . . 5. Binet

devitalize . . . 3. sap 6. weaken

devoid . . . 4. free, void 5. empty 6. faulty, vacant 7. without 9. destitute 11. nonexistent

devoid of . . .
feeling . . 9. apathetic, insensate
interest . . 6. jejune

devote . . . 3. use, vow 5. apply 6. employ, hallow, resign 7. address, consign, destine 8. dedicate, set apart 10. consecrate 11. appropriate

devoted . . . 5. loyal, pious, vowed 6. doomed, loving 7. betaken, zealous 8. addicted, constant, faithful, friendly, obedient 9. dedicated, engrossed, patriotic

devotee . . . **3.** fan, ist, nun **4.** monk
6. votary **7.** epicure, fanatic, Pietist
8. aesthete (esthete), partisan
devotion . . . **4.** love, zeal **5.** ardor, piety
6. novena, prayer **7.** pietism, worship
8. idolatry **9.** addiction, adoration,
constancy **10.** attachment, dedication,
devoutness, friendship **11.** devotedness,
earnestness, engrossment
12. consecration **13.** appropriation,
religiousness
devour . . . **3.** eat **4.** bolt, gulp, wolf
5. gorge, use up, waste **6.** absorb,
engulf **7.** consume, engorge, swallow
(up) **8.** prey upon **9.** devastate
10. annihilate
devout . . . **4.** holy, warm **5.** godly, pious
6. hearty, solemn **7.** cordial, devoted,
saintly, sincere, zealous **8.** reverent
9. religious, righteous **10.** worshipful
dew . . . **4.** rime **5.** bedew, bloom, roris
dewy . . . **5.** roral, roric
dexterity . . . **3.** art **5.** knack, magic,
skill **7.** ability, address, aptness,
finesse, sleight **8.** aptitude, deftness,
facility **9.** smartness **10.** adroitness
15. right-handedness
dexterous . . . **3.** apt **4.** deft, yare **5.** adept,
handy, quick, ready **6.** adroit, artful,
clever **7.** skilful **8.** skillful **11.** right-
handed
dextral . . . **5.** right (to the) **9.** favorable
diabolical . . . **5.** cruel **6.** wicked **7.** beastly,
demonic, hellish, satanic, ungodly
8. damnable, demoniac, devilish,
fiendish, infernal
diacritic . . . **4.** mark **5.** point **7.** symptom
10. diagnostic **14.** distinguishing
diacritical mark . . . **5.** breve, tilde **6.** tittle
9. diaeresis (dieresis)
diadem . . . **5.** crown, tiara **6.** anadem,
circle, emblem, empire, fillet **7.** coronet
8. headband, insignia, ornament
11. sovereignty
diaeresis, dieresis . . . **4.** mark **5.** break
8. division **10.** resolution
diagnose . . . **7.** analyze **8.** construe
9. interpret
diagnosis . . . **8.** analysis, decision,
nosology **9.** prognosis **14.** interpretation
diagonal . . . **4.** bias **7.** oblique **8.** bendwise
(Her) **10.** transverse **11.** cater-corner
13. cater-cornered
diagram . . . **4.** draw, icon, plan, plot,
tree **5.** chart, epure, gamut, graph
6. design **7.** drawing **9.** blueprint
dial . . . **4.** disk **5.** plate **8.** horologe
9. indicator, timepiece **11.** chronometer
dialect . . . **5.** idiom, lingo **6.** patois,
speech **7.** diction **8.** language, locution,
parlance **10.** vernacular
dialect (pert to) . . .
Afrikaans . . **4.** Taal
Aramaic . . **6.** Syriac
Aryan . . **4.** Pali
provincial . . **6.** patois
Semitic . . **4.** Geez
diameter . . . **2.** pi (3.1416) **4.** bore **5.** width
6. module, radius **7.** breadth, caliber
(calibre) **9.** thickness
diametric, diametrical . . . **6.** averse

7. adverse **8.** antipode, opposite
9. antipodal, diametral
diamond . . . **3.** gem, ice **5.** cards, field
(baseball), jager, jewel, plane **6.** carbon
7. adamant, infield, lozenge, rhombus
8. treasure
diamond (pert to) . . .
base . . **5.** culet
crystal . . **7.** glassie
cutting . . **4.** bort
cutting cups . . **3.** dop
famed . . **4.** pitt **5.** Sancy **6.** Orloff
7. Lesotho (601 carat) **8.** Cullinan, Koh-
i-noor **9.** Excelsior **10.** Great Mogul
14. Star of the South
surface . . **5.** facet
weight . . **5.** carat (karat)
Diamond State . . . **8.** Delaware
diaphanous . . . **4.** fine, thin **5.** filmy,
gauzy, lucid, sheer **6.** flimsy
9. gossamery **11.** translucent,
transparent
diaphragm . . . **4.** wall **6.** middle, septum
7. midriff **9.** partition
diary . . . **3.** log **6.** record **7.** journal
8. register **9.** chronicle
13. autobiography
diaskeuast . . . **6.** editor **7.** reviser
diatribe . . . **6.** screed, tirade **7.** lecture
8. berating, harangue **9.** invective,
philippic **10.** discussion (prolonged)
dice . . . **3.** cog, die (sing) **4.** cube, game,
sice (6's) **5.** bones, craps, cubes
7. ivories, tessera
Dickens characters . . . **3.** Tim **4.** Dora,
Nell **5.** Fagin, Miggs, Sikes **6.** Cuttle
7. Barnaby, Scrooge **9.** Pecksniff
10. Chuzzlewit **11.** Oliver Twist
Dickens pseudonym . . . **3.** Boz
dictate . . . **3.** law **4.** rule **5.** maxim,
order, utter **6.** advise, dictum, enjoin,
impose **7.** command, deliver, require,
suggest **9.** prescribe **10.** injunction
dictatorial . . . **5.** bossy **6.** lordly
7. pompous **8.** absolute, arrogant,
despotic, dogmatic, oracular, positive
9. imperious, masterful, pragmatic
10. autocratic, dogmatical, imperative,
peremptory **11.** categorical,
domineering, magisterial, opinionated,
overbearing **13.** authoritative
diction . . . **5.** style **8.** language, parlance,
phrasing **9.** elocution **10.** vocabulary
11. enunciation, phraseology
14. expressiveness
dictionary . . . **5.** words **7.** calepin, lexicon
8. wordbook **9.** reference **10.** vocabulary
11. terminology
dictionary compiler . . . **7.** Webster
(Noah) **13.** lexicographer
dictum . . . **3.** saw **5.** adage, maxim
6. saying **7.** opinion, precept, proverb
8. aphorism, apothegm **11.** declaration
didactic . . . **8.** teaching **9.** mentorial
10. preceptive **11.** instructive
dido . . . **5.** antic, caper, prank, trick **6.** frolic
Dido (also Elissa) . . . **5.** Queen (of
Carthage) **8.** Princess (Tyrian)
die . . . see also *dice* **4.** fade, mold, pass,
seal, wane **5.** stamp **6.** expire, perish,
recede, vanish, wither **7.** decease,

succumb **8.** languish **12.** extinguished (to be)
die-hard ... **4.** Tory **11.** British Army **12.** Conservative
dies ... **3.** day
dies atri ... **9.** black days
dies faustus ... **13.** favorable omen (day of)
diet ... **4.** fare **5.** board **6.** Hoftag, ration, viands **7.** Council, Landtag, regimen **8.** assembly, Kreistag **9.** allowance, nutrition, Reichstag **10.** Parliament
Diet (of) ... **5.** Worms (1521) **6.** Speyer (1529), Spires **8.** Augsburg (1530)
dietetics ... **8.** sitology **9.** nutrition **12.** biochemistry, dietotherapy
differ ... **4.** vary **5.** clash **7.** dispute, dissent, quarrel **8.** disagree
difference ... **3.** sum **5.** shade **6.** nuance **8.** variance **10.** inequality, unlikeness **11.** contrariety, distinction, distinguish **12.** disagreement, discriminate **13.** differentiate, dissimilarity
different ... **4.** many **5.** novel, other **6.** divers, sundry, unlike **7.** diverse, several, unequal, unusual, variant **8.** assorted, contrary, distinct, manifold, opposite, separate, variform **9.** divergent, otherwise **10.** dissimilar, variegated **11.** diversified **13.** heterogeneous
different place ... **9.** elsewhere **10.** otherwhere
difficulty ... **3.** bar, rub **4.** clog, crux, knot, snag **5.** cavil, check, demur, nodus **6.** plight, scrape, strait **7.** barrier, problem, trouble **8.** obstacle **9.** hindrance **10.** impediment, ruggedness **11.** obstruction **12.** disagreement
difficulty in swallowing ... **9.** dysphagia
diffidence ... **5.** doubt, qualm **7.** anxiety, modesty **8.** distrust, humility, timidity **10.** hesitation **11.** bashfulness **12.** apprehension
diffident ... **3.** coy, shy **5.** timid **6.** modest **7.** anxious **8.** doubtful, reserved, retiring **9.** shrinking, unwilling **11.** distrustful **12.** apprehensive
diffuse ... **4.** full, shed **5.** strew **6.** expand, extend, prolix **7.** copious, perplex, pervade, publish, radiate, refract, verbose **8.** disperse **9.** redundant **10.** widespread
diffused ... **5.** loose **6.** sparse **7.** flowing **9.** dispersed
diffusion ... **7.** osmosis **9.** pervasion, radiation **10.** dispersion, refraction
dig ... **3.** jab **4.** find, grub, mine, open, pion, prod, root **5.** delve, dwell, spade **6.** exhume, loosen, pierce, plunge, search, thrust **7.** extract, unearth **8.** excavate **10.** understand
digamy ... **11.** deuterogamy **12.** twice married (legally)
digest ... **4.** code **5.** brief **6.** abrégé, codify **7.** epitome, Pandect **8.** abstract, classify, synopsis **10.** assimilate, compendium
digestion ... **6.** pepsis **8.** eupepsia **9.** dyspepsia, ingestion **10.** absorption **12.** alimentation, assimilation

digestive secretions ... **4.** bile, gall **6.** pepsin, rennin **7.** chalone, gastric, glucase, hormone, maltase **8.** salivary, thyroxin **9.** endocrine **10.** intestinal, pancreatic
digestive tract ... **7.** enteron **15.** alimentary canal
digger ... **3.** loy, pal **4.** plow, wasp **5.** spade **6.** Indian, sapper **7.** comrade, soldier **8.** Levelers **9.** excavator **12.** New Zealander
digit ... **3.** toe **4.** unit **5.** thumb **6.** finger, number (under 10) **7.** dewclaw, integer, measure
digits repeated ... **8.** repetend
digitus ... **6.** finger, tarsus **8.** dactylus
dignified ... **5.** grand, lofty, manly, sober, staid **6.** august, graced, sedate **7.** courtly, pompous, togated **8.** decorous, ennobled, imposing, majestic **9.** venerable **11.** ceremonious **12.** aristocratic
dignify ... **5.** exalt, grace, honor **7.** elevate, ennoble **9.** solemnize **11.** distinguish
dignitary ... **3.** don **4.** rank **5.** mogul **6.** priest, sachem **7.** magnate, notable, prelate **9.** clergyman
dignity ... **4.** rank **5.** grace, honor **6.** status **7.** decorum, majesty **8.** nobility, prestige, standing **9.** loftiness, nobleness **10.** excellence, sedateness
diagraph ... **8.** ligature **9.** diphthong
digress ... **4.** veer **5.** shift **6.** swerve, wander **7.** deviate **9.** turn aside **10.** transgress
digression ... **4.** loop **6.** ecbole **7.** circuit, episode **8.** excursus **9.** deviation, excursion, obliquity **10.** discussion
digressive ... **8.** rambling **9.** deviative, excursive, wandaring **10.** circuitous, discursive
dike, dyke ... **3.** bar, dig, gap **4.** bank, gulf, ha-ha, mole, pond, pool **5.** ditch, levee, mound **7.** barrier, channel **8.** causeway, estacade **9.** earthwork **10.** embankment **11.** watercourse **13.** fortification
diked land ... **6.** polder
dike rock ... **7.** odinite
dik-dik ... **8.** antelope
dilapidation ... **4.** ruin **5.** decay, waste **7.** breakup **9.** disrepair **10.** impairment **11.** dissolution **13.** decomposition **14.** disintegration
dilate ... **5.** bulge, swell, widen **6.** expand **7.** distend, enlarge, inflate **9.** expatiate
dilation ... **7.** ectasia, ectasis **8.** swelling **9.** expansion **10.** dilatation, distension
dilatory ... **3.** lax **4.** slow **5.** slack, tardy **6.** fabian, remiss **8.** backward, delaying, inactive, sluggish **10.** behindhand **13.** lackadaisical **15.** procrastinating
dilemma ... **4.** trap **5.** brike (obs), snare **8.** argument, quandary **10.** perplexity **11.** alternative, predicament
dilettante ... **7.** amateur, dabbler, devotee, esthete (aesthete)
diligence ... **4.** care, heed **6.** effort **7.** caution **8.** industry, sedulity **9.** assiduity, attention, constancy

10. stagecoach 11. application,
earnestness, painstaking
12. heedlessness, perseverance,
sedulousness 15. industriousness
diligent . . . 4. busy 6. active 7. operose
8. sedulous 9. assiduous, attentive,
laborious 11. industrious, persevering
dill, dill seed . . . 4. anet, herb 5. anise
(Bib) 6. fennel
dillydally . . . 3. lag 6. linger, loiter,
trifle 9. vacillate 12. shilly-shally
13. procrastinate
dilute . . . 3. cut 4. thin 6. debase, rarefy,
reduce, weaken 8. lengthen 9. attenuate
10. adulterate 12. denaturalize
diluted . . . 4. thin, weak 7. reduced,
thinned, watered 10. attenuated
dim . . . 4. dull, fade, pale 5. bleak,
blear, faint 6. darken 7. darkish,
dimness, eclipse, obscure 8. overcast
10. caliginous, indistinct, mysterious
dimension . . . 4. size 6. extent, height,
length 7. breadth 9. magnitude,
thickness 11. measurement
13. circumference
diminish . . . 3. ebb 4. bate, fade, pare,
ploy, wane 5. abase, abate, lower,
peter, taper 6. lessen, recede, reduce,
weaken 7. curtail, dwindle 8. decrease,
subtract 9. disparage
diminution . . . 5. abate, taper 7. litotes
8. decrease, lowering 9. decrement,
lessening, reduction 10. moderation
diminutive . . . 3. wee 4. runt, slip
5. minny, small 6. bantam, little,
peewee, petite 7. bendlet
diminutive suffix . . . 2. el, ie 3. ole, ule
4. ette
dimmer . . . 8. rheostat
din . . . 4. ding 5. clang, noise 6. clamor,
hubbub, racket, rattle, tumult, uproar
7. clatter, turmoil 9. commotion
diner . . . 5. eater
dingle . . . 4. dale, dell, glen, ring, vale
6. jingle, tingle, tinkle, valley 7. tremble
9. storm door
dining room . . . 4. hall 5. salon 6. spence
7. cenacle 8. mess hall 9. refectory
12. salle à manger
dining science . . . 10. aristology
dinosaur . . . 7. reptile 8. sauropod
9. Sauropoda 10. Diplodocus,
Morosaurus 11. Ornithopoda,
Stegosaurus 12. Brontosaurus,
Ceratosaurus, Megalosaurus,
Palaeosaurus 13. Atlantosaurus,
Tyrannosaurus
diocese . . . 3. see 6. parish 8. district,
province 9. bishopric 12. jurisdiction
Diocletian martyr (Rome) . . . 5. Agnes
Dionysian . . . 4. wild 8. frenzied, sensuous
9. orgiastic
Dionysus (pert to) . . .
birthplace . . 6. Thebes
father . . 4. Zeus
festival . . 8. Dionysia
god of (Gr) . . 4. wine (Bacchus, later)
10. vegetation
lover . . 6. Selene
mother . . 6. Semele
Dioscuri, The (Gr Myth) . . . 4. cult

5. twins (Castor and Pollux) 8. Castores
10. Polydeuces
dip . . . 3. dap, dib, sop 4. bail, dunk,
lade 5. merge, merse, pitch, rinse,
scoop, slope, souse 6. candle, plunge
7. baptize, immerse 9. declivity
10. pickpocket 11. hors d'oeuvre
diphthong, dipthong . . . 5. sound
7. digraph 8. ligature
diploma . . . 8. testamur 9. sheepskin
10. credential 11. certificate, testimonial
diplomacy . . . 4. tact 7. address, cunning
9. dexterity 10. artfulness, discretion
11. arbitration, diplomatism,
negotiation, savoir-faire
diplomat . . . 5. doyen (head), envoy
6. consul 7. attaché 8. emissary,
minister 10. ambassador, politician
15. chargé d'affaires, plenipotentiary
diplomatic . . . 6. crafty 7. cunning
8. consular 11. mediatorial
diplomatic corps, staff . . . 7. embassy
8. legation 17. corps diplomatique
dipsomania . . . 9. addiction, oenomania,
potomania 10. alcoholism 15. delirium
tremens
dipthong . . . see *diphthong*
dire . . . 3. bad 4. base, evil, rank, want
5. awful, fatal, needy 6. deadly, dismal,
funest, odious 7. baneful, doleful,
fearful, ghastly 8. dreadful, horrible,
terrible, ultimate 10. oppressive
12. inauspicious, overpowering
direct . . . 3. ain, bid, con 4. bend,
boss, head, lead, turn 5. order, pilot,
refer, steer, teach 6. govern, manage
7. avigate, command, conduct, marshal
8. instruct, straight 9. influence
direction . . . 3. way 4. airt, bent,
care, east, west 5. avast, belay,
north, route, south, trend 6. advice,
course 7. address, command, pointer
8. guidance 10. management
11. instruction 15. superintendence
directly . . . 4. soon 6. pronto 7. shortly
8. as soon as, promptly 9. forthwith,
instantly, presently 11. immediately
directly opposite . . . 9. antipodal,
diametric 10. antipodean
director . . . 4. boss 5. aimer (gunner)
6. conner, leader 7. manager, teacher
8. governor, producer
14. superintendent
director's cry . . . 3. Cut!
direful . . . 4. dire 6. woeful 8. dreadful,
terrible 10. calamitous
dirge . . . 4. keen, Mass, song 5. psalm,
rites 6. lament 7. requiem 8. coronach
dirigible . . . 4. Roma 5. blimp 7. balloon
10. Shenandoah 12. Graf Zeppelin
Dirigo . . . 5. I Lead 7. I Direct (Maine
motto)
dirk . . . 4. snee, stab 5. knife, sword
6. dagger
dirt . . . 3. mud 4. dust, foul, land, muck,
soil 5. earth, filth, grime, stain 6. gossip,
refuse 7. scandal, slander 9. obscenity
dirty . . . 4. foul, mean 5. dingy, foggy,
gusty, mucky, nasty 6. bemire, filthy,
soiled, stormy, untidy 7. clouded,
muddied, squalid, sullied

dis (pert to) . . .
Greek . . **5.** Pluto
Norse . . **5.** Freya **7.** spirits **9.** Valkyries **11.** superhumans
prefix . . **5.** twice **6.** double
Roman . . **3.** Dis **8.** Dis pater **12.** realm of Pluto
disable . . . **4.** maim **5.** unfit **6.** impair, weaken **7.** cripple **9.** disparage, hamstring **10.** disqualify **12.** incapacitate
disadvantage . . . **3.** out **4.** harm, hurt **6.** damage, injury **7.** penalty, trouble **8.** drawback, handicap **9.** detriment, liability, prejudice **12.** inexpedience **13.** inconvenience
disagreeable . . . **4.** edgy **5.** cross, nasty **7.** fulsome **8.** unsavory **9.** dissonant, invidious, irritable, offensive, repugnant **10.** ill-humored, unpleasant **11.** displeasing, ill-tempered, incongruous **13.** uncomfortable
disagreement . . . **5.** clash **7.** detente, discord, dispute, dissent, wrangle **8.** variance **9.** diversity **10.** contention, difference, dissension, unlikeness **11.** contrariety, controversy, discrepancy, incongruity **13.** nonconformity **16.** misunderstanding
disappear . . . **3.** die **4.** face, pass **5.** cease **6.** be lost, perish, vanish **7.** dwindle **8.** evanesce **9.** evaporate
disappoint . . . **4.** balk, bilk, fail, fall, foil **6.** baffle, thwart **7.** let down **9.** frustrate **10.** disenchant, dissatisfy **11.** disillusion
disappointment . . . **3.** rue **6.** defeat **7.** failure **10.** bafflement **11.** frustration **15.** dissatisfaction
disapprobation . . . **5.** odium **11.** disapproval **12.** condemnation **13.** disparagement
disapproval . . . **3.** boo **4.** hiss, veto **7.** censure, protest **9.** objection, rejection **12.** condemnation **14.** disapprobation
disarrange . . . **4.** muss **5.** upset **6.** foul up, jumble **7.** disturb **8.** disorder, unsettle **10.** discompose **11.** disorganize
disarray . . . **5.** strip **6.** unrobe **7.** despoil, undress, unkempt **8.** disorder **9.** confusion, ungarment **10.** disarrange, dishabille **12.** discomposure, dishevelment
disaster . . . **4.** evil, ruin **6.** mishap **8.** accident, calamity, casualty, fatality **9.** cataclysm, mischance **10.** misfortune **11.** catastrophe **12.** misadventure
disastrous . . . **4.** dire **7.** unlucky **8.** ill-fated **9.** ill-boding **10.** calamitous **11.** destructive, unfortunate **12.** unpropitious
disavow . . . **4.** deny **6.** abjure, disown, recant, refuse **7.** decline, retract **8.** disclaim, renounce **9.** disaffirm, repudiate
disbeliever . . . **5.** pagan **7.** atheist, heathen, heretic, infidel **8.** agnostic
disburse . . . **5.** spend **6.** defray, expend, pay out
disbursement . . . **5.** outgo **6.** outlay **7.** payment **8.** spending **11.** expenditure

disc . . . see also disk **3.** man **4.** dial, puck **5.** medal, plate, quoit, wheel **6.** circle, record **7.** discoid **8.** artifact **9.** gyroscope, medallion
discard . . . **4.** drip, shed **5.** scrap, sluff **6.** disuse, reject, remove **7.** abandon, cast off, dismiss, forsake **9.** eliminate, eradicate, throw away
discern . . . **3.** see, spy **4.** espy, know, read, view **5.** sight **6.** behold, descry, detect **7.** witness **8.** discover, perceive **10.** understand **11.** distinguish **12.** discriminate **13.** differentiate
discernible . . . **7.** evident, obvious, visible **8.** apparent, distinct, knowable, manifest **11.** conspicuous, perceptible **15.** distinguishable
discerning . . . **4.** sage **5.** acute, sharp **6.** astute, shrewd **9.** sagacious **14.** discriminating, discriminative
discernment . . . **4.** tact **5.** taste **6.** acumen **7.** insight **8.** sagacity **9.** sharpness **10.** astuteness, perception, shrewdness **12.** perspicacity **14.** discrimination
discharge . . . **2.** do **4.** bang, cass, fire, sack, shot **5.** blast, egest, eject, erupt, expel, exude, flash, salvo, shoot, speed **6.** acquit, bounce, defray, exempt, pay off, report, unload, volley **7.** dismiss, execute, explode, payment, quietus, release **8.** emission, eruption **9.** acquittal, dismissal, excretion, execution, explosion, fusillade **10.** accomplish, detonation, observance **11.** performance
disciple . . . **5.** chela, Judas, pupil **7.** apostle, convert, learner, scholar, student **8.** adherent, believer, follower
disciples (Bib) . . . **6.** twelve (72, Vulgate) **10.** Christians
disciplinarian . . . **7.** Puritan, teacher, trainer **8.** martinet
discipline . . . **4.** rule, whip **6.** govern, punish **7.** chasten, control, culture, educate, penance, scourge **8.** training **9.** education, restraint **10.** correction, punishment **11.** castigation, instruction, self-control **12.** chastisement **13.** regimentation
disclaim . . . **4.** deny **6.** abjure, cry out, disown, recant, refuse, reject **7.** disavow **8.** abnegate, disallow, renounce **9.** repudiate
disclose . . . **4.** bare, open, show, tell **5.** utter **6.** expose, impart, reveal, unmask, unveil **7.** divulge, uncloak, unclose **8.** discover, indicate
disclosure . . . **6.** exposé **8.** exposure **9.** discovery, revealing, unmasking, unveiling **10.** appearance, revealment, revelation
discolor . . . **4.** spot **5.** stain **6.** bruise **7.** distain (anc), tarnish **9.** ecchymose (by blood)
discolored . . . **4.** doty (by decay) **5.** faded **7.** altered **8.** ustulate **10.** variegated
discomfit . . . **4.** balk, rout **5.** upset **6.** baffle, defeat, dismay **7.** confuse **9.** embarrass, frustrate, overthrow **10.** disconcert
discomfiture . . . **4.** rout **6.** defeat, flurry

7. letdown 9. confusion, overthrow
10. bafflement 11. frustration
13. embarrassment, inconvenience
14. disappointment
discomfort . . . 4. pain 6. sorrow
7. misease 8. distress 9. annoyance
10. uneasiness 11. displeasure
13. embarrassment, inconvenience
discommode . . . 6. bother, molest,
put out 7. trouble 9. incommode
13. inconvenience
discompose . . . 4. fret 5. upset 6. excite,
flurry, rubble 7. agitate, confuse,
derange, disturb, fluster 8. unsettle
9. embarrass 10. disarrange, disconcert
disconcert . . . 5. abash, alarm 6. rattle,
thwart 7. confuse, disturb, fluster,
nonplus 8. bewilder 9. discomfit,
embarrass 10. disarrange
disconnect . . . 5. sever 6. detach, unyoke
7. disjoin 8. disunite, separate, uncouple
disconnected . . . 6. broken 8. detached,
rambling 9. desultory, scattered
10. disjointed, incoherent
11. unconnected
disconsolate . . . 3. sad 6. gloomy,
woeful 7. forlorn 8. desolate, hopeless
9. sorrowful 10. despairing, despondent,
melancholy 12. inconsolable
discontent . . . 6. misery, unrest
8. disquiet 10. unquietude, uneasiness
11. displeasure, unhappiness
14. discontentment 15. dissatisfaction
discontinue . . . 3. end 4. drop, quit, stop
5. cease 6. desist, give up 7. abandon,
refrain 8. intermit 9. terminate
discord . . . 3. din 5. noise 6. strife
7. dissent 8. disunity, variance
9. cacophony, Discordia, harshness
10. antagonism, contention, difference,
discordant, disharmony, dissension,
dissonance 11. altercation
12. disagreement
discord (goddess of) . . . 3. Ate 4. Eris
discordant . . . 5. harsh 7. grating, jarring
8. contrary, jangling 11. cacophonous,
disagreeing, incongruous, quarrelsome,
unmelodious 12. inconsistent,
inharmonious 14. irreconcilable
discordant (pert to) . . .
music . . 8. scordato
serenade . . 9. charivari 10. callithump
sound . . 6. jangle
discount . . . 3. cut 4. agio 6. rebate,
reduce 8. mark down 9. abatement,
allowance, reduction 10. concession,
percentage
discourage . . . 4. damp 5. check, daunt,
deter 6. deject, dismay, oppose
7. depress 8. dispirit, dissuade
10. dishearten
discourse . . . 4. talk, tell 5. essay,
paper (written), prose, speak, spiel
6. homily, lesson, screed, sermon
7. account, address, article, declaim,
discant, dissert, expound, lecture,
narrate, oration 8. converse, treatise
9. expatiate, narrative 10. exposition,
recitation 12. conversation, dissertation
discourteous . . . 4. rude 7. uncivil
8. impolite, insolent 9. ungallant

10. ungracious 13. disrespectful
discover . . . 3. see 4. espy, find 5. learn
6. descry, detect, expose 7. exhibit, find
out, uncover, unearth 9. apprehend,
ascertain
discoverer . . . 3. spy 5. scout
discoverer of . . .
America . . 4. Eric (the Red) 7. Vikings
8. Columbus (1492)
blood circulation . . 6. Harvey
electric light . . 6. Edison
North Pole . . 5. Peary (1909)
radium . . 5. Curie (Madame)
South Pole . . 8. Amundsen (1911)
telegraph . . 5. Morse (Samuel)
telephone . . 4. Bell (Alexander)
vaccination . . 6. Jenner
discovery, logic of . . . 8. heuretic
discredit . . . 5. doubt 7. asperse, falsify,
scandal 8. disgrace, dishonor, disprove,
distrust 9. disbelief, disparage,
disrepute, misgiving, suspicion
10. invalidate 11. discredence
discreet . . . 4. wary 5. civil 6. polite
7. careful, mindful, politic, prudent
8. cautious 9. judicious, selective
11. circumspect 12. noncommittal
13. discretionary
discrepancy . . . 8. variance 9. disaccord,
disparity, diversity 10. difference
11. contrariety 12. disagreement
13. inconsistency 15. incompatibility
discretion . . . 4. tact, will 6. option
7. caution, reserve 8. judgment,
prudence, wariness 11. disjunction
12. cautiousness, discreetness
13. discontinuity, judiciousness,
secretiveness 14. circumspection,
discrimination
discretionary . . . 7. politic, prudent
8. discreet 9. arbitrary, judicious,
voluntary 10. prudential 11. considerate
14. discriminating
discriminate . . . 6. divide, screen, secern
8. separate, set apart 11. distinguish
13. differentiate
discrimination . . . 5. taste 6. acumen,
option 9. prejudice 10. discretion
11. discernment, distinction,
penetration, segregation
discursive . . . 6. roving 7. cursory
9. desultory, diffusive, wandering
10. circuitous, digressive
discus . . . 4. disk 5. plate, quoit
discuss . . . 3. air, rap 4. moot 5. argue,
treat 6. confer, debate, parley
7. bargain, canvass, dispute, dissert,
mention 8. talk over 9. discourse,
thrash out
discus thrower . . . 10. discobolus
disdain . . . 5. pride, scorn 7. askance,
contemn, despise 8. contempt
9. arrogance 11. haughtiness
16. contemptuousness
disease . . . 6. malady 7. ailment, illness,
trouble 8. disorder, sickness 9. affection,
infirmity 10. affliction, disability
11. derangement
disease (of) . . .
animals (Afr) . . 5. nenta
apoplexy . . 4. esca

apples.. **7.** stippen **9.** bitter pit
blood.. **6.** anemia **8.** leukemia
(leukaemia, leucemia)
cattle.. **5.** hoose (hooze) **6.** nagana,
wheeze **7.** anthrax
chickens.. **3.** pip **4.** roup
diet.. **7.** rickets **8.** pellagra, rachitis
divers.. **5.** bends **7.** caisson
dog.. **5.** lyssa **6.** rabies **11.** hydrophobia
eye.. **6.** caligo **7.** pinkeye **8.** cataract,
glaucoma, trachoma **9.** amaurosis
14. conjunctivitis
fungus.. **6.** mildew **9.** elm blight
Oriental.. **8.** beriberi
painful.. **7.** lumbago **9.** arthritis
plant.. **4.** rust, smut **5.** ergot, scald
6. Panama (banana) **7.** erinose (grape)
potato, tomato.. **8.** dartrose
skin.. **5.** hives, psora **6.** eczema, herpes,
tetter **7.** scabies **8.** impetigo, shingles
9. psoriasis, urticaria **10.** erysipelas
stonecutter's.. **9.** silicosis
sugar cane.. **5.** sereh
disease (pert to)...
classification.. **8.** nosology
10. nosography
decline.. **9.** catabasis
determination of.. **9.** diagnosis
germ transfer.. **7.** vection
native to.. **7.** endemic
outlook.. **9.** prognosis
science of.. **8.** etiology, medicine
spread of.. **8.** epidemic
suffix.. **4.** itis, osis
treatment.. **7.** therapy **12.** kinesiatrics
disembark... **4.** land **6.** alight, debark
7. deplane, detrain, pile out (sl)
disembowel... **3.** gut **10.** eviscerate
disengage... **5.** clear **6.** detach, loosen
7. release **8.** liberate, unfasten
9. extricate **11.** disencumber,
disentangle **12.** disembarrass
disentangle... **4.** card, comb **5.** clear,
loose, ravel, solve **6.** evolve, sleave,
sleeve **7.** unravel, unsnare, untwine,
untwist **8.** simplify **9.** disengage,
extricate **10.** disinvolve, unscramble
disfavor... **7.** dislike **8.** distaste
9. detriment, disrepute **10.** alienation
11. disapproval, displeasure
14. discountenance
disfigure... **3.** mar **4.** scar **6.** deface,
deform, injure, mangle, uglify
7. blemish **8.** mutilate
disgorge... **4.** barf (sl), spew, vent
5. eject, eruct, erupt, expel, heave,
vomit **7.** exhaust **9.** discharge
10. relinquish **11.** regurgitate
disgrace... **5.** abase, odium, shame,
shend, sully **7.** attaint, degrade, distain,
obloquy, upbraid **8.** dishonor, ignominy,
reproach **9.** discredit, disesteem,
disrepute, humiliate **10.** opprobrium
11. abomination, humiliation
13. disparagement
disguise... **3.** mum (mumm) **4.** mask,
veil **5.** cloak, feign **6.** covert, masque
7. conceal, costume, falsify, pretend
9. dissemble, incognito, inebriate
10. camouflage, masquerade
11. dissimulate **12.** misrepresent

disgust... **6.** nausea **7.** offense, quarrel
8. aversion, loathing, nauseate
9. animosity, annoyance, antipathy,
revulsion **10.** abhorrence, repugnance
11. abomination
disgusting... **5.** gross, nasty **6.** filthy,
odious **9.** loathsome, obnoxious,
offensive, repellent, repulsive, revolting,
sickening
dish... **3.** jar, pot **4.** boat (gravy) **5.** cruse,
nappy, paten, plate **6.** patera, saucer,
tureen **7.** charger (anc), platter, ramekin
9. casserole
dish (food)... **5.** kibbe (kibbeh), pilaf,
pilau, salmi **6.** hachis, haslet, omelet,
potage, ragout **7.** bok choy, chowder,
falafel (felafel), pudding, soufflé **10.** egg
foo yong, shish kabob **11.** ratatouille
dishabille... **6.** kimono **7.** négligé,
undress **8.** bathrobe, negligee, peignoir
9. housecoat, nightgown
dishearten... **5.** amate (anc), appal,
daunt, deter, unman **6.** deject, dismay
7. depress, unnerve **8.** dispirit
10. disconcert, discourage
disheveled... **5.** tousy **6.** frowzy,
mussed, shaggy, untidy **7.** ruffled,
tousled, tumbled, unkempt **8.** deranged,
uncombed **10.** disarrayed, disordered
11. disarranged
dishonest... **4.** base **5.** false, lying
6. crafty, unjust **7.** corrupt, crooked,
knavish **8.** rascally, scheming
9. deceitful, truthless **10.** fraudulent,
mendacious, perfidious, untruthful
12. dishonorable
dishonor... **5.** shame **6.** defame,
infamy **7.** debauch, degrade, obloquy
8. disgrace, ignominy, reproach
9. desecrate, disrepute, improbity
10. disrespect, opprobrium
13. disparagement
dishonorable... **7.** ignoble **8.** infamous,
shameful **9.** dishonest **10.** inglorious
11. disesteemed, disgraceful
12. disreputable
disillusion... **10.** disquixote
disillusioned... **8.** thwarted
12. disappointed, disenchanted
disinclination... **7.** dislike **8.** aversion,
distaste **10.** reluctance, repugnance
12. disaffection **13.** indisposition
disinclined... **6.** averse **8.** indolent
9. reluctant, unwilling **10.** indisposed
disinfectant... **5.** Lysol **6.** cresol,
iodine, phenol **7.** alcohol **9.** germicide
10. antiseptic **12.** formaldehyde
disintegrate... **5.** decay, erode **7.** break
up, corrode, crumble, disband, resolve
8. dissolve **9.** decompose
11. disorganize
disinter... **5.** dig up **6.** exhume, reveal
disjoin... **4.** part, undo **5.** sever,
untie **6.** detach, sunder, unhook
7. unhitch **8.** disunite, separate,
unbutton **9.** disengage **10.** disconnect,
dissociate
disk, disc... **4.** puck **5.** medal, paten,
plate, quoit, wafer, wheel **6.** harrow,
record, sequin **7.** discoid, medalet
9. faceplate, gyroscope, medallion

dislike . . . 4. mind 5. odium 6. detest
8. aversion, distaste 9. antipathy,
disrelish 12. disaffection
dislike of children . . . 9. misopedia
dislike of home . . . 9. ecophobia
disloyal . . . 5. false 6. fickle, untrue
9. faithless 10. inconstant, perfidious,
unfaithful 11. treacherous
dismal . . . 3. sad, wan 4. dark 5. black,
bleak, drear, lurid 6. dreary, gloomy,
somber 7. doleful, joyless, Stygian,
unhappy, unlucky 8. dolorous, dreadful,
funereal, lonesome, mournful, overcast,
sinister 9. ill-omened, sorrowful
10. calamitous, depressing, lugubrious
11. pessimistic, unfortunate
dismantle . . . 4. raze, undo 5. strip
6. divest 7. deprive, destroy, disrobe,
uncloak 8. demolish 11. disassemble
dismay . . . 4. fear 5. alarm, daunt
6. appall, fright, terror 8. affright,
bewilder 9. dejection 10. depression,
disconcert 12. apprehension
13. consternation 14. discouragement
dismiss . . . 4. drip, fire 5. amand, amove,
eject, exile, remue 6. acquit, bounce,
depose, recall, refute, shelve 7. forgive,
release 8. relegate 9. discharge,
disregard 10. relinquish
dismount . . . 6. alight 7. descend,
unhorse, unmount 11. disassemble
disobedient . . . 7. forward, froward,
wayward 8. mutinous 10. rebellious,
refractory 11. intractable
12. contumacious
disorder . . . 3. tic 4. mess, riot 5. chaos,
deray, snarl 6. malady, tumult
7. ailment, anarchy, derange, illness,
misdeed 8. disarray, paranoia, sickness
9. confusion, craziness, distemper,
paranomia 10. discompose, revolution
11. lawlessness, misdemeanor
12. irregularity 13. indisposition
14. disarrangement 15. disorganization
disorderly . . . 3. bad 5. mussy, rowdy
6. unruly 7. chaotic, naughty, violent
8. confused, rowdyish, slipshod
9. irregular, offensive, turbulent
12. ungovernable, unmanageable
disorganization . . . 5. decay 7. anarchy,
breakup, split-up 8. disorder
10. separation 11. destruction,
dissolution 13. disbandonment
14. disarrangement, disintegration
disown . . . 4. deny 5. expel 6. recant,
reject 7. disavow 8. disclaim, renounce
9. disaffirm, repudiate 10. disinherit
disparage . . . 3. dis 4. slam, slur 5. decry,
lower 6. lessen, slight 7. degrade,
detract, run down 8. bad-mouth,
belittle, dishonor, minimize 9. discredit
10. depreciate, disapprove, disrespect,
undervalue
disparagement . . . 7. diasyrm 8. disgrace
9. indignity 10. detraction
12. depreciation
disparaging . . . 8. decaying
10. defamatory, pejorative
11. unfavorable
disparity . . . 3. gap 7. deficit 8. shortage
10. deficiency, difference, inequality

dispart . . . 4. open, rend, rive 5. break,
sever, split 6. cleave, divide
dispassionate . . . 4. cool, fair 6. serene
8. composed, moderate 9. collected,
impartial, temperate, unruffled
11. unemotional 12. unprejudiced
dispatch . . . 4. kill, mail, post, send,
slay 5. haste, speed 6. hasten
7. message 8. celerity, conclude,
expedite 9. diligence 10. accelerate,
accomplish, promptness
dispatch boat . . . 5. aviso 6. packet
Dis pater (Rom) . . . 3. god (underworld)
5. Pluto (Gr) 12. realm of Pluto
dispel . . . 6. vanish 7. scatter 8. disperse
9. dissipate
dispensation . . . 6. scheme 7. economy
9. exemption, remission 10. dispersion,
management, misericord (misericorde)
11. arrangement 12. distribution
13. apportionment 14. administration
dispense . . . 4. deal, dole, give, vend
6. effuse, excuse, exempt 7. absolve
8. disperse 9. apportion 10. administer
dispenser of alms . . . 7. almoner
disperse . . . 3. sow 4. rout 5. strew
6. branch, spread, vanish 7. diffuse,
refract, scatter 9. apportion, dissipate
10. distribute 11. disseminate
dispirit . . . 3. cow 4. damp 5. daunt
6. deject 7. depress 10. discourage,
dishearten, intimidate
displace . . . 6. depose, mislay, remove
8. misplace 9. discharge, dislocate,
supersede 10. substitute
display . . . 3. air 4. pomp, show,
wear 5. array 6. evince, flaunt,
parade, set out 7. exhibit, pageant,
splurge 8. emblazon 9. advertise
10. appearance 11. demonstrate,
ostentation 13. manifestation
display (pert to) . . .
case . . 10. show window
in public . . 5. stage
of emotion . . 10. enthusiasm
of force (distant) . . 9. telenergy
of temper . . 5. scene 9. spectacle
displease . . . 3. vex 4. miff, roil 5. anger,
annoy, pique 6. offend 7. provoke
8. irritate 10. dissatisfy
displeasure . . . 5. anger 7. disgust,
dislike, offense, trouble 8. disfavor,
distaste 10. resentment, uneasiness
11. indignation, unhappiness
14. disapprobation 15. dissatisfaction
dispose (of) . . . 3. set 4. give, mind, sell,
tend 5. order, place 6. adjust, assign,
bestow, settle 7. arrange, destroy,
discard, testate 8. give away, regulate
9. eliminate 10. distribute, relinquish
disposed . . . 5. prone 7. settled, willing
8. arranged, assigned, inclined
11. distributed
disposed (pert to) . . .
favorably . . 7. propend
to cling together . . 8. clannish
to doubt . . 9. skeptical
to please . . 11. complaisant
disposition . . . 3. use 4. bent, bias,
mood, turn 6. animus, giving, morale,
nature, temper 7. control 8. tendency

9. character 10. management,
settlement 11. arrangement,
elimination, temperament
12. organization 13. apportionment

dispossess . . . 5. eject, evict 6. divest,
refute 8. disseize

dispossessed . . . 6. bereft, ousted
7. ejected, evicted 8. deprived, divested

disproof . . . 6. answer, denial 8. negation,
rebuttal 10. refutation 11. confutation
12. invalidation

disprove . . . 5. belie, rebut 6. refute
7. confute 9. discredit 10. invalidate

disputation . . . 6. debate 7. polemic
8. argument 10. contention
11. controversy 12. conversation

disputatious . . . 7. eristic, polemic
11. contentious, quarrelsome
13. argumentative, controversial

dispute . . . 4. deny, feud, moot, spar
5. brawl, broil 6. bicker, debate, haggle,
higgle, naggle 7. contest, dissent,
protest, quarrel, wrangle 8. argument,
squabble 11. altercation, controversy

disqualify . . . 5. debar 9. indispose
10. invalidate 12. incapacitate

disquiet . . . 3. vix 4. fret 5. alarm 6. excite
7. agitate, concern, disturb 8. distress,
frighten 12. apprehension

disquisition . . . 5. essay 10. discussion
12. dissertation

disregard . . . 4. snub 6. ignore, slight
7. neglect 8. defiance 9. unconcern
11. inattention

disreputable . . . 3. low 4. base 5. seamy
7. raffish 8. shameful, unworthy
13. discreditable 15. persona non grata

disrespect . . . 7. affront 9. disesteem,
insolence 10. incivility 11. discourtesy

disrespectful . . . 7. uncivil 8. impudent,
insolent 10. irreverent 12. discourteous

disrupt . . . 4. part (forcibly), rend, tear
5. upset 6. thwart 11. disorganize

dissatisfaction . . . 8. vexation
10. discontent 11. displeasure,
unsatisfied

dissect . . . 3. cut 6. divide 7. analyze
8. separate 9. anatomize

disseize (law) . . . 4. oust 5. evict 6. depose
10. dispossess 11. expropriate

dissemble . . . 4. hide 5. cloak, feign
7. conceal 8. disguise 9. disregard
11. counterfeit

disseminate . . . 3. sow 6. effuse,
spread 7. publish, scatter 8. disperse
9. circulate, propagate

dissension . . . 7. discord 8. brouille,
friction 10. dissidence 12. disagreement

dissent . . . 3. nay 8. apostasy, disagree
10. separation 12. disagreement,
nonagreement 13. nonconformity
14. nonconcurrence

dissenter . . . 7. heretic, Sectary
8. apostate, recusant 9. protester
10. Protestant 13. nonconformist

dissertation . . . 5. essay, tract 6. debate,
thesis 7. article, lecture 8. treatise
9. discourse 10. discussion, exposition
12. disquisition

dissidence . . . 7. dissent 8. variance
9. cacophony 10. difference, dissension

12. disagreement

dissimilarity . . . 7. variety 9. disparity,
diversity 10. difference, unlikeness,
unsameness 13. dissimilation,
heterogeneity 17. heterogeneousness

dissipate . . . 5. spend, waste 6. dispel,
expend 7. consume, scatter, shatter
8. dispense, dissolve, squander
9. disappear

dissipation . . . 4. loss 9. decrement,
diffusion 10. dispersion, profligacy
11. consumption, prodigality
12. intemperance 13. disappearance,
dissoluteness 14. disintegration

dissolute . . . 3. lax 4. lewd, wild 5. loose
6. loosed, rakish, wanton, wicked
7. lawless, vicious 8. reckless, uncurbed
9. abandoned, debauched, unbridled
10. dissipated, licentious, profligate
11. demoralized 12. unrestrained

dissolve . . . 4. fuse, melt 5. solve
7. adjourn, liquefy 9. decompose,
disappear 11. disorganize
12. disintegrate

dissolved . . . 6. solute 7. soluble

dissonant . . . 5. harsh 7. grating, jarring
8. jangling 9. deviative, different,
differing 10. discordant, discrepant
11. disagreeing, unmelodious
12. inconsistent, inharmonious
13. contradictory

dissuade . . . 5. deter 6. advise, dehort,
divert 8. admonish 10. discourage,
disincline 11. expostulate

distaff side . . . 5. women 6. female

distain . . . 5. stain, tinge 6. define
7. tarnish 8. discolor

distance . . . 4. step, yond 5. depth,
range, space 6. offing 7. mileage,
reserve, yardage 8. coldness, outstrip
9. aloofness, antiquity, dimension
10. remoteness

distant . . . 3. far, tel, yon 4. afar, cold,
tele (pref) 5. aloof 6. remote, utmost,
yonder 7. foreign 8. ulterior

distaste . . . 7. disgust 8. aversion
9. disrelish 10. repugnance
11. displeasure 14. disinclination
15. dissatisfaction

distasteful . . . 7. hateful 8. nauseous,
unsavory 9. loathsome, offensive
10. disgusting, unpleasant
11. displeasing, unpalatable
12. disagreeable

distemper . . . 3. vex 4. soak 5. anger,
color, steep 6. dilute, malady, ruffle
7. ailment, disease, disturb 8. painting
(process), sickness 13. indisposition

distend . . . 4. grow 5. bulge, swell
6. dilate, expand, spread 7. enlarge,
inflate, stretch 8. lengthen

distended . . . 5. tumid 7. bloated, swollen
8. inflated, patulous, puffed up

distich . . . 7. couplet 8. two lines

distill, distil . . . 4. leak 6. decoct, infuse
7. extract, squeeze, trickle 8. vaporize

distilling device . . . 5. flask 6. retort
7. alembic 10. distillery

distinct . . . 4. fair 5. clear 7. audible,
obvious, precise, several 8. explicit,
manifest 9. different 10. individual

13. distinguished

distinction . . . **4.** rank **5.** honor **6.** repute
8. nobility **9.** clearness, greatness,
variation **10.** difference
14. discrimination **15.** differentiation

distinctive . . . **7.** typical **8.** peculiar
9. prominent **14.** characteristic,
discriminative

distinctive mark . . . **4.** sign **5.** badge
6. cachet, emblem, symbol

distinctive quality . . . **6.** genius, talent
9. specialty

distinguish . . . **6.** secern **7.** discern
8. perceive, separate **9.** recognize
12. discriminate **13.** differentiate

distinguished . . . **5.** great, noted
6. famous, marked **7.** defined, eminent,
honored, special **8.** laureate, renowned,
superior **9.** different, egregious,
prominent **10.** celebrated
11. conspicuous, illustrious
13. extraordinary **14.** characteristic

distort . . . **4.** skew, warp **5.** screw, twist,
wrest **6.** deform **7.** contort, falsify,
pervert **10.** camshackle **12.** misrepresent

distorted . . . **4.** awry **6.** rubato **7.** twisted

distortion . . . **5.** loxia **10.** perversion
12. malformation

distract . . . **5.** craze **6.** divert, harass,
madden, puzzle **7.** confuse, perplex
10. distraught

distracted . . . **3.** mad **7.** frantic **8.** distrait,
diverted, rambling **9.** disturbed
10. distraught **11.** overwrought

distraction . . . **6.** frenzy, tumult **7.** despair,
madness **8.** disorder **9.** agitation,
confusion, diversion **10.** dissension,
perplexity **11.** derangement,
disturbance, inattention **12.** perturbation

distrain . . . **5.** seize

distress . . . **3.** ail **4.** pain **5.** agony, annoy,
grief, worry **6.** danger, grieve, harrow,
misery **7.** anguish, anxiety, perplex,
poverty, trouble **8.** distrain, vexation
9. necessity **10.** affliction, discomfort

distress call . . . **3.** SOS

distribute . . . **3.** dot, sow **4.** deal, dole,
mete **5.** allot, share **6.** assign, assort,
divide, spread **7.** deal out, prorate,
scatter **8.** allocate, classify, dispense,
disperse **9.** apportion, broadcast
10. administer

distribution . . . **8.** disposal **9.** allotment
10. dispersion **11.** arrangement,
disposition **12.** dispensation
13. apportionment **14.** classification

distribution of favors . . . **9.** patronage
11. benefaction

distributor . . . **5.** agent **6.** agency
8. merchant **11.** broadcaster

district . . . **4.** pale, slum, ward **5.** realm
6. canton, domain, ghetto, region
7. circuit, demesne, quarter **8.** province
9. bailiwick, territory

District of Columbia . . . see *Washington,
DC*

distrust . . . **5.** doubt, qualm **8.** jealousy,
mistrust, wariness **9.** misgiving,
suspicion, treachery

disturb . . . **3.** vex **4.** riot, roil **5.** alarm,
annoy, rouse, roust, upset **6.** excite,

molest, ruffle **7.** agitate, derange,
fluster, perturb, trouble **8.** disorder,
distract **9.** interrupt **10.** discompose,
disconcert

disturbance . . . **5.** alarm, brawl **6.** hubbub,
rumpus, static, tumult, uproar
7. anxiety, clatter **8.** stramash
9. agitation, annoyance, commotion,
confusion **10.** excitement, turbulence
11. derangement **12.** perturbation

disturbed . . . **6.** uneasy **7.** annoyed,
excited, inquiet, unquiet **8.** agitated
10. bewildered **12.** disconcerted

disunion . . . **9.** severance **10.** alienation,
detachment, dissension, separation
11. disjunction **13.** disconnection

disunite . . . **3.** rip **4.** part **5.** sever, untie
6. divide, sunder, unteam, unyoke
7. discerp, disjoin, unravel **8.** alienate,
separate **9.** dismember

disuse . . . **6.** misuse, nonuse **7.** abandon,
discard **8.** disusage **9.** desuetude
11. antiquation, discontinue
12. obsolescence

ditch . . . **3.** sap **4.** dike, hole, moat,
rine **5.** canal, evade, fossa, fosse,
rhine **6.** escarp, furrow, relais, trench
7. abandon, acequia, channel

dithyramb . . . **3.** ode **4.** hymn **6.** poetry
7. epithet (of Dionysus)

ditty . . . **3.** lay **4.** poem, sing, song **5.** carol
6. saying **7.** canzone **8.** canticle

diurnal . . . **5.** daily **8.** everyday
9. quotidian

divan . . . **4.** sofa **5.** couch **6.** leewan,
settee **9.** davenport **12.** Chesterfield

diva's forte . . . **4.** aria

dive . . . **4.** swim **6.** plunge, resort, saloon
7. brothel, descend, descent, explore
8. submerge

divergence . . . **7.** theorem **9.** deviation,
obliquity **10.** difference, separation
12. disagreement, divarication

divers . . . **5.** cruel **6.** sundry **7.** several,
various **8.** perverse **9.** different

diver's disease . . . **5.** bends **7.** caisson

diverse . . . **6.** sundry, unlike **7.** several,
various **8.** distinct, separate **9.** different,
multiform

diver's gear . . . **8.** flippers
12. respirometer

diversify . . . **4.** vary **6.** change **7.** variate
9. variegate **10.** distribute
13. differentiate

diversion . . . **4.** game, play **5.** hobby,
sport **6.** change **7.** pastime **8.** apostasy
9. amusement **10.** deflection, recreation
11. distraction **13.** entertainment

diversity . . . **7.** variety **10.** difference
11. variegation **12.** multiformity

divert . . . **5.** amuse, avert, parry **7.** deflect,
delight **8.** dissuade, distract, recreate
9. entertain **10.** disincline

divest . . . **4.** doff, reft, tirl **5.** strip
6. debunk, depose **8.** unclothe
10. dispossess

divide . . . **3.** lot **4.** fork, part **5.** cleft,
halve, sever, share, slice, space, split
6. bisect, cleave, septum, sunder
7. prorate **8.** alienate, classify, separate
9. apportion, bifurcate, calculate,

dismember, partition, segregate, watershed **11.** distinguish
divide (pert to) . . .
areas (small) . . **8.** areolate
feet . . **4.** scan
four parts . . **4.** paly (Her) **7.** quarter
many parts . . **8.** fraction **9.** multisect
seven parts . . **9.** septimole
steps . . **8.** graduate
transversely . . **12.** cross-section
two parts . . **6.** bisect
divided . . . **4.** enté (Her), reft **5.** bifid, split, zoned **6.** halved, parted **7.** partial, partite, septate **8.** aerolate, bifidate, unjoined **9.** alienated, disunited **11.** distributed
dividend . . . **5.** bonus, share **6.** number **7.** payment
divination . . . **3.** art (magic) **4.** omen, sors **6.** augury, sortes **7.** presage **9.** intuition
divination by . . .
ashes (sacrificial) . . **11.** tephromancy
cards . . **10.** cartomancy
dead spirits . . **10.** necromancy
dreams . . **11.** oneiromancy
eggs . . **7.** oomancy
fig leaf . . **9.** sycomancy
figures . . **8.** geomancy
fire . . **9.** pyromancy
footprints . . **10.** ichnomancy
forehead . . **11.** metapomancy
fountains . . **9.** pegomancy
letters of a name . . **7.** nomancy **8.** onomancy
mice . . **8.** myomancy
moon . . **10.** seleomancy
neighing horse . . **10.** hippomancy
oracles . . **9.** theomancy
palmistry . . **10.** chiromancy
pebbles . . **9.** thrioboly
romantic medium . . **5.** daisy
salt . . **9.** halomancy
serpents . . **10.** ophiomancy
smoke (sacrificial) . . **10.** capromancy
stars . . **11.** sideromancy
straws (burning) . . **11.** sideromancy
sword . . **13.** machairomancy
verses . . **13.** rhapsodomancy
wands, rods . . **11.** rhabdomancy
water . . **10.** hydromancy
weather . . **9.** aeromancy
wild animals . . **11.** theriomancy
wine . . **9.** oenomancy
divine . . . **5.** divus, guess, pious **6.** priest, sacred, superb **7.** foresee, godlike, predict **8.** forebode, foretell, heavenly, minister, prophecy **9.** beautiful, celestial, clergyman, religious **10.** anticipate, superhuman, theologian **12.** supernatural
divine (pert to) . . .
being . . **4.** deva
breath . . **4.** soul
force . . **5.** deity, numen **6.** spirit
gift . . **8.** blessing
inspiration . . **8.** afflatus
messenger . . **7.** apostle
opinion . . **14.** theologoumenon
power . . **7.** entheos (obs)
utterance . . **8.** prophecy

wisdom . . **8.** theogamy
word . . **5.** grace, logos
work . . **7.** theurgy
divining rod . . . **4.** wand **6.** dowser **9.** doodlebug
divinity . . . **3.** God, Ler **4.** Deus, Lord **5.** Allah, deity, Khuda, Mazda **6.** Brahma, Christ **7.** Jehovah, Saviour, Taranis, Trinity **8.** Almighty
division . . . **4.** part, sect, unit **5.** share **6.** schism, sector **7.** faction, section **8.** cleavage, disunion, variance **9.** allotment, bisection, partition **10.** alienation, department, separation **11.** compartment, disjunction **12.** distribution **13.** apportionment, disconnection, dismemberment **14.** classification
division (pert to) . . .
center (Biol) . . **9.** centriole
city . . **4.** ward **5.** block **8.** precinct
French . . **6.** canton **7.** Commune **10.** department **14.** arrondissement
mankind . . **4.** race
poem . . **5.** canto, verse **6.** stanza
time . . **3.** Age, Eon (Aeon), Era **6.** Eogaea (Zool)
zone (earth) . . **6.** frigid, torrid, tropic **9.** temperate
divorce, Mohammedan law . . . **5.** talak
divot . . . **3.** sod **4.** clod, turf
divulge . . . **4.** tell **6.** expose, impart, reveal **7.** confide, publish, uncover **8.** disclose, discover, proclaim **11.** communicate
Dixie, Dixieland . . . **4.** song **6.** utopia **7.** Sunbelt **8.** The South (US)
dizziness . . . **5.** whirl **7.** vertigo **9.** giddiness **10.** fickleness
dizzy . . . **5.** crazy, giddy, tipsy **6.** fickle, stupid **7.** foolish **8.** confused, swimming, unsteady **9.** delirious **10.** capricious **11.** vertiginous
Djibouti, east Africa . . .
city . . **5.** Obock **6.** Dikkil
gulf . . **4.** Aden
do . . . **2.** ut (Mus) **3.** act, pay **4.** dost, fare, make, suit, work **5.** avoid, cause, cheat, exert, serve, solve **6.** answer, effect, finish **7.** achieve, deceive, execute, perform, produce, prosper, suffice **8.** transact **9.** discharge **10.** administer
docile . . . **4.** calm, tame **6.** gentle **7.** duteous **9.** compliant, teachable, tractable
dock . . . **4.** clip, pier, slip **5.** basin, jetty, plant, wharf **6.** cut off, deduct, hangar **7.** curtail, shorten **8.** waterway **9.** anchorage **12.** witness stand
docket . . . **4.** list, mark **6.** record, ticket **8.** calendar, schedule **11.** certificate
docking post . . . **7.** bollard
dock worker . . . **6.** loader **7.** laborer **9.** stevedore **12.** longshoreman
doctor . . . **3.** cut, fly (angling) **4.** dose **5.** spike, title, treat **6.** degree, dilute, healer, intern (interne) **7.** surgeon, teacher **9.** physician **10.** adulterate, veterinary **12.** psychiatrist
doctrine . . . **3.** ism, ist **4.** rule **5.** credo, creed, dogma, logic, maxim, tenet **6.** gospel **7.** article, opinion, precept

8. position **9.** principle
doctrine (pert to) ...
existence (Philos) .. **6.** henism
finality (Theol) .. **11.** eschatology
good .. **8.** agathism
inevitability .. **8.** fatalism
philosophy .. **10.** pragmatism
secrecy .. **6.** cabala **8.** esoteric
selfishness .. **6.** egoism
doctus ... **7.** learned
document ... **4.** deed, writ **5.** paper,
proof, scrip **6.** escrow **7.** archive
11. corroborate
document (pert to) ...
copy (true) .. **5.** Xerox **7.** estreat
8. syngraph **9.** duplicate, photostat
depository .. **8.** archives
file, report .. **7.** dossier
hamper .. **7.** hanaper
dodecade ... **5.** dozen **6.** twelve (series)
dodge ... **4.** duck, jouk, snub **5.** avoid,
cheat, elude, evade, parry, trick
6. escape, palter **7.** deceive **8.** artifice
9. expedient
dodger ... **7.** biscuit, shirker **8.** deceiver,
handbill
dodo ... **3.** moa **4.** bird (extinct)
doe ... **3.** tag, teg **4.** deer, hind
doer ... **5.** actor, agent, maker **6.** author,
factor, worker **7.** manager **8.** attorney,
executor, producer **9.** performer
doff ... **4.** shed, vail **5.** strip **6.** divest,
remove **7.** take off, undress
dog ... **3.** cur, pug **4.** foot, lyam
(lyme) **5.** canis, hound, pooch,
whelp **6.** canine, fallow, shadow,
wretch, yelper **7.** mongrel **9.** carnivore
13. constellation
dog (breed) ... **3.** pom **4.** chow, Dane
5. boxer, husky **6.** basset, beagle, collie,
lucern, nootka, poodle, Saluki, setter,
Sussex **7.** bulldog, griffon, mastiff,
pointer, Samoyed, Shih Tzu, spaniel,
terrier, whippet **8.** Airedale, Doberman,
Keeshong,Labrador,Malemute,Pekinese,
Sealyham, shepherd **9.** Chihuahua,
dachshund, Dalmatian, greyhound,
Pekingese, retriever, schnauzer, St
Bernard, wolfhound **10.** bloodhound,
Pomeranian, schipperke **11.** Skye terrier
12. gazelle hound **13.** Boston terrier
dog (pert to) ...
Buster Brown .. **4.** Tige
Cape (hunting) .. **8.** cynhyena
days .. **8.** canicule
F D R's .. **4.** Fala (Falla)
ferocious .. **7.** agoura
fictional .. **4.** Asta, Toby **6.** Lassie **9.** Rin
Tin Tin
heroic .. **5.** Balto
house .. **6.** kennel
howl .. **9.** ululation
like .. **6.** cynoid
mythical .. **7.** Cerebus
part .. **5.** flews **7.** dewclaw
short-eared (Her) .. **4.** alan (aland)
star .. **6.** Sirius **8.** Canicula
Victor records .. **6.** Nipper (His Master's
Voice)
wild .. **5.** dhole, dingo **6.** bandog, kolsun
8. cimarron

Doge's barge ... **9.** Bucentaur
dogfish ... **5.** shark **6.** burbot **9.** blackfish
10. nursehound
dogma ... **4.** code **5.** tenet **6.** belief,
dictum (pl dicta), ritual **7.** precept
8. doctrine **9.** Levitical, principle
dogmatic ... **7.** certain **8.** absolute,
positive **9.** assertive, canonical,
doctrinal, pragmatic **11.** dictatorial,
doctrinaire, magisterial, opinionated
dogmatism ... **10.** pragmatism
11. intolerance
dogwood ... **5.** osier **6.** cornel **7.** boxwood
do it again ... **5.** itero
dole ... **4.** alms, mete **5.** grief **6.** sorrow
8. pittance **9.** allotment **10.** distribute,
misfortune **12.** distribution
doleful ... **3.** sad **4.** dree **5.** drear
6. dismal, dreary, rueful, woeful
8. doloroso, dolorous, grievous,
jeremiad, mournful **10.** lugubrious,
melancholy
doll ... **3.** toy **4.** baby (toy), girl **6.** moppet,
puppet **9.** miniature, plaything
dolmen ... **8.** cromlech
dolphin ... **4.** fish, inia **5.** bouto **6.** dorado,
dugong, sea pig **8.** Cetacean, porpoise
9. goosebeak **10.** bottlenose
dolt ... **3.** ass, oaf **4.** clod, dope,
loon, lout, moke **5.** dunce, idiot
7. dullard, half-wit **8.** clodpate,
dumbbell, numskull **9.** blockhead, dumb
bunny **10.** ignoramous
domain ... **5.** realm **6.** empery, empire,
sphere **7.** country, demesne **8.** dominion
dome ... **4.** arch, head, roof (Astron)
5. spire, tower **6.** cupola, turret
Domesday, doomsday ... **4.** Book (Eng
Hist) **11.** Judgment Day **13.** Great
Domesday **14.** Little Domesday
17. Domesday of St Paul's
domestic ... **4.** tame **5.** domal **7.** servant
9. enchorial, home-grown, intestine
(not foreign)
domestic establishment ... **6.** ménage
9. household
domicile ... **5.** abode, house **7.** habitat
8. dwelling **9.** residence **10.** habitation
dominant ... **5.** chief, chord **6.** ruling
7. regnant, supreme **8.** superior
9. ascendant, governing, imperious,
paramount, principal **10.** pre-eminent,
prevailing **11.** influential, outweighing,
overtopping **12.** preponderant
13. authoritative, overbalancing
dominate ... **4.** boss, rule, sway **5.** reign
6. govern **7.** command, control, overtop,
possess **11.** predominate
domineering ... **6.** lordly **7.** haughty
8. arrogant, blustery **9.** imperious,
masterful **10.** oppressive
11. overbearing
Dominican Republic ...
capital .. **12.** Santo Domingo
city .. **14.** Ciudad Trujillo
discoverer .. **8.** Columbus
island site .. **10.** Hispaniola
oldest city (W Hem) .. **12.** Santo Domingo
(1496)
dominion ... **4.** rule, sway **5.** realm
6. empery, empire, sphere **7.** control

9. authority, hierarchy (celestial)
12. jurisdiction

domino . . . 3. pip (spot) 4. game (in pl), hood, mask 5. amice, cloak, ivory 7. costume

dominoes, galloping . . . 7. ivories

donate . . . 3. tip 4. give 6. bestow 7. present

done . . . 4. fini 5. baked, ended, finis 6. agreed, cooked 7. through 8. finished, tired out 9. completed, concluded, exhausted

done (pert to) . . .
by stealth . . 13. surreptitious
by word of mouth . . 5. parol
for pay . . 9. mercenary
with effort . . 5. labor

Don Juan's lover . . . 6. Haidee

donkey . . . 3. ass 4. moke 5. burro, neddy 6. onager

donna . . . 4. Dona, lady, wife 5. madam, woman 8. mistress

Don Quixote's steed . . . 9. Rosinante

doom . . . 3. fey, lot 4. fate, ruin 5. death 7. condemn, destine, destiny 8. sentence 11. destruction

doomed . . . 3. fey 5. death, fated, goner 9. sentenced

doomsayer . . . 9. Cassandra

doomsday . . . 8. Ragnarok 11. Judgment Day (see *Domesday)*

door . . . 4. gate 6. portal 7. doorway, opening, passage, postern 11. entranceway 12. porte-cochere

doorframe . . . 3. dar 4. jamb, rail, sash, sill 5. janua, panel, stile 6. lintel 9. threshold

doorkeeper . . . 4. hasp 5. tiler 6. porter 7. durwaum, ostiary 8. chokidar 9. concierge

dope . . . 3. hop, LSD 4. hemp 6. mescal, opiate, peyoti (peyote) 7. fathead 8. narcotic 9. marijuana

Dorian Festival (Sparta) . . . 6. carnea (carneia)

Dorian magistrates . . . 6. ephors

Doric Order (Gr Arch) . . .
capital . . 6. abacus
frieze fillet . . 6. taenia
frieze space . . 6. metope
history . . 6. oldest 8. simplest

dormant . . . 5. inert 6. asleep, latent, torpid 7. resting 8. inactive, sleeping 9. quiescent

dormer window . . . 5. oriel 6. gablet 7. dormant (obs), lucarne

dormeuse . . . 5. couch 8. carriage (sleeping), nightcap

dormouse . . . 4. Glis, loir 5. lerot 6. rodent

dorsal (pert to) . . .
back . . 5. notal, notum 6. dorsum, lumbar, neural, tergal, tergum
column . . 6. spinal

dose . . . 5. bolus, draft, treat 6. potion 7. portion

Dos Passos trilogy . . . 3. USA

dot . . . 3. jot 4. clot, code, lump 5. dowry, fleck, point, speck, telia (fungus) 6. period 7. stipple

dote . . . 3. rot 5. decay, dowry 6. babble, dotage, dotard, drivel, stupor 7. portion

(marriage) 8. imbecile

dotted . . . 5. pinto 7. piebald, specked, studded 8. stippled 9. sprinkled 11. diversified

dotty . . . 5. crazy 6. feeble, senile

Douay Bible . . . 4. Aree

double . . . 2. di (pref) 4. dual, fold, twin 5. duple, plait, twice 6. binary, binate, duplex, folded 7. twofold 8. artifice, two-faced 9. deceitful, duplicate, insincere, intensify 11. counterpart

double (pert to) . . .
bars (Her) . . 5. gemel
cross . . 7. deceive, two-time
dagger . . 6. diesis
edged . . 9. ancipital
ghost (live person) . . 11. counterpart 12. Doppelgänger, doubleganger
meaning . . 9. equivocal

doubt . . . 5. demur, waver 8. hesitate, mistrust, question 9. misgiving, suspicion 10. Pyrrhonism, skepticism 11. uncertainty

doubter . . . 5. cynic 6. Humist 7. skeptic 10. Pyrrhonist

doubtful . . . 7. dubious 8. wavering 9. ambiguous, equivocal, uncertain, undecided 10. hesitating, improbable, precarious 11. distrustful, vacillating 12. questionable, unbelievable, undetermined 13. problematical

doubtful authority . . . 6. mythic, unreal 10. apocryphal

dough . . . 4. cash, mash 5. money, paste 6. leaven, noodle

doughnut . . . 6. sinker 7. cruller, simball 9. friedcake

dour . . . 5. harsh, stern 6. gloomy, severe 9. obstinate 10. inflexible

dove . . . 3. nun 4. blue (color), Inca 5. color 6. culver, pigeon 7. Columba, tumbler 8. pacifist, peacenik

Dove, the . . . 6. symbol (Relig) 10. Holy Spirit

dovefoot . . . 8. geranium (wild)

dovekey, dovekie . . . 3. auk 4. Alle 6. rotche 9. guillemot

dowdy . . . 3. pie (deep-dish) 6. pastry, shabby, untidy 7. pudding 8. slovenly 10. slatternly

dowel . . . 3. pin 4. coak 5. tenon 6. fasten, pintle

dower . . . 3. dos 5. dowry, endow, grant 6. dotate 7. bequest 8. dotation, jointure

down . . . 2. de (pref) 3. nap 4. fuzz, hair 5. adown, below, floor 7. descent 8. softness

downcast . . . 3. low, sad 7. lowered 8. dejected 9. bowed down, depressed 10. despondent, dispirited 11. discouraged, downhearted

downright . . . 4. flat 5. blunt, plain, sheer, stark, utter 6. arrant, candid 8. positive, thorough 10. absolutely, forthright 11. unqualified 13. unceremonious

down source . . . 5. eider

downy . . . 4. soft, wary 5. nappy, pilar, quiet 6. placid 7. villous 8. feathery 10. flocculent, lanuginose, lanuginous

dowry . . . 3. dos, dot 4. gift 5. dower, sulka 6. talent 9. endowment

dowser's tool . . . **4.** wand **6.** willow
Doxology . . . **4.** hymn **6.** praise **7.** Kaddish
doze . . . **3.** nap, nod **5.** sleep **6.** catnap, drowse, snooze **7.** stupefy (obs)
Dracula (pert to) . . .
actor . . **6.** Lugosi (Bela)
author . . **6.** Stoker (Bram)
film (Murnau) . . **9.** Nosferatu
homeland . . **12.** Transylvania
inspiration for . . **4.** Vlad (Tepes) **14.** Vlad the Impaler
draft, draught . . . **3.** map, nip **4.** dose, dram, draw, plan, pull, swig **5.** drink, epure **7.** current, diagram, drawing, outline **8.** protocol, recruits, traction **9.** conscript **10.** money order
drag . . . **3.** lag, lug, tow, tug **4.** clog, draw, hale, haul, pull, sing, tump **5.** drawl, scent (hunt), smoke, trail **6.** drogue, harrow **7.** grapnel **8.** dragrope, linger on, obstacle **9.** conveyance
dragoman . . . **11.** interpreter (official)
dragon . . . **4.** lung **5.** drake, Rahab (Bib) **6.** animal, duenna, lizard, musket (anc), pigeon **7.** dragoon, monster (Her), serpent **10.** earthdrake **14.** Dragon of Komodo
drain . . . **3.** gaw, sap **4.** lade, loss, sink, sump **5.** ditch, dreen, empty, rhine, sewer, siver **6.** filter, trench **7.** acequia, alberca, channel, consume, exhaust, outflow **11.** watercourse
dram . . . **3.** nip **4.** mite, slug **5.** draft, drink **6.** drachm **8.** potation **11.** indifferent
drama (pert to) . . .
beginning . . **8.** Dyonysia (anc)
form . . **4.** play **5.** opera **6.** comedy **7.** tragedy **10.** peripeteia **11.** composition
parts . . **8.** epitasis, protasis **12.** introduction
scenery . . **7.** diorama
dramatic . . . **4.** wild **5.** stagy, vivid, vocal **6.** poetic, scenic **8.** thespian **10.** histrionic, theatrical **11.** pretentious, spectacular **12.** melodramatic
dramatic piece . . . **4.** skit
drastic . . . **5.** stern **6.** fierce, severe **7.** intense, radical **8.** rigorous
draught . . . see *draft*
Dravidian (pert to) . . .
country (anc) . . **5.** India
ghost . . **4.** bhut
language . . **5.** Tamil **8.** Kanarese **12.** Dravido-Munda
native . . **5.** Croat **8.** Croatian
people . . **4.** Nair **6.** Slavic
soldier . . **8.** Croatian
draw . . . **3.** lug, tie, tow, tug **4.** drag, etch, haul, limn, lure, plot, pull, tole **5.** draft, smoke **6.** allure, arroyo, convey, entice **7.** attract, conduct, extract, lottery **9.** delineate **10.** attraction
draw (pert to) . . .
away . . **6.** abduce, divert **7.** detract
close . . **4.** loom, near **5.** hover **8.** approach
forth . . **5.** educe **6.** elicit, ferret **7.** extract
off . . **6.** siphon **7.** extract **8.** abstract, withdraw
through an eye . . **4.** rove

together . . **4.** coul, frap, lace, rake **8.** assemble
drawback . . . **5.** fault, wince **6.** defect, resile, retire **8.** obstacle **9.** objection **12.** disadvantage
drawing . . . **3.** art **5.** draft **7.** diagram, hauling, picture, pulling **8.** doodling **9.** animation **10.** attracting, extracting
drawing back . . . **9.** retrahent
drawing room . . . **6.** parlor, saloon
drayage . . . **6.** charge **7.** cartage, haulage **8.** truckage **14.** transportation
dread . . . **3.** awe **4.** fear **5.** timor **6.** dismay, horror, terror **7.** anxiety **8.** affright, disquiet **9.** reverence **12.** apprehension
dreadful . . . **4.** dire **6.** horrid **7.** awesome, fearful, hideous **8.** horrible, terrible, terrific **9.** frightful **10.** formidable, outrageous
dreadnaught, dreadnought . . . **5.** cloth **7.** garment **8.** fearless **10.** battleship, fearnought
dream . . . **4.** muse, rêve **5.** fancy **6.** bubble, vision **7.** imagine, reverie, romance, suppose **8.** illusion, stargaze **11.** contemplate
dream (pert to) . . .
interpretation . . **10.** oneirology
interpreter . . **12.** oneirocritic
tranquility . . **3.** kef (keef) **7.** reverie
dreamer . . . **4.** seer **7.** fantast **8.** idealist, puffbird **9.** visionary **11.** romanticist **13.** castle-builder
dreamy . . . **3.** kef (keef) **6.** poetic **7.** languid **8.** soothing **9.** visionary **11.** imaginative
dreary . . . **3.** sad **4.** dull, gray **5.** bleak, ourie **6.** dismal, elenge, gloomy, remote **7.** doleful, tedious **9.** cheerless **10.** depressing, foreboding, melancholy, monotonous **11.** comfortless
dredge . . . **4.** tong (for oysters) **5.** scoop **6.** burrow, deepen, grains, tunnel **8.** excavate
dregs . . . **4.** faex, lees, marc, silt **5.** draff, dross, magma **6.** refuse, scoria, sludge **7.** grounds, hogwash, residue **8.** riffraff, sediment **9.** settlings **10.** faex populi
drench . . . **4.** hose, soak **5.** douse, draft, imbue, purge, scour, souse **6.** potion **7.** immerse **8.** inundate, permeate, saturate, submerge
drenched . . . **4.** asop **5.** asoak **6.** doused, soaked **9.** saturated
dress . . . **3.** rig, tog **4.** deck, garb, gown, suit, trim **5.** getup, mufti, preen **6.** attire, clothe, enrobe, livery, toilet **7.** apparel, threads (sl) **8.** clothing, decorate, negligee **10.** habiliment **13.** mother hubbard
dress (pert to) . . .
flax . . **3.** ted
gaudily . . **5.** prank **7.** bedizen, spangle
leather . . **3.** taw, tew **5.** curry
of Mecca pilgrims . . **5.** ihram
riding . . **5.** chaps, habit **7.** hacking (jacket) **8.** jodhpurs **10.** chaparajos
stone . . **3.** dab, nig **5.** nidge
surgically . . **5.** dight, panse **7.** bandage **8.** ligature
up . . **4.** dude **5.** preen, primp **6.** spruce **8.** titivate

dressed loosely ... 8. discinct, ungirded
dressing ... 4. lint 5. sauce 7. bandage, pledget, raiment, reproof 8. attiring, scolding 9. condiment, neatsfoot (leather) 11. castigation
drew ... see *draw*
Dreyfus defender ... 4. Zola
dried ... 4. sere 5. wiped 6. seared, wasted 7. drained, parched, wizened 9. shriveled 10. dehydrated, desiccated, exsiccated
dried meat ... 7. biltong (biltongue), charqui 8. pemmican 10. jerked beef
dried tubers (orchids) ... 5. salep
drift ... 3. aim, sag 4. idle, pile, sail, soar, tide, tool 5. float, stray, tenor, trend 6. course, intent 7. deposit, impetus, meaning 8. crescent (sidewise), movement, seaweeds, tendency 9. deviation
drill ... 3. gad, row (seeds), tap 4. bore 5. auger, borer, train 6. baboon, pierce 7. machine 8. excavate, exercise, practice, rehearse 9. perforate
drilling ... 5. denim 7. nurture 8. training 11. inculcation
drink ... 3. ade, ale, bib, lap, nip, pop, rum, sip, tea, tot 4. flip, fram, grog, shot, slug, soda, soma, swig, tope 5. bouse, draft, julep, negus, posca, punch, quaff, skink, toast, toddy, water 6. caudle, coffee, imbibe, liquor, mai tai, mao-tai, posset, potion, ptisan, tipple 8. beverage, cocktail, highball, sillabub 9. decoction 10. intoxicant, mixed drink
drink (pert to) ...
ancient .. 5. morat
Arabian .. 4. boza
English .. 7. wassail 8. champers
fond of .. 8. bibulous
frozen .. 6. frappé
gods (of the) .. 6. nectar
honey .. 4. mead 5. morat
hot .. 5. salep, toddy 6. posset, saloop
Irish .. 10. shandygaff
Japanese .. 4. sake
mix .. 5. setup 8. vermouth 9. grenadine
rum .. 5. bumbo
Russian .. 5. vodka 6. kumiss (koumiss)
Spanish .. 7. tequila
together .. 9. symposium
tropical .. 7. sangria 8. sangaree
Turkish .. 4. raki 5. airan, arrak
drinking salutation ... 5. skoal, toast 6. prosit 7. propine, slainte
drinking vessel ... 3. mug 4. bowl, tass 5. cylix (anc), glass, gourd, jorum, mazer, stein 6. goblet, rhyton 7. tankard 8. schooner 10. Vaphio cups (gold)
drip ... 4. bore, drop, leak 5. droop 7. dribble, falling, trickle
drive ... 3. caa 4. herd, ride, slog, urge 5. force, guide, impel, pilot, press, rouse 6. attack, compel, energy, propel, thrust 7. crusade, operate 8. campaign 10. compulsion
drive (pert to) ...
away .. 4. rout 5. chase, exile, expel, repel 6. banish, dispel, rebuff 7. repulse

8. disperse
down .. 4. tamp
frantic .. 4. loco 6. madden 7. bedevil
obliquely .. 3. toe 5. slice
stakes .. 4. camp, park 6. locate, settle
drivel ... 4. dote 5. drool 6. slaver 7. slobber, twaddle 8. nonsense
driveler ... 4. fool 5. doter, idiot 6. dotard, prater 8. jabberer 9. blatherer, chatterer
driver ... 4. club (golf), jehu 6. drover, hammer, mahout, sarwan 7. speeder 8. coachman, engineer, motorist, operator, overseer, reinsman 9. propeller 10. charioteer, taskmaster
drizzle ... 4. mist, rain, smur 6. mizzle (misle)
droll ... 3. odd 4. zany 5. comic, merry, queer, witty 6. jester 7. amusing, buffoon, waggish 8. farcical, humorous 9. diverting, laughable, whimsical 10. ridiculous 11. merry-andrew
drollery ... 3. wit 4. jest 5. farce, humor 6. puppet 9. absurdity 10. buffoonery
dromedary ... 4. oont 5. camel (one-hump) 6. hageen 7. Camelus 8. Bactrian (two-hump)
drone ... 3. bee, dor, hum 4. male (bee) 5. idler, snail 6. loafer 7. bagpipe, humming, slacker 8. sluggard 9. non-worker, slow mover
drool ... 6. drivel, slaver 7. dribble, slabber, slobber
droop ... 3. lop, sag 4. flag, hang, loll, pine, sink, tire, wilt 6. nutate, slouch 7. decline, languish
drooping ... 4. alop, weak 5. loose 7. hanging, nodding, sinking 8. dejected, fatigued 11. languishing
drooping eyelids ... 6. ptosis
drop ... 4. bead, blob, dose, dram, drib, drip, fall, omit, shed, sink, slot, stop, tear 5. candy, dreep, droop, gutta, lower, minim, remit 6. letter, plunge 7. abandon, descent, distill (distil), earring, globule, pendant, trickle 8. ornament, trapdoor 9. declivity 10. relinquish
drop (pert to) ...
anchor .. 4. moor
by drop .. 7. guttate 9. guttation
measure .. 7. pipette 11. stactometer
nautical .. 5. hance
serene .. 9. amaurosis (Med)
vowel .. 5. elide
dropsy ... 5. edema 8. hydropsy, swelling
dross ... 4. lees, scum, slag 5. chaff, dregs, scobs, sprue, waste 6. refuse, scoria, sinter (iron)
drove ... 4. herd 5. crowd, drive, flock
drover ... 4. boat 6. dealer (cattle), driver 8. herdsman
drowse ... 3. nid, nod 4. doze 5. dover (Eng), sleep 6. snooze
drowsiness ... 7. languor 8. dullness, lethargy 9. lassitude, oscitance 10. narcolepsy, sleepiness 12. listlessness, sluggishness
drowsy ... 4. logy 6. sleepy 8. oscitant, soothing 9. somnolent, soporific
drudge ... 3. fag 4. grub, hack, mail,

plod, toil **5.** labor, slave **6.** toiler
7. plodder
drug . . . **4.** alum, dope, dull, numb
6. opiate **7.** stupefy **8.** narcotic, sedative
10. medication **11.** anesthetize
drug (pert to) . . .
action . . **7.** synergy
addict . . **6.** junkie
analgesic . . **6.** Anacin **7.** aspirin
10. acetanilid, phenacetin
anesthesia . . **3.** gas **5.** ether **8.** Novocain
10. chloroform
dangerous . . **11.** thalidomide
emetic . . **6.** ipecac **11.** ipecacuanha
eye . . **8.** atropine **10.** belladonna
forgetfulness . . **8.** nepenthe
narcotic . . **3.** hop, kif **4.** hemp **5.** bhang,
daggo, opium **6.** codein **7.** cocaine
9. marijuana
sedative . . **7.** bromide, Seconal, Veronal
8. barbital, Nembutal **11.** scopolamine
13. phenobarbital
drugget . . . **3.** mat, rug **5.** cloth
druggist . . . **8.** gallipot **10.** apothecary,
pharmacist
Druids (anc) . . . **5.** Order (Relig)
9. conjurers **12.** philosophers
drum . . . **4.** beat **5.** naker, snare, tabor,
tombe **6.** atabal, barrel, tambor
(tambour), tom-tom, tympan **7.** taboret,
timbrel, timpany **8.** cylinder, tympanum
(ear)
drum (pert to) . . .
call . . **4.** dian (diana) **6.** rappel, tattoo
8. rataplan
Indian . . **6.** nagara
nautical term . . **7.** capstan
Oriental . . **6.** tom-tom **7.** anacara
drumming fingers . . . **12.** devil's tattoo
drunkard . . . **3.** sot **4.** soak, wino
5. souse, toper **6.** addict, barfly, boozer
7. guzzler, tippler **9.** alcoholic, inebriate
11. dipsomaniac
dry . . . **3.** sec, ted **4.** arid, blot, brut,
dull, keen, seco, sere, wipe **5.** drain,
parch, vapid **6.** aerify, barren, jejune,
shrewd **7.** insipid, sterile, thirsty, xerotic
8. solidify, tiresome **9.** dehydrate,
fruitless, pointless **12.** unprofitable
13. uninteresting
dryad . . . **5.** deity, Napea, nymph, oread
duck . . . **3.** dip **4.** flee, fowl **5.** dodge,
douse **6.** plunge **7.** bob down
duck (breed) . . . **4.** Anas, coot, pato,
skua, smee, smew, teal **5.** Anser, eider,
scaup **6.** Aythya, Nyroca, Peking, scoter
7. mallard, Muscovy, pintail, pochard,
Spatula, widgeon **8.** Anatinae, bluebill,
shoveler (shoveller) **9.** harlequin,
merganser, sheldrake **10.** bufflehead,
canvasback, ring-necked
duck (pert to) . . .
baby . . **8.** duckling
class . . **3.** sea **5.** river **7.** Muscovy
crested . . **4.** smew
disabled . . **4.** lame
ducklike . . **5.** decoy **8.** duckbill
fabric . . **5.** cloth
flock (mallards) . . **4.** sord
flower . . **12.** lady's slipper
game . . **6.** tenter

hawk . . **6.** falcon **7.** harrier
litter . . **4.** team
male . . **5.** drake
ruddy . . **5.** noddy
duct . . . **3.** vas **4.** main, pipe, race, tube
5. canal **7.** channel, passage, trachea
8. aqueduct
ductile . . . **6.** docile, facile, pliant **7.** elastic,
plastic, tensile **8.** flexible, tractile,
yielding **9.** compliant, complying,
malleable, tractable **10.** manageable
dude . . . **3.** fop **5.** dandy **7.** coxcomb,
Johnnie **10.** tenderfoot
dudeen . . . **4.** pipe (tobacco)
due . . . **4.** debt, duty, just, meed, owed
5. owing **6.** charge, lawful **7.** exactly
8. adequate, directly, expected, rightful
9. appointed **10.** ascribable, sufficient
duel . . . **4.** tilt **5.** fence **6.** combat
7. contest **8.** conflict **9.** monomachy
12. satisfaction
duelist's aide . . . **6.** second
duet . . . **3.** duo **8.** duettino
dug . . . see *dig*
dugong . . . **7.** manatee, Sirenia **8.** Halicore
dugout . . . **4.** abri, cave, shed **5.** canoe
6. cavity **7.** pirogue, shelter
dulcet . . . **5.** sweet **6.** ariose **7.** tuneful
8. pleasant, soothing **9.** agreeable,
melodious **10.** harmonious
dulcimer . . . **6.** citole **7.** bagpipe, cembalo
8. psaltery **10.** instrument
dull . . . **3.** dim, dry, dun **4.** dead, drab,
gray, logy, poky **6.** barren, cloudy,
deaden, dismal, dreary, drowsy,
jejune, leaden, muffle, obtund, obtuse,
sleepy, somber, stupid **7.** doltish,
irksome, prosaic, tedious **8.** lifeless,
listless, overcast, sluggish, stagnant,
tiresome **9.** apathetic, inanimate,
saturnine, unfeeling **10.** insensible,
lackluster, melancholy, slow-witted
13. unimaginative
dull (pert to) . . .
finish . . **3.** mat (matte)
heavy . . **4.** logy **5.** leady **6.** stodgy
of cloth . . **6.** starry (Eng)
statement . . **9.** platitude
dullard . . . **3.** oaf **4.** dope, mope **5.** dunce
8. dumbbell, numskull **9.** dumb
bunny
dumb . . . **4.** mute **6.** aphony, silent,
stupid **7.** aphonia **8.** ignorant, taciturn
9. inanimate, irregular **10.** speechless
12. inarticulate
dumbfounded . . . **6.** amazed **7.** crabbed
9. staggered, surprised **10.** astonished,
bewildered **11.** overwhelmed
13. flabbergasted
dummy . . . **3.** pel **4.** copy, dolt, mort
(cards), sham **5.** model **6.** pontic, silent
9. imitation, mannequin, nonentity
10. figurehead, substitute **11.** counterfeit
dump . . . **3.** tip **4.** bump, game (Eng),
jail, sell, thud, tune **5.** empty,
hovel **6.** plunge, unload **7.** discard
10. rendezvous
dumpling . . . **7.** biscuit, gnocchi
10. appleberry
dupe . . . **3.** fox **4.** bilk, cull, tool
5. cheat, fraud, trick **6.** delude, sucker

7. cat's-paw, deceive, mislead

duplicate ... **4.** copy, game (cards), twin **6.** double, duplex **7.** estreat, mislead, replica, twofold **8.** likeness **9.** analogous, facsimile, identical, replicate **10.** transcript **11.** counterpart **12.** reproduction

duplicated ... **7.** dittoed **8.** repeated **10.** repetitive

duplicity ... **5.** fraud, guile **6.** deceit **7.** duality **9.** deception, duplexity, falsehood, treachery **13.** dissimulation, double-dealing

durable ... **4.** firm **5.** stout, tough **6.** staple **7.** lasting **8.** constant, enduring **9.** permanent **10.** continuing, persistent **11.** everlasting, substantial

duration ... **3.** age **4.** date, span, term, time **6.** period **8.** eternity, lifetime **10.** durability, permanence **11.** continuance

during ... **4.** time **5.** while **6.** whilst **7.** pending, through **10.** throughout

dusk ... **4.** dark **5.** dusky, gloom, slate (color) **8.** gloaming, twilight

dusky ... **3.** dim, sad **4.** dark, dusk **5.** murky, tawny, umbra **6.** gloomy, somber **7.** swarthy **8.** blackish **10.** melancholy

dust ... **4.** cash, coom (coomb), dirt, gold, pilm, soil **5.** briss, brush, chaff, clean, color, earth, money, stive, stour (dial), trash **6.** corpse, pollen, powder **7.** dryness, turmoil **9.** commotion, confusion, sweepings

dust (pert to) ...
flax .. **5.** pouce
flour .. **5.** stive
glacier .. **10.** kryokonite
reduce to .. **4.** mull
speck .. **4.** mote

Dutch (pert to) ... see also *Netherlands*
cheese .. **4.** Edam **7.** cottage
country .. **7.** Germany, Holland **11.** Netherlands
man .. **10.** Hogen-Mogen
news agency .. **5.** Aneta
painter .. **3.** Dou **4.** Hals **7.** van Gogh, van Eyck, Vermeer **8.** Mondrian, Ruisdael (Ruysdael) **9.** Rembrandt (van Rijn)
poet .. **7.** Da Costa
pottery .. **4.** delf (delft) **9.** delftware
river .. **3.** Eem **4.** Maas **5.** Meuse
scholar .. **7.** Erasmus (Humanist)
woman, wife .. **4.** frow
uncle .. **3.** eme (dial), oom

Dutch East Indies (Indonesia) ...
capital .. **7.** Batavia (former), Jakarta (Djakarta)
islands (3,000), largest .. **4.** Bali, Java **6.** Borneo (part) **7.** Celebes, Sumatra **8.** Malaysia (part) **9.** New Guinea (part)
renamed .. **9.** Indonesia

Dutch Guiana (Netherlands Antilles) ...
capital .. **10.** Paramaribo
mountain .. **10.** Tumuc Humac
renamed .. **7.** Surinam

dutiful ... **6.** devout, docile **7.** duteous **8.** obedient, reverent **9.** compliant

10. respectful, submissive **11.** deferential, reverential

duty ... **3.** job, tax **4.** care, onus, rite, task, toll **5.** chore, stint, trick **6.** devoir, dharma, excise, heriot (anc), impost, tariff **7.** payment, respect **9.** reverence **10.** imposition, obligation

duvet ... **9.** comforter

dwale ... **5.** sable (Her) **6.** opiate, potion **9.** soporific **10.** belladonna, nightshade

dwarf ... **3.** elf, urf **4.** grig, puny, runt **5.** crile, gnome, midge, pygmy (pigmy), small, stunt, troll **6.** droich, durgan, midget **7.** manikin, Pacolet, stunted **9.** dandiprat, micrander **10.** diminished, homunculus

dwarfish ... **6.** nanoid

dwarfishness ... **6.** nanism

Dwarfs, The Seven ... **3.** Doc **5.** Dopey, Happy **6.** Grumpy, Sleepy, Sneezy **7.** Bashful

dweeb ... **4.** nerd

dwell ... **4.** bide, harp, live, stay **5.** abide, delay, lodge, pause, tarry **6.** linger, remain, reside

dwelling ... **3.** hut **4.** flat **5.** abode, hotel, house, hovel **6.** duplex, shanty **7.** trailer **8.** abidance, domicile, tenement **9.** apartment, residence **10.** habitation

dwelling (pert to) ...
house (law) .. **8.** messuage
in field .. **10.** arvicoline
in groves .. **10.** nemoricole
of dead (Bab) .. **5.** Aralu
of souls (Polyn) .. **2.** Po
Oriental .. **3.** dar

dwindle ... **4.** melt, wane **5.** taper, waste **6.** lessen, shrink, sicken **8.** decrease, diminish **10.** degenerate

dyad ... **3.** two **4.** duad, pair **6.** couple, dyadic

Dyak, Dayak ... **6.** Borneo **7.** blowgun **8.** sumpiter **9.** aborigine

dye ... **4.** anil **5.** color, imbue, stain, tinge **7.** pigment **8.** colorant

dyeing method ... **5.** batik

dye stuff (pert to) ...
blue .. **4.** woad (wad, wade)
brown .. **5.** erika, sumac
indigo .. **4.** anil
mulberry .. **3.** aal
red .. **4.** chay **5.** aurin, eosin, henna **6.** isatin, madder, relbun **7.** annatto, magenta **8.** morindin **9.** rhodamine **10.** orseilline
violet .. **5.** murex **6.** archil
yellow .. **7.** xanthic **8.** luteolin, orpiment **10.** quercitron

dyke ... see *dike*

dynamic ... **4.** keen **5.** acute, vivid **6.** potent **7.** intense, kinetic **8.** forceful, forcible **9.** energetic, strenuous

dynamite inventor ... **5.** Nobel (1866)

dynamo (pert to) ...
attachment .. **10.** commutator
inventor .. **7.** Faraday
machine .. **9.** generator
part .. **5.** rotor **8.** armature

dynast ... **5.** ruler **6.** prince **8.** governor

dynasty . . . **4.** race **8.** dominion, lordship **10.** succession **11.** sovereignty
dynasty (pert to) . . .
Chinese . . **2.** Fo **3.** Han, Yin **4.** Isin, Ming, Sung, Tang
Spanish . . **6.** Ommiad
dysphoria . . . **7.** illness **8.** debility
dyvour . . . **6.** beggar **8.** bankrupt
dzeren . . . **8.** antelope

E

E . . . **7.** Epsilon (Gr)
Ea (Bab) . . . **3.** God **5.** deity
each . . . **3.** all, per **5.** alike, every **6.** apiece, singly **10.** separately **12.** individually **14.** distributively
eager . . . **3.** apt **4.** agog, avid, keen, yare **5.** agasp, sharp **6.** ardent, greedy, intent **7.** anxious, burning, excited, thirsty, willing, zealous **8.** desirous, spirited **9.** strenuous
eager beaver . . . **7.** hustler **8.** go-getter **10.** enthusiast
eagerness . . . **4.** élan, zeal **5.** ardor **6.** fervor **7.** avidity **8.** alacrity, cupidity, fervency **9.** alertness, readiness **10.** enthusiasm, impatience **13.** impetuousness
eagle . . . **4.** erne (ern), gier (Bib), seal **6.** bergut, eaglet, emblem **8.** standard (Rom) **13.** constellation (Milky Way)
eagle (pert to) . . .
American . . **4.** bald
brood . . **5.** aerie, eyrie
coin . . **4.** gold
European . . **3.** sea **5.** harpy **6.** golden **8.** imperial
genus . . **6.** Aquila
heraldry . . **8.** allerion
male . . **6.** tercil
sacred to Jupiter . . **9.** Jove's bird
S America . . **9.** eagle hawk
scout badge . . **5.** merit
Eagles . . . **14.** Fraternal Order
eagre (acker) . . . **4.** bore, flow, wave **5.** flood (tidal)
ear . . . **4.** head **5.** auris **7.** auricle, hearing **8.** orillion **9.** appendage, attention, orecchion (obs)
ear (pert to) . . .
anvil . . **5.** incus
bone . . **6.** stapes, tegman **7.** stirrup
canal . . **7.** cochlea **9.** labyrinth **10.** Eustachian, scala media
drum . . **8.** tympanum
external . . **6.** concha
grain . . **3.** epi **5.** spica **6.** mealie, rizzom (ressum)
hammer . . **7.** malleus
inflammation . . **6.** otitis
part . . **5.** helix, pinna **6.** tragus
science . . **7.** otology
shell . . **5.** ormer **7.** abalone
specialist . . **6.** aurist **9.** otologist
stone . . **7.** otolith
term . . **4.** otic **5.** aural **9.** auricular
wax . . **7.** cerumen
earache . . . **6.** otalgy **7.** otalgia

early . . . **4.** soon **7.** ancient, betimes, matinal **9.** premature, primitive **10.** beforehand, beforetime
earn . . . **3.** get, win **4.** gain **5.** ettle, merit **7.** acquire, deserve
earnest . . . **5.** arles (pledge), grave, sober, staid **6.** ardent, hearty, pledge, sedate, solemn **7.** handsel (money), serious, sincere, zealous **8.** resolute **9.** heartfelt, important **10.** thoughtful **12.** wholehearted
earnestly . . . **8.** solemnly **9.** intensely, zealously **10.** resolutely
earphone . . . **7.** trumpet (double) **8.** otoscope **9.** auriphone, topophone (double) **11.** stethescope
earring . . . **4.** hoop **6.** earbob, pendle **7.** earstud, pendant **9.** girandole (girandola)
earth . . . **3.** erd **4.** clay, clod, dirt, land, marl, muck, sand, soil, vale **5.** geest, loess, sloam, terra **6.** ground, planet, rideau **7.** topsoil **8.** alluvium
earth (pert to) . . .
center . . **10.** geocentric **12.** centrosphere
comb form . . **3.** geo
deformation . . **10.** epeirogeny
formed beneath . . **8.** hypogene, plutonic
formed by ores . . **9.** supergene
formed on surface . . **7.** epigene
god (Egypt) . . **3.** Geb (Keb)
goddess . . **4.** Erda, Gaea (Gaia), Tari **6.** Semele **7.** Demeter
produced by . . **6.** mortal **11.** terrigenous
satellite . . see *satellite*
volcanic . . **5.** trass
earthdrake . . . **6.** dragon
earthly . . . **7.** mundane, secular, terrene, worldly **8.** temporal **11.** terrestrial, universally, unspiritual **13.** materialistic
earthmover . . . **6.** digger **7.** backhoe, leveler **9.** bulldozer, excavator **11.** steam shovel
earth pig . . . **8.** aardvark
earthquake . . . **5.** quake, seism **7.** temblor **12.** diastrophism
earthstar . . . **6.** fungus **7.** Geaster
earthworm . . . **7.** annalid, dew worm, ipokoea **9.** Lumbricus
earthy . . . **3.** low **5.** gross, marly **6.** coarse **7.** worldly **8.** material **9.** unrefined
ease . . . **4.** calm, rest **5.** abate, allay, peace, quiet, relax **6.** pacify, relief, repose, soothe **7.** assuage, comfort, content, leisure, relieve, slacken **8.** facility, mitigate **9.** alleviate, disburden, enjoyment **10.** prosperity,

relaxation, solicitude **11.** informality, tranquilize **12.** tranquillity (tranquility)

easily . . . **4.** eath (eith) **6.** gently, slowly, softly **7.** readily **8.** smoothly **11.** comfortably, dexterously **12.** effortlessly

easily (pert to) . . .
broken . . **6.** shelly **7.** fragile, friable
frightened . . **8.** skittish
managed . . **6.** docile
moved . . **6.** mobile
offended . . **9.** sensitive
split . . **8.** schistic
understood . . **5.** lucid

east . . . **4.** Asia, dawn **6.** Levant, Orient **7.** sunrise **8.** eastward

East Africa . . .
hartebeest . . **4.** tora
house (mud) . . **5.** tembe
republic . . **5.** Kenya **7.** Somalia
island . . **8.** Zanzibar
people . . **3.** Luo **4.** Embu, Teso **5.** Bantu, Masai **6.** Kikuyu, Mau Mau **7.** Nilotes
vessel . . **4.** dhow

East India . . . see also *East Indian*
drink . . **4.** nipa
fan . . **6.** punkah (punka)
gateway (temple) . . **5.** toran (torana)
hat, helmet . . **5.** topee (topi)
money of account . . **4.** anna
mountain pass . . **4.** ghat (ghaut)
musical instrument . . **4.** vina **5.** ruana, saron
police station . . **5.** thana (tanna)
sailing vessel . . **5.** dhoni (doni) **7.** patamar
sugar, molasses . . **3.** gur **10.** massecuite
water vessel (brass) . . **4.** lota (lotah)

East Indian animal . . .
antelope . . **5.** bongo, takin **6.** impala, nilgai **8.** axis deer
cattle . . **4.** gaur, zebu **5.** gayal, tsine **7.** banteng
civet . . **6.** musang **10.** paradoxure
goat (wild) . . **4.** tahr **7.** markhor
lemurlike . . **7.** tarsier
raccoonlike . . **3.** wah **5.** panda
rat . . **9.** bandicoot
swine . . **8.** babirusa (babiroussa)

East Indian bird . . .
broadbill . . **4.** raya
bulbul . . **4.** kala
falcon . . **5.** besra
fruit pigeon . . **6.** treron
thrush . . **5.** shama
weaverbird . . **4.** baya

East Indian people . . .
boatswain . . **6.** serang
chief . . **6.** sirdar
groom . . **4.** syce
harem . . **6.** zenana
native sailor, soldier . . **5.** sepoy **6.** lascar
nurse . . **4.** amah, ayah
peasant . . **4.** ryot
poet . . **6.** Tagore
princess . . **4.** rani (ranee)
robber . . **6.** dacoit
title . . **4.** raja **5.** rajah, sahib
warrior . . **5.** singh

East Indian tree, plant . . .
bark . . **4.** lodh **5.** niepa

cedar . . **6.** deodar
cotton . . **5.** simal
fiber . . **4.** jute
fruit . . **3.** bel **6.** lanseh (lansa)
gum . . **4.** kino
herb . . **5.** tikor **6.** sesame **7.** roselle
mahogany . . **4.** toon
mulberry . . **4.** tapa
palm . . **3.** tal (fiber) **4.** nipa (thatch) **5.** sural (juice), toddy **7.** palmyra
pea . . **4.** dhak **5.** Butea
rubber . . **3.** saj
shade . . **6.** banyan
timber . . **3.** saj, sal (saul) **4.** poon, teak **5.** siris **6.** sissoo
walnut . . **6.** lebbek

east wind . . . **5.** Eurus

easy . . . **4.** calm, slow **5.** loose, suave **6.** cinchy, facile, gentle, simple **7.** natural **8.** gullible, informal, moderate, tranquil, unforced **9.** leisurely, unhurried **10.** manageable, nonchalant, unaffected **11.** comfortable, complaisant, unconcerned

easy-going . . . **4.** calm **11.** unflappable

easy job . . . **8.** sinecure

easy mark . . . **4.** dupe, gull **6.** sucker, victim **7.** cat's-paw

eat . . . **3.** sup **4.** dine, etch, feed, gnaw **5.** board, erode **6.** devour, ravage **7.** consume, corrode, destroy

eat (pert to) . . .
between meals . . **4.** nosh **5.** bever, snack
by rule . . **4.** diet
earth, clay . . **8.** geophagy **12.** chthonophagy
greedily . . **3.** lab **4.** glut **5.** gorge, scarf (down) **6.** gobble, pig out (sl) **7.** edacity **8.** voracity

eatable . . . **6.** edible **8.** esculent, gustable **10.** comestible

eater . . . **5.** diner **7.** epicure, glutton, gourmet **8.** gourmand

eating (pert to) . . .
alone . . **9.** monophagy
comb form . . **7.** phagous
decay . . **12.** saprophagous
fish . . **11.** piscivorous **13.** icthyophagous
flesh, raw . . **9.** omophagia
flesh-eating . . **9.** creophagy **10.** zoophagous **11.** carnivorous
man-eating . . **12.** androphagous **13.** anthropophagy
nuts . . **10.** nucivorous **11.** nuciphagous
plants, herbs . . **11.** herbivorous **12.** phytophagous
roots . . **12.** rhizophagous

savesdrop . . . **3.** bug **4.** drip **6.** harken, listen **7.** wiretap **10.** stillicide **14.** listen secretly

ebb . . . **3.** low **4.** neap, sink, tide, wane **5.** abate, decay **6.** recede, reflux, retire **7.** decline, dwindle, shallow, subside **8.** decrease

ebb and flow . . . **5.** surge **6.** aestus (estus) **11.** alternation

ebb tide . . . **8.** low water

ebullition . . . **7.** boiling, ferment **8.** bubbling **9.** agitation, commotion **12.** fermentation **13.** effervescence

eccentric ... 3. cam (shaft), odd 5. flaky, kinky 6. weirdo 7. erratic, strange 8. abnormal 9. erratical, irregular 13. nonconformist 15. idiosyncratical

eccentricity ... 6. oddity 9. queerness 10. aberration, erraticism 11. abnormality, peculiarity, strangeness 12. idiosyncrasy, irregularity 13. nonconformity 17. unconventionality

Ecclesiastes ... 8. Koheleth (Gr)

echidna ... 7. monster (Gr Myth) 8. anteater

echinoderm ... 8. starfish 9. sea urchin

echo ... 4. mute, stop (organ) 5. nymph (Myth), reply 6. repeat 7. imitate, resound, respond 8. resemble, response 9. duplicate 10. repetition 13. reverberation

echoism ... 12. onomatopoeia

Eciton ... 4. ants (legionary)

eclipse ... 5. cloud, sully 6. darken 7. obscure, surpass 10. extinguish

ecliptic term ... 5. lagna, orbit 6. circle 9. penumbral

ecology, oecology ... 4. sere 6. botany 7. biology 9. bionomics, sociology 10. bioecology

economical ... 5. canny, chary 6. frugal, saving 7. careful, thrifty 8. domestic 9. provident 12. parsimonious

economics terms ... 5. T-bill 7. bailout 8. bankable, cash flow, rollover 9. plutology 10. monetarism, production (wealth)

economize ... 4. save 5. skimp, stint 6. scrimp 7. husband, utilize 8. retrench

economy ... 4. care 6. saving, thrift 7. cutback 8. prudence 9. canniness, husbandry 10. providence

ecru ... 3. tan 5. beige

ecstasy ... 5. bliss 6. trance 7. emotion, rapture

ecstatic ... 4. rapt 7. rapture 9. rapturous, rhapsodic

ectad ... 7. outward

ecto (comb form) ... 7. outside, without 8. external

Ecuador (pert to) ...
capital .. 5. Quito
export .. 7. bananas
hat .. 6. Panama 8. 'Jipijapa'
island .. 9. Galapagos
mountain .. 5. Andes
reptile .. 6. iguana 8. tortoise
volcano .. 10. Chimborazo

ecumenical ... 7. general, liberal 8. catholic, tolerant 9. universal, world-wide 12. cosmopolitan

eczema ... 6. herpes, tetter 8. eruption 9. salt rheum

edacity ... 5. greed 7. avarice 8. appetite, gulosity, voracity 10. greediness

eddy ... 4. bore, gulf 5. gurge, surge, swirl, whirl 6. vortex 7. current, wreathe 9. whirlpool

Edentate (Zool) ... 6. sloths 7. mammals 9. aardvarks, anteaters 10. armadillos

edge ... 3. hem, jag, lip, rim 4. brim, brow, side 5. arris, brink, crest, marge, sharp, sidle (to), splay, verge 6. border, flange,

labrum, margin 7. ambitus, selvage 8. acrimony, pungency, selvedge 9. advantage, sharpness 10. escarpment

edged ... 5. erose 7. crenate 8. bordered, invected (Her)

edging ... 3. hem 4. lace, welt 5. frill, ruche 6. border, fringe, ruffle 7. binding, bordure (Her), flounce, tatting

edgy ... 5. sharp 7. angular, nervous 8. critical, snappish 9. excitable, impatient 13. sharp-cornered

edict ... 3. act, ban 4. Bull (Pope's), fiat 5. arret, dicta (pl), irade, order, ukase 6. assize, decree, dictum, firman 7. command, mandate 8. decretal 9. ordinance 12. proclamation

edification ... 8. learning 9. knowledge 11. improvement, instruction

edifice ... 5. house 6. church, palace, temple 7. Capitol 8. building 9. structure 10. tabernacle

edify ... 5. build, teach 7. educate, improve 8. instruct, organize 9. construct, enlighten, establish

Edinburgh ...
burgh .. 5. Leith
capital of .. 8. Scotland
county .. 10. Midlothian
famed street .. 9. Royal Mile
Gaelic name .. 7. Dun Edin (Dunedin)
nickname .. 16. Athens of the North
site .. 12. Firth of Forth

Edison's workplace ... 9. Menlo Park

edit ... 5. emend 6. direct, excise, redact, revise, reword 7. arrange, correct, prepare

edition ... 4. copy 5. issue 6. number 7. version

editions (Bib) ...
eight texts .. 7. octapla
four texts .. 8. tetrapla
six texts .. 7. hexapla
style and type .. 7. Elzevir (1583)

editor ... 7. analyst, newsman, reviser 8. arranger, redactor 9. annotator, gazetteer 10. journalist, supervisor 11. commentator 12. newspaperman

editor's word ... 4. dele, stet

Edom ... 5. Teman (Bib) 7. Idumaea

Edomite ... 4. Esau 5. Isaac, Jacob 8. Idumaean

educate ... 4. rear 5. teach, train 6. inform 7. develop 8. instruct 9. cultivate, enlighten 10. discipline 12. indoctrinate

educated ... 6. taught 7. erudite, learned, trained 8. cultured, informed, lettered, literate 11. enlightened

education ... 8. breeding, literacy, training 9. opsimathy (late in life), schooling 10. discipline

educe ... 4. draw 6. deduce, elicit, evolve, obtain, secure

eel (pert to) ...
colorful .. 5. moray 7. Muraena
genus .. 8. Anguilla 13. Leptocephalus
marine .. 5. elver 6. conger
mud .. 5. siren
sand .. 4. grig
young .. 5. elver

eellike ... 4. lant, ling 7. eelpout, lamprey 8. Ophidion 10. anguilloid

11. Lepidosiren
eels, fishing for ... 7. sniggle
eels, migration of ... 7. eelfare
eelworm ... 4. nema 8. Nematoda
9. roundworm 10. vinegar eel
eerie, eery ... 5. scary, timid, weird
6. gloomy, spooky 7. awesome,
fearful, uncanny 9. deathlike, unearthly
10. frightened
efface ... 5. erase 6. cancel, delete 7. blot
out, expunge 10. obliterate
effect ... 4. does 5. close, éclat,
force, mneme 6. mirage, obtain,
result 7. achieve, compass, conjure,
execute, fulfill, meaning, operate,
outcome, perform, reality, realize
8. complete 9. discharge, execution,
influence 10. accomplish, appearance,
consummate, impression
11. consequence, performance
effective ... 4. able 6. active, actual,
cogent 7. capable, telling 8. adequate,
eloquent, equipped, striking 9. brilliant,
competent, effectual, efficient,
operative, trenchant 11. efficacious,
influential
effects ... 5. goods, wares 8. movables,
property
effeminate ... 3. sop 5. sissy 6. female,
tender 7. cockney, epicene, womanly
8. feminine, womanish 9. Sybaritic
11. mollycoddle 12. overdelicate
13. overemotional
effervescent ... 5. fizzy 6. bubbly,
lively 7. boiling, hissing 8. bubbling,
mousseux 9. ebullient, sparkling
10. boisterous
effete ... 4. aged, idle 5. spent 6. barren
7. worn out 9. exhausted, fruitless
11. ineffectual
efficacious ... 4. able 5. valid 6. potent
9. effective, effectual, operative
11. influential
efficacy ... 4. dint 5. force, power
6. virtue 7. ability, potency 10. efficiency
efficiency ... 5. power, skill 7. ability,
utility 8. efficacy 10. capability,
competence 11. proficiency
12. productivity 13. effectiveness
15. efficaciousness
efficient ... 4. able 7. capable, operant
9. competent, effective, effectual,
operative 10. productive
12. businesslike
effigy ... 4. copy, icon 5. image 8. likeness
9. facsimile, jackstraw, semblance
11. resemblance
effluvium ... 4. aura, fume, odor
9. ectoplasm, emanation
efflux ... 3. end 6. expiry, runoff
7. outflow 8. effusion 9. effluence,
emanation
effodient ... 9. burrowing, fossorial
effort ... 3. try, tug 4. dint, jump, toil,
will, work 5. assay, burst, labor, nisus,
pains, trial 7. attempt, conatus,
trouble 8. endeavor, exertion, struggle
11. application
effrontery ... 5. brass 8. audacity,
boldness 9. arrogance, impudence,
sauciness 11. presumption

effulgence ... 5. aglow, glory 6. luster
8. radiance, rutilant, splendor
10. brightness, brilliance
effusive ... 7. gushing 9. exuberant,
rhapsodic 13. demonstrative
eft ... 4. evet, newt 6. lizard, triton
7. urodele 10. salamander
egest ... 4. emit, void 7. excrete
9. discharge, ejaculate, eliminate
egg ... 3. nit, ova (pl) 4. goad,
ovum, prod, urge 5. ovule 6. incite
9. instigate
egg (pert to) ...
bird's .. 7. chalaza (white of), treadle
(embryo)
case .. 6. ovisac
comb form .. 2. oo 3. ovi
part .. 7. latebra
shaped .. 4. ooid, oval 5. ovate, ovoid
6. ooidal 9. ovaliform
shell .. 5. shard 6. ovisac
undeveloped .. 5. addle
white .. 5. glair 7. albumen
yolk, yelk .. 7. liaison 8. lecithin
eggplant ... 9. melongena
eggs (pert to) ...
feeding on .. 9. ovivorous
fish .. 3. roe 5. berry, spawn
preserved .. 5. pidan
tester of .. 7. candler
two at a time .. 8. ditokous
egis, aegis ... 4. care 5. guard 6. shield,
symbol (anc) 7. backing, defense
8. advocacy, auspices, guidance,
tutelage 9. fosterage, patronage
10. protection 11. sponsorship
ego ... 3. man 4. self 5. atman (Hind)
6. psyche, spirit 7. conceit, jivatma
(Hind) 11. selfishness
egress ... 4. exit 5. issue 6. outlet
8. issuance 9. departure
egret ... 5. heron, plume 8. aigrette
Egypt, UAR ... see also *Egyptian*
capital .. 5. Cairo
Christian .. 4. Copt
city (ruined) .. 5. Luxor, Tanis 6. Karnak,
Thebes
dam .. 5. Aswan
desert .. 5. Dakla
gulf .. 4. Suez 5. Aqaba
king .. 6. Farouk (Faruk)
language (anc) .. 6. Coptic
lighthouse (anc) .. 6. Pharos
mother .. 3. Mut
peninsula .. 5. Sinai
philosopher .. 8. Plotinus
port .. 4. Said, Suez 10. Alexandria
president .. 5. Sadat 6. Nasser
queen .. 9. Cleopatra
river .. 4. Nile
ruler .. 5. pasha 6. caliph 7. khedive
ruler .. 7. Busiris (Myth), Pharaoh,
Ptolemy, Rameses
sea .. 3. Red 13. Mediterranean
Egyptian (pert to) ...
abode of dead .. 4. Aaru (fields of)
6. Amenti
antelope .. 7. bubalis
ape (sacred) .. 4. Aani
beetle .. 6. scarab
bird (crocodile) .. 6. sicsac

bird (sacred) . . **4.** Benu, ibis **7.** phoenix
bull . . **4.** apis
cobra . . **4.** haje
cross . . **3.** tau **4.** ankh (emblem of life)
   10. crux ansata
crown . . **4.** atef
dancing girl . . **4.** alma (alme, Almeh)
   7. ghawazi **8.** Baramika
dog . . **6.** saluki (gazelle hound)
headdress of ruler . . **6.** Uraeus
heaven . . **4.** Aaru
lizard . . **4.** adda **5.** skink
lute . . **5.** nable
paper . . **7.** papyrus
solar disk . . **4.** aten
soul . . **2.** Ba **4.** khet, sahu
stone (famed) . . **7.** Rosetta
symbol . . **3.** asp **6.** scarab (beetle)
tomb . . **6.** serdab (cell) **7.** mastaba
watchman . . **6.** ghafir (ghaffir)
writing . . **13.** hieroglyphics
Egyptian god of . . .
day . . **5.** Horus
earth . . **3.** Geb, Keb
life . . **4.** Ptah
pleasure . . **3.** Bes
primeval fluid . . **2.** Nu
sea . . **5.** Aegir
sun . . **2.** Ra **3.** Tem (Tum) **4.** Atmu
   5. Mentu (Ment) **7.** Khepera
   11. Harpocrates
supreme . . **4.** Amon (Amun) **6.** Amon-Re
underworld . . **6.** Osiris **7.** Hershef
unknown . . **2.** Ka
wisdom . . **5.** Thoth **6.** Dhouti
Egyptian goddess of . . .
arms . . **4.** Anta
fertility . . **4.** Isis
gods . . **4.** Sati
motherhood . . **4.** Apet
sea . . **3.** Ran
truth . . **4.** Maat
eidolon . . . **5.** image **7.** phantom **8.** illusion
   10. apparition
eight, eighth (pert to) . . .
day (every) . . **5.** octan
feast day . . **4.** utas
group . . **5.** octad, octet **6.** octave
   7. octette
heaven . . **5.** stars (fixed)
number . . **4.** ocho **6.** ogdoad
philosophy . . **8.** Diagrams
sided . . **9.** octagonal
tone, note . . **4.** unca **6.** quaver (8th)
   8. diatonic
eighteen inches . . . **5.** cubit
Eire . . . **4.** Erin **7.** Ireland
ejaculate . . . **4.** emit, oust, void **5.** blurt,
   eject, evict, expel **7.** exclaim **8.** dislodge
eject . . . **4.** emit, oust, spew, void **5.** evict,
   expel, spout, spurt **6.** banish **7.** extrude
   9. discharge, eliminate
ejection . . . **6.** ouster **8.** eviction
   9. expulsion **11.** elimination
eke (out) . . . **3.** add, imp, tab **4.** also, etch
   8. addition, appendix (dial), increase,
   piece out **10.** postscript
El . . . **3.** God **5.** deity
elaborate . . . **6.** ornate, refine **7.** develop,
   improve, perfect, studied **9.** embellish,
   perfected, superfine **11.** complicated,

high-wrought
Elam capital . . . **4.** Susa (anc)
élan . . . **4.** dash **5.** ardor **6.** spirit
   9. eagerness **10.** enthusiasm
elapse . . . **2.** go **3.** die, fly, run **4.** flit,
   pass, slip **5.** lapse **6.** expire
elastic . . . **6.** pliant, rubber **7.** buoyant,
   ductile, springy **8.** flexible, stretchy
   9. expansive, resilient **12.** recuperative
elasticity . . . **4.** give **6.** elater, spring
   7. pliancy, rebound **9.** ductility
   10. resilience
elated . . . **6.** jovial **7.** gleeful **8.** exultant,
   jubilant **9.** overjoyed
Elbe tributary . . . **4.** Eger, Iser
elbow . . . **5.** ancon, joint, nudge **6.** jostle
   8. chelidon (hollow of)
El Camino Real . . . **9.** Royal Road
   12. King's Highway (Pac Hwy)
elder . . . **3.** iva **4.** ainé, blue (color)
   5. berry, judge, ruler **6.** Mormon, senior
   7. ancient **8.** ancestor **10.** forefather
eldest . . . **5.** eigne **6.** oldest **8.** earliest
   9. firstborn
eldritch . . . **4.** wild **5.** eerie (eery), weird
   9. frightful
Eleatic philosopher . . . **4.** Zeno
   10. Parmenides
elect . . . **3.** ort **4.** name **5.** elite, choose,
   select **9.** designate
election . . . **6.** choice **11.** alternative
   13. determination **14.** discrimination
Electra (pert to) . . .
brother . . **7.** Orestes
father . . **9.** Agamemnon
mother . . **12.** Clytemnestra
electric (pert to) . . .
atom . . **8.** electron
condenser (anc) . . **9.** Leyden jar
conductor . . **6.** ohmage
current . . **2.** AC, DC **7.** circuit
force . . **4.** elod
generator . . **6.** dynamo
light . . **3.** arc **4.** neon **12.** incandescent
meter . . **7.** ammeter **9.** voltmeter,
   wattmeter
particle . . **3.** ion **6.** cation (kation)
power . . **7.** wattage
safety device . . **4.** fuse
unit . . **3.** ohm, rel **4.** volt, watt
   5. farad, henry, joule **6.** ampere, proton
   7. coulomb, oersted **8.** kilowatt
electricity . . . **5.** juice, power
   10. illuminant
eleemosynary . . . **4.** alms, free **7.** charity
   10. almsgiving
elegance . . . **5.** charm, grace, taste
   6. beauty, polish **9.** propriety
   10. ornateness, politeness, refinement
   13. sumptuousness
elegant . . . **4.** rich **6.** dressy, ornate,
   soigné, urbane **7.** courtly, genteel
   refined **8.** graceful, handsome, polished,
   tasteful **9.** admirable, beautiful,
   excellent **10.** fastidious **11.** fashionable
   13. grandiloquent
element . . . **3.** air **4.** fire **5.** earth, water
elementary . . . **5.** basic **6.** simple
   7. primary **8.** inchoate, original
   9. beginning **11.** fundamental
elephant . . . **3.** cow **4.** bull, calf **5.** hathi,

rogue 6. tusker 8. behemoth
9. pachyderm
elephant (pert to) . . .
apple . . 7. Feronia
boy . . 4. Sabu
call, cry . . 4. barr 7. trumpet
enclosure, trap . . 6. keddah
extinct . . 7. mammoth
goad . . 5. ankus
keeper . . 6. mahout
seat . . 6. howdah
tusk . . 5. ivory 9. scrivello
young . . 4. calf
elevate . . . 4. lift, rear 5. elate, exalt, raise
6. refine, uplift 7. advance, dignify,
ennoble, glorify, inspire, promote
10. exhilarate
elevated . . . 2. el 5. lofty, risen 6. elated
7. exalted, sublime 8. eminence
elevation . . . 4. hill 6. height (highth)
9. promotion 10. exaltation
11. composition (Eccl), distinction
13. glorification
elevation of the mind . . . 7. anagoge
elevator . . . 3. bin 4. cage, lift, silo
9. ascenseur
elevator name . . . 4. Otis
eleven . . . 7. hendeca (comb form)
elf . . . 3. fay, hob, imp, nix 4. peri 5. fairy,
gnome, ouphe, pixie 6. goblin, sprite
7. brownie
elfish . . . 5. elfin 6. elvish, impish 7. elflike,
tricksy 8. eldritch 11. mischievous
Elgin Marbles . . . 10. sculptures (by
Phidias)
Elia . . . 4. Lamb (Charles)
Eli alma mater . . . 4. Yale
elicit . . . 3. get 4. draw, pump 5. claim,
educe, evoke, exact, wrest, wring
6. deduce, demand, entice, extort,
induce, obtain 7. extract
elide . . . 4. dele, omit 5. annul 6. ignore
7. destroy, nullify, shorten 8. demolish,
suppress 9. eliminate
eligible . . . 3. apt, fit 4. meet 6. worthy
8. entitled, suitable 9. competent,
desirable, qualified 10. acceptable,
admissible
Elijah . . . 7. prophet 8. oratorio 14. John
the Baptist (Bib)
eliminate . . . 3. rid 4. kill 5. erase, expel
6. detach, remove 7. discard, divulge,
exclude, excrete, release 8. evacuate,
separate 9. segregate 11. exterminate
Eliot, George (pseud) . . . 12. Mary Ann
Evans
Elisha . . . 7. prophet 8. disciple (of Elijah)
elision . . . 7. syncope 9. severance
10. abridgment, shortening
11. suppression (vowel)
elite . . . 5. stars 6. flower, galaxy
7. fashion, society 9. beau monde
10. upper crust
elixir . . . 6. remedy 7. cure-all, essence,
extract, heal-all, panacea 8. medicine,
tincture 10. catholicon 12. quintessence
elixir of life . . . 11. elixir vitae
Elixir of Love . . . 13. L'Elisir d'Amore
elk . . . 4. deer 5. Alces, eland, moose
6. sambar, wapiti
ellipse . . . 5. curve, focus (foci), ovoid

ellipsis . . . 4. dots 6. points 8. omission
elliptical . . . 5. ovoid, vague 7. obscure
10. incomplete
elm (pert to) . . .
borer . . 6. beetle, lamiid
fruit . . 6. samara
genus . . 5. Ulmus
rock, wing (kinds) . . 5. wahoo
Elm City . . . 8. New Haven
Elmo . . . 11. patron saint (sailors)
elocution . . . 7. oratory 8. rhetoric
9. eloquence 10. expression
elocutionist . . . 6. reader 7. reciter
11. elocutioner 13. recitationist
eloge . . . 6. eulogy 7. address, oration
8. encomium, eulogium
eloign . . . 6. convey, remove 7. conceal
elongate . . . 6. extend, remove 7. stretch
8. continue, lengthen, protract
elongated . . . 4. lank, long 6. linear,
oblong 7. prolate, slender 8. extended
9. stretched 10. attenuated
elope . . . 6. decamp 7. abscond, skip out
8. slip away
eloquence . . . 7. fluency, oratory
9. discourse, elocution
14. expressiveness
eloquence, teacher of . . . 6. rhetor
eloquent . . . 5. vivid 10. Ciceronian,
expressive, meaningful, oratorical
11. significant
else . . . 2. or 4. ense (ens) 5. if not,
other 9. otherwise 10. additional
12. accompanying
elsewhere . . . 4. away 5. alibi (law)
elucidate . . . 5. clear, lucid 7. clarify, clear
up 8. simplify 9. interpret 10. illustrate
elude . . . 4. flee, foil, mock, shun 5. avoid,
dodge, evade 6. baffle, befool, escape
10. circumvent
elusive . . . 4. eely 6. subtle 7. elusory,
evasive 8. baffling 9. equivocal
10. impalpable
elves . . . see *elf*
Elysium (Myth) . . . 8. paradise
em . . . 2. en (half) 4. unit (Elec)
emaciated . . . 4. lean 5. gaunt 6. peaked,
wasted 7. pinched 10. attenuated,
cadaverous
emanation . . . 4. aura, odor 5. light,
niton (radium), vapor 7. outcome
8. creation, effluvia 9. ectoplasm,
radiation 10. exhalation, generation
11. consequence
emancipation . . . 6. rescue 7. freedom,
release 10. liberation 11. manumission
15. enfranchisement
emancipator, famous . . . 7. Lincoln
emasculate . . . 4. geld, spay 5. unman
6. soften 8. castrate 9. expurgate,
sterilize 10. effeminize
embalmer . . . 5. cerer 9. mortician,
preserver 10. undertaker
embankment . . . 3. dam 4. bund, dike
5. levee, revet, shore 7. barrier, pilapil
(rice field) 8. buttress 10. breakwater
13. fortification
embargo . . . 5. edict, order 7. exclude
8. blockade, prohibit, stoppage
9. exclusion 10. impediment
11. prohibition, requisition

embark . . . **4.** sail, ship **5.** begin **6.** depart, invest, set off (out), unmoor **7.** cast off, entrain

embarrass . . . **5.** abash, shame **6.** hamper, hinder, impede **7.** confuse, fluster, involve, mortify, nonplus **8.** bewilder, confound, encumber, handicap **9.** discomfit, dumbfound **10.** complicate, disconcert

embarrassed . . . **8.** red-faced

embarrassment . . . **5.** shame **9.** abashment, confusion **11.** involvement, predicament **12.** discomfiture, entanglement **13.** inconvenience, mortification

embellish . . . **3.** gem **4.** deck, gild **5.** adorn, array, dress, gouge, grace **6.** bedeck, enrich **7.** bedrape, enhance, garnish **8.** beautify, emblazon, furbelow, ornament **9.** embroider **10.** exaggerate

embellishment . . . **9.** garniture **10.** decoration, furbishing **12.** exaggeration **13.** ornamentation

ember . . . **3.** ash **4.** coal (live), izle **5.** gleed **6.** cinder **7.** residue

embers . . . **5.** ashes **8.** emotions (past), memories

embezzle . . . **5.** steal, swipe **6.** lessen, thieve, weaken (obs) **7.** purloin **8.** peculate, squander **9.** dissipate **11.** appropriate

embitter . . . **4.** sour **5.** anger **7.** envenom **8.** acerbate **10.** antagonize, exacerbate

emblazon . . . **4.** laud **5.** color, extol **6.** praise **7.** display, exhibit, glorify **9.** celebrate, embellish

emblem . . . **3.** rue **4.** mace, sign, type **5.** badge, crown, image, token, totem **6.** device, figure, symbol **7.** balance (justice), coronet, sceptor **9.** prototype

emblematic . . . **5.** typal **7.** typical **8.** symbolic **10.** figurative **14.** characteristic

embodiment . . . **4.** Apis **6.** avatar, matter **7.** epitome **9.** inclusion **10.** enfoldment **11.** combination, composition, incarnation **12.** organization **13.** incorporation **14.** representative **15.** personification

embolden . . . **5.** nerve **6.** assure **7.** hearten **8.** reassure **9.** encourage

embosom . . . **6.** foster **7.** cherish, embrace, enclose **8.** surround

embrace . . . **3.** hug **4.** fold, gain, hold, love, wrap **5.** adopt, clasp, cling, grasp, inarm, seize **6.** accoll (obs), caress, enfold **7.** cherish, contain, enclose, espouse, include, involve, welcome **8.** comprise, encircle, greeting, surround **9.** encompass

embroider . . . **7.** falsify **8.** decorate, ornament **9.** embellish **10.** exaggerate

embroidery . . . **8.** appliqué **9.** hardanger

embroidery frame . . . **7.** taboret (tabouret)

embroil . . . **5.** upset **6.** jumble **7.** agitate, disturb, perplex, trouble **8.** convulse, disorder, distract **9.** commingle, implicate **10.** complicate, discompose

emcee . . . **4.** host

eme . . . **5.** uncle **6.** friend, gossip

emend . . . **4.** edit, mend **5.** amend, right **6.** better, remedy, revise **7.** correct, improve, rectify

emerald . . . **5.** beryl, color, green **7.** smaragd

Emerald Isle . . . **4.** Erin **7.** Ireland

emerge . . . **3.** dip **4.** pend, rise **5.** hatch, issue **6.** appear **7.** debouch, emanate **10.** disembogue

emergency . . . **5.** pinch **6.** clutch, crisis, strait **8.** exigency, juncture **9.** extremity, necessity **10.** substitute

emery . . . **6.** pumice **8.** abradant, abrasive, corundum **9.** sandpaper

emesis . . . **6.** puking **7.** spewing **8.** vomiting **12.** disgorgement **13.** regurgitation

emeute . . . **4.** riot **6.** Putsch **8.** outbreak **10.** insurgence **12.** insurrection

emigrant . . . **6.** emigré **7.** migrant, outgoer, settler **8.** colonist, stranger **9.** immigrant, migratory (of birds)

eminence . . . **4.** hill **5.** title **6.** height, rideau **7.** dignity **9.** authority, elevation, greatness, loftiness **10.** famousness, importance, projection **11.** superiority **13.** transcendency

eminent . . . **4.** arch, high **5.** great, lofty, noted **6.** famous, marked, signal **8.** renowned, superior, towering **9.** important **10.** celebrated, protruding **11.** illustrious **13.** distinguished

emissary . . . **3.** spy **5.** agent, scout **8.** delegate, diplomat

emit . . . **4.** glow, reek, shed **5.** eject, eruct, exude, issue, pluff, voice **6.** exhale **7.** distill (distil), emanate, publish, radiate **8.** opalesce (colors), transmit **9.** discharge, irradiate

emmet . . . **3.** ant **7.** pismire **8.** formicid

emollient . . . **4.** balm **8.** ointment, soothing **9.** lubricant, softening

emolument . . . **4.** fees, gain **5.** wages **6.** profit, salary **7.** stipend, tribute **9.** allowance **12.** compensation

emotion . . . **5.** agony, stoic **6.** pathos **7.** feeling, passion **9.** agitation, gratitude, sensation, sentiment **10.** excitement **11.** disturbance, sensibility

emotional seat . . . **5.** bosom

emotionless . . . **9.** apathetic, impassive, unfeeling **10.** spiritless **11.** unemotional **12.** unresponsive

emperor . . . **4.** czar, tsar **5.** Mogul **7.** monarch **9.** commander, imperator, sovereign

emphasis . . . **6.** accent, stress **7.** cadence **8.** salience **10.** insistence **14.** impressiveness

emphasize . . . **6.** accent, insist, stress **7.** point up **9.** punctuate **10.** accentuate

emphatic . . . **7.** earnest **8.** forcible, positive, striking **9.** energetic, insistent **10.** expressive **11.** significant

empire . . . **4.** rule, sway **5.** green (color), reign, state **6.** domain **7.** control, country

Empire (pert to) . . .
of the Rising Sun . . **5.** Japan
State . . **7.** New York

State of the South .. **7.** Georgia

empiric ... **4.** fake **5.** cheat, quack
8. impostor **9.** charlatan **10.** mountebank

employ ... **3.** use **4.** busy, coax,
hire **5.** apply, exert **6.** devote,
occupy **7.** concern, entrust, service
10. occupation

employees ... **4.** crew, gang, help **5.** force,
hands, staff **9.** personnel **10.** associates

employer ... **4.** user **5.** hirer **6.** master
8. consumer **12.** entrepreneur

employment ... **3.** use **4.** work **5.** trade
7. calling, purpose, service **8.** business,
vocation **10.** occupation, profession

emporium ... **4.** fair, mart **5.** store
6. bazaar, market **10.** exposition

empower ... **6.** enable **7.** entitle
8. delegate, deputize **9.** authorize
10. commission

empty ... **4.** idle, toom, vain, void **5.** blank,
clear, drain, inane **6.** hollow, hungry,
jejune, vacant, vacate **7.** deplete,
foolish, vacuous **8.** evacuate, unfilled
9. insincere **10.** unburdened,
unoccupied

empusa (Gr Myth) ... **5.** fungi **7.** specter
9. hobgoblin

empyrean ... **3.** sky **5.** ether **6.** Caelus,
welkin **7.** heavens, the blue

emulate ... **5.** equal, outdo, rival
7. compete, imitate, vie with
11. competition

emulsion ... **9.** demulcent **10.** semiliquid,
suspension

enable ... **5.** equip **6.** clothe **7.** empower,
qualify **9.** authorize **10.** capacitate

enact ... **4.** pass, play **6.** decree,
enjoin, ordain, record **7.** actuate,
appoint, perform **9.** legislate, represent
10. constitute **11.** impersonate

enactment ... **3.** law **4.** veto **5.** canon,
edict, usage **6.** decree **7.** statute
9. ordinance **11.** legislation

encamp, encampment ... **4.** camp, tent
5. siege **7.** bivouac, camping

enchant ... **5.** charm **6.** delude **7.** bewitch,
delight **8.** ensorcel **9.** captivate,
enrapture, fascinate

enchantment ... **5.** charm, magic, spell
7. sorcery **8.** witchery **10.** allurement,
necromancy, witchcraft
11. bewitchment, fascination,
incantation

enchantress ... **5.** Circe, Medea
7. charmer **9.** bewitcher, sorceress,
temptress

encina ... **7.** live oak

encircle ... **3.** orb **4.** gird, ring, zone
5. belay, inorb, twist **6.** enfold
7. besiege, circuit, enclose, environ,
include, wreathe **8.** surround
12. circumscribe

encircled ... **4.** girt **5.** orbed, paled,
zoned **6.** belted, forded, hooped, ringed
7. enlaced **8.** enclosed, enfolded,
wreathed **10.** surrounded

enclose ... **3.** hem, mew **5.** bound, fence
6. corral, encase, engulf **7.** enclave,
envelop, harness, include **8.** imprison,
surround **9.** encompass
12. circumscribe

enclosed ... **4.** pent, sept (area)
7. encased **8.** confined **10.** surrounded

enclosure ... **3.** pen **4.** bawn, cage, yair
(yare), yard **5.** carol (cloister), kraal
(craal), sekos **6.** corral **8.** contents,
poundage, stockade

encomium ... **4.** hymn **5.** eloge **6.** eulogy,
praise **7.** tribute **8.** accolade **9.** panegyric

encompass ... **4.** ring **5.** hem in **6.** begird,
effect **7.** besiege, circuit, compass,
contain, enclose, environ, include
8. encircle, surround **10.** accomplish
12. circumscribe

encompassing ... **7.** ambient
13. circumambient

encore ... **3.** bis **4.** echo, over **5.** again
8. applause, once more

encounter ... **4.** bout, meet **5.** brave,
brush, fight, incur, onset **6.** attack,
breast, oppose **7.** collide, meeting
8. conflict **10.** engagement, experience

encourage ... **4.** abet, urge **5.** boost,
cheer, impel, nerve, rally **6.** assure,
exhort, foster, incite **7.** advance,
comfort, console, hearten, inspire,
promote **8.** embolden, inspirit
9. instigate, stimulate **11.** countenance

encouragement ... **3.** aid **7.** comfort
9. fosterage, incentive **10.** inducement
11. emboldening

encroach upon ... **5.** poach **6.** invade,
trench **7.** impinge, intrude **8.** infringe,
overstep, trespass

encumber ... **4.** clog, load **5.** check
6. burden, hamper, hinder, retard,
saddle **7.** involve, oppress **8.** entangle,
handicap, obstruct, overload
9. embarrass **10.** overburden

encumbrance ... **5.** alien (law), claim
6. burden **9.** dependent **10.** impediment

encyclic ... **6.** letter **7.** pandect **8.** circular,
treatise **10.** encircling
13. comprehensive

encyclopedic learning, person of ...
10. polyhistor **13.** encyclopedist

end ... **3.** aim, neb, tip, toe **4.** fate,
kill, ruin, tail **5.** amend, close, death,
finis, limit, omega, point, telos, upend
6. expire, finale, finish, result, thirty
7. destroy, purpose **8.** complete,
conclude, dissolve **9.** cessation,
determine, extremity, intention,
objective, terminate **10.** completion
11. termination

end (pert to) ...
arrow .. **4.** nock
boundary .. **5.** bourn **7.** abuttal
cloth .. **7.** remnant
game .. **4.** goal
man .. **8.** minstrel
news .. **6.** thirty
timber .. **5.** tenon

endanger ... **4.** risk **6.** expose, hazard
7. imperil **10.** compromise, jeopardize

endeavor ... **3.** aim, try, vie **4.** seek
5. essay, ettle, nisus, tempt **6.** effort,
strive **7.** attempt **8.** struggle

endemic ... **6.** native **10.** indigenous
14. characteristic

ending ... **5.** death **6.** result **9.** cessation,
desinence **10.** completion, conclusion

11. destruction, termination

endless ... **4.** many **6.** eterne **7.** eternal, undying **8.** eternity, infinite, numerous, unending **9.** boundless, continual, incessant, perpetual, unceasing, unstinted **10.** continuous **11.** everlasting **12.** interminable **13.** uninterrupted

endorse, indorse ... **4.** sign **6.** attest, second **7.** approve, support **8.** sanction **9.** authorize, guarantee

endorsement ... **4.** fiat, visa (vise) **8.** approval, sanction **9.** provision, signature **10.** acceptance, validation **12.** ratification **14.** authentication

endow ... **3.** dow, due **4.** dote, vest **5.** dower, endue, indue **6.** bestow, clothe, enrich, give to, invest **7.** empower, furnish, provide

endowment ... **4.** gift **5.** dower, grant **7.** talents **8.** appanage (apanage) **9.** insurance, provision **11.** empowerment, instruction (Mormon)

endue ... **5.** endow, teach **6.** clothe, digest, invest, supply **7.** empower

endurable ... **8.** bearable **9.** tolerable **10.** sufferable **11.** supportable

endurance ... **7.** stamina **8.** patience, strength **9.** fortitude, suffering **10.** durability, permanence, sufferance **11.** continuance, resignation **12.** perseverance

endure ... **4.** bear, bide, dree, last, live, tide, wear **5.** abide, allow, brook, stand **6.** afford, remain, suffer **7.** condone, persist, sustain, undergo **8.** continue, tolerate **9.** persevere, withstand

enduring ... **7.** durable, lasting, patient **9.** permanent **11.** persevering, substantial, unforgotten **13.** long-suffering

enemy ... **3.** foe **5.** devil, force, fremd (frenne), hater, rival, Satan **6.** foeman **8.** opponent **9.** adversary **10.** antagonist

energetic ... **5.** fresh **6.** active **8.** forceful, forcible, vigorous **9.** strenuous **11.** industrious

energy ... **2.** go **3.** erg, pep, vim **4.** bent **5.** force, nerve, power, vigor **6.** spirit **7.** potency, sthenia **8.** strength **9.** animation

energy (pert to) ...
lack of .. **5.** atony **6.** anergy **7.** aneuria, inertia **8.** asthenia
mental .. **9.** psychurgy
personified .. **6.** Shakti
potential .. **5.** ergal
unit .. **3.** erg **5.** ergon

enervate ... **3.** sap **5.** drain, unman **6.** weaken **7.** exhaust, unnerve **8.** enfeeble **10.** debilitate

enfeeble ... **4.** numb **6.** sicken, soften, weaken **7.** depress **8.** enervate **9.** attenuate **10.** debilitate

enfilade ... **4.** rake **5.** vista **7.** barrage **9.** broadside **11.** arrangement (in rows)

enfold, infold ... **4.** fold, wrap **5.** clasp, cover **6.** infold **7.** embrace, envelop **8.** surround

enforce ... **5.** drive **6.** assail, compel **7.** execute, inspire **9.** constrain,

encourage, intensify, reinforce **10.** invigorate

enfranchise ... **4.** free **5.** admit **7.** deliver, set free **8.** liberate **10.** emancipate

engage ... **4.** bind, draw, hire, rent **5.** lease **6.** absorb, embark, employ, enlist, induce, occupy, pledge **7.** attract, betroth, engross, involve, promise **8.** contract, entangle **9.** interlock, intermesh

engaged ... **4.** busy **5.** hired **6.** bonded, meshed **7.** earnest, entered, pledged, versant **8.** embedded, employed, involved, occupied, promised **9.** affianced, betrothed, engrossed **10.** contracted

engaged in controversy ... **9.** disputant

engagement ... **4.** date **6.** battle **7.** promise **9.** betrothal, encounter **10.** attachment **11.** appointment, involvement

engaging ... **5.** sapid **6.** taking **8.** alluring, duelling **10.** attractive, delightful **11.** interesting

engender ... **3.** sow (seeds) **5.** beget, breed, cause **6.** excite **7.** develop, produce **8.** generate, occasion **9.** call forth, procreate, propagate

engine ... **3.** gin, ram **5.** mogul, motor **6.** onager **7.** machine, robinet, turbine **10.** locomotive

engine (type) ... **3.** gas **5.** motor, solar, steam **6.** Diesel, rocket **8.** gasoline **10.** combustion

engineer ... **4.** plan **7.** manager **8.** computer, contrive, designer, inventor, maneuver, operator, therblig **9.** construct **11.** constructor, superintend

engineer (type) ... **5.** civil, corps, sales **6.** driver, mining **7.** planner **8.** chemical, geodetic, military, railroad, research, sanitary **9.** hydraulic **10.** electrical, industrial, mechanical, structural **11.** electronics **12.** aeronautical, construction **14.** administrative

engird ... **6.** begird, circle, girdle **7.** envelop **8.** encircle, ensphere

England ... see also *English*
called .. **6.** Albion (anc) **7.** Britain **9.** Britannia
capital .. **6.** London
city .. **3.** Ely **4.** Hull, York **5.** Derby, Leeds **6.** Exeter **7.** Bristol, Croydon **8.** Brighton, Coventry, Hastings, Plymouth **9.** Liverpool, Sheffield **10.** Birmingham, Epsom Downs, Manchester, Nottingham, Portsmouth **11.** Southampton
college (famed) .. **6.** Oxford **9.** Cambridge, Sandhurst (military)
conqueror .. **5.** Danes **6.** Angles, Saxons **7.** Normans
constitution .. **10.** Magna Carta (1215) **12.** Bill of Rights (1688)
county .. **4.** Kent **5.** Devon, Essex **6.** Dorset, Sussex **9.** Yorkshire
emblem .. **4.** lion, rose
House of .. **4.** York **5.** Blois, Tudor **6.** Stuart **7.** Hanover, Windsor **8.** Normandy **9.** Lancaster **11.** Plantagenet

island .. **5.** Wight **6.** Scilly, Virgin
7. Bahamas, Bermuda, Channel,
Solomon **8.** Falkland, Windward **9.** Isle
of Man
king (anc) .. **6.** Arthur (legend), Egbert
8. Ethelred **9.** Ethelwulf
native (anc) .. **4.** Celt, Dane, Jute
5. Saxon **8.** Anglican **9.** Sassenach
10. Anglo-Saxon
river .. **3.** Exe **4.** Avon, Ouse **5.** Trent
6. Thames
royal residence .. **7.** Windsor
school .. **4.** Eton **5.** Rugby **6.** Harrow
street (London) .. **10.** Piccadilly
12. Threadneedle
English (pert to) ...
bride's gift .. **3.** dos
court .. **4.** eyre (circuit), leet (anc)
dislike of .. **11.** Anglophobia
district .. **4.** Soho
estate (feudal) .. **4.** fief
excuse (legal) .. **6.** essoin
festival (country) .. **3.** ale
field .. **5.** croft
forest .. **5.** Arden **8.** Sherwood
freeman .. **5.** ceorl, thane, thegn
hamlet .. **4.** dorp
heather .. **4.** ling
lawyer .. **9.** barrister, solicitor
leave of absence (school) .. **5.** exeat
lover of .. **10.** Anglophile
Marbles .. **6.** Oxford **7.** Arundel
money of account .. **3.** ora
news agency .. **6.** Reuter
Parliament process .. **7.** Hansard
political party .. **4.** Tory, Whig **8.** Laborite
12. Conservative
porcelain .. **5.** Spode **8.** Wedgwood
prehistoric site .. **8.** Piltdown
race course .. **5.** Ascot **9.** Newmarket
10. Epsom Downs
races (famed) .. **5.** Derby **7.** The Oaks
sheep (blackface) .. **4.** Lonk
song (mock) .. **12.** lillibullero
stolen article (on thief) .. **7.** mainour
subway .. **4.** tube **11.** underground
symbol .. **4.** bull, lion, rose
thicket .. **5.** copse **7.** spinney
tract (sandy) .. **4.** dean (dene)
trolley .. **4.** tram
uplands .. **5.** downs
wren .. **6.** tomtit
English Channel ... **8.** La Manche
English, famed ...
architect .. **4.** Wren
composer .. **4.** Arne, Byrd **5.** Elgar
6. Handel, Tallis **7.** Dowland, Stainer
15. Vaughan Williams
diarist .. **5.** Pepys
dramatist .. **6.** Jonson, Pinter **7.** Marlowe
8. Sheridan
engraver .. **3.** Pye **7.** Hogarth
essayist .. **4.** Elia (Charles Lamb), Lang
6. Arnold, Steele **7.** Addison
explorer .. **4.** Ross **5.** Cabot **6.** Baffin,
Beatty, Hudson **7.** Raleigh
10. Shackleton
financier .. **7.** Gresham
historian .. **4.** Bede **7.** Spelman, Toynbee
8. Macaulay
humorist .. **4.** Lear (Edward)

navigator .. **4.** Cook **5.** Drake **6.** Nelson
painter .. **6.** Turner **7.** Millais **8.** Reynolds,
Rossetti **9.** Constable **12.** Gainsborough
philosopher .. **7.** Russell, Spencer
poet .. **4.** Pope **5.** Byron, Keats
6. Dryden **7.** Bridges, Chaucer, Shelley,
Skelton, Southey, Spenser **8.** Browning,
Tennyson **10.** Wordsworth
printer .. **6.** Caxton
reformer .. **4.** Owen **6.** Spence
saint .. **6.** George (patron saint)
7. Alphege, Swithin
satirist .. **5.** Swift
scientist .. **4.** Davy **5.** Boyle **6.** Dalton,
Darwin, Halley, Harvey, Huxley, Jenner,
Kelvin, Lister, Newton **7.** Faraday,
Fleming **9.** Cavendish, Priestley
10. Rutherford
spy (in Am Rev) .. **5.** André
statesman .. **4.** Peel, Pitt **7.** Baldwin,
Balfour, Walpole **8.** Cromwell, Disraeli,
Thatcher **9.** Churchill **11.** Chamberlain,
Lloyd George
theologian .. **5.** Booth **6.** Becket **7.** Tyndall
8. Wycliffe **10.** Whitefield
thesaurus compiler .. **5.** Roget
writer .. **5.** Hardy, Woolf **6.** Austen,
Barrie **7.** Boswell, Dickens, Johnson
8. Fielding, Lawrence, Trollope
9. Thackeray
engrave ... **3.** cut **4.** etch, rist **5.** carve,
chase, hatch, infix **6.** chisel, incise
7. enchase, impress, imprint, stipple
9. sculpture
engraver's tool ... **5.** burin
engraving ... **3.** cut **5.** print **7.** etching,
chasing, tooling **8.** celature, incising,
intaglio **9.** stippling **10.** xylography
(wood) **11.** lithography **12.** glyptography
engross ... **6.** absorb, engage
10. monopolize **11.** concentrate
engrossed ... **4.** busy, rapt **6.** intent
8. absorbed, employed **10.** interested
engulf ... **4.** gulf, gulp **5.** swamp **6.** absorb
7. swallow **8.** inundate, submerge
9. overwhelm
enhance ... **4.** lift **5.** exalt, extol, raise
7. advance, augment, elevate, enlarge,
magnify **8.** increase **9.** aggravate
10. exaggerate
enigma ... **3.** why **5.** rebus **6.** puzzle,
riddle **7.** charade, mystery
9. conundrum **11.** mind-boggler
enigmatic ... **6.** arcane, mystic **8.** puzzling
12. inexplicable
enjoin ... **3.** bid **5.** order **6.** advise, charge,
decree, direct, forbid **7.** command
8. admonish, prohibit
enjoy ... **4.** bask, have **5.** savor **6.** relish
10. appreciate
enjoyment ... **4.** ease, zest **6.** relish
7. delight **8.** felicity, fruition, pleasure
9. amusement, happiness
enlarge ... **3.** eke **4.** ream **5.** swell **6.** dilate,
expand, extend, spread **7.** amplify,
augment, develop, distend **8.** increase
9. expatiate **10.** exaggerate
enlargement ... **8.** increase **9.** expansion,
extension **12.** augmentation
13. amplification
enlighten ... **5.** teach **6.** inform **7.** educate,

explain **8.** enkindle, instruct
10. illuminate **11.** disillusion
enlightened person ... **10.** illuminate
enlist ... **4.** join, list **6.** engage, enroll,
induce, muster
enliven ... **5.** amuse, cheer, rouse
7. animate, comfort, inspire, refresh
8. brighten, energize, inspirit
9. encourage, stimulate **10.** exhilarate,
invigorate
enmity ... **3.** war **4.** feud **6.** hatred,
malice, rancor **7.** discord **8.** aversion
9. antipathy, disaccord, hostility
10. antagonism, repugnance
11. malevolence **14.** unfriendliness
ennead ... **4.** gods (nine), nine **18.** Ennead
of Heliopolis (famed)
ennoble ... **5.** exalt, honor, raise **6.** uplift
7. elevate, glorify, promote
ennui ... **4.** bore, bored **6.** tedium
7. boredom, fatigue, languor
9. weariness **15.** dissatisfaction
enormous ... **4.** huge, vast **5.** great
6. wicked **7.** immense, massive,
titanic **8.** abnormal, colossal, gigantic,
infamous **9.** atrocious, excessive,
monstrous **10.** inordinate, prodigious,
stupendous
Enos' father ... **4.** Seth
enough ... **4.** enow **5.** ample, basta, fully,
quite **6.** plenty **8.** adequate **9.** amplitude
10. sufficient **12.** satisfactory
enounce ... **5.** state, utter **8.** proclaim
9. enunciate, pronounce
enow ... **9.** presently
enrage ... **5.** anger **6.** madden **7.** incense,
inflame **9.** infuriate
enraged ... **5.** irate **7.** angered
8. maddened **10.** infuriated
enraptured ... **6.** enrapt **8.** ecstatic
9. delighted, entranced **10.** enravished
enravished ... **4.** rapt **9.** enchanted,
entranced, rapturous **10.** enraptured
enrich ... **4.** lard **5.** adorn, endow **6.** fatten
7. improve **8.** increase, ornament
9. embellish, fertilize
enroll ... **4.** coil, join, list, roll **5.** enter
6. enlist, induct, unfurl, wrap up
7. engross, impanel **8.** initiate, register
11. matriculate
ens ... **5.** being **6.** entity **7.** essence
ensconce ... **4.** hide **5.** cover **6.** settle
7. conceal, protect, shelter **9.** establish
ensemble ... **3.** all **5.** decor, group, whole
7. costume
enshroud ... **4.** wrap **6.** clothe, swathe
7. conceal, enclose **8.** enshrine
ensiform ... **12.** xiphisternum
ensign ... **4.** flag **6.** banner **7.** officer
8. gonfalon, standard **9.** oriflamme
(oriflamb, anc)
ensign of Othello ... **4.** Iago
enslave ... **8.** enthrall
ensnare ... **3.** web **4.** trap **5.** benet,
catch, innet, noose **6.** allure, enmesh,
entrap, seduce **7.** involve
ensorcell, ensorcel ... **7.** bewitch,
enchant
ensue ... **6.** follow, pursue, result
7. imitate, succeed **8.** come next
ensuing ... **4.** next **9.** resultant

10. subsequent, succeeding
ensure ... **6.** assure, insure, secure
7. protect, warrant **9.** guarantee
entad ... **6.** inward (opp of ectad)
ental ... **5.** inner (opp of ectal)
entangle ... **3.** mat, web **4.** mesh, mire
5. afoul, ravel, snarl, twist **6.** enlace,
enmesh, puzzle, raffle **7.** confuse,
ensnare, involve, perplex **8.** bewilder
9. embarrass **10.** interweave
entanglement ... **4.** knot **5.** snare, snarl
6. abatis **8.** obstacle **9.** barricade,
imbroglio **10.** barbed wire, complexity
11. involvement
enter ... **4.** join, list **5.** begin, start, train
6. come in, engage, enlist, enroll, insert,
record **8.** initiate, inscribe, register
9. introduce, penetrate **11.** participate
enter (pert to) ...
career .. **6.** incept
legal objection .. **5.** demur
with hostility .. **6.** invade
without permission .. **7.** intrude
8. encroach, infringe
enterprise ... **4.** firm **5.** essay **6.** daring
7. attempt, crusade, exploit, venture
10. initiative **11.** undertaking
enterprising ... **4.** bold **6.** daring
9. energetic **11.** up-and-coming
entertain ... **4.** fete **5.** amuse, treat
6. divert, regale **7.** beguile, cherish
8. interest
entertainer ... **5.** actor **6.** dancer,
singer **7.** actress, speaker **8.** magician
9. performer **11.** pantomimist
12. impersonator
entertainment ... **4.** play **5.** party, revue,
sport **6.** kermis (kermess), repast
7. pastime, ridotto, theater **8.** entr'acte,
musicale **9.** amusement, diversion,
reception, wayzgoose **10.** recreation
12. Roman holiday
enthralled ... **10.** captivated, fascinated,
spellbound
enthusiasm ... **4.** élan, fire, zeal, zest
5. ardor, craze, estro, furor (furore),
mania, verve **6.** fervor **7.** ecstasy
8. interest **9.** animation, eagerness,
transport **10.** exaltation
enthusiast ... **3.** fan **5.** bigot **6.** rooter,
zealot **7.** devotee, fanatic
enthusiastic ... **5.** eager, nutty, rabid
6. active, ardent **7.** zealous
10. interested
entice ... **4.** bait, coax, lure, tole **5.** decoy,
tempt **6.** allure, cajole, incite, seduce
7. attract, wheedle **8.** inveigle, persuade
enticement ... **9.** seduction
10. allurement, attraction, incitement,
inducement, persuasion, temptation
12. inveiglement
entire ... **3.** all **5.** cover (Philat),
sound, total, utter, whole **6.** intact
7. perfect, sincere, upright **8.** complete,
faithful, stallion **9.** integrate, undivided
10. unimpaired **11.** unqualified
12. undiminished
entirely ... **3.** all **5.** clean, fully, stark
6. solely, wholly **7.** totally **9.** every inch,
perfectly, sincerely **10.** completely
entitle ... **3.** dub **4.** call, name, term

5. style 6. assign, enable, impute
7. empower, qualify 9. authorize,
designate 10. denominate

entity ... 3. ens 4. soul, unit 5. being,
entia, thing 7. integer 8. infinity (Math)
9. existence

entomb ... 4. bury 5. inter, inurn
6. hearse, inhume 7. confine
9. sepulture

entourage ... 5. suite, train 7. retinue
10. associates, attendants
12. surroundings

entr'acte ... 3. act 5. dance, music
7. interim 9. interlude

entrails ... 4. guts 6. bowels 7. insides,
viscera 8. interior 10. intestines

entrance ... 3. way 4. adit, door,
gate 5. entry, inlet 6. access, portal
7. gateway, ingress, postern
9. admission, insertion, threshold,
vestibule 10. admittance

entrance (pert to) ...
church (Eastern) .. 5. Great 6. Little
formal .. 5. debut 12. introduction
hostile .. 9. incursion
temple (Buddh) .. 5. toran (torana)

entranced ... 4. rapt 7. charmed
8. dreaming 9. delighted, overjoyed
10. fascinated, hypnotized, spellbound
11. overpowered

entrap ... 3. net 4. trap 5. catch, decoy,
noose, snare 6. tangle 7. beguile,
ensnare 8. entangle, inveigle

entreat ... 3. ask, beg, woo 4. pray
5. crave, halse (obs), plead 6. adjure,
appeal 7. beseech, implore, solicit
8. petition 9. importune 10. supplicate

entreaty ... 4. plea, suit 6. appeal, prayer
7. request 8. petition 10. invitation
11. importunity 12. solicitation,
supplication

entree, entrée ... 4. dish 6. access
7. ingress, opening 9. admission
10. permission (to enter)

entrench ... 6. invade 7. enter on,
fortify, intrude 8. encroach, trespass
9. establish

entrenchment ... 7. defense, parapet
9. intrusion 10. protection
12. encroachment, infringement
13. establishment

entrepot ... 5. depot, store 9. warehouse
10. depository

entrepreneur ... 7. provost 9. executive
10. impresario 13. administrator

entrust ... 6. commit 7. confide, consign
8. delegate 10. commission

entry ... 4. hall, item, lane, post 7. ingress
8. entrance, register 9. admission,
vestibule 10. contestant, memorandum
12. introduction

entwine ... 4. lace 5. clasp, twine, twist,
weave 6. enlace 7. wreathe 9. interknit

enumerate ... 4. list, tell 5. count 6. detail,
number, reckon, relate 7. compute
8. estimate, name over, rehearse
9. calculate, catalogue (catalog)
12. recapitulate 13. particularize

enumeration ... 4. list 5. count 6. census
10. numeration 14. recapitulation

enunciate ... 3. say 5. utter 6. affirm

7. declare 8. announce, proclaim
9. postulate, pronounce 10. articulate

enunciation ... 9. statement, utterance
11. affirmation, attestation, declaration
12. announcement 13. pronouncement,
pronunciation

envelop ... 4. case, wrap 5. cover
6. clothe, encase, enwrap, infold,
invest, sheath, shroud 7. conceal,
enclose, sheathe 8. encircle, surround
9. encompass, enwreathe
10. integument

envelope ... 3. bur (burr) 5. cover, curve
6. jacket 7. conceal, rampart, vesicle,
wrapper 8. membrane 10. integument

enveloped ... 6. amidst 7. covered
10. surrounded

envenom ... 5. taint 6. poison 8. embitter

envious ... 7. jealous 8. covetous,
grudging, spiteful 9. green-eyed
10. begrudging

environ ... 3. hem 6. suburb 7. compass,
envelop, hedge in, involve, purlieu
8. encircle, outskirt, surround
9. encompass

environment ... 4. area 6. medium,
milieu 7. setting, suburbs, terrain
8. environs 10. background
12. neighborhood, surroundings
13. encompassment

environmental ... 10. ecological

envisage ... 4. face 8. confront 9. visualize
11. contemplate 12. meet squarely

envision ... 5. dream 7. picture
9. visualize 11. contemplate 12. meet
squarely

envoy ... 5. agent 6. legate, l'envoi,
stanza 7. refrain 8. ablegate, delegate,
diplomat 9. messenger 10. ambassador,
postscript 12. commissioner

envy ... 5. covet 6. grudge 8. jealousy
12. covetousness

enwrap, inwrap ... 4. roll, wrap 6. clothe,
enfold, infold 7. engross 8. surround

enzyme ... 3. ase (suff) 5. bread (Eccl)
6. lotase, olease, pepsin, rennin,
urease 7. amylase, ferment, laccase,
ptyalin, trypsin 8. diastase, protease
9. digestant

enzyme activator ... 11. biocatalyst

eoan ... 7. auroral 8. daybreak, easterly

eon, aeon ... 3. age, era 4. time 5. cycle
8. eternity 10. generation

ephemeral ... 7. diurnal 9. chickweed,
deciduous, transient 10. short-lived

ephemeris ... 5. diary 7. almanac, journal
8. calendar 10. periodical 11. publication

Ephesus (pert to) ...
city of .. 6. Greece (anc)
famed for .. 5. ruins 12. Christianity
site .. 9. Aegean Sea
temple .. 7. Artemis
visitor (early) .. 6. St Paul

Ephraim ... 4. bear (grizzly) 5. tribe
8. fruitful

epi ... 6. finial

epic ... 3. cid 4. epos, poem, saga
5. epode 6. Aeneid (by Vergil), epopee,
heroic 9. narrative

epicene ... 7. neutral, sexless
10. effeminate

epicure . . . **6.** friand (obs) **7.** glutton, gourmet **8.** gourmand, Sybarite **9.** bon vivant **10.** gastronome, voluptuary **11.** connoisseur

epidemic . . . **4.** pest **6.** plague **8.** pandemic **9.** prevalent, spreading **10.** contagious, pestilence

epidermis . . . **4.** skin **7.** cuticle **8.** ectoderm **9.** scarfskin

epigram . . . **3.** mot, saw **4.** poem, quip **5.** adage, maxim **6.** dictum, saying **7.** distich **11.** inscription (obs)

epigraph . . . **5.** motto, title **9.** quotation **11.** inscription

Epiphany (Eccl) . . . **5.** Feast (Jan 6)

Epirus, oracle of . . . **6.** Dodona (Mt Tomarus, Gr)

episode . . . **5.** event, story **8.** incident **10.** digression (Mus), occurrence

epistle . . . **4.** note, post **6.** billet, lesson, letter **7.** message, missive, writing **8.** dispatch, rescript **13.** communication

epitaph . . . **7.** writing (monument) **8.** hic jacet **11.** inscription

epithet . . . **4.** name, term **5.** label **6.** byname **7.** agnomen **9.** sobriquet **11.** appellation (significant)

epitome . . . **6.** digest **7.** summary **8.** abstract **9.** comprisal **10.** abridgment, compendium

epitomize . . . **7.** abridge, curtail **8.** abstract, compress, condense, contract, diminish **9.** capsulize

epoch . . . **3.** age, day, eon, era **4.** date, time **5.** event **6.** period

epopee . . . **4.** epic, epos, poem **5.** genre (epic) **6.** poetry (epic)

epoptic . . . **6.** mystic, secret

Epstein-Barr . . . **4.** mono **5.** virus

equable . . . **4.** even **6.** steady **7.** uniform

equal . . . **3.** iso (pref), par, tie **4.** both, even, fere (obs), just, pari (pref), peer, same **5.** match, rival **7.** compeer, emulate, equable, uniform **8.** adequate, parallel **9.** equitable, identical **10.** coordinate, equivalent, substitute **11.** counterpart **12.** commensurate **13.** proportionate

equal day and night . . . **11.** equidiurnal, equinoctial

equal density (atmospheric) . . . **8.** isoteric

equality . . . **3.** par, tie **6.** equity, owelty (payment), parity **7.** egalite, isonomy (law) **8.** adequacy, evenness, fairness, identity, sameness **10.** uniformity **12.** impartiality

Equality State . . . **7.** Wyoming (first with Woman Suffrage)

equalize . . . **4.** even **5.** equal, level, match **6.** equate, smooth **7.** balance **10.** symmetrize

equally . . . **2.** as **4.** equi (pref) **5.** alike **6.** evenly, justly **11.** identically **15.** correspondingly

equanimity . . . **5.** poise **6.** aplomb **7.** balance **8.** calmness, evenness, serenity **9.** assurance, composure **10.** confidence, equability **11.** tranquility **12.** tranquillity

equilibrium . . . **5.** poise **6.** stasis **7.** balance **8.** equality **9.** stability

10. equanimity

equine . . . **3.** ass **4.** colt, foal, mare **5.** filly, horse, steed, zebra **6.** donkey

equine cry . . . **5.** neigh **6.** whinny

equip . . . **3.** arm, fit, imp, rig **4.** deck, gear, gird **5.** dress, endow **7.** costume, furnish, qualify **8.** accouter

equipment . . . **4.** gear **5.** armor **6.** outfit, tackle, traits (personal) **7.** ability, panoply (warriors) **8.** equipage **9.** apparatus **11.** preparation **12.** accouterment, accoutrement

equitable . . . **4.** fair, just **5.** right **6.** honest **7.** upright **9.** impartial **10.** bonitarian (Rom law), reasonable

equity . . . **4.** laws **6.** rights **7.** honesty, justice **8.** fairness **9.** rectitude **11.** uprightness

equivalence . . . **3.** par **7.** valence **8.** equality, sameness **10.** relativity **11.** correlation

equivalent . . . **5.** alike, equal **9.** identical **10.** tantamount

equivocal . . . **7.** dubious, obscure **8.** doubtful, puzzling **9.** ambiguous, enigmatic, uncertain **10.** amphibolic, mysterious, perplexing **11.** problematic **13.** indeterminate

equivocate . . . **3.** lie **5.** dodge, evade, fence, shift **6.** palter, trifle **7.** quibble, shuffle **11.** prevaricate **12.** tergiversate

era . . . **2.** AD, BC **3.** age, eon **4.** date, time **5.** cycle, epoch **6.** period **10.** Anno Domini **12.** Before Christ

eradicate . . . **4.** dele, root, weed **5.** annul, erase **6.** remove, uproot **7.** abolish, destroy, epilate, extract, root out **9.** eliminate, extirpate **10.** annihilate **11.** exterminate

erase . . . **4.** dele, kill **5.** arase (obs) **6.** cancel, delete, efface, excise **7.** expunge, relieve **10.** obliterate

Erasmus satire . . . **16.** The Praise of Folly

Erastus (Swiss) . . . **9.** physician **10.** theologian

ere . . . **4.** also, soon **5.** early, prior **6.** before, erenow, sooner **7.** earlier, ere long **8.** erewhile, formerly **10.** before long, previously, sooner than

Erebus (pert to) . . .
brother . . **3.** Nox
father of . . **3.** Day **6.** Aether
Greek myth . . **8.** darkness (nether)
native of . . **5.** Hades
son . . **5.** Chaos

erect . . . **4.** lift, rear, stay **5.** build, found, raise, stand, upend **6.** raised **7.** elevate, upright **8.** uplifted, vertical **9.** construct, establish, institute **13.** perpendicular

eremite . . . **6.** hermit **7.** recluse **8.** anchoret, solitary **9.** anchorite

erenow . . . **5.** prior **8.** erewhile, formerly **10.** heretofore

ergo . . . **5.** hence **9.** therefore

Erin . . . **4.** Eire **7.** Ireland

Eritrea, Africa . . .
capital . . **6.** Asmara
formerly part of . . **8.** Ethiopia
site . . **6.** Red Sea

ermine . . . **3.** fur **4.** robe (emblem)

5. stoat (stot) 6. clothe, lasset, weasel 7. ermelin

erode . . . 3. eat 4. gnaw, wear 7. corrode, decline, destroy 11. deteriorate 12. disintegrate

erotic . . . 6. loving, sexual 7. amative, amatory, amorous, sensual

err . . . 3. sin 4. miss, slip 5. stray 6. bungle 7. blunder, deviate 10. transgress 12. miscalculate, misinterpret

Er Rai . . . 5. stars 8. shepherd

errand . . . 4. task, trip 7. journey, mission 8. business (special) 10. commission

errand boy . . . 4. page 7. bellboy, bellhop, courier 9. messenger

errant . . . 6. erring, roving 7. peccant 8. fallible 9. deviating, erroneous, itinerant, wandering 10. journeying

erratic . . . 5. queer, rogue 6. whacky 7. nomadic, strange 8. abnormal 9. eccentric, irregular, planetary, wandering 10. capricious, changeable

erroneous . . . 5. false, wrong 6. untrue 7. peccant 8. illusory, mistaken 9. wandering

error . . . 3. sin 4. flub, muff, slip 5. boner, lapse 6. errata (pl), miscue 7. blunder, falsity, misstep, mistake 8. iniquity 11. anachronism, misjudgment 14. miscalculation

ersatz . . . 5. proxy, token 9. vicarious 10. equivalent, substitute 11. alternative, replacement 12. substitution

Erse . . . 5. Irish 6. Celtic, Gaelic

erst, erstwhile . . . 4. also, once 5. first 6. former, sooner 8. earliest, formerly 10. heretofore, previously

erudite . . . 4. wise 7. learned 8. cultured, educated, literate 9. scholarly

erudition . . . 4. lore 6. finish, wisdom 7. letters 8. learning, pedantry 9. knowledge

eruption . . . 4. rash 6. geyser 7. volcano 8. ejection, outbreak, outburst 9. commotion, exanthema 10. nettlerash 13. efflorescence

Esau (pert to) . . .
Bible ref . . 7. Genesis
brother . . 5. Jacob
father . . 5. Isaac
home . . 4. Seir
mother . . 7. Rebekah
name (later) . . 4. Edom

escape . . . 4. flee 5. dodge, elope, elude, evade, spill 7. evasion 9. avolation 13. circumvention

escargot . . . 5. snail

escarpment . . . 5. cliff, slope 9. precipice 13. fortification

eschar . . . 4. scab, sore 5. crust 6. slough

escharotic . . . 7. caustic, mordant 8. stinging 9. corrosive

escheat . . . 4. fall 5. lapse 6. revert (land) 7. forfeit 9. reversion 10. forfeiture

eschew . . . 4. shun 5. avoid 7. abstain, refrain

escolar . . . 4. fish 8. mackerel (like)

escort . . . 3. see 4. beau 5. guard (honor), usher 6. attend, convoy, gigolo, squire 7. conduct, retinue 8. chaperon 9. accompany 13. accompaniment

escritoire . . . 4. desk 6. bureau 7. dresser 9. secretary 10. secretaire

escrow . . . 4. bond, deed (deposit) 9. muniments

esculent . . . 6. edible 7. eatable 8. gustable 10. comestible

escutcheon . . . 4. fess (band), orle (voided) 5. crest 6. shield

esker, eskar . . . 2. os 4. osar (pl) 5. drift, hills, mound, ridge

Eskimo . . . 3. Ita 4. Yuit 5. Aleut 6. Innuit 10. skraelling 11. Yikirgaulit (Diomede Isles)

Eskimo (pert to) . . .
boat, canoe . . 5. kayak, umiak (oomiac)
boot (sealskin) . . 5. kamik
coat (bird skin) . . 5. parka 6. temiak
color . . 5. brown (rustic)
dog . . 5. Husky 8. Malemute
family . . 9. Eskimauan
fish . . 4. Atka 8. mackerel
hut, house . . 5. igloo, tupek (tupik)
jacket . . 6. temiak
knife (woman's) . . 3. ulu
memorial post . . 3. xat
settlement . . 4. Etah
totem . . 4. pole, post 6. symbol

esne . . . 4. serf 5. slave 8. hireling

esophagus, oesophagus . . . 4. crop, gula 6. gullet, throat 7. pharynx

esoteric . . . 5. inner 6. occult, secret 7. private 8. abstruse, initiate, personal 9. recondite 12. confidential

esoteric doctrine . . . 6. cabala

esoteric wisdom . . . 6. gnosis

espalier . . . 7. epaulet, railing, trellis

Español . . . 7. Spanish

especial . . . 5. chief 7. special 8. peculiar, uncommon

Esperanto . . . 3. Ido 8. language (Internat)

espionage . . . 4. espy 6. spying 11. observation (secret) 14. reconnaissance

esplanade . . . 4. walk 5. drive, level, Prado, praya 6. strand 7. walkway

espousal . . . 7. wedding 8. adoption, ceremony 10. acceptance 11. embracement

espouse . . . 3. wed 4. bind, mate 5. adopt, marry 6. defend, pledge 7. betroth, embrace, support 8. maintain, plead for

esprit de corps . . . 3. wit 6. spirit 8. devotion 10. enthusiasm, fellowship 11. partisanism

esprit fort (Relig) . . . 11. freethinker

espy . . . 3. see 5. watch 6. behold, descry, detect 7. discern 8. discover 9. look about

esquire . . . 5. title 6. escort, gentry 7. armiger 8. escudero, nobleman 11. armor-bearer 12. shield-bearer

essay . . . 3. try 4. test 5. assay, chris (Rhet), paper, theme, tract, trial 6. effort, thesis 7. attempt 8. endeavor, treatise 11. composition 12. disquisition, dissertation

esse . . . 5. being (real) 9. existence

essence . . . 3. ens 4. core, gist, odor, pith 5. attar, being, scent 6. kernel, nature 7. element, extract, perfume

9. principle, substance 12. quintessence
essential . . . 5. vital 6. mortal 7. needful
8. existent, inherent 9. necessary,
necessity 13. indispensable
essential oil . . . 8. volatile 12. attar of
roses
essential part . . . 4. core, crux, gist, pith
7. element 8. inherent 10. inwardness
establish . . . 3. fix 4. base, seat 5. build,
enact, erect, found, plant, prove, set
up 6. create, ground, locate, ordain,
settle 7. confirm, pre-empt 8. ensconce,
legalize, radicate (rare) 9. ascertain,
originate
established . . . 5. fixed 6. proved, rested,
stable 11. naturalized, traditional
12. conventional
established (pert to) . . .
church . . 9. Episcopal (Eng)
rule . . 8. standard
thing . . 4. fact
truth . . 8. verified
establishment . . . 4. mill 5. plant
6. custom, menage 7. factory
9. structure 12. organization
establishment of cordial relations . . .
13. rapprochement
establishment of new plant home . . .
6. ecesis
estate . . . 4. alod, fief (feudal), rank
(social) 5. manor, title 6. assets,
equity 7. alodium, demesne, fortune
8. freehold, interest, property
9. situation
esteem . . . 4. dear 5. adore, honor, judge,
pride, value 6. admire, regard, repute,
revere 7. respect 8. appraise, venerate
10. appreciate 13. consideration
ester of . . .
silicic acid . . 8. silicate
stearic acid . . 7. stearin 8. stearate
tropic acid . . 7. tropate
vinegar . . 7. acetate
esthetic, aesthetic . . . 6. essene
8. artistic, tasteful 9. beautiful
estimable . . . 6. worthy 8. valuable
9. admirable, honorable, reputable,
venerable 10. measurable
12. praiseworthy
estimate . . . 3. aim, set 4. gage, rank,
rate 5. audit, gauge, guess, prize, think
6. assess, repute 7. adjudge, compute,
measure, opinion 8. appraise, judgment
9. calculate, statement, valuation
Estonia . . .
capital . . 5. Revel 7. Tallinn
industry . . 3. oil
island . . 5. Oesel
estop . . . 3. bar 4. fill, halt, plug, stay
6. impede, stop up 7. prevent 8. prohibit
estrange . . . 4. part, wean 6. divert,
divide 8. alienate, disunite, separate
estreat . . . 4. copy 6. amerce, sconce
7. extract 9. duplicate, penalties (law)
estuary . . . 3. bay 4. Pará 5. firth, frith,
Plata
etch . . . 3. cut 4. bite 5. infix 7. corrode,
engrave, impress (upon)
eternal . . . 6. eonian 7. aeonian, ageless,
endless, lasting 8. enduring, immortal,
timeless 9. boundless, ceaseless,

immutable, incessant, unceasing
10. unchanging 11. everlasting
12. imperishable, interminable,
unchangeable
Eternal City . . . 4. Rome
eternal death . . . 9. perdition
eternal home . . . 6. heaven 12. The
Hereafter
eternity . . . 3. eon 4. aeon, ages, olam
8. Olam haba
etesian . . . 4. wind (Aegean Sea) 6. annual
8. seasonal 10. periodical
Ethan Frome author . . . 7. Wharton
ether . . . 3. air, sky 5. ester, space
6. anisol, heaven (anc) 8. empyrean
10. anesthetic
ethereal . . . 4. rare 5. aerie (aery), light
7. fragile, slender, tenuous 8. delicate,
heavenly, vaporous 9. celestial
10. atmosphere (earth's), spiritlike
11. phantomlike 13. unsubstantial
ethereal (pert to) . . .
being . . 5. sylph
color . . 7. sky blue
fluid . . 5. ichor (icor)
poetic . . 4. aery
salt . . 5. ester
ethical . . . 5. moral, right 7. upright
8. virtuous
ethics . . . 6. morals 8. hedonics
10. principles (moral) 11. highest good,
summum bonum 12. Magna Moralia
(Aristotle)
Ethiopia (Abyssinia) . . .
capital . . 10. Addis Ababa
city . . 5. Adowa
empress . . 7. Zauditu
king (Myth) . . 5. Negus 6. Memnon
people . . 6. Hamite 10. Abyssinian
people (anc) . . 5. Bejas, Galla 6. Hamite,
Semite
river . . 3. Omo 4. Juba 5. Abbai (Blue
Nile)
ruler . . 7. Menelik 13. Haile Selassie
tribes (anc) . . 5. Bejas, Galla 7. Hamites,
Semites
Ethiopian (pert to) . . .
ape . . 6. gelada
banana . . 6. ensete
dialect . . 4. Geez
lily . . 5. calla
Torah . . 5. tetel
ethnic . . . 5. pagan 6. racial 7. gentile,
heathen
ethnology . . . 5. races (Man)
ethology . . . 7. manners 9. bionomics,
character
ethos (opp of pathos) . . . 9. attitudes
(moral), esthetics
etiquette . . . 4. form 5. label, mores
6. ticket 7. decorum, manners
9. amenities, propriety 10. civilities
etiquette, breach of . . . 8. solecism
Etruria, Italy . . . see *Etruscan*
Etruscan (pert to) . . .
bookbinding (anc) . . 9. classical
deity . . 3. Lar, Uni
pottery . . 8. bucchero (black)
race . . 7. Rasenna 8. Tursenoi, Tyrrheni
soothsayer . . 8. haruspex (a)
soothsayer's function . . 8. extispex

ettle... **3.** try **4.** plan **6.** aspire, design, intent **8.** consider, endeavor
etui, etwee... **4.** case **7.** trousse
etymology... **10.** word origin
eucalyptus... **4.** lerp (laap, juice) **7.** gum tree **8.** eucalypt
eucalyptus eater... **5.** koala
Eucharist (pert to)...
  administer to.. **6.** housel **8.** viaticum (dying)
  plate.. **5.** paten
  rite.. **9.** Communion (Holy) **11.** Lord's Supper
  wafer.. **4.** host
  wafer vessel.. **8.** ciborium
  wine.. **5.** krama
  wine vessel.. **3.** ama **5.** amula
Euclid (Gr)... **8.** geometer (BC)
eulogist... **9.** encomiast **10.** panegyrist
eulogize... **4.** laud **5.** boost, extol **6.** praise **7.** commend, glorify **9.** celebrate **10.** panegyrize
eulogy... **5.** eloge **6.** hesped (Heb), praise **7.** oration **8.** citation, encomium **9.** laudation, panegyric
euphony... **5.** meter **6.** melody, rhythm, speech (ease of) **7.** harmony
Eurafrica... **5.** Egypt **6.** Europe **7.** Algeria **9.** Abyssinia (anc)
Eurasia... **4.** Asia **6.** Europe **7.** Scythia (anc)
Eurasian (pert to)...
  herb.. **6.** yarrow **7.** gosmore
  mint.. **6.** Nepeta
  people.. **5.** Finns **7.** Ugrians **9.** Armenians, Turanians
eureka... **3.** aha **11.** exclamation **12.** I Have Found It (Calif motto)
Euripedes (Gr)... **4.** poet (BC)
Europe... see also *European*
  basin (coal).. **4.** Saar
  battlefield.. **5.** Marne **6.** Verdun **8.** Normandy, Waterloo **11.** Belleau Wood
  capitals.. **4.** Bonn, Oslo, Riga, Rome **5.** Berne, Paris, Sofia **6.** Athens, Berlin, Dublin, Lisbon, London, Madrid, Moscow, Prague, Warsaw **8.** Belgrade, Brussels, Budapest, Helsinki **9.** Amsterdam, Bucharest, Stockholm **10.** Bratislava, Copenhagen, Monte Carlo
  country (anc).. **4.** Elis (Gr) **7.** Etruria (It)
  country (modern).. **5.** Italy, Spain **6.** France, Greece, Latvia, Monaco, Norway, Poland, Russia, Sweden **7.** Belgium, Denmark, England, Finland, Germany, Hungary, Ireland, Rumania **8.** Bulgaria, Portugal, Slovakia **10.** Yugoslavia **11.** Netherlands, Switzerland **13.** Czech Republic **14.** Czechoslovakia
  economic union.. **7.** Benelux
  gulf.. **4.** Riga **7.** Bothnia
  invaders.. **4.** Huns **5.** Arabs, Turks **7.** Mongols
  kingdom (anc).. **5.** Arles **6.** Aragon **8.** Burgundy
  lancer.. **5.** uhlan **6.** hussar
  mountain region.. **4.** Alps **5.** Tirol (Tyrol)

8. Pyrenees **9.** Apennines
  race (anc).. **5.** Goths **7.** Teutons **9.** Visigoths **10.** Ostrogoths
  river.. **4.** Elbe, Isar **5.** Loire, Meuse, Rhine, Rhone, Seine, Volga **6.** Danube **7.** Dneiper, Moselle
  sea.. **4.** Azov **5.** North **6.** Baltic
  strait.. **8.** Bosporus
  valley.. **4.** Ruhr
  volcano.. **4.** Etna **8.** Vesuvius **9.** Stromboli
European (pert to)...
  antelope... **7.** chamois
  bat.. **8.** serotine
  bird.. **3.** ani, daw, mew (gull) **4.** kite, stag **5.** glede, mavis, ousel, serin **6.** godwit, linnet, marten, merlin (falcon) **7.** bittern, jackdaw, ortolan, starnel **8.** dotterel, garganey **9.** brambling, gallinule **10.** turtledove **11.** lammergeier **12.** capercaillie
  bison.. **7.** aurochs
  clover.. **6.** alsike
  dog.. **7.** griffin
  fish.. **3.** gar **4.** dace, rudd, spet, tope (shark) **5.** sprat **6.** allice, barbel, brasse, morgay, turbot
  grape.. **6.** muscat
  linden.. **4.** teil
  mint.. **6.** hyssop **9.** horehound
  mouse.. **4.** loir, vole
  polecat.. **7.** fitchew
  rodent.. **3.** erd **4.** loir **6.** leriot **7.** hamster
  sandpiper.. **4.** ruff **5.** terek
  squirrel.. **5.** sisel **10.** polatouche
  tree.. **4.** cade (juniper), sorb (apple) **5.** carob **9.** terebinth
  weasel.. **5.** stoat
  wheat.. **5.** emmer (speltz) **7.** einkorn
evacuant... **6.** emetic **8.** diuretic **9.** cathartic, purgative
evacuate... **4.** void **5.** empty, expel **6.** depart, vacate **7.** deprive, exhaust **8.** withdraw **9.** discharge
evade... **3.** gee **4.** duck, foil, shun **5.** avoid, dodge, elude, parry, shirk, shunt **6.** baffle, escape, illude **7.** beguile, quibble **8.** sidestep, slip away **10.** circumvent
evaluate... **5.** judge, weigh **6.** assess **8.** appraise
evanescent... **8.** fleeting **9.** ephemeral, transient, vanishing **11.** impermanent **12.** disappearing **13.** infinitesimal
evangelical... **7.** Gospels **8.** orthodox **10.** Protestant, scriptural
Evangeline (pert to)...
  home.. **6.** Acadia
  lover.. **7.** Gabriel
  poem by.. **10.** Longfellow (1847)
evangelist... **6.** Graham, Sunday (Billy) **7.** apostle, Roberts **9.** McPherson
evaporate... **3.** dry **5.** steam **6.** escape, exhale **7.** avolate **8.** vaporize **9.** cease to be, dehydrate, disappear
evasion... **5.** dodge, shift **6.** escape **8.** avoiding **9.** avoidance, quibbling, shuffling **12.** equivocation **13.** circumvention, secretiveness
evasive... **3.** sly **4.** eely **6.** shifty **7.** elusive, elusory **9.** deceitful,

quibbling, secretive

eve . . . **3.** iva (herb), wet **4.** dusk, thaw **6.** sunset **12.** on the brink of, on the verge of

even . . . **3.** e'en, tie **4.** just, tied **5.** equal, exact, level, match, plane **6.** placid, smooth, square, steady **7.** abreast, balance, equable, neutral, regular, uniform **8.** directly, parallel **9.** impartial, precisely **11.** symmetrical

even (if) . . . **8.** although **12.** nevertheless **15.** notwithstanding

even (so) . . . **3.** yes **12.** nevertheless

evener . . . **9.** equalizer **10.** doubletree

evenglow . . . **3.** red (color) **8.** twilight

evening . . . **5.** Abend **8.** sunset

evening dress . . . **4.** gown **6.** jewels, tuxedo **8.** slippers (high heel) **9.** full dress, headdress **10.** dinner coat **11.** tie and tails **17.** swallow-tailed coat

event . . . **4.** fate (obs), game **5.** drama, issue **6.** result **7.** contest, episode, scandal **8.** incident **9.** adventure, happening, milestone **10.** conclusion, occurrence **11.** consequence, termination **12.** circumstance

event (pert to) . . .
extraordinary . . **10.** phenomenon
supernatural . . **7.** miracle
theater . . **6.** opener **8.** premiere
turning point . . **6.** crisis **8.** decision, landmark

eventide . . . **4.** dusk **6.** sunset, vesper **7.** evening, sundown **8.** twilight **9.** nightfall

eventually . . . **3.** yet **6.** lastly **7.** finally **10.** ultimately

ever . . . **3.** e'er **4.** anon **5.** at all **6.** always **7.** forever **10.** constantly **11.** perpetually

Everest peak . . . **6.** Lhotse (28,100 ft)

evergreen shrub . . . **4.** Ilex, moss, Olax, titi **5.** heath, holly, savin, toyon **6.** laurel **7.** baretta, jasmine **9.** perennial **12.** rhododendron

evergreen tree . . . **3.** fir, yew **4.** pine **5.** carob, cedar, larch, olive, Taxus **6.** balsam, deodar, spruce, tarata **7.** conifer, hemlock, madrona, redwood

everlasting . . . **6.** eterne **7.** aeonian, agelong, durable, endless, eternal, forever, lasting, tedious **8.** enduring, evermore, immortal, infinite **9.** continual, incessant, perpetual, unceasing, wearisome **10.** immortelle, indefinite **11.** never-ending, strawflower **12.** Eternal Being, imperishable **13.** unintermitted, uninterrupted

every . . . **3.** all, any, ilk **4.** each, ilka **6.** entire **8.** complete

every one, everyone . . . **3.** all **4.** each **9.** everybody **10.** individual

everything . . . **3.** all, sum **5.** total

evict . . . **4.** oust **5.** eject, expel, prove **6.** remove **7.** confute **8.** force out

eviction . . . **6.** ouster **9.** ejectment **11.** dislodgment **13.** dispossession

evidence . . . **4.** clue, sign **5.** proof, token **6.** attest, evince **7.** constat (law), probate, support **8.** argument, manifest, rebuttal **9.** testimony **10.** indication **15.** circumstantiate

evident . . . **5.** clear, plain **6.** patent **7.** obvious, visible **8.** apparent, manifest, palpable **9.** notorious **11.** indubitable

eviscerate . . . **3.** gut **10.** disembowel

evil . . . **3.** bad, ill, mal (pref) **4.** bane, vile **6.** injury, sinful, wicked **7.** adverse, baleful, corrupt, hurtful, immoral, malefic, misdeed, satanic, unsound, vicious **8.** depraved, iniquity, sinister **9.** injurious, malignant, offensive **10.** calamitous, malevolent, pernicious, wrongdoing **12.** unpropitious

evil (pert to) . . .
child . . **3.** imp
deed . . **3.** sin **4.** harm
devil (little) . . **9.** deevilick (Scot)
doer . . **5.** cheat **9.** miscreant, wrongdoer **10.** malefactor
omen . . **5.** knell
spirit . . **5.** bugan, demon, devil, ghoul, Satan **6.** Belial **7.** Ahriman, Amaimon **8.** Asmodeus **9.** cacodemon, demonkind, lost souls

evils . . . **4.** ills, mala

evince . . . **4.** show **7.** display, exhibit, express, provoke **8.** convince, evidence, indicate, manifest

evoke . . . **4.** call (out) **5.** educe, voice **6.** elicit, prompt, summon **7.** conjure

evolution . . . **7.** biogeny, cosmism **8.** heredity, maneuver, movement **9.** Darwinism, phylogeny, unfolding, unrolling **10.** evolvement **11.** development **13.** manifestation, Spencerianism

evolve . . . **4.** emit **5.** educe **6.** create, deduce, derive, unfold, unroll **7.** develop, grow out **9.** disengage, expatiate, extricate **11.** disentangle

ewe . . . **3.** keb **4.** lamb **5.** crone (old), sheep **6.** theave

ewer . . . **3.** jug **5.** crock **7.** pitcher

exacerbate . . . **5.** anger **6.** incite **8.** embitter, irritate **9.** aggravate

exact . . . **4.** just, levy, nice **6.** assess, demand, elicit, extort, formal, minute, oblige, strict **7.** careful, correct, literal, precise, regular, require **8.** accurate **10.** methodical, meticulous

exact (pert to) . . .
opposite of . . **8.** antipode **9.** antipodal
penalty . . **4.** fine **7.** estreat
thinking . . **13.** ratiocination
vengeance . . **6.** avenge

exacting . . . **6.** severe, strict **7.** arduous **8.** critical **9.** demanding, elicitory **10.** fastidious **12.** extortionate

exacting devotion (exclusive) . . . **7.** jealous

exactly . . . **3.** due **5.** spand **6.** nicely **7.** quite so **8.** as you say **9.** precisely **10.** accurately

exaggerated . . . **5.** outré **8.** enhanced, enlarged, overdone, romanced **9.** excessive, increased, magnified **10.** overstated **11.** exceptional **13.** overestimated **14.** misrepresented

exaggerated comedy . . . **5.** farce

exalt . . . **5.** elate, extol, raise **6.** praise **7.** elevate, ennoble, glorify, inspire, promote, worship 8. enthrone, increase, sanctify 10. aggrandize

exalted . . . 5. grand, noble, sheen 6. elated 7. refined, sublime 8. elevated, extolled 9. dignified 11. illustrious

examination . . . 4. test 5. audit, trial 7. inquiry 8. research, scrutiny, specimen 10. discussion, inspection 11. inquisition 13. investigation

examine . . . 3. pry, spy, try (law) 4. pore, scan, sift, test 5. audit, probe, quest 6. censor, debate, ponder 7. analyze, collate, discuss, explore, inspect 8. consider 10. scrutinize 11. interrogate

examiner . . . 6. censor, conner, tester 7. auditor, officer (court) 9. inspector

example . . . 4. case, norm, type 5. bysen (obs), model 6. sample 7. pattern, warning 8. instance, paradigm, specimen 9. exemplify, precedent 12. illustration 15. exemplification

ex animo . . . 9. sincerely 12. from the heart

Excalibur . . . 5. sword

excavate . . . 3. dig 4. cave, mine 5. dig up, scoop, stope 6. dredge, exhume, quarry 9. hollow out

excavation . . . 3. pit 4. hole, mine 5. stope 6. cavity, dugout 7. digging 8. opencast

exceed . . . 3. top 4. pass 5. excel, outdo 6. outvie, overdo 7. eclipse, outrank, surpass 8. outstrip, overstep 9. overshoot, transcend 11. predominate

exceedingly . . . 4. many, very 9. extremely 13. extraordinary

excel . . . 3. cap, top 4. beat, best 5. outdo, outgo, rival 6. better, exceed, precel 7. surpass 8. dominate, outshine 9. transcend

excellence . . . 4. meed 5. merit 6. desert, virtue 7. classic, probity 9. supremacy 13. inimitability

excellent . . . 4. A-one, best, fine, good 5. bravo, prime, super 6. choice, select, tiptop, worthy 7. capital, corking, stellar 8. skillful (skilful), stunning, valuable 9. admirable, exquisite, first-rate 12. transcendent

except . . . 3. bar, but 4. omit, save 6. exempt, reject, unless 7. besides 9. eliminate, other than

exception . . . 4. plea 5. cavil, doubt 6. oddity 7. dissent 8. demurrer 9. condition, exclusion, exemption, objection, rejection 11. restriction

exceptional . . . 4. rare 7. notable, unusual 8. superior, uncommon 9. exclusive, wonderful 10. remarkable 11. outstanding 13. extraordinary

excerpt . . . 4. cite 5. quote, scrap 6. choice 7. extract, passage (selected) 9. selection

excess . . . 3. too 4. over, plus 5. luxus 7. nimiety, overage, profuse, surplus 10. indulgence (undue), redundancy 11. superfluity 12. intemperance 14. immoderateness, superabundance

excess (solar over lunar month) . . . 5. epact

excessive . . . 3. too 5. undue 6. overly 7. extreme, profuse 8. overmuch 9. fanatical, plethoric 10. exorbitant, immoderate, inordinate, redundancy 11. exaggerated, extravagant 12. unreasonable

excessive (pert to) . . .
development . . 11. hypertrophy
fear . . 5. panic 6. phobia
gushing . . 8. effusion
waste . . 12. extravagance

excessively . . . 3. too 5. enorm 6. unduly 12. exorbitantly, inordinately 13. intemperately

exchange . . . 4. swap 5. bandy, trade 6. barter, resale, rialto 7. dealing, traffic 9. transpose 10. substitute 11. interchange, reciprocate

exchange (pert to) . . .
discount . . 4. agio
for money . . 4. cash, sell
letters . . 10. correspond
place . . 4. mart 5. store 6. bourse, market, shoppe
premium . . 4. agio
visits . . 3. gam

exchequer . . . 4. fisc (fisk) 5. funds, purse 8. finances, treasury 11. possessions (money)

excise . . . 3. tax 4. toll 6. impost

exciseman . . . 5. gager 7. officer 8. revenuer

excision . . . 7. erasure, removal 10. cutting off, cutting out, mutilation 11. destruction, extirpation

excite . . . 4. fire, roil, spur, stir, urge 5. elate, impel, rouse 6. arouse, awaken, bestir, incite, kindle, prompt, stir up 7. agitate, animate, inflame, provoke, psych up 8. energize, interest 9. electrify, impassion, instigate, stimulate

excited . . . 4. agog 6. hoopla 7. aroused, fevered, keyed up 8. agitated, startled 10. interested 11. impassioned

excited, not easily . . . 6. stolid 7. stoical 9. impassive

excitement . . . 3. ado 4. stir 5. fever 6. furore 7. emotion, ferment 9. agitation, commotion 10. incitement, irritation 11. disturbance, stimulation

exciting . . . 5. kicky 6. gung-ho, hectic 7. parlous 8. alluring 9. desirable, thrilling 10. delightful 11. interesting, provocative

exciting compassion . . . 7. piteous

exclamation . . . 2. ah, lo, oh, so 3. aha, bah, boo, fic, hep, oho, tut, ugh, yah 4. ahem, alas, drat, egad, evoe, phew, pish, rats, yech 5. bravo, humph, pshaw 6. indeed, shezam 7. kerwham 9. alackaday 11. ejaculation 12. interjection

exclude . . . 3. bar 4. omit 5. debar, eject, expel 6. banish 7. shut out 8. disallow, preclude, prohibit 9. eliminate 13. excommunicate

exclusive . . . 5. aloof, ritzy 6. select 7. special 8. limiting, snobbish 9. seclusive 10. definitive, unsociable 11. prohibitive, restrictive

exclusive right . . . **6.** patent
   10. concession **11.** restriction
excoriate . . . **4.** flay, gall, peel **5.** strip
   6. abrade **9.** criticize
excrescence . . . **4.** boss (Arch), lump
   6. growth, nodule **9.** appendage,
   outgrowth **10.** protrusion
excrete . . . **5.** egest **9.** discharge, eliminate
excruciating . . . **7.** painful, racking
   9. agonizing, torturing **11.** distressing
excursion . . . **3.** row **4.** ride, sail, tour,
   trek, trip **5.** jaunt, sally **6.** junket, outing,
   ramble **7.** circuit, journey, outlope
   8. circuity **10.** expedition
excusable . . . **6.** venial **9.** allowable,
   justified **10.** defensible, exemptible,
   pardonable, remissible **11.** justifiable
excuse . . . **4.** plea **5.** alibi, remit **6.** acquit,
   essoin, pardon **7.** absolve, apology,
   condone, forgive, pretext **8.** overlook
   9. exonerate, extenuate
execrate . . . **4.** hate **5.** abhor, curse
   6. detest, loathe **8.** denounce
execute . . . **2.** do **3.** act **4.** hang, kill,
   vest **6.** direct, effect, finish, manage
   7. conduct, enforce, perform **8.** carry
   out, complete, transact **10.** accomplish,
   administer
execution . . . **4.** writ **7.** hanging
   10. production, punishment
   11. achievement, performance,
   transaction **14.** accomplishment
exegate . . . **6.** leader **7.** adviser
   8. dragoman **11.** interpreter
exegesis . . . **7.** explain **9.** interpret
   10. exposition, expounding
exemplar . . . **5.** ideal, model **7.** example,
   paragon, pattern **8.** specimen
   9. archetype
exemplary . . . **8.** laudable, monitory
   11. commendable **12.** exemplifying,
   praiseworthy **14.** representative
exemplify . . . **4.** copy **6.** typify **7.** explain
   10. illustrate, transcribe
exempt . . . **4.** exon **5.** clear **6.** immune
   7. absolve, release **8.** dispense,
   excepted, excluded, released, set apart
   10. privileged
exemption . . . **6.** essoin **7.** freedom
   8. immunity, impunity, navicert
   12. dispensation
exercise . . . **3.** ply, ure (anc), use
   4. task, yoga **5.** drill, étude, exert,
   train **6.** action, employ, lesson, praxis,
   school, tai chi **7.** display, jogging,
   problem, workout **8.** activity, aerobics,
   ceremony, practice, training **9.** athletics
   10. exhibition, gymnastics, isometrics
exertion . . . **5.** essay, trial **6.** effort
   7. attempt **8.** endeavor
exhalation . . . **4.** aura, fume **5.** steam
   6. breath **7.** halitus **9.** effluvium,
   emanation **10.** expiration
   11. evaporation **12.** vaporization
exhale . . . **4.** emit **6.** vanish **7.** exhaust,
   respite **9.** transpire **10.** breathe out
exhaust . . . **3.** fag, sap **4.** emit, jade, tire
   5. drain, empty, spend, waste, weary
   6. exhale, overdo, weaken **7.** consume,
   deplete, fatigue **9.** discharge
   10. impoverish

exhausted . . . **4.** done, worn **5.** spent,
   tired **6.** used up **7.** emptied, petered
   (out) **8.** dog-tired, forspent
exhaustion . . . **6.** effete **7.** burnout, fatigue
   9. depletion, lassitude **11.** prostration
   14. impoverishment
exhibit . . . **3.** air **4.** fair, shew (anc),
   show, wear **5.** stage, state **6.** evince,
   expose, flaunt, parade, reveal **7.** display
   8. disclose, evidence, manifest
   9. spectacle **11.** demonstrate
   15. circumstantiate
exhibit (pert to) . . .
   colors (change of) . . **8.** iridesce, opalesce
   pleasure . . **5.** gloat, revel (in)
   taste (refined) . . **6.** ostent **7.** elegant
exhibition . . . **4.** fair, show **9.** spectacle
   10. exposition **11.** ostentation
   13. manifestation
exhibition room . . . **10.** panopticon
exhilaration . . . **6.** gaiety **7.** jollity
   8. gladness, hilarity **9.** animation,
   merriment **10.** excitement, joyousness
   11. gleefulness, refreshment
   12. cheerfulness, invigoration
exhort . . . **4.** urge, warn **6.** advise, dehort,
   incite, preach **7.** caution **9.** encourage,
   stimulate
exhume . . . **3.** dig **5.** delve **7.** unearth
   8. disinter, exhumate
exigeant . . . **8.** exacting **11.** importunate
exigency . . . **4.** need, urge **6.** crisis
   7. demands, urgency **8.** juncture,
   pressure **9.** emergency, extremity,
   necessity **12.** requirements
exigent . . . **4.** writ **6.** strict, urgent
   8. critical, exacting, pressing
   9. demanding, necessary **10.** compelling
   13. indispensable
exile . . . **6.** banish, deport **7.** outcast
   8. outlawry, relegate **9.** expulsion
   10. banishment, expatriate
   12. expatriation, proscription
exist . . . **2.** am, be, is **3.** are **4.** live
   5. alive **6.** abound **9.** be present
existence . . . **3.** ens **4.** esse, life **5.** actus,
   being, entia **6.** extant **7.** essence, reality
   8. presence **9.** actuality
   13. manifestation
existing (pert to) . . .
   fancifully . . **9.** imaginary **10.** transitory
   name only (in) . . **7.** nominal, titular
   now . . **6.** extant **7.** current, present
   9. immediate
   same time . . **15.** contemporaneous
   way of . . **9.** lifestyle
exit . . . **3.** die **4.** door, gate, vent **5.** going,
   go out, issue **6.** egress, outlet **7.** leaving,
   passage (out), walkout **9.** departure
exitus . . . **5.** death, issue **6.** exodus, outlet
   7. outcome
exlex . . . **6.** outlaw
ex libris . . . **8.** colophon **9.** bookplate
exodus . . . **4.** Book (Bib), exit **5.** going
   6. flight, hegira **9.** departure
Exodus author . . . **4.** Uris
exonerate . . . **4.** free **5.** clear **6.** acquit
   7. absolve, release, relieve **9.** disburden
   (obs), exculpate
exorbitant . . . **5.** undue **9.** excessive
   10. high-priced

exorbitant interest ... 5. usury
exorcism ... 5. spell 7. formula
9. expulsion (of evil spirits)
11. conjuration, incantation
exordium ... 5. proem 7. preface, prelude
8. overture 9. beginning 12. introduction
exoteric ... 8. exterior, external, outsider
14. comprehensible
exotic ... 5. alien 7. foreign, strange
8. colorful, ulterior 9. not native,
peregrine, unrelated 10. extraneous,
outlandish
expand ... 4. grow, open 5. sheet, splay,
tract 6. dilate, spread 7. broaden,
develop, distend, enlarge 9. expatiate,
intumesce
expanse ... 3. sea 4. main (broad)
5. ocean, plain, reach, tract 6. desert,
extent, spread 7. stretch 8. eternity
(time) 9. expansion
expansion ... 4. size 6. extent, growth,
spread 8. dilation, increase
10. distention 11. development,
enlargement, expatiation
expansive ... 4. wide 5. broad, large
7. elastic, liberal 8. effusive, spacious
9. bombastic, grandiose 11. extensional,
sympathetic 12. unrestrained
13. comprehensive
expatiate ... 5. dwell 6. dilate 7. descant,
enlarge 10. widespread
expatriate ... 5. exile, expel 6. banish,
outlaw 7. exclude, outcast 9. ostracize
13. excommunicate
expect ... 4. deem, hope, wait 5. await,
think 6. intend 7. suppose 10. anticipate
expectation ... 4. hope 9. imminence,
intention 12. anticipation
expedience ... 6. wisdom 7. fitness
10. adaptation, timeliness 11. suitability
expedient ... 4. wise 5. shift 6. timely
7. fitting, politic, ressort, stopgap
8. artifice, resource 9. advisable
10. profitable 12. advantageous
expedite ... 3. hie 4. easy, free 5. hurry,
light, speed 6. hasten 7. further, quicken
8. dispatch 10. accelerate, facilitate
expedition ... 5. drave, foray, haste,
speed 6. safari 7. Crusade, entrada,
journey 8. Crusades 9. excursion,
hastening
expel ... 4. oust, void 5. eject, evict,
exile 6. banish, exhale 7. extrude
9. discharge, eliminate 10. dispossess
expend ... 3. pay, use 5. spend, waste
7. consume 8. disburse 10. distribute
expenditure ... 5. outgo, price 6. outlay
7. expense, payment 11. consumption
12. disbursement
expense ... 4. cost 5. price 6. outlay
9. allowance 11. consumption
12. disbursement
expensive ... 4. dear, high 5. fancy, steep
6. costly, lavish 7. liberal 10. high-priced
11. extravagant
experience ... 3. see, try 4. feel, have,
know, test 5. maxim, sense, skill
6. ordeal, suffer, wisdom 7. emotion,
undergo 8. facility 9. knowledge,
sensation 10. occurrence
experience (pert to) ...

pleasure .. 5. enjoy
regret .. 6. repent
suffering .. 7. calvary
worldly .. 14. sophistication
experiment ... 3. try 4. test 5. essay,
proof, prove, trial 6. verify
11. observation
expert ... 3. ace 4. deft, whiz (whizz)
5. adept 6. adroit, clever, habile,
master 7. casuist (in conscience), dab
hand 8. artistic, skillful 10. proficient
11. connoisseur, experienced
12. professional
expiate ... 5. atone, purge 6. purify,
shrive (anc)
expiation ... 4. rite 6. amends 7. redress
8. piacular 9. atonement 10. redemption
12. compensation, propitiation
expire ... 3. die, end 4. pass 5. cease,
lapse 6. elapse, perish 7. breathe (out)
9. terminate
explain ... 5. clear, solve 6. define
7. expound, premise 8. describe
9. elucidate, interpret 11. demonstrate
explanation ... 6. theory 7. meaning
8. exegesis, scholium, solution
10. exposition 11. description,
explication 13. clarification
14. interpretation 15. exemplification
expletive ... 3. gee 4. egad, gosh,
oath 5. curse, there, voilà 6. behold
8. addition 9. added word
11. exclamation
explicit ... 4. open 5. exact, fixed
6. candid 7. express, precise 8. absolute,
distinct, implicit, manifest, positive
9. outspoken 11. unambiguous,
unequivocal, unqualified
13. unconditional 14. discriminating
explode ... 3. pop 4. fail 5. blast, burst
6. blow up 7. implode 8. backfire,
detonate
exploit ... 3. act (heroic) 4. dare,
deed, feat, gest, milk 5. bleed
7. heroism 9. advantage 10. overcharge
11. achievement
explore ... 4. look, view 5. probe 6. search
7. examine 8. discover 9. penetrate
11. investigate
explorer ... 5. diver 7. pioneer
10. discoverer
explorer ... 4. Byrd, Cook, Dias, Polo
(Marco), Ross 5. Cabot, Drake, Peary,
Scott 6. Balboa, Cortes (Cortez), De
Soto, Hudson, Pinzón 7. Cartier,
Pizarro, Raleigh (Ralegh) 8. Columbus,
Coronado, Magellan 9. Champlain
10. Shackleton 11. Ponce de León
explosion ... 3. pop 4. bank 5. blast,
noise 6. report 7. failure 8. outburst
10. detonation
explosive ... 3. cap, TNT 4. mine
5. niter, shell 6. amatol, petard,
powder, tittle, tonite 7. cordite, grenade,
lyddite 8. dynamite 9. cartridge,
cellulose, fulgurite, guncotton, pyroxylin
11. firecracker 13. nitroglycerin
15. trinitrotoluene
exponent ... 4. note 5. index 7. symptom
9. explainer, expounder 10. explaining
11. interpreter

expose ... **3.** air **4.** bare, open **6.** divest, reveal, unmask **7.** exhibit, unearth **8.** disclose, discover, endanger **9.** ventilate **10.** exposition

expose·to danger ... **11.** periclitate

expose to scorn ... **6.** satire **7.** pillory

exposition ... **4.** fair **6.** bazaar, expose, lesson **7.** display **8.** exposure, treatise **9.** discourse, spectacle **10.** disclosure, exhibition **11.** abandonment, explanation **12.** dissertation **14.** interpretation

expostulate ... **5.** orate **6.** advise, demand **7.** call for, discuss, protest **8.** complain, dissuade **11.** remonstrate

exposure ... **8.** disproof, jeopardy, openness, snapshot **9.** liability **10.** appearance, disclosure, exposition, visibility

express ... **3.** say **4.** mean, show **5.** exude, speak, state, train, utter, voice **6.** depict, evince, extort, phrase **7.** betoken, carrier, declare, exhibit, expound, extract, signify, testify **8.** describe, dispatch, indicate, intimate, manifest **9.** delineate, messenger, posthaste, utterance **11.** declaration

express (pert to) ...
censure .. **10.** animadvert
disapproval .. **9.** deprecate
fervor .. **7.** enthuse
gratitude .. **5.** thank
indirectly .. **5.** imply
in words .. **6.** phrase
numerically .. **8.** evaluate
regard .. **6.** praise **10.** compliment
regret .. **9.** apologize
sympathy .. **7.** condole, console **10.** grieve with **11.** commiserate

expressing ...
doubt .. **10.** dubitative
extra phrase (Gram) .. **12.** periphrastic
feeling .. **7.** emotive
past tense .. **11.** preteritive
pique .. **5.** pouty
praise .. **9.** laudatory

expression ... **4.** grin, show, term **5.** scowl, smile **6.** aspect, oracle, phrase **7.** diction, meaning **8.** locution **9.** statement, utterance **10.** extraction, indication **11.** delineation **13.** manifestation **14.** representation

expression (pert to) ...
mathematics .. **8.** equation
of approval .. **4.** clap **7.** ovation **8.** applause
of contempt .. **3.** fie **5.** pshaw, sneer
of disapproval .. **6.** rebuke
of ideas .. **4.** mode **5.** style **7.** fashion
of politics .. **4.** vote
of weariness .. **4.** sigh
peculiar .. **5.** idiom
without .. **7.** deadpan

expressive motion ... **7.** gesture **13.** gesticulation

expulsion ... **5.** exile **10.** banishment, expiration **11.** elimination

expunction ... **4.** blot **7.** erasure **10.** effacement **12.** obliteration

expunge ... **4.** dele **5.** erase **6.** cancel, delete, efface, excise, rub out **7.** blot

out, destroy **9.** strike out **10.** annihilate, obliterate

expurgate ... **5.** bathe, purge **6.** censor, excise, purify **7.** cleanse

exquisite ... **4.** fine, rare **6.** dainty, superb **7.** perfect, refined **8.** delicate **9.** beautiful, delicious, matchless **10.** delightful, fastidious

exsanguine ... **6.** anemic **9.** bloodless

exsiccate ... **3.** dry **4.** arid, sear **5.** dry up, parch **7.** exhaust **9.** evaporate

extant ... **5.** being **7.** in vogue, present, visible **8.** existent, existing

extempore ... **7.** offhand **8.** ad-libbed **9.** impromptu **10.** improvised **14.** unpremeditated

extend ... **2.** go **3.** eke, jut, lie, run **4.** give, span **5.** bulge, reach, renew, steal, widen **6.** deepen, deploy, expand, spread **7.** amplify, broaden, draw out, proffer, prolong, radiate, stretch **8.** continue, increase, lengthen, postpone, protract, protrude **10.** exaggerate, straighten

extended ... **4.** open **5.** broad **6.** valued **7.** assured, diffuse **8.** expanded, spacious **10.** lengthened **12.** outstretched

extended view ... **8.** panorama

extension ... **4.** area **5.** range, scope **6.** extent **8.** addition, duration, increase, sequence **9.** expansion **10.** denotation **11.** continuance, enlargement, lengthening **12.** augmentation **13.** extensiveness

extension of time ... **4.** stay **7.** respite

extensive ... **4.** vast, wide **5.** broad, large **7.** immense, titanic **8.** expanded, spacious **9.** expansive, wholesale **10.** widespread **11.** far-reaching

extent ... **4.** area, bulk, room, side, writ **5.** areal, range, reach, scope **6.** amount, degree, length **7.** breadth, compass, expanse, measure **8.** distance, frontage **9.** dimension **10.** assessment (Hist), denotation, proportion

extenuate ... **4.** thin **6.** excuse, lessen, reduce, sicken, weaken **7.** justify **8.** diminish, palliate **9.** attenuate

extenuating ... **10.** justifying, qualifying

exterior ... **5.** ectad (toward), ectal, outer **7.** outside **8.** external **10.** extraneous

exterminate ... **4.** kill **5.** expel **7.** abolish, destroy **8.** get rid of **9.** eradicate, extirpate **10.** annihilate

extermination ... **9.** expulsion **11.** destruction, eradication

extern ... **7.** outward **8.** exterior, external **9.** extrinsic

external ... **4.** ecto **5.** outer, outre **6.** nonego **7.** outside **8.** cortical **10.** extraneous

external appearance ... **5.** guise, image, looks **6.** aspect **8.** features **9.** semblance

extinct ... **4.** dead, past **5.** passé **7.** defunct, died out, expired **8.** quenched **11.** nonexistent **12.** extinguished

extinct bird ... **3.** moa **4.** dodo

extinction ... **5.** death **9.** quenching

11. destruction 12. annihilation
extinct reptile . . . 11. pterodactyl
extinguish . . . 5. annul, choke, douse,
  quell 6. put out, quench, stifle 7. destroy
  8. suppress
extirpate . . . 4. dele, root, stub 5. erase,
  expel 6. excise, uproot 7. destroy
  9. eradicate 11. exterminate
extol . . . 4. laud 5. exalt, kudos 6. praise
  7. applaud, commend, elevate, glorify
  8. emblazon 9. celebrate
extort . . . 5. bleed, exact, steal, wrest,
  wring 6. compel, elicit, wrench
  7. extract 10. overcharge
extortion . . . 7. robbery, seizure
  8. exaction, rapacity 10. extraction,
  oppression, overcharge
extortionist . . . 5. harpy 7. vampire,
  vulture 9. profiteer 11. blackmailer
extra . . . 3. bye 4. over 5. added, spare,
  super 7. surplus 8. superior 9. accessory
  10. additional
extra cache . . . 5. stock, store 7. reserve
  9. reservoir
extract . . . 4. cite, pull 6. deduce, elicit,
  select 7. essence, estreat, excerpt
  8. withdraw
extract (pert to) . . .
  balsam . . 7. toluene
  Bible . . 7. passage 8. pericope
  forcibly . . 6. evulse
  newspaper . . 8. clipping
  orchid (climbing) . . 7. vanilla
extraction . . . 5. birth, stock 6. origin
  7. essence, excerpt 8. tincture
  9. parentage 10. withdrawal
extraneous . . . 5. outer 6. exotic 7. foreign
  9. extrinsic, separated, unrelated
  11. unessential
extraordinary . . . 3. odd 4. rare, unco
  5. great 7. notable, special, unusual
  8. singular 9. irregular, marvelous,
  wonderful 10. noteworthy, remarkable
  11. exceptional 13. distinguished
extravagance . . . 5. waste 6. excess
  8. wildness 9. abundance 10. fanaticism,
  lavishness 11. exorbitance, prodigality
  12. exaggeration, intemperance,
  recklessness
extravagant . . . 3. E la 4. ee la (Mus), high
  (priced) 5. outré 6. absurd 7. baroque,
  bizarre, diffuse, fanatic 8. boastful,
  prodigal, wasteful 9. excessive,
  fanatical, fantastic, luxurious, plentiful
  10. digressive 11. intemperate
  12. unrestrained
extreme . . . 3. end 4. last, sore 5. final,
  great, ultra 6. excess, severe, utmost
  7. drastic, intense, outward, radical
  8. farthest, greatest, ultimate
  9. excessive, extremity, fanatical,
  outermost 10. conclusive, immoderate
extreme degree . . . 3. nth
extreme fear . . . 5. panic 6. horror
extreme unction . . . 5. anele 9. last
  rites, sacrament

extremist . . . 7. radical 8. ultraist
extremity . . . 3. end, tip 4. foot, limb
  (body), pole 5. verge 6. border,
  crisis, summit 8. terminal 9. necessity
  11. termination
extricate . . . 4. free 5. loose 6. evolve,
  rescue, wangle 7. extract 8. liberate
  9. disengage 10. disembroil
  11. disentangle 12. disembarrass
extrinsic . . . 7. foreign, outward
  8. external 9. objective 10. accidental
  (Log), contingent, extraneous, incidental
  12. adventitious, nonessential
extrovert . . . 11. personality (opp of
  introvert)
exuberance . . . 6. excess, plenty
  8. overflow, rankness, vivacity
  9. abundance, animation, profusion
  10. friskiness, liveliness, luxuriance
  11. copiousness 14. superabundance
exuberant . . . 6. frisky, lavish 7. fertile,
  profuse 8. effusive, fruitful, thriving
  9. luxuriant, plentiful 11. overflowing
  13. superabundant
exudation . . . 3. gum, lac, tar 5. pitch,
  resin 6. oozing 8. emission, sweating
  9. discharge, excretion
exude . . . 4. emit, ooze, reek 5. sweat
  7. excrete, give out 9. discharge
exult . . . 3. joy 4. crow, leap (obs), rave
  5. boast, elate, ovare, pride 7. rejoice
  8. jubilate
exultant . . . 5. ovant 6. elated
exultation . . . 3. joy 7. delight 8. boasting
  9. jubilance, rejoicing 10. jubilation
exults . . . 5. leaps 7. glories, springs
  9. jubilates
eye . . . 2. ee 3. orb, see 4. auge, glim, hole,
  ogle 5. optic, organ (human), sight,
  watch 6. look at, peeper 7. observe,
  witness 10. scrutinize
eye (pert to) . . .
  absence of pupil . . 6. acorea
  black . . 5. mouse 6. shiner
  brow . . 4. arch 6. eebree 11. supercilium
  cavity . . 5. orbit 6. hippus, socket
  disease . . 8. cataract, glaucoma,
    hypopyon, trachoma 9. amblyopia
    14. conjunctivitis
  disorder . . 6. squint 7. walleye
    9. exotropia 10. strabismus
  dropper . . 7. pipette
  glass . . 4. lens 7. lorgnon, monocle
    8. pince-nez 10. spectacles
  inflammation . . 6. ititis 7. uveitis
  lash, lashes . . 5. cilia (pl) 6. cilium
  lid . . 8. palpebra
  part . . 4. iris, uvea 5. pupil 6. cornea,
    retina
  to blind (falconry) . . 4. seel
eyelet . . . 7. cringle, grommet, ocellus
  8. loophole, peephole
eyetooth . . . 6. cuspid 8. dogtooth
eyot . . . 3. ait 4. holm 5. islet
eyra . . . 7. wildcat
eyrie, eyry . . . 4. nest 5. aerie, nidus

F

F . . . **6.** letter (6th)
fabes . . . **10.** gooseberry
fabian . . . **7.** caution **8.** dilatory, inaction
    15. procrastination
Fabian . . . **7.** General (Rom), Society
fable . . . **3.** lie **4.** myth **5.** story **6.** legend
    7. fabliau, fantasy, fiction, Marchen,
    parable **8.** allegory, apologue, folk tale
    9. falsehood
fable (pert to) . . .
    being . . **5.** troll
    king . . **3.** Log
    monster . . **4.** ogre **7.** centaur
    narrator . . **10.** parabolist
    writer . . **5.** Aesop
fabric . . . **5.** build, cloth **6.** tissue **7.** texture
    8. erection, material **9.** framework
    11. workmanship **12.** construction
fabric (types of) . . . **3.** rep **4.** alma, duck,
    felt, gros, jean, lamé, lawn, leno, silk
    5. baize, batik, beige, crash, crepe,
    denim, linen, nylon, pekin, rumal,
    satin, scrim, serge, suede, toile, tulle,
    tweed, twill, voile, wigan **6.** agaric,
    alpaca, burlap, calico, canvas, chintz,
    cotton, damask, dimity, étoile, madras,
    mohair, moreen, muslin, penang,
    pongee, poplin, ratiné, sateen, tricot
    7. batiste, brocade, bunting, challis,
    chiffon, delaine, elastic, etamine,
    flannel, galatea, gingham, hernani,
    paisley, percale, satinet, ticking,
    worsted **8.** cashmere, chambray,
    chenille, corduroy, cretonne, drilling,
    prunella, sarcenet, Shantung, sheeting,
    whipcord **9.** bombazine, crinoline,
    gabardine, grenadine, lansdowne,
    matelassé, paramatta **10.** broadcloth,
    seersucker, terry cloth
fabric (pert to) . . .
    dealer . . **6.** mercer
    ornamental . . **4.** lace **8.** fagoting
    silk, watered . . **5.** moiré
    silk and gold . . **4.** acca (anc) **7.** brocade
    twill . . **6.** caddis (cadis)
    velvet . . **5.** panne, terry **6.** velure
    7. velours
    waste . . **5.** mungo
    window shade . . **7.** Holland
    woven . . **6.** tricot
fabricate . . . **4.** coin, form, make, mint
    5. build, frame, weave **6.** create,
    devise, invent, scheme **7.** falsify,
    fashion, produce, trump up **9.** construct
    11. manufacture
fabrication . . . **3.** lie, web **5.** guile
    6. cogger, deceit, making **7.** fiction,
    forging, untruth **9.** falsehood, invention
    12. construction
fabulist . . . **4.** liar **5.** Aesop **11.** storyteller
fabulous . . . **6.** absurd **7.** feigned
    8. mythical **9.** fictional, imaginary,
    legendary **10.** fictitious, remarkable
    11. astonishing **12.** mythological
fabulous (pert to) . . .

animal . . **7.** unicorn **9.** rosmarine (walrus)
beast . . **4.** lung **6.** dragon, wivern
    7. griffon, serpent **10.** earthdrake
being . . **6.** Lapith, Nessus **7.** centaur
bird . . **3.** moa, roc **4.** rukh
facade . . . **4.** face **5.** facia, front **7.** frontal
face . . . **3.** mug **4.** dare, defy, dial, line,
    meet, moue, phiz **5.** brave, cover, front
    6. answer, obvert, oppose, phizog,
    visage **7.** grimace **8.** boldness, confront,
    envisage, exterior, features, pretense
    9. encounter, impudence **10.** effrontery
    11. countenance, physiognomy, self-
    respect
face (pert to) . . .
    bone . . **6.** zygoma (cheek) **7.** maxilla
    (jaw)
    card . . **4.** jack, king **5.** queen
    east . . **9.** orientate
    gem . . **5.** facet
    lifting . . **13.** rhytidoplasty
    masonry . . **5.** revet
    nose . . **11.** rhinoplasty
    pains . . **4.** ague **13.** tic douloureux
    surgery . . **14.** blepharoplasty (eyelid)
    to face . . **6.** afront **7.** vis-à-vis **8.** opposite
    value . . **3.** par
faces (twelve) . . . **12.** dodecahedron
facet . . . **4.** face **5.** bezel, culet **6.** aspect,
    collet **8.** exterior
facetious . . . **5.** droll, funny, witty
    6. facete, jocose **7.** comical, jesting
    8. laughter **9.** whimsical
facia . . . **5.** plate **6.** tablet
facial pain . . . **3.** tic **4.** ague **9.** neuralgia
    13. tic douloureux
facient . . . **4.** doer **5.** agent **10.** multiplier
facile . . . **4.** easy **5.** quick, ready **6.** expert,
    fluent, gentle, pliant **7.** affable, lenient,
    pliable **9.** compliant, teachable
facilitate . . . **3.** aid **4.** ease, help **6.** assist
facility . . . **3.** art **4.** ease, help **5.** éclat,
    means, skill **7.** address, pliancy
    8. easiness **9.** readiness **10.** adroitness,
    expertness, pliability **11.** convenience,
    furtherance **13.** accommodation
facing . . . **6.** lining, veneer **7.** coating,
    surface **8.** opposite
facing (pert to) . . .
    glacier direction . . **5.** stoss
    inward . . **8.** introrse
    outward . . **8.** extrorse
facsimile . . . **4.** copy **5.** match **7.** replica
    9. duplicate **11.** counterpart
fact, facts . . . **4.** data, deed, feat,
    fiat **5.** datum, event, posit, truth
    6. really **7.** keynote, lowdown, paradox
    9. actuality
fact collector . . . **7.** statist **12.** statistician
faction . . . **4.** bloc, camp, sect, side
    5. cabal, junto, party **6.** clique
    7. machine (Polit) **11.** combination,
    partisanism
factious . . . **9.** demagogic, seditious,
    turbulent

F

factitious ... **4.** made (by art), mock, sham **5.** phony **9.** unnatural **10.** artificial **11.** make-believe

factor ... **4.** ager, gene **5.** agent, cause **6.** detail **9.** component **11.** constituent

factotum ... **4.** maid **5.** do-all **7.** servant **8.** busybody

faculties ... **4.** wits **6.** senses **7.** talents **9.** abilities, aptitudes **12.** capabilities

faculty ... **3.** art **4.** body, ease, gift **6.** talent **7.** ability, know-how **8.** aptitude, teachers **9.** endowment (mental) **12.** professorate

fad ... **4.** rage, whim **5.** craze, fancy, hobby, mania **6.** custom **7.** caprice, fashion

faddist ... **10.** monomaniac

fade, fade out ... **3.** age, dim, dow, wan **4.** flat, pale, wilt **5.** daver, decay, peter **6.** perish, vanish, weaken, wither **7.** decline, insipid **8.** discolor, dissolve, languish **9.** disappear **11.** deteriorate

faded ... **3.** dim **4.** dull, pale **5.** faint, passé **8.** impaired

Faerie Queene (pert to) ...
author .. **7.** Spenser
character .. **3.** Ate, Una **5.** Guyon, Truth **7.** Acrasia **8.** Gloriana
theme .. **8.** chivalry **10.** knighthood
type work .. **4.** poem **8.** allegory

fag ... **4.** flag, hack, jade, tire, toil, work **5.** droop, slave, weary **6.** drudge, menial **7.** exhaust, fatigue, untwist (rope end) **8.** drudgery **9.** cigarette

fag end ... **3.** end **4.** tail **6.** scraps, tag end **7.** remnant **8.** last part, leavings

Fagin ... **3.** Jew (Oliver Twist)

Fagin's pupil ... **12.** Artful Dodger (John Dawkins)

fagot, faggot ... **4.** bind **5.** bunch **6.** bundle, emblem (Her) **8.** firewood, slattern

fail ... **3.** ebb, err **4.** flop, lack, miss, sink **5.** decay, flunk, lapse **6.** defect, desert, weaken **7.** decline, exhaust **8.** unbetide **9.** fall short **10.** disappoint, go bankrupt **11.** deteriorate

failed admission ... **11.** blackballed

failed to follow suit ... **7.** reneged

failure ... **3.** dud **4.** flop, foil, lack, lose, miss **5.** decay, fault, lapse **6.** defeat, fiasco **7.** default **10.** bankruptcy, deficiency, insolvency, nonsuccess, suspension **11.** delinquency

faint ... **3.** dim, ill **4.** pale, soft, weak **5.** swelt, swoon, timid **6.** feeble, sickly **7.** languid **8.** cowardly, fatigued, listless, timorous **10.** indistinct, oppressive

faintness ... **5.** qualm (sudden) **7.** dimness, syncope **8.** paleness, weakness **10.** feebleness

fair ... **4.** just, mart **6.** bazaar, blonde, comely, honest, kermis **8.** festival, mediocre, rainless, unbiased **9.** impartial **10.** auspicious, reasonable **12.** unprejudiced **13.** dispassionate

fairy, faery ... **3.** elf, fay **4.** peri, pixy **5.** genie, magic, nymph, ouphe, pixie **6.** elfkin, sprite **7.** brownie, gremlin **8.** illusion

fairy (pert to) ...

abode (Scot) .. **4.** shee (sidhe)
death spirit .. **7.** banshee
evil .. **4.** ogre, puck **9.** hobgoblin
fort .. **3.** lis (liss)
German .. **6.** kobold
Irish .. **10.** cluricaune, leprechaun
king .. **6.** Oberon
Persian .. **4.** peri
queen .. **3.** Mab, Una **7.** Titania
Scandinavian .. **5.** nisse
tale .. **3.** fib **7.** Marchen **8.** allegory **9.** narrative

faith ... **4.** hope **5.** creed, piety, troth, trust **6.** belief, credit, verily, virtue **7.** loyalty **8.** credence, fidelity **9.** assurance, authority, orthodoxy **10.** confidence **11.** credibility

faithful ... **4.** fast, feal, leal, true **5.** liege, loyal, pious **6.** devout, steady, truly **7.** devoted, sincere, staunch **8.** constant, obedient, reliable **9.** believers, steadfast, veracious

faithful friend ... **7.** Achates (Vergil's Aeneid)

faithless ... **5.** false, punic **6.** fickle, untrue **8.** apostate, disloyal, shifting **9.** deceptive, mercurial, skeptical **10.** perfidious, unfaithful **11.** incredulous, irreligious, treacherous, unbelieving **12.** falsehearted

fake ... **3.** rob **4.** faux, sham **5.** cheat, fraud, trick **6.** ersatz **7.** trump up **8.** doctor up **9.** deception, fabricate, imitation **10.** artificial **11.** counterfeit

faker ... **5.** cheat, fraud **7.** bluffer **8.** impostor **9.** hypocrite, pretender

fakir ... **4.** sect (Muslim, Islam), yogi **7.** dervish **9.** mendicant

falcon ... **4.** hawk **5.** besra, saker **6.** laggar, lanner, luggar, merlin, shahin (shaheen), sorage, tercel **7.** kestrel, sakeret **8.** lanneret, Raptores **9.** gyrfalcon (gerfalcon), peregrine

falcon, military ... **8.** ordnance

falconry term ... **4.** hood, jess, lure, seel **6.** rebate **7.** hawking

fall ... **3.** ebb **4.** bang, drop, plop, ruin, sink, slip **5.** crash, spill **6.** autumn, defeat, perish, plunge, tumble **7.** descend, descent, devolve, failure, plummet, relapse **8.** collapse, commence, downfall, rainfall **9.** abatement, overthrow, surrender, waterfall **10.** depreciate, subversion **11.** degradation, precipitate

fall (pert to) ...
asleep .. **6.** nod off
back .. **6.** recede, recoil **7.** relapse, retreat **10.** retrogress
behind .. **3.** lag **4.** lose **7.** regress
guy .. **5.** patsy
in .. **4.** cave **5.** agree, lapse **6.** concur, line up **8.** collapse **9.** terminate
rhythmical .. **6.** cadent
short .. **4.** lack, want **10.** disappoint

fallacious ... **4.** wily **5.** false **6.** crafty, untrue **8.** delusive, guileful **9.** deceitful, deceptive, erroneous, illogical, insidious **10.** fraudulent, misleading **13.** disappointing

fallacy ... **5.** error **6.** idolum **7.** sophism

9. deception, falseness, sophistry
13. deceitfulness
false . . . **4.** sham, tale **5.** bogus, paste
  6. betray, impugn, pseudo, untrue
  7. mislead **8.** apostate, spurious
  9. deceitful, deceptive, erroneous,
  faithless, incorrect, insincere,
  pretended, unfounded **10.** fictitious,
  mendacious, traitorous, unfaithful,
  unreliable, untruthful **11.** counterfeit
  12. illegitimate
false (pert to) . . .
  friend . . **5.** Judas **7.** traitor
  front . . **8.** disguise **11.** affectation
  fruit . . **10.** pseudocarp
  god . . **4.** idol
  hearted . . **9.** deceitful **10.** perfidious
    11. treacherous
  items . . **6.** spuria
  jewelry . . **5.** paste **6.** strass
  reasoning . . **10.** paralogism
  report . . **5.** rumor **6.** canard **7.** slander
  show . . **6.** tinsel
  wing (bird's) . . **5.** alula
falsehood . . . **3.** lie **4.** tale **7.** falsity,
  fiction, perjury, untruth **9.** imposture,
  mendacity **11.** counterfeit, fabrication
  12. exaggeration
falseness . . . **5.** error **8.** illusion
  9. deception, falsehood **10.** infidelity
falsetto . . . **5.** voice (false) **10.** artificial
  11. high-pitched
falsify . . . **3.** lie **5.** belie, forge **7.** distort,
  pervert **8.** disprove **10.** adulterate
  11. counterfeit **12.** misrepresent
Falstaff . . . **5.** opera (Verdi) **9.** character
  (Shaksp)
falter . . . **3.** lag **4.** fail **5.** demur,
  pause, waver **6.** flinch, quaver, totter
  7. stagger, stammer, stumble, tremble
  8. hesitate, lose hope
fame . . . **4.** note **5.** éclat, glory, kudos
  6. renown, repute **9.** celebrity
famed . . . **7.** eminent, honored, popular
  8. renowned **9.** notorious **10.** celebrated
familiar . . . **4.** easy **5.** usual **6.** common,
  versed **7.** affable **8.** domestic, frequent,
  friendly, habitual, informal
  9. companion, customary, well-known
  10. accustomed, colloquial, conversant
  12. domesticated, presumptuous
  13. unconstrained
familiarity . . . **8.** intimacy **9.** awareness,
  knowledge, liberties **10.** affability
  12. acquaintance (close), friendliness
familiarize . . . **6.** inform **8.** accustom
  9. habituate
family . . . **3.** ilk, kin **4.** clan, line, race
  5. class, group, house, tribe **6.** stirps
  7. kindred, lineage **9.** community,
  household, posterity **10.** kith and kin
family (pert to) . . .
  bees . . **5.** apina **7.** Apoidea
  favoritism . . **8.** nepotism
  herbs . . **7.** Ranales
  Italians (famed) . . **4.** Este
  kings . . **7.** dynasty
  name . . **7.** surname
famous . . . **5.** named, noted **7.** eminent,
  namable, notable **8.** renowned
  9. excellent, notorious **10.** celebrated,

remarkable **13.** distinguished
famous murderer . . . **4.** Aram, Cain
  9. Bluebeard
famous pirate . . . **4.** Kidd (Capt)
fan . . . **4.** blow, cool, vane, whip
  5. punka (punkah) **6.** blower, foment,
  incite, rooter, spread, thresh, winnow
  7. admirer, devotee, refresh
  9. stimulate, strike out (baseball),
  ventilate **10.** enthusiast
fanatic, fanatical . . . **3.** mad **5.** bigot,
  crank, crazy, rabid **6.** maniac, zealot
  7. devotee, frantic, lunatic **8.** frenzied
  9. energumen, phrenetic **10.** enthusiast,
  unbalanced **11.** extravagant,
  overzealous **12.** enthusiastic
  13. nonconformist, overreligious
fanatical partisan . . . **6.** zealot
fancied . . . **6.** unreal **7.** dreamed, ideated
  8. favorite, imagined **9.** well-liked
  10. ornamental
fanciful . . . **3.** odd **5.** queer **7.** bizarre,
  strange **8.** romantic **9.** fantastic,
  grotesque, visionary, whimsical
  10. capricious, chimerical
  11. imaginative **13.** grandiloquent
fancy . . . **3.** fad **4.** idea, like, love, ween,
  whim **5.** dream, freak **6.** design, desire,
  devise, humour, ideate, megrim, notion,
  ornate, vagary **7.** caprice, conceit,
  fantasy, imagine, impulse, suppose,
  thought **8.** illusion, phantasy, superior
  9. expensive **10.** conception, impression
  11. extravagant, imagination, inclination
  12. ostentatious
fandango . . . **3.** hop **4.** ball, prom **5.** dance
  7. cantico
fandango bird . . . **7.** manakin
Faneuil Hall (1742) . . . **4.** hall **6.** market
  (Boston) **15.** Cradle of Liberty
fanion . . . **4.** flag **6.** guidon, marker
fanon . . . **4.** cape (Pope's) **5.** orale
  6. banner **7.** maniple
fan-shaped . . . **10.** flabellate
fan sticks (radiating) . . . **4.** brin
  7. panache
fantastic . . . **3.** odd **5.** outré, queer
  6. absurd, rococo, unreal **7.** baroque,
  bizarre, caprice, foppish, unusual
  8. fanciful, freakish, illusory **9.** eccentric,
  grotesque, visionary **10.** capricious,
  chimerical, irrational **11.** extravagant,
  imaginative **12.** phantastical
fantastic imitation . . . **6.** parody
  8. travesty
fantasy . . . **5.** dream, fancy, story **6.** vision
  7. caprice, phantom, romance **8.** illusion
  10. apparition **13.** hallucination
far . . . **3.** tel (pref) **4.** afar, long, tele
  (pref) **6.** marked, remote **9.** separated
  10. abstracted
farce . . . **4.** mime, play **5.** drama
  (humorous), exode, humor, stuff
  6. comedy **7.** mockery **8.** stuffing
  9. burlesque, forcemeat
farceur . . . **5.** joker **8.** comedian
  9. dramatist
fare . . . **3.** eat **4.** diet, food, rate **5.** crowd,
  going, swarm, table **7.** conduct, journey,
  passage, prosper, succeed **9.** passenger
  10. expedition

farewell . . . 3. ave 4. vale 5. adieu, adios, aloha, congé (formal) 7. good-bye, leaving, parting 8. au revoir, Godspeed 9. bon voyage 11. leave-taking

farinaceous drink . . . 6. ptisan

farinaceous food . . . 4. sago 5. flour, grain, salep, wheat 7. cereals

farm . . . 4. plot, till, torp 5. croft, ranch 6. grange, rancho 7. acreage, cotland 9. cultivate

farm (pert to) . . .
English . . 6. barton
laborer . . 4. hind 6. farmer, tiller
prefix . . 4. agro
repairer . . 10. plowwright
Spanish . . 8. hacienda
steward . . 7. granger
tenant . . 6. cotter

farmer . . . 4. ryot 5. kulak 6. grower, tiller 7. cropper, metaver, peasant, planter, rancher 10. agronomist, cultivator 13. agriculturist

faro term . . . 4. bank 5. monte, stuss 6. cathop, layout

Faroe (Faeroe) **Islands** . . .
called also . . 12. Sheep Islands
capital . . 9. Thorshavn
magistrate . . 4. foud
rule . . 5. Norse (anc) 7. Denmark
whirlwind . . 2. oe

far-reaching . . . 4. deep, long 5. scope 7. intense 9. extensive

farrow . . . 3. pig 6. litter

farsighted . . . 6. shrewd 9. provident, sagacious 10. presbyopic 11. foresighted 12. clearsighted

farther, further . . . 4. also 7. thither 8. moreover 10. additional

farthest . . . 5. final 6. inmost, utmost 7. endmost, extreme, longest

farthest point . . . 6. apogee

fascia . . . 4. band, sash 6. fillet, ribbon 7. bandage

fascinate . . . 5. charm 6. allure, enamor, thrill 7. bewitch, delight, enchant 8. entrance, interest 9. captivate, enrapture

fascinating . . . 5. siren 8. alluring, charming 10. attractive, bewitching, delightful 11. interesting

Fascist (1919) . . . 6. Pareto 9. Mussolini 10. Black Shirt

fashion . . . 3. fad, fit, ton, way 4. make, mode, mold, rage 5. adapt, carve, craze, feign, forge, frame, guise, model, shape, style, vogue 6. create, custom, invent 7. compose 8. contrive 9. construct, fabricate, smartness 10. appearance

fashionable . . . 5. smart 6. formal, modish 7. a la mode, in vogue, stylish 8. up-to-date 10. conforming 13. well-appearing

fast . . . 5. agile, fixed, fleet, hasty, quick, rapid, sound, space, stuck, swift 6. lively, speedy, staple 7. abiding, soundly 8. enduring, securely 10. profligate, stationary, unyielding 11. expeditious

fasten . . . 3. bar, pin, tie 4. bind, clip, lace, lash, moor, nail, rope, seal, tack,

wire 5. affix, belay, chain, clamp, clasp, latch, paste, rivet 6. attach, secure, solder, staple, tether, toggle 7. padlock

fastening . . . 5. desmo (comb form)

fastest (pert to) . . .
animals . . 6. coyote 7. cheetah 8. antelope
birds . . 5. eagle, goose 7. ostrich

fast horse . . . 6. pelter

fastidious . . . 4. nice 6. dainty 7. elegant, finical, precise 8. critical, delicate, exacting, overnice 9. squeamish 10. meticulous, particular, scrupulous

fastness . . . 4. fort 6. fixity 7. citadel 8. celerity, firmness, velocity 9. stability 10. profligacy, stronghold

fat . . . 4. lard, oily, suet 5. adeps, fatty, lipin, obese, olein, stout 6. axunge (goose), grease, portly, steato (pref), stocky, tallow 7. adipose, lanolin, opulent, paunchy, stearin, wealthy 9. corpulent, plentiful 10. profitable

fatal . . . 5. fated 6. deadly, doomed, lethal, mortal 7. fateful, ominous 8. destined 9. condemned, prophetic 10. calamitous, disastrous 11. destructive

fatality . . . 4. fate 5. death 8. disaster 10. deadliness

fatally . . . 8. mortally 9. ruinously

fate . . . 3. end, lot 4. doom, luck, ruin 5. karma 6. chance, kismet 7. destiny, fortune 8. disaster, downfall 13. inevitability

fateful . . . 5. fated 6. deadly 9. momentous 10. inevitable, portentous 11. destructive, predestined

Fates (Gr) . . . 6. Clotho, Moirae (group of Three) 7. Atropos 8. Lachesis

Fates (Norse) . . . 4. Urth 5. Norns (group of three), Skuld 9. Verthandi

Fates (Rom) . . . 4. Fata, Mona 5. Morta 6. Decuma, Parcae (group of three)

father . . . 2. pa 3. Abu, dad 4. abba, papa, père, sire 5. adopt, friar, padre, pater, vater 6. priest, senior 7. creator 8. generate 9. confessor, procreate 11. acknowledge

Father (of) . . .
Ajax . . 7. Telamon
Christmas . . 10. Santa Claus
English learning . . 4. Bede
engraving . . 3. Pye
Evil . . 5. Satan
his country . . 6. Cicero (Rom), Medici (It) 10. Washington (US)
history . . 9. Herodotus
Mankind (Myth) . . 7. Iapetus
New York . . 13. Knickerbocker
Ocean . . 7. Neptune
the Gods . . 6. Amen-Ra
Time . . 10. Methuselah
Waters . . 11. Mississippi

father (pert to) . . .
land . . 6. native
land, love of . . 10. philopater
term . . 6. agnate 8. paternal
wise . . 6. mentor

fatherless . . . 6. orbate 7. forlorn 8. helpless, orphaned

fathom . . . 3. try 4. test 5. delve, plumb,

solve, sound **7.** measure, plummet
8. encircle **9.** penetrate **10.** understand
13. take soundings
fatigued . . . **5.** bored, faint, jaded, spent,
tired, weary **6.** fagged **7.** languid,
wearied **9.** exhausted
Fatima (pert to) . . .
character in . . **13.** Arabian Nights
father . . **8.** Mohammed
husband . . **9.** Bluebeard
fatten . . . **4.** feed **6.** batten, enrich
7. improve, prosper **8.** pinguefy
fatty . . . **5.** suety **6.** greasy **7.** adipose
9. aliphatic
fatty (pert to) . . .
acid . . **6.** adipic **7.** valeric
degeneration . . **8.** adiposis
substance, sheep . . **5.** suint
tumor . . **6.** lipoma
fatuous . . . **4.** vain **5.** inane, silly **6.** vacant
7. foolish, idiotic, witless **8.** demented,
illusory, imbecile **9.** insensate
11. thoughtless
faucet . . . **3.** peg, tap **4.** cock **6.** spigot
7. fixture, hydrant, petcock
fault . . . **4.** hade, lode, slip, vice
5. cavil, cleft, culpa (law), error,
lapse, tache (anc) **6.** defect, foible
7. blemish, blunder, demerit, failing,
frailty, misdeed, offense **8.** fracture
10. peccadillo **11.** delinquency
12. imperfection
faultfinder . . . **6.** carper, nagger **7.** caviler
10. complainer, criticizer
faultfinding . . . **7.** carping, nagging
8. captious, caviling, critical **9.** censorial
faultless . . . **4.** pure **5.** right **7.** correct,
paragon, perfect **8.** flawless, innocent
9. blameless **10.** impeccable
13. unimpeachable **14.** irreproachable
faultlessness . . . **8.** accuracy **9.** innocence
10. perfection **11.** preciseness
faulty . . . **3.** ill **5.** amiss, unfit **6.** guilty
8. culpable **9.** blemished, defective,
deficient, erroneous, imperfect
11. blameworthy
faun . . . **3.** Pan **5.** deity, satyr **6.** Faunus
10. Praxiteles
Faust . . . **4.** hero **5.** drama (Goethe),
opera
faux pas . . . **4.** slip **5.** error, gaffe
6. booboo, slip-up **7.** blunder, misstep,
mistake
favor, favour . . . **3.** aid **4.** boon,
gift, help **5.** bless, grace, token
6. esteem, letter, regard **8.** good
will, kindness, leniency, resemble
9. patronage, patronize, privilege
10. assistance, concession, favoritism,
partiality, permission **11.** approbation
favorable . . . **4.** good, kind, rosy **6.** benign,
timely **7.** helpful, hopeful, popular
8. friendly, gracious, pleasing
9. approving, opportune **10.** auspicious,
beneficial, propitious **11.** complaisant
12. advantageous
favorite . . . **3.** pet **4.** lamb (pet) **6.** minion
7. darling **10.** preference
favoritism . . . **4.** bias **7.** leaning
8. nepotism **10.** partiality
12. predilection

fawn . . . **3.** doe **4.** buck, coax, deer,
faon (color) **5.** color, cower, crawl,
creep, toady **6.** cringe, grovel, shrink
7. truckle **10.** ingratiate
fawning . . . **7.** servile **8.** toadyish
9. truckling **10.** obsequious
11. bootlicking, sycophantic
fawnskin (classic art) . . . **6.** nebris
fay . . . **3.** elf **5.** fairy **6.** sprite
fealty . . . **4.** duty **6.** homage **7.** loyalty,
respect **8.** fidelity **9.** constancy
10. allegiance, obligation
fear . . . **3.** awe **5.** alarm, dread, panic
6. dismay, fright, horror, phobia, terror
7. anxiety **8.** venerate **9.** apprehend,
cowardice, reverence **11.** nervousness
13. consternation
fear (of) . . .
animals . . **9.** zoophobia
bees . . **9.** apiphobia
being alone . . **10.** autophobia,
monophobia
blood . . **10.** hemophobia
cats . . **12.** aelurophobia
crossing streets . . **11.** dromophobia
crowds . . **11.** ochlophobia
darkness . . **11.** nyctophobia, scotophobia
death . . **11.** necrophobia
disease . . **10.** nosophobia
enclosures . . **14.** claustrophobia
fire . . **10.** pyrophobia
food . . **10.** cibophobia
heights . . **10.** acrophobia
11. hypsophobia
holy things . . **11.** hagiophobia
men . . **11.** androphobia
new things . . **9.** neophobia
open spaces . . **11.** agoraphobia
pain . . **10.** algophobia
places (certain) . . **10.** topophobia
poison . . **10.** toxiphobia
reptiles . . **13.** herpetophobia
sea . . **14.** thalassophobia
strangers . . **10.** xenophobia
sunlight . . **11.** heliophobia
thirteen . . **13.** tridecaphobia
weeds . . **11.** runcophobia
fear (pert to) . . .
for fear that . . **4.** lest
fearful . . . **4.** dino (pref) dire **5.** awful,
pavid, timid **6.** afraid, craven **7.** anxious,
nervous **8.** dreadful, horrible, timorous
9. appealing, frightful **11.** distressing,
frightening **12.** apprehensive
fearless . . . **4.** bold **5.** brave **6.** daring
7. impavid **8.** harmless, intrepid
9. audacious, confident, dauntless,
undaunted **10.** courageous
feast . . . **4.** fete, meal **5.** agape, epulo,
revel **6.** junket, picnic, regale, repast
7. banquet, gratify **8.** carousal, festival
9. carrousel
Feast (of) . . .
Lanterns (Jap) . . **3.** Bon
Lots . . **5.** Purim
Nativity . . **9.** Christmas
Pentecost (weeks) . . **8.** Shabuoth
Tabernacles . . **7.** Succoth
feasting . . . **6.** dining **9.** epulation
feat . . . **3.** act **4.** deed **5.** stunt **7.** exploit
11. achievement, performance

14. accomplishment
feather . . . 4. deck, flaw (jewel), tuft
5. adorn, penna, plume, quill 6. clothe,
fletch, hackle, trifle 7. plumage
9. lightness
feather (pert to) . . .
an arrow . . 6. fledge, fletch
barb . . 7. pinnula 8. barbicel
bird (area) . . 7. pteryle
featherlike . . 7. pinnate
filament . . 4. dowl
key (machine) . . 6. spline
molt . . 3. mew
repair (falconry) . . 3. imp
shaft . . 5. scape
feathered . . . 5. swift 6. plumed, winged
7. fledged 8. pennated, plumaged
10. ornamented
feature . . . 4. face 5. motif, trait
6. aspect 7. special 8. headline,
resemble 9. component, lineament
10. appearance, comeliness
11. countenance 14. characteristic
features . . . 3. mug 4. face 5. looks
6. visage 7. outline 9. geography
February birthstone . . . 8. amethyst
federal agent . . . 4. G-man, T-man
Federalist Papers . . . 3. Jay 7. Madison
8. Hamilton
federation . . . 5. union 6. league
8. alliance 10. government 11. affiliation
13. confederation
fed up . . . 5. bored, jaded 7. wearied
8. satiated 9. surfeited
fee . . . 3. feu, tip 4. fief, rate, wage
5. bribe 6. charge, estate (law)
8. gratuity, retainer 9. emolument
10. honorarium
feeble . . . . 4. aged, lame, puny, weak
5. dotty 6. infirm 10. indistinct
11. debilitated
feeble-minded . . . 5. anile 9. infirmity
10. irresolute, weak-willed
11. vacillating
feed . . . 4. dine, meal, sate 5. stoke
6. fodder, gavage 7. engorge, foldage,
furnish, indulge, nourish, nurture,
pannage (swine) 9. encourage,
provision
feel . . . 3. ail, air 4. palp 5. grope, sense,
touch 6. handle, suffer 7. examine,
explore, quality, texture 8. perceive
10. atmosphere, experience
feel (pert to) . . .
compunction . . 6. repent
dejection . . 6. repine
fear . . 2. ug
melancholy . . 6. grieve
worth of . . 10. appreciate
feeler . . . 4. palp, test 6. barbal, palpus
7. antenna 8. question, tentacle
feeling . . . 4. feel, tact, view 5. hunch,
touch 7. emotion, opinion, passion
8. attitude 9. sensation, sentiment
10. atmosphere, experience,
perception 11. sensibility
13. consciousness
feeling (pert to) . . .
capable of . . 5. emote 8. sentient
9. sensitive
displeasure . . 9. resentful

hostility . . 6. animus 9. animosity
ill . . 7. malaise 10. discomfort
impassive . . 8. stoicism
joyful . . 6. jocund
offense . . 5. pique
superiority . . 9. arrogance
without . . 6. apathy, steely 7. callous
8. numbness 9. unfeeling
13. insensibility
feet . . . see also *foot*
designating . . 5. podal
having . . 6. pedate
number . . 7. footage
two (Pros) . . 6. dipody 7. dimeter
9. ditrochee
without . . 4. apod 6. apodal 8. footless
feign . . . 3. act 4. sham 5. fable 6. affect,
assume, gammon, garble, invent
7. connive, imagine, pretend 8. malinger
(illness), simulate 9. dissemble
11. counterfeit, make-believe
feint . . . 5. appel (fencing), blind, shift,
trick 6. attack (mock), thrust 7. mislead,
pretext 8. artifice, pretense
Felicia . . . 7. thistle 9. happiness
felicitate . . . 4. laud 5. bless 8. macarize
10. compliment 12. congratulate
felicity . . . 5. bliss, grace 7. aptness,
success 8. aptitude 9. happiness,
well-being 11. achievement (happy),
blessedness 12. blissfulness
Felidae . . . 4. cats, lion, lynx, pard, puma
5. tiger 6. jaguar 7. cheetah, leopard,
wildcat
feline . . . 3. sly 5. Felis 6. animal 7. catlike,
furtive 8. stealthy 11. treacherous
Felis . . . 3. cat
fell . . . 3. cut, hem, hew 4. beat, hill,
kill, pelt, ruin, skin 5. cruel, level
6. fierce, fleece, lay low, mighty,
savage 7. brutish, tumbled
9. barbarous, ferocious, overthrow,
prostrate
fellow . . . 3. lad, man 4. beau, chap,
peer 5. equal 6. member, person
7. comrade 8. neighbor 9. associate,
companion 10. sweetheart
11. confederate
fellow (pert to) . . .
accomplice . . 7. abettor 9. accessory
11. confederate
awkward . . 4. boor, gawk
clumsy . . 3. oaf 4. lout, pleb 5. yahoo
7. bumpkin
coward . . 3. cad, fop 4. drip 7. bounder
8. spalpeen
droll . . 3. wag 4. card
old . . 6. geezer 7. callant
small . . 6. shaver
smart . . 5. aleck
young . . 4. chap 5. blade, youth
7. younker 9. stripling
fellowman . . . 7. brother 11. fellow being
fellowship . . . 4. sect 5. guild, union
7. company 8. alliance, sodality
9. communion 10. membership
11. affiliation, comradeship, partnership,
scholarship 12. friendliness
13. companionship
felon . . . 3. bum 4. wild 5. cruel 6. wicked
7. convict, culprit, outcast, villain,

whitlow **8.** criminal, disloyal **9.** infection, malignant, murderous **10.** malefactor, paronychia, traitorous

felony . . . **3.** sin **5.** crime, wrath **6.** daring, deceit **8.** baseness, burglary, outlawry **9.** treachery **10.** illegality, wickedness **11.** misdemeanor

female . . . **4.** bibi, dame, doña, girl, gyne, lady, miss **5.** donna, femme, rhyme, squaw, woman **6.** maiden, matron **7.** distaff, dowager, fair sex, Sahibah **8.** mistress **9.** weaker sex

female (pert to) . . .
  architecture . . **8.** Caryatid
  comb form . . **5.** gyneo, thely
  erudite . . **10.** pedantress
  fox . . **5.** vixen
  government . . **8.** gynarchy
  hormone . . **8.** estrogen
  monster . . **6.** gorgon
  prayerful . . **5.** orant
  spirit . . **7.** banshee **8.** succubus
  suffix . . **4.** ette
  term . . **7.** distaff **8.** gynecoid
  warrior . . **6.** Amazon

feminine . . . **4.** soft, weak **6.** female, gender, tender **7.** womanly **8.** maidenly **10.** effeminate

femme fatale . . . **4.** vamp **5.** siren **7.** Lorelei, vampire

femur . . . **3.** hip (bone) **4.** bone (thigh), coxa

fen . . . **3.** bog **4.** moor, pool **5.** marsh, swale **7.** The Fens

fence . . . **3.** aha **4.** bank, duel, ha-ha, pale, rail, wall **5.** close, ditch, fight, hedge, stile **6.** paling, picket, secure **7.** barrier, confine, enclose, fortify, protect, railing **8.** palisade, prohibit **9.** enclosure, swordplay **11.** self-defense

fencing (pert to) . . .
  breastplate . . **8.** plastron
  defense . . **5.** carte, parry, prime, sixte **6.** octave, quinte, tierce **7.** seconds, septime
  master . . **7.** lanista
  position . . **9.** pronation **10.** supination
  sword . . **4.** epee, foil, tuck **5.** extoc **6.** rapier
  term . . **4.** volt **7.** corrida **8.** estocado
  thrust . . **6.** remise **7.** riposte

fend . . . **4.** ward **5.** avert, parry, shift **6.** defend, resist **7.** prevent, repulse, ward off

fender . . . **5.** guard **6.** buffer, bumper, shield, sluice **7.** cushion **9.** fireguard **10.** firescreen **11.** splashboard

fenestra . . . **6.** window **7.** foramen, opening, orifice

Fenian (Ir) . . . **4.** hero **11.** nationalist

fennel . . . **4.** herb **6.** Seseli **7.** Azorian, Nigella

feral . . . **4.** wild **6.** deadly, ferine, savage **7.** bestial, untamed **8.** funereal, unbroken **9.** malignant **12.** uncultivated

feretory . . . **4.** bier **6.** chapel, shrine (saint's) **8.** feretrum

ferment . . . **4.** barm, brew, fret, sour, stum, zyme **5.** anger, fever, yeast **6.** enzyme, foment, leaven, rennin, seethe, uproar **7.** glucase, maltase

8. diastase, disorder **9.** agitation **10.** effervesce, turbulence

fermentation . . . **6.** unrest **9.** agitation, chemistry, leavening **10.** ebullition **13.** effervescence

fermented drink . . . **3.** ale **4.** beer, mead **6.** kumiss (koumiss) **9.** hard cider **10.** malt liquor

fermenting vat . . . **4.** gyle

fern . . . **4.** tara **5.** brake, heath, holly **6.** osmund, spider **7.** bracken **8.** polypody **10.** maidenhair **11.** elephant-ear

fern (pert to) . . .
  family . . **12.** pteridophyte
  genus . . **6.** Anemia
  leaf . . **5.** frond
  scale . . **8.** ramentum
  seedlike part . . **5.** spore

ferocious . . . **4.** grim, wild **5.** cruel, feral **6.** bloody, brutal, fierce, savage **7.** acharne, inhuman **8.** pitiless, ravenous, ruthless **9.** barbarous, malignant, merciless, murderous, rapacious, truculent **10.** implacable, malevolent, relentless, sanguinary **11.** remorseless **12.** bloodthirsty

ferret . . . **3.** hob **4.** hunt, jill, tape **5.** worry **6.** badger, harass, search, weasel **7.** polecat

ferrotype . . . **7.** tintype **10.** photograph

ferrum . . . **2.** Fe (sym) **4.** iron

ferry . . . **7.** traject **9.** transport **10.** sail across

ferryboat . . . **3.** bac **4.** pont **6.** wherry

ferryman . . . **6.** Charon (River Styx) **7.** ferrier

fertile . . . **4.** rank, rich **7.** teeming **8.** abundant, fruitful, prolific **9.** exuberant, inventive, plenteous, plentiful **10.** productive

fertilizer . . . **4.** marl **5.** guano **6.** pollen **7.** compost, nitrate **8.** bone meal, dressing **9.** phosphate

ferule . . . **3.** rod **5.** ruler **6.** fennel **10.** punishment

fervency . . . **4.** heat, keen, zeal **5.** ardor, eager, fiery, gusto, verve **6.** fervor, warmth **7.** ardency, passion **9.** eloquence, vehemence **12.** empressement **15.** impassionedness

fervent . . . **3.** hot **4.** keen, warm **5.** eager, fiery **6.** ardent, fervid **7.** excited, intense, zealous **8.** eloquent, vehement **10.** passionate **11.** impassioned

fervid . . . **3.** hot **5.** fiery **6.** ardent, tropic **7.** boiling, fervent, zealous **8.** vehement **11.** impassioned

fervor . . . **4.** rage, zeal, zest **5.** ardor **7.** ecstasy, passion **11.** earnestness

fester . . . **6.** rankle **7.** abscess, pustule, putrefy **9.** suppurate

festival . . . **3.** ale, bal **4.** fete, gala **5.** Delia (Apollo), feast, revel, Seder **6.** Easter, Kermis **7.** holiday, uphelya **8.** apodosis (Church) **9.** Christmas, Mardi gras **10.** Parentalia, Saturnalia

festive . . . **3.** gay **4.** gala **5.** merry **6.** joyous **8.** mirthful, sportive **9.** convivial

festivity . . . **3.** joy **4.** fete, gala **5.** mirth, revel **6.** gaiety **7.** jollity, whoopee

8. festival, jamboree 10. joyfulness
11. celebration, merrymaking
12. conviviality
festoon . . . 4. loop 5. adorn 6. wreath
7. garland
fetch . . . 3. get 5. bring, reach 6. attain,
deduce, revive 7. achieve 8. go and
get, retrieve
fetching . . . 8. alluring, charming,
pleasing 10. attractive, delightful
11. fascinating
fete . . . 4. gala 5. feast, party 6. fiesta
8. carnival, festival 10. Saturnalia
13. entertainment
fetid . . . 4. olid, rank 5. fusty 7. noisome
10. maladorous 11. ill-smelling
fetish . . . 3. obi 4. idol, joss, juju 5. charm,
image, totem 6. amulet, avatar, mascot
7. Dahoman 8. talisman
fetter . . . 4. band, bond, gyve, iron
5. chain 6. hamper, hobble, hopple,
thrall 7. enchain, manacle, shackle
feud . . . 4. fief, fray 5. broil 6. affray,
estate, strife 7. contest, dispute, quarrel
8. vendetta 9. hostility
feudal (pert to) . . .
estate . . 3. fee 4. fief, soke
French . . 4. feod
lord . . 6. tenure 8. overlaid, suzerain
payment . . 6. socage
service . . 5. banal
tenant . . 5. leud 6. vassal
tribute . . 6. heriot
fever . . . 4. ague 5. ardor 6. frenzy
8. delirium, sickness 9. calenture
10. excitement
fever (pert to) . . .
heat . . 9. sunstroke
intermittent . . 5. octan 7. quartan
malarial . . 4. ague
marsh . . 6. elodes 7. helodes
subsidence . . 12. defervescent
term . . 7. febrile, pyretic
tropical . . 6. dengue 9. calenture
feverish . . . 5. hasty 7. excited, febrile,
fervent, fevered 8. restless 9. delirious,
overeager 10. disordered
fey . . . 4. dead 5. dying, elfin, fatal, spell
9. enfeebled, visionary 12. otherworldly
fez . . . 3. cap 5. busby, shako 8. tarboosh
9. headdress
fiat . . . 3. act 5. edict, order 6. decree
7. command 8. decision, sanction
fiber . . . 3. nap, nep, tal 4. bast, eruc,
hemp, imbe, jute, lint, pile, pita, silk,
yarn 5. datil, istle, kapok, linen, nerve,
rayon, sisal 6. fibril, raffia, staple,
thread 7. filasse, texture 8. fibrilla,
filament
fiber plant . . . 4. hemp, imbe, palm
5. abaca, agave 6. ambary, cotton,
linaga
fibers . . . 5. hairs 7. strands 9. filaments
fibula . . . 4. bone (arm) 5. class 6. brooch
(anc), buckle 9. safety pin
fickle . . . 5. false 6. mobile 7. mutable
8. unstable, unsteady, variable,
wavering 9. changeful, deceitful,
faithless, unsettled 10. capricious,
changeable, inconstant, irresolute,
unfaithful 11. vacillating

fiction . . . 4. tale 5. false, fancy,
novel, story 6. legend 7. coinage,
figment, forgery, romance 9. falsehood,
invention 11. fabrication
fictitious . . . 5. false 6. poetic, pseudo
(pref) 7. assumed, feigned 8. chimeric
9. imaginary, imitative, pretended
10. artificial
fictitious name . . . 5. alias 6. anonym
7. pen name 8. nickname
9. pseudonym, stage name 10. nom
de plume 11. nom de guerre
Fidel (eg) . . . 8. caudillo
Fidelio (eg) . . . 5. opera
fidelity . . . 5. topaz, troth, truth 6. fealty
7. honesty 8. accuracy, devotion,
veracity 9. adherence, constancy,
exactness 10. allegiance 12. faithfulness
fidget . . . 4. fuss 5. worry 6. twitch
9. dysphoria 10. uneasiness
12. restlessness
fidgety . . . 5. jerky 6. uneasy 7. nervous,
restive, twitchy 8. bustling, restless
9. excitable, impatient
fiducial . . . 4. firm 5. solid, sound
6. secure, stable 7. trusted 8. trustful
9. confident 11. trustworthy
fiduciary . . . 4. held (in trust) 5. trust
7. founded, holding, in trust, trustee
12. confidential
fief . . . 3. fee 4. feud 6. estate
field . . . 3. lea, lot 4. acre, ager, land,
mead, rand 5. croft, glebe, range,
tract 6. campus, ground, meadow,
sphere 7. compass, diamond, expanse,
pasture, savanna (savannah), terrain
8. clearing, gridiron 11. battlefield
field (pert to) . . .
athletic . . 4. oval 5. arena, court, track
6. course, sphere 7. diamond, stadium
8. gridiron
bloodshed . . 8. Aceldama (Akeldama)
13. Ager Sanguinis
duck . . 7. bustard
god of . . 4. Faun
mouse . . 4. vole
snow . . 4. neve
stubble . . 5. rowen
term . . 5. agral 8. agrarian 10. campestral
fiend . . . 3. foe 5. demon, devil, enemy,
Satan 6. addict, wizard 7. Amaimon
(Amamon) 9. archfiend 10. evil spirit
fiendish . . . 5. cruel 6. wicked 7. Avernal,
demonic 8. demoniac, devilish, diabolic
fierce . . . 4. grim 5. cruel, eager 6. raging,
savage 7. furious, racking, violent
9. ferocious, impetuous, truculent
10. catawampus, forbidding, passionate
11. belligerent, overwrought
12. overpowering
fierceness . . . 7. cruelty 8. violence
10. truculence
fiery . . . 3. hot, red 4. sore 5. angry
6. ardent 7. burning, excited, fervent,
flaming, glowing, igneous, parched,
violent 8. choleric, feverish, inflamed,
spirited, vehement 9. impetuous,
irascible 10. mettlesome, passionate
11. hot-tempered, inflammable
fiery cross . . . 5. alarm 6. emblem, signal,
symbol 8. crantara 10. call to arms

fiesta ... 5. color 7. holiday 8. festival 9. festivity

fifish ... 6. cranky 9. half crazy

fig ... 4. fico 5. eleme, gruit 6. Carica, Fiscus, Smyrna, trifle

fig basket ... 5. cabas, seron

fight ... 3. row, war 4. bout, duel, fray, mell, tilt 5. brawl, melee, scrap, set-to 6. affray, attack, barney, battle, combat, oppose, strife, strike, strive 7. contest, quarrel, warfare 8. conflict, struggle 9. pugnacity 13. combativeness

fighter ... 7. battler, duelist, soldier, warrior 8. champion, pugilist, scrapper 9. combatant

fighting ... 3. war 4. game 6. plucky 7. warlike 8. militant 10. contention, pugnacious 11. belligerent

fig leaf ... 6. symbol (modesty) 8. clothing (Bib), covering

figment ... 5. fancy 7. fiction 9. falsehood, invention

figurative ... 6. florid 7. flowery, typical 8. allusive 9. numerical 12. emblematical, metaphorical

figure ... 4. body, dash, dope, form, nude, rank, type 5. digit, image, judge, price, shape, solve 6. aspect, emblem, entail, number, symbol 7. diagram, numeral, outline, pattern 8. ornament, phantasm 9. calculate, celebrity, character, personage 10. appearance, impression, similitude 11. distinction

figure (pert to) ...
  column .. 6. elamon 7. telamon 8. Atlantes, Caryatid, pilaster
  geometric .. 4. cone, lune 5. prism, rhomb 6. isagon, isogen, isogon (rare) 7. ellipse, rhombus 8. pentagon, triangle 13. parallelogram, quadrilateral 16. parallelepipedon
  praying .. 5. orant
  repeated digits .. 8. repetend
  speech .. 5. trope 6. aporia, simile 8. metaphor
  star-shaped .. 8. pentacle

figured ... 4. rich 6. ornate 7. façonné 10. ornamented

figurine ... 4. doll 7. carving, tanagra 9. sculpture, statuette

Fiji Island, Viti Levu ...
  capital .. 4. Suva
  export .. 5. sugar
  mountain .. 8. Victoria
  people .. 11. Melanesians
  ruler .. 7. British

filament ... 4. barb, dowl (dowle), hair 5. fiber (fibre), harle 6. strand, thread

filament lamp ... 12. incandescent

filbert ... 3. nut 5. brown, hazel 7. Corylus 8. hazelnut

filch ... 3. nim, rob 4. beat 5. steal, theft 6. pilfer 7. purloin

file ... 3. row 4. list, rasp, rate 5. enter, march, store 6. abrade, smooth 7. sharpen 8. classify 9. catalogue 10. pickpocket 11. triggerfish (filefish)

file (combmaking) ... 5. grail (graille) 6. carlet 7. quannet

filibeg ... 4. kilt 5. skirt

filibuster ... 6. pirate 7. impeder

8. thwarter 9. legislate 10. freebooter, obstructer 14. obstructionist

filicide ... 6. murder (child by parent)

filigree ... 4. lace 5. adorn (with) 7. pattern 8. fanciful 10. decorative 13. unsubstantial

Filipino, Filipina (pert to) ...
  homeland (mostly) .. 5. Luzon
  people .. 5. Bikol (Bicol) 7. Malayan (Christian), Tagalog (Tagal), Visayan (see also *Philippine*)

fill ... 3. pad 4. calk, feed, glut, hold, plug 5. block, close, gorge, stuff 6. occupy, stop up 7. execute, fulfill, pervade, satiate, satisfy, suffuse 8. complete, compound, permeate 10. accomplish 11. superabound

fille ... 4. girl 8. daughter

filled ... 5. dated, laden 7. replete 8. suffused 9. saturated

filled with crevices ... 7. areolar

fillet ... 4. band, orle, ring, tape 5. snood, tiara 6. anadem, border, ribbon, taenia 7. bandage 8. headband, insignia 9. lemniscus, scantling 10. tenderloin

fillet (Arch) ... 5. stria 6. cimbia, listel, reglet, regula, taenia 7. chaplet, molding (part)

filly ... 4. colt, foal, girl, mare

film ... 4. brat, haze, scum, skin, veil 5. cover, layer 6. lamina, patina 7. coating 8. pellicle 10. photograph

film fan ... 8. cinéaste

filmy ... 3. dim 4. fine 5. gauzy, misty 6. cloudy, opaque 7. clouded 9. laminated 10. indistinct

fils ... 3. son

filter ... 4. ooze 5. clean, drain 6. purify, strain 7. trickle 8. colature 9. percolate

filth ... 4. dirt, muck, slut 5. lucre 6. vermin 7. squalor 9. excrement, obscenity, scoundrel

filthiness ... 8. cenosity 9. fetidness, obscenity 10. odiousness

filthy ... 3. low 4. foul, vile 5. dirty, fetid, gross 6. impure, odious, putrid 7. obscene, squalid, unclean 9. polluting 10. licentious

filthy lucre ... 4. gain (shameful) 5. money

fimbriated ... 5. edged 7. fringed 8. bordered (Her), margined

fin ... 3. arm 4. five, keel

fin (pert to fish) ...
  median .. 4. anal 6. caudal, dorsal
  paired .. 6. pelvic 7. ventral 8. pectoral

final ... 3. end 4. last 5. be-all, telic 7. dernier 8. decisive, definite, eventual, ultimate 9. mandatory, ultimatum 10. conclusive, definitive 11. unqualified 13. determinating

final argument ... 11. ultima ratio

finale ... 3. end 4. coda 5. close 6. result 8. swan song 10. completion, conclusion 11. termination

finality ... 5. finis 6. finale, finish, windup 10. conclusion 11. termination 12. decisiveness 14. conclusiveness

finally ... 10. eventually, ultimately 12. conclusively

final notice ... 4. obit

final outcome . . . 5. issue 6. upshot
10. denouement
financial . . . 6. fiscal 8. monetary
9. pecuniary
finch . . . 4. moro 5. Junco, serin, spink,
tarin 6. burion, linnet, siskin, towhee
7. chewink, redpoll 9. brambling,
chaffinch, Fringilla
find . . . 3. get 4. gain 5. learn 6. detect,
locate, summon, supply 7. procure,
provide 8. discover, meet with, perceive
9. determine, discovery, good thing
10. experience 11. acquisition
find fault . . . 4. beef, carp 5. cavil
8. complain 9. criticize
finding . . . 7. verdict 8. solution
9. discovery 11. serendipity
find out . . . 5. learn, solve 6. detect
8. discover 9. ascertain
fine . . . 3. fit 4. good, lacy, pure, rare, thin
5. dandy, filmy, frail, gaudy, noble,
sharp, sheer 6. ornate, slight, smooth
7. elegant, fragile, healthy, perfect,
powdery, precise, slender 8. absolute,
ethereal, handsome, polished, skillful,
superior 9. beautiful, excellent, sensitive
10. fastidious, pulverized, surpassing
finery . . . 6. beauty 7. clothes, gaudery,
gewgaws 8. elegance, fineness,
frippery, ornament 10. decoration,
lavishness 11. refinements
finesse . . . 5. skill 6. purity, serene
7. cunning 8. artifice, card play,
subtlety, thinness 9. clearness, good
taste, stratagem 10. refinement
14. discrimination (subtle)
finger . . . 3. toy (with) 4. hook 5. digit,
touch 6. dactyl, handle, pilfer
7. measure, purloin 8. identify
finger (pert to) . . .
alphabet . . 11. dactylology
cymbal . . 8. castanet
fish . . 8. starfish
flower . . 8. foxglove
foods . . 12. hors d'oeuvres
fore . . 5. index 7. pointer
little . . 6. pinkie 7. minimus 9. auricular
middle . . 6. medius
ring . . 7. annular
stall . . 3. cot
term . . 7. digital
Finger Lakes . . . 6. Cayuga, Seneca
fingernail moon . . . 6. lunule
fingernail overgrowth . . . 10. onychauxis
fingerprint (term) . . . 4. arch, loop
5. whorl 9. composite 11. dactylogram
12. dactyloscopy
finial . . . 3. epi, tee
finical . . . 4. nice 5. fussy 6. dainty,
dapper, jaunty, spruce 7. finicky,
foppish, mincing, prudish 8. delicate
9. finicking, squeamish 10. fastidious,
meticulous 11. overprecise
14. overscrupulous
finis . . . 3. end 4. goal 6. finale 8. finality
10. conclusion 11. culmination
finish . . . 3. end 4. kill 5. chare, close,
matte (mat), style 6. enamel, polish
7. destroy, perfect, surface, texture
8. complete, conclude 9. terminate
10. completion, consummate, perfection

finished . . . 3. o'er 4. done, fine, over, ripe
5. ended 6. closed 7. refined, stopped
8. climaxed, complete, lustered,
polished 9. completed, concluded,
perfected 10. terminated
finite . . . 7. fleshly, limited 9. definable
10. restricted, terminable 11. conditional
fink . . . 3. spy 4. scab 5. finch 8. informer
13. strikebreaker
Finland . . . see also *Finnish*
capital . . 8. Helsinki (Helsingfors)
Finnish for Finland . . 5. Suomi
government . . 8. republic
island . . 5. Aland
language . . 6. Magyar 7. Swedish
8. Estonian
legislature . . 9. Eduskunta
port . . 3. Abo 5. Turku 9. Mariehamn
Finnish (pert to) . . .
bath . . 5. sauna
dramatist . . 4. Kivi 7. Waltari
people . . 5. Finns, Suomi 9. Karelians
10. Tavastians
fire . . . 4. heat, zeal 5. blaze, fever,
flame 6. excite, fervor, igneus,
ignite, incite, kindle 7. barrage,
explode, inspire 8. detonate, illumine
9. discharge, eloquence 11. inspiration
12. inflammation 13. conflagration
fire (pert to) . . .
basket . . 5. grate 7. cresset
comb form . . 4. igni
cracker . . 6. petard
dog . . 7. andiron
fear of . . 10. pyrophobia
god . . 6. Vulcan
opal . . 7. girasol (girasole)
power over . . 10. ignipotent
worshiper . . 5. Parsi 9. pyrolater
10. ignicolist
firearm . . . 3. BAR, gat, gun, rod,
Uzi 4. heat 5. luger, piece, rifle
6. musket, pistol 7. handgun, shotgun,
sidearm 8. ordnance, petronel, repeater,
revolver, tommy gun 9. flintlock,
harquebus (arquebus) 10. six-shooter
11. Springfield (rifle)
firearms discharge . . . 9. fusillade
firearms maker . . . 4. Colt 7. Beretta
8. Browning 9. Remington
10. Winchester 14. Smith and Wesson
fired . . . 3. lit 4. shot 5. baked 6. on
fire (Her) 7. excited 8. inspired
10. discharged
fireman . . . 4. vamp 6. fueler, stoker
8. trainman 9. fire-eater 11. firefighter
fireplace . . . 5. fogon, forge, ingle
6. hearth 9. inglenook 13. Franklin
stove
fireside (home) . . . 11. hearthstone
firewood . . . 6. billet
fireworks . . . 4. caps, gerb 6. flares
7. fizgigs, gunfire, rip-raps, rockets
8. serpents 9. pinwheels, sparklers,
torpedoes 10. girandoles
12. firecrackers, Roman candles
firm . . . 4. fast, hard, safe, sure, trig
5. dense, fixed, rigid, solid, sound,
stout, tight 6. secure, stable, stanch,
steady, strict, strong 7. compact,
company, decided, devoted, staunch

8. faithful **9.** immovable, steadfast
10. determined, unslipping, unyielding
11. substantial
firmament . . . **3.** sky **5.** vault **6.** Caelus,
welkin **7.** heavens **8.** empyrean
firmly set . . . **5.** fixed, solid **6.** rooted
10. inveterate
firmness . . . **8.** fidelity, rigidity, solidity,
strength, tenacity **9.** constancy, stability
10. immobility, steadiness **11.** reliability
15. indissolubility
firmness, want of . . . **5.** loose **6.** laxity
8. weakness **11.** instability, vacillation
firn . . . **3.** ice **4.** neve, snow
firs . . . **5.** Abies, pines
first . . . **5.** chief, front, prime **6.** maiden,
primal, primus **7.** highest, initial,
leading, primary **8.** earliest, foremost,
original **9.** beginning, elemental,
principal **10.** primordial
first (pert to) . . .
appearance . . **5.** debut **8.** premiere
born . . **5.** eigne **6.** eldest
Christian martyr . . **7.** Stephen
coin (silver) . . **8.** sesterce
days of Rom month . . **7.** calends
(kalends)
fruits (Eccl) . . **7.** annates
letter . . **4.** Alif **5.** Aleph
stages . . **8.** inchoate **9.** rudiments
world navigator . . **8.** Magellan
fish . . . **3.** dib **4.** food **5.** angle, drail,
seine, troll **6.** Pisces **13.** constellation
fish (types of) . . . **2.** id **3.** cat, cod, gar, ray
4. bass, carp, char, chub, cusk, dace,
goby, hake, ling, opah, parr, peto, pike,
ruff, scup, shad, sisi, sole, tuna, ulua
5. bream, cisco, fluke, guppy, perch,
porgy, shark, skate, smelt, snook, sprat,
trout, tunny, wahoo **6.** barbel, bonito,
bowfin, burbot, conger, darter, marlin,
minnow, puffer, redfin, salmon, shiner,
sucker, tarpon, tautog, turbot **7.** alewife,
anchovy, catfish, crappie, croaker,
dogfish, garfish, grouper, haddock,
halibut, herring, hogfish, jewfish,
lamprey, mudfish, oquassa, pollack,
pompano, redfish, sardine, sawfish,
sunfish, torpedo, walleye **8.** albacore,
blue fish, bluegill, bonefish, bullhead,
chimaera, filefish, flatfish, flounder,
goldfish, grayling, kingfish, lumpfish,
mackerel, menhaden, pickerel, pilchard,
sailfish, sergeant, sting ray, sturgeon,
toadfish, weakfish **9.** barracuda,
cigarfish, devilfish, jellyfish, namaycush,
sheatfish, whitefish **10.** barramunda,
butterfish, candlefish, hammerhead,
yellowtail **11.** muskellunge (see also
mammal)
fish (pert to) . . .
adhering . . **4.** pega **6.** remora
ascending rivers . . **7.** anadrom
10. anadromous
bait . . **4.** chum **5.** chack **6.** minnow
9. killifish (killy)
basket . . **4.** caul **5.** creel, slath (slarth)
bivalve, mollusk . . **4.** clam, slug **5.** snail,
whelk **6.** limpet, mussel, oyster
7. abalone, Ocypode (crab), scallop
caviar-yielding . . **7.** sterlet

climbing, jumping . . **5.** saury **6.** anabas
7. skipper
club . . **6.** muckle
codfish . . **4.** cusk **5.** torsk **7.** bacalao,
buffalo
comb form . . **7.** ichthyo
crustacean . . **3.** Uca **4.** crab **6.** shrimp
7. lobster **8.** Decapoda
devil . . **3.** ray **5.** manta
eaters . . **12.** ichthyophagi
eating . . **11.** piscivorous
14. ichthyophagous
fabled (Pers) . . **4.** Mahi (Mah)
gaff (through ice) . . **5.** ching
game . . **4.** tuna **5.** chiro, sword, trout
6. marlin, salmon, tarpon **8.** grayling
11. muskellunge
genus . . **4.** Amia (bowfin), Mola
(sunfish) **5.** Elops (tarpon), Perca
(perch) **8.** Haliotis (abalone), Octopoda
(octopus)
hook . . **5.** Kirby, snell (part) **8.** Aberdeen,
barbless, Carlisle, Limerick
largest (freshwater) . . **8.** arapaima
like . . **8.** ichthyic
line . . **6.** nossel (norsel) **7.** spillet
living by . . **9.** piscatory
living on . . **12.** ichthyophagy
man-eating . . **6.** caribe **7.** piranha
mollusk . . see _bivalve_
nest building . . **5.** acara
net . . **4.** fyke **5.** seine, snell, trawl
7. boulter, spiller
pond . . **7.** piscina **8.** aquarium
roe . . **6.** caviar
salmon . . **3.** fog **4.** masu, parr **5.** sprod
6. alevin **7.** gilling
sauce . . **4.** alec
spear . . **3.** gig
taboo . . **13.** ichthyophobia
treatise . . **11.** ichthyology
worship . . **12.** ichthyolatry
young brood . . **3.** fry
fisherman . . . **6.** angler **8.** piscator
fishery . . . **7.** piscary
fishing . . . **4.** chug (through ice) **8.** snelling
9. halieutic, piscation
fishing vessel . . . **5.** smack **6.** seiner
7. trawler
fishy . . . **4.** dull **6.** vacant **8.** fishlike
9. deceptive, dishonest **10.** improbable,
lusterless, suspicious, unreliable
11. extravagant **14.** expressionless
fissure . . . **3.** gap **4.** leak, lode, open,
rent, rift, rima, seam, slit, vein **5.** break,
chasm, chine, chink, cleft, crack, sever,
split **7.** crevice
fissured . . . **5.** cleft **6.** rimate, rimose
fist . . . **4.** duke, hand (closed) **5.** nieve
6. clench **8.** tightwad **11.** handwriting
fit . . . **3.** due, fay, pat **4.** able, gear,
meet, mesh, ripe, suit, whim **5.** adapt,
equip, fancy, ready, spasm, train
6. attack, enmesh, frenzy, proper,
stroke, suited **7.** adapted, caprice,
conform, healthy, prepare, tantrum
8. disposed, dovetail, eligible, outbreak,
suitable **9.** competent, qualified
11. accommodate, appropriate
fit (pert to) . . .
an arrow (archery) . . **4.** nock

fury .. **4.** rage
groove (Arch) .. **4.** dado
resentment .. **4.** huff, mood **5.** pique
7. tantrum
to eat .. **6.** edible
to till .. **6.** arable
fitchew ... **5.** skink, zoril **7.** foumart,
polecat
fitful ... **8.** restless, unstable, variable
9. impulsive, irregular, orderless,
spasmodic **10.** capricious, convulsive
12. intermittent
fitly ... **4.** duly **5.** right **6.** timely
8. properly, suitably **10.** decorously
fitness ... **7.** decorum **9.** congruity
10. expedience, timeliness **11.** eligibility,
suitability **12.** preparedness
fitting ... **3.** apt, pat **4.** just, meet
6. proper, seemly, timely **8.** adapting,
suitable **9.** expedient **11.** appropriate
five (pert to) ...
Books of Moses .. **10.** Pentateuch
children (born at once) .. **11.** quintuplets
Civilized Tribes (Ind) .. **5.** Creek
7. Choctaw **8.** Cherokee, Seminole
9. Chickasaw
comb form .. **5.** penta
cornered .. **11.** pentagonous
divided by .. **11.** quinquesect
dollar bill .. **1.** V **3.** fin **5.** fiver
feet .. **10.** pentameter
five-year period .. **6.** pentad **7.** lustrum
(census) **12.** quinquennial
fold .. **9.** quintuple
group .. **6.** pentad **8.** fivesome
lines (nonsense) .. **8.** limerick
Nations (Ind Confed) .. **7.** Cayugas,
Mohawks, Oneidas, Senecas
9. Onondagas
trump card (auction pitch) .. **5.** pedro
fix ... **3.** peg, pin, set **4.** mend, moor,
nail **5.** amend, brace, bribe, imbed,
limit, stamp **6.** adjust, anchor, cement,
define, fasten, ossify, punish, repair,
settle **7.** arrange, confirm, delimit,
dilemma, prepare, rectify **8.** organize,
solidify **9.** condition, establish, stabilize,
stipulate **10.** prearrange
fixed ... **3.** set **4.** firm **5.** rigid **6.** formal,
intent, nailed, static **7.** assured, limited,
settled, special **8.** arranged, habitual
9. immovable, permanent, unwinking
11. established, prearranged, traditional
fixed (pert to) ...
allowance .. **4.** diet **6.** ration **7.** stipend
10. remittance
beforehand .. **13.** predetermined
by choice .. **8.** elective
idea .. **8.** idée fixe **9.** obsession
manner .. **9.** immovably
routine .. **4.** rote
star .. **4.** Veda
time .. **3.** era **4.** date, fast
fizgig ... **9.** fireworks, whirligig
flabellate ... **9.** fan-shaped
flabrum ... **3.** fan **9.** flabellum
flaccid ... **4.** limp, weak **6.** flabby
8. yielding
flag ... **3.** sag **4.** fail, fane, iris, pave,
pine, sign, weak, wilt **5.** Roger
(pirate) **6.** banner, burgee, colors,

cornet, ensign, fanion, flower, guidon,
pennon, signal **7.** bunting, calamus,
decline, pennant **8.** gonfalon, masthead,
standard, streamer, vexillum
9. banderole **16.** Quincunx of Heaven
flagging ... **4.** weak **7.** languid
8. pavement **10.** flagstones, spiritless
11. languishing
flagging in energy ... **9.** lassitude
flagitious ... **6.** wicked **7.** corrupt, heinous
8. criminal, flagrant **10.** scandalous,
villainous
flag maker ... **9.** Betsy Ross
flagon ... **3.** jug **4.** ewer **5.** stoup **6.** bottle,
carafe **7.** canteen **8.** demijohn
flagpole standard ... **7.** bracket
9. bracciale
flagrant ... **4.** rank **5.** great **6.** absurd,
wanton, wicked **7.** glaring, hateful,
heinous, obvious, scarlet, violent
8. infamous, terrible **9.** abandoned,
atrocious, monstrous, nefarious
10. profligate, villainous
flail ... **4.** beat, flag, whip **6.** thrash,
weapon (anc) **7.** swingle
flam ... **4.** hoax **5.** cheat, spoof, trick
6. cajole **7.** pretext **8.** drumbeat,
flimflam **9.** deception, falsehood
flambeau ... **5.** torch (flaming) **7.** cresset
11. candlestick
flamboyant ... **4.** wavy (Arch) **6.** florid,
ornate **9.** brilliant, flamelike
11. resplendent
flame ... **3.** arc **4.** beam, burn, fire,
glow, leye (obs), love, zeal **5.** ardor,
blaze, flare, flash, glare, ingle, light,
lover **6.** redden **7.** scarlet **8.** flammule
(small) **10.** brightness, sweetheart
flamen ... **6.** priest (anc)
flamenco ... **5.** dance (gypsy)
Flaminian Way ... **4.** Rome
Flanders, Belgium ...
brick .. **4.** Bath
capital .. **5.** Ghent (East) **6.** Bruges
(West)
city .. **5.** Alost **6.** Ostend **7.** Dixmude
(Dixmuide)
people (anc) .. **5.** Celts **6.** Franks
11. Burgundians
poppy .. **9.** corn poppy
flâneur ... **5.** idler
flap ... **3.** tab **4.** blow, slap, sway,
wave **5.** skirt **6.** dangle, lappet, stroke
7. flapper, flutter **9.** appendage
flare ... **3.** blaze, flame, flash, fusee,
glare, light **6.** signal, spread **7.** display,
flicker **8.** outburst **10.** illuminate
flaring ... **5.** gaudy **6.** spread **7.** burning,
glaring **8.** dazzling, flashing
flash ... **4.** show **5.** blaze, burst, gleam,
glint, shine, spark **6.** glance, signal
7. display, glimmer, glisten, glitter,
instant, shimmer, sparkle **8.** dispatch
9. telegraph
flashing ... **5.** showy **6.** flashy **8.** meteoric,
snapping **9.** transient
flashy ... **3.** gay **5.** fiery, gaudy, showy
6. frothy, garish, sporty **7.** raffish
8. vehement **9.** flaunting, impetuous
13. grandiloquent
flask ... **4.** ewer, olpe **5.** betty **6.** flagon

7. ampulla, canteen **9.** aryballus
(aryballas, anc)
flask-shaped . . . **10.** lageniform
flat . . . **3.** low **4.** palm **5.** banal, blunt,
level, molle, plain, plane, prone, stale,
suite, tract, vapid **6.** boring, dreary,
wholly **7.** insipid, uniform **8.** tenement,
unbroken **10.** horizontal
flat (pert to) . . .
  boat . . **3.** ark **4.** punt, scow **5.** barge
  breastbone . . **6.** ratite
  canopy . . **6.** tester
  flatfoot . . **9.** pes planus **13.** talipes planus
  iron . . **7.** sadiron
  nosed . . **6.** simous
  piece . . **4.** slab
  surface . . **4.** area **6.** pagina **7.** tabular
  worm . . **9.** planarian, trematode
flatfish . . . **3.** dab **4.** sole **5.** brill, fluke
6. acedia, turbot **7.** flounder
flatten . . . **4.** even **5.** level **6.** deject,
smooth **7.** depress **8.** dispirit
9. prostrate **10.** discourage, dishearten
flattened . . . **6.** evened, oblate **7.** leveled
8. smoothed **9.** applanate
flatter . . . **3.** oil **4.** coax, palp **5.** charm,
float **6.** cajole, caress, please, praise,
smooge, soothe **7.** adulate, beguile,
blarney, flutter **8.** blandish **9.** encourage
10. compliment, ingratiate
flatterer . . . **6.** flunky, glozer **7.** Jenkins
8. adulator, courtier, parasite
9. sycophant
flattering . . . **9.** adulatory, gnathonic,
insincere **10.** obsequious
13. complimentary
flattery . . . **5.** gloze, taffy **6.** praise
7. blarney, eyewash, fawning, palaver
8. cajolery **9.** adulation **10.** compliment,
sycophancy **14.** obsequiousness
flaunt . . . **4.** wave **5.** boast, vaunt
6. parade **7.** display, flutter **8.** brandish
Flavian, House of Flavius, Emperors . . .
5. Titus **8.** Domitian **9.** Vespasian
Flavian Amphitheater . . . **9.** Colosseum
(Rome)
flavor . . . **4.** gust, odor, tang, zest
5. aroma, imbue, sapid, sapor,
sauce, savor, scent, taste **6.** season
7. perfume **8.** piquancy **9.** flavoring
14. characteristic
flaw . . . **3.** gap, mar **4.** rase, rift
5. cleft, fault **6.** breach, defect
7. blemish, fissure, sophism **8.** fracture
12. imperfection
flawless . . . **5.** ideal **7.** perfect **8.** unmarked
11. unblemished
flax . . . **3.** lin, tow **5.** linen
flax (pert to) . . .
  capsule . . **4.** boll
  dust . . **5.** pouce
  filaments . . **4.** harl
  process plant . . **7.** rettery
  refuse . . **3.** pob, tow **5.** hurds
  seed . . **7.** linseed
  soak . . **3.** ret
  weed . . **8.** toadflax
flaxweed . . . **8.** toadflax
flay . . . **4.** peel, skin **6.** fleece **7.** censure,
reprove, scarify **9.** criticize, excoriate
flea . . . **4.** puce **5.** pulex **6.** beetle,

chigoe **7.** chigger, cyclops **8.** reminder
13. Ctenocephalus
fleam . . . **6.** lancet, stream **10.** millstream
fleck . . . **4.** flea, mark, spot **5.** flake
6. blotch, dapple, streak, stripe
7. freckle, speckle, stipple **8.** particle
9. variegate
flection, flexion . . . **7.** bending, turning
flee . . . **3.** fly, run **4.** shun **5.** avoid, elope,
evade, speed **6.** vanish **7.** abandon,
forsake **9.** disappear
fleece . . . **3.** abb, nap **4.** flay, pile,
skin, wool **5.** fleck, mulct, sheer,
strip **6.** divest **7.** despoil, swindle
10. overcharge
fleer . . . **4.** gibe, jeer, mock **5.** flout, scoff,
sheer, taunt
fleet . . . **4.** fast, flit, flow, navy, sail,
swim **5.** drift, group, quick, rapid, swift
6. armada, hasten, nimble, speedy
9. transient **10.** evanescent, transitory
fleeting . . . **7.** passing **9.** transient
10. evanescent, transitory
Fleet Street . . . **5.** Fleta (book written in
prison) **6.** prison (London) **11.** London
press
Flemish painter . . . **5.** David **6.** Rubens
7. Van Dyke
flesh . . . **3.** kin **4.** body, meat, pink,
pulp, race (human) **6.** family, fatten,
muscle **7.** kindred, kinsmen, mankind
8. humanity **9.** mortality **10.** sensuality
flesh (pert to) . . .
  eating . . **8.** omophagy (raw)
  9. omophagia **10.** omophagous,
  zoophagous **11.** carnivorous,
  creophagous
  fond of . . **12.** sarcophilous
  like . . **7.** carnose
  lust for . . **9.** carnality
  resembling . . **7.** sarcoid
  slain animals . . **7.** carnage
fleshpots . . . **6.** plenty, wealth **10.** high
living, prosperity **12.** fat of the land
fleshy . . . **3.** fat **5.** beefy, human, obese,
plump, pulpy, stout **6.** carnal **7.** adipose,
carnose **9.** corpulent
fleshy fruit . . . **4.** pear, pome **5.** bacca,
berry, drupe
fleur-de-lis . . . **3.** lis (Her) **4.** iris, lily,
luce **6.** emblem
flew . . . see *fly*
flexible . . . **4.** limp **5.** lithe **6.** limber,
pliant, supple **7.** elastic, lissome
flexion, flection . . . **9.** anaclasis
flexure . . . **4.** genu **5.** crook **7.** bending
flick (sl) . . . **4.** film **5.** movie
flicker . . . **4.** burn, flit **5.** blaze, glare,
waver **7.** flutter, high-hoe
10. woodpecker
flickering . . . **7.** burning, lambent
8. flickery **9.** irregular
flier, flyer . . . **3.** ace **4.** bird **5.** pilot,
train **6.** airman, gamble, insect
7. aviator, speeder, sunfish, venture
11. speculation
flight . . . **3.** hop **4.** rout **5.** arrow
(volley), flock, skein (wild fowl), speed
6. exodus, fletch (arrows), flying,
hegira, perron, stairs, throng **7.** soaring
8. escapism, mounting, stampede,

swarming 9. excursion, formation,
migration 10. volitation
flightless bird . . . see *bird, flightless*
flighty . . . 5. barmy, swift 6. fickle, fitful
7. foolish 8. fanciful, freakish, volatile
9. frivolous 10. capricious
flimflam . . . 5. freak, hocus, trick
6. humbug 7. caprice, swindle
8. nonsense, trifling 9. deception,
deceptive 11. nonsensical
flimmer . . . 7. flicker, glimmer
flimsy . . . 4. limp, rare, thin, vain, weak
5. frail 6. feeble, paltry, sleazy, slimsy
7. flaccid, shallow, trivial 9. illogical
11. superficial 13. unsubstantial
flinch . . . 4. game 5. quail, start, wince,
wonde 6. blench, cringe, falter, flense,
recoil, shrink, swerve
fling . . . 3. shy 4. dart, dash, gibe, hurl,
toss 5. cheat, dance, flock (sandpipers),
revel, sling, sneer, throw 6. baffle,
spirit 7. cast off, sarcasm 9. prostrate
flint . . . 5. chert, clint, silex 6. quartz
7. lighter 8. hardness 9. firestone,
skinflint
flip . . . 3. hop, tap 4. flap, glib, snap, toss
5. drink (spiced), flick, flirt, throw 6. fillip
8. flippant, turn over 10. somersault
11. impertinent
flippant . . . 4. flip, glib, pert 5. cocky
6. chatty, fluent 8. impudent
10. persiflate 11. impertinent
flipper . . . 3. arm, fin, paw 4. hand
5. panel 8. flapjack
flirt . . . 3. toy 4. dart, fike, flip, jerk, jilt,
mash, play, toss 5. dally 6. coquet,
fillip, masher, trifle 7. trifler 8. coquette
11. philanderer
flirtation . . . 5. dance 8. coquetry, trifling
10. love affair
flit . . . 3. fly 4. dart 5. glide, hover
6. nimble 7. flicker, flutter, migrate
flitter . . . 3. rag 5. hover, piece 6. tatter
7. flicker, flutter, fritter 8. fragment
flittermouse . . . 3. bat
float . . . 4. buoy, cork, hove, lure, raft,
ride, sail, soar, swim, waft 5. balsa,
drift, hover, ladle 6. launch 7. support
8. navigate, undulate 9. transport
10. inaugurate
floating . . . 4. free 5. awash, loose
6. adrift, natant 7. buoyant, movable,
rumored 8. changing, drifting, shifting
9. launching, wandering
floating herb . . . 7. frogbit
16. Hydrocharitaceae
flock . . . 4. bevy, fold, herd, pack,
raft 6. flight, hirsel 7. company
9. multitude 10. assemblage, collection
11. aggregation
flock (pert to) . . .
bees . . 4. hive 5. swarm 6. colony
cattle . . 4. herd
fish . . 5. shoal
geese . . 5. skein 6. gaggle
herons . . 5. sedge
insects . . 5. swarm
like . . 6. gregal
lions . . 5. pride
partridge . . 5. covey
pheasants . . 4. nide (nid)

sandpipers . . 5. fling
walrus . . 3. pod
flocks, god of . . . 3. Pan
floe . . . 3. ice 4. berg
flog . . . 3. cat, tan 4. beat, cane, goad,
lash, wale, welt, whip 6. larrup, punish,
strike, thrash 8. chastise
flogging . . . 4. toco (toko) 7. beating
8. whipping 9. thrashing 10. punishment
12. chastisement
flood . . . 3. sea 5. eagre, spate 6. deluge,
drench, excess 7. freshet, torrent
8. cataract, inundate, overflow
9. cataclysm 10. oversupply
14. superabundance
flood (pert to) . . .
disaster . . 9. Galveston (1900),
Johnstown (1889)
gate . . 4. gool, lock, slow 6. sluice
8. penstock
lights . . 5. klieg
tidal . . 5. eagre
floor . . . 4. base, pave, sill 5. chess
(pontoon), story 6. baffle, bottom,
defeat 7. coaming, silence 9. overthrow
10. substratum
floor leader . . . 4. whip
flora . . . 6. plants 11. florilegium
flora and fauna . . . 5. biota
Florence gallery . . . 5. Pitti 6. Uffizi
Florentine (pert to) . . .
color . . 7. scarlet
family (famed) . . 6. Medici
lily . . 6. giglio
school . . 6. Tuscan
sculptor . . 8. Ammanati, Ghiberti
florid . . . 3. red 5. ruddy 6. ornate, rococo
7. flowery, flushed 8. enriched, rubicund
10. figurative, melismatic, rhetorical
11. embellished 13. grandiloquent
Florida . . .
cape . . 9. Canaveral
capital . . 11. Tallahassee
city . . 5. Miami, Tampa 7. Daytona, Key
West, Orlando 8. Sarasota 9. Pensacola
11. St Augustine (1565) 12. Jacksonville,
St Petersburg 14. Fort Lauderdale
discoverer . . 11. Ponce de Leon (1513)
fish . . 6. mullet, shrimp, tarpon, testar,
tetard 8. blue crab
flower . . 13. orange blossom
Indian . . 8. Seminole
lake . . 10. Okeechobee
museum . . 10. Circus Hall (Ringling)
plant . . 7. coontie
river . . 8. Suwannee
State motto . . 22. Liberty and
Independence
State nickname . . 8. Sunshine
swamp, park . . 10. Everglades
trail . . 7. Tamiami
flounce . . . 4. flap, fold, jerk, trim 5. caper,
frill, twist 6. edging, frolic 8. flounder,
struggle
flounder . . . 4. roll 6. bungle, muddle,
welter 7. stumble 8. struggle 9. fluctuate
flounder (fish) . . . 3. dab 5. fluke 6. plaice,
turbot 8. flatfish
flour . . . 4. bran, meal 6. farina, pinole,
powder 9. middlings, pulverize
flour (pert to) . . .

diabetic . . **9.** aleuronat
gravy . . **4.** roux
maker . . **6.** miller
pudding . . **4.** duff
flourish . . . **4.** grow, show, wave **5.** vaunt
  6. flaunt, paraph (signature), thrive
  7. display, fanfare, prosper, roulade
  8. arpeggio, brandish, ornament
  9. embellish, luxuriate **11.** ostentation
flout . . . **4.** defy, gibe, jeer, mock **5.** fleer,
  scoff, scout, sneer, taunt **6.** insult
  8. ridicule
flow . . . **3.** jet, run **4.** bore, flow, flux,
  gush, ooze, pour, roll, teem **5.** glide,
  issue, river, spout **6.** abound, afflux,
  course, stream **7.** current, fluency,
  flutter **9.** streaming **10.** outpouring
flow (pert to) . . .
along . . **4.** lave
back . . **7.** redound
jet . . **4.** gush **5.** spurt
out . . **5.** exude, issue, spill
over . . **5.** slosh, spill **6.** deluge, engulf
  8. inundate **9.** overwhelm
tide . . **3.** ebb **4.** flow, neap
flower . . . **3.** bud **4.** best, blow **5.** bloom
  6. unfold **7.** blossom, develop, essence,
  produce **8.** choicest, ornament **11.** Four
  Hundred (Society)
flower (types of) . . . **3.** gul (rose) **4.** iris,
  ixia, lily, pink, rose **5.** aster, calla,
  canna, daisy, pansy, peony, phlox,
  poppy, stock, tulip **6.** azalea, cosmos,
  crocus, dahlia, lupine, maypop, orchid,
  oxalis, violet, zinnia **7.** arbutus,
  begonia, fuchsia, gentian, passion,
  petunia, rhodora, verbena **8.** amaranth,
  arethusa, camomile, cyclamen, daffodil,
  geranium, hepatica, hyacinth, larkspur,
  magnolia, marigold, Mariposa (lily),
  primrose, sweet pea **9.** amaryllis,
  calendula, carnation, edelweiss,
  gladiolus, hollyhock, mayflower,
  narcissus, water lily **10.** cornflower,
  delphinium, fleur-de-lis, marguerite,
  mignonette, nasturtium, periwinkle,
  poinsettia, snapdragon **11.** forget-me-
  not, strawflower **13.** chrysanthemum
  15. lily of the valley
flower (pert to) . . .
arranging . . **7.** ikebana
bed, garden . . **8.** floretum, parterre
bloom (full) . . **8.** anthesis
bud (sauce) . . **5.** caper
bunch . . **4.** posy **7.** bouquet, corsage,
  nosegay
bursting into . . **12.** efflorescent
cluster, clustered . . **4.** cyme **5.** umbel
  8. racemose **9.** glomerule **10.** paniculate
largest . . **9.** rafflesia (3-ft diameter)
like . . **7.** anthoid
meadow-grown . . **6.** pratal
part . . **4.** stem **5.** bract, calyx, petal,
  sepal, spike, torus **6.** carpel, pistil,
  stamen **7.** corolla, petiole **8.** epicalyx,
  peduncle, perianth
poet's . . **8.** asphodel **9.** narcissus
sacred . . **5.** lotus
seed . . **5.** ovule
shaped . . **7.** fleuron
small . . **7.** fleuret

stand . . **7.** epergne
flower, shrub . . . **5.** lilac **6.** azalea,
  laurel **7.** dogwood, heather, jasmine,
  spiraea, syringa **8.** bayberry, hawthorn
  9. jessamine, mistletoe, sagebrush
  10. bitterroot **12.** rhododendron
flower, vine . . . **8.** clematis, wisteria
  11. honeysuckle **12.** morning glory
flower, wild . . . **5.** bluet, daisy **6.** cactus,
  clover, myrtle, pasque **7.** anemone,
  cowslip **8.** bluebell, camellia
  9. buttercup, goldenrod, mayflower,
  sunflower **10.** bluebonnet **12.** lady's-
  slipper
flowering again . . . **9.** remontant
flowers . . . **9.** flowerage
flowers, goddess of . . . **5.** Flora (Rom)
Flowery Kingdom . . . **5.** China
flowing . . . **5.** fluid **6.** afflux, fluent
  7. copious, cursive, emanant, fluxing
  8. coursing, eloquent **9.** streaming
  10. transitive
flowing (pert to) . . .
from source . . **6.** rising **9.** emanating
together . . **9.** confluent
veil . . **5.** colet (anc)
well . . **6.** gusher
fluctuate . . . **4.** roll, vary, veer **5.** waver
  7. vibrate **8.** intermit, undulate,
  unsteady **9.** oscillate, vacillate
  10. irresolute **12.** undetermined
flue . . . **4.** barb **5.** fluke **6.** funnel, tunnel
  7. chimney
fluent . . . **4.** glib **5.** fluid, ready **6.** facile,
  smooth, solute **7.** copious, elegant,
  flowing, gliding, verbose, voluble
  8. eloquent **9.** talkative **10.** loquacious
fluff . . . **4.** down, girl, lint, yarn **5.** floss
  6. bungle **8.** softness **9.** lightness
fluffy . . . **4.** soft **5.** downy, drunk,
  fuzzy, linty **8.** feathery **9.** forgetful
  12. undependable
fluid . . . **3.** gas, ink, oil **4.** bile, milk
  5. ichor, serum, water **6.** fluent, liquid,
  plasma, watery **7.** flowing **8.** floating,
  nonsolid
fluke . . . **4.** fish, worm **5.** blade (whale)
  8. accident, flatfish, flounder
flume . . . **5.** shoot **6.** raving, sluice
  7. channel, conduit
flummox . . . **7.** confuse, perplex
flunk . . . **4.** fail, miss, slip **5.** shirk **6.** flinch
  7. back out
flunky, flunkey . . . **4.** snob **5.** toady
  6. cookee, lackey **7.** footman, servant
  8. henchman **9.** stagehand
flurry . . . **3.** ado **4.** fret, gust **5.** haste,
  hurry **6.** bustle, squall **7.** bluster,
  fluster, flutter **8.** snowfall **9.** agitation,
  commotion, confusion **10.** excitement
flush . . . **3.** hot, jet **4.** full, glow, gush,
  rush **5.** blush, cards, color, drunk, fever,
  rinse, ruddy **6.** drench, lavish, redden,
  thrill **7.** healthy, wealthy **8.** abundant,
  affluent, prodigal, rosiness, squarely,
  unbroken **10.** prosperous
flushed . . . **3.** hot, red **4.** ruby **5.** aglow,
  drunk **6.** elated, florid **7.** excited,
  fervent **8.** blushing, exultant, feverish,
  reddened
fluster . . . **4.** move **5.** shake **6.** bustle,

excite, flurry, pother **8.** distract
10. excitement **11.** distraction
flute . . . **5.** crimp, twill **6.** furrow, groove
7. magadis **9.** organ stop, wineglass
10. instrument
flute (pert to) . . .
  bagpipe part . . **7.** chanter
  nose . . **3.** bin **5.** pungi
  player . . **6.** aulete **7.** tootler
  shrill . . **7.** piccolo
  stop . . **7.** ventage
  transverse . . **4.** fife
fluting . . . **5.** strix **7.** gadroon, shading
10. decoration
flutter . . . **4.** flap, flit, wave **5.** float, haste,
hover, waver **6.** bustle, ruffle **7.** agitate,
pitapat **8.** disorder **9.** agitation,
confusion, palpitate
flux . . . **4.** flow, fuse, melt **5.** flood, purge,
resin, rosin, smalt, smear **6.** course
7. flowing, liquefy, outflow, solvent
fly . . . **3.** hop **4.** flee, flit, leap, melt,
soar, wave, whir, wing **5.** alate, float,
glide, speed **6.** aviate, elapse, escape,
insect, spring, vanish **7.** avigate, avolate
8. fishhook **9.** cease to be, disappear
fly (types of) . . . **3.** bot **4.** gnat **5.** cadew,
horse, house, midge **6.** Asilus, caddis,
gadfly, punkie, tsetse **7.** Diptera, nosee-
um **8.** dipteron, lacewing, mosquito
11. caterpillar
fly (pert to) . . .
  African . . **4.** zimb (zebub) **6.** tsetse
  agaric . . **8.** mushroom (poisonous)
  artificial . . **4.** harl **5.** alder, sedge **6.** Cahill,
  claret **7.** grannom
  blow . . **4.** eggs **5.** larva
  catcher . . **4.** tody **6.** peewee (pewit),
  phoebe **8.** kingbird
flying . . . **5.** a-wing, brief, hasty, yarak
(falcon) **6.** volant, waving **7.** fleeing
8. fleeting, floating **9.** temporary,
transient **12.** aeronautical
flying (pert to) . . .
  adder . . **9.** dragonfly
  boat . . **8.** airplane, seaplane **9.** amphibian
  cat . . **5.** lemur **6.** marmot
  Dutchman . . **5.** opera **7.** mariner (fabled)
  8. wanderer
  fox . . **3.** bat **6.** kalong
  island . . **6.** Laputa (Gulliver's Travels)
  machine . . **9.** gyroplane, orthopter
foal . . . **4.** colt **5.** filly **8.** Equuleus (Astron)
9. youngling
foam . . . **4.** barm, boil, fume, rage, scum,
suds **5.** froth, spume, yeast **6.** trivia
7. bubbles
foaming . . . **7.** spumous **8.** bubbling
10. fermenting, infuriated
11. overwrought
fob . . . **4.** sham **5.** cheat, trick **6.** impose,
pocket **7.** palm off **8.** ornament
focal point . . . **8.** omphalos
focus . . . **6.** center **8.** converge, omphalos
10. adjustment **11.** concentrate
fodder . . . **3.** hay **4.** corn, feed **5.** straw,
vetch **6.** forage, silage, stover **7.** stubble
8. ensilage **9.** pasturage, provender
fodder (pert to) . . .
  pit . . **4.** silo
  storage . . **6.** haymow

store . . **6.** ensile
stored . . **6.** silage
foe . . . **4.** army **5.** enemy, rival **8.** opponent
9. ill-wisher
fog . . . **4.** blur, daze, haar, haze, mist,
roke, smog **5.** brume, cloud, vapor
6. nebula, opaque, stupor **7.** aerosol,
confuse, pogonip (Sierras) **9.** confusion
fogdog . . . **5.** stubb **8.** fogeater
foggy . . . **3.** dim **4.** dull, hazy, roky
5. dense, misty, vague **6.** cloudy,
opaque **7.** muddled, obscure
8. confused, nubilous **9.** beclouded,
uncertain **10.** indistinct
12. muddleheaded
foghorn . . . **5.** siren, voice (hoarse)
6. signal
fogle . . . **12.** handkerchief (thieves')
fogy . . . **4.** dull, slow **6.** dotard, fogram,
Hunker **8.** mossback **10.** Barnburner
12. conservative, old-fashioned
16. overconservative
foible . . . **5.** blade (part), fault **7.** failing,
frailty **8.** weakness **9.** infirmity
12. imperfection
foil . . . **4.** balk **5.** actor, metal, sheet,
stump, sword **6.** defeat, offset, outwit,
stooge, thwart, weapon **7.** failure,
repulse **9.** frustrate **10.** disappoint
11. frustration
Foism . . . **8.** Buddhism
foist . . . **4.** palm **5.** cheat **7.** intrude
9. interpose **11.** interpolate
fold . . . **3.** end, lap, pen, ply **4.** coil
(serpent), fail, furl, loop, pile, reef, ruga,
sile, tuck, wrap **5.** clasp, close, crimp,
drape, laity, plait, pleat, plica **6.** crease,
dewlap, double, infold, lamina, lappet,
rimple, suffix **7.** entwine, envelop,
plicate (fanlike) **8.** collapse **9.** plicature
10. go bankrupt
folded, not . . . **8.** eplicate
folder . . . **7.** booklet, leaflet **8.** pamphlet
13. advertisement
foliage . . . **5.** spray **6.** leaves, ramage
7. bouquet, leafage, umbrage
8. ornament (Arch)
folio . . . **4.** case, leaf **5.** paper (folded)
6. folder, number (serial)
folk . . . **4.** race **5.** tribe **6.** nation, people
8. servants **9.** followers, relatives,
retainers **11.** aggregation
folk (pert to) . . .
  learned . . **7.** pedants
  lore . . **6.** legend **9.** mythology, tradition
  12. superstition
  song . . **4.** fado, lied **7.** art song, lullaby
  9. Kunstlied, Volkslied
  tale . . **4.** myth, saga **5.** fable, Nancy
  6. legend, mythos, mythus **7.** fantasy,
  parable
follow . . . **3.** dog, tag **4.** heed, heel, next,
nose, obey, seek, tail **5.** after, ensue,
trace, trail **6.** pursue, result, shadow
7. conform, draggle, emulate, imitate,
observe, replace, succeed **8.** come
next, practice, supplant **9.** persevere,
supervene **10.** understand
follower . . . **3.** fan, ist (suff), ite (suff), son
4. aper **5.** lover (of) **6.** copier, ensuer,
votary, zealot **7.** devotee, pursuer,

sequent **8.** adherent, believer, disciple, henchman, partisan **9.** Christian, dependent, satellite **10.** enthusiast **11.** cuadrillero

follower of . . .
Arius . . **5.** Arian
Buddha . . **8.** Buddhist
Confucius . . **9.** Confucian
Falstaff . . **3.** Nym
Mohammed . . **6.** Moslem **8.** Islamite

following . . . **4.** next, sect **5.** suant **7.** ensuing, pursuit, sequent **8.** trailing **9.** resultant **10.** subsequent, succeeding, successive **13.** accompaniment

following (pert to) . . .
exact words . . **7.** literal
one's death . . **10.** posthumous
stories . . **6.** sequel, series

folly . . . **3.** sin **5.** crime **6.** levity, lunacy **7.** blunder, foolery, madness **8.** lewdness, unwisdom **9.** silliness **10.** desipience, imprudence, wantonness **11.** foolishness **12.** indiscretion

foment . . . **3.** egg **4.** abet, brew, spur **5.** bathe, rouse **6.** arouse, excite, incite **7.** agitate, cherish **9.** encourage, instigate

fomentation . . . **6.** lotion, stupes **10.** excitement **11.** instigation **13.** encouragement

Fomoriana (Celt Myth) . . . **10.** sea robbers (race of)

fonda . . . **3.** inn **5.** hotel **6.** fonduk

fondle . . . **3.** pet **4.** neck **5.** ingle **6.** caress, coddle, cosset, foster, pamper **7.** cherish **8.** blandish

fondling . . . **3.** pet **4.** fool **5.** ninny **9.** caressing, simpleton **10.** love-making

fondly . . . **6.** dearly **8.** tenderly **14.** affectionately

fondness . . . **3.** gra **4.** love **6.** desire, doting, liking, relish **8.** appetite **9.** affection **10.** attachment, propensity

fond of . . .
hunting . . **7.** venatic
sea . . **15.** thalassophilous
wife (overly) . . **8.** uxorious

font . . . **3.** jet **4.** fons, lava **5.** stoup **6.** source, spring **7.** piscina **8.** fountain **9.** reservoir

food . . . **3.** cud, pap **4.** cate, chow, diet, eats, fare, grub, junk (food), meat, tofu **5.** bread, manna, scran **6.** bulgur (wheat), cereal, gluten, quiche, snacks, Tex-Mex, viands **7.** aliment, cuisine, edibles, tapioca **8.** chili dog, fast-food, kreplach, munchies, victuals **9.** nutriment, nutrition, provender **10.** sustenance **11.** charcuterie, comestibles, nourishment

food (pert to) . . .
animal . . **6.** forage **9.** provender
bit . . **4.** bite **6.** morsel **7.** munchie
devotee . . **7.** epicure, gourmet
digestant . . **5.** chyle
digested (partly) . . **5.** chyme
dislike of . . **9.** sitomania **10.** cibophobia
element . . **7.** protein, vitamin
fasting (Lenten) . . **9.** xerophagy
gods, the . . **6.** amrita **8.** ambrosia

heavenly . . **5.** manna
impure . . **4.** tref
provide . . **5.** cater, scaff **6.** tucker
room . . **5.** ambry **6.** pantry, spence **7.** butlery, pantler

fool . . . **3.** ass, toy **4.** butt, dolt, dupe, jerk, nerd, nizy, raca (Bib), simp **5.** clown, idiot, moron, ninny **6.** dotard, jester, noodle, trifle, turkey **7.** buffoon, deceive, dingbat, fathead **9.** ignoramus, simpleton

foolhardy . . . **4.** rash **7.** Icarian **8.** reckless **11.** adventurous

fool hen . . . **6.** grouse

foolish . . . **3.** mad **4.** daft, raca, rash, zany **5.** inane, inept, silly **6.** absurd, harish **5.** palty **6.** simple, stupid, unwise **7.** asinine, fatuous, idiotic, puerile, witless **9.** brainless, desipient, imprudent, ludicrous, senseless **10.** illadvised, irrational, ridiculous **12.** preposterous **13.** insignificant

foolish fancy . . . **7.** chimera (chimaera)

foolishness . . . **5.** folly **6.** levity **9.** absurdity, stupidity **10.** triviality

fool's bauble . . . **7.** marotte

fool's gold . . . **6.** pyrite

foot . . . **3.** pad **6.** paw pes (pref) **4.** base, hoof, inch (part), sole, step, walk **5.** sum up, tread **6.** reckon **7.** residue **9.** calculate, extremity

foot (pert to) . . .
bone . . **6.** tarsus **10.** metatarsus
care of . . **8.** pedicure, podiatry **9.** chiropody **11.** chiropodist
combining form . . **4.** pede, pedi
lever . . **5.** pedal **7.** treadle
like . . **8.** pediform
measure . . **4.** inch
part . . **3.** toe **4.** arch, heel, sole
prefix . . **4.** pedi
race course (anc) . . **7.** diaulos
reference to . . **5.** pedal, podal
rest . . **4.** rail **7.** cricket, hassock, ottoman, support **8.** footrail **9.** footstool
sole . . **7.** plantar
unstressed part (Pros) . . **5.** arsis

foot, feet (metric) . . . **4.** iamb, mora, unit **6.** dactyl, dipody, iambus **7.** anapest, dimeter, pyrrhic, spondee, tripody **8.** trimeter **9.** hexameter **10.** heptameter, pentameter

footed . . . **5.** biped **7.** bipedal, megapod (large), metered

footing . . . **4.** lace, rank **5.** basis, dance, tread **6.** status **7.** support **8.** foothold, progress, standing **9.** condition **11.** calculation

footlike part . . . **3.** pes

footman . . . **6.** varlet, walker **7.** servant **9.** attendant **10.** pedestrian

footprint mold . . . **7.** moulage

footway . . . **7.** catwalk (Naut)

fop . . . **3.** nob **4.** Adon, buck, dude **5.** dandy, puppy, sport, swell **6.** Adonis, masher **7.** coxcomb, gallant **9.** exquisite, pretender **12.** boulevardier

foppish . . . **6.** dapper, spruce **7.** finical, foplike **8.** dandyish **9.** conceited, dandified

for . . . **2.** to **3.** pro **5.** spite **7.** because,

instead **8.** behalf of **9.** intending
10. indicating **11.** preparation
for (pert to)...
each.. **3.** per
example.. **2.** as, eg **4.** vide **13.** exempli
gratia
fear.. **4.** lest
most part.. **6.** mostly **7.** chiefly, usually
9. generally
nothing.. **6.** gratis, naught **9.** lagniappe
(lagnappe)
this reason.. **4.** ergo **5.** hence
forage... **4.** food, mast, raid **5.** spoil
6. browse, ravage **7.** plunder
9. pasturage
foramen... **4.** pore **7.** opening, orifice,
passage **8.** fenestra
foray... **4.** raid **6.** ravage, sortie **7.** pillage
9. incursion
forbear... **4.** lose, shun **5.** avoid **6.** desist,
endure **7.** abstain, decline, refrain
8. part with **9.** be patient
forbearance... **5.** mercy **6.** disuse,
lenity **8.** leniency, mildness, patience
9. tolerance **10.** abstinence, temperance
11. forgiveness, placability
forbid... **3.** ban **4.** deny, tabu, veto
5. debar, taboo **6.** disbar, hinder,
impede, oppose **7.** exclude, inhibit,
prevent **8.** disallow, preclude, prohibit
9. interdict, proscribe **11.** countermand
forbiddance... **3.** ban **4.** veto
11. unallowable **12.** illiberality,
interdiction, proscription
forbidden city... **5.** Lhasa (Tibet), Pekin
(walled)
forbidden food (Bib)... **4.** tref
8. terephah
forbidding... **4.** grim, ugly **5.** plain,
stern **6.** fierce, odious **9.** offensive,
revolting **10.** prevention, unpleasant
11. displeasing, prohibitive
force... **3.** vim, vis **4.** dint, make, urge
5. drive, impel, power, press, repel
staff, vigor **6.** coerce, compel, effect,
energy, extort, hasten, strain **7.** impetus,
meaning **8.** eloquent, momentum,
pressure, validity, violence **9.** constrain,
influence, puissance **10.** compulsion,
constraint **11.** necessitate
force (pert to)...
alleged.. **2.** od
armed.. **4.** army **5.** posse
by seizure.. **5.** usurp
down.. **7.** detrude
full.. **5.** amain
substance.. **8.** catalyst
unit.. **4.** dyne **5.** staff, tonal **7.** poundal
forced... **7.** labored **9.** reluctant, unwilling
10. artificial, compulsory, farfetched
11. constrained
forced feeding... **6.** gavage
forceful... **5.** valid **6.** mighty, potent,
strong **7.** dynamic **8.** eloquent,
emphatic, vigorous **9.** effective,
energetic **10.** compulsory
forces... **4.** army **5.** armed **6.** troops
forcible... **6.** cogent, mighty, potent
7. violent, weighty **8.** eloquent,
emphatic, positive, puissant **9.** energetic
10. compulsory, impressive

11. influential
forcible entry... **10.** effraction
forciform... **6.** forked **7.** furcate
11. forficulate **14.** scissors-shaped
ford... **4.** wade **5.** cross **6.** stream
fore... **3.** way **5.** front, prior, track
6. former **7.** journey
forebear... **4.** sire **5.** elder **6.** parent
8. ancestor **10.** antecedent, forefather,
progenitor
forebode... **5.** augur **7.** betoken,
portend, predict, presage **8.** foretell
15. prognostication
foreboding... **6.** augury **8.** croaking,
sinister **11.** pessimistic, presagement
12. apprehension, presentiment
forecast... **4.** bode, plan **6.** scheme
7. foresee, fortune, predict **8.** foretell,
prophecy **9.** calculate, foresight,
foretoken **10.** foreordain, prediction
12. predetermine
forecaster... **4.** seer **5.** vates **6.** oracle
7. diviner, palmist, prophet **8.** dopester,
presager **10.** astrologer, soothsayer
11. Nostradamus **13.** meteorologist
14. prognosticator
foreclose... **5.** debar **6.** hinder **7.** prevent,
shut out **8.** preclude **10.** dispossess
foredoom... **4.** doom **7.** predict
12. predestinate
foredoomed... **3.** fey **5.** fatal **8.** accursed
forefather... **4.** sire **5.** elder **6.** parent
8. ancestor, forebear **10.** progenitor
forefinger... **5.** index
foregather... **4.** meet **7.** convene
8. assemble **9.** encounter
forego, forgo... **6.** pass by **7.** neglect,
precede **8.** renounce
foregoing... **4.** past **5.** above **6.** former,
prefix **7.** leading **10.** antecedent
foregone... **4.** past **8.** previous
11. predestined, preordained,
preresolved **13.** predetermined
foregone conclusion... **9.** certainty
forehead... **4.** brow **8.** calvaria, glabella,
sinciput **9.** assurance **10.** effrontery
forehead, divination by...
11. metopomancy
forehead, frontal... **7.** metopic
foreign... **4.** xeno (comb form) **5.** alien,
fremd **6.** exotic, remote **7.** distant,
outside (of country), strange **8.** excluded
9. extrinsic, peregrine, unrelated
10. extraneous, outlandish
11. incongruous **12.** adventitious
foreign (pert to)...
accent.. **4.** burr **6.** brogue, patois
7. dialect
crystals (Geol).. **7.** epigene
disease.. **7.** ecdemic
insertion.. **13.** interpolation
place.. **6.** forane
quarter.. **4.** Para **5.** Latin **6.** French
7. enclave
service residence.. **9.** consulate
foreigner... **5.** alien **6.** gringo **8.** outsider,
stranger **9.** outlander, uitlander
10. tramontane **12.** ultramontane
foreland... **8.** headland **10.** promontory
forelock... **4.** bang **7.** cowlick, fetlock
8. linchpin **9.** cotter pin, fastening

(armor)
foreman . . . **4.** boss **5.** chief **6.** leader
7. juryman, overman **10.** supervisor
14. superintendent
foremost . . . **5.** chief, first, front **7.** leading,
supreme **8.** headmost **13.** most
important
forensic . . . **10.** rhetorical
13. argumentative
foreordain . . . **7.** destine **9.** predicate,
preordain **12.** foreordinate, predestinate,
predetermine
forerun . . . **6.** herald **7.** advance, prelude,
presage **8.** announce, antecede
9. forestall, introduce, prefigure
10. anticipate, foreshadow
forerunner . . . **4.** omen, sign **6.** augury,
herald **8.** ancestor **9.** harbinger,
messenger, precursor **10.** forefather,
foreganger, progenitor, prognostic
11. predecessor
foreshadow . . . **6.** shadow (beforehand)
7. presage **9.** adumbrate, prefigure
foresight . . . **8.** sagacity **9.** prevision
10. precaution, prediction, prescience,
prevoyance, providence
11. omniscience **13.** foreknowledge
forest . . . **4.** wold, wood **5.** grove,
woods **6.** jungle, timber **8.** woodland
9. greenwood **10.** timberland,
wilderness
forest (pert to) . . .
deity . . **3.** Pan **7.** Aegipan
fire . . **5.** crown, stand **6.** ground
7. surface
fire-finding instrument . . **7.** alidade
glade . . **6.** camass (camas, cammas)
love of, lover of . . **9.** nemophile,
nemophily
regarding . . **6.** sylvan **7.** nemoral
tilled . . **7.** thwaite
warden . . **6.** ranger
forestall . . . **6.** hinder **7.** exclude, head
off, prevent **9.** intercept **10.** anticipate,
monopolize
foretell . . . **4.** bode, spae **5.** augur, insee
7. portend, predict, presage **8.** forebode,
forecast, prophesy **10.** vaticinate
13. prognosticate
foretelling . . . **6.** augury **7.** fatidic
9. fatidical, prophetic **10.** vaticinant
forethought . . . **8.** prepense, prudence
9. foresight, provident **10.** deliberate,
precaution **12.** aforethought,
anticipation **13.** premeditation
foretoken . . . **4.** omen **7.** presage
8. foreshow, indicant **10.** presignify
13. preindication, prognosticate
foretooth . . . **5.** biter **6.** cutter **7.** incisor
9. milk tooth
forever . . . **3.** ake (Maori), aye (ay)
4. olam, ever **6.** always, eterne
7. endless **8.** infinity **9.** continual,
perpetual **10.** constantly, invariably
11. ceaselessly, continually, incessantly,
perpetually, unceasingly
12. interminably, unchangeably
13. everlastingly
forewarning . . . **4.** omen **7.** caution,
portent **9.** informing **10.** admonition,
foreboding

foreword . . . **5.** proem **7.** preface, prelude
8. exordium, preamble, prologue
12. introduction
forfeit . . . **4.** fine, lose, loss **5.** forgo,
mulct **6.** forego, pledge **7.** deodand,
penalty
forfeiture . . . **4.** fine, loss **5.** dédit, mulct
7. penalty **10.** amercement
forfend . . . **5.** avert **6.** forbid **7.** prevent,
protect **8.** preserve, prohibit
forfex . . . **6.** shears
forgather . . . **4.** meet **7.** consort, convene
8. assemble **9.** encounter **10.** fraternize
forge . . . **4.** coin, form, mint **5.** feign
6. create, smithy, stithy, swinge
7. falsify, imitate **8.** bloomery, smithery
11. counterfeit
forgery . . . **4.** sham **7.** fiction **9.** falsehood,
invention **11.** counterfeit, fabrication
13. falsification
forget . . . **4.** omit **5.** lapse, remit **6.** slight
7. neglect **9.** disregard **11.** disremember
forgetfulness . . . **5.** Lethe (Myth), lotus
(legend) **7.** amnesia, amnesty
8. Manassah, oblivion **12.** carelessness,
heedlessness **13.** obliviousness
forgive . . . **5.** remit, spare **6.** acquit,
excuse, pardon **7.** condone
forgiveness . . . **6.** pardon **9.** remission
10. absolution **11.** condonation,
exoneration, magnanimity
forgiving . . . **6.** humane **8.** merciful,
placable **9.** remissive **11.** magnanimous
forgo . . . **4.** quit **5.** leave, waive **6.** give
up, resign **7.** abstain, forbear, forfeit,
forsake, neglect, refrain **8.** overlook,
renounce **9.** do without **10.** relinquish
forhoo . . . **7.** abandon, despise
fork . . . **6.** expend, pay out **7.** dilemma,
diverge **10.** divaricate, divergence,
headstream **11.** bifurcation
fork (pert to) . . .
feature . . **4.** tine **5.** prong
garden . . **5.** graip
pickle . . **13.** runcible spoon
table . . **5.** salad **6.** dinner, oyster
7. dessert **8.** ice-cream
forked . . . **5.** bifid **6.** horned, ramous
7. divided, furcate **8.** branched, crotched
9. ambiguous, equivocal **10.** bifurcated,
branchlike
forlorn . . . **4.** reft **5.** alone **6.** abject,
bereft **8.** deserted, desolate, forsaken,
helpless, pitiable **9.** abandoned,
destitute, miserable **10.** friendless
12. disconsolate
form . . . **4.** body, cast, idea, mold,
rite **5.** build, guise, model, shape
6. beauty, create, figure, invent,
ritual **7.** compose, contour, formula,
outline, pattern, profile, species, variety
8. ceremony, conceive, document
9. establish, formality **10.** appearance
11. arrangement **12.** conformation
13. configuration, questionnaire
15. conventionality
form (pert to) . . .
bust . . **6.** taille
chainlike . . **8.** catenate
deceptive . . **5.** ghost **7.** specter
8. phantasm

display . . **4.** rack
good . . **4.** chic **6.** fettle
government . . **6.** polity
hollow . . **5.** shell
into fabric . . **4.** knit, spin **5.** weave
primitive . . **9.** prototype
spiral . . **5.** helix
suffix . . **5.** shape **10.** resembling
formal . . . **4.** prim **5.** exact, stiff **6.** solemn
   7. orderly, outward, precise, regular,
   stilted **8.** affected, apparent, starched
   9. formative **10.** ceremonial, methodical
   11. pharisaical, ritualistic, superficial
   12. conventional
formal introduction . . . **5.** debut
   12. presentation
formalities . . . **5.** rites **9.** etiquette
   10. ceremonies
formal warning . . . **5.** alarm **6.** caveat
   12. caveat emptor
format . . . **4.** size **5.** shape, style
formation . . . **4.** form **5.** order **9.** structure
   11. arrangement, composition
   12. construction
formation (pert to) . . .
   chain (twisted) . . **9.** torquated
   geologic . . **7.** terrain, terrane
   military . . **4.** line **5.** herse **7.** echelon
   sand . . **4.** dene, dune
formed . . . **4.** made **5.** built **7.** created,
   decided, matured, settled **8.** arranged
   9. fashioned, organized **11.** constructed
formed (pert to) . . .
   by law . . **9.** corporate
   by lips . . **6.** labial
   mountain foot . . **8.** piedmont
   on earth's surface . . **7.** epigene
   plates (two) . . **11.** bilamellate
formed into . . .
   chain . . **8.** catenate **9.** torquated
   fabric . . **5.** spun **7.** woven **9.** knitted
   mass (hard) . . **4.** iced **5.** caked **6.** frozen
   9. congealed
   mosaic . . **9.** tessellar **11.** tessellated
former . . . **2.** ex **3.** old **4.** erst, late,
   once, past **5.** front, prior **6.** passed,
   whilom **7.** ancient, earlier **8.** previous
   9. erstwhile, foregoing, preceding
   10. antecedent
former days . . . **3.** eld, old **4.** yore
formerly . . . **3.** nee **4.** erst, once,
   then **6.** before, whilom **7.** one-time
   8. sometime **9.** aforetime, erstwhile
   10. heretofore, previously
formicary . . . **7.** anthill **8.** ant's nest
formicid . . . **3.** ant **5.** emmet **7.** Formica
formidable . . . **7.** fearful **8.** alarming,
   dreadful, menacing, terrible **9.** difficult
   11. redoubtable, threatening
formless . . . **5.** arupa **7.** anidian, chaotic
   9. amorphous, shapeless
   13. indeterminate
Formosa, Taiwan . . .
   capital . . **6.** Taipei
   city . . **6.** Tainan **7.** Hualien, Keelung
   9. Kaohsiung
   group . . **6.** Penghu (64 Isls)
   island . . **5.** Matsu **6.** Quemoy
formula . . . **3.** law **4.** form, rule **5.** axiom,
   creed, lurry, maxim, model **6.** method,
   recipe, ritual **12.** prescription

forsake . . . **4.** deny, quit, shun **5.** avoid,
   leave **6.** depart, desert, refuse, reject
   7. abandon **8.** renounce, withdraw
   9. surrender
forsaken . . . **4.** lorn **6.** vacant **7.** forlorn
   8. deserted, lovelorn, rejected
   9. abandoned
forspeak . . . **5.** curse **6.** forbid **7.** asperse,
   bewitch **8.** renounce **10.** relinquish
fort . . . **5.** redan, tower **6.** abatis, castle,
   escarp, glacis (bank of) **7.** bastion,
   bulwark, castlet **8.** bastille, fastness,
   fortress **10.** stronghold **13.** fortification,
   propugnaculum
Fort (Fr Ind War) . . . **9.** Necessity
forte . . . **4.** loud **5.** skill **8.** strength
   10. strong suit
forth . . . **3.** out **4.** away **6.** abroad, onward
   7. forward, outward
forthright . . . **5.** ahead **7.** frankly
   8. forwards **9.** downright
   11. immediately, straightway
   13. straightforth
forthwith . . . **3.** now **6.** pronto **8.** promptly
   9. summarily **11.** immediately,
   straightway
fortification . . . **4.** wall **5.** redan **6.** abatis
   7. bastion, citadel, defense, parados,
   ravelin, redoubt **8.** barbette (part),
   fortress **10.** stronghold
   13. corroboration, strengthening
fortify . . . **3.** arm, man **4.** gird **5.** add
   to, spike, stank **6.** defend, secure
   7. confirm, refresh **8.** embattle
   10. adulterate (drink), invigorate,
   strengthen, vitaminize **11.** corroborate
fortitude . . . **6.** virtue **7.** bravery, courage
   8. strength **9.** endurance **10.** resolution
   12. resoluteness **14.** impregnability
fortress . . . see *fort*
fortuitous . . . **3.** hap **6.** chance
   10. accidental **12.** unexpectedly
fortunate . . . **5.** happy, lucky **6.** timely
   7. favored **10.** auspicious, prosperous,
   successful **12.** providential
fortune . . . **3.** hap, lot **4.** doom, fate,
   luck **6.** chance, estate, riches, wealth
   7. destiny, success **8.** accident
   10. prosperity **13.** circumstances
fortune (pert to) . . .
   gypsy . . **4.** bahi
   ill . . **9.** mischance
   place . . **6.** cookie
   planet (Astrol) . . **5.** Venus **7.** Jupiter
   teller . . **4.** seer **5.** sibyl, Tyche **6.** oracle
   7. spaeman
fortuneteller's deck . . . **5.** tarot (cards)
forum fashion . . . **4.** toga
forward . . . **2.** on, to **3.** aid **4.** abet,
   bold, fore, help, pert, send, ship,
   vain **5.** ahead, along, eager, front,
   impel, ready, relay, saucy, ultra
   6. active, bright, hasten, onward
   7. deliver, earnest, extreme, further,
   radical, willing **8.** advanced, immodest,
   impudent, transmit **9.** audacious,
   encourage **10.** precocious
   11. progressive **12.** presumptuous
forward moving (Zool) . . . **5.** proal
   (digestion) **11.** mastication
fosse, foss . . . **3.** pit **4.** moat **5.** canal,

ditch, fossa, grave **6.** cavity, trench
10. depression
fossil, fossils . . . **5.** relic, stone **7.** antique,
remains
fossil (pert to) . . .
egg . . **7.** ovulite
footprint . . **7.** ichnite
resin . . **5.** amber
shell . . **6.** dolite **8.** ammonite
site . . **8.** Badlands
study of . . **12.** paleontology
toothlike . . **8.** conodont
worm track . . **7.** nereite
foster . . . **4.** rear **5.** breed, nurse **7.** cherish,
gratify, indulge, promote **9.** cultivate
fosterage . . . **7.** nurture **11.** development
foster child . . . **4.** dalt **5.** norry (nurry)
7. stepson **8.** nursling **12.** stepdaughter
fought . . . see *fight*
foul . . . **3.** bad **4.** olid, ugly **5.** dirty,
fetid, grimy, nasty, reeky, spoil,
sully **6.** defame, filthy, malign,
odious, putrid, rotten, thwart, unfair
7. abusive, confuse, noisome, obscene,
profane, unclean **8.** entangle, indecent,
infamous, shameful, stagnant, stinking
9. dishonest, obnoxious **10.** complicate,
malodorous, scurrilous **11.** contaminate,
ill-smelling, unfavorable
12. inauspicious, unpropitious
foul play . . . **6.** murder, unfair (play)
7. perfidy **8.** violence **9.** deception,
treachery **10.** unfairness
found . . . **3.** fix **4.** base, cast **5.** endow,
set up **6.** attach, create **9.** establish,
institute, originate
foundation . . . **3.** bed **4.** base, plot,
sill **5.** basal, basis **6.** legacy, riprap
7. bedding, charity, premise, support
8. cosmetic, creation, donation, pedestal
9. placement **11.** corporation
13. justification
found by chance (thing) . . .
11. serendipity
founded on . . .
base . . **10.** predicated
evidence . . **10.** evidential
experience . . **7.** empiric **9.** empirical
imagination . . **7.** Utopian
founder . . . **4.** fail, fall, sink **6.** author
7. capsize, creator, stumble **8.** miscarry
9. break down, organizer **10.** originator
foundling . . . **3.** oaf **4.** waif **5.** child
(unclaimed) **6.** orphan **8.** derelict,
nursling
fountain . . . **3.** jet, spa **4.** font, head, well
6. spring **9.** reservoir **11.** scuttlebutt
(ship's) **12.** fountainhead
fountain (pert to) . . .
god of . . **4.** Fons
Muse (Gr) . . **8.** Aganippe
nymph . . **5.** naiad **8.** Egeria
of Lions . . **8.** Alhambra (Spain)
four (pert to) . . .
bits . . **7.** quarter (silver)
Books . . **8.** Classics (Chin)
footed . . **8.** tetrapod
genii, of Amenti . . **13.** Horus' children
group . . **6.** tetrad
Hundred . . **5.** elect, elite **7.** society
letters, word of . . **9.** tetragram

seas . . **13.** Great Britain's
senses (Bib) . . **15.** interpretations
four-flusher . . . **5.** cheat, fraud **7.** bluffer
8. impostor **9.** pretender
four-in-hand . . . **3.** tie **4.** team (horses)
6. cravat **7.** necktie
fourth (pert to) . . .
Caliph . . **3.** Ali
century martyr . . **8.** St Blaise
estate . . **5.** press **10.** newspapers
part . . **6.** fardel **7.** quarter
stomach (cow) . . **8.** abomasum
fowl . . . **3.** hen **6.** bantam, Gallus **7.** Blue
Hen, broiler, chicken, Dorking, leghorn,
Minorca, poultry, rooster, seafowl
8. pheasant **9.** guinea hen, waterfowl
11. chanticleer
fox . . . **3.** cub, tod **4.** stag **5.** vixen
fox (pert to) . . .
African . . **4.** asse
Asian . . **5.** adive **6.** corsac
fabled . . **7.** Reynard
female . . **5.** vixen
genus . . **6.** Vulpes
hedge (hunter's) . . **4.** oxer
foot . . **3.** pad
Indian . . **10.** Algonquian
Russian . . **6.** corsac **7.** karagan
foxglove . . . **9.** digitalis
foxy . . . **3.** sly **4.** sexy, wily **6.** artful,
crafty **7.** cunning, vulpine
foyer . . . **5.** lobby **8.** anteroom, entrance
9. greenroom
fracas . . . **3.** row **5.** brawl, melee, set-
to **6.** uproar **7.** quarrel **9.** commotion
11. disturbance
fraction . . . **3.** bit **4.** part **5.** piece, scrap
6. sector **7.** element, ruction **8.** division,
fragment **9.** commotion
fractious . . . **4.** ugly **5.** cross **6.** unruly
7. peevish, waspish **8.** perverse,
snappish **9.** irritable **10.** ill-humored
11. disobedient
fracture . . . **4.** rend **5.** break, cleft, crack
6. breach, injury **7.** rupture
fragile . . . **4.** weak **5.** brash, frail **6.** frough
(obs), infirm, slight **7.** brittle **8.** delicate,
slattery **9.** frangible
fragment . . . **3.** bit, ort **4.** chip, grot, part,
snip **5.** groat, piece, relic, scrap, shard,
sherd, shred, torso (art) **6.** morsel,
sippet **7.** flinder **8.** fraction
fragments . . . **3.** ana **6.** fardel, groats,
rubble **8.** buttings, excerpts, flinders
10. miscellany **11.** smithereens
fragrance . . . **4.** odor **5.** aroma, elemi,
smell **7.** incense, perfume **9.** redolence
fragrant . . . **4.** nard **5.** balmy, olent,
spicy, sweet **7.** odorous **8.** aromatic,
redolent **9.** ambrosial **11.** odoriferous
12. sweet-scented **13.** sweet-smelling
frail . . . **4.** girl, thin, weak **5.** woman
6. basket (fig), feeble, sickly, slimsy
7. brittle, fragile **8.** strumpet, unchaste
10. weak-willed **12.** destructible
frailty . . . **5.** fault **6.** defect **7.** failing
8. thinness, weakness **9.** fragility,
infirmity **12.** imperfection
frame . . . **4.** body, make, plan, rack, sess,
sill **5.** build, easel, grate, herse, knape
6. abacus, border, charge (falsely),

direct, tenter **7.** carcass, chassis,
cresset (torch), fashion, prepare,
setting, taboret **8.** conceive, skeleton
9. construct **10.** prearrange
framework . . . **4.** rack, sill **5.** cadre,
shell **6.** cradle **7.** trestle **8.** skeleton
11. scaffolding
France . . . see also *French*
anc name . . **4.** Gaul **6.** Gallia
Bay . . **6.** Biscay
Botanical Gardens . . **16.** Jardin des
Plantes
capital . . **5.** Paris
city . . **4.** Nice **5.** Lyons **7.** LeHavre
8. Bordeaux, Toulouse **9.** Marseille
10. Strasbourg
dread of . . **11.** Gallophobia
12. Francophobia
island . . **6.** Comoro (Afr), Tahiti
7. Corsica, Réunion **10.** Guadeloupe
(Leeward), Martinique (Windward)
12. New Caledonia
lover of . . **10.** Gallophile **11.** Francophile
mountain . . **4.** Alps, Jura **5.** Pelat
8. Pyrenees **9.** Mont Blanc **11.** Pic
Montcalm
port . . **4.** Caen **5.** Brest **6.** Calais, Toulon
7. Dunkirk (Dunkerque), Le Havre
8. Bordeaux
resort . . **3.** Pau **5.** Vichy **6.** Cannes,
Menton (Mentone) **7.** Riviera **9.** Côte
d'Azur **11.** Aix-les-Bains (anc)
river . . **3.** Lys **4.** Yser **5.** Aisne, Eiser,
Loire, Meuse, Rhône, Seine
Southern . . **4.** Midi
Verdun battle site . . **4.** Vaux
wine region . . **8.** Bordeaux, Burgundy
franchise . . . **4.** vote **5.** right **6.** patent
7. freedom, license **8.** immunity,
suffrage **9.** exemption
frank . . . **4.** free, mail, open **5.** blunt,
naive, plain **6.** candid, direct, honest
7. artless, liberal, sincere **8.** generous
9. ingenuous, outspoken **10.** unreserved
11. frankfurter **15.** straightforward,
unsophisticated
frankincense . . . **4.** thus **8.** gum resin,
olibanum **9.** fragrance
Frankish (pert to) . . .
dynasty . . **11.** Carolingian, Merovingian
king . . **5.** Pepin **6.** Clovis
law . . **5.** Salic
people (anc) . . **6.** Salian
site . . **4.** Gaul
Franklin, Benjamin . . . **11.** Poor Richard
frantic . . . **3.** mad **4.** mang **5.** moved,
rabid **7.** furious **8.** frenetic, frenzied
9. delirious, desperate, turbulent
10. distracted, distraught
11. overwrought
frappé . . . **3.** ice **5.** chill **6.** freeze **7.** dessert,
mixture (sweet) **8.** beverage
fraternal . . . **4.** kind **5.** order, twins
7. society **8.** friendly **9.** brotherly
fraud . . . **4.** fake, sham, wile **5.** cheat,
covin, craft, guile **6.** deceit, ringer
7. defraud, roguery **8.** artifice, cozenage,
impostor, subtlety, swindler, trickery
9. deception, imposture, stratagem
10. imposition **13.** circumvention
fraudulence . . . **9.** improbity

10. subreption
fraudulent . . . **4.** fake, wily **5.** snide
6. crafty, quacky **7.** cunning, knavish
8. cheating, guileful, spurious
9. deceitful, deceiving, deceptive,
designing, dishonest, insidious
10. fallacious **11.** counterfeit,
treacherous
fraught . . . **4.** lade, load **5.** cargo, equip,
laden **6.** burden, filled **7.** freight
9. freighted, transport
fray . . . **4.** fret (cloth), wear **5.** broil,
dread, melee, panic, ravel **6.** affray,
combat, fright, hassle, terror, tumult
7. contest, frazzle, ruction **9.** commotion
12. apprehension
freak . . . **4.** flam, lune, whim **5.** fancy,
prank, sport **6.** streak, vagary **7.** caprice,
checker, crochet, monster **9.** eccentric,
variegate **11.** monstrosity
12. whimsicality
freakish . . . **7.** curious **9.** eccentric,
fantastic, whimsical **10.** capricious,
changeable
freck . . . **4.** bold, hale **5.** eager, frack,
lusty, ready, stout **6.** strong **7.** forward
8. desirous
freckle . . . **4.** mark, spot **7.** blemish,
ephelis, lentigo, speckle **10.** ferntickle
free . . . **3.** rid **4.** easy, open **5.** clear,
frank, loose **6.** acquit, candid, exempt,
gratis, immune, vacant **7.** absolve,
inexact, manumit, not busy, release,
relieve, unbound **8.** liberate **9.** extricate,
footloose, voluntary **10.** autonomous,
gratuitous, unconfined, unhampered
11. emancipated **12.** uncontrolled,
unrestrained, unrestricted
free (pert to) . . .
bacteria . . **7.** aseptic, sterile
difficulty . . **9.** extricate
doubt . . **7.** resolve
flesh (dietary) . . **6.** maigre
knots . . **7.** enodate, unravel
reproach . . **9.** blameless
slavery . . **7.** manumit **10.** emancipate
suspicion . . **5.** clear, purge **6.** acquit
7. absolve **9.** exculpate, exonerate
sweetness . . **3.** sec
freebooter . . . **5.** rover **6.** pirate **8.** pillager
9. plunderer **10.** filibuster
freed . . . **3.** rid **6.** loosed, spared, untied
8. released **9.** delivered, liberated
10. manumitted **11.** emancipated
freedom . . . **6.** candor **7.** leisure, liberty,
license **8.** latitude **9.** exemption,
privilege **11.** manumission
12. emancipation, independence
freedom (pert to) . . .
abused . . **7.** liberty (excess), license
from doubt . . **9.** assurance, certitude
from sepsis . . **7.** asepsis
Freedom Our Rock (motto) . . .
7. Tammany (1789)
free enterprise . . . **6.** policy **8.** commerce
10. capitalism **15.** noninterference
freely . . . **6.** gratis **7.** largely, readily
9. bountiful, copiously, liberally,
willingly **10.** abundantly, generously
11. bounteously, plenteously,
plentifully, voluntarily **12.** gratuitously

freeze ... **3.** ice **5.** be-ice, chill **6.** steeve
7. congeal, terrify **8.** preserve, solidify
9. stabilize **11.** anesthetize, refrigerate
freezing, science of ... **10.** cyrogenics
freight ... **4.** load, ship **5.** cargo,
laden, train **6.** burden, charge, lading
7. fraught, rattler **8.** shipment
9. transport **14.** transportation
freight boat ... **5.** barge **9.** freighter
freit, freet ... **4.** omen **5.** charm
fremd (obs) ... **5.** alien **7.** foreign, hostile
9. unrelated
French (people) ...
  artist .. **4.** Dore **5.** Corot, David, Degas,
  Leger, Manet, Monet, Rodin **6.** Braque,
  Gerome, Greuze, Renoir, Seurat
  7. Courbet, Gauguin, Matisse, Watteau
  8. Daubigny, Pissarro, Rousseau
  9. Delacroix, Fragonard
  author .. **4.** Hugo, Loti, Zola **5.** Camus,
  Dumas, Verne **6.** Balzac, Proust
  8. Flaubert, Rabelais
  cardinal, famed .. **7.** Mazarin **9.** Richelieu
  caricaturist .. **7.** Daumier, Gavarni
  chemist .. **7.** Gautier, Holbach, Pasteur
  composer .. **4.** Lalo **5.** Bizet, D'Indy,
  Ravel, Satie **6.** Gounod **7.** Berlioz,
  Debussy, Delibes, Poulenc **8.** Couperin
  conqueror (anc) .. **6.** Clovis
  crusader .. **7.** Godfrey (of Bouillon)
  dramatist .. **6.** Favart, Racine **7.** Molière
  8. Quinault **12.** Beaumarchais
  dynasty .. **5.** Caput **6.** Valois **7.** Bourbon
  emperor .. **8.** Napoleon (Bonaparte)
  encyclopedist .. **7.** Diderot **9.** D'Alembert
  film director .. **6.** Renoir **8.** Truffaut
  film star .. **6.** Bardot **7.** Deneuve
  9. Depardieu
  Foreign Legion creator, 1831 .. **8.** Philippe
  (Louis)
  historian .. **5.** Renan, Taine **7.** Braudel
  8. Michelet **9.** Froissart
  marshal .. **3.** Ney **4.** Foch, Niel, Saxe
  5. Murat
  naturalist .. **8.** Audebert
  navigator .. **9.** Freycinet
  officer, famed .. **7.** Dreyfus
  pantomimist .. **7.** Pierrot
  patron saint .. **5.** Denis **6.** Martin
  philosopher .. **5.** Bayle **6.** Pascal,
  Sartre **7.** Abelard **8.** Rousseau,
  Voltaire **9.** Descartes, Montaigne
  11. Montesquieu
  physician .. **7.** Laveran
  physicist .. **5.** Binet **6.** Ampere
  poet .. **6.** Villon **7.** Mistral, Rimbaud
  10. Baudelaire
  radical .. **7.** Jacobin
  revolutionary ... **5.** Marat **6.** Danton
  11. Robespierre
  scientist .. **5.** Curie **7.** Pasteur
  statesman .. **4.** Coty **5.** Laine, Laval,
  Morny **6.** Carnot **7.** Briande, Herriot
  8. DeGaulle **9.** Lafayette
French (pert to) ...
  academic rank .. **6.** agrégé
  Academy .. **12.** The Institute
  and .. **2.** et
  annuity .. **5.** rente
  anthem .. **12.** Marseillaise
  article .. **2.** la, le, un **3.** les, une

beast .. **4.** bête
bread .. **4.** pain
calender (Rev) .. **6.** Nivose **7.** Ventose
cathedral .. **8.** Chartres **9.** Notre Dame
champagne .. **2.** Ay
cheese .. **4.** Brie **6.** Chevre **9.** Camembert
chorus (male) .. **7.** orpheon
coach .. **6.** fiacre
coat-of-arms .. **10.** fleur-de-lis
coffee (black) .. **8.** café noir
company (Bus) .. **3.** cie
crown (gold coin) .. **3.** ecu
cult (art) .. **7.** Dadaism
daisy .. **10.** marguerite
dance .. **3.** bal **5.** gavot **6.** cancan
decree, edict .. **5.** arrêt
dialect .. **6.** patois
dugout .. **4.** abri
father .. **4.** père
fortification .. **7.** parados
friend .. **3.** ami **4.** amie
fugitive .. **6.** émigré
God .. **4.** Dieu
hairdresser .. **7.** friseur
hat .. **5.** beret **7.** chapeau
here .. **3.** ici
inn .. **6.** hostel
king .. **3.** roi
lace .. **5.** Cluny
language (Provence) .. **9.** Provençal
laugh .. **3.** ris
legal code .. **10.** Napoleonic
liquor .. **8.** absinthe (banned 1915)
love .. **5.** amour
lover .. **5.** amant
mask .. **4.** loup
morning .. **5.** matin
mountain peak .. **3.** pic
museum .. **6.** Louvre
narcissus .. **10.** polyanthus
native .. **8.** Gallican
nursemaid .. **5.** bonne
ornaments (set of) .. **6.** parure
outcast .. **5.** Agote, Cagot **6.** pariah
pancake .. **5.** crepe
parliament .. **5.** Sénat
pastry .. **7.** dariole, galette
plane .. **5.** avion
poem, poetry .. **3.** dit **6.** aubade, rondel
police .. **6.** Sûreté **8.** gendarme
political club .. **7.** Jacobin
porcelain .. **6.** Sèvres **7.** Limoges
priest .. **4.** abbe, père
prison, famed .. **8.** Bastille
racecourse .. **7.** Auteuil
restaurant .. **4.** café **6.** bistro
revolutionary government .. **7.** Commune
sauce .. **8.** ravigote **9.** allemande
school .. **5.** école, lycée
school of painting .. **8.** Barbizon
securities .. **6.** rentes
smoking room .. **9.** estaminet
soldier .. **5.** poilu **6.** Zouave
stable .. **6.** écurie
state .. **4.** état
stock exchange .. **6.** Bourse
storm .. **5.** orage
street .. **3.** rue
summer .. **3.** été
theater .. **16.** Comédie Française
university .. **8.** Sorbonne

uprising . . **6.** Fronde
verse . . **3.** lai **4.** alba **6.** rondel **7.** ballade, virelay
wall . . **3.** mur
water . . **3.** eau
wind . . **7.** mistral
wine . . **5.** Medoc **6.** Barsac, brandy, claret, Cognac, masdeu **8.** Bordeaux, Burgundy, sauterne **10.** Beaujolais
world . . **5.** monde
Frenchy . . . **6.** Gallic
frenzied . . . **4.** amok **5.** rabid **7.** enraged, frantic, madding **8.** maddened **9.** turbulent **11.** overwrought
frenzy . . . **3.** mad **5.** furor, mania **7.** frantic, madness **8.** delirium **9.** agitation **10.** excitement, turbulence
frequent . . . **3.** oft **5.** haunt, often, usual **6.** common **7.** current **8.** familiar, habitual, intimate (with) **9.** recurrent **10.** persistent
frequenter . . . **7.** habitué, visitor **8.** attender
frère . . . **5.** friar **7.** brother
fresh . . . **3.** new **4.** good, lush **5.** relay, ruddy, sound, sweet **6.** florid, lively, strong, unused **7.** healthy, unfaded, untried **8.** impudent, original **10.** additional, refreshing, unimpaired **13.** inexperienced
freshen . . . **4.** cool **5.** renew **6.** revive **7.** refresh, sweeten
freshet . . . **4.** gush **5.** flood, spate **6.** stream **7.** outflow, torrent **10.** inundation (sudden)
freshman . . . **5.** frosh **6.** novice **7.** student
freshness . . . **7.** newness, novelty **8.** verdancy **9.** impudence **11.** originality
freshwater fish . . . **2.** id (ide) **4.** chub, dace, inid (porpoise) **6.** anabas **7.** herring **8.** drumfish
fret . . . **3.** eat, nag, orp, rub, vex **4.** fray, fume, gall, gnaw, stew **5.** adorn, annoy, chafe, grate, tease, worry **6.** abrade, grieve, harass, plague, strait **7.** agitate, consume, disturb, network, roughen **8.** diminish, irritate, ornament
fretful . . . **5.** angry **6.** repine **7.** peevish, pettish **8.** captious, petulant **9.** impatient, irascible, irritable, plaintive, querulous **10.** ill-humored, ill-natured
Freud (pert to) . . .
birthplace . . **6.** Vienna
complex . . **7.** Electra, Oedipus
concept . . **2.** id **3.** ego **8.** superego
topic . . **3.** sex **5.** dream **7.** anxiety **8.** hysteria, neurosis **9.** sexuality **10.** repression **11.** unconscious **12.** subconscious **14.** psychoanalysis
friable . . . **5.** crisp, frail, mealy, short **7.** brittle **8.** fragible
friar . . . **3.** fra **4.** fish (small), monk **5.** abbot, Minor **6.** lister (obs) **7.** brother **8.** cenobite, Minorite, Teresian (anc) **9.** Carmelite, Dominican **10.** Franciscan **11.** Augustinian
friction . . . **7.** erasure, rubbing **8.** clashing **9.** attrition, disaccord **10.** resistance **12.** disagreement **13.** counteraction
friend . . . **3.** ami, pal **4.** ally, amie, chum,

kith, sect **5.** amigo, crony **7.** comrade **8.** promoter **9.** associate, attendant, companion, supporter **10.** benefactor, sweetheart, well-wisher
Friend . . . **6.** Quaker
friendless . . . **5.** alone **7.** forlorn **8.** helpless **9.** destitute (friends)
friendly . . . **3.** sib **4.** kind **7.** affable **8.** amicable, homelike, sociable **9.** favorable **10.** harmonious, hospitable **11.** comfortable
Friendly Islands . . . **5.** Tonga
friendship . . . **4.** kelt **5.** amity **7.** harmony **8.** good will, relation **9.** affection, right hand **10.** attachment **12.** friendliness
frieze . . . **4.** band (sculptured) **5.** adorn, chase **6.** taenia (Doric) **8.** ornament, trimming **10.** decoration, embroidery
Frigga, Norse Myth (pert to) . . .
goddess . . **3.** sky
maid . . **5.** Fulla
named for . . **6.** Friday
wife of . . **4.** Odin
fright . . . **3.** awe **4.** fear, ogre **5.** alarm, panic, scare, shock **6.** terror **7.** eyesore **13.** consternation
frighten . . . **3.** cow **5.** alarm, appal, scare **7.** startle, terrify **10.** intimidate
frightened . . . **3.** rad **5.** eerie, timid **6.** afraid **8.** skittish
frightful . . . **5.** awful, great **6.** horrid **7.** hideous **8.** alarming, dreadful, horrible, shocking, terrible, terrific **11.** frightening
frightfulness . . . **13.** atrociousness **15.** Schrecklichkeit
frigid . . . **3.** icy **4.** cold **5.** stiff **6.** formal **8.** freezing, impotent, reserved
frijol, frijole . . . **4.** bean
frill . . . **4.** purl **5.** jabot, ruche (rouche) **6.** border, edging, ruffle **8.** furbelow **9.** frillback (pigeon) **11.** superfluity
fringe . . . **4.** lace, loma, tuft **5.** thrum **6.** border, edging, margin **8.** ciliella, trimming
frisk . . . **4.** skip **5.** brisk, caper **6.** frolic, gambol, lively, search **7.** disport, rejoice
frisky . . . **3.** gay **6.** lively **7.** playful **8.** sportive **10.** frolicsome
frisson . . . **5.** chill **6.** quiver, shiver, thrill **7.** shudder **10.** excitement
frivolous . . . **5.** giddy, petty **6.** fickle, slight **7.** fatuous, trivial **9.** worthless **13.** shallow-witted
frock . . . **4.** gown, wrap **5.** dress, tunic **6.** jersey, kirtle (anc), mantle **7.** garment, soutane
frog . . . **3.** pad (horse's) **4.** Rana, toad **5.** Anura **6.** peeper **7.** croaker, paddock, tadpole **8.** Amphibia, pollywog **9.** Batrachia, Frenchman, Salientia **10.** hoarseness
froglike . . . **6.** ranine
frogman . . . **5.** diver **6.** seaman **7.** swimmer **9.** Frenchman
frog pond . . . **8.** ranarium
frolic . . . **3.** fun **4.** lark, ogle, play, ramp, romp **5.** binge, caper, frisk, prank, spree, trick **6.** gambol, shindy **7.** disport, marlock, shindig, wassail **8.** carousal
frolicsome . . . **3.** gay **5.** merry **6.** frisky

7. playful, waggish 8. sportive
from . . . 2. at, de (pref), of 3. apo (pref)
4. away 5. above, out of 6. source
8. away from, downward
from (pert to) . . .
  beginning to end . . 4. over 7. through
  egg to apple . . 16. ab ovo usque ad
    mala
  head to foot . . 7. cap-a-pie
  slang . . 10. soup to nuts 11. stem to
    stern
front . . . 3. bow, van 4. face, fore 5. aface,
  afore, blind (false), forne (obs) 6. before,
  facade 7. obverse 8. confront, mediator
  9. forefront 10. appearance, figurehead
  11. affectation 12. intermediary
frontier defense . . . 11. arcifinious
frontiersman . . . 5. Boone 6. Carson
  (Kit)
frost . . . 3. ice, mat 4. cold, foam, hoar,
  rime 5. chill 6. freeze, whiten 7. failure
  8. severity (manner) 14. unfriendliness
frosty . . . 3. icy 4. cold, gray, rimy 5. chill,
  hoary, white 6. frigid 8. freezing,
  inimical 10. unfriendly
froth . . . 4. foam, scum, suds 5. spume,
  yeast 6. lather 7. bubbles
frothy . . . 5. foamy, light, sudsy
  7. spumous 8. sillabub
frow . . . 4. froe (tool), wife 5. woman
  6. maenad 8. slattern
froward . . . 5. cross 7. peevish, wayward
  8. perverse, petulant, scolding,
  shrewish, untoward 9. obstinate
  10. refractory, unyielding
  11. disobedient 12. ungovernable
frowl . . . 9. guillemot
frown . . . 5. gloom, lower, scowl 6. glower
frowsey, frowzy . . . 5. musty 7. unkempt
  8. slovenly 9. offensive 10. discordant,
  disordered
frozen . . . 4. cold 5. frore (anc), froze,
  gelid, glacé 6. chilly, mousse 7. chilled
  9. congealed, terrified, unfeeling,
  unmovable 10. unyielding
  11. coldhearted 12. refrigerated
frugal . . . 5. chary 6. meager, saving
  7. careful, sparing, thrifty 9. provident
  10. economical, unwasteful
  11. inexpensive 12. parsimonious
frugality . . . 6. thrift 7. economy
  9. parsimony
fruit (types of) . . . 3. fig 4. lime, pear,
  plum, pome 5. apple, berry, drupe,
  grape, guava, lemon, mango, melon,
  olive, peach, pomum 6. banana,
  cherry, orange, papaya, pawpaw,
  pomelo 7. apricot, azarole, genipap,
  tangelo 8. shaddock 9. persimmon,
  tangerine 10. grapefruit, watermelon
  11. pomegranate
fruit . . . 4. diet, food 5. yield, young
  7. benefit, product 9. offspring,
  outgrowth, posterity 11. consequence
fruit (pert to) . . .
  aggregate . . 7. etaerio
  astringent . . 4. sloe
  basket . . 6. pottle
  buttercup . . 6. achene 8. achenium
  class . . 6. simple 9. aggregate
  10. collective

cordial . . 7. ratafia (ratafee)
decay . . 4. blet
dried . . 6. raisin 7. apricot
drink . . 3. ade 6. nectar
Goddess . . 6. Pomona
gourd . . 4. pepo 7. chayote
grapefruit . . 6. pomelo
imperfect . . 6. nubbin
jelly substance . . 6. pectin
Jove's . . 9. persimmon
part . . 7. epicarp 8. mesocarp, pericarp
  9. sarcocarp
preserve . . 7. compote 9. marmalade
pulpy . . 3. uva
rose . . 3. hip
study of . . 9. carpology
tree . . 4. date, nuts 5. regma 6. camato,
  samara (winged)
tropical . . 3. fig 4. date 5. guava, mango,
  papaw (pawpaw) 6. papaya
fruitful . . . 7. fertile, uberous 8. abundant,
  prolific 9. plenteous
fruitfulness, goddess of . . . 7. Demeter
fruitless . . . 4. vain 6. barren 7. sterile,
  useless 10. profitless 11. ineffectual
  12. unprofitable, unsuccessful
frump . . . 3. vex 4. mock, snub 5. crone,
  flout, shrew 6. gossip, insult 7. provoke
  8. irritate
frustrate . . . 4. balk, bilk, foil 5. block,
  cross, elude 6. baffle, blight, defeat,
  outwit, thwart 7. nullify 8. confound
  9. checkmate 10. circumvent,
  disappoint, disconcert
frustrater . . . 7. marplot 8. thwarter
frustration . . . 4. balk 6. defeat, fiasco
  13. circumvention 14. disappointment
  15. disillusionment
fry . . . 4. cook 5. brood (fish), group,
  saute, young 7. stir-fry 9. offspring
frying pan . . . 6. spider 7. skillet
fubsy . . . 5. plump, short 6. chubby
fuddle . . . 4. bout (drinking) 5. drink
  (strong), spree 6. muddle, tipple
  7. confuse 9. confusion, inebriate
fudge . . . 4. fake 5. candy, cheat
  6. bungle, humbug 7. trump up
  8. nonsense 9. makeshift 10. substitute
  11. counterfeit
Fuegian . . . 3. Ona 6. Indian, Yakgan
  8. Alikuluf 14. Tierra del Fuego (pert
  to)
fuel . . . 3. gas, log, oil 4. coal, coke, peat
  6. butane, diesel, elding 7. gasohol,
  nuclear, synfuel 8. gasoline, kerosene
  9. petroleum 11. combustible
fugie . . . 4. cock (nonfighter) 6. coward
fugient . . . 7. fleeing 8. retiring
fugitive . . . 5. exile 6. outlaw, roving
  7. fleeing, refugee, roaming, runaway
  8. fleeting, unstable, vagabond, volatile
  9. fugacious, strolling, uncertain
  10. evanescent
fugue . . . 5. theme, tonal 7. amnesia,
  stretto (stretta) 9. psychosis, ricercare
fulcrum . . . 4. axis, bait, prop 5. pivot,
  scale (fish), thole 7. support
fulfill . . . 4. meet 6. finish, redeem
  7. execute, satisfy 8. complete
  10. accomplish, effectuate
fulfillment . . . 8. fruition 9. execution,

flowering **10.** completion
11. performance **14.** accomplishment
full . . . **3.** fat **4.** fill **5.** drunk, sated **6.** entire,
filled, rotund **7.** perfect, plenary,
replete, satiety **8.** abundant, adequate,
complete, occupied, resonant, satiated,
thorough **9.** satisfied
full (pert to) . . .
 authority . . **12.** carte blanche
 blooded . . **4.** pure, rich **5.** lusty **6.** virile
  7. genuine **8.** purebred, vigorous
  9. authentic
 bloom . . **8.** anthesis, blooming, maturity
 bodied . . **4.** rich **5.** large **6.** robust
 control . . **7.** mastery **10.** domination
 force . . **5.** amain
 house . . **3.** SRO
full of . . .
 cracks . . **6.** rimose
 hollows . . **8.** lacunose
 love . . **7.** amative, amatory
 meaning . . **5.** pithy **10.** meaningful
 openings (tiny) . . **6.** porous
 sand . . **7.** arenose **8.** sabulous
 substance . . **5.** meaty
 suffix . . **3.** ose
 thorns . . **6.** briary
 vigor . . **5.** lusty
fulness, fullness . . . **4.** much **7.** orotund,
pleroma, satiety, surfeit **9.** abundance,
greatness, plenitude, repletion,
resonance **10.** perfection
12. completeness
fulsome . . . **3.** bad, fat **4.** base, foul, full
5. nasty, plump, suave **7.** copious,
overfed **8.** abundant **9.** offensive,
overgrown, repulsive **10.** disgusting
Fulton's Folly . . . **8.** Clermont
fumble . . . **5.** grope **6.** bungle, huddle,
mumble **7.** confuse
fume . . . **4.** odor, rage, rant, reek **5.** anger,
smoke, steam, vapor **8.** outburst
10. excitement, exhalation
fun . . . **4.** gell, jest, joke, play **5.** chaff,
sport **9.** amusement, merriment
function . . . **3.** act, use **4.** duty, rite,
role, work **5.** party **6.** office **7.** calling,
operate, purpose, service **8.** ceremony,
province **10.** providence
function (pert to) . . .
 math . . **4.** sine **6.** cosine
 mind . . **8.** ideation
 social . . **3.** tea
functional . . . **8.** official **9.** operative
11. ceremonious, utilitarian
fund . . . **5.** basis, money **6.** bottom,
supply **7.** capital, provide, revenue
10. foundation, groundwork
fundamental . . . **4.** tone **5.** basal, basic,
vital **7.** basilar, organic, primary, radical
8. original, rudiment **9.** elemental,
essential, principle **10.** elementary
Fundamental Orders (US Hist) . . .
8. document (1639) **12.** Constitution
(first, 1639 Conn)
funds . . . **5.** means **6.** assets, moneys
8. finances
funeral . . . **5.** rites **6.** burial **8.** exequies
9. obsequies **10.** procession
funeral (pert to) . . .
 bell . . **5.** knell

ceremony . . **6.** exequy
hymn, song . . **5.** dirge, éloge, elogy
  7. requiem **8.** threnody
oration, poem . . **5.** elegy
pile . . **4.** pyre
procession . . **6.** exequy **7.** cortege
vase . . **3.** urn
funereal . . . **3.** sad **4.** dark **6.** dismal,
solemn **8.** exequial, mournful
9. dirgelike
fungi . . . **5.** rusts, Uredo **6.** mildew
7. Boletus
fungoid . . . **6.** fungal, fungus
fungus . . . **4.** bunt, mold, rust, smut
5. ergot, morel, uredo **6.** agaric, lichen,
mildew **7.** aminita, blewits, boletus,
geaster, truffle **8.** mushroom, puffball
9. toadstool
fungus, edible . . . **5.** morel **7.** truffle
8. mushroom
funguslike . . . **6.** agaric
funk . . . **4.** kick, odor, rage **5.** panic, smell
(bad), smoke, spark **6.** flinch, fright,
shrink, terror **8.** frighten **9.** cowardice,
touchwood
funnel . . . **4.** cone, flue, pipe, tube
6. hopper **7.** channel
funnel-shaped . . . **8.** choanoid
funny . . . **3.** odd **5.** comic, droll, queer,
witty **7.** comical, rowboat (Eng), strange
8. humorous **9.** eccentric, laughable
fur . . . **3.** fox **4.** mink, pelt, seal, vair
5. coypu, fitch, genet, otter, sable,
skunk **6.** badger, ermine, martin, nutria
7. miniver (anc) **8.** squirrel **10.** chinchilla
fur (pert to) . . .
 collective . . **6.** peltry
 cover . . **4.** pelt **6.** pelage
 garment . . **4.** robe **5.** stole **6.** tippet
  7. pelisse
 tippet . . **8.** palatine
furbish . . . **3.** rub **4.** vamp **5.** clean,
scour **6.** polish **7.** burnish, touch up
8. renovate **9.** embellish
Furies . . . **5.** Dirae **6.** Alecto, ghosts,
Semnae **7.** Erinyes (Erinys), Magaera,
spirits (avenging) **9.** Eumenides,
Tisiphone
Furies, The Three . . . **6.** Alecto
7. Magaera **9.** Tisiphone
furious . . . **5.** angry, hasty **6.** fierce
7. frantic, violent **8.** frenzied, vehement
9. impetuous, turbulent **10.** boisterous,
passionate, tumultuous
11. overwrought
furl . . . **4.** roll, wrap **6.** bundle, inroll
furlough . . . **5.** leave **14.** leave of absence
furnace . . . **4.** etna, kiln, oven **5.** forge,
stove **6.** boiler **7.** caldron, reactor,
rotator, smelter
furnish . . . **3.** fit **4.** bear, give, lend
5. adorn, cater, endow, equip, indue
6. afford, fit out, render, supply
7. appoint, provide
furnishing . . . **7.** fitting **8.** fixtures,
ornament **9.** adornment, apparatus,
furniture, provision **10.** enrichment
furnish with . . .
 funds . . **5.** endow
 meals . . **5.** board, cater
 Mil equipment . . **8.** accoutre

tapestry . . **5.** arras
wings . . **3.** imp
furniture . . . **4.** Adam **5.** Eames, Louis,
Phyfe, suite (matched set) **6.** Empire,
graith (obs) **7.** mission **8.** Sheraton,
Stickley **9.** Queen Anne **10.** Directoire
11. Chippendale, Hepplewhite
13. Mediterranean **16.** French
Provincial
furor . . . **4.** fury, rage **5.** anger, craze
6. fervor, flurry, frenzy, furore, tumult
7. madness **10.** excitement, turbulence
furrow . . . **3.** rut **4.** plow **6.** groove,
gutter, trench **7.** channel, wrinkle
furrowed . . . **5.** rutty **6.** rivose **7.** grooved
further . . . **3.** aid, and, new, yet **4.** abet,
more **7.** advance, develop, improve,
promote, remoter, thither **10.** additional
furtherance . . . **3.** aid **4.** help **6.** relief,
succor **8.** progress **9.** promotion
11. advancement, development
furtherer . . . **7.** abettor **8.** promoter
furthermore . . . **3.** and, yet **4.** then
5. again **7.** au reste, besides
8. moreover **10.** in addition
12. additionally
furtive . . . **3.** sly **4.** wary **6.** covert, secret,
sneaky, stolen **8.** skulking, stealthy
9. deceitful **11.** clandestine
fury . . . **3.** ire **4.** rage **5.** anger, wrath
6. frenzy **7.** madness **8.** violence
10. excitement, turbulence
13. desperateness

Fury . . . **6.** Erinys, Spirit (avenging)
7. Atropos
furze . . . **4.** Ulex, whin **5.** gorse, shrub
fuse . . . **4.** flux, frit (partly), melt
5. blend, smelt, unite **6.** anneal, mingle,
solder **7.** combine, liquefy **8.** dissolve
9. detonator
fusee . . . **5.** flair, torch **6.** signal
fusion . . . **5.** alloy, blend, union **7.** melting,
mixture, nuclear **8.** fluidity **9.** coalition
fuss . . . **3.** ado **4.** spat, to-do **5.** busle
6. bother, bustle, pother, tumult
7. bombast, dispute, quarrel, trouble
8. brouhaha **9.** confusion
fussy . . . **7.** finical **8.** overnice
10. fastidious, meticulous
fustian . . . **4.** rant **5.** cloth, tumid
7. bombast, pompous **8.** claptrap,
inflated **9.** bombastic, worthless
fustic . . . **3.** dye **5.** amber, morin
7. dyewood
futile . . . **4.** idle, vain **6.** otiose **7.** trivial
8. hopeless **11.** ineffectual
futility . . . **8.** nugacity **10.** invalidity
11. uselessness **12.** bootlessness
future . . . **3.** yet **4.** to be **5.** later, still,
tense **6.** fiancé **8.** expected, intended
9. hereafter **11.** prospective
fuzzy . . . **5.** downy, hairy **6.** fluffy
7. blurred, frizzly **9.** imperfect
10. indistinct
fyke . . . **3.** net **6.** bag net
fylfot . . . **8.** swastika **9.** gammadion

G

G . . . **4.** tone (scale) **6.** letter (7th)
gab . . . **3.** lie **4.** mock, talk **5.** boast,
mouth, prate, scoff, taste **6.** tongue
7. chatter, deceive **9.** utterance
gabardine . . . **6.** cotton, woolen
gabble . . . **4.** chat **6.** babble, jabber,
mumble **7.** chatter **8.** nonsense
gabelle . . . **3.** tax **5.** likin (imports)
6. excise, impost
gaberdine . . . **4.** gown **5.** frock **6.** mantle
7. garment (loose) **8.** covering, pinafore
9. gabardine
gable . . . **4.** roof (part) **7.** aileron (half)
8. pediment
gablock . . . **4.** gaff, spur **5.** spear **6.** gaffle
7. crowbar **8.** gavelock
Gabon, Africa . . .
capital . . **10.** Libreville
Gabriel (pert to) . . .
astrology . . **10.** moon spirit
New Test . . **6.** herald **11.** good tidings
Old Test . . **5.** angel
tradition . . **9.** archangel (one of seven),
messenger
gaby . . . **4.** fool **9.** simpleton
gad . . . **3.** bar, God (oath), rod **4.** goad,
roam, rove, whip **5.** ingot, spear, staff
6. billet, chisel, wander **7.** on the go,
run wild, traipse (trapes) **8.** gadabout

9. gallivant
Gad (pert to) . . .
Bib . . **7.** prophet
deity (Bib) . . **7.** Fortune
father . . **5.** Jacob
tribe . . **6.** Gadite, Israel (one of seven)
gadabout . . . **3.** gad **6.** roving **7.** dogcart,
gadding, on the go
Gaddang, Gaddan . . . **7.** Malayan
8. language (Indonesia)
gadfly . . . **6.** botfly, insect **8.** horsefly
gadget . . . **6.** device, jigger **7.** gimmick
8. gimcrack **11.** contrivance,
thingumajig
Gadsden Purchase (1853) . . . **5.** tract
7. Arizona **9.** New Mexico
gadwall . . . **4.** duck
Gaea, Gaia . . . **12.** Earth Goddess
Gael . . . **4.** Celt, Kelt, Manx, Scot
10. Highlander
Gaelic (pert to) . . .
for John . . **3.** Ian
hero . . **6.** Ossian
language . . **4.** Erse
native . . **4.** Erse **5.** Irish **6.** Celtic, Keltic,
Scotch
pagan god . . **5.** Dagda (harpist)
sea god . . **3.** Ler
spirit . . **7.** banshee

warriors . . **7.** Fenians

gaff . . . **4.** hoax, hook, scam, spar, spur, talk **5.** fraud, spear, trick **6.** deceit, fleece, gamble **7.** chatter, prating **8.** trickery **9.** spearhead

gaffer . . . **4.** hick, rube **6.** old man **11.** electrician (TV)

gag . . . **4.** hoax, joke **5.** choke, retch **7.** closure, prevent, shackle **8.** obstruct, one-liner, restrain, silencer **9.** imposture **10.** instrument **13.** interpolation

gage, gauge . . . **4.** rule, test **5.** scale **6.** device, pledge **7.** measure **8.** capacity, defiance, diameter (firearm), mortgage, security **9.** challenge **11.** measurement

gaggle . . . **5.** flock (geese), group (women) **6.** cackle

gaiety, gayety . . . **4.**, glee, show **5.** mirth **6.** finery **7.** jollity **8.** vivacity **9.** festivity, merriment, showiness **10.** liveliness **12.** colorfulness, conviviality

gain . . . **3.** get, net, win **4.** earn, pelf, reap **5.** booty, clear, lucre, reach **6.** attain, come by, obtain, profit, secure, trover **7.** acquire, benefit, procure, realize **8.** addition, arrive at, increase **9.** advantage **11.** acquisition **12.** accumulation **13.** amplification

gainsay . . . **4.** deny **6.** forbid, impugn, oppose, refute **7.** dispute **10.** contradict, controvert

gait . . . **3.** run, way **4.** lope, pace, trip, trot, walk **5.** amble, order, strut, tread **6.** canter, gallop **8.** slowness, velocity

gaiter . . . **4.** boot, spat **5.** strad **6.** puttee **7.** legging **8.** overshoe **11.** galligaskin

gala . . . **4.** fete, pomp **6.** festal, fiesta, gaiety **8.** festival **9.** festivity **11.** celebration

Galago . . . **5.** lemur

Galahad's quest . . . **9.** Holy Grail

Galatea . . . **7.** heroine **8.** sea nymph **9.** Pygmalion (sculptor) **11.** shepherdess

galaxy . . . **6.** throng **8.** Milky Way **10.** assemblage **11.** celebrities

gale . . . **4.** gust, wind **5.** storm **8.** outburst **9.** hurricane

galea . . . **6.** helmet

galeate . . . **12.** helmet-shaped

Galen (Gr) . . . **9.** physician

Galilean (pert to) . . .
province . . **9.** Palestine
religion . . **9.** Christian
town . . **4.** Cana **6.** Tiberias

gall . . . **3.** vex **4.** bile, fret **5.** annoy, chafe, grate, spite **6.** bitter, harass, rancor **8.** irritate **9.** impudence, secretion, virulence

gallant . . . **4.** hero **5.** dandy, lover, noble, spark, swain **6.** escort, suitor **7.** stately **8.** cavalier, cicisbeo **9.** attentive, courteous **10.** chivalrous, courageous

gallantry . . . **7.** bravery, courage, display **8.** courtesy **9.** courtship **11.** intrepidity

galleon . . . **6.** vessel (sailing)

gallery . . . **3.** poy **4.** hall **5.** salon **6.** dedans, loggia, museum **7.** passage, veranda **8.** audience, corridor, platform **9.** promenade **10.** ambulatory **11.** observatory

galley . . . **4.** boat, tray **6.** vessel

7. caboose, caravel (caravelle), dromond, kitchen **8.** cookroom

galley, Roman . . .
one-bank oared . . **7.** unireme
two-bank oared . . **6.** bireme
three-bank oared . . **7.** trireme
six-bank oared . . **7.** hexeris
slave . . **5.** rower **6.** drudge

Gallic . . . **4.** Gaul **6.** French

Gallic chariot . . . **5.** essed

gallimaufry . . . **4.** hash, olio, stew **6.** jumble, medley, ragout **9.** potpourri **10.** hodgepodge

gallipot . . . **6.** vessel (Medit) **8.** druggist

gallo . . . **7.** rooster **12.** fighting cock

gallop . . . **3.** run **4.** lope, ride **6.** canter **7.** tantivy

gallopade . . . **5.** dance, galop **6.** curvet

gallows humor, like . . . **6.** morbid

gam . . . **3.** leg **4.** herd **5.** visit **6.** school

Gambia, Africa . . .
capital . . **6.** Banjul

gambit . . . **4.** move **7.** comment, opening (chess) **8.** maneuver **9.** launching **10.** concession

gamble . . . **3.** bet **4.** dice, game, risk **5.** stake, wager **6.** chance, exacta, hazard, plunge **8.** perfecta **9.** speculate, totalizer **10.** parimutuel, superfecta **11.** daily double, uncertainty

gambler . . . **5.** shill **7.** sharper

gambol . . . **3.** hop **5.** bound, caper, prank **6.** cavort, curvet, frolic

Gambrinus (King) . . . **6.** brewer (1st)

game . . . **4.** lark, play, prey **5.** brave, dodge, prank, sport **6.** frolic, gamble, gritty, plucky, quarry **7.** contest, pastime **8.** resolute **9.** amusement, diversion **10.** courageous

game, ball . . . **4.** golf, polo, pool **5.** rugby **6.** hockey, pelota, soccer, squash, tennis **7.** cricket, croquet **8.** baseball, football **11.** racquetball

game, beans . . . **6.** fan-tan **8.** beanbags

game, board . . . **4.** keno **5.** bingo, chess, lotto **7.** pachisi (parchesi) **8.** checkers, cribbage, Monopoly **10.** backgammon

game, card . . . **3.** gin, pam **4.** bank, faro, skat **5.** pitch, poker, rummy, whist **6.** bridge, écarté, flinch, hearts **7.** bezique, canasta, cassino, old maid, seven-up

game, club . . . **4.** golf **6.** hockey **7.** cricket

game, court . . . **6.** pelota, squash, tennis **7.** jai alai **9.** badminton

game, parlor . . . **5.** jacks **7.** marbles **8.** charades, dominoes **11.** tiddlywinks

game plan . . . **6.** scheme **8.** strategy

game, ring . . . **6.** quoits

gamin . . . **3.** tad **4.** serf **6.** urchin **7.** mudlark **10.** street Arab

gamut . . . **5.** orbit, range **6.** extent **7.** compass

gamy . . . **4.** game **7.** lustful **8.** sporting **12.** high-flavored

gander . . . **5.** goose **6.** stroll **9.** simpleton

Gandhi (Hind) . . . **6.** Indira, leader **7.** Mahatma (Mohandus)

gang . . . **3.** mob, set **4.** band, crew, pack, team, walk (cattle) **5.** group, horde, sheet (Print), shift **6.** clique **7.** company

9. pasturage
gangling . . . **5.** lanky **9.** spindling
gangrene . . . **5.** decay **6.** slough
8. necrosis **9.** sphacelus
13. mortification
gangster . . . **4.** thug **5.** thief **6.** bandit
7. mobster **8.** criminal, hireling
9. racketeer
gannet . . . **4.** ibis, Sula **5.** booby, goose,
solan **6.** gander
gap . . . **3.** col **4.** hole, pass **5.** break,
chasm, cleft, fault, meuse, shard, space,
split **6.** breach, hiatus, lacuna, lacune,
ravine **7.** opening
gaping . . . **5.** agape **6.** chappy **7.** ringent,
yawning **9.** expectant
garb . . . **5.** array, dress, habit, mufti
(civilian), style **6.** attire, clothe
7. apparel, costume, fashion, raiment,
uniform **8.** clothing **10.** appearance,
habiliment
garbage . . . **5.** trash, waste **6.** refuse
garbanzo . . . **8.** chickpea
garbed . . . **4.** clad **7.** attired, dressed,
habited
garble . . . **5.** alloy **6.** mangle **7.** distort,
falsify, pervert **8.** mutilate
12. misinterpret, misrepresent,
sophisticate
garden . . . **3.** bed **4.** yard **5.** hardy, patch
6. jardin, verger **7.** topiary **8.** outfield
9. arboretum, cultivate, enclosure,
herbarium
garden (pert to) . . .
Berlin . . **10.** Tiergarten
Bible . . **4.** Eden
city . . **4.** Kent **6.** Sicily **7.** Chicago
8. Touraine
colony . . **5.** Natal
Colorado . . **9.** of the Gods
Kansas . . **9.** of the West
kind of . . **5.** truck **8.** kaleyard **9.** botanical
10. zoological
State . . **9.** New Jersey
garden implement . . . **3.** hoe **4.** fork,
rake **5.** graip, mower **6.** scythe, sickle,
trowel, weeder
Garfield's assassin . . . **7.** Guiteau
Gargantua (pert to) . . .
character . . **4.** King (Rabelais romance)
son . . **10.** Pantagruel (giant)
gargantuan . . . **4.** huge **7.** titanic
garish . . . **5.** gaudy, showy **7.** flighty,
glaring **8.** dazzling
garland . . . **3.** lei **6.** anadem, circle,
corona, fillet, rosary, trophy, wreath
7. chaplet, coronal, festoon **8.** headband
9. anthology **11.** compilation
garlic . . . **4.** herb, moly **5.** clove **6.** ramson
garment . . . **4.** cape, coat, gown, robe,
suit, vest, wrap **5.** cloak, dress,
frock, shift, simar, smock, stole, tunic
6. coatee, duster **7.** pelisse, raiment,
surcoat, topcoat **8.** overcoat, vestment
garment (pert to) . . .
African . . **6.** kaross
ancient . . **5.** burel
Arab . . **3.** aba
clerical . . **3.** alb **5.** amice **6.** chimer
7. cassock, zimarra **8.** surplice
cover . . **5.** apron **8.** overalls, pinafore

9. coveralls
Eskimo . . **5.** parka
Jewish . . **5.** ephod
knight's . . **6.** tabard
patchwork . . **5.** cento
thin . . **8.** gossamer
garner . . . **4.** reap **5.** amass, store **6.** gather
7. collect **10.** accumulate
garnet . . . **3.** gem, red **5.** color **6.** aplome,
pyrope **7.** olivine (green) **8.** cinnamon
(stone), essonite (yellow), melanite
(black) **9.** almandine (almandite, dark
red), uvarovite (green)
garnish . . . **4.** trim **5.** adorn **6.** attach,
bedeck **7.** fetters **8.** decorate, ornament
garnishment . . . **4.** lien **7.** summons
8. ornament **10.** attachment, decoration
garret . . . **4.** loft **5.** attic **6.** turret **8.** cockloft
10. watchtower
garrot . . . **9.** goldeneye (duck)
10. tourniquet
garrote, garrotte . . . **8.** strangle
9. execution **10.** throttling
13. strangulation
garrulous . . . **5.** gabby, wordy **6.** chatty
7. diffuse **9.** talkative **10.** loquacious
gas . . . **4.** brag, talk **5.** vapor **6.** poison
7. chatter **8.** gasoline, nonsense
10. anesthesia, asphyxiate, illuminant
11. anesthetize
gas . . . **3.** air **4.** neon **5.** argon,
ether, ozone, radon, xenon **6.** arsine,
butane, ethane, helium, ketene, nebula
(luminous), oxygen **7.** methane
8. chlorine, cyanogen, etherion,
hydrogen, nitrogen **9.** butadiene
gascon . . . **7.** boaster **8.** braggart
11. braggadocio **12.** swashbuckler
gasconade . . . **4.** brag **5.** boast **7.** bluster,
bravado **11.** fanfaronade, rodomontade
gaseous . . . **4.** smog, thin **5.** smoke
7. tenuous **9.** vaporous
13. unsubstantial
gash . . . **3.** cut **5.** cleft, notch, sever,
slash **6.** furrow, gossip, injury, tattle
8. incision
gasp . . . **3.** say **4.** pant, yawn **5.** utter
7. breathe
gasping . . . **5.** agasp **7.** panting
gastropod . . . **4.** slug **5.** Harpa, Murex,
Oliva, snail, whelk **6.** Nerita, volute
7. abalone, mollusk **8.** sea snail
gat . . . **3.** gun, rod **7.** channel, passage
8. revolver
gate . . . **3.** dar **4.** door, hole, pass **5.** start
(racing), toran, valve **6.** defile, portal
7. barrier, opening, postern **8.** Lion-
Gate **9.** floodgate, turnstile **10.** Needle's
Eye (Jerusalem), portcullis
gateau . . . **4.** cake
gather . . . **4.** bale, brew, fold, meet, reap
5. amass, glean, pleat, rally, shirr
6. bundle, deduce, garner, muster,
pucker **7.** acquire, collect, compile,
convene, convoke, harvest, procure,
suppose **8.** assemble **10.** accumulate
gatherer, collector of . . .
coins . . **11.** numismatist
money . . **5.** miser
news . . **8.** reporter **10.** journalist
stamps . . **11.** philatelist

gathering ... 3. sum 4. stag 5. crowd, party, troop 6. galaxy, smoker 7. abscess, meeting 8. swelling 10. assemblage, harvesting 11. contraction 12. accumulation, congregation 14. conglomeration

gaucho ... 6. cowboy (pampas) 8. herdsman, horseman

gaucho weapon ... 4. bola

gaud ... 4. jest, joke 5. adorn, fraud, paint, sport, trick 6. finery, flashy, gewgaw 7. trinket 8. artifice, ornament

gaudy ... 4. fine, loud 5. cheap, feast, showy 6. flashy, flimsy, garish, tawdry, tinsel 7. glaring, trinket 9. flaunting 11. pretentious 12. meretricious, ostentatious 13. overdeveloped

gaufre ... 4. iron (waffle) 6. waffle

gauge, gage ... 4. norm, rate, rule, size 5. judge, scale, value 6. assess 7. measure 8. estimate

gauge (pert to) ...
airplane .. 10. tachometer
distance .. 10. micrometer
miles .. 8. odometer
pointer .. 3. arm
rain .. 8. udometer
velocity .. 11. speedometer
wind .. 10. anemometer

Gaul ... 5. Aedui 6. France, Gallia 9. Frenchman

Gauls ... 4. Remi 5. Celts, Cymry

gaunt ... 4. bony, lank, lean, thin, ugly 5. spare 7. haggard 8. desolate

gauntlet ... 4. cuff 5. armor (part), glove 7. bandage

gaur ... 2. ox 5. gayal 7. buffalo

gauss ... 4. unit (Elec)

Gauss ... 13. mathematician

Gaussian curve, like a ... 10. bell-shaped

gauze ... 4. haze, leno 5. crape, lisse, marli (marly) 6. barege, filter, tissue 8. dressing

gauze film on wine ... 8. beeswing

gavage ... 7. feeding

gave ... see *give*

Gavia ... 4. loon

gavial ... 11. crocodilian

gaw ... 4. gape 5. drain 6. trench

gawk ... 4. dolt, gowk, left, lout 5. booby, stare 9. simpleton

gawky ... 6. clumsy, cuckoo, stupid 7. awkward, foolish 8. clownish

gay ... 4. airy, glad 5. drunk, gaudy, jolly, merry, riant, showy 6. blithe, cheery, jovial, joyful, joyous, lively 7. dashing, festive, gleeful 8. cheerful, colorful, rory-tory, sportive 9. convivial, sprightly, vivacious 10. frolicsome, profligate 12. lighthearted

gay time ... 4. lark 5. spree 8. jamboree

gazabo, gazebo ... 4. cony 6. rabbit, turret 7. balcony, blunder, whopper 11. summerhouse

gaze ... 3. con, eye 4. gape, look, moon, peer, pore, scan 5. glare, gloat, stare 6. glower, regard

gazelle ... 3. ahu, goa 4. admi, cora, dama, kudu, mohr, oryx 5. ariel, brown, korin 7. chikara (4-horn), corinne, dibatag 8. antelope 9. springbok

gazette ... 7. journal, publish 8. announce 9. newspaper 15. Arkansas Gazette (1819)

gazetteer ... 7. newsman 9. newspaper 10. dictionary

gear ... 3. cam, rig 5. equip, goods, tools, wheel 6. things 7. baggage, conform, harness, rigging 8. adjust to, clothing, cogwheel, garments 9. equipment, mechanism, trappings, vestments 10. appliances, implements

gecko ... 6. lizard 7. tarente

geese ... 5. brant, quink, solan

geese (pert to) ...
fat .. 6. axunge
flock .. 4. raft 6. gaggle
formation .. 3. vee
genus .. 4. Chen 5. Anser 6. Branta

gecko ... 6. lizard

Geisel ... 7. Dr Seuss (pseud)

gelatin, gelatine ... 4. agar, food, jell 5. jelly 6. collin 7. protein 8. agar-agar

gelid ... 3. icy 4. cold 6. frozen

gem ... 4. jade, onyx, opal, ruby, sard, type 5. agate, beryl, bijou, jewel, pearl, stone, topaz 6. garnet, ligure, spinel, zircon 7. cat's-eye, diamond, emerald, jacinth 8. amethyst, hawk's-eye, sapphire 9. carnelian, moonstone 10. aquamarine 11. alexandrite, lapis lazuli 12. star sapphire

gem (pert to) ...
artificial .. 5. paste
base .. 5. culet
carver .. 8. lapidary
Egyptian .. 6. scarab
flaw .. 8. gendarme
food .. 6. muffin
imperfect .. 5. loupe
semiprecious .. 5. cameo 8. intaglio
six rays .. 7. asteria
surface .. 5. bezel, facet
weight .. 5. carat
with many facets .. 9. brilliant

gemel ... 4. bars (Her), twin 6. paired 7. coupled, doubled

gemsbok ... 4. goat, oryx 7. chamois

Gem State ... 5. Idaho

gendarme ... 4. blue, flaw (gem) 5. guard 6. police 7. officer, soldier, trooper 9. policeman 10. cavalryman

gender ... 3. sex 5. breed, genus 7. grammar (term) 8. engender

genealogy ... 4. tree 5. order (of descent) 6. family 7. account, history, lineage, peerage, progeny 8. pedigree, register 9. offspring

genealogy of the gods ... 8. theogony

gener ... 8. son-in-law

general ... 5. gross, usual, vague, whole 6. common, public 7. officer 8. catholic, communal 9. extensive, prevalent, universal, well-known 10. encyclical, indefinite 11. approximate

general (pert to) ...
agreement .. 5. chief, court
aspect .. 6. facies
chief .. 6. Führer, Il Duce 9. president 10. Grand Mogul 13. Generalissimo
court .. 5. Synod
direction .. 5. tenor, trend 6. course

favor . . **7.** popular **10.** popularity
feature . . **5.** motif
group . . **8.** ensemble
orders . . **7.** routine
rule . . **5.** canon
summary . . **8.** synopsis
type . . **7.** average
generalize . . . **5.** widen **6.** extend, reason, spread **7.** broaden **12.** universalize
General Sherman (pert to) . . .
Civil War march . . **15.** Atlanta to the Sea
giant trees . . **8.** sequoias
tree . . **10.** eucalyptus
generate . . . **5.** beget, breed, cause **6.** create **8.** develop, produce **8.** engender **9.** originate, procreate, propagate
generation . . . **3.** age **7.** descent **8.** lifetime **9.** epigonous (later), formation, genealogy **10.** production **11.** abiogenesis, procreation
generosity . . . **10.** liberality **11.** hospitality, magnanimity, munificence
generous . . . **4.** free **5.** large **7.** liberal **8.** tolerant **9.** indulgent, plentiful, unstinted **10.** hospitable **11.** magnanimous
genesis . . . **4.** Book **5.** birth **6.** origin (of races) **8.** nascency **9.** beginning, ethnology, etymology, inception **10.** generation
genet . . . **3.** fur **5.** civet
genethliac . . . **5.** stars (influence) **9.** birthdays
genetics term . . . **3.** DNA, RNA **4.** gene **8.** dominant, heredity **9.** recessive **10.** chromosome, hereditary **11.** recombinant
Geneva Cross . . . **8.** Red Cross
genial . . . **4.** warm **5.** bland **6.** jovial, kindly **7.** amiable, festive, nuptial **8.** cheerful, friendly, pleasant **9.** expansive **10.** enlivening
geniculate . . . **5.** kneel
genie . . . **4.** jinn **6.** genius
genius . . . **5.** deity, jinni **6.** talent **7.** ability, prodigy **9.** endowment (supreme) **11.** inspiration **12.** intelligence
Genoa lace . . . **4.** tape **6.** bobbin **7.** macramé **13.** gold and silver
genos . . . **4.** clan, gens, race
genre . . . **3.** art (style) **4.** kind, sort **5.** genus **6.** gender **7.** species **8.** category
genteel . . . **6.** polite **7.** refined **8.** wellborn, well-bred
Gentiles . . . **6.** goyims **10.** Christians, non-Moslems **14.** non-Mohammedans
gentle . . . **4.** calm, easy, meek, mild, soft, tame **5.** bland, quiet **6.** docile, humane, kindly, tender **7.** amabile (Mus), clement, genteel, refined, subdued **8.** moderate, peaceful, soothing, tranquil, wellborn **9.** courteous, honorable, temperate, tractable **10.** chivalrous **11.** considerate **13.** compassionate
gentleman . . . **3.** sir **6.** knight **7.** esquire, shoneen (would-be), younker **8.** nobleman
gentleness . . . **6.** lenity **8.** elegance,

leniency, meekness, softness **9.** lightness **10.** kindliness, moderation **11.** genteelness
genuflect . . . **5.** kneel **6.** curtsy
genuine . . . **4.** pure, real, true **5.** frank, pucka (pukka) **7.** germane, sincere **8.** existent **9.** authentic, simon-pure, unalloyed, veritable **10.** unaffected **13.** unadulterated
genus . . . **4.** kind, sort **5.** class, order
genus, animal life . . .
animals (one-celled) . . **6.** Amoeba **8.** Protozoa **9.** Rhizopoda
ants . . **6.** Eciton
apes . . **5.** Simia
armadillos . . **9.** Glyptodon
auks . . **4.** Alle
bears . . **5.** Ursus
bees (honey) . . **4.** Apis
beetles . . **10.** Coleoptera
birds . . **7.** Ratitae
bivalve mollusks . . **6.** Anomia **8.** Estheria
bugs (long-legged) . . **5.** Emesa
cats . . **5.** Felis
cattle . . **3.** Bos
crabs . . **4.** Maia
dogs . . **5.** Canis
ducks . . **3.** Aix **4.** Anas **7.** Harelda **8.** Clangula
elks . . **5.** Alces
fish . . **6.** Cybium, Remora **7.** Girella, Muraena
flies . . **6.** Asilus **8.** Glossina (tsetse)
frogs . . **4.** Rana **5.** Anura **8.** Amphibia **9.** Batrachia
geese . . **4.** Chen **5.** Anser
goats . . **5.** Capra
gulls . . **4.** Xema
herons . . **7.** Egretta
hogs . . **3.** Sus
horses . . **5.** Equus
insects . . **10.** Coleoptera
lemurs . . **6.** Galago
lizards . . **3.** Uta **5.** Agama
mammals . . **4.** Homo
Man . . **11.** Homo sapiens
marten . . **7.** Mustela
mice . . **3.** Mus
monkeys (spider) . . **6.** Ateles
moose . . **5.** Alces
moths . . **5.** Tinea
oysters . . **6.** Ostrea
peacocks . . **4.** Pavo
pigeons (crowned) . . **5.** Goura
porcupines . . **7.** Hystrix
porpoise . . **4.** Inia
rats . . **6.** Spalax
roadrunners . . **9.** Geococcyx
scorpions . . **4.** Nepa
seabirds . . **4.** Sula
sloths . . **11.** Megatherium
slugs . . **5.** Arion
snails . . **5.** Mitra **6.** Nerita, Triton **8.** Geophila
snakes . . **4.** Eryx (sand) **7.** Ophidia
spiders . . **7.** Agalena
squirrels . . **7.** Sciurus
swans . . **4.** Olar **6.** Cygnus
ticks . . **6.** Ixodes
tortoises . . **4.** Emys
turkeys . . **9.** Meleagris

wasps . . **5.** Vespa
whales . . **4.** Orca **5.** Areta **9.** Sibbaldus
　(blue)
genus, plant life . . .
algae (blue-green) . . **10.** Gloeocapsa
apple trees . . **5.** Malus
cabbage . . **3.** Cos
currant . . **5.** Ribes
elms . . **5.** Ulmus
evergreen, heaths . . **5.** Erica
fern . . **6.** Anemia
fungi . . **7.** Boletus **10.** geoglossum
grasses . . **3.** Poa (blue) **5.** Avena
　6. Elymus **7.** Setaria
herbs . . **4.** Arum **6.** Asarum, Asitis
　(mustard), Cassia, Seseli **7.** Hedeoma,
　Linaria **8.** Solidago
holly . . **4.** Ilex
ipecac . . **4.** Evea
ivy . . **11.** Hedera helix
lily . . **7.** Bessera
maples . . **4.** Acer
olives . . **4.** Olea
orchids . . **5.** Vanda **7.** Listera
palms . . **5.** Areca, Assai **6.** Bacaba
poplar . . **5.** Alamo
rhubarb . . **5.** Rheum
vines (woody) . . **6.** Hedera
geode . . . **3.** vug (vugg, vugh, voog)
　5. druse **6.** nodule
geological (pert to) . . .
division . . **3.** eon, era
era . . **6.** Eocene **7.** Miocene **8.** Cenozoic
　Mesozoic **9.** Paleozoic **11.** Archaeozoic
period . . **4.** Dyas, Lias **5.** Trias
prelife . . **5.** Azoic
zone (fossil) . . **6.** assise
geologist . . . **6.** Strabo (anc Gr)
　8. geognost **12.** mineralogist
geometric (pert to) . . .
angle . . **9.** incidence
axis . . **8.** abscissa
contact . . **10.** osculation
curve . . **6.** spiral **7.** evolute
pottery . . **7.** Dipylon (anc)
geometric figure . . . **4.** cone, cube,
　lune **5.** prism **6.** gnomon, oblong,
　square **7.** hexagon, octagon, polygon,
　rhombus **8.** heptagon, pentagon,
　triangle **9.** rectangle, trapezoid
　10. quadrangle **13.** parallelogram
geometric proposition (pert to) . . .
ratio . . **2.** pi (3.1416)
surface . . **4.** tore **5.** nappe
term . . **4.** sine **5.** locus **6.** secant
　7. tangent **11.** asses' bridge
geometry (pert to) . . .
figure . . **6.** conoid **9.** ellipsoid
　10. paraboloid
mathematician . . **6.** Euclid, Pascal
proposition . . **6.** porism
geoponic . . . **5.** rural **6.** rustic
Georgia . . .
capital . . **7.** Atlanta
city . . **5.** Macon **7.** Augusta **8.** Columbus,
　Marietta, Savannah **9.** Brunswick
holiday . . **11.** Georgia Day (Feb 12)
memorial . . **11.** Warm Springs **16.** Little
　White House (FDR)
mountain . . **7.** Lookout **9.** Blue Ridge
　11. Alleghenies

peak . . **9.** High Point **13.** Brasstown Bald
river . . **8.** Savannah, Suwannee
settler (1st) . . **10.** Oglethorpe
State admission . . **6.** Fourth
State nickname . . **5.** Peach **7.** Cracker
　16. Empire of the South
swamp . . **10.** Okefenokee
Georgian of the Caucasus . . . **4.** Svan
georgic . . . **4.** poem (rural)
geosphere . . . **5.** earth
Geraint, Sir . . . **6.** Knight (Round Table)
germ . . . **3.** bud **4.** ovum, seed **5.** spore
　6. embryo, origin **7.** microbe **8.** bacteria
　(pl) **9.** bacterium **13.** microorganism
germ (free) . . . **7.** aseptic **10.** antiseptic
German (pert to) . . . see also *Germany*
air force . . **9.** Luftwaffe
art . . **5.** kunst
art movement . . **13.** Sturm und Drang
article . . **3.** das, der, ein
battleship . . **8.** Graf Spee
beverage . . **5.** lager
book . . **4.** buch, heft
cake . . **5.** torte
castle . . **7.** schloss
Christmas . . **11.** Weihnachten
dance . . **9.** allemande
deity . . **5.** Donar (thunder)
drinking salute . . **6.** prosit
folklore . . **5.** gnome **6.** kobold
guild member . . **13.** Meistersinger
gun . . **9.** Big Bertha
hail . . **4.** heil
highway . . **8.** autobahn
language . . **7.** Deutsch
league . . **4.** Bund **6.** Verein **9.** Hanseatic
　10. Turnverein
letter . . **4.** rune
lyric poems . . **6.** lieder
mister . . **4.** Herr
ox (wild) . . **4.** urus
parliament . . **9.** Bundestag, Reichstag
　(formerly)
people . . **5.** Goths, Quadi **6.** Franks,
　Saxons **7.** Teutons, Vandals
　8. Lombards **9.** Prussians
　10. Herminones
police . . **7.** Gestapo
prison camp . . **6.** stalag
ruler . . **6.** kaiser
society . . see *league (above)*
song . . **4.** lied
teacher . . **6.** docent **12.** privatdocent
title . . **3.** Von **4.** Graf, Herr **6.** Ritter
tribal group . . **4.** gau
vowel change . . **6.** umlaut
wheat . . **5.** spelt
wine . . **4.** hock, wein **5.** Rhine **7.** Moselle
　(Mosel) **8.** Riesling **11.** Niersteiner
woman . . **4.** frau **8.** fraulein
yes . . **2.** ja
germane . . . **4.** akin **6.** allied **7.** kindred
　8. relevant **11.** appropriate
Germanic language . . . **5.** Dutch
　6. Danish, German, Gothic **7.** English,
　Frisian, Swedish, Yiddish **8.** Old Norse
　9. Icelandic, Norwegian
German people (famed) . . .
actor . . **8.** Jannings (Emil)
archaeologist . . **10.** Schliemann
artist . . **5.** Dürer, Ernst, Grosz **8.** Kollwitz

9. Friedrich
astrologer.. **5.** Faust
astronomer.. **5.** Galle **6.** Kepler
author.. **4.** Böll, Mann **5.** Grass,
  Grimm, Hesse, Kafka, Zweig **6.** Goethe
  7. Fontane, Wieland **8.** Brentano
auto engineer.. **4.** Benz **5.** Bosch
  6. Diesel **7.** Daimler, Porsche
bacteriologist.. **4.** Koch (Nobel Prize,
  1905)
chemist.. **5.** Haber **6.** Bunsen, Liebig
composer.. **4.** Bach **5.** Gluck, Weber
  (Carl Maria) **6.** Handel, Schütz,
  Wagner **8.** Schumann **9.** Beethoven
  11. Stockhausen
dramatist.. **6.** Brecht, Kleist **7.** Lessing
  8. Schiller **9.** Hauptmann, Sudermann
Egyptologist.. **5.** Ebers
general.. **6.** Moltke, Rommel **7.** Steuben
  (Rev War) **10.** Hindenburg, Ludendorff
geographer.. **6.** Ritter
Gestapo chief.. **7.** Himmler
goldsmith (anc).. **5.** Faust
hero.. **8.** Arminius
historian.. **4.** Dahn **5.** Ranke **7.** Meineke,
  Mommsen **8.** Spengler
industrialist.. **5.** Krupp
leader.. **7.** Bismark, Wilhelm (William)
  9. Frederick (the Great) **10.** Hindenburg
mathematician.. **5.** Gauss
military expert.. **10.** Clausewitz
mystic.. **5.** Bohme **7.** Eckhart (Meister)
naturalist.. **8.** Humboldt **9.** Ehrenberg
neurologist.. **11.** Krafft-Ebing
pathologist.. **6.** Eberth
philologist.. **5.** Grimm, Heyne
philosopher.. **4.** Kant, Marx **5.** Hegel
  6. Engels, Fichte, Herder **7.** Liebniz
  8. Schlegel **9.** Feuerbach
  12. Schopenhauer
physicist.. **3.** Ohm **5.** Weber (Wilhelm)
  6. Planck **10.** Fahrenheit
poet.. **5.** Heine, Rilke **6.** Goethe
  9. Holderlin
president (first).. **5.** Ebert
socialist.. **10.** Liebknecht
sociologist.. **5.** Weber (Max)
teller of tall tales.. **10.** Munchausen
  (Baron)
theologian.. **6.** Luther
Germany...
capital.. **6.** Berlin
capital, former.. **4.** Bonn (W Ger)
  6. Berlin (E Ger)
city.. **5.** Essen, Halle, Mainz **6.** Bremen
  7. Cologne, Dresden, Hamburg, Leipzig,
  Munster **9.** Frankfurt, Nuremberg,
  Stuttgart
coal region.. **4.** Ruhr, Saar
lake.. **8.** Konstanz (Constance)
mountain range.. **4.** Harz
mountain region.. **11.** Black Forest
  (Schwarzwald)
Nazi state.. **10.** Third Reich
region, annexed.. **7.** Sudeten
  (Sudetenland)
region, state.. **6.** Anhalt, Saxony
  7. Bavaria, Hanover, Prussia **8.** Saarland
  9. Rhineland, Thuringia **10.** Palatinate,
  Westphalia
republic.. **6.** Weimar

river.. **4.** Elbe, Main, Oder **5.** Rhine,
  Weser **6.** Danube, Neisse **7.** Moselle
  (Mosel)
secondary school.. **9.** gymnasium
germicide... **6.** iodine (iodin), phenol
  10. antiseptic **12.** disinfectant
germinate... **3.** bud **4.** grow **5.** beget
  6. sprout **7.** develop **8.** vegetate
  10. effloresce
Geronimo... **6.** Apache (Chief)
gerrymander (Polit)... **6.** divide (unfairly)
  10. manipulate
gesticulation... **6.** motion **7.** gesture
gesture... **3.** act **4.** gest (geste), sign
  5. sanna **6.** beckon, behave, motion
  7. perform, pretext **8.** carriage (body)
  11. gesticulate **13.** gesticulation
get... **3.** pen, win **4.** earn, hear, pain,
  take, trap **5.** beget, fetch, incur, learn
  6. attain, become, derive, induce,
  obtain, profit, secure **7.** achieve,
  acquire, capture, prepare, procure,
  receive **8.** contract, contrive, discover
  9. ascertain, determine **10.** understand
get along... **3.** age **4.** fare **5.** hurry
  6. begone, depart, manage, move on
  7. advance, prosper
get around... **5.** evade **6.** cajole,
  outwit, spread **7.** deceive **9.** circulate
  10. circumvent
get off... **5.** start, utter **6.** alight, depart,
  escape, go free **8.** dismount
get out... **4.** exit **5.** scram **6.** elicit,
  escape, reveal **7.** draw out, leak out,
  publish **8.** evacuate **9.** extricate
get over... **4.** move **5.** cover **6.** bridge,
  finish **7.** recover **8.** surmount **9.** make
  clear
Ghana, capital of... **5.** Accra (Gold
  Coast)
ghastly... **3.** wan **4.** grim, pale
  5. lurid **6.** dismal, grisly, pallid
  7. deathly, hideous **8.** gruesome,
  horrible, shocking, terrible **9.** deathlike,
  frightful **10.** cadaverous
ghost... **3.** Ker **5.** larva (Rom Relig),
  lemur, shade, spook **6.** daemon,
  spirit, wraith **7.** banshee (banshie),
  eidolon, phantom, specter **8.** phantasm,
  revenant **10.** apparition, glimmering,
  substitute **11.** ghostwriter, poltergeist
ghostly... **5.** eerie (eery) **8.** spectral
  9. spiritual
giant... **4.** huge, ogre **5.** Titan **6.** afreet,
  nozzle, thurse **7.** monster **8.** colossus
  9. monstrous **10.** gargantuan,
  prodigious, tremendous
giant (pert to)...
Biblical.. **7.** Goliath, Rephaim
crafty.. **5.** Cacus
Greek.. **5.** Atlas, Mimas, Titan
  7. Antaeus, cyclops
hundred-armed.. **9.** Enceladus
land, country.. **9.** Utgarthar
  10. Jotunnheim **11.** Brobdingnag
Norse.. **4.** Ymir (Ymer) **5.** Mimir
  6. Jotunn (Jotun) **12.** Utgartha-Loki
one-eyed.. **5.** Arges **7.** Brontes, Cyclops
  10. Polyphemus
primeval.. **4.** Ymir **12.** Utgartha-Loki
Rabelais'.. **9.** Gargantua **10.** Pantagruel

sea god.. **5.** Aegir

seer.. **5.** Mimir

strong.. **6.** Samson, Targan **7.** Antaeus **8.** Hercules

Teutonic.. **4.** Wade **5.** Aegir

thousand-armed.. **4.** Bana

three-hundred handed, many-handed.. **8.** Briareus

giantess (Teut Myth)... **4.** Norn

gibbed... **9.** castrated (cat)

gibber... **4.** chat, hump, talk (rapid) **5.** stone (loose) **6.** mumble **7.** boulder, chatter **8.** swelling

gibberish... **4.** talk **5.** lingo **6.** jargon, patois, patter **8.** nonsense

gibbet... **3.** jib **4.** hang **7.** gallows **9.** execution

gibbon... **3.** ape, lar **6.** wou-wou **7.** hoolock, siamang **10.** anthropoid

gibe... **4.** jape, jeer, jibe, quip **5.** fleer, flirt, flout, scoff, sneer, taunt **6.** heckle

Gibraltar...

named for (legend).. **5.** Gobir

ruled by.. **12.** Great Britain

site.. **5.** Spain (coast)

giddy... **4.** reel **5.** dizzy, tipsy, whirl **6.** fickle **7.** flighty **8.** gyratory, heedless **9.** delirious **14.** scatterbrained

gift... **4.** alms, bent, boon, dole, free **5.** bribe, grant, knack, token **6.** legacy, talent **7.** aptness, faculty, largess (largesse), present **8.** aptitude, blessing, donation, gratuity **9.** endowment, lagniappe (lagnappe), readiness **11.** serendipity **12.** contribution

gifted... **7.** endowed **8.** talented

gigantic... **4.** huge **5.** giant, large, titan **7.** immense, mammoth **8.** colossal, enormous **9.** colossean, monstrous **10.** prodigious

giggle... **5.** laugh (silly), te-hee **6.** tee-hee, titter **7.** chuckle, snicker, snigger

Gila monster... **4.** Gila **6.** lizard

gild... **4.** coat, lure **5.** adorn, paint, tempt **7.** aureate, falsify **8.** brighten **9.** embellish

gilding... **4.** gilt, gold **6.** ormolu **7.** coating **8.** ornament, painting

gill... **5.** brook, leach, organ, penny **6.** tipple, valley, wattle **7.** measure **10.** sweetheart

gimcrack... **3.** fob, toy **5.** showy **6.** bauble, gewgaw, paltry, trifle **7.** trinket **8.** trumpery, whimwham **15.** Jack-of-all-trades

gimlet... **3.** awl **4.** tool **5.** drink (mixed) **6.** wimble

gimp... **5.** orris (upholstery) **6.** fabric, thread **7.** galloon **8.** fishline, trimming

gin... **4.** game, sloe, tool, trap, whim **5.** snare, trick **6.** device, liquor, scheme, thresh **7.** machine **8.** artifice, schnapps **11.** contrivance

ginger... **3.** pep **5.** color **6.** Asarum, energy, lively, mettle, spirit **8.** pungency, Zingiber **9.** rootstalk

gingerbread... **4.** cake **5.** money **6.** flimsy, frills, wealth **8.** ornament (tawdry) **11.** superfluity

gingerly... **6.** warily **7.** charily **9.** carefully, finically, guardedly **10.** cautiously

12. fastidiously

gingham... **5.** cloth **8.** umbrella (cheap)

gipsy... see *gypsy*

giraffe... **5.** okapi **6.** mammal, spinet **10.** camelopard **13.** constellation

girasol, girasole... **4.** opal **9.** artichoke, sunflower

gird... **4.** belt, bind, gibe, girt, sill **5.** brace, equip, scoff, sneer **6.** fasten, girdle, secure **7.** enclose, environ **8.** surround **10.** strengthen

girder... **4.** beam **5.** truss **6.** timber **7.** support

girdle... **3.** obi **4.** band, belt, cest, ring, sash **6.** cestus, cingle, circle, corset **8.** cincture, encircle **10.** cummerbund

girdle bone... **12.** sphenethmoid

Girdle of Venus (pert to)...

bridal.. **11.** power of love

palmistry line.. **8.** hysteria **11.** nervousness

girl... **3.** sis **4.** bint, chit, dame, lass, minx, miss **5.** filly, sissy, skirt **6.** damsel, female, giglet, hoyden (hoiden), lassie, maiden, shiver, thrill, tomboy **7.** colleen, damosel, fillock, ingénue, roebuck **10.** sweetheart **11.** maidservant

girlish... **4.** pert **5.** sissy **7.** artless **8.** immature, maidenly **10.** flapperish

girt... **4.** band **6.** fasten, saddle **7.** besiege **9.** encircled

girth... **4.** band, hoop, size **5.** brace, strap **6.** girdle, saddle **7.** measure **8.** encircle **13.** circumference

gist... **3.** nub **4.** core, crux, meat, pith **5.** heart, point (main) **7.** essence, meaning

give... **3.** gie **4.** hand **5.** endow, grant, yield **6.** accord, afford, bestow, confer, devote, donate, impart, remise, render, supply **7.** present, proffer, provide **9.** attribute, vouchsafe **10.** administer, elasticity

give (pert to)...

and take.. **11.** reciprocity

authority.. **7.** empower

away.. **5.** break, grant, marry, yield **6.** bestow, betray **7.** discard, divulge, succumb **8.** disclose **9.** sacrifice **10.** relinquish

back.. **4.** echo **5.** remit **6.** recede, remand, remise, retire, return **7.** replace, restore, retreat

birth to.. **4.** foal **5.** calve **6.** farrow, mother **9.** originate

expectation.. **7.** promise

forth.. **4.** emit **5.** blaze **6.** afford, exhale **7.** publish

information.. **4.** tell **6.** inform, report **7.** divulge, publish **8.** disclose **9.** advertise

out.. **4.** deal, emit **5.** exude, issue, print, utter (publicly) **6.** report, weaken **7.** declare, publish, release **8.** allocate, announce **9.** apportion, circulate **10.** distribute

prominence.. **4.** star **7.** feature **8.** headline

up.. **4.** cede, emit, fail, quit **5.** demit, waive, yield **6.** betray, disuse, resign, vacate **7.** abandon, despair, succumb

8. abdicate, part with, renounce, swear off 9. sacrifice, surrender 10. capitulate, relinquish

given . . . 5. dated, datum, fixed 6. stated 7. assumed, granted 8. accorded, addicted, bestowed, inclined, set forth 10. determined, disposed to

given (pert to) . . .
by word of mouth . . 4. oral 5. parol
name . . 7. surname
particularly . . 9. specified

given (to) . . .
experiment . . 7. empiric
expression . . 13. demonstrative
meditation . . 13. contemplative
suspicion . . 9. querulent

giving . . . 6. ceding 7. largess (largesse) 9. bestowing 10. conferring, liberality 12. philanthropy, presentation 13. administering

giving up . . . 8. yielding 10. abandoning, despairing 11. sacrificing 12. surrendering 13. relinquishing

glacial (pert to) . . .
deposit . . 6. placer 7. moraine
direction . . 5. stoss (opp to lee)
drift . . 8. diluvium
dust . . 10. kryokonite
erosion wall . . 6. cirque
mill . . 6. moulin
ridge . . 2. os (pl osar) 4. kame (Scot) 5. esker (eskar)
snow . . 4. neve

glaciarium . . . 4. rink (skating)

glacis . . . 5. slope 7. incline 13. fortification

glack . . . 4. fork (road) 6. defile, ravine, valley

glad . . . 3. gay 4. fain 5. merry 6. elated, joyful, joyous 8. animated, cheering, pleasing 9. animating, beautiful, delighted, gratified 11. exhilarated, well-pleased 12. exhilarating

gladden . . . 5. cheer, elate 6. please 7. gratify

gladdy . . . 12. yellowhammer

glade . . . 4. dell, nemo (comb form), vale 5. laund 6. valley 8. clearing 9. everglade, open space

gladiator . . . 6. fencer 7. lanista

gladiator's arena . . . 4. ludi

gladly . . . 4. fain, lief 5. fitly 6. freely 7. eagerly, readily 8. joyfully, properly 9. willingly 10. cheerfully, preferably

gladsome . . . 4. glad 6. blithe, joyful 7. festive, jocular, pleased 8. cheerful

Gladstone . . . 3. bag (travel) 4. wine 7. Liberal (Party) 8. carriage, Irishman 11. portmanteau

glad tidings . . . 3. joy 6. gospel 7. evangel

glamorous . . . 8. alluring, charming 10. bewitching 11. fascinating

glance . . . 3. eye 4. hint, leer, look, ogle, scry, skew 5. flash, gleam, glint, touch 6. allude, signal 7. glimpse

gland . . . 5. gonad, liver, lymph, ovary 6. spleen, thymus 7. adrenal, carotid, parotid, thyroid 8. pancreas, salivary 9. pituitary 10. suprarenal

gland (pert to) . . .
enlargement . . 6. ademia
full of . . 7. adenose

glandlike . . 7. adenoid 9. glandular
inflammation . . 8. adenitis
secretion . . 7. hormone
tumor . . 7. adenoma

glaring . . . 5. clear, plain 6. bright, garish 7. evident, flaring, obvious, staring, visible, vividly 8. apparent, distinct, flagrant, manifest 9. barefaced 11. conspicuous

glass . . . 4. lens, pony 5. glaze, purex 6. goblet, liquor, mirror, seidel 7. binocle, crystal, reflect, tumbler 9. barometer, binocular, hourglass, telescope 10. microscope, opera glass 11. stactometer, thermometer

glass (pert to) . . .
blue . . 5. smalt
cabinet . . 7. vitrine
component . . 6. silica
French for . . 5. verre
furnace, oven . . 4. lehr (leer) 5. bocca, siege, tisar 7. drosser (part)
jeweler's . . 5. paste 6. strass
like . . 6. vitric 7. hyaline, hyaloid 8. vitreous
material . . 4. frit (fritt)
mineral . . 7. hyalite 8. feldspar
molten . . 7. parison
mosaic . . 7. tessera
red . . 7. schmelz (schmelze)
scrap . . 6. cullet
sheet . . 4. pane 5. slide 7. platten
showcase . . 7. vitrine
volcanic . . 6. pumice 8. obsidian
worker . . 7. glazier

glass (type of) . . . 3. cut 4. milk, spun 5. crown, plate, Pyrex 6. ground, safety 7. Corning, frosted, Lalique, stained, Steuben, Tiffany 8. Sandwich, Venetian 9. Waterford 10. Depression

glass blowing (pert to) . . .
annealing term . . 4. fuse, heat
glass content . . 4. sand, zinc 6. potash, temper 7. soda ash
oven . . 4. lehr (leer)
rod . . 5. punty (pontil)

glass container . . . 3. jar 4. vial (phial) 5. ampul (ampoule, ampule), flask 6. beaker, bottle, carboy 7. matrass 8. test tube

glazier's diamond . . . 5. emery (emeril)

glazing machine . . . 8. calender

gleam . . . 3. ray 4. glow 5. flash, glint, gloze, light 7. glimmer, shimmer 8. radiance 9. coruscate 10. brightness

glean . . . 4. reap 5. sheaf (of hemp) 6. bundle, deduce, gather 7. collect, harvest, procure

glee . . . 3. joy 4. club, song 5. mirth 7. delight 8. pleasure 9. merriment 12. cheerfulness

glen . . . 4. dale, dell, vale 6. dingle, ravine, valley 10. depression

glib . . . 4. easy, oily 5. suave 6. facile, fluent, smooth 8. castrate, flippant, slippery 9. talkative 10. loquacious

glide . . . 4. sail, skid, slip, soar 5. coast, slide

gliding over . . . 7. lambent 10. slithering

glimmer . . . 3. bit 4. hint, leam 5. blink, flash, gleam, glint 7. glimpse, glitter

10. perception (slight)

glimpse . . . 4. view (quick) 5. flash, tinge, trace 6. glance, luster 7. glimmer, inkling

glisten . . . 5. flash, shine 7. glister, sparkle 9. coruscate

glitter . . . 5. glare, gleam, shine 7. glimmer, glisten, sparkle 9. coruscate, showiness 14. attractiveness

gloaming . . . 4. dusk 8. twilight 9. darkening 11. candlelight

globe . . . 3. map, orb 4. ball, moon 5. earth 6. sphere 10. hemisphere (half)

Globe, The . . . 7. Theater (London, first to play Shakespeare)

globular . . . 5. beady 7. globose 9. orbicular, spherical 10. orbiculate 11. globe-shaped

globule . . . 4. bead, blob, drop, pill, tear 5. minim 6. bubble 8. spherule

glochis . . . 4. hair (barbed) 7. bristle

glockenspiel . . . 4. lyra, stop (organ) 8. carillon 10. instrument

gloom . . . 5. cloud, frown, scowl 7. dimness, sadness 8. darkness 9. dejection, heaviness, obscurity 10. cloudiness, depression, melancholy, sullen look

gloomy . . . 3. dim, sad, wan 4. dark, dour, glum 5. drear, eerie, lurid, moody, murky 6. cloudy, droopy, lowery, morose 7. obscure 8. darkling, dejected, dolesome, downcast 9. darkening, depressed, tenebrous 10. depressing, foreboding, tenebrific 11. pessimistic 12. disheartened

Gloomy Dean . . . 4. Inge

gloomy person . . . 7. killjoy

Gloria . . . 4. rite 8. doxology

glorification . . . 6. praise 7. worship 8. doxology, honoring 9. festivity 10. apotheosis 13. jollification 14. sanctification

glorify . . . 4. laud 5. adore, bless, exalt, extol, honor 6. praise 7. elevate, worship 8. beautify, sanctify 9. celebrate

glorious . . . 3. sri 5. grand, noble 6. elated, superb 7. eminent, radiant 8. ecstatic, renowned, splendid 9. beautiful, hilarious 10. celebrated, delightful 11. illustrious, magnificent, resplendent 12. praiseworthy

glory . . . 4. fame, halo 5. bliss (celestial), boast, éclat, honor 6. heaven, nimbus (cloud of), praise, renown 8. grandeur 10. admiration, brilliancy, effulgence 11. distinction 13. glorification

gloss . . . 4. glow, note 5. color, sheen, shine 6. enamel, luster, polish, remark 7. burnish, comment, pretext 8. glossary, palliate 9. extenuate 10. annotation, brightness, commentary 14. interpretation

gloss over . . . 4. fard (obs), wink 5. blink, color 6. excuse 8. palliate

glossy . . . 5. glacé, nitid, shiny, sleek 6. luster, sheeny, smooth 7. radiant, shining 8. lustrous, polished 10. reflecting

glove . . . 3. mit 4. mitt 5. trank (shaped) 6. boxing, ceatus, mitten 7. gantlet

8. gauntlet 12. mousquetaire

glow . . . 4. burn 5. ardor, flame, flush, glean, shine 6. beauty, redden 7. redness 9. eloquence 10. luminosity 13. incandescence

glower . . . 4. gaze 5. glare, scowl, stare

glowing . . . 3. red 4. warm 5. drunk 6. ardent, cadent 7. burning, excited, fervent, flushed 8. eloquent, luminous 9. beautiful 12. enthusiastic

glucose . . . 5. rutin, sugar 8. dextrose

glue . . . 3. fix 4. join 5. paste, stick 6. adhere, cement, fasten, sizing 7. gelatin 8. adhesive, fastener 9. viscosity

glum . . . 3. sad 5. moody 6. dismal, gloomy, sullen 8. frowning

glut . . . 4. cloy, fill, sate 5. gorge, stuff 6. pamper 7. engorge, satiate, satisfy, surfeit 8. overfill, overload, plethora, saturate

gluten . . . 3. gum 4. glue 6. fibrin 7. gliadin 8. adhesive

glutinous . . . 4. sizy 5. gluey 6. viscid 8. adhesive

glutton . . . 6. rascal, wretch 7. epicure 8. gourmand 9. cormorant, scoundrel, wolverine 11. gormandizer, greedy eater

gluttony . . . 5. greed 7. edacity 8. voracity 12. intemperance 13. voraciousness

glycerine machine man . . . 8. effetman

gnar, gnarr (of dogs) . . . 5. growl, snarl

gnarl . . . 4. knot 5. growl, snarl, twist 6. tangle 7. contort, distort, roughen 10. contortion 12. protuberance (tree)

gnarled . . . 5. rough 6. knotty, rugged 7. complex, knotted, twisted 12. cross-grained

gnash . . . 4. bite 5. grate, grind (teeth)

gnat . . . 3. fly 5. nidge 6. insect 8. mosquito

gnaw . . . 3. eat 4. bite, chew 5. grind, waste 6. rankle 7. corrode 8. wear away

gnede . . . 6. scanty 7. lacking, miserly, sparing

gnib . . . 5. ready, sharp 6. clever

gnome . . . 3. elf, imp, saw 5. bodie, bogey, dwarf, maxim, nisse 6. goblin, kobold, sprite 8. aphorism

gnomic . . . 8. didactic 10. aphoristic

gnomic poets (Gr) . . . 5. Solon 8. Theognis (of Megara) 10. Phocylides (of Miletus)

gnostic . . . 4. wise 6. shrewd 7. knowing 9. sagacious

Gnostic . . . 6. Ophite 7. Abraxas (Abrasax), Sethite

gnu . . . 6. kokoon 8. antelope

go . . . 3. act, die, gae, run 4. fail, fare, game, move, pass, turn, walk, wane, wend, work 5. leave, sally 6. betake, decamp, depart, elapse, embark, energy, extend, result, retire, travel, weaken 7. advance, entrain, journey, proceed 8. continue, diminish, withdraw 9. eventuate, harmonize

go (pert to) . . .
around . . 6. detour 7. circuit 8. surround
ashore . . 4. land 9. disembark

astray . . **3.** err
at . . **6.** attack **9.** undertake
away . . **4.** exit, scat, shoo **5.** scoot,
scram **6.** begone, depart **9.** disappear
back . . **3.** ebb **6.** recede, repass, retire,
return, revert
7. regress, retrace
before . . **7.** precede **8.** antecede
11. participate
down, under . . **4.** fail, sink **7.** capsize,
descend, founder, succumb, undergo
8. submerge **11.** deteriorate
easily . . **4.** lope **5.** amble
furtively . . **5.** steal **6.** tiptoe
over . . **5.** renew **6.** revise **7.** retrace
8. rehearse, traverse **9.** backtrack,
re-examine
through . . **4.** pass **5.** spend **6.** suffer
7. exhaust (fortune), persist, undergo
9. persevere **10.** experience
up . . **4.** fail, rise **5.** arise, raise **6.** ascend
with . . **4.** suit **5.** agree, court **6.** accord
8. coincide **9.** accompany
10. understand
goa . . . **8.** antelope (Tibet)
goad . . . **3.** egg **4.** poke, prod, prog, spur,
urge **5.** ankus (elephant), decoy, impel,
prick, sting, thorn, valet (manège)
6. incite **7.** inflame **8.** irritate, stimulus
9. incentive
goal . . . **3.** aim, end **4.** base, fate, home,
mark **5.** bourn (bourne), Mecca, reach,
score, Thule (Myth) **6.** object **7.** purpose
9. objective **11.** destination
goanna . . . **6.** iguana, lizard **7.** monitor
goat . . . **4.** buck, dupe **5.** brown **6.** engine,
lecher **9.** scapegoat **13.** laughingstock
goat (pert to) . . .
astronomy . . **9.** Capricorn
fig . . **8.** caprifig
fish . . **6.** mullet
get one's . . **3.** irk, vex **4.** rile **5.** pique
6. nettle
god . . **3.** Pan
haircloth . . **5.** Tibet (Thibet) **6.** camlet
hair cord (Bedouin) . . **4.** agal
goat (type of) . . . **3.** kid, ram, tur, zac
4. ibex, tahr, urus **5.** Capra, goral,
pasan (pasang), serow, takin **6.** Alpine,
Angora, chamal, Jemlah, mammal
7. aurochs, markhor **8.** Cashmere,
ruminant
goatsucker . . . **4.** bird **7.** dorhawk, grinder
9. nighthawk **12.** whippoorwill
gob . . . **4.** lump, mass **5.** choke, mouth
6. sailor **8.** mouthful, quantity
goby . . . **4.** fish, mapo
go-by . . . **4.** snub **7.** evasion, passing
13. circumvention
god (Myth, Relig) . . .
Babylonian . . **2.** Zu **3.** Anu, Sin **4.** Adad,
Enzu, Nama, Nebo (Nebu) **5.** Aruru,
Cirru, Dagan, Nintu **8.** Ningirsu
10. Ninkhursag **11.** Ningishzida
Celtic . . **6.** Aengus
Cymric . . **4.** Lleu (Llew)
Egyptian . . **2.** Ra **3.** Bes, Dis, Geb
(Keb), Min, Seb **4.** Amen, Amon, Ptah
5. Horus, Thoth **6.** Dhouti, Osiris
false . . **4.** Baal, idol **6.** Mammon
Greek . . **4.** Ares, Zeus **5.** Comus, Hymen,

Momus, Pluto **6.** Hermes, Somnus
7. Bacchus **8.** Dionysus
Hebrew . . **6.** Yahweh (Jahveh, Jahweh,
Yahveh)
Hindu . . **4.** Agni, Deva, Kama, Siva
(Shiva) **6.** Varuna
household . . **3.** Lar **5.** Lares **6.** Penate
Irish . . **5.** Dagda (pagan)
love of, for . . **5.** piety **6.** bhakti
9. theophile
Muslim . . **5.** Allah
Norse . . **2.** Er, Ve **3.** Tyr, Ull, Van
4. Loki, Odin, Thor, Ymir **5.** Aesir,
Donar, Vanir, Wodin
Roman . . **4.** Jove **5.** Comus, Janus, Orcus
7. Bacchus, Mercury **8.** Dis pater
Semitic . . **5.** Hadad **6.** Nergal
Supreme . . **3.** Dei, Deo, Dio **4.** Deus,
Soul, Zeus **6.** Elohim, Spirit **12.** Infinite
Mind, Supreme Being
Teutonic . . **3.** Tiu **4.** Hoth
god (of) . . .
agriculture . . **4.** Nebo **6.** Faunus
beauty . . **6.** Aengus (Oengus)
beginnings, creation . . **4.** Ptah, Zeus
5. Janus **6.** Varuna
commerce . . **5.** Vanir **7.** Mercury
darkness, evil . . **3.** Set, Sin **6.** Nergal
day . . **5.** Horus
dead . . **5.** Orcus **6.** Osiris
discord . . **4.** Loki
earth . . **3.** Geb (Keb), Seb **5.** Dagan
east wind . . **5.** Eurus
evil . . **2.** Zu **3.** Set, Sin **6.** Nergal
fate . . **5.** Moira (Moera)
fire . . **4.** Agni **5.** Girru **6.** Vulcan
flocks . . **3.** Pan
January . . **5.** Janus
joy . . **5.** Comus
justice . . **7.** Forseti (Forsete)
law . . **5.** Zeus
lightning . . **4.** Agni
love . . **4.** Amor, Ares, Eros, Kama
5. Bhaga, Cupid **6.** Aengus (Oengus)
March . . **4.** Mars
marriage . . **5.** Hymen
medicine . . **11.** Ningishzida
mountains . . **5.** Atlas **7.** Olympus
music . . **6.** Apollo
Northmen . . **5.** Aesir
oceans . . **7.** Oceanus
poetry . . **5.** Bragi
ridicule . . **5.** Momus
sea . . **7.** Neptune, Proteus
sky . . **3.** Anu
sleep, dreams . . **6.** Somnus **8.** Morpheus
storm . . **2.** Zu **6.** Teshup
sun . . **2.** Ra (Re) **6.** Apollo, Nergal
thunder . . **4.** Thor **7.** Jupiter
Thursday . . **4.** Thor
Tuesday . . **3.** Tiu, Tyr
underworld . . **3.** Dis **5.** Pluto **6.** Osiris
7. Serapis **8.** Dis pater **11.** Ningishzida
war . . **3.** Ira, Tyr **4.** Mars **5.** Woden
8. Ningirau
wealth . . **5.** Bhaga **6.** Plutus
Wednesday . . **5.** Woden
wind . . **4.** Adad **5.** Eolus, Eurus, Hadad
6. Aeolus, zephyr **8.** Favonius
wine . . **7.** Bacchus **8.** Dionysus
wisdom . . **4.** Nebo **5.** Thoth **6.** Dhouti

woods . . **7.** Silenus
youth . . **6.** Apollo
goddess . . . **3.** Ate, Dea, Eir, Eos, Nox,
Nyx, Ops, Pax, Uni **4.** Apet, Eris, Fury,
Gaea, Hera, Isis, Leda, Maat, Nike, Nina,
Sati **5.** Aruru, Damia, Diana, Doris,
Epona, Freya, Hygea, Irene, Pakht,
Salus, Venus, Vesta **6.** Allatu, Athena,
Aurora, Cybele, Hecate, Hestia, Ningal,
Pietho, Selene, Semele, Tellus, Vacuna
7. Artemis, Demeter, Minerva, Parvati
9. Aphrodite, Eumenides, Mnemosyne
10. Persephone, Proserpina
goddess of . . .
agriculture . . **3.** Ops **7.** Demeter
arts . . **6.** Athena, Pallas
beauty . . **3.** Sri **5.** Freya, Venus
7. Lakshmi
dawn . . **3.** Eos **5.** Ushas **6.** Aurora,
Matuta
destiny . . **4.** Fate **5.** Moira, Parca
discord . . **3.** Ate **4.** Eris
earth . . **4.** Gaea **5.** Aruru **6.** Ishtar, Tellus
Eskimos . . **5.** Sedna
fertility . . **4.** Isis **7.** Demeter
fire . . **6.** Hestia
fortune . . **5.** Tyche
freedom . . **7.** Feronia
fruit . . **6.** Pomona
grain, harvest . . **3.** Ops **5.** Ceres
Hawaiians . . **4.** Pele
healing . . **3.** Eir **4.** Gula
health . . **5.** Damia, Hygea, Salus
hearth . . **5.** Vesta
history . . **4.** Saga
horses . . **5.** Epona
hunt . . **5.** Diana **6.** Vacuna
infatuation . . **3.** Ate
justice . . **7.** Nemesis
light . . **6.** Lucina
love . . **5.** Venus **6.** Ishtar **9.** Aphrodite
magic, witchcraft . . **6.** Hecate
marriage . . **4.** Hera
maternity . . **4.** Apet
mischief . . **3.** Ate **4.** Eris
moon . . **4.** Luna **5.** Diana **6.** Phoebe,
Selene (Selena)
mother of the gods . . **4.** Rhea
nature . . **4.** Rhea **5.** Nymph **6.** Cybele
night . . **3.** Nox, Nyx
peace . . **3.** Pax **5.** Irene **6.** Athena
poetry . . **5.** Erato
rainbows . . **4.** Iris
sea . . **5.** Doris
seasons . . **5.** Horae
summer . . **6.** Aestus
sun . . **5.** Pakht (Pacht)
trees . . **6.** Pomona
truth . . **4.** Maat
underworld . . **4.** Fury **6.** Allatu
10. Persephone, Proserpina
vengeance . . **3.** Ara, Ate **7.** Nemesis
victory . . **4.** Nike
virtue . . **5.** Fides
war . . **5.** Anath, Bella
wealth . . **3.** Sri **7.** Lakshmi
wisdom . . **6.** Athena **7.** Minerva
youth . . **4.** Hebe
Godforsaken . . . **6.** vacant **7.** forlorn
8. desolate, wretched **9.** neglected
godly . . . **5.** pious **6.** devout, divine

7. saintly **9.** religious, righteous
godmother . . . **6.** cummer (kimmer)
7. sponsor
God's . . .
abode . . **7.** Olympus
acre . . **10.** churchyard
board . . **14.** communion table
country . . **4.** home **8.** homeland
9. Vaterland **10.** fatherland
cupbearer . . **8.** Ganymede
fluid (vein) . . **5.** ichor (icor)
food . . **8.** ambrosia
gods, The (pert to) . . .
death of . . **9.** theoktony
marriage of . . **8.** theogamy
messenger of . . **6.** Hermes
mother of . . **4.** Rhea
Twilight of . . **8.** Ragnarok
worship of . . **9.** theolatry
Goetae . . . **7.** wizards (anc) **9.** sorcerers
14. thaumaturgists
Goethe (pert to) . . .
home . . **6.** Weimar (Ger)
masterpiece . . **5.** Faust
talent . . **4.** poet **8.** novelist **9.** dramatist
goffer, gauffer . . . **5.** crimp, flute, plait
(lace, paper)
gog . . . **3.** bog **4.** stir **9.** agitation
Gog (Bib) . . . **5.** Ruler (of Magog)
goggle . . . **3.** eye **4.** roll **5.** state **6.** squint
11. roll the eyes
goggler . . . **4.** fish (oceanic)
goggles . . . **6.** screen **7.** glasses **8.** blinkers,
eyeshade **10.** spectacles
going . . . **6.** moving, travel **7.** current,
working **9.** departure **10.** obtainable
11. in operation
gola . . . **7.** granary **9.** storeroom **11.** Indian
caste
golach, goloch . . . **6.** beetle, earwig
9. centipede
Golconda . . . **6.** wealth **8.** rich mine
gold . . . **2.** Au **3.** oro **4.** gelt, gilt **5.** aurum,
color, lucre, metal, money **6.** riches,
wealth **7.** bullion
gold (pert to) . . .
alloy . . **4.** asem **6.** oroide
artificial . . **8.** Mannheim
assayer cup . . **5.** cupel
bar . . **5.** ingot
braid, lace . . **5.** orris
brick . . **7.** swindle
coin . . **5.** eagle **10.** Krugerrand (So Afr)
compound . . **6.** auride
containing . . **4.** doré
discoverer (US) . . **6.** Sutter (1849)
field (Bib) . . **5.** Ophir
fish . . **9.** shubunkin
fool's . . **6.** pyrite
gilding . . **6.** ormolu **9.** imitation
Heraldry . . **2.** or
King (Myth) . . **5.** Midas
land of (Bib) . . **5.** Ophir
like . . **5.** auric **7.** aureate
measure . . **5.** carat
Rush . . **8.** Klondike (1897) **10.** California
(1849)
seekers (Calif) . . **9.** Argonauts (1849)
11. Forty-Niners
symbol . . **2.** Au
vein . . **4.** lode

washing pan . . **5.** cupel
gold and silver . . **11.** noble metals
golden . . . **4.** gilt **5.** auric, blest **6.** blonde,
yellow **7.** aureate, aureous, halcyon
8. metallic, precious, valuable
9. Pactolian **10.** auspicious
11. flourishing
golden (pert to) . . .
Age . . **9.** Saturnian, siècle d'or
apple . . **3.** bel **4.** Eris (goddess) **5.** Paris
(giver) **6.** tomato
bird . . **6.** oriole
bough . . **9** mistletoe
Fleece seeker . . **5.** Jason **8.** Argonaut
Fleece ship . . **5.** Argos
rod . . **8.** solidago
goldenrod (pert to) . . .
genus . . **8.** Solidago
State Flower of . . **7.** Alabama
8. Kentucky, Nebraska
goldfish . . . **4.** carp **9.** shubunkin
Goldfish (Astron) . . . **6.** Dorado
golf (pert to) . . .
club . . **4.** iron, wood **5.** baffy, spoon,
wedge **6.** driver, mashie, putter
7. brassie, midiron, niblick
hazard . . **4.** trap **5.** stymy **6.** bunker
11. restriction
score . . **3.** par **4.** bogy (bogie) **5.** eagle
6. birdie
stroke . . **4.** baff, chip, fade, hook, loft,
putt **5.** drive, slice **8.** approach, mulligan
term . . **3.** ace, par, tee **4.** baff, fore
5. bogey, divot, eagle, green, links,
rough, slice **6.** birdie, dormie, sclaff,
stymie (stimy) **7.** fairway, gallery
Golgotha . . . **7.** Calvary **8.** cemetery
goliath . . . **4.** frog **5.** crane, giant, heron
Goliath (pert to) . . .
Bib . . **5.** giant (Philistine)
death site . . **4.** Elah
home . . **4.** Gath
slayer . . **5.** David
Gomorrah (Bib) . . . **5.** Sodom **13.** wicked
country
Gomuti palm . . . **5.** areng
gondola race (Venice) . . . **7.** regatta
gone . . . **3.** ago, off **4.** dead, left, lost,
past, yore **5.** since **6.** absent, passed,
ruined **8.** departed, past hope, vanished
9. forgotten **10.** infatuated
goober . . . **6.** peanut
good . . . **2.** eu (pref) **3.** bon, fit **4.** able,
full, gain, just, kind **5.** ample, godly,
moral, nifty, pious, sound, valid
6. benign, devout, expert, profit, savory
7. genuine, helpful, liberal, trained,
upright **8.** decorous, interest, pleasing,
salutary, suitable, virtuous **9.** admirable,
competent, enjoyable, estimable,
excellent, favorable, honorable,
indulgent, reputable **10.** auspicious,
beneficial, courageous, gratifying,
profitable, sufficient **11.** commendable,
well-behaved **12.** considerable,
satisfactory, stouthearted
good (pert to) . . .
bye . . **4.** ta-ta **5.** adieu, adios, ciaou
6. so long **7.** cheerio **8.** farewell
for nothing . . **4.** mean **5.** idler **6.** wretch
7. useless **8.** indolent **9.** worthless

11. rapscallion
health . . **5.** skoal **6.** prosit
management . . **6.** eutaxy
mighty . . **7.** skookum
ordinarily . . **8.** mediocre
spirit . . **6.** daemon **8.** Eudaemon
12. agathodaemon
tidings . . **6.** gospel **7.** evangel
will . . **5.** favor **9.** affection, readiness
11. benevolence **12.** friendliness
Good Book . . . **5.** Bible
goodness . . . **5.** piety **6.** virtue **8.** kindness,
validity **9.** godliness, propriety
10. excellence, generosity, savoriness
goods . . . **5.** wares **7.** ability **8.** chattels,
property **11.** information, merchandise
goods cast overboard, sunk . . . **5.** lagan
(lagend) **6.** jetsam **7.** flotsam
10. contraband
goose . . . **4.** bean, dupe, fool, gull, iron,
snow, tule **5.** Anser, brant, solan
6. Canada, gander, gannet, goslet
7. gosling, graylag (greylag) **8.** barnacle
12. white-fringed
goose (pert to) . . .
egg . . **4.** zero
grease . . **6.** axunge
group . . **6.** gaggle
pygmy . . **6.** goslet
relating to . . **8.** anserine
story character . . **5.** ganza
gooseberry . . . **5.** fabes (color) **6.** escort,
groser (groset), thapes **8.** chaperon,
feaberry
gopher . . . **5.** snake **6.** rodent **7.** burglar
8. squirrel, tortoise **10.** salamander
Gopher State . . . **9.** Minnesota
gore . . . **3.** mud **4.** dirt, dung, stab **5.** blood,
cloth (triang), filth, slime **6.** pierce
8. heraldry **9.** bloodshed, penetrate
gorge . . . **3.** eat **4.** bolt, glut, sate **5.** chasm,
gully **6.** canyon, coulee, defile, nullah,
ravine, valley **7.** choke up, overeat,
pitcher, satiate **8.** overfill
gorgeous . . . **5.** grand, showy **8.** colorful,
dazzling **9.** beautiful **10.** delightful
11. magnificent, resplendent
gorgon . . . **4.** ogre, ugly **7.** Jezebel (Bib),
monster
Gorgons (Gr Myth) . . . **6.** Medusa, Stheno
7. Euryale **9.** sentinels
gorilla . . . **3.** ape **4.** thug **5.** brute
6. monkey **8.** assassin
gorilla man . . . **9.** Du Chaillu (brought
ape from Africa)
gormandizer . . . **9.** chowhound
11. trencherman
gorse . . . **5.** furze **7.** juniper
goshawk . . . **5.** Astur **6.** tercel
gospel . . . **5.** faith, truth **6.** belief **7.** epistle,
evangel **8.** doctrine **9.** orthodoxy,
selection (Bib) **10.** revelation **11.** glad
tidings **12.** proclamation
Gospels (Four) . . . **11.** diatessaron
gossip . . . **3.** cat, eme, gup **4.** chat, news,
talk **5.** on-dit **6.** claver, gabble, norate,
report, tattle **7.** clatter **8.** idle talk,
quidnunc **9.** chatterer **10.** newsmonger,
talebearer
gossoon . . . **3.** boy, lad (serving) **5.** youth
6. garçon

got ... see *get*
Gotham ... **9.** Newcastle (Eng) **11.** New York City
Gothamite ... **9.** New Yorker
Gothic (pert to) ...
  alphabet .. **11.** Moeso-Gothic
  architecture .. **6.** French
  design .. **7.** writing **12.** architecture
  era .. **10.** Middle Ages
  people .. **4.** rude **5.** Goths **6.** fierce **7.** Teutons
  printing type .. **5.** Doric **9.** square-cut
gouge ... **4.** tool **5.** cheat **6.** chisel, groove **7.** defraud, swindle **8.** impostor **10.** imposition
Gounod's opera ... **5.** Faust
gourd ... **4.** pepo **5.** color, flask, melon **6.** squash **8.** calabash, cucurbit **9.** Cucurbita **11.** calabazella
gourmand ... **5.** eater (luxurious) **6.** taster **7.** epicure, glutton, gourmet **10.** fastidious, gluttonous, voluptuary **11.** connoisseur
gourmet ... **7.** epicure **8.** gourmand **11.** connoisseur
gout ... **4.** clot, drop **6.** blotch **7.** disease **9.** arthritis
govern ... **3.** run **4.** curb, lead, rein, rule **5.** reign **6.** bridle, direct, manage **7.** conduct, control, preside **8.** dominate, regulate, restrain **9.** influence, supervise
governess ... **4.** ayah **5.** nurse **6.** abbess, duenna **8.** guardian **12.** instructress
government ... **4.** rule, sway **6.** polity **7.** control, regimen **10.** management **12.** jurisdiction **14.** administration
government (pert to) ...
  absence of .. **6.** acracy **7.** anarchy
  centralized .. **12.** totalitarian
  church .. **9.** hierarchy **10.** heirocracy
  science of .. **8.** politics
  system .. **6.** regime
government by ...
  church, clergy .. **9.** theocracy **10.** hierocracy
  few .. **9.** oligarchy
  God .. **8.** theonomy
  holy body .. **9.** hagiarchy **10.** hagiocracy
  law .. **9.** nomocracy
  men .. **9.** andocracy
  mob .. **10.** ochlocracy
  no one .. **6.** acracy
  rich .. **10.** plutocracy
  seven .. **9.** heptarchy
  six .. **12.** sextumvirate
  slaves .. **10.** doulocracy
  ten .. **8.** decarchy (dekarchy)
  three .. **8.** triarchy **11.** triumvirate
  women .. **8.** gynarchy **11.** gynecocracy
  worst men .. **12.** kakistocracy
governor ... **4.** woon **5.** chief, nabob, ruler **6.** dynast, regent **7.** alcalde, decarch (of 10 men), viceroy **8.** decurion, director **9.** mechanism **10.** magistrate
gown ... **4.** robe, toga **5.** cloak, dress, frock **6.** chiton, clothe, cyclas, invest, kimono, mantle **7.** cassock, college, garment, matinee, soutane (Eccl), sultane **8.** negligee, peignoir **9.** nightgown
gozell, gozill ... **10.** gooseberry

gozzard ... **9.** gooseherd
gra ... **4.** love **5.** agrah **6.** liking **8.** fondness **10.** sweetheart
grab ... **3.** nab **4.** game (cards), take **5.** grasp, seize **6.** arrest, clutch, snatch, vessel
grabble ... **4.** feel **5.** grope **6.** grovel, sprawl **7.** harvest **11.** appropriate
grace ... **4.** fate, luck, note, tact **5.** adorn, charm, favor, honor, mercy, title **6.** beauty, become, bedeck, polish, prayer, virtue **7.** dignify, enhance **8.** clemency, easiness, elegance, kindness, reprieve **10.** comeliness, refinement, seemliness **12.** graciousness, thanksgiving
graceful ... **4.** airy, easy, feat **6.** comely, seemly **7.** elegant, fitting, tactful **8.** charming, debonair **9.** beautiful, courteous, sylphlike **11.** appropriate
Graces, The Three (Gr Myth) ... **5.** Aegle (Mother) **6.** Aglaia (Brilliance), Thalia (Bloom) **9.** Euphrosyne (Joy)
gracile ... **4.** slim, thin **6.** slight **7.** slender
gracious ... **4.** kind **5.** suave **6.** benign, urbane **7.** affable **8.** generous **9.** courteous, favorable
grackle ... **3.** daw **4.** bird, myna **7.** jackdaw **9.** blackbird
gradation ... **4.** step **5.** scale, steps **6.** ablaut, nuance, series, stages **7.** degrees **10.** graduation, succession
grade ... **4.** even, rank, rate, size, sort, step **5.** level, order **6.** assort, degree, school, smooth **7.** arrange, incline **8.** classify, gradient, graduate
gradual ... **4.** easy, slow **6.** gentle **9.** leisurely
graduate ... **4.** pass, size **5.** grade, taper **6.** alumna **7.** alumnus, promote, student **8.** shade off
graffito (scratched crudely) ... **7.** drawing **10.** scratching **11.** inscription
Graf Spee blown up ... **7.** Uruguay (1939)
graft ... **3.** dig **4.** cion (scion), join, toil, work **5.** ditch, fraud, labor, spade, unite **6.** boodle, fasten, inarch, trench **7.** bribery, implant, joining
grafted (Her) ... **4.** enté
Grail ... see *Holy Grail*
grain ... **3.** jot, rye **4.** atom, bran, corn, dram, food, grit, iota, malt, meal, mite, oats, rice, whit **5.** fiber, maize, scrap, spark, trace, wheat **6.** barley, millet, sesame **8.** particle
grain (pert to) ...
  Bible .. **4.** ador
  bundle .. **5.** sheaf **7.** sheaves
  chaff .. **4.** bran, grit
  cracked .. **6.** groats
  ear of .. **5.** spike **6.** ressum (rizzom)
  exchange (Finan) .. **3.** pit
  feeding on .. **11.** granivorous
  fungus, disease .. **4.** rust, smut **5.** ergot **6.** mildew
  goddess of .. **5.** Ceres
  ground .. **4.** meal **5.** flour, grist
  husks .. **4.** bran **5.** straw
  measure .. **6.** thrave
  mill .. **5.** quern

mixture.. **6.** fodder **7.** farrage
9. bullimong
small.. **7.** granule
spike.. **3.** ear **6.** rizzom
stack.. **4.** rick
storage, warehouse.. **3.** mow **4.** silo
5. hutch **8.** elevator
grammar (pert to)... **5.** parse **6.** gender,
simile, syntax **7.** diction, parsing,
prosody, synesis, wordage **8.** enallage,
language, metaphor, paradigm
9. accidence, etymology, phonology
10. conformity, declension, inflection
11. conjugation
grammatical case... **6.** dative
8. ablative, genitive, vocative
9. objective **10.** accusative, nominative
grampus... **3.** arc **4.** orca **5.** whale
6. killer **7.** dolphin **8.** cetacean
granada... **11.** pomegranate
Granada Moorish Castle site...
8. Alhambra (Sp)
granary... **3.** bin **6.** grange **8.** cornloft
10. repository, storehouse (grain)
grand... **4.** epic **5.** great, large, lofty,
money, noble, piano **6.** august, epical,
famous, superb, swanky **7.** eminent,
sublime **8.** gorgeous, majestic, splendid,
thousand **9.** dignified, grandiose,
important, sumptuous **11.** illustrious,
magnificent
Grand Canyon State... **7.** Arizona
grandchild... **2.** oe, oy
grandchild, great... **5.** ieroe
grandee... **7.** magnate **8.** nobleman
10. clarissimo
grandeur... **5.** glory **7.** dignity, majesty
8. elegance, eminence, vastness
9. greatness, immensity, sublimity
10. augustness **11.** stateliness
grandeval... **4.** aged **7.** ancient
grandfather... **4.** aiel (obs), avus
6. atavus **8.** gudesire
grandiloquent... **5.** grand, lofty **6.** turgid
7. pompous **9.** bombastic
12. magniloquent
grandiose... **4.** epic **5.** grand **6.** turgid
8. imposing **9.** bombastic, flaunting
12. ostentatious
Grandma Moses... **17.** Anna Mary
Robertson
grandmother... **6.** beldam (beldame),
granny, gudame **7.** grandam
(grandame), grandma **8.** babushka
grandparent (pert to)... **4.** aval
grandson... **6.** nepote
Grand Teton peak... **7.** Wyoming
grange... **4.** farm **7.** granary **9.** farmhouse
11. association (1867) **18.** Patrons of
Husbandry
granite... **4.** rock **5.** stone **6.** aplite,
marble, quartz **8.** feldspar **9.** pegmatite
Gran Quivira... **5.** ruins (mission)
16. National Monument (N M)
grant... **4.** cede, deed, enam, gift,
give, lend, loan, mise **5.** admit, allow,
bonus, jagir (jaghar), spare **6.** accord,
bestow, confer, demise, permit,
remise **7.** appease, concede, confess,
subsidy **8.** appanage, sanction, transfer
10. conveyance **11.** acknowledge

granulated... **5.** rough **6.** coarse
7. grained **8.** granular, hardened
12. crystallized
grape... **3.** fox, uva **5.** Tokay **6.** Malaga,
Muscat **7.** Catawba, Concord, Hamburg,
Mission, Niagara **8.** Delaware, grenache,
Isabella, Thompson **9.** Chasselas,
muscadine **10.** sweetwater
11. scuppernong
grape (pert to)...
cluster.. **6.** raceme
color.. **7.** blue-red **9.** cathedral
conserve.. **5.** uvate
cultivation.. **11.** viticulture
dried.. **4.** pasa **6.** raisin
family, genus.. **5.** Vitus **8.** Vitaceae
juice.. **4.** dibs, must, sapa, stum
military.. **4.** shot
pomace.. **4.** marc, rape
preserve.. **7.** raisine
residue.. **4.** marc, rape **6.** pomace
seed.. **6.** acinus
sugar.. **7.** maltose **8.** dextrose
grapefruit... **6.** pomelo **8.** shaddock
12. Citrus Maxima
grapevine... **4.** caro **5.** rumor **6.** canard,
report **8.** maneuver (wrestling), pipeline
9. dance step **11.** information,
underground
graph... **5.** chart **7.** contour, diagram,
drawing
graphic... **5.** clear, drawn, vivid **7.** written
8. engraved **9.** pictorial **11.** descriptive,
picturesque, significant
12. diagrammatic
grasp... **4.** grip, hent (obs), hold,
take **5.** catch, clasp, gripe, seize
6. clinch, clutch, gowpen (gowpin)
7. control **8.** handgrip **9.** apprehend
10. comprehend, understand
grasping... **4.** avid **5.** close **6.** greedy
7. holding, miserly **8.** covetous
9. rapacious **10.** avaricious, prehensive
11. acquisitive **13.** comprehending,
understanding
grass... **3.** eel, hay, Poa, rye **4.** cane, Coix,
crab, gama, herb, oats, reed, rice, rush,
tare, wire **5.** ankee, Avena, Briza, brome,
chess, goose, grain, grama, hedge,
otate, spart, spear **6.** bamboo, barley,
darnel, fescue, marram, millet, redtop,
sesame, switch **7.** alfalfa, Bermuda,
buffalo, esparto, Hordeum, Poeceae,
timothy **8.** mesquite **9.** blue-grass,
Boutelous
grasshopper... **4.** grig **6.** cicada, locust
7. katydid
grassland... **3.** lea, sod **4.** mead, veld
(veldt) **5.** llano, range, sward **7.** pasture,
prairie, savanna (savannah)
grasslike plant... **5.** sedge
grate... **3.** rub **4.** fret, grid, grit, rasp
5. annoy, chafe, grind **6.** abrade, scrape
7. network **8.** irritate
grateful... **7.** cumshaw (beggar's
phrase), welcome **8.** pleasing, thankful
10. gratifying **12.** appreciative
gratification... **6.** relish, reward
8. gratuity, pleasure **10.** indulgence,
recompense
gratified... **4.** glad **7.** pleased

gratify ... **5.** favor, grace, humor **6.** arride, foster, pamper, please **7.** appease, delight, flatter, indulge, requite, satisfy **10.** remunerate

grating ... **4.** grid **5.** grate, grill, harsh, raspy **6.** grille **7.** lattice, network **8.** strident **9.** partition **10.** irritating **11.** latticework **12.** nerve-racking

gratis ... **4.** free **6.** freely **9.** on the cuff **10.** for nothing, gratuitous, on the house **12.** gratuitously

gratitude ... **5.** grace **6.** praise, thanks **12.** appreciation, gratefulness, thankfulness

gratuitous ... **4.** free **5.** given **6.** gratis, wanton **7.** assumed **8.** baseless, needless **9.** voluntary **10.** groundless **11.** superfluous, unwarranted

gratuity ... **3.** fee, tip **4.** dole, gift, give, vail **5.** bonus, bribe **6.** bounty **7.** cumshaw, pension, present **9.** baksheesh (bakshish), buonamano, lagniappe (lagnappe), pourboire

grave ... **3.** pit, urn **4.** bier, tomb **5.** fosse (foss), sober, staid **6.** sedate, solemn, trench **7.** earnest, engrave, serious **8.** sermonic **9.** important, momentous, ponderous, sculpture, sepulcher

grave (pert to) ...
cloth .. **6.** shroud **8.** cerement **9.** cerecloth
coffin .. **4.** pall
comb form .. **5.** serio
mound (anc) .. **6.** barrow **7.** hillock, tumulus
person .. **10.** sobersides
robber .. **5.** ghoul

gravel ... **5.** geest, grain, stone **6.** baffle, defeat, refute **7.** calculi, erratic (boulder), pebbles **10.** meerschaum (color)

graven ... **6.** etched **7.** infixed **8.** engraved **10.** sculptured

gravestone ... **5.** stele (stela) **6.** cippus, marker, pillar **8.** monument **9.** tombstone **11.** sarcophagus

gravitation ... **7.** descent, gravity **10.** attraction

gravity ... **6.** weight **7.** dignity, sadness **8.** enormity, grimness, sobriety **9.** formality, solemnity **10.** attraction, importance **11.** earnestness, seriousness, weightiness **12.** significance **13.** momentousness

gravity law, discoverer ... **6.** Newton

gray, grey ... **3.** dim, old, sad **4.** aged, dark, dull, gris, obex **5.** dingy, hoary, polio (comb form), sober **6.** animal (gray), dismal, somber **7.** hueless, neutral, silvery **9.** cheerless **10.** achromatic

gray, grey (color) ... **3.** ash, bat, dun **4.** ashy, dove, iron, lead, mole, zinc **5.** acier, ashen, dusty, mouse, pearl, slate, smoke, steel, taupe **6.** French, Oxford, Quaker, reseda, silver **7.** cesious, dappled, grizzle **8.** charcoal, cinereal, gunmetal **10.** battleship, dapple-gray **13.** pepper-and-salt

graze ... **3.** eat, rub **4.** drab, rase, skim **5.** brush, shave **6.** browse, feed on, scrape **7.** scratch

grease ... **3.** fat, oil, tip **4.** daub, lard, mort, saim, soil **5.** bribe, smear, suint **6.** axunge **7.** fatness, fawning, lanolin **8.** flattery **9.** lubricate

greasy ... **4.** oily **5.** dirty, gross, thick **6.** smooth **8.** slippery, unctuous **10.** indelicate

great ... **3.** big **4.** good, huge, vast **5.** ample, chief, large, major, stout, whole **6.** famous, grande **7.** drastic, eminent, extreme **8.** intimate, numerous **9.** elaborate, important **11.** magnanimous **12.** considerable **13.** distinguished

great (comb form) ... **5.** macro, megal

Great (pert to) ...
Barrier (NZ) .. **4.** Otea (Isl) **9.** coral reef
Beyond .. **5.** grave **9.** afterlife, hereafter **10.** after world, The Unknown **11.** eternal home **14.** beyond the grave
Cham of Literature .. **13.** Samuel Johnson (Dr)
Circle sailing .. **10.** orthodromy
Commoner .. **4.** Clay, Pitt **7.** Stevens (Thaddeus) **9.** Gladstone
Divide .. **7.** Rockies **8.** Rocky Mts **9.** watershed (US) **14.** Rocky Mountains **17.** Continental Divide
Fire .. **6.** London (1666) **7.** Chicago (1871)
Lakes .. **4.** Erie **5.** Huron **7.** Ontario **8.** Michigan, Superior
Mogul .. **5.** Akbar (Hind) **7.** diamond
Names .. **6.** Hector **8.** Hercules, Lysander **9.** Alexander
Pyramid .. **6.** Cheops
Spirit (Ind) .. **4.** Mana, Zemi **5.** Wakan **6.** Manito (orenda), Pokunt
White Way .. **8.** Broadway (NY)

Great Britain ... **5.** Wales **7.** England **8.** Scotland **12.** Commonwealth **13.** United Kingdom **15.** Northern Ireland

greatest ... **6.** utmost **7.** extreme, noblest

greatness ... **9.** largeness **10.** importance **11.** magnanimity

Greco, Graeco (comb form) ... **5.** Greek **7.** Grecian

Greece ... see also *Greek*
ancient .. **4.** Elis **5.** Argos, Doris, Ionia **6.** Attica, Epirus, Hellas **7.** Argolis, Boeotia **8.** Thessaly
cape .. **5.** Melea **7.** Matapan
capital .. **4.** Elis (anc) **6.** Athens
citadel .. **9.** Acropolis
city .. **6.** Patras, Sparta **7.** Corinth, Piraeus **8.** Salonika
island .. **5.** Chios, Corfu, Crete, Samos **6.** Ithaca, Lesbos, Patmos, Rhodes **10.** Dodecanese (group), Samothrace
mountain .. **3.** Ida **5.** Athos **6.** Peleon, Pindus **7.** Olympus **9.** Parnassus
peninsula .. **6.** Balkan
river .. **4.** Arta **7.** Hellada **9.** Archelous
sea .. **6.** Aegean, Ionian
seaport .. **4.** Enor, Volo **5.** Corpu, Pylos **8.** Salonika

Greek, Grecian (pert to) ...
abbess .. **4.** amma
alphabet .. see *Greek alphabet*
altar .. **7.** eschara

architecture .. **5.** Doric, Ionic **6.** xystus (part) **10.** Corinthian
assembly .. **4.** pynx **5.** agora
avenging spirit .. **3.** Ate, Ker **6.** Erinys
boat .. **6.** caique
bowl (golden) .. **5.** depas
breath .. **6.** pneuma
chariot .. **4.** biga
church section .. **6.** andron, bemata
citadel .. **9.** Acropolis
city (Greek for) .. **5.** polis
commander (anc) .. **7.** navarch
commune .. **4.** deme, nome
contest .. **4.** agon (anc) **6.** Delian **7.** Pythian, Olympic **8.** marathon
courtesan (Athen) .. **5.** Thais
culture, literature .. **7.** classic **9.** classical
cup, bowl .. **5.** depas **6.** cotula
cupid .. **4.** Eros
dance (anc) .. **6.** hormos **7.** pyrrhic, strophe **9.** dithyramb
department .. **8.** nomarchy
dessert .. **7.** baklava
dish .. **8.** moussaka **9.** souvlakia
early .. **5.** Arius **6.** oecist
epic .. **5.** Iliad **7.** Odyssey
female worshipper .. **5.** orant
garment .. **5.** tunic **6.** chiton, peplos
gravestone .. **5.** stele
horse (talking) .. **5.** Arion
hospitality .. **5.** zenia
judge .. **6.** dicast
language .. **6.** Romaic
lawgiver .. **5.** Minos, Solon
magistrate .. **6.** archon, eparch **7.** nomarch
mistress .. **7.** hetaera (hetaira)
monster .. **8.** Minotaur, Typhoeus (100-headed)
note .. **4.** nete **5.** neume **6.** pneuma **9.** hexachord **10.** tetrachord
Old Testament .. **10.** Septuagint
platform .. **4.** bema **7.** logeion
poem .. **5.** Iliad **7.** Odyssey
portico .. **4.** stoa, xyst
sacred enclosure .. **5.** sekos
sacred object .. **6.** sacrum
sacrificial offering .. **5.** hiera **8.** sphagion
sandwich .. **4.** gyro
school .. **7.** Eleatic
serpent .. **4.** seps **6.** Python
slave .. **5.** Baubo, helot, iambe **6.** penest
soldier .. **7.** hoplite
song .. **5.** melos
sorceress .. **5.** Circe
spirit .. **5.** Momus (evil)
temple .. **4.** naos **5.** cella (part)
theater .. **5.** odeon
war cry .. **5.** alala
youth (would-be citizen) .. **7.** ephebus
Greek alphabet ... **2.** Mu, Nu, Pi, Xi **3.** Chi, Eta, Phi, Psi, Rho, Tau **4.** Beta, Iota, Zeta **5.** Alpha, Delta, Gamma, Kappa, Omega, Sigma, Theta **6.** Lambda **7.** Digamma (obs), Epsilon, Omicron, Upsilon
Greek Furies ... **6.** Alecto, Erinys **7.** Magaero **9.** Tisiphone
Greek god of ...
atmosphere .. **5.** Hadad
chief .. **4.** Zeus

dreams .. **8.** Morpheus
fire .. **6.** Vulcan
flocks .. **3.** Pan
heavens .. **6.** Uranus
love .. **4.** Eros
lower world .. **5.** Hades
ridicule .. **5.** Momus
river .. **8.** Eridanus
sea .. **6.** Nereus
storm .. **6.** Teshup **7.** Hittite
sun .. **6.** Apollo, Helios **7.** Phoebus
vegetation .. **8.** Dionysus
war .. **4.** Ares **8.** Enyalius
winds .. **5.** Eurus **6.** Aeolus
youth .. **6.** Apollo, Pothos (winged)
Greek goddess of ...
agriculture .. **7.** Artemis, Demeter
beauty .. **9.** Aphrodite
chase .. **7.** Artemis
clouds .. **5.** Niobe
dawn .. **3.** Eos **7.** Alcmene, Ariadne
discord .. **4.** Eris
earth .. **2.** Ge **4.** Gaea
fate .. **5.** Moira
fortune .. **5.** Tyche
heaven .. **4.** Hera
infatuation .. **3.** Ate
magic .. **6.** Hecate (3-headed)
memory .. **9.** Mnemosyne
moon .. **2.** Io **5.** Diana **6.** Selene
nature .. **7.** Artemis
night .. **3.** Nyx **4.** Leto **6.** Hecate
peace .. **5.** Irene
phallus .. **5.** Baubo
retribution .. **7.** Nemesis
underworld .. **6.** Hecate (Hekate)
vengeance .. **3.** Ara **7.** Nemesis
victory .. **4.** Nike
wisdom .. **6.** Pallas **7.** Minerva
youth .. **4.** Hebe
Greek Myth ...
character .. **5.** Niobe, Sinon **6.** Adonis, Gorgon, Rhesus **7.** Calchus, Icarius, Pandora, Phrixos **8.** Atalanta, Endymion, Meleager, Tantalus **12.** Erichthonius
deity .. **5.** Satyr, Titan **6.** Cronus
enchantress .. **5.** Circe, Medea
giant .. **7.** Antaeus **9.** Enceladus (100-armed)
huntress .. **8.** Atalanta
monster .. **8.** Typhoeus (100-headed)
nymph .. **5.** Oread **6.** Nereid
serpent .. **6.** Python
spirit (evil) .. **5.** Momus
Greek personalities ...
astronomer .. **12.** Eratosthenes
biographer .. **8.** Plutarch
counselor .. **6.** Nestor
dramatist .. **9.** Aeschylus, Euripides, Sophocles **12.** Aristophanes
fabulist .. **5.** Aesop
geographer .. **6.** Strabo
hero .. **4.** Ajax **5.** Talos **6.** Nestor **7.** Cecrops, Theseus **8.** Achilles, Odysseus **10.** Hippolytus
historian .. **8.** Xenophon **9.** Dionysius, Herodotus **10.** Thucydides
mathematician .. **6.** Euclid **10.** Archimedes
painter .. **7.** Apelles

patriarch .. **5.** Arius
philosopher .. **4.** Zeno **5.** Galen,
Plato, Timon **6.** Nestor **8.** Diogenes,
Epicurus **9.** Aristotle **10.** Heraclitus,
Parmenides, Pythagorus, Xenophanes
11. Anaximander
physician .. **5.** Galen
poet .. **5.** Arion, Homer **6.** Hesiod, Pindar
7. Thespis **8.** Anacreon **9.** Aeschylus
poetess .. **6.** Erinna, Sappho **7.** Corinna
sage .. **6.** Thales
satirist .. **6.** Lucian
sculptor .. **5.** Myron **7.** Phidias
statesman .. **8.** Pericles **9.** Aristides
green ... **3.** raw **4.** vert **5.** fresh, mossy
6. callow, praseo (comb form), unripe
7. emerald, verdant **9.** malachite,
unskilled, untrained **11.** flourishing
13. inexperienced **15.** unsophisticated
green (pert to) ...
back .. **4.** frog **11.** legal tender (US)
blue .. **4.** cyan, saxe **7.** sistine
comb form .. **6.** praseo
eyed .. **7.** jealous
famous .. **6.** Gretna (Scot)
film .. **6.** patina
gray .. **5.** olive **6.** reseda
pale .. **7.** celadon
pigment .. **10.** terre-verte
quartz .. **5.** prase
sickness .. **9.** chlorosis
tea .. **5.** Hyson
green-back herring ... **5.** cisco
Greenland ...
Bay .. **6.** Baffin
capital .. **8.** Godthaab
Danish word .. **8.** Crönland
explorer .. **9.** Frobisher (1576) **10.** Eric
the Red
natives .. **6.** Eskimo (mostly)
settlement .. **4.** Etah
strait .. **5.** Davis
whale .. **5.** right
Green Mt Boys' leader ... **10.** Ethan
Allen (1775)
Green Mt State ... **7.** Vermont
greenness ... **5.** color **8.** sourness
9. ignorance **10.** immaturity
11. gullibility **12.** inexperience
Greenwich time (London) ... **8.** absolute,
standard **16.** Royal Observatory
Greenwich Village ... **9.** Manhattan
11. New York City
greeting ... **3.** ave, how **4.** hail **5.** hallo
6. accoil, halloa, salute **7.** address,
welcome **8.** saluting **9.** reception
10. compliment, salutation
14. correspondence
gregarious ... **6.** common, social
7. affable **8.** sociable **12.** social-minded
13. communicative
grego ... **5.** cloak **6.** jacket **9.** greatcoat
Gregory ... **4.** Code (Rom law), Pope,
year **5.** chant, staff (Mus) **6.** church
8. calendar
grenier ... **5.** attic
grey ... see *gray*
grid ... **5.** grill **7.** grating, griddle, network
8. gridiron **13.** football field
grief ... **3.** rue, woe **4.** care, pain,
ruth **5.** abuse, dolor, trial **6.** mishap,

sorrow **7.** anguish, offense, remorse,
sadness **8.** disaster, distress, document
9. grievance, suffering **10.** affliction
11. bereavement, lamentation
grieve ... **3.** cry, rue **4.** erme, pain
5. mourn, wound **6.** lament, sorrow
7. afflict **8.** complain, distress
10. discomfort
grievous ... **4.** sore **6.** bitter, severe
7. doleful, heinous, intense **8.** terrible
9. sorrowful **10.** disastrous, oppressive
11. distressing, gravaminous
griff ... **4.** claw, glen **6.** griffe, ravine
griffe ... **4.** spur (Arch) **7.** mulatto
griffin, griffon ... **6.** charge (Her)
7. monster **10.** decoration
grig ... **2.** eel **5.** annoy, dwarf **7.** cricket,
heather **8.** irritate **9.** tantalize
11. grasshopper
grill ... **4.** cook **5.** broil **7.** griddle, network,
torture **8.** gridiron **10.** restaurant
11. interrogate **12.** cross-examine
grille ... **6.** window (ticket) **7.** grating,
network
grilse ... **6.** salmon **7.** botcher
grim ... **4.** dour, sour **5.** gaunt, harsh,
stern **6.** grisly, horrid, savage, sullen
7. ghastly, hideous **8.** horrible, pitiless,
ruthless, sinister **9.** ferocious, frightful,
merciless, repellent **10.** forbidding,
inexorable, relentless, unyielding
grimace ... **3.** mop, mow, mug **4.** face,
mock, moue, pout, sham **8.** pretense
10. distortion **11.** affectation
grimalkin ... **3.** cat **5.** vixen **6.** feline
8. old woman
grime ... **4.** dirt, smut, soot **5.** sully
9. blackness
grin ... **5.** fleer, smile, smirk
grind ... **3.** dig, rub, vex **4.** bray, grit,
mull, whet **5.** crush, gnash, grate,
study **6.** abrade, drudge, harass,
polish, powder, satire, school, squash
7. operate, routine, sharpen **8.** drudgery
9. comminute, masticate, pulverize,
triturate
grinder ... **5.** molar, tooth, tutor
8. sideshow **9.** announcer **10.** flycatcher,
goatsucker
grinding ... **6.** boning **7.** grating
9. attrition **10.** burdensome, irritating,
tyrannical **12.** excruciating
grinding (pert to) ...
mental .. **6.** boning **8.** cramming,
studying
stone .. **4.** mano **6.** metate, muller
9. millstone
substance .. **5.** emery **8.** abrasive
gringo ... **5.** alien **8.** American **9.** foreigner
10. Englishman
grip ... **3.** bag **4.** hold **5.** clasp, cleat,
ditch, drain, grasp, seize, spasm
6. clench, clutch, furrow, grippe, handle,
obsess, trench, valise **7.** control, illness
8. gripsack, handfast
gripe ... **4.** grip, hold, pain **5.** annoy,
brake, colic, grasp, pinch, spasm
6. clutch, harass **7.** afflict, control,
mastery, vulture **8.** complain, distress
9. complaint **10.** affliction, oppression
griskin ... **4.** chop, loin **5.** steak

grisly . . . **4.** grim **5.** harsh **7.** ghastly, hideous **8.** gruesome, terrible **9.** deathlike **10.** forbidding

grist . . . **3.** lot **4.** malt **5.** grain, grind **8.** quantity (bees)

grit . . . **4.** sand **5.** nerve, pluck **6.** gravel **7.** bravery, courage, Liberal **9.** sandstone **11.** persistence **12.** perseverance

grivet . . . **4.** tota, waag **6.** monkey

grizzly bear . . . **7.** Ephraim (hunter's) **15.** Ursus horribilis

groats . . . **5.** grain, wheat (cracked) **6.** cereal

grog . . . **3.** rum **5.** rumbo **8.** beverage **9.** firewater

groggy . . . **5.** dazed, drunk, shaky, tipsy **8.** unsteady, wavering **9.** tottering

groin . . . **4.** lisk **6.** inguen

groom . . . **4.** syce, tidy **5.** brush, curry, dress, preen, train **7.** hostler, servant, shopboy **9.** assistant, stableman **10.** bridegroom, manservant

groove . . . **3.** rut **4.** dado **5.** chase, croze, flute, scarf, stria, track **6.** furrow, rabbet, raggle, scrobe, sulcus **7.** channel, rifling, routine **8.** philtrum **10.** excavation **11.** canaliculus

grooved . . . **6.** fluted **7.** striate, sulcate **11.** canalicular **12.** canaliculate

grope . . . **4.** feel **6.** fumble, search **7.** grabble, grubble

groper . . . **4.** fish **7.** grouper

grosbeak . . . **5.** finch **8.** hawfinch

gros point . . . **4.** lace (Venetian) **6.** stitch (Aubusson) **8.** tapestry (Gobelin) **11.** cross-stitch

gross . . . **3.** fat **5.** obese **6.** brutal, coarse, earthy, greasy, impure, vulgar **7.** brutish, massive, obscene, sensual, witless **8.** flagrant, indecent, receipts **9.** aggregate, unrefined **10.** indefinite, indelicate, scurrilous

grotesque . . . **3.** odd **5.** antic, clown, freak **6.** unique **7.** awkward, baroque, bizarre **8.** deformed, fanciful **9.** fantastic **11.** incongruous

grotesque figure (Chin) . . . **5.** magot

grotto . . . **3.** den **4.** blue, cave, grot **5.** crypt, speos, vault **6.** cavern, recess **8.** catacomb

ground . . . **3.** bog **4.** acre, area, base, clay, clod, farm, land, moor, park, plot, root, soil **5.** basis, cause, earth, field, hurst, marsh, ridge, solum, swale, train **6.** belief, bottom, milled, region **7.** country, gritted, opinion, premise, terrain (terrane) **8.** initiate, instruct **9.** establish, territory, viewpoint **10.** background, foundation, substratum

ground (pert to) . . .
beetles . . **5.** Amara
berry . . **9.** cranberry **12.** checkerberry
grain . . **4.** bran, meal **5.** flour, grist
nut . . **5.** chufa, gobbe **6.** goober, peanut
squirrel . . **5.** Xerus **6.** gopher, hackee, rodent **8.** chipmunk **11.** spermophile

groundhog (pert to) . . .
American . . **6.** marmot
day . . **9.** Candlemas (Feb 2)
home . . **8.** Puxatori

termed . . **6.** marmot, rodent **8.** aardvark, whistler **9.** woodchuck **10.** whistlepig

groundless . . . **4.** idle **8.** false **9.** unfounded **11.** unwarranted **13.** unsubstantial

grounds . . . **4.** lees, park **5.** basis, dregs **7.** residue **8.** scruples

group . . . **3.** set **4.** band, bevy, clan, crew, gang, herd, pack, sect, sept, team, unit **5.** batch, bunch, class, clump, corps, flock, genus, order, panel, shift, tribe **6.** legion, troupe **7.** arrange, bracket, cluster, company, species **8.** assemble, category, classify, division **10.** assemblage **11.** aggregation

group (pert to) . . .
actors . . **6.** troupe
animal . . **3.** gam (whales), pod (seals, whales) **4.** herd, pack **5.** drove, flock, pride (lions)
beautiful women . . **4.** bevy
birds . . **4.** bevy, nest, nide (pheasants) **5.** covey (quail), flock **6.** clutch (eggs), flight, gaggle (geese)
celebrities . . **6.** galaxy
church . . **5.** laity **6.** clergy, parish **12.** congregation
fish . . **6.** school
followers . . **4.** cult, sect
insects . . **4.** hive **5.** swarm **6.** colony
musicians . . **3.** duo **4.** band, trio **5.** combo, nonet (nonette), octet (octette) **6.** septet (septette), sextet (sextette) **7.** quartet (quartette), quintet (quintette) **9.** orchestra
offspring . . **5.** brood **6.** clutch, litter
political . . **4.** bloc, ring **5.** junta, party **7.** machine
secret . . **5.** cabal
singers . . **3.** duo **4.** trio **5.** choir **6.** chorus **7.** quartet (quartette)
trees . . **4.** tope **5.** copse, grove, woods **7.** alameda, orchard, pinetum (pines)
witches . . **5.** coven

group (quota of) . . .
eight . . **5.** octad, octet (octette)
five . . **6.** pentad **7.** quintet (quintette)
four . . **6.** tetrad **7.** quartet (quartette)
nine . . **6.** ennead
seven . . **6.** heptad, septet (septette)
six . . **6.** sextet (sextette)
ten . . **5.** decad **6.** decade
three . . **4.** trio **5.** triad, trine **7.** Trinity
two vowels . . **6.** digram **7.** digraph **9.** diphthong

grouped . . . **7.** classed **8.** agminate, arranged, gathered **9.** assembled, collected, organized **10.** classified

grouper . . . **4.** fish **5.** guasa **6.** groper **8.** rock hind

grouse . . . **4.** bird **6.** repine **7.** grumble **8.** complain **9.** ptarmigan **12.** capercaillie

grouse (pert to) . . .
courtship . . **3.** lak
red . . **7.** Lagopus
ruffed . . **6.** Bonasa

grouty . . . **5.** cross, sulky **6.** crabby, grumpy **7.** grouchy

grove (pert to) . . .
living in . . **7.** nemoral

mango . . **4.** tope
pine . . **7.** pinetum
poplar . . **7.** alameda
sacred . . **5.** Altis (Gr), Nemus (to Diana)
small trees . . **5.** copse
grovel . . . **4.** fawn, roll **5.** crawl, creep
  6. cringe, crouch, shrink, tumble,
  wallow, welter **7.** debauch, truckle
  8. flounder
groveling, grovelling . . . **6.** abject
  7. fawning **9.** prostrate, truckling
  11. bootlicking
grow . . . **3.** bud, wax **4.** come **5.** raise
  6. accrue, expand, mature, thrive
  7. augment, develop, enlarge, improve,
  produce **8.** increase, vegetate
  9. cultivate
grow (pert to) . . .
dark . . **6.** darkle
dim . . **5.** blear
intense, profound . . **6.** deepen
thin . . **8.** emaciate
tiresome . . **4.** bore, pall
together . . **7.** accrete
worse . . **11.** deteriorate
growing (pert to) . . .
angry . . **8.** irascent
from without . . **9.** ectogenic
  10. ectogenous
in . . **6.** linose
on trees . . **10.** epidendral, epidendric
  11. xylophilous (fungus)
out from . . **3.** bud **4.** stem **5.** enate
  6. sprout
spontaneously . . **9.** adventive
together . . **7.** accrete, joining **8.** adhering
growing in . . .
clusters . . **8.** racemose
fields . . **8.** agrestal **9.** agrestial
  10. campestral
ground . . **9.** geogenous
mud . . **9.** uliginose
pairs . . **6.** binate
rubbish . . **7.** ruderal
snow . . **5.** nival
water . . **7.** aquatic
growl . . **4.** girn, gnar, rome **5.** snarl
  6. mutter **7.** grumble **8.** complain
growler . . . **3.** cab, can **4.** bass (black)
  7. iceberg, pitcher **8.** clarence
growth . . . **3.** bud, wen **4.** rise **5.** felon,
  shoot, tumor **6.** effect, result **8.** increase,
  swelling **9.** expansion **10.** vegetation
  11. consequence, development,
  enlargement **12.** augmentation
growth (pert to) . . .
from within . . **8.** endogeny
from without . . **9.** ectogenic
  10. ectogenous
fungus . . **4.** mold, moss **6.** mildew
marine . . **7.** seaweed
of wood . . **5.** copse **7.** coppice
  9. brushwood
premature . . **9.** precocity
process of . . **8.** nascency
retarding . . **9.** paratonic
grub . . . **3.** dig **4.** food, plod, root, spud
  5. larva, mathe, slave, stump **6.** assart,
  drudge, maggot, search **7.** plodder
  8. victuals
grubby . . . **5.** dirty, grimy, small

  8. dwarfish, infested, slovenly, toadfish
grudge . . . **4.** envy **5.** covet, spite **6.** hatred
  7. grumble **8.** begrudge **10.** resentment
grudging spender . . . **8.** tightwad
gruel . . . **4.** diet **6.** cereal, liquid **7.** disable
  8. porridge
grueling, gruelling . . . **6.** trying
  9. demanding, punishing, weakening
  10. exhausting
gruesome . . . **4.** ugly **6.** grisly, horrid,
  sordid **7.** ghastly, hideous, macabre
  9. deathlike
gruff . . . **4.** deep, rude, sour **5.** bluff,
  harsh, surly **6.** clumsy, hoarse, morose,
  severe **7.** austere, bearish, brusque
grum . . . **4.** glum, sour **6.** sullen **8.** gutteral
  13. harsh-sounding
grumble . . . **4.** fret, hone, kick **5.** growl,
  snarl **6.** grouse, mumble, mutter, repine,
  rumble **7.** maunder **8.** complain
guacharo . . . **6.** owlish **7.** oilbird
  10. goatsucker
Guam . . .
capital . . **5.** Agana
discoverer . . **8.** Magellan (1521)
idol, fetish . . **5.** anito
island . . **7.** Mariana
mountain peak . . **6.** Lamlam
port . . **4.** Apra
guanaco . . . **5.** llama (like) **6.** alpaca
guarantee . . . **6.** avouch, ensure, insure,
  surety **7.** endorse, promise, warrant
  8. guaranty, security, warranty
  9. agreement
guaranty . . . **4.** bond **6.** pledge **8.** security,
  warranty **9.** agreement, assurance,
  guarantee
guarapucu . . . **5.** wahoo
guard . . . **3.** van **4.** care, curb, keep, tend,
  tile **5.** tiler, watch **6.** bantay, bridle,
  convoy, defend, escort, fender, gaoler,
  jailer, keeper, patrol, picket, police,
  sentry, shield, warden **7.** defense,
  protect **8.** restrain, sentinel, watchman
  9. attention, protector **10.** cowcatcher,
  precaution, protection
guarded . . . **4.** wary **7.** careful **8.** cautious,
  defended, discreet, vigilant, watchful
  9. protected **10.** restrained
  11. circumspect, sentinelled
guardhouse . . . **4.** brig
guardian . . . **5.** angel, tutor **6.** helper,
  keeper, patron, warden **7.** trustee
  8. defender, tutelary **9.** custodian,
  protector **10.** mystagogue (Church
  relics)
guardian (Gr) . . . **5.** Argus (100-eyed)
  8. Cerberus (3-headed)
guardianship . . . **4.** care **6.** charge
  7. custody, tuition **8.** guidance, tutelage
  13. protectorship
Guatemala . . .
ant . . **5.** kelep
bird (sacred) . . **7.** quetzal (quezal)
capital . . **13.** Guatemala City
coin (gold) . . **7.** quetzal
fruit (avocadolike) . . **4.** anay
Indian people . . **4.** Inca
port . . **7.** San José **10.** Champerico
  13. Puerto Barrios
ruins . . **5.** Mayan

volcano . . **4.** Agua **5.** Fuego
gudgeon . . . **4.** bait, dupe, goby **9.** killifish **10.** allurement
gue . . . **5.** rogue **7.** sharper
guenon . . . **6.** monkey (long-tailed)
guerdon . . . **5.** crown, prize **6.** reward **8.** requital **10.** recompense
guereza . . . **6.** monkey
Guernsey . . . **6.** brandy, cattle, Island (Channel) **7.** garment
guess . . . **5.** fancy, think **6.** divine **7.** imagine, presume, surmise, suspect **8.** estimate **10.** conjecture
guest . . . **6.** caller, inmate, lodger, patron **7.** visitor **9.** inquiline (insect)
Guiana . . .
  British capital . . **10.** Georgetown
  Dutch (Surinam) capital . . **10.** Paramaribo
  French capital . . **7.** Cayenne
guide . . . **3.** con, key **4.** clew, clue, lead, rein, sign, sley **5.** order, pilot, steer, teach, tutor, usher **6.** advise, beacon, direct, dirigo, govern, guidon **7.** adviser, conduct, courier, marshal **8.** Baedeker (book), cicerone, director, polestar, regulate **9.** regulator
Guido (scale) . . . **2.** ut **3.** alt, A re, B mi, E la (highest) **5.** E la mi, gamut **7.** alamire
guild . . . **5.** hanse **7.** society **10.** fellowship **11.** association, brotherhood
Guildhall statue (London) . . . **3.** Gog **5.** Magog (1708)
guile . . . **5.** craft **6.** deceit **9.** duplicity, falseness, treachery **11.** furtiveness
guileless . . . **5.** naive **6.** simple **7.** artless, natural, sincere **8.** innocent
guillemot . . . **3.** auk **4.** coot **5.** murre
guilt . . . **3.** sin **4.** sake **5.** culpa **8.** iniquity, peccancy **10.** guiltiness, wickedness **11.** criminality, culpability **14.** impeachability
guilty . . . **6.** nocent **8.** culpable
Guinea, W Afr . . .
  capital . . **7.** Conakry (Konakri)
  city . . **4.** Boke, Labe
  export . . **7.** bananas **10.** pineapples
  government . . **8.** republic
  mineral . . **4.** gold **7.** bauxite **8.** diamonds
  people . . **6.** Fullah **7.** Malinke, Soussou
  tree . . **4.** akee
guinea fowl . . . **3.** hen **4.** keet **6.** turkey **7.** pintado **8.** pheasant
guinea pig . . . **4.** boar, cavy **5.** Cavia **8.** capybara
guise . . . **3.** way **4.** form, garb, mask, mien, mode **5.** cloak, cover **6.** aspect, custom **7.** fashion, pretext **8.** behavior **9.** semblance **10.** appearance
guitar (pert to) . . .
  Hindu . . **4.** vina
  like . . **4.** lute **7.** bandore
  octaves . . **5.** three
  Oriental . . **5.** sitar
  pitch (term) . . **5.** dital
  ridge . . **7.** samisen
  small . . **7.** ukulele
gula . . . **4.** cyma, neck, ogee **6.** gullet **7.** cavetto, molding
gulch . . . **5.** cleft, gorge **6.** arroyo, coulee, ravine

gulf . . . **3.** bay, pit, sea (landlocked) **4.** eddy **5.** abyss, basin, chasm, cleft, inlet **6.** vorago **7.** opening **9.** whirlpool **10.** separation (wide)
gull . . . **4.** dupe, fool, gray **5.** brick, cheat, cully, fraud **7.** cheater, deceive, defraud, mislead **8.** impostor
gull (bird) . . . **3.** cob (cobb), mew **4.** Lari, pirr, skua, tern, Xema **5.** pewit (laughing) **7.** Larinae **8.** seedbird **9.** kittiwake
gullet . . . **3.** maw **4.** tube **5.** gully **6.** throat **7.** channel, harness (part) **9.** esophagus
gullible one . . . **4.** dupe, fool **8.** easy mark
Gulliver, Lemuel (pert to) . . .
  brutes . . **6.** Yahoos (race of)
  character, story by . . **5.** Swift
  voyage . . **6.** Laputa **8.** Lilliput **9.** Houyhnhnm **11.** Brobdingnag
gully . . . **3.** gut **4.** wadi (wady) **5.** drain, gorge, gulch **6.** arroyo, gutter, ravine **7.** couloir **11.** watercourse
gum . . . **3.** ase **4.** chew, lerp (larp, laarp) **5.** elemi, myrrh, xylan **6.** acacia, arabic, chicle, conima, thwart, tupelo **7.** camphor, deceive, elastic, gingiva **8.** bdellium (Bib), mucilage **12.** frankincense
gum (pert to) . . .
  Africa . . **4.** kino **7.** catechy
  Asia . . **6.** Storax **8.** galbabum
  Australia . . **5.** tuart
  Central America . . **6.** chicle
  Egypt . . **5.** kikar
  India . . **5.** amrad
  Philippines . . **8.** galagala
  United States . . **5.** Nyssa **6.** tupelo
gumbo . . . **3.** mud **4.** okra (ocra), sail, soup **6.** patois
gumboil . . . **7.** abscess, parulia
gummy . . . **5.** lumpy **6.** viscid **7.** viscous **8.** adhesive, resinous
gumption . . . **8.** sagacity **10.** enterprise, initiative, shrewdness
gums . . . **3.** ula **6.** resins **8.** gingivae
gun . . . **3.** gat, rod **4.** iron, pump, roer **5.** Maxim, rifle, thief, tommy **6.** ack-ack, Archie, barker, Bertha, cannon, mortar, pistol, Rodman **7.** bazooka, carbine, firearm, Gatling, machine, shotgun **8.** amusette, ordnance, revolver
gun (pert to) . . .
  blow . . **8.** sumpitan
  caliber . . **4.** bore
  case (leather) . . **7.** holster
  chamber . . **5.** gomer
  cleaner . . **6.** ramrod
  cotton . . **5.** nitro **9.** explosive, pyroxylin
  mount . . **6.** turret
  platform . . **11.** emplacement
gunfire . . . **5.** salvo **6.** strafe **8.** enfilade
gunner . . . **10.** bombardier **12.** artilleryman
guppy . . . **6.** minnow **8.** Lebistes **9.** killifish
gurnard . . . **4.** fish **6.** rochet, Trigla **8.** dragonet, sea robin
guru (Ind) . . . **7.** teacher
gush . . . **3.** jet **4.** flow, pour, spew **5.** emote, spurt **7.** chatter **10.** outpouring **14.** sentimentalize
gushing . . . **7.** flowing **8.** diffused, effusive,

spurting **9.** exuberant **11.** sentimental
13. demonstrative

gusset . . . **4.** gore **7.** bracket **9.** abatement
(Her)

gust . . . **4.** blow, gale, scud, wind **5.** berry,
blast, storm **6.** flurry, squall **8.** outburst
10. excitement

gusto . . . **4.** élan, zest **5.** savor, taste
6. fervor, liking, relish **9.** eagerness
12. appreciation

gut . . . **3.** sac (silkworm) **5.** gully **6.** bowels,
catgut, defile, strait **7.** destroy, plunder
8. entrails **9.** intestine **10.** disembowel,
eviscerate

guts . . . **5.** belly, force, pluck **6.** vitals
7. courage, insides, stamina, stomach
8. backbone, gluttony **10.** intestines

gutta . . . **4.** drop, spot **5.** latex **7.** campana,
marking **8.** ornament

guttate . . . **7.** spotted **8.** droplike

gutter . . . **4.** rone **5.** brook, ditch,
drain, eaves, gully, siver **6.** cullis,
groove **7.** channel, conduit, scupper
11. watercourse

gutteral . . . **3.** dry **4.** burr **5.** husky, velar
6. hoarse **7.** rasping, throaty

guttersnipe . . . **4.** Arab **5.** gamin **6.** poster
9. ragpicker, sandpiper, vulgarian

guy . . . **3.** rod **4.** flee, rope, stay, vang
5. chaff, chain, guide **6.** banter,

decamp, effigy (Guy Fawkes), fellow,
person

Guy Fawkes Day . . . **13.** Gunpowder
Plot (Eng, Nov 5, 1605)

guzzle . . . **3.** tun **4.** tope **5.** drain, drink,
spree **6.** gutter, liquor, throat, tipple
7. debauch, swallow

gymnast . . . **7.** acrobat, athlete, teacher

gymnastics . . . **9.** exercises **10.** acrobatics
12. calisthenics

gypsy (pert to) . . .
book . . **3.** lil
devil . . **5.** theng
Dutch . . **8.** Heidenen
horse . . **3.** gri (gry)
Hungarian . . **7.** Czigany
husband . . **3.** rom
India . . **7.** Bazigar
language . . **6.** Romany
man . . **4.** chal
sea . . **6.** Selung
Spanish . . **6.** gitano **7.** Zincalo
Syrian . . **5.** Aptal
term . . **4.** calo **5.** nomad
woman . . **4.** chai (chi)

gyrate . . . **4.** spin **5.** twirl, whirl **6.** rotate
7. revolve

gyre . . . **5.** demon, whirl **10.** revolution

gyves . . . **5.** irons **6.** chains **7.** fetters
8. shackles

H

H . . . **5.** aitch, zygal (shaped) **6.** letter
(8th), symbol **8.** aspirate

haab . . . **8.** calendar (Mayan)

haar . . . **3.** fog

haba . . . **4.** bean **8.** lima bean

Habakkuk . . . **4.** Book (Old Test)
7. prophet

habble . . . **5.** brawl **6.** gabble, hobble,
uproar **9.** confusion **10.** difficulty

habeas corpus . . . **4.** writ **7.** summons
(you have the body)

habile . . . **3.** apt, fit **4.** able **6.** adroit,
clever, expert **8.** skillful (skilful), suitable
9. dexterous

habiliment . . . **4.** garb **5.** dress, habit
6. attire **7.** apparel, costume, raiment
8. clothing, vestment **11.** furnishings

habilitate . . . **5.** dress, equip **6.** clothe,
fit out **7.** entitle, quality (for teaching)

habit . . . **3.** rut, use **4.** garb, suit, vice,
wont **5.** array, dress, haunt, usage
6. attire, clothe, custom, joseph (riding),
nature **7.** costume **8.** clothing, habitude,
practice **9.** mannerism **10.** deportment,
habiliment

habitat . . . **4.** home **5.** abode, house, hovel
6. harbor, reside **7.** exhibit (museum),
lodging, station

habitation . . . **4.** ecad, home **5.** hovel
6. ghetto, warren (rabbit) **7.** lodging
8. domicile, dwelling, tenement
9. occupancy, residence

habitual . . . **5.** usual **6.** common, wonted

7. orderly, regular **9.** customary
10. accustomed, inveterate

habituate . . . **5.** enure, inure **6.** addict,
inborn, season, settle **8.** accustom,
frequent, inherent **9.** acclimate
11. acclimatize, familiarize

habitué . . . **8.** attender **10.** frequenter

hacendero . . . **6.** farmer **10.** proprietor

hache . . . **2.** ax **7.** hatchet

hacienda . . . **4.** farm **5.** abode, croft
6. estate **7.** revenue **13.** establishment

hack . . . **3.** cut, hew **4.** chop, jade, rent
5. coach, cough, devil, horse (rented),
sever **6.** drudge, mangle, writer
8. carriage, mutilate **9.** mercenary
11. chronometer

hackberry . . . **6.** Celtis **8.** hapberry,
oneberry **10.** sugarberry

hackee . . . **8.** chipmunk

hackle . . . **3.** fly (angling) **4.** comb, hack
6. shiner, temper **7.** feather, hatchel,
plumage **11.** stickleback

hackneyed . . . **3.** saw **5.** banal, corny,
stale, trite **6.** cliché **8.** timeworn
10. threadbare **11.** commonplace,
stereotyped **13.** platitudinous

Hades . . . **3.** pit **4.** hell **5.** abyss, limbo
7. inferno **9.** perdition **10.** lower world,
underworld **11.** netherworld

Hades (pert to) . . .
Babylonian . . **5.** Aralu
capital . . **11.** Pandemonium
ferryman . . **6.** Charon

god .. **5.** Pluto
guide .. **6.** Hermes
Hebrew .. **5.** Sheol **7.** Abaddon, Gehenna **8.** Apollyon
Hindu .. **6.** Naraka
mother .. **4.** Rhea
region, lowest .. **8.** Tartarus
river .. **4.** Styx **5.** Lethe **7.** Acheron
Roman .. **3.** Dis **5.** Orcus
hadj, hajj ... **10.** pilgrimage (Mecca)
haft ... **4.** ansa, grip, hold **6.** handle **8.** dwelling
hag ... **4.** Fury, goad **5.** crone, ghost, Harpy, vixen, witch **6.** beldam (beldame), goblin **8.** harridan, old woman **9.** hobgoblin
hageen, hagein ... **9.** dromedary
hagfish ... **5.** borer **6.** Mysine **7.** lamprey (lowest existing craniate vertebrate)
haggard ... **4.** bony, lank, lean, pale, thin, wild **5.** gaunt, spare **6.** wanton **7.** anxious, untamed **8.** harrowed, unchaste, wild-eyed **9.** deathlike, suffering, untrained **10.** cadaverous **11.** intractable, overwrought
haggle ... **3.** cut, hew **4.** hack, prig **5.** cavil **6.** chisel, dicker, higgle, palter **7.** bargain, chaffer, stickle, wrangle
Hague, The ... **7.** capital (Neth)
Haida (pert to) ...
famed for .. **6.** totems **7.** carving **10.** seamanship
people .. **11.** Skittagetan
hail ... **3.** ave, ice **4.** ahoy, call **5.** avast, greet, skoal **6.** accost, health, signal **7.** acclaim, address, graupel, pellets
hair ... **3.** cue, fur, mop **4.** lock, mane, seta, shag **5.** pilus, plume, tress **6.** thread **7.** bristle **8.** filament **10.** narrowness
hair (pert to) ...
accessory .. **3.** net, pin **8.** barrette
Angora .. **6.** mohair
band .. **5.** snood **6.** fillet
braid .. **3.** cue **4.** fall **5.** queue **7.** pigtail
cell .. **12.** Organ of Corti
cloth .. **3.** aba **5.** shirt **6.** cilice
comb form .. **4.** pilo
curly .. **10.** cymotrichy
disease .. **8.** dandruff, psilosis
dresser .. **7.** friseur (Fr), stylist
dryness .. **7.** xerasia
excessive growth .. **7.** pilosis
flaxen .. **5.** linus
horse's foot .. **7.** fetlock
intestinal .. **6.** villus
liquid for .. **3.** set **5.** spray **6.** lotion **7.** relaxer
lock .. **5.** tress **7.** earlock, ringlet **8.** lovelock **9.** dreadlock
loss of .. **8.** alopecia, baldness
of the .. **6.** crinal
remover .. **9.** decalvant, epilatory **10.** depilatory
straight .. **10.** leiotrichy
style .. **3.** set **4.** Afro, tete, updo **6.** hairdo **7.** chignon, cornrow **8.** coiffure
tuft .. **4.** coma **5.** beard **6.** goatee **7.** cirrose, Galways, Vandyke **8.** whiskers **9.** sideburns
wave .. **4.** perm **6.** marcel

wig .. **6.** peruke **7.** periwig
wooly .. **9.** ulotrichy
hairiness ... **7.** villous **9.** villosity
hairless ... **4.** bald **5.** acoma **7.** acomous, epilose **8.** depilous, glabrous
hairpin ... **6.** bodkin **8.** bobby pin
hairsplitting ... **9.** quibbling **11.** distinction **13.** hypercritical **14.** hypercriticism, overparticular
hairy ... **4.** noil **5.** pilar **6.** comate, comoid, comose, crinal, pilose, shaggy **7.** bristly, crinose, hirsute **8.** trichoid
Haiti, Haitian ...
bandit .. **4.** caco
capital .. **12.** Port-au-Prince
dance .. **5.** mambo
dictator .. **7.** Papa Doc **8.** Duvalier
discoverer .. **8.** Columbus (1492)
evil spirit .. **4.** baka (boko)
island .. **10.** Hispaniola **15.** Greater Antilles
language .. **6.** Creole, French, patois
liberator .. **9.** Toussaint
product .. **6.** coffee
sweet potato .. **6.** batata
hake ... **4.** fish **5.** idler, tramp **6.** loiter **7.** handgun **8.** kingfish
halberd ... **4.** bill **5.** frame (flogging) **6.** glaive, weapon (Mil)
halcyon ... **4.** bird, calm **8.** peaceful, tranquil **10.** auspicious, kingfisher
Halcyone (pert to) ...
changed to .. **10.** kingfisher
daughter of .. **5.** Aeolus
wife of .. **4.** Ceyx (Gr)
hale ... **3.** tug **4.** drag, draw, haul, pull, well **6.** hearty, robust, strong **7.** healthy **8.** vigorous **9.** strapping
half ... **4.** demi, hemi, part, semi, term **5.** share **6.** moiety **7.** divided, partial **8.** division, semester **9.** equal part, bisection **11.** imperfectly
half (pert to) ...
and half .. **5.** equal, mixed **6.** halved **7.** neutral
boot .. **3.** pac (pack) **6.** buskin
man, half bull .. **8.** minotaur
man, half horse .. **7.** centaur
mask .. **6.** domino
moon-shaped .. **9.** semilunar
nelson (wrestling) .. **4.** hold
stem to stem .. **8.** midships
turn (manège) .. **8.** caracole (caracol)
wit .. **4.** dolt **5.** dunce **9.** blockhead
Half Moon ship (pert to) ...
captain .. **11.** Henry Hudson
country .. **11.** Netherlands
first to sail .. **11.** Hudson River (1609)
Halicarnassus, famed for ...
Historians (Gr) .. **9.** Dionysius, Herodotus
monument .. **9.** Mausoleum (Tomb of Mausolus, 325 BC)
hall ... **4.** aula, room, sala **5.** entry, foyer, odeum (odeon) **6.** atrium, lyceum **7.** hallway, passage, theater **8.** corridor **9.** vestibule **10.** auditorium, passageway
hallow ... **5.** bless **8.** dedicate, sanctify, venerate **9.** celebrate **10.** consecrate
hallowed place ... **4.** fane, holy **5.** altar **6.** bethel, church, shrine, temple **9.** cathedral, synagogue

hallucination ... **4.** trip **6.** mirage
  7. chimera, fantasy **8.** delusion
  9. nightmare
hallucinogen ... **3.** LSD **4.** acid **6.** mescal,
  peyote **9.** mescaline **10.** psilocybin
  12. lysergic acid
hallux ... **3.** toe **5.** digit
halo ... **3.** arc **4.** aura, glow, nimb, ring
  5. glory, light **6.** areola, brough, circle,
  corona, nimbus **7.** aureole (aureola)
  8. encircle, halation
halt ... **3.** end **4.** camp, lame, limp,
  stop **5.** cease, check, pause, stand
  6. arrest, desist, hold up, maimed
  7. limping **8.** blockage, crippled,
  lameness **9.** mutilated **10.** standstill
halter ... **4.** hang, rope **5.** noose, strap
  6. hamper **7.** shackle **8.** cavesson,
  restrain **9.** hackamore
halting ... **4.** lame **6.** maimed **7.** limping
  8. spavined **10.** hesitating, stammering
halting place ... **4.** camp **5.** étape
  7. bivouac **10.** encampment
halved ... **9.** dimidiate
Hamburg, Germany ...
  color .. **5.** white **6.** yellow **7.** carmine
    11. carmine lake
  fowl .. **11.** Leghornlike
  fruit .. **5.** grape
  lace .. **6.** edging
  root (edible) .. **7.** parsley
  steak .. **4.** beef
hamiform ... **6.** curved, hooked
  7. hamulus **8.** aquiline **10.** hook-shaped
Hamilton (pert to) ...
  killed by .. **4.** Burr
  party .. **10.** Federalist
  secretary (lst) .. **8.** Treasury
Hamite (No Afr) ... **5.** Fulah **6.** Berber,
  Somali (Somal)
hamlet ... **4.** dorp, vill **5.** aldea (aldee),
  casal (casale), thorp (thorpe) **7.** grouper
  (fish), village
Hamlet (pert to) ...
  author .. **11.** Shakespeare
  country .. **7.** Denmark
  friend .. **7.** Horatio
  site .. **8.** Elsinore
hammer ... **4.** beat, claw, jack, maul,
  peen, tack, tamp **5.** gavel, kevel, madge,
  pound **6.** beetle, martel, oliver, sledge,
  strike, swinge **7.** belabor **8.** malleate
hammer (pert to) ...
  bird .. **8.** umbrette
  blacksmith's .. **6.** fuller, oliver
  bricklayer's .. **6.** scutch
  end .. **4.** poll
  face .. **4.** trip
  head .. **4.** peen **5.** shark
  medical .. **6.** plexor **7.** plessor
  out .. **5.** anvil, forge
  smite .. **5.** skite
  stone .. **5.** kevel, spall
hamper ... **3.** ped **4.** clog, curb,
  load, slow **5.** cramp, crate, maund
  6. basket, burden, fetter, hinder, hopple,
  impede, seroon **7.** confine, hanaper,
  manacle, shackle, trammel **8.** encumber,
  restrain, restrict **9.** container, embarrass
  10. impediment
Ham's son ... **4.** Cush

hamster ... **6.** rodent **8.** Cricetus
hamus ... **4.** hook **7.** process (Zool)
hanaper ... **6.** basket, hamper
hand ... **3.** paw **4.** fist, give, mano, palm,
  part, pass, side, till **5.** claut, grasp,
  index, manus, power, share, skill
  6. agency, worker **7.** ability, pointer,
  workman **8.** applause, tendency,
  transmit **9.** craftsman, handiwork,
  signature **10.** metacarpus
  11. handwriting, performance
  15. instrumentality
hand (pert to) ...
  back of .. **10.** opisthenar
  bag .. **4.** etui, grip **5.** cabas, purse
    8. reticule
  book .. **4.** tome **5.** codex **6.** manual
    9. vade mecum
  cuffs .. **7.** darbies **8.** manacles
    9. bracelets
  handful .. **4.** kirn **6.** gowpen **7.** maniple
    8. quantity
  measure .. **8.** fistmele
  me-down .. **4.** used, worn **5.** cheap
    9. ready-made **10.** secondhand
  of the .. **6.** chiral, manual
  palm .. **4.** loof **6.** thenar
  picked .. **5.** eleme **6.** choice **8.** selected
  script .. **5.** Neskhi (Neski)
  stone (grinding) .. **4.** mano
  without .. **7.** amanous
  writing .. **11.** chirography
  writing on walls .. **4.** doom, mene (Bib),
    omen **8.** graffito
handicap ... **4.** lisp, race **6.** burden,
  hamper, hinder, impede **8.** encumber,
  equalize, penalize **9.** advantage
  10. impediment, stuttering
  11. encumbrance **12.** disadvantage
handicraftsman ... **7.** artisan
handkerchief ... **7.** malabar **8.** mouchoir
  9. neckcloth **11.** neckerchief
handle ... **3.** ear, paw, ply, use **4.** ansa,
  bail, deal, feel, haft, hilt, knob, maul,
  name, toat, tote **5.** helve, pilot, snath,
  swipe, title, touch, treat, wield **6.** deal
  in, direct, manage, rounce, second,
  sneath, tiller **7.** control, operate
handle (pert to) ...
  awkwardly .. **6.** fumble, mumble
  carelessly .. **6.** cajole **7.** tweedle
  roughly .. **4.** maul **6.** bruise, injure,
    mangle
  shaped .. **6.** ansate
  skillfully .. **6.** manage **7.** control
    10. manipulate
hands (pert to) ...
  nautical .. **4.** crew, gang
  off .. **4.** don't, quit, stop **5.** taboo **6.** desist
    9. interdict
  on hips .. **6.** akimbo
  without .. **7.** amanous
handsome ... **5.** ample **6.** comely,
  heppen (dial) **7.** elegant, gallant, liberal
  8. generous, gracious, pleasing, suitable
  9. agreeable, beautiful **10.** jimpricute
  11. appropriate, magnanimous
  12. considerable
handwriting on the wall ... **4.** mene
  (Bib) **8.** graffito, upharsin
handy ... **4.** deft **5.** adept, ready

6. adroit, heppen, nearby, wieldy
8. skillful (skilful) 9. dexterous, versatile
10. accessible, convenient
hang . . . 3. sag 4. pend, rest, sway 5. cling,
drape, droop, hover, knack 6. cleave,
dangle, depend 7. execute, meaning,
suspend
hang (pert to) . . .
around . . 4. loaf, wait 6. loiter 8. frequent
back . . 3. lag 5. demur, loath 6. falter
9. reluctant
down . . 3. lop 4. lave 5. droop 6. depend
loosely . . 3. lop 4. flag, loll 6. bangle,
dangle
on, onto . . 5. cling 6. adhere, depend
9. persevere
over . . 6. impend
together . . 4. loin 6. cohere 9. co-operate
hanger-on . . . 3. bur 5. toady 6. heeler
8. follower, loiterer, parasite
9. appendage, dependent, sycophant,
toadeater (menial) 10. blackguard
hanging . . . 5. arras, drape, loose
7. curtain, pendant (pendent), pensile,
valance 8. downcast, pendency
9. execution, suspended
hanging (pert to) . . .
Eccl . . 6. dorsal, dossal (dossel)
Gardens of Babylon, builder . .
14. Nebuchadnezzar (Nebuchadrezzar)
ornament . . 6. bangle 7. pendant
stage . . 7. scenery
hangman . . . 8. carnifex 9. Jack Ketch
11. executioner
hangman's noose . . . 4. rope 6. hempen
hangnail . . . 6. agnail 7. whitlow
hangout . . . 5. joint 10. rendezvous
hank . . . 3. ran (twine) 4. coil 5. skein
hanker after . . . 5. crave, yearn 6. aspire,
desire, hunger 7. long for
Hannibal (pert to) . . .
accomplishment . . 8. Punic War (2nd)
father . . 13. Hamilcar Barca
native of . . 8. Carthage
rank . . 7. General (genius)
victory at . . 6. Cannae
Hanover, House of . . . 8. Victoria
Hanukkah, Hanukka . . . 7. holiday (Jew)
16. Festival of Lights (Bib) 17. Feast
of Dedication (Jew)
haphazard . . . 6. chance, random
8. accident, careless 9. orderless
haply . . . 9. perchance
happen . . . 4. come, fall, fare 5. evene
(obs), occur 6. arrive, befall, betide,
chance, mayhap 9. eventuate, transpire
happening . . . 4. fact 5. event (chance)
6. tiding 7. episode 8. incident, periodic,
sporadic 10. occurrence
happily . . . 5. fitly, haply 6. gladly
9. tactfully, willingly 10. blissfully,
cheerfully, gracefully 11. contentedly,
opportunely 12. auspiciously,
felicitously, prosperously, successfully
13. appropriately
happiness, science of . . .
11. eudaemonics
happy . . . 3. apt 4. cosh, glad 5. blest,
faust, lucky, ready, seely, sunny
6. joyful, timely 7. blessed, content,
fitting 8. cheerful 9. contented,

fortunate, pertinent 10. auspicious,
felicitous, propitious, prosperous
Happy Valley . . . 8. paradise (of Rasselas,
Andrew Jackson)
hara-kiri (Jap) . . . 7. seppuku, suicide
harangue . . . 3. nag 4. rant 5. orate,
spiel, spout 6. screed, speech, tirade
7. address, declaim, expound, lecture,
oration
harass . . . 3. din, fag, nag, try, vex
4. bait, fret, gall, haze, jade, raid, tire
5. annoy, beset, bully, chafe, grind,
harry, tease, weary, worry 6. badger,
bother, heckle, hector, molest, pester,
plague 7. agitate, disturb, hagride,
perplex, provoke, torment, trouble
8. distress, irritate 9. persecute, tantalize
harbinger . . . 4. host, omen 5. usher
6. herald 7. presage, shelter 8. fourrier,
harborer 9. informant, messenger,
precursor 10. forerunner
harbinger of Spring . . . 5. robin, tulip
6. crocus
harbor, harbour . . . 3. bay 4. cave,
port 5. haven 6. covert, foster, refuge
7. lodging, outport, retreat, shelter
hard . . . 3. fit 4. cold, dour, firm, iron,
mean 5. close, harsh, rigid, stern, stony
6. knotty, robust, steely, stingy, strict,
strong 7. callous, onerous 8. diligent,
rigorous, toilsome 9. difficult, heartless,
intricate, strenuous, stringent,
wearisome 10. inflexible, relentless,
unyielding 12. impenetrable,
incorrigible 13. unsympathetic
hard (pert to) . . .
boiled . . 4. hard 5. tough 6. strict
7. callous 8. hardened 10. solidified
13. sophisticated
coal . . 10. anthracite
money . . 6. silver 8. metallic
prefix . . 3. dys
question . . 5. poser
rubber . . 7. ebonite 9. vulcanite
shell . . 6. lorica
stone . . 7. adamant (diamond)
wood . . 4. mabi, teak 5. maple 6. walnut
8. mahogany
harden . . . 3. gel, set 4. cake, kern
5. enure, inure, steel 6. freeze, ossify,
temper 7. toughen 8. indurate, solidify
9. habituate 10. strengthen
hardened . . . 4. hard 5. caked 6. frozen,
wicked 7. callous, steeled 8. indurate,
obdurate, ossified 9. heartless,
reprobate, unfeeling 10. impenitent,
impervious, inveterate, solidified
12. impenetrable
hardening of the arteries . . .
16. arteriosclerosis
hardening of the eyeball . . . 8. glaucoma
hardheaded . . . 6. shrewd, strict
9. obstinate, sagacious
hardhearted . . . 4. mean 5. cruel
7. callous 8. pitiless 9. unfeeling
13. unsympathetic
hardship . . . 5. rigor 6. injury 7. trouble
8. hardness 9. adversity, privation
hardtack . . . 5. bread 7. galette 10. sea
biscuit
hardwood . . . 3. ash, oak 4. ipil, mabi,

teak **5.** maple **6.** walnut **8.** mahogany
hardy . . . **4.** bold, hale, rash **5.** brave,
lusty, stout **6.** daring, strong **7.** healthy,
spartan **8.** intrepid, resolute
9. audacious, confident **10.** courageous
Hardy heroine . . . **4.** Tess
hare . . . **3.** doe, wat (watt) **4.** buck, cony,
pika (tailless) **5.** lapin, Lepus **6.** rabbit,
rodent, tapeti **7.** leveret
hare (pert to) . . .
   constellation . . **5.** Lepus
   harelike . . **6.** agouti **8.** leporine
   tail . . **4.** scut
   track . . **4.** slot
   type . . **10.** cottontail, jack rabbit
harem . . . **5.** serai **6.** purdah, zenana
8. seraglio **9.** gynaeceum
harem room . . . **3.** oda (odah)
harem slave . . . **9.** odalisque (odalisk)
hark . . . **4.** heed, hist **6.** listen **7.** hearken,
whisper **9.** attention
harkened . . . **5.** heard **6.** heeded
8. listened **9.** hearkened
harlequin . . . **4.** duck (sea) **5.** clown,
color **7.** buffoon **9.** fantastic, trickster
11. masquerader **12.** multi-colored,
parti-colored
Harlequin (comedy) . . . **11.** pantomimist
harm . . . **3.** mar **4.** bane, dere, evil,
hurt, pain **5.** grief, wrong **6.** damage,
impair, injure, injury, scathe (scath),
sorrow **10.** misfortune, wickedness
12. disadvantage
harmful . . . **3.** bad **4.** evil, upas **6.** nocent
7. baneful, hurtful, malefic, noisome,
noxious **8.** damaging, sinister
9. injurious **10.** pernicious
11. deleterious, detrimental
12. insalubrious
harmless . . . **5.** seely **6.** unhurt
8. dehorned, unharmed **9.** innocuous,
undamaged, uninjured **11.** unoffending
harmonious . . . **6.** syntax **7.** harmony,
musical, orderly, spheral, tuneful
9. accordant, agreeable, congruous,
consonant, eurythmic (eurhythmic),
melodious **10.** compatible, concordant,
euphonious **11.** conformable,
symmetrical
harmonize . . . **2.** go **3.** gee **4.** tone
5. agree, blend, chime **6.** attune
7. conform, consist **9.** reconcile
10. correspond, symmetrize, sympathize
harmony . . . **4.** tone, tune **5.** music,
order, triad, unity **6.** accord, cosmos,
melody, unison **7.** concord, euphony
8. symmetry **9.** agreement, harmonics
10. conformity, consonance
harness . . . **4.** gear **5.** armor, equip
6. graith, tackle **7.** uniform **8.** accouter,
ornament **9.** caparison, parachute
harness part . . . **3.** tug **4.** hame,
rein **5.** trace **6.** collar, halter, terret
7. apparel **9.** hackamore **10.** breastband,
martingale
harp . . . **4.** arpa, koto, lyre, Lyra (Astron)
5. nanga **8.** Irishman **11.** clairschach
harp (pert to) . . .
   key . . **5.** C Flat
   octaves (number) . . **11.** six and a half
   pedals . . **5.** seven

   star . . **12.** Harp of Arthur
   strings . . **8.** forty-six
harping . . . **7.** humdrum, tedious
9. iterating, repeating **11.** repetitious
harpoon . . . **5.** spear **7.** javelin **8.** lily
iron
harpsichord . . . **6.** spinet **8.** clavecin
9. lyrichord **12.** clavicembalo
harpy . . . **3.** bat **5.** eagle, fiend **9.** plunderer
12. extortionist
Harpy (Myth) . . . **5.** Aello, ghoul
7. Celaeno, monster (part bird, woman),
Ocypete, Podarge (The Iliad)
harridan . . . **3.** hag **5.** vixen, witch
6. virago **7.** Jezebel **8.** strumpet
9. termagant
harrier . . . **3.** dog **4.** hawk **5.** bully, hound
7. heckler **8.** badgerer **9.** tormentor
harrow . . . **4.** dish, pain **5.** harry, herse
(Hist), wound **7.** oppress, torment,
torture **8.** distress, lacerate **9.** cultivate,
formation (geese), implement
harrowing . . . **7.** painful, racking, tilling
9. agonizing, torturous **11.** cultivating,
distressing **12.** heart-rending
harry . . . **3.** vex **4.** sack **5.** annoy, hound,
worry **6.** harass, hector, plague,
ravage, ravish **7.** agitate, besiege,
pillage, plunder, violate **8.** lay waste
9. persecute
Harry . . . **5.** Devil (Shaksp)
harsh . . . **3.** raw **4.** dure, grim **5.** acerb,
acrid, asper, crude, gruff, raspy, stern,
stiff **6.** bitter, coarse, severe, unkind
7. drastic, painful, pungent, rasping
8. clashing, gutteral, jangling, rigorous,
strident **9.** inclement, offensive,
repellent **10.** discordant, relentless
11. acrimonious, disagreeing
harshness . . . **5.** rigor **7.** raucity
8. acrimony, pungency, severity
9. gruffness **11.** raucousness
hart . . . **4.** deer, stag **5.** spade
hartebeast . . . **4.** asse, tora **5.** caama
(kaama) **6.** lecama **7.** bubalis **8.** antelope
10. Alcelaphus
Harvard College honor . . . **4.** book
5. detur **12.** let it be given
harvest . . . **4.** crop, gain, rabi, reap
5. fruit, yield **6.** autumn, gather, reward
7. acquire, produce
harvest (pert to) . . .
   god . . **6.** Cronus, Saturn
   goddess . . **3.** Ops **5.** Ceres
   home . . **4.** kirn, mell **6.** hockey
   moon . . **4.** full **15.** autumnal equinox
   second . . **9.** aftermath
   tick . . **6.** acarid
hash . . . **4.** food **5.** mince **6.** jumble,
medley, ragout **7.** mixture
10. hodgepodge **11.** gallimaufry, olla
podrida
hashish . . . **4.** hemp **5.** bhang (bang)
8. cannabis, narcotic
hassle . . . **4.** fray **5.** brawl, melee
hasten . . . **3.** hie **4.** scud, urge **5.** amain,
apace, hurry, scamp, speed **7.** further
8. expedite **10.** accelerate **11.** precipitate
hastened . . . **3.** ran **4.** hied, sped
5. raced **6.** rushed **7.** hurried, scooted
8. galloped **9.** expedited **11.** accelerated

12. precipitated

hasty . . . **4.** fast, rash **5.** brash, eager,
fleet, quick, swift **6.** speedy, sudden,
urgent **7.** cursory, hurried **8.** reckless
9. impetuous, impulsive, premature
11. expeditious, precipitate

hasty pudding . . . **4.** mush **9.** stirabout

hat . . . **3.** fez, tam, top **4.** felt, hood, silk
5. beret, derby, gibus, opera, straw,
terai, toque **6.** bonnet, cloche, cocked,
fedora, Panama, sailor, topper, turban
7. chapeau, picture, pillbox, porkpie,
tricorn **8.** sombrero **9.** headdress,
sou'wester, stovepipe, ten-gallon
11. mortarboard **13.** three-cornered

hat (pert to) . . .
antique . . **7.** bycoket (bycocket), petasos
(petasus)
covering . . **8.** havelock
crown . . **4.** poll
defensive . . **4.** coif
Eccl . . **7.** biretta **9.** Cardinal's
military . . **5.** shako
opera . . **4.** tile **5.** gibus **6.** topper
pass (the hat) . . **10.** collection
slang . . **4.** plug **5.** dicer
stovepipe . . **8.** caroline
under one's . . **6.** secret **9.** to oneself

hatch . . . **4.** door, gate, line (art),
plot **5.** breed **6.** invent **7.** concoct,
produce **8.** contrive, hatchway, incubate
9. floodgate, originate **10.** bring forth,
sluice gate

hatchet . . . **2.** ax (axe) **3.** adz (adze)
4. mogo **8.** tomahawk

hate . . . **4.** miso (comb form) **5.** abhor,
odium **6.** detest, hatred, loathe, rancor
7. despise, dislike **9.** abominate,
antipathy

hateful . . . **6.** odious **7.** heinous **8.** terrible
9. abhorrent, execrable, invidious,
loathsome, malicious, obnoxious,
offensive, revolting **10.** abominable,
detestable, disgusting **11.** distasteful
12. disagreeable

hater of . . .
children . . **10.** misopedist
mankind . . **11.** misanthrope
marriage . . **10.** misogynist
mathematics . . **8.** misomath
newness . . **9.** misoneist
sights . . **11.** misoscopist
strangers . . **8.** misoxene
work . . **11.** ergophobiac

hatred . . . **5.** odium **6.** animus, enmity,
rancor **8.** aversion, loathing
9. animosity, malignity **10.** abhorrence,
repugnance **11.** detestation,
malevolence

hatred of . . .
argument . . **8.** misology
change . . **9.** misoneism
children . . **9.** misopedia
God, gods . . **10.** misotheism
mankind . . **11.** misanthropy
marriage . . **8.** misogamy
strangers . . **8.** misoxeny **10.** xenophobia
war . . **9.** polemical **11.** misopolemic
wisdom . . **9.** misosophy
women . . **8.** misogyny

hauberk . . . **5.** armor **9.** habergeon

haughty . . . **4.** airy, bold, high **5.** lofty,
noble, proud **6.** snooty **7.** fatuous,
stately **8.** arrogant, cavalier, orgulous,
scornful **10.** disdainful, hoity-toity
11. domineering, highfalutin
12. contemptuous, supercilious

haul . . . **3.** lug, tow, tug **4.** cart, drag,
draw, pull **5.** booty, bouse, catch,
check, shift **9.** reprimand, transport

haul down a flag . . . **6.** strike

haunch . . . **3.** hip **4.** huck **10.** leg and
loin **12.** hindquarters

haunch bone . . . **10.** innominate

haunt . . . **3.** den **4.** dive, nest **5.** ghost,
habit **6.** infect, obsess, resort **7.** torment
8. frequent, practice

hautboy . . . **4.** oboe

have . . . **3.** get, hae, own **4.** hold, keep,
know **5.** beget, trick **6.** accept, effect,
retain **7.** cherish, perform, possess,
swindle **10.** experience, understand,
suffer from

have (pert to) . . .
ambition . . **6.** aspire
charge . . **4.** tend
on . . **4.** wear
thoughts of . . **6.** ideate
to do with . . **4.** deal
weight . . **8.** militate

haven . . . **3.** bay **4.** port **5.** hithe (small),
inlet **6.** asylum, harbor, recess, refuge
7. shelter **9.** sanctuary

havier . . . **4.** deer

having (pert to) . . .
blind end . . **6.** caecal
branches . . **6.** ramose
clamp, pincers . . **7.** chelate
dignity . . **8.** majestic
equal sides . . **9.** isosceles
eyes . . **7.** oculate
faith . . **8.** trusting
featherlike petals . . **7.** pinnate
feelers . . **9.** antennate
fingers . . **8.** digitate
foreknowledge . . **9.** prescient
four feet . . **11.** quadrupedal
harmful quality . . **9.** innocuous
leaves . . **6.** foliar **7.** foliate
limits . . **6.** finite
local designation . . **7.** topical
lumps . . **7.** noduled
more than one mate . . **9.** polyandry
no angles . . **6.** agonic
no interest . . **6.** supine
no teeth . . **7.** edental **8.** edentate
nothing to do . . **6.** otiose
one foot . . **6.** uniped
pits, depressions . . **7.** foveate **9.** foveolate
plane surfaces . . **7.** faceted
pointed end . . **6.** peaked **7.** cuspate
8. aristate
power over fire . . **10.** ignipotent
power to believe . . **9.** creditive
reflecting surface . . **8.** specular
same ending . . **11.** conterminal
same parents . . **7.** germane
sawlike edge . . **7.** serrate
scales . . **8.** perulate
scalloped edge . . **7.** crenate
taste . . **5.** sapid
thorns . . **7.** spinate

three broods yearly .. **11.** trigoneutic
two feet .. **5.** biped **7.** bipedal
two horns .. **6.** bicorn
two meanings .. **9.** ambiguous
unequal sides .. **7.** scalene
web feet .. **8.** pinniped
wings .. **4.** alar
having a ...
backbone .. **10.** vertebrate
beak .. **8.** rostrate
beard .. **8.** aristate
handle .. **6.** ansate
large nose .. **6.** nasute
shield .. **9.** clypeated
stem .. **9.** petiolate
tail .. **7.** caudate
tuft .. **6.** comose
veil .. **6.** velate
will .. **7.** testate
havoc ... **4.** harm **5.** botch, waste
7. destroy **11.** destruction, devastation
12. annihilation
haw ... **4.** sloe **5.** fence, hedge **6.** eyelid
(3rd) **7.** stammer **8.** hawthorn,
messuage, turn left **9.** enclosure
11. exclamation
Hawaii ... see also *Hawaiian*
capital .. **8.** Honolulu
city .. **4.** Hilo **7.** Wailuku
district .. **7.** Lahaina
explorer .. **4.** Cook (Capt)
harbor .. **5.** Pearl (bombed 12/7/41)
islands (major) .. **4.** Maui, Oahu **5.** Kauai,
Lanai **6.** Hawaii, Niihau **7.** Molokai
9. Kahoolawe
lake .. **5.** Waiau
native .. **10.** Polynesian
old name .. **15.** Sandwich Islands
peak .. **8.** Mauna Kea, Mauna Loa
9. Waialeale
resort .. **7.** Waikiki
Southernmost point (US) .. **5.** Ka Lae
State admission .. **8.** Fiftieth
State bird .. **13.** Hawaiian goose
State flower .. **8.** hibiscus
State nickname .. **5.** Aloha **20.** Paradise
of the Pacific
volcano .. **7.** Kilauea **8.** Mauna Loa
(largest active)
Hawaiian ... **6.** Kanaka **10.** Melanesian,
Polynesian **16.** South Sea islander
Hawaiian (pert to) ...
banquet, feast .. **7.** ahaaina
basket .. **2.** ie
beverage .. **4.** kava **8.** kavakava
bird .. **2.** io, o-o **3.** iwa **4.** iiwi, mamo
(ext), noio, o-o-a-a **6.** olomao (thrush)
8. drepanis
canoe .. **5.** waapa
chant .. **4.** mele
cloth, clothes .. **4.** kapa, tapa
coffee .. **4.** kona
dance .. **4.** hula
fern .. **4.** pulu
fibre (pine) .. **2.** ie
fish .. **3.** awa **4.** ulua **5.** akule, lania
flower wreath, garland .. **3.** lei
food .. **3.** poi **4.** kalo, taro
garment .. **6.** holoku, muumuu
god .. **5.** Wakea **7.** Kanaloa (Pantheon)
goddess .. **4.** Pele (volcanoes, fire)

gooseberry .. **4.** poha
grass .. **6.** emoloa
greeting .. **5.** aloha
herb .. **3.** pia (starch root)
king (first) .. **10.** Kamehameha
lava .. **2.** aa **8.** pahoehoe
loincloth, girdle .. **4.** malo
musical instrument .. **7.** ukulele
newcomer .. **8.** malihini
pepper .. **3.** ava **4.** kava **8.** kavakava
precipice .. **4.** pali
Queen .. **8.** Kamamalu
royalty .. **4.** alii
seaweed (edible) .. **4.** limu
shampoo, massage .. **8.** lomi-lomi
shrub .. **3.** pia **4.** akia, pulu **5.** olona
temple .. **5.** heiau
tern .. **4.** noio
tree .. **3.** koa
veranda .. **5.** lanai
windstorm .. **4.** kona
woman .. **5.** haole **6.** wahine
yam .. **3.** hoi
hawfinch ... **8.** grosbeak
hawk ... **3.** cry **4.** hunt, sell, vend
6. peddle **7.** canvass **9.** plunderer,
warmonger
hawk (bird) ... **2.** io **3.** hen **4.** eyas,
kahu, kite, nyas, seel (blind) **5.** Astur,
Buteo **6.** falcon, osprey, tercel (tiercel)
7. buzzard, Cooper's, goshawk, harrier,
kestrel, puttock, sparrow, vulture
8. caracara **9.** Accipiter, red-tailed
hawker of fruit (Eng) ... **6.** coster
12. costermonger
hawk-eyed deity ... **2.** Ra
Hawkeye State ... **4.** Iowa
hawking ... **7.** hunting, vending
8. falconry
hawk's cage ... **3.** mew
hawk moth ... **6.** sphinx **8.** sphingid
hawksbill ... **4.** pawl **6.** turtle **8.** tortoise
hawkshaw ... **6.** sleuth **9.** detective
11. sleuthhound
hawk's nest ... **5.** aerie (aery)
hawk's opposite ... **4.** dove
hawser ... **4.** line, rope
hawser post ... **4.** bitt **7.** bollard
hawthorn ... **3.** may **5.** hazel (fruit) **6.** red
haw **7.** haw tree **9.** mayflower
Hawthorne's ...
adultress .. **6.** Hester (Prynne)
House of .. **11.** Seven Gables
Letter .. **7.** Scarlet
reverend .. **10.** Dimmesdale
hay ... **6.** fodder **7.** timothy
hay (pert to) ...
bird .. **7.** hay jack **8.** black cap
9. sandpiper (pectoral)
bundle .. **3.** mow **4.** bale, cock, rick
5. stack
fork .. **5.** pikel (pikle), pitch
herb .. **8.** sainfoin
mown .. **5.** swath
second cutting .. **5.** rowen
spreader .. **6.** tedder
stack .. **4.** rick **7.** hayrick
storage site .. **3.** mow **4.** barn, loft, silo
haywire ... **4.** awry **5.** crazy
hazard ... **3.** fog **4.** dare, game, jump,
risk **5.** peril **6.** gamble, sanger, stroke

7. imperil, jeopard, presume, venture
8. cabstand, casualty, endanger,
jeopardy 11. restriction
hazardous ... 5. hairy (sl), jumpy,
risky 6. chancy, queasy, unsafe
7. unsound 8. perilous 9. uncertain,
venturous 10. fortuitous 11. speculative,
venturesome
haze ... 3. fog 4. beat, film, glin (at sea),
mist, smog 5. scold, smoke, vapor
7. dimness, drizzle 8. frighten
hazy ... 3. dim 5. filmy, foggy, misty,
smoky, thick, vague 6. cloudy, opaque,
stupid 7. muddled, nebular, obscure
8. overcast 9. invisible, uncertain
10. indistinct
he ... 2. il 3. man 4. ipsi, male 6. any
one, letter 7. pronoun
head ... 3. aim, nob 4. lead, pate, poll,
tête (Fr) 5. caput, chief, skull 6. noggin,
noodle (sl), source 7. cranium
head (pert to) ...
  abbey .. 5. abbot 6. abbess
  back of .. 7. occiput
  bald .. 6. acomia 9. pilgarlic
  bone .. 8. parietal 9. occipital
  Gorgon .. 6. Medusa (Myth)
  hard .. 5. boche
  of hair .. 5. crine
  pert to .. 8. cephalic
  proportion .. 14. mesitacephalic
  shaven .. 7. tonsure
  shrunken .. 7. tsentsa
headache ... 6. megrim 8. migraine
11. cephalalgia
head covering ... 3. cap, hat, tam, wig
4. hair, hood, veil 5. beret, miter, scalp
6. bonnet, peruke, toupee, wimple
7. biretta 8. sombrero 10. fascinator
headdress ... 3. wig 4. pouf, tête
5. busby, miter, shako, tiara 6. coiffe,
diadem, hennin, peruke, pinner
7. bandore, buzz wig, coronet, periwig
8. coiffure, headtire
headdress (Egypt) ... 6. uraeus (with
sacred asp)
headhunters (Luzon) ... 7. Igorots
heading ... 3. top 5. front, title, topic
6. pillow 7. bolster, caption 8. headline
9. direction 12. decapitation
headland ... 4. cape, mull, ness 5. morro,
ridge 10. promontory
headless ... 6. stupid 7. acephal, topless
9. acephalus (monster) 10. acephalous
headline ... 6. banner 7. caption, display,
heading 8. streamer
headliner ... 4. star 7. feature 8. composer
headlong ... 4. rash 5. hasty, steep
6. head-on, sudden 8. reckless
9. headfirst, impetuous, impulsive
10. recklessly 11. impulsively,
precipitate, precipitous
headpiece ... 3. cap, hat, top 4. atef
5. crown 6. halter, helmet, lintel
7. fitting 8. covering, ornament, skull
cap 9. headboard, headdress, headstall
head-shaped ... 8. capitate
headstrong ... 4. rash, entêté, unruly
7. violent, wayward 9. obstinate
11. intractable, opinionated
12. contumacious, ungovernable

heal ... 4. cure, knit, mend 6. doctor,
pacify, remedy, repair 7. correct, restore
9. cicatrize
healing (pert to) ...
  agent .. 6. balsam
  compound .. 4. balm
  goddess .. 3. Eir
  magic .. 6. powwow
  plant .. 4. aloe (vera)
  process .. 4. scar 8. cicatrix
  remedy .. 8. curative, sanative
  science .. 9. iatrology
  suffix .. 7. iatrics
health (pert to) ...
  care .. 7. welfare
  comb form .. 4. sani
  conditions .. 8. sanitary
  goddess .. 5. Salus 6. Hygeia 7. Minerva
  Latin .. 5. salus
  neurotic .. 13. hypochondriac
  resort .. 3. spa 7. springs
  symbol .. 5. pansy
healthful ... 7. healthy 8. curative,
salutary, sanatory 9. medicinal
10. salubrious
healthy ... 4. hale, sane, well 6. hearty,
robust 8. salutary, vigorous 9. healthful,
wholesome 10. salubrious
heap ... 3. cop 4. dess, load, lump,
pile, pyre, raff, raft 5. amass, cairn,
crowd, stack 6. plenty, sorite, throng
7. cumulus 9. multitude 10. accumulate
heaped ... 5. piled 7. stacked 8. acervate
9. collected
hear ... 3. see 4. feel, heed, oyez (oyes)
5. favor, judge, learn 6. attend, listen
7. hearken (harken) 8. listen to, perceive
9. attention 10. adjudicate
hearer ... 7. audient, auditor 8. disciple,
listener 9. hearkener (harkener)
12. eavesdropper
hearing (pert to) ... 3. act, aid, ear
4. otic, oyer 5. aural, sense (special),
sound, trial 6. otosis, tryout 7. earshot
8. audience, audition, auditory
9. attention, auricular, interview,
knowledge
hearken, harken ... 4. hear, heed
6. attend, listen 7. give ear, inquire
hearsay ... 4. talk 5. bruit, rumor
6. gossip, report 8. evidence
heart ... 3. cor 4. card, core, gist, life, love,
mood, soul 5. cheer, organ 6. center,
depths, kardia, middle, spirit, vitals
7. courage, emotion, essence, feeling
9. affection, substance 10. conscience
11. temperament
heart (pert to) ...
  ache .. 4. grief 6. sorrow 7. anguish
  active .. 7. sthenic
  artery .. 5. aorta
  beat .. 5. pulse, throb 7. systole
  8. diastole 9. pulsation 10. palmoscopy
  bleeding (flower) .. 8. dicentra
  burn .. 4. envy 6. enmity 7. burning,
  pyrosis 8. jealousy 10. cardialgia,
  discontent, heartscald (heart-scaud)
  cavity .. 6. atrium
  chamber .. 6. atrium 7. auricle 9. ventricle
  11. ventriculum
  contraction .. 7. systole

disease . . **14.** angina pectoris
Egypt . . **2.** Ab **4.** hati
expansion . . **8.** diastole
felt . . **4.** dear, deep, real, true **7.** genuine, sincere
shaped . . **7.** cordate
valve . . **6.** mitral **8.** bicuspid **9.** tricuspid
hearten . . . **5.** cheer **7.** comfort **8.** embolden, inspirit, reassure **9.** encourage
hearth . . . **4.** home **5.** ingle **6.** astrer (pert to) **8.** fireside **9.** fireplace
hearth goddess . . . **5.** Vesta **6.** Hestia
hearty . . . **4.** hale, real, rich, warm **5.** heavy, lusty **6.** active, robust, stanch **7.** cordial, earnest, fervent **8.** friendly, vigorous **9.** convivial, energetic, unfeigned **10.** nourishing **11.** substantial
heat . . . **4.** fire, race, warm, zeal **5.** ardor, calor, cauma, fever, tepor **6.** degree, warmth **7.** inflame, passion **10.** excitement **11.** temperature
heat (pert to) . . .
heating . . **9.** calorific
measure . . **5.** therm (therme) **7.** calorie (calory), Celsius **10.** centigrade, Fahrenheit
pert to . . **7.** thermic
plaster . . **4.** mull **7.** steatin
principle . . **7.** caloric
white . . **13.** incandescence
heater . . . **4.** etna, kiln, oven **5.** forge, stove, tisar **6.** boiler, retort **7.** brazier, furnace **8.** annealer, register **12.** electron tube
heath . . . **4.** moor **5.** Erica, plain, savin, waste **8.** tamarisk **10.** underbrush
heathen . . . **5.** pagan **6.** ethnic, paynim **7.** gentile, godless, infidel **10.** unbeliever **11.** irreligious **13.** unenlightened
heathen deity . . . **4.** idol **5.** image **6.** symbol
heather . . . **5.** color, Erica, plant **9.** crowberry **12.** poverty plant
heaume . . . **6.** helmet (armor)
heave . . . **4.** cast, draw, hurl, lift, toss **5.** fling, hoist, pitch, raise, retch, scena, throw **11.** rise and fall
heaven . . . **3.** sky **4.** ciel, Eden **5.** ether **6.** utopia, welkin **7.** arcadia, Elysium, Nirvana **8.** empyrean, Paradise, Valhalla (Valhall) **9.** firmament
heavenly . . . **5.** godly **6.** divine, sacred **7.** angelic, blessed, uranian **8.** supernal **9.** beautiful, celestial **10.** delightful
heavenly (pert to) . . .
being . . **5.** angel, saint **6.** cherub, seraph **7.** Madonna **8.** cherubim, Dei Mater, seraphim
belt . . **6.** galaxy, zodiac
body . . **3.** sun **4.** luna, moon, star **5.** comet **6.** planet **8.** luminary
city . . **4.** Zion **12.** New Jerusalem
food . . **5.** manna
path . . **5.** orbit
solar apparatus . . **6.** orrery
sphere . . **8.** empyrean
twins (Gemini) . . **6.** Castor, Pollux
heavens . . . see *heaven*
heaves . . . **9.** emphysema

heavy . . . **3.** sad **4.** deep, dull, hard, role **5.** actor, dense, grave, great, inert, massy **6.** coarse, gloomy, leaden, sleepy, strong, viscid **7.** doleful, onerous, serious, villain, violent, weighty **8.** burdened, grievous, overcast, pregnant, profound **9.** difficult, ponderous **10.** afflictive, burdensome, encumbered, oppressive **11.** substantial **13.** consequential
heavy (pert to) . . .
handed . . **6.** clumsy **7.** awkward, unhandy **8.** bungling **9.** maladroit **10.** oppressive
headed . . **4.** dull, logy **6.** drowsy, stupid
hearted . . **3.** sad **10.** despondent, melancholy
laden . . **6.** loaded **8.** careworm **9.** oppressed **12.** weighted down
with moisture . . **6.** sodden
Hebrew . . . **3.** Jew **4.** Zion **6.** Habiri, Habiru, Semite **7.** Semitic
Hebrew (pert to) . . .
abode of the dead . . **5.** Sheol
acrostic . . **4.** agla
amulet . . **4.** agla
demon . . **8.** Asmodeus
eternity . . **4.** Olam **8.** Olam haba
excommunication form . . **5.** herem
festival . . **5.** Purim, Seder **8.** Passover
flute (Bib) . . **8.** nehiloth
forbidden . . **4.** tref
God . . **2.** El **5.** Eloah **6.** Adonai, Elohim, Yahweh (Yahveh) **7.** Jehovah
grammar . . **7.** stative
greeting . . **6.** Shalom
instrument (lyrelike) . . **4.** asor
kinsman . . **4.** goel
law book . . **5.** Torah (Tora) **6.** Talmud **7.** Mishnah (Mishna) **8.** Tosephta **10.** Pentateuch
lesson (Nebiim) . . **9.** haphtarah
marriage custom . . **8.** levirate
month (Spring) . . **4.** Abib **5.** Nisan
Order (Cenobite) . . **6.** Essene
plural ending . . **2.** im
prayer shawl . . **7.** tallith
proselyte . . **3.** ger
psalm of praise . . **6.** hallel
quarters . . **6.** ghetto
rabbis, teachers . . **6.** sabora **7.** amoraim, tannaim **8.** saboraim
sacred objects . . **4.** Urim **7.** Thummin
school . . **5.** heder (cheder)
spice (anc) . . **6.** stacte
town . . **6.** Mizpah (Mizpeh)
trumpet . . **7.** shophar (shofar)
underworld . . **5.** Sheol
Hebrew alphabet . . . **2.** he, pe **3.** mem, nun, sin, tav, vau **4.** ayin, beth, caph, koph, resh, shin, yodh **5.** aleph, cheth, gimel, sadhe, zayin **6.** daleth, lamedh, samekh
Hebrides, New . . .
administrators . . **6.** French **7.** British
church . . **6.** Celtic (early)
islands . . **4.** Iona, Skye **5.** Banks **6.** Torres
people . . **10.** Melanesian
type rule . . **11.** Condominium
hecatomb . . . **9.** sacrifice **11.** hundred oxen
hecco . . . **8.** hickwall **10.** woodpecker

heckle . . . **4.** gibe **6.** badger, hackle, harass

hectic . . . **5.** fever, flush **7.** excited **8.** feverish, restless **9.** reddening **11.** consumptive

hector . . . **5.** bully, worry **6.** harass **7.** bluster, swagger **8.** browbeat **9.** roisterer **10.** intimidate

Hector (pert to) . . .
character in . . **5.** (The) Iliad
companion . . **8.** Diomedes
father . . **5.** Priam
mother . . **6.** Hecuba
slain by . . **8.** Achilles
wife . . **10.** Andromache

heddle . . . **4.** loom **5.** blade (with eyelet) **7.** weaving

hedge . . . **3.** bar, haw, hem, pen **4.** boma **5.** fence **6.** hinder, raddle **7.** barrier, enclose, quibble **8.** boundary, obstruct, sidestep, surround

hedgehog . . . **6.** animal, tenrec, urchin **7.** dredger, echidna, echinus, pudding (fruit) **8.** herisson, hurcheon **9.** porcupine **11.** transformer

hedge trimmer . . . **7.** plasher, topiary

hedonism (pert to) . . .
advocate . . **8.** Cyrenaic **9.** Epicurean
doctrine of . . **8.** pleasure

heed . . . **3.** ear **4.** care, hear, mind, note, obey **6.** attend, listen, notice, regard **7.** caution, observe **8.** consider **9.** attention, be careful, diligence **10.** cognizance, solicitude **11.** observation

heedful . . . **4.** wary **5.** alert **6.** attent **7.** careful, mindful **8.** cautious, vigilant **9.** advertent, attentive **11.** considerate

heedless . . . **6.** remiss **8.** careless **9.** desperate, impulsive, negligent **10.** insouciant, regardless **11.** improvident, inadvertent, inattentive, thoughtless, unobservant, without heed **13.** inconsiderate

heehaw . . . **4.** bray

heel . . . **3.** cad, tip **4.** cant, foot (part), knob, tilt **5.** stern **6.** careen, follow **7.** bounder, deviate, incline **9.** scoundrel **12.** protuberance

Heidi author . . . **12.** Johanna Spyri

heifer . . . **3.** cow **4.** quey **5.** stirk, woman **6.** bovine **8.** terrapin (fem) **10.** colpindach

height . . . **3.** alt, top **4.** apex **5.** crest, pitch **6.** summit **7.** stature **8.** altitude, eminence, highness **9.** elevation **10.** The Heavens

heighten . . . **5.** raise **7.** augment, elevate **8.** increase **9.** aggravate, intensify **10.** exaggerate

height of action, drama . . . **10.** catastasis

heimlich . . . **10.** reticently **12.** mysteriously

Heimweh . . . **9.** nostalgia **12.** homesickness

heinous . . . **3.** bad **6.** odious, wicked **7.** beastly (Brit), hateful **8.** flagrant, infamous, terrible **9.** atrocious, malicious **10.** outrageous

heir . . . **5.** scion **7.** heritor, legatee **8.** atheling (apparent), parcener (joint) **9.** firstborn, inheritor, successor

11. beneficiary

Hejaz . . .
city . . **5.** Islam, Mecca **6.** Medina
monument . . **14.** Tomb of Mohammed (Mosque of the Prophet)
district of . . **11.** Saudi Arabia
shrine . . **5.** Kaaba

helcos . . . **5.** ulcer

helcos (pert to) . . .
repair . . **11.** helcoplasty
science . . **9.** helcology
ulceration . . **8.** helcosis

held . . . see hold

Helen of Troy (pert to) . . .
abductor, lover . . **5.** Paris
brother-in-law . . **9.** Agamemnon
famed for . . **6.** beauty
husband . . **8.** Menelaus (King)
mother . . **4.** Leda
sister of . . **11.** The Dioscuri

helical . . . **5.** helix (formed) **6.** spiral

helical year . . . **6.** Sothic

helicoid . . . **6.** curved, ear rim (like) **10.** snail shell (like)

helicon . . . **4.** tuba

helicopter (pert to) . . . **5.** rotor **7.** chopper **8.** autogiro (autogyro), heliport **9.** eggbeater **10.** whirlybird

helicopter developer . . . **8.** Sikorsky

heliophobia . . . **14.** fear of sunlight **16.** sensitivity to sun

Heliopolis . . . **12.** City of the Sun (Egypt)

Helios . . . **3.** Sol **6.** sun god **16.** Colossus of Rhodes

helix . . . **4.** coil **5.** snail **6.** spiral

hell . . . **7.** dungeon, inferno **9.** perdition, purgatory **10.** underworld **11.** nether world

hell (pert to) . . .
bottomless pit . . **9.** barathrum
capital of . . **11.** Pandemonium
Greek . . **5.** Hades **8.** Tartarus
Hebrew . . **5.** Sheol
Hindu . . **6.** Naraka
Jewish . . **6.** Tophet **7.** Gehenna
Norse . . **7.** Niflhel (Neflheim)
Queen . . **3.** Hel
Roman . . **3.** Dis **5.** Orcus

hellbent . . . **7.** dead set, like mad **8.** full tilt, reckless **10.** determined, recklessly **12.** determinedly

Hellene . . . **5.** Greek

Hellenistic school (Sculp) . . . **9.** Pergamene

Hellespont . . .
city . . **6.** Abydos (legend), Sestos
legend . . **4.** Hero **7.** Leander (swimmer)
modern name . . **11.** Dardanelles (The)
peninsula . . **9.** Gallipoli
port . . **8.** Gelibola (Gallipoli)
sea . . **6.** Aegean **7.** Marmara

helm . . . **5.** wheel **6.** helmet, rudder, summit, tiller **7.** control **10.** management **12.** steering gear

helmet . . . **5.** armet, armor, galea, topee (topi) **6.** casque, heaume, morion, sallet, sconce **7.** basinet, hard hat

helmet (pert to) . . .
flap . . **8.** aventail
lower part . . **6.** beaver
nose guard . . **5.** nasal

opening .. **3.** vue
part .. **4.** bell **5.** crest, visor (vizor)
7. ventail **8.** aventail
shaped .. **7.** galeate
helminth ... **4.** worm
helmsman ... **5.** pilot **6.** conner, guider
8. coxswain **9.** steersman
helot ... **4.** esne, serf **5.** slave **6.** thrall,
vassal **7.** servant
help ... **3.** aid **4.** abet, back, cure **5.** avail,
boost, serve, stead **6.** assist, relief,
remedy, succor **7.** benefit, forward,
further, improve, prevent, relieve,
servant, serving, subsidy, support,
sustain
helper ... **3.** aid (aide) **8.** teammate
9. assistant, paramedic **10.** apprentice,
benefactor
helpful ... **6.** useful **7.** helping **8.** salutary
10. beneficial, tiding over
12. contributory, instrumental
helpless ... **4.** limp, weak **7.** forlorn
8. impotent, unaiding **9.** destitute,
powerless, spineless **10.** bewildered,
unsupplied **11.** defenseless, unprotected
12. irremediable
helpmate ... **4.** wife **6.** helper, spouse
7. husband **8.** helpmeet **9.** assistant,
companion
Helsinki, Finland ... **7.** capital
helter-skelter ... **5.** haste, hurry **7.** hastily
8. disorder **9.** confusion **10.** carelessly,
recklessly
helve ... **5.** lever **6.** handle
hem, hem in ... **3.** pen **4.** edge **5.** beset
6. border, margin **7.** environ, stammer
8. hesitate, surround **9.** hem and haw
11. exclamation **12.** circumscribe
hemal, haemal (pert to) ... **5.** blood
12. blood vessels
hemeralopia ... **12.** day blindness (opp
of nyctalopia)
hemi ... **4.** half, semi (pref)
hemiplegia ... **9.** paralysis (body half)
hemlock ... **3.** kex **5.** Tsuga **6.** conium
(fruit) **9.** evergreen, poisoning
hemophilia ... **8.** bleeding
10. hemorrhage (uncontrollable)
hemp ... **3.** ife, kef **4.** flax, keef, kief,
rine, sunn **5.** abaca, bhang, istle, sisal
(sizal) **6.** fennel, Manila **7.** hashish,
lhiamba (liamba) **8.** cannabis
hemp (pert to) ...
bagasse .. **6.** linaga
cannabis .. **5.** ganja (smoking)
fabric .. **6.** burlap
filament .. **4.** harl
leaves .. **5.** sabzi
like .. **9.** cannabine
loose .. **5.** oakum
resin (narcotic) .. **6.** charas
seed .. **5.** rogue, scamp
short .. **3.** tow
hen ... **4.** fowl, wife **6.** pullet
hen (pert to) ...
clam .. **4.** surf **5.** pismo
hawk .. **7.** buzzard, harrier
heath .. **4.** gray **6.** grouse (black)
of Reynard the Fox .. **7.** Partlet
poison .. **7.** hebenon, henbane
water .. **9.** gallinule

hence ... **2.** so **4.** away, ergo, thus
8. away from **9.** therefore
henchman ... **4.** page **5.** groom **6.** gillie,
squire **7.** mafioso **8.** follower, hanger-on
9. attendant, supporter **12.** right-hand
man
hend, hende ... **4.** fair, kind, near
5. civil **6.** clever, comely, gentle, kindly
8. gracious, pleasant, skillful (skilful)
9. dexterous **10.** convenient
Henley event ... **7.** Regatta
henpeck ... **3.** nag
heortology, science of ... **14.** liturgical
year
hepar ... **5.** liver **8.** compound (Chem)
hepatitis ... **12.** liver disease
Hephaestus (Gr Relig) ... **9.** god of Fire
Hepplewhite ... **9.** furniture
heptad ... **5.** seven (group of)
Hera (pert to) ...
husband .. **4.** Zeus
mother of .. **4.** Ares, Rhea
rival .. **2.** Io **4.** Leto
herald ... **5.** crier **6.** tabard **7.** presage,
usher in **8.** announce, point man,
proclaim **9.** harbinger, messenger
10. forerunner
heraldic (pert to) ...
balls .. **5.** palle (6 balls of Medici)
band .. **3.** bar **4.** fess, fill
barnacle .. **4.** brey
bearing .. **4.** ente, gore, orle **5.** pheon
6. charge **8.** tressure
boss .. **5.** rumbo
charge .. **5.** fusil, gyron **7.** bearing,
humetty (humettee)
circle (gold) .. **6.** bezant
cross .. **4.** nowy, paty, urde **6.** cleche,
pattée (patté), raguly **7.** patonce, saltier
(saltire)
decoration .. **4.** seme **5.** crest
design (fur) .. **4.** pean, vair
division .. **4.** ente, paly **5.** barry **6.** canton
7. compone **11.** counterpaly
embattled .. **8.** bretessé
end (metal) .. **7.** boterol (boteroll)
large .. **5.** pavis
lozenge (voided) .. **6.** mascle
opening .. **6.** rustre
panel .. **9.** hatchment (death)
sardonyx .. **8.** sanguine
scalloped, edged .. **8.** invected
segment .. **6.** flanch
ship .. **7.** lymphad
star .. **6.** mullet **7.** estoile
stripe .. **4.** pale
swallow .. **10.** hirondelle
winged .. **4.** aile
wreath .. **5.** torse **7.** chaplet, garland
heraldic (pert to animals) ...
head .. **8.** caboshed (caboched)
bear .. **5.** grise
beast, running .. **7.** courant
beast, sitting .. **5.** assis **6.** sejant
beasts .. **6.** enurny
beast's leg .. **4.** gamb (gambe)
bird .. **7.** issuant (half visible), martlet
9. half eagle
duck (footless) .. **6.** cannet (cannette)
fish, swimming .. **6.** naiant
headless .. **5.** etète

heraldic (pert to color) . . .
black . . **5.** sable
blue . . **5.** azure
brown . . **5.** tenne
gold, yellow . . **2.** or
green . . **4.** vert
purple . . **7.** purpure
red . . **5.** gules
heraldic shield (pert to) . . .
back . . **8.** aversant
back to back . . **8.** addorsed
bent . . **9.** debruised
broken . . **5.** rompu
Danes . . **5.** raven
England . . **14.** lilies of France
facing each other . . **8.** affronté
savages . . **6.** tattoo
toward spectator . . **4.** gaze **7.** gardant
tribe of Judah . . **4.** lion
herb . . . **3.** pia, rue **4.** aloe, anet,
balm, dill, hemp, mint, moly, sage,
woad, yamp **5.** anise, basil, nondo,
sedge, senna, tansy, thyme **6.** arnica,
borage, catnip, cicely, clover, endive,
fennel, hyssop, jacoby, madder,
yarrow **7.** boneset, caraway, chervil,
chicory, figwort, gentian, ginseng,
henbane, parsley, ragwort **8.** abelmosk,
licorice, marjoram, rosemary, samphire,
tarragon **9.** coriander, digitalis,
spikenard **10.** elecampane, pennyroyal,
turtlehead
herb (pert to) . . .
bitter . . **3.** rue **4.** aloe **5.** tansy **7.** boneset
8. centaury **9.** snakehead **10.** turtlehead
dill . . **4.** anet
genus . . **3.** Iva **4.** Arum, Ruta **5.** Galax,
Inula, Lemna, Rubia **6.** Cassia, Mentha,
Oxalis, Sagina **7.** Alpenia, Anemone,
Freesia, Hedeoma, Tellima, Tovaria
8. Hepatica, Psorales **9.** Grundelia
living on . . **11.** herbivorous
12. phytophagous
mythical . . **4.** moly
narcotic . . **4.** hemp
onionlike . . **5.** chive
poisonous . . **4.** loco **6.** conium
7. hemlock, henbane **9.** hellebore
salad . . **6.** endive **7.** chicory
10. watercress
Hercules (pert to) . . .
captured . . **8.** Cerberus
father . . **4.** Zeus
hero of . . **8.** strength **12.** twelve labors
killed . . **5.** Hydra
mother . . **7.** Alcmene
stables . . **6.** Augean
statue . . **7.** Farnese
stone . . **9.** loadstone
sweetheart . . **4.** Iole
wife . . **4.** Hebe
herd . . . **3.** mob **5.** crowd, drive, drove,
flock, guard **6.** gregis, rabble **7.** shelter
11. aggregation
herd's grass . . . **7.** timothy
herdsman . . . **4.** senn **6.** drover **7.** vaquero
(vaciero) **8.** Damoetas, ranchero,
wrangler
herdsman's god . . . **5.** Pales
here . . . **3.** ici, now **6.** hereat, hither
7. present **8.** vicinity **9.** this place

11. in this place
here and now . . . **8.** thisness **9.** haecceity
11. specificity
here and there . . . **5.** about **6.** passim
10. everywhere
hereditary . . . **6.** inborn, innate, lineal
8. heirship **9.** ancestral, descended,
lineality **11.** inheritable, inheritance,
patrimonial
heredity . . . **4.** gene **5.** birth **7.** atavism
8. heritage **10.** Mendel's law
11. inheritance
heretic . . . **9.** dissenter, sectarian
10. schismatic **13.** nonconformist
heretofore . . . **6.** erenow **7.** prior to
8. formerly, hitherto, previous
heritage . . . **3.** lot **9.** cleronomy
10. birthright **11.** inheritance
heritrix, heretrix . . . **7.** heiress
herl, harl . . . **3.** fly (angling) **4.** barb
hermeneutics . . . **14.** interpretation
(Scriptures)
Hermes (pert to) . . .
birthplace . . **7.** Cyllene
character . . **6.** herald **9.** messenger
father . . **4.** Zeus
god of . . **5.** youth **7.** science **9.** eloquence,
invention
mother . . **4.** Maia
Roman equivalent . . **7.** Mercury
shoes (winged) . . **7.** talaria
hermetic . . . **6.** closed, sealed **7.** magical
8. airtight **10.** alchemical
hermetic art . . . **7.** alchemy
hermit . . . **4.** monk **5.** cooky **7.** ascetic,
eremite, recluse, stylite (Hist)
8. headsman **9.** anchorite, pillarist
11. hummingbird
hermitary . . . **3.** hut **4.** cell
hern, herne . . . **4.** hers, hook **5.** heron
6. corner
hero . . . **4.** idol, star **5.** model **7.** demigod,
warrior **8.** champion **9.** celebrity,
conqueror **11.** protagonist
hero (pert to) . . .
American . . **5.** Allen (Ethan), Bowie
6. Bonham, Travis **8.** Crockett
Babylonian . . **5.** Etana
deified . . **7.** demigod
genealogy . . **9.** heroogony
Greek . . **3.** Ion **4.** Ajax
legendary . . **6.** Amadis, Roland
7. Paladin, Tancred
lore . . **9.** heroology
Persian . . **6.** Rustam (Rustum)
romantic . . **4.** Erec **6.** Amadis **7.** Leander
Russian . . **4.** Igor
heroic . . . **4.** bold, epic, huge **5.** brave,
great, noble **6.** epical, poetic, viking
7. extreme, gallant, valiant **8.** fearless,
intrepid, powerful **10.** courageous
11. magnanimous, venturesome
heroic poem, story . . . **4.** epic, epos
6. epopee
heroine . . . **4.** Tess **5.** actor **6.** Esther,
Europa **8.** Atalanta **9.** celebrity
11. demigoddess
heroism . . . **5.** valor **7.** bravery, courage
9. fortitude **11.** magnanimity
13. unselfishness
heron . . . **5.** Ardea, crane, egret, herle

7. Bittern 8. Ardeidae, heronsew
9. Great Blue 10. Great White, Little
Blue
heron flock ... 5. sedge
herpes ... 6. eczema 8. cold sore, shingles
herring ... 3. cob 4. alec, brit, raun (fem),
sile 5. cisco, matie, sprat 7. alewife,
anchovy, shadine 8. scuddawn
herring (pert to) ...
barrel .. 4. cade, cran
bone .. 7. pattern 11. arrangement
fry .. 4. sile
herringlike .. 5. cisco 7. anchovy
young .. 4. brit 5. sprat (sprot)
Herse (Gr) ... 7. goddess (dew)
Hersey setting ... 5. Adano 9. Hiroshima
Hershef (Egypt) ... 5. deity (tutelary)
hesitate ... 3. haw, hem 4. wait 5. delay,
demur, pause, stall 6. falter, loiter
7. stammer 13. procrastinate
hesitation ... 5. doubt, pause, waltz
9. faltering, hesitancy 10. reluctance,
stammering 11. uncertainty, vacillation
15. procrastination
hesped (Heb) ... 6. eulogy 7. funeral
Hesperides (pert to) ...
group name .. 10. Atlantides
guards of .. 12. golden apples (Hera)
nymph .. 5. Aegle 6. Hestia 7. Hespera
8. Arethusa, Erytheia
Hesperus ... 4. poem (Wreck of the
Hesperus) 5. Venus 6. Hesper
11. evening star
Hessian ... 3. fly 5. boots, Hesse
6. German 9. mercenary 10. adventurer
hest ... 6. behest 7. command, precept,
promise 10. injunction
Hestia (pert to) ...
goddess of .. 6. hearth
guard of .. 12. golden apples
mother .. 4. Rhea
hetaera, hetaira (Gr) ... 4. Lais 6. Phryne
8. mistress, paramour
hetaerocracy, governed by ...
8. hetaerae 10. college men
Heterodontus ... 5. shark
heterodox ... 9. heretical 10. unorthodox
11. nonorthodox
heterogeneous (opposed to
homogeneous) ... 5. mixed 6. unlike
7. diverse 9. different 10. dissimilar
11. diversified 13. miscellaneous
hew ... 3. cut 4. chop, fell, hack 5. carve,
sever
hex ... 3. hag, six 4. jinx 5. lamia, spell
7. bewitch 9. sorceress, witchwife
hexad ... 3. six 6. sestet
hexameter verse ...
meter .. 7. six feet
terms .. 7. iams 8. dipodies, trochees
9. anapaests
hexapod ... 7. six feet 9. six-footed
hexarchy ... 9. six States (group)
hexastich, poem or stanza ... 8. six
lines 9. six verses
heyday ... 3. joy 4. acme 8. wildness
11. high spirits 12. highest vigor
14. frolicsomeness
heyrat ... 8. kinkajou (obs)
Hezekiah (pert to) ...
Biblical .. 4. King (12th)

kingdom .. 5. Judah
mother .. 3. Abi
hiatus ... 3. col, gap 5. break, chasm,
pause, space 6. lacuna 7. fissure,
opening 8. interval 12. interruption
Hiawatha (pert to) ...
character, poem by .. 10. Longfellow
grandmother .. 7. Nokomis
mother .. 7. Wenonah
people .. 8. Iroquois
hibernate ... 6. hole up (summer in
torpor), winter 8. estivate 10. latibulize
Hibernia ... 4. Erin 7. Ireland
Hibernian (pert to) ...
color .. 5. green
native .. 8. Irishman
secret society (US 1832) .. 24. Ancient
Order of Hibernians
hickory ... 4. cane 5. Carya, pecan
6. switch 8. kiskatom 9. shellbark
hidalgo ... 5. title 8. nobleman (lower
class)
hidden ... 4. dern, lurk 5. inner, perdu
6. arcane, buried, cached, closed,
covert, latent, masked, occult, secret
7. covered, cryptic, obscure, unknown
8. abstruse, screened, secluded,
secreted 9. concealed, latescent
10. mysterious 11. clandestine
hide ... 3. kip 4. bury, cyst, dern
(derne), lurk, mask, pelt, skin, veil
5. cache, cloak, cover, skulk 6. screen,
shroud 7. conceal, eelskin, rawhide,
secrete 8. carucate, disguise, ensconce,
suppress 9. dissemble 10. camouflage
hidebound ... 5. bound, petty 6. little,
narrow 7. bigoted 9. barkbound
10. restrained (opinion) 11. strait-
laced 12. conventional, narrow-minded
13. hyperorthodox
hideous ... 4. grim, ugly 6. grisly, horrid,
odious 7. ghastly 8. scabrous, terrible
9. frightful, revolting 10. detestable,
terrifying
hiding place ... 3. mew 4. lair 5. cache
9. latibulum
hi-fi devotee ... 10. audiophile
high ... 3. alt, dry, ela (note) 4. tall
5. aloft, drunk, great, noble, steep
6. costly, shrill 7. eminent, haughty
8. elevated, foremost, stranded,
towering 9. excessive, expensive
high (pert to) ...
and mighty .. 8. arrogant 9. imperious
brow .. 7. snob 7. Brahmin, egghead,
high-hat, learned 12. intellectual
14. intelligentsia
flown diction .. 8. euphuism
flying .. 7. Icarian 9. visionary
11. extravagant, pretentious
12. ostentatious 13. grandiloquent
handed .. 9. arbitrary 10. autocratic,
imperative 11. domineering,
overbearing
hat .. 8. snobbish 12. aristocratic
priest .. 3. Eli (Israel) 11. Melchezedek
(Mormon)
sounding .. 4. loud 7. fustian 9. high-
toned 13. grandiloquent
spirited .. 4. edgy 5. fiery 6. lively
9. excitable 10. mettlesome 11. high-

mettled
strung . . **4.** taut **5.** tense **7.** nervous
9. excitable
time . . **3.** fun **5.** binge, spree **8.** carousal
11. opportunity
toned . . **5.** tense **7.** stylish **8.** elevated
9. dignified **11.** fashionable
highest . . . **3.** top **4.** best **6.** utmost
7. maximum, supreme, topmost
8. bunemost, dominant **9.** nth degree,
uppermost
highest (pert to) . . .
comb form . . **4.** acro
dice number . . **3.** six **4.** sise (sice)
point . . **3.** top **4.** acme, apex **5.** crest
6. apogee, climax, summit, vertex,
zenith **7.** ceiling, noonday **8.** meridian,
noontide, pinnacle **11.** ne plus ultra
Highlands, the (pert to)
heavy pole . . **5.** caber
inhabitant . . **4.** Scot
sword . . **8.** claymore
highway . . . **3.** via, way **4.** bahn, iter, path,
pike, road, toby **6.** artery, course, street
7. beltway, freeway, parkway, thruway
(throughway) **8.** arterial, autobahn,
turnpike **9.** boulevard, concourse
10. expressway **12.** thoroughfare
highwayman . . . **5.** thief **6.** bandit, robber
7. brigand, footpad, ladrone **8.** hijacker
9. bandolero **10.** bushranger, highjacker
hike . . . **4.** jerk, toss, walk **5.** hitch,
march, raise, throw, tramp **8.** backpack,
increase
hilarious . . . **3.** mad **5.** merry, noisy
7. festive **8.** mirthful **9.** ludicrous
hilarity . . . **4.** glee **5.** mirth **6.** gaiety,
levity **7.** jollity, whoopee **8.** laughter
9. joviality **10.** jocularity, joyousness
12. cheerfulness, exhilaration
hill . . . **3.** kop, tor **4.** dene, dune, heap,
holt, kame, knob, loma, mesa, paha,
rath **5.** bargh, butte, esker, morra,
mound **6.** barrow, summit **9.** acclivity,
elevation, monadnock
hill myna . . . **8.** starling
hillside . . . **4.** bank, brae, hill, knop, ramp
5. cleve (cleeve), cliff, knoll, scarp,
slope **6.** glacia
hilt . . . **4.** haft **6.** handle
hilum . . . **3.** eye (bean) **5.** hilar, notch
7. opening (kidney)
Himalaya (pert to) . . .
antelope . . **5.** goral, serow
bear . . **5.** bhalu
bearcat . . **5.** panda
bird . . **5.** monal (pheasant) **6.** chough
(crow)
cat . . **5.** ounce
country . . **5.** Nepal
dweller . . **8.** Nepalese
formations . . **7.** Siwalik
goat . . **4.** ibex, kail, tahe
kingdom . . **5.** Hunza
mountain peak . . **3.** Api **7.** Everest, The
Hump
pass . . **7.** Nathula
plant . . **4.** nard (Med)
sheep (wild) . . **6.** bharal, nahoor
swamp . . **5.** Terai
tree . . **3.** fir (silver) **5.** Neoza (pine)

6. Bhutan, deodar (cedar)
himself . . . **4.** ipse
hind . . . **3.** doe **4.** back, deer, rear, stag
6. caudal, haunch, rustic **7.** peasant,
servant **8.** domestic **9.** posterior
11. hindquarter
hind (red fish) . . . **7.** grouper **8.** cabrilla
hinder . . . **3.** bar **5.** block, check, cramp,
debar, delay, deter, embar **6.** cumber,
hamper, impede, retard **7.** prevent
8. restrain **9.** posterior
hindrance . . . **3.** bar, rub **4.** clog, snag,
stop **5.** check, delay **8.** obstacle
9. deterrent, restraint, stricture
10. impediment **11.** obstruction
12. interruption
Hindu, Hindoo . . . **4.** Koli, Sikh **5.** Tamil
6. Indian **9.** Hindustan
Hindu (pert to) . . .
alphabet . . **6.** Sarada
apartment . . **5.** mahal
ascetic . . **4.** yati, yogi **5.** fakir, sadhu
atheist . . **7.** nastika
author of law . . **4.** Manu (Code)
bird . . **5.** Munia **6.** garuda
Buddha's mother . . **4.** Maya
caravansary . . **8.** choultry
carriage . . **6.** gharry (gharri)
caste . . **4.** Bhil **5.** Palli, Sudra, Tamil
7. Brahman
ceremony . . **7.** sraddha
city (sacred) . . **5.** Mecca **7.** Benares
9. Allahabad
coin . . **4.** anna
cymbals . . **3.** tal
dancing girl . . **8.** bayadere
darkness (spiritual) . . **5.** tamas
deity . . **4.** Devi, Rama, Siva (Shiva),
Yama **5.** Ahura, Asura **6.** Brahma,
Vishnu **7.** Krishna **8.** Trimurti
deity consort . . **5.** sakti
dialect . . **5.** Tamil
division . . **5.** Patti, Taraf **6.** zillah
7. Pargana
Dravidian . . **5.** Tamil
drink (sacrificial) . . **4.** soma
evil spirit . . **4.** Mara **5.** asura **6.** yaksha
festival . . **4.** Holi, tali **6.** Dewali, Pongal
9. Dashahara
first mortal to die . . **4.** Yama
flute . . **3.** bin **5.** pungi
garment . . **4.** sari (saree)
Gautama's wife . . **6.** Ahalya
gentleman (Mr) . . **5.** baboo (babu), sahib
giant . . **4.** Bana (thousand-armed)
government . . **6.** sircar
guitar . . **4.** vina **5.** sitar
hero . . **4.** Nala
incarnation . . **4.** Rama **5.** asura **6.** yaksha
jackal . . **4.** kola
king . . **5.** Rajah
language (oldest) . . **5.** Tamil
language (sacred) . . **4.** Pali
loincloth . . **5.** dhoti
magic . . **4.** jadu (jadoo), maya
magician . . **4.** yogi **5.** fakir
meal (wheat) . . **4.** atta (ata)
mendicant . . **4.** naga **8.** sannyasi
merchant . . **6.** banian (banya) **7.** goladar
mind . . **5.** manas
monkey god . . **7.** Hanuman

mountain .. **4.** Meru
mystic .. **4.** yogi
nursemaid .. **4.** ayah
paradise .. **7.** Nirvana
patriarch .. **5.** Pitri
peasant .. **4.** ryot
philosophy .. **4.** yoga, Yuga **5.** tamas
physicist .. **5.** Raman (Nobel 1930)
pillar .. **3.** lat
poet .. **5.** rishi **6.** Tagore (Nobel 1913)
prince .. **4.** raja
reign .. **3.** raj
sacred river .. **6.** Ganges
sage .. **5.** rishi **6.** Dharma **7.** Gautama,
  Mahatma
savant .. **5.** swami
scarf .. **4.** sari (saree)
serpent (semi-human) .. **4.** Naga
servant .. **5.** hamal
slave .. **4.** dasi (fem)
soldier .. **4.** sikh **5.** sepoy
supernatural being .. **6.** Garuda
swan .. **5.** hansa
syllable of assent .. **2.** om
Taraf ruler .. **8.** tarafdar
title .. **3.** Sri **4.** Raja, Rana, Rani **5.** Rajah,
  Ranee **6.** sirdar **8.** maharaja (maharajah)
tree (sacred) .. **5.** pipal **6.** bo tree
tunic .. **4.** jama (jamah)
underworld (series) .. **6.** Patala
village .. **5.** abadi
virtue .. **6.** sharma
widow (cremation) .. **6.** suttee
woman (first) .. **6.** Ahalya
Hindu Ages, Yoga ...
  1st .. **5.** Krita
  2nd .. **5.** Treta
  3rd .. **7.** Dvapara
  4th .. **4.** Kali
  end .. **7.** Pralaya
  total .. **4.** Maha **10.** Manvantara
Hindu goddess ... **3.** Sri, Uma **4.** Devi,
  Kali **5.** Durga, Gauri **6.** Chandi, Shakti
  7. Lakshmi, Parvati **9.** Haimavati (Durga)
Hindu god of ...
  ancestors .. **5.** Pitri
  dead .. **4.** Yama
  fire .. **4.** Agni
  love .. **4.** Kama
  spirit .. **5.** Asura
  unknown .. **2.** Ka
  wisdom (elephant-headed) .. **6.** Ganesa
    (Ganesha)
Hindu religion ...
  abode of gods .. **4.** Meru
  call to prayer .. **4.** azan (adan)
  ceremony, rite .. **7.** araddha
  congregation .. **5.** samaj
  convert (to Islam) .. **6.** shaikh
  creator .. **6.** Brahma
  cremation .. **4.** sati **6.** suttee
  doctrine, destiny .. **5.** karma
  first human to die (deified) .. **4.** Yama
  hell .. **6.** Naraka
  Hinduism .. **5.** Agama **6.** Tantra
    7. Jainism **8.** Buddhism **10.** Brahmanism
  holy man .. **5.** Sadhu (Sadh)
  image worship .. **5.** arati
  incarnation .. **4.** Rama **6.** avatar
    11. Ramachandra
  literature (sacred) .. **4.** Veda **7.** Shastra

lord of the world .. **9.** Jagannath
  (Jagannatha)
monastery .. **4.** math
philosophy (life) .. **5.** artha, atman, prana
  6. tattva
prayer, call to .. **4.** azan (adan)
prayer rug .. **5.** asana, Melas
religion .. **5.** Agama **6.** Tantra **7.** Jainism
  8. Buddhism **10.** Brahmanism
scripture .. **4.** Veda **5.** Agama **6.** Tantra
  7. Shastra
sect .. **4.** Jain (Jaina), Sikh **6.** tantra
Shastra (4 parts) .. **5.** aruti **6.** purana,
  smriti, tantra
Siva worshiper .. **5.** Saiva
Supreme Spirit .. **5.** atman **7.** jivatma
teacher .. **4.** guru **5.** swami
Trimurti (Triad) .. **4.** Siva **6.** Brahma,
  Vishnu
trinity, triad .. **8.** Trimurti (Siva, Brahma,
  Vishnu)
unorthodox .. **7.** Jainism
widow (cremation) .. **6.** suttee
Hindustan (pert to) ...
  dialect .. **4.** Urdu **10.** Hindustani
  people .. **9.** Dravidian
  poet .. **5.** Siraj (Beng)
  rice .. **7.** aghanee
hinge ... **3.** pan (part) **4.** axis, axle,
  hang, knee, turn **5.** joint, pivot, stand
  6. depend, fasten, lamina, pintle
hint ... **3.** cue **5.** imply, refer, tinge, trace
  6. allude, glance **7.** eyewink, inkling,
  suggest **8.** allusion, innuendo, intimate,
  reminder **9.** insinuate **10.** intimation,
  suggestion **11.** insinuation, supposition
hip ... **3.** hop, pod **4.** coxa, limp, miss,
  skip **6.** haunch **8.** greeting
hip, hips (pert to) ...
  bone .. **4.** coxa **5.** ilium **7.** os coxae
    10. innominate
  muscle .. **9.** iliopsoas
  nerve .. **7.** sciatic (largest)
  rose fruit .. **10.** pseudocarp
Hippocrates (pert to) ...
  drug .. **5.** mecon (possibly opium)
  famed as .. **9.** physician (Gr)
  oath .. **11.** Hippocratic
hippopotamus ... **5.** hippo **6.** seacow,
  zeekoe **8.** behemoth (Bib)
hippopotamus, thong of hide ...
  7. chicote
Hiram ... **9.** most noble **10.** King of Tyre
  (Bib)
hire ... **3.** let, use **4.** hack, rent **5.** bribe,
  lease, price, wages **6.** employ, engage,
  reward, salary **7.** charter, stipend
  9. allowance **12.** compensation
hireling ... **4.** esne, serf **5.** slave, venal
  8. employee **9.** mercenary
hirmos ... **4.** hymn **8.** canticle **9.** troparion
hirondelle (Her) ... **7.** swallow
hirsel ... **4.** herd **5.** flock **7.** pasture
hirsute ... **5.** hairy, rough **6.** coarse,
  shaggy **7.** boorish, bristly, uncouth
Hispania (anc) ... **16.** Spain and Portugal
Hispanic ... **6.** Latino **7.** Spanish **13.** Latin
  American **15.** Spanish American
hispid ... **5.** rough **7.** grooved **8.** strigose
hiss ... **3.** boo, tst **4.** fizz **7.** condemn
  8. derision, sibilate **10.** effervesce,

sibilation
historian ... **5.** actor **6.** writer **8.** annalist
   10. chronicler
history ... **5.** drama **6.** annals, events,
   memoir **7.** account **8.** relation, treatise
   9. chronicle, narrative
history (pert to) ...
   Father of .. **9.** Herodotus
   muse of (Gr Myth) .. **4.** Clio
   period .. **3.** era
   personal .. **7.** memoirs **9.** biography,
   genealogy **13.** autobiography
histrio ... **5.** actor
histrion ... **5.** actor
histrionics ... **6.** acting, actors **9.** theatrics
   11. theatricals
hit ... **3.** bop, lob, rap, tap **4.** blow, bunt,
   slam, slap, slog, suit, swat **5.** flick,
   knock, shoot, smite **6.** buffet, larrup,
   please, strike **7.** succeed, success
   9. collision
hitch ... **3.** hop, tie, tug **4.** halt, jerk, knot,
   limp, pull, yoke **5.** catch, cling, crick,
   marry, unite **6.** enlist, fasten, hobble
   8. obstacle **9.** hindrance **10.** enlistment
hitherto ... **3.** ago, yet **5.** as yet **7.** prior
   to **8.** formerly, until now
hit or miss ... **6.** casual **8.** at random,
   by chance, careless **9.** haphazard
Hittite (pert to) ...
   ancestor (Bib) .. **4.** Heth
   city .. **6.** Hamath, Pteria (ruins)
   country .. **6.** Khatti (Asia Minor)
   people (anc) .. **8.** Hittites **10.** aborigines
   storm god .. **6.** Teshup (Teshub)
hoagie, hoagy ... **3.** sub **4.** hero
hoar ... **4.** aged, gray, rime **5.** hoary,
   white **7.** ancient **9.** hoarfrost, venerable
hoard ... **5.** amass, lay up, store **6.** garner,
   supply **7.** husband **8.** treasure, treasury
   10. accumulate, collection
hoarder ... **5.** miser **6.** storer **9.** treasurer
hoarfrost ... **3.** rag **4.** hoar, rime
   7. needles (ice) **9.** Jack Frost
hoarse ... **3.** old **4.** aged, gray **6.** remote
   (in time) **7.** ancient **9.** canescent
hoatzin, hoactzin ... **4.** anna **5.** hanna
   8. pheasant **9.** stinkbird **11.** Opisthocomi
   (group)
hoax ... **3.** bam **4.** bilk, ruse, sham
   5. bluff, cheat, spoof, trick **6.** canard
   7. deceive **8.** artifice **9.** deception
hob ... **3.** elf, hub, peg, pin **4.** game,
   mark **5.** clown, fairy, havoc **6.** ferret,
   rustic, sprite **7.** hobnail **8.** mischief
   9. fireplace, hobgoblin
hobble ... **4.** clog, gait (unequal), halt,
   limp **5.** dance **6.** fetter, tether,
   wabble **7.** dilemma, pastern, shackle
   11. predicament
hobbledehoy ... **4.** gawk **5.** youth
hobbler ... **5.** pilot **7.** boatman, hoveler,
   laborer, soldier **8.** retainer
hobby ... **3.** fad, nag **5.** dolly, horse
   6. falcon **7.** bicycle, pastime
   9. avocation, plaything **10.** hobbyhorse
   12. rocking horse
hobgoblin ... **3.** elf, imp **4.** bogy, pixy,
   Puck **5.** scrat **6.** sprite **7.** bugaboo
   9. coltpixie **10.** apparition **15.** Robin
   Goodfellow

hobnob ... **9.** associate (with), drink with,
   hit or miss
hobo ... **3.** bum **5.** tramp **6.** beggar
   7. vagrant **8.** vagabond
hock ... **3.** ham **4.** pawn, wine **5.** ankle,
   joint, thigh (man) **6.** pledge **7.** disable
   9. hamstring
hockey (pert to) ...
   ball, disk .. **3.** nur **4.** knur, puck
   cup .. **7.** Stanley (prize)
   goal .. **4.** cage
   stick .. **6.** shinny **7.** cammock
   team number .. **5.** seven
hocus ... **4.** drug **5.** cheat **6.** liquor
   (drugged) **7.** deceive, falsify **8.** cheating,
   trickery **10.** adulterate
hocus-pocus ... **5.** cheat, trick **6.** bunkum,
   humbug **7.** juggler **8.** flimflam,
   nonsense, quackery **9.** deception,
   trickster **11.** incantation **12.** charlatanism
   13. sleight of hand **15.** juggler's formula
hod ... **3.** tub **4.** hide **6.** barrow, trough
   7. scuttle
hodgepodge ... **4.** hash, mess, olio, stew
   5. cento **6.** jumble, medley **7.** mélange,
   mixture **10.** miscellany **11.** gallimaufry,
   olla-podrida
hog ... **3.** pig, sow, Sus **4.** bene, boar, galt,
   gilt **5.** sheep (unshorn), shoat, swine
   6. barrow **8.** babirusa (babiroussa),
   javelina **9.** boschvark, razorback
hog ... **6.** corner (the market) **7.** glutton
   8. slattern **9.** take it all **10.** locomotive,
   monopolist
hog (pert to) ...
   breed .. **5.** Essex **9.** Hampshire
   food .. **4.** mast
   ground .. **6.** marmot
   hoglike .. **7.** porcine
   salted side .. **5.** bacon **6.** flitch
   shears (snout) .. **7.** snouter
   thigh (cured) .. **3.** ham
hogfish ... **7.** capitan, pigfish **8.** scorpene
hoggerel ... **5.** sheep **6.** hogger
hoggery ... **4.** hogs **5.** greed
   11. beastliness **14.** hoggish manners
hoggish ... **6.** filthy, greedy **7.** porcine,
   selfish, swinish **10.** gluttonous
hogshead ... **4.** cask **6.** barrel **7.** measure
hogwash ... **5.** swill, waste
hoi polloi ... **3.** mob **5.** herde **6.** masses,
   rabble **7.** the many **8.** populace
   9. multitude
hoist ... **4.** lift, sail **5.** boost, heave,
   hoise, raise **7.** elevate **8.** elevator
hoisting device ... **3.** gin **4.** jack
   5. crane, davit, lewis **7.** capstan, derrick
   8. elevator, windlass **9.** parbuckle
hoity-toity ... **5.** giddy, proud **6.** snooty
   7. flighty, haughty **8.** arrogant
   11. exclamation, harum-scarum,
   patronizing, thoughtless
   13. irresponsible
hold ... **3.** own **4.** bind, have, keep,
   lien, seat, stow **5.** avast, cling,
   delay, grasp, judge **6.** adhere, arrest,
   cleave, clench, defend, detain, endure,
   harbor, regard, retain **7.** contain,
   control, custody **8.** consider, foothold,
   maintain, thurrock (ship's), treasury
   9. anchorage, constrain, entertain,

prosecute **11.** compartment
hold (pert to) . . .
  back . . **3.** dam **4.** last, stem **5.** delay,
  deter, stint **6.** detain, hinder, refuse,
  retard **7.** abstain, inhibit, repress
  8. restrain
  belief . . **7.** suppose
  dear . . **7.** cherish
  fast . . **5.** cling **6.** adhere **9.** persevere
  forth . . **5.** offer, speak **7.** declaim,
  descant, exhibit, expound **8.** continue,
  maintain, propound
  off . . **5.** avert, delay **7.** repulse, ward
  off **9.** stay aloof, temporize
  on . . **4.** stop, wait **6.** endure, retain
  7. forbear **8.** continue
  opinion . . **4.** deem
  out . . **4.** last **6.** endure, refuse, resist
  7. exclude **8.** continue
  session . . **3.** sit **7.** convene **8.** assemble
  together . . **6.** adhere, cohere **8.** be joined
  9. co-operate
  up . . **3.** rob **4.** buoy, halt, lift, rein
  5. check, delay, raise **6.** hinder, resist,
  retard **7.** display, exhibit, pillory (to
  scorn), robbery, support, sustain
  water . . **5.** sound **10.** consistent
holder . . . **3.** cop (yarn) **4.** file **5.** owner,
  payee **6.** bearer, binder, lienor, tenant
  7. trustee **8.** endorsee **9.** mortgagor,
  possessor, recipient **10.** receptacle
hold in . . .
  check . . **4.** curb, rein **6.** arrest, bridle
  7. control **8.** restrain
  custody . . **4.** jail **6.** detain, intern
  hand . . **6.** assure **7.** control, promise,
  toy with
  mind . . **6.** harbor **7.** cherish **9.** entertain
holding . . . **5.** asset, claim, stake, tenet,
  title, trust **6.** belief, equity, estate,
  tenure **8.** interest, property **9.** retention
  10. possessing, possession, supporting
holding fast . . . **9.** tenacious **10.** persistent
holding sway . . . **7.** regnant **8.** dominant,
  reigning
hole . . . **3.** den, pit **4.** bore, cave, cove,
  dive, flaw, gulf, lair, nook, slot,
  vent **5.** abyss, chasm, fault, hovel,
  place, shaft **6.** burrow, cavern, cavity,
  cellar, hollow, prison **7.** impasse,
  opening, orifice, ostiole **10.** excavation
  11. predicament
hole (pert to) . . .
  bowling ball . . **4.** grip
  cable (ship's) . . **5.** hawse
  enlarger . . **6.** reamer
  implement . . **3.** awl, eye **4.** bore **5.** drill
  8. stiletto
  metal mold . . **5.** sprue
  mud . . **6.** wallow
  wall . . **5.** niche
  water . . **5.** oasis
  whirlpool . . **5.** gourd (obs)
Holi (or Hoolee) . . . **8.** festival (Hind)
holia . . . **6.** salmon (humpback)
holiday . . . **4.** fete **5.** feria, merry **6.** fiesta,
  jovial, outing **7.** festive, playday
  8. festival, vacation **9.** convivial, festivity
  10. recreation
holiness . . . **5.** piety, title (Pope) **8.** sanctity
  9. godliness **10.** sacredness

11. saintliness **13.** righteousness
Holland . . . **11.** Netherlands (which see)
Holland . . .
  capital . . **8.** The Hague (Court)
  9. Amsterdam
  city . . **3.** Ede **5.** Doorn **6.** Leyden
  9. Amsterdam, Rotterdam
  government . . **8.** monarchy
  liquor . . **3.** gin **8.** schnapps
  oddity . . **5.** dikes **6.** canals, tulips
  painter . . **6.** Rubens **7.** Van Eyck
  people . . **5.** Dutch
  port . . **4.** Edam
  pottery . . **5.** delft (delf)
  province . . **4.** Edam **7.** Drenthe, Zeeland
  river . . **3.** Ems, Lek **5.** Meuse, Rhine
  7. Scheldt (Schelde)
  sea . . **5.** North
  village . . **3.** Ede
hollow . . . **3.** den, pit **4.** thin, void
  5. bight, empty, false, gaunt, sinus
  6. cavern, cavity, cirque, corrie,
  groove, hungry, socket, sunken, vacant
  7. concave, unsound **8.** capsular,
  specious **9.** cavernous, depressed,
  faithless, insincere, worthless
  10. sepulchral **12.** unsatisfying
hollowed . . . **6.** cavate **7.** concave, glenoid
holly . . . **4.** holm, hull, Ilex **5.** yapon
  6. hulver, laurel **8.** Eryngium
  9. blackjack, Ilicaceae **10.** Sapindales
hollyhock . . . **5.** color **7.** Althaea, blue-red
  9. perennial
holm . . . **3.** oak **5.** holly, islet, marsh
  7. bottoms, low land
holobaptist . . . **12.** immersionist
holocaust . . . **9.** sacrifice (by fire)
  11. destruction **13.** burnt offering
holy . . . **5.** godly, pious **6.** chaste, devout,
  sacred **7.** epithet (Relig), sainted
  8. hallowed **9.** venerated
Holy, holy (pert to) . . .
  Alliance name . . **10.** Metternich
  Bottle (Rabelais) . . . **6.** Bacbuc
  carpet . . **5.** kiswa (kiswah)
  comb form . . **5.** hagio
  Communion . . **9.** Eucharist
  cow (smoke, Toledo, etc.) . . **3.** wow
  Father . . **4.** Pope
  Island . . **11.** Lindisfarne
  Joe . . **8.** sky pilot **9.** clergyman
  Land . . **9.** Palestine
  oil . . **6.** chrism **7.** unction
  Ones . . **9.** Innocents (slain by Herod)
  orders . . **10.** ordination
  Roman Empire name . . **4.** Otto **7.** Francis
  9. Frederick (Barbarossa)
  11. Charlemagne
  Scripture(s), Writ . . **5.** Bible
  water, et al . . **11.** sacramental
  water sprinkler . . **11.** aspergillum
  war . . **5.** jihad
  Willie's Prayer . . **4.** poem **5.** Burns
Holy Grail (pert to) . . .
  castle . . **9.** Monsalvat (Mt)
  guardian . . **8.** Amfortas
  knight . . **7.** Galahad
  legend . . **8.** Sangraal (Sangreal)
  quest by . . **4.** Bors **7.** Galahad **9.** Percivale
  terms . . **7.** platter, wine cup
homage . . . **5.** dulia, honor, liege **6.** fealty,

latria **7.** loyalty, ovation, respect,
worship **9.** deference, obeisance,
reverence **10.** allegiance
12. commendation
homard ... **7.** Homarus, lobster
hombre ... **3.** man **4.** homo, male **6.** fellow
home ... **4.** care, goal (games), kern
(kirn), nest **5.** abode, astre, grave,
heart **6.** asylum, estate, hearth
7. habitat, village **8.** domicile, dwelling
9. residence **10.** fatherland, habitation
home (pert to) ...
base .. **3.** den **5.** plate
dislike .. **9.** ecophobia
Home Sweet Home author .. **5.** Payne
(John Howard 1823)
Irish King's .. **4.** Tara
of the gods .. **7.** Olympus
of the Golden Fleece .. **7.** Colchis
homely ... **4.** ugly **5.** plain **6.** humble,
kindly, simple **7.** plainly **8.** domestic,
homelike, informal, plebeian, uncomely
9. unsightly **10.** intimately
11. comfortable **13.** unpretentious
homemade ... **5.** plain **6.** simple
8. domestic, handmade, homespun
Homer (pert to) ...
birthplace .. **5.** Chios (claimed)
book .. **5.** Iliad **7.** Odyssey
burial place .. **3.** Ios (Isl)
hero .. **6.** Aeneas
Homer's poems (pert to) ...
rhapsodists .. **9.** Homeridae
student, reciter of .. **7.** Homerid
8. Homerist
study of .. **10.** Homerology
style .. **7.** Homeric
homesickness ... **7.** Heimweh **9.** mal
du pays, nostalgia
homespun ... **5.** cloth, plain, rough
6. coarse, russet **8.** domestic,
homemade **10.** not elegant, unpolished
(person)
homicide ... **5.** morth **6.** murder **7.** killing
12. manslaughter
homily ... **5.** adage **6.** sermon
8. assembly, converse **9.** communion,
discourse
homing pigeon ... **13.** carrier pigeon
hominy ... **4.** samp **5.** maize **10.** hulled
corn
Homo sapiens ... **3.** man **4.** homo
9. anthropos
Honduras ...
capital .. **11.** Tegucigalpa
city .. **4.** Tela **6.** Roatan **8.** Trujillo
12. Puerto Cortes
discoverer .. **8.** Columbus
gulf .. **7.** Fonseca
Indian people .. **5.** Lenca
language .. **7.** Spanish
river .. **4.** Ulua **5.** Negro **6.** Patuca
hone ... **4.** long, pine **5.** delay, dress,
stone (sharpening), strop, yearn
6. lament **7.** grumble, sharpen
8. oilstone **9.** whetstone
honest ... **4.** open **5.** frank **6.** candid,
chaste **7.** genuine, up and up, upright
8. faithful, suitable, virtuous **9.** guileless,
honorable, ingenuous, integrity
10. creditable **13.** unadulterated

15. straightforward
honesty ... **5.** honor **6.** equity **7.** justice
8. fairness **9.** integrity, rectitude
11. genuineness, uprightness
12. truthfulness **15.** trustworthiness
honey ... **3.** mel **5.** melli (comb
form), sweet **6.** nectar **7.** sweeten
10. endearment
honey (pert to) ...
bear (sloth) .. **8.** Melursus
bearing .. **11.** melliferous
bee .. **4.** Apis **6.** dingar **7.** deseret
9. mellifera
bird .. **3.** iao **6.** manuao **10.** honey eater
brew .. **4.** mead
buzzard .. **4.** kite, pern
comb .. **4.** raat **5.** favus **8.** alveolus
drink .. **4.** mead **5.** morat
flowing .. **11.** mellifluent, mellifluous
pert to .. **8.** melissic
sucking .. **11.** mellisugent, mellivorous
yellow .. **6.** dorado **10.** melichrous
Hong Kong ...
capital .. **8.** Victoria
government .. **11.** Crown Colony
island .. **12.** Stonecutters
peninsula .. **7.** Kowloon
Honolulu ...
capital of .. **6.** Hawaii
island site .. **4.** Oahu
port .. **11.** Pearl Harbor
suburb .. **3.** Ewa
honorable, honourable ... **5.** moral, title
7. upright **8.** honorary **9.** estimable,
reputable, venerable **10.** creditable
11. commendable, illustrious,
meritorious, respectable
honorably ... **5.** nobly **6.** fairly, justly
8. worthily **9.** equitably, reputably,
uprightly
honorarium ... **7.** douceur
honored ... **5.** famed, feted **6.** graced
7. awarded, revered **8.** knighted
9. accoladed
hood ... **4.** corf, cowl, hide, mail (armor)
5. amice, blind, cloak **6.** bonnet,
camail, capote **7.** capuche (capouch)
8. babushka, burnoose (burnous),
capsheaf, covering, liripipe, mozzetta,
tapadera **12.** strong-arm man
hood (suff) ... **9.** condition
hooded ... **9.** cucullate
hooded seal ... **11.** bladdernose
hoodwink ... **4.** dupe, fool, hide, wile
5. blear, blind, cheat, cover, cozen
6. befool, delude **7.** deceive, mislead
9. blindfold
hooey ... **4.** blah, bunk **5.** tripe **7.** baloney,
hogwash **8.** buncombe, malarkey,
nonsense **13.** horsefeathers
hoof ... **4.** clee, frog, walk **5.** cloof (clufe,
cluve) **6.** ungula **7.** pastern (part)
8. periople (part), pododerm
hoof-paring tool ... **8.** butteris
hoof-shaped ... **8.** ungulate
hoof track ... **5.** piste
hook ... **4.** gaff, lure **5.** catch, chape,
cleek, crome, curve, hamus, snare,
steal **6.** anchor, clevis, fasten, hangle,
tenter **7.** hamulus
hookah, hooka ... **4.** pipe **8.** narghile

hooked ... 6. curved, hamate 7. angular, cleeked 8. aduncous (adunc), anchoral, aquiline, uncinate
Hooker (Thomas) ... 9. clergyman 18. Luther of New England
hooks (group) ... 5. Party (Neth) 9. pulldevil, scrodgill 10. Kabbeljaws (Nobles)
hookworm ... 7. Necator 9. Uncinaria
hooligan ... 6. loafer 7. gorilla, hoodlum, ruffian 8. larrikin
hoop ... 4. bail, band, ring 5. clasp 6. circle, wicket 7. circlet 8. surround
hoop skirt ... 9. crinoline 11. farthingale
Hoosier poet ... 5. Riley (J Whitcomb)
Hoosier State ... 7. Indiana
hop ... 3. fly 4. drug, halt, jump, leap, limp, trip, vine 5. bound, caper, dance, frisk, opium 6. flight, gambol, spring 8. narcotic
hope ... 3. bay 4. opal, spes, Spes (Goddess) 5. haven, inlet, trust 6. aspire, desire, expect 7. cherish, promise 8. optimism, reliance 11. expectation 12. anticipation
hoped for ... 7. sperate
hopeful ... 8. probable, sanguine 9. confident, expectant 10. propitious
hopeless ... 4. vain 6. futile 7. forlorn, useless 8. downcast 9. desperate, incurable 10. despairing, despondent 11. ineffectual 12. disconsolate, irremediable 13. irrecoverable, irretrievable
hopelessness ... 7. despair 8. futility 13. impossibility
hop kiln ... 4. oast (ost)
hoplite ... 7. soldier
hopper ... 3. box 5. chute 6. dancer, jumper, leaper 7. penguin (rock) 10. receptacle 11. grasshopper
hopscotch ... 6. pebble, peever 7. pallall
Horace ... 4. poet 10. Ars Poetica
Horae (Gr Relig) ... 4. dike (justice) 6. Eirene (peace) 7. Eunomia (wisdom) 9. goddesses 11. Book of Hours
horal ... 6. hourly
horde ... 4. army, camp, clan, pack 5. crowd, swarm, tribe, troop
Horde, Golden ... 6. Tatars (Mongol)
Horde, Great (Anthrop) ... 5. Kazak 7. Kirghiz
horizon ... 4. blue 5. limit, range 6. circle, sea rim 7. azimuth, sea line, sky line 8. junction (earth and sky), boundary
horizon glass ... 7. sextant
horizontal ... 4. flat 5. level 8. parallel (to horizon)
hormone ... 8. estrogen 9. cortisone
horn ... 4. Cape, cusp, gore, peak, tuba 5. alarm, bugle, cornu, keras, siren 6. antler, beaker, cornet, vessel 7. buccina, process (animal), trumpet 8. tentacle 9. appendage
horn (pert to) ...
  blare .. 4. toot 7. fanfare, tantara 9. tantarara
  comb form .. 5. kerat 6. kerato
  crescent moon .. 4. cusp
  drinking (anc) .. 6. rhyton
  insect's .. 7. antenna

Jewish .. 7. shophar (shofar)
player .. 6. bugler 9. cornetist, trumpeter
producing .. 11. keratogenic
trumpet .. 6. kerana (kerrana)
unbranched (antler) .. 3. dag 7. pricket
hornbeam ... 8. ironwood
hornbill ... 4. bird, tock 6. homrai, toucan 7. Buceros
horned animal (Myth) ... 7. Unicorn 9. Monoceros
horned rattlesnake ... 3. asp 5. viper 8. cerastes 10. sidewinder
horned toad ... 6. lizard 9. Iguanidae
hornet ... 4. wasp 5. Vespa 6. crabro
horny tissue ... 7. keratin 8. keratoid (ceratoid), keratose (ceratose)
horologe ... 4. dial 5. clock, watch
horoscope ... 3. map 5. chart 6. scheme 7. diagram
horrendous ... 7. fearful 8. horrible
horrible ... 4. dire, grim 6. grisly, horrid, odious 7. ghastly, hideous 8. dreadful, shocking, terrible 9. atrocious, frightful, revolting 10. detestable, horrendous
horror ... 3. awe 4. fear 5. dread 6. aghast, terror 8. aversion, distress 10. abhorrence 11. abomination, detestation 13. consternation
hors d'oeuvre ... 6. canapé, relish 8. aperitif 9. antipasto, appetizer
horse ... 3. cob, nag 4. colt, foal, mare, mule, plug, pony, prad, race, stud 5. beast, burro, draft, filly, genet (jennet), hobby, mount, pacer, steed 6. bronco (broncho), cheval, dobbin, donkey, equine, garran, hippos, maiden, pelter, rouncy 7. caballo, cavalry, charger, courser, Equidae, gelding, hackney, harness, mustang, prancer, quarter, stepper, trotter 8. roadster, stallion, trotting 9. broomtail
horse (pert to) ...
  ankle .. 4. hock
  arena .. 10. hippodrome
  Australian .. 5. dingo, myall 8. warragal, yarraman
  blanket .. 5. manta
  breastplate .. 7. poitrel (peytrel)
  broken-down .. 6. garran, gleyde
  buyer (of nags) .. 5. coper 7. knacker
  calico .. 5. pinto
  collar .. 7. bargham
  comb form .. 4. hipp 5. hippo 6. hippus
  command .. 3. gee, haw, hup 4. whoa 6. giddap
  covering .. 9. caparison
  cry .. 5. neigh 6. whinny
  dealer .. 7. chanter, scorser
  disease .. 5. surra (surrah) 6. heaves, lampas, spavin 7. founder, lampers
  draft .. 9. Percheron
  family .. 7. Equidae 9. Miohippus, Orohippus
  fast .. 6. pelter
  feed box .. 6. manger
  female .. 4. mare, yaud 5. filly
  fly .. 4. cleg (clegg) 6. botfly
  foot .. 4. frog, hoof 7. fetlock, pastern
  forehead .. 8. chanfrin
  gait .. 3. run 4. lope, pace, trot, walk 6. canter, gallop

genus . . **5.** Equus
giant (Norse) . . **7.** Goldfax
goddess . . **5.** Epona
gray . . **8.** schimmel
hide . . **8.** cordovan
hired . . **4.** hack
hoof (part) . . **7.** caltrop **8.** periople
laugh . . **5.** snort **6.** guffaw, heehaw
leap . . **6.** curvet, hurdle **9.** ballotade
lover . . **10.** hippophile
mackerel . . **5.** atule, tunny **6.** bonita
male . . **4.** stud **7.** gelding **8.** stallion
manège term . . **5.** longe, mount
　6. pesade **7.** piaffer, saccade **8.** caracole
　9. estrapage
measure . . **4.** hand
miracle (Myth) . . **5.** Arion
monster (fabled) . . **11.** Hippocampus
old . . **4.** jade, yaud **5.** skate **8.** harridan,
　old paint
opera . . **7.** Western
pace . . **4.** lope, trot **5.** amble **6.** canter
pack . . **7.** sumpter
pair . . **4.** span, team
pasturage right . . **9.** horsegate
piebald . . **5.** pinto
pole . . **5.** poler, wheel
prehistoric . . **8.** Eohippus
　10. Mesohippus, Pliohippus
　13. Protorohippus
racer . . **4.** pony **6.** mudder, plater, staker
ref to . . **6.** equine, equoid, hippic
　9. caballine
relay (remounts) . . **6.** remuda
riding . . **3.** cob
rope . . **5.** longe **6.** halter
roundup . . **5.** rodeo
saddle . . **3.** cob **5.** mount **7.** palfrey
shoer . . **7.** farrier **10.** blacksmith
slang . . **3.** nag **4.** hack, plug **6.** dobbin
　8. bangtail
small . . **3.** cob, tit **4.** pony **5.** bidet,
　genet (jennet) **8.** Galloway, Shetland
sorrel . . **4.** roan **6.** chestnut
spirited . . **4.** Arab **5.** steed **6.** rearer
　7. courser
stable of . . **6.** string
study of . . **9.** hippology
swift . . **6.** pelter **7.** Pacolet
talking (Myth) . . **5.** Arion
three (harnessed) . . **6.** tandem **7.** unicorn
track, arena . . **10.** hippodrome
trappings . . **5.** manta **6.** tackle **7.** harness
　9. caparison
trotting . . **6.** Morgan
turn . . **7.** passade
war . . **5.** steed **7.** charger **8.** destrier
　(anc)
white-streaked face . . **4.** shim
wild . . **6.** bronco, tarpan **7.** mustang
　8. warragal (warrigal)
winged . . **7.** Pegasus
horse, breed . . . **4.** Arab, Barb **5.** Shire,
　Waler **6.** Cayuse, Morgan **7.** Arabian,
　Belgian, Hackney, Mustang, Suffolk
　8. Galloway, Normandy, Palomino,
　Shetland **9.** Appaloosa, Miohippus,
　Percheron **10.** Clydesdale
horse, color . . . **3.** bay, tan **4.** pied,
　roan **5.** cream, pinto **6.** calico, sorrel
　7. brindle, dappled, piebald **8.** chestnut,

palomino, schimmel, skewbald **10.** flea-
bitten
horse, famed (and rider) . . . **4.** Tony
　(Tom Mix) **5.** Grani (Sigurd) **6.** Bayard
　(Rinaldo), Rienzi (Gen Sherman),
　Silver (Lone Ranger), Trojan (legend),
　Whitey (Zachary Taylor) **7.** Alborak
　(Mohammed), Morengo (Napoleon),
　Pegasus (Gr Myth), Trigger (Roy
　Rogers), Xanthus (Achilles)
　8. Comanche (Gen Custer), Sleipnir
　(Odin), Soapsuds (Will Rogers) **9.** Black
　Bess (Dick Turpin), Houyhnhnm
　(Gulliver's Travels), Incitatus (Caligula),
　Rosinante (Don Quixote), Traveller
　(Gen Robt E Lee) **10.** Bootlegger
　(Will Rogers), Bucephalus (Alexander
　the Great), Cincinnati (Gen Grant),
　Copenhagen (Wellington at Waterloo),
　King Philip (Gen Forrest) **11.** Black
　Beauty (legend), Vegliantino (Orlando)
　12. Little Sorrel (Stonewall Jackson)
horseman . . . **5.** rider **6.** cowboy
　7. centaur, vaquero **8.** buckaroo
　10. cavalryman, equestrian
　12. broncobuster
horsemanship . . . **6.** manège
horseradish tree . . . **3.** ben (oil) **5.** behen
　(behn) **7.** Moringa
Horus (pert to) . . .
bird . . **6.** falcon
father . . **6.** Osiris
hawk-headed god of . . **3.** day
mother . . **4.** Isis
slayer of . . **4.** Seth
hospice . . . **3.** inn **6.** asylum, imaret
　9. hospitium, infirmary
hospitable . . . **6.** kindly **7.** cordial
　8. friendly, gracious **9.** receptive,
　welcoming **10.** neighborly
hospital . . . **6.** crèche, refuge
　9. ambulance (mobile), infirmary
　10. nosocomium, sanatorium,
　sanitarium **11.** institution, xenodochium
　12. ambulatorium
hospitality . . . **7.** accueil, welcome **8.** open
　door **9.** open house, xenodochy
　10. cordiality **13.** receptiveness
host . . . **3.** sum (obs) **4.** army **5.** swarm
　6. legion, throng **8.** assemble, landlord
　9. multitude, sacrifice **11.** entertainer
hostel . . . **3.** inn **5.** hotel, motel **6.** tavern
　8. lodgings **9.** residence (student)
hostelry . . . **3.** inn **5.** hotel **6.** hostel,
　tavern **11.** caravansary
hostile . . . **5.** enemy **7.** adverse (law),
　opposed **8.** contrary, inimical
　10. malevolent, unfriendly
　11. belligerent **12.** antagonistic
　13. unsympathetic
hostilities . . . **3.** war **5.** feuds, raids
hostility . . . **5.** anger **6.** animus, enmity,
　hatred, rancor **7.** ill will, warfare
　8. opponent **9.** animosity, antipathy
　10. antagonism, bitterness, opposition,
　resentment **11.** contrariety
　13. antisocialism **14.** unfriendliness,
　vindictiveness
hostler . . . **5.** groom **7.** equerry
　9. innkeeper, stableboy, stableman
Host vessel . . . **3.** pyx **5.** paten

10. monstrance
hot ... 3. red 5. calid, eager, fiery
6. fervid, raging, recent, torrid, urgent
7. burning, calidus, excited, fervent,
glowing, peppery, violent 8. feverish,
sizzling, vehement 10. hot-blooded,
passionate
hot cakes ... 8. kneepads (army sl)
hotel ... 3. inn 5. lodge 6. hostel, tavern
7. albergo 11. caravansary
hot-tempered ... 5. angry, breth, fiery
7. enraged, iracund 8. choleric, wrathful
10. hot-blooded
Hottentot, S Africa (pert to) ...
cloak .. 6. kaross
hut .. 5. kraal
language .. 7. Khoisan
mixed native .. 6. Griqua
musical instrument .. 4. gora (gorah)
nickname .. 9. Khoi-Khoin (Koi-Koin)
(men of men)
people .. 5. Bantu 7. Bushman
hound ... 4. hunt 5. chase, track 6. follow,
pursue 7. devotee 9. scoundrel
hound (animal) ... 4. alan 6. Afghan,
basset, beagle, setter 7. harrier, skirter
8. Cerberus (Myth), elkhound, foxhound
9. boarhound, dachshund, deerhound,
greyhound, staghound, wolfhound
10. bloodhound, otterhound
hounds, relay of ... 8. avantlay
hour (pert to) ...
astrology .. 7. inequal 9. planetary
by the .. 5. horal 6. horary
Eccl .. 4. sext 9. canonical
Latin .. 4. hora 5. Horae (Book of Hours)
measure .. 9. hourglass
term .. 4. time 6. period 7. measure
8. interval
houri ... 5. nymph (Muslim)
Hours, Book of ... 5. Horae
house ... 3. eco (comb form) 4. casa,
firm, home 5. abode, cover, lodge,
tribe 6. billet, family 7. cottage,
enclose, lineage, mansion, quarter,
shelter, theater 8. audience, bungalow,
Congress, domicile, dwelling
9. playhouse, residence, workhouse
10. habitation, Parliament
house (pert to) ...
astrology .. 7. mansion, mundane
9. planetary
boarding .. 3. inn 5. hotel 6. tavern
9. dormitory
comb form .. 3. eco 4. oeco, oiko
correction .. 9. Bridewell (Eng)
11. reformatory
dog .. 6. kennel
government .. 5. Lords 7. Commons
15. Representatives
ranch .. 4. casa 6. casita 8. hacienda
roof .. 9. penthouse
small .. 3. hut 4. nest 5. cabin, shack
stately .. 5. villa 6. palace 7. mansion
summer .. 6. casino, gazebo 9. belvedere
warming .. 6. infare
household (pert to) ...
deity .. 5. Lares 7. Penates
domestic .. 6. family, menage
fairy .. 4. Puck
linen .. 6. napery

housekeeping ... 8. oikology
10. management 11. hospitality
House of ... 4. Keys (Isle of Man) 5. David,
Lords, Peers 7. Bishops, Commons,
Windsor 11. Seven Gables
housewarming ... 6. infare
11. merrymaking
Houston, Texas ...
capital .. 8. Republic (Texas, 1837)
college .. 4. Rice
named for .. 10. Sam Houston (Gen)
nickname .. 12. Space City USA
site .. 11. Ship Channel
site of .. 4. NASA
hovel ... 3. den, hut 4. shed 5. cabin,
hutch, shack 6. dugout 7. shelter
hover ... 4. flit, soar 5. brood, drift,
float 6. linger 7. shelter 9. hang about
12. be irresolute
however ... 3. but, how, tho, yet
6. anyhow, though 7. at least
8. although 11. at all events
12. nevertheless 15. notwithstanding
howl ... 3. bay, cry 4. wail, yell, yowl
6. lament 7. ululate
howling monkey ... 5. araba
hoyden, hoiden ... 4. rude 5. a romp
6. tomboy 7. ill-bred
Hoyle's forte ... 5. cards, games
hub ... 3. hut 4. axle, nave 6. center
(centre) 7. hummock 12. protuberance
(rough)
Hub (The) ... 6. Boston
hubbub ... 3. ado, din 4. game (US Ind),
stir 6. bustle, clamor, outcry, racket,
rumpus, tumult, uproar 8. rowdy-dow
9. agitation, commotion, confusion
10. turbulence
hubristic ... 8. arrogant, insolent
12. contemptuous
huck ... 3. hip 4. hook, howk 6. haunch,
higgle, hollow 7. bargain
Huck Finn (pert to) ...
con man .. 4. Duke 7. Dauphin
creator .. 5. Twain 7. Clemens
friend .. 9. Tom Sawyer
feud family .. 7. Granger
11. Shepherdson
raft mate .. 3. Jim
huckleberry ... 5. bacca 9. blueberry
12. Vacciniaceae
huckleberry endocarp ... 6. pyrene
huckster ... 6. broker, hawker, vendor
7. peddler 8. pitchman, retailer
9. middleman
huddle ... 3. hug 5. crowd 6. bustle,
confer, jumble, mingle 7. confuse
8. assemble, disorder, grouping
(football) 9. confusion, skinflint
10. conference 14. conglomeration
Hudson (pert to) ...
boat .. 8. Half Moon (Henry Hudson's)
explorer .. 11. Henry Hudson
River School .. 8. Painters (19th Cent)
River seal .. 7. muskrat
hue ... 4. form, tint, tone 5. color, guise,
shade, shout, swart, tinge 6. outcry
7. swarthy 8. shouting 10. complexion
huff ... 4. puff 5. anger, bully, swell
6. offend 7. inflate
hug ... 4. hold 5. clasp, seize 6. adhere

7. embrace, welcome 8. greeting

huge . . . 3. big 4. vast 5. giant, great, large 7. immense, mammoth, massive, monster, titanic 8. colossal, enormous, gigantic 9. monstrous 10. gargantuan

Huguenot . . . 10. Protestant

Huguenot leader . . . 6. Adrets (Baron)

hui (Chin) . . . 4. firm 5. guild 7. society (secret) 11. partnership

huisache . . . 4. wabe (wabi) 5. shrub 7. popinac

huissier . . . 5. usher 7. bailiff, sheriff 10. doorkeeper

huitre . . . 6. oyster

hulky . . . 5. bulky, large 6. clumsy 7. hulking, loutish

hull . . . 3. pod 4. free, husk 5. calyx, frame (ship), shell, shoot, strip 8. covering

hullabaloo . . . 3. din 6. clamor (clamour), hubbub, outcry, racket, tumult, uproar 9. confusion

hulled corn . . . 4. samp 5. maize 6. hominy

hulver . . . 5. holly

hum . . . 4. buzz, sing (with closed lips) 5. croon, drone 6. murmur 7. deceive

human . . . 3. man 4. homo, kind 6. humane, mortal 7. Adamite 8. merciful

human (pert to) . . .
being . . 3. man 6. mortal, person 7. Adamite 8. creature
bondage . . 7. slavery
race . . 3. man 7. mankind
skull . . 10. death's-head
structure . . 7. anatomy
trunk . . 5. torso

humble . . . 3. low 4. mean, meek, mild, poor 5. abase, abash, demit, lower, lowly, plain 6. modest, simple, subdue 7. degrade, mortify 8. chastise, deferent, disgrace, plebeian, reverent 9. humiliate 10. unassuming 12. unpretending

humbug . . . 4. bosh, fake, flam, guff, hoax, sham 5. cheat, fraud, guile, trick 7. deceive, mislead 8. pretense 9. deception, imposture, stratagem

humid . . . 4. damp, dank 5. moist 6. sultry 8. vaporous

humiliate . . . 5. abase, abash, shame 6. humble, nither 7. affront, degrade, mortify 8. disgrace

humiliation . . . 7. subdual 9. abasement 11. disgraceful 13. mortification

humility . . . 6. humble (spirit) 7. modesty 8. meekness, mildness 9. lowliness (mind) 10. humbleness

hummingbird . . . 3. ava 4. star 5. sylph, topaz 6. rufous, Sappho 7. colibri, Lucifer 8. calliope 9. sheartail, thornbill, thorntail 10. rackettail 11. Trochilidae

humor, humour . . . 3. fun, wit 4. baby, mood, whim 5. blood, cater, fancy, fluid, freak, quirk 6. comedy, levity, nature, please 7. caprice, gratify, indulge 8. drollery 10. comicality 11. inclination, temperament

humorist . . . 3. wag 5. comic, droll 8. comedian 11. entertainer

humorist (famed) . . . 3. Ade, Nye 4. Cobb, Ward (Artemus) 5. Dunne (Peter

Finley), Twain (Clemens) 6. Rogers (Will) 7. Lardner, Leacock, Thurber 8. Benchley, Perelman 9. Wodehouse

humorous . . . 5. funny, humid, moist, witty 6. jocose 7. amusing, jocular 9. facetious, laughable, whimsical 10. capricious

hump . . . 4. arch, hunk, lump 5. bulge, exert, hurry, mound, sulks 7. hummock 8. shoulder 12. protuberance

humpbacked . . . 6. humped, kyphos 8. deformed, kyphosis 9. camel back 11. hunchbacked

humpbacked fish . . . 5. whale 6. salmon, sucker 9. whitefish

humus . . . 4. mold, soil 5. humin, mulch

Hun . . . 6. Attila, vandal 7. soldier 9. barbarian 10. Ephthalite

hunch . . . 4. bend, hump, lump 5. crook, fudge, shove 6. chilly, crouch, frosty, thrust 9. intuition 12. protuberance

Hunchback of Notre Dame (pert to) . . .
actor . . 6. Chaney 8. Laughton
author . . 4. Hugo
character . . 9. Esmeralda (gypsy), Quasimodo (The Hunchback)
French name . . 16. Notre Dame de Paris

hunched . . . 7. gibbous

hundred (pert to) . . .
comb form . . 5. centi, hecto 7. hecaton
eyed being . . 5. Argus
fold . . 8. centuple 12. centuplicate
historian (of centuries) . . 11. centuriator
Latin . . 6. centum
men, soldiers . . 7. century 12. centumvirate
number . . 7. ten tens 9. five score
symbol . . 1. C
victim sacrifice . . 8. hecatomb
weight . . 6. cental 7. centner
years . . 7. century 9. centenary, centurial

Hundred Days (pert to) . . . 8. Napoleon, Waterloo (Battle 1815)

hundred percent . . . 5. quite 8. entirely 10. altogether 14. unquestionable

hundredth of a right angle . . . 4. grad

Hundred Years War . . . 5. Crécy (Cressy)

hung . . . see *hang*

Hungarian (pert to) . . . see also *Hungary*
army . . 6. Honvéd 9. Honvédség
cavalryman . . 6. hussar
Communist leader . . 4. Nagy 5. Kádár
composer . . 5. Lehár, Liszt 6. Bartók, Kodály
dance . . 7. czardas
ethnic group . . 6. Magyar
gypsy . . 7. tzigane
hash . . 7. goulash
hero . . 5. Arpad 7. Kossuth
Hungarian name . . 12. Magyarország
language . . 6. Magyar, Uralic 10. Finno-Ugric
legislature . . 8. Felsohaz
measure . . 5. antal, itcze
partridge . . 6. Perdix
Pretender to the throne . . 4. Otto
turnip . . 8. kohlrabi
wine . . 5. Tokay
writer . . 6. Molnár

Hungary . . .
capital . . 8. Budapest

city . . **6.** Szeged **8.** Debrecen
lake . . **7.** Balaton
plain . . **6.** Alfold
river . . **6.** Danube
hunger . . . **4.** long, want **6.** acoria, desire, famine, thirst **7.** craving **8.** appetite, coveting, voracity **9.** esurience
hungry . . . **4.** avid, poor **5.** eager **6.** barren, hollow, jejune **7.** starved **8.** esurient, famished, indigent **10.** avaricious
Hung Society (secret) . . . **5.** Triad (Man, Earth, Heaven) **6.** Deluge
hunt . . . **3.** dig **4.** seek **5.** chase, delve, hound, probe, quest, track, trail **6.** ferret, follow, pursue, search, shikar
hunter . . . **3.** dog **5.** green, horse, jager, Jason, Orion **6.** cuckoo, Nimrod **7.** shikari (shikaree), stalker, trapper, venerer **8.** huntsman
hunting (pert to) . . .
act of . . **6.** venery **7.** pursuit **10.** cynegetics
coyotes . . **7.** wolfing
dog . . **5.** dhole **6.** basset, beagle, setter **7.** pointer
Dogs (Astron) . . **13.** Canes Venatici
expedition . . **6.** safari
fond of . . **7.** venatic
horn . . **5.** bugle
leopard . . **7.** cheetah
hurdy-gurdy . . . **4.** lire, rota **5.** organ (street) **7.** sambuke **10.** instrument (lutelike), waterwheel
hurl . . . **4.** cast, pelt, rush, toss **5.** fling, pitch, sling, throw **6.** elance (dart), hurtle **9.** overthrow
hurlbarrow . . . **11.** wheelbarrow
hurled . . . **4.** cast, sent **5.** flung, slung, threw **6.** pelted, tossed **7.** hurtled, twisted **8.** betossed
hurly-burly . . . **5.** storm **6.** tumult, uproar **9.** agitation, confusion **10.** excitement
huron . . . **6.** grison (animal) **9.** black bass
Huron . . . **4.** lake **6.** Indian **9.** Iroquoian
hurrah . . . **3.** joy **4.** viva **5.** cheer, huzza, shout **7.** triumph **8.** applause **10.** hallelujah **11.** exclamation **13.** encouragement
hurricane . . . **5.** storm **6.** baguio **7.** cyclone, Hurakan (god), tornado, typhoon (in China Sea)
hurry . . . **3.** hie **4.** rush, scud **5.** chase, haste, impel, sessa, speed **6.** hasten, scurry, tumult, urge on **7.** quicken **8.** dispatch, expedite **9.** agitation, commotion **10.** expedition **11.** disturbance, precipitate
hurst . . . **4.** hill, wood **5.** copse, grove, knoll **7.** hillock (wooded)
hurt . . . **4.** harm, maim, pain **5.** lesed, parry **6.** damage, grieve, impair, injure, injury, offend **8.** distress, mischief **9.** detriment **10.** impairment
hurtful . . . **6.** malign, nocent **7.** baneful, harmful, malefic, nocuous, noisome, noxious, painful **9.** injurious **10.** pernicious **11.** destructive, detrimental, prejudicial **15.** disadvantageous
hurtle . . . **4.** dash, push **5.** clash, fling **6.** assail, jostle **7.** collide, resound

8. brandish
husband . . . **3.** eke **4.** mate, save **5.** marry, store **6.** direct (frugally), farmer, spouse, tiller **7.** espouse, granger, manager, steward **8.** conserve **9.** cultivate, economize **10.** husbandman
husbandry . . . **6.** thrift **7.** economy, farming, tillage **10.** management (domestic) **11.** agriculture, cultivation
husband's brother . . . **5.** levir
hush . . . **3.** tut **4.** calm, hist, lull **5.** allay, quiet, still **6.** soothe **7.** appease, silence **10.** keep secret
husk . . . **4.** bran, leam, rind **5.** shood, shuck, straw
husky . . . **3.** dry **5.** burly, harsh **6.** hoarse, strong **7.** raucous **8.** powerful
Husky . . . **3.** dog **6.** Eskimo **8.** Malemute
huss . . . **7.** dogfish
hussar . . . **4.** fish (banded) **6.** dolman (jacket) **10.** cavalryman, skirmisher
hussy . . . **4.** girl, jade **8.** strumpet **9.** housewife
hustings . . . **5.** court **8.** platform (Guildhall)
hut . . . **3.** cot **4.** cote, isba, shed, skeo (fisherman's) **5.** cabin, hogan, hovel, igloo, jacal, scale **6.** lean-to, shanty, wigwam
hutch . . . **3.** bin, box, car, hut, pen **4.** coop **5.** chest, hoard, hovel **6.** coffer, humped, shanty, warren
hyacinth (pert to) . . .
color . . **5.** tenne **7.** blue-red
genus . . **10.** Hyacinthus
mineral . . **6.** zircon
myth . . **4.** iris, lily (Turk's cap)
of Peru . . **9.** Cuban lily
precious stone . . **8.** sapphire (legend)
wild . . **6.** camass
hybrid . . . **7.** mongrel **9.** half-breed
hybrid (pert to) . . .
buffalo . . **7.** cattalo
dog . . **5.** Husky **7.** mongrel
fruit . . **7.** plumcot, tangelo **8.** citrange
horse . . **4.** mule **5.** hinny, jenny
vegetable . . **6.** pomato
zebra . . **7.** zebrass, zebrula **8.** zebrinny
hydra . . . **4.** evil **6.** polyps **11.** thermometer
Hydra (Gr) . . . **6.** island **7.** serpent **13.** constellation
hydraulic (pert to) . . .
brake . . **8.** cataract
element . . **5.** water
engine . . **3.** ram **6.** tremie
product . . **5.** power
hydria . . . **3.** jar **6.** kalpis
hydrocarbon . . . **5.** tolan (tolane) **6.** ethane, octane, pinene, pyrene, tolane, toluol **7.** benzene, methane, terpene **9.** acetylene
hydrocarbon radical . . . **4.** amyl **6.** pentyl
hydrocyanic acid . . . **7.** cyanide, prussic **8.** fumigant
hydrogen . . . **1.** H **3.** gas **7.** element (univalent)
hydroid . . . **9.** polyplike
hydrophobia . . . **5.** lyssa **6.** rabies
Hydrus . . . **12.** water serpent (fabled) **13.** constellation
hyena . . . **6.** mammal **8.** aardwolf

9. earthwolf 13. Tasmanian wolf
hygienic . . . 7. sterile 8. sanitary
9. healthful 10. uninfected
12. prophylactic
hylophagous . . . 10. wood-eating
hymenopter, hymenopteron . . . 3. ant,
bee, fly 4. wasp 9. ichneumon
hymn . . . 3. ode 4. song (of praise)
5. dirge, music, paean (pean) 6. anthem,
hirmos, Te Deum 7. chorale 8. doxology
9. Trisagion 11. recessional
hymn (pert to) . . .
book . . 6. hymnal
composer . . 7. hymnist
12. hymnographer
science of . . 9. hymnology
singing of . . 7. hymnody
victory . . 9. epinicion
hypnotic . . . 6. opiate, sleepy 8. mesmeric,
narcotic, sedative 9. soporific
12. somnifacient 13. sleep-inducing
hypnotist . . . 6. Mesmer 9. mesmerist
10. hypnotizer
hypnotize . . . 5. charm 6. dazzle
8. entrance 9. fascinate, mesmerize,
spellbind
hypochondriac . . . 4. hypo 6. insane
7. invalid (imaginary) 8. dejected,
neurotic 9. depressed, psychotic
10. nosomaniac

hypocrisy . . . 4. cant 6. deceit 8. feigning
9. falseness 10. sanctimony, simulation
11. outward show
hypocrite . . . 4. fake 5. cheat 7. tartufe
(tartuffe) 8. deceiver 10. dissembler
hypocritical . . . 5. false 8. specious,
two-faced 9. insincere 10. Janus-faced
11. pharisaical 13. sanctimonious,
self-righteous
hypodermic glass vessel . . . 7. ampoule
(ampule)
hypodermic injection . . . 4. shot
11. inoculation
hypothesis . . . 3. ism 6. theory 7. premise,
theorem 8. proposal 9. condition,
postulate 10. assumption
11. proposition, supposition
hypothetical . . . 8. academic
11. conditional, conjectural, speculative,
theoretical
hypothetical (pert to) . . .
being . . 3. ens 5. entia (pl) 6. entity
biological unit . . 2. id
force . . 2. od
medium . . 5. ether
hyrax . . . 8. procavia
hyssop . . . 4. mint 11. aspergillum
hysteria . . . 7. anxiety 12. emotionalism
hysterical . . . 7. frantic 8. frenzied,
wild-eyed 9. emotional 12. uncontrolled

I

I . . . 2. me 3. eye 4. iota (Gr), self 6. letter
(9th), myself 7. pronoun
I (pert to) . . .
big . . 3. ego
excessive . . 8. iotacism
love . . 3. amo
Iago . . . 7. villain (Othello)
iambus . . . 4. foot, iamb
iatrics (comb form) . . . 11. treatment of
iatrology . . . 7. healing 8. treatise
Iberia . . . 5. Spain 7. Georgia (anc)
ibex . . . 3. sac, tur, zac 4. kail (kyl)
6. sakeen 8. antelope
ibid . . . 6. lizard 7. monitor
ibidem . . . 4. ibid 9. same place
ibis . . . 5. guara, stork 9. gourdhead
Ibsen drama . . . 6. Ghosts 8. Peer Gynt
11. A Doll's House, Hedda Gabler
ice . . . 4. rime 5. frost, glacé, glaze
6. freeze 7. congeal, diamond, jewelry
11. refrigerant, refrigerate
ice (pert to) . . .
bartender's . . 5. rocks (sl)
cream dish . . 4. cone, soda 6. frappé,
mousse, sundae 7. parfait
dessert . . 5. glacé 6. frappé 7. sherbet
fine, slushy . . 4. grue, hail, sish, snow
5. flake, frost, sleet
fishing . . 4. chug
glacier . . 4. neve 5. serac
mass . . 4. berg, calf, floe 5. serac
6. icecap 7. glacier, growler
pendent . . 6. icicle

sea . . 6. sludge
Iceland . . .
airport . . 9. Kopavogur
assembly . . 7. Althing
bird . . 4. gull 6. falcon 10. gyrofalcon
capital . . 9. Reykjavik
city . . 3. Hof 8. Akureyri
dramatist . . 12. Siguryonsson
epic . . 4. Edda
first discoverer . . 8. Norseman (about
870)
giant . . 4. Atli
glacier . . 6. Jökull 11. Orafajökull
god . . see *Norse god(s), goddess*
government . . 8. republic (1944)
legends . . 5. Eddas, Sagas 12. Volsunga
Saga
Parliament . . 7. Althing (world's oldest)
product . . 7. herring
sculptor . . 9. Sveinsson
volcano . . 5. Askja, Hekla, Katla
ichneumon . . . 3. fly 8. mongoose
9. Herpestes 12. hymenopteron
ichor . . . 5. fluid (of the gods)
ichthus . . . 4. fish 6. amulet, symbol
8. talisman
ichthyophagy . . . 10. fish eating
icicle . . . 7. shoggle 10. stalactite,
stalagmite
icing . . . 8. frosting, meringue
icterus . . . 6. oriole 7. disease 8. jaundice
10. yellowness
ictus . . . 4. beat (rhythm), blow 6. accent,

stress, stroke

icy . . . **4.** cold **5.** algid, gelid **6.** frigid, frosty, frozen **7.** glacial **8.** chilling

id . . . **4.** idem, unit **5.** idant **6.** libido, psyche, suffix **7.** the same

Idaean (pert to) . . .
dweller of . . **5.** Mt Ida
goddess . . **4.** Rhea (Crete) **6.** Cybele (Asia Minor)
nature goddess . . **6.** Cybele **11.** Great Mother

Idaho . . .
capital . . **5.** Boise
city . . **7.** Orofino **9.** Pocatello
crop (famed) . . **8.** potatoes
dam . . **5.** Oxbow **8.** Brownlee
famed citizen . . **5.** Borah (Sen)
monument . . **16.** Craters of the Moon
mountain . . **8.** Sawtooth **11.** Bitterroots
river . . **5.** Snake
salmon (landlocked) . . **7.** kokanee
State admission . . **10.** Forty-third
State bird . . **8.** bluebird
State flower . . **7.** syringa
State motto . . **11.** Live Forever **12.** Esto Perpetua
State nickname . . **8.** Gem State

ide (id) . . . **3.** orf (orfe) **4.** fish **7.** the same

idea . . . **4.** clue, idée, ideo (comb form) **5.** ethic, motif **6.** belief, notion **7.** concept, meaning, opinion, wrinkle **10.** impression **11.** supposition

ideal . . . **4.** type **5.** dream, model, Thule (Myth) **6.** unreal **7.** paragon, pattern, perfect, typical, Utopian **8.** complete, exemplar, fanciful **9.** faultless, imaginary, visionary **10.** conceptual, consummate, idealistic **11.** mental image, theoretical **12.** intellectual

idealist . . . **7.** dreamer **8.** romancer **9.** visionary **11.** illusionist

idealistic . . . **9.** fictional, visionary **10.** starry-eyed **13.** philosophical

ideate . . . **5.** think **6.** invent **7.** imagine **8.** conceive **9.** prefigure

identical . . . **4.** same, self, twin **5.** alike, equal **10.** equivalent, tantamount

identification . . . **3.** tag **4.** disk, sign **5.** badge, brand **6.** naming **7.** earmark **11.** recognition, unification

identify . . . **4.** name **5.** place, prove **8.** coalesce **9.** designate, establish **13.** associate with

identity . . . **5.** unity **7.** oneness **8.** equality, sameness **9.** exactness **11.** homogeneity **13.** individuality

ideologist . . . **7.** dreamer **8.** theorist **9.** visionary

idiocy . . . **7.** amentia, anoesia, fatuity, idiotry **10.** deficiency (mental) **11.** foolishness

idiograph . . . **9.** trademark

idiom . . . **6.** phrase **7.** diction **8.** language **11.** peculiarity

idiosyncrasy . . . **9.** mannerism **11.** peculiarity **12.** eccentricity **14.** characteristic

idiot . . . **3.** oaf **4.** dolt, fool **5.** booby, dunce, moron **6.** cretin, nitwit **7.** dullard, half-wit **8.** imbecile **9.** blockhead, simpleton

idiotic . . . **4.** daft **5.** crazy **7.** foolish **9.** senseless **12.** feeble-minded

idle . . . **4.** laze, lazy, loaf, sorn, vain **5.** drone, empty, inert **6.** loiter, otiose, tiffle, truant, unused, vacant **7.** leisure, loafing, trivial, useless **8.** baseless, inactive, indolent, slothful, trifling **9.** unfounded, worthless **10.** groundless, unemployed, unoccupied **11.** ineffectual, unwarranted

idleness . . . **5.** folly, sloth **6.** vanity **7.** inertia **8.** delirium, faniente, laziness **9.** silliness **10.** inactivity, triviality **15.** lightheadedness

idler . . . **4.** hobo **5.** drone **6.** loafer **7.** dawdler, lounger **8.** loiterer

idol . . . **3.** god (sacred) **4.** Baal, icon, zemi **5.** afgod, deity (heathen), eikon, satyr **6.** effigy, fetish, idolum, statue **7.** darling, fallacy, phantom, picture **8.** impostor **9.** pretender

idolater . . . **5.** pagan **6.** adorer **7.** admirer, Baalist, Baalite, heathen **8.** idolizer **9.** worshiper

idolize . . . **5.** adore **6.** esteem, revere **7.** worship **10.** idolatrize

idyl, idyll . . . **4.** poem **5.** image **7.** bucolic, eclogue, picture **8.** pastoral

i.e. . . . **5.** id est **6.** that is

if . . . **2.** si **3.** gif **8.** granting, provided **9.** supposing

if ever . . . **4.** once

if not . . . **4.** else, nisi (law) **6.** unless

igneous rock . . . **4.** boss, dike, trap **5.** magma **6.** basalt **7.** peridot **10.** granophyre **11.** molten magma

ignis . . . **4.** fire

ignite . . . **4.** burn, fire, heat **5.** light **6.** kindle **7.** blaze up, flare up **9.** set fire to

ignoble . . . **3.** low **4.** base, mean, vile **6.** menial **8.** plebeian, shameful **11.** disgraceful **12.** dishonorable, disreputable

ignoramus . . . **4.** dolt, fool **5.** dunce **6.** nitwit, no bill (law) **11.** know-nothing

ignorance . . . **5.** tamas (Hind) **9.** nescience **12.** inexperience

ignorant . . . **7.** unaware **8.** nescient **9.** unknowing, untutored **10.** illiterate, unlettered **13.** inexperienced, unintelligent

ignore . . . **3.** cut **4.** omit, snub **7.** condone, disobey, neglect **8.** overlook **9.** disregard, eliminate

Igorot . . . **6.** Bontok **7.** Nabaloi **8.** Kankanai **10.** Indonesian

iguana . . . **6.** goanna (goana), lizard **7.** monitor, tuatara **9.** Iguanidae **10.** lace lizard

I Have Found It . . . **6.** Eureka (Calif motto)

ihi (Maori) . . . **7.** skipper **8.** halfbeak **10.** stitchbird

IHS . . . **5.** Jesus **6.** symbol **10.** in hoc signo

iiwi . . . **4.** bird

ikbal . . . **7.** arrival **8.** prestige **10.** prosperity

Iknaton . . . **9.** Amenhotep, Amenophis (IV)

ikona . . . **9.** greenhorn, simpleton
ileum . . . **9.** intestine (small)
ilex . . . **5.** holly **7.** holm oak **11.** Paraguay
    tea
Iliad (pert to) . . .
    founder (anc) . . **4.** Troy **5.** Ilium
    poem author . . **5.** Homer
    poem character . . **4.** Ajax **6.** Hector
    7. Stentor **8.** Achilles, Brisseis
    9. Agamemnon, Cassandra
ilium . . . **4.** bone (pelvic)
ilium . . . **4.** Troy (anc)
ilk . . . **4.** kind, sort, type **6.** nature
    9. character
ill . . . **3.** bad, mal (comb form) **4.** evil,
    hard, poor, rude, sick **5.** badly, wrong
    6. ailing, malice, poorly, savage,
    unkind **7.** noxious, painful, unlucky
    9. dangerous, difficult **10.** disastrous,
    indisposed, iniquitous, malevolent,
    unpolished, unskillful **11.** unfavorable,
    unfortunate, unwholesome
    12. disagreeable, inauspicious
ill (pert to) . . .
    at ease . . **7.** awkward **9.** graceless,
    maladroit
    bred . . **4.** rude **7.** uncivil **8.** impolite
    9. bourgeois
    hap . . **10.** misfortune
    humored . . **5.** cross, moody
    natured . . **4.** dour **5.** cross, moody,
    surly **6.** morose, sullen **7.** crabbed
    10. crosspatch
    tempered . . **7.** bilious **8.** choleric
    timed . . **5.** inapt **8.** untimely **9.** premature
    10. malapropos **11.** inexpedient,
    inopportune
    will . . **6.** enmity, malice
    11. malevolence
illegal . . . **4.** foul **7.** illicit **8.** outlawry,
    unlawful, wrongful **10.** contraband,
    unofficial **12.** illegitimate, unauthorized
illegal entry . . . **6.** ringer
illimitable . . . **4.** vast **8.** infinite
    9. boundless **11.** measureless
    12. immeasurable, unrestricted
Illinois . . .
    airport . . **5.** O'Hare
    capital . . **8.** Vandalia (first) **11.** Springfield
    city . . **5.** Elgin **6.** Peoria **7.** Chicago,
    Decatur **8.** Evanston, Waukegan
    9. Centralia
    lake . . **8.** Michigan
    slogan . . **13.** Land of Lincoln
    State admission . . **11.** Twenty-first
    State nickname . . **7.** Prairie
illiterate . . . **6.** unread **8.** ignorant,
    untaught **9.** inerudite, unlearned,
    unrefined, untutored, unwritten
ill-mannered . . . **4.** rude **7.** boorish
illness . . . **6.** malady **8.** cachexia, sickness
    9. complaint, distemper **10.** affliction
    13. indisposition
illuminant . . . **3.** gas **4.** lamp **9.** petroleum
    10. Kleig light
illuminate . . . **5.** adorn, color, light
    6. illume **7.** explain, lighten, miniate
    8. emblazen, illumine **9.** elucidate,
    enlighten, irradiate, rubricate
    10. illustrate
illumination, unit of . . . **3.** lux **4.** phot

illusion . . . **5.** fancy **6.** mirage **7.** chimera,
    fallacy, mockery, phantom **8.** delusion,
    phantasy **9.** deception, false show
    10. apparition **13.** hallucination,
    misconception
illusive . . . **5.** false **6.** unreal **8.** spectral
    9. deceitful, deceptive, imaginary
    10. phantasmal, transitory
illusory . . . **5.** false **8.** delusory, illusive
    9. deceptive, erroneous, imaginary,
    unfounded **10.** fallacious
illustrate . . . **4.** cite, draw **5.** adorn
    7. explain, picture **8.** beautify
    9. elucidate, exemplify, represent
    10. illuminate
illustrious . . . **5.** noble, noted **6.** famous,
    heroic **7.** eminent, exalted, radiant
    8. glorious, luminous, renowned,
    splendid **9.** brilliant, honorable
    10. celebrated
image . . . **3.** god **4.** copy, icon, idea,
    idol, ikon, type **6.** alraun, aspect,
    effigy, idolon, mirror, recept, sphinx,
    statue, typify **7.** eidolon, phantom,
    picture, portray **8.** illusion, likeness,
    phantasm **9.** semblance **10.** apparition,
    conception, simulacrum **11.** counterpart
    12. reproduction
imaginary . . . **5.** ideal **7.** fancied **8.** fanciful,
    illusory, mythical **10.** fictitious
imaginary disease . . . **9.** nosomania
imagination . . . **5.** dream, fancy
    8. phantasy, poetical
imagine . . . **5.** dream, fancy, opine, think
    6. ideate **7.** suppose **8.** conceive
    10. conjecture
imam . . . **6.** caliph, priest (Muslim)
imbecile . . . **4.** dolt, weak **5.** anile,
    idiot, inane, moron **6.** cretin, dotard,
    feeble, stupid, witlet **7.** fatuous, idiotic,
    witling **9.** driveling **10.** half-witted
    12. feeble-minded
imbed . . . **5.** embed, inset **6.** cement
    9. establish
imberbe . . . **9.** beardless
imbibe . . . **4.** soak **5.** drink, imbue,
    learn **6.** absorb, inhale **8.** saturate
    10. assimilate
imbroglio . . . **5.** brawl **11.** embroilment,
    predicament **16.** misunderstanding
imbrue . . . **3.** fig, wet **4.** soak **5.** color,
    stain (with blood), steep **6.** defile,
    drench **7.** moisten **8.** saturate
imbue . . . **3.** dye **5.** steep, teach,
    tinge **6.** infuse, leaven **7.** ingrain,
    inspire **8.** permeate, saturate, tincture
    9. inculcate **10.** impregnate
imitant . . . **9.** imitation **11.** counterfeit
imitate . . . **3.** ape **4.** copy, mime,
    mock **5.** mimic **6.** borrow **7.** emulate
    8. pastiche, resemble, simulate
    9. dissemble, reproduce
imitation . . . **4.** copy, echo, sham **5.** apery,
    apism, paste **6.** ectype, olivet (pearl),
    parody **7.** mimesis, mimicry **8.** travesty
    9. burlesque **10.** caricature, simulation
    12. onomatopoeia
imitative . . . **5.** apish **8.** apatetic
    9. emulative, imitation **10.** simulative
    11. counterfeit
immaculate . . . **4.** pure **5.** clean **6.** chaste

8. spotless, unsoiled 9. faultless, undefiled, unstained, unsullied

immanence ... 7. inbeing 9. inherence 10. indwelling, innateness

immanent ... 5. inner 6. inward 8. internal 9. intrinsic 10. indwelling

immaterial ... 6. slight 8. trifling 9. spiritual 10. impalpable, intangible 11. disembodied, incorporeal, unimportant 12. supernatural 13. insignificant, unsubstantial

immature ... 5. crude, green 6. callow, unripe 7. untried 8. untimely, youthful 9. premature 10. unfinished 11. undeveloped

immeasurable ... 7. endless 8. infinite 9. boundless, unlimited 10. indefinite 11. illimitable, innumerable 12. immeasurable, incalculable, unfathomable 13. indeterminate 16. incomprehensible

immediacy ... 9. awareness, closeness 10. directness 11. punctuality

immediate ... 4. next, stat 6. direct, prompt 7. instant, nearest, present 10. continuous, succeeding

immediately ... 3. now 4. anon 7. closely 8. directly, promptly 9. instantly, therewith 11. straightway 12. without delay

immemorial ... 3. old 7. ageless, ancient 8. dateless 9. out of mind 11. prehistoric, traditional

immense ... 4. huge, vast 5. grand, great 6. superb 7. mammoth, titanic 8. enormous, infinite 9. monstrous 10. prodigious, unmeasured

immerge ... 3. dip 4. sink 5. merge 6. engulf, plunge 7. immerse 8. inundate, submerge

immerse ... 3. dip 4. bury, dunk, sink 5. douse, souse 6. absorb, plunge 7. baptize, engross 9. overwhelm

imminent ... 7. nearing 8. menacing, upcoming 9. impending 10. near at hand 11. approaching, forthcoming, overhanging, threatening

immobile ... 3. set 5. fixed, inert 6. stable 8. moveless 9. immovable, obstinate, unfeeling 10. inflexible, motionless, stationary

immoderate ... 5. ultra, undue 7. extreme 9. excessive 10. exorbitant, inordinate 11. extravagant, intemperate 12. unreasonable

immolation ... 8. oblation, offering 9. sacrifice

immoral ... 3. bad 6. wicked 7. corrupt, vicious 8. depraved, indecent 9. dissolute 10. licentious, misconduct

immortal ... 6. divine 7. abiding, endless, eternal, godlike, undying 8. enduring 9. ambrosial, ceaseless, celebrity, perpetual 10. superhuman 11. amaranthine, everlasting 12. imperishable 13. incorruptible

Immortal (Taoism) ... 8. Chang Kuo

immortality ... 4. fame 6. amrita (conferring) 9. anathasia 11. lasting fame 13. deathlessness 15. everlastingness

immovable ... 3. pat 4. fast, firm 5. fixed, rigid 6. stable 7. adamant 8. immobile, obdurate 9. obstinate, unfeeling 10. inflexible, stationary

immunity ... 7. freedom 8. impunity 9. exemption 10. resistance (power of) 11. unrestraint

immure ... 4. wall 6. entomb 7. confine 8. imprison, surround 9. encompass 11. incarcerate

immutable ... 4. firm 6. stable 7. eternal 8. constant 9. obstinate 10. inflexible, invariable 12. unchangeable 13. unadulterated

imp ... 3. bud, elf, fay 4. brat, cion, pixy, slip 5. child, demon, devil, fairy, graft, rogue, scion, shoot, youth 6. repair (falconry), spirit, sprite 7. progeny 9. offspring

impact ... 4. pack, slam 5. brunt, force, shock, wedge 6. effect, stroke 7. contact, impulse, meaning 8. striking 9. collision, fix firmly, impinging

impair ... 3. mar 4. harm, hurt, ruin, rust, wear 5. break, spoil 6. damage, debase, injure, lessen, reduce, weaken 7. vitiate 8. decrease, enfeeble 11. deteriorate

impale ... 4. edge, gore, join (Her), spit, stab 5. hem in, spike 6. border, pierce, punish 7. confine, torture 8. encircle, surround

impalement ... 5. calyx 8. stabbing 10. punishment 11. coats of arms (united)

impalpable ... 4. fine 10. immaterial, intangible 13. infinitesimal

impart ... 3. say 4. give, lend, tell 5. grant, share, yield 6. confer, convey, inform, reveal 7. divulge 8. disclose, discover 9. partake of 10. distribute 11. communicate

impartial ... 4. even, fair, just 7. neutral 8. unbiased 9. equitable 12. unprejudiced 13. disinterested, dispassionate

impartiality ... 7. justice 8. fairness 10. neutrality 11. unprejudice 17. disinterestedness

impassable ... 6. stolid 9. impassive 10. impervious, unpassable 11. impermeable, unnavigable 12. impenetrable

impasse ... 8. cul-de-sac 9. stalemate 10. blind alley

impassible ... 9. impassive, unfeeling

impassioned ... 6. ardent 7. amorous, zealous 8. eloquent, vehement 10. passionate

impassive ... 4. calm 5. stoic 6. serene 7. passive 9. apathetic 10. impassable 12. invulnerable 13. insusceptible

impatient ... 5. eager, testy 6. uneasy 7. anxious, fretful, itching, peevish, restive 8. choleric, petulant, restless 9. impetuous, irascible, irritable 10. intolerant

impavid ... 8. fearless

impeach ... 4. harm 6. accuse, charge, hinder, impair, impede, indict 7. arraign, censure, prevent 9. challenge, criminate, discredit, disparage

impeccable . . . **8.** flawless, innocent **9.** faultless **10.** immaculate

impede . . . **3.** bar, let **4.** clog **5.** block, debar, estop **6.** hamper, hinder, retard, stymie (stimy) **8.** encumber, obstruct, restrict

impediment . . . **3.** bar, rub **4.** snag **5.** hitch **6.** defect, malady **7.** baggage, barrier **8.** obstacle **9.** hindrance **10.** difficulty **11.** encumbrance, obstruction

impel . . . **3.** put **4.** move, urge **5.** drive, force, forge **6.** compel, incite, induce, obsess, prompt, propel **7.** actuate **9.** constrain, influence

impel a boat . . . **3.** oar, row **4.** pole **5.** scull

impelling force . . . **7.** impetus **8.** momentum

impending . . . **7.** nearing **8.** awaiting, imminent, menacing **9.** hindering **11.** overhanging, threatening

impenetrable . . . **5.** dense **10.** impervious **11.** impregnable, inscrutable **12.** inaccessible, unfathomable **13.** unimpressible **14.** unintelligible

impenitent . . . **8.** obdurate **10.** uncontrite **11.** unrepentant, unrepenting

imperative . . . **4.** mood (Gram) **6.** needed, urgent **7.** binding **8.** pressing **9.** directive, imperious, mandatory, necessary **10.** compulsory, obligatory, peremptory **13.** authoritative

imperceptible . . . **6.** subtle **9.** invisible **10.** insensible **13.** inappreciable, indiscernible, infinitesimal **14.** unintelligible

imperfect . . . **3.** mal (pref) **4.** cull **5.** frail **6.** faulty, second **7.** errable **8.** fallible, immature, impaired **9.** blemished, defective **10.** inadequate, incomplete

imperfection . . . **4.** flaw, vice **5.** fault **6.** defect **7.** blemish, failing **8.** fraility, weakness **10.** deficiency **11.** shortcoming **14.** incompleteness

imperfectly . . . **8.** slightly **12.** inadequately

imperial . . . **5.** regal, royal **6.** kingly, lordly, purple **8.** majestic **9.** imperious, masterful, monarchal, sovereign

imperial (pert to) . . .
Academy . . **6.** Han-lin (Chin)
blue . . **5.** smalt
cap . . **5.** crown
city (anc) . . **4.** Rome
domain . . **6.** empire
legislature . . **4.** Diet (Jap)
officer . . **8.** palatine

imperil . . . **4.** risk **6.** expose **8.** endanger **10.** jeopardize

imperious . . . **6.** lordly **7.** haughty **8.** arrogant, despotic, dominant, pressing **10.** commanding, compelling, tyrannical **11.** dictatorial, domineering, overbearing

imperishable . . . **7.** eternal, undying **8.** enduring, immortal **11.** everlasting **14.** indestructible

impermanent . . . **8.** fleeting, temporal, unstable **9.** ephemeral, momentary, temporary, transient **10.** evanescent, short-lived

impersonate . . . **3.** ape **4.** pose **6.** pose

as, typify **7.** portray **9.** exemplify, personate (law), personify, represent, symbolize

impertinence . . . **4.** sass **9.** impudence, insolence, unfitness **10.** incivility **11.** impropriety, irrelevance

impertinent . . . **4.** rude **5.** saucy **7.** ill-bred **8.** impudent, insolent **9.** frivolous, officious **10.** inapposite, irrelevant **12.** inapplicable, inconsequent **13.** disrespectful

imperturbability . . . **8.** ataraxia (ataraxy), serenity

imperturbable . . . **4.** calm, cool **6.** placid, serene, steady **8.** tranquil **9.** impassive **10.** phlegmatic **13.** dispassionate

impervious . . . **5.** tight **6.** opaque **7.** callous **10.** impassable **12.** impenetrable, inaccessible

impetuosity . . . **5.** ardor **6.** fougue **8.** rashness

impetuous . . . **3.** hot **4.** rash **5.** eager, hasty, heady, sharp **6.** ardent, bensel (motion), fervid, sudden **7.** furious, violent **8.** forcible, headlong, reckless, vehement **9.** impulsive **10.** passionate **11.** precipitate

impetus . . . **4.** birr **7.** impulse **8.** momentum, stimulus **9.** incentive

impi (Zulu) . . . **8.** armed men, warriors

impignorate . . . **4.** pawn **6.** pledge **8.** mortgage

impious . . . **7.** godless, profane **9.** nefandous, undutiful **10.** irreverent **11.** irreligious

impish . . . **5.** elvan **6.** elfish **7.** puckish **9.** malignant **11.** mischievous

implacable . . . **6.** enmity **11.** immitigable **12.** unappeasable **14.** uncompromising

implant . . . **4.** root **5.** infix, inset, plant **6.** enroot, infuse, insert **7.** enforce, engraft, impress, inspire, instill **9.** establish, inculcate, inoculate, insinuate, introduce

implement . . . **3.** kit **4.** peel, tool **5.** dolly, knife, means, scoop, tongs **6.** pestle, petard **7.** fulfill, utensil **8.** carry out, complete, material, scissors **9.** equipment **10.** accomplish, instrument

implement (pert to) . . .
ancient . . **4.** celt **6.** eolith **9.** paleolith (stone)
cleaning . . **3.** mop **5.** broom, brush **6.** vacuum **7.** sweeper
hide flesher . . **6.** slater
holding . . **5.** tongs **6.** pliers **8.** tweezers
lifting . . **3.** pry **5.** crane, lever, tongs
lumbering . . **4.** tode **6.** peavey (peavy)
nap . . **6.** teasel
printing . . **5.** biron, press **6.** brayer
reaping . . **5.** mower **6.** reaper, scythe, shears, sickle
surgical . . **7.** scalpel **9.** tenaculum
threshing . . **5.** flail

implicate . . . **5.** imply **7.** embroil, entwine, involve **8.** entangle **10.** interweave **11.** incriminate

implicit . . . **5.** tacit **7.** implied, virtual **8.** complete, inherent **9.** entangled, potential **11.** unqualified

12. constructive 13. unquestioning

implied ... 5. tacit 11. inferential 12. not expressed

implore ... 3. ask, beg 4. pray 5. crave 7. beseech, entreat, solicit 8. petition 10. supplicate

imply ... 4. hint, mean 5. argue 6. infold 7. connote, involve, suggest, suppose 9. predicate

impolite ... 4. rude 5. crude, rough 7. uncivil 10. ill-behaved, mannerless, ungracious, unmannerly, unpolished 12. discourteous 13. disrespectful

impolitic ... 6. unwise 9. untactful 10. indiscreet 11. inexpedient 12. undiplomatic

import ... 5. drift, sense, value 6. denote, weight 7. betoken, meaning, signify 8. commerce, indicate 9. introduce, of concern 10. importance 11. consequence, implication, importation, merchandise

importance ... 6. moment, stress, weight 8. prestige 9. influence 10. famousness 11. consequence, importunity 12. solicitation

important ... 3. key 5. grave 6. famous, urgent 7. pompous, weighty 8. material 9. momentous 11. considerate, influential, significant, substantial 12. considerable, ostentatious 13. consequential

import tax ... 4. duty 6. tariff

importune ... 3. beg, ply, tax, woo 4. coax, push, urge 5. beset, impel, plead, press 6. appeal, cajole 7. entreat, press on

importunity ... 11. importunate, pertinacity 12. solicitation

impose ... 3. tax 4. duty, levy 6. burden, entail 7. command, confirm (Eccl), exploit, inflict, intrude, obtrude, penalty, presume 10. discommode

imposing ... 5. noble, regal 6. august 7. stately 9. dignified, grandiose 10. commanding, impressive 11. ceremonious 13. grandiloquent

impossible ... 6. absurd 8. hopeless, terrible 9. insoluble 10. outlandish 11. unthinkable 12. unimaginable 13. contradictory, impracticable

impost ... 3. tax 4. levy, task, toll 5. abwab 6. custom, excise, surtax, tariff, weight 7. tribute 8. handicap

impostor ... 4. fake 5. fraud, phony, quack 6. humbug 7. empiric 9. charlatan, pretender 10. mountebank

imposture ... 5. fraud, trick 8. delusion, quackery 9. deception 10. imposition

impotent ... 4. weak 6. barren 7. cripple, sterile 9. deficient, incapable, powerless 13. uninfluential

impound ... 5. pen in, seize, store 6. freeze 7. collect 8. imprison 9. reservoir 10. confiscate 11. appropriate

impoverish ... 4. ruin 6. beggar 7. despoil, exhaust 8. bankrupt, make poor 11. make sterile

imprecation ... 4. oath 5. curse 8. anathema 10. execration

11. malediction

impregnable ... 4. hard 10. inviolable 12. inexpugnable, invulnerable 13. unconquerable

impregnate ... 5. imbue 6. infuse 8. fructify 9. fertilize, inculcate

impresa ... 5. maxim, motto 6. device, emblem

impresario ... 7. manager 9. conductor, projector (opera) 12. entrepreneur

impress ... 3. awe, fix 4. bite, dent, levy, mark, seal 5. press, print, stamp 6. affect, effect, enlist, indent 7. engrave, imprint 8. printing, shanghai 9. conscript, engraving, inculcate 10. commandeer, impression 11. indentation 14. characteristic

impressed ... 4. awed 7. infixed, stamped 8. affected, engraved 9. imprinted

impression ... 4. form, idea, mark 5. hunch, print, stamp 6. macule, signet 7. emotion, opinion 8. printing 9. engraving, sensation 10. appearance 11. inculcation, indentation, supposition

impressionable ... 6. pliant 7. plastic 9. sensitive, teachable 10. responsive 11. suggestible, susceptible

impressive ... 6. solemn 8. dramatic, eloquent 9. arresting, grandiose 10. convincing

imprint ... 3. fix 4. dint 5. infix, press, stamp 6. indent 7. edition, engrave 8. printing 9. engraving

imprison ... 4. bond, cage, gaol, jail 5. limit 6. arrest, detain, immure, intern, lock up 7. confine, impound 8. restrain 11. incarcerate

imprisonment ... 4. band 6. duress 8. coercion 9. restraint 10. constraint, immurement, internment 11. confinement, impoundment 13. incarceration

impromptu ... 6. extemp 7. offhand 11. extemporary 13. improvisation 14. extemporaneous 15. autoschediastic

improper ... 3. ill, pah 4. evil 5. amiss, wrong 6. vulgar 7. illegal, naughty 8. indecent, unseemly, unsuited, untoward 9. incorrect, inelegant 10. inaccurate, indecorous, indelicate, unbecoming, unsuitable

impropriety ... 5. wrong 8. solecism 9. indecency, vulgarity 11. malapropism, misbehavior

improve ... 4. mend 5. amend, edify, emend, moise, train 6. better, employ, uplift 7. advance, augment, correct, enhance, perfect, promote, recover, rectify, upgrade 9. cultivate, get better, intensify, meliorate 10. ameliorate, recuperate

improvident ... 4. rash 8. prodigal, wasteful 9. negligent 10. thriftless 11. thoughtless

improvise ... 5. ad lib 6. invent 7. ad libit 9. ad libitum 11. extemporize 13. autoschediaze

imprudence ... 5. brass 8. rashness 9. hardihood 12. indiscretion, recklessness

impudence ... 5. cheek 8. rudeness

9. flippancy, indecency, insolence
10. brazenness, disrespect
12. impertinence **13.** shamelessness
impudent . . . **4.** bold, pert, rude **5.** brash,
saucy **6.** brazen **8.** flippant, insolent,
malapert **9.** audacious, shameless
11. impertinent **13.** disrespectful
impugn . . . **4.** deny **5.** blame **6.** assail
(by words), oppose, refute **7.** asperse,
censure, gainsay
impulse . . . **3.** ate **4.** rush, urge **5.** force
6. motive **7.** impetus **8.** instinct
9. incentive **11.** instigation
impulsive . . . **5.** hasty, quick **6.** moving
9. impellent, impetuous **10.** motivating
11. instinctive **13.** ill-considered
impure . . . **4.** foul, lewd **5.** dirty,
mixed **6.** filthy, unholy **7.** bastard,
defiled, obscene, unclean **8.** unchaste
10. inaccurate, unhallowed
11. adulterated, unwholesome
impure metal . . . **5.** alloy, matte **6.** speiss
impure rock . . . **5.** chert **9.** flintlike
imputation . . . **7.** censure **8.** charging
9. aspersion, criticism **10.** accusation,
ascription **11.** attribution, insinuation
impute . . . **6.** accuse, charge, credit,
impart, reckon, regard **7.** arraign,
ascribe **8.** consider **9.** attribute
impy . . . **11.** mischievous
in . . . **2.** at **4.** amid, into **5.** among **6.** at
home, inside, within
in (pert to) . . .
abundance . . **5.** store **6.** galore
accordance . . **8.** pursuant
addition . . **3.** too, yet **4.** also, more,
plus **11.** furthermore
all directions . . **8.** everyway
12. everywhither
an undertone . . **9.** sotto voce
as much as . . **3.** for **5.** since **6.** seeing
7. because, insofar
back . . **3.** aft **5.** arear **6.** astern **7.** postern
behalf of . . **3.** for, pro **7.** favor of
camera . . **9.** in private **10.** in chambers
common . . **4.** same **5.** alike
concert . . **8.** together
contact . . **8.** touching **9.** attingent
current style . . **3.** a la **7.** alamode,
popular
existence . . **6.** extant
fact . . **5.** truly **6.** indeed **7.** de facto
favor of . . **3.** aye, pro, yea
good health . . **3.** fit **4.** hale **7.** healthy
love . . **7.** smitten **9.** enamoured
name only . . **7.** nominal, titular
need . . **7.** straits **8.** distress
open air . . **7.** outdoor **8.** al fresco
passing . . **9.** en passant
place of . . **3.** for **5.** stead **7.** instead
possession . . **5.** title **6.** seizin
private . . **8.** in camera
regard to . . **5.** anent
rows . . **4.** arow **6.** serial **7.** aligned
(alined)
so far as . . **3.** qua
spite of . . **6.** mauger **7.** despite, however
11. nonetheless
standing position . . **7.** statant
store . . **5.** ready **7.** waiting **8.** awaiting
straight lines . . **8.** e regione

succession . . **6.** series **8.** serially, seriatim
the future . . **5.** hence, later **6.** mañana
12. subsequently
the know . . **3.** hep
the same place . . **4.** ibid **6.** ibidem
the year of . . **4.** anno
truth . . **6.** certes, indeed, verily
8. forsooth
what way . . **3.** how **7.** quo modo
inability . . . **9.** impotence **10.** inadequacy,
incapacity **12.** incapability,
incompetence
inability to . . .
articulate . . **7.** inaudia
chew . . **8.** amasesis
comprehend . . **11.** acatalepsia
move . . **7.** apraxia
name objects . . **9.** paranomia
read . . **6.** alexia
stand erect . . **7.** astasia
swallow . . **7.** aphagia
inaccessible . . . **8.** reserved
10. unsociable **11.** out-of-the-way
12. unattainable **14.** unapproachable
inaccurate . . . **5.** loose **6.** faulty **7.** inexact
9. defective, erroneous, imperfect,
incorrect **13.** ungrammatical
inaction . . . **6.** torpor **7.** inertia
8. abeyance, idleness **9.** inertness
10. suspension
inactive . . . **4.** idle **5.** inert **7.** abeyant,
neutral, not busy **8.** sluggish
9. sedentary **10.** indisposed
inadequacy . . . **9.** inability **10.** deficiency,
inequality **11.** inferiority
12. incompetence **13.** insufficiency
14. incompleteness
inadvertence . . . **5.** error **7.** neglect
11. inattention **12.** carelessness,
heedlessness **15.** thoughtlessness
inadvertent . . . **9.** negligent, unwitting
11. inattentive
inadvertently . . . **10.** heedlessly
11. unwittingly **12.** neglectfully
inane . . . **4.** vain, void **5.** empty,
inept, silly **6.** famous **7.** fatuous,
foolish, puerile, trivial **8.** trifling
9. frivolous **11.** ineffectual, thoughtless
13. characterless
inappropriate . . . **5.** inept, undue
8. untimely **10.** irrelevant, unsuitable
11. inexpedient
inapt . . . **5.** inept **10.** unsuitable
inattentive . . . **3.** lax **6.** absent, remiss
8. careless, heedless **9.** negligent,
unheeding, unmindful **10.** distracted,
regardless **11.** inadvertent
inaugurate . . . **5.** admit, begin, start
6. induct **7.** install, instate, usher
in 8. initiate **9.** auspicate, institute,
introduce **10.** consecrate
inauspicious . . . **7.** adverse, ominous,
unlucky **8.** sinister, untimely **9.** ill-
omened **12.** unpropitious
inborn . . . **6.** allied, inbred, innate,
native **7.** cognate, natural **8.** inherent
10. connatural
inbred . . . **6.** inborn, innate **9.** endogamic
10. bred within **15.** to the manner
born
Inca (pert to) . . .

descent.. **6.** the sun
empire.. **4.** Peru (11th cent)
government.. **11.** communistic
king.. **9.** Atahualpa (15th cent)
prince.. **7.** Huascar (16th cent)
incalculable ... **8.** infinite **9.** boundless, uncertain, very great **11.** illimitable **12.** immeasurable **13.** unforeseeable
incandescent ... **5.** clear, light, white **7.** glowing, shining
incantation ... **5.** magic, spell **6.** powwow **7.** sorcery **8.** exorcism **10.** hocus-pocus, mumbo jumbo
incapable ... **6.** unable **8.** impotent **11.** incompetent, inefficient, unqualified **12.** disqualified
incapacitate ... **7.** cripple, disable, invalid **10.** disqualify **11.** render unfit
incapacitated ... **8.** crippled, disabled **9.** hamstrung, paralyzed **11.** invalidated **12.** disqualified **13.** superannuated (retired)
incarcerate ... **5.** hem in **6.** immure, intern, lock up, retire **7.** confine, impound **8.** imprison **10.** disqualify
incarnate ... **4.** rosy **6.** embody **9.** enshrined **11.** incorporate, personified **12.** impersonated
incarnation ... **6.** avatar, Christ **10.** embodiment
Incarnation of Vishnu (eight) ... **4.** Apis, Rama **7.** Krishna (8th)
incase ... **3.** box, can **4.** pack **5.** box up, cover, crate **6.** carton **7.** enclose, package **8.** surround
incaution ... **4.** rash **6.** unwary **8.** careless, heedless, reckless **9.** impolitic, imprudent **10.** indiscreet
incendiarism ... **5.** arson **9.** pyromania
incendiary ... **5.** firer **7.** exciter **8.** agitator, arsonist, incitive **9.** seditious **10.** instigator **12.** inflammatory
incense ... **3.** ire **5.** anger **6.** arouse, enrage, incite **7.** inflame, provoke **8.** irritate **9.** instigate
incense (pert to) ...
burner.. **6.** censer **8.** thurible **9.** incensory
carrier.. **8.** thurifer
Hebrew for.. **7.** keturah
pert to.. **5.** aroma, spice **7.** perfume **9.** fragrance, redolence
product.. **5.** matti, myrrh **6.** storax **7.** linaloa **8.** gum resin, olibanum, pastille, thurible **9.** lignaloes, tacamahac **12.** frankincense
sacrifice.. **8.** oblation
spice.. **6.** balsam, stacte
tree bearing.. **7.** linaloa **8.** agalloch, calambac **9.** Boswellia
vessel.. **6.** censer **7.** navette
incensed ... **3.** mad **5.** angry, irate, vexed, wroth **6.** peeved, piqued **7.** angered, enraged, nettled **8.** wrathful **11.** exasperated
incentive ... **4.** brod, call, goad, spur, urge, whet **5.** spark **6.** motive **7.** impulse, rousing **8.** inciting, stimulus **9.** influence **10.** incitement, inducement **11.** provocation, stimulative **13.** encouragement

inception ... **6.** origin, source **9.** reception **10.** inchoation, initiation **12.** commencement **15.** intussusception
inceptive ... **9.** beginning **10.** inchoative
incessant ... **7.** endless **8.** constant **9.** ceaseless, continual, perpetual **10.** continuous **11.** unremitting **13.** unintermitted
inch (pert to) ...
barometric.. **6.** degree
forward.. **4.** edge **7.** crowhop
inch by inch.. **9.** gradually, piecemeal
meal.. **9.** gradually
three parts.. **11.** barleycorns (anc)
twelve parts.. **5.** lines
twelve seconds.. **6.** a prime (anc)
verb.. **5.** creep **7.** measure
inches ... **4.** hand (4), nail (2 1/4), span (9)
inchoate ... **6.** partly **8.** initiate, recently **9.** beginning, incipient **10.** incomplete
inchpin ... **10.** sweetbread
incident ... **5.** event **7.** episode, subject **8.** accident, casualty **9.** befalling, happening **10.** incidental, occurrence **11.** contingency **12.** circumstance, slight matter
incidental ... **3.** bye **6.** casual, chance, liable **8.** episodic **9.** accessory, extrinsic **10.** accidental, contingent, fortuitous, occasional **11.** subordinate **12.** nonessential **13.** parenthetical
incidentally ... **6.** obiter **8.** by chance, by the way **9.** en passant, in passing
incinerate ... **4.** burn **7.** consume, cremate
incipient ... **4.** seat **6.** induct **7.** initial **8.** inchoate **9.** beginning, embryonic **10.** commencing, inaugurate **11.** rudimentary
incise ... **3.** cut **4.** open **5.** carve, lance, sever **6.** furrow **7.** engrave
incised ... **6.** carved **7.** notched **8.** engraved, furrowed **9.** laciniate **10.** laciniated
incision ... **3.** cut **4.** gash, slit **5.** cleft **6.** furrow, injury **7.** cutting **9.** engraving **10.** laceration, separation **11.** penetration
incisor ... **5.** tooth
incite ... **3.** egg, tew **4.** abet, fire, goad, prod, spur, urge **5.** impel, sting **6.** arouse, foment, stir up, suborn **7.** agitate, animate, inflame, provoke **9.** encourage, stimulate
inclement ... **4.** foul **5.** harsh, rough **6.** severe, stormy **9.** merciless
inclination ... **3.** dip, nod **4.** bent, bias, love, urge **5.** fancy, grade, slant, slope, taste, trend **6.** animus, bowing, desire, liking, nature **8.** aptitude, penchant, tendency **9.** affection, attention, deviation, direction, intention, obeisance, proneness **10.** attachment, proclivity, propensity **11.** disposition **12.** predilection **13.** prepossession
incline ... **3.** dip, tip **4.** bend, cant, heel, lean, tend, tilt **5.** alist, bevel, grade, slant, slide, slope, trend **9.** be willing, gravitate
inclined ... **3.** apt, dip **4.** wont **5.** prone

6. sloped 7. leaning, pronate, willing
8. disposed 11. predisposed
inclined (pert to) . . .
plane . . 4. ramp 7. oblique
to believe . . 9. credulous
to droop . . 3. sag
to sin . . 13. transgressive
inclose . . . see also *enclose* 3. hem, pen,
pin 4. case, mure 5. embar 6. encase,
encave, incase 7. enclose, environ
inclosure . . . 3. pen, ree, sty 4. cage, cote,
sept 5. hutch, kraal 6. corral 8. sepiment
9. enclosure 10. impalement
include . . . 6. shut up 7. confine, contain,
embrace, enclose, inclose, involve
8. comprise 9. encompass
including . . . 8. covering 10. comprising,
containing 12. encompassing
13. comprehensive
incognito . . . 6. veiled 7. feigned
8. disguise, not known 10. camouflage
incoherent . . . 5. loose 6. broken
8. detached, inchoate 9. delirious,
illogical 11. incongruous
12. disconnected, inconsequent,
inconsistent
income . . . 4. gain 5. rente, wages
6. profit, return, usance 7. annuity,
pension, produce, revenue, tontine
8. interest, proceeds, receipts
9. emolument
incommensurate . . . 7. unequal
12. insufficient 14. unsatisfactory
16. disproportionate
incommode . . . 3. vex 5. annoy 6. molest,
plague, put out 7. disturb, trouble
8. disquiet 13. inconvenience
incomparable . . . 7. eminent, unalike
8. peerless 9. matchless, unrivaled
10. surpassing 11. superlative
12. transcendent, without equal
incompatible . . . 9. differing 10. intolerant
11. disagreeing 12. inconsistent,
inharmonious 13. contradictory,
unsympathetic 14. irreconcilable
incompetence . . . 9. inability, unfitness
10. disability, inadequacy
13. insufficiency 15. unqualification
incompetent . . . 5. inept, unfit 7. wanting
8. impotent 9. incapable 10. unskillful
11. inefficient 12. disqualified,
insufficient 14. incommensurate
incomplete . . . 5. crude 6. undone
7. lacking 8. immature, inchoate
9. defective, deficient, imperfect,
partially 10. unfinished
incomprehensible . . . 8. infinite
9. wonderful 10. miraculous,
mysterious, unreadable 11. unthinkable
12. unfathomable, unimaginable
13. inconceivable, unconceivable
14. unintelligible
incongruity . . . 9. inharmony
10. dissonance 11. incoherence
12. disagreement, inexpedience
13. inconsistency 14. unsuitableness
incongruous . . . 5. alien 6. absurd,
motley 8. off-color 9. differing,
illogical 10. solecistic, unsuitable
12. disagreeable, inconsistent,
inharmonious 13. inappropriate

inconsequent . . . 7. invalid 8. unproved
9. illogical 10. irrelevant 11. impertinent,
unimportant 12. inconsistent
13. inconsecutive
inconsiderate . . . 4. rash 5. hasty
6. unkind 8. careless, heedless
9. imprudent, impulsive 10. ill-advised,
incautious, indiscreet, neglectful
11. improvident, injudicious,
thoughtless
inconsistent . . . 9. differing, dissonant,
fanatical, illogical 10. discordant,
discrepant, incoherent, inconstant
11. incongruous 12. incompatible,
inharmonious 13. contradictory
14. irreconcilable
inconspicuous . . . 9. unseeable 10. out
of sight, unapparent 12. not prominent
13. imperceptible, indiscernible
incontestable . . . 7. certain
10. undeniable 11. indubitable,
irrefutable 13. unimpeachable
14. unquestionable
inconvenience . . . 6. bother 8. disquiet
9. incommode 10. uneasiness
11. awkwardness, disturbance
12. disadvantage, untimeliness,
unwieldiness
inconvenient . . . 5. unfit 7. unhandy
8. annoying, improper, unwieldy
10. unsuitable 11. inexpedient,
inopportune, troublesome
12. unreasonable 15. disadvantageous
incorporate . . . 3. mix 4. fuse 5. blend,
merge, unite 6. embody 7. combine,
include 8. embodied 10. assimilate
incorporation . . . 5. union 9. inclusion
10. embodiment 11. affiliation,
association, combination, composition,
incarnation 12. assimilation
incorporeal . . . 7. phantom 8. bodiless
9. spiritual 10. immaterial
13. unsubstantial
incorrect . . . 5. wrong 6. faulty
8. improper 9. erroneous, inelegant
10. inaccurate, solecistic, unbecoming
13. ungrammatical
incorrect naming of objects . . .
9. paranomia
incorruptible . . . 4. just 7. upright
8. immortal 11. trustworthy
14. indestructible
increase . . . 3. add, eke, wax 4. gain,
grow, rise 5. add to, amass, raise, swell
6. accrue, dilate, enrich, expand, extend
7. accrete, advance, augment, enhance
(inhance), inflate, promote, upswing
8. heighten, multiply 9. accession,
aggravate, crescendo, expansion,
extension, increment, intensify
10. accelerate 11. aggravation,
enlargement 13. amplification
15. intensification
incredible . . . 8. fabulous, unlikely
9. fantastic, marvelous, wonderful
10. improbable, remarkable
12. unbelievable
increment . . . 6. growth 8. addition,
increase 11. enlargement
12. augmentation
incriminate . . . 6. accuse 7. involve

9. implicate, inculpate
incubator . . . **8.** couveuse, isolette
incubus . . . **4.** ogre **5.** demon, dream
6. burden **9.** nightmare **10.** evil spirit
13. hallucination
inculcate . . . **5.** imbue, infix **7.** implant,
impress, instill (instil) **12.** indoctrinate
incumbent . . . **5.** vicar **6.** rector **8.** resident
9. clergyman, impending, overlying
10. burdensome, obligatory (upon)
11. threatening **12.** superimposed
incumbents . . . **3.** ins
incunabula . . . **7.** infancy **10.** beginnings
incur . . . **5.** bring **6.** accrue, entail **7.** bring
on **8.** be liable, contract, fall into **10.** be
involved
incurable . . . **8.** hopeless **9.** apathetic
11. inattentive, indifferent, unconcerned,
uninquiring **12.** uninterested
13. uninquisitive
incur hostility . . . **10.** antagonize
11. contend with
incursion . . . **4.** raid **5.** foray **6.** attack,
influx, inroad **8.** invasion **9.** intrusion
incus . . . **4.** bone (ear) **5.** anvil **6.** hammer
indecency . . . **8.** impurity **9.** immodesty,
indecorum, obscenity, vulgarity
10. indelicacy, unchastity
indecent . . . **5.** gross **6.** impure, vulgar
7. obscene **8.** immodest, improper,
uncomely **9.** offensive **10.** ill-looking,
indecorous, indelicate **11.** inexpedient
indecision . . . **5.** doubt **10.** hesitation
11. uncertainty, vacillation
12. irresolution
indecisive . . . **7.** dubious **8.** formless
9. uncertain **10.** hesitating, indefinite,
indistinct, irresolute **11.** unsupported,
vacillating **12.** inconclusive
indecorous . . . **4.** rude **5.** wrong **6.** coarse,
vulgar **7.** uncivil **8.** impolite, improper,
indecent, unseemly **9.** inelegant **10.** out
of place, unbecoming **11.** inexpedient
indefatigable . . . **6.** active **8.** sedulous,
tireless, untiring **9.** unwearied, weariless
10. unwearying **11.** persevering
indefinite . . . **5.** loose, vague **7.** general,
inexact, neutral **8.** formless
9. ambiguous, equivocal, uncertain
10. inexplicit, unmeasured
12. undetermined **13.** indeterminate
indefinite amount . . . **3.** any **4.** some
5. about **10.** more or less
indehiscent (pert to) . . .
fruit . . **3.** uva **4.** pepo (gourd) **5.** apple,
grape **6.** orange, samara **9.** sunflower
legume . . **3.** pea **4.** bean **6.** loment
vegetable . . **5.** melon **6.** squash, tomato
7. pumpkin **8.** cucumber
indelible . . . **4.** fast **5.** fixed **8.** deepfelt
9. permanent **10.** inerasable
12. ineffaceable, ineradicable,
inexpungible **13.** unforgettable
indelicate . . . **5.** gross **6.** coarse, vulgar
7. fulsome **8.** impolite, improper,
indecent, unseemly **9.** offensive,
unrefined **10.** indecorous, unbecoming
indemnification . . . **9.** atonement
10. recompense **11.** restitution
12. compensation **13.** reimbursement
indemnify . . . **3.** pay **6.** recoup, secure

8. make good **9.** reimburse
10. compensate, recompense
indent . . . **3.** cut, jag **4.** dent **5.** inlay,
notch, press, stamp, tooth **6.** emboss,
furrow, recess, zigzag **7.** impress,
imprint, press in **8.** contract, covenant,
draw upon **9.** indenture **11.** requisition
indentation . . . **3.** jab **4.** dint, nick **5.** choil,
notch **6.** crenel, furrow, hollow, recess
7. imprint **8.** crenelet **10.** depression,
impression
indented . . . **6.** dented, jagged, milled
7. notched, sinuous **8.** serrated (Her)
9. impressed **10.** undulating
indenture . . . **4.** dent **5.** notch **8.** contract,
document **9.** agreement **10.** depression
11. indentation
independence . . . **7.** freedom
9. exemption **10.** competency,
neutralism, Urania blue
13. unrelatedness **14.** nonpartisanism
15. self-subsistence
independent . . . **4.** free **5.** Party (Polit)
7. neutral, wealthy **8.** separate
9. competent, exclusive, free-lance,
isolative, sovereign, uncoerced,
unrelated **12.** irrespective, uncontrolled,
unrestricted **13.** self-governing
independent land . . . **7.** alodium (law)
indescribably . . . **9.** ineffably
11. wonderfully
indeterminate . . . **5.** vague **7.** apeiron,
general, neutral, obscure **8.** formless,
infinite
index . . . **4.** face, file, fist, list **5.** guide,
ratio, table **6.** gnomon **7.** pointer
8. exponent **9.** indicator **10.** forefinger,
indication
India . . . see also *Indian*
anc . . **9.** Hindustan
Bay . . **6.** Bengal
Cape . . **7.** Comorin
capital . . **4.** Agra (anc) **5.** Simla (summer)
8. New Delhi
city . . **4.** Agra, Gaya **5.** Delhi, Poona,
Surat **6.** Bombay, Jaipur, Madras,
Madura, Mysore, Nagpur **8.** Calcutta,
Kolhapur, Mandalay, Mirzapur,
Shahpura **9.** Bangalore **10.** Darjeeling
city, sacred . . **5.** Nasik **7.** Benares
Coast . . **7.** Malabar
kingdom . . **5.** Asoka, Nepal
mountain . . **5.** Ghats **8.** Sulaiman (Throne
of Solomon) **9.** Himalayas, Hindu Kush
12. Vindhya Hills
Persian name (anc) . . **9.** Hindustan
region . . **3.** Goa **5.** Assam, Surat
6. Baroda, Bengal **7.** Benares, Kashmir
relics (famed) . . **8.** Taj Mahal (Agra)
10. Kutab Minar **11.** Ajanta Caves
river . . **6.** Ganges **7.** Krishna (Kristna)
State . . **4.** Rewa **5.** Delhi **6.** Baroda,
Indore, Jaipur, Madras, Marwar, Punjab,
Rampur, Sakkim **7.** Manipur
Indian (pert to) . . .
aeon . . **5.** kalpa
animal . . **4.** gaur, zebu **5.** sasin **6.** nilgai
apartment . . **6.** zenana
army officer . . **4.** naik (naig) **7.** jemadar
attorney . . **6.** muktar
bandit . . **6.** dacoit

bard . . **4.** bhat
bird . . **4.** baya, kala, koel, kyak **5.** sarus, shama **6.** seesee, shahin **8.** amadavat
boat . . **5.** dhoni (doni)
book (sacred) . . **6.** Avesta
bracelet . . **6.** sankha
bread (unleavened) . . **4.** naan **7.** chapati
breakfast . . **5.** hazri
buffalo . . **4.** arna (arnee)
carpet . . **4.** Agra
carriage . . **4.** ekka **5.** tonga **6.** gharry (gharri)
caste . . **3.** Jat, Meo **4.** Ahir **5.** Sudra, Varna **6.** Lohana, Rajput, Vaisya **7.** Brahman (Brahmin) **9.** Kahatriya
cavalryman . . **5.** sowar **7.** ressala
charm . . **6.** mantra
chief . . **4.** Raja **5.** Rajah **6.** sirdar **7.** Gaekwar
cigarette (cheap) . . **4.** biri
claim (legal) . . **3.** hak (hakh)
college (Sanskrit) . . **3.** tol
Court, Supreme . . **6.** Sudder
crocodile . . **6.** gavial, mugger (muggar, muggur)
cymbal . . **3.** tal
dagger . . **5.** katar
dam . . **6.** anicut (annicut)
dancer (fem) . . **8.** bayadere
dancing girls . . **6.** nautch
deer . . **4.** axis **5.** kakar **6.** sambur
deity . . **4.** Deva
demon . . **4.** bhut **5.** asura **6.** daitya
devil's tree . . **4.** dita
dialect . . **4.** Urdu **5.** Hindi, Tamil **7.** Prakrit
disciple . . **5.** chela
dog . . **5.** dhole **6.** pariah
drama . . **6.** nataka
drink . . **4.** soma **5.** bhang (bang) **6.** arrack
dust storm . . **7.** peesash, shaitan (sheitan)
elephant . . **5.** hathi
elephant driver . . **6.** mahout
elephant trappings . . **5.** jhool
epic . . **8.** Ramayana **11.** Mahabharata
falcon . . **6.** shahin (shaheen)
father . . **4.** babu
festival . . **4.** Holi, Mela **6.** Dewali **10.** Rathayatra
fig tree (sacred) . . **5.** pipal **6.** banian, banyan
garment . . **4.** sari **7.** luhinga
gateway . . **5.** toran
ghost . . **4.** bhut
god . . **4.** Deva, Yama **5.** Shiva
goddess . . **4.** Amma
governor . . **5.** nazim
grove . . **5.** Sarna
guard . . **7.** daloyet
hall . . **6.** durbar
handkerchief . . **7.** malabar
harem . . **5.** serai **6.** zenana **8.** seraglio
heiress . . **5.** Begum
herb . . **6.** sesame **7.** curcuma, tumeric, zeodary
holy . . **3.** sri (shri)
holy powder . . **4.** abir (perfumed)
hunt . . **6.** shikar
intoxicant . . **4.** soma
jungle . . **5.** shola
king . . **4.** Shah

king of serpents (Myth) . . **6.** Shesha (Sesha)
king's son . . **8.** shahzada
knife . . **3.** dah **5.** kukri
lady . . **7.** sahibah
language . . **4.** Urdu **5.** Hindu, Tamil **8.** Sanskrit (anc)
leader . . **13.** Mahatma Gandhi
legal claim . . **3.** hak (hakh)
leopard . . **7.** cheetah
licorice . . **9.** jequirity (bean)
loincloth . . **5.** dhoti
lover of . . **9.** Indophile
mahogany . . **4.** toon
mail . . **3.** dak (dawk)
medicine man . . **6.** Shaman
mendicant . . **5.** fakir
merchant . . **8.** soudagar
midwife . . **4.** dhai
Minister of Finance . . **5.** Dewan
mountain pass . . **4.** ghat
musical instrument . . **5.** ruana
narcotic . . **4.** bang **5.** bhang **7.** hashish
native . . **5.** Hindu, Sepoy, Tamil **8.** Assamese **10.** Hindustani
ox . . **4.** gaur
palanquin (conveyance) . . **6.** palkee (palhi)
palm . . **7.** Calamus, malacca
peasant . . **4.** ryot
pheasant . . **5.** monal (monaul)
philosopher . . **4.** Yogi
pillar . . **3.** lat
pipe . . **6.** hookah
police . . **4.** peon **5.** sepoy
police station . . **5.** thana
priest . . **5.** mobed **6.** shaman
prince . . **4.** rana
princess . . **4.** rani (ranee) **5.** Begum
queen . . **4.** rani (ranee) **8.** maharani
religious body . . **5.** samaj **7.** ajivika (anc)
resort . . **3.** Abu **5.** Mt Abu
rope dancer . . **3.** nat
rubber . . **10.** caoutchouc
ruler . . **4.** rana **5.** nabob, nawab, nizam
sage . . **6.** pundit
sailor . . **6.** lascar
sarsaparilla root . . **7.** nunnari
servant . . **3.** par **4.** amah, maty
sheep . . **5.** urial **6.** nahoor
shrine . . **6.** dagoba
silkworm . . **3.** eri
snake . . **5.** krait **6.** bongar, katuka
soldier . . **4.** peon **5.** sepoy, singh
split pea . . **3.** dal
steps (to a river) . . **4.** ghat
study of . . **8.** Indology
sugar (crude) . . **3.** gur **9.** tabasheer (bamboo)
Supreme Court . . **6.** Sudder
sword (short) . . **5.** kukri
syllable of assent . . **2.** om
tapir . . **8.** saladang
tariff . . **6.** zabeta
teacher . . **6.** mullah (mulla)
temple . . **4.** rath **12.** Seven Pagodas (of Madras)
title of respect . . **3.** sri (shri) **4.** mian
tower . . **5.** minar, sikar **7.** sikhara
tree . . **3.** saj **4.** dita, teak **5.** dhava **6.** banyan, sissoo

umbrella . . **6.** chatta
water carrier . . **7.** bheesty (bheestie)
wheat . . **4.** suji
wine . . **5.** shrab
yellow (color) . . **5.** piuri **7.** majagua
Indian, American (pert to) . . .
chief . . **5.** Logan **6.** Joseph, Philip,
sachem **7.** Cochise, Pontiac
8. Geronimo, Red Cloud, Tecumseh
9. Massasoit **10.** Crazy Horse **11.** Sitting
Bull, Spotted Tail
dance . . **7.** cantico
festival . . **8.** potlatch
hatchet . . **8.** tomahawk
hero . . **4.** Rama (So Am)
lodge . . **5.** hogan, igloo, tepee **6.** wigwam
7. wickiup
married . . **5.** squaw (fem) **6.** sannup
(male)
Mexico . . **4.** Maya **5.** Aztec **7.** Tehueco
money . . **5.** sewan (beads) **6.** wampum
Newfoundland . . **6.** Micmac
pipe (peace) . . **7.** calumet
pony . . **6.** cayuse
richest tribe . . **5.** Osage
S America . . **3.** Ona **4.** Cara (anc), Inca,
Peru, Tupi **5.** Carib **6.** Arawak, Aymara
7. Quechua
Spirit, Great . . **6.** Manito **7.** Manitou
12. Gitchi Manito
squaw . . **6.** mahala
symbol . . **5.** totem
tax, impost . . **5.** abwab
village . . **6.** pueblo
water lily . . **5.** wokas (wocas)
Indiana . . .
capital . . **12.** Indianapolis
city . . **4.** Gary **6.** Muncie **7.** Hammond
9. Vincennes **10.** Terre Haute
industrial region . . **7.** Calumet
monument (Hist) . . **7.** Lincoln **12.** Indian
Mounds **13.** Wyandotte Cave
post office (famed) . . **10.** Santa Claus
river . . **6.** Maumee, Wabash
10. Tippecanoe
State admission . . **10.** Nineteenth
State bird . . **8.** cardinal
State flower . . **5.** peony
State motto . . **19.** Crossroads of America
State nickname . . **7.** Hoosier
Indian people . . . **3.** Aht, Fox, Oto (Otoe)
Ree, Sac, Ute **4.** Cree, Crow, Erie, Hano,
Hopi, Iowa, Maya, Mono, Sauk, Yuma,
Zuni **5.** Aleut, Cadoo, Carib, Coree,
Creek, Haida, Huron, Miami, Moqui,
Omaha, Osage, Piute, Ponca, Sioux,
Sooke, Teton, Yazoo **6.** Ahtena (Alaska),
Apache, Biloxi, Cayuga, Dakota,
Eskimo, Isleta, Lenape, Mohawk,
Mojave, Navaho, Nootka, Oneida,
Paiute (Piute), Pawnee, Santee, Seneca,
Siwash **7.** Amerind, Bannock, Catawba,
Chinook, Ojibway, Tlingit, Yavanai
8. Arapahoe, Cherokee, Chippewa,
Comanche, Iroquois, Kickapoo, Nez
Percé, Onondaga, Sagamore, Seminole,
Shoshone **9.** Algonquin, Athabasca,
Blackfoot, Chickasaw, Winnebago
10. Muskhogean **12.** Narragansett
indicate . . . **4.** cite, hint, mark, mean,
show **5.** point **6.** denote, evince,

reveal, sketch **7.** bespeak, betoken,
connote, declare, display, signify,
specify **8.** disclose, evidence, intimate,
manifest, point out, register
9. designate, foretoken
indicated . . . **6.** marked, signed
7. denoted, implied **8.** presumed
9. betokened, portended, suggested
indicating succession . . . **7.** ordinal
indication . . . **4.** clue, hint, mark, note,
omen, sign **5.** proof, token, trace
6. signal **7.** reading (a) **8.** evidence
10. suggestion **13.** manifestation
indicative . . . **7.** ominous **10.** evidential,
indication, meaningful, suggestive
11. connotative **13.** significative
indicator . . . **4.** dial, hand, sign, vane
5. arrow, gauge, index, level **6.** gnomon
7. indices (pl), pointer **9.** grape fern
(belief) **10.** instrument **11.** annunciator,
thermometer **15.** telethermometer
indicia (sing indicium) . . . **5.** marks,
signs **6.** tokens **8.** markings (PO)
11. appearances, indications, metered
mail
indict . . . **6.** accuse, charge, decree
7. arraign, impeach **8.** proclaim
indictive . . . **8.** declared **9.** appointed
10. proclaimed
indictment . . . **6.** charge **10.** accusation,
imputation **11.** arraignment
indifference . . . **5.** shrug **6.** apathy
7. inertia **8.** coldness **9.** unconcern
10. mediocrity, negligence, neutrality
12. carelessness, heedlessness,
unimportance **13.** insensibility
14. insignificance
indifferent . . . **3.** ill **4.** cold, cool,
sick **5.** blasé **6.** casual, poorly
7. neutral, stoical, uneager **8.** careless,
heedless, listless, mediocre **9.** apathetic
10. nonchalant, regardless
11. adiaphorous, unimportant
12. nonessential, uninterested
indigence . . . **4.** lack, need, want **6.** penury
7. poverty **10.** deficiency
indigene . . . **6.** native **8.** habitant
9. primitive **10.** autochthon
indigenous . . . **6.** inborn, innate, native,
rooted **7.** edaphic, endemic, natural
8. endemism, inherent
13. autochthonous
indigent . . . **4.** free, poor, void **5.** needy
6. bereft **7.** lacking, wanting **8.** beggarly
9. destitute, penniless **10.** pauperized
11. impecunious, necessitous
15. poverty-stricken
indigestion . . . **8.** disorder, phthisis
9. dyspepsia **10.** immaturity
indignant . . . **3.** hot **5.** angry, irate,
wroth **7.** annoyed **8.** incensed, wrathful
9. resentful **11.** exasperated
indignation . . . **3.** ire **4.** base, fury
5. anger, wrath **7.** disdain **8.** contempt
indignity . . . **7.** affront, dudgeon
10. uncivility
indigo . . . **3.** dye **4.** anil, blue
indigo (pert to) . . .
bale of . . **6.** seroon
compound . . **6.** isatin
plant . . **4.** anil

source . . **7.** indican **9.** indigotin
wild . . **8.** Baptisia
indirect . . . **7.** devious, oblique
  9. deceitful, dishonest **10.** circuitous,
  contingent, misleading, roundabout
indirect expense . . . **8.** overhead
indiscreet . . . **4.** rash **5.** hasty, silly
  6. unwise **7.** foolish, witless **8.** careless,
  heedless **9.** imprudent **10.** incautious
  11. injudicious **12.** undiscerning
  13. inconsiderate
indiscriminate . . . **5.** mixed **7.** mingled
  9. extensive, haphazard, orderless,
  wholesale **13.** heterogeneous
indispensable . . . **5.** basic, vital **6.** needed
  7. exigent **8.** integral **9.** essential,
  requisite, right-hand **10.** imperative
  13. irreplaceable
indisposed . . . **3.** ill **4.** sick **6.** averse
  9. unwilling **10.** disordered, unfriendly
  11. disinclined
indisposition . . . **7.** ailment, illness,
  malaise **10.** averseness, reluctance
  13. unwillingness
indisputable . . . **4.** sure **7.** certain,
  evident **8.** positive **10.** undeniable
  11. indubitable **12.** irrefragable
  13. incontestable
indistinct . . . **3.** dim **4.** hazy **5.** vague
  7. blurred, obscure, unclear **8.** confused
  9. ambiguous, undefined **10.** indefinite
  16. undiscriminating
  17. indistinguishable
indite . . . **3.** pen **5.** write **6.** phrase
  7. compose **8.** describe, inscribe
individual . . . **3.** man, one **4.** bion, idio
  (comb form), self, sole, unit, zoon
  6. egoist, person, single **7.** special
  8. organism, selfsame **9.** identical
  11. inseparable, personality
individuality . . . **5.** being, seity **6.** nature
  7. oneness **8.** ethology, identity,
  selfness
individually . . . **9.** severally **10.** personally
  12. each by itself **14.** distributively
Indo-Aryan (pert to) . . .
  deity . . **5.** Indra
  native of . . **5.** India
  speech . . **5.** Aryan
  type . . **4.** Jats **7.** khatris, Rajputs
Indochina . . . **4.** Laos **5.** Burma **6.** Malaya
  7. Myanmar (formerly Burma), Vietnam
  8. Cambodia, Thailand
indoctrinate . . . **5.** coach, edify, imbue,
  teach **8.** instruct **12.** rehabilitate
indolence . . . **5.** scorn, sloth **7.** inertia,
  languor **8.** inaction, laziness
  10. ergophobia **11.** lotus-eating, spring
  fever **13.** indisposition
indolent . . . **4.** idle, lazy **5.** inert
  6. otiose **8.** inactive, slothful, sluggish
  10. unemployed
indomitable . . . **10.** invincible
  11. intractable, "never say die"
  13. unconquerable
Indonesia . . .
  capital . . **7.** Jakarta (Djakarta)
  formation . . **11.** archipelago (once
    world's largest)
  former name . . **7.** Batavia **15.** Dutch
    East Indies

government . . **8.** Republic (1950)
islands (3,000 in all) . . **4.** Bali, Java
  7. Sumatra **8.** Sulawesi (Celebes)
  9. New Guinea (W half) **10.** Kalimantan
  (W Borneo)
president . . **7.** Sukarno
race . . **5.** Dyaks (Dayaks) **7.** Battaks
  (Bataks), Igorots **8.** Balinese, Javanese
religion . . **6.** Moslem
shrine . . **6.** dagoba
indorse, endorse . . . see *endorse*
indorsement, endorsement . . . **4.** visa,
  visé (passport)
Indra (Hindu) . . . **3.** God **5.** Deity, Sakra
  (Sakka)
indubitable . . . **4.** fact, sure **7.** evident
  10. infallible, undeniable **11.** irrefutable
  12. irrefragable, unanswerable
  13. incontestable **14.** unquestionable
  16. incontrovertible
induce . . . **4.** lead, move, urge **5.** cause,
  impel, infer **6.** allure, elicit, entice, incite
  8. persuade **9.** influence, instigate,
  prevail on
inducement . . . **6.** motive, reason
  8. stimulus **9.** incentive, influence
  10. persuasion **13.** consideration
induct . . . **6.** enroll **7.** bring in, install
  8. initiate **9.** conscript, introduce
inductance unit . . . **5.** henry
inductile . . . **10.** inflexible, unyielding
induction . . . **5.** logic **7.** causing
  8. entrance **9.** accession, beginning,
  deduction **10.** conclusion, initiation,
  production **12.** commencement,
  conscription, installation, introduction
indue . . . **5.** endow **6.** assume, clothe,
  draw on, invest, supply (spiritual)
  7. furnish
indulge . . . **3.** pet **5.** grant, humor, yield
  6. pamper **7.** cherish, gratify
indulgences . . . **8.** excesses **10.** tolerances
indulgent . . . **4.** easy **7.** lenient, patient
  8. tolerant, yielding **9.** compliant
  10. permissive **11.** considerate,
  intemperate
indurate . . . **6.** harden **7.** callous
  10. solidified
indurated . . . **3.** set **5.** fixed **9.** calloused
  10. solidified
industrial magnate . . . **6.** shogun, tycoon
industrious . . . **4.** busy **6.** active **7.** zealous
  8. diligent, sedulous **9.** assiduous
  11. intentional, painstaking
  13. indefatigable
industry . . . **4.** toil, work **5.** labor, trade
  7. concern **8.** commerce **9.** diligence
  12. perseverance, sedulousness
indweller . . . **6.** native **7.** denizen
  8. indigene
indwelling . . . **7.** inbeing **8.** immanent,
  inherent **9.** immanence, inherence
  10. inhabiting
inearth . . . **5.** inter **6.** inhume
inebriacy . . . **11.** drunkenness
  12. intemperance
inebriate . . . **3.** sot **5.** addle, drunk,
  toper **7.** stupefy, tippler **8.** drunkard
  10. exhilarate (by liquor), intoxicate
ineffable . . . **4.** surd **6.** sacred **9.** wonderful
  11. unspeakable, unutterable

13. indescribable, inexpressible
15. unpronounceable
ineffaceable . . . 9. indelible 10. inerasable
12. ineradicable
ineffectual . . . 4. vain, weak 6. futile
7. useless 9. fruitless 10. unavailing
11. inefficient 12. unsuccessful
13. inefficacious, uninfluential
inefficient . . . 6. unable 10. indisposed
11. incompetent 12. unproficient
inelegant . . . 6. clumsy, vulgar 8. indecent
9. deficient (in beauty) 11. unbeautiful
inept . . . 4. null, void 5. silly, unfit
6. absurd, clumsy 7. foolish 8. unsuited
10. out of place, unbecoming, unskillful,
unsuitable 11. inexpedient
inequality . . . 9. disparity, diversity
10. inadequacy, unevenness
12. disagreement, variableness
13. disproportion
ineradicable . . . 7. lasting 9. indelible,
permanent 12. ineffaceable
inerrant . . . 8. unerring 10. infallible
inert . . . 4. dead, lazy 6. latent, stupid,
supine, torpid 7. passive 8. inactive,
lifeless, listless, slothful, sluggish
9. apathetic, inanimate, lethargic
10. motionless, phlegmatic
inertia . . . 9. indolence, inertness
10. immobility
inesculant (rare) . . . 9. indelible
inestimable . . . 9. priceless 10. invaluable
12. incalculable
inevitable . . . 3. due 5. fated 7. nemesis
9. necessary 11. unavoidable
inexorability . . . 5. rigor 9. obstinacy
10. strictness
inexorable . . . 6. strict 9. obstinate
10. inflexible, relentless, unyielding
inexpedience, inexpedient . . . 6. unwise
8. untimely 9. ignorance, impolitic,
imprudent, unfitting 10. indiscreet,
unwiseness 11. inadvisable
15. disadvantageous
inexperience . . . 6. unwise 9. ignorance,
imprudent 10. immaturity, indiscreet
11. inadvisable 12. unprofitable
14. unskillfulness 15. disadvantageous
inexperienced . . . 3. raw 4. naif 5. green,
naive 6. callow 8. ignorant, immature,
prentice 9. unskilled 10. amateurish
11. unpracticed
inexplicable . . . 11. undefinable
12. supernatural 13. preternatural,
unaccountable, unexplainable
inextricable . . . 4. mazy 5. stuck
8. involved 9. intricate 10. insolvable
infallible . . . 4. sure, true 6. gospel
7. certain 8. inerrant, unerring
9. inerrable 11. indubitable
infamous . . . 4. base 6. odious, wicked
8. shameful, terrible 9. negarious
10. detestable 11. ignominious
12. contemptible, disreputable
infamy . . . 5. shame 8. disgrace, dishonor,
ignominy, reproach 9. disrepute
10. opprobrium 11. abomination
infancy . . . 8. babyhood, minority
9. beginning
infant . . . 4. babe, baby 5. child, minor
6. novice 8. bantling 9. foundling

infantryman . . . 6. Zouave 7. dog-face
8. chasseur 9. musketeer
11. footslogger, foot soldier 14. gravel
agitator
infatuated . . . 7. foolish, smitten
8. enamored, obsessed 9. bewitched
10. captivated, enraptured
12. enthusiastic
infatuation . . . 3. ate, mad 4. love 5. craze,
folly 10. enthusiasm 11. foolishness
infeasible . . . 8. unlikely 10. improbable,
unsuitable 13. impracticable
infect . . . 5. taint 6. defile, excite,
poison 7. corrupt, deprave, pollute
11. contaminate
infection . . . 7. disease 8. epidemic
9. pollution 11. implication (law),
inspiration 13. contamination
infelicity . . . 6. misery 9. inaptness
10. misfortune 11. unhappiness
12. inexpedience, untimeliness
wretchedness
infer . . . 4. hint 5. drive, guess, imply
6. deduce 7. presume, suppose, surmise
8. conclude, construe
inference . . . 5. truth 8. illation
9. corollary, deduction 10. assumption,
conclusion 11. implication, proposition
inferential . . . 8. illative 9. deductive,
inducible 10. deductible, suggestive
15. inconsequential
inferior . . . 3. bad 4. less, poor 5. baser,
lower, minor, petit, petty 6. lesser,
menial, nether 7. humbler, unequal
8. anterior, mediocre 10. inadequate,
low-blooded 11. subordinate
inferior lawyer . . . 9. leguleian
11. pettifogger
infernal . . . 6. cursed, plaguy, wicked
7. hellish, satanic 8. damnable, devilish
9. chthonian, execrable, malignant,
Tartarean 10. demoniacal, detestable,
outrageous
inferno (pert to) . . .
Bib . . 4. Hell 5. abyss, limbo
Buddah . . 6. Naraka
Egypt . . 6. Amenti
ferry to . . 4. Styx
Hebrew . . 5. Sheol 7. Abaddon, Gehenna
myth . . 5. Aralu, Hades, Orcus
7. Acheron, Niflhel 8. Tartarus
infest . . . 3. vex 5. annoy, beset 6. assail,
molest, plague 7. overrun, torment
8. frequent
infidel . . . 5. deist, pagan 7. atheist,
Saracen, skeptic 8. agnostic
10. unbeliever 11. freethinker 12. non-
Christian 13. non-Mohammedan
infidelity . . . 6. deceit 7. perfidy 8. unbelief
9. misbelief, treachery 10. disloyalty
11. incredulity 13. faithlessness
infinite . . . 4. vast 5. vague 6. divine
7. endless, eternal, immense, perfect
9. boundless, limitless, unlimited
10. indefinite 11. illimitable, interminate,
omnipresent, The Absolute 12. all-
embracing, interminable, undetermined
13. inexhaustible, The Omnipotent
16. all-comprehensive
Infinite Being . . . 3. God
Infinite knowledge . . . 11. omniscience

infinitesimal . . . 5. small 7. minimum
9. invisible 10. evanescent
11. microscopic
infirm . . . 4. weak 5. anile, frail 6. senile
7. fragile 8. decrepit 9. doddering
10. irresolute 11. vacillating
infirmity . . . 6. defect, foible, malady, old
age 7. disease, failing, frailty, illness
8. debility, weakness 10. feebleness
inflame . . . 4. burn, fire 5. anger 6. arouse,
enrage, excite, ignite, kindle, madden,
rankle, redden 7. incense 8. irritate
10. exasperate
inflammable . . . 5. fiery 6. tinder
7. piceous 8. burnable 9. excitable,
irascible, irritable 10. accendible
11. combustible
inflammable substance . . . 6. ethane,
tinder 7. acetone, bitumen
inflammation . . . 8. ignition, soreness
10. congestion, excitement, incitement
inflammation (pert to) . . .
  bladder . . 8. cystitis
  bone . . 7. rickets 8. osteitis
    13. osteomyelitis
  ear . . 6. otitis
  eye . . 6. iritis 7. uveitis
  joints . . 4. gout 9. arthritis
    10. rheumatism
  spinal cord . . 13. poliomyelitis
  stomach . . 9. gastritis
  suffix . . 4. itis
  vein . . 9. phlebitis
inflect . . . 3. bow 4. bend 5. curve
7. decline, deflect 8. modulate
inflection, inflexion . . . 4. tone 5. angle,
curve 7. bending 8. paradigm
9. accidence 10. modulation
inflexible . . . 4. iron 5. rigid, stiff 6. strict
8. obdurate, rigorous 9. immovable,
immutable, obstinate, unbending
10. implacable, inexorable, relentless,
unyielding 11. unalterable
14. uncompromising
inflict . . . 3. add 4. deal 5. wreak
6. impose, punish
inflorescence . . . 4. cyme 5. whorl
6. cymose 7. budding, flowers
8. racemose 9. flowerage, flowering
10. unfoldment 13. efflorescence
inflow . . . 6. influx 9. inpouring
11. inspiration
influence . . . 3. win 4. lead, move, pull,
sway 5. aegis (egis), bribe, force,
impel, lobby 6. affect, effect, induce,
influx, leaven, obsess 7. control,
inspire, mastery 8. dominate, effusion,
persuade, prestige 9. authority,
determine
influence (world-wide) . . . 8. ecumenic
influenced . . . 6. biased 7. induced,
pliable (easily) 8. affected 10. prejudiced
influential . . . 6. potent, strong 7. weighty
8. momentus, powerful 9. effective
13. authoritative
influx . . . 4. tide 5. firth, mouth (river)
6. import, inflow 7. estuary, illapse
9. influence, inpouring
11. debouchment
infold . . . see *enfold*
inform . . . 4. tell 5. teach, train 6. advise,

notify, report 7. animate, apprise,
inspire 8. instruct 9. enlighten
informal . . . 7. offhand 9. irregular
information . . . 3. air, tip 4. data, lore,
news 5. aviso, datum, facts 6. digest
7. advices, tidings 9. knowledge
10. annotation 11. instruction
12. intelligence
informed . . . 2. up 3. hep 4. up on,
wise 5. aware 6. posted 8. apprised,
educated, versed in, well-read
10. instructed 11. enlightened
informer . . . 3. spy 4. tout 6. gossip,
snitch, teller 7. delator 8. affirmer,
betrayer, mouchard, reporter, telltale
9. informant, spokesman 10. talebearer,
tattletale
informer (sl) . . . 4. fink, nark 6. canary,
snitch 7. stoolie 8. snitcher, squealer
9. blabberer 11. stool pigeon
12. blabbermouth
infraction . . . 6. breach 8. fracture,
trespass 9. intrusion, violation
12. encroachment, infringement,
overstepping 13. transgression
infrequency . . . 6. rarity 7. fewness
8. rareness, solitude 9. isolation
12. uncommonness
infrequent . . . 4. rare 6. scarce, seldom,
sparse 8. uncommon 9. spasmodic
10. occasional
infrequently . . . 6. rarely, seldom 8. not
often, sparsely
infringe . . . 6. defeat, refute 7. confute,
destroy, violate 8. encroach, overstep,
trespass 9. frustrate
infringement . . . 6. breach, piracy
(copyright) 9. intrusion, violation
10. infraction 12. overstepping
14. nonfulfillment
infundibulum . . . 4. cone, lura 10. gray
matter (brain)
infuriate . . . 5. anger 6. enrage, incite,
madden 8. irritate 10. antagonize
infuscate . . . 6. darken 7. obscure
infuse . . . 4. fill, shed 5. steep 6. drench
7. implant, instill 9. insinuate, introduce
infusion . . . 3. tea 4. wort 8. affusion,
tincture 9. admixture, decoction,
inpouring 12. instillation
ingang . . . 5. porch 8. entrance
10. intestines
ingenious . . . 5. sharp, smart, witty
6. adroit, clever, daedal, gifted, shrewd,
subtle 8. skillful, talented 9. Daedalian,
deviceful 11. intelligent, resourceful
ingenuity . . . 5. skill 6. candor, genius
10. adroitness 11. originality
13. inventiveness
ingenuous . . . 4. naif, open 5. frank, naive,
noble, plain 6. candid, innate 7. artless,
sincere 8. freeborn, innocent 9. guileless
10. unreserved 15. unsophisticated
ingest . . . 3. eat 5. learn 6. take in
7. consume, swallow
ingot . . . 3. gad, pig 4. mold 5. metal,
sycee 7. bullion
ingratiate . . . 4. fawn 7. commend, flatter
9. insinuate, introduce
ingredient . . . 6. factor 7. element
9. component 11. constituent

ingress . . . **4.** go in **5.** entry **6.** access,
portal **8.** entrance **9.** reception
11. entranceway
ingrowing nail . . . **7.** acronyx
inhabitant . . . **3.** cit **6.** inmate, people,
tenant **7.** citizen, denizen **8.** resident
inhabitant (pert to) . . .
Alaska . . **9.** sourdough
desert . . **4.** Arab **5.** nomad
earliest . . **9.** aborigine
foreign . . **5.** alien
Maine . . **10.** down-easter
moon . . **8.** selenite
northern . . **6.** Yankee **11.** Septentrion
(Lowell)
inhabitants, equator's other side . . .
8. antiscii **10.** antiscians
inhabited . . . **5.** lived **7.** dwelled, peopled
8. occupied, tenanted **9.** populated
inhabiting (pert to) . . .
caves . . **8.** spelaean (spelean)
10. troglodyte
ground . . **9.** terricole **11.** terricolous
groves . . **7.** nemoral **10.** nemoricole
islands . . **7.** nesiote
lakes . . **9.** lacustral
sea . . **7.** pelagic **15.** thalassophilous
seashore . . **8.** littoral
inhale . . . **4.** suck **5.** smell, smoke, sniff
7. breathe, inspire, respire
inharmonious . . . **7.** jarring **9.** differing,
dissonant, unmusical **10.** discordant
11. conflicting, disagreeing
inherent . . . **6.** inborn, innate **7.** infixed
8. immanent **9.** immanence, intrinsic
10. indwelling, subsistent **11.** instinctive
13. indispensable
inheritance . . . **6.** legacy **7.** bequest,
legitim **8.** heirship, heredity, heritage,
Salic law **9.** cleronomy **10.** birthright
inheritance diminisher . . . **6.** abator
inheritor . . . **4.** heir **6.** coheir **7.** heiress,
legatee **10.** coparcener **11.** beneficiary
inhibit . . . **5.** check **6.** forbid, hinder
8. prohibit, restrain **9.** interdict
inhibition . . . **3.** ban, bar **4.** writ
7. embargo **8.** checking **9.** hindrance,
restraint **10.** impediment **11.** prohibition
12. interdiction
inhuman . . . **4.** fell **5.** cruel **6.** brutal,
savage **7.** bestial, brutish **8.** devilish,
nonhuman **9.** barbarous, ferocious
10. demoniacal, diabolical
inhumation . . . **6.** burial **9.** arenation,
interment
inhume . . . **4.** bury **5.** inter, inurn
7. deposit, inearth
inimical . . . **7.** adverse, hostile, opposed
8. contrary **10.** unfriendly
11. belligerent, unfavorable
iniquity . . . **3.** sin **4.** evil, vice **5.** crime
7. misdeed **9.** injustice **10.** immorality,
wickedness
initial . . . **6.** paraph **9.** incipient **11.** large
letter **12.** commencement
initiate . . . **4.** open **5.** admit, begin,
epopt (anc) **6.** induct **7.** install,
instate **8.** inchoate **10.** inaugurate
11. preinstruct
initiation . . . **8.** ceremony **9.** admission
10. admittance **12.** inauguration,

introduction
injection . . . **4.** hypo **5.** enema **7.** clyster
9. immission
injudicious . . . **4.** rash **6.** unwise
9. impolitic, imprudent **11.** inexpedient
injunction . . . **3.** ado **4.** writ **5.** order,
union **6.** behest **7.** mandate, precept
9. direction **11.** prohibition
injure . . . **3.** mar **4.** harm, hurt, lame, maim
5. wound, wrong **6.** assail, damage,
grieve, impair, scathe **7.** affront,
slander, tarnish
injurious . . . **3.** bad **4.** evil **7.** abusive,
harmful, hurtful, noxious
10. defamatory, slanderous
11. detrimental, mischievous
injury . . . **3.** ill, mar **4.** dere (obs), evil,
harm, hurt, loss, pain, tort **5.** wound,
wrong **6.** damage, lesion, mayhem,
trauma **7.** slander **9.** detriment,
indignity, injustice **10.** impairment
injustice . . . **5.** wrong **6.** injury **7.** umbrage
8. hardship, inequity, iniquity
10. imposition, unfairness
ink . . . **3.** jet **5.** black **7.** blacken
8. atrament, blacking
ink (pert to) . . .
bag . . **3.** sac (fish)
berry . . **5.** holly **6.** indigo
black . . **10.** atramental **11.** atramentous
cap . . **8.** mushroom
fish . . **5.** squid **6.** cuttle
pad . . **7.** tompion (tampion)
ref to . . **10.** atramental
source . . **7.** inkweed, oak gall **8.** inkstone,
pokeweed **9.** gallberry
spreader . . **6.** brayer
inkle . . . **4.** hint, tape, yarn **5.** braid, twist
6. thread **8.** intimate
inkling . . . **4.** hint **5.** rumor **6.** desire,
report **10.** intimation **11.** supposition
inlaid . . . **6.** mosaic **7.** adorned, set into
9. champleve, decorated
inlay . . . **4.** buhl, line **5.** inset **6.** insert,
mosaic, niello, tarsia **7.** filling, implant
8. buhlwork, intarsia **9.** champleve
inlet . . . **3.** bay, ria, voe **4.** cove, slew,
sump **5.** admit, bayou, bight, creek,
fiord (fjord), firth , inlay **6.** estero,
recess, strait **7.** estuary, orifice
8. entrance, waterway
inn . . . **3.** pub **4.** khan **5.** abode,
fonda, hotel, motel, serai **6.** hostel,
imaret, posada, tavern **7.** albergo,
cabaret, hospice, locanda, osteria,
pension, shelter **8.** alehouse, hostelry
9. roadhouse **11.** caravansary
innate . . . **4.** born **6.** inborn, inbred,
native **7.** natural **9.** ingrained, inherited,
intrinsic **10.** congenital, hereditary,
inveterate **11.** instinctive
14. constitutional
innate ability . . . **6.** genius, talent
innate idea (Philos) . . . **11.** immortality
inn courts . . . **11.** Inner Temple
inner . . . **4.** ento (comb form) **5.** ental
6. inside, inward, secret **7.** obscure
8. esoteric, interior, internal **9.** intestine
10. indistinct **14.** intramolecular
inner circle . . . **3.** set **4.** clan, club, ring
5. group, junta, junto **6.** clique

inner man . . . 4. mind, self, soul 6. psyche 7. stomach
innermost coating . . . 6. intima
Inner Temple . . . 11. Inns of Court
Innisfail . . . 4. Eire, Erin 7. Ireland 15. Island of Destiny
innocence . . . 6. purity 7. diamond 11. sinlessness 12. harmlessness 13. guiltlessness, innocuousness
innocent . . . 4. Holy, pure 5. idiot, naive, seely 6. benign, lawful 7. artless, sinless, upright 8. spotless 9. destitute, guiltless, ingenuous, permitted, simpleton, stainless, unsullied 10. unblamable 12. simple-minded 13. free from guilt
innocuous . . . 8. harmless, hurtless, innocent 9. innoxious 11. inoffensive, unoffending
innovation . . . 3. new 6. change 7. novelty 13. prolification
Inns of Court name . . . 4. Gray 7. Lincoln
innuendo . . . 4. hint, slur 6. change 7. meaning 9. aspersion 10. intimation 11. implication, indirection, insinuation
Innuit . . . 4. Yuit (Eskimo)
innumerable . . . 6. legion, myriad 7. umpteen 8. infinite, numerous 9. countless 10. numberless
inodorous . . . 8. odorless 9. scentless
inopportune . . . 8. ill-timed, untimely 10. malapropos, unsuitable 11. contretemps, inexpedient 12. embarrassing, unseasonable
inordinate . . . 5. undue 9. excessive, fanatical 10. disordered, disorderly, exorbitant, immoderate 11. unregulated 12. unrestrained
inorganic . . . 7. mineral 9. inanimate 13. nonbiological
inquest . . . 4. jury 5. quest, trial 6. assize, search 7. inquiry 11. examination 13. investigation
inquire . . . 3. ask 4. seek 5. query 7. examine 8. question 11. interrogate, investigate
inquirer . . . 6. seeker 7. querier, student, zetetic 8. searcher
inquiry . . . 5. query 6. examen, tracer 7. examine, seeking 8. question, research 11. examination 13. investigation
inquisition . . . 5. trial 6. search 7. inquiry 8. tribunal 11. examination 13. investigation
Inquisition figure . . . 10. Torquemada
inquisitive . . . 4. nosy 5. peery 6. prying 7. curious 8. meddling 10. meddlesome
inquisitor . . . 6. tracer 7. coroner, sheriff 8. examiner
in re . . . 10. concerning 13. in the matter of
inroad . . . 4. raid 5. foray 8. invasion, trespass 10. incursion, intrusion, irruption 12. overstepping 13. transgression
insane . . . 3. mad 4. daft, loco, luny 5. batty, crazy, loony 6. crazed 7. cracked, foolish, frantic, rammish, touched, witless 8. demented, deranged 9. non compos 15. non compos mentis
insane urge to steal . . . 11. kleptomania

insanity . . . 5. mania 6. frenzy, lunacy, trance 7. madness 8. delirium, dementia 10. alienation 11. derangement 16. mental deficiency
inscribe . . . 4. draw, etch 5. infix, stamp, write 6. blazon, enroll 7. address, engrave, impress 8. dedicate, depencil
inscribed . . . 5. runed 7. written 8. engraved, recorded 10. registered, rupestrian (on rocks)
inscription . . . 4. text 5. motto, title 6. legend 7. epitaph, writing 8. colophon, epigraph, graffito 9. lettering, sgraffito 10. dedication 14. superscription
inscrutable . . . 6. secret 8. abstruse 10. mysterious 12. impenetrable, inexplorable, unfathomable 16. incomprehensible
insect . . . 3. ant, bee, bug, dor, fly 4. flea, gnat, lerp, lice, mite, moth, tick, wasp 5. aphid, borer, cadew, emmet, leech, louse, roach, Vespa 6. acarid, beetle, cicada, earwig, hornet, locust, mantis, sawfly, scarab, spider 7. ant lion, chigger, firefly, gallfly, katydid, ladybug, pismire, termite 8. bullhead, glowworm, mosquito, stinkbug, turicata 9. bumblebee, butterfly, caddis fly, centipede, cockroach, dragonfly, ichneumon, tsetse fly, tumblebug 10. silverfish 11. caterpillar, grasshopper 12. yellow jacket
insect (pert to) . . .
adult . . 5. imago
aquatic . . 7. Ranatra
arboreal . . 7. katydid
back . . 5. notum
Bible . . 7. ant lion
butterfly . . 11. Lepidoptera
egg . . 3. nit
eyes . . 6. ocelli 7. stemmas
feelers . . 5. palps 8. antennas 9. tentacles
fly . . 4. zimb 7. Diptera
hymenopterous . . 3. ant, bee 4. wasp 6. sawfly 7. gallfly
immature . . 4. grub, pupa 5. larva 6. maggot 9. chrysalis
immature covering . . 6. cocoon
leg . . 6. proleg
like . . 8. entomoid
long-legged . . 5. emesa 10. harvestman 13. daddy-longlegs
mature . . 5. imago
molting . . 6. instar 7. ecdysis
parasitic . . 4. lice 5. louse
plant . . 5. aphid, aphis , borer, thrip
plate . . 6. scutum
praying . . 6. mantis
reference to . . 11. entomologic
relationship to host . . 7. metochy 10. parasitism
science . . 10. entomology
sound . . 5. chirr 7. stridor
stage . . 4. pupa 5. imago, larva 6. instar 9. chrysalis
stinging . . 3. ant, bee 4. wasp 6. hornet 7. sciniph (Bib) 12. yellow jacket
wingless . . 4. flea 6. aptera
wing vein . . 5. media
Insectivora (mammals) . . . 5. moles

6. shrews 7. desmans, tenrecs
9. hedgehogs

insecure . . . 5. risky, shaky 6. infirm,
unsafe, unsure 7. dubious, rickety,
unsound 8. unstable 9. dangerous,
hazardous 10. precarious

insensate . . . 5. blind, harsh 6. brutal,
unwise 7. fatuous, foolish 8. lifeless
9. inanimate, unfeeling, untouched
10. insensible, insentient 11. insensitive
13. unintelligent

insensibility . . . 4. coma 8. neurosis
9. analgesia 13. lack of feeling

insensible . . . 4. numb, slow 7. gradual,
unaware 9. apathetic, inanimate,
insensate, senseless 11. indifferent,
unconscious 13. inappreciable

insert . . . 4. gore 5. foist, graft, immit,
inset, panel, wedge 7. ingraft 8. interact,
ornament 9. interface, interpose,
introduce 11. intercalate, interpolate

insertion . . . 5. inset 9. injection
10. embroidery, needlework

insertion (pert to) . . .
cords in cloth . . 5. shirr
day in calendar . . 13. intercalation
newspaper . . 2. ad 13. advertisement
phrases, words . . 11. parenthesis
sound in a word . . 9. anaptyxis
10. epenthesis

inset . . . 5. panel 6. inflow, influx
10. phenocryst

inside out, turning . . . 5. evert 8. aversion
9. evertible

insidious . . . 4. deep, wily 7. cunning
8. guileful 9. deceitful, dishonest 11. full
of plots, treacherous

insight . . . 3. ken 6. acumen, aperçu
9. intuition 11. discernment, penetration
12. clairvoyance 13. understanding

insignia . . . 3. bar 4. ankh, flag 5. badge,
cross, crown 6. banner, emblem,
symbol 7. chevron, regalia, scepter
8. caduceus, swastika 15. hammer and
sickle

insignificance . . . 6. trifle 9. smallness
10. slightness 12. unimportance

insignificant . . . 4. puny 5. minor, petit,
petty, small, zilch 6. paltry 7. trivial
8. inferior 9. senseless 11. meaningless,
unimportant 12. contemptible
13. inconsiderate

insignificant object . . . 8. molehill

insincere . . . 5. false 8. affected
9. deceptive 12. hypocritical

insinuate . . . 4. hint 5. enter, imply
6. allude, infuse 8. intimate 9. penetrate
10. ingratiate

insinuation . . . 4. hint 5. sneer
8. innuendo 9. aspersion, insertion,
intrusion 10. intimation 12. ingratiation,
interjection

insipid . . . 3. dry 4. dead, dull, flat, tame
5. heavy, prosy, stale, vapid, wimpy (sl)
6. jejune 7. prosaic 8. lifeless, mediocre
9. tasteless 10. monotonous, namby-
pamby, spiritless, unanimated, wishy-
washy 11. indifferent 13. uninteresting

insisted . . . 5. urged 6. held to 7. pressed
8. demanded 9. persisted
10. maintained, stipulated

insnare . . . see *ensare*

insolence . . . 5. serve 6. insult 8. defiance
9. arrogance, contumely, impudence
11. haughtiness

insolent . . . 4. pert, rude 7. abusive,
defiant 8. arrogant, impudent
9. insulting 10. disdainful
11. extravagant, impertinent,
overbearing 12. contemptuous,
contumelious 13. disrespectful

insolvent . . . 8. bankrupt

insouciant . . . 8. carefree 11. indifferent,
unconcerned

inspect . . . 3. pry, spy 4. view 5. grade
7. examine 10. scrutinize

inspector . . . 4. ager 6. conner, grader,
police, sealer, tester 8. examiner,
overseer

inspiration . . . 6. sprite 8. afflatus,
hiccough 9. influence, intuition
10. exhalation, inhalation, motivation

inspire . . . 4. fire 5. cheer, exalt 6. infuse,
inhale 7. animate, breathe, enliven
8. motivate 9. encourage, infatuate
11. communicate (to the spirit)

inspired power . . . 7. entheos

inspiring . . . 8. cheering, eloquent
11. provocative

inspiring (pert to) . . .
awe . . 4. fear 5. awful, eerie
confidence . . 11. encouraging
favor . . 13. prepossessing
horror . . 6. grisly

inspirit . . . 5. cheer, elate, rouse
7. animate, enliven, hearten, inspire,
quicken 9. encourage 10. ingratiate,
invigorate

instability . . . 8. weakness 10. changeable,
insecurity, mutability, unsafeness
11. inconstancy 12. irresolution,
unsteadiness 13. changeability,
unreliability

install . . . 4. seat 6. induct, ordain
7. instate 8. initiate 9. establish
10. inaugurate

instance . . . 4. case, suit 6. motive
7. example, request, urgency
8. occasion 10. suggestion
11. instigation

instant . . . 3. pop 4. time, urge 5. flash,
trice 6. direct, minute, moment,
second, urgent 7. current, solicit
8. pressing 9. immediate, importune
11. importunate

instantly . . . 3. now 8. directly, in a flash,
in a trice

instate . . . 5. admit, endow 6. invest
7. install 9. establish

instead of . . . 4. else 5. stead 6. in lieu,
rather 10. equivalent, substitute

instigate . . . 3. egg 4. abet, goad, move,
prod, spur, urge 5. impel 6. foment,
incite, suborn 7. provoke 8. motivate
9. stimulate

instigator . . . 5. urger 7. abettor, exciter,
inciter 8. agitator, fomenter, inflamer,
provoker 10. ringleader

instill, instil . . . 5. imbue 6. impart,
infuse, pour in 7. pervade 9. inculcate,
insinuate

instinct . . . 5. knack 6. libido, talent

7. impulse 8. aptitude 11. instigation, orientation

instinctive . . . 6. innate 7. natural 8. inherent, original 9. automatic, intuitive 11. involuntary, spontaneous

institute . . . 5. erect, found 6. create, ordain, school 7. academy, college, precept, society 8. initiate, organize, seminary 9. originate, principle 10. inaugurate 12. organization

Institute (The) . . . 5. Gaius 6. France 8. Politics 10. Technology

institute a suit . . . 3. sue 7. go to law 8. litigate 9. prosecute

Institution, International (maritime) . . . 7. Veritas 13. Bureau Veritas

instruct . . . 4. show 5. coach, edify, order, teach, train 6. advise, direct, inform 7. command, confirm, educate, nurture 9. enlighten 10. discipline 12. indoctrinate

instruction . . . 3. act 4. lore, news 6. lesson, report 7. precept, tuition 8. pedagogy, teaching, tutorage 9. paideutic 11. information 13. propaedeutics

instructive . . . 8. didactic, sermonic 10. commanding, preceptive 11. educational, informative 12. propaedeutic

instructor . . . 5. tutor 6. mentor 7. adviser, teacher, trainer 8. lecturer 9. preceptor, professor

instrument . . . 4. barb, bill, deed, tool, writ 5. agent, means 6. medium 7. utensil, writing 8. document 9. implement 11. contrivance

instrument, musical (pert to) . . .
ancient . . 4. asor, lyre 5. rebab, rocta, shawn 7. bandore, cithern, theorbo 8. penorcon, psaltery
brass . . 4. horn 6. cornet 7. helicon
keyboard . . 5. organ, piano 6. spinet 7. celesta (celeste), cembalo 8. virginal 10. clavichord 11. harpsichord
percussion . . 4. drum, gong 5. bells, conga 6. bongos, chimes, claves 7. cymbals, marimba 8. carillon 9. castanets, xylophone 10. vibraphone 12. glockenspiel
sacred (Mormon) . . 4. Urim 7. Thummim
stringed . . 4. asor, harp, lute, lyre, rota 5. banjo, cello, dobro, ribec (ribeck), sitar, viola 6. fiddle, guitar, violin 7. ukulele 8. dulcimer, mandolin 10. hurdy-gurdy
wind . . 3. sax 4. horn, oboe, reed, tuba 5. flute, organ 6. cornet 7. althorn, bassoon, ocarina, piccolo, trumpet 8. clarinet, trombone 9. accordion, flageolet, harmonica, saxophone 10. concertina

instrument, others (pert to) . . .
astronomical . . 5. armil
Biblical . . 4. Urim
butcher's . . 5. steel 7. cleaver
communication . . 9. telegraph, telephone 10. hydrophone
cooking (eggs) . . 7. oometer
cutting . . 5. knife, razor 6. scythe, shears, sickle 7. cutlery 8. scissors, strickle

drawing . . 10. pantograph
gripping . . 4. vise 5. clamp, tongs 7. pincers 8. tweezers
legal . . 4. deed, writ 6. escrow
mathematics . . 6. abacus 8. mesolabe
measure . . 7. ammeter 8. odometer, otoscope, rheostat 9. barometer, koniscope, rheometer 11. pyronometer
medical . . 6. trocar (trochar) 7. dilator, levator, ligator, scalpel 8. trephine
mining . . 6. jumper
music . . 4. bell 9. ergograph, metronome
navigating . . 7. pelorus, sextant
optical . . 7. alidade (alidad) 9. periscope, telescope
pointed . . 3. awl 6. stylet, stylus 8. stiletto
time . . 11. chronometer, chronoscope
two-pronged . . 6. bident

instrumental . . . 6. useful 7. helpful 9. conducive, promoting, symphonic 10. orchestral 11. implemental, serviceable

instrumental (pert to) . . .
composition . . 5. fugue, rondo 6. sonata 7. cantata 8. symphony
grammar . . 4. case
introduction . . 7. intrada

instrumentality . . . 5. means 6. agency, medium 7. organon 9. mechanism

insubordinate . . . 8. mutinous 10. unresigned 11. disobedient 12. contumacious, unsubmissive

insubstantial . . . 5. frail 6. flimsy 9. illogical 10. unreliable 12. apparitional

insufficient . . . 5. short 6. scanty, scarce 7. unequal, wanting 9. deficient 10. inadequate 14. incommensurate, unsatisfactory

insular . . . 5. alone 6. narrow 7. nesiote 8. detached, islander, isolated, secluded 9. illiberal, insulated, sclerosis, separated, unrelated 10. contracted 12. Island of Reil (Anat)

insulated . . . 5. isled, taped 8. isolated 9. separated 10. segregated

insulating material . . . 4. tape 5. kapok 6. balata, Kerite 7. okonite 10. fiber glass 12. friction tape

insult . . . 3. cag 4. mock, slur 5. flout 6. offend, revile 7. affront, assault, offense, outrage 8. contempt 9. contumely, indignity

insulting . . . 8. arrogant, insolent 9. offensive 10. affrontive 13. disrespectful

insurance . . . 4. risk 7. annuity, promise 8. guaranty, security, warranty 9. assurance 10. protection

insurance group . . . 7. tontine

insurance personnel . . . 5. agent 6. broker 7. actuary 8. adjuster

insurgent . . . 5. rebel 8. agitator, mutineer, revolter 10. rebellious 13. insubordinate

insurmountable . . . 10. impassable, invincible 11. insuperable 13. beyond control

insurrection . . . 4. riot 6. mutiny, revolt 8. sedition, uprising 9. rebellion 10. insurgence, revolution

intact ... 5. sound, whole 9. unchanged, undefiled, undivided, uninjured, untouched 10. unimpaired

intaglio ... 3. die, gem 6. relief 7. carving 9. engraving

intangible ... 5. vague 7. phantom 10. immaterial, impalpable 13. imperceptible, insubstantial, unsubstantial

integer ... 3. one 5. whole 6. entity, number 8. integral

integral ... 3. all 5. inner, whole 8. totality 9. component, essential

integration ... 5. whole 10. adjustment 11. unification 12. coordination, equalization 13. accommodation

integrity ... 5. unity 6. purity, virtue 7. honesty, probity 9. innocence, soundness 12. completeness

integument ... 4. aril, coat, derm, skin 5. testa 8. covering, envelope 10. investment

intellect ... 3. wit 4. mind, nous 5. inwit, mahat 6. genius, noesis, reason 7. noetics, wise man 9. mentality 12. intelligence 13. understanding

intellectual ... 6. brainy, mental, noetic, sophic 7. egghead, learned 8. highbrow 11. intelligent

intelligence ... 4. mind, news 5. sense, spies 6. acumen, spirit 8. capacity 9. intellect, knowledge 11. information 13. understanding

intelligent ... 3. apt 4. sane 5. acute, aware, smart 6. astute, bright, versed 7. knowing, skilled 8. rational, sensible 9. cognizant 13. understanding

intelligentsia ... 8. literati 9. illuminati 11. the educated 13. intellectuals

intelligible ... 5. clear, plain 8. knowable 10. cognizable, conceptual, explicable, fathomable 11. perspicuous 13. suprasensuous 14. comprehensible, understandable

intelligibly ... 6. simply 7. clearly, lucidly, plainly 13. unequivocally 14. comprehensibly, understandably

intemerate ... 4. pure 9. inviolate, undefiled

intemperance ... 6. excess 8. bibacity, gluttony, severity, tippling 10. debauchery, inclemency 11. drunkenness 12. inabstinence, incontinence

intemperate ... 6. Frigid (Zone), severe, Torrid (Zone) 7. extreme 8. addicted, bibulous 9. excessive, inclement, indulgent 10. gluttonous, immoderate, inordinate 12. ungovernable, unrestrained

intend ... 3. aim 4. mean, plan 5. serve 6. design, direct, expect, regard, set out, strive 7. proceed, propose 8. aspire to, attend to, consider

intended ... 5. meant 8. designed, purposed, remedial 9. affianced, betrothed, meditated 10. calculated, considered 11. deliberated, intentional 12. contemplated

intense ... 4. deep 5. great, vivid 6. strong 7. violent 8. powerful 9. energetic

10. high degree

intensely ... 4. very 5. quite 7. acutely

intensify ... 6. deepen 7. enhance 8. condense, heighten, increase 9. aggravate

intensity ... 5. ardor, depth 6. deepen, degree, energy 7. density 8. loudness, softness, strength 9. greatness, vehemence 12. colorfulness

intent ... 4. rapt 5. eager, tense 6. design 7. earnest, meaning, purpose 9. intention

intention ... 3. aim, end 4. will 6. animus, design, motive, object 7. concept, healing, meaning, purpose 8. intentio 13. determination

intentional ... 5. aimed, meant 7. knowing 8. designed, intended 9. voluntary 10. calculated, deliberate 12. contemplated

intently ... 7. eagerly, fixedly 9. earnestly, zealously 10. diligently, sedulously 11. attentively, steadfastly

inter (pref) ... 5. among, intra 6. mutual, within 7. between 10. reciprocal

inter (verb) ... 4. bury 5. inurn 6. entomb, inhume 7. inearth

intercalary month ... 6. Veadar 8. leap year 10. bissextile

intercalate ... 6. insert 11. interpolate

intercede ... 6. umpire 7. bargain, mediate, referee 9. arbitrate, go between, interpose, intervene

intercessor ... 5. agent, front 6. bishop, Christ 8. mediator 9. middleman 10. interceder 11. internuncio

interchange ... 5. trade 6. barter 7. permute 8. commerce, exchange 9. alternate 10. transposal 11. alternation, reciprocate, retaliation

intercourse ... 7. dealing 8. commerce 10. connection, fellowship 12. conversation 13. communication

interdependence ... 9. mutuality 13. interrelation 16. interaffiliation

interdict ... 3. ban 4. veto 5. debar, taboo (tabu) 6. forbid 7. inhibit 8. prohibit 9. proscribe

interest ... 4. hold, weal 5. savor, share, usury 6. behalf, engage 7. attract, concern 9. entertain

interested ... 4. rapt 7. partial 8. a party to, involved, partisan 9. attentive 10. prejudiced

interesting ... 8. exciting 10. attractive 11. provocative

interfere ... 5. clash 6. hinder, meddle, molest, tamper 7. intrude 9. interpose, intervene 11. intermeddle

interim ... 7. respite 8. interval, meantime 9. interlude, meanwhile 12. intermission

interior ... 5. inner 6. center, inland, inside, secret 8. internal 9. enclosure

interjection ... 2. eh, lo 3. bah 4. ahem, alas, egad, haha, whew 7. heavens 11. ejaculation, exclamation

interlace ... 3. mix 5. braid, unite 9. alternate, interlink 10. intertwine, interweave 11. interpolate, intersperse

interlock ... 4. knit, mesh 5. unite, weave 6. device, engage 7. connect

9. interjoin, interlace **11.** interrelate
interlope . . . **6.** insert **7.** intrude, obtrude
 9. interfere, intervene **11.** intermeddle,
 interpolate
interloper . . . **8.** intruder **10.** trespasser
 11. gate crasher
interlude . . . **5.** farce, pause, truce
 6. verset **7.** interim, respite **8.** entr'acte,
 overture, versicle **10.** intermezzo
 11. performance **13.** entertainment
intermediary . . . **5.** agent **6.** medium,
 middle **8.** mediator **9.** go-between
 10. interagent **11.** intervening,
 mediatorial
intermediate . . . **5.** mesne **6.** grades,
 medial, medium, middle **7.** aniline
 (dye), mediate **8.** mediator **9.** naphthols
 11. interjacent, intervening
 12. intermediary
interminable . . . **4.** aeon, long **7.** endless,
 eternal **8.** infinite, unending
 9. boundless, limitless, perpetual,
 unlimited **10.** continuous, protracted
intermission . . . **4.** rest **5.** pause **6.** recess
 7. respite **8.** entr'acte, interval
 9. cessation **10.** suspension
 12. interruption
intermit . . . **4.** stop **5.** cease, recur
 7. suspend **9.** interpose, interrupt
 11. discontinue
intermittent . . . **6.** broken, fitful
 8. periodic **9.** irregular, recurrent,
 spasmodic **11.** alternating
internal . . . **5.** inner **6.** inside, inward,
 mental, within **7.** revenue **8.** domestic,
 esoteric, interior **9.** intrinsic, spiritual
internal organs . . . **6.** vitals **7.** viscera
international (pert to) . . .
 agreement . . **4.** pact **6.** accord, treaty
 7. entente **8.** suzerain
 business combine . . **6.** cartel
 fixed calendar . . **9.** Cotsworth
 language . . **2.** Ro **3.** Ido **5.** Arulo
 7. Volapük **9.** Esperanto **10.** Occidental
 11. Interlingua
interpolate . . . **5.** alter **6.** insert **7.** corrupt,
 implant **11.** intercalate
interpose . . . **7.** intrude, mediate
 9. intercede, interfere, interject,
 intervene, introduce
interpret . . . **4.** read, rede, scan **6.** define
 7. explain, expound **8.** construe,
 diagnose, exegesis **9.** elucidate,
 translate
interpretation . . . **5.** sense **8.** solution
 9. rendering **10.** definition
 11. explanation, translation
interpretation, science of . . . **7.** anagoge
 (Bib) **8.** exegesis **9.** dittology
 12. hermeneutics
interpreter . . . **5.** ulema **6.** gnomon
 7. exegete, latiner **8.** dragoman,
 exponent **9.** catechist, exegetist,
 explainer, go-between, hermeneut
 12. oneirocritic (dreams)
interrogate . . . **3.** ask **4.** pump, quiz,
 test **5.** grill, query **7.** examine, inquire
 8. question **9.** catechize
interrogation . . . **7.** eroteme (question
 mark) **8.** erotisis, question, quizzing
 11. examination, questioning

interrupt . . . **4.** stop **5.** break, check
 6. arrest, hinder, thwart **7.** break
 in, intrude **8.** obstruct **9.** intercept
 11. interpolate
interrupter (electric) . . . **8.** rheotome
interruption . . . **3.** gap **5.** pause **6.** hiatus
 7. interim **8.** interval **9.** cessation,
 hindrance **10.** suspension
 11. obstruction **12.** intermission,
 intervention **13.** interposition
intersect . . . **3.** cut **4.** meet **5.** cross
 6. divide, pierce **9.** decussate
 10. intercross
intersperse . . . **6.** insert, thread **7.** scatter
 9. diversify
interstice . . . **4.** mesh, pore **5.** chink, crack,
 space **6.** areola **7.** crevice **8.** interval
 10. interspace
intertwine . . . **5.** unite, weave **8.** entangle
 9. interknit, interlace **10.** intertwist
interval . . . **3.** gap **4.** rest **5.** break, lapse,
 pitch, space **6.** degree, period, recess
 7. diastem, interim, respite **8.** diastema,
 distance, half step **10.** interspace
 12. intermission, interruption
intervals, at . . . **8.** brokenly, fitfully
 11. haphazardly, irregularly
 12. occasionally **14.** intermittently
 15. longo intervallo
intervene . . . **6.** step in **7.** intrude, mediate
 9. interlude, interpose **10.** lie between
 11. come between
intervening (pert to) . . .
 between, among . . **11.** interjacent
 law . . **5.** mesne
 space . . **8.** distance
 time . . **7.** interim **9.** interlude
interweave . . . **3.** mat **4.** plat **5.** braid,
 plait, plash **6.** enlace, raddle, splice,
 wattle **8.** intermix **9.** interlace **13.** twist
 together
intestinal . . . **7.** enteric **8.** visceral
intestine (pert to) . . .
 coating . . **4.** caul
 comb form . . **6.** entero
 part . . **5.** colon, ilium, large, small
 6. caecum, rectum **7.** jejunum
 8. appendix, duodenum **15.** alimentary
 canal
intestines . . . **4.** guts **6.** bowels **8.** entrails
intimacy . . . **9.** closeness **10.** connection,
 friendship **11.** association, familiarity,
 sociability
intimate . . . **3.** sib **4.** hint, near **6.** friend,
 united **8.** familiar, friendly, informal,
 personal, sociable **9.** confidant,
 innermost **12.** confidential
intimation . . . **3.** cue **4.** clue, hint **5.** trace
 7. inkling **9.** reference **10.** foreboding,
 indication, suggestion **11.** supposition
 12. announcement, notification
intimidate . . . **3.** awe, cow **5.** abash,
 bully, daunt, deter **7.** overawe, terrify
 8. browbeat, frighten, threaten
intolerance . . . **7.** bigotry **9.** dogmatism,
 prejudice **10.** impatience, narrowness
 12. illiberality
intolerant . . . **6.** narrow **7.** bigoted
 8. dogmatic **9.** impatient **10.** prejudiced
 11. not enduring
intolerant person . . . **5.** bigot **7.** fanatic

intone ... **4.** sing **5.** chant, croon, sound
   7. introit

intoxicated ... **3.** lit, sot **4.** tosy **5.** drunk,
   heady, tipsy **6.** boiled **7.** fervent,
   fuddled, maudlin **8.** besotted, temulent
   9. befuddled **10.** inebriated

intractable ... **5.** tough **6.** sullen, unruly
   7. restive, willful (wilful) **8.** indocile,
   perverse, stubborn **9.** obstinate,
   unbending, unpliable **10.** headstrong,
   inflexible, refractory **11.** unteachable
   12. ungovernable

intransitive ... **6.** neuter, verbal
   8. confined **10.** in transitu

intrenchment ... **2.** pa (pah) **4.** fort
   7. defense, parapet **8.** stockade
   12. encroachment, infringement

intrepid ... **4.** bold **5.** brave **6.** heroic
   7. doughty, valiant **8.** fearless, resolute
   9. dauntless, undaunted **10.** courageous

intrepidity ... **5.** nerve, valor **7.** courage,
   prowess **8.** boldness, valiancy
   9. gallantry

intricacy ... **9.** sinuosity **10.** complexity,
   involution, perplexity **11.** complexness
   12. complication, entanglement

intrigue ... **4.** plot **5.** amour, cabal
   6. brigue, scheme **8.** artifice, cheating
   9. fascinate **10.** conspiracy
   11. machination

intrinsic ... **4.** real, true **5.** inner **6.** inborn,
   inbred, inward, native **7.** genuine,
   natural **8.** immanent, implicit, inherent
   9. essential, necessary **11.** inseparable
   13. indispensable

intrinsically ... **5.** truly **6.** really
   10. internally **11.** essentially

intrinsic being ... **7.** essence

introduce ... **5.** immit, start, usher
   6. broach, herald, infuse, insert, submit
   7. bring in, preface, present, sponsor
   8. acquaint, approach, initiate, innovate
   10. inaugurate **11.** preinstruct

introduced from foreign country ...
   6. exotic **10.** extraneous

introduced serum ... **10.** inoculated

introduction ... **5.** debut, guide, proem
   7. introit, isagoge, preface **8.** exordium,
   foreword, preamble **9.** insertion
   10. innovation **11.** instruction,
   preparation **12.** inauguration,
   presentation

introduction (pert to) ...
   Biblical .. **9.** isagogics
   drama (anc) .. **8.** protasis
   new words .. **7.** neology
   spurious matter .. **13.** interpolation

introductory ... **9.** prefatory, prelusive
   11. preliminary

introit ... **4.** hymn, rite **5.** psalm
   8. entrance **12.** introduction

introrse ... (opp of extrorse) **12.** facing
   inward

introversion ... (opp of extroversion)
   9. inversion, reticence

intrude ... **5.** enter **6.** invade, meddle
   8. encroach, infringe, overstep, trespass
   9. interfere, interlope

intruder ... **7.** invader **8.** outsider
   9. buttinsky **10.** interloper, trespasser

intrust, entrust ... **6.** commit **7.** confide,

consign **8.** delegate **10.** commission

intuition ... **5.** hunch **6.** noesis, regard
   7. insight **9.** knowledge, reference
   13. contemplation

intuitive ... **6.** noetic, seeing **7.** sensing
   10. perceiving **11.** instinctive

inulase ... **6.** enzyme

inunction ... **7.** unguent **8.** inunctum,
   ointment

inundate ... **3.** dip **4.** dunk **5.** douse,
   drunk, flood **6.** deluge, engulf **7.** baptize,
   immerse **8.** overflow, submerge
   9. overwhelm **10.** oversupply

inure ... **6.** harden, season **7.** benefit,
   callous, toughen **8.** accustom
   9. habituate

inurn ... **4.** bury **5.** inter **6.** entomb

invade ... **4.** raid **5.** enter (foeman), usurp
   6. attack, infest **7.** intrude, overrun,
   violate **8.** encroach, trespass

invader ... **4.** Pict **8.** attacker, intruder
   9. aggressor, assailant **10.** trespasser

invalid ... **4.** null, sick, void, weak **5.** frail
   6. feeble, infirm, sickly **8.** nugatory
   11. ineffectual **14.** valetudinarian

invalidate ... **4.** undo **5.** annul, quash
   7. abolish, nullify, vitiate **8.** disprove
   10. disqualify, neutralize

invalidism ... **13.** indisposition
   17. valetudinarianism

invaluable ... **6.** useful **8.** precious
   9. priceless, worthless **11.** inestimable

invariable ... **7.** uniform **8.** constant
   10. unchanging **12.** unchangeable

invasion ... **4.** raid **5.** foray **6.** attack,
   breach, inroad **8.** entrance (hostile)
   9. incursion, intrusion, irruption
   10. infraction **11.** infestation

invective ... **5.** abuse, curse **6.** tirade
   7. inveigh, railing **8.** diatribe
   10. revilement **11.** malediction
   12. vituperation

inveigle ... **4.** lure, rope **5.** snare **6.** allure,
   entice, entrap, seduce **7.** deceive,
   wheedle **10.** lead astray

invent ... **4.** coin **5.** frame **6.** create,
   design, devise **7.** concoct **8.** discover
   9. fabricate (mentally), originate

inventive ... **6.** adroit **7.** fertile **8.** creative,
   original **9.** ingenious

inventor ... **7.** creator **8.** imaginer
   10. discoverer, originator

inventor, discoverer of ...
   adding machine .. **9.** Burroughs
   air brake .. **12.** Westinghouse
   airplane .. **6.** Wright (Bros)
   automobile (gasoline) .. **7.** Daimler
   ballpoint pen .. **4.** Biro
   baseball (reputed) .. **9.** Doubleday
   bifocal lens .. **8.** Franklin
   brake (safety) .. **4.** Otis
   calculating machine .. **7.** Babbage
   camera .. **4.** Land **7.** Eastman
   cotton gin .. **7.** Whitney
   dynamite .. **5.** Nobel
   electric light .. **6.** Edison
   elevator .. **4.** Otis
   frozen food .. **8.** Birdseye
   gun .. **4.** Colt **5.** Maxim **7.** Gatling
   8. Browning **9.** Remington
   harp (Bib) .. **5.** Jubal

helicopter.. **8.** Sikorsky
lamp (safety).. **4.** Davy
lightning rod.. **8.** Franklin
lock, cylinder.. **4.** Yale
locomotive.. **6.** Cooper **10.** Stephenson
phonograph.. **6.** Edison
printing.. **9.** Gutenberg
radio.. **8.** De Forest
reaper.. **9.** McCormick
safety razor.. **8.** Gillette
sewing machine.. **4.** Howe
sleeping car.. **7.** Pullman
steamboat.. **5.** Fitch **6.** Fulton
steam engine.. **4.** Watt **8.** Newcomen
telegraph.. **5.** Morse
vulcanized rubber.. **8.** Goodyear
wireless.. **7.** Marconi
X-ray.. **8.** Roentgen
inventory ... **4.** list **5.** index, stock
  6. supply **7.** account , catalog
  (catalogue) **8.** register **10.** tally sheet
inverse ... **8.** inverted, opposite, reversed
inversely club-shaped ... **9.** obclavate
inversely oval ... **7.** obovate
inversion ... **8.** overturn, reversal
  9. overthrow, reversion **10.** conversion
  12. introversion
invert ... **7.** capsize, convert, pervert
  (obs), reverse, tip over **8.** overturn
  9. transpose **10.** turn turtle
invertebrate ... **5.** polyp **6.** insect, sponge
  7. mollusk **9.** spineless **10.** weak-willed
invest ... **3.** don **4.** vest, wrap **5.** array,
  dress, endow, indue, spend **6.** clothe
  7. empower, envelop, instate
  8. surround
invest (pert to) ...
  authority.. **8.** accredit, sanction
  ministry.. **6.** ordain
  sovereignty.. **8.** enthrone
investigate ... **3.** pry **4.** sift **5.** probe,
  study, track **6.** excuse, search **7.** discuss,
  explore **8.** indagate **10.** scrutinize
investigation ... **6.** examen **7.** inquiry,
  zetetic **8.** research **9.** discovery, heuristic
  10. discussion **11.** examination
investiture ... **7.** clothes, vesture
  8. clothing, covering **9.** induction
  10. holy orders, investment (money),
  ordination **11.** instatement
  12. installation **15.** enfranchisement
investment ... **5.** siege **7.** finance,
  garment **8.** blockade, clothing, covering,
  purchase, vestment **9.** endowment
  11. empowerment
investment list ... **9.** portfolio
inveterate ... **3.** old **6.** rooted **7.** chronic
  8. habitual, hardened **9.** confirmed,
  ingrained **10.** deep-rooted
  11. established, traditional **15.** long-
  established
invidious ... **6.** odious, ornery **7.** envious,
  hateful **9.** malignant **14.** discriminating
  (unjustly)
invigorate ... **3.** pep **5.** brace, cheer,
  nerve, renew **6.** vivify **7.** animate,
  enliven, fortify, refresh **8.** energize
  9. stimulate **10.** exhilarate, strengthen
invigorating ... **4.** cool **5.** tonic
  8. cheering **10.** energizing, life-giving,
  refreshing **11.** stimulating

invincible ... **10.** unbeatable
  11. indomitable **13.** unconquerable
inviolate ... **6.** sacred, secret **8.** faithful,
  unbroken **9.** unchanged, undefiled,
  unstained **10.** inviolable, unimpaired,
  unprofound **13.** incorruptible
invisible ... **3.** hid **6.** hidden **10.** indistinct,
  unapparent **13.** infinitesimal,
  undiscernible, unperceivable
Invisible, The ... **3.** God **11.** Rosicrucian
  16. German Protestant
invisible emanation ... **4.** aura
invitation ... **3.** bid **4.** call **7.** bidding,
  summons **10.** allurement, inducement
  12. solicitation
invite ... **3.** ask, beg, bid, try **4.** bade
  5. court, order, tempt **6.** allure, entice,
  induce **7.** request, solicit **9.** encourage
invocation ... **4.** call, plea, rite **6.** appeal,
  prayer, sermon **7.** summons **8.** entreaty
  11. conjuration, incantation
  12. supplication
invoice ... **4.** bill **7.** account (written)
  8. manifest **9.** reckoning **12.** bill of
  lading
invoke ... **3.** beg **4.** pray **6.** appeal
  7. address, conjure, entreat, implore,
  solicit **8.** draw down **10.** supplicate
involuntary ... **9.** not willed, reluctant,
  unwilling, unwitting **11.** instinctive,
  spontaneous **13.** unintentional
involve ... **3.** lap **4.** coil, wind, wrap
  5. imply **6.** employ, entail, evince, infold
  7. concern, ensnare, entwine, envelop,
  include **8.** interest **9.** embarrass,
  implicate **10.** complicate **11.** incriminate
involved ... **7.** complex, implied
  8. involute, tortuous **9.** engrossed
  10. implicated
involving punishment ... **8.** punitive
invulnerable ... **10.** invincible
  11. impregnable, insuperable
  12. impenetrable, unassailable
inward ... **4.** into **5.** entad, inner **6.** inside
  7. ingoing, muffled **8.** interior, internal
  9. spiritual **10.** internally
inwards ... **8.** entrails **10.** intestines
Io ... **7.** goddess (Gr) **9.** butterfly, satellite
  (of Jupiter)
iodine, iodin (pert to) ...
  comb form.. **3.** iod **4.** iodo
  compound.. **6.** iodide
  containing.. **5.** iodic **6.** iodous
  poisoning.. **6.** iodism **9.** iododerma
  source.. **4.** kelp **8.** sea water **9.** salt
    peter **12.** thryoid gland
  standard.. **9.** idiometry
  substitute.. **7.** Aristol
ion ... **5.** anion **6.** cation (kation)
  8. electron, particle (Elec)
Ionian (pert to) ...
  city.. **4.** Teos (birthplace of Anacreon)
  islands.. **5.** Greek **9.** Asia Minor
  mode (Mus).. **6.** Lydian
Ionic (pert to) ...
  architecture.. **5.** Order
  dialect.. **5.** Greek
  poetry.. **4.** foot **5.** meter
  printing.. **4.** type
iota ... **3.** ace, jot **4.** atom, mite, star
  (9th brightest), whit **6.** letter (Gr), tittle

8. particle
Iowa . . .
capital . . **9.** Des Moines
city . . **4.** Ames **8.** Waterloo **9.** Davenport,
Fort Dodge, Marquette, Sioux City
10. West Branch **11.** Cedar Rapids
famed attractions . . **10.** Hoover home
12. Effigy Mounds **17.** Little Brown
Church
famed first . . **12.** apple orchard (1799)
famed names . . **6.** Joliet **7.** Dubuque
9. Marquette
flower . . **8.** wild rose
locale . . **8.** farm belt (Midwest)
river . . **8.** Missouri **11.** Mississippi
State admission . . **11.** twenty-ninth (1846)
State nickname . . **7.** Hawkeye
ipecac . . . **4.** evea **6.** emetic **7.** emetive
9. purgative
irade . . . **6.** decree (Turk)
Iran . . . see also *Iranian, Persia*
capital . . **6.** Tehran (Teheran)
city . . **6.** Abadan, Shiraz **7.** Isfahan
conqueror . . **6.** Darius **9.** Alexander
lake . . **7.** Rezaieh
mountain . . **6.** Elburz, Zagros
8. Damavand (peak)
old name . . **6.** Persia
parliament . . **6.** Majlis (Mejlis)
people (anc) . . **5.** Medes **6.** Aryans
8. Persians
ruins . . **10.** Persepolis (Shiraz)
Iranian (pert to) . . .
almond . . **5.** badam
Ayatollah . . **8.** Khomeini
books . . **5.** Koran, Yasma **6.** Avesta
country . . **4.** Elam **5.** Media
demigod . . **4.** Yima
demon . . **7.** Ahriman
diadem . . **3.** taj
dynasty . . **6.** Safavi, Seljuk **8.** Sassanid
fire worshiper . . **5.** Parsi (Parsee)
god . . **6.** Ormazd (Supreme) **7.** Mithras
Koran student . . **5.** hafiz
language . . **5.** Farsi **7.** Avestan, Pehlevi
(Pahlavi), Persian
poet . . **4.** Omar **5.** Saadi
Relig founder . . **9.** Zoroaster
Shah . . **7.** Pahlavi
tapestry . . **7.** susanee
tentmaker . . **4.** Omar
Iraq, Mesopotamia . . .
capital . . **6.** Bagdad (Baghdad)
culture (anc) . . **8.** Sumerian
historic city . . **2.** Ur **5.** Eridu **7.** Babylon,
Nineveh
historic Valley . . **15.** Tigris-Euphrates
port . . **5.** Basra (Busrah)
product . . **3.** oil **4.** date **5.** sheep
river . . **6.** Tigris **9.** Euphrates **11.** Shatt-
al-Arab
irascibility . . . **3.** ire **6.** choler **9.** crossness,
testiness **10.** perversity **11.** waspishness
12. churlishness, irritability
irate . . . **3.** hot **5.** angry, wroth **7.** enraged
8. incensed **9.** irascible
ire . . . **5.** anger, wrath **7.** madness
8. vexation **9.** vehemence
10. enragement, resentment
12. exasperation
ireful . . . **5.** angry, wroth **7.** iracund

9. irascible **10.** passionate
Ireland . . . **4.** Eire, Erin **5.** Irena **6.** Old
Sod, Ulster **8.** Hibernia **9.** Innisfail
11. Emerald Isle, Erin go brath
14. Ireland Forever
Ireland (pert to) . . . see also *Irish*
Bay . . **6.** Bantry, Dingle, Galway
7. Donegal
capital . . **4.** Tara (old) **6.** Dublin
channel . . **5.** North **9.** St George's
city . . **4.** Cork, Tara **6.** Galway, Tralee,
Ulster **7.** Belfast, Donegal, Kildare,
Wexford **8.** Kilkenny, Limerick
9. Tipperary
county . . **4.** Cork, Mayo **5.** Kerry,
Sligo **6.** Dublin, Galway **7.** Wicklow
8. Kilkenny, Limerick
islands . . **4.** Aran
legislature . . **4.** Dail
mountain . . **7.** Errigal **13.** Carrantuohill
northern province . . **6.** Ulster
river . . **3.** Lee **4.** Erne, Suir **6.** Liffey
7. Shannon
sea . . **5.** Irish
seat of archbishops . . **6.** Armagh
irenic . . . **7.** henotic **8.** peaceful
11. harmonizing **12.** conciliatory
iridescent . . . **7.** opaline **9.** prismatic
10. opalescent
iris . . . **4.** flag **6.** flower **7.** rainbow
iris (pert to) . . .
astronomy . . **8.** asteroid (7th)
color . . **11.** reddish-blue
eye part . . **4.** uvea **5.** irian
Florentine . . **5.** orris (orrice)
inflammation . . **6.** iritis
mineral . . **6.** quartz (iridescent)
Iris, goddess . . . **7.** rainbow
Irish (pert to) . . .
alphabet (early) . . **4.** ogam (ogham)
battle cry . . **3.** abu (aboo) **9.** To Victory
11. Erin go brath
cattle . . **5.** Kerry
Celtic, chief's heir . . **6.** tanist
churchman . . **7.** erenach (herenach)
club, cudgel . . **10.** shillalagh (shillalah)
convention (anc) . . **4.** Feis **10.** Feis of
Tara
cordial . . **10.** usquebaugh
dagger (anc) . . **5.** skean
dance . . **3.** jig **4.** rink **10.** rinkafadda
emblem . . **8.** shamrock
exclamation . . **3.** aru **5.** arrah
fairy, spirit . . **4.** shee (sidhe) **7.** banshee
(banshie) **10.** leprechaun
festival . . **4.** feis
goblin . . **5.** pooka
god . . **3.** Ler (sea)
goddess . . **4.** Dana
hero, warrior . . **9.** Cuchulain (Cuchullin)
king's home . . **4.** Tara
landholding . . **7.** rundale
legislature . . **10.** Oireachtas (House)
11. Dail Eireann (Chamber) **13.** Seanad
Eireann (Senate)
liquor house (illegal) . . **7.** shebeen
love, sweetheart . . **3.** gra
moss . . **9.** carrageen
peasant . . **4.** kern (lerne)
pig . . **5.** bonav
policeman . . **8.** spalpeen

potato city.. **7.** Youghal
queen (folklore).. **4.** Medb
Society (secret).. **6.** Fenian
soldier.. **4.** kern (kerne) **10.** galloglass
tenant.. **4.** saer
theatre, famed.. **5.** Abbey
verse.. **4.** rann
whisky, whiskey (illegal).. **6.** poteen
(poteheen)
Irish (people) ...
ancestor (fabled).. **3.** Mil **6.** Miledh
author.. **5.** Behan, Joyce, Synge, Yeats
6. O'Casey **7.** Beckett
chemist.. **5.** Boyle
clan subdivision.. **4.** sept
composer.. **7.** Herbert
family.. **5.** cinel
Irishman.. **4.** Aire, Celt, Gael **6.** Teague
8. Milesian **9.** Hibernian, Orangeman
10. Eireannach
lawyer.. **6.** brehon
Nuns (Order).. **15.** Ladies of Loretto
patriot.. **5.** Emmet, Tandy **6.** Oakboy
refugee.. **7.** fuidhir
saint.. **7.** Columba, Patrick
Saxon.. **8.** Sasanach
sea robbers (Myth).. **9.** Fomorians
surgeon.. **6.** Colles
irk ... **3.** vex **4.** bore, tire **5.** annoy,
weary **6.** nettle **7.** disgust, trouble
10. exasperate
irksome ... **5.** vexed, weary **7.** operose,
painful, tedious **8.** annoying **9.** fatiguing,
vexatious, wearisome **10.** burdensome,
exhausting, monotonous
12. disagreeable
iron ... **2.** Fe (symbol) **5.** harsh, metal,
power, press **6.** ferrum, fetter, mangle,
pistol, severe **7.** firearm, manacle,
shackle, sideros **8.** firmness, handcuff,
hardness, strength **10.** inflexible,
unyielding **11.** unrelenting
iron (pert to) ...
casting.. **5.** mitis
comb form.. **5.** ferro **6.** sidero
compound.. **5.** steel
containing.. **6.** ferric
dog.. **7.** firedog
dross.. **6.** sinter
herb.. **8.** Vernonia **9.** ironweeds
lump.. **3.** pig
magnet.. **8.** armature
meteoric.. **8.** siderite
ore.. **7.** turgite **8.** hematite, siderite
11. sesquioxide
ref to.. **6.** ferric **7.** ferrous **8.** siderous
rod.. **5.** punty (puntee)
salts of.. **10.** chalybeate
sand.. **7.** iserine
science of.. **10.** siderology
symbol.. **2.** Fe
tailor's.. **5.** goose
tool.. **6.** lifter
vessel, basket.. **7.** cresset
ironclad ... **6.** severe **7.** armored, Monitor
(ship) **8.** exacting, rigorous **9.** stringent
ironic, ironical ... **3.** dry **7.** cynical,
satiric **9.** sarcastic **10.** figurative
11. Rabelaisian
irons ... **5.** gyves **6.** chains **7.** fetters
8. manacles, shackles **9.** handcuffs

Ironsides ... **7.** cavalry (Cromwell's)
8. Cromwell
ironwood ... **4.** acle **5.** olive **6.** colima
7. breakax **8.** hornbeam **9.** stavewood
irony ... **6.** banter, satire **7.** lampoon,
sarcasm **8.** ridicule
Iroquoian Indian ... **4.** Erie **5.** Huron
6. Cayuga, Mohawk, Oneida, Seneca
7. Wyandot **8.** Cherokee, Onondaga
9. Conestoga, Tuscarora
Iroquois (pert to) ...
Five Nations.. **6.** Cayuga, Mohawk,
Oneida, Seneca **8.** Onondaga
native of.. **7.** New York **9.** Wisconsin
irrational ... **6.** stupid **9.** fanatical,
illogical, senseless **10.** ridiculous
11. impractical **12.** preposterous,
unreasonable **13.** unintelligent
irregular ... **4.** wild **5.** erose, rough
6. fitful, rugged, uneven **7.** atactic,
crooked, devious, erratic, mutable,
styptic, unequal **8.** aberrent, abnormal,
atypical, informal, variable
9. anomalous, desultory, distorted,
eccentric, haphazard, orderless,
unsettled **10.** changeable, immoderate,
inconstant **11.** intemperate
12. unsystematic
irregularity ... **6.** ataxia (muscular)
7. anomaly **8.** disorder **9.** deviation
10. distortion **11.** abnormality,
informality **12.** eccentricity
irrelevant ... **7.** foreign **9.** unrelated
10. extraneous **11.** impertinent,
unessential **12.** inconsequent
13. insignificant
irreligious ... **5.** pagan **7.** godless,
impious, profane **11.** unreligious
irreparable ... **4.** gone, lost **6.** ruined
11. irrevocable **12.** incorrigible,
irremediable **13.** irrecoverable,
irretrievable
irrepressible ... **7.** Homeric (laughter)
12. ungovernable, unrestrained
irrepressible conflict ... **8.** civil war
irreproachable ... **7.** perfect **9.** blameless
10. impeccable, inculpable
irresolute ... **6.** fickle, unsure **8.** doubtful,
unstable **9.** uncertain, undecided
10. capricious, changeable, inconstant
12. undetermined
irresolution ... **10.** fickleness, indecision
11. fluctuation, uncertainty, vacillation
14. capriciousness
irresponsible ... **6.** fickle **7.** lawless
8. carefree **9.** insolvent
12. independable **13.** unaccountable,
untrustworthy
irretrievable ... **8.** hopeless **9.** incurable
11. irreparable **12.** irremediable,
unchangeable **13.** irrecoverable
irreverence ... **7.** impiety **8.** dishonor
9. profanity **10.** disrespect
irrevocable ... **3.** end **4.** past **5.** final
10. inevitable, past recall **11.** unalterable
12. beyond recall, unchangeable
irrigate ... **3.** wet **5.** water **6.** dilute,
sluice **7.** moisten, refresh
irritable ... **4.** edgy **5.** cross, techy, testy
6. cranky, ornery, touchy **7.** fretful,
iracund, peevish, tempery, twitchy

8. snappish
irritate ... **3.** irk, nag, vex **4.** fret, gall, rasp, rile **5.** anger, annoy, chafe, cross, grate, peeve, pique, rouse, sting, tease **6.** excite, incite, madden, needle, nettle, rankle **7.** incense, provoke **10.** exacerbate, exasperate **14.** rub the wrong way
irritated ... **4.** sore **5.** afret, testy **6.** peeved **7.** annoyed, nettled, rankled **8.** provoked
irritation ... **4.** itch **5.** pique **6.** temper **9.** annoyance **10.** resentment **12.** exasperation
irruption ... **5.** foray **6.** inroad **8.** invasion **9.** incursion
Irving pseudonym ... **13.** Knickerbocker (Diedrich)
is ... **6.** exists **10.** represents **11.** personifies
Isaac (pert to) ...
    Bib .. **9.** patriarch (Heb)
    father of .. **4.** Esau **5.** Jacob
    grandfather of .. **4.** Edom
    husband of .. **7.** Rebekah
    son of .. **5.** Sarah **7.** Abraham
Ishmael (pert to) ...
    ancestor .. **11.** Ishmaelites
    Bib .. **6.** pariah **7.** outcast
    father of .. **8.** Nebaioth
    son of .. **5.** Hagar **7.** Abraham
isinglass ... **4.** huso, mica **7.** gelatin **8.** agar-agar
Isis (pert to) ...
    daughter of .. **3.** Geb, Nut
    goddess of .. **9.** fertility **10.** motherhood
    identified with .. **7.** Dog Star
    mother of .. **4.** Sept (Horus)
    represented (at times) .. **9.** cow-headed
    shrine of .. **5.** Iseum (Iseium)
    wife of .. **6.** Osiris
Islam, Islamic (pert to) ...
    adherent .. **6.** Muslim (Moslem) **10.** Mohammedan
    convert .. **5.** ansar
    founder, prophet .. **8.** Mohammed (Mahomet)
    God .. **5.** Allah
    holy city .. **5.** Mecca **6.** Medina
    holy war .. **5.** jihad (jehad)
    leader .. **9.** ayatollah
    mosque .. **6.** masjid
    praying position .. **6.** kiblah
    rules for living .. **5.** Sunna
    sacred place .. **5.** Kaaba (Caaba) **10.** Black Stone
    sacred text .. **5.** Koran
    scholarly group .. **5.** ulema
    teacher .. **4.** alim **6.** mullah (mulla)
Islamic (pert to) ...
    convert .. **5.** ansar
    holy city .. **5.** Mecca **6.** Medina
    mosque .. **6.** masjid
    pilgrimage .. **5.** Kaaba (Caaba) **10.** Black Stone
    Supreme Being .. **5.** Allah
    teacher .. **4.** alim **5.** ulema **6.** mullah (mulla)
island ... **3.** ait, cay, ile, key **4.** calf, cayo, eyot, holm, isle, reef **5.** atoll, islet **7.** isolate **8.** insulate

island (pert to) ...
    city .. **8.** Montreal
    coral .. **5.** atoll **8.** Zanzibar
    enchanted .. **4.** Bali
    fabled .. **4.** Meru **6.** Avalon, Bimini **8.** Atlantis
    fabulous .. **7.** Zangbar
    group .. **8.** Antilles, Marshall **11.** archipelago
    inhabitant, native .. **7.** nesiote **8.** islander
    universe (Astron) .. **6.** galaxy
Island of ...
    Langerhans .. **8.** pancreas
    Odysseus .. **6.** Ithaca
    Reil .. **5.** brain
    Saints .. **4.** Erin
Isle of Man ...
    Celtic name .. **4.** Manx
    city .. **4.** Peel **6.** Ramsey **7.** Douglas
    division .. **5.** Treen
    judge .. **8.** deemster (dempster)
    legislature .. **7.** Tynwald
    mountain peak .. **8.** Snaefell
    Northern point .. **4.** Ayre
    site .. **8.** Irish sea
Isle of Wight ...
    Queen's summer home .. **12.** Osborne House
    site .. **10.** English Sea
    sport (famed) .. **9.** yacht race
    town .. **7.** Newport
    watering place .. **4.** Ryde
Isles of Galway Bay ... **4.** Aran
ism ... **4.** cult **5.** dogma, ideal, tenet **6.** belief, school, system **8.** doctrine, practice **11.** abnormality
isochromatic ... **9.** same color
isochronal ... **9.** equal time **11.** uniform time
isocracy ... **9.** equal rule **10.** equal power
isodont (Zool) ... **10.** alike teeth
isogonal ... **11.** equal angles
isolate ... **4.** isle **6.** enisle **7.** seclude **8.** insulate, separate **9.** segregate, sequester **10.** quarantine
isolation ... **8.** escapism, solitude **9.** seclusion **10.** insulation, loneliness, separation **11.** segregation
isomer ... **7.** metamer **8.** compound (Chem)
isonomy ... **11.** equal rights
isonym ... **7.** paronym **8.** same name
isosceles ... **10.** equal sides (triangle)
Israel (Bib) ... **4.** Jews **5.** Jacob, Zions **13.** Hebrew Kingdom
Israel (pert to) ... see also *Israelite*
    appellation .. **8.** Jeshurun
    capital .. **9.** Jerusalem
    city .. **4.** Acre **5.** Elath, Haifa, Jaffa **7.** Galilee, Jericho, Tel Aviv
    desert .. **5.** Negev
    dust storm .. **7.** khamsin
    lawgiver .. **5.** Moses
    Plain of .. **6.** Sharon
    priest .. **3.** Eli
    river .. **6.** Jordan
    sea .. **4.** Dead **7.** Galilee
    song (Zionist) .. **8.** Hatikvah
    statesman .. **4.** Meir **5.** Begin
Israelite (pert to) ...
    hero .. **6.** Gideon

judge.. **4.** Elon **8.** Jephthah
king.. **4.** Ahab, Jehu, Saul (1st) **5.** David (2nd) **7.** Solomon
lawgiver.. **5.** Moses
priest.. **3.** Eli
tribe.. **3.** Dan **5.** Asher **6.** Reuben
tribe, priestly.. **4.** Levi
issue... **3.** son **4.** come, emit, flow, gush **5.** arise, child, sally, spout, stock, topic, utter **6.** effect, emerge, escape, sortie, source, upshot **7.** edition, emanate, proceed, product, progeny **8.** question **9.** emergence, offspring, posterity **11.** consequence, publication
Istanbul (Constantinople)...
ancient name.. **9.** Byzantium
capital of.. **6.** Turkey (to 1923)
foreign quarter.. **4.** Pera
Greek quarter.. **5.** Fanar
site.. **8.** Bosporus **10.** Golden Horn
isthmus (pert to)...
American.. **6.** Panama
anatomy.. **6.** fauces
Greek (anc).. **7.** Corinth
Siam.. **3.** Kra
it... **5.** charm, thing **6.** itself, person **7.** egotist, pronoun
Ita... **4.** Acta **7.** Negrito
Italian (pert to)... see also *Italy*
card game.. **5.** tarot
carriage.. **7.** vettura
cathedral.. **5.** duomo
cheese.. **6.** Romano **8.** Parmesan **10.** mozzarella
condiment.. **6.** tamara (tamarind)
deity.. **4.** faun
dish.. **5.** pizza **7.** calzone **8.** braciola **11.** saltimbocca
dome, peak.. **4.** cima
entertainment.. **5.** festa **7.** ridotto
food.. see *pasta*
grape.. **6.** verdea
hamlet.. **5.** casal
house.. **4.** casa **6.** casino (summer)
inlay.. **6.** tarsia
inn.. **7.** locanda
innkeeper.. **7.** padrone
lady.. **5.** donna **7.** signora
lake.. **4.** lago
law.. **6.** Latium **8.** Jus Latii
lover.. **7.** amoroso
magistrate (anc).. **8.** podestra
marble.. **4.** Neri **7.** carrara, cipolin
marsh.. **7.** maremma
opera house.. **7.** La Scala (1778)
peasant.. **7.** paesano **9.** contadino
photographers.. **9.** paparazzi (press)
porridge.. **7.** polenta
pottery.. **8.** majolica
secret society.. **5.** Mafia (Maffia) **7.** Camorra
sheep.. **6.** merino
unification.. **12.** Risorgimento
vessel.. **9.** trabacolo
wind (hot).. **7.** sirocco
wine.. **4.** Asti **5.** Capri, Soave **6.** Barolo **7.** Chianti, Orvieto **9.** Bardolino **12.** Asti Spumante, Valpolicella
Italian (pert to people)...
anti-Fascist.. **6.** Sforza
architect.. **7.** Bernini **8.** Bramante

artist.. **6.** Titian **7.** Cellini, da Vinci, Raphael **9.** Donatello **10.** Botticelli, Caravaggio, Tintoretto, Modigliani **12.** Michelangelo
astronomer.. **6.** Secchi **7.** Galileo
author.. **5.** Dante **9.** Boccaccio **11.** Machiavelli
biographer (artists).. **6.** Vasari
composer.. **5.** Verdi **7.** Puccini, Rossini, Vivaldi **9.** Scarlatti **10.** Palestrina
deity.. **6.** Faunus
dictator.. **9.** Mussolini
educator.. **10.** Montessori
explorer.. **8.** Columbus, Vespucci **9.** Marco Polo
family (princely).. **4.** Este **5.** Doria **6.** Medici
family (violin).. **5.** Amati
friend (outside).. **10.** Italophile
geographer.. **8.** Amoretti
goddess.. **3.** Ops **4.** Juno **5.** Diana
hero.. **7.** Orlando
historian.. **4.** Dion **5.** Cantu
king.. **7.** Umberto
naturalist.. **4.** Poli
noblewoman.. **8.** Marchesa **11.** Marchioness
people.. **5.** Aequi (anc) **7.** Italici **8.** Umbrians **9.** Etruscans, Ligurians
philosopher.. **4.** Vico **5.** Croce **7.** Aquinas
physician.. **5.** Abano **9.** Eustachio
physicist.. **5.** Volta **7.** Galvani, Marconi
poet.. **4.** Redi **5.** Dante, Tasso **7.** Manzoni **8.** Annunzio, Casanova, Petrarch **9.** Boccaccio
saint.. **4.** Neri **7.** Aquinas (Thomas)
sculptor.. **5.** Dupre, Leoni **8.** Ammanati **12.** Michelangelo
singer.. **5.** Patti **6.** Caruso
statesman.. **5.** Rossi **8.** Gioberti **11.** Machiavelli
theologian.. **7.** Peronne
violinist.. **8.** Paganini
Italy...
Alps.. **5.** Cozie **6.** Carnac, Julian **7.** Atesine, Letiche, Pennine **8.** Maritime **9.** Lepontine
capital.. **4.** Rome
city.. **4.** Lodi, Pisa **5.** Anona, Fiume, Genoa, Milan, Padua, Pavia, Trent, Turin **6.** Mantua, Modena, Naples, Spezia, Venice, Verona **7.** Messina, Palermo, Pompeii, Ravenna, Trieste **8.** Brindisi, Florence, Sorrento
commune.. **6.** Rivoli (Hist) **7.** Trieste
country (anc).. **7.** Etruria, Lucania, Tuscany
gulf.. **7.** Salerno
historical site.. **10.** Blue Grotto **18.** Leaning Tower of Pisa
island.. **4.** Elba **5.** Capri, Leros **6.** Eschia, Sicily **8.** Sardinia
lake.. **4.** Como **6.** Albano, Lugano **8.** Maggiore
mountain.. **4.** Alps, Rosa **5.** Blanc **12.** Gran Paradiso
port (fishing).. **6.** Amalfi
resort.. **4.** Lido **5.** Capri **6.** Agnone **7.** Riviera
river.. **2.** Po **4.** Arno **5.** Tiber

sea .. **6.** Ionian **8.** Apennine
10. Tyrrhenian
strait .. **7.** Messina, Obranto
volcano .. **4.** Etna **8.** Vesuvius
9. Stromboli
itch ... **4.** reef, riff **5.** mange, psora
6. desire, eczema **7.** scabies, sycosis
9. cacoethes, hankering, psoriasis,
sensation **10.** irritation
ite ... **8.** adherent, disciple, follower
item ... **3.** bit **4.** news **5.** asset, entry,
scrap, topic **6.** detail **7.** article, integer
9. commodity **10.** memorandum
11. information
iter ... **4.** eyre, road (Rom) **7.** circuit
iterate ... **6.** recite, repeat, retell, review
7. recount **8.** rehearse
iteration ... **5.** recap **10.** repetition
11. restatement
ithand ... **8.** constant, diligent
14. unintermittent
itinerant ... **5.** mover, nomad **6.** roamer
7. nomadic **8.** gadabout **9.** traveling,
unsettled, wandering, wayfaring
itinerary ... **4.** gest (royal), plan **5.** route
6. prayer, record **8.** register, roadbook
9. directory, guidebook

Ivanhoe (pert to) ...
author .. **5.** Scott
character .. **5.** Boeuf **6.** Cedric, Rowena,
Ulrica
hero .. **7.** Ivanhoe
ivories (pert to) ...
anatomy .. **5.** teeth
game .. **4.** dice
piano .. **4.** keys
ivory (pert to) ...
anatomy .. **5.** tooth **7.** dentine
block .. **4.** dice **7.** tessera
carving .. **9.** toreutics
color .. **5.** white (off)
Latin .. **4.** ebur
mixture (dust, cement) .. **7.** eburine
plum .. **11.** wintergreen
tower .. **7.** retreat
ivy ... **5.** Rheus, sumac **11.** Hedera helix
iwa ... **11.** frigate bird
IWW ... **6.** wobbly
izar (Hind) ... **4.** star **7.** garment **9.** loin
cloth
izle ... **4.** root **5.** ember, spark
Izmir ... **6.** Smyrna
izzat ... **5.** honor **6.** credit **8.** prestige
10. reputation

J

J ... **3.** Jay **6.** letter (10th)
ja (Ger) ... **3.** yes
jaal goat ... **4.** ibex **5.** beden
jab ... **3.** dig, hit, jag **4.** poke, prod, stab
5. punch **6.** strike, thrust
jabber ... **4.** chat **5.** prate **6.** babble,
gabble, jargon **7.** chatter, twaddle
8. nonsense **9.** gibberish
Jabberwock ... **6.** Jubjub **7.** monster
(Through the Looking Glass)
Jabberwocky ... **4.** poem **6.** prolix
8. nonsense **10.** double talk
jabble ... **6.** splash **7.** dashing **8.** rippling
9. agitation, confusion, splashing
jabiru ... **5.** stork
jack ... **3.** can, jug, man **4.** card, coat, flag,
male, pump **5.** hoist, knave, money
6. lifter, sailor **7.** mariner **8.** nickname
jackal ... **3.** dog (wild) **4.** dieb, kola,
Thos **7.** cat's-paw **8.** henchman
jackass ... **3.** ass **4.** deer (mule), dolt,
fool, hare, nerd **6.** clover, donkey,
rabbit **7.** morwong, penguin, witling
9. blockhead
jackdaw ... **3.** daw, kae **4.** crow **7.** grackle
jacket ... **4.** coat, Eton, pelt **5.** cover
(book) **6.** blazer, blouse, bolero, casing,
jerkin, jumper, reefer **7.** garment, Mae
West, wrapper
jacket (pert to) ...
Arctic .. **6.** anorak
armor .. **5.** acton
Eskimo .. **6.** temiak
horseback riding .. **7.** hacking (jacket)
knitted .. **6.** jersey, sontag **7.** sweater

8. cardigan
Levant .. **5.** grego
Scottish .. **4.** jupe
Spanish .. **8.** chaqueta
jack-in-the-pulpit ... **4.** arum
Jack Ketch ... **7.** hangman (Eng)
11. executioner (public)
jackknife ... **6.** barlow **8.** penknife
11. toadstabber, toadsticker
jack-of-all-trades ... **8.** handyman
jackstones ... **4.** dibs, game **7.** pebbles
Jacob ... **6.** Israel **9.** patriarch
Jacob (pert to) ...
brother .. **4.** Edom, Esau
daughter .. **5.** Dinah
father-in-law .. **5.** Laban
parents .. **5.** Isaac **7.** Rebekah
retreat .. **5.** Haran
son .. **3.** Gad, Dan **4.** Levi **5.** Asher,
Judah **6.** Reuben (oldest)
wife .. **4.** Leah **6.** Rachel
Jacobin ... **4.** Club **5.** Friar (Dominican)
7. plotter, radical, Society **8.** Democrat
(Fr 1789)
Jacob's ladder ... **4.** herb **8.** hyacinth
10. belladonna **11.** bittersweet
12. Solomon's seal
jade ... **4.** bore, tire **5.** green, horse,
stone, wench **7.** fatigue **8.** strumpet
jaded ... **8.** fatigued, shopworn
9. dissolute **10.** bedraggled
jaeger (jager) ... **4.** gull (like), skua
6. teaser
jager ... **6.** hunter **7.** diamond
8. huntsman, rifleman

jagged ... **5.** erose, rough, sharp
  6. barbed, pinked, ragged, rugged
  7. cutting, notched, pointed, slashed
  8. serrated **10.** saw-toothed
jagua ... **4.** palm **7.** genipap
jaguar ... **3.** cat **4.** puma **5.** ounce
  6. cougar **7.** panther **11.** snow leopard
Jah (Heb) ... **3.** God **7.** Jehovah
jai alai ... **4.** game **5.** cesta **6.** pelota
  7. fronton
jail ... **3.** jug **4.** brig, gaol **5.** clink
  6. cooler, lockup **7.** slammer (sl)
  8. hoosegow **9.** Bridewell (London),
  calaboose **11.** incarcerate
jailer, jailor ... **5.** guard **6.** gaoler, keeper,
  warden **7.** alcaide, turnkey
jail sentence ... **3.** rap
jalousie ... **5.** blind **7.** shutter
Jamaica ...
  beverage .. **3.** rum **4.** jake
  capital .. **8.** Kingston
  cucumber .. **7.** gherkin
  ebony .. **10.** crocuswood
  island .. **10.** West Indies
  pepper .. **8.** allspice
  tree (drug) .. **7.** quassia
jangle ... **5.** brawl, chide, noise, prate
  6. babble, gossip **7.** chatter, grate on,
  quarrel, ringing, whimper
Janizary (anc) ... **5.** slave **7.** soldier
Janus (Rom) ... **3.** god (two-faced)
Japan ... **5.** Jipun (Chin), Nihon, Nisei
  6. Nippon **7.** Cipango (of Marco Polo)
Japan ... see also *Japanese*
  capital .. **4.** Nara (anc) **5.** Kyoto (anc),
  Tokyo
  city .. **4.** Kobe **7.** Sapporo **8.** Kawasaki,
  Kumamoto, Nagasaki, Yokohama,
  Yokosuka **9.** Hiroshima **10.** Kitakyushu
  current .. **8.** Kuroshio
  islands .. **6.** Honshu, Kyushu **7.** Shikoku
  9. Haikkaido (Yezo)
  mountain .. **8.** Fujiyama
  naval base .. **8.** Yokosuka
  port .. **4.** Kobe **5.** Osaka **6.** Nagoya
  8. Yokohama
  protectorate .. **9.** Manchukuo
  river .. **4.** Yalu (Annock)
  shrine .. **7.** Toshogu (at Nikko)
  spring (hot) .. **6.** Hakone
  volcano .. **9.** Asamayama
Japanese (pert to) ...
  airplane .. **4.** Zero
  annals, chronicles .. **7.** Nihongi
  apricot .. **3.** ume
  army (conscription) .. **6.** geneki
  army officer .. **7.** samurai
  art of self-defense .. **4.** judo **7.** jujitsu
  (jujutsu, jiujutsu)
  badge (family) .. **3.** mon
  banjo .. **7.** samisen
  battle cry .. **6.** banzai
  brazier .. **7.** hibachi
  button (carved) .. **7.** netsuke
  cape .. **4.** mino
  cedar .. **4.** sugi
  chess .. **5.** shogi
  church (Buddhist) .. **4.** tera
  circle, ship (suffix) .. **4.** maru
  deer .. **4.** sika
  dog .. **6.** tanate

drama .. **2.** no **6.** no-gaku
drink .. **4.** sake (saki)
entertainer .. **6.** geisha
festival .. **3.** Bon **15.** Feast of Lanterns
fish .. **3.** ayu, tai **4.** fugu
flower arranging .. **7.** ikebano
flower design .. **10.** Shin, Soe, Tai
  (Heaven, Man, Earth)
game (forfeits) .. **3.** ken
gateway .. **5.** torii
girdle .. **3.** obi
girdle box .. **4.** inro
greeting .. **6.** banzai
herb (edible) .. **3.** udo
legislature .. **4.** Diet
litter (covered) .. **7.** norimon
monster (film) .. **8.** Godzilla
news agency .. **5.** domei
newspaper (Tokyo) .. **12.** Asahi Shimbun
outlaw .. **5.** ronin
pagoda .. **3.** taa
painting school .. **4.** Kano
palanquin, litter .. **4.** pago **7.** norimon
paper-folding art .. **7.** origami
partition .. **5.** shoji
persimmon .. **4.** kaki
plant .. **3.** udo (edible) **6.** sugamo
porgy .. **3.** tai (fish)
pottery .. **7.** Satsuma
prefecture .. **2.** fu
radish .. **6.** daikon
religion .. **6.** Shinto **8.** Buddhism
  9. Shintoism
robe .. **6.** kimono
sash .. **3.** obi
salmon .. **4.** masu
screen (partition) .. **5.** shoji
seaweed .. **4.** nori
self-defense, art of .. **4.** judo **7.** jujitsu
  (jujutsu, jiujutsu)
ship suffix .. **4.** maru
shout (greeting) .. **6.** banzai
shrine .. **7.** Toshogu (at Nikko)
silk .. **7.** habutai **8.** chirimen (crepe)
silkworm .. **4.** eria **7.** yamamai
sock (separate big toe) .. **4.** tabi
song .. **3.** uta
suicide .. **7.** seppuku **8.** hara-kiri
  (hari-kari)
tree .. **5.** akeki, kiaki **7.** camphor, hinooki
verse .. **5.** hokku, tanka **6.** haikai
wrestling .. **4.** sumo
Japanese people ...
  aborigine .. **4.** Ainu (Aino)
  admiral .. **3.** Ito **4.** Togo
  admirer .. **11.** Japanophile
  American-born .. **5.** Issei, Nisei
  army officer .. **7.** samurai
  baron .. **6.** daimio
  Buddha, Great .. **8.** Daibutsu
  caste (nobility) .. **7.** kwazoku
  clan .. **7.** Satsuma **8.** Fujiwara, Minamoto
  deity .. **5.** Amita (Amida) **8.** Amitabba
  Emperor .. **8.** Hirohito
  Emperor, founder .. **5.** Jimmu (660 BC)
  Emperor, title .. **5.** Tenno **6.** Mikado
  God of Happiness .. **7.** Jurojin **10.** Fuku-
  roku ju
  governor .. **6.** shogun
  nobility (caste) .. **7.** kwazoku
  outlaw .. **5.** ronin

J

paradise (of Amita) .. **4.** Jodo
race .. **4.** Ainu
jape ... **4.** fool, jeer, jest, jipe, mock
  5. fraud, trick **6.** banter, deride
japery ... **4.** jest, joke **7.** jesting **8.** trickery
  10. buffoonery
jar ... **4.** jolt **5.** grate, shake **6.** incase,
  rattle **7.** startle, vibrate **8.** preserve
  9. vibration
jar ... **3.** jug, urn **4.** ewer, lute (rubber),
  olla **5.** cadus (anc), crock, cruse
  6. dolium, goglet, hydria **7.** amphora,
  terrine **10.** jardiniere
jararaca ... **7.** serpent **10.** fer-de-lance
  11. jararacussu
jardiniere ... **3.** jar, jug, urn **4.** vase
  5. stand (plant) **9.** flowerpot
jargon ... **4.** cant **5.** argot, idiom, lingo,
  slang **6.** drivel, patois, patter, zircon
  7. Chinook, Yiddish **8.** nonsense
  9. gibberish **10.** vocabulary (secret)
jasmine, jasmin ... **4.** bela **5.** color,
  papaw **7.** jessamy **9.** jessamine
Jason (pert to) ...
  friend, sweetheart .. **5.** Medea
  heroes .. **9.** Argonauts
  quest .. **12.** Golden Fleece
  ship .. **4.** Argo
  son .. **5.** Aeson
  uncle .. **6.** Pelias
jaundice ... **7.** disease, icterus **8.** jealousy
  9. prejudice **10.** yellowness
jaunt ... **4.** ride, trip **6.** ramble **7.** journey
  9. excursion
jaunty ... **4.** airy **5.** perky, showy, smart
  6. dapper, rakish **7.** finical, stylish
  12. lighthearted
Java ... see also *Javanese*
  city .. **7.** Batavia, Jakarta (Djakarta)
  8. Samarang, Surabaya **9.** Surakarta
  island group .. **10.** East Indies
  Java Man (anc) .. **15.** Pithecanthropus
  (erectus)
  location .. **7.** equator **16.** Malay
  Archipelago
Javanese (pert to) ...
  arrow poison .. **4.** upas
  badger .. **5.** ratel **6.** teledu
  carriage .. **4.** sado (sadoo)
  cotton .. **5.** kapok
  dancers .. **6.** bedoyo
  dog (wild) .. **5.** adjag
  ox (wild) .. **5.** banteng
  pantomime .. **6.** topeng
  plum .. **5.** jambo (jambul) **6.** lomboy
  puppet show .. **6.** wajang (wayang)
  rice field .. **5.** sawah
  squirrel .. **8.** jelerang
  temple .. **6.** chandi (candi)
  tree .. **4.** upas **5.** ligas **7.** gondang
javelin ... **3.** bat **4.** dart, pike **5.** lance,
  spear **6.** jereed (jirid) **7.** assagai
  (assegai)
javelina ... **4.** boar **7.** peccary
jaw ... **3.** maw **4.** chop **5.** scold **6.** berate,
  splash **7.** chatter, orifice **8.** scolding
jaw (pert to) ...
  angle of .. **6.** gonion
  bone .. **7.** maxilla **8.** mandible
  comb form .. **6.** gnatho
  disease .. **7.** lump jaw **13.** actinomycosis

formation .. **8.** gnathism
Greek for .. **7.** gnathos
muscle .. **8.** masseter
ref to .. **5.** malar **7.** gnathic
without .. **8.** agnathic
jawab ... **5.** reply **6.** answer, mosque
  (false Arch)
jay ... **3.** gae **4.** bird, blue, dupe
  9. chatterer
jayhawker ... **6.** Kansan, spider **7.** soldier
  8. guerilla
Jayhawker State ... **6.** Kansas
jazz ... **4.** jive **5.** dance, music, swing
  9. syncopate **11.** syncopation
jealous ... **7.** envious, zealous **8.** doubtful,
  grudging, vigilant, watchful **9.** jaundiced
  10. solicitous **11.** distrustful
  12. apprehensive
jealousy ... **4.** envy **5.** doubt **7.** rivalry
  8. distrust, jaundice, mistrust
  12. covetousness
jeans ... **8.** overalls, trousers
jeer ... **4.** gibe, hoot, jape, mock **5.** flout,
  scoff, sneer, taunt **6.** deride **8.** ridicule
Jehovah ... **3.** God, Jah **4.** Lord **6.** Yahweh
  (Yahwe) **8.** Almighty (The) **12.** Supreme
  Being
Jehovah's comfort ... **8.** Nehemiah
jehu (humorous) ... **8.** coachman **10.** fast
  driver
Jehu's father (Bib) ... **11.** Jehoshaphat
jejune ... **3.** dry **4.** arid **5.** banal, empty,
  stale, trite **6.** barren, hungry, meager
  7. insipid **8.** foodless **12.** unproductive
jelly ... **3.** jam, rob (rhob) **4.** food, sapa
  5. aspic **6.** pectin **7.** gelatin **8.** gelatine,
  Kei Apple **10.** semiliquid
jellyfish ... **5.** quarl **6.** coward, medusa
  7. acaleph **8.** weakling **9.** Acalephae
jellyfish (pert to) ...
  class .. **9.** Acalephae
  group .. **10.** discophora
  part .. **6.** pileus **8.** umbrella
  10. exumbrella
  stinging .. **9.** sea nettle
  swim organ .. **5.** stene
jemmy ... **4.** boot (riding) **5.** jimmy, lever
  7. crowbar **9.** greatcoat
Jena (Ger) ... **5.** glass **6.** battle (1806)
jenna ... **8.** Paradise (Muslim)
jennet ... **3.** ass **5.** horse **6.** donkey
jenny ... **3.** ass **5.** crane (moving)
  6. female **8.** airplane **13.** spinning
  wheel
jenny (pert to) ...
  billiards .. **6.** hazard
  folklore .. **4.** wren
  howlet .. **5.** owl **6.** owlet
  machine .. **13.** spinning wheel
  spinner .. **3.** fly (angling)
jeopardize ... **4.** risk **6.** expose, hazard
  7. imperil **8.** endanger
jeopardy ... **4.** risk **5.** peril **6.** hazard,
  menace
jeremiad ... **3.** woe **6.** lament, plaint,
  tirade **9.** complaint
jerk ... **3.** tic **4.** flip, jolt, push, yank
  5. shake, tweak **6.** chorea, thrust, twitch
  7. charqui
jerkin ... **4.** coat **6.** jacket, salmon
  9. gyrfalcon, waistcoat

jeroboam ... **4.** bowl **6.** battle, goblet
Jeroboam ... **4.** King (of Israel)
jerry ... **5.** aware **6.** flimsy, Geremy,
German **7.** knowing **9.** beer house,
conscious
jersey ... **5.** cloth **6.** cattle, jacket
Jersey Red ... **5.** swine **11.** Duroc-Jersey
Jersey tea ... **11.** wintergreen
12. checkerberry
Jerusalem ... **5.** Ariel, Salem **8.** Holy
City **11.** City of David
Jerusalem (pert to) ...
artichoke .. **7.** girasol **10.** topinambou
capital of .. **6.** Israel
corn .. **5.** durra
Garden .. **10.** Gethsemane
haddock .. **4.** opah
hill .. **6.** Olivet **13.** Mount of Olives
historic site .. **11.** Wailing Wall
12. Mosque of Omar **13.** Mount
of Olives (Olivet) **18.** Garden of
Gethsemane
mosque .. **4.** Omar
pool .. **6.** Siloam **8.** Bethesda
region .. **5.** Perea **6.** Gilead
Relig .. **7.** Judaism **12.** Christianity
13. Mohammedanism
spring .. **5.** Gihon **6.** Siloam
star .. **7.** salsify
Sunday .. **11.** Refreshment
thorn .. **7.** catechu **12.** Christ's-thorn
willow .. **8.** oleaster
jess ... **5.** strap (hawk's leg) **6.** ribbon
jessamy ... **3.** fop **5.** dandy **7.** jasmine
jessant (Her) ... **7.** issuing **9.** lying over
jessur ... **5.** viper (Russell's)
jest ... **3.** fun, mot, wit **4.** fool, jape, jeer,
joke, quip **5.** droll, prank, sport, taunt,
trick **6.** banter, rail at, trifle **8.** ridicule
jester ... **4.** fool, mime **5.** clown
7. buffoon, goliard **8.** humorist
11. merry-andrew
jester's cap ... **7.** coxcomb
Jesuit ... **5.** Order **7.** casuist, sectary
8. explorer **9.** intriguer **10.** missionary
14. Society of Jesus (S J)
jet ... **3.** jut **4.** gush, spew **5.** black,
ebony, ladle, raven, spout, spray, spurt
6. burner, nozzle, stream **7.** mineral,
outpour **8.** spouting **9.** black onyx
jet coal ... **6.** cannel
jetty ... **4.** mole, pier **5.** wharf **8.** buttress
Jew ... **6.** Essene, Hebrew, Semite
9. Israelite
jewel ... **3.** gem **4.** naif, opal, ruby **5.** beryl,
stone **6.** garnet **7.** bearing, diamond,
emerald **8.** ornament **9.** bespangle,
brilliant **10.** rhinestone **13.** precious
stone, precious thing
jewel cutter ... **10.** lapidarist
jeweled headdress ... **5.** tiara **7.** coronet
jeweler's glass ... **5.** loupe
jeweler's weight ... **4.** tola **5.** carat
(karat, kerat)
jewelry ... **3.** ice **4.** ring **5.** paste **6.** parure,
strass **7.** costume **10.** bijouterie
Jewish ... **6.** Hebrew **7.** Yiddish **9.** Israelite
Jewish (pert to) ...
academy (Talmudic) .. **8.** Yeshinah
adherent .. **7.** Zionist
benediction .. **5.** Shema

Bible .. **5.** Torah (Tora) **6.** Gemara,
Talmud **7.** Haggada, Halakah
10. Pentateuch
calendar .. **4.** Adar, Ahab, Elul, Iyar
5. Nisan, Sivan, Tebet **6.** Kislev, Shebat,
Tammuz, Tishri, Veadar (leap year)
7. Heshvan
Day of Atonement .. **9.** Yom Kippur
Dispersion .. **8.** Diaspora
divorce .. **3.** get (gett)
doctrine .. **7.** Mishnah (Mishna)
enemy (Bib) .. **5.** Haman
faction .. **7.** Zealots
father, patriarch .. **7.** Abraham
festival .. **5.** Purim, Seder (Sedar)
7. Sukkoth
greeting, peace .. **6.** Shalom
high priest .. **3.** Eli **4.** Ezra **5.** Aaron,
Annas **8.** Caiaphas
high priest costume .. **4.** urim **5.** abnet
7. petalon, tallith, yamilke
historian .. **8.** Josephus
holiday .. **7.** Sukkoth **8.** Hanukkah
(Hannukka), Tishabov **11.** Rosh Hashana
(Rosh Hashonoh)
horn .. **7.** shophar (shofar)
lawgiver .. **5.** Moses
leader .. **8.** Nehemiah
liturgy .. **6.** minhah (PM) **9.** shaharith
(AM)
loaves (unleavened) .. **9.** shewbread
(showbread)
mystical writing .. **6.** atbash
patriots .. **9.** Maccabees
prayer book .. **6.** siddur
prophet .. **6.** Elijah
psalms of praise .. **6.** hallel
quarter (living) .. **6.** ghetto
ram's horn .. **7.** shophar (shofar)
slaughter (Relig) .. **8.** shehitah
song (Zionist anthem) .. **8.** Hatikvah
(Hattikvah)
jew's harp ... **8.** guimbard **9.** crembalum
Jezebel (pert to) ...
epithet .. **5.** vixen **6.** virago **8.** strumpet
father .. **7.** Ethbaal
husband .. **4.** Ahab (King)
murdered (caused to be) .. **6.** Naboth
jib ... **3.** gib, jaw **4.** balk, boom, sail,
spar, tack **5.** crane, shift **6.** fleece
8. underlip
jibe ... **3.** fit **4.** gibe **5.** agree, shift
9. harmonize
jiff, jiffy ... **5.** trice **6.** moment **7.** instant,
quickly **9.** instantly, twinkling
jig ... **4.** jerk, jolt **5.** dance **6.** ballad,
twitch **8.** fishhook
jigger ... **4.** club, dram
jiggle ... **5.** sauce, shake
jimmy ... **3.** pry **5.** handy, smart
6. spruce **7.** coal car, crowbar, pry
open **10.** sheep's head
jimson weed ... **6.** dature
10. stramonium, thorn apple **11.** apple
of Peru
jingle ... **4.** poem, rime **5.** clink, rhyme
6. tinkle **13.** two-wheeled car
jinn, jinnee ... **5.** demon, Eblis, genie
6. afreet **8.** jenniyeh
jinx ... **3.** hex **5.** Jonah **6.** hoodoo,
whammy

jitters ... **6.** nerves **7.** dithers, fidgets **8.** trembles

jittery ... **4.** edgy **5.** jumpy **7.** nervous

jivatma (Hind) ... **4.** soul **9.** life force **10.** life energy **11.** human spirit

Joan of Arc's appellation ... **7.** pucelle **13.** Maid of Orleans

job ... **3.** act **4.** hire, task **5.** chare, chore, stint **8.** position, sinecure

Job (pert to) ...
Book .. **9.** patriarch **12.** Old Testament
friend .. **6.** Zophar
home .. **2.** Uz
literally .. **9.** afflicted **10.** persecuted

jockey ... **3.** pad **5.** cheat, racer, rider **6.** outwit **7.** cushion **8.** cavalier, horseman, minstrel, vagabond **9.** Earl Sande (famed)

jocose ... **3.** dry **5.** droll, lepid, merry **7.** jocular **8.** humorous **9.** facetious

jocular ... **3.** gay **4.** airy, loco **5.** droll, funny, merry, witty **6.** elated, jocund, lively, ribald **7.** comical, festive, gleeful, jesting, playful, waggish **8.** animated, mirthful **9.** convivial, facetious, hilarious, laughable, vivacious **10.** frolicsome

jocund ... **3.** gay **4.** airy **5.** merry **6.** lively **7.** jocular **8.** cheerful, sportive

jog ... **4.** gait, jolt, lope, plod, push, trot, walk **6.** canter, notify, remind, trudge **8.** slow pace **9.** suggest to

John ... **3.** Ian **4.** Ivan, Jack, Juan **8.** Chinaman, Johannes **9.** policeman

John (pert to) ...
Bull .. **10.** Englishman
Company .. **9.** East India
Crow .. **7.** buzzard (turkey)
Doe (law) .. **7.** unknown **9.** false name
Hancock .. **9.** autograph, signature
Q Public .. **6.** people **8.** populace

johnnycake ... **4.** pone **7.** hoecake **9.** corn bread

join ... **3.** add, mix, pin, tie, wed **4.** ally, fuse, link, lock, meet, pair, seam, team, weld, yoke **5.** annex, blend, enter, graft, group, hitch, marry, merge, unite **6.** adjoin, attach, cement, concur, couple, engage, enlist, fasten, mingle, solder, splice, suture, syzygy **7.** combine, conjoin, connect **8.** assemble, coalesce, compound **9.** associate **11.** incorporate

joint ... **3.** ell, hip **4.** dive (sl), knee, node, seam **5.** alula, elbow, hinge, miter, nexus, tenon, wrist **6.** rabbet, resort **7.** hangout, pastern **8.** coupling, dovetail **12.** articulation

joint (pert to) ...
cavity .. **5.** bursa
firs .. **7.** ephedra
fluid .. **7.** synovia **8.** synovial
grass stem .. **4.** culm
pert to .. **5.** nodal **9.** articular
put out of .. **6.** lucate **9.** dislocate
without .. **10.** acondylous

joke ... **3.** fun, gag, pun **4.** fool, hoax, jape, jest, quip **5.** prank, rally, sport **6.** banter, humbug **7.** bromide **8.** chestnut, one-liner

joker ... **3.** dor, wag, wit **4.** card

7. buffoon, farceur, gagster **8.** humorist **9.** mistigris

jollity ... **4.** jest **5.** mirth **6.** gaiety **8.** hilarity **9.** enjoyment, festivity, joviality, merriment **12.** conviviality

jolly ... **6.** banter, jovial, joyful, mellow **7.** flatter, jocular **9.** make merry

Jolly Roger ... **5.** Roger **10.** pirate flag

jolt ... **3.** jar, jig, jut **4.** blow, butt, stun **5.** shake, shock **6.** jostle, jounce **7.** startle **8.** astonish, jail term (thieves)

Jonah (pert to) ...
Bib .. **7.** prophet (Heb)
Book .. **12.** Old Testament
slang .. **4.** jinx
swallowed by .. **5.** whale

Jordan ...
capital .. **5.** Amman
city .. **7.** Jericho, Samaria **9.** Bethlehem
historic trove .. **14.** Dead Sea Scrolls
official name .. **9.** Hashemite (The)
people (anc) .. **7.** Essenes
region .. **5.** Perea **6.** Basham
river .. **6.** Jordan

Jorth (pert to) ...
goddess .. **5.** Earth
husband .. **4.** Odin
named also .. **6.** Forgyn
son .. **4.** Thor

Joseph (pert to) ...
Bib .. **9.** patriarch
buyer of .. **8.** Potiphar
coat of .. **10.** many colors
father .. **5.** Jacob
mother .. **6.** Rachel
son .. **5.** Jesus **7.** Ephraim

josh ... **3.** guy, kid **5.** chaff, spoof, tease **6.** banter

Joshi (Ind) ... **10.** astrologer, astronomer

Joshua (pert to) ...
associate .. **5.** Caleb
Book .. **12.** Old Testament
burial place .. **5.** Gaash
successor to .. **5.** Moses
tree .. **5.** yucca

jostle ... **4.** jolt, push, rush **5.** crowd, elbow, joust, shake, shove **6.** hustle, joggle, jounce, thrust

jot ... **3.** ace, bit **4.** atom, iota, item, mite, whit **5.** minim, point, speck **6.** tittle **7.** smidgen **8.** particle

jouk ... **4.** dart, duck, fawn, hide **5.** cheat, dodge, evade, perch, roost, skulk **6.** cringe **9.** obeisance

Joule, James P ... **9.** physicist

journal ... **3.** log **5.** diary, paper **6.** record **7.** daybook, diurnal, logbook, support **8.** magazine, register **9.** chronicle **10.** periodical **11.** account book

journalist ... **6.** editor, legman **7.** newsman **8.** reporter **9.** columnist, gazetteer **11.** interviewer **13.** correspondent

journey ... **3.** run **4.** fare, iter, ride, tour, trek, trip, wend **5.** jaunt **6.** travel, voyage **7.** odyssey **8.** traverse **9.** excursion **10.** expedition, pilgrimage **13.** peregrination

journey (pert to) ... **4.** eyre (circuit) **6.** viatic **8.** anabasis (upward) **9.** itineracy, itinerary, traveling

10. travelling
joust . . . **4.** bout, spar, tilt **6.** combat
  10. tournament
Jove . . . **7.** Jupiter
jovial . . . **5.** jolly, merry **6.** elated,
  joyous **7.** festive, jocular **8.** Jovelike
  9. convivial, hilarious **14.** mirth-inspiring
jowl . . . **3.** jaw **4.** chop **5.** cheek **6.** dewlap,
  wattle **7.** jawbone
joy . . . **4.** glee **5.** bliss, exult, gelid **6.** gaiety
  7. delight, ecstasy, rapture, rejoice
  8. felicity, gladness, hilarity, pleasure
  9. beatitude, happiness, merriment,
  transport **10.** exultation **12.** exhilaration
joyous . . . **3.** gay **4.** glad **5.** happy, merry
  6. blithe, elated, festal, joyful **7.** festive,
  gleeful, jocular **8.** cheerful, mirthful
jubilant . . . **6.** elated **8.** exultant, exulting
  9. overjoyed, rejoicing **10.** triumphant
Judah (pert to) . . .
  ancestry . . **12.** tribe of Judah
  brother . . **4.** Levi **6.** Reuben, Simeon
  father . . **5.** Jacob
  kingdom . . **9.** Palestine
  son . . **2.** Er **6.** Shelah
  translation (Heb) . . **10.** celebrated
Judas (pert to) . . .
  Bible . . **7.** apostle, traitor **8.** betrayer,
  deceiver, disciple
  called . . **8.** Iscariot
  historic . . **13.** Paschal candle
  kiss . . **8.** betrayal **11.** double-cross,
  treacherous
  priest . . **4.** oath
  suicide site . . **8.** Aceldama
Judea (pert to) . . .
  governor . . **6.** Pilate
  king . . **3.** Asa **5.** Herod **7.** Jehoram
  11. Jehoshaphat
  location . . **5.** Berea
  people . . **4.** Jews
  province of . . **9.** Palestine
judge . . . **3.** try **4.** deem, rate **5.** opine,
  think **6.** critic, puisne **7.** arbiter,
  referee, suppose **8.** deemster, estimate,
  mediator, sentence **9.** arbitrate, criticize
  10. adjudicate, magistrate
  11. connoisseur
judge (pert to) . . .
  bench . . **4.** banc (bancus)
  chamber . . **6.** camera
  circuit . . **4.** iter
  gavel . . **4.** mace
  group . . **5.** bench **9.** judiciary
  of the dead . . **6.** Osiris
  opinion . . **12.** obiter dictum
  sittings . . **7.** assizes
  summary . . **6.** postea
judgment . . . **4.** doom **5.** arrêt, award,
  sense, taste **7.** censure, opinion
  8. decision, judicium, sentence
  9. criticism **10.** conclusion, discretion,
  persuasion (Relig), punishment
  11. arbitration, sensibility
judgment (pert to) . . .
  creditor . . **13.** quasi contract
  day . . **7.** last day **8.** Dies Irae, doomsday
  left to one's . . **13.** discretionary
  note . . **10.** promissory
  seat . . **3.** bar **5.** mercy **8.** tribunal,
  woolsack

judicial . . . **5.** legal **8.** critical **9.** judicious
  10. judicatory
judicial (pert to) . . .
  council . . **5.** cabal, junta, junto **7.** coterie
  hearing . . **5.** trial
  order . . **4.** writ **6.** elegit, venire **7.** precept
  security . . **7.** custody
judicious . . . **4.** wise **7.** politic, prudent
  8. cautious, discreet **9.** sagacious
  10. discerning **11.** circumspect, well-
  advised
jug . . . **4.** ewer, jail, olpe, toby **5.** askos,
  buire, cruse, gotch **6.** flagon, gomlah,
  lockup, prison, tinaja, urceus **7.** pitcher
  13. Schnabelkanne
Juggernaut . . . **6.** Vishnu (Hind)
juggler . . . **5.** cheat, trick **7.** buffoon
  8. deceiver **13.** sleight of hand
  14. legerdemainist
Jugoslavia, Yugoslavia . . .
  area . . **6.** Kosovo **8.** Dalmatia
  brandy . . **5.** rakia **9.** slivovitz
  capital . . **8.** Belgrade
  language . . **7.** Slovene **10.** Macedonian,
  Serbo-Croat
  leader . . **4.** Tito
  monarch . . **5.** Peter
  money . . **5.** dinar
  organization . . **9.** Comitadji
  people . . **4.** Serb **5.** Croat **7.** Slovene
juice . . . **3.** rob, sap **4.** milk (plant),
  must, stum **5.** fluid, latex, syrup
  (sirup) **7.** essence, hebenon, moisten
  10. succulence **11.** electricity
jujitsu, jiujitsu . . . **11.** self-defense
juju . . . **5.** charm, magic **6.** amulet, belief,
  fetish, voodoo
jujube . . . **3.** ber **5.** fruit, jelly **7.** lozenge
  8. Zizyphus
Jules Verne's captain . . . **4.** Nemo (the
  Nautilus)
Julian Emperors (first Five) . . . **4.** Nero
  8. Augustus, Caligula, Claudius, Tiberius
jumble . . . **2.** pi **3.** mix **4.** cake, hash, heap,
  mess, raff, stir **5.** blend, botch, chaos,
  shake **6.** medley, muddle **7.** agitate,
  confuse, mixture **8.** disorder, riffraff
jumble type . . . **3.** pie (pi)
jump . . . **3.** hop, lep **4.** leap, move
  (checkers) **5.** bound, caper, halma, salto,
  scold, start, vault **6.** chorea, escape,
  hurdle, spring, twitch **7.** saltary, saltate
  8. increase **9.** advantage **10.** transition
jumping (pert to) . . .
  adjective . . **7.** saltant
  Frog, tale by . . **9.** Mark Twain
  music . . **7.** saltato
  rodent . . **5.** mouse **6.** jerboa **11.** kangaroo
  rat
  stick . . **4.** pogo, pole
junction . . . **4.** axil, seam **5.** union
  6. suture **7.** joining, meeting
  11. combination, concurrence
juncture . . . **4.** pass **5.** joint, pinch **6.** crisis,
  strait **8.** exigency, quandary
  9. emergency **10.** connection
  11. conjuncture, predicament
  12. articulation
June bug . . . **3.** dor **6.** beetle, May bug
  8. figeater
jungle . . . **4.** camp **7.** thicket **8.** woodland

11. dense growth 12. complication
jungle (pert to) . . .
  dweller . . **5.** beast **6.** savage
  fever . . **7.** malaria
  grass . . **3.** poa
  ox . . **4.** gaur **5.** gayal **7.** timarau
  sheep . . **7.** muntjac
junior . . . **5.** cadet, petty **6.** puisne,
  recent **7.** student, younger **8.** inferior
  9. unskilled
juniper . . . **4.** cade, puny **5.** cedar, gorse,
  retem (raetem), savin
junket . . . **4.** dish (milk), food, meal
  5. feast **7.** banquet **8.** festival
  9. excursion, sweetmeat
Juno (pert to) . . .
  consort . . **7.** Jupiter
  goddess (Rom) . . **3.** sky **5.** light
  identified with . . **4.** Hera
  messenger . . **4.** Iris
junta, junto . . . **5.** cabal **6.** circle, clique
  7. coterie, council, faction **8.** intrigue
  11. combination
jupe . . . **4.** coat **5.** jupon, shirt, skirt, tunic
  6. bodice, jacket
Jupiter (pert to) . . .
  angel . . **7.** Zadkiel
  astronomy . . **6.** planet (largest)
  daughter . . **4.** Bura
  deity . . **4.** Jove **9.** Father Sky
  festival . . **14.** Vinalis sustica
  god of . . **7.** Heavens
  heraldry . . **5.** azure
  lover . . **2.** Io
  son . . **6.** Castor, Pollux
  triad . . **4.** Juno **7.** Minerva
  wife . . **4.** Juno
Jupiter, god of . . .
  law . . **6.** Fidius **10.** Dius Fidius
  lightning . . **6.** Fulgur
  rain . . **7.** Pluvius
  thunder . . **6.** Tonans
jurat . . . **5.** juror **8.** recorder **10.** magistrate
  (Channel Isis)
jure . . . **3.** jus (ius), law **5.** right
  13. jurisprudence
jurisprudence . . . **3.** law, soc **4.** soke

5. power (legal) **6.** charge, sphere
  7. control, custody, emirate **9.** authority,
  consulate **10.** government, judicature,
  patriarchy
juror . . . **6.** dicast **7.** assizer, juryman
  9. venireman
jury . . . **5.** panel, tales (additions) **6.** venire
jus . . . **3.** law **5.** gravy, juice **10.** legal
  power, legal right
just . . . **4.** fair, tilt **5.** equal, exact, valid
  7. logical, upright **8.** provided, unbiased
  9. equitable, righteous **10.** legitimate
just begun . . . **8.** inchoate
justice . . . **4.** doom **5.** right **6.** equity,
  virtue **8.** fairness, fair play, justness
  9. rectitude **10.** judicature **11.** give and
  take **12.** rightfulness
justice of the peace . . . **6.** squire
  10. magistrate
justification . . . **7.** apology, defense
  11. vindication
justify . . . **5.** clear **6.** defend, excuse
  7. absolve, support, warrant **8.** maintain,
  sanction, underpin **9.** authorize,
  exculpate, vindicate **12.** substantiate
justly . . . **5.** truly **6.** fairly **7.** equally
  8. honestly **9.** equitably **10.** deservedly
justness . . . **7.** fitness, justice **8.** accuracy,
  validity **9.** exactness **11.** correctness
Justus . . . **4.** just
jute . . . **5.** fiber, gunny **6.** burlap **7.** sacking
Jute . . . **5.** Dane **9.** Jutlander
jutty . . . **4.** mole, pier **5.** jetty **7.** project
  8. buttress, protrude
juvenile . . . **5.** actor, young, youth
  8. immature, youthful **9.** youngling,
  youthlike **11.** undeveloped
juvia . . . **9.** Brazil nut
juxta . . . **4.** near **6.** nearby
juxtaposition . . . **5.** touch **7.** contact
  8. nearness **9.** proximity **10.** contiguity,
  side by side
jynx . . . **5.** charm, spell **7.** wryneck
  10. woodpecker
Jynx . . . **11.** woodpeckers
J'y suis, j'y reste . . . **18.** I am here;
  here I remain

K

K . . . **5.** kappa (Gr) **6.** letter (11th)
Ka . . . **3.** God (Hind)
Kaaba, Caaba (pert to) . . .
  content . . **10.** Black Stone (of Mecca)
  location . . **11.** Great Mosque (Mecca)
  pilgrimage . . **7.** Islamic
  praying direction . . **6.** Kiblah
  shape . . **7.** cubical
kaama . . . **10.** hartebeest
kachina worshipper . . . **4.** Hopi, Zuni
  6. Pueblo
Kaddish . . . **8.** Doxology
Kadiak, Kodiak, bear . . . **5.** brown

  7. Alaskan
Kaiser brown . . . **6.** ginger
Kaiser's residence . . . **5.** Doorn
kaka . . . **6.** parrot
kakapo . . . **6.** parrot **9.** owl parrot
kakar . . . **7.** muntjac
kakariki . . . **6.** lizard
kaki . . . **5.** stilt (bird) **9.** persimmon
kakkak . . . **5.** heron **7.** bittern
kakke . . . **8.** beriberi
kala . . . **6.** bulbul (bird)
kale . . . **4.** cole **5.** money **7.** cabbage,
  collard **8.** colewort, corecole

kaleidoscopic . . . **7.** varying
  10. changeable, variegated
Kali (pert to) . . .
  Hindu . . **10.** evil genius
  Persian . . **6.** carpet
  Vedic Myth . . **12.** tongue of Agni
    (fire-god)
kallah . . . **5.** bride (Jew)
kamavachara . . . **6.** heaven (Buddh)
Kamchatka . . .
  capital . . **13.** Petropavlovsk
  peninsula . . **7.** Siberia
  people . . **7.** Russian **9.** Mongolian
  sea . . **6.** Bering **7.** Okhotsk
Kamehameha Day . . . **7.** holiday (Haw)
Kamerad . . . **7.** comrade **9.** surrender
kamik . . . **12.** sealskin boot
Kammerspiel . . . **5.** drama **7.** theater
Kanaka . . . **3.** man **8.** Hawaiian
  10. Melanesian, Polynesian **16.** South
  Sea islander
Kanaloa . . . **3.** God (Pantheon)
kangaroo (pert to) . . .
  class . . **9.** marsupial
  family . . **12.** Macropodidae
  female . . **3.** doe, gin, 'roo
  giant . . **8.** forester
  leaping . . **6.** jeroba **7.** bettong (bettonga)
  male . . **5.** bilby (bilbi)
  rat . . **7.** pototoo
  reference to . . **7.** wallaby
    11. macropodine
  small . . **7.** wallaby
  young . . **4.** joey
kangaroo court . . . **9.** mock court, moot
  court **14.** irregular court
Kansas . . .
  capital . . **6.** Topeka
  city . . **5.** Dodge **7.** Abilene, Wichita
    10. Hutchinson, Kansas City
    11. Leavenworth
  Eisenhower home . . **7.** Abilene
  military post . . **9.** Fort Riley
  penitentiary . . **11.** Leavenworth
  State admission . . **12.** Thirty-fourth
  State motto . . **16.** Ad Astra per Aspera
    (To the Stars Through Difficulties)
  State nickname . . **9.** Sunflower
kapok tree . . . **7.** God tree **9.** Ceiba tree
  10. silk-cotton
kappa . . . **1.** K (Gr) **4.** star **6.** letter (10th)
karakul, karakule . . . **5.** sheep
  9. astrakhan, broadtail
karma . . . **4.** fate **7.** destiny **8.** casualty
Kartvelian people . . . **4.** Svan (Svane)
  9. Georgians **10.** Imeritians, Svanetians
kasha . . . **4.** mush (Russ)
Kashmir, India . . .
  alphabet . . **6.** Sarada
  capital . . **8.** Srinagar
  deer . . **6.** hangul
  official . . **6.** pundit
Kashyapa (Vedic Myth) . . . **8.** tortoise
Kaskaskia . . . **5.** epoch **6.** Indian
  10. Algonquian
kat . . . **5.** shrub **8.** narcotic
katar . . . **6.** dagger
katchung . . . **6.** peanut
katogle . . . **8.** eagle owl
kava, kavakava . . . **6.** Kawaka, pepper
kayak . . . **5.** canoe

kea . . . **6.** parrot
Keat's poem . . . **8.** Endymion, Hyperion
keek . . . **3.** spy (of rival fashions) **6.** peeper
keel . . . **4.** cool, seel, ship, skeg, tilt
  6. careen, ruddle, timber (ship's)
  7. capsize **8.** overturn, red ocher, turn
  over **10.** guinea fowl
keelbill, keelbird . . . **3.** ani
keeling . . . **7.** codfish
keel-shaped . . . **6.** carina **7.** carinal
keen . . . **4.** avid, cute, gare, good, nice,
  tart **5.** acute, alert, eager, sharp, smart,
  snell, vivid, witty **6.** astute, bitter,
  clever, shrewd, shrill **7.** caustic, fervent
  9. sensitive, trenchant **11.** acrimonious,
  penetrating
keenness . . . **4.** edge **5.** acies (of sight),
  nifty **6.** acuity, acumen **8.** acrimony,
  pungency **9.** acuteness, eagerness,
  sharpness, smartness, wittiness
keep . . . **4.** save **6.** detain, retain
  7. confine, custody, fulfill, husband,
  reserve **8.** conserve, maintain, preserve,
  restrain, withhold **14.** accommodations
keep (pert to) . . .
  account . . **5.** score
  afloat . . **4.** buoy
  apart . . **7.** seclude **8.** separate
  back, out . . **3.** bar, dam **4.** save **5.** debar,
    delay **6.** detain, except, hinder, retard
    7. exclude, reserve **8.** restrain, withhold
  from . . **5.** avoid, delay **7.** abstain, boycott,
    prevent
  hidden . . **7.** secrete
  in . . **6.** retain
  off . . **4.** fend **7.** prevent, repulse, ward
    off
  on . . **6.** endure **9.** persevere
keeper . . . **5.** guard **6.** warden **9.** constable,
  custodian, possessor **10.** maintainer
keeper of . . .
  birds . . **8.** aviarist
  borders . . **8.** margrave
  door . . **5.** tiler
  elephant . . **6.** mahout
  golden apples (Myth) . . **6.** Ithunn (Ithun)
  parks . . **6.** ranger
  prison . . **6.** gaoler, jailer, jailor, warden
    7. turnkey
keeping . . . **4.** care **5.** board, guard, trust
  7. custody **8.** tutelage **9.** retention
  10. caretaking, conformity, possession,
  preserving, protection **11.** maintenance
  12. guardianship
keeve . . . **3.** tub **4.** tuft **5.** knoll, plume
  8. haystack
kef . . . **6.** dreamy **7.** languor **12.** tranquillity
  (tranquility)
keg . . . **3.** tun, vat **4.** cade, cask **6.** firkin
kelly . . . **5.** derby, killy (fish)
kelp . . . **4.** game **5.** sight, wrack **7.** insight,
  seaweed **9.** water lily
ken . . . **4.** lore **9.** recognize **10.** cognizance,
  prescience **13.** understanding
Kentish freedman . . . **4.** laet
Kentucky . . .
  bluegrass . . **3.** poa
  capital . . **9.** Frankfort
  city . . **7.** Paducah **9.** Lexington
    10. Louisville **12.** Bowling Green
  famed road . . **15.** Wilderness Trail

K

famed sights.. **7.** Obelisk (J Davis)
8. Fort Knox, Log Cabin (Lincoln)
11. Federal Hill (My Old Ky Home),
Mammoth Cave
famed sport.. **13.** Kentucky Derby
(Churchill Downs)
mountain.. **4.** Pine **10.** Cumberland
pioneer.. **11.** Daniel Boone
river.. **4.** Ohio **10.** Cumberland
State admission.. **9.** Fifteenth
State name meaning (Indian)..
8. tomorrow
State nickname.. **9.** Bluegrass
Kenya...
capital.. **7.** Nairobi
leader.. **3.** Moi **8.** Kenyatta
mountain, volcano.. **5.** Kenya
people.. **5.** Masai **6.** Kikuyu
secret society.. **6.** Mau Mau
kept... see *keep*
ker (Gr)... **4.** doom, fate **5.** ghost **6.** spirit
kermis, kermess... **4.** fair **8.** festival
kernel... **3.** nut **4.** core, gist, meat, pith,
seed **5.** grain, heart **6.** acinus, nutmeg
7. nucleus
ketch... **4.** Jack, saic, ship **6.** vessel
ketone... **5.** irone **6.** carone **7.** acetone,
camphor **8.** deguelin
kettle... **3.** pot **4.** drum, pail **6.** kibble
7. caldron **8.** cauldron **9.** teakettle
10. kettledrum
kettledrum... **4.** drum **5.** naker, tabor
6. atabal **7.** anacara **8.** tympanon
key... **4.** clue, crib, isle, quay, reef,
tone **5.** islet, pitch, tasto **6.** clavis,
cotter, fasten, island, opener, switch,
tapper **7.** digital **8.** mainstay, solution
11. explanation, fundamental,
translation
keyed up... **4.** agog **5.** eager, fired
7. aroused, stirred **8.** hopped up,
worked up **10.** stimulated
Keys, House of... **9.** Isle of Man, officials
Keystone State... **12.** Pennsylvania
khan... **3.** inn **4.** lord **6.** prince
9. resthouse **11.** caravansary
kiang... **5.** diver **6.** onager **7.** wild ass
kick... **4.** blow, boot, funk, punt
6. energy, object, thrill **7.** grumble,
protest **8.** complain, pungency, sixpence
9. complaint **10.** calcitrate, enthusiasm
Kickapoo... **6.** Indian **10.** Algonquian
kickshaw... **3.** toy **6.** trifle **7.** trinket
8. delicacy
kid... **3.** guy **4.** fool, goat, hoax, joke,
josh, twit **5.** child, jolly, suede **6.** banter,
humbug **8.** antelope (young), yeanling
9. youngling
kidang... **4.** deer **7.** muntjac
kidney... **4.** neer **5.** gland, reins
7. nephros
kidney (pert to)...
comb form.. **6.** nephro
disease.. **7.** nephria **9.** nephritis
pyramid.. **9.** reniculus
reference to.. **4.** reni **5.** renal **6.** vitals
7. nephric
shaped.. **8.** reniform
stone.. **6.** pebble **8.** nephrite
kiki... **14.** castor oil plant
kill... **4.** slay, veto **5.** blast, creek **6.** defeat,

murder **7.** channel, destroy, execute,
silence **8.** dispatch, immolate, lapidate,
massacre, overbeat **9.** slaughter
11. assassinate, exterminate
killer... **4.** Cain **6.** gunman, slayer
7. butcher **8.** cannibal, man-eater,
mongoose, murderer **9.** cutthroat
12. assassinator
killer whale... **3.** orc **4.** orca **7.** grampus
killing... **5.** fatal **6.** deadly, murder
7. amusing, carnage, cleanup
(speculation), garrote **8.** homicide
9. execution **10.** euthanasia
11. captivating **12.** overpowering
killing of...
brother.. **10.** fratricide
cats.. **8.** felicide
father.. **9.** patricide
man.. **8.** homicide
mother.. **9.** matricide
old men (tribal).. **8.** senicide
self.. **7.** suicide **9.** martyrdom
sister.. **10.** sororicide
wolf.. **8.** lupicide
kiln... **4.** oast, oven **5.** clamp, stove,
tiler **7.** furnace
kilo (pref)... **8.** thousand
kind... **3.** ilk **4.** good, race, sort, type
5. class, genre, genus, order, seely,
style **6.** benign, gender, humane,
loving, strain **7.** kindred, lenient, species
8. gracious **9.** benignant **10.** benevolent
11. sympathetic **12.** well-disposed
kindle... **4.** burn, fire **5.** brood, light,
rouse, young **6.** excite, ignite, incite,
litter **7.** animate, inflame, provoke
kindly... **4.** mild **6.** benign, blithe, genial,
humane **7.** natural **8.** benignly, heartily
9. agreeably, benignant, indulgent
10. beneficent, legitimate, pleasantly
11. sympathetic
kindness... **5.** favor **8.** clemency,
goodness, humanity, mildness
9. benignity **10.** compassion, generosity,
gentleness, indulgency, tenderness
kindred... **3.** sib, tie **4.** akin, clan, kith
5. blood **6.** allied, family **7.** cognate,
descent, kinship, kinsmen, related
8. kinsfolk **9.** relations **12.** relationship
14. consanguineous
kine... **4.** cows **6.** cattle
kinetic... **6.** active, moving
king... **3.** rex, rey, roi **4.** rank **5.** chief,
ruler **6.** master **7.** regulus **8.** chessman
9. potentate, sovereign
king (pert to)...
beasts.. **4.** lion
birds.. **5.** eagle
chamber.. **9.** camarilla
cheeses.. **4.** Brie
child.. **6.** prince **8.** princess
dwarfs.. **8.** Alberich (Ger)
fairies.. **7.** Oberon
family.. **7.** dynasty
gods.. **7.** Jupiter
heaven.. **3.** God **6.** Christ
herrings.. **4.** opah **7.** oarfish **8.** chimaera
mackerel.. **4.** cero
March (The).. **5.** Sousa
metals.. **4.** gold
monkeys.. **7.** guereza

murder of .. **8**. regicide
myth .. **4**. Atli **5**. Midas
myth (classical) .. **4**. Zeus **7**. Jupiter
rivers .. **6**. Amazon
serpents (race of) .. **6**. Shesha (Sesha)
symbol .. **7**. scepter (sceptre)
vultures .. **4**. papa
waters .. **7**. Neptune, Pacific
Woods (The) .. **13**. Rex Nemorensis
King Arthur (pert to) ...
abode .. **6**. Avalon **7**. Camelot
battleground (fatal) .. **6**. Camlan
father .. **5**. Uther (Pendragon)
home .. **8**. Caerleon (on the Usk)
Knights of the Round Table .. **3**. Kay
6. Gawain **7**. Galahad **8**. Lancelot,
Tristram (Tristan) **9**. Percivale
Lady of the Lake .. **6**. Vivian
magician .. **6**. Merlin
Queen .. **9**. Guinevere
quest of .. **9**. Holy Grail (The)
shield .. **7**. Pridwin
sister .. **11**. Morgan le Fay
son .. **7**. Mordred (Modred)
sword .. **9**. Excalibur
kingdom ... **5**. realm **6**. empire, estate
8. dominion, kingship, monarchy
kingdom (pert to) ...
ancient .. **4**. Elam, Moab
Asia .. **5**. Nepal
between Spain, France .. **7**. Navarra
(Navarre)
confusion .. **5**. Babel
divisions .. **4**. animal **7**. mineral
9. vegetable
Indo-China .. **5**. Annam (Anam)
kingfish ... **4**. cero, haku, opah **7**. kingpin,
pintado **8**. big wheel **9**. threadfin
kingly ... **5**. grand, noble, regal, royal
6. august **7**. leonine **8**. imperial,
majestic, princely **9**. dignified, sovereign
11. monarchical
King of ...
Albania .. **3**. Zog
Bashan .. **2**. Og
Bulgaria .. **5**. Boris
Greece (anc) .. **9**. Agamemnon
Israel .. **4**. Ahab, Jehy, Saul **5**. David
7. Solomon **8**. Jeroboam
Judea .. **3**. Asa
Kings .. **3**. God **6**. Christ
Men .. **4**. Odin, Zeus **7**. Jupiter
Oriental .. **11**. King of Kings
Persia (Iran) .. **5**. Cyrus **6**. Xerxes
Troy .. **5**. Priam
Tyre .. **5**. Hiram
Visigoths .. **6**. Alaric
Kipling, Rudyard (pert to) ...
award .. **10**. Nobel Prize (1907)
birthplace .. **6**. Bombay
book .. **3**. Kim **10**. Jungle Book
poem (for Queen Victoria) ..
11. Recessional
kissing, science ... **13**. philematology
knee (pert to) ...
bend .. **9**. genuflect
bent .. **10**. geniculate
bone .. **6**. rotula **7**. kneepan, patella
britches .. **6**. smalls **8**. knickers
on bended .. **7**. humbled **8**. obeisant
10. submissive, worshipful

12. supplicatory
kneeling desk ... **8**. prie-dieu
knew ... see *know*
Knickerbocker, Father ... **9**. New Yorker
(Hist)
knickknack ... **3**. toy **6**. bauble, gewgaw,
trifle **7**. trinket **8**. gimcrack
knife ... **4**. bolo, snee, stab **5**. corer,
prune **6**. cutter, weapon
knife (pert to) ...
Burmese .. **3**. dah
Hindu .. **5**. kukri
Irish .. **5**. skean **8**. skean dhu
Malay .. **4**. kris **6**. barong, creese
New Zealand .. **4**. patu
one-bladed .. **6**. barlow
Scottish .. **4**. dirk
Spanish .. **7**. machete
surgical .. **7**. scalpel **10**. greffotome
Turkish .. **8**. yataghan (yatagan)
US Navy .. **7**. cutlass
knife maker ... **6**. cutler
knife-throwing game ...
11. mumbletypeg **12**. mumble-the-peg
knight (pert to) ...
adventure .. **8**. errantry
adventurer .. **8**. cavalier **9**. caballero,
chevalier
cloak .. **6**. tabard
combat .. **5**. joust
ensign .. **8**. gonfalon, gonfanon
errant .. **7**. Paladin
hero .. **7**. Paladin
servant .. **4**. page **6**. varlet
title .. **3**. Sir **8**. banneret
wife .. **4**. Dame, Lady
wreath (with crest) .. **4**. orle
Knight of the Round Table ... **3**. Kay
6. Gawain **7**. Galahad **8**. Lancelot,
Tristram (Tristan) **9**. Percivale
Knight of the Rueful Countenance ...
10. Don Quixote
knit ... **4**. bind, heal, join, seam **5**. plait,
unite, woven **6**. cement, couple, fasten
7. conjoin, connect, wrinkle **8**. contract
9. interlace **11**. consolidate
knitting machine guide ... **4**. sley
knitting stitch ... **4**. knit, purl
knob ... **3**. nub **4**. boss, head, hill, lump,
node, stud, umbo **5**. bulge, knurl
6. croche (antler), pommel **8**. tubercle
12. protuberance
knobkerrie ... **4**. club, kiri **5**. stick
knock ... **3**. hit, rap, tap **4**. bang, bash,
beat, bump, dash, glow, hill, pass,
slay, snop **5**. pound, thump **6**. hammer,
jostle, strike **7**. collide **9**. criticism,
criticize, disparage **12**. faultfinding
knock (pert to) ...
about .. **6**. travel, wander
down .. **4**. fell, raze **6**. deject, strike
8. vanquish
off .. **3**. die **6**. deduct, recess **9**. improvise
out .. **2**. KO **4**. kayo
knocking ... **6**. rat-tat **7**. rapping, tapping
9. rat-tat-tat
knock-knee ... **6**. in-knee
knoll ... **4**. bank, clod, hill, knap, knob,
lump **5**. bunch, hurst, knell, mound
7. hillock
knot ... **3**. bow, nep, tie **4**. burl, knar,

knob, knur, lump, node, noil, snag
5. gnarl, noose **6.** clique, nodule,
tangle **7.** dilemma, lanyard, problem,
rosette **9.** sandpiper **10.** sheepshank
12. complication, protuberance

knotted . . . **3.** nep **5.** noded, nowed (Her)
6. knotty **7.** clotted, complex, gnarled,
knitted, nodated **8.** abstruse, puzzling
9. difficult, entangled

knotty . . . **5.** nodal, rough **7.** gnarled,
knarred, knobbed, knurled, nodular
9. difficult, entangled, intricate
10. perplexing

know . . . **3.** ken, wis, wot **5.** sense
6. regard, reveal **8.** perceive
9. apprehend, be certain, recognize
11. be cognizant, distinguish

knowing . . . **3.** hep **6.** artful, crafty,
scient, shrewd **7.** cunning **8.** informed
9. cognitive, conscious, wide-awake
10. perceptive **11.** intelligent,
intentional **12.** familiar with
13. comprehension

know-it-all . . . **6.** gossip **8.** quidnunc,
wiseacre

knowledge . . . **3.** ken **4.** kith, lore
5. ology **6.** wisdom **7.** science
8. learning, scientia **9.** erudition
11. familiarity, information, instruction
12. acquaintance

knowledge (pert to) . . .
acquisition of . . **7.** organon
ancestral . . **9.** tradition
epithet of Muses . . **7.** Pierian
exhibition of . . **6.** pedant
instrument . . **7.** organon
lack of . . **9.** ignorance, nescience
object of . . **7.** scibile
pert to . . **7.** gnostic **8.** instinct
9. epistemic, intuition, sciential
12. epistemology
pretender to . . **7.** aeolist (eolist) **8.** sciolist
seeker of . . **10.** philonoist
slight . . **7.** inkling, smatter **10.** smattering
summarized . . **12.** encyclopedia
(encyclopaedia)
superficial . . **9.** sociology
system . . **7.** science
universal . . **9.** pantology
without . . **8.** atechnic

know-nothing . . . **5.** dunce **8.** agnostic
9. ignoramus

kobird . . . **6.** cuckoo
kobold . . . **3.** elf, imp **5.** gnome **8.** folklore
9. hobgoblin
Kodiak, Kadiak bear . . . **7.** Alaskan
Kohinoor . . . **7.** diamond (700 carats)
kohl . . . **5.** horse **8.** antimony, cosmetic
kola . . . **3.** nut **6.** jackal
kooky . . . **7.** offbeat
kopje . . . **5.** mound **7.** hillock
Koran, Alcoran (pert to) . . .
author . . **8.** Mohammed
division . . **4.** Sura (chapter)
learned man . . **5.** ulema
recording angel . . **6.** sijill (sijil)
scriptures . . **10.** Mohammedan
teacher . . **5.** ulema **7.** alfaqui (alfaquin)
Korea . . .
capital . . **5.** Seoul (South) **9.** Pyongyang
(North)
city . . **6.** Gensan
dynasty . . **2.** Yi
leader . . **9.** Kim Il-Sung (North)
11. Syngman Rhee (South)
mountain peak . . **6.** Paekdu
old name . . **6.** Chosen **13.** Hermit
Kingdom
peninsula . . **6.** Ongjin
province . . **5.** Fusan (Fuzan)
river . . **4.** Yalu **5.** Tuman **7.** Naktong
Korean dish . . . **6.** kimchi
Krakatoa, et al . . . **7.** volcano
kosher . . . **5.** clean **8.** kashruth
10. sanctioned
kra . . . **3.** ape (long-tailed)
krimmer . . . **8.** lambskin
Krishna (Hind) . . . **5.** deity (of Vishnu)
6. avatar (8th), Goloka
Krupp steel works, site . . . **5.** Essen
(Ger)
kudu . . . **8.** antelope **9.** gray-brown
kusimansel . . . **6.** mangue **8.** mongoose
kvetch . . . **3.** nag
Kwantung capital . . . **6.** Dairen
kwazoku (Jap) . . . **8.** nobility (modern)
kyah . . . **9.** partridge
kyaung . . . **9.** monastery
kymatology, science of . . . **5.** waves
10. wave motion
kyphosis . . . **8.** humpback **9.** hunchback
15. spinal curvature
kyte . . . **5.** belly **7.** stomach
Kyushu (Jap) . . . **6.** Island (southernmost)

L

L . . . **5.** fifty (Rom num) **6.** lambda, letter
(12th) **7.** lammedh
laager, lager . . . **4.** camp
laagte . . . **6.** bottom, valley **8.** riverbed
Laban (pert to) . . .
daughter . . **4.** Leah **6.** Rachel
father . . **7.** Bethuel
son-in-law . . **5.** Jacob
label . . . **3.** tab, tag **4.** band, name
6. fillet, lappet, tassel, ticket **8.** insignia
9. designate

labellum . . . **3.** lip **6.** labium, labrum
labia . . . **4.** lips
labial stop . . . **9.** organ stop
labial teeth . . . **6.** canine **7.** incisor
labile . . . **8.** shifting, unstable
labium . . . **3.** lip
La Boheme . . . **4.** Mimi **7.** Puccini
labor, labour . . . **4.** moil, task, toil, work
5. sweat **6.** strive **7.** travail, work
for **8.** drudgery, endeavor, exertion,
industry

labored . . . **5.** heavy **6.** forced, strove
7. not easy, operose **8.** strained
9. difficult, elaborate, laborious
11. painstaking
laborer . . . **4.** hind, peon, toty **5.** navvy
6. coolie, toiler, worker **7.** bracero,
wetback, workman
laborious . . . **4.** hard **7.** arduous, operose
8. toilsome **9.** difficult **11.** hard working,
industrious, painstaking
labor leader . . . **5.** Hoffa, Lewis, Meany
7. Gompers (1st), Reuther **8.** Petrillo
labor letters . . . **3.** AFL, CIO, ILO, UAW
Labrador (pert to) . . .
 Arctic flow . . **7.** Current
 dog . . **9.** retriever **12.** Newfoundland
 missionary . . **8.** Grenfell (Dr)
 part . . **12.** Newfoundland
 tea . . **5.** Ledum **8.** gowiddie
labyrinth . . . **4.** maze **7.** circuit, cochlea
10. perplexity **12.** complication
labyrinths . . . **7.** complex **8.** involved
9. intricate **10.** circuitous
11. complicated
lac . . . **4.** milk **5.** resin **7.** lacquer, shellac
lace . . . **3.** net, tat, tie, web **4.** band, beat,
cord, flog, lash, line, trim **5.** braid, filet,
lacis, snare **6.** fasten, string, tissue
7. network **9.** embroider **10.** intertwine,
shoestring **13.** dash of spirits
lace (pert to) . . .
 Antwerp . . **7.** pot lace
 bobbin . . **3.** val **12.** Valenciennes
 cape, scarf . . **8.** mantilla
 edge . . **5.** picot
 Flemish . . **7.** malines, Mechlin
 French . . **5.** filet **7.** guipure
 frill . . **5.** ruche
 front . . **5.** jabot
 gold, silver . . **5.** orris
 make . . **3.** tat **5.** weave **7.** crochet,
 entwine
 needlepoint . . **7.** Alencon
 opening . . **6.** eyelet
 patterned . . **7.** guipure
lacerate . . . **3.** cut, rip **4.** pain, rend, tear
6. harrow, injure, mangle **7.** afflict,
torture
lachryma . . . **4.** tear **5.** fluid **8.** teardrop
lachrymal, lachrymose . . . **5.** teary,
weepy **7.** tearful **8.** tearlike
lack . . . **4.** need, want **6.** dearth **7.** absence,
lacking, missing, require **8.** have
need, scarcity **9.** fall short, neediness
10. deficiency
lack (pert to) . . .
 blood cells (red) . . **6.** anemia
 correspondence . . **13.** nonconformity
 energy . . **5.** atony, tepid **6.** energy
 7. aimless, sapless
 feeling . . **10.** insensible **13.** insensibility
 firmness . . **4.** limp **8.** boneless
 9. spineless
 interest . . **6.** apathy **9.** apathetic
 knowledge . . **9.** ignorance, nescience
 melody . . **6.** atonic **9.** atonality
 preparation . . **8.** unfitted
 reasoning . . **7.** idiotic
 refinement . . **5.** gross **9.** grossness,
 inelegant **10.** inelegance
 vigilance . . **6.** unwary

lackadaisical . . . **7.** languid **8.** listless
10. spiritless
Laconia (anc) . . .
 capital . . **6.** Sparta
 clan . . **3.** obe
 inhabitant . . **5.** Lacon
 location . . **12.** Peloponnesus
 race . . **6.** Dorian
laconic . . . **5.** brief, pithy, short, terse
7. concise, pointed, summary
8. succinct, taciturn
lacquer . . . **3.** lac, red (color) **5.** japan,
resin **6.** enamel **7.** shellac, varnish
lacrimando . . . **9.** lamenting, plaintive
lactarium . . . **5.** dairy
lacteal . . . **5.** milky
lacune, lacuna . . . **3.** gap, pit **5.** break
6. hiatus **7.** opening (small)
10. depression
ladder . . . **3.** run, sty **5.** scale **7.** scalade
8. escalade **10.** stepladder
lade . . . **3.** dip **4.** bail, draw, fill, load,
ship **5.** drain, ladle **6.** burden
laden . . . **6.** loaded **8.** burdened
9. freighted
lading . . . **4.** load **5.** cargo **6.** burden
7. freight
ladle . . . **3.** dip **4.** bowl **5.** scoop, spoon
6. dipper
lady . . . **4.** burd (anc), dame **5.** donna
6. domina, female, senora **7.** signora
8. ladylove **13.** harlequin duck
lady (pert to) . . .
 bird . . **6.** beetle **7.** Vedalia
 fish . . **6.** wrasse
 killer . . **4.** wolf **5.** shiek **7.** Don Juan
 8. Casanova
 like . . **6.** female, polite **7.** genteel
 8. feminine
Lady Godiva's town . . . **8.** Coventry
Lady of the Lake character (legend) . . .
6. Merlin, Vivian
Lady's Book author . . . **5.** Godey
lady's-slipper . . . **6.** balsam, orchid
8. Noah's ark **9.** nerveroot
lady's-thumb . . . **9.** peachwort, persicary
lag . . . **4.** slow **5.** delay, tardy **6.** dawdle,
linger, loiter **7.** belated **10.** dillydally,
fall behind
lagarto . . . **9.** alligator **10.** lizard fish
laggard . . . **4.** slow **5.** idler **7.** lagging
8. backward, dilatory, indolent, loiterer,
sluggish **9.** loitering, straggler
La Gioconda . . . **8.** Mona Lisa
lagniappe, lagnappe . . . **5.** pilon
7. largess (largesse), present (trifling)
8. gratuity
lagoon . . . **4.** lake, pond, pool **5.** atoll
laic . . . **3.** lay **5.** civil **6.** layman **7.** secular
8. temporal
lair . . . **3.** bed, den, pen **4.** cave, shed, trap
5. abode, couch **6.** cavern **7.** retreat
Lais (Gr) . . . **7.** hetaera (of Corinth)
8. mistress **14.** beautiful woman
laissez faire, laisser faire . . . **5.** let
go **7.** let pass **8.** inaction, inactive
9. do-nothing, passivism, unconcern
12. indifference **15.** noninterference
Laius' son . . . **7.** Oedipus (of Thebes)
lake . . . **4.** loch, mere, pond, pool, tarn
5. lacus **6.** lagoon **7.** carmine (color)

L

lake (pert to) . . .
  bass . . **4.** rock **6.** calico
  deposit . . **5.** trona
  duck . . **5.** scaup **7.** mallard
  dweller . . **10.** lacustrian
  dwelling . . **7.** crannog
  growing in . . **10.** lacustrine
  Hades (of) . . **7.** Avernus
  highest . . **8.** Titicaca
  pert to . . **9.** lacustral
  poet (Eng) . . **6.** lakist **7.** Southey
    9. Coleridge **10.** Wordsworth
  State . . **8.** Michigan
lama . . . **4.** monk **5.** Dalai
Lamaism . . . **8.** Buddhism
Lamaism, Buddhism (pert to) . . .
  convent . . **8.** lamasery
  dignitary . . **8.** hutukhtu
  palace site . . **5.** Lhasa
  priest, monk . . **4.** lama **6.** Getsul **9.** Dalai
    Lama, Grand Lama
  reliquary, stupa . . **7.** chorten
lamb . . . **3.** ean, ewe **4.** cade, yean **5.** gigot,
    sheep **6.** cosset **7.** eanling, lambkin
    8. yearling **9.** youngling **10.** endearment
Lamb, Charles . . . **4.** Elia (pen name)
lambaste . . . **4.** beat, whip **6.** thrash
    7. reprove
lambent . . . **7.** glowing, radiant
    8. wavering **10.** flickering **11.** gliding
    over
Lambeth (London) . . . **6.** palace (of
    Archbishops) **15.** religious center
Lamb of God . . . **7.** paschal **8.** Agnus
    Dei
lame . . . **4.** halt **7.** halting, limping
    8. crippled, disabled, hobbling
    9. defective **11.** inefficient
lame (pert to) . . .
  brains . . **9.** balminess, daffiness,
    goofiness, wackiness
  duck . . **7.** session **9.** insolvent
    10. politician, speculator
Lamech (pert to) . . .
  descendant of . . **4.** Cain
  father of . . **5.** Jabal, Jubal **9.** Tubal-cain
lament . . . **3.** rue **4.** keen, moan, sigh,
    wail, weep **5.** mourn **6.** bemoan, bewail,
    grieve, plaint, regret, repine, yammer
    7. condole, deplore, elegize, weeping
    8. jeremiad
lamentation . . . **3.** cry, woe **5.** dolor, grief,
    tears **6.** sorrow **7.** anguish, wailing
Lamentations . . . **4.** Book (Old Test)
lamia . . . **5.** witch **7.** monster, vampire
    (Myth) **8.** cub shark **9.** sorceress
lamina . . . **4.** obex (brain) **5.** blade, flake,
    hinge, layer
lamp . . . **4.** davy, etna **5.** light, torch
    6. crusie **7.** lantern, lucigen **9.** veilleuse
lamp (pert to) . . .
  black . . **4.** soot
  holder . . **11.** candelabrum
  lighter . . **5.** spill
  safety . . **4.** davy **7.** Geordie
  slang . . **6.** look at
  waving of . . **5.** arati
lampadedromy (Gr) . . . **8.** foot race (with
    torch)
lampoon . . . **4.** skit **5.** squib **6.** iambic
    8. ridicule, satirize **10.** pasquinade

lampoon writer . . . **8.** satirist
lamprey . . . **3.** eel **6.** ramper
Lamps of the Lord . . . **5.** yucca (blooms)
Lancashire (Eng) . . . **6.** Eccles
lance . . . **3.** cut **4.** dart, hurl, stab **5.** blade,
    spear **6.** incise, launch, pierce, weapon
    7. javelin
lance (pert to) . . .
  battle . . **5.** joust
  head . . **5.** morne
  knight . . **10.** lansquenet (Hist)
  officer . . **4.** Jack
  surgical . . **6.** lancet
Lancelot . . . **6.** Knight **13.** Lancelot du
    Lac
Lancelot's beloved . . . **6.** Elaine
lancer . . . **5.** uhlan **6.** Hussar **7.** cossack,
    soldier, spearer
land . . . **3.** lot **4.** acre, farm **5.** arada,
    downs, field, range, tilth **6.** alight,
    debark, ground, region **7.** country,
    pasture **9.** disembark
land (pert to) . . .
  absolute ppty . . **4.** alod **7.** alodium
  alluvial . . **5.** delta
  ancestral . . **5.** ethel
  assessor . . **8.** cadastre (cadaster)
  church . . **5.** glebe
  heritable . . **4.** odal, udal
  holding . . **6.** tenure **9.** leasehold
  leasehold . . **5.** feoff
  locked in . . **13.** mediterranean
  mythical . . **4.** Eden **6.** Utopia **9.** Shangri-
    La
  northernmost . . **5.** Thule (Greenland)
  open . . **4.** moor, wold **5.** heath
  pile . . **5.** cairn
  prefix . . **4.** agro
  reversion . . **7.** escheat
  sandy . . **4.** dene
  surveyor . . **9.** arpenteur
  Sussex tract (Eng) . . **5.** laine
  treeless . . **5.** llano **6.** steppe **7.** prairie
  verb . . **3.** win **4.** gain **5.** catch **6.** secure
    7. capture
  waste . . **5.** heath
landed estate . . . **5.** manor **7.** demesne
landing place . . . **4.** deck, dock, pier, quay
    5. field, levee, strip, wharf **7.** airport
    8. platform **9.** staircase
landmark . . . **4.** copa, tree **5.** senal
Land of (the) . . .
  bondage . . **5.** Egypt
  Cush . . **8.** Ethiopia
  Eden (East of) . . **3.** Nod
  Enchantment . . **9.** New Mexico
  Leal . . **6.** Heaven
  Little Sticks (Canada) . . **19.** Barren Islands
    border
  Midnight Sun . . **6.** Alaska, Norway
  O'Cakes . . **8.** Scotland
  Opportunity . . **8.** Arkansas
  Plenty . . **6.** Goshen
  Promise . . **6.** Canaan
  Regrets . . **5.** India
  Rising Sun . . **5.** Japan
  Rose . . **7.** England
  Shamrock . . **4.** Eire **7.** Ireland
  sleep . . **3.** Nod
  Steady Habits . . **11.** Connecticut
  Thistle . . **8.** Scotland

Thousand Lakes.. **7.** Finland
White Elephant.. **4.** Siam
landscape ... **7.** paysage, scenery, topiary
landslide ... **9.** avalanche **10.** éboulement
Landsmaal, Landsmal ... **8.** language
(Norway)
Landstag ... **4.** Diet **8.** assembly
11. legislature
lane ... **4.** path, road **5.** alley, route,
track **6.** airway, course, gullet, throat
7. channel, red land **8.** footpath
10. passageway
language ... **6.** langue, speech, tongue
7. dialect, diction **8.** parlance
9. utterance **11.** linguistics
language (pert to)...
acquiring.. **12.** chrestomathy
ancient.. **4.** Pali **5.** Aryan, Greek, Latin
6. Hebrew **7.** Chinese **8.** Sanskrit
artificial.. **2.** Od, Ro **3.** Ido **7.** Volapük
9. Esperanto
classical.. **5.** Greek, Latin
conversant in.. **9.** pantoglot
dead.. **4.** Pali
deaf-mute.. **11.** dactylology
expression, peculiar.. **5.** idiom, lingo
6. jargon **7.** dialect **13.** colloquialism
international.. **2.** Od, Ro **3.** Ido
7. Volapük **9.** Esperanto
pert to.. **8.** semantic
pretentious.. **7.** bombast **11.** highfalutin
Romance.. **5.** Latin **6.** French **7.** Catalan,
Italian, Spanish **9.** Provencal
10. Portuguese
sacred.. **4.** Pali
sign.. **11.** dactylology
thieves.. **5.** argot
languid ... **4.** slow, weak **5.** faint, inert,
weary **6.** dreamy, feeble, sickly, supine,
torpid **7.** passive **8.** careless, drooping,
flagging, heedless, indolent, sluggish
9. apathetic **10.** spiritless
languish ... **3.** die **4.** fade, fail, flag, pine,
wilt **5.** droop, faint **6.** repine, sicken,
weaken, wither **7.** decline
languor ... **3.** kef (kief) **7.** fatigue
8. dullness, weakness **9.** indolence,
lassitude **10.** dreaminess, drowsiness,
stagnation **12.** listlessness, sluggishness
lanky ... **4.** lean, tall, thin **5.** gaunt, spare
12. loose-jointed
lanner ... **6.** falcon
Lanterns, Feast of (Jap) ... **3.** Bon
Laodicean ... **8.** lukewarm **9.** apathetic
11. indifferent
Laos ...
aborigine.. **3.** Kah
capital.. **9.** Vientiane **12.** Luang Prabang
native.. **7.** Chinese **14.** Thai-Indonesian
religion.. **8.** Buddhism
river.. **6.** Mekong
lap ... **3.** sip **4.** fold, lick, wrap **5.** drink
6. ripple, tipple **7.** circuit
lapel ... **4.** fold **5.** rever **6.** facing, lappet
lapicide ... **11.** stonecutter
lapidary's forte ... **4.** gems
lapin ... **6.** rabbit
lapis lazuli ... **4.** blue **5.** stone **8.** lazurite,
sapphire **10.** azure stone
Lapland ...
people.. **5.** Lapps **10.** Laplanders

11. Ural-Altaics **12.** tent-dwellers
sledge (traveling).. **5.** pulka (pukk)
sledge puller.. **8.** reindeer
town.. **6.** Kiruna
waterfalls.. **11.** Harspranget
lappet ... **4.** flap, fold, lobe **5.** lapel
6. wattle **9.** appendage
lapse ... **3.** err **4.** fall, slip **5.** error, fault,
pause **6.** expiry **7.** decline, misstep,
relapse **8.** apostasy **9.** reversion
lapsus ... **4.** slip **5.** error **12.** inadvertence
lapsus calami ... **10.** lipography **12.** slip
of the pen
lapsus linguae ... **15.** slip of the tongue
lapwing ... **4.** gull **5.** pewee, pewit
6. plover
larceny ... **5.** theft **7.** robbery **8.** burglary,
stealage **10.** scrounging
larch ... **5.** Larix **8.** tamarack
lard ... **3.** fat **4.** line, pork **5.** adeps, bacon,
baste, enarm **6.** axunge, cerate, enrich,
fatten, grease **7.** garnish **8.** saindoux
9. lubricate
larder ... **6.** pantry **7.** buttery **8.** cupboard
12. commissariat
lares (Rom) ... **4.** gods (household)
7. spirits
large ... **3.** big, nth **4.** bold, huge, much,
vast **5.** ample, bulky, burly, giant, great,
loose, scads **7.** copious, immense,
leonine, liberal, massive, titanic,
weighty **8.** colossal, enormous, gigantic,
spacious **9.** excessive, extensive,
plentiful **11.** exaggerated
12. considerable **13.** comprehensive
large (pert to)...
artery.. **5.** aorta
comb form.. **5.** macro
fish.. **4.** opah, tuna **9.** swordfish
intestine.. **5.** colon **6.** caecum, rectum
knife.. **4.** bolo, snee
lettered.. **6.** uncial
number.. **4.** slew **6.** myriad
pulpit.. **4.** ambo
volume.. **4.** tome
largess, largesse ... **4.** gift **6.** bounty
7. charity, present **10.** generosity,
liberality **11.** beneficence
largest bird ... **6.** condor **7.** ostrich
13. whooping crane
largest fish (freshwater) ... **8.** arapaima
larghetto ... **9.** slow tempo
larghissimo ... **8.** very slow
lariat ... **4.** rope **5.** honda (part), lasso,
noose, reata, riata
lark ... **5.** ghost (anc), prank, revel
6. frolic **7.** skylark, titlark **8.** songbird
9. adventure, Alaudidae, parchment
(color)
larrigan ... **8.** moccasin
larrikin ... **5.** rough, rowdy **6.** loafer
10. street Arab
larrup ... **3.** hit **4.** beat, blow, flog, whip
larva ... **3.** bot (bott) **4.** grub, pupa
5. redia **6.** embryo, maggot **7.** atrocha
8. cercaria **9.** chrysalis, doodlebug
11. caterpillar
lascivious ... **4.** lewd **5.** bawdy **6.** erotic,
wanton **7.** lustful, sensual **9.** lecherous,
salacious **10.** libidinous, licentious
laser ... **9.** light beam

lash . . . **3.** tie **4.** beat, bind, flag, whip **5.** scold, smite **6.** splice, strike **7.** scourge

lass . . . **4.** girl **6.** lassie, maiden **7.** colleen **11.** maidservant

lassitude . . . **7.** languor **8.** debility, lethargy, weakness **9.** weariness

lasso . . . **4.** lash, rope **5.** noose, reata (riata), snare **6.** lariat **8.** cabestro

last . . . **3.** end **5.** final, omega **6.** endure, latest, lowest, newest, penult, ultima, utmost **7.** extreme, supreme **8.** eventual, rearmost, terminal, ultimate **9.** penultima **10.** antepenult, conclusive, most recent

last (pert to) . . .
at last . . **6.** Eureka
but one . . **6.** penult
cry . . **10.** dernier cri
evening . . **9.** yesterday
long . . **7.** outwear, perdure **9.** perendure
month . . **3.** ult **6.** ultimo
offer . . **9.** ultimatum
person in contest . . **4.** mell
shoe . . **5.** block
syllable but one . . **6.** penult
syllable but two . . **10.** antepenult

Last (pert to) . . .
Assize . . **11.** Last Inquest **12.** Last Judgment
Days of Pompeii character . . **4.** Ione **5.** Nydia **7.** Glaucus
Gospel . . **4.** Mass
of the Gothic Kings . . **8.** Roderick
of the Mohicans . . **5.** Uncas (Chief)
Supper . . **6.** Christ **9.** disciples

lasting . . . **4.** long **6.** stable **7.** abiding, durable, eternal **8.** constant **9.** continual, lingering, permanent, steadfast **11.** substantial, unforgotten

lasting briefly . . . **9.** ephemeral, temporary

lat . . . **6.** column, pillar

latchet . . . **3.** tap **4.** lace (leather) **5.** strap, thong **9.** fastening

late . . . **3.** neo (comb form), new **4.** sero **5.** tardy **6.** former, recent **7.** belated, overdue **8.** neoteric **10.** behindhand

latent . . . **5.** inert **6.** hidden **7.** dormant **9.** disguised, potential, quiescent, suspended **10.** underlying

later . . . **4.** anon, soon **5.** after **6.** future, mañana, puisne **9.** posterior, presently **12.** subsequently

lateral . . . **5.** flank, raphe **8.** indirect, sideward

lath . . . **4.** slat **9.** wood strip

lathe . . . **4.** tool **7.** mandrel

lather . . . **4.** foam, suds **5.** froth

Latin (pert to) . . .
alphabet letters . . **9.** twenty-one
and . . **2.** et
bath . . **7.** balneum
behold . . **4.** ecce
booth . . **7.** taberna
bowl . . **6.** patina
bronze . . **3.** aes
church . . **8.** Catholic
couch . . **9.** accibutum
country . . **6.** French **7.** Italian, Spanish
dish . . **4.** lanx **6.** patina

foot . . **3.** pes
God . . **3.** Dei, Deo **4.** Deus **7.** Mercury
goddess . . **3.** Dea
grammar (case) . . **6.** dative **8.** ablative, genitive, vocative **10.** accusative, nominative
historian . . **6.** Justin
holidays . . **5.** feria
hymn . . **13.** Adesti Fideles
javelin . . **5.** aclys, pilum
land . . **4.** ager
law . . **3.** lex **6.** Latium
life . . **4.** vita
people . . **6.** Romans
poet . . **4.** Ovid **6.** Horace
pronoun . . **2.** tu **3.** ego, hic **4.** ille, ipse, iste
quarter (section) . . **5.** Paris **10.** New Orleans
ram . . **5.** aries
rite . . **4.** orgy **5.** sacra
seat . . **5.** sella
trumpet . . **4.** tuba **7.** buccina
Way . . **9.** Via Latina

latite . . . **4.** lava

latitude . . . **4.** zone **5.** scope, width **6.** extent **7.** breadth, freedom **8.** distance **10.** liberality

latrant . . . **7.** barking

latter . . . **4.** last **5.** final **6.** latest **9.** foregoing **10.** more recent

Latter-day Saint . . . **6.** Mormon

lattice . . . **6.** grille **7.** trellis **8.** cancelli **9.** crossbars, framework **12.** crossed slats

latticelike . . . **7.** grating **8.** espalier **9.** clathrate **10.** cancellate

Latvia . . .
capital . . **4.** Riga
city . . **6.** Dvinsk, Libava (Libau)
money unit . . **3.** lat (gold)
people . . **4.** Lett **7.** Lettish
river . . **2.** Aa

laud . . . **4.** sing **5.** extol **6.** praise **7.** applaud, commend, glorify, magnify **8.** eulogize

laudable . . . **9.** admirable, estimable **11.** commendable, meritorious **12.** praiseworthy

laudatory . . . **9.** panegyric **10.** flattering **11.** approbatory, encomiastic **12.** commendatory

laugh . . . **4.** roar **5.** fleer, smile, snort **6.** cackle, deride, giggle, guffaw, hawhaw, tee-hee **7.** chortle, chuckle **8.** ridicule **10.** cachinnate

laughable . . . **3.** odd **5.** droll, funny, merry, queer, witty **7.** amusing, comical, jocular, risible, strange, waggish **8.** humorous, sportive **9.** burlesque, diverting, facetious, ludicrous **10.** ridiculous

laughing . . . **3.** gay **5.** merry, riant **6.** rident

laughing (pert to) . . .
bird . . **4.** loon **10.** woodpecker
falcon . . **4.** hawk
gas . . **12.** nitrous oxide
jackass . . **10.** kingfisher, kookaburra
pert to . . **8.** gelastic

laughter . . . **4.** gelo (comb form) **5.** gelos, mirth, risus **6.** guffaw **12.** cachinnation

launch . . . **4.** hurl **5.** begin, float, lance, shove, start, throw **6.** plunge **7.** descant **9.** undertake **10.** inaugurate
laureate . . . **4.** poet **6.** decked (with laurel) **7.** drowned, honored **13.** distinguished
laurel . . . **3.** bay, ivy, oak, oil **6.** daphne, Kalmia, salmon **8.** magnolia **9.** sassafras, spoonwood
laurel wreath . . . **7.** Iresine
lava . . . **2.** aa, oo **3.** ash **5.** ashes **6.** coulee, latite, scoria **8.** lapillus, pahoehoe
lava field . . . **8.** pedregal
lavaliere, lavalier . . . **7.** pendant **8.** ornament
lavatory . . . **5.** basin **7.** piscina **8.** washroom **9.** washbasin
lave . . . **4.** lade, pour, wash **5.** bathe, rinse **6.** drench **8.** absterge
lavender . . . **4.** mint **6.** purple **7.** blue-red, perfume **9.** fragrance
laver . . . **4.** bowl **5.** basin **6.** trough, vessel **7.** cistern, seaweed
Lavinia (pert to) . . .
　father . . **7.** Latinus
　husband . . **6.** Aeneas
　mother . . **5.** Amata
　myth . . **5.** Roman
lavish . . . **4.** free, lush, rank, wild **5.** spend **7.** profuse **8.** abundant, generous, prodigal, reckless, squander **9.** bountiful, exuberant, impetuous, luxuriant, plentiful, unstinted **10.** immoderate **11.** extravagant **12.** unrestrained **13.** superabundant
law . . . **3.** act, jus, lex **4.** bill, code, jure, nisi, rule **5.** axiom, canon, droit, edict, mercy, mesne **6.** decree, equity, Latium, police **7.** justice, precept, statute **9.** enactment **12.** constitution **13.** jurisprudence
law (pert to) . . .
　action . . **3.** res **4.** suit **5.** actus **6.** trover **7.** impeach, implead **8.** gravamen, replevin **9.** ademption
　Bible . . **6.** Mosaic **12.** Old Testament
　claim . . **4.** lien
　code . . **8.** Napoléon **9.** Hammurabi **10.** codex juris **16.** Codex Justinianus
　decree . . **4.** nisi **5.** edict
　degree . . **3.** LLD
　divine . . **11.** commandment
　document . . **4.** deed, writ **6.** capias, elegit
　drafting . . **10.** nomography
　evidence . . **7.** constat
　expert (US) . . **5.** Moore (John B)
　for fourth offender (NY) . . **6.** Baumes
　German Franks . . **5.** Salic
　goddess . . **4.** Maat (Egypt)
　heredity . . **8.** Gresham's
　Manu . . **5.** sutra
　mathematics . . **7.** formula
　morals . . **7.** conduct
　Moses . . **5.** Torah (Tora) **10.** Pentateuch
　offender . . **5.** felon **6.** sinner **8.** criminal **9.** wrongdoer
　offense . . **4.** tort **5.** crime, malum **6.** delict
　pert to . . **3.** res **9.** judiciary
　philology . . **6.** Grimm's
　science . . **8.** nomology **13.** jurisprudence
　student . . **8.** stagiary

　thought . . **7.** noetics
　warning . . **6.** caveat
　within the . . **5.** licit **8.** judicial
　wrong . . **4.** tort
lawful . . . **3.** due **5.** legal, licit, valid **9.** permitted **10.** legitimate **11.** permissible
lawgiver . . . **5.** Moses
lawless . . . **4.** lewd **6.** unruly **7.** illegal **10.** anarchical, disorderly
lawlessness . . . **4.** riot **6.** mutiny **7.** anarchy, license **12.** disobedience
lawmaker . . . **5.** solon **7.** senator **10.** legislator **11.** congressman
lawn . . . **5.** green **7.** batiste **9.** grassplot **12.** village green
lawyer . . . **5.** agent **6.** jurist, legist **7.** abogado, shyster **8.** advocate, attorney, lawgiver **9.** barrister, counselor (counsellor), leguleian, solicitor **11.** intercessor, pettifogger
lawyer group . . . **3.** ABA
lax . . . **4.** dull, free, limp, open, slow **5.** loose, slack, tardy **6.** remiss **7.** lenient **8.** backward, dilatory, inactive, indolent, not tense **9.** dissolute, scattered **10.** licentious, unconfined **12.** unrestrained
lay . . . **3.** bet, put **4.** lair, pave, poem, song **5.** allay, ditty, place, quiet, stake, still **6.** ballad, hazard, impose, impute, pacify **7.** appease, ascribe, deposit, relieve, store up **9.** direction **10.** profession
lay (pert to) . . .
　aside . . **5.** table **6.** remove, shelve **7.** dismiss, reserve **8.** postpone **9.** segregate
　away . . **4.** heap, hive **5.** amass, cache, hoard, store **7.** husband **8.** treasure **10.** accumulate
　bare . . **5.** strip **6.** denude, expose, reveal **7.** uncover
　down . . **3.** bet, set **5.** level **6.** give up **7.** declare, deposit **9.** postulate, prescribe, stipulate, surrender
　off . . **4.** don't, stop **5.** cease **6.** recess **7.** dismiss, measure
　out . . **4.** plan **5.** set up **6.** design **7.** pattern
　waste . . **6.** ravage **7.** destroy **8.** desolate **9.** depredate, devastate
layer . . . **3.** bed **4.** coat, derm, tier, uvea **5.** sloam (earth) **6.** lamina **7.** stratum (strata, pl) **10.** substratum
lazar . . . **5.** leper **9.** loathsome
lazaretto, lazaret . . . **8.** hospital **9.** pest house **10.** lazar house
laziness . . . **5.** sloth **7.** inertia **8.** oisivity, vagrancy **9.** indolence **10.** ergophobia, remissness **12.** slothfulness **13.** shiftlessness
lazy . . . **3.** lax **4.** idle, slow **5.** slack **6.** otiose, remiss **7.** dronish, laggard **8.** dilatory, inactive, indolent, slothful, sluggish **9.** shiftless **13.** lackadaisical
lazy man . . . **3.** bum **4.** lusk **5.** drone, idler **6.** rotter **9.** lazybones **11.** Weary Willie
lea . . . **4.** mead **5.** haugh **6.** meadow **7.** pasture **9.** grassland
leach . . . **3.** wet **7.** moisten **9.** lixiviate,

percolate

lead . . . 3. cue, key, van 4. cart, clue, head, lode 5. begin, guide, pilot, plumb, usher 6. direct, entice, escort, govern, induce 7. conduct, pioneer, precede 8. antecede, guidance 9. direction, influence, precedent 10. precedence

lead (mineral) . . . 4. came (rod), gray, shot 6. ceruse, fother, galena, leaden, strass (glass) 7. bullets, plummet 8. graphite, litharge, plumbago

lead astray . . . 4. lure, mang 6. allure, delude, entice, induce 7. deceive, pervert 8. inveigle

leader . . . 4. head 5. chief, guide, sinew 6. cantor, tendon 7. special 8. choragus, director 9. chieftain, conductor 10. forerunner

leader (Eccl) . . . 3. fra 4. pope 5. rabbi 6. bishop, vicar 7. cardinal, minister, preacher 10. evangelist

leading . . . 5. chief, first 6. ruling 7. guiding 8. foremost, in the van 9. directing, governing 11. controlling

leaf . . . 3. ola 4. gear, page 5. blade, frond, petal, sepal 6. areola, ligula, spathe 7. tendril

leaf (pert to) . . .
book . . 5. folio
bud . . 5. gemma
curvature . . 8. epinasty (down) 9. hyponasty (upward)
floating . . 3. pad
green . . 11. chlorophyll
heart-shaped . . 9. obcordate
mold . . 5. humus
network . . 6. areola
part . . 5. bract, costa, stoma 6. pagina, stipel 7. petiole 9. petiolule
point, pointed . . 5. mucro 9. mucronate 13. mucroniferous
pore . . 8. lenticel
secretion . . 4. lerp
stalk . . 7. petiole 8. petiolus
vein . . 3. rib 5. costa

leafless . . . 9. aphyllous

leaflet . . . 5. pinna, tract 6. folder 7. booklet 8. pamphlet 13. advertisement

league . . . 4. band, Bund 5. Hanse, union 7. combine 8. alliance 9. coalition 10. federation 11. affiliation, combination 13. confederation

League of Nations site . . . 5. Paris (1920) 6. Geneva (Secretariat)

League of the Iroquois . . . 11. Five Nations

Leah (pert to) . . .
Bible book . . 7. Genesis
sister . . 6. Rachel
son . . 4. Levi
wife of . . 5. Jacob

leak . . . 4. drip, hole, seep 5. crack 6. escape, run out 7. crevice, fissure 10. be revealed

leal . . . 4. just, real, true 5. legal, loyal 6. lawful 7. correct, genuine 8. accurate, faithful

lean . . . 4. bare, cant, lank, poor, rely, slim, tend 5. gaunt, slope, spare 6. barren, meager 7. scraggy, slender

8. not plump 9. deficient, gravitate

lean (pert to) . . .
animal, person . . 4. ribe (Scot)
emaciated . . 6. marcid
make . . 8. macerate
towards . . 6. prefer

Leander's love . . . 4. Hero

leaning . . . 5. slope 6. desire 7. pronate, tending 8. aptitude, enclitic, penchant, tendency 9. prejudice 10. partiality

Leaning Tower . . . 4. Pisa 6. Venice 7. Bologna 8. Zaragoza

lean-to . . . 4. roof, shed, wing 5. shack 9. extension (bldg)

leap . . . 3. dive, jump, ramp, skip 5. bound, caper, lunge, salto, spang, vault 6. spring 7. saltary 8. capriole

leaping . . . 7. jumping, salient, saltant 8. bounding, salience 9. saltation

learn . . . 4. lere (anc) 6. master 8. memorize 9. ascertain, determine

learned . . . 3. wot 4. read, sage 6. legist 7. erudite 8. lettered, literate, schooled 9. scholarly 12. well-informed

learned person . . . 6. master, pundit 7. scholar, teacher 9. professor

learning . . . 3. art, ken, wit 4. lore 7. culture 8. pedantry 9. education, erudition, knowledge, philology (love of), philomath 11. scholarship

lease . . . 3. let 4. hire, rent 5. weave 6. demise, remise, tenure 8. contract

leasehold . . . 6. rental, tenure

leash . . . 4. bind, cord, lash, lune (hawking) 5. reins, three 6. fasten, string, tierce 9. restraint 11. subjugation

leash hound . . . 5. limer

least . . . 5. grain 6. little, lowest, merest 7. minimum 8. minority, shortest, simplest, smallest 9. slightest

leather . . . 4. hide, skin 5. aluta, leder (old spelling) 6. vellum 7. canepin 8. cheveril (cheverel) 9. toughness

leather (kinds) . . . 3. kid, kip 4. calf, napa, vici 5. Mocha, suede 6. patent, saddle, skiver 7. chamois, Morocco 8. cordovan 9. sheepskin

leather (pert to) . . .
artificial . . 7. keratol
bookbinding . . 4. roan 6. levant
bottle . . 4. olpe 6. matara
cuirass . . 6. lorica
glove . . 5. suede, trank 8. capeskin
pare . . 5. skive
patch . . 5. clout
piece of . . 5. strap, thong 6. latigo
pouch (Highlander's) . . 7. sporran
process . . 3. tan, taw
strap . . 5. thong 6. latigo
term . . 8. efflower
tool . . 6. skiver
worker . . 6. chamar, tanner 8. chuckler

leatherneck . . . 6. marine

leave . . . 2. go 4. quit 6. depart, retire, vacate 7. liberty 9. allowance 10. permission

leave (pert to) . . .
desolate . . 7. bereave
empty . . 6. vacate
isolated . . 6. desert, maroon
of absence . . 5. exeat 8. furlough

off.. **4.** don't, stay **5.** cease **6.** desist

out.. **4.** omit, skip **5.** elide **8.** pass over

taking.. **5.** adieu **6.** congee **7.** vamoose **9.** departure

leaven ... **4.** barm **5.** imbue, yeast **6.** enzyme **7.** corrupt (implied), ferment, pervade **10.** impregnate

leaves ... **5.** pages, shaws **6.** sepals **7.** foliage

leaves, feeding on ... **13.** phyllophagous

leavings ... **4.** left, orts, rest **5.** culls, dregs, dross, waste **6.** refuse **7.** remains, residue **8.** remnants

leban, lebban ... **5.** drink **8.** beverage, sour milk

Lebanon city ... **5.** Sidon **6.** Beirut (capital) **7.** Tripoli

lech (anc) ... **4.** slab **8.** capstone, monument

lecher ... **7.** glutton **8.** gourmand, parasite **9.** debauchee, libertine

lectern ... **4.** ambo, desk **6.** pulpit **10.** escritoire

lecture ... **4.** jobe, rate **5.** scold **6.** lesson **7.** declaim, expound, lection, reproof, reprove **8.** instruct, scolding **9.** discourse **10.** admonition

lecturer ... **6.** docent, reader **7.** teacher **9.** prelector

Leda (pert to) ...
geology.. **4.** clay (marine)
husband.. **9.** Tyndareus
lover.. **4.** Zeus (swan)
mother of.. **6.** Castor, Pollux **11.** Helen of Troy **12.** Clytemnestra
zoology.. **7.** mollusk

ledge ... **4.** berm, edge, lode, reef, sill **5.** shelf **7.** retable, stratum

leechlike ... **8.** bdelloid

lees ... **5.** draff, dregs **8.** sediment

leeward ... (opp of windward) **9.** protected, sheltered

Leeward Islands ... **5.** Nevis **7.** Antigua, Barbuda, Redonda **8.** Anguilla, Sombrero **10.** Montserrat **13.** St Christopher

Leeward Islands group ... **6.** Virgin **7.** Society

leeway ... **4.** room **5.** drift

left ... see also *leave* **3.** haw, kay **8.** departed, larboard **9.** abandoned, remaining

left (pert to) ...
aground.. **6.** neaped **8.** beneaped
animal (motherless).. **4.** cade **5.** dogie
comb form.. **8.** sinistro
hand (Mus).. **8.** sinistra
hand page.. **5.** verso
hand pitcher.. **8.** southpaw
out.. **7.** omitted **8.** excluded **10.** eliminated
spirally.. **11.** sinistrally
to one's judgment.. **13.** discretionary
toward the.. **5.** aport **9.** sinistrad, sinistral **12.** levorotatory (Chem)

left-handed ... **6.** clumsy, gauche **7.** oblique **8.** southpaw **9.** insincere, insulting **14.** sinistromanual **16.** counterclockwise

left-handed marriage ... **10.** morganatic

leftist ... **7.** liberal, radical **10.** left-winger,

liberalist **11.** progressive

leg (pert to) ...
armor.. **4.** jamb **6.** greave **7.** jambeau
bone.. **4.** shin **5.** tibia **6.** fibula
calf.. **5.** sural
insect.. **4.** coxa
joint.. **4.** hock, knee **5.** thigh
longest bone.. **5.** femur
of lamb (cooked).. **5.** gigot
term.. **4.** crus **5.** jambe **6.** crural

legacy ... **4.** gift, will **6.** devise **7.** bequest, codicil **9.** testament **10.** bequeathal

legal ... **4.** leal **5.** licit, valid **6.** lawful **10.** authorized, legitimate

legal (pert to) ...
abstract.. **6.** précis
act, thing.. **5.** actus
action.. **3.** res **4.** case **7.** detinet, lawsuit, summons
case, postponed.. **7.** remanet
claim.. **4.** lien
confirmation.. **10.** validation
contestant.. **6.** suitor **8.** litigant **9.** plaintiff
critic.. **6.** censor
decree, divorce.. **10.** decree nisi
defense.. **5.** alibi
delay.. **4.** mora
denial, stoppage.. **8.** estoppel
extract.. **7.** estreat
matter.. **3.** res
order.. **4.** writ
paper.. **4.** deed, writ **5.** lease **6.** escrow
possession.. **6.** seizin (seisin)
power (to take).. **7.** prender (prendre)
process.. **6.** caveat **7.** detinet
right, by.. **6.** ex jure
security.. **4.** bond
surrender.. **6.** remise

legally competent ... **5.** capax

legate ... **5.** envoy **8.** bequeath, delegate **10.** ambassador, diplomatic

legend ... **4.** Edda, myth, saga, tale **5.** fable **7.** history **9.** narrative, tradition **11.** inscription

legendary ... **8.** fabulous **9.** imaginary, narrative **11.** traditional **12.** mythological

legendary (pert to) ...
goddess (slave).. **5.** Baube, lambe
primate.. **6.** Dubric
water sprite.. **6.** undine

legendry ... **7.** legends (collectively)

leggings ... **5.** chaps, spats **6.** strads **7.** gaiters, greaves, puttees **8.** gamashes, gambados **12.** galligaskins

legislate ... **3.** act **5.** elect, enact **8.** pass laws **10.** put through

legislative (pert to) ...
agent.. **8.** lobbyist
assembly.. **4.** diet **6.** assize, senate **8.** congress **10.** parliament
group.. **4.** bloc

legislator ... **5.** solon **7.** senator **8.** lawgiver, lawmaker **9.** statesman **11.** congressman **14.** representative

legislature ... **4.** Diet **5.** House **6.** Senate **8.** Congress **9.** bicameral (2 branches)

legitimate ... **4.** real, true **5.** legal, licit, valid **6.** cogent, lawful **7.** genuine **9.** permitted **11.** efficacious, justifiable

legman . . . 8. newshawk
legume . . . 3. pea, pod, uva 4. bean, soya 6. clover, lentil, loment 7. alfalfa
leisure . . . 4. ease, time, toom 5. otium 6. otiose 7. freedom 9. spare time 11. convenience, opportunity
lemming . . . 4. maki, vari 5. mouse 6. rodent
lemur . . . 5. indri, loris, makis, potto 6. anguid, aye-aye, colugo, galago, macaco, monkey 7. tarsier 8. Anguidae, mongoose 10. angwantibo
Lenape . . . 6. Indian (Del)
lend . . . 4. loan 5. grant 6. devote (to) 7. advance
length (pert to) . . .
  measure . . 4. area 5. gauge 6. linear, volume
  ten meters . . 9. decameter
  three-quarters inch . . 5. digit
  time . . 3. age, eon, era 6. moment, period
  two and one-quarter inches . . 4. nail
  unit . . 6. micron, parsec (Astron)
lengthen out . . . 7. prolong, stretch 8. continue, elongate, protract
lengthwise . . . 5. along 12. horizontally 14. longitudinally
lenient . . . 3. lax 4. easy, mild 7. clement, patient 8. merciful, relaxing, tolerant 9. assuasive, emollient, softening
Lenin (pert to) . . .
  leader of . . 10. Bolsheviks
  real name . . 7. Ulyanov (Ulianov)
  Revolution . . 7. October, Russian
Leningrad (Russ) . . . 9. Petrograd 12. St Petersburg 15. Window on the West
lenis . . . 4. soft 6. gentle, smooth
lenitive . . . 4. mild 6. gentle 8. mitigant, ointment, remedial 9. assuasive, emollient, mitigator, relieving, softening 10. palliative, qualifying
lens . . . 5. toric 7. bifocal, lentoid 8. meniscus, sunglass 9. lenticula 10. anastigmat 13. apochromatism
Lent . . . 6. carême 9. Forty days, Great Fast 12. Quadragesima
lentamento . . . 6. slowly
lentando . . . 9. retarding 14. becoming slower
lenticula . . . 7. freckle, lentigo (freckly)
lento . . . 4. slow
Leo constellation star . . . 7. Regulus, the Lion
leopard . . . 4. pard 5. ounce 6. jaguar, ocelot 7. cheetah, panther
leper . . . 5. lazar, mesel 6. Naaman (Bib)
lepidopteran . . . 4. moth 9. butterfly
Lepontine Alps . . . 10. Monte Leone (peak)
lepra . . . 7. leprosy 14. Hansen's disease
Lesbos . . . 5. Assos (Aristotle's) 6. Island (Sappho's) 8. Mytilene
Les Miserables author . . . 4. Hugo (Victor)
lessen . . . 4. bate, wane 5. abate, lower, peter, relax 6. impair, minify, narrow, reduce, shrink, weaken 7. cut down, relieve 8. decrease, diminish, mitigate, moderate, palliate 11. deteriorate
lesser . . . 4. less 5. minor (Mus) 7. smaller

8. inferior
Lesser Bear (Astron) . . . 9. Ursa Minor
Lesser Dog (Astron) . . . 10. Canis Minor
Lesser Lion (Astron) . . . 8. Leo Minor
let . . . 4. hire, rent 5. allow, lease, leave 6. hinder, impede, permit 7. prevent
let (pert to) . . .
  down . . 5. lower 8. comedown, drawback, relaxing 10. slackening 14. disappointment
  fall . . 4. drop, slip 5. spill 7. mention
  in . . 5. admit, enter 6. insert
  it be given . . 5. detur
  it stand . . 3. sta (Mus) 4. stet
  up . . 4. rest 5. cease, pause, relax 6. slow up 7. slacken 8. decrease
lethal . . . 5. fatal, feral 6. deadly, mortal 7. deathly, killing 11. destructive 12. death-dealing
lethargic . . . 4. dull 5. heavy, inert 6. drowsy, sleepy, torpid 8. comatose, listless 9. apathetic
lethargy . . . 4. coma 5. sleep, sopor 6. apathy, stupor, torpor 7. languor 8. hebetude, neurosis 9. lassitude 10. drowsiness (morbid)
Lethe . . . 5. abyss, Hades, river 8. oblivion 13. forgetfulness
lethiferous . . . 6. deadly 11. destructive
Leto (pert to) . . .
  mother of . . 6. Apollo 7. Artemis
  Roman name . . 6. Latona
  wife of . . 4. Zeus
letter . . . 4. note, type 7. epistle, message 9. character 13. communication
letter (pert to) . . .
  bright star . . 4. Beta
  carrier . . 6. correo 7. mailman, postman
  cross stroke . . 5. serif
  first . . 7. initial
  letter for letter . . 9. literatim
  marks . . 5. breve
  of advice . . 11. lettre d'avis
  of challenge . . 6. cartel
  representation . . 10. literation
  short . . 4. line, note 6. billet
  sloping . . 6. italic
  sound loss (last) . . 7. apocope
  two letters (one sound) . . 7. digraph 9. diphthong
  writer . . 13. correspondent
letters (pert to) . . .
  decorate with . . 7. miniate 10. illuminate
  man of . . 9. literatus
  ref to . . 8. literary
lettuce . . . 3. cos 4. head 7. Lactuca, romaine
leukocyte . . . 9. corpuscle (white)
Levant . . . 4. East 6. Orient 7. leather (Morocco) 8. East wind
Levantine (pert to) . . .
  country . . 13. Mediterranean
  garment . . 6. caftan
  herb . . 6. madder
  ketch . . 3. bum 4. jerm, saic 5. xebec 6. settee 8. levanter
  valley . . 4. wadi (wady)
  wind . . 7. Morocco
levee . . . 4. bank, dike, pier, quay 5. ridge 6. durbar, trench 8. assembly 9. reception 10. embankment

level . . . **4.** even, fell, flat, just, raze
5. equal, grade, plane, plani (comb
form), point **6.** peavey (peavy), smooth,
steady, topple **7.** flatten, terrace,
uniform **8.** demolish, equalize, parterre
12. well-balanced

lever . . . **3.** bar, lam, pry **5.** crank, jimmy,
pedal, prise **6.** peavey (peavy), tappet,
tiller **7.** crowbar, treadle

leveret . . . **4.** hare

leviathan (pert to) . . .
animal (Bib) . . **5.** whale **6.** dragon
9. crocodile
embroidery . . **6.** canvas **11.** cross-stitch
political . . **12.** (the) commonwealth
size . . **4.** huge **7.** titanic **10.** formidable

Levi's father (Bib) . . . **5.** Jacob

levitate . . . **4.** rise **5.** float

Levite . . . **5.** tribe **10.** descendant

Levitical . . . **7.** Aaronic **9.** Aaronical
10. priesthood (Mormon)

Leviticus . . . **10.** Pentateuch

levity . . . **6.** gaiety **8.** buoyancy **9.** frivolity,
lightness **10.** triviality, volatility

levy . . . **3.** tax **4.** fine, wage (war) **5.** rally,
stent **6.** assess, impose **7.** collect,
estreat **9.** recruital

lex . . . **3.** law **7.** statute

lexicon . . . **4.** book (of words)
10. dictionary, vocabulary

lex loci . . . **13.** law of the place

lex non scripta . . . **12.** unwritten law

liability . . . **4.** debt **5.** debit **8.** cessavit
9. proneness **10.** likelihood, obligation
11. possibility **14.** responsibility

liable . . . **3.** apt **5.** bound **6.** likely
7. exposed, subject **10.** answerable,
chargeable **11.** responsible

liable (pert to) . . .
likely to . . **3.** apt **5.** prone **11.** predisposed
not liable . . **6.** exempt
to objection . . **13.** exceptionable
to penalty . . **6.** guilty

Lia Fail . . . **12.** Stone of Scone
15. Coronation Stone (Ir)

liaison . . . **4.** link **7.** joining **8.** intimacy,
intrigue **11.** co-operation
18. intercommunication

liana . . . **4.** cipo **5.** vines (woody) **9.** wild
grape

liar . . . **5.** cheat **6.** fibber **7.** Ananias,
wernard (obs) **8.** deceiver, fabulist,
perjurer **12.** prevaricator

Lias system . . . **8.** Jurassic

libation . . . **5.** drink **8.** oblation, offering,
potation

libel . . . **4.** bill **6.** defame **7.** lampoon,
request, slander **8.** circular (obs),
handbill, roorback **10.** defamation
11. certificate, declaration
12. supplication

liberal . . . **4.** free, Whig **5.** ample,
frank **7.** copious, profuse **8.** eclectic,
generous **9.** bountiful, extensive,
plentiful **10.** hospitable, munificent
11. broad-minded, magnanimous
12. uncontrolled

liberate . . . **4.** flee, free **5.** loose **6.** redeem
7. deliver, manumit, release **8.** separate,
unfetter **9.** disengage **10.** emancipate

Liberia . . .

capital . . **8.** Monrovia
city . . **8.** Buchanan **10.** Greenville
gulf . . **5.** Sidra
language . . **3.** Kru **7.** English
people . . **3.** Vai (Vei)

libertine . . . **4.** rake, roué

liberty . . . **4.** ease, free **5.** leave
7. freedom, license **9.** exemption,
privilege **10.** permission **11.** opportunity

librarian . . . **7.** bookman **10.** bibliosoph,
bibliothec **13.** bibliothecary

Libya, Africa . . .
astronomy . . **4.** Mars (portion)
capital . . **7.** Tripoli **8.** Benghazi
district . . **6.** Fezzan **9.** Cyrenaica
12. Tripolitania
language . . **7.** Hamitic
oasis (saline) . . **6.** Sebkha (Sebka)
people . . **5.** Arabs
sea . . **13.** Mediterranean

Libya, Gr (pert to) . . .
children . . **5.** Belus **6.** Agenor
heroine of . . **5.** Libya
husband . . **8.** Poseidon

license . . . **5.** right **6.** bandon, permit
7. dismiss, freedom, liberty **8.** sanction
9. approbate, authority, authorize,
privilege **10.** permission **11.** lawlessness
13. authorization

licentious . . . **3.** lax **4.** lewd **5.** loose
7. immoral, lawless **9.** debauched,
dissolute **10.** lascivious, profligate
12. uncontrolled, unrestrained

licet . . . **6.** lawful **7.** granted **12.** it is
conceded

lichens (pert to) . . .
abounding in . . **9.** lichenose
derivative . . **4.** moss **5.** usnic **6.** litmus
genus . . **5.** Usnea **7.** Evernia
study of . . **11.** lichenology

licit . . . **3.** sue **4.** just **5.** legal **6.** lawful
9. permitted

lick . . . **3.** lap, win **4.** flog, whip **5.** lap
up, taste **6.** baffle, defeat, thrash
7. conquer **8.** overcome, vanquish

licorice . . . **5.** abrin **9.** jequirity

licorice-flavored liqueur . . . **7.** sambuca

lid . . . **3.** cap, hat **4.** bred, case,
roof **5.** cover **6.** eyelid **7.** stopper
9. operculum

lid, put on the . . . **3.** end **6.** hush up
7. license **8.** complete, suppress

lie . . . **3.** fib **4.** rest **7.** falsify, falsity,
recline, untruth **9.** deception, falsehood,
mendacity **10.** equivocate
13. prevarication

lie (pert to) . . .
at ease . . **4.** loll **5.** droop **6.** dangle
face down . . **7.** pronate
hidden, in ambush . . **4.** lurk, plot **6.** in
wait **9.** insidiate **11.** concealment
in warmth . . **4.** bask **9.** luxuriate
low . . **6.** abased **9.** prostrate
prostrate . . **4.** flat **5.** creep **6.** grovel

Liebestraum composer . . . **5.** Liszt

Liechtenstein, Europe . . .
capital . . **5.** Vaduz
government . . **12.** principality
language . . **6.** German
religion . . **8.** Catholic

lief (anc) . . . **4.** dear, fain, glad **7.** willing

8. disposed 9. agreeably, favorably

lieutenant . . . 6. deputy 10. substitute
11. locum tenens

life . . . 3. vie 4. bios 5. being 6. always,
energy, spirit 8. vitality, vivacity
9. animation, existence

life (pert to) . . .
after death . . 8. Olam-haba
animal . . 4. bios 5. biota (flora, fauna)
biology . . 4. bios
comb form . . 3. bio
giving . . 9. animative 11. procreative
god of . . 6. Faunus
insurance . . 7. tontine
jacket (sl) . . 7. Mae West
later, older . . 8. autumnal
lifelike . . 5. alike, vital 6. biotic 9. realistic
plant . . 4. bios 5. biota
principle . . 5. atman, prana, tenet 6. spirit
prolonger . . 6. elixir
science of . . 7. anatomy, biology, zoology
12. paleontology
sea . . 5. coral 8. plankton
staff of . . 5. bread
without . . 4. dead 5. azoic 8. lifeless
9. inanimate

lifeless . . . 4. abio (comb form), dead, dull,
flat 5. amort, azoic, heavy, inert, vapid
6. jejune, torpid 8. inactive, listless
9. bloodless, exanimate, inanimate,
powerless, tasteless 10. lackluster,
spiritless, unanimated

lifetime . . . 3. age, day, eon (aeon)
6. always 8. duration 10. generation

lift . . . 3. aid, pry 4. jack, perk 5. boost,
exalt, heave, hoist, raise, steal,
theft 6. puff up, thrill 7. derrick,
elevate, improve, inspire 8. elevator
11. inspiration

lifting device . . . 4. jack, pump 5. crane,
davit, lever, tongs 7. capstan, derrick,
erector 8. elevator, heighten, windlass

lifting muscle . . . 7. erector, levator

ligament . . . 4. bond, cord 6. tendon
7. bandage

ligan, lagan . . . 6. debris, jetsam
7. flotsam

ligature . . . 3. tie 4. band, bond, cord, note
6. amulet, binder, taenia 7. bandage

light . . . 3. arc, gay, sun 4. dawn,
easy, glim, lamp, lume, mild, pale,
soft 5. flare, flood, klieg, laser, taper
6. alight, aspect, blonde, bright,
candle, gentle, ignite, illume, medium,
window 7. cresset, fragile, glimmer,
glowing, trivial 8. buoyancy, daylight,
delicate, illumine, lambency, radiance,
trifling 9. effulgent 10. brightness,
luminosity, weightless 11. information
12. incandescent

light (pert to) . . .
apparatus . . 9. holophote
circle . . 4. halo, nimb 6. corona, nimbus
7. aureola, aureole
cloud . . 6. nimbus
coating . . 4. film
footed . . 4. fast 5. agile
globe . . 4. bulb
god . . 6. Balder (Baldr)
handed . . 4. deft
headed . . 5. dizzy 6. fickle 9. beeheaded

image . . 8. spectrum
leading . . 8. luminary
reflector . . 4. lens 6. mirror
refractor . . 5. prism
science . . 6. optics
source . . 3. sun
touch . . 3. dab
unit . . 3. lux, pyr 4. phot, watt 5. lumen
6. carcel, Hefner
without . . 4. dark 7. aphotic, obscure
8. starless 9. pitch-dark 10. caliginous
yellow . . 5. amber

light and airy . . . 7. tenuous 8. delicate,
ethereal

light and quick . . . 6. nimble, volent

light dress fabric . . . 6. merino
8. cashmere 9. bombazine, paramatta
(parramatta)

lighten . . . 4. ease 5. allay, cheer, clear
6. reduce 7. gladden, relieve 8. brighten,
illumine, jettison 9. alleviate, disburden
10. illuminate

lighter . . . see also *light* 4. scow 5. barge
7. gabbard, igniter, pontoon 8. chopboat
(Chin)

lighthearted . . . 3. gay 6. upbeat
7. buoyant 8. carefree, cheerful, jubilant
9. vivacious

Light Horse Harry . . . 3. Lee (Gen Henry
Lee)

lighthouse . . . 5. tower 6. beacon, pharos
7. seamark 10. watchtower

lightness . . . 6. gaiety, levity 8. airiness,
buoyancy, sobriety 9. flippancy,
frivolity, giddiness 10. fickleness,
triviality, volatility, wantonness
11. flightiness, inconstancy, instability
12. unsteadiness 14. weightlessness
15. thoughtlessness

lightning . . . 4. lait 5. flash, levin 6. stroke
8. flashing 9. discharge

lightning (pert to) . . .
bug . . 6. beetle 7. firefly
discharge . . 4. bolt 11. thunderbolt
form . . 4. fork 5. chain, sheet
reference to . . 8. fulgural
rod . . 8. arrester
stone . . 9. fulgurite
war . . 10. blitzkrieg

lightsome . . . 3. gay 4. airy 5. agile, clear,
light, lucid, merry 6. fickle, nimble
7. lighted 8. cheerful, cheering, graceful,
luminous, unsteady 9. frivolous
12. lighthearted

lights out . . . 4. taps

ligneous . . . 5. woody 6. wooden, xyloid
8. firewood

lignite . . . 4. coal

like . . . 2. as 4. copy, love 5. enjoy, equal,
liken, savor 6. admire, desire 7. similar
10. comparable 11. counterpart,
homogeneous

like (pert to) . . .
bone . . 6. osteal
fern . . 8. frondose, frondous
gland . . 7. adenose
gold . . 7. aureate
house, dome . . 5. domal
kneecap . . 7. rotular 10. rotuliform
sea lion . . 7. otarian, otarine
suffix . . 2. ar, ic 3. ine, oid, ose

likeable, likable . . . 6. genial 8. charming, pleasant
likelihood . . . 8. prospect 10. good chance 11. possibility, probability 14. apparently true
likely . . . 3. apt, fit 5. prone 6. comely 8. credible, feasible, probable, suitable 9. promising 11. verisimilar
likeness . . . 4. copy, icon, twin 5. clone, guise, image 6. effigy, statue 7. parable, picture, replica 8. parallel, portrait 9. imitation, semblance 10. comparison, photograph, similarity 11. counterfeit 12. reproduction 14. representation
likewise . . . 3. too 4. also 5. ditto 8. moreover 11. furthermore
liking . . . 4. like, love, lust 5. fancy 6. comely 7. delight 8. pleasing 10. preference 12. predilection
lilac . . . 5. lilas, mauve 6. purple 7. syringa
lilac throat . . . 11. hummingbird
Lilliputian . . . 4. tiny 5. dwarf, minim 6. midget 7. dwarfed 10. diminutive
lilt . . . 3. air 4. song, tune 5. swing 6. poetic, rhythm 7. rejoice
lily . . . 2. ti 3. lis 4. aloe, ixia, sego 5. calla, lotus, onion, water, wokas (wocas), yucca 6. Allium, Nuphar 8. daffodil, mariposa, martagon, soaproot 9. narcissus
lily (pert to) . . .
family, genus . . 4. aloe 6. Tulipa 7. Bessera 9. Liliaceae 10. Hyacinthus
grass . . 10. cuckoopint
iron . . 7. harpoon
of France . . 10. fleur-de-lis
shaped . . 7. crinoid 9. crinoidal
water . . 8. Castalia, Nymphaea
lily of the valley (pert to) . . .
bud . . 3. pip
Cape Cod . . 13. barney-clapper
English . . 6. mugget
family . . 15. Convallariaceae
liliaceous plant . . 5. yucca
shrub . . 10. fetterbush
tree . . 6. sorrel
lima bean disease . . . 6. mildew 9. yeast spot
liman . . . 5. marsh 6. lagoon
limb . . . 3. arm, fin, imp, leg 4. wing 5. bough, scamp 6. branch, member 7. flipper 9. anaclasis
limber . . . 4. limp, weak 5. agile, lithe, loose 6. flabby, pliant, supple 7. flaccid, lissome 8. flexible, yielding
limbo . . . 4. hell, jail 6. prison 9. purgatory
limbs, absence of . . . 6. amelia 7. acolous
lime . . . 4. calx 5. color, fruit 8. chlorine, fumigant 9. deodorant, quicklime 11. green-yellow 12. linden yellow
limen . . . 9. threshold
limestone . . . 4. calp, malm 5. chalk 6. marble, oolite 8. pisolite
lime tree . . . 6. linden, tupelo
limey . . . 6. sailor 7. soldier
limit . . . 3. end, fix, ori (comb form) 4. term 5. allot, bourn 6. summit 7. confine 8. boundary, capacity, restrain, restrict, terminal 11. restriction, termination 12. consummation
limited . . . 3. few 5. local, scant 6. finite,

narrow, scanty 7. bounded, topical 8. confined, reserved 9. astricted, parochial 10. restricted 11. conditional, topopolitan 13. circumscribed
limiting . . . 7. hedging 10. qualifying, relational 11. restraining, restricting, restrictive
limn . . . 4. draw 5. paint 6. depict 7. portray 8. decorate 9. delineate 10. illuminate
limp . . . 3. hop, lax 4. halt, soft, thin, weak 5. loose 6. flabby, limber 7. flaccid 8. drooping, flexible 9. inelastic 13. unsubstantial
limpid . . . 4. pure 5. lucid 6. bright 7. crystal 8. pellucid 11. translucent, transparent 12. intelligible
Lincoln, Abraham (pert to) . . .
assassin . . 15. John Wilkes Booth
birthplace . . 8. Kentucky (1809)
debater . . 7. Douglas (Stephen A)
dog . . 4. Fido
mother . . 10. Nancy Hanks
Secy of State . . 6. Seward
Secy of War . . 7. Stanton
son . . 10. Robert Todd
wife . . 8. Mary Todd
Lincoln (pert to) . . .
color . . 9. Carthamus 11. yellow-green
sheep (breed) . . 7. English
Lindbergh, Charles A (pert to) . . .
birthplace . . 7. Detroit (1902)
flight field . . 9. Roosevelt (LI)
flight to (1927) . . 5. Paris (1st)
retreat . . 10. Illiec Isle (Fr)
wife . . 10. Anne Morrow
linden . . . 3. lin 4. lime, teil 5. Tilia
line . . . 3. row 4. arow, axis, cant, ceil, clew, cord, face, mark, race, rail, rein, rule, seam, side 5. agone, align, raphe, ridge, route, stria, track 6. crease, isobar, policy, series, streak, stripe 7. engrave, outline 8. boundary, vocation, wainscot 9. delineate
line (pert to) . . .
adjusting . . 9. alinement
central . . 4. axis
comb form . . 4. lino
conceptual, geological . . 6. agonic, isotac, tropic 7. equator 8. isothere, isotherm, latitude, meridian 9. longitude
equidistant . . 8. parallel
fine (type) . . 5. leger, serif
fishing . . 5. snell 7. ratline (ratlin)
imaginary . . 7. equator, Maginot
mathematics . . 4. sine 5. agone 6. secant 7. tangent
measure . . 3. gry 4. rule
meteoric . . 6. isobar
nautical . . 6. earing 7. halyard, hawsing
poetic . . 5. stich, verse
racing . . 4. wire
raised . . 4. weal, welt 5. ridge
selling . . 11. merchandise
soldiers . . 4. file, rank 6. cordon
transport . . 5. stage 7. carrier 8. carriage
type . . 5. agate, serif
up, lineup . . 4. plan 5. align 6. muster 7. arrange 8. schedule 9. formation 11. arrangement, parallelize
lineage . . . 3. kin 4. race 5. birth, blood,

stock, tribe **6.** family, strain **7.** descent
8. pedigree **9.** offspring **10.** extraction,
progenitor

lineal ... **6.** racial **10.** continuous,
delineated **12.** genealogical

lineman ... **3.** end **5.** guard **6.** center,
tackle **7.** wireman **11.** electrician

linen ... **4.** crea, duck, lawn, lint **5.** crash,
gulix, inkle (tape), toile **6.** barras,
damask, dowlas, napery, sheets
7. cambric, Holland, lockram

ling ... **4.** fish, hake **5.** heath **6.** burbot
7. eelpout, Gidadae, heather **8.** chestnut

linger ... **3.** lag **4.** drag, idle, wait
5. dally, defer, delay, dwell, hover,
tarry **6.** dawdle, go slow, loiter, remain
8. continue, hesitate **13.** procrastinate

lingerie ... **9.** underwear **11.** underthings
14. unmentionables

lingering ... **5.** delay **7.** chronic **8.** dilatory,
slowness **10.** protracted

lingo ... **4.** cant **6.** jargon, lingua, patois,
patter, tongue **8.** language

lingua ... **5.** lingo **6.** jargon, tongue
11. hypopharynx

lingual ... **7.** glossal **9.** lingulate
10. linguiform, tonguelike

linguistics ... **6.** syntax **7.** grammar
8. language **9.** phonology, semantics
10. lexicology

link ... **3.** tie **4.** bond, join, loop, yoke
5. annex, nexus, torch, unite **6.** couple,
member, relate **7.** connect, liaison,
passage **8.** catenate **12.** intermediary

linkage ... **5.** tie-up, union **6.** hookup
7. joinder, joining **8.** junction
11. conjunction

linking ... **7.** liaison **9.** annectent

links in a chain ... **7.** hundred

linseed ... **8.** flaxseed

lion ... **3.** cat, cub, leo **4.** puma **5.** simba
6. cougar, Lionel, lionet **8.** Felis leo
9. celebrity **12.** King of Beasts

Lion (pert to) ...
England .. **8.** heraldry
God .. **3.** Ali
Lucerne .. **11.** Switzerland (Sculpture)
St Mark .. **6.** Venice (winged)
the North .. **6.** Sweden (King Adolphus)

lionlike ... **6.** feline **7.** catlike, leonine

lip ... **3.** jib, rim **4.** edge, kiss, talk **5.** cheil,
words **6.** flange, labium, labrum, speech
7. cheilos **8.** labellum **10.** mouthpiece
12. impertinence

lip (pert to) ...
comb form .. **5.** chilo, labio
formed .. **6.** labial
inflammation .. **9.** cheilitis
ornament .. **6.** labret
service .. **9.** hypocrisy **10.** sanctimony
12. unctuousness
surgery .. **9.** chilotomy **11.** chiloplasty
tumor .. **7.** chiloma

lipped ... **6.** labial **7.** labiate

liquefy ... **4.** fuse, melt, thaw **6.** reduce
8. dissolve, fluidify **10.** deliquesce

liqueur ... **4.** anis, ouzo **5.** crème,
noyau, sirup **6.** cognac, genepi,
kummel, Pernod **7.** cordial, curaçao,
ratafia **8.** absinthe, anisette, Drambuie
9. Cointreau **11.** Benedictine

liquid ... **5.** clear, fluid **6.** watery **7.** flowing
8. beverage, manifest, not solid

liquid (pert to) ...
assets .. **4.** cash **5.** money **9.** resources
chemical .. **7.** acetone **8.** furfural
inflammable .. **3.** gas **5.** ether **7.** alcohol
8. gasoline
oily .. **5.** olein **7.** aniline, picamar
soap .. **6.** napalm
thick .. **3.** tar **4.** dope **5.** syrup (sirup)
weak .. **5.** blash

liquidate ... **4.** kill **6.** depose, pay
off, settle **8.** amortize **9.** discharge
11. exterminate

liquor ... **3.** ale, dew, gin, rum, rye **4.** beer,
brew, grog, lush, sake, wine **5.** hooch,
kefir, punch, stout, vodka **6.** arrack
(arak), arrope, elixir, whisky (whiskey)
8. cocktail, highball **9.** applejack,
moonshine **10.** chasse-café

liquor container ... **3.** keg **5.** flask
6. barrel, bottle **8.** cellaret, decanter

liquor maker ... **6.** abkari (Ind), brewer
7. vintner **9.** distiller

liquor server ... **6.** barman **7.** barmaid,
skinker (anc), tapster

liquor shop ... **3.** bar **6.** saloon, tavern
7. barroom, cabaret, shebeen (Scot),
taproom **8.** alehouse **9.** groghouse,
honky-tonk **11.** rathskeller (ratskeller)

liripipe, liripoop (Hist) ... **4.** hood **5.** scarf
6. dotard, tippet

lissom ... **5.** layer **7.** stratum **8.** platform
12. strand of rope

lissome ... **5.** agile, lithe **6.** limber,
nimble, supple **7.** willowy **8.** flexible

list ... **3.** tip **4.** edge, file, roll, rota, rote
5. index, limit, panel, table **6.** careen,
edging, enlist, record, roster, stripe
7. catalog, incline **8.** calendar, classify,
manifest, register, schedule, tabulate
9. catalogue, enclosure, inventory,
repertory **10.** repertoire **11.** enumeration

list (pert to) ...
actors .. **4.** cast
competitors .. **5.** entry, slate
foods .. **4.** menu **5.** carte
investments .. **9.** portfolio
memoranda .. **5.** scrip
officers .. **6.** roster
references .. **5.** index

listen ... **3.** ear **4.** hear, heed **6.** attend
7. give ear, hearken (harken) **8.** overhear
9. eavesdrop

listening ... **7.** audient **9.** attentive

listing ... **4.** list **6.** strips **7.** selvage
10. enlistment, enrollment

listless ... **4.** dull **6.** abject, drowsy,
moping, supine **7.** languid **8.** careless,
heedless, sluggish **9.** apathetic
10. spiritless **11.** unconcerned
13. uninteresting

litchi nut ... **8.** rambutan

literary ... **6.** versed **8.** lettered **9.** classical
11. book-learned

literary (pert to) ...
composition .. **5.** cento, essay, opera
8. rhetoric
criticism .. **9.** epicrisis
drudge .. **4.** grub, hack
extracts .. **9.** anthology

fragments . . **3.** ana **5.** notes **8.** analecta, analects
laws . . **9.** copyright
piracy . . **10.** plagiarism
selection . . **7.** excerpt
style . . **5.** prose **6.** purism **8.** pedantic
literature . . . **4.** book, epic, Veda **5.** drama, lyric, novel **6.** ballad, poetry **7.** fiction, writing **10.** nonfiction **13.** belles-lettres
lithe . . . **4.** slim **6.** limber, supple, svelte **7.** lissome, slender **8.** flexible
Lithuania . . .
capital . . **5.** Vilna (Vilnius) **6.** Kaunas (Kovno)
Jew . . **6.** Litvak
people . . **5.** Balts, Letts **6.** Aestii
port . . **8.** Klaipeda (Memel)
river . . **6.** Niemen
litigant . . . **6.** suitor **9.** defendant, disputant, litigator, plaintiff
litigation . . . **4.** suit **7.** contest, dispute, lawsuit **10.** contention, discussion
litigious . . . **10.** disputable **11.** belligerent, contentious
litten . . . **7.** lighted **8.** cemetery **10.** churchyard
litter . . . **3.** bed, hay **4.** bier, mess **5.** couch, dooly (doolie), mulch, straw, young **6.** coffin, jumble **7.** clutter, rubbish **9.** palanquin, stretcher
litter of pigs . . . **6.** farrow
little . . . **3.** sma, wee **4.** puny, tiny, weak **5.** brief, petit, petty, scant, short, small **6.** dapper, petite, slight **7.** not much **8.** trifling **9.** niggardly **11.** unimportant **12.** narrow-minded **14.** inconsiderable
little (pert to) . . .
bethel . . **6.** chapel (seaman's), church
by little . . **6.** slowly **7.** peu à peu **9.** piecemeal, poco a poco
comb form . . **5.** steno
devil . . **3.** imp **4.** minx **5.** rogue **7.** ruffian **13.** mischief-maker
fellow . . **6.** shaver
finger, toe . . **7.** minimus
flag . . **9.** banderole
music term . . **4.** poco
ring . . **7.** annulet
Little Rhody . . . **11.** Rhode Island
Little Women, author . . . **6.** Alcott (Louisa)
littoral . . . **4.** zone (marine) **5.** shore **7.** coastal **9.** bordering
liturgical . . . **10.** ceremonial **11.** ritualistic
liturgy . . . **4.** rite **6.** ritual **8.** ceremony **14.** consuetudinary
live . . . **5.** dwell, exist **6.** reside **7.** breathe **8.** continue, have life
live (pert to) . . .
by sponging . . **5.** cadge
by stratagems . . **5.** shark
by wits . . **5.** cheat **7.** deceive, falsify **13.** Machiavellize
earlier . . **8.** pre-exist
in . . **7.** inhabit
in tents . . **5.** nomad **7.** scenite
in the country . . **9.** rusticate
live . . . **5.** alert, alive, vital, vivid **6.** bright, lively, living, virgin (mineral) **7.** charged, not dead **8.** vigorous **9.** energetic **11.** electrified

lively . . . **3.** gay, vif **4.** airy, grig, keen, pert, spry, yare **6.** active, blithe, bright, snappy **7.** animate, buoyant, pungent, tittupy (tittuppy) **8.** spirited **9.** energetic, sprightly, vivacious **10.** enlivening, rebounding **11.** interesting **12.** effervescent
liver (pert to) . . .
comb form . . **6.** hepato
disease . . **9.** cirrhosis, hepatitis
duct . . **4.** bile
pert to . . **5.** hepar **7.** hepatic
resembling . . **8.** hepatoid
Liverpool native . . . **12.** Liverpudlian
liverwort . . . **6.** Riccia **8.** agrimony, hepatica **9.** bryophyte
living . . . **4.** life **5.** alive, being, quick **6.** extant **7.** animate, organic, topical **8.** benefice, existent, lifelike **10.** livelihood **11.** subsistence
living (in, on, near) . . .
currents . . **5.** lotic
ground . . **7.** epigeal
holes . . **11.** latebricole
leaves . . **13.** phyllophagous
oxygen . . **7.** aerobic
plane (same) . . **8.** coplanar
poverty . . **11.** necessitous
river bank . . **9.** riparious
rivers, streams . . **9.** rheophile
seas (deep) . . **8.** bathybic
shores . . **8.** littoral
solitude, seclusion . . **10.** eremitical **11.** eremiticism
tents . . **7.** scenite
together . . **11.** contubernal
living (pert to) . . .
again . . **6.** Buddha **7.** revived **8.** Hutukhtu **9.** redivivus
being . . **5.** wight **6.** animal **8.** organism
capable of . . **6.** viable
dull . . **10.** vegetation
individual . . **4.** bion
near the ground . . **7.** epigeal
together . . **8.** intimate **11.** contubernal (contubernial)
lixivium . . . **3.** lye **6.** bleach **8.** cleanser
lizard . . . **3.** dab, eft **4.** adda, gila, newt, seps, uran **5.** agama, anoli, gecko, skink, varan **6.** dragon, hardim, iguana, moloch **7.** monitor, saurian, tuatera **8.** basilisk **9.** chameleon **10.** chuckwalla, salamander
llama . . . **6.** alpaca, vicuna **7.** guanaco
load . . . **3.** jag **4.** fill, lade, onus **5.** cargo **6.** burden, charge, weight **7.** fraught, freight, oppress, prepare **8.** contents, encumber **10.** imposition **11.** encumbrance
loaded . . . **5.** drunk, flush, laden, ready **7.** charged, fraught **8.** burdened, weighted **10.** in the chips
loader of vessels . . . **9.** stevedore
loadstone, lodestone . . . **6.** magnet **8.** terrella **9.** magnetite
loaf . . . **4.** idle, lump **5.** bread **6.** loiter, lounge **9.** Eucharist
loafer . . . **5.** idler **6.** beggar **7.** lounger **8.** vagabond
loam . . . **3.** rab **4.** clay, lime, malm, silt, soil **5.** chalk, loess, regur

loan ... **4.** lend **6.** borrow **7.** advance
10. provisions **13.** accommodation
loath ... **6.** averse **7.** hostile **9.** disliking,
reluctant, unwilling
loathe ... **4.** hate **5.** abhor **6.** detest
7. despise, dislike **9.** abominate
loathsome ... **4.** foul, vile **5.** nasty
6. odious **7.** cloying, hateful
9. abhorrent, offensive, repellant
10. abominable, disgusting
lob ... **3.** box, cop **4.** step, till, toss, vein
5. stair, throw **7.** lugworm, pollack
9. chandelle
lobby ... **4.** hall, room **5.** foyer
8. anteroom, corridor, coulisse
9. enclosure, vestibule **10.** wirepuller
13. pressure group
lobe ... **5.** alula **6.** earlap, lappet, lobule
7. pendant
lobster (pert to) ...
claw .. **5.** chela **6.** nipper, pincer
eggs .. **3.** roe **5.** coral
French .. **6.** homard
genus .. **7.** Homarus, Macrura
8. Nephrops
part .. **6.** thorax
tail .. **6.** telson
trap .. **3.** pot **4.** corf **5.** creel **6.** bow
net
local ... **7.** edaphic, topical **8.** regional
9. parochial **10.** epichorial (epichoric)
13. autochthonous
local court ... **5.** gemot (gemote)
locale ... **4.** site **5.** place, scene, venue
locality ... **4.** area, spot **5.** place, situs
7. endemic, habitat **8.** position
locate ... **4.** find, spot **6.** settle **7.** situate
9. establish
locatio ... **7.** leasing, letting
location ... **4.** seat, site, spot **5.** locus,
place, situs **6.** ubiety **7.** habitat **8.** district
9. situation **12.** neighborhood
locator of forest fires ... **7.** alidade
loch ... **3.** bay **4.** lake, pond **5.** inlet,
lough
lock ... **4.** bolt, hasp, hold **5.** Gatun,
latch **6.** cotter, detent, fasten, fetter
8. fastener **9.** floodgate
lockjaw ... **7.** tetanus, trismus
11. ankylostoma
lockman ... **8.** summoner (Isle of Man)
11. executioner
lock of hair ... **4.** curl **5.** tress **6.** berger
7. daglock, ringlet **8.** lovelock, spit
curl
lockup ... **3.** jug **4.** jail **5.** clink **6.** cooler
8. hoosegow (hoosgow) **9.** calaboose
loco ... **3.** mad **4.** daft **5.** craze, crazy
6. crazed **7.** disease **10.** moonstruck
15. non compos mentis
locomotion ... **6.** lation (Astrol), moving,
travel **7.** transit **8.** progress
locomotive ... **3.** hog **5.** dolly, mogul
6. diesel, dinkey, engine, mikado **9.** iron
horse
locomotive cowcatcher ... **5.** pilot
locus ... **4.** area, drug, site **5.** place
8. locality
locus (pert to) ...
in quo .. **5.** where **12.** place in which
sigilli .. **14.** place of the seal

locust ... **4.** weta **6.** beetle, cicada,
cicala, kowhai **7.** Locusta **9.** wetapunga
11. grasshopper
locust (pert to) ...
berry .. **5.** drupe **9.** glamberry
bird .. **4.** dial **7.** grackle **8.** starling
10. white stork
like .. **6.** mantis
plant .. **5.** senna
sound .. **7.** stridor **10.** stridulate
tree .. **5.** carob, honey **6.** acacia
lode ... **3.** vug (vugg) **4.** path, road,
vein **5.** canal, drain, ledge **6.** course
7. deposit **8.** waterway
lodestar ... **8.** cynosure, polestar
11. guiding star
lodestone, loadstone ... **6.** magnet
8. terrella **9.** magnetite
lodge ... **3.** hut, lie **4.** camp, tent
5. cabin, hovel **6.** billet, encamp, reside
7. deposit, quarter **11.** brotherhood
lodge doorkeeper ... **5.** tiler
lodging ... **3.** inn **4.** gite, room **5.** abode,
hotel, roost **6.** billet, harbor (harbour),
tavern **8.** barracks, dwelling, hostelry,
quarters **9.** dormitory, harborage
(harbourage) **10.** habitation
loess ... **4.** loam, silt, soil
lof ... **6.** praise **7.** measure
loft ... **3.** bin **4.** balk **5.** attic
loftiness ... **6.** height **7.** dignity
8. eminence **9.** eloquence
11. distinction, magnanimity
Lofting's doctor ... **8.** Dolittle
lofty ... **4.** high, tall **5.** proud **6.** aerial,
Alpine, Andean **7.** eminent, exalted,
haughty, stately, sublime **8.** arrogant,
elevated, eloquent, majestic, towering
9. dignified **11.** magisterial,
magnanimous **13.** distinguished
lofty place ... **4.** peak **5.** aerie, eyrie
(eyry) **6.** summit **8.** eminence, pinnacle
log ... **4.** birl, slab **5.** diary **6.** record
8. firewood, mountain, puncheon,
register **11.** speedometer
log (pert to) ...
cock .. **10.** woodpecker
gin .. **6.** jammer
hauler (sled) .. **4.** tode
implement .. **6.** nigger, peavey (peavy),
rosser
measure .. **7.** scalage
noser .. **6.** sniper
rolling .. **7.** birling
section .. **5.** spalt
support .. **3.** nog
logarithmic terms ... **3.** bel **4.** base
5. power **8.** mantissa **14.** characteristic
logarithm inventor ... **6.** Napier
loge ... **3.** box **5.** booth, stall
loggerhead ... **4.** tool **6.** turtle **7.** fathead
8. bonehead, numskull **9.** blockhead
10. thickskull
loggerheads, be at ... **8.** disagree
loggia ... **7.** gallery
logging (pert to) ...
boots .. **4.** pacs
rock .. **6.** loggan
sled .. **4.** tode **7.** travois (travoise)
wheels .. **7.** katydid
logic ... **9.** reasoning **13.** argumentation

logic (pert to)...
fallacy.. **6.** idolum
induction.. **7.** epagoge
proposition.. **5.** lemma **7.** ferison
  9. enthymeme, obvertend
specious.. **7.** sophism
term.. **5.** Darii, Ferio **8.** Celarent
logical... **4.** sane **5.** sound, valid
  8. coherent, credible, rational
  9. plausible **10.** consistent, reasonable
logician... **8.** reasoner
logograph... **5.** rebus **6.** riddle **7.** anagram
  8. logogram
logy... **4.** dull **6.** drowsy **8.** sluggish
Lohengrin (pert to)...
character.. **4.** Elsa **8.** Parsifal
composer.. **6.** Wagner (1850)
Knight.. **15.** Knight of the Swan
loin (pert to)...
beef.. **10.** tenderloin
mutton.. **4.** rack **5.** chump
pork.. **7.** griskin
loincloth... **5.** dhoti, pagne **7.** G-string
  11. breechcloth
loir... **8.** dormouse
Loire, France...
Dept capital.. **12.** Saint Etienne
river's old name.. **5.** Liger
town.. **6.** Nantes
tributary.. **5.** Indre
loiter... **3.** lag **5.** dally, delay, tarry
  6. dawdle, linger **7.** saunter
loiterer... **4.** slug **5.** drone, idler **6.** lagger
  7. dawdler, laggard **8.** sluggard
Loki (pert to)...
god.. **7.** Discord **8.** Mischief
wife.. **5.** Sigyn
loll... **4.** hang **5.** droop **6.** dangle,
  frowst (froust), lounge, repose, sprawl
  7. recline
loma, lomita... **4.** hill
Lombard (pert to)...
ancient.. **6.** cannon
historic.. **4.** bank, loan
King.. **6.** Alboin (legend)
school.. **11.** Renaissance
street.. **6.** London
Lombardy province... **4.** Como
lomboy... **8.** Java plum
lomilomi (Haw)... **3.** rub **7.** massage,
  shampoo
London, England...
art gallery.. **4.** Tate
bank.. **27.** Old Lady of Threadneedle
  Street
borough.. **6.** Ealing **11.** Westminster
bridge.. **5.** Tower **6.** London **7.** Chelsea
  8. Waterloo
bridle path.. **9.** Rotten Row
brown.. **9.** carbuncle
cathedral.. **7.** St Paul's
clock.. **6.** Big Ben
club (Whigs).. **6.** Kit-Kat
concert hall.. **11.** Royal Albert
district.. **3.** Kew **7.** Chelsea, Mayfair
  8. Vauxhall **9.** Southwark
  10. Bloomsbury, Kensington,
  Marylebone
hawker.. **6.** coster
monument (Guildhall).. **3.** Gog **5.** Magog
Opera Company.. **12.** Sadler's Wells

palace.. **10.** Buckingham
park.. **4.** Hyde **7.** Regent's
  10. Kensington
porter.. **6.** George
press.. **11.** Fleet Street
prison.. **7.** Newgate **9.** Bridewell
quarter.. **8.** Vauxhall
roisterer (Hist).. **3.** mum
Roman name.. **6.** Agusta
square.. **9.** Trafalgar
stables.. **4.** mews
stock exchange.. **17.** Throgmorton Street
street.. **5.** Fleet **6.** Strand **8.** Pall Mall
  9. Cheapside, Whitehall **10.** Piccadilly
  11. Throgmorton **12.** Threadneedle
subway.. **4.** tube **11.** underground
train station.. **6.** Euston **8.** Victoria,
  Waterloo **9.** St Pancras **10.** King's
  Cross, Paddington
Londoner... **7.** Cockney
Londres... **5.** cigar
lone... **3.** one **5.** alone **6.** lonely, single
  7. forlorn **8.** solitary **9.** unmarried
  12. unfrequented
loneliness... **8.** loneness, solitude
  9. aloneness, dejection, isolation
  10. depression, desolation
  12. lonesomeness
lonely... **4.** lorn **6.** dreary **8.** desolate,
  lonesome, secluded, solitary
  10. friendless **11.** sequestered
  12. unfrequented
Lone Star State... **5.** Texas
long... **3.** yen **4.** pine **5.** crave, wordy,
  yearn **6.** aspire, prolix, thirst **7.** lengthy,
  tedious **8.** tiresome **9.** prolonged,
  wearisome **10.** protracted
long (pert to)...
ago, since.. **3.** eld **4.** yore
beard.. **9.** graybeard **10.** bellarmine
  (jug)
discourse, speech.. **6.** screed, tirade
  7. descant **9.** philippic, rigmarole
dog.. **9.** dachshund, greyhound
dozen.. **8.** thirteen
established.. **8.** habitual **10.** inveterate
  11. traditional
for.. **4.** hope, pine **5.** covet, crave
horn.. **6.** cattle (Tex)
inlet.. **3.** ria
journey.. **4.** trek **7.** odyssey
jump.. **5.** halmo
letters.. **7.** screeds
life.. **9.** longevity
limbed.. **5.** rangy
lived.. **9.** macrobian
periods.. **4.** ages, eons
scarf.. **4.** sari
suffering.. **7.** patient **10.** forbearing
Tom.. **3.** gun **8.** titmouse
windedness.. **9.** garrulity, prolixity
  13. longiloquence
longing... **3.** yen **6.** desire, pining
  7. craving, wistful **8.** yearning
  9. hankering, nostalgia
longitudinal... **10.** euthytatic (stress),
  lengthwise
longshoreman... **6.** docker, loader,
  lumper, stower **9.** stevedore
  10. roustabout
loo... **3.** pam **4.** game

look . . . 3. con, ken, pry, see 4. haze,
heed, leer, peep, scry, seek, seem
5. point, stare, watch 6. appear, expect
7. examine, inspect, observe 8. indicate,
perceive 9. search for

look (pert to) . . .
after . . 4. tend 5. serve 6. follow 7. care
for 9. keep vigil, supervise
at . . 3. eye 4. face, scan, upon 6. regard
7. examine
back . . 6. recall 7. retrace 8. remember
9. recollect 10. call to mind
down upon . . 4. leer, snub 5. fleer,
gloat 7. askance, despise
forward to . . 5. await 6. expect 7. foresee
10. anticipate
like . . 8. resemble
obliquely . . 4. skew
slyly . . 4. leer, ogle, peer
sullen . . 5. frown, lower 6. glower
toward . . 4. face
upon . . 2. at 4. deem 6. behold
11. contemplate

lookout . . . 4. view 5. guard, watch
6. conner 7. outlook 9. vigilance

looks . . . 4. cons, face, kens, sees 5. peers,
pores, pries, seeks, seems 6. visage
8. features 9. resembles 10. appearance
11. countenance

loom . . . 3. auk 4. loon, tool 6. appear,
puffin, vessel, weaver 7. machine
9. guillemot, implement 10. receptacle

loom part . . . 3. lam 4. caam, leaf, sley
5. easer, lathe, lever 6. heddle

loon . . . 5. diver (great Northern), Gavia,
grebe, wabby 10. Gavia immer

loon . . . 4. dolt 6. menial (anc), rascal
7. lunatic

loony . . . 3. mad 4. daft 5. crazy, silly
8. demented

loop . . . 3. eye, tab 4. ansa, clew, kink
5. bight, bride, honda, noose, picot,
sling, wootz (iron) 6. becket 7. folding
8. doubling

loophole . . . 4. hole, plea 5. mense, oilet
6. escape, eyelet, outlet 7. opening,
pretext 8. aperture

loop-shaped . . . 9. fundiform 11. sling-
shaped

loose . . . 3. lax 4. free, limp 5. slack
6. detach, remiss, unlash, wanton,
wobbly 7. escaped, immoral, movable,
relaxed, slacken, unbound, unleash
8. insecure, unstable 9. discharge (gun,
arrow) 10. unconfined 11. improvident
12. loose-moraled 14. unconventional

loose (pert to) . . .
ends . . 4. dags 5. slack 7. tagrags
8. restless
garment . . 5. simar 6. banion, chimar,
kimono 7. zimarra 8. peignoir
jointed . . 5. lanky, rangy 6. wobbly
7. rickety 10. ramshackle

loosely dressed . . . 8. discinct

loosen . . . 4. ease, free, undo 5. pried,
relax 6. soften 7. slacken

looseness . . . 7. laxness 8. limpness
9. slackness, vagueness 10. remissness,
wantonness

loot . . . 3. rob 4. gelt, haul, sack, swag
5. booty 6. spoils 7. pillage, plunder,

seizure 10. contraband

looter . . . 6. rifler, sacker 7. ravager,
spoiler 8. marauder, pillager

lop (off) . . . 3. bob, cut 4. oche, sned,
trim 5. droop, prune 6. cut off, snathe
8. truncate

lopsided . . . 4. alop 7. leaning 8. top-heavy
10. unbalanced 13. unsymmetrical

loquacious . . . 4. glib 6. chatty 7. voluble
9. garrulous, talkative 10. chattering

loquacity . . . 7. fluency, leresis 8. glibness
9. gabbiness, garrulity 12. effusiveness

lord . . . 3. aga (agha), bey, God 4. earl,
peer, rule, tsar 5. liege, ruler, title
6. master, prince 7. Jehovah, marquis,
Saviour 8. governor, nobleman,
seignior, suzerain, viscount
10. proprietor 11. Jesus Christ

Lord (pert to) . . .
Buddhism . . 6. Buddha
Jacobite . . 3. Mar
of Heaven . . 7. Tien Chu (Chin)
of Lords . . 8. Demiurge (Plato) 11. King
of Kings 13. Prince of Peace
of Wisdom . . 5. Mazda 6. Ormazd

Lord have mercy upon us . . . 12. Kyrie
eleison 14. Christe eleison

lordly . . . 6. uppish 8. arrogant, despotic
9. dignified, masterful 10. tyrannical
11. domineering, overbearing

Lord's Prayer . . . 11. Pater Noster

lore . . . 4. lear 6. advice, wisdom
7. counsel 8. learning 9. erudition,
mythology, tradition 12. superstition

lorgnette . . . 7. lorgnon 8. eyeglass
10. opera glass

lorica . . . 5. shell 7. cuirass 11. Breastplate
(St Patrick's)

lorikeet . . . 6. lories, parrot

loris . . . 5. lemur

lorn . . . 6. bereft 7. forlorn 8. deserted,
desolate, forsaken 9. abandoned
11. Godforsaken

loro . . . 10. monk parrot, parrot fish

lose . . . 4. fail, miss, omit 5. leese (obs),
spill, waste 6. forget, mislay, perish
7. forfeit, let slip 8. estrange, squander
9. incur loss 10. wander from

lose (pert to) . . .
balance . . 4. trip 7. stumble
courage . . 7. despair, despond
flesh . . 8. emaciate
freshness . . 4. fade, wilt 6. wither
ground . . 7. regress 8. slow down 9. fall
short 10. fall behind
luster . . 7. tarnish
vigor . . 3. fag, sag 4. fail, flag, pine
6. weaken 7. decline

loser . . . 6. victim 7. also ran 8. defeatee,
underdog

loss . . . 4. ruin, weak 6. damage, injury
9. decrement, detriment, privation
10. forfeiture 11. bereavement,
destruction

loss of . . .
commodities . . 6. ullage
eyebrows, lashes . . 9. madarosis
feeling . . 7. agnosia 10. anesthesia
(anaesthesia)
hair . . 8. alopecia
loved one . . 11. bereavement

memory . . **7.** amnesia
reason . . **7.** amentia
smell . . **7.** anosmia
speech . . **4.** mute **6.** alalia **7.** aphasia
  10. laloplegia
voice . . **7.** aphonia
willpower . . **6.** abulia
lost . . . **4.** asea, gone, lorn **5.** unwon
  6. hidden, ruined, sinful, wasted
  7. mislaid **8.** absorbed, confused,
  defeated, obscured, vanished
  9. abandoned, forfeited, forgotten,
  perplexed, reprobate, subverted
  10. abstracted, bewildered, dissipated,
  overthrown, parted with
  11. preoccupied **13.** irreclaimable,
  irretrievable
lost (pert to) . . .
cause . . **8.** Civil War
color . . **5.** faded, paled
consciousness . . **7.** fainted, swooned
life fluid . . **4.** bled
to view . . **5.** perdu
tribes (ten) . . **10.** Israelites
lot . . . **3.** tax **4.** doom, fate, luck, much,
  plat **5.** share **6.** chance, hazard, studio
  7. destiny, fortune, portion **9.** allotment,
  great deal **13.** apportionment
Lot (pert to) . . .
father . . **5.** Haran
penalty . . **12.** pillar of salt
sister . . **6.** Milcah
son . . **4.** Moab
uncle . . **7.** Abraham
lots, divination by . . . **9.** sortilege
lottery . . . **4.** game **5.** bingo, lotto
  6. chance, raffle **7.** Genoese, grab bag
  11. sweepstakes
lottery prize . . . **4.** tern (from three
  numbers)
lotus . . . **7.** nelumbo **10.** chinquapin
lotus (pert to) . . .
bird . . **6.** jacana
eaters . . **9.** indolents, Lotophagi
  11. daydreamers
tree . . **4.** sadr **6.** jujube, nettle
  9. persimmon
loud . . . **5.** crass, gaudy, noisy, showy
  6. coarse, flashy, garish, vulgar
  7. blatant, booming **8.** vehement
  9. clamorous, turbulent, unrefined
  10. blustering, boisterous, tumultuous,
  vociferous **11.** stentorious
  12. obstreperous
loudmouthed . . . **10.** scurrilous, stentorian
  11. thersitical
Louise de la Ramée (novelist) . . . **5.** Ouida
  (pen name)
Louisiana . . .
bird . . **7.** pelican
capital . . **10.** Baton Rouge
city . . **10.** New Orleans, Shreveport
county . . **6.** parish
dialect . . **6.** Creole
dish (cooked) . . **9.** jumbalaya
flower . . **8.** magnolia
hero . . **6.** De Soto, de Vaca, Pineda
  7. La Salle
native . . **5.** Cajun **6.** Creole, French
  7. Acadian, Spanish
purchased from . . **8.** Napoleon (1803)

river . . **5.** Pearl **6.** Sabine **11.** Mississippi
State admission . . **10.** Eighteenth
State motto . . **22.** Union, Justice,
  Confidence
State nickname . . **7.** Pelican
tradition . . **10.** pirate lore
Louis Viaud (author) . . . **10.** Pierre Loti
  (pen name)
lounge . . . **4.** loaf, loll, sofa **5.** divan
  6. frowst, repose **7.** recline
louse . . . **5.** aphis **6.** cootie, insect, slater
  8. Anoplura, arachnid **9.** Hemiptera,
  scoundrel
lout . . . **3.** oaf **4.** boor, clod, dolt **6.** lubber,
  rustic **7.** bumpkin
loutish . . . **4.** rude **7.** awkward, boorish,
  ill-bred **8.** clownish **11.** countrified
lovable . . . **7.** amiable **8.** adorable,
  charming **9.** desirable, endearing
love . . . **3.** amo, gra, woo **4.** like **5.** adore,
  amore, fancy **6.** liking **7.** charity
  8. fondness, good will **9.** affection
  10. endearment, sweetheart
love (pert to) . . .
affair . . **7.** liaison, romance **10.** flirtation
apple . . **6.** tomato
bird . . **6.** parrot
call . . **3.** coo
feast . . **5.** agape
flower . . **4.** lily
full of . . **4.** dote **6.** doting, erotic
  7. amative **9.** idolizing
god of . . **4.** Amor, Ares, Eros, Kama
  5. Bhaga, Cupid
goddess of . . **5.** Athor, Freya (Freyja),
  Venus **6.** Ishtar **9.** Aphrodite
intrigue . . **5.** amour
knot, token of . . **6.** amoret
meeting . . **5.** tryst **10.** rendezvous
of . . **5.** phile (comb form)
parental . . **6.** storge
potion . . **7.** philter
science . . **9.** erotology
song . . **6.** serena (evening) **8.** madrigal
lover . . . **4.** beau **5.** amant, Romeo
  6. minion **7.** amorist, Don Juan
  8. paramour **9.** enamorato
  10. sweetheart
lover of . . . see also *craze for*
animals . . **10.** zoophilist
beauty . . **8.** aesthete (esthete)
wealth . . **9.** plutocrat
work . . **9.** ergophile
Lover's Leap . . . **10.** Cape Ducato
Lovers' Quarrels . . . **12.** amantium Irae
loving . . . **4.** fond **5.** phile (comb
  form) **6.** ardent, erotic **7.** adoring,
  amative, amatory, amorous, devoted
  8. charming, enamored, romantic
  11. sentimental **12.** affectionate
loving cup . . . **3.** tyg (tig)
low . . . **3.** bas, moo **4.** base, deep,
  neap, orra **5.** faint **6.** humble, menial,
  sneaky, vulgar, wicked **8.** dejected,
  indecent, infamous, inferior, plebeian
  9. inelegant **11.** unfavorable
low (pert to) . . .
born . . **4.** rude **5.** lowly **6.** common
  7. lowbred **8.** plebeian
bred . . **5.** crude **6.** coarse, vulgar
brow . . **9.** ignoramus

church.. **11.** evangelical
comedy.. **8.** travesty
country.. **7.** Belgium, Holland
  9. Luxemburg **11.** Netherlands
German.. **5.** Saxon **8.** Frankish
  12. Plattdeutsch
in spirits.. **4.** blue **6.** megrim **8.** dejected,
  downcast **10.** dispirited, melancholy
  11. crestfallen
Roman wall.. **5.** spina
shrubs, plants.. **4.** moss **5.** Erica
syllable (Mus).. **2.** ut
tide.. **3.** ebb **4.** neap **8.** low water
wall.. **7.** parapet
lower... **3.** dip **4.** vail, vase **5.** abase,
  demit, frown, neath **6.** bemean,
  debase, deepen, demean, demote,
  humble, lessen, meaner, nether, reduce
  7. cheapen, degrade, depress, descent
  8. diminish, inferior **10.** depreciate
lower (pert to)...
case letter.. **5.** small
Empire.. **9.** Byzantine
geology.. **5.** Chalk (Eng) **6.** strata
  7. stratum
most.. **6.** bottom, lowest **7.** bedrock
  10. nethermost
world.. **4.** hell **5.** earth, Hades, limbo,
  orcus, Sheol **7.** Abaddon, Gehenna
  8. Cerberus **9.** perdition, purgatory
lowering... **4.** dark **6.** gloomy, sullen
  7. ominous **8.** frowning **9.** deepening
  10. cheapening **11.** threatening
lowery... **6.** cloudy, gloomy **8.** lowering
lowest (pert to)...
animal life.. **6.** amoeba (ameba)
deck.. **5.** orlop
least.. **5.** minim **6.** bottom **7.** minimum
pedestal member (Arch).. **6.** plinth,
  quadra
peer (ranking).. **5.** baron
point.. **5.** depth, nadir **6.** bottom
  10. nethermost
point, planet.. **7.** perigee
lowing... **6.** mooing **7.** mugient
  9. bellowing
lowland... **4.** flat, holm, spit **5.** plain,
  terai **6.** bottom **8.** molehill
lowly... **4.** mean, meek **6.** humble,
  humbly, meekly, menial, modest
  8. inferior, modestly, plebeian
  12. unpretending
loxia... **7.** wryneck **9.** crossbill
loy... **5.** slick (tool), spade
loyal... **4.** feal, leal, true **5.** liege **6.** stanch
  7. staunch **8.** constant, faithful, obedient
loyalty... **5.** faith **6.** fealty, homage
  8. devotion, fidelity **9.** constancy
  10. allegiance, stanchness (staunchness)
  12. faithfulness **13.** steadfastness
Loyolite... **6.** Jesuit
lozenge... **5.** candy, facet **6.** jujube,
  tablet, troche **7.** diamond, molding
  8. pastille (pastil, pastile) **11.** perforation
lubber... **4.** boor, dolt, gawk, lout
  5. churl, drone, idler, thick **6.** sailor
  8. landsman **11.** grasshopper
lubricity... **8.** lewdness **10.** smoothness
  12. slipperiness
lubricous... **4.** lewd **6.** tricky, wanton
  7. elusive **8.** unstable **10.** lascivious

lucban... **8.** shaddock
luce... **4.** pike **10.** fleur-de-lis
lucent... **5.** clear **6.** bright **7.** shining
  11. translucent, transparent
lucern... **3.** dog **4.** lynx
lucerne... **4.** herb **6.** fodder **7.** alfalfa
  11. purple medic
lucet, luce... **4.** pike (fish)
Lucia's home... **10.** Lammermoor
lucid... **4.** sane **5.** clear, vivid **6.** bright,
  lucent **7.** shining **8.** luminous, pellucid
  11. translucent **12.** intelligible
Lucifer... **5.** Satan
luck... **3.** hap **4.** cess **5.** deuce **6.** chance
  7. ambsace **8.** fortuity **11.** good fortune
lucky... **5.** canny, happy **6.** timely
  9. fortunate **10.** auspicious **11.** good
  fortune
lucky animal... **6.** mascot
lucky token... **4.** mojo **5.** charm
  6. amulet **7.** periapt **8.** talisman
  9. alectoria **10.** rabbit foot
  12. antinganting
lucrative... **3.** fat **6.** paying **7.** gainful
  10. productive, profitable, worthwhile
  12. remunerative
lucre... **4.** gain, pelf **6.** profit, riches
  9. emolument **11.** acquisition
lucubrate... **18.** burn the midnight oil
ludicrous... **5.** antic, comic, droll,
  funny **6.** absurd **7.** amusing, comical,
  jesting, risible **9.** burlesque, laughable
  10. ridiculous
Ludolphian... **2.** pi (3.14159)
  14. Ludolph's number
Luftpost... **7.** airmail, air post
lug... **3.** box, ear, hug **4.** drag, hale,
  haul, loop, pull, tote **5.** carry **6.** basket
  9. container
luge... **4.** sled
lugs... **4.** airs **7.** clothes (showy), tobacco
  10. affections
lugubrious... **3.** sad **6.** woeful **7.** doleful
  8. grievous, mournful **9.** plaintive
  10. lamentable
lugworm... **3.** lob **7.** annelid **9.** Arenicola
luhinga... **9.** petticoat
lukewarm... **4.** cool **5.** tepid **6.** tepefy
  8. tepidity **9.** not ardent **10.** irresolute
  11. indifferent
lumber... **4.** wood **6.** bungle, litter, refuse,
  rumble, timber, trudge **7.** lombard
  9. rough wood **10.** pawnbroker
  11. impedimenta
lumberman... **6.** logger, sawyer, scorer
  9. timberman **10.** lumberjack,
  woodcutter
lumberman's half boot... **3.** pac
lumberman's sled... **4.** tode **7.** go-devil,
  travois (travoise)
luminary... **3.** sun **4.** fire, star **5.** light
  7. wise man **9.** celebrity **12.** illumination,
  leading light
luminescence... **7.** foxfire
  12. fluorescence **15.** phosphorescence
luminous... **5.** clear, lucid **6.** bright
  7. shining **9.** brilliant **11.** enlightened,
  illuminated, intelligent, transparent
  14. phosphorescent
luminous circle... **4.** halo
luminous impression... **9.** phosphene

10. afterimage
lummox . . . 3. oaf 4. boor, dolt,
lout 5. yahoo 7. bumpkin, bungler
12. clumsy fellow
lump . . . 3. gob, lob, wad 4. beat, blob,
clot, hunk, loaf, mass 5. bulge 6. nodule,
nubble, nugget, thresh 7. cluster
8. swelling 12. protuberance
lump (pert to) . . .
butter . . 3. pat
clay . . 4. clag, clod
metal . . 3. pig 5. ingot
lumpish . . . 4. dull 5. bulky, inert
6. clumsy, stolid, stupid 7. boorish
8. sluggish 9. heaviness, inertness,
ponderous 11. countrified
13. shapelessness
lumpy . . . 5. drunk, rough 6. choppy
7. gnarled, nodular
lumpy jaw . . . 6. big jaw
13. actinomycosis
luna . . . 6. silver 11. moon goddess
lunacy . . . 4. moon 5. mania 7. madness
8. insanity 9. craziness
11. derangement, foolishness
lunar . . . 5. orbed 6. lunate 8. crescent,
moonlike 9. celestial, satellite 10. moon-
shaped
lunar (pert to) . . .
appulse . . 7. eclipse
bone . . 7. lunatum
cycle . . 7. Metonic 9. Callippic
deity . . 6. Selene (Selena)
halo . . 6. corona, nimbus 7. aureola
surface feature . . 6. crater
lunatic . . . 3. mad 5. crazy, idiot, loony
6. insane, madman 8. demoniac
10. moonstruck
lunatic asylum . . . 9. Bethlehem (London)
lunch . . . 5. snack 6. brunch, repast, tiffin
8. brown-bag, luncheon, nuncheon
9. collation 11. refreshment
lunchroom . . . 6. eatery 10. coffee shop,
restaurant 12. luncheonette
lundyfoot . . . 5. snuff (by Lundy Foot)
lunge . . . 3. cut, jab 4. grab, pass, stab
5. feint, swing 7. thrust
lungs (pert to) . . .
ailment . . 9. emphysema 10. chalicosis
12. tuberculosis
having . . 9. pulmonate
part . . 5. lobes 6. lights 7. bronchi,
trachea
sound . . 4. rale 6. rattle
lunula . . . 8. crescent, half moon
lurch . . . 4. joll, roll, sway 5. lunge
6. careen, topple 7. deceive 8. flounder
10. disappoint
lure . . . 4. bait, trap 5. decoy, snare,
tempt 6. allure, entice, invite 7. attract,
beguile, trumpet, tweedle
10. enticement
lurid . . . 3. wan 4. dark, pale 5. color,
vivid 6. dismal, gloomy 7. ghastly,
obscene 9. deathlike 11. sensational
lurk . . . 4. hide, lote (obs) 5. creep,
prowl, skulk, slink, sneak 9. lie in wait,
pussyfoot
luscious . . . 4. rich 5. sweet 6. creamy,
wanton 7. cloying, honeyed 8. sensuous
9. delicious 10. lascivious, voluptuous

lush . . . 4. soft 5. drink, drunk, juicy
6. lavish, limber, liquor, mellow
7. verdant 8. flexible 9. luxuriant,
succulent 11. intoxicated
lusory . . . 7. playful 8. sportive
lust . . . 5. greed 6. desire, libido
7. craving, longing, passion 8. virility
14. lasciviousness
luster, lustre . . . 4. naif 5. glory,
gloss, sheen, shine 6. beauty, polish
7. glitter, lustrum 8. radiance, schiller,
splendor 10. brightness 11. distinction,
iridescence
lusterless . . . 3. dim, mat 4. dead, dull,
flat 14. expressionless
lustful . . . 4. lewd 5. randy 9. lecherous
10. lascivious
lustrous . . . 4. naif 5. nitid 6. agleam,
bright 7. radiant, shining 11. illustrious,
transparent
lustrous mineral . . . 4. spar
lustrum (Roman) . . . 6. census, luster
12. purification (5 yrs), quinquennium
lusty . . . 6. active, robust, strong, sturdy
7. healthy 8. vigorous 9. corpulent
lute . . . 4. clay, ring (rubber), seal
6. cement
lute, lutelike . . . 4. asor 6. guitar
7. bandore, pandore, theorbo, ukulele
8. archlute (architute)
lute tablature . . . 7. lyraway
lutjanoid fish . . . 4. sesi 7. snapper
Luxembourg . . .
capital . . 10. Luxembourg
government . . 10. Grand Duchy
language . . 6. French, German
13. Letzeburgesch
river . . 7. Moselle
luxuriant . . . 4. lush, rank, rich 6. ornate,
uberty 7. fertile, opulent, profuse,
teeming 8. abundant, prolific
9. bounteous, Sybaritic
luxuriate . . . 4. bask 5. revel 8. flourish
luxurious . . . 5. plush, ritzy 6. ornate,
superb 8. imposing 9. expensive,
grandiose, sumptuous 10. impressive
11. extravagant
luxury . . . 4. lust 7. lechery 8. elegance,
pleasure, richness 10. prosperity,
sensuality 11. superfluity
12. extravagance 13. gratification,
sumptuousness 14. voluptuousness
luxury lover . . . 7. reveler 8. Sybarite
Luzon . . .
dialect . . 6. Itaves
mountain . . 3. Iba 6. Pagsan (Sicapoo)
people . . 5. Malay 6. Igorot (Igorrote)
7. Tagalog 8. Tinggian (Tinguian)
seaport . . 5. Vigan 6. Aparri, Cavite
volcano . . 5. Mayon
lyam . . . 5. leash (Her) 10. bloodhound
lycanthrope . . . 8. werewolf 9. loup-garou
Lycia (pert to) . . .
citizen . . 6. Lycian
city . . 4. Myra
district of . . 9. Asia Minor
language . . 5. Greek 6. Lycian
Lydia . . .
capital . . 6. Sardis
dynasty of . . 5. Gyges 7. Croesus
13. Cyrus the Great

name, later .. **6.** Persia
name, old .. **5.** Ionia
queen .. **7.** Omphale
river .. **8.** Pactolus
ruins .. **6.** temple
lye ... **4.** buck **6.** bleach, potash
　8. lixivium
lying ... **5.** false **6.** deceit **7.** fudging
　9. decumbent, mendacity, reclining,
　recumbent **10.** untruthful
lying (pert to) ...
　across .. **10.** transverse
　at mountain base .. **8.** piedmont
　hidden .. **6.** latent **11.** delitescent
　in .. **12.** accouchement
　near earth's axis .. **5.** polar
　on the back .. **5.** prone **6.** supine
　　7. passive
lymph ... **3.** sap **5.** chyle, fluid, serum,
　water **6.** plasma **7.** cassein
lynch ... **4.** hang **6.** murder, punish
　(lawlessly) **7.** execute
lynx ... **6.** bobcat, lucern **7.** caracal,

　wildcat **8.** carcajou **13.** constellation
lynx-eyed ... **7.** oxyopia
lyre ... **4.** asor, harp **6.** kissar, sabeca,
　trigon, zither **7.** cithara, cittern, testudo
　8. phorminx
lyre (pert to) ...
　bird .. **6.** Menura **8.** lyretail, pheasant
　shaped .. **6.** lyrate
　tree .. **5.** tulip
　turtle .. **11.** leatherback
lyric (pert to) ...
　Arabic .. **5.** gazel
　Muse .. **5.** Erato **10.** Polyhymnia
　music, poetry .. **3.** lay, ode **4.** epic, poem
　　5. epode, melic, rhyme (rime), verse,
　　vocal **6.** epopee, poetic **7.** canzone,
　　musical, rondeau **8.** operatic, palinode
　　9. dithyramb
　poet .. **5.** odist
lyrical ... **6.** epodic
lyrichord ... **11.** harpsichord
lyssa ... **6.** rabies **11.** hydrophobia
lyssophobia ... **17.** fear of hydrophobia

M

M ... **2.** Mu (Gr) **6.** letter (13th) **8.** thousand
Ma (Ma Bellona) ... **7.** goddess (fertility)
maarib (Jew) ... **7.** liturgy
Maat (Egypt) ... **7.** goddess (justice)
Mab (Queen Mab) ... **4.** poem **10.** fairy
　queen
mabolo ... **4.** plum **7.** camagon
macabre ... **4.** grim **5.** lurid, weird
　6. grisly **7.** ghastly **8.** gruesome
　12. Dance of Death
macaco ... **5.** lemur **6.** Macaca
　7. macaque **10.** Barbary ape
macan ... **4.** rice
macao ... **4.** game (gambling)
Macao ... **6.** Island **7.** seaport
macaque ... **6.** machin, monkey
Macassar ... **7.** seaport (Celebes)
macaw ... **3.** ara **5.** arara **6.** parrot
　7. maracan **8.** aracanga (blue and red),
　ararauna (blue and yellow)
Macbeth (pert to) ...
　author .. **11.** Shakespeare (1605)
　character .. **4.** Duff, Ross **5.** Angus
　　6. Banquo, Hecate, Lennox **7.** Macduff
　murder victim .. **6.** Duncan
　play type .. **7.** tragedy
　rival .. **7.** Macduff
McBurney's Point (Med) ...
　13. abdominal wall
Maccabees ... **11.** Hasmonaeans
　14. fraternal order, Jewish patriots
maccaboy ... **5.** snuff
mace ... **4.** maul **5.** baton, gavel, spice
　(nutmeg), staff **6.** ensign, mallet
　7. scepter (sceptre)
mace bearer ... **5.** macer **6.** beadle
Macedonia, Balkans ...
　capital (anc) .. **5.** Pella
　city .. **5.** Berea **6.** Edessa **8.** Salonika

　people .. **6.** Greeks **8.** Serbians
　　9. Albanians **10.** Bulgarians
　ruler .. **6.** Philip **9.** Alexander (the Great)
　site .. **15.** Balkan Peninsula
macerate ... **3.** ret, vex **4.** soak **5.** steep
　6. soften **7.** mortify, oppress, torture
　8. emaciate **9.** waste away
machete ... **4.** bolo, fish **5.** knife **6.** guitar
　11. cutlass fish
Machiavellian, Machiavelian ... **4.** wily
　6. crafty **7.** cunning **8.** guileful,
　scheming **9.** deceitful **12.** falsehearted
machila ... **7.** hammock
machin ... **6.** monkey **7.** macaque
machinate ... **4.** plan, plot **6.** scheme
　8. contrive, maneuver
machination ... **6.** design, device, scheme
　7. machine **8.** intrigue **9.** stratagem
　10. conspiracy
machine ... **3.** car **4.** auto **6.** device,
　engine **7.** vehicle **9.** apparatus,
　automaton **10.** automobile
　11. association, standardize
machine (pert to) ...
　cloth maturing .. **4.** ager
　cloth stretching .. **6.** tenter
　cotton .. **3.** gin **4.** mule **5.** baler
　glazing .. **8.** calender
　hay .. **5.** baler **6.** tedder
　hoisting .. **3.** gin, pry **4.** pump **5.** crane,
　　davit, lever, tongs **7.** derrick
　hummeling .. **5.** awner
　hydraulic .. **9.** telemotor
　imitating .. **9.** automaton
　military .. **3.** ram **6.** onager
　mixing .. **9.** malaxator
　ore .. **6.** vanner
　planing .. **8.** surfacer
　planting .. **6.** seeder

political . . **5.** party **6.** system **7.** faction
reckoning . . **6.** abacus **9.** tabulator
　10. calculator
rubber shaping . . **8.** extruder
stage effect . . **13.** deus ex machina
tool . . **5.** drill, lathe
machine gun . . . **4.** nest (hidden place)
　5. Maxim **6.** cannon **7.** Gatling
　9. Hotchkiss **10.** chatterbox
machine-made . . . **11.** stereotyped
machine power, energy . . . **5.** input
　6. output
machinist . . . **7.** artisan **8.** mechanic
mackerel . . . **5.** atule, spike, tunny
　6. sierra, tinker
mackerel (pert to) . . .
　bait . . **9.** jellyfish
　bird . . **7.** wryneck **9.** kittiwake
　genus . . **7.** Scomber
　goose . . **9.** phalarope
　like . . **4.** cero **6.** bonito **7.** escolar
　net . . **7.** spiller
　shark . . **9.** porbeagle
　sky . . **6.** clouds **9.** striation
　small (allowable size) . . **5.** spike **6.** tinker
　7. blinker
mackle . . . **4.** blur, spot **6.** blotch, macule
macrobiotic . . . **9.** long-lived
mad . . . **4.** vain, wild **5.** angry, crazy,
　irate, rabid, vexed **6.** insane, maniac
　7. enraged, foolish, frantic, furious
　8. demented, frenetic, maniacal,
　reckless **9.** hilarious, turbulent
　10. distraught, infatuated, infuriated
　12. arreptitious
Madagascar, Malagasy . . .
　animal . . **5.** indri, lemur **6.** aye-aye,
　tenrec (tendrac) **9.** babacoote
　capital . . **10.** Tananarive
　cattle . . **4.** zebu (humped)
　city . . **7.** Majanga **8.** Tamatave
　civet . . **7.** fossane
　government . . **8.** Republic (1960)
　language . . **16.** Malayo-Polynesian
　native . . **4.** Hova **8.** Sakalava
　palm . . **6.** raffia
　religion . . **7.** Animist **9.** Christian
Madam . . . **3.** Mrs **4.** Frau, lady, Ma'am
　5. donna, hussy **6.** Madame, Señora
　8. goodwife, mistress **9.** courtesan
madcap . . . **3.** wag **4.** rash, wild
　5. blood **6.** madman **7.** hotspur, violent
　8. reckless **9.** daredevil, foolhardy
madden . . . **3.** vex **5.** craze **6.** enrage, incite
　7. incense **9.** infuriate **10.** antagonize
madder . . . **2.** al **3.** aal, red **4.** herb, rose
　(color) **5.** brown, Rubia **6.** orange,
　violet, yellow **7.** crimson, xanthin
　9. turkey-red
made . . . **5.** built **7.** created, trained
　8. invented, prepared, produced,
　rendered **10.** artificial, successful
　11. constructed **12.** enfranchised,
　manufactured
made (pert to) . . .
　accurate . . **5.** trued
　believe . . **7.** feigned **9.** pretended,
　simulated
　blind . . **6.** seeled
　clear . . **9.** explained **10.** elucidated
　destitute . . **6.** bereft

fun of . . **6.** jeered, mocked **7.** derided
　9. ridiculed
hard, obdurate . . **7.** steeled
light of . . **7.** dwarfed **9.** belittled
　10. disparaged
over . . **8.** reformed, revamped
　9. remodeled
plain . . **9.** evidenced, exhibited
　10. manifested
public . . **5.** aired **7.** accused, delated
　8. reported
scalloped edges . . **6.** pinked
sound . . **7.** bleated, rumbled, swished
tart . . **7.** euchred
up . . **9.** composite **10.** artificial, fabricated
　12. manufactured
up mind . . **7.** decided
valid . . **6.** proved **9.** confirmed
　13. authenticated
whole again . . **7.** renewed **10.** reconciled
　13. redintegrated, re-established
Madeira Islands . . .
　capital . . **7.** Funchal
　embroidery . . **6.** eyelet
　nut . . **6.** walnut
　owner of Islands . . **8.** Portugal
　wind . . **5.** leste
　wine . . **4.** bual **5.** tinta (red) **7.** malmsey,
　sercial **8.** verdelho
　wood . . **8.** ironwood (white), mahogany
madhouse . . . **5.** chaos **6.** asylum, bedlam
　8. nuthouse
madman . . . **3.** nut **4.** coot, loon **6.** maniac
　7. lunatic **9.** phrenetic
madness . . . **3.** ire **4.** fury, rage **5.** anger,
　mania **6.** frenzy, lunacy **8.** insanity
　9. agitation, theomania (Relig)
　11. foolishness, inspiration
Mad Parliament (1258) . . . **18.** Provisions
　of Oxford
Madras, India . . .
　capital . . **6.** Madras
　city . . **5.** Adoni, Arcot **7.** Calicut
　export . . **4.** lace **7.** fabrics **9.** kerchiefs
　(for turbans)
　government . . **10.** presidency
madrepore . . . **5.** coral **6.** fossil, marble
　8. Acropora **12.** Madreporaria
Madrid, Spain . . .
　architecture . . **7.** Moorish
　boulevard . . **5.** Prado **12.** Salon de Prado
　noted buildings . . **7.** Armeria **11.** Prado
　Museum, Royal Palace
madrigal . . . **3.** ode **4.** glee, poem **5.** lyric,
　music **6.** verses
maduro . . . **5.** cigar **6.** mature **11.** dark-
　colored
maelstrom . . . **5.** churn **6.** foment
　7. turmoil **9.** whirlpool (Norway)
maestro . . . **6.** master **7.** teacher
　8. composer, musician **9.** conductor
　13. Kapellmeister
maestro-di-cappela . . . **11.** choirmaster
Mae West . . . **8.** life belt
Mafia . . . **9.** syndicate **10.** Cosa Nostra,
　underworld **12.** organization (Sicilian)
maffle . . . **6.** muddle, mumble **7.** confuse,
　stammer **8.** squander
mafoo, mafu (Chin) . . . **5.** groom **9.** stable
　boy
mag . . . **6.** magpie **7.** chatter **8.** titmouse

M

9. halfpenny
magadis ... **5.** flute **9.** monochord
magazine ... **4.** shop **5.** depot, store
6. review **7.** arsenal, chamber (gun),
tabloid **9.** ephemeris, reservoir,
warehouse **10.** periodical, repository,
storehouse
magazine rifle ... **6.** Mauser **8.** repeater
mage ... **5.** Magus **6.** Merlin **7.** Houdini
8. conjurer, magician
magenta ... **3.** dye **7.** fuchsia
maggot ... **4.** grub, mawk **5.** larva,
mathe **6.** notion **7.** caprice, Diptera
12. eccentricity
Magi (Three Wise Men) ... **6.** Gaspar
8. Melchior **9.** Balthasar
magic ... **3.** art **4.** juju, mana, maya, rune,
show **5.** charm, fairy, spell **6.** voodoo
10. necromancy **11.** conjuration,
enchantment, legerdemain
magic (pert to) ...
art (black) .. **7.** demonry **9.** diablerie,
diabolism
art (white) .. **5.** turgy **7.** theurgy
ejaculation .. **2.** om (um) **6.** sesame
goddess .. **5.** Circe **6.** Hecate
image .. **5.** sigil **8.** sigillum
lantern .. **11.** epidiascope
12. stereopticon
lantern slide .. **6.** tinter
staff, wand .. **6.** rhabdo **8.** caduceus
symbol .. **5.** charm **6.** caract, fetish
8. pentacle **9.** pentalpha
word .. **2.** om (um) **5.** voilà **6.** presto,
sesame **10.** abacadabra
magical ... **6.** goetic (goety) **8.** charming
magician ... **4.** mage **5.** magus **6.** Merlin,
wizard **7.** Houdini, juggler **8.** conjurer,
mandrake, sorcerer **9.** archimage,
charlatan, enchanter **11.** entertainer,
necromancer, thaumaturge
13. thaumaturgist **15.** prestidigitator
magician (pert to) ...
attendant .. **7.** famulus
command .. **6.** presto **11.** abracadabra
manual .. **8.** grimoire
magirics ... **7.** cookery
magirist ... **4.** cook
magisterial ... **5.** lofty, proud **6.** august,
lordly **7.** haughty, stately **8.** arrogant,
dogmatic, judicial, official **9.** dignified,
imperious, masterful **10.** commanding
11. dictatorial, domineering,
overbearing **13.** authoritative
magistrate ... **4.** cadi, doge **5.** ephor,
judge **6.** aedile (edile), archon, bailli,
puisne, syndic **7.** alcaide (alcaid),
alcalde, bailiff
magistrate's orders ... **4.** acta
magma ... **5.** dregs **8.** sediment
10. molten rock, suspension (Pharm)
magna cum laude ... **14.** with great
honor
magnanimous ... **4.** free **5.** lofty,
noble **7.** exalted, liberal **8.** generous
9. honorable, unselfish, unstinted
10. high-minded **11.** great of mind
13. disinterested
magnate ... **4.** lord **5.** baron, mogul, noble
6. bashaw, bigwig, tycoon **7.** grandee,
richman **9.** personage **11.** millionaire

magnesium (pert to) ...
limestone .. **8.** dolomite
nitrate .. **9.** saltpeter
silicate .. **4.** talc
sulphate .. **10.** Epsom salts
magnet ... **7.** terella **8.** solenoid
9. loadstone, lodestone
magnet (type) ... **3.** bar **9.** horseshoe
10. artificial
magnetic ... **10.** attractive, electrical
14. attractiveness
magnetism ... **5.** oomph **8.** polarity
magnificence ... **4.** pomp **5.** glory
8. grandeur, splendor
15. superexcellence
magnificent ... **5.** grand, regal **6.** lavish,
superb **7.** exalted, pompous, sublime
8. imposing, palatial, splendid, striking
9. brilliant, grandiose, sumptuous
10. munificent
magnify ... **4.** laud **5.** exalt, extol
6. expand, praise **7.** enlarge, glorify,
worship **8.** increase **9.** intensify,
overstate **10.** exaggerate
magnitude ... **4.** size **6.** extent **7.** bigness
8. grandeur, nobility **9.** extension,
greatness
Magnolia State ... **11.** Mississippi
magnum ... **4.** bone (wrist) **6.** bottle
9. capitatum
magnum opus ... **9.** great work
11. achievement
magpie ... **3.** daw, mag, pie **4.** Pica,
piet (pyet) **5.** madge, scold **6.** pigeon,
talker **9.** chatterer **10.** chattermag
magpie type ...
diver .. **4.** smew
shrike .. **7.** tanager
maguari ... **5.** stork
magus ... **8.** magician **9.** one of Magi
Magyar ... **3.** Hun **9.** Hungarian
Mah (Persian) ... **9.** moon angel
maha ... **10.** sambar deer
Mahabharata (blind king, Hind) ...
13. Dhritarashtra
mahajan, mahajun (Ind) ... **8.** great man
11. moneylender
mahal ... **8.** Taj Mahal **9.** residence
(summer) **10.** apartments, Natal brown
mahala ... **5.** squaw
maharaja, maharajah ... **5.** ruler
6. prince
maharani, maharanee ... **5.** queen
mahatma ... **4.** sage **7.** wise man
9. great soul, occultist **21.** Great White
Brotherhood (member)
mahi-mahi ... **7.** dolphin
mah-jongg piece ... **4.** tile
mahogany ... **3.** roe (burl) **4.** toon, wood
5. brown **6.** totara **7.** ratteen
maholi ... **5.** lemur
Mahomet ... see *Mohammedan*
Mahound ... **5.** Devil **8.** Mohammed
mahout ... **6.** driver (elephant), keeper
Mah to Mahi ... **10.** Fish to Moon
Maia (pert to) ...
mountain nymph .. **7.** Arcadia
son .. **6.** Hermes
star .. **8.** Pleiades
maid ... **4.** girl, lass **5.** bonne, woman
6. damsel, maiden, virgin **7.** abigail,

servant **8.** spinster **9.** tirewoman
Maid (of) . . .
  Astolat . . **6.** Elaine
  Athens . . **12.** Theresa Macri
  Lydia . . **7.** Arachne (changed to a spider)
  Orléans . . **9.** Joan of Arc
  Zeus . . **2.** Io (changed to heifer)
maidenhair . . . **4.** fern **8.** Adiantum
  10. Venus's hair
maidenhair tree . . . **6.** gingko
maidenly . . . **6.** gentle, modest **7.** girlish
  9. unmarried
maigre . . . **4.** diet, fish
mail . . . **3.** dak (dawk) **4.** post **5.** armor
  7. consign, letters, plumage **8.** dispatch
mail, coat of . . . **5.** armor **6.** byrnie
  (brinie) **7.** broigne, cuirass (part),
  hauberk, panoply
mail boat . . . **6.** packet
maim . . . **6.** injure, mangle, mayhem
  7. disable **8.** mutilate **9.** tear apart
main . . . **3.** sea **4.** duct **5.** chief, first, great,
  prime, sheer, utter **6.** mighty, potent
  7. chiefly, conduit, leading **8.** foremost
  9. conductor, essential, principal **10.** on
  the whole **11.** essentially **13.** most
  important
main (pert to) . . .
  act (drama) . . **8.** epitasis
  beam . . **6.** girder **7.** walking
  part . . **4.** body
  point . . **3.** jet, nub **4.** crux, gist, pith
  post . . **9.** sternpost
  sea (poet) . . **11.** Spanish Main (Caribbean
    Sea)
Maine . . .
  bay . . **5.** Casco **13.** Passamaquoddy
  capital . . **7.** Augusta
  city . . **4.** Saco **5.** Hiram, Orono **6.** Bangor
    8. Lewiston, Portland **11.** Millinocket
  college . . **5.** Bates, Colby **7.** Bowdoin
  Easternmost city . . **8.** Eastport
  Easternmost point . . **19.** West Quoddy
    Head Light
  Easternmost town . . **5.** Lubec
  lake . . **6.** Sebago **9.** Moosehead
  mountain . . **5.** Kineo **8.** Cadillac, Katahdin
  resort . . **9.** Bar Harbor
  resort island . . **8.** Mt Desert
  river . . **8.** Kennebec **9.** Penobscot
  State admission . . **11.** Twenty-third
  State motto . . **6.** Dirigo **7.** I Direct
  State nickname . . **8.** Pine Tree
  trout . . **7.** oquassa
Maine, The . . . **10.** battleship (Sp-Am
  War)
maintain . . . **4.** aver, hold, keep **5.** claim
  6. affirm, allege, assert, avouch, defend,
  endure, insist, retain **7.** justify, support,
  sustain **8.** continue, preserve
maintainable . . . **7.** tenable
maintenance . . . **3.** aid **6.** upkeep
  7. alimony, defense, support
  9. retention **10.** livelihood, sustenance
  11. continuance **12.** conservation,
  preservation, sustentation
maison . . . **5.** house
Maison Carrée . . . **12.** Norman Temple
  (Nimes)
maison de santé . . . **6.** asylum **8.** hospital
  10. sanatorium

maître d'hôtel (famed) . . . **5.** Oscar
maize . . . **3.** Zea **4.** corn **7.** mealies
maja, majo . . . **5.** belle, dandy
majestic . . . **5.** grand, great, lofty,
  noble, regal, royal **6.** august, kingly
  7. stately, sublime **8.** elevated,
  eloquent, imperial, splendid **9.** dignified,
  grandiose **11.** ceremonious, magnificent
majesty . . . **5.** title **7.** crowned (Her),
  dignity **8.** grandeur **9.** eloquence,
  greatness, loftiness, sceptered (Her)
major . . . **3.** dur (Mus) **6.** course (study),
  ditone **7.** greater, officer **8.** legal age,
  majority
major-domo . . . **6.** butler **7.** bailiff, steward
  9. seneschal
majority . . . **3.** age **4.** most **6.** quorum
  7. greater **8.** maturity **9.** majorship,
  plurality, seniority **12.** more than half
make . . . **2.** do **4.** earn, form, gain, kind
  5. shape **6.** compel, create, induce,
  render **7.** compose, execute, produce
  8. contrive, generate **9.** structure
  10. accomplish **11.** composition,
  manufacture
make (pert to) . . .
  affidavit . . **4.** affy
  allowance . . **5.** abate, admit **7.** concede
  allusion to . . **7.** mention
  amends . . **5.** atone **7.** redress
  as if . . **7.** pretend **8.** as though
  bare . . **5.** strip **6.** balden, denude
  believe . . **4.** sham **5.** feign **7.** pretend
    8. pretense
  better . . **5.** widen **6.** soften **7.** broaden,
    improve **9.** meliorate **10.** ameliorate
  book . . **10.** record bets
  buoyant . . **8.** levitate
  calm . . **5.** allay, quiet **6.** serene
    7. appease, compose
  certain . . **6.** assure, ensure
  cheerful . . **6.** solace **7.** comfort, console
  choice . . **3.** opt **4.** cull **6.** choose, select
    7. pick out
  clean breast of . . **7.** confess **8.** disclose
  clear . . **7.** explain **9.** elucidate
  coins . . **4.** mint
  counterchange . . **11.** recriminate
  crisp . . **9.** embrittle
  deduction . . **6.** rebate
  desolate . . **5.** strip **7.** bereave
  diminutive . . **9.** bantamize
  do . . **3.** eke **5.** get by **6.** manage **8.** piece
    out **9.** improvise
  eccentric . . **8.** decenter
  edging . . **3.** tat **7.** crochet
  effective . . **6.** compel **7.** enforce
  enduring . . **6.** anneal, temper
  equal . . **6.** equate
  evident . . **6.** evince
  familiar . . **8.** accustom
  famous . . **8.** eternize **11.** immortalize
  fast . . **4.** snub **5.** belay **6.** batten, secure
  faulty . . **6.** impair **7.** vitiate
    11. contaminate
  firm . . **3.** fix **5.** brace **6.** cement
  fit . . **4.** suit **5.** adapt **6.** adjust **7.** conform
  foolish, stupid . . **4.** daff **8.** stultify
    10. ridiculous
  fun of . . **3.** rib **5.** scoff **8.** ridicule
  glass . . **7.** platten

good .. **7.** absolve, justify, succeed
9. indemnify, vindicate
happy .. **5.** elate **7.** beatify **8.** felicify
(obs)
hard, harsh .. **5.** steel **6.** freeze **7.** roughen
harmonious .. **6.** attune
headway .. **4.** gain **7.** advance **8.** progress
holy .. **5.** bless **6.** hallow **10.** consecrate
honorable .. **5.** exalt **6.** uplift **7.** ennoble
ineffective .. **4.** void **5.** annul
insensible to pain .. **11.** anesthetize
(anaesthetize)
into law .. **5.** enact **9.** legislate
known .. **6.** impart, reveal **7.** divulge,
publish, uncover **8.** disclose, discover,
proclaim
lace .. **3.** tat **7.** crochet
less dense .. **4.** thin **6.** rarefy
less smooth .. **7.** roughen
level .. **4.** true
light .. **6.** jetsam **8.** illumine, jettison
like .. **7.** imitate **11.** impersonate
lively .. **8.** energize
love .. **3.** coo, woo **5.** court
merry .. **5.** laugh **6.** banter **7.** disport
mild .. **8.** mitigate, modulate
moral .. **8.** ethicize
much of .. **6.** praise **7.** enthuse, lionize
10. exaggerate
muddy .. **4.** roil
notes .. **8.** annotate
off with .. **5.** steal
out .. **4.** know **5.** solve **6.** decode, draw
up **7.** analyze, discern **8.** contrive,
decipher **10.** understand
over .. **4.** redo **6.** revamp **7.** convert
8. renovate, transfer **9.** refashion,
reproduce
pale, sickly .. **8.** etiolate
possible .. **6.** enable
pottery .. **7.** spattle
precious .. **6.** endear
pretentious .. **7.** buckram
public .. **3.** air **5.** bruit, noise **6.** delate
7. publish **9.** divulgate **11.** acknowledge
ready .. **4.** gear **5.** coach, prime
7. prepare
reparation .. **5.** atone
resistance .. **5.** rebel **6.** mutiny, revolt
secure .. **3.** fix, pin **4.** nail, snub **5.** belay
6. batten, fasten
shift .. **9.** temporary
short work of .. **6.** hasten **7.** destroy
10. accomplish
shrill noise .. **10.** stridulate
smooth .. **4.** buff, iron **5.** sleek, slick
6. scrape
spruce .. **4.** perk **7.** smarten
strong .. **7.** stouten
thin .. **9.** attenuate
three-cornered .. **11.** triangulate
unhappy .. **8.** embitter **10.** exacerbate
up .. **5.** atone, build **6.** invent, settle
7. compose, concoct, prepare
8. assemble, cosmetic **9.** construct,
improvise, reconcile **10.** compensate
use of .. **5.** apply **6.** borrow, employ
7. utilize **11.** appropriate
waste (law) .. **7.** estrepe
watertight .. **4.** calk, seal
white .. **6.** blanch, bleach

worse .. **9.** aggravate
zealous .. **7.** enthuse
maker of ...
arrows .. **8.** fletcher
barrels .. **6.** cooper
bundles .. **5.** baler
infusion .. **7.** steeper
knives .. **6.** cutler
pottery .. **6.** potter **8.** ceramist
makeshift ... **7.** stopgap
maki ... **5.** lemur
mal (comb form) ... **3.** bad, ill **5.** badly
7. disease **8.** sickness
Malabar (pert to) ...
bark .. **5.** ochna
nutmeg .. **10.** Bombay mace
palm .. **7.** talipot
rat .. **9.** bandicoot
Malacca ... **7.** seaport (Malaya)
Malachi ... **4.** Book (Old Test) **7.** prophet
malachite ... **4.** bice **5.** green **6.** copper
7. pigment
maladroit ... **6.** clumsy **7.** awkward,
unhandy **8.** bungling **9.** all thumbs,
graceless **10.** blundering, left-handed,
ungraceful
maladventure ... **6.** mishap **8.** escapade
12. ill adventure
malady ... **4.** amok **7.** ailment, disease,
illness **8.** disorder, sickness
9. complaint, distemper
13. indisposition
mala fide ... **10.** in bad faith
Malaga ... **4.** city (Sp), wine **10.** oxblood
red
Malagasy lemur ... **6.** aye-aye
Malagasy region ... **10.** Madagascar
malaise ... **4.** pain **10.** discomfort,
uneasiness
malapert ... **4.** bold, pert **5.** saucy
8. impudent
malaria ... **5.** miasm **6.** miasma
10. strophulus
malaxation ... **7.** massage **9.** softening
Malay Archipelago ...
animal .. **4.** mias **5.** tapir, tsine **6.** gibbon,
taguan **7.** banteng
apparel .. **4.** baju **5.** banju **6.** sarong
buffalo .. **4.** gaur **7.** carabao, seldang
canoe .. **4.** proa **5.** prahu
chief (tribal) .. **4.** dato (datto)
crane .. **5.** sarus
dagger, knife .. **6.** creese (kris), parong
disease (jumping) .. **4.** Lata (Latah)
gentleman .. **3.** sir **4.** tuan
island .. **4.** Bali, Java **5.** Timor **7.** Celebes,
Sumatra **9.** New Guinea **11.** Philippines
isthmus .. **3.** Kra
language .. **7.** Tagalog
native .. **5.** Bajau **6.** Ifugao **8.** Filipino
9. Samal Laut **10.** sea gypsies
palm .. **6.** Arenga, gomuti (gomuto)
8. Saguerus
pygmy .. **4.** Aeta
rice field .. **5.** sawah
seaport .. **7.** Malacca
state .. **5.** Kedah, Perak **6.** Jahore
tree .. **5.** upas **6.** kapur, niepa, terap
6. durian (fruit)
vessel .. **4.** toup **6.** lugger
Malaysia ...

capital.. **11.** Kuala Lumpur
malcontent... **5.** rebel **6.** Fenian,
   uneasy **7.** repiner **8.** agitator, grumbler
   10. rebellious **12.** discontented
male... **2.** he **3.** cob, him, tom **4.** bull,
   dude, galt, jack, stud **5.** andro (comb
   form), macho, manly **6.** tercel, virile
   7. rooster **8.** stallion **9.** masculine
male (pert to)...
   column (Arch).. **7.** Telamon **8.** Atlantes
   One Hundred eyes.. **5.** Argus
malediction... **5.** curse **6.** threat
   7. malison, slander **8.** anathema
   11. imprecation **12.** denunciation
malefaction... **5.** crime **7.** offense
   9. malum in se
malefactor... **5.** felon **7.** culprit
   8. criminal, evildoer **9.** wrongdoer
malevolence... **4.** hate **5.** pique, spite
   6. grudge, malice, rancor **7.** ill will
   8. inimical **9.** animosity, malignity
   10. bitterness
malevolent... **4.** evil **6.** hating **7.** envious,
   hateful **8.** spiteful **9.** malicious,
   rancorous **11.** ill-disposed
malfeasance... **7.** misrule **8.** impolicy
   10. wrongdoing **11.** evil conduct, illegal
   deed
malfeasant... **8.** criminal, evildoer
malgré... **9.** in spite of
   15. notwithstanding
malheur... **10.** misfortune
Mali, Africa...
   capital.. **6.** Bamako
malice... **4.** envy, evil **5.** malum,
   pique, spite, wrong **6.** rancor **7.** ill
   will **9.** animosity, malignity, malintent
   10. bitterness **11.** malevolence
malicious... **4.** evil, mean **6.** bitter,
   malign, ornery **7.** hateful **8.** sinister,
   spiteful **9.** rancorous, resentful, vitriolic
   11. ill-disposed **12.** cantankerous,
   unpropitious
malicious (pert to)...
   destruction.. **5.** arson **8.** sabotage
   9. vandalism
   gossip.. **4.** dirt **7.** scandal, slander
   intention.. **6.** animus
maliform... **11.** apple-shaped
malign... **4.** evil **5.** abuse, libel **6.** deadly,
   defame, revile, vilify **7.** asperse, baleful,
   harmful, slander, traduce **8.** badmouth,
   virulent **10.** calumniate **12.** unpropitious
malignancy... **6.** malice **9.** virulence
   10. deadliness **11.** harmfulness,
   noxiousness
malignant... **3.** ill **4.** evil **5.** felon
   6. deadly, wicked **7.** harmful, heinous,
   vicious **8.** spiteful, virulent **9.** felonious,
   invidious, malicious, poisonous,
   rancorous **10.** rebellious **11.** deleterious
maligner... **8.** libelist **9.** slanderer
malignity... **4.** evil, hate **5.** spite, venom
   11. harmfulness, heinousness
maline(s)... **3.** net **11.** Mechlin lace
malingerer... **6.** truant **7.** quitter, shirker,
   slacker, welsher
malison... **5.** curse **11.** malediction
malkin... **3.** cat, mop **4.** drab, hare
   6. sponge **8.** slattern **9.** scarecrow
mall... **4.** gull, walk **5.** alley, plaza,

prado **6.** arcade, mallet **7.** alameda
   8. assembly **9.** esplanade, promenade
   14. shopping center
mallangong... **8.** duckbill
mallard... **4.** Anas, duck **5.** drake
malleable... **4.** soft **6.** pliant **7.** ductile,
   plastic **9.** teachable
mallemuck... **6.** fulmar, petrel
   9. albatross
mallet... **3.** tup **4.** club, mace, maul
   5. gavel, madge **6.** beater, beetle,
   driver, hammer
malm... **4.** marl **5.** chalk
malmsey... **4.** wine
malodorous... **4.** foul, rank **5.** fetid
   6. rotten, smelly **7.** noisome, odorous
   11. ill-smelling, odoriferous
malt (pert to)...
   froth.. **4.** barm
   ground.. **5.** grist
   infusion.. **4.** wort **9.** sweetwort
   kiln.. **4.** oast
   liquor.. **4.** beer, suds **6.** Scotch (whisky)
   mixture.. **6.** zythum **7.** maltate
   source.. **5.** grain **6.** barley
   vinegar.. **4.** wort **6.** alegar
Malta, Mediterranean Isle...
   capital.. **8.** Valletta
   fever.. **8.** undulent
   group island.. **4.** Gozo **6.** Comino
Maltese... **3.** cat **5.** cross **6.** Knight,
   native (of Malta)
maltreat... **5.** abuse **6.** misuse **8.** ill
   treat **9.** do wrong by
malty... **5.** drunk
malum... **4.** evil **5.** wrong **7.** offense
malversation... **9.** extortion (in office)
   10. corruption **11.** evil conduct,
   fraudulence, misbehavior
mammal... **3.** ape, man **4.** homo **5.** whale
   10. vertebrate
mammal... **2.** ai, ox **3.** ape, bat, cat,
   cow, dog, hog, orc, pig, rat, yak
   4. bear, bull, deer, lion, mink, mole,
   paca, seal, tait, zebu **5.** camel, coati,
   daman, koala, lemur, llama, moose,
   mouse, okapi, otter, ounce, panda,
   ratel, rhino, sable, shark, sheep, swine,
   tapir, tayra, whale **6.** alpaca, badger,
   desman, dugong, marten, monkey,
   ocelot, rytina (ext), tenrec (tendrac),
   walrus, weasel **7.** dolphin, manatee,
   opossum, peccary, raccoon **8.** aardvark,
   anteater, antelope, elephant, kangaroo,
   mongoose, reindeer **10.** chevrotain,
   rhinoceros **12.** hippopotamus
mammal (pert to)...
   coat.. **4.** hide, skin **6.** pelage
   cud-chewing.. **8.** ruminant
   edentate.. **8.** anteater, pangolin,
   tamandua (anteater)
   extinct.. **6.** rytina **8.** mastodon
   9. Glyptodon
   flying.. **3.** bat
   largest.. **5.** whale
   man.. **6.** Bimana (group)
   meat-eating.. **9.** carnivore
   nipple.. **4.** teat **8.** mammilla
   omnivorous.. **3.** hog, pig **5.** swine
   Order.. **7.** Cetacea **8.** Edentata, Rodentia
   Order, highest.. **7.** Primata **8.** Mammalia

Order, lowest.. **9.** Marsupial
plantigrade.. **7.** raccoon
primate (except Man).. **10.** Quadrumana
scaled.. **8.** pangolin
shelled.. **9.** armadillo
smallest.. **5.** shrew
snake-eating.. **8.** mongoose
toothless.. **8.** edentate
web-footed.. **6.** aliped
wing-footed.. **6.** aliped
zebralike.. **6.** quagga
mammock... **4.** tear **5.** break, scrap
   8. fragment
mammon... **5.** money **6.** riches, wealth
   11. fallen angel (Bib) **15.** demon of
   cupidity
mammoth... **5.** giant, large (very)
   7. titanic **8.** behemoth, elephant,
   gigantic, mastodon **9.** pachyderm
   11. Dinotherium **12.** hippopotamus
man... **3.** arm, fit, rig **4.** homo, male
   5. adult, equip, fit up, human, staff
   6. outfit, person **7.** fortify, furnish,
   mankind, prepare, someone **9.** human
   race **10.** human being
man (of)...
all work.. **4.** mozo **6.** Friday **8.** factotum
   9. assistant
Blood and Iron.. **8.** Bismarck
Destiny.. **9.** Bonaparte (Napoleon)
Galilee... **11.** Jesus Christ
God.. **5.** saint **6.** priest **9.** clergyman
   12. ecclesiastic
law.. **6.** lawyer **7.** counsel **8.** attorney
   9. counselor (counsellor)
learning.. **6.** pundit, savant **7.** scholar
   9. literatus **11.** litterateur
quackery.. **7.** buffoon **9.** trickster
   10. mountebank
the sea.. **3.** tar **6.** merman, sailor
the signs.. **12.** homo signorum
the woods.. **6.** rustic **8.** silvanus,
   woodsman **9.** orangutan
the world.. **6.** layman **11.** cosmopolite
   12. sophisticate
war.. **7.** frigate, soldier, warrior
man (pert to)...
aged.. **3.** vet **9.** patriarch
   12. octogenarian
bachelor.. **4.** stag **8.** celibate
bald.. **9.** pilgarlic
conceited.. **7.** coxcomb
cunning.. **5.** rogue **6.** rascal **7.** shyster
   10. mountebank
dissolute.. **4.** roué
eccentric, elderly.. **4.** sire **5.** uncle
   6. codger, gaffer **11.** grandfather
effeminate.. **9.** androgyne
entire (soul and body).. **3.** ego
fashionable.. **3.** fop **4.** dude **5.** dandy
   11. Beau Brummel **12.** boulevardier
fungus.. **9.** earthstar (the)
handsome.. **6.** Adonis
hardheaded.. **5.** Boche
hard-pressed.. **3.** Job
important.. **4.** hero, lion **5.** chief, nabob
   6. tycoon **7.** mugwump
isle of, capital.. **7.** Douglas
lady's.. **4.** beau **6.** fiancé
lawless.. **7.** ruffian
learned.. **6.** pundit, savant **7.** erudite,

scholar **9.** literatus **11.** philologist
like.. **7.** android **10.** anthropoid
little.. **6.** mankin, shrimp, squirt
   10. homunculus
loud-voiced.. **7.** stentor
lowbred.. **4.** serf **5.** churl **6.** rustic
   7. peasant **8.** plebeian
medicine, magic.. **6.** shaman
millionaire.. **7.** Croesus **10.** capitalist,
   Corinthian
newspaper.. **6.** editor **8.** reporter
   10. journalist
old.. **5.** elder **7.** veteran **12.** octogenarian
prehistoric.. **4.** cave **6.** Ice Age **8.** eolithic,
   Grimaldi, Piltdown **9.** neolithic
   11. paleolithic
red.. **6.** Indian
strong.. **6.** Samson **8.** ironside
wise.. **4.** sage, seer **5.** solon **6.** nestor
   7. Solomon
without a country.. **5.** Nolan (Philip)
manacle... **4.** gyve, iron **5.** chain **6.** fetter
   7. shackle **8.** handcuff **9.** restraint
manada... **4.** herd **5.** drove, flock
manage... **3.** man, run **4.** boss, head,
   lead, tend **5.** cater, dight, guide, pilot,
   wield **6.** direct, govern **7.** control,
   husband, operate **8.** contrive, engineer
   10. administer, manipulate
manageable... **4.** easy, tame, yare
   6. docile, wieldy **7.** ductile **9.** compliant,
   tractable **10.** governable **12.** controllable
management... **4.** care **6.** charge,
   menage **7.** conduct, control, gestion
   9. direction **10.** government
   11. negotiation
manager... **4.** boss **6.** gerent **7.** steward
   8. director, governor, operator, overseer
   9. economist **12.** entrepreneur
   13. administrator
managery... **7.** cunning **8.** artifice
   9. frugality, husbandry **10.** management
   12. manipulation **14.** administration
mañana... **8.** tomorrow **10.** before long
manas (Hind)... **3.** ego **4.** mind
Manasseh... **5.** tribe (Israel) **11.** King
   of Judah
Manchuria...
capital.. **6.** Mukden (old) **9.** Changchun
government.. **5.** China
Japanese name.. **9.** Manchukuo
native.. **9.** Mongolian
river.. **4.** Amur, Liao, Yalu
manciple... **5.** slave **7.** servant, steward
   8. purveyor
mandarin (pert to)...
bird.. **4.** duck
city.. **9.** Chungking
color.. **3.** red
dialect.. **7.** Chinese
figure in Chinese dress, seated..
   9. grotesque
fruit.. **6.** orange **9.** tangerine
official.. **8.** governor **10.** bureaucrat
residence.. **5.** yamen
ware.. **9.** porcelain
mandate... **5.** edict, order **6.** behest,
   charge, decree, mandat **7.** bidding,
   command, precept **9.** direction
   10. injunction, referendum
mandatory... **10.** imperative, obligatory,

preceptive
mandible . . . **3.** jaw **4.** beak **5.** chops,
   molar (part) **9.** chelicera
mandrel, mandril . . . **3.** hob **4.** axle, pick
   (miner's) **5.** arbor **7.** spindle
mandriarch . . . **9.** monk ruler
mandrill . . . **6.** baboon
mane . . . **4.** hair, juba, shag **6.** thatch
manege . . . **6.** school (riding) **7.** academy
   (riding) **8.** cavesson (halter)
manes (Rom) . . . **4.** gods (lower world)
   7. spirits
maneuver, manoeuvre . . . **4.** ruse
   5. trick **6.** device, jockey, scheme,
   tactic **7.** operate **8.** artifice, intrigue,
   strategy **9.** stratagem **10.** manipulate
   13. Immelmann turn
mangabey . . . **6.** monkey
manger . . . **3.** bin **4.** crib, meal, rack
   6. bunker, trough **7.** banquet
mangle . . . **3.** cut, mar **4.** hack, maim
   5. press **6.** bruise, injure, ironer
   8. calender, demolish, lacerate, mutilate
   9. dismember
mango (pert to) . . .
   bird . . **6.** oriole **11.** hummingbird
   fish . . **9.** threadfin
   fruit . . **5.** amini, bauno, drupe, melon
   9. muskmelon
   grove . . **4.** tope
mangy . . . **4.** mean **5.** itchy, seedy
   6. ronyon, scurvy, shabby **7.** squalid
   12. contemptible
manhandle . . . **4.** maul **5.** abuse **7.** rough
   up **8.** maltreat, mistreat
mania . . . **4.** rage **5.** craze, furor
   6. frenzy, furore, lunacy **7.** madness,
   passion **8.** delirium **10.** alienation
   11. fascination, infatuation
mania (for) . . .
   buying . . **9.** oniomania
   drink . . **9.** potomania **10.** dipsomania
   foreign customs . . **9.** xenomania
   narcotics . . **10.** narcomania
   religion . . **9.** theomania
   stealing . . **10.** erotomania
   11. kleptomania
   wandering . . **10.** dromomania
   work . . **9.** ergomania
manifest . . . **4.** list, open, show **5.** clear,
   index, overt **6.** evince, liquet, patent
   7. declare, evident, express, obvious,
   visible **8.** apparent, disclose
   11. indubitable **12.** indisputable,
   unmistakable
manifestation . . . **4.** aura **5.** phase
   7. display **8.** evidence **10.** appearance,
   disclosure, exhibition, indication,
   revelation **13.** demonstration
manifestation of . . .
   deity . . **4.** Apis **7.** serapis
   divinity . . **6.** Christ **8.** Epiphany
   Vishnu . . **6.** avatar
manifesto . . . **5.** edict **6.** decree
   8. evidence, rescript **11.** declaration
   (public) **12.** announcement
   13. demonstration
manikin . . . **5.** dwarf, model, pygmy
   6. figure **7.** phantom **9.** mannequin
Manila . . .
   boat . . **6.** bilalo

capital of . . **11.** Philippines
hemp . . **5.** abaca
hero . . **5.** Dewey (Adm)
island site . . **5.** Luzon
native . . **7.** Chinese, Tagalog **9.** Filipinos
manioc . . **7.** cassava
maniple . . . **5.** fanon, orale **7.** handful,
   phalanx, platoon
manipulate . . . **3.** rig, use **4.** work
   5. pilot, treat, wield **6.** handle, manage
   7. operate
manipulation . . . **5.** using **8.** handling,
   intrigue **9.** operation, stratagem
   10. management, use of hands
Manitoba, Canada . . .
   capital . . **8.** Winnipeg
   Indian . . **4.** Cree
   lake . . **8.** Manitoba
   river . . **3.** Red
mankind . . . **3.** man **4.** Adam, folk
   7. menfolk **8.** humanity **9.** human race
mankind (pert to) . . .
   division . . **4.** race **5.** tribe
   group (kindred) . . **6.** ethnos, socius
   hater . . **11.** misanthrope
   science . . **9.** ethnogeny, ethnology
   12. anthropology
manly . . . **4.** bold **5.** adult, brave, hardy,
   noble **6.** daring **8.** resolute **9.** honorable,
   masculine, undaunted **10.** courageous
manna . . . **4.** food (miracle), lerp (laap,
   laarp) **7.** godsend **10.** gazangabin
manner . . . **3.** air, way **4.** kind, mien,
   mode, sort **5.** guise, style **6.** aspect,
   custom, method **7.** fashion **8.** behavior
   10. appearance, deportment
manner (pert to) . . .
   frenzied . . **4.** amok, amuck, huffy
   7. haughty
   law . . **5.** modus
   like . . **4.** thus **6.** in kind **8.** parallel
   meddlesome . . **9.** officious
   meditative . . **13.** contemplative
   rough . . **7.** brusque **10.** irreverent
mannerism . . . **4.** mode **8.** elegance
   11. affectation
mannerly . . . **4.** nice **5.** moral, suave
   6. seemly **8.** decorous, politely
   9. courteous **10.** well-spoken
   12. ingratiating
manner of . . .
   making something . . **7.** facture
   pronouncing . . **6.** accent, brogue
   speaking . . **7.** grammar
manners . . . **7.** mores **8.** behavior
   9. amenities, etiquette
Mannheim gold . . . **5.** brass
mano (comb form) . . . **4.** hand
manoc . . . **4.** fowl (jungle) **7.** chicken,
   rooster
manor . . . **4.** hall **5.** abode **6.** estate
   7. demesne, mansion
manred . . . **4.** homage **9.** vassalage
   10. leadership (in war)
mansion . . . **4.** seat **5.** house, manor,
   manse **8.** dwelling **9.** astrology
manta . . . **3.** ray (fish) **4.** wrap **5.** cloak,
   cloth **7.** blanket **8.** mantelet (mantlet)
   9. devilfish
mantilla . . . **4.** cape, veil **5.** cloak
mantis . . . **4.** Cagn (deity) **6.** insect

7. mantoid 9. rearhorse
mantis crab . . . 7. squilla
mantle . . . 4. cape, cope, robe 5. cloak,
cover 6. capote, kittel 7. garment
8. filament, insignia, mantelet, mantling
(Her), vestment 10. witzchoura
11. mantelletta
manto . . . 3. ore 4. gown 5. cloak
6. mantle, mantua
mantoid . . . 6. mantis
Mantua (pert to) . . .
birthplace of . . 6. Vergil (Virgil)
capital . . 7. Mantova
walled by . . 11. Charlemagne
Manu (Myth) . . .
laws . . 8. creation, religion
progenitors of . . 3. Man
Seventh Age, author of . . 10. Code of
Manu (Hind laws)
manual . . . 4. book 7. clavier (Mus),
didache 8. exercise, handbook
14. consuetudinary
manual (pert to) . . .
alphabet (deaf) . . 11. dactylology
arts . . 6. crafts
crafts . . 5. sloyd (sloid, slojd)
10. handicraft
digit . . 3. toe 5. thumb 6. finger
8. dactylar
ritual . . 7. rituale 8. breviary 9. formulary
manufacture . . . 4. make 6. invent
7. produce, trump up 9. fabricate
manufacturer of drugs, liquors . . .
6. abkari (abkary)
manumission . . . 7. freeing 10. liberation
(slave) 12. emancipation
manumit . . . 4. free 5. let go 6. unhand
7. dismiss, release 8. liberate
manuscript (Ms, Mss) . . . 4. copy
(author's), opus 5. codex, folio
7. writing 8. document 11. composition,
handwriting 13. written by hand
manuscript (pert to) . . .
back . . 5. dorso
blank space . . 6. lacuna
copier . . 6. scribe
mark (old) . . 6. obelus
many . . . 6. divers 7. diverse, several,
various 8. frequent, manifold, numerous
9. different, multitude 10. multiplied
many (pert to) . . .
footed . . 8. multiped
prefix . . 4. poly, vari 5. multi
sided . . 9. versatile 12. multilateral
times . . 5. often 10. frequently
manyplies . . . 12. third stomach
(ruminant)
Manx cat characteristic . . . 6. no tail
8. tailless
mao . . . 7. peacock
Maori (pert to) . . .
Adam, ancestor . . 4. Tiki
bird . . 3. tui 4. weka (flightless)
canoe, raft . . 4. moki, waka
charm (grotesque) . . 7. heitiki
compensation . . 3. utu
fish . . 4. hiku 7. rainbow 9. trumpeter
hero . . 4. Maui
people . . 3. Ati 4. Hapu
priest . . 7. tuhunga
sect . . 7. Ringatu

tatooing . . 4. moko
tree . . 5. mapau
village . . 4. kaik (kaika)
weapon . . 4. mere, patu, rata 6. marree
Maoriland . . . 10. New Zealand
map . . . 4. plat 5. chart, image 6. charte,
design, isobar (weather line), sketch,
survey 7. diagram, epitome, explore,
picture 9. delineate 10. embodiment
14. representation
maple (pert to) . . .
bowl . . 5. mazer, rogan (sap)
flowering . . 8. abutilon
genus . . 4. Acer 9. Aceraceae
insect scale . . 10. pulvinaria
seed . . 6. samara
sugar tube . . 5. stile
tree . . 8. box elder 9. moosewood
map maker . . . 4. Eric (Father) 7. charter
8. Mercator 12. cartographer
mapo . . . 4. goby (fish)
mar . . . 4. ruin, scar 5. botch, spoil
6. damage, deface, impair, mangle
7. blemish 8. mutilate 9. disfigure
Mar . . . 4. Lord (Jacobite)
marabou, marabout . . . 5. stork 6. argala,
covert 8. adjutant
maracan . . . 5. macaw
maranon . . . 6. cashew
marasca, maraschino . . . 6. cherry
marasma . . . 5. waste 7. disease
10. emaciation 12. malnutrition
maraud . . . 3. rob 4. loot, raid, rove, sack
6. forage 7. brigand, cateran, pillage,
plunder 10. plundering
marble . . . 3. mib, mig, taw 4. cold,
hard 5. agate, white 6. basalt, marmor
7. pattern (mottled) 8. dolomite
9. limestone, sculpture, unfeeling
marble (pert to) . . .
Belgian . . 5. rance
Catalonia . . 8. brocatel (brocatelle)
cork (tree) . . 9. tambookie
famous . . 6. Parian 7. Carrara 8. Pentelec
game . . 3. taw 5. alley
group (famed) . . 5. Elgin (Marbles)
made of . . 9. marmoreal
mosaic . . 7. tessera
Roman . . 7. cipolin
slab . . 5. dalle, stele
marbled . . . 9. marmorate
Marbles . . . 5. Elgin 7. Arundel
marc . . . 6. refuse, spirit 7. residue 14. eau
de vie de marc
marcato (Mus) . . . 6. marked 8. accented,
emphatic
march . . . 4. fill, hike, step, trek 5. troop
6. border, parade 7. advance, proceed
8. boundary, drumbeat, frontier,
lockstep, movement, progress, smallage
9. cavalcade, quickstep
March King . . . 5. Sousa (John Philip)
marcid . . . 4. weak 7. decayed, tabetic
8. withered 9. exhausted 10. emaciating
Marcobrunner . . . 4. wine (White Rhine)
Mardi Gras . . . 8. carnival 10. fat Tuesday
(literal) 13. Shrove Tuesday
Mardi Gras King . . . 3. Rex
mare . . . 4. yaud 5. filly, horse 6. goblin,
grasni (gypsy) 7. incubus, specter,
trestle 8. the blues 9. nightmare 10. blue

marge, margent . . . **3.** rim **4.** brim, edge,
side **5.** brink, shore **6.** border, fringe,
margin **8.** marginal
margin . . . **3.** rim **4.** brim, edge, rand,
room, side **5.** brink, limit **6.** amount,
border, reward **10.** collateral
margin (pert to) . . .
  business . . **5.** gross
  notched . . **5.** erose
  note . . **7.** apostil **8.** scholium
    10. annotation
  scalloped . . **7.** crenate
  set in . . **6.** indent
  straighten (to) . . **5.** align
marginal note . . . **4.** kere (kri, keri)
  7. apostil **8.** scholium **10.** annotation
marigold . . . **5.** aster, boots, caper,
finch **6.** orange (cadmium) **7.** cowslip,
Tagetes
marijuana . . . **3.** hay **4.** hemp **6.** reefer
  7. tobacco (wild) **8.** locoweed
  9. cigarette
marikina . . . **7.** tamarin **8.** marmoset
marimba . . . **9.** xylophone
marina . . . **4.** dock **5.** basin **9.** esplanade,
promenade (seaside)
marinal . . . **6.** marine, sailor, saline
marine . . . **3.** tar **5.** jolly, naval **7.** mariner,
oceanic, pelagic **8.** maritime, nautical
  11. leatherneck
marine (pert to) . . .
  animal . . **3.** orc **4.** brit, seal **5.** coral,
polyp **6.** dugong, Otaria, teredo, walrus
7. manatee, mollusk, octopus
  clam . . **8.** shipworm
  crustacean . . **4.** brit **8.** barnacle
  fauna, flora . . **7.** benthos
  fish . . **5.** shark **8.** menhaden
  gastropod . . **5.** conus (snail), murex
7. terebra
  growth . . **4.** kelp **5.** algae **6.** enalid
7. seaweed **10.** ditch grass
  individual . . **6.** merman **7.** mermaid
  skeleton . . **5.** coral
  slogan . . **6.** gung-ho
mariner . . . **3.** gob, tar **4.** salt **5.** Jacky
  6. sailor, seaman **8.** waterman
mariner's card . . . **5.** chart
mariner's compass points . . . **6.** rhumba
marionette . . . **4.** doll, duck **6.** figure,
puppet
maritime . . . **5.** naval **6.** marine **7.** oceanic
  8. nautical
marjoram . . . **3.** dot **4.** mint **6.** origin
  8. origanum **9.** flavoring
mark . . . **3.** aim, tee **4.** heed, line, note, rist,
seal, sign **5.** brand, label, notch, score,
stain, stamp, trait **6.** denote, symbol,
target **7.** betoken, blemish, earmark,
engrave, impress, imprint, insigne
8. evidence, identify, insignia, landmark
9. emphasize, objective, punctuate,
signature, trademark **10.** indication
11. distinction, distinguish
14. characteristic
mark (pert to) . . .
  bad . . **7.** demerit
  bounds . . **7.** delimit **9.** demarcate
  contest (in a) . . **5.** bogey (bogie)
  critical . . **6.** obelus

  diacritical . . **5.** hacek, tilde **6.** tittle,
umlaut **7.** cedilla
  disgrace . . **6.** stigma
  fingerprint . . **5.** whorl
  logic . . **11.** differentia
  misconduct . . **7.** demerit
  off . . **4.** plot **6.** assign **7.** measure
12. characterize, circumscribe
  of homage . . **7.** ovation
  of whip . . **4.** wale, welt
  on a seed . . **5.** hilum (pl hila)
  out . . **6.** cancel **10.** obliterate
  possessive . . **10.** apostrophe
  printing . . **4.** dele, stet **5.** caret **6.** dagger,
diesis, obelus **7.** obelisk **10.** apostrophe
  pronunciation . . **5.** breve **6.** macron
  proofreading . . **4.** dele **5.** caret
  prosody . . **7.** caesura, triseme
9. diaeresis, tetraseme
  punctuation . . **4.** dash **5.** colon, comma
6. period **9.** diaeresis (dieresis),
semicolon **10.** apostrophe
  question . . **7.** eroteme (erotema)
  reference . . **4.** star **6.** dagger, diesis
8. asterisk
  with bars . . **5.** grill
  with dots, spots . . **6.** dapple **7.** stipple
  with pointed instrument . . **6.** scrive
  with ridges . . **3.** rib
marked by . . .
  dispute . . **13.** controversial
  maneuvering . . **8.** tactical
  nicety . . **7.** elegant
  small areas . . **9.** areolated
  time . . **5.** dated
marked with . . .
  colors . . **7.** mottled **10.** variegated
11. psychedelic
  depressions . . **7.** dimpled
  furrows . . **6.** rivose
  grooves . . **6.** lirate
  lines . . **5.** ruled **6.** linear, notate
  sables (Her) . . **8.** pelleted
  spots . . **6.** notate **7.** mottled
  stripes . . **7.** lineate
  zones . . **6.** zonate
marker . . . **4.** buoy **5.** pylon **6.** scorer,
signal **7.** brander, counter, monitor
8. bookmark, marksman, monument,
recorder **9.** indicator
market . . . **4.** mart, sale, sell, shop
5. forum, trade **6.** rialto, square
9. clientele
market (pert to) . . .
  bonds . . **5.** float
  day (Rom) . . **7.** nundine
  French . . **8.** débouché
  place . . **4.** sook **5.** agora, plaza, store
6. bazaar, rialto **8.** emporium, exchange
marketable . . . **6.** staple **7.** salable **8.** in
demand, vendible **12.** merchantable
markhor . . . **4.** goat
marking (crescent) . . . **6.** lunula, lunule
7. lunulet **9.** engraving
markings . . . **7.** rasceta
marksman . . . **4.** shot **6.** gunner, sniper
  7. shooter **9.** Orangeman
Mark Twain (pert to) . . .
  character . . **9.** Tom Sawyer
15. Huckleberry Finn
  pseud of . . **13.** Samuel (Langhorne)

Clemens
tale . . **9**. Gilded Age **10**. Roughing It **15**. Innocents Abroad
marl . . . **4**. malm **5**. earth, fiber **6**. manure **7**. deposit (earthy), marlite **9**. greensand **10**. fertilizer, overspread
marli . . . **4**. lace **5**. gauze, tulle **6**. border (raised on dish)
marlin . . . **6**. curlew, godwit **8**. sailfish **9**. spearfish
marlinspike . . . **3**. fid **4**. bird, tool **6**. jaeger **8**. skua gull
marmalade . . . **3**. jam **6**. Achras, sapote **8**. plum tree, preserve **12**. mammee sapota
marmit . . . **6**. kettle **7**. soup pot
marmite (Mil) . . . **4**. bomb (soup kettle) **5**. shell
marmor . . . **6**. marble
marmoset . . . **4**. mico (black-tailed) **6**. monkey, sagoin **7**. tamarin
marmot . . . **5**. bobac **6**. rodent **7**. Marmota **8**. Arctomys, whistler **9**. ground hog, woodchuck
maroon . . . **5**. slave **7**. abandon, cast off, forsake, isolate **8**. chestnut **13**. leave helpless
marquee . . . **4**. tent **6**. canopy
Marquis, infamous . . . **4**. Sade
marriage . . . **5**. union **7**. wedding, wedlock **9**. matrimony **10**. nuptiality **11**. espousement
marriage (pert to) . . .
absence of . . **5**. agamy
age . . **6**. mature, nubile
broker . . **9**. schatchen **10**. matchmaker
forswearer . . **8**. celibate
god . . **5**. Hymen
goddess . . **4**. Hera
hater . . **10**. misogamist
late in life . . **8**. opsigamy
more than one . . **6**. bigamy, digamy **8**. polygamy **9**. polyandry, tetragamy (4th) **11**. deuterogamy
notice . . **5**. banns
of the gods . . **8**. theogamy
outside the tribe . . **7**. exogamy
pert to . . **7**. marital, spousal **8**. hymeneal **9**. connubial, endogamic
portion . . **3**. dot **5**. dotal, dowry
promise . . **7**. betroth **8**. affiance
secret . . **9**. elopement
married . . . **5**. wived **6**. wedded **8**. espoused **9**. connubial
married (pert to) . . .
more than once at a time . . **9**. polyandry (woman)
once at a time . . **8**. monandry
person . . **4**. wife **6**. spouse **7**. husband **8**. benedict
twice . . **6**. bigamy, digamy **11**. deuterogamy
marrow . . . **4**. pith **6**. center **7**. essence, medulla **9**. substance
Mars . . . **3**. god (of War) **4**. Ares **6**. planet, war-god
Mars (pert to) . . .
altar . . **13**. Campus Martius (field of Mars)
constellation . . **3**. Ara
festival . . **5**. March **7**. October

pert to . . **5**. Arean **7**. Martian
priests . . **5**. Salii
red . . **5**. totem
satellites . . **6**. Deimos, Phobos
ship . . **8**. moon ship **9**. spaceship
sons (twin) . . **5**. Remus **7**. Romulus
spot . . **5**. oasis
Marseillaise . . . **4**. song (1792)
Marseille, France . . .
capital of Dept . . **14**. Bouches du Rhone
church . . **9**. Notre Dame
fort . . **11**. Rue Noailles **13**. Rue Cannebière
old name . . **8**. Massilia
seaport site . . **13**. Mediterranean
marsh . . . **3**. bog, fen **4**. meer, mire, moor, slue **5**. bayou, liman, swale, swamp **6**. morass, saline, slough **7**. maremma
marsh (pert to) . . .
bird . . **4**. rail, sora **5**. crane, snipe, stilt **7**. bittern
crocodile . . **3**. goa
elder . . **3**. Iva
fever . . **7**. helodes
gas . . **7**. methane **8**. firedamp
grass . . **5**. sedge, spart
hawk . . **5**. harpy **7**. harrier
hen . . **4**. rail
inhabiting . . **12**. limnophilous
mallow . . **5**. altea
marigold . . **5**. boots, calla **7**. cowslip
pert to . . **8**. paludine
shrub . . **4**. reed **5**. sedge **7**. bulrush, cattail **8**. moorwort **12**. pickerelweed
marshal . . . **3**. Ney (Fr) **4**. lead **5**. align, aline, array, groom, guide, range, usher **6**. direct, parade **7**. farrier, officer **8**. official
Marshall Islands . . .
chains (two) . . **6**. Ralick (eleven isls) **7**. Rattach (13 isls)
government . . **11**. trusteeship
WWII scene . . **6**. Bikini **8**. Eniwetok **9**. Kwajalein
marshberry, marshwort . . . **9**. cranberry
marshy . . . **3**. wet **5**. boggy, fenny, liman **7**. moorish **8**. morassey, paludine
marsupial . . . **4**. frog, tait **5**. kaola **6**. wombat **7**. opossum, wallaby **8**. kangaroo **9**. bandicoot, phalanger, tapoatafa **10**. Diprotodon **11**. Marsupialia
marsupium . . . **5**. pouch
martel (Hist) . . . **6**. hammer
martel-de-fer . . . **6**. weapon **12**. hammer of iron
marten . . . **3**. fur **4**. pelt **5**. sable **6**. mammal **7**. Mustela
martial . . . **4**. Mars (pert to) **5**. brave **7**. warlike **8**. fighting, militant, military
Martinique . . .
capital . . **8**. St Pierre (former) **12**. Fort de France
formation . . **8**. volcanic
mountain peak . . **9**. Mont Pelée
martyr . . . **4**. kill **5**. title **7**. Stephen (Christian), torture **8**. sufferer
marvel . . . **4**. gape **6**. wonder **7**. miracle, portent, prodigy **8**. astonish
marvelous . . . **6**. superb **7**. strange **9**. wonderful **10**. improbable, incredible,

remarkable **11.** astonishing
13. extraordinary
Maryland ...
bay .. **10.** Chesapeake
capital .. **9.** Annapolis
city .. **9.** Baltimore
Hist site .. **8.** Antietam **10.** State House
(nation's oldest) **11.** Fort Mc Henry
mountain .. **8.** Backbone, Piedmont
11. Appalachian
race (famed) .. **9.** Preakness
12. Steeplechase
race track .. **5.** Bowie **6.** Butler, Laurel
7. Pimlico
school .. **9.** Annapolis (Acad) **12.** Johns
Hopkins
settler .. **7.** Calvert (Leonard)
State admission .. **7.** Seventh
State motto .. **22.** Manly Deeds,
Womanly Words
State nickname .. **4.** Free **7.** Old Line
mash ... **4.** feed, ogle, pulp **5.** crush, flirt,
press, smash, steep **6.** jumble, soften
7. mixture **9.** pulverize **11.** infatuation
mashal ... **7.** parable, proverb
masher ... **5.** dandy, flirt, ricer **7.** utensil
10. pulverizer **11.** philanderer
masjid ... **6.** mosque
mask ... **4.** ball, loup, veil **5.** cloak,
cover, dance, drama, onkos **6.** domino,
screen **7.** conceal, pretext **8.** disguise
10. subterfuge
masked ... **6.** comedy, cowled, hidden,
veiled **7.** larvate, obscure **8.** shrouded
9. concealed, disguised
masker ... **5.** mimer **6.** mummer
11. masquerader
maslin ... **5.** brass **6.** kettle **7.** mixture
(grain) **9.** potpourri
Masonic doorkeeper ... **5.** tiler
Mason, Perry (pert to) ...
actor .. **4.** Burr (Raymond, TV) **6.** Larkin
(John, radio) **7.** William (Warren, film)
author .. **18.** Erle Stanley Gardner
detective ... **5.** Drake (Paul)
secretary .. **6.** Street (Della)
title words .. **9.** The Case of
masonry ... **6.** ashlar **9.** revetment
mass ... **3.** cob, dab, gob, mop, pat, wad
4. blob, body, bulk, load, loaf, lump,
roll, size **5.** solid **8.** quantity **9.** large
part, magnitude **11.** large amount
12. accumulation, congregation
mass (pert to) ...
book .. **6.** missal
collection .. **9.** aggregate
directory (RCCh) .. **4.** ordo
for dead .. **7.** requiem
matter .. **5.** molar
molten glass .. **7.** parison
nerve tissue .. **8.** ganglion
tangled .. **3.** mop **4.** shag
vestment (Eccl) .. **5.** amice
Massachusetts ...
capital .. **6.** Boston (1630)
city .. **5.** Salem **7.** Concord **8.** Plymouth
9. Cambridge, Lexington **10.** Gloucester,
New Bedford **12.** Provincetown
college (oldest, US) .. **7.** Harvard
explorer .. **5.** Cabot **7.** Gosnold **9.** Capt
Smith (John)

hero .. **10.** Paul Revere
island .. **9.** Nantucket **15.** Martha's
Vineyard
mountain .. **3.** Tom **8.** Greylock
10. Berkshires
river .. **10.** Housatonic **11.** Connecticut
school (first free) .. **6.** Dedham (1649)
settlers .. **8.** Pilgrims, Puritans
State admission .. **5.** Sixth
State nickname .. **8.** Bay State **9.** Old
Colony
massacre ... **5.** havoc **6.** pogrom
7. carnage **8.** butchery, decimate,
genocide **9.** slaughter
massage ... **3.** rub **5.** knead **6.** stroke
7. therapy
masses, the ... **4.** folk **6.** rabble **9.** hoi
polloi, multitude **11.** proletariat, rank
and file **12.** common people **13.** great
unwashed
massive ... **3.** big **4.** bold **5.** bulky,
large, massy **7.** weighty **8.** imposing
9. ponderous **10.** impressive
11. substantial
mast ... **3.** cue, fid **4.** pole, spar **5.** stick,
stuff (oneself)
master ... **3.** man, rab **4.** lord, mian, rule
5. chief, judge, rabbi, tutor **6.** expert,
humble, subdue **7.** captain, conquer,
maestro, padrone, subject, teacher
8. dominate, overcome, regulate,
surmount, vanquish **9.** commander,
conqueror, craftsman, preceptor,
subjugate
master (pert to) ...
African .. **5.** bwana
Eton .. **4.** beak
fencing .. **7.** lanista
hard .. **6.** despot
Indian .. **5.** sahib
music .. **7.** maestro
of a house .. **13.** paterfamilias
of ceremonies .. **2.** M C **5.** emcee
of Heaven .. **16.** Celestial Teacher
of the horse .. **7.** equerry
stroke .. **4.** coup
masterful ... **6.** lordly **7.** haughty
8. arrogant, skillful **9.** arbitrary,
imperious **10.** commanding
11. dictatorial, domineering, magisterial,
overbearing **13.** authoritative
masterpiece ... **10.** magnum opus
11. chef d'oeuvre **17.** pièce de
rèsistance
mastery ... **4.** gree **5.** power, skill
7. control, victory **8.** dominion
10. ascendancy **11.** proficiency
12. vanquishment
mastic ... **3.** asa, gum **5.** resin **6.** liquor
8. adhesive **9.** red-yellow
masticate ... **4.** chew **5.** crush, grind
8. macerate
mastiff ... **3.** dog **5.** burly, matin
7. massive
mastodon ... **5.** giant **6.** animal, Mammut
7. mammoth **8.** behemoth **9.** dinothere
10. Dinotheres, Mammutidae
11. Dinotherium
mat ... **3.** rug **4.** dull (finish) **5.** doily,
platt, twist **7.** webbing **8.** entangle,
material **10.** interweave, lusterless

matador ... see *bullfighting*
matagasse ... 11. butcherbird
match ... 3. pit 4. copy, game, mate, pair, peer, sort 5. equal, fusee, marry, tally, vesta 7. compare, contest, lighter, lucifer 8. coincide, marriage, parallel 10. correspond 11. counterpart
matched ... 5. mated 6. paired, pitted, teamed 7. equaled (equalled)
matchless ... 5. alone 6. unlike 7. unequal 8. peerless 9. unequaled 10. inimitable 12. incomparable
matchlock ... 3. gun 7. gunlock
mate ... 4. pair, wife 5. equal, marry, match 6. seaman, spouse 7. comrade, husband, mariner, partner 9. companion 11. confederate, counterpart
matelassé ... 6. fabric 8. quilting (imitation) 13. ornamentation
material, materiel ... 4. data 5. goods, stuff 6. fabric, matter, plasma, staple, swatch 7. weighty 8. relevant, supplies, tangible 9. apparatus, corporeal, equipment, essential 11. substantial 12. nonspiritual 13. materialistic
material (pert to) ...
 building .. 4. frit, lime, tile, wood 5. adobe, brick, rabat, tapia 6. cement, thatch 7. plywood 8. asbestos, Masonite 9. wallboard
 discard .. 4. slag 5. scrap 6. refuse 7. rubbish
 dress .. 4. silk, wool 5. crepe, linen, satin, surah, tulle, tweed 6. baleen, faille, sennit, tricot, velvet 8. corduroy
 household .. 5. scrim 6. carpet, damask, lampas, mohair, napery 7. drapery 8. tapestry
 needlework .. 4. lace, yarn 6. thread 8. arrasene, chenille
 paper .. 3. wax 4. bond, news, note, rice 6. letter, tissue, vellum 7. drawing, writing 8. wrapping 9. cardboard, onionskin, parchment 11. papier-mâché
 polishing .. 11. rottenstone
materia medica ... 7. acology 10. leechcraft
maternal ... 7. enation 8. motherly 10. motherlike
math ... 6. mowing 9. aftermath, monastery
mathematician ... 6. Euclid 7. actuary 9. physicist, Whitehead
mathematics (pert to) ...
 abbreviation .. 3. QED
 arbitrary .. 5. radix 9. parameter
 deduction .. 8. analysis
 diagram .. 5. graph
 element .. 4. cube, root 6. factor 7. decimal, divisor, formula, minuend 8. dividend, fraction, quotient, repetend 10. multiplier, subtrahend 12. multiplicand
 equation .. 2. pi 4. cosh, sine, surd 6. cosine
 factor .. 10. quaternion
 instrument .. 6. sector 7. compass 8. arbalest
 number .. 5. digit
 operation, operator .. 5. nabla 6. scalar 7. operand 10. quaternion
 proposition .. 7. theorem
 quantity .. 6. addend, augend, scalar
 sheets of .. 4. cone 5. nappe
 symbol .. 5. digit 7. facient, operand 12. multiplicand
 type .. 4. pure 6. higher 7. algebra, physics 8. abstract, calculus, geometry 10. arithmetic, elementary, quadratics 12. trigonometry
mathemeg ... 7. catfish
matie ... 7. herring
matin ... 6. aubade (song) 7. morning, service 8. watchdog 11. morning song 13. morning prayer
matinee ... 5. levee, party, salon 6. soiree 8. negligee 9. reception 13. conversazione, entertainment
matipo ... 4. wood (fuel) 5. napau
matka, matkab ... 4. seal
matlow ... 6. sailor
matrass ... 4. tube 5. flask 6. bottle, carafe 8. bolthead
matriculate ... 4. list 5. admit, adopt, enter 6. enroll 8. register 10. naturalize
matrimonial ... 7. marital, nuptial, spousal 8. conjugal, hymeneal 9. connubial
matrimony ... 7. wedlock 8. marriage
matrix ... 3. bed 4. cast, form, mold, womb 5. cutis 6. gangue 10. foundation, impression
matron ... 4. dame, wife 5. widow 11. housekeeper
matter ... 3. gas, pus 4. body, gear, malm, pith 5. atoms, fluid, vapor 6. affair, amount, solids 7. problem, trouble 8. business, elements, material 10. importance 11. constituent 12. circumstance
matter (pert to) ...
 alluvial .. 5. geest
 celestial .. 6. nebula
 coloring .. 5. eosin 10. endochrome
 fatty .. 5. sebum
 noxious .. 6. miasma
 of doubt .. 7. dubiety
 of fact .. 7. literal, prosaic 9. practical, pragmatic
 of law .. 3. res
 of note .. 8. notandum
 particle .. 4. atom
 perfume .. 7. essence
 spinal cord .. 4. alba
 uniform (physics) .. 7. inertia
 volcanic .. 2. aa, oo 4. lava
mattress ... 3. bed, pad 5. futon 7. cushion
mature ... 3. age, due, old 4. ripe 5. adult, grown, ripen 6. digest, mellow, season 7. develop, fall due, grow old, perfect 8. complete 9. full-grown, perfected, ratheripe
maturity ... 8. ripeness 9. adulthood, readiness 10. falling due 11. development
matutinal ... 5. early, matin 7. morning 12. antemeridian
maty ... 7. servant
maud ... 3. rug 5. plaid, shawl
maudlin ... 5. beery, drunk, silly, tipsy

7. tearful, weeping **10.** lachrymose
11. sentimental (overly)
maul, mall . . . **4.** beat, bung, club, mace,
   mall, moth **5.** abuse, gavel, staff
   6. beetle, bruise, mallet
maumet . . . **3.** god (false), guy **4.** doll,
   idol **5.** image **6.** puppet **9.** scarecrow
maund, maun . . . **3.** beg **6.** basket,
   hamper **7.** begging, measure
Maundy . . . **4.** alms **8.** ceremony **10.** Last
   Supper
Maundy Thursday (Bib) . . . **8.** Holy Week
   13. washing of feet
Mauritius, Ile de France . . .
   capital . . **9.** Port Louis
   government . . **7.** British
   product . . **5.** coral, sugar
   site . . **11.** Indian Ocean
Mauser . . . **5.** rifle **7.** firearm
mauve . . . **5.** lilac **6.** mallow, purple,
   violet **10.** atmosphere (color)
maven . . . **6.** expert **11.** connoisseur
maverick . . . **4.** calf (unbranded) **5.** dogie
   (dogy), stray **11.** independent
   13. nonconformist
mavis, mavie . . . **6.** thrush
maw . . . **4.** craw, crop **6.** gullet, mallow
   7. gizzard, stomach
mawk . . . **6.** maggot
mawkish . . . **5.** vapid **6.** sickly **8.** nauseous
   9. squeamish **10.** disgusting
   11. sentimental
maxilla . . . **7.** jawbone
maxim . . . **3.** saw **4.** dict, rule **5.** adage,
   axiom, gnome, motto, tenet, truth
   6. saying **7.** precept, proverb
   8. aphorism, apothegm **10.** apophthegm
maxims . . . **5.** logia **9.** moralisms
maximum . . . **4.** most **5.** limit **7.** highest,
   supreme **8.** greatest **12.** consummation
maximus . . . **7.** largest
may . . . **3.** can **6.** be able **9.** be allowed
   11. in one's power, opportunity
May (pert to) . . .
   apple . . **8.** mandrake
   bird . . **6.** thrush
   cock . . **5.** melon **6.** plover
   curlew . . **8.** whimbrel
   Duke . . **6.** cherry
   festival . . **7.** Beltane (anc)
   First . . **7.** Beltane **14.** May-day festival
   fish . . **9.** killifish
   flower . . **7.** arbutus **8.** hawthorn,
   marigold **9.** calla lily **10.** stitchwort
   12. cuckooflower
   fly . . **3.** dun **7.** shad fly **9.** ephemerid
   goddess . . **4.** Maia
   gowan . . **5.** daisy
Maya . . . **3.** Mam (people) **6.** Indian
   8. Pokonchi
Mayan calendar . . .
   five added days . . **5.** uayeb
   no leap year . . **5.** solar
   twenty-day month . . **5.** uinal
   year . . **4.** haab
Mayan underworld . . . **7.** xibalba
maybe . . . **2.** if **7.** perhaps **8.** possibly
   9. perchance **11.** conceivably,
   possibility, uncertainty
Mayday . . . **3.** SOS **4.** help **8.** distress
Mayfair . . . **6.** London (fashionable)

Mayflower (pert to) . . .
   boat of . . **8.** Pilgrims (1620)
   Compact . . **9.** agreement (1620)
   sister ship . . **9.** Speedwell
mayhap . . . **7.** perhaps **12.** peradventure
mayor . . . **5.** maire **7.** alcalde
   10. magistrate **11.** burgomaster
mazarine . . . **4.** blue (color from Cardinal
   Mazarin)
maze . . . **5.** fancy **7.** stupefy **8.** confound,
   delirium, delusion **9.** confusion,
   deception, labyrinth **12.** bewilderment,
   complication
mazed . . . **4.** lost **7.** in a maze **9.** stupefied
   10. bewildered
mazuma . . . **5.** money
mead . . . **5.** drink **6.** meadow **8.** hydromel
   9. metheglin
meadow . . . **3.** lea **4.** mead **5.** field, haugh,
   pampa, swale **7.** pasture, savanna
   (savannah) **9.** grassland **10.** agostadero
meadow (pert to) . . .
   chicken . . **8.** sora rail
   crocus . . **7.** saffron
   crowfoot . . **9.** buttercup
   hen . . **4.** coot, rail **7.** bittern
   mouse . . **4.** vole **8.** arvicole
   part . . **5.** swale
   sage . . **6.** salvia
   saxifrage . . **6.** seseli
   sweet . . **7.** Spiraea
meager, meagre . . . **4.** arid, bare, lank,
   poor, slim **5.** gaunt, scant, spare
   6. barren, jejune, lenten, narrow, sparse
   7. starved, sterile, trivial **9.** emaciated
   10. inadequate
meal . . . **3.** tub **4.** bran, dune, mess
   5. feast, grout, salep, snack **6.** bucket,
   fodder, powder, ration, repast, tiffin
   7. banquet **8.** sandbank **9.** collation,
   pulverize
mealy . . . **4.** pale **7.** friable, powdery
   10. soft-spoken **11.** farinaceous
   12. mealymouthed
mealy (pert to) . . .
   Amazon . . **6.** parrot
   back . . **6.** cicada
   bird, duck . . **5.** squaw
   bug . . **4.** pest **5.** scale **10.** pear blight
   mouth . . **7.** warbler
   tree . . **9.** arrowwood, wayfaring
mealy-mouthed . . . **5.** suave **10.** flattering
   12. hypocritical **13.** sanctimonious
mean . . . **3.** low **4.** base **5.** petty,
   small, snide, solar (time), sorry
   6. common, denote, design, humble,
   intend, medium, menial, middle,
   midway, paltry, shabby, sordid, stingy
   7. average, ignoble, purport, purpose,
   servile, squalid **8.** beggarly, ordinary,
   plebeian, shameful, wretched
   9. difficult, malicious, niggardly,
   penurious **10.** despicable, ill-humored,
   spiritless **11.** closefisted, disgraceful
   12. contemptible, dishonorable, narrow-
   minded, parsimonious
mean clef (Mus) . . . **5.** C clef
meander . . . **4.** wind **6.** ramble, wander
meaning . . . **4.** null (without) **5.** sense
   6. import, intent, spirit **7.** purport
   8. semantic **9.** intending, intention,

knowledge 10. understand
12. significance 13. signification
14. interpretation
meaningless . . . 4. rote 5. banal, derry
7. aimless 9. senseless 10. designless
11. purposeless 13. insignificant
meanness . . . 6. infamy, malice
8. baseness, ill-humor 9. servility
10. humbleness, paltriness, sordidness,
stinginess 11. inferiority
means . . . 5. funds 7. capital 8. averages
9. resources 11. wherewithal
means of . . .
  access . . 4. adit 5. inlet 7. ingress
  8. aperture
  communication . . 4. note 5. flags, phone,
  radio, smoke 6. letter, postal, tom-tom
  8. telegram 9. telegraph, telephone
  livelihood . . 4. work 5. labor, trade
  8. vocation 10. profession
  outlet . . 4. door, exit 6. egress 8. aperture
  support . . 5. funds 6. assets 7. aliment
  11. maintenance
meantime . . . 5. while 7. interim
8. interval, same time 9. meanwhile
measles . . . 7. rubella, rubeola 8. morbilli
measure (pert to) . . .
  area . . 2. ar 3. are, rod 4. acre, area, mile,
  rood 6. square 7. geodesy, hectare,
  section 8. township
  Bible . . 3. cab (kab), kor, log 4. epha
  5. cubit, homer
  gauge . . 3. erg, lea (yarn) 5. ergon,
  level, plumb, scale, stone 6. denier,
  square 7. calorie (calory), compass,
  sextant 8. calipers, quadrant
  length . . 3. ell, mil, rod 4. foot, hand,
  inch, knot, mile, nail, pace, rule, tape,
  yard 5. chain, cubit, meter 6. league
  7. furlong 9. kilometer, yardstick
  10. centimeter, micrometer, millimeter
  nautical . . 4. knot 6. fathom, league
  paper . . 4. page, ream 5. quire, sheet
  poetry . . 6. dipody, iambic, rhythm,
  sestet 7. anapest, couplet, distich,
  tripody 8. quatrain 9. hexameter
  10. ottava rima, pentastich, tetrameter,
  tetrastich 11. Alexandrine
  printer . . 2. em, en 4. pica 5. agate
  volume, weight . . 3. ton, tun (wine)
  4. bale, butt, cord 5. carat, liter,
  minim, ounce, pound, quart 6. barrel,
  bushel, finger, gallon, magnum, pottle
  8. hogshead, teaspoon 9. kiloliter
  10. tablespoon
measurement . . . 4. size 6. amount,
alnage, extent, metage 7. azimuth
8. abscissa, capacity, quantity
9. substance 11. calculation,
mensuration
measuring instrument . . . 6. stadia
7. alidade, caliper 8. odometer
12. perambulator (surveyor)
meat . . . 4. beef, fish, food, lamb, pork
5. flesh 6. fillet, kernel, mutton, quarry
7. brisket 9. aitchbone (icebone),
spareribs
meat (pert to) . . .
  ball . . 7. rissole 9. croquette, hamburger
  cured, dried . . 3. ham 5. bacon
  6. flitch, jerked 7. biltong (biltongue)

8. pemmican
  jellied . . 5. aspic
  minced, roll . . 7. rissole
  roasted . . 5. cabob (kabob) 9. barbecued
  slaughterhouse . . 8. abattoir
  smoking place . . 6. buccan (bucan)
  stew . . 8. mulligan 9. lobscouse
meatus . . . 4. burr (ear) 5. canal
7. opening, passage
meaty . . . 5. pithy, solid 11. substantial
Mecca, Arabia . . . 8. Holy City 16. City
of the Prophet
Mecca (pert to) . . .
  birthplace of . . 8. Mohammed
  capital . . 5. Hejaz
  color . . 11. Tuscan brown
  famed for . . 5. Kaaba (Caaba, Kaabeth)
  10. Black Stone 11. Great Mosque
  governor . . 6. sherif (shereef)
  pilgrimage . . 4. hadj
  pilgrim's dress . . 5. ihram
  rug . . 6. Shiraz
mechanic . . . 7. artisan, workman
8. operator 9. artificer, craftsman,
machinist, operative
mechanical . . . 8. machinal 9. automatic,
practical, technical 11. involuntary,
stereotyped
mechanical (pert to) . . .
  adjustment . . 9. tentation
  drawing . . 8. drafting
  law, motion . . 8. dynamics, kinetics
  lever . . 6. tappet
  part . . 5. rotor 6. stator
mechanics . . . 9. technique
11. mechanology
mechanism . . . 4. gear, tool 5. means
6. tackle 7. control, rigging 9. apparatus,
machinery, technique
medal . . . 4. coin, disk (disc) 5. badge
6. plaque 9. medallion 10. decoration
medallion . . . 4. coin 5. cameo, medal,
panel 6. tablet 8. ornament
meddle . . . 3. pry 4. nose 6. dabble,
tamper 7. obtrude 9. interfere
meddler . . . 8. busybody 9. pragmatic
meddlesome . . . 7. Paul Fry 8. meddling
9. officious 11. inquisitive, pragmatical
Mede . . . 6. Median 7. Persian
medial, median . . . 4. mean 5. mesne,
raphe (valve) 6. medium, middle
7. average 11. intervening
12. intermediate
Median . . . 4. Magi, Mede 5. Medic
mediate . . . 5. opine 9. intercede,
interpose, reconcile
mediator . . . 5. muser 7. arbiter 9. go-
between 10. interagent 11. intercessor
medic . . . 3. doc 6. clover, doctor, median,
medico 9. physician
medical (pert to) . . .
  comb form . . 3. oma 4. itis 6. iatric
  7. iatrics
  compound . . 5. hepar
  fluid . . 5. blood, lymph, serum
  man . . 5. medic 6. shaman, voodoo
  monster . . 5. teras
  officer . . 7. coroner
  practitioner . . 2. MD 6. doctor, intern
  (interne) 7. surgeon 8. sawbones
  system . . 7. therapy 9. allopathy

10. homeopathy, psychiatry
term . . **8.** curative **9.** medicinal
medical terms . . .
chicken pox . . **9.** varicella
flat feet . . **9.** pes planus
headache . . **11.** cephalalgia
heartburn . . **7.** pyrosis
hives . . **9.** urticaria
measles . . **7.** rubella, rubeola
mumps . . **9.** parotitis
whooping cough . . **9.** pertussis
medicinal (pert to) . . .
agent . . **3.** tea **6.** tisane **9.** decoction
bark . . **6.** cartex
dropper . . **7.** pipette
equal parts . . **3.** ana
herb, plant . . **3.** rue **4.** aloe **5.** ergot,
   jalap, orris, senna, tansy **6.** arnica,
   cohosh, ipecac **7.** boneset, chirata,
   comfrey **8.** licorice, valerian
pain allaying . . **7.** anodyne **8.** sedative
   9. goofballs, paregoric **11.** barbiturate
patent . . **7.** nostrum
remedy . . **5.** drops, salve **6.** elixir, iodine
   7. panacea **8.** antidote, ointment
science . . **7.** biology **10.** physiology,
   psychology
tablet . . **4.** pill **6.** troche **7.** lozenge
term . . **4.** drug **11.** therapeutic
mediety . . . **6.** loiety **10.** moderation,
   temperance
medieval, mediaeval . . . **7.** archaic
   10. Middle Ages
medieval (pert to) . . .
contest . . **4.** tilt **5.** joust **10.** tournament
empire . . **9.** Holy Roman **11.** Carolingian
emperor . . **4.** Otto **11.** Charlemagne
estate . . **4.** fief **5.** manor
freeholder . . **8.** franklin
galley (ship's) . . **3.** nef **5.** xebec **6.** bireme,
   galiot (galliot) **7.** dromone (dromon),
   trireme, unireme
garment . . **6.** tabard
headdress . . **6.** abacot, wimple
helmet . . **5.** armet
holy wars . . **8.** Crusades
instrument (stringed) . . **5.** rebec (rebeck)
knights' system . . **8.** chivalry
land system . . **9.** feudalism
   11. manorialism
legend . . **9.** Holy Grail **12.** Wandering
   Jew
merchant guild . . **5.** hanse
money of account . . **3.** ora
musical form . . **7.** organum **9.** plainsong
   (plainchant), polyphony **14.** Gregorian
   chant
musical instrument . . **4.** rote **5.** rebec
   (rebeck), shawm **7.** clarion, sackbut
papal seat (temporary) . . **7.** Avignon
peasants' overseer . . **5.** reeve
philosopher . . **9.** alchemist, Schoolman
   (Scholastic)
pilgrim . . **6.** palmer
plague . . **10.** Black Death (1347)
poem . . **3.** lay **7.** fabliau (pl fabliaux)
   14. chanson de geste (epic)
poet, singer . . **7.** gleeman **8.** jongleur,
   minstrel, trouvère **9.** troubador
preacher . . **8.** pardoner
secular movement . . **8.** Humanism

shield . . **3.** ecu **5.** pavis (pavise) **6.** scutum
tax . . **8.** Danegeld
title, teacher . . **8.** magister
wandering student . . **7.** goliard
weapon . . **4.** mace **5.** oncin **8.** falchion
Medina, Saudi Arabia (pert to) . . .
anc name . . **9.** Lathrippa
Mohammed supporters . . **6.** ansars
sacred city of . . **5.** Islam
tombs . . **4.** Omar **6.** Fatima
   8. Mohammed
mediocre . . . **4.** mean, so-so **6.** medium
   7. average **8.** middling, ordinary,
   passable **9.** tolerable **11.** indifferent
meditate . . . **4.** muse, plan, pore **5.** brood,
   study, watch, weigh **6.** ponder
   7. purpose, reflect, revolve **8.** cogitate,
   consider **11.** contemplate
meditation . . . **4.** yoga **7.** thought
   8. devotion **10.** rumination
   11. thanatopsis **13.** contemplation
   14. omphaloskepsis
mediterranean . . . **6.** inland **7.** midland
   10. landlocked
Mediterranean (pert to) . . .
boat . . **3.** nef **4.** saic **5.** xebec (zebec)
   6. galiot (galliot), mistic (mistico),
   settee (setee) **7.** felucca, hexeris
cat . . **5.** genet
coast . . **7.** Riviera
falcon . . **6.** lanner
fish . . **6.** remora
fowl . . **7.** leghorn
fruit . . **5.** olive **7.** azarole
gulf . . **5.** Tunis
herb . . **4.** Ammi
inland . . **3.** sea
island . . **4.** Elba, Gozo **5.** Crete, Malta
   6. Candia, Cyprus, Ebusis, Sicily
   7. Majorca **8.** Belearic (group), Sardinia
island, volcanic . . **6.** Lipari, Salina
   7. Vulcano **9.** Stromboli
port . . **5.** Tunis **7.** Tunisia
region . . **6.** Levant
storm . . **7.** borasca (borasco, borasque)
tree . . **5.** carob **7.** azarole
wind . . **6.** solano **7.** etesian, gregale,
   mistral, sirocco **8.** levanter
   10. euroclyden
medium . . . **4.** agar (cultured), doer, mean
   5. color, organ **6.** degree, medial,
   oracle **7.** average, psychic **8.** mediator,
   mediocre **10.** instrument, interagent
   11. environment **12.** intermediary,
   spiritualist
medium's meeting . . . **6.** séance
medley . . . **4.** olio **5.** relay **6.** jumble
   7. ferrago, mélange, mixture **8.** fantasia,
   mingling **9.** potpourri **10.** hodgepodge,
   salmagundi
medrick . . . **4.** gull (Bonaparte's), tern
   (Wilson's)
medulla . . . **4.** pith **6.** marrow **7.** summary
   9. oblongata **10.** compendium
Medusa (Myth) . . . **6.** Gorgon, Stheno
   (sister) **9.** gorgoneum
Medusa's head (pert to) . . .
constellation (cluster) . . **7.** Perseus
star . . **5.** Algol
vegetable . . **8.** mushroom
Zool . . **10.** basket fish

meed ... 5. bribe, merit, repay, share
6. desert, reward 7. bribery
10. recompense

meek ... 4. mild 6. docile, gentle, humble,
modest 7. pacific, patient 8. moderate,
yielding 10. spiritless, submissive

meerkat ... 6. monkey

meerschaum ... 4. pipe 6. gravel (color)
7. seafoam 9. sepiolite

meet ... 3. fit 4. face, game, join 5. equal,
match, touch 6. battle, combat, concur
7. collide, conform, contact, contest,
convene, fulfill, satisfy 8. assemble,
confront 9. encounter 10. congregate,
experience, rendezvous

meet halfway ... 7. mediate
10. compromise

meeting ... 4. mall, race 5. court,
gemot (gemote), joint, synod, tryst,
union 6. caucus, powwow, séance
7. contact, joining 8. assembly,
conclave, junction 9. encounter,
gathering, in contact 10. conference,
convention, converging, rendezvous
11. convergence 12. congregation,
intersection

mega, meg (comb form) ... 5. great
6. mighty

megalith ... 5. stone (huge) 6. dolman
7. boulder 8. monument (Prehist)

megapode, megapod ... 6. leipoa
9. mound bird 10. jungle fowl 11. brush
turkey

megascope ... 12. magic lantern

megaseism ... 10. earthquake

megrim, megrims ... 4. whim 5. fancy,
freak, humor 8. headache 9. dizziness
12. hypochondria

Mehitabel, Mehetabel ... 3. cat

Mekong River people ... 3. Moi (Asian)

mel ... 5. honey

melancholia ... 7. sadness 8. neurosis
9. nostalgia, psychosis 10. depression

melancholy ... 3. sad 4. blue, dark, glum
5. drear, gloom 6. sombre, sorrow
7. doleful, sadness 8. atrabile, liverish,
tristful 9. dejection 10. depressing,
depression, dispirited, lamentable
11. despondency, downhearted,
pensiveness 12. hypochondria,
mournfulness

Melanesia ... 14. Pacific Islands

Melanesian (pert to) ...
island .. 4. Fiji 7. Solomon 11. New
Hebrides
native .. 4. Fiji 6. Papuan 10. Polynesian
superbeing .. 5. adaro

mélange ... 4. olio 6. jumble, medley
7. mixture 9. pasticcio 10. miscellany
14. conglomeration

melee ... 3. row 4. fray 5. fight
6. affray 7. contest, diamond (small
cut) 8. skirmish 9. commotion

melicocca ... 5. genip 9. soapberry

melicratum ... 4. mead 8. beverage,
hydromel

melilotus ... 6. clover

meliorate ... 6. soften 7. improve
10. ameliorate

melisma ... 6. melody 7. cadenza

Melissa ... 4. balm 12. Old World mint

mell ... 3. mix 4. maul 5. grain (last
cut), honey 6. beetle, hammer, mallet,
meddle, mingle

mellow ... 4. rich, ripe, soft 5. drunk
6. genial, jovial, mature, tender
7. amiable, matured 9. melodious

melodic ... 6. ariose 7. cadenza, melisma
9. melodious

melodious ... 6. ariose, arioso, dulcet
7. musical, tunable, tuneful
10. harmonious

melodist ... 6. singer 8. composer,
musician 9. harmonist

melodramatic ... 8. dramatic, romantic
11. sensational

melody ... 3. air 4. aria, tune 5. canto,
charm, dirge, melos, music 6. rhythm,
strain 7. harmony, melisma, rosalia
9. cantilena, cantilene 11. tunefulness

melon ... 4. musk, pepo 6. casaba
7. Persian 8. honeydew 9. muskmelon,
red-yellow 10. cantaloupe, paddymelon,
watermelon

melon (pert to) ...
financial .. 4. plum 8. dividend
like .. 5. gourd
pear .. 6. pepino
political .. 5. graft 6. spoils

melongena ... 7. brinjal (brinjaul)
8. eggplant

melos ... 4. song 6. melody

melt ... 3. run 4. frit, fuse, thaw 5. smelt,
swale 6. render, soften 7. liquefy
8. diminish, dissolve 9. disappear
12. disintegrate

Melville (pert to) ...
character .. 4. Ahab, Babo 5. Billy (Budd)
6. Cereno (Benito), Delano 7. Ishmael
8. Bartleby, Queequeg, Starbuck
work .. 4. Omoo 5. Typee 6. Pierre
8. Moby Dick

member ... 4. limb, part 5. organ
6. branch, fellow, joiner 7. section
8. belonger, district, enlistee, enroller
9. associate

member (pert to) ...
boy's club .. 3. cub 5. scout
Caliph dynasty .. 6. Omniad
chapter (Eccl) .. 9. capitular
crew .. 4. hand
diplomatic staff .. 6. consul 7. attaché
8. minister 10. ambassador
Jewish brotherhood .. 6. Essene
laity .. 6. layman
literary club .. 9. academist
11. academician
oldest .. 4. dean
regiment .. 8. legioner 9. grenadier,
legionary 11. legionnaire
religious sect .. 5. Amish 6. Quaker,
Shaker
Roman Catholic society .. 6. Jesuit
State .. 7. citizen
swing band .. 6. hepcat 7. swinger

membrane ... 4. caul, skin, tela 5. lemma
6. lamina 8. ectoderm, striffin

membrane (pert to) ...
brain .. 13. meninges mater
diffusion .. 7. osmosis
ear .. 7. eardrum
fold .. 5. plica

optical . . **6.** retina
weblike . . **4.** tela
memento . . . **5.** relic, token **6.** trophy
  8. keepsake, memorial, souvenir
  11. remembrance
Memnon (pert to) . . .
  famed statue . . **11.** vocal Memnon
  father . . **8.** Tithonus
  Greek name . . **9.** Amenhotep
  king of . . **8.** Ethiopia
  mother . . **3.** Eos (Aurora)
  war hero . . **6.** Trojan
memoir . . . **4.** hint, note **5.** éloge, essay
  6. record, report **7.** account, history
  9. biography, narrative, reminding
  10. memorandum **12.** dissertation
  13. autobiography
memorabilia . . . **3.** ana **5.** notes **6.** record
  7. memoirs **8.** memories
memorable . . . **7.** namable, notable
  9. reminding **11.** reminiscent
memorandum . . . **4.** chit, note **5.** diary
  6. minute, record **7.** tickler **8.** protocol,
  reminder
memoria . . . **4.** tomb **6.** chapel, church,
  shrine **8.** monument **9.** reliquary
memorial . . . **6.** memoir, memory, record,
  trophy **8.** mnemonic, monument
  10. memorandum **11.** celebrative,
  remembrance **12.** recollection
  13. commemorative
memorial mound . . . **5.** cairn (stone),
  totem (carved)
memory . . . **4.** mind **6.** recall **9.** retention
  11. remembrance **12.** recollection,
  reminiscence **13.** commemoration
memory (pert to) . . .
  aid . . **8.** mnemonic **10.** anamnestic
  book . . **5.** diary **9.** scrapbook
  jog . . **6.** remind
  loss of . . **5.** lethe **7.** amnesia, aphasia
  (partial) **13.** forgetfulness
  term . . **6.** mnesic **8.** mnemonic
Memphis, Egypt (pert to) . . .
  deity . . **2.** Ra (Re) **3.** Shu, Tem
  dynasty . . **8.** Memphite
  god, chief . . **4.** Ptah
men (pert to) . . .
  armed body . . **5.** posse
  gymnasts . . **8.** acrobats
  learned . . **8.** erudites, literati
  mechanical . . **6.** robots
  of same tongue . . **6.** langue
  old . . **7.** gaffers **10.** patriarchs
  party of . . **4.** stag **6.** smoker
  section, Gr Church . . **6.** andron
  single . . **5.** stags **9.** bachelors, celibates
  slang . . **6.** blokes
  Three Wise . . **4.** Magi (Gaspar, Melchior,
  Balthazar)
  wild . . **7.** savages **9.** cannibals
menace . . . **6.** threat **8.** forebode, threaten
  10. intimidate **11.** fulmination
menacing . . . **7.** ominous **8.** imminent
  11. threatening
menage . . . **4.** club **7.** society
  9. homestead, household, husbandry
  10. management **12.** housekeeping
menagerie . . . **3.** zoo **10.** collection,
  Tiergarten
menald (said of horses) . . . **8.** speckled

  10. variegated
Menaspis . . . **5.** shark (crescent-shaped)
mend . . . **3.** fix, sew **4.** cure, darn, heal,
  knit **5.** alter, amend, botch, emend,
  moise, patch **6.** better, cobble, reform,
  repair **7.** correct, improve **9.** reconcile
  10. ameliorate
mendacious . . . **5.** false, lying **6.** untrue
  7. in error **9.** truthless **10.** fallacious
mendacity . . . **3.** lie **5.** lying **6.** deceit
  7. falsity, fibbery, untruth
mendicant . . . **5.** fakir **6.** beggar
  7. begging
mendicant order . . . **10.** Carmelites,
  Dominicans **11.** Franciscans
  12. Augustinians
mendole . . . **4.** fish **8.** cackerel
Menelaus' wife . . . **11.** Helen of Troy
menhaden . . . **4.** pogy **7.** sardine
  8. bonyfish **10.** mossbunker
menhir . . . **5.** stone (standing) **8.** monolith
menial . . . **6.** flunky, varlet **7.** servant,
  servile, serving, slavish
meninges membrane . . . **8.** pia mater
  9. arachnoid, dura mater
meniscus . . . **4.** lens **8.** crescent
  12. crescent moon
Mennonite leader . . . **11.** Menno Simons
Mennonite sect . . . **5.** Amish
meno . . . **4.** less **5.** month (comb form)
menology (Eccl) . . . **8.** calendar, register
Menominee, Menomini . . . **5.** Falls (Wis),
  river **6.** Indian **9.** whitefish
Menorah . . . **11.** candelabrum (Jew)
  12. organization
mensk . . . **5.** adorn, favor, grace, honor
  6. credit **8.** ornament **9.** reverence
  12. graciousness
mental . . . **7.** phrenic **9.** of the mind,
  psychotic **11.** intelligent **12.** intellectual
mental (pert to) . . .
  alienation . . **8.** insanity
  deficiency, deficient . . **5.** ament, idiot,
  moron **6.** idiocy **8.** imbecile
  discipline . . **8.** mathesis
  disorder . . **7.** aphasia **8.** insanity,
  neurosis, paranoia **9.** psychosis
  11. megalomania **12.** hypochondria
  13. forgetfulness, schizophrenia
  faculties . . **4.** mind, wits
  feeling . . **7.** emotion
  image, picture . . **4.** idea **6.** idolus
  8. phantasm **10.** conception
  peculiarity . . **12.** idiosyncracy
  science, study . . **10.** New Thought,
  psychiatry
  state . . **6.** morale **7.** doldrum (doldrums)
  8. euphoria
  strain . . **7.** tension
mentality . . . **4.** mind **5.** sense **6.** acumen,
  sanity **9.** endowment, intellect
  11. mental power **12.** intelligence
mention . . . **4.** cite, mind, name **5.** refer,
  speak, trace **6.** denote, notice, record,
  remark **7.** specify, vestige **8.** citation,
  indicate **9.** make known, statement
  10. indication
mentor . . . **7.** adviser, teacher, wise man
  10. instructor
mentum . . . **4.** chin
menu . . . **4.** card, list **5.** carte **8.** schedule

10. bill of fare

Mephistopheles . . . 5. devil, Faust, Satan

mephitis . . . 4. odor 5. skunk, smell
6. stench 7. polecat 10. exhilation
(earth)

mercantile . . . 5. trade 7. trading
10. commercial, industrial

mercenary . . . 4. hack 5. hired, venal
6. sordid 7. Hessian 8. hireling, salaried,
vendible

merchandise . . . 4. ware 5. goods, wares
7. effects 9. vendibles 10. emporeutic
(pert to) 11. commodities 12. stock in
trade

merchant . . . 5. buyer 6. trader 7. vintner
10. shopkeeper, trafficker
11. storekeeper

merchant (pert to) . . .
group . . 5. guild, hanse 6. cartel
Indian . . 4. seth
League . . 9. Hanseatic
ship . . 6. argosy 8. Indiaman
wine . . 7. vintner

Merchant of Bagdad . . . 7. Sindbad

Merchant of Venice character . . .
6. Portia 7. Antonio, Shylock

merci . . . 6. thanks

merciful . . . 4. kind, mild 6. humane,
tender 7. clement, lenient 9. benignant
10. charitable 13. compassionate

merciless . . . 5. cruel 8. pitiless
9. unsparing 10. relentless
13. unsympathetic

mercurial (pert to God Mercury) . . .
4. fast 5. swift 6. active, clever, fickle
8. metallic 9. saturnine 11. money-
making

mercurous chloride . . . 7. calomel

mercury . . . 5. azoth, guide, metal
7. chibrit, element 9. barometer
11. quicksilver, temperature,
thermometer

Mercury (pert to) . . .
astronomy . . 6. planet (smallest)
god of . . 8. commerce
Greek name . . 6. Hermes
staff . . 8. caduceus
statue, image . . 5. herma
winged cap . . 7. petasos (petasus)
winged shoes . . 7. talaria

mercy . . . 4. pity, ruth 5. grace 6. blithe,
lenity 7. charity 8. clemency, lenience,
leniency 9. tolerance 10. compassion,
indulgence 11. forbearance

mercy killing . . . 10. euthanasia

mercy seat . . . 5. bench 11. golden
plate (on the Ark), Throne of God
12. judgment seat 13. seat of justice

mere . . . 3. sea 4. bare, lake, only, pool,
sole, such, wisp 5. bound, limit, sheer,
small 6. divide, simple 8. absolute,
boundary, landmark, only this

mère . . . 6. mother

merely . . . 4. also, just, only 5. quite
6. barely, purely, simply, singly,
solely 7. utterly 8. entirely, scarcely
9. unmixedly 10. absolutely

mere show . . . 4. airs 5. front 8. pretense
9. formality 10. pretension
11. affectation

mere taste . . . 3. nip, sip 4. gulp

7. draught

merganser . . . 3. nun 4. duck, smee,
smew 6. Mergus 7. bec-scie 8. Merginae
9. goosander

merge . . . 4. sink 5. blend, unite 6. mingle
7. combine, immerse 8. coalesce
11. consolidate

merger . . . 4. pool 5. union 6. cartel,
fusion 8. monopoly 10. absorption
12. amalgamation

meridian . . . 3. top 4. apex, noon 5. plane
6. midday, summit, zenith 8. latitude,
southern 9. celestial 11. culmination
12. highest point

meringue . . . 5. icing 8. egg white, frosting

Merino . . . 4. wool, yarn 5. sheep

merit . . . 4. earn, meed 5. worth 6. desert,
reward 7. deserve 10. excellence

merited . . . 3. fit 4. just 6. worthy
8. adequate, deserved, suitable
9. warranted

meritorious . . . 5. valid 6. worthy
7. merited 9. deserving, honorable
12. praiseworthy

merlin . . . 6. falcon

Merlin . . . 7. prophet, romance 8. magician

mermaid . . . 5. siren 6. merrow
7. Oceanid, swimmer 8. sea nymph
9. sea spirit 14. marine creature

mermaid's hair . . . 4. alga

mero . . . 4. fish 5. guasa 7. grouper
8. rock hind

merogenesis . . . 12. segmentation

meropia . . . 9. blindness (partial)

meros . . . 5. thigh 10. meropodite

merriment . . . 3. fun 4. glee 5. mirth
6. gaiety (gayety) 8. laughter
9. amusement, diversion
11. merrymaking

merrow . . . 7. mermaid

merry . . . 3. gai, gay 4. glad 5. funny,
happy 6. blithe, bonnie, jocose, jovial,
joyous 7. comical, festive, gleeful,
jocular 8. cheerful, mirthful, sportive
9. favorable, hilarious, sprightly
13. sweet-sounding

merry-andrew . . . 4. mime, zany 5. antic,
clown, joker 6. jester 7. buffoon
8. merryman

merry-go-round . . . 8. carousel (carrousel)
17. revolving platform

merrymaking . . . 4. reel 5. momus,
revel 7. festive, wassail 9. festivity,
merriment 12. conviviality

merrythought . . . 8. wishbone

merrytrotter . . . 5. swing 6. seesaw

merrywing . . . 4. duck 9. goldeneye
10. bufflehead

merse . . . 3. dip 5. marsh 6. plunge
7. immerse

merycism . . . 7. chewing 10. rumination

mesa . . . 5. butte 7. mesilla, oakwood
(color), plateau, terrace 9. tableland
14. flat-topped hill

mescal . . . 6. cactus, liquor, peyote

mesel . . . 5. leper

mesh . . . 3. net, web 5. catch 6. areola
7. complex, ensnare, netting, network
10. crisscross 11. interaction

mesial plane . . . 5. meson (Zool)
6. median, middle

mesmeric . . . **11.** fascinating, hypnotizing **12.** irresistible, spellbinding
mesmeric force . . . **2.** od
Mesopotamia . . .
  ancient city . . **2.** Ur **5.** Eridu **7.** Babylon, Ninevah
  city . . **5.** Basra, Mosul **6.** Edessa
  colloquialism . . **6.** Mespot
  culture . . **8.** Sumerian
  export . . **3.** oil
  language . . **6.** Arabic
  people (anc) . . **8.** Aramaean (Aramean)
  river . . **6.** Tigris **9.** Euphrates
  wind . . **6.** shamal
Mesopotamian . . . **5.** Iraqi
Mesozoic era . . . **7.** reptile **8.** dinosaur **10.** evergreens, ganoid fish
mesquin . . . **4.** mean **6.** shabby, sordid
mesquita . . . **6.** mosque
mesquite . . . **5.** pacay **7.** thicket **8.** Prosopis **9.** algarroba
mesquite bean flour . . . **6.** pinole
mess . . . **4.** meal **5.** batch, share, spoil **6.** bungle, jumble, litter **7.** eyesore, failure, mixture **8.** disorder **9.** confusion **11.** predicament **12.** kettle of fish
mess (up) . . . **5.** botch, spoil **6.** muss up **7.** clutter, derange, shuffle **10.** disarrange
message . . . **4.** news, note, wire, word **5.** cable **6.** brevet, letter, notice **7.** epistle, evangel, tidings **8.** dispatch, telegram **10.** communiqué **13.** communication
message medium . . . **5.** Ouija
messenger . . . **4.** Iris, page, sand, toty **5.** angel, envoy **6.** herald, nuncio, Revere (Paul) **7.** apostle, carrier, courier, prophet, totyman **8.** delegate, minister **9.** estafette (estafet) **10.** forerunner
messenger bird . . . **9.** secretary
Messenger of the Gods . . . **6.** Hermes (Gr) **7.** Mercury (Rom)
Messiah . . . **6.** Christ **7.** Saviour (Savior) **8.** Oratorio (Handel) **9.** deliverer
Messina Rock . . . **6.** Scylla
messy . . . **5.** dirty **6.** untidy **7.** jumbled **8.** slovenly **10.** disordered
mestive . . . **8.** mournful
mesto . . . **3.** sad **7.** pensive
met . . . **3.** sat **7.** equaled, measure **11.** measurement (see also *meet*)
metabolism . . . **9.** anabolism **10.** catabolism **12.** assimilation **13.** dissimilation, metamorphosis **14.** transformation
metacarpus . . . **4.** bone
metad . . . **3.** rat
metagnomy . . . **10.** divination
metagnostic . . . **10.** unknowable
metal . . . **3.** tin **4.** gold, iron, lead, zinc **5.** steel **6.** cobalt, copper, erbium, nickel, radium, silver, sodium **7.** cadmium, calcium, element, gallium, iridium, lithium, mercury, terbium **8.** cast iron **9.** potassium **11.** quicksilver
metal . . . **6.** mettle, spirit **8.** material **9.** substance
metal (pert to) . . .
  bar . . **3.** gad **5.** ingot
  cake . . **4.** slag

casting . . **3.** pig
cement . . **6.** solder
clippings . . **7.** scissil
coarse . . **5.** matte
coat . . **6.** patina
color . . **9.** pearl blue
content . . **3.** ory
crude . . **5.** matte
deposit . . **4.** lode
disc . . **5.** paten
dross . . **4.** slag
electric . . **6.** magnet
filings . . **5.** lemel
forging term . . **5.** sprue
goldlike . . **6.** oroide
impurity . . **7.** regulus
layer . . **4.** seam, vein **5.** stope
lightest . . **7.** lithium
lump . . **3.** pig **4.** slug **6.** nugget
patch . . **6.** solder
plate . . **4.** foil, shim
rare . . **6.** erbium **7.** iridium, terbium, yttrium **8.** platinum
refuse . . **4.** slag **5.** dross **6.** scoria
rock . . **3.** ore
science of . . **10.** metallurgy
tag . . **5.** aglet (aiglet)
test . . **5.** assay
tool . . **5.** swage **7.** stemmer
ware . . **4.** tole **6.** Revere
worker . . **6.** welder **7.** riveter **9.** goldsmith **11.** silversmith
metamerism . . . **12.** segmentation (Zool)
metamorphosis . . . **6.** change **9.** oxidation **10.** hydrolysis **12.** degeneration, ossification **14.** transformation
metaphor . . . **5.** trope **6.** simile **10.** comparison **11.** tralalition
metaphysics . . . **5.** being **6.** nature **8.** ontology, theology **9.** cosmology **10.** psychology
mete . . . **4.** dole, give, goal **5.** allot, award **7.** measure **8.** boundary **9.** apportion **10.** distribute
meteor . . . **5.** bolis **6.** Bielid, bolide, Leonid, Lyraid **7.** Arietid, Perseid **8.** fireball **9.** Andromede
meteorite (pert to) . . .
  iron . . **10.** siderolite
  shower . . **6.** Leonid **9.** Andromede (Andromedid)
  stony . . **8.** aerolite
meteor mark . . . **6.** crater
meteorology . . . **9.** astronomy **10.** atmosphere **11.** climatology
meter, metre . . . **5.** gauge **6.** rhythm **7.** cadence, measure **8.** measurer
meter (pert to) . . .
  cubic . . **5.** stere
  measure . . **5.** litre
  millionth . . **6.** micron
  prosody . . **4.** mora
  square . . **7.** centare
  ton . . **5.** tonne
  unit term . . **3.** are **6.** decare **9.** decameter, decastere
  weight . . **4.** gram
methane . . . **8.** paraffin
metheglin . . . **4.** mead **8.** beverage
mether . . . **3.** cup
method . . . **3.** way **4.** mode, plan, rule

5. means, order, usage **6.** course, manner, system **7.** fashion, process **9.** procedure **11.** arrangement **14.** classification

methodic, methodical ... **6.** formal **7.** orderly, regular **10.** systematic

Methuselah (pert to) ...
Bib .. **7.** aged man **9.** Patriarch
father .. **5.** Enoch

metic ... **5.** alien **7.** settler **9.** immigrant

meticulous ... **4.** nice, prim **5.** fussy **7.** careful, fearful, precise **8.** exacting **9.** selective **10.** fastidious, scrupulous **14.** discriminating

métier ... **4.** line **7.** calling **8.** business **10.** occupation, profession

metis, metisse ... **7.** mulatto **8.** octoroon **9.** half-breed

Metis ... **8.** asteroid **9.** Zeus's wife

metrical ... **8.** measured, poetical, rhythmic

metrical composition ... **4.** poem **5.** poesy **6.** poetry

metrical foot ... **4.** iamb **6.** iambus **7.** anapest, spondee, trochee **8.** choriamb

metrical stress ... **4.** scan **5.** arsis, ictus **6.** thesis

metronome (Maelzel's) ... **5.** timer

metropolis ... **4.** city, seat, town **6.** center **8.** district **9.** metropole

metropolitan ... **5.** chief, urban **6.** bishop, center **7.** leading **9.** principal

mettle ... **5.** ardor, honor, nerve, pluck, spunk **6.** spirit **7.** courage **9.** fortitude **11.** temperament

meuse, muse ... **3.** gap **4.** hole **7.** opening **8.** loophole

Meuse River ... **4.** Maas

mew ... **3.** cob, den **4.** cage, cast, coop, gull, molt, shed **5.** miaow, miaul **6.** change **7.** seagull, stables **8.** spicknel **11.** concealment, confinement

mewl ... **3.** cry, mew **6.** squall **7.** whimper

Mexican (pert to) ... see also *Mexico*
agave .. **5.** datil **6.** zapupe **8.** henequen
almond .. **7.** malabar
American .. **6.** gringo
ancient .. **4.** Maya **5.** Aztec, Nahua **6.** Mixtec, Toltec **7.** Zapotec
antelope .. **9.** pronghorn
asphalt .. **9.** chapapote
bean .. **6.** frijol **7.** frijole
bedbug .. **8.** conenose
beverage (alcoholic) .. **6.** mescal, pulque **7.** tepache, tequila
bird .. **6.** jacana, towhee **7.** jacamar, tinamou **8.** zopilote
blanket .. **6.** serape
brigand .. **7.** ladrone
bull .. **4.** toro
cactus .. **6.** chaute, mescal
cape .. **6.** serape
cat .. **6.** margay
cherry tree .. **7.** capulin
cheif .. **4.** jefe **12.** jefe politico
cloak .. **5.** manta
cockroach .. **9.** cucaracha
common land (law) .. **6.** ejidos
coral drops (lily) .. **7.** Bessera
cottonwood .. **5.** alamo

dance (solo) .. **8.** guaracha
dish .. **4.** taco **5.** atole, chili (chile) **6.** tamale **7.** burrito **8.** frijoles, tortilla **9.** enchilada **13.** chili con carne
dog .. **9.** Chihuahua
dollar .. **4.** peso **5.** adobe
dove .. **4.** Inca
drug .. **7.** damiana
elm .. **6.** mezcal **8.** Ulmaceae
estate, farm .. **8.** hacienda
fever .. **10.** tabardillo
fish (food) .. **6.** salema **7.** totuava
game (card) .. **4.** frog
grass .. **3.** mat **5.** otate **6.** petate **8.** henequen
herdsman .. **8.** ranchero
hog .. **7.** peccary
hut, house .. **5.** jacal
insect .. **8.** turicata
labor system .. **7.** peonage
landmark .. **5.** senal
masonry .. **5.** adobe
moon god (Aztec) .. **6.** Meztli
mullet .. **4.** bobo
musical instrument .. **6.** clarin (anc) **7.** maracas
Noah .. **6.** Coxcox
onyx .. **6.** tecali
orange .. **7.** Choisya
peasant .. **4.** peon
persimmon .. **7.** chapote
phlox .. **6.** cobaea
plant, shrub .. **4.** pita **5.** agave, amole, datil, istle, sisal, sotol, yucca **6.** maguey **8.** ocotillo **10.** candlewood, Dasylirion
rose .. **9.** portulaca
saloon .. **7.** cantina
sandal .. **8.** huaracho (huarache)
sauce .. **7.** Tabasco
scarf .. **6.** tapalo
shawl .. **6.** serape
stirrup .. **7.** estribo
stirrup hood .. **8.** tapadera (tapadero)
sugar .. **7.** panocha
tea .. **6.** basote **7.** apasote
thong .. **5.** romal
throwing stick .. **6.** atlatl
tree .. **3.** ule **5.** alamo, ocote **6.** colima, poplar **7.** capulin **10.** cottonwood
war god .. **7.** Mexitli
yucca .. **5.** izote (isote)

Mexican people ...
artist .. **6.** Orozco, Posada, Rivera
composer .. Chavez
conqueror .. **6.** Cortés (Cortez)
dictator .. **4.** Díaz **9.** Santa Anna
emperor .. **10.** Maximilian
president .. **6.** Huerta, Juárez, Madero **7.** Obregón **8.** Cárdenas, Carranza
revolutionary .. **6.** Madero, Zapata **11.** Pancho Villa
writer .. **3.** Paz **6.** Azuela **7.** Fuentes

Mexican War (1846) ...
battle site .. **11.** Chapultepec
general .. **5.** Scott (Winfield) **6.** Taylor (Zachary) **9.** Santa Anna (Mex)
president .. **4.** Polk

Mexico ...
battleground .. **6.** Puebla
capital .. **10.** Mexico City
city .. **6.** Merida, Puebla **7.** Durango,

Tampico **8.** Mazatlan, Monterey, Vera Cruz **11.** Guadalajara
conqueror . . **6.** Cortes (Cortez)
hero . . **6.** Juarez **11.** Poncho Villa
lake . . **7.** Chapala
mountain . . **12.** Popocatepetl
peninsula . . **4.** Baja **7.** Yucatan
people . . **5.** Mayas **6.** Aztecs **7.** Toltecs **10.** Cuitlateco
river . . **9.** Rio Grande
volcano . . **6.** Colima **7.** Jorullo, Orizaba **12.** Ixtaccihuatl, Popocatepetl
mezzanine . . . **8.** entresol, low story
miaow, miaou . . . **3.** mew
mias . . . **9.** orangutan
miasma . . . **4.** fume **6.** poison **7.** malaria, malodor **9.** contagion
mib . . . **7.** a marble
mica . . **4.** talc **5.** glist **7.** biotite **8.** chlorite, silicate **9.** damourite, hydromica, isinglass, muscovite **10.** lepidolite
Micah . . **4.** Book (Old Test) **7.** prophet
mice . . . **3.** Mus **5.** voles **7.** rodents
miche . . . **5.** skulk, sneak **6.** lie hid **7.** conceal
micher . . . **5.** sneak, thief **6.** truant
Michigan . . .
  capital . . **7.** Lansing
  city . . **5.** Flint **7.** Detroit, Lansing **8.** Ann Arbor **9.** Marquette
  explorer . . **7.** Jolliet, Nicolet **9.** Marquette **13.** Sault Ste Marie
  river . . **4.** Cass **5.** Huron
  State admission . . **11.** Twenty-sixth
  State motto . . **6.** Tuebor **11.** I Will Defend
  State nickname . . **9.** Wolverine
mickey finn . . . **5.** drink **8.** narcotic
mico . . . **6.** monkey **8.** marmoset
micraner . . . **3.** ant (small)
micro (comb form) . . . **4.** moth **5.** petty, small
microbe . . . **4.** germ **5.** virus **8.** organism **9.** bacterium **13.** microorganism
microcosm . . . **4.** body (humerous) **5.** world (small) **8.** universe
microscopic (pert to) . . .
  algae . . **6.** amoeba, diatom
  anatomy . . **9.** histology
  size . . **5.** small **6.** minute **9.** very small **13.** infinitesimal
microspores . . . **6.** pollen
microwave (sl) . . . **4.** nuke
Midas (Gr) . . . **13.** King of Phrygia
midday . . . **4.** noon **7.** noonday **8.** meridian, noontide
midday nap . . . **6.** siesta
middle . . . **5.** mesne, midst **6.** center, centry, median, medium, mesial **7.** central **8.** interior **11.** intervening **13.** intermediator
middle (pert to) . . .
  Age . . **8.** Medieval
  class . . **9.** bourgeois **11.** proletarian
  comb form . . **3.** mes **4.** medi, meso
  finger . . **6.** medius **10.** third digit
  ground . . **4.** mean **7.** average **9.** mid-course
  man . . **5.** agent **6.** broker, medium **8.** mediator **9.** go-between **11.** intercessor **12.** intermediary

middling . . . **4.** fair **6.** medium, middle **7.** average, between, midland **8.** mediocre, moderate, ordinary **10.** middle-aged
midge . . . **3.** fly **4.** gnat **6.** midget, punkie **7.** minutia
Midi . . . **8.** The South (France)
Midian king . . . **3.** Evi **4.** Reba
Midian priest . . . **6.** Jethro
midriff . . . **9.** diaphragm
midshipman . . . **5.** cadet **6.** reefer **8.** toadfish
Midsummer Night's Dream (play) . . . **4.** Puck, Snug **6.** Bottom, Oberon **7.** Titania
midwife . . . **4.** baba, dhai **6.** cummer (kimmer) **11.** accoucheuse
mien . . . **3.** air, eye **4.** look **5.** guise **6.** aspect, manner, ostent **7.** bearing, posture **8.** behavior, carriage, demeanor **10.** appearance, deportment
miff . . . **3.** vix **4.** tiff **5.** anger **6.** offend **7.** dudgeon, quarrel **9.** displease, sulkiness **10.** sullenness
mig . . . **4.** duck **7.** a marble
might . . . **3.** arm **5.** force, power **7.** ability **8.** efficacy, strength **9.** greatness
mighty . . . **4.** huge, vast, very **6.** potent, strong **7.** eminent, violent **8.** enormous, forcible, powerful, puissant **9.** extremely **10.** omnipotent **11.** efficacious **13.** authoritative
migniard . . . **6.** dainty, minion **7.** mincing **8.** delicate, mistress
mignon . . . **5.** small **6.** dainty, petite **7.** blue-red **8.** delicate, graceful
mignonette (pert to) . . .
  color . . **5.** green **6.** reseda
  emblem of . . **6.** Saxony
  herb . . **6.** reseda
  tree . . **5.** henna
  vine . . **7.** Madeira, tarweed
migraine . . . **6.** megrim **8.** headache **10.** hemicrania
migrate . . . **4.** move, trek **8.** resettle, transfer **12.** transmigrate
migration . . . **4.** trek **5.** exode **6.** exodus **7.** passage **8.** shifting (Chem) **10.** relocation
migratory . . . **6.** moving, roving **7.** nomadic **9.** peregrine, wandering
migratory (pert to) . . .
  ant . . **6.** driver
  cell . . **9.** leucocyte
  thrush . . **5.** robin
mihrab . . . **4.** slab **5.** niche **7.** chamber (mosque)
Mikado . . . **5.** dairi, opera, title **9.** red-yellow, sovereign
Mikado character . . . **4.** Ko-Ko **6.** Yum-Yum **7.** Pooh-Bah
Mikania . . . **7.** dogbane, thistle **11.** Willugbaeya (Willugheia) **12.** Ancylocladus
mike . . . **4.** loaf **6.** loiter **10.** microphone
mil . . . **5.** mille **8.** thousand
milady . . . **5.** woman **6.** madame **10.** noblewoman **11.** gentlewoman
Milan (pert to) . . .
  hat . . **5.** straw
  opera house . . **7.** La Scala

point.. **10.** bobbin lace **12.** point de
Milan
mild ... **4.** calm, kind, meek, soft, warm
5. balmy, bland **6.** benign, gentle
7. clement, insipid, lenient **8.** benedict,
favonian, gracious, lenitive, moderate,
soothing, tranquil **9.** assuasive,
indulgent, temperate **10.** mollifying
11. considerate
mild (pert to) ...
attack.. **5.** touch (flu)
burn.. **11.** first-degree
cheese.. **10.** mozzarella
cigar.. **5.** claro
illness.. **7.** ailment
nausea.. **11.** butterflies
oath.. **4.** darn, drat, heck **5.** shoot
6. shucks
reproof.. **10.** admonition
mildew ... **4.** mold, must, rust, smut
6. blight, fungus **8.** honeydew
mild expression ... **9.** euphemism
mild offense ... **6.** delict
mile (term) ... **3.** sea **7.** statute **8.** nautical
9. Admiralty **12.** geographical
Miledh ... **8.** ancestor (fabled)
Milesian ... **4.** Celt **8.** Irishman
10. Miledh's son
milestone ... **5.** stele **7.** waymark
8. landmark, milepost
milfoil ... **4.** herb **6.** yarrow
milieu ... **7.** ecology **8.** ambience
11. environment **12.** surroundings
militant ... **7.** hawkish, warlike **8.** battling,
fighting **9.** combating, combative
11. contentious
military ... **7.** martial **8.** soldiers
military (pert to) ...
advance.. **8.** anabasis
aide.. **7.** attaché
base.. **4.** camp **5.** depot, field **7.** billets
8. barracks, firebase, quarters
10. encampment
call.. **6.** tattoo **8.** reveille
cap.. **4.** kepi **5.** busby, shako
cap, hat cover.. **8.** havelock
cloak.. **5.** sagum (anc)
commission.. **6.** brevet
defense.. **4.** fort **6.** abatis
depot.. **4.** base
division.. **4.** unit **5.** corps, squad
7. company, platoon **8.** regiment
engine.. **6.** onager **7.** robinet
expedition to Holy Land.. **7.** Crusade
force.. **4.** army **5.** ranks, troop **6.** legion
7. reserve **8.** soldiery
guard.. **6.** patrol
horsemen.. **7.** cavalry, hussars
infraction.. **4.** AWOL
inspection.. **5.** drill **6.** parade, review
instrument.. **5.** bugle **7.** althorn
landing point.. **9.** beachhead
maneuver.. **6.** tactic
messenger.. **7.** estafet
night attack.. **8.** camisade
obstruction.. **6.** abatis
officer.. **4.** major **7.** captain, colonel,
general **8.** corporal, sergeant
9. brigadier, subaltern **10.** lieutenant
operations.. **8.** campaign, strategy
order.. **7.** command

organization.. **5.** cadre
pit.. **10.** trou-de-loup
police.. **2.** MP **9.** gendarmes
12. constabulary
punishment.. **4.** brig **9.** strappado
quarters.. **4.** camp **7.** billets **8.** barracks
10. cantonment
salute (artillery).. **5.** salvo
science.. **3.** war **7.** war game **8.** warcraft
9. logistics
service stripes.. **9.** hashmarks
signal.. **7.** chamade (anc)
staff.. **5.** cadre
storehouse.. **5.** étape **7.** arsenal
supplies.. **8.** materiel, ordnance
survey.. **11.** reconnoiter
testament, will.. **11.** nuncupative
tool (hook-shaped).. **4.** croc (anc)
truck (cannon).. **6.** camion
vehicle.. **4.** jeep, tank **6.** camion
7. caisson
militate ... **5.** fight **6.** debate, rebuff
7. contend **8.** conflict
milk ... **3.** lac **5.** cream, drain, fluid
6. elicit, suckle **7.** despoil, draw out,
exploit, extract **8.** beverage
milk (pert to) ...
beverage.. **4.** whig **10.** buttermilk
coagulator.. **4.** ruen **6.** rennet
curd.. **5.** zeiga **6.** casein
curdled.. **6.** yogurt **7.** clabber
fermented.. **5.** kefir **6.** kumiss (koumiss)
7. matzoon
fish.. **3.** awa **6.** Chanos, sabalo
food (fasting).. **10.** lacticinia
glass.. **7.** opaline **8.** cryolite
mouse.. **6.** spurge
pail.. **5.** bowie, eshin
pert to.. **6.** lactic **7.** lactary, lacteal
product.. **6.** cheese, yogurt
sap.. **5.** latex
sop.. **5.** sissy **11.** mollycoddle
sour.. **4.** curd, whey, whig **6.** blinky
store.. **5.** dairy **9.** lactarium
strainer.. **6.** milsey (milsie)
sugar.. **7.** lactose
watery part.. **4.** whey
with (milk).. **6.** au lait
milkweed ... **6.** spurge **7.** dogbane
10. sow thistle **14.** Asclepiadaceae
milkwood ... **8.** Moraceae **9.** paperbark
milky ... **4.** mild, tame, weak **5.** timid,
white **6.** gentle, liquid **7.** lacteal
8. emulsion, emulsive, lactesce (to
become), timorous **10.** effeminate
Milky Way ... **6.** Galaxy **9.** Via Lactea
14. galactic circle
Milky Way black spaces ... **9.** Coalsacks
mill ... **3.** box **4.** beat, coin (to) **5.** crush,
dress, fight, grind, knurl, quern, shape
6. finish, powder, thrash **7.** factory,
machine, serrate **8.** arrastra, snuffbox,
vanquish, workshop **9.** comminute,
pulverize, transform **10.** move around
12. housebreaker
mill (pert to) ...
beetle.. **9.** cockroach
bill.. **3.** adz
clapper.. **10.** chatterbox
course.. **4.** lade **8.** millrace, tailrace
end.. **7.** remnant

grain . . **5.** grist
run of . . **7.** average **8.** millrace, ordinary
millefleurs . . . **7.** perfume
millenarian . . . **8.** chiliast
millennium . . . **6.** period, utopia
　　9. millenary **13.** thousand years
millepede . . . **6.** insect **7.** myriapod
millepore . . . **5.** coral **9.** madrepore
miller . . . **3.** ray **4.** moth **5.** boxer **7.** harrier
　　8. pugilist **10.** flycatcher
miller's thumb . . . **4.** bird, fish **7.** warbler
　　8. titmouse (long-tailed) **9.** goldcrest
millesimal . . . **10.** thousandth
millet . . . **4.** moha **5.** bajra, grass, hirse,
　　milly **8.** cenchrus **9.** broomcorn **10.** hirse
　　grass **14.** non-Moslem group
millimeter . . . **6.** micron **14.** thousandth
　　part
millions, one thousand . . . **7.** billion
millions of millions . . . **9.** trillions
Mills grenade . . . **4.** bomb
Milne character . . . **6.** Eeyore (donkey),
　　Piglet, Winnie (the Pooh)
　　16. Christopher Robin
milo . . . **5.** durra **12.** grain sorghum
Milvus . . . **4.** kite
mime . . . **3.** ape **4.** aper, copy **5.** actor,
　　clown, mimic **6.** jester, mummer
　　7. buffoon, imitate
mimesis . . . **7.** mimicry **9.** imitation
mimic . . . **3.** ape **4.** aper, copy, mime,
　　mimo, mock **5.** actor **6.** mummer, parrot
　　7. buffoon, copying, imitate, mimetic
　　8. imitator **9.** imitative **11.** counterfeit
mimicry . . . **5.** apery, apism **7.** mimesis,
　　mockery **8.** parrotry
mimic thrush . . . **11.** mockingbird
Mimidae, Miminae . . **7.** catbird
　　8. thrasher **11.** mockingbird
Mimir . . . **5.** giant
mimsey . . . **4.** prim **7.** prudish
min . . . **5.** ruler **6.** memory, prince, remind
　　8. remember **11.** remembrance
Min (Egypt) . . . **3.** god (procreation)
　　5. deity
Minar . . . **4.** myna **5.** Kutab (Delhi), tower
minaret . . . **4.** lamp **5.** tower **10.** lighthouse
minaway . . . **6.** minuet
mince . . . **3.** cut **4.** chop, dice, hash
　　5. slash **8.** diminish, prim step
　　9. subdivide **10.** short steps
minced meat . . . **7.** rissole
minced oath . . . **4.** drat, egad
minchen . . . **3.** nun
minchery . . . **7.** nunnery
minchiate . . . **5.** tarot
mind . . . **4.** care, heed, mens, obey,
　　reck, tend, will **6.** desire, memory,
　　psyche **7.** opinion **9.** intellect, intention
　　11. remembrance **12.** intelligence
mind (pert to) . . .
　　development . . **13.** psychogenesis
　　peace of . . **8.** ataraxia, calmness
　　　　16. imperturbability
　　picture . . **4.** idea **5.** image
　　reader . . **8.** telepath
　　set . . **8.** attitude
　　split . . **13.** schizophrenic
Mindanao . . .
　　language . . **3.** Ata
　　people . . **3.** Ata **4.** Moro **5.** Lutao

　　6. Bagobo, Illano
site . . **11.** Philippines
town . . **4.** Dapa **5.** Davao **9.** Zamboanga
volcano . . **3.** Apo **9.** Malindany
mindful . . . **8.** disposed **9.** observant,
　　regardful **11.** remembering
mine . . . **2.** my **3.** bal, dig, mio, pit, sap
　　4. meum **5.** stope **6.** cavity, quarry
　　7. gallery, passage **10.** excavation
　　12. entrenchment
mine (pert to) . . .
　　basket, tub . . **4.** corf
　　ceiling . . **5.** astel
　　coal . . **3.** rob
　　deviation (lode) . . **4.** hade
　　device (sweeper) . . **3.** gad **8.** paravane
　　entrance, passage . . **4.** adit **5.** stulm
　　excavation . . **5.** stope
　　floor . . **4.** sill
　　guardian (Myth) . . **5.** gnome
　　holes . . **7.** gophers
　　prop . . **5.** sprag, stull
　　reservoir . . **4.** sump **8.** standage
　　shack . . **3.** doe
　　shaft . . **4.** sump **6.** upcast
　　signalman . . **5.** cager **7.** cageman
　　step . . **7.** stemple (stempel)
　　surface . . **6.** placer
　　thrower . . **6.** minnie **11.** minenwerfer
　　tunnel . . **5.** stulm
　　vein . . **4.** lode
　　waste . . **3.** gob **4.** goaf
　　worker . . **5.** cager, miner **8.** onsetter
miner (pert to) . . .
　　disease . . **8.** phthisis
　　instrument . . **4.** dial
　　lamp . . **4.** davy
　　pick . . **3.** gad **7.** mandrel
　　sieve . . **6.** dillue
　　worm . . **8.** hookworm
mineral . . . **3.** ore, tin **4.** alum, iron
　　5. pitch **6.** barite, egeran, gangue,
　　iolite, pinite, quartz **7.** apatite, asphalt,
　　ataxite, bullion, epidote, felsite, felspar
　　8. danalite, edentite, misenite
　　9. uraninite
mineral (ore) . . .
　　black . . **3.** jet **6.** cerine, yenite (Elba)
　　　　7. niobite **8.** graphite **10.** minguetite
　　blue-green . . **5.** beryl
　　brittle . . **7.** euclase
　　brown . . **6.** cerine, egeran, rutile
　　　　9. elaterite
　　calcium, plus . . **7.** calcite **8.** calespar,
　　　　diopside
　　crosslike . . **10.** staurolite
　　dark . . **7.** minette
　　fibrous . . **8.** asbestos (abeston)
　　flaky . . **4.** mica
　　gray white . . **5.** trona
　　green . . **7.** alalite, erinite **9.** malachite
　　gunpowder . . **5.** niter **7.** thorite
　　hard . . **4.** ruby **6.** spinel (spinelle)
　　　　7. adamant
　　jelly . . **8.** vaseline
　　jewelry . . **8.** diopside
　　lustrous . . **4.** spar **7.** blendes
　　magnetic . . **9.** lodestone (loadstone)
　　nonmetallic . . **5.** boron **6.** iodine
　　plaster of Paris . . **6.** gypsum
　　rare, brittle . . **7.** euclase, thorite

red .. **4.** ruby **6.** garnet
soft .. **4.** talc
waxlike .. **9.** ozocerite **11.** hatchettine
white, colorless .. **6.** barite, gypsum
yellow .. **5.** topaz **6.** pyrite **7.** epidote
mineral (pert to) . . .
  cavity .. **3.** vug (vugg, vugh, voog)
  dark spot .. **5.** macle
  deposit .. **4.** lode **6.** placer
  greasy .. **7.** atopite
  oil .. **5.** colza
  pitch .. **7.** asphalt
  pocket .. **4.** nest
  salt .. **4.** alum
  spring .. **3.** spa **4.** well
  tallow, wax .. **9.** ozocerite **11.** hatchettine
  tar .. **6.** maltha
  water .. **6.** lithia **7.** Seltzer **8.** alkaline
Minerva (pert to) . . .
  feast .. **11.** Quinquatrus
  flower, plant .. **6.** azalea
  goddess of .. **5.** civic **6.** health
  11. handicrafts
  shield .. **5.** aegis (egis)
  temple site .. **8.** Aventine (Rome)
ming . . . **6.** remind **7.** mention, recount
  8. remember
Ming (Chin) . . . **7.** dynasty
mingle . . . **3.** mix **4.** fuse, meld **5.** admix,
  blend, merge, unite **7.** combine, concoct
  8. coalesce, intermix **9.** associate
  10. amalgamate **11.** consolidate
mingle-mangle . . . **6.** jumble, medley
  7. mixture **9.** potpourri **10.** hodgepodge,
  miscellany
minhag (Jew) . . . **6.** custom, manner
  7. liturgy
miniate . . . **5.** paint **8.** decorate, luminate
  9. rubricate
minikin . . . **4.** type **5.** baize **6.** dainty
  7. elegant, mincing **8.** affected, delicate
  10. diminutive
minim . . . **3.** jot **4.** drop **5.** Order (RCCh)
  6. minute **8.** smallest **11.** small amount
minimize . . . **6.** reduce **7.** detract
  8. belittle **9.** disparage **10.** depreciate
  13. underestimate
minimum . . . **3.** jot **5.** least **6.** lowest
minion, minionette . . . **4.** idol, neat
  5. lover **6.** dainty, pretty **7.** darling,
  elegant **8.** delicate, favorite, ladylove,
  mistress, paramour
minister . . . **4.** tend **5.** angel, cater, serve
  6. afford, attend, curate, parson, pastor,
  priest, supply **7.** furnish **8.** diplomat,
  executor, preacher **9.** clergyman,
  officiate
ministerial . . . **7.** serving **9.** executive
  12. instrumental **14.** administrative,
  ecclesiastical
minister's home . . . **5.** manse
  9. parsonage
Minnesota . . .
  capital .. **6.** St Paul
  city .. **6.** Duluth **11.** Minneapolis
  hero .. **14.** Father Hennepin
  lake .. **3.** Red **10.** Minnewaska
  land of .. **16.** Ten Thousand Lakes
  mountain .. **6.** Cayuna, Mesabe
  9. Vermilion
  river .. **3.** Red **10.** St Lawrence

  11. Mississippi
  State admission .. **12.** Thirty-second
  State motto .. **13.** L'Etoile du Nord
  14. Star of the North
  State nickname .. **6.** Gopher **9.** North
  Star
Minoan . . . **6.** Cretan **7.** culture (Prehist)
  8. language
minor . . . **3.** key **4.** less, mode **5.** friar
  (Franciscan), petit, petty, scale, youth
  6. course, infant, league, lesser
  7. smaller **8.** inferior, interval, underage
  9. youngling
minority . . . **3.** few **6.** nonage **7.** smaller
  8. underage **10.** immaturity
  11. inferiority
Minos (pert to) . . .
  daughter .. **7.** Ariadne
  father .. **4.** Zeus
  king of .. **5.** Crete
  mother .. **6.** Europa
Minotaur (Gr) . . . **7.** monster (half man,
  half bull)
minster . . . **6.** church **9.** monastery
minstrel . . . **3.** lay **4.** bard, poet, show
  6. end man, troupe **7.** gleeman, goliard
  8. jongleur, musician **9.** troubador
  11. entertainer
minstrel show (pert to) . . .
  end man .. **5.** bones
  middleman .. **12.** interlocutor
  part .. **4.** olio
mint . . . **3.** aim **4.** blow, coin, sage **5.** basil,
  feint, money **6.** hyssop, intend, invent,
  mentha, ramona **7.** attempt, purpose,
  venture **8.** endeavor **9.** fabricate
mint (pert to) . . .
  charge, levy .. **8.** brassage
  11. seigniorage
  drink .. **5.** julep
  family .. **5.** basil **6.** catnip **8.** calamint
  9. Lamiaceae
  genus .. **6.** Ramona **7.** Melissa
  geranium .. **8.** costmary
  hog .. **8.** shilling
  sauce .. **5.** money
minuet . . . **5.** dance **7.** scherzo
minus . . . **4.** lack, less **6.** absent, bereft,
  defect **7.** short of, without **8.** subtract
  10. deficiency
minuscule . . . **4.** type **5.** petty, small
  6. letter (lower case) **10.** diminutive
minute . . . **3.** jot, wee **4.** mite, note,
  tiny **5.** draft, petty, small **6.** atomic,
  little, moment, period, record, slight,
  tittle **7.** instant **8.** atomical, trifling
  10. memorandum **11.** unimportant
  12. sixty seconds **14.** circumstantial
minute (pert to) . . .
  animal .. **10.** animalcule
  details .. **11.** particulars
  difference .. **5.** shade
  glass .. **9.** hourglass
  Jack .. **10.** timeserver
  opening .. **4.** pore **5.** stoma
  organism .. **5.** monad, spore **8.** zoospore
  part .. **6.** tittle
  particle .. **4.** atom, iota, mote
  record .. **8.** protocol
minutely . . . **9.** continual, unceasing
  11. every minute

minutes ... **4.** acta **6.** record
minutia ... **6.** detail, minute **11.** minor detail, petty matter
minx ... **4.** brat, doll, miss **6.** pet dog **7.** colleen **8.** pert girl **9.** saucy girl, saucy jade **13.** mischief-maker
minyan ... **6.** quorum **7.** pottery
Miohippus ... **5.** horse
miqra ... **9.** Bible text (Heb)
mir (Pers) ... **4.** head **5.** chief, title **9.** president
miracle ... **4.** feat, play **5.** anomy **6.** marvel, wonder **10.** occurrence, phenomenon **17.** supernatural event
miracle drug ... **6.** elixir **7.** cure-all, panacea
miracle scene ... **4.** Cana
miracle wheat ... **7.** poulard
miracle worker ... **8.** magician **11.** thermaturge
miraculous ... **9.** marvelous, wonderful **12.** supernatural **13.** wonder-working
mirador ... **5.** brown, oriel **6.** loggia, turret **7.** balcony **9.** bay window **10.** watchtower
mirage ... **5.** serab **7.** chimera, reflect **8.** illusion **10.** phenomenon
mire ... **3.** bog, mud, wet **4.** glar, moil, ooze, slud **5.** addle, dirty, marsh, slush, stall **7.** sludder
mirror ... **5.** glass **7.** crystal, paragon, pattern, reflect **8.** exemplar, speculum **9.** reflector **11.** image worker **12.** looking glass
mirror iron ... **12.** spiegeleisen
mirth ... **3.** fun, joy **4.** glee **6.** gaiety (gayety), levity, spleen **7.** delight, jollity **8.** gladness, hilarity **9.** happiness, merriment, rejoicing **10.** joyousness **12.** cheerfulness
mirthful ... **3.** gay **5.** happy, jolly
miry ... **4.** oozy **5.** boggy, muddy, slimy **6.** filthy, lutose
mis (comb form) ... **5.** amiss, wrong
misadventure ... **6.** mishap **8.** accident, calamity, casualty, disaster **9.** mischance **10.** misfortune
misandry (opp of misogyny) ... **12.** dislike of man (by woman)
misanthrope ... **5.** cynic, Timon (Shaksp) **8.** man hater **9.** pessimist **12.** mankind hater
misapply ... **5.** misdo **6.** misuse **12.** misinterpret
misapprehend ... **7.** mistake **8.** misapply **11.** misconceive **13.** misunderstand
misbegotten ... **8.** deformed **12.** illegitimate
miscalculate ... **3.** err **8.** misjudge **9.** misreckon, overshoot
miscall ... **5.** abuse **6.** revile **7.** misname **9.** read amiss **12.** mispronounce
miscarriage ... **5.** lapse **6.** mishap **7.** failure, misdeed, mistake **8.** abortion **9.** mischance **11.** misdemeanor **13.** mismanagement **14.** premature birth
miscellaneous ... **5.** mixed **6.** medley, varied **7.** blended, diverse, mingled **8.** combined **12.** conglomerate **13.** heterogeneous **14.** indiscriminate

miscellany ... **6.** medley **7.** mixture **8.** excerpts **9.** anthology **10.** collection **11.** odds and ends
mischance ... **6.** mishap **8.** calamity, disaster **10.** misfortune **12.** misadventure
mischief ... **3.** ill **4.** evil, harm **5.** wrack **6.** damage **7.** trouble **9.** devilment
mischief (pert to) ...
   god .. **4.** Loki
   goddess .. **3.** Ate **4.** Eris
   maker .. **8.** agitator **12.** troublemaker
mischievous ... **4.** arch **6.** elfish (elvish), impish **7.** harmful, mocking, naughty, parlous, roguish, waggish **8.** sportive
misconduct ... **7.** offense **10.** wrongdoing **11.** delinquency, misbehavior **12.** misdemeanor **13.** mismanagement
miscreant ... **6.** rascal, wretch **7.** heretic, villain **8.** polisson **9.** reprobate **10.** unbeliever, villainous **11.** fallen angel, misbeliever **12.** unscrupulous
miscue ... **3.** err **4.** miss, slip **5.** error **6.** bungle **7.** mistake
misdeed ... **5.** crime, wrong **7.** offense **8.** wrongful **11.** misdemeanor
misdemeanor ... **3.** sin **4.** tort **5.** crime **7.** misdeed, offense **10.** illegality, wrongdoing **11.** misbehavior
mise ... **4.** levy **5.** grant **6.** layout, treaty **8.** expenses (law), immunity **9.** privilege
miser ... **5.** hunks, Nabal (Bib) **6.** nipper, wretch **7.** boarder, niggard
miserable ... **3.** sad **6.** abject, paltry **7.** forlorn, pitiful, unhappy **12.** disconsolate, disreputable
misericord, misericorde ... **4.** hall, pity **5.** mercy **6.** dagger **9.** refectory **10.** compassion **12.** dispensation
miserly ... **4.** mean **5.** close, tight **6.** stingy **7.** chintzy (sl) **8.** churlish, covetous **9.** niggardly, penurious **10.** avaricious **12.** parsimonious
misery ... **3.** woe **5.** grief **7.** anguish, avarice, poverty, sadness **8.** calamity, distress **9.** heartache, privation **10.** affliction, misfortune **11.** despondency, Pandora's box, unhappiness **12.** covetousness, wretchedness **13.** niggardliness
misfeasance ... **5.** wrong **8.** trespass **10.** wrongdoing
misfortune ... **3.** ill **4.** evil, harm **6.** mishap **7.** bad luck, reverse, setback **8.** calamity, disaster **9.** adversity, holocaust, mischance **11.** catastrophe **12.** misadventure
misgiving ... **5.** doubt, qualm **7.** anxiety **10.** foreboding **12.** apprehension
mishap ... **4.** slip **6.** accident, casualty **10.** misfortune **11.** contretemps, miscarriage **12.** misadventure
Mishnah, Mishna ... **4.** Moed **5.** tenet **6.** Nashim **7.** Nezikim **8.** doctrine, Halakoth, Kodashim, Tohoroth **9.** tradition
misinterpret ... **3.** err **4.** warp **7.** distort, misread **8.** misjudge
misjudge ... **3.** err **11.** misconstrue **12.** miscalculate
misky ... **5.** foggy, misty

mislay ... **4.** lose **8.** displace, misplace
misle ... **4.** mist, rain **6.** mizzle **7.** drizzle
mislead ... **4.** fool **5.** blear **6.** delude,
 seduce **7.** deceive **8.** misguide
 9. deception, misbehave, misinform
misleading ... **5.** false **7.** crooked
 8. illusory **9.** deceptive **10.** fallacious,
 fraudulent **12.** misinforming
 14. misinformation
mislippen ... **6.** delude **7.** neglect, suspect
 10. disappoint
mismanage ... **5.** blunk, misdo **6.** bungle,
 misuse **9.** mishandle
misogynist ... **8.** celibate **10.** woman
 hater
misplace ... **4.** lose **6.** mislay, misset
 8. displace **9.** dislocate, mislocate
 11. anachronism
misplay ... **3.** err **5.** error **6.** renege
 7. mismove **9.** wrong play
misprise, misprize ... **5.** scorn **6.** slight
 7. despise, disdain, mistake **8.** contempt
 9. underrate **10.** misprision, undervalue
 13. underestimate
misprision ... **5.** scorn **7.** mistake
 8. contempt, misprize **10.** misconduct
 11. misdemeanor **12.** depreciation
 16. misunderstanding
mispronunciation ... **8.** cacology **10.** bad
 diction
misrepresent ... **5.** belie **7.** deceive,
 distort, falsify **8.** disserve
miss ... **2.** Ms. **3.** err **4.** chit, fail, girl, lack,
 lose, omit, skip **5.** evade, lapse, title
 7. failure, mistake **8.** mistress **9.** fall
 short **10.** prostitute **12.** mademoiselle
missal ... **4.** book (Eccl) **8.** breviary
missel ... **9.** mistletoe
misshapen ... **4.** ugly **8.** deformed
 9. distorted, monstrous, unshapely
missile ... **2.** MX **4.** ICBM, Nike, Thor
 5. Atlas, Snark, Titan **6.** rocket
 7. grenade, matador **8.** Redstone
 9. Minuteman
missing ... **3.** out **4.** gone, lost **6.** absent
 7. lacking, wanting **8.** vanished
 11. nonexistent
missing part ... **3.** gap **4.** void **5.** space
 6. hiatus, lacuna **8.** omission
mission ... **3.** job **4.** body, duty, task
 5. Alamo **6.** charge, church, errand
 7. calling, embassy **8.** legation,
 outreach **10.** assignment, commission,
 delegation, deputation, missionary
missionary ... **7.** apostle **8.** emissary,
 preacher **10.** evangelist
Missionary Ridge ... **11.** Chattanooga
 (Tenn)
Mississippi ...
 capital .. **7.** Jackson
 city .. **6.** Biloxi **7.** Natchez **8.** Gulfport
 9. Vicksburg **13.** Pass Christian
 explorer, colonizer .. **6.** De Soto
 9. Iberville
 festival .. **9.** Mardi gras (Biloxi)
 king crop .. **6.** cotton
 kite (bird) .. **9.** everglade
 mountain .. **6.** Woodal
 river .. **5.** Yazoo **11.** Mississippi
 State admission .. **9.** Twentieth
 State bird .. **11.** mockingbird

State flower .. **8.** magnolia
State motto .. **14.** Virtute et Armis (By
 Valor and Arms)
State nickname .. **5.** Bayou
Mississippian (Geol) ...
 15. Eocarboniferous (system)
Mississippi River head ... **10.** Lake
 Itasca (Minn)
Mississippi River nickname ... **10.** Great
 River **14.** Father of Waters
missive ... **4.** note **6.** billet, letter
 7. message, missile **8.** document
Missouri ...
 capital .. **13.** Jefferson City
 city .. **7.** Sedalia, St Louis **8.** Hannibal,
 St Joseph
 famed native .. **6.** Carver (G W), Truman
 (Pres) **9.** Mark Twain **10.** Jesse James
 gourd .. **11.** calabazilla
 mountains .. **6.** Ozarks
 river .. **8.** Big Muddy, Missouri
 11. Mississippi
 skylark .. **13.** Sprague's pipit
 State admission .. **12.** Twenty-fourth
 State bird .. **8.** bluebird
 State flower .. **8.** hawthorn
 State nickname .. **6.** Show Me
 sucker (fish) .. **10.** black horse
misspelling ... **10.** cacography
misspend ... **4.** lose **5.** waste **8.** squander
 10. spend amiss
misstep ... **4.** slip, trip **7.** faux pas
mist ... **3.** dim, fog **4.** blur, film, gray,
 haze, rain, smur **5.** bedim, brume, cloud
 7. droplet **9.** obscurity **11.** uncertainty
mistake ... **3.** err **4.** bull, goof, slip
 5. boner, botch, error, fault, folly
 7. blooper, blunder, erratum, violate
 8. miscount, solecism **11.** anachronism
 12. inadvertence **13.** misconception
 15. misapprehension
mistaken ... **5.** wrong **9.** erroneous
 12. misconceived **13.** misunderstood
 14. judging wrongly
mistletoe ... **6.** emblem (Okla), missel,
 Viscum **9.** Loranthus
mistonusk ... **6.** badger
mistreat ... **5.** abuse, wrong **6.** ill-use
mistress ... **4.** bibi (beebee) **5.** title,
 woman **6.** matron **7.** control, teacher
 8. Dulcinia, ladylove **9.** concubine,
 governess, patroness **10.** proprietor,
 sweetheart
Mistress of ...
 Adriatic .. **6.** Venice
 Charles II .. **4.** Nell
 Seas .. **12.** Great Britain
 World .. **4.** Rome (anc)
misty ... **3.** dim **4.** hazy, roky **5.** foggy,
 rouky, vague **6.** blurry, cloudy, hoarse
 7. obscure, shadowy **10.** indistinct
 13. unenlightened, unilluminated
misuse ... **5.** abuse **6.** revile **7.** pervert
 8. maltreat, misapply, wrong use
 9. misemploy **12.** misrepresent
misuse of words in speech ...
 11. heterophemy, malapropism
mite ... **3.** bit, jot **4.** atom, coin, mote
 5. child, speck **6.** acarus, insect
 7. bdellid, chigger, smidgen (smidge)
 8. acaridan, particle

miter, mitre . . . **4.** belt **5.** frank, joint, tiara **6.** fillet, girdle, gusset, tavern **7.** petalon (Eccl) **8.** dovetail, headband, insignia **9.** headdress

mithridate . . . **8.** antidote **9.** electuary **12.** alexipharmic

mitigate . . . **4.** ease, tone **5.** abate, allay, mease, relax, remit, slake **6.** lessen, reduce, soften, temper **7.** appease, mollify, qualify, relieve **8.** diminish, lenitive, moderate, palliate **9.** alleviate, extenuate, meliorate

mitigation . . . **6.** relief **9.** abatement **10.** diminution, moderation **11.** extenuation **13.** mollification

mix . . . **3.** pug (clay) **4.** ease, join, meng, stir **5.** addle, blend, cross, knead, unite **6.** jumble, mingle, muddle **7.** combine, fluster **8.** coalesce **9.** associate **10.** complicate

mixable . . . **8.** miscible

mixed (pert to) . . .
bag . . **6.** medley **10.** assortment, hodgepodge, miscellany
breed . . **7.** mongrel
type . . **2.** pi
with water . . **6.** slaked
with yeast . . **6.** barmed, frothy

mixer . . . **5.** whisk **6.** beater **7.** mingler **9.** eggbeater, (food) processor

mixture . . . **4.** hash, mash, olio **5.** blend, chaos, mixed **6.** batter, medley, miscue **7.** amalgam, mélange **8.** compound, solution **9.** admixture, potpourri **10.** hodgepodge **11.** combination, preparation

mixture (pert to) . . .
beverage . . **5.** clary **10.** shandygaff
cement . . **5.** putty
medicinal . . **5.** hepar **6.** potion **12.** prescription
metallic . . **6.** speiss
sand and clay . . **4.** loam

mix-up . . . **5.** melee, snafu **6.** muddle, tangle **8.** conflict **9.** confusion

Mizar . . . **4.** Zeta (Great Dipper)

mizmaze . . . **9.** confusion **12.** bewilderment

mizzenmast . . . **9.** aftermast, third mast

mizzle . . . **4.** mist, rain **5.** misle **6.** decamp **9.** slink away

mizzy . . . **3.** bog **8.** quagmire

Mnenosyne (pert to) . . .
ancestor . . **5.** Titan
goddess . . **6.** memory
mother of . . **8.** The Muses

moa . . . **6.** ratite (flightless) **8.** Dinornis

moab . . . **3.** hat (anc)

Moabite (pert to) . . .
dwelling (Bib) . . **7.** Dead Sea
language . . **7.** Semitic
mountain . . **4.** Nebo
people . . **4.** Emim
stone (Bib) . . **11.** black basalt

moan . . . **3.** cry **4.** suum, wail **5.** groan, sough **6.** bemoan, bewail, grieve, lament, suffer **9.** complaint **11.** lamentation

moat . . . **4.** foss (fosse) **5.** ditch **6.** trench **13.** fortification

mob . . . **3.** set **4.** gang, herd, mass **5.** crowd, drove, flock, group, Mafia, taunt **6.** clique, rabble, throng **7.** company **8.** canaille, populace

mobile . . . **7.** movable **8.** not fixed **9.** versatile **10.** changeable

Mobile Bay hero . . . **8.** Farragut (Adm)

mobile home . . . **3.** van **6.** camper **7.** caravan (Brit), trailer

mob member . . . **6.** rioter **7.** Mafioso **8.** criminal, mobocrat **9.** roisterer

mobocracy . . . **7.** mob rule

Moby Dick (pert to) . . .
author . . **8.** Melville (Herman)
character . . **4.** Ahab **7.** Ishmael **8.** Queequeg, Starbuck
ship . . **6.** Pequod

moccasin . . . **3.** pac **4.** shoe **5.** snake **6.** Flower (Minn State), orchid **8.** larrigan **10.** argus brown **11.** cottonmouth

moch . . . **4.** moth

mocha . . . **4.** bark, town (Arab) **6.** coffee, dollar **7.** leather **9.** moss agate

mock . . . **3.** ape **4.** defy, gibe, jape, jibe, sham **5.** feign, fleer, flout, mimic, scoff, sneer, taunt **6.** delude, deride **7.** imitate, mockery, pretend **8.** ridicule **10.** disappoint **11.** counterfeit

mock (pert to) . . .
brawn . . **10.** headcheese
cucumber . . **11.** balsam apple
duck . . **4.** meat **8.** pork chop
hero . . **5.** comic
jewelry . . **5.** logie, paste **9.** imitation
lead, ore . . **10.** sphalerite
moon . . **10.** paraselene
nightingale . . **7.** warbler **8.** blackcap
olive . . **9.** axbreaker **12.** cherry laurel
orange . . **7.** syringa (seringa)
plane . . **8.** sycamore
sun . . **7.** parhelion
turtle . . **9.** calf's head

mockage . . . **7.** mimicry, mockery **9.** imitation

mocker . . . **5.** mimic **7.** scoffer **8.** deceiver **11.** mockingbird

mockernut . . . **7.** hickory

mockery . . . **5.** farce **6.** satire **7.** mimicry, sarcasm **8.** derision **9.** imitation **11.** counterfeit

mockingbird . . . **5.** Mimus

mode . . . **3.** fad, way **4.** form **5.** flair, style, vogue **6.** manner, method **7.** fashion, variety

mode (pert to) . . .
expression . . **10.** vernacular
government . . **6.** regime, system
logic . . **7.** Ferison (3rd figure)
procedure . . **5.** order **6.** system
speech . . **8.** parlance **11.** phraseology
standing . . **4.** pose **6.** stance **7.** posture **8.** position

model . . . **3.** act **4.** form, idea, mold, norm, plan, plat, pose **5.** ideal, image, shape **7.** example, manikin, measure, paragon, pattern, templet **8.** ensample, paradigm, standard, template **9.** archetype, mannequin, precedent **11.** meritorious **12.** reproduction

model (of) . . .
a word . . **8.** paradigm

a work . . 9. archetype
excellence . . 7. paragon 8. exemplar
solar system . . 6. orrery 11. planetarium
moderate . . . 4. bate, ease, slow, some
   5. abate, lower, slake 6. frugal,
   lessen, soften, temper 7. control,
   lenient, mediate, modesto 8. mediocre,
   modulate, slow down 9. temperate
   10. reasonable 11. inexpensive
   12. conservative 14. inconsiderable
moderation . . . 7. control 9. abatement,
   restraint 10. diminution, governance,
   limitation, mitigation 11. restriction
   13. temperateness
moderator . . . 5. judge 6. umpire 7. arbiter
   8. mediator 10. arbitrator, controller
modern . . . 3. neo (pref), new 4. late
   6. latter 7. present 8. neoteric
modernize . . . 6. update 10. streamline
Modern School of Art . . . 4. Dada
   7. Dadaism (1920)
modern Syriac script . . . 5. serta
   8. peshitta
modest . . . 3. coy, mim, shy 6. chaste,
   demure, humble, seemly 8. reserved,
   retiring, virtuous 9. diffident 11. well-
   behaved 13. unpretentious
   14. inconsiderable
modesty . . . 7. decency, reserve, shyness
   8. chastity, humility, pudicity
   10. diffidence, humbleness 11. self-
   control
modicum . . . 3. bit 4. drop 5. minim, share
   6. little 11. small amount 12. small
   portion
modification . . . 4. tone 6. change,
   umlaut 9. variation 10. adaptation,
   alteration, limitation 13. qualification
   15. differentiation
modify . . . 4. vary 5. alter, limit 6. change,
   master, temper 7. assuage, qualify
   8. attemper, mitigate, moderate,
   quantify 9. influence 13. differentiate
modish . . . 4. chic, trim 5. smart 7. in
   vogue, stylish 8. vogueish (voguish)
   11. fashionable
modiste . . . 8. milliner 9. couturier
   10. couturière, dressmaker
modulated . . . 5. toned 6. merged
   7. adapted, attuned, changed, intoned
   8. softened, tempered 9. inflected,
   regulated
modulation . . . 4. tone 6. change
   8. shifting 9. tempering 10. alteration,
   inflection, moderation
moggan . . . 8. stocking 10. knit sleeve
moggy . . . 3. cat, cow 4. calf 7. pet name
   8. slattern 9. scarecrow
mogo . . . 7. hatchet
mogul . . . 4. lord 5. nabob 6. tycoon
   7. magnate 8. autocrat 9. dignitary
   10. locomotive, panjandrum 14. great
   personage
Mogul . . . 6. Empire, Mongol 7. dynasty
   9. Mongolian
Mohammed (pert to) . . .
   birthplace . . 5. Mecca
   daughter . . 5. Fatima
   flight to Mecca . . 6. hegira
   horse . . 5. Fadda (white mule) 7. Alborak
   names . . 7. Mahomet, Mahound

son-in-law . . 3. Ali
Mohammedan (pert to) . . .
   angel of death . . 6. Azrael
   ascetic . . 4. Sufi 5. fakir (fakeer)
   8. Marabout
   caliph . . 3. Ali 4. Omar 6. Othman 7. Abu
   Bekr
   chief . . 3. aga (agha) 4. dato (datto)
   5. sayid 6. Caliph
   crier (for prayer) . . 7. muezzin
   crusader's enemy (Muslim) . . 7. Saracen
   deity . . 5. Allah 9. Termagant
   demon . . 5. afrit, eblis, jinni (jinnee)
   7. Shaitan (Sheitan)
   Malay (Javanese) . . 6. Sassak
   Moslem . . 5. hanif 9. Mussulman
   noble . . 4. amir (ameer), emir
   nymph . . 5. houri
   officer . . 3. aga 5. diwan 6. vizier (vizir)
   princess, queen . . 5. begum
   saint . . 3. pir 6. santon
   scholars, body of . . 5. ulema
   sect . . 6. Wahabi (Wahabee, Wahhabi)
   student (Theol) . . 5. softa
   successor . . 6. Caliph (Calif)
   teacher . . 5. mufti 6. mullah (mollah)
Mohammedanism (pert to) . . .
   Bible, book . . 5. Koran 7. Alcoran
   bier, tomb . . 5. tabut
   cap . . 3. taj
   caravansary . . 6. imaret
   crusade . . 5. jihad (jehad)
   custom, tradition . . 6. sunnah
   divorce . . 5. talak 7. mubarat
   dome, over tomb . . 6. turbeh
   Easter . . 3. Eed
   Fast (annual) . . 7. Ramadan
   festival . . 6. Bairam
   garment . . 4. izar 6. jubbah
   house (men's part) . . 8. selamlik
   instrument . . 5. rebab
   marriage custom . . 5. iddat
   marriage settlement . . 4. mahr
   Messiah, priest . . 4. Imam (Imaum)
   5. Mahdi
   monastery . . 5. ribat
   platform, porch . . 7. mastaba
   prayer . . 4. azan (adan) 5. namaz
   property (law) . . 6. mushaa
   religion . . 6. Moslem 8. Islamism
   saber . . 8. yataghan (yatagan)
   salutation . . 6. salaam (salam)
   shrine (Mecca) . . 5. Kaaba (Caaba,
   Kaabeh) 10. Black Stone
   veil . . 7. yashmak (yashmac)
   war (Relig) . . 5. jihad (jehad)
moho . . . 4. rail 9. gallinule 10. honey
   eater
mohr . . . 7. gazelle
moider . . . 4. toil 5. crowd, worry
   6. wander 7. smother 8. bewilder,
   encumber
moiety . . . 4. half, part (small) 7. portion
moil . . . 4. spot, tire, toil 5. labor, taint
   6. seethe 7. torment, trouble, turmoil
   8. drudgery 9. confusion 10. defilement
moiré . . . 7. clouded, watered
moist . . . 3. wet 4. damp, dank, dewy,
   uvid 5. humid, rainy 7. tearful
moisten . . . 3. wet 4. hose, moil 5. bedew,
   spray 6. anoint, dampen, sparge

8. humidify, sprinkle
moisture . . . **3.** dew, fog **5.** vapor, water
  6. liquid **8.** dampness, dankness,
  dewdrops, humidity
moisture (pert to) . . .
  body . . **6.** humors **9.** exudation
  condensed . . **4.** drip, drop
  excess, swelling . . **5.** edema
  expose to . . **3.** ret
  remove . . **4.** wipe **5.** wring
mojo . . . **4.** Moxo **5.** charm (voodoo)
  6. amulet **7.** majagua
moke . . . **4.** dolt, mesh **5.** horse **6.** donkey
  7. network **8.** minstrel **9.** performer
moki . . . **4.** raft
moko . . . **9.** tattooing
moky . . . **5.** foggy, misty
molar . . . **5.** tooth **6.** molary **7.** chopper,
  grinder **8.** grinding
molarimeter . . . **11.** thermometer
molasses . . . **5.** sirup **7.** treacle **8.** theriaca
mold, mould . . . **3.** die **4.** cast, form,
  must **5.** humus, knead, nowel, plasm,
  sprue **6.** blight, growth (fungus),
  matrix, mildew **7.** moulage **9.** sculpture
  12. reproduction
Moldavia, Rumania . . .
  balm . . **4.** mint
  capital . . **5.** Balta **8.** Tiraspol
  govt . . **9.** Socialist
molding . . . **3.** ess **4.** bead, beak, cyma,
  ogee, reed, tori **5.** conge, gulla,
  ovolo, splay, torus **6.** fascia, fillet,
  listel, reglet, scotia **7.** cavetto, cornice,
  reeding, shaping **8.** astragal, bezantee
  12. reproduction
molding (pert to) . . .
  convex . . **5.** torus
  decoration . . **4.** dado
  egg and dart . . **9.** arrowhead
  series . . **7.** surbase
  suit of . . **8.** ledgment (ledgement)
moldy, mouldy . . . **5.** fusty, mucid, musty,
  stale **8.** mildewed
mole (rat) . . . **4.** gray **5.** fault, nevus
  (naevus), shrew, snake, Talpa, taupe
  6. rodent **7.** blemish, Nesokia
  9. birthmark **12.** imperfection
molecule . . . **3.** ion **4.** atom, unit **6.** steric
  8. particle
molest . . . **4.** harm **5.** annoy, tease
  6. bother, harass, pester **7.** disturb
  8. mistreat **9.** incommode **13.** interfere
  with
Molière (pert to) . . .
  author of . . **5.** drama, Miser, plays
  6. comedy, satire **8.** Tartuffe
  11. Misanthrope
  character (story) . . **5.** Damis **6.** Eraste,
  Scapin **7.** Dorante
mollify . . . **4.** calm **5.** allay, relax,
  sleek **6.** pacify, relent, soften, temper
  7. appease, lighten, qualify, relieve
  9. alleviate **10.** conciliate
mollitious . . . **8.** sensuous **9.** luxurious,
  softening
mollusk . . . **3.** asi **4.** clam, pipi, slug,
  spat **5.** chama, snail, squid, whelk
  6. cockle, limpet, mussel, oyster
  7. abalone, bivalve, octopus, scallop,
  veliger **8.** univalve **10.** cuttlefish

mollusk . . . **5.** Anoma, Chama, Murex
  6. Chiton **7.** Astarte, Etheria
  8. Buccinum, Mollusca, Nautilus
mollusk (pert to) . . .
  bait . . **6.** limpet
  eight-armed . . **7.** octopus
  freshwater . . **7.** etheria
  marine . . **7.** abalone, scallop **8.** nautilus
  shell . . **4.** test **5.** testa **6.** cockle, cowrie
  (cowry)
  shell, without . . **4.** slug
  shell concretion . . **5.** pearl
  teeth . . **6.** radula
  ten-armed . . **5.** squid
  young . . **4.** spat
mollycoddle . . . **6.** coddle, pamper
  8. weakling **12.** spoiled child
  13. effeminate boy
Moloch (pert to) . . .
  Bible . . **5.** deity
  doctrine . . **4.** evil
  zoology . . **6.** agamid, lizard
Molotov cocktail . . . **4.** bomb
molt, moult . . . **3.** mew **4.** cast, mute,
  shed **7.** ecdysis **8.** exuviate
molten rock . . . **2.** aa
Moluccas, Spice Islands . . .
  capital . . **7.** Amboina
  island . . **5.** Banda
  product . . **5.** spice
  site . . **9.** Indonesia
moly . . . **4.** herb (fabled) **6.** garlic
momble . . . **6.** jumble, tangle
mome (anc) . . . **4.** fool **7.** buffoon
  9. blockhead
moment . . . **4.** time **5.** avail, flash, nonce,
  point, trice, value **6.** crisis, minute,
  second, weight **7.** impetus, instant
  9. influence, twinkling **10.** importance
  11. consequence **13.** consideration,
  signification
momentary . . . **9.** ephemeral, transient
  10. transitory **13.** instantaneous
momentous . . . **7.** weighty **8.** eventful
  9. important **11.** influential
  13. authoritative
momo . . . **3.** owl
Momus (Gr) . . . **3.** god (of ridicule) **6.** critic
  11. faultfinder
mon . . . **5.** badge (imperial) **7.** kikumon
  13. chrysanthemum
monachal . . . **8.** celibate, monastic
  9. claustral
monad . . . **3.** one **4.** atom, unit **5.** deity,
  monas **8.** particle **10.** individual
  12. Supreme Being
monadnock . . . **4.** hill **8.** mountain (NH)
Mona Lisa (pert to) . . .
  famed for . . **5.** smile (subtle)
  named also . . **10.** La Gioconda
  painter . . **7.** da Vinci
  site (of picture) . . **6.** Louvre
monandry . . . **10.** one husband (at a
  time)
monarch . . . **4.** czar, king, shah **5.** chief,
  queen, ruler **6.** dynast, kaiser, sultan
  7. czarina, emperor **9.** potentate,
  sovereign **13.** royal highness
monarch . . . **9.** butterfly **13.** constellation
monastery . . . **5.** abbey **6.** friary, priory
  7. convent, hospice, nunnery **8.** cloister

monastery (pert to)...
head.. **3.** dom **5.** abbot
Pavia.. **10.** Carthusian
room.. **4.** cell
Tibet.. **8.** lamasery
monastic... **4.** monk **5.** friar **7.** monkish
8. celibate **9.** claustral
monde... **5.** globe, world (fashion)
6. circle (fashion) **7.** coterie, société,
society **9.** beau monde
monetary... **7.** coinage **8.** currency
9. financial, pecuniary
monetary unit (sl)... **3.** bob (Brit), fin
4. buck **7.** sawbuck, smacker, ten spot
8. simoleon
money... **3.** wad **4.** cash, coin, grig, mina,
pelf **5.** frank, funds, lucre, maneh, uhllo
(ullo) **6.** mazuma, talent, wampum,
wealth **8.** currency **10.** spondulics
(spondulix) **11.** legal tender
money (pert to)...
ancient.. **3.** aes
bank (Eur).. **5.** banco
box, chest.. **4.** arca, safe, till, tray
5. chest **6.** drawer **7.** brazier **8.** register
changer.. **6.** banker, broker, shroff
(saraf), usurer **7.** cambist
coinage.. **4.** mint
English slang.. **7.** ooftish (oof)
found.. **5.** trove
gamblers'.. **6.** barato
gift.. **4.** alms **7.** bequest **9.** endowment
lender.. **6.** banker, usurer **7.** Shylock
10. pawnbroker
luck.. **6.** barato **7.** handsel
maker.. **6.** coiner, minter
13. counterfeiter
manual.. **7.** cambist
matters.. **6.** fiscal **9.** economics
of account.. **3.** ora
paper.. **4.** bill, kale **7.** lettuce
pledge.. **5.** arles
premium.. **4.** agio
roll (coins).. **7.** rouleau
shell.. **5.** uhllo (ullo) **6.** cowrie (cowry)
slang.. **4.** gilt, jack, lour **5.** rhino
6. boodle, wampum
spinner.. **6.** usurer **10.** speculator
substitute.. **5.** scrip
to coin.. **4.** mint
wildcat.. **9.** yellow dog
worthless.. **4.** pelf **11.** shinplaster
moneyed... **4.** rich **5.** flush **7.** opulent,
wealthy **8.** affluent, well-to-do
10. prosperous, well-heeled
monger... **6.** dealer, mercer, trader,
vendor **7.** peddler **8.** merchant
9. tradesman
mongler... **9.** sandpiper
Mongol... see also *Mongolian* **5.** Asian,
Tatar **9.** yellow man
Mongolian (pert to)...
ass (wild).. **8.** chigetai
capital.. **4.** Urga
conjurer.. **6.** shaman
conqueror.. **9.** Tamerlane
desert.. **4.** Gobi
dynasty.. **4.** Yuan
monk, priest.. **4.** lama
people.. **3.** Lai **4.** Lapp **5.** Ordos
7. Khalkas, Tsaktar **9.** Ouryantai

religion.. **9.** Shamanism, Shintoism
12. Confucianism
river.. **3.** Pei **4.** Onon
mongoose... **4.** urva **5.** lemur
9. ichneumon
mongrel... **3.** cur **5.** mixed **6.** hybrid
10. crossbreed **14.** stilt sandpiper
mongrel fish... **5.** skate (angelfish)
8. tullibee (whitefish)
monial... **3.** nun
moniker... **4.** name **8.** nickname
monition... **6.** advice, notice
7. summons, warning **10.** admonition,
dissuasion, intimation **11.** forewarning
monitor... **4.** ship (Civil War), uran
5. varan **6.** lizard, manual, mentor,
nozzle **7.** adviser, student, warning
8. conenose (bug), director, recorder,
reminder **9.** informant
monk... **3.** fra **4.** bede, lama, saki **5.** fakir,
friar, padre **6.** ferret, monkey **7.** ascetic,
caloyer, dervish **8.** anchoret, capuchin,
celibate, cenobite **9.** anchorite, bullfinch,
touchwood
monkey (pert to)...
African.. **4.** waag **5.** potto **6.** grivet,
vernet
American.. **4.** saki **5.** acari **7.** ouakari
8. marmoset **9.** beelzebub
bearded.. **8.** entellus
bonnet.. **4.** zati **5.** toque
bread.. **6.** baobab
chimpanzee.. **6.** nchega
crying.. **4.** kaha
cups.. **9.** nepenthes **12.** pitcher plant
family.. **10.** Catarrhina
flower.. **7.** mimulus (herb)
genus.. **5.** Cebus **6.** Ateles **7.** Colobus,
Saimiri, Tarsius **8.** Alouatta
handsome.. **4.** mona
house.. **5.** apery
howling.. **4.** mono **5.** araba **7.** stentor
8. alouatte
large.. **5.** sajou
Madagascar.. **8.** mangabey (mangaby)
organ grinder.. **5.** Cebus **8.** capuchin
Oriental.. **7.** macaque
puzzle.. **5.** piñon
small.. **8.** marmoset
South American.. **4.** titi **6.** grison
9. beelzebub
spider.. **7.** sapajou
squirrel.. **7.** saimiri
tailless.. **3.** ape
wrench.. **7.** spanner
monk's hood... **4.** cowl
monkshood... **4.** atis **7.** aconite
9. dandelion
monoceros... **4.** fish (one-horned)
7. sawfish, Unicorn **9.** swordfish
13. Constellation
monochord... **7.** concord, harmony
9. sonometer **10.** clavichord, instrument
monocle... **8.** eyeglass
monocleid, monocleide... **4.** desk (one
key) **7.** cabinet
monocracy... **9.** autocracy **13.** undivided
rule
Monodelphia... **7.** mammals **8.** Eutheria
monody... **3.** ode **4.** poem (lament),
song **5.** dirge **6.** melody **9.** homophony

monogamy . . . **11.** one marriage
monogram . . . **6.** cipher, sketch **7.** outline
　8. initials **9.** character
monolith . . . **5.** stone **6.** menhir, pillar,
　statue **8.** monument
monologue . . . **6.** speech **9.** soliloquy
monomachy . . . **4.** duel **6.** combat
monopoly . . . **5.** grant, right, trust
　6. corner **7.** charter, control **9.** privilege,
　syndicate **10.** possession (exclusive)
monotonous . . . **4.** dead, drab, dull
　5. drone, thrum **6.** dreary, samely
　7. humdrum, tedious **8.** singsong
　9. wearisome **11.** repetitious
monotony . . . **6.** tedium **8.** sameness
　9. wearisome **10.** sameliness, uniformity
　15. repetitiousness
monoxylon, monoxyle . . . **4.** boat
　5. canoe
monseigneur . . . **5.** title **6.** My Lord
monster . . . **4.** ogre **5.** fiend, harpy,
　teras **6.** dragon, ellops, geryon,
　gorgon, sphinx **8.** behemoth, Cerberus
　11. monstrosity
monster (pert to) . . .
　abode (Scot) . . **8.** Loch Ness
　actor . . **6.** Chaney **7.** Karloff
　classic . . **8.** minotaur
　comb form . . **6.** terato
　desert . . **4.** Gila
　eight-headed . . **6.** Scylla
　fabled . . **5.** harpy **6.** kraken, sphinx
　　7. centaur **9.** bucentaur
　flame-breathing . . **7.** chimera (chimaera)
　half man, half bull . . **8.** minotaur
　headless . . **9.** acephalus
　like . . **8.** teratoid
　man-eating . . **4.** ogre **5.** lamia
　medical . . **5.** teras
　Shelley's . . **12.** Frankenstein
　three-bodied . . **6.** Geryon (slain by
　　Hercules)
　Tokyo's . . **8.** Godzilla
　twin . . **10.** xiphopagus
　two-bodied . . **7.** disomus
　two-headed . . **10.** dicephalus,
　　opodidymus
　winged . . **5.** harpy
monstrous . . . **4.** huge, ugly, vast
　5. enorm (anc) **6.** absurd, wicked
　7. strange, titanic **8.** deformed, gigantic,
　infamous **9.** fantastic, monstrous,
　unnatural **10.** prodigious, stupendous
　12. overpowering, overwhelming
　13. extraordinary
Montaigne (pert to) . . .
　translator . . **6.** Florio
　writer of . . **6.** essays
Montana . . .
　capital . . **6.** Helena
　city . . **5.** Butte **8.** Anaconda, Billings
　　10. Great Falls
　Historic site . . **14.** Custer Cemetery
　lake . . **8.** Flathead
　mountain . . **7.** Rockies **17.** Continental
　　Divide
　park . . **7.** Glacier **11.** Yellowstone
　peak . . **7.** Granite
　reservation (Ind) . . **4.** Cree, Crow **5.** Sioux
　　8. Cheyenne, Chippewa **9.** Blackfeet
　State admission . . **10.** Forty-first

　State motto . . **13.** Gold and Silver
　State nickname . . **8.** Treasure
montanto . . . **6.** rising **10.** broadsword
Monte Cristo, Count of (pert to) . . .
　author . . **5.** Dumas (Alexandre)
　hero . . **6.** Dantès
Montenegro . . . **10.** Yugoslavia
montero . . . **3.** cap (hunter's) **6.** ranger
　8. forester, huntsman, mountain
Montezuma (pert to) . . .
　Chief of . . **6.** Aztecs
　cypress . . **9.** ahuehuete
　hero of . . **6.** Mexico
　prisoner of . . **6.** Cortez
　ruins, site of . . **6.** Pueblo
month (pert to) . . .
　astronomy . . **5.** lunar, solar
　half . . **9.** fortnight
　revolution . . **8.** sidereal **9.** synodical
　term . . **5.** epact **6.** ultimo **7.** proximo
　twelfth part . . **8.** calendar
monticule . . . **4.** cone (volcano) **5.** mount
　7. hillock **10.** prominence (small)
montilla . . . **6.** sherry
Montmorency . . . **6.** cherry
monture . . . **5.** frame, horse (saddle),
　mount
monument . . . **4.** tomb **5.** cairn, stele
　(stela), tower, vault **6.** bilith, dolmen
　7. obelisk **8.** cenotaph, cromlech,
　monolith **9.** sepulcher **10.** gravestone
　11. commemorate, remembrance
monumental . . . **4.** high **5.** great
　7. mammoth, massive, notable
　8. colossal **10.** impressive, sculptural,
　stupendous
Monumental City . . . **9.** Baltimore
moo . . . **3.** low (of a cow) **6.** lowing
mooch . . . **4.** loaf **5.** skulk, sneak, steal
　6. loiter, pilfer **7.** vagrant
moocha . . . **6.** girdle **9.** loincloth
mood . . . **3.** tid **4.** tone, vein, whim
　5. freak, humor **6.** nature **7.** caprice
　11. disposition
moody . . . **3.** sad **4.** glum **5.** sulky
　6. gloomy, sullen **7.** pensive
　9. whimsical **10.** capricious
mool . . . **4.** bury, mold, soil **5.** earth,
　grave **6.** mingle **7.** crumble
mools . . . **10.** chilblains
moon . . . **4.** idle, Luna **5.** Diana **6.** Phoebe
　wander **7.** Cynthia **8.** crescent **9.** satellite
　13. celestial body
moon (pert to) . . .
　age (first of year) . . **5.** epact
　area . . **4.** mare
　Astrol . . **6.** Cancer (mansion), planet
　autumn . . **7.** harvest
　beam . . **3.** ray **9.** pearl blue
　bird . . **11.** goldencrest
　blindness . . **10.** nyctalopia
　calf . . **4.** dolt **7.** monster **8.** born fool,
　　imbecile
　comb form . . **5.** selen
　fern . . **8.** moonwort
　festival . . **8.** neomenia
　fish . . **4.** opah **6.** minnow **7.** sunfish
　　9. spadefish
　flower . . **10.** oxeye daisy
　gazing . . **16.** absent-mindedness
　geographer . . **13.** selenographer

god.. **3.** Sin **6.** Nannar
heraldry.. **6.** argent
inhabitant.. **8.** Selenite
instrument.. **11.** selenoscope
lighter.. **9.** serenader **10.** moonshiner
  11. night worker
lily.. **10.** moonflower
mad.. **7.** lunatic
mock.. **10.** paraselene
month.. **5.** lunar
new.. **6.** phasis
phase.. **7.** gibbous, horning
picture of.. **11.** selenograph
point.. **4.** cusp, horn **5.** apsis **6.** apogee
  7. perigee
position.. **6.** octant
raker.. **10.** stupid lout **12.** woolgatherer
stone.. **3.** gem **8.** feldspar **10.** hecatolite
struck.. **7.** lunatic **8.** obsessed
Uranus's.. **5.** Ariel
valley.. **4.** rill (rille) **5.** cleft
moon goddess...
  Greek.. **6.** Hecate, Phoebe **7.** Artemis,
    Cynthia
  Italian.. **5.** Diana
  Phoenician.. **6.** Tanith (Tanit) **7.** Astarte
  Roman.. **3.** Dea **5.** Virgo **9.** Caelestis
moonish... **7.** flighty **10.** capricious
moonshine... **5.** empty **6.** liquor, poteen,
  whisky (whiskey) **7.** bootleg **8.** egg
  sauce, nonsense **10.** balsamweed
moony... **5.** round **6.** dreamy
  9. moonlight **10.** abstracted
  14. crescent-shaped
moor... **3.** bog, fen **4.** hill, root **5.** heath,
  marsh, swale **6.** anchor, fasten, secure
  9. fix firmly
Moor... **6.** Berber, Moslem **7.** Moorman,
  Othello (Shaksp), Saracen **8.** goldfish
  (black), Moroccan
moor (pert to)...
  berry.. **9.** cranberry
  bird.. **6.** grouse
  blackbird.. **5.** ouzel
  buzzard.. **5.** harpy **7.** harrier
  cock.. **9.** blackcock
  dance.. **7.** morisco
  grass.. **5.** heath **6.** sundew
  hen.. **4.** coot **9.** gallinule
  monkey.. **7.** macaque
  stone.. **7.** granite
Moorish... **6.** Moslem **8.** Moresque
Moorish (pert to)...
  garment.. **5.** jupon
  horse.. **4.** barb (Barbary)
  judge.. **4.** cadi
  kettledrum.. **5.** tabor **6.** atabal
  Order.. **7.** Alcazar **8.** Alhambra
    9. horseshoe, Saracenic
  palace.. **7.** Alcazar
moose... **3.** elk **4.** alce **5.** eland **7.** society
  (Loyal Order)
moose bird... **9.** Canada jay
moot... **4.** pose **5.** argue, plead, speak
  6. debate **7.** discuss, propose
mop... **4.** swab, wipe **5.** scrub **6.** merkin
  7. drink up, grimace **9.** blindfold,
  implement
mope... **4.** sulk **5.** dumps, idler **6.** grieve
moppet... **3.** tot **4.** baby, doll, tike
  7. darling, toddler **9.** youngster

mora... **4.** tree (Trinidad) **5.** delay,
  stool **7.** default **8.** syllable **9.** footstool
  11. Spartan army **12.** postponement
moral... **4.** good, pure **5.** maxim **6.** lesson
  7. epimyth, ethical, upright, virtual
  8. likeness, virtuous **9.** righteous
moral (pert to)...
  excellence.. **6.** virtue
  fault.. **4.** vice
  law.. **9.** Decalogue
  obligation.. **4.** duty
  poem.. **3.** dit
  principle.. **7.** precept
  story.. **5.** fable **7.** parable **8.** apologue
morale... **4.** hope, zeal **6.** morals, spirit
  8. morality **10.** confidence
moralist... **4.** prig **7.** teacher **9.** moralizer
  10. sermonizer
morality... **6.** amoral, ethics, virtue
  13. righteousness
morals... **8.** morality **10.** ethography
morass... **3.** bog, fen **4.** moor **5.** marsh,
  swamp **6.** slough **8.** quagmire
  9. everglade
moratorium... **5.** delay **10.** suspension
Moravia, capital... **5.** Brünn (Brno)
Moravian... **9.** Christian **10.** Herrnhuter
  13. Unitas Fratrum **19.** Church of the
  Brethren
moray... **3.** eel **6.** hamlet **7.** Muraena
  8. food fish **10.** Muraenidae
morbid... **4.** sick **6.** gloomy **7.** ghastly,
  unsound **8.** diseased **9.** unhealthy
  11. unwholesome
morbid (pert to)...
  appetite.. **10.** adephagous
  complex.. **11.** inferiority
  condition.. **8.** ochlesis
  desire for music.. **9.** melomania
  displacement.. **7.** ectopia
morbus... **7.** disease, illness
morceau... **3.** bit (Mus) **6.** morsel
mordant... **4.** acid, keen **6.** biting
  7. burning, caustic, pungent **8.** scathing
  9. corrosive, sarcastic **11.** acrimonious
more... **3.** yea **4.** also, mair, plus, some
  5. again, extra **6.** plural **7.** greater
  10. additional **13.** approximately
more (pert to)...
  cunning.. **5.** slyer **6.** tricky
  difficult.. **6.** harder
  distant.. **8.** ulterior
  mature.. **5.** older, riper
  miserly.. **6.** closer, meaner, nearer
  not any.. **4.** dead, past **8.** vanished
    11. nonexistent
  or less.. **4.** some **8.** somewhat
    13. approximately
  over.. **3.** and **4.** also, else **7.** besides,
    further, thereto
  precious.. **6.** dearer
  relative.. **11.** comparative
  severe.. **7.** sterner
  so.. **3.** yea
  than.. **4.** over **5.** above **6.** beyond
    9. exceeding **10.** in excess of
  than enough.. **3.** too
  than one.. **4.** many **6.** plural **7.** several
  than this.. **3.** yes
  unusual.. **5.** rarer
  vapid.. **6.** staler

morel ... **6.** fungus **8.** mushroom
morello ... **4.** ruru **6.** cherry **7.** boobook
  8. morepork, mulberry (color)
morena ... **8.** brunette
mores ... **7.** customs, manners **9.** etiquette
  11. conventions
Moreton Bay ... **9.** Australia
Morgan ... **5.** horse **10.** sea dweller
morganatic marriage ... **10.** left-handed
  (royal)
morgay ... **7.** dogfish
morglay ... **5.** sword
morgue ... **8.** mortuary **9.** deadhouse,
  stolidity **11.** haughtiness, impassivity
Morgue (The) ... **17.** Library of Congress
moribund ... **4.** sick **5.** dying **9.** near
  death
moriform ... **14.** mulberry-shaped
morindin dye ... **2.** al
morion ... **6.** helmet, quartz **8.** cabasset
Mormon Church (pert to) ...
  Band (Polit) .. **6.** Danite (1837)
  cricket .. **11.** grasshopper
  emblem .. **3.** bee
  Indian .. **8.** Lamanite
  instrument .. **4.** Urim **7.** Thummin
  officer .. **5.** Elder
  official name .. **36.** Church of Jesus
    Christ of Latter Day Saints
  patriarch .. **11.** Joseph Smith **12.** Brigham
    Young
  prophet .. **6.** Moroni
  State .. **4.** Utah
  tea plant .. **7.** Brigham
  tree .. **11.** black poplar
morning (pert to) ...
  clouds .. **4.** velo
  coat .. **7.** cutaway
  concert .. **6.** aubade
  glory .. **3.** nil **7.** ipomoea
    14. Convolvulaceae
  goddess .. **3.** Eos
  performance .. **7.** matinee
  prayer .. **5.** matin
  reception .. **5.** levee
  star .. **4.** Mars **5.** Venus **6.** Saturn
    7. Daystar, Jupiter, Lucifer, Mercury
    8. Phosphor
  term .. **2.** AM **4.** dawn **5.** matin, wight
    6. Aurora **7.** sunrise **9.** matutinal
moro ... **5.** finch
moro (comb form) ... **6.** stupid
Moro ... **6.** Muslim
Morocco ...
  capital .. **5.** Rabat
  city .. **3.** Fez **7.** Tangier **9.** Marrakech
    (Marrakesh) **10.** Casablanca
  color .. **3.** red
  enclave .. **4.** Ifni
  famed site .. **5.** Casba
  hat .. **3.** fez
  island .. **7.** Madeira
  Jewish quarter .. **8.** El Millah
  language .. **6.** Arabic
  leather imitation .. **4.** roan
  military expedition .. **5.** harka
  millet .. **12.** Johnson grass
  mountains .. **5.** Atlas
  people .. **4.** Arab, Moor **6.** Berber
  plateau .. **6.** mesata
  ruler .. **4.** king **5.** malek **6.** sultan

  soldier .. **5.** askar
morology ... **5.** folly **8.** nonsense
moron ... **4.** dull **5.** ament, idiot, zombi
  6. nitwit, stupid **8.** imbecile, sluggish
  12. stupid person
morose ... **4.** blue, dour, glum, grum,
  sour **5.** moody, surly **6.** crusty, gloomy,
  sullen **7.** crabbed, unhappy **9.** splenetic
  10. embittered
Morpheus (Gr) ... **10.** god of Sleep
  11. god of Dreams
morphine ... **6.** heroin **8.** hypnotic
  9. analgesic, calmative
morphology ... **7.** anatomy **8.** cytology
  9. histology **10.** embryology
  12. organography
morris ... **4.** game **5.** chair, dance
morro ... **4.** hill **6.** Castle (Havana)
  7. hillock **11.** point of land
Mors (Rom) ... **5.** Death, deity
Morse ... **4.** code, lamp **8.** alphabet
morsel ... **3.** ort **4.** bite, chip **5.** piece,
  scran (sl), scrap, snack **6.** tidbit, titbit
  7. morceau **8.** delicacy, fragment
  11. small amount
mort ... **4.** dead, lard **5.** death, fatal
  6. deadly, grease, salmon **9.** abundance
mortacious ... **4.** very **9.** extremely
mortal ... **5.** fatal, human **6.** deadly,
  lethal **10.** perishable
mortally ... **5.** amort **6.** deadly **7.** à
  la mort, deathly, fatally **9.** extremely
  10. grievously
mortar ... **3.** rab **4.** bowl **5.** putty
  6. cannon **7.** mortier **10.** night light
  (Hist)
mortarboard ... **3.** cap (Acad)
mortgage ... **4.** bond, pawn **6.** pledge
mortician ... **8.** embalmer **10.** undertaker
  15. funeral director
mortification ... **5.** decay, shame
  7. chagrin **8.** gangrene, vexation
  11. humiliation
mortify ... **5.** abase, abash, abuse, shame,
  spite **6.** ashame, deaden, humble
  7. chagrin **9.** embarrass, humiliate
mortis causa ... **15.** by reason of death
mortise, mortice ... **6.** cavity, insert
  8. amortize **10.** foundation
mortuary ... **4.** gift (burial) **6.** morgue
  7. funeral **8.** funereal **9.** deadhouse,
  sepulcher **10.** cinerarium
  12. corsepresent (offering, Hist)
mosaic ... **5.** virus **6.** design **7.** ceramic,
  picture **10.** decoration, variegated
  11. tessellated
mosaic (pert to) ...
  apply .. **7.** incrust
  gold .. **6.** ormolu
  law .. **5.** Torah (Moses)
  piece .. **7.** tessera
Moscow ...
  capital of .. **6.** Russia
  citadel .. **7.** Kremlin
  river .. **6.** Moskva
  shrine .. **9.** Lenin Tomb, Red Square
  Third Internat .. **9.** Comintern
Moselle ... **4.** Saar, wine **5.** river, Ruwer
  9. Rhine wine
Moses (pert to) ...
  Bible .. **7.** prophet **8.** lawgiver

brother.. **5.** Aaron
emissary.. **5.** Caleb
father.. **5.** Amram
father-in-law.. **6.** Jethro
law.. **5.** Torah (Tora) **10.** Pentateuch
mother.. **8.** Jochebed
mountain.. **4.** Nebo
sister.. **6.** Miriam
successor.. **6.** Joshua
wife.. **8.** Zipporah
mosey... **6.** depart, stroll **7.** shuffle
Moslem... see *Muslim*
mosque... **4.** Omar **5.** Kaaba (Caaba)
6. masjid **11.** Great Mosque
mosque tower... **7.** minaret
mosque warden... **5.** nazir
mosquito (pert to)...
bite preventive.. **10.** culicifuge
coast.. **8.** Honduras **9.** Nicaragua
comb form.. **6.** culici
destroyer.. **8.** culicide
disease.. **7.** malaria **11.** yellow fever
family.. **9.** Culicidae
fish.. **8.** gambusia
genus.. **5.** Aedes, Culex **7.** Diptera
8. Mansonia **9.** Anopheles, Culicidae
10. Psorophora
hawk.. **9.** dragonfly, nighthawk
Indian drink.. **6.** mushla
larvae.. **8.** wigglers
plant.. **4.** mint **10.** pennyroyal
shaped.. **10.** culiciform
term.. **7.** culicid **11.** gallinipper
moss... **3.** bog, rag **4.** agar **5.** Maium,
money, Musci, swamp **6.** lichen, morass
7. skeeter **8.** agar-agar **9.** treebeard
moss (pert to)...
back.. **4.** dodo, fogy (fogey) **9.** old turtle
10. fuddy-duddy, Southerner (1861)
12. conservative
berry.. **9.** cranberry
capsule.. **9.** operculum
color.. **5.** green
coral.. **8.** bryozoan
duck.. **7.** mallard **8.** moss-head
9. merganser
fish.. **8.** menhaden **10.** mossbunker
grown.. **10.** antiquated
kind.. **4.** peat **7.** Spanish
like.. **6.** mnioid
mossy... **4.** dull **5.** boggy, downy
6. marshy, stupid **9.** crumbling
most... **7.** highest, maximum **8.** greatest,
main part, majority **9.** nearly all
most favorable... **7.** optimum
Most High... **3.** God **12.** Supreme Being
most northerly land... **5.** Thule
mot... **5.** adage, maxim, motto **7.** opinion
9. witticism
mote... **4.** atom, hill, iota **5.** match,
speck, squib **6.** barrow, height, trifle
7. tumulus **8.** eminence, particle
mote nut... **5.** carap
motet... **4.** hymn **6.** anthem, choral
moth... **2.** io **5.** egger, tinea **6.** lappet,
miller **7.** noctuid, Tineina **8.** forester
(8-spotted), Tineidae **9.** Tineoidea
11. Lepidoptera
moth (pert to)...
hawk.. **10.** goatsucker
kind.. **5.** gypsy **6.** carpet **9.** browntail

spot (Med).. **8.** chloasma
spot (wing).. **8.** fenestra
mother... **2.** ma **3.** dam **4.** amma
5. adopt, mamma, mater **6.** abbess,
parent **7.** care for, creator **8.** ancestor,
begetter, genetrix, producer
10. procreator
mother (pert to)...
church.. **9.** cathedral **16.** Christian
Science
goddess.. **6.** matris **7.** Shaktis **10.** sapta-
matri (7 mothers)
goddess of motherhood (Egypt).. **4.** Isis
godmother.. **4.** Rhea **6.** cummer
(kimmer) **9.** Brigantia
Goose character.. **5.** Simon, Sprat
6. Bo-peep
Govt.. **10.** matriarchy, metrocracy
house.. **7.** convent **9.** monastery
Hubbard.. **4.** gown **5.** dress
lode.. **3.** ore
Maid.. **10.** Virgin Mary
Mother Carey's chickens.. **7.** petrels
(stormy)
Myth (Gr).. **5.** Niobe
related.. **6.** enatic
spiritual.. **4.** amma
Tagalog.. **3.** Ina
motherly... **8.** maternal
mother of...
Castor.. **4.** Leda
gods.. **4.** Rhea **9.** Brigantia
Graces.. **5.** Aegle
Nature.. **6.** Cybele
Night.. **3.** Nox, Nyx
pearl.. **5.** nacre **7.** abalone
presidents.. **8.** Virginia
States.. **8.** Virginia
the month.. **4.** Moon
motif... **5.** theme, topic **6.** edging
7. subject
motion... **3.** bob **4.** lipe, move **5.** impel,
trend **6.** seesaw, travel, tremor, unrest
7. gesture, propose, request, suggest
8. kinetics, mobility, movement, petition
motionless... **5.** inert, rigid, still **6.** static
8. immobile, stagnant **10.** stationary,
stock-still
motion picture terms... **4.** film,
show **5.** flick, klieg (light), movie,
rerun **6.** cinema **7.** cartoon, feature
9. filmstrip, videotape **11.** golden oldie
12. silver screen
motivate... **4.** move **5.** force, impel
6. compel, incite, induce, propel
7. actuate, animate, promote, trigger
9. stimulate
motive... **4.** sake, spur **5.** cause,
motif, topic **6.** reason **7.** pretext
8. stimulus **9.** incentive, influence,
intention **10.** incitement, inducement
11. instigation **13.** consideration
motley... **5.** mixed **6.** fabric **7.** diverse,
mixture, mottled **9.** checkered, diversity
10. variegated **12.** parti-colored
13. heterogeneous
motor... **5.** mover, rotor **6.** Diesel,
dynamo, engine **7.** turbine **8.** motor
car **9.** locomotor **10.** automobile
motor speed control... **8.** governor,
rheocrat

mottled . . . 3. roe 4. pied 5. pinto 6. calico
  7. dappled, marbled, piebald, spotted
  13. pepper-and-salt
mottled soap . . . 7. castile
motto . . . 3. mot 5. adage, axiom, gnome,
  maxim 6. advice 7. empresa (impresa),
  precept 8. aphorism 9. principle
  11. inscription
motto of . . .
  Boy Scouts . . 10. Be Prepared
  Coast Guard . . 11. Always Ready
    13. Semper paratus
  Order of the Garter . . 20. Honi soit qui
    mal y pense
  Queen Elizabeth . . 11. Semper Eadem
    13. Always the Same
mouche . . . 5. patch (black)
mouchoir . . . 12. handkerchief
mouflon, moufflon . . . 5. sheep
mould, mold . . . 5. knead 6. matrix
moulrush . . . 7. pollack (food fish)
mound . . . 3. dam, dun, tee 4. bank, dene,
  doon, dune, heap, hill, terp, tomb,
  tump 5. knoll 6. bounds 7. barrier,
  bulwark, rampart, tumulus 8. boundary
  9. elevation 10. embankment
  13. fortification
mound (pert to) . . .
  bird . . 8. megapode
  City . . 7. St Louis
  lily . . 5. yucca
  memorial . . 5. cairn
  of light . . 8. Kohinoor (diamond)
  Polynesian . . 3. ahu
  prehistoric . . 5. matte
  Scottish . . 5. toman
mount . . . 3. fly, set (jewel) 4. glue, hill,
  lift, pony (polo), rise 5. arise, climb,
  horse, paste, steed 6. ascent 7. elevate
  8. increase, mountain 10. promontory
Mount (pert to) . . .
  Etna city . . 7. Catania
  Everest peak . . 6. Lhotse
  Parnassus fountain, spring . . 8. Castalia
  S Dakota . . 8. Rushmore
mountain . . .
  Africa . . 11. Kilimanjaro
  Alaska . . 8. McKinley
  Asia . . 7. Everest 9. Himalayas
  Babylonia . . 6. Ararat
  California . . 6. Shasta 7. Whitney
  Crete . . 3. Ida
  Europe . . 4. Ural 8. Pyrenees
  fabled . . 4. Meru
  Greek (Myth) . . 7. Helicon
  Japan . . 8. Fujiyama
  legendary . . 3. Kaf, Qaf (Muslim) 4. Meru
  Mexico . . 12. Popocatepetl
  Montana . . 6. Tetons
  South America . . 5. Andes
  Switzerland . . 4. Alps 10. Matterhorn
  Thessaly . . 4. Ossa 6. Pelion
  U S Chain . . 5. Rocky 7. Sawback,
    Sierras 9. Blue Ridge 11. Appalachian
  Yukon . . 5. Logan
mountain (pert to) . . .
  ash . . 5. rowan
  badger . . 6. marmot
  balsam . . 3. fit
  banana . . 3. fei
  barometer . . 8. orometer

beaver . . 8. sewellel
blackbird . . 5. ouzel
cat . . 4. lynx 6. bobcat, cougar
  10. cacomistle
comb form . . 3. oro
cowslip . . 8. auricula
crest, spur . . 5. arête
curassow (pheasant) . . 10. oreophasis
defile . . 3. gap 4. gate, ghat (ghaut),
  pass 5. gorge
depression . . 3. col
dew . . 6. whisky
eagle . . 6. golden
goat . . 4. ibex
highest . . 7. Everest
ice . . 4. berg 7. glacier
ivy . . 6. laurel
lake . . 4. tarn
lion . . 4. puma 6. cougar
lodge . . 4. gite
low . . 5. butte
nymph . . 5. oread
oak . . 8. chestnut
peak . . 3. tor
raspberry . . 10. cloudberry
rose . . 6. laurel
sheep . . 7. bighorn 13. Rocky Mountain
shrub . . 10. fetterbush
sickness . . 7. soroche
State . . 7. Montana
sunset . . 9. alpenglow
Tatars . . 5. Tauli
witch . . 9. quail dove
mountaineer . . . 7. climber 11. backsettler
mountains, science of . . . 7. orology
  9. orography
mountant . . . 6. raised, rising 8. mounting
  9. ascendant
mountebank . . . 4. gull 5. cheat, quack
  7. buffoon, empiric 8. impostor
  9. charlatan, pretender 11. quack doctor
mounted men . . . 7. knights
mounting . . . 6. ascent 7. rimbase,
  seating, setting 9. adjusting, equipment
  13. embellishment
mourn . . . 3. rue 4. erme, long, sigh,
  wail, weep 6. bemoan, bewail, grieve,
  lament, murmur, repine, sorrow
  7. deplore
mourner . . . 6. keener, wailer 7. griever
  8. lamenter
mournful . . . 3. sad 6. repine 7. elegiac
  8. grievous 9. elegiacal, plaintive,
  saddening, sorrowful, threnodic,
  woebegone
mournful poem . . . 5. elegy
mourning . . . 3. sad 4. garb 5. crape,
  weeds (dress) 6. lament, sorrow
  7. drapery 9. sorrowing 10. black badge
  11. lamentation
mourning dress . . . 5. weeds 6. sables
mouse . . . 3. erd, Mus 4. buck, vole
  5. prowl, shrew 6. jerboa, migale
  7. harvest, toy with
mouse (pert to) . . .
  bird . . 4. coly 6. shrike
  color . . 4. gray
  deer . . 7. plandok 10. chevrotain
  ear . . 8. hawkweed 9. bloodwort,
    chickweed 11. forget-me-not
  fish . . 9. sargassum

hare.. **4.** pika
hound.. **6.** weasel
kind.. **6.** pocket **7.** harvest, jumping
leaping.. **6.** jerboa
milk.. **6.** spurge
mouselike.. **6.** murine
web.. **6.** cobweb, phlegm **8.** gossamer
mousse ... **7.** dessert **9.** moss green
   12. gelatine dish
moutan ... **5.** peony
mouth ... **2.** os **3.** mow, mun **4.** boca,
   dupe, lade, lick **5.** inlet, stoma **6.** cavity,
   rictus **7.** declaim, opening, orifice
   8. aperture, lorriker **9.** impudence
mouth (pert to) ...
away from.. **6.** aboral
deformity.. **7.** harelip
disease.. **6.** canker **10.** stomatitis
furnace.. **5.** bocca
glands.. **8.** salivary
muscle.. **7.** caninus
organ.. **4.** harp **7.** Pandean **8.** jew's-harp
   9. crembalum, harmonica
part.. **3.** lip **5.** uvula **6.** palate **7.** pharynx
pert to.. **4.** oral **6.** rictal, stomal
   8. stomatic
piece (Mus).. **10.** embouchure
through the.. **7.** peroral
tissue.. **3.** gum
toward.. **4.** orad
wide, gaping.. **6.** rictus
mouthed, loud ... **11.** thersitical
mouton ... **5.** sheep **9.** prison spy
movable ... **6.** mobile **10.** changeable
   12. transferable
movable property ... **8.** chattels
move ... **3.** act, gee, mog, say **4.** goad,
   sell, spur, stir **5.** budge, cause,
   impel, rouse, shift **6.** excite, incite,
   induce, kindle, motion, prompt, travel
   7. actuate, advance, animate, propose,
   provoke **9.** instigate, recommend,
   stimulate
move (pert to) ...
about.. **8.** locomote
along.. **5.** mosey, scram **7.** maunder
back.. **3.** ebb **6.** recede, retire, revert
   7. retreat **10.** retrogress
back and forth.. **6.** teeter, wigwag
   7. shuttle **9.** oscillate
clumsily.. **4.** joll
false.. **4.** balk **5.** feint
forward.. **4.** edge, scud **5.** drive
   7. advance **8.** progress
furtively.. **5.** slink, sneak
heavily.. **3.** lug **6.** fidget, lumber, trudge
in circles.. **4.** purl
place to place.. **7.** migrate **8.** emigrate
quickly.. **3.** ply **4.** dart, dash, scud,
   shot **5.** scoot, spank **6.** bustle, gallop,
   hurtle
restlessly.. **6.** kelter
rhythmically.. **5.** dance
sideways, sidewise.. **4.** slue **5.** sidle
slowly.. **3.** jog, lag **4.** edge, inch, pant
smoothly.. **4.** slip **5.** glide, skate, slide
spasmodically.. **6.** twitch
to and fro.. **3.** wag **4.** flap, sway
together.. **5.** unite **8.** converge
towards each other.. **8.** converge
towards the east.. **9.** orientate

unsteadily.. **4.** reel **6.** wabble **7.** stagger
up and down.. **3.** bob **6.** teeter
with exertion.. **5.** heave
with measured tread.. **5.** march
moved by entreaty ... **8.** exorable
moved easily ... **5.** loped **6.** mobile
   8. affected **9.** emotional
movement ... **5.** cause, trend **6.** action,
   motion, rhythm, travel **7.** emotion,
   gesture, impulse **8.** activity, maneuver,
   progress
movement (pert to) ...
backwards.. **13.** retrogression
dance step.. **4.** lilt **6.** chassé **9.** pirouette
music.. **4.** moto **7.** con moto
of ships.. **5.** heave, pitch, scend
of waves.. **4.** roll, toss **5.** surge
   6. tumble, welter
vibratory.. **7.** tremor
moving ... **6.** active, motile **7.** nomadic
   8. eloquent, exciting, pathetic
   9. affecting, impelling, traveling
   10. motivating
moving stairway ... **9.** escalator
mow ... **3.** cut, lay, mew **4.** dess, fell,
   heap, mass, math, mock, raze, stow
   5. mouth, stack **6.** garner, smooth
   7. cut down, grimace, harvest, shorten
   9. cornfield
mowana ... **6.** baobab
mowing ... **7.** cutting, mockery **8.** derision
   9. grimacing **10.** harvesting,
   meadowland
mowing machine ... **5.** mower **6.** scythe,
   sickle
moxieberry ... **9.** snowberry
moy ... **4.** mild **6.** demure, gentle
   8. affected
moyen ... **3.** way **5.** means **6.** agency,
   course **8.** property **9.** influence
Mozambique ...
Bay.. **8.** Mossuril
capital.. **15.** Lourenco Marques
native.. **3.** Yao
port.. **10.** Mozambique
mozo ... **10.** manservant
Mrs ... **5.** madam **8.** goodwife, Mistress
mucaro ... **3.** owl
much ... **3.** lot **4.** high, many **5.** great
   7. greatly **8.** abundant, uncommon
   9. great deal **10.** indefinite
   12. considerable
muchacha ... **4.** girl, lass
muchacho ... **3.** boy, lad **7.** servant
mucid ... **5.** musty, slimy **6.** clammy,
   mucous **8.** muculent
mucilage ... **3.** gum **5.** paste **6.** mucago
   8. adhesive **9.** lubricant
mucilaginous ... **5.** moist **6.** sticky, viscid
muckender ... **12.** handkerchief
mucker ... **4.** fall (from a horse),
   mess **6.** muddle, wretch **8.** disorder
   9. confusion, vulgarian
muckle ... **4.** club, fret **6.** bother, putter
muckraker ... **7.** defamer **8.** vilifier
   9. slanderer
mud ... **4.** mire, muck, silt, slop **5.** abuse,
   gumbo, limus, shine **6.** gobbet, sludge
   12. offscourings **14.** abusive charges
mud (pert to) ...
bath.. **10.** illutation

dab.. **8.** flounder
dauber.. **4.** wasp
devil.. **10.** hellbender
eel.. **5.** siren
hole.. **6.** puddle **8.** quagmire
lark.. **5.** gamin, horse **6.** magpie, urchin
like.. **7.** luteous
living in.. **10.** limicolous
peep.. **9.** sandpiper **11.** meadow pipit
pike.. **5.** saury
puppy.. **10.** hellbender, salamander
rake.. **5.** claut
shoveler.. **13.** spoonbill duck
snipe.. **8.** woodcock
sunfish.. **4.** bass **8.** warmouth
teal.. **9.** greenwing
volcano.. **5.** salse
Mudcat State... **11.** Mississippi
muddle... **3.** mix **4.** daze, mess, soss,
  stir **5.** addle, botch, snafu **6.** bemuse,
  bollix, jumble **7.** confuse, perplex,
  stupefy **8.** befuddle, bewilder, confound,
  disorder, squander **10.** intoxicate
  11. predicament
muddled... **3.** ree **5.** drunk, muzzy,
  tipsy **7.** burbled, fuddled **8.** confused
  9. befuddled, entangled
muddlehead... **4.** dolt **9.** blockhead
muddy... **4.** base, miry **5.** dingy, dirty,
  roily, slaky **6.** lutose, opaque, slushy,
  turbid **7.** clouded, obscure **8.** confused
  9. besmeared
muddy places... **7.** wallows
muezzin... **4.** azan (adan) **5.** crier
  (Muslim)
muff... **5.** beard, cover **6.** bungle
  7. bungler, failure **8.** feathers
  11. mollycoddle, whitethroat
muffed... **5.** vexed **7.** crested **9.** irritated
muffet... **11.** whitethroat
muffetee... **7.** muffler **8.** wristlet
muffin... **3.** cob, gem **5.** bread, hazel,
  plate, scone **7.** biscuit, crumpet, English,
  popover
muffle... **3.** gag **4.** damp, dull, mute,
  wrap **6.** deaden, mumble, shroud,
  stifle **7.** conceal **8.** decorate, envelope
  9. blindfold, soft-pedal
muffler... **3.** gag **4.** mute **5.** scarf
  6. muzzle, tippet **8.** silencer
  10. suppressor
mufflin... **8.** titmouse
mufti... **5.** dress (civilian)
mufti (Muslim)... **4.** alim **5.** judge
  6. priest **8.** assessor, official
mug... **3.** cup **4.** cram, dupe, face, fool,
  Toby **5.** mungo, pulse, sheep, study
  6. noggin **7.** drizzle, grimace **8.** quantity
  10. photograph
muga... **4.** moth, silk **11.** caterpillar
mugger... **3.** goa **6.** robber, tinker
  7. peddler **9.** crocodile
mugget... **8.** woodruff **15.** lily of the
  valley
muggins (game)... **5.** cards **7.** penalty
  8. dominoes
muggy... **4.** damp, warm **5.** humid,
  moist, moldy **6.** sticky, stuffy, sultry
  10. sweltering **11.** whitethroat
mug house... **6.** tavern **7.** barroom
  8. alehouse, pothouse

mugient... **6.** lowing **9.** bellowing
mugwump... **5.** chief **8.** apostate,
  objector **11.** independent, nonpartisan
  16. Republican bolter
Muhammed... see *Mohammed*
muir... **4.** wall
muirfowl... **9.** red grouse
muishond... **5.** zoril **6.** weasel
mujer... **4.** wife **5.** woman
mulberry... **2.** al **5.** Morus **6.** murrey
  10. blackberry **12.** thimbleberry
mulberry (pert to)...
  bark (paper).. **4.** tapa (tappa)
  beverage.. **5.** morat
  bird.. **8.** starling
  dye.. **3.** aal **8.** morindin
  fig.. **8.** sycamore
  purple.. **7.** blue-red **8.** camerier
  tree.. **5.** Morus
  wild.. **7.** yawweed
mulch... **5.** straw **6.** ground, leaves
  7. sawdust
mulct... **4.** fine, scot **6.** amerce, defect,
  punish **7.** blemish, deceive, penalty,
  swindle **11.** amercement
mulcter... **7.** amercer
mule... **4.** mewl, mool, mute **5.** coble,
  hinny, jenny **6.** acemia, hybrid
  7. slipper, tractor **9.** chilblain
  10. crossbreed, locomotive **15.** obstinate
  person
mule (pert to)...
  chair.. **7.** cacolet
  driver.. **7.** skinner **8.** muleteer
  drove.. **5.** atajo
  killer.. **6.** mantis
  leading.. **8.** cencerro
  skinner.. **6.** driver
  untrained.. **9.** shavetail
muleteer... **4.** peon **6.** driver
mulga... **6.** acacia, shield
muliebria... **8.** feminine
muliebriety... **9.** womanhood
  10. femininity **11.** womanliness
mulier... **4.** wife **5.** woman **6.** mother
mulish... **6.** hybrid, sullen **7.** asinine,
  sterile **8.** stubborn **9.** obstinate
mull... **3.** cow **4.** crag, dust, heat,
  mess, mold **5.** crush, grind, snout,
  spice **6.** fumble, muddle, muslin,
  muzzle, ponder **7.** failure, rubbish,
  squeeze, steatin, sweeten **8.** cogitate,
  consider, ointment, ruminate, snuffbox
  9. pulverize **10.** promontory
  11. contemplate
mullah... **6.** priest **7.** teacher (Muslim)
mullet... **4.** bobo, fish, star **6.** puffin
mullet hawk... **6.** osprey
mulligan... **4.** stew
mulligatawny... **4.** soup
mulligrubs... **5.** blues, colic, sulks
mullock... **5.** spoil, waste **6.** refuse
  (mine) **7.** rubbish
mulloway... **7.** jewfish
multi (comb form)... **4.** many
multifarious... **8.** manifold **9.** multifold,
  multiplex **10.** multiphase
multifold... **7.** diverse **8.** manifold,
  multiple, numerous
multilingual... **8.** polyglot
multiped... **10.** many-footed

multiplier . . . 6. bulbil 7. facient
8. operator
multiply . . . 5. breed 6. spread 7. amplify,
magnify 8. increase 9. calculate,
pluralize, procreate
multitude . . . 3. mob 4. host, many,
mass, much 5. crowd, horde, shoal,
swarm 6. legion, throng 7. myriads
8. populace 9. profusion 11. bourgeoisie
12. numerousness
multitudinous . . . 6. myriad
mum . . . 3. ale 4. mute 6. silent 8. taciturn
11. not speaking
mumble . . . 4. chew, mump 6. chavel,
fumble, mutter, patter
mumbo jumbo . . . 6. genius 7. bugaboo
12. superstition 13. awesome person
mummer . . . 5. actor 6. guiser 7. buffoon
9. performer
mummy . . . 5. brown, Congo (color), relic
6. corpse, mother 7. cadaver, carcass
mummy apple . . . 6. papaya
mump . . . 3. beg 5. cheat, sulks
6. mumble, sponge 7. deceive, grimace
10. impose upon
mumpish . . . 4. dull, glum 5. sulky
6. sullen
mumruffin . . . 8. titmouse
mundane . . . 6. cosmic 7. earthly, horizon,
secular, terrene, worldly 8. temporal
11. unspiritual
mundatory . . . 9. cleansing 11. purificator
mundil . . . 6. turban (embroidered)
mungo . . . 4. herb, wool (reclaimed)
8. mongoose, mung bean
13. mongoose plant
municipal . . . 5. civic, urban 7. oppidan
9. political 10. municipium
munificence . . . 6. bounty 7. largess
(largesse) 10. generosity, liberality
13. bounteousness, unselfishness
muniment . . . 6. record 7. defense
8. evidence, writings 9. valuables
10. furnishing 13. fortification
munity . . . see *immunity* 9. privilege
munshi (Hind) . . . 6. writer 7. teacher
9. secretary 11. interpreter
muntjac, muntjak . . . 5. kakar, ratwa
6. kidang
mura (Jap) . . . 7. village 9. community
Mura . . . 6. Indian
mural . . . 4. wall (pert to) 5. crown
8. painting
murder . . . 4. kill, slay 7. carnage
8. homicide 9. slaughter 11. assassinate
12. manslaughter
murder of . . .
brother . . 10. fratricide
father . . 9. patricide
king . . 8. regicide
mother . . 9. matricide
own child . . 9. prolicide
parent . . 9. parricide
prophet . . 8. vaticide
sister . . 10. sororicide
spouse (by the other) . . 10. mariticide
wife . . 9. uxoricide
woman . . 8. femicide
murderous . . . 4. gory 5. cruel 6. bloody,
deadly, savage 7. killing 10. sanguinary
12. bloodthirsty

mure . . . 4. meek, soft, wall 6. gentle,
immure, modest 8. imprison
murk, mirk . . . 3. fog 4. dark, mist
5. gloom 6. opaque 7. blacken
8. darkness 9. dark color 11. dark-
colored
murky, mirky . . . 4. dark 5. dense,
foggy, thick 6. gloomy, opaque
7. obscure, stained 11. dark-colored
12. impenetrable
murmur . . . 3. coo, hum 4. blow, curr,
fret, purl 6. babble, mutter, repine
7. trickle, whisper 8. complain
muscle . . . 4. beef, thew 5. brawn, sinew,
teres 6. flexor, lacert, tensor 8. lacertus,
retentor
muscle (pert to) . . .
affection . . 5. crick 6. ataxia
bending . . 6. flexor
chemistry . . 6. inosic 8. inosinic
chest . . 8. pectoral
column . . 10. sarcostyle
contracting . . 7. agonist
expander . . 7. dilator
extending . . 8. extensor
eyeball . . 6. rectus
lifting . . 7. levator
loin, tenderloin . . 5. psoas
lower . . 9. depressor
raising . . 7. deltoid, erector, levator
recording . . 8. ergogram 9. ergograph
round . . 5. teres
segment . . 8. myocomma
sense . . 11. kinesthesia
separating . . 11. divaricator
spasm . . 5. cramp, tonus 12. charley
horse
stretching . . 6. tensor
sugar . . 8. inositol
thigh . . 10. quadriceps
trapezius . . 10. cucullaris
triangular . . 7. deltoid
turning . . 7. evertor, rotator
two-headed . . 6. biceps
muscovite . . . 4. mica 11. yellow-green
Muscovite . . . 7. Russian
muscular . . . 4. wiry 5. beefy, thewy
6. brawny, mighty, sinewy, strong,
torose 8. athletic, stalwart, vigorous
muscular (pert to) . . .
contraction (involuntary) . . 3. tic 5. spasm
co-ordination . . 7. synergy
in-co-ordination . . 6. ataxia 15. locomotor
ataxia
non-co-ordination in walking . . 6. abasia
spasm . . 5. tonus
stomach . . 7. gizzard
muse . . . 4. mull, poet, rune 5. dream
6. ponder 7. bagpipe, reverie 8. cogitate,
consider, meditate, ruminate
Muse of . . .
astronomy . . 6. Urania
choral song . . 11. Terpsichore
comedy . . 6. Thalia
dancing . . 11. Terpsichore
eloquence . . 8. Calliope
history . . 4. Clio
joy . . 4. Tara
music . . 7. Euterpe
poetry . . 5. Erato (lyric) 6. Thalia (bucolic)
8. Calliope (heroic)

tragedy . . **9.** Melpomene
Muses . . . **4.** Clio **5.** Erato **6.** Thalia,
   Urania **7.** Euterpe **8.** Calliope, Polymnia
   (Polyhymnia) **9.** Melpomene
   11. Terpsichore
Muses (pert to) . . .
   epithet . . **7.** Pierian
   fountain . . **8.** Aganippe (near Thebes)
   mother of . . **9.** Mnemosyne
   mountain . . **6.** Pierus **7.** Helicon
   9. Parnassus
   number . . **4.** nine
   sacred place . . **5.** Aonia (Boeotia)
   spring . . **7.** Pierian
   The Muses (Gr) . . **8.** Pierides
musette . . . **3.** air, bag **4.** oboe **7.** bagpipe,
   gavotte
museum, famed . . .
   Florence . . **6.** Uffizi
   London . . **4.** Tate **14.** Madame Tussaud's
   Madrid . . **5.** Prado
   New York . . **4.** MOMA **10.** Guggenheim
   12. Metropolitan
   Oxford . . **9.** Ashmolean
   Paris . . **6.** Louvre
   St Petersburg (Russia) . . **9.** Hermitage
   Washington, DC . . **9.** Hirshhorn
   11. Smithsonian
museum keeper . . . **7.** curator
   9. custodian
mush . . . **3.** cut **4.** call, face, pulp **5.** atole,
   march (over snow), notch **6.** cereal,
   indent, sepawn **8.** flattery, umbrella
   12. hasty pudding **14.** sentimentality
mushroom . . . **5.** morel, plant **6.** agaric,
   anchor, fungus **7.** parvenu, upstart
   8. umbrella **11.** beaver brown
mushroom (pert to) . . .
   circle . . **9.** fairy ring
   disease . . **5.** flock
   edible . . **5.** morel **11.** chanterelle
   poisoning . . **8.** mycetism
   poisonous . . **7.** amanita **9.** toadstool
   stem . . **5.** stipe
   umbrella top . . **6.** pileus
music (pert to) . . .
   abridgment . . **7.** ridotto
   accompaniment . . **9.** obbligato
   aftersong . . **5.** epode
   all voices . . **5.** tutti
   as written . . **3.** sta
   chapel . . **9.** a cappella
   character . . **3.** bar, key **4.** clef, rest, slur
   5. cleft, neume, segno
   chord . . **8.** arpeggio
   clear-cut . . **8.** staccato
   closing measure . . **4.** coda
   comic . . **6.** bouffe
   do . . **2.** ut
   drama . . **5.** opera
   duet . . **3.** duo
   encore . . **3.** bis
   flourish . . **7.** cadenza
   half note . . **5.** minim
   half tone . . **8.** semitone
   impassioned, emotional . .
   12. appassionato
   interlude . . **6.** verset
   interval . . **6.** octave **7.** tritone
   introduction . . **7.** prelude
   it proceeds . . **2.** va

knowledge . . **10.** musicology
lead cue . . **5.** presa
left-handed . . **8.** sinistra
light notes . . **6.** ottava
low pitch . . **5.** grave
lutelike . . **10.** hurdy-gurdy
major . . **3.** dur
major third . . **6.** ditone
melodious . . **6.** arioso
melody . . **5.** melos
nine-piece composition . . **5.** nonet
one performer (choral) . . **4.** soli
opera (comic) . . **6.** bouffe
organization . . **4.** band **5.** Ascap, choir
   6. chorus **8.** symphony **9.** orchestra
organ stop . . **6.** dulcet, tromba **7.** celesta
pause . . **4.** rest
performance . . **7.** recital
phrase . . **9.** leitmotiv (leitmotif)
pick . . **8.** plectrum
pitch C . . **2.** du
pompous . . **7.** orotund
refrain . . **5.** epode **8.** repetend
repetition . . **5.** rondo
scale . . **5.** gamut
sestet . . **7.** sestuor
sextuplet . . **7.** sestole (sestolet)
soprano part . . **5.** canto
speaking part . . **8.** parlando
study . . **5.** étude
tenor part . . **5.** canto (original)
theme . . **4.** tema
third . . **6.** tierce
three-chord note . . **5.** triad
thrice . . **3.** ter
time . . **4.** temp **6.** giusto
timing device . . **9.** metronome
twice . . **3.** bis
variations, set of . . **7.** partita
whimsical . . **8.** bizzarro **9.** capriccio
musical direction (pert to) . . .
   accented . . **8.** sforzato **9.** sforzando
   bold . . **6.** audace
   brisk . . **5.** tanto **7.** animato
   detached . . **8.** spiccato, staccato
   dying away . . **7.** calendo
   emphatic . . **7.** marcato
   evenly . . **10.** egualmente
   fantastic . . **11.** carpiccioso
   fast . . **4.** vivo **5.** tosto **6.** presto, vivace
   10. tostamente
   faster . . **7.** stretto
   fluctuating . . **6.** rubato
   gay . . **7.** giocoso **10.** brilliante
   gentle . . **5.** dolce
   half . . **5.** mezzo
   held firmly . . **6.** tenuto
   high . . **3.** alt
   hurried . . **7.** agitato
   less . . **4.** meno
   let it stand . . **3.** sta
   lightly . . **10.** con agilita
   little by little . . **9.** poco a poco
   lively . . **6.** vivace **7.** allegro, animato
   loud . . **5.** forte **10.** fortissimo
   louder . . **9.** crescendo
   lutelike . . **10.** hurdy-gurdy
   more rapid . . **7.** stretto (stretta)
   movement (with) . . **7.** con moto
   muted . . **5.** sorda, sordo
   narrating . . **8.** narrante

one by one . . **7.** uno a uno
quick . . **6.** presto
quickening . . **11.** affrettando
quicker than . . **7.** andante **9.** andantino
repeat . . **3.** bis **6.** da capo **7.** ripresa
sadly . . **7.** dolente **8.** doloroso
shake . . **5.** trill
silent . . **5.** tacet
sliding . . **9.** glissando
slow . . **5.** largo, lento, molto, tardo
6. adagio **7.** andante
slow (very) . . **5.** molto
slowing . . **9.** allentato **10.** ritardando
11. rallentando
smooth . . **6.** legato
soft . . **5.** dolce, piano
softer . . **10.** diminuendo
spirited . . **7.** con moto
strict tempo . . **6.** giusto
sustained . . **6.** tenuto **9.** sustenuto
tenderly . . **10.** affettuoso, con affetto
turn . . **5.** verte **9.** gruppetto
vivacious . . **7.** con brio
musical form . . . **3.** jig, ode, pop, rap
4. aria, folk, jazz, jive, olio, opus, punk
(rock), scat, song, soul **5.** derry, dirge,
disco, elegy, fugue, melos, motet,
opera, salsa **6.** arioso, ballad, fusion,
hip-hop, medley, melody, minuet,
New Age, reggae, sonata **7.** ragtime,
toccata **8.** carillon (bells), hornpipe,
operetta, oratorio, serenade, symphony
9. barcarole, bluegrass, interlude,
polonaise **10.** heavy metal, rockabilly
11. rock and roll **12.** boogie woogie
musical instruments . . . **3.** sax **4.** asor,
drum, fife, harp, horn, lute, lyre,
oboe, pipe, reed, tuba, viol **5.** banjo,
bugle, cello, Dobro, flute, organ, piano,
rebec (rebeck), rocta, tabor, vibes,
viola **6.** atabal, cither, citole, cornet,
fiddle, guitar, spinet, tabret, violin,
zither **7.** althorn, bagpipe, bandore,
bassoon, celesta, clarion, clavier,
gittern, helicon, marimba, musette,
ocarina, pandora, piccolo, theorbo,
timpani (tympani), trumpet, ukulele
8. castanet, clarinet, dulcimer, keyboard,
mandolin, trombone **9.** flageolet,
saxophone **10.** concertina, pianoforte,
sousaphone (tuba), tambourine
11. harpsichord, synthesizer, violoncello
musical instruments (foreign) . . .
Africa . . **5.** nanga **7.** kalimba (thumb
piano), sistrum
China . . **3.** kin
E Indies . . **4.** bina
Egypt . . **7.** sistrum
Greece . . **7.** cithara (anc)
Hindu . . **4.** vina (anc)
India . . **5.** ruana
Italy . . **6.** tromba
Japan . . **7.** samisen (shamisen)
10. shakuhachi
Java . . **8.** gamelang (gamelan)
Mexico . . **6.** clarin **7.** maracas
Spain . . **6.** atabal **9.** castanets
musician . . . **4.** bard **5.** piper **6.** hepcat,
lyrist, singer **7.** chorist, crooner,
drummer, fiddler, flutist, harpist,
pianist, reedman, yodeler **8.** bandsman,

composer, minstrel, organist
9. conductor, serenader, troubador,
violinist **10.** prima donna, trombonist
11. clarinetist, keyboardist, minnesinger,
saxophonist **12.** interlocutor
13. Kapellmeister, percussionist
musicians' group . . . **4.** band, duet, trio
5. nonet **6.** septet, sextet **7.** nonetto,
quartet **8.** ensemble, septette, sextette,
symphony **9.** orchestra, quartette
musicians' patron saint . . . **7.** Cecilia
musk . . . **4.** deer **7.** perfume
musk (pert to) . . .
beaver . . **7.** muskrat
cat . . **5.** civet
cattle . . **4.** oxen
cucumber . . **11.** cassabanana
deer . . **10.** chevrotain
duck . . **7.** Muscovy
hog . . **7.** peccary
melon . . **10.** cantaloupe
okra . . **8.** abelmosk
shrew . . **6.** desman
weasel . . **5.** civet
muskellunge . . . **4.** fish, pike
musket . . . **4.** hawk **5.** rifle **7.** firearm
9. flintlock
Musketeers, Three . . . **5.** Athos **6.** Aramis
7. Porthos **9.** D'Artagnon
muskmelon . . . **6.** atimon, casaba
10. cantaloupe
muskrat . . . **5.** shrew **6.** desman **7.** ondatra
Muslim . . . **5.** Hanif, Islam, Salar
7. Saracen **9.** Mussulman
10. Mohammedan
Muslim (pert to) . . .
ablution . . **4.** wudu (widu, wuzu)
cap . . **3.** fez, taj
capturer of Jerusalem . . **4.** Omar
caste . . **5.** mopla (moplah)
chief . . **4.** dato (datto), rais
city (holy) . . **5.** Mecca
college, school . . **8.** madrasah (madrasa,
madrasseh)
dagger . . **7.** khanjar
deity . . **5.** Allah, Eblis
devil . . **5.** Eblis
devotee . . **6.** santon **7.** dervish
Easter . . **3.** Eed
guide (spiritual) . . **3.** pir
interpreter . . **5.** ulema
invocation . . **9.** bismillah
javelin . . **6.** jereed
judge . . **4.** cadi
lawyer . . **5.** mufti
market, booth . . **4.** sook
monastery . . **5.** ribat **7.** khankah
mosque . . **6.** masjid
noble . . **4.** amir (ameer), emir
officer . . **5.** dewan (diwan)
people . . **4.** Moro
pilgrimage to Mecca . . **4.** hadj
prayer . . **4.** azan (adan)
priest . . **4.** imam (imaum)
saint . . **3.** pir **6.** santon **8.** Marabout
sect . . **6.** Senusi (Senousi, Senussite)
shrine, Mecca . . **5.** Kaaba (Caaba,
Kaabeh)
teacher . . **4.** Alim **8.** mujtahid
title . . **3.** Sid **5.** Sayid (Said)
tradition . . **7.** Al Sirat (Bridge to Paradise)

Turkish.. **5.** Salar
university.. **8.** madrasah (madrasa)
viceroy.. **7.** Saracen
muslin... **3.** ban, cap **4.** mull **5.** doria,
shela **6.** canvas, gurrah **7.** organdy
8. nainsook, sheeting, tarlatan
muss... **4.** mess, soil **5.** chaos, dirty
6. bitter, muddle, rumple, tousle
7. confuse, wrinkle **8.** dishevel,
scramble, squabble **10.** disarrange
mussel... **4.** food, naid, unio **5.** horse,
moule, naiad **6.** byssus, mucket, nerita
7. mollusk, Mytilus
Musselman... **6.** Moslem **7.** Saracen
10. Mohammedan
must... **4.** mold, musk, sapa, stum
5. juice, ought, shall **6.** blight,
mildew, refuse **7.** malodor **9.** necessity
10. obligation
mustang... **5.** horse, pinto **6.** bronco,
sphinx
mustard... **5.** nigra, senvy **7.** sinapis
8. charlock
mustard (pert to)...
chemistry.. **8.** sinapine
gas.. **7.** yperite
genus.. **7.** Sinapis **8.** Brassica
plaster.. **8.** sinapism
Mustelidae... **5.** minks **7.** badgers,
martens, weasels
muster... **4.** levy **5.** erect **6.** gather,
summon **7.** collect, marshal
8. assemble, comprise **10.** assemblage
muster out... **7.** disband
musty... **3.** bad, old **4.** damp, hoar,
rank **5.** fetid, fusty, moist, moldy, rafty,
stale, trite **6.** rancid **7.** pungent
mutable... **6.** fickle **7.** erratic **8.** variable
9. alterable, changeful
mute... **3.** mum **4.** dumb, lene, surd
6. muffle, silent **8.** deadener, silencer,
taciturn **9.** voiceless **10.** speechless
mutilate... **3.** mar **4.** geld, hack, maim
6. deface, deform, garble, injure,
mangle **7.** cripple, destroy **8.** castrate
9. dismember, tear apart
mutinous... **6.** unruly **9.** seditious,
turbulent **10.** rebellious, refractory
11. intractable
mutiny... **6.** Putsch (Swiss), revolt,
strife, tumult **9.** commotion, rebellion
12. insurrection **15.** insubordination
mutter... **5.** growl **6.** murmur, patter,
plaint **7.** grumble, maunder **8.** complain
9. mussitate
mutton... **4.** meat **5.** cabob (kabob),
gigot, sheep **6.** candle
muttonfish... **4.** sama **5.** pargo
7. abalone, eelpout, mojarra, snapper
mutual... **4.** plan **5.** joint **6.** common
8. intimate **9.** symbiotic **10.** reciprocal,
responsive **15.** interchangeable
mutual understanding... **9.** agreement,
unanimity **12.** consentience, coordination **13.** interrelation
17. interrelationship
mux... **4.** mess **5.** batch
muy... **4.** very **7.** greatly
muzhik, muzjik... **7.** peasant
muzzle... **3.** gag **4.** cope, maul, nose
5. mouth, snout **6.** clevis, thrash

7. shackle, sheathe, silence **8.** restrain
10. respirator
my... **3.** mes, mon **4.** mine **7.** due to
me **11.** exclamation
myall... **4.** wild, wood (fragrant) **6.** acacia
11. uncivilized
Myanmar... see *Burma, Burmese*
mycoderma... **5.** fungi **6.** mother (formed
on wine) **8.** membrane (ferment)
mycophagy... **11.** eating fungi **15.** eating
mushrooms
myna, mynah... **4.** bird **7.** grackle
8. starling
Mynheer... **8.** Dutchman
myo (comb form)... **6.** muscle
myomancy, divination by... **14.** muscle
movement
myopic... **11.** nearsighted
myriad... **11.** innumerable, ten thousand
13. multitudinous
myriapod... **9.** centipede
myrmicid... **3.** ant
myrtle... **8.** ramarama **10.** periwinkle
11. candleberry
mysterious... **4.** dark **6.** arcane,
mystic, occult, secret **7.** cryptic
8. abstruse, esoteric **9.** recondite,
sphinxian **10.** cabalistic **12.** inexplicable,
unfathomable
mystery... **4.** cult, rune **6.** arcane, cabala,
enigma, puzzle, secret **7.** arcanum,
esotery, miracle **8.** whodunit
9. sacrament **13.** inexplainable
19. incomprehensibility
mystery writer's award... **5.** Edgar
mystic... **4.** seer, yogi **5.** magic, runic
6. occult, orphic, secret **7.** cryptic,
Mahatma **8.** cabalist, esoteric, symbolic
9. enigmatic, recondite **10.** cabalistic,
mysterious
mystic (pert to)...
cry.. **4.** evoe
doctrine.. **5.** cabal **7.** esotery **8.** esoteric
initiate.. **5.** epopt (Gr Antiq)
ocean isle.. **6.** Avalon
theosophy.. **6.** cabala
word.. **2.** om **7.** abraxas **11.** abracadabra
mystical... **6.** muddle, puzzle **7.** confuse,
cryptic, furtive, obscure **9.** enigmatic,
obfuscate
mystical (pert to)...
character (Teut Myth).. **8.** Eckehart
meaning.. **7.** anagoge
word.. **11.** abracadabra
mystify... **5.** befog **6.** muddle, puzzle
7. becloud, confuse, perplex
8. befuddle, bewilder **9.** bamboozle,
obfuscate
myth... **4.** tale **5.** fable, fancy, story
6. legend **7.** figment, parable
9. apocrypha, falsehood
mythical... **7.** fancied **8.** fabulous
9. fictional, imaginary, legendary
10. fictitious **12.** mythological
mythical (pert to)...
being.. **6.** Garuda, Icarus **7.** centaur,
griffin
bird.. **3.** roc
deity.. **6.** Moloch (tyrant)
demon.. **4.** Rahu (tail called Kehu)
hero.. **4.** Ajax **8.** Achilles

heroine.. **4.** Leda **6.** Europa
  8. Atalanta
hunter.. **5.** Orion
island.. **8.** Atlantis
king (Hind).. **4.** Nala
monster.. **4.** ogre **7.** chimera
mother.. **5.** Niobe

river.. **4.** Styx
serpent.. **5.** Apepi
winged creature.. **7.** Alborak
woman.. **6.** Gorgon, Medusa, Stheno
  7. Euryale
mythogony, science of... **5.** myths
mythologist... **9.** mythmaker

N

N... **2.** en, Nu **8.** nitrogen (symbol)
nab... **4.** grab **5.** catch, seize **6.** arrest,
  nibble, snatch **7.** capture **9.** apprehend
Nabal's wife (Bib)... **7.** Abigail
nabob... **5.** nawab **6.** bigwig, tycoon
  7. viceroy **8.** governor **9.** plutocrat
  10. viceregent
Nabokov nymphet... **6.** Lolita
nacelle... **4.** boat **7.** shelter
nacket... **3.** boy **4.** cake **5.** lunch **6.** caddie
  8. saucy boy
nacre... **9.** shellfish **10.** conchiolin
  13. mother-of-pearl
Nadab (Bib)... **12.** King of Israel
nadir... **4.** pole **11.** lowest point (opp
  zenith)
nag... **4.** pony, twit **5.** annoy, cobra,
  horse, scold, snake, tease **6.** heckle,
  hector, peck on, pester, plague
  7. henpeck **8.** harangue
nagor... **8.** antelope, reedbuck
nahoor... **5.** sheep **6.** bharal
naiad... **5.** nymph **6.** mussel, Nereid
  7. limniad, Oceanid
nail... **3.** cut, hob **4.** brad, claw,
  spad, stud, tack, wire **5.** clout, spike,
  sprig, talon **6.** fasten, secure, unguis,
  ungula **7.** capture, measure **8.** sparable
  9. finishing, intercept **12.** upholstering
nail (pert to)...
  headless.. **5.** sprig
  ingrowing.. **7.** acronyx
  marking, fingernail.. **6.** lunule
  size.. **8.** tenpenny
  slanted.. **4.** toed
naissance... **5.** birth **6.** origin
naive... **5.** frank **6.** simple **7.** artless,
  ingenue **8.** childish, gullible, untaught
  9. guileless, ingenuous, unworldly
  10. simplicity **13.** unphilosophic
  15. unsophisticated
naked... **4.** bald, bare, mere, nude,
  open **5.** clear, plain **6.** barren,
  meager **7.** exposed, literal, obvious
  8. manifest, stripped **9.** unadorned,
  uncovered **11.** defenseless, unprotected,
  unsupported
nakoo... **6.** gavial **9.** crocodile
namaycush... **5.** togue, trout
namby-pamby... **5.** inane, silly, vapid
  7. insipid **10.** wishy-washy
  11. sentimental
name... **3.** dub, nom **4.** call, cite, term
  5. clepe, nomen, style, title **6.** y-
  clepe **7.** appoint, entitle, mention

  8. cognomen, identify **9.** celebrity,
  enumerate, personage **10.** denominate,
  reputation **11.** appellation, designation
  12. denomination
name (pert to)...
  added.. **7.** agnomen
  assumed.. **3.** pen **5.** alias **7.** John Doe
    9. incognito, pseudonym, sobriquet
    10. nom de plume
  bad.. **7.** caconym
  binomial.. **8.** teutonym
  by location.. **7.** toponym
  derivation.. **7.** eponymy
  family (father's).. **7.** eponymy
    9. patronymy
  fictitious.. **9.** pseudonym
  first.. **9.** baptismal, Christian, praenomen
  Japanese.. **4.** maru
  known.. **9.** onomatous
  nickname.. **7.** moniker (monicker)
    8. cognomen
  nominate.. **9.** designate
  secret.. **9.** cryptonym
  spelled backwards (real name)..
    6. ananym
  surname.. **7.** eponymy
  technical.. **4.** onym
  unknown.. **9.** anonymous
  wrong.. **8.** misnomer
name as agent... **6.** depute
named... **5.** cited **6.** called, y-clept
  (y-cleped)
named for a god... **11.** theophorous
nameless... **7.** bastard, obscure **8.** not
  known **9.** aforesaid, anonymous,
  unnamable **10.** unrenowned
  12. illegitimate **13.** indescribable,
  inexpressible **15.** undistinguished
namelessness... **9.** anonymity
namely... **5.** to wit **9.** expressly,
  nominally, videlicet (viz)
names, divination by... **8.** onomancy
names, science of... **11.** onomatology
namesake... **6.** eponym **7.** homonym
nanga... **4.** harp
nanism... **12.** dwarfishness (opp of
  gigantism)
Nanking...
  capital.. **5.** China (1932--1937)
  color.. **12.** Naples yellow
  province.. **7.** Kiangsu
  river site.. **7.** Yangtze
nanoid... **8.** dwarfish
nanpie... **6.** magpie
naos... **5.** cella **6.** shrine, temple

Naos ... **4.** star
nap ... **3.** nod **4.** doze, pile, shag, wink
  5. fluff, grasp, seize, sleep, steal
  6. duffel, siesta, snooze
nape ... **5.** nucha, nuque, scrag **6.** scruff,
  turnip **7.** niddick **9.** auchenium
napellus ... **9.** monkshood
napery ... **5.** linen (table)
napiform ... **12.** turnip-shaped
napkin ... **5.** doily, towel **6.** diaper
  8. kerchief **9.** serviette **11.** neckerchief
Naples ...
  biscuit .. **10.** ladyfinger
  famed building .. **9.** Cathedral (Gothic,
  1272)
  red .. **5.** ochre **6.** Indian
  site .. **11.** Bay of Naples
napoleon ... **4.** game **6.** pastry **7.** top
  boot **11.** reddish-blue, sweet cherry
  13. crimson clover
Napoleon I (pert to) ...
  birthplace .. **7.** Ajaccio (Corsica)
  brother-in-law .. **5.** Murat
  death site .. **8.** St Helena
  exiled to .. **4.** Elba
  father .. **7.** Charles
  island .. **5.** Capri
  marshal .. **3.** Ney (executed)
  title .. **7.** Emperor (of France)
  warfare site .. **5.** Ligny, Malta **7.** Marengo
  8. Waterloo **10.** Alexandria, Austerlitz
napped (short) ... **3.** ras
nappy ... **3.** ale **4.** dish **5.** downy,
  heady, wooly **6.** liquor, shaggy, sleepy
  7. foaming **10.** inebriated
napu ... **10.** chevrotain
Naraka (Hind) ... **4.** hell
Narcissus (Gr) ... **6.** egoist **14.** beautiful
  youth
narcosis ... **5.** sleep **10.** drowsiness
narcotic ... **4.** dope, drug, hemp,
  junk **5.** bhang (bang), ether, opium
  6. heroin **7.** anodyne, cocaine, hashish
  8. hypnotic, mandrake, morphine
  9. soporific **10.** belladonna,
  hyoscyamus, stramonium
narcotic (pert to) ...
  dose .. **3.** fix **5.** locus
  package .. **6.** bindle
  seller .. **6.** pusher **7.** peddler
  user (group) .. **6.** love-in **9.** snow party
nard ... **6.** anoint **8.** matgrass, ointment,
  rhizomes
nardoo, nardu ... **6.** clover
nares ... **8.** nostrils
narghile, nargile, nargileh ... **4.** pipe
  6. hookah
nargil ... **7.** coconut
nark ... **3.** spy **5.** annoy **8.** informer
  11. stool pigeon
Narragansett ... **3.** Bay **5.** horse **6.** Indian,
  turkey
narrate ... **4.** tell **6.** detail, recite, relate
  7. recount **8.** describe
narration ... **4.** tale **5.** drama (acted), story
  6. detail **7.** account, recital **8.** relation
  9. discourse, narrative, rehearsal
narrative ... **4.** epic, epos, myth, poem,
  saga, tale **5.** conte, drama, fable,
  story **6.** legend **7.** account, episode,
  history, parable **8.** allegory, anecdote

9. narration, statement
narrator ... **9.** raconteur **11.** storyteller
narrow ... **4.** mean, poor **5.** inlet,
  scant, taper **6.** linear, strait **7.** closely,
  slender **8.** strictly **9.** confining, illiberal,
  niggardly **10.** restricted, straighten
  11. reactionary **12.** parsimonious
  13. circumscribed
narrow (pert to) ...
  comb form .. **4.** sten **5.** steno
  leather strip .. **5.** thong
  minded .. **5.** petty **6.** biased **7.** bigoted
  10. intolerant, prejudiced
  opening .. **4.** rima, slot **9.** stenopaic
  souled .. **10.** ungenerous
narrowly incised ... **9.** laciniate
narrows ... **5.** sound **6.** strait
narthex ... **7.** portico **9.** asafetida
  (asafoetida)
narwhal, narwal ... **5.** whale **8.** cetacean
nasab (Muslim Law) ... **7.** kinship
  13. consanguinity
nasal ... **4.** nose **5.** sound **6.** narine,
  rhinal, twangy **11.** inspiratory
nascency ... **5.** birth **6.** origin **7.** genesis
  9. beginning
naseberry ... **9.** sapodilla
Nasi ... **6.** prince **8.** Gamaliel **9.** patriarch
Nasicornia ... **10.** rhinoceros
Naso, famed ... **4.** Ovid
nasology ... **9.** nose study
Nassau ...
  capital .. **7.** Bahamas
  hamlet .. **7.** grouper
  sports .. **4.** golf
nastika ... **7.** atheist
nasty ... **4.** foul, mean **5.** dirty **6.** filthy,
  odious **7.** obscene **8.** indecent,
  unsavory **9.** offensive **12.** disagreeable,
  dishonorable
Nasua ... **5.** coati **6.** coatis
nasute ... **10.** large-nosed
nasutiform ... **8.** noselike
natal ... **6.** inborn, native **7.** gluteal,
  nascent **9.** from birth
Natal ... **7.** seaport (Braz) **8.** Province
  (So Afr)
natator ... **7.** swimmer
natatorium ... **4.** pool **6.** plunge
  12. swimming hole
natchbone ... **9.** aitchbone
Natchez ... **4.** city (La) **6.** Indian
nation ... **4.** host, race **5.** caste, class,
  state **6.** people, polity **7.** country
  9. community, multitude
national ... **4.** blue **6.** racial **7.** citizen,
  federal
nationality ... **4.** race **6.** nation **8.** nativity
  9. statehood **11.** nationalism
national salute ... **13.** Twenty-one guns
native ... **3.** ite, son **5.** natal **6.** innate,
  normal, simple **7.** genuine, natural,
  primary **8.** inherent, original, primeval
  9. unbranded **10.** aboriginal,
  indigenous, unaffected **11.** not acquired
native (pert to) ...
  agent .. **9.** comprador (compradore)
  bear .. **5.** koala
  cat .. **7.** dasyure
  dog .. **5.** dingo
  Indian .. **4.** Arab

juniper . . **9.** blueberry
Madagascan . . **4.** Hova
naturalized person . . **7.** denizen
plant, animal . . **8.** indigene
salt . . **6.** halite
nativity . . . **5.** birth **9.** beginning,
horoscope, sculpture
Nativity, The . . . **8.** festival **9.** Christmas
13. birth of Christ
natterjack . . . **4.** toad
natty . . . **4.** chic, neat, tidy, trim **6.** spruce
10. fastidious
Natty Bumppo's alias . . . **7.** Hawkeye
10. Deerslayer, Pathfinder
15. Leatherstocking
natural . . . **3.** raw **4.** born **5.** flesh, usual
6. common, cretin, expert, inborn,
inbred, innate, normal **7.** genuine,
regular, typical **8.** informal, inherent,
lifelike, ordinary **9.** character (Mus),
dice throw, unassumed, unfeigned
10. unaffected
natural (pert to) . . .
capacity . . **9.** endowment
condition . . **4.** norm
group . . **4.** race **6.** ethnic, family
location, position . . **4.** site **5.** situs
not (natural) . . **5.** alien **8.** acquired
10. artificial
philosophy . . **7.** physics
science . . **10.** physiology
voice (Mus) . . **7.** dipetto
naturalist . . . **4.** Muir (John) **7.** Burbank
(Luther)
naturalize . . . **5.** adapt **8.** accustom
9. acclimate **11.** domesticate, familiarize
nature . . . **4.** kind, self, sort, soul, type
6. cosmos **7.** essence **8.** tendency,
universe **11.** naturalness, temperament
14. characteristic
nature (pert to) . . .
concealed . . **7.** latency
divinity of . . **5.** dryad, naiad, nymph
god . . **3.** Pan
goddess . . **6.** Cybele **7.** Artemis
in the raw . . **6.** nudity
of the case . . **9.** ipso facto
worship . . **11.** physiolatry
natus . . . **4.** born
nausea . . . **4.** pall **5.** qualm **8.** loathing, mal
de mer **10.** queasiness **11.** seasickness
nauseous . . . **7.** fulsome, mawkish
9. loathsome, offensive, sickening,
squeamish **10.** disgusting
nautical . . . **5.** naval **6.** marine **7.** oceanic
8. maritime
nautical (pert to) . . .
almanac . . **9.** ephemeris
direction . . **5.** avast, belay
hail . . **4.** ahoy
instrument . . **3.** aba **7.** compass, pelorus,
sextant
measure . . **3.** ton **4.** knot **6.** fathom
7. sea mile
nautilus . . . **7.** mollusk **8.** argonaut
9. submarine **10.** diving bell
Navaho, Navajo . . . **5.** hogan **6.** Indian
7. blanket **9.** red-yellow
naval . . . **6.** marine **8.** nautical
naval (pert to) . . .
brigade . . **7.** militia

commander . . **7.** navarch
depot . . **4.** base
device . . **6.** dolter
officer . . **5.** bosun **6.** ensign, yeoman
7. admiral, captain **9.** boatswain
(bosun), commander **10.** lieutenant
nave . . . **3.** hob, hub, nef **4.** apse, fist
5. nieve **7.** apsidal
navel . . . **6.** middle, orange **8.** omphalos
9. umbilicus **10.** depression
navigate . . . **4.** keel, sail **7.** avigate **11.** ship
science
navigator . . . **5.** navvy **12.** third command
(or 4th)
navy (fleet) . . . **7.** tankers **8.** cruisers,
flattops, gunboats **10.** destroyers,
submarines **11.** battleships **12.** mine
sweepers **13.** hospital ships **16.** aircraft
carriers
navy (pert to) . . .
bean . . **6.** kidney
coffee . . **3.** mud
color . . **4.** blue **10.** marine blue
drinking fountain . . **11.** scuttlebutt
fleet . . **6.** armada **13.** combat vessels
plug . . **7.** tobacco
ships, collectively . . **5.** fleet **6.** armada
song . . **13.** Anchors Aweigh
training camp . . **8.** boot camp
underwear . . **8.** skivvies
nawab, nabob . . . **5.** ruler, title **7.** viceroy
nay . . . **2.** no **4.** deny **5.** flute, never
6. denial, naysay, refuse **7.** refusal
8. negative **11.** prohibition
nayaur . . . **5.** sheep
nayword . . . **6.** byword **7.** proverb (of
reproach) **9.** watchword
Nazarene (pert to) . . .
artist . . **8.** Overbeck (of Rome)
disciple . . **9.** Christian
native . . **11.** Jesus Christ
native of . . **8.** Nazareth
Nazi . . . **9.** Hitlerite
Nazi emblem . . . **6.** fylfot **8.** swastika
nchega . . . **6.** monkey **10.** chimpanzee
neanic . . . **8.** immature, youthful
neap . . . **4.** tide **6.** tongue (vehicle) **7.** low
tide **8.** low water
Neapolitan (pert to) . . .
dance . . **10.** tarantella
fever . . **8.** undulent
Italian . . **6.** Naples
medlar . . **5.** fruit **7.** azarole
music . . **5.** chord (6th)
ointment . . **9.** mercurial
yellow . . **6.** Naples
near . . . **2.** at **4.** nigh **5.** about, close,
handy **6.** around, within **7.** closely,
related **8.** adjacent, approach, imminent,
intimate **11.** approximate
13. propinquitous
nearby, near-by . . . **3.** gin **4.** nigh **5.** anent,
handy **6.** beside, nearly **7.** close by,
close to, vicinal **8.** adjacent **9.** adjoining
10. convenient
Nearctic . . . **9.** Greenland, Holarctic
11. Palaearctic **13.** Arctic America
Near East . . . **7.** Balkans **12.** Balkan States
Near East valley . . . **4.** wadi (wady)
5. oasis **6.** ravine
nearest . . . **4.** next **7.** closest **9.** proximate

nearly ... **5.** about **6.** almost **7.** closely
   8. narrowly **10.** similarity
   13. approximately
nearness ... **8.** affinity, intimacy, likeness,
   relation **9.** closeness **11.** propinquity
near of kin ... **7.** germane
nearsighted ... **6.** myopic **8.** purblind
   12. narrow-minded, shortsighted,
   undiscerning
neat ... **3.** pat **4.** prim, smug, snod, tidy,
   trig, trim **5.** natty **6.** adroit, dapper,
   spruce **7.** orderly, perjink, precise
   9. shipshape **10.** meticulous, perjinkety
   12. spick-and-span
neatherd ... **7.** cowherd **8.** herdsman
neathmost ... **6.** lowest
neb ... **3.** tip **4.** beak, bill, face, kiss,
   nose **5.** point, snout
Nebo, Nebu ... **8.** mountain (Bib) **11.** god
   of wisdom
Nebraska ...
   capital .. **7.** Lincoln
   city .. **5.** Omaha **8.** Hastings
     11. Scottsbluff
   Indian .. **4.** Otoe **5.** Omaha **6.** Pawnee
   meaning .. **11.** water valley
   railroad (1865) .. **12.** Union Pacific
   river .. **6.** Nemaha, Platte **8.** Missouri
   State admission .. **13.** Thirty-seventh
   State motto .. **20.** Equality Before the
     Law
   State nickname .. **4.** Beef **10.** Cornhusker
nebula ... **3.** sky **4.** mist **5.** cloud, vapor
   10. atmosphere
Nebula of ... **4.** Lyra **5.** Orion
   9. Andromeda
nebulous ... **4.** hazy **5.** misty, vague
   6. cloudy **7.** clouded, nebular
   8. nebulose
nebulous envelope ... **4.** coma
   9. chevelure
necessarily ... **8.** perforce
   11. unavoidably **12.** consequently
   13. indispensably
necessary ... **5.** vital **7.** needful
   9. essential, mandatory, requisite
   11. requirement, unavoidable
   13. indispensable
necessitate ... **5.** force, impel **6.** compel,
   entail, oblige **7.** require **9.** constrain
necessity ... **4.** food, need, want
   5. drink **7.** aliment, poverty, urgency
   9. neediness **10.** constraint
   14. inevitableness
neck ... **4.** hals (halse) **5.** crane, scrag,
   swire **6.** cervix, fondle, strait **7.** channel,
   embrace, isthmus
neck (pert to) ...
   armor .. **6.** gorget **8.** gorgerin
   artery .. **7.** carotid
   back of .. **4.** nape **5.** nucha, nuque
     6. scruff
   frill .. **5.** jabot, ruche **6.** wimple
   land .. **6.** strake **9.** peninsula
   muscle .. **8.** scalenus
   pendant .. **6.** locket **9.** lavaliere
   piece .. **3.** boa **5.** amice, rabat, scarf,
     stole **6.** collar
   water .. **6.** strait
   zoology .. **4.** gula **6.** wattle **7.** withers
neckcloth ... **6.** cravat **7.** muffler

9. barcelona **11.** neckerchief
neckerchief ... **7.** belcher **8.** kerchief
   12. handkerchief
necklace ... **5.** beads **6.** torque **7.** baldric,
   chaplet, rivière **11.** shark's-teeth
neckpiece ... **3.** boa **5.** ascot, rabat,
   scarf, stole **6.** collar **8.** kerchief
necktie ... **3.** tie **4.** band **5.** ascot, scarf
   6. cravat **10.** four-in-hand
necrology ... **9.** death roll **13.** death
   register **14.** obituary notice
necromancy ... **5.** goety, magic **7.** sorcery
   9. sortilege **11.** conjuration,
   enchantment
necropolis ... **8.** cemetery
necropsy ... **7.** autopsy **10.** post-mortem
nectar ... **3.** red **5.** drink, honey
   8. beverage
nectar of the gods ... **8.** ambrosia
neddy ... **6.** donkey **13.** life preserver
need ... **4.** lack, poor, thar, want
   7. poverty, require, urgency **8.** exigency
   9. extremity, necessity **10.** compulsion,
   deficiency **11.** requirement
needle ... **3.** sew **4.** acus, goad,
   sail **5.** tease, thorn **6.** bodkin,
   pierce **7.** darning, obelisk **9.** astatizer
   10. upholstery
needle (pert to) ...
   bath .. **3.** jet **9.** sprinkler
   bird .. **9.** phalarope **10.** needlebill
   bug .. **4.** Nepa **7.** Ranatra
   case .. **4.** etui (etwee)
   fish .. **3.** gar **8.** pipefish
   gun .. **11.** Dreyse rifle
   kind .. **5.** blunt, sharp **7.** between,
     crochet, darning **8.** knitting
   long-eyed .. **10.** embroidery
   medical .. **10.** hypodermic
   needlelike body .. **7.** spicule
   needlework .. **7.** crochet, sampler
     8. knitting **10.** embroidery
   record .. **10.** phonograph
   shaped .. **6.** acuate **7.** acerose **8.** acicular
   under the skin .. **5.** seton
needy ... **4.** poor **7.** almoner **8.** indigent
   9. necessary, penniless, requisite
   10. distressed
neel-bhunder ... **8.** wanderoo **10.** blue
   monkey
neep ... **6.** turnip
ne'er-do-well ... **5.** idler **6.** wretch
   8. poltroon **9.** schlemiel **14.** good-for-
   nothing
nef ... **4.** nave **5.** clock (ship-shaped)
nefarious ... **6.** wicked **7.** heinous,
   impious **8.** horrible, infamous, terrible
   9. atrocious **10.** detestable, iniquitous,
   villainous
nefas ... **6.** sinful
negate ... **4.** deny **6.** refuse, refute
   7. nullify **8.** disprove **10.** counteract
negative ... **2.** ir, ne, no **3.** nay, non,
   nor, not **4.** deny, film, veto **5.** minus
   6. refuse **7.** neutral **8.** disprove, negation
   9. privative **13.** contradiction
negative (pert to) ...
   electrode, pole .. **7.** cathode (kathode)
   eyepiece .. **8.** Campani's **9.** Huygenian
   ion .. **5.** anion
   sign .. **5.** minus

neglect . . . **4.** fail, omit, slip, snub
5. shirk **6.** slight **7.** failure **8.** omission
9. disregard, negligent, pretermit
11. inattention
negligee . . . **4.** gown, robe **6.** attire
8. peignoir
negligence . . . **7.** laxness **9.** oversight,
unconcern **10.** remissness
11. inattention **12.** carelessness,
inadvertence
negligent . . . **3.** lax **4.** lash **6.** remiss,
supine **8.** careless, heedless
10. neglectful **11.** unconcerned
negotiate . . . **4.** deal, pass **5.** treat
6. manage, treaty **7.** bargain, mediate
8. transact
Negrito (pert to) . . .
 African . . **4.** Akka **5.** Batwa, Pygmy
 7. Bambute, Bushman
 Dutch New Guinea . . **6.** Tapiro
 Indonesian . . **3.** Ata **4.** Aeta (Ita)
 Malay . . **6.** Semang
neigh . . . **4.** akin **6.** whinny **7.** whicker
neighborhood . . . **7.** purlieu **8.** environs,
vicinity **9.** proximity **10.** thereabout
neither right nor wrong . . .
 11. adiaphorous, indifferent
Nemesis . . . **7.** avenger, goddess, penalty
nemoral . . . **6.** sylvan **14.** living in a
grove
neology . . . **8.** new words **9.** neologism
11. new doctrine **14.** new expressions
neonate . . . **7.** new baby, newborn
neophobia (fear of) . . . **6.** the new
neophyte . . . **4.** tyro **6.** novice **7.** convert
8. beginner **9.** proselyte **10.** catechumen
neoplasm . . . **5.** tumor
neosology (study of) . . . **10.** young birds
neoteric . . . **3.** new **4.** late **6.** modern,
recent
nep . . . **6.** catnip
Nepal . . .
 aborigines . . **10.** Mongolians
 capital . . **8.** Katmandu
 district . . **7.** Mustang
 mountain . . **7.** Everest **9.** Himalayas
 ruler . . **9.** Maharajah
nepesh . . . **4.** soul **10.** animal soul
12. divine breath
nephew . . . **4.** neve **6.** nepote
nephrite . . . **4.** jade **7.** mineral **11.** kidney
stone
nephroid . . . **8.** reniform **12.** kidney-
shaped
nephros . . . **6.** kidney
nepote . . . **6.** nephew **8.** grandson
nepotism . . . **9.** patronage **10.** favoritism,
preference
Neptune . . . **3.** sea **5.** ocean **6.** sea god
Neptune (pert to) . . .
 Astron . . **6.** planet (3rd largest)
 Celtic . . **3.** Ler
 consort . . **7.** Salacia
 emblem . . **7.** trident
 Greek . . **8.** Poseidon
 Roman . . **6.** sea god
 son . . **6.** Triton
 wife . . **6.** Medusa
Nereid (Gr) . . . **8.** sea nymph
Nero (pert to) . . .
 excesses . . **7.** cruelty **13.** burning of

Rome (64 AD)
 mother . . **9.** Agrippina
 Roman title . . **7.** Emperor
 wife . . **6.** Sabina **7.** Octavia
nerve . . . **4.** pulp **5.** cheek, fiber, pluck,
sinew **6.** aplomb, energy, tendon,
tissue **7.** courage, nervure **8.** audacity,
coolness, strength **10.** resolution
nerve (pert to) . . .
 action . . **9.** neurergic
 cell . . **4.** axon **6.** neuron
 center . . **8.** ganglion
 comb form . . **5.** neuro
 fiber . . **5.** motor **7.** sensory **8.** afferent,
efferent
 force . . **7.** neurism
 gray matter . . **7.** cinerea
 inflammation, medical . . **8.** neuritis,
neurosis **9.** neurotomy **10.** neurectasy,
neurolysis, neuropathy **11.** neurologist
13. tic douloureux
 network . . **4.** rete **6.** plexus
 of Wrisberg . . **6.** facial
 operation . . **10.** neurolysis
 passage . . **4.** rete **5.** hilum **8.** ganglion
 ref to . . **6.** neural, neuric **7.** neuroid
 8. neurotic
 root . . **5.** radix
 science . . **9.** neurology
 sheath . . **9.** medullary
 tissue . . **7.** cinerea, neurine **9.** neuroglia
 tumor . . **6.** glioma **7.** neuroma
nerveless . . . **4.** dead **5.** inert **9.** foolhardy,
powerless **10.** courageous
nervous . . . **5.** tense, timid **6.** neural,
touchy **7.** fearful, jittery **8.** eloquent,
neurotic, timorous **9.** excitable, sensitive
10. high-strung **12.** apprehensive
nervous (pert to) . . .
 affliction . . **3.** tic **6.** ataxia, chorea
 7. aphasia **8.** neurosis
 energy deficiency . . **7.** aneuria
 seizure . . **4.** amok (amuck)
 system, center . . **5.** brain, spine
 system, description . . **11.** neurography
 system, name . . **9.** neuronymy
 system, science . . **9.** neurology
 system, specialist . . **12.** neuropathist,
psychiatrist
 tissue tumor . . **11.** neurocytoma
ness . . . **4.** cape **8.** headland
10. promontory
nest . . . **3.** bed, den, nye, web **4.** inro
5. abode, aerie, eyrie, group, haunt,
nidus **6.** cuddle, series (graduated)
7. lodging, retreat **9.** residence
10. nidificate **13.** breeding place
nest (pert to) . . .
 boxes . . **4.** inro
 eagle's . . **5.** aerie, eyrie (eyry)
 pheasant's . . **4.** nide
 spider's . . **3.** web
 squirrel's . . **4.** dray (drey)
 swallow's . . **9.** nidus avis
 to build . . **6.** nidify
nestle . . . **3.** pet **4.** nest **6.** cuddle, pettle,
settle **7.** protect, shelter, snuggle
nestling . . . **4.** bird **5.** child **9.** fledgling,
youngling
Nestor (pert to) . . .
 famed for . . **6.** wisdom

King of . . **5.** Pylos
known as . . **4.** sage **7.** adviser **8.** The Elder **9.** Patriarch
net . . . **3.** gin, web **4.** mesh, toil, trap, weir **5.** clear, lacis, score, seine, snare, weave **6.** profit **7.** enclose, network, trammel **8.** receipts **9.** reticulum
net (pert to) . . .
fishing . . **4.** fyke **5.** seine, trawl **7.** trammel
hair . . **5.** snood
lacemaking . . **5.** lacis
silk . . **5.** tulle **6.** maline
winged (lacy) . . **12.** neuropteroid
Netherlands . . . see also *Dutch, Holland*
capital . . **9.** Amsterdam
cheese . . **4.** Edam
city . . **5.** Delft **7.** Utrecht **9.** Eindhoven, Rotterdam
gin . . **8.** schnapps
government . . **8.** monarchy
government seat . . **8.** The Hague
inhabitant . . **5.** Dutch **7.** Flemish
lake . . **7.** Haarlem
legislative body . . **4.** Raad
low land . . **6.** polder
port . . **9.** Rotterdam
possession . . **7.** Surinam (Dutch Guiana) **8.** Antilles (W Ind)
river . . **3.** Eem **5.** Meuse, Rhine **6.** Ijssel (Yssel), Kromme
sea (inland) . . **9.** Wadden Sea, Zuider Zee **10.** Ijssel Lake, Ijsselmeer
nettle . . . **3.** vex **4.** fret, herb, line, whip **5.** anger, annoy, pique, rouse **6.** incite, Urtica **7.** provoke **8.** irritate **10.** Parietaria, Urticaceae
nettle (pert to) . . .
bird . . **11.** whitethroat
geranium . . **6.** coleus
rash . . **5.** hives, uredo **9.** urticaria
sea . . **5.** cnida
network . . . **3.** web **4.** caul, fret, kell, lace, mesh, moke, rete **5.** chain **6.** cobweb, plexus, reseau, sagene **7.** webwork
neume . . . **5.** neuma **6.** pneuma
neurad . . . **12.** to neural side
neural . . . **6.** dorsal, nerval **7.** ventral **9.** posterial
neuralgia . . . **3.** tic **4.** pain **8.** face ague **13.** tic douloureux
neuter . . . **6.** gender **7.** neither, neutral, sexless **9.** impartial
neutral . . . **7.** antacid **8.** mediocre, middling, negative, unbiased **10.** achromatic **11.** indifferent, nonpartisan **12.** noncombatant, noncommittal
neutral equilibrium . . . **7.** astatic
neutralize . . . **5.** annul **6.** offset **7.** nullify, vitiate **9.** frustrate **10.** counteract **11.** countervail **14.** counterbalance
Nevada . . .
capital . . **10.** Carson City
city . . **3.** Ely **4.** Elko **6.** Sparks **7.** Boulder **8.** Las Vegas
lake . . **4.** Mead **6.** Mohave **7.** Pyramid
mine (famed) . . **12.** Comstock Lode (1859)
mountain . . **7.** Rockies, Wasatch **13.** Sierra Nevadas

native Indian . . **6.** Digger
resort . . **4.** Reno **8.** Las Vegas (The Meadows) **9.** Lake Tahoe
State admission . . **11.** Thirty-sixth
State motto . . **16.** All For Our Country
State nickname . . **6.** Silver **9.** Sagebrush
neve . . . **4.** firn, snow **6.** nephew **7.** glacier
nevel, nevell . . . **9.** fisticuff
never . . . **4.** nary **6.** nowise **7.** not ever **8.** at no time, not at all **9.** by no means, nevermore
nevertheless . . . **3.** but, yet **5.** still **6.** anyhow **7.** however **15.** notwithstanding
nevus . . . **4.** mark, mole **5.** tumor **7.** blemish **9.** birthmark
new . . . **3.** neo (pref) **4.** anew, late, nova (star) **5.** fresh, novel **6.** growth, modern, recent **8.** neoteric, original, untested **9.** recreated, renovated **12.** unaccustomed **13.** inexperienced
New Brunswick . . .
capital . . **11.** Fredericton
city . . **6.** St John
gulf . . **10.** St Lawrence
new but yet old . . . **10.** novantique
Newfoundland . . .
city . . **7.** St John's **9.** Grand Bank
discoverer . . **9.** John Cabot (1497)
gulf . . **10.** St Lawrence
New Guinea, Papua Island . . .
capital . . **6.** Rabaul
hog (wild) . . **4.** bene
island size (world) . . **5.** third
native . . **6.** Papuan
parrot . . **4.** lory
port . . **4.** Daru **7.** Moresby
region . . **10.** Melanesian
river . . **3.** Fly
New Hampshire . . .
capital . . **7.** Concord
city . . **6.** Durham **7.** Hanover **8.** Merrimac **10.** Manchester, Portsmouth
cog rail (first) . . **12.** Mt Washington
lake . . **13.** Winnipesaukee
mountains . . **5.** White
Our Town . . **13.** Grover's Corner
park . . **13.** Crawford Notch, Dixville Notch
range . . **12.** Presidential
river . . **8.** Merrimac **11.** Connecticut
sculpture . . **14.** Great Stone Face (Profile Peak)
State admission . . **5.** Ninth
State motto . . **13.** Live Free or Die
State nickname . . **7.** Granite
New Jersey . . .
capital . . **7.** Trenton
city . . **6.** Camden, Newark **7.** Raritan **9.** Montclair **12.** Fort Monmouth, New Brunswick
college . . **9.** Princeton (1746)
inventor . . **6.** Edison
naval air station . . **9.** Lakehurst
poet . . **11.** Walt Whitman
resort . . **7.** Cape May **8.** Wildwood **9.** Ocean City **10.** Asbury Park **12.** Atlantic City
river . . **7.** Raritan
State admission . . **5.** Third
State motto . . **20.** Liberty and Prosperity

State nickname .. **6**. Garden
New Mexico . . .
  capital . . **7**. Santa Fe
  city . . **4**. Taos **7**. Roswell **11**. Albuquerque
  Fort . . **5**. Tejon
  Indian Reservation . . **5**. Acoma (Sky
    City) **11**. Chaco Canyon
  peak . . **7**. Wheeler
  river . . **4**. Gila **5**. Pecos **8**. Canadian
  space center . . **6**. Sandia **8**. Holloman,
    Kirtland **9**. Los Alamos **10**. White Sands
  State admission . . **12**. Forty-seventh
  State bird . . **10**. road runner
  State flower . . **5**. yucca
  State motto . . **12**. Crescit Eundo **15**. It
    Grows as it Goes
  State nickname . . **17**. Land of
    Enchantment
  State wonder . . **15**. Carlsbad Caverns
new moon festival . . . **8**. neomenia
news . . . **5**. flash, scoop **6**. report
  7. courier, evangel, tidings
news agency . . . **2**. AP **3**. DNB, UPI
  4. Tass **5**. Aneta, Domei **7**. Reuters
  9. syndicate
newspaper (pert to) . . .
  editor . . **7**. reviser **8**. redactor
  file . . **6**. morgue
  popular name . . **7**. gazette
  writer . . **8**. reporter **9**. columnist
  10. newscaster **13**. correspondent
newsstand . . . **5**. booth, kiosk, stall
new star . . . **4**. nova
newt . . . **3**. eft **6**. lizard, triton
  10. salamander
New Testament . . . **6**. Gospel **8**. Epistles
  15. Pauline Epistles
new wine . . . **4**. must
new word, usage . . . **7**. neology
  9. neologism, neoterism
New York . . .
  borough . . **5**. Bronx **6**. Queens
  8. Brooklyn, Richmond (formerly)
  9. Manhattan **12**. Staten Island
  buyer (for $24) . . **11**. Peter Minuit
  capital . . **6**. Albany
  city . . **5**. Utica **7**. Buffalo, New York
  8. Saratoga **9**. Rochester
  11. Schenectady **12**. Poughkeepsie
  college . . **7**. Colgate, Cornell **8**. Columbia
  9. West Point
  Falls . . **7**. Niagara
  Indian . . **6**. Oneida, Seneca **8**. Iroquois
  Irving's home . . **9**. Tarrytown
  island . . **6**. Staten **9**. Manhattan
  monument . . **7**. Obelisk **10**. Grant's
    Tomb **15**. Statue of Liberty
  mountains . . **9**. Catskills
  name, old . . **12**. New Amsterdam
  nickname . . **6**. Gotham **8**. Big Apple
  river . . **4**. East **6**. Harlem, Hudson
  river channel . . **8**. Hell Gate
  section (famed) . . **4**. SoHo **16**. Greenwich
    Village
  State admission . . **8**. Eleventh
  State bird . . **8**. bluebird
  State flower . . **4**. rose
  State motto . . **9**. Excelsior **10**. Ever
    Upward
  State nickname . . **6**. Empire
New Yorker . . . **8**. Dutchman **9**. Gothamite

  13. Knickerbocker
New Zealand . . .
  capital . . **10**. Wellington
  city . . **7**. Dunedin **8**. Auckland, Hamilton
  12. Christchurch
  discoverer . . **6**. Tasman
  explorer . . **4**. Cook (Captain James)
  location . . **12**. South Pacific
  native . . **3**. Ati **5**. Maori **10**. Polynesian
  peak . . **6**. Mt Cook
  sect . . **7**. Ringatu
  soldier . . **5**. Anzac
  volcano . . **7**. Ruapehu
New Zealand (pert to) . . .
  bird . . **3**. kea, moa, poe **4**. titi, weka, kiwi
  7. apteryx, boobook, wrybill, Xenicus
  caterpillar . . **5**. aweto
  club, weapon . . **4**. mere
  mahogany . . **6**. totara
  mollusk . . **4**. pipi
  myrtle . . **8**. ramarama
  morepork . . **4**. peho, ruru
  palm . . **5**. nikau
  parrot . . **6**. kakapo **9**. owl parrot
  pigeon . . **4**. kuku
  reptile . . **7**. tuatara
  white pine . . **5**. kauri (kaury)
next . . . **4**. then **5**. aware, neist **7**. closest,
  nearest, proximo **9**. adjoining,
  immediate **10**. contiguous, succeeding
next to . . . **6**. almost, beside, nearly
  8. adjacent
next to last syllable . . . **6**. penult
  11. penultimate
nexus . . . **3**. tie **4**. bond, link **5**. group
  6. series **10**. connection
  15. interconnection
Nez Percé . . . **6**. Indian **11**. pierced nose
Niagara . . . **5**. flood, grape (green)
Niagara Falls (pert to) . . .
  cataract . . **8**. American, Canadian
  9. Horseshoe
  division between . . **10**. Bridal Veil, Goat
    Island
  point of interest . . **14**. Cave of the Winds
nib . . . **3**. end **4**. beak, bill **5**. point (pen),
  prong **6**. tongue
nibble . . . **3**. eat, nab, nip **4**. gnaw, peck
  5. champ, munch **6**. browse
Nicaragua . . .
  capital . . **7**. Managua
  city . . **7**. Granada
  lake . . **7**. Managua
  mountain range . . **10**. Cordillera
  river . . **4**. Coco, Tuma **7**. San Juan
nice . . . **4**. fine, good, kind, neat
  6. dainty, proper, queasy, subtle, tickle
  7. elegant, finical, genteel, prudish,
  refined **8**. exacting, pleasant, pleasing,
  suitable **9**. agreeable, squeamish
  10. appetizing, delightful, fastidious,
  particular, scrupulous **11**. considerate,
  punctilious, well-behaved
  13. hypercritical **14**. discriminating,
  discriminative
Nicene Creed . . . **10**. Confession
nicety . . . **7**. finesse, modesty **8**. accuracy,
  delicacy **9**. precision **11**. preciseness
  13. squeamishness
niche . . . **4**. apse, nook **5**. space (recessed)
  6. alcove, covert, recess **7**. retreat,

secrete **10.** tabernacle
nick . . . **3.** gap **4.** dent, dint, slit **5.** notch, steal **7.** swindle
Nick Charles . . . see *Thin Man*
nickel (pert to) . . .
  alloy . . **5.** Invar
  bronze . . **11.** cupranickel
  coin . . **13.** five-cent piece
  color . . **4.** gray **6.** nimbus
  compound . . **8.** argenton **11.** maillechort
  silver . . **6.** German
  symbol . . **2.** Ni
nickelodeon . . . **4.** juke **7.** jukebox, theater (5-cent)
nickname . . . **3.** pun **6.** monica **7.** agnomen, epithet, misname, moniker (monicker), pet name **8.** cognomen, misapply **10.** soubriquet
nicknaming pun . . . **12.** prosonomasia
nictate . . . **4.** wink **5.** blink **7.** twinkle **9.** nictitate
nid . . . **3.** nod **10.** bend and bob
nide . . . **4.** nest **5.** brood
nidge . . . **3.** nig **5.** shake **6.** quiver
nidificant . . . **12.** nestbuilding
nidology, science . . . **10.** birds' nests
nidor . . . **5.** aroma, scent
nidus . . . **4.** nest **5.** abode **7.** nucleus **13.** breeding place
Nietzsche . . . **11.** philosopher
nieve . . . **4.** fist, hand
niffer . . . **7.** bargain **8.** exchange
niffy-naffy . . . **7.** finical **8.** trifling
Niflheim, Nifelheim (Norse Myth) . . . **8.** Universe (division of) **10.** Nine Worlds
nifty . . . **5.** smart **7.** stylish **8.** very good
Nigeria . . .
  capital . . **5.** Abuja, Lagos (formerly)
  city . . **3.** Ede **6.** Ibadan
  people . . **3.** Ibo **6.** Yoruba
  plains . . **5.** Bornu
niggardly . . . **5.** scant **6.** paltry, sordid, stingy **9.** penurious, scrimping **10.** avaricious **12.** parsimonious
nigh . . . **2.** at **3.** nei **4.** left, near **5.** about, anear, close **6.** almost, direct, nearly **8.** adjacent **10.** contiguous **11.** neighboring
night . . . **4.** nuit **5.** death **7.** evening **8.** darkness, wee hours **9.** adversity, nightfall **11.** concealment
night (pert to) . . .
  bird . . **5.** potoo **8.** nightjar **9.** nighthawk **10.** goatsucker, nightchurr, owl swallow, shearwater **11.** nightingale
  blindness . . **10.** nyctalopia
  cap . . **6.** biggin
  club . . **4.** café **5.** disco **6.** bistro **7.** cabaret **11.** discotheque
  goddess . . **3.** Nox, Nyx
  jasmine . . **10.** hursinghar
  Norse . . **4.** Nott
  sight (only) . . **11.** hemeralopia
  wandering . . **11.** noctivagant
nightfall, at . . . **6.** sunset **9.** acronical (achronical) (opp of cosmical)
nightingale . . . **6.** thrush **8.** philomel **9.** bed jacket
night jar . . . **5.** potoo **10.** goatsucker
nightmare . . . **3.** alp **4.** Mara, ogre

5. dream **7.** incubus **9.** cauchemar **13.** hallucination
nightshade . . . **5.** morel (moril) **7.** henbane **10.** belladonna **11.** bittersweet
nigrescent . . . **8.** blackish
nihil . . . **7.** nothing, no value
nihil debet . . . **13.** he owes nothing
nihil ex nihilo . . . **7.** nothing (comes) **11.** from nothing
Nihilist . . . **9.** anarchist, Socialist
Nile (pert to) . . .
  bird . . **4.** ibis **7.** wryneck
  boat . . **5.** baris **6.** nuggar **8.** dahabeah
  branch . . **4.** Blue **5.** White
  city . . **7.** Rosetta
  color . . **3.** boa **5.** green
  dam . . **5.** Aswan
  Falls . . **5.** Ripon
  fish . . **5.** bagre **8.** mormyrid (sacred)
  god . . **4.** Hapi
  headstream . . **6.** Kagera
  houseboat . . **8.** dahabeah
  island . . **4.** Roda (Rhoda)
  waste . . **4.** sudd
nilgai . . . **8.** antelope
nimble . . . **4.** deft, fast, flit, gleg, lish, spry **5.** agile, alert, brisk, fleet, quick, smart, swift **6.** active, adroit, clever, lively, prompt, volant
nimbose . . . **6.** cloudy, stormy **7.** clouded **8.** nebulous, nubilous, overcast
nimbus . . . **4.** disk, halo **5.** cloud, vapor **6.** fabric, gloria, nickel **7.** aureole **10.** atmosphere
nimiety . . . **6.** excess **10.** redundancy
niminy-piminy . . . **7.** mincing, refined **10.** effeminate
nimmer . . . **5.** thief
Nimrod (Bib) . . . **5.** ruler **6.** hunter **8.** Cush's son
nimshi . . . **4.** fool **7.** half-wit **11.** silly person
Nimshi's son (Bib) . . . **11.** Jehoshaphat
nine (pert to) . . .
  angles . . **7.** nonagon
  banded armadillo . . **4.** peba
  based on . . **8.** novenary
  Books of nine chapters . . **7.** Enneads
  comb form . . **6.** ennead
  composition for nine . . **5.** nonet
  days' devotion . . **6.** novena
  eyes . . **7.** lamprey
  gems . . **7.** Vikrama
  gods . . **9.** Etruscans
  group . . **6.** ennead, nonary **18.** Ennead of Heliopolis
  headed monster . . **5.** Hydra
  inches . . **4.** span
  number . . **5.** ennea, nueve
  pert to . . **8.** enneadic
  players . . **8.** baseball
  poetic . . **8.** ninefold
Nineteenth amendment . . . **14.** Woman's Suffrage
Nineveh (Bib) . . .
  capital . . **7.** Assyria
  famed for . . **11.** excavations (1814)
Nine Worlds (Norse) . . . **3.** Hel **6.** Asgard **7.** Alfheim, Midgard **8.** Niflheim, Vanaheim **10.** Jotunnheim

12. Muspellsheim 13. Svartalfaheim
Nine Worthies . . . 5. David, Judas
  6. Arthur, Caesar, Hector, Joshua
  7. Godfrey 9. Alexander
  11. Charlemagne
ninny . . . 4. clod, dolt, fool, nerd
  9. blockhead, simpleton
ninth . . . 5. nones (day before Ides)
  8. enneatic, ninefold 11. ennea-eteric
  (year)
Ninth of Ab (Jew) . . . 7. fast day
ninut . . . 6. magpie
Niobe (pert to) . . .
  changed by Zeus to . . 5. stone
  father . . 8. Tantalus
  husband . . 12. King of Thebes
nip . . . 3. bit, cut, sip 4. bite, clip, dram,
  peck 5. blast, cheat, check, chill, clamp,
  draft, drink, hurry, pinch, seize, sever,
  steal, thief 6. benumb, blight, catnip,
  cut off, freeze, snatch, tipple 7. shorten,
  squeeze 8. compress 10. pickpocket
nipa (pert to) . . .
  drink . . 9. alcoholic
  mat . . 6. thatch
  palm . . 4. atap
  palm sap . . 5. sugar 7. alcohol
nipcheese . . . 5. miser 6. purser
nipper . . . 3. boy, lad 4. claw, grab 5. biter,
  drink, miser, thief 6. cunner, mitten,
  urchin 7. gripper, incisor, pincers
  12. costermonger
nippers . . . 6. pliers 7. pincers 8. leg
  irons, pince-nez 9. handcuffs
nipple . . . 3. pap 4. teat 7. mamelon,
  papilla 8. mammilla 10. projection
  12. protuberance
nippy . . . 4. cold 5. brisk 6. active,
  biting 7. nipping, pungent 8. grasping,
  vigorous
Nirvana . . . 4. rags 6. heaven 8. oblivion
  12. emancipation
Nisan (Jew calendar) . . . 10. first month
  (Mar-Apr)
nisi . . . 5. if not 6. unless
nissen . . . 6. goblin, kobold 7. brownie
nisus . . . 7. impulse 8. endeavor, striving
nit . . . 3. egg 4. mite 8. parasite
nitency . . . 6. luster 10. brightness
niter, nitre . . . 6. natron 9. saltpeter
  13. sodium nitrate 16. potassium nitrate
nither . . . 5. blast 6. debase, shiver
  7. oppress, tremble 9. humiliate
nithing (anc) . . . 6. coward 7. niggard
nitid . . . 3. gay 6. bright 8. lustrous
nitric acid . . . 10. aqua fortis
nitrogen . . . 3. azo (comb form), gas
  5. azote 7. element 10. atmosphere
nitrogen compound . . . 7. ammonia
nitroglycerin, nitroglycerine . . .
  8. dynamite (1846) 9. explosive,
  guncotton
nitrous oxide . . . 3. gas 10. anesthetic
  11. laughing gas
nitty-gritty . . . 4. base, crux, gist
  7. essence
Niue, Pacific island . . .
  territory of . . 10. New Zealand
niveau . . . 5. level
niveous . . . 5. snowy, white (shining)
nix . . . 2. no 5. no one 6. forbid, nobody,

sprite 7. nothing
Njorth, Njord (Norse) . . . 3. god (fertility)
  5. Vanir
Njorth's daughter . . . 5. Freya (Freyja)
  7. goddess (love and beauty)
Njorth's son . . . 3. god 4. Frey
no . . . 3. naw, nay, nit 4. baal, dead, gone,
  none 5. not so 6. denial, no-gaki, not
  any 8. not at all
Noah, Bib (pert to) . . .
  boat . . 3. Ark
  dove . . 7. Columba
  father . . 6. Lamech
  flood . . 6. Deluge
  Genesis . . 9. patriarch
  grandson . . 4. Aram
  landing, the Ark . . 6. Ararat
  raven . . 6. Corvus
  son . . 3. Ham 4. Shem 7. Japheth
nob . . . 4. head, nave 6. hobnob
  8. nobleman 9. personage
nobby . . . 4. boat 5. smart 7. stylish
Nobel powder . . . 10. Ballistite
noble . . . 4. epic, fine, peer 5. ducal,
  grand, lofty, manly 6. epical 7. eminent,
  grandee, liberal, stately, sublime
  8. elevated, generous, imposing,
  renowned, splendid 9. dignified,
  high birth, honorable 10. impressive
  11. illustrious, magnanimous,
  magnificent 12. aristocratic
nobleman . . . 3. sir 4. duke, earl, lord,
  peer 5. baron 6. barony, flaith,
  thakur 7. baronet, grandee, marquis
  8. margrave, optimate, viscount
  9. blueblood, patrician 10. aristocrat,
  chess piece
nobleness of birth . . . 6. eugeny
noblewoman . . . 4. lady 5. begum
  7. duchess, peeress 8. baroness,
  contessa, countess, marquise
  11. marchioness
nobody . . . 4. none 5. no one 7. nebbish
  8. no person 9. jackstraw, nonentity
  10. not anybody
nocent . . . 6. guilty 7. harmful, hurtful
  8. criminal (opp of innocent)
nocturnal . . . 5. night 7. nightly
  8. darkness, nocturne
nocturnal (pert to) . . .
  animal . . 3. bat 4. coon 5. lemur, ratel
  6. possum 7. opossum
  astronomy . . 9. astrolabe
  bird . . 3. owl
  signs . . 8. zodiacal
nocturne . . . 7. lullaby 8. serenade
  10. night scene (art)
nocuous . . . 7. hurtful, noxious
nod . . . 3. bow 4. bend, bock, doze,
  tend, wink 6. beckon, signal 7. bidding
  8. greeting
Nod (Bib) . . . 9. Land of Nod 10. East
  of Eden
nodding . . . 6. nutant 7. annuent, weeping
  (as a willow) 8. cernuous, drooping
noddy . . . 3. auk 4. fool 6. drowsy, fulmar,
  noodle, sleepy 7. foolish, hackney
  9. simpleton
node . . . 4. knob, knot, knur, plot
  5. joint, nodus 7. dilemma 8. swelling
  10. difficulty 12. complication,

protuberance

nodule . . . **4.** auge, bump, knot, lump, mass **5.** geode **7.** granule, nablock **8.** tubercle **12.** complication

nodus . . . **4.** knot, node **10.** difficulty **12.** complication

noel . . . **5.** carol (Xmas), shout **9.** sign of joy

Noel . . . **6.** Natale **9.** Christmas

noeud . . . **3.** bow **4.** knot

nog . . . **3.** peg, pin **5.** block **6.** eggnog, noggin **8.** treenail **9.** brickwork

nogada . . . **10.** pecan candy

nogal . . . **5.** pecan

noggin . . . **3.** cup, mug **4.** head, pate

noise . . . **3.** din, pop, rap **4.** bang, boom, klop, roar, rout **5.** blare, blast, bruit, chang, clang, click, rumor, sound **6.** clamor, outcry, racket, report, strife, uproar **7.** brattle, chortle, discord, quarrel, rapping **9.** shoutings

noise (pert to) . . .
ghost . . **11.** poltergeist
harsh . . **4.** bray **7.** stridor **9.** caterwaul
respiration . . **4.** rale
rustling . . **5.** swish
Scotch . . **5.** chang
water . . **5.** plash **6.** ripple, splash
whirring . . **4.** burr

noised . . . **6.** dinned **7.** rumored **8.** reported

noisemaker . . . **4.** horn **5.** siren **6.** rattle **7.** clacker, whistle **8.** whiz-bang

noisome . . . **3.** bad **4.** foul **5.** fetid, nasty **7.** harmful, noxious **8.** stinking **9.** offensive **10.** malodorous, pernicious **11.** destructive, unwholesome **12.** insalubrious

noisy . . . **4.** loud **7.** blatant **8.** brawling, clattery **9.** clamorous, turbulent **10.** blustering, boisterous, vociferous **12.** obstreperous, rattley-bang

nom . . . **4.** name

nomad . . . **4.** arab **5.** gypsy **6.** roamer, Romany **7.** Bedouin, Saracen, scenite, zingaro **8.** wanderer

nomadic . . . **9.** itinerant

nomarchy (Gr) . . . **4.** nome **8.** province **10.** department

nom de plume . . . **7.** pen name **9.** pseudonym

nomen . . . **4.** gens, name **7.** agnomen **8.** cognomen **9.** praenomen

nomenclature . . . **4.** name **5.** onymy **8.** glossary, onymatic, register **10.** dictionary, Latin names, vocabulary **11.** designation, terminology

nominal . . . **3.** par **6.** unreal **7.** not real, titular, topical **8.** so-called

nominal recognizance (law) . . . **3.** Doe

nonage . . . **6.** neanic **8.** immature, minority, pupilage, youthful

nonary . . . **9.** nine group **10.** base of nine **11.** group of nine

nonbeliever . . . **5.** pagan **7.** atheist, heathen, infidel **8.** agnostic **11.** disbeliever **12.** non-Christian

nonce . . . **3.** now **8.** meantime **11.** temporarily

nonchalant . . . **4.** cool **6.** casual **8.** careless **10.** insouciant **11.** indifferent,

unconcerned **13.** imperturbable

noncompliance . . . **7.** refusal **12.** disobedience **13.** recalcitrance

non compos mentis . . . **7.** unsound **8.** demented, deranged **11.** disoriented

nonconformist . . . **7.** heretic, sectary **8.** objector, recusant **9.** dissenter, protester

nondescript . . . **11.** exceptional **13.** indescribable **14.** indeterminable

none . . . **2.** no **4.** nary **5.** nones, no one **6.** nobody, not any, not one **10.** nobody else

nonentity . . . **7.** a nobody, nullity **8.** nihility, nonbeing **9.** res nihili **11.** nothingness **12.** nonexistence

nonessential . . . **8.** needless **9.** extrinsic **10.** adiaphoron, incidental, irrelevant **11.** superfluous **12.** adventitious

non licit . . . **8.** unlawful

nonmetallic . . . **4.** spar **5.** argon, boron **6.** carbon, helium, iodine, oxygen **7.** bromine **8.** chlorine, nitrogen

nonpareil . . . **4.** type **7.** paragon **8.** nonesuch, peerless **9.** unrivaled **11.** unsurpassed **14.** painted bunting

nonplus . . . **4.** stop **5.** blank, stump **6.** baffle, puzzle, thwart **7.** mystify, perplex **8.** quandary

nonproductive . . . **6.** barren **7.** sterile **9.** fruitless

nonprofessional . . . **3.** ham, lay **4.** laic **5.** laity **7.** amateur **10.** apprentice

nonsense . . . **3.** bah **4.** bosh, bunk, tosh **5.** folly, stite **6.** drivel, humbug, jargon **7.** blarney, foolery, rubbish, trifles, twaddle **8.** falderal, flimflam, tommyrot, trumpery **9.** absurdity, frivolity, poppycock, silliness **10.** balderdash, tomfoolery, triviality

nonsense verse . . . **9.** amphigory (amphigouri), rigmarole

non tanto (Mus) . . . **9.** non troppo, not as much

noodle . . . **4.** fool, head **5.** brain, ninny **9.** blockhead, simpleton **12.** stupid person

nook . . . **4.** cant, cove **5.** angle, herne, niche **6.** corner, cranny, recess **7.** crevice **10.** promontory

noon . . . **6.** midday, summit **8.** meridian, noontide **9.** ninth hour **11.** noon of night (poet)

noonday rest . . . **6.** siesta

noose . . . **3.** tie **4.** bond, hang, loop **5.** snare **6.** circle, halter **7.** laniard (lanyard) **12.** hangman's rope

Nootka . . . **3.** Aht, dog **6.** Indian

norati . . . **5.** noise **6.** gossip

Norbertine . . . **12.** Premonstrant

Nordic . . . **8.** Germanic **12.** Scandinavian

norie . . . **9.** cormorant

norm . . . **4.** rule, type **5.** model, norma **7.** average, measure, pattern **8.** standard, template

norma . . . **4.** rule **5.** gauge, model **6.** square **7.** pattern **8.** standard, template **13.** constellation

normal . . . **3.** par **4.** just, mean, sane **5.** usual **6.** common **7.** average, logical, natural, orderly, regular, typical

8. everyday, ordinary 9. customary
Norman ... 6. French 7. crimson
8. Northman 10. Romanesque
17. conquest of England (1066)
Normandy ...
beach .. 5. Omaha
capital .. 4. Caen 5. Rouen (old)
city .. 5. Havre 6. Dieppe 7. Alençon
9. Cherbourg
conqueror .. 5. Rollo 8. William I
governed by .. 6. France (1940)
Viking duke (anc) .. 5. Rollo
Norn (Teut Myth) ... 4. Urth, Wyrd
5. Skuld 9. Verthandi
Norse ... 9. Norwegian 12. Scandinavian
Norse (pert to) ...
abode of gods .. 6. Asgard 8. Valhalla
alphabet .. 6. runics
ash tree, universe .. 10. Yddrasill
bard .. 5. scald (skald) 7. sagaman
collected songs, myths .. 4. Edda
demon (Fire) .. 4. Surt (Surtr)
earth .. 7. Midgard
epic .. 4. saga
explorer .. 11. Leif Ericson
first man .. 4. Askr
giant .. 4. Loki, Ymir (Ymer) 5. Jotun
6. Fafnir
horse .. 8. Brimfaxi 9. Skinfaksi
horse (Odin's) .. 10. Yggdrasill
king .. 4. Atli
language (old) .. 9. Icelandic
maidens (Odin's) .. 8. Valkyrie
man .. 8. Northman
monster .. 6. kraken 7. Midgard
patron saint .. 4. Olaf
poem .. 4. rune
toast .. 5. skoal
warrior .. 9. berserker
watchdog (Hel's) .. 4. Garm (Garmr)
wolf .. 6. Fenrir
Norse goddess of ...
death, underworld .. 3. Hel, Ran
fate .. 4. Norn, Urth, Wyrd
flowers .. 5. Nanna
giantess .. 4. Nott
love, beauty .. 5. Freya
peace, healing .. 3. Eir
sky .. 5. Frigg (Frigga)
Norse God of ...
day .. 3. Dag
evil .. 4. Loki
fertility .. 4. Frey (Freyr) 6. Njorth (Njord)
giants .. 4. Ymir
justice .. 4. Frey 7. Forseti
light .. 6. Balder
night .. 4. Nott
poetry .. 4. Odin 5. Bragi
primeval (the world) .. 4. Ymir (Ymer)
sea .. 5. Aegir
thunder .. 4. Thor
war, wisdom .. 4. Odin (Wodin)
watchfulness .. 8. Heimdall
Norse gods, chief ... 3. Tyr (Tiu) 4. Frey,
Jarl, Loki, Odin (Othin, Wodin), Thor
(Donar), Vali, Ymir 5. Aesir (group)
6. Balder, Njorth 7. Asynjur (group),
Forseti 8. Heimdall
North (far) ... 6. Arctic
North Africa ... see also Africa
country .. 7. Algeria, Tunisia

fruit .. 3. fig 4. date
people .. 4. Moor 6. Berber, Hamite,
Libyan
port .. 4. Sfax
North America ... see also America
Indian blanket .. 6. stroud
mountain, highest .. 8. McKinley
orchid .. 8. arethusa
owl .. 7. wapacut
rail .. 4. sora
reindeer .. 7. caribou
river, longest .. 5. Yukon 8. Missouri
11. Mississippi
snake .. 5. adder
North Atlantic (pert to) ...
cape .. 5. Sable
island .. 7. Britain, Iceland, Ireland
9. Greenland, Manhattan
sea gull .. 4. skua
North Carolina ...
cape .. 4. Fear 7. Lookout 8. Hatteras
capital .. 7. Raleigh
city .. 6. Durham 9. Asheville, Charlotte
12. Winston-Salem
explorer .. 6. De Soto 9. Verrazano
famed person .. 12. Virginia Dare 16. Sir
Walter Raleigh
first flight .. 9. Kitty Hawk
mountain .. 10. Mt Mitchell
pine .. 8. loblolly
river .. 3. Tar 5. Neuse 6. Peedee (Yadkin)
State admission .. 7. Twelfth
State bird .. 8. cardinal
State flower .. 7. dogwood
State motto .. 14. Esse Quam Videri
20. To Be Rather Than To Seem
State nickname .. 7. Tarheel 8. Old
North
North Dakota ...
capital .. 8. Bismarck
city .. 5. Fargo, Minot
fort .. 6. Mandan 7. Lincoln
11. Abercrombie
historic site .. 24. International Peace
Garden
mountain .. 10. White Butte
reservoir .. 8. Garrison
State admission .. 8. Fortieth (or
Thirty-ninth)
State bird .. 10. meadowlark
State flower .. 11. prairie rose
State nickname .. 5. Sioux 11. Flickertail
northeaster ... 4. gale, wind 5. storm
Northern ... 6. boreal 11. hyperborean
13. septentrional
Northern constellation ... 3. Cor 4. Lyra
9. Andromeda
northernmost world (inhabitable) ...
5. Thule 9. Trondheim
North Pole ... 10. boreal pole
North Sea ... 6. Baltic, German
North Sea arm ... 8. Kattegat
9. Skagerrak (Skager-Rak)
North Sea canal ... 4. Kiel
North Star ... 7. Polaris 8. Cynosure,
lodestar (loadstar), polestar
north wind ... 6. Boreas 10. tramontane
Norway ... see also Norwegian
capital .. 4. Oslo 11. Christiania (old)
city .. 6. Bergen 7. Drammen
9. Trondheim

county.. **5.** fylke
inlet.. **5.** fiord (fjord)
mountain.. **6.** Kjolen
parliament.. **8.** Storting (Storthing)
patron saint.. **4.** Olaf (Olaus)
phenomenon.. **11.** midnight sun
   14. Northern Lights
plateau.. **5.** fjeld
river.. **2.** Oi **4.** Tana **7.** Glommen
Norwegian (pert to)...
bird.. **4.** rype **9.** ptarmigan
cart.. **11.** stolkjaerre
dance.. **7.** halling
duck.. **7.** widgeon
embroidery.. **9.** hardanger
goblin.. **5.** Nisse **6.** kobold
guardian spirit.. **6.** fylgia **8.** hamingja
haddock.. **8.** rosefish
language.. **5.** Norse **8.** Rigsmaal
   9. Landsmaal
liquor.. **7.** akevitt
sea monster.. **6.** kraken
tales.. **4.** Edda
Norwegian people...
author.. **6.** Hamsun, Undset
composer.. **5.** Grieg
dramatist.. **5.** Ibsen
explorer.. **6.** Nansen (Nobel Prize)
   8. Sverdrup
king.. **6.** Harold (The Fairhaired)
   15. Harold Hardraade
philologist.. **5.** Assen
raiders.. **7.** Vikings
saint.. **4.** Olaf (Olaus)
violinist.. **7.** Ole Bull
zoologist.. **4.** Sars
nose... **3.** neb, pry **4.** conk, prow
   5. nasus, scent, smell, snout **6.** meddle,
   muzzle, nuzzle **8.** olfactor **9.** detective,
   proboscis **11.** investigate
nose (pert to)...
ailment.. **6.** coryza **8.** rhinitis
bees, birds.. **4.** lore **5.** lorum
bleeding.. **9.** epistaxis
cartilage.. **6.** septum
glasses.. **8.** pince-nez
large.. **6.** nasute
muscle.. **7.** nasalis
opening.. **5.** naris (nares, pl) **7.** nostril
partition.. **5.** vomer
plug.. **12.** rhineurynter
relating to.. **5.** nasal **6.** narial, rhinal
snub.. **6.** simous
surgery.. **11.** rhinoplasty
noseband (bridle)... **6.** misrol
nosegay... **4.** posy **7.** bouquet, perfume
   9. fragrance **10.** frangipani (tree)
nosh... **3.** eat
nosocomium... **8.** hospital
nosography, nosology (science of)...
   7. disease
nostalgia... **8.** yearning **11.** wistfulness
   12. homesickness **14.** sentimentality
nostology (study of)... **8.** senility
   10. geriatrics **11.** gerontology
Nostradamus... **4.** seer **7.** prophet
   10. astrologer
nostril... **5.** naris (nares, pl) **6.** narial
   9. olfactory
nostril-shaped... **8.** nariform
nosy... **5.** nasal **6.** prying **7.** curious

8. fragrant **10.** malodorous
   11. inquisitive
Nosy, Old (nickname)... **16.** Duke of
   Wellington
not (pert to)...
any.. **2.** no **4.** nane, nary, none **7.** no
   trace
at all.. **5.** nohow **6.** nowise
easy.. **7.** labored
either.. **7.** neither
feral.. **4.** tame
harmed.. **9.** unscathed
having a will.. **9.** intestate
hollow.. **5.** solid
in motion.. **5.** fixed **6.** stable, static
   7. stabile **10.** stationary
in the least.. **6.** nowhit
moral.. **6.** amoral **7.** immoral
open (fruit).. **11.** indehiscent
prefix.. **2.** il, im, in, ir, un **3.** non
professional.. **4.** laic **7.** amateur
qualified.. **5.** unfit
running (stream).. **8.** stagnant
separable.. **11.** indivisible
settled.. **4.** moot
subjugated.. **7.** unbowed
suitable.. **5.** inept
the same.. **5.** other **9.** different
to know.. **5.** unken **10.** unfamiliar
notable... **6.** famous **8.** historic
   9. celebrity, important, memorable,
   notorious **10.** noteworthy, remarkable
   13. distinguished, extraordinary
notandum... **4.** note **5.** entry
   10. memorandum
notary... **5.** notar **8.** attestor, notebook,
   official **9.** scrivener **12.** notary public,
   stenographer
notation... **4.** memo, note **5.** entry
   7. comment, marking **9.** etymology
   10. annotation
notator... **5.** noter **8.** recorder
   9. annotator
notch... **3.** gap, jap **4.** dent, dint,
   kerf, nick, nock **5.** cleft, crena, score
   6. defile, dentil (Her), indent **7.** passage
   8. undercut **9.** indenture **11.** indentation
notched bar (door)... **4.** risp
notched opening (Anat)... **5.** hilum
note... **2.** ut **3.** jot **4.** chit, heed,
   mark, memo, sign, sole, song, tone,
   tune **5.** breve, gloss, sound, token
   6. billet, notice, postil, record, remark,
   report **7.** apostil (apostille), comment,
   epistle **8.** dispatch, eminence, indicate,
   marginal, scholium **9.** character
   10. annotation, importance, indication,
   memorandum, reputation **11.** certificate,
   observation
note (pert to)...
death sound.. **4.** mort
explanatory.. **5.** gloss **8.** scholium
half.. **5.** minim
high.. **3.** alt, E la
marginal.. **6.** postil **7.** apostil (apostille)
musical.. **5.** breve **6.** ecbole **7.** punctus
stem of.. **5.** filum
notebook... **6.** street **7.** estreat
   8. ratebook **10.** adversaria,
   memorandum
noted... **4.** seen **5.** famed **6.** famous,

marked 7. eminent, notable 8. far-
famed, renowned 9. distingué,
prominent, well-known 10. celebrated

notes . . . 5. duole 6. strain 7. tiralee
11. solmization

nothing . . . 3. nil, nox 4. luke, rien,
void, zero 5. nihil 6. naught, nichil,
nought, trifle 7. a nobody 9. nonentity
11. empty-handed 12. nonexistence

nothing doing . . . 4. calm 6. hushed, no
dice, no soap, placid 7. I refuse 9. by
no means, God forbid, quiescent

notice . . . 2. ad 3. see 4. heed, idea, mark,
mind, news, note, sign 5. blurb, edict,
quote 6. advice, espial, notion, regard,
remark 7. affiche, mention, observe,
warning 8. bulletin, citation 9. attention
10. commentary 11. information,
observation 12. announcement,
intelligence 13. advertisement

notice (pert to) . . .
advance . . 8. ballyhoo
death . . 4. obit 8. obituary
marriage . . 4. bans 5. banns

notify . . . 4. cite, page, tell, warn 6. inform,
remind 7. apprise, declare, publish
8. announce

notion . . . 4. idea, view, whim 5. freit
6. belief, theory, vagary 7. caprice,
impulse, opinion 9. intention
10. conception, denotation, knickknack
11. supposition

notionable . . . 8. fanciful 9. whimsical

notional . . . 6. unreal 9. imaginary,
visionary, whimsical

notions . . . 5. goods, wares
11. commodities, merchandise

notoriety . . . 4. fame, plug 5. éclat
8. ballyhoo 9. limelight, publicity,
spotlight

notorious . . . 5. known, noted 6. arrant,
famous, notour 8. flagrant, infamous,
talked of 10. recognized 11. conspicuous

notorious character . . . 5. James (Jesse)
7. Cochise, Younger 8. Geronimo,
Jennings, Murietta 9. Jack Ketch, Wyatt
Earp 11. Billy the Kid, Poncho Villa,
Sitting Bull 12. Calamity Jane 13. John
Dillinger 14. Wild Bill Hickok

notum . . . 4. back

notus . . . 4. back (comb form)

notwithstanding . . . 3. but, yet 5. still
6. mauger (maugre), though 7. despite,
however 8. although 9. in spite of
12. nevertheless

nought, naught . . . 3. bad, nil 4. zero
5. wrong 7. nothing, useless
9. worthless

noughty . . . 3. bad 9. worthless

noumenal . . . 4. real 5. ontal (opp of
phenomenal)

noun . . . 7. subject

noun (pert to) . . .
gender, common . . 7. epicene
indeclinable . . 6. aptote
irregular . . 5. pecus 11. heteroclite
suffix . . 2. et, ia 3. ent, ery, ier, ion,
ior, ist, ite 4. ence
verbal . . 6. gerund

nourish . . . 4. feed, grow 5. nurse 6. foster,
suckle, supply 7. support, sustain

9. cultivate 13. promote growth

nourishing . . . 6. alible 8. nutrient
9. nutritive 10. alimentary

nourishment . . . 3. aid 4. food 5. manna,
meats 7. aliment, pabulum 9. nutriment,
nutrition 10. sustenance
13. nutritiveness 14. nutritiousness

nous . . . 4. mind 8. ready wit 9. intellect
11. world spirit

Nova . . . 4. star

Nova Scotia . . .
bay . . 5. Fundy 10. Chedabucto
cape . . 5. Canso
capital . . 7. Halifax
greens . . 11. sea plantain
island . . 10. Cape Breton
lake, salt . . 7. Bras d'Or
native . . 7. Acadian 8. Bluenose
poetic name . . 6. Acadia (Acadie)
settlement, first . . 9. Port Royal

novel . . . 3. new 4. book, rare 5. fresh,
story 7. fiction, romance, strange,
unusual 8. original

novelty . . . 3. fad 7. newness 9. freshness
10. innovation, recentness
11. originality

novice . . . 3. nun 4. tyro (tiro) 5. chela
6. rookie, tyrone 7. amateur, learner
8. beginner, freshman, initiate,
neophyte, newcomer 9. fledgling,
greenhorn, postulant 10. apprentice,
catechumen 11. abecedarian

novitiate . . . 6. novice 9. probation
14. apprenticeship

now . . . 3. noo 4. here 6. at once
7. present 9. at present, forthwith,
instantly 10. very lately 12. at this
moment

nowhere . . . 5. limbo 6. absent 7. no place
8. oblivion 9. nowhither 11. nonexistent,
not anywhere, nullibicity

nowhere else . . . 5. there

nowise . . . 8. not at all

Nox (pert to) . . .
brother . . 6. Erebus
daughter . . 10. Hesperides
goddess (Rom) . . 5. Night
husband . . 5. Chaos

noxious . . . 4. evil 5. nasty, yucky
(sl) 6. nocent, odious 7. baneful,
harmful, hurtful, noisome 9. injurious,
miasmatic 10. corruptive, pernicious
11. destructive, unwholesome
12. insalubrious

nozzle . . . 3. tew 4. nose, vent 5. giant,
snout 6. nuzzle, outlet, tuyère 7. conduit
9. sprinkler

nuance . . . 5. shade 9. gradation, variation
10. refinement

nub . . . 4. gist, knob, knot, knub,
lump, neck, snag 9. main point
12. protuberance

Nubia (pert to) . . .
afterglow . . 14. second twilight
animal . . 4. goat 5. horse
autonym . . 6. Berber 7. Barabra
harp . . 5. nanga
people . . 4. Nuba

nubia . . . 4. wrap 5. cloud

nucha . . . 4. nape, neck

nuclear complex . . . 7. Oedipus

nuclear energy (terms)... **4.** mass **6.** fusion, ionize **7.** fission, neutron, reactor, tokamak **8.** hydrogen, meltdown

nuclear network fiber... **5.** linin

nucleus... **4.** core **5.** cadre, focus, umbra **6.** center, kernel **8.** rudiment

nude... **4.** bare **5.** color, naked **6.** Season (color) **7.** denuded **8.** stripped, undraped **9.** unadorned, unclothed, undressed

nudge... **3.** jog, nog **4.** knub, lump, poke, prod, push **5.** block, elbow **6.** jostle, remind, signal

nudibranch... **7.** mollusk

nugatory... **4.** vain **7.** invalid, trivial **8.** trifling **9.** worthless **11.** ineffectual

nuisance... **4.** bane, bore, harm, hurt, pest **6.** injury **9.** annoyance

nuit... **5.** night

null... **4.** void **6.** vacant **7.** invalid **8.** nugatory **11.** nonexistent **13.** inefficacious, insignificant

nullifidian... **7.** skeptic **9.** nullibist, skeptical **10.** unbeliever **11.** disbeliever

nullify... **4.** undo, void **5.** annul **6.** cancel, negate **7.** abolish, destroy **8.** abrogate **10.** counteract, neutralize

numb... **6.** clumsy, freeze, stupid, torpid **8.** benumbed, deadened, helpless **9.** apathetic, incapable, rigescent **10.** insensible **12.** anesthetized

number... **3.** sum **5.** count, digit, limit **7.** integer, numeral **8.** quantity **9.** aggregate, enumerate **10.** complement **11.** information

number (pert to)...
added.. **6.** encore
again.. **10.** renumerate
by tens.. **7.** decimal
cardinal.. **7.** primary (one, two)
consecutively.. **5.** folio
copies (printed).. **7.** edition
describable.. **6.** scalar
irrational.. **4.** surd
least whole.. **4.** unit
lucky.. **5.** seven
many.. **4.** herd **6.** myriad **7.** several **9.** multitude **12.** considerable
ordinal.. **5.** first **6.** second (etc)
third power.. **4.** cube
votes.. **4.** poll
whole.. **7.** integer

numbles, nombles... **6.** umbles **7.** inwards **8.** entrails

numbness... **6.** torpor **10.** rigescence

numeral... **5.** Roman **6.** Arabic, figure **9.** character

numerous... **4.** lots, many **7.** copious, crowded **8.** abundant, measured, thronged **9.** plentiful

Numidia (pert to)...
city.. **5.** Hippo
crane.. **10.** demoiselle
language (written).. **5.** Punic **6.** Tuareg **7.** Hamitic
modern kingdom.. **7.** Algeria

numskull... **4.** dolt, nerd **5.** dunce

nun... **4.** moth, smew **5.** Clare (Franciscan), Vesta **6.** monial, pigeon, sister **8.** titmouse, votaress **9.** priestess **13.** Lady of Loretto

nun bird... **6.** Monasa **8.** puffbird

nunciate... **9.** announcer, messenger

nuncio... **6.** legate **8.** delegate **9.** messenger **11.** internuncio

nuncupate... **7.** declare **8.** dedicate, inscribe, proclaim **9.** designate

nuncupative... **4.** oral **9.** unwritten (will) **11.** designative

nun headdress... **6.** wimple

nunnari root... **12.** sarsaparilla

nunnery... **5.** abbey **7.** convent **8.** cloister

nunnery head... **6.** abbess

nunni... **7.** blesbok (blesbuck) **8.** antelope

Nuphar... **11.** spatterdock

nuptial... **6.** bridal **7.** marital **9.** connubial **11.** matrimonial

nurse... **4.** amah, ayah, feed, rear, tend **5.** bonne, mammy **6.** caress, suckle **7.** care for, cherish, nourish, nurture, nutrice **9.** nursemaid

nursed... **3.** fed **6.** tended **7.** cradled, suckled **8.** nurtured **9.** nourished

nursery... **6.** crèche, school **7.** day care (center)

nurse shark... **4.** gata

nurture... **3.** aid **4.** feed, rear **5.** nurse **6.** foster **7.** care for, cherish **8.** breeding, training **9.** education, encourage, nutriment

nut... **4.** anta, kola (cola) **5.** acorn, betel, pecan, piñon **6.** almond, Brazil, cashew, litchi, peanut, walnut **7.** filbert, hickory, maranon **8.** beechnut, chestnut **9.** butternut

nut (pert to)...
bearing.. **10.** nuciferous
brown.. **5.** hazel **6.** walnut **8.** chestnut
coal.. **10.** anthracite
collectively.. **4.** food **5.** shack **9.** beechnuts
confection.. **8.** marzipan
cracker.. **4.** crow
eating.. **10.** nucivorous **11.** nuciphagous
edible part.. **6.** kernel
grass.. **5.** sedge
Med.. **4.** kola **5.** bichy **9.** gourounut
odd.. **8.** eccentric
palm.. **5.** betel, lichi **7.** coconut
ref to.. **5.** nucal
shell.. **4.** case, hull **6.** trifle

Nut (pert to)...
consort of.. **3.** Geb
daughter.. **4.** Isis **8.** Nephthys
goddess of.. **5.** earth
son.. **2.** Ra

nutation... **3.** nod **7.** nodding

nuthatch... **4.** bird **5.** sitta **6.** xenops **8.** titmouse **9.** nutpecker

nutmeg... **4.** mace **5.** drupe **6.** beaver (color)

nutmeg (pert to)...
bird, finch.. **5.** cowry **10.** weaverbird
family.. **13.** Myristicaceae
tree.. **6.** camara

Nutmeg State... **11.** Connecticut

nutpecker... **8.** nuthatch

nut quad... **6.** en quad

nutria... **3.** fur **5.** grège **10.** beaverlike

nutria fur bearer... **5.** coypu

nutrice... **5.** nurse

nutriment... **4.** food **7.** aliment, pabulum

9. nutrition 11. nourishment
nutritious . . . 9. alimental 10. alimentary, nourishing
nuts . . . 4. food, mast 5. shack 9. beechnuts
nut's partner . . . 4. bolt
nutty . . . 4. gaga, zest 5. queer, smart, spicy 7. amorous, piquant 10. unbalanced 11. fascinating 14. cracker-brained
nuzzle . . . 5. nurse 6. burrow, cuddle, foster, nestle 7. cherish 8. make snug
nyctalopia . . . 14. night blindness
nye . . . 4. eyas, nest, nide 5. brood
nymph . . . 4. nais 5. deity, dryad, naiad, oread, siren, sylph 6. Nereid 7. Oceanid 9. hamadryad
nymph (pert to) . . .
  Arcadian . . 6. Syrinx
  beloved of Narcissus . . 4. Echo
  color . . 4. pink
  Cretan . . 8. Cynosura
  fountain, river . . 4. nais 5. naiad 6. Egeria
  German legend . . 7. Lorelei
  Greek . . 4. Echo 6. Daphne 8. Arethusa
  Hesperides (one of) . . 5. Aegle 7. Hespera

  hills, mountain . . 5. oread
  laurel tree . . 6. Daphne
  Messina Strait . . 6. Scylla
  monster . . 6. Scylla
  Mt Ida . . 6. Oenone
  Muslim paradise . . 5. houri
  ocean . . 5. siren 6. Nereid 7. Galatea, Oceanid 10. Callirrhoe
  pursued by Apollo . . 6. Daphne, Syrinx 8. Arethusa
  Queen . . 3. Mab
  sea bird . . 6. Scylla
  tree . . 5. Dryad 9. Hamadryad
  water . . 5. Naiad 6. Undine 7. Hydriad
  woods . . 5. Dryad 8. Arethusa 9. Hamadryad
  young . . 7. nymphet
Nymphaea . . . 8. Castalia 11. water lilies
nymphs . . . 10. Atlantides, Hesperides
nystagmus . . . 14. eyeball disease
Nyx, Nox (pert to) . . .
  daughter . . 4. Eris
  father . . 5. Chaos
  goddess of . . 5. Night
  mother of . . 11. Day and Night
Nzambi . . . 7. goddess (Afr) 11. earth mother

O

O (pert to) . . .
  interjection . . 11. exclamation
  letter . . 5. tenth
  mathematics . . 4. zero 6. cipher
  pref (family) . . 5. Irish
oaf . . . 4. boor, dolt, lout 5. idiot, ouphe, yokel 9. blockhead, simpleton 10. changeling
oafish . . . 6. simple, stupid
oak . . . 4. club 5. brave, color, oaken, stout 6. strong 7. Quercus 8. hardness, strength 13. artificial fly
oak (pert to) . . .
  apple . . 4. gall 10. she-oak cone
  beauty . . 4. moth
  California . . 5. roble 6. encina
  comb form . . 6. querci
  evergreen . . 4. holm, ilex 5. holly
  family . . 8. Fagaceae
  fern . . 8. polypody
  fruit . . 5. acorn 6. camata
  fungus . . 10. armillaria
  gall . . 8. oak apple
  Jerusalem . . 7. ambrose
  kinds . . 3. bur, red 5. black, white 6. ground, poison, willow 8. chestnut 10. canyon live
  plantation . . 9. quercetum
  resembling . . 9. roboreous
  tannin . . 7. quercic 9. quercinic
  thicket . . 9. chaparral
  Turkey . . 6. cerris
  web . . 10. cockchafer
  young . . 8. flittern
oam . . . 5. steam 7. warm air

Oannes (Bab) . . . 5. deity (part man, part fish)
oar . . . 3. row 5. blade, remus, rower, scull 6. paddle, propel 7. oarsman
oar (pert to) . . .
  blade . . 4. palm, peel
  feather . . 5. remex
  fulcrum, lock . . 5. pivot, thole
  lop . . 6. rabbit
  shaft . . 4. loom
  shaped . . 7. remiped 8. remiform
oars (pert to) . . .
  collective . . 6. oarage, sculls
  one bank . . 7. unireme
  reverse . . 6. sheave
  three banks . . 7. trireme
  two banks . . 6. bireme
oasis . . . 3. ojo 4. wadi (wady) 5. Gafsa 6. Dakhla 11. fertile spot
oast . . . 4. kiln, oven
oat (pert to) . . .
  cake . . 5. caper
  ear (Old World) . . 4. bird 7. wagtail
  fowl . . 11. snow bunting
  genus . . 5. Avena 6. oathay
  grass . . 4. ulla 9. chaparral
  husks . . 5. shood (shude)
  like . . 10. avenaceous
  rent (paid as) . . 7. avenage
oath . . . 3. God 4. aith, drat, egad 5. bedad, curse 6. pledge 7. serment 9. affidavit, holy smoke, profanity 10. deposition 11. affirmation
Obadiah (Bib) . . . 6. Quaker 7. prophet
obbligato . . . 8. required

13. accompaniment, indispensable

obduction . . . 7. autopsy 8. covering

obdurate . . . 4. firm, hard 5. rough, stony
6. mulish, rugged 7. adamant, callous
8. stubborn 9. heartless, obstinate,
unbending, unfeeling 10. impenitent,
inflexible, insensible, unyielding
11. hardhearted, intractable

obedient . . . 6. docile 7. duteous,
dutiful, orderly 8. amenable, yielding
9. attentive, compliant 10. submissive
11. conformable

obeisance . . . 3. bow 5. binge, congé
6. curtsy, fealty, homage 9. deference
10. respectful 14. obsequiousness

obeisance, to make . . . 3. bow 6. congee,
curtsy, salaam

obelisk . . . 5. pylon 6. guglia (guglio),
needle, obelus, pillar 16. Cleopatra's
Needle

Oberon (pert to) . . .
  Astron . . 9. satellite
  character of . . 11. Shakespeare
  classic . . 4. poem 5. opera
  husband of . . 7. Titania
  Myth . . 13. King of Fairies

obese . . . 3. fat 5. puffy, pursy, squab,
stout 6. fleshy, turgid 8. liparous
9. corpulent

obey . . . 3. ear 4. hear, mind 5. yield
6. comply, submit

obfuscate . . . 3. dim 6. darken, opaque
7. confuse, perplex 8. bewilder

obi . . . 4. sash 6. girdle

obit . . . 4. rest 5. death 6. notice
7. decease, release 8. obituary
9. obsequies 10. necrologue
11. Requiem Mass 12. mortuary roll

obiter . . . 9. in passing 12. incidentally

obiter dictum . . . 7. opinion (of judge)

object . . . 3. aim, end 4. goal, hulk 5. cavil,
demur, scoff, thing 6. appose, expose,
motive, oppose 7. article, grammar,
protest, purpose 9. intention

object (pert to) . . .
  bulky . . 4. hulk
  circular . . 7. trundle
  cloudlike . . 6. nebula
  illustrative . . 6. realia (pl)
  rare . . 5. curio 7. antique
  rational . . 8. noumenon
  sacred . . 4. Urim 7. Thummim
  small . . 4. mite

object for . . .
  devotion, worship . . 4. icon, idol 5. totem
  6. fetish
  dread . . 5. bogey (bogie) 6. goblin 8. the
  Devil
  going and coming . . 6. errand
  greed . . 5. lucre, money 6. wealth
  knowledge . . 7. scibile

objection . . . 3. bar 5. cavil 7. protest,
quarrel 8. demurrer, obstacle
9. exception 11. disapproval

objectionable . . . 9. offensive
11. exceptional, inexpedient
13. uncommendable

objective . . . 3. aim, end 4. goal 6. motive,
target 7. purpose

objector, conscientious . . . 6. conchy

objects (Bib) . . . 4. Urim 7. Thummim

objects (floating) . . . 7. flotsam

objurgate . . . 5. abuse, chide, scold
6. rebuke 7. reprove, upbraid
9. reprimand

oblate . . . 5. oblat 7. devoted 9. dedicated,
flattened (opp of prolate)

obligated . . . 5. bound 6. in debt
7. obliged 8. beholden 9. obstringe

obligation . . . 3. tie, vow 4. bond, debt,
duty, oath, onus 7. promise 8. civility,
contract 9. agreement, necessity
10. compulsion 11. obstriction

obligatory . . . 7. binding 8. imposing,
required 9. mandatory, necessary
10. compulsory

oblige . . . 4. bind, pawn 5. favor
6. compel, engage 7. gratify 8. obligate
9. constrain, obstringe
11. accommodate

obliged . . . 7. favored 8. beholden,
grateful 9. duty bound

obliging . . . 4. kind 7. helpful 9. agreeable,
courteous, indulgent 11. complaisant,
considerate 13. accommodating

oblique . . . 4. cant, skew 5. bevel, slant,
slope 7. obscure, scalene 8. inclined,
perverse, sidelong, sidewise, sinister,
slanting 9. underhand 10. circuitous,
collateral, transverse 12. disingenuous

oblique angle . . . 5. acute 6. obtuse

obliquely . . . 4. skew 6. aslant 7. askance
8. sideways, sidewise 9. on the bias
10. slantingly

obliterate . . . 4. blot, dele 5. erase
6. cancel, delete, efface, sponge
7. expunge

obliteration . . . 6. rasure 7. erasure
8. deletion 10. extinction

oblivion . . . 7. nirvana, silence 9. unfeeling
13. forgetfulness 15. unconsciousness

oblivion, producing . . . 8. nepenthe

oblivion, river of . . . 5. Lethe

oblivious . . . 6. asleep 8. heedless
9. forgetful, unfeeling 10. abstracted
11. unconscious

oblong . . . 8. elliptic 9. elongated
11. rectangular 12. quadrangular

obloquy . . . 5. abuse 6. infamy 7. calumny
9. criticism 11. malediction
12. reprehension

obnoxious . . . 4. vile 5. nasty 6. odious,
rancid 7. hateful 8. amenable, infamous,
terrible 9. offensive 13. objectionable

oboe . . . 4. reed 5. shawm (anc)
7. hautboy, musette 8. schalmei
(schalmey) 9. chalumeau

obscene . . . 4. lewd 6. vulgar 8. indecent,
prurient 9. offensive, repulsive
10. disgusting 12. pornographic

obscuration . . . 7. eclipse 9. darkening,
vagueness

obscure . . . 3. dim, fog 4. dark, hazy, slur
5. bedim, blind, mirky, misty, murky
6. cloudy, darken, delude, mystic,
opaque, remote 7. becloud, conceal,
eclipse, shadowy, unknown 8. darkling,
formless, nameless, nubilous, obstruse,
oversile (obs) 9. enigmatic, undefined
10. indistinct, unrenowned

obscurity . . . 3. fog 5. gloom 7. dimness,
opacity, unknown 8. darkness

9. nonentity, vagueness
12. formlessness **13.** imperspicuous
14. insignificancy, uncomprehended
obsecrate ... **7.** beseech, entreat
10. supplicate
obsequies ... **5.** wakes **8.** funerals **9.** last
rites
obsequious ... **5.** slick **6.** abject
7. devoted, dutiful, fawning, servile,
slavish **8.** cringing, funereal, obedient,
toadying **9.** attentive, compliant
11. subservient
observance ... **3.** act **4.** form, rite
6. custom **8.** behavior, ceremony,
practice **9.** attention, deference,
sacrament, vigilance **10.** conformity
11. celebration
observant ... **7.** careful, heedful, mindful
8. faithful, vigilant, watchful **9.** attentive,
regardant, regardful
observation ... **4.** idea **6.** espial, remark
7. opinion **9.** attention
observatory ... **4.** Lick **6.** Yerkes
7. lookout, Palomar **8.** Mt Wilson
11. planetarium
observe ... **2.** lo! **3.** eye, see, spy **4.** espy,
heed, keep, nark, note, obey, tout
6. behold, notice, remark **7.** conform,
examine, witness **8.** preserve
9. celebrate, solemnize
observed, to be ... **8.** notandum
10. memorandum
observer ... **4.** eyer, nark **7.** aviator,
student, witness **8.** beholder, informer,
looker-on, onlooker **9.** spectator
11. stool pigeon
obsess ... **5.** beset, haunt **6.** harass
7. bewitch, possess **8.** demonize
9. influence, preoccupy
obsession ... **5.** mania **8.** impelled
11. bewitchment **13.** spirit control
obsignate ... **4.** seal **5.** stamp **6.** ratify
obsolete ... **3.** old **5.** passé **6.** effete
7. archaic, disused, effaced, outworn,
worn out **9.** out of date **10.** antiquated
12. old-fashioned
obstacle ... **3.** dam **4.** snag **6.** hurdle
9. hindrance **10.** difficulty, impediment
11. obstruction
obstetrician ... **6.** doctor **10.** accoucheur
obstetrix ... **7.** midwife
obstinate ... **3.** set **5.** balky, tough
6. dogged, mulish, sullen **7.** willful
8. perverse, stubborn **9.** pigheaded
10. determined, headstrong, self-willed
11. opinionated
obstreperous ... **5.** noisy **6.** unruly
7. blatant **9.** clamorous, turbulent
10. vociferous **11.** disobedient
12. ungovernable
obstruct ... **3.** bar, dam, dit **4.** clog, ditt,
stop **5.** beset, block, check, choke,
delay **6.** arrest, hamper, oppose, stop
up **7.** occlude **9.** barricade, embarrass,
interfere, interrupt
obstruction ... **3.** ban, dam **4.** clog, reef,
snag **7.** barrier **8.** obstacle **9.** hindrance
10. difficulty, filibuster, impediment
11. retardation
obtain ... **3.** buy, eke, get, win **4.** earn,
fang, gain **5.** fetch, reach **6.** attain,

derive, elicit, secure **7.** achieve, acquire,
capture, prevail, procure, receive
obtain (pert to) ...
by intimidation .. **9.** blackmail
by threats .. **6.** extort
control of .. **6.** corner **8.** overcome
equivalent .. **6.** recoup
obtest ... **6.** beg for **7.** beseech
10. supplicate
obtrude ... **5.** eject, expel **6.** impose
7. intrude
obtrusive ... **7.** forward, pushing
9. intrusive, officious
obtund ... **4.** dull **5.** blunt, quell **6.** deaden
8. moderate
obtuse ... **4.** dull, slow **5.** blunt,
crass, dense **6.** stupid **9.** unfeeling
11. insensitive
obvelation ... **7.** veiling **10.** concealing
obverse ... **5.** front **8.** converse
10. complement **11.** counterpart
obviate ... **7.** head off, rule out
8. preclude **9.** forestall **10.** anticipate
obvious ... **5.** clear, gross, plain
7. evident, patient **8.** apparent, distinct,
manifest, palpable **11.** conspicuous,
open and shut
obvolute ... **7.** twisted **9.** contorted,
convolute **11.** overlapping
occasion ... **4.** sele, time **5.** cause, event,
nonce **6.** excuse, motive **7.** pretext
8. ceremony, exigency, function,
incident **9.** condition, happening
11. opportunity **12.** circumstance
occasional ... **3.** odd **4.** orra **5.** stray
6. casual **10.** incidental, infrequent
occasionally ... **7.** at times **9.** sometimes
10. now and then **11.** at intervals
12. sporadically
occasive ... **8.** westward **10.** setting sun
Occident ... **4.** West **6.** sunset **17.** Western
Hemisphere (opp of Orient)
Occidental ... **6.** ponent **7.** The West,
Western **9.** Hesperian
occiput ... **10.** back of head **11.** back
of skull
occlude ... **3.** dam **4.** shut **5.** close **6.** shut
up **8.** obstruct
occult ... **5.** magic **6.** hidden, mystic
7. alchemy, cryptic **8.** esoteric
9. concealed, recondite **10.** mysterious,
necromancy **11.** supernormal
12. supernatural
occultation ... **4.** gone, lost **7.** eclipse
11. concealment
occultism ... **6.** cabala **7.** mystery
occult science ... **9.** esoterics
occupant ... **6.** inmate, tenant
10. inhabitant
occupation ... **3.** job **4.** call, note,
work **5.** hobby, trade **6.** career,
tenure **7.** calling, pursuit **8.** business,
vocation **9.** avocation **10.** employment,
habitation, possession, profession
11. engrossment
occupied ... **3.** sat **4.** busy, held **6.** filled
7. engaged **8.** employed, pervaded
9. engrossed, inhabited
occupy ... **3.** use **4.** fill, hold **6.** employ,
engage, expend, invest **7.** engross,
inhabit, oversit, pervade, possess

8. interest
occur ... 4. come, fall, meet 5. clash
6. appear, befall, betide, happen
occurrence ... 3. hap 5. event 8. incident,
presence, scenario 9. existence,
happening 10. appearance
11. eventuality 12. circumstance
occurring (pert to) ...
after death .. 10. posthumous
at nightfall .. 9. acronical
often .. 8. frequent 10. frequently
ocean ... 3. sea 4. brim, deep, main
5. brine 6. depths, pelago 8. great sea
ocean (pert to) ...
approach .. 7. sea gate
bottom .. 3. bed
crop cultivation .. 11. mariculture
deep .. 7. bathyal
deepest, lowest .. 5. hadal 8. bathybic
12. bathypelagic
division .. 6. Arctic, Indian 7. Pacific
8. Atlantic 9. Antarctic
floating matter .. 5. algae 7. flotsam
geography .. 12. oceanography
mammal .. 4. seal 5. whale
on (the ocean) .. 4. asea
periodic motion .. 4. tide
person .. 8. aquanaut, oceanaut 9. skin
diver 10. scuba diver
ref to .. 7. pelagic 9. Neptunian
route .. 4. lane
sealing .. 7. pelagic
vessel .. 6. Sealab 9. submarine
10. bathyscaph 11. bathysphere
Oceania, Oceanica ... 9. Melanesia,
Polynesia 10. Micronesia 12. Pacific
lands
Oceanids (Gr Myth, pert to) ...
father .. 7. Oceanus
mother .. 6. Tethys
nymphs .. 13. three thousand
Oceanus (Gr Myth, pert to) ...
children .. 5. Doris 8. Eurynome
(goddess), Oceanids
god of .. 6. rivers
wife .. 6. Tethys
ocellus ... 3. eye 6. stemma 7. eyespot
ocelot ... 3. cat 7. leopard
ocher, ochre (pert to) ...
red .. 5. tiver 7. almagra 8. hematite
9. faded rose
yellow .. 3. sil 7. Chinese 8. limonite
9. ochrolite
ochlocracy ... 7. mob rule
ochlophobia (fear of) ... 6. crowds
ocotillo ... 5. shrub 10. candlewood
ocracy ... 9. group rule
octad ... 5. eight (group)
octameron ... 12. eight-day fast
octagon ... 8. octangle 11. eight angles
octahedron ... 10. eight faces
octameter ... 8. octapody 9. eight feet
octarchy ... 11. rule by eight
octastich ... 6. octave 10. eight lines
11. eight verses
Octateuch (Old Test) ... 10. Eight Books
(1st)
octave ... 4. utas 5. eight 6. eighth
8. wine cask 10. eight notes
Octavia (pert to) ...
sister of .. 8. Augustus

wife of .. 10. Mark Antony
Octavian ... 7. Library (Rome's 1st)
16. committee of eight (one of)
octet, octette ... 7. huitain 12. group
of eight
October (pert to) ...
bird .. 8. bobolink
birthstone .. 4. opal 5. beryl
Club .. 9. political
drink .. 3. ale
month .. 5. tenth
octogenarian ... 13. eighty-year-old
octopod ... 9. eight arms, eight legs
Octopoda (Roder) ... 8. mollusks (8-
armed) 9. argonauts, octopuses
octopus ... 5. poulp (poulpe)
octroi, octroy ... 3. tax 9. privilege
10. concession
ocular ... 3. eye (pert to) 5. optic, sight
6. visual 10. ophthalmic
oculus ... 3. eye 14. Corona Borealis
odd ... 4. orra, rare 5. droll, extra, outré,
queer 6. uneven, unique 7. azygous,
bizarre, strange, unequal, unusual
8. unpaired 9. eccentric, remaining,
unmatched 10. occasional
oddity ... 9. queerness 11. peculiarity,
singularity 12. eccentricity, idiosyncrasy
odds ... 6. gamble 7. dispute, quarrel
8. gambling, variance 9. advantage
10. difference, dissension, inequality
11. probability 12. disagreement
13. probabilities
odds and ends ... 4. orts 6. refuse,
scraps 7. mixture, remains 8. remnants
10. miscellany
ode ... 4. like (suff), poem 5. psalm
8. canticle, serenata
ode (type) ... 7. Lesbian, regular
8. Horatian, Pindaric 9. irregular
odeon ... 4. hall 7. gallery, theater
Odin (pert to) ...
attendants .. 9. Valkyries
god of .. 3. war 6. poetry, wisdom
hall .. 8. Valhalla
horse .. 8. Sleipner
son .. 3. Tyr 4. Thor 6. Balder
Teutonic name .. 5. Woden (Wotan)
wife .. 5. Frigg (Frigga)
odious ... 4. foul, vile 5. nasty 7. hateful
8. infamous, terrible
odium ... 6. hatred, infamy 9. antipathy
10. abhorrence, opprobrium
11. detestation
odontist ... 7. dentist
odontology (science of) ... 5. teeth
9. dentistry
odor, odour ... 4. fume, funk, nose
5. aroma, fetor, nidor, scent, smell
6. flavor 7. essence, malodor, perfume
9. fragrance, redolence
odor, meat cooking ... 5. fumet
(fumette)
odorous ... 8. aromatic, fragrant, redolent,
smelling
Odysseus (pert to) ...
chieftain .. 9. Trojan War
dog .. 5. Argos
father .. 7. Laertes
hero of .. 10. The Odyssey (Homer)
king of .. 6. Ithaca (Gr)

magic herb.. **4.** moly
modern name.. **7.** Ulysses
wife.. **8.** Penelope
oecist... **9.** colonizer
oecodomic... **13.** architectural
Oedipus (pert to)...
daughter.. **8.** Antigone
father.. **5.** Laius (King of Thebes)
mother.. **7.** Jocasta
oeno (comb form)... **4.** wine
oenomancy... **12.** wine prophecy
oenophilist... **9.** wine lover
oenopoetic... **10.** wine making
oestrus... **4.** fury **5.** sting **6.** desire,
frenzy **7.** impulse **8.** stimulus
of... **2.** in, on **4.** over, upon, with **5.** about,
avent **10.** indication
of (pert to)...
a chamber.. **7.** cameral
a class (related).. **7.** generic
a father.. **6.** agnate
a flock.. **6.** gregal
a forefather.. **9.** ancestral
a grandfather.. **4.** aval
all.. **3.** ava
a mother.. **7.** cognate
an epoch.. **4.** eral
an order.. **7.** ordinal
a wife.. **7.** uxorial
common gender.. **7.** epicene
each.. **3.** ana
earth.. **4.** geal
equal value.. **10.** comparable
French.. **2.** du **3.** des
great importance.. **7.** capital
9. momentous
high standing.. **8.** sterling
little importance.. **5.** petty **7.** trivial
morning.. **5.** matin **7.** matinal
New Stone Age.. **9.** Neolithic
no avail.. **6.** futile
nostrils.. **6.** narine
old age.. **8.** gerontal
planet's path.. **7.** orbital
recent times.. **6.** lately **9.** latter-day
reign.. **6.** regnal
river banks.. **8.** riparian
same family.. **7.** cognate, germane
sound.. **5.** tonal
summer.. **7.** estival
tears.. **8.** lacrimal
the country.. **5.** rural
the ear.. **4.** otic
the eye.. **6.** ocular
the mouth.. **4.** oral
the skin.. **6.** dermal
the third degree.. **7.** cubical
the throat.. **5.** gular
the tongue.. **7.** glossal
the wrist.. **6.** carpal
this day.. **9.** hodiernal
thread color.. **7.** ficelle
winter.. **6.** hiemal
yore.. **5.** olden
off... **3.** ill **4.** agee, away, doff **5.** aside
6. begone, insane, remote **7.** distant,
tainted **9.** dissonant, erroneous,
imperfect, right-hand **10.** unemployed
offal... **5.** filth **6.** ordure, refuse **7.** carrion,
garbage, rubbish
offbeat... **14.** unconventional

off-color... **6.** risqué **7.** dubious
8. inferior
offend... **3.** cag, sin, vex **4.** miff **5.** anger,
annoy, pique, wound **6.** assail, insult,
revolt **7.** affront, do wrong, mortify
9. displease
offender... **6.** sinner **8.** criminal
9. wrongdoer **10.** malefactor
12. transgressor
offense... **3.** sin **5.** crime, delit, fault,
grief, malum **6.** delict, felony, insult
7. outrage, umbrage **8.** trespass
9. indignity **10.** resentment
11. delinquency, misdemeanor,
stellionate
offensive... **4.** foul, ugly **6.** attack,
odious, ribald, vulgar **7.** abusive,
eyesore, fulsome, harmful, obscene
8. invading, shocking **9.** assailant,
attacking, insulting, obnoxious,
repugnant, revolting **10.** aggressive,
malodorous, scurrilous **11.** approbrious,
displeasing, distasteful **12.** disagreeable
13. transgressive
offer... **3.** bid **6.** adduce, tender **7.** proffer,
propine, propose **8.** immolate, overture
9. ultimatum
offering... **4.** gift **6.** corban **7.** deodate,
present **8.** oblation **9.** sacrifice
offering resistance... **8.** renitent
offhand... **8.** careless, informal, slapdash
9. extempore, impromptu **10.** carelessly,
nonchalant **11.** extemporary
12. nonchalantly **15.** autoschediastic
office... **4.** duty, post, rite, wike (obs)
5. place, trust **7.** station **8.** ceremony,
function, position **9.** situation
11. appointment
office (pert to)...
chief.. **7.** manager
divine.. **9.** akoluthia
for the dead.. **7.** trental
holder.. **8.** placeman
of a datary (Roman Curia).. **7.** dataria
of a ruler.. **7.** regency
relinquish (to).. **5.** demit
third hour.. **6.** tierce
officer... **6.** tindal **7.** bailiff, command,
conduct, general, manager, marshal,
sheriff **8.** adjutant, avigator, director
9. constable, policeman, president
officer (pert to)...
assistant.. **4.** aide
Brit Royal Guard.. **4.** exon
chief executive.. **3.** dey **4.** czar
5. mayor **7.** emperor, monarch, premier
8. governor **9.** president **10.** chancellor
church.. **5.** elder **6.** sexton
civil law.. **6.** notary, police **7.** bailiff,
marshal, sheriff **9.** constable, policeman
10. magistrate
club.. **7.** steward
corrupt.. **7.** grafter
despotic.. **6.** satrap
diplomatic.. **7.** attaché
Jewish Relig.. **6.** parnas
King's stables.. **6.** avener
monastic.. **5.** prior
naval.. **6.** ensign, yeoman
parish.. **6.** beadle, bedral
ship's.. **9.** boatswain (boson)

weights, measures.. **6.** sealer
official ... **6.** formal **9.** authentic
  10. functional **13.** authoritative
official (pert to) ...
  command.. **5.** edict
  despotic.. **6.** satrap
  game.. **5.** judge **6.** umpire **7.** referee
  government.. **10.** bureaucrat
  insurance.. **7.** actuary **8.** adjuster
  intinerant (Hist).. **6.** missus
  mark.. **5.** stamp
  order (RCCh).. **8.** rescript
  proclamation.. **5.** ukase **6.** decree
  record.. **5.** actum
  state.. **8.** governor **9.** secretary
officious ... **4.** cool, pert **5.** saucy
  6. formal **8.** arrogant, impudent,
  official **9.** pragmatic **10.** meddlesome
  11. efficacious, impertinent, pragmatical
  12. contemptuous
officiousness ... **10.** pragmatism
offing ... **10.** background
offshoot ... **3.** rod **5.** scion **6.** branch,
  member **8.** addition **9.** by-product
  10. descendant **12.** organization
offspring ... **3.** son **4.** brat, seed **5.** child,
  fruit, issue, sprig **6.** origin, result
  7. produce, product, progeny **8.** fountain
  9. posterity **10.** descendant
oficina ... **5.** works **6.** office **7.** factory
  10. laboratory
often ... **3.** oft **9.** many times
  10. frequently, repeatedly **11.** over and
  over **13.** time after time
ogdoad ... **5.** eight **10.** eight group
ogee ... **4.** gula **5.** talon **7.** molding
  9. cyma recta **11.** cyma reversa
ogle ... **3.** eye **4.** gaze, leer **5.** stare
  7. examine
Ogpu ... **8.** Gay-Pay-Oo (Russ secret
  service)
O Henry ... **6.** Porter (Wm Sydney)
Ohio ...
  capital.. **8.** Columbus
  city.. **5.** Akron **6.** Dayton, Toledo
  9. Cleveland **10.** Cincinnati
  first settlement.. **8.** Marietta
  hero.. **12.** Anthony Wayne (Gen)
  lake.. **4.** Erie
  name meaning (Indian).. **14.** Beautiful
  River
  State admission.. **11.** Seventeenth
  State motto.. **27.** With God All Things
  are Possible
  State nickname.. **7.** Buckeye
oil ... **3.** ben, fat **4.** balm, ghee **5.** bribe,
  oleum **6.** aceite, anoint, asarum, grease,
  olanin **8.** flattery, medicate, painting
  9. lubricant, lubricate, petroleum
  10. illuminant
oil (pert to) ...
  beetle.. **5.** meloe
  berry.. **5.** olive
  bird.. **8.** guachare
  cartel.. **4.** OPEC
  cask.. **4.** rier
  class.. **5.** fatty, fixed **6.** animal **7.** mineral
  8. volatile **9.** essential, vegetable
  cloth.. **8.** linoleum
  coal.. **8.** photogen
  comb form.. **2.** ol **3.** ole

fish.. **7.** escolar
flask.. **4.** olpe
gauge.. **9.** oleometer
glands (birds).. **9.** uropygial
  11. elaeodochon
lamp.. **7.** lucigen
mineral.. **7.** naphtha
plant.. **6.** sesame **9.** castor-oil
prefix.. **2.** ol
rock.. **5.** shale **9.** limestone
seed.. **3.** til (teel) **6.** sesame **7.** linseed
  8. rapeseed **10.** castor bean, cottonseed
skin.. **5.** sebum
stone.. **4.** hone **9.** whetstone
term.. **5.** oleic
tree.. **4.** eboe (ebo), tung **5.** mahua
  6. illupi **7.** oil palm **9.** candlenut,
  castor-oil
tube.. **5.** vitta
whale.. **5.** sperm
oil of ...
  cloves.. **7.** eugenol
  myrcia.. **6.** bay oil
  orange blossoms.. **6.** neroil
  roses.. **4.** otto **5.** attar (atar)
  salt.. **7.** bittern
oils ... **10.** elaeoptene (elaeopten) (opp
  of stearoptene)
oily ... **3.** fat **4.** glib **5.** bland, oleic, suave
  6. olease, supple **7.** pinguid **8.** unctuous
  9. compliant, plausible **10.** flattering,
  oleaginous **11.** insinuating, subservient
  12. hypocritical
oily liquids ... **3.** tar **6.** cresol, octane
  7. aniline, picamar **8.** creosote
oily tissue ... **3.** fat
ointment ... **4.** balm, cere, lard, nard
  5. salve **6.** balsam, carron, cerate,
  ceroma, grease **7.** pomatum, unguent
  8. liniment **9.** spikenard, xeromyron
  10. petrolatum **11.** embrocation
Oise (France) ... **5.** Aisne (tributary), river
  10. department
Ojibway secret order ... **4.** mide (meda)
  9. midewiwin
ojo ... **5.** oasis
OK ... **6.** righto **7.** correct
Okinawa ...
  capital.. **4.** Naha
  island group (64).. **6.** Ryukyu
  prefecture of.. **5.** Japan
Oklahoma ...
  capital.. **12.** Oklahoma City
  city.. **3.** Ada **4.** Enid **5.** Tulsa **6.** Lawton
  8. Muskogee **9.** Claremore
  12. Bartlesville
  Five Civilized Tribes.. **5.** Creek
  7. Choctaw **8.** Cherokee, Seminole
  9. Chickasaw
  lake.. **6.** Texoma
  migrant from.. **4.** Okie
  mountain.. **5.** Ozark **8.** Ouachita
  museum.. **6.** Indian **8.** Woolaroc
  native son (famed).. **10.** Will Rogers
  old name.. **15.** Indian Territory
  State admission.. **11.** Thirty-third
  State bird.. **10.** flycatcher
  State flower.. **9.** mistletoe
  State motto.. **16.** Labor Omnia Vincit
  (Labor Conquers All)
  State nickname.. **6.** Sooner

okra . . . **5.** bendy, gumbo **6.** mallow
old . . . **3.** ald, eld **4.** aged **5.** anile **6.** infirm, senile **7.** ancient, antique, archaic **8.** obsolete **9.** doddering, senescent, venerable **10.** antiquated
old (pert to) . . .
age . . **6.** senile **7.** geratic **8.** gerontic, senility **10.** geriatrics (Med), senescence **11.** gerontology
ancient (very) . . **7.** Ogygian
billy, granny . . **5.** squaw
fashioned . . **4.** fogy **7.** antique **9.** primitive **12.** conservative
hat . . **5.** trite **9.** out-of-date
maid . . **5.** prude **10.** fussbudget
man . . **5.** elder **6.** codger, gaffer, geezer, Nestor **7.** oldster **8.** old-timer **10.** fuddy-duddy
sailor . . **3.** tar **4.** salt
saying . . **3.** saw **5.** adage, maxim
time . . **3.** eld **4.** syne
woman . . **3.** hag **5.** crone **6.** dotard, gammer
womanish . . **5.** anile
Old (pert to) . . .
Bailey . . **12.** English court
Bay State . . **13.** Massachusetts
Dominion . . **8.** Virginia
Empire . . **4.** Maya
English alphabet . . **10.** Anglo-Saxon
Faithful . . **6.** geyser
Franklin State . . **9.** Tennessee
Gentleman Harry . . **5.** Devil
Gooseberry . . **5.** Devil, Satan
Glory . . **15.** Stars and Stripes
Guard (Waterloo) . . **9.** Napoleon's
Hickory . . **13.** Andrew Jackson
Ironsides . . **15.** USS Constitution
Kingdom . . **7.** Memphis (Egypt)
Lady of Threadneedle Street . . **13.** Bank of England
Line State . . **8.** Maryland
Man of the Mountain . . **7.** Profile (The)
Noll . . **14.** Oliver Cromwell
North Church . . **12.** Christ Church
North State . . **13.** North Carolina
Rough and Ready . . **13.** (Gen) Zachary Taylor
Serpent . . **5.** Satan
Sod . . **4.** Erin **7.** Ireland
Sol . . **3.** sun
Stone Age . . **11.** Paleolithic
Three Stars . . **5.** (Gen) Grant
World . . **7.** Eastern
olden . . . **6.** bygone
older . . . **5.** elder **6.** senior **8.** ancestor
oldest . . . **4.** dean **6.** eldest **7.** stalest
Old Testament (pert to) . . .
Books (number) . . **10.** Thirty-nine
Elohim . . **3.** God (The Hexateuch)
Hexateuch . . **13.** first Six Books
Land of riches . . **5.** Ophir
objects (sacred) . . **4.** Urim **7.** Thummim
Pentateuch . . **10.** Law of Moses **14.** first Five Books
writer . . **7.** Elohist (The Hexateuch)
Old World (pert to) . . .
ape . . **7.** Primate **10.** Catarrhina
carnivore . . **5.** genet
falcon . . **5.** saker
herb . . **5.** tansy

lizard . . **5.** Agama
shrub . . **4.** Olax
oleaginous . . . **4.** oily **5.** oleic **8.** unctuous
oleander . . . **6.** Nerium **11.** rhododaphne **12.** rhododendron
oleoresin . . . **5.** anime, elemi **6.** balsam **7.** copaiba
oleum . . . **3.** oil
olfaction . . . **7.** osmesis **8.** smelling **12.** sense of smell
olfactory organ . . . **4.** nose **8.** olfactor
olid . . . **4.** foul **5.** fetid **6.** rancid, smelly **10.** malodorous **11.** strong smell
oligarchy . . . **10.** rule by a few
olinda bug . . . **6.** weevil
olio . . . **4.** olla, stem **6.** medley **7.** mixture **8.** chowchow **9.** burlesque, potpourri **10.** collection, hodgepodge **11.** olla-podrida
oliphant . . . **8.** elephant **9.** ivory horn
oliprance . . . **4.** romp, show **7.** jollity **11.** merrymaking, ostentation
olive (pert to) . . .
branch . . **5.** child, peace **6.** symbol (peace)
color . . **11.** yellow-green
dun . . **3.** fly (fishing)
enzyme . . **6.** olease
family . . **8.** Oleaceae
fly . . **3.** dun **4.** gnat **5.** quill
gray . . **10.** Scotch gray
gum . . **6.** olivil
overripe . . **5.** drupe
stuffed . . **6.** pimola
true . . **4.** Olea
wild . . **8.** oleaster
yard . . **6.** olivet
yellow . . **9.** moss green **10.** chartreuse
olla . . . **3.** jug, pot **4.** olio **8.** palm leaf (palmyra) **11.** olla-podrida
olla-podrida . . . **4.** hash, olio **6.** medley **10.** hodgepodge
oloroso . . . **6.** sherry
olpe . . . **5.** flask **8.** oenochoë **11.** wine pitcher
olycook, olykoek . . . **7.** cruller **8.** doughnut
Olympia . . . **4.** ship **7.** capital (Wash) **8.** heavenly **9.** sanctuary (anc)
Olympiad . . . **14.** four-year period
Olympian god . . . **4.** Ares, Zeus **5.** Apollo, Hermes **8.** Dionysus, Hercules, Poseidon **10.** Hephaestus
Olympian goddess . . . **4.** Hera **6.** Athena, Hestia **7.** Artemis, Demeter **8.** Aphrodite
Olympic cupbearer . . . **8.** Ganymede
Olympic Games (pert to) . . .
honor of . . **4.** Zeus
period . . **14.** four years apart
revival site . . **6.** Athens (1896)
site (first) . . **4.** Elis **7.** Olympia
time of games . . **8.** four days
Olympieion, Olympium . . . **6.** temple (Athens)
Olympus (Gr) . . . **3.** sky **5.** Mount **6.** heaven **8.** mountain
Olympus (Hind) . . . **4.** Meru
Omaha . . . **4.** city (Neb) **5.** Sioux **6.** Indian
Omar Khayyam (pert to) . . .
country . . **4.** Iran **6.** Persia
fish (fabled) . . **3.** mah

poem . . **8.** Rubaiyat
omasum . . . **9.** manyplies **10.** psalterium
   12. third stomach
ombro (comb form) . . . **4.** rain
ombrometer . . . **9.** rain gauge
omega . . . **3.** end **4.** last **5.** final **6.** letter
   (Gr)
omen . . . **4.** bode, sign **5.** abode,
   knell, token **6.** augury **7.** auspice,
   portent, presage **8.** forebode, foreshow
   9. abodement **10.** divination
   15. prognostication
omer . . . **5.** ephah, sheaf **9.** fifty days
   (Passover to Pentecost)
ominous . . . **4.** dour, trim **8.** sinister
   9. ferocious **10.** inexorable, portentous
   12. inauspicious
omission . . . **4.** want **5.** caret, error
   7. neglect **9.** oversight **10.** deficiency,
   leaving out **13.** nonobservance
omission of end syllables . . . **7.** apocope
omission of words . . . **8.** ellipsis
omit . . . **4.** dele, pass, skip **5.** elide
   6. delete, ignore **7.** exclude **11.** leave
   undone
omitting . . . **7.** elision **9.** excepting,
   excluding **10.** precluding
omneity . . . **7.** allness **16.** all-
   comprehensive
omnipotent . . . **6.** divine **8.** almighty
   9. unequaled, unlimited **11.** all-powerful
omniscient . . . **4.** wise **6.** divine **7.** learned
   10. all-knowing
omnitude . . . **7.** allness **8.** totality
   12. universality
omnivorous . . . **6.** greedy **9.** all-eating
   10. gluttonous
omoplate . . . **7.** scapula
omphalos . . . **3.** hut **4.** knob **5.** altar,
   navel **6.** center **9.** umbilicus
on . . . **2.** at **4.** atop, upon **5.** above, ahead,
   along **6.** toward **7.** against, forward
   10. concerning **13.** juxtaposition
On (Bib) . . . **7.** Baalbek **8.** holy city
   10. Heliopolis (Egypt) **12.** City of the
   Sun
on (pert to) . . .
   account of . . **3.** for
   all sides . . **5.** about **6.** around
   and on . . **7.** forever, tedious **9.** tediously
   behalf of . . **3.** for
   dit . . **5.** rumor **6.** report
   going . . **7.** forward **10.** proceeding
   grand scale . . **4.** epic
   hand . . **4.** here **7.** present **9.** available
   high . . **5.** aloft
   other side . . **4.** over **6.** across
   sheltered side . . **4.** alee
   this side . . **3.** cis (pref) **9.** cisalpine
   10. cismontane, cispontine
   windward side . . **8.** aweather
onager . . . **3.** ass **5.** kiang **8.** catapult
once in a while . . . **9.** erstwhile **10.** now
   and then **12.** occasionally
once upon a time . . . **6.** one day **7.** the
   past, time was **8.** formerly **10.** the
   long ago
Oncorhynchus . . . **6.** salmon
ondoyant . . . **4.** wavy (art)
one . . . **2.** an, un **3.** ace, ain, ein **4.** unit
   5. alone, unity, whole **6.** person, single

9. unmarried **10.** individual
one (pert to) . . .
   after the other . . **8.** serially, seriatim
   12. successfully
   bearing heraldic arms . . **7.** armiger
   behind the other . . **6.** tandem
   born in serfdom . . **4.** neif
   bringing good luck . . **6.** mascot
   by one . . **6.** apiece, singly **10.** one at
   a time **12.** individually
   comb form . . **3.** uni **4.** mono
   curious . . **6.** gossip **8.** quidnunc
   despondent in views . . **9.** pessimist
   fond of women . . **11.** philogynist
   footed . . **6.** uniped
   frantic for freedom . .
   15. eleutheromaniac
   gigantic in size . . **5.** giant, titan
   happy in views . . **8.** optimist
   horse . . **5.** petty **6.** little **8.** inferior
   10. second-rate **13.** insignificant
   in a thousand . . **6.** oddity **7.** paragon,
   prodigy
   in second childhood . . **6.** dotard
   instructed in secret system . . **5.** epopt
   8. initiate
   living on another . . **8.** parasite
   moving stealthily . . **7.** prowler
   sided . . **5.** askew **7.** partial **10.** prejudiced,
   unilateral
   thousand . . **3.** mil
   time . . **7.** quondam **8.** formerly
   undergoing change . . **6.** mutant
oneberry . . . **9.** hackberry
   14. partridgeberry
one devoted to . . .
   deviltry . . **7.** hellion
   fast driving . . **4.** jehu **7.** speeder
   indolence . . **10.** daydreamer, lotus-eater
   own opinion . . **5.** bigot
   physical feats . . **7.** athlete
   pursuit . . **3.** ist (suff)
   table delicacies . . **7.** epicure
onefold . . . **6.** simple, single **7.** sincere
   9. guileless
onegite . . . **8.** amethyst
Oneida . . . **6.** Indian **8.** Iroquois
   9. Community (NY)
oneiros . . . **5.** dream
oneirotic . . . **6.** dreams (pert to)
oneism . . . **6.** egoism, monism
oneness . . . **5.** union, unity **7.** concord
   8. identity, sameness **9.** agreement,
   aloneness, constancy **10.** loneliness,
   singleness, uniformity, uniqueness
   11. singularity **13.** undividedness
one of . . .
   ancient race . . **4.** Mede **7.** Iberian
   Buddhist precepts . . **6.** nidana
   Persian dynasty . . **8.** Sassanid
   religious sect . . **10.** Anabaptist
   the Bears . . **4.** Ursa
   the Greek Wise Men . . **6.** Thales
   the initiated . . **5.** epopt
   twins . . **5.** gemel (Her)
onerous . . . **4.** load **5.** heavy **6.** burden
   7. onerose **9.** difficult, laborious,
   ponderous **10.** burdensome, oppressive
   12. impedimental
one versed in . . .
   children's diseases . . **12.** pediatrician

law.. **6.** legist
literature.. **6.** savant **9.** literatus
memory.. **9.** mnemonist
politics.. **9.** statesman
religious law.. **8.** canonist
resources, wealth.. **9.** economist
one who...
absconds.. **6.** eloper **8.** decamper,
 deserter
appropriates.. **9.** pre-emptor
attacks.. **9.** aggressor
believes in all religions.. **6.** omnist
believes in personal God.. **5.** deist
believes in self.. **9.** solipsist
beseeches.. **7.** pleader
brings meat to royal table.. **7.** dapifer,
 steward
cherishes.. **8.** fosterer
collects voluntary taxes.. **6.** tither
conveys property.. **7.** alienor
dies for a cause.. **6.** martyr
differs.. **4.** anti **9.** dissenter, dissident
disowns.. **10.** repudiator
displays learning.. **6.** pedant
disposes by will.. **7.** devisor
edits.. **7.** reviser
feigns illness.. **10.** malingerer
fights for cause.. **8.** crusader
forsakes faith principles.. **8.** apostate
frustrates a plan.. **7.** marplot
gives up.. **9.** abnegator
grants by deed.. **7.** remiser
hates argument.. **10.** misologist
hates people.. **11.** misanthrope
holds office.. **2.** in **9.** incumbent
inculcates.. **7.** infuser **9.** instiller
inflicts retribution.. **7.** nemesis
misuses authority.. **6.** satrap
plunders.. **6.** sacker **8.** pillager
practises palmistry.. **11.** chiromancer
prevents entrance.. **5.** hajib
quarrels.. **5.** rowdy
removes nuisance.. **6.** abator
rules, manages.. **6.** gerent
sells provisions to troops.. **6.** sutler
shoots from ambush.. **6.** sniper
sponges.. **6.** cadger **8.** parasite
stays.. **5.** bider
summons spirits.. **8.** evocator
testifies.. **8.** deponent
transfers property.. **7.** alienor
ongall... **5.** onset **6.** attack
onion... **3.** set (bulbs) **4.** boll, bulb,
 cepa, leek **5.** chive, cibol, pearl, reeve
 6. Allium **7.** Bermuda, onionet, shallot
 8. eschalot, rareripe, scallion
onkos (Gr)... **7.** topknot
only... **4.** just, lone, mere, sole **5.** chief
 6. lonely, merely, simple, simply, single,
 singly, solely **8.** uniquely **11.** exclusively
 13. companionless **14.** above all others
onocentaur... **3.** ape **5.** demon (fabled)
onomasticon... **7.** lexicon **10.** dictionary,
 vocabulary (Gr)
onomatology (science of)... **5.** names
 11. terminology
onomatopoeic... **6.** echoic **9.** imitative
 (of natural sound)
onset, onslaught... **6.** attack **7.** assault
 11. rushing upon, setting upon
Ontario...

Bay.. **6.** Hudson
capital.. **7.** Toronto
city.. **6.** Ottawa **7.** Timmins **8.** Hamilton
lake.. **9.** Great Lake (one of five)
province.. **6.** Canada
river.. **6.** Ottawa, Thames **7.** Niagara
 10. St Lawrence
ontogeny... **9.** evolution
ontology (science of)... **5.** being **7.** reality
onus... **4.** duty, load **6.** burden, charge
 10. impediment, imposition, obligation
onus probandi... **13.** burden of proof
onward, onwards... **5.** ahead, forth
 6. future, moving **7.** forward
 8. forwards, progress **9.** in advance
onychauxis... **14.** nail overgrowth
onyx... **6.** nicolo (niccolo), tecali
ooid... **9.** egg-shaped
oology (science of)... **8.** bird eggs
oomancy (divination by)... **4.** eggs
oont... **5.** camel **13.** beast of burden
oop... **4.** join **5.** unite
oopak, oopack... **3.** tea (black)
oorial... **3.** sha **5.** sheep, urial
ooze... **3.** bog **4.** drip, leak, seep, sipe,
 soak **5.** exude, marsh **6.** be damp
 7. leather **8.** transude **9.** percolate
oozy... **4.** miry **5.** muddy, slimy
opah... **4.** fish, soko **8.** kingfish
 9. Lampridae
opal... **3.** gem **4.** blue **5.** stone **7.** hyalite
 10. pearliness
opal, variety of... **4.** wood **5.** black,
 noble, pitch, resin **6.** common **7.** girasol,
 hyalite **8.** menilite, precious
 9. cacholong, geyserite, harlequin
 10. chalcedony
opalescent... **6.** pearly **7.** opaline
 8. irisated **10.** iridescent
opaque... **4.** dark **6.** obtuse, stupid
 7. obscure **8.** eyeshade **10.** not shining
 13. unilluminated **14.** not transparent
open... **3.** ope **4.** ajar, bare, free, undo
 5. agape, begin, clear, frank, overt,
 plain, start, untie **6.** candid, honest,
 patent, public, reveal, unbolt, unfold,
 unfurl, unlock, unseal, unstop, vacant
 7. artless, evident, exposed, natural,
 obvious, sincere, unbosom, unclose
 8. apparent, commence, disclose,
 expanded, initiate, patulous, revealed,
 unclosed, unfasten **9.** spreading,
 uncertain, uncovered, unfeigned
 10. accessible, unreserved
 11. unprotected **12.** questionable
open (pert to)...
acknowledgment.. **6.** avowal
air.. **8.** alfresco
and shut.. **7.** assured, obvious
 11. prearranged
bursting.. **10.** dehiscence
cabinet.. **7.** étagère
country.. **5.** veldt, weald
court.. **4.** area **5.** patio
door.. **6.** policy **11.** hospitality
eyed.. **7.** curious **8.** vigilant **9.** attentive,
 expectant
for discussion.. **4.** moot
fully.. **4.** wide **9.** dehiscent, full-blown
land.. **4.** moor **5.** heath **6.** desert, plains
out.. **6.** deploy (Mil)

partly . . **3.** mid **4.** ajar
passage in forests . . **5.** glade
to scorn . . **9.** derisible
to view . . **5.** overt
opening . . . **2.** os **3.** bay, gap **4.** door,
gate, hole, loop, pore, rift, slot,
vent **5.** cleft, mouth, sinus, start
6. breach, eyelet, hiatus, outlet,
portal **7.** display, foramen, initial,
orifice, vacancy **8.** aperture, fenestra,
position **9.** admission, beginning
10. passageway, unfoldment
11. entranceway, opportunity
opening (pert to) . . .
chess . . **6.** gambit
ear . . **4.** burr
enlarge . . **4.** ream
from third ventricle (Anat) . . **4.** pila
having . . **10.** fenestrate
in a mold . . **6.** ingate
minute . . **5.** stoma
narrow . . **4.** rima, slot **7.** crevice
9. stenopaic
nasal . . **4.** nare
small . . **4.** pore **5.** chink **6.** cranny, eyelet,
lacuna **7.** foramen, orifice, pinhole
wide (Bot) . . **9.** dehiscent
openings . . . **3.** ora **7.** stomata
openwork . . . **6.** eyelet **7.** Madeira, tracery
10. decoration
opera (pert to) . . .
comic (singer) . . **5.** buffa, buffo
7. buffoon
glass . . **7.** binocle **9.** binocular, lorgnette
hat . . **5.** crush, gibus **6.** topper
kind . . **4.** soap **5.** horse **8.** burletta
singer . . **4.** bass, diva **5.** buffa, buffo,
tenor **7.** buffoon, soprano **10.** basso
buffo, coloratura
solo . . **4.** aria **5.** scena
star . . **4.** diva **10.** prima donna
text . . **8.** libretto
opera, composer . . . **5.** Bizet, Gluck,
Haydn, Verdi **6.** Glinka, Gounod,
Handel, Mozart, Wagner **7.** Puccini,
Rossini **9.** Donizetti, Meyerbeer
11. Deems Taylor **14.** Rimski-Korsakov
(Korsakoff)
opera, drama . . . **4.** Aida **5.** Boris,
Faust, Orfeo, Thais, Tosca **6.** Bohême,
Carmen, Coq d'or, Daphne, Isolde
7. Alceste, Fidelio **9.** Lohengrin,
Pagliacci, Rigoletto **10.** Magic Flute,
Prince Igor, Tannhäuser **11.** Don
Giovanni, Il Travatore **13.** Peter Ibbetson
14. Tales of Hoffman **15.** Hansel and
Gretel, Madame Butterfly **16.** Marriage
of Figaro
operation . . . **6.** action, agency **7.** surgery
8. creation **9.** influence **11.** functioning,
transaction
Operation Overlord . . . **4.** D-Day
16. Normandy invasion
operation, surgical . . . **6.** trepan
8. excision **9.** resection **10.** amputation,
castration **11.** exploratory
12. appendectomy, hysterectomy
13. tonsillectomy
operative . . . **6.** worker **7.** artisan, working
8. mechanic **9.** detective
operative, become . . . **5.** inure (enure)

operator . . . **5.** agent, quack **6.** dealer,
worker **7.** creator, handler, surgeon
10. mountebank, speculator
operculum (Bot) . . . **3.** cap, lid **7.** stopper
8. covering
operose . . . **4.** busy **8.** diligent **9.** difficult,
laborious **11.** painstaking
Ophidia . . . **6.** snakes **8.** reptiles, serpents
9. Serpentes
ophidian . . . **5.** snake, viper **7.** serpent
ophiolatry . . . **12.** snake worship
ophthalmic . . . **6.** ocular **7.** optical **9.** eye
region
ophthalmology, science . . . **6.** the eye
opiate . . . **4.** drug, hemp, snow **5.** opium
6. heroin **7.** anodyne, cocaine, hashish
(hasheesh), soother **8.** narcotic
9. analgesic, paregoric **11.** somniferous
12. somnifacient
opine . . . **4.** deem **5.** judge, think **6.** remark
7. opinion, suppose **10.** conjecture
opinion . . . **4.** idea, view **6.** belief, esteem,
notion, report **7.** feeling **8.** judgment,
two cents **9.** sentiment **10.** estimation,
impression, ober dictum, reputation
opinion (pert to) . . .
expert . . **9.** expertise
expression, common . . **5.** theme
expression, formal . . **4.** vote
religious, unorthodox . . **6.** heresy
opinions (pert to) . . .
collection . . **9.** anthology, symposium
professed . . **5.** credo
opium . . . **4.** drug **8.** narcotic **10.** intoxicant
opium (pert to) . . .
concentrate . . **6.** heroin
derivative (Chem) . . **7.** meconic
Egyptian . . **8.** thebaine
extract . . **7.** chandoo (chandu), codeine
8. morphine **9.** narcotine **10.** papaverine
overuse . . **8.** opiumism
poppy seed . . **3.** maw
source . . **5.** poppy
tincture . . **9.** paregoric
variety . . **6.** Indian, Smyrna, Turkey
7. Chinese, Persian
opodeldoc . . . **7.** plaster **8.** liniment
opodidymus . . . **7.** monster (two-headed)
opossum . . . **7.** Marmosa **9.** didelphid,
marsupial, phalanger
opossum (pert to) . . .
S America . . **5.** quica **7.** sarigue
variety . . **5.** mouse, water, wooly
water . . **5.** yapok (yapock)
wood . . **10.** silver bell
opponent . . . **3.** foe **4.** anti **5.** enemy, rival
7. adverse **8.** opposite **9.** adversary,
combatant **10.** antagonist
opportune . . . **3.** fit, pat **5.** ready
6. timely **7.** apropos **8.** suitable
9. expedient, well-timed **10.** convenient
11. appropriate
opportunist . . . **10.** politician, vacillator
opportunity . . . **4.** turn **6.** chance
7. opening **8.** occasion **12.** circumstance
16. suitable occasion
oppose . . . **3.** pit **4.** deny, face **5.** fight,
rebel **6.** expose, oppugn, refute, resist
7. contest, exhibit, gainsay **8.** confront
10. antagonize, contradict, contravene,
counteract

opposed . . . 3. met 4. anti, vied
5. coped 6. averse, pitted 7. adverse,
fronted 8. contrary, renitent, resisted
9. contested, withstood 12. oppositional
opposed (pert to) . . .
against . . 6. pitted
lee . . 5. stoss
to change . . 7. die-hard 11. reactionary
12. conservative
to entad (inward) . . 5. ectad
zenith . . 5. nadir
opposite . . . 5. polar 6. facing 7. adverse,
antonym, hostile, opposed, reverse
8. contrary, converse 9. different,
repugnant 10. opposition
12. antagonistic 13. contradictory
14. contrapositive
opposite (pert to) . . .
directly . . 10. antipodean
exact . . 8. antipode
in action, in nature . . 5. polar 7. inverse
prefix . . 6. contra
science . . 3. art
to spring tide . . 4. neap
opposition . . . 9. hostility, opponency
10. antagonism, antithesis, refutation,
resistance 11. contrariety, disapproval
13. contradiction
oppress . . . 4. rape 5. crush 6. burden,
harass, nither (Scot), ravish 7. depress,
swelter 8. distress, macerate, suppress
9. overpower, overwhelm, persecute,
tyrannize 10. extinguish
oppressive . . . 5. harsh 6. severe,
stuffy, sultry 7. onerous 8. rigorous
9. ponderous 10. burdensome,
depressing, tyrannical
oppressor . . . 4. czar (tsar), Nero
6. despot, tyrant 8. autocrat, burdener
11. Simon Legree
opprobrious . . . 7. abusive 8. despised,
infamous 9. insulting, offensive
10. scurrilous 11. disgraceful
12. contumelious
opprobrium . . . 5. odium 6. infamy
8. disgrace 11. malediction
oppugn . . . 6. assail, oppose
10. controvert, counteract
oppugnant . . . 7. hostile, opposed
8. contrary 12. antagonistic
13. counteractive
Ops (pert to) . . .
called also . . 10. Ops Consiva
consort of . . 6. Consus, Saturn
Festival . . 6. Opalia
Greek counterpart . . 4. Rhea
Roman goddess of . . 7. Harvest
opsigamy . . . 14. old-age marriage
opt . . . 4. pick 5. elect 6. choose 11. make
a choice
optic . . . 6. ocular, visual 11. optological
optical (pert to) . . .
device . . 9. stenopaic
glass . . 4. lens
illusion . . 6. mirage
instrument . . 5. prism 7. alidade, reticle
9. eriometer, optometer 10. microscope
membrane . . 6. retina
organ . . 3. eye
optic defect . . . 6. myopia
optimistic . . . 4. rosy 7. hopeful, roseate

8. cheerful, sanguine 9. expectant
10. auspicious
optimum . . . 4. best 7. maximum 13. most
favorable
option . . . 6. choice, future (Finan)
7. refusal 8. free will 11. alternative
13. right to choose
optional . . . 8. elective 9. voluntary
10. permissive 13. not compulsory
opulence . . . 6. plenty, riches, wealth
9. abundance, affluence, amplitude,
profusion
opulent . . . 4. rich 6. lavish 7. profuse,
wealthy 8. abundant, affluent
9. luxuriant
opulus . . . 11. guelder-rose 13. cranberry
tree
opus . . . 4. work 5. étude 10. embroidery,
needlework 11. composition
oquassa . . . 5. trout
oracle . . . 4. seer 5. sibyl 6. Dodona,
medium, mentor 7. prophet, wise man
8. Delphian (Delphic) 10. revelation
oracular . . . 4. wise 5. vatic (vatical)
9. prophetic 10. predictive
11. forecasting
orage . . . 5. storm 7. tempest
oral . . . 5. parol, vocal 6. spoken, verbal
10. not written 11. nuncupative
orang . . . 9. orangutan (orangutang)
orange (pert to) . . .
Bowl site . . 5. Miami
bird . . 7. tanager
color . . 5. ocher, peach 6. carrot 7. apricot
8. mandarin
covering . . 4. rind
flower oil . . 6. meroli
genus . . 6. Citrus
heraldry . . 5. tenné
kind . . 4. mock 5. hedge, navel, Osage
8. bergamot, mandarin, Valencia
9. tangerine
leaf . . 6. karamu
marigold . . 9. tangerine
membrane . . 4. zest
mock . . 7. seringa
seed . . 3. pip
Orangeman . . . 14. North Irelander
orangutan . . . 4. mias 5. orang, Pongo,
satyr, Simia
orate . . . 5. plead, speak, spiel 8. harangue
oration . . . 5. éloge 6. eulogy, prayer,
sermon, speech 7. lecture 8. encomium,
petition 9. discourse
orator . . . 6. rhetor 7. speaker 9. perorator
10. petitioner 11. rhetorician,
spellbinder
orator, famed . . . 5. Bryan (Wm Jennings)
6. Cicero 9. Churchill 11. Demosthenes
oratory . . . 6. chapel 7. chantry
9. elocution, eloquence
orb . . . 3. eye, sun 4. ball, moon, star
5. earth, globe, world 6. bereft, circle,
planet, sphere 7. enclose 8. encircle,
insignia, surround
orbed . . . 5. lunar, round
orbit . . . 4. path 5. globe, route 6. sphere
7. circuit 10. trajectory
orbit (pert to) . . .
cavity . . 9. eye socket
curve . . 10. trajectory

of a planet.. **7.** ellipse
point.. **5.** apsis **6.** apogee (farthest)
　　7. perigee (nearest)
orc, Orca ... **5.** whale **7.** grampus
orchestra (pert to) ...
　bells.. **12.** glockenspiel
　circle.. **7.** parquet **8.** parterre
　small.. **11.** symphonette
orchestra instrument group ...
　brass.. **4.** horn, tuba **6.** cornet **7.** trumpet
　　8. trombone
　percussion.. **4.** drum **7.** cymbals, timpani
　　(tympani) **8.** triangle
　strings.. **5.** cello, viola **6.** violin
　　10. contrabass **11.** violoncello
　wind.. **4.** oboe **5.** flute **7.** bassoon
　　8. clarinet
orchid ... **4.** Disa **5.** vanda **6.** Ophrys
　　7. Listera, lycaste, pogonia **8.** arethusa,
　　Cattleya, Oncidium **9.** cymbidium,
　　puttyroot **10.** letterleaf
orchid (pert to) ...
　appendage.. **8.** caudicle
　handsomest.. **4.** Disa
　largest.. **10.** letterleaf
　meal.. **5.** salep
　petal.. **8.** labellum
　tuber, root.. **5.** salep **7.** cullion
Orcus ... **3.** God (Rom) **5.** Hades, Pluto
　　(Gr) **10.** lower world
ordain ... **4.** plan **5.** allot, enact,
　　equip **6.** decree **7.** appoint, arrange,
　　command, destine, install **8.** canonize
　　9. institute **10.** predestine
ordeal ... **4.** gaff, test **5.** trial **7.** sorcery
　　8. judgment **10.** experience (painful)
order ... **3.** bid **4.** fiat, ordo, rank,
　　rule, sect, will **5.** array, class, edict,
　　genus, money **6.** cosmos, decree,
　　direct, enjoin, genera (pl), manage,
　　system **7.** arrange, command, dispose,
　　mandate, prepare, verdict **8.** regulate,
　　sequence **9.** condition, procedure
　　10. injunction **11.** arrangement
order (pert to) ...
　back.. **6.** remand
　connecting.. **6.** in turn **8.** seriatim
　cosmic.. **3.** tao **4.** rita
　for writ.. **7.** precipe
　good.. **6.** eutaxy
　grammar.. **5.** taxis
　judicial.. **4.** fiat, writ **7.** summons
　proper.. **6.** kilter
　written.. **6.** billet
Order, architecture ... **5.** Doric, Ionic
　　6. Tuscan **8.** Etruscan **10.** Corinthian
Order, association ... **4.** Club **5.** Guild
　　7. DeMolay, Society, St Clare
　　8. Sodality, Sorority **9.** The Garter,
　　Trappists **10.** Fellowship, Fraternity,
　　Sisterhood **11.** Brotherhood, Eastern
　　Star, Purple Heart **12.** The Rising Sun
ordered ... **4.** bade, trim **7.** regular
　　8. arranged, measured, ordained
　　9. regulated
orderly ... **4.** neat, tidy, trim **7.** regular,
　　uniform **8.** obedient, peaceful
　　9. attendant, regularly, shipshape
　　10. methodical, systematic
order of ...
　amphibians.. **5.** Anura

aquatic animals.. **7.** Cetacea
holy beings.. **9.** hierarchy
insects.. **7.** Diptera
mammals.. **8.** Edentata, Primates
mites.. **6.** acarid
the day.. **8.** schedule **12.** instructions
whales.. **4.** Cete
ordinal ... **6.** number, ritual, serial
　　10. succession **11.** Book of Rules (Eccl),
　　categorical
ordinance ... **3.** law **4.** rite **5.** bylaw, edict
　　6. assize, decree **7.** control, statute
　　8. decretum **9.** allotment, direction,
　　enactment, sacrament **10.** management,
　　regulation
ordinarily ... **7.** plainly, usually
　　8. commonly **9.** generally, naturally
　　11. customarily
ordinary ... **4.** ruck, so-so **5.** judge,
　　nomic, plain, prosy, usual **6.** common,
　　normal, tavern **7.** average, natural,
　　prosaic, vulgate **8.** everyday, habitual,
　　mediocre, plebeian, workaday **9.** of
　　the Mass **10.** table d'hôte
ordinate ... **6.** ordain **7.** appoint, orderly,
　　regular **8.** moderate **9.** harmonize
　　10. co-ordinate
ordination ... **5.** order **11.** appointment,
　　arrangement, disposition
　　12. organization
ordnance ... **4.** guns **5.** armor, orgue
　　7. petards, rabinet, weapons
　　8. armament, firearms, supplies
　　9. artillery, torpedoes **10.** ammunition
　　14. apparatus belli
ordo ... **5.** order **11.** publication
ore ... **3.** tin **4.** gold, iron, lead, paco
　　5. brass, metal, ochre **6.** copper,
　　silver, speiss **7.** mercury, mineral,
　　seaweed, uranium **8.** cinnabar, tungsten
　　9. loadstone (lodestone) **11.** quicksilver
ore (pert to) ...
　box.. **6.** sluice
　deposit.. **4.** lode, mine **7.** bonanza
　fuser.. **7.** smelter
　horizontal layer.. **5.** stope
　impure.. **6.** speiss
　iron.. **5.** ocher **8.** hematite **9.** magnetite
　lead.. **6.** galena
　loading platform.. **4.** plat
　machine separator.. **6.** vanner
　refuse.. **6.** scoria **8.** tailings
　roller.. **9.** edgestone
　silver.. **5.** noble (metal)
　sluice.. **5.** trunk
　stirrer.. **5.** dolly
　tin.. **5.** scove
　trough.. **5.** strake
　vein.. **4.** lode **5.** scrin, stope
　worthless.. **5.** matte
oread ... **5.** nymph **7.** seamaid
Oregon ...
　capital.. **5.** Salem
　caves.. **11.** Marble Halls
　city.. **6.** Eugene **7.** Astoria, Medford
　　8. Portland **12.** Klamath Falls
　crab apple.. **7.** powitch
　emigrant route.. **11.** Oregon Trail
　famed persons.. **4.** Gray (Capt) **5.** Astor,
　　Clark, Lewis
　Indian.. **5.** Modoc **7.** Chinook, Klamath

8. Nez Percé
mountain . . **4.** Hood **5.** Coast **8.** Cascades
native nickname . . **7.** webfoot
river . . **5.** Rogue **7.** Klamath **8.** Columbia
  10. Willamette
State admission . . **11.** Thirty-third
State motto . . **8.** The Union
State nickname . . **6.** Beaver **13.** Sawdust
  Empire
wind . . **7.** chinook
oremus . . . **9.** let us pray
Oreortyx . . . **5.** quail
Orestes (pert to) . . .
father . . **9.** Agamemnon
friend . . **7.** Pylades
mother . . **12.** Clytemnestra
sister . . **7.** Electra
wife . . **8.** Hermione
orf, orfe . . . **3.** ide **4.** fish
orfevrerie . . . **7.** jewelry **9.** gold plate
organ (pert to) . . .
anatomy . . **3.** ear, eye **4.** lung, nose
  5. brain, heart, liver **6.** kidney, syrinx,
  tongue, tonsil **7.** viscera (pl)
bristlelike . . **4.** seta
desk . . **7.** console
fish . . **8.** drumfish
honey-secreting . . **7.** nectary
plant . . **5.** stoma **7.** tendril
motion . . **6.** muscle
respiratory . . **4.** lung
secretion . . **5.** gland
spider's spinner . . **9.** spinneret
stop (music) . . **8.** register
tactile . . **6.** feeler **8.** tentacle
organic . . . **5.** state, vital **6.** innate
  8. inherent **9.** organized **10.** structural
  11. fundamental **14.** constitutional
organic (pert to) . . .
compound . . **5.** amine, ester **6.** enzyme,
  ketone
disease . . **11.** organopathy
memory . . **5.** mneme
radical . . **5.** ethyl
remains . . **5.** azoic
soil . . **5.** humus
organism (pert to) . . .
bacterial . . **4.** germ **7.** microbe
body of . . **4.** soma
elementary . . **5.** monad
minute . . **5.** spore **6.** amoeba
pelagic . . **6.** nekton
plant . . **5.** spore
potential . . **7.** idorgan
sea . . **6.** nekton **7.** benthos **8.** plankton
type . . **5.** plant **6.** animal **9.** vegetable
vegetable . . **4.** tree **5.** plant
organization . . . **4.** bloc, sect, unit
  5. cadre, guild, party, setup **6.** empire
  11. association, corporation
  12. constitution **13.** establishment
  14. classification
organized body . . . **5.** corps, posse
organized matter . . . **5.** fauna, flora
  6. living, nekton **7.** animate, benthos
  8. plankton
organology, science . . . **10.** phrenology
  13. splanchnology
organoscopy . . . **10.** phrenology
orgueil . . . **5.** pride **11.** haughtiness
orgy . . . **4.** lark, romp **5.** binge, revel,

rites (anc), spree **6.** frolic, ritual,
shindy **7.** debauch, revelry, shindig,
wassail **8.** carousal **11.** celebration,
merrymaking
oribi . . . **7.** bleebok, Ourebia **8.** antelope
oriel . . . **3.** bay **6.** recess, window
  7. balcony, gallery, portion **8.** corridor
  10. moucharaby **11.** meshrabiyeh
  (Muslim)
orient . . . **4.** dawn **7.** eastern, shining,
  sunrise **8.** oriental, pellucid
  11. resplendent
Orient . . . **4.** Asia, East **6.** Levant
oriental (pert to) . . .
abode, gateway . . **3.** dar
animal . . **4.** zebu
archangel . . **5.** Uriel
beverage . . **6.** arrack
building . . **6.** pagoda
burden bearer . . **5.** hamal
cap (sheepskin) . . **6.** calpac (calpack)
caravansary . . **4.** khan **5.** serai **6.** imaret
carpet . . **4.** kali
carriage . . **10.** jinrikisha (jinricksha)
cart, wagon . . **5.** araba
chief . . **4.** Khan **6.** Mikado
Christian . . **5.** Uniat
corn . . **4.** para
cosmetic . . **4.** kohl
council . . **5.** Divan
cymbals . . **4.** zels
deity . . **3.** Bel
destiny . . **6.** Kismet
disease . . **8.** beriberi
dish . . **4.** rice **5.** pilau (pilaw) **6.** pilaff
  8. chop suey, chow mein
drug . . **5.** opium **6.** heroin **7.** hashish
  (hasheesh)
drum . . **6.** tom-tom
dulcimer . . **6.** santir
fan . . **3.** ogi
food . . **4.** rice **5.** salep
garment . . **3.** aba **6.** sarong
guitar . . **5.** sitar
head cover . . **6.** turban
hospice . . **6.** imaret
inn . . **5.** serai
instrument (Mus) . . **7.** samisen
laborer . . **6.** coolie (cooly)
leader . . **4.** amir (ameer)
liquor . . **4.** sake, saki
litter . . **5.** dooly (doolie) **9.** palanquín
lute . . **3.** tar
maid . . **4.** amah, ayah, eyah
manservant . . **5.** hamal **6.** coolie
marketplace . . **6.** bazaar
monkey . . **7.** macaque
nurse . . **4.** amah, ayah (governess)
obeisance . . **6.** salaam (salam)
pagoda . . **3.** taa
people . . **4.** Sere (anc) **5.** Asian, Malay
  6. Indian **7.** Chinese, Eastern, Tartars
  (Tatars) **8.** Japanese **10.** Mohammedan
pipe . . **8.** narghile
rice paste . . **3.** ame
rug . . **8.** sedjadeh **11.** Baluchistan
ruler . . **4.** Khan, Shah **5.** sahib (saheb)
  6. caliph (calif), sultan
sabre . . **8.** scimitar
sailor . . **6.** lascar
sash . . **3.** obi

tambourine . . **5.** daira
taxi . . **7.** ricksha (rickshaw) **10.** jinrikisha
trousers (women) . . **9.** shaksheer
vessel (sailing) . . **4.** dhow, saic
wagon . . **5.** araba
warehouse . . **6.** godown
wind . . **7.** monsoon
worker . . **6.** coolie (cooly)
orifice . . . **4.** hole, lura, pore, vent **5.** inlet,
   mouth, porus, stoma **6.** outlet, porule
   7. chimney, opening, ostiole **8.** aperture,
   bunghole, spiracle
origin . . . **3.** nee **4.** germ, rise, root,
   seed **5.** alpha, birth, cause, start
   6. nature, parent, source **7.** genesis
   9. beginning, etymology, inception,
   parentage **10.** inconabula, provenance
   11. provenience **12.** commencement,
   fountainhead
original . . . **3.** new **5.** basic, first, novel
   6. fontal, native, primal, primer,
   unused **7.** genuine, pattern, primary
   8. pristine **9.** aborigine, beginning,
   inventive, primitive **10.** inimitable
   11. fundamental, origination
   12. commencement
original copy . . . **6.** ectype
originate . . . **4.** coin, open, rise, stem
   5. arise, begin, breed, start **6.** author,
   create, derive, invent **7.** emanate,
   produce **8.** generate, initiate
   11. etymologize
originator . . . **5.** cause, maker **7.** creator
   8. inventor, producer **9.** contriver
   10. discoverer
oriole . . . **5.** pirol **6.** golden, hooded,
   loriot, Mimeta **7.** orchard **8.** Bullock's
   9. Baltimore, Icteridae
Orion (pert to) . . .
   Astron . . **7.** Dog Star **10.** Canis Major
      11. Orion's Hound **13.** constellation
   color . . **11.** Holland blue
   Gr Myth . . **6.** hunter
   Jacob's Staff . . **10.** Yard and Ell
      13. Golden Yardarm
   slain by . . **7.** Artemis
   star . . **5.** Rigel
orison . . . **6.** prayer
Orkney Islands, Scotland . . .
   capital . . **8.** Kirkwall
   Firth . . **8.** Pentland
   fishing grounds . . **4.** haaf
   island, largest . . **6.** Pomona
   President, Supreme Court . . **4.** foud
   stone tower (Prehist) . . **5.** broch
orle (Her) . . . **6.** border, fillet, wreath
   7. bearing, chaplet **10.** escutcheon
   (voided)
Orloff . . . **5.** horse **7.** diamond (Russ,
   194 3/4 carats)
orlop . . . **4.** deck (lowest)
Ormazd (Pers) . . . **5.** deity (supreme)
ormer . . . **7.** abalone **8.** ear shell
ornament . . . **4.** ouch, semé **5.** adorn,
   decor, gutta, honor **6.** amulet, brooch,
   emboss, finery, sequin **7.** antefix
   8. appliqué, decorate **9.** embellish
   10. decoration **13.** embellishment
ornament (pert to) . . .
   apex . . **6.** finial
   ball . . **6.** pompon

bell-shaped . . **9.** clochette
Bible . . **4.** Urim
boat-shaped . . **3.** nef
brilliant . . **4.** gaud **5.** spang **6.** sequin,
   tinsel **7.** spangle
circular . . **7.** rosette
delicate . . **7.** tracery
diamond-shaped . . **11.** epigonation
dress . . **5.** jabot **9.** stomacher
   10. embroidery
egg-shaped . . **3.** ove
hair, head . . **4.** comb **5.** tiara **8.** barrette
indented . . **5.** chase
Japanese girdle . . **4.** inro
leaves and grapes . . **6.** pampre
magical . . **6.** amulet
mantel . . **7.** bibelot, trinket
pendant . . **6.** bangle, tassel **7.** earring
   9. lavaliere (lavalier)
pretentious . . **6.** rococo
protuberant . . **4.** boss
raised design . . **7.** brocade
scroll-like . . **6.** volute
set of . . **6.** parure
setting in . . **5.** inlay **7.** emblema
silverware . . **7.** gadroon
spiral . . **5.** helix
terminal . . **6.** finial
wall . . **6.** plaque, sconce
ornamental (pert to) . . .
   bottle . . **8.** decanter
   button . . **4.** stud
   description . . **5.** fancy **10.** decorative
   lace edge . . **5.** picot **7.** tatting
   metal . . **6.** niello
   raised . . **7.** brocade
   stand . . **7.** étagère
   vase . . **3.** urn
ornamented . . . **6.** chased, etched, tooled
   8. engraved
ornate . . . **3.** gay **5.** fancy **6.** florid, tawdry
   7. adorned **9.** decorated
ornery . . . **8.** perverse, stubborn
   9. malicious **11.** ill-tempered
ornithoid . . . **8.** birdlike
ornithology (study of) . . . **5.** birds
ornithon . . . **6.** aviary
oro . . . **4.** gold **5.** money
Oro . . . **3.** God (Tahiti)
oro (comb form) . . . **5.** month, serum
   8. mountain
orology (science of) . . . **9.** mountains
orotund . . . **7.** pompous **9.** bombastic
orp . . . **4.** fret, weep
Orpheus (pert to) . . .
   astronomy . . **6.** Cygnus
   eighteenth century . . **6.** Handel
   father . . **6.** Apollo
   mother . . **8.** Calliope
   poet . . **8.** Thracian
   reference . . **6.** Orphic
   river . . **6.** Hebrus
   wife . . **8.** Eurydice
Orphic . . . **3.** egg (Creation's) **5.** hymns
   7. tablets (gold) **13.** Book of the Dead
   (rites)
orphrey . . . **10.** embroidery (gold)
orpit (Scot) . . . **7.** fretful
orra . . . **3.** odd **5.** oddly **10.** not
   matched, occasional, unemployed
   13. miscellaneous

ort . . . **3.** end **4.** bits **5.** scrap **6.** refuse, scraps **7.** remnant **8.** leavings, leftover

orthodox . . . **7.** Trinity **8.** accepted, approved, believer, standard **9.** canonical, customary **12.** conventional

Orthodox Moslem . . . **5.** hanif

orthography . . . **8.** spelling

ortolan . . . **7.** bunting **8.** bobolink, sora rail, wheatear

Oryx . . . **5.** beisa **7.** gazelle, gemsbok **8.** antelope, leucoryx

os . . . **4.** bone **5.** mouth, osker (Geol) **7.** opening

Osage . . . **5.** river **6.** Indian (Sioux) **10.** orange tree

Osaka, Japan . . . **7.** capital **10.** prefecture

oscillate . . . **3.** wag **4.** rock, sway, vary **5.** swing, waver, weave **7.** vibrate **9.** fluctuate

Oscines . . . **12.** singing birds

oscitancy . . . **6.** gaping **7.** yawning **8.** dullness, lethargy **10.** drowsiness

oscitant . . . **4.** dull **6.** drowsy, gaping, sleepy **7.** yawning **8.** careless, sluggish **9.** apathetic

osculate . . . **4.** buss, kiss

osier . . . **3.** rod **4.** wand **6.** sallow, willow **7.** dogwood

Osiris, Egypt (pert to) . . .
brother . . **3.** Set (Seth)
crown . . **4.** atef
enemy . . **3.** Set **7.** brother
father . . **3.** Geb
god . . **9.** fertility **10.** underworld
god (Gr) . . **8.** Dionysus
husband of . . **4.** Isis
king of . . **5.** Egypt
mother . . **3.** Nut
seat . . **6.** Abydos
son . . **5.** Horus **6.** Anubis

Osmanli . . . **4.** Turk **8.** language

osmesis . . . **8.** smelling **9.** olfaction

osmosis . . . **10.** absorption **12.** infiltration

osprey . . . **4.** hawk **7.** feather (hat) **8.** fish hawk **9.** ossifrage **10.** breakbones

ossature . . . **8.** skeleton **9.** framework (Arch)

osse . . . **4.** dare **7.** attempt, presage, promise **8.** prophecy

osseous . . . **4.** bony, hard **10.** ossiferous

ossifrage . . . **5.** eagle **6.** osprey **11.** lammergeier

ossuary . . . **3.** urn **4.** tomb **10.** depository **12.** charnel house **13.** burial chamber

ostend . . . **6.** reveal **7.** exhibit **8.** manifest **11.** demonstrate

ostensible . . . **5.** shown **6.** avowed **7.** alleged, seeming **8.** apparent, declared, specious **9.** exhibited, plausible, professed

ostent . . . **3.** air **4.** mien **5.** token **7.** portent **10.** appearance

ostentatious . . . **4.** arty, vain **5.** dashy **6.** sporty **7.** pompous **11.** conspicuous, pretentious

ostiole . . . **4.** pore **5.** stoma **7.** orifice **8.** aperture

ostler . . . **7.** hostler **9.** stableman

ostracize . . . **5.** exile, expel **6.** banish, deport **7.** cast out, exclude **9.** extradite **10.** expatriate

ostrich . . . **3.** emu **4.** Rhea **5.** nandu **8.** Struthio **9.** cassowary

ostrichlike . . . **11.** struthiform

ostrich tail feather . . . **3.** boo

Otaheite . . . **6.** Tahiti

otalgia . . . **7.** earache

Othello (pert to) . . .
opera by . . **5.** Verdi
tragedy by . . **11.** Shakespeare
villain . . **4.** Iago
wife . . **9.** Desdemona

other . . . **2.** or **5.** alter, ither **6.** either, second **8.** one of two **9.** different **10.** additional

others . . . **7.** the rest **9.** remaining

otherwise . . . **2.** or **5.** alias, ossia, other **6.** or else **9.** different **10.** contrarily **11.** differently

Othman . . . **4.** Turk **5.** Osman **6.** sultan **7.** Osmanli, Ottoman, Turkish

Othman's successor . . . **3.** Ali

otiant . . . **4.** idle **8.** in repose **10.** unemployed

otiose . . . **4.** idle **6.** at ease, futile **7.** sterile, useless **8.** indolent **12.** functionless

otium . . . **7.** leisure

otkon . . . **4.** okee (oki) **5.** demon (Iroquois)

otologist . . . **6.** aurist **9.** ear doctor

ottava . . . **6.** eighth, octave

ottava rima . . . **15.** eight-line stanza

ottavino . . . **7.** piccolo

ottoman . . . **4.** seat **5.** couch, stool **7.** cricket **9.** footstool

Ottoman (pert to) . . . see also Othman
color . . **9.** vermilion
court . . **5.** Porte **12.** Sublime Porte
Empire . . **7.** Turkish
fabric . . **6.** ribbed **10.** corded silk
governor . . **3.** bey, dey **5.** pasha
leader . . **5.** Osman
native . . **4.** Turk
poetry (couplet) . . **4.** beyt
province . . **6.** eyalet (former) **7.** vilayet
Turkish . . **7.** Osmanli

oubliette . . . **7.** dungeon (top opening)

ouch . . . **5.** bezel, clasp, jewel **6.** brooch **8.** ornament **11.** exclamation

ought . . . **4.** duty, must, zero **5.** at all, aught, owned **6.** cipher, should **7.** behoove, nothing **8.** anything, in need of **9.** possessed **10.** obligation

Ouija board . . . **10.** planchette

ouk . . . **4.** week

ouphe . . . **3.** elf **6.** goblin

Our (pert to) . . .
Father . . **11.** Lord's Prayer
French . . **5.** notre
Lady . . **10.** Virgin Mary
Lady's-mint . . **9.** spearmint
Lady's Wand (Astron) . . **10.** Orion's Belt
Lady's Way . . **6.** Zodiac

ourie . . . **4.** cold **5.** dingy **6.** dreary

ousia . . . **6.** nature **7.** essence **9.** substance, true being

oust . . . **3.** bar **5.** eject, evict **6.** depose, remove, unseat **7.** turn out

out . . . **3.** odd **4.** away **5.** drunk **6.** absent, beyond, excuse, issued, outlet **9.** published **10.** dislocated, extinguish **11.** unconscious

12. extinguished, not available

out and out ... **6.** arrant **8.** absolute,
complete, outright, thorough
9. downright **13.** thoroughgoing

outbreak ... **4.** rash, riot **5.** burst,
spurt **6.** emeute, tumult **7.** outcrop,
ruction **8.** eruption, hysteria, outburst
12. insurrection **13.** recrudescence

outburst ... **4.** gale **5.** blast, flare, flash
8. ejection, eruption **9.** explosion
10. ebullition

outcast ... **5.** exile, leper, ronin **6.** pariah
7. quarrel **8.** castaway, derelict,
vagabond **10.** expatriate

outclass ... **5.** excel, outdo **6.** outvie
7. outrank, surpass **8.** outshine
10. outperform

outcome ... **5.** issue **6.** effect, outlet,
result, sequel, upshot **7.** emanate,
product **8.** solution **10.** denouement
11. consequence

outcry ... **4.** wail, yell **5.** alarm, shout
6. clamor, plaint **7.** suction **8.** proclaim
11. exclamation

outdated ... **7.** archaic **8.** obsolete
10. antiquated **12.** old-fashioned

outdo ... **5.** excel **6.** defeat, exceed,
outwit

outdoor game ... **4.** polo **6.** hockey,
tennis **7.** cricket, croquet

outer ... **5.** ectad, ectal **7.** outside, outward
8. exterior, external **9.** objective
10. extraneous

outer (pert to) ...
boundary .. **9.** perimeter
coat .. **4.** coat, hull **5.** testa **6.** extine,
jacket **8.** tegument
garment .. **4.** suit, wrap **5.** cloak, dress
7. paletot, sweater **8.** mackinaw,
mantilla, overcoat, raincoat
layer of roots .. **7.** exoderm
opposed to .. **5.** ental
shell .. **4.** test
skin .. **9.** epidermis

Outer Mongolia ...
capital .. **4.** Urga **14.** Ulan Bator Khoto
desert .. **4.** Gobi

outermost ... **6.** utmost **7.** extreme,
outmost **8.** far-flung, farthest

outfit ... **3.** kit, rig **4.** gear, suit,
unit **5.** equip, group **7.** company,
costume **8.** wardrobe **12.** organization
13. paraphernalia

outflow ... **4.** gush, teem **6.** deluge, efflux
7. freshet, outflux, outpour **8.** effusion
10. ebullience

outgate ... **4.** exit, vent **6.** egress, outlet
7. outcome

outknee ... **6.** bowleg

outlander ... see *outsider*

outlandish ... **3.** odd **6.** remote **7.** bizarre,
foreign, strange, uncouth **8.** freakish
9. barbarous, inelegant, unrelated
10. extraneous, impossible, tramontane

outlaw ... **5.** horse, ronin **6.** bandit,
banish **7.** brigand, outcast **8.** criminal,
fugitive **9.** ostracize, proscribe

outlet ... **4.** exit, vent **5.** bayou **6.** stream
7. culvert, opening, outcast, passage

outline ... **3.** map **5.** chart, draft, frame,
shape **6.** sketch **7.** contour, drawing,

summary **8.** scenario **9.** adumbrate,
delineate, lineament, perimeter,
summarize **10.** compendium
11. delineation **13.** configuration

outlook ... **5.** scope, vista, watch
7. purview **8.** frontage, prospect
9. viewpoint **10.** perception
11. probability **12.** watchfulness

outmoded ... **5.** passé **7.** offbeat
8. outdated **10.** superseded

outmost ... **5.** final, utter **6.** remote,
utmost **8.** farthest **9.** extremest,
outermost, uttermost **15.** farthest
outward

out of ...
agreement .. **6.** dehors
danger .. **4.** safe
date, style .. **3.** old **5.** passé
10. antiquated
place .. **5.** inept
sorts .. **5.** nohow **7.** peevish
the ordinary .. **7.** unusual
the question .. **10.** impossible
the way .. **5.** aside **6.** afield

outpeer ... **5.** excel **7.** surpass

output ... **3.** cut **5.** expel, power,
yield **6.** amount, energy **7.** turnout
10. production

outraged ... **6.** abused, harmed
8. insulted, offended **9.** affronted
10. infuriated, mistreated

outrageous ... **6.** absurd **7.** furious,
heinous, obscene **8.** flagrant
9. atrocious, excessive, monstrous
10. exorbitant, scandalous
11. disgraceful, unwarranted

outré ... **3.** odd **6.** absurd **7.** bizarre
10. immoderate **11.** extravagant

Outre-Mer ... **13.** Book of Travels
(Longfellow, 1835)

outremer ... **12.** beyond the sea, foreign
parts

outrigger ... **4.** proa, spar **5.** canoe

outright ... **8.** thorough **10.** completely
11. unqualified **12.** unreservedly

outrival ... **5.** excel **6.** outvie **7.** eclipse,
outrank **8.** outclass, outshine, outsmart,
outstrip

outside ... **3.** exo (pref) **4.** ecto (comb
form) **8.** exterior, external, outdoors
10. extraneous **11.** superficial

outsider ... **5.** alien **8.** stranger
9. auslander, foreigner, Uitlander

outspoken ... **4.** free **5.** blunt, frank
6. candid, direct **10.** unreserved
13. communicative

outstanding ... **3.** due **5.** famed,
noted **6.** famous, unpaid **7.** eminent,
obvious **8.** exterior **9.** important,
principal, prominent **10.** projecting
11. conspicuous, uncollected

outstrip ... **4.** best, lead **5.** excel, outdo
7. surpass **8.** outrival

outward ... **5.** ectad, evert, outer,
overt **6.** formal, spiral **8.** apparent,
exterior, external, manifest **9.** extrinsic
11. superficial

outwit ... **4.** balk, best, foil **5.** block, check,
cross **6.** baffle, thwart **9.** checkmate,
frustrate **10.** circumvent, disappoint

outwork (Fort) ... **7.** ravelin **8.** tenaille

(tenail)
ouvrage . . . 4. work
ouzel, ousel . . . 4. piet 6. thrush
  8. whistler 9. blackbird
oval . . . 5. ovate, ovoid 6. circle 7. ellipse
  10. elliptical 11. ellipsoidal
ovale . . . 3. egg
ovate . . . 4. bard, oval 7. obovate
  (inversely)
oven . . . 3. umu 4. kiln, oast (oste)
  7. furnace 8. hot place 9. microwave
  12. brick chamber
oven (pert to) . . .
  glass annealing . . 4. lehr (leer)
  hop drying . . 4. oast
  mop . . 6. scovel
over . . . 3. o'er, too 4. also, anew, atop
  5. above, again, ended, super, supra
  8. finished
overact . . . 3. haw 5. emote, spout
overalls . . . 5. chaps 8. trousers
  10. chaparajos
overbearing . . . 7. haughty 8. arrogant,
  cavalier, snobbish, subduing
  9. imperious 10. highhanded
  11. domineering 12. overpowering
overcast . . . 3. dim 4. dark 6. cloudy,
  darken, gloomy 10. overturned (Geol)
overcoat . . . 5. benny, parka 6. capote,
  raglan, slip-on, ulster 7. paletot,
  surtout, topcoat 9. greatcoat, inverness
  (sleeveless)
overcome . . . 3. awe, win 4. beat
  5. crush 6. beaten, defeat, exceed
  7. conquer 8. outstrip, overbear,
  overturn, persuade, surmount,
  unnerved, vanquish 9. overpower,
  overthrow, overwhelm, prostrate
overcrowded . . . 9. congested
overdue . . . 4. late 5. tardy 7. belated
  8. mistimed
overfeed . . . 4. glut 6. agrote, pamper
  7. satiate, surfeit 8. overfill 9. crapulate,
  overstuff
overflow . . . 4. teem 5. spate 6. abound,
  deluge, outlet 7. copious, overrun
  8. inundate, opulence, overload,
  plethora, teem with 9. abundance,
  pour forth 10. ebullience
overfond of . . . 4. dote 5. silly
overfull . . . 8. inflated, satiated 9. plethoric
  10. overloaded
overhang . . . 3. jut 6. beetle 7. project,
  suspend 9. advantage 11. over and
  over
overlapping . . . 8. obvolute 9. imbricate,
  syphering
overloaded . . . 6. turgic 8. inflated, overfill
  9. bombastic, plethoric
overlook . . . 4. face, miss, scan, skip,
  snub 6. acquit, excuse, ignore, slight,
  survey 7. absolve, condone, forgive,
  neglect, overtop 9. disregard, oversight,
  rise above, supervise
overlord . . . 6. master 8. domineer,
  governor 9. tyrannize
overly . . . 3. too 8. careless 9. negligent
  11. overbearing, superficial
  12. supercilious
overmodest . . . 7. prudish 8. priggish
  11. puritanical, strait-laced

overnice . . . 5. fussy 6. purist 7. elegant,
  finicky 8. affected 10. fastidious
overpower . . . 3. awe 4. rout, stun
  5. crush 6. dazzle, defeat, master,
  subdue 7. conquer 8. overbear,
  overcome, vanquish 9. overthrow,
  overwhelm
overpowering . . . 6. fierce 8. exciting
  12. overwhelming
overreach . . . 4. dupe 5. cheat 6. exceed,
  nobble, outwit, overgo, strain 7. deceive
  10. circumvent
overrun . . . 5. crush, swarm 6. abound,
  desert, exceed, infest, outrun, ravage,
  spread 7. destroy, pervade, run over,
  trample 8. overflow 9. overwhelm
  11. superabound
overscrupulous . . . 7. prudish
  9. overexact 10. overstrict
  14. overfastidious
overshadow . . . 5. excel 6. darken
  7. eclipse, obscure, shelter 8. dominate
  9. overcloud
overshoe . . . 3. gum 6. arctic, galosh
  (galoshe)
oversight . . . 4. care 5. error, lapse,
  watch 6. charge 7. control, neglect
  8. omission 9. direction 10. inspection
  11. supervision 12. guardianship,
  surveillance 13. nonobservance
overskirt . . . 7. pannier (anc) 10. upper
  skirt
oversleeve . . . 6. armlet
overspread . . . 5. cover 6. infest
  7. overrun, pervade 8. disperse,
  suffused
overt . . . 4. open 6. patent, public
  7. obvious 8. apparent, manifest
  10. open to view
overtake . . . 5. catch, reach, seize
  6. detect, rejoin 7. ensnare
  9. apprehend, captivate
overthrow . . . 4. down, rout, ruin
  5. worst 6. defeat, depose, refute,
  unseat 7. conquer, deposal, destroy,
  ruinate, unhorse 8. demolish, disprove,
  overcome, overturn, vanquish
  9. prostrate 10. revolution
overthrown . . . 6. fallen, ruined
  8. defeated 9. disproved
overtones . . . 5. tones 8. partials
  9. harmonics
overtop . . . 5. dwarf, excel 7. obscure,
  surpass 8. go beyond, overhead,
  override 9. transcend 10. tower above
overture . . . 5. offer, proem 7. opening,
  prelude 8. aperture, proposal
  11. composition, proposition 13. peace
  offering
overturn . . . 3. tip 4. tilt 5. throw, upset
  6. topple 7. capsize, conquer, destroy,
  overset, reverse, subvert 9. overthrow,
  overwhelm
overweight . . . 7. obesity 11. overbalance
  13. preponderance
overwhelm . . . 4. bury, rout 5. crush
  6. defeat, deluge, engulf 7. confute,
  conquer, engross, immerse, oppress
  8. overturn, submerge 9. overpower,
  overthrow .
Ovidae, Ovinae . . . 5. goats, sheep

oviparous . . . **11.** ovoviparous **12.** egg producing (opp of viviparous)
ovoid, ovoidal . . . **7.** egglike **9.** egg-shaped
ovule . . . **3.** egg **4.** seed **6.** embryo, ovulum
ovum . . . **3.** egg **4.** seed **5.** spore **6.** gamete **8.** germ cell
owe . . . **3.** due, own **7.** possess **9.** be obliged **10.** be indebted
ower . . . **6.** debtor
owl (pert to) . . .
  barn . . **4.** lulu **5.** padge
  breed . . **6.** pigeon
  eagle . . **7.** katogle **14.** Tiger of the Wood
  eye . . **4.** disc
  family . . **9.** Strigidae
  female . . **3.** hen
  genus . . **4.** Bubo **5.** Ninox, Strix **7.** Syrnium
  horned . . **4.** Bubo **6.** aziola (small) **8.** Hush-wing
  light . . **4.** dusk
  like . . **4.** owly **8.** strigine
  parrot . . **6.** kakapo
  Puerto Rican . . **6.** mucaro
  short-eared . . **8.** marsh owl
  tawny . . **8.** billywix
  term . . **4.** hoot **11.** bird of night **13.** bird of Minerva
  white . . **7.** wapacut
  young . . **4.** utum **5.** owlet
own . . . **4.** have **5.** admit **7.** confess, possess **11.** acknowledge
owner . . . **6.** master **7.** planter (plantation) **8.** landlady, landlord **10.** proprietor
ownership . . . **4.** oadl (anc law) **5.** claim **7.** tenancy **8.** dominium, interest, property **10.** possession **11.** seigniorage **12.** seignioralty **14.** proprietorship
ox . . . **5.** beeve, steer **6.** bovine **8.** strength **13.** beast of burden
ox (pert to) . . .
  Celebes . . **4.** anoa

  genus . . **3.** Bos
  harness . . **4.** yoke
  horned . . **4.** reem
  India . . **4.** gaur
  like . . **5.** bison **6.** bovine **7.** taurine
  stall . . **5.** boose
  Tibetan . . **3.** yak
  type . . **4.** zebu
  wild . . **4.** urus **7.** banteng
  working . . **4.** aver
  yoke . . **4.** span
oxeye . . . **4.** boce (fish) **5.** daisy **6.** dunlin, plover
oxford . . . **4.** gray, shoe **5.** cloth
Oxford (pert to) . . .
  college accts . . **6.** battel
  color . . **4.** blue, gray
  Marbles . . **7.** Arundel
  Museum . . **9.** Ashmolean (1683)
  officer . . **6.** beadle (bedel at Oxford) (bedell at Cambridge)
  scholarship . . **6.** Rhodes
  school . . **10.** University (1570)
  sheep (hornless) . . **4.** Down
oxide of iron . . . **4.** rust
oxide of sodium . . . **4.** soda
oxidize . . . **4.** rust **5.** erode **9.** sulphuret (Philat)
oxter . . . **3.** arm **6.** armpit **7.** embrace
oxtongue . . . **5.** plant **7.** biltong, bugloss
oxwort . . . **9.** butterbur
oxygen . . . **3.** gas **5.** oxide, ozone **7.** element
oxyopia . . . **10.** extra sight
oyez, oyes . . . **6.** hear ye
oyster . . . **6.** huitre **7.** bivalve, mollusk
oyster (pert to) . . .
  gatherer . . **7.** tongman
  rake . . **5.** tongs
  shell . . **4.** husk, test **5.** shuck
  spawn . . **6.** cultch
  type . . **9.** bluepoint
  young . . **4.** spat
Ozark State . . . **8.** Missouri
Oz author . . . **4.** Baum (L Frank)
ozone . . . **3.** air **6.** oxygen

P

P . . . **2.** Pi **6.** letter (16th)
pa . . . **4.** Papa **6.** father
pa, pah . . . **4.** fort **7.** village **10.** settlement (fortified)
paauw . . . **7.** bustard
pabulum . . . **4.** food, fuel **7.** aliment, support **9.** nutriment **10.** sustenance **11.** nourishment
pac, pack . . . **8.** half boot, moccasin
paca . . . **6.** rodent **9.** Cuniculus
pace . . . **3.** run **4.** gait, lope, rate, step, trot, walk **5.** speed **7.** measure **8.** movement, velocity
pace (L) . . . **5.** peace
Pace . . . **5.** Pasch **6.** Easter
pachyderm . . . **8.** elephant **10.** rhinoceros **12.** hippopotamus, Pachydermata

pachydermous . . . **11.** thick-walled **12.** thick-skinned
pacific . . . **4.** calm **6.** irenic, serene **8.** irenical, peaceful, tranquil **9.** peaceable, quiescent **12.** conciliatory
Pacific (pert to) . . .
  Coast tree . . **7.** madrona **8.** knob pine
  Highway . . **10.** Camino Real
  island bird . . **4.** kagu
  island shark . . **4.** mako **11.** blue pointer
  island tree . . **4.** ipil
  islands . . **4.** Guam, Wake **5.** Samos **7.** Oceania **8.** Caroline, Tasmania **9.** Melanesia, Polynesia **10.** Micronesia
  shrub . . **5.** salal
  States . . **6.** Oregon **10.** California, Washington

P

stepping stones.. **9**. Aleutians (Russia to America)

Pacific Ocean discoverer ... **6**. Balboa

pacifier ... **3**. sop **4**. ring (baby's) **6**. nipple **7**. soother **8**. sedative **10**. peacemaker

pacify ... **4**. calm, ease, lull **5**. abate, allay **6**. soften, soothe **7**. appease, assuage, mollify, placate **8**. mitigate, palliate **9**. alleviate **10**. conciliate, propitiate **11**. tranquilize (tranquillize)

pack ... **3**. ram, set, wad **4**. cram, fill, load, stow, tamp **5**. carry, flock, horde, steve, truss **6**. bundle, embale **8**. assemble, encumber, quantity, send away

pack (pert to) ...
animal.. **3**. ass **5**. burro, camel, llama **6**. donkey
back.. **8**. knapsack
horse.. **7**. sumpter
horse bag.. **5**. kyack **7**. pannier
of hounds.. **6**. kennel

package ... **3**. pad **4**. bale **5**. fadge **6**. bundle, packet, parcel, robbin (peppers), seroon **11**. combination

packing ... **4**. lute, seal **7**. stowage **9**. packaging **10**. rubber ring

paco ... **3**. ore **6**. alpaca

Pacolet ... **10**. swift horse

pact ... **6**. pactum **7**. bargain **8**. contract **9**. agreement

Pactolian ... **6**. golden

Pactolus, Myth (pert to) ...
famed for.. **5**. Midas **11**. gold-bearing
river (Asia Minor).. **5**. Lydia

pad ... **3**. mat, paw **4**. fill, foot, frog, line, path, walk **5**. quilt, stuff, track, tramp **6**. tablet, trudge **7**. bedding, bolster, cushion, footpad **8**. notebook, protract, saturate **9**. footprint, pulvillus **10**. highwayman

pad (pert to) ...
cloth.. **7**. housing **11**. saddlecloth
hair.. **3**. rat
harness, part.. **5**. panel **6**. terret **7**. housing **10**. horsecloth
perfume.. **6**. sachet

padding ... **6**. lining **7**. wadding **8**. softness, stuffing **11**. superfluity

paddle ... **3**. oar, row **4**. beat, stir, wade, whip **5**. blade, board, scull, spank, spoon **6**. dabble, propel **7**. flipper **8**. lumpfish

paddle (pert to) ...
English.. **7**. trample **8**. lumpfish **9**. tread upon **10**. paddlecock
Scotch.. **3**. hoe **4**. spud

paddock (pert to) ...
paddockstool.. **9**. toadstool
piper.. **9**. horsetail
stone.. **10**. greenstone

paddy ... **4**. rice, soft **7**. padlike **8**. cushiony **9**. rice field **10**. hod carrier

Paddy ... **7**. Patrick **8**. Irishman

paddymelon ... **7**. wallaby

Paddy's hurricane (Naut) ... **4**. calm

paddywhack ... **4**. beat, blow **6**. temper **9**. ruddy duck, thrashing

padge ... **7**. barn owl

padmasana ... **11**. cross-legged (Buddha style), lotus-shaped

padre ... **4**. monk **6**. Father, priest

8. chaplain, minister

padrona ... **8**. landlady, mistress

padrone ... **8**. master, patron **8**. landlord **9**. innkeeper

paedarchy ... **14**. rule by children

pagan ... **6**. ethnic, paynim **7**. heathen **10**. heathenism, idolatrous, unbeliever **11**. irreligious

Paganalia ... **8**. festival (Rom)

pagan god ... **4**. idol

page ... **3**. boy **4**. leaf **5**. child, folio **6**. summon **7**. attendant, messenger

page (pert to) ...
beginning.. **7**. flyleaf
book.. **5**. folio **6**. cahier, sheets
lady's.. **7**. esquire **8**. escudero
left-hand.. **5**. verso
number.. **5**. folio
right-hand.. **5**. recto
title.. **5**. unwan **6**. rubric **12**. frontispiece

pageant ... **4**. pomp, show **5**. drama **6**. parade **7**. tableau **8**. aquacade **9**. spectacle **10**. exhibition **11**. ostentation

pages ... **7**. paginal **8**. paginate

Pagliacci ... **5**. opera **9**. character

pagne ... **9**. loincloth, petticoat

pagoda ... **2**. ta **3**. taa **4**. idol **5**. booth **6**. temple **11**. summerhouse

pagoda (pert to) ...
finial.. **3**. tee
sleeve.. **12**. funnel-shaped
stone.. **12**. Agalmatolite
tree.. **6**. banyan **10**. frangipani

paha ... **4**. hill **5**. ridge (glacial)

pahi ... **4**. ship **5**. canoe (seagoing)

pahmi ... **5**. bobac **6**. marmot

paho ... **7**. pahutan **11**. prayer stick

pahutan ... **5**. mango

paid ... **5**. hired **6**. cashed **7**. content, settled, yielded **9**. satisfied **10**. discharged

paideutics ... **8**. pedagogy, teaching

paid office (without work) ... **8**. sinecure

paid out ... **5**. spent **8**. expended **9**. disbursed

paigle ... **7**. cowslip **8**. crowfoot **10**. stitchwort **12**. cuckooflower

pail ... **3**. can, pan **4**. beat **5**. bucket, harass, situla, thrash, vessel **8**. cannikin

paillasse, palliasse ... **3**. bed (masonry) **8**. mattress (straw)

pailles ... **6**. straws (cookery)

paillou, pailoo ... **7**. archway (memorial)

pain ... **3**. ail **4**. ache, agra, pang **5**. agony, labor, thraw, throb, wound **6**. grieve, stitch **7**. afflict, ailment, gnawing, torture, trouble **8**. disquiet, distress **9**. suffering **10**. affliction, punishment

painful ... **4**. sore **7**. careful **8**. diligent **9**. difficult, laborious **10**. afflictive, unpleasant **11**. industrious, painstaking

painkiller ... **7**. anodyne **8**. medicine, sedative **9**. analgesic, calmative **10**. depressant

painstaking ... **5**. fussy **7**. careful, labored **8**. diligent, thorough **9**. assiduity, assiduous, laborious

paint ... **4**. coat, draw, limn **5**. adorn, color, rouge, stain **6**. depict, parget, sketch **7**. picture, pigment, portray

8. cosmetic, describe 9. delineate, embellish 11. application (Med)
paint (pert to)...
blue, green.. 4. bice
comb form.. 5. picto
face.. 4. fard
glossy.. 6. enamel
Latin.. 6. pinxit
spreader.. 7. spatula
through pattern.. 7. stencil
with vermilion.. 7. miniate
paintbrush... 8. hawkweed 10. painted cup 11. St John's wort
painted... 6. coated 7. colored, feigned 9. disguised, portrayed 10. artificial, variegated
painted (pert to)...
bat.. 11. Vespertilio
beauty.. 9. butterfly
bunting.. 5. finch
duck.. 8. mandarin 9. harlequin
enamel.. 7. Limoges
hyena.. 14. Cape hunting dog
lady.. 7. thistle 8. sweet pea 9. butterfly
process.. 7. scumble
trillium.. 9. wake-robin
turtle.. 8. carapace
painter... 4. puma 6. cougar 7. panther
painter... 4. Dali 5. Monet 6. Millet, Rubens 7. da Vinci, El Greco, Picasso, van Gogh 8. Reynolds, Whistler 9. Rembrandt 12. Gainsborough, Grandma Moses, Michelangelo
Painter's Easel... 6. Pictor (constellation)
painting... 3. oil 5. genre, mural, Pietà (sacred), secco 6. fresco, marine 7. impasto, tempera 9. encaustic, grisaille, landscape 10. cerography 11. portraiture 12. illustration
pair... 3. duo, two 4. dyad, mate, span, team, yoke 5. brace, unite 6. couple
paired... 5. gemel (Her) 7. coupled, leagued
pairs, growing in... 6. binate, double
paisano... 7. peasant 10. countryman, road runner
pal... 4. chum, pard 5. buddy, crony 6. cobber 7. partner 9. companion 10. accomplice
palace... 5. court, Doges, house (Astrol) 6. palais 7. palazzo 10. praetorium (pretorium)
paladin... 4. hero 6. knight (Round Table)
Paladins of France... 9. The Twelve
palais... 6. palace 10. courthouse
Palamedes... 4. hero (Trojan War)
palampore... 7. hanging (cotton) 8. bedcover
palanquin, palankeen... 4. kago 5. dooly (doolie), palki 6. litter, palkee 10. conveyance
palanquin bearer... 5. hamal 6. sirdar
palas... 4. dhak, tree (yellow dye)
palatable... 5. sapid, tasty 6. savory 8. pleading, seasoned 10. acceptable
palate... 4. cion 5. taste, uvula, velum 6. relish 10. epipharynx
palatine... 4. bone 6. artery, county 8. palatial
Palatine Confession... 10. Heidelberg

palaver... 4. talk 6. confer 7. chatter 8. converse, flattery 10. conference 12. conversation
pale... 3. dim, wan 4. ashy, fade, lily 5. ashen, fence, lurid, pasty, stake, white 6. blanch, bounds, paling, pallid, pallor, sallow, sickly, sphere 7. haggard, obscure, whitish 8. palisade 9. deathlike 10. indistinct
palea, palet... 4. fold 5. bract, scale 6. dewlap 8. ramentum
paleo (comb form)... 3. old 7. ancient
paleolithic culture... 8. Stone Age
Paleozoic... 10. Appalachia
Palestine (pert to)...
ancient name.. 6. Canaan
animal.. 4. cony (Bib) 5. daman
conqueror.. 5. David, Turks 11. Constantine
country (anc).. 4. Edom 5. Endor (Indur) 8. Nazareth 9. Philistia
lake.. 7. Dead Sea, Galilee
language.. 7. Aramaic
mountain (Bib).. 4. Zion 6. Carmel, Gilead, Hermon 13. Mount of Olives
plain, steppe.. 5. Negeb 6. Sharon
river.. 6. Jordan
town, district.. 4. Gaza 5. Haifa 7. Samaria 8. Jerusalem
paletot... 4. coat 8. overcoat
pali... 9. precipice 10. steep slope
pali (comb form)... 5. again 8. backward
Pali... 7. dialect (anc) 12. dead language
palimpsest... 9. parchment, rewritten 10. re-engraved 15. codex rescriptus
palindrome (same backward, forward)... 8. wordplay 9. inversion
paling... 5. fence, limit, palis, stake 6. fading, picket 7. fencing 9. enclosure
palisade... 5. cliff, fence, stake 6. picket 7. defense, enclose, fortify 8. espalier, palisado, surround 9. precipice 10. impalement 13. fortification
pall... 4. pale 5. cloak, cover, faint, qualm 6. coffin, mantle, nausea 7. secrecy 12. graveclothes
pallall... 9. hopscotch
palle... 5. balls 8. six balls (Medici)
pallet... 3. bed 4. pate 5. quilt 7. blanket 8. mattress 9. headpiece, paillasse
palliard... 6. beggar, lecher, rascal 8. vagabond
palliate... 4. hide 5. abate, cloak, cover, gloss 6. excuse, lessen, soften 7. conceal, qualify, relieve, shelter 8. disguise, mitigate, moderate 9. alleviate, extenuate
pallid... 3. wan 4. gray, pale 5. pasty, white 6. anemic, sallow
Pallu... 10. Reuben's son (Bib)
palm... 4. hand (part) 5. areca, bribe, steal 6. bacaba, handle, rattan, stroke, trophy
palm (pert to)...
civet.. 6. musang
cockatoo.. 5. arara
down.. 7. pronate
drink.. 5. assai
drink (alcoholic).. 4. beno, nipa
hand.. 6. palmus, thenar
handlike.. 7. palmate

house .. **8.** palmetum
lily .. **2.** ti
mat .. **6.** petate
off .. **5.** foist
ref to .. **10.** palmaceous
sap (fermented) .. **5.** toddy
starch .. **4.** sago
sugar .. **7.** jaggery
thatch .. **4.** nipa
palm (tree) ...
  African .. **7.** palmyra (sugar, wine)
  Arab .. **4.** doum (doom)
  Asiatic .. **4.** atap, nipa
  betel .. **5.** areca, bonga **6.** pinang
  book .. **4.** tara **7.** taliera
  Brazil .. **7.** urucuri (urucury)
  bussu, thatching .. **7.** troolie (trooly)
  cabbage .. **5.** Sabal **8.** palmetto
  Ceylon .. **4.** tala **7.** talipot (fanleaf)
  climbing, flexible .. **6.** rattan
  dwarf .. **5.** Sabal
  E Indies .. **4.** atap, nipa **7.** jaggery
   (sugar), tokopat (hat)
  fan .. **7.** talipot **8.** palmetto
  fiber .. **3.** tal **6.** raffia **8.** piassava
   (piassaba)
  Florida .. **5.** royal
  gingerbread tasting .. **4.** doum (doom)
  leaf .. **3.** tal **4.** olla (ola) **12.** chiquichiqui
  Malayan, feather .. **4.** irok **6.** gomuti
  palmyra .. **4.** brab, olla **6.** ronier
  Philippine (coconut) .. **4.** niog
  pinnate .. **5.** assai, nikau **7.** calamus,
   feather
  S America .. **5.** bussu, datil **6.** tooroo
   12. chiquichiqui
  spiny .. **6.** grugru
palmate ... **6.** antler, webbed **10.** hand-
  shaped
palmer ... **6.** ferule **7.** pilgrim (Holy Land)
  8. date palm **15.** prestidigitator
Palmetto State ... **13.** South Carolina
palmistry ... **10.** chirognomy, chiromancy
palmodic (Med) ... **5.** jerky
palp ... **6.** feeler, palpus **8.** tentacle
palpable ... **5.** plain **6.** patent **8.** manifest,
  tangible **9.** touchable **10.** noticeable,
  ponderable
palpebra ... **6.** eyelid
palpebrate ... **4.** wink
palpitate ... **4.** beat, drum **5.** throb
  7. flutter, pulsate
palpitation ... **7.** flutter, tremble
  9. pulsation, quivering, throbbing
  10. excitement
palsied ... **5.** shaky **9.** paralyzed, tottering
palter ... **5.** shift **6.** babble, haggle,
  mumble, parley **7.** bargain, chatter,
  quibble **9.** vacillate **10.** equivocate
  11. prevaricate
paltry ... **4.** mean, vile **5.** petty, trash
  6. trashy **7.** pitiful, rubbish **8.** picayune,
  trifling **9.** worthless **10.** despicable
  12. contemptible
pampass ... **5.** Pampa **6.** plains (treeless)
pamper ... **3.** pet **4.** cram, glut **5.** humor,
  spoil **6.** caress, coddle, cosset, cuddle,
  dandle, posset **7.** gratify, indulge
  11. mollycoddle
pamphagous ... **10.** omnivorous
pamphlet ... **5.** tract **6.** folder **7.** booklet,

  leaflet **8.** brochure
pan ... **3.** tab **4.** part, tina (mining),
  wash **5.** basin, roast, title (nobility)
  6. frying, lappet, spider, vessel
  7. cranium, hardpan, portion, skillet,
  subsoil **8.** ridicule, saucepan **9.** criticize
  10. acetabulum
pan (comb form) ... **3.** all **5.** every
Pan (pert to) ...
  animal .. **3.** ape **10.** chimpanzee
  god (Gr) .. **6.** flocks
  instrument .. **4.** pipe, reed
  music .. **9.** Pan's pipes
  Pipes of .. **6.** syrinx **8.** Panpipes
  Roman identity .. **6.** Faunus
  seat of worship .. **7.** Arcadia
  son .. **7.** Silenus
panacea ... **4.** cure **6.** elixir, remedy
  7. allheal (plant), cure-all **8.** nepenthe
  10. catholicon **11.** panchreston
panache ... **4.** tuft (feathered) **5.** plume
  7. swagger
Panama ...
  bay .. **5.** Limon
  capital .. **10.** Panama City
  city .. **5.** Colon **6.** Balboa **9.** Cristobal
  engineer .. **8.** Goethals
  gulf .. **6.** Darien
  Indian .. **4.** Cuna
  isthmus of .. **6.** Darien (old name),
   Panama **7.** San Blas
  redwood .. **5.** quira
  river .. **7.** Chagres
Panama Canal Lock ... **5.** Gatun
  10. Miraflores
panarchy ... **13.** universal rule
panaris ... **5.** felon **7.** whitlow
  10. paronychia
panary ... **5.** bread **11.** breadmaking
panatela ... **5.** cigar
pancake ... **6.** froise (fraise) **7.** fritter
  8. flapjack **11.** griddlecake
Pancake Day ... **13.** Shrove Tuesday
pancreas ... **5.** gland **10.** sweetbread
  16. Isle of Langerhans
panda ... **7.** bearcat
pandemonium ... **4.** hell **5.** noise
  6. tumult, uproar
Pandemonium (pert to) ...
  abode of .. **6.** demons
  capital of .. **4.** Hell
  palace of .. **5.** Satan
  pert to .. **15.** infernal regions
pander ... **4.** bawd, pimp **5.** cater, serve
  7. toady to **12.** administer to
pandle ... **7.** a shrimp
Pandora's Box ... **6.** plague **9.** human
  ills
Pandora's husband ... **10.** Epimetheus
panegyric ... **5.** éloge, elogy **6.** eulogy
  7. oration, writing **8.** encomium
  9. discourse, laudation
pang ... **3.** fit **4.** pain **5.** throe **6.** twinge
  8. paroxysm
pangolin ... **5.** Manis **8.** anteater
  9. Pholidota
panhandle ... **3.** beg
Panhellenic ... **5.** games (Isthmian)
  6. Greece **10.** fraternity (Greek-letter)
panic ... **4.** fear, fray **5.** alarm, chaos,
  scare **6.** fright **8.** stampede

pannier ... **6.** basket, dosser (dorser)
    7. corbeit **9.** overskirt
panoply ... **7.** defense **11.** suit of armor
panorama ... **4.** view **5.** scene **7.** picture,
    scenery **9.** cyclorama
pant ... **4.** beat, gasp **5.** heave, throb
    7. breathe, pulsate **11.** palpitation
Pantagruel (pert to) ...
    character (romantic) .. **5.** giant
    companion .. **7.** Panurge
    father .. **9.** Gargantua
pantaloon, pantaloons ... **5.** pants
    6. dotard, old man **8.** breeches, trousers
    11. Patron Saint (Venice)
Pantheon (pert to) ...
    aggregate .. **4.** gods **7.** deities
    builder .. **7.** Hadrian (120 AD)
    building .. **6.** shrine, temple **10.** le
    Pantheon (Paris) **16.** Westminster Abbey
    Rome .. **15.** Temple of the Gods
panther, painter ... **4.** pard, puma
    6. cougar, jaguar, ocelot **7.** leopard
pantler ... **6.** butler **7.** servant
pantry ... **5.** ambry **6.** larder **7.** buttery,
    pannier, pantler **8.** cupboard
pants ... **5.** chaps **7.** drawers **8.** trousers
    10. chaparajos (chaparejos), pantaloons
panuelo ... **6.** collar **8.** kerchief
    9. neckcloth
pap ... **4.** teat **6.** nipple **8.** mammilla,
    soft diet
papa ... **3.** dad **4.** clay, Pope **6.** baboon,
    father, potato, priest **7.** vulture
papal ... **9.** apostolic **10.** pontifical
papal (pert to) ...
    book of decrees .. **8.** decretal
    chancery .. **6.** datary
    Court .. **3.** See **5.** Curia
    envoy .. **8.** ablegate
    legate .. **6.** nuncio
    letter .. **4.** bull
    reformer .. **7.** Gregory
    residence .. **7.** Vatican
    seal .. **5.** bulla
    vestment .. **5.** fanon, orale
paper (pert to) ...
    absorbent .. **7.** blotter
    broken .. **5.** casse
    brown .. **6.** manila
    coated .. **6.** charta
    collection .. **7.** dossier
    copy .. **6.** carbon
    crinkled .. **5.** crepe
    crisp .. **6.** pelure
    currency .. **5.** scrip
    cutlet wrap .. **8.** papilote
    damaged .. **5.** casse, salle **6.** retree
    design .. **9.** watermark
    fine .. **5.** linen **6.** vellum **9.** parchment
    flower .. **11.** strawflower
    folded .. **5.** folio
    for pounding gold sheets .. **7.** cutches
    gummed .. **5.** label, stamp **7.** plaster,
    sticker
    legal .. **4.** writ **5.** title
    measure .. **4.** page, ream **5.** quire, sheet
    nautilus .. **8.** argonaut
    official .. **5.** targe **8.** document
    pad .. **6.** tablet
    postage stamp .. **6.** pelure
    size .. **3.** cap **4.** copy, demy, pott, quad

    5. atlas, crown, folio, legal **6.** octavo
    8. foolscap, imperial **9.** colombier
    small piece .. **5.** scrip
    thin .. **4.** rice **6.** pelure, tissue **9.** onionskin
    transfer .. **12.** decalcomania
    untrimmed .. **6.** deckle (deckel) **10.** deckle
    edge **11.** deckle-edged
    writing size .. **3.** cap
paper chase ... **13.** hare and hounds
papilla ... **6.** nipple **10.** projection
papule ... **6.** papula, pimple
papyra (comb form) ... **5.** paper
papyrus ... **4.** pith, reed **5.** paper, sedge
    6. scroll
par ... **2.** by **5.** value **7.** average, by
    way of, strokes, through **8.** equality,
    superior
parable ... **4.** myth, tale **5.** fable, story
    8. allegory, apologue **10.** comparison,
    similitude
parabola ... **5.** curve
parade ... **4.** pomp, show **5.** march
    6. flaunt **8.** flourish, grandeur, splendor
    9. pageantry, promenade, spectacle
    10. pretension, procession
    11. ostentation **12.** magnificence
    13. formal display
paradigm ... **5.** model **7.** example, pattern
paradisaic ... **6.** Edenic
Paradise ... **4.** Eden **5.** Jenna **6.** Aidenn,
    heaven, Utopia **7.** Elysium
Paradise (pert to) ...
    apple .. **5.** dwarf
    Arabic form .. **6.** Aidenn
    Buddhist, Western .. **4.** Jodo
    fool's .. **5.** limbo
    grosbeak .. **9.** cutthroat (bird)
    Mohammedan .. **5.** Jenna
    plumage .. **14.** bird of paradise
    poem (Milton) .. **12.** Paradise Lost
    16. Paradise Regained
    river .. **5.** Gihon (Bib)
    tree .. **9.** China tree
paragon ... **4.** type **5.** ideal, match,
    model **7.** diamond (100 carats), paladin,
    pattern **8.** parallel **9.** nonpareil
paragram ... **3.** pun
Paraguay ...
    capital .. **8.** Asunción
    city .. **9.** Paraguari **10.** Concepcion,
    Villarrica
    language .. **7.** Guarani, Spanish
    river .. **6.** Paraná **8.** Paraguay
    tea .. **4.** maté **5.** yerba **11.** yerba de
    maté
parakeet ... **5.** green **6.** parrot, puffin
    11. budgereegah (budgerygah)
paralysis ... **5.** palsy **7.** paresis
    10. hemiplegia, paraplegia **11.** loss of
    power
paralyze ... **5.** scram **6.** benumb, deaden
    7. astound, terrify, unnerve
paramount ... **3.** top **5.** chief, liege
    6. ruling **7.** supreme **8.** dominant,
    superior **9.** principal **10.** preeminent
    13. most important
paramour ... **5.** amour, leman, lover,
    wooer **8.** mistress **9.** gallantry
    10. sweetheart
paranoia ... **9.** catatonia, monomania,
    nosomania

parapet . . . **5.** redan **7.** barrier, bulwark, rampart

parasite . . . **3.** bur, sug **5.** drone, toady **6.** Gnatho, insect, sponge **7.** entozoa **8.** hanger-on **9.** entophyte, sycophant

parasite (pert to) . . .
animal . . **6.** cuckoo **7.** cowbird, entozoa
external . . **12.** ectoparasite
internal . . **7.** entozoa
marine . . **6.** remora, sponge
plant . . **9.** entophyte
slang . . **6.** flunky
trout . . **3.** sug

parasitic (pert to) . . .
fish . . **6.** remora
fungus . . **4.** rust **6.** lichen
worm . . **8.** trichina (larva)

parcel . . . **3.** lot **4.** mete, part **5.** piece, solum (law) **6.** bundle, packet **7.** package, portion **8.** fragment

parch . . . **3.** dry **4.** burn **5.** dry up, roast, toast **6.** scorch **7.** shrivel, torrefy

parched . . . **4.** sere **5.** burnt, dried **7.** thirsty **8.** withered

parchment (pert to) . . .
bookcover . . **5.** forel (forrel)
fine . . **6.** vellum
manuscript . . **10.** palimpsest
roll . . **4.** pell **6.** scroll
school . . **7.** diploma

pard . . . **4.** chum **5.** tiger **7.** comrade, leopard, panther, partner **10.** camelopard **11.** confederate

pardesi (Hind) . . . **9.** foreigner, outlander

pardie, parde, pardi (anc) . . . **4.** oath **6.** indeed, surely, verily **9.** certainly

pardon . . . **5.** mercy, remit, spare **6.** acquit, excuse **7.** absolve, amnesty, condone, forgive **8.** tolerate **9.** acquittal, remission **10.** absolution, indulgence (Eccl) **11.** forgiveness

pardonable . . . **6.** venial **8.** expiable **9.** excusable **10.** forgivable

pardon chair, stall . . . **12.** confessional

pare . . . **3.** cut **4.** peel, skin **5.** shave **6.** cut off, remove, resect

parent . . . **3.** dad **4.** sire **5.** pater **6.** father, mother, source **7.** genitor **8.** begetter **10.** progenitor

parental affection (animal) . . . **6.** storge

parget . . . **4.** coat **5.** paint **7.** plaster **8.** decorate, ornament **9.** whitewash

parhelion . . . **3.** sun (mock)

pariah . . . **3.** dog (half-wild) **7.** outcast **8.** commoner, low caste

parian . . . **6.** marble, market

Parian . . . **5.** Paros **6.** marble (sculptural) **9.** porcelain

parimutuel machine . . . **9.** totalizer **11.** totalizator

Paris (pert to) . . .
blue . . **6.** cobalt **8.** Prussian
daisy . . **10.** marguerite
Garden (London) . . **10.** bear garden
green . . **11.** insecticide

Paris, France . . .
anc name . . **7.** Lutetia (Lutice)
airport . . **4.** Orly
capital of . . **6.** France
criminal . . **6.** apache
famed sites . . **6.** Louvre **8.** Pantheon
9. Notre Dame **10.** Montmartre **11.** Eiffel Tower **13.** Champs Elysées, Napoleon's Tomb
native . . **8.** Parisian
patron saint . . **5.** Denis (Denys)
racecourse . . **7.** Auteuil
river . . **5.** Seine
subway . . **5.** Metro

Paris, Gr legend . . .
brought about . . **9.** Trojan War **10.** Fall of Troy
father . . **5.** Priam (King of Troy)
killer of . . **8.** Achilles
mother . . **6.** Hecuba
wife . . **6.** Oenone

parish . . . **5.** laity **7.** diocese **8.** district **9.** parochial

paristhmion . . . **6.** tonsil

park . . . **4.** area (enclosed) **5.** place, tract **6.** claire, common, settle **7.** pasture (Eng) **8.** woodland **9.** grassland, pleasance **10.** playground **11.** reservation, set and leave

Park, Highway . . .
Avenue . . **9.** Manhattan
Lane . . **6.** London
Row . . **9.** Manhattan

Park, Historical . . . **6.** Shiloh **8.** Pea Ridge, Saratoga **9.** Minute Man **10.** Gettysburg, Morristown **12.** Harper's Ferry, Independence

Park, US . . . **4.** Zion **7.** Glacier, Olympic (rain forests) **8.** Sequoyah (Sequoja), Yosemite **9.** Haleakala, Mesa Verde **10.** Everglades, Mt McKinley, Shenandoah **11.** Grand Canyon, Kings Canyon, Yellowstone **12.** Harper's Ferry **15.** Petrified Forest

parlay, parley . . . **4.** chat **5.** parle, treat **6.** confer **7.** discuss **8.** converse **10.** conference, discussion **11.** arbitration

parliament . . . **4.** Diet **8.** Congress **11.** legislature

parlous . . . **4.** keen **5.** risky **6.** shrewd **7.** cunning **8.** shocking **9.** dangerous

Parnassian . . . **4.** muse, poet **9.** butterfly **10.** Parnassius

Parnassus, Greece . . .
mountain . . **6.** Phocis
site of . . **6.** Delphi **8.** Castalia (fountain) **13.** Delphic Apollo
symbol of . . **6.** poetry

parody . . . **5.** farce **6.** satire **7.** mockery, take-off **9.** burlesque, imitation **10.** caricature

paroemia . . . **7.** proverb

parol, parole . . . **4.** oral, word **6.** speech **7.** freedom, promise, release **8.** pleading **11.** word of mouth

paronomasia . . . **3.** pun **7.** punning **8.** wordplay **9.** assonance **12.** agnomination

paroxysm . . . **3.** fit **4.** pang **5.** throe **6.** access, attack, frenzy **7.** illness **9.** agitation **10.** fit of anger **12.** exacerbation

paroxysm of grief . . . **5.** agony

parricide (murder of) . . . **7.** kinsman

parrot . . . **3.** ara, hia, kea **4.** jako, kaka, loro, lory **5.** arara, cagit, macaw,

polly **6.** kakapo, tiriba **7.** corella,
lorilet **8.** cockatoo, lorikeet, lovebird,
parakeet **9.** Psittacus (Old World)
   14. Psittaciformes
parrot (pert to) . . .
   disease . . **11.** psittacosis
   genus . . **6.** Nestor **9.** Psittacus
   gray . . **4.** jako
   green . . **5.** cagit
   hawk . . **3.** hia
   long-tailed . . **5.** macaw
   monk . . **4.** loro
   New Zealand . . **4.** kaka
   owl . . **6.** kakapo
   parrot fish . . **4.** loro, scar **5.** lauia **6.** scarid
      7. labroid **8.** Labridae, Scaridae
   parrotlike (tongued) . . **12.** anthropoglot
   sheep-killing . . **3.** kea
   short-tailed . . **7.** lorilet
parry . . **4.** fend, ward **5.** avert, avoid,
   elude, evade, shift **6.** refute, thwart
pars . . . **4.** part
Parsee Bible . . . **10.** Zend Avesta
Parsei, Parsi . . **6.** Gheber (Ghebre)
   11. Zoroastrian **13.** fire worshiper
Parsifal (pert to) . . .
   character . . **6.** Knight
   healer of . . **8.** Amfortas
   son . . **9.** Lohengrin
parsimonious . . . **4.** near **5.** close
   6. frugal, meager, skimpy, sordid,
   stingy **7.** miserly, sparing **8.** covetous,
   grasping **9.** illiberal, mercenary,
   penurious **10.** avaricious
parsley . . . **4.** herb **5.** cumin **7.** garnish
   9. Ammiaceae, flavoring
parsley camphor . . . **6.** apiole
parson . . . **6.** rector **8.** minister, preacher,
   reverend **9.** clergyman
parsonage . . . **5.** gleve, manse, tithe
   7. rectory **8.** benefice, vicarage
   9. pastorate **10.** presbytery
parson bird . . . **3.** tui
part . . . **3.** cut, die **4.** open, role, twin
   5. allot, break, piece, sever, share
   6. depart, divide, member, sunder
   7. analyze, disband, disjoin, divorce,
   portion, section, segment **8.** dissever,
   disunite, division, fragment, function,
   separate **9.** component
part (pert to) . . .
   basic . . **4.** core, pith **7.** essence, nucleus
   choice . . **5.** cream, elite **6.** marrow
   coarse . . **5.** dregs
   composite . . **7.** section
   corresponding . . **7.** isomere
   essential . . **4.** core, gist, pith **5.** heart
   extra . . **5.** spare
   greater . . **4.** bulk
   hardest . . **5.** brunt
   infinitesimal . . **4.** atom, mite
   insignificant . . **3.** bit **4.** iota **6.** trifle
   kept . . **6.** retent
   main . . **4.** body **5.** trunk
   narrow . . **4.** neck
   proportional . . **5.** quota
   rootlike . . **7.** radicle
   sawlike . . **5.** serra
   segment . . **5.** tmema
   small . . **3.** bit, jot **4.** iota **6.** detail
      7. snippet

   smallest . . **4.** whit **5.** minim
   solo accompaniment . . **9.** obbligato
   tenth . . **5.** tithe
   unpaid . . **6.** arrear **9.** arrearage
   uppermost . . **3.** top **4.** peak **6.** upside
      7. topside
   winglike . . **3.** ala
   with . . **7.** discard **10.** relinquish
partage . . . **4.** part **5.** share **7.** portion
   8. division
partake . . . **3.** eat **5.** share **7.** receive
   11. participate
partan . . . **4.** crab
parted . . . **5.** cleft **6.** cloven **7.** divided,
   severed **9.** separated **11.** apportioned
parterre . . . **10.** level space **12.** theater
   boxes, theater space **17.** ornamental
   gardens
parthogenesis . . . **7.** apogamy
   10. thelyotoky **12.** reproduction
partial . . . **6.** biased, unfair, unjust
   7. limited **8.** not total, one-sided,
   partisan **9.** imperfect **10.** fractional,
   incomplete, prejudiced **11.** predisposed
   13. foolishly fond
partiality . . . **4.** bias **6.** desire **9.** injustice,
   prejudice **10.** preference **11.** inclination,
   partisanism **12.** partisanship,
   predilection
participant . . . **6.** sharer **7.** entrant
   8. partaker **9.** accessory, colleague
   12. participator
particle . . . **3.** ace, bit, ion, jot **4.** atom,
   drop, iota, mite, mote, whit **5.** grain,
   piece, shred, spark **6.** tittle **7.** globule,
   granule, smidgen
particle (pert to) . . .
   electric . . **3.** ion **5.** anion **6.** proton
   least possible . . **5.** minim
   minute . . **3.** jot, ray **4.** atom, iota **5.** grain,
      speck **7.** granule
   negative . . **3.** nor, not
   nuclear . . **5.** gluon, meson, quark
      6. baryon, hadron
parti-colored . . . **4.** pied, roan **5.** pinto
   6. motley **7.** piebald **9.** harlequin
   10. variegated **11.** polychromic
particular . . . **4.** item, nice, part, sole
   5. event, fussy **6.** detail **7.** precise,
   special, topical **8.** detailed, especial,
   peculiar, separate, specific **9.** attentive
   10. fastidious, individual, overminute
   11. persnickety **12.** circumstance,
   technicality
partisan, partizan . . . **4.** pike **5.** staff
   6. zealot **7.** partial **8.** adherent, advocate,
   follower **9.** supporter **10.** fractional,
   prejudiced
partition . . . **4.** wall **5.** allot **6.** divide,
   screen, septum **7.** scantle **8.** set apart
   9. apportion, severance **10.** distribute,
   separation **13.** apportionment
partitioned . . . **7.** septate
partly . . . **6.** in part **9.** partially
partly illuminated . . . **6.** shaded
   8. adumbral **9.** penumbral
partly open . . . **4.** ajar
partner . . . **3.** pal **4.** ally, mate, wife
   6. sharer, spouse **7.** comrade, husband
   9. associate, coadjutor, colleague
   10. accomplice **11.** confederate,

participant
partnership . . . **4.** firm **7.** cahoots, co-mated **8.** business, contract **10.** fellowship **11.** affiliation **13.** participation
part of . . .
anchor . . **4.** palm
bird wing . . **5.** alula
cannon . . **5.** chase
church . . **4.** apse, nave **5.** altar **7.** chancel **8.** transept
circle . . **3.** arc **6.** degree **7.** segment
compass . . **6.** needle
ear . . **4.** lobe **5.** pinna **6.** tragus **8.** tympanum **9.** labyrinth
eye . . **4.** iris, uvea **5.** pupil **6.** cornea, retina
flower . . **4.** stem **5.** calyx, petal, sepal
foot lever . . **5.** pedal **7.** treadle
fort . . **5.** redan **7.** bastion
head . . **4.** pate **5.** scalp, skull **7.** cranium
minstrel show . . **4.** olio **5.** bones **6.** end man **12.** interlocutor
newspaper . . **3.** ear **4.** item, page **6.** by-line **9.** editorial
optical measure . . **7.** alidade
printing press . . **6.** platen
rifle (anc) . . **4.** tige
ship . . **3.** bow **4.** brig, deck, helm, keel, mast **5.** stern, wheel **6.** anchor, bridge, rudder **8.** steerage
step . . **5.** riser, tread **6.** nosing
theater . . **3.** box **4.** loge **5.** foyer, stage **7.** balcony, curtain, gallery, parquet **8.** parterre **9.** orchestra
turtle . . **7.** calipee **8.** calipash
partridge . . . **4.** hill, snow, yutu **5.** covey (flock) **6.** bamboo, chukar (chukor), Perdix, seesee **7.** cinerea, tinamou **8.** raw umber **9.** francolin **11.** Francolinus **12.** ruffed grouse
party . . . **3.** tea **4.** ball, drum, sect, side **6.** clique, fiesta, person **7.** company, faction **8.** sociable **9.** reception **10.** detachment **11.** association, combination **12.** participator
party (pert to) . . .
deserter . . **6.** bolter
evening . . **6.** soiree
lawn . . **4.** fete
man . . **8.** partisan
member . . **8.** Democrat, Federate **9.** Communist, Dixiecrat, Greenback (Hist), Socialist **10.** Republican **11.** Independent
men's . . **4.** stag **6.** smoker
Parvati (pert to) . . .
consort . . **4.** Siva
father . . **7.** Himavat
goddess . . **8.** mountain
parvenu . . **4.** snob **7.** upstart **12.** nouveau riche
Pasch, pasch . . . **4.** lamb, moon **6.** candle, Easter, supper **8.** Passover **10.** Good Friday **11.** candlestick, celebration
pascual . . . **8.** pascuage, pastures
pasear . . . **4.** walk **6.** parade, stroll **9.** promenade **11.** perambulate
pasha, pacha . . . **3.** dey **4.** emir **5.** title **6.** bashaw (early) **8.** nobleman **10.** magistrate

pashalik (pashalic) . . . **9.** territory (pasha's) **12.** jurisdiction
pashm . . . **6.** fleece (Tibetan goat)
pasigraphy . . . **6.** system (Universal) **7.** symbols **8.** language
Pasiphae (pert to) . . .
mother of . . **7.** Ariadne
son . . **8.** minotaur (monster)
wife of . . **5.** Minos
pasquinade . . . **5.** squib **6.** satire **7.** lampoon, pasquil
pass . . . **2.** go **3.** die, end, gap **4.** ghat, hand, lane, pace, step **5.** canto, enact, gorge, lapse, occur, relay, spend, throw **6.** convey, crisis, defile, elapse, exceed, happen, passus, perish, permit, ratify, ticket **7.** excrete, passage **8.** hand over, passport, surmount, transfer **10.** permission **11.** Annie Oakley **13.** complimentary
pass (pert to) . . .
Alpine . . **3.** col
around . . **5.** skirt **6.** detour
as genuine . . **5.** cheat, foist **11.** interpolate
away . . **3.** die, end **6.** perish, vanish **9.** cease to be, disappear, obsolesce
by . . **4.** cote, omit, skip, snub **6.** elapse, forego, ignore **7.** proceed **8.** overlook **9.** disregard
hurriedly . . **7.** scamper, skitter **9.** skim along
into . . **5.** glide, merge **6.** become **7.** get to be **9.** penetrate
judgment . . **4.** rule **6.** decree, ordain **8.** sentence
on . . **3.** die **6.** confer, ratify **7.** advance **8.** bequeath, continue
out . . **3.** die **4.** exit **5.** faint **7.** be dazed **9.** disappear **11.** be dead drunk **13.** be unconscious
over . . **4.** omit, skip **5.** cross **6.** elapse, excuse, exempt, ignore, slight **7.** condone, exclude, neglect **8.** overlook, transfer, traverse
sudden . . **5.** lunge
through . . **5.** cross, reeve (cringle) **6.** pierce **7.** pervade, undergo **8.** traverse **9.** penetrate **10.** comprehend, experience
up . . **4.** snub **5.** evade **6.** reject **7.** decline **9.** disregard
without touching . . **5.** clear
passable . . . **4.** so-so **7.** current **8.** mediocre, moderate, traveled **9.** navigable, tolerable, traversed **10.** acceptable, accessible, admissible **12.** satisfactory
passado (fencing) . . . **6.** thrust
passage . . . **4.** adit, exit, flue, ford, gang, hall, iter **5.** aisle, allay, allée, canal, death **6.** atrium, avenue, egress, travel, voyage **7.** channel, excerpt, journey, transit **8.** corridor, incident, progress, sanction **9.** enactment, migration **10.** transition **11.** altercation, negotiation, preterition **12.** thoroughfare
passage (pert to) . . .
book . . **7.** excerpt
brain . . **4.** iter
closed end . . **7.** impasse **8.** cul-de-sac

covered.. **4.** pawn
history.. **5.** alure
mine.. **4.** sill **5.** stope
narrow.. **3.** gut **5.** aisle, alley, gully,
slype **6.** defile, strait
river.. **7.** estuary
passageway . . . **4.** hall, lane, ramp, slip
5. aisle, alley, lumen **6.** access, arcade,
avenue, defile, outlet, strait, tunnel
7. gangway **8.** corridor
passant . . . **7.** cursory, walking (Her)
8. passer-by **9.** ephemeral, excelling
10. surpassing, transitory
passé . . . **4.** aged, past, worn **5.** faded
6. gone by **8.** obsolete **10.** antiquated
13. superannuated
passed (pert to) . . .
by .. **6.** bygone, former **8.** preterit
(preterite)
over .. **7.** fleeted **11.** preterition
through pores .. **7.** osmosed **8.** dialyzed
9. permeated, transuded
passenger . . . **4.** fare **6.** pigeon, trekku
7. pilgrim, tourist **8.** commuter, traveler,
wayfarer **9.** sightseer, transient
passerine bird . . . **5.** finch **7.** sparrow
8. songbird
passing . . . **7.** cursory **8.** elapsing,
fleeting **9.** departing, enactment,
ephemeral, exceeding, happening,
transient, vanishing **10.** surpassing,
transitory **11.** preterition
passion . . . **3.** ire, yen **4.** love, lust, rage,
zeal **5.** anger, craze, wrath **6.** desire
7. emotion, feeling **9.** eloquence,
martyrdom **10.** enthusiasm, excitement
passion (pert to) . . .
flower.. **6.** maypop **11.** passionwort
flower family .. **10.** Passiflora
for doing great things .. **11.** megalomania
music .. **8.** oratorio
Play .. **14.** Christ's Passion
(Oberammergau)
Week .. **8.** Holy Week
passionate . . . **3.** sad **5.** angry **6.** ardent
7. amorous, excited, fervent, pitiful,
violent **8.** agitated, eloquent, vehement
9. emotional, irascible **10.** passionato
11. hot-tempered, impassioned
passionless . . . **4.** calm **8.** painless
9. heartless, unfeeling **10.** spiritless
11. unemotional **13.** dispassionate
passive . . . **5.** inert, quiet, stoic **6.** stolid
7. languid, patient **8.** inactive
9. apathetic **10.** submissive
11. acquiescent, indifferent, unresisting
Passover (pert to) . . .
festival .. **5.** Seder **6.** Jewish
lamb .. **7.** paschal
psalm .. **6.** hallel **14.** Egyptian Hallel
sacrifice .. **11.** paschal lamb
The (Passover) .. **5.** Pasch
passport . . . **4.** pass, visa (vise) **5.** congé
6. congee, permit **8.** document **11.** safe
conduct
passus . . . **5.** canto
password . . . **9.** watchword **10.** mot de
passé, open sesame **11.** countersign
past . . . **2.** by **3.** ago **4.** date, dead, gone,
over, yore **5.** after, since **6.** beyond,
ultimo **7.** elapsed, outworn **9.** foregoing,

yesterday
pasta . . . **7.** gnocchi, lasagna, ravioli
8. linguini, macaroni **9.** fettucini,
manicotti, spaghetti **10.** vermicelli
paste . . . **3.** pap, poi **4.** glue, sham
5. dough, stick **6.** mastic, strass
8. adhesive, frippery, mucilage
10. confection **13.** stick together
pastel . . . **5.** light **6.** crayon, sketch **9.** pale
color
pastille . . . **6.** troche **7.** lozenge
pastime . . . **4.** game **5.** hobby, sport
9. amusement, diversion **10.** recreation
13. entertainment
pastor . . . **5.** rabbi **6.** curate, divine,
keeper, parson, priest, rector
8. chaplain, guardian, minister,
Reverend, shepherd
pastoral . . . **4.** poem **5.** drama, rural
6. poetic **7.** romance **14.** ecclesiastical
pastoral (pert to) . . .
cantata .. **8.** serenata
crook, staff .. **5.** pedum **7.** crosier
god .. **3.** Pan
oboe .. **7.** musette
pert to .. **6.** rustic **8.** agrestic, herdsman,
shepherd
pipe .. **3.** oat **4.** reed
poem .. **5.** idyll (idyl) **7.** bucolic, eclogue
pastry . . . **3.** pie **4.** tart **6.** Danish,
éclair **7.** dariole, strudel **8.** napoleon,
pandowdy, turnover **9.** cream puff,
shortcake **10.** pâtisserie
past tense . . . **8.** preterit (preterite)
pasturage, right of . . . **9.** horsegate
pasture . . . **3.** ham, lea **4.** feed, food
5. agist, grama, grass, graze **6.** meadow
9. grassland **10.** agostadero
pasture bird . . . **6.** plover **7.** sparrow
pat . . . **3.** dab, fit, paw, tap **4.** blow,
lump **5.** fixed, impel, known, throw
6. caress, smooth, stroke **7.** flatten
9. immovable **10.** seasonable
Patagonia (So Am) . . .
city .. **11.** Punta Arenas
deity .. **7.** Setebos
Indian people .. **9.** Tehuelche
nearby island .. **14.** Tierra del Fuego
race (said of) .. **6.** giants **7.** Big Feet,
tallest **9.** Patagones
rodent .. **4.** cavy **8.** capybara, Caviidae
strait .. **8.** Magellan (Magallanes)
patamar (pattamar) . . . **6.** vessel (Naut)
7. courier **9.** messenger
patata . . . **6.** potato **11.** sweet potato
patch . . . **4.** mend, vamp **5.** bodge, botch,
clump, cover, field **6.** blotch, cobble,
parcel **8.** addition, appliqué **9.** reconcile
patch (pert to) . . .
cloth .. **5.** clout
imprinting .. **5.** friar
metal .. **6.** solder
of trees .. **4.** mott
patcher (humorous) . . . **6.** sartor
patchwork . . . **5.** quilt **6.** jumble, pillow,
scraps **7.** mixture **9.** checkered,
fancywork, fragments **10.** hodgepodge
pate . . . **3.** pie, top **4.** head **5.** brain,
crown, pasty, patty **6.** badger
patella . . . **3.** pan **4.** bone, dish, vase
7. kneecap, kneepan

paten ... **4.** disc, dish, disk **5.** plate
  7. patener (bearer of)
patent ... **4.** open **5.** berat (Turk), right
  7. license, warrant **8.** document,
  manifest **9.** available, copyright,
  privilege, trademark **10.** accessible,
  protection, university **12.** unobstructed
pater ... **6.** father, priest
Pater Noster ... **11.** Lord's Prayer
Paternoster Row ... **6.** street (London)
Pater Patriae ... **18.** Father of his country
  (Cicero, Marius, Trajan, Washington,
  etc)
path ... **3.** way **4.** lane, line **5.** piste,
  route, swath, track, trail **6.** course
  7. footway
path (pert to) ...
  along a slope .. **4.** berm (berme)
  animal .. **5.** piste, spoor **6.** roddin
    7. rodding
  of energy .. **7.** ergodic
  of moving parts .. **5.** locus
  of planets .. **5.** orbit
  Spanish .. **6.** camino, comino
pathetic ... **3.** sad **5.** teary **8.** dolorous,
  grievous, stirring **9.** affecting
  10. lamentable
pathological ... **6.** morbid **9.** unhealthy
pathological reaction ... **7.** allergy
patience ... **9.** endurance, fortitude,
  solitaire, tolerance **10.** submission,
  sufferance **11.** forbearance, resignation
  12. acquiescence, perseverance
patient ... **4.** calm, meek **6.** client
  8. tolerant **9.** unsettled **11.** persevering
  13. long-suffering
patio ... **5.** court **9.** courtyard
patriarch ... **4.** Noah, sire **5.** elder,
  pater **6.** bishop, father **7.** aged man,
  veteran **9.** churchman **10.** Methuselah
  13. paterfamilias
patrimonial ... **9.** inherited **10.** hereditary
patrimony ... **8.** heritage **10.** birthright
  11. ancient rite, inheritance
patriot ... **4.** Cato (Rom), Otis (Am)
  5. jingo **7.** chauvin **9.** flag-waver
  10. chauvinist, countryman
patriotism ... **10.** chauvinism
  11. nationalism **13.** love of country
patrol ... **5.** guard **7.** protect **8.** traverse
  9. keep guard **13.** perambulation
patron ... **5.** buyer, guest **6.** backer,
  seller, trader **8.** customer, guardian
  9. financier, protector, supporter
  10. benefactor
patronage ... **5.** aegis (egis), favor
  6. defend **7.** support **8.** auspices
  9. clientele, fosterage **10.** assistance
  13. condescension, encouragement
patronizing ... **8.** deigning **9.** financing,
  revealing **10.** sponsoring
  13. condescending
patrons (group) ... **7.** backers, masters
  9. clientele, customers
Patron Saint of ...
  beggars .. **5.** Giles
  boys .. **8.** Nicholas
  England .. **4.** Anne **6.** George
  fishermen .. **5.** Peter
  France .. **5.** Denis
  Ireland .. **7.** Patrick

  lawyers .. **4.** Ives
  motherhood .. **6.** Gerard
  musicians .. **7.** Cecilia
  Pueblo Indians .. **7.** Stephen
  sailors .. **4.** Elmo
  Scotland .. **6.** Andrew
  shoemakers .. **7.** Crispin
  swineherds .. **7.** Anthony
  Venice .. **4.** Mark **9.** Pantalone
  Wales .. **5.** David
patten ... **4.** clog **5.** skate **8.** footgear,
  overshoe, snowshoe
pattern ... **4.** norm, seme **5.** habit, model
  6. design, format **7.** diagram, paragon
  8. paradigm, parterre, template
pavilion ... **4.** tent **5.** cover, kiosk
  6. canopy **8.** covering **9.** gloriette
  10. tabernacle
pavis ... **5.** cover **6.** screen, shield
  7. protect
paw ... **3.** pad, pud **4.** foot, hand **5.** patté,
  pedal **6.** handle, stroke **7.** foreleg (Her)
  8. forefoot **10.** manipulate
pawl ... **4.** bolt, sear, trip **5.** click **6.** detent,
  pallet, tongue **7.** ratchet **9.** mechanism
pawn ... **4.** gage, hock, tool **6.** pledge
  7. counter, peacock **8.** chessman,
  guaranty, hockshop **9.** put in pawn
  10. pawnbroker
Pawnee ... **6.** Indian
pawnie ... **7.** peacock
pay ... **3.** aby (abye), fee, tip **4.** ante,
  meet, wage **5.** remit, repay **6.** defray,
  reward, salary, suffer **7.** requite, satisfy
  9. indemnify, reimburse, retaliate
  10. compensate, punishment,
  recompense, remunerate **11.** retribution
  12. compensation
pay (pert to) ...
  attention .. **4.** heed **6.** listen
  back .. **6.** rebate, refund **9.** reimburse,
    retaliate
  dirt .. **3.** ore
  envelope .. **5.** wages **6.** salary **7.** stipend
  extra .. **5.** bonus **8.** kickback
  for .. **3.** aby (abye) **5.** atone **6.** suffer
  off .. **6.** punish **7.** requite **9.** pay in full,
    retribute **10.** compensate
  out .. **5.** spend **6.** expend, settle
    7. hand out **8.** disburse **10.** distribute
    12. exorbitantly **14.** through the nose
  up .. **4.** ante **6.** settle **9.** liquidate
paymaster ... **6.** burser, purser **7.** cashier
payment ... **3.** cro, fee **4.** dues,
  mail **6.** return **8.** defrayal, requital
  10. punishment, recompense
  12. chastisement, compensation
payment (pert to) ...
  for homicide, murder .. **3.** cro **4.** eric
    (Brehon Law) **7.** galanas (Welsh),
    wergild (weregild)
  immediate .. **4.** cash
  upon delivery .. **3.** COD **14.** cash on
    delivery
paynim ... **5.** pagan **7.** heathen, infidel
  8. Pagandom **10.** Mohammedan
payong ... **8.** umbrella (golden)
paysage ... **7.** picture (landscape)
  9. landscape
pea (pert to) ...
  bird .. **6.** oriole

chick.. **4.** gram **5.** Cicer
everlasting (Bib).. **9.** vetchling
family.. **8.** Fabaceae
flour (seasoned).. **9.** Erbswurst
heath.. **7.** carmele
pigeon.. **3.** dal **5.** arhar
sausage.. **9.** Erbswurst
shaped.. **8.** pisiform
soup.. **3.** fog (dull yellow)
split.. **3.** dal
tree.. **8.** laburnum
tropical.. **4.** dove **7.** Zenaida
   12. mourning dove
vine.. **8.** earthpea
peace... **3.** pax **5.** amity, quiet, truce
   6. accord, repose **7.** harmony, Nirvana,
   silence **8.** ataraxia (ataraxy), serenity
   9. stillness **10.** quiescence **11.** tranquility
peaceable... **5.** quiet, still **6.** irenic,
   silent **7.** henotic, pacific **8.** amicable,
   tranquil **9.** quiescent **10.** concordant,
   harmonious **11.** undisturbed
peaceful... **4.** calm **5.** irene **6.** irenic,
   placid, serene **7.** halcyon, pacific
   8. tranquil **11.** comfortable
peace pipe... **7.** calumet
peach... **5.** fruit **6.** accuse, betray, brandy,
   indict, inform **7.** impeach **8.** quandong
   9. red-yellow
peach (pert to)...
cordial.. **7.** persico **8.** persicot
family.. **12.** Amygdalaceae
French.. **8.** persicot
grafted (quince).. **9.** melocoton
like.. **6.** almond
origin.. **5.** China
stone.. **7.** putamen
variety.. **7.** Elberta **8.** Crawford
   9. freestone, nectarine **10.** clingstone
peacock... **3.** mao **4.** Pavo (Astron),
   pawn, pose **5.** strut **9.** swaggerer
peacock (pert to)...
blue (color).. **4.** paon
butterfly.. **2.** io
fan.. **9.** flabellum
feather part.. **4.** marl
female.. **6.** peahen
fish.. **6.** wrasse
flower.. **9.** poinciana
heron.. **7.** bittern
ref to.. **7.** peafowl **8.** pavonine
tail spot.. **3.** eye
peak... **3.** alp, epi, pic, top, tor **4.** acme,
   apex, cone, crag, cusp, dent, dolt
   5. crown, piton, slink, sneak, steal
   6. finial, shrink, summit **8.** headland,
   mountain **9.** simpleton **10.** promontory
Peak... **5.** Borah, Logan **7.** Everest,
   St Elias **8.** McKinley **9.** Mont Blanc
   10. Matterhorn **11.** Kilimanjaro
   12. Popocatepetl
peal... **4.** boom, clap, echo, ring, toll
   6. appeal, shovel **7.** resound, summons,
   thunder **8.** carillon
peanut... **5.** pinda (pindal, pindar)
   6. goober, trifle **8.** earthnut, earthpea,
   katchung
pear (pert to)...
alligator.. **7.** avocado
cider.. **5.** perry
Latin.. **5.** pirum

prickly.. **4.** tuna **5.** nopal **7.** Opuntia
shaped.. **8.** pyriform
shaped vessel.. **6.** aludel
squash.. **7.** chayote
type.. **4.** Bosc **8.** Bartlett
pearl... **3.** gem **4.** drop **5.** nacre, tooth,
   white **9.** margarite
pearl (pert to)...
bird.. **10.** guinea fowl
color.. **4.** blue **13.** mother-of-pearl
eye.. **8.** cataract
imitation.. **6.** olivet
of great luster.. **6.** orient
opal.. **9.** cacholong (opaque)
oyster.. **7.** Avicula
seed.. **7.** aliofar (obs)
vegetable.. **5.** onion
pearly... **5.** milky, quick, smart **7.** opaline,
   whitish **8.** pellucid **10.** opalescent
   11. flourishing
Pearly Gates (Bib)... **6.** heaven, twelve
peasant... **4.** boor, hind, peon, serf
   5. clown, knave, swain **6.** carlot,
   cotman, cottar, rascal, rustic
   10. countryman
peasant (pert to)...
Arab, Syria.. **6.** fellah
cropsharer.. **7.** metayer
English.. **4.** hind **5.** churl
Indian.. **4.** ryot
Irish.. **4.** kern (kerne) **7.** cottier
like.. **4.** base, rude **8.** clownish
Russian.. **5.** kulak (rich)
Scottish.. **4.** tyke (tike) **6.** cotter (cottar)
pease... **5.** quiet **6.** pacify **7.** appease
   9. reconcile
peasecrow... **4.** tern
peat... **3.** bog, pet **4.** coal, fuel, moor,
   moss, turf **6.** minion **7.** darling
   8. favorite **11.** combustible
peat (pert to)...
cutter.. **5.** piner
moss.. **8.** sphagnum
turf spade.. **5.** slave
wood.. **11.** loosestrife
peau... **4.** skin (silks) **6.** fabric
peba... **9.** armadillo
pebble... **5.** scree, stone, talus **6.** quartz
   7. chuckie (chucky), crystal, psephos
   11. gravelstone, pebblestone
peccadillo... **4.** slip **5.** error, fault, lapse
   12. indiscretion
peccant... **3.** bad **5.** wrong **6.** guilty,
   morbid, wicked **7.** corrupt, sinning,
   spoiled **9.** incorrect, unhealthy
   12. insalubrious
peccary... **6.** mammal (piglike)
   7. Tagassu, Tayassu **8.** javelina
pech... **4.** pant **11.** breathe hard
pecht (Scot)... **5.** fairy, gnome, pygmy
peck... **3.** dab, dot, eat, nag **4.** food,
   hole, jerk, kiss **5.** pitch, prick, throw
   6. peggle, stroke **7.** measure **8.** quantity
   11. large amount
peck at... **3.** nag **4.** carp, twit **5.** tease
   6. attack, harass
pectase... **6.** enzyme
peculiar... **3.** odd **4.** idio (comb form)
   5. queer **6.** oddish, unique **7.** curious,
   special, strange, typical **8.** distinct,
   separate, singular **9.** different, eccentric

10. particular 14. characteristic
peculiar expression ... 5. idiom
peculiarity ... 4. kink 5. quirk, trait
6. oddity 7. oddness 9. mannerism
10. partiality 11. singularity
12. eccentricity 14. characteristic
peculiar to a district ... 7. endemic
pecuniary ... 6. fiscal 8. monetary
9. financial
pedagogue ... 5. tutor 6. pedant
7. teacher 12. schoolmaster
pedal ... 4. foot 5. lever 6. driver 7. treadle
9. propeller
pedant ... 4. prig 5. tutor 6. dorbel, purist
9. formalist, pedagogue 10. conformist
12. bluestocking, precisionist,
schoolmaster
peddle ... 4. hawk, sell, vend 6. piddle,
retail 11. disseminate
peddler, pedlar ... 6. cadger, coster,
hawker, mugger, sutler 7. chapman
8. huckster 9. vivandier
12. costermonger
peddler's French ... 6. jargon (thieves')
9. gibberish
pedestal ... 7. support 10. foundation
pedestal part ... 3. die 4. base, dado
5. socle 6. plinth, quadra
pedestrian ... 3. ped 4. dull, slow 5. hiker
6. hoofer, walker 11. commonplace
12. foot traveler 13. unimaginative
pedicel ... 3. ray (of an umbel) 4. stem
5. stalk 8. peduncle
pediculosis ... 9. lousiness
Pediculus ... 4. lice
pedigree ... 6. stemma 7. descent, lineage
8. ancestry, register 9. genealogy
10. family tree
pedio (comb form) ... 4. sole 6. instep
pedology ... 9. soil study 10. child study
pedometer ... 5. watch 8. odograph
10. instrument, passometer
pedregal ... 9. lava field
pedum ... 5. crook, staff (pastoral)
peduncle ... 4. stem 5. scape, stalk
7. pedicel, pedicle, sessile
peek ... 3. pry 4. peep 5. chirp, flash
6. glance 7. glimpse 9. look slyly
peekaboo ... 4. game 6. bopeep
peel ... 4. bark, pare, rind, skin 5. slipe,
stake, strip 6. cut off, lamina, shovel
8. car blade, palisade, stockade
peel (off) ... 4. harl, pare, tear 7. come
off 8. get loose 11. decorticate
peeler ... 4. crab (shedding), yarn 5. corer
7. hustler 8. pillager 9. policeman
peep ... 3. pry 4. peek, peer, pule, skeg
5. cheep, chirp, pipit, sight (firearms)
6. glance, squeak 7. crevice 8. peephole
9. sandpiper
peephole ... 4. hole 6. eyelet 8. aperture
9. sighthole
peer ... 4. duke, earl, fere, gaze, mate
5. baron, equal, match, noble, stare,
stime (styme) 7. marquis 8. nobleman,
superior, viscount
Peer Gynt (pert to) ...
drama, poem by .. 5. Ibsen
mother .. 3. Ase
music suite by .. 5. Grieg
peerless ... 9. matchless, nonpareil,

paper size, unequaled, unmatched
10. unexcelled 11. ne plus ultra,
superlative
peesweep, peeseweep ... 7. lapwing
10. greenfinch
peetweep ... 9. sandpiper (spotted)
peeved ... 4. sore 7. annoyed, nettled
9. irritated
peevish ... 3. coy 4. sour 5. cross, sulky,
techy, testy 6. crusty, morose, touchy
7. fretful, pettish, spleeny, waspish
8. captious, choleric, contrary, perverse,
petulant, snappish 9. irascible, irritable,
querulous, splenetic
peg ... 3. hob, leg, nob, nog, pin 4. dram,
skeg 5. drink, stake, tooth 6. drudge,
fasten, reason 7. pretext, support
9. persevere, recognize
peg (pert to) ...
cribbage .. 4. game
iron .. 5. piton
out .. 7. croquet
shoe .. 5. cleat
wood .. 5. spill, thole 8. treenail
pega ... 5. shark 6. remora
Pegasus ... 5. horse (winged), steed
13. constellation
Pegasus's rider ... 11. Bellerophon
pegomancy, divination by ... 7. springs
9. fountains
peho ... 8. morepork
peignoir ... 8. negligee 12. dressing
gown, dressing sack
pejorative ... 11. disparaging
12. depreciatory
Peking, Pekin ... 4. blue, city, duck
7. spaniel
pelagic ... 6. marine 7. oceanic
9. underseas
pelagic organism ... 6. nekton 7. benthos
8. plankton
Pele ... 7. goddess (volcanoes)
pêle-mêle ... 8. pellmell
Peleus (pert to) ...
father .. 4. Aeacus
King of .. 9. Myrmidons
son .. 8. Achilles
wife .. 6. Thetis
pelf ... 3. fur, rob 4. gain 5. booty,
lucre, money, spoil, trash 6. pilfer,
profit, refuse, riches, wealth 7. rubbish
10. ne'er-do-well
Pelias (pert to) ...
daughter .. 5. Medes
King of .. 6. Iolcus
nephew .. 5. Jason
son .. 7. Acastus
pelican (pert to) ...
heraldry .. 10. in her piety
symbolic of .. 6. Christ 7. charity
Pelican State ... 9. Louisiana
pell ... 3. fur 4. hide, pelt, skin 5. hurry
6. hasten 13. parchment roll
pellagra ... 5. zeism
pellar, peller ... 6. wizard 8. conjurer
pellet ... 4. ball, pill 6. bullet 7. granule,
missile, pallion
pellicle ... 4. film, scum 6. lamina
7. coating 8. membrane
pell-mell, pellmell ... 10. vehemently
12. furious haste 13. helter-skelter

pellock ... **8.** porpoise
pellucid ... **5.** clear **6.** bright, limpid
  8. luminous **11.** translucent, transparent
  12. intelligible
pelmet ... **7.** valance (short)
Peloponnesus ...
  capital .. **7.** Corinth
  city .. **7.** Argolis
  League .. **11.** Confederacy
  peninsula (Gr) .. **5.** Morea
    12. Peloponnesos (old), Peloponnesus
    (modern)
  race (anc) .. **6.** Dorian **7.** Spartan
  School .. **6.** Dorian **9.** Sculpture
  War .. **12.** Athens-Sparta (BC)
Pelops (pert to) ...
  father .. **8.** Tantalus
  son .. **6.** Atreus **8.** Thyestes
  wife .. **10.** Hippodamia
pelota ... **4.** ball, game **5.** cesta **7.** fronton,
  jai alai
pelt ... **3.** fur **4.** blow, fell, hide, push,
  skin **5.** stone **6.** hurl at, pelage, refuse,
  strike, thrust **7.** apparel (of skins),
  rubbish **8.** woolfell
peltry ... **4.** furs, pelt **5.** skins
peludo ... **9.** armadillo (six-banded)
pelvic bone ... **5.** ilium **7.** ischium **8.** seat
  bone
pelvic-shaped ... **11.** basin-shaped
pemmican ... **4.** meat (dried) **7.** buffalo,
  venison
pen ... **3.** cot, sty **4.** bolt, coop,
  gaol **5.** abode, hutch, quill, write
  6. fasten, indite **7.** confine **9.** enclosure
  12. penitentiary
pen (pert to) ...
  like .. **7.** styloid
  name .. **6.** anonym **9.** pseudonym
    10. nom de plume
  point .. **3.** neb, nib **4.** stub
  text .. **5.** ronde
penalize ... **4.** fine **5.** mulct **6.** punish
  8. handicap
penalty ... **4.** fine, loss **7.** forfeit
  8. handicap, hardship **10.** punishment,
  repentance
Penang Islands capital ...
  10. Georgetown
penchant ... **4.** bent **6.** desire, liking
  7. leaning **8.** tendency **10.** attraction
  11. inclination **12.** decided taste
pendant ... **3.** bob, tag **4.** tail **5.** aglet
  (aiglet), queue **6.** tassel **7.** eardrop,
  earring, hanging **8.** appendix, pendulum
  9. lavaliere **10.** chandelier
pendent ... **3.** lop **4.** pend **7.** hanging
  8. appended **9.** impending, pendulous
  11. jutting over, overhanging
pendent cone (limestone) ... **10.** stalactite
pendulous fold, skin ... **6.** dewlap
Penelope (pert to) ...
  father .. **7.** Icarius
  husband .. **7.** Ulysses **8.** Odysseus
  island .. **6.** Ithaca
  suitor .. **7.** Agelaus
penetrate ... **4.** bore, gore, stab **5.** delve,
  elbow, enter **6.** pierce **7.** pervade
  8. permeate **9.** perforate **10.** move
  deeply
penetrating ... **4.** cold, deep **5.** acute,

sharp **6.** shrill, subtle **7.** caustic, odorous
  8. incisive **9.** pervading, sagacious,
  searching
penetration ... **6.** acumen **7.** ingress,
  insight **9.** acuteness, sharpness
  11. discernment, perforation
  14. discrimination
Peneus (pert to) ...
  father of .. **6.** Daphne
  genus of .. **6.** prawns
  god of .. **11.** Peneus River (Thessalia)
penguin ... **3.** auk **6.** Johnny **10.** rock
  hopper
penguin (pert to) ...
  aviation .. **13.** training plane
  duck .. **12.** Indian Runner (duck)
  genus .. **8.** Eudyptes
  nest .. **7.** rookery **10.** penguinery
  type .. **4.** king **6.** Adelie **7.** emperor,
    jackass
peninsula ... **4.** neck **6.** penile
  10. chersonese
Peninsula ...
  Asia .. **5.** Malay
  Cimbrian, Cimbric .. **7.** Jutland
  Iberia .. **5.** Spain
  Seward .. **6.** Alaska
  Tauric .. **6.** Crimea
  Thracian .. **9.** Gallipoli
penitent ... **5.** sorry **8.** contrite
  9. repentant
penitential discipline ... **7.** penance
penitential period ... **4.** Lent
pennant ... **4.** fane, flag, whip **6.** banner,
  burgee (yacht), ensign, pennon, pinion
  9. banderole
pennant fish ... **11.** cobblerfish
pennate ... **6.** winged **7.** pinnate
  9. feathered, penniform
pennon ... **4.** flag, wing **6.** banner, pinion
  8. streamer
Pennsylvania ...
  capital .. **10.** Harrisburg
  city .. **4.** Erie **7.** Reading **8.** Scranton
    10. Pittsburgh **12.** Philadelphia
  famed site .. **10.** Gettysburg **11.** Liberty
    Bell, Valley Forge **16.** Independence
    Hall
  founder .. **11.** William Penn
  mountain .. **5.** Davis **11.** Alleghenies
  named, first .. **10.** Penn's Woods
  river .. **4.** Ohio **8.** Delaware **10.** Schuylkill
    11. Susquehanna
  State admission .. **6.** second
  State motto .. **28.** Virtue, Liberty, and
    Independence
  State nickname .. **8.** Keystone
penny ... **4.** cent, coin **5.** pence **6.** copper,
  stiver **8.** denarius (Bib)
penologist, famed ... **5.** Lawes
penology, study of ... **11.** criminology
  18. punishment for crime
pensive ... **3.** sad **5.** mesto, sober
  6. dreamy, musing **7.** wistful
  10. meditative, melancholy, reflective,
  thoughtful **13.** contemplative
pentastich ... **4.** poem **5.** stanza
  7. strophe **10.** five verses
Pentateuch ... **5.** Torah (Tora) **10.** Law
  of Moses **14.** First Five Books (Old
  Test) **16.** Five Books of Moses

Pentecost . . . **8.** festival **10.** Whitsunday
Pentheus (pert to) . . .
grandson of . . **6.** Cadmus
King of . . **6.** Thebes
mother . . **5.** Agave
penthouse . . . **6.** lean-to **7.** leaning,
pentice **9.** apartment (roof)
11. overhanging
penury . . . **4.** want **7.** poverty **9.** indigence,
privation **10.** scantiness **11.** destitution,
miserliness
peon . . . **4.** pawn (chess), serf **7.** laborer,
peasant, soldier **9.** attendant, constable,
messenger, policeman
peony . . . **4.** piny **6.** moutan **7.** Paeonia
11. Burmese ruby
people . . . **3.** kin, men **4.** folk, ones, race,
Rais **5.** demos, laity **6.** family, nation,
public **7.** kinsmen, persons **8.** populace,
subjects **9.** citizenry **10.** population
people (pert to) . . .
Am Indian, Eskimo . . **7.** Amerind
ancient . . **5.** Medes **6.** Greeks, Romans
7. Sabines **9.** Egyptians, Etruscans
class, lowest . . **8.** canaille
common . . **6.** vulgar **7.** tilikum (tilicum)
headless (Myth) . . **8.** Acephali
old-fashioned . . **6.** prudes **7.** squares
13. antediluvians
ref to . . **4.** laic **6.** ethnic **7.** demotic
Spanish . . **5.** gente
wild young . . **10.** rantipoles
people (of) . . .
culture (earliest) . . **8.** Grecians
gentle birth . . **6.** gentry
one government . . **6.** nation
rank . . **11.** aristocracy, aristocrats
the people . . **6.** ethnic
peopled . . . **5.** abadi (Ind village)
8. occupied, populous **9.** populated
pep . . . **2.** go **3.** vim **4.** dash **6.** energy
7. quicken **9.** stimulate **10.** initiative,
liveliness
pepper . . . **4.** pelt **5.** shoot **6.** energy
7. bombard **8.** sprinkle **9.** condiment
pepper (pert to) . . .
betel . . **4.** siri (sirih)
black . . **11.** Piper nigrum
box . . **5.** tower **8.** spitfire
Capsicum, source of . . **7.** cayenne, chilies
(chili), paprika
climbing . . **5.** betel **6.** nigrum
condiment . . **7.** cayenne, paprika
dulse . . **7.** seaweed (red)
genus . . **8.** Capsicum
grass . . **5.** crass **8.** pillwort
sauce . . **7.** Tabasco
turnip . . **15.** jack-in-the-pulpit
pepper (pert to country) . . .
Australia . . **4.** kava (cava) **8.** kavakava
Borneo . . **4.** kava (cava)
Guinea . . **5.** chili **8.** Capsicum
Malay . . **4.** siri (sirih)
Spain . . **7.** paprika, pimento **8.** allspice,
pimiento
pepper-and-salt . . . **4.** gray **17.** harbinger-
of-spring
peppermint . . . **3.** oil **4.** herb **6.** spirit
7. essence, gum tree, lozenge, menthol
(camphor)
peppery . . . **5.** fiery **7.** piquant, pungent

8. choleric, spirited, stinging
10. passionate **11.** hot-tempered
per . . . **2.** by **7.** for each, through **9.** by
means of **11.** according to
peradventure . . . **3.** hap **5.** doubt **7.** it
may be **8.** possibly **11.** uncertainty
perambulate . . . **4.** walk **6.** ramble, stroll
8. traverse **9.** promenade, walk about
perceive . . . **3.** see **4.** hear, know, note
5. sense **6.** behold, descry, detect,
divine, notice, remark **7.** discern,
observe, sensate **9.** apprehend
10. comprehend, understand
11. distinguish **12.** discriminate
perceptible . . . **5.** faint **7.** tactile, visible
8. knowable, manifest, tangible
10. cognizable **11.** appreciable,
discernible, perceivable
perception . . . **3.** ear **4.** tact **5.** sense,
taste **6.** acumen, seeing **8.** sagacity
9. awareness, sensation **10.** cognizance
11. discernment **13.** consciousness
14. discrimination
perceptive . . . **7.** knowing **8.** sensible
9. sagacious **14.** discriminative
perch . . . **3.** bar, peg, rod, sit **4.** fish,
pole **5.** aerie, barse, roost, sit on,
staff **6.** alight, aviary, sauger, settle,
weapon **7.** measure **9.** trumpeter
Percheron . . . **5.** horse **15.** Percheron
Norman
perchers . . . **5.** birds **7.** candles **8.** Passeres
10. Insessores
percolate . . . **4.** ooze, seep, sift, silt, sipe
5. exude, leach, steep **6.** filter, strain
7. trickle **8.** permeate, transude
percussion . . . **9.** collision **10.** concussion,
detonation
percussion instrument . . . **4.** drum, gong
5. bells, bones, conga, snare, traps
6. Becken, bongos, chimes, tom-tom
7. celesta, cymbals, marimba, potlids,
timpani (tympani) **8.** carillon, clappers,
triangle **9.** castanets, xylophone
10. kettledrum, tambourine, vibraphone
12. glockenspiel
perdition . . . **4.** hell, loss (soul), ruin
5. wreck **9.** damnation **11.** destruction
peregrinate . . . **6.** travel, wander **7.** go
about, migrate, sojourn
peregrine . . . **5.** alien **6.** exotic, falcon
7. foreign, pilgrim, strange **9.** foreigner
perempt . . . **5.** quash **6.** defeat **7.** destroy
peremptory . . . **5.** final **7.** express
8. absolute, arrogant, decisive,
dogmatic, positive, resolute **9.** arbitrary,
mandatory **10.** compulsory, conclusive,
imperative, obligatory **11.** dictatorial
13. authoritative **16.** incontrovertible
perennial . . . **7.** lasting **8.** constant,
enduring **9.** continual, evergreen,
permanent, perpetual, unceasing
10. continuous **12.** never-failing
perennial (pert to) . . .
climbing . . **5.** liana (liane)
grass . . **4.** lyme **6.** Elymus (genus) **7.** wild
rye
herb . . **4.** Geum **5.** avens
weed . . **8.** toadflax
perfect . . . **4.** holy, pure, sole **5.** ideal,
model, teleo (comb form), whole

6. entire 7. correct, develop, improve
8. finished 9. blameless, faultless,
inviolate, righteous 10. consummate,
satisfying 11. unqualified
perfection . . . 4. acme 5. ideal 7. paragon
8. accuracy, maturity 10. completion,
excellence 13. faultlessness
perfectly . . . 5. quite 7. ideally, rightly,
utterly 9. correctly 10. absolutely,
accurately, altogether, completely,
flawlessly, thoroughly
perfecto . . . 5. cigar (tapering)
perficient . . . 6. actual 9. effective,
effectual
perfidious . . . 6. shifty 8. disloyal
9. faithless 11. disaffected, treacherous
12. falsehearted
perfidy . . . 7. treason 8. apostasy
9. duplicity, treachery 10. disloyalty
13. faithlessness
perforate . . . 4. bore, dock 5. drill, punch
6. pierce, pounce, riddle 9. penetrate
10. umbilicate
perforated . . .
block . . 3. nut
initials (Philat) . . 10. stamp marks
nozzle . . 4. rose
space . . 5. brain
sphere . . 4. bead
perforation . . . 4. bore, hole 6. eyelet
8. aperture, piercing, punching
perform . . . 2. do 3. act 4. play 5. enact,
exert 6. effect 7. execute, fulfill, produce
8. complete, transact 9. officiate
10. accomplish, bring about, perpetrate
performance . . . 3. act 4. test, work
6. action 7. exploit 8. ceremony
9. operation 10. completion, exhibition,
observance, production
12. consummation 14. accomplishment
performance (pert to) . . .
clumsy . . 6. bungle
daytime . . 7. matinee
for one . . 4. solo
notable . . 4. feat
of duty . . 8. feasance
performer . . . 4. doer 5. actor 6. dancer,
worker 8. magician, musician, thespian
9. pretender 15. prestidigitator
perfume . . . 4. balm, odor 5. aroma, attar,
orris, savor, scent, smell 7. bouquet,
cologne, essence, rose oil 9. fragrance,
redolence 10. frangipani
perfume (pert to) . . .
base . . 4. musk 9. ambergris
cherry . . 7. mahaleb
essence . . 4. attar 8. bergamot
medicated . . 8. pastille (pastil)
musky . . 5. civet
oriental . . 5. myrrh 7. incense
12. frankincense
scent . . 7. jasmine 8. lavender
10. heliotrope
toilet . . 6. bay rum 12. eau de Cologne
unguent . . 6. pomade
violet . . 5. irone
pergola . . . 5. arbor, bower, kiosk
6. pandal 7. balcony, trellis 9. colonnade
11. summerhouse
perhaps . . . 5. maybe 6. ablins (Scot),
belike, mayhap 8. doubtful, possibly,

probably 9. perchance 10. contingent
peri . . . 3. elf 5. about (pref), fairy 6. beauty
periapt . . . 5. charm 6. amulet
pericarp . . . 3. pod 5. berry, shell
8. seedcase
Pericles (Gr) . . . 9. statesman
periculum (Rom law) . . . 4. risk 5. peril
6. danger
perigee (Astron) . . . 12. nearest earth
(opp of apogee)
peril . . . 4. risk 6. danger, hazard, menace
8. jeopardy
perilously high . . . 7. Icarian (flying)
perimeter . . . 5. ambit 6. border 7. outline
8. boundary 9. periphery
period . . . 3. age, day, dot, end, eon,
era, eve 4. stop, term, time, year
5. cycle, epoch, limit, spell 6. degree,
moment, season 8. duration, sentence
10. conclusion 11. termination
period (pert to) . . .
historical . . 4. eral 6. Eocene 7. Neocene
penitential . . 4. Lent
statutory . . 10. limitation
Tertiary . . 6. Eocene 7. Miocene, Neocene
8. Pliocene
periodic . . . 4. eral 6. annual 7. etesian
8. seasonal 9. recurrent 10. rhythmical
12. intermittent
periodic (pert to) . . .
sea motion . . 4. tide
wind . . 2. oe 7. chinook, etesian,
monsoon
windstorm . . 2. oe 7. tornado
9. whirlwind
periodical . . . 5. paper 6. review
7. etesian, journal 8. magazine
9. recurring 11. publication
periodical cicada . . . 6. locust (17 yrs)
period of . . .
delay . . 10. moratorium
dryness . . 7. drought
evolution . . 6. hemera
fifty days . . 13. quinquagesima
five years . . 6. pentad
holding . . 6. tenure
instruction . . 7. session
possession . . 5. lease
probation . . 6. parole
prosperity . . 4. boom 6. golden
recovery . . 13. convalescence
14. reconstruction
sleep . . 11. hibernation
ten years . . 6. decade
time . . 3. age, day, eon 4. span
work . . 4. turn 5. shift, spell, watch
youth . . 6. nonage
peripatetic . . . 7. walking 8. rambling
Peripatetic (pert to Aristotle) . . . 6. school
8. disciple 10. Philosophy
peripheral . . . 6. distal 7. outmost
8. external 9. outlinear 10. round about
periphery . . . 3. lip, rim 4. brim
5. ambit 6. areola, border 8. confines
9. perimeter 10. borderland
13. circumference
perique . . . 7. tobacco (strong) 10. otter
brown
perish . . . 3. die, rot 4. fade 5. decay,
waste 8. pass away, squander 9. cease
to be, disappear 11. be destroyed

perissodactyl ... **15.** odd-numbered toes
peristyle ... **7.** columns (range of)
  8. corridor **9.** colonnade **10.** peripteral
peritoneum fold ... **7.** omentum
periwig ... **3.** wig **6.** frizzy, peruke
  9. shellfish **10.** periwinkle
periwinkle ... **4.** blue **5.** snail, vinca
  6. mussel, myrtle **9.** evergreen
perjink ... **4.** neat, nice **7.** precise
perjure ... **7.** violate **8.** forswear
perjury ... **9.** violation **12.** breech of oath
  13. false swearing
perk ... **5.** preen, prink **7.** smarten
  9. percolate **10.** perquisite
perkin ... **5.** cider
perk up ... **7.** cheer up, improve, raise
  up, refresh **10.** recuperate
permanent ... **5.** fixed **6.** innate, stable
  7. abiding, durable, lasting **8.** constant,
  enduring, inherent **9.** perpetual
  10. changeless, continuing
  12. unchangeable
permeate ... **5.** imbue **7.** pervade
  8. saturate
permission ... **5.** grace, leave **7.** consent,
  license **9.** allowance **10.** sufferance
  13. authorization
permissive ... **8.** optional **9.** allowable,
  permitted, tolerated **10.** consenting,
  permitting **13.** power of choice
permit ... **3.** let **4.** leve **5.** allow, grant,
  leave **6.** suffer **7.** consent, license,
  warrant **8.** tolerate **9.** authorize
  10. permission
permit to live ... **5.** spare **8.** reprieve
permutate ... **6.** change **9.** rearrange
  11. interchange
permutation ... **6.** barter **11.** interchange
  13. transmutation **14.** transformation
pérn ... **6.** Pernis **7.** buzzard (honey)
pernicious ... **4.** bane **5.** fatal **6.** anemia,
  deadly, malign, wicked **7.** baleful,
  baneful, harmful, hurtful, noisome,
  noxious, ruinous, vicious **10.** villainous
  11. deleterious
pernio ... **9.** chilblain
perorate ... **5.** speak (at length) **7.** declaim
  8. harangue **9.** expatiate
perpendicular ... **4.** sine **5.** erect, plumb,
  sheer, steep **7.** apothem, upright
  8. binormal, vertical **9.** rectitude
  10. standing up **11.** precipitous
perpetrate ... **6.** commit **7.** perform
  12. carry through
perpetual ... **7.** endless, eternal
  8. constant, unending **9.** continual,
  perennial, permanent, unceasing
  10. continuous **11.** everlasting
perpetually ... **9.** endlessly, eternally
  11. ceaselessly **12.** interminably
perpetuity ... **7.** annuity **8.** eternity
  11. endless time
perplex ... **3.** vex **4.** cark **5.** amaze
  6. puzzle, riddle **7.** confuse **8.** bewilder,
  entangle **9.** obfuscate **10.** complicate
perplexity ... **3.** fog **6.** tangle **7.** anxiety,
  dilemma, problem **8.** question
  9. confusion, situation **10.** complexity
  11. distraction **12.** bewilderment,
  complication
perquisite ... **3.** tip **4.** gain **6.** boodle

8. appanage, gratuity
perquod ... **7.** whereby
Perry Mason ... see *Mason, Perry*
per se ... **6.** itself **8.** directly **11.** essentially
  13. intrinsically
perse ... **4.** blue
persecute ... **5.** annoy, harry, hound
  6. harass **7.** afflict, oppress, torment
  8. hunt down **9.** martyrize
persecution ... **9.** treatment
  10. harassment, oppression
  12. mistreatment
Persephone (pert to) ...
  abductor .. **5.** Hades
  Attica, name .. **4.** Kore (Cora)
  deity of .. **11.** agriculture
  father .. **4.** Zeus
  Greek name .. **11.** Persephassa
  mother .. **7.** Demeter
  Orphic literary name .. **8.** Despoina
  queen of .. **15.** infernal regions
  Roman name .. **10.** Proserpine
  (Proserpina)
Perseus (pert to) ...
  Astron .. **13.** Constellation
  father .. **4.** Zeus
  mother .. **5.** Danae
  slayer of .. **6.** Medusa
perseverance ... **8.** patience, tenacity
  9. constancy **10.** resolution, steadiness
  11. persistence, pertinacity
  13. steadfastness
persevere ... **5.** abide **6.** endure, insist,
  keep on **7.** carry on, persist **8.** continue
Persia (Iran, Irani) ... see also *Persian*
  capital .. **6.** Tehran (Teheran)
  city .. **5.** Niriz **6.** Abadan, Shiraz, Tabriz
  7. Hamadan, Ispahan
  country (anc) .. **4.** Elam **7.** Chaldea
  gulf .. **4.** Oman **7.** Persian
  gulf port .. **7.** Bushire **9.** Mohamerah
  gulf province .. **6.** Kuwait
  gulf wind .. **6.** shamal
  lake .. **7.** Rezaieh, Urumidh (Salt)
  mountain .. **6.** Ararat, Elburz, Zagros
  9. Hindu Kush
  pert to .. **6.** Persic
  river .. **5.** Safid **9.** Euphrates
  ruins .. **10.** Persepolis (Shiraz)
Persian (pert to) ... see also *Iranian*
  blue .. **10.** regimental
  calendar reformer .. **9.** Jalalaean
  (Jalalian)
  carpet, rug .. **4.** kali **5.** Herat (Herati),
  Senna **6.** Kerman, Tabriz **11.** Baluchistan
  cushion .. **6.** musnud
  diadem .. **3.** taj
  door .. **3.** dar
  evergreen .. **4.** olax
  grass .. **6.** millet
  gum .. **10.** tragacanth
  hat .. **3.** fez **6.** turban
  idiom .. **7.** persism
  javelin .. **6.** jereed (jerid)
  rose .. **3.** gul
  rug .. see *carpet (above)*
  screen .. **6.** purdah
Persian animals, birds, fruit ...
  apple .. **6.** citron
  bird .. **6.** bulbul
  cat .. **6.** Angora

deer .. **5.** maral **6.** fallow
gazelle .. **4.** cora
lamb .. **9.** astrakhan, broadtail
lynx .. **7.** caracul
tick (venomous) .. **8.** Miana bug

Persian Myth, Religion ...
angel .. **3.** Mah
deity .. **6.** Ormazd (Supreme)
demigod, hero .. **4.** Yima
demon .. **7.** Apaosha
fairy .. **3.** elf, fay **4.** peri
fire worshiper .. **5.** Parsi (Parsee)
god of light .. **7.** Mithras
mystic .. **4.** sufi
nymph .. **5.** houri
religion founder .. **9.** Zoroaster
religious doctrine .. **6.** Babism (Babiism)
sacred books (Zoroastrian) .. **6.** Avesta
scriptures (Muslim) .. **5.** Koran
spirit .. **7.** Ahriman

Persian people, government ...
assembly (1906) .. **6.** Majlis (Mejlis)
caste (priestly) .. **4.** Magi **7.** Wise Men
chief .. **3.** mir **4.** Shah
chief's wife, lady .. **4.** bibi
civil officer .. **4.** khan
dynasty .. **5.** Kajar **7.** Arsacid **8.** Selencid
  10. Sassanidae (Sassanid)
governor (anc) .. **4.** satrap
King .. **4.** Shah **5.** Cyrus (the Great)
  6. Darius, Xerxes
language (anc) .. **4.** Zend **7.** Pahlavi
  (Pahlevi)
New Year's Day .. **7.** Nowroze
people .. **4.** Leks, Lurs **5.** Arabs,
  Kurds, Medes, Mukri, Perse **6.** Aryans
  7. Gypsies, Hadjemi, Iranics **8.** Baluchis,
  Iranians
poet .. **4.** Omar **5.** Hafiz, Saadi
ruler .. **4.** Shah **6.** atabeg (atabek), Sultan
student (Koran) .. **5.** hafiz
trader .. **4.** Sart
Wise Men .. **4.** Magi

persiflage ... **6.** banter **8.** raillery
persimmon ... **4.** kaki **7.** chapote
persist ... **4.** last, urge **6.** endure **7.** prevail
  9. persevere
persistent ... **7.** durable **8.** constant,
  habitual **10.** determined, inveterate
  11. persevering **13.** indefatigable
persistently opposed ... **8.** renitent
  9. obstinate **12.** recalcitrant
person ... **3.** one **4.** body, soul **5.** being,
  wight **6.** figure **8.** creature **9.** character
  10. individual
person (pert to) ...
accuser, challenger .. **9.** appellant
acting for another .. **5.** proxy **9.** alternate
baptized (anc) .. **11.** illuminatus
base .. **7.** caitiff, hangdog
bringing bad luck .. **4.** jinx **5.** Jonah
bringing good luck .. **6.** mascot
canonized .. **5.** saint
careless .. **7.** trifler **11.** pococurante
charged with high mission .. **7.** apostle
charitable .. **9.** samaritan
cheerful .. **8.** optimist
clumsy .. **3.** oaf **5.** staup **6.** lummox
  7. bungler
common .. **3.** lay **8.** roturier
conceited .. **4.** prig

contemptible .. **3.** cad **4.** heel, toad
  7. bauchle (Scot)
crazed .. **6.** maniac **10.** monomaniac,
  psychopath
credulous .. **5.** Simon
cruel .. **5.** fiend
dishonorable .. **6.** rotter
dissolute .. **4.** roué
drunken .. **4.** lush
dull .. **4.** dolt **5.** dunce, moron, stock
  6. dorbel **9.** blockhead
dwarf .. **5.** shurf
educated .. **6.** pedant, pundit, savant
  7. erudite, learned, student **8.** cultured,
  highbrow **9.** literatus **12.** intellectual
emitting smoke .. **7.** whiffer
enterprising .. **8.** go-getter
fabulously rich .. **5.** Midas
foolish .. **3.** sop **4.** zany **5.** clown, idiot,
  nutty **6.** dotard **7.** bonkers, buffoon
  9. simpleton
gigantic .. **5.** giant, titan **7.** monster
gloomy .. **7.** killjoy **10.** crosspatch
good luck .. **6.** mascot
grotesque .. **9.** golliwogg
guilty .. **7.** culprit **12.** transgressor
held as pledge .. **7.** hostage
image of .. **4.** doll, idol **5.** clone **6.** poppet,
  puppet
impatient .. **6.** fidget **7.** hotspur
important .. **3.** VIP **5.** mogul **7.** magnate,
  notable **9.** personage
indifferent .. **5.** stoic
inexperienced .. **9.** greenhorn
insignificant .. **5.** sprat **6.** little, nobody
lazy .. **5.** drone **8.** sluggard
learned .. see *educated (above)*
left-handed .. **6.** clumsy **8.** sinister
  9. portsider
loud-voiced .. **7.** stentor **8.** blowhard
low-bred .. **3.** cad **6.** vulgar
miserly .. **9.** skinflint **10.** curmudgeon
non-Jewish .. **5.** Aryan **7.** Gentile
overmodest .. **5.** prude **8.** bluenose
perfidious .. **5.** snake **7.** traitor **9.** faithless
rapacious .. **4.** wolf **5.** harpy
relaxed .. **4.** calm **8.** laid-back
representing another .. **5.** proxy **7.** stand-
  in **9.** alternate
respondent to appeal .. **8.** appellee
rich .. **7.** wealthy **9.** plutocrat **10.** capitalist
  11. millionaire
rude, ill-mannered .. **4.** boor **5.** yahoo
scatterbrained .. **6.** madcap
self-centered .. **6.** egoist **7.** egotist
  9. extrovert, introvert
self-righteous .. **8.** pharisee
sharp-eyed .. **5.** alert, Argus
sick .. **9.** aegrotant, bedridden
skilled .. **6.** artist, master **7.** artisan
  8. mechanic
staff (Mil) .. **10.** aide-de-camp
stupid .. **3.** ass **4.** dolt, gump, nerd
  5. moron, stock
supercilious .. **4.** snob **9.** conceited
thankless .. **7.** ingrate
unclassified .. **11.** nondescript
unique .. **4.** oner
unknown .. **7.** inconnu **8.** inconnue
unmarried .. **6.** maiden, single
  8. bachelor, celibate, spinster

untidy . . **5.** messy **6.** grungy **8.** slipshod, slovenly **9.** litterbug
valorous . . **4.** hero **8.** champion
violent-tempered . . **6.** tartar
wealthy . . **5.** nabob, pluto (comb form) **10.** capitalist **11.** millionaire
who reads, writes . . **8.** literate
witty . . **3.** wag **7.** punster **8.** comedian **10.** comedienne
worthless . . **5.** lorel, losel
writ serving . . **6.** elisor
young . . **9.** stripling **14.** whippersnapper
personage . . . **5.** image, mogul **7.** bearing, stature **8.** great man, one's body, portrait **13.** impersonation
persona grata . . . **13.** welcome person **16.** acceptable person
personal (pert to) . . .
appearance . . **8.** presence
comb form . . **4.** idio
history . . **6.** memoir
ornament . . **6.** parure
ownership, land . . **6.** estate **7.** demesne **8.** chattels, property
personality . . . **3.** ego **5.** being **6.** person **8.** identity **13.** individuality **15.** distinctiveness
persona non grata . . . **18.** unacceptable person
personate . . . **5.** enact **7.** feigned **9.** represent **10.** personated **11.** counterfeit
personification . . . **3.** Una (truth) **10.** embodiment **11.** attribution **14.** representation
person of . . .
age . . **5.** major
courage . . **7.** Spartan
eighty years . . **12.** octogenarian
encyclopedic learning . . **10.** polyhistor
fifty years . . **15.** quinquagenarian
forty years . . **14.** quadragenarian
great intellect . . **6.** genius
nervous disorders . . **8.** neurotic
ninety years . . **12.** nonagenarian
one hundred years . . **11.** centenarian
seventy years . . **14.** septuagenarian
sixty years . . **12.** sexagenarian
skill . . **6.** master, talent **7.** magnate
persons of . . .
a familiar set . . **7.** coterie
a family tree . . **6.** stirps
groups . . **4.** army, band, team **6.** chorus, troupe **7.** company **8.** assembly **9.** orchestra
organized bodies . . **5.** corps, posse
perspicacity . . . **6.** acumen, vision **8.** sagacity **9.** acuteness **11.** discernment, penetration
perspicuity . . . **8.** lucidity, sagacity **12.** translucency, transparency
perspiration . . . **5.** sudor, sweat **7.** sudoric **8.** hard work **11.** evaporation, saline fluid **13.** transpiration
persuade . . . **4.** coax, sway, urge **6.** entice, induce, reason **7.** convert, suasion **8.** convince, inveigle **9.** influence, plead with, stonewall
persuasible . . . **6.** pliant **11.** persuadable **14.** open-mindedness
persuasive . . . **8.** eloquent **9.** impelling

10. convincing, persuading
pert . . . **3.** gay **4.** bold, keen **5.** brash, sassy, saucy **6.** clever, comely, dapper, daring, lively, nimble **7.** forward **8.** handsome, skillful **9.** exquisite, officious, sprightly **11.** impertinent **12.** presumptuous
pert (girl) . . . **4.** chit, minx
pertain . . . **5.** belie **6.** belong, relate **7.** adjunct **8.** function, peculiar **9.** accessory, appendage, appertain, attribute
pertaining to . . .
act of rising . . **6.** ortive **7.** eastern
agriculture . . **7.** georgic
ancestral type . . **9.** atavistic
ancient Nile city . . **4.** Sais (Saite)
ancient Troy . . **5.** Iliac
anything remote . . **6.** forane
apostles . . **7.** Petrine
Asiatic (old) . . **8.** Chaldean
Asiatic mountain . . **6.** Altaic
Athens . . **5.** Attic
authorized doctrine . . **8.** dogmatic **10.** dogmatical
birthmark . . **6.** nevoid (naevoid)
body . . **5.** somal
body of land . . **11.** continental
book description . . **13.** bibliographic
both ears . . **8.** binaural
both sexes . . **6.** unisex **7.** epicene
breadmaking . . **6.** panary
breastbone . . **7.** sternal
bristles . . **5.** setal
bunch . . **5.** comal
canonical hours . . **7.** matinal
carving . . **6.** glypic **7.** glyptic
cheek . . **5.** malar
church, part . . **7.** apsidal
city . . **5.** civic, urban
cod family . . **6.** gadoid
coins . . **12.** numismatical
colors . . **9.** chromatic
construction . . **8.** geodesic, tectonic
cork . . **7.** suberic
cough . . **7.** tussine
court . . **5.** aulic **9.** judiciary
crown . . **7.** coronal
dance . . **6.** gestic **13.** terpsichorean
daughter . . **6.** filial
dawn . . **4.** eoan
day (ordinary) . . **6.** ferial
desert wastes . . **6.** eremic
diaphragm . . **7.** phrenic
dogma . . **9.** levitical
doves . . **9.** columbine
downward air . . **9.** katabatic
downy . . **5.** dotal
dreams . . **7.** oneiric **9.** oneirotic
ducks . . **7.** anatine
early church . . **9.** patristic
early culture . . **8.** eolithic
earth . . **4.** geal **5.** terra **7.** teluric **9.** planetary
earthquake . . **7.** seismic
east . . **4.** dawn, eoan **7.** auroral
elms . . **9.** ulmaceous
engraving . . **7.** glyptic
equal rights . . **3.** ERA **6.** libber
essence . . **5.** basic
exhaustion . . **7.** burnout **9.** tiredness

fallow deer.. **6.** damine
fashion.. **5.** modal **6.** preppy, trendy
fasting.. **8.** anorexic **9.** abstinent
fats.. **6.** adipic, sebaic **9.** cellulite
feet.. **5.** pedal
fields.. **8.** agrarian
fine arts.. **9.** aesthetic (esthetic)
fingers.. **7.** digital
first principles.. **9.** elemental
fissure.. **5.** rimal
flood.. **8.** diluvian
flowers.. **9.** floscular **10.** florescent
forehead.. **7.** metopic
frogs.. **6.** anuran, ranine
funeral music.. **10.** threnodial
funerals.. **8.** exequial
gospel.. **9.** evangelic
gulls.. **6.** larine
gums (Anat).. **8.** gingival
hair.. **5.** pilar **7.** blow-dry
hands.. **6.** chiral, manual
head.. **8.** cephalic
heaths.. **8.** ericetal
holiday.. **6.** ferial (Eccl), festal
honey.. **10.** melaginous
horse.. **6.** equine
house.. **5.** domal (Astrol)
hypothetical force.. **4.** odic
infernal regions.. **7.** avernal
ink.. **10.** atramental
insects.. **11.** entomologic
intellect.. **6.** noetic
iron.. **6.** ferric
islands.. **7.** insular
jaw.. **10.** mandibular
kidney.. **5.** renal
knots.. **5.** nodal
land.. **8.** praedial (predial)
language meaning.. **8.** semantic
laughter.. **8.** risorial
leg.. **6.** crural **7.** fibular
lips.. **6.** labial
liver.. **7.** hepatic
living organism.. **13.** parasitologic
lockjaw.. **7.** tetanic
love.. **6.** erotic **7.** amatory **8.** erotical
male.. **5.** macho, manly **7.** agnatic
marriage.. **7.** marital **8.** hymeneal
marsh.. **8.** paludine
meaning, in language.. **8.** semantic
medicine.. **6.** iatric **8.** iatrical
medulla oblongata (brain).. **6.** bulbar
memory.. **6.** mnesic **7.** mnestic
     8. mnemonic **13.** retrospective
midday.. **8.** meridian
milk.. **7.** lactary, lacteal
mind.. **6.** mental **7.** phrenic
money matters.. **5.** T-bill **7.** bailout
     8. economic
morning.. **5.** matin, sunup **7.** matinal
     9. matutinal
motion.. **7.** kinetic
mouth.. **4.** oral **7.** oscular, palatal
     8. stomatic
mustard family.. **11.** cruciferous
nephew.. **7.** nepotal
north wind.. **6.** boreal
nose.. **5.** nasal **6.** narial, rhinal
nut.. **5.** nucal
ocean.. **7.** pelagic
old age.. **6.** senile **7.** geratic **8.** gerontic

9. geriatric
Old World.. **13.** gerontogenous
peacock.. **8.** pavonine
people.. **4.** laic **7.** demotic
pigs.. **7.** porcine
pleasure.. **7.** hedonic
priests.. **10.** sacerdotal
prophecy.. **9.** vaticinal
public.. **7.** cameral
public prayer.. **8.** liturgic **10.** liturgical
punishment.. **5.** penal **8.** punitive
queen.. **7.** reginal
rainbow.. **6.** iridal
reason.. **6.** noetic
region without earthquakes..
     11. peneseismic
rhubarb.. **7.** rheumic
river.. **5.** amnic
river bank.. **8.** riparian
rock.. **7.** petrean
royal court.. **5.** aulic
salvation.. **8.** soterial **9.** soterical
sarcasm.. **8.** ironical
school of philosophy.. **7.** Eleatic
sea.. **6.** marine **7.** oceanic, pelagic
     9. thelassic
seacoast.. **8.** littoral
sense of taste.. **9.** gustatory
sepulchral mound.. **7.** tumular
shin, shinbone.. **7.** cnemial
ship's sails.. **5.** velic
singing birds.. **6.** oscine
skull.. **5.** inial
sole of foot.. **7.** plantar
spring.. **6.** vernal
stars.. **6.** astral **7.** stellar **8.** sidereal
state affairs.. **9.** pragmatic
stepmothers.. **8.** novercal
storks.. **7.** pelagic
summer.. **7.** estival (aestival)
     8. festival
sun.. **5.** solar **6.** heliac
tail.. **6.** caudal
teaching.. **9.** pedagogic
tears.. **8.** lacrimal
tempo.. **6.** agogic
the plague.. **6.** loimic
the skin.. **5.** deric **6.** dermic
thread.. **5.** filar
tile.. **7.** tegular
time.. **7.** chronic
tin.. **7.** stranic
tissue.. **5.** telar
tongue.. **7.** glossal, lingual
tortoises.. **9.** chelonian
touch.. **7.** tactile
travel.. **6.** viatic
trees.. **8.** arboreal
verse stress.. **5.** ictic
walls.. **5.** mural **8.** parietal
wax.. **5.** ceral
weight.. **5.** baric **8.** ponderal
whales.. **5.** rotal
wife.. **7.** uxorial
wine.. **5.** vinic
wine making.. **10.** oenopoetic
wings.. **5.** alary
winter.. **6.** hiemal
womanhood.. **9.** muliebral
woods.. **6.** sylvan
wrist.. **6.** carpal

pertaining to country...
Asiatic.. **8.** Chaldean
Asiatic mountain.. **6.** Altaic
Athens.. **5.** Attic
Carthage.. **5.** Punic
Celts.. **4.** Erse
Cretan language.. **6.** Minoan
Dissenters meeting house.. **7.** pantile
  (from the roofing)
England.. **8.** Anglican
Ethiopian religion.. **6.** Coptic
France.. **6.** Gallic
Franks.. **5.** Salic
Gentiles.. **6.** ethnic
German State.. **8.** Bavarian
Greek epic.. **9.** Homerical
Greek philosophy.. **7.** Eleatic **8.** Platonic
Greek race (anc).. **6.** Aeolic
Greek valley.. **6.** Nemean **8.** Argolian
Hindu books, writing.. **5.** Vedic **7.** Tantric
Hindu philosophy, inertia.. **5.** tamas
Irish.. **6.** Celtic, Gaelic
Isle of Man.. **4.** Manx
Mars.. **5.** Arean
Mediterranean.. **6.** Levant
Moses.. **6.** Mosaic
Nile city (anc).. **4.** Sais (Saite)
Norse poem.. **5.** runic
Passover.. **7.** Paschal
Red Sea colony.. **8.** Eritrean
Rhine.. **7.** Rhenish
Scotch Highlander.. **6.** Gaelic
Spice Islands.. **7.** Molucca
Troy (anc).. **5.** Iliac **6.** Trojan
Vulcan.. **11.** Mulcibirian
West Indies.. **9.** Antillean
pertenencia... **10.** concession **11.** mining
  claim
Perth... **6.** Atholl (Athole) **7.** Ontario
  9. Australia
pertinacious... **4.** firm **8.** adhering,
  resolute **9.** tenacious **10.** determined,
  inflexible, persistent, unyielding
  11. persevering
pertinacity... **9.** obstinacy
  11. persistency
pertinent... **3.** fit **6.** timely **7.** germane
  8. apposite, relevant
perturb... **5.** alarm **6.** excite **7.** agitate,
  derange, disturb, fluster, trouble **8.** bewilder, disorder, distress **9.** confusion
perturbation... **5.** alarm **7.** anxiety,
  fluster **9.** agitation, confusion
  10. excitement **11.** fearfulness
  12. bewilderment, irregularity
pertusion... **8.** piercing, punching
  11. perforation, punched hole
pertussis... **5.** cough **13.** whooping
  cough
Peru... see also *Peruvian*
capital.. **4.** Lima **5.** Cuzco (Inca) **14.** City
  of the Kings
hero.. **7.** Bolivar, Pizarro
lake.. **8.** Titicaca
mountain.. **5.** Andes **10.** Cordillera
port.. **6.** Callao **7.** Iquitos **8.** Mollendo
river.. **4.** Sama **5.** Santa **6.** Amazon
  7. Maranon, Ucayali **8.** Urubamba
ruins.. **4.** Inca **5.** huaco (relics)
Peruvian (pert to)...
animal.. **4.** paco **5.** llama **6.** alpaca

bark.. **8.** cinchona
goddess of fertility.. **4.** Mama
inn, tavern.. **5.** tambo
king (petty).. **7.** cacique
plant.. **3.** oca
rodent.. **10.** chinchilla
tinamou.. **4.** yutu
tree.. **8.** cinchona
university.. **9.** San Marcos
volcano.. **7.** El Misti
wind (cold).. **4.** puna
pervade... **4.** fill **5.** imbue **6.** extend
  8. permeate, traverse **9.** penetrate
pervading... **9.** prevalent, universal
perverse... **3.** awk **4.** awry, wogh
  5. wrong **6.** cranky, erring **7.** corrupt,
  forward, froward, wayward, willful
  (wilful) **8.** contrary, petulant **9.** obstinate
  10. ill-humored
perversion... **5.** error **6.** misuse
  8. apostasy **9.** sophistry **10.** corruption,
  distortion **13.** falsification
  17. misinterpretation, misrepresentation
perversion of taste... **7.** malacia
pervert... **4.** ruin **5.** upset **6.** divert,
  misuse **7.** corrupt, distort, falsify,
  heretic **8.** apostate, overturn, renegade
  9. turn aside **10.** degenerate, lead
  astray **12.** misinterpret, misrepresent
pervulgate... **7.** publish
Pesach, Pesah... **8.** Passover (Feast)
pesante... **5.** heavy **10.** impressive
peshkash... **3.** tax **7.** present, tribute
  8. offering
peskar... **5.** agent **7.** steward **8.** minister
  10. accountant
pesky... **6.** plaguy **7.** teasing **9.** harassing
  10. tormenting
pes planus... **8.** flatfoot **13.** talipes
  planus
pess... **7.** hassock (church)
pessimist... **5.** cynic **6.** malist **9.** defeatist,
  worrywart
pessimistic... **6.** gloomy **7.** cynical
  8. cowardly, hopeless **10.** despairing,
  foreboding, uncheerful
pest... **3.** nag **4.** bane **6.** plague
  7. ragweed **8.** epidemic, nuisance
  9. annoyance **10.** pestilence
pester... **3.** nag, rib **5.** annoy, tease,
  worry **6.** badger, harass, impede, infest
  7. torment **8.** entangle **9.** importune
  10. overburden
pestilence... **4.** bane **7.** disease, scourge
  8. epidemic **13.** bubonic plague
pestilent... **6.** deadly **7.** noxious
  8. annoying **9.** pestering, poisonous
  10. contagious, infectious, pernicious
  11. mischievous, troublesome
pestle... **4.** club **6.** muller **7.** crusher,
  pounder
pes valgus... **9.** bowlegged **13.** talipes
  valgus
pet... **4.** dear, tiff **5.** humor **6.** caress,
  coddle, cosset, dandle, fondle, pamper
  7. darling, dudgeon, indulge **8.** cade
  lamb, favorite **10.** endearment
petals (pert to)...
flower.. **7.** corolla
having.. **8.** petalous
orchid.. **8.** labellum

ref to . . **5.** whorl **8.** petaline, petaloid
without . . **9.** apetalous
petard . . . **9.** explosive **11.** firecracker
peteman (thieves' sl) . . . **5.** thief **7.** burglar
   8. peterman **9.** cracksman, fisherman
   (Hist) **10.** safeblower
Peter (pert to) . . .
  Bell . . **4.** poem
  Bible . . **5.** Simon (also called) **7.** epistle
  (New Test)
  the Great . . **4.** Czar
  the Great's father . . **6.** Alexis
  the Hermit . . **8.** Crusader (1st)
peter out . . . **4.** fade, fail, tire, wane
  6. weaken **7.** dwindle **9.** cease to be
Peter Pan (pert to) . . .
  author . . **6.** Barrie
  children . . **4.** John **5.** Wendy **7.** Michael
  fairy . . **10.** Tinker Bell
  family . . **7.** Darling
  Indian princess . . **9.** Tiger Lily
  pirate . . **11.** Captain Hook
  place . . **14.** Never-Never Land
petiole . . . **4.** stem **5.** stalk **8.** peduncle
  9. leafstalk **10.** mesopodium
petit . . . **4.** mean **5.** petty, small **6.** little
  13. insignificant
petite . . . **5.** small **6.** demure, little
petition . . . **3.** ask, beg, sue **4.** plea, pray
  5. apply, plead **6.** prayer **7.** entreat,
  relator, request, solicit **8.** entreaty
  10. supplicate
peto . . . **5.** wahoo
petrified . . . **8.** hardened **9.** terrified
  15. carved from stone
petrified body . . . **6.** fossil
petrify . . . **4.** numb **6.** deaden, harden
  7. astound, stupefy **8.** paralyze
  11. become stone
petroglyph . . . **11.** rock carving **15.** rock
  inscription
Petrograd . . . **9.** Leningrad **12.** St
  Petersburg
petroleum product . . . **6.** butane, diesel
  7. naphtha, propane **8.** gasoline
petrology (science of) . . . **5.** rocks
petrosal . . . **4.** bone **6.** sinus, stony
  7. petrous **8.** ganglion
petticoat . . . **4.** girl, kilt **5.** jupon,
  pagne, woman **6.** kirtle **8.** basquine
  9. undercoat, waistcoat **10.** fustanella,
  underskirt
petticoat tails . . . **7.** teacake **9.** shortcake
pettifogger . . . **4.** tyro **5.** quack **6.** lawyer
  7. shyster **8.** attorney
pettish . . . **7.** fretful, peevish **9.** irritable
pettle . . . **6.** cuddle, nestle, potter
  7. cherish
petto . . . **12.** in one's breast **15.** in
  contemplation
petty . . . **4.** mean, orra **5.** minor,
  small **6.** paltry **7.** trivial **8.** childish,
  inferior, nugatory, trifling **9.** miniscule
  10. diminutive **11.** small-minded,
  subordinate, unimportant **12.** narrow-
  minded **13.** insignificant
  14. inconsiderable
petty (pert to) . . .
  captain . . **9.** centurion
  fault . . **10.** peccadillo
  larceny . . **10.** scrounging

mullein . . **7.** cowslip
objection . . **5.** cavil
prince . . **6.** satrap
petulance . . . **8.** ill humor, pertness
  9. insolence, sauciness **10.** wantonness
  11. peevishness, pettishness
petulant . . . **4.** pert **5.** cross, huffy, saucy,
  testy **6.** wanton **7.** forward, fretful,
  peevish, wayward, willful **8.** contrary,
  immodest, insolent **9.** querulous
peu à peu . . . **9.** by degrees **14.** little by
  little
pewee . . . **5.** pewit **6.** phoebe **8.** woodcock
  10. flycatcher
pewit . . . **5.** pewee **7.** lapwing **12.** laughing
  gull
Pfefferkuchen . . . **11.** gingerbread
Phaëthon, Class Myth (pert to) . . .
  bird . . **4.** swan
  car . . **3.** sun
  father . . **6.** Helios
  sun god . . **6.** Helios
phagomania . . . **8.** insanity **16.** insatiable
  hunger
Phalacrocorax . . . **5.** coots **10.** cormorants
phalacrosis . . . **8.** alopecia, baldness
phalanger . . . **5.** tapoa **9.** marsupial
phalanx . . . **4.** bone **5.** pawns **6.** troops
  7. company (Mil) **8.** infantry
phalera . . . **4.** boss **5.** cameo
phantasm . . . **5.** dream, fancy, ghost
  6. idolum, spirit **7.** eidolon, fantasy,
  phantom, specter (spectre) **8.** delusion,
  illusion **10.** apparition
phantasy, fantasy . . . **5.** fancy, image
  6. autism **8.** daydream **11.** imagination
phantom . . . **5.** fairy, ghost **7.** eidolon,
  specter (spectre) **10.** simulacrum
Pharaoh (Bib) . . . **4.** faro, king
Pharaoh (pert to) . . .
  ancestor . . **2.** Ra
  chicken, hen . . **7.** vulture (Egypt)
  fig . . **8.** sycamore
  mouse . . **9.** ichneumon
phare . . . **6.** beacon, pharos **10.** lighthouse
pharisee . . . **7.** pietist **9.** hypocrite
pharmacology . . . **5.** drugs **13.** materia
  medica
pharos . . . **5.** cloak **6.** beacon
  10. chandelier (Eccl), lighthouse,
  watchtower
phase . . . **5.** facet, stage **6.** aspect
  7. caprice, chapter, horning (moon)
phases, having many . . . **11.** Hydra-
  headed
phasm . . . **6.** meteor **7.** phantom
pheasant . . . **5.** cheer, monal **6.** pukras
  7. kallege **8.** tragopan **12.** ruffed grouse
pheasant (pert to) . . .
  brood . . **3.** nye **4.** nide (nid) **5.** flock
  cuckoo . . **6.** coucal
  duck . . **7.** pintail **9.** merganser
  finch . . **7.** waxbill
  genus . . **10.** Oreophasis
  wren . . **7.** emu wren
pheasant species . . . **5.** argus, blood
  6. golden, silver **7.** kallege **8.** curassow
  9. Mongolian **10.** ring-necked **12.** Lady
  Amherst's
phenomenal . . . **7.** unusual **8.** eventful,
  sensible **9.** objective, wonderful

13. extraordinary
phenomenon ... **4.** fact **5.** event (unusual)
  7. prodigy
phial ... **3.** cup **4.** bowl, vial **6.** bottle,
  vessel
phiale ... **5.** laver **6.** vessel **8.** fountain
  (Eccl)
Phi Beta Kappa (pert to) ...
  badge .. **8.** watch key
  founding .. **21.** William and Mary College
  (1776)
  meaning .. **24.** Philosophy the guide of
  life
  society .. **11.** Greek-letter (oldest)
philabeg (filibeg) ... **4.** kilt
Philadelphia ...
  City of .. **13.** Brotherly Love
  fleabane .. **7.** skevish
  lawyer .. **6.** shrewd
  ref to .. **12.** Philadelphus (Ptolemy II)
  sport team .. **6.** Eagles **8.** Phillies
philander ... **5.** flirt, lover **7.** opossum
  10. flirtation, love-making, lover of
  men
philanthropic ... **6.** humane
  10. benevolent **12.** eleemosynary
philanthropist ... **5.** donor **8.** altruist, do-
  gooder **9.** Robin Hood **10.** benefactor,
  benevolist, Montefiore, Rothschild
  12. humanitarian
philanthropy ... **7.** charity **8.** good
  will **10.** almsgiving **11.** beneficence,
  benevolence (opp of misanthropy)
philatelist's concern ... **5.** stamp
  (postage)
Philippic ... **6.** screed, tirade **7.** oration
  8. diatribe **9.** Philippus
Philippine, Philippines ...
  archipelago .. **4.** Sulu **5.** Malay
  bay .. **6.** Manila
  capital .. **6.** Baguio (summer), Manila
  10. Quezon City
  city .. **5.** Albay, Davao **6.** Cavite
  7. Dagupan
  district .. **7.** Lepanto
  fort .. **4.** Gota **10.** Corregidor
  island .. **4.** Cebu **5.** Leyte, Luzon, Panay,
  Samar, Ticao **6.** Negros **7.** Palawan,
  Paragua **8.** Mindanao
  mountain .. **3.** Apo, Iba **5.** Mayon
  river .. **4.** Abra, Agno **5.** Pasig
  8. Mindanao, Pampanga
  university .. **10.** Santo Tomas (1611)
  volcano .. **3.** Apo **5.** Mayon
Philippine (pert to) ...
  animal .. **5.** civet, lemur
  ant, termite .. **4.** anay (anai)
  barracks .. **7.** cuartel
  boat, canoe, raft .. **5.** balsa, banca
  breadfruit .. **7.** camansi
  buffalo .. **7.** carabao, timarau (timerau)
  chair (on poles) .. **7.** talabon
  dagger .. **4.** itac
  drink .. **4.** beno **5.** bubud
  fabric .. **4.** pina **9.** pineapple
  fetish, idol .. **5.** anito
  food .. **3.** poi **4.** Musa, saba, taro
  hemp .. **5.** abaca **6.** Manila
  house .. **5.** bahay
  knife .. **4.** bolo
  litter, pole chair .. **7.** talabon

lizard .. **4.** ibid (monitor)
mango .. **5.** bauno **7.** pahutan
market day .. **7.** tiangue
melon .. **6.** atimon
mudfish .. **5.** dalag
palm .. **4.** nipa **6.** anahau (anahao)
parrot (green) .. **5.** cagit
reptile .. **6.** python
rice .. **4.** paga **5.** macan
rice field bank .. **7.** pilapil
river .. **4.** ilog
shrub .. **4.** alem
sweetsop .. **4.** ates
town .. **4.** agoa
tree .. **3.** tui **4.** ipil (ypil) **5.** asana, ligas,
  narra, yacal **6.** molave **7.** Eugenia,
  tindalo **8.** macaasim
turnip .. **7.** cincoma
vehicle (public) .. **9.** carromata
water jar .. **5.** banga
wood .. **4.** teak **5.** ebony **6.** sandal
  8. mahogany
Philippine people (pert to) ...
  discoverer .. **8.** Magellan (1521)
  farmer .. **3.** tao
  headman .. **4.** datu
  language .. **4.** Moro **7.** Tagalog (Tagal)
  8. Pilipino
  Muslim, Moslem .. **4.** Moro
  native worker .. **7.** polista
  Negrito .. **3.** Ati **4.** Aeta
  patriot .. **5.** Rizal
  peasant .. **3.** tao
  people .. **3.** Ati, Lao **4.** Aeta, Moro, Sulu
  5. Bikol (Chr) **7.** Tagalog, Visayan
  president .. **5.** Roxas **6.** Aquino, Marcos,
  Quezon
  priest (Moro) .. **7.** pandita
  servant .. **4.** bata **5.** alila
Philistine ... **5.** enemy **7.** prosaic
  9. philister **10.** conformist, uncultured
  12. antagonistic **13.** prosaic person,
  unenlightened
Philistine (pert to) ...
  anc name .. **9.** Palestine, Philistia
  assimilated by .. **7.** Semites
  city .. **4.** Gaza **5.** Ekron (Bib)
  god .. **4.** Baal **5.** Dagon
philo (comb form) ... **6.** fond of, loving
philogeant ... **12.** lover of earth
philogyny ... **11.** love of women
philology ... **11.** linguistics **14.** love of
  learning
Philomela (pert to) ...
  father .. **7.** Pandion (King of Athens)
  sister .. **6.** Procne
  turned into .. **7.** swallow **11.** nightingale
philosopher ...
  American .. Dewey, James (William),
  Royce **6.** Peirce **9.** Santayana
  Arab .. **8.** Averroes (Averrhoes)
  Chinese .. **6.** Lao-tzu **9.** Confucius
  Christian .. **7.** Abelard, Aquinas
  9. Augustine
  Danish .. **11.** Kierkagaard
  Dutch .. **7.** Spinoza
  English .. **4.** Mill **5.** Bacon, Locke
  6. Hobbes **7.** Bentham, Russell, Spencer
  9. Whitehead
  French .. **6.** Pascal **8.** Rousseau, Voltaire
  9. Descartes

German . . **4.** Kant **5.** Hegel **9.** Heidegger,
Nietzsche **12.** Schopenhauer
Greek . . **4.** Zeno **5.** Plato **8.** Epicurus,
Socrates **9.** Aristotle
Indian . . **6.** Buddha
Italian . . **5.** Bruno
Scottish . . **4.** Hume
Seven Sages (7 Wise Men of Greece) . .
4. Bias **5.** Solon **6.** Chilon, Thales
8. Pittacus **9.** Cleobulus **10.** Epimenides
(or Periander)
Philosopher of . . .
Farney . . **8.** Voltaire
Malmesbury . . **6.** Hobbes
Sans Souci . . **17.** Frederick the Great
Syracuse . . **4.** Dion
Wimbledon . . **14.** John Horne Tooke
philosopher's school . . . **7.** Eleatic
philosophical . . . **4.** wise **7.** erudite,
logical, sapient **8.** rational **9.** temperate,
unruffled
philosophical being . . . **6.** entity
philosophy (pert to) . . .
choice of . . **11.** eclecticism
of law . . **13.** jurisprudence
of pantheists . . **5.** Stoic
sublimated . . **17.** Transcendentalism
theory . . **4.** yoga **9.** pantheism, Platonism,
solipsism **12.** epistemology
phlegmatic . . . **4.** calm, dull, slow **5.** inert
6. mucous, watery **7.** viscous **8.** sluggish
9. apathetic
phlogistic . . . **5.** fiery **6.** heated **7.** burning
11. impassioned **12.** inflammatory
Phoebad . . . **7.** seeress **9.** priestess
(Delphian) **10.** prophetess
Phoebe (pert to) . . .
daughter . . **4.** Leto
epithet of . . **7.** Artemis
mother . . **4.** Gaea (earth goddess)
poetic . . **4.** moon
phoebe . . . **4.** fish **5.** craps, pewit
6. peewee **9.** satellite (Saturn)
10. flycatcher
Phoebus . . . **3.** Sol **6.** sun god
Phoenicia . . .
capital city . . **4.** Tyre **5.** Sidon
Colony . . **5.** Hippo **8.** Carthage
deity . . **4.** Baal
famed for . . **9.** purple dye **10.** navigation
goddess of fertility . . **6.** Baltis **7.** Astarte
god of healing . . **6.** Eshmun (Eshmoun)
king . . **6.** Agenor
region . . **5.** Syria
Phoenix . . . **4.** bird (fabled), palm **7.** capital
(Ariz)
phonetic (pert to) . . .
science . . **9.** phonology
sound . . **7.** phoneme
stop . . **9.** occlusive
system . . **5.** romic
phonic . . . **6.** spoken, voiced **7.** sounded
8. auditory **9.** accoustic, vibration
phony (comb form) . . . **5.** sound, voice
phony . . . **4.** fake **9.** contrived, simulated
11. counterfeit
photograph . . . **4.** film **5.** image, photo
7. picture **8.** likeness, portrait
9. ferrotype, pictorial, portrayal
10. centerfold, heliograph
12. photogravure

photographic bath . . . **5.** toner **7.** reducer
9. developer
photography, science of . . . **5.** light
6. optics **7.** photics
photography inventors . . . **4.** Land
6. Niepce, Talbot **8.** Daguerre
photometric unit . . . **3.** pyr, rad
phrase . . . **5.** idiom **6.** remark, saying,
slogan **7.** diction, epigram, epithet,
passage **8.** flattery **9.** catchword
10. expression **11.** phraseology
phraseology . . . **5.** style **6.** jargon
7. diction, wording **8.** parlance
phratry (Hist) . . . **4.** clan **5.** group
phrenetic . . . **3.** mad **5.** crazy **6.** madman
7. fanatic, frantic, violent **9.** delirious
10. passionate
phrenology, science of . . . **5.** skull
10. craniology
Phrygia, Asia Minor . . .
cap (comical) . . **10.** liberty cap
deity . . **5.** Attis
Eccl Hist . . **9.** Montanist
founder . . **7.** Gordius (800 BC)
King . . **5.** Midas
marble (anc) . . **9.** pavonazzo
(pavonazzetto)
music . . **4.** mode
river . . **7.** Meander
phylactery (Eccl) . . . **4.** case **5.** charm,
chest, miter **6.** amulet, infula, record,
scroll
phylarchy . . . **12.** rule by tribes
phyletic . . . **6.** racial **7.** descent, species
12. phylogenetic
phyllophagous . . . **15.** feeding on leaves
physical . . . **6.** bodily **7.** natural, somatic
8. material **9.** corporeal
physical force . . . **10.** attraction
physical unit . . . **3.** erg
physician . . . **5.** medic **6.** doctor, healer,
intern **7.** coroner **8.** restorer
physician (pert to) . . .
ancient . . **5.** Galen
comb form . . **5.** iatro
French Nobel Prize . . **7.** Laveran
Greek (anc) . . **5.** Galen **11.** Asclepiades
quack . . **10.** medicaster
symbol . . **8.** caduceus
physicist . . . **4.** Bohr, Mach, Rabi
5. Fermi, Pauli **6.** Dalton, Pascal,
Teller **7.** Feynman, Hawking, Marconi,
Maxwell **8.** Chadwick, Einstein,
Sakharov **11.** Oppenheimer,
Schrödinger
physiognomy . . . **3.** mug **4.** face
11. countenance **14.** external aspect,
interpretation
physique . . . **4.** body **6.** figure
physis (Gr) . . . **6.** nature
phytology, science of . . . **6.** botany,
plants
piacle . . . **3.** sin **5.** crime, guilt **7.** offense
15. sacrificial rite **17.** expiatory offering
pian . . . **5.** tumor **9.** frambesia
piano (pert to) . . .
direction . . **10.** pianissimo (softly)
duet, upper part . . **5.** primo
dumb keyboard . . **10.** digitorium
early . . **6.** spinet
Italian . . **10.** Cristofori

keyboard . . **7.** clavier **8.** pedalier
pedal . . **7.** celeste
pianolike . . **7.** celesta
player . . **7.** pianola
slang . . **11.** eighty-eight
small . . **8.** pianette
piatti . . . **7.** cymbals
piazza . . . **5.** campo, porch **6.** square
  7. gallery, portico, veranda
pic . . . **4.** peak **8.** picayune
picacho . . . **4.** hill **5.** butte
picador . . . **3.** wit **6.** jester **7.** debater
  8. horseman (with lance), toreador
  11. bullfighter
picaro . . . **5.** knave, rogue **7.** sharper
  8. vagabond **10.** picaresque
picaroon . . . **5.** rogue, thief **6.** pirate,
  rascal **7.** brigand, corsair **8.** prey upon
pick . . . **4.** cull, gaff, peck, sort **5.** elect,
  pluck, strum **6.** assort, choose, indent,
  pickax, pierce, select **7.** diamond (card),
  harvest, the best **8.** plectrum, the elite
  9. toothpick
pick (pert to) . . .
  flaws . . **5.** cavil
  out . . **6.** pilfer, select **7.** acquire,
  procure, specify **9.** eliminate, segregate
  11. distinguish
  pick-me-up . . **5.** tonic **6.** bracer
  9. kittiwake, stimulate **11.** restorative
  up . . **4.** tidy **6.** arrest **7.** improve
  9. stimulant **10.** recuperate
picked . . . **4.** trim **5.** piked, spiny **6.** choice,
  chosen, culled, dainty, peaked, spruce
  7. adorned, plucked, pointed **8.** stripped
  10. fastidious
pickerel . . . **4.** fish, pike **9.** Esox niger
  12. walleyed pike
picket . . . **3.** peg **4.** pale, post, tern
  5. fence, guard, stake **6.** bullet, fasten,
  paling, sentry, tether **7.** enclose, fortify,
  shackle **8.** sentinel **10.** go on strike
pickle . . . **4.** alec, peck **5.** achar, brine
  6. dawdle, nibble, piddle, pilfer, trifle
  7. chutney, vitrial
pickled . . . **5.** drunk **6.** soused
  9. marinated
pickled pig's feet . . . **5.** souse
pickle fork . . . **8.** runcible
pickle-herring . . . **7.** buffoon **11.** merry-
  andrew **12.** Pickelhering
pickpocket . . . **4.** wire **5.** thief **6.** bulker
picnic . . . **3.** fun **4.** camp, play **6.** junket,
  outing **9.** festivity
Pict (anc) . . . **4.** Scot **5.** Aryan **9.** aborigine
Pictland . . . **8.** Scotland
pictorial . . . **8.** painting **11.** illustrated,
  picturesque
Pict's house (Archaeol) . . . **8.** dwelling
  (subterranean)
picture . . . **3.** oil **4.** copy, draw, icon
  5. image, print, scene **6.** chromo,
  depict, pastel **7.** diorama, etching,
  portray, porture, tableau **8.** describe,
  likeness, painting, portrait **9.** engraving,
  paintings, represent, visualize
  10. photograph **11.** description
  14. representation
picture (pert to) . . .
  mounting, border . . **3.** mat **5.** frame
  8. kakemono, makimono (scroll)

moving . . **4.** film **5.** movie **6.** cinema
positive . . **5.** print
puzzle . . **5.** rebus
small . . **5.** cameo **9.** miniature
stand . . **5.** easel
viewer . . **11.** alethoscope, stereoscope
  12. magic lantern, stereopticon
picturesque . . . **5.** vivid **6.** scenic
  7. graphic **9.** pictorial
picuda . . . **9.** barracuda (great), picudilla
  (small)
picudo . . . **6.** weevil **10.** boll weevil
piddle . . . **3.** toy **4.** pick, play **6.** putter,
  trifle **9.** waste time
pie . . . **4.** food, mess **5.** chaos, patty
  6. jumble, magpie, pastry **7.** cobbler,
  dessert, measure **9.** confusion
piebald . . . **4.** pied **5.** mixed, pinto
  6. motley **7.** mongrel, mottled, pintado
  10. variegated **13.** heterogeneous
piece . . . **3.** bit **4.** join, part, role
  5. crumb, drama, piece, scrap, shred
  6. sample **7.** measure, portion, writing
  8. chessman, fragment, specimen,
  treatise
piece (pert to) . . .
  armor . . **5.** tasse (tace) **8.** corselet
  de résistance . . **6.** entrée **8.** main dish
  door, jamb . . **6.** lintel
  eccentric . . **3.** cam
  fastening . . **3.** gib
  fitted . . **4.** shim **5.** tenon
  flat . . **4.** slab, slat **5.** flake, strip
  meal . . by degrees, fragments
  12. piece by piece **14.** little by little
  metal . . **3.** sow
  neck . . **3.** boa **5.** rabat, scarf, stole
  8. kerchief
  of one's mind . . **6.** rebuke **7.** reproof
  13. candid opinion
  out . . **3.** eke **6.** cantle
  preventing slippage . . **5.** cleat
  short . . **4.** skit
  side . . **3.** rib **5.** stave
  split off . . **6.** sliver, splint **8.** splinter
  tapering . . **4.** gore **6.** gusset
  work (art) . . **4.** pavé **6.** mosaic, niello
pieces of . . .
  eight . . **6.** dollar, escudo
  meat . . **5.** cabob
  silk waste . . **4.** noil
pied . . . **4.** foot **5.** pinto **7.** colored (2
  or more colors), dappled, piebald
  10. variegated **12.** parti-colored
pied (pert to) . . .
  blackbird . . **6.** thrush
  brant . . **5.** goose
  diver . . **4.** smew
  duck . . **8.** Labrador
  Friar (Eccl Hist) . . **9.** mendicant
  monk . . **10.** Bernardine, Cistercian
  Piper of Hamelin . . **8.** musician **10.** rat
  charmer
  widgeon . . **8.** garganey **9.** goldeneye
Piedmont, Italy . . . **7.** capital (Turin)
pieplant . . . **7.** rhubarb
pier . . . **4.** anta, dock, mole, quay **5.** groin,
  wharf **6.** pillar **7.** landing **8.** buttress,
  gatepost **9.** promenade **10.** breakwater
pierce . . . **4.** bore, cold, gore, pain, tart
  5. enter, gride, lance, probe, spear,

spike, sting, wound **6.** riddle, tunnel **7.** discern **8.** puncture **9.** penetrate, perforate **10.** comprehend
piercing . . . **4.** keen, loud **5.** acute **6.** shrill **7.** caustic, clearly, painful, piteous, pungent, sharply, shrilly, spiking, violent **8.** deep-felt, poignant, spearing, stabbing **9.** searching.
Pieria, Macedonia (pert to) . . .
epithet of . . **5.** Muses
native . . **7.** Pierian
reference to . . **6.** poetry **9.** knowledge
seat of . . **5.** Muses
piet . . . **5.** ouzel **6.** magpie **7.** piebald **10.** chatterbox, chattering **11.** saucy person
Pietà (It) . . . **9.** sculpture **10.** Virgin Mary
pietose (Mus) . . . **11.** sympathetic **13.** compassionate
piety . . . **4.** pity, zeal (worship) **6.** filial **8.** devotion, holiness, religion **9.** reverence **10.** compassion, devoutness, sanctimony **11.** dutifulness
pig . . . **3.** car (RR), ham, hog, sow **4.** boar, pork **5.** bacon, crosk, flask, swine **6.** farrow **7.** casting, dogboat, glutton **8.** pressman, sixpence, slattern **9.** policeman **11.** stoolpigeon
pig (pert to) . . .
bed . . **3.** pen, sty **5.** reeve **6.** pigsty
female . . **3.** sow **4.** gilt
guinea . . **4.** cavy
headed . . **6.** stupid **9.** obstinate
iron . . **5.** ingot
iron, ballast (Naut) . . **9.** kentledge
iron, cast . . **9.** kentledge (Mil)
last of litter . . **4.** runt
lead, weight . . **6.** fother
litter . . **6.** farrow
piglike . . **7.** hoglike, porcine, suiform
piglike animal . . **7.** peccary **8.** babirusa
potato . . **7.** cowbane
rat . . **9.** bandicoot
skin . . **6.** saddle **8.** football
yoke . . **7.** sextant **8.** quadrant
young . . **5.** grice, shoat **6.** farrow, piglet **9.** gruntling
pigdan . . . **8.** spittoon
pigeon . . . **3.** nun **4.** barb, dove, dupe, fowl, girl, gull, ruff **5.** heart, piper, pluck, sweet **6.** coward, fleece, pouter, roller, turbit **7.** fantail, jacobin, pintail, tumbler **9.** trumpeter
pigeon, pidgin (pert to) . . .
Australia . . **5.** wonga **10.** wonga-wonga
berry . . **7.** dogwood **9.** Juneberry, wild elder
blood . . **6.** garnet
carrier . . **5.** homer **6.** homing **10.** scandaroon
extinct . . **4.** dodo
food . . **7.** saltcat
genus . . **5.** Goura **7.** Columba
hawk . . **5.** falcon, merlin
house . . **7.** dovecot **9.** columbary
ref to . . **12.** peristeronic
short-beaked . . **4.** barb
wood . . **6.** cushat **8.** ringdove
young . . **5.** piper
pigment . . . **3.** red **4.** blue, gray, pink **5.** black, brown, color, green, ocher

(ochre), paint, white **6.** orange, purple, yellow **8.** colorant
pigment (pert to) . . .
arsenic, yellow . . **8.** orpiment
black . . **3.** tar **5.** sepia **7.** melanin
blue . . **5.** smalt
blue-green . . **4.** bice
brown . . **5.** sepia, umber **6.** bister (bistre), sienna (burnt) **7.** cypress
brownish yellow . . **6.** sienna
calico yellow . . **7.** canarin (canarine)
coal tar . . **7.** aniline
cuttlefish . . **5.** sepia
madder root . . **7.** rubiate
orange red . . **7.** realgar
oxide of lead . . **8.** massicot
red . . **7.** turacin
yellow . . **5.** ocher (ochre) **7.** etiolin
pigmy . . . see *pygmy*
pignus . . . **4.** pawn **6.** pledge
pig's feet . . . **9.** pettitoes
pigtail . . . **5.** braid, queue **7.** tobacco (rolled) **8.** rope's end (Naut)
pika . . . **6.** rodent
pike . . . **3.** ged (gedd) **4.** fish, luce, pick **6.** beacon, pickax
pike (pert to) . . .
North American . . **11.** muskellunge
perch . . **6.** sauger
pikelike . . **3.** gar **4.** luce **5.** lucet **6.** robalo **8.** robalito **9.** barracuda
walleyed . . **4.** doré
pikel, pikle . . . **7.** hayfork **9.** pitchfork
pikelet . . . **7.** crumpet
piker . . . **5.** thief, tramp **6.** coward **7.** gambler, quitter, shirker, vagrant **8.** tightwad
pilar . . . **5.** downy, hairy
pilaster . . . **4.** anta **6.** alette (part), column
Pilate (Bib) . . . **10.** procurator (Judean)
pilchard . . . **7.** sardine
pile . . . **3.** awn, mow, nap **4.** heap, load, mole, pier, rick, shag **5.** amass, slack, spile, stake **6.** heap up, pillar, wealth **7.** fortune, store up, texture
pile (pert to) . . .
burning . . **4.** pyre
defense . . **8.** estacade
driver . . **7.** fistuca
of hay . . **3.** mow **4.** dess, rick **5.** stack
up . . **4.** heap **7.** smashup, store up **9.** shipwreck **10.** exaggerate
pilfer . . . **3.** rob **4.** lift, loot **5.** filch, steal, swipe **6.** rustle (cattle), snitch **7.** purloin
pilgrim . . . **5.** exile (Relig) **6.** palmer **8.** crusader, newcomer, traveler, wanderer, wayfarer **9.** immigrant, sojourner **10.** tenderfoot **12.** peregrinator
Pilgrim (pert to) . . .
father . . **9.** John Alden
Fathers . . **11.** Separatists (1620)
garment . . **5.** ihram (Mecca)
landing . . **12.** Plymouth Rock (1620)
Scotch . . **6.** palmer
ship . . **9.** Mayflower, Speedwell
pilgrimage to Mecca . . . **4.** hadj
Pilgrim's bottle . . . **7.** ampulla, costrel
Pilgrim's Progress . . . **8.** allegory (Bunyan)
pill . . . **3.** rob **4.** ball, bore, pare, pell, pool

5. bolus, creek 6. bullet, pellet, pilule
8. medicine 9. cigarette 11. decorticate
pillage . . . 4. flay, loot, prey, sack
5. booty, harry, spoil, strip 6. rapine,
ravage 7. despoil, plunder, robbery
9. depredate, extortion 10. spoliation
pillar . . . 4. post, slab 5. shaft, stele
(stela), tower 6. column 7. support
8. mainstay, monument, pedestal
pillar (pert to) . . .
airfield . . 5. pylon
Buddhist . . 3. lat
carved . . 9. totem pole
little . . 8. pillaret
of society . . 9. personage
pillarlike . . 6. stelar
saint . . 7. recluse, stylite
tall, slender . . 7. obelisk
with front figure . . 7. osiride
Pillars of Hercules site . . . 5. Abila,
Calpe 17. Strait of Gibralter
pillbox . . . 3. cap, hat 8. brougham,
fortress 13. fortification
pillory . . . 4. yoke 5. stock, trone
6. cangue, punish
pillow . . . 3. pad 5. block 7. cushion,
support
pillow (pert to) . . .
case, cover . . 4. sham, slip
long . . 7. bolster
stuffing . . 5. kapok 8. feathers
pilose . . . 5. hairy 6. pilous
pilot . . . 4. lead 5. flyer, guide, steer
6. aviate, direct, leader 8. director,
helmsman, preacher 9. clergyman,
navigator 10. cowcatcher
pilot (pert to) . . .
bird . . 6. plover
expert . . 3. ace
fish . . 6. remora 9. amberfish, whitefish
house . . 10. wheelhouse
jacket . . 9. pea jacket
sky . . 8. preacher 9. clergyman
snake . . 10. copperhead
weed . . 9. rosinweed
whale . . 9. blackfish
pilotless plane . . . 5. drone
Piltdown, England (pert to) . . .
Hist yield . . 7. Dawn Man, fossils
Prehist station . . 6. Sussex
piltock . . . 8. coalfish
pilum . . . 6. pestle 7. javelin
pilus . . . 4. hair
Pima . . . 5. Opata
pimento . . . 6. pepper 7. paprika
8. allspice, pimiento
pin . . . 3. hob, peg, pen 4. axle, bolt,
coak (coag), join 5. affix, badge,
dowel, rivet, thole 6. brooch, cotter,
fasten, secure, trifle 7. confine, enclose,
gudgeon, jewelry, spindle, stopper,
trenail 8. linchpin, ornament, transfix
10. chatelaine
pin (pert to) . . .
axle . . 8. linchpin
dial . . 5. style
fish . . 11. stickleback
game . . 7. skittle
grass . . 9. alfilaria (forage)
jackstraw (game) . . 8. spilikin (spillikin)
meat fastener . . 6. skewer

quoits . . 3. hob
sailmaker's . . 3. fid
small . . 3. peg 4. lill
with looped head . . 7. eyebolt
pinafore . . . 5. apron, smock 7. tablier
8. sun dress
Pinafore . . . 5. opera (Gilbert & Sullivan)
pinag . . . 4. lake (rain season)
piñata . . . 5. globe (swinging, with gifts)
pinax . . . 4. dish 5. table 6. plaque,
scheme, tablet 7. picture 9. catalogue
pinbone . . . 7. hipbone
pince-nez . . . 7. glasses, nippers
10. eyeglasses
pincers . . . 3. tew 5. chela, tongs 6. pliers
7. forceps, pinette
pinch . . . 3. nip, rob 4. pain, raid 5. cramp,
gripe, pugil (anc), steal, stint, tweak
6. arrest, crisis, extort, scrimp, snatch,
snitch, strait, twinge 7. afflict, confine,
squeeze, urgency 8. compress, contract,
exigency, straiten
pinchbeck . . . 4. sham 5. alloy (cheap
jewelry) 8. frippery, spurious
11. counterfeit
pinched . . . 4. poor, thin 8. squeezed
10. compressed, contracted, distressed,
straitened
pinchem . . . 8. titmouse
pinda . . . 6. peanut
Pindar . . . 4. poet (lyric)
pindaric . . . 3. ode 9. irregular
12. unrestrained
pine . . . 4. flag 5. waste, yearn 6. grieve,
lament, needle, repine, sicken, weaken,
wither 8. languish 11. deteriorate
pine (pert to) . . .
Brazil . . 5. paraná
chemical . . 5. pinic
exudation . . 5. resin, rosin
family . . 3. fir 5. larch, piñon 6. spruce
finch . . 6. siskin
fir . . 6. balsam 12. Balm of Gilead
fruit . . 4. cone
genus . . 5. Pinus
gum . . 8. sandarac
knot . . 7. dovekie
leaf . . 6. needle
low-growing . . 5. piñon
mahogany . . 6. totara
New Zealand . . 5. kauri (kaury)
Pacific coast . . 8. knobpine
Philippine . . 7. Amboina 8. galagala
screw . . 3. ara 6. pandan
tar extract . . 6. retene
tulip . . 10. pipsissewa
pineal . . . 5. brain, gland 8. pine cone
pineapple . . . 4. bomb, pina 5. fiber, fruit
6. ananas 8. pine cone 12. Bromeliaceae
pineapple (pert to) . . .
cheese . . 7. Cheddar
cloth . . 4. pina
segment . . 3. pip
weed . . 8. marigold
Pina Tree State . . . 5. Maine
pinguescent . . . 9. fattening
pinguid . . . 3. fat 4. oily, rich 5. fatty
8. unctuous
pinguitude . . . 7. fatness, obesity
8. oiliness 10. greasiness
pink . . . 3. cut, Red 4. deck, rose, stab

5. adorn, blink, color, coral, smart, wound **6.** flower, indent, minnow, pierce, salmon, vessel **7.** radical, serrate **8.** decorate, grayling **9.** carnation **11.** fashionable

pink (pert to) . . .
coat . . **10.** foxhunter's
eye . . **4.** duck **14.** conjunctivitis
family . . **7.** Campion **9.** Carnation **15.** Caryophyllaceae
fish . . **8.** gobylike
genus . . **6.** Silene
lady . . **3.** fly (fishing) **8.** cocktail
needle . . **9.** alfilaria
Pearl . . **6.** azalea
pill . . **7.** cure-all
root . . **8.** wormroot

pinkeen . . . **6.** minnow **19.** insignificant person

pinna . . . **3.** fin **4.** wing **7.** auricle, feather, leaflet

pinnace . . . **4.** boat **5.** woman **6.** tender (Naut) **9.** procuress **10.** prostitute

pinnacle . . . **3.** epi, tee, tor **4.** acme, apex, peak **5.** crest, crown, serac, spire **6.** finial, needle, summit

pinnate . . . **11.** featherlike

pinniped . . . **4.** seal **6.** walrus

pinochle term . . . **3.** dix **4.** meld

piñon . . . **4.** pine, seed **8.** pignolia **12.** monkey puzzle

pintado . . . **4.** cero, fish, sier (fish) **5.** pinto **6.** chintz, pigeon, sierra

pintail (pert to) . . .
duck . . **4.** smee **5.** river, ruddy
grouse . . **4.** sand **11.** sharp-tailed

pinto (horse) . . . **4.** pied **6.** calico **7.** mottled, painted, piebald, spotted

pinwing . . . **7.** penguin

pioneer . . . **4.** lead **5.** guide, miner **6.** digger, open up **7.** settler **8.** colonist, explorer **9.** excavator **10.** forerunner

Pioneer's Day . . . **4.** Utah (July 24) **5.** Idaho (June 15)

pious . . . **5.** godly, loyal **6.** devout, worthy **9.** excellent, religious **11.** reverential **13.** sanctimonious

pip . . . **3.** ace **4.** paip, peep, roup, seed, spot, trey **7.** disease **12.** officer's star

pipe . . . **2.** TD **3.** see, tee **4.** blow, clay, duct, reed, tube **5.** spout, voice **6.** convey, dudeen, hookah (hooka), outlet **7.** channel **9.** brierwood

pipe (pert to) . . .
connection . . **3.** ell, tee **5.** cross, elbow
dream . . **8.** illusion **10.** bemusement
end . . **4.** taft **6.** nozzle
line . . **9.** grapevine
Oriental . . **8.** narghile (nargile)
pastoral, shepherd's . . **3.** oat **4.** reed **7.** larigot **9.** flageolet
peace . . **7.** calumet
player . . **5.** fifer **8.** shepherd
short . . **6.** dudeen
smoke . . **5.** tewel
steam . . **5.** riser
tobacco . . **10.** meerschaum
wood . . **5.** brier (briar) **9.** brierwood
wrench . . **8.** Stillson

pipette . . . **6.** taster, tubule **7.** dripper

pipit . . . **7.** titlark

piquancy . . . **4.** zest **5.** spice **8.** pungency, raciness, tartness **11.** conciseness

piquant . . . **4.** racy, tart **5.** salty, sharp, spicy, zesty **7.** concise, cutting, pungent **11.** interesting, provocative

pique . . . **4.** dive, fret, goad **5.** anger, annoy, sting, tempt **6.** grudge, incite, nettle, offend **7.** dudgeon, offense, provoke, umbrage **8.** irritate **9.** displease **10.** irritation, resentment **11.** displeasure

pir (Muslim) . . . **4.** tomb **5.** guide, saint

pirate . . . **6.** robber **7.** corsair, mariner **8.** marauder, picaroon **9.** buccaneer **10.** freebooter **11.** appropriate

pirate (famed) . . . **4.** Kidd **6.** Morgan **7.** Lafitte **10.** Blackbeard (Capt Teach)

pirate (pert to) . . .
base, famed . . . **7.** Barbary (Coast)
bird . . **10.** jaeger gull
flag . . **10.** Jolly Roger
gallows . . **7.** yardarm
perch . . **8.** Xenarchi
ship . . **5.** rover **7.** corsair **8.** picaroon
weapon . . **4.** snee

piraya . . . **6.** caribe (fish) **7.** piranha

pirogue . . . **5.** canoe **7.** piragua

pirol . . . **6.** oriole

Pisa, Italy . . .
capital of . . **7.** Tuscany
famed for . . **9.** campanile **12.** Leaning Tower
river . . **4.** Arno

pis aller . . . **10.** last resort

piscary . . . **7.** fishery **12.** fishing place **13.** fishing rights

piscatology (science of) . . . **7.** angling, fishing **10.** halieutics

Pisces . . . **4.** fish **6.** fishes **13.** constellation

piscina . . . **4.** tank **5.** basin (Eccl) **8.** fishpond **9.** reservoir

Piscis Volans . . . **10.** flying fish **13.** constellation

Pisgah (pert to) . . .
site . . **4.** Nebo **8.** mountain (top)
view . . **12.** Land of Canaan **13.** Land of Promise
viewer . . **5.** Moses

pismire . . . **3.** ant **5.** emmet

pistachio . . . **3.** nut **5.** green

piste . . . **4.** path **5.** spoor, track, trail **10.** racecourse

pisteology, pistiology . . . **5.** faith **6.** belief

pistil . . . **5.** ovary **6.** carpel **9.** gynoecium

pistol . . . **3.** dag **7.** firearm **9.** derringer

pistol (pert to) . . .
case . . **7.** holster
lock . . **5.** rowet
slang . . **3.** gat, rod **6.** barker, cannon, heater

pistology (Theol) . . . **5.** faith

piston . . . **7.** plunger

pit . . . **4.** cave, hole, mine, pool, sump, tomb, trap, well **5.** abyss, arena, grave, sluig, snare **6.** cavity, slough **7.** alveola, cockpit, dungeon **8.** audience **9.** waterhole **10.** excavation **13.** Stock Exchange

pit (pert to) . . .
anatomy . . **5.** fossa, fovea
botany . . **7.** alveola, pitamen **8.** endocarp
bottomless . . **7.** Abaddon

fodder.. **4.** silo
Hades.. **4.** hell
Hawaiian.. **3.** imu
theater.. **7.** parquet
viper.. **9.** Viperidae **11.** rattlesnake
pitch ... **3.** key, tar **4.** camp, hurl, tilt,
tone, toss **5.** black, color, erect, fling,
heave, lurch, resin, sense, slope, throw
6. degree, encamp, plunge, settle,
topple **7.** incline **8.** flounder **9.** sales
talk
pitch (pert to)...
high.. **6.** shrill
identity.. **6.** unison
inflammable.. **7.** piceous
mineral.. **7.** asphalt, bitumen
music.. **4.** flat **6.** accent, stress
8. paranete **9.** tonometer
pitchlike.. **7.** piceous
pitchblende ... **6.** radium **7.** uranium
pitched ball, curving away ...
8. outshoot
pitcher ... **3.** jug **4.** ewer, olla, olpe,
toby **5.** gorge **8.** cruisken (cruiskeen),
oenochoe (wine), southpaw (left-
handed)
pitcher (pert to)...
plant, genus.. **9.** Nepenthes
10. Cephalotus, Sarracenia
plus catcher.. **7.** battery
shaped.. **9.** urceolate
shaped vessel.. **8.** aiguière
piteous ... **5.** pious **6.** devout, paltry,
tender **7.** pitiful, pitying **8.** pitiable
13. compassionate
pitfall ... **3.** pit **4.** lure, trap **5.** decoy,
snare **6.** danger **10.** difficulty
pith ... **3.** jet, nub **4.** gist, meat, pulp
6. center, kernel, marrow **7.** essence,
meaning, nucleus **9.** substance
pith helmet ... **3.** cap, hat **5.** topee (topi)
pith tree (Nile) ... **7.** ambatch (ambash)
pithy ... **4.** soft **5.** crisp, meaty, pulpy,
terse **7.** laconic **10.** meaningful
12. epigrammatic
pithy (pert to)...
expression.. **7.** epigram
saying.. **3.** mot
sentence.. **5.** motto
pitiable ... **3.** sad **6.** woeful **7.** piteous
8. grievous, terrible **9.** miserable,
sorrowful **10.** lamentable
pitiful ... **4.** mean **6.** paltry **7.** piteous
8. pathetic, shameful **10.** despicable
12. contemptible **13.** compassionate,
tenderhearted
pitiless ... **5.** cruel **8.** ruthless **9.** merciless
10. relentless **13.** unsympathetic
pitpit ... **8.** guitguit **12.** honey creeper
Pitri, Hindu (pert to)...
ancestor of.. **4.** gods **6.** demons **10.** four
castes
Prajapatis, one of.. **10.** progenitor
(human race)
semidivine.. **6.** father **9.** patriarch
10. forefather
pittance ... **4.** alms, dole, gift, scat
7. bequest **8.** donation **9.** allowance
11. small amount
pity ... **4.** ruth **5.** mercy, yearn **7.** remorse
8. clemency, sympathy **10.** compassion,

condolence, repentance
13. commiseration
pivot ... **3.** toe **4.** slew, slue, turn **5.** hinge
6. pintle, swivel
pivotal ... **4.** crux **5.** polar **7.** turning
pixy, pixie ... **3.** elf, imp **5.** fairy **6.** goblin,
sprite **13.** mischief-maker
Pizarro (pert to) ...
adventurer.. **7.** Spanish
conqueror of.. **4.** Peru
founder of.. **4.** Lima (capital)
placable ... **8.** peaceful **9.** agreeable,
forgiving, peaceable **10.** appeasable
placard ... **4.** bill, post **5.** edict **6.** notice,
poster **7.** affiché **9.** manifesto,
stomacher **12.** proclamation
placate ... **4.** calm **6.** pacify, soothe
7. appease **10.** conciliate **11.** tranquilize
place ... **3.** put **4.** lieu, site, spot **5.** abode,
locus, posit, situs, stead **6.** locale,
locate, region, street **7.** arrange,
demesne, deposit **8.** classify, location,
position **9.** recognize, situation
place (of) ...
amusement.. **4.** park **6.** casino, midway
bliss.. **4.** Eden **8.** paradise
confinement.. **3.** pen **4.** brig, cage,
coop, gaol, jail, stir **6.** asylum, corral,
prison **7.** dungeon **9.** calaboose
12. penitentiary
confusion.. **5.** Babel
content.. **7.** Arcadia
darkness.. **6.** Erebus
exit.. **6.** egress
honor.. **9.** right hand
origin.. **6.** cradle, source
refuge.. **3.** ark **4.** port **5.** haven
resort.. **7.** purlieu
rest.. **3.** bed, den **4.** lair, nook **5.** chair,
couch, grave, niche
sleep.. **3.** bed **4.** doss **5.** berth, couch
6. pallet **7.** hammock
suffering.. **10.** Armageddon,
Gethsemane
trial.. **5.** venue
place (pert to) ...
apart.. **6.** enisle **7.** isolate **9.** sequester
beneath.. **9.** infrapose
between.. **9.** interpose
burial.. **5.** grave **8.** catacomb, cemetery
9. graveyard **10.** necropolis
by itself.. **7.** isolate
camping.. **5.** étape
confidence in.. **7.** entrust
different.. **10.** otherwhere
for boats.. **7.** portage
for candles.. **9.** chandlery
forest (open).. **5.** glade
for keeping animals.. **3.** zoo **4.** barn
7. pasture **9.** menagerie
frequented.. **4.** dive **5.** haunt **6.** resort
from which jury is taken.. **5.** venue
hallowed.. see *sacred (below)*
hiding.. **3.** mew **4.** lair **5.** niche
high.. **7.** eminent **8.** eminence
horse training.. **4.** ring **5.** longe
in a row.. **5.** align, aline
in bondage.. **7.** enslave
in order.. **7.** arrange **11.** systematize
in statu quo.. **7.** put back, replace,
restore

interpretation on .. **8.** construe
landing .. **4.** dock, pier **5.** wharf **7.** airport
market .. **4.** mart **5.** agora **6.** rialto
meeting .. **5.** tryst
of .. **4.** lieu **5.** stead
on mound .. **3.** tee
opposite .. **6.** appose
over .. **11.** superimpose
sacred .. **4.** fane **5.** altar **6.** chapel,
   church, shrine, temple **9.** synagogue
   10. tabernacle
side-by-side .. **9.** collocate, juxtapose
sleeping .. **3.** bed **4.** bunk **5.** berth,
   couch **6.** pallet **7.** hammock
under .. **9.** infrapose
under restraint .. **6.** arrest, intern
value upon .. **5.** price **6.** assess
   8. appraise, estimate
wet .. **4.** slew **5.** marsh **6.** slough
wrestling .. **5.** arena **9.** palaestra
   (palestra)
placed ... **3.** put **7.** located **8.** arranged,
   situated **10.** classified
placed in lodgings ... **6.** roomed
   8. billeted
placid ... **4.** calm **5.** quiet, suant
   6. demure, gentle, serene **8.** composed,
   peaceful **9.** agreeable, quiescent,
   unruffled **11.** undisturbed
pladaroma ... **5.** tumor (eyelid)
plafond ... **7.** ceiling **14.** contract bridge
plage ... **5.** beach
plagiarism ... **6.** piracy **8.** cribbing,
   stealing **10.** purloining **13.** appropriation
plague ... **3.** dun, vex **4.** bane, pest, twit
   5. harry, tease, worry **6.** harass, hector,
   infest **7.** scourge, torment **8.** epidemic,
   nuisance **10.** Black Death, pestilence
   11. infestation
plaguy ... **6.** vexing **8.** annoying
   9. difficult, harassing **10.** tormenting
   11. troublesome
plaice ... **8.** flatfish, flounder
plaid ... **4.** maud **6.** tartan
plain ... **3.** lea **4.** chol, mesa, moor, wold
   5. blunt, camas, clear, frank, heath
   6. lenten **7.** artless, evident, genuine,
   legible, obvious, prairie **8.** apparent,
   distinct, explicit, ordinary **9.** downright,
   primitive, unadorned **10.** unaffected
plain (pert to) ...
clothes .. **10.** unofficial
dealing .. **4.** open **5.** frank
knitting .. **12.** garter stitch
of Mars .. **9.** palmistry
spoken .. **15.** straightforward
Plains (pert to) ...
Arctic .. **6.** tundra
Europe .. **6.** steppe
Florida .. **7.** savanna (savannah)
Italy .. **8.** campagna
Russia .. **6.** steppe, tundra
S African .. **6.** pampas
Sp American .. **4.** vega **5.** llano **6.** salada
   (salt-covered)
Plains Indians ... **6.** Kiowan, Siouan
   7. Caddoan **10.** Algonquian,
   Athapascan, Uto-Aztecan
plainsman ... **6.** cowboy **7.** llanero
   8. herdsman
Plains of Abraham ... **10.** Quebec City

plaint ... **6.** bewail, lament **9.** complaint
   11. lamentation
plaintiff ... **4.** suer **6.** orator **7.** accuser
   8. claimant, libelant (libellant)
   10. complainer **11.** complainant
plaintive ... **3.** sad **5.** cross **7.** elegiac,
   fretful, peevish, pettish, wailful, wistful
   8. mournful, petulant, repining
   9. lamenting, sorrowful **10.** melancholy
   11. complaining **12.** discontented
plait ... **4.** fold, hair, knit, lace, plat
   5. braid, pleat, weave **6.** pleach, wimple
   9. corrugate, interlace **10.** interweave
plaited ... **5.** Milan (straw) **6.** folded,
   kilted, sennit (palm leaves) **8.** pleached
   10. interlaced **11.** intertwined
plan ... **3.** map, way **4.** form, idea, line,
   plat, plot **5.** chart, draft, ettle, frame,
   setup **6.** design, devise, intend, layout,
   method, scheme **7.** arrange, diagram,
   outline, pattern, project **8.** engineer,
   strategy **9.** calculate, procedure
   11. arrangement, contemplate,
   preconceive, premeditate
plan (pert to) ...
architecture .. **5.** draft, épure
frustrator of .. **7.** marplot
preliminary .. **4.** idea **6.** map out
   8. proposal
secretly .. **4.** plot **7.** connive **8.** conspire
planate ... **5.** plane **9.** flattened
plancher ... **3.** bed **5.** board (occult), floor,
   plank **6.** pallet **8.** planking, platform
plancier ... **6.** soffit **7.** cornice
plandok ... **9.** mouse deer
plane ... **3.** fly **4.** even, flat, ramp, scar, tool
   5. level **6.** degree, smooth **7.** jointer,
   surface **8.** airplane **10.** smoothness
plane (pert to) ...
block .. **5.** stock
boundary .. **9.** perimeter
four-angled .. **6.** square **7.** rhombus
   8. tetragon **10.** quadrangle
handle .. **4.** tote (bench plane)
inclined .. **4.** ramp **5.** chute
iron .. **5.** blade
kind .. **3.** mig **5.** stuka **6.** router
measure .. **10.** planimeter
smoothing, chamfering .. **5.** howel
tree .. **6.** chinar (Orient) **8.** Platanus
type .. **5.** bench, block, stock **6.** trowel
   7. jointer, routing
planet ... **4.** Mars, star **5.** Earth, Pluto,
   Venus **6.** Saturn, Uranus **7.** Jupiter,
   Mercury, Neptune **8.** wanderer
planet (pert to) ...
astrology .. **9.** alfridary
brightest .. **5.** Venus
cone .. **8.** strobile
course .. **5.** orbit
minor .. **9.** satellite
nearest sun .. **7.** Mercury
orbit .. **7.** ellipse
red .. **4.** Mars
remotest .. **5.** Pluto (1930)
resembling .. **8.** asteroid
ringed .. **6.** Saturn
satellite .. **4.** moon
shadow .. **5.** umbra
small .. **8.** asteroid
sphere .. **6.** oblate

planet (solar system) **by size** . . . **7.** Jupiter
 6. Saturn **7.** Neptune **6.** Uranus **5.** Earth,
 Venus, Pluto **4.** Mars **7.** Mercury
planetarium . . . **5.** Zeiss **6.** orrery
planetary . . . **7.** earthly, erratic **9.** celestial,
 wandering, worldwide
planetology (study of) . . . **7.** planets
 10. satellites
plangor . . . **4.** wail **11.** lamentation
planisphere . . . **7.** sextant **9.** astrolabe
plank . . . **3.** sny **4.** deal, slab **5.** board,
 shole, stone **6.** timber **7.** pay down
 8. planking **10.** gravestone
plank down . . . **3.** pay **7.** advance, deposit
planner . . . **8.** designer, engineer,
 gardener **9.** architect, projector
plant . . . **3.** fix, sow, spy **4.** ache, bury,
 herb, seed, trap **5.** cache, decoy, shrub
 6. clover **7.** falsify **8.** colonize, workshop
 9. deception, detective, equipment,
 vegetable
plant (pert to) . . .
 abnormal environs . . **4.** ecad
 adjustment . . **6.** ecesis
 air . . **8.** epiphyte
 appendage . . **7.** stipula
 biggest . . **10.** Aspidistra
 body . . **6.** cormus **7.** thallus
 bud . . **4.** cion **5.** scion
 climbing . . **4.** vine **5.** liana
 coloring matter . . **11.** chlorophyll
 crossbred . . **6.** hybrid
 cross-fertilization . . **9.** phytogamy
 disease . . **4.** gall, rust, smut **5.** ergot
 7. blister **8.** ramentum
 embryo . . **8.** plantule
 enchantment-proof . . **7.** haemony
 (Milton's Comus)
 flowerless . . **4.** fern **6.** lichen
 9. cryptogam **11.** Cryptogamia (opp
 of phanerogam)
 growing on rock . . **6.** lichen
 growing on sea bottom . . **6.** enalid
 growing wild . . **9.** agrestial
 history . . **12.** phytogenesis
 legendary, forgetfulness . . **5.** lotus
 male . . **3.** mas
 mosslike . . **6.** orpine
 mushroom type . . **6.** fungus
 native . . **8.** indigene
 orifice . . **5.** stoma
 pigment lacking . . **6.** albino
 poisonous . . **4.** atis **6.** datura **7.** amanita
 8. oleander
 poisonous to cattle . . **4.** loco **8.** locoweed
 pore . . **8.** lenticel
 round-leaved . . **9.** pennywort
 science of . . **6.** botany
 seedless . . **6.** agamic
 stem, stalk . . **4.** bine **5.** haulm **6.** caulis
 tequila-yielding . . **5.** agave
 tissue . . **7.** tapetum
 without chlorophyll . . chlorophyll
 6. albino
 without petals . . **9.** apetulous
 woody . . **6.** xyloid
plant (type of) . . .
 aconite . . **4.** bikh
 agave, century plant . . **4.** aloe, pita
 9. amaryllis
 ammoniac . . **5.** oshac

anise . . **4.** dill
aquatic . . **6.** sugamo **7.** frogbit
 8. plankton
aromatic . . **4.** mint, nard **5.** basil, tansy,
 thyme **8.** tarragon
arum . . **4.** sago **6.** starch **9.** arrowroot
aster family . . **5.** daisy **8.** fleabane
bitter . . **3.** rue
bitter vetch . . **3.** ers
box . . **5.** Buxus **7.** boxwood
broom . . **5.** spart **6.** Canary **7.** genista
bryophytic . . **4.** moss
burdock . . **5.** elite **8.** Xanthium
burning bush . . **5.** wahoo
butter-and-eggs . . **8.** ranstead
cactus . . **5.** dildo **6.** cereus, chaute,
 mescal **7.** saguaro **9.** xerophyte
century . . **4.** aloe **5.** agave **6.** maguey
dill . . **4.** anet
evergreen . . **3.** ivy **5.** holly **6.** laurel
 8. conifers **9.** mistletoe
everlasting . . **6.** orpine **11.** live-forever
furze . . **4.** ulex **5.** gorse
garlic (wild) . . **4.** moly
leguminous . . **3.** pea **4.** bean **6.** Cassia,
 clover, lentil
lilaceous . . **4.** aloe, iris, leek **5.** lotus,
 onion, tulip, yucca
linen . . **4.** flax
medicinal . . **4.** alem, aloe **5.** anise,
 wahoo **6.** arnica, cacoon, catnip, ipecac
 7. aconite, boneset, gentian, lobelia,
 rhatany **8.** camomile
pea family . . **7.** Cytisus
perennial . . **4.** Geum **5.** avens
 10. sneezewort
poisonous . . **6.** datura **8.** oleander
poisonous to cattle . . **8.** locoweed
poisonous to fowl . . **7.** henbane
prickly, thorny . . **5.** brier **6.** cactus, nettle,
 teasel **7.** thistle
satinpod (transparent) . . **7.** honesty
soap . . **5.** amole
tapioca . . **7.** cassava
thorny . . see *prickly* **6.** fatsia
trifoliate . . **6.** clover **8.** shamrock
plant, typical of . . .
 Africa . . **5.** argel (arghel)
 Alps . . **9.** edelweiss
 Arabia . . **3.** kat (stimulant)
 Australia . . **5.** Hakes, lilac **6.** Correa
 7. columba, fuchsia **8.** Rutaceae
 China . . **5.** ramie
 Egypt . . **5.** anise, cumin **7.** aniseed
 8. nepenthe
 Hawaii . . **5.** olona
 Japan . . **3.** tea **5.** acuba **6.** quince
 7. cydonia **8.** japonica
 Japan (vine) . . **8.** Bignonia **14.** trumpet
 creeper
 Mexico . . **4.** chia **5.** datil **6.** salvia
 9. sabadilla
 Peru . . **3.** oca **7.** rhatany
 Philippines . . **4.** alem (Med) **6.** agamid
 Spain . . **3.** aji **6.** pepper **8.** Capsicum
 Syria . . **5.** cumin
 tropical vine . . **8.** redwithe **10.** tillandsia
 tropics . . **4.** arum, palm, taro **5.** agave,
 zamia **7.** dasheen, hamelia **8.** mangrove
plantain . . . **6.** banana
plantation pines . . . **7.** pinetum

plantation trees ... **4.** holt **6.** forest
   7. nopalry (cactus), orchard
planters, Govt of ... **11.** plantocracy
plantigrade mammal ... **5.** panda
plaque ... **5.** medal, patch **6.** brooch,
   tablet **8.** ornament, platelet (Anat)
plash ... **4.** plop, pool **5.** swash **6.** puddle,
   ripple, splash
plasm ... **4.** mold **6.** matrix
plasma ... **4.** cell, whey **5.** blood (fluid)
   10. protoplasm
plaster ... **4.** teer **5.** gesso, grout, salve
   6. gypsum, parget, stucco **8.** adhesive,
   poultice **9.** inebriate
plastered ... **5.** drunk **7.** crocked, smeared
   8. mortared
plasterer ... **5.** mason
plaster of Paris ... **5.** gesso **6.** gypsum
   15. calcium sulphate
plastic ... **3.** pug **5.** gesso, vinyl **6.** slurry
   7. ductile, fictile, pliable, viscose
   8. creative **9.** compliant, formative,
   teachable **14.** impressionable
plastic, commercial ... **6.** Lucite
   7. Formica **8.** Bakelite, Vinylite
   9. Plexiglas
plasty (pert to) ...
   comb form .. **7.** molding
   eyelid .. **14.** blepharoplasty
   face lift .. **13.** rhytidoplasty
   nose .. **11.** rhinoplasty
plat ... **3.** map **4.** flat, plan, plot
   5. braid, chart, field, level, plain, plait,
   pleat **6.** flatly, scheme **7.** outline,
   plateau **8.** absolute, directly, straight
   9. tableland **10.** interweave
   15. straightforward
platanist ... **4.** fish, susu
plate ... **3.** gib **4.** disc, dish, shoe (horse)
   5. paten **6.** lamina, patera **7.** coating,
   denture, overlay **9.** bookplate,
   engraving **10.** receptacle
plate (pert to) ...
   armor .. **6.** cuisse (cuish)
   battery .. **4.** grid
   bone (Anat) .. **7.** scapula
   cooking .. **4.** grid
   culture .. **8.** bacteria
   Eccl .. **5.** paten **6.** patina
   graduated .. **4.** dial
   holder .. **8.** cassette
   horny .. **5.** scute
   horse .. **6.** plater
   insect (bony) .. **6.** scutum
   mark .. **8.** hallmark **9.** engraving
   numbered .. **4.** disc
   of glass .. **5.** slide
   perforated metal .. **3.** dod
   ship-shaped .. **3.** nef
plateau ... **4.** dish, mesa, puna **5.** plain
   6. plaque, salver **9.** tableland
platform ... **3.** map **4.** dais, deck, k'ang,
   plan **5.** arena, chart, plank, stage
   6. lissom, lyceum, podium, policy,
   pulpit, scheme **7.** estrade, outline,
   rostrum, soapbox, tribune **8.** hustings
   9. bandstand **14.** public speaking
platform (pert to) ...
   fort .. **8.** barbette
   gun .. **11.** emplacement
   mining .. **6.** sollar (soller)

nautical .. **7.** foretop, maintop
   9. gangplank
scaffold (funeral) .. **10.** catafalque
wheeled .. **5.** float
platic (Astrol) ... **8.** not exact **9.** imperfect
plating ... **5.** armor **6.** lamina **7.** shoeing
platinum wire ... **4.** oese
platitude ... **6.** cliché, old hat, truism
   7. bromide **8.** banality **9.** staleness,
   triteness **11.** commonplace
   15. commonplaceness
Plato (pert to) ...
   famed for .. **9.** Dialogues **10.** philosophy
   founder of .. **7.** Academe, academy
   name, real .. **10.** Aristocles
   pupil of .. **8.** Socrates
platoid ... **4.** flat **5.** broad
Platonic (pert to) ...
   idea .. **5.** eidos
   love .. **4.** pure **5.** ideal **6.** chaste
   8. virtuous **10.** idealistic
   11. comradeship
   philosophy .. **8.** idealism **9.** Platonism
   11. theoretical
   solids .. **10.** hexahedron, octahedron
   11. icosahedron, tetrahedron
   12. dodecahedron
platoon ... **3.** set **4.** unit **5.** squad
   7. company, coterie **11.** subdivision
platoon school ... **4.** Gary (Ind)
platter ... **4.** dish, lanx **5.** grail, plate
   6. record **9.** scutellum
platter-shaped ... **10.** scutellate
platyfish ... **8.** moonfish
platypus ... **8.** duckbill
plaudit ... **5.** cheer, éclat **6.** encore
   8. applause, approval, clapping,
   encomium **10.** plaudation
   11. acclamation, approbation
plausible ... **8.** credible, probable,
   specious **10.** applausive, believable,
   ostensible, plauditory, reasonable
   11. conceivable
plausible excuse ... **5.** alibi
play ... **3.** act, fun, toy **4.** game, jest,
   romp **5.** dally, drama, enact, feign,
   sport, wager **6.** affect, frolic **7.** disport,
   operate, pretend **9.** amusement,
   diversion, melodrama, pantomime
   10. recreation **11.** impersonate
   13. entertainment
play (pert to) ...
   exhibit a .. **5.** stage
   for time .. **5.** stall
   house .. **5.** movie **6.** cinema **7.** theater
   9. dollhouse
   musical .. **5.** opera **8.** burletta, operetta
   outline .. **8.** scenario
   part .. **4.** role **7.** prelude **8.** epilogue,
   epitasis, prologue
   pranks .. **4.** haze
   silent .. **9.** pantomime
   story .. **8.** scenario
   stupid .. **5.** boner
   the bagpipe .. **5.** skirl **6.** doodle
   the buffoon .. **5.** droll
   the coquette .. **5.** flirt
   tricks .. **4.** hoax, shab
   truant .. **5.** miche
   unskillfully .. **5.** strum
   upon words .. **3.** pun **11.** paronomasia

playa . . . **5.** beach, shore **7.** salt pan
playboy . . . **4.** fool **5.** clown, cutup
  7. buffoon, reveler **8.** carouser
  10. merrymaker **12.** Jack of Trumps
  (Spoilfive)
player . . . **3.** dub **4.** star **5.** actor, idler,
  piper **7.** gambler, trifler **8.** gamester,
  musician, stroller, thespian **9.** frolicker,
  performer **11.** barnstormer
player on words . . . **7.** punster
playful . . . **3.** gay **6.** lusory **7.** jocular
  8. humorous, playsome, sportive
  9. facetious, kittenish **11.** mischievous
playing cards . . . **4.** deck, pack **6.** tarots
playlet . . . **4.** skit **9.** short play
plaything . . . **3.** die, toy **4.** dupe **6.** bauble
  7. cat's-paw
plea . . . **4.** suit **5.** claim **6.** abater, appeal,
  excuse, prayer **7.** apology, defense,
  pretext **8.** argument, entreaty, pretense
  10. advocation, allegation **13.** nolo
  contendre
plead . . . **3.** beg, sue **5.** argue **6.** adduce,
  allege **7.** entreat, implore
plead (for) . . . **7.** entreat, justify, solicit
  10. supplicate
pleader . . . **4.** suer **6.** lawyer **8.** advocate
  9. entreater, justifier **11.** intercessor
pleading . . . **4.** oyer **8.** advocacy,
  demurrer, entreaty **9.** imploring,
  objection **10.** litigation **12.** intercession,
  supplication
pleasant . . . **3.** fun, gay **4.** nice **5.** merry,
  sweet **6.** genial **7.** affable, amusing,
  leesome, winsome **8.** cheerful, friendly,
  humorous, pleasing, sportive
  9. agreeable, diverting, laughable,
  sprightly
pleasant (pert to) . . .
  manners . . **9.** amenities
  sound . . **6.** dulcet **8.** euphonic
  9. melodious **10.** harmonious
  to peruse . . **8.** readable
  weather . . **4.** fair, fine **6.** bright **8.** rainless
  9. cloudless
please . . . **4.** like, suit **5.** fancy **6.** arride
  7. appease, content, delight, gratify,
  indulge, placate, satisfy **9.** vouchsafe
pleased . . . **4.** fain, game, glad **5.** happy
  9. contented, gratified
pleasing . . . **4.** cool, lief, nice **5.** sooth
  6. comely, eesome, savory **7.** amiable,
  roseate, welcome **8.** pleasant
  9. agreeable, desirable **10.** delectable
  11. pleasureful
pleasurable . . . **7.** hedonic **8.** pleasant
  10. gratifying
pleasure . . . **3.** joy **4.** gree, will, wish
  5. mirth, sport **6.** choice, gaiety
  7. delight, purpose **8.** gladness,
  hedonism, hilarity **9.** amusement,
  diversion, enjoyment, happiness,
  merriment **11.** delectation
  12. satisfaction **13.** gratification
pleasure (pert to) . . .
  god . . **3.** Bes
  ground . . **4.** park **9.** pleasance
  pert to . . **7.** hedonic
  philosophy . . **8.** Hedonism
  seeker . . **5.** sport **7.** epicure, playboy
  8. hedonist

pleat . . . **4.** fold **5.** braid, plait
pleater . . . **8.** plicator
plebeian . . . **4.** pleb (Rom) **6.** common,
  vulgar **7.** ignoble, ill-bred, lowborn
  8. ordinary
plebiscite . . . **4.** vote **6.** decree
  10. referendum
pleck . . . **4.** plot (ground), spot **5.** speck,
  stain **9.** enclosure
plectrum . . . **4.** pick **5.** uvula **6.** tongue
  7. malleus **8.** plectron
pledge . . . **3.** bet, vas, vow **4.** bond,
  gage, gate, oath, pawn, seal, wage
  5. swear, toast, troth **6.** engage, parole,
  plight **7.** chattel, earnest, promise
  8. guaranty, mortgage, obligate,
  security **9.** assurance **10.** collateral
  11. impignorate
pledget . . . **4.** swab **8.** compress
Pleiad (pert to) . . .
  Alexandria . . **10.** Seven Poets
  French . . **10.** The Pléiade
  lost Pleiad . . **6.** Merope **7.** Electra
  philosophical (Gr) . . **12.** Seven Wise
  Men
Pleiades (pert to) . . .
  Seven Daughters of Atlas . . **10.** Atlantides
  star . . **4.** Maia **7.** Sterope **8.** Asterope
  star cluster . . **8.** in Taurus (Constellation)
plenary . . . **4.** full **5.** great **6.** entire
  7. perfect **8.** absolute, complete
  9. unlimited **11.** unqualified
plenipotentiary . . . **5.** envoy **8.** diplomat,
  minister **10.** ambassador
plenteous . . . **6.** plenty **7.** copious, fertile,
  liberal **8.** abundant, fruitful, generous
  9. bounteous, bountiful, plentiful
  10. productive
plentiful . . . **4.** full, rich, rife **5.** ample
  6. lavish **7.** copious, fertile, liberal,
  opulent, profuse **9.** abounding,
  bounteous, bountiful **13.** superabundant
plentifully . . . **6.** galore **9.** abounding,
  abundance
plenty . . . **4.** enow **6.** enough, galore,
  uberty **8.** fullness **9.** abundance,
  plenitude **10.** perfection **11.** copiousness
  12. completeness, considerable
  14. superabundance
plenum . . . **5.** space **8.** assembly, fullness
  (of space) (opp of vacuum)
pleon . . . **6.** telson **7.** abdomen
pleonasm . . . **8.** fullness **10.** redundancy
  11. diffuseness, reiteration
plethora . . . **4.** glut **6.** excess **9.** repletion
  14. superabundance
plethoric . . . **6.** turgid **8.** inflated, overfull
  9. bombastic **10.** overloaded
plexiform . . . **4.** rete **7.** network
  11. complicated
plexus . . . **4.** rete **5.** solar **7.** network
pliable . . . **4.** limp **6.** limber, pliant,
  supple **7.** plastic **8.** flexible, suitable
  9. compliant, teachable
pliant . . . **7.** bending, pliable, tensile,
  willowy **8.** flexible, workable, yielding
  9. adaptable, compliant
plicate . . . **4.** fold **5.** pleat **6.** folded
  7. plaited
plight . . . **4.** fold **5.** braid, plait **6.** status
  7. embrace, promise **8.** position

9. condition, situation (bad)
11. predicament
plinth . . . **4.** orlo **7.** subbase
Pliosaurus (extinct) . . . **7.** reptile
plod . . . **3.** dig, mog **4.** slog, toil, tore
6. drudge, trudge
plodder . . . **3.** fag **4.** grub, hack **5.** slave
6. drudge
plot . . . **3.** lot, map **4.** acre, area, brew,
burn, pack, plan, plat **5.** cabal, frame,
tract, trick **6.** design, scheme, scorch,
secret **7.** diagram, project **8.** conspire,
intrigue **10.** conspiracy, prearrange
11. machination
plot (of ground) . . . **3.** lot **4.** acre, area,
plat **5.** grave, tract **7.** terrain
Plotinus . . . **11.** philosopher (Alexandrian
School)
plotted . . . **7.** charted, hatched **8.** lineated
9. conspired **10.** delineated
11. prearranged
plotter . . . **5.** Haman **7.** Jacobin, planner,
schemer **8.** agitator **9.** contriver
11. conspirator
ploughshare (plowshare) **part** . . . **6.** colter
(coulter)
plover . . . **4.** dupe **5.** piper, sandy
7. lapwing **9.** courtesan, sandpiper,
shorebird
plover (pert to) . . .
crab . . **5.** drome
crested . . **7.** lapwing
egg . . **11.** darning ball
genus . . **12.** Charadriidae
Old World . . **8.** dotterel, killdeer
page . . **6.** dunlin **9.** sandpiper
quail . . **13.** plain wanderer
ring . . **5.** pandy
plow . . . **4.** rove, till **5.** break, miner,
scaut **6.** furrow, turn up **7.** break up
8. reinvest **9.** cultivate
plow (pert to) . . .
fish . . **3.** ray
gang . . **6.** oxgang **7.** measure
light . . **10.** Plow Monday **13.** hoggler's
light
man . . **6.** rustic **10.** countryman,
husbandman
part . . **4.** buck, chip, hale **5.** share, slade,
stilt **6.** clevis, colter
type . . **5.** sulky **8.** mole plow
plowed land . . . **5.** arada, arado
pluck . . . **3.** pug, rob, tug **4.** grab, jerk,
pick, pull **5.** nerve, spunk, steal, strip,
strum **6.** avulse, divest, fleece, gather,
twitch **7.** courage, harvest, pick off,
plunder, strip of, swindle **10.** resolution,
straighten (wool)
plucky . . . **4.** game **5.** brave, nervy
6. spunky, sticky **8.** adhesive, resolute,
spirited **10.** courageous
plug . . . **3.** peg, tap, top **4.** blow, bung
5. horse, knock, punch, shoot, spile,
wedge **7.** commend, hydrant, stopper,
stopple, tobacco **9.** persevere, publicity,
publicize **12.** commendation
plug (pert to) . . .
board . . **11.** switchboard
cannon muzzle . . **7.** tampion (tampeon,
tampoon)
dentistry . . **7.** filling

hat . . **4.** tile **5.** gibus **6.** topper
medical . . **4.** clot **6.** fibrin, tampon
7. embolus
slender . . **5.** spill
up . . **4.** calk (caulk)
plum . . . **5.** drupe, money, prune **6.** Prunus
8. dividend **9.** good thing, sugarplum
plum (pert to) . . .
beetle . . **8.** curculio
bitter . . **4.** sloe
California (wild) . . **5.** islay
coco . . **5.** icaco
England . . **6.** damson
Europe . . **7.** bullace
hybrid . . **7.** plumcot
India . . **7.** hog plum
Java . . **7.** jambool (jambul) **8.** jambolan
type . . **4.** gage **6.** damson **9.** greengage,
wild-goose **11.** Reine Claude
plumage . . . **4.** down **6.** hackle **7.** floccus
(first down) **8.** feathers, ornament
plumb . . . **4.** seal, true **5.** delve, gauge,
sound, utter **6.** adjust, fathom, sinker,
weight (lead) **7.** examine, measure,
plummet **8.** absolute, complete, vertical
9. downright **13.** perpendicular
plumbage . . . **8.** leadwork
plumbog . . . **9.** raspberry (dwarf)
plumcot . . . **6.** hybrid **11.** plum apricot
plume . . . **5.** crest, egret, preen, pride
6. plumet **7.** feather, panache
8. decorate, plumelet
plummet . . . **4.** dive, drop, fall, lead, plop,
test **5.** pitch, sound, swoop **6.** fathom,
plunge, weight **9.** criterion
plump . . . **3.** fat **4.** drop, dull, fall, plop,
rude, sink, tidy **5.** blunt, buxom, flock,
fubsy, obese **6.** chubby, dilate, fatten,
flatly **7.** distend **8.** blurt out, straight
9. corpulent, filled out **10.** vertically
11. well-rounded
plumpness of person . . . **9.** stoutness
10. embonpoint
plunder . . . **3.** rob **4.** boot, loot, pelf,
prey, raid, rape, sack **5.** booty, poach,
raven, reave, rifle, strip **6.** boodle,
fleece, maraud, profit, rapine, ravage,
spoils **7.** despoil, pillage **8.** spoliate
9. depredate
plundered . . . **4.** reft **6.** looted, robbed
plunderer . . . **5.** thief **6.** looter, pirate,
preyer, raider, robber **7.** spoiler, stealer
8. pillager **10.** freebooter
plunge . . . **3.** bet, dip **4.** dash, dive,
fall, pool, risk, sink **5.** douse, drive,
lunge, plumb, souse **6.** gamble,
thrust **7.** baptize, immerse **8.** flounder
9. gravitate, overwhelm, speculate
plunge (into) . . . **4.** clap, dive **5.** begin
7. immerge, immerse **9.** set to work,
undertake
plunger . . . **5.** diver **6.** risker **7.** gambler
10. speculator
plunk . . . **4.** blow, drop, pull, push, sink,
thud **5.** drive, plump, strum, throw
7. a dollar **10.** play truant
plurality . . . **8.** majority **9.** multitude
11. greater part, large number
plural marriage . . . **8.** polygamy
Plutarch (Gr) . . . **10.** biographer
Pluto (pert to) . . .

Astron.. **6.** planet (most remote)
god of.. **10.** lower world
Greek name.. **5.** Hades
kingdom.. **5.** Hades
Roman name.. **3.** Dis **5.** Orcus
wife.. **10.** Proserpina
plutocracy ... **13.** rule by wealthy
  17. dominion of the rich
Plutus (pert to) ...
  god of.. **6.** wealth
  son of.. **6.** lasion **7.** Demeter
pluvia ... **4.** rain **9.** pluviosus
pluviometer, pluvioscope ... **9.** rain
  gauge
pluvious ... **5.** rainy **7.** pluvial
ply ... **4.** bend, fold, mold, sail, urge
  5. exert, plait, wield **6.** employ, handle,
  lamina **8.** navigate **9.** importune,
  thickness
pneuma ... **4.** soul **5.** neume **6.** breath,
  spirit **9.** breathing, life force, vital soul
pneumology (science of) ... **5.** lungs
  17. respiratory organs
poach ... **3.** mix, ram **4.** poke, push,
  sock, stir **5.** drive, force, shirr (egg),
  steal **6.** thrust **7.** trample **8.** encroach,
  trespass
poacher ... **7.** lurcher, stalker, widgeon
Poblacht ... **8.** Republic
Pocahontas (pert to) ...
  father.. **8.** Powhatan (Chief)
  husband.. **9.** John Rolfe
  Indian title.. **8.** Princess
  name.. **12.** Rebecca Rolfe
  rescuer of.. **9.** John Smith (Capt)
pocket ... **3.** bag, bin, cly, fob, sac
  4. poke, sack, take **5.** money, pouch,
  purse **6.** cavity, hollow **7.** conceal,
  confine, enclose **8.** envelope
pocketbook ... **3.** bag, lil **5.** pouch,
  purse **6.** income, wallet **8.** notebook
  9. resources
pod ... **3.** bag, kid, sac **4.** aril, boll **5.** belly,
  carob, chili, pouch, shuck **6.** legume
poem ... **3.** dit, lay, ode **4.** Edda, epic,
  epos, hymn, rune, saga **5.** elegy,
  epode, idyll, psalm, verse **6.** ballad
  (ballade), jingle, rondel (roundelle),
  sonnet **7.** eclogue, erotics, rondeau
  8. limerick, rondelet **9.** dithyramb
  10. villanelle **11.** acatalectic
poem (pert to) ...
  bad ... **8.** doggerel
  division.. **5.** canto, epode, verse
  6. stanza **7.** refrain
  eight lines.. **7.** triolet
  foot.. **6.** iambic **7.** anapest, pyrrhic
  imitation.. **6.** parody
  Japanese.. **5.** haiku
  line.. **5.** stich **6.** octave, septet, sestet
  tercet **7.** couplet, triplet **8.** cinquain,
  quatrain **11.** alexandrine
  meter.. **6.** iambic **8.** spondaic, trochaic
  9. dactyllic, hexameter **10.** anaepestic
  (anapestic), pentameter
  ref to.. **5.** meter, rhyme, verse
  7. cadence, helicon **8.** feminine,
  scansion **9.** masculine
  religious.. **4.** hymn **5.** psalm
  rhythmic break.. **7.** caesura
  satirical.. **3.** dit **6.** parody

poem, famed ...
  Homer.. **5.** Iliad **7.** Odyssey
  Khayyám.. **8.** Rubáiyát
  Milton.. **12.** Paradise Lost
  Ovid.. **13.** Metamorphoses
  Poe.. **8.** The Raven
  Poem in Marble.. **8.** Taj Mahal
  poem of declaration.. **8.** Invictus
  Shakespeare.. **7.** Macbeth
  Spenser.. **12.** Faerie Queene
poems ... **5.** poesy, sylva **6.** poetry
poet ... **4.** bard **5.** odist, rimer **6.** lyrist
  7. dreamer **8.** laureate **9.** poetaster,
  rhymester, versifier
poetic word ... **3.** ere, 'tis **4.** ne'er, 'twas
  5. 'twere, 'twixt
Poet Laureate (a few) ... **6.** Dryden
  7. Spenser **8.** Tennyson **9.** Ben Jonson,
  Masefield **10.** Wordsworth
poetry (pert to) ...
  Muse of.. **5.** Erato **6.** Thalia **8.** Calliope
  Norse god of.. **5.** Bragi
  School of (anc).. **9.** Parnassus
  type.. **4.** epic **5.** lyric **6.** ballad **8.** didactic
  9. free verse, narrative **10.** blank verse
pogoniate ... **7.** bearded
pogonip ... **3.** fog (Sierras)
pogonology (study of) ... **6.** beards
pogrom ... **8.** massacre
poi ... **4.** food, taro, then (Mus)
poignant ... **4.** keen **5.** acute **6.** biting,
  bitter **7.** cutting, pungent
point ... **3.** aim, dot, jab, jot, neb, nib, pin
  4. apex, barb, cape, gaff, gist, node,
  peak, stop, tack **5.** focus, prong, quill,
  spike **6.** bodkin, direct, needle, period,
  summit, tenet **7.** apicula, punctum
  10. breakwater, promontory
point (pert to) ...
  antler, branch.. **4.** snag
  astronomy.. **5.** apsis **6.** syzygy
  central, pivotal.. **4.** crux
  farthest from earth.. **6.** apogee
  focal.. **9.** epicenter
  geometry.. **6.** acnode **7.** crunode
  highest.. **4.** acme, apex, peak **6.** summit,
  zenith **8.** meridian, pinnacle
  lace.. **10.** petit point **11.** needlepoint
  law.. **3.** res **5.** locus
  lowest.. **5.** nadir **6.** bottom
  mathematics.. **5.** unode
  nearest earth.. **7.** perigee
  of contact.. **5.** focus
  of debate.. **5.** issue, topic
  of honor.. **7.** scruple
  of view.. **5.** angle, slant **8.** attitude
  opposite zenith.. **5.** nadir
  reference to.. **6.** apical
  salient.. **7.** feature
  starting, golf.. **3.** tee
  strong.. **5.** forte
  utmost.. **7.** extreme
  weak.. **4.** flaw **5.** fault **6.** foible
pointed ... **5.** aimed, noded, piked,
  sharp, terse **6.** acuate, marked, peaked
  7. angular, concise, conical **8.** aculeate,
  piercing, poignant, spicated, stinging
  9. acuminate, pertinate, spiculate
  10. emphasized **11.** conspicuous,
  significant **12.** epigrammatic
pointed (pert to) ...

architecture.. **5.** ogive **6.** Gothic
end.. **4.** cusp
fox.. **3.** red
instrument.. **3.** awl, gad **4.** prod
  6. gimlet, stylet
rod.. **4.** goad
pointer ... **3.** arm, dog, tip **4.** sign **5.** index
  6. fescue, gnomon
pointless ... **4.** dull **5.** blunt, inane, silly,
  vapid **6.** stupid **7.** insipid, witless
poise ... **6.** aplomb **7.** balance, ballast
  8. carriage **9.** composure, equipoise,
  stability
poison (pert to) ...
  arrow.. **4.** inee, upas **5.** urari **6.** curare
    (curari)
  deadly.. **4.** bane, upas **5.** arrow
    7. arsenic, cyanide, hemlock
    10. strychnine
  study of.. **10.** toxicology
poissarde ... **8.** fishwife, low woman
poisson ... **4.** fish
poisson bleu ... **7.** catfish **8.** bluefish,
  grayling
poitrel ... **5.** armor, plate **9.** stomacher
  11. breastplate
poke ... **3.** bag, jab, jog, pry **4.** bore,
  goad, prod, root, sack **5.** grope, nudge,
  probe, purse **6.** dawdle, potter, search,
  thrust, wallet **7.** project, tobacco
poker ... **3.** rod **6.** beadle **7.** bugbear,
  pochard **9.** hobgoblin
poker (pert to) ...
  face.. **8.** immobile
  form of.. **4.** draw, stud
  painting.. **10.** pyrography
  picture.. **11.** pyrogravure
  stake.. **3.** pot **4.** ante **6.** roodle
poky, pokey ... **4.** dull, mean, slow
  5. dowdy, small **6.** bonnet, narrow,
  shabby **7.** cramped, tedious
Poland ... see also *Polish*
  ancestors.. **5.** Lakha, Slavs
  ancient name.. **7.** Polonia
  capital.. **6.** Warsaw
  city.. **4.** Lodz **6.** Gdynia, Krakow, Lublin
  river.. **7.** Dnieper, Vistula
Poland China ... **5.** swine
polar ... **5.** curve **6.** Arctic **7.** guiding
  8. opposite **9.** Antarctic, magnetism
Polar base (exploration) ... **4.** Etah
Polaris ... **5.** Alpha **9.** North Star
  11. guiding star
Polaroid inventor ... **4.** Land
pole ... **3.** bar, oar, pew, poy, rod, xat
  4. axle, beam, mast, prop, spar **5.** shaft,
  sprit, staff, stool, totem
pole (pert to) ...
  bad end.. **7.** raw deal
  burn.. **7.** disease (tobacco)
  cat.. **5.** skunk, zoril **6.** ferret, musang
    7. fitchew **8.** Putorius **9.** scoundrel
  cat weed.. **12.** skunk cabbage
  electric.. **5.** anode, pitch **7.** cathode
    8. magnetic **9.** electrode
  Gaelic.. **5.** caber
  head.. **7.** tadpole
  Spanish.. **4.** pale, palo
  star.. **5.** guide **7.** polaris **8.** lodestar
    9. North Star **13.** l'Etoile du Nord
  vehicle.. **4.** cope, crab **5.** thill

well.. **5.** sweep
polemic ... **9.** disputant **11.** contentious
  13. argumentative, controversial
polenta ... **8.** porridge
poles of cold ... **7.** Siberia (Verkhoyansk)
  12. Grinnell Land (Fort Conger)
police (pert to) ...
  badge.. **6.** buzzer, shield
  club.. **8.** spontoon
  man.. **3.** cop **5.** guard **6.** bobbie, copper,
    peeler, Ranger **7.** officer, sheriff, trooper
    9. constable, detective, N W Mounted
    11. carabinière (carabineer)
  station.. **5.** thana **6.** lockup **8.** bargello
policy ... **3.** wit **4.** plan **6.** wisdom
  8. regulate, sagacity **9.** insurance
  10. government, management,
  shrewdness **11.** contrivance
  13. judiciousness **14.** administration
policy of segregation ... **9.** apartheid
polish ... **3.** rub **4.** buff **5.** glaze, gloss,
  rabat, scour, shine **6.** finish, luster,
  smooth **7.** burnish, culture, furbish
  8. brighten, civilize, elegance, lapidate,
  levigate, urbanity **10.** refinement
Polish (pert to) ...
  Bull.. **13.** Constellation
  cake.. **4.** baba
  carriage.. **7.** britska
  composer, pianist.. **6.** Chopin
    10. Paderewski
  dance.. **7.** mazurka **9.** polonaise
    11. cracovienne (krakowiak)
  nobleman.. **7.** starost
  premier.. **10.** Paderewski (pianist)
  president (1st).. **10.** Philsudski
  scientist.. **5.** Curie (Madame)
polishing material ... **5.** emery, rabat,
  rouge **6.** pumice **11.** rottenstone
polite ... **4.** neat, tidy **5.** civil, suave,
  urban **6.** gentle, smooth, urbane
  7. gallant, genteel, refined **8.** polished
  9. courteous, debonaire (debonair,
  debonnaire) **10.** cultivated
  11. complaisant
politesse ... **10.** politeness (formal)
  11. cleanliness, courtliness
  12. decorousness
politic ... **4.** wary **7.** cunning, tactful
  8. cautious, discreet **9.** judicious,
  political, politique, provident
  10. diplomatic
political (pert to) ...
  boss.. **7.** cacique
  district.. **4.** city, ward **5.** State **6.** canton,
    county, parish **7.** borough **10.** palatinate
  economy.. **9.** economics
  faction.. **4.** bloc, ring **5.** junta, party
    7. machine
  hanger-on.. **6.** heeler **10.** ward heeler
  influence.. **5.** lobby, rally **6.** caucus
  party (old).. **4.** Tory, Whig **9.** Politique
politician ... **7.** schemer **9.** intriguer,
  statesman **11.** gerrymander
  12. politicaster
politics ... **7.** cunning **8.** scheming
  10. government, profession **15.** partisan
  rivalry **16.** political affairs
Polizei ... **9.** the police
poll ... **3.** cut, tax **4.** clip, head, roll,
  vote **5.** shear, skull **6.** fleece, survey

7. despoil **8.** election, schedule
pollan ... **9.** whitefish
polled ... **5.** shorn **6.** shaved **8.** hornless
pollen ... **4.** seed **6.** anther **8.** fine dust
  11. microspores **13.** fertilization
pollen brush (bee's) ... **5.** scopa
pollenization ... **5.** xenia **13.** fertilization
pollent ... **6.** strong **8.** powerful
poller ... **5.** voter **6.** barber **9.** plunderer
  11. extortioner, taxgatherer
pollex ... **5.** thumb **11.** bastard wing
  (bird) **13.** dactylopodite
pollex impression ... **10.** thumbprint
polliwog ... **7.** tadpole
pollute ... **4.** soil **5.** taint **6.** befoul, defile,
  ravish **7.** corrupt, debauch, profane
  9. desecrate, inebriate **11.** contaminate
pollution ... **8.** impurity **9.** infection
  10. corruption, defilement
  13. contamination
Pollux (pert to) ...
  brother (twin) .. **6.** Castor
  father .. **4.** Zeus
  mother .. **4.** Leda
  protector of .. **7.** sailors
  star .. **13.** Beta Geminorum
Polly's request ... **7.** cracker
Polonius ... **8.** courtier (Shaksp)
polony ... **7.** sausage
poltergeist (folklore) ... **5.** ghost **6.** spirit
poltfoot ... **8.** clubfoot
poltroon ... **4.** idle, lazy **6.** coward,
  craven, wretch **7.** buffoon, dastard
  8. cowardly **9.** dastardly **10.** ne'er-do-
  well, scaramouch
polverine ... **6.** potash (of Levant)
  8. pearlash
polyandrium (Gr) ... **8.** cemetery
polyandry ... **8.** polygamy **14.** plural
  husbands (Tibet)
polychromatic ... **10.** variegated
polyglot ... **6.** jargon **9.** languages
  (confusion of) **10.** dictionary
  11. philologist **21.** Complutensian
  Polyglot (Bib)
polygon ... **6.** isagon **7.** decagon,
  hexagon, nonagon, octagon
  8. heptagon **9.** dodecagon
polygyny ... **8.** polygamy **11.** plural wives
polyhedron ... **5.** solid **6.** figure
  14. trisoctahedron **17.** triakisoctahedron
polymny ... **10.** sacred song
Polynesia ...
  native .. **5.** Maori **6.** Kanaka **8.** Hawaiian
  10. Melanesian
  ocean .. **7.** Pacific
  origin (probable) .. **7.** Savaiki (Isl)
  South Sea Island group .. **5.** Samoa
  6. Hawaii, Tahiti **7.** Savaiki **10.** New
  Zealand
Polynesian (pert to) ...
  butterfly .. **2.** io
  chestnut .. **4.** rata
  cloth .. **4.** tapa
  demon .. **4.** atua
  dragon .. **3.** ati
  goddess of volcanoes .. **4.** Pele
  god of forests .. **4.** Tane
  hero .. **4.** Maui
  homeland (fabled) .. **7.** Havaiki
  loincloth .. **5.** pareu

memorial .. **3.** ahu
oven .. **3.** umu
people .. **3.** Ati
social tradition .. **6.** tattoo
wages, reward .. **3.** utu
polyp ... **5.** coral, Hydra, tumor **10.** sea
  anemone **12.** invertebrate
polyphone ... **4.** lute
polytropic ... **9.** versatile
pomade ... **6.** anoint **7.** pomatum,
  unguent **8.** ointment
pome ... **4.** pear **5.** apple, fruit **6.** quince
  11. pomegranate
pomelo ... **8.** shaddock **10.** grapefruit
Pomerania (pert to) ...
  animal .. **3.** dog
  capital .. **7.** Stettin
  formerly .. **5.** duchy (Prussia)
  river .. **4.** Oder
pomme de terre ... **6.** potato
Pomona ... **4.** city (Calif) **7.** college,
  goddess (of fruit)
pomp ... **5.** pride, state **6.** parade
  7. cortege, display, pageant **8.** grandeur
  9. pageantry, spectacle **10.** ceremonial
  11. ostentation **12.** magnificence
pompano ... **7.** alewife
Pompeii, Italy (pert to) ... **10.** earthquake,
  excavation, Mt Vesuvius (site)
pompous ... **5.** budge **6.** august,
  stilty **7.** Podsnap (Dickens), stilted
  9. bombastic, grandiose
  11. ceremonious **12.** high-sounding,
  ostentatious, stuffed shirt
Ponce de Leon (pert to) ...
  discoverer of .. **7.** Florida **15.** Fountain
  of Youth
  famed as .. **8.** explorer
  landing site, America .. **11.** St Augustine
pond ... **4.** pool **5.** ocean (humorous)
  6. lagoon **7.** lakelet
pond (pert to) ...
  apple .. **9.** evergreen
  crow, hen .. **4.** coot
  dogwood .. **10.** buttonbush
  duck .. **7.** mallard
  fish .. **7.** sunfish
  frog .. **8.** ranarium
  glass .. **8.** aquarium
ponder ... **4.** mull, muse, pore **5.** brood,
  opine, weigh **7.** perpend, reflect
  8. appraise, cogitate, consider, evaluate,
  meditate, ruminate
ponderous ... **4.** dull, huge **5.** bulky,
  heavy **7.** weighty **8.** ungainly
  9. important, momentous
  11. elephantine
pongee ... **4.** silk **6.** tussah **8.** shantung
poniard ... **4.** dirk, kill **5.** sword **6.** dagger,
  pierce
ponica ... **8.** gardener
pont ... **5.** ferry, float **6.** bridge **7.** caisson,
  pontoon **9.** ferryboat
Pontiac ... **4.** city (Mich) **5.** Chief (Ottawa
  Indian) **6.** Indian
pontiff ... **4.** pope **6.** bishop **8.** pontifex
pony ... **3.** cab, nag **4.** crib **5.** glass, horse,
  pinto **6.** bronco **7.** Express (mail, 1860),
  piebald **8.** Shetland **11.** translation
pooch ... **3.** dog **5.** pouch
pooka ... **6.** goblin **7.** specter

pool . . . **3.** lin, pot **4.** carr, fund, game, linn, mere, pond, tank, tarn **5.** kitty, stake **6.** cartel, lagoon, league, puddle **7.** alberca, plashet **9.** billiards, reservoir, resources **10.** natatorium **11.** aggregation

pool ball . . . **3.** cue **4.** spot **6.** ringer

poon tree . . . **5.** domba, keena

poor . . . **3.** bad **4.** mean, thin **5.** needy **6.** feeble, humble, meager, paltry, shabby, sickly **7.** hapless, unlucky **8.** indigent, inferior **9.** destitute, illogical, imperfect, infertile **10.** unskillful (unskilful) **11.** impecunious, unfavorable, unfortunate **12.** impoverished, inauspicious, insufficient **14.** unsatisfactory

poor (pert to) . . .
creature . . **9.** pilgarlic
joe . . **5.** heron
John . . **3.** cod **4.** hake **8.** mean fare
man's remedy . . **8.** valerian
Richard . . **8.** Saunders (Richard)
section of city . . **4.** slum **6.** ghetto **7.** skid row **10.** shantytown
soldier . . **9.** friarbird

poorly . . . **3.** ill **5.** badly **8.** abjectly, meagerly, shabbily **10.** indisposed **11.** defectively **13.** disparagingly

pop . . . **4.** bang, snap, soda **5.** bulge, burst, crack **6.** bubble **7.** concert **8.** beverage

popadam . . . **5.** water (fried) **10.** popper cake

popdock . . . **8.** foxglove

pope . . . **3.** fin **4.** ruff **6.** bishop, puffin, shrike, weevil **8.** beverage **9.** bullfinch **14.** painted bunting

Pope (pert to) . . .
cathedral . . **7.** Lateran
collar . . **5.** orale
court officer . . **6.** datary
crown . . **5.** tiara **6.** triple
first . . **5.** Peter
headdress . . **5.** miter (mitre)
name . . **4.** Pius **5.** Ratti **7.** Gregory
palace . . **7.** Vatican
scarf . . **5.** fanon

Pope, Alexander (pert to) . . .
essay . . **10.** Essay on Man
poem . . **13.** Rape of the Lock
satire . . **7.** Dunciad
translation . . **5.** Iliad **7.** Odyssey

popeler . . . **7.** sea gull **9.** spoonbill

popinac . . . **8.** huisache

popinjay . . . **6.** parrot

poplar . . . **5.** abele, alamo, aspen, bahan, white **10.** cottonwood **12.** balm of Gilead

poplar (pert to) . . .
Arabic . . **5.** bahan, garab
balsam . . **9.** tacamahac
Fr black . . **4.** liar **10.** cottonwood
N. American . . **7.** Populus **8.** Lombardy
white . . **5.** abele, bolle

poppy . . . **3.** maw **7.** Papaver (opium), ponceau **8.** foxglove

poppycock . . . **3.** rot **4.** bosh **8.** nonsense

populace . . . **3.** mob **4.** mass **5.** demos, plebs **6.** people **11.** inhabitants **12.** common people

popular . . . **3.** lay, pop **5.** cheap, liked, usual **6.** famous, simple, vulgar **7.** crowded, demotic, secular **8.** accepted, epidemic, favorite, populous **9.** prevalent, well-known, well-liked **11.** fashionable, proletarian **12.** nontechnical

popular belief . . . **4.** lore **7.** opinion **9.** tradition **12.** old wives' tale, superstition

popularity . . . **4.** fame **5.** vogue **10.** reputation **15.** fashionableness

popular success . . . **3.** hit

population study . . . **10.** larithmics

porcelain . . . **4.** frit **5.** china **6.** kaolin **7.** ramekin (mold)

porcelain (kind) . . . **5.** Spode **6.** Sèvres **7.** celadon, Dresden, Limoges **8.** Haviland

porch . . . **4.** door, stoa **5.** stoop **6.** harbor, loggia **7.** galilee, gallery, portico, veranda **8.** entrance **9.** colonnade

porcine animal . . . **3.** hog, pig, sow **5.** shoat, swine **6.** porker **7.** peccary **8.** babirusa (babiroussa) **9.** razorback

porcupine (pert to) . . .
anteater . . **7.** echidna
Canada . . **5.** urson **7.** cawquaw
disease . . **10.** ichthyosis
grass . . **5.** stipa
species . . **6.** rodent, tenrec (tendrac) **8.** hedgehog, quill pig

pore . . . **3.** con **4.** duct, gaze, vent **5.** stare, stoma, study **6.** ponder **7.** eporose (without), opening, orifice, ostiole **8.** lenticel

porgy . . . **4.** fish, scup **5.** bream, pargo **6.** pagrus, red tai

pork (pert to) . . .
barrel . . **4.** fund (Polit) **6.** boodle
chop . . **7.** griskin
fish . . **4.** sisi

porker . . . **3.** hog, pig **5.** swine, sword (obs)

porpoise . . . **4.** Inia **6.** seahog **7.** dolphin, pellock **8.** cetacean, Phocaena

porr . . . **4.** cram, kick, poke, push, stir **5.** poker **6.** thrust

porrect . . . **6.** tender **7.** present

porridge . . . **3.** pob **4.** pobs, samp **5.** atole, brose, grout, gruel **6.** cereal **7.** oatmeal, polenta, pottage **9.** stirabout

port . . . **4.** gate, left, mien, wine **5.** armor, haven **6.** harbor, portal **7.** airport, bearing, opening, posture **8.** carriage, demeanor, larboard, porthole, portside **10.** deportment **11.** destruction

portable . . . **6.** mobile **7.** movable

portable altar . . . **10.** altar stone, superaltar (Hist)

portal . . . **4.** door, gate **5.** porch **7.** gateway **8.** entrance **9.** vestibule **12.** porte-cochere

portcullis . . . **3.** bar **4.** shut **5.** herse **7.** barrier, grating, lattice (Her) **13.** fortification

Porte . . . **12.** Ottoman court (anc), Sublime Porte

porte-bonheur . . . **5.** charm **6.** amulet

porte-cochere . . . **5.** porch (carriage) **7.** gateway

portefeuille . . . **9.** portfolio

portend ... **4.** bode **5.** augur **7.** betoken, predict, presage **8.** forebode, foreshow, foretell, prophecy **9.** foretoken
portent ... **4.** omen, sign **6.** marvel, ostent **7.** prodigy **11.** forewarning
portentous ... **4.** dire **5.** fatal, grave **6.** solemn **7.** fateful, ominous **8.** sinister **9.** monstrous, wonderful **10.** impressive **13.** extraordinary
porter ... **3.** ale **4.** beer **5.** hamal (hammal), stout (drink) **6.** bearer **7.** carrier, janitor **9.** attendant **10.** doorkeeper
Porter's pseudonym ... **6.** O Henry
Portia (pert to) ...
  character (Merchant of Venice) .. **7.** heiress
  husband .. **8.** Bassanio
  husband's friend .. **7.** Antonio
  maid .. **7.** Nerissa
portico ... **4.** stoa **6.** atrium, xystus (xyst) **7.** pteroma, veranda **9.** colonnade, peristyle, vestibule
portion ... **3.** bit, cut, dab, lot **4.** dole, dose, dunt, fate, half, mete, part, some **5.** piece, share, whack **6.** moiety, parcel **7.** section, segment **8.** quantity **9.** allotment, apportion, partition
portion (pert to) ...
  curve .. **3.** arc **7.** segment
  detached .. **6.** coupon
  inheritance .. **7.** legitim **9.** dead's part
  marriage .. **5.** dowry
  sectional .. **5.** curve
  widow's .. **5.** dower
Portland (pert to) ...
  arrowroot, sago .. **4.** arum
  beds (Eng) .. **11.** Upper Oolite **13.** Upper Jurassic
  city of .. **5.** Maine **6.** Oregon
  stone .. **6.** cement **8.** concrete
  vase .. **9.** Barberini (Rom palace) **10.** cameo glass
portmanteau ... **3.** bag **4.** word (blended) **5.** cloak **6.** mantle, valise
portoise ... **7.** gunwale **8.** portlast
Porto Rico ... see *Puerto Rico*
portrait ... **4.** copy **5.** image **7.** picture **8.** likeness, painting **10.** similitude **11.** description, portraiture **12.** lifelikeness **14.** representation
portrait on dollars ...
  fifty .. **5.** Grant
  five .. **7.** Lincoln
  five hundred .. **8.** McKinley
  five thousand .. **7.** Madison
  one .. **10.** Washington
  one hundred .. **8.** Franklin
  one hundred thousand .. **6.** Wilson
  one thousand .. **9.** Cleveland
  ten .. **8.** Hamilton
  ten thousand .. **5.** Chase
  twenty .. **7.** Jackson
  two .. **9.** Jefferson
portray ... **3.** act **4.** draw, form, limn **5.** enact, frame, image, paint **6.** depict, fashion, picture **8.** describe **9.** delineate, represent
portrayal ... **3.** act **5.** drama **7.** process **8.** portrait **9.** depiction **11.** delineation, description

portreeve ... **5.** mayor **7.** bailiff
Port Royal ... **15.** Cistercian abbey (Versailles)
Portugal ... see also *Portuguese*
  bridge .. **7.** Salazar
  capital .. **6.** Lisbon
  city .. **5.** Braga **6.** Aveiro, Guarda, Oporto **7.** Granada
  island .. **6.** Azores **7.** Madeira **8.** Principe
  mountain .. **15.** Serra da Estrella
  peninsula .. **7.** Iberian
  port .. **6.** Aveiro
  province .. **3.** Goa **5.** Macao, Timor **9.** Cape Verde **10.** Mozambique
  resort .. **7.** Estoril
  river .. **5.** Tagus (Tajo)
Portuguese (pert to) ...
  author .. **9.** de Lobeira
  bird, fish .. **8.** man-of-war
  ceremonial (Inquisition) .. **8.** auto de fe
  coin (gold) .. **6.** escudo **7.** milreis (old)
  lady .. **4.** dona
  legislature .. **6.** Cortes **12.** Cortes Geraes
  money of account .. **4.** reis
  navigator .. **6.** da Gama **8.** Magellan
  wine .. **5.** porto
Portunus (Rom Relig) ... **10.** god of gates
posada ... **3.** inn **5.** hotel
Posaune ... **8.** trombone **9.** organ stop
posca ... **5.** drink (Hist)
pose ... **3.** put, sit **5.** model **6.** baffle, puzzle, stance **7.** nonplus, posture, pretend, propose **8.** attitude, position, pretense, propound **9.** postulate **11.** affectation, impersonate
Poseidon (pert to) ...
  attributes .. **5.** horse **7.** dolphin, trident
  cult site .. **7.** Corinth
  father .. **6.** Cronus
  god of .. **3.** sea **6.** waters
  mother .. **4.** Rhea
  Roman name .. **7.** Neptune
  wife .. **10.** Amphitrite
poser ... **5.** facer **6.** puzzle **7.** problem, sticker **14.** attitudinarian
posh ... **5.** smart **6.** spruce **7.** elegant **9.** luxurious
position ... **3.** job, lie **4.** pose, rank, seat, site **5.** coign (coigne), place, situs, stand, state **6.** manner, stance, ubiety **7.** opinion, posture, premise **8.** attitude, location, prestige, proposal **9.** viewpoint **11.** affirmation, supposition
position (pert to) ...
  anchorlike .. **5.** apeak
  fencing .. **7.** septime
  finder (gun) .. **13.** triangulation
  golf .. **6.** stance
  inescapable .. **7.** impasse
  of affairs .. **6.** status
  relative .. **8.** standing
  secure .. **7.** footing
  with no responsibility .. **8.** sinecure
positive ... **4.** plus, sure **5.** exact **6.** actual, thetic **7.** certain **8.** dogmatic, emphatic **9.** assertive, convinced, downright **11.** dictatorial
positive (pert to) ...
  charge (Elec) .. **8.** positron
  evidence .. **7.** constat

pole .. **5.** anode
saying .. **6.** dictum
school, criminology .. **10.** Lombrosian (by Lombroso)
positivism ... **7.** Comtism **9.** certainty, dogmatism **10.** confidence **11.** materialism
positure ... **7.** posture **11.** arrangement, disposition **13.** configuration
posnet ... **3.** pot (3-footed) **8.** saucepan
poss ... **4.** beat, dash, push **5.** drive, knock, pound, stamp **6.** thrust
posse ... **5.** crowd **6.** throng **7.** company **9.** armed band **10.** detachment (police)
possess ... **3.** own **4.** have, know, take **5.** haunt **6.** inform, occupy **7.** bewitch, inhabit **8.** convince, demonize, persuade
possessed ... **5.** hadst, owned **6.** insane **7.** haunted **8.** demoniac, obsessed **9.** bewitched
possessing (pert to) ...
feeling .. **6.** souled
flavor .. **5.** sapid, tasty
land .. **5.** acred
pincer claws .. **8.** chelated
power .. **11.** plenipotent
sensation .. **8.** sentient
special ability .. **6.** gifted **8.** talented
possession ... **4.** hold **5.** asset **6.** taking, wealth **7.** control, country, mastery **8.** dominion, property **9.** obsession, ownership **10.** equanimity **11.** bewitchment
possession (pert to) ...
again .. **6.** revest
law .. **6.** seizin (seisin)
not in (possession) .. **6.** devoid
suffix .. **3.** ose
possessions ... **6.** assets, estate, wealth **7.** effects **8.** property
posset ... **4.** turn **6.** curdle, pamper **8.** beverage, infusion **9.** coagulate
possibility ... **4.** bare **7.** latency **9.** liability, potential **10.** good chance, likelihood **11.** contingency **13.** improbability **16.** prospective value
possible ... **6.** latent, liable, likely **8.** feasible **9.** plausible, potential **11.** practicable
possibly ... **5.** maybe **7.** perhaps **9.** perchance **11.** conceivably
post ... **3.** bet, dak (dawk), xat **4.** bitt, fort, list, mail, trot **5.** enter, newel, opium, place, stake, totem **6.** alette, assign, hasten, inform, marker, office, pillar, pledge **7.** bollard, placard, station, upright **8.** dispatch, position **9.** messenger, sternpost **12.** enter account
post (pert to) ...
adverb .. **5.** after, later **9.** afterward
boat .. **4.** mail **5.** stage **6.** packet
boy .. **7.** courier **9.** postilion (postillion)
dance (army sl) .. **8.** struggle
goal (anc) .. **4.** meta
Indian memorial .. **3.** xat **5.** totem
meridian .. **8.** afternoon
mortem .. **7.** autopsy **8.** necropsy **10.** after death
office .. **6.** correo
prefix .. **5.** after **6.** behind **10.** subsequent

stair .. **5.** newel
postage stamp paper (pert to) ...
design .. **8.** spandrel
paper .. **6.** pelure
pattern .. **6.** burele **8.** burelage
poster ... **4.** bill, card **7.** placard, sticker **8.** bulletin **9.** messenger **10.** billposter
posthumous ... **5.** after **10.** after death, post-mortem
postiche ... **9.** false hair **10.** artificial **11.** counterfeit
postilion ... **5.** guide **7.** postboy **9.** postrider
postimpressionist ... **6.** cubist, Derain **7.** Cezanne, Matisse
postpone ... **4.** wait **5.** defer, delay, remit, table **6.** put off, shelve **7.** adjourn, reserve, suspend **8.** hold over, prorogue **10.** pigeonhole **11.** subordinate **13.** procrastinate
postponement ... **7.** remanet, respite **8.** deferral, reprieve **9.** deferment **11.** prorogation
postprandial ... **11.** after dinner
postulate ... **6.** assume **7.** prelude, premise **9.** condition, predicate, stipulate **10.** hypothesis **11.** stipulation, supposition
posture ... **4.** pose **6.** stance **8.** attitude, position, pretense **9.** viewpoint **11.** frame of mind
pot ... **3.** jug, pan **4.** olla **5.** belly, crock, cruse **6.** aludel, kettle, liquor, teapot **7.** amphora (anc), caldron **9.** flowerpot **10.** jardiniere
potash ... **6.** potass, saline **7.** potassa **8.** pearlash **18.** potassium carbonate
potassium (pert to) ...
bitartrate .. **13.** cream of tartar
bromide .. **8.** sedative
carbonate .. **6.** potash
compound .. **4.** alum
dichromatic .. **6.** chrome
iodide .. **8.** medicine
nitrate .. **5.** niter **9.** saltpeter
permanganate .. **8.** oxidizer **12.** disinfectant
sulphate .. **4.** alum
potate ... **9.** liquefied
potation ... **5.** draft, drink **6.** liquor **8.** beverage, tippling **12.** drinking bout
potato ... **3.** oca, yam **4.** papa, spud **5.** tuber
potato (pert to) ...
beetle .. **8.** hardback
bogle .. **9.** scarecrow
French .. **12.** pomme de terre
French style .. **9.** lyonnaise
genus .. **10.** Solanaceae
Indian .. **4.** yamp
moss .. **9.** pondgrass
So Am .. **7.** Uruguay
sweet .. **6.** patata
potator ... **5.** poter **7.** tippler
potboiler ... **4.** book **6.** writer **8.** painting (for quick money) **9.** potwaller
potdar ... **7.** assayer, cashier, weigher
potence, potency ... **3.** vis **4.** élan **5.** cross, power **6.** energy, gibbet **7.** gallows **8.** virility **9.** authority, influence

potent . . . **4.** able **6.** cogent, mighty, strong, virile **7.** dynamic, warrant (Mil) **8.** forcible, heraldry, powerful, puissant, virulent **9.** effective, efficient **11.** efficacious, influential **13.** authoritative

potentate . . . **4.** amir (ameer), emir (emeer) **5.** mogul, ruler **6.** dynast, prince **7.** emperor, monarch **8.** syzerain **9.** sovereign

potential . . . **4.** mood (Gram) **5.** ergal **6.** latent, mighty **8.** possible **11.** influential, in the making, possibility, undeveloped

potentiality . . . **5.** power **7.** latency **11.** possibility

poter . . . **5.** toper **7.** drinker

potgun . . . **5.** rumor **6.** cannon, mortar, pistol **8.** braggart

pothead . . . **7.** dullard **8.** terminal (Elec) **9.** blackfish

pother . . . **3.** ado, row **4.** fuss, stir **5.** worry **6.** bother, bustle, harass **7.** fluster, perplex, trouble **9.** commotion **10.** excitement, perplexity **11.** disturbance **12.** perturbation

potherb . . . **4.** mint **6.** greens **7.** spinach

pothook . . . **3.** rod **4.** hook (S-shaped) **5.** crook **6.** scrawl, stroke (S-like) **9.** pot lifter **10.** iron collar (penalty)

pothouse . . . **3.** bar, low **6.** saloon, tavern, vulgar **7.** barroom **8.** alehouse, grogshop, mughouse **11.** public house

potiche . . . **4.** vase **7.** ceramic

potion . . . **4.** dose, dram, drug **5.** draft, drink **7.** draught, philter **8.** nepenthe

potlatch . . . **4.** gift **5.** feast **8.** Festival

pot mender . . . **6.** tinker

potomania . . . **10.** dipsomania **15.** delirium tremens

potong . . . **5.** crown **6.** wreath **9.** head cloth

potoroo . . . **11.** rat kangaroo

potpourri . . . **4.** olio, stew **6.** medley **7.** mixture, perfume **8.** anthology **11.** olla-podrida, salamagundi

potrero . . . **4.** farm **7.** pasture **10.** cattle farm

pottage . . . **4.** soup **6.** brewis **8.** porridge

pottah . . . **5.** lease **6.** tenure **9.** title deed

potter . . . **3.** pry **4.** mess, poke, push **6.** dawdle, doodle, meddle, putter, tamper, trifle **7.** saunter **8.** ceramist

potter's clay, earth . . . **4.** slip **5.** argil **6.** galena, kaolin **8.** alquifou **10.** terra cotta

potter's wheel . . . **4.** disk **5.** lathe, throw **6.** jigger, pallet (palet)

pottery . . . **5.** Delft **6.** Samian **7.** celadon (Chin), keramos (Gr) **8.** Arretine (It), ceramics, Majolica (It) **9.** delftware (Holland), keramikos (Gr) **11.** earthenware **14.** terra sigillata (anc)

pottery (pert to) . . .
  black . . **6.** basalt
  broken . . **5.** shard (sherd)
  decorate . . **6.** stamps **9.** sigillate
  decoration . . **11.** sigillation
  firing box . . **6.** sagger
  glasslike . . **8.** vitreous
  glaze . . **6.** enamel

  mineral . . **8.** feldspar
  oven . . **4.** kiln
  paste . . **9.** barbotine
  red . . **7.** aretine

pottle . . . **3.** pot **6.** basket, vessel **7.** tankard

potty . . . **3.** pot **5.** crazy **7.** foolish, haughty **8.** trifling **12.** supercilious **13.** insignificant

pot-valiant . . . **10.** courageous (when drunk)

pouch . . . **3.** bag, pod, sac **4.** cyst, poke, sack **5.** bulge, bursa, purse **6.** gipser (Hist), pocket **7.** bladder, mailbag, silicle, sporran (sporan) **10.** pocketbook

pouch bone . . . **9.** marsupial

pouched (pert to) . . .
  dog . . **9.** thylacine **13.** Tasmanian wolf
  frog . . **9.** marsupial
  gopher . . **9.** pocket
  mouse . . **9.** marsupial
  rat . . **8.** kangaroo
  rodent (cheek-pouched) . .
    11. spermophile
  stork . . **8.** adjutant

poultry . . . **4.** fowl, hens **5.** cocks, ducks, geese **6.** capons **7.** Bantams, peahens, pigeons, turkeys **8.** chickens, peacocks, roosters, volaille **9.** cockerels, pheasants **10.** guinea fowl

poultry (breeds) . . . **6.** Ancona, Bantam, Brahma **7.** Cornish, Dorking, Hamburg, Leghorn, Minorca **9.** Wyandotte **12.** Plymouth Rock **14.** Rhode Island Red

poultry (pert to) . . .
  disease . . **3.** pip **4.** roup, tick
  dish . . **9.** galantine
  farm . . **7.** hennery

pounamu . . . **4.** jade **6.** weapon **8.** nephrite **10.** greenstone

pound . . . **3.** hit, ram **4.** beat, ding, drum, maul, pond, quid (Brit money), tamp **5.** money, pen up, thump **6.** bruise, hammer, kennel, prison **7.** impound **9.** enclosure, pulverize

pounding instrument . . . **6.** hammer, pestle

Pound of poetry . . . **4.** Ezra

pounds (100) . . . **6.** cental **13.** hundredweight

pour . . . **4.** flow, gush, rain, teem, vent, well **5.** flood **6.** abound, effuse, stream **7.** niagara, radiate, torrent **8.** downpour **9.** discharge **11.** extravasate

pour (pert to) . . .
  molten glass . . **7.** dagrade
  molten steel . . **4.** teem
  off . . **5.** drain **6.** decant
  oil upon . . **6.** anoint, pacify
  out . . **11.** extravasate
  sacrificial liquid . . **6.** libate

pouring hole (mold) . . . **5.** sprue

pout . . . **3.** bib, mop **4.** fish, moue, sulk **5.** pique **7.** catfish, eelpout, grimace **9.** sulkiness

poverty . . . **4.** lack, need, want **5.** illth (opp of wealth) **6.** dearth, penury **8.** leanness, poorness, scarcity **9.** indigence, pearlweed **11.** destitution

powder . . . **4.** dust, talc **5.** boral **6.** pollen,

yttria **7.** crumble **8.** cosmetic, sprinkle
9. explosive, pulverize
powder (pert to) . . .
antiseptic . . **6.** formin **7.** aristol
bag . . **6.** sachet
festival (Ind) . . **4.** abir (perfumed)
goa . . **7.** araroba
heater, melter . . **6.** sinter
insecticide . . **9.** hellebore
medical . . **8.** tannigen
perfumed . . **6.** empasm
polishing . . **5.** emery **7.** tripoli
smokeless . . **6.** poudre **8.** amberite
stamping . . **6.** pounce
powdered (Her) . . . **4.** semé
power . . . **3.** arm, art, can, jet, vis
4. dint, gift, iron, sway, will **5.** force,
magic, might, steam, vigor **6.** degree,
energy **7.** control, faculty, magnate,
potency **8.** capacity, efficacy, strength
9. authority, eloquence, influence,
magnetism, puissance **10.** efficiency,
government **11.** mathematics (term)
power (pert to) . . .
creative . . **6.** Shakti
device . . **9.** telemotor
hammer . . **4.** trip
inherent . . **6.** energy
of attorney . . **5.** agent **10.** procurator
of feeling . . **7.** sensate
of mind . . **4.** wits
of resistance . . **7.** stamina
persuasive . . **8.** rhetoric **9.** political
sovereign . . **6.** throne
spiritual . . **8.** divinity
superior . . **10.** prepotency
under one's . . **10.** subjugated
unit . . **3.** erg **4.** dyne **8.** kilowatt
powerful . . . **4.** loud **5.** great **6.** cogent,
mighty, potent, strong **7.** drastic,
intense, leonine, skookum **8.** eloquent,
forcible, puissant **9.** effective, effectual,
efficient **10.** armipotent, convincing
11. efficacious, influential
13. authoritative
powerful force . . . **6.** libido
powerful man, businessman . . . **5.** titan
6. tycoon **7.** magnate
powerless . . . **4.** weak **8.** impotent
pownie . . . **7.** peacock
powwow . . . **6.** frolic, priest **7.** meeting
8. assembly, ceremony, congress,
conjurer **9.** gathering **10.** conference,
convention
poyou . . . **9.** armadillo
prabble . . . **7.** chatter, quarrel **8.** squabble
practic . . . **6.** artful, shrews **7.** cunning,
skilled **9.** difficult, practical, practiced
11. experienced
practicable, practical . . . **5.** utile
6. usable, useful **7.** virtual, working
8. feasible, possible, workable
9. available, expedient, operative,
pragmatic, realistic **11.** pragmatical,
utilitarian
practical (pert to) . . .
Christianity . . **10.** New Thought
example . . **6.** praxis
joke . . **4.** hoax **5.** trick **6.** humbug
judgment . . **7.** ethical (Kant)
practically . . . **9.** virtually **11.** essentially

13. approximately
practice, practise . . . **2.** do **3.** ply,
ure, use **4.** plot, rite **5.** drill, habit,
train, usage **6.** action, addict, custom,
scheme, tryout **7.** perform **8.** ceremony,
exercise, intrigue, rehearse, training,
vocation **9.** procedure **10.** experience,
experiment, observance
practice (pert to) . . .
corrupt . . **5.** abuse
established . . **5.** canon **6.** custom
fraud . . **5.** cheat, shark **8.** trickery
specific . . **6.** praxis
voice . . **8.** intonate
witchcraft . . **3.** hex
practicer of evasions . . .
13. tergiversator
practicer of palmistry . . .
11. chiromancer
prad . . . **5.** horse
pragmatic . . . **7.** meddler, skilled
8. busybody, dogmatic, meddling
9. conceited, officious, practical
10. systematic **11.** opinionated
pragmatical . . . **8.** dogmatic **9.** officious,
practical **10.** meddlesome
11. commonplace
Prague, Praha . . .
capital of . . **14.** Czechoslovakia
famed bldg . . **10.** University (1st in Cent
Eur, 1348)
famed teachers (anc) . . **4.** Huss **6.** Jerome
founder . . **14.** Duchess Libussa (722)
prairie . . . **3.** bay **5.** llano, plain **6.** camass
(camas, cammas), meadow, steppe
7. quamash (camass) **9.** grassland
10. prairillon
prairie (pert to) . . .
anemone, crocus . . **12.** pasque flower
antelope . . **9.** pronghorn
apple . . **9.** breadroot
artichoke . . **9.** sunflower
berry . . **9.** trompillo
chicken . . **6.** grouse
dog . . **6.** marmot
mud . . **5.** gumbo
pigeon . . **6.** plover **9.** sandpiper
rose . . **14.** Baltimore belle
schooner . . **12.** covered wagon
squirrel . . **11.** spermophile
tree (clump) . . **5.** motte
weed . . **10.** cinquefoil
wolf . . **6.** coyote
Prairie State . . . **8.** Illinois
praise . . . **4.** laud **5.** bless, extol, honor,
kudos **6.** eulogy **7.** acclaim, applaud,
commend, glorify, magnify, plaudit
8. applause, encomium, eulogize,
macarize **9.** adulation, celebrate,
panegyric **11.** approbation
12. commendation
praise (pert to) . . .
continual . . **5.** chant
high . . **5.** extol **8.** encomium
hymn of . . **8.** doxology
insincere . . **4.** bull **7.** flatter **8.** flattery
of another's blessing . . **8.** macarism
9. Beatitude
to God . . **7.** Laus Deo
Ye The Lord . . **8.** Alleluia (Alleluiah)
10. Hallelujah (Halleluiah)

praiseworthy ... **8.** laudable **11.** commendable, meritorious

prana (Hind) ... **6.** spirit **9.** life force **10.** life breath

prance ... **4.** gait **5.** caper, dance **6.** cavort, spring **7.** swagger

prank ... **3.** jig **4.** fold, joke, prat **5.** antic, caper, pleat, shine, trick **6.** frolic, prance **7.** caprice, dress up **8.** escapade **11.** monkeyshine

prankish ... **9.** facetious **10.** frolicsome **11.** mischievous

prate ... **3.** gab **4.** chat, talk **6.** gossip **7.** chatter, twaddle **8.** nonsense

prattle ... **3.** gab **4.** chat, talk **5.** clack, prate **6.** babble **7.** blather **12.** impudent talk, trifling talk

prawn ... **6.** shrimp **10.** crustacean, shrimp pink

pray ... **3.** ask, beg, sue **7.** entreat, implore, request, worship **8.** devotion **10.** supplicate

praya ... **4.** bund, road **5.** beach **6.** strand

prayer ... **3.** ave **4.** bead, bene, plea, suit **5.** credo, grace, matin **6.** litany, orison, vesper **7.** request, worship **8.** petition **12.** intercession, supplication

prayer (pert to) ...
book .. **4.** ordo **6.** missal **7.** portass (portas) **8.** breviary
call (Muslim) .. **4.** azan (adan)
call tower .. **7.** minaret
cloak .. **6.** zizith (fringed) **7.** tallith
desk, ledge .. **8.** prie-dieu
evening .. **7.** complin (compline) **9.** night song
figure .. **5.** orant
incarnation .. **7.** Angelus **11.** Angelus Bell
liturgical .. **6.** litany **7.** complin
Lord's (prayer) .. **11.** Paternoster
morning .. **5.** matin
nine days' devotional .. **6.** novena
response .. **8.** antiphon
short .. **5.** grace
stick .. **4.** paho

praying ... **8.** entreaty **9.** precation **12.** supplication

praying cricket ... **6.** mantis

praying figure ... **5.** orant

preach ... **6.** exhort **7.** expound, lecture **8.** advocate, homilize **9.** discourse, sermonize

preacher ... **6.** parson, rector **7.** evangel, teacher **8.** homilist, lecturer, minister **9.** clergyman, pulpiteer

preaching ... **6.** sermon **7.** kerygma (kerugma) **10.** preachment **11.** exhortation

preaching friar ... **9.** Dominican

Preaching of Peter ... **9.** Apocrypha

preamble ... **5.** proem **7.** preface, prelude **11.** preliminary **12.** introduction

prebellum ... **7.** antewar **12.** before the war

prebend ... **7.** stipend **8.** benefice **9.** allowance

precarious ... **7.** assumed, dubious **8.** insecure, unstable **9.** hazardous, uncertain, unsettled **10.** unreliable

preceded ... **3.** led **8.** prefaced, was prior

9. anteceded, antedated **10.** introduced, went before **13.** had precedence, occurred first

precedence ... **3.** pas **4.** lead, rank **8.** priority **12.** anteposition

precedent ... **4.** sign **5.** model, usage **7.** example, leading **8.** anterior, decision, standard **10.** antecedent, forerunner **11.** going before

preceding others ... **5.** first **7.** leading, ternary (by threes) **10.** antecedent

precept ... **4.** rule, writ **5.** adage, axiom, maxim, order, sutra (sutta), torah (tora) **6.** belief **7.** command **8.** doctrine **9.** direction **11.** commandment, instruction

preceptor ... **4.** guru **5.** guide, tutor **6.** master, mentor, mullah, pundit **7.** teacher **8.** educator **10.** instructor

precinct ... **5.** ambit, space **6.** region **8.** boundary, district, environs

precious ... **4.** dear, rare **5.** great **6.** costly, valued **7.** beloved, elegant, perfect **8.** complete, esteemed, overnice, valuable **9.** downright **10.** beloved one, fastidious, particular

precious (pert to) ...
Blood (RCCh) .. **5.** Feast (July 1)
garnet .. **6.** pyrope
stone .. **3.** gem **4.** opal, ruby **5.** pearl, topaz **6.** garnet, ligure **7.** diamond, emerald, jacinth (Bib) **8.** hyacinth, sapphire
stone, sometimes .. **7.** cat's-eye **11.** alexandrite

precipice ... **4.** crag, linn, pali **5.** bluff, cliff **9.** declivity

precipitancy ... **5.** haste **8.** rashness

precipitation ... **3.** gel **4.** fall, hail, mist, rain, snow **5.** haste, sleet **8.** downpour **9.** hastening **11.** prematurity **12.** acceleration, condensation, recklessness

precipitous ... **4.** rash **5.** hasty, steep **6.** abrupt, sudden **7.** rushing (headlong) **9.** very rapid **11.** precipitate

précis ... **6.** sketch **7.** epitome, pandect, summary **8.** abstract, synopsis **9.** summarize

precise ... **4.** prim **5.** exact **7.** correct, literal, special **8.** accurate, definite, detailed, overnice **10.** meticulous, overminute, particular, scrupulous **11.** ceremonious, punctilious

preciseness ... **9.** exactness **10.** strictness **12.** definiteness **14.** fastidiousness

precision ... **6.** nicety **8.** accuracy **9.** exactness, formality **11.** preciseness **12.** definiteness

preclude ... **3.** bar **4.** omit, stop **5.** avert, debar, estop **6.** hinder, impede **7.** head off, prevent, shut out **8.** prohibit

precocious ... **7.** forward **8.** advanced **9.** premature

preconceive ... **6.** ideate, precox **7.** presume **8.** foreknow, prejudge **9.** predecide **10.** presuppose

predatory ... **7.** looting **9.** marauding, pillaging, piratical **10.** plundering, predaceous (predacious) **11.** destructive

predatory bird ... **3.** owl **4.** hawk, kite

6. falcon
predatory raid ... **5.** foray
predestine ... **4.** doom, fate **6.** decree, ordain **7.** appoint **9.** determine, foretoken **10.** foreordain
predetermine ... **4.** bias **7.** destine **8.** prejudge **9.** prejudice, preordain **10.** prepossess **11.** premeditate
predicament ... **3.** fix **4.** pass **5.** state **6.** plight, scrape **7.** dilemma, impasse **8.** quandary **9.** condition, situation
predicator ... **4.** seer **5.** friar **7.** prophet **8.** preacher **9.** predicter
predict ... **4.** bode, dope, omen **7.** foresee, portend, presage **8.** forecast, foretell, prophecy **13.** prognosticate
prediction ... **6.** augury **8.** prophecy **9.** foresight **10.** foreboding **11.** foretelling **15.** prognostication
predilection ... **4.** bias **6.** desire **8.** tendency **9.** prejudice **10.** favoritism, partiality, preference, propensity **11.** disposition **13.** preconception **14.** predisposition
predominant ... **5.** chief **6.** ruling **8.** reigning, superior **9.** hegemonic **11.** controlling, influential, outstanding
predominate ... **5.** excel **7.** prevail **8.** dominate **10.** be superior **12.** preponderate
pre-eminent ... **3.** top **4.** only, star **5.** chief **7.** palmary, ranking **8.** superior **9.** excellent, principal **11.** outstanding
pre-emption ... **8.** monopoly, purchase **10.** prior right **13.** appropriation
preen ... **3.** pin, sew **4.** perk **5.** clasp, dress, groom, plume, primp **6.** bodkin, brooch, stitch **9.** make sleek
preface ... **5.** front, proem **6.** herald, prayer **7.** prelude, problem **8.** exordium, foreword, preamble, prologue **10.** paraphrase **12.** introduction
prefect, praefect ... **4.** dean (Jesuit) **6.** chin fu **7.** monitor, officer **8.** director, minister, official **9.** president **10.** magistrate
prefecture ... **7.** eparchy
prefer ... **5.** elect, offer **6.** choose, select **7.** outrank, present, proffer, promote **9.** be partial **12.** give priority
preference ... **6.** choice **8.** favorite, priority **9.** advantage **10.** favoritism **11.** alternative, prior choice **12.** predilection
prefiguration ... **4.** omen **9.** foretoken, prototype **12.** typification **13.** preindication
prefigure ... **7.** imagine, suggest **8.** foretell **10.** foreshadow
prefix for ...
about .. **3.** amb **4.** peri
above .. **3.** epi, sur **5.** hyper, super, supra
across .. **3.** dia **4.** tran **5.** trans
again .. **2.** re
against .. **4.** anti
ahead .. **3.** pre
all .. **4.** omni
alongside .. **3.** par **4.** para
an .. **2.** al
apart .. **2.** se **3.** dia, dis

appearing to .. **5.** quasi
around .. **4.** peri
away .. **3.** aph, apo
back .. **2.** re **3.** ana
backward .. **5.** retro
bad .. **3.** dys, mal
badly .. **3.** mis
beauty .. **5.** calli (kalli)
before .. **2.** ob **3.** pre, pro **4.** ante, prae
beside .. **3.** par **4.** para
between .. **3.** dia **4.** meta **5.** inter
beyond .. **4.** para **5.** ultra
black .. **4.** atra
blood .. **4.** haem, hemo
bone .. **4.** oste **5.** osteo
both .. **4.** ambi
Chinese .. **4.** Sino **5.** Chino
clear .. **4.** delo
dawn .. **2.** eo
difficult .. **3.** dys
distant .. **3.** tel **4.** tele
double .. **2.** di
down .. **2.** de **4.** cata
ear .. **3.** oto
earnest .. **5.** serio
earth .. **3.** geo
eight .. **3.** oct **4.** octa, octo
English .. **5.** Anglo
equal .. **3.** iso
equally .. **4.** equi
evil .. **3.** mal
far .. **3.** tel **4.** tele
faulty .. **3.** mis
fictitious .. **6.** pseudo
fire .. **3.** pyr
five .. **5.** penta
for .. **3.** pro
former .. **2.** ex
four .. **5.** tetra **6.** quadri
from .. **2.** ab, de, ec
from away .. **3.** apo
gas .. **4.** aero
good .. **2.** eu
half .. **4.** demi, hemi, semi
hard .. **3.** dys **6.** stereo
ill .. **3.** mal, mis
in, into .. **2.** en **4.** endo
iron .. **5.** ferro
lizard .. **5.** saura, sauro
many .. **4.** mult, poly **5.** multi
middle .. **4.** meso **5.** medio
modern .. **3.** neo
mountain .. **3.** oro
nail .. **4.** helo
negative .. **2.** il, ir, un **3.** mon
new .. **3.** neo
not .. **2.** il, im, ir, un **3.** non
numerical .. **3.** uni
one .. **3.** uni **4.** mono
oneself .. **4.** auto
out of, outer .. **2.** ec, ex **3.** ect, epi, exo **4.** ecto
over .. **3.** epi, sur **5.** super, supra
possession .. **3.** ose
pray .. **3.** ora
priority .. **3.** pre
recent .. **3.** neo
release .. **2.** un
reversed .. **2.** di
same, equal .. **3.** iso **4.** equi, homo
separation .. **2.** di **3.** dis

shoulder.. **6.** humero
single.. **4.** mono
son of.. **3.** Mac
ten.. **3.** dec **4.** deca
this side of.. **3.** cis
three, thrice.. **3.** ter, tri **4.** tris
through.. **3.** dia, per
to.. **2.** ap
together.. **3.** com, con, cor, syn
toward.. **2.** ob, oc
turning.. **4.** roto
twice.. **2.** bi, di
twofold.. **2.** bi, di **3.** dua
under.. **3.** sub
upon.. **2.** ep **3.** epi
upward.. **3.** ana, ano
very much.. **3.** eri
well.. **2.** eu
with.. **3.** col, com, pro, syl, syn
within.. **3.** eso **4.** endo, ento **5.** intra
without.. **2.** se **3.** ect **4.** ecto
wood.. **4.** xylo
wrong.. **3.** mis
pregnant... **7.** fertile **8.** fruitful
   9. expecting, with child **10.** parturient
prehistoric (pert to)...
animal.. **7.** reptile **8.** dinosaur, mastodon
   9. phytosaur
continent.. **8.** Atlantis (Atalantis)
man.. **4.** cave, Dawn **11.** lake dweller
ref to.. **9.** primitive
tool.. **6.** eolith
prejudiced... **6.** biased **7.** partial
   8. partisan **11.** opinionated
   12. prepossessed
prejudicial... **9.** injurious **11.** detrimental
   15. disadvantageous
prelate... **4.** head, pope **5.** abbot, chief
   6. bishop, priest **7.** primate, red-blue
   8. minister, superior **9.** Monsignor
   (Monsignore)
prelector, praelector... **6.** reader
   7. teacher **8.** lecturer **9.** professor
preliminary... **5.** prior **7.** preface,
   prelude **8.** entrance, previous, proemial
   9. precedent, prefatory, threshold
   10. antecedent **11.** preparatory
   12. introduction, introductory
preliminary memo... **8.** protocol
preliminary plan... **4.** idea
prelude... **5.** proem **6.** verset **7.** preface
   8. overture, ritornel (ritornelle)
premature... **6.** infant **8.** too early,
   untimely **10.** precocious
premier... **3.** bet (gambling) **5.** chief
   7. leading **8.** earliest **9.** principal
   13. prime minister
premiere... **4.** show **10.** first night
   12. presentation **16.** first performance
premium... **4.** agio **5.** bonus, prize,
   stake **6.** reward **8.** gratuity, interest
   10. recompense
premonition... **5.** hunch **6.** notice
   7. warning **8.** forecast **10.** foreboding
   11. forewarning, information
   12. presentiment
preoccupied... **4.** lost **6.** absent, filled
   8. absorbed, observed **9.** engrossed
   10. abstracted, pre-engaged **13.** lost
   in thought
preparation... **8.** training **9.** equipment,

study hour **10.** groundwork **11.** making
   ready **12.** introduction
preparation (pert to)...
of a dress.. **7.** fitting
place.. **10.** laboratory, paratorium
sugar, for candy.. **7.** fondant
without.. **5.** ad lib **9.** impromptu
prepare... **3.** fit, fix, get **4.** cook, gird,
   make, pave, yark **5.** adapt, equip,
   ready, train **6.** adjust **7.** arrange
prepare (pert to)...
by boiling.. **6.** decoct
for golf game.. **3.** tee
for melting glass.. **4.** frit
for publication.. **4.** edit
for seasoning.. **8.** marinate
skins.. **3.** taw
prepared... **5.** armed, ready **7.** adapted,
   groomed, skilled, trained **8.** equipped,
   provided
prepared instruction...
   13. propaedeutics
preponderance... **6.** weight **8.** dominion,
   majority **9.** influence **11.** outweighing,
   superiority
prepose... **6.** prefix **7.** preface **11.** place
   before
preposition... **2.** at, by, ex, in, of, on,
   to, up **3.** off, out, tae **4.** into, onto,
   over, unto, upon, with
prepossession... **4.** bent, bias
   9. obsession, prejudice **10.** preference
   11. inclination **12.** predilection
   13. appropriation, preconception
   14. predisposition
presage... **4.** bode, omen, osse, sign
   5. token **6.** augury, betide, divine
   7. portend, predict **8.** forebode,
   foretell **10.** prediction, prognostic
   11. preindicate **13.** foreknowledge
presager... **7.** prophet **9.** foreboder
presbytery... **6.** church, clergy **7.** council
   8. ministry **9.** parsonage **10.** presbyters
prescribe... **3.** set **5.** allot, guide, limit,
   order **6.** advise, bestow, direct, ordain
   7. control, dictate **9.** designate
presence... **4.** mien, port **7.** bearing,
   posture, specter **8.** phantasm
   9. existence, proximity **10.** apparition,
   appearance, attendance **11.** personality
present... **3.** now **4.** boon, gift, give
   5. grant, nonce, offer **6.** bestow, bounty,
   donate **7.** largess (largesse) **8.** donation,
   gratuity **9.** introduce **10.** contribute
   11. benefaction
present (pert to)...
for acceptance.. **6.** tender
pupil to teacher.. **8.** minerval
time.. **3.** now **5.** nonce, today **7.** current
   8. juncture
to customers.. **7.** freebie, premium
   8. giveaway **9.** lagniappe (lagnappe)
to foreign ambassador.. **6.** xenium
presentation... **4.** gift, plan **5.** debut,
   offer **7.** present **8.** bestowal, donation,
   offering **10.** appearance, exhibition
   12. introduction
presently... **4.** anon, soon **6.** at once
   7. shortly **8.** nowadays **9.** forthwith
   10. before long **11.** immediately
preservation... **6.** saving **9.** retention,

safeguard 10. protection
11. maintenance, safekeeping
12. conservation, perpetuation
preservative ... 4. salt 5. spice 7. alcohol,
vinegar 10. protective 14. sodium
benzoate
preserve ... 3. can, jam, tin 4. corn,
cure, keep, salt, save 5. guard, jelly,
spare, store 6. defend, pickle, retain,
secure, shield, uphold 7. compote,
protect, sustain 8. conserve, maintain
9. freeze-dry, safeguard
preserve (pert to) ...
by drying .. 9. desiccate
fruit .. 7. compote 9. marmalade
grape .. 5. uvate (conserve)
in brine .. 4. corn, cure, salt
in oil .. 8. marinate
president ... 4. head 5. ruler 8. governor
14. chief executive
President (US) ... 4. Ford, Polk, Taft
5. Adams (John), Adams (John Q),
Grant, Hayes, Nixon, Tyler 6. Arthur
(Chester), Carter, Hoover, Monroe,
Pierce, Reagan, Taylor, Truman, Wilson
7. Harding, Jackson, Johnson (Andrew),
Johnson (L B), Kennedy, Lincoln,
Madison 8. Buchanan, Coolidge,
Fillmore, Garfield, Harrison (Benj),
Harrison (Wm Henry), McKinley,
Van Buren 9. Cleveland, Jefferson,
Roosevelt (Theo), Roosevelt (F D)
10. Eisenhower, Washington
President (pert to) ...
place .. 10. Oval Office, White House
power .. 4. veto
press ... 3. dun 4. cram, iron, urge
5. crowd, force, wedge 6. compel,
hasten, smooth, throng, thrust
7. impress, squeeze 8. compress,
condense, insist on 9. extractor,
importune 10. compulsion, journalism,
newspapers 12. conscription
press (pert to) ...
ancient .. 6. Aldine
bookbinder .. 7. smasher
corrector .. 11. proofreader
critic .. 6. censor 8. reviewer
ranks .. 5. serry
pressed (pert to) ...
amber .. 8. amberoid
cheese .. 7. cheddar
grapes, residue .. 4. marc (mark)
into a mass .. 7. kneaded
together .. 5. dense 6. mashed
7. compact, crowded, serried
pressing ... 6. urgent, urging 7. exigent
9. insistent 10. compelling, extraction,
motivating 11. importunity
pressure ... 4. urge 5. force 6. compel,
stress, weight 7. squeeze, urgency
8. exigency, instancy 9. authority,
influence 10. compulsion, constraint,
harassment 11. compression
pressure (pert to) ...
barometer .. 7. mesobar
boiler, cooker .. 9. autoclave
instrument (for liquids) .. 9. manometer
10. piezometer 11. Bourdon tube
of necessity .. 7. urgency
resisting .. 8. renitent

unit .. 5. barad
prestidigitation ... 8. juggling
11. legerdemain 13. sleight of hand
prestige ... 4. bias, face, sway 5. clout,
éclat 6. renown, repute 7. sorcery
8. illusion 9. authority, deception,
influence 10. importance 11. superiority
presto ... 5. magic 7. command, passing,
quickly 8. suddenly 9. instantly
10. rapid tempo 11. immediately
13. instantaneous
presumably ... 7. no doubt 8. probably
10. ostensibly, supposedly
presume ... 4. dare, hope 5. imply, judge,
think 6. assure, impose 7. suppose,
venture 10. presuppose 11. preconceive
14. take for granted
presumption ... 4. hope 6. daring
7. opinion 8. audacity 9. arrogance,
impudence, insolence 10. effrontery
11. implication, probability, supposition
presumptive ... 5. brash 7. assumed,
Icarian 8. arrogant, inferred, probable
10. evidential
presumptuous ... 5. undue 7. forward,
haughty 8. arrogant, insolent
9. foolhardy 11. venturesome
pretend ... 3. act, aim 4. fake, sham
5. claim, feign, feint 6. affect,
allege, assume, pose as 7. presume,
pretext, profess 8. disguise, simulate
11. impersonate, make believe
pretended ... 4. sham 7. alleged
8. affected, intended, proposed,
so-called 10. ostensible
pretended omission (Rhet) ...
9. apophasis 11. paraleipsis (paralepsis)
pretender ... 4. idol, snob 5. cowan,
quack 6. seemer 7. Aeolist (Eolist)
8. claimant, impostor 9. charlatan
10. mountebank 11. fourflusher
pretense, pretence ... 3. act 4. flam,
ruse, sham, show 5. claim, cloak,
cover, feint, horse, study 6. excuse,
tinsel 7. pretext 8. artifice, stalking
10. appearance, masquerade,
subterfuge 11. affectation, fabrication,
ostentation
pretentious ... 4. arty 5. showy 6. rococo
7. elegant, pompous 8. affected,
boastful 9. high-flown 12. ostentatious
13. grandiloquent
pretentious words, use of ...
9. bombastic 10. lexiphanic
pretermit ... 4. omit 6. pass by
7. neglect, suspend 8. intermit, pass
over 9. interrupt
pretext ... 4. flam, plea 5. cloak, cover,
trick 6. excuse 8. pretense (pretence)
9. deception, semblance
pretty ... 3. toy 4. cute, fair, joli, very
5. bonny (bonnie) 6. clever, comely,
lovely, rather 7. dollish, finical, foppish
8. handsome 9. ingenious, tolerably
10. attractive, knickknack 11. good-
looking, interesting 15. pulchritudinous
prevail ... 3. win 5. exist 6. induce,
subdue 7. succeed, triumph
8. dominate, frequent 9. prevalent
11. predominate
prevailed ... 3. got, won 5. urged

9. succeeded, triumphed
prevailing ... 4. rife 5. chief, usual
6. common 7. current, general
8. abundant, dominant 9. prevalent
10. widespread 11. predominant
prevail upon ... 4. urge 6. induce
8. persuade
prevalent ... 4. rife 6. potent 7. current
8. dominant, powerful 9. extensive
10. prevailing, successful, victorious,
widespread 11. efficacious, influential
prevaricate ... 3. lie 5. evade 7. deviate,
quibble, shuffle
prevene ... 7. prevent 9. forestall
10. anticipate
prevent ... 4. warn 5. avert, debar,
deter, estop 7. ward off 8. preclude
9. forestall, frustrate 10. circumvent
preventative, preventive ... 8. antidote
9. deterrent 12. prophylactic
previous ... 4. past 5. prior 6. before,
former 7. earlier 8. untimely
9. foregoing, preceding, premature
11. unwarranted
previously ... 4. erst 6. before 7. earlier
8. formerly 9. aforesaid 10. heretofore
prey ... 3. rob 5. booty, spoil 6. quarry,
victim 7. plunder
prey (to seize) ... 9. raptorial
prey upon ... 3. eat 4. feed 5. ravin
(raven) 7. plunder, torment 9. predacity
Priam (pert to) ...
daughter .. 8. Polyxena 9. Cassandra
grandfather .. 4. Ilus
King of .. 4. Troy
servant .. 7. Agelaus
son .. 5. Paris 6. Hector 7. Troilus
wife .. 6. Hecuba
price ... 3. sum 4. cost, fare, odds,
rate 5. offer, value, worth 6. charge
7. expense 10. estimation, excellence,
recompense 12. preciousness
priceless ... 7. amusing 8. precious
10. high-priced, invaluable, not salable
prick ... 4. goad, pain, pang 5. sting,
wound 6. pierce 7. prickle, remorse
8. distress
pricked ... 6. dotted, pinked 7. pointed
9. punctured
prickle ... 4. burr, prod, seta 5. spike,
thorn 6. pierce, tingle 7. acantha
8. stinging
prickly ... 6. tingly 7. pointed 8. echinate
prickly (pert to) ...
flower .. 4. burr
pear .. 4. tuna 5. nopal 6. cactus
7. Opuntia
plant .. 3. ash 5. briar, elder 6. teasel
7. juniper, lettuce, thistle 12. Hercules-
club
pride ... 6. vanity 7. conceit, egotism
9. arrogance, proudness 11. self-respect
priest ... 3. Eli, fra 4. abbé, curé, lama,
père 5. clerk, druid, padre 6. cleric,
father 7. prester 9. oratorian
priest (pert to) ...
assistant .. 7. acolyte
Brit order (anc) .. 5. Druid
cap .. 5. miter (mitre) 7. biretta
fish .. 8. rockfish
mantle .. 4. cope

priest-in-the-pulpit .. 10. cuckoopint
relating to .. 10. sacerdotal
tribe (Israel) .. 4. Levi
vestment .. 3. alb 5. amice, ephod (Jew),
stole 7. cassock, maniple 8. chasuble,
surplice
priestly caste ... 4. Magi 7. wise men
prig ... 3. beg, fog, pan 4. buck, snob
5. dandy, filch, plead, prink, prude,
steal, thief 6. haggle, pilfer, purist, tinker
7. bargain, entreat, pitcher 8. pilferer
priggish, prim ... 7. prudish 8. snobbish,
thievish
prim ... 4. fish, neat, smug 5. primp,
smelt 6. demure, formal 7. precise,
prudish 8. decorous
prima donna ... 4. diva 6. singer
prima facie ... 7. at sight 9. first view
10. apparently
primal ... 5. basic, chief, first 7. primary
8. original 9. elemental, primitive
primary ... 5. basic, color, first 6. primal
7. initial 8. election, primeval, pristine
9. elemental, essential, firsthand,
primitive, principal 10. elementary
11. fundamental
primary (pert to) ...
armament .. 6. cannon
circles .. 7. equator, horizon 8. ecliptic,
galactic
colors .. 3. red 4. blue 6. yellow
primate, bishop ... 10. Archbishop
Primates (Order of) ... 3. ape, man
5. lemur 6. mammal, monkey
8. marmoset 9. orangutan
(orangoutang)
prime ... 4. best, dawn 5. first, paint
7. primary, the best 8. original, primeval
9. primitive
prime minister ... 7. premier
primer ... 5. paint 8. hornbook, textbook,
type size 9. detonator 10. battledore
primeval ... 6. primal 7. primary
8. original, pristine
primeval deity ... 5. Titan
primitive ... 5. basic, first 6. embryo,
native, quaint 7. ancient, priscan
8. pristine 10. aboriginal, antiquated
11. fundamental
primitive (pert to) ...
area .. 5. Idaho 8. Colorado
art objects .. 9. artifacts
group .. 6. ethnos
self .. 2. id 8. instinct
primness ... 8. neatness, niceness
9. stiffness 11. preciseness
primo ... 5. chief, first 12. leading tenor
primordial ... 7. primary 8. original
9. elemental, primitive 10. prototypal
11. rudimentary 12. first created
primrose (pert to) ...
called .. 10. an innocent 13. flower of
youth
color .. 6. yellow 10. snapdragon
genus .. 7. Primula 11. Primulaceae
green .. 5. color
League .. 13. Conservatives (Eng)
path .. 7. sensual
prince ... 4. knez 5. prinz 7. dynasty,
monarch 8. archduke 9. potentate,
princekin, sovereign 10. princeling

prince (pert to)...
Albert.. **9.** frock coat
allowance.. **8.** appenage
petty.. **6.** satrap
princely... **5.** noble, regal, royal **6.** kingly
    10. munificent **11.** magnificent
princely Italian family... **4.** Este
Prince of...
Afghanistan.. **4.** amir
apostate angels.. **5.** Eblis
Apostles.. **6.** St Paul **7.** St Peter
darkness.. **5.** devil, Satan **7.** Ahriman
demons.. **5.** devil **9.** Beelzebub
destruction.. **9.** Tamerlane
evil spirits.. **7.** Sammael
liars.. **5.** Pinto
Peace.. **7.** Messiah **11.** Jesus Christ
Spanish poetry.. **4.** Vega
the Church.. **8.** cardinal
the ode.. **7.** Ronsard
the sonnet.. **6.** Bellay **15.** Joachim du
    Bellay
this world (Bib).. **5.** Satan
Tunis.. **3.** bey
princess (pert to)...
literally.. **5.** Sarah
loved by Cupid.. **6.** Psyche
loved by Zeus.. **6.** Europa
Mohammed.. **5.** begum
mythical.. **5.** Danae **8.** Atalanta
royal.. **14.** eldest daughter
Tyrian.. **4.** Dido (Elissa)
principal... **3.** top **4.** arch, head, main
    5. chief, major, prime **6.** Führer, leader,
    master, origin, source **7.** captain,
    leading, palmary, primary **8.** foremost
    9. important, organ stop, preceptor
    10. capital sum **11.** outstanding
principality... **6.** Monaco
principal meal (Rom)... **4.** cena
principle... **4.** rule **5.** axiom, canon,
    prana, tenet **6.** dictum **7.** precept,
    theorem **9.** essential **10.** foundation
principle (pert to)...
active in tobacco.. **8.** nicotine
distance.. **11.** perspective
Hindu.. **5.** Sakti
life, theosophy.. **5.** prana, tenet
musical.. **8.** tonality
vital.. **4.** soul **5.** anima
principles... **5.** creed **9.** generalia
    10. essentials **12.** generalities
princox, princock... **7.** coxcomb **9.** pert
    youth
prink... **4.** deck, wink **5.** adorn, preen,
    primp **6.** bedeck, glance **7.** dress up
print... **5.** stamp **7.** edition, engrave,
    impress, picture, publish **11.** indentation
printed (pert to)...
defamation.. **5.** libel
fabric.. **4.** silk **6.** calico **7.** percale
sheets.. **8.** pamphlet
printer... **8.** pressman **9.** publisher
    11. typographer **12.** lithographer
printer (pert to)...
aid.. **5.** devil **10.** apprentice
dauber.. **5.** biron
direction.. **4.** stet
hand ink roller.. **6.** brayer
ink pad.. **6.** dabber
manuscript.. **4.** copy

mark.. **4.** dash, stet **5.** caret, serif, tilde
    8. asterisk
measure.. **2.** em, en **4.** pica
type, mixed.. **3.** pie (pi)
printing (pert to)...
blur.. **6.** mackle, macule
cylinder.. **6.** rounce
error.. **7.** erratum
form.. **3.** die
for the blind.. **7.** braille
mark.. **4.** dele **6.** diesis **8.** ellipsis
measure.. **2.** em, en **5.** agate
metal block.. **4.** quad
press part.. **6.** platen, rounce **7.** frisket
prion... **6.** petrel **7.** sea bird
prior... **3.** ere **4.** fore, past **6.** before,
    former **8.** previous, priorate
    9. preceding **10.** antecedent
priority... **10.** precedence **11.** order of
    time
priory... **5.** abbey **8.** cloister
priscan... **9.** primitive
Priscian... **7.** grammar **10.** grammarian
Priscilla (pert to)...
Bib.. **16.** Christian convert
color.. **7.** fog blue
Hist.. **7.** Puritan
husband.. **9.** John Alden
tale.. **24.** Courtship of Myles Standish
prism (optical device)... **5.** Porro
prismatic... **10.** iridescent, variegated
prison... **3.** jug **4.** brig, gaol, jail, keep,
    quod **5.** clink **6.** carcer **10.** guardhouse
    12. penitentiary
prison (pert to)...
courtyard.. **4.** quad
English (old).. **7.** Newgate **9.** Bridewell
French.. **8.** Bastille
guarded.. **10.** panopticon
keeper.. **5.** guard **6.** gaoler, jailer,
    keeper, warden **7.** turnkey
Russian.. **5.** gulag
slang.. **3.** jug **4.** quod, rock **5.** clink,
    limbo **6.** cooler **7.** slammer **8.** big
    house, hoosegow
spy.. **6.** canary, mouton
Prisoner of...
Chillon.. **16.** Francois Bonivard
Vatican.. **4.** Pope
prisoner's release... **6.** parole
pristine... **7.** primary **8.** original
    9. primitive
prittle-prattle... **7.** chatter, prattle
    8. chitchat **9.** chatterer, empty talk
privacy... **7.** privity, retreat, secrecy
    8. solitude **9.** seclusion
private... **5.** privy **6.** covert, secret
    7. one's own **8.** esoteric, eyes-
    only, hush-hush, personal, secluded,
    separate, solitary **11.** sequestered
    12. confidential **15.** uncommunicative
privateer... **4.** Kidd (Capt) **5.** caper
    6. pirate **7.** corsair, soldier (not enlisted)
    9. freelance
privately... **5.** aside **6.** secret **8.** in secret
    10. personally, unofficial **12.** unofficially
privation... **4.** loss, want **6.** misery
    7. poverty **8.** hardship **10.** divestment
    11. destitution
privilege... **3.** soc, use **5.** favor, right
    7. charter **8.** easement **9.** advantage

10. concession 12. carte blanche
privileged . . . 6. exempt 8. licensed
priveleged ones . . . 5. haves
prix . . . 5. prize
prize . . . 3. cup 5. award, booty, Detur
(Harvard), medal, plate, price, purse,
stake, value 6. assess, esteem, ribbon,
trophy 7. premium, respect 8. treasure
prize fight . . . 2. go, KO 3. TKO 4. bout,
spar 6. boxing 7. contest 8. knockout,
pugilism 10. fisticuffs
pro . . . 3. aye, for 6. before 8. behalf of
9. in front of 12. professional
probability . . . 4. odds 6. chance, shoo-in
(sl) 7. vantage 9. liability 10. conclusion,
good chance, likelihood, likeliness
11. credibility
probe . . . 3. dig 4. prod, tent 5. sound
6. feeler, pierce, search, stylet
7. examine, explore, feel out, inquiry
10. instrument, scrutinize
probity . . . 6. virtue 7. honesty 9. integrity,
rectitude 11. uprightness
problem . . . 3. nut 4. crux, knot
6. enigma, riddle 7. theorem 8. question
9. situation
pro bono publico . . . 16. for the public
good
proboscis . . . 4. beak, nose 5. snout,
trunk
procaccia . . . 4. cart (carrier's) 7. carrier
procacious . . . 4. pert 8. insolent, petulant
procacity . . . 8. pertness 9. insolence,
petulance
Procavis . . . 4. cony 5. hyrax 6. rabbit
procedure . . . 4. step 5. order 6. custom,
method, policy, system 7. process
8. behavior 11. continuance
proceed . . . 2. go 4. fare, move,
pass, wend 5. arise, issue 6. derive
7. emanate 8. continue, progress
9. originate
proceed (pert to) . . .
hastily . . **5.** speed
leisurely . . **5.** amble, mosey (mosy)
on one's way . . **4.** wend
rapidly . . **4.** zoom 6. gallop
proceeding . . . 4. step 5. actum 6. course
7. conduct, measure, process 8. activity,
behavior 9. procedure 11. transaction
proceeding (pert to) . . .
by threes . . **7.** ternary
from earth . . **8.** telluric
from the sun . . **5.** polar
proceedings . . . 4. acta 5. trial 6. doings
7. affairs, lawsuit, minutes 8. activity
proceeds . . . 4. gain, goes 6. income
7. marches, profits, returns
procerity . . . 4. height 8. tallness
process . . . 4. cook, writ 5. lapse (of time),
order 6. course, notice 7. advance,
mandate, summons 8. progress
9. emanation, operation, outgrowth,
procedure, sterilize
process (pert to) . . .
beak (small) . . **9.** rostrulum
electroplating, steeling . . **8.** acierage
fabric coloring . . **5.** batik
fish (winglike) . . **3.** fin
in organisms . . **6.** moisis
of development . . **7.** nascent

pointed . . **3.** awn
steel making . . **8.** Bessemer
11. cementation
surveying . . **13.** triangulation
transferring pictures . . **5.** decal
12. decalcomania
procession . . . 4. file 5. train 6. parade
7. cortege 8. sequence 9. formation
prochein, prochain . . . 4. next 7. nearest
proclaim . . . 4. nype (sl), tout 5. blaze,
voice 6. herald 7. declare, enounce,
presage, publish 8. announce
10. promulgate
proclamation . . . 4. fiat 5. bando, banns
(bans), blaze, edict, ukase 6. decree,
notice 9. manifesto 12. announcement,
promulgation
proclivity . . . 4. bent 6. desire 7. leaning
8. tendency 10. propensity
11. disposition, inclination
procrastinate . . . 5. defer, delay, stall
7. soldier 8. postpone
procrastination . . . 5. delay, stall
7. laxness 10. hesitation 11. vacillation
12. dilatoriness
procrastinator . . . 7. delayer, trifler
8. deferrer
procreant . . . 8. fruitful 9. producing
10. generating 11. propagative
Procrustes (Gr legend) . . .
10. highwayman (Attica)
14. Procrustean bed
procurator . . . 5. agent 6. lawyer
7. proctor, steward
procure . . . 3. get 4. gain 5. bring, fetch
6. effect, elicit, induce, obtain 7. acquire
8. contrive, purchase
prod . . . 3. egg, jab 4. goad, poke, urge
6. thrust
prodigal . . . 4. cloy 6. lavish 7. spender
9. plentiful 10. squanderer
11. extravagant, intemperate,
spendthrift, squandering
prodigality . . . 5. waste 9. abundance
12. extravagance, intemperance
13. superabundant
prodigious . . . 4. huge 5. great 7. amazing,
immense 8. enormous 9. marvelous,
monstrous, wonderful 10. miraculous,
portentous, tremendous 11. astonishing
13. extraordinary
prodigy . . . 4. omen, sign 6. genius,
marvel, oddity, wonder 7. miracle
prodition . . . 7. treason 8. betrayal
produce . . . 2. do 4. bear, make, show,
wage 5. carry, cause, stage, yield
6. author, create, effect 7. exhibit,
product 8. engender, generate, receipts
9. originate 10. accomplish
11. merchandise
produce (pert to) . . .
copy of . . **4.** type
effect . . **3.** act
ideas . . **6.** ideate
noise . . **5.** sound
produced . . . 8. extended 9. elongated,
prolonged
produced (pert to) . . .
by heat . . **7.** igneous 8. volcanic
by kitchen gardens . . **7.** olitory
8. potherbs

by wind .. **7.** aeolian
regularly .. **6.** staple
producer ... **4.** doer **6.** farmer, parent
  7. creator **10.** theaterman
  12. manufacturer
producing (pert to) ...
  cold .. **7.** algific
  fire .. **8.** sparking
  illusions .. **15.** phantasmagorial
  poison .. **6.** septic
product ... **3.** sum **4.** crop **5.** fruit
  6. result **7.** hormone **8.** artifact, creation
  9. commodity, outgrowth
production ... **3.** hit **4.** book, work **5.** fruit
  7. produce **8.** creation **9.** execution,
  extension **14.** accomplishment
productive ... **4.** rich **7.** fertile, gainful
  8. creative, fruitful **9.** inventive
  10. generative
proem ... **7.** preface, prelude **8.** foreword,
  preamble **12.** introduction
profane ... **6.** misuse, unholy, wicked
  7. godless, impious, ungodly, worldly
  8. temporal **9.** desecrate **10.** unhallowed
  11. blasphemous, unspiritual
  12. unsanctified
profess ... **4.** avow **5.** claim, feign
  6. affirm, allege **7.** declare
  11. acknowledge
profession ... **5.** claim, faith, trade
  6. avowal, career, metier **7.** calling,
  pretext **8.** vocation **9.** testimony
  10. occupation **11.** affirmation
  14. acknowledgment
professional ... **4.** paid **5.** hired **6.** expert
  7. skilled, trained **8.** finished
professional, non ... **3.** lay **4.** laic
  7. amateur **8.** unskilled
proffer ... **3.** bid **4.** give **5.** offer **6.** tender
proficient ... **3.** apt **5.** adept **6.** expert,
  versed **7.** skilled **12.** accomplished
profile ... **4.** draw, form **7.** contour,
  diagram, outline, picture **9.** biography
  14. representation
profit ... **3.** net **4.** boot, gain, good,
  mend **5.** avail **6.** return **7.** benefit, rake-
  off, results **8.** interest **9.** advantage
  11. share of gain **12.** remuneration
profitable ... **6.** paying, useful **7.** helpful
  8. repaying **9.** expedient, lucrative
  10. beneficial **12.** remunerative
profligate ... **6.** wicked **7.** corrupt,
  spender, vicious **8.** depraved, prodigal,
  wasteful **9.** abandoned, dissolute,
  reprobate **10.** overthrown
  11. extravagant
profound ... **4.** deep, wise **5.** heavy
  7. abysmal, intense, learned **8.** abstruse,
  complete, deep-felt, poignant
  9. downright, recondite, sagacious
  11. far-reaching **12.** encompassing,
  unfathomable **13.** thoroughgoing
profundity ... **5.** depth **6.** wisdom
  8. deepness **12.** abstruseness
profuse ... **6.** galore, lavish **7.** diffuse,
  liberal, palaver **8.** abundant, generous,
  numerous, prodigal, wasteful
  9. bountiful **10.** munificent
  11. extravagant, overflowing
profusion ... **6.** plenty **9.** abundance
  11. diffuseness, prodigality

  12. extravagance, lavish supply
progenitor ... **4.** sire **6.** parent **8.** ancestor
  9. precursor **10.** forefather
progenitor of giants (Norse Myth) ...
  4. Ymir **8.** rime-cold
progeny ... **3.** son **4.** race **5.** issue
  6. family **7.** outcome **8.** children,
  daughter, outbirth **9.** offspring,
  parentage, resultant **11.** descendants
prognosis ... **7.** outlook **8.** forecast
  9. diagnosis **10.** prediction
  14. interpretation
prognosticate ... **4.** bode, omen
  7. betoken, predict, presage **8.** forebode,
  foreshow, foretell, prophecy
  9. foretoken
program, programme ... **4.** bill (printed),
  card, plan **5.** edict **6.** notice, policy
  7. outline **8.** bulletin, platform,
  schedule, syllabus **9.** broadcast,
  catalogue, programma **10.** prospectus
  12. proclamation, prolegomenon
  13. advertisement
programma ... **5.** edict **6.** decree, notice
  7. preface **12.** prolegomenon
progress ... **4.** fare, tour, wend **5.** march
  6. course, travel **7.** advance, journey
  10. expedition **11.** progression
progress (pert to) ...
  chart .. **5.** Gantt
  clumsily .. **8.** scramble
  intelligently .. **6.** egress **7.** telesis (telesia)
  laborious .. **4.** plod, wade
  outward .. **6.** egress
  weakly .. **6.** feebly
progressive ... **6.** modern, onward
  7. forward, gradual, liberal
  9. advancing, improving **11.** consecutive
  12. enterprising
prohibit ... **3.** ban, bar, bid **5.** debar,
  estop, taboo (tabu) **6.** enjoin, forbid,
  hinder **7.** prevent **9.** interdict
prohibited ... **7.** illegal, illicit **8.** unlawful
prohibition ... **3.** ban **7.** embargo
  8. estoppel **9.** exclusion **10.** prevention,
  temperance **11.** forbiddance
  12. interdicting
project ... **3.** jet, jut **4.** abut, cast, idea,
  plan **5.** shoot **6.** beetle, design, device,
  scheme **7.** pattern, problem **8.** contrive,
  proposal, protrude **9.** intention
  10. conception **11.** undertaking
projectile ... **4.** bomb **5.** shell **6.** bullet,
  rocket **7.** missile, torpedo **8.** parabola
  9. cartridge
projection ... **3.** arm, ear, fin, jag,
  toe **4.** barb, cape, lobe, ness, prop,
  snag **5.** apsis, bulge, ledge, prong,
  redan, socle, tenon **6.** lobule, tappet
  8. headland
prolific ... **6.** fecund **7.** fertile, teeming
  8. fruitful **9.** inventive **10.** generative
  11. propagative **12.** reproductive
prolix ... **5.** wordy **7.** diffuse, verbose
  8. tiresome **9.** prolonged, rigmarole,
  wearisome **10.** long-winded, pleonastic,
  protracted
prolocutor ... **6.** orator **7.** speaker,
  teacher **8.** chairman **9.** spokesman
  10. mouthpiece **11.** Lord Speaker (Eng)
prolong ... **4.** spin **7.** draw out **8.** continue,

lengthen, postpone, protract
prolonged ... **7.** chronic, delayed
8. extended **9.** continued, postponed
10. lengthened, protracted
promenade ... **4.** mall, walk **6.** airing,
marina, pasear **7.** alameda, gallery
Prometheus (pert to) ...
famed as .. **5.** Titan (a)
poem (Shelley) .. **17.** Prometheus
Unbound
tale, tragedy .. **15.** Prometheus Bound
16. Prometheus Loosed **24.** Prometheus
the Fire Bringer
prominence ... **4.** cusp **6.** height
8. eminence, prestige, salience
9. greatness **10.** famousness,
importance **11.** distinction, obviousness,
prosiliency **12.** distinctness,
protuberance
prominent ... **4.** high, star **5.** great
6. famous, marked **7.** obvious, salient
8. distinct, manifest **9.** important
10. celebrated, noticeable, prosilient,
protruding **11.** conspicuous, distinctive,
outstanding **13.** distinguished
promiscuous ... **5.** mixed **8.** careless
9. haphazard, orderless
14. indiscriminate
promise ... **3.** vow **4.** hope, oath **5.** swear
6. engage, parole, pledge, plight, votive
(by vow) **7.** betroth, predict **8.** affiance,
contract, give hope **9.** assurance, ray
of hope **11.** declaration
Promised Land ... **6.** heaven, utopia
8. Paradise **9.** millenium, Shangri-La
11. Happy Valley **13.** Celestial City
promontory ... **3.** tor **4.** cape, naze
(nase), ness, scaw **5.** mount, point
8. headland **10.** projection
promote ... **4.** help **5.** exalt, nurse
6. extend, prefer **7.** actuate, advance,
dignify, elevate, finance, further,
improve **8.** increase **9.** advertise,
encourage, patronize
promoter ... **5.** agent **6.** backer **7.** planner
8. lobbyist **9.** financier, publicist
promotion ... **6.** brevet **7.** advance
10. preferment **11.** advertising,
furtherance, improvement
prompt ... **3.** cue **4.** easy, hint, soon,
tell, yare (anc) **5.** alert, early, quick,
ready **6.** advise, remind **7.** animate,
suggest **8.** punctual **11.** expeditious
prompter ... **3.** aid **4.** cuer **6.** pit man,
reader **7.** inducer, reciter **8.** reminder
promptly ... **4.** tite (anc) **6.** at once
7. quickly **9.** willingly
promulgate ... **7.** declare, publish
8. proclaim **9.** make known
prone ... **3.** apt **4.** bent, flat **5.** apish
6. supine **7.** willing **8.** downward
9. prostrate, recumbent
13. ventricumbent
prone to sin ... **8.** peccable
prong ... **3.** nib, peg **4.** fang, fork, tine
5. spike, tooth **6.** branch
pronghorn ... **6.** cabree (cabrie) **9.** prong
buck, springbok
prong key ... **7.** spanner
pronoun ... **2.** he, it, me, my, us, we, ye
3. her, him, one, she, thy, who, you

4. that, thee, them, they, thou, what,
your **5.** these, those **6.** itself, myself
7. herself, himself, oneself, ourself
8. one's self, yourself **9.** ourselves
10. themselves
pronoun (possessive) ... **2.** my **3.** her,
his, its, our **4.** hers, mine, one's, ours,
your **5.** their, yours **6.** theirs
pronounce ... **3.** say **5.** bless (holy),
speak, utter **6.** affirm, assert **7.** adjudge,
declare, deliver **8.** announce
9. enunciate **10.** adjudicate, articulate,
assibilate
pronouncement ... **6.** decree **8.** judgment
9. manifesto **11.** affirmation, declaration
12. announcement
pronto ... **5.** quick **7.** quickly **8.** promptly
11. immediately
pronunciation ... **4.** burr **8.** orthoepy
9. utterance (clear) **11.** enunciation
pronunciation mark ... **5.** tilde **7.** cedilla
8. dieresis
proof ... **4.** test **5.** trial **6.** result **7.** outcome
8. evidence **9.** testimony **11.** galley
proof **12.** confirmation, verification
13. certification
proofreader's mark ... **4.** dele, stet
5. caret, space
prop ... **3.** beg, gib, nog **5.** brace, shore,
sprag, staff, stell **6.** shorer **7.** fulcrum,
support **9.** stanchion
propagate ... **5.** breed **6.** extend,
spread **7.** diffuse, publish **8.** disperse,
engender, generate, increase, multiply,
transmit
propel ... **3.** row **4.** pole, push, urge
5. drive, impel **7.** project
propeller ... **3.** fan, gun, oar **4.** vane
5. screw **6.** driver **9.** plane part
propensity ... **4.** bent **6.** desire **7.** leaning
8. aptitude, tendency **9.** proneness
10. proclivity **11.** disposition, inclination
proper ... **3.** fit **4.** fine, just, meet,
prim, smug **5.** exact, right **6.** chaste,
decent, goodly, honest, kilter **7.** correct
8. decorous, inherent, orthodox,
suitable **9.** excellent, expedient
11. appropriate, grammatical,
respectable **12.** conventional
properly ... **5.** fitly **7.** rightly, utterly
8. decently, strictly, suitably **9.** correctly
11. expediently **14.** conventionally
proper sense of worth ... **5.** pride
property ... **3.** res **4.** bona, gear
5. asset, goods, trait **6.** estate, nature,
realty, wealth **7.** holdings **8.** attribute,
copyright, ownership **10.** real estate
11. peculiarity, possessions
14. characteristic
property (pert to) ...
act to regain .. **8.** replevin (repleven)
destruction of .. **8.** sabotage **9.** vandalism
landed property .. **9.** cadastral
light without heat .. **15.** phosphorescence
movable .. **4.** gear **8.** chattels
no private ownership .. **11.** aspheterism
of matter .. **7.** inertia
one's own .. **7.** alodium
right .. **4.** lien
stolen .. **4.** loot, pelf **5.** lucre, spoil
suit for recovery .. **6.** trover

transferrer.. **7.** alienor, grantor
wife to husband.. **3.** dos
woman's (Hindu).. **9.** stridhana
(stridhan)
prophecy... **6.** oracle **9.** utterance
10. divination, prediction **11.** foretelling
prophesy... **4.** osse **5.** augur **6.** divine
7. predict, presage **8.** forecast,
foreshow, foretell **10.** vaticinate
11. preindicate **13.** prognosticate
prophet... **4.** seer **6.** medium, oracle
7. psychic **8.** Mohammed, preacher,
presager **9.** John Smith, predictor
10. soothsayer **11.** Joseph Smith
(Mormon)
prophet (Bib)... **4.** Amos **5.** Cyrus, Hosea
6. Elijah (Elias) **7.** Malachi, Obadiah
prophet, murder of... **8.** vaticide
prophetess... **5.** sibyl **7.** seeress
9. Cassandra (of evil)
prophetic, prophetical... **5.** vatic
6. mantic **7.** fateful, vatical **8.** oracular
9. vaticinal **10.** divinatory, presageful
11. predicative
propinquity... **7.** kinship **8.** nearness
9. proximity **12.** neighborhood,
relationship **13.** consanguinity
propitiate... **5.** atone **6.** pacify **8.** atone
for **10.** conciliate
propitiation... **9.** atonement, expiation
12. pacification, satisfaction
14. reconciliation
propitious... **4.** rosy **5.** happy, lucky
6. benign, timely **7.** helpful **9.** favorable,
opportune, promising **10.** auspicious,
benevolent, prosperous
12. advantageous, well-disposed
proponent... **8.** advocate **10.** propounder
proportion... **4.** part, rate **5.** quota, ratio,
share **6.** adjust, extent **7.** analogy,
compare, euphony, prorate **8.** equalize,
symmetry **9.** apportion
proportional... **4.** rate **8.** relative
10. comparable, respective
11. dimensional
proportionate... **5.** equal **8.** adequate,
relative **9.** analogous **10.** respective
11. comparative **13.** corresponding
proposal... **3.** bid **4.** plan **5.** offer
6. feeler, motion **8.** marriage **9.** intention
10. nomination, suggestion
11. proposition, supposition
propose... **5.** image, offer, state,
toast **6.** intend, submit **7.** purpose
8. nominate, propound **9.** postulate
proposed (pert to)...
for consideration.. **9.** suggested
for debate.. **6.** mooted
international language.. **2.** Ro **3.** Ido
9. Esperanto
proposition... **4.** plan **5.** axiom, lemma
6. porism, thesis **7.** project **8.** empirema,
proposal **9.** corollary **11.** supposition,
undertaking
proposition, proof of... **18.** reductio
ad absurdum
propound... **6.** submit **7.** propose **8.** set
forth **9.** postulate
proprietary... **5.** owner, title **8.** interest,
medicine (secret) **9.** ownership
10. proprietor **12.** landed estate

propriety... **7.** decency, decorum,
fitness **8.** standard **9.** ownership
10. convention, expedience, properness
11. correctness, suitability
12. tastefulness **13.** possessorship
propugnaculum... **7.** bulwark, defense
8. fortress
prorogue... **5.** defer **6.** extend **7.** adjourn,
prolong **8.** postpone, protract
prosaic... **4.** drab, dull, flat **5.** plain,
prosy **6.** prolix, stupid **7.** humdrum,
insipid, tedious **8.** ordinary, tiresome
10. unexciting **11.** commonplace
12. matter-of-fact **13.** unimaginative
proscribe... **3.** ban **6.** forbid, outlaw
7. condemn (to death) **8.** prohibit,
restrain **9.** interdict, ostracize
proscription... **5.** exile **8.** outlawry
11. prohibition **12.** interdiction
prosecute... **3.** sue **4.** urge **5.** chase
6. intend (law), pursue **7.** carry on,
enforce, execute
prosecutor... **6.** lawyer **7.** accuser,
relator **8.** attorney
proselyte... **3.** ger (to Judaism)
7. convert
proseuche, proseucha... **7.** oratory
9. synagogue **13.** place of prayer
prosody... **13.** versification
prospect... **4.** view **5.** buyer, scene, vista
6. survey **7.** explore, foresee, outlook
8. customer **9.** applicant, candidate,
foresight, intention **10.** contestant
11. probability **12.** anticipation
prosper... **4.** fare **5.** cheve, speed
6. thrive **7.** succeed **8.** flourish
prosperity... **3.** hap, ups **4.** boom, weal
6. thrift **7.** success, welfare **9.** well-being
11. good fortune
Prospero (pert to)...
character.. **9.** Ferdinand
daughter.. **7.** Miranda
servant.. **5.** Ariel
slave.. **7.** Caliban
The Tempest.. **11.** Duke of Milan
prosperous... **4.** weal **5.** lucky, palmy,
sonsy (sonsie) **7.** wealthy **8.** thriving
9. favorable, fortunate **10.** auspicious,
successful **11.** flourishing
prostitute... **4.** drab **5.** venal **6.** harlot
7. corrupt **8.** infamous **12.** street walker
prostrate... **4.** flat, raze **5.** abase, prone
6. fallen, grieve, supine **7.** exhaust
8. helpless, supinate **9.** flattened,
recumbent **10.** obsequious, submissive
prosy... **3.** dry **4.** dull **6.** jejune
7. prosaic, tedious **11.** commonplace
13. plain-speaking
protagonist... **4.** hero, lead (theater)
5. actor **6.** leader **8.** advocate,
champion, defender **9.** contender,
principal, spokesman **11.** participant
Protagoras (Gr)... **7.** Sophist, teacher
11. philosopher
protasis... **5.** maxim **9.** drama part
11. proposition **12.** introduction
protect... **3.** arm **4.** save **5.** guard
6. defend, insure, police, screen, sheath,
shield **7.** cherish, shelter **8.** enshield,
preserve **9.** safeguard
protected... **5.** armed **6.** shaded

7. aproned, guarded 8. shielded
12. invulnerable

protection . . . 3. bib, lee 4. coat, fort,
moat 5. aegis (egis), apron, armor,
guard, shade, shell, smock 6. glacis,
refuge, safety 7. defense, parapet,
shelter 8. havelock, passport, security
11. safekeeping 12. preservation

protector . . . 6. patron, regent
8. defender, guardian 10. safekeeper

protector of vineyards (Gr) . . . 7. Priapus

protégé . . . 4. ward 6. charge 9. dependent

Proteida . . . 7. Proteus 10. amphibians
11. salamanders

protein . . . 6. casein 7. albumin, mucedin,
peptone 8. globulin, lecithin, nutrient
9. protamine 11. chlorophyll

protein (pert to) . . .
  blood . . 6. fibrin 8. globulin
  castor oil bean . . 5. ricin (poison)
  egg . . 7. albumin
  milk . . 6. casein
  muscles . . 8. creatine
  seeds . . 7. edestin 8. aleurone, prolamin

Proteles . . . 8. aardwolf

protest . . . 4. aver, beef, deny 6. assert
7. declare 9. objection, stipulate
10. asseverate 11. expostulate
13. expostulation

protestation . . . 6. avowal (public)
7. protest 11. affirmation, obtestation
12. asseveration, supplication

Proteus (pert to) . . .
  biology . . 3. olm 6. amoeba 8. bacteria
  10. salamander
  Gr Myth . . 6. sea god
  Shakespeare . . 17. Gentleman of Verona

protocol . . . 5. rules (official) 7. compact
8. schedule 9. agreement, etiquette
10. memorandum (diplomatic)
12. original copy

protograph . . . 9. holograph
12. illustration (of species)

protoplasm . . . 5. spore 7. nucleus
9. archetype, cytoplasm 10. primordium
11. basis of life

protoplasmic (pert to) . . .
  body . . 8. ectosark 9. ectoplasm,
  endoplasm
  cell . . 6. amoeba (ameba)
  cell contents . . 9. metaplasm
  substance . . 3. gel

protozoan . . . 6. amoeba (ameba),
Lobosa, phylum 11. unicellular

protract . . . 4. spin 5. defer, delay
6. extend 7. prolong, stretch 8. continue,
elongate, lengthen, postpone, protrude
9. expatiate

protrude . . . 3. jut 5. bulge 6. exsert
7. project 9. thrust out

protuberance . . . 3. jag, nub, wen 4. boss,
bump, cere, hump, knob, knot, lobe,
lump, node, snag, wart 5. bulge,
caput, inion, knurl, torus 8. eminence,
swelling 9. extrusion 10. projection

proud . . . 4. vain 5. grand, lofty, noble
6. elated, lordly 7. haughty, pleased,
stately, valiant 8. arrogant, boastful,
imposing, splendid 9. conceited,
gratified 10. impressive
11. independent, magisterial,

magnificent 12. presumptuous,
supercilious

prove . . . 3. try 4. test 5. check, nurse
6. evince, try out, verify 7. confirm,
justify, probate 8. identify, manifest
9. ascertain, establish 11. corroborate,
demonstrate

prove false . . . 6. refute

Provencal dialect . . . 9. langue d'oc

provender . . . 3. hay 4. food 5. grain
6. fodder 8. ensilage

proverb . . . 3. saw 5. adage, axiom
6. byword, enigma, saying 8. aphorism,
link verb, paroemia

proverbial . . . 10. aphoristic
11. sententious 12. epigrammatic

provide . . . 4. give 5. cater, endow, endue,
equip, stock, treat, yield 6. afford,
ration, supply 7. care for, finance
9. make ready 10. contribute

provided . . . 2. if, so 5. boden 6. sobeit
8. afforded, equipped, prepared,
supplied 11. on condition
13. conditionally

Providence founder . . . 13. Roger
Williams (1636)

provident . . . 4. wise 6. frugal, saving
7. prudent, thrifty 9. judicious
10. economical 11. precautious,
preparatory

providential . . . 5. lucky 7. prudent
9. opportune, provident 10. miraculous
11. foresighted

province . . . 4. area, beat, nome 5. arena,
range, shire, tract 6. colony, domain,
empire, eparch, region, sphere 7. circuit,
diocese, kingdom 8. district 9. territory
10. palatinate (royal) 12. jurisdiction

provincial . . . 4. rude 5. crude, local,
rural 6. narrow 7. insular, limited
8. suburban 10. restricted, uncultured
11. countrified 12. narrow-minded
15. unsophisticated

provincialism (diction) . . . 6. patois
10. patavinity

provision . . . 4. fare, food 5. board, stock,
store 6. vivres 7. proviso 9. condition
11. preparation

provisional . . . 9. makeshift, temporary,
tentative 10. promissory, substitute
11. conditional, preparatory
12. experimental 14. circumstantial

provision seller (Mil) . . . 6. sutler

proviso . . . 5. salvo 6. clause

provocative . . . 9. desirable, provoking
10. appetizing, stirring up, suggestive
11. interesting

provoke . . . 3. ire, vex 4. bate, goad,
move, rile, spur, stir 5. anger, annoy,
start 6. arouse, incite, induce, invite,
invoke, nettle, offend, stir up, summon
7. incense 8. irritate 9. challenge
10. antagonize, exasperate

provoking . . . 8. annoying, exciting
10. suggestive 11. interesting
12. antagonizing

provoking laughter . . . 7. risible

prow . . . 3. bow 4. beak, duty, good, proa,
stem 5. brave, honor, prore 6. steven
7. courage, gallant, gun deck

prowess . . . 5. valor 9. gallantry

proximal... **9.** immediate (opp of distal)
proximate... **4.** next **6.** direct **7.** closest,
  nearest **9.** immediate **10.** succeeding
proximity... **8.** nearness, nighness,
  relation, vicinity **9.** adjacence, closeness
  11. propinquity
proxy... **5.** agent, power **6.** agency,
  ballot, deputy **7.** proctor **9.** authority
  10. procurator, substitute
prudence... **6.** virtue, wisdom **7.** caution,
  economy **8.** sagacity **9.** foresight
  11. calculation, forethought
  13. judiciousness **14.** circumspection
prudent... **4.** wary, wise **5.** canny
  6. frugal **8.** cautious, discreet
  9. judicious, penny-wise, provident
  10. economical **11.** circumspect,
  considerate
prudish... **4.** prim **8.** priggish
prune... **3.** cut, lop **4.** clip, food, frog,
  plum, trim, weed **5.** dress, plume,
  preen, purge, shape **6.** anoint **7.** cut
  down, tonsure **9.** simpleton
prunelike fruit... **9.** myrobalan
pruning knife... **8.** serpette
prurient... **7.** itching, longing, lustful
  10. lascivious
Prussia...
  bay.. **4.** Kiel **6.** Danzig **10.** Pomeranian
  cathedral city.. **5.** Essen **7.** Cologne
    10. Düsseldorf
  city.. **6.** Aachen
  color.. **4.** blue **12.** gold pheasant
  Knight.. **8.** Noachite
  lagoon.. **4.** haff **12.** Frisches Haff
  lancer.. **5.** Uhlan
  land aristocracy.. **6.** Junker
  legislature.. **7.** Landtag
  mountain.. **4.** Harz
  resort.. **3.** Ems
  river.. **3.** Ems **4.** Elbe, Oder, Saar
  seaport.. **4.** Kiel **5.** Emden **7.** Stettin
  State.. **6.** German
pry... **4.** nose, peek **5.** lever, mouse,
  snoop **6.** meddle, search
prying... **7.** curious, peeking, peeping,
  peering **8.** snooping **9.** searching
  10. meddlesome **11.** inquisitive
psalm (pert to)...
  book.. **7.** Psalter
  Fiftieth, Vulgate.. **8.** Miserere
  Mass opening.. **7.** introit
  Ninety-fourth, Vulgate.. **6.** Venite
Psalms (Old Test)... **7.** Psalter
psalterium... **4.** lyra **6.** omasum
  7. stomach **9.** manyplies
psammite... **4.** rock **9.** sandstone
psephology... **7.** pebbles (study of)
psephomancy... **19.** divination by
  pebbles
pseudatoll... **9.** coral reef
pseudo... **4.** sham **5.** bogus, false
  6. untrue **7.** feigned **8.** spurious
  9. deceptive, imitation, pretender
pseudologist... **4.** liar (humorous)
pseudology... **5.** lying **9.** falsehood
pseudonym... **5.** alias **6.** anonym **7.** pen
  name **10.** nom de plume
pseudonym (famed)...
  C L Dodgson.. **12.** Lewis Carroll
  Mary Ann Evans.. **11.** George Eliot

Samuel Clemens.. **9.** Mark Twain
W S Porter.. **6.** O Henry
psychagogic... **9.** inspiring **10.** attractive,
  persuasive
psyche... **4.** mind, self, soul **6.** spirit
psychedelic psychologist... **5.** Leary
psychic... **6.** mental **9.** spiritual
  10. Gnosticism **11.** incorporeal
  12. spiritualist, supernatural
  13. psychological
psychic (pert to)...
  emanation.. **4.** aura
  devotion.. **6.** autism
  monism.. **10.** one reality
psychotic... **3.** mad **6.** insane **8.** neurotic
  12. psychopathic
Ptah (pert to)...
  Egypt Relig.. **8.** chief god (of Memphis)
  father of.. **3.** men **4.** gods
  representation.. **5.** mummy
  symbolic of.. **4.** life **8.** strength
ptarmigan... **4.** rype **6.** grouse
pterodactyl... **7.** reptile (extinct)
  9. pterosaur **11.** ornithosaur
pterography (description of)...
  8. feathers
pteroid... **8.** fernlike, winglike
pteropod... **6.** Clione (Arctic) **7.** mollusk
ptilosis... **7.** plumage **9.** madarosis
  10. loss of hair **15.** loss of eyelashes
ptisan... **3.** tea **5.** drink **6.** coddle
  9. decoction
Ptolemy (pert to)...
  author of.. **8.** Almagest
  birthplace.. **5.** Egypt (130 AD)
  famed as.. **10.** astronomer, geographer
public... **3.** inn **4.** open **5.** state **6.** people,
  vulgar **8.** communal **9.** clientele,
  community
public (pert to)...
  assembly.. **4.** Diet
  conveyance.. **3.** bus, cab, car **4.** taxi,
    tram **5.** train **10.** jinrikisha (jinricksha)
  display.. **10.** exhibition **13.** exhibitionism
  edict.. **3.** ban **12.** proclamation
  entertainment.. **7.** ridotto
  hangman (Eng).. **9.** Jack Ketch
  lands.. **4.** ager (Hist) **6.** domain
  official.. **6.** notary
  position.. **8.** official
  storehouse.. **5.** étape
  walk.. **4.** mall **7.** alameda **9.** esplanade,
    promenade
publication... **4.** book **8.** pamphlet,
  printing **12.** notification, proclamation,
  promulgation
publication (pert to)...
  article.. **7.** feature
  condensed.. **7.** tabloid
  make-up.. **6.** format
  prelim.. **9.** prodromus
publicist... **5.** solon **6.** Gallup, lawyer,
  writer **10.** journalist, publicizer
  11. commentator
publish... **4.** edit, vent **5.** issue, print
  6. blazon, delate **7.** divulge **8.** proclaim
  10. promulgate **11.** disseminate
publish (pert to)...
  abroad.. **8.** promulge
  after death.. **10.** posthumous
  banns.. **7.** betroth **8.** marriage

far and wide.. **6.** blazon
without authority.. **6.** pirate
10. plagiarize
publisher's description (book)...
5. blurb **13.** advertisement
publisher's inscription (book)... **5.** facts
8. colophon
Puccini heroine... **4.** Mimi
pucker... **4.** fold **5.** bulge, purse **6.** crease
7. anxiety, fluster, wrinkle **8.** contract
puckered... **7.** bullate **8.** wrinkled
10. contracted
puckish... **6.** impish **8.** Pucklike
10. mysterious **11.** mischievous
pud... **3.** paw **4.** hand **8.** forefoot
pudding... **4.** duff, mush, plum, sago
6. junket **7.** custard, dessert, tapioca
8. roly-poly, softness, stuffing (game)
9. Yorkshire
puddle... **3.** mud **4.** mess, pond, pool
5. plash, swamp **6.** muddle **7.** plashet,
pollute
puddle duck... **7.** mallard
puddock... **4.** kite, toad **7.** buzzard
9. enclosure (paddock)
pueblo... **4.** town **7.** village
Pueblo (pert to)...
ceremonial chamber.. **4.** kiva
Indian (American).. **4.** Hopi, Piro, Tano,
Zuni **5.** Acoma **7.** Keresan **12.** cliff
dweller
water jar.. **4.** olla
puerile... **4.** weak **5.** young **7.** babyish,
trivial **8.** childish, juvenile, youthful
12. simple-minded
Puerto Rican (pert to)...
bark, beverage.. **4.** mabi
dove.. **4.** rola
fish.. **4.** sama, sisi **8.** porkfish
Puerto Rico... see also *Puerto Rican*
capital.. **7.** San Juan
city.. **5.** Ponce **7.** Arecibo
discoverer.. **8.** Columbus
first settlement.. **7.** Caparra
government.. **12.** Commonwealth
Indian name.. **9.** Borinquen
island (off shore).. **4.** Mona **7.** Culebra
island group.. **15.** Greater Antilles
politically.. **12.** Commonwealth
program (Polit).. **18.** Operation Bootstrap
sea.. **9.** Caribbean
puff... **4.** blow, blub, chug, flam, pant,
pegh (Scot), pouf, waff **5.** elate **7.** efflate
puffbird... **6.** barbet **8.** barbacou
pug... **3.** dog, elf **4.** moth, puck, snub
5. chaff, dwarf **6.** harlot, refuse (grain),
sprite **8.** bargeman, mistress, pugilist
9. footprint, hobgoblin
pugging... **8.** grasping, thieving
pugilistic... **6.** fistic **10.** pugnacious
pugnacious... **9.** combative
11. belligerent, quarrelsome
pugnacious man... **12.** fighting cock
pug-nosed... **5.** camus (camuse)
puisne... **4.** puny **5.** judge, later,
petty **6.** feeble, junior **9.** associate,
unskilled **10.** law student, subsequent
11. subordinate
puissance... **3.** force, might, power
8. strength **9.** authority
puissant... **6.** mighty, potent **7.** mastery

8. forcible, powerful **13.** authoritative
pulchritude... **5.** grace **6.** beauty
10. comeliness, loveliness
pule... **4.** peep **5.** cheep, whine **7.** ululate,
whimper
pulicat... **8.** bandanna (bandana)
puling... **6.** sickly **7.** babyish, howling,
whining **8.** childish, delicate
Pulitzer prizes... **6.** awards
10. journalism, literature
pull... **2.** pu **3.** lug, tow, tug **4.** drag,
draw, haul, yank **5.** bouse, drink,
tweak **6.** effort, strain **7.** attract, extract
9. influence **10.** attraction
pull (pert to)...
apart.. **4.** rend, tear **7.** destroy
8. demolish, enfeeble, separate
back.. **5.** demur **6.** recoil **7.** retract
8. withdraw
down.. **4.** fell, raze **9.** dismantle
off.. **3.** pug **6.** avulse, commit **8.** carry
out **10.** accomplish
one's leg.. **4.** hoax, joke **7.** deceive,
flatter **8.** hoodwink **9.** make fun of
out.. **5.** leave **6.** secede **7.** extract
9. eradicate
up.. **4.** stop **5.** elate **6.** aviate **7.** arraign,
extract
pullet... **4.** fowl **5.** child **7.** bivalve
8. poullard
pulley (pert to)...
groove.. **5.** gorge
grooved.. **5.** fusee (fuzee)
part.. **4.** arse
wheel.. **6.** sheave (grooved)
pulp... **3.** pap **4.** marc, mash, mass
5. chyme **8.** magazine **10.** fleshy part
pulpit... **4.** ambo, bema, dais, desk
5. stage **6.** clergy **7.** rostrum **8.** platform,
scaffold
pulpy... **5.** mushy **7.** squashy
pulpy (pert to)...
dregs.. **5.** magma
fruit.. **3.** uva **4.** pome **6.** sidder (siddow)
state.. **4.** mash, soft **6.** fleshy
pulsate... **4.** beat, drum **5.** throb
7. vibrate
pulsation... **5.** ictus **6.** moving, rhythm
7. impulse, systole **8.** acrotism (failure),
vitality **9.** throbbing, vibrating
pulsatory... **8.** rhythmic, systolic
9. throbbing
pulse... **3.** dal (split) **5.** seeds (edible),
throb **6.** rhythm **7.** beating **8.** resonate
9. pulsation, throbbing
pulse family... **3.** pea **8.** Fabaceae
pulverize... **4.** bray, mull **5.** crush,
grind **6.** abrade, powder **7.** atomize
8. levigate **9.** triturate **12.** disintegrate
pulverulent... **5.** dusty **7.** crumbly
8. powdered
puma... **6.** cougar **7.** Quechua (Kochua)
pummel... **4.** beat, maul **5.** thump
6. batter, buffet, hammer, pommel,
strike
pump... **3.** gin, ram **4.** draw, emit, quiz
5. eject **6.** elicit, propel **7.** extract
10. pulsometer **11.** interrogate
pumpernickel... **5.** bread (Westphalian)
pump handle... **5.** sweep, swipe
pumpkin (pert to)...

head.. **4.** dolt **7.** Puritan **9.** blockhead, Roundhead
seed.. **7.** sunfish **8.** sailboat
yam.. **11.** sweet potato
pun... **4.** yoke **8.** paragram **9.** assonance, equivoque (equivoke), witticism **11.** paronomasia
punch... **3.** die **4.** blow, poke, prod, tool **5.** douse, drink, negus, paste **6.** liquor, pierce **7.** mattoir (etcher's) **8.** beverage, puncture **9.** perforate **11.** punch cattle
Punch and Judy dog... **4.** Toby
Punch Bowl... **6.** crater **9.** graveyard (Honolulu), hot spring (Yellowstone)
puncheon... **3.** die **4.** cask **5.** punch, stamp **6.** dagger
puncher... **6.** cowboy **10.** cowpuncher, perforator
punching... **8.** piercing **9.** pertusion
punctilious... **4.** nice **5.** exact **6.** formal, strict **7.** correct, precise **8.** exacting **9.** observant **10.** meticulous, scrupulous
punctuation mark... **3.** dot **4.** dash, star **5.** brace, breve, colon, comma, tilde **6.** dagger, hyphen, period, tittle, umlaut **8.** brackets, ellipsis **9.** ampersand, semicolon **10.** apostrophe, circumflex **11.** exclamation **12.** question mark
pundit... **6.** nestor, savant **7.** Brahmin, scholar, teacher **10.** learned man
pung... **4.** sled **6.** sleigh
pungent... **4.** keen, racy, sour, tart **5.** acrid, acute, sharp, smart, snell **6.** biting, bitter **7.** caustic, odorous, painful, peppery, piquant **8.** piercing, poignant, stabbing **11.** stimulating
pungent herb... **6.** Asarum
punish... **4.** fine **5.** mulct, spank, wreak **6.** amerce **7.** chasten, correct **8.** chastise, penalize **9.** castigate **10.** discipline
punishment (pert to)...
Brehon law.. **4.** eric
by torture.. **9.** strappado
church.. **15.** excommunication
condign.. **11.** retributive
law.. **5.** peine
term.. **5.** penal **7.** penalty, revenge **8.** punitive
Turk, Chin.. **9.** bastinade
Welsh law (anc).. **3.** cro **7.** galanas
punitive... **5.** penal **10.** revengeful, vindictive **11.** castigatory
Punjab, India...
capital.. **6.** Lahore (West) **8.** Amritsar (East)
language.. **7.** Panjabi
name meaning.. **10.** Five Rivers
soldier.. **4.** Sikh
summer capital.. **5.** Simla
punk... **3.** bad **5.** child **6.** amadou **7.** lighter **8.** inferior **9.** touchwood
punto... **3.** hit **5.** joint (fencing) **6.** stitch (needle)
puny... **4.** weak **5.** frail, petty **6.** little, meager, puisne, sickly **8.** delicate **14.** inconsiderable
pupa... **5.** shell **9.** chrysalis
pupil... **3.** eye, son **4.** tyro **5.** élève, youth **7.** écolier, learner, scholar **8.** disciple, neophyte

puppet... **3.** guy **4.** doll **5.** image **6.** maumet **9.** miniature, nonentity **10.** figurehead, marionette
puppeteer, famed... **4.** Sarg
puppy... **3.** dog, fop **5.** shark, whelp
purblind... **10.** dim-sighted **11.** partly blind **12.** narrow-minded, undiscerning
purchasable... **5.** venal **8.** bribable, hireling **9.** mercenary **11.** corruptible
purchase... **3.** buy, win **4.** earn, hold **5.** bribe **6.** buying, obtain **7.** acquire, bribery, procure **8.** barratry, foothold, leverage
purchaser... **5.** buyer **6.** patron, vendee **8.** customer **9.** acquéreur **13.** adjudicataire
purdah (Ind)... **4.** veil **6.** screen **7.** curtain
pure... **4.** neat, real **5.** clean, fresh, godly, sheer, utter **6.** candid, chaste, simple, vestal **7.** genuine, perfect, refined, unmixed **8.** absolute, filtered, innocent **9.** downright, faultless, inviolate, stainless, undefiled, unsullied **11.** pure-blooded, uncorrupted, unqualified **13.** unadulterated
purga (Russ)... **8.** blizzard **9.** snowstorm
purgative... **5.** jalap **6.** physic **8.** absterge **9.** catharsis, cathartic, cleansing
purgatory... **4.** hell **5.** limbo **6.** erebus **7.** torment
purified... **10.** elutriated
purified wool fat... **7.** lanolin (lanoline)
purify... **5.** clean, purge **6.** filter, refine, spurge **7.** cleanse, epurate **8.** lustrate, renovate, sanctify **9.** elutriate
purifying... **7.** smectic **8.** depurant **9.** cathartic, cleansing **10.** distilling
Purim... **7.** holiday **8.** festival (Jew) **11.** Feast of Lots
puritan... **5.** prude **7.** ascetic **9.** precisian **10.** Separatist
puritan clergyman... **10.** Cartwright
puritanical... **6.** strict **7.** ascetic **11.** strait-laced **13.** hyperorthodox
purity... **8.** chastity **9.** innocence
purl... **4.** eddy **5.** frill **6.** murmur, ripple **7.** trickle
purloin... **5.** filch, steal, swipe **6.** finger **11.** appropriate
purple... **4.** bice, lake, plum, puce **5.** lilac, mauve, pansy, regal, showy **6.** damson, orchid, ornate, Tyrian, violet **7.** Cassius, magenta, mollusk, pigment **8.** amaranth, Burgundy, imperial, mulberry **9.** brilliant, cathedral **11.** sovereignty
purple (pert to)...
bottle.. **4.** moss
cactus.. **8.** Missouri
death adder.. **10.** black snake
emperor.. **9.** butterfly
Forbidden City.. **5.** Lhasa
granadilla.. **13.** passion flower
haw.. **7.** capulin (Mex) **8.** bluewood
Heart, Order of.. **5.** medal (Mil) (est by Washington, re-est. 1932)
laurel.. **12.** rhododendron
lily.. **8.** Turk's cap
martin.. **7.** swallow
navy.. **10.** marine blue
nightshade.. **9.** trompillo

purport... 4. feck, gist, mean 5. sense, tenor 6. allege, import, intent 7. meaning 9. substance

purpose... 3. aim, end 4. goal, idly, main, plan, sake 5. avail 6. design, intend, intent, motive 7. meaning, resolve 8. function 9. determine, discourse, intention, objective, predesign

purposive... 5. telic

purse... 3. bag, cly 5. pouch 6. pucker, wallet 7. wrinkle 8. crumenal (obs) 10. pocketbook 12. porte-monnaie

purser... 5. clerk (ship's) 6. bursar 7. boucher, cashier 9. paymaster

purse rat... 12. pocket gopher

pursue... 3. run 4. hunt, seek, tack 5. chase, court 6. follow 7. carry on, proceed 9. persecute 10. specialize

pursuit... 5. chase, quest, scent 9. objective 10. occupation

purvey... 5. cater 6. supply 7. foresee, provide

purveyor of untruth (Bib)... 7. Ananias

purview... 4. body (statute) 5. field (law), range, scope 7. compass 8. province

push... 2. go 4. bunt, butt, gang, ping, pole, prod, urge 5. crowd, elbow, impel, nudge, press, shove 6. attack, energy, propel, thrust 9. importune, offensive (Mil) 10. forge ahead, propulsion 12. press forward

pusillanimous... 4. base, weak 5. timid 6. craven 8. cowardly 12. fainthearted, mean-spirited

put... 3. set 4. butt, dupe, fool, sail 5. place, throw 6. impose, option, phrase, repose, rustic 7. deposit 8. invest in 9. attribute

put (pert to)...
an end to.. 5. quash (law)
away.. 4. kill 5. store 6. murder
back.. 6. demote 7. replace, restore
before.. 6. appose
down.. 6. humble 7. degrade, deposit, depress 8. suppress
forth.. 5. exert 7. propose 9. circulate
off.. 4. doff, haft, sail 5. defer, delay, evade 8. postpone
on alert.. 5. alarm 6. alarum
out.. 3. vex 4. oust 5. eject 9. ostracize 10. expatriate
over.. 4. bilk 5. cheat, trick 7. deceive

put in, into...
action.. 6. excite
holy place.. 8. enshrine
motion.. 6. arouse
opposition.. 3. pit
order.. 4. trim 5. mense 6. settle 7. arrange 8. organize 11. systematize
rapture.. 8. entrance
relation to.. 9. correlate 10. coordinate, co-ordinate
rhythm.. 5. meter
scabbard.. 7. sheathe

putrefaction... 3. rot 5. decay 13. decomposition 14. disintegration

puttee... 6. gaiter 7. legging

put to...
flight.. 4. rout
strain.. 3. tax
trouble.. 10. discommode

use.. 5. apply
wrong use.. 8. misapply

put up... 3. pay 4. ante, hang 5. build, offer 6. pledge 7. install 8. nominate 9. construct

put up with... 4. bear 5. stand 6. endure, permit 7. stomach 8. tolerate

puzzle... 3. cap 4. crux, pose 5. griph (griphus), poser, rebus 6. enigma, riddle 7. anagram, confuse, mystify, nonplus, paradox, perplex, problem 8. entangle 9. conundrum 10. complicate, disconcert

puzzle (pert to)...
monkey.. 5. piñon
picture.. 5. rebus
word.. 7. charade 9. crossword 10. anacrostic

puzzling... 6. knotty 10. perplexing 11. enigmatical, paradoxical

pygarg, pygargus... 5. addax 8. sea eagle 9. quadruped (Bib)

Pygmalion (pert to)...
color.. 5. brown
endowed with life.. 7. Galatea (statue)
king of.. 6. Cyprus
sister.. 4. Dido
talented as.. 8. sculptor

pygmy, pigmy... 3. elf 4. Akka, Doko, pixy 5. atomy, Batwa, dwarf, gnome, minim, short 6. Abongo, Achuas 7. manikin 9. dandiprat

pygmy (pert to)...
hog.. 7. Porcula
musk deer.. 10. chevrotain
owl.. 8. gnome owl
rattlesnake.. 10. massasauga
squirrel (smallest known).. 9. Sciuridae

pyic... 8. purulent, virulent

pyknic... 3. fat 5. round, stout

pylon... 4. post 5. tower 6. marker 7. gateway 14. monumental mass

pyosis... 4. pus 4. boil 11. suppuration

pyramid... 4. cone, heap, pile, tomb 5. tower 8. monument 9. speculate

pyramid (pert to)...
builder, largest.. 6. Cheops (khufu)
Egypt.. 9. The Sphinx 12. Great Pyramid, Tomb of Cheops
group.. 5. Gizeh 7. Menkare 8. Chephren 9. Mycerinus
kidney (Anat).. 7. Perrein 10. Malpighian
Mexico.. 7. Benares
site of Cheops.. 4. Giza (Gizeh)
texts.. 12. inscriptions 13. Book of the Dead
world wonder.. 12. Great Pyramid, Tomb of Cheops

pyramidal... 4. huge 7. angular, conical 8. enormous, imposing

pyre... 4. bier, heap, pile 9. cremation, death fire

Pyrenees (pert to)...
bandit.. 8. Miquelet
mountain chain.. 11. France-Spain
peak.. 9. Pic d'Aneto 11. Pic de Méthou
resort.. 3. Pau
State.. 7. Andorra (Fr)

pyriform... 10. pear-shaped

pyrology (study of)... 4. heat

pyromaniac... 7. firebug 8. arsonist

10. incendiary
pyrope . . . **3.** red **6.** garnet **7.** mineral
pyrophobia . . . **11.** dread of fire
pyrotechnics . . . **7.** oratory, science
   9. fireworks
pyrrhic . . . **4.** foot (Pros) **5.** dance
Pyrrhic victory . . . **11.** at great cost
pyrrho (comb form) . . . **3.** red **5.** tawny
Pyrrho (Gr) . . . **7.** teacher (Pyrrhonism)
pyrrhotist . . . **7.** redhead
Pyrrhulexia . . . **5.** finch **8.** grosbeak
Pythagorus (Gr) . . .
   birthplace . . **5.** Samos
   daughter . . **4.** Camo
   famed as . . **11.** philosopher
   friend . . **5.** Damon
   teacher of . . **8.** theorems **18.** influence
      of numbers
Pythian (pert to) . . .
   contests . . **6.** Delphi

Festival . . **11.** Panhellenic
patron . . **6.** Apollo
term . . **8.** ecstatic **9.** phrenetic
python . . . **3.** boa **8.** anaconda
Python (pert to) . . .
   home . . **11.** Mt Parnassus
   myth . . **14.** monster serpent
   slaver . . **6.** Apollo
   survivor of . . **10.** muddy earth (anc)
pythonic . . . **4.** huge **6.** Pythia
   (Delphi), python **8.** oracular
   9. monstrous
pythonism, art of . . . **8.** prophecy
   10. divination
pyx, pix . . . **3.** box **4.** test, veil **5.** chest
   6. coffer, vessel (Eccl) **8.** binnacle,
   ciborium **10.** tabernacle
pyxie . . . **5.** shrub **9.** evergreen
pyxis . . . **3.** box **4.** Argo (Astron), vase
   9. jewel case

Q

Q . . . **5.** queue **6.** letter (17th)
QED . . . **21.** Quod Erat Demonstrandum
Q-ship (Eng) . . . **11.** mystery ship
qua, quabird . . . **10.** night heron
quachil . . . **12.** pocket gopher
quack . . . **3.** cry (duck) **5.** faker **7.** empiric
   8. impostor **9.** charlatan, pretender
   10. medicaster, mountebank
quack medicine . . . **6.** patent **7.** nostrum
quad (pert to) . . .
   printing . . **5.** crown **7.** quadrat
   school . . **4.** yard **6.** campus
   10. quadrangle
   slang (Brit) . . **5.** horse
quadra . . . **6.** fillet, listel, plinth
quadragenarian . . . **12.** forty-year-old
   (person)
Quadragesima . . . **4.** Fast, Lent **6.** Sunday
   (1st in Lent) **7.** Holy Day **9.** Forty Days
quadrangle . . . **5.** plane (four-angles)
   6. square **7.** rhombus **8.** tetragon
quadrant . . . **4.** gill **6.** fourth **7.** measure,
   quarter **8.** farthing, six hours
   10. instrument, semicircle
quadrate . . . **4.** suit **5.** adapt, agree,
   ideal **6.** square **7.** conform, perfect,
   squared **8.** balanced **10.** correspond
   13. correspondent
quadriga . . . **3.** car **7.** chariot (4-horse)
   10. four horses
quadrumane . . . **3.** ape **6.** mammal
   7. gorilla, Primate (except Man)
   10. chimpanzee **13.** feetlike hands
quadruped . . . **3.** ass, cat, cow, dog
   4. bull, calf, colt, foal, lion, mule
   5. burro, horse, jenny, panda, tiger
   6. badger, donkey, mammal **7.** bullock
   10. four-footed
quaff . . . **5.** draft, drink **6.** tipple
quag . . . **5.** quake **6.** quiver **8.** quagmire
quagga . . . **5.** zebra **7.** wild ass
quaggy . . . **5.** boggy, fenny **6.** spongy
   7. queachy **8.** yielding

quagmire . . . **3.** bay, fen **4.** lair **5.** marsh,
   swamp **6.** morass **11.** predicament
quahog . . . **4.** clam
quail . . . **3.** cow **4.** bird **5.** colin,
   cower, quake, shake **6.** blench,
   curdle, flinch, shrink, tremor, Turnix
   7. massena, tremble **8.** bobwhite,
   Coturnix **9.** coagulate, courtesan, eddish
   hen
quail (pert to) . . .
   button . . **6.** Turnix
   call . . **4.** pipe
   color . . **9.** hair brown
   flock . . **4.** bevy
   French . . **6.** caille
   hawk . . **6.** falcon
   quailhead . . **11.** lark sparrow
   snipe . . **9.** dowitcher
quaint . . . **3.** odd **4.** wise **5.** proud
   6. expert, pretty, proper **7.** curious,
   prudent, refined, strange, uncouth
   8. fanciful, peculiar
quake . . . **5.** shake **6.** quiver, shiver,
   tremor **7.** shudder, tremble, vibrate
   10. earthquake
Quaker (pert to) . . .
   bird . . **9.** albatross (sooty)
   city . . **12.** Philadelphia
   colonizer . . **4.** Penn (Wm)
   color . . **4.** drab, gray **5.** acier
   poet . . **6.** Barton **8.** Whittier
   sect . . **16.** Society of Friends
   sect founder . . **9.** George Fox
   State . . **12.** Pennsylvania
   word . . **4.** thee
qualified . . . **3.** fit **4.** able **6.** fitted
   7. adapted, capable, enabled, limited
   8. eligible, entitled, equipped, modified,
   prepared, tempered **9.** competent
   10. restrained, restricted **11.** conditional
qualify . . . **3.** fit **4.** name **5.** abate, adapt,
   be fit, equip, limit, train **6.** enable,
   modify, soften, temper **7.** assuage,

prepare **8.** diminish, mitigate, modulate, quantify, regulate, restrain, restrict
quality . . . **5.** prime, trait, value **6.** nature, pathos, strain **7.** caliber, texture **8.** accident, capacity, inferior, nobility, property **9.** attribute, character, specialty **10.** difference, excellence **14.** characteristic
quality of heredity . . . **9.** lineality
qualm . . . **4.** pall **5.** demur, doubt, spasm **6.** nausea, regret **7.** scruple **9.** faintness, misgiving **11.** compunction **12.** apprehension
quandary . . . **3.** fix **6.** pickle, plight, strait **7.** dilemma **10.** perplexity **11.** predicament
quandy . . . **9.** squaw duck
quant . . . **11.** punting pole
quantity . . . **3.** ace, any, gob, lot, sea, sum **4.** bulk, dose, drop, mass, much, raff, raft, scad, size, some **5.** batch, scads, store **6.** amount, cupful, degree, extent, hatful, number, oceans **7.** handful
quantity (pert to) . . .
fixed . . **5.** quota **8.** constant
mathematics . . **4.** surd **5.** graph **6.** scalar, vector
minute . . **4.** atom, dram, iota, mill
standard . . **4.** unit **9.** allotment
time unit . . **4.** rate
quantum . . . **4.** body **5.** share **6.** amount, energy, theory **7.** atomics, portion **8.** quantity
quap . . . **5.** heave, throb **6.** quaver **9.** palpitate
Quapaw . . . **5.** Sioux **8.** Arkansas
quarantine . . . **7.** confine, isolate **8.** pratique (marine) **9.** forty days (law), isolation, segregate **11.** confinement
quarantine flag . . . **6.** yellow **7.** warning **10.** yellow jack
quarenden . . . **5.** apple (deep red)
quarentene . . . **4.** rood **7.** furlong
quark . . . **3.** caw **5.** croak, quawk
quarl, quarle . . . **4.** sour, tile **5.** brick **6.** cundle, medusa **9.** jellyfish
quarred . . . **6.** soured **7.** curdled (beer)
quarrel . . . **3.** row **4.** spat, tiff, tile **5.** arrow, brawl, broil, cavil, flite (flyte), gnarr, scene, scrap **6.** affray, bicker, chisel, dustup, hassle **7.** diamond, wrangle **8.** argument, squabble **9.** complaint **10.** accusation, Donnybrook, free-for-all **11.** altercation **12.** disagreement **16.** misunderstanding
quarrel (pert to) . . .
hereditary . . **4.** feud **8.** vendetta
noisy . . **6.** fracas, jangle, uproar
over . . **6.** bicker **7.** contend, dispute
petty . . **4.** miff, spat, tiff
quarrelsome . . . **8.** choleric, petulant **9.** irascible, irritable, litigious **10.** discordant, pugnacious **11.** belliferent, contentious **13.** argumentative
quarry . . . **4.** delf, game, heap, mine, prey **6.** victim **8.** entrails, excavate **12.** object hunted
quart . . . **5.** gills (eight) **6.** fourth **7.** measure **8.** schooner
quarter . . . **4.** coin, side **5.** house **6.** fourth,

region **7.** measure, two bits **8.** insignia, semester **9.** direction, dismember **10.** quadrature (Astron), quadrisect
quarter (pert to) . . .
acre . . **4.** rood
animal . . **5.** horse
astronomy . . **9.** quadrature
fathom . . **6.** fourth
military . . **8.** clemency (to enemy)
music . . **4.** note **8.** crotchet
nautical . . **4.** deck, lift **6.** galley
pint . . **4.** gill
sports . . **4.** back **11.** quarterback
quartered . . . **8.** billeted **12.** quartersawed (wood)
quarters (living) . . . **4.** camp, room **5.** abode **7.** housing, lodging, shelter **8.** barracks, diggings, lodgings, lodgment **9.** dormitory
Quartodeciman . . . **10.** paschalist
quartz . . . **4.** onyx, sard **5.** flint **6.** silica **7.** mineral
quartz (pert to) . . .
banded, spotted . . **4.** onyx **5.** agate **6.** jasper **8.** sardonyx
blue-red . . **10.** bloodstone, heliotrope
brown . . **5.** smoky **9.** cairngorm
brownish-red . . **7.** sinople
chalcedony . . **4.** sard **9.** carnelian **11.** chrysoprase
flint . . **9.** hornstone **10.** touchstone
glass . . **6.** silica
green . . **5.** prase (dull) **6.** plasma (bright) **11.** chrysoprase
hard . . **5.** flint
opaque . . **6.** jasper
purple . . **8.** amethyst
red . . **4.** sard **9.** carnelian
ruby-red . . **7.** rubasse
silica . . **5.** silex
transparent . . **11.** rock crystal
violet . . **8.** amethyst
yellow . . **5.** topaz (false) **7.** citrine
quash . . . **4.** cass, void **5.** abate, annul, crush, quell, shake **6.** hush up, subdue **7.** shatter **8.** suppress **9.** overthrow **10.** extinguish
quasi . . . **4.** as if **6.** pseudo **8.** as it were, as though **9.** seemingly
Quasimodo . . . **9.** Hunchback (Notre Dame), Low Sunday (first after Easter)
quatern . . . **8.** fourfold **10.** quadrangle **12.** four quarters (having)
quaver . . . **5.** shake, trill **6.** quiver **7.** tremble, tremolo, vibrate **11.** trepidation **13.** tremulousness
quawk . . . **3.** caw **5.** heron (night) **7.** screech **8.** quagmire
quay, key . . . **4.** pier **5.** levee, wharf **7.** landing
queachy . . . **5.** boggy, bushy, fenny **6.** marshy, swampy
quean . . . **4.** girl, jade, slut **5.** vixen, wench **6.** harlot
queasy . . . **4.** sick **8.** delicate, qualmish, ticklish, troubled **9.** hazardous, ill at ease, nauseated, squeamish, uncertain, unsettled
Quebec . . .
battle site . . **15.** Plains of Abraham
capital . . **6.** Quebec (province)

city . . **6.** Verdun **8.** Montreal **11.** Three Rivers
founder . . **9.** Champlain (1608)
river . . **10.** St Lawrence
vehicle . . **7.** calèche (2-wheeled)
quebrada . . . **3.** gap **5.** brook, gorge **7.** fissure
qued, quede . . . **3.** bad **4.** evil **8.** The Devil
queen . . . **3.** ant, bee, cat **7.** empress, goddess, monarch **8.** chessman, honeybee **9.** sovereign **10.** chess piece **11.** playing card
queen (pert to) . . .
bee . . **8.** honeybee
cactus . . **7.** Mexican **10.** ornamental
conch . . **5.** shell
fern . . **5.** royal
pigeon . . **7.** crowned
Queen (pert to) . . .
Bernice's Hair (Astron) . . **13.** Coma Berenices
City of the Lakes . . **7.** Buffalo
City of the West . . **10.** Cincinnati
Mab . . **11.** Fairie Queen (Rom/Juliet)
Victoria . . **14.** Widow of Windsor (nickname by Kipling)
Queen Anne's . . .
lace . . **6.** carrot (wild)
melon . . **6.** dudaim
War . . **17.** Spanish Succession
War treaty . . **14.** Peace of Utrecht
queen of . . .
chess . . **4.** fers
fairies . . **3.** Mab **7.** Titania **8.** Gloriana
gods . . **4.** Hera (Gr), Juno (Rom)
Hearts . . **9.** Elizabeth
heaven . . **10.** Virgin Mary
Isles (Brit) . . **6.** Albion
night . . **4.** moon
Scots . . **4.** Mary
Sheba . . **6.** Balkis (Koran)
Spades (solo) . . **5.** basta
the Adriatic . . **6.** Venice
the Antilles . . **4.** Cuba
the East . . **7.** Antioch (Syria), Batavia (Java), Zenobia
the tides . . **7.** the moon
the underworld . . **3.** Hel
queen's (pert to) . . .
arm . . **6.** musket
flower . . **9.** bloodwood
hub . . **7.** tobacco
July flower . . **8.** damewort
ware . . **9.** Wedgewood
Queensland (Austral) . . .
animal . . **8.** kangaroo **9.** koala bear (teddy bear)
bean . . **8.** snuffbox
capital . . **8.** Brisbane
fire tree . . **5.** tulip
fish . . **9.** trumpeter
hemp . . **4.** sida **6.** lucern **9.** jellyleaf **11.** paddy lucern
plum . . **8.** Burdekin
tree (timber) . . **3.** box **4.** pine **5.** beech, ebony **10.** sandalwood **12.** Dundathu pine
queer . . . **3.** odd, rum **4.** sham **5.** false, funny **6.** insane, thwart **7.** strange **8.** peculiar, singular, spurious

9. eccentric, fantastic, interfere **10.** disconcert, suspicious **11.** counterfeit **12.** questionable
queer fellow . . . **4.** coot, goop **6.** galoot, geezer **9.** character
queersome . . . **3.** odd **7.** strange **8.** abnormal
Queer Street . . . **9.** imaginary
queest . . . **8.** ringdove
queet . . . **4.** coot **5.** ankle
quell . . . **3.** end **4.** calm **5.** allay, crush, quash, quiet **6.** pacify, reduce, soothe, stifle, subdue **7.** destroy, repress **8.** suppress **9.** overpower **10.** extinguish
quench . . . **4.** cool, damp, sate **5.** allay, check, slake, still **6.** stifle, subdue **7.** assuage, gratify **8.** suppress **10.** discourage, extinguish **11.** clamp down on
quenelle . . . **8.** meatball
Quercus . . . **4.** oaks
queriman . . . **4.** fish **6.** mullet
quern . . . **4.** mill (grain)
quernal . . . **5.** crown (oak leaves)
querulous . . . **7.** fretful, peevish **9.** plaintive **11.** complaining **12.** faultfinding
query . . . **5.** doubt **6.** murmur **7.** inquire, inquiry, whining **8.** question
quest . . . **3.** bay (dog's) **4.** hunt, seek **6.** desire, pursue, search **7.** inquest, request **8.** seek alms **9.** adventure **12.** solicitation
question . . . **3.** ask **4.** quiz **5.** cavil, doubt, grill, poser, query, scout, topic **6.** riddle **7.** dispute, inquire, inquiry, problem **8.** erotesis **9.** catechize (catechise) **11.** interrogate, uncertainty **12.** interpellate (formally) **13.** interrogation
question, out of the . . . **6.** absurd **7.** refused **8.** hopeless, rejected **10.** impossible, prohibited **11.** unthinkable
questionable . . . **4.** moot **7.** dubious **8.** doubtful **9.** debatable, dishonest, uncertain **10.** disputable, improbable **12.** unbelievable **13.** problematical
questioning (prolonged) . . . **11.** inquisition
question mark . . . **7.** erotema, eroteme
quet . . . **3.** auk **5.** murre **9.** guillemot
quethe . . . **3.** say **4.** call, tell, will **5.** quoth, speak **6.** clamor **8.** bequeath **9.** testament
quetzal, quezal . . . **6.** trogon **14.** national emblem (Guatemala)
Quetzalcoatl . . . **10.** god of winds (Aztec)
queue . . . **3.** cue **6.** hair, line (waiting), tail **7.** pigtail **9.** lance rest
quey . . . **6.** heifer
quia-quia . . . **9.** cigarfish
quib, quibble . . . **3.** pun **4.** carp, quip **5.** argue, cavil, cheta, evade **7.** shuffle
Quiche, Indian . . . **5.** Mayan
quick . . . **3.** apt **4.** deft, fast, yare **5.** agile, alert, brisk, fiery, fleet, hasty, rapid, ready, smart, swift **6.** lively, nimble, presto, prompt, pronto, speedy, sudden **7.** animate **9.** dexterous, impatient, impulsive, sprightly, vital

part **10.** passionate **11.** expeditious, hot-tempered

quicken . . . **5.** hurry, rouse, speed **6.** excite, hasten, incite, revive, vivify **7.** animate, further, refresh, sharpen **8.** energize, expedite **9.** stimulate **10.** accelerate **11.** resuscitate **12.** reinvigorate

quickly . . . **4.** cito, fast, soon **5.** apace **6.** presto, pronto **7.** briefly, hastily, rapidly **8.** promptly, speedily, vigorous

quickness . . . **4.** nous (humor) **5.** haste **6.** acumen **7.** acidity, agility **8.** alacrity, celerity, dispatch, pungency, rapidity **9.** acuteness, briskness, fleetness, sharpness, smartness **10.** expedition, promptness **13.** impulsiveness

quicksand . . . **3.** bog **4.** syrt **6.** Syrtis

quickset . . . **5.** hedge **7.** thicket **8.** hawthorn

quicksilver . . . **5.** metal **7.** mercury

quid . . . **3.** cud, fid **6.** guinea **7.** essence, tobacco **9.** sovereign

quidam . . . **8.** somebody **10.** one unknown

quidnunc . . . **6.** gossip **7.** what now **11.** inquisitive

quid pro quo . . . **9.** tit for tat **10.** equivalent, substitute **11.** interchange

quiescent . . . **5.** quiet, still **6.** at rest, latent, silent, static **8.** sleeping **10.** motionless

quiet . . . **2.** sh **3.** pet **4.** calm, ease, hush, lull, mild **5.** peace, sober, still **6.** gentle, hushed, modest, placid, smooth, soothe **7.** halcyon, restful, silence **8.** peaceful, tranquil **9.** contented, peaceable, quiescent, reposeful, unruffled **10.** unmolested **11.** undisturbed

quietist . . . **6.** mystic (Quietism)

quietive . . . **8.** sedative

quietly . . . **6.** calmly, gently, simply **8.** modestly, silently **9.** patiently, peaceably, privately **10.** composedly **11.** noiselessly **16.** unostentatiously

quietude . . . **4.** rest **5.** peace **6.** repose **7.** silence **10.** quiescence **12.** tranquillity (tranquility)

quietus . . . **4.** mort, obit **5.** death **6.** defeat **7.** release **9.** acquittal, deathblow, discharge (of debt)

quiff . . . **4.** coif, puff **5.** whiff

quilkin . . . **4.** frog, toad

quill . . . **3.** cop, pen **5.** remex **6.** bobbin **7.** spindle

quilt . . . **3.** pad **4.** flog, gulp **5.** duvet **6.** caddow **7.** swallow **8.** coverlet **9.** patchwork **11.** comfortable, counterpane

quin . . . **7.** scallop

quincentenary . . . **11.** anniversary **13.** commemoration **16.** five hundred years

quindecemvir (Rom) . . . **10.** custodians (Sibylline Books), fifteen men

quink . . . **5.** brant, goose

quinoa . . . **6.** cereal **7.** pigweed

Quinquagesima Sunday . . . **10.** before Lent **12.** Shrove Sunday

quinque (comb form) . . . **4.** five

quinsy . . . **10.** sore throat **11.** tonsillitis

quint . . . **3.** tax (one 5th) **7.** E string **8.** interval, schooner (5-masted) **9.** organ stop

quintal . . . **13.** hundredweight

quintessence . . . **3.** col **5.** elite **6.** elixir **7.** essence, the best **10.** perfection

quip . . . **3.** mot **4.** gibe, jest **5.** sally, taunt **6.** oddity **7.** caprice, quibble **8.** gimcrack **9.** witticism **12.** equivocation

quires, twenty . . . **4.** ream **6.** sheets (20)

quirk . . . **4.** quip, turn **5.** clock, shift, twist **7.** caprice, evasion, quibble **8.** flourish **9.** deviation, mannerism, witticism **12.** eccentricity

quirt . . . **4.** whip **5.** romal

quis . . . **8.** woodcock

quisby . . . **5.** idler, queer **8.** bankrupt **10.** down and out

quit . . . **3.** rid **4.** free, stop **5.** cease, clear, leave, pay up, repay, yield **6.** depart, resign **7.** abandon, discard, forsake, release, relieve, requite **8.** abdicate, liberate, renounce **9.** surrender **10.** relinquish **11.** discontinue

quitclaim . . . **6.** acquit **7.** release **12.** convey a claim **13.** deed of release **14.** relinquishment

quite . . . **3.** all, yes **4.** very **5.** stark, truly **6.** really, wholly **7.** totally **8.** entirely, somewhat **10.** absolutely, completely, positively

quite so . . . **8.** that is so, very true, very well

quite some . . . **12.** considerable

quittance . . . **5.** repay **6.** return **7.** requite **8.** reprisal, requital **9.** atonement, departure, repayment **10.** recompense **11.** acquittance

quitter . . . **5.** piker **6.** coward, truant **7.** shirker, welsher

quiver . . . **4.** case **5.** quake, shake **6.** quaver, sheath, shiver, tremor **7.** flicker, tremble, tremolo, vibrate **11.** trepidation

quiver leaf . . . **5.** aspen

Quivira (pert to) . . . *famous for* . . **6.** wealth *sought by* . . **8.** Coronado (1541) *town site* . . **6.** Kansas

Quivira, Gran . . . **12.** mission ruins **16.** National Monument (N Mex)

qui vive . . . **5.** alert **7.** excited **9.** challenge **12.** who goes there

quixotic . . . **7.** utopian **9.** visionary **10.** Don Quixote (like) **11.** impractical

quiz . . . **4.** hoax, jest, joke, mock **5.** coach **6.** banter **8.** ridicule **11.** examination, inquisitive, interrogate, questioning

quizzical . . . **3.** odd **7.** amusing, teasing **9.** bantering, eccentric, inquiring, perplexed

quizzing . . . **6.** banter **11.** questioning

quizzing glass . . . **7.** monocle **8.** eyeglass

quod . . . **3.** jug **6.** prison **8.** imprison

quoddies . . . **7.** herring

quod erat demonstrandum . . . **3.** QED **24.** which was to be demonstrated

quodlibet . . . **6.** medley **8.** fantasia, subtlety **13.** what you please

quoit . . . **4.** disc **6.** discus

quoit pin . . . **3.** hob
quoits . . . **4.** game **8.** cromlech **10.** stone cover
quo modo . . . **5.** means **6.** manner, method
quondam . . . **6.** former **8.** formerly, sometime
quorum . . . **7.** council **8.** majority **10.** select body
quota . . . **4.** part **5.** share **6.** ration **10.** proportion
quotable . . . **7.** citable
quotation . . . **5.** chria, cital, motto, price, stock **7.** passage **8.** citation **10.** memorandum, repetition

quotation mark . . . **9.** guillemet
quote . . . **4.** cite, name **5.** price **6.** adduce, repeat **7.** extract **9.** quotation, reference
quoth . . . **4.** said **5.** spoke
quotha . . . **6.** indeed **8.** forsooth
quotidian . . . **5.** daily **8.** day by day, every day, ordinary **9.** recurring **11.** commonplace
quotient . . . **6.** number, result
quotity . . . **5.** group, quota **7.** integer **10.** collection
quotum . . . **5.** quota, ratio
quo vadis . . . **16.** whither goest thou
Quo Vadis tyrant . . . **4.** Nero

R

R . . . **3.** rho (Gr) **6.** letter (18th)
Ra, Egypt Relig (pert to) . . .
 atmosphere . . **3.** Shu
 god of . . **3.** sun
 morning sun . . **7.** Chepera, Khepera
 night sun . . **7.** Sokaris
 representation . . **3.** cat **4.** lion **5.** Bacis (bull) **6.** falcon **9.** solar disk
 rising sun . . **5.** Horus **9.** Marmachis
 setting sun . . **3.** Tem
 solar disk . . **4.** Aten
 son . . **6.** Khonsu
 son of . . **3.** Nut (the sky)
 wife . . **3.** Mut
raad . . . **15.** electric catfish
raad . . . **7.** council (So Afr) **9.** volksraad
raadzaal . . . **11.** council hall (So Afr)
rab . . . **5.** mixer (mortar) **6.** beater
Rab . . . **5.** title **6.** master, rabban **7.** teacher **8.** Gamaliel
rabato, rebato . . . **4.** ruff **6.** collar **9.** piccadill
rabbet . . . **4.** weld **5.** miter **6.** groove, recess **7.** channel **8.** dovetail
rabbi . . . **4.** lord **5.** rabat, title **6.** master **7.** teacher **9.** clergyman **11.** breastpiece
rabbi (pert to) . . .
 examiners . . **8.** sabaraim (saboraim)
 interpreters . . **7.** amoraim
 teachers . . **7.** tannaim
rabbit . . . **4.** cony (coney), hare, tyro **5.** bunny, lapin **6.** animal, novice, rodent **10.** cottontail **11.** Belgian hare
rabbit (pert to) . . .
 breeding ground . . **6.** warren **8.** rabbitry
 ear . . **7.** antenna **8.** toadflax
 female . . **3.** doe
 fever . . **9.** tularemia
 fiction . . **6.** Harvey
 fish . . **8.** chimaera **9.** globefish, porcupine
 foot . . **5.** charm **8.** talisman
 fur . . **4.** cony (coney) **5.** lapin
 genus . . **5.** Lepus
 male . . **4.** buck
 mouthed . . **10.** harelipped
 rat . . **9.** bandicoot
 S America . . **6.** tapeti

 shelter . . **5.** hutch
 stew . . **12.** hasenpfeffer
 tail . . **3.** fud **4.** scut
rabbitry . . . **5.** hutch **6.** warren
rabble . . . **3.** mob **4.** herd, raff, rout, skim, stir **5.** crowd **6.** ragtag, tumult **7.** bobtail **8.** canaille, riffraff **9.** confusion, rigmarole, the masses **12.** accumulation (chaotic)
rabble rouser . . . **6.** ragtag
Rabelais (Fr) . . . **6.** author **8.** satirist **9.** Gargantua (1st work)
rabid . . . **3.** mad **6.** raging **7.** frantic, furious, rampant, violent **8.** frenzied **9.** fanatical **10.** infuriated
rabies . . . **5.** lyssa **11.** hydrophobia
raccoon, ally of . . . **5.** coati, panda
race . . . **3.** cut, hie, run **4.** flow, lane, line, rush, slit, sort, stem **5.** breed, caste, flume, relay, speed **6.** course, family, nation, people, strain **7.** contest, regatta, running, scratch **10.** passageway **11.** competition, watercourse
race (pert to horses) . . .
 chariot . . **13.** Circus Maximus
 gait . . **4.** lope, pace, trot
 horse . . **4.** pony **5.** racer **6.** maiden, mantis, plater **8.** bangtail
 handicap . . **6.** impost
 open . . **10.** Donnybrook, free-for-all
racecourse, racetrack (pert to) . . .
 3. lap **4.** heat, oval, tout, turf **5.** track **6.** circus (anc), colors **7.** raceway, tipster **8.** dopester
Rachel (pert to) . . .
 daughter of . . **5.** Laban
 mother of . . **6.** Joseph **8.** Benjamin
 sister of . . **4.** Leah
 wife of . . **5.** Jacob
racing colors . . . **5.** silks
rack . . . **3.** gin **4.** gait, gear, pain, ruin **5.** agony, frame **6.** punish, strain, wrench **7.** agonize, support, torment, torture **9.** framework **10.** excruciate
rack (pert to) . . .
 barrel . . **3.** job
 comb . . **9.** toothcomb

corn . . **4.** crib
floating . . **5.** vapor
plate . . **5.** creel
skin of . . **6.** rabbit
racket . . . **3.** bat, din **5.** fraud, noise,
revel **6.** bustle, clamor, crosse, outcry,
scheme **8.** vocation **9.** commotion
15. illicit business
rackety . . . **5.** noisy **8.** clattery, exciting
9. turbulent **10.** boisterous
racy . . . **5.** brisk, fresh, naive, smart,
spicy **6.** lively, risqué **7.** piquant,
pungent, zestful **8.** eloquent, spirited,
stirring **11.** interesting **12.** exhilarating,
full-flavored
rad . . . **4.** unit **5.** eager, quick, ready
6. afraid, elated **11.** exhilarated
radar (pert to) . . .
beacon . . **4.** buoy **5.** racon **6.** ramark
navigation . . **5.** navar
range (Navig) . . **5.** loran **6.** shoran
sight . . **5.** scope **6.** radome, screen
7. display
signal . . **3.** pip **4.** beam, blip **5.** pulse
11. transceiver, transponder
sounding . . **5.** rawin **9.** ionosonde
television . . **7.** teleran
raddle . . . **3.** rod **4.** beat, twig **5.** cheat,
color, fence, hedge **6.** branch, hurdle,
ruddle, thrash **7.** wheedle
10. interweave
radeau . . . **4.** raft **5.** gloat
radial . . . **3.** ray **8.** quadrant **9.** diverging
radiance . . . **5.** beamy, glare, light, nitor,
sheen **6.** beauty, luster **7.** beaming,
glitter, glowing, lambent, shining
8. splendor **9.** brilliant, radiation
10. brilliancy, effulgence
12. cheerfulness
radiant . . . **5.** aglow, beamy, sheen
7. beaming, glowing, lambent, shining
8. glorious **9.** beautiful, diverging,
effulgent **11.** resplendent
radiate . . . **4.** beam, emit, shed **5.** gleam,
shine **7.** diffuse, diverge, emanate
9. irradiate **10.** illuminate
radiation . . . **5.** alpha (particle), light, polar
(point) **10.** divergence **12.** illumination
13. radiant energy
radiation unit . . . **3.** rad, rem **8.** roentgen
radical . . . **3.** red **4.** atom, left, root,
surd **5.** basic, radix, ultra, vital
7. capital, drastic, extreme **8.** cardinal,
reformer **9.** extremist **10.** foundation
11. fundamental
radicated . . . **6.** rooted **11.** established
radicle . . . **4.** root **5.** radix **6.** etymon
7. rootlet
radio (pert to) . . .
activity . . **7.** fallout **9.** radiation
antenna . . **6.** aerial
detector . . **5.** radar **11.** transceiver
frequency . . **5.** audio
interference . . **6.** static
operator . . **2.** CB **3.** ham (amateur)
11. dit-da-artist **12.** citizens' band
rays . . **5.** beams
receiver, interfering . . **7.** blooper
tube . . **4.** grid **5.** diode
radium (pert to) . . .
discoverer . . **5.** Curie (1898)

emanation . . **5.** niton, radon
paint . . **8.** luminous
source of . . **7.** uranite **9.** carnotite
radius . . . **4.** area, bone **5.** spoke **6.** circle,
extent **8.** diameter
radix . . . **4.** root **6.** etymon, source
7. radical, radicle
raff . . . **4.** heap, rake, scum **5.** sweep, trash
6. jumble, litter **7.** rubbish **8.** leavings,
riffraff
raffia . . . **4.** palm **5.** fiber **6.** jupati
raffish . . . **3.** low **6.** common, flashy,
frowsy **7.** unkempt **9.** worthless
12. disreputable
raffle . . . **6.** chance, rabble, tangle
7. confuse, crumple, lottery, perplex,
serrate **8.** entangle, plucking, riffraff
9. stripping **10.** plundering
raft . . . **3.** lot **4.** spar **5.** balsa, float **6.** rafter
7. to flock **10.** collection (large)
raft-breasted (Ornith) . . . **6.** ratite
raft duck . . . **5.** scoup **7.** redhead
8. bluebill
rag . . . **3.** fog **4.** mist, sail **5.** cloth,
scold, shred **6.** berate, catkin, lichen,
tatter **7.** ragtime, remnant **8.** farthing
9. hoarfrost **11.** syncopation
rag (pert to) . . .
bag . . **10.** depository
doll . . **3.** toy **6.** moppet, puppet
10. marionette
fish . . **10.** Icosteidae
rag picker . . **5.** tramp
weed . . **3.** Iva
wool . . **5.** mungo **6.** shoddy
ragamuffin . . . **8.** titmouse **9.** ragged
boy **14.** tatterdemalion
rage . . . **3.** fad **4.** fume, fury, gret, ramp,
rant, tear **5.** anger, chafe, craze,
furor (furore), storm, wrath **6.** fervor,
frenzy **7.** bluster, passion **8.** violence
9. vehemence **10.** excitement
ragged . . . **5.** harsh, rough **6.** jagged,
raguly (Her), scoury, shabby, uneven
7. shreddy **9.** defective, dissonant,
irregular **10.** straggling **11.** dilapidated
raging . . . **4.** grim **5.** rabid **7.** acharne
8. storming **9.** ferocious, turbulent
10. blustering, infuriated
11. overwrought
raglan . . . **8.** overcoat **11.** sleeve style
Ragnarok, Norse (pert to) . . .
leader . . **4.** Loki
meaning . . **16.** world destruction
repeopler of the world . . **3.** Lif
10. Lifthrasir
ragout . . . **4.** beef, stew **5.** civet, salmi
6. mutton **7.** goulash, haricot
rahdar . . . **14.** tollroad keeper
raid . . . **4.** tata **5.** foray, seize **6.** inroad
8. invasion **9.** incursion
rail . . . **3.** bar, jaw **4.** coot, jest, rant,
sora, weka **5.** cloak, crake, dress, scoff,
scold **6.** banter, revile, septum (altar)
7. courlan, garment, inveigh, limpkin,
ortolan **8.** reproach
railbird . . . **9.** spectator **12.** horse watcher
railing . . . **5.** fence, rails **7.** barrier, parapet
10. balustrade
raillery . . . **5.** chaff, sport **6.** banter
7. asteism (Rhet) **8.** badinage, ridicule

10. persiflage
railroad (pert to) . . .
flare . . **5.** fusee
signal . . **9.** semaphore
sleeper . . **3.** tie **7.** pullman
switch . . **4.** frog
torpedo . . **9.** detonator
worker . . **6.** dinger **8.** strapper **11.** gandy
dancer
Rail Splitter . . . **14.** Abraham Lincoln
raiment . . . **4.** garb **5.** amice, dress
7. apparel, clothes, vesture **8.** clothing,
garments
rain (pert to) . . .
cloud . . **6.** nimbus
coat . . **3.** mac **4.** mino **6.** poncho **7.** slicker
10. mackintosh
comb form . . **5.** hyeto, ombro **6.** pluvio
fine . . **4.** mist **6.** serein
fowl . . **6.** cuckoo **10.** woodpecker
11. channelbill
gauge . . **8.** udometer **10.** hyetometer
glass . . **9.** barometer
icy . . **4.** hail **5.** sleet
protection . . **9.** ombrifuge
short . . **6.** shower
storm . . **5.** spate **13.** precipitation
study . . **9.** hyetology, ombrology
sudden . . **5.** plash, spate **6.** deluge
7. torrent **8.** downpour
rainbow . . . **3.** arc **4.** arch, iris, omen
rainbow (pert to) . . .
bridge (Norse Myth) . . **7.** Bifrost (to
Asgarth)
chaser . . **9.** visionary **11.** doctrinaire
flower . . **4.** iris
goddess . . **4.** Iris
term . . **6.** iridal
tree . . **5.** saman **8.** genisaro
unit . . **4.** inch
worm . . **8.** nematode **9.** earthworm
rainy . . . **3.** wet **7.** showery
rais, reis (Muslim) . . . **5.** chief, title
7. captain (ship's)
Rais . . . **10.** Mongoloids
raise . . . **3.** end **4.** grow, levy, lift, rear,
stir **5.** boost, breed, erect, exalt,
heave, hoist, rouse **6.** awaken, excite,
gather, leaven, muster, remove, uplift
7. collect, elevate, enhance, lighten,
present, produce, provoke, recruit
8. heighten, increase **9.** construct,
cultivate, promotion, propagate
10. aggrandize
raise (pert to) . . .
a nap . . **5.** tease **6.** teasel
Cain . . **3.** Ned **4.** hell **5.** cut up **7.** be
noisy **10.** vociferate
the dead . . **13.** lift the anchor
vegetables . . **12.** olericulture
raised . . . **4.** bred, hove **6.** buoyed,
enlève, hefted, lifted, reared **7.** hoisted
8. elevated, leavened, produced,
promoted
raised (pert to) . . .
spirits . . **6.** elated
to 3rd power . . **5.** cubed
troops . . **6.** levied **7.** drafted
11. conscripted
type . . **7.** braille
uproar . . **6.** rioted

with a bar . . **7.** levered
raisin . . . **4.** pasa **5.** grape, lexia
raja, rajah . . . **4.** king, rana **5.** title **6.** prince
9. dignitary
raja's consort . . . **4.** rani (ranee)
8. princess
Rajmahal hemp . . . **5.** fiber **9.** jiti fiber
Rajput . . . **5.** caste **9.** Kshatriya
rake . . . **3.** rut **4.** comb, path, raff,
roué **5.** slope, teeth, track **6.** lecher
7. debauch, seducer **8.** enfilade,
Lothario **9.** cultivate, implement,
libertine
rakehell . . . **4.** free, rake **9.** debauched,
debauchee, dissolute **10.** dissipated,
licentious, profligate
rakh . . . **3.** hay **8.** hayfield **9.** grassland
raki, rakee . . . **7.** spirits (distilled)
rale . . . **6.** rattle **8.** rhonchus **11.** morbid
sound
rallentando . . . **9.** direction (Mus)
10. ritardando, slackening
Rallidae . . . **5.** birds, coots, rails, wekas
6. crakes **10.** gallinules
rally . . . **6.** banter **7.** recover, reunite
8. assemble, recovery, ridicule
10. assemblage, call to arms
rallying cry . . . **4.** call **6.** slogan **9.** battle
cry, bugle call
ralph . . . **5.** raven
ram . . . **3.** hit, pun, tup **4.** buck, butt,
tamp **5.** Aries, crash, sheep **6.** rancid,
wether **7.** collide
Rama . . . **11.** Ramachandra (7th of fame)
19. incarnation of Vishnu
ramada . . . **5.** arbor **7.** pergola
Ramadan (Muslim) . . . **7.** fasting **10.** ninth
month (for fasting)
ramage . . . **4.** wild **5.** rough **6.** branch
(tree), unruly **7.** untamed **8.** frenzied
ramage hawk . . . **8.** brancher
ramass . . . **6.** gather **7.** collect
ramberge . . . **6.** galley (swift)
ramble . . . **3.** gad **4.** roam, rove, walk
5. jaunt, prowl, range **6.** stroll, wander
7. deviate, digress, saunter **8.** straggle
rambling . . . **7.** devious **9.** desultory,
deviation, deviative, wandering
10. circuitous, discursive, distracted
14. discursiveness
rambunctious . . . **4.** wild **6.** unruly
10. rampageous **12.** obstreperous
14. uncontrollable
ramentum . . . **5.** palea (palet) **6.** scales
8. a shaving, particle (minute)
Rameses Dynasties (pert to) . . .
famed for . . **5.** ruins **7.** papyrus
kings . . **6.** twelve
site . . **5.** Egypt
ramex . . . **6.** hernia **10.** varicocele
ram-headed goat . . . **5.** Ammon
ramie . . . **4.** hemp, rhea **5.** plant (fiber)
7. garment **9.** Boehmeria **10.** China
grass
ramification . . . **3.** arm **5.** ramus **6.** branch
8. offshoot **9.** branching **10.** divergence
12. embranchment
rammack . . . **4.** gawk, romp **5.** scamp
rammel . . . **4.** hard **6.** coarse **7.** new milk,
raw milk **9.** brushwood **11.** undergrowth
Ramona (pert to) . . .

heroine.. **9.** half-breed (Ind)
novel by.. **7.** Jackson (Helen Hunt)
shrub.. **4.** mint
ramp... **3.** rob **4.** rage, romp, walk
   5. bound, climb, crawl, creep, storm
   6. dupery, unruly **7.** incline, rampage,
   swindle **8.** gradient, platform
   9. helicline, impetuous **10.** cuckoopint
rampant... **6.** fierce, unruly, vallum (anc)
   7. ramping **8.** abundant, reared up (Her)
   9. exuberant, prevalent, unchecked
   10. rampageous **12.** high-spirited,
   unrestrained **13.** perpendicular
rampart... **4.** wall **5.** agger, mound, redan
   6. escarp **7.** barrier, bulwark, defense,
   parapet, ravelin **8.** buttress **9.** earthwork
   10. embankment **13.** fortification
ram's horn (Heb)... **7.** shophar (shofar)
ran... **4.** fled, sped **6.** flowed **7.** coursed,
   managed, trotted **8.** operated
ran (pert to)...
   aground.. **8.** decamped, levanted,
   stranded
   away.. **4.** fled **6.** eloped **9.** absconded
   out.. **5.** spilt **7.** petered, spilled
rana (Ind)... **5.** title **6.** prince
Rana... **5.** frogs **10.** amphibians (tailless)
ranarium... **8.** frog pond
rance... **4.** prop **6.** marble **7.** support
ranch... **4.** casa, farm **6.** estate
   8. estancia, hacienda
ranchero... **6.** cowman **7.** vaquero
   8. herdsman **9.** cattleman
rancid... **4.** rank **5.** musty, stale **6.** reechy
   9. obnoxious, offensive **10.** unpleasant
rancor, rancour... **3.** ire **4.** gall **5.** spite
   6. enmity, hatred, malice, rankle **7.** ill
   will **9.** animosity **10.** resentment
rand... **4.** edge, rant **5.** ridge, storm
   6. border, margin
random... **5.** stray **6.** casual, chance
   7. aimless **8.** casually **9.** at liberty,
   haphazard, orderless **10.** accidental,
   fortuitous **11.** haphazardly
randy... **4.** wild **5.** revel, spree **6.** beggar,
   coarse, frolic, virago **7.** canvass
   8. carousal **9.** festivity **10.** disorderly
   11. ill-mannered **12.** unmanageable
rang (pert to)... see also *ring*
   loudly.. **7.** clanged
   mournfully.. **6.** tolled **7.** knelled
   slowly.. **6.** tolled
range... **3.** row **4.** ally, area, line, rank,
   roam, size **5.** align, gamut, orbit,
   scope **6.** limits, ramble, region, series,
   wander **7.** arrange, compass, earshot,
   habitat, pasture **8.** classify, mountain
   9. cookstove
range (pert to)...
   finder.. **9.** mekometer, telemeter
   10. trekometer
   man.. **5.** rider **6.** warden
   of hills.. **5.** ridge
   of knowledge.. **3.** ken
   of stables.. **4.** mews
rangle... **5.** stray **6.** wander **8.** entangle,
   straggle
rani, ranee (Hind)... **4.** wife **5.** queen
   7. empress **8.** princess
rani (Romany)... **4.** lady, wife
Ranier, Mt... **10.** Washington (State)

ranine... **5.** frogs **7.** Raninae **8.** mink
   frog
rank... **3.** bad, row **4.** file, foul, line, rate,
   size, tier **5.** caste, class, grade, gross,
   order, range **6.** degree, estate, rancid,
   status, wicked **7.** arrange, glaring,
   tainted **8.** absolute, abundant, classify,
   eminence, flagrant, indecent, infamous,
   nobility, palpable, position, prestige,
   unsavory **9.** downright, formation,
   luxuriant, plentiful **10.** malodorous
   11. distinction
rank (pert to)...
   and file.. **4.** army **8.** regulars
   10. commonalty **11.** third estate
   celestial.. **9.** hierarchy
   exalted.. **8.** eminence
   military (old).. **8.** banneret
   noble.. **10.** patriciate
   rider.. **8.** reckless **10.** highwayman
   social.. **5.** caste
rankle... **5.** chafe **6.** fester **7.** putrefy
   8. make sore **9.** suppurate **10.** be
   inflamed
rann... **5.** verse **6.** stanza, strain
ransack... **4.** rake, sack **5.** rifle **6.** search
   7. plunder, rummage
ransom... **4.** fine **6.** redeem, rescue
   7. expiate **8.** recovery
ranstead... **8.** toadflax (yellow)
   13. butter-and-eggs
rant... **4.** rage, rail, rave **5.** boast **6.** steven
   7. bluster, bombast, declaim **9.** gay
   frolic **10.** get excited
rantipole... **4.** wild **6.** rakish, unruly
   9. termagant
ranula... **4.** cyst
Ranunculaceae... **7.** anemone
   8. aconitum, clematis, crowfoot
   10. delphinium, ranunculus
rap... **3.** bop, hit **4.** bang, blow,
   gibe, grab, knap, tirl **5.** knock, steal
   6. rascal, snatch, trifle **8.** betrayal,
   sentence (prison) **9.** criticism, reprimand
   10. punishment **11.** skein of yarn
rapacious... **6.** greedy, rapine
   8. grasping, ravenous **9.** devouring,
   voracious **10.** avaricious, predacious
rapacity... **5.** greed, ravin (raven)
   6. rapine **8.** appetite **9.** predacity
rapid... **4.** fast **5.** fleet, quick, swift
   7. stretto (stretta)
rapidity... **5.** haste, speed **8.** celerity,
   velocity **9.** fleetness, quickness
rapidly... **5.** amain, apace **7.** quickly,
   swiftly **8.** snappily
rapids... **5.** rifts **6.** dalles
rapier... **5.** bilbo, sword **6.** verdun
   7. ricasso (part)
rapine... **7.** pillage, plunder **8.** spoiling
   10. ravishment, spoliation
rapport... **6.** accord **7.** empathy,
   harmony **8.** relation **9.** agreement
   11. co-operation (hypnotism)
rapt... **8.** absorbed, ecstatic
   10. enraptured, interested
   11. preoccupied, transported
rapture... **3.** joy **4.** love **5.** bliss
   6. trance **7.** delight, ecstasy **8.** rhapsody
   9. transport **10.** exultation
rapturous... **8.** ecstatic

rara avis . . . **6.** rarity **8.** rare bird
rare . . . **3.** odd, raw **4.** thin **6.** scarce,
   seldom, sparse **7.** notable, unusual
   8. rarefied, uncommon **10.** infrequent
   11. undercooked
rare (pert to) . . .
   bird . . **8.** rara avis
   earth . . **6.** cerium **7.** terbium, yttrium
   metallic element . . **7.** yttrium
   object . . **5.** curio **6.** oddity **7.** antique
Rare Ben, inscription . . . **15.** tomb of
   Ben Jonson (Westminster Abbey)
rarebit . . . **10.** cheese dish **11.** Welsh
   rabbit
rarefy . . . **4.** thin **6.** dilute, expand
   9. attenuate
rarely . . . **6.** finely, seldom **8.** not
   often, scarcely **9.** extremely, unusually
   11. beautifully **12.** infrequently
rarity . . . **6.** oddity **7.** fewness, tenuity
   8. scarcity, thinness **11.** infrequency
ras . . . **4.** cape **6.** prince **11.** short-napped
   13. Fascist leader
rasa . . . **3.** sap (tree) **5.** fluid, taste
   6. amrita, flavor **7.** essence **11.** living
   water
rascal . . . **3.** cad, imp **5.** knave, rogue,
   scamp **6.** varlet **9.** miscreant
rascally . . . **4.** mean **6.** impish **7.** knavish,
   roguish **8.** scampish **11.** mischievous
rase . . . **3.** cut, rub **4.** tear **5.** graze, level
   6. scrape **7.** scratch
rash . . . **3.** mad **4.** wild **5.** giddy, hasty,
   heady, hives, scamp **6.** unwary, wanton
   7. Icarian **8.** careless, eruption, heedless
   9. desperate, exanthema, impetuous
   10. headstrong, incautious, indiscreet
   11. temerarious, thoughtless
rasher . . . **5.** piece, slice **7.** portion **9.** thin
   slice
rashness . . . **6.** acrisy **7.** acrisia **8.** temerity
   9. hastiness
rasion . . . **6.** filing **7.** erasing, rasping,
   shaving **8.** scraping
Rasores . . . **4.** fowl **5.** birds **6.** quails
   7. turkeys **8.** Columbae, Gallinae
   9. pheasants **10.** partridges
rasp . . . **3.** rub **4.** file **5.** belch, chafe,
   erupt, grate **6.** abrade, offend, scrape
   8. irritate **9.** raspberry
raspberry . . . **3.** red **5.** apple, Rubus
   6. raspis **7.** plumbog **8.** blackcap
rasping . . . **5.** harsh **7.** chafing, grating,
   raucous **8.** grinding, scraping, very
   fast **9.** offensive **10.** irritating
raspings . . . **6.** refuse **7.** filings, remains
rasse . . . **5.** civet
rasure . . . **3.** cut **5.** shave **7.** erasure,
   polling, scratch, tonsure **8.** scraping
   12. obliteration
rat . . . **3.** rut **4.** scab, snob, wart **5.** track
   6. desert, ratton, rodent **7.** scratch,
   traitor **8.** deserter **9.** hairpiece,
   scoundrel
rat (pert to) . . .
   fish . . **8.** chimaera
   goose . . **11.** common brant
   hare . . **4.** pika
   kangaroo . . **7.** Potorus **9.** marsupial
   pineapple . . **7.** pinguin
   poison . . **8.** ratsbane

ratlike . . **4.** vole
rhyme . . **6.** jargon **13.** doggerel verse
ratafia . . . **7.** biscuit (almond), curacao,
   liqueur (Danzig)
ratchet . . . **4.** pawl **5.** click **6.** bobbin,
   detent
rate . . . **4.** fare, pace **5.** price, ratio, style,
   tempo, value **6.** assess, berate, charge,
   reckon, regard **7.** account, deserve,
   premium, reprove **8.** appraise, classify,
   estimate, evaluate, interest
rate (of exchange) . . . **4.** agio **5.** batta
rath (anc) . . . **4.** hill, home (walled)
rath, ratha . . . **3.** car **6.** temple (Seven
   Pagodas, Madras) **7.** chariot
Rathaus . . . **8.** town hall
rathe, rath . . . **4.** soon **5.** eager, quick,
   speed **7.** betimes, quickly **8.** speedily
rather . . . **3.** ere, yes **6.** before **7.** earlier,
   however, instead **9.** somewhat **10.** more
   truly, tolerably **10.** especially, preferably
   11. immediately **14.** on the other hand
ratification . . . **4.** amen **5.** logic
   8. sanction **9.** reasoning
   11. endorsement **12.** confirmation
ratify . . . **4.** amen, pass, seal **6.** enseal,
   verify **7.** approve, confirm, consent,
   endorse **8.** roborate, sanction
   9. authorize
ratio . . . **2.** pi **4.** rate, sine **5.** share
   6. cosine, ration **7.** portion
   10. proportion
ratiocination . . . **5.** logic **7.** thought
   9. reasoning
ration . . . **5.** share **6.** budget **8.** relation
   9. allotment, allowance, provision
   11. calculation
rational . . . **4.** sane, wise **5.** sober
   7. logical **8.** sensible **9.** reasoning
   10. reasonable **11.** philosophic
rationale . . . **6.** reason **11.** explanation
   12. the how and why
ratio scripta . . . **13.** written reason
ratite . . . (opp of carinate)**7.** Ratitae
   8. unkeeled **14.** flat breastbone
ratite bird . . . **3.** emu (emeu), moa
   7. ostrich **9.** cassowary
ratoon . . . **5.** shoot, stalk **6.** spring, sprout
rattan, ratan . . . **4.** cane, palm, sega,
   whip **6.** switch **7.** calamus
ratteen . . . **8.** mahogany
rattle . . . **3.** toy **4.** herb, rale, rick,
   tirl **5.** annoy, clack **6.** assail, prison
   (Nav), racket, uproar **7.** agitate,
   chatter, clapper, clatter, confuse,
   fluster, maracas, prattle **8.** nonsense
   9. chatterer, rapid talk **10.** disconcert,
   noisemaker
rattle (pert to) . . .
   bones . . **8.** clappers, snappers
   9. castanets
   headed . . **8.** confused **11.** empty-headed
   13. rattlebrained
   mouse . . **3.** bat
   nut . . **10.** chinquapin
   pate . . **3.** ass
   root . . **7.** bugbane
rattlesnake . . . **7.** rattler **8.** belltail,
   Crotalus, pit viper **9.** Sistrurus
rattlesnake (pert to) . . .
   bean . . **6.** cedron

bite . . **9.** meadow rue
fern . . **9.** chain fern, sporangia
flag (Maine) . . **13.** Don't Tread on Me (Hist)
herb . . **9.** baneberry
leaf . . **8.** plantain
pilot . . **10.** copperhead
plantain . . **6.** orchid
variety . . **3.** red **6.** banded, timber **7.** prairie **11.** diamondback
venom . . **8.** crotalus
rattletrap . . . **6.** gewgaw **7.** rickety **8.** claptrap, the mouth **10.** knickknack, ramshackle
ratton . . . **3.** rat
ratwa . . . **7.** muntjac
raucous . . . **3.** dry **4.** bray, loud **5.** harsh, noisy **6.** hoarse, raucid, rauque **8.** strident **11.** cacophonous
rauk, roke . . . **4.** poke, stir **5.** vapor **7.** scratch
raun . . . **3.** roe **4.** fish **5.** spawn
ravage . . . **4.** loot, ruin, sack **5.** havoc, spoil, waste **6.** damage, infest **7.** debauch, destroy, overrun, pillage, plunder **9.** devastate **10.** desolation **11.** despoilment, devastation, infestation
ravages of time . . . **13.** deterioration **14.** disintegration
rave . . . **4.** rage, rant **5.** crush, storm **7.** bluster, declaim, enthuse **8.** be insane, harangue
ravel . . . **4.** fray **6.** runner, slough, unwind **7.** involve, unravel, untwist, unweave **8.** entangle, separate **11.** disentangle, loose thread
ravelin . . . **7.** railing **8.** demilune, half-moon **13.** fortification
Ravel opus . . . **6.** Bolero
raven . . . **4.** bird, crow **6.** Corvus **8.** standard (vikings) **10.** raven-black **11.** Corvus corax
Raven (The) . . . **4.** poem (Edgar Allan Poe)
ravening . . . **3.** mad **5.** rabid **6.** greedy, prying **8.** desirous **9.** rapacious, turbulent
ravenous . . . **6.** greedy **8.** edacious **9.** rapacious, voracious **10.** gluttonous **11.** catawampous
ravine . . . **3.** gap **4.** dell, linn (lin), wadi (wady) **5.** chine, gorge, gulch, slade, strid **6.** arroyo, clough, gulley, nullah **8.** barranca
ravish . . . **3.** rob **4.** rape **5.** seize **7.** corrupt, debauch, delight, despoil, plunder, violate **8.** deflower, entrance **9.** enrapture, transport
raw . . . **4.** cold, sore **5.** bleak, crude, naked **6.** chilly, unripe, vulgar **7.** natural, not spun, untried **8.** immature, indecent, uncooked **9.** inclement, unskilled, wind-swept **10.** unprepared **11.** undeveloped, unprocessed **13.** inexperienced
rawboned . . . **4.** lank **5.** gaunt **7.** angular **8.** skeletal
rawbones . . . **5.** Death **8.** skeleton
raw-flesh-eating . . . **9.** omophagia
rawhide . . . **4.** skin (untanned), whip
rawhide whip . . . **5.** knout, quirt, thong

7. sjambok
raw sugar . . . **9.** cassonade
rax . . . **5.** reach **6.** become, strain **7.** stretch
ray . . . **4.** beam, dorn, soil, X-ray **5.** array, dress, gamma, order, skate (fish) **6.** defile, radius, stripe, vision **7.** besmear, raiment **8.** particle, radiance, stingray **11.** arrangement, irradiation
raya . . . **9.** broadbill
rayless . . . **4.** dark **5.** blind
rayon . . . **3.** ray **5.** fiber **6.** radius **14.** postal district (Switz)
raze, rase . . . **3.** cut **4.** fell, ruin **5.** erase, graze, level, shave **6.** efface, scrape **7.** destroy **8.** demolish **9.** dismantle, prostrate **10.** obliterate
razee . . . **3.** cut (Naut) **5.** prune **7.** abridge
razor (pert to) . . .
back . . **3.** hog **4.** boar **5.** ridge **10.** roustabout (circus)
bill . . **3.** auk **7.** skimmer
billed auk . . **4.** falk **5.** murre, noddy
clam . . **5.** Solen **11.** chopa blanca
grinder . . **10.** goatsucker
sharpen . . **4.** hone **5.** strop
stone . . **9.** whetstone **10.** novaculite
strap . . **5.** strop
type . . **6.** safety **7.** rattler
razz . . . **5.** chaff, tease **6.** banter, deride **8.** ridicule **9.** raspberry
razzle-dazzle . . . **5.** cinch (game), spree **6.** dazzle **7.** confuse **8.** bewilder **9.** commotion **10.** noisemaker
re . . . **4.** back (pref) **5.** about, again, anent, tone D (Mus) **8.** syllable (Mus) **10.** concerning
Re . . . **2.** Ra (Egypt) see also *Ra*
reach . . . **4.** come, gain, hawk, ryke, spar, spit **5.** equal, retch **6.** advene, arrive, attain, extend, length **7.** achieve, compass, earshot, expanse, possess, stretch **8.** distance, overtake **9.** influence **10.** understand
reach (pert to) . . .
across . . **4.** span
for applause . . **9.** captation
high point . . **9.** culminate
out . . **6.** extend **7.** stretch
under . . **7.** subtend
up . . **6.** aspire
reaction . . . **4.** kick **6.** change (Chem) **7.** tropism **8.** response **9.** influence **10.** opposition
reactionary . . . **4.** Tory **10.** malcontent **12.** conservative, recalcitrant
read . . . **3.** con **4.** pore, scan, skim, tell **5.** guess, solve **6.** advise, browse, peruse, recite, relate **7.** counsel, declare, discern, foresee, prelect (praelect) **8.** decipher, describe, foretell **9.** interpret **10.** understand
readable . . . **7.** legible **12.** decipherable
reader . . . **6.** lector, lister, primer (McGuffey) **7.** browser, license, reciter, speaker, teacher **8.** anagnost (anagnostes), literate, textbook **9.** churchman, prelector (praelector) **10.** pocketbook **11.** proofreader **12.** elocutionist
readily . . . **6.** at once, easily **7.** quickly

8. probably 9. willingly 10. very likely
readjust . . . 7. readapt, restore
    9. rearrange 11. reconstruct
    12. rehabilitate
ready . . . 3. apt, fit, fix 4. bain, free,
    here, ripe, yare 5. alert, apert, eager,
    handy, point, quick 6. facile, fitted,
    prompt 7. willing 8. cheerful, disposed,
    inclined, prepared, skillful 9. dexterous
    12. unhesitating
ready acceptance . . . 11. embracement
ready for . . . 6. awaits 8. liable to 10. in
    store for 11. prepared for
ready-to-wear . . . 12. haute couture
real . . . 4. true, very 5. pucka (pukka)
    6. actual 7. factual, genuine, sincere
    8. absolute, existent, handmade,
    tangible 9. authentic, veritable
    10. unaffected 11. substantial
real (pert to) . . .
    being . . 6. entity
    estate . . 5. lands 6. domain, houses,
    realty 7. demesne 8. easement,
    freehold, property 9. tenements
    13. hereditaments
    map . . 4. plot
    name (backwards) . . 6. ananym
    school . . 10. Realschule
realistic . . . 5. vivid 8. lifelike 9. practical
    11. descriptive
reality . . . 5. truth 7. realism
    11. genuineness
reality, non-existent . . . 8. nihilism
realize . . . 3. get, win 4. gain, know
    5. sense 7. convert 8. conceive
    10. accomplish
realm . . . 6. domain, empire, region,
    sphere 7. country, demesne, kingdom
    8. division, province 10. department
    12. jurisdiction
realm (of) . . .
    darkness (Myth) . . 2. po
    Jamshid . . 6. Persia
    perfection . . 6. Utopia
ream . . . 4. bore, foam, scum 5. widen
    6. bundle 7. enlarge 8. bevel out
    11. countersink 14. enormous amount
reanimate . . . 5. rally 6. revive 7. refresh
    11. resuscitate 12. reinvigorate
rear . . . 3. aft 4. back, grow, hind, lift,
    loom, rise, rump 5. breed, build, erect,
    raise, stern, train 6. behind, foster
    7. arriere, educate, elevate, produce
    8. instruct 9. construct, establish,
    posterior 10. background
rear (pert to) . . .
    admiral . . 7. two bars (silver)
    commodore, yacht club . . 7. officer
    end . . 6. breech 7. hind end 9. afterpart,
    posterior
    horse (insect) . . 6. mantis
    most . . 4. last
    toward . . 3. aft 5. abalt 6. astern
    8. backward, rearward
rearing up (horse) . . . 5. stend 6. pesade
rearrange . . . 4. sort 8. readjust
    10. reordinate, reorganize
reason . . . 5. argue, cause, logic, sense,
    think 6. deduce, ground, motive, sanity
    7. discuss 8. argument, conclude,
    judgment, question, solution

9. discourse, intellect 11. explanation,
    ratiocinate, rationalize 13. justification,
    understanding
reason (pert to) . . .
    discursively . . 11. ratiocinate
    doctrine of, author . . 10. Anaxagoras
    higher . . 4. mind, nous 5. logic
    Latin . . 5. causa
    ostensible . . 7. pretext
    pert to . . 6. noetic
    proof of . . 8. argument
    want of . . 7. amentia
    why . . 5. cause 6. motive
reasonable . . . 4. fair, just, sane 6. proper
    7. logical 8. rational 9. equitable,
    plausible, practical 10. fair-minded
    11. inexpensive, intelligent, justifiable
reasoning (pert to) . . .
    basis of . . 7. premise
    delusive . . 7. fallacy
    exact . . 5. logic
    harmonize . . 11. rationalize
    plausible . . 8. specious
reassure . . . 6. assure, solace 7. comfort,
    console, hearten 8. embolden, give
    hope
reata . . . 4. rope 5. lasso, riata 6. lariat
reave . . . 3. rob 4. rend, tear 5. break,
    burst, seize, split 7. plunder
reb . . . 5. rebel
rebate . . . 5. check 6. reduce, weaken
    8. diminish, discount 9. abatement,
    deduction, remission
rebato (Hist) . . . 4. ruff 6. collar, rabato
    9. piccadill
Rebekah (pert to) . . .
    husband . . 5. Isaac
    sister . . 5. Laban
    son . . 4. Esau 5. Jacob
rebel . . . 3. reb 4. rise 6. resist, revolt
    8. renounce, turncoat 9. insurgent
    13. revolutionist
rebellion . . . 5. Great (Eng 1642-49)
    6. mutiny, revolt 8. American (Civil
    War 1861-65) 10. resistance, revolution
    12. insurrection, renunciation
rebellious . . . 8. mutinous 9. insurgent
    10. refractory 12. contumacious
    13. insubordinate, revolutionary
rebirth . . . 7. revival 9. salvation
    10. conversion 11. renaissance
    13. reincarnation
rebound . . . 4. stot 5. carom 6. bounce,
    recoil, re-echo, spring 7. resound
    8. rebounce, ricochet 11. reverberate
rebuff . . . 4. slap, snub 5. chide, scold
    6. defeat, lesson, recoil, refuse, reject,
    resist 7. censure, refusal (brusque),
    reprove, repulse 9. reprimand
rebuke . . . 3. nip 4. slap 5. check,
    chide, rebuff 7. repress, reproof,
    reprove 8. admonish, reproach, restrain
    9. criticize, reprehend, reprimand
    11. comeuppance
recalcitrant . . . 5. rebel 8. renitent
    9. obstinate, recoiling, resistant
    10. rebellious, refractory 11. disobedient
    12. ungovernable
recall . . . 5. annul 6. encore, recant,
    remind, repeal, revoke, summon
    7. retract 8. remember, withdraw

9. recollect, reminisce 11. recantation
12. recollection

recant . . . 6. abjure, revoke 7. disavow,
retract 8. renounce, withdraw
9. repudiate 10. contradict

recapitulate . . . 5. essay, sum up
6. repeat, review 7. restate 8. argument
9. reiterate, summarize

recapture . . . 6. recall, regain, retake
7. recover

recede . . . 3. ebb 4. wane 6. depart, retire
7. deviate, regress, retreat 8. withdraw
10. retrograde

receipt . . . 5. axiom 6. acquit, answer,
recipe 7. formula 12. prescription
14. acknowledgment

receipts . . . 7. the take

receive . . . 3. get 4. hold, take 5. admit,
greet, learn, reset 6. accept, assent,
derive, obtain, take in 7. acquire,
contain, procure 9. apprehend

receive (pert to) . . .
a confession . . 6. shrive
a reward . . 4. reap
stolen property . . 5. reset

receiver . . . 5. donee, fence 7. catcher
8. believer 9. recipient, treasurer
10. receptacle

receiver (pert to) . . .
fixed income . . 7. rentier
profits (law) . . 6. pernor
property in trust . . 6. bailee
stolen property . . 5. fence

recension . . . 6. review 8. revising,
revision 9. reviewing 11. enumeration,
examination

recent . . . 3. new 4. late, past 5. fresh
6. former, modern 7. current, newborn
8. neonatal, neoteric

receptacle . . . 3. bag, bin, box, can,
cup, pan 4. case, cask, cyst (anc),
etui, pail, tank, tray, vase 5. basin,
crock 6. basket, bottle, bucket, carton,
holder, hopper 7. compote, hanaper,
platter 8. canister, catchall 9. container
10. repository

receptacle (pert to) . . .
assayer's, stonecutter's . . 7. sebilla
botany . . 5. torus
coal . . 3. bin
corporal (RCCh) . . 5. burse
grain . . 3. bin 8. elevator
holy water . . 5. stoup
vote . . 6. situla

reception . . . 3. tea 5. levee, salon
6. infare, soiree 7. accueil, ovation,
receipt, welcome 8. ceremony, sociable
9. admission, interview, intuition
12. housewarming 13. entertainment

reception hall, room . . . 5. salon
6. atrium, parlor 9. vestibule

receptionist . . . 4. host 7. hostess
8. landlord

receptive . . . 6. pliant 8. sensible
9. acceptant, admissive, teachable
10. hospitable, open-minded
11. persuasible

receptor . . . 5. basin 8. receiver
10. dispositor (Astron), sense organ

recess . . . 3. ala, bay, pan (leaf) 4. apse,
nook, rest 5. crypt, niche, pause,

sinus, space 7. adjourn, respite, retreat
9. recession, seclusion 11. indentation
12. intermission

recipe . . . 5. axiom 7. formula, receipt
12. prescription

recipient . . . 4. heir 5. donee 7. legatee
8. receiver

reciprocal . . . 5. joint 6. mutual, shared
8. exchange 9. alternate 11. convertible,
correlative, retaliatory
15. interchangeable

reciprocate . . . 5. bandy 6. accord, concur
8. exchange 9. alternate, retaliate
10. correspond 11. interchange

recision . . . 6. repeal 7. pruning
9. canceling (cancelling) 10. rescinding

recital . . . 4. tale 5. story 6. lesson,
speech 7. account, concert (exhibition)
8. musicale 9. narration, narrative,
rehearsal 10. recitation, repetition
11. enumeration, reiteration

recitation . . . 6. lesson, speech 7. reading
10. exhibition

recite . . . 4. tell 5. quote, speak,
state 6. relate, repeat 7. declaim,
narrate, recount 8. rehearse, tell over
9. enumerate, pronounce
12. recapitulate

recite (pert to) . . .
in monotone . . 6. intone
metrically . . 4. scan
rhetorically . . 7. declaim
to music . . 5. chant 10. cantillate

reciter . . . 4. book (of extracts) 5. roter
7. relator, speaker 8. narrator

reck . . . 4. care, deem, heed, mind
6. regard 7. concern 8. estimate

reckless . . . 4. rash 5. perdu (perdue)
6. madcap 7. hotspur 8. careless,
heedless 9. desperate, hotheaded,
imprudent 10. neglectful, regardless
11. indifferent, thoughtless,
unconcerned 13. inconsiderate

reckon . . . 4. aret (arette), date, deem,
tell 5. class, count, judge, tally,
think 6. impute, number, regard,
repute 7. account, compute, include,
suppose 8. consider, estimate, evaluate
9. calculate, enumerate

reckoning . . . 3. sum 4. bill, shot 5. score,
tally 6. esteem 7. account, verdict
8. counting 9. summation 10. estimation
11. calculation

reckoning instrument . . . 6. abacus
9. tabulator 10. calculator

reclaim . . . 4. tame 5. renew, train
6. ransom, recall, redeem, revoke
7. convert, recover, restore 8. civilize
10. regenerate 12. rehabilitate

recline . . . 3. lay, lie, sit 4. lean, loll, rest
6. repose 7. incline, lie down

reclining . . . 4. flat 5. prone 6. supine
7. lolling 8. couchant, reposing
9. prostrate, recumbent

recluse . . . 3. fra, nun 4. monk 6. hermit,
hidden, secret, shut up 7. ascetic,
eremite, retired (from world)
8. anchoret, isolated, solitary
9. anchorite 10. cloistered
11. sequestered

recognition . . . 4. fame 6. recall

9. detection 10. cognizance
11. discernment 14. acknowledgment
recognize . . . 3. see 4. know 5. admit
6. detect 7. consent 8. identify,
perceive 10. appreciate, recognosce
11. acknowledge
recoil . . . 3. shy 4. funk 5. quail 6. flinch,
resile, shrink 7. rebound, retreat
8. reaction, withdraw
recollect . . . 6. recall, revive 7. think of
8. remember 10. call to mind
recollection . . . 4. mind 6. memory
9. anamnesis 11. remembrance
12. reminiscence
recommence . . . 5. renew 6. resume
8. return to 9. begin anew
recommend . . . 4. tout, urge 6. advise,
commit, denote, praise 7. commend,
consign, entrust 8. advocate
recompense . . . 3. fee, pay 4. meed
5. repay 6. reward 8. requital
9. indemnify, reimburse
10. compensate, remunerate
11. reciprocate
recompense (pert to) . . .
Brehon Law . . 4. eric
Germanic law . . 7. wergild
Scot law . . 3. cro
Welsh law . . 7. galanas
reconcile . . . 4. suit, wean 5. atone
6. adjust, pacify, settle 7. cleanse
(Eccl), conform, reunite 9. harmonize
10. conciliate, propitiate
reconciliation . . . 7. harmony, reunion
10. adjustment, conformity
12. pacification 13. reconcilement
reconciliator . . . 10. arbitrator, reconciler
13. intermediator
recondite . . . 4. dark, deep 6. hidden,
mystic, occult 7. cryptic 8. abstract,
abstruse, esoteric 9. concealed
reconnaissance . . . 6. survey 8. scouting
11. examination
reconnoiter . . . 5. scout 6. survey
reconstruct . . . 6. recast, remake
7. rebuild, remodel 9. reproduce
11. reestablish
record . . . 3. log, tab 4. disc, file, list,
memo 5. annal, diary, enter, entry,
score 6. agenda, legend, memoir,
postea 7. archive, estreat, history
8. memorial, register 9. chronicle
10. chronology, transcribe, transcript
record (pert to) . . .
criminal investigation . . 7. dossier
document . . 8. protocol
earth tremor . . 11. seismograph
formal . . 4. vita 8. register
historic . . 6. annals 7. rotulet
keeper . . 9. registrar 10. chartulary
of events . . 5. annal, fasti 7. history
official . . 5. actum
pictorial . . 5. graph
ship's voyage . . 3. log
year's . . 5. diary 8. calendar
recording terms . . . 2. LP 4. reel, tape
5. album, Dolby 6. needle, stereo, stylus
7. capstan 8. cassette 9. cartridge,
videotape
recount . . . 3. min 4. tell 5. sum up
6. reckon, relate, repeat, retail 7. narrate

8. rehearse 9. enumerate, reiterate
12. recapitulate
recoup . . . 4. gain 7. recover 8. retrieve
9. indemnity, reimburse 10. compensate
recourse . . . 3. use 5. recur 6. access,
betake, refuge, resort, return, revert
7. retreat
recover . . . 3. get 4. cure, gain, heal
5. rally, reach, upset 6. obtain, recoup,
redeem, regain, rescue, resume 7. get
well, reclaim, recruit 8. overcome,
retrieve 9. repossess 10. convalesce,
recuperate
recovery . . . 6. return 7. salvage
9. retrieval 11. reclamation, reformation,
restoration
recreant . . . 6. coward, wretch 7. dastard,
knavish 8. apostate, betrayer, cowardly,
deserter 9. reprobate 10. unfaithful
recreation . . . 4. food, game, meal,
play 5. sport 7. holiday, renewal
8. vacation 9. amusement, diversion
11. refreshment 12. reproduction
14. reconstruction
recrement . . . 5. dross 6. refuse, scoria
recruit . . . 5. raise 6. enlist, gather, muster,
novice, revive, rookie 7. recover,
refresh, restore 8. assemble, inductee,
newcomer 9. conscript, reinforce,
replenish 12. reinvigorate
rectangle . . . 10. quadrangle
13. parallelogram
rectangular . . . 6. oblong
12. quadrangular
rectify . . . 5. amend, emend, right
6. adjust, better, reform, remedy
7. correct, justify 8. emendate, regulate,
set right 10. straighten
rector . . . 5. chief 6. leader, master
(Oxford), pastor 8. director, governor
9. churchman, clergyman
10. headmaster
rectory . . . 8. benefice 9. personage
recumbent . . . 4. idle 5. lying, prone
7. leaning, resting 8. inactive, reposing
9. reclining
recuperate . . . 4. rest 6. recoup, regain
7. improve, recover, restore 9. get
better, reimburse
recur . . . 5. again 6. repeat, return
7. persist, reoccur 8. reappear
recurrent . . . 10. repetitive
recurring (pert to) . . .
continually . . 8. constant 10. habitually,
repeatedly
ninth day . . 5. nonan
seventh day . . 6. septan
third day . . 7. tertian
red . . . 4. rosy 5. color, ruddy 7. radical
8. blushing, inflamed, rutilant, sanguine
9. bloodshot 12. bloodstained
13. revolutionary
red (color) . . . 4. fire, lake, pink, puce,
rose, ruby, tile, wine 5. blood,
brick, canna, coral, flame, flesh,
henna, poppy 6. auburn, cerise,
cherry, claret, damask, maroon,
minium, raddle, salmon, titian, Turkey
7. anemone, annatto, carmine, Chinese,
crimson, lobster, magenta, nacarat,
scarlet, stammel 8. cardinal, cinnabar

9. carnation, carnelian, vermilion
red (pert to) . . .
cap (Turk) . . **8.** tarboosh
cell . . **11.** erythrocite
corpuscle . . **10.** hemoglobin (source of)
dog . . **4.** game **8.** banknote
dye . . **3.** aal, lac **4.** chay (choy) **5.** aurin
   (aurine), eosin (eosine) **8.** morindin
gum . . **10.** strophulus
hair . . **6.** titian
herring . . **4.** ruse **9.** diversion
minded . . **7.** radical
planet . . **4.** Mars
race . . **7.** Indians
robbin . . **14.** scarlet tanager
truffle . . **12.** melanogaster
viper . . **10.** copperhead
Red (pert to) . . .
Book . . **7.** Austria **13.** Royal Kalendar
Crescent . . **8.** Red Cross (Turk)
Cross . . **9.** St George's (Eng)
Friar . . **13.** Knight Templar
Guard . . **4.** Army **7.** Russian
Hand . . **13.** Badge of Ulster
Horse . . **10.** Kentuckian
Planet . . **4.** Mars
Polled . . **6.** cattle (hornless)
Prince . . **7.** Russian (Frederick Charles)
Ribbon . . **14.** Order of the Bath
Rose . . **16.** House of Lancaster
Russian . . **9.** Bolshevik
Sea . . **14.** Erythraean main
Sea city . . **9.** Leningrad
Sea colony . . **7.** Eritrea
Sea gulf . . **5.** Aqaba
Square . . **6.** Moscow
The Red . . **4.** Eric (Scand)
Triangle . . **4.** YMCA (symbol)
redact . . . **4.** edit **5.** draft, frame **6.** revise
redactor . . . **6.** editor **7.** reviser
   9. redacteur
reddish (pert to) . . .
blue . . **5.** smalt **9.** damascene
brown . . **3.** bay **4.** roan **5.** henna
   6. auburn, russet, sorrel **8.** chestnut
dye . . **7.** annatto
yellow . . **5.** amber **6.** orange
rede . . . **6.** advice, relate **7.** counsel,
   explain, predict **9.** interpret
redeem . . . **3.** pay **6.** ransom, regain,
   rescue **7.** convert, fulfill, reclaim,
   recover **8.** liberate **10.** repurchase,
   substitute
redeemer . . . **4.** goel (Heb) **7.** saviour
   (savior) **9.** deliverer, liberator
   11. emancipator
Redeemer, The . . . **8.** Son of God **10.** The
   Messiah, The Saviour **11.** Jesus Christ
redintegrate . . . **5.** renew, unite **7.** restore
   9. reconcile **11.** re-establish
redness . . . **4.** glow **8.** blushing
   10. erubescent, rubescence
redolence . . . **4.** odor **5.** aroma, scent
   9. fragrance, sweetness
redolent . . . **5.** balmy **7.** odorous, scented
   8. aromatic, fragrant **11.** impregnated,
   reminiscent
redouble . . . **6.** re-echo, repeat **7.** reflect,
   reprise (fencing) **9.** intensify
   10. ingeminate, repetition
   11. reduplicate

redoubt . . . **4.** fear **5.** doubt **6.** reduit
   7. defense, ravelin
redound . . . **5.** surge **6.** abound, return
   7. conduce, resound **8.** flow back,
   overflow **10.** contribute (to)
   11. reverberate
redpoll . . . **5.** finch **6.** linnet **7.** warbler
Red Polled cattle . . . **8.** hornless
redress . . . **4.** help **5.** amend, emend
   6. reform, remedy **7.** correct, relieve
   8. atone for, reprisal **9.** atonement
   10. correction, recompense, reparation
   11. reformation, restitution
reduce . . . **3.** cut **4.** bant, bate, pare,
   thin **5.** abase, abate, lower, razee
   6. demote, derate, humble, lessen,
   subdue, weaken **7.** abridge, analyze,
   cheapen, conquer, curtail, deplete,
   qualify, relieve, shorten **8.** decrease,
   diminish, discount, minimize, moderate
   9. subjugate **10.** impoverish, slenderize
reduce in flesh . . . **8.** emaciate
reduce in rank . . . **6.** demote
reduce to . . .
ashes . . **7.** cremate
average . . **4.** mean **6.** equate
bondage . . **7.** enslave
common measure . . **12.** commensurate
half . . **9.** dimidiate
lower grade . . **6.** demote **7.** degrade
mean time . . **6.** equate
spray . . **7.** atomize
reduction . . . **6.** rebate **7.** subdual
   8. decrease, demotion, discount,
   lowering **9.** weakening **10.** abridgment,
   cheapening, conversion, moderation
reduction (pert to) . . .
in value . . **12.** depreciation
to absurdity . . **18.** reductio ad absurdum
to common level . . **15.** standardization
to compactness . . **12.** condensation
to standard . . **15.** standardization
redundancy . . . **6.** excess **7.** profuse
   8. pleonasm, verbiage **9.** prolixity,
   talkative, tautology, verbosity
   10. repetition **11.** periphrasis
   13. diffusiveness **14.** circumlocution
redundant . . . **6.** lavish **7.** copious, diffuse,
   verbose **9.** excessive, exuberant,
   plethoric **10.** pleonastic **11.** overflowing,
   repetitious, superfluous
   13. superabundant
ree . . . **3.** dam **4.** sift, wild **5.** crazy, drunk,
   river **6.** harbor, riddle **7.** channel,
   fuddled **8.** coalyard **9.** enclosure,
   sheepfold
re-echo . . . **7.** resound **11.** reverberate
reechy . . . **5.** fetid **6.** rancid
reed . . . **4.** stem, tube **5.** arrow, straw
   6. thatch **10.** instrument
reed (pert to) . . .
bird . . **4.** wren **7.** babbler, warbler
   8. bobolink
buck . . **5.** bohor, nagar **8.** antelope
bunting . . **7.** sparrow **8.** reedling
instrument . . **4.** oboe **7.** bagpipe
   8. clarinet **9.** accordion, saxophone
loom . . **4.** sley
mace . . **7.** cattail, matreed
measure (Jew) . . **9.** six cubits
pipe . . **5.** kazoo **8.** mirliton

reef . . . **3.** bar, cay (cayo), key (quay)
4. itch, lode, sail, vein **5.** islet, mange,
shoal **6.** island **7.** shorten **8.** eruption
reef (pert to) . . .
coral . . **3.** key
knot . . **6.** square
mining . . **4.** lode, vein
nautical . . **5.** sails
sand . . **3.** bar
reefer . . . **5.** miner **6.** jacket, oyster
9. cigarette **10.** midshipman
reek . . . **3.** fug, rig **4.** fume **5.** equip,
exude, smell, smoke, steam **7.** malodor,
seaweed **8.** fetid air, smell bad, vaporize
10. exhalation
reel . . . **4.** eddy, pirn, rock, sail, sway,
wind **5.** dance, lurch, spool, swift
(yarn), swing, waver, wince **6.** tatter
7. scrieve, stagger **8.** flounder, titubate,
windlass **12.** Virginia reel
reeling . . . **5.** drunk **7.** swaying, winding
8. rotating
reem (Bib) . . . **6.** animal (horned), wild
ox **7.** unicorn
re-embody . . . **7.** combine, reshape
10. reorganize **11.** reincarnate
13. reincorporate
reeve . . . **3.** pen **4.** ruff **5.** strip **6.** thread
8. official (Eng Hist) **9.** enclosure,
sheepfold
refect . . . **7.** refresh, restore
refectory . . . **6.** frater (monastery) **8.** mess
hall **10.** dining hall
refer . . . **4.** cite **5.** apply, recur **6.** allude,
appeal, charge, impute, relate, return
7. ascribe **9.** appertain, attribute
refer (to) . . . **4.** harp **6.** advert **7.** consult,
mention
referee . . . **5.** judge **6.** umpire **7.** arbiter
8. attorney **9.** moderator **10.** arbitrator
reference . . . **6.** regard **7.** respect
8. allusion, relation **9.** character,
relevance **10.** connection, pertinence
14. recommendation
reference (pert to) . . .
book . . **5.** atlas **8.** handbook, syllabus
9. thesaurus **10.** dictionary
12. encyclopedia
referendum . . . **4.** vote **7.** mandate
8. politics **10.** plebiscite
refine . . . **5.** smelt **6.** rarefy **7.** clarify,
elevate, improve, sublime **9.** elaborate,
sensitize, sublimate
refined . . . **4.** fine, nice, pure, rare
5. urban **6.** chaste **7.** elegant, smelted
8. cleansed, highbred, purified, well-
bred **9.** clarified, courteous, perfected
10. cultivated, fastidious, meticulous
refined spirit . . . **5.** grace **6.** elixir
refinement . . . **5.** taste **6.** polish **7.** finesse
8. delicacy, elegance, fineness
9. gentility **11.** cultivation, rarefaction
13. clarification
refinery (ore) . . . **7.** smelter
refining cup . . . **5.** cupel
reflect . . . **3.** say **4.** muse, pore **5.** radar,
think **6.** divert, mirror, ponder **7.** deflect
8. cogitate, consider, meditate,
ruminate, turn back **9.** reproduce
11. reverberate
reflecting . . . **6.** musing **9.** judicious

10. reflective, ruminating, thoughtful
11. insinuating **13.** reverberatory
15. casting reproach
reflection . . . **4.** idea **5.** image, light
6. musing **7.** bending, thought
8. reaction, thinking **10.** cogitation,
meditation, rumination **12.** afterthought,
recollection **13.** consideration,
contemplation
reflex . . . **4.** bent **6.** turned **8.** allusion,
reaction, reversed **9.** duplicate, reflected
13. introspection
reflux . . . **3.** ebb **6.** ebbing, reflow
8. backflow, reaction **9.** refluence,
returning
reform . . . **4.** mend **5.** amend, emend,
renew **6.** better, remake, remass, repair
7. convert, rebuild, reclaim, rectify,
restore **9.** amendment **10.** regenerate
11. reformation
reformation . . . **7.** rebirth **10.** conversion,
emendation **12.** regeneration,
reproduction **15.** re-establishment
Reformation leaders (Hist) . . . **4.** Knox
6. Calvin, Luther, Ridley **7.** Cranmer,
Latimer, Zwingli **8.** Campbell
11. Melanchthon
reformer . . . **7.** amender, reviser
9. reformado, reformist **10.** politician
refraction . . . **7.** rebound **9.** dioptrics
10. deflection, dispersion **11.** anaclastics
refractor . . . **5.** prism **9.** telescope
refractory . . . **7.** restive **8.** indocile,
stubborn **11.** disobedient
12. ungovernable
refrain . . . **4.** curb, shun **5.** avoid,
cease, derry, epode **6.** chorus, govern
7. abstain, forbear **8.** response, restrain
refrain from using . . . **5.** spare **7.** boycott
refresco . . . **4.** food **5.** drink
11. refreshment
refresh . . . **3.** air, dew **4.** cool **5.** cheer,
renew, slake **6.** repose, revive
7. freshen, relieve **8.** recreate, renovate
9. reanimate, replenish **10.** invigorate,
strengthen **11.** refreshment
12. reinvigorate
refreshing . . . **5.** balmy **7.** bracing
8. regaling **10.** heartening
11. stimulating **12.** exhilarating
refrigerant . . . **3.** ice **6.** cooler **7.** ammonia,
coolant, cryogen
refrigeration . . . **7.** cooling **8.** cryogeny
10. anesthetic, cryogenics
12. preservation
refuge . . . **3.** ark **4.** plea **5.** haven
6. asylum, covert, excuse **7.** retreat,
shelter **8.** hospital, recourse, resource
9. sanctuary **10.** protection, safety zone
refugee . . . **5.** exile, fleer **6.** émigré
7. escapee, evacuee **8.** fugitive,
renegade
refulgence . . . **6.** luster **8.** radiance,
splendor **10.** brilliancy
refund . . . **5.** repay **6.** rebate **9.** reimburse
refurbish . . . **4.** vamp **5.** renew **8.** brighten,
renovate **11.** recondition
refusal . . . **3.** nay **6.** denial **9.** rejection
11. declination
refuse . . . **3.** cot (wool), ort **4.** balk, coom
(coomb), culm, deny, junk, marc, scum

5. attle, chaff, dregs, dross, repel, scrap, trash, waste, weeds **6.** debris, give up, litter, midden, naysay, reject, renege, scoria, scraps **7.** abandon, bagasse, cast off, decline, garbage, hogwash, repulse **8.** disclaim, leavings, oddments, renounce, withhold **9.** excrement, repudiate **11.** odds and ends

refuse to ...
accept .. **6.** reject
acknowledge .. **7.** disavow **9.** repudiate
comply .. **12.** recalcitrant
proceed .. **4.** balk

refutation ... **6.** answer **8.** disproof, elenchus, rebuttal **11.** confutation

refute ... **4.** deny, meet **5.** rebut, refel **6.** assoil **8.** disprove, elenctic, redargue **9.** overthrow **10.** contradict

regain ... **6.** recoup **7.** get back, recover **8.** retrieve **9.** get back to **10.** reach again

regal ... **5.** royal **6.** groove, kingly **7.** channel, stately **8.** imperial, majestic, splendid **9.** dignified, sovereign

regale ... **4.** dine, fete **5.** amuse, feast, treat **7.** gratify, refresh **9.** entertain **11.** refreshment

regalia ... **6.** finery **7.** costume, emblems, symbols **8.** insignia **11.** decorations **12.** special dress **13.** paraphernalia

regard ... **3.** air, awe **4.** care, deem, gaze, heed, hold, look, love, mind, obey (law), rate, sake, view **5.** honor, judge, think, treat **6.** aspect, behold, esteem, remark, repute **8.** attitude, consider, estimate, hold dear, listen to **9.** attention, relevance, viewpoint **10.** appearance, estimation **11.** contemplate, observation **13.** consideration

regard (pert to) ...
for others .. **8.** altruism
for other's wish .. **9.** deference
highly .. **6.** admire **7.** lionize
with approval .. **6.** admire
with deference .. **5.** honor **7.** respect
with veneration .. **6.** revere

regardful ... **7.** careful, mindful **8.** cautious **9.** attentive, observant **10.** altruistic, respectful, thoughtful **11.** considerate

regarding ... **2.** re **4.** as to **5.** anent **10.** concerning, respecting

regardless ... **6.** anyhow **8.** careless, heedless, slighted **9.** negligent **10.** neglectful **11.** inattentive, indifferent, unconcerned, unobservant **15.** notwithstanding

regards ... **8.** respects **9.** greetings **11.** compliments

regatta cup ... **5.** Platt **8.** Carnegie, Grimoldi

regency ... **4.** rule **8.** dominion **10.** government

regenerate ... **5.** shape **6.** redeem, reform, revive **7.** convert, restore **8.** re-create **9.** reproduce **11.** fashion anew

regeneration ... **7.** renewal, revival **9.** reversion **10.** re-creation **11.** reformation **12.** reproduction **14.** divine function

regent ... **5.** ruler **6.** deputy, ruling **7.** regnant **8.** governor

Regent diamond, 137 carats (pert to) ...
included in .. **11.** State jewels (France)
named for .. **14.** Regent of France
placed in .. **6.** Louvre
sold (1717) to .. **4.** Pitt (Gov of Madras, Ind)

regime, regimen ... **4.** diet, rule **6.** system **7.** therapy **10.** government, regulation **14.** administration

regiment ... **4.** unit, wing **6.** outfit **8.** organize **11.** systematize

regiment, framework of ... **5.** cadre

regina ... **5.** queen

region ... **4.** area, belt, zone **5.** clime, place, realm, space, tract **6.** sphere **7.** climate, cockpit, country, demesne, kingdom, section **8.** district, province

region (pert to) ...
beyond Jordan .. **5.** Perea **6.** Basham
blissful .. **4.** Eden
comb form .. **5.** nesia
desert .. **3.** erg **5.** waste
indefinite .. **5.** tract
infernal .. **7.** Avernal **8.** Tartarus
meteorological .. **6.** pleion
wooded .. **4.** wold
woodless .. **5.** weald

region of ...
contentment .. **6.** Arcady
dead (Egypt Myth) .. **6.** Amenti
fabled wealth .. **8.** Eldorado
nether darkness .. **6.** Erebus
opposite side earth .. **9.** Antipodes
Solomon's gold (Bib) .. **5.** Ophir

register ... **3.** act **4.** list, roll **5.** annal, entry, index **6.** docket, enlist, enroll, record **7.** rotulet **8.** archives, recorder, schedule **9.** catalogue, chronicle, necrology, registrar **11.** account book, matriculate

registrar ... **8.** recorder **9.** accounter

regius ... **5.** royal **13.** professorship

regret ... **3.** rue **4.** ruth **5.** grief, sorry **6.** repent, repine, sorrow **7.** deplore, remorse **9.** penitence **10.** repentance **11.** compunction **12.** self-reproach

regretful ... **5.** sorry **8.** repining **9.** repentant

regular ... **4.** even **5.** usual **6.** formal, normal, smooth, stated **7.** correct, orderly, typical, uniform **8.** constant, habitual, ordinary, ordinate, rhythmic, standard **9.** isometric **10.** systematic

regularity ... **5.** order **8.** symmetry **9.** constancy **10.** smoothness, uniformity

regularly ... **6.** always **7.** usually **8.** properly, smoothly **9.** correctly **10.** constantly, habitually **12.** methodically, periodically **13.** symmetrically

regulate ... **3.** set **4.** rule **6.** adjust, direct, govern, manage, ordain, remedy **7.** arrange, control, dispose **8.** organize **9.** influence, methodize **11.** standardize

regulation ... **3.** law **4.** rule **5.** bylaw, order **6.** system **7.** control, precept **9.** direction, principle

regulator . . . **7.** control **8.** governor,
rheostat **9.** rheometer
Regulus . . . **4.** king, star **5.** Alpha
8. warblers **9.** Cor Leonis (star)
rehabilitate . . . **7.** restore **9.** reeducate,
reinstall
rehash . . . **7.** restate **9.** réchauffé
rehearse . . . **3.** say **4.** tell **5.** speak, sum
up, train **6.** detail, recite, relate, repeat,
try out **7.** mention, narrate, recount
8. describe **9.** enumerate, reiterate
12. recapitulate
rehoboam . . . **3.** hat **4.** bowl **6.** flagon
8. jeroboam
Rehoboam (Bib) . . . **11.** King of Judah
(1st) **12.** King of Israel (last)
reif . . . **7.** plunder, robbery
reign . . . **3.** raj **4.** rule, sway **5.** guide,
realm **6.** empire **7.** kingdom, prevail
8. dominion, flourish **11.** sovereignty
12. supreme power
Reign of Terror (Fr Hist) . . . **7.** anarchy
9. bloodshed, despotism
12. confiscation
reimburse . . . **3.** pay **5.** repay **6.** refund
7. pay back, replace **9.** indemnify
10. recompense
Reims, Rheims (pert to) . . .
capital (anc) . . **4.** Remi
famed building . . **9.** Cathedral (Gothic)
famed site . . **15.** crowning of kings (Fr)
rein . . . **4.** curb, stop **5.** check, leash
6. direct, retard **7.** control **8.** reindeer,
restrain **9.** hindrance **10.** bridle part
reina . . . **8.** rockfish
reindeer . . . **6.** tarand **7.** caribou
13. constellation
reindeer (pert to) . . .
age, epoch . . **11.** Paleolithic
flower . . **9.** buttercup (white)
genus . . **8.** Rangifer
reinforce . . . **4.** back **5.** add to, brace,
reman **7.** restore, support **9.** intensify,
replenish **10.** strengthen
reinforcement . . . **7.** adjunct, support
8. addition **13.** replenishment,
strengthening
reins . . . **5.** loins **7.** harness, kidneys
9. restraint
reis . . . **6.** escudo **7.** milreis **14.** money
of account
reit . . . **5.** sedge **7.** seaweed
reiterate . . . **4.** drum, harp **6.** repeat
8. rehearse **12.** recapitulate
reject . . . **5.** repel, spurn **6.** disown, recuse
(law), refuse **7.** decline, discard, dismiss
8. athetize, disallow **9.** repudiate
rejectamenta . . . **5.** wrack **6.** refuse,
reject **7.** rubbish **9.** excrement
rejection . . . **6.** heresy **7.** discard, refusal
8. ejection **9.** exclusion, objection
11. disapproval, repudiation
rejoice . . . **5.** cheer, elate **7.** delight,
gladden **8.** jubilate
rejoinder . . . **5.** reply (law) **6.** answer,
retort, return **8.** comeback
rejuvenate . . . **6.** revive **7.** restore
9. stimulate **12.** reinvigorate
relâche . . . **10.** relaxation **12.** intermission
13. no performance (Theat)
relapse . . . **4.** sink **5.** lapse **7.** subside

8. slip back **9.** backslide, reversion
10. recurrence, regression **11.** falling
back **12.** recidivation
relate . . . **4.** tell **5.** state **6.** assert, detail,
recite, report **7.** narrate, pertain, recount
8. describe, rehearse **9.** appertain,
associate
related (pert to) . . .
by blood . . **3.** sib **4.** akin **7.** cognate
on father's side . . **6.** agnate **7.** cognate
8. agnation
on mother's side . . **5.** enate **6.** enatic
7. cognate, enation **9.** umbilical
story . . **7.** sidebar
to land . . **8.** praedial (predial)
relating to . . .
bread . . **6.** panary
Chinese . . **7.** Sinitic
dancing . . **6.** gestic **13.** choreographic
fruit jelly . . **7.** pectous
grandparents . . **4.** aval
Hindu literature . . **5.** Vedic
life . . **5.** vital
morn . . **7.** matinal **8.** forenoon
motion . . **7.** kinetic **9.** kinematic
realities . . **7.** factual **9.** entelechy
soft palate . . **5.** velar
vascular fluid . . **5.** hemic
relation . . . **3.** kin **4.** mode, tale **6.** status,
ubiety **7.** account, analogy, kinship,
kinsman, recital, telling **8.** relative
9. character, narration, reference,
rehearsal, rishtadar (Hind law)
10. connection **13.** consanguinity
relationship . . . **4.** outs **7.** kinship,
kinsman, metochy **8.** affinity, relative
13. consanguinity
relative . . . **3.** eme, kin, sib, son **4.** aunt
5. niece, uncle **6.** allied, cousin, father,
mother, nephew, sister **7.** brother,
kindred **8.** apposite, daughter, kinsfolk
9. pertinent **11.** comparative, correlative
13. corresponding, proportionate
relative (pert to) . . .
favor to . . **8.** nepotism
rank . . **6.** degree
to . . **7.** apropos **12.** in proportion
relax . . . **4.** ease, open, rest **5.** abate,
loose, remit **6.** divert, loosen, soften,
unbend **7.** detente, slacken **8.** mitigate,
slow down
relaxed . . . **4.** calm, cool **6.** casual
8. laid-back **9.** easygoing
relay . . . **3.** dak (dawk) **4.** race **5.** shift
6. remuda **7.** relieve **8.** avantlay
10. television (station)
release . . . **4.** drop, free, trip, undo
5. death, let go, loose, undam, unpen,
untie **6.** acquit, escape, exempt, loosen,
parole, remise **7.** deliver, freedom,
manumit, receipt, relieve, unleash,
unloose **8.** liberate **9.** discharge
10. liberation, relinquish
11. acquittance, deliverance
relegate . . . **5.** exile, refer **6.** assign,
banish, commit, deport, depute, remove
7. ascribe, consign, discard, dismiss,
exclude **8.** delegate
relent . . . **5.** abate, yield **6.** regret, soften,
submit **7.** slacken
relentless . . . **6.** strict **9.** merciless

10. inflexible, unyielding
11. persevering, unremitting
relevant . . . 7. germane 9. pertinent
10. sufficient 11. referential
reliable . . . 4. safe, sure 5. tried
6. stable, trusty 7. solvent 8. true-blue
11. trustworthy
reliance . . . 4. hope 5. trust 6. belief
8. mainstay 10. confidence, conviction,
dependence
relic . . . 5. curio, huaca, huaco, ruins
7. antique, memento, remains
8. artifact, fragment, memorial,
souvenir, survival 9. antiquity
relic cabinet . . . 7. étagère, whatnot
relict . . . 5. widow 7. widower 8. survivor
relied . . . 6. banked 7. counted, reposed,
trusted 8. confided, depended, reckoned
relief . . . 3. aid 4. bote (bot), dole,
ease, fret (Arch), help 5. spell
6. remedy, succor 7. comfort, outline,
redress, relieve, welfare 8. easement
10. assistance, embossment, mitigation,
substitute, sustenance 11. alleviation,
deliverance 15. indemnification
relieve . . . 3. aid 4. cure, ease, free,
help 5. abate, allay, clear, raise, spell
6. assist, remedy, remove, succor
7. assuage, lighten, redress, refresh,
support, sustain, unloose 8. diminish
10. substitute
religion (pert to) . . . 4. sect 5. creed,
deism, faith, piety, trust 6. belief,
hermit, schism, theism, voodoo
8. monastic, theology 9. solipsism
10. conformity, persuasion
religion, type . . . 5. Islam 6. Taoism
7. Jainism, Judaism 8. Buddhism,
Hinduism 9. Mormonism, Moslemism,
Muslimism, Shintoism 11. Anglicanism,
Catholicism 12. Christianity,
Confucianism 13. Mohammedanism,
Protestantism
religious . . . 4. holy 5. exact, godly, pious,
rigid 6. devout, sacred 7. devoted,
fervent, zealous 9. born-again,
pharasaic, spiritual 10. devotional,
meticulous, scrupulous 11. theological
13. conscientious
religious (pert to) . . .
assembly . . 12. congregation
belief . . 5. deism 6. omnist
10. monotheism
brotherhood . . 8. sodality 9. ecumenism
10. fellowship 11. ecumenicism
center . . 7. Lambeth (Eng)
composition . . 5. motet
cult, sect . . 5. fakir 6. Shaker, Shinto
7. Pietism, Sikhism 8. cenobite
9. anchorite 11. Hare Krishna
devotee . . 5. fakir
devotion . . 6. novena
division . . 6. schism
expedition (Mil) . . 7. crusade
fasting . . 4. Lent 9. Ember Days
10. Ember Weeks
festival . . 4. mela (Ind) 5. Purim (Jew)
image . . 4. icon
madness, mania . . 9. theomania
metaphysics . . 7. gnostic
musical . . 6. anthem

offering . . 7. deodate 8. oblation
Order member . . 6. Marist 7. Templar
poem . . 5. psalm
psalm . . 4. hymn, poem, song
publication (RCCh) . . 4. ordo
relinquish . . . 3. let 4. cede, quit
5. forgo, leave, waive, yield 6. desert,
desist, forego, give up, remise, resign
7. abandon, forsake, release 8. abdicate,
renounce 9. surrender 11. leave behind
12. withdraw from
relinquishment . . . 9. surrender
11. abandonment 12. renunciation
reliquary, reliquiae (pl) . . . 3. box 4. arca,
tomb 5. chest 6. casket, chasse, shrine
8. monument
relish . . . 4. gust, tang, zest 5. achar,
enjoy, gusto, sauce, taste 6. canape,
caviar, degust, flavor, liking 8. pleasure
9. condiment, degustate, enjoyment,
flavoring, seasoning 11. hors d'oeuvre
13. gratification
relucent . . . 5. lucid 6. lucent 7. radiant,
shining 8. lightish 9. refulgent
reluctance . . . 8. aversion 10. repugnance
13. indisposition, unwillingness
14. disinclination
reluctance unit (Elec) . . . 3. rel
reluctant . . . 5. chary, loath 6. averse
8. hesitant, not ready 9. resisting,
unwilling 11. disinclined
reluctate . . . 5. repel 6. oppose
9. repudiate
rely . . . 4. hold, lean, rest 5. count, trust
6. cleave, depend, reckon, repose
7. confide
rely on, upon . . . 4. hope 5. trust
6. depend, lippen 7. believe
remain . . . 3. lie 4. bide, last, rest,
stay 5. abide, tarry 6. endure, reside
8. continue
remainder . . . 4. rest, stub 5. relic, stump
6. estate 7. balance, remnant, residue,
surplus 8. fragment, leavings, residual,
residuum
remaining . . . 4. left, over 6. ledger (leger)
7. durable, remnant, staying, surplus
8. residual 9. permanent
remaining stationary . . . 6. static
7. waiting 8. awaiting
remains . . . 5. ashes, ruins, stays
6. corpse, relics 7. cadaver, fossils
9. remainder
remanent . . . 4. left 7. further, lasting,
remains, remnant, residue 8. enduring,
leftover, residual 9. permanent,
remainder 10. additional
13. supplementary
remark . . . 3. say, see 4. heed, note
5. gloss, state 6. notice, regard
7. comment, observe 8. perceive,
point out 9. statement 10. annotation,
commentary, indication 11. observation
12. interjection
remark (pert to) . . .
amusing, witty . . 3. gag 4. quip
clever . . 3. mot
commonplace . . 9. platitude
smarting . . 7. sarcasm, stinger
upon . . 7. explain
witless . . 5. boner

remarkable ... 5. great 7. notable, strange, unusual 8. uncommon 9. wonderful 10. noteworthy, noticeable, observable 11. conspicuous 13. extraordinary

Rembrandt (pert to) ...
birthplace .. 6. Leyden (Neth)
color .. 5. brown
famed as .. 6. etcher (Dutch) 7. painter
style .. 14. Rembrandtesque

remedial ... 6. remedy (pert to) 7. healing 8. curative, panacean 10. corrective 11. therapeutic

remedy ... 3. aid, fix 4. bote (bot), cure, gain, help 5. amend 6. doctor, relief 8. antidote, medicine 10. assistance, reparation

remedy (pert to) ...
cure-all .. 6. elixir
mysterious (of Paracelsus) .. 7. arcanum
quack .. 7. nostrum
soothing .. 4. balm 6. balsam
universal .. 7. panacea

remember ... 3. min 9. recollect, reminisce 10. keep in mind

remembrance ... 4. fame 5. token 6. memory, Minnie, trophy 7. memento 8. allusion, memorial, reminder, souvenir 12. recollection 13. commemoration

remex ... 12. quill feather

remind ... 6. prompt, recall 8. remember 13. call attention

reminder ... 4. memo, twit 7. memento 8. souvenir 10. memorandum 11. remembrance

reminiscence ... 3. act 4. fact 5. power 6. memory 8. anecdote 10. experience 11. memorabilia 12. recollection

remise ... 6. giving, return 7. release, replace, respite 8. granting 9. remission, surrender

remiss ... 3. lax 5. slack 7. lenient 8. careless, dilatory, heedless 9. negligent 10. neglectful 11. inattentive, thoughtless

remissness ... 7. neglect 9. indolence 10. negligence 12. improvidence

remit ... 3. pay 5. relax 6. acquit, assign, cancel, excuse, pardon, reduce, resign 7. absolve, forgive, release, restore, suspend 8. abrogate, liberate, mitigate, recommit 9. surrender

remnant ... 3. ash, end, ort, rag 4. dreg, left, rest, stub 5. piece, relic, scrap, shred, trace 7. oddment, remains, yet left 8. fragment 9. remainder, remaining 10. suggestion

remolade ... 5. sauce 8. dressing, ointment

remonstrate ... 5. plead 7. protest 8. point out 11. expostulate

remontant ... 14. flowering again

remora ... 4. fish, pega (pegora)

remord ... 5. taint 6. ponder, rebuke 7. afflict, censure, remorse

remorse ... 4. pity 6. regret, sorrow 8. distress 9. penitence, repentent 10. compassion 11. compunction

remorseful ... 5. sorry 7. pitiful 8. contrite, merciful, penitent, pitiable

9. regretful 13. compassionate

remorseless ... 8. pitiless 9. merciless, unpitying 10. implacable, inflexible, relentless, unmerciful 11. unregretful

remote ... 3. far, off 5. alien, vague 6. elenge, forane, ultima 7. distant, foreign 8. abstruse, reserved, secluded, ulterior 10. farfetched, unsociable 11. out-of-the-way

remote control ... 10. pushbutton, tele-action

remote region ... 5. Thule (Greenland)

remotest ... 7. endmost, very end 8. farthest 14. ghost of a chance

removal ... 8. ejection 9. deduction 10. divestment, evacuation, extraction 11. elimination 12. transference

remove ... 3. rid 4. dele, doff, move, void, weed 5. erase, evict, expel, strip 6. change, debunk, delete, depose, divest, eloign (law) 7. dismiss, extract, relieve 8. abstract, displace, evacuate, put aside, transfer 9. eliminate, eradicate, translate 11. assassinate

remove (pert to) ...
cover .. 5. uncap
from office .. 4. oust 6. depose, recall
moisture .. 3. dry 5. wring 9. dehydrate
point of origin .. 6. distal
seed from flax .. 6. ribble
seeds .. 3. gin, pit
stalk .. 5. strig
to another place .. 8. transfer 9. translate
whole blubber .. 6. flense

removed ... 4. took 5. apart 6. betook, remote 7. distant, far away 8. reserved, secluded 9. separated, unrelated 10. unsociable

remover ... 6. porter 7. carrier, drayman, solvent 9. scavenger 10. contractor, eradicator

remunerate ... 3. pay 5. repay 6. reward 7. requite, satisfy 9. reimburse 10. compensate, recompense

remuneration ... 3. pay 6. reward 7. payment 8. pittance, requital 9. emolument 10. recompense 12. compensation, satisfaction 13. reimbursement

Remus (pert to) ...
brother .. 7. Romulus
father .. 4. Mars
legendary founder of .. 4. Rome (with brother)
slayer .. 7. Romulus

renable ... 4. glib 5. ready 6. fluent 8. eloquent

renaissance ... 7. rebirth, revival

Renaissance (pert to) ...
Archit .. 12. Roman classic
art .. 10. neoclassic
associated with .. 8. Petrarch
furniture .. 6. carved 7. English, Flemish
Italian reference .. 12. Resorgimento (new arising)
lace .. 10. Battenburg

renal ... 6. kidney 7. nephric

renascence ... 7. rebirth, revival 14. The Renaissance

rencounter ... 4. duel 5. clash 6. action, combat, flight 7. contest, meeting

8. conflict 9. collision

rend ... 3. rip 4. rive, tear 5. break, burst, sever, split, wrest 7. extract, rupture 8. fracture

render ... 3. pay, put 4. give, make, melt 6. return 7. clarify, convert, deliver, execute, extract, narrate, present, requite 8. transmit 9. translate 10. understand 11. communicate

render (pert to) ...
accessible . . 4. open
agreeable . . 7. dulcify
angry, choleric . . 6. enrage
conformable to Eng . . 7. Anglify 9. Anglicize
divine . . 5. deify
dull . . 8. hebetate
enduring . . 6. anneal
fat . . 3. try out
fertile . . 6. enrich
free from bacteria . . 9. sterilize
ineffective . . 4. void 5. annul 10. invalidate
intelligible . . 9. elucidate
less pliant . . 7. stiffen
muddy, turgid . . 4. roil
oblique . . 5. splay
obscure . . 6. darkle 9. obfuscate
sharp . . 9. acuminate
unconscious . . 4. stun

rendezvous ... 5. tryst 6. refuge 7. meeting, retreat 11. appointment

rendition ... 7. account 8. delivery 9. surrender 10. extraction 11. performance, translation 14. interpretation

renegade ... 3. rat 5. rebel 7. pervert, traitor 8. apostate, deserter, fugitive, turncoat

renege ... 4. deny 6. desert, revoke 7. decline 8. renounce

renew ... 6. resume, revamp, revive 7. convert, refresh, restore 8. renovate 10. invigorate, regenerate 12. redintegrate

renewal ... 10. conversion, renovation, resumption 11. restoration

renitent ... 7. opposed 9. reluctant, resistant 12. recalcitrant

rennet ... 3. lab 5. apple 6. curdle, rennin 7. extract 9. coagulate

rennin ... 6. enzyme

renommé ... 8. renowned 10. celebrated

Renommist ... 8. braggart, renowner 9. swaggerer

renounce ... 4. cede, deny 5. forgo (forego), waive 6. abjure, desert, disown, recant, reject, renege, resign 7. abandon, forsake, retract 8. abnegate, forswear, swear off 9. repudiate, surrender 10. relinquish 12. abrenunciate

renouncement ... 9. rejection 10. temperance 11. abandonment, recantation

renovate ... 5. renew 6. repair, resume, revive 7. restore 10. regenerate

renown ... 4. fame, note 5. éclat, glory 10. reputation

renowned ... 5. famed, noted 6. famous 10. celebrated 11. illustrious

13. distinguished

rent ... 3. let, pay 4. dues, hire, hole, slit, tear, toll, tore, torn 5. break, cleft, lease, share, split 6. reward 7. revenue, rupture, slitted, tribute 8. tattered

rent (pert to) ...
asunder . . 5. rived
harvest . . 7. onstand
in oats . . 7. avenage
paid . . 3. tac

renter ... 6. lessee, lodger, tenant

renunciation ... 6. denial 9. disavowal, rejection, surrender 10. abjuration, disclaimer, temperance 11. abandonment, recantation 14. relinquishment

repaid in kind ... 10. retaliated

repair ... 3. fix 4. darn, heal, mend 5. amend, patch, renew 6. doctor, remedy, resort 7. correct, rebuild, restore 8. atone for 9. condition 13. betake oneself

reparation ... 6. amende, amends, remedy, repair, reward 7. damages, redress 8. reprisal, requital 9. atonement, indemnity 10. recompense 11. restitution 12. compensation, satisfaction

repartee ... 3. wit 5. reply 6. retort 7. riposte

repast ... 3. tea 4. feed, meal 5. feast, lunch, treat 6. tiffin 8. mealtime, prandial 9. collation

repatriate ... 5. exile 6. banish 10. expatriate

repay ... 4. meed 6. answer, avenge, refund, return 7. requite, restore 9. reimburse, retaliate 10. compensate, recompense, remunerate

repeal ... 5. annul, emend, forgo (forego) 6. appeal, cancel, recall 7. abandon, abolish, rescind, retract, reverse 8. abrogate, renounce, withdraw

repeat ... 4. copy, echo, rame 5. recur 7. iterate, restate 8. remember 9. duplicate, reiterate

repeat (pert to) ...
mathematics . . 8. repetend
mechanically . . 6. parrot
noisily . . 3. din
performance . . 6. encore
twice (pref) . . 3. bis

repeating ... 4. rote 10. repetitive 11. repetitious

repel ... 5. avert, check 6. offend, oppose, rebuff, refuse, reject, resist, revolt 7. disgust, repulse 9. drive back, force back

repellent ... 5. harsh 6. odious 9. repulsive, resistant, revolting

repent ... 3. rue 6. reform, regret 9. do penance

repentance ... 4. ruth 5. shame 6. regret 9. penitence 10. contrition 11. compunction

repercussion ... 4. blow 6. impact 9. afterclap, aftermath 10. reflection

repertory ... 4. list 5. index, store 8. calendar, magazine, treasure 9. catalogue 10. collection, repertoire, storehouse

repetition ... **4.** rote **5.** troll **6.** encore
8. iterance **9.** iteration **11.** reiteration
14. recapitulation
repetition (pert to) ...
biology .. **6.** merism
music .. **5.** rondo **7.** tremolo
rhetoric .. **8.** anaphora **9.** tautology
sound .. **4.** echo
sounds (slight) .. **6.** patter
repetitive ... **8.** habitual **9.** redundant
11. repetitious
repine ... **4.** fret **6.** lament, regret
7. grumble **8.** complain
replace ... **4.** stet **5.** reset, stead **6.** repone
7. restore **8.** supplant **9.** discharge,
supersede **10.** substitute
replaceable ... **10.** expendable
replenish ... **4.** feed, fill **5.** store **6.** refill
7. perfect, provide **8.** complete
replete ... **3.** fat **4.** full **5.** sated
6. filled, gorged **7.** bloated **8.** abundant
9. surfeited
replevin ... **4.** bail, writ **8.** recovery
replica ... **3.** bis **4.** copy **6.** repeat
9. duplicate, facsimile
reply ... **4.** echo **5.** rebut **6.** answer,
oracle, rejoin, retort **7.** defense, epistle,
respond **8.** reaction, repartee, response
9. rejoinder **11.** retaliation
report ... **3.** cry, pop **4.** bang, note **5.** bruit,
rumor, sound, state, story **6.** delate,
recite, relate, repute **7.** account,
hearsay, recital, verdict **8.** describe
9. narration, narrative, statement
10. accounting, commentary,
responsory **11.** information, publication
report (pert to) ...
common .. **6.** gossip
false, absurd .. **5.** rumor **6.** canard
7. slander
following lightning .. **7.** thunder
for duty .. **14.** present oneself
official .. **7.** hansard
of proceedings .. **6.** cahier
reporter ... **3.** cub **6.** legman, pistol
7. newsman **8.** newshawk **9.** informant
12. newspaperman
reporter's rounds ... **8.** newsbeat
reporter's sign off ... **6.** thirty
repose ... **3.** lie, sit **4.** ease, rely, rest
5. peace, place, sleep **7.** deposit, recline
9. quiescent, quietness **10.** quiescence,
relaxation
repository ... **3.** ark **4.** file **5.** vault
6. chapel (RCCh), museum **8.** treasury
9. confidant, sepulcher **10.** depository,
storehouse **11.** auction room
reposoir ... **5.** altar
repoussé ... **7.** art work
reprehensible ... **8.** blamable, culpable
9. accusable, obnoxious **10.** censurable,
reprovable **11.** blameworthy
reprehension ... **5.** blame **7.** censure,
reproof **9.** reprimand **11.** reprobation
12. condemnation, denunciation
represent ... **5.** enact **6.** denote, depict,
typify **7.** betoken, exhibit, portray,
produce **8.** describe **9.** delineate
representation ... **3.** art **4.** copy, icon,
idea, idol, show **5.** drama **6.** avowal,
symbol **7.** picture **9.** depiction,

enactment, portrayal, spectacle
10. exhibition, profession
11. delineation, description, portraiture
12. reproduction
representation (pert to) ...
by characters (Mus) .. **8.** notation
graphic .. **5.** chart
Medusa's head .. **9.** gorgoneum
mental .. **5.** image **7.** eidolon, phantom
of scene .. **7.** tableau
of solar system .. **6.** orrery
of star .. **7.** estoile
small .. **5.** model **9.** miniature
representative ... **4.** heir, type **5.** agent,
envoy **6.** deputy, legate **7.** example,
tribune, typical **8.** delegate, exponent,
symbolic **9.** successor **10.** ambassador,
legislator, lieutenant, substitute
12. illustrative
repress ... **4.** curb, rein, stop **5.** check,
crush, quell **6.** hush up, muffle, stifle
7. put down **8.** restrain, suppress
9. overpower
reprieve ... **5.** delay **6.** pardon, relief
7. relieve, respite **8.** postpone
reprimand ... **5.** chide, scold, slate
6. rebuke **7.** censure, reprove
reprisal ... **7.** revenge, revenue **8.** requital
11. retaliation
reproach ... **4.** taca, twit **5.** abuse, blame,
chide, shend, taunt **6.** accuse, revile,
vilify **7.** censure, condemn, reproof,
sarcasm, upbraid **8.** disgrace, dishonor
9. disrepute, invective **10.** accusation,
opprobrium **12.** vilification
reproach, free of ... **9.** blameless
reprobate ... **6.** disown, reject, wicked
7. abandon, corrupt, knavish, vicious
8. depraved, hardened, recreant
9. condemned, miscreant, reprehend,
scoundrel **10.** black sheep
12. unprincipled **13.** reprehensible
reproduce ... **4.** copy **6.** recite, remake,
repeat **8.** multiply **9.** duplicate,
propagate
reproduction ... **4.** copy **6.** ectype,
recall **7.** picture, replica **8.** likeness
10. repetition **11.** counterpart,
duplication **14.** representation
reproductive ... **5.** gamic, spore
10. recreative **12.** regenerative
reproof ... **5.** roast **6.** rebuke **7.** chiding
8. disgrace, reproach **9.** reprimand
10. admonition, censurable, refutation
11. blameworthy, confutation
12. reprehension **13.** reprehensible
reprove ... **4.** rate **5.** blame, chide,
scold **6.** berate, rebuke **7.** censure,
correct, upbraid **8.** admonish, reproach
9. objurgate, reprehend, reprimand
reproving ... **10.** admonitive
reptile ... **4.** toad, worm **5.** snake,
viper **6.** dragon, iguana, lizard, turtle
7. monitor, serpent **8.** creeping, Reptilia
9. scoundrel
reptile (pert to) ...
class .. **8.** Reptilia
crocodile .. **6.** mugger
extinct .. **9.** pterosaur **10.** diplodocus
11. pterodactyl, Pterosauria
group .. **6.** Sauria

hard-shelled.. **6.** iguana, turtle
8. terrapin, tortoise
iguanalike.. **7.** tuatara
large.. **3.** boa **9.** alligator, crocodile
10. salamander
lizard.. **3.** eft **4.** adda, newt, seps **5.** skink
(scink) **6.** Anolis, iguana, moloch
7. monitor **9.** chameleon **10.** chuckwalla
11. Gila monster
Mesozoic.. **8.** dinosaur
myth.. **6.** dragon **8.** basilisk
10. cockatrice, salamander
oldest.. **9.** sea turtle
salamander.. **3.** eft **4.** newt
scale.. **5.** scute
snake.. **3.** asp **5.** adder, cobra,
krait **6.** garter, python **8.** anaconda,
Squamata **10.** copperhead
reptilian ... **7.** saurian
Reptilian Age ... **8.** Mesozoic
Republic ... **5.** State **6.** France **7.** Andorra
(Andorre) **9.** San Marino
10. commonweal, government
12. United States
Republican Party ... **3.** GOP
7. mugwump (bolter 1884)
Republic of Plato ... **4.** Book (famed)
8. dialogue **10.** ideal State
repudiate ... **4.** deny **6.** abjure, disown,
recant, reject **7.** disavow, discard,
exclude **8.** renounce
repugnance ... **4.** hate **5.** odium **6.** nausea
7. disgust, opposed **8.** aversion,
loathing **9.** antipathy, hostility
10. abhorrence, antagonism, opposition,
reluctance **12.** disagreement
repugnant ... **6.** odious **7.** adverse,
hostile, opposed **8.** inimical **9.** offensive,
repellent, repulsive **10.** refractory
11. distasteful **12.** incompatible
14. irreconcilable
repulse ... **5.** repel **6.** denial, rebuff
7. refusal **9.** rejection
repulsive ... **4.** ugly, vile **5.** nasty
6. odious **7.** fulsome **9.** offensive,
repellent, resistant, revolting
10. disgusting, forbidding, malodorous
repurchase ... **6.** redeem
reputable ... **6.** worthy **9.** estimable,
honorable **10.** creditable **11.** respectable
reputation ... **4.** fame, name, note
5. glory, honor **9.** celebrity, notoriety
11. distinction **13.** consideration
repute ... **4.** hold, word **5.** éclat, honor
6. credit, esteem, regard, report, revere
8. prestige **9.** reputable **10.** popularity,
reputation
reputed ... **6.** deemed **7.** assumed
8. accepted, presumed, putative,
supposed **10.** understood
request ... **3.** ask, beg **4.** plea, pray, suit
6. appeal, behest, demand **7.** entreat,
solicit **8.** entreaty, petition, rogation
12. supplication
requiescat in pace ... **11.** rest in peace
requiescence ... **6.** repose
requin ... **5.** shark **8.** man-eater
require ... **3.** ask **4.** need **5.** claim, exact,
force **6.** charge, compel, demand,
enjoin, entail, oblige **8.** obligate
11. necessitate

requisition ... **5.** order **6.** demand
11. application, requirement
requital ... **7.** payment, revenge
8. reprisal **10.** recompense
11. retaliation, retribution
12. compensation
requite ... **3.** pay **5.** atone, repay
6. avenge, return, reward **7.** revenge,
satisfy **9.** retaliate **10.** compensate,
recompense **11.** interchange
reredos ... **4.** wall **6.** screen **9.** back-plate
(armor), partition
reremouse ... **3.** bat
res ... **5.** point, thing **6.** matter
rescind ... **5.** annul **6.** cancel, recall,
recant, repeal, revoke **7.** abolish
8. abrogate
rescue ... **3.** aid **4.** free, save **6.** ransom,
redeem, regain **7.** deliver, reclaim,
recover, release **8.** delivery, liberate
9. extricate **11.** deliverance
rese ... **4.** rage, rush **5.** hurry, onset,
quake, shake **7.** impulse, tremble
8. rashness
resemblance ... **6.** ringer **7.** analogy
8. affinity, likeness **9.** agreement,
semblance **10.** similarity, similitude
resembling (pert to) ...
bark.. **11.** corticiform
comb.. **8.** pectinal
goose.. **8.** anserine
gypsum.. **11.** alabastrine
horse.. **6.** equoid
man.. **7.** android
minute animals.. **11.** animalcular
rind.. **8.** cortical
salt.. **6.** haloid
seed.. **6.** ovular
snakes.. **7.** elapine **8.** viperine
star.. **7.** stellar **8.** stellate **9.** stellated
turf.. **5.** soddy
wall.. **5.** mural
resentment ... **3.** ire **5.** pique, spite
6. choler, enmity, hatred, malice, rancor
7. dudgeon, umbrage **9.** animosity,
malignity **11.** displeasure, indignation
reservation ... **5.** tract **8.** preserve
9. reticence **10.** engagement, limitation
11. withholding **13.** qualification
reserve ... **4.** bank, fund, keep, save
5. allot, spare, stock, store **6.** engage,
refuge **7.** backlog, modesty, shyness
8. coldness, distance, postpone,
withhold **9.** exception, restraint,
retention, reticence, sanctuary
10. constraint, diffidence, limitation,
substitute **11.** self-control, taciturnity
reserved ... **3.** coy **4.** cool, kept,
unco **5.** aloof, saved, staid, taken
6. modest, sedate **7.** distant **8.** reticent
15. uncommunicative
reservoir ... **4.** font, pool, sump **5.** store
6. cavity, cenote, supply **7.** piscina,
reserve **8.** fountain
reservoir of Pecquet (Anat) ... **12.** lymph
channel **13.** cisterna chyli
res gestae ... **5.** deeds, facts **8.** exploits
10. things done
resiant ... **7.** present **8.** resident
reside ... **4.** bide, live, room, stay **5.** abide,
dwell, lodge **6.** remain **7.** sojourn

8. habitate
residence . . . 4. home, seat, stay 5. abode
  6. palace 7. deanery 8. domicile,
  dwelling 9. consulate, residency
  10. habitation
residencia . . . 5. court, trial
resident . . . 3. cit 6. intern, tenant
  7. burgess, citizen 8. diplomat, occupant
  10. inhabitant
residual . . . 7. remnant 8. residuum
  9. remainder
residue . . . 3. ash, ort 4. coke, dreg, marc,
  rest, silt, slag 5. ashes 6. pomace,
  relics 7. balance, remains, remnant
  8. leavings, sediment 9. remainder
residuum . . . 7. residue 8. hangover,
  leavings 9. remainder
resign . . . 4. cede, quit 5. demit,
  waive, yield 6. give up, submit
  7. abandon, consign 8. abdicate,
  renounce 9. surrender 10. relinquish
resignation . . . 5. demit 8. patience
  9. demission, endurance 10. abdication,
  submission 12. renunciation
  14. relinquishment
resigned . . . 9. contented 10. submissive
  11. acquiescent 13. uncomplaining
resilient . . . 7. buoyant, elastic 8. cheerful
  9. recoiling 10. rebounding 11. returning
  to 12. recuperative
resin . . . 3. gum, lac 4. aloe, tolu 5. amber,
  anime, copal, jalap, rosin 6. dammar,
  mastic
resin (pert to) . . .
  aromatic . . 4. balm 5. elemi, myrrh
   6. balsam 7. acouchi, camphor, copaiba
   8. sandarac 12. frankincense
  Bib . . 8. bdellium
  bitter . . 8. labdanum (ladanum)
  brown (mineral) . . 9. elaterite
  Chian turpentine . . 3. alk
  fossil . . 5. amber 8. retinite
  gum . . 5. gugal (googul)
  hard . . 5. rosin
  medicinal . . 7. aroeira 9. asafetida
   (asafoetida)
  narcotic . . 6. charas
  pine . . 7. galipot
  soft . . 5. animé, copal, elemi
  translucent . . 8. sandarac
  tropical . . 5. copal
  varnish ingredient . . 6. dammar
  yellowish . . 5. amber 7. gamboge
resinous substance . . . 3. gum, lac
  5. copal 7. shellac
resist . . . 4. fend, stem 5. rebel, repel
  6. defeat, oppose 7. prevent, ward off
  8. outstand 9. withstand 10. counteract
resistance . . . 6. rebuff 7. defense
  8. rheostat 9. hostility 10. opposition
resistance unit . . . 3. ohm
resistant . . . 5. tough 8. obdurate
  9. resisting 10. unyielding
  13. counteractive
resisting . . . 7. hostile 8. opposing
  9. oppugnant, tenacious
  12. antagonistic
resisting (pert to) . . .
  description . . 11. indefinable
  power . . 4. wiry
  pressure . . 8. renitent

pressure bar . . 5. strut
resolute . . . 4. bold, firm 5. fixed, stern
  6. gritty, steady 7. decided 8. constant,
  positive, resolved, unshaken
  9. desperado, obstinate, steadfast
  10. determined, inflexible, unyielding
  11. perseverant, persevering
resolution . . . 4. firm 5. nerve 6. motion,
  steady 7. courage, purpose, resolve,
  verdict 8. analysis, decision, resolved,
  strength 9. assurance, constancy,
  fortitude 10. conversion, conviction,
  relaxation, separation 11. persevering
  12. perseverance 13. determination,
  steadfastness 15. disentanglement
resolve . . . 4. melt 5. lapse (law), parse,
  relax, solve 6. assure, decide, dispel,
  inform, reduce, settle 7. analyze,
  explain, purpose, unravel 8. convince,
  dissolve, separate 9. determine,
  transform 11. disentangle
resonance . . . 8. sonority, vibrance
  10. resounding
resonant . . . 7. echoing, ringing, vibrant
  8. sonorous, sounding 10. resounding
  11. reverberant
resort . . . 3. spa 4. dive 5. haunt
  6. betake, casino, refuge 7. finagle,
  purlieu 8. frequent, recourse, resource
  9. expedient, fainaigue, honky-tonk
resound . . . 4. echo, peal, ring 6. be loud,
  re-echo 8. proclaim 11. reverberate
resounding . . . 4. loud 13. reverberating
resource . . . 5. means, skill 6. refuge,
  resort, supply 9. expedient
  10. capability 11. contrivance
resourceful . . . 5. sharp 9. Daedalian,
  ingenious
resources . . . 5. funds, means, money
  6. assets, supply 7. resorts
  10. expedients 12. contrivances
respect . . . 3. awe 4. heed 5. defer,
  favor, honor 6. aspect, detail, esteem,
  homage, regard, repute, revere
  7. concern, observe, regards 8. attitude,
  venerate 9. attention, deference,
  relevance, reverence, viewpoint
  10. politeness 13. consideration
respectable . . . 6. decent 9. estimable,
  honorable, reputable, tolerable
  11. presentable
respectful . . . 5. civil 6. polite 7. careful,
  duteous, heedful 8. reverent
  11. deferential
respective . . . 6. mutual 7. careful,
  heedful, several, special 9. attentive,
  regardful 10. particular 12. distributive
respiration . . . 4. rale, sigh 7. eupnoea
  9. breathing
respire . . . 7. breathe
respite . . . 4. rest 5. delay, first, pause
  6. breath 7. leisure 8. postpone, reprieve
  9. extension (time) 10. suspension
  11. opportunity, short shrift
  12. intermission
resplendent . . . 5. grand 7. aureate,
  radiant, shining 8. lustrous, splendid
  9. beautiful, brilliant, refulgent
  10. epiphanous 11. illustrious
respond . . . 4. echo 5. react, reply
  6. accord, answer, retort 8. response

10. correspond 11. reciprocate
response... 4. echo 5. reply 6. answer, anthem, chorus 7. rapport, refrain 8. antiphon (Mus), reaction
responsibility... 4. care, duty, onus 6. charge 8. solvency 11. reliability 14. accountability 15. trustworthiness
responsible... 6. liable 7. solvent 8. amenable, reliable 10. answerable 11. accountable, respectable, trustworthy
responsive... 6. pliant 7. elastic 8. reactive 9. answering, sensitive, teachable 10. open-minded 11. persuasible, sympathetic
res publica... 5. state 8. republic 10. commonweal 12. commonwealth
rest... 3. lay, set, sit 4. base, calm, ease, lair, lean, prop, seat, slip, stay, stop 5. cease, death, found, pause, peace, quiet, relax, renew 6. depend, desist, ground, repose, settle 7. balance, leisure, recline, refresh, remains, remnant, reposal, respite, silence, support, surplus 8. at anchor, interval, lodgment, residuum 9. cessation, quietness, remainder, stillness 10. quiescence, remain idle 12. intermission, peacefulness, tranquillity
rest (pert to)...
assured.. 9. be certain, believe me
at rest.. 4. abed, dead 6. otiose 11. comfortable
day.. 7. Sabbath
foot.. 4. rail 7. hassock, ottoman
house (Orient).. 5. serai
reading.. 7. caesura (cesura)
restaurant... 4. café, deli (sl) 5. diner 6. eatery 7. automat, beanery, tearoom 8. fast-food, pizzeria, snack bar 9. cafeteria 10. coffee shop 11. rathskeller 12. luncheonette
resting... 4. abed 7. dormant 8. drowsing 9. quiescent
resting place... 4. tomb 5. étape, roost 6. hearth 7. lairage, landing, support 8. quarters
restitution... 6. return 9. atonement, repayment 10. recompense, reparation 12. compensation 13. reinstatement
restless... 5. antsy, hyper, itchy 6. roving, uneasy 7. agitato, fidgety, fretful, unquiet, restive, wakeful 8. agitated 9. impatient, sleepless, unceasing, unrestful, unsettled, wandering 10. changeable, reposeless 12. discontented
restoration... 6. repair, return 7. renewal, revival 8. recovery 10. renovation, reparation 11. improvement, restitution 14. redintegration 15. reestablishment
restorative... 6. acopon 7. anodyne 8. remedial 10. reparative
restore... 4. cure, heal 5. renew, repay 6. redeem, refund, repone, revive 7. rebuild, recover, replace 8. renovate 9. reinstate 11. reconstruct, reestablish 12. redintegrate, rehabilitate
restore (pert to)...
after cancelling.. 4. stet

certainty, confidence.. 8. reassure
to former position.. 9. reinstate
to original condition.. 9. refurbish
to proper position.. 5. right
restrain... 3. dam 4. bate, bind, curb, rein, stay 5. check, cramp, deter, limit, stint 6. arrest, bridle, fetter, halter, hinder, tether 7. abridge, confine, control, inhibit, overawe, qualify, repress 8. restrict, suppress, withhold 9. constrain, detention
restraint... 4. bit 5. curb, stop 5. check, force 7. durance, modesty, reserve 9. condition, hindrance, reticence 10. abridgment, constraint, inhibition, limitation, moderation, repression, temperance 11. confinement, deprivation, self-control 12. tastefulness
restraint, lack of... 9. looseness
restrict... 3. tie 4. bind, curb 5. bound, cramp, limit, scant, stint 6. censor, coerce, modify 7. confine, qualify, repress 10. specialize 12. circumscribe
restricted... 5. local 6. narrow 7. limited, topical 9. exclusive 10. restrained 11. specialized
restriction... 5. stint 9. restraint 10. limitation, narrowness, regulation, tightening 11. reservation 12. constriction 13. qualification
resty... 5. quiet 7. restive 8. sluggish
result... 3. end, sum 4. rise 5. arise, ensue, event, fruit, issue, total 6. accrue, answer, effect, follow, sequel, spring, upshot 7. proceed, product 8. solution 9. aftermath, deduction, eventuate, terminate 10. conclusion 11. achievement, consequence, termination
resume... 5. recur, renew 6. reopen 7. recover 8. reoccupy 9. epitomize, reiterate, summarize 10. recommence
résumé... 8. abstract 10. compendium 11. work history
resurrection... 6. rising 7. revival 10. apotheosis 11. restoration
resuscitate... 6. revive 7. restore 8. revivify
ret... 3. rot 4. soak 5. steep 6. expose, impute 7. ascribe
retable... 5. ledge, shelf 6. gradin (gradine) 8. predella
retail... 4. sale, sell 6. repeat 8. dispense, disperse
retain... 4. hold, keep, save, stet 6. employ 8. maintain, preserve, remember 9. recollect
retainer... 3. fee 4. cage 6. menial, minion, vassal, yeoman 7. servant 9. attendant, bodyguard
retaining wall... 9. revetment
retaliate... 5. repay 6. avenge 7. requite 12. make requital
retaliation... 6. talion (Mosaic law, eye for eye, tooth for tooth) 7. revenge 8. reprisal, requital 10. punishment 11. comeuppance, retribution
retard... 4. clog, drag, slow 5. defer, delay, laten 6. belate, deaden, detain, hinder, impede 8. keep back, obstruct, postpone, slow down

retardant ... **4.** clog, drag **6.** remora **8.** obstacle

retardate ... **6.** impede **8.** retarded

retch ... **3.** gag **4.** barf (sl), hawk, spit **5.** reach, vomit **6.** expand, extend, strain **7.** stretch, upchuck

rete ... **3.** net **6.** plexus **7.** network

retention ... **6.** memory **7.** custody, holding, keeping **8.** tenacity **11.** maintenance, self-control

retentive ... **6.** memory **7.** keeping **9.** tenacious **12.** recollective

retenue ... **7.** reserve **10.** discretion **11.** self-control **13.** self-restraint

rethe ... **5.** cruel **6.** ardent, fierce, severe

retiary ... **6.** spider **7.** netlike **9.** gladiator, retiarius

reticence ... **7.** reserve, silence **9.** restraint **13.** secretiveness

reticulated ... **3.** web **6.** meshed, netted **7.** network **12.** intercrossed

reticule ... **3.** bag **4.** etui **5.** cabas (caba) **7.** handbag, reticle, workbag

reticulum ... **7.** network, stomach (2nd) **9.** neuroglia

retinue ... **4.** crew **5.** harem, suite, train **6.** escort **7.** cortege, service **8.** equipage **9.** entourage, retainers **10.** attendants

retire ... **6.** depart, depose, pay off, recede, vanish **7.** go to bed, retreat **8.** withdraw **9.** disappear, discharge

retired ... **4.** abed, left, lone, paid **7.** receded **8.** departed, emeritus, recessed, resigned, secluded, solitary, vanished, withdrew **9.** pensioned **10.** disengaged **11.** disappeared, sequestered

retirement ... **7.** deposal, payment, privacy, retreat **8.** solitude **9.** departure, recession, reticence **10.** withdrawal **11.** resignation **13.** disemployment

retiring ... **3.** shy **6.** modest **8.** reserved, reticent **9.** diffident **10.** not forward, retreating **11.** unobtrusive

retort ... **3.** mot **4.** quip **5.** reply **6.** answer **7.** riposte (ripost) **8.** repartee **9.** retaliate **11.** retaliation

retract ... **6.** abjure, disown, draw in, recent, repeal **7.** disavow, rescind, swallow **8.** take back **9.** repudiate

retraction ... **6.** repeal **8.** palinode **10.** revocation, withdrawal **11.** recantation

retrad ... **8.** backward **11.** posteriorly

retral ... **8.** backward **9.** posterior **10.** retrograde

retreat ... **3.** den **4.** abri, lair, nest, nook, rout **6.** asylum, recede, recoil, refuge, retire **7.** privacy, retiral, sanctum, shelter **8.** fallback, solitude **9.** departure, katabasis, seclusion **10.** retirement, withdrawal

retrench ... **6.** cut off, excise, lessen, reduce **7.** abridge, curtail, cut down **8.** decrease, diminish **9.** economize, intercept

retrenchment ... **3.** cut **8.** excision **9.** lessening, reduction **10.** abridgment **11.** curtailment, economizing

retribution ... **3.** pay **6.** return, reward **7.** nemesis **8.** reprisal, requital

9. vengeance **10.** punishment **11.** restitution **12.** Last Judgment

retrieve ... **5.** fetch **6.** redeem, regain, rescue, revive **8.** make good

retrograde ... **4.** slow **6.** recede, retral, revert **7.** regress **8.** backward, decadent, rearward **10.** regressive **11.** deteriorate **12.** reversionary

retroussé ... **6.** pugged (nose) **8.** turned up

retund ... **4.** beat, dull **5.** blunt **6.** refute, subdue **9.** attenuate, drive back **10.** render weak

return ... **5.** recur, repay, reply **6.** answer, render, repeat, report, revert **7.** regress, relapse, requiet, respond, restore **9.** repayment **11.** restitution, retaliation

return (pert to) ...
day . . **12.** answer to writ
evil for evil . . **7.** revenge **9.** retaliate
tennis term . . **3.** lob
thrust (fencing) . . **7.** riposte (ripost)
to . . **6.** resume **7.** relapse, revisit
to first theme (Mus) . . **7.** reprise

returns ... **5.** gains, polls **8.** receipts

reune ... **4.** join **7.** reunite **10.** reassemble

reunion ... **7.** joining **8.** sociable **14.** reconciliation

re-up ... **8.** re-enlist

reus ... **9.** defendant

Reuter's News Agency ... **6.** London

reveal ... **3.** bid **4.** bare, jamb, open, tell, wray **6.** impart, unveil **7.** divulge, exhibit, uncover **8.** disclose, discover, evidence, indicate, manifest **11.** communicate

reveal (in trust) ... **7.** confide

reveal intentionally ... **4.** tell **6.** betray, expose **7.** divulge, mislead

reveille ... **4.** call **5.** levet **6.** signal (sunrise)

revel ... **3.** joy **4.** orgy, riot, wake **5.** feast, spree, watch **6.** frolic **7.** carouse, delight, rejoice, revelry, wassail **8.** carousal, festival **11.** celebration, merrymaking **12.** conviviality

revelant ... **5.** clear **8.** manifest **12.** intelligible

revelation ... **6.** oracle, vision **8.** The Bible **9.** discovery **10.** appearance, disclosure **13.** communication, manifestation

Revelation (Bib) ... **10.** Apocalypse

revelry ... **3.** joy **4.** evoe, orgy, riot **6.** revels **8.** carnival, carousal **9.** revelment, revelrout **11.** merrymaking

revenant ... **5.** ghost **7.** eidolon, specter (spectre) **9.** recurring **10.** apparition

revendicate ... **7.** reclaim, recover **10.** real action

revenge ... **6.** avenge **7.** requite **8.** reprisal, requital **9.** retaliate, vengeance **10.** punishment **11.** retribution

revenue ... **3.** tax **5.** yield **6.** income, profit **7.** annates

reverberate ... **4.** echo, ring **5.** repel, reply **6.** return **7.** rebound, reflect, resound

reverberation ... **4.** echo **9.** reboation **10.** reflection, resounding

revere ... **4.** love **5.** adore, honor

6. esteem, regard, repute 7. respect, worship 8. venerate

reverence ... 3. awe 5. dread, honor, piety 7. respect, worship 8. venerate 9. adoration, deference 10. veneration

reverent ... 5. pious 6. devout 7. dutiful 10. respectful, worshipful

reverie ... 4. muse 5. dream 6. notion, trance, vision 7. fantasy

reversal ... 6. defeat, repeal 9. inversion, reversion 14. tergiversation

reverse ... 4. back 5. upset 6. back up, defeat, invert, repeal, revert, revoke 7. relapse 8. contrary, converse, opposite, overturn 9. transpose 10. misfortune

reversion ... 6. estate 7. revival 8. transfer 9. inversion 10. regression 11. inheritance

reversion (pert to) ...
ancestral .. 7. atavism 9. atavistic
insurance .. 7. annuity
land .. 7. escheat

revert ... 5. react, recur 6. advert, return 7. regress, relapse 11. antistrophe

revest ... 4. robe 5. dress 6. attire, clothe 8. reinvest 9. reinstate

review ... 4. edit 6. parade, relate, survey 8. critique, remember 9. criticism, criticize, re-examine 10. certiorari, commentary, compendium, discussion, inspection, periodical, reconsider 11. examination, reiteration 12. recollection 15. reconsideration

reviewer ... 6. critic, writer 11. commentator

revile ... 4. rail 5. abuse, curse 6. berate, debase, vilify 7. asperse 8. reproach, ridicule

revise ... 4. edit 5. amend, emend 6. redact 7. correct, rewrite 8. readjust

revision ... 7. revisal 10. correction, emendation 11. rebeholding 13. re-examination

revival ... 7. rebirth, renewal 10. quickening 11. reanimation, renaissance, restoration 12. resurrection

revive ... 4. stum (wine) 5. rally, renew, rouse 6. come to 7. enliven, recover, refresh, respire, restore 8. rekindle, remember 9. resuscitate

revocate ... 6. recall, revoke 7. repress

revocation ... 6. repeal 8. reversal 10. retraction, withdrawal 11. recantation

revoke ... 5. adeem, annul 6. abjure, cancel, recall, recant, renege, repeal, revive 7. abolish, retract 8. abrogate 9. fainaigue 11. countermand

revolt ... 5. rebel 6. mutiny, offend, strike 8. nauseate, sedition, uprising 9. rebellion 10. revolution 12. insurrection

revolting ... 4. ugly 7. hideous 8. shocking 9. offensive, repellent 10. disgusting, nauseating

revolution ... 4. gyre, turn 5. cycle, epoch, orbit, round 6. revolt 7. circuit 8. disorder, rotation 9. rebellion

revolutionary ... 3. new 7. radical 12. catastrophic 15. insurrectionary

Revolutionary hero ... 5. Allen (Ethan), Gates 6. Revere 8. Burgoyne 10. Cornwallis, Washington 15. Lighthorse Harry (Gen Lee)

revolve ... 4. pirl, roll, spin, turn 5. recur, wheel, whirl 6. circle, gyrate, ponder, rotate 7. trundle 8. meditate 9. circulate 10. deliberate

revolver ... 3. gat, gun, rod 6. pistol 7. firearm 10. six-shooter

revolving ... 3. orb 4. cowl (metal cap) 6. rotary

revolving (pert to) ...
in thought .. 8. perusing
light .. 10. lighthouse
part .. 3. cam 5. rotor
storm .. 7. cyclone

revue ... 6. medley, review 9. burlesque 13. musical comedy

reward ... 3. pay, utu 4. meed 5. award, bonus, merit, Oscar, yield 6. hallow (to hounds) 7. guerdon 8. reprisal 10. recompense, remunerate 11. retribution 12. compensation, remuneration

reword ... 5. alter 7. restate 8. rephrase 9. reiterate 10. paraphrase

rex ... 4. king

rey ... 4. king

Reynard ... 3. fox (epic character)

rezai ... 8. coverlet (quilted)

rhamn ... 7. Rhamnus 9. buckthorn

rhapontic ... 7. rhubarb 8. knapweed, pieplant

rhapsodic ... 6. poetic 8. ecstatic

rhapsodist ... 4. poet 8. minstrel 9. visionary 10. enthusiast

rhapsody ... 6. jumble, medley 9. utterance (ecstatic) 10. recitation 11. composition

rhea ... 3. emu (emeu) 5. nandu 7. ostrich

Rhea (pert to) ...
called .. 15. Mother of the Gods
father .. 6. Uranus
home .. 5. Mt Ida (Crete)
mother .. 4. Gaea
mother of .. 4. Hera, Zeus 5. Hades 8. Poseidon
wife of .. 6. Cronus

rhebok ... 5. peele 8. antelope

Rheims ... see *Reims*

rhema ... 4. term, verb, word

rheophile ... 15. living in streams

rhetoric ... 7. diction, oratory 9. eloquence 11. composition

rhetorical term ... 6. aporia, simile 10. antithesis, oratorical 11. catachresis

rhetoric digression ... 6. ecbole

rheumatism root ... 7. wild yam

rheumatism weed ... 10. Indian hemp, pepsissewa

rhexis ... 7. rupture

rhinal ... 5. nasal 6. narial

rhine ... 5. ditch, drain 6. runnel

Rhine (pert to) ...
breed .. 7. rabbits
native .. 11. Rhinelander
nymph .. 7. Lorelei
ref to .. 7. Rhenish
tributary .. 4. Ruhr 6. Neckar
wine .. 7. Moselle

rhino . . . **4.** cash, nose (comb form)
 5. money **10.** rhinoceros
rhinoceros (pert to) . . .
 Bib . . **4.** reem
 bird . . **8.** hornbill **9.** beefeater
 black . . **6.** borele **7.** keitlos
 Malay . . **5.** abada
 viper . . **5.** snake (poisonous)
rhizopod . . . **6.** amoeba **8.** Protozoa
Rhoda . . . **4.** rose
Rhode Island . . .
 bay . . **12.** Narragansett
 capital . . **10.** Providence
 city . . **7.** Newport **9.** Pawtucket
 10. Woonsocket
 famed cotton mill . . **6.** Slater
 first U.S. synagogue . . **5.** Touro
 founder . . **13.** Roger Williams (1636)
 Rebellion . . **5.** Dorr's (1842)
 resort . . **7.** Newport **11.** Block Island
 river . . **9.** Pawtucket **10.** Blackstone
 settlers . . **8.** Puritans
 State admission . . **10.** Thirteenth
 State motto . . **4.** Hope
 State nickname . . **11.** Little Rhody
Rhode Island Red . . . **4.** fowl
Rhodesia . . . see *Zimbabwe*
rhododaphne . . . **8.** oleander
Rhoeadales . . . **5.** poppy **11.** Papaverales
rhomb . . . **7.** rhombus **10.** magic wheel
 11. spinning top
rhomboid . . . **13.** parallelogram
rhombus . . . **5.** rhomb **13.** parallelogram
 (equilateral)
Rhone tributary . . . **5.** Isere
rhubarb . . . **5.** clash, Rheum **6.** hassle
 7. citrine, dispute, yawweed
 8. argument, pieplant **9.** rhapontic
 10. discussion
Rhus . . . **5.** sumac **7.** wax tree
rhyme, rime . . . **4.** poem **6.** poetry,
 rhythm **7.** measure **9.** assonance
rhythm . . . **4.** beat, lilt **5.** meter, pulse,
 swing, tempo **6.** poetry **7.** cadence,
 euphony, measure, pattern
 8. movement, rhythmus, symmetry
rhythmical break . . . **7.** caesura
ria . . . **5.** creek, inlet
rial . . . **4.** coin, king **5.** great, noble, royal
 6. prince **8.** splendid **9.** excellent, stag's
 horn **11.** magnificent
rialto . . . **4.** mart **6.** Bridge (Venice),
 market **7.** theater **8.** exchange
riant . . . **3.** gay **6.** blithe, bright **7.** smiling
 8. laughing
riata . . . **4.** rope **5.** lasso **6.** lariat
rib . . . **4.** bone, meat, vein **5.** costa, ridge
 6. lierne
ribald . . . **3.** low **4.** lewd **6.** coarse,
 erotic, harlot, risqué, vulgar **7.** obscene
 10. scurrilous **11.** blasphemous
 12. ribble-rabble
riband . . . **6.** ribbon
ribbed . . . **3.** rep **5.** piqué **6.** corded,
 ridged **7.** costate
ribble-rabble . . . **6.** gabble, rabble, ribald
 7. chatter **10.** incoherent
ribbon . . . **3.** bow **4.** band, sash **5.** strip
 6. cestus, fillet, riband **10.** decoration
ribbon (pert to) . . .
 badge . . **6.** cordon

 band . . **5.** corse **9.** banderole
 fish . . **7.** oarfish **8.** dealfish
 inked . . **10.** typewriter
 knot . . **7.** rosette
 ribbonlike . . **8.** taenioid
 snake . . **6.** garter
 Society . . **7.** Ireland
 worm . . **8.** tapeworm **9.** nemertine
ribwort . . . **8.** plantain
rice (pert to) . . .
 bird . . **4.** rail, sora **8.** bobolink
 dish . . **5.** pilaf (pilau, pilaw) **7.** risotto
 8. kedgeree **9.** jambalaya, ricetable
 drink . . **5.** bubud
 feeding on . . **11.** oryzivorous
 field . . **5.** paddy
 hen . . **9.** gallinule
 inferior . . **4.** chit, pago
 paste . . **3.** ame
 rat . . **8.** Oryzomys
 refuse . . **5.** shood (shud)
 Spanish . . **5.** arroz
 wild . . **4.** reed
 wine . . **4.** sake
rich . . . **3.** fat **5.** opime **6.** creamy, fecund,
 fruity, mighty, ornate, potent **7.** copious,
 fertile, moneyed, opulent, wealthy
 8. abundant, affluent, colorful, powerful,
 resonant, valuable **9.** bountiful,
 expensive, luxuriant, sumptuous **10.** in
 the chips **13.** grandiloquent
rich (pert to) . . .
 English slang . . **4.** oofy **6.** oofier
 man . . **5.** Dives (Bib), Midas, nabob
 7. Croesus **9.** plutocrat **10.** capitalist
 11. millionaire
richard . . . **9.** plutocrat
riches . . . **5.** lucre, means **6.** mammon
 (Bib), wealth **7.** bonanza **8.** big bucks
 (sl), opulence **9.** affluence, megabucks
 (sl) **10.** prosperity
riches, demon of . . . **6.** Mammon
rick . . . **4.** heap, pile **5.** noise, scold,
 stack, twist **6.** pile up, rattle, sprain,
 wrench **7.** chatter
rickets . . . **7.** disease **8.** rachitis
rickety . . . **4.** weak **5.** crazy, shaky **6.** senile
 7. unsound **8.** unstable, unsteady
 9. tottering **10.** ramshackle
rickle . . . **4.** heap, pile, rick **5.** stack
 6. jingle, rattle
rickrack . . . **5.** braid **6.** edging **9.** insertion
ricksha, rickshaw . . . **10.** jinrikisha
ricochet . . . **5.** carom **7.** rebound
 10. bounce back
rid . . . **4.** doff, free, kill **5.** clear, empty
 6. remove, rescue **7.** deliver, destroy,
 discard **9.** dispose of, drive away,
 eliminate **11.** disencumber
riddance . . . **6.** escape **7.** discard
 11. elimination **14.** relinquishment
riddle . . . **3.** ree **4.** crux, sift **5.** rebus,
 sieve **6.** enigma, pierce **7.** perplex
 8. separate **9.** conundrum, perforate
ride . . . **4.** twit **5.** drive, float **6.** pester,
 travel **7.** be borne, journey, overlap
 8. domineer, ridicule **9.** carrousel
 (carousel), cavalcade, excursion
 10. forest road **12.** merry-go-round
 13. roller coaster
ride (pert to) . . .

herd.. **9.** guard over
off.. **4.** polo (term)
roughshod over.. **9.** tyrannize
shank's mare.. **4.** walk
to hog, pig.. **11.** boar hunting
to line.. **4.** herd
rident... **5.** riant **7.** smiling **8.** laughing
rider... **5.** ryder **6.** clause, knight
  7. allonge, codicil **8.** addition, horseman
  9. performer **10.** freebooter,
  highwayman **11.** endorsement,
  mosstrooper
Rider Haggard's novel... **3.** She
ridge... **3.** aas, rib **4.** hill, rand, wale,
  weal, welt **5.** arête, bulge, chine, crest
  7. wrinkle
ridge (pert to)...
  anatomy.. **4.** ruga **6.** carina
  barrier.. **5.** parma
  between furrows.. **7.** porcate **8.** porcated
  coral.. **4.** reef
  glacial.. **2.** os **5.** esker (eskar)
  military.. **6.** rideau
  mountain.. **4.** loma **5.** arête **6.** sierra
  narrow, raised.. **4.** wale
  oak.. **9.** blackjack
  raised by stroke.. **5.** wheal, whelk
  short.. **4.** kame
  sloping.. **6.** cuesta
  steep.. **7.** hogback
  stony.. **4.** rand
  zoology term.. **5.** varix
ridicule... **3.** guy, pan **4.** butt, gibe, jeer,
  mock, quiz, twit **5.** chaff, irony, sneer,
  taunt **6.** banter, deride, satire **7.** asteism,
  mockery, sarcasm **8.** derision, raillery
  9. burlesque
ridiculous... **5.** funny **6.** absurd
  7. amusing **8.** farcical **9.** grotesque,
  laughable, ludicrous **10.** impossible,
  outrageous **12.** preposterous,
  unbelievable
ridiculous failure... **6.** fiasco
riding (pert to)...
  bitts.. **11.** anchor cable
  breeches.. **8.** jodhpurs
  dress, costume.. **5.** habit
  knot.. **8.** slipknot
  rhyme.. **7.** couplet
  school.. **6.** manège
  whip.. **4.** crop **5.** quirt
rife... **7.** replete, rumored **8.** abundant
  9. abounding, plentiful, prevalent
  10. prevailing, widespread
riff... **6.** rapids, riffle, ripple **7.** midriff
  9. diaphragm **13.** improvisation
riffle... **7.** shallow, shuffle, wavelet
riffraff... **3.** mob **4.** mean **5.** offal
  6. rabble, refuse, trashy **7.** rubbish
  9. sweepings
rifle... **3.** rob **5.** reeve, steal, strip
  6. Mauser, search, snider **7.** carbine,
  despoil, firearm, pillage, plunder,
  ransack
rifle (pert to)...
  accessory.. **6.** ramrod
  ball.. **5.** Minié **6.** bullet
  bird.. **14.** bird of paradise
  bomb.. **7.** grenade
  French.. **9.** chassepot
  old form.. **4.** tige

rifler... **4.** hawk **6.** robber
rift... **3.** gap, lag **4.** rima, rive **5.** break,
  cleft, split **6.** cleave, divide **10.** falling
  out
rig... **3.** fit **4.** gear, suit **5.** dress, equip
  6. lateen **7.** bedizen, costume, rigging,
  vehicle **9.** Bermudian (Naut)
Riga (pert to)...
  balsam.. **5.** resin (Swiss pine)
  capital of.. **6.** Latvia
  native.. **4.** Lett **7.** Latvian
  rine.. **4.** hemp
rigging (ship)... **4.** gear, rope, spar
  6. tackle **9.** equipment
right... **3.** fit, pat **4.** fair, true **6.** adjust,
  dexter, proper, remedy **7.** correct,
  justice, upright **8.** becoming, suitable
  9. equitable, faultless, franchise,
  privilege, propriety **10.** put in order
  11. appropriate, prerogative
  13. justification
right (pert to)...
  angled.. **10.** orthogonal
  comb form.. **6.** dextro
  exclusive.. **6.** patent **10.** concession
  hand.. **6.** dexter
  hand page.. **5.** recto
  law.. **5.** droit
  neither right nor wrong..
    11. adiaphorous
  of belligerent (Naut).. **6.** angary
  of ownership.. **5.** title
  of procedure.. **3.** pas
  real estate.. **8.** easement
  royal.. **7.** regalia
  time.. **3.** tid
  to choice.. **6.** option
  to pasture.. **6.** eatage
  turn.. **3.** gee
righteous... **4.** holy, just **5.** godly,
  moral, pious **6.** worthy **7.** upright
  8. virtuous **9.** believers, blameless,
  equitable, guiltless
righteousness... **6.** equity, virtue
  8. holiness **9.** godliness, rectitude
  11. uprightness
rightful... **4.** just, true **5.** legal, right
  6. honest, lawful, proper **7.** fitting,
  genuine **9.** equitable **11.** appropriate
rigid... **3.** set **4.** firm, hard **5.** exact,
  stern, stiff, tense **6.** formal, narrow, not
  lax, severe, strict **7.** ascetic, austere
  8. rigorous **9.** obstinate, stringent,
  unbending **10.** inflexible, meticulous,
  unyielding
rigidity... **7.** tensity **8.** hardness, severity
  9. exactness, obstinacy, stiffness
rigol... **4.** ring **6.** circle, groove **7.** channel
Rigoletto... **5.** dance, opera (Verdi)
rigor, rigour... **4.** cold, fury **7.** cruelty
  8. asperity, rigidity, severity, violence
  9. exactness, harshness, rigidness
  10. shuddering, strictness
  13. inflexibility
rigor mortis... **10.** stiffening (death)
  12. rigor of death
rigorous... **4.** cold **5.** exact, harsh, rigid,
  stern, stiff **6.** severe, strict **7.** austere,
  drastic, violent **8.** accurate **9.** inclement,
  obstinate, puritanic **10.** inexorable,
  inflexible, relentless

rikk ... **10.** tambourine
rile ... **3.** vex **4.** roil **5.** anger, muddy
  6. offend **7.** agitate **8.** irritate **9.** turbidity
rill ... **5.** brook **6.** course, runnel **7.** rillock,
  rivulet **9.** streamlet
rim ... **3.** lip, web **4.** band, brim, edge,
  orle, tire **5.** bezel, brink, felly (felloe),
  verge **6.** border, flange, margin, shield
  7. enclose, horizon, rimrock **8.** boundary
  9. perimeter
rima ... **5.** cleft **7.** fissure **8.** aperture
  10. breadfruit
rima oris ... **16.** space between lips
rim ash ... **9.** hackberry
rimate ... **8.** fissured
rime ... **4.** hoar, poem, rent **5.** chink,
  cleft, crack, frost, rhyme **6.** poetry
  7. fissure **8.** aperture **9.** assonance,
  hoarfrost **10.** ladder step
rime-cold giant (Norse) ... **4.** Ymir
  (Ymer)
rimple ... **4.** fold **6.** ripple, rumple
  7. wrinkle
rimption ... **3.** lot **9.** abundance
Rinaldo's steed ... **6.** Bayard
rind ... **4.** bark, husk, peel, skin **5.** crust
  6. cortex **7.** epicarp **9.** hoarfrost
rindle ... **5.** brook **6.** runnel **7.** rivulet
ring ... **3.** rim, set **4.** band, halo,
  hoop, peal, toll **5.** arena, bague,
  chime, group, knell **6.** circle, clique,
  collar **7.** annulus, circlet, coterie,
  resound **8.** encircle, insignia, ornament,
  surround **9.** encompass **11.** association
ring (pert to) ...
  around .. **7.** environ
  around the sun .. **6.** corona
  barrel .. **4.** hoop
  bill .. **4.** duck
  bird .. **11.** reed bunting
  comb form .. **4.** gyro
  dove .. **6.** cushat
  finger .. **5.** third
  fruit jar .. **4.** lute
  gem crown .. **5.** bezel
  gem setting .. **6.** chaton
  gun carriage .. **7.** lunette (lunet)
  harness part .. **6.** terret
  horse training .. **5.** longe
  Latin .. **7.** annulus
  leader .. **6.** rouser **9.** demagogue
  12. rabble-rouser
  little .. **7.** annulet, circlet
  ornament (metal) .. **3.** bee (angling)
  ouzel .. **6.** thrush
  rope .. **7.** grommet
  sail .. **4.** hank **8.** ringtail
  tail .. **3.** cat **4.** coon **5.** lemur **6.** godwit,
  marlin **10.** cacomistle **11.** golden eagle
  (young)
ringed boa ... **5.** aboma
ringed worm ... **7.** annelid
ringhals ... **5.** snake (spitting)
ringing ... **7.** clangor, orotund, pealing,
  tolling **8.** clanging, resonant
  10. resounding
ringle-eye ... **7.** walleye
ringlet ... **4.** curl, lock **5.** tress **6.** circle
  7. circlet **9.** fairy ring
ringworm ... **5.** tinea **6.** tetter **7.** disease,
  serpigo **9.** millepede

rink ... **4.** hero, race, ring **6.** circle,
  course **7.** warrior **8.** encircle, ice sheet
  (skating) **9.** encounter
rinse ... **4.** lave, sind, wash **5.** flush
  6. sluice **7.** cleanse **8.** absterge
rinthereout, rintherout (Scot) ...
  5. tramp **7.** vagrant **8.** vagabond
rio ... **5.** river **6.** coffee, stream
Rio de Janeiro ... **7.** capital (old, Braz)
Rio Grande ... **5.** river **7.** disease (lettuce)
riot ... **3.** din **5.** brawl, melee **6.** clamor,
  excess, pogrom, revolt, tumult, uproar
  7. dispute, quarrel, revelry **8.** carousal,
  disorder, violence **9.** commotion
riotous ... **4.** raid **5.** aroar **6.** wanton
  7. violent **9.** dissolute, luxuriant,
  seditious **10.** profligate, tumultuous
  12. unrestrained
riotous jollity ... **9.** dissolute
  11. saturnalian
rip ... **3.** cut **4.** rend, rent, tear **5.** break,
  horse (old) **7.** riptide **9.** debauchee,
  libertine, reprobate **10.** fish basket,
  laceration
ripe ... **3.** fit **5.** ready, rifle **6.** mature,
  mellow **7.** plunder **8.** finished, prepared,
  rareripe **9.** developed, full-grown,
  perfected **10.** consummate
ripen ... **3.** age **5.** addle **6.** digest, mellow,
  nature **7.** develop, perfect, prepare
  8. complete, grow ripe
riposte, ripost ... **5.** reply **6.** answer,
  retort, thrust **8.** repartee
ripping ... **5.** bully, grand, swell
  9. admirable, hunky-dory **12.** fine and
  dandy
rippit ... **9.** fist fight
ripple ... **3.** cut, lap **4.** fret, purl, riff, tear,
  wave **5.** acker, eagre, graze **6.** dimple,
  murmur **7.** crinkle, disturb, scratch,
  trickle, wavelet **11.** corrugation
ripple grass plantain ... **7.** ribwort
ris de veau ... **10.** sweetbread
rise ... **4.** grow, soar, well **5.** arise,
  begin, climb, get up, mount, raise,
  reach, rebel, start, surge, tower
  6. ascend, ascent, attain, be high,
  emerge, growth, height, revolt, spring,
  thrive **7.** succeed **8.** eminence,
  flourish, increase, levitate, reaction
  9. acclivity, ascension, beginning,
  elevation, originate **11.** development
rise (pert to) ...
  above .. **4.** loom **8.** surmount **11.** triumph
  over
  again .. **7.** resurge **11.** resurrected
  and fall of the sea .. **5.** scend, tidal
  6. welter
  by buoyancy .. **8.** levitate
  gradually .. **4.** loom
  hawk's .. **6.** mounty
  high .. **5.** tower
risible ... **5.** funny **6.** absurd **9.** laughable
rising ... **6.** ascent, ortive, revolt
  7. growing, montant, sloping, surgent
  8. elevated, emergent, gradient (by
  degrees), swelling **9.** acclivity,
  advancing, ascending, ascension
rising and falling ... **5.** tidal **7.** surging
  8. undulant
risk ... **4.** dare **5.** peril **6.** chance, danger,

expose, gamble, hazard, injury, plight
7. venture **8.** endanger **10.** investment
12. disadvantage
risky ... **6.** risqué **9.** hazardous
11. venturesome
risp ... **3.** rub **4.** file, rasp, tirl **5.** stalk
7. bulrush, scratch
risper ... **11.** caterpillar
risqué ... **4.** racy **5.** risky, salty **8.** off-color
9. hazardous **10.** suggestive
rissle ... **4.** pole **5.** staff, stick
risus ... **5.** laugh **8.** laughter
rit (rare) ... **3.** cut, rip **4.** slit, tear **5.** split
6. pierce **7.** scratch
ritardando ... **9.** direction, retarding
10. slackening **11.** rallentando
rite ... **4.** cult, form **6.** ritual, sacrum
7. formula, liturgy, tonsure **8.** ceremony
9. solemnity **10.** ceremonial, initiation,
observance **12.** patriarchate
ritratto ... **7.** picture **8.** portrait
Ritter ... **6.** knight
ritual ... **4.** book, code, cult, form,
rite **5.** feast, salat **6.** novena, prayer
7. liturgy **8.** ceremony **10.** ceremonial
ritus ... **5.** usage **6.** custom
ritzy ... **5.** smart (vulgarly), swank
6. swanky **11.** pretentious **16.** ultrafashionable
rivage ... **4.** bank, duty **5.** coast, green,
shore
rival ... **3.** foe, vie **4.** even, peer **5.** excel,
match **7.** compete, emulate **8.** emulator,
opponent **10.** antagonist, competitor
11. compete with
rivalry ... **4.** feud **9.** emulation
11. competition
rive ... **3.** rip **4.** bank, open, rent, rift, tear
5. cleft, sever, shore, split **6.** cleave
8. lacerate
rive droite ... **9.** Right Bank (Seine)
rive gauche ... **8.** Left Bank (Seine, Paris,
including Latin Qtr)
rivel ... **6.** shrink **7.** shrivel, wrinkle
river ... **2.** ea **3.** ria, rio, run **4.** ilog
5. amnis, brook, creek **6.** stream
7. rivulet, torrent **8.** riverlet **9.** streamlet
river (pert to) ...
arm (of sea) .. **7.** estuary
bank .. **4.** ripa **5.** levee
bank, pert to .. **8.** riparian
bed .. **4.** holm **6.** alveus, bottom
7. channel
bend .. **5.** oxbow
boat .. **3.** ark
delta branch .. **5.** bayou
dog .. **10.** hellbender
dragon .. **9.** crocodile
duck .. **4.** teal
fish (spawning, from sea) ..
10. anadromous
horse .. **5.** hippo **12.** hippopotamus
inlet .. **4.** slew **5.** fiord (fjord) **6.** slough
islet .. **3.** ait **4.** holm
mouth .. **4.** lade **5.** delta **7.** estuary
mussel .. **4.** unio
Near East .. **4.** wadi (wady)
Nile measure .. **9.** Nilometer
nymph .. **4.** nais **5.** naiad
rat .. **5.** thief
ref to .. **5.** amnic

region (near) .. **8.** riverine
siren .. **7.** Lorelei
thief .. **3.** rat **6.** ackman
winding .. **3.** ess
river in ...
Africa .. **4.** Nile, Tana **5.** Niger
Austria .. **4.** Iser **5.** Drava
Bavaria .. **4.** Eger, Isar
Belgium .. **4.** Yser
Bohemia .. **4.** Elbe, Iser
Brazil .. **3.** Rio
Bulgaria .. **5.** Mesta
China .. **3.** Wei **6.** Yellow **7.** Hwang Ho
England .. **4.** Isis **6.** Thames
France .. **5.** Seine
Germany .. **6.** Danube
Italy .. **4.** Arno **5.** Tiber
Netherlands .. **3.** Eem **4.** Maas (Meuse)
S America .. **6.** Amazon
Siberia .. **2.** Ob **4.** Lena
Switzerland .. **3.** Aar **5.** Reuss
river of ...
Annie Laurie .. **4.** Nith
Caesar .. **7.** Rubicon
lower regions .. **4.** Styx **5.** Lethe
7. Acheron
woe .. **7.** Acheron
rixy ... **4.** tern
road ... **3.** via, way **4.** iter, path, raid
5. agger **7.** estrada, highway, journey,
passage **8.** pavement **9.** incursion,
roadstead **10.** expedition
road (pert to) ...
block .. **3.** dam **4.** weir
goose .. **5.** brant
hog .. **8.** motorist **10.** monopolist
horse .. **6.** saddle (horse)
impassable .. **7.** impasse
man .. **7.** drummer, peddler **8.** salesman
9. canvasser
map .. **5.** chart, globe **9.** directory
master .. **10.** supervisor **11.** trackmaster
nautical .. **9.** roadstead
no outlet .. **8.** cul-de-sac
paving .. **6.** Tarmac **7.** ballast, macadam
runner .. **6.** cuckoo
scraper .. **4.** harl
weed .. **8.** plantain
roam ... **2.** go **3.** err, gad **4.** rove
5. prowl, range **6.** ramble, stroll, wander
7. meander **9.** gallivant
roan ... **5.** horse (bay, gray, chestnut)
8. antelope **9.** sheepskin, yellow-red
roanoke ... **6.** wampum
Roanoke ...
city .. **8.** Virginia
famed as .. **11.** First Colony (1584)
famed for .. **12.** Virginia Dare (1st white
child, 1587)
settler .. **16.** Sir Walter Raleigh **19.** Sir
Richard Grenville
roar ... **4.** bell, blow, boom, rote (surf)
5. brool, laugh, shout **6.** bellow, steven
7. ululate **8.** cry aloud **9.** loud sound
roaring ... **5.** aroar, great **7.** booming,
riotous **10.** disorderly
Roaring (pert to) ...
Forties .. **8.** Broadway (NYC)
game .. **7.** curling (Scot)
Twenties .. **14.** Golden Twenties **16.** Age
of Red Hot Mamas

roast . . . **4.** beef, cook **5.** cabob, parch **6.** assate, banter **7.** torrefy **8.** ridicule **9.** criticize

roasting (pert to) . . .
ear . . **4.** corn
jack . . **9.** smokejack
stick . . **4.** spit

rob . . . **4.** loot, pelf **5.** pinch (sl), reave, rifle, steal, touch **6.** pilfer, ravish, snatch, snitch **7.** despoil, pillage, plunder **10.** plagiarize

robbed . . . **5.** stole **6.** rubato (Mus) **8.** snatched, snitched

robber . . . **4.** yegg **5.** crook (sl), thief **6.** bandit, reaver, rifler **7.** brigand, burglar, yeggman **8.** pillager **9.** despoiler, embezzler, larcenist, peculator **10.** depredator, highwayman, shoplifter

robber (pert to) . . .
grave . . **5.** ghoul
high seas . . **6.** pirate **7.** corsair **9.** privateer
highway . . **7.** footpad, ladrone
Indian . . **6.** dacoit

robber baron . . . **4.** Fisk **5.** Gould

robbery . . . **4.** reif **5.** theft **6.** burgle, piracy **7.** larceny, pillage, plunder **8.** burglary **10.** spoliation **11.** depredation

robe . . . **5.** array, cover, dress, tunic **6.** invest, mantle **7.** costume, garment **8.** clerical, vestment

robe (pert to) . . .
ancient Roman's . . **4.** toga
bishop's . . **6.** chimer
camel's hair . . **3.** aba
long . . **5.** talar
loose . . **5.** cymar (symar)
royal . . **6.** ermine, purple

robin . . . **4.** bird, lout, tody **6.** thrush **7.** bumpkin **8.** trimming **9.** redbreast **10.** toxalbumin

robin (pert to) . . .
dipper . . **14.** bufflehead duck
runaway . . **7.** dewdrop
sandpiper . . **4.** knot **5.** snipe **9.** dowitcher
songbird . . **8.** accentor

Robin Bluestring . . . **13.** Robert Walpole

robinet . . . **6.** cannon **9.** chaffinch

Robin Goodfellow . . . **4.** Puck **6.** sprite **9.** hobgoblin

Robin Hood (pert to) . . .
famed as . . **6.** archer, outlaw, yeoman
followers . . **9.** Friar Tuck **10.** Little John, Maid Marian
forest . . **8.** Sherwood (Eng)
habit . . **11.** robbing rich (for the poor)

Robinson Crusoe's man . . . **6.** Friday

roborant . . . **4.** drug **5.** tonic **6.** bracer **8.** pick-me-up **9.** stimulant

roborean . . . **5.** oaken, stout **6.** strong

robot . . . **9.** automaton

Rob Roy . . . **5.** canoe **6.** outlaw (Scot) **15.** Robert MacGregor

robust . . . **4.** hale **5.** hardy, lusty, rough, sound, stout, wally **6.** hearty, sinewy, strong, sturdy **7.** healthy **8.** muscular, vigorous

roc . . . **4.** bird (Arabian Nights) **7.** simurgh (simurg)

rocca . . . **4.** hold **6.** donjon **8.** fortress

rock . . . **3.** orc **4.** lull, peak, sway, trap, tufa, tuff **5.** agate, chert, cliff, quiet, shake, slate, stone **6.** basalt, egeran, gneiss, refuge, schist, teeter **7.** diamond, missile **8.** dolomite, porphyry, strength **9.** whinstone **10.** promontory

rock (pert to) . . .
black . . **6.** basalt
brittle . . **5.** shale
broken . . **4.** sand **5.** attle
cavity . . **5.** druse
chain . . **4.** reef
coarse . . **8.** psammite, psephite
crystal . . **6.** silica
crystalline . . **6.** gneiss, schist
decomposed . . **6.** gossan
fluid . . **4.** lava
fragments . . **5.** scree **8.** detritus, xenolith
geyser deposit . . **6.** sinter
glacial . . **7.** moraine
granitelike . . **6.** gneiss
granular . . **6.** oolite, quartz **7.** diorite **10.** rockallite
gray . . **5.** slate **8.** andesite
igneous . . **4.** boss, trap **6.** basalt **7.** peridot
jutting . . **3.** tor **4.** crag
nodule . . **5.** geode
pinnacle . . **4.** scar **6.** needle
porous . . **4.** tufa, tuff
rounded . . **6.** rognon
science . . **9.** petrology
Sicilian . . **8.** Scylla (opp Charybdis)
stratified . . **5.** shale
suffix . . **3.** ite, yte
volcanic . . **4.** tufa **6.** basalt, domite, latite

rock, animal . . .
badger . . **4.** cony
cavy . . **6.** rodent
dassie . . **6.** rabbit
goat . . **4.** ibex
kangaroo . . **7.** wallaby
squirrel . . **11.** spermophile

rock, bird . . .
blackbird . . **9.** ring ouzel
dove . . **9.** guillemot **10.** rockpigeon
duck . . **9.** harlequin
goose . . **9.** kelp goose
grouse . . **9.** ptarmigan
hawk . . **6.** falcon, merlin
hopper . . **7.** penguin
lark . . **5.** pipit
pigeon . . **10.** sand grouse
sandpiper . . **5.** pipit, snipe
shrike . . **10.** rock thrush
starling . . **5.** ouzel
swallow . . **10.** rock martin

rock, fish . . .
bass . . **5.** black **7.** striped
clam . . **5.** borer
cod . . **7.** grouper
cook . . **6.** wrasse **7.** whiting
eel . . **6.** gunnel
gurnet . . **9.** fortescue
hind . . **7.** grouper (spotted)
lobster . . **8.** crayfish
salmon . . **7.** codfish **9.** amberfish
sucker . . **7.** lamprey
trout . . **9.** greenling

rock, flora ...
bell .. **9.** columbine
brake .. **8.** polypody
candytuft .. **8.** gold-dust
cedar .. **7.** juniper
cranberry .. **8.** mountain
elm .. **11.** slippery elm
garden .. **6.** alpine
geranium .. **8.** alumroot
hair .. **6.** lichen
lily .. **9.** columbine **12.** pasqueflower
maple .. **5.** sugar
melon .. **10.** cantaloupe
shrub .. **9.** buckthorn
rocket ... **5.** lance **6.** ascend, ascent, fire
at **8.** aircraft, firework **9.** skyrocket,
spaceship
rocket (famed) ... **5.** Titan **6.** Apollo,
Gemini, Saturn **7.** Jupiter, Mercury
8. Redstone
Rock of Chickamauga ... **6.** Thomas
(Gen) (Civil War)
rocks ... **5.** money
rocks, on the ... **7.** aground **8.** bankrupt,
stranded **10.** saxicoline
rocky ... **4.** hard **5.** stony **6.** rugged
7. sickish **8.** obdurate, unsteady
9. unfeeling
Rocky Ford ... **9.** muskmelon
Rocky Mountain ...
group .. **5.** Coast **8.** Cascades **12.** Sierra
Nevada
park .. **5.** Estes
peak .. **6.** Elbert **8.** McKinley
popular name .. **7.** Rockies
range .. **5.** Teton, Uinta
rococo ... **6.** florid **7.** baroque, bizarre
9. fantastic, grotesque
13. ornamentation
rod ... **3.** gat, gun **4.** pole, wand, whip
5. baton, perch, power, scion, staff
7. measure, scepter
rod (pert to) ...
comb form .. **5.** rhabd **6.** rhabdo
fibrous .. **5.** lytta
flat .. **6.** ferula, ferule
grooved .. **4.** came (stained glass)
knitting .. **6.** needle
meat-holding .. **4.** spit
mechanical .. **6.** piston
metal .. **7.** stemmer
mixing .. **3.** rab
pointed .. **4.** goat, spit
rodlike .. **9.** vergiform
rotating .. **7.** spindle
short .. **6.** toggle
spinning .. **7.** spindle
rodd ... **8.** crossbow, stonebow
rodent ... **4.** cony, hare, paca, vole
5. hutia (jutia), mouse, stoat **6.** agouti
(agouty), beaver, gerbil, gopher,
marmot, murine **7.** lemming, leveret
8. chipmunk, hedgehog, mongoose,
squirrel **9.** guinea pig, porcupine
rodent (pert to) ...
Andes .. **8.** abrocome
aquatic .. **6.** beaver **7.** muskrat
Belgian .. **8.** leporide
burrowing .. **6.** marmot **8.** sewellel
disease .. **9.** tularemia
European .. **4.** cony **5.** lerot

fur-bearing .. **6.** beaver
genus .. **3.** Mus **5.** Lepus
gnawing .. **3.** rat **4.** mole
hare .. **6.** rabbit
jumping .. **6.** jerboa
largest .. **8.** capybara (capibara)
migrating .. **7.** lemming
Mongoloid .. **3.** rat **6.** gopher **12.** pocket
gopher
mouselike .. **4.** vole
rabbitlike .. **4.** pika
reference to .. **7.** gnawing **8.** rosorial
S American .. **4.** degu **5.** coypu **6.** agouti
8. capybara **10.** chinchilla
spiny .. **9.** porcupine
rodeo ... **4.** show **7.** roundup **9.** spectacle
11. performance (public)
rodomontade ... **4.** brag, rant **5.** boast
7. bluster **8.** boastful, boasting,
braggart, bragging
roe ... **2.** ra **3.** doe **4.** deer, hind, raun
5. coral (lobster) **8.** fish eggs
Roentgen, Röntgen (Wilhelm) ...
famed as .. **9.** physicist
famed for .. **5.** X-rays **10.** Nobel Prize
(1901) **12.** Roentgen rays
rogan ... **4.** bowl (wooden) **10.** receptacle
(maple sap)
Roger's plane (Will) ... **9.** Winnie May
rogue ... **3.** imp, wag **4.** kite **5.** cheat,
knave, scamp, shark, tramp **6.** beggar,
pirate, rascal **7.** corsair, vagrant,
villain **8.** elephant, picaroon, vagabond
13. mischief-maker
roguish ... **3.** sly **4.** arch **5.** pawky
7. knavish **8.** espiegle, rascally
10. frolicsome, picaresque
11. mischievous
roguishly ... **5.** slyly **8.** impishly, trickily
10. prankishly
roid ... **5.** rough **6.** severe **7.** riotous
10. frolicsome **12.** unmanageable
roil ... **3.** vex **4.** foul, roam, romp
5. anger, annoy, horse (Flemish),
muddy **6.** fidget, ruffle, wander
7. agitate, disturb **8.** irritate
roister ... **4.** brag, rude **5.** bully **7.** bluster
boorish, swagger, violent **9.** gilravage
roisterer (Hist) ... **3.** mun
roke ... **3.** fog **4.** stir **5.** moist, smoke,
steam, vapor **8.** moisture
roker ... **3.** ray **8.** rockling **9.** thornback
roky ... **4.** damp **5.** foggy, misty, smoky
6. hoarse
role ... **4.** duty, part **6.** office **8.** capacity,
function **9.** character **13.** impersonation
roll ... **3.** bun, rob **4.** coil, film, food,
furl, list, pell, rota, sway, wind, wrap
5. trill, troll **6.** billow, bundle, rotate,
rumble, scroll **8.** bankroll, cylinder,
rotation
roll (pert to) ...
along .. **7.** trundle
back .. **7.** reduce **8.** retrench
bread .. **3.** bap
butter .. **3.** pat
cloth .. **4.** bolt
coins .. **7.** rouleau
fish .. **7.** rissole
hair .. **3.** rat **7.** chignon
military .. **5.** cadre **6.** roster

the bones.. **4.** dice **10.** shoot craps
tobacco.. **5.** cigar
to one side.. **5.** lurch
up.. **4.** furl **6.** bundle **10.** accumulate
roller... **4.** wave **5.** inker, skate, towel
  6. canary, caster, fillet, pigeon, platen
  7. bandage, rotator, sirgang **8.** cylinder
  10. Holy Roller, pulverizer
rolling (pert to)...
  movement.. **6.** welter
  pin.. **6.** roller **8.** cylinder
  stock.. **7.** coaches, engines **8.** cabooses,
    Pullmans **9.** motor cars **11.** locomotives
  stone.. **8.** wanderer
  weed.. **10.** tumbleweed
rollix... **4.** play **6.** frolic **7.** rollick
romaine... **10.** cos lettuce
romal... **5.** quirt, thong
Roman... **5.** brave, Latin **6.** frugal, honest,
  simple **7.** Italian
Roman (pert to)... see also *Rome*
  afterpiece (theater).. **5.** exode, farce
    8. travesty
  alcove.. **8.** tablinum
  apostle (Bib).. **4.** Neri
  assembly.. **5.** forum **7.** comitia
  augur.. **6.** auspex
  awning.. **8.** velarium
  barrack, hut.. **6.** canaba (cannaba)
  basilica.. **7.** Lateran
  booth, shelter.. **7.** taberna
  bowl.. **6.** patina
  boxing glove.. **6.** cestus
  breastplate.. **6.** lorica
  bronze.. **3.** aes
  building.. **5.** aedes (worship)
  case.. **5.** bulla (for amulets)
  cathedral.. **7.** Lateran
  chariot.. **5.** essed (esseda)
  chest.. **4.** cist
  circus post.. **4.** meta
  circus wall.. **5.** spina
  cistern.. **9.** impluvium
  citadel.. **3.** arx
  citizen (nonvoting).. **8.** aerarian
  clan.. **4.** gens
  cloak.. **5.** sagum (Mil) **6.** abolla **7.** planeta
  concert hall.. **5.** odeum
  court (Pope's).. **5.** Curia
  cuirass.. **6.** lorica
  Curia office.. **6.** datary **7.** dataria
  date.. **4.** ides **5.** nones **7.** calends
  dish.. **6.** patera
  division (Polit).. **5.** curia
  earthwork (Mil).. **5.** agger
  Empire district.. **5.** Pagus
  era.. **5.** Varro
  farce.. **5.** exode
  festival days.. **5.** feria **10.** feriae Jovi
    (festivals of Jupiter)
  fish sauce.. **4.** alec **5.** garum
  foot coverage, sock.. **3.** udo
  galley.. **6.** bireme **7.** trireme
  garment.. **4.** toga **5.** palla, stole, tunic
  general's cloak.. **12.** paludamentum
    (paludament)
  Govt of two men.. **10.** duumvirate
  Hades.. **5.** Orcus **10.** lower world
  hairpin.. **4.** acus
  hall (concert).. **5.** odeum
  helmet.. **5.** galea

highway.. **3.** via **4.** iter
highway, famed.. **9.** Appian Way
hills.. **7.** Viminal **8.** Aventine, Palatine,
  Quirinal **9.** Esquiline **10.** Capitoline
javelin.. **5.** pilum
land (public).. **4.** ager
language.. **5.** Latin
law.. **3.** jus **4.** cern
law, divine.. **3.** fas
market day.. **7.** nundine
marriage.. **13.** confarreation
matron's garment.. **5.** stola, stole
meal (chief).. **4.** cena (coena)
military cloak.. **5.** sagum
military machine.. **7.** terebra
military unit.. **6.** legion **7.** maniple
money.. **3.** aes
ornament (neck).. **5.** bulla
palace.. **7.** Lateran
peace.. **3.** pax
provisions (free).. **6.** annona
ram (battery).. **5.** aries
religious law.. **3.** fas
religious rite.. **5.** sacra
road.. **4.** iter **6.** Appian (paved)
robe.. **4.** toga
room.. **3.** ala **6.** atrium **8.** tablinum
seat.. **5.** sella
shelter, shop.. **7.** taberna
shield.. **6.** scutum
soldier's protection.. **7.** testudo
spirits (group).. **5.** lares (sing lar),
  manes **7.** lemures
tablet (writing).. **7.** diptych
temple.. **4.** naos **5.** cella
tent.. **7.** taberna
theater.. **5.** odeum
travesty.. **5.** exode
vase.. **7.** amphora (wine) **8.** murrhine
warship.. **6.** bireme **7.** trireme
Way (famed).. **6.** Appian
wine shop.. **7.** taberna
romance... **5.** fancy, novel, story
  7. fantasy, fiction, romanza, romaunt
  8. idealize **9.** falsehood, sentiment
  11. imagination
romance (pert to)...
  language.. **6.** French **7.** Catalan, Italian,
    Spanish **9.** Provençal **10.** Portuguese
  ref to.. **8.** knightly **10.** chivalrous
  verse.. **7.** sestina
Roman god (of)...
  chief.. **4.** Jove **7.** Jupiter
  dead.. **5.** Orcus
  fire.. **6.** Vulcan
  Hades.. **3.** Dis **5.** Pluto **8.** Dispater
  households.. **5.** Lares **7.** Penates
  husbandry, animals.. **6.** Faunus
  love.. **4.** Amor **5.** Cupid
  mirth.. **5.** Comus
  sun.. **3.** Sol
  Supreme.. **4.** Jove **7.** Jupiter
  two-faced.. **5.** Janus
  underworld.. **3.** Dis **5.** Pluto **8.** Dispater
  war.. **4.** Mars **8.** Quirinus
Roman goddess (of)...
  agriculture.. **3.** Ops **5.** Ceres
  beauty.. **5.** Venus
  burials.. **8.** Libitina
  childbirth.. **6.** Lucina
  crops.. **6.** Annona

dawn . . **6.** Aurora
earth . . **6.** Tellus
fertility . . **6.** Annona
handicrafts . . **7.** Minerva
harvests . . **3.** Ops
health . . **7.** Minerva
hearth . . **5.** Vesta
horses . . **5.** Epona
love . . **5.** Venus
moon . . **4.** Luna **7.** Phoebus
mothers, nursing . . **6.** Rumina
night . . **3.** Nox
peace . . **3.** Pax **5.** Irene
religion . . **4.** Maia
strife . . **9.** Discordia
victory (war) . . **6.** Vacuna
womanhood . . **4.** Juno
Romania . . .
capital . . **9.** Bucharest
city . . **4.** Cluj, Iasi **7.** Ploesti
mountains . . **10.** Carpathian
port . . **6.** Galati (Galatz)
privileged class . . **5.** boyar (boyard)
river . . **6.** Danube
Romanian(-born) person . . .
dramatist . . **7.** Ionesco
gymnast . . **8.** Comaneci (Nadia)
hero . . **7.** Michael (the Brave)
king . . **5.** Carol
president, dictator . . **9.** Ceausescu
violinist . . **6.** Enesco
writer . . **6.** Wiesel (Elie)
Roman people . . .
author . . **5.** Pliny, Varro
biographer . . **5.** Nepos
Bishop . . **4.** Pope
boy (free birth) . . **8.** camillus
Catholic priest . . **8.** sacerdos
Catholic Society . . **6.** Jesuit
consul . . **6.** Scipio
Cupid . . **4.** Eros
deity . . **4.** faun
Diana . . **7.** Artemis
dictator . . **5.** Sulla **11.** Cincinnatus
diviner . . **5.** augur **6.** auspex
divinity (chief) . . **4.** Jove
Emperor . . **4.** Nero, Otto **5.** Titus
   7. Maximus **8.** Tiberius **11.** Constantine
   12. Heliogabalus
Eros . . **5.** Cupid
farmer . . **7.** colonus
Fates . . **4.** Nona **5.** Morta **6.** Decuma
General . . **5.** Sulla, Titus **6.** Antony,
   Marius, Scipio
ghosts . . **7.** lemures
gladiator . . **7.** Samnite **9.** retiarius
gladiator trainer . . **7.** lanista
governor . . **9.** proconsul
guard . . **6.** lictor
historian . . **4.** Livy **5.** Nepos **7.** Sallust
   8. Appianus (Appian)
king (1st) . . **7.** Romulus
king's adviser (Myth) . . **6.** Egeria
magistrate, official . . **5.** augur **6.** aedile
   (edile), censor, consul **7.** praetor
   (pretor), tribune
maiden, betrayer to Sabrines . . **7.** Tarpeia
military officer . . **9.** proconsul
Naturalist . . **5.** Pliny
nun . . **6.** vestal
nymph (fountain) . . **6.** Egeria

officer . . **6.** lictor **8.** triumvir (one of
   three)
official of public games . . **6.** aedile
   (edile) **7.** Asiarch
orator . . **5.** Pliny **6.** Cicero
palace officer . . **8.** palatine
patriot . . **4.** Cato
people (anc) . . **7.** Sabines **8.** Samnites
   9. plebeians **10.** patricians
philosopher . . **4.** Cato **6.** Seneca
   7. Rosmini
physician . . **11.** Aesculapius
poet . . **4.** Ovid **5.** Lucan **6.** Horace,
   Vergil **7.** Juvenal (satirical)
politician, courtier . . **7.** Sejanus
priest . . **5.** epulo **8.** tresviri (10 in all)
   9. decemviri **10.** septemviri
priest, serving a god . . **6.** flamen
priestess . . **6.** vestal
priests of Faunus . . **7.** Luperci
race (conquered) . . **6.** Sabine
saint . . **4.** Neri
scholar . . **5.** Varro
serf . . **6.** colona (fem) **7.** colonus (male)
slave (befriended lion) . . **9.** Androcles
   (Androclus)
soldiers (body of) . . **6.** cohort
statesman . . **4.** Cato **6.** Caesar, Cicero,
   Seneca
Tarquin rulers . . **9.** Etruscans
tenant farmer . . **7.** colonus
triumvirate, first . . **6.** Caesar, Pompey
   7. Crassus
triumvirate, second . . **6.** Antony
   7. Lepidus **8.** Octavius
troops . . **6.** alares
tyrant . . **4.** Nero
virgin . . **6.** vestal
writer (comic) . . **7.** Terence
Romany, Rommany . . . **5.** gypsy
   10. mascot blue
Rome . . .
cathedral (world's largest) . . **8.** St Peter's
churches . . **7.** Lateran **8.** Castello,
   Gandolfo
conqueror . . **6.** Alaric
founder (legendary) . . **7.** Romulus
hills . . **5.** Seven **6.** Sabine **7.** Viminal
   8. Aventine, Palatine, Quirinal
lake . . **4.** Nemi
original city . . **12.** Roma Quadrata
palace (world's largest) . . **7.** Vatican
peak (Capitoline) . . **8.** Tarpeian
port (anc) . . **5.** Ostia
prairie . . **8.** Campagna
river . . **5.** Tiber
seat of . . **7.** Holy See **11.** Vatican City
site, ancient . . **13.** Campus Martius
site, founding . . **12.** Palatine Hill
street (famed) . . **5.** Corso
Romulus (pert to) . . .
brother . . **5.** Remus
city site . . **12.** Palatine Hill
father . . **4.** Mars
founder (Myth) . . **4.** Rome
king (1st) . . **4.** Rome
mother . . **6.** Sylvia
rescued from . . **5.** Tiber
suckled by . . **7.** she-wolf
ronde . . . **6.** script (heavy) **9.** round hand
rondeau . . . **4.** game, poem **5.** rondo

6. rondel
rondel, rondelle . . . **4.** poem **5.** tower
(Fort) **8.** round gem
rondure . . . **9.** plumpness, roundness
ronier . . . **7.** palmyra
ronin . . . **6.** outlaw **7.** outcast, samurai
rood . . . **5.** cross (holy), goose **7.** measure
8. crucifix
roodebok . . . **6.** impala **9.** duikerbok
roof . . . **3.** hip **4.** dome, eave, flat, nave, tile
5. cover, gable, slate, spire **6.** cupola,
lean-to **7.** chopper, gambrel, mansard,
pitched, shingle **8.** housetop, thatched
9. penthouse **10.** jerkinhead
roof (pert to) . . .
boards (thin) . . **4.** sark
brain cover . . **4.** tela **14.** telachorioidea
frame (raised) . . **7.** coaming
material . . **3.** tin **4.** tile **5.** paper, slate
6. copper, shakes **7.** roofage **8.** shingles
mouth . . **6.** palate
ornament . . **3.** epi
tile . . **7.** pantile
timber . . **6.** rafter
tin (coating) . . **5.** terne
tool . . **3.** zax
Roof of the World, Asia . . . **6.** Pamirs
(The) **9.** Bam i Dunya
rook . . . **4.** bird, crow, dupe **5.** cheat
6. castle **7.** defraud, sharper
8. chessman **9.** ruddy duck
rookery . . . **4.** slum **9.** confusion
13. breeding place (rooks, herons,
penguins) **14.** breeding ground (seals)
rookie, rooky . . . **6.** novice **7.** recruit
8. beginner, newcomer
rooky . . . **4.** roky **5.** foggy
room . . . **3.** ala (anc), den **4.** aula, cell, hall,
sala, seat, shed **5.** attic, lodge, place,
salon, scope, space **6.** cellar, leeway,
pantry, parlor, reside **7.** chamber,
drawing, laundry, nursery, quarter
8. capacity **9.** apartment, storeroom
11. opportunity
room (pert to) . . .
church (bishop's) . . **4.** apse
convent . . **9.** parlatory
dining . . **7.** cenacle, dinette **9.** refectory
harem . . **3.** oda
household . . **5.** ewery
inner . . **3.** ben
large . . **4.** aula, hall **7.** rotunda, theater
10. auditorium
monastery . . **4.** cell
outer . . **3.** but
pantry . . **6.** larder **8.** cupboard
prayer . . **7.** oratory
Pueblo Ind ceremonial . . **4.** kiva
Roman . . **6.** atrium
ship's . . **4.** brig **5.** cabin, salon
sleeping . . **5.** lodge **6.** dormer **7.** barrack,
bedroom, chamber **9.** dormitory
tower (bell) . . **6.** belfry
roomy . . . **4.** airy **5.** ample **8.** spacious
9. capacious, expansive
10. commodious **11.** large-framed
roon . . . **5.** shred **6.** border **7.** darling
8. treasure
roorback, roorbach . . . **3.** lie **6.** canard
7. lampoon **9.** falsehood
roose . . . **5.** boast, vaunt **6.** praise

Roosevelt . . .
president, 26th . . **8.** Theodore
president, 32nd . . **8.** Franklin
roost . . . **3.** bed, sit **4.** jouk, pole, rest
5. perch **6.** settle **7.** lodging, support
rooster . . . **4.** cock, male (animal) **5.** gallo
7. percher **11.** chanticleer **12.** fighting
cock
root . . . **4.** bulb, word **5.** cheer, plant,
radix, tuber **6.** source **7.** radical **8.** take
root **9.** establish
root (pert to) . . .
aromatic . . **9.** sassafras
edible . . **3.** oca, yam **4.** beet, eddo,
taro **6.** carrot, potato, radish, turnip
7. parsnip **8.** rutabaga
food (Maori) . . **3.** roi
medicinal . . **4.** atis **5.** jalep **6.** ipecac,
senega **7.** Senegal
out . . **4.** seek **7.** extract **9.** eliminate,
eradicate
perfume . . **5.** orris
pungent . . **6.** ginger
starch . . **7.** cassava
stock . . **7.** rhizome
stringy . . **5.** watap (watape)
taro . . **4.** eddo
word . . **4.** etym **6.** etymon
rooted . . . **8.** habitual **9.** implanted
10. deep-seated **11.** established,
traditional
rootlet . . . **7.** radical, rhizoid, taproot
rope . . . **3.** tew, tie, tye **4.** bind, cord, line,
rood **5.** cable, cigar, lasso, longe, noose,
reata, wanty **6.** fasten, halter, hawser,
lariat, string, tether **7.** cordage, lanyard,
measure **8.** hangman's, inveigle
rope (pert to) . . .
boat's . . **4.** rode **6.** hawser **7.** painter
chain . . **3.** tye **9.** stern fast
dancer, walker . . **8.** balancer
11. equilibrist, funambulist
fiber . . **4.** bast, hemp, jute **5.** sisal
flag raising . . **7.** halyard
gun carriage . . **8.** prolonge
guy . . **4.** stay, vang
nautical . . **3.** tye **4.** vang, wapp **6.** parrel
(parral) **7.** snotter
of onions . . **5.** reeve
security device . . **4.** butt **5.** cleat
ship's . . **3.** tye **4.** stay, vang **6.** hawser,
shroud **7.** painter, ratline, snotter
splicer's tool . . **3.** fid
straw, twisted . . **5.** sugan (soogan)
two strand . . **7.** marline
walker . . **11.** funambulist
ropery . . . **6.** banter **7.** roguery
roral . . . **4.** dewy, rory **5.** roric
rorqual . . . **5.** whale **7.** finback
Ros . . . **10.** Slav rulers (Russ), Varangians
rosary . . . **4.** aves **5.** beads (prayer)
7. chaplet (of roses), garland **8.** devotion
roscoe . . . **3.** gat, gun
rose . . . **3.** cut (jewelry) **5.** color, flush,
Rhoda **6.** emblem, flower, nozzle,
symbol, window **7.** fixture
rose (pert to) . . .
apple . . **4.** plum **6.** cherry **7.** jambool
8. poma rosa
beetle . . **6.** chafer, weevil
City . . **8.** Portland (Oreg)

colored .. **8.** alluring **10.** auspicious, optimistic
cross .. **6.** symbol **11.** Rosicrucian **14.** cross in a circle
genus .. **4.** Rosa **6.** Acaena **8.** Rosaceae
hiller .. **7.** rosella **8.** parakeet
moss .. **9.** portulaca
of Sharon .. **6.** Althea
petal oil .. **4.** otto **5.** attar
rash .. **7.** roseola
under the rose .. **6.** secret **7.** sub rosa
wild .. **9.** eglantine
Rosetta Stone (pert to) ...
decipherer .. **11.** Champollion
famed for .. **11.** inscription **13.** hieroglyphics
site found .. **4.** Nile (1799)
type .. **11.** black basalt
roster ... **4.** list, roll, rota **5.** slate **8.** schedule
rostrum ... **4.** beak, dais, prow **5.** snout, stage **6.** pulpit **8.** platform **9.** proboscis
rosy ... **3.** red **4.** pink **7.** flushed, roseate **8.** blooming, blushing **9.** rosaceous **10.** auspicious, optimistic
rot ... **3.** die **5.** decay, spoil **6.** blight **7.** corrupt, disease, putrefy **8.** nonsense **9.** decompose **10.** degenerate **12.** putrefaction **13.** decomposition
rota ... **4.** Club (Eng), list, roll **5.** court, round (Mus) **6.** roster **15.** Sacra Romana Rota
rotate ... **4.** roll, spin, turn, whiz **5.** recur, wheel **6.** gyrate **7.** rabatte, revolve, trundle **8.** rotiform
rotation ... **4.** spin, turn **5.** round **7.** turning **8.** sequence **10.** revolution, succession
rotator ... **5.** rotor **6.** muscle **7.** whirler **9.** carrousel **12.** merry-go-round
rotche, rotch ... **5.** goose, rotge **7.** dovekie
rote ... **6.** course, custom, system **7.** by heart, routine **8.** par coeur, practice **9.** condition
roti ... **5.** roast **7.** roasted
rotor ... **5.** wheel **6.** roller, stator **7.** rotator, turbine **8.** impeller
rotten ... **3.** bad **4.** foul, punk **5.** doted, fetid **6.** putrid, wicked **7.** decayed, tainted, unsound **8.** depraved, unstable **9.** dishonest, offensive, putrefied **10.** putrescent, undermined **13.** disintegrated
Rotten Row (Hyde Park, London) ... **12.** thoroughfare (equestrian)
rottenstone ... **6.** polish **7.** tripoli
rotter ... **3.** cad **7.** bounder, shirker, slacker **10.** blackguard
rottgoose ... **5.** brant
rotund ... **3.** fat **5.** obese, plump, round, stout **6.** chubby **7.** rounded **8.** roly-poly **9.** corpulent, spherical
Rotwelsch ... **5.** argot, slang **6.** jargon **14.** secret language
roué ... **4.** rake, wolf **7.** rounder **9.** debauchee, libertine
rouge ... **5.** blush, flush **6.** polish, redden **7.** radical **8.** cosmetic
rough ... **4.** hard, rude **5.** crude, draft, harsh, raspy, rowdy, seamy, stern

6. broken, choppy, coarse, hoarse, rugged, severe, shaggy **7.** boorish, inexact, jarring, jolting, ruffled **8.** scabrous, unsmooth **9.** imperfect, turbulent **10.** incomplete, tumultuous, unfinished **11.** approximate
rough (pert to) ...
avens .. **6.** bennet (herb)
cloth .. **5.** terry
footed (bird) .. **9.** feathered
hair .. **4.** shag
hewn .. **6.** brutal **10.** unpolished **12.** uncultivated
house .. **5.** cut up **9.** rowdiness **10.** disorderly, noisy sport
jest (Mus) .. **9.** charivari
neck .. **4.** boor **5.** rowdy, tough
rider .. **9.** Roosevelt (Teddy) **10.** cavalryman
rock .. **4.** crag
shod (to ride) .. **7.** trample **8.** dominate **9.** tyrannize
rough and ...
hoarse .. **7.** raucous
lean .. **6.** craggy
ready .. **4.** rude **10.** unpolished
Ready .. **6.** Taylor (Gen Zachary)
roughen ... **4.** chap, shag **8.** asperate
roughly ... **4.** or so **6.** rudely **7.** harshly **8.** coarsely, severely, unevenly, vulgarly **9.** brusquely **10.** unsmoothly **13.** approximately
roughness ... **6.** lipper (of the sea) **8.** acrimony, asperity, pungency, unfinish **9.** gruffness, harshness, vulgarity **10.** hoarseness
roughsome ... **5.** rough **6.** rustic **7.** uncouth
roulade ... **3.** run **8.** arpeggio, division, flourish **13.** vocal flourish
roulette ... **3.** bas (bet) **4.** disk, game **5.** wheel **6.** roller **8.** wagering
rounceval ... **5.** giant, large **6.** strong, virago **9.** termagant
round ... **4.** beat, bout, rota, rung, turn **5.** cycle, orbed, rondo **6.** circle, curved, rotate, rotund, series, sphere **7.** circuit, routine **8.** circular, globular **9.** in a circle, spherical **11.** cylindrical
round (pert to) ...
bone .. **3.** hip
building .. **7.** rotunda
clam .. **6.** quahog
fish .. **9.** whitefish
head .. **5.** Swede **7.** Puritan
house .. **5.** cabin, coach **6.** lockup, prison **10.** watch house
of applause .. **7.** plaudit
regular .. **4.** beat
robin .. **6.** angler, letter **7.** pancake, request **9.** cigarfish
worm .. **4.** nema **7.** ascarid, Ascaris, eelworm
roundabout ... **5.** about, dance **6.** detour, jacket **7.** ambient, devious **8.** indirect **10.** circuitous **13.** approximately **14.** circumlocution
rounded (pert to) ...
heap of stone .. **5.** cairn
irregularly .. **7.** gibbous
leaf .. **6.** retuse

molding . . **5.** ovolo
projection . . **4.** lobe **5.** tooth
scalloped . . **7.** crenate
Round Table (pert to) . . .
knight . . **7.** Galahad **8.** Lancelot
seating . . **7.** knights (King Arthur's)
site . . **7.** Camelot
type . . **6.** marble
roundup . . . **5.** rodeo
roup . . . **4.** cold **6.** clamor **7.** auction
   8. shouting **10.** hoarseness
rouse . . . **3.** hie **4.** stir, wake **5.** alarm,
   raise, start, upset, waken **6.** awaken,
   bestir, elicit, excite, kindle **7.** disturb
   9. stimulate
rouser . . . **7.** stirrer **8.** surprise
   9. demagogue (demagog) **10.** instigator
roussette . . . **5.** shark **7.** dogfish **8.** fruit
   bat
roust . . . **4.** roar, stir **5.** rouse **6.** bellow,
   tumult **7.** current (tidal), roaring
   9. bellowing
roustabout . . . **6.** lumper **7.** laborer
   8. handy man **12.** longshoreman
rout . . . **3.** low, mob **4.** bray, roar
   5. crowd, snort **6.** bellow, defeat,
   rabble **7.** debacle, scatter **8.** disperse,
   stampede, vanquish **9.** agitation,
   discomfit, overpower, overthrow **11.** put
   to flight
route . . . **3.** way **4.** line, path **5.** march
   6. detour **7.** circuit
routh . . . **6.** plenty **8.** abundant
   9. abundance, plentiful
routier . . . **6.** robber **7.** brigand **9.** free
   lance, plunderer
routine . . . **3.** rut **5.** grind, habit, order,
   round, troll **6.** course, system **7.** regular
   8. everyday **9.** treadmill
rove . . . **3.** gad **4.** flit, part, roam **5.** range,
   stray **6.** maraud, ramble, stroll, swerve,
   wander, washer **7.** deviate **8.** straggle
rover . . . **5.** nomad **6.** bandit, pirate, viking
   7. corsair, pilgrim, vagrant **8.** marauder,
   wanderer
roving . . . **8.** errantry **9.** desultory,
   deviative **10.** discursive
row . . . **3.** air, oar **4.** file, fuss, live, spat,
   tier **5.** align, brawl, broil **6.** lineup,
   paddle, propel, series **7.** quarrel, ruction
   9. commotion
rowboat . . . **3.** cog, gig **4.** dory **5.** canoe,
   coble, skiff **6.** randan
rowdy . . . **5.** cutup, rough, tough
   7. boorish, ruffian **8.** larrikin, plug-ugly
   10. boisterous, disorderly
rowdy contention . . . **10.** donnybrook
rowel . . . **4.** spur **5.** wheel
rowen . . . **4.** crop (secondary) **5.** field
   7. stubble **9.** aftermath
rowing . . . **5.** sport **6.** randan **7.** regatta
   8. sculling
rox . . . **3.** rot **5.** decay
royal . . . **4.** real, rial, stag, true **5.** basil,
   noble, regal **6.** august, kingly **7.** stately
   8. imperial, majestic, princely, splendid
   9. dignified, sovereign **11.** magnificent
royal (pert to) . . .
agaric . . **8.** mushroom
bay . . **6.** laurel
color . . **4.** blue **5.** smalt

court . . **5.** aulic **6.** ermine
crest . . **10.** fleur-de-lis (Fr)
deer's antler . . **8.** tres-tine
fur . . **6.** ermine
mace . . **7.** scepter (sceptre)
martyr . . **8.** Charles I (Eng. 1649)
maundy . . **4.** alms
officer . . **7.** naperer
rights . . **7.** regalia
rock snake . . **6.** python
stables . . **4.** mews
stars (Astrol) . . **7.** Antares, Regulus
   9. Aldebaran, Fomalhaut
Royal (pert to) . . .
Academy . . **4.** Arts (1768)
Arcanum . . **7.** Society (1877)
Canadian Mounted Police . . **8.** Mounties
   16. Northwest Mounted
Castle . . **8.** Balmoral
Crown . . **5.** tiara
Highlanders . . **10.** Black Watch
Highness . . **5.** title **6.** prince **8.** princess
House . . **5.** Tudor **6.** Stuart, Valois
   7. Bourbon, Hanover, Windsor
Oak (Eng Hist) . . **7.** lottery **10.** Shropshire
Psalmist . . **9.** King David
Scot . . **16.** Lothian Regiments
royet . . . **4.** wild **6.** unruly **7.** romping
   11. mischievous
rub . . . **4.** crux, fret, wipe **6.** abrade, polish,
   scrape, smooth, stroke **7.** burnish,
   massage **8.** friction, irritate **9.** hindrance,
   triturate
rub (pert to) . . .
away . . **6.** abrade
down . . **4.** comb **5.** curry, groom
   7. massage
elbows . . **9.** associate **10.** fraternize
off . . **5.** erase **6.** abrade, remove
   10. obliterate
out . . **4.** kill **5.** erase **6.** cancel,
   efface, excise **7.** expunge, wipe out
   10. obliterate
wrong way . . **6.** ruffle **8.** irritate
   9. displease **10.** antagonize
rub-a-dub . . . **6.** clamor **7.** clatter, pit-a-pat,
   rat-a-tat **8.** rattatoo **9.** drumbeats
Rubáiyát (pert to) . . .
author . . **11.** Omar Khayyám
stanza form . . **8.** quatrain
translator . . **10.** Fitzgerald (1859)
rubber . . . **4.** para **5.** stare **6.** eraser
   7. ebonite, elastic **8.** massager,
   sight-see **10.** caoutchouc
rubber (pert to) . . .
city . . **5.** Akron
hard . . **7.** ebonite
India (pure) . . **10.** caoutchouc
plant . . **5.** Ficus
ring . . **4.** lute **6.** gasket
sap . . **5.** latex
shoe . . **6.** galosh (galoshe)
tree . . **3.** ule **7.** guayule
wild . . **5.** Ceara **6.** caucho
rubbish . . . **4.** junk, ross **5.** attle, dross,
   stent, trash, waste **6.** debris, refuse,
   rubble, trashy **8.** nonsense, riffraff,
   trumpery **9.** worthless
rubble . . . **5.** brash, chalk, stone, trash
   7. rubbish **8.** nonsense **11.** foolishness
rube . . . **4.** dolt **6.** rustic **7.** hayseed

rubedity ... **7.** redness **9.** ruddiness

rubella ... **7.** measles, rubeola

rubescent ... **3.** red **8.** flushing **9.** reddening **10.** erubescent

rubiator ... **4.** rake **5.** bully **6.** rascal

Rubicon ... **5.** river (Caesar's) **9.** Fiumicino (modern)

rubicund ... **3.** red **4.** ruby **5.** ruddy **6.** florid **7.** redness

rubric ... **3.** rod **6.** paraph, ritual **8.** category, red chalk **14.** title page in red

rubrics (book of) ... **4.** ordo

ruby (pert to) ...
  bird .. **11.** hummingbird
  heraldry .. **5.** gules
  stained quartz (red) .. **6.** Ancona **7.** rubasse **9.** Mont Blanc
  stone .. **3.** gem **5.** balas **6.** spinel
  type .. **4.** size

ruck ... **3.** rut, sit (on eggs) **4.** heap, pile, rick **5.** cower, crowd, squat, stack **6.** crease, crouch, furrow, horses (race), pucker **7.** wrinkle **9.** multitude **10.** generality

ruckus ... **3.** ado, row **5.** fight **6.** rumpus, uproar **7.** quarrel, ruction **8.** outbreak **9.** commotion

rudd ... **3.** hue **4.** carp, fish **6.** redden **7.** azurine, redness **10.** complexion

rudder ... **4.** helm **5.** guide

rudder part ... **8.** bearding **9.** whipstaff

rude ... **3.** raw **4.** curt **5.** rough, rowdy **6.** clumsy, coarse, rugged, simple, vulgar **7.** boorish, uncouth **8.** ignorant, insolent **9.** barbarous, inclement, makeshift, turbulent, unlearned, unskilled, untrained **10.** boisterous, unpolished **11.** impertinent, uncivilized **12.** discourteous

rudeness ... **6.** ferity **8.** curtness **9.** impudence, insolence, vulgarity **11.** raucousness **12.** impertinence

rudiment ... **7.** vestige

rudimentary ... **5.** basic **7.** initial **8.** original **9.** beginning, elemental, embryonic, vestigial **11.** undeveloped

rudimentary digit ... **7.** dewclaw

rudiments ... **4.** ABCs **6.** basics

rue ... **4.** rake, Ruta **6.** grieve, regret, repent, sorrow **8.** afflict, deplore **10.** bitterness, compassion, repentance **14.** disappointment

ruff ... **3.** ree **5.** pride, reeve, ruche, trump **6.** collar, fringe, rebato **7.** sunfish **8.** drumbeat **9.** sandpiper, vainglory

ruffian ... **4.** fish, pimp, thug **5.** rowdy, tough **6.** brutal, cuttle, pander **8.** assassin, paramour, the Devil **9.** cutthroat, desperado, murderous, vulgarian

ruffle ... **3.** vex **4.** fret, roil **5.** anger, annoy, frill, jabot **6.** edging, muddle, nettle, rumple, tousle **7.** agitate, disturb, flounce, fluster, shuffle **8.** dishevel, disorder, drumbeat, irritate **9.** balayeuse **10.** disarrange, discompose

ruffler ... **5.** bully **7.** boaster, ruffian **8.** braggart **9.** swaggerer **10.** attachment (sewing)

rug ... **3.** mat **4.** maud, shag **5.** Senna, throw **6.** carpet, hooked, petate **7.** Chinese, drugget, steamer **8.** coverlet, Oriental **9.** Samarkand

ruga ... **4.** fold **7.** wrinkle **8.** membrane

rugby ... **5.** Fives **6.** Rugger, school (Eng) **8.** football

rugby term ... **9.** scrum half, scrummage

rugged ... **4.** rude **5.** asper, hardy, harsh, rough, surly **6.** craggy, fierce, robust, seamed, shaggy, strong, sturdy **7.** austere, crabbed, healthy, uncivil **8.** vigorous, wrinkled **9.** irregular, not smooth, turbulent **11.** substantial

rugged mountain crest ... **5.** arête

ruin ... **4.** bane, doom, fate, loss **5.** blast, havoc, spoil, wrack, wreck **6.** defeat **7.** debauch, destroy, subvert **8.** bankrupt, demolish, downfall **9.** perdition **10.** desolation, subversion **11.** destruction, devastation

ruined ... **4.** gone **7.** spoiled, wrecked **8.** bankrupt, defeated **9.** destroyed **11.** dilapidated **12.** irremediable

ruinous ... **6.** deadly **7.** baneful, decayed **10.** demolished, disastrous, pernicious, submersive, tumbledown **11.** destructive

ruins ... **5.** relic, wreck **7.** remains

rukh ... **6.** forest, jungle

rule ... **3.** law **4.** norm, sway **5.** axiom, canon, guide, habit, order, regle, reign **6.** decree, govern, manage, method, regime, screed **7.** counsel, measure, precept, prevail, regency, regimen **8.** dominate, persuade, standard **9.** criterion, direction, influence, principle **12.** jurisdiction **15.** totalitarianism

rule by ...
  children .. **9.** paedarchy
  ecclesiasts .. **9.** hierarchy
  one .. **8.** monarchy
  race .. **10.** ethnocracy
  ten .. **8.** decarchy
  the mob .. **9.** mobocracy
  the people .. **9.** democracy
  tribes .. **9.** phylarchy

rule out ... **6.** cancel, excise **7.** obviate

ruler ... **3.** min **4.** amir (ameer), czar, emir, lord **5.** queen **6.** despot, dynast, ferule, gerent, prince, regent, satrap, sultan, tyrant **7.** emperor, monarch **8.** autocrat, governor, hierarch, measurer **9.** potentate

ruling ... **3.** law **6.** decree **7.** average, regnant, statute, verdict **8.** decision, reigning **9.** governing, prevalent **11.** predominant **12.** drawing lines

rullion ... **4.** shoe **6.** sandal

rum ... **3.** dye (blue), odd **4.** good **5.** queer, tafia (taffia) **6.** liquor **8.** Demon rum

rumal ... **6.** fabric **8.** kerchief (man's)

Rumania ... see *Romania*

rumble ... **4.** boom, seat (back) **5.** rumor **6.** murmur, ripple, stir up **9.** complaint **11.** rolling tone

rumen ... **3.** cud **5.** tripe **6.** gullet, paunch **7.** stomach (1st)

ruminant ... **2.** ox **3.** cow, yak **4.** bull, deer, gaur, goat, oryx, zebu **5.** bison, camel, eland, gayal, llama, moose,

okapi, sheep, steer **6.** alpaca, nilgai, vicuna, wapiti **7.** banteng, buffalo, caribou, chamois, gemsbok, giraffe **8.** antelope, elephant, reindeer, seladang **9.** dromedary, nannygoat, pronghorn **10.** cud-chewing, hartebeest, meditative, rhinoceros, thoughtful
ruminant (pert to) . . .
  division . . **8.** Ungulata **10.** Ruminantia
  first stomach . . **5.** rumen **6.** paunch
  fourth stomach . . **8.** abomasum **9.** rennet bag
  second stomach . . **9.** reticulum
  third stomach . . **6.** omasum **9.** manyplies **10.** psalterium
ruminate . . . **4.** chew, muse **6.** ponder **7.** reflect **8.** consider, meditate
rummage . . . **4.** junk **6.** litter, search **7.** collect (by search), ransack
rumor, rumour . . . **4.** Fama, talk **5.** bruit, noise, story **6.** norate, report **7.** hearsay, tidings **11.** scuttlebutt
rump . . . **4.** bone **6.** breech, sacrum **7.** meat cut **8.** bankrupt, buttocks **9.** remainder
rumpade . . . **3.** rob **6.** hold up
rumple . . . **4.** muss **5.** touse **6.** crease, ruffle, tousle **7.** crinkle, crumple, wrinkle **8.** dishevel **10.** disarrange
rumpus . . . **3.** row **6.** fracas, hubbub, uproar **9.** commotion, confusion **11.** disturbance
rumtytoo . . . **8.** ordinary **11.** commonplace
run . . . **2.** go **3.** fly, gad, hie **4.** dart, flee, flow, lope, melt, race, scud, tend, trot **5.** blend, hurry, speed, trend **6.** charge, course, elapse, endure, extend, manage, pursue, sprint, stream **7.** average, liquefy, operate, proceed, roulade, routine, smuggle, stretch, trickle **8.** continue **9.** discharge, suppurate
run (pert to) . . .
  about . . **5.** wagon **6.** gadder **8.** roadster, runagate, vagabond
  after . . **5.** chase, fetch, toady **6.** pursue **7.** lionize
  aground . . **6.** strand **7.** founder
  along the edge . . **5.** skirt
  away . . **4.** bolt, flee **5.** elope **6.** decamp, escape **8.** stampede
  before the wind . . **4.** scud
  between ports . . **3.** ply
  down . . **3.** hit **4.** find **5.** seedy, trace **7.** run over **9.** exhausted **11.** dilapidated **12.** deteriorated
  out . . **3.** end **5.** lapse, waste **6.** elapse, emerge, escape **7.** exhaust **8.** squander
  over . . **6.** browse, exceed, ponder **7.** trample **8.** overflow **9.** reiterate
  quickly, swiftly . . **4.** dart, race, scud **5.** scoot **6.** gallop, sprint **7.** scuttle
  stocking . . **6.** ladder
  through . . **4.** stab **6.** pierce **7.** inspect, pervade **8.** rehearse, squander, transfix **11.** superabound
  up against . . **4.** find **9.** encounter, stumble on **10.** experience
runagate . . . **7.** runaway **8.** apostate, fugitive, renegade, vagabond, wanderer
rundle . . . **4.** ball, coil, rung, step **5.** round

6. circle, roller, sphere, stream
rune . . . **5.** magic **6.** secret, symbol **7.** mystery **9.** character (anc)
rung . . . **4.** step **5.** round, spoke, stair, tread **6.** degree, rundle **7.** girdled, ratline
runic . . . **5.** verse **6.** poetic **7.** writing **8.** alphabet (anc), Norsemen
runner . . . **3.** ski (skee) **4.** sled **5.** miler, racer, stolo **6.** stolon **7.** tendril **8.** operator, procurer, salesman, smuggler, sprinter **9.** messenger, solicitor
running . . . **7.** current, cursive, fleeing, flowing, melting **9.** advancing, prevalent, smuggling **10.** continuous
running knot . . . **5.** noose
running race . . . **5.** relay **6.** sprint
running toad . . . **10.** natterjack
runt . . . **3.** elf **4.** chit (letter), wrig **5.** dwarf, pygmy **6.** pigeon **10.** diminutive
runway . . . **4.** file, ramp **8.** airstrip
rupa . . . **4.** body, form (visual)
rupee . . . **4.** anna, coin **14.** money of account
rupestrian . . . **14.** composed of rock **15.** inscribed on rock
ruption . . . **7.** ruction, rupture **8.** bursting
rupture . . . **4.** rent **5.** break, burst **6.** hernia, injury, rhexis **7.** quarrel **9.** hostility **10.** disruption, falling out, separating
rural . . . **6.** rustic **7.** bucolic **8.** agrestic, pastoral **12.** agricultural
rural (pert to) . . .
  deity . . **3.** Pan **6.** Faunus
  genus . . **6.** potato
  life . . **8.** pastoral
  poem . . **7.** eclogue, georgic
  Spanish . . **9.** policeman
  term . . **8.** agrestic
Rusa . . . **4.** deer **6.** sambar
ruse . . . **4.** fall, slip, wile **5.** fraud, trick **6.** deceit **8.** artifice **9.** stratagem **10.** subterfuge
rush . . . **3.** jet **4.** dart, dash, flow, scud **5.** brook, haste, hurry, plant, press, scoot, spate, speed, surge **6.** charge, course, defeat, demand, hasten, runlet, sortie **7.** cattail, repulse **8.** outburst, reed mace, stampede **9.** attention, thronging
rush (pert to) . . .
  forth . . **5.** sally
  hour . . **4.** peak
  light . . **6.** candle, feeble
  nut . . **5.** chufa
  Scot . . **5.** sprat (herb) **6.** Juncus
  toad . . **10.** natterjack
  wheat . . **10.** couch grass
rusk . . . **5.** bread **7.** biscuit
rusma . . . **9.** quicklime **10.** depilatory
Russia . . . see also *Russian*
  Asian part . . **7.** Siberia
  capital . . **6.** Moscow **9.** Petrograd (old)
  citadel . . **7.** Kremlin
  city . . **4.** Baku, Kiev, Omsk **5.** Minsk **6.** Rostov **7.** Kharkov **8.** Smolensk **9.** Petrograd **10.** Sevastopol (Sebastopol) **11.** Vladivostok **12.** St Petersburg (Leningrad)
  coal fields . . **6.** Donets (Ukraine)

fleet base.. **10.** Sevastopol, Stalingrad
former name.. **7.** Muscovy
founder.. **4.** Ivan **15.** Ivan the Terrible
gulf.. **4.** Azov
isthmus.. **7.** Karelia
lake.. **5.** Onega **6.** Baykal **7.** Aral Sea
  10. Caspian Sea
mountains.. **4.** Ural **8.** Caucasus
peninsula.. **4.** Kola **6.** Crimea
resort.. **5.** Yalta **6.** Crimea
river.. **2.** Ob **4.** Amur, Lena, Neva,
  Ural **5.** Volga **6.** Donets **7.** Dneiper,
  Yenisei
sea.. **4.** Azov **5.** Black, White
  6. Baltic **7.** Caspian
strait.. **6.** Bering
Russian (pert to)...
antelope.. **5.** saiga
aristocratic order.. **4.** knez **5.** Boyar
assembly.. **4.** duma, rada **7.** zemstoo
association, guild.. **5.** artel
bank.. **4.** game
beer, beverage.. **5.** kvass, vodka
boat.. **6.** baidak (baydak)
braid (trim).. **8.** soutache
calendar (to 1918).. **6.** Julian
cap (peasant).. **4.** aska
carriage.. **6.** drosky, troika **9.** tarantass
  (tarantas)
cart, wagon.. **6.** telega
cathedral.. **5.** sober
cloak (fur).. **5.** shuba
council.. **4.** duma, rada **6.** soviet
dance (rustic).. **7.** ziganka
decree.. **5.** ukase
dog (wolfhound).. **6.** borzoi **7.** owtchah
dress (peasant).. **7.** sarafan
duke, prince.. **4.** knez (kniaz)
edict.. **5.** ukase
fur (lamb).. **7.** karakul (karakule)
  9. astrakhan
guild.. **5.** artel
hemp.. **4.** rine
hut.. **4.** isba
leather.. **5.** jufti (jufts) **6.** Bulgar
  8. shagreen
marsh, lagoon.. **5.** liman
massacre.. **6.** pogrom
monetary unit.. **5.** ruble (rouble)
  6. kopeck (kopek)
musical instrument.. **5.** gudok, gusla
  9. balalaika
naval academy.. **6.** Frunze
news agency.. **4.** Tass
no.. **4.** nyet
parliament.. **4.** duma
peasant.. **4.** Slav **5.** kulak **6.** muzhik
  (muzjik)
peasant village.. **3.** mir
plain (treeless).. **6.** steppe, tundra
police (secret).. **5.** Cheka
pound.. **4.** pood
prince, duke.. **4.** knez (kniaz)
ruler.. **4.** czar (tsar)
satellite.. **7.** sputnik
soup (cabbage).. **5.** stchi (shchi)
  6. borsch
stockade.. **5.** etape
synod.. **5.** sobor
tea urn.. **7.** samovar
turnip.. **8.** rutabaga

villa.. **5.** dacha
wagon (springless).. **6.** telega
wheat.. **5.** emmer
whip.. **4.** plet (plete) **5.** knout
wolfhound.. **6.** borzoi
yes.. **2.** da
Russian people...
author.. **5.** Gogol, Gorki (Gorky)
  7. Tolstoy (Tolstoi) **8.** Turgenev
  10. Dostoevski (Dostoyevsky)
  12. Solzhenitsyn
chess champ (1892).. **8.** Alekhine
composer.. **3.** Cui **7.** Borodin
  10. Rubenstein, Stravinsky
  12. Tschaikovsky **14.** Rimsky-Korsakov
conqueror.. **6.** Tatars **7.** Mongols
Cossack.. **5.** Tatar
czar.. **4.** Ivan **13.** Peter the Great
duke.. **5.** kniaz (knez, knyoz)
empress.. **7.** Czarina, Tsarina
General.. **10.** Timoshenko
grand duke.. **8.** Nicholas
language deviser.. **8.** Zamenhof
  9. Esperanto (pseudonym)
leader.. **5.** Lenin **6.** Stalin **7.** Molotov,
  Yeltsin **8.** Brezhnev **9.** Gorbachev
  10. Khrushchev
little Russian.. **7.** Russene (Ruthene)
monk.. **8.** Rasputin
people.. **4.** Lett, Slav **7.** Cossack
  8. Russniak **9.** Muscovite, Ruthenian
poet.. **7.** Pushkin, Yesenin **9.** Pasternak
premier.. **5.** Lenin **7.** Kosygin, Molotov
  8. Bulganin **10.** Khrushchev
saint.. **4.** Olga
teacher, monk.. **7.** starets
rust... **3.** eat **5.** erode **6.** aerugo, patina
  7. erosion, oxidize **9.** corrosion
rustic... **4.** boor, carl, rube, rude
  5. churl, clown, Damon, rough, rural,
  swain, yokel **6.** coarse, simple, sturdy,
  sylvan **7.** artless, awkward, boorish,
  bucolic, Corydon, plowboy **8.** agrestic,
  pastoral **9.** agrestian **10.** clodhopper,
  countryman, unpolished
rustic (pert to)...
lover.. **5.** swain
maiden.. **9.** Thestylis
peasant.. **4.** boor
pipe.. **4.** reed
poetic.. **4.** carl
verse.. **4.** idyl (idyll)
rustle... **4.** flow **5.** steal, swish, whisk
  7. crinkle **11.** sound softly
rut... **5.** ditch, track **6.** furrow, groove,
  strake **7.** routine, wrinkle
Ruth (pert to)...
Book.. **12.** Old Testament
country.. **4.** Moab
husband.. **4.** Boaz
mother-in-law.. **5.** Naomi
ruthless... **5.** cruel **8.** pitiless **9.** merciless
  10. ironfisted
rye... **5.** bread, grain, grass **6.** cereal,
  whisky **9.** gentleman (gypsy)
rye bread... **5.** black **10.** knackebrod
  12. pumpernickel
ryot... **6.** farmer, tenant **7.** peasant
Rytina... **6.** dugong, sea cow **7.** manatee
  12. Hydrodamalis **14.** Steller's sea cow
Ryukyu Islands... **7.** Okinawa

S

S (pert to)...
curve.. **4.** ogee
letter.. **10.** nineteenth
shaped.. **7.** sigmate, sigmoid
suffix.. **6.** plural
Saal... **4.** hall, room (large)
sabalo... **6.** tarpon **8.** milkfish
sabana... **5.** plain **7.** plateau, savanna (savannah)
sabbat... **8.** assembly (demons), festival (orgies)
Sabbatarian... **9.** ritualist **11.** Russian sect
Sabbath... **6.** Sunday **7.** holy day
sabbatical year... **7.** seventh **8.** vacation **14.** leave of absence
sabbatism... **4.** rest **9.** ritualism **12.** intermission (labor)
Sabbatist (pert to)...
devotee of.. **4.** cult (Oriental)
member.. **6.** Semite
named for.. **5.** Sabbe (goddess) **8.** Sambathe
saber, sabre (pert to)...
bean.. **4.** jack
bill.. **6.** curlew
fish.. **7.** cutlass
knot.. **8.** military
legged (horse).. **12.** sickle-hocked
Mohammedan.. **8.** yataghan (yatagan)
oriental.. **8.** scimiter
toothed.. **3.** cat **5.** tiger **12.** machairodont
wing.. **11.** hummingbird
sabino... **9.** ahuehuete, rock cedar
sabio... **4.** sage **6.** priest **7.** wise man
sable... **4.** ebon, pelt **5.** black, brush **6.** mammal, marten **8.** antelope **10.** mysterious, Russia iron
sabotage... **6.** damage, mayhem **9.** undermine **11.** destruction (malicious)
Sabrina... **10.** river nymph **11.** River Severn
sabuline, sabulous... **5.** sandy **6.** gritty **8.** psammous **10.** arenaceous
sabutan... **5.** fibre, straw
sac... **3.** bag **4.** cyst, sack **5.** ascus, bursa, pouch, purse, theca **6.** cavity, pocket, saccus **7.** saccule, vesicle **8.** sacculus
sacalait... **7.** crappie **8.** warmouth **9.** killifish
saccadic... **5.** jerky **9.** twitching **11.** eye movement
saccharine... **5.** sweet **7.** honeyed **10.** sweetening
saccos... **7.** tunicle **8.** vestment
sacerdocy... **10.** priesthood **13.** priestly order
sacerdos... **6.** priest
sachem... **5.** chief (Indian) **8.** governor (Tammany)
sachet... **3.** bag **5.** pouch **6.** powder **7.** perfume **8.** reticule **11.** perfumed pad
sack... **3.** bag **4.** loot, poke, wine **5.** ascus, bursa, catch, pouch, purse **6.** defeat, ravage, secure **7.** pillage, plunder **8.** desolate **9.** discharge, dismissal
sack (pert to)...
baseball.. **3.** bag **4.** base
Bible.. **8.** mourning
but.. **4.** butt, cask **8.** trombone (anc)
cloth.. **7.** penance, sacking **15.** garb of penitence
dress.. **4.** robe **6.** jacket, sacque
sacrament... **3.** act **4.** oath **5.** token **6.** pledge, symbol **7.** mystery **8.** ceremony, covenant, practice **9.** communion, Eucharist **10.** intinction (to administer)
Sacramento (pert to)...
capital, river.. **10.** California
cat.. **10.** horned pout
pike.. **9.** squawfish
salmon.. **7.** quinnat
sacrarium (anc)... **6.** chapel, shrine **7.** oratory **8.** sacristy **9.** sanctuary, synsacrum
sacred... **4.** holy **6.** divine **7.** blessed **8.** hallowed, reverend **9.** dedicated, inviolate, religious, venerable **10.** inviolable, sacrosanct **11.** consecrated **13.** sanctimonious
sacred (pert to)...
bark.. **7.** cascara **14.** cascara sagrada
bean.. **11.** Indian lotus
beetle.. **10.** scarabaeus
bird.. **4.** ibis
book.. **5.** Bible, Koran
bo tree.. **3.** fig **5.** pipal
bull.. **4.** apis, zebu
chest.. **4.** arca **9.** reliquary
comb form.. **5.** hagio, hiero
dialect (Buddh writings).. **4.** Pali
grove.. **5.** Altis (Olympia)
image.. **4.** icon (ikon) **5.** Pietà
instrument.. **4.** Urim **7.** Thummim
malady.. **8.** epilepsy
monkey.. **6.** baboon, rhesus **8.** entellus
most.. **10.** sacrosanct
music.. **4.** hymn **5.** chant, motet **8.** oratorio
river (Ind).. **6.** Ganges (Ganga)
room.. **8.** sacristy
traffic (in sacred things).. **6.** simony
weed.. **7.** vervain
wine vessel.. **3.** ama
writ.. **10.** Scriptures
sacrifice... **4.** lose, loss **5.** offer **6.** give up, victim **8.** chiliomb (1,000 oxen), hecatomb (100 oxen), immolate, libation, oblation, offering **9.** atonement, holocaust, martyrdom, privation, surrender **11.** crucifixion, destruction
sacrificer... **6.** martyr
sacrificial fire... **5.** ignis
sacrilege... **7.** robbery (church) **9.** blasphemy **11.** desecration, profanation
sacrilegious... **7.** impious **10.** irreverent

11. blasphemous, irreligious
sacrosanct ... 4. holy 6. sacred 8. ironical, most holy
sad ... 3. bad 4. blue, dark, dire, dull 5. dusky, sorry 6. solemn, somber, triste, wicked 7. doleful, pensive, unhappy 8. dejected, downcast, grievous, pathetic, shameful, terrible 9. cheerless, depressed, sorrowful 10. calamitous, deplorable, depressing, melancholy 11. distressing, unfortunate
saddle ... 4. meat (cut of), ride, seat 5. cinch, ridge 6. burden 7. harness (part) 8. encumber, straddle
saddle (pert to) ...
back .. 4. hill 5. ridge
bag .. 7. alforja, pannier
blanket .. 6. corona, tilpah
boot .. 7. gambado
cloth .. 6. cover 7. housing 8. shabrack 9. appendage 10. horsecloth
elephant .. 6. howdah
girth .. 5. cinch
horse .. 5. mount 6. remuda 7. palfrey
light .. 5. pilch 7. pillion
pack .. 7. aparejo
part .. 6. cantle, crutch, pommel 7. stirrup 8. tapadera (tapadero) 9. saddlebow
place behind .. 5. croup
rock .. 6. oyster
strap .. 5. girth 6. latigo
saddler ... 4. seal 5. horse 6. cozier 7. cobbler, lorimer 8. merchant 9. shoemaker
sadness ... 5. dolor 6. pathos, sorrow 9. dejection 10. gloominess, melancholy 11. unhappiness 13. sorrowfulness
sad tree ... 10. hursinghar (dye yield)
safari ... 4. tour, trip 6. junket 7. caravan, journey 10. expedition, pilgrimage
safe ... 4. pete (thieves' sl), sane, sure 5. chest, vault 6. closet, secure, unhurt 8. cautious, cupboard, unharmed 9. protected, strongbox 11. trustworthy
safeblower ... 7. burglar, peteman 8. peterman
safe conduct ... 4. pass 5. cowle, guard 6. convoy, escort 8. passport 10. precaution, protection
safecracker ... 4. yegg
safekeeping ... 4. care 7. custody, storage 10. protection 12. preservation
safety lamp (miner's) ... 4. Davy
safety rail ... 9. guardrail
saffron ... 6. crocus, yellow 10. colchicine
sag ... 4. bend, hang, reed, rush, sink, wilt 5. drift, droop, sedge, slump 6. weaken 10. depreciate
saga ... 4. Edda, epic, tale 5. story, witch 6. legend 7. recital, sagaman 9. narrative
Saga ... 7. goddess, seeress
sagacious ... 4. sage, wise 5. aware, witty 6. argute, astute, shrewd 7. politic, sapient 9. judicious 10. discerning, farsighted 11. penetrative 13. perspicacious
sagacity ... 3. ken 6. acumen, wisdom 9. acuteness, quickness 10. shrewdness 11. discernment, penetration 13. judiciousness

sage ... 4. mint, wise 5. solon 6. astute, Salvia, shrewd 7. sapient 9. counselor, judicious, sagebrush 10. discerning 11. philosopher
Sage (of) ...
Chelsea .. 7. Carlyle (Thomas)
Concord .. 7. Emerson (Ralph W)
Emporia .. 5. White (Wm Allen)
Ferney .. 8. Voltaire
Monticello .. 9. Jefferson (Thomas)
Pylos .. 6. Nestor
sage (pert to) ...
Bethlehem .. 9. spearmint
cheese .. 7. Cheddar
chippy .. 14. Brewer's sparrow
cock, hen .. 6. grouse
family .. 4. mint
rose .. 5. alder (yellow)
tea .. 5. tonic
Sagebrush State ... 6. Nevada
sagene ... 5. seine 7. measure, network
sagitta ... 7. otolith 8. keystone (Arch), The Arrow
Sagittarius ... 6. bowman 9. The Archer 13. constellation
sago (pert to) ...
palm .. 6. gebang, gomuti
plant .. 10. cuckoopint
product .. 6. starch
tree .. 7. coontie
sagoin ... 8. marmoset
saguaro ... 6. cactus, flower
saguing ... 6. banana
Sahara ... 5. cocoa (color), leste (wind) 6. desert
sahib ... 5. title 6. master 9. gentleman
sai ... 6. monkey 8. capuchin
said ... 6. stated 7. uttered 9. aforesaid 15. before-mentioned
said to be ... 7. reputed, rumored 8. reported
saiga ... 8. antelope
Saigon nickname ... 14. Paris of the East
sail ... 3. jib, lug 4. luff, tack 5. craft, float 6. vessel, voyage 8. navigate
sail (pert to) ...
around .. 14. circumnavigate
close to wind .. 4. luff
end .. 7. yardarm
fish .. 12. basking shark 15. quillback sucker
fore and aft .. 7. spanker
foresail .. 9. spinnaker
part .. 4. clew, yard 5. leech
rope .. 5. sheet 6. earing
secure, lash .. 7. trice up
strings .. 10. reef points
type .. 3. jib, lug, top, try 4. main, reef, stay 6. lateen, mizzen, square 7. topsail 8. mainsail, save-alls 12. mutton-legger
sailboat ... 4. yawl 5. ketch, skiff, sloop, yacht 7. caravel (caravelle)
sailing term ... 3. leg, run 4. asea, beat, jibe, scud, tack 5. hoist (sail), point, reach 7. gliding
sailing vessel ... 4. bark (barque), brig, saic, yawl 5. sloop 7. frigate 8. schooner 10. barkentine (barquentine), windjammer
sailor ... 3. gob, tar 4. salt, wave 5. middy

6. lascar, matlow 7. mariner, voyager
8. seafarer 10. bluejacket, lobscouser
(sl)
sailor (pert to)...
associate at meals.. 8. messmate
clothes.. 11. bell-bottoms
kit.. 8. ditty bag 9. housewife
knot.. 8. geranium
mess tub.. 3. kid
patron saint.. 4. Elmo
song.. 7. chantey 9. barcarole
Saimiri... 4. titi 6. monkey 8. squirrel
sain doux... 4. lard 6. grease
saint... 3. Ste 5. angel 7. apostle, pietist
8. canonize, enshrine, sanctify 10. holy
person 11. godly person
Saint (pert to)...
Anthony's fire.. 10. erysipelas
Buddhist.. 5. arhat
Elmo's fire (or light).. 6. corona, Helena
9. corposant
Esprit.. 9. holy ghost
Francis of Assisi.. 11. il Poverello
13. little poor man
Gaudens.. 8. sculptor
George's flag.. 14. national emblem
Helena's hemlock.. 7. jellica
John Lateran.. 12. Mother Church
John's bread.. 5. carob 9. algarroba
Leger (Eng).. 9. horse race
Luke's summer.. 12. Indian summer
Martin.. 13. Bishop of Tours
Martin's feast.. 9. Martinmas
Mary-le-Bow.. 15. Cheapside Church
(Cockney area)
Mohammedan.. 3. pir
Patrick's breastplate.. 6. lorica
Paul.. 12. Saul of Tarsus
Paul's Church (London), designer..
18. Sir Christopher Wren
Peter's dome architect..
12. Michelangelo
Vitus' dance.. 6. chorea
Saint, patron...
children's.. 8. Nicholas (Santa Claus)
desperate person's.. 4. Jude
English.. 6. George
French.. 5. Denis
hospitals.. 9. John of God 10. Juan
Ciudad
Irish.. 7. Patrick
Italian.. 7. Anthony
lawyer's.. 4. Ives
lover's.. 9. Valentine
sailor's.. 4. Elmo
Scottish.. 6. Andrew
Spanish.. 5. James
Welsh.. 5. David
saints (pert to)...
biography.. 9. hagiology
11. hagiography
symbol.. 4. halo 6. nimbus
tomb.. 6. shrine
worship of.. 10. hagiolatry
sajou... 6. monkey 7. sapajou
sake... 4. beer 6. motive, reason
7. purpose 8. beverage (rice)
salacious... 4. lewd 5. horny (sl)
7. lustful, obscene 8. unchaste
9. lecherous
salad plant, vegetable... 4. bibb 5. cress

6. celery, endive 7. cabbage, lettuce,
romaine 10. watercress
salamander... 3. eft 4. newt 5. poker
6. triton 7. axolotl, Caudata, urodela
9. fire-eater 10. hellbender 12. pocket
gopher
salary... 3. fee, pay 4. hire, wage
5. wages 6. reward 7. stipend 8. pittance
9. allowance, emolument, salt money
(anc) 10. honorarium 12. compensation,
remuneration
salat... 6. prayer (facing Mecca)
sale... 4. deal, vend 6. barter, demand,
market 7. auction, handsel (1st in
morning) 8. contract 11. black market
salesman... 5. agent 6. vendor
7. drummer 9. solicitor
14. representative 18. commercial
traveler
salient... 4. bold 6. trench 7. eminent,
jetting, jumping, leaping, obvious
8. bounding, extended 9. prominent
10. noticeable, protruding
11. conspicuous
salient angle... 5. arris, Doric
Salientia... 5. Anura, frogs, toads
8. Amphibia (tailless)
salient point... 7. feature (detail)
saline... 5. salty 6. salina 8. solution
10. saliferous
Salinger, J. D. (pert to)...
character.. 6. Phoebe 15. Holden
Caulfield
work.. 13. Franny and Zooey 15. Catcher
in the Rye
saliva... 7. spittle 8. digester, ptyalism
salivary gland... 8. racemose
sallow... 3. wan 4. gray, pale 5. muddy,
pasty 6. pallid 9. yellowish
sally... 4. jest, leap, trip 5. issue, jaunt,
start 6. sortie 7. journey 8. escapade,
outburst 9. witticism
salmagundi... 4. hash, olio, stew
6. medley 7. mixture 9. potpourri
10. periodical (old)
salmon... 4. fish 5. color 6. orlean,
sauqui 7. annatto, saumont
salmon (pert to)...
adult.. 7. gilling
after spawning.. 4. kelt
cured.. 6. kipper
dog.. 4. keta
family.. 10. Salmonidae
female.. 4. raun 6. baggit
genus.. 12. Oncorhynchus
herring.. 8. milkfish
humpbacked.. 5. haddo, holia
kind.. 7. quinnat
landlocked.. 7. kokanee
male.. 3. gib 6. kipper
newly hatched.. 4. pink
second year.. 6. hepper
silver.. 4. coho
small.. 4. peal 6. grilse
third year.. 4. mort
trout.. 5. sewen
young.. 3. fog 4. parr 5. smolt 6. grilse
samlet 7. essling
Salome (pert to)...
Bib.. 6. dancer
father.. 8. Herodias

grandfather . . **5.** Herod
opera, by . . **7.** Strauss
salon . . . **7.** gallery **8.** New Salon (Paris),
Old Salon **9.** reception **10.** assemblage,
exhibition **11.** drawing room
Salon del Prado (Madrid) . . .
9. promenade
saloon . . . **3.** bar **4.** deck **6.** tavern
7. barroom, cantina, gallery
8. dramshop, groggery **11.** drawing
room
saloop . . . **8.** hot drink **9.** sassafras
salt . . . **3.** sal **4.** cure **5.** brine, taste
6. flavor, halite, sailor, saline
8. piquancy **9.** seasoning **10.** antiseptic,
corrective **14.** sodium chloride
salt (pert to) . . .
acetic acid . . **7.** acetate
alkaline . . **5.** borax
astringent . . **4.** alum
block, rock . . **3.** pig
boric acid . . **6.** borate
cat . . **4.** lump **10.** pigeon food
comb form . . **4.** sali
cracker . . **7.** saltine
dish for . . **10.** saltcellar
ethereal . . **5.** ester
flat . . **5.** playa
lake . . **5.** shott (chott)
marsh, pond . . **6.** salina
native . . **6.** halite
nature of, like . . **6.** haloid
of the earth . . **7.** the best **10.** commonalty
peter, petre . . **5.** niter
rock, block . . **3.** pig
spring . . **4.** lick
tax . . **7.** gabelle
tree . . **4.** atle (atlee) **5.** cedar **7.** tamarix
8. tamarisk
working . . **7.** halurgy
works . . **7.** saltern, saltery **9.** salthouse
saltant . . . **7.** dancing, jumping, leaping
8. bouncing, bounding
salted . . . **5.** briny, cured **6.** corned
7. treated **8.** brackish, hardened,
seasoned **11.** experienced
salty . . . **3.** reh **5.** briny, salic, witty
6. risqué, saline
salubrious . . . **4.** good **8.** salutary
9. healthful, wholesome **10.** beneficial
salutary . . . **7.** healthy **8.** curative
9. medicinal **10.** salubrious
11. restorative
salutation . . . **2.** hi **3.** ave **4.** hail **5.** aloha,
hello, howdy, skoal **6.** curtsy, homage,
kowtow, Mizpah (Mizpeh), prosit,
salaam (salam) **7.** Dear Sir **8.** greeting,
serenade
salute . . . **4.** hail, kiss **5.** greet **6.** homage,
signal **7.** address
salvage . . . **4.** save **6.** redeem, rescue
10. redemption **11.** reclamation
salvation . . . **8.** soterial **10.** liberation,
redemption **11.** deliverance, soteriology
12. preservation
Salvation Army founder . . . **5.** Booth
salve . . . **3.** tip **4.** balm, cure **5.** allay,
quiet **6.** anoint, cerate **7.** assuage,
relieve **8.** flattery, medicate, ointment
9. gloss over, lubricate, mitigator
10. medication

salver . . . **4.** tray **9.** flatterer **11.** serving
dish
salvo . . . **6.** excuse **7.** gunfire, pretext,
proviso, quibble, rockets **8.** applause
9. discharge, exception **11.** projectiles,
reservation
Samaria (pert to) . . .
capital (anc) . . **6.** Israel
deity . . **6.** Nibhaz
destroyer . . **6.** Romans
founder . . **4.** Omri (925 BC)
people . . **9.** Assyrians
province of . . **9.** Palestine
rebuilder . . **5.** Herod (the Great)
Samaritan, good . . . **5.** aider **6.** helper
10. befriender, benefactor **11.** helping
hand
Sambal (Zambal) **language** . . . **4.** Tino
sambar (sambur) . . . **4.** deer, maha, rusa
same . . . **2.** id **3.** ilk, one **4.** ibid, idem,
self **5.** alike, ditto **7.** cognate, identic
8. selfsame **9.** identical **10.** equivalent
sameness . . . **6.** parity, tedium **7.** analogy,
oneness **8.** identity, monotony
9. alikeness **10.** similarity, uniformity
11. equivalence **14.** correspondence
Samian (pert to) . . .
island . . **5.** Samos
Sage . . **10.** Pythagoras
sea . . **6.** Aegean
ware . . **8.** Arretine
samlet . . . **4.** parr **6.** salmon (young)
Samoa . . .
anthropologist who studied . . **4.** Mead
capital . . **4.** Apia
councilor . . **7.** faipule
islands . . **8.** American
islands, main . . **5.** Manua, Upolu **6.** Savaii
7. Tutuila
natives . . **10.** Polynesian
owl (barn) . . **4.** lulu
political council . . **4.** fono
town . . **8.** Pago Pago
warrior . . **3.** toa
samovar . . . **3.** urn **6.** teapot
Samoyed, Samoyede . . . **3.** dog (Arctic)
8. Siberian
sample . . . **4.** test **5.** model, taste **6.** swatch
7. example, pattern **8.** specimen
sampler . . . **8.** original **9.** archetype
10. needlework
Samson (pert to) . . .
Bib . . **5.** judge (Israelite)
death site . . **4.** Gaza (Syria)
famed as . . **9.** strong man
opera . . **16.** Samson and Delilah
tribe . . **3.** Dan
wife . . **7.** Delilah (betrayer)
Samuel . . . **4.** Book (Old Test) **5.** judge
7. prophet
samurai . . . **6.** vassal **7.** officer
Sana native . . . **8.** Yemenite
San Andreas rift . . . **15.** earthquake fault
(Calif)
San Antonio mission . . . **5.** Alamo
sanative . . . **7.** healing **8.** curative,
sanatory
Sancho's master . . . **10.** Don Quixote
Sancta Sanctis . . . **20.** Holy things for
the holy
sanctify . . . **5.** honor **6.** hallow

10. consecrate 11. free from sin
sanctimonious . . . 4. holy 6. sacred
   7. saintly 8. affected 12. hypocritical
sanction . . . 4. abet, amen, fiat, okay
   6. assent, permit, ratify 7. approve,
   condone, endorse, support 8. approval
   9. approbate, authority, authorize
   11. countenance, endorsement
   12. ratification 13. authorization
sanctity . . . 8. holiness 9. godliness,
   solemnity 10. sacredness 11. saintliness
   13. inviolability
sanctuary . . . 4. bema, fane, holy, naos
   5. abbey, bamah, cella, haven 6. priory,
   refuge, temple 7. Alsatia, convent,
   retreat, shelter 8. cloister 9. monastery
   10. penetralia
sanctum . . . 3. den 5. study 6. adytum,
   office 7. retreat
sand . . . 4. grit 5. arena, nerve, pluck,
   stone
sand (pert to) . . .
   applied to body . . 9. arenation
   bog . . 4. syrt 9. quicksand
   eel . . 4. grig 6. launce
   flea . . 6. chigoe, red bug 7. chigger,
      sandboy
   fluke . . 7. sand dab 8. flounder
   hill, mound . . 4. dene, dune
   hog . . 7. laborer (in compressed air)
      8. tunneler (tunneller)
   inhabiting . . 11. arenicolous
   like (sand) . . 9. arenulous 10. arenaceous
   man . . 5. genie
   mixture (clay) . . 4. loam 9. sandstone
   pear . . 5. Pyrus
   submerged bank . . 3. bar 5. hurst, shoal
   sugar . . 5. niter
   widgeon . . 7. gadwall
sandal . . . 4. boat, shoe, sock 7. talaria
sandpiper . . . 3. ree 4. knot, pume,
   ruff, stib 5. stint (long-toed) 6. dunlin
   8. pectoral, triddler
sandstone . . . 7. sarsens 8. ganister
Sandwich Islands . . . 6. Hawaii
   8. Hawaiian
sandy . . . 6. desert, gritty 7. arenose
   8. granular, sabulous, Scotsman
   9. sandpiper 10. arenaceous, ring
   plover
sane . . . 5. lucid, sound 7. logical
   8. rational, sensible 9. practical
   10. reasonable
San Francisco Mil Post . . . 8. Presidio
sang . . . 5. blood, sheng 7. chanted,
   ginseng, Society
sang-froid . . . 8. coolness 9. cold blood,
   composure 11. insouciance
sanguinary . . . 3. ant (slave) 4. gory
   5. cruel 6. bloody, yarrow 8. sanguine
   9. bloodroot, murderous
   12. bloodthirsty
sanguine . . . 4. warm 5. ruddy 6. ardent
   7. hopeful 8. blood-red 9. confident
   10. optimistic 12. bloodthirsty
sanity . . . 4. wits 6. reason 8. lucidity,
   saneness 9. soundness
   13. wholesomeness
San Juan Hill . . . 4. Cuba (Battle, 1898)
San Juan Indian . . . 4. Tewa
San Kuo . . . 13. Three Kingdoms (Shu,
Wei, Wu)
San Marino, Europe (pert to) . . .
   famed as . . 11. oldest State (Eur)
   government . . 8. Republic (smallest)
   mountains . . 8. Appenine
   site . . 8. Mt Titano
sannup . . . 6. Indian (married male) (opp
   of squaw)
Sanskrit (pert to) . . .
   college . . 3. tol
   dialect . . 4. Pali
   drama . . 9. Sakuntala (Shakuntala)
   epic . . 8. Ramayana
   god . . 4. Kama (Cupid), Vayu (wind)
      5. Indra (Great) 6. Aditya
   goddess . . 3. Uma (Splendor) 4. Devi
      (Mother) 5. Aditi, Gauri
   human spirit . . 7. jivatma
   literature . . 5. sruti (shruti)
   period . . 5. Vedic
   Phonet (sounds) . . 6. sandhi
   poem (epic) . . 11. Race of Raghu,
      Raghuvamsha
   poet . . 8. Kalidasa
   sacred books . . 4. Veda
   soul . . 5. atman
   treatise . . 9. Upanishad
Santo Domingo . . . 7. capital (Dominican
   Republic)
sap . . . 3. gum 4. boob, dupe, fool, mine,
   seve, upas 5. drain, fluid, lymph, sapor
   6. juices, trench, weaken 7. essence,
   schnook 8. unsettle 9. simpleton,
   undermine
sapid . . . 5. tasty 7. zestful 8. flavored
   9. palatable, toothsome
sapient . . . 4. sage, wise 6. shrewd
   7. knowing 8. profound 9. sagacious
   10. discerning
sapiutan . . . 4. anoa 6. wild ox
sapodilla . . . 5. chico 6. chicle, zapote
   7. nispero 9. naseberry
sapor . . . 5. savor, taste 6. flavor, relish
sapper . . . 5. miner 6. digger 9. excavator
Saracen . . . 4. Arab 5. nomad, pagan
   6. Muslim (Moslem) 7. heathen, infidel,
   ragwort 9. Moor's head (Her)
Saracen Knight . . . 8. Ruggiero
Sarah (pert to) . . .
   bird . . 9. wake-robin
   husband . . 7. Abraham
   mother of . . 5. Isaac
   slave of . . 5. Hagar
sarcasm . . . 4. gibe 5. irony, taunt 6. satire
   8. ironical, ridicule
sarcastic . . . 3. dry 6. biting, ironic
   7. caustic, cutting, satiric 8. ironical,
   sardonic 9. malicious 10. mordacious
sarcophagic . . . 10. sarcophagy 11. flesh-
   eating 13. sarcophageous
sarcophagus . . . 5. chest 6. coffin
   9. limestone 11. Assian stone, lapis
   Assius
sardine . . . 4. bang 7. alewife, anchovy,
   herring (young) 8. pilchard
Sardinia, Italy . . .
   capital . . 8. Cagliari
   island . . 13. Mediterranean
   sheep . . 7. mouflon (moufflon)
   tower (Prehist) . . 6. nuragh
sardonic . . . 3. dry 6. ironic, morose

7. cynical, satiric 8. derisive 9. sarcastic
11. Rabelaisian
sartor ... 6. tailor
sash ... 3. obi 4. band, belt, benn, tobe
6. girdle 8. casement 10. cummerbund
sash pulley weight ... 5. mouse
Saskatchewan, Canada ...
capital .. 6. Regina
city .. 8. Moose Jaw 9. Saskatoon
sassaby ... 8. antelope
sassafras (pert to) ...
nut .. 8. pichurim
oil of (part) .. 6. safrol
tea .. 6. saloop
tree .. 4. ague
sassy ... 4. pert 5. saucy 8. impudent
Satan ... 5. Demon, Devil, Eblis, fiend
6. Belial 7. Lucifer, Scratch, Tempter
9. archfiend 14. Mephistopheles
16. Prince of Darkness
Satan (pert to) ...
angel (bottomless pit) .. 8. Apollyon
associate .. 6. Azazel 9. Beelzebub
before his fall .. 7. Lucifer
Jewish .. 8. Asmodeus
Scottish .. 4. deil
son .. 3. Imp (jocular)
satanic ... 5. cruel 6. wicked 7. demonic
8. devilish, infernal 10. diabolical
satchel ... 3. bag 4. case, etui, grip,
sack 5. cabas 6. valise
sate ... 4. cloy, glut 5. gorge 7. gratify,
satiate, satisfy, surfeit 8. saturate
sated ... 4. full 5. blasé 6. gorged
satellite ... 4. Echo, luna, moon 5. Atlas
6. comsat, planet 7. aerosat, Landsat,
Sputnik, Telstar 8. Explorer, follower,
Vanguard 9. companion, dependent
satellite of Jupiter ... 2. Io (1st)
6. Europa (2nd) 8. Callisto, Ganymede
satellite of Saturn ... 4. Rhea 5. Dione,
Mimas, Titan 6. Phoebe, Tethys
8. Hyperion 9. Enceladus
satellite of Uranus ... 5. Ariel 6. Oberon
7. Titania, Umbriel
satellite's orbit ... 4. path
14. geosynchronous
Sati (Egypt) ... 5. Queen
satiate ... 4. cloy, glut, pall, sate 5. gorge
7. gratify, satisfy, surfeit
satin ... 4. silk 6. étoile, fabric, sateen,
satiny 9. satinette 10. smoothness
satire ... 3. wit 5. irony, spoof 6. parody
7. lampoon
satiric, satirical ... 3. dry 6. bitter,
ironic 7. abusive, caustic, cutting
8. ironical, poignant 9. burlesque,
sarcastic 11. reproachful
satisfaction ... 3. cro 4. duel 6. amends
7. comfort, content, payment, satiety
8. adequacy, pleasure, reprisal
9. atonement 10. recompense,
reparation 11. contentment, fulfillment
12. compensation, propitiation,
remuneration 15. indemnification
satisfied ... 5. proud, sated 7. content,
pleased 8. satiated 9. contented,
convinced, gratified 10. paid in full
satisfy ... 2. do 3. pay 4. fill, sate, suit
5. atone, solve 6. pay off, please, supply
7. assuage, content, fulfill, gratify,

indulge, requite, satiate 8. atone for,
convince
satrap (anc) ... 5. ruler 6. despot, prince
8. governor, overlord
saturate ... 3. ret, sop, wet 4. fill, soak
5. imbue, souse, steep 6. drench,
seethe 7. satiate 8. overfill, permeate
10. impregnate
saturated ... 4. full 6. soaked, sodden
Saturday ... 6. Samedi 9. sabbatine
13. Jewish Sabbath
Saturn (pert to) ...
Astron .. 6. planet
consort .. 3. Ops
god of .. 4. seed
Latin .. 8. Saturnus
rings .. 7. moonlet 9. particles
rings, part .. 4. ansa
satellite .. 4. Rhea 5. Dione, Titan
7. Iapetus 8. Hyperion
Temple treasury (State) .. 8. aerarium
saturnalia ... 4. orgy 7. debauch
8. Festival (of Saturn) 11. pandemonium
saturnine ... 6. dismal, gloomy, somber
8. funereal
satyr ... 4. faun 5. deity 7. demigod,
silenus 9. butterfly, capripede,
orangutan
sauce ... 3. soy 4. alec, pulp 5. caper,
curry, garum, gravy, pesto 6. gansel,
tahini 7. catchup (catsup), soubise,
Tabasco, veloute 8. amandine, dressing,
marinara 9. espagnole, insolence,
seasoning 11. beurre blanc
12. impertinence
saucy ... 4. bold, pert, vain 5. brash,
cocky, sassy, smart 7. forward
8. impudent, malapert 9. officious
11. impertinent 13. disrespectful
Saudi Arabia ...
city .. 5. Islam
founder .. 7. Ibn Saud (1913)
gulf .. 7. Persian
Mohammed's tomb .. 6. Medina
mosque .. 5. Kaaba
peninsula .. 7. Arabian
provinces .. 4. Asir, Nejd 5. Hejaz 6. El
Hasa
sea .. 3. Red
sect .. 6. Wahabi (Wahabee, Wahhabi)
sauerbraten ... 8. pot roast
sauger ... 9. pike perch
Saul (pert to) ...
concubine .. 6. Rizpah
daughter .. 6. Michal
father .. 4. Kish
herdsman .. 4. Doeg
of Tarsus .. 4. Paul
uncle .. 3. Ner
wife .. 7. Ahinoam
witch of .. 5. Endor
Sault Ste Marie ... 3. Soo 6. rapids
9. ship canal
saumont ... 6. salmon
sauna ... 4. bath (Finnish)
saunter ... 3. jog, lag, mog 4. roam,
rove, walk 5. range, stray 6. dawdle,
loiter, lounge, potter, ramble, stroll,
wander 8. ruminate
sauqui ... 6. salmon
saurian ... 6. lizard, Sauria 7. reptile

9. crocodile
sausage . . . **6.** banger, salami **7.** bologna, chorizo, saveloy **8.** kielbasa (kolbasi), rolliche **9.** bratwurst, pepperoni **10.** knackwurst
sausage-shaped . . . **9.** allantoid **10.** botuliform
savage . . . **3.** att **4.** rude, wild **5.** brute, cruel, feral, yahoo **6.** ferine, fierce, Indian **7.** brutish, howling **8.** cannibal, pitiless **9.** atrocious, barbarian, ferocious, merciless, primitive **11.** uncivilized **12.** uncultivated
savanna, savannah . . . **5.** plain **9.** grassland **11.** level region
savant . . . **4.** sage **6.** pundit **7.** scholar **9.** scientist **10.** classicist **12.** intellectual, man of letters
save . . . **3.** but **4.** keep **5.** catch, hoard, lay by **6.** except, redeem, rescue, scrimp **7.** prevent, protect, reserve, salvage **8.** conserve **9.** economize, excepting, safeguard **10.** accumulate
savin, savine . . . **5.** cedar **7.** juniper **9.** evergreen
savior, Saviour . . . **8.** Redeemer **9.** deliverer, liberator **11.** emancipator, Jesus Christ
savoir-faire . . . **4.** tact **5.** poise, savvy (sl) **7.** culture **9.** gentility **12.** ease of manner, mannerliness
savor, savour . . . **4.** odor, zest **5.** nidor, sapor, scent, smack, smell, taste **6.** flavor, relish **9.** degustate
savory, savoury . . . **5.** sapid, tasty **7.** piquant **8.** gustable **9.** agreeable **10.** appetizing, delightful
saw . . . **3.** cut **4.** dict **5.** adage, maxim **6.** cliché, saying, truism **7.** noticed, proverb **9.** platitude, serration
saw (kind) . . . **3.** jig, rip **4.** band, buzz, hack, whip **5.** crown, power **7.** keyhole **8.** crosscut
saw (pert to) . . .
back . . **6.** sierra
bill . . **6.** motmot **9.** merganser
buck . . **8.** sawhorse **13.** ten-dollar bill
crosscut . . **5.** briar
fish . . **3.** ray
grass . . **5.** sedge
horse . . **4.** buck, rack **7.** sawbuck
log . . **5.** edger
of sawfish . . **5.** serra
surgeon's . . **6.** trepan (trephine)
teeth . . **5.** tines
two-bladed . . **6.** stadda
sawmill gate . . . **4.** sash
saw-whet . . . **10.** Acadian owl
saxhorn . . . **4.** tuba **7.** althorn **8.** bass tuba **9.** saxcornet
saxifrage . . . **6.** Seseli
Saxon (pert to) . . .
color . . **5.** smalt **8.** Saxe blue **10.** Bremen blue **13.** indigo carmine
king . . **6.** Egbert **8.** Ethelred **14.** Alfred the Great
language . . **10.** Anglo-Saxon **12.** Plattdeutsch
people . . **7.** English **9.** Sassenach **10.** Anglo-Saxon **11.** Lowland Scot
serf . . **4.** esne

swineherd . . **5.** Gurth (Ivanhoe)
warrior . . **5.** thane
Saxony capital . . . **7.** Dresden **10.** Wittenburg (anc)
say . . . **4.** aver, cite, tell **5.** gnome, speak, state, utter **6.** affirm, answer, assert, assume, recite, remark, speech **9.** authority **11.** declaration **12.** conversation
say (pert to) . . .
a blessing . . **5.** bensh
again . . **6.** repeat **7.** restate **9.** reiterate
further . . **3.** add
no (to) . . **6.** negate, refuse **8.** prohibit **10.** disapprove
one thing, mean another . . **6.** palter **7.** falsify **9.** fluctuate **10.** equivocate **12.** be capricious
uncle . . **4.** cede **9.** surrender **10.** capitulate **15.** throw in the towel
saying . . . **3.** dit, mot, saw **4.** quip **5.** adage, axiom, maxim **6.** byword, enigma, phrase, remark **7.** proverb **8.** aphorism, apothegm **11.** declaration
saying, sayings (pert to) . . .
collection of . . **9.** gnomology
criterion, party cry . . **10.** shibboleth
dogmatic . . **6.** dictum
religious . . **5.** logia
scab . . . **3.** rat **4.** sore **5.** crust, mange **6.** rotter **7.** blemish **8.** deserter **9.** scoundrel **12.** incrustation **13.** strikebreaker
scabbard . . . **6.** sheath **7.** holster, pilcher **13.** emblem of peace
scabbard fish . . . **7.** cutlass **9.** frostfish
scaddle . . . **5.** cruel, timid **6.** fierce **7.** nervous **8.** skittish, thievish **11.** mischievous
scads . . . **4.** gobs, wads **5.** heaps, money, piles **6.** oodles **11.** great number **12.** considerable
scaffold, scaffolding . . . **5.** easel, stage **7.** staging, support **8.** platform **9.** grain loft
scalawag, scallawag . . . **5.** scamp **6.** rascal **7.** sculpin **10.** scapegrace
scale . . . **3.** hut **4.** husk, peel, rate, shed, size **5.** climb, crust, flake, gamut **6.** ascend, degree, ladder, lamina, rustre (anc armor), series, weight **7.** compare, measure **12.** incrustation
scale (pert to) . . .
botany . . **5.** palea
color . . **10.** tintometer
comb form . . **4.** cten **5.** cteno, lepis
duck . . **9.** merganser, sheldrake
fish . . **6.** ganoid **8.** scabbard
grand . . **4.** epic
music . . **3.** E la (highest note) **5.** gamut, minor **9.** chromatic, hexachord **10.** tetrachord
slide . . **7.** vernier
tail . . **6.** rodent
Zool . . **6.** scutum
scallop . . . **4.** quin **5.** crena, notch **7.** mollusk **9.** serration, shellfish **12.** summer squash
scalloped . . . **6.** cooked **7.** notched **8.** invected (Her) **9.** crenulate
scalpel . . . **5.** knife **6.** lancet **7.** dissect

8. bistoury
scaly . . . **5.** flaky **6.** crusty, scabby, scurfy
7. leprose **8.** squamous
scamp . . . **3.** imp **5.** cheat, knave, rogue
6. rascal, slight **7.** bacalao, codfish
8. scalawag, spalpeen **9.** scoundrel
15. worthless fellow
scamper . . . **3.** hie, run **4.** dash, race, scud
5. haste **6.** hasten **7.** brattle **9.** hasten
off, skedaddle **11.** hasty flight
scan . . . **3.** eye **6.** browse, peruse
7. examine **10.** scrutinize
11. contemplate **16.** recite metrically
scance . . . **5.** blame, shine **6.** glance
7. comment, glitter
scandal . . . **5.** odium, shame **6.** gossip
7. calumny, offense, slander **8.** disgrace,
ignominy **10.** defamation, detraction,
opprobrium **11.** abomination
scandalous . . . **6.** wicked **8.** libelous,
terrible **10.** defamatory, slanderous
11. disgraceful, opprobrious
Scandinavia, countries . . . see also
Scandinavian **6.** Norway, Sweden
7. Denmark, Iceland
Scandinavian (pert to) . . .
alphabetical character . . **4.** rune
ash tree . . **10.** Yggdrasill
author . . **8.** Andersen (Hans C)
bay . . **5.** fjord
explorer . . **4.** Eric
goblin, brownie . . **5.** nisse **6.** kobold
god . . **4.** Lake, Thor
goose . . **5.** nisse
hall of Odin (heroes' souls) . . **8.** Valhalla
legend . . **4.** Edda, saga
maiden of Odin . . **8.** Valkyrie
navigator . . **4.** Eric
people . . **4.** Dane, Lapp **5.** Swede
8. Norseman **9.** Norwegian
people, type . . **8.** Teutonic
pert to . . **5.** runic
plateau . . **5.** field
rulers . . **10.** Varangians
saga narrator . . **7.** sagaman
sea monster (fabled) . . **6.** kraken
supernatural being (dwarf or giant) . .
5. troll
scant . . . **3.** few **5.** chary **6.** meager,
narrow, scarce, slight, sparse **7.** slender,
sparing **12.** parsimonious
scanty . . . **4.** rare **6.** meager (meagre),
narrow, scarce, sparse **7.** scrimpy
12. insufficient **14.** inconsiderable
scapegoat . . . **4.** goat (Bib) **9.** sacrifice
10. substitute
scapegrace . . . **5.** scamp **8.** scalawag
(scallawag) **9.** reprobate **10.** profligate
12. incorrigible
scar . . . **3.** arr, shy **4.** seam, sear **5.** cliff,
mound **7.** blemish **8.** cicatrix
scarce . . . **4.** rare **5.** short **6.** scanty
7. sparing **8.** uncommon **9.** deficient
10. infrequent
scarcely . . . **6.** barely, hardly **7.** but just
12. infrequently
scarcity . . . **4.** lack, want **6.** dearth,
famine, rarity **7.** paucity **8.** rareness
11. infrequency **13.** insufficiency
scare . . . **3.** cow **5.** alarm, panic **7.** startle,
terrify **8.** affright, frighten

scarecrow . . . **4.** ogre **5.** bogle **6.** effigy,
goblin, malkin, shewel (sewel)
9. jackstraw **10.** frightener **11.** hide-
and-seek
scarf . . . **3.** boa, tie **4.** sash **5.** ascot, cloud,
nubia **6.** tippet **7.** muffler **9.** rigolette
10. fascinator
scarf (pert to) . . .
bird . . **9.** cormorant
broad . . **5.** shawl
clerical . . **5.** fanon, orale, rabat, stole
feather . . **3.** boa
head . . **10.** fascinator
Hindu . . **4.** sari
India . . **7.** dopatta
Mexico . . **6.** tapalo
skin . . **7.** cuticle **9.** epidermis
Scarlet Letter . . . **5.** novel (Hawthorne)
Scarlet O'Hara's home . . . **4.** Tara
scarp . . . **5.** cliff, pitch **7.** descent, incline
9. declivity
scary . . . **5.** eerie, timid, weird **7.** ghostly,
uncanny **8.** alarming **12.** easily scared
scat . . . **4.** hiss **5.** burst, smash **6.** buffet
7. scatter
scat, scatt (Orkney Isls) . . . **3.** tax
7. tribute
scathe . . . **4.** flay, harm, hurt **6.** assail,
damage, injury, scorch **7.** scarify
9. excoriate **10.** misfortune
scatter . . . **3.** sow, ted **4.** deal, rout
5. spray, strew **6.** dispel, litter, shower,
splash, spread **7.** bestrew, diffuse,
radiate **8.** disperse, separate, squander
9. circulate, dissipate **10.** disarrange,
strew about
scattered . . . **4.** semé **5.** dealt **6.** sparse,
strewn **8.** confused, sparsile, sporadic
9. broadcast, dispersed, separated,
sprinkled **10.** widespread **11.** distributed
scattering . . . **3.** few **8.** Diaspora
10. dispersion, separating
13. dissemination
scatty . . . **7.** showery
scaup . . . **4.** duck **8.** bluebill **9.** blackhead,
broadbill
scavenger . . . **4.** bird **8.** organism
10. saprophyte **16.** garbage collector
scaw . . . **8.** headland **10.** promontory
scene . . . **4.** site, view **5.** anger, sight,
vista **6.** locale **7.** diorama, picture,
tableau
scene (pert to) . . .
behind the . . **8.** secretly **9.** backstage,
invisible
inside . . **7.** neorama
last . . **6.** finale
of action . . **5.** arena, stage **6.** sphere
of confusion . . **5.** babel
of miracle (Bib) . . **4.** Cana
opera . . **5.** scena
wright . . **6.** artist **8.** designer (scenery),
stageman
scenic . . . **8.** dramatic **9.** panoramic
11. picturesque
scenic (pert to) . . .
enigma . . **7.** charade
pert to . . **5.** stage **7.** episode, scenery
representation . . **7.** diorama **13.** motion
picture
scent . . . **4.** aura, clue, nose, odor

5. aroma, flair, nairn, nidar, smell, spoor **6.** detect **7.** perfume **9.** fragrance

scented . . . **5.** olent **6.** odored **8.** perfumed, smelling **11.** odoriferous

scepter, sceptre . . . **3.** rod **4.** mace **5.** baton, staff **6.** emblem (royal) **8.** insignia **11.** sovereignty

schedule . . . **4.** card, list **5.** slate **7.** program **8.** calendar, document **9.** catalogue, inventory

scheme . . . **3.** aim **4.** lark, plan, plot **5.** cabal **6.** device, devise, racket, system **7.** complot, concoct, diagram, epitome, outline, project, purpose **8.** artifice, contrive **9.** boomerang **10.** conspiracy, enterprise **11.** machination

schemer . . . **7.** plotter **8.** conniver, finagler **9.** intriguer

schism . . . **4.** rent, sect **5.** split **6.** breach **7.** dissent, faction **8.** division **10.** falling-out, separation

schismatic . . . **7.** heretic, sectary **8.** apostate **9.** dissenter, sectarian **10.** factionist

schist . . . **4.** mica, rock **5.** slate **10.** hornblende

scholar . . . **6.** pedant, savant **7.** learner, student **8.** disciple **11.** philologist

scholarly . . . **7.** erudite, learned **8.** academic, studious **9.** philomath **10.** scholastic

scholarship . . . **5.** burse **8.** learning **9.** education, erudition, knowledge **10.** foundation **11.** instruction

school . . . **4.** cult, sect **5.** class, drill, flock, order, teach, train **7.** convent, educate, seminar **8.** instruct, seminary **9.** institute

school (pert to) . . .
  book . . **6.** primer, reader **7.** speller
  English . . **4.** Eton **6.** Oxford **9.** Cambridge
  French . . **5.** ecole, lycée
  German . . **6.** schule
  head, inspector . . **9.** scholarch
  master . . **7.** dominie **9.** pedagogue (pedagog)
  ref to . . **10.** scholastic
  riding . . **6.** manège
  teacher . . **4.** marm
  term . . **8.** semester
  wrestling . . **9.** gymnasium, palaestra (palestra)

school of . . .
  art . . **4.** Dada
  divinity . . **8.** seminary
  Fine Arts . . **9.** Wagnerian
  fishes . . **5.** shoal
  philosophers . . **7.** Eleatic
  philosophy . . **7.** Gnostic
  seals . . **3.** pod
  thieves . . **4.** gang
  whales . . **3.** gam, pod

schooner . . . **4.** boat, brig, tern **5.** glass **6.** vessel **7.** measure, prairie (Hist)

schuit, schuyt . . . **5.** sloop **6.** vessel **7.** eelboat

science . . . **3.** art **5.** ology, skill **9.** knowledge **11.** proficiency

science of . . .
  agriculture . . **8.** agronomy
  better living . . **9.** euthenics

  better working . . **10.** ergonomics
  breeding . . **8.** eugenics
  character . . **8.** ethology
  children's diseases . . **10.** pediatrics (paediatrics)
  controversy . . **8.** polemics
  creatures . . **10.** entomology
  dining . . **10.** aristology
  doctrines . . **9.** esoterics
  ears . . **7.** otology
  family symbols . . **8.** heraldry
  forest trees . . **7.** silvics (sylvics)
  good . . **6.** ethics **9.** euthenics **10.** agathology
  government . . **8.** politics
  happiness . . **11.** eudaemonics
  healing . . **9.** iatrology
  health . . **7.** hygiene
  kissing . . **13.** philematology
  language . . **9.** philology, semantics **11.** linguistics
  life . . **7.** biology **10.** entomology
  light . . **6.** optics
  mind . . **10.** psychology
  moral conduct . . **6.** ethics
  organism behavior . . **7.** ecology (oecology) **9.** bionomics
  philosophy . . **6.** noesia
  reality . . **10.** philosophy
  reasoning . . **5.** logic
  rocks . . **9.** petrology
  sea (the) . . **12.** oceanography
  self-defense . . **4.** judo **7.** jujitsu
  sound . . **9.** acoustics
  theology interpretation . . **8.** exegesis **12.** hermeneutics
  verse . . **7.** prosody
  virtue . . **8.** aretaics
  words . . **9.** semantics

scientific . . . **5.** exact **8.** clinical **9.** realistic, technical **16.** precise knowledge

scimitar, scimiter . . . **4.** snee **5.** saber **8.** billhook

scintilla . . . **4.** atom, iota, whit **5.** spark, trace **7.** modicum

scintillate . . . **5.** flash, gleam, spark **7.** be witty, glitter, twinkle **9.** coruscate **10.** be eloquent

scion, cion . . . **3.** son **4.** slip **5.** graft, shoot **10.** descendant

scold . . . **3.** jaw, nag **4.** carp, rail, rate **5.** chide, shrew **6.** berate, chider, rebuke **7.** reprove, upbraid **8.** admonish **9.** reprimand

scolding . . . **7.** froward **8.** reproach, shrewish **10.** upbraiding **12.** admonishment, reprimanding

sconce . . . **3.** top **4.** head **5.** brain, mulct, skull **6.** screen **7.** bulwark, lantern, redoubt, skelter **11.** candlestick, counterfort

scoop . . . **4.** bail, beat, lade, news **5.** empty, ladle, spoon **6.** bucket, hollow, shovel **8.** excavate, gather in

scoop out . . . **3.** dig **5.** gouge **6.** chisel, hollow **7.** fashion

scope . . . **4.** area, room **5.** ambit, arena, range, reach **6.** degree, domain **7.** compass, freedom, liberty **8.** latitude **9.** gyroscope, intention, periscope, telescope **10.** microscope

11. stethoscope 12. kaleidoscope, spectroscope

scorch . . . **4.** burn, char, sear, sere **5.** parch, singe, speed **7.** shrivel **9.** criticize

scordato . . . **9.** out of tune **14.** made discordant

score . . . **3.** peg, run, sum, tab **4.** debt, gain, goal, rate **5.** corge, judge, notch, scold, slash, tally **6.** berate, furrow, groove, points, reason, twenty **7.** account, arrange, scratch **8.** incision **9.** calculate, tally mark **10.** obligation **11.** arrangement, composition, orchestrate **12.** indebtedness

scoria (volcano) . . . **4.** lava, slag **5.** dross **6.** refuse **7.** residue

scorn . . . **4.** defy, geck, mock **5.** spurn **6.** deride, reject **7.** contemn, despise, disdain **8.** contempt, derision, disgrace **9.** contumely

scornful . . . **8.** derisive, insolent **10.** disdainful **12.** contemptuous, contumelious

Scorpio (pert to) . . .
constellation in . . **8.** Milky Way
genus . . **8.** Scorpius
night mansion of . . **4.** Mars
pictured as . . **8.** scorpion
star (brightest) . . **7.** Antares
zodiac sign . . **6.** eighth

scorpion . . . **4.** nepa **7.** alacran, scourge (Bib) **8.** arachnid, catapult **10.** pine lizard, vinaigrier **11.** vinegarroon (vinagron) **15.** blue-tailed skink

Scot . . . **3.** Mac **4.** Celt, Gael **5.** Saxon **6.** Sawney **7.** bluecap **8.** Scotsman **10.** Caledonian, Highlander

Scotland . . . see also *Scottish*
capital . . **9.** Edinburgh
city . . **3.** Ayr **5.** Perth **6.** Atholl (Athole), Dundee **7.** Glasgow (largest), Renfrew **8.** Aberdeen **9.** Inverness
congress (musical) . . **3.** Mod
district . . **6.** Argyll, Atholl **10.** Midlothian
famed site . . **9.** Trossachs (Lady of the Lake) **10.** Loch Lomond **11.** Loch Katrine
firth . . **3.** Tay **4.** Loch **5.** Clyde, Forth, Moray, Tweed
islands . . **7.** Orkney **8.** Hebrides, Shetland
Latin name (anc) . . **9.** Caledonia
moors . . **10.** Lochar Moss
mountain . . **9.** Grampians
poetic name . . **6.** Scotia **9.** Caledonia
resort . . **4.** Oban
river . . **3.** Ayr, Dee, Tay **5.** Afton, Clyde, Forth, Tweed **6.** Teviot **7.** Deveron
seaport . . **5.** Leith **6.** Dundee

Scotland Yard headquarters . . .
6. London **18.** Metropolitan Police

Scott, Sir Walter (pert to) . . .
estate . . **10.** Abbotsford (Scot)
famed as . . **4.** poet **8.** novelist
novel . . **7.** Ivanhoe, Waverly **8.** Talisman **10.** Kenilworth **14.** Quentin Durward
poem . . **13.** Lady of the Lake

Scottish (pert to) . . .
accent . . **4.** birr
alder . . **3.** arn
attendant (hunter's) . . **6.** gillie (gilly)

bagpipe music . . **7.** pibroch
beret . . **3.** tam **11.** tam-o'-shanter
bird . . **3.** gae (blue) **6.** grouse **7.** snabbie (snabby) **9.** swinepipe
blessing . . **6.** rebuke **8.** scolding
blood money . . **3.** cro **7.** galanas
blue . . **6.** homage **8.** infernal **11.** reddish-blue
bluebell . . **8.** harebell
boat . . **4.** zulu **7.** coracle, skaffie
bonnets . . **8.** mushroom
brandy . . **6.** Athole
breeches . . **5.** trews
brier, briar . . **4.** rose
broth . . **5.** brose
bull, ox . . **4.** stot
cake (tea) . . **5.** scone
cap . . **3.** tam **8.** Balmoral **9.** Glengarry **11.** tam-o'-shanter
carpet . . **13.** Kidderminster
cattle . . **8.** Aberdeen, Ayrshire
celebration . . **4.** kirn (harvest)
child . . **5.** bairn **6.** scuddy (naked)
church . . **4.** kirk
cloth . . **4.** kelt **6.** tartan
coalfish . . **7.** glashan, sillock
court officer . . **5.** macer
cup . . **4.** tass
dagger (anc) . . **4.** dirk
dagger, knife . . **8.** skean dhu
dance . . **4.** reel **5.** fling **9.** ecossaise **10.** strathspey **13.** Highland fling
devil . . **4.** deil **6.** Hornie
dirge . . **8.** coronach (as on bagpipes)
duck . . **4.** coot **6.** scoter
earth . . **4.** eard
elder . . **7.** tobacco
elm . . **7.** wych-elm
excuse . . **6.** sunyie
eye . . **2.** ee
family (same) . . **3.** ilk
festival . . **3.** Mod **7.** uphelya (Epiphany)
fish . . **4.** sile **7.** sillock **8.** spalding
fog . . **4.** haar
Gaelic . . **4.** Erse
ghost . . **6.** taisch
girl . . **4.** lass **6.** lassie, towdie **7.** winklot
goblin . . **8.** barghest
godmother . . **6.** cummer (kimmer)
grandchild . . **2.** oy (oye)
grandfather . . **8.** gudesire
hill, hillside . . **4.** brae **6.** strone
icicle . . **7.** shoggle
kilt . . **7.** filibeg
kiss (stolen) . . **8.** smoorich
lake . . **4.** loch
language . . **4.** Erse **6.** Lallan (Lalland)
liquor . . **5.** scour **6.** Athole **7.** whitter
lovage . . **10.** sea parsley
money, silver . . **6.** siller
nephew . . **6.** nepote
New Year's Day . . **7.** Cake Day **8.** hogmanay
nightingale . . **7.** warbler
ox, bullock . . **4.** nowt
plaid . . **4.** maud **6.** tartan
porridge . . **5.** brose
pouch, purse (kilt front) . . **7.** sporran
pudding . . **6.** haggis
reel (fishing) . . **4.** pirn
rod, over the door . . **10.** willow wand

sausage.. **9.** whitehass (whitehawse)
schoolmaster.. **3.** dux
shawl (plaid).. **4.** maud
stream, brook.. **4.** sike
sweetheart.. **2.** jo
sword.. **8.** claymore
toad.. **3.** ted **4.** taed
tobacco.. **5.** elder
topaz.. **9.** cairngorm
townhall.. **8.** tolbooth (tollbooth)
uncle.. **3.** eme
village.. **3.** rew
waistcoat (under).. **6.** fecket
whirlpool.. **7.** swilkie
whisky.. **9.** Glenlivet (Glenlivat)
    10. usquebaugh
window.. **7.** winnock
youth.. **6.** chield (chiel) **7.** callant (callan)
Scottish person (pert to)...
    author.. **5.** Scott **9.** Stevenson (Robert
    Louis)
    biographer, famed.. **7.** Boswell
    dynasty.. **6.** Stuart
    economist.. **5.** Smith (Adam)
    engineer, inventor.. **4.** Watt
    geneticist.. **7.** Haldane
    king.. **6.** Robert (the Bruce)
    physicist.. **7.** Maxwell
    poet.. **5.** Burns
scoundrel... **3.** cad **5.** cheat, knave,
    scamp **6.** varlet **7.** villain **8.** scalawag
    9. miscreant **10.** blackguard
    11. rapscallion
scoup... **3.** run **4.** leap, skip **7.** scamper
scourge... **4.** bane, flog, lash, whip
    6. punish, swinge, switch **8.** chastise
    10. affliction, infliction, punishment
Scourge of God... **6.** Attila (King of
    Huns)
Scourge of Princes... **7.** Aretino (It
    satirist)
scout... **3.** spy **5.** flout, scoff **7.** lookout,
    servant **8.** emissary, watchman
    9. guillemot **11.** reconnoiter **14.** razor-
    billed auk
scow... **4.** acon **6.** garvey **7.** lighter
scowl... **5.** frown, lower **6.** aspect
    (gloomy), glower **7.** wrinkle (brow)
    10. sullen look
scraggly... **5.** rough **6.** ragged
    7. unkempt **9.** irregular
scraggy... **4.** bony **5.** rough **6.** meager,
    rugged, skinny **7.** knotted, scrawny,
    stunted
scram... **6.** begone, benumb, decamp
    7. vamoose
scramble... **4.** push **5.** climb, crowd,
    crush **6.** jostle, strive **7.** clamber, scatter
    8. struggle
scrap... **3.** bit, end, ort, rag **4.** chip, junk
    5. fight, melee, piece, waste **6.** morsel,
    refuse **7.** cutting, discard, excerpt,
    extract, quarrel, remnant **8.** fragment,
    ramentum
scrape... **3.** row, rub **4.** rake, rasp
    5. grate, graze, shave **6.** abrade, eke
    out, injure, sclaff **7.** collect, scratch
    9. economize, obeisance **10.** difficulty
    11. predicament
scraper... **4.** harl (wool), tool **6.** barber,
    rasper **7.** abrader, fiddler, strigil

    8. grattoir
scrappy... **9.** irregular **10.** pugnacious
    11. contentious, fragmentary,
    quarrelsome
scratch... **3.** mar, rit, rub **4.** claw, draw,
    itch, mark, rake, rist, tear **5.** erase
    6. cancel, injury, scrape **7.** blemish,
    roughen, scarify **8.** scribble, withdraw
scrawl... **6.** doodle **7.** scratch **8.** scribble
scrawny... **4.** lean, poor, thin **5.** spare
    6. skinny **7.** scranny **8.** rawboned
scream... **3.** cry **4.** wail, yell **6.** shriek,
    squeal **7.** screech
screamer... **5.** swift (bird) **7.** blunder
    8. headline
scree... **5.** stone, talus **6.** debris, pebble
screech... **3.** cry, say **6.** outcry, scream,
    shriek, squeal **7.** ululate
screech (pert to)...
    hawk.. **10.** goatsucker
    martin.. **5.** swift
    owl.. **4.** barn **5.** Scops
screed... **4.** list, rend, tear **5.** shred
    6. tirade **7.** lecture **8.** fragment
    12. dissertation
screen... **3.** net **4.** hide, laun, mask, sift,
    sort, veil **5.** arras, blind, cloak, pavis,
    shade, sieve, spier **6.** defend, grille,
    riddle, sifter, sorter **7.** conceal, curtain,
    protect, reredos, shelter **8.** parclose
    9. partition, safeguard **10.** protection
    12. discriminate
screw... **3.** key **4.** coil, turn **5.** horse,
    twist **6.** fasten, gimlet, rotate, spiral
    7. contort, distort, tighten, turnkey
    9. bargainer, propeller, skinflint
    10. contortion, thumbscrew
screwlike... **6.** spiral **7.** spiroid
scribble... **6.** doodle, scrawl **7.** scratch
    8. scrabble
scribe... **5.** clerk **6.** author, jurist,
    lawyer, penman, writer **8.** recorder
    10. amanuensis, cuttlefish, journalist
    13. bibliographer
scriggle... **5.** twist **6.** squirm **7.** wriggle
    8. curlicue
scrimmage... **3.** row **5.** fight **6.** tussle
    8. football (term), practice, skirmish,
    struggle
scrimp... **4.** save **5.** scant, stint **6.** scanty,
    scrape, sparse **7.** sparing **9.** economize
scrip... **3.** bag **4.** list **5.** money **6.** wallet
    7. writing **8.** document, schedule
script... **5.** ronde **6.** letter **7.** writing
    8. scenario **10.** manuscript, typescript
    11. handwriting
scriptural... **7.** written **8.** Biblical,
    orthodox
scriptural interpreter... **7.** exegete
scripture... **4.** writ **5.** motto, truth
    7. passage, writing **8.** document
    10. manuscript **11.** inscription **13.** sacred
    writing
Scripture, Scriptures... **4.** text **5.** Bible
    6. lesson **7.** Oracles, passage, Vulgate
Scripture interpretation... **8.** exegesis
    12. hermeneutics
scrivello... **4.** tusk (elephant's)
scrivener... **6.** notary, scribe, writer
    8. recorder **10.** amanuensis
scroll... **4.** list, roll **5.** draft **6.** record,

spiral, volute **7.** engross, writing
8. document, inscribe, schedule,
streamer **9.** parchment
scroll roll . . . **8.** makimono
scrub . . . **3.** mop, rub **4.** halt, mean, runt,
tree, wash **5.** abort, clean, dwarf, scour
6. cancel, drudge, paltry **7.** cleanse
8. inferior **10.** undersized
scrubby . . . **4.** base **6.** paltry, shabby,
stubby **7.** bristly, shrubby, stunted
10. underbrush **13.** insignificant
scruff . . . **4.** nape, scum, slur **5.** crust,
dross, scuff **6.** refuse **7.** surface
8. dandruff
scruple . . . **4.** coin **5.** demur, qualm
6. object, weight **9.** small part
10. hesitation **13.** unwillingness
scrupulous . . . **4.** nice **5.** exact **6.** formal,
proper, strict **8.** qualmish **10.** fastidious,
meticulous **11.** punctilious
13. conscientious
scrutinize . . . **3.** eye, pry **4.** scan **5.** probe
7. examine, inspect, observe
scud . . . **4.** dash, foam, gust, rain, sail,
skim **5.** speed **6.** clouds, shower
scuffle . . . **4.** fray **5.** melee **6.** strive,
tussle **7.** contend, contest, shamble,
shuffle **8.** struggle
sculduddery . . . **9.** grossness, obscenity
scull . . . **3.** oar **4.** gull **5.** shoal, skate
6. basket, paddle, propel **7.** rowboat
scullion . . . **4.** base **6.** menial **7.** servant
10. dishwasher, kitchenman
scullog, scullogue . . . **6.** farmer, rustic
7. laborer
sculp . . . **5.** carve **7.** engrave **8.** seal skin
9. engraving, sculpture
sculptor . . . **6.** artist, carver, imager,
molder **8.** chiseler **13.** constellation
19. Apparatus Sculptoris (constellation)
sculptor (famed) . . . **5.** Rodin **7.** Cellini,
Phidias **10.** Praxiteles **12.** Michelangelo,
Saint Gaudens
sculptor's tool . . . **6.** chisel, graver
9. ébauchoir
sculpture . . . **4.** form **5.** carve, model
6. figure, statue **9.** engraving **11.** alto-
relievo
scum . . . **4.** film, foam **5.** cover, dross,
froth, scurf, spume **6.** refuse, scoria
7. coating **8.** riffraff **10.** impurities
scup . . . **5.** bream, porgy
scurrility . . . **5.** abuse **9.** indignity,
obscenity
scurrilous . . . **3.** low **4.** vile **5.** gross
6. vulgar **7.** abusive **8.** indecent,
scurrile **9.** insulting **11.** foulmouthed,
opprobrious
scurry . . . **3.** hie **4.** dash **5.** scoot, speed
6. flurry, hasten **7.** scamper, scuttle
9. skedaddle
scurvy . . . **4.** base, mean **7.** disease
12. contemptible, discourteous
scuttle . . . **3.** hod, run **4.** dish, sink
5. haste, scoot **6.** basket, hasten, scurry,
shovel **7.** octopus, platter **8.** hatchway
10. cuttlefish
scutum . . . **5.** scute **6.** shield
13. constellation (Milky Way)
15. Scutum Sobieskii
Scylla (pert to) . . .

father . . **5.** Nisus
home . . **4.** rock (coast of Italy)
lover . . **5.** Minos
menace to . . **9.** seafarers
Myth . . **7.** monster
transformed to . . **7.** sea bird
scythe . . . **2.** sy (sye) **5.** swath
scythe handle . . . **5.** snath, snead
sea . . . **3.** Red **4.** Aral, Azov, Ross, wave
5. Black, brine, China, ocean, swell,
water **6.** aequor **7.** Caspian **8.** seashore
9. Caribbean
sea (pert to) . . .
adder . . **8.** pipefish **11.** stickleback
anemone . . **5.** polyp
Antarctic . . **4.** Ross
arm . . **4.** gulf, meer, mere **5.** bayou,
firth **7.** estuary
bird . . **3.** auk **4.** erne (ern), gull, smew,
tern **5.** booby, cahow, solan **6.** gannet,
petrel, puffin **9.** albatross **10.** shearwater
comb form . . **3.** mer
cow . . **6.** dugong, rytina (Steller's),
walrus **7.** manatee **8.** sirenian
12. hippopotamus
cucumber . . **7.** trepang
devil . . **9.** angelfish, devilfish
dog . . **4.** seal (Her) **6.** fogdog, sailor
dragon . . **8.** dragonet, sea horse
dread of . . **14.** thalassophobia
duck . . **5.** eider, scaup **6.** scoter
eagle . . **4.** erne (ern) **6.** osprey
ear . . **7.** abalone
eel . . **6.** conger
farer . . **3.** tar **6.** sailor, seaman **7.** mariner
foam . . **5.** froth **9.** sepiolite
10. meerschaum
fowl . . **3.** auk **4.** gull, tern **6.** gannet,
petrel
fox . . **5.** shark
god, deity . . **3.** Lar **5.** Aegir **6.** Triton
7. Neptune, Phorcus, Proteus
8. Poseidon
goddess . . **4.** Nina **5.** Doris **10.** Amphitrite
gull . . **3.** cob, mew **9.** kittiwake
hare . . **7.** mollusk
hen . . **4.** skua **9.** guillemot
hog . . **8.** porpoise
holly root . . **6.** eryngo (eringo)
ladder . . **6.** Jacob's
lion . . **4.** seal
mammal . . **4.** seal **5.** whale **6.** dugong
7. manatee **11.** bladdernose
mouse . . **4.** duck (harlequin) **6.** dunlin
7. annelid
nymph . . **5.** naiad, siren **6.** nereid
7. oceanid
onion . . **6.** squill
otter . . **5.** kalan
owl . . **6.** puffin **8.** lumpfish
pig . . **6.** dugong **7.** dolphin **8.** porpoise
pumpkin . . **8.** cucumber
quail . . **6.** auklet **9.** turnstone
raven . . **7.** sculpin **9.** cormorant
10. squaretail
reference to . . **5.** naval **6.** marine
7. oceanic, pelagic **8.** maritime
9. Neptunian, thalassic
robber . . **6.** jaeger, pirate **7.** corsair
9. buccaneer, privateer
serpent . . **5.** Hydra **8.** snake eel

shell.. **5.** conch
sickness.. **8.** mal de mer **9.** naupathia
spider.. **10.** spider crab
turtle.. **5.** green **9.** hawksbill
  10. loggerhead, thalassian
  11. leatherback
unicorn.. **7.** narwhal
urchin.. **5.** heart **10.** echinoderm,
  Spatangina **13.** cushionflower
wolf.. **4.** seal **6.** pirate **9.** privateer,
  submarine
sea king... **3.** Ler **5.** chief **6.** pirate,
  Viking **7.** Neptune
seal (pert to)...
bearded.. **5.** ursuk **6.** makluk
breeding ground.. **7.** rookery
eared.. **5.** otary
flock.. **3.** pod
fur (fem).. **5.** matka (matkah)
harp (male).. **7.** saddler
leather.. **3.** pin
limb.. **7.** flipper
skin.. **5.** sculp
type.. **3.** fur **7.** sea lion **8.** elephant,
  pinniped
young.. **3.** pup
sealed instrument... **6.** escrow
seam... **4.** line, load, scar **5.** joint, ridge,
  strip **6.** burden, groove, stitch, streak,
  suture **7.** crevice, stratum **9.** horseload
  10. interstice, packsaddle
seaman... **3.** gob, tar **6.** sailor, Seabee
  7. mariner
seaman's chapel... **6.** bethel, church
seamark... **6.** beacon **10.** lighthouse
seamy... **5.** rough **8.** wrinkled
  12. disreputable
séance... **7.** session, sitting **9.** treatment
séance holder... **6.** medium
sear, sere... **3.** dry **4.** burn, cook
  5. parch **6.** braise, scorch, wither
  7. dried up, shrivel **8.** deadened,
  withered **9.** cauterize **10.** threadbare
  11. deteriorate
search... **4.** comb, fish, hunt, look, seek
  5. frisk, ghoom, grope, probe, quest
  6. ferret, forage, survey **7.** inquire,
  ransack, rummage, zetetic **9.** expiscate
  10. scrutinize **11.** investigate
searchlight... **4.** beam **10.** flashlight
seashell... **4.** clam **5.** conch, snail
  7. scallop
season... **3.** age **4.** fall, salt, tide,
  time **5.** devil, inure, spice **6.** flavor,
  mature **7.** qualify **8.** accustom, preserve
  11. acclimatize
season (pert to)...
Astron.. **5.** Aries, Libra **6.** Cancer
  11. Capricornus
Eccl.. **4.** Lent **6.** Advent, Easter
  7. Trinity **8.** Epiphany **9.** Christmas
  11. Whitsuntide
Lent.. **6.** carême
Scot.. **4.** sele
yearly.. **6.** Autumn, Spring, Summer,
  Winter
seasonable... **6.** timely **7.** apropos
seasoning... **4.** sage, salt **5.** spice, thyme
  6. cloves, garlic, pepper **7.** mustard,
  paprika **8.** allspice, estragon, marjoram,
  rosemary, turmeric **9.** condiment

Seasons, goddesses of...
justice.. **4.** Dike
order (Universe).. **5.** Horae
peace.. **6.** Eirene
wise laws.. **7.** Eunomia
seat... **3.** pew **4.** root, site **5.** bench,
  chair, embed, sella, stool **6.** settee,
  settle **7.** install **9.** establish
seat (pert to)...
church.. **3.** pew **6.** sedile
of justice.. **4.** banc
of self.. **3.** ego
on elephant.. **6.** howdah
outdoor.. **6.** exedra
privileged.. **6.** curule
series (one of).. **6.** gradin (gradine)
seaweed... **4.** kelp **5.** algae, dulse, laver,
  varec, wrack **6.** Alaria **8.** agar-agar
secco... **3.** dry
secern... **7.** secrete **8.** separate
  11. distinguish **12.** discriminate
Secessionist (S Carolina)... **5.** Rhett
secluded... **5.** aloof, apart **6.** hidden,
  lonely, remote, secret **7.** private,
  retired **8.** debarred, expelled, isolated,
  recessed, retiring, screened, solitary
  9. cloistral, concealed
seclusion... **7.** privacy, retreat **8.** solitude
  9. aloofness, exclusion **10.** quarantine,
  retirement, separation
second... **3.** aid **4.** abet, back, echo,
  time **5.** jiffy, trice **6.** assist, attend,
  backer, double, moment **7.** instant,
  support, sustain **8.** inferior **9.** assistant,
  encourage, imperfect, prototype,
  reinforce **11.** corroborate, subordinate
second (pert to)...
childhood.. **6.** dotage, dotard **8.** senility
crop.. **5.** rowen
lieutenant.. **9.** shavetail
number.. **6.** addend
person.. **3.** you
rate.. **8.** inferior, mediocre
Republic.. **6.** French (1848-52)
sight.. **6.** myopia **7.** psychic **9.** intuition
  12. clairvoyance
team.. **5.** scrub **9.** Yannigans
thought.. **6.** sequel **12.** afterthought
  15. reconsideration
secondary... **4.** less **5.** minor **6.** deputy
  8. inferior, offshoot **9.** auxiliary,
  dependent, satellite **10.** contingent,
  derivative, second-rate, subsequent,
  substitute **11.** subordinate, unessential
  12. nonessential, quill feather
secondary color... **5.** green **6.** orange,
  purple
secondary school... **4.** prep **5.** lycée
  7. academy **10.** Realschule
secrecy... **4.** tile **6.** hiding **7.** mystery,
  privacy, privity **8.** velation **9.** reticence,
  seclusion **10.** confidence
  11. concealment
secret... **3.** key **4.** dern **5.** close, inner,
  privy **6.** arcane, covert, hidden, mystic,
  occult **7.** arcanum, cryptic, mystery,
  private, unknown **8.** esoteric, intimate
  (armor), reticent, secluded, skullcap
  9. concealed, recondite, secretive,
  underhand **10.** confidence, mysterious
  11. clandestine **12.** confidential

13. surreptitious

secret (pert to) . . .
agent . . **3.** spy **5.** scout **6.** espier **7.** spotter **8.** emissary **13.** undercover man
council . . **5.** by-end, junto **7.** purpose
language . . **5.** argot **7.** dialect
meeting . . **5.** tryst
movement . . **7.** stealth
name . . **9.** cryptonym
place . . **5.** cache **6.** adytum **7.** sanctum **9.** sanctuary
society . . **3.** hui (Chin) **4.** tong **7.** Camorra (It)

secretary . . . **4.** bird, desk **5.** agent **6.** scribe **7.** officer **8.** recorder **9.** confidant **10.** amanuensis, escritoire

secrete . . . **4.** bury, hide, stow **5.** exude **7.** conceal

secretion (pert to) . . .
gland . . **7.** hormone
inflammation . . **3.** pus
liver . . **4.** bile
mammal gland . . **9.** lactation
mouth . . **6.** saliva
nasal . . **10.** secernment
scale, insect . . **3.** lac
shrubs . . **4.** lerp
whale . . **9.** ambergris

secretly . . . **5.** aside, slyly **7.** sub rosa **8.** covertly **9.** not openly **13.** clandestinely

sect . . . **4.** clan, cult, part **5.** Alogi (Hist), class, group, order, party **6.** essene, school, Yezidi (Kurdish) **9.** following, Mennonite **10.** shibboleth (Bib) **12.** denomination

sectarian . . . **7.** heretic **8.** partisan **9.** dissenter, heterodox **13.** nonconformist **14.** denominational

section . . . **4.** area, part, plot **5.** panel, piece, slice, tmema, torso **6.** region **7.** portion, segment, ternion **8.** parabola, surgical **9.** paragraph, signature **11.** subdivision

secular . . . **3.** lay **4.** laic **5.** civil **6.** laical **7.** earthly, profane, worldly **8.** temporal **9.** centuried, temporary

secure . . . **3.** fix, get, pin **4.** bind, easy, fast, firm, moor, nail, safe, tape **5.** fetch, spike, trice (sail) **6.** elicit, ensure, fasten, obtain, stable **7.** acquire, assured, certain, procure, receive **8.** make fast **9.** confident, guarantee **10.** dependable **11.** undisturbed

security . . . **4.** bail, gage **5.** guard **6.** pledge, safety, vadium **7.** defense, shelter **8.** guaranty **9.** guarantee, insurance, stability **10.** protection

sedate . . . **4.** calm **5.** douce, quiet, sober, staid **6.** demure, proper, serene, solemn **7.** serious, settled **8.** composed, decorous **9.** dignified, unruffled **11.** unobtrusive **13.** contemplative, dispassionate

sedative . . . **6.** remedy **7.** anodyne, bromide, chloral, veronal **8.** atropine, barbital, lenitive, soothing **9.** calmative, mitigator, paregoric **10.** palliative, phenacetin **12.** tranquilizer (tranquillizer) **13.** phenobarbital

sedent . . . **7.** sitting (statue)

sediment . . . **4.** lees, silt **5.** dregs **7.** deposit, grounds, siltage **9.** settlings

sedition . . . **6.** revolt, strife, tumult **7.** treason **9.** commotion **10.** dissension, turbulence

seditious . . . **7.** riotous **8.** factious **9.** turbulent **11.** treasonable **15.** insurrectionary

seduce . . . **4.** lure **5.** decoy, tempt **6.** allure, enamor, entice **7.** corrupt, mislead **8.** inveigle

seducer . . . **7.** enticer, tempter **8.** Lothario **9.** debaucher

seduction . . . **5.** charm **10.** allurement, corruption, temptation **11.** debauchment

sedulous . . . **4.** busy **6.** steady **8.** diligent, untiring **9.** assiduous, laborious, unwearied **10.** persistent **11.** persevering, unremitting

see . . . **3.** spy **4.** espy, heed, know, look, scry, seat, view **5.** visit **6.** behold, descry, detect **7.** diocese, discern, witness **8.** discover, perceive **9.** apprehend, interview, visualize **10.** comprehend, understand **11.** contemplate

seed . . . **3.** egg, pip, pit, sow **4.** germ **5.** grain, ovule, plant, sperm, spore **6.** kernel, origin **7.** lineage, progeny **8.** rudiment **9.** beginning **11.** descendants

seed (pert to) . . .
apple . . **3.** pip
aromatic . . **5.** anise **7.** aniseed, caraway
coat . . **3.** pod **4.** aril, burr, husk **5.** testa **6.** carpel **8.** pericarp
container, envelope . . **3.** bur (burr), pod **6.** loment, vessel **7.** capsule
edible . . **3.** pea **4.** bean **5.** grain **6.** lentil
enclosing soft fruit . . **5.** drupe
flower . . **6.** pistil
immature . . **5.** ovule
lemon, orange, apple . . **3.** pip
licorice . . **9.** jequerity
medicinal . . **8.** flaxseed
Moringa, tropical . . **3.** ben
naked (one-seeded fruit) . . **6.** achene (akene)
oak . . **5.** acorn
one-called . . **6.** carpel
part . . **6.** tunica
poppy, opium . . **3.** maw
underground . . **6.** peanut
winged . . **6.** samara

seeds (pert to) . . .
cocoa . . **5.** cacao
feeding on . . **11.** granivorous
perfume . . **8.** abelmosk
rudiments . . **3.** ova **4.** eggs, pips, pits **6.** ovules, sperms

seedy . . . **5.** dingy, lousy, tacky **6.** shabby **7.** worn out **8.** slovenly **10.** spiritless **11.** spawn-filled **12.** bearing seeds

seek . . . **3.** beg **4.** hunt **5.** essay **6.** pursue, search **7.** explore, solicit **8.** endeavor **9.** neologize (new words) **11.** investigate

seeker . . . **6.** prober, tracer **7.** pursuer, zetetic **8.** aspirant, searcher **9.** applicant **10.** petitioner

seeker of . . .
knowledge . . **10.** philonoist

new words . . **9.** neologist
pleasure . . **7.** epicure **8.** hedonist
seem . . . **4.** look **6.** appear **7.** pretend
   8. resemble
seeming . . . **5.** guise, quasi **8.** apparent,
   illusion, illusory, pretense, specious
   9. befitting
seeming contradiction . . . **7.** paradox
seeming truth . . . **14.** verisimilitude
seemly . . . **3.** fit **4.** meet **6.** comely,
   decent, proper, suited **7.** elegant, fitting
   8. decorous, tasteful **9.** expedient
seep . . . **4.** leak, ooze **5.** exude **6.** filter
   8. transude **9.** percolate
seer, seeress . . . **5.** sibyl **6.** oracle, scryer
   7. Phoebad, prophet **9.** predictor,
   visionary **10.** forecaster, prophetess,
   soothsayer **11.** Nostradamus
   14. prognosticator
seesaw . . . **6.** teeter, tilter **7.** pastime
   9. alternate, crossruff, fluctuate,
   vacillate **11.** oscillation **12.** teeter-totter
seethe . . . **4.** boil, stew, teem **5.** be hot,
   steep **6.** bubble **7.** be angry
segment . . . **3.** pip **4.** part **5.** tmema
   6. cantle **7.** portion, section **8.** fragment
   12. cross section
segment (pert to) . . .
  botany . . **5.** tmema **7.** lacinia
  corresponding part . . **7.** isomere
  curve . . **3.** arc
  shaped . . **5.** toric
  Zool . . **6.** somite, telson **8.** metamere,
  somatome
seine . . . **3.** net **5.** trawl **6.** sagene
   7. dragnet, network
seism . . . **10.** earthquake
seize . . . **3.** bag, cly, cop, nab, net **4.** bind,
   bite, grab, grip, take, trap **5.** annex,
   catch, grasp, ravin, reave, usurp,
   wrest **6.** arrest, clutch, collar, fasten,
   ravish, snatch **7.** capture, embargo,
   grapple **8.** distrain **9.** apprehend, lay
   hold of **10.** confiscate, understand
   11. appropriate
seizin . . . **9.** occupancy **10.** possession
seizing . . . **4.** cord **7.** lashing **9.** arresting,
   raptorial
seizure . . . **3.** fit **4.** grip, hold **5.** spasm
   6. arrest, attack, frenzy, seizin
   9. ownership **10.** convulsion, occupation
   11. manucapture
seladang . . . **4.** gaur **7.** buffalo
selah (Bib) . . . **4.** sign **5.** pause
select . . . **4.** cull, name, pick, take
   5. elect, elite **6.** choice, choose,
   picked **7.** appoint, pick out, specify
   9. exclusive, segregate **10.** registrate
   11. distinguish, outstanding
selection . . . **5.** piece **6.** choice **7.** analect,
   excerpt, passage **10.** collection
   11. appointment
selective . . . **5.** draft **8.** eclectic
   9. exclusive **10.** particular
   14. discriminative
self . . . **3.** ego, own **4.** same **5.** being
   6. person, psyche **7.** oneself
   10. individual **11.** personality
self (pert to) . . .
  acting . . **9.** automatic, voluntary
  assertion . . **6.** egoism, vanity

centered . . **7.** selfish **9.** egotistic
  10. egocentric **11.** independent **12.** self-
  absorbed
comb form . . **4.** auto
complacent . . **13.** self-satisfied
confidence . . **5.** poise **6.** aplomb
  9. assurance **11.** self-reliant
contained . . **8.** reserved **10.** controlled,
  sufficient (in itself) **11.** independent
  15. uncommunicative
control . . **8.** stoicism **9.** restraint
  10. automation, discipline, equanimity,
  temperance
defense . . **6.** karate, jung fu **7.** jujitsu
determination . . **8.** autonomy
  12. independence
enjoyment . . **13.** gratification
esteem . . **5.** pride **6.** vanity **7.** concept,
  ego-trip
evident . . **5.** clear **9.** axiomatic
examination . . **13.** introspection,
  introspective
French . . **3.** soi
love of . . **6.** egoism
ref to . . **8.** personal
reproach . . **7.** remorse
righteous . . **5.** pious **9.** Pharisaic
  13. sanctimonious **14.** holier-than-thou
same . . **9.** identical
satisfied . . **4.** smug **6.** jaunty
Scottish . . **3.** sel (sell)
worship . . **8.** idolatry **9.** autolatry
selfish . . . **6.** grabby (sl) **11.** egotistical,
   self-seeking **12.** self-centered
sell . . . **4.** vend **5.** scalp, trade **6.** barter,
   market, retail **7.** auction, bargain
   8. convince, exchange, persuade
   9. negotiate
sell (out) . . . **6.** betray, desert **8.** inform
   on **9.** victimize
seller . . . **6.** dealer, vender, vendor
   7. peddler **8.** merchant, salesman
   9. tradesman **10.** saleswoman
semantics . . . **8.** meanings
   11. semasiology
semblable . . . **4.** like **5.** alike **7.** seeming,
   similar **8.** apparent, suitable
   10. ostensible, resembling
   11. conformable
semblance . . . **4.** copy, face, form **5.** guise,
   image **6.** aspect, figure **7.** pretext,
   umbrage **8.** illusion **10.** appearance,
   similarity **11.** countenance,
   presumption, resemblance
semeiology, semeiotics . . . **5.** signs
   (signaling) **11.** diagnostics
   14. interpretation, symptomatology
semester . . . **4.** term **6.** course, period
Seminole chief . . . **7.** Osceola (1804--38)
Semitic (pert to) . . .
  deity . . **4.** Baal
  dialect . . **4.** Geez
  god (evil) . . **6.** Moloch
  language . . **5.** Iraqi **6.** Syrian **7.** Arabian,
  Aramaic **8.** Egyptian **11.** Palestinian
  people . . **6.** Harari , Shagia (Shaikiyeh)
  8. Moabites
semper eadem . . . **13.** always the same
   (motto of Queen Elizabeth)
semper fidelis . . . **14.** always faithful
semper idem . . . **13.** always the same

semper paratus . . . **11.** always ready
senate . . . **5.** boule **7.** council (Rom)
   8. assembly **11.** legislature
   18. administrative body
send . . . **4.** mail, ship **5.** drive, grant,
   issue, speed **6.** bestow, convey, export,
   launch, propel **7.** forward **8.** dispatch,
   transmit **10.** commission
send (pert to) . . .
   back . . **5.** remit **6.** remand, return
      11. reverberate
   by different person . . **5.** relay
   off . . **5.** start **6.** launch **7.** impulse
      8. dispatch **11.** consignment
      13. demonstration
   out . . **4.** emit, spew **5.** shoot
   out rays . . **7.** radiate
   payment . . **5.** remit
   to an address . . **7.** deliver
Seneca . . . **6.** Indian **9.** Iroquoian
Senegal, Africa . . .
   capital . . **5.** Dakar
   ebony . . **9.** blackwood
   gazelle . . **5.** korin
   gum . . **9.** gum arabic
   mahogany . . **9.** cailcedra
   native . . **10.** Senegalese
senescence . . . **5.** aging **10.** growing old
senicide . . . **13.** killing old men (tribal)
senility . . . **6.** dotage, old age **8.** caducity,
   dementia **10.** feebleness
senior . . . **4.** aine, dean **5.** chief, elder
   7. ancient, student **8.** superior
senior member . . . **5.** doyen
sensation . . . **5.** sense **6.** thrill, uproar,
   wonder **7.** emotion **8.** rhigosis (cold)
   10. perception **12.** great success
sensational . . . **5.** lurid **6.** superb
   8. dramatic, exciting **9.** emotional
   12. melodramatic
sense . . . **4.** feel, mind, sane **5.** flair, sight,
   smell **7.** feeling, meaning **8.** sapience
   9. awareness, intuition, sensation,
   sentience **10.** perception, understand
   11. discernment, recognition
   12. intelligence
senseless . . . **5.** inept **6.** insane, stupid,
   unwise **7.** fatuous, foolish, idiotic,
   inanity **9.** illogical, inanimate, insensate,
   unfeeling **10.** irrational **11.** meaningless,
   purposeless, unconscious
   12. unreasonable **13.** unintelligent
sense of . . .
   beauty . . **8.** aesthete (esthete), tasteful
      9. aesthetic
   dignity . . **5.** pride
   distance . . **11.** telesthetic
   hearing . . **8.** audition **12.** auscultation
   humor . . **10.** risibility
   sight . . **6.** vision
   smell . . **7.** osmatic **9.** olfaction
   taste . . **6.** palate
sense organ . . . **3.** ear, eye **4.** nose, skin
   6. tongue **8.** receptor, sensilla
senses . . . **4.** wits **6.** sanity **7.** sensory
   9. sensation
sensible . . . **4.** sane **5.** aware, privy,
   sound **7.** logical, prudent **8.** rational
   9. cognizant, practical, sensitive
   10. reasonable, responsive
   11. intelligent, susceptible

sensitive . . . **4.** nice, sore **5.** acute
   6. pliant, tender, touchy **7.** sensory
   8. sensible **9.** receptive **10.** responsive
   11. susceptible **14.** discriminating,
   impressionable
sensitivity . . . **9.** emotional, hebetated
   (blunted) **11.** sensibility **12.** irritability
   14. discrimination
sentence . . . **4.** doom **5.** maxim, motto
   6. phrase, remark, saying **7.** condemn,
   passage, thought, verdict **8.** decision,
   judgment, proposal **9.** statement
   12. condemnation
sentence (pert to) . . .
   balance . . **7.** parison
   clause (concluding) . . **8.** apodosis
   concluding . . **8.** epilogue (epilog)
   construction . . **6.** syntax
   difficult articulation . . **13.** tongue twister
   introductory . . **8.** protasis
   judicial . . **5.** futwa
   pithy . . **5.** motto **8.** aphorism
   punishment . . **11.** year and a day
   subordinate part . . **6.** clause, phrase
sententious . . . **5.** pithy, terse **7.** concise,
   laconic **10.** aphoristic **13.** grandiloquent
sentient . . . **4.** mind **5.** aware **7.** feeling
   8. sensible **9.** conscious, sensitive
   10. perceptive **13.** consciousness
sentiment . . . **5.** toast **7.** emotion, feeling,
   opinion **8.** attitude **10.** perception,
   sentimento **11.** sensibility
   14. sentimentality
sentimental . . . **6.** loving **7.** maudlin,
   mawkish **8.** romantic **9.** emotional
   13. lackadaisical
sentimental song . . . **11.** strephonade
sentinel . . . **5.** guard **6.** picket, sentry
   7. vedette (mounted) **8.** watchman
   10. lookout man, watchtower
sepad . . . **5.** think **7.** believe, suppose
sepal . . . **4.** leaf **5.** petal
separate . . . **4.** open, part, shed, sift, sort
   5. alone, apart, sever, space **6.** cleave,
   detach, divide, secern, single, sleave,
   sunder, winnow **7.** disband, diverge,
   diverse, divided, divorce, isolate
   8. alienate, discrete, distinct, peculiar,
   secluded **9.** disjoined, partition,
   segregate, sequester, unrelated
   10. dissociate, particular, respective
   11. disembodied, unconnected
separate (pert to) . . .
   Chem . . **11.** fractionate
   from others . . **5.** aloof **8.** isolated
   metal from ore . . **5.** smelt
   thread . . **6.** sleave
separation . . . **6.** tmesis **7.** divorce
   8. autotomy **9.** partition, secession,
   seclusion **10.** alienation **11.** disjunction,
   segregation **13.** sequestration
   14. discontinuance, discrimination
separatist . . . **7.** heretic, seceder
   8. apostate **9.** dissenter **12.** secessionist
   13. nonconformist
sepia . . . **3.** dun, ink **5.** color **7.** pigment
   10. cuttlebone, cuttlefish
sepiment . . . **5.** hedge **7.** defense
   9. enclosure
Sepiola . . . **10.** cuttlefish
sepiolite . . . **10.** meerschaum

sepoy ... **7.** soldier **9.** policeman
seps ... **6.** lizard **7.** serpent
sept ... **4.** clan **5.** class, seven, tribe
7. lineage
septic ... **6.** morbid, pyemia (pyaemia)
8. diseased, infected, poisoned
9. gangrened, mortified, poisonous
10. septicemia (blood poison)
sepulcher, sepulchre ... **4.** bury, tomb
5. crypt, grave, vault **6.** entomb
9. sepulture **10.** repository
sepulchral ... **5.** urnal **6.** gloomy, hollow
7. charnel **8.** funereal **9.** deep-toned
sepulchral (pert to) ...
chest .. **4.** cist
mound .. **7.** tumulus
vault .. **6.** burial **8.** catacomb, monument
9. interview
sequel ... **5.** issue **6.** effect, series, upshot
7. outcome **8.** follow up, sequence,
sequitur **9.** posterity **10.** succession
sequela ... **7.** disease (resulting)
8. adherent **9.** inference **10.** conclusion
11. concomitant, consequence
15. morbid condition
sequence ... **5.** gamut **6.** course (usual),
series, tierce (three cards) **8.** straight
10. succession
sequential ... **9.** deducible, resultant
10. continuous, succeeding
11. consecutive
sequestered ... **6.** lonely, secret
7. private, recluse, retired **8.** isolated,
secluded, solitary, withdraw
9. concealed, separated
12. unfrequented
sequitur ... **9.** inference, influence, it
follows **14.** natural sequent
sequoia, Sequoia ... **4.** Park (Calif)
6. Indian (famed for alphabet) **7.** big
tree, conifer, redwood
seraglio ... **5.** harem, serai **6.** zenana
9. enclosure
serape ... **5.** shawl **7.** blanket
seraph ... **5.** angel **6.** cherub
seraphic ... **7.** angelic, sublime
8. cherubic **9.** unworldly
Serb ... **4.** Slav **7.** Serbian (Servian)
Serbia, Yugoslavia ...
church .. **8.** Orthodox
conqueror .. **5.** Turks
hero .. **6.** Dushan, Nemaya (1159)
queen .. **7.** Natalie
Revolutionary .. **7.** Chetnik
sere ... **4.** claw, sear, worn **5.** talon
6. effete, yellow **8.** withered
10. desiccated
serenade ... **4.** sing **5.** music **8.** serenata
9. charivari, entertain **10.** callithump
11. celebration
serene ... **4.** calm, cool **5.** clear, quiet
6. placid **8.** peaceful, serenity, tranquil
9. collected, unruffled **11.** undisturbed
12. tranquillity (tranquility)
serenity ... **5.** peace **6.** repose
8. calmness, coolness **9.** composure
10. quiescence
serf ... **4.** esne, neif (fem), peon **5.** helot,
slave **6.** thrall, vassal **7.** captive, villein
series ... **3.** set **4.** nest **5.** class,
gamut, group **8.** sequence **9.** seriation

10. succession
series, connected ... **5.** chain, suite
6. catena
series of ...
discussions .. **9.** symposium
heroic events .. **4.** epos
meetings .. **7.** session
pictures .. **8.** panorama
races .. **7.** regatta
rings .. **4.** coil
six .. **5.** hexad
steps .. **5.** scale
syllogisms .. **7.** sorites
travels .. **7.** odyssey
serious ... **4.** keen **5.** grave, serio (comb
form), sober, staid **6.** demure, sedate,
solemn **7.** capital, earnest, weighty,
zealous **8.** resolute **9.** important
10. thoughtful
seriousness ... **4.** zeal **7.** gravity
10. importance **11.** earnestness
sermon ... **4.** talk, text **5.** psalm **6.** homily,
lesson, preach **7.** address, lecture,
reproof **8.** harangue **9.** discourse,
preaching **10.** admonition
seron ... **5.** crate **6.** hamper **7.** boxwood,
spanner
serotine ... **3.** bat **4.** adda **9.** late bloom
serpent ... **3.** asp **4.** seps (anc) **5.** cobra,
krait, racer, snake
serpent (pert to) ...
deity, of good .. **12.** agathodaemon
13. agathos daemon
fabulous .. **5.** Hydra **6.** dragon **8.** basilisk
11. amphisbaena
large .. **3.** boa **5.** aboma **6.** python
8. jararaca
monster .. **6.** ellops
Old .. **5.** Satan
semihuman (Hind Myth) .. **4.** Naga
sky (Vedic Myth) .. **3.** Ahi
worshipers (Gnostic) .. **7.** Ophites
serpentine ... **4.** wily **5.** snaky **6.** subtle,
zigzag **7.** sinuous, winding **8.** diabolic,
tempting **9.** snakelike **10.** circuitous,
meandering
serpigo ... **8.** ringworm **11.** skin disease
serrano ... **12.** squirrelfish
serrate ... **7.** notched, toothed **8.** indented
10. saw-toothed
serried ... **5.** dense **7.** compact, concise,
crowded
serum ... **4.** whey **5.** blood, fluid **6.** serous
9. antitoxin
servant ... **3.** gyp **4.** bata, cook, maid,
maty, mozo, serf, syce **5.** agent, boots,
chela, nurse, slave, valet **6.** bildar,
butler, flunky, garçon, gillie (gilly),
menial, servus, vassal, wallah (walla)
7. equerry (nobleman's) **8.** coistrel,
domestic, handmaid **9.** assistant
11. chamberlain
servant of God ... **6.** bishop
serve ... **2.** do **3.** act, aid **4.** deal, help,
wait **5.** avail, cater **6.** assist, succor
7. advance, bestead, forward, further,
suffice, work for **8.** bear arms, fight for
9. officiate **10.** administer, distribute
serve (pert to) ...
as accomplice .. **4.** abet
as escort .. **6.** squire

food.. **4.** wait **5.** cater **7.** dish out
one's sentence.. **6.** do time
religion.. **4.** obey **7.** worship
server... **4.** tray **6.** player, salver
7. acolyte
Servia... see *Serbia*
service... **3.** aid, use **4.** help, mail,
Mass, rite **5.** favor, matin **6.** employ,
ritual **7.** benefit, nocturn, utility
8. ceremony, evensong, kindness,
ministry **9.** servitude **10.** attendance,
employment **12.** ministration
service tree... **4.** sorb **5.** rowan
serviette... **6.** napkin
servile... **4.** mean **6.** abject, menial,
minion **7.** fawning, slavish **8.** cringing,
faithful **9.** dependent, parasitic, truckling
10. obsequious, submissive
11. subservient, sycophantic
Servite... **9.** mendicant **13.** Order of
Friars (1233)
servitude... **7.** bondage, serfdom,
service, slavery **8.** servitus **9.** vassalage
14. apprenticeship
sesame... **3.** oil **4.** herb **5.** benne **7.** gingili
(seed), teel oil **8.** ajonjoli, sesamine
Sesame, Open... **10.** magical key
12. magic command (Arab Nights)
sess... **4.** heap, pile **9.** soap frame
session... **5.** court **6.** séance **8.** assembly
11. legislature
set... **3.** lay **4.** form, heal, laid, pose, post
5. brood, class, fixed, group, place,
posit, ready, staid, stand **6.** adjust,
clique, define, fasten, formal, ossify,
series, settle **7.** confirm, congeal,
coterie, station, stiffen **8.** regulate,
solidify **9.** coagulate, designate,
direction, obstinate, stabilize
10. collection, determined, solidified
11. established, prepared for
set (pert to)...
afloat.. **6.** launch
against.. **6.** oppose **10.** antagonize
apart.. **5.** allot, elect, taboo **6.** exempt
7. isolate, reserve, seclude **8.** allocate,
separate **9.** segregate, sequester
11. distinguish **13.** differentiate
aside.. **4.** void **5.** annul **6.** except, reject
7. abolish, discard, dismiss, earmark,
exclude **8.** overrule, postpone
at an angle.. **4.** cant
back.. **4.** loss **5.** check **6.** demote,
hinder, recess **7.** relapse **8.** restrain,
slow down
exclusive.. **5.** elect, taboo **6.** clique
fire to.. **6.** ignite, kindle **7.** emblaze,
inflame **8.** irritate
firmly.. **5.** embed, plant, posit **6.** cement,
ossify
forth.. **5.** adorn **6.** depart, expose, lay
out **7.** arrange, commend, display,
enounce, exhibit, explain, expound,
present, promote, propone, publish
8. announce, decorate, indicate,
manifest **9.** translate **10.** promulgate
11. demonstrate
free.. **6.** acquit **7.** absolve, release,
unloose **8.** liberate **10.** emancipate
11. disillusion
off.. **6.** incite, offset **7.** measure

8. beautify, detonate **9.** demarcate,
embellish **11.** distinguish
on firm basis.. **9.** establish
out.. **4.** plot **5.** allot, begin **7.** arrange
right.. **5.** teach **6.** adjust, direct, remedy
11. disillusion
up.. **3.** rig **4.** plan **5.** build, cause, erect,
exalt, hoist, print, raise **7.** elevate,
finance, install **9.** construct, establish
10. inaugurate, prearrange
set (pert to in)...
a groove.. **5.** dadoe
a row.. **4.** tier **5.** align, aline, range
columns.. **7.** tabular **8.** tabulate
from margin.. **6.** indent
operation.. **4.** move **5.** start **6.** launch
opposition.. **3.** pit
order.. **5.** align **6.** adjust **7.** arrange
set (pert to of)...
eight.. **6.** ogdoad
friends.. **7.** coterie
jeweled ornaments.. **6.** parure
laws.. **4.** code **8.** statutes
on end.. **5.** upend **10.** topsy-turvy
opinions.. **5.** credo
organ pipes.. **5.** stops
rules.. **4.** code
sheets (paper).. **5.** quire
seta... **4.** hair **5.** spine **7.** bristle, feather
Seth (pert to)...
brother.. **4.** Abel, Cain
father.. **4.** Adam
son.. **4.** Enos
wife.. **8.** Nephthys
setting... **5.** scene **6.** locale **8.** mounting,
planting **10.** background
settle... **3.** fix, pay **4.** nest, root, seat,
sink **5.** agree, clear, lodge, order, prove,
quiet, solve **6.** assign, assure, decide,
locate, pay off, purify, secure, soothe
7. arrange, clarify, confirm, mediate,
resolve **8.** colonize, ensconce, regulate
9. designate, determine, establish,
reconcile **10.** strengthen **11.** tranquilize
settled... **4.** paid **5.** ended, fixed
6. proved, sedate **7.** assured, decided,
located **9.** steadfast **10.** unchanging
11. established
settled in advance... **13.** predetermined
settled in mind... **10.** equanimity
settlement... **3.** dos **4.** camp **6.** colony,
hamlet **7.** payment **8.** fixation, sediment,
showdown **9.** community, endowment
10. adjustment **12.** colonization,
conciliation, satisfaction
13. determination, establishment
Settlement House... **9.** Hull House
(Chicago) **10.** University (NY)
11. Toynbee Hall (London)
settler... **6.** Sooner (Okla) **7.** pioneer,
planter, Puritan **8.** colonist **9.** immigrant
settlings... **4.** lees **5.** dregs **8.** sediment
10. settlement **12.** precipitates
seven (pert to)...
angles.. **8.** heptagon **9.** septangle
arts.. **5.** logic, music **7.** grammar
8. geometry, rhetoric **9.** astronomy
10. arithmetic
comb form.. **5.** hepta, septi
days and nights.. **8.** sennight
fold.. **8.** septuple

gods of happiness .. **5.** Ebisu, Hotei
6. Benten **7.** Daikoku, Jurojin
8. Bishamon **10.** Fuku-roku-ju
group .. **6.** heptad, septet **8.** septuple
12. septemvirate
Hills .. **4.** Rome
languages .. **9.** heptaglot
Latin .. **6.** septum
number .. **8.** hebdomad **9.** septenary
Old Test Books (1st seven) ..
10. Heptateuch
Seas .. **11.** world oceans
Stars .. **8.** Pleiades
tones .. **10.** heptachord, heptatonic
seventy . . . **12.** septuagenary
seventy-day period . . . **12.** septuagesima
seventy-year-old . . . **14.** septuagenarian
sever . . . **3.** cut, lop **4.** part, rend **5.** break
6. behead, cleave, detach, divide,
except, exempt **7.** disjoin **8.** accurate,
disunite, separate **9.** interpose,
segregate **10.** decapitate, disconnect,
dissociate **12.** disassociate
several . . . **4.** many **6.** divers, sundry
7. diverse, various **8.** distinct **9.** different
10. respective
severe . . . **3.** bad **4.** dure, hard, keen,
sore, tart **5.** acute, cruel, exact, grave,
harsh, rigid, snell, sober, stern **6.** biting,
bitter, chaste, sedate, simple, solemn,
strict, taxing, trying **7.** arduous, austere,
condign, drastic, extreme, intense,
painful, serious, violent **8.** accurate,
rigorous **9.** draconian, strenuous,
stringent **10.** censorious, restrained
severe critic (of Alexandria) . . .
9. Aristarch
severity . . . **5.** rigor **7.** cruelty **8.** hardness,
pungency, violence **9.** austerity,
exactness, gruffness, harshness,
solemnity, sternness, stiffness
10. bitterness, difficulty, inclemency,
simplicity, strictness **12.** rigorousness
Seville cathedral tower . . . **7.** Giralda
Seville orange . . . **9.** red-yellow **12.** bitter
orange
Sèvres blue . . . **5.** color **9.** bleu de roi,
porcelain **11.** bleu céleste
sew . . . **4.** mend **5.** baste, unite **6.** fasten,
needle, secure, stitch
sewan . . . **5.** beads, money **6.** wampum
sewing . . . **6.** sutile **8.** suturing **9.** stitching
10. needlework
sewing case . . . **4.** etui
sewing machine inventor . . . **9.** Elias
Howe
sexagenarian . . . **13.** a sixty-year-old
sexagesimal . . . **5.** sixty
sexes, common to both . . . **6.** unisex
7. epicene
sexless . . . **6.** neuter **7.** epicene
sextet, sextette . . . **6.** sestet **8.** six parts
10. group of six **13.** six-line stanza
sexton . . . **6.** beetle **7.** sacrist **9.** sacristan
12. underofficer
sextuplet . . . **7.** sestole (sestolet) **8.** six
notes
sha . . . **5.** sheep, urial (oorial)
shabbash . . . **5.** bravo **8.** well done
Shabbath . . . **7.** Sabbath (Jew)
shabbiness . . . **8.** baseness, slovenry

9. seediness
shabby . . . **4.** base, mean, worn **5.** dowdy,
faded, ratty, seedy, tacky, yucky
6. grungy, paltry, ragged, scurvy,
scuzzy, sleazy **7.** outworn, shagrag,
squalid **10.** despicable, ragamuffin,
threadbare **12.** contemptible
shack . . . **3.** coe, hut **4.** husk, plug
5. chase, hutch, tramp **6.** shanty
7. stubble **8.** vagabond **9.** hibernate
shackle . . . **3.** tie **4.** band, bind, bond,
gyve, iron, ring **5.** chain **6.** fetter,
hobble, hogtie, impede, pinion
7. manacle, trammel **8.** restrain
shackled . . . **4.** tied **5.** bound, gyved
6. curbed, ironed **7.** hobbled **8.** fettered,
hampered, hindered, manacled
10. restrained
shad . . . **4.** fish **5.** Alosa **7.** crappie,
mojarra
shade . . . **3.** hue **4.** dull, roof, tint, tone,
veil **5.** ghost, tinge, visor **6.** awning,
canopy, darken, degree, follow, nuance,
screen, shadow, shield, sprite **7.** eclipse,
foliage, parasol, protect, shelter,
umbrage **10.** overshadow, protection
11. adumbration
shade, affording . . . **9.** umbratile
shadow . . . **3.** dim, dog, spy **4.** hide,
tail **5.** cloud, image, umbra **6.** attend,
screen **7.** blacken, conceal, protect,
remains **8.** follower, hanger-on, illusion,
penumbra **9.** adumbrate, detective
10. protection
shadow fighting . . . **9.** sciamachy
shadowless . . . **6.** ascian
Shadrach (pert to) . . .
enemy .. **14.** Nebuchadnezzar
name once .. **7.** Ananias **9.** Hannaniah
one of three Hebrew youths ..
7. Meshach **8.** Abednago, Shadrach
shady . . . **4.** dark **5.** faint, fishy **6.** umbral
7. shadowy **9.** deceitful, dishonest,
underhand **10.** indistinct, unreliable
12. questionable
shaft . . . **3.** pit, rod **4.** axle, fust, mine, orlo
(part), stem, tige, tole **5.** arrow, scape,
shank, spire, stalk, thill, tower, trunk
6. column, tongue **7.** feather, missile,
obelisk **8.** monument **9.** flagstaff
shag . . . **3.** nap **4.** hair, mane, pile
5. chase, dance **6.** follow, rascal
7. tobacco **9.** cormorant, make rough
10. blackguard
shaggy . . . **5.** bushy, furry, nappy, rough
6. ragged **7.** hirsute, unkempt, villous
8. confused (of thought), uncombed
10. unpolished
shagrag . . . **6.** ragged, tagrag **7.** unkempt
8. rascally
shake . . . **3.** jar, jog, wag **4.** jolt, rock,
stir, sway, toze **5.** swing, trill **6.** dither,
dodder, quiver, shimmy, shiner,
weaken **7.** agitate, flutter, shingle,
shudder, tremble, tremolo **8.** enfeeble
10. earthquake
Shakespeare (pert to) . . .
actor .. **4.** Ward **7.** Gielgud, Olivier,
Sothern **8.** Modjeska
called .. **10.** Bard of Avon
character, female .. **6.** Juliet, Portia

7. Ophelia **9.** Cleopatra
character, male .. **5.** Romeo, Timon
6. Antony, Hamlet **7.** Macbeth, Othello
8. Falstaff
forest .. **5.** Arden
river .. **4.** Avon
site .. **6.** Verona **8.** Elsinore
villain .. **4.** Iago
wife .. **12.** Anne Hathaway
shaky ... **6.** infirm, wabbly, wobbly
7. fearful, nervous, unsound **8.** agitated,
unsecure **9.** tottering, trembling,
uncertain, unsettled **10.** precarious,
unreliable **12.** questionable
shale ... **4.** rock **5.** flake, scale **8.** dandruff
Shalimar Gardens ... **6.** Lahore
shallow ... **5.** shoal **6.** lagoon (lagune)
7. cursory, trivial **9.** depthless, frivolous,
insincere **11.** superficial
sham ... **3.** ape **4.** fake, hoax, mock
5. dummy, false, fraud, trick **6.** deceit,
humbug **7.** feigned **8.** pretense
9. imitation, imposture, pretended
Shamash (pert to) ...
centers of worship .. **5.** Larsa **6.** Sippar
consort .. **3.** Aya (Ai)
deity (Babylon) .. **6.** sun god
messenger .. **6.** Bunene
Sumerian equivalent .. **3.** Utu (Utug)
6. Babbar
shame ... **5.** abash **7.** mortify **8.** disgrace,
dishonor **9.** humiliate **11.** abomination,
humiliation, impropriety
shameful ... **4.** mean, vile **5.** gross
6. wicked **8.** flagrant, improper,
indecent, infamous, terrible
9. degrading **10.** outrageous,
scandalous **11.** disgraceful, ignominious
12. dishonorable, disreputable,
vituperative
shameless ... **6.** arrant, brazen
8. immodest, impudent **9.** audacious
10. unblushing **11.** brazenfaced
shammer ... **8.** impostor
shanghai ... **6.** abduct, to drug
9. slingshot
shank ... **3.** leg **4.** crus, gamb (gambe)
7. meat cut **12.** travel on foot
shape ... **4.** bend, form, mold (mould),
plan **5.** frame, model **6.** adjust,
create, cut out, design, devise,
figure **7.** arrange, conform, contour,
develop, fashion, incline **8.** phantasm
10. appearance, figuration
11. arrangement
shaped like a ...
comb .. **9.** pectinate
shield .. **7.** peltate, scutate
strap, thong .. **6.** lorate
urn .. **9.** urceolate
shapeless ... **7.** lumpish **8.** deformed,
formless **9.** amorphous, contorted,
distorted, unshapely
shapely ... **3.** fit **4.** neat, trim **6.** comely,
gainly **10.** well-formed **11.** symmetrical
16. well-proportioned
shapes (ornamental, garden) ... **5.** topia
7. topiary
share ... **3.** cut, lot **4.** dole, part **5.** enter,
quota **6.** ration **7.** partake, portion
8. take part **9.** allowance, apportion

11. co-operative, participate
sharecropper ... **7.** metayer
shark ... **5.** fraud **6.** lawyer **8.** parasite,
swindler **9.** trickster
shark (fish) ... **4.** gata, mako, tope
5. lamia (cub), Rhina **6.** Galeos, Galeus,
requin **7.** dogfish, tiburon **8.** man-
eater, Mustelus, Selachii, sharklet,
Squatina **9.** porbeagle **10.** Carcharias,
hammerhead **11.** Carcharodon,
Galeorhinus
shark-clinger ... **4.** pega **6.** remora
sharp ... **4.** acid, curt, edgy, keen, tart
5. acerb, acrid, acute, alert, brisk,
crisp, edged, harsh, quick, smart,
steep, witty **6.** abrupt, astute, bitter,
crafty, shrill **7.** angular, caustic,
cutting, nipping, painful, pointed,
pungent, sharper **8.** incisive, poignant
9. penetrant, sagacious, sarcastic,
trenchant **10.** discerning, proficient
11. acrimonious, penetrating, well-
dressed
sharp (pert to) ...
answer .. **6.** retort
blow .. **4.** slap
cornered .. **7.** angular
edged .. **5.** arris
flavor .. **4.** tang
make .. **10.** cacuminate
pointed .. **5.** acute
saw .. **8.** titmouse
Scot .. **5.** snell **6.** snelly
sighted .. **4.** keen **6.** astute **7.** lyncean
sound .. **4.** ping
Tuesday .. **13.** Shrove Tuesday
witted .. **6.** shrewd **10.** discerning
11. intelligent
sharpen ... **3.** nib, ted **4.** edge, hone,
whet **5.** grind, point, strop **6.** acuate
7. enhance, quicken **9.** intensify
10. cacuminate
sharper ... **5.** cheat, knave, rogue
6. keener **8.** deceiver, swindler
9. trickster
shatter ... **5.** blast, break, crash, smash,
split **8.** splinter
shave ... **3.** cut **4.** pare **5.** cheat, strip
6. cut off **7.** swindle, tonsure **9.** cut
prices, thin slice
shaver ... **3.** boy, lad **4.** tool **5.** cheat
6. barber **8.** swindler **9.** youngster
11. extortioner
shavetail ... **4.** mule **6.** ensign
10. lieutenant
shawl ... **5.** manta **6.** serape **7.** paisley
8. cashmere
Shawnee (pert to) ...
chief .. **8.** Tecumseh
Indian people .. **9.** Algonquin
location (present) .. **8.** Oklahoma
sheaf ... **4.** kern, omer **6.** bundle **7.** cluster
11. hyperpencil
shear ... **3.** cut **4.** clip, snip, trim **5.** sever
6. fleece, remove **7.** scissor, whittle
shears ... **5.** lewis **6.** forfex **8.** secateur
sheatfish ... **4.** wels **7.** catfish
sheath ... **4.** case **5.** forel (book), glove,
ocrea, theca **6.** sleeve, spathe **7.** stipule
8. scabbard
sheathe ... **4.** wrap **5.** cover, drape

6. encase 7. envelop 8. enshroud
sheave . . . 5. wheel 6. pulley 9. back
water, eccentric
shebang . . . 6. affair, boodle, outfit
7. concern 11. contrivance
13. establishment 14. kit and caboodle
she-cat . . . 4. elle 9. grimalkin
shed . . . 3. hut 4. abri, cote, lair, molt
5. hovel, scale, spill 6. effuse, hangar,
lean-to, slough 7. cottage, diffuse,
radiate, shelter
shed (light) . . . 4. glow 7. explain, radiate
10. illuminate
shedding . . . 7. ecdysis (Zool), molting
sheen . . . 5. glint, gloss, shine 6. luster
7. glitter, shimmer 8. splendor
9. shininess 10. brightness
sheep . . . 3. ewe, ram, sha, teg, tup
4. buck, lamb, Ovis, zenu 5. bidet,
dumba, oudad 6. argali, cosset,
gimmer, hogget, mutton, sheder,
wether 8. ruminant, shearhog, yeanling
9. blackface
sheep (pert to) . . .
cry . . 3. baa 5. bleat
disease . . 3. coe, gid, rot 4. bane 5. braxy
7. anthrax
faced . . 3. shy 7. bashful 8. sheepish
female . . 3. ewe, teg 6. sheder
flock leader . . 10. bellwether
fold . . 3. ree 4. cote 5. kraal, reeve,
stell 6. church
head . . 5. jimmy 8. powsowdy
headed . . 5. silly 6. stupid 12. simple-
minded
kidney extract . . 5. renes
laurel . . 6. Kalmia
leg wool . . 4. gare
male . . 3. ram, tup 4. buck 5. heder
6. wether
owner's mark . . 4. smit 6. ruddle
pet . . 6. cosset
sheeplike . . 5. ovine 9. tractable
skin, leather . . 4. pelt, roan 5. basil
7. chamois, diploma 8. woolfell
stealing . . 7. abigest
tick . . 3. ked
wild . . 3. sha 4. Ovis 5. urial 6. aoudad,
argali, bharal, nayaur 7. bighorn,
mouflon (moufflon) 9. Thian Shan
(Marco Polo's)
sheep, breeds . . . 6. Merino, Romney
7. Cheviot, Delaine, Dishley, Karakul,
Suffolk, Targhee 8. Cotswold, Dartmoor
9. Kerry Hill, Leicester, Southdown,
Teeswater 10. Corriedale, Dorset
Horn, Oxford Down, Shropshire
13. Hampshire Down
sheepish . . . 3. shy 5. timid 7. bashful
9. chagrined
sheeplike . . . 5. ovine
sheer . . . 4. mere, pure, thin, turn 5. brant,
steep, utter 6. abrupt, swerve 7. deviate,
unmixed 8. absolute 9. deviation,
downright, undiluted 10. completely,
diaphonous 11. transparent
13. perpendicular
sheet . . . 4. leaf, rope, sail 5. paper
6. shroud 9. cover with, duodecimo
(12-fold), newspaper, sheathing
sheik, sheikh . . . 4. Arab 5. chief 6. prince

shelf . . . 4. berm (berme), reef, sell
5. ledge, shoal 6. mantel 7. stratum
8. postpone, put aside
shell . . . 3. pod 4. boat, bomb, husk
5. conch, crust, shard, shuck 6. cowrie
(cowry) 7. bombard, capsule, grenade,
missile 8. carapace, exterior, shrapnel
9. cartridge 10. projectile
shell (pert to) . . .
button source . . 5. troca 6. lorica, mucket
cone . . 7. admiral
ear . . 7. abalone
explosive . . 3. dud 4. bomb 7. grenade
fish . . 4. clam, pipi 6. cockle, limpet,
mussel, oyster 7. abalone, lobster,
mollusk, scallop 8. barnacle 9. trunkfish
fossil . . 8. ammonite
game . . 10. thimblerig 13. sleight of
hand
marine . . 6. cowrie (cowry)
money . . 5. hawok, sewan, uhllo (ulo)
6. cowrie, wampum
out . . 4. give 6. expend, pay out
protective . . 6. lorica
ridge . . 4. lira 5. varix
seaweed . . 8. frustule
spiral . . 5. chank, whelk 8. caracole
trumpet (Triton's) . . 5. conch
shelter . . . 3. lee, pad 4. abri, camp,
cote, digs, port, roof, shed, skug,
tent 5. condo, cover, haven, house,
hutch, shack, shade 6. asylum,
burrow, dugout, hangar, harbor,
refuge, screen, shield 7. defense,
hospice, pillbox, protect, retreat
8. mantelet (mantlet), quarters, security
9. coverture, sanctuary 10. protection
sheltered side . . . 3. lee 4. alee 7. leeward
shelve . . . 5. slope, table, waive 6. retire
7. dismiss, incline 8. postpone, put
aside 10. pigeonhole
Shem (pert to) . . .
brother . . 3. Ham
descendant . . 6. Semite
father . . 4. Noah
son . . 3. Lud 4. Aram, Elam
shenanigan . . . 7. foolery 8. trickery,
zaniness 9. horseplay 10. hanky-panky
11. monkeyshine
shend . . . 3. mar 4. harm, ruin 5. spoil
6. injure, revile 7. destroy, stupefy
8. confound, disgrace, reproach
Sheol . . . 4. Hell 5. Aralu, grave, Hades
6. the pit, Toppet 7. Abaddon, Gehenna
10. underworld 11. nether world
14. abode of the dead
shepherd . . . 5. guide 6. direct, escort,
feeder, herder, pastor, shadow
8. guardian, herdsman 9. clergyman
shepherd, shepherds (pert to) . . .
band of . . 10. pastoureau
dog . . 5. sheep 6. collie
flute . . 7. musette 9. flageolet
god . . 3. Pan
pipe . . 3. oat 4. reed 7. larigot
spider . . 13. daddy longlegs
staff . . 4. Kent 5. crook
sheriff (pert to) . . .
aide . . 5. posse
deputy . . 6. elisor 7. bailiff
jurisdiction . . 9. bailiwick

sheriffdom . . **10.** shrievalty
sherry . . . **5.** jerez, Xeres **7.** oloroso
8. montilla
Shetland Island (pert to) . . .
fishing grounds (deep-sea) . . **4.** haaf
kingdom of . . **8.** Scotland
land, fee simple . . **4.** udal
promontory . . **4.** noup
Supreme Court Pres . . **4.** foud
viol . . **3.** gue
shewbread, showbread (Bib) . . . **6.** ritual
10. unleavened
shibboleth (Bib) . . . **4.** mode **5.** habit
6. saying, slogan **9.** criterion,
watchword **11.** peculiarity (speech)
shield . . . **3.** écu **4.** boss, umbo **5.** aegis
(egis), armor, cover, pavis, pelta,
scute, shade, shell, targe (anc)
6. defend, scutum, target **7.** defense,
protect, shelter **8.** insignia **9.** protector
10. escutcheon, protection
shield (pert to) . . .
Athena's . . **5.** aegis (egis)
bearer . . **8.** escudero
border . . **4.** orle **7.** bordure
emblem . . **7.** impresa
French (anc) . . **8.** rondache
heraldry . . **4.** enté **6.** points
part . . **4.** enté, orle, umbo
Roman . . **6.** scutum
sacred . . **6.** ancile (Rom)
shaped . . **7.** peltate, scutate **8.** aspidate
shift . . . **4.** eddy, fend, jibe, move,
ruse, stir, tack, veer **5.** shunt, smock,
trick **6.** baffle, change, device, rustle
7. deviate, pretext, quibble **8.** artifice,
mutation, transfer **9.** deviation,
expedient, fluctuate, vacillate
10. conversion, subterfuge
12. redistribute **13.** transposition
shifty . . . **6.** crafty, tricky **7.** devious,
evasive, furtive **9.** deceitful, makeshift
10. changeable **11.** treacherous
shill, shillaber (circus term) . . . **5.** decoy
8. employer, hanger-on **10.** accomplice
shillalagh, shillalah . . . **4.** club **6.** cudgel
7. sapling
shilly-shally . . . **8.** hesitate **9.** vacillate
10. hesitation, indecision **11.** vacillation
Shiloh . . . **4.** town (anc) **6.** Seilun (modern)
9. sanctuary (the ark) **10.** battle site
(Tenn)
shimmy . . . **5.** quake **6.** quiver **7.** chemise,
tremble, vibrate **9.** jazz dance, vibration
shin . . . **5.** climb, tibia **6.** cnemis **7.** foreleg
shindy . . . **3.** row **4.** lark, orgy, riot,
romp **5.** dance, party, revel, spree,
wince **6.** frolic, uproar **7.** wassail
8. carousal **9.** commotion, festivity
11. merrymaking
shine . . . **3.** ray **4.** beam, beek, star
5. excel, gloss, prank **6.** polish
7. furbish, glisten, glister, glitter,
radiate, splurge **8.** rutilate **9.** irradiate
shiner . . . **6.** bruise **8.** black eye
9. bootblack **10.** dollarfish
shingle . . . **4.** sign, wood **6.** hairdo
7. haircut, overlap **8.** chastise, coiffure,
detritus **9.** signboard
shining . . . **5.** aglow, lucid, nitid, shiny
6. glossy, lucent **7.** beaming, glowing,

radiant **8.** luminous, lustrous, nitidous,
rutilant, splendid **9.** refulgent
10. glistening, glittering **11.** illustrious,
irradiating, resplendent
Shinto (pert to) . . .
adherent . . **9.** Shintoist
cult . . **8.** Japanese
deity . . **8.** Hachiman
temple . . **3.** sha **5.** jinja (jinsha) **7.** yashiro
temple gateway . . **5.** torii
temple deity . . **5.** Jinja (Jinsha)
shiny . . . **5.** nitid, sleek **6.** bright
7. radiant, shining **8.** luminous, nitidous
9. unclouded
ship . . . **3.** ark **4.** lade, load, send
5. liner, tramp **6.** argosy, vessel
7. freight, steamer **9.** freighter, transport
10. watercraft
ship (pert to) . . .
abandoned . . **8.** derelict
apparatus . . **5.** crane, davit, winch
7. bollard, capstan **8.** windlass
Argonaut's . . **4.** Argo
armored . . **7.** carrack, cruiser
9. destroyer, submarine
attendant . . **7.** steward
auxiliary . . **4.** dory, life **6.** dinghy (dingy),
tender
biscuit . . **8.** hardtack **10.** pilot bread
cabin . . **6.** saloon **9.** stateroom
cargo . . **5.** oiler **6.** tanker **7.** oreboat
11. supertanker
deck . . **4.** main, poop **5.** orlop, upper
deck, cut down . . **5.** razee
deserter . . **3.** rat
duck shooting . . **4.** skag
flat bottom . . **4.** keel **5.** barge
fleet . . **6.** armada
invoice . . **8.** manifest
jail . . **4.** brig
kitchen . . **6.** galley **7.** caboose
Levantine . . **4.** saic
loader . . **9.** stevedore **12.** longshoreman
Mediterranean . . **5.** xebec **6.** galiot
(galliot) **7.** polacre
officer . . **4.** mate **6.** purser **7.** steward
9. boatswain (bosun)
one-masted . . **5.** sloop
part . . **4.** brig, keel, skeg **5.** stern, waist
6. bridge, rudder **8.** binnacle, taffrail
permit to enter . . **8.** pratique
platform (boarding) . . **9.** gangplank
privateer . . **10.** brigantine
prow . . **5.** prore (Poet)
quarters . . **5.** berth **8.** steerage
10. forecastle (fo'c's'le)
record . . **3.** log
rope . . **4.** line **6.** hawser **7.** halyard,
lanyard, painter, ratline
sailing . . **4.** bark (barque), dhow, proa,
saic **5.** ketch, sloop, xebec **6.** caique,
cutter, galley, lugger **7.** Geordie,
pinnace, polacre
side . . **3.** lee **4.** port **9.** starboard
three-oar bank . . **7.** trireme
twin-hulled . . **9.** catamaran
two-oar bank . . **6.** bireme
Venetian . . **9.** frigatoon
voyage record . . **3.** log
war . . **3.** sub **7.** cruiser, flattop
9. destroyer, submarine

11. dreadnaught
window.. **4.** port **8.** porthole
worm.. **5.** borer **6.** teredo
ship, famed... **4.** Nina **5.** Maine,
Pinta **6.** Bounty **7.** Monitor, Titanic
8. Clermont, Half Moon, Merrimac
9. Mayflower **10.** Golden Hind, Santa
Maria **12.** Constitution (Old Ironsides)
15. Bonhomme Richard
shipment... **5.** cargo **7.** carload
shippage... **3.** fee **4.** levy **8.** shipping
shipshape... **3.** nef (clock) **4.** neat, tidy,
trim **7.** orderly
shipwreck, cargo overboard...
6. jetsam **7.** flotsam
shire... **5.** horse **6.** county **8.** district,
province **11.** subdivision
shirk... **4.** duck, pike **5.** avoid, dodge,
evade, slink **7.** goof off **9.** fainaigue
(finagle)
shirker... **5.** piker **6.** truant **7.** quitter,
slacker **8.** embusqué **10.** malingerer
shirt... **4.** polo, sark **6.** blouse, camisa,
cilice, skivvy, T-shirt **8.** pullover
shiver... **5.** quake, shake **6.** be cold
7. shatter, shudder, tremble, vibrate
8. fragment **11.** trepidation
shivering... **4.** cold **6.** creepy **7.** nervous,
shaking **8.** fragment **9.** agitation,
twitching **10.** chilliness
shoal... **3.** bar **4.** bank, reef, spit **5.** crowd,
flock **6.** throng **8.** sand bank (shallow)
9. multitude
shock... **3.** jar **4.** blow, heap (grain),
jolt, stun **5.** appal, brunt, bushy (hair),
shake, stack, start **6.** appall, impact,
offend, stroke, trauma **7.** disgust,
horrify, startle, terrify **8.** calamity,
frighten, paralyze **9.** collision, electrify
10. concussion
shock absorber... **7.** cushion, snubber
shocking... **3.** bad **5.** awful, lurid
6. horrid **7.** ghastly, hideous **8.** horrible,
terrible **9.** appalling, frightful, offensive,
revolting, startling **10.** abominable
shoe (pert to)... **4.** boot, clog, geta, mule,
pump **5.** horse, moyle, sabot, scuff
6. ballet, bootee, brogan, buskin, gillie,
loafer, Oxford, patten, planch (planche),
sandal, secque **7.** chopine, rullion,
slipper, sneaker, talaria **8.** moccasin,
sabotine, solleret **10.** clodhopper
shoe (pert to)...
form.. **4.** last, tree
grip.. **5.** cleat
lace.. **3.** tie **5.** aglet (aiglet), lacet
6. lacing **7.** latchet **8.** bootlace
10. shoestring
maker.. **5.** sutor **7.** cobbler, Crispin
(patron saint) **8.** zapatero
part.. **3.** cap **4.** rand, vamp, welt **6.** insole
7. counter **9.** inner sole
shoebill, shoebird... **5.** stork
shoemaker's patron saint... **7.** Crispin
shogun... **5.** chief, title (Jap) **6.** tycoon
7. shikken
shoneen... **4.** snob **5.** toady
shoot... **3.** rod **4.** bine, dart, film, fine,
hunt, kill, plug, twig, weft **5.** bough,
craps, eject, gemma, plant, scion,
snipe, spear, sprig, throw, tuber, vimen

6. branch, sprout, stolon **7.** execute,
project **9.** discharge **10.** descendant,
photograph
shooting (pert to)...
fish.. **10.** archer fish
iron.. **6.** pistol **7.** firearm **8.** revolver
match.. **3.** tir **5.** skeet
objective.. **6.** target
star.. **5.** comet **6.** meteor **7.** cowslip
shop... **4.** mart **5.** burse, store **6.** market,
saloon **7.** atelier **8.** boutique, emporium
shopping mania... **9.** oniomania
shore... **4.** bank, prop **5.** beach,
coast, marge, playa **6.** rivage, strand
7. support **9.** foreshore, waterside
10. run aground, waterfront
shore (pert to)...
bird.. **3.** ree **5.** snipe **6.** avocet, curlew,
plover, wading **9.** Limicolae
inhabiting.. **8.** littoral
pine.. **4.** sand **8.** tamarack **9.** lodgepole
10. hack-me-tack
recess.. **3.** bay **4.** cove **5.** bayou, inlet
short... **4.** curt, rude **5.** brief, brusk,
scant, terse **6.** abrupt, scanty **7.** curtate,
friable, summary **8.** abridged, succinct
12. insufficient
short (pert to)...
and pointed.. **5.** terse
and stout.. **5.** dumpy **6.** stocky, stodgy
8. roly-poly, thickset
essay.. **5.** tract
legged.. **8.** breviped
letter.. **4.** chit
lived.. **9.** ephemeral
stop.. **5.** delay, pause **7.** respite
8. interval **9.** cessation
shortage... **4.** want **6.** ullage
10. deficiency **13.** insufficiency
shorten... **3.** bob, cut, lop **4.** clip, dele,
dock **5.** elide **6.** lessen, reduce, reef in
7. abridge, curtail **8.** condense, contract,
decrease, hold back **9.** decurtate
10. abbreviate
shortening a syllable... **7.** systole
shorthand... **5.** Gregg **6.** Pitman
8. Tironian (Rom) **11.** stenography
12. brachygraphy, speed writing
shortly... **4.** soon **6.** curtly, not
far **7.** harshly, quickly **8.** abruptly
9. presently
shortsighted... **4.** dull **6.** myopic, obtuse
8. purblind **11.** nearsighted
Shoshone Indian... **3.** Ute **4.** Hopi
5. Piute **7.** Bannock **8.** Comanche
shot... **4.** dram **5.** carom, speed **6.** birdie,
bullet, gamble, pellet, ruined **7.** gunfire,
missile, worn out **8.** marksman,
unnerved **9.** discharge **10.** detonation,
photograph, projectile **11.** dilapidated,
vaccination
shoulder... **5.** carry, shelf **6.** épaule
7. meat cut, scapula, support
8. buttress, omoplate
shoulder (pert to)...
armor.. **9.** épaulière
badge, ornament.. **7.** epaulet
blade.. **7.** scapula **8.** omoplate
comb form.. **3.** omo **6.** humero
inflammation.. **6.** omitis **7.** omalgia
of a road.. **4.** berm (berme)

reference.. **7.** humeral **8.** scapular
shout ... **3.** cry **4.** call, hoop, hoot, root, yell **5.** cheer **7.** acclaim **8.** applause, laughter
shouting ... **6.** clamor, crying **7.** calling, hooting, yelling **9.** bellowing
shove ... **4.** push **5.** drive, eject, elbow **6.** propel, thrust
shovel ... **4.** peel, spud **5.** scoop, skeet, spade **7.** scooper **8.** strockle **10.** antler part
show ... **4.** lead **5.** movie, prove, revue, teach **6.** cinema, escort, evince, reveal **7.** betoken, display, divulge, exhibit **8.** evidence, indicate, instruct, manifest **11.** demonstrate **13.** demonstration
show (pert to) ...
case (glass).. **7.** vitrine
deference.. **3.** bow **6.** salaam
disapproval.. **3.** boo **4.** hiss, pout
house.. **4.** hall **5.** odeum, opera **6.** circus **8.** coliseum, showboat
musical.. **5.** revue
off.. **6.** flaunt **10.** grandstand
of learning.. **6.** pedant
pompous.. **6.** parade **7.** display, pageant **9.** cavalcade **10.** exhibition
to a seat.. **5.** guide, usher **6.** escort **7.** conduct
up.. **6.** appear, arrive, attend, expose
shower ... **4.** bath, give, rain **6.** abound **8.** sprinkle
shower of meteorites ... **6.** Leonid (from Leo) **9.** Andromede
showing ...
animal remains.. **6.** zootic
care.. **9.** attentive, regardful **11.** considerate
display.. **10.** exhibition **12.** presentation
envy.. **9.** invidious
first.. **8.** premiere
good judgment.. **6.** astute **8.** sensible
showy ... **3.** gay **4.** arty, loud **5.** gaudy **6.** flashy, garish, sporty, tinsel **7.** pompous **8.** gorgeous, splendid, striking **9.** sumptuous **12.** ostentatious **13.** grandiloquent
shred ... **3.** rag **4.** snip **5.** piece, strip **6.** sliver, tatter **7.** vestige **8.** fragment, particle
shrew ... **3.** erd **4.** tana **5.** satan, scold, Sorex, vixen **6.** mammal, migale, tartar **7.** Blarina, outcast, villain **9.** scoundrel, termagant, Xanthippe
shrewd ... **3.** sly **4.** cagy, foxy, sage, wily **5.** acute, canny, harsh, sharp, smart, stern **6.** artful, astute, biting, clever, crafty **7.** cunning, knowing, practic, sapient, subtile **8.** shrewish **9.** sagacious **10.** discerning **11.** penetrating, sharp-witted **13.** perspicacious
shrewdness ... **6.** acumen **9.** smartness **10.** craftiness
shriek ... **3.** cry, yip **4.** yell **5.** laugh **6.** holler, outcry, scream **7.** screech
shrievalty ... **7.** sheriff (office of)
shrill ... **4.** keen, pipy **5.** acute, clear, sharp **6.** biting, squeak **7.** screech **8.** piercing, strident **11.** high-pitched, penetrating
shrimp ... **4.** pink **5.** dwarf, prawn

7. artemia **8.** crevette **10.** crustacean
shrine ... **3.** box **4.** case, tomb **5.** altar, chest **6.** chapel, temple **8.** monument **9.** holy place, reliquary **10.** receptacle
shrine (pert to) ...
ancient.. **4.** naos
Buddhist.. **4.** tope **5.** stupa **9.** Amaravati
India.. **6.** dagoba (dagaba) **7.** chaitya
Mecca.. **5.** Kaaba (Caaba) **11.** Great Mosque
secret, of goddesses.. **9.** anaktoron
shrink ... **5.** cower, parch, quail, rivel, wince **6.** blench, cringe, flinch, huddle, recoil **7.** dwindle, shrivel **8.** contract, draw back **9.** constrict **10.** depreciate
shrinking ... **3.** coy, shy **5.** timid **6.** afraid **9.** recoiling, sensitive **10.** withdrawal **11.** contraction
shrivel ... **3.** age, dry **5.** parch, wizen **6.** shrink, wither **11.** deteriorate
shroud ... **4.** cowl, hide, mask, veil, wrap **5.** cloak, cover, sheet **6.** clothe, screen **7.** conceal, curtain, foliage, protect **8.** cerement **9.** cerecloth **12.** graveclothes
Shrove (pert to) ...
cake.. **7.** pancake
Sunday.. **13.** Quinquagesima
tide.. **9.** pre-Lenten (3 days)
Tuesday.. **9.** Mardi gras **10.** Pancake Day
shrub ... **4.** bush **5.** plant (woody) **6.** frutex **8.** beverage
shrub (pert to) ...
Adam's needle.. **5.** yucca **9.** lady's comb
Arabian tea, narcotic.. **3.** kat
aromatic.. **3.** tea **4.** mint, sage **5.** thyme **6.** Aralia **7.** jasmine (jasmin) **8.** lavender, rosemary
Asian.. **5.** musky **8.** abelmosk
cherry.. **6.** Prunus **7.** Cerasus **12.** laurocerasus
Chinese.. **6.** Kerria
climbing.. **5.** grape, liana, Vitis **8.** Bignonia, clematis **14.** trumpet creeper
creeping.. **5.** pyxie
dogwood.. **6.** aucuba, Cornus
evergreen.. **3.** box, yew **4.** ilex, moss, titi **5.** erica, heath, pyxie, salal, savin **6.** laurel, myrtle **7.** jasmine, juniper **8.** camellia, oleander **9.** mistletoe
flowering.. **5.** lilac **6.** azalea, laurel **7.** spiraea, syringa **10.** mignonette
fragrant.. see aromatic (above)
Hawaiian.. **5.** akala
Mexican.. **7.** guayule **9.** coyotillo
New Zealand.. **4.** tutu **6.** myrtle **8.** ramarama
ornamental.. **8.** hawthorn
parasitic.. **9.** mistletoe
pea.. **5.** broom
pepper.. **4.** kava **8.** kavakava
poisonous.. **4.** tutu **5.** sumac
prickly.. **5.** Rubus **6.** smilax **8.** barberry, dewberry **9.** raspberry **10.** blackberry
S America.. **5.** ceibo
tropical.. **4.** sida, titi **5.** henna **7.** lantana **8.** Oacaceae, tamarisk **10.** frangipani (frangipane)

shrunken . . . **4.** lank, thin **5.** dried
  6. shrunk, wasted **8.** puckered, withered
  9. atrophied, shriveled
shudder . . . **4.** grue **5.** abhor, dread,
  quake **6.** agrise, loathe, quiver, shiver,
  tremor **7.** frisson, tremble
shuffle . . . **3.** mix **5.** scuff, shift **6.** huddle,
  juggle, riffle **7.** confuse, evasion,
  quibble, scuffle **10.** equivocate **12.** walk
  slovenly
shuffle off . . . **5.** evade, shirk **6.** put off
  7. push off **10.** mosey along (sl)
shun . . . **5.** avoid, evade, evite **6.** eschew
  10. escape from **11.** keep clear of
  12. cold shoulder
shut . . . **3.** bar **4.** stop **5.** close **7.** close
  in, exclude **8.** prohibit
shut (pert to) . . .
  in . . **3.** hem **5.** embar **6.** fenced,
    hemmed **7.** bottled, confine, impound,
    invalid, recluse **8.** confined, enclosed
    10. surrounded
  out . . **3.** ban, bar **6.** defeat **7.** exclude,
    lockout, occlude **8.** obstruct, preclude,
    prohibit
  up . . **3.** dam, end **4.** cage, pent
    5. close, mewed, pen in **6.** refute
    7. confine, enclose **8.** conclude,
    imprison **9.** terminate
shutter . . . **3.** lid **4.** gate **5.** blind **6.** screen
  7. seclude **8.** jalousie **9.** diaphragm
shuttle . . . **5.** train **6.** looper, weaver
  7. type bar **9.** alternate, vacillate
  10. oscillator **11.** money drawer
shy . . . **3.** coy, mim **4.** wary **5.** aloof,
  dodge, throw, timid **6.** demure,
  modest, recoil, shrink **7.** bashful,
  evasive, fearful, quibble, rabbity
  8. hesitant, reserved, retiring, secluded,
  sheepish, skittish **9.** diffident, reluctant,
  shrinking **10.** shamefaced, unassuming
  11. distrustful, unobtrusive
Shylock (pert to) . . .
  character in . . **16.** Merchant of Venice
  coin . . **5.** ducat
  daughter . . **7.** Jessica
  famed as . . **6.** usurer **11.** money lender
    12. extortionist
  friend . . **5.** Tubal
shyness . . . **7.** coyness, reserve **8.** timidity
  10. diffidence **11.** bashfulness
Siam . . . **8.** Thailand
Siamese (pert to) . . .
  group . . **3.** Kui, Lao
  temple . . **3.** wat
  twins . . **9.** pygopagus (joined at spine)
    11. Chang and Eng
sib . . . **4.** akin **6.** allied **7.** kinsman, related
  (by blood)
Siberia . . . see also *Siberian*
  city . . **7.** Irkutsk **11.** Novosibirsk
  conqueror . . **9.** Timafeyev **11.** Genghis
    Khan
  government . . **7.** Russian
  gulf . . **2.** Ob (Arctic)
  Mongoloid . . **6.** Tartar
  mountains . . **4.** Ural **5.** Altai
  people . . **5.** Yakut **6.** Tartar (Tatar)
    7. Samoyed **9.** Mongolian
  plain . . **6.** steppe, tundra
  river . . **2.** Ob, Om **4.** Lena **5.** Vitim

  6. Abakan **7.** Yenisei
  squirrel . . **7.** miniver
  storm . . **5.** buran
Siberian (pert to) . . .
  antelope . . **5.** saiga
  hunters, fishers (people) . . **6.** Giliak
    (Gilyak)
  mammal . . **5.** sable
  sled dog . . **7.** Samoyed
  squirrel fur . . **7.** calaber (calabar)
  swamp . . **5.** urman
  tent . . **4.** yurt (yurta)
  windstorm . . **5.** buran (bura)
sibilate . . . **4.** hiss, lisp **8.** aspirate
sibling . . . **5.** child
Sibyl (Gr) . . . **6.** oracle **7.** seeress
  10. prophetess **13.** fortuneteller
Sibylline Books (3) . . . **7.** oracles
  16. prophetic sayings (BC)
sic . . . **4.** thus
siccity . . . **7.** aridity, drought, dryness
sice . . . **3.** six (dice) **8.** sixpence
Sicilian Vespers (pert to) . . .
  Bull (anc) . . **8.** Phalaris
  massacre of . . **6.** French (1282)
Sicily . . .
  aborigines . . **6.** Sicani
  anc name . . **9.** Trinacria
  capital . . **7.** Palermo **8.** Syracuse (anc)
  composer . . **7.** Bellini
  harbor . . **7.** Palermo
  port . . **7.** Messina
  island . . **6.** Lipari (group) **11.** Pantelleria
  river . . **4.** Acis
  secret society . . **5.** Mafia
  volcano . . **4.** Etna **7.** Vulcano **9.** Stromboli
  whirlpool . . **9.** Charybdis
sick . . . **3.** ill, sad, wan **4.** pale **5.** weary
  6. sickly, unwell **9.** disgusted, nauseated
  10. indisposed
sick (pert to) . . .
  be . . **3.** ail
  deathly . . **5.** amort **7.** à la mort, fatally
    10. terminally
  flag . . **6.** yellow **10.** quarantine
  headache . . **8.** migraine
  of . . **7.** tired of **8.** satiated **9.** disgusted
  person . . **7.** patient **9.** aegrotant
  terms . . **3.** bay **7.** hospice **8.** syndrome
    9. infirmary **10.** dispensary **13.** intensive
    care
  worker . . **5.** nurse **11.** nursekeeper
sicken . . . **4.** tire **5.** weary **6.** impair,
  weaken **7.** afflict, depress, surfeit
  8. languish **10.** impoverish
sickly . . . **4.** pale, sick, weak **5.** faint
  6. ailing, feeble, infirm, weakly
  7. languid, mawkish **8.** diseased
  9. unhealthy
Siddhartha, Siddhattha . . . **6.** Buddha
side . . . **4.** face, team, wall **6.** behalf,
  border, region **7.** faction, lateral,
  support, surface **9.** declivity
side (pert to) . . .
  board . . **5.** table **6.** buffet **8.** dressoir,
    whiskers
  by side . . **8.** parallel
  ditch . . **6.** escarp
  drum . . **5.** snare
  hog (salted) . . **6.** flitch
  kick . . **3.** pal **7.** comrade, partner

9. assistant 11. confederate
left.. 4. port 8. larboard
long.. 7. lateral, oblique, sloping
  8. indirect, slanting
meat.. 5. bacon 8. salt pork
of head.. 6. temple
of triangle.. 3. leg
on the side.. 5. apart
sheltered.. 3. lee 4. alee 8. windless
sidewalk salesman.. 8. pitchman
step.. 4. duck 5. dodge, evade, hedge
  6. astral, starry 7. quibble
view.. 7. profile
ways, wise.. 7. athwart, lateral
  9. laterally, obliquely
whiskers.. 9. sideburns 10. sideboards
windy.. 4. port 9. starboard
sidereal... 6. astral, starry 7. stellar
  9. celestial
sidero (comb form)... 4. iron
siderography... 14. steel engraving
siderology (science of)... 4. iron
sides, unequal... 7. scalene
sidle... 4. cant, edge, skew, tilt 7. advance
  (furtive)
siècle... 3. age 7. century
siècle d'or... 9. Golden Age
siege... 7. besiege 8. assieger 9. besetting
  11. besiegement 12. wearying time
  13. beleaguerment
Siegfried (pert to)...
  hero of.. 5. opera (Wagner's)
  slayer.. 5. Hagen
  sword.. 7. Balmung
  wife.. 9. Kriemhild
Sierra Leone...
  capital.. 8. Freetown
  lingua franca.. 4. Krio
  people.. 5. Mende, Temne
Sierra Nevada fog... 7. pogonip
Sierra poet... 13. Joaquin Miller
siesta... 3. nap 4. lull, rest 6. cat nap,
  midday, snooze 10. forty winks
sieve... 3. lue 4. bolt, sift, sile 5. purée
  6. bolter, filter, riddle, semmet, sifter,
  sorter, strain 7. dilluer 8. strainer
  9. segregate, separator
sievelike... 8. cribrate
Sif (Norse), (pert to)...
  goddess of.. 4. home
  wife of.. 4. Thor
sift... 3. lue 4. bolt 5. sieve 6. dredge,
  filter, riddle, screen, sorter, winnow
  7. refiner 8. cribrate
sigh... 3. sob 5. mourn, sithe, yearn
  6. bemoan, bewail, exhale, grieve,
  lament 7. deplore 10. lament over
  11. suspiration
sight... 3. see 4. espy, gaze, view
  5. scene, sense 6. behold, descry,
  vision 7. discern, display 8. aperture
  10. exhibition 11. observation
sight (pert to)...
  acuteness of.. 7. oxyopia
  come into.. 4. loom 5. issue
  disorder.. 7. anopsia 8. paropsis
  imaginary.. 6. vision
  offensive.. 7. eyesore
  out of.. 5. range 6. absent 8. vanished
  9. invisible 10. exorbitant
  11. disappeared

second.. 3. ESP 7. psychic
sigil... 4. seal 5. image (magic), stamp
  8. sigillum 9. signature 11. endorsement
sigmoid... 3. ess 5. curve 9. intestine
sign... 3. cue, nod 4. code, hire,
  mark, neon, omen 5. token, trace
  6. emblem, engage, intone, motion,
  notice, signal, symbol 7. endorse,
  execute, insigne, portent, presage,
  symptom, vestige, warning 8. evidence,
  password 9. semaphore, subscribe,
  watchword 10. forerunner, indication,
  underwrite 11. countersign
  13. advertisement, constellation
sign (pert to)...
  astrological.. 5. Aries 6. Gemini, Pisces,
  Taurus 8. Aquarius 9. Capricorn
  11. Sagittarius
  briefly.. 7. initial
  by the same.. 8. likewise, moreover
  11. accordingly
  diacritical.. 5. tilde 7. cedilla
  language.. 11. dactylology
  music.. 5. presa
  off.. 8. withdraw 10. Yours truly
  11. discontinue
  ref to.. 5. semic 7. semeion
  representing a word.. 8. logogram
  spiritual.. 9. sacrament
  up.. 4. join 6. enlist 8. register
  zodiac.. see *astrological (above)*
signal... 3. cue 4. code, fire, flag,
  sign 5. alarm, flare, token 6. beacon,
  emblem, notify, wigwag 7. eminent,
  lantern, notable, warning 8. striking
  9. memorable, prominent, semaphore,
  watchword 10. lighthouse, remarkable
  11. communicate, conspicuous
  13. extraordinary
signal (pert to)...
  aviator's.. 5. roger
  danger, warning.. 4. bell 5. alert, fusee
  flag.. 6. ensign, wigwag
  night.. 6. beacon, curlew, pharos
  10. lighthouse
  preceding taps.. 6. tattoo
  railroad.. 5. fusee 9. semaphore
signature... 4. mark, sign, visa (vise)
  5. prima, sigil, stamp 6. signum
  9. autograph 11. endorsement
signed by writer... 9. onomatous (opp
  of anonymous)
signet... 4. mark, seal 5. sigil, stamp
  9. signature 10. impression
  11. endorsement
significance... 6. import, moment,
  weight 7. anagoge, meaning
significant... 4. sign 5. token 6. symbol
  7. ominous 8. sinister 9. important,
  momentous 10. expressive, indicative,
  meaningful, portentous, suggestive
  13. consequential
signification... 6. import 7. meaning
  10. indication 11. consequence
  12. notification 13. comprehension,
  specification
signify... 4. hint, mean, sign 5. imply,
  utter 6. denote, import, matter, signal
  7. betoken, connote, declare, specify
  8. announce, evidence, foreshow,
  indicate, intimate, manifest

11. communicate
signum . . . **4.** bell (tower), mark, sign **5.** cross **9.** signature
sika . . . **4.** deer
sike . . . **4.** rill **5.** brook, ditch, gully **6.** ravine, stream, trench
sikhara, sikhra . . . **5.** tower (pyramidal)
silage . . . **4.** feed **6.** fodder **9.** pasturage, provender
Silas (pert to) . . .
  Bib . . **7.** prophet **8.** Silvanus
  character . . **4.** Wegg
  companion of . . **4.** Paul (Bib)
  novel . . **11.** Silas Marner
sile . . . **3.** fry **4.** beam, drip, drop, fall, flow, pass, pour, sink, skim **5.** cheat, cover, glide, sieve, spawn **6.** betray, filter, strain, stream **7.** conceal, deceive, herring (young), subside **8.** strainer
silence . . . **3.** gag **4.** hush, kill, lull, mute, rest **5.** quiet, shush, still, tacet **6.** defeat, muffle **7.** confute, repress, secrecy **8.** oblivion, preclude, restrain, suppress **9.** eliminate, stillness **10.** silentness **11.** taciturnity **13.** noiselessness, tacit omission
silent . . . **3.** mum **4.** mute, tace **5.** quiet, still, tacet, tacit **8.** reserved, reticent, taciturn **9.** soundless **10.** speechless **11.** unexpressed **15.** uncommunicative
silhouette . . . **6.** shadow **7.** contour, outline, picture, profile **9.** delineate, hourglass
silica . . . **4.** opal **5.** silex
silicate . . . **4.** mica **8.** calamine, wellsite
silk (pert to) . . .
  ancient . . **6.** Mantua, sendal
  artificial . . **5.** nylon, rayon
  Assam . . **4.** eria
  black . . **5.** crape (mourning), crepe
  brown . . **4.** muga **6.** tussah
  corded . . **6.** faille **7.** Ottoman
  embroidery thread . . **5.** floss **8.** arrasene
  fiber . . **5.** floss
  gland . . **9.** serictery
  gland of . . **7.** spiders **9.** silkworms **11.** insect larva **12.** caterpillars
  gold . . **4.** tash **6.** samite **7.** brocade
  heavy . . **4.** crin
  kind of . . **5.** China, crepe, moiré, ninon, satin, surah, tabby, tulle **6.** pongee, tobine, tussah **7.** taffeta
  lining . . **8.** sarcenet (sarsenet)
  muslin . . **16.** mousseline de soie
  raw . . **8.** marabout
  rustle of . . **6.** scroop
  source . . **6.** cocoon
  thin, glossy . . **7.** alamode
  thread (for velvets) . . **4.** tram (trame)
  unspun . . **6.** sleave
  upholstery . . **7.** tabaret
  waste . . **4.** noil **6.** strass
  watered . . **5.** moiré
  yarn . . **4.** tram **7.** schappe
  yarn size . . **6.** denier
silken . . . **5.** seric, silby, sleek, suave **6.** gentle, smooth, tender **7.** elegant **8.** delicate, lustrous, silklike **9.** luxurious **10.** effeminate **12.** ingratiating
silkworm (pert to) . . .
  Assam . . **3.** eri **4.** eria

China . . **6.** pernyi **9.** Ailanthus
cocoon . . **4.** clew
disease . . **7.** pebrine
genus (moth) . . **6.** Bombyx
India . . **6.** tussah
Japan . . **7.** yamamai
silky . . . **4.** soft **5.** quiet **6.** glossy, smooth **8.** delicate **9.** sericeous **11.** filamentary **12.** ingratiating
silky fabric . . . **6.** barège
sill . . . **4.** base, beam, seat, sile **5.** basis **6.** timber **9.** threshold **10.** foundation
silly . . . **3.** mad **4.** daft, fond **5.** anile, apish, dazed, dense, inane **6.** dottle, simple **7.** asinine, fatuous, foolish, shallow, trivial **9.** brainless **10.** indiscreet **12.** simple-minded
silver . . . **2.** Ag **4.** gray **5.** metal, money, plate, white **6.** argent **7.** bullion **8.** argentum, eloquent, metallic, sterling
silver (pert to) . . .
  alchemy . . **4.** luna **6.** occamy
  alloy . . **6.** billon
  ball . . **4.** pome
  coin . . **6.** tester
  containing . . **5.** lunar
  German . . **6.** albata
  gilded . . **7.** vermeil
  ingots . . **5.** sycee
  jackal . . **9.** silver fox
  lace (with gold) . . **5.** orris **8.** filigree
  leaf . . **4.** foil **8.** hardback **9.** hydrangea, jewelweed **12.** buffalo berry
  oak . . **11.** flannelbush
  tongued . . **7.** musical **8.** eloquent
  uncoined . . **7.** bullion
silversides . . . **5.** smelt **6.** minnow **12.** silver salmon
Silver State . . . **6.** Nevada
silverware . . . **5.** vases **6.** dishes **8.** flatware **9.** ornaments, tableware
silvery . . . **7.** frosted, musical **8.** lustrous, metallic **9.** argentine
simian . . . **3.** ape **6.** monkey **7.** apelike
similar . . . **4.** akin, like, such **5.** alike **7.** uniform **8.** analogic **9.** analogous **11.** homogeneous
similarity . . . **7.** analogy **8.** likeness **11.** homogeneity, resemblance **13.** approximation
simile . . . **8.** allegory, metaphor
simper . . . **5.** smirk **10.** silly smile **13.** affected smile
simple . . . **4.** easy, mere **5.** naive **6.** dorian, oafish **7.** artless **8.** innocent **9.** ingenuous **10.** elementary **11.** open and shut **15.** unsophisticated
simpleton . . . **3.** ass, daw, oaf **4.** boob, dolt, dupe, fool, gaby, gawk, gump, simp, zang **5.** dunce, goose, idiot, ikona, moron, Simon, yokel, zombi **6.** dawkin, gander, nitwit **7.** half-wit **8.** Abderite **9.** greenhorn **10.** nincompoop **11.** Simple Simon
simplicity . . . **6.** purity **7.** modesty, naiveté **9.** clearness, ignorance, innocence, plainness, rusticity **10.** homeliness, humbleness, simpleness **11.** gullibility, informality **13.** ingenuousness **14.** unaffectedness
simplify . . . **7.** clarify, explain, expound

9. elucidate, interpret
simply . . . **5.** alone, truly **6.** barely, easily, merely, purely, really, solely **7.** plainly **10.** informally
simulate . . . **3.** act, ape **4.** sham **5.** feign **6.** affect, assume **7.** imitate **11.** counterfeit
simulated . . . **4.** aped, sham **5.** acted **7.** assumed, feigned, shammed **9.** pretended **10.** fictitious
simurgh, simurg (Myth) . . . **3.** roc **12.** gigantic bird
sin . . . **3.** err **4.** evil, vice **5.** crime, error, guilt, wrong **6.** felony, heresy **7.** offense **8.** iniquity, peccancy **9.** deviation **10.** immorality, wickedness **11.** misdemeanor **13.** transgression
Sinai (pert to) . . .
famed for . . **5.** Moses **15.** Ten Commandments
location . . **6.** Red Sea **11.** Gulf of Aqaba (Akaba)
mountain (Bib) . . **5.** Horeb **6.** Serbal **9.** Catharine, Umm Shomer
sinapis . . . **7.** mustard
sinawa . . . **10.** Ceylon hemp
sinay bean . . . **8.** rice bean
since . . . **2.** as **3.** ago, for **4.** ergo, gone, past, syne **5.** hence, later **7.** already, because, whereas **8.** inasmuch, until now **9.** therefore, thereupon **10.** seeing that **11.** considering **12.** subsequently
sincere . . . **4.** open, pure **5.** frank **6.** candid **7.** correct, earnest, genuine, intense, unmixed, upright, zealous **9.** authentic, unfeigned, veracious **10.** unaffected **11.** unvarnished **13.** unadulterated **15.** straightforward
sincerity . . . **4.** zeal **6.** candor **7.** honesty **10.** heartiness **11.** genuineness, sincereness
sincerity symbol . . . **8.** amethyst
sind . . . **5.** rinse **6.** drench, quench **7.** rinsing
Sind (Ind) . . .
capital . . **7.** Karachi
ibex . . **8.** wild goat
prince . . **5.** ameer
Sindbad's bird . . . **3.** roc
Sindbad the Sailor . . . **9.** character (Arabian Nights)
sindico . . . **7.** trustee **8.** assignee, receiver
sine . . . **7.** without
sinew . . . **4.** thew **5.** nerve, power **6.** muscle, string, tendon
sinewy . . . **4.** firm, wiry **5.** thewy, tough **6.** brawny, strong **7.** fibrose, stringy **8.** powerful, vigorous
sinful . . . **3.** bad **4.** evil **5.** wrong **6.** wicked **7.** vicious **10.** iniquitous **11.** unrighteous
sing . . . **3.** hum, say **4.** hymn, lilt **5.** carol, chant, croon, yodel **6.** intone, warble **7.** rejoice **8.** proclaim, vocalize **9.** celebrate
sing (pert to) . . .
exultantly . . **4.** lilt **7.** chortle **10.** cheerfully
jovially . . **5.** troll
off key . . **4.** flat
or whistle . . **7.** tweedle
shrilly . . **4.** pipe
softly . . **5.** croon

sorrowfully . . **7.** despond **8.** complain
Swisslike . . **5.** yodel
with trills . . **6.** warble **7.** roulade
singe . . . **4.** burn, sear **6.** scorch **8.** discolor
singer . . . **4.** bard, bird, diva, poet **5.** blues, siren, tenor, torch **6.** cantor, hymner **7.** caroler, crooner, warbler, yodeler **8.** minstrel, songster, vocalist **9.** chanteuse, descanter **10.** cantatrice, prima donna **11.** minnesinger
Singhalese tree . . . **4.** poon **5.** domba
singing (pert to) . . .
birds . . **6.** Oscine
canary . . **10.** white whale
fish . . **8.** toadfish
group . . **5.** choir **6.** chorus
Memnon . . **9.** Amenhotep (statue)
ref to . . **5.** melic
single . . . **3.** ace, odd, one **4.** lone, only, sole, unit **6.** simple, unique **8.** sporadic **9.** unmarried
single (pert to) . . .
algebra . . **6.** nomial
comb form . . **3.** uni
odd . . **7.** azygous
racing term . . **4.** heat
tones (one of two) . . **10.** monotonous
singleness . . . **5.** unity **8.** celibacy **9.** sincerity, unmarried
singly . . . **4.** once, only, solo **5.** alone, apart **6.** simply **8.** uniquely **9.** severally **12.** individually, particularly, single-handed
singular . . . **3.** odd **4.** each, rare, sole, unit **5.** queer **6.** unique **7.** eminent, special, strange, unusual **8.** peculiar, separate, uncommon **9.** eccentric, fantastic, whimsical **10.** individual, remarkable, unexampled **11.** exceptional **12.** unparalleled **13.** extraordinary, unprecedented **14.** characteristic
singularity . . . **6.** oddity **7.** oddness, oneness **8.** peculiar **11.** peculiarity **12.** eccentricity **13.** individuality **15.** distinctiveness
Sinic . . . **7.** Chinese, Sinitic
sinister . . . **4.** evil, grim, left **7.** adverse, corrupt, ominous **9.** dishonest, injurious, malicious, underhand **10.** disastrous, portentous **11.** unfortunate
sinistral . . . **7.** baneful **10.** left-handed **12.** illegitimate, inauspicious (opp of dextral)
sink . . . **3.** age, bog, dip, ebb, sag **4.** cave, drop, fall, mire, sump **5.** drain, droop, lapse, lower, quail **6.** cavity, deject, engulf, go down, recede, settle, sicken, weaken **7.** decline, depress, descend, despond **8.** decrease, diminish, submerge **10.** degenerate
sinuous . . . **4.** wavy **7.** winding **9.** deviating, intricate **10.** circuitous
Sioux (pert to) . . .
division . . **5.** Teton **6.** Santee
famed as . . **8.** warriors
people . . **3.** Oto (Otoe) **4.** Crow, Iowa **5.** Omaha, Osage **6.** Dakota, Plains **9.** Winnebago
sip . . . **3.** lap, sup **4.** gulp **5.** drink, quaff, taste **6.** tipple

sircar ... **5.** ruler **6.** master **7.** servant
  8. province (Mogul) **10.** government
sire ... **5.** beget
siren ... **5.** alarm, Circe, deity, lurer, vixen
  7. charmer, enticer, foghorn, Lorelei,
  mermaid **9.** bewitcher, Cleopatra,
  temptress
Sirenia ... **6.** dugong, mammal
  7. manatee **14.** Steller's sea cow
siriasis ... **9.** sunstroke
Sirius ... **4.** star **7.** Dog Star **10.** Canis
  Major, dog of Orion (Gr Myth)
sissy ... **5.** softy **6.** prissy, sister
  10. effeminate, pantywaist
  11. mollycoddle
sister ... **3.** kin, nun, sib **5.** nurse, soror
sisterhood ... **4.** nuns **8.** sorority
Sistrurus ... **11.** rattlesnake
sit ... **3.** fit **4.** isle, loll, pose, rest **5.** brood,
  perch, press, roost, squat **6.** repose
  7. convene **8.** incubate
site ... **4.** ruin, seat **5.** place, scene, venue
  6. locale, locate **8.** location, position
site of Taj Mahal ... **4.** Agra (Ind)
sitting ... **4.** seat **6.** séance, sedent
  7. posture, sessile, session
  10. incubation **11.** convocation
situated ... **3.** lie, set **4.** case, seat **5.** fixed
  6. clutch, placed, plight **9.** ensconced,
  stationed **11.** established
situated (pert to) ...
  at back .. **6.** astern **7.** postern **9.** posterior
  at base .. **5.** basal
  between folds .. **11.** interplical
  in middle .. **6.** medial, median
  on left hand .. **9.** sinistrad
  on right hand .. **6.** dexter
situation ... **3.** job **4.** case, post
  5. place, situs, state **6.** office, plight
  7. station **8.** locality, location, position
  9. condition, placement
situation (pert to) ...
  approximate .. **11.** whereabouts
  difficult .. **6.** scrape **7.** dilemma
  8. quandary **9.** imbroglio
  11. predicament **12.** circumstance
  doomed .. **7.** rattrap
  favorable .. **7.** vantage
  Latin .. **5.** situs
  perplexing .. **6.** strait
  three choices .. **8.** trilemma
Siva, Shiva (pert to) ...
  consort .. **3.** Uma **4.** Devi
  dancer .. **8.** Natajara
  god, deity .. **8.** Hinduism **9.** Destroyer
  title .. **8.** Mahadeva
  trident .. **6.** trisul (trisula)
six (pert to) ...
  balls (Medici) .. **5.** palle
  dice number .. **4.** sice
  eyed .. **9.** senocular
  feet of earth .. **5.** grave
  fold .. **8.** sextuple
  footed .. **7.** hexaped **9.** hexapodal
  group .. **5.** hexad
  lines .. **6.** sestet **7.** sextain
  pence .. **6.** bender **7.** fiddler
  pert to .. **6.** senary
  pointed figure .. **4.** star
  square .. **9.** hexagonal
sixty, sixties ... **5.** cycle, saros **7.** numeral

size ... **3.** cap **4.** area, bulk, pica,
  pope, pott **5.** agate, grade **6.** adjust
  7. arrange, measure, portion **8.** classify
  9. magnitude **10.** gargantuan
  11. measurement
sizzle ... **3.** fry **4.** hiss **5.** speed **7.** be
  angry **10.** effervesce
sjambok ... **4.** flog, whip
skate ... **3.** jag, ray (fish) **4.** plug, skim
  5. glide, horse, scull, spree
skean ... **4.** dirk **6.** dagger
skedaddle ... **4.** bolt, flee, flit **6.** scurry
  7. run away, scamper
skein ... **3.** rap (120 yds), web **4.** hank,
  yarn **6.** thread **7.** spireme **12.** flight
  of fowl
skelder ... **5.** cheat **7.** vagrant
  9. panhandle
skeleton ... **4.** cage **5.** bones, frame,
  mummy **6.** sketch **7.** contour, diagram,
  outline **8.** thinness **9.** framework
skeleton (pert to) ...
  at the feast .. **7.** kill-joy **10.** wet blanket
  11. crapehanger
  English dialect .. **4.** reme
  framework .. **5.** cadre
  in the closet .. **4.** evil **6.** secret
  13. mortification
  key .. **6.** master
  marine animal .. **6.** sponge
  polyp .. **5.** coral
skeptic, sceptic ... **7.** doubter, infidel
  8. aporetic **10.** Pyrrhonist, unbeliever
  11. freethinker, irreligious, nullifidian
skeptical, sceptical ... **8.** doubtful,
  doubting **11.** incredulous, unbelieving
sketch ... **3.** jap, jot **4.** draw, idea, limn,
  plan, skit **5.** draft, trace **6.** apercu,
  design **7.** diagram, drawing, outline
  8. esquisse, treatise **9.** delineate
  11. delineation, description
sketchy ... **5.** rough, vague **10.** unfinished
skewer ... **3.** pin, rod **5.** truss **6.** fasten,
  pierce **9.** brochette
skid ... **4.** clog, shoe, slip, trig **5.** brake,
  check, slide **7.** travois **8.** sideslip
skiff ... **4.** boat, skim **5.** canoe, glide,
  graze **6.** caique **7.** rowboat **11.** slight
  touch
skill ... **3.** art **5.** craft, knack **6.** gifted,
  talent **7.** ability, address, aptness,
  cunning, finesse, mastery **8.** aptitude,
  deftness, facility **9.** adeptness, dexterity,
  expertise, readiness, smartness
  10. adroitness, cleverness, proficient
  11. proficiency
skilled ... **5.** adept **6.** expert **7.** endowed,
  trained **8.** talented **10.** conversant,
  proficient
skilled (pert to) ...
  in government .. **9.** statesman
  in mechanics .. **5.** sloyd
  in strategy .. **7.** finesse
skillful, skilful ... **3.** apt **4.** able, deft, fine
  6. adroit, clever, crafty, daedal, expert
  7. capable **8.** artistic, dextrous, tactical
  9. daedalian, dexterous, ingenious
  10. proficient, well-versed
  12. accomplished
skim ... **4.** flit, sail, scan, scud **5.** glide,
  graze, scoon, skirr **6.** slight **8.** pass

over
skin . . . **4.** bark, derm, fell, flay, hide,
pare, peel, pelt, rind, scum **5.** cheat,
cutis, derma, fraud, scalp **6.** fleece,
lamina, scrape **7.** callous, cuticle,
defraud, swindle **8.** covering, tegument
9. epidermis **10.** integument
11. decorticate
skin (pert to) . . .
animal . . **4.** coat, hide, pelt **7.** pellage
animal's neck fold . . **6.** dewlap
beaver . . **4.** plew
comb form . . **4.** derm **5.** derma
decoration . . **6.** tattoo
destitute of . . **8.** apellous
disease . . **4.** acne **5.** hives, mange, uredo
6. eczema, herpes, tetter **8.** ringworm
9. urticaria
drying frame . . **5.** herse
dryness . . **7.** xerosis
fawnskin (of Dionysus) . . **6.** nebris
fold . . **5.** plica **6.** dewlap
fruit . . **7.** epicarp
gobbler's throat . . **3.** tar
layer . . **5.** cutis, derma
layer, outer . . **7.** epicarp
opening . . **4.** pore
pert to . . **6.** dermal **7.** dermoid
piece . . **5.** blype
pigment, excess . . **8.** melanism
protuberance . . **4.** mole, wart
salting bin . . **5.** kench
squirrel . . **4.** vair
tan . . **3.** taw
tanned . . **5.** suede
unsheared . . **8.** woolfell
skinflint . . . **5.** cheat, miser **9.** bargainer
skink . . . **4.** adda **6.** lizard
skinned . . . **6.** bested **7.** euchred, fleeced
skinned (pert to) . . .
dark . . **7.** melanic, swarthy
pert to . . **5.** bared **7.** denuded **8.** stripped
slang . . **7.** euchred, fleeced
thick . . **9.** pachyderm **11.** pachydermic
skinny . . . **4.** lean, thin **5.** scant **6.** stingy
8. skinlike **9.** emaciated, niggardly
skip . . . **3.** dap **4.** gait, jump, leap, omit
5. bound, caper, elide, frisk, salto, vault
6. gambol, lackey, spring **7.** abscond
8. ricochet
skipjack . . . **3.** fop **4.** pike **5.** saury
6. bonito **7.** bounder, parvenu, upstart
8. bluefish, sailboat **9.** stripling
(conceited) **10.** butterfish **14.** snapping
beetle
skipper . . . **5.** saury **6.** locust, maggot,
master, serang **8.** skipjack **9.** butterfly
11. grasshopper
ski race (obstacle) . . . **6.** slalom
ski resort . . . **4.** Vail **5.** Aspen
skirling . . . **5.** trout **6.** salmon
skirmish . . . **4.** fray **5.** brush, clash,
melee **6.** combat **8.** conflict, flourish
9. encounter **10.** velitation
skirt . . . **5.** dress, evade, woman **6.** border,
edging, fringe **9.** appendage,
baseboard, periphery, petticoat **10.** pass
around, saddle part
skirt (pert to) . . .
armor . . **5.** tasse (tace) **7.** lamboys
attached to blouse . . **6.** peplum

chaser . . **9.** libertine **11.** philanderer
dance . . **6.** ballet
short . . **4.** kilt
skit . . . **4.** joke, play **5.** caper **6.** parody,
shower, sketch
skittish . . . **3.** coy, shy **5.** jumpy **6.** fickle,
frisky, tricky **7.** bashful **8.** unstable,
volatile **9.** excitable **10.** capricious
13. irresponsible
skittles . . . **4.** game, play **8.** ninepins
9. enjoyment (not all beer and skittles)
skoal . . . **5.** toast **10.** salutation
11. exclamation **14.** pledge of health
skulk . . . **4.** lurk **5.** cower, dodge, hedge,
sneak **8.** malinger
skull . . . **4.** bean, head, mind **5.** brain
7. cranium, harnpan **8.** brain box
skull (pert to) . . .
cap . . **6.** beanie **7.** calotte **9.** zucchetto
10. berrettino
cavity . . **5.** fossa
measure . . **11.** craniometer
monk's . . **6.** pileus
operation . . **6.** trepan
part . . **5.** inion **6.** bregma **7.** calotte,
occiput
ref to . . **5.** inial **6.** cranic **7.** cranial
science of . . **10.** craniology
skull and crossbones . . . **5.** death (symb)
10. danger sign
skunk . . . **5.** zoril **6.** defeat **7.** fitchew,
polecat, stinker **8.** conepate (conepati)
zorrillo **9.** scoundrel
sky . . . **4.** blue **5.** ether, vault **6.** caelum,
canopy, heaven, welkin **7.** heavens,
the blue **8.** empyrean **9.** firmament
10. blue yonder
sky (pert to) . . .
color . . **4.** blue **5.** azure **7.** celeste
8. cerulean
god . . **3.** Anu
lark . . **5.** pipit **6.** Alauda, frolic **7.** titlark
light . . **6.** window **8.** abatjour
lure . . **7.** horizon
parlor . . **6.** attic **6.** garret
pilot . . **8.** chaplain **9.** clergyman
10. missionary
serpent . . **3.** Ahi
slab . . . **3.** mud **4.** tile **5.** board, dalle,
plank, slime **6.** lamina, ledger, pillar
(stone), puddle **7.** portion **8.** monument
9. flagstone
slab (pert to) . . .
grave . . **5.** stele (stela)
marble . . **5.** dalle **6.** tablet
slablike . . **6.** stelar
slack . . . **3.** lax **4.** lull, slow **5.** chaff, inert,
let up, loose, shirk, tardy **6.** abated,
remiss **7.** relaxed **8.** careless, dilatory,
inactive, indolent, sluggish **9.** reluctant,
secondary **10.** diminished, inadequate
11. inattentive
slacken . . . **5.** abate, delay, relax **6.** loosen,
reduce, repose, retard **7.** let down,
relieve **8.** hold back
slackening of strained relations . . .
7. detente (Internat)
slag . . . **4.** lava **5.** dross **6.** cinder, scoria
7. residue **9.** recrement **11.** agglomerate
slain . . . **4.** dead **6.** fallen, killed
8. murdered **12.** assassinated

slake . . . **4.** cool, sate **5.** abate, allay, slack **6.** quench **7.** assuage, crumble, hydrate, refresh, relieve, satisfy, slacken **8.** decrease, mitigate, moderate **10.** extinguish **12.** disintegrate

slam . . . **4.** bang, blow, give, shut, vole **5.** abuse, score **6.** impact **9.** criticism, criticize

slander . . . **5.** belie, libel, smear **6.** defame, malign, vilify **7.** asperse, blacken, distort, traduce **8.** derogate, disgrace, reproach **10.** defamation, scandalize **12.** misrepresent

slang . . . **4.** cant **5.** argot **6.** jargon, patois **7.** hep talk **10.** vernacular

slant . . . **4.** bend, cant, skew **5.** angle, bevel, slope **6.** aslant, aspect, biased, glance **7.** incline, opinion **8.** attitude, occasion **9.** obliquely, viewpoint **10.** hypotenuse **11.** inclination, opportunity

slap . . . **3.** hit **4.** blow, clap, cuff, snub **5.** crack, skelp, sound, twank **6.** buffet, rebuff, slight, strike **8.** chastise **12.** chastisement

slash . . . **3.** cut **4.** gash, lash, slit **5.** marsh, sever **6.** attack, reduce, stripe **7.** censure, scourge **8.** price cut **9.** criticize, reduction

slate . . . **4.** list, rock **5.** color, scold, sculp **6.** ballot, enroll, record, roster, tablet, thrash **7.** censure, roofing, writing **8.** register, schedule, slattern **9.** criticize, reprimand

slate (pert to) . . .
 ax . . **7.** mattock
 black . . **4.** gray
 blue . . **9.** Swiss blue
 gray . . **7.** Russian **9.** red-yellow **10.** sandy beige **13.** oriental pearl
 roof . . **3.** rag
 tool . . **3.** zax **7.** scantle

slater . . . **6.** critic **7.** hellier

slattern . . . **4.** slut **5.** frump, idler, mopsy **6.** sloppy **7.** trifler, trollop **8.** careless, slovenly **9.** litterbug

slaughter . . . **4.** kill, slay **6.** battue, murder, pogrom **7.** butcher, carnage, killing **8.** butchery, hecatomb, massacre, occision **9.** bloodshed **10.** butchering **11.** destruction

slaughterhouse . . . **8.** abattoir, Aceldama, butchery, matadero, shambles **9.** stockyard **12.** field of blood

Slav . . . **4.** Pole, Slav, Sorb, Wend **5.** Croat, Czech **6.** Slovak **7.** Russian, Serbian, Servian **8.** Bohemian, Croatian, Moravian **9.** Bulgarian

slave . . . **4.** boor, esne, peon, serf **5.** chela, helot, thane **6.** drudge, lascar, minion, thrall, vassal **7.** bondman, captive, chattel, enslave, odalisk, servant **8.** slave ant **9.** bondslave

slave (pert to) . . .
 block (selling) . . **7.** catasta
 born . . **4.** neif
 comedy (stock name) . . **5.** Davus
 dealer . . **5.** bichy, mango (obs)
 Eleusinian (Gr Relig) . . **5.** Baubo, lambe
 female . . **9.** concubine, odalisque (odalisk)

free . . **5.** thane (thegn)
fugitive . . **8.** marooner
Indian . . **10.** Athapascan
The Tempest . . **7.** Caliban

slavery . . . **4.** bond **7.** bondage, service **8.** drudgery **9.** captivity, servitude, thralldom, vassalage **11.** enslavement **12.** enthrallment

Slave States . . . **5.** Texas **7.** Alabama, Florida, Georgia **8.** Arkansas, Delaware, Kentucky, Maryland, Missouri, Virginia **9.** Louisiana, Tennessee **11.** Mississippi **13.** North Carolina, South Carolina

slay . . . **4.** kill **5.** amuse, burke, knock, lynch, smite **6.** murder, strike **7.** butcher, destroy **9.** slaughter **10.** annihilate **11.** assassinate, destroy life, exterminate

slayer . . . **6.** killer **8.** criminal, murderer, regicide, vaticide **9.** matricide, patricide **10.** fratricide, sororicide

sleave . . . **4.** sley **5.** floss **6.** tangle **8.** separate **9.** floss silk **11.** disentangle **13.** untwisted silk

sled . . . **4.** luge, pung **6.** sledge, sleigh, travoy, troika **8.** toboggan

sledge . . . **4.** sled **6.** hammer, sleigh, strike **7.** seven-up (game), vehicle

sleep . . . **3.** nap, nod **4.** dorm, doss, doze, wink **5.** death, sopor **6.** drowse, snooze, somnus **7.** slumber **10.** narcolepsy, somnipathy **11.** hibernation

sleep (pert to) . . .
 comb form . . **5.** somni
 deep . . **6.** stupor **8.** lethargy **10.** narcolepsy
 dreaming stage . . **3.** REM
 hypnotic . . **10.** somnipathy
 inducing . . **5.** dwale **6.** opiate, potion **8.** sedative **9.** soporific **10.** anesthesia, belladonna
 insensible . . **4.** coma
 midday . . **6.** siesta
 prolonged . . **5.** sopor
 upon . . **8.** consider, postpone

sleeper . . . **3.** tie **4.** beam **6.** rafter, rester, timber **7.** Pullman, reposer, support **8.** dormouse **9.** slumberer **10.** slow seller **11.** sleeping car

sleeping . . . **4.** dead **5.** inert **6.** asleep, latent **7.** dormant **8.** dormient, inactive **9.** quiescent **10.** quiescence **11.** inattentive

sleeping (pert to) . . .
 pill . . **9.** soporific
 place . . **3.** bed, cot **4.** bunk, doss **5.** berth, couch **6.** pallet **7.** cubicle **9.** dormitory
 sickness . . **6.** nagana, tsetse **9.** lethargus

sleepwalking . . . **8.** neurosis **12.** nightwalking, somnambulism

sleepy . . . **4.** dull **5.** tired **6.** drowsy **8.** soporose **9.** lethargic, somnolent **11.** somniferous

sleeve . . . **3.** arm **5.** gigot (leg-ó-mutton) **10.** copper tube **14.** British channel

sleigh . . . **4.** pung **6.** cutter

sleight of hand performer . . . **4.** mage **8.** magician **14.** legerdemainist **15.** prestidigitator

slender . . . **4.** lank, lean, slim, thin **5.** gaunt, lanky, leger, reedy **6.** lissom, narrow, svelte 7. gracile, tenuous, trivial, willowy 9. elongated

slender pinnacle . . . 3. epi

sleuth . . . 6. tracer 8. hawkshaw 9. detective, sleuthdog 11. sleuthhound 12. investigator

slice . . . 3. cut, saw 4. gash, slab 5. piece, share, shave 6. rasher, sliver, stroke 7. portion 8. golf term, splinter 12. cross section

slick . . . 4. neat, tidy 5. alert, sleek, smart 6. clever, smooth 8. slippery, unctuous 9. first-rate, lubricate 10. glistening 12. accomplished

slide . . . 3. ski 4. rule, skid, slip, slue 5. chute, clasp, glide, plane (sloping), scoot, skate 6. elapse 7. lantern, slither 8. toboggan 9. avalanche 11. deteriorate

slight . . . 3. cut 4. defy, rare, snub, thin 5. faint, frail, leger, minor, oligo (comb form), scorn, small 6. flimsy, ignore, little, meager 7. disdain, fragile, neglect, nominal, scantly, shallow, trivial 8. contempt, delicate 9. disregard, indignity 10. immaterial 11. unimportant 13. imperceptible, unsubstantial 14. inconsiderable

slight (pert to) . . .
  convexity . . 6. camber
  sound . . 4. peep
  variation . . 6. nuance 7. shading

slightest . . . 5. least 6. barest

slightly (pert to) . . .
  damaged paper . . 6. retree
  sour . . 8. acescent
  tapering . . 6. terete

slim . . . 3. sly 4. lean, mean, thin 5. small, spare 6. adroit, scanty, sparse, svelte 7. slender, tenuous 9. worthless

slime . . . 3. mud 4. ooze 5. filth, gleet 6. mucous

slip . . . 3. err, pew, sin 4. dock, fail, pier, skid, slue 5. boner, cover, error, fault, glide, lapse, slide, strip 6. bungle, elapse 7. blunder, cutting, failure, faux pas, misdeed, mistake, slither 9. youngling 10. pillowslip 12. undergarment 13. transgression

slipknot . . . 5. noose

slipper . . . 4. mule, neap, shoe 5. apron, moyle, Romeo 6. pinson, sandal 7. scuffer 8. babouche (baboosh), covering

slippery . . . 3. sly 4. eely, glib 5. slick 6. crafty, fickle, shifty, tricky, wanton 7. cunning, elusive, evasive 8. unctuous, unstable 9. deceitful, uncertain 10. intangible, precarious, unreliable 11. treacherous 13. untrustworthy

slit . . . 4. kerf 5. cleft, slash, split 6. furrow 7. severed

slither . . . 5. crawl, glide, sidle, slide

sliver . . . 3. cut 5. shred, slice, split 8. fragment, splinter

sloe . . . 3. haw 4. plum

sloe (pert to) . . .
  berry . . 7. juniper
  bush . . 10. blackthorn
  color . . 9. blue-black
  fruit (blackthorn) . . 3. haw 4. sloe
  gin . . 12. sloe-flavored

slogan . . . 3. cry 5. motto 6. phrase 9. catchword, watchword 10. shibboleth (Bib)

sloop . . . 5. yacht 6. cutter, schuit (schuyt) 7. eelboat

slope . . . 3. dip, lie 4. bank, hade, ramp 5. bevel, scarp, slant, talus 6. calade, decamp, escarp, glacis 7. terrace 9. declivity 10. declension 11. inclination

sloping bank . . . 4. brae 7. terrace

sloth . . . 2. ai 4. pack (bears), pazy, unau 6. acedia, mammal 7. inertia 8. idleness, slowness 9. indolence

slothful . . . 4. lazy 8. inactive, indolent, sluggish

sloth monkey . . . 5. lemur, loris

slough . . . 3. bog 4. husk, mire, molt, shed, skin 5. bayou, swamp 7. channel, discard

sloughing . . . 7. ecdysis, molting 8. shedding 10. discarding

slovenly . . . 5. dowdy, messy, tacky 6. frowzy, sloppy, untidy 8. careless, slattern, slipshod 9. negligent 10. disheveled, disorderly, slatternly

slow . . . 4. dull, late, poky 5. delay, inert, relax 6. boring, hinder, retard, stupid 7. slacken 8. boresome, dilatory, inactive, moderate 9. lingering 20. inch by inch phlegmatic 13. unprogressive

slow (pert to) . . .
  action . . 6. dawdle 10. deliberate
  adverb . . 10. behindhand
  down . . 4. idle 6. retard 8. wind down 10. decelerate
  music . . 5. largo, lento, molto, tardo 6. adagio 7. andante 8. lentando 10. lentamento
  poke . . 5. snail 7. dawdler
  up . . 3. lag 6. retard 7. decline
  witted . . 4. dull 6. stupid

sludge . . . 3. mud 4. gunk, mire, ooze 5. slime 8. sediment

slug . . . 3. hit 4. blow, dose 5. Arion, drink, drone, idler, Limax, space, token 6. bullet, loiter, nugget 7. trepang 8. sluggard 9. gastropod

sluggish . . . 4. logy, slow 5. dopey, inert 6. drowsy, stupid, supine 7. dronish, languid 8. dilatory, inactive, indolent, listless, stagnant 9. stagnancy, stupidity, torpidity

sluice . . . 4. race 5. flush 6. drench, stream 7. channel 9. floodgate

slumber . . . 4. doze 5. sleep 6. catnap, drowse, repose, snooze, somnus 14. arms of Morpheus

slump . . . 4. drop, fall 7. decline, descend, dessert, sinkage 9. fall short 10. depreciate, depression

slur . . . 4. blur 5. elide 6. defame, insult, mackle, slight, stigma 7. calumny, traduce 8. disgrace, innuendo, reproach, skim over 9. aspersion, disparage 10. calumniate, stigmatize

slush . . . 3. mud 4. mire, snow 5. slime 14. sentimentality

sly . . . 4. arch, foxy, wary, wily, wink 5. cagey, catty, snaky 6. covert, crafty, feline, shrewd, sneaky, subtle 7. cunning, furtive 8. craftily

9. underhand **11.** mischievous,
underhanded **15.** surreptitiously
smack . . . **3.** bit, bop **4.** bang, belt, buss,
glow, kiss, tang **5.** clout, taste **6.** strike,
vessel, wallop **8.** chastise, sailboat
smacking . . . **5.** brisk **6.** lively **7.** dashing
8. spanking, vigorous **9.** energetic
small . . . **3.** tot, wee **4.** thin, tiny, wisp
5. dwarf, petty **6.** humble, little, meager,
minute, modest, petite **7.** faintly, trivial
8. picayune, trifling **9.** miniature,
minuscule, thumbnail **10.** diminutive,
undersized **11.** unimportant
13. insignificant **14.** contemptuously,
inconsiderable
small (pert to) . . .
amount . . **3.** dab **4.** dram **5.** minim
6. morsel **7.** modicum **8.** pittance
anvil . . **5.** teest
area . . **6.** areola (areole)
armadillo . . **4.** peba
arms . . **3.** bow **5.** rifle, sword **6.** pistol
7. carbine, grenade
attractive . . **4.** cute **5.** dainty
bomb . . **6.** petard **7.** grenade
bottle . . **4.** vial **5.** phial
case, handbag . . **4.** etui
comb form . . **5.** lepto, micro
dab . . **3.** pat, wad **5.** chunk
deer . . **4.** fawn, napu
delicately . . **6.** mignon
distance . . **3.** hop **4.** step
drink . . **3.** nip **4.** pony, swig
drum . . **5.** bongo, tabor
field . . **5.** croft
fish . . **3.** ide
flag . . **6.** fanion
fruits . . **10.** low growing
fry . . **4.** fish, kids, tots **8.** children
10. youngsters
insect . . **4.** flea **5.** midge
island . . **3.** ait **4.** isle
lake . . **4.** mere, pond
law . . **5.** petit
minded . . **4.** mean **5.** petty **6.** biased
10. prejudiced, vindictive
neat . . **6.** dapper
number . . **3.** few **7.** paucity
opening . . **4.** pore **5.** stoma **7.** orifice
ox . . **4.** anoa
part . . **4.** iota **6.** detail **7.** snippet
particle . . **4.** atom, mote **8.** molecule
people . . **5.** elves **6.** common **7.** fairies,
midgets, Pygmies
piece . . **3.** mot **4.** chip, tate **5.** speck
7. driblet, morceau
post . . **9.** paper size
quantity . . **4.** drop, mite **5.** trace
7. handful
rope (Naut) . . **7.** marline (marling)
Scot . . **3.** sma, wee
shield . . **3.** écu **9.** scutellum
stream . . **3.** run **4.** rill **6.** rillet
surface . . **5.** facet
talk . . **6.** babble **7.** prattle **8.** chitchat
task . . **5.** chore **6.** odd job
things . . **3.** fry
tower . . **6.** turret **7.** minaret
very . . **3.** wee **8.** picayune **11.** Lilliputian
world . . **9.** microcosm
smallpox . . . **7.** variola

smaragd . . . **7.** emerald
smart . . . **3.** apt **4.** chic, perk, posh, trig,
trim, wise **5.** acute, alert, natty, nifty,
quick, sting **6.** astute, clever, shrewd,
spruce, trendy **7.** dashing, painful,
pungent, stylish **8.** impudent, poignant,
pricking **9.** competent, ingenious
10. precocious **11.** fashionable,
intelligent
smash . . . **4.** blow, mash, pulp, ruin
5. break, crush, drink (spirits), stave,
wreck **6.** defeat **7.** collide, debacle,
destroy, failure, shatter, success
8. accident, beverage **9.** collision,
pulverize
smear . . . **3.** dab, rub **4.** daub, gaum
5. slake, stain, sully **6.** anoint, bedaub,
defame, defile, grease, malign, smirch,
smudge **7.** besmear, plaster, pollute,
slander **8.** besmirch
smear with . . .
egg white . . **5.** glair **8.** meringue
mud . . **5.** slime
ointment . . **6.** anoint
smell . . . **4.** odor, olid, reek **5.** aroma,
fetor, scent, sense, sniff, stink **6.** detect
7. perfume **9.** fragrance, redolence
10. atmosphere
smell (pert to) . . .
acute . . **8.** oxyrhine
loss of sense of . . **7.** anosmia
offensive . . **3.** bad **4.** foul, olid **5.** fetor
6. stench
sense of . . **6.** osmics **7.** osmesis
9. olfaction
smelling salts . . . **9.** hartshorn
17. ammonium carbonate
smelt . . . **4.** fish, fuse, melt **6.** tomcod
7. scorify **10.** silverside
smilax . . . **8.** catbrier **10.** greenbrier
smile . . . **4.** grin **5.** laugh, smirk, sneer
6. simper **8.** greeting
smiling . . . **5.** agrin, merry, riant **6.** rident
8. gleaming, grinning
smirch . . . **4.** blot **5.** smear, stain, sully,
taint **6.** blotch, smutch, stigma, vilify
7. begrime, blacken, blemish, tarnish
8. discolor **10.** blackening
smirk . . . **4.** grin, leer **6.** simper
smite . . . **4.** kill, slap **6.** lay low, strike
7. chasten, impress, inflict, trouble
8. chastise
smithy . . . **6.** forger, stithy **7.** farrier
8. smithery **10.** blacksmith
smock . . . **5.** kamis, shift, tunic, woman
(obs) **7.** chemise **9.** philander
11. overgarment
smoke . . . **4.** burn, cure, floc, fume, pipe
5. cigar, cloud, cubeb, flume, smook,
vapor **6.** smudge **7.** incense, tobacco
8. fumigate, preserve **9.** cigarette
smokestack . . . **6.** funnel **7.** chimney
8. fumiduct
smoking apparatus (Orient) . . . **7.** tabagie
8. narghile (nargile)
smolder, smoulder . . . **4.** burn **5.** choke,
smoke **6.** smudge **7.** smother
9. suffocate
smooth . . . **4.** comb, ease, even, iron,
lene, pave **5.** bland, clear, level, plane,
press, sleek, slick, suave **6.** glossy,

mangle, pacify, urbane **7.** uniform
8. hairless, unctuous **10.** facilitate,
flattering **12.** frictionless, ingratiating
smooth (pert to) . . .
breathing . . **13.** spiritus lenis
comb form . . **3.** lio
feathers, hair . . **5.** preen
hard, transparent . . **6.** glassy
phonetically . . **4.** lene
tare . . **12.** slender vetch
tongued . . **4.** glib **5.** suave
12. hypocritical
smooth and . . .
soft . . **5.** furry, silky, soapy **7.** velvety
soothing . . **5.** bland
sweet . . **11.** mellifluent
white . . **11.** alabastrine
smother . . . **4.** daub, kill **5.** befog, choke,
cover **6.** deaden, hush up, muffle, stifle,
welter **7.** overlie, smolder **8.** suppress
9. suffocate, to blanket **11.** exterminate
smudge . . . **4.** blot, smut, soil, spot
5. smear, smoke, stain **6.** smutch
7. begrime, smolder
smug . . . **4.** neat, tidy, trim **5.** smart,
suave **6.** pilfer **7.** correct **9.** confident
10. complacent **13.** self-satisfied
smuggler . . . **6.** runner **9.** rumrunner
13. contrabandist
smur . . . **4.** mist **5.** cloud, smurr **7.** drizzle
Smyrna . . . **5.** Izmir (present name)
Smyrna fig . . . **5.** eleme (elemi)
Smyrna melon . . . **6.** casaba
snack . . . **4.** nosh
snail . . . **4.** slug **5.** drone, Helix, Mitra,
whelk **6.** Nerita, Triton **7.** mollusk
9. gastropod **10.** periwinkle
snake . . . **3.** asp, ess **4.** tree, worm
5. adder, cobra, coral, racer, viper
6. garter, gopher **7.** hognose, rattler,
reptile **8.** Micrurus, moccasin
9. Heterodon **10.** bushmaster,
copperhead, sidewinder
11. cottonmouth, diamondback,
rattlesnake **12.** schaapsteker
snake (pert to) . . .
African . . **5.** mamba
bird . . **6.** darter
black . . **5.** racer
cobra . . **3.** nag (naga)
comb form . . **5.** ophio, ophis **6.** herpes
crusher . . **6.** python **8.** anaconda **14.** boa
constrictor
dance . . **4.** Hopi **6.** ophism
division (serpents) . . **7.** Ophidia
9. Serpentes
expert . . **13.** herpetologist
fear of . . **13.** herpetophobia
Florida . . **8.** moccasin
front-fanged . . **5.** cobra, mamba **6.** elapid
8. Elapinne
garter . . **5.** Elaps
genus . . **7.** Ophidia
heraldic . . **5.** bisse
horned . . **8.** cerastes
India . . **5.** krait **6.** bongar
killer . . **8.** mongoose
like . . **7.** ophioid **9.** colubrine
mouth . . **6.** orchid
movement . . **4.** coil, drag, wind **5.** crawl,
sneak, twist

mythical . . **6.** Python (on Mt Parnassus)
nonpoisonous . . **4.** king **6.** garter, gopher
9. Colubrina
pert to . . **5.** ophic **7.** anguine **8.** viperine
9. colubrine, scoundrel
poisonous . . **3.** asp **5.** adder, coral
7. rattler **8.** moccasin **10.** copperhead
11. cottonmouth **13.** thanatophidia
python . . **8.** anaconda
python deity . . **5.** zombi (zombie)
reptilelike . . **9.** herpetoid
Russell's viper . . **6.** daboia, jessur
sacred . . **6.** Shesha
S America . . **5.** aboma
sand snake . . **4.** Eryx
semihuman, race of . . **4.** Naga
shaped . . **9.** anguiform
skin . . **6.** exuvia
spitting . . **8.** ringhals
snaky . . . **3.** sly **4.** wavy **7.** anguine,
sinuous, wriggly **8.** spiteful, twisting,
venomous **9.** snakelike **10.** perfidious,
serpentine **11.** treacherous
snaky sisters . . . **6.** Erinys **17.** snaky-
haired Furies
snap . . . **3.** bit **4.** bite, flip **5.** break, crack,
flick, quick, snarl, thump **6.** energy,
fasten, fillip (fingers) **7.** bargain, crackle
8. easy task, handcuff, snapshot
9. crispness, fastening, smartness
10. gingersnap, photograph, resilience
11. sharp retort
snapper . . . **4.** bean, sesi **5.** error, pargo
6. beetle, bonbon, tamure, turtle
7. cracker, grouper **8.** fastener, rosefish
9. countfish **10.** stitchwort, stringbean,
woodpecker **11.** firecracker
snappy . . . **4.** cold, fast **5.** quick **6.** lively,
sudden **7.** pungent **8.** snappish
9. crackling, energetic
snare . . . **3.** beg, gin, net, web **4.** lure,
mesh, trap **5.** benet, catch, noose, steal
6. entoil, trepan **7.** pitfall **9.** deception
snark . . . **3.** nag **5.** snort **6.** boojum
8. creature (fabled)
snarl . . . **4.** gnar, knot **5.** gnarr, growl,
scold, snare **6.** tangle **7.** confuse,
ensnare, grumble, quarrel **8.** complain,
entangle **9.** confusion **10.** complicate
12. complication
snatch . . . **4.** grab, jerk, take **5.** catch,
erept, grasp, gripe, pluck, seize, steal,
wrest **6.** clutch, kidnap, rescue **7.** seizure
sneak . . . **4.** lead (game), lurk **5.** cower,
creep, knave, slink, snoop **6.** coward,
cringe, tattle **7.** smuggle **11.** furtive
move
sneaking . . . **3.** sly **4.** mean, poor
6. craven, hidden, paltry, secret
7. furtive **8.** cowardly, stealthy
9. dastardly, niggardly, underhand
12. contemptible **13.** surreptitious
sneer . . . **4.** gibe, jeer, mock **5.** fleer,
flout, laugh, scoff, scorn
sneer, expressive . . . **8.** sardonic
snell . . . **4.** keen **5.** acute, eager, quick,
sharp, snood, swift **6.** active, biting,
severe **7.** caustic, pungent **8.** piercing
snicker . . . **5.** laugh, neigh, sneer **6.** giggle,
nicker, tittle, whinny **7.** snigger
8. laughter

sniff ... **4.** nose **5.** scent, smell, snuff
  6. detect, inhale **7.** sniffle **8.** sibilate,
  smell out **14.** show of contempt
snifter ... **3.** nip **4.** dram, good **5.** drink,
  sniff, snort **6.** snivel **9.** excellent
snip ... **3.** bit, cut **4.** clip, snap **5.** notch,
  piece, shred **8.** fragment, particle
snipe (pert to) ...
  eel .. **6.** thread
  flock .. **4.** wisp
  game .. **6.** godwit
  hawk .. **7.** harrier
  verb .. **7.** shoot at **10.** sharpshoot
snippy ... **4.** curt, tart **5.** brief, sharp
  8. snippety, snobbish **11.** fragmentary
  12. supercilious
snirl ... **5.** gnarl, snare **6.** tangle **7.** wrinkle
snitch ... **5.** pinch, steal **6.** betray, inform,
  pilfer, snatch, tattle **8.** informer, particle
snob ... **4.** prig **7.** cobbler, parvenu
  8. bluenose, commoner, courtier
  9. sycophant
snobby, snobbish ... **5.** proud **6.** uppish
  7. haughty **8.** arrogant **9.** exclusive
  11. overbearing
snood ... **5.** snell **6.** fillet **7.** hairnet
snook ... **4.** fish **5.** smell **6.** robalo, search
  9. barracuda
snoop ... **3.** pry **4.** nose **5.** prowl, sneak
  6. meddle **7.** meddler **8.** busybody
  10. sneak thief
snooze ... **3.** nap **4.** doze **5.** sleep
  6. cuddle, nuzzle, siesta **7.** snoozle,
  snuggle
snore, snoring ... **4.** rale **5.** sleep
  7. stertor **8.** rhonchus, sibilate
  10. sibilation, stertorous **15.** hoarse
  breathing
snort ... **5.** drink, grunt, laugh, snore
snotty ... **5.** dirty, nasty **6.** offish,
  snooty **7.** high-hat **9.** offensive
  12. contemptible, supercilious
snow ... **4.** firn, neve **5.** opium **8.** narcotic
  12. interference
snow (pert to) ...
  bunting .. **5.** finch **9.** snowflake
  glacial .. **4.** firn, neve
  grouse, quail .. **9.** ptarmigan
  house .. **5.** igloo
  leopard .. **5.** ounce
  lily .. **6.** violet (white)
  living in .. **5.** nival
  mouse .. **4.** vole **7.** lemming
  ref to .. **5.** nival
  ridges .. **8.** sastrugi (zastrugi)
  runner .. **3.** ski **4.** sled
  shoe .. **3.** pac **7.** webfoot
  sliding .. **9.** avalanche
  slope .. **8.** glissade
snub ... **3.** cut **5.** check, quell, scold
  6. cut off, ignore, rebuff, rebuke,
  slight **7.** neglect, shorten **8.** restrain
  9. reprimand **10.** inhalation
snuff (pert to) ... **5.** scent, smell, sniff
  6. draw in, inhale, snoose **7.** tobacco
  (pulverized), umbrage **10.** extinguish,
  inhalation
snuff (pert to) ...
  a candle .. **4.** snot
  box .. **4.** mull **9.** tabatière
  color .. **10.** mummy brown

type .. **6.** rappee **8.** Maccaboy
  10. Copenhagen
snug ... **4.** cozy, neat, safe, trim **5.** close,
  tight **6.** secure **7.** compact **8.** homelike,
  reticen**9.** concealed, secretive **10.** prosperous
  11. comfortable
snuggle ... **6.** cuddle, nestle
sny (shipbuilding) ... **5.** curve (of plank)
so ... **2.** as **3.** how **4.** ergo, thus,
  very **5.** hence **6.** if only **7.** because
  8. likewise, provided **9.** therefore
  11. accordingly, in order that
  12. consequently
so (pert to) ...
  far .. **3.** yet **7.** thus far **8.** until now
  Latin .. **3.** sic
  so be it .. **4.** Amen
  to speak .. **8.** as it were **12.** figuratively
soak ... **3.** dip, sog, sop, wet **4.** sock
  5. souse, steep **6.** drench, imbrue, strike,
  tipple **7.** extract, immerse **8.** drunkard,
  macerate, marinate, permeate, saturate
  9. percolate **10.** overcharge
soap ... **4.** sapo, suds, wash **5.** bribe
  6. lather **7.** bribery **8.** cleanser, flattery
  9. slush fund
soap (pert to) ...
  box .. **4.** dais **5.** stage **8.** platform
  convert to .. **8.** saponify
  fish .. **10.** lizard fish
  frame bar .. **4.** sess
  ingredient .. **3.** lye
  liniment (camphorated) .. **9.** opodeldoc
  making .. **14.** saponification
  mottled .. **8.** Eschwege (Eschweg)
  opera .. **6.** serial **9.** broadcast **13.** network
  serial
  plant .. **5.** amole
  soft .. **8.** flattery
soar ... **3.** fly **4.** flit, rise, wing **5.** float,
  plane **6.** ascend, aspire, be high
  9. transcend
soaring ... **6.** flight **7.** gliding, planing,
  winging **8.** essorant **9.** skyriding
  10. ballooning
sob ... **3.** cry **4.** bawl, weep **6.** boohoo,
  simper **7.** whimper **9.** shed tears
sobeit ... **4.** amen **8.** provided
sober ... **4.** calm, cool, dark, sane
  5. grave, quiet, staid **6.** gentle, sedate,
  solemn, somber, subdue, temper
  7. chasten, earnest, regular, serious
  8. composed, moderate, sensible
  9. abstinent, collected, dignified,
  temperate **10.** abstemious, thoughtful
  11. impassioned **13.** unintoxicated
sobriety ... **6.** sanity **9.** composure,
  restraint, soberness **10.** abstinence,
  moderation, temperance
  11. seriousness
sobriquet ... **5.** alias, title **6.** byname
  7. epithet **8.** cognomen, nickname
  11. appellation
soccer ... **19.** association football
soccer great ... **4.** Pele
sociable ... **5.** party **7.** affable **8.** familiar,
  friendly, informal **9.** reception
  10. accessible, gregarious
  13. communicative, companionable
social ... **3.** tea **5.** party **6.** smoker
  9. convivial, gathering

13. companionable
social (pert to)...
career.. **5.** debut
class.. **4.** clan, sept **5.** caste **6.** estate
ethics.. **6.** morals **9.** standards
   10. principles
function.. **3.** bee, tea **4.** ball **5.** party
   6. soiree **7.** reunion **9.** reception
gathering, men.. **4.** stag **6.** smoker
group.. **4.** sept **5.** tribe **6.** ethnos **8.** smart
   set **10.** upper crust **11.** cafe society
   13. kaffeeklatsch
insect.. **3.** ant, bee
outcast.. **5.** leper **6.** pariah
standing.. **6.** estate
system.. **6.** regime
socialist... **3.** Red **8.** Nihilist **9.** anarchist,
   communist **10.** Bolshevist
   12. collectivist
society... **5.** union **7.** company
   8. alliance, populace **9.** community
   10. fellowship **11.** association,
   partnership **13.** companionship,
   confederation, participation
society (pert to)...
bud.. **3.** deb
Chinese.. **4.** Tong
German.. **6.** Verein
high.. **5.** elite **10.** upper crust
Italian.. **5.** Mafia (Maffia)
of Friends.. **7.** Quakers
secret.. **5.** lodge, Order
Society Islands...
capital.. **7.** Papeete
chief island.. **6.** Tahiti
site.. **12.** South Pacific
Socrates (pert to)...
birthplace.. **6.** Athens
disciple of.. **5.** Plato
famed as.. **7.** teacher **11.** Grecian sage
wife.. **9.** Xanthippe (Xantippe)
sod... **4.** soil, turf **5.** divot, glebe, sward
   7. stratum **10.** greensward
soda... **3.** sal **8.** beverage **9.** saleratus,
   saltpeter
sodden... **5.** drunk, moist, soggy
   6. soaked, stewed, stupid **7.** drunken,
   steeped **9.** saturated **11.** intoxicated
sodium (pert to)...
carbonate.. **4.** soda **5.** borax, trona
   7. sal soda, saltcat
chloride.. **3.** sal, tar **4.** NaCl, salt
nitrate.. **5.** niter
salicylate.. **8.** medicine
symbol.. **2.** Na
sofa... **5.** couch, divan **6.** lounge, settee
   7. dos-à-dos **8.** causeuse, love seat
   9. davenport, tête-à-tête **12.** chesterfield
soft... **4.** easy, limp, weak **5.** bland,
   downy, mushy, pulpy **6.** dreamy,
   gentle, placid, silken, supple, tender
   7. clement, ductile, lenient, lightly,
   quietly, squashy, velvety **8.** flexible,
   gullible, merciful, tranquil **9.** temperate,
   tractable **10.** effeminate, peacefully
   11. comfortable, sentimental,
   sympathetic **13.** compassionate
soft (pert to)...
cancer.. **11.** encephaloma
coal.. **10.** bituminous
food.. **3.** pap

head.. **9.** simpleton
job.. **4.** snap **8.** sinecure
mass.. **4.** pulp
music.. **5.** dulce, piano
palate.. **4.** cion **5.** uvula, velum
pedal.. **3.** ban **4.** curb **6.** subdue **8.** tone
   down
soap.. **7.** blarney **8.** blandish, flattery
   9. wheedling
spoken.. **4.** mild **5.** suave
soften... **4.** melt, thaw **5.** allay, malax,
   relax **6.** affect, lenify, pacify, relent,
   soothe, temper, weaken **7.** appease,
   assuage, cushion, mollify, relieve
   8. emoliate, enervate, enfeeble,
   macerate, mitigate, modulate
   9. alleviate, meliorate **11.** tranquilize
soften (pert to)...
by kneading.. **5.** malax
by soaking.. **8.** macerate
leather.. **5.** sammy (sam)
skins.. **3.** taw
temper.. **6.** relent
softening... **7.** lenient **8.** emulsive
   9. relenting, relieving, tempering
   10. lightening, mitigating
softening of the brain... **8.** dementia
softhearted... **4.** kind **6.** tender
   8. merciful
softly... **3.** low **5.** sotto **6.** easily, gently
   10. delicately **13.** unobtrusively
soggy... **3.** wet **4.** damp **5.** heavy
   6. soaked, sodden, watery **9.** saturated
soil... **4.** clay, daub, dirt, land, loam,
   sand, spot **5.** adobe, dirty, earth,
   glebe, gumbo, humus, stain, sully
   6. bedaub, bemire, ground, region,
   smirch, vilify **7.** begrime, besmear,
   corrupt, debauch, pollute, tarnish
   8. alluvium **9.** bedraggle, bespatter
   11. contaminate **12.** fuller's earth
soil (pert to)...
barren.. **4.** arid, gall **8.** lifeless
goddess of.. **7.** Demeter
kind of.. **4.** clay, lair, loam, malm
   5. adobe, humus
oneself.. **4.** moil
poetic.. **5.** glebe
sojourn... **4.** bide, stay, stop **5.** abide
   6. reside **8.** abidance, stop over
   11. peregrinate
solace... **5.** allay, amuse, cheer **6.** soothe
   7. assuage, comfort, console
   9. alleviate, entertain **10.** relaxation
   11. consolation
solan... **5.** goose **6.** gannet
solar (pert to)...
deity.. **2.** Ra **3.** Shu (Su) **6.** Helios
disk.. **4.** aten
exposure.. **9.** sunstroke **10.** heatstroke
halo.. **6.** nimbus **7.** aureole **12.** vesica
   piscis
plexus.. **10.** stomach pit
system.. **6.** bodies, planet **15.** celestial
   bodies
system apparatus.. **6.** orrery
year.. **5.** epact
soldier... **3.** ant **5.** cadet, poilu **6.** galoot
   7. fighter, private, regular, trooper,
   veteran, warrior **8.** gendarme, servitor
   9. combatant, grenadier, musketeer

11. enlisted man
soldier (pert to)...
Algeria.. **6.** Zouave
cavalryman.. **6.** lancer **7.** dragoon,
  trooper
Croatian.. **5.** Croat
field worker.. **6.** sapper
flask.. **7.** canteen
French.. **5.** poilu
Gaelic.. **4.** Kern
girl.. **3.** WAC (Army)
Gr Myth.. **8.** Myrmidon
hireling.. **9.** mercenary
Ind (Brit).. **5.** sepoy
Ind (Brit), with own horse.. **8.** silladar
Moroccan.. **5.** askar
of fortune.. **7.** Hessian **9.** mercenary
  10. adventurer
Prussian.. **5.** uhlan
slang.. **6.** galoot **7.** chicken **8.** shackman
soldiers, soldier's...
body of.. **5.** troop **6.** cohort **7.** brigade,
  company, platoon
captured, wounded.. **6.** losses
flask.. **7.** canteen
Maryland (Rev War).. **10.** macaronies
overcoat.. **6.** capote
quarters.. **7.** billets **8.** barracks
Three.. **5.** tales (by Kipling)
vacation.. **4.** pass **5.** leave **8.** furlough
sole... **3.** one **4.** base, fish, only **5.** alone,
  slade **6.** entire, lonely, single, unique
  8. desolate, isolated, solitary, unshared
  9. exclusive, unmarried, unmatched
  10. underframe
sole (pert to)...
cookery.. **8.** Marguéry
foot.. **4.** vola **6.** planta
hand (palm).. **4.** vola
pert to.. **7.** plantar
plow.. **5.** slade
toward the sole.. **7.** plantad
solecism... **5.** error **7.** blunder
  9. barbarism, deviation **11.** impropriety
solemn... **3.** sad **5.** grave, pious,
  sober **6.** august, devout, formal,
  gloomy, ritual, silent **7.** earnest,
  serious, stately, sublime **8.** funereal
  9. dignified **10.** ceremonial, devotional
  11. ceremonious, reverential **12.** awe-
  inspiring
solemnity... **4.** pomp **7.** dignity, sadness
  8. ceremony **9.** formality **10.** importance
solicit... **3.** ask, beg **4.** lure, seek, tout
  5. claim, court, crave, plead **6.** accost,
  demand, invite, obtain **7.** beseech,
  canvass, entreat, implore, request
  8. campaign, petition **9.** challenge,
  importune, panhandle, prosecute
  10. supplicate
solicitor... **6.** barker, lawyer **8.** attorney
  9. canvasser **10.** petitioner
solicitude... **4.** care, coda, heed
  7. anxiety, caution, concern **9.** attention
  11. carefulness **12.** apprehension
  15. considerateness
solid... **4.** cone, cube, firm, full, good,
  hard **5.** dense, level, sound, stiff
  6. stable, strong **7.** uniform **8.** complete,
  resolute, sensible, sterling **9.** estimable,
  unanimous **10.** dependable, inflexible

11. homogeneous, responsible,
  substantial, trustworthy
solid (pert to)...
comb form.. **6.** stereo
geometrical.. **5.** prism
seven-faced.. **11.** heptahedron
six-faced.. **4.** cube
tapering.. **4.** cone **7.** pyramid
solidarity... **5.** unity **10.** correality
  11. nationality **12.** completeness
solidity... **5.** unity **6.** volume **7.** density
  8. firmness, hardness, solvency,
  strength **9.** solidness, stability
  11. compactness **12.** completeness
  13. dependability **14.** substantiality
solidum... **4.** dado **9.** entire sum
soliloquy... **4.** poem **9.** discourse,
  monologue **16.** talking to oneself
solitaire... **8.** Canfield
solitary... **3.** one **4.** lone, only, sole
  5. alone, eremo (comb form) **6.** hermit,
  lonely, single **7.** recluse **8.** deserted,
  desolate, lonesome **10.** individual
  12. unfrequented
solitude... **6.** desert **7.** privacy, retreat
  9. aloneness, isolation, seclusion
  10. loneliness, wilderness
solo accompaniment... **9.** obbligato
Solomon (pert to)...
author of (reputed).. **8.** Proverbs
  9. Canticles **12.** Ecclesiastes **15.** Wisdom
  of Solomon
called also.. **8.** Koheleth **11.** The
  Preacher
famed as.. **4.** sage **7.** wise man **12.** King
  of Israel
father.. **5.** David
literally.. **9.** peaceable
mother.. **9.** Bathsheba
Solomon Islands site... **9.** South Seas
solon... **4.** sage **8.** lawmaker **9.** statesman
solstice... **5.** limit **13.** farthest point
  (from equator)
solution... **3.** key **6.** answer **7.** solving
  8. analysis **10.** denouement, resolution
  11. explanation **13.** disentanglement
solution (pert to)...
alkaline.. **3.** lye
saline.. **5.** brine
strength.. **5.** titer (titre)
Somalia...
capital.. **9.** Mogadishu
people.. **6.** Somali **7.** Hamitic
port.. **5.** Zeila **6.** Bulhar
somber, sombre... **3.** sad **4.** dark
  5. grave **6.** solemn **7.** austere
  9. depressed **10.** depressing,
  foreboding, lackluster, melancholy
  11. dark-colored, dispiriting
some... **3.** any, one **5.** about **6.** plural,
  suffix **7.** several **10.** indefinite, more
  or less **13.** approximately
somebody... **6.** person **7.** big name
  8. luminary **9.** celebrity, personage
somersault... **4.** flip, leap **8.** somerset
  9. cartwheel **10.** end over end
something... **6.** object **8.** somewhat
  9. personage **12.** in some degree
something (pert to)...
abnormal.. **5.** freak **6.** mutant
  11. monstrosity **12.** malformation

else.. **10.** irrelevant
extra.. **5.** bonus **6.** bounty **7.** premium **9.** lagniappe
found.. **5.** cache, trove **11.** serendipity **13.** treasure-trove
frightening.. **7.** bugbear
heavy.. **4.** onus **9.** ponderant
illogical.. **7.** alogism
imagined.. **5.** story **7.** figment
inserted.. **4.** gore **5.** inset, wedge
like.. **7.** related, similar **8.** somewhat
similar.. **4.** analogue **11.** counterpart
small.. **3.** dot, jot **4.** atom, iota, whit **5.** speck **6.** sliver, tittle
soothing.. **7.** unction
superfluous.. **5.** luxus **6.** luxury
unexplained.. **5.** poser **7.** mystery
unfinished.. **4.** quab
somewhat ... **4.** part **6.** little, partly, rather **12.** in some degree
somnifacient ... **4.** drug **8.** hypnotic, sedative **9.** soporific
somniloquy ... **12.** sleep talking
somnolence ... **8.** dormancy **10.** drowsiness, sleepiness
somnus ... **5.** sleep
Somnus (pert to) ...
brother.. **4.** Mors (Death)
known also as.. **6.** Hypnos
son of.. **3.** Nox (Night)
son, son of (pert to) ...
a gun.. **5.** rogue **6.** fellow, wretch
Anak.. **5.** giant
a Scot.. **3.** Mac
God.. **11.** Jesus Christ
Heaven (China).. **7.** Emperor
in-law.. **5.** gener
in Trinity.. **6.** second (person)
Jacob.. **4.** Levi
man.. **4.** male **6.** mortal
Odin.. **2.** Ve
Odysseus.. **9.** Telegonus
Priam.. **5.** Paris
reference to.. **3.** ben **4.** fils **5.** scion **6.** filial **9.** offspring **10.** descendant
Seth.. **4.** Enos
the soil.. **6.** farmer **7.** peasant
youngest.. **5.** cadet
sonance ... **4.** tune **5.** sound **7.** sonancy
sonant ... **5.** sound, tonic, vocal **6.** voiced **8.** sounding **9.** intonated
song ... **3.** air, lay, ode **4.** aria, leed, lilt, noel, poem, tune **5.** carol, chant, ditty, melos, troll, verse **6.** ballad, melody, strain, trifle **7.** chantey (chanty), descant **8.** canticle, pittance **9.** cabaletta
song (pert to) ...
after.. **5.** epode
Bib.. **8.** canticle **11.** Song of Songs **13.** Song of Solomon
boat, gondolier.. **7.** chantey (chanty)
choral Muse.. **11.** Terpsichore
collection.. **9.** anthology **10.** cancionero
college.. **4.** glee
depressing.. **5.** blues
evening.. **6.** vesper **8.** evensong, serenade
French.. **7.** chanson
funeral.. **5.** dirge, elegy **6.** lament **8.** threnody **9.** epicedium
gay.. **4.** lilt

German.. **4.** lied **9.** Kunstlied
gypsy.. **10.** zingaresca
Italian.. **7.** canzone
lament.. **8.** threnody
love.. **5.** lyric **6.** ballad **8.** madrigal, serenade
merry.. **4.** lilt
morning.. **5.** matin
mountaineer.. **5.** yodel
pert to.. **5.** melic
praise.. **5.** carol, paean (pean)
sacred.. **4.** hymn **5.** chant, motet, psalm **6.** anthem
sailor's.. **7.** chantey (chanty) **9.** barcarole
short.. **7.** arietta
simple.. **6.** ballad
words.. **6.** lyrics
songbird ... **4.** lark **5.** mavis, robin, veery **6.** canary, oriole, thrush **8.** throstle **11.** mockingbird
sonic recorder ... **9.** echograph
sonnet ... **4.** poem, song **5.** verse
sonnet (pert to) ...
first eight lines.. **5.** octet
last six lines.. **6.** sestet
two quatrains.. **10.** Petrarchan
sonorous ... **4.** loud **6.** tonous **7.** ringing **8.** resonant **9.** melodious **10.** impressive, resounding
sonsy, sonsie ... **5.** buxom, happy **6.** comely **11.** good-natured
sontag ... **4.** cape **6.** jacket
soon ... **3.** ere **4.** anon **5.** early, later **6.** at once **7.** betimes, erelong, quickly, readily, shortly **8.** promptly, speedily **9.** certainly, presently **11.** immediately
Sooner State ... **8.** Oklahoma
sooner than ... **3.** ere **6.** before
soot ... **4.** smut, stup **5.** black, grime, smoke **6.** carbon, smudge **7.** residue **9.** lampblack
soothe ... **3.** pet **4.** calm, lull **5.** allay, quiet **6.** pacify, please, solace **7.** assuage, compose, mollify, relieve, satisfy **8.** mitigate, palliate **9.** alleviate **11.** tranquilize
soother ... **4.** balm **6.** luller **7.** anodyne, placebo **8.** lenitivo, pacifier, sedative **9.** flatterer
soothing ... **5.** balmy, sirup (syrup) **6.** dulcet, gentle **7.** calming **8.** lenitive, sedative **9.** appeasing, demulcent **13.** tranquilizing
soothsayer ... **4.** seer **5.** augur, vatis **6.** mantis **7.** diviner, prophet **8.** Chaldean, haruspex **9.** Cassandra **13.** praying insect **14.** prognosticator
sooty (pert to) ...
brown.. **6.** bister **8.** teakwood
color.. **5.** black
mangabey.. **6.** monkey
pert to.. **9.** albatross **10.** fuliginous
petrel.. **7.** skimmer **10.** shearwater
sophistical ... **8.** captious **9.** deceptive, sophistic
sophistication ... **9.** sophistry **10.** corruption, experience **11.** worldliness **13.** ungullibility
soporific ... **4.** drug **6.** drowsy, opiate **7.** anodyne **8.** hypnotic, narcotic, sedative **11.** somniferous **12.** sleep

inducer, somnifacient
soprano (operatic) . . . **4.** Alda, Bori, Lind, Pons **5.** Calvé, Eames **6.** Callas, Steber
sora . . . **4.** rail **5.** crake
sorcerer . . . **4.** mage **5.** Magus **6.** wizard **7.** diviner **8.** conjurer, magician **11.** necromancer
sorceress . . . **3.** hex **5.** Circe, lamia, Medea, witch **6.** Gorgon **7.** vampire **12.** Witch of Endor
sorcery . . . **5.** magic, obeah, spell **6.** voodoo **8.** pishogue **9.** diablerie, diabolism **10.** black magic, necromancy, witchcraft
sordid . . . **3.** low **4.** base, mean, vile **5.** gross **6.** filthy, menial **7.** ignoble, servile, squalid **8.** sluttish, wretched **10.** despicable, slatternly **12.** contemptible
sore . . . **4.** pain, sair **5.** angry, vexed, wound **6.** tender **7.** painful **8.** abrasion, inflamed, offended **9.** irritated, vexatious **11.** distressing **12.** inflammation
soreness . . . **4.** ache **5.** anger **8.** vexation **10.** bitterness, tenderness **11.** painfulness **12.** irritability
sorghum . . . **4.** milo **5.** durra (dari), grain, sorgo **6.** imphee, shallu **8.** feterita
sorority . . . **4.** club **7.** society **10.** fellowship, sisterhood
sorrel . . . **3.** oca **4.** buck, herb **5.** color (horse), Rumex **7.** roselle
Sorrento, Italy (pert to) . . .
  anc name . . **9.** Sorrentum
  famed as . . **6.** resort
  famed for . . **9.** cathedral
  site . . **11.** Bay of Naples
sorrow . . . **3.** rue, woe **4.** sigh, teen, weal **5.** dolor, grief, mourn **6.** grieve, lament, misery, repent **7.** remorse, trouble **8.** calamity, distress, egrimony, mourning **9.** adversity, penitence **10.** affliction, contrition **11.** lamentation, tribulation **12.** disconsolate, wretchedness
sorrowful . . . **3.** sad **4.** blue **5.** drear, sadly **6.** dismal, dolent, dreary, rueful **7.** doleful, grieved, tearful, unhappy **8.** mournful **9.** plaintive **10.** afflictive, melancholy **11.** distressing **12.** disconsolate
sorry . . . **3.** sad **4.** hurt **5.** vexed **6.** dismal, gloomy, rueful **7.** painful, pitiful, unhappy **8.** contrite, grievous, mournful, penitent, shameful, wretched **9.** afflicted, chagrined, mortified, regretful, repentant, worthless **10.** displeased, melancholy **12.** disappointed
sort . . . **3.** ilk, way **4.** cull, kind, rank **5.** blend, class, grade, group **6.** assort, manner, nature, strain **7.** quality, species, variety **8.** classify, separate **9.** character **11.** description
sortie . . . **4.** raid **5.** foray, onset, sally **6.** attack, thrust
sottish . . . **4.** dull **6.** stupid **7.** doltish, drunken, foolish **8.** bibulous **9.** senseless
sotto (It) . . . **5.** below, under

sotto voce . . . **5.** aside **8.** secretly **9.** privately, undertone **14.** under the breath
soubrette . . . **9.** lady's maid **10.** intrigante **11.** maidservant
soudagur . . . **8.** merchant **10.** shopkeeper
soul . . . **2.** ba, ka **3.** ego, God **4.** life **5.** anima **6.** pneuma, spirit **7.** essence **8.** inspirer **9.** substance **10.** embodiment **15.** exemplification, personification
soul (pert to) . . .
  beatified . . **5.** saint
  destiny of . . **8.** theodicy
  dwelling place . . **2.** Po **6.** heaven
  Egypt . . **2.** Ba
  Hindu . . **5.** atman **7.** jivatma
  lost . . **9.** âme damnée, the damned
  maligners . . **7.** Harpies
  music . . **14.** rhythm and blues
  personified . . **6.** Psyche
  transmigration . . **7.** rebirth **13.** reincarnation
sound . . . **3.** bam, cry, hum **4.** beep, bong, hale, honk, rale, ring, sane, test, tone, toot **5.** drone, noise, plumb, probe, snore, valid, whole **6.** intact, jingle, report, robust, stable, sturdy **7.** feel out, perfect, resound **8.** flawless, reliable, susurrus **9.** undamaged **10.** scrutinize **11.** trustworthy
sound (pert to) . . .
  addition to word end . . **8.** paragoge
  atonic . . **4.** surd
  dashing . . **5.** swash **6.** splash
  discordant . . **6.** jangle **9.** cacophony
  drum, beating . . **8.** rataplan
  explosion . . **4.** boom **6.** report
  fixed . . **5.** toned
  harsh . . **3.** caw **4.** bray **5.** creak, twang **7.** stridor **9.** cacophony
  insect's . . **5.** chirr
  loud . . **4.** peal **5.** blare, clang
  low . . **3.** hum **4.** moan **5.** drone
  metallic . . **4.** ping, ting **5.** clank, clink, twank **6.** tinkle
  pert to . . **5.** tonal **6.** sonant **10.** acoustical
  prosody . . **4.** rime (rhyme)
  reflected . . **4.** echo
  sharp . . **3.** pop **7.** rat-a-tat, tapping
  shrill . . **5.** reedy
  sibilant . . **4.** hiss
  similar . . **8.** assonant
  small . . **4.** peep **6.** rustle
  surf . . **4.** rote **5.** swish
  throwing . . **8.** abat-sons
  trumpet . . **7.** clarion
  unit . . **7.** decibel
  warning . . **5.** alarm, siren **6.** tocsin
  whispering . . **8.** susurrus
  with rhythm . . **5.** music
sounding . . . **5.** depth, rawin **6.** sonant **7.** ringing **8.** sonation **10.** resounding
soundness . . . **5.** truth **6.** sanity **8.** solidity, solvency, strength **9.** integrity, rectitude, stability **10.** heartiness **11.** healthiness
soup . . . **3.** fog **5.** broth, chili, purée **6.** bisque, potage, won ton **7.** borscht, chowder, pottage **8.** bouillon, consommé, gazpacho, julienne **10.** oyster stew **11.** vichyssoise **12.** mulligatawny

soupçon . . . **5.** taste **7.** portion **9.** suspicion
10. suggestion
soup dish . . . **6.** tureen
sour . . . **3.** wry **4.** acid, tart **5.** acerb,
acrid **6.** acetic, bitter, morose, off key,
rancid **7.** acetose, acidify, crabbed,
pungent, tainted **8.** acescent, embitter
9. acidulous **10.** astringent, unpleasant
sour (pert to) . . .
apple . . **9.** crab apple
aspect . . **4.** dour, hard **6.** sullen
berry . . **9.** cranberry
bread . . **8.** leavened
cherry . . **7.** morello
stomach . . **4.** acor
turn sour . . **5.** prill **6.** bleeze
source . . . **4.** font, germ, mine, rise,
root, seed **5.** cause, fount **6.** origin,
parent, quarry **8.** fountain **9.** beginning
10. wellspring **12.** fountainhead
source (pert to) . . .
income . . **7.** revenue
insecticides . . **9.** sabadilla
iodine . . **4.** kelp
ipecac . . **4.** evea
metal . . **3.** ore **7.** bonanza
opium . . **5.** poppy
rubber . . **3.** ule
South Africa . . . see also South African
capital . . **8.** Cape Town, Pretoria
city . . **6.** Durban **9.** Germiston
12. Johannesburg
division . . **5.** Natal **9.** Transvaal **14.** Cape
of Good Hope **15.** Orange Free State
exports . . **4.** gold **8.** diamonds
legislature seat location . . **8.** Cape Town
people . . **5.** Boers, Zulus **6.** Bantus
7. British **10.** Hottentots **11.** Afrikanders
(Dutch)
river . . **4.** Vaal **6.** Orange
South African (pert to) . . .
antelope . . **3.** gnu **5.** eland, oribi, peele
6. rhebok **7.** sassaby
armadillo . . **4.** para
ass (wild) . . **6.** quagga
bird . . **4.** taha
camp . . **6.** laager
Cape ash . . **9.** essenhout
cocktail . . **9.** sundowner
cony . . **3.** das
council . . **4.** Raad
dialect . . **4.** Taal **9.** Afrikaans
diamond (blue-white) . . **5.** jager
fox . . **4.** asse **5.** caama
grass hut . . **8.** rondawel (rondavel)
grassland . . **4.** veld (veldt) **8.** bushveld
mountain, hill . . **3.** kop
snake . . **8.** eggeater
tableland . . **5.** karoo
tree (dogwood) . . **7.** assagai (assegai)
village . . **5.** kraal
war . . **4.** Boer
warrior . . **4.** impi
weaverbird . . **4.** taha
whip . . **7.** sjambok
South American (pert to) . . .
animal . . **2.** ai **4.** paca **5.** llama, sloth,
tapir **6.** jaguar, tapeti **7.** agouara (dog)
8. anteater **9.** armadillo
armadillo . . **4.** apar (apara) **10.** pichiciago
(burrowing)

arrow poison . . **6.** curare (curari)
balsam . . **4.** tolu
bellbird . . **8.** arapunga **9.** campanero
bird . . **4.** rara, taha **5.** agami, arara,
chaja, macaw **6.** barbet **7.** oilbird,
seriema, tinamou **8.** bellbird, boatbill,
caracara, guacharo, puffbird
blanket . . **6.** serape
city section . . **6.** barrio
cloth . . **4.** crea
country . . **4.** Peru **5.** Chile **6.** Brazil
7. Bolivia, Ecuador, Uruguay
8. Paraguay, Suriname (Surinam)
9. Argentina, Venezuela
drink . . **5.** assai
fiber . . **6.** yachan
fish . . **4.** paru **7.** piranha, scalare
8. arapaima
Indian . . **2.** Ge (Gesan) **3.** Ona **4.** Inca
5. Carib **6.** Tapuya
knife . . **7.** machete
leader . . **6.** Franko **7.** Pizarro
liberator . . **7.** Bolivar
mammal . . **5.** llama, tapir **6.** alpaca
8. kinkajou **10.** chinchilla
marmoset . . **7.** tamarin
monkey . . **3.** sai **4.** saki, titi **5.** araba
8. orabassu **9.** barrigudo
mountain range . . **5.** Andes
native . . **5.** Carib **6.** Arawak
ostrich . . **4.** rhea
palm . . **5.** assai **12.** chiquichiqui
parrot . . **5.** macaw
plains . . **6.** llanos, pampas
plainsman . . **7.** llanero
plant . . **6.** ipecac **11.** ipecacuanha
poison . . **6.** curare
river . . **3.** Apa **4.** Acre, Pará **5.** Plata
6. Amazon, Paraná
rodent . . **5.** coypu **6.** agouti (agouty)
8. capibara, viscacha **10.** chinchilla
snake . . **4.** lora **5.** aboma **8.** anaconda
10. bushmaster
stork . . **7.** maguari
tinamou . . **7.** tataupa
toucan . . **7.** aracari
trumpeter . . **5.** agami
tuber . . **3.** oca
vulture . . **6.** condor
weapon . . **4.** bola
wild cat . . **4.** eyra
wind . . **7.** pampero
South Carolina . . .
capital . . **8.** Columbia
city . . **8.** Beaufort **10.** Charleston
11. Spartanburg
monument . . **10.** Fort Sumter
mountain . . **9.** Blue Ridge, Sassafras
resort . . **1.** Myrtle Beach
State admission . . **6.** Eighth
State bird . . **4.** wren
State flower . . **9.** jessamine
State motto . . **13.** Dum Spiro, Spero
(While I Breathe, I Hope)
State nickname . . **8.** Palmetto
State secession . . **5.** First (1860)
South Dakota . . .
capital . . **6.** Pierre
city . . **5.** Huron **8.** Deadwood **9.** Rapid
City **10.** Sioux Falls
Indians . . **5.** Brule, Sioux

mine (US largest).. **9.** Homestake
monument.. **10.** Crazy Horse, Mt
   Rushmore
mountain.. **10.** Black Hills, Harney Peak
river.. **5.** White **8.** Cheyenne, Missouri
State admission.. **8.** Fortieth (or
   Thirty-ninth)
State bird.. **8.** pheasant
State flower.. **12.** pasqueflower
State motto.. **21.** Under God the People
   Rule
State nickname.. **6.** Coyote **8.** Sunshine
topography.. **8.** Bad Lands **10.** Black
   Hills
southeast wind ... **5.** Eurus
southern ... **7.** austral
Southern (pert to) ...
Buddhism.. **8.** Hinayana
Cross.. **4.** Crux **12.** Stars and Bars
Crown.. **15.** Corona Australis
dish.. **3.** yam **4.** okra, pone **5.** gumbo
   7. catfish, hoecake **8.** chess pie, ham
   hocks **9.** cornbread **11.** hush puppies
   12. chitterlings, turnip greens
shrub.. **8.** magnolia, oleander
States.. **5.** Dixie **7.** Sunbelt
southernmost city ... **12.** Puerto Arenas
   (Chile)
South Pole bird ... **4.** skua **7.** penguin
South Pole constellation ... **4.** Pavo
South Sea ... **12.** Pacific Ocean
South Sea Bubble ... **6.** scheme (1720)
   10. stock fraud (Eng)
South Wales people ... **7.** Silures
southwest wind ... **4.** afer
south wind ... **5.** Notus
souvenir ... **5.** relic, token **6.** memory,
   trophy **7.** memento **8.** keepsake,
   memorial, reminder **11.** remembrance
   12. recollection, remembrancer
sovereign ... **5.** chief, liege, regal, ruler
   6. divine, prince, ruling **7.** empress,
   monarch, supreme **8.** princely, superior,
   suzerain **9.** effectual, gold piece,
   paramount, potentate **11.** controlling,
   independent
sovereign (pert to) ...
claim.. **11.** seigniorage
coin.. **4.** skiv
decree.. **5.** arrêt
pardon.. **7.** amnesty
petty.. **8.** tetrarch
power.. **6.** throne
sovereignty ... **5.** realm **6.** diadem,
   empery, empire **7.** dynasty, scepter
   (sceptre) **8.** dominion **9.** supremacy
Soviet, Russian (pert to) ...
committee.. **9.** presidium
farm.. **7.** sovkhoz (sovkhose)
government.. **9.** Communism, Sovietism
   10. Bolshevism
hero.. **5.** Lenin
newspaper.. **6.** Pravda **8.** Izvestia
police, secret service.. **3.** KGB
sow ... **3.** pig **4.** gilt, seed **5.** plant
   7. implant, scatter **8.** disperse, squander
   9. broadcast **10.** salamander
   11. disseminate
sow bug ... **6.** slater
sow thistle ... **7.** Sonchus
soybean ... **4.** Soja **8.** soya bean

soybean enzyme ... **6.** urease
spa ... **3.** Ems **4.** Bath **5.** Baden **6.** Bilina
   (Bilin), hot tub **7.** Jacuzzi (tm)
space ... **3.** gap **4.** area, rank, room,
   time, void **5.** blank, inane, niche, place,
   range **6.** areola, areole, degree, extent,
   vacuum **7.** arrange, expanse **8.** capacity,
   distance, interval **9.** concourse, elbow
   room
space (pert to) ...
architectural.. **6.** metope **8.** pediment
blank.. **5.** chasm **6.** hiatus, lacuna
botany (leaves).. **6.** areola
environment.. **5.** ambit **8.** ambiance
larynx.. **7.** glottis
occupied.. **6.** volume
ref to.. **5.** areal, outer **6.** cosmos, galaxy,
   pulsar **7.** heavens, lacunal, spatial
   8. galactic, infinity **9.** black hole, deep
   space
storage.. **4.** shed **5.** attic, depot **6.** cellar,
   garage **9.** storeroom, warehouse
theory.. **7.** plenism
time.. **8.** interval
travel.. **4.** NASA **7.** reentry, swingby
   8. time warp
traveler.. **5.** alien **6.** cyborg **8.** aeronaut
   9. astronaut, cosmonaut
vehicle.. **6.** rocket, Skylab **7.** shuttle,
   sputnik
void.. **5.** chasm **7.** inanity
wall.. **5.** niche
spacious ... **5.** ample, broad, roomy
   9. capacious, expansive, extensive
   10. commodious, far and wide,
   widespread **13.** comprehensive
spadassin ... **5.** bravo **7.** duelist
   9. swordsman
spade ... **3.** dig, loy **4.** spud, stag (3-yr
   old), suit (cards) **5.** slade **6.** shovel
   11. playing card
spade (pert to) ...
bone.. **13.** shoulder blade
fish.. **5.** porgy **10.** paddlefish
foot.. **4.** toad
grass.. **4.** rush
Irish.. **5.** slane
money.. **7.** Chinese (early)
peat.. **5.** slade
triangular.. **5.** didle
spae ... **6.** divine **8.** foretell
Spain ... see also *Spanish*
cape.. **9.** Trafalgar
capital.. **6.** Madrid
city.. **4.** Irun **5.** Cadiz, Lorca **6.** Malaga
   7. Cordoba, Granada, Seville **8.** Valencia
   9. Barcelona
city cathedral.. **9.** Saragossa
islands.. **5.** Ceuta **6.** Canary **7.** Melilla
   8. Balearic
kingdom, region.. **4.** Léon **6.** Aragon,
   Basque (Provinces) **7.** Castile, Navarre
   8. Asturias **9.** Catalonia
mountain.. **8.** Asturias, Pyrenees
old name.. **6.** Iberia
palace.. **8.** Escorial
plain, plateau.. **6.** Meseta
river.. **4.** Ebro, Muga **5.** Tagus
span ... **3.** two **4.** arch, join, pair, team
   6. bridge, extend, length, period (time)
   7. breadth, measure, stretch **8.** overarch

9. encompass

spangle ... **6.** aiglet, sequin **7.** glitter, sparkle **8.** ornament, zecchino

spaniel ... **5.** trasy **6.** cocker **8.** Brittany, springer

Spanish (pert to) ...
alcazar (palace) .. **8.** Alhambra
arbor .. **6.** ramada
art museum .. **5.** Prado
battle .. **6.** Armada (1588)
bayonet .. **5.** yucca
boat .. **5.** aviso **7.** galleon (ship)
Christmas .. **7.** Navidad
cloak .. **4.** capa **5.** manta **6.** mantle **7.** zamarra (zamarro)
corral .. **5.** atajo
dance .. **5.** tango **6.** bolero, gitano **8.** fandango, flamenco, saraband
fabric .. **4.** crea (cotton) **5.** tiraz (silk)
fleet, famed .. **6.** Armada
fortress chief .. **4.** caid **7.** alcaide
friend .. **5.** amigo
fruit .. **8.** pimiento
game .. **6.** pelota **7.** jai alai
garment .. **6.** serape **8.** mantilla
gift holder .. **6.** piñata
gold .. **3.** oro **8.** El Dorado
governor .. **10.** gobernador
grass .. **5.** spart **7.** esparto
gruel .. **5.** atole
gypsy .. **7.** zincalo
holiday .. **6.** fiesta
horse .. **5.** genet **6.** jennet **7.** caballo
hotel .. **6.** posada
house .. **4.** casa **6.** casita
jar .. **4.** olla, tina **6.** tinaja
knight .. **8.** cavalier **9.** caballero
lake .. **4.** lago
language .. **6.** Basque **7.** Catalan, Spanish **8.** Galician **9.** Castilian
light opera .. **8.** zarzuela
mausoleum .. **8.** Escorial
musical instrument .. **6.** atabel, guitar **8.** castanet
plant .. **3.** aji **8.** capsicum
porridge .. **5.** atole
promenade .. **5.** paseo
raisin .. **4.** pasa
river .. **3.** ria, rio
road .. **6.** camino
room .. **4.** sala
shawl .. **5.** manta **6.** serape
sheep .. **6.** merino
sherry .. **5.** Xeres **7.** oloroso
sorcerer .. **5.** brujo
street .. **5.** calle
three .. **4.** tres
title .. **3.** don **5.** señor **6.** señora **7.** hidalgo **8.** señorita
trail .. **6.** camino
vehicle .. **7.** tartana
watch .. **5.** reloj
watchtower .. **7.** atalaya
watchword .. **6.** alerta
watercourse .. **6.** arroyo
wind .. **6.** solano
window .. **7.** ventana
witchcraft .. **8.** brujeria
year .. **3.** ano

Spanish people ...
architect .. **5.** Gaudi **11.** Churriguera

artist .. **4.** Dali, Goya, Gris, Miró **6.** Ribera **7.** Murillo **8.** Zurbarán **9.** Velázquez (Velásquez)
author .. **9.** Cervantes **11.** García Lorca, Pérez Galdos
cellist .. **6.** Casals
chaperone .. **6.** duenna
composer .. **5.** Falla
conqueror .. **6.** Cortés (Cortez) **7.** Pizarro
dictator, general .. **6.** Franco
dramatist .. **9.** Echegaray (Nobel Prize 1904)
explorer .. **6.** Balboa **11.** Ponce de León
gentleman .. **5.** señor **8.** cavalier **9.** caballero
God .. **4.** Dios
guitarist .. **7.** Segovia
herdsman .. **7.** llanero **8.** ranchero
hero .. **3.** Cid
justice of the peace .. **7.** entrada
king .. **7.** Alfonso, Charles **9.** Ferdinand
lady .. **4.** doña **6.** señora **8.** señorita
letter carrier .. **6.** correo
man .. **3.** don **6.** hombre
missionary .. **5.** Serra
monk .. **5.** padre
peasant .. **7.** paisano
people .. **5.** genta
pianist .. **6.** Iturbi
pretender to throne .. **6.** Carlos (Don)
Queen .. **8.** Isabella
singer, tenor .. **7.** Domingo (Placido)
soldier .. **8.** miquelet
soprano .. **4.** Bori (Lucrezia)

spar ... **3.** box **4.** beam, boom, gaff, mast, rung, yard **5.** sprit, steve **6.** timber **7.** dispute, quarrel, topmast, yardarm

spare ... **4.** lean, thin **5.** chary, lanky **6.** afford, exempt, frugal, meager, scanty **7.** sparing, surplus **8.** preserve **9.** duplicate, parsimony **10.** economical, occasional **11.** superfluous **12.** parsimonious

spare time ... **7.** leisure

sparing ... **5.** chary **6.** frugal, meager, saving, scanty **7.** scrimpy, thrifty **8.** merciful, reticent, stinting **9.** scrimping **12.** parsimonious

spark ... **4.** beau, fire, funk **5.** aizle, court, dandy, lover **6.** incite **7.** diamond, gallant, glitter, modicum, sparkle **8.** humorist **10.** sweetheart **11.** scintillate

sparkle ... **5.** flash, gleam, glint, shine, trace **7.** be smart, be witty, glisten, glister, glitter, radiate, reflect, spangle, twinkle **8.** be lively **9.** coruscate **10.** effervesce, illuminate **11.** scintillate **13.** scintillation

sparkling ... **4.** dewy **5.** crisp, witty **6.** bright, starry **7.** shining **8.** cheerful, eloquent, glittery, gorgeous, mousseux (wine) **9.** twinkling **10.** glittering, reflecting **12.** effervescent

sparoid fish ... **4.** scup **5.** porgy **8.** sea bream **10.** sheepshead

Sparta, Greece ... see also *Spartan*
capital .. **7.** Laconia (anc)
kingdom .. **12.** Peloponnesus
river .. **7.** Eurotas

spartan ... **5.** hardy, stoic **10.** courageous **13.** uncomplaining

Spartan (pert to)...
army division.. **4.** mora **6.** lochus
cipher writing.. **7.** scytale
class (anc).. **8.** perioeci
commander.. **7.** lochage
dog.. **10.** bloodhound
festival.. **6.** Carnea **7.** Carneia
king.. **8.** Leonidas, Menelaus
lawgiver.. **8.** Lycurgus
magistrate.. **5.** ephor
native.. **8.** Laconian **9.** Spartiate
serf.. **5.** helot
spasmodic... **6.** fitful **7.** snatchy
   9. excitable, irregular **10.** convulsive
   12. intermittent **13.** highly wrought
spasmodic (pert to)...
disease.. **5.** croup **7.** tetanus
inspiration.. **8.** hiccough
twitch.. **3.** tic
spat... **3.** row **4.** slap, tiff **5.** spawn
   6. gaiter, oyster, strike **7.** dispute,
   legging, quarrel **10.** oysterseed
spate... **4.** gush **5.** flood **7.** freshet, torrent
   9. overwhelm, rainstorm **10.** waterspout
spatial... **5.** areal **8.** sterical
   11. dimensional
spatter... **3.** wet **4.** soil, spot **5.** spurt
   6. dabble, splash **7.** sputter **8.** splutter,
   sprinkle
spawn... **3.** ova, roe **4.** eggs, germ, seed
   7. lay eggs **8.** generate **13.** numerous
   issue
speak... **3.** say **4.** chat, lisp, talk, tell
   5. orate, utter **6.** reveal **7.** address,
   chatter, declaim, sputter **8.** converse,
   proclaim **9.** discourse, pronounce
   10. articulate **11.** tell in words
speak (pert to)...
affectedly.. **4.** mime **5.** mince
against.. **6.** oppose
boastfully.. **4.** brag **5.** vaunt **7.** enlarge
   10. exaggerate
from memory.. **6.** recite
ill of.. **5.** decry **8.** backbite **9.** disparage
noisily.. **4.** rant, rime **8.** harangue
offhand.. **11.** extemporize
slowly.. **5.** drawl
softly.. **7.** whisper
under breath.. **5.** mouth **6.** mumble,
   murmur, mutter **7.** grumble
speaker... **5.** sayer **6.** lisper, orator,
   proser **8.** lecturer **9.** demagogue
   10. mouthpiece, prolocutor
   11. spellbinder
speaker of languages... **8.** linguist,
   polyglot
speaking (pert to)...
generally.. **7.** as a rule, roughly **12.** in
   the long run **13.** approximately
of.. **7.** apropos **12.** incidentally
offhand.. **13.** extemporizing
privately.. **7.** whisper **9.** in one's ear
   11. into one's ear
publicly.. **7.** oratory **11.** declamation
style.. **8.** fluently
spear... **4.** dart, pike, stab **5.** catch, lance
   6. pierce, weapon **7.** javelin, missile
   9. penetrate
spear (pert to)...
anc Teutons.. **6.** framea (fram)
fish.. **3.** gig **4.** gaff

iron-tipped.. **7.** assagai
shaped.. **7.** hastate
three-pronged.. **7.** trident
two-pronged.. **6.** bident
spearfish... **6.** marlin **9.** quillback
special... **4.** rare **5.** extra **6.** unique
   7. notable, unusual **8.** concrete,
   detailed, favorite, specific, uncommon
   10. individual, noteworthy, particular,
   restricted **11.** distinctive, exceptional
   13. extraordinary
special (pert to)...
ability.. **5.** forte **6.** talent **7.** charism
   8. charisma
commodity.. **6.** leader **7.** feature **10.** best
   seller
edition.. **5.** extra
favor.. **9.** influence, privilege
train.. **5.** flier **7.** express **10.** cannonball
specialist (pert to)...
atomic.. **9.** physicist
ear.. **6.** aurist **9.** otologist
eye.. **7.** oculist **15.** ophthalmologist
medical.. **6.** doctor **7.** surgeon
money.. **9.** economist
specialty... **5.** skill **8.** aptitude, contract
   13. particularity **14.** characteristic
specie... **4.** cash, coin **5.** money (hard)
species... **4.** kind, sort, type **5.** class,
   genre, genus, group **7.** general, isotope,
   mankind, variety **8.** category, humanity
   11. Homo sapiens **12.** nomenclature
specific... **5.** exact, virus **6.** remedy
   7. limited, precise, special **8.** definite,
   detailed, explicit, peculiar
specificity... **9.** haecceity
specify... **4.** name **5.** limit, state
   6. define, detail **8.** indicate **9.** be precise,
   designate, enumerate, stipulate
specimen... **4.** copy **5.** model, piece,
   taste, token **6.** person, sample, swatch
   7. example, pattern **14.** representative
specious... **4.** fair **5.** showy **7.** alleged
   8. illusory, pleasing **9.** plausible
   10. ostensible **12.** hypocritical
speck... **3.** bit, dot, jot, nit **4.** blot, iota,
   mark, mite, mote, spot, whit **5.** fleck,
   stain **7.** blemish **8.** particle **10.** sand
   darter
speckled... **6.** menald **7.** mottled
   9. sprinkled **10.** variegated
spectacle... **4.** show, view **5.** scene, sight
   6. wonder **7.** diorama, display, pageant
   8. panorama, spyglass **10.** exhibition
   14. representation
spectacles... **7.** glasses
spectator... **6.** espier, viewer **7.** watcher,
   witness **8.** audience, beholder, kibitzer,
   looker-on, observer, onlooker
   9. bystander
specter, spectre... **4.** bogy (bogey,
   bogie) **5.** ghost, shade, spook **6.** idolum,
   spirit, wraith **7.** eidolon, phantom
   8. illusion, phantasm, revenant
   10. apparition
spectral... **5.** eerie (eery) **6.** ghosty,
   spooky **7.** ghostly, phantom
   12. apparitional
speculate... **5.** guess, think **6.** gamble,
   ponder, wonder **8.** consider, meditate,
   ruminate, theorize **10.** deliberate,

doctrinize, philosophy **11.** contemplate
speculative . . . **5.** risky **9.** uncertain
10. thoughtful **11.** inquisitive, theoretical
12. experimental **13.** contemplative
speculator . . . **7.** lookout, scalper
8. explorer, observer, theorist
12. investigator
speculum . . . **7.** diopter **9.** reflector
sped . . . **4.** hied **5.** raced **6.** darted,
dashed, let fly **8.** galloped, hastened
10. discharged
speech . . . **5.** spiel **6.** dilogy, orison
7. address, chatter, diction, oration
8. colloquy, harangue, language
9. elocution, utterance **12.** conversation
speech (pert to) . . .
abusive . . **6.** tirade
blunder . . **8.** improper, solecism
comb form . . **4.** logo
conclusion . . **10.** peroration
conversational . . **13.** colloquialism
defective . . **10.** disphrasia
difficulty . . **9.** baryphony **10.** baryphonia
famous . . **9.** Philippic (Demosthenes)
goddess . . **3.** Vac
hasty . . **7.** stammer, stumble, stutter
impediment . . **4.** lisp **8.** betacism,
mytacism
intemperate . . **6.** tirade
loss of . . **6.** alalia **7.** aphasia
movements . . **9.** vocimotor
parts . . **4.** verb **6.** adverb **9.** adjective
11. conjunction, preposition
12. interjection
pompous . . **12.** magniloquent
provincial . . **6.** patois **7.** dialect
set speech (drama) . . **6.** rhesis
term . . **6.** zeugma **9.** syllepsis
understatement . . **7.** litotes
vitriolic . . **6.** tirade
voiceless . . **7.** spirate
without . . **4.** mute **6.** alogia
world . . **7.** Volapük **9.** Esperanto
speechless . . . **4.** dumb, mute **6.** silent
7. aphasic **8.** taciturn **9.** voiceless
speed . . . **3.** fly, hie, run **4.** flit, race,
zoom **5.** haste, hurry, spurt **6.** assist,
go fast, hasten **8.** celerity, dispatch,
expedite, promptly, rapidity, velocity
9. posthaste, quickness, swiftness
10. accelerate, expedition, facilitate
12. precipitance
speedily . . . **4.** soon **5.** apace **6.** presto
7. betimes, quickly, rapidly, swiftly
8. promptly **13.** expeditiously
speedy . . . **4.** fast **5.** apace, fleet, hasty,
quick, rapid, swift **6.** prompt, racing,
sudden
spell . . . **4.** bout, mean, snap, tell, turn
5. charm, magic, relay, shift **6.** glamor,
relate, relief, trance **7.** explain,
relieve, sorcery, syncope **9.** take turns
11. abracadabra **12.** entrancement
13. substitute for
spell (pert to) . . .
binder . . **6.** orator **7.** charmer, spieler
bound . . **4.** rapt **9.** enchanted
10. astonished, interested **11.** under
a spell
brief . . **4.** snap
in another alphabet . . **13.** transliterate

out . . **7.** explain, itemize
pretended . . **11.** abracadabra
under a spell . . **9.** in a trance
10. hypnotized, mesmerized
with loss of letter . . **7.** syncope
spend . . . **3.** use **4.** pass **5.** waste
6. employ, expend, lavish, weaken
7. consume, exhaust **8.** disburse,
squander **9.** dissipate, sacrifice
10. distribute
spend the summer . . . **8.** estivate
(aestivate)
spendthrift . . . **4.** daft **6.** waster
7. spender, wastrel **8.** prodigal
10. profligate, squanderer
Spenser, Edmund (pert to) . . .
character . . **3.** Una
famed as . . **4.** poet
famed work . . **12.** Faerie Queene
poetic stanza . . **10.** Spenserian
Spenser's Ireland personified . . .
5. Irene
spent . . . **4.** paid **5.** weary **6.** effete, used
up, wasted **7.** worn out **8.** consumed,
lavished, tired out **9.** exhausted
10. squandered
speos . . . **4.** cave, tomb **6.** grotto
sphenoid . . . **11.** wedge-shaped
sphere . . . **3.** orb **4.** ball, star **5.** arena,
earth, field, glove, orbit, realm,
scope **6.** extent, planet **7.** circuit,
heavens **8.** terrible **10.** atmosphere
12. jurisdiction
sphere of . . .
action . . **6.** domain
life . . **5.** world
making . . **7.** orbific
spherical (pert to) . . .
aberration, free from . . **9.** aplanatic
geometry . . **10.** magnitudes
lune . . **7.** portion
magnet . . **8.** terrella (terella)
nearly . . **8.** obrotund
reference to . . **6.** rotund **7.** globose
9. orbicular **15.** celestial bodies
ungula . . **5.** wedge
sphericity . . . **9.** globosity, rotundity,
roundness
sphinx (pert to) . . .
builder (Great Sphinx) . . **6.** Khafre (IV
Dynasty)
Great Sphinx site . . **4.** Gaza (Egypt)
Greek myth . . **7.** monster (sphinxlike)
reference to . . **9.** enigmatic
11. inscrutable
Zool . . **8.** hawk moth
spice . . . **4.** dill, herb, mace, sage **5.** chili,
clove **6.** cassia, nutmeg, pepper,
season, stacte **7.** mustard **8.** marjoram,
pungency **9.** condiment, flavoring,
fragrance, seasoning
spicy . . . **3.** hot **4.** keen, racy, sexy
5. balmy, natty, smart **6.** risque
7. gingery, peppery, piquant, pungent
8. aromatic, fragrant, spirited
spider . . . **3.** cob, pan **5.** arain **6.** Epeira,
katipo, tripod, trivet **7.** pokomoo, retiary,
skillet, spinner **8.** arachnid, attercop,
telarian **9.** tarantula **10.** black widow
spider (pert to) . . .
comb form . . **7.** arachno

crab . . **4.** Maia (genus)
fly . . **4.** tick
genus . . **4.** Maia **6.** Aranea **7.** Agalena,
Attidae, Pholcus **9.** Drassidae
Gr Myth . . **7.** Arachne (Lydian girl)
Latin . . **6.** aranea
leaping . . **10.** saltigrade
monkey . . **6.** ateles, coaita
nest . . **5.** nidus
scorpion . . **8.** pedipalp
scorpion appendage . . **10.** pedipalpus
study of . . **10.** araneology
web (anc) . . **8.** attercop
weblike . . **9.** arachnoid
web-spinning organ . . **9.** spinneret
spieler . . . **5.** crier **6.** barker, talker
7. sharper, speaker **8.** lecturer
9. solicitor **10.** ballyhooer
spiffy . . . **4.** fine, neat **5.** smart **8.** splendid
9. excellent
spigot . . . **3.** peg, tap **5.** spile, spout
6. dossil, faucet **7.** stopper
spike . . . **3.** cob, ear **4.** brob, stab,
tine, umbo **5.** ament, piton, prong,
thorn **6.** antler, flower, pierce, spadix
7. amentum, disable, spinule, trenail
10. adulterate **12.** tenpenny nail
spikenard . . . **3.** phu (Cretan) **4.** herb,
nard **8.** ointment
spile . . . **3.** pin, rod **4.** plug, tube **5.** spill,
spout, stake **6.** Aralia, spigot
spill . . . **4.** blab, fall, shed, slop **5.** flosh,
waste **6.** let out, splash, tumble
7. divulge, scatter **8.** downpour,
overflow, overture **11.** tell secrets
spin . . . **4.** birl, fish, reel, ride, turn **5.** swirl,
twirl, twist, whirl **6.** extend, gyrate,
rotate **7.** prolong, revolve
spinach (wrinkled) . . . **5.** savoy
spinal (pert to) . . .
column . . **9.** vertebrae
cord . . **4.** alba **6.** myelon (marrow)
16. medulla oblongata
disease . . **8.** myelitis **10.** meningitis
muscle (attached) . . **5.** psoas
spindle . . . **3.** pin, rod **4.** axis, axle, hasp
5. pivot, xeres **6.** swivel **7.** capstan,
mandrel
spindle-legged . . . **4.** lean **5.** lanky
14. spindle-shanked
spindling . . . **4.** long **5.** gawky, leggy
6. skinny **7.** slender **11.** ineffectual
spine . . . **3.** awn **4.** axis, seta **5.** chine,
ridge, thorn **6.** spirt **7.** acicula,
courage, process **8.** backbone, spiculum
9. scoliosis (curvature) **12.** spinal
column
spinel . . . **5.** balas (ruby) **7.** mineral
8. spinelle
spineless . . . **4.** limp, weak **5.** frail
10. weak-willed **12.** invertebrate
spinet . . . **5.** piano **7.** giraffe **8.** virginal
10. clavichord **11.** couched harp,
harpsichord
spinnaker . . . **4.** sail
spinner . . . **3.** top **4.** liar **6.** spider, weaver
8. narrator **9.** nighthawk **10.** goatsucker
11. storyteller **12.** whippoorwill
spinning . . . **6.** rotary **7.** strobic **8.** telarian,
whirling **9.** revolving
spinning device . . . **5.** jenny **7.** distaff,

spindle **8.** throstle
spiracle . . . **4.** pore, vent **7.** orifice
8. aperture, blowhole
spiral . . . **4.** coil, curl **5.** helix **6.** galaxy,
volute **7.** helical, winding **8.** circling,
helicoid **9.** corkscrew
spire . . . **4.** coil, surl **5.** tower, twist, whorl
6. ascend, finial, summit **7.** steeple
spire finial . . . **3.** épi
spirit . . . **3.** imp, pep, vim **4.** dash,
élan, fire, life, mood, pixy, soul
5. demon, devil, fairy, genie, ghost,
heart, metal, pluck, Satan, shade,
spook, verve **6.** animus, breath, energy,
fervor, goblin, intent, morale, pneuma,
sprite **7.** bravery, courage, essence,
extract, gremlin, specter **8.** spiritus
9. animation **10.** enterprise, individual
11. real meaning **12.** cheerfulness
13. consciousness
spirit, spirit of (pert to) . . .
avarice . . **6.** Mammon
bad . . **6.** afreet **7.** Amaimon (Amaymon)
Egypt . . **2.** ba, ka **3.** akh
English folklore . . **2.** po
evil . . **4.** jinn **5.** Aecto, jinni (jinnel)
6. Azazel, Belial, Erinys **7.** Tempter
(The) **9.** Beelzebub
female . . **6.** undine **7.** banshee
good . . **8.** Eudaemon
household . . **5.** Lares **15.** Lares and
Penates
infatuation . . **3.** Ate
knights . . **8.** errantry
malignant . . **3.** Ker
mockery . . **5.** Momus
people . . **5.** ethos
refined . . **6.** elixir
tapping (theory) . . **9.** typtology
the age . . **9.** Zeitgeist
the air . . **5.** Ariel
the sea . . **5.** siren **6.** Triton **7.** mermaid,
Neptune **9.** Davy Jones
spirited . . . **3.** gay **4.** gamy, racy **5.** brisk,
eager, fiery **6.** lively, plucky, spunky
7. dashing, fervent **8.** eloquent,
generous, vigorous **9.** audacious,
energetic, spiritoso, sprightly
10. mettlesome
spiritless . . . **4.** dead, dull, meek **5.** amort,
vapid **6.** gloomy **8.** dejected, lifeless,
listless **9.** depressed, heartless
10. despondent, dispirited
spirits (pert to) . . .
Babylonian . . **5.** Igigi
dwelling . . **2.** po **5.** Hades **7.** Elysium
low . . **5.** blues, dumps, gloom
8. doldrums
of the dead . . **5.** Manes (Rom) **7.** lemures
9. chthonian (Gr)
spiritual . . . **4.** holy, pure, song **5.** pious
6. devout, divine, sacred **7.** psychic
8. churchly, internal, platonic, spectral
9. unworldly **10.** immaterial
11. disembodied, incorporeal
12. supernatural **14.** ecclesiastical,
heavenly minded
spiritual (pert to) . . .
affinity . . **8.** soul mate
apathy . . **6.** acedia
being . . **3.** ens **5.** angel **6.** seraph

darkness .. **4.** Hell **5.** tamas
director .. **9.** confessor
meaning of words .. **7.** anagoge
meeting .. **6.** séance
shrine .. **6.** adytum **7.** sanctum
spirt ... **3.** jet **4.** gush **5.** flare, spurt
6. squirt
spit ... **3.** rod **4.** rain **5.** eject, image,
stick **6.** impale, pierce, saliva, skewer,
sputum **7.** hissing, spindle, sputter
8. likeness, sprinkle, turnspit
9. exsputory **11.** expectorate
spite ... **3.** vex **4.** hate **5.** pique, shame,
venom **6.** enmity, malice, offend,
rancor, thwart **7.** dislike, ill will
8. disgrace, dishonor **9.** animosity,
cattiness, humiliate **10.** resentment
11. malevolence **12.** spitefulness
spiteful ... **4.** mean **5.** catty **7.** cattish
8. annoying, venomous **9.** malicious,
malignant **10.** irritating, vindictive
spittoon ... **6.** pigdan **8.** crachoir,
cuspidor
splash ... **3.** lap, wet **4.** spot **5.** spray,
swash **6.** blotch, flouse (floush), ripple
7. scatter, spatter, splurge **8.** cut a dash,
splatter **9.** dashingly **14.** ostentatiously
splashboard ... **4.** gate (false) **5.** plank
6. fender, screen **9.** dashboard
10. flashboard, flushboard
splay ... **3.** hem **4.** turn **5.** adorn, carve,
slant, slope **6.** clumsy, expand, spread
7. awkward, display **9.** dislocate,
displayed, expansion
spleen ... **3.** fit **4.** fire, mood, whim
5. anger, ardor, freak, gland **6.** malice,
temper **7.** impulse **8.** ill humor
10. low spirits, melancholy, resentment
11. impetuosity
spleen (pert to) ...
amarinth .. **4.** weed
excision .. **13.** splenectomize
reference to .. **6.** lienal **7.** splenic
splendid ... **4.** braw, fine **5.** grand, regal,
showy **6.** costly, superb **7.** gallant,
shining, sublime **8.** glorious, gorgeous
9. beautiful, brilliant, excellent,
sumptuous **10.** brilliance, effulgence
11. illustrious, magnificent
splendor ... **4.** gite, pomp **5.** éclat, glory
6. beauty, luster **7.** display **8.** grandeur,
radiance, richness **9.** pageantry,
showiness **10.** brilliance
12. gorgeousness, magnificence,
resplendence
splint ... **4.** scob, tace **5.** brace, plate,
strip **6.** fasten, tasset **7.** confine
splinter ... **4.** chip **5.** break, broom
6. shiver, sliver **7.** shatter **8.** fragment
9. matchwood
split ... **3.** cut, rit **4.** chap, open, rend,
rent, rive, tear **5.** break, burst, cleft,
crack, laugh, leave (sl), riven, wedge
6. bisect, cleave, cloven, depart (sl),
divide, sunder **7.** dispart, divided,
rupture, shatter **8.** separate **9.** apportion,
partition **10.** separation
split (pert to) ...
hairs .. **7.** quibble **12.** discriminate
13. differentiate
into two parts .. **5.** bifid **6.** cloven

pea .. **3.** dal **5.** dahll
the difference .. **5.** share **7.** average
10. compromise **12.** go fifty-fifty
up .. **5.** cleft **7.** disband, divorce
8. separate **9.** apportion, partition
spoil ... **3.** mar, rot **4.** loot, prey, ruin,
sack **5.** botch, decay, harry **6.** coddle,
impair, injure, pamper **7.** destroy,
estrepe, louse up (sl), pillage, plunder,
vitiate **9.** frustrate
spoilation ... **6.** rapine **7.** pillage
10. plundering, spoliation
spoiled ... **3.** bad **5.** moldy, musty
6. addled, marred, molded, preyed,
rancid, wasted **7.** botched, bungled,
decayed, tainted **8.** pampered, pillaged
9. plundered **12.** deteriorated
spoiler ... **6.** robber **7.** marplot **8.** pillager
9. despoiler, plunderer
spoils ... **4.** loot, prey, swag **5.** booty,
perks (sl) **11.** perquisites
spoilsport ... **7.** marplot **10.** wet blanket
11. party-pooper
spoke ... **3.** bar, pin, ray, rod **4.** rung,
said **5.** check, round, spake, stake
6. radius, speech **7.** uttered **9.** hindrance
10. impediment
spoke monotonously ... **6.** droned
spoken ... **4.** oral **5.** parol **9.** declaimed,
ideophone (word)
spoliation ... **6.** rapine **7.** pillage
8. ravaging **10.** spoilation
sponge ... **3.** dry, wet **4.** bath, swab
5. erase, mooch **6.** absorb, animal,
efface, eraser, extort **7.** badiaga,
cleanse, sponger, zimocca **8.** drunkard,
parasite **9.** absorbent, sycophant
10. obliterate, porousness
sponge (pert to) ...
Europe .. **7.** badiaga
fruit .. **5.** luffa (loofah)
Mediterranean .. **7.** zimocca
opening .. **7.** apopyle
orifice .. **7.** osculum
young .. **5.** ascon **6.** rhagon
sponger ... **4.** sorn **5.** leech **6.** cadger
7. moocher **8.** parasite **9.** scrounger
10. freeloader
sponsor ... **5.** angel **6.** backer, patron
7. finance **9.** financier, godparent,
guarantee, guarantor, patronize
sponsorship ... **5.** aegis (egis) **7.** subsidy
8. auspices
spontaneous ... **4.** free **6.** native
8. untaught **9.** automatic, voluntary
10. self-acting **11.** instinctive,
involuntary
spontoon ... **4.** club, pike **7.** halberd,
pantoon **9.** espantoon, truncheon
spoof ... **3.** guy **4.** fool, hoax, joke
5. trick **7.** deceive, swindle **8.** nonsense
9. deception
spook ... **5.** ghost **6.** spirit, zombie (zombi)
7. specter **8.** frighten **9.** hobgoblin
10. apparition
spooky ... **5.** eerie, weird **7.** ghostly,
haunted, uncanny **8.** spectral
spool ... **4.** reel, wind **6.** bobbin **7.** spindle
8. cylinder
spoon ... **4.** club **5.** labis, ladle **6.** shovel
7. fish for **8.** cochlear, make love,

runcible
spoonbill . . . **5.** ajaja (ayaya) **9.** sandpiper
Spoon River poet . . . **7.** Masters (E L)
spore (pert to) . . .
  capsule, sac. . **5.** ascus, theca
    10. sporangium
  cluster. . **5.** sorus
  formation. . **6.** tetrad
  fruit. . **7.** asocarp
sport . . . **3.** fun, toy **4.** game, hunt,
  jest, joke, play, romp, wear **5.** dandy,
  mirth **6.** banter, flaunt, frolic, gamble,
  racing, skiing **7.** contest, gambler,
  jesting, mockery, pastime **8.** raillery
  9. amusement, bon vivant, diversion,
  good loser, plaything, sportsman
  10. pleasantry, recreation
  13. entertainment
sport (pert to) . . .
  art of (contests). . **10.** agonistics
  cheap. . **5.** piker
  of kings. . **6.** racing **7.** the turf
sportive . . . **3.** gay **5.** merry **7.** jocular,
  playful **8.** frolicky, playsome **9.** facetious
  10. frolicsome
sports . . . **5.** Rugby, track **6.** hockey, jai
  lai, soccer, squash, tennis **7.** cricket
  8. baseball, football, la crosse, softball
  9. athletics, palaestra **10.** acrobatics,
  gymnastics **11.** racquetball
sports attendance . . . **4.** gate
sports official . . . **5.** coach, judge
  6. umpire **7.** referee **8.** linesman
  10. timekeeper
sporty . . . **5.** rorty, showy **6.** dressy,
  flashy
spot . . . **3.** dot **4.** blet, blot, espy, flaw,
  mark, site, soil **5.** fleck, place, point,
  speck, stain, taint **6.** detect, locate,
  macula, macule, stigma **7.** asperse,
  blemish, freckle, observe, speckle,
  splotch **8.** discolor, disgrace, locality,
  location, position **9.** bespatter, limelight,
  recognize **11.** predicament, small
  amount
spot (pert to) . . .
  cards. . **3.** pip
  fertile. . **5.** oasis
  fish. . **7.** pinfish
  high. . **4.** apex **6.** climax
  mineral. . **5.** macle
  on the spot. . **3.** now **4.** here **7.** imperil,
    present **8.** promptly
  payment. . **4.** cash
  secluded. . **6.** alcove
  sun. . **6.** lucule **7.** granule
  wood. . **3.** wem
spotless . . . **4.** pure **5.** clean **6.** chaste
  8. innocent **9.** blameless, faultless,
  unsullied **10.** immaculate
  11. unblemished, untarnished
  14. irreproachable
spotted . . . **6.** espied, marked, soiled
  7. dappled, guttate (droplike), mottled,
  stained, sullied **8.** speckled
  9. blemished, sprinkled, tarnished
  11. diversified
spouse . . . **4.** mate, wife **5.** bride
  7. consort, partner **9.** companion
  10. better half
spout . . . **3.** jet, jut, lip **4.** dale,

gush, pawn, rant, spew **5.** erupt,
  spile, spurt **6.** pledge, recite, spigot,
  squirt, trough **7.** chatter, conduit,
  declaim **8.** downpour, gargoyle (carved)
  9. discharge, waterfall **10.** waterspout
spouter . . . **5.** whale **6.** geyser **7.** oil well,
  speaker **9.** declaimer **11.** speechifier
sprat . . . **6.** garvie **7.** herring **8.** sixpence
spray . . . **3.** jet **4.** foam **5.** stour, water
  6. squirt **7.** atomize, flowers, gunfire
  8. perfumer, sprinkle **9.** spindrift
  10. spoondrift
spread . . . **3.** ted **4.** meal **5.** bruit, feast,
  flare, strew, widen **6.** expand, extent,
  sprawl, unfurl **7.** divulge, radiate, scatter
  8. disperse **10.** broadcast **11.** disseminate
  13. advertisement
spread (pert to) . . .
  by defamation. . **5.** libel
  by report. . **6.** norate
  by rumor. . **5.** noise
  eagle. . **8.** boastful, insignia **9.** patriotic
    12. exaggeration
  out. . **3.** fan **4.** open, span **5.** flare
    6. deploy
  over. . **5.** cover, smear
  thickly. . **7.** slather
  thin. . **4.** bray
spree . . . **4.** lark, orgy, romp **5.** binge,
  revel **6.** bender, frolic, shindy **7.** wassail
  8. carousal
sprig . . . **4.** trim, twig **5.** scion, shoot,
  smart **6.** active, spruce **8.** ornament
  9. youngling
sprightly . . . **3.** gay **4.** airy, pert **5.** alive,
  brisk, peart **6.** blithe, lively **7.** briskly,
  ghostly **8.** vigorous **10.** enlivening,
  spiritedly **11.** incorporeal
spring . . . **3.** fly, hop, spa **4.** dart, font,
  jump, leap, well **5.** shoot, spurt, vault,
  vigor **6.** bounce, energy, geyser, origin,
  season, source **9.** saltation **10.** elasticity,
  resilience
spring (pert to) . . .
  back. . **6.** recoil, resile **7.** rebound
  of the Muses. . **7.** Pierian
  ref to. . **6.** vernal
  up. . **4.** grow **5.** arise, occur **6.** appear,
    ascend **9.** originate
springing into being . . . **9.** renascent
springs . . . **4.** spas **5.** baths, fonts **6.** resort
  (health) **7.** thermae
sprinkle . . . **3.** deg, dot, wet **4.** rain
  5. bedew, spray, strew, water **6.** bedrop,
  sparge, spreng **7.** baptize, scatter
  9. bespatter
sprinkler . . . **11.** aspergillum (Eccl)
sprinkle with . . .
  flour. . **6.** dredge
  grit. . **4.** sand
  heraldic. . **4.** semé
  powder. . **4.** dust
  water. . **3.** deg
sprint . . . **3.** run **4.** dash, race
sprite . . . **3.** elf, fay, hob, imp, nix **4.** peri
  5. fairy, ghost, gnome, pixie, sylph
  6. goblin, spirit **7.** brownie **9.** hobgoblin
  10. apparition
sprite (pert to) . . .
  fiction. . **5.** Ariel
  Irish. . **10.** leprechaun

mischievous . . **4.** Puck
ref to . . **6.** elfish

sprocket . . . **5.** tooth, wheel **8.** cylinder (toothed) **10.** projection

sprout . . . **3.** bud, son **4.** cion, grow **5.** scion, shoot, spire, sprit **6.** branch, ratoon, tiller **7.** burgeon, upstart **8.** offshoot **9.** germinate **10.** descendant

spruce . . . **4.** chic, neat, posh, smug, tree, trig, trim **5.** adorn, natty, smart **6.** dapper **7.** finical, smarten **8.** titivate

spruce (pert to) . . .
beverage . . **4.** beer
black . . **7.** yew pine
fir . . **6.** Norway
genus . . **5.** Abies, Picea
Japanese . . **6.** Alcock
type . . **7.** Douglas, hemlock
white . . **8.** épinette

sprue . . . **5.** dross, waste **6.** thrush **7.** disease **8.** psilosis **9.** asparagus

spry . . . **5.** agile, brisk, quick, smart **6.** active, nimble **8.** vigorous **9.** sprightly

spud . . . **5.** drill, knife, spade **6.** dagger, paddle, potato, reamer, shovel

spume . . . **4.** foam, scum **5.** froth

spunky . . . **4.** game **5.** quick **6.** plucky, touchy **9.** spirited **10.** courageous, mettlesome **13.** quick-tempered

spur . . . **3.** egg **4.** goad, move, urge **5.** drive, press, ridge, rowel, spine **6.** calcar, excite, griffe, incite, needle **7.** provoke **8.** stimulus **9.** instigate, stimulate **10.** incitement

spur (pert to) . . .
badge . . **10.** knighthood
fowl . . **5.** quail **9.** partridge
gamecock's . . **4.** gaff **7.** gablock
mountain . . **5.** arête
pert to . . **7.** spicate
railroad . . **5.** track
wheel . . **5.** rowel

spurious . . . **4.** fake, sham **5.** false **6.** pseudo **7.** bastard **10.** adulterate, apocryphal, artificial, fictitious, fraudulent **11.** counterfeit **12.** illegitimate **14.** supposititious

spurious (pert to) . . .
fruit . . **10.** pseudocarp
olive . . **9.** heartwood
rainbow . . **8.** faint arc
wing . . **7.** bastard

spurn . . . **4.** defy **5.** scorn **6.** reject, strike **7.** contemn, disdain

spurt . . . **3.** jet, jut **4.** dash, gush, spew **5.** burst, spout **7.** outpour, upsurge **8.** outbreak

spy . . . **3.** pry, see **4.** espy, note, tout **5.** scout, sneak, snoop, watch **6.** behold, descry, detect, search **7.** examine, snooper **8.** discover, emissary, informer, perceive **10.** scrutinize **11.** reconnoiter

spy (pert to) . . .
city . . **7.** Belgium
in clothing circles . . **4.** keek
Man of . . **14.** paleolithic man
prison . . **6.** mouton

squab . . . **3.** fat **4.** fowl, sofa **5.** piper, plump **6.** fat man, pigeon **7.** cushion **8.** nestling **9.** fledgling

squabble . . . **5.** brawl **6.** bicker, jangle

7. contend, quarrel, wrangle **10.** disarrange (Print) **13.** collieshangie

squad . . . **4.** team, unit **5.** posse **7.** company

squalid . . . **4.** foul, mean, poor **5.** dirty **6.** filthy, sordid **7.** unclean **8.** slovenly **9.** repellent, repulsive **11.** squalidness **15.** poverty-stricken

squall . . . **3.** cry, row **4.** blow, gale, gust, wail, wind, yell **6.** squawk, squeal **9.** commotion **11.** disturbance

squalor . . . **4.** dirt, mire **5.** filth **8.** slovenry **9.** dirtiness **10.** filthiness **11.** squalidness **16.** unkempt condition

squamate, squamous . . . **5.** scaly **6.** scaled

squander . . . **5.** waste **6.** lavish **7.** scatter **8.** disperse, misspend **9.** dissipate, throw away **10.** run through

squanderer . . . **5.** loser **7.** wastrel

square . . . **4.** even, meal **5.** bribe, plaza **6.** common, honest, settle **7.** exactly, obelisk, old fogy **8.** absolute, cube face, directly, equalize, quadrate **9.** city block, divergent **11.** unequivocal **13.** parallelogram **14.** unsophisticate **15.** straightforward

squash . . . **4.** mash, pepo, pulp **5.** crush, gourd, press **6.** cushaw, refute, simlin, simnel, soften **7.** cymling (cymbling), Hubbard, squeeze **8.** pattypan, suppress **9.** crookneck **10.** extinguish **11.** calabazilla

squat . . . **3.** low **5.** dumpy, pudgy, quash, stoop **6.** crouch, hunker, settle, stubby **7.** sit down **8.** squatter, thickset

squatter . . . **6.** nester (illegal) **7.** pioneer **9.** sandpiper **11.** homesteader

Squatter State . . . **6.** Kansas

squaw . . . **6.** coween, Indian, mahala (mahaly)

squeal . . . **6.** betray, inform **7.** protest, quarrel

squealer . . . **4.** fink **6.** grouse, pigeon, plover **7.** traitor **8.** informer

squeamish . . . **4.** nice **5.** dizzy **6.** dainty, queasy **7.** prudish **8.** overnice, qualmish **9.** nauseated **10.** fastidious, scrupulous

squeeze . . . **3.** hug, jam, nip **4.** cram, crux **5.** crowd, crush, pinch, press, wring **6.** crisis, extort **7.** embrace **8.** compress **9.** constrict, influence **10.** constraint **11.** compression

squeezer, fruit . . . **6.** juicer, reamer

squelch . . . **5.** crush, quash, quell **6.** rebuke, refute, subdue **7.** repress, silence **8.** suppress **10.** disconcert

squib . . . **4.** bomb, fuse, pipe, skit, tube **6.** speech, squirt **7.** explode, lampoon, writing **9.** bespatter **10.** pasquinade **11.** firecracker

squire . . . **4.** beau **5.** court, lover **6.** escort **7.** gallant **8.** henchman, nobleman **9.** attendant, gentleman, landowner

squirm . . . **5.** twist **6.** wiggle, writhe **7.** wriggle

squirrel (pert to) . . .
African . . **5.** xerus
American . . **5.** bunny **7.** assapan **8.** chipmunk **9.** chickaree
American, flying . . **7.** assapan

Asian.. **5.** sisel **6.** suslik
Austral, flying.. **9.** phalanger
burrowing.. **6.** gopher
cage.. **9.** treadmill
color.. **4.** lead
E Ind, flying.. **6.** taguan
fish.. **7.** serrano
fur (Her).. **4.** vair
genus.. **6.** Tamias **7.** Sciurus
Java.. **8.** jelerang
like.. **8.** sciuroid
nest.. **4.** dray, drey
shrew.. **4.** tana **6.** Tupaia
skin.. **4.** vair
Spanish.. **7.** ardilla
squirrellike mammal... **8.** banxring, dormouse
stab... **4.** gore, pang, pink **5.** knife, knive, lunge, wound **6.** attack, injury, pierce, thrust **7.** poniard, slander **8.** puncture, stoccado
stability... **5.** poise **7.** balance **8.** firmness, strength **9.** constancy **10.** permanence, stableness, steadiness **11.** reliability **12.** immovability, immutability **13.** steadfastness
stabilize... **3.** set **5.** poise **6.** steady **7.** ballast **8.** regulate
stable... **3.** mew (Royal) **4.** barn, byre, firm, safe **5.** fixed, solid, sound, stall **6.** steady, strong **7.** durable, lasting, paddock, support **8.** constant, reliable **9.** confirmed, permanent, steadfast **10.** stationary, unwavering **11.** established, trustworthy
stableman... **5.** groom **7.** hostler (ostler)
staccato... **7.** détaché **8.** ricochet **12.** disconnected
stack... **4.** heap, load, pile, rick **5.** mound, shock **6.** pile up **7.** chimney, conduit **8.** quantity
stacked... **11.** accumulated, prearranged
stacked pack, cards... **8.** cold deck
stadium... **5.** stage **6.** course, dromos **8.** foot race (anc)
stadium race, start... **7.** aphesis
staff... **3.** rod **4.** club, mace, pole **5.** baton, music, stave **7.** scepter, support **8.** caduceus, insignia, pastoral **9.** personnel **10.** assistants, associates
staff (pert to)...
Bacchus.. **7.** thyrsus
bearer.. **5.** macer
magician's.. **7.** rhabdos
marshal's.. **5.** baton
member, officer.. **4.** aide **7.** attaché
mountain climbing.. **10.** alpenstock
pastoral.. **5.** pedum **7.** baculus, crosier (crozier)
shepherd's.. **5.** crook, pedum
sovereign's.. **7.** scepter (sceptre)
stag... **4.** colt, deer (red), hart **5.** party, royal, spade **7.** male fox, pollard **8.** gamecock, informer
stage... **4.** dais, tier **5.** arena, phase, scene **6.** degree **7.** display, estrade, perform, rostrum **8.** platform, scaffold **9.** dramatize, gradation **10.** proscenium, stagecoach
stage (pert to)...
call (trumpet).. **6.** sennet

direction.. **5.** aside, manet **6.** sennet
of disease.. **9.** catabasis
of insects.. **5.** imago, larva
part.. **5.** stair **8.** dutchman (patch) **10.** proscenium
scene (side).. **8.** coulisse
scenery.. **3.** set
stagger... **4.** reel, stot, stun, sway, walk **5.** lurch **6.** excite, totter, zigzag **7.** be drunk, tremble, vibrate **8.** astonish, flounder, frighten, titubate, unsettle **9.** alternate, fluctuate
staggering... **5.** areel **9.** startling **10.** astounding **11.** the staggers **12.** unbelievable
Stagirite, The... **9.** Aristotle
stagnant... **4.** dull, foul **5.** inert, stale, still **8.** inactive, sluggish, standing **10.** motionless, not flowing **13.** unprogressive
stagnate... **3.** rot **4.** dull **5.** inert **8.** stagnant, vegetate **10.** motionless
staid... **5.** grave, sober **6.** demure, sedate, solemn **7.** serious, settled **8.** composed, decorous, sensible **9.** steadfast
stain... **3.** dye **4.** blot, soil, spot, tint **5.** color, paint, smear, sully **6.** infamy, smudge, stigma **7.** blemish, corrupt, pigment, tarnish **8.** discolor, disgrace, dishonor, maculate **9.** pollution **10.** stigmatize **11.** contaminate **13.** discoloration
stained by decay... **4.** doty
stained glass rod (lead)... **4.** came
stair... **4.** step **5.** riser, stage, tread **6.** degree, flight (series)
staircase (pert to)...
French.. **8.** escalier
moving.. **9.** escalator
outdoor.. **6.** perron
post.. **5.** newel
ship's.. **12.** companionway
spiral.. **8.** caracole
stairs to bath (Ind)... **4.** ghat (ghaut)
stake... **3.** bet, peg, pel, pin **4.** ante, pale, pile, post, risk, spit **5.** sowel, teest, wager **6.** chance, estate, gamble, hazard, picket, pledge **7.** finance, venture
stale... **3.** old **5.** banal, fusty, trite, vapid **7.** insipid, spoiled **9.** hackneyed, tasteless **10.** flavorless **11.** commonplace
stalemate... **6.** corner **7.** impasse **8.** cul-de-sac, deadlock **10.** blind alley, standstill
stalk... **4.** axis, hunt, risp, stem, walk **6.** pursue, stride **7.** pedicel **8.** peduncle **11.** reconnoiter
stalk (pert to)...
cotton, sugar cane.. **6.** ratoon
dry.. **3.** hay, kex **5.** haulm (halm)
flower.. **7.** petiole
grain, grass.. **4.** culm **5.** straw **6.** ressum
strawberry.. **4.** risp
stalkless... **7.** sessile
stall... **3.** cot, pew **4.** crib, fail, loge, mire, stop **5.** booth, check, choir, stick **6.** hinder, manger, stable **7.** disgust **9.** temporize **10.** dillydally **11.** compartment, play for time

12. parking space 13. procrastinate

stalwart . . . 5. brave, stout 6. strong, sturdy 7. valiant 8. partisan, resolute 9. corpulent 10. courageous, unyielding

stamen part . . . 6. anther, pollen 8. filament

stamina . . . 5. pluck, vigor 7. courage 8. backbone, strength 9. endurance, fortitude 12. staying power

stammer . . . 3. haw, hem 4. mant 6. falter 7. stumble, stutter 8. hesitate

stammering . . . 8. psellism

stamp . . . 3. die 4. date, dink, form, mark, seal, sign, tool 5. brand, infix, label 6. signet 7. engrave, impress, imprint, postage, trading 8. tressure (tressour) 11. endorsement 14. characteristic

stamp (pert to) . . .
border . . 8. tressure (tressour)
collecting . . 9. philately
collector . . 11. philatelist
madness . . 11. timbromania
paper . . 6. pelure
postage . . 6. timbre
space . . 8. spandrel

stampede . . . 3. run 4. rout, rush 5. panic 6. flight 7. debacle 11. wild scamper

stance . . . 4. pose 7. posture, station 8. position

stanch . . . 5. allay, check, quell 6. steady, strong 7. zealous 8. faithful 9. steadfast 10. extinguish 11. substantial

stanchion . . . 3. bar 4. post, prop 5. brace, piton 6. secure 7. support, upright

stand . . . 4. bear, bier, halt, rack, stop, zarf 5. abide, arise, booth, easel, store, table 6. endure, tripod 7. coaster, étagère, footing, impasse, sustain, taboret 8. attitude, foothold, pedestal, position, tolerate 9. withstand 10. standstill

stand (pert to) . . .
against . . 6. resist
by . . 3. aid 6. defend 7. support 9. be present
cost of . . 5. treat
Eccl . . 4. ambo
for . . 6. permit, typify 9. represent, symbolize
for candles . . 7. epergne 10. candelabra
in . . 6. deputy 10. substitute
it . . 4. bear 5. brook 6. suffer
offish . . 4. cold 5. aloof 8. reserved 10. not cordial
opposite . . 4. face
three-legged . . 6. teapoy, tripod, trivot
up to . . 5. brave 6. resist

standard . . . 3. par 4. flag, norm 5. grade, model, usual 6. ensign 7. average, classic, paragon, precept 8. orthodox 9. customary, principle 13. authoritative

standard (pert to) . . .
battle . . 9. oriflamme (oriflamb)
bearer . . 6. leader 7. officer 10. politician
chem test . . 5. titer (titre)
ensign . . 8. gonfalon, gonfanon
flag (Rom) . . 8. vexillum
of excellence . . 4. idea
of intelligence . . 5. Binet
of light . . 6. carcel
of quantity . . 4. unit
Ottoman Emp . . 4. alem

standardize . . . 9. calibrate, normalize

standing . . . 4. rank 5. fixed, state 6. at rest, status 7. footing, settled, station, upright 8. duration, prestige 9. permanent 10. durability, reputation

standing (pert to) . . .
long . . 7. durable 8. duration 11. traditional
mode of . . 6. stance
out . . 7. eminent, salient
room only . . 3. SRO
social . . 6. estate, status 8. prestige
upright . . 11. orthostatic

stannum . . . 2. Sn 3. tin

stanza . . . 4. rann, unit 5. stave, verse 6. octave, sestet 7. strophe, triolet (8-lined)

stanza scheme . . . 6. ballad 10. Gray's Elegy, Spenserian

star . . . 3. sun 4. hero, lead 5. actor, shine 6. étoile 7. destiny, fortune 8. asterisk, insignia, ornament 9. emphasize, principal 11. hummingbird 12. heavenly body, luminous body

star (pert to) . . . see also *Stars*
brightest . . 3. Cor, sun 5. Deneb 6. Altair, Lucida, Sirius
Bull's Eye . . 9. Aldebaran
divination . . 9. astrology
Dog . . 4. Sept 6. Sirius 8. Canicula 12. Canis Majoris
evening . . 5. Venus 6. Hesper, Vesper 7. evestar 8. Hesperus
feather . . 9. comatulid
five-pointed . . 9. pentagram, pentalpha
French . . 6. étoile
gazer . . 4. fish 10. astronomer
giant . . 10. Betelgeuse (Betelgeux)
group (fixed) . . 13. constellation
guiding . . 5. Alpha, North 7. Polaris 8. Cynosure, loadstar, lodestar, polestar
large . . 5. Rigel
morning . . 4. Mars 5. Venus 6. Saturn 7. daystar, Jupiter, Mercury 8. Phosphor
North . . 7. Polaris 8. loadstar, lodestar
of Africa . . 15. Cullinan diamond
of Bethlehem (Bib) . . 11. guide of Magi
of the sea . . 11. Maris Stella (Stella Maris)
ornament . . 4. semé
path . . 5. orbit
ref to . . 6. astral, starry 7. sideral, stellar 8. sidereal 9. planatoid
representation . . 6. étoile
shooting . . 5. comet 6. Leonid, meteor
variable . . 4. nova 7. cepheid, R R Lyrae
wars . . 3. SDI

starch . . . 3. vim 4. sago 5. hilum, vigor 6. amidin, energy, farina, fecula 7. cassava 8. glycogen 9. arrowroot, formality, stiffness

starchy . . . 5. stiff 6. formal, viscid 7. amyloid, precise 9. unbending

stare . . . 4. gape, gawk, gaze, look, ogle, peer 5. glare 6. glower, goggle, wonder

starfish . . . 7. asteria 10. echinoderm

stark . . . 4. bare, mere 5. rigid, tense 6. barren, wholly 7. violent 8. absolute, complete, entirely 9. downright, unadorned 10. absolutely

starling . . . 4. myna, sali 6. pastor

Stars (pert to) . . .
  and Bars . . **15.** Confederate flag
  belt, tract (luminous) . . **6.** Galaxy **8.** Milky
    Way
  circumpolar group . . **5.** Draco **6.** Dragon
  four (famed) . . **4.** Crux **13.** Southern
    Cross
  North Pole group . . **9.** Great Bear
    10. Little Bear **11.** Septentrion
  Ursa Major . . **9.** Big Dipper, Great Bear
  Ursa Minor . . **10.** Little Bear **12.** Little
    Dipper
start . . . **4.** dart, dash, jerk, rush **5.** begin,
  enter, sally **6.** broach, origin, twitch
  7. get away, startle **8.** commence
  9. advantage, beginning, departure,
  originate **10.** inaugurate
starting point . . . **4.** text (sermon)
  7. scratch **9.** departure
startle . . . **5.** alarm, rouse, scare, shock
  6. excite, fright **8.** astonish **9.** electrify
starve . . . **3.** die **4.** kill **5.** crave **6.** famish,
  perish, scrimp **7.** atrophy, destroy
  10. be indigent
starved . . . **4.** thin **5.** empty **6.** frozen,
  hungry **8.** famished, ravenous
starwort . . . **5.** aster **9.** colicroot
stash . . . **5.** cache, plant, store **7.** lay
  away **8.** hide away
state . . . **3.** say **4.** aver, case, état, mode,
  tell **5.** utter **6.** affirm, allege, assert,
  plight, recite, remark, report **7.** country,
  declare, expound, express, narrate
  8. announce, propound **9.** condition,
  enunciate, postulate, pronounce,
  territory **10.** government, possession
  11. body politic **12.** circumstance,
  commonwealth
state (pert to) . . .
  a fact . . **4.** aver **5.** posit **6.** avouch
    7. declare
  agitated . . **9.** disturbed, perturbed
  disordered . . **9.** cluttered
  formally . . **8.** propound **9.** enunciate,
    pronounce
  French . . **4.** état
  hypnotic . . **6.** trance
  ideal . . **6.** Utopia
  office . . **8.** governor **11.** secretariat
  on oath . . **6.** depose
  police . . **7.** trooper
  reference . . **6.** statal
  secret . . **7.** arcanum
  specifically . . **6.** define **7.** itemize
    13. particularize
  treasury . . **4.** fisc **6.** fiscus
  ultimate . . **3.** end
  under foreign control . . **12.** protectorate
  without proof . . **6.** allege
stately . . . **5.** grand, largo, lofty, regal,
  royal **6.** august, coldly, kingly
  7. haughty, queenly, togated
  8. eloquent, imperial, imposing,
  majestic **9.** dignified, grandiose
  11. magnificent
statement . . . **4.** bill, list **5.** audit, dixit
  6. dictum, remark, report, resumé
  7. account, invoice, premise **8.** abstract,
  proposal, schedule **9.** affidavit,
  assertion, manifesto **10.** accounting,
  expression, recitation **11.** declaration

12. announcement, presentation
statement (pert to) . . .
  abridged . . **6.** precis, resumé **7.** summary
    10. abridgment **11.** abridgement
  assumed true . . **7.** premise
  contradictory . . **7.** paradox
  defamatory . . **5.** libel
  detailed . . **8.** schedule
  dogmatic . . **6.** dictum
  introductory . . **5.** proem **7.** preface,
    prelude **8.** foreword, prologue
  legal . . **11.** declaration
  mathematical . . **7.** theorem
  of belief . . **5.** credo, creed
  of introduction . . **8.** prologue
  precise . . **8.** aphorism
  self-evident . . **6.** truism
  sworn . . **9.** affidavit
State nicknames . . .
  Alabama . . **6.** Cotton **12.** Heart of Dixie,
    Yellowhammer
  Alaska . . (no official)
  Arizona . . **11.** Grand Canyon
  Arkansas . . **17.** Land of Opportunity
  California . . **6.** Golden
  Colorado . . **10.** Centennial
  Connecticut . . **6.** Nutmeg
  Delaware . . **5.** First
  Florida . . **8.** Sunshine
  Georgia . . **5.** Peach
  Hawaii . . **5.** Aloha
  Idaho . . **3.** Gem
  Illinois . . **7.** Prairie
  Indiana . . **7.** Hoosier
  Iowa . . **7.** Hawkeye
  Kansas . . **9.** Sunflower
  Kentucky . . **9.** Bluegrass
  Louisiana . . **7.** Pelican
  Maine . . **8.** Pine Tree
  Maryland . . **4.** Free **7.** Old Line
  Massachusetts . . **3.** Bay **9.** Old Colony
  Michigan . . **9.** Wolverine
  Minnesota . . **6.** Gopher **9.** North Star
  Mississippi . . **8.** Magnolia
  Missouri . . **6.** Show Me
  Montana . . **8.** Treasure
  Nebraska . . **4.** Beef **10.** Cornhusker
  Nevada . . **6.** Silver **9.** Sagebrush
  New Hampshire . . **7.** Granite
  New Jersey . . **6.** Garden
  New Mexico . . **17.** Land of Enchantment
  New York . . **6.** Empire
  North Carolina . . **7.** Tarheel **8.** Old North
  North Dakota . . **5.** Sioux **11.** Flickertail
  Ohio . . **7.** Buckeye
  Oklahoma . . **6.** Sooner
  Oregon . . **6.** Beaver
  Pennsylvania . . **8.** Keystone
  Rhode Island . . **11.** Little Rhody
  South Carolina . . **8.** Palmetto
  South Dakota . . **6.** Coyote **8.** Sunshine
  Tennessee . . **9.** Volunteer
  Texas . . **8.** Lone Star
  Utah . . **7.** Beehive
  Vermont . . **13.** Green Mountain
  Virginia . . **11.** Old Dominion
  Washington . . **9.** Evergreen
  West Virginia . . **8.** Mountain
  Wisconsin . . **6.** Badger
  Wyoming . . **8.** Equality
state of . . .

dissension .. **8.** scission
disuse .. **9.** desuetude
ecstasy .. **6.** trance **7.** rapture **8.** paradise
hostility .. **6.** feudal
mind .. **4.** mood **5.** humor **6.** morale
  8. attitude
unconsciousness .. **4.** coma **5.** faint
state of being ...
a layman .. **9.** laicality
artless .. **7.** naiveté
a son .. **7.** sonship
a woman .. **10.** muliebrity
behindhand .. **9.** in arrears
beyond natural laws .. **12.** supernatural
complete .. **9.** plenitude
confined .. **10.** internment
free from error .. **9.** inerrancy
married twice, illegally .. **6.** bigamy
married twice, legally .. **6.** digamy
overfull .. **8.** plethora
passive .. **9.** stolidity
poison .. **5.** toxic **8.** toxicity
voiced .. **7.** sonancy
worse .. **8.** pejority
wrong .. **7.** errancy
static ... **5.** inert, noise **6.** stable **7.** resting
  8. electric, inactive **9.** quiescent
  10. stationary **12.** atmospherics,
  interference
station ... **4.** fire, post, rank, seat,
  stop **5.** berth, depot, place, radio,
  serai **6.** health, police **7.** calling,
  dignity **8.** location, position, prestige
  9. situation **11.** institution
stationary ... **3.** set **5.** fixed, still **6.** stable,
  static, stator **8.** immobile **9.** immovable
  10. motionless, unchanging
stationery ... **3.** pen **5.** paper **6.** pencil
  9. onionskin, papeterie **12.** writing
  páper
statue ... **4.** bust **5.** image **8.** acrolith,
  figurine, monument **9.** sculpture,
  statuette
statue (pert to) ...
at Thebes .. **6.** Memnon
gigantic .. **8.** Colossus
Guildhall (London) .. **3.** Gog **5.** Magog
holy .. **4.** icon (ikon)
male figure (support) .. **7.** telamon
part .. **5.** socle, trunk **6.** plinth
primitive .. **6.** xoanon
Pygmalion's .. **7.** Galatea
world wonder .. **6.** Helios (Rhodes)
status ... **4.** rank **5.** class, state **7.** station
  8. position, prestige, standing
status symbol ... **11.** swivel chair
statute ... **3.** act, jus, law, lex **5.** bylaw,
  canon, edict, title **6.** decree, rubric,
  treaty **8.** statutum **9.** enactment,
  ordinance **10.** regulation **11.** legislation
staunch, stanch ... **4.** firm, true
  6. hearty **7.** devoted **8.** faithful,
  resolute **9.** steadfast **10.** dependable
  11. trustworthy
stave ... **3.** bar, leg **4.** fend, pole, rung,
  slat **5.** staff, stick **6.** cudgel, lathee,
  letter, stanza **7.** baculus, support, ward
  off **8.** overcome **11.** set of verses
stave off ... **4.** fend **7.** prevent
  8. postpone
staves, bundle of ... **5.** shook

stay ... **3.** guy, leg, rib **4.** prop,
  rely, stop, wait **5.** abide, brace,
  cease, check, pause, tarry **6.** adhere,
  arrest, linger, remain, retard, status
  7. prevent, respite **8.** postpone, restrain
  9. cessation, hindrance **10.** impediment
  12. postponement
stead ... **4.** help, lieu **5.** place **6.** assist,
  behalf **7.** replace, service, support
  9. advantage, farmstead, homestead
steadfast ... **4.** firm, true **5.** fixed **6.** stable
  7. durable, staunch **8.** constant, faithful,
  reliable **9.** unwinking **10.** unchanging,
  unswerving **11.** unalterable
steadiness ... **5.** nerve **7.** balance
  9. constancy, stability **10.** uniformity
  11. reliability
steady ... **4.** firm **5.** fixed, grave, sober,
  staid **6.** stable, sturdy **7.** assured,
  equable, regular, uniform **8.** constant,
  resolute **9.** incessant, steadfast
  10. invariable, unswerving
  11. unfaltering, unmitigated
  13. uninterrupted
steal ... **3.** cly, cop, gyp, nim, rap,
  rob **4.** crib, lift, loot **5.** filch, pinch,
  poach, swipe **6.** finger, kidnap, pilfer,
  snitch **7.** purloin **8.** embezzle, peculate
  10. plagiarize **11.** appropriate
steal (pert to) ...
a march on .. **5.** evade **7.** precede
  10. anticipate **13.** gain advantage
away .. **5.** creep, slink, sneak
cattle .. **6.** rustle
feloniously .. **6.** ratten
game .. **5.** poach **8.** trespass
insane desire to .. **11.** kleptomania
nautical .. **7.** manavel
stealer ... **5.** crook, thief **6.** lifter, pirate
  7. abactor, abigens, filcher, rustler
  8. pilferer **9.** embezzler, peculator,
  purloiner **10.** pickpocket, plagiarist
  11. biblioklept **12.** kleptomaniac
stealthy ... **3.** sly **6.** artful, feline,
  secret **7.** catlike, cunning, furtive
  11. clandestine
steam ... **4.** boil, fume, heat, mist, reek
  5. force, power, smoke, stufa, vapor
  6. energy, pother (puther) **8.** vaporize
  9. evaporate
steam (pert to) ...
boat .. **5.** liner **7.** steamer **9.** steamship
  11. side-wheeler
jet .. **5.** stufa **8.** suffione
organ .. **8.** calliope
steamboat cabin (officer's) ... **5.** texas
steamy ... **5.** misty **7.** excited **8.** vaporous
  9. steamed up
steatite ... **4.** talc **9.** soapstone
steed ... **3.** nag **5.** horse **7.** charger,
  courser, Pegasus (winged)
steel ... **5.** inure **6.** harden, smooth
  10. strengthen
steel (pert to) ...
armor plate .. **4.** tace **5.** tasse
color .. **4.** gray **9.** steel blue **12.** Prussian
  blue
conversion to .. **10.** acieration
India .. **5.** wootz **10.** wootz steel
metallurgy of .. **9.** siderurgy
process .. **8.** Bessemer **11.** cementation

type . . **6.** damask, Toledo **8.** Damascus

steep . . . **3.** ret, sop **4.** brae, buck, high, soak, stew, tall **5.** cleve (cleeve), hilly, lofty, scarp, sharp, sheer **6.** abrupt, clifty, escarp, imbrue, infuse, seethe **7.** extract, extreme **8.** elevated, headlong, macerate **9.** difficult, excessive, expensive, precipice **10.** exorbitant **11.** precipitous **13.** perpendicular

steeple . . . **5.** spire, tower **6.** flèche **7.** minaret **8.** pinnacle

steer . . . **2.** ox **3.** cow, ply, yaw **4.** helm, luff, stot **5.** guide, pilot **6.** bovina, direct, govern, manage **7.** bullock, control, operate

steer clear of . . . **4.** snub **5.** avert, avoid **9.** sidetrack, step aside **14.** be inhospitable

steer close to wind . . . **4.** luff

steeve . . . **4.** lade, pack, spar (a) **5.** store, stuff **6.** freeze

stein . . . **3.** mug **4.** Toby

stellar . . . **6.** astral, starry **7.** leading, starlit **8.** starlike, stellate **10.** theatrical

Steller's sea cow . . . **6.** Rytina

stem . . . **3.** dam **4.** axis, base, cion, corm, prow, root, stop, tige **5.** check, shaft, stalk, tuber **6.** branch, breast, oppose, scapel, stanch **7.** lineage, petiole **8.** ancestry, peduncle **9.** originate

stem (pert to) . . .
   bulblike . . **4.** corm, drub
   cylinder . . **5.** stele
   grass . . **4.** culm
   joint . . **4.** cane, node
   mushroom . . **5.** stipe
   plant . . **4.** bine
   seedling . . **7.** tigella (tigelle) **9.** hypocotyl
   strawberry . . **4.** risp
   twining . . **7.** tendril
   underground . . **5.** tuber

stemless herb (evergreen) . . . **5.** Galax **11.** acaulescent

stench . . . **4.** odor **5.** fetor, smell, stink

stenographer of Cicero . . . **4.** Tiro

step . . . **3.** pas, way **4.** gait, pace, rung **5.** dance, grise, phase, riser, stair, stalk, strut, tread **6.** degree, stride **7.** advance, imprint, measure, process **8.** distance, footstep **9.** footprint, gradation **10.** stepladder

step (pert to) . . .
   arrangement of troops . . **7.** echelon
   clumsy . . **5.** stamp
   dance . . **3.** pas **6.** chassé
   mincingly . . **6.** sashay
   mother . . **7.** noverca
   stately . . **5.** stalk
   up . . **8.** approach **9.** intensify **10.** accelerate

steppe . . . **5.** plain **9.** grassland

steps (outdoor flight) . . . **6.** perron

stereotyped . . . **5.** banal, corny, trite **6.** common, old hat **9.** hackneyed **11.** cut and dried

sterile . . . **4.** arid **6.** barren **7.** useless **8.** impotent **9.** fruitless **10.** unfruitful **11.** ineffective, ineffectual **12.** unproductive

stern . . . **4.** dour, grim, hard, rear, rump

5. harsh **6.** gloomy, severe, strict, sullen, unkind **7.** austere **8.** buttocks, hind part, rigorous **9.** harshness, unfeeling **10.** strictness, unyielding **11.** hardhearted **14.** uncompromising

sternutation . . . **8.** sneezing

sternutative . . . **7.** errhine

stertorous . . . **7.** snoring **15.** hoarse breathing

stevedore . . . **5.** lader **6.** loader, stower **7.** carrier **8.** unloader **12.** longshoreman

stew . . . **3.** pot **4.** boil, cook, food, fret, fume, mess, olio, olla **5.** anger, imbue, steep, worry **6.** bustle, ragout, seethe, simmer **7.** haricot, swelter **8.** meat dish **9.** Brunswick **10.** excitement, hodgepodge **11.** predicament

steward . . . **5.** agent, reeve **6.** seaman, waiter **7.** dapifer, erenach, foreman, granger, manager, servant **8.** manciple **9.** custodian, major-domo, seneschal, treasurer **10.** magistrate **11.** chamberlain, fiscal agent

Stewart, Stuart sovereigns (last) . . . **4.** Anne **5.** Henry

stewed fruit . . . **7.** compote

stick . . . **3.** bar, bat, bow, gad, gum, rod **4.** cane, dolt, glue, mast, pogo, ship, stab, wand, wood **5.** baton, cling, fagot, paste, shaft, staff, stall, stave, stilt **6.** adhere, baffle, ballow, cleave, cohere, mallet, pierce, puzzle, thrust **7.** defraud **8.** chatwood, revolver, transfix **9.** drumstick, persevere **10.** matchstick, overcharge **13.** stick-in-the-mud

stick (pert to) . . .
   bamboo . . **6.** lathee (lathi)
   bundle . . **5.** fagot **6.** fasces
   crooked . . **5.** caman **7.** cammock, gambrel
   insects . . **5.** Emesa
   mountain climbing . . **10.** alpenstock

sticker . . . **4.** burr **5.** label, poser, thorn **6.** poster, puzzle, weapon **7.** bramble **8.** adherent

sticky . . . **3.** goo **5.** gluey, humid, moist, woody **6.** clammy, slushy, viscid **7.** viscous **8.** adhesive **9.** difficult, glutinous, tenacious **10.** saccharine

stiff . . . **4.** dead, hard, hobo, limp, taut **5.** harsh, horse, idler, rigid, stark, tense **6.** corpse, formal, proper, severe, strict **7.** awkward, cadaver, starchy **8.** resolute, rigorous, starched **9.** dead-drunk, obstinate, unbending **14.** uncompromising

stiff-necked . . . **8.** stubborn **9.** ankylotic, obstinate **11.** strait-laced **12.** contumacious

stiffness . . . **8.** rigidity **9.** formality, toughness **10.** strictness **11.** starchiness

stifle . . . **3.** gag **4.** stop **5.** choke **6.** deaden, muffle, quench **7.** repress, smother **8.** strangle, throttle **9.** suffocate **10.** extinguish

stigma . . . **4.** blot, mark, scar, slur **5.** brand, odium, stain, stamp, taint **6.** defect **7.** blemish **8.** disgrace, reproach

stigmatism . . . **7.** blemish **10.** refraction

(eye)
stigmatize . . . **5.** brand **6.** defame
8. denounce
still . . . **3.** but, mum, yet **4.** calm, even,
lull, moot **5.** allay, check, inert, quiet
6. always, hushed, pacify, silent,
soothe, subdue **7.** silence, subdued
8. inactive, restrain, suppress, tranquil,
until now **9.** quiescent **10.** distillery,
motionless, photograph **11.** continually
12. nevertheless **15.** notwithstanding
still water . . . **4.** pond, pool **6.** lagoon
stilt . . . **6.** crutch **7.** yeguita (black-necked)
stilted . . . **6.** formal **7.** pompous
8. elevated, inflated, on stilts
9. bombastic, inelegant
stimulant . . . **3.** tea **5.** salts, tonic
6. bracer, coffee **7.** alcohol **8.** caffeine,
stimulus **9.** digitalis, sassafras
10. adrenaline, strychnine
11. epinephrine
stimulate . . . **3.** jog, pep **4.** goad, stir,
urge, whet **5.** elate, impel, rouse, sting
6. excite, fillip (filip), incite, spur on
7. animate, enliven, quicken, refresh
8. energize, motivate **9.** encourage,
instigate, sensitize **10.** exhilarate,
invigorate
stimulating . . . **4.** cool **7.** piquant
8. exciting **10.** energizing, refreshing
stimulus . . . **4.** spur **5.** sting **6.** motive
7. impetus **9.** incentive, stimulant
sting . . . **4.** bite, pain **5.** smart **6.** offend,
tingle **8.** irritate
sting of conscience . . . **5.** pangs, voice
6. qualms, twinge **11.** compunction
sting organ . . . **10.** nematocyst
stingy . . . **4.** dree, mean, near **5.** close
6. scanty **7.** miserly, selfish **8.** covetous
9. niggardly **10.** avaricious
11. closefisted **12.** parsimonious
stinkbird . . . **7.** hoatzin
stint . . . **4.** duty, task **5.** limit **6.** scrimp
7. confine **8.** be frugal, restrict **9.** be
sparing
stipend . . . **3.** ann, fee, pay **5.** annat,
wages **6.** salary **7.** annates, pension,
subsidy **9.** allowance **12.** compensation,
remuneration
stipulate . . . **5.** agree **6.** demand
7. bargain, specify **8.** contract, indicate
9. designate, guarantee, postulate
stipulation . . . **4.** bond **6.** clause, demand,
detail **7.** compact, proviso **8.** contract,
covenant **9.** agreement, condition
11. arrangement **13.** specification
stir . . . **3.** ado, mix **4.** fuss, jail, move, poke,
roil, to-do **5.** budge, churn, rally, rouse,
shake, stoke, waken **6.** arouse, awaken,
bestir, bustle, excite, flurry, hubbub,
pother, prison, rustle, tumult **7.** agitate,
animate, disturb, inflame, provoke
8. activity, movement **9.** commotion
12. penitentiary
stir (pert to) . . .
colors (calico) . . **4.** teer
fire . . **5.** stoke
together . . **3.** mix **6.** stodge
up . . **3.** mix **4.** rile, roil **5.** anger, awake,
rouse **6.** arouse, foment, incite
stirring . . . **6.** moving **7.** rousing

8. bustling, eventful, exciting
9. animating, inspiring **11.** stimulating
stirrup . . . **4.** ring **5.** strap **6.** saddle
(part), stapes **7.** support **8.** footrest,
tapadera
stitch . . . **3.** bit, hem, sew **4.** mend, pain
5. baste, piece, ridge **6.** suture, tailor
8. particle **9.** embroider
stitch (type) . . . **3.** hem **5.** chain, coral,
cross **6.** carpet, damask, suture
7. glover's **11.** needlepoint, over-and-
over
stitchbird . . . **3.** ihi **10.** honey eater
stithy . . . **5.** anvil, forge **6.** smithy
8. smithery
stoa . . . **7.** portico **9.** colonnade
stoat . . . **6.** ermine, weasel
stob . . . **4.** post, stab, stub **5.** stake
6. gibbet, pierce
stoccado, stoccata . . . **4.** stab **6.** thrust
(rapier)
stock . . . **4.** fund, line, race, stem **5.** breed,
broth, hoard, store, trunk **6.** assets,
cravat, pillar, strain, supply **7.** capital,
lineage, provide, rhizome **8.** credence,
original **9.** livestock, provision, replenish
10. progenitor
stock (pert to) . . .
book . . **6.** ledger
breeding . . **5.** brood
certificate . . **5.** scrip **8.** document
flower . . **11.** gillyflower
hawk . . **15.** peregrine falcon
in trade . . **6.** assets, supply
11. merchandise
market . . **6.** Bourse **8.** Exchange **10.** Wall
Street
of goods . . **4.** line
owl . . **8.** eagle owl
payment . . **8.** dividend
pile . . **7.** reserve **12.** accumulation
theater . . **5.** plays
type . . **6.** common **9.** preferred
stockade . . . **3.** pen **5.** étape, pound
6. corral, kennel, laager **7.** barrier,
bulwark, parapet, rampart, redoubt
8. palisade **9.** barricade, earthwork,
enclosure
stocking . . . **4.** hose, sock **6.** anklet,
argyle **7.** bandage, fortune, hosiery
8. seamless **9.** livestock **12.** bluestocking
15. Leatherstocking (Natty Bumppo)
stocks . . . **7.** pillory, shackle **10.** securities
stoic, stoical . . . **7.** passive, Spartan
8. enduring **9.** impassive **11.** unflinching
Stoic School founder . . . **4.** Zeno
stoker . . . **5.** firer **6.** seaman, teaser
7. fireman, greaser **8.** trainman
stolen (pert to) . . .
goods receiver . . **5.** fence **7.** smasher,
swagman
property . . **4.** pelf **5.** booty, spoil
stolid . . . **4.** dull, slow **5.** beefy **6.** stupid
7. adamant, passive **9.** impassive,
inanimate **11.** inexcitable, unexcitable
stoma . . . **4.** pore **5.** mouth **7.** opening,
orifice
stomach . . . **3.** gut, maw **4.** craw, crop,
vell **5.** belly, rumen, taste **6.** desire,
endure, gaster, paunch **7.** abdomen,
gizzard **8.** tolerate **10.** resentment

stomach (pert to) . . .
ache . . **5.** colic, cramp **7.** gullion
8. rumbling **11.** borborygmus
acidity . . **4.** acor
animal . . **3.** maw
bird . . **4.** craw, crop
comb form . . **6.** gaster **7.** gastero
ref to . . **7.** gastric, pyloric
ruminant . . **5.** rumen **6.** omasum
8. abomasum, roddikin **9.** manyplies,
reticulum **10.** psalterium
stone . . . **3.** gem, pit **4.** kill, pelt, rock,
seed **5.** agate, block, geode, jewel,
lapis, shale, slate, spall **6.** attack,
pebble **7.** diamond, peridot, sharpen
8. monument, pavement **9.** hailstone,
sculpture, whetstone **10.** gravestone,
grindstone **12.** philosopher's
stone (pert to) . . .
abrasive . . **5.** emery
Age . . **8.** Eolithic **9.** Neolithic
11. Paleolithic
alchemy . . **6.** carmot **12.** philosopher's
arch (top stone) . . **8.** keystone
Bib . . **4.** ezel
broke . . **4.** flat **8.** strapped
broken . . **6.** rubble
carved . . **5.** cameo **8.** intaglio
chisel . . **4.** celt
cutters' disease . . **9.** silicosis
10. chalicosis
famed . . **4.** Hope, Pitt **5.** Mogul, Sancy
6. Jonker, Orloff, Regent **7.** Blarney,
Rosetta **8.** Cullinan, Kohinoor (Kohinur)
9. Excelsior **10.** Great Mogul
12. Plymouth Rock, Star of Africa
flat . . **4.** flag, slab **5.** slate
fruit . . **3.** pip **4.** paip, seed **5.** cling
7. putamen **8.** endocarp
gem . . **4.** jade, opal, ruby, sard
5. agate, pearl, topaz **6.** garnet, ligure,
spinel **7.** diamond, emerald, peridot
8. amethyst, sapphire **9.** turquoise
11. alexandrite
gem cutting . . **6.** adamas
hammer . . **5.** kevel
hard . . **7.** adamant **9.** chatoyant (cat's-
eye)
heap . . **5.** cairn
instrument . . **8.** lapideon
masonry . . **6.** ashlar
medical . . **4.** gall **5.** renal **7.** biliary,
otolith **8.** calculus
oil . . **4.** hone
ornamental . . **9.** scagliola
pert to . . **7.** lithoid
pillar . . **8.** monolith
pyramid . . **6.** benben
quarry . . **6.** latomy
small . . **6.** pebble **8.** lapillus
special . . **3.** key, lap, oil, rub **4.** curb,
flag, head, lime, lode, mile, tomb, whet
5. birth, flint, grave, grind **6.** cobble,
corner **8.** stepping
statue (part wood) . . **8.** acrolith
to dress . . **3.** nig
uncut . . **4.** naif
woman turned to stone by Zeus . .
5. Niobe
stonecutter (pert to) . . .
disease of . . **9.** silicosis **10.** chalicosis

receptacle . . **7.** sebilla
tool . . **6.** eolith
type . . **6.** jadder **7.** jeweler **8.** lapidary
worker . . **5.** mason
stonecutting art . . . **10.** stereotomy
stoning, death by . . . **10.** lapidation
stony . . . **4.** cold, hard **5.** rigid, rocky
6. rugged **7.** adamant **8.** lapidose,
obdurate, pitiless **9.** petrified
10. inflexible, relentless, unyielding
15. uncompassionate
stooge . . . **4.** foil **5.** toady **6.** flunky
7. cat's-paw **8.** henchman
stool . . . **4.** seat **5.** bench **6.** pigeon,
tripod **7.** taboret **8.** informer
stop . . . **2.** ho **3.** bar, dam, end **4.** balk,
foil, halt, kill, quit, stay, stem, whoa
5. avast, block, cease, check, choke,
close, delay **6.** arrest, desist, detain
7. impasse, prevent, silence **8.** preclude,
swear off **10.** standstill **11.** discontinue,
obstruction, punctuation **12.** lower the
boom
stop (pert to) . . .
close . . **8.** obturate
debate . . **7.** cloture
fermentation . . **4.** stum
gap . . **7.** stopper **9.** expedient, makeshift
momentarily . . **5.** pause
nautical . . **5.** avast
organ . . **5.** viola **7.** gemsbok **8.** dulsiana
seams (boat) . . **4.** calk
short . . **5.** pause **7.** respite **8.** interval
12. intermission
unintentional . . **5.** stall
watch . . **5.** timer
with clay . . **3.** pug
stopper . . . **4.** bung, cork, plug **5.** spile
7. bouchon
storage (pert to) . . .
bin . . **3.** mow **4.** loft, shed, silo **7.** granary
8. elevator
fodder (in silo) . . **6.** ensile
hidden . . **5.** cache
place . . **3.** bin **4.** barn **5.** attic, depot,
étape **6.** cellar, closet **7.** arsenal,
granary **8.** cupboard, elevator, magazine
10. promptuary, repository
stork . . . **4.** ibis **6.** jabiru **7.** Maguari,
marabou **8.** adjutant
storklike . . . **8.** pelargic
storm . . . **4.** blow, fume, fury, rage,
rain, rave, snow, wind **5.** orage
6. attack, shower, simoom (simoon),
tumult **7.** bluster, disturb, tempest,
trouble **8.** calamity, eruption, outbreak,
upheaval, violence **9.** agitation
11. disturbance
storm (pert to) . . .
cold . . **11.** northeaster
evil storm god . . **2.** Zu **9.** blackbird
(symb), Hlorrithi
extreme . . **4.** gale **7.** cyclone, monsoon,
tempest, tornado **9.** hurricane
occidental . . **6.** wester
recorder (thunder) . . **11.** brontometer
sand . . **6.** tebbad
snow . . **5.** buran
stormy . . . **5.** rainy **7.** furious, riotous,
violent **8.** agitated **9.** inclement,
turbulent **10.** tumultuous

11. tempestuous

story . . . 3. fib, lie 4. hoax, joke, lore, saga, tale, tier, yarn 5. fable, floor 6. gossip, legend, serial 7. mystery, narrate, parable, romance 8. anecdote 9. chronicle, falsehood, tradition

story (pert to) . . .
absurd . . 4. hoax, yarn 6. canard
doleful . . 8. jeremiad
exclusive . . 4. beat, news 5. scoop
part . . 6. serial
short . . 5. conte 7. novella

storyteller . . . 4. liar 5. Aesop 6. fibber 7. relater 9. raconteur

stot . . . 2. ox 4. bull 5. steer 6. bounce 7. paunchy, stammer, stumble, stutter

stout . . . 3. fat 4. bold 5. brave, bulky, burly, hardy, obese, plump 6. fleshy, rotund, stocky, strong 7. haughty, violent 8. forcible, powerful, resolute, thickset 9. corpulent, undaunted 10. courageous, persistent

stoutness . . . 7. courage 8. strength 10. corpulence, embonpoint

stove . . . 4. etna, kiln, oven 5. grate, plate, range 6. heater 7. Coleman, furnace, smelter

stove part . . . 4. oven, pipe 6. burner 7. firebox, griddle

stow . . . 4. cram, hide, mass, pack 5. crowd, lodge, store, stuff 6. steeve 7. arrange, secrete

straddle . . . 5. salvo 6. option 7. astride 8. bestride 9. be neutral, go halfway

straggle . . . 4. rove 6. wander 7. deviate, meander

straight . . . 5. cards, erect, exact, rigid, stern 6. candid, direct, honest 7. correct, exactly, unmixed 8. directly, reliable, sequence, unbroken, vertical 9. authentic 10. horizontal, racing term 11. straightway, undeviating 13. uninterrupted 15. straightforward

straight (pert to) . . .
baseball . . 5. liner
course . . 7. beeline
edge . . 5. ruler
line . . 6. secant 8. enfilade 9. asymptote
Math . . 8. vinculum
out . . 6. candid 9. downright 11. unqualified 13. thoroughgoing 14. uncompromising
shooter . . 11. on the square
way . . 4. anon 8. directly 9. forthwith 11. immediately

straighten . . . 5. align, aline, level, order, plumb 6. tidy up 7. rectify, unravel 11. disentangle

straightforward . . . 5. frank 6. candid, direct, honest 7. sincere 8. outright 9. outspoken 10. forthright 11. undeviating

straightway . . . 4. anon 8. directly 9. downright, forthwith 10. forthright 11. immediately

strain . . . 3. sye, tax, try, tug 4. bend, dash, kind, mood, ooze, race, sort, tone, vein 5. breed, shade, stock, tense, touch 6. filter, melody, overdo, poetry, refine, sprain, streak, stress, strive 7. descent, fatigue, lineage, progeny, stretch, tension, variety 8. ancestry, endeavor, exertion 9. constrain, overheave, percolate 10. generation

strained . . . 4. taut 5. tense 6. forced 7. intense, labored 8. wrenched 9. stretched 10. farfetched

strainer . . . 4. sile 5. sieve, tamis 6. filter, screen, sifter 8. colander, filterer 17. Hippocrates' sleeve

strait . . . 3. gut 4. neck, need 5. inlet 6. angust, narrow, strict 7. channel, limited 8. rigorous 9. difficult 10. restricted, scrupulous 11. distressful, predicament

Strait . . . 6. Bering 7. Surigao 8. Bosporus 9. Belleisle

Strait of Gibraltar . . . 17. Pillars of Hercules

Straits Settlements . . .
capital, Penang . . 10. Georgetown
capital, Singapore . . 9. Singapore
city . . 7. Malacca
peninsula . . 5. Malay
port . . 4. Prai

strand . . . 3. sea 4. bank, quay 5. beach, shore 6. maroon, thread 7. channel, current 8. filament

strange . . . 3. coy, new, odd, shy 4. rare, xeno (comb form) 5. alien, eerie, novel, queer, timid 6. exotic, quaint 7. curious, erratic, unknown, unusual 8. peculiar, singular, uncommon 9. eccentric, unrelated 10. extraneous, outlandish, tramontane, unfamiliar 12. unaccustomed, unacquainted 13. extraordinary, preternatural

stranger . . . 3. ger 5. alien, guest 7. visitor 8. intruder 9. foreigner, outlander

strangle . . . 5. choke 6. stifle 7. execute, garrote, repress, squeeze 8. suppress, throttle 9. suffocate

strap . . . 3. tie 4. belt, bind, hang, jess, rein, riem, whip 5. leash, strop, thong 6. enarme, latigo, oxreim 7. lanyard (laniard) 8. chastise

strap-shaped . . . 6. lorate 8. ligulate

strass . . . 5. glass, paste 10. silk refuse

strata . . . 6. layers 7. classes 10. formations

stratagem . . . 4. coup, ploy, ruse, trap, wile 5. trick 6. device, gambit 7. finesse 8. artifice

strategy . . . 7. tactics 8. artifice, intrigue, maneuver

stratum . . . 3. bed 4. coat 5. layer

straw . . . 4. stem 5. mulch 6. fodder, sennit, trifle 7. remains, sabutan

straw (pert to) . . .
bid . . 5. fraud 7. auction 9. worthless
coat (Jap peasant) . . 4. mino
color . . 6. flaxen
flower . . 11. everlasting
hat . . 4. baku 5. milan 6. panama
like . . 6. chaffy 11. stramineous
vote . . 5. Roper 6. Gallup

stray . . . 3. err, gad, sin 4. cavy, roam, rove, waif 5. range 6. swerve, wander 7. deviate, digress 8. aberrant, aberrate, go astray 9. wandering 10. occasional

streak . . . 3. roe 4. line, seam, vein 5. fleck, layer, stria 6. groove, strain,

strake, stripe
streaked . . . **4.** liny **6.** banded **7.** brindle, striped **8.** brindled, striated
stream . . . **3.** run **4.** burn, flow, rill, sike (syke) **5.** brook, creek, river **6.** abound, course, rillet, runlet, runnel, throng **7.** current, rivulet, torrent **9.** streamlet **11.** watercourse
stream (pert to) . . .
dry . . **6.** arroyo, spruit
gold . . **6.** placer
of consciousness . . **8.** thoughts **10.** psychology **11.** abstraction
of forgetfulness . . **5.** Lethe
underground . . **3.** aar
street . . . **4.** road **5.** calle **6.** avenue **7.** highway, roadway **8.** chaussée **9.** boulevard **12.** thoroughfare
street (pert to) . . .
car . . **4.** tram
famed . . **4.** Beal, Main, Wall **5.** Canal **6.** Beacon **7.** Downing **8.** Broadway **9.** Peachtree **12.** Threadneedle
French . . **3.** rue
narrow . . **4.** lane **5.** alley
show . . **4.** peep **5.** raree
Spanish . . **5.** calle
urchin . . **4.** Arab **5.** gamin **7.** outcast **8.** vagabond **11.** guttersnipe
Street called Straight (Bib) . . . **8.** Damascus
strength . . . **3.** vis **4.** iron, thew **5.** brawn, force, might, nerve, power, rally, sinew, titer, vigor **6.** energy, health **7.** potency, stamina, sthenia, support **8.** firmness **9.** endurance, lustiness, stoutness, toughness, vehemence, willpower **10.** robustness, stronghold
strengthen . . . **4.** grow, prop **5.** brace, nerve **6.** deepen **7.** confirm, fortify, nourish, toughen **8.** increase, roborate **9.** encourage, intensify, reinforce **10.** invigorate **11.** consolidate
strengthening . . . **7.** bracing **8.** roborant **12.** invigorating, invigoration
strenuous . . . **6.** ardent, severe **7.** zealous **8.** vigorous **9.** difficult, energetic, laborious **11.** industrious
strepent . . . **4.** loud **5.** noisy
streperous . . . **4.** loud **5.** harsh **7.** noisily **9.** turbulent **10.** boisterous
strepor . . . **5.** noise
stress . . . **5.** arsis, ictus, labor **6.** accent, insist, strain, weight **7.** urgency **8.** emphasis, exigency, pressure **9.** emphasize **10.** elasticity, exaggerate **12.** exaggeration
stretcher . . . **3.** bar, lie **6.** litter, racker **9.** falsehood
stretch out . . . **6.** be long, extend **9.** expatiate
strew . . . **3.** ted **6.** spread **7.** diffuse, overlay, scatter **8.** disperse **10.** distribute **11.** disseminate
strewn . . . **4.** semé **6.** littered **9.** scattered **12.** disseminated
stria . . . **4.** line **5.** ridge, strip **6.** fillet, furrow, groove, hollow, streak, stripe **7.** channel **9.** striation
stricken . . . **7.** smitten, worn out, wounded **8.** unnerved **13.** incapacitated

strickle . . . **5.** rifle **7.** pattern **8.** template **10.** sweepboard **13.** striking board
strict . . . **4.** hard **5.** exact, harsh, rigid, stern **6.** severe **7.** ascetic, austere, precise **8.** accurate, rigorous **9.** puritanic, stringent **10.** forbidding, inexorable, inflexible, meticulous, relentless, scrupulous **11.** strait-laced, undeviating **13.** conscientious **14.** uncompromising
strict disciplinarian . . . **8.** martinet
strict discipline . . . **13.** regimentation
stricture . . . **7.** binding, censure **9.** criticism, narrowing **11.** contraction **12.** constriction
stride . . . **4.** gait, pace, step, walk **8.** bestride, progress, straddle, velocity
strident . . . **6.** shrill **7.** grating, raucous **11.** cacophonous
strife . . . **3.** war **4.** feud **5.** fight **6.** battle, combat, stasis **7.** contest, quarrel **8.** conflict, exertion, struggle **9.** logomachy **11.** altercation
strike . . . **3.** hit, pat, rap **4.** bump, bunt, slap, swat **5.** clout, labor, smite, whack **6.** attack, revolt **7.** impinge **9.** discovery
strike (pert to) . . .
a balance . . **5.** weigh **7.** average **8.** equalize **10.** compromise
against . . **7.** collide **8.** illision
and rebound . . **5.** carom (carrom) **9.** carambole
breaker . . **4.** fink, scab
dumb . . **4.** stun
heavily . . **3.** lam, ram **4.** bash, slam, slog, sock, wham **5.** punch, smite
obliquely . . **5.** carom **6.** glance
out . . **3.** fan **4.** dele **5.** elide, erase **6.** cancel, delete **9.** eliminate
to and fro . . **5.** bandy
with beak . . **4.** peck
with fist . . **5.** pound, punch
with head . . **4.** butt
with weapon . . **5.** crunt
with wonder . . **3.** awe **7.** astound
striking . . . **7.** salient **8.** dramatic, eloquent, exciting **9.** arresting, wonderful **10.** noticeable, remarkable, surprising
striking effect . . . **5.** éclat
striking part . . . **7.** clapper
string . . . **3.** ran, set **4.** bind, cord **5.** lacet, snare, twine **6.** fasten, series, thread **10.** succession
string (pert to) . . .
alphabet . . **5.** knots (for blind)
of beads . . **6.** rosary **8.** necklace
of horses . . **6.** stable
out . . **6.** line up **8.** lengthen **9.** expatiate
pottery . . **13.** Schnurkeramik (neolithic)
stringed instrument . . . **4.** harp, lute, lyre **5.** banjo, piano, recta, viola **6.** fiddle, guitar, violin, zither **7.** bandore, mandore, ukulele **8.** mandolin, psaltery **9.** mandolute **11.** harpsichord
stringed instrument bridge . . . **5.** magas
stringent . . . **4.** ropy **5.** rigid, tight **6.** cogent, severe, strict **10.** convincing **11.** acrimonious, restrictive
stringy . . . **4.** ropy **5.** gluey, tough **6.** sinewy, viscid **7.** fibrous

10. threadlike 11. filamentous

strip . . . 4. bare, belt, live, pare, peel, skin, slat 5. cleat, shred, unrig 6. denude, divest, remove, strake 7. deprive, plunder, pull off, uncloak, uncover, undress 9. dismantle 10. dispossess, impoverish 11. decorticate

strip (pert to) . . .
blubber . . 6. flense
curved . . 5. stave
lead (stained glass) . . 4. came
leather . . 4. welt 5. thong 6. latido 7. belting
narrow . . 4. lath, slat, tape, welt 5. reeve, stave, strap
off skin . . 4. flay
of possessions . . 4. milk 5. bleed, bunko (bunco), shear 6. fleece 7. despoil, swindle 10. dispossess
raised . . 5. ridge
tease dancer . . 8. stripper 9. ecdysiast
wood . . 5. stave 6. reglet, spline

stripe . . . 3. bar, pin 4. band, beat, line, mark, sort, type, wale, weal, welt, whip 5. chalk, strip, vitta 6. streak 7. chevron 8. insignia 9. striation

striped (pert to) . . .
alder . . 11. winterberry
antelope . . 5. bongo
gillyflower . . 9. carnation
longitudinally . . 7. vittate

stripling . . . 3. boy, lad 5. youth 8. juvenile 9. youngster

strive . . . 3. aim, try, tug 4. toil 5. labor 6. battle, buffet, strain 7. compete, contend, emulate 8. endeavor, struggle

strive (pert to) . . .
for . . 3. aim 4. seek
to equal ... 5. rival 6. strain 7. emulate
to overtake . . 5. ensue
with . . 3. vie 7. compete

strobile . . . 4. cone 8. pine cone

strockle . . . 6. shovel

stroke . . . 3. fit, pat, pet, rub 4. beat, blow, coup, flip, line, putt, shot 5. ictus, serif, spasm, trait, whisk 6. caress, fondle 7. illness, solidus

stroll . . . 4. roam, walk 5. range, stray 6. go slow, ramble, wander 7. meander, saunter 8. ambulate 9. promenade 11. perambulate

stroller . . . 5. actor, tramp 6. beggar 7. peddler, vagrant 8. wanderer 9. saunterer 12. perambulator

strolling . . . 7. nomadic 8. rambling 10. meandering 13. perambulation

strong . . . 3. fit, hot 4. able, firm, hale, hard, wiry 5. fetid, hardy, lusty, solid, sound, stout, tough 6. potent, robust, sinewy, stable, sturdy, virile 7. healthy, intense, odorous, tainted 8. accented, forceful, forcible, muscular, resonant, stalwart, vigorous 9. effective, energetic 10. outrageous, persuasive, pronounced, remarkable 11. substantial 12. concentrated

strong (pert to) . . .
drink . . 6. liquor 7. spirits 9. distilled
flavor . . 4. racy 5. acrid 7. pungent
hold . . 4. fort 7. citadel 8. fastness, Fort Knox, fortress, muniment, treasury

man . . 5. Atlas 6. Samson (Sampson)
muscles . . 5. brawn, thewy
music . . 4. loud 5. forte 7. saccade
willed . . 8. resolute 9. obstinate 10. determined
wind . . 7. pampero

stroygood . . . 7. wastrel 11. spendthrift

strubbly . . . 6. untidy 7. unkempt

struck . . . 4. smit 5. smote 7. smitten, swatted 8. shutdown (see also *strike*)

struck (pert to) . . .
an attitude . . 5. posed
out . . 5. deled 6. elided, erased, fanned 7. deleted
with fear . . 6. aghast 7. alarmed
with missiles . . 6. pelted

structure . . . 3. dam 4. dais, form, pier 5. frame, house, jetty, kiosk, stage, tower 6. bridge, make-up, pagoda 7. edifice 8. building, platform 9. formation 10. tabernacle 11. composition 12. constitution, construction

structure (pert to) . . .
calcareous . . 5. coral
conical . . 7. pyramid
crownlike . . 6. corona
filamentous . . 4. hair
human . . 8. physique
monumental . . 5. pylon
roof . . 6. cupola, dormer
tall . . 5. tower 7. steeple 9. campanile
tentlike . . 10. tabernacle

struggle . . . 3. tug, vie 4. cope, wade 5. labor 6. effort, Peniel (Bib) 7. strife, strike, strive, tussle 8. contend, contest, scuffle, wrestle 8. endeavor, flounder, scramble 10. contention, difficulty

strumpet . . . 5. belie 6. harlot 8. harridan 10. prostitute

stub . . . 3. end 4. dock, tail 5. squat, stump 6. coupon, stocky 7. remnant 8. thickset 11. counterfoil

stubble . . . 5. beard, stump 6. arrish 7. bristle 8. eelgrass

stubborn . . . 3. set 4. rude 5. fixed, hardy, rough, tough 6. coarse, mulish, sturdy 7. restive 8. perverse, resolute, starkish, vigorous 9. obstinate, pigheaded 10. determined, headstrong, inflexible, refractory, unyielding 11. intractable 12. recalcitrant

stuck . . . 4. fast 7. baffled, cohered 8. coherent, stranded (see also *stick*)

stuck-up . . . 4. vain 8. arrogant 9. conceited 10. egocentric 12. supercilious 13. self-important

stud . . . 3. dot, pin 4. boss, knob 5. haras 6. enstar 7. hobnail 8. ornament, stallion 9. studhorse

student . . . 4. co-ed 5. cadet, eleve, plebe, pupil 6. tosher 7. learner, scholar 8. disciple 9. collegian

student of . . .
behavior (human) . . 12. psychologist
birds . . 13. ornithologist
birds' eggs . . 8. oologist
Eton . . 7. Etonian
law . . 8. stagiary
medical . . 6. intern (interne)
military . . 5. cadet, plebe

natural history.. **10.** naturalist
navy.. **5.** cadet **10.** midshipman
Oxford.. **8.** commoner
proverbs.. **14.** paroemiologist
punishment.. **10.** penologist
reptiles.. **13.** herpetologist
spiders.. **13.** arachnologist
students, advanced group... **7.** seminar
13. upperclassmen
studied... **5.** boned, pored **6.** formal
7. learned, planned, weighed
8. designed, measured, reasoned
10. well-versed **11.** intentional
12. premeditated
studio... **4.** shop **7.** atelier, bottega
8. workshop **11.** working room
study... **3.** con, den **4.** bone, muse,
pore, scan **5.** étude, grind, learn, weigh
7. discuss **6.** peruse, ponder **7.** analyze,
examine, pegging, reverie, science,
subject, thought **8.** endeavor, learning,
treatise **10.** discussion, inspection
11. contemplate **13.** contemplation
study of...
animals.. **7.** zoology **9.** zoography
bees.. **8.** apiology
birds' eggs.. **6.** oology
disease.. **8.** nosology
fingerprints.. **13.** dactylography
handwriting.. **10.** graphology
insects.. **10.** entomology
man.. **12.** anthropology
mountains.. **7.** orology
old age.. **9.** nostology **10.** geriatrics
11. gerontology
population.. **10.** demography, larithmics
12. demographics
punishment.. **8.** penology
sacred images.. **9.** iconology
temples.. **7.** naology
words.. **9.** etymology **12.** lexicography
stuff... **3.** goo, pad, ram, wad **4.** cram, fill,
stow **5.** gorge, trash **6.** fabric, matter,
potion **7.** content, element, rubbish,
satiate **8.** marinate, material, nonsense,
overfill, trumpery **9.** principle, substance
10. gluttonize
stuffiness... **7.** prudery **8.** dullness
9. obstinacy **10.** sullenness, sultriness
11. pompousness
stuffing... **6.** lining **7.** padding
8. contents, dressing **9.** forcemeat
stuffy... **3.** fat **4.** dull, prim **5.** close,
stout **6.** stodgy, sullen, sultry **7.** airless,
pompous, prudish **8.** resolute
9. bombastic, obstinate **10.** old-
fogyish **11.** strait-laced **12.** conservative
13. ill-ventilated
stulm... **4.** adit **7.** passage **8.** entrance
stumble... **3.** err **4.** fall, trip **5.** lurch
6. boggle, bungle, chance, falter,
happen **7.** blunder, perplex, stagger,
stammer **8.** confound, flounder
stump... **4.** butt, dare, skeg, snag,
stab, stub **5.** clump, scrab **6.** baffle,
trudge **7.** declaim, nonplus **8.** platform
9. challenge, remainder, tortillon
11. electioneer
stun... **4.** bowl, daze **5.** amaze, daunt
6. benumb, bruise, deaden **7.** astound,
stupefy, terrify **8.** astonish, bewilder

9. overpower, overwhelm
stunning... **8.** striking **9.** beautiful
10. astounding, stupefying, terrifying
stunt... **4.** feat **5.** blunt, check, cramp,
crowl, dwarf, whale (2-yr) **6.** hinder
7. curtail, exploit, shorten
10. tomfoolery
stunted... **7.** blunted, checked, dwarfed
9. curtailed, shortened
stupa... **4.** tomb **5.** mound, tower
6. shrine **8.** monument
stupefied... **5.** doped **6.** aghast,
sotted **7.** drugged, shocked, stunned
8. benumbed **9.** petrified
stupefy... **4.** daze, dope, drug, numb,
pall, stun **5.** beset, blunt, shock
6. bedaze, bemuse, muddle **7.** astound,
confuse, petrify, terrify **8.** bewilder,
confound **10.** incrassate, make stupid
11. flabbergast (sl)
stupid... **4.** clod, dull, dumb **5.** blunt,
crass, dense, inane **6.** oafish, obtuse,
simple, stolid **7.** asinine, doltish, foolish,
witless **8.** blockish, Boeotian, gullible
9. brainless, senseless **11.** heavywitted
13. unintelligent
stupid (pert to)...
grossly.. **7.** asinine **9.** imbecilic
person.. **3.** ass, oaf **4.** clod, coot, dolt,
loon, lout, nerd **5.** goose, klutz, stirk
7. tomfool **11.** gillygaupus
render.. **8.** hebetate
stupidity... **7.** fatuity **8.** dullness,
hebetude **11.** foolishness
12. indifference **13.** foolish remark
stupor... **4.** coma, daze **5.** sleep, sopor
6. apathy, torpor, trance **8.** lethargy,
neurosis, numbness **9.** lassitude
15. unconsciousness
sturdy... **4.** firm **5.** burly, hardy, lusty,
stout **6.** robust, stable, steady, strong
8. resolute, stalwart, stubborn, vigorous
10. courageous, determined, unyielding
11. substantial
sturgeon... **6.** beluga, caviar **7.** sterlet
9. Acipenser **10.** hackleback
stutter... **6.** falter **7.** stammer
sty... **3.** pen **4.** boil **5.** hovel, stair,
steps, stile **6.** ladder, pimple **7.** pustule
8. swelling **9.** enclosure
style... **3.** air, pen, way **4.** form, kind,
mode, name **5.** get-up, gusto, trend,
vogue **6.** gnomon, graver, phrase,
stylus **7.** alamode, diction, fashion
8. elegance **9.** execution **10.** appearance
12. characterize, presentation
style (pert to)...
architecture.. **5.** Doric, Greek, Ionic,
Roman **6.** Gothic, Norman **7.** Italian
8. Colonial, Georgian **9.** Byzantine
10. Corinthian, Romanesque
11. Renaissance
painting.. **5.** genre **11.** Renaissance
type.. **5.** roman, runic **6.** italic
styled... **5.** named **6.** called, termed,
y-clept (y-cleped) **7.** phrased
stylet... **5.** probe **6.** trocar **7.** poniard
8. stiletto **9.** specillum
stylish... **3.** mod **4.** chic, cool, neat, tony
5. nifty, ritzy, sharp, smart, swank **6.** chi-
chi, dressy, jaunty, modish, preppy,

snazzy, trendy **7.** alamode, voguish **11.** fashionable

styptic ... **4.** alum **10.** astringent, tannic acid **12.** constringent

Styx ferryman ... **6.** Charon

suant ... **4.** even **6.** demure, smooth, steady **7.** equable, regular

suave ... **4.** oily, smug **5.** bland **6.** urbane **7.** fulsome **8.** unctuous **9.** agreeable **12.** ingratiating, mealy-mouthed **13.** smooth-talking

suavity ... **7.** amenity **8.** civility, courtesy, urbanity **10.** gentleness

subdue ... **3.** cow **4.** calm, tame **5.** allay, crush, lower, quash, quell, sober **6.** disarm, muffle, reduce, soften **7.** conquer, repress, squelch **8.** mitigate, overcome, suppress, surmount, vanquish **9.** overpower, subjugate **11.** subordinate

subdued ... **4.** meek, soft **7.** muffled, quelled **8.** disarmed, relieved, tempered **9.** conquered, toned down **10.** made gentle, subjugated **11.** soft colored, unperturbed

subject ... **4.** text, word **5.** cause, prone, theme, topic **6.** matter, motive, submit, vassal **7.** citizen, servant **8.** inferior **9.** subjugate, substance **10.** predispose **11.** subordinate **12.** part of speech

subjective ... **6.** mental **7.** topical **8.** fanciful, illusory **9.** of the mind **10.** nominative **11.** introverted

subject of ...
discourse .. **5.** theme, topic
disease .. **4.** case **7.** patient
lawsuit .. **3.** res **7.** grounds
sentence .. **4.** noun

subject to ...
abuse .. **6.** revile
analysis .. **7.** titrate
argument .. **4.** moot
change .. **7.** mutable **8.** amenable
choice .. **8.** elective
control .. **7.** rulable
death .. **6.** mortal
depression .. **5.** moody
dislike .. **8.** aversion
mistakes .. **7.** erratic
outbursts .. **9.** irritable
tension .. **8.** strained
vassalage .. **5.** feoff

sublimation ... **9.** underling **12.** underscoring

sublime ... **4.** high **5.** grand, great, lofty, noble, proud **6.** refine **7.** exalted, haughty **8.** elevated, eloquent, empyreal, majestic, splendid, upraised, vaporize **9.** beautiful, expletive **11.** magnanimous

Sublime Porte ... **12.** Ottoman Court **17.** Turkish government

sublimity ... **4.** acme **5.** glory **6.** beauty **7.** majesty **8.** grandeur **9.** greatness **10.** excellence **11.** distinction **12.** magnificence

submarine ... **3.** sub **4.** boat, ship **8.** Nautilus, Scorpion, Thresher **11.** submersible

submarine eye ... **9.** periscope

submission ... **5.** kneel **8.** fatalism, meekness, patience, yielding **9.** deference, obedience, surrender **10.** compliance, confession **11.** resignation **13.** nonresistance

submissive ... **4.** meek, tame **6.** humble **7.** dutiful, patient **8.** obedient, resigned, uxorious (to wife), yielding **9.** compliant **11.** acquiescent, conformable

submit ... **3.** bow **4.** obey **5.** defer, remit, stoop, yield **6.** soften, temper **7.** succumb **8.** moderate **9.** acquiesce, postulate, surrender **10.** condescend

submit to ... **4.** obey **6.** endure **11.** acknowledge

subordinate ... **4.** exon **5.** minor **6.** subdue **7.** servant, subject **8.** inferior, parergon **9.** appendage, assistant, dependent, secondary **10.** collateral, incidental, submissive **11.** subservient

subsequent ... **5.** later **7.** ensuing **9.** following, postnatal **10.** succeeding **11.** consecutive

subservient ... **6.** vassal **7.** servile, subject **9.** assistant, truckling **10.** obsequious, submissive **11.** subordinate **12.** instrumental

subside ... **3.** ebb **4.** bate, fall, lull, sink, wane **5.** abate **6.** settle **7.** descend, relapse **8.** decrease, languish **9.** gravitate **11.** deteriorate

subsidiary ... **8.** inferior **9.** assistant, auxiliary, extrinsic, tributary **10.** collateral **11.** stipendiary **12.** nonessential **13.** supplementary

subsist ... **2.** be **4.** live **5.** abide, exist **6.** endure, remain **7.** prevail, survive **8.** continue

subsist on prey ... **9.** rapacious

substance ... **3.** sum **4.** gist, meat **5.** stuff **6.** import, matter, wealth **7.** aliment, element, essence, meaning, purport, summary **8.** hardness, material **9.** actuality, affluence, solidness **11.** consistency

substance (pert to) ...
absorbent .. **5.** fomes
aeriform .. **3.** gas **5.** argon
amorphous .. **7.** ferrite
antitoxic .. **5.** serum
aromatic .. **5.** myrrh, spice **6.** balsam
basic .. **7.** element
bitter .. **5.** aloes, aloin, linin **7.** amarine, emetine **8.** elaterin
brittle .. **5.** glass
cleansing, purifying .. **8.** depurant **10.** abstergent, clarifiant
corrosive .. **4.** acid **7.** caustic
dissolved .. **6.** solute
dissolving .. **9.** resolvent
electrical .. **3.** ion
elemental .. **5.** metal
expanding .. **8.** dilatant
fatty .. **5.** lipin, suint
ferment .. **9.** activator
flocculent .. **4.** wool
food .. **7.** protein
fruit jellying .. **6.** pectin
gelatinous .. **4.** agar
hard .. **4.** bone **5.** ivory **7.** adamant
hypnotic .. **4.** ural
inflammable .. **6.** tinder **7.** bitumen

inorganic.. **7.** mineral
ipecac root.. **7.** emetine
light.. **4.** cork
milk curdling.. **6.** rennet
moss (Ceylon).. **4.** agar **8.** agar-agar
neutralizing.. **6.** alkali
resinous.. **3.** gum, lac **5.** copal **7.** shellac
rubberlike.. **5.** gutta
soapmaking.. **3.** lye
stabilizing.. **7.** ballast
sulphur.. **5.** hepar
tar.. **6.** cresol
unctuous.. **3.** fat, oil **7.** pinguid
vegetable.. **5.** resin, rosin
wax, waxy.. **5.** cerin **7.** suberin
  8. paraffin
whale (perfume).. **9.** ambergris
wood ash.. **6.** potash
substantial ... **4.** firm, real, true **5.** pucka
  (pukka), solid, stout **6.** actual, bodily,
  hearty, stable, strong, sturdy **7.** genuine
  8. abundant, tangible **9.** corporeal,
  essential, important **10.** nourishing
  12. considerable
substantiate ... **6.** embody, verify
  7. confirm, justify **8.** underpin
  9. establish **11.** corroborate
substantive ... **4.** firm, noun **5.** sound
  6. actual, entity **7.** pronoun **9.** essential
  11. substantial **13.** self-contained
substitute ... **5.** proxy, vicar **6.** deputy,
  ersatz **7.** apology, replace **8.** exchange,
  nominate **9.** alternate, surrogate
  10. understudy, viceregent
  11. replacement
subterfuge ... **4.** ruse **5.** blind, trick
  6. refuge **7.** evasion, pretext **8.** artifice,
  pretense **9.** expedient **13.** prevarication
subterranean ... **6.** hidden, secret
  8. hypogeal, plutonic **10.** in the earth
  11. underground
subtile ... **3.** sly **4.** rare, wily **6.** crafty,
  subtle **7.** cunning, elusive **9.** beguiling
subtle ... **3.** sly **4.** fine, nice, rare,
  thin **6.** artful, clever, crafty, shrewd
  7. cunning, refined, subtile **8.** analytic,
  delicate **9.** beguiling, designing,
  ingenious **10.** mysterious
  14. discriminating
subtle (pert to) ...
  emanation (invisible).. **4.** aura
  10. atmosphere
  sarcasm.. **5.** irony
  variation.. **6.** nuance
subtlety ... **5.** guile **7.** cunning, finesse,
  slyness **8.** delicacy, fineness
  9. quodlibet **10.** shrewdness
subtraction, terms ... **7.** minuend
  9. deduction **10.** difference, subtrahend
subversion ... **4.** ruin (utter) **9.** overthrow
  10. corruption, revolution
  11. destruction
subvert ... **4.** ruin **5.** evert, upset **6.** refute,
  uproot **7.** corrupt, destroy, pervert
  8. alienate, overturn **9.** overthrow,
  undermine
subvertive ... **8.** eversive
subway ... **4.** tube **5.** train **6.** tunnel
  11. underground **18.** underground
  railway
succade ... **8.** preserve **10.** confection

succeed ... **5.** ensue, occur **6.** attain,
  follow, thrive **7.** achieve, devolve,
  prosper, replace, triumph **8.** come next,
  flourish, supplant **10.** accomplish
succeeding ... **4.** next **7.** ensuing, sequent
  9. following **10.** subsequent, successful
  11. in the wake of
success ... **2.** go **3.** hit **4.** luck **5.** elate
  7. fortune, outcome **8.** accolade, smash
  hit **10.** prosperity **11.** consequence
successful ... **5.** lucky **8.** thriving
  9. fortunate **10.** prosperous, succeeding,
  triumphant **11.** flourishing
succession ... **3.** row, run **5.** music
  (rhythmic) **6.** series **7.** dynasty, lineage
  8. sequence **9.** posterity
succin ... **5.** amber
succinct ... **4.** curt **5.** brief, hasty,
  short, terse **7.** compact, concise,
  laconic, summary **10.** compressed
  11. compendious, sententious
succor, succour ... **3.** aid **4.** abet,
  help **6.** brandy (Alpine), relief, rescue
  7. comfort, deliver, relieve, sustain
  8. befriend, mitigate **10.** assistance
succulent ... **3.** uva **4.** lush **5.** juicy,
  pappy, tasty **6.** cactus, tender
succumb ... **3.** die **5.** faint, yield **6.** perish,
  submit **7.** give way **8.** get tired
such (as) ... **3.** sic **4.** like **7.** certain,
  similar **8.** analogue **9.** analogous
suction (as in clicks of Bantu) ...
  9. implosive
Sudan, Africa ...
  capital.. **8.** Khartoum
  desert.. **6.** Libyan, Nubian
  export.. **9.** gum arabic
  gazelle.. **4.** dama
  gum forests.. **8.** Kordofan
  lake.. **4.** Chad
  language.. **2.** Ga **6.** Arabic
  people.. **4.** Arab, Sere **5.** Fulah (Fula)
  6. Nubian
  Plain.. **6.** Gezira
  river.. **8.** Blue Nile **9.** White Nile
  town.. **5.** Segou
sudden ... **4.** rash **5.** hasty, swift
  6. abrupt, prompt, speedy **7.** violent
  8. headlong **9.** impetuous, impromptu,
  impulsive **10.** unexpected, unforeseen
  11. precipitate, precipitous
sudden (pert to) ...
  all of a.. **5.** short **6.** presto **8.** suddenly
  and brilliant.. **8.** meteoric
  fear.. **13.** consternation
  sally.. **6.** sortie
  shock.. **4.** jolt
  stroke.. **4.** coup, dash
  thrust.. **3.** jab **5.** lunge
sudor ... **5.** sweat **8.** sudation **9.** exudation
  12. perspiration
Sudra caste ... **3.** mal (low) **5.** palli
sue ... **3.** beg, woo **4.** plea, urge
  5. court, plead **6.** appeal, pursue
  7. entreat, request **8.** continue, petition
  9. prosecute, seek after
suet ... **6.** tallow **8.** leaf lard
Suez Canal builder ... **9.** de Lesseps
  (Ferdinand)
suffer ... **3.** let **4.** bear, dree **5.** admit,
  allow **6.** endure, permit, submit

7. undergo 8. tolerate 10. experience
suffer (pert to) . . .
 distress . . 5. gripe, groan, smart 6. starve
 from heat . . 7. swelter
 remorse . . 3. rue
 ruin . . 5. wreck
sufferance . . . 4. pain 6. misery
 9. endurance, passivity 10. permission
 11. forbearance
suffering, scene of . . . 10. Gethsemane
suffice . . . 2. do 5. avail, serve 6. answer
 7. appease, content, satisfy
 11. sufficiency
sufficiency . . . 4. fill 7. ability, conceit
 8. adequacy, capacity, validity
 9. abundance 10. competency 14. self-
 confidence
sufficient . . . 3. due, fit 4. enow, full,
 good 5. ample, valid 6. enough, plenty
 7. suffice 8. adequate 9. qualified
 11. responsible 12. satisfactory
suffix, for or denoting . . .
 abounding in . . 5. ulent
 abundant . . 3. ose
 act of . . 3. ure 4. ance, tion
 advocate . . 3. ite
 alcohol . . 2. ol
 being . . 3. ure
 capable of . . 3. ile
 chemical . . 2. ac 3. ane, ene, ile, ine,
  iol, ole, ose 4. alic, idin, itol
 diminutive . . 2. el 3. cle, ole, ule 4. ette
 disease . . 4. itis
 doer . . 4. ator
 enzyme . . 3. ase
 feminine . . 3. ess
 follower . . 3. ist, ite
 full of . . 3. ose
 geological age . . 4. cene
 inflammation . . 4. itis
 inhabitants of . . 3. ese 4. ites
 jurisdiction . . 3. ric
 law . . 2. ee
 medicine . . 2. ia 3. oma 4. itis
 profession . . 3. eer
suffocate . . . 5. burke, choke 6. stifle
 7. smother 8. strangle, suppress,
 throttle 10. asphyxiate, extinguish
 12. deprive of air
suffrage . . . 4. vote 5. voice 6. assent,
 ballot, prayer 7. witness 8. petition
 9. franchise 10. assistance 11. right
 to vote 12. intercession, supplication
sugar . . . 4. cane 5. biose, bribe, candy,
 maple, money 6. doctor, season
 7. sucrose, sweeten 9. sugarcoat
 10. endearment, saccharose,
 sweetening 12. carbohydrate,
 disaccharide 14. monosaccharide
sugar (pert to) . . .
 and molasses . . 6. melada
 burnt . . 7. caramel
 chemical . . 6. acrose 7. osamine, sucrose
  8. fructose 10. saccharose
 crude . . 3. gur 5. maple 10. massecuite,
  piloncillo
 fruit, honey . . 8. levulose
 plant . . 7. sorghum
 raw . . 9. cassonade, muscovado
 sand . . 5. niter
 simple . . 6. ketose, triose 7. glucide

substitute . . 5. honey
 syrup . . 7. treacle 8. molasses
 tree . . 5. maple
 without . . 3. sec
 wood . . 6. xylose
sugar cane (pert to) . . .
 disease . . 5. sereh
 pulp, refuse . . 4. marc 7. bagasse
 stalk . . 6. ratoon
sugared . . . 5. sweet 7. honeyed
 9. sweetened 11. mellifluous,
 sugarcoated
Sugar Loaf Mt locale . . . 3. Rio
suggest . . . 4. hint, mean, move 5. imply
 6. advise, allude, prompt 7. connote,
 inspire, propose 8. indicate, intimate
 9. insinuate
suggestion . . . 4. clue, hint, idea, plan
 5. tinge, trace 6. advice, symbol
 7. soupçon 8. proposal 9. hypnotism
 10. indication, intimation 11. small
 amount, supposition
Suidae . . . 5. swine
sui generis . . . 6. unique
suit . . . 3. fit 4. plea 5. befit, cards,
 dress, habit, match, serve, tally
 6. adjust, answer, attire, become,
 prayer, wooing 7. clothes, comport,
 conform, costume, lawsuit, retinue
 8. petition, sequence 9. courtship
 10. litigation 11. accommodate
suit (pert to) . . .
 at law . . 10. litigation
 for property . . 6. trover
 maker . . 6. sartor, tailor
 starter . . 7. relator
 the occasion . . 6. timely
suitability . . . 7. fitness 9. propriety
 10. expedience, timeliness 11. eligibility
 13. qualification
suitable . . . 3. apt, due, fit, pat 4. meet
 6. proper, timely 8. adequate, apposite,
 eligible, idoneous 9. accordant,
 agreeable, competent, congruent,
 congruous, consonant, expedient
 10. compatible, consistent
 11. appropriate 12. commensurate
 13. correspondent
suitably proportioned . . .
 13. commensurable
suite . . . 3. set 5. music, staff 7. retinue
 8. sequence 9. apartment
 10. attendance, succession
 11. consequence
suitor . . . 5. swain, wooer 7. amoroso
 10. petitioner 12. party to a suit
sulk . . . 3. pet 4. mope, plow, pout
 6. furrow
sulky . . . 3. gig 4. dull, glum, plow
 5. moody, pouty, surly 6. gloomy,
 go-cart, sullen 8. carriage 9. obstinate
sullen . . . 4. dour, glum, grim, sour
 5. cross, gruff, harsh, moody, pouty,
 sulky, surly 6. crusty, gloomy, morose
 7. austere, cynical, fretful, peevish,
 pettish 8. chumpish, churlish, petulant,
 spiteful 9. obstinate, saturnine
sully . . . 4. foul 5. dirty, smear, stain,
 taint 6. defile, smirch, vilify 7. blemish,
 corrupt, debauch, disdain, pollute
 9. bespatter, denigrate 10. stigmatize

11. contaminate
sulphur (pert to)...
alchemy.. **7.** chibrit
alloy.. **6.** niello
butterfly.. **7.** clouded **9.** cloudless
color.. **6.** yellow
comb form.. **5.** thion
element.. **11.** nonmetallic
reference to.. **7.** thionic **9.** brimstone
sultan (pert to)...
decree.. **5.** irade
fowls.. **5.** breed
home.. **5.** serai
Mohammedan State.. **5.** ruler **6.** prince
　9. sovereign
Turkish ruler.. **6.** Caliph **8.** Padishah
　13. Grand Seignior
wife.. **7.** sultana
sultana ... **4.** roll (dessert), wife **5.** grape
　8. mistress **9.** gallinule
sultry ... **3.** hot **5.** humid, lurid **6.** torrid
　7. dog days, sensual **10.** oppressive,
　sweltering
sum ... **3.** add, tot **4.** loot **5.** count,
　gross, total, whole **6.** amount, number,
　result **7.** summary **8.** addition, quantity
　9. aggregate, summarize, summation
　12. recapitulate
sum (pert to)...
forfeited.. **5.** dédit
of money.. **6.** budget
total.. **8.** entirety
unexpended.. **7.** savings
up.. **3.** tot **5.** count **8.** perorate
sumac ... **5.** Rheus **7.** dogwood
　8. shadbush **9.** squawbush
　13. Toxicodendron **14.** buckthorn brown
Sumatra ...
harbor.. **6.** Padang **9.** Palembang
island of.. **16.** Malay Archipelago
kingdom.. **5.** Achin, Jambi
mountain.. **12.** Bukit Barisan
raft (bamboo).. **5.** rakit
river.. **4.** Musi **5.** Jambi, Rokan **6.** Asahan
squirrel shrew.. **4.** tana
wildcat.. **4.** balu
sumless ... **11.** inestimable
　12. incalculable **13.** unaccountable
summary ... **5.** brief, short **6.** digest,
　prompt, resume **7.** epitome **8.** abstract
　10. compendium **11.** abridgement,
　enumeration, reiteration
　14. recapitulation
summary (pert to)...
book.. **5.** blurb
concise.. **6.** précis
of facts.. **7.** roundup
of knowledge.. **12.** encyclopedia
　(encyclopaedia)
of principles.. **5.** creed
of speech.. **5.** notes
summer ... **3.** été **6.** season
summer (pert to)...
bird.. **7.** cuckold, sparrow, tanager,
　wryneck
coot.. **9.** gallinule
house.. **6.** gazebo **9.** belvedere
lilac.. **8.** damewort
pert to.. **7.** estival
rash.. **11.** prickly heat
resort.. **4.** camp

squash.. **7.** cymling, scallop **9.** crookneck
summit ... **3.** top **4.** acme, apex, knap,
　peak **5.** crest, crown, knoll, spire
　6. height **7.** Everest **8.** pinnacle
　9. fastigium **10.** perfection
　11. culmination, mountaintop
summon ... **4.** call, cite, page, sist
　5. evoke **6.** call up, demand, elicit,
　invite, muster **7.** conjure, evocate
　8. remember **9.** conscript
sumpter ... **4.** mule **9.** pack horse
sun ... **3.** orb, Sol **4.** bask **6.** Helios
　7. Phoebus **12.** heavenly body
　13. celestial body
sun (pert to)...
clock.. **6.** gnomon (part) **7.** sundial
comb form.. **5.** helio
crossing the equator.. **7.** equinox
disk.. **4.** aten
down.. **3.** eve **8.** twilight
farthest from.. **8.** aphelion
fish.. **4.** mola, opah **5.** bream
god.. **2.** Ra **4.** Amen, Baal, Lier (Llew)
　6. Apollo, Helios **7.** Khepera (Chepera),
　Shamash, Sokaris **8.** Hyperion
mock.. **9.** parhelion
nearest to.. **10.** perihelion
outer layer.. **6.** corona
over the equator.. **7.** equinox
path.. **4.** halo **6.** circle **8.** ecliptic
pert to.. **5.** solar **6.** heliac **9.** heliology
poetic.. **5.** glory, power **6.** sunset
　7. daystar, sunrise **8.** splendor
satellite.. **6.** planet
spot.. **6.** facula **7.** freckle
squall.. **9.** jellyfish
stroke.. **8.** siriasis **9.** calenture
sundang ... **4.** bolo **5.** knife
sunder ... **4.** part, rend, rive **5.** sever, split
　6. cleave, divide **7.** divorce **8.** dissever,
　disunite, sejugate
sundry ... **6.** divers **7.** several, various
　8. frequent, manifold, numerous
　9. different **10.** multiplied
　12. multifarious **13.** miscellaneous
sunflower ... **8.** marigold, rockrose
　10. heliotrope
Sunflower State ... **6.** Kansas
sunk ... **4.** turf **7.** baffled, concave,
　lowered **8.** dejected, overcome
　9. depressed (see also *sink*)
sunk fence ... **4.** ha-ha (haw-haw)
sunny ... **4.** warm **5.** clear, merry **6.** bright,
　sunlit **8.** cheerful **9.** sparkling, vivacious
sunrise ... **4.** dawn
sunset ... **3.** eve **4.** dusk **7.** evening,
　sundown **8.** twilight
Sunset State ... **6.** Oregon **7.** Arizona
Sunshine State ... **9.** New Mexico
　11. South Dakota
supawn ... **4.** mush **12.** hasty pudding
superabundance ... **5.** flood **6.** excess,
　plenty **7.** surplus **8.** plethora
　10. exuberance **11.** superfluity
superabundant ... **4.** rank **6.** lavish
　7. profuse **9.** excessive, exuberant,
　luxuriant, plentiful **11.** overflowing
　14. oversufficient
superannuate ... **6.** retire **9.** antiquate
　10. pension off **13.** prove obsolete
superb ... **4.** rich **5.** grand, noble

6. lordly 7. elegant, stately 8. majestic, splendid 9. sumptuous 11. magnificent 13. extraordinary 14. superexcellent

supercilious ... 5. proud 7. haughty 8. arrogant 9. arbitrary 11. overbearing 12. contemptuous 13. hypercritical

supercilious person ... 4. snob

superficial ... 4. glib 6. slight, square 7. cursory, shallow, smatter, surface, trivial 8. apparent, external 9. frivolous, insincere

superfluity ... 6. excess, luxury, wealth 7. overset 8. frippery 10. redundancy 11. prodigality 14. superabundance

superfluous ... 4. over 5. luxus, spare 6. excess 7. surplus, useless 8. needless, wasteful 9. redundant 10. inordinate 11. extravagant 12. nonessential 13. superabundant 14. supererogatory

superhuman ... 6. divine 9. Herculean 12. supernatural 13. extraordinary

superimposed ... 4. over, upon 5. above 7. covered, layered 8. overlaid 9. overlying

superintend ... 4. boss 5. guide 6. direct, manage 7. oversee 8. overlook 9. look after, supervise 10. administer, have charge

superintendent ... 4. boss 7. curator, manager 8. director, overseer 9. inspector, straw boss 10. supervisor 11. chamberlain

superior ... 4. over, peer 5. above, chief, upper 6. higher, senior 7. exalted, mastery, ranking 8. goodness, priority 9. advantage, paramount, seniority 10. ascendancy, excellence, pre-eminent, surpassing 11. pre-eminence 12. predominancy

superlative ... 4. acme, best, peak 6. utmost 7. elative, extreme, supreme, the best 8. peerless 9. hyperbole 12. exaggeration

supernatural ... 5. eerie, magic 6. divine 10. miraculous, superhuman 13. hyperphysical, preternatural

supernatural (pert to) ...
being .. 3. God 4. atua 5. jinni (jinnee) 7. banshee (banshie), specter (spectre)
event .. 7. miracle
power .. 4. ngai 6. fetish 8. talisman 11. incantation

superscribe ... 6. direct 7. address (a letter), engrave 8. inscribe

supersede ... 4. omit 7. replace, succeed 8. displace, make void, supplant

superstition ... 6. notion, voodoo 8. folklore, idolatry 9. tradition 10. Aberglaube 12. old wives' tale

superstitious ... 6. goetic 7. magical 10. idolatrous 11. fetishistic (fetichistic)

supervene ... 5. occur 6. accrue, happen 7. be added 12. be subsequent

supervise ... 4. boss, read, scan 5. check 6. direct, govern, peruse, revise 7. inspect, oversee 11. superintend

supervisor ... 4. boss 7. foreman, proctor 9. inspector, straw boss

supine ... 5. inert, prone 6. abject, drowsy 7. servile, unalert 8. careless, inclined,

indolent, listless, sluggish 9. apathetic, lethargic, recumbent 11. inattentive, indifferent, thoughtless

supplant ... 5. upset, usurp 6. remove, uproot 7. replace 8. displace, drive out 9. eradicate, extirpate, overthrow, supersede

supple ... 3. sly 4. bent 5. agile, lithe 6. limber, nimble, pliant 7. fawning, lissome 8. flexible, yielding 9. compliant, resilient 10. obsequious, responsive 11. complaisant

supplement ... 3. add, eke 5. add to 6. sequel 7. ripieno 8. addition, appendix, complete 9. accessory 10. complement 12. nonessential 13. reinforcement

supplementary, music ... 7. ripieno

supplicate ... 3. beg 4. pray 5. crave, plead 6. appeal, obtest 7. beseech, conjure, entreat, implore, solicit 8. petition 9. importune, obsecrate

supplication ... 4. plea 6. litany, prayer 7. craving 8. entreaty, petition, rogative 11. obtestation 12. solicitation

supplies ... 6. hoards, relays, stocks, stores 8. estovers, ordnance 9. provender

supply ... 4. fund, give 5. cache, cater, hoard, relay, stock, store, yield 6. purvey, remuda 7. provide, reserve 9. provision, reservoir 10. administer, contribute

supply (pert to) ...
food .. 4. feed 5. cater 9. alimental
fuel .. 5. stoke
funds .. 5. endow
horses .. 5. relay
provisions .. 6. purvey

support ... 3. aid, arm, fid, guy, leg, peg, rib 4. abet, ally, back, base, buoy, limb, mast, prop 5. brace, cleat, shore, spile, stell, strut, tenon 6. backer, pillar, second, uphold 7. bolster, fulcrum, trestle 8. buttress, underlie 9. auxiliary, encourage, reinforce, stanchion 10. assistance, foundation 11. corroborate 12. substantiate 13. corroboration

support (pert to) ...
anatomy .. 3. rib 5. spine
cannon .. 4. trunnion
coffin .. 4. bier
mast .. 4. bibb
resilient .. 6. spring
three-legged .. 5. easel 6. tripod, trivot
upright .. 8. baluster 9. stanchion
wedge-shaped .. 5. cleat

supporters ... 6. allies, braces 7. backers, bracers, garters 10. suspenders 15. ministerialists

suppose ... 3. wis 4. deem, trow 5. allow, imply, judge, opine, think 6. assume, expect, repute 7. presume 8. conclude, consider 9. apprehend, intention 10. conjecture 11. supposition

supposed ... 8. putative

supposition ... 2. if 6. theory 7. surmise 8. supposed 9. postulate 10. assumption, conjecture, hypothesis 11. connotation, implication

suppress . . . **4.** kill, stop **5.** check, crush, elide, quash, quell **6.** hush up, muffle, retard, stifle **7.** abolish, exclude, oppress, smother **8.** hold back, prohibit, restrain, withhold **9.** interdict, overpower **10.** extinguish

suppression . . . **6.** hush up **7.** reserve **8.** hush-hush **9.** overthrow, restraint **10.** inhibition

supremacy . . . **5.** power **7.** control, mastery, primacy **8.** dominion **9.** influence **10.** ascendancy, domination, first place **11.** sovereignty **12.** championship

supreme . . . **3.** top **4.** last **5.** chief, final **6.** divine, ruling **7.** crucial, highest **8.** foremost, greatest, peerless **9.** paramount **10.** preeminent

supreme being . . . **3.** God **4.** Lord **5.** Allah, Deity, monad **6.** Brahma, Buddha **7.** Creator, Jehovah **8.** autocrat

surcease . . . **3.** end **4.** rest, stop **5.** defer, delay **6.** desist, relief **7.** respite **8.** drop work, postpone **9.** cessation

surd . . . **4.** deaf, mute **7.** aphonic, radical **9.** voiceless

sure . . . **3.** yes **4.** fast, firm, safe, true **5.** bound **6.** indeed, secure, stable, steady, strong **7.** assured, certain **8.** positive, reliable **9.** confident, steadfast, unfailing **10.** guaranteed, inevitable, infallible **11.** trustworthy **12.** indisputable **13.** incontestable **14.** unquestionable

surety . . . **4.** bail, bond, fact **6.** backer, pledge, safety **7.** sponsor **8.** security, sureness **9.** certainty **10.** confidence, engagement

surf . . . **4.** foam, rote, wave **5.** bathe, spray, surge, swell **7.** breaker

surface . . . **4.** area, face, orlo, pave, plat, skin **5.** facet, meros **6.** facing, patina **7.** outside **9.** exterior **9.** periphery

surface (pert to) . . .
artificial . . **4.** rink
front (coin) . . **7.** obverse
gem . . **5.** facet
geometric . . **6.** toroid
medical . . **7.** acrotic
toward . . **4.** ectad
under . . **6.** latent **10.** internally
water . . **4.** ryme

surfeit . . . **4.** cloy, feed, glut, jade, sate **6.** excess **7.** replete, satiate, satisfy **9.** satiation **11.** overindulge, superfluity

surge . . . **4.** eddy, flow, rush, wave **5.** swarm, swell, whirl **6.** billow, thrill **7.** estuate **9.** gurgitate **11.** rise and fall

surgeon (pert to) . . .
ancient . . **10.** chirurgeon
case (instrument) . . **6.** tweeze (tweese)
slang . . **8.** sawbones

surgery . . . **7.** aciurgy **8.** medicine **9.** operation, resection

surgery (pert to) . . .
chin . . **11.** mentoplasty
ears . . **9.** otoplasty
face lift . . **13.** rhytidoplasty
    14. blepharoplasty (eyelids)
fractures . . **10.** agmatology
mouth, lip . . **12.** cheiloplasty (chiloplasty)

nose . . **7.** nose job **11.** rhinoplasty
organ . . **10.** transplant
skin . . **12.** dermabrasion
vein . . **10.** phlebotomy
vertebra . . **11.** laminectomy

surgical (pert to) . . .
compress . . **4.** swab **5.** stupe
counterirritant . . **5.** seton
equpment . . **4.** X-ray **6.** splint **7.** CAT scan, scanner **8.** iron lung **10.** respirator, tomography, tourniquet **11.** stethoscope **12.** resuscitator
hook . . **9.** tenaculum
instrument . . **3.** saw **5.** fleam, lance, probe **6.** catlin, lancet, stylet, trepan, xyster **7.** forceps **8.** hemostat, keratome, speculum, tweezers
knife . . **7.** scalpel
puncture . . **8.** céntesis
saw . . **6.** trepan
stitch . . **5.** seton **6.** suture

Suriname (pert to) . . .
capital . . **10.** Paramaribo
former name . . **11.** Dutch Guiana
mountain . . **10.** Tumuc-Humac
toad . . **4.** pipa

surly . . . **4.** glum, grum, rude **5.** gruff **6.** abrupt, grumpy, morose, sullen **7.** crabbed **8.** arrogant, growling **10.** ill-natured **11.** intractable

surmise . . . **4.** deem **5.** fancy, guess, judge, opine, think **7.** imagine, presume **8.** mistrust **9.** suspicion **10.** assumption, conclusion, conjecture **11.** supposition

surmount . . . **3.** top **4.** pass, rise **5.** climb, excel, mount **6.** subdue **7.** conquer, surpass **8.** overcome **9.** transcend

surname . . . **6.** eponym, family, maiden **7.** agnomen **8.** cognomen **10.** patronymic **11.** appellation

surpass . . . **3.** cap, top **4.** best **5.** excel, outdo **6.** better, exceed, outvie, outwit **7.** outrank, outride **8.** go beyond, outrange, outreach, outshine, outsmart, outstrip, surmount **9.** transcend

surpassing . . . **12.** transcendent

surplice . . . **3.** fee **5.** cotta, ephod **6.** collar **7.** pelisse

surplus . . . **4.** over, rest **5.** epact **6.** excess **7.** overage, reserve **8.** overplus **9.** remaining **10.** additional, redundancy **11.** superfluous

surprise . . . **3.** awe **5.** alarm, amaze, seize, shock **6.** wonder **7.** astound, capture, perplex, startle **8.** astonish, bewilder, confound, dumfound **9.** amazement, dumbfound, overwhelm, surprisal **10.** wonderment **11.** flabbergast **12.** astonishment

surprising . . . **7.** amazing **8.** striking **9.** startling **10.** unexpected **11.** astonishing, unlooked for **13.** extraordinary

surrealism (pert to) . . .
film director . . **6.** Buñuel
founder, poet . . **6.** Breton
painter . . **4.** Dali **5.** Ernst **8.** Magritte

surrender . . . **4.** cede, give **5.** yield **6.** give up, remise, resign **7.** abandon, cession, deliver **8.** dedition, remittal **9.** extradite **10.** relinquish, submission

11. abandonment, divestiture
12. cancellation **14.** relinquishment
surreptitious ... **3.** sly **6.** hidden, secret
8. stealthy **9.** concealed, deceitful
10. fraudulent **11.** clandestine
surround ... **4.** gird, isle, wrap **5.** beset,
hem in, inarm **6.** circle, encase, incase,
invest **7.** besiege, enclave, enclose,
envelop, environ **8.** encircle, inundate,
overflow **9.** encompass **12.** circumscribe
14. circumnavigate
surrounding ... **5.** about, beset, midst
7. ambient, setting **9.** hemming in,
perioptic **10.** encircling, enveloping
11. circumpolar **12.** circumjacent
survey ... **4.** plan, poll, scan **5.** study,
vista **6.** regard, review **7.** examine,
inspect, oversee **8.** traverse **9.** delineate,
determine **10.** scrutinize
11. examination, reconnoiter,
superintend **14.** reconnaissance
surveying (pert to) ...
instrument .. **7.** alidade (alidad), transit
9. stadia rod **10.** throdolite
mathematics .. **7.** geodesy
process .. **13.** triangulation
surveyor (pert to) ...
helper .. **6.** rodman **7.** lineman, poleman
land .. **8.** measurer, overseer **9.** arpenteur
measure .. **7.** chain
mine .. **6.** dialer
survival ... **5.** relic **9.** endurance, outliving
10. durability
survivor ... **6.** relict **8.** outliver, remainer,
survival **11.** joint tenant
susceptibility ... **5.** sense **7.** emotion,
feeling, pliancy **11.** sensibility
12. teachability **13.** affectibility,
vulnerability **14.** sentimentality
susceptible ... **4.** easy **6.** liable, pliant
7. exposed, subject **8.** sensible
9. receptive, sensitive, teachable
10. responsive, vulnerable
11. softhearted **13.** tenderhearted
14. impressionable
suslik ... **5.** sisel **8.** squirrel
11. spermophile
suspect ... **4.** fear **5.** doubt, fancy,
guess **7.** imagine, presume, suppose
8. distrust, mistrust **9.** discredit
10. disbelieve, suspicious
suspecting ... **4.** wary **8.** doubtful,
doubting **11.** incredulous, mistrusting
suspend ... **4.** hang, oust, stay, stop
5. cease, debar, defer, expel, remit
6. dangle, depose, recess **7.** adjourn,
pensile **8.** intermit, postpone, set aside,
withhold **9.** pretermit
suspended ... **4.** hung **5.** inert **6.** barred,
latent **8.** abeyant, pendent **8.** inactive
9. pendulous **11.** inoperative,
interrupted
suspenders ... **4.** pegs **5.** belts, hooks,
rings **6.** braces, straps **7.** gallows,
garters **8.** galluses **9.** bretelles
10. supporters **11.** clothespins
suspense ... **5.** pause **7.** anxiety
10. expectancy **11.** uncertainty
12. apprehension, irresolution
14. indecisiveness
suspension ... **4.** stop **5.** delay **7.** deposal,

failure, hanging, respite **8.** abeyance,
buoyancy **11.** withholding
12. intermission, interruption
suspicious ... **4.** fear, hint **5.** doubt,
hunch, trace **7.** askance, inkling,
soupcon **8.** distrust, jealousy, mistrust,
wariness **9.** mere trace, misgiving
10. diffidence, intimation, skepticism,
suggestion **11.** incredulity, supposition
12. apprehension
Sussex (pert to) ...
breed (Eng) .. **4.** fowl **6.** cattle
kingdom (anc) .. **7.** English
land measure .. **4.** wist
land tract (Downs) .. **5.** laine
man .. **8.** Piltdown (Prehist)
spaniel .. **6.** gun dog
sustain ... **4.** bear, buoy, feed, prop
5. abide, carry **6.** endure, foster, keep
up, uphold **7.** confirm, justify, nourish,
prolong, support, undergo **8.** continue,
maintain, preserve **9.** encourage,
establish **10.** strengthen **11.** corroborate
sustained ... **6.** tenuto, upheld
9. permanent, prolonged, supported
10. unflagging
suttee ... **5.** widow **9.** cremation, sacrifice
14. self-immolation
suture ... **5.** unite **6.** stitch **7.** pterion
12. synarthrosis
swagger ... **4.** brag, gait, walk **5.** bluff,
boast, bully, strut, swell **6.** prance
7. bluster, dashing, roister, stagger,
stylish **8.** domineer **11.** braggadocio,
ostentation **16.** ultrafashionable
swain ... **3.** boy, lad **4.** beau **5.** lover
6. suitor **7.** admirer, gallant, peasant
8. shepherd **10.** countryman
swallow ... **3.** sip **4.** gulp **5.** drink
6. absorb, englut, engulf, imbibe,
ingest, recant **7.** consume, engorge,
retract **8.** tolerate **10.** bear meekly
swallow (pert to) ...
chimney .. **5.** swift
European .. **6.** martin
hawk .. **4.** kite
plover .. **10.** pratincole
sea .. **4.** tern
tail .. **4.** coat **9.** butterfly
the anchor .. **10.** quit the sea
swamp ... **3.** bog, fen **4.** mire, muck,
sink, slue, sump **5.** flood, marsh
6. deluge, engulf, morass, slough
7. cienaga, pocosin **8.** quagmire,
submerge **9.** everglade, overwhelm
swamp (pert to) ...
boggy .. **7.** queachy **8.** muskeggy
earth .. **4.** muck
gas .. **6.** miasma
grass .. **5.** sedge
marsh .. **5.** slash **8.** paludine
tract .. **10.** Everglades
swan ... **3.** cob, pen **4.** Olor **5.** swear
6. cygnet, cygnus **7.** declare
9. trumpeter
swan (pert to) ...
astronomy .. **6.** Cygnus
flower .. **6.** orchid
goose .. **7.** Bewick's, Chinese
myth (Hind) .. **5.** hansa
poem .. **12.** Swan of Thames (Pope)

15. Sweet Swan of Avon (Jonson)
star (brightest).. **5.** Deneb
trumpeter.. **4.** wild
type.. **4.** mute **5.** black **8.** whooping
11. black-necked
swap... **4.** beat **5.** trade **6.** barter, thrash
8. exchange **11.** give-and-take
sward... **3.** sod **4.** lawn, turf **5.** grass
10. greensward
swarm... **3.** fry **5.** crowd, flock, horde
6. abound, infest, throng **7.** pervade
9. migration, multitude **10.** congregate
11. aggregation
swarthy... **3.** dun **4.** dark **5.** dusky
8. bistered (bistred), blackish
swashbuckler... **5.** bravo **6.** gascon
7. ruffian **8.** Almanzor **9.** blusterer,
daredevil, swaggerer **10.** Drawcansir
swastika (swastica)... **6.** fylfot, symbol
(since 1918) **9.** gammadion
10. hakenkreuz
swat... **3.** bat, hit **5.** clout **6.** strike **7.** hit
hard
swathe... **4.** band, bind, wrap **6.** enfold
7. envelop, swaddle
sway... **4.** bend, bias, rock, rule, veer,
wave **5.** lurch, power, shake, swing,
waver, wield **6.** direct, empire, govern,
induce, totter, waddle **7.** command,
control, deflect, incline **8.** flounder
9. fluctuate, influence, oscillate, vacillate
10. ascendancy **11.** fluctuation
swayback... **8.** lordosis
swaying... **7.** pensile, sagging
8. swinging, waddling **11.** influential,
oscillating
swear... **3.** vow **4.** oath **5.** curse, vouch
6. adjure, pledge (sacred) **7.** confirm,
declare, promise **10.** asseverate,
deposition **11.** bear witness
swear (pert to)...
at.. **5.** clash (colors), curse **8.** disagree
by.. **5.** bet on **7.** count on **8.** take oath
falsely.. **7.** perjure
off.. **4.** stop **6.** eschew, give up
7. abandon **8.** renounce
sweat... **4.** work **5.** exude, grill,
sudor **6.** drudge **7.** excrete, ferment
8. perspire, transude **9.** exudation
10. impatience **11.** nervousness
Sweden... see also *Swedish*
capital.. **9.** Stockholm
city.. **5.** Malmö **7.** Uppsala (Upsala)
8. Göteborg
dynasty (1st).. **8.** Ynglings
gulf.. **7.** Bothnia
lake.. **6.** Vanern **7.** Vattern
mountain.. **5.** Kölen (Kjölen)
parliament.. **7.** Riksdag
peninsula.. **11.** Scandinavia
port.. **8.** Göteborg **9.** Stockholm
river.. **4.** Klar **7.** Götaalv
sea.. **6.** Baltic
university (oldest).. **7.** Uppsula (Upsula,
1477)
Swedish (pert to)...
actress.. **5.** Garbo
artist.. **4.** Zorn
botanist.. **8.** Linnaeus
bread.. **10.** knäckebröd
clover.. **6.** alsike

dance.. **6.** polska
diplomat.. **12.** Hammarskjöld (Dag)
dramatist.. **10.** Strindberg
explorer.. **5.** Hedin
film director.. **7.** Bergman (Ingmar)
fir.. **10.** Scotch pine
hero (WWII).. **10.** Wallenberg
idiom.. **7.** Suecism
manual training.. **5.** sloyd (slojd)
northern inhabitants.. **5.** Lapps
novelist.. **8.** Lagerlöf (Pulitzer prize,
1909)
opera singer.. **9.** Jenny Lind (Swedish
Nightingale) **7.** Nilsson (Birgit)
philosopher.. **10.** Swedenborg
religion (State).. **8.** Lutheran
turnip.. **8.** rutabaga
sweep... **3.** oar **4.** scan **5.** clean, clear,
cover, curve, glide, strip, surge, swish,
trail **6.** course, vision **7.** contour
8. traverse
sweeping... **8.** complete, thorough
9. extensive **12.** all-embracing
13. comprehensive
sweet... **5.** bonny, candy **10.** dolce douce
5. fresh, spicy **6.** dulcet, gentle, sugary,
syrupy **7.** caramel, honeyed, lovable
8. aromatic, fragrant, luscious, pleasant,
preserve **9.** agreeable, ambrosial,
melodious, nectarine **10.** confection,
saccharine **11.** mellifluous, mellisonant
sweet (pert to)...
and fair.. **5.** bonny
bread.. **4.** food **6.** thymus **8.** pancreas
9. ris de veau
brier.. **4.** rose **9.** eglantine
drink.. **6.** nectar
meat.. **4.** cake **5.** candy **6.** comfit, éclair,
pastry **7.** caramel, dessert **8.** marzipan
10. confection
potato.. **3.** yam **6.** batata
potato, musical.. **7.** ocarina
sop.. **4.** ates, atta **6.** Annone **14.** Annona
squamosa
sounding.. **11.** mellisonant
wine.. **4.** port **5.** Lunel
sweetheart... **2.** jo **3.** gra **4.** beau, lass
5. flame, leman, lover, spark, swain
7. darling **8.** dowsabel, honeybun
(sl), ladylove **9.** Amaryllis, inamorata,
valentine
swell... **3.** fob, nob **4.** grow, rise, surf,
wave **5.** bulge, dandy, grand, heave,
mound, surge **6.** billow, dilate, expand,
growth, puff up, tiptop **7.** distend,
inflate, stylish **8.** increase, protrude
9. sumptuous **10.** aristocrat, prominence
11. enlargement **12.** augmentation
swell (pert to)...
ocean.. **4.** surf **6.** billow, expand, roller
rolling.. **7.** seagate
slang.. **3.** nob **5.** dandy, grand
9. first-rate
swelled (pert to)...
head.. **3.** ego **7.** conceit **9.** cockiness
14. self-importance
out.. **4.** lump, node **5.** tumid **6.** bulged,
podded, turgid **9.** grandiose
swelling... **4.** sore **5.** bulge, edema
6. dropsy **9.** bombastic **10.** distention,
increasing **12.** protuberance

swelter . . . **4.** fret **5.** exude, roast, sweat **8.** perspire **10.** sultry heat

swerve . . . **4.** veer **5.** dodge, sheer, shift **6.** recoil **7.** deflect, deviate **9.** deviation, turn aside

swift . . . **4.** bird, fast, racy, reel **5.** alert, fleet, hasty, quick, rapid, ready **6.** lizard, prompt, speedy, sudden, winged **8.** headlong

swift (pert to) . . .
astronomer . . **5.** Lewis (Swift)
bird . . **4.** crin **7.** chimney
boat . . **7.** flyboat **10.** Hovercraft
footed . . **5.** ariel (gazelle) **7.** Mercury
satirist . . **8.** Jonathan (Swift)

swiftness . . . **5.** haste, speed **8.** celerity, velocity **9.** quickness **10.** promptness

swimmer . . . **5.** diver **6.** bather **7.** Cloelia (Tiber Riv), Leander (Hellespont), natator

swimming . . . **5.** crawl **6.** natant **7.** vertigo **9.** dizziness, freestyle, skinny-dip **10.** sidestroke **12.** breast stroke

swimming (pert to) . . .
birds . . **9.** natatores
bladder . . **10.** air bladder (fish)
pert to . . **5.** dizzy **7.** aquatic **8.** natatory
pool . . **4.** hole, tank **10.** natatorium
sandpiper . . **9.** phalarope

swindle . . . **3.** con, gyp **4.** dupe, fake, sell **5.** bunco, cheat **6.** trepan **7.** defraud **8.** flimflam **9.** gold brick

swindler . . . **3.** gyp **5.** biter, cheat, crook, knave, rogue, shark **6.** gypper **7.** sharper **9.** defrauder

swindling . . . **6.** estafa

swine . . . **3.** hog, pig, sow, Sus **4.** boar **7.** Anthony (smallest), peccary **8.** slattern **9.** scoundrel

swine, breed of . . . **8.** Cheshire, Tamworth **9.** Berkshire, Hampshire, razorback, Yorkshire **11.** Duroc-Jersey, Poland China **12.** Chester-White

swineherd (pert to) . . .
patron saint . . **7.** Anthony
reference to . . **7.** sybotic

swinelike . . . **7.** porcine

swing . . . **4.** hang, jazz, jive, lilt, sway **5.** shake, trend, waver, wield **6.** dangle, manage, rhythm, totter **7.** suspend, trapeze, vibrate **8.** pendulum, undulate **9.** fluctuate, oscillate

swingtree . . . **11.** whippletree

swinish . . . **5.** gross **6.** carnal, filthy, greedy **7.** beastly, porcine, sensual **8.** gluttony

swipe . . . **4.** gulp **5.** draft, drink, lever, steal, swape, swath, sweep **6.** handle, pilfer, snatch **7.** purloin

swipes . . . **4.** beer (Eng sl)

swirl . . . **4.** curl, eddy **5.** curve, gurge, surge, twist, whirl, whorl

swirly . . . **7.** knotted, tangled, twisted

Swiss (pert to) . . . see also *Switzerland*
artist . . **4.** Klee
ax (ice) . . **6.** piolet
bell . . **9.** alpenhorn (alphorn)
cabin . . **6.** chalet
composer . . **4.** Raff
flower, emblem . . **9.** edelweiss
herdsman . . **4.** senn

hero . . **11.** William Tell
language . . **6.** French, German **7.** Italian **8.** Romansch
legislature . . **9.** Bundesrat (Bundesrath), Grosse Rat (Grossrat)
mathematician . . **5.** Euler
physician, alchemist . . **10.** Paracelsus
pine . . **6.** arolla
psychologist . . **4.** Jung
scientist . . **6.** Haller (von)
surgeon . . **6.** Kocher (Nobel Prize)
theologian . . **5.** Vinet **7.** Zwingli
warble . . **5.** yodel
warbler . . **7.** yodeler (yodeller)
wind . . **4.** bise
wine . . **7.** Dezaley

switch . . . **4.** lash, turn (on or off), whip **5.** shift, shunt **6.** change, divert, siding **8.** exchange, transfer

switchback (Brit) . . . **13.** roller-coaster

Switzerland (pert to) . . .
ancient . . **8.** Helvetia
canton . . **5.** Aarau
capital . . **5.** Berne (Bern)
city . . **5.** Basel **6.** Geneva, Zurich **7.** Locarno, Lucerne **8.** Lausanne **9.** Constance
famed for . . **5.** banks (Finan)
lake . . **3.** Uri **6.** Brienz, Geneva, Zurich **7.** Lucerne **8.** Maggiore **9.** Constance, Neuchâtel **10.** Stattersee
mountain . . **4.** Alps, Jura **5.** Blanc **8.** Jungfrau **9.** Monte Rosa (peak) **10.** Matterhorn
resort . . **7.** Urseren, Yverdon
river . . **3.** Aar **5.** Reuss, Rhine, Rhone
tunnel . . **5.** Cenis **7.** Gothard, Simplon **11.** Loetschberg
university (oldest) . . **5.** Basel
valley . . **3.** Aar

swollen . . . **5.** pursy, tumid **6.** turgid **7.** bloated, bulbous, bulging, pompous **8.** enlarged, inflated, puffed up, varicose **9.** bombastic, distended, plethoric, tumescent **11.** protuberant

swoon . . . **3.** fit **5.** faint, spell **7.** ecstasy, syncope **8.** languish **10.** heavy sleep

swoop . . . **5.** seize, sweep **6.** attack, pounce **7.** descend

sword (pert to) . . .
ancient . . **5.** estoc **6.** glaive
cavalry . . **5.** saber (sabre)
curved . . **7.** cutlass, Ferrara **8.** Claymore, scimitar
fencing . . **4.** foil, epee **6.** rapier
fine . . **6.** Toledo **8.** Damascus
handle . . **4.** haft, hilt
India . . **5.** kukri
like . . **7.** xiphoid
Mohammedan's . . **8.** scimitar
part . . **5.** forte, talon **6.** foible
practice . . **5.** fence
scabbard tip . . **7.** crampit
Scot Highlander's . . **4.** dirk
seaman's . . **6.** hanger
shaped . . **6.** ensate **7.** xiphoid (xyphoid) **8.** ensiform, gladiate
sheik's . . **4.** pata
Siegfried's . . **4.** Gram **7.** Balmung
Sir Bevis' . . **7.** Morglay
Spanish . . **5.** bilbo

support . . **7.** baldric
two-handed . . **7.** espadon
type . . **4.** epee, pata **5.** blade, degen, estoc, gully, saber **6.** barong, creese, parang, rapier **7.** cutlass **9.** gladiolus
swordfish . . . **6.** dorado, Dorado (constellation), espada **7.** espadon, Xiphias **9.** broadbill
sword of . . .
Damocles . . **12.** fateful thing
God . . **6.** Khaled (Muslim hero)
mercy . . **7.** Curtana (pointless)
Sir Bevis . . **7.** Morglay (death)
St George . . **7.** Askelon
the Cid . . **6.** Colada
swordsman . . . **6.** fencer **7.** duelist, epeeist, saberer, sabreur **9.** gladiator **11.** Beau Sabreur
sworn statement . . . **9.** affidavit
sworn to secrecy . . . **5.** tiled
sybarite . . . **7.** epicure **10.** voluptuary **11.** luxury lover
sybil (sibil) . . . **4.** seer **5.** witch **7.** seeress **10.** prophetess **13.** fortuneteller
syce . . . **5.** groom
sycophant . . . **5.** toady **7.** fawning, spaniel **8.** hanger-on, informer, parasite **9.** charlatan, flatterer, toadeater **10.** talebearer
sycophantic . . . **7.** fawning, servile, slavish **8.** obedient, toadying **10.** obsequious **11.** bootlicking
syllable . . .
accented . . **5.** arsis
by syllable . . **11.** syllabation
charm . . **2.** om **6.** mantra
last . . **6.** ultima
last, omission of . . **7.** apocope
last but one . . **6.** penult
last but two . . **10.** antepenult
lengthening of . . **7.** ectasis
ref to . . **5.** affix **6.** prefix, suffix **8.** dactylic, syllabic
short . . **4.** mora
shortening . . **7.** systole
stress . . **5.** ictus
table . . **9.** syllabary
unaccented . . **4.** lene **6.** thesis
syllabled, three . . . **7.** triseme (3 moras) **11.** trisyllabic
syllabus . . . **6.** aperçu, digest **8.** abstract, synopsis **10.** compendium, conspectus
syllogism . . . **7.** premise, sorites **9.** deduction, reasoning **11.** epicheirema (epichirema) **18.** deductive reasoning
sylvan, silvan . . . **5.** woody **6.** groved, rustic, wooded **8.** forested **10.** forestlike
sylvan deity . . . **3.** Pan **4.** faun **5.** Satyr, Vidar **6.** Faunus
symbol . . . **2.** om **4.** icon, palm, sign, type **5.** badge, crest, cross, image, token, totem **6.** emblem, ensign, figure, letter, number **9.** character (graphic), prototype, trademark **12.** abbreviation
symbol (pert to) . . .
authority . . **4.** mace
bondage . . **4.** yoke
ecclesiastic . . **4.** ring
England . . **4.** lion
France . . **4.** lily
mathematics . . **7.** operand

military . . **3.** bar **4.** star **5.** eagle, wings **6.** stripe **7.** chevron, epaulet (epaulette) **8.** caduceus
peace . . **4.** dove
power . . **4.** mace
prayer figure (anc) . . **5.** orant
royal . . **3.** rod **5.** crown, tiara **6.** corona **7.** scepter (sceptre)
Tammany Hall . . **5.** tiger
tribal . . **5.** totem (pole)
victory . . **4.** palm
symbol for . . .
arsenic . . **2.** As
calcium . . **2.** Ca
chromium . . **2.** Cr
copper . . **2.** Cu
gold . . **2.** Au
iron . . **2.** Fe
lead . . **2.** Pb
neon . . **2.** Ne
nickel . . **2.** Ni
radium . . **2.** Ra
silver . . **2.** Ag, Ar
sodium . . **2.** Na
tin . . **2.** Sn
symbolic, symbolical . . . **7.** typical **9.** imagerial **10.** figurative, relational **11.** allegorical, significant **12.** emblematical **14.** representative
symbolism . . . **7.** mystery, writing **9.** mysticism, ritualism, symbolics **10.** figuration **11.** hieroglyphy **14.** representation
symmetric, symmetrical . . . **7.** orderly, regular, spheral, uniform **8.** balanced **10.** euphonious
symmetry . . . **5.** order **7.** balance, euphony, harmony **8.** equality **9.** congruity **10.** conformity, proportion **11.** consistency
sympathetic . . . **4.** kind **6.** humane, tender **7.** empathy, pitying **8.** dewy-eyed **10.** responsive **13.** compassionate, understanding
sympathy . . . **4.** pity **5.** favor **7.** consent, harmony, support **8.** affinity, interest **9.** agreeable, agreement, tolerance **11.** sensitivity **13.** commiseration, understanding
sympathy, lack of . . . **8.** dyspathy **9.** antipathy
symphony . . . **6.** accord **7.** concert, harmony **8.** ritornel **9.** orchestra **10.** consonance **11.** composition
symposium . . . **4.** book, talk **7.** banquet **8.** dialogue, tippling **10.** collection, discussion **11.** compotation
symptom . . . **4.** mark, note, omen, sign **5.** alarm, token **7.** warning **10.** indication
synagogue . . . **6.** temple **10.** tabernacle **12.** congregation
synagogue (pert to) . . .
founder (anc) . . **4.** Ezra
platform . . **7.** almemar
singer . . **6.** cantor, chazan (chazzan)
synchronize . . . **5.** agree **6.** concur **8.** coincide **9.** harmonize **12.** contemporize
syncopation . . . **5.** tempo **7.** ragtime, syncope
syncope . . . **5.** faint, swoon **7.** elision

8. fainting, swooning 9. haplology
11. contraction, hyphaeresis
syndicate . . . 5. chain (journalistic), group,
trust 6. cartel, school 7. combine,
council 9. committee 10. underworld
11. association 12. organization
synonym . . . 7. antonym, homonym,
metonym 8. identity 9. heteronym
synonymous . . . 4. like 5. alike 7. similar
10. equivalent, homonymoùs
synopsis . . . 6. digest, manual 7. epitome,
summary 8. abstract, syllabus
9. statement 10. abridgment
(abridgement), compendium,
conspectus, tabulation
synthesis . . . 5. logic 11. combination,
composition 13. incorporation
14. identification
Syracuse (pert to) . . .
ancient name . . 8. Siracusa
city of . . 6. Sicily
famed for . . 6. battle (BC)
founded by . . 6. Greeks
tyrant of . . 9. Dionysius
Syria, Arab Republic . . . see also *Syrian*
ancient name . . 4. Aram
capital . . 8. Damascus
city . . 4. Hama, Homs 6. Aleppo, Beirut
7. Antioch, Latakia 8. Damascus
language . . 6. Arabic
organization, party . . 5. Baath
river . . 6. Barada, Jordan 7. Orontes
9. Euphrates
Syrian (pert to) . . .
antiquarian . . 11. Syriologist
deity . . 2. El 4. Baal 6. Mammon
7. Resheph
goat . . 6. Angora
grass . . 7. Johnson
leader . . 5. Assad
mallow . . 4. okra
·people . . 7. Ansarie (Ansarieh)
script . . 8. Peshitta (Peshito)
10. estrangelo 11. Syro-Chaldee
sect . . 5. Druse
wind (hot) . . 6. simoom (simoon)

syrinx . . . 4. tomb 6. larynx 7. Panpipe
10. mouthpiece (anc lute) 13. Arcadian
nymph
syrup, sirup . . . 4. Karo, sapa 5. maple
6. orgeat 7. dhebbus, glucose, sorghum,
treacle 8. molasses 9. grenadine
system . . . 3. ism, way 4. code, plan
5. order 6. regime, theory 8. religion,
universe 9. procedure 10. hypothesis,
regularity 11. arrangement,
orderliness
system (pert to) . . .
conduct . . 4. code
eating . . 4. diet 7. dietary
geological . . 5. Trias
management . . 6. regime
manual training . . 5. sloyd
mystic . . 6. cabala
numbering . . 7. decimal
pitch (Mus) . . 5. neume
religious . . 4. cult 6. cultus
solar . . 6. planet
weights . . 4. long, troy 5. cubic 6. liquid
11. avoirdupois 12. apothecaries
systematic . . . 4. neat 6. formal 7. orderly,
regular 9. organized, schematic
10. methodical
systematics . . . 8. taxonomy
14. classification
systematize . . . 4. code 6. codify
7. arrange 8. classify, organize,
regiment 9. catalogue (catalog),
formulate
systematized knowledge . . . 7. science
systole (pert to) . . .
correlative . . 8. diastole
medical . . 11. contraction (heart)
14. coming and going
rhyme . . 10. shortening (syllable)
syzygy (pert to) . . .
astronomy . . 7. appulse 11. conjunction
Gnosticism . . 5. aeons (pair)
rhyme . . 11. coupled feet (group)
zoology . . 5. union 7. segment
szlachta . . . 8. nobility (Poland)
szopelka . . . 4. oboe (Russ)

T

T . . . 3. tau (Gr) 6. letter (20th)
taa . . . 6. pagoda
Taal . . . 8. language 9. Afrikaans
taar . . . 10. tambourine
Taaroa . . . 3. God
tab . . . 3. pan, tag 4. bill, cost, flap, loop
5. aglet (aiglet), label, strip 6. eartab,
record 7. account, latchet, pendant
(pendent) 9. afterpart, appendage,
reckoning 10. accounting
tabac . . . 5. brown, snuff 7. tobacco
tabard . . . 4. cape 5. cloak 6. chimer,
jacket, mantle
Tabard . . . 3. Inn (Canterbury Tales)
tabatière . . . 8. snuffbox
tabby . . . 3. cat 4. gown, silk 5. dress
6. fabric, gossip 7. old maid, taffeta

tabernacle . . . 4. tent 5. abode, niche
6. church, temple 7. shelter, support
8. enshrine 9. sanctuary 10. habitation
table . . . 4. fare, list, slab 5. board, panel,
plate, stand 6. lamina, repast, tablet,
teapoy 7. console, plateau, weights
8. postpone, put aside, synopsis,
tabulate 9. reference 10. collection
14. multiplication
table (pert to) . . .
calculating . . 6. abacus
centerpiece . . 7. epergne
communion . . 5. altar 8. credence,
credenza
contents . . 5. index
cover . . 5. baize, tapis
dish . . 6. tureen

land . . **4.** mesa **6.** karroo (karoo), plains **7.** plateau
linen . . **6.** napery
philosophy . . **13.** deipnosophism
salt . . **4.** NaCl
talk (versed in) . . **13.** deipnosophist
type . . **3.** tea **4.** turn **6.** coffee, gaming **7.** dinette, dresser, gate-leg, kitchen, taboret **8.** captain's, drop-leaf
tableau . . . **5.** drama, scene **7.** picture **8.** schedule **14.** representation
tablet . . . **3.** pad **4.** pill, slab **5.** facia, slate, stele **6.** troche **7.** lozenge **8.** monument, notebook
taboo, tabu . . . **3.** ban **4.** deny **5.** debar **6.** forbid **7.** embargo **8.** disallow, prohibit **9.** forbidden, interdict, proscribe **11.** prohibition **12.** interdiction
tabulate . . . **4.** list **6.** record **7.** tabular **8.** classify, schedule
tabulation . . . **7.** listing **8.** calendar, paradigm **12.** registration
taccada . . . **9.** fanflower
tacit . . . **6.** silent **7.** implied **8.** unspoken, wordless **9.** indicated, noiseless **10.** understood
taciturn . . . **6.** silent **8.** reserved, reticent **9.** saturnine
tack . . . **4.** brad, gear, jibe, join, rope, sail, trip **5.** baste, lease, route **6.** course, fasten, secure, staple, tackle **7.** clothes **9.** fastening **10.** supplement
tackle . . . **3.** cat, rig **4.** gear, tack **5.** davit, seize **6.** burton, collar, garnet **7.** cordage, grapple, harness, rigging **8.** football (term) **9.** encounter, equipment, undertake
tacky . . . **5.** crude, dowdy, seedy **6.** shabby, sticky, untidy **8.** adhesive, slovenly
tact . . . **5.** grace, poise, taste **7.** address, finesse **8.** delicacy **9.** diplomacy **10.** adroitness, cleverness, discretion **11.** discernment, savoir-faire **14.** discrimination
tadpole . . . **4.** frog, toad **8.** polliwog, porwigle **9.** youngling
tag . . . **3.** add, end, rag, tab **4.** flap, game, loop, name **5.** aglet (aiglet), label, sheep, strip **6.** fasten, follow **7.** earmark, frazzle, pendant, taglock **9.** appendage **11.** aiguillette (ornamental)
Tagalog, Tagal (pert to) . . .
child, servant . . **4.** anac, bata
deity . . **6.** Batala
game (gambling) . . **10.** panguingui
native of . . **5.** Luzon **11.** Philippines
peasant . . **3.** tao
race . . **4.** Aeta (dwarf) **7.** Malayan
Tahiti . . .
arrowroot . . **3.** pia
boat . . **4.** pahi
capital . . **7.** Papeete (of all Society Isles)
food plant . . **4.** taro
god . . **3.** oro **6.** Taaroa (Supreme)
old name . . **8.** Otaheite
robe (coronation) . . **4.** malo
woman . . **6.** wahine (vahine)
Tai, Thai people . . . **4.** Laos, Shan **7.** Siamese
tail . . . **3.** bun, cue, end **4.** arse, back,

hair, last, rear **5.** cauda, stern **6.** follow, shadow **7.** pendant **8.** entailed, streamer **9.** afterpart, appendage, extremity
tail (pert to) . . .
aircraft's . . **9.** empennage
boar's . . **6.** wreath
coin . . **5.** verso **7.** reverse
dog's . . **5.** plume, stern, twist
having a . . **7.** caudate
peacock's . . **5.** train
pert to . . **6.** caudal **9.** coccygeal
rabbit's . . **4.** scut
rudimentary . . **6.** coccyx
tailrace . . **5.** flume **7.** channel
tailing . . . **5.** chaff, waste **6.** refuse
tailless . . . **6.** tenrec (mammal) **7.** acaudal, anurous, Ranidae **8.** acaudate, ecaudate
tailor . . . **3.** cut, fit **4.** form **6.** darzee, draper, sartor **7.** fashion **8.** tailleur
tailor (pert to) . . .
goose . . **4.** iron **12.** pressing iron
made . . **6.** fitted **9.** fashioned
reference to . . **9.** sartorial
twist . . **10.** silk thread (stout)
taint . . . **3.** due, hue **5.** color, imbue, spoil, stain, sully, tinge **6.** defile, infect, poison, stigma **7.** blemish, corrupt, deprave, pollute, vitiate **8.** disgrace **9.** denigrate, infection **10.** corruption, stigmatize **11.** contaminate
tainted . . . **3.** bad **6.** soiled **7.** stained **8.** diseased **9.** corrupted
taintless . . . **4.** good **5.** clean **6.** chaste **8.** flawless, innocent
Taiwan . . .
capital . . **6.** Taipai
Taj Mahal (pert to) . . .
architecture . . **9.** Saracenic
builder . . **9.** Shah-Jahan
mausolem site . . **4.** Agra
named for . . **4.** wife
take . . . **2.** go **3.** get, win **4.** deem, doff, gain, shut **5.** atone, booty, carry, catch, seize, snare, steal, usurp **6.** accept, borrow, deduce, endure, obtain **7.** capture, conduct, control, detract, receive **8.** proceeds, receipts, subtract, tolerate **9.** apprehend **11.** appropriate
take (pert to) . . .
a chair . . **3.** sit
a direction . . **5.** steer
advantage of . . **5.** abuse **6.** misuse
apart . . **8.** demolish **11.** disassemble
as one's own . . **5.** adopt **6.** borrow
away . . **5.** adeem, clear, reave, steal, wrest **6.** adempt, deduct, remove **7.** deprive, detract, retract **8.** derogate, subtract, withdraw **11.** expropriate
back . . **6.** recant, repeal, return
by storm . . **5.** seize **6.** attack
by stratagem . . **4.** trap **8.** outsmart
care of . . **4.** mind **5.** guard, nurse, serve, watch **6.** beware **7.** support **10.** provide for
charge of . . **8.** attend to **9.** look after
down . . **4.** fell, raze **5.** lower, write **6.** humble, record **7.** reprove, swallow **8.** emaciate
first . . **7.** pre-empt
for granted . . **5.** infer **6.** assume, expect

7. believe, presume, suppose
in .. 3. eat, see 4. hear 5. admit, annex, learn 6. absorb, attend 7. embrace, include, involve, receive, shorten 9. encompass
notice .. 2. NB 3. see
off .. 5. leave 6. deduct, depart, launch, parody, remove 8. subtract 9. imitation
on .. 4. hire 6. assume, employ, oppose 9. undertake
out .. 4. dele 5. elide 6. delete, efface 7. expunge
place of .. 8. supplant 9. supersede
the floor .. 5. speak 7. address 9. legislate
to flight .. 4. flee 7. run away, scamper 9. skedaddle
up .. 4. fill, lift 5. adopt, begin, raise 6. absorb, assume, gather, occupy 8. engage in 9. undertake
without authority .. 5. usurp
talapoin ... 6. monkey (guenon) 8. poonghie 12. Buddhist monk
talc ... 6. powder, talcum 7. agalite 8. steatite 9. soapstone
tale ... 3. lai, lay, lie 4. myth, saga, yarn 5. conte, fable, story 6. gossip, legend 7. romance 8. anecdote 9. discourse, falsehood, narration, narrative 11. declaration 12. conversation
tale (pert to) ...
adventure .. 4. gest
bearer .. 6. gossip 7. blabber, tattler 8. informer 13. scandalmonger
chivalry .. 7. romance
doleful .. 8. jeremiad
fatality .. 5. drama 7. tragedy
symbolic .. 8. allegory
traditional .. 4. saga 8. folktale
talent ... 4. gift 5. dower, flair, forte, money (anc), skill 6. genius 7. ability, faculty 8. aptitude, artistry 9. attribute 11. disposition 14. accomplishment
talesman ... 5. juror 8. narrator
talisman ... 4. juju, mojo, tara 5. charm, karma 6. amulet, fetish, grigri (greegree), scarab 7. periapt 12. antinganting
talk ... 3. gab, gas, rap, yak, yap 4. blab, blat, chat, chin, harp, rant, rave 5. lingo, orate, parle, prate, rumor, speak, spiel, utter 6. babble, confab, confer, gabble, gossip, jargon, lesson, speech 7. address, blabber, chatter, declaim, discuss 8. causerie, chitchat, colloquy, converse, language, parlance 9. dalliance, discourse 11. communicate 12. conversation
talk (pert to) ...
about .. 5. rumor 6. gossip
affected, pretentious .. 4. cant, rant
ancient .. 5. parle
back .. 4. sass 6. retort 7. riposte 8. feedback, repartee
flattering .. 7. palaver
fluent .. 7. verbose, voluble
idiotically .. 6. drivel
long .. 9. gibberish, rigmarole
loud .. 5. blate
promoting .. 4. hype 8. ballyhoo
running .. 6. patter
silly .. 5. drool 6. drivel, footle 7. blather,

prattle, twaddle
slang .. 3. gab, gas 4. sass 5. spiel
slowly .. 5. drawl
small .. 3. gab 4. chat, chin 7. prattle 8. chitchat
Spanish .. 7. palabra
talkative ... 4. glib 6. fluent 7. verbose, voluble 9. garrulous 10. loquacious 13. communicative
talker ... 6. gasser, proser, ranter 7. speaker, spieler 10. chatterbox 17. conversationalist
tall ... 4. high, long 5. lofty 6. seemly 7. procere, sky-high 8. towering, yielding 10. incredible, statuesque 11. exaggerated
tall (pert to) ...
order .. 9. falsehood 10. difficulty
person .. 10. hypermeter
structure .. 7. steeple
talk .. 4. brag 12. exaggeration 14. grandiloquence
tallest known people ... 10. Patagonian
Talleyrand's affair ... 3. XYZ
tallow source ... 4. suet
tally ... 3. run, sum, tab 4. goal, list, mark 5. agree, check, count, match, notch, score 6. accord, reckon, record 7. account, compare, count up 8. coincide, estimate 9. reckoning 10. bottom line, correspond
Talmud ... 9. Jewish law
Talmud (pert to) ...
academy .. 8. Yeshivah (Yeshiva)
commentary .. 6. Gemara
student .. 5. bahur
text .. 7. Mishnah
talon ... 3. paw 4. claw, fang, nail 6. clutch, finger, pincer
talus ... 5. ankle 8. clubfoot
tamarisk ... 4. atle (atlee) 8. salt tree
tambo ... 3. inn 6. corral, stable, tavern 10. tambourine
tambor ... 6. puffer 8. rockfish
tambour ... 4. desk, drum, lace 5. frame 6. stitch 7. drummer 8. ornament, stockade 9. embroider
tambourine ... 4. dove, drum, taar 5. daira 7. timbrel 8. minstrel
tambourine effect (Mus) ... 7. travale
tambreet ... 8. duckbill
tamburone ... 4. drum 8. bass drum
tame ... 4. dull, meek, mild 5. inert 6. docile, gentle, humble, subdue 7. crushed, insipid, subdued 8. tone down 9. tractable 10. cultivated 11. domesticate 12. domesticated
Tamil ... 5. Hindu 8. language (oldest Dravidian) 9. Dravidian
tamis ... 5. sieve, tammy 8. strainer
Tammany (pert to) ...
Hall .. 14. Democratic Club
man .. 10. politician
officer .. 8. Wiskinky (Wiskinkie)
scandal .. 9. Tweed Ring
Society site .. 11. New York City (1789)
symbol .. 5. tiger
tamper with ... 4. plot 5. alter, bribe 6. meddle, monkey, scheme, tinker 7. falsify 9. influence, interfere
tampion, tampon ... 4. plug 6. tympan

7. stopper, turnpin **9.** rhynobyon
tan . . . **3.** dun, taw **4.** buff, ecru, tent, whip **5.** beige, brown, color, tawny **6.** rabbit, suntan, thrash **7.** sunburn
tanager . . . **4.** yeni **5.** lindo **7.** Piranga, redbird
tanbark . . . **3.** oak **7.** hemlock
Tancred . . . **6.** leader (1st crusade)
Tanganyika . . . see *Tanzania*
tangible . . . **4.** real **7.** tactile **8.** palpable **9.** objective, touchable **11.** perceptible, substantial
tangle . . . **3.** mat, mop **4.** kink, shag **5.** ravel, snare, snarl, weave **6.** entrap, medley, muddle, sleave, tousle **7.** ensnare, involve **8.** quandary **9.** interlock **10.** complicate, interweave
tank . . . **3.** vat **4.** lake, pond, pool **5.** basin **6.** hot tub **7.** cistern, stomach **9.** reservoir **11.** army vehicle, hard drinker
tanker . . . **4.** ship **5.** oiler **8.** fuel ship
tanner's bath . . **4.** bate
tanning shrub . . . **5.** alder, sumac (sumach)
tantalize . . . **3.** vex **5.** taunt, tease **6.** harass, plague **7.** torment
tantalum symbol . . . **2.** Ta
Tantalus (pert to) . . .
  father . . **4.** Zeus
  father of . . **5.** Niobe **6.** Pelops
  genus of . . **4.** ibis
  king (rich) . . **6.** Greece
tantamount . . . **5.** equal **9.** identical **10.** equivalent **13.** corresponding
tantara . . . **7.** fanfare **9.** tantarara **12.** trumpet blare
tantrum . . . **3.** fit **4.** rage **7.** caprice **8.** tirrivee (tirrivie) **10.** conniption
Tanzania, Africa . . .
  capital . . **11.** Dar es Salaam (Haven of Peace)
  famed Mt. . . **11.** Kilimanjaro
  famed plains . . **9.** Serengeti
  famed town . . **5.** Ujiji (Stanley found Livingstone, 1871)
  formerly . . **8.** Zanzibar **10.** Tanganyika
  language . . **7.** Swahili
  natives . . **5.** Bantu
Taoism, names . . . **6.** Kwanti, Laotze **7.** Yu Hwang
tap . . . **3.** dum, hit, hob, rap **4.** plug, tamp **5.** sound, spile **6.** faucet, liquor, siphon, spigot, strike **7.** censure, petcock, reprove
tape . . . **3.** gin, tie **4.** band, wick **5.** strip **6.** fillet, ribbon, secure **7.** bandage, measure **9.** recording
taper . . . **4.** ream, wick **5.** point, snape, spire **6.** candle, cierge, narrow **7.** conical **8.** decrease, diminish **9.** acuminate **11.** pyramidical
tapering (pert to) . . .
  blades . . **6.** spires
  pert to . . **6.** spired, terete **7.** conical, pointed **8.** fusiform **9.** narrowing
  piece . . **4.** gore **5.** miter **6.** gusset
  pillar . . **7.** obelisk
  solid . . **4.** cone
tapestry . . . **5.** arras, tapis **6.** Bayeux, dosser **7.** Gobelin

tapeworm . . . **6.** Taenia
tapeworm (pert to) . . .
  embryonic . . **10.** oncosphere
  like . . **8.** taenioid
  segment . . **8.** strobila
tapioca, source . . . **5.** salep **7.** cassava (casava)
Tapirus . . . **6.** tapirs
tapster . . . **7.** barmaid, skinker
tar . . . **3.** gob **4.** brea, pave, salt **5.** black, pitch **6.** cresol, maltha, sailor, seaman **7.** mariner **8.** telegram **10.** bluejacket
tarantula . . . **6.** spider **7.** mygalid **10.** wolf spider
tarboosh . . . **3.** fez **6.** red cap
tardy . . . **3.** lag, lax **4.** late, slow **5.** slack **6.** remiss **7.** belated, lagging, overdue **8.** dilatory **10.** behindhand **11.** cunctatious
tare . . . **4.** weed (Bib) **5.** vetch **8.** discount **9.** allowance, deduction
target . . . **3.** aim, tee **4.** butt, goal, goat, mark, prey **5.** sight **6.** object, shield, tassel **8.** bull's-eye, ridicule **9.** objective
tariff . . . **4.** duty, list, rate **6.** charge **7.** tribute **8.** schedule
tariffist . . . **8.** advocate **13.** protectionist
tarnish . . . **3.** dim **4.** dull, soil, spot **5.** cloud, stain, sully, taint **6.** smirch, stigma, vilify **7.** blemish, destroy, obscure **8.** besmirch, discolor **10.** lose luster, stigmatize
taro . . . **3.** poi **4.** eddo, food, gabi (gabe) **5.** cocco, tania (tanier) **12.** elephant's-ear
tarot . . . **14.** fortunetelling (cards)
tarried . . . **6.** waited **7.** dallied **8.** lingered, remained
tarry . . . **3.** lag **4.** bide, stay, wait **5.** abide, await, dally, delay, pause, stall **6.** dawdle, linger, loiter, retard **7.** outstay
tarsus . . . **5.** ankle **7.** segment
tart . . . **4.** acid, sour **5.** acrid, sharp **6.** pastry, severe **7.** caustic, pungent, waspish **8.** poignant, turnover **10.** astringent **11.** acrimonious
tartan . . . **4.** wool **5.** plaid **7.** pattern (plaid) **10.** Highlander
tartar . . . **5.** argol (argal), shrew, valet **12.** incrustation
Tartar, Tatar . . . **4.** Turk **6.** Mongol
Tartar, Tatar (pert to) . . .
  domain . . **7.** Khanate
  horseman . . **7.** Cossack
  lancer . . **5.** uhlan
  nobleman . . **5.** murza
  people . . **2.** Hu **3.** Hun **6.** Mongol
  people of . . **6.** Turkey **8.** Mongolia
  title . . **4.** Khan
tartarean . . . **5.** cruel **7.** hellish **8.** infernal
Tartarus (Myth) . . . **4.** hell **5.** Hades **15.** infernal regions (Iliad)
Tarzan (pert to) . . .
  actor . . **7.** Lincoln (Elmo) **11.** Weissmuller
  creator . . **9.** Burroughs (Edgar Rice)
  Lord . . **9.** Greystoke
  mate . . **4.** Jane
task . . . **3.** job **4.** duty, snap, test, toil **5.** chore, labor, stent, stint **6.** burden, dargue, impost, strain **10.** assignment,

employment 11. undertaking
Tasmania (pert to) . . .
animal (burrowing) . . 6. wombat
discoverer . . 6. Tasman (1642)
marsupial . . 9. phalanger
mountain . . 6. Cradle 9. Ben Lomond
strait . . 4. Bass
taste . . . 3. sip, sup 4. tang 5. flair,
  sapor, savor, sense, smack, style
  6. liking, palate, relish, sample
  7. soupçon 8. delicacy, elegance,
  fondness, judgment 9. gustation
  10. experience 14. discrimination
  15. aesthetic liking
taste (pert to) . . .
bite . . 4. nosh 5. snack
decided . . 8. fondness, penchant
French . . 7. soupçon
fundamental . . 4. acid, salt 5. sweet
  6. bitter
lacking . . 4. rude 5. bland, gross, stale
  10. unpolished
ref to . . 7. palatal 9. gustatory
sharp . . 4. acid, tang
tasteless . . . 4. dull, flat 5. vapid 6. vulgar,
  watery 7. insipid 8. lifeless 9. savorless
  10. inartistic
tasty . . . 5. sapid 6. savory 8. saporous,
  tasteful 9. delicious, palatable,
  toothsome
Tatar . . . see *Tartar*
tatouay . . . 9. armadillo
tatter . . . 3. rag 4. tags, tear 5. patch,
  piece, shred 6. ribbon
tatterdemalion . . . 5. gamin 9. ragpicker
  10. ragamuffin
tattle . . . 4. blab, tell 5. prate 6. gossip
  7. chatter, divulge, prattle 8. idle talk,
  inform on
tattler . . . 6. gossip, willet 8. quidnunc,
  redshank, telltale 10. alarm clock,
  talebearer, yellowlegs
tattoo . . . 4. call (drum, bugle), pony,
  scar 13. entertainment
tau . . . 4. ankh, crux, rood 5. cross 6. letter
  (Gr) 7. T-shaped
tau cross . . . 4. ankh 6. symbol 8. crucifix,
  insignia 10. St Anthony's
taunt . . . 4. gibe, jeer, mock, twit 5. sneer,
  tease 6. deride 7. provoke 8. reproach,
  ridicule 9. aggravate
Taurus . . . 4. bull 8. Pleiades
  13. constellation
taut . . . 4. firm, snug, tidy 5. tense, tight
  6. severe, strict 7. nervous 9. distended
tautology . . . 8. pleonasm 10. redundancy,
  repetition
tavern . . . 3. inn, pub 5. hotel 7. barroom,
  cabaret, Gasthof, taberna 8. alehouse,
  Gasthaus, hostelry
taw . . . 4. game, whip 6. marble 7. tanning
tawdry . . . 4. loud 5. cheap, gaudy, showy
  6. garish 7. blatant
tawny, tawney . . . 3. tan 5. dusky, olive,
  tenne 6. tanned 7. jacinth 8. brindled
  9. bullfinch
tax . . . 4. cess, duty, geld, levy, scat
  (scatt), task, toll 5. stent 6. assess,
  burden, custom, excise, impose,
  income, octroi, strain 7. doomage,
  license, tribute 8. exaction, overtire

  9. prescribe 10. assessment
tax (pert to) . . .
ancient . . 3. cro 4. geld 7. galanas
assessment . . 4. rate 5. ratal 7. doomage
church . . 5. tithe
commodity . . 6. octroi
French history . . 6. taille
kind . . 5. tithe 6. excise, surtax, taille
  7. boscage 8. auxilium, carucage
  9. surcharge
liquor . . 6. abkari (abkary)
pasturage (Shetland Isls) . . 4. scat (scatt)
taxi . . . 3. cab 4. hack
tea . . . 5. dance, party, shrub 6. supper
  8. beverage, function, sociable
  9. collation, reception
tea (pert to) . . .
cake . . 5. scone
chemical content . . 6. tannin, theine
  (thein) 8. caffeine
Chinese . . 5. black, hyson
Formosa . . 6. oolong
Ind Ceylon . . 5. pekoe
infusion . . 6. ptisan, tisane
Labrador . . 5. Ledum 8. gowiddie
Paraguay . . 5. yerba
receptacle . . 5. caddy 8. canister
table . . 6. teapoy (tepoy)
type . . 3. cha 4. tsia 5. Assam, black,
  green, hyson, Ledum, oopak, pekoe
  6. oolong 7. cambric 8. gowiddie
urn . . 3. pot 7. samovar
weak . . 7. cambric
teach . . . 4. show 5. coach, drill, edify,
  guide, prime, train, tutor 6. direct,
  impart, preach, school 7. educate,
  show how 8. instruct 9. enlighten
  11. demonstrate
teacher . . . 5. coach, guide, rabbi, tutor
  6. doctor, mentor, pastor, pedant, priest,
  pundit, reader, regent, rhetor, scribe
  7. edifier, starets 8. educator, preacher
  9. pedagogue, preceptor 10. instructor
teacher (pert to) . . .
Alexandrian . . 6. Origen
Indian . . 4. guru
Jewish . . 5. rabbi
Mohammedan . . 3. pir 4. imam 6. mullah
of the deaf . . 7. oralist
Russian . . 7. starets
teaching . . . 5. moral 6. docent 7. precept
  8. doctrine 11. instruction
Teaching of the Twelve . . . 10. The
  Didache
team . . . 3. two 4. haul, join, pain, span,
  yoke 5. brood, chain, wagon 7. vehicle
  8. carriage 9. yannigans
teamster . . . 6. carter, driver 7. carrier
Teapot Dome (pert to) . . .
known as . . 8. Scandals (Teapot Dome)
leased by . . 4. Fall (Sec'y of Interior)
lease of . . 8. oil field
site . . 8. Elk Hills (Wyo)
tear . . . 3. rip 4. rend, rent, rive 5. revel,
  sever, speed, split, spree 6. cleave,
  hasten 7. destroy, shatter, torment
  8. lacerate, separate 10. dilacerate
tear (pert to) . . .
apart . . 7. disjoin 8. demolish
asunder . . 10. dilacerate
down . . 4. rase, raze

limb from limb . . **6.** punish **9.** dismember
to shreds . . **6.** tatter
up . . **3.** rip **6.** damage
up the roots . . **6.** arache
teardrop lace design . . . **5.** larme
tearful . . . **3.** sad **7.** maudlin, weeping
9. lachrymal (lacrimal)
tears . . . **5.** drops (lachrymal), grief, rheum
6. lament **9.** teardrops
tease . . . **3.** guy, nag, rag, vex **4.** twit
5. annoy, devil, taunt **6.** bother,
harass, heckle, needle, pester, plague
7. provoke, torment **8.** irritate
9. aggravate, tantalize
teaser . . . **4.** gull **6.** carder, curler, sniper,
stoker **7.** curtain, fireman, problem
8. pesterer, willower **9.** tormentor
13. advertisement
technical . . . **7.** skilled, trained **8.** specific
11. specialized **12.** professional
technocracy . . . **12.** organization **17.** rule
by technicians
technology . . . **3.** art **7.** science
9. technique **10.** agrotechny, virtuosity
11. terminology **12.** nomenclature
13. ethnotechnics
technophobe . . . **7.** Luddite
techy . . . **6.** touchy, vexing **7.** fretful,
peevish **9.** irascible, irritable, sensitive
tedious . . . **3.** dry **4.** dull **5.** bored,
prosy **6.** boring, prolix **7.** irksome,
noxious **11.** displeasing, repetitious
13. uninteresting
tedium . . . **5.** ennui **7.** boredom
10. melancholy **11.** tediousness
teeming . . . **4.** full **6.** aswarm **7.** pouring,
replete **8.** crowding, numerous, prolific
9. abounding **10.** productive
11. overflowing
teeter . . . **4.** rock **5.** waver **6.** jiggle, seesaw
9. alternate, fluctuate, sandpiper,
vacillate **12.** teeter-totter
teeth . . . **5.** bucks, fangs **6.** molars, tushes
7. canines, ivories **8.** grinders, incisors
teeth (pert to) . . .
all alike . . **7.** isodont
cleaning . . **5.** brush, floss **10.** dentrifice,
toothpaste
covering . . **6.** enamel
crustation . . **6.** tartar
destitute of . . **5.** morné (Her) **8.** edentate
10. edentulous
elephant's . . **9.** scrivello **11.** scrivelloes
false . . **8.** choppers (sl), dentures
few . . **12.** oligodontous
large . . **8.** megadont **9.** macrodont
pointed . . **5.** fangs, tusks **6.** tushes
ref to . . **4.** pulp **5.** molar **6.** dental
7. dentine **8.** odontoid
science . . **10.** odontology
teething . . . **6.** growth **9.** dentition,
odontosis **10.** odontogeny
teetotaller . . . **3.** dry **7.** non-user
9. abstainer, nephalist, Rechabite (Bib)
11. teetotalist
teg, tag . . . **3.** doe **5.** sheep (young),
woman **6.** fleece (sheep's)
teguexin . . . **4.** teju **6.** lizard
tegument . . . **4.** bark, coat, skin **5.** cover
6. cortex **10.** integument
tekke . . . **3.** rug **6.** carpet **7.** convent

9. monastery
tela . . . **6.** tissue **8.** membrane
Telamon (Gr Myth, pert to) . . .
brother . . **6.** Peleus
companion . . **8.** Hercules
expedition . . **8.** boar hunt **10.** Argonautic
male figure . . **6.** column **7.** support
son . . **4.** Ajax **6.** Teucer
telegraph (pert to) . . .
code, inventor . . **5.** Morse (Samuel F)
key . . **6.** tapper
service . . **5.** cable **8.** dispatch
telephone (pert to) . . .
inventor . . **4.** Bell (Alexander)
term . . **3.** PBX **4.** buzz, call, dial, hold,
horn (sl), ring, toll **5.** trunk **6.** call
up **7.** collect, hotline **8.** exchange,
intercom **10.** push-button, videophone
11. switchboard **12.** speakerphone
14. radiotelephone
telescope . . . **4.** Lick **6.** Yerkes **7.** Palomar
8. Galilean (1609) **9.** Gregorian (Scot
1663)
telescopic . . . **9.** farseeing
television . . . **2.** TV **3.** box, set **4.** tube
5. telly (Brit) **8.** boob tube, idiot box
11. small screen
television (pert to) . . .
person . . **6.** anchor, viewer **7.** sponsor
9. superstar **10.** newscaster
program . . **4.** show **6.** sitcom **7.** variety
8. newscast **9.** docudrama, soap opera
term . . **3.** air **5.** audio, bleep, cable,
rerun **7.** channel, minicam **8.** telecast
10. commercial, laugh track
tell . . . **3.** say **4.** talk **5.** count, peach, utter
6. assail, impart, inform, recite, reckon,
relate, repeat, report, reveal **7.** divulge,
narrate, recount **8.** acquaint, disclose,
rehearse **9.** recognize **11.** communicate
teller . . . **6.** banker **8.** informer, narrator
9. describer, informant
telling . . . **6.** cogent, potent **8.** forceful,
striking **9.** affective, narration, pertinent
11. influential, significant
telltale . . . **4.** blab, clue, hint **6.** bearer,
device, gossip **7.** tattler **8.** informer
9. indicator, informing **10.** indication,
talebearer
tellurian . . . **2.** Te **7.** earthly **11.** terrestrial
12. earth dweller
temeritous, temerarious . . . **4.** rash
8. heedless, reckless **10.** headstrong
temerity . . . **4.** gall **5.** cheek, nerve
8. audacity, rashness **10.** effrontery
12. recklessness
temper . . . **4.** mood **5.** humor **6.** adjust,
animus, anneal, attune, dander, harden,
nature, season, soften **7.** assuage,
mollify, tantrum **8.** hardness, mitigate,
moderate **9.** composure **10.** equanimity,
irritation **11.** disposition, temperament
temper (pert to) . . .
bad . . **4.** fury, rage **5.** anger **6.** choler,
spleen
clay . . **6.** puddle
even . . **4.** calm **5.** staid **6.** sedate
in a . . **4.** huff, rage, stew **5.** tizzy
metal . . **6.** anneal, harden **7.** toughen
temperament . . . **4.** mood **6.** crasis,
nature **8.** artistic **11.** disposition

temperance . . . **6.** virtue **8.** calmness, sobriety **10.** abstinence, moderation **11.** self-control **13.** self-restraint **14.** abstemiousness
temperate . . . **4.** calm, cool **5.** sober **8.** moderate **10.** abstemious, restrained **14.** self-controlled
tempered . . . **5.** angry **6.** sedate **8.** annealed, disposed, moderate **9.** moderated, mollified, qualified
tempest . . . **4.** gale, wind **5.** blast, orage, storm **6.** tumult **7.** turmoil **9.** agitation, commotion, windstorm **10.** excitement **12.** thunderstorm
Tempest (pert to) . . .
Cuban . . **6.** bayamo
in a teapot . . **10.** triviality **12.** exaggeration
The (character) . . **5.** Ariel (spirit) **7.** Caliban, Miranda **8.** Prospero
tempestuous . . . **5.** windy **6.** stormy **7.** excited, violent **9.** turbulent
temple . . . **4.** fane, naos **5.** cella, ratha, speos **6.** aedile, church, pagoda **7.** edifice
temple (pert to) . . .
Anglo-Ind . . **5.** kovil (covil)
approach . . **5.** toran (torana)
Assyrian . . **8.** ziggurat (anc)
Aztec temple site . . **12.** Tenochtitlan
Chinese . . **6.** pagoda
Hawaiian . . **5.** heiau
Mexico . . **8.** teocalli
Muslim . . **6.** mosque
part . . **4.** naos **5.** cella **6.** adytum **7.** narthex, sanctum **10.** penetralia
ref to . . **6.** hieron
sanctuary . . **10.** penetralia
Shinto . . **3.** Sha **5.** jinja (jinsha) **7.** yashiro
Temple Bar (London) . . . **7.** gateway
Temple Butte site . . . **11.** Grand Canyon
Temple of Heaven . . . **7.** Peiping
Temple of Onias . . . **5.** Egypt
Temple of Reason . . . **9.** Notre Dame
Temple of the Sphinx . . . **5.** Egypt
tempo . . . **4.** pace, time **5.** grave, largo, speed **6.** adagio, presto, rhythm **7.** allegro, andante **8.** moderato **11.** synchronism
temporal . . . **4.** bene, laic **5.** civil **7.** earthly, secular, worldly **9.** ephemeral, temporary **10.** transitory **11.** present time **13.** chronological
temporize . . . **5.** delay **6.** demand, parley **9.** negotiate **13.** procrastinate
tempt . . . **4.** lead, lure **5.** decoy **6.** allure, entice, induce, seduce **7.** attract **8.** persuade **9.** seduction **10.** inducement
Tempter, The . . . **5.** Devil, Satan **7.** Evil One **10.** Evil Spirit, Old Serpent **14.** Prince of Devils
temptress . . . **5.** siren **7.** Delilah (Bib), mermaid **11.** enchantress
ten (pert to) . . .
ace . . **10.** bridge game
Commandments . . **9.** Decalogue
dollars . . **7.** sawbuck
fold . . **6.** denary **7.** decuple
footed . . **7.** decapod
gallon hat . . **7.** Stetson **8.** sombrero
geometric figure . . **7.** decagon

10. decahedron
measure . . **4.** acre, bath **6.** decare
number . . **5.** decad **7.** several
physics . . **3.** bel
poetic . . **9.** decameter (decametre)
prefix . . **4.** deca (deka)
stringed . . **9.** decachord
thousand . . **6.** myriad
year period . . **6.** decade **9.** decenniad, decennium
tenable . . . **10.** defensible **12.** maintainable
tenacious . . . **5.** tough **6.** dogged, viscid **7.** viscous **8.** adhesive, cohesive, sticking, stubborn **9.** glutinous, obstinate, retentive **10.** persistent **12.** pertinacious
tenant . . . **4.** saer **5.** ceile, dreng (drengh) **6.** holder, leaser, lessee, renter, vassal **7.** cottier, dweller, villein **8.** occupant **10.** inhabitant
tenant's tribute . . . **4.** cens
tend . . . **4.** care, heed, lean, mind, wait **5.** nurse, offer, serve, watch **6.** attend, manage **7.** incline, oversee **8.** converge, minister **9.** cultivate, gravitate, look after
tendency . . . **4.** bent, bias, tide **5.** drift, drive, trend **6.** course, object **7.** bearing, leaning **8.** aptitude, relation **9.** direction, proneness **10.** proclivity, propensity **11.** disposition, inclination
tender . . . **3.** bed, pay **4.** boat, fond, gift, give, kind, soft, sore **5.** offer, young **6.** extend, gentle, humane, waiter **7.** pitiful, present, rail car **8.** delicate, merciful **9.** attendant, sensitive **10.** effeminate **11.** softhearted, sympathetic, warmhearted **12.** affectionate **13.** compassionate
tender (pert to) . . .
animal . . **6.** cowboy, herder
farm . . **10.** husbandman
feeling . . **9.** sentiment
foot . . **4.** dude **6.** novice **8.** newcomer **10.** raw recruit
hearted . . **4.** kind **8.** merciful
horse . . **5.** groom **6.** ostler **7.** hostler
regard . . **4.** love **6.** tendre
ship . . **7.** pinnace
style . . **7.** amoroso
tenderloin . . . **4.** meat **7.** brothel **12.** city district, vice district
tenderness . . . **4.** love, pity **8.** sympathy **9.** affection **10.** compassion, gentleness
tending to . . .
arouse . . **7.** emotive
assist memory . . **8.** mnemonic
check . . **10.** repressive
clear of guilt . . **11.** exculpatory
control . . **10.** regulating
drive away . . **9.** repellant
evade . . **7.** elusory
lateness . . **7.** tardive
separate . . **8.** divisive
tear . . **10.** lacerative
wear away . . **8.** abrasive
tendon . . . **4.** cord, thew **5.** sinew **8.** ligament **11.** aponeurosis
tendril . . . **4.** coil, curl **5.** shoot, sprig **6.** branch, cirrus **7.** stipule **8.** filament
tenet . . . **3.** ism **4.** rule **5.** canon, creed,

dogma, maxim **6.** belief **7.** precept
8. doctrine **9.** principle
tenne . . . **5.** brown, color
Tennessee . . .
  battle . . **11.** Chattanooga **14.** Above the
  Clouds
  capital . . **9.** Nashville (Athens of the
  South)
  city . . **7.** Memphis **8.** Oak Ridge
  9. Knoxville **11.** Chattanooga
  first State . . **8.** Franklin
  Mts . . **7.** Lookout **10.** Cumberland, Great
  Smoky **13.** Clingman's Dome
  museum . . **9.** Hermitage, Parthenon
  12. Atomic Energy (Oak Ridge)
  13. Ancestral Home (Pres Polk)
  park . . **6.** Shiloh
  river . . **9.** Tennessee
  State admission . . **9.** Sixteenth
  State motto . . **16.** America At Its Best
  State nickname . . **9.** Volunteer
tennis (pert to) . . .
  four persons . . **7.** doubles
  player . . **6.** netman
  score . . **3.** ace **4.** love (zero) **5.** deuce
  (tie)
  series . . **3.** set
  site . . **5.** court
  stroke . . **3.** cut, lob
  term . . **3.** ace, lob, net, set **5.** serve
  6. hazard **7.** receive
  two persons . . **7.** singles
tenon . . . **3.** cog **4.** tusk **5.** tooth **7.** mortise
tenor . . . **4.** alto (violin), copy, mode,
  tone **5.** drift, trend **6.** course, intent,
  singer **7.** meaning, purport **8.** tenoreno
  9. male voice, procedure **10.** transcript
tense . . . **4.** edgy, rapt, taut **5.** rigid, tight
  6. intent **7.** intense, nervous, stretch
  8. strained **9.** stretched **10.** breathless
tense (grammar) . . . **4.** past **6.** future
  7. perfect, present **9.** preterite
  10. pluperfect **11.** past perfect,
  progressive
tensile . . . **6.** pliant **7.** ductile **8.** tensible
tension . . . **6.** strain, stress **7.** detente,
  nervous **9.** disaccord, stiffness
tent . . . **3.** hut **4.** camp, show **5.** cover,
  lodge **6.** dossil **7.** marquee **8.** pavilion
tent (pert to) . . .
  covering . . **4.** tilt
  Eskimo . . **5.** tubik (skin)
  general's . . **10.** praetorium (pretorium)
  India . . **4.** pawl
  Indian . . **5.** tepee **6.** teepee, wigwam
  occupant . . **5.** nomad **6.** camper **7.** tourist
  Russian . . **7.** kibitka
  Scottish . . **6.** pulpit
  surgical . . **6.** screen
  type . . **3.** fly, pup **4.** bell, wall **6.** Sibley
  8. pavilion
tentacle . . . **4.** hair, palp **6.** feeler **7.** tendril
tentative . . . **7.** feeling, testing
  9. makeshift, temporary **10.** substitute
  11. making trial, provisional
  12. experimental
tenterhooks . . . **6.** strain **8.** suspense
  10. uneasiness
tenth . . . **5.** decim, tithe **6.** decima **9.** organ
  stop
tenth Muse . . . **6.** Sappho

Tent Maker . . . **4.** Omar
tenuity . . . **6.** rarity **7.** poverty **8.** delicacy,
  subtlety, thinness **9.** indigence, unreality
tenuous . . . **4.** rare, thin **6.** subtle
  7. slender **8.** delicate, ethereal
  13. unsubstantial
tenure . . . **4.** term **5.** lease **6.** socage
  7. holding **10.** possession
tepee, teepee . . . **4.** tent **6.** wigwam
tepid . . . **4.** mild, warm **8.** lukewarm
tequila . . . **6.** liquor **12.** century plant
teraphim . . . **5.** idols **6.** images
teras . . . **7.** monster
tergiversate . . . **3.** lie **5.** evade, shift
  10. apostasize, equivocate
term . . . **3.** age, end, era **4.** date, name,
  time, word **5.** epoch, limit, style
  6. estate, period, tenure **7.** premise
  8. duration, semester, terminus
  12. nomenclature
term (pert to) . . .
  connotation . . **6.** intent **11.** designation
  death . . **4.** doom, mort
  for years . . **10.** real estate
  glacial . . **5.** stoss
  golf . . **4.** hook **5.** bogey (bogie), divot,
  eagle, slice **6.** birdie
  grammar . . **6.** phrase, syntax
  11. phraseology
  logic . . **4.** mode **5.** major, minor
  of life . . **3.** age **5.** sands (hourglass)
  Rugby . . **5.** scrum
  sea . . **4.** ahoy **5.** avast, belay
  tennis . . **4.** love **5.** deuce, serve
termagant . . . **5.** scold, shrew, vixen
  6. Amazon, virigo **7.** furious **8.** scolding
  9. turbulent **10.** boisterous, tumultuous
  11. quarrelsome
Termagant . . . **5.** deity **14.** imaginary
  being
terminal . . . **3.** end **4.** goal **5.** anode,
  depot, final, limit **6.** finish **7.** limital,
  station **8.** desinent, terminus, ultimate
  9. end of life, extremity **10.** concluding
  11. desinential, destination, termination
terminal (pert to) . . .
  battery . . **5.** anode **7.** cathode **9.** electrode
  leaf . . **8.** apiculus
  ornament . . **6.** finial
  town (end of line) . . **8.** terminus
terminate . . . **3.** end **4.** halt **5.** abort,
  cease, close, limit **6.** expire, result
  7. end with **8.** complete, conclude
termination . . . **3.** end **4.** amen **5.** close,
  limit **6.** ending, result **7.** outcome
  8. terminus **9.** desinence **10.** completion,
  conclusion, expiration
termite . . . **3.** ant (white) **4.** anay (anai)
  8. Isoptera (Order)
tern . . . **4.** darr (black), gull **6.** Sterna
  (genus) **8.** schooner (Naut) **9.** threefold
  10. sea swallow
ternary . . . **5.** three, triad **6.** tercet (Poet),
  triple **7.** ternion, trinity **9.** threefold
ternate . . . **5.** tern **9.** threefold
  12. trifoliolate
terpsichore . . . **5.** dance **6.** dancer
  7. dancing
Terpsichore (Myth) . . . **13.** Muse of
  dancing
terra . . . **5.** earth **10.** terra firma

terrace ... **4.** flaw (marble), mesa, step
7. balcony, gallery, plateau, portico
8. platform (earth) **9.** colonnade
terrain, terrane ... **4.** land **5.** tract
6. region **11.** environment
terrapin ... **4.** Emys **6.** turtle **8.** Chelonia,
Emydinae, tortoise **9.** cheloniid
terrapin, turtle (pert to) ...
color .. **9.** grapenuts
type .. **6.** potter, slider **10.** red-bellied
11. diamondback **13.** yellow-bellied
War .. **14.** Eighteen Twelve (1812)
terrene, terrestial ... **4.** land **5.** earth,
realm **6.** earthy, mortal **7.** earthly,
mundane, worldly
terrestrial planets ... **4.** Mars **5.** Venus
7. Mercury
terrible ... **3.** bad **4.** dire **5.** awful
6. tragic **7.** fearful, ghastly, hideous,
painful **8.** dreadful, horrible, terrific
9. appalling, frightful **10.** formidable,
terrifying, unpleasant
Terrible, The ... **4.** Ivan (Russ Czar)
terrier ... **3.** fox **4.** bull, Skye **5.** Cairn,
Irish, Welsh **6.** Boston **8.** Airedale,
Scottish, Sealyham **9.** Kerry blue,
schnauzer **10.** Bedlington, Clydesdale
13. Dandie Dinmont
terrific ... **5.** great **6.** superb **7.** extreme
8. dreadful, exciting, terrible
9. appalling, excessive, frightful
10. tremendous
terrify ... **3.** awe, cow **4.** stun **5.** alarm,
appal, haunt, scare, shock **6.** appall,
freeze **7.** horrify, petrify **8.** affright,
frighten
territory ... **4.** area, land **5.** banat, field
6. canton, region **7.** country **8.** district,
environs, Pashalic (Pasha's), province
10. palatinate
terror ... **3.** awe **4.** fear **5.** alarm, dread,
panic **6.** fright, horror **7.** hellion, Reign
of (Hist) **13.** consternation
terrorism ... **11.** subjugation
12. intimidation
terse ... **4.** curt, neat **5.** pithy **6.** smooth
7. compact, concise, laconic, pointed,
refined **8.** succinct **11.** sententious
12. accomplished, epigrammatic
Tertiary period ... **6.** Eocene **7.** Miocene
8. Pliocene **9.** Oligocene **12.** Age of
Mammals
tertium quid ... **12.** third someone
13. third somewhat
tertulia ... **4.** club **5.** party **7.** meeting
tessellated ... **6.** mosaic **9.** checkered
tessera ... **3.** die **4.** cube, tile **5.** token
6. marble, ticket **8.** password
11. certificate
test ... **3.** try **4.** exam, feel **5.** assay,
proof, prove, taste, tempt, trial
6. ordeal, sample **7.** examine, witness
8. evidence, standard **9.** criterion,
testimony **10.** experience, experiment
11. examination, performance
12. authenticate
test (pert to) ...
fineness .. **3.** pyx
orally .. **7.** examine
ore, value .. **5.** assay
pot .. **8.** crucible

severe .. **6.** ordeal
testa ... **7.** coating **8.** covering, tegument
testament ... **3.** New, Old **4.** will
8. covenant
testator ... **7.** legator, witness **9.** testatrix
tester ... **6.** canopy, helmet, prover,
taster **7.** assayer, candler, sampler
testify ... **4.** avow **6.** affirm, depone,
depose **7.** declare, profess, protest
8. indicate, manifest **11.** bear witness
testimonial ... **5.** token **7.** tribute, warrant
8. evidence **9.** reference **10.** compliment
11. certificate
testimony ... **7.** witness **8.** evidence
10. Scriptures **11.** affirmation,
attestation, declaration
testy, tetchy ... **6.** touchy **7.** fretful,
peevish **8.** petulant, snappish
9. irascible, obstinate **10.** headstrong
tetched in the head ... **9.** pixilated
tetrad ... **4.** four **7.** quartet (quartette),
quatern **8.** foursome **10.** quaternion
tetragon ... **4.** park **6.** square **7.** rhombus
9. courtyard **10.** quadrangle
Tetragrammaton ... **7.** Jehovah
12. Supreme Being **14.** four consonants
(unpronounced)
Teuton ... **4.** Goth **6.** German
Teutonic (pert to) ...
alphabet character .. **4.** rune
deity .. **2.** Er **3.** Tiu (Tiwaz), Tyr **4.** Frea,
Odin, Thor **5.** Aesir, Bragi, Wodin
6. Balder, Frigga **7.** Forseti **8.** Heimdall
demon .. **3.** alp
giantess .. **4.** Norn **11.** demigoddess
goddess .. **3.** Eir, Hel, Ran **4.** Norn, Urth
(Urthr), Wyrd
homicide (tribal) .. **5.** morth
land .. **4.** odal
law .. **5.** Salic
nymph (water) .. **3.** nis
race .. **5.** Goths, Jutes **6.** Franks, Saxons
7. Vandals **8.** Lombards **10.** Norwegians
13. Scandinavians
supernatural being .. **5.** troll
Teutonic goddess of ...
death .. **3.** Hel, Ran
healing .. **3.** Eir
peace .. **7.** Nerthus
Teutonic god of ...
justice .. **7.** Forseti (Forsete)
pantheon .. **5.** Aesir (group)
peace .. **6.** Balder
sea .. **5.** Aegir
skill .. **3.** Ull (Ullr)
sky .. **2.** Er **3.** Tiu (Tiwaz), Tyr
thunder .. **4.** Thor **5.** Donar
war .. **3.** Tiu (Tiwaz), Tyr
Texas ...
birthplace of Pres .. **10.** Eisenhower
capital .. **6.** Austin
cattle .. **8.** longhorn
city .. **4.** Waco **6.** Dallas, El Paso
7. Abilene, Denison, Houston
9. Arlington, Fort Worth, Galveston
10. San Antonio **13.** Corpus Christi
flags (six) .. **5.** Spain **6.** France, Mexico
8. Republic (of Texas) **11.** Confederate
12. United States
flower .. **10.** bluebonnet, yellow rose
Indian people .. **5.** Caddo

monument (Battle).. **10.** San Jacinto
police.. **7.** Rangers
river.. **3.** Red **5.** Pecos **9.** Rio Grande
shrine, mission.. **5.** Alamo
State admission.. **12.** Twenty-eighth
State motto.. **5.** Tejas **10.** Friendship
State nickname.. **8.** Lone Star
text... **4.** book **5.** topic, verse **7.** passage
  8. libretto, textbook **11.** letterpress
textile screw pine... **3.** ara
textile shop... **7.** mercery
texture... **3.** web **4.** wale, warp, wooz
  5. grain, weave **6.** cobweb, fabric
  7. textile **9.** roughness, structure
  10. smoothness
Thailand (Siam), **capital**... **7.** Bangkok
Thames River town... **4.** Eton
thana... **13.** police station
thanador... **7.** officer (Hind)
thanatology doctrine... **5.** death
thane... **5.** baron (anc) **7.** servant, warrior
  9. Scots peer
thankless... **7.** ingrate **10.** ungrateful
  13. unappreciated
thanks... **5.** grace **6.** prayer **8.** gramercy
  9. gratitude **12.** appreciation
  14. acknowledgment
Thanks to God... **10.** Deo gratias
that (pert to)...
  is.. **2.** ie **5.** id est
  is to say.. **3.** viz **5.** to wit **6.** namely
  9. videlicit
  pronoun.. **3.** who **4.** what
thatch (pert to)...
  grass.. **4.** rope **6.** slough
  hair.. **3.** mop **4.** crop, mane
  palm.. **5.** Sabal **7.** Thrinax
  roofing.. **5.** reeds, straw **6.** rushes
  support.. **6.** wattle
thatcher... **7.** hellier
thaumaturgy... **5.** magic **7.** sorcery
  8. wizardry **11.** legerdemain
the (pert to)...
  end.. **5.** omega **6.** thirty
  French.. **2.** la, le **3.** les
  German.. **3.** das, der, die
  Italian.. **2.** il, la, le **4.** ella
  same.. **4.** idem **5.** ditto
  Spanish.. **2.** el, la **3.** las, los
theater, theatre... **5.** arena, drama,
  odeum, stage **6.** lyceum **8.** coliseum
  9. playhouse **12.** amphitheater
theater (pert to)...
  actress.. **7.** heroine, ingénue
  box.. **4.** loge
  curtain.. **4.** drop **6.** teaser
  district.. **6.** Rialto **8.** Broadway
  floor (lower).. **7.** parquet
  full house.. **3.** SRO
  Greek.. **5.** odeum (odeon)
  part.. **3.** box, pit **4.** loge **5.** foyer, stage
  7. balcony, gallery, parquet **8.** parterre
  9. orchestra **10.** proscenium
theatrical... **5.** showy, stagy **8.** affected,
  dramatic **10.** artificial, histrionic
  12. melodramatic
theatrical (pert to)...
  art.. **10.** histrionic
  company.. **6.** troupe
  machine.. **9.** eccyclema
  spectacle.. **5.** revue **7.** pageant

star.. **4.** hero, lead **7.** heroine
Theban (pert to)...
  bard.. **6.** Pindar
  deity.. **4.** Amen (Amon) **6.** Amen-Ra
  god.. **5.** Ammon (Zeus)
  king.. **5.** Laius **7.** Amphion, Oedipus
  8. Pentheus
  queen.. **5.** Niobe **7.** Jocasta
  soothsayer (blind).. **8.** Tiresias
  triad.. **3.** Mut **6.** Amen-Ra, Khonsu
Thebes...
  capital of.. **10.** Upper Egypt (anc)
  famed avenue.. **8.** Sphinxes
  famed for.. **5.** ruins
  location.. **4.** Nile
  ruined temple.. **5.** Ammon **6.** Karnak
  Seven against (one of).. **6.** Tydeus
theca... **3.** pod **4.** case, cell **7.** capsule
theft... **6.** holdup, piracy **7.** larceny,
  robbery **8.** burglary, stealing
  10. plagiarism **12.** embezzlement
theftlike... **7.** piratic **9.** piratical
theme... **4.** text **5.** essay, lemma, motif,
  thema, topic **6.** matter, thesis **7.** subject
  9. discourse, leitmotiv
then... **3.** poi (Mus) **4.** also, next,
  when **5.** hence **7.** besides **8.** formerly
  9. therefore **12.** subsequently
thence... **4.** away **5.** hence **9.** after that,
  elsewhere, therefore **10.** henceforth,
  thereafter
theogamy... **14.** marriage of gods
theologian... **5.** Arius (Bib) **6.** Luther
  7. Abelard, Aquinas, Erasmus
  9. Augustine
theology... **7.** irenics **8.** canonics, religion
  9. depositum **10.** doctrinism
theorem... **3.** law **4.** rule **5.** axiom,
  topic **7.** premise **9.** principle, statement
  11. proposition
theoretical... **5.** ideal **8.** academic,
  platonic **11.** conjectural, impractical,
  speculative **12.** hypothetical, not
  practical
theorize... **6.** reason **9.** postulate,
  speculate
theory... **3.** ism **4.** plan **6.** scheme
  7. formula, opinion **8.** analysis,
  doctrine **10.** hypothesis **11.** speculation,
  supposition **13.** contemplation
theory of...
  evolution.. **9.** Darwinism **10.** Lamarckism
  13. Spencerianism
  knowledge.. **12.** epistemology
  language.. **6.** bowwow **8.** ding-dong,
  pooh-pooh
  philosophy.. **13.** phenomenalism
  relativity.. **8.** Einstein
theosophist... **7.** Mahatma
theosophy... **4.** yoga **6.** cabala **7.** Nirvana
  8. kamarupa (Kama)
therapeutic... **7.** healing **8.** curative,
  remedies
therapy... **4.** cure **5.** faith **9.** dietetics,
  medicines, treatment **12.** hydrotherapy,
  therapeutics **13.** psychotherapy
there... **3.** yon **5.** ready **6.** yonder
  7. thereat, thither **11.** at that place
therefore... **2.** as, so **4.** ergo **5.** hence,
  since **6.** thence **9.** thereupon, to
  that end, wherefore **11.** accordingly

12. consequently

thermometer . . . **5.** Hydra **7.** Reaumur **10.** Centigrade, Fahrenheit

Thesaurus compiler . . . **5.** Roget

thesis . . . **5.** essay, theme, topic **6.** accent **7.** premise **8.** treatise **9.** postulate **10.** assumption **11.** affirmation **12.** dissertation

thespian . . . **3.** art **5.** actor **6.** player, tragic **7.** actress, Thespis (founder) **8.** dramatic

Thessaly, Greece . . .
ancient name . . **9.** Thessalia
famed for . . **6.** horses **8.** horsemen
mountain . . **4.** Ossa **6.** Pelion
native . . **5.** Greek **10.** Thessalian
town . . **7.** Larissa

thew . . . **5.** brawn, sinew **6.** manner, muscle, virtue **8.** strength

they go out . . . **6.** exeunt

thick . . . **4.** burr, dull, hazy **5.** broad, bushy, close, crass, dense, gross, husky, plump, solid, squat **6.** coarse, espeso, stodgy, stupid **7.** crowded, grumous, muffled **8.** familiar, friendly, intimate, numerous, thickset **9.** luxuriant **10.** indistinct **11.** inspissated **12.** impenetrable

thicken . . . **3.** gel **4.** clot, curd **5.** cloud, flock **6.** curdle, deepen, harden **7.** congeal, stiffen **8.** increase, solidify **9.** intensify **10.** incrassate, inspissate, strengthen

thicket . . . **4.** bosk, rone **5.** copse, grove, hedge, shola **6.** bosket (bosquet) **7.** boscage, coppice, spinney **9.** brushwood, chaparral **10.** underbrush

thickheaded . . . **4.** dull **5.** dense **6.** stupid **7.** doltish

thickness . . . **3.** ply **5.** layer **7.** density **8.** diameter, intimacy **10.** opaqueness **11.** consistency, measurement

thickset . . . **5.** squat, stout **6.** stocky, stodgy, stubby **14.** closely planted

thick-skinned . . . **7.** callous **11.** hardhearted, insensitive, pachydermic **14.** pachydermatous

thick soup . . . **5.** purée

thief . . . **5.** scamp **6.** ackman, bandit, looter, pirate, rascal, robber **7.** burglar, filcher, rustler, stealer **8.** gangster, larcener **9.** larcenist, scoundrel **10.** freebooter, pickpocket, plagiarist

thieves (famed) . . . **5.** Fagin **9.** Robin Hood **10.** Dick Turpin, Jesse James **11.** Claude Duval **12.** Jonathan Wild **13.** Thief of Bagdad

thieves' Latin . . . **4.** cant **5.** slang **12.** secret jargon

thigh (pert to) . . .
animal's . . **3.** ham **4.** hock **5.** flank
armor plate . . **6.** cuisse (cuish)
bone . . **5.** femur, ilium
ref to . . **5.** groin, meros (merus) **6.** crural

thimble . . . **3.** cap **4.** ring **5.** cover, watch

thimble (pert to) . . .
berry . . **9.** raspberry **10.** blackberry
eye . . **12.** chub mackerel
flower . . **8.** foxglove
rig . . **5.** cheat **7.** swindle **13.** sleight of hand

weed . . **6.** clover

thin . . . **4.** bony, lank, lean, poor, rare, slim, weak **5.** gaunt, lanky, lathy, reedy, sheer, spare, washy **6.** dilute, meager, rarefy, shrill, sleazy, slinky, sparse, watery **7.** haggard, insipid, scraggy, scrawny, slender **8.** araneous, rarefied **10.** attenuated, diaphanous **11.** transparent

thin (pert to) . . .
air . . **5.** smoke, vapor **6.** bubble
and delicate . . **8.** araneous **10.** diaphanous
and haggard . . **5.** gaunt
and withered . . **7.** wizened **9.** shriveled
fabric . . **8.** gossamer
out . . **5.** peter
plate, bone . . **6.** tegmen
plate, metal . . **4.** leaf
plate, Zool . . **6.** lamina **7.** lamella
skinned . . **6.** gentle, tender, touchy
Thin Man's dog . . **4.** Asta

thine . . . **4.** tuum

thing . . . **3.** act, res **4.** deed, fact, idea, unit **5.** being, event **6.** affair, entity, gadget, object **7.** article, reality **8.** anything, creature **9.** happening, situation, something

thing (pert to) . . .
added . . **6.** insert **8.** addendum **9.** insertion **10.** supplement
assumed . . **7.** premise **11.** implication
complete . . **4.** unit
cursed . . **8.** anathema
done . . **5.** actum
following . . **6.** sequel
found . . **5.** trove
hard to classify . . **11.** nondescript
huge . . **7.** monster
indefinite . . **7.** so-and-so **10.** thingumbob (thingumabob) **12.** what's-its-name
nonexisting . . **9.** nonentity
of little worth . . **6.** stiver, trifle **7.** trinket
the (thing) . . **7.** the rage
unique . . **4.** sole

things (pert to) . . .
added . . **7.** addenda **11.** additaments
brought into being . . **9.** creations
found, surprise . . **11.** serendipity
intricate . . **9.** involutes
little . . **16.** inconsequentials
moving to and fro . . **7.** wigwags
of like nature . . **8.** cognates
suitable to eat . . **9.** esculents
theoretical . . **7.** noumena
to be done . . **6.** agenda
to be learned . . **7.** lessons
to follow . . **7.** sequels **8.** sequelae
to sharpen . . **10.** whetstones
widely separated . . **8.** extremes

think . . . **3.** wis **4.** deem, muse, trow **5.** opine **6.** reason **7.** believe, imagine, reflect, suppose **8.** cogitate, conceive, meditate **11.** contemplate

think (pert to) . . .
better of . . **6.** repent **10.** reconsider
bring to mind . . **6.** recall **7.** imagine **10.** conjecture
logically . . **6.** reason
of . . **5.** judge **6.** intend, recall **8.** consider, remember **9.** recollect **10.** call to mind

over.. **3.** wis **4.** mull, muse **5.** brood
  6. ponder **8.** meditate
up.. **6.** devise, scheme **7.** concoct
thinker, religious freedom...
  14. latitudinarian
Thin Man (pert to)...
  actor.. **3.** Loy (Myrna) **6.** Powell (William)
  character.. **11.** Nick Charles, Nora
    Charles
  dog.. **4.** Asta
thinness... **6.** rarity **7.** tenuity **8.** rareness
  11. slenderness
third (pert to)...
  comb form.. **3.** tri **4.** trit
  day (Quakers).. **7.** Tuesday
  estate.. **6.** people
  figure.. **7.** ferison
  in number.. **8.** tertiary
  music.. **6.** tierce
  ordinal of.. **5.** three
  person.. **6.** escort **7.** grammar
  8. chaperon
  power.. **4.** cube
  Republic.. **6.** French (1871)
thirst... **6.** desire, hunger **7.** craving,
  dryness, longing
this... **4.** near **9.** the nearer
Thisbe's lover (Bab)... **7.** Paramus
thisness... **9.** haecceity
thistle (pert to)...
  bird.. **9.** goldfinch
  color.. **6.** violet (cobalt)
  emblem.. **8.** Scotland
  genus.. **6.** Arnica, Cosmos **7.** Carlina
  star.. **7.** caltrop (caltrap)
thistledown... **6.** pappus **12.** thistlebeard
thither... **3.** yon **5.** hence **6.** yonder
thong... **4.** lash, riem, whip **5.** knout,
  lorum, quirt, romal, strap **6.** lorate
  7. amentum, lanyard (laniard)
Thor (pert to)...
  father.. **4.** Odin
  German.. **5.** Donar
  god of.. **7.** thunder
  other name.. **9.** Hlorrithi
  stepson.. **3.** Ull (Ullr)
  wife.. **3.** Sif
thorax... **5.** chest **6.** cavity **7.** cuirass
  8. pectoral **11.** breastplate
thorn... **4.** bane **5.** briar (brier), spine
  7. acantha, bramble, prickle
thorn (pert to)...
  apple.. **3.** haw **6.** Datura
  back.. **3.** ray **4.** dorn **5.** skate **10.** spider
    crab **11.** stickleback
  bill.. **11.** hummingbird
  comb form.. **5.** spini
  full of.. **6.** briary
  letters.. **2.** th **3.** edh
  lizard.. **6.** moloch
  pert to.. **6.** spinal
  small.. **7.** spinule
thornless... **5.** inerm **8.** inermous
thorny... **5.** sharp, spiny **7.** brambly,
  prickly **9.** acanthoid, bristling, difficult
thorough... **4.** full **8.** absolute, complete
  9. downright, intensive **10.** exhaustive
  11. painstaking
thoroughfare... **4.** road **6.** artery,
  street **7.** highway, parkway, passage,
  roadway, thruway **8.** arterial, autobahn,

highroad, pent road, turnpike, waterway
  9. boulevard, concourse **10.** autostrada
thoroughgoing... **4.** zeal **7.** extreme
  9. downright **11.** painstaking
thoroughly... **3.** all **9.** intensive, out-and-
  out **11.** intensively **13.** letter-perfect
thorp, thorpe... **4.** dorp, town **6.** hamlet
  7. village
those (pert to)...
  adept at table talk.. **14.** deipnosophists
  brought to terms.. **11.** transients
  in office.. **3.** ins
  in the stock market.. **5.** bears, bulls
  7. traders **9.** investors
  of a habit.. **7.** addicts
  of the same goal.. **6.** rivals
  outside a profession.. **5.** laity
those who...
  read and write.. **9.** literates
  ridicule.. **8.** deriders
  verify.. **13.** corroborators
  work together.. **13.** collaborators
thou... **3.** tha **7.** pronoun **8.** thousand
thought... **4.** care, heed, idea, view
  5. logic **6.** deemed, opined **7.** anxiety,
  opinion **9.** attention, cogitated,
  reasoning **10.** cogitation, meditation,
  reflection **11.** cerebration
  12. deliberation, recollection
  13. consideration, ratiocination
thought (pert to)...
  continuous.. **10.** meditation
  deep in.. **10.** cogitabund
  form.. **6.** ideate
  laws of.. **7.** noetics
  reader.. **11.** telepathist
thoughtful... **4.** kind **5.** moody
  7. mindful, museful, pensive, prudent,
  serious **9.** attentive **10.** cogitative,
  meditative, reflective, ruminative,
  solicitous **11.** circumspect, considerate
  13. contemplative
thoughtless... **4.** rash **6.** stupid **7.** foolish
  8. careless, heedless, reckless
  9. brainless, impulsive **11.** harum-
  scarum, inattentive, thought-free
  12. unreflecting **13.** inconsiderate
thousand... **3.** mil **5.** mille **7.** chiliad
  10. ten hundred
Thousand and One Nights...
  13. Arabian Nights
thousand men, command of...
  11. chiliarchia
thousandth... **9.** chiliadal **10.** millesimal
thousand years... **7.** chiliad **9.** millenary
  10. millennium
thrall... **4.** esne, serf **5.** slave **7.** bondage,
  bondman, captive, slavery **9.** thralldom
  10. oppression
thrash... **3.** lam, tan **4.** beat, cave,
  drub, flog, whip **5.** flail, pound, twist
  6. defeat, punish, strike, swinge, thresh
  7. belabor, trounce **8.** urticate, vanquish
  9. pulverize, toss about
thrashing... **7.** beating, milling
  8. drubbing, flogging, whipping
  10. punishment
thread... **4.** flax, jute, line, silk, vein, wire,
  yarn **5.** fiber, floss, linen, lisle, rayon
  6. cotton, dacron, sleave **8.** arrasene,
  filament

thread (pert to) . . .
ancient . . **4.** byss
a needle . . **5.** reeve
ball . . **4.** clew (clue)
cell . . **5.** cnida
coiled . . **3.** cop
comb form . . **3.** nem **4.** nema **5.** nemat
6. nemato
fish . . **7.** cutlass **9.** threadfin
11. cobblerfish
herring . . **11.** gizzard shad
like . . **5.** filar **6.** filose
loose . . **4.** lint **7.** raveled
medical . . **5.** seton
metal . . **4.** wire
mystery lead . . **4.** clue
shoemaker's (obs) . . **6.** lingel (lingle)
silk . . **5.** floss **9.** filoselle
tangle . . **6.** sleave
tape, braid (thread) . . **5.** inkle
tester . . **9.** serimeter
weaving term . . **4.** warp, weft, woof
5. leash
threadbare . . . **4.** sere, worn **5.** trite
6. shabby
threaten . . . **4.** warn **5.** curse **6.** menace
7. portend **8.** forebode **9.** comminate
10. intimidate **12.** anathematize
threatening . . . **4.** dark **7.** ominous
8. imminent, lowering, menacing
three (pert to) . . .
banded armadillo . . **4.** apar **5.** apara
comb form . . **3.** ter
dimensional . . **5.** bruit, cubic
12. stereoscopic
fold . . **4.** tern **6.** ternal, treble, triple
7. ternate
group of . . **4.** trio **5.** triad **7.** triplet
8. triplets
hundredth anniversary . .
13. tercentennial
in one . . **6.** triune **7.** trinity **10.** The
Godhead
legged stand . . **6.** teapoy, tripod, trivet
lined . . **9.** trilinear
masted vessel . . **5.** xebec **7.** frigate
8. schooner
math term . . **2.** pi (3.1416)
prefix . . **3.** tri
R's . . **7.** reading, writing **10.** arithmetic
seeded . . **11.** trispermous
sided figure . . **6.** trigon **8.** triangle
spot . . **4.** trey
styled . . **10.** trystylous
toed sloth . . **2.** ai
Three Kingdoms (Chin) . . . **2.** Wu **3.** Shu,
Wei
Three Kings of Cologne . . . **6.** Gaspar
8. Melchior **9.** Balthasar **12.** Three
Wise Men
Three Musketeers . . . **5.** Athos **6.** Aramis
7. Porthos **9.** D'Artagnan (friend)
Three Sisters (Myth) . . . **5.** Fates **6.** Clotho
7. Atropos **8.** Lachesis
Three Wise Men (Kings of Cologne) . . .
6. Gaspar **8.** Melchior **9.** Balthasar
threnody . . . **5.** dirge **7.** requiem
8. coronach
threshold . . . **3.** eve **4.** gate, sill **5.** limen
6. portal **8.** doorsill
threw . . . see also *throw* **4.** cast **5.** flung,

slung **6.** bunged, heaved, hurled, pelted,
tossed **7.** pitched
thrice . . . **3.** ter, tri **5.** fully **6.** highly
10. repeatedly, three times
thrift . . . **7.** economy **8.** prudence
9. husbandry **10.** providence
11. thriftiness
thriftless . . . **6.** lavish **8.** prodigal, wasteful
11. extravagant, improvident
thrifty . . . **6.** frugal, saving **7.** careful,
prudent, sparing **9.** provident
10. economical, forehanded, prosperous
11. flourishing
thrill . . . **4.** tirl **6.** dindle, thrush,
tingle, tremor **7.** delight **9.** electrify
10. excitement
thrive . . . **4.** grow **5.** moise (Eng) **6.** batten
7. prosper, succeed **8.** flourish, increase
throat . . . **3.** maw **4.** crop, neck **5.** gular,
halse, mouth, voice **6.** groove,
gullet, larynx, mutter **7.** channel,
glottis, jugular, orifice, pharynx,
trachea **9.** esophagus **10.** passageway
12. constriction
throb . . . **4.** ache, beat, drum, pant **5.** pulse
7. pulsate, vibrate **9.** palpitate
throe . . . **4.** pang **5.** agony **7.** anguish
8. struggle
Throgmorton Street . . . **13.** Stock
Exchange (London)
throne . . . **3.** see **4.** apse **5.** exalt
8. enthrone **9.** royal seat
11. sovereignty, supreme rank **12.** Chair
of State
throng . . . **4.** crew, host, push **5.** crowd,
horde, press, swarm **6.** bustle, stress
7. hurried **9.** confusion, multitude
throttle . . . **5.** choke, lever, seize **6.** throat
7. garrote **8.** strangle, suppress,
windpipe
through . . . **2.** by **3.** dia, per **4.** into,
thru **5.** ended **7.** perpend **8.** finished
9. because of, by means of, completed
throughout . . . **5.** about **6.** during
8. thorough **10.** completely, everywhere
throw . . . **3.** cob, don, lob, peg, shy
4. bear, cast, hurl, kist, pelt, toss, yerk
5. chuck, fling, heave, pitch, sling,
twist, whirl **6.** baffle, strike, thwart
7. discard, project **9.** prostrate
throw (pert to) . . .
a scare . . **7.** terrify
away . . **7.** discard **8.** handbill, squander
back . . **5.** repel **6.** reject, revert
dice (term) . . **4.** sise **7.** ambsace
in the towel . . **4.** cede, quit **9.** surrender
into confusion . . **7.** disturb, perturb,
trouble **8.** stampede **10.** demoralize
into ecstasy . . **9.** enrapture
into shade . . **7.** eclipse
off . . **4.** cast, shed **6.** derail, reject
7. abandon, discard
out . . **4.** emit, lade **5.** egest, eject,
expel **6.** bounce **7.** discard, project
9. eliminate
over . . **4.** jilt **5.** build **6.** give up, refute
7. abandon, discard **9.** eliminate
overboard . . **8.** jettison
water upon . . **5.** douse
throwback . . . **7.** setback **9.** reversion
10. misfortune, regression

throwing (pert to) . . .
rope . . **5.** lasso, reata, riata **6.** lariat
science . . **10.** ballistics
stick (anc) . . **6.** womera (woomera)
thrum . . . **3.** bit, hum **4.** drum, tuft **5.** strum
   6. fringe, repeat
thrush . . . **5.** brown, mavis, robin, veery
   7. disease **8.** shagbark, songbird
   9. blackbird
thrush (pert to) . . .
American . . **5.** robin, veery **12.** hermit
   thrush
European . . **5.** ouzel (ousel) **6.** missel
   7. redwing **11.** nightingale
golden . . **6.** oriole
Hawaiian . . **4.** omao
Ind . . **5.** shama
Scot . . **8.** throstle
thrust . . . **3.** dig, jab **4.** gird, poke,
   push, stab **5.** lunge **6.** extend, pierce
   7. intrude, obtrude, riposte **8.** protrude
   9. interject, interpose
thrust (pert to) . . .
aside . . **5.** shove **7.** dismiss **8.** brush
   off
down . . **7.** detrude
fencing term . . **5.** lunge **7.** allonge,
   riposte **8.** estocade
one's self in . . **5.** enter **7.** intrude
out . . **5.** eject **6.** extend **8.** protrude
thug . . . **4.** goon, yegg **6.** cuttle, gunman
   7. ruffian **8.** assassin **9.** cutthroat,
   roughneck
thumb . . . **6.** pollex, thenar
thumb (pert to) . . .
a ride . . **9.** hitchhike
bird . . **9.** goldcrest
lady's (herb) . . **9.** peachwort, persicary
mark . . **4.** soil **10.** impression
   11. fingerprint **14.** identification
nail . . **5.** small **6.** complete
over . . **4.** skim **6.** browse
part . . **6.** thenar
thump . . . **4.** bang, beat, blow, drum,
   thud, whip, yerk **5.** knock, pound
   6. hammer, pummel, strike, thrash
   8. chastise **10.** pound along
thunder . . . **4.** boom, peal, roar **5.** storm
   9. fulminate
thunder (pert to) . . .
bolt . . **5.** speed **6.** Caesar **8.** surprise
   9. lightning **11.** fulmination
fish . . **4.** raad **5.** loach **7.** catfish (electric)
god . . **4.** Thor **6.** Manito
of applause . . **5.** cheer **7.** ovation
peal . . **4.** clap **5.** crash
smitten goddess . . **6.** Semele **8.** Keraunia
thurible . . . **6.** censer
thurifer . . . **12.** censer bearer
Thursday . . . **4.** Thor **8.** fifth day **12.** god
   of thunder
thus . . . **2.** so **3.** sic **4.** ergo **5.** hence
   7. this way **9.** therefore **11.** for instance
   12. consequently
thwack . . . **3.** rap **4.** bang, blow, club
   5. crush, knock, whack **6.** defeat,
   pommel, strike, thrash **7.** belabor
thwart . . . **4.** balk, foil **5.** block, clash,
   cross, parry, spite **6.** defeat, gaffle,
   oppose, outwit **7.** oblique, prevent
   8. obstruct, stubborn **9.** frustrate,

interpose **10.** across from, disappoint
thymus . . . **5.** gland **10.** sweetbread
   (lambs, calves)
tiara . . . **5.** crown **6.** diadem **7.** coronet
   8. ornament
Tibbett opera . . . **12.** Emperor Jones
   (1932)
tibert . . . **3.** cat
Tibet, Asia . . . see also *Tibetan*
animal . . **3.** goa, sus **5.** panda
capital . . **5.** Lhasa
dialect . . **9.** Bhutanese
kingdom . . **5.** Nepal
Mts . . **8.** Himalaya **9.** Karakoram
religion . . **7.** Lamaism
river . . **5.** Hwang, Indus **7.** Yangtze
   11. Brahmaputra
ruler . . **9.** Dalai Lama
Tibetan (pert to) . . .
beer (barley) . . **5.** chang
deer . . **4.** shou
food (barley) . . **6.** tsamba
gazelle . . **3.** goa
monk, priest . . **4.** lama
ox . . **3.** yak
sheep . . **3.** sha **5.** urial **6.** bharal, nahoor,
   nayaur
wild ass . . **5.** kiang
wildcat . . **5.** manul
tibia . . . **4.** bone, shin **5.** flute **6.** cnemis
Tibur (anc) . . . **6.** Tivoli
tiburon . . . **5.** shark
Tiburtine . . . **12.** Sibyl of Tibur
tic . . . **5.** spasm **6.** twitch
tick . . . **3.** ked, tap **4.** beat, mark,
   mite, pest **5.** Argas **6.** acarid, Ixodes
   7. instant **8.** carapato, function, ticktock
   10. pajahuello (pajaroello)
ticket . . . **3.** tag **4.** note, pass, slip
   5. check, ducat, label, token **6.** ballot,
   billet, permit, record **7.** license, voucher
   8. document **11.** certificate
ticket dealer . . . **7.** scalper
tickle . . . **5.** amuse **6.** thrill, tingle
   7. delight **9.** titillate, vellicate
ticklish . . . **5.** risky **6.** fickle, queasy,
   touchy **7.** comical **8.** unstable, unsteady
   9. uncertain **10.** precarious, unreliable
tidal (pert to) . . .
creek . . **6.** estero **7.** estuary
current . . **8.** tiderace
flood . . **5.** eagre
flow . . **3.** ebb **4.** bore, neap **5.** surge
tidbit, titbit . . . **5.** goody **6.** morsel
   7. saynete **8.** delicacy
tide . . . **3.** ebb, rip **4.** high, neap, time
   5. drift **6.** period, stream **7.** current
   8. low water **9.** be carried
tide (pert to) . . .
gate . . **9.** floodgate
go with . . **5.** drift, float **7.** proceed **13.** be
   fashionable
out with . . **3.** ebb **6.** recede **8.** diminish,
   fade away
over . . **6.** endure **8.** surmount **11.** live
   through
tidings . . . **4.** news, word **6.** gospel, report,
   rumors **7.** message **10.** evangelist
   11. information
tidy . . . **4.** neat, trig, trim **5.** groom, natty,
   plump **6.** spruce **7.** orderly **9.** shipshape

10. put in order 12. antimacassar, considerable

tie . . . **4.** bind, bond, draw, even, knot, lash, link **5.** ascot, equal, nexus, noose, trice, truss **6.** cravat, enlace, fasten, relate, tether **7.** confine, necktie, sleeper **8.** equality, fastener, restrain, shoelace **10.** allegiance, obligation

tie (pert to) . . .
off . . **5.** belay
ornament . . **3.** pin
ready-made . . **4.** teck
securely . . **7.** trammel
sports . . **8.** dead heat
uniting . . **4.** bond **5.** tache
up . . **4.** bind, wrap **5.** truss **6.** fasten **8.** restrain

tier . . . **3.** row **5.** grade, layer **6.** series

Tiergarten . . . **4.** park **16.** Zoological Garden

tiff . . . **3.** sip **4.** huff, spat **5.** drink **7.** dudgeon, quarrel **8.** outburst **10.** fit of anger

tiffin . . . **3.** tea **5.** brown, lunch **6.** repast **8.** luncheon

tiger . . . **5.** bully **6.** emblem, savage **9.** swaggerer

tiger (pert to) . . .
American . . **6.** jaguar
bird . . **5.** finch **8.** amadavat
family . . **3.** cat **6.** mammal **11.** Felis tigris
hunting dog . . **5.** dhole
S African . . **7.** leopard
Tasmania . . **9.** thylacine **13.** Tasmanian wolf
wolf . . **5.** hyena
young . . **3.** cub

tight . . . **4.** fast, snug, taut, trim **5.** alert, close, drunk, tense **6.** narrow, stingy **7.** exactly, shapely **9.** condensed **11.** closefisted **12.** close-fitting, parsimonious

tight (pert to) . . .
fisted . . **6.** stingy **12.** parsimonious
lipped . . **5.** terse **9.** secretive
wad . . **5.** miser **10.** curmudgeon

tighten . . . **4.** frap, lace **5.** brace, tense **6.** fasten, tauten **7.** squeeze **9.** constrict

Tigris River city of ruins . . . **7.** Nineveh (anc)

til . . . **4.** tree **6.** sesame

tilde . . . **4.** dash, mark, sign **6.** accent, tittle **15.** diacritical mark

tile . . . **3.** red **5.** slate **6.** domino, mosaic, pament (pamment), tegula **7.** ceramic, pantile, tessera **8.** pavement

tiler . . . **5.** thief **6.** slater **7.** hellier **10.** doorkeeper

till . . . **3.** box **4.** farm, plow, tray, when **5.** labor, while **6.** before, casket, drawer, whilst **7.** develop **9.** cultivate

tillable . . . **6.** arable

tiller . . . **4.** helm **5.** stalk **6.** farmer, sprout **7.** plowman, rancher **8.** harrower **10.** cultivator, husbandman

tilt . . . **3.** tip **4.** cant, heel, list **5.** joust, pitch, slant, slope **6.** careen, oliver (hammer), seesaw, unload **7.** incline **8.** log house **10.** tournament **11.** altercation

timber . . . **3.** log **4.** beam, tree, wood **6.** forest, lumber **7.** support **9.** underpier

timber (pert to) . . .
bend . . **3.** sny
building . . **4.** sill, stud **5.** joist **6.** purlin, rafter **8.** stringer
convex . . **6.** camber
cribs (logging) . . **4.** dram
cut . . **6.** lumber **7.** fallage
decay . . **4.** doty (doaty)
end . . **5.** tenon
hard, heartwood . . **7.** duramen
Naut . . **3.** rib **4.** bitt, keel, mast, spar, wale **8.** sternson
support . . **6.** corbel
upright . . **8.** puncheon
wolf . . **4.** lobo

timbre . . . **4.** tone **5.** clang, crest (Her), miter **7.** coronet **9.** resonance, tone color

timbrel . . . **4.** drum **5.** tabor **7.** sistrum **10.** tambourine

time . . . **3.** age, day, eon, era **4.** aeon, date, hour, term, turn, week, year **5.** clock, epoch, shift, tempo **6.** decade, minute, moment, period, season, second **7.** century **8.** duration, occasion, schedule **9.** fortnight, millenium

time (pert to) . . .
accurate . . **10.** isochronon
before Christmas . . **6.** Advent
before Easter . . **4.** Lent
equal . . **10.** isochronal
geologic . . **5.** azoic
granted . . **4.** stay **5.** delay **8.** reprieve
legal . . **6.** usance **11.** year and a day
limit . . **8.** deadline
long ago . . **4.** once, yore **8.** formerly
medical . . **3.** tid **8.** ter in die (three times a day)
of vigor . . **6.** heyday
one . . **4.** once
present . . **5.** nonce **12.** contemporary
prior . . **9.** antedated **11.** retroactive
right . . **3.** tid
same . . **7.** however **9.** meanwhile **10.** concurrent **11.** synchronous **14.** simultaneously
spare . . **7.** leisure
waste . . **4.** idle, loaf **5.** dally **6.** loiter
wrong . . **11.** anachronism **13.** anachronistic

timeless . . . **7.** ageless, eternal, undated **8.** dateless, unending, untimely **9.** premature **11.** everlasting **12.** interminable

timely . . . **3.** apt, pat **4.** soon **5.** early **6.** prompt **9.** opportune **10.** seasonably **11.** opportunity

timepiece . . . **4.** dial **5.** clock, watch **6.** gnomon **8.** egg glass, horologe **9.** clepsydra, hourglass, metronome **10.** isochronon, wristwatch **11.** chronometer

times . . . **3.** ago, eld **4.** yore **5.** often **10.** frequently, yesterdays **11.** ups and downs

timid . . . **3.** shy **4.** meek **5.** eerie, henny, mousy, pavid, scary **6.** afraid, trepid **7.** bashful, fearful, nervous, not bold **8.** cowardly, retiring, timorous

9. diffident, shrinking 12. fainthearted
13. pusillanimous
timocracy (pert to) . . .
defined by . . **5.** Plato
principle . . **11.** love of honor
State . . **6.** Sparta (anc)
Timon of Athens . . . **5.** Cynic (The)
11. misanthrope
timorous . . . **5.** timid **6.** afraid **7.** bashful,
fearful **8.** hesitant **9.** shrinking
Timothy (pert to) . . .
Bib . . **7.** convert **8.** Epistles
grass . . **3.** hay **10.** herd's grass
timpani . . . **11.** kettledrums
tin . . . **3.** can, pan **5.** money, plate
7. element, stannum **8.** preserve **10.** not
genuine
tin (pert to) . . .
alloy (copper) . . **6.** pewter
box . . **7.** trummel
coat with . . **5.** terne **10.** terneplate
comb form . . **6.** stanni
extract . . **8.** prillion
foil, plate . . **4.** tain
mine . . **8.** stannary
ref to . . **7.** stannic
sheet . . **6.** latten
symbol . . **2.** Sn
tinamou . . . **4.** yutu **7.** tataupa **9.** partridge
tincture . . . **4.** dash **5.** color, imbue, myrrh,
tinge, trace **6.** iodine **7.** extract, vestige
8. solution **9.** paregoric, suspicion
10. extraction
tinder . . . **4.** punk **5.** spunk **6.** amadou
9. touchwood
tine . . . **3.** nib **5.** prong, spike, tooth
tinea . . . **7.** sycosis **8.** ringworm
tinge . . . **3.** dye **4.** tint **5.** color, imbue,
shade, stain, taint **6.** flavor **8.** coloring,
tincture **10.** suggestion
tingle . . . **4.** ring **5.** sting **6.** dingle, thrill
7. prickle **9.** sensation, stimulate
tinkle . . . **5.** clink **6.** dingle, tingle
tint . . . **3.** due, hue **4.** tone **5.** blush,
color, tinge **6.** nuance
tintinnabulum . . . **4.** bell **6.** tinkle
9. rhymester
tintype . . . **9.** ferrotype **12.** old-fashioned
tiny . . . **3.** wee **5.** small, teeny **6.** atomic,
infant, minute, petite **9.** miniature
10. diminutive **13.** infinitesimal
tip . . . **3.** cue, end, fee, neb, top **4.** apex,
cant, heel, hint, lean, list, tilt **5.** crown,
point, slant, spire, upset **6.** careen,
inform, summit, tiptop **7.** cumshaw,
incline **8.** bonamano, gratuity, overturn
9. extremity, overthrow
tip (pert to) . . .
end . . **3.** neb
French . . **9.** pourboire
Italian . . **8.** bonamano
near . . **6.** apical
Near East . . **9.** baksheesh (bakshish)
scabbard . . **5.** chape **7.** crampet
(crampette)
slender . . **6.** arista
to one side . . **4.** list, tile **5.** alist **6.** careen
up and over . . **4.** cant
tippet . . . **4.** cape, hood **5.** amice, scarf
6. almuce **7.** muffler **8.** liripipe, palatine
9. comforter

tipple . . . **3.** bib, nip, pot, sip **4.** suck
5. drink, quaff **6.** fuddle, guzzle, liquor,
tumble **7.** spirits **8.** beverage, overturn
tippler . . . **3.** sot **5.** souse, toper **7.** drinker
9. draftsman
tipster . . . **4.** tout **8.** dopester **9.** informant,
predictor **10.** forecaster, speculator
tipsy . . . **4.** awry **5.** drunk, shaky **6.** groggy
7. fuddled, muddled **10.** staggering
11. intoxicated
tiptoe . . . **5.** alert **6.** warily **7.** eagerly,
quietly **8.** cautious, stealthy
10. cautiously
tirade . . . **6.** screed, speech **8.** berating
9. philippic
tire . . . **3.** fag, lag, rim **4.** bore, jade
5. dress, weary **6.** attire **7.** exhaust,
fatigue
tired . . . **5.** bored, jaded, spent, weary
6. aweary
tireless . . . **8.** untiring **9.** unwearied
10. unwearying **13.** indefatigable
tiresome . . . **3.** dry **4.** dull, tame **6.** boring,
prolix **7.** irksome, tedious **8.** annoying
9. fatiguing, vexatious, wearisome
10. irritating
tissue . . . **3.** web **4.** bast, tela **5.** fiber,
paper **6.** fabric **7.** culture **8.** meshwork
tissue (pert to) . . .
Biol . . **4.** bone **5.** nerve **6.** muscle
8. ganglion **10.** epithelium
cell . . **8.** meristem
cellular . . **10.** epithelium
connecting . . **6.** stroma, tendon
8. ligament
decay . . **6.** caries
fatty . . **3.** fat **4.** suet
hardening of . . **9.** sclerosis
horny . . **7.** keratin
layer . . **7.** stratum
lymphoid . . **7.** tonsils
nerve . . **8.** ganglion
ref to . . **4.** tela **5.** telar
spinal . . **4.** alba
vegetable . . **4.** bast **7.** endarch
8. meristem
wood . . **6.** lignin, lignum
Titan . . . **4.** Rhea, Thea **5.** Coeus, Creus,
deity, Dione, giant, Theia **6.** Phoebe,
Tethys, Themis **7.** Cronius, Iapetus,
Oceanus **8.** Hyperion **9.** Mnemosyne
titanic . . . **4.** huge **5.** great **7.** immense
8. colossal, enormous, gigantic
Titan War (Thessaly) . . . **11.** Titanomachy
tithe . . . **3.** tax **4.** part **5.** teind, tenth
11. frank pledge
titi . . . **6.** monkey **7.** sea bird **8.** ironwood
9. buckwheat
Titian . . . **3.** red **6.** artist **7.** red hair
9. red-haired
titillate . . . **5.** amuse **6.** thrill, tickle
7. delight **8.** interest
titlark . . . **5.** pipit
title . . . **3.** sir **4.** dame, deed, earl, lord,
name, sire, term, type **5.** claim, right
6. knight, madame, squire **7.** caption,
epithet, esquire, heading **8.** muniment
9. designate **11.** appellation, designation
titled member, Stock Exchange . . .
6. orchid (sl)
titmouse . . . **3.** mag, tit **4.** wren

5. Parus **6.** parine, tomtit **7.** jacksaw
9. mumruffin
titter ... **5.** laugh, te-hee **6.** giggle, tee-hee
7. snicker
tittle ... **3.** dot, jot **4.** iota, mark, whit
5. tilde **6.** gossip, tattle **8.** particle
tittle-tattle ... **6.** gossip **8.** idle talk
16. scandalmongering
tittupy ... **3.** gay **5.** shaky **6.** lively
8. prancing, unsteady
titubate ... **4.** reel **6.** totter **7.** stagger,
stammer
titular ... **7.** nominal **9.** incumbent (of
a title)
Tlingit ... **6.** Indian (Alaska)
TNT ... **6.** trotol **9.** explosive
15. trinitrotoluene
to ... **2.** at **4.** into, till, unto **5.** until
6. toward **7.** as far as, thither
11. preposition
to (pert to) ...
to be .. **4.** esse, être
to-do .. **3.** ado **4.** fuss, stir **6.** bustle
9. commotion
to each his own .. **10.** suum cuique
to which .. **7.** whereto
to wit .. **3.** viz **6.** namely **8.** scilicet
9. videlicet
toad ... **4.** agua, Bufo, frog, pipa
6. anuran, peeper **7.** crapaud
9. amphibian, Batrachia, spadefoot
10. natterjack
toad (pert to) ...
eater .. **5.** toady **8.** hanger-on, parasite
fish .. **6.** puffer, slimer **8.** frogfish
head .. **6.** plover (golden)
lily .. **9.** waterlily
stabber .. **9.** jackknife
tree .. **4.** Hyla
toadflax ... **8.** flaxweed, ranstead
13. butter-and-eggs
toadstool ... **5.** morel **6.** fungus
8. mushroom, puffball
toady ... **4.** ugly **8.** parasite, truckler
9. repulsive, sycophant, toadeater
toast ... **3.** tan **4.** cook, leep **5.** bread,
brede, brown, parch, roast, skoal
6. pledge, sippet **7.** drink to **8.** cinnamon
tobacco (pert to) ...
ash .. **6.** dottle (dottel)
Cuban .. **4.** capa **6.** Vuelta (leaf)
disease .. **6.** calico, mosaic **7.** walloon
English .. **8.** bird's-eye
epithet .. **12.** Lady Nicotine
French .. **7.** caporal
Greek .. **7.** Knaster
hookah smoking .. **7.** goracco
Indian .. **7.** uppowoc
introduced by .. **7.** Raleigh (Sir Walter)
Kentucky .. **6.** Burley
kind .. **4.** capa, shag **5.** tabac **6.** Burley,
Vuelta **7.** caporal, henbane, Latakia,
perique, Turkish **8.** Virginia **9.** salvadora
paste .. **7.** goracco
Persian .. **6.** tumbak (tumbaki)
pipe .. **7.** calumet, chibook (chibouque)
principle (active) .. **8.** nicotine
receptacle .. **4.** pipe **7.** humidor
S American .. **8.** canaster
small cut .. **3.** cud **4.** plug, quid **6.** dottle
(dottel) **7.** carotte

Turkish .. **7.** Latakia
wrapping .. **9.** broadleaf
toboggan ... **4.** sled **5.** coast, glide
7. coaster **12.** sharp decline **14.** downhill
course
toby ... **3.** dog (Punch's), jug, mug, rob
5. cigar **7.** highway, pitcher
tocsin ... **5.** alarm **9.** alarm bell
13. warning signal
toe ... **3.** tae, tip **5.** digit **6.** dactyl, hallux
7. minimus
toehold ... **7.** footing **8.** foothold,
purchase
toes, odd-numbered ... **13.** perissodactyl
toe the line ... **4.** obey
together ... **3.** com, con, syn **4.** mass,
with **5.** union **10.** conjointly
11. unanimously **12.** coincidently,
concurrently, continuously
toggery ... **3.** set **4.** garb, togs **5.** dress
7. clothes, harness **9.** trappings
12. haberdashery
tolerable ... **4.** so-so **8.** bearable, passable
9. endurable **10.** acceptable, fairly well,
sufferable **11.** supportable
tolerance ... **8.** patience **10.** indulgence,
permission
tolerant ... **7.** lenient, patient **9.** indulgent
10. forbearing, permissive
tolerate ... **4.** bear, bide **5.** abide, allow,
brook, stand **6.** endure, permit, suffer
9. put up with
toll ... **3.** due, tax **4.** call, duty,
peal, ring **5.** knell **6.** allure, charge,
custom, entice, impost, invite, strike
7. ringing **8.** exaction **10.** assessment
12. compensation
Tolypeutes ... **4.** apar **9.** armadillo
tomahawk ... **3.** axe **4.** kill **6.** attack
7. hatchet
tomb ... **4.** cist, lair **5.** crypt, grave, speos,
vault **6.** shrine **7.** mastaba (mastabah),
orruary, tritaph **8.** catacomb, cenotaph
9. mausoleum, sepulcher
tombé ... **4.** drum
tomboy ... **3.** meg **4.** romp **5.** rowdy
6. hoyden (hoiden), tomrig
tomcat ... **3.** gib
tomcod ... **8.** bocaccio
tome ... **4.** book, opus **5.** atlas **6.** volume
11. papal letter, publication
tomorrow ... **5.** later **6.** mañana **9.** the
morrow
tonant ... **7.** blatant **10.** thundering
tone ... **4.** mode, mood, note, tang,
tune **5.** pitch, reedy, sound, trend,
twang, vigor **6.** accent, energy, melody,
nuance, timbre **7.** cadence **8.** modulate,
monotone, tonology **9.** harmonize
10. inflection, intonation, modulation
tone (pert to) ...
down .. **3.** dim **6.** mellow, modify, soften
8. moderate
lacking .. **5.** atony **6.** atonal
quality, color .. **6.** timbre
series .. **5.** scale
single .. **8.** monotone
succession .. **5.** melos
thin .. **7.** sfogato
vibrant .. **5.** twang
toneless ... **4.** weal **5.** stony **6.** silent

9. colorless
tonga ... **7.** vehicle (2-wheeled)
Tonga ... **15.** Friendly Islands
tongue ... **3.** gab **4.** meat **5.** lingo,
speak **6.** speech **7.** clapper, lingula
8. language, lorriker, parlance
9. utterance
tongue (pert to)...
classical.. **5.** Greek, Latin **6.** Hebrew
fish.. **4.** sole
Jesus.. **7.** Aramaic
lash.. **5.** scold **8.** scolding
pivoted.. **4.** pawl
reference to.. **7.** glossal, lingual
sacred.. **4.** Pali
shaped.. **9.** lingulate
tied.. **4.** mute **8.** taciturn
wagon.. **4.** neap, pole
tongueless ... **4.** dumb, mute
10. speechless
tonic ... **6.** bracer, catnip, liquor **7.** bracing
8. medicine, remedial, roborant
9. stimulant **10.** refreshing
11. corroborant **12.** invigorating
tonsil ... **8.** amygdala
tonsorialist ... **6.** barber
tonsured ... **4.** bald **5.** shorn **6.** shaven
7. clipped **10.** baldheaded
too ... **3.** and **4.** also, over, very **6.** overly
7. besides **8.** likewise **9.** extremely
11. excessively **12.** additionally
too (pert to)...
bad.. **4.** alas
much.. **4.** trop **6.** excess **7.** nimiety
small.. **13.** unappreciable
soon.. **9.** premature
tool ... **3.** axe, saw **4.** dupe, file **5.** agent
6. device, gadget, puppet **7.** engrave,
gimmick, utensil, utility **9.** appliance
11. contrivance
tool (type) ... **2.** ax (axe) **3.** adz (adze),
awl, bit, hob, hoe, saw, sax, tap **4.** file,
jack, pick, tong, vise **5.** brush, burin,
drill, knife, lathe, level, plane, punch,
razor, spade **6.** chisel, gimlet, hammer,
lifter, peavey (peavy), pliers, reamer,
shears, slater, slicer, square, trepan,
wrench **7.** cleaver, mattock, mattoir,
scalpel, spatula **11.** screwdriver
tools (pert to)...
category.. **5.** power, speed **7.** cutlery,
machine, medical **9.** precision **11.** labor-
saving **12.** straightedge
prehistoric.. **4.** celt **6.** eolith **9.** paleolith
stone.. **6.** banner
theft of.. **6.** ratten
toosh ... **4.** gown (short), robe
9. nightgown
toot ... **3.** pry, spy **4.** fool, gaze, peep
5. blare, drink, revel, shout, spree
6. sprout **7.** whistle **8.** carousal,
eminence, proclaim **9.** blow a horn,
elevation
tooth ... **3.** cog **4.** dent, fang, snag,
tine, tusk **5.** ivory, molar, point,
prong, taste **6.** canine, cuspid, wisdom
7. grinder, incisor **8.** bicuspid, eyetooth
10. projection
tooth, teeth (pert to) ...
ache.. **8.** dentagra **9.** dentalgia
comb form.. **5.** denti, odont **6.** odonto

7. odontia
covering.. **6.** enamel
cutting of.. **8.** teething **9.** dentition
decay.. **6.** caries, cavity **11.** saprodontia
destitute of.. **8.** edentate
irregularity.. **11.** odontoloxia
molar.. **4.** wang
ref to.. **6.** dental **7.** odontic
science.. **10.** odontology
Scot.. **3.** gam
socket.. **8.** alveolus
toothlike.. **8.** odontoid **9.** dentiform
toothless ... **8.** decrepid, edentate
toothsome ... **5.** tasty **9.** delicious,
palatable
top ... **3.** cap, fid, lid, tip, toy **4.** acme,
apex, pate, roof **5.** crest, criss,
crown, excel, mensa, outdo, ridge,
scalp **6.** finial, summit, vertex, zenith
7. highest, supreme, surpass, topmost
8. dominate, pinnacle, teetotum
9. uppermost
topaz ... **3.** gem **5.** color **7.** mineral
11. hummingbird **13.** precious stone
tope ... **4.** tomb, wren **5.** drink, grove,
shark, stupa, tower **6.** guzzle, shrine
7. dogfish
toper ... **3.** sot **4.** tope **5.** shark **6.** barfly,
boozer **7.** guzzler, tippler, tosspot
8. drunkard **9.** alcoholic, inebriate
12. bacchanalian
tophet, topheth ... **4.** hell **5.** chaos
8. darkness
topi, topee ... **3.** cap, hat **8.** antelope
topiary ... **6.** garden **9.** gardening
topic ... **4.** plot, text **5.** theme **6.** reason,
remedy **7.** subject **8.** argument
11. application
topical ... **5.** local **9.** temporary
10. thematical
topknot ... **5.** crest, onkos **6.** pigeon
8. flounder **9.** headdress
topmost ... **6.** apical **7.** highest, supreme
8. foremost **9.** uppermost
topnotcher ... **3.** ace **4.** hero, star
6. tiptop **7.** supreme **9.** first-rate
11. unsurpassed
topography ... **7.** mapping **8.** location
9. surveying **11.** description **15.** regional
anatomy
topple ... **3.** tip **4.** fall, tilt **5.** pitch,
upset **6.** totter, tumble **8.** overturn
9. overthrow **10.** somersault
topsail ... **5.** raffe (raffee)
topsy-turvy ... **8.** confused **10.** contrarily,
disordered **11.** withershins
toque ... **3.** hat **6.** monkey (bonnet)
9. headdress
tor ... **4.** crag, peak **5.** mound **8.** pinnacle
torah, tora ... **3.** law **7.** precept **10.** Law
of Moses, Pentateuch, revelation
torch ... **4.** lamp **5.** blaze, flare, fusee
(fuzee), light **7.** lighter, lucigen
8. flambeau **10.** flashlight
torero ... **11.** bullfighter
torment ... **3.** rib, vex **4.** bait, pain, rack
5. agony, devil, harry, tease, worry
6. badger, harass, harrow, hector,
pester, plague, stir up **7.** afflict, anguish,
bedevil, torture **8.** distress, vexation
9. suffering, tantalize **10.** punishment

11. persecution

torn . . . 4. rent 5. riven, split 6. ripped
7. severed 8. tattered 9. alienated,
lacerated (see also *tear)*

tornado . . . 4. wind 7. cyclone, twister
8. blizzard, outburst 9. hurricane,
whirlwind, windstorm 12. thunderstorm

toro . . . 4. bull 7. cavalla, cowfish

torpedo . . . 3. ray 4. boat, mine 5. shoot
6. attack, gunman 7. explode 8. fire
upon, firework, numbfish 9. crampfish,
detonator, submarine

torpid . . . 4. dull, numb 5. inert 6. stupid
7. dormant 8. benumbed, inactive,
lifeless, listless, sluggish 9. apathetic,
lethargic

torpor . . . 4. coma 6. acedia, apathy,
stupor 7. languor 8. dormancy,
lethargy 9. inertness 10. inactivity
12. sluggishness 13. insensibility

torque . . . 5. chain 6. collar 7. torsion
8. necklace, ornament

torrefy . . . 5. parch, roast 6. scorch

torrent . . . 5. flood, spate 6. stream
7. current, roaring 8. downpour,
outburst

torrential . . . 12. overwhelming

torrid . . . 3. hot 4. arid 7. burning, parched
8. scorched, tropical 10. oppressive,
passionate

tortilla cooking dish . . . 5. comal

tortoise . . . 4. emyd, Emys 6. gopher,
turtle 7. hicatee 8. Chelonia, matamata
9. ellachick

tortuous . . . 6. spiral 7. devious, sinuous,
winding 8. twisting 10. circuitous,
roundabout 12. labyrinthine

torture . . . 4. flay, pain, rack 5. agony,
twist 6. impale, punish, wrench
7. crucify, distort, torment
10. punishment

tory, Tory . . . 6. bandit, outlaw, Papist
8. loyalist, marauder, partisan, Royalist
11. reactionary 12. Conservative

toss . . . 3. lob 4. cast, flip, hurl 5. bandy,
chuck, fling, flirt, heave, pitch, throw
6. billow, thrash 7. disturb 8. flounder,
scramble 9. commotion 10. excitement

toss (pert to) . . .
a coin . . 4. flip
and turn . . 6. thrash 8. flounder
9. vacillate
off . . 5. drink 6. tipple 9. dispose of,
improvise
out . . 5. eject 8. trick out
together . . 8. scramble

tosspot . . . 3. sot 5. drunk, toper 6. flagon
8. drunkard

tossup . . . 6. gamble 10. even chance
11. uncertainty

tota . . . 6. grivet, monkey

total . . . 3. add, all, sum, tot 5. gross,
utter, whole 6. amount, entire 7. perfect,
summary 8. absolute, complete, entirety
9. aggregate

totally . . . 5. quite 6. wholly 8. entirely
10. completely

totem . . . 4. pole, post 6. fetish, pillar,
symbol

totem pole . . . 3. xat

toto . . . 3. all 4. baby 5. totum

totter . . . 4. reel, rock, sway 5. pitch,
shake, waver 6. falter, seesaw 7. stagger
8. titubate 9. fluctuate, vacillate

toucan . . . 4. toco 7. aracari 8. hornbill
13. constellation (opp Southern Cross)

touch . . . 3. dab, tag, tap, tig 4. abut,
feel, meet 5. taste, trait 6. adjoin,
border 7. contact 9. acuteness

touch (pert to) . . .
acuteness of . . 8. oxyaphia
bound . . 4. abut
closely . . 7. impinge 8. osculate
examine . . 7. palpate
light, lightly . . 3. pat 5. brush 7. attinge,
lambent
off . . 4. fire 6. incite
ref to . . 7. tactile, tactual
stone . . 8. basanite 9. criterion 11. Lydian
stone
wood . . 4. punk 6. amadou, tinder

touching . . . 6. moving 7. contact, feeling,
tangent 8. pathetic 9. affecting, attingent
10. concerning 11. interesting

touchy . . . 4. sore 5. cross, testy 7. peevish
8. ticklish 9. irascible, irritable, sensitive
10. precarious 13. oversensitive

tough . . . 4. hard, wiry 5. hardy, rowdy,
stiff 6. robust, sinewy, strong 7. ruffian
8. adhesive, hardened, leathery,
stubborn 9. difficult, obstinate, resistant,
tenacious 10. unyielding

toupee . . . 3. wig 6. peruke 7. periwig
9. false hair

tour . . . 4. trip 5. shift 6. travel 7. circuit,
journey 9. barnstorm, excursion

tourmaline . . . 3. gem 6. schorl 9. rubellite
10. indicolite

tournament . . . 4. tilt 5. games, joust, trial
6. battle 7. contest, regatta, tourney
8. Olympics 9. encounter 11. Turnierfest

tourniquet . . . 6. binder, garrot
7. bandage

tousle, tousel . . . 4. pull, tear 6. rumple,
tussle 8. dishevel

tout . . . 3. spy 5. scout, watch 6. praise
7. canvass, lookout, tipster 8. give a
tip, informer, smuggler 9. predictor,
solicitor

tow . . . 3. tew, tug 4. drag, draw, haul,
pull, rope 5. chain 6. hawser 8. cordelle

toward . . . 2. ad, at, to 4. near 5. anent
6. facing 7. forward, towards, willing
8. imminent 9. compliant, headed for
11. approaching

toward (pert to) . . .
blood vessels . . 5. hemad (haemad)
center . . 5. entad 6. inward
direction . . 7. leeward, seaward
8. homeward, landward, windward
9. earthward 10. heavenward
exterior . . 5. ectad
front . . 8. anterior
left . . 3. haw 5. aport 9. sinistrad,
sinistral
mouth . . 4. orad
right . . 7. dextrad 9. dextrally
stern . . 3. aft 5. abaft 6. astern

towards . . . 7. ynesche

tower . . . 3. tor 4. boom, silo, soar
5. exalt, pylon, spire, stupa 6. belfry,
height, turret, uplift 7. bulwark, defense,

elevate, steeple, surpass 8. domineer,
fortress 9. campanile 10. stronghold,
watchtower
tower (pert to) . . .
astrology . . 7. mansion 14. planetary
house
bell . . 9. campanile
chess . . 6. castle
church . . 5. spire 6. belfry, cupola
glacial . . 5. serac
India . . 5. minar 7. sikhara
marker . . 5. pylon
of . . 4. Pisa 5. Babel, Minar 6. Eiffel,
Hunger, London 7. silence (dakhma)
10. Kutab Minar
Oriental . . 7. minaret
watch . . 7. mirador
towering . . . 4. high, huge, tall 5. great,
lofty 6. Alpine 7. eminent, soaring
11. overweening
towhee . . . 5. finch 7. bunting, chewink
town . . . 4. burg, deme 6. ciudad, hamlet,
Podunk, suburb 7. borough, commune,
village 8. boom town, township 9. ghost
town
townsman . . . 3. cit 7. citizen, oppidan
(Eton student) 8. resident 9. selectman
toxic . . . 7. noxious 8. poisoned,
venomous, virulent 9. poisonous
toxicology (science of) . . . 7. poisons
9. antidotes
toxology . . . 7. archery
toxophilite . . . 6. archer
toy . . . 3. pet, top 4. doll, hoop, play,
whim 5. dally, fancy, flirt 6. bauble,
gewgaw, hoople, rattle, trifle 7. cat's
paw, trinket 8. flirting 9. plaything
10. knickknack
trace . . . 4. clew (clue), copy, find, hint,
mark, nose, seek, sign 5. refer, shade,
tinge, track, trail 6. deduce, derive,
detect, follow, sketch 7. glimpse,
outline, thought, vestige 8. evidence,
traverse 9. delineate, footprint
11. investigate, small amount
trachea . . . 4. duct 8. windpipe
tracing . . . 4. copy 6. record 8. ergogram
10. cardiogram 12. reproduction
track . . . 3. rut, way 4. path, rail, slot,
spur, wake 5. route, spoor, trail,
tread 6. follow, pursue 7. nereite
(worm), vestige 8. traverse 9. footprint,
spectacle
tract . . . 4. area, plot, zone 5. essay,
range 6. estate, region 7. booklet,
country, expanse, leaflet, quarter,
stretch 8. brochure, district, pamphlet,
treatise 9. territory 10. exposition
11. subdivision 12. dissertation
tract (pert to) . . .
arid . . 4. dene 6. desert
boggy, swampy . . 6. morass
10. Everglades
grassland . . 7. prairie
lava . . 8. pedregal
treeless . . 5. llano 6. steppe 7. prairie
tractable . . . 4. easy 6. docile, gentle,
pliant 7. ductile 8. amenable, flexible
9. adaptable, compliant, malleable
10. governable 11. conformable
trade . . . 3. buy 4. deal, sell, swap,

wind 5. craft 6. barter, merger,
metier 7. bargain, calling, dealing,
pursuit, traffic 8. business, commerce,
exchange, practice, purchase, vocation
10. handicraft, occupation, profession
11. intercourse
trade-mark, trademark . . . 4. logo
5. brand, label 8. logotype
trader . . . 6. dealer, monger, sutler
8. merchant 9. tradesman
10. shopkeeper
trading association . . . 5. hanse (hansa)
trading station (Mil) . . . 2. PX 4. fort,
post
tradition . . . 4. lore, myth 5. usage
6. custom, legend 7. culture 8. folklore
10. convention (established)
12. superstition
traditional . . . 3. old 9. legendary
10. historical 12. conventional, long-
standing 15. long-established
traditional tale . . . 4. sage 6. legend
traduce . . . 4. slur 5. abuse, belie
6. debase, defame, malign, vilify
7. asperse, pervert, slander 8. disgrace
10. calumniate
traffic . . . 3. buy 4. sell 5. trade 6. barter,
simony (sacred) 8. business, carriage,
commerce, dealings 11. familiarity,
intercourse
tragedy . . . 6. misery 8. calamity, disaster
10. misfortune
tragic . . . 3. sad 4. dire 5. fatal 8. dramatic,
pathetic 10. calamitous, disastrous,
fatal event
tragopan . . . 8. pheasant
trail . . . 3. lag 4. drag, hunt, path, slot,
spur 5. blaze, piste, route, scent, spoor,
trace, track 6. camino, follow 7. draggle
8. be behind, footpath 9. lag behind
Trail (famed) . . . 6. Mormon, Oregon
7. Santa Fe, Spanish 8. Chisholm,
El Camino, Heritage 10. Lewis-Clark,
Wilderness 11. Appalachian 12. Natchez
Trace, Pacific Crest
trail (pert to) . . .
blazer . . 7. pioneer
deer . . 4. slot
mark a . . 5. blaze
marker . . 5. cairn
mountain . . 4. pass
Spanish . . 6. camino
Trail of Tears people . . . 8. Cherokee
train . . . 2. el 4. line, load, tail 5. breed,
chain, coach, drill, flier, focus, shape,
suite 6. direct, school, series 7. caravan,
cortege, educate, retinue 8. accustom,
instruct, railroad, rehearse 9. afterpart,
entourage, following 10. attendants,
conveyance, discipline, line of cars,
procession 11. progression, streamliner
13. accommodation
trained mechanic . . . 7. artisan
trainee . . . 6. rookie 7. recruit, student
8. enrollee
traipse . . . 3. gad 5. trail, tramp 6. trudge,
wander 8. gadabout
trait . . . 5. habit, touch 6. streak 7. feature,
quality 9. lineament, mannerism
11. peculiarity 13. individuality
14. characteristic

traitor . . . **3.** rat **8.** informer, Quisling, turncoat **10.** treasonist **13.** double-crosser, Judas Iscariot **14.** Benedict Arnold

traject . . . **3.** way **4.** sage **5.** ferry, route **6.** course **7.** passage **8.** crossing

trajectory . . . **5.** route **6.** rocket **9.** celestial **10.** fixed orbit

tram . . . **3.** car **4.** limb **5.** wagon **7.** carrier, railway, tramcar, trolley, vehicle **9.** streetcar **10.** conveyance

tramontane . . . **5.** alien **8.** polestar **9.** foreigner, North Star **11.** transalpine

tramp . . . **3.** bum **4.** hike, hobo, hoof, step, walk **5.** jaunt, nomad, tread **6.** beggar, trudge, wander **7.** sponger, traipse, trample, vagrant **8.** vagabond **9.** sundowner **10.** landlouper (landloper), pedestrian **11.** bindle stiff **12.** foot traveler

trample . . . **5.** crush, tread **6.** bruise, subdue **7.** conquer, destroy, run over **9.** press down

trance . . . **4.** coma, doze **5.** dream, spell, swoon **6.** raptus, stupor **7.** amentia, ecstasy, rapture **8.** hypnosis **9.** catalepsy, enrapture, hypnotize, spellbind

tranchant . . . **5.** sharp **7.** cutting **9.** trenchant

tranquil . . . **4.** calm, cool, easy, mild **5.** quiet, still **6.** gentle, placid, serene **7.** pacific, restful **8.** composed, peaceful **9.** quiescent **11.** undisturbed **13.** imperturbable

tranquility . . . **3.** keg **5.** peace, quiet **8.** calmness, serenity **9.** composure **10.** quiescence **12.** peacefulness

tranquilize . . . **4.** calm, lull **5.** allay, quiet, still **6.** pacify, settle, soothe **7.** appease, assuage, compose

transaction . . . **4.** deal, sale **6.** action, affair **7.** bargain **8.** business **9.** discharge, execution **10.** proceeding **11.** negotiation, performance, proposition **16.** buying and selling

transcend . . . **3.** cap **5.** excel, mount **6.** ascend, exceed **7.** surpass **8.** go beyond, outstrip, surmount

transcendent . . . **5.** above **8.** ethereal, heavenly, superior **9.** recondite **10.** superhuman, surpassing **12.** metaphysical, supernatural, transmundane **13.** extraordinary **14.** transcendental **15.** beyond knowledge

transcribe . . . **4.** copy **5.** write **6.** record **9.** reproduce, translate **10.** paraphrase

transcript . . . **4.** copy **6.** record **8.** apograph **9.** duplicate, imitation **12.** reproduction

transfer . . . **4.** cede, deed, pass, sale **5.** grant, shift **6.** assign, attorn, change, convey, depute, remove **7.** removal **8.** alienate, delivery **9.** transport **10.** conveyance, transcript

transfer (pert to) . . .
conveyance (estate) . . **5.** lease **6.** demise
crown to successor . . **6.** demise
design . . **5.** decal **12.** decalcomania
medical . . **10.** transplant

of ownership . . **6.** attorn **10.** abalienate, alienation, conveyance

of property . . **8.** disposal

transfigure . . . **5.** exalt **6.** change **7.** glorify **8.** idealize **9.** irradiate, transform, transmute **12.** metamorphose

transfix . . . **3.** pin **4.** hold **5.** spear **6.** fasten, impale, pierce **9.** hold fixed **11.** transpierce **14.** hold motionless

transform . . . **4.** turn **5.** alter **6.** change, revamp **7.** convert **9.** transmute **10.** assimilate **11.** transfigure **12.** metamorphose, transmogrify **16.** transubstantiate

transformation . . . **3.** wig **6.** change **8.** mutation **10.** conversion, false front **13.** metamorphosis, transmutation **17.** anthropomorphosis

transgress . . . **3.** err, sin **5.** cross **6.** exceed, offend, thwart **7.** disobey, infract, violate **8.** overstep, trespass **9.** break a law

transgression . . . **3.** sin **5.** crime, fault **7.** misdeed, offense **8.** trespass **9.** violation **10.** effrontery, infraction **11.** lawbreaking **12.** infringement **13.** nonconformity

transgressor . . . **6.** sinner **8.** offender **9.** wrongdoer **10.** delinquent, malefactor

transient . . . **5.** brief **6.** lodger **7.** flighty **8.** fleeting, fugitive, traveler **9.** ephemeral, migratory, momentary **10.** evanescent, short-lived, transitory

transit . . . **6.** travel **7.** passage **9.** metabasis **10.** conveyance **12.** transference

transition . . . **5.** shift **7.** passage **9.** anabolism, evolution, metabasis **10.** catabolism (katabolism), conversion, metabolism, modulation **11.** transfusion

transitory . . . **5.** brief, fleet **8.** fleeting, temporal **9.** ephemeral, temporary, transient **10.** evanescent **11.** not enduring

transitory things . . . **8.** ephemera

translate . . . **4.** read, rede **6.** decode, render **7.** convert **8.** construe, transfer **9.** interpret **10.** paraphrase

translation . . . **4.** pony, trot **7.** version **9.** rendition **10.** paraphrase **12.** transference **14.** interpretation **15.** transliteration

translucent . . . **6.** limpid **8.** luminous **11.** transparent **14.** shining through

transmit . . . **4.** send **6.** convey, render **7.** devolve, forward **8.** bequeath, hand down, transfer **11.** communicate

transmutation . . . **9.** evolution

transmute . . . **6.** change **7.** convert, resolve **9.** transform **11.** transfigure **12.** metamorphose **16.** transubstantiate

transparent . . . **4.** open **5.** clear, gauzy, lucid, sheer **6.** bright, candid, glassy, lucent **7.** crystal, pelucid, shining **8.** luminous, lustrous **9.** guileless **10.** diaphanous **11.** crystalline, perspicuous, translucent, unconcealed

transparent thing . . . **4.** mica, silk, veil **5.** beryl, water **6.** quartz, tissue **7.** crystal, diamond **8.** gossamer **9.** isinglass

transport ... **3.** dak **4.** boat, move, raft, send, ship **5.** bring, carry, truck **6.** banish, convey, deport, vessel **7.** ecstasy, freight, passion, rapture, smuggle **8.** carriage, emigrate, entrance, palander, transfer **9.** enrapture, troopship

transpose ... **5.** shift **6.** change, convey, invert **7.** convert, reverse **8.** transfer **9.** rearrange, translate, transmute **11.** interchange

transposition of sounds, words ... **10.** metathesis, spoonerism

Transvaal (pert to) ...
capital .. **8.** Pretoria
city .. **12.** Johannesburg
daisy .. **7.** gerbera
discovery .. **4.** gold, Rand (The)
famed emigration .. **9.** great trek (1836)
legislature .. **4.** raad
policeman .. **4.** zarp
settlers .. **5.** Boers
War .. **4.** Boer (1899-1902)

transverse ... **6.** across **7.** oblique, transom **8.** diagonal **9.** crosswise **10.** crosspiece

trap ... **3.** gin, net, pat, web **4.** cage, door, lure, rock, tipe, tree, weir **5.** catch, creel, mouth, snare **6.** ambush, corner, device, eelpot, enmesh, recess **7.** dragnet, ensnare, pitfall, springe **8.** carriage, deadfall, trapping, trickery **9.** caparison, road block, stratagem

trapper ... **5.** lurer **6.** hunter, netter, snarer **7.** decoyer

trappings ... **4.** gear, tack **5.** props **7.** scenery **8.** wardrobe **9.** apparatus, caparison, ornaments **10.** horse cloth **13.** paraphernalia

trash ... **4.** bosh, dirt, junk **5.** waste **6.** debris, refuse, rubble **7.** rubbish **8.** nonsense, riffraff, trumpery **10.** balderdash

trashy ... **5.** cheap, toshy **6.** paltry **7.** useless **8.** rubbishy **9.** worthless **11.** nonsensical

trauma ... **5.** shock, wound **6.** injury

travail ... **4.** pain, toil **5.** agony, labor **7.** journey, trouble **9.** suffering **11.** parturition

trave ... **9.** crossbeam

travel ... **2.** go **4.** fare, move, mush, post, ride, taxi, tour, trek, wend **5.** coast **6.** motion **7.** commute, journey, migrate, sojourn **8.** progress, traverse **9.** gallivant **11.** peregrinate

travel (pert to) ...
equipment .. **7.** baggage **9.** viaticals
expense .. **8.** viaticum
group .. **7.** caravan
over obstacles .. **9.** roughshod
pert to .. **6.** viatic
place to place .. **9.** itinerate

traveler, travelers ... **5.** farer **6.** viator **7.** caravan, tourist **8.** salesman, wayfarer **9.** journeyer

travels ... **7.** odyssey **8.** journeys **14.** peregrinations

traverse ... **4.** deny, pass **5.** cross **6.** refute, thwart **7.** athwart, oblique, parados **8.** navigate **10.** counteract

travesty ... **5.** drama **6.** parody, satire **7.** lampoon **8.** disguise **9.** burlesque **10.** caricature **11.** incongruity

tray ... **6.** salver, server **7.** ashtray, coaster

treacherous ... **5.** false, Judas, punic, snaky **8.** disloyal, plotting, unstable **9.** deceitful, faithless, insidious **10.** perfidious, traitorous, unreliable **11.** disaffected **13.** Machiavellian (Machiavelian), untrustworthy

treachery ... **5.** guile **6.** deceit **7.** perfidy, treason **8.** betrayal **10.** disloyalty

treacle ... **4.** cure **6.** remedy **7.** claggum, sweeten **8.** molasses **10.** sweetening

treacle water ... **7.** cordial

tread ... **3.** rut **4.** gait, mark, pace, step, volt, walk **5.** crush, stair **6.** course **7.** conquer, set foot, trample **8.** footstep, shoe sole **9.** footprint

treadle ... **5.** lever, pedal **7.** chalaza

tread underfoot ... **5.** crush **6.** subdue **7.** oppress, run over **8.** domineer **9.** tyrannize

treason ... **7.** perfidy **8.** betrayal, sedition **9.** treachery

treasonable, treasonous ... **10.** perfidious, traitorous **11.** treacherous

treasure ... **4.** fisc (fisk), fund, roon **5.** cache, chest, hoard, prize, purse, store, trove, value **6.** coffer, fiscus, riches, wealth **7.** cherish **8.** hold dear **9.** exchequer, thesaurus **10.** appreciate, depository, repository, storehouse

treasurer ... **6.** bursar, purser **7.** cashier, curator, officer **8.** receiver **9.** paymaster **11.** chamberlain

Treasure State ... **7.** Montana

treasure-trove ... **5.** money (hidden) **7.** bullion **9.** discovery **14.** buried treasure

treat ... **4.** dose **5.** Dutch, feast **6.** doctor, handle, regale, repast **7.** delight, discuss, process **8.** consider **9.** discourse, entertain, negotiate **10.** manipulate

treat (pert to) ...
improperly .. **4.** snub **5.** flout, spite **6.** insult, misuse, offend **9.** humiliate
maliciously .. **5.** frame, spite
of morals .. **6.** ethics
royally .. **6.** regale **9.** with honor
silk (for rustle) .. **6.** scroop
snobbishly .. **7.** high hat, high-hat
surgically .. **7.** operate
tenderly .. **6.** coddle, pamper
with contempt .. **5.** flout, scorn, scout, spurn **7.** contemn
with deference .. **7.** respect

treatise ... **5.** essay, study, tract **6.** thesis **7.** article **9.** discourse **10.** discussion **12.** dissertation

treatise on ...
forests .. **5.** silva
fruit trees .. **6.** pomona
language .. **7.** grammar
pines .. **7.** pinetum

treatment (pert to) ...
application (Med) .. **5.** stupe
compassionate .. **5.** mercy
harsh .. **5.** abuse **8.** misusage, severity

ill . . **5.** abuse

preparatory . . **8.** training **10.** ground work, processing

term . . **5.** usage **8.** addition (to soil), handling

treaty . . . **4.** mise, pact **6.** cartel **7.** compact, entente **8.** contract **9.** agreement **10.** convention **11.** arrangement, negotiation **12.** capitulation **13.** understanding

treaty (pert to) . . .

bound nations . . **6.** allies

Elm . . **12.** Philadelphia (1682)

first draft . . **8.** protocol

peace . . **5.** truce **6.** Pax Dei **9.** armistice **10.** pax in bella

secret . . **13.** the Engagement (1647)

treble . . . **5.** three, voice **6.** latten, triple **7.** soprano **9.** threefold **11.** high-pitched

treble clef . . . **3.** Gee **5.** G clef, staff (G clef)

tree . . . **5.** plant **6.** corner, timber **7.** gallows **9.** genealogy

tree (pert to) . . . see also *trees*

antidote for snakebite . . **6.** cedron

aromatic . . **9.** sassafras

bear . . **7.** raccoon

cactus . . **7.** saguaro

camphor . . **5.** kapur

cat . . **9.** palm civet

cobra . . **6.** mambra

cone-bearing . . **3.** fir, yew **5.** alder, cedar, larch **7.** conifer

dwarf . . **6.** bonsai

evergreen fruit . . **5.** lemon **6.** orange

exudation . . **3.** gum, lac, sap

India . . **4.** dita **10.** devil's tree

lotus . . **4.** sadr

mineral (formed on) . . **8.** dendrite

of Buddha . . **2.** bo

of chastity . . **11.** agnus castus

of life . . **10.** arbor vitae

of strength . . **3.** oak

rain . . **5.** saman (zaman) **8.** genisaro

resin . . **3.** fir **4.** pine **6.** balsam

sacred (Bib) . . **7.** asherah

salt . . **4.** atle (atlee) **8.** tamarisk

snake . . **4.** gimp, lora

sprout . . **5.** copse, sprig **7.** coppice

sugar . . **5.** maple

Texas . . **5.** alamo **6.** poplar

tiger . . **7.** leopard

toad . . **4.** hyla

trunk . . **4.** bole **5.** caber, stock

umbrella . . **5.** wahoo

victor's crown . . **6.** laurel

worshiper . . **5.** dryad, nymph (wood)

trees (pert to) . . .

grove . . **5.** copse

plantation . . **6.** forest **7.** orchard, pinetum

poem . . **6.** Kilmer (Joyce)

ref to . . **8.** arboreal **9.** cacuminal

science . . **7.** silvics **12.** silviculture

service (rowan) . . **5.** sorbs

trefoil . . . **6.** clover **8.** shamrock **10.** black medic, clover leaf (Her)

tregetour (anc) . . . **7.** juggler **8.** magician

trek . . . **6.** travel **7.** journey, migrate **10.** expedition

trellis . . . **5.** arbor **7.** lattice, pergola **8.** espalier **11.** latticework

tremble . . . **5.** quake, shake **6.** doddle, falter, quaver, quiver, shiver, tatter, thrill, tremor **7.** shudder, tremolo, twitter, vibrate **8.** be afraid **9.** be excited, trepidate

trembling . . . **5.** aspen **6.** dither, trepid **7.** fearful, nervous, quaking, quavery, shaking **9.** vibrating

tremendous . . . **3.** big **4.** huge **5.** awful, giant, great **6.** superb **8.** horrible, powerful, terrific **9.** frightful, momentous, monstrous **10.** terrifying **13.** extraordinary

tremolo . . . **6.** quaver **10.** fluttering

tremor . . . **5.** palsy, quake, shake **6.** quiver, thrill **7.** tremble **9.** vibration

tremulous . . . **5.** aspen, quaky, timid **7.** excited, fearful, nervous, palsied, shaking, shivery **9.** quavering, sensitive, trembling, vibratory **11.** palpitating

trench . . . **3.** gaw **4.** bury, gash, leat, moat **5.** canal, carve, ditch, drain, fosse **6.** furrow, groove, gutter **7.** acequia, intrude **8.** aqueduct, encroach, entrench, infringe, trespass **10.** excavation **12.** entrenchment

trenchant . . . **4.** keen **5.** acute, sharp **6.** biting **7.** cutting **8.** clear-cut, incisive **11.** penetrating

trencherman . . . **5.** eater **7.** sponger **8.** gourmand **9.** chowhound **11.** gormandizer

trend . . . **4.** tone, turn, vein **5.** drift, skirt, swing, tenor **6.** strike **7.** deviate, revolve **8.** movement, tendency **9.** direction **11.** inclination

trepan . . . **3.** saw **4.** lure, tool **5.** snare, trick **6.** entrap **7.** deceive, swindle **8.** deceiver, trephine **9.** stratagem, trickster

trepang . . . **10.** bêche-de-mer **11.** sea cucumber **14.** sea caterpillar

trepid . . . **7.** quaking **8.** timorous **9.** trembling

trepidation . . . **4.** fear **5.** alarm **6.** dismay **7.** quaking **9.** agitation, confusion **10.** excitement **11.** disturbance, oscillation **12.** perturbation **13.** consternation

trespass . . . **3.** sin **4.** tort **5.** poach **6.** breach, invade, trench **7.** intrude, offense **8.** encroach, entrench, infringe, overstep **10.** infraction, transgress **11.** misfeasance **12.** infringement **13.** transgression

tress . . . **4.** curl, hair **5.** braid, plait **7.** ringlet **10.** lock of hair

tressure . . . **4.** band **6.** border, fillet, ribbon **9.** headdress

trestle . . . **5.** bench **7.** support, viaduct

tret . . . **9.** allowance

triad . . . **5.** chord, three, trine **7.** trinary, trinity **9.** trivalent **12.** ternary group

trial . . . **2.** go **4.** bout, case, test **5.** venue **6.** assize, ordeal **7.** attempt, contest, empiric **8.** evidence, hardship **9.** prolusion, trying out **10.** experiment **11.** examination, tribulation

triangle . . . **6.** trigon **8.** virginal **13.** constellation

triangle (pert to) . . .

connection . . **5.** delta
draw circle within . . **7.** escribe
military . . **10.** punishment
music instrument . . **10.** percussion,
  triquetrum (anc)
side . . **3.** leg
three acute angles . . **6.** oxygon
two equal sides . . **9.** isosceles
unequal sides . . **7.** scalene
triangular (pert to) . . .
  decoration . . **8.** pediment, triqueta
  muscle . . **7.** deltoid
  pert to . . **10.** trilateral
  piece . . **4.** gore **5.** miter, wedge **6.** gusset
  sail . . **6.** lateen **9.** spinnaker
  shaped . . **7.** deltoid **8.** oxygonal
tribal custom . . . **7.** couvade (childbirth)
tribal symbol . . . **5.** totem **9.** totem pole
tribe . . . **4.** clan, kind, race, sept
  5. class, group **6.** family **7.** company
  11. aggregation **14.** classification
tribe (pert to) . . .
  birds . . **5.** flock
  head of . . **5.** chief **6.** sachem **9.** patriarch
  Israel . . **3.** Dan **4.** Levi **6.** Reuben
  migrated . . **5.** Aryan
  New Zealand . . **3.** ati
  of Ben . . **5.** poets (Ben Jonson)
Tribes, Five Civilized . . . **5.** Creek
  7. Choctaw **8.** Cherokee, Seminole
  9. Chickasaw
Tribes, Five Nations (Iroquois) . . .
  6. Cayuga, Mohawk, Oneida, Seneca
  8. Onondaga
tribulation . . . **5.** trial **6.** ordeal, sorrow
  8. distress **9.** suffering
tribunal . . . **3.** bar **4.** banc, seat **5.** bench,
  court, curia, forum **8.** Areopagus (anc)
tributary . . . **4.** fork, vein **6.** branch, feeder
  8. affluent, effluent, influent **9.** auxiliary
  11. subordinate **12.** contributary
tribute . . . **3.** fee, pay, tax **4.** cain, duty,
  levy, scat **5.** allow, grant **6.** assign,
  bestow, homage, impost, praise,
  rental **7.** chevage (Hist), ovation,
  payment, pension, respect **8.** encomium
  9. attribute, gratitude **10.** allegiance,
  contribute, obligation **11.** retribution
tricar . . . **8.** tricycle **10.** motorcycle (with
  extra car)
trice . . . **5.** jiffy **6.** moment **7.** instant
  9. twinkling
trick . . . **3.** fob, gag **4.** dido, dupe, feat,
  flam, gull, jest, ruse, wile **5.** cheat,
  child, dodge, fraud, guile, knack, prank,
  shift, stunt **6.** deceit, delude **7.** deceive,
  defraud, finesse, pretext **8.** artifice,
  delusion, flimflam, illusion **9.** chicanery,
  deception, imposture **10.** subterfuge
  11. contrivance, legerdemain
trickery . . . **5.** fraud, hocus **6.** deceit
  7. roguery **8.** artifice, cheating, trumpery
  9. chicanery, deception, duplicity
  10. hanky-panky **11.** amenability,
  legerdemain
trickle . . . **4.** drip, drop, flow, leak **7.** distill
  (distil), dribble, dripple, leakage
tricks . . . **4.** shab **5.** ruses **7.** roguery
  10. deceptions
trickster . . . **3.** fox **5.** cheat, rogue **6.** rascal
  7. slicker **8.** deceiver **12.** Artful Dodger

tricky . . . **3.** sly **5.** snide **6.** artful, clever,
  crafty, shrewd **7.** cunning, devious
  8. rascally **9.** deceitful **13.** Machiavellian
trident . . . **5.** curve, spear **6.** symbol
  7. leister
tried . . . **4.** true **6.** proved, tested
  7. devoted **8.** faithful, reliable
  11. trustworthy
tries . . . **5.** tests **6.** assays **8.** attempts,
  contests
trifle . . . **3.** ace, bit, fig, toy **4.** doit,
  fico, fool, jest **5.** dally, fable, straw
  6. bauble, dabble, dawdle, doodle,
  fiddle, gewgaw, palter, pewter, potter,
  wanton **7.** dessert, nothing, traneen
  8. flimflam, gimcrack, make love
  9. bagatelle **10.** knickknack, peccadillo,
  triviality **11.** small amount **12.** treat
  lightly
trifler . . . **7.** dallier, flaneur **8.** palterer,
  putterer **10.** dilettante
trifles . . . **4.** toys **6.** trivia **7.** gewgaws,
  palters **8.** minutiae, trumpery
trifling . . . **4.** idle, mere **5.** inane,
  petty **6.** little **7.** trivial **8.** badinage,
  frippery **9.** nugacious **10.** immaterial
  13. insignificant
trifolium . . . **6.** clover **8.** shamrock
trig . . . **4.** chic, neat, prim, tidy, trim
  5. natty, smart **6.** lively, spruce
  7. precise **10.** methodical
trigo . . . **5.** wheat
trigon . . . **4.** game, harp, lyre (anc)
  8. triangle
trigonometry term . . . **4.** sine **6.** cosine,
  secant **7.** tangent **8.** spherics
  10. goniometry
trihoral . . . **11.** three-hourly **15.** every
  three hours
trill . . . **4.** move, sing **5.** shake, twirl
  6. quaver, ripple, warble **7.** mordent,
  tremolo, trickle, vibrate **8.** grupetto
  12. pralltriller
trillion . . . **5.** trega (comb form) **14.** million
  million
trim . . . **3.** bob, cut, lop **4.** chic,
  clip, crop, neat, perk, snod, tidy,
  trig, whip **5.** adorn, natty, nifty,
  panel, preen, prune, shear, shrag
  6. border, dapper, defeat, punish,
  reduce **7.** compact, orderly **8.** decorate,
  ornament **9.** embellish, shipshape
  10. decoration
trimming . . . **4.** gimp, lace **5.** braid,
  jabot, ruche **6.** edging, frieze, fringe,
  piping **7.** falbala, ruching **8.** furbelow,
  ornament **9.** chicanery, garniture
  10. decoration **11.** accessories
  13. passementerie
trinity . . . **5.** three, triad **6.** triune
Trinity (Eccl) . . . **7.** Godhead (Father,
  Son, Holy Ghost) **8.** Trimurti
trinket . . . **3.** toy **4.** gaud, tali (tahli)
  5. bijou, jewel **6.** bangle, gewgaw,
  trifle **7.** bibelot **8.** gimcrack, ornament
  10. knickknack
trip . . . **3.** err, run **4.** halt, skip, slip,
  trap **5.** caper, dance, jaunt, speed
  6. bungle, cruise, errand, flight, frolic,
  voyage **7.** journey, misstep, stumble
  8. obstruct **9.** excursion **10.** expedition

triple ... **3.** tri **5.** trine **6.** tercet, treble **9.** intensify, threefold **12.** three-base hit
triple crown ... **5.** tiara (Pope's)
triplet (one of) ... **4.** trin
tripletail ... **4.** fish, sama **9.** berrugate, spadefish
tripod ... **3.** cat (6-legged) **5.** easel, stand, three **6.** trivet
Tripoli, Libya ...
  capital of .. **12.** Tripolitania
  caravan route to .. **5.** Wadai **8.** Lake Chad, Timbuktu
  famed arch to .. **14.** Marcus Aurelius
  people .. **4.** Arab, Turk **6.** Berber
  ruler .. **3.** bey, dey
triptych ... **5.** volet (part) **10.** altarpiece, writing pad **13.** writing tablet (3-part)
trismus ... **7.** lockjaw, tetanus **16.** gnashing the teeth
trist ... see *tryst*
Tristan and Isoide ... **5.** opera (Wagner)
triste ... **3.** sad **4.** full **6.** dismal **10.** depressing
tristful ... **3.** sad **10.** melancholy
tristich group ... **10.** three lines **11.** three verses (stanza)
Tristram & Iseult ... **4.** poem (Arnold)
trite ... **5.** banal, corny, petty, stale, vapid **6.** betide, cliché, common, jejune **7.** bromide **9.** hackneyed, well-known **10.** threadbare, unoriginal **11.** commonplace, stereotyped **13.** platitudinous
triton ... **3.** eft **4.** newt **5.** shell, snail **10.** salamander
Triton (pert to) ...
  art figure .. **7.** demigod
  Gr Myth .. **10.** sea demigod
  symbol .. **7.** trumpet
triumph ... **3.** win **5.** exult, glory **6.** defeat **8.** ceremony (anc), conquest **10.** exultation **11.** achievement
trivia ... **5.** trash **7.** trifles **8.** trumpery
trivial ... **5.** banal, petty, small, trite **6.** common, paltry, slight **7.** nominal, piperly, shallow **8.** doggerel, ordinary, trifling **9.** frivolous, nugacious **11.** commonplace, unimportant **13.** insignificant
triviality ... **3.** toy **6.** bauble, gewgaw, trifle **8.** falderal, nugacity **9.** bagatelle, frivolity **10.** knickknack **14.** insignificance
troche ... **4.** pill **6.** button, rotula, tablet **7.** lozenge **8.** pastille (pastil) **9.** cough drop **10.** deer's tines
trochee ... **4.** foot (2-syllable) **5.** meter **7.** choreus
trod ... see *tread*
trogger ... **7.** peddler, vagrant
trogon ... **7.** quetzal
Troilus (pert to) ...
  butterfly genus .. **7.** Papilio
  legendary hero of .. **7.** Chaucer
  son of .. **5.** Priam
Trojan (pert to) ...
  astronomy .. **9.** asteroids
  epic .. **5.** Iliad **8.** Aeneid **7.** Odyssey
  expedition hero .. **4.** Ajax **8.** Achilles
  founder of .. **4.** Troy
  hero .. **5.** Paris **6.** Aeneas, Hector

  9. Palamedes
  horse .. **6.** wooden
  horse builder .. **5.** Epeus
  king .. **5.** Priam
  native .. **6.** Dardan
  soothsayer .. **7.** Helenus
  war cause .. **5.** Helen (of Troy)
  war leader .. **9.** Agamemnon
  warrior .. **6.** Agenor
troll (Myth) ... **5.** dwarf, giant, gnome
troll ... **4.** bowl, fish, roll, sing **5.** angle (fishing), rondo **6.** allure, entice, propel **7.** revolve, trundle **9.** circulate
trolley ... **4.** cart, tram **5.** truck **6.** barrow, sledge **7.** tramcar **8.** handcart **9.** streetcar
trolley, off his ... **4.** nuts **5.** balmy, batty, daffy, dippy, dotty, goofy **6.** cuckoo
trollop ... **5.** slump **6.** slouch **8.** slattern
trombone (pert to) ...
  ancient .. **7.** sackbut, sambuke
  instrument .. **5.** brass
  mouthpiece .. **5.** bocal
  popular size .. **5.** tenor
troop ... **4.** army, band, unit **5.** crowd **7.** company, march on, ressala **8.** quantity, soldiers **9.** go forward **10.** armed force
troop (pert to) ...
  arrangement .. **7.** echelon
  encampment .. **5.** étape
  formation .. **4.** line
  one of .. **7.** peltast **8.** chasseur
  ship .. **9.** transport
troops (pert to) ...
  assemble .. **6.** muster
  German .. **6.** Panzer
  hidden .. **6.** ambush
  Hungary .. **7.** Hussars
  mounted .. **7.** cavalry
  sally .. **6.** sortie
  term for .. **4.** army **5.** squad **6.** forces **7.** battery, militia, phalanx **9.** commandos **11.** armed forces
trophy ... **3.** cup **4.** palm **5.** award, medal, Oscar, prize **6.** reward **7.** laurels, memento **8.** memorial
tropical (pert to) ...
  animal .. **4.** eyra **5.** araba, coati, potto **6.** agouti **7.** peccary
  bird .. **3.** ani **4.** tody **5.** jalap **6.** motmot **7.** jacamar
  dolphin .. **4.** inia
  fish .. **4.** toro **5.** remora, salema
  fruit .. **3.** fig **4.** date **5.** guava, mango, papaw **6.** banana, papaya
  lizard .. **5.** agama
  rodent .. **6.** agouti
  tree .. **4.** coco, palm **5.** balsa, seron **6.** sapota **8.** tamarind
  vine .. **7.** cowhage, lantana **14.** trumpet creeper
trot ... **3.** jog, run **4.** gait, pony **5.** hurry **7.** routine **11.** translation
trotting horse ... **6.** Morgan **7.** Hackney **12.** Hambletonian
trottoir (rare) ... **8.** footpath, pavement, sidewalk
troubadour ... **4.** bard, poet **8.** jongleur, minstrel, musician **9.** trovatore
trouble ... **3.** ado, ail, irk **4.** fuss, harm,

stir **5.** annoy, grief, worry **6.** bother,
effort, grieve, harass, pester, plague,
sorrow **7.** agitate, anxiety, concern,
disturb, perturb, torment **8.** calamity,
disorder, disquiet, distress, mischief
9. adversity, annoyance, commotion
10. affliction, difficulty, misfortune
11. disturbance **13.** inconvenience,
interfere with
troubled . . . **6.** queasy **7.** annoyed,
anxious **8.** agitated **9.** disturbed
10. distressed
troublemaker . . . **8.** agitator, gossiper
13. mischief-maker
troublesome . . . **5.** pesky **8.** annoying,
perverse **9.** difficult, laborious,
turbulent, vexatious, wearisome
10. bothersome, burdensome,
disturbing, oppressing **11.** distressing
12. inconvenient
trough . . . **3.** bin **4.** bosh, bowl, dale,
tank **5.** basin, chute, drain, toper
6. coffin, gutter, manger, sluice, trench
7. channel, conduit
trounce . . . **4.** beat, flog **5.** scald **6.** indict,
punish, thrash **7.** censure, journey
trout . . . **4.** char, peal **7.** oquassa
9. namaycush **11.** Dolly Varden
trout (pert to) . . .
genus . . **5.** Salmo **6.** Trutta
lake . . **9.** namaycush
Maine . . **7.** oquassa
parasite (external) . . **3.** sug
ref to . . **11.** truttaceous
type . . **3.** sea **4.** rock **5.** brook, brown,
river **7.** oquassa, rainbow **8.** speckled
9. cutthroat
trovatore . . . **10.** troubadour
trove . . . **4.** find **8.** treasure (buried)
9. discovery **10.** thing found
13. treasure-trove
trow . . . **4.** boat, hope **5.** barge, think,
trust **6.** expect **7.** believe, suppose
9. catamaran
trowing . . . **5.** creed **6.** belief **7.** opinion
Troy, or Ilium . . .
capital of . . **5.** Troad (anc)
defender . . **6.** Aeneas
famed for . . **5.** ruins
founder (Myth) . . **4.** Ilus (son of Tros),
Tros
king . . **5.** Priam **9.** Agamemnon
king's wife . . **5.** Helen
mountain . . **3.** Ida
name, present . . **9.** Hissarlik
pert to . . **5.** Iliac **6.** Trojan
site . . **9.** Asia Minor
troy weight . . . **5.** grain, ounce, pound
11. pennyweight
truant . . . **4.** idle **7.** shirker, trivant, vagrant
8. absentee
truant, to play . . . **5.** miche
truce . . . **5.** pause, peace, trêve
9. armistice, cessation **10.** brief quiet
12. intermission
truck . . . **3.** van **4.** deal, dray, haul
5. bogie, dance, lorry, trade **6.** barter,
peddle **7.** flatcar, traffic **8.** commerce,
exchange, nonsense **9.** groceries
truckle . . . **4.** fawn **5.** toady **6.** cringe,
submit **7.** knuckle

truculent . . . **4.** base, mean **5.** cruel
6. fierce, savage **8.** ruthless, scathing
9. barbarous, ferocious **11.** destructive
trudge . . . **4.** pace, plod, slog, walk
5. tramp **6.** go slow **7.** traipse
true . . . **2.** so **4.** fact, leal, pure, real
6. gospel, honest, lawful **7.** certain,
devoted, germane, precise, sincere,
upright **8.** faithful, orthodox, reliable,
straight, unerring **9.** authentic,
steadfast, veracious, veritable
10. legitimate **11.** trustworthy,
unfaltering
true (pert to) . . .
blue . . **5.** loyal **8.** faithful, orthodox
10. man of honor
copy . . **7.** estreat
not . . **5.** false **10.** figurative
poetic . . **4.** leal
skin . . **4.** derm (suff) **5.** derma
to fact . . **7.** literal
to life . . **8.** lifelike **11.** descriptive
truffle . . . **5.** fungi, tuber **8.** earthnut
10. ascus fruit
truism . . . **5.** axiom, truth **9.** platitude
11. commonplace
trull . . . **4.** girl, lass **5.** demon, fiend,
giant, wench **7.** trollop **8.** strumpet
truly . . . **3.** yea **4.** amen **5.** sooth
6. indeed, justly, verily **7.** exactly, rightly
8. properly **9.** certai y **10.** accurately,
positively, truthfully
trump . . . **3.** pam **4.** card, ruff (cards),
suit **7.** surpass **10.** good fellow
12. masterstroke
trumpery . . . **5.** fraud, trash **6.** deceit
7. rubbish **8.** nor ense
trumpet . . . **4.** horn o. blare **6.** summon
7. clarion **8.** proclaim **9.** organ stop
12. elephant's cry **14.** wind instrument
trumpet (pert to) . . .
blare . . **7.** fanfare, tantara
call (stage) . . **6.** sennet
creeper . . **6.** tecoma
fish . . **7.** bellows **10.** flutemouth
lily . . **5.** calla **7.** Bermuda
trumpeter . . . **4.** bird, fish, swan **5.** agami,
perch **6.** pigeon **7.** whiting **8.** musician
9. messenger
truncheon . . . **4.** club **5.** baton, staff
6. cudgel **8.** splinter
trunk . . . **3.** box, log **4.** body, bole, pool,
soma, tank **5.** chest, stalk, torso **6.** coffer
7. railway **8.** main stem **9.** proboscis
10. lobster pot
trunkfish . . . **4.** toro **7.** cowfish
truss . . . **3.** tie **4.** bind, gird, pack **6.** bundle,
fasten **7.** support **10.** strengthen
trust . . . **4.** hope, rely, task **5.** faith **6.** belief,
commit, credit, dartle, depend, estate
7. believe, confide, consign, custody,
entrust, loyalty **8.** credence, reliance,
security **9.** assurance, syndicate
10. confidence, dependence, give credit,
investment **12.** organization
trustee . . . **6.** bailee **7.** sindico **9.** fiduciary,
treasurer **10.** depository
13. administrator
trustful . . . **5.** liege **7.** reliant **8.** trusting
9. confiding, credulous
13. unquestioning

trustworthiness . . . 9. axiopisty
12. trustability 13. dependability
trustworthy . . . 4. safe 5. solid 6. honest
7. certain 8. reliable 9. authentic
10. dependable
trusty . . . 7. convict 8. faithful, prisoner
10. dependable 11. trustworthy
truth . . . 3. tao 4. fact, real 5. sooth (anc)
6. verity 7. honesty, reality 8. fidelity,
veracity 9. constancy, exactness,
orthodoxy, sincerity 11. correctness
14. verisimilitude
truth (pert to) . . .
ancient term . . 5. sooth 6. certes
Chinese Philos . . 3. tao
goddess . . 4. Maat
personified . . 3. Una 4. Maat
ref to . . 6. verily 11. verisimilar
14. verisimilitude
self-evident . . 5. axiom 6. truism
truthful . . . 6. honest 7. veridic
9. veracious, veridical
truthfulness . . . 5. truth 7. honesty
8. accuracy, veracity 13. veraciousness
try . . . 2. do 3. say 4. test 5. annoy,
assay, ettle, prove, taste, trial 6. purify,
refine, render, sample, strive 7. attempt,
contest, torment 8. audition, endeavor,
irritate 9. prosecute, undertake
10. experiment 11. demonstrate,
investigate
trying . . . 7. irksome, painful, tasting
8. annoying, sampling 10. attempting
12. exasperating 13. experimenting
tryst . . . 6. invite, market 7. beguile,
meeting 9. agreement, betrothal
10. engagement, rendezvous
11. appointment 12. meeting place
tsamba . . . 5. flour 6. barley
tsar . . . 4. czar, tzar 6. despot 8. autocrat
tsetse, tsetse fly . . . 4. kivu 8. Glossina,
parasite
tsetse fly disease . . . 6. nagana
16. sleeping sickness
T-shaped . . . 3. tau
tsine . . . 6. wild ox 7. banteng
tsunami . . . 4. wave (tidal)
tuatara, tuatera . . . 7. reptile (iguanalike)
tub . . . 3. hod, keg, kid, soe, tun, vat
4. cask, ship, wash 5. barge, bathe,
bowie, keeve 6. barrel, firkin, piggin,
vessel 7. bathtub, cistern, washtub
9. container, fat person
tuba . . . 6. liquor (palm) 7. helicon,
trumpet (anc) 9. bombardon
10. contrabass 11. bass saxhorn
12. mythical tree
Tubal-cain's father . . . 6. Lamech
Tubal's father . . . 7. Japheth
tube . . . 3. cop 4. bulb, duct, hose, pipe
5. auget, chute, diode 6. siphon, tunnel
7. burette, cannula, conduit, fistula,
matrass, railway, salpinx 8. cylinder,
electron, stenosis 9. spaghetti,
telescope
tuber . . . 3. oca, yam 4. beet, bulb, eddo,
root, taro 5. jalap, salep 6. potato
12. protuberance
tubular . . . 4. pipy 5. round 6. tubate
8. cannular, fistular, tubiform
11. cylindrical

tuck . . . 3. eat, nip 4. cram, fold, poke
5. feast, pinch, pleat, press 7. shorten,
tighten 9. appendage
tucker . . . 3. bib 4. food, meal 5. board
6. ration
Tuesday (pert to) . . .
French . . 5. Mardi
Norse god . . 3. Tyr (Tiu)
Shrove . . 9. Mardi gras
Teutonic . . 10. Martis dies
tufa . . . 4. rock, toph, tuff 5. trass
tuft . . . 4. coma, doss, hair 5. beard,
bunch, clump, crest 6. button, goatee,
pompon, tassel 7. cluster, fetlock
8. aigrette, feathers
tug . . . 3. tow 4. drag, draw, haul, pull,
toil 5. labor 6. drudge, effort, strain,
tussle 7. contend, contest, wrestle
8. struggle
tulip (pert to) . . .
center (World) . . 7. Holland
color . . 6. auburn 9. tulipwood
genus . . 6. Tulipa
Mexican . . 6. orchid
military slang . . 9. explosive
tree . . 6. timber 7. majagua, waratah
type . . 6. Darwin, parrot 7. breeder,
cottage
tumble . . . 4. fall, flop, trip, veer 5. pitch,
spill 6. jumble, rumple, topple, tousle,
wallow 7. stumble 8. collapse, disorder,
flounder, roll over 9. break down,
confusing 10. handspring, somersault
11. precipitate
tumbler . . . 3. dog 4. cart, drum 5. glass
6. Dunker, pigeon, vessel 7. acrobat,
gymnast, tippler, tumbrel 8. lock part
13. contortionist
tumbleweed . . . 6. indigo 7. bugseed,
pigweed, thistle 10. amaranthus
tumbrel, tumbril . . . 4. cart 5. wagon
8. dumpcart 12. cucking stool (Hist)
tumescent, tumid . . . 6. turgid 7. bloated,
bulging, pompous 8. inflated
9. bombastic, disturbed, plethoric
11. protuberant
tumor . . . 3. wen 4. cyst, wart 6. cancer,
goiter, growth, lipoma, struma
7. adenoma, sarcoma 8. ganglion,
swelling 11. excrescence
12. protuberance
tumor, eyelid . . . 9. pladaroma
tumult . . . 3. din, mob 4. fray, riot 5. Babel,
brawl, noise 6. affray, babble, bustle,
émeute, hubbub, uproar 7. bluster,
ferment, turmoil 8. disorder, outbreak,
uprising 9. agitation, commotion,
confusion 10. excitement, turbulence
11. disturbance
tumultuous . . . 4. wild 5. noisy, rough
7. lawless, riotous, violent 8. agitated,
confused 9. disturbed, turbulent
10. boisterous, disorderly, hurly-burly
tumulus . . . 5. mound, stump 6. barrow
7. hillock
tun . . . 3. cup (anc), jar, tub, vat 4. cask,
year (Mayan, 360-day) 5. drink 6. guzzle,
vessel 7. measure
tuna . . . 5. tunny 8. albacore
tune . . . 3. air, key 4. aria, lilt, port, song
5. pitch 6. adjust, melody 7. chorale,

harmony, sonance **9.** harmonize
10. adjustment, intonation
tune (pert to) . . .
correctly . . **3.** key
down . . **6.** reduce, soften **8.** moderate
musical instrument . . **6.** string
out of . . **9.** dissonant **11.** inaccordant
12. unconforming
tungsten . . . **7.** wolfram
Tunisia . . .
cape . . **3.** Bon
capital . . **5.** Tunis
famed ruins . . **8.** Carthage
gulf . . **5.** Gabes
oasis . . **5.** Gafsa
people . . **5.** Arabs **7.** Berbers
resort island . . **6.** Djerba
river . . **8.** Medjerda
ruler . . **3.** dey **5.** pasha
seaport . . **4.** Sfax **5.** Bizorte
tunnel . . . **4.** adit, bore, cave, tube **5.** drift
6. burrow, dig out, funnel, subway
10. excavation, smokestack
tunny . . . **4.** tuna **8.** albacore
tup . . . **3.** ram **4.** beat, butt **5.** sheep
6. mallet **7.** cuckold
turban . . . **6.** entrée, fillet, Moslem,
mundil, squash **8.** bandanna, seerband
9. headdress
turbid . . . **4.** dark, dull **5.** dense, muddy,
roily **6.** cloudy, impure, opaque
7. clouded, muddled **8.** confused,
feculent, polluted
turbot . . . **5.** brill **8.** flatfish
turbulence . . . **4.** fury **6.** tumult, uproar
7. bluster, rioting, turmoil **9.** agitation,
commotion **10.** excitement, unruliness
11. disturbance, impetuosity
14. tumultuousness
turbulent . . . **4.** loud, wild **5.** noisy, rough
6. stormy **7.** excited, furious **8.** virulent
10. tumultuous
turf . . . **3.** sod **4.** peat, slab **5.** divot, glebe,
grass, sward, track **10.** race course
turgid . . . **5.** tumid **7.** bloated, pompous,
swollen **8.** inflated **9.** bombastic,
distended, grandiose, redundant
12. magniloquent, ostentatious
13. grandiloquent
Turk . . . **5.** Tatar **6.** Tartar **7.** Osmanli,
Ottoman **9.** Kizilbash
Turkestan people . . . **5.** Uzbek (Uzbeg)
turkey . . . **4.** fowl **5.** poult **7.** bustard,
gobbler, vulture
Turkey . . . see also *Turkish*
capital . . **6.** Angora (anc), Ankara
city . . **5.** Adana, Izmir (Smyrna) **6.** Edessa,
Samsun **7.** Scutari **8.** Istanbul
(Constantinople) **10.** Adrianople
founder . . **6.** Othman
mountain . . **6.** Ararat
peninsula . . **9.** Anatolian
river . . **5.** Mesta **6.** Seyhan
Turkish (pert to) . . .
army corps . . **4.** ordu **8.** seraglio
commander, ruler . . **3.** aga (agha), bey
4. wali **5.** pasha **6.** atabeg (atabek)
court (Ottoman) . . **5.** Porte **12.** Sublime
Porte
dignitary . . **5.** pasha
dish (food) . . **5.** cabob **6.** pilaff (pilau)

drink . . **4.** boza (bozah), raki **5.** airan
6. mastic **9.** lion's milk
dynasty . . **6.** seljuk
emblem . . **8.** crescent
Empire . . **7.** Ottoman
flag . . **4.** alem, toug (former)
harem girl . . **6.** kadein (kadine)
hat, cap . . **3.** fez **6.** calpac (calpack)
hospice, inn . . **6.** imaret
infidel . . **6.** giaour
javelin . . **6.** jereed (jerid)
judge . . **4.** cadi (kadi)
minister of state . . **6.** vizier
money of account . . **5.** asper
mosque . . **4.** jami
music . . **8.** janizary
native . . **6.** Edesan (anc)
palace . . **5.** serai
pavilion . . **5.** kiosk
people . . **5.** Ersar, Tatar **7.** Bashkir,
Viddhal
pipe (long-stemmed) . . **7.** chibouk
(chibouque)
regiment . . **4.** alai
religious war . . **5.** jihad (jehad)
robe . . **6.** dolman
rug . . **5.** Melas, Tekke, Yomud, Yuruk
6. Afghan **8.** Turkoman **9.** Kurdistan
ruler . . **3.** bey, dey **4.** khan **6.** sultan
7. chambul
sailing vessel . . **4.** saic **6.** mahone
sailor . . **9.** galiongee (galionji)
soldier . . **5.** nizan, redif **6.** Arnaut
(Arnaout) **8.** Janizary **11.** bashi-bazouk
statute . . **8.** Tanzimat (1839)
sultan . . **5.** Ahmed, Selim **7.** Ilderim,
Saladin
sultan's title . . **6.** caliph (calif)
sword . . **8.** yataghan (yatagan)
tambourine . . **5.** daira
tax (from Christians) . . **6.** avania
title . . **3.** aga (agha), ali **4.** amir (ameer)
tobacco . . **7.** chibouk (chibouque), Latakia
Turkoman . . **11.** tribal group
veil (double) . . **7.** yashmak (yashmac)
vest . . **6.** jelick
whip, lash . . **7.** kurbash
turmeric . . . **3.** rea **4.** ango, herb **5.** olena
8. curcumin
turmoil . . . **3.** ado, din **5.** upset, worry
6. tumult, unrest **7.** ferment, tempest,
trouble **8.** disquiet **9.** agitation,
commotion, confusion **10.** excitement,
turbulence **12.** perturbation
turn . . . **3.** bow, lap **4.** bend, deed,
gyre, roll, slew, slue, spin, tour, veer,
vert **5.** curve, lathe, pivot, quirk,
round, shift, spell, wheel, whirl, whorl
6. abvert, change, crisis, gyrate, rotate,
swivel, zigzag **7.** deflect, deviate,
reverse, revolve **8.** aptitude, circuity,
maneuver, persuade, rotation, tendency
9. deviation, pirouette, reversion
11. convolution **12.** metamorphose
turn (pert to) . . .
about . . **9.** alternate
aside, away . . **4.** slew, slue **5.** avert,
deter, repel, shunt **6.** divert, swerve
7. deflect, deviate, digress, diverge
back . . **5.** repel **6.** coward, revert
7. evolute, head off, reflect

coat . . **7.** traitor **8.** apostate, deserter, renegade
comb form . . **5.** tropo
down . . **4.** veto **6.** refuse, reject **7.** decline
gate . . **5.** stile **9.** turnstile
inside out . . **5.** evert **6.** invert **7.** ransack
inward . . **8.** introrse **9.** introvert
left . . **3.** haw **4.** port
of duty . . **5.** spell, trick
off . . **5.** shunt **7.** dismiss, execute **10.** extinguish
on axis . . **6.** obvert, rotate
one's back upon . . **4.** flee, snub **5.** avoid **6.** ignore, oppose, refuse, reject
on pivot . . **6.** swivel
out . . **4.** fare, oust **5.** array, evert, expel, track **6.** detour, output, siding **7.** dismiss **8.** assemble, clearing **9.** eventuate, gathering **10.** accomplish, extinguish
outward . . **5.** evert, splay **8.** extrorse **9.** extrovert
over . . **3.** pie **4.** keel, tart **5.** sales, shift, spill **6.** assign, pastry **7.** capsize **8.** hand over, overturn
over a new leaf . . **6.** change, reform
over pages . . **4.** leaf **5.** thumb
over to others . . **4.** farm **7.** farm out
to left . . **3.** haw **4.** port
to right . . **3.** gee **9.** starboard
up . . **4.** find, keel **5.** occur **6.** appear, arrive **7.** be found
upside down . . **4.** roll **6.** invert, whelve **7.** ransack **8.** overturn
turned up (nose) . . . **9.** retroussé
turning . . . **6.** rotary **7.** bending, crooked, winding **8.** rotation, twisting, whirling **9.** deviating, deviation **10.** circuitous, revolution **11.** convolution, sinistrorse
turning (pert to) . . .
left to right . . **9.** dextrorse
machine . . **5.** lathe
point . . **6.** crisis **8.** decision, landmark **11.** climacteric **13.** crucial period
right to left . . **11.** sinistrorse
turnip . . . **4.** neep, rape, root **8.** rutabaga
turnip (pert to) . . .
large . . **7.** Russian, Swedish **8.** rutabaga
shaped . . **8.** napiform
wild . . **5.** navew
Turnix . . . **4.** bird (3-toed) **5.** quail **10.** Hemipodius
Turpentine State . . . **13.** North Carolina
turpentine tree . . . **4.** pine **6.** tarata **9.** terebinth
turpid . . . **3.** low **4.** base, vile **8.** cowardly
turpitude . . . **6.** fedity **8.** baseness, vileness **9.** decadence, depravity **10.** corruption
turquoise . . . **3.** gem **4.** blue **7.** mineral, Turkish
turret . . . **4.** loom, soar **5.** tower **6.** cupola (revolving), height **9.** structure **10.** stronghold, watchtower
turtle (pert to) . . .
edible . . **8.** terrapin
freshwater . . **4.** emyd **8.** tortoise
genus . . **4.** Emys
hawklike . . **5.** carat **9.** hawk's-bill
large . . **5.** arrau **6.** jurara, mamata
largest . . **11.** leatherback
ref to . . **9.** chelonian

sea . . **10.** thalassian
shell . . **8.** carapace
snapping . . **6.** cooter **8.** shagtail
Tuscany . . .
birthplace of . . **7.** Galileo (Astronomer)
capital . . **8.** Florence
city . . **4.** Pisa **7.** Leghorn
color . . **9.** colcothar
famed tower . . **4.** Pisa (1174)
island . . **4.** Elba (1st exile, Napoleon)
native . . **6.** Tuscan
marble . . **7.** Carrara
province . . **4.** Pisa
river . . **4.** Arno **6.** Cecina **7.** Ombrone
wine . . **7.** chianti
tusk . . . **4.** fang **5.** ivory, tooth **6.** canine **7.** incisor **9.** scrivello (elephant's)
Tussaud, Madame's London district . . . **8.** Waxworks (Museum) **10.** Marylebone
tussis . . . **5.** cough
tussle . . . **7.** contend, contest, scuffle, wrestle **8.** struggle
tutelage . . . **7.** nurture **8.** teaching, tutorage **9.** oversight, tutorship **11.** instruction **12.** guardianship
tutelary gods (Rom) . . . **5.** lares **7.** penates
tutor . . . **5.** coach, teach **6.** docent, ground, mentor, school **7.** teacher **8.** instruct **9.** pedagogue (pedagog), preceptor
twaddle . . . **3.** rot **6.** drivel, gabble **7.** chatter, fustian, prattle **8.** claptrap, nonsense **9.** absurdity, silly talk **10.** flapdoodle **16.** trash and nonsense
twang . . . **4.** tang **5.** strum **6.** accent **7.** dialect **8.** pungency
tweak . . . **4.** jerk, pain **5.** pinch **6.** snatch, twitch
tweeg . . . **10.** hellbender, salamander
tweezers . . . **7.** pincers **10.** instrument
twelfth . . . **5.** twait, uncia **8.** duodenal **9.** duodenary
Twelfth Night character . . . **5.** Viola **6.** Olivia, Orsino **7.** Sir Toby **8.** Malvolio **12.** Sir Toby Belch
Twelfthtide . . . **8.** Epiphany **10.** Twelfth-day
twelve (pert to) . . .
amount . . **5.** dozen
angles . . **9.** dodecagon
prefix . . **5.** dodec **6.** dodeca
rule of . . **9.** dodecarch
series . . **8.** dodecade
Twelve, The . . . **8.** Apostles
twenty (pert to) . . .
Anglo-Ind . . **5.** carge, score
comb form . . **4.** icos **5.** icosa, icosi
faces . . **11.** icosahedron
pert to . . **7.** icosian **8.** vicenary
quires . . **4.** ream
symbol . . **5.** XX
years . . **9.** vicennial
twenty-fourth part (gold alloy) . . . **5.** carat (karat)
twibil (twibill) . . . **2.** ax (axe) **6.** pickax (pickaxe) **7.** mattock **8.** battle-ax (battle-axe)
twice . . . **2.** bi, di **6.** doubly **7.** twofold **8.** two times
twig . . . **4.** reis **5.** besom, birch, bough **6.** branch, sallow, switch, twitch, wattle
twigs, bundle of . . . **5.** fagot **6.** barsom

(sacred)
twilight . . . 3. dim 4. blue, dusk 6. shaded
7. obscure 8. foredawn, gloaming
9. cocklight 10. crepuscule
Twilight of the Gods . . . 8. Ragnarok
twill . . . 3. rib 5. flute, weave 6. fabric
9. tricotine
twilled . . . 3. rep 5. reedy, ridgy, sedgy,
serge 6. corded, fluted
twin . . . 3. two 4. dual, mate, pair
5. gemel, macle 6. couple, double
7. didymus, Siamese 8. didymous,
matching 9. duplicate, identical
11. counterpart 12. accompanying
Twin Cities (Minn) . . . 6. St Paul
11. Minneapolis
twine . . . 4. bend, coil, turn, wind, wrap
5. braid, snarl, twist, weave 6. enfold,
enlace, tangle 7. embrace, enclasp,
entwine, wreathe 8. convolve, encircle
9. interlace 10. intertwine, interweave
11. intermingle
twine (pert to) . . .
color . . 4. dune 7. anamite
hank of . . 3. ran
left to right . . 9. dextrorse
right to left . . 11. sinistrorse
Scot . . 4. part
twinge . . . 4. ache, pain, pang 5. pinch,
qualm 6. twitch
twin stars . . . 6. Castor, Pollux
twin stock . . . 4. bees 7. beehive (two
colonies)
twirl . . . 4. coil, eddy, gyre, spin
5. pitch, querl, twist, whirl 6. gyrate,
writhe 7. revolve 8. flourish, rotation
11. convolution
twist . . . 3. cue, ply 4. coil, curl,
slew, slub, slue, spin, turn, warp,
wind 5. braid, quirk, tweak, wrest
7. contort, deflect, distort, falsify,
meander, pervert, wreathe, wriggle
8. convolve 9. insinuate, interlace,
prejudice 10. distortion 12. eccentricity,
misrepresent
twisted . . . 3. wry 4. awry, cued
5. askew, kinky, torse, wrung 6. warped
7. complex, torqued, tortile, wrested,
writhed
twisted cord . . . 7. torsade
twister . . . 3. lie 7. cruller, tornado
8. doughnut 9. dust whirl 10. sand
column, somersault, waterspout
twit . . . 4. gibe, josh 5. blame, taunt,
tease, tweet 6. banter 7. upbraid
8. reproach, ridicule
twitch . . . 3. nip, tic, tug 4. hurt, jerk,
yank 5. pluck, shake, tweak 6. snatch
9. be excited, quick pull, vellicate
11. contraction
twitter . . . 5. chirp 6. giggle, titter
7. chatter, tremble 9. agitation
two (pert to) . . .
chambered . . 9. bicameral
colored . . 9. dichromic
edged . . 9. ancipital
faced . . 5. false 6. double 9. deceitful
11. treacherous 12. falsehearted
fisted . . 6. virile
fold . . 4. dual, twin 6. binary, double,
duplex 8. didymous

forked . . 6. bident 9. bifurcate
11. dichotomous
handed . . 7. bimanal 8. bimanous
10. secondhand 12. ambidextrous
headed . . 9. ancipital 11. dicephalous
masted ship . . 4. yawl, zulu
parts . . 3. duo 4. duad, dyad 7. duality
poetic . . 5. twain
prefix . . 2. bi, di
Scot . . 3. twa
Spanish . . 3. dos
spot . . 5. deuce
time . . 7. deceive
wheeled carriage, chariot . . 3. gig
6. esseda 10. jinrikisha (jinriksha)
Tyche . . . 7. Fortuna 16. goddess of
Fortune
tycoon . . . 6. shogun 7. magnate
9. financier 13. industrialist
tylopod . . . 5. camel
tympanum . . . 7. eardrum 9. middle ear
10. water wheel
tympany . . . 6. tympan 7. bombast
9. inflation 10. distention
typal . . . 7. typical 8. symbolic
type . . . 2. pi 4. font, form, kind, norm,
sign, sort 5. genre, genus, model,
print, Roman, token 6. emblem, italic,
minion, symbol 7. measure, pattern,
species 8. boldface, classify, standard
9. archetype, character 10. transcribe
11. Baskerville 14. characteristic,
representative
type (pert to) . . .
assortment . . 4. font, kern
block of . . 4. quad 7. quadrat
bold style . . 4. text
bridge . . 7. bascule
classic . . 5. Roman 6. italic 11. black
letter (Gothic)
line . . 4. slug
measure . . 2. em, en
mixed . . 2. pi
mold . . 6. matrix
perfection . . 7. paragon
set . . 7. compose
setter . . 8. linotype, monotype
10. compositor
size . . 4. norm, pica, ruby 5. agate,
canon, pearl 6. minion 7. diamond
stroke . . 5. serif
tray . . 6. galley
typewriter (pert to) . . .
bar . . 6. spacer
cylinder . . 6. platen, spacer
type . . 4. pica 5. elite
type of . . 6. ticker 8. teletype
9. stenotype
typhoon . . . 4. wind 5. storm 7. cyclone
typhus fever . . . 10. tabardillo
typical . . . 4. norm 5. typal 6. normal
7. regular 10. conforming, emblematic,
figurative 11. precedental
14. characteristic, representative
typify . . . 6. embody 9. prefigure,
represent, symbolize
Tyr (Norse) . . . 3. Tiu 6. sky-god, war-god
tyrannical . . . 5. cruel 6. lordly 8. despotic
9. imperious 10. oppressive
11. domineering
tyrannize . . . 7. oppress 8. domineer

tyranny ... **8.** severity **9.** despotism
tyrant ... **4.** czar, Ivan, Nero, tsar, tzar
  6. despot **7.** monarch
Tyre ... see also *Tyrian*
  capital of .. **9.** Phoenicia (anc)
  famed for .. **9.** purple dye
  seaport of .. **7.** Lebanon
  site .. **9.** peninsula **13.** Mediterranean
Tyrian (pert to) ...
  alphabet .. **7.** Moabite
  Cynosure .. **9.** Ursa Minor
  god (Teut) .. **2.** Er
  king .. **5.** Hiram
  princess .. **4.** Dido (Elissa)

tyro, tiro ... **5.** pupil **6.** novice **7.** amateur
  8. beginner, neophyte **9.** commencer,
  fledgling, greenhorn **10.** apprentice
  11. abecedarian
Tyrol ...
  capital .. **9.** Innsbruck
  dialect .. **5.** Ladin
  district .. **8.** Trentino
  mountain .. **4.** Alps **9.** Dolomites
  province of .. **7.** Austria
  river .. **4.** Isar
tzar, tsar, czar ... **4.** king **5.** ruler
  6. tyrant
tzigane ... **5.** gypsy

U

U ... **6.** letter (21st)
uang ... **6.** beetle
uberous ... **7.** copious **8.** abundant,
  fruitful **9.** plentiful
uberty ... **6.** plenty **12.** fruitfulness
ubiety ... **8.** location, position, relation
  9. whereness
ubiquity ... **8.** doctrine (Luther)
  10. everywhere **12.** omnipresence
U-boat ... **3.** sub **9.** submarine
  base .. **4.** Kiel
Uca ... **11.** fiddler crab
Uchean Indian ... **5.** Yuchi (Uchee)
udometer ... **9.** rain gauge
Uffizi Gallery ... **8.** Florence
Uganda (pert to) ...
  capital .. **7.** Kampala
  Falls .. **4.** Owen **9.** Murchison
  lake .. **8.** Victoria
  lake explorer .. **7.** Stanley
  mountain .. **9.** Ruwenzori **18.** Mountains
  of the Moon
  people .. **5.** pygmy
ugly ... **5.** cross, surly **6.** cranky,
  homely **7.** crabbed, hideous, vicious
  8. gruesome, uncomely, unlovely
  9. frightful, loathsome, offensive,
  repulsive, unsightly **10.** ill-favored, ill-
  natured, unpleasant **11.** ill-tempered,
  quarrelsome **12.** disagreeable
uhlan ... **6.** lancer **7.** militia, soldier
  10. cavalryman
uhllo ... **6.** wampum **8.** currency (shell)
uitlander ... **9.** foreigner, outlander
ukase ... **5.** edict, order **12.** proclamation
Ukraine (pert to) ...
  capital .. **4.** Kiev **7.** Kharkov
  legislature .. **4.** rada
  official name .. **12.** Ukrainian SSR
  Relig .. **9.** Ruthenian **13.** Little Russian
  scientist .. **10.** Bogomolets
  sea .. **5.** Black
  seaport .. **6.** Odessa
  statesman .. **7.** Mazeppa
  writer .. **6.** Franko
ullage ... **5.** dregs **7.** deficit, wantage
  8. shortage **9.** shrinkage **10.** deficiency
Ulmas ... **3.** elm
ulna ... **4.** bone **5.** elbow **7.** cubitus

ulster ... **8.** overcoat
Ulster, to some ... **15.** Northern Ireland
ulterior ... **6.** future **7.** further, remoter,
  thither **10.** additional, extraneous,
  subsequent, succeeding **11.** undisclosed
ultima ... **4.** last **5.** final **8.** farthest
  10. most remote **12.** last syllable
ultimate ... **3.** end **4.** dire, last **5.** final,
  telus **6.** future, latest, result **7.** extreme,
  maximum **8.** eventful, eventual,
  farthest, terminal **9.** elemental
  10. conclusive, end product
ultimatum ... **5.** offer **6.** demand
  13. ultimate point **14.** final objective
ultimo ... **3.** ult **9.** past month (opp of
  proximo)
ultra ... **6.** beyond **7.** extreme, radical
  9. excessive, extremist, fanatical
  11. extravagant **14.** uncompromising
ultramarine ... **11.** blue pigment, lapis
  lazuli **12.** beyond the sea
ultramontane ... **5.** alien **6.** beyond
  9. foreigner **10.** tramontane **13.** beyond
  the Alps, Roman Catholic
ulu (Esk) ... **5.** knife
ululate ... **4.** hoot, howl, wail, yelp
  6. bellow, lament
Ulysses (pert to) ...
  antagonist .. **4.** Irus
  dog .. **5.** Argos
  enchantress .. **5.** Circe
  father .. **7.** Laertes
  Greek name .. **8.** Odysseus
  hero .. **7.** Odyssey (Homer's)
  literally .. **5.** hater
  son .. **9.** Telegonus
  wife .. **8.** Penelope
umber ... **3.** raw **5.** brown, burnt
  6. shadow, Turkey **8.** grayling, umbrette
  10. brown earth
umbilicus (pert to) ...
  anatomy .. **5.** navel
  botany .. **5.** hilum
  geometry .. **5.** focus
  paleology .. **5.** stick (papyrus)
  zoology .. **3.** pit **10.** depression
umbra ... **4.** fish **5.** ghost, shade
  6. shadow **7.** phantom, vestige
umbrage ... **5.** doubt, pique, shade, trace

6. offend, resent 7. foliage, offense, shelter 8. disfavor 9. semblance, suspicion 10. overshadow, resentment 11. displeasure

umbrella ... 4. gamp 5. cover, guard, shade 6. chatta, payong, pileus (of a jellyfish) 7. parasol, shelter 9. parachute, sea anchor 11. bumbershoot

umbrella tree ... 5. bendy 7. dogwood, ginseng 8. magnolia

umbrette ... 4. bird, fish 5. omber (ombre) 9. hammerkop

umpire ... 5. judge 7. arbiter, referee 8. mediator 9. moderator 10. arbitrator, negotiator

Umpqua ... 6. Indian 10. Athapascan

unable ... 6. cannot 8. helpless, impotent 9. incapable 11. incompetent, inefficient, unqualified 13. incapacitated

Una boat ... 7. catboat

unabridged ... 8. complete 11. uncondensed

unaccented ... 4. lene 6. atonic

unaccountable ... 7. lawless, strange 9. fantastic 10. mysterious 12. inexplicable, unfathomable 13. irresponsible, unpredictable

unacknowledged ... 9. anonymous, forgotten, unthanked 10. unrewarded

unadorned ... 4. bald, bare, form 5. grace, naked, stark 7. austere 13. plain-speaking

unadulterated ... 4. pure 5. naked 6. honest 7. unmixed 9. unalloyed, undiluted 11. uncorrupted

unaffected ... 4. naif, real 5. naive, plain 6. simple 7. artless, genuine, natural, sincere 8. informal 9. unaltered, untouched 12. uninfluenced 13. plain-speaking

Unalaska ... 5. Aleut 9. Eskimauan

unanimous ... 5. solid 6. agreed, mutual, united 8. agreeing 9. of one mind 10. concordant 11. consentient 12. with one voice

unanimously ... 7. una voce 12. with one voice

unapproachable ... 8. reserved 10. unsociable 12. inaccessible

unapt ... 4. dull, slow 5. inapt 8. backward 10. unskillful, unsuitable 13. inappropriate

unaroused ... 6. latent 7. dormant 8. inactive 9. unstirred

unaspirated ... 4. lene 6. smooth

unassuming ... 3. shy 6. modest 7. genuine, natural 8. informal, retiring 9. diffident 11. undeceptive 14. unostentatious

unau ... 5. sloth (2-toed)

unavailing ... 6. futile 8. gainless

unbalanced ... 6. insane, uneven, unjust 7. unequal 8. deranged, lopsided, one-sided 9. off center 10. disordered

unbecoming ... 4. rude 5. inept 8. unseemly 10. indecorous, unsuitable 12. unattractive

unbelievable ... 9. fantastic, untenable 10. incredible, unreliable 11. implausible, unthinkable

13. inconceivable

unbeliever ... 5. pagan 7. atheist, doubter, heretic, infidel, skeptic 8. agnostic

unbend ... 4. rest, thaw 5. frese, relax, yield 6. loosen 7. slacken 8. be pliant, unfasten 10. condescend, straighten

unbending ... 5. rigid, stern, stiff 8. resolute 10. inexorable, inflexible, unyielding

unbiased ... 4. fair, just 9. impartial 12. free from bias, unprejudiced

unbind ... 4. free, undo 5. loose, untie 6. loosen 7. absolve, deliver, release 8. dissolve, unfasten

unbound ... 4. free 5. loose 10. unconfined

unbounded ... 8. infinite 9. limitless, unchecked, unlimited 10. unconfined 11. measureless 12. uncontrolled, unrestrained

unbridled ... 4. free 5. loose 7. lawless, violent 10. licentious 12. uncontrolled, unrestrained

unbroken ... 4. even 5. undug, whole 6. direct, entire, intact, smooth 7. untamed 8. constant, straight, unplowed 10. continuous 13. uninterrupted

uncanny ... 5. eerie (eery), weird 6. spooky 7. ghostly, strange 8. careless 9. unnatural 10. mysterious

unceasing ... 6. eterne 7. endless, eternal 9. continual, incessant 11. everlasting

unceremonious ... 4. curt 5. blunt 6. abrupt, casual 7. offhand 8. informal 14. unconventional

uncertain ... 4. hazy 5. vague 6. chancy, fickle, fitful, shifty, unsure 7. dubious 8. doubtful, unsteady, variable 9. ambiguous, irregular, undecided 10. changeable, indefinite, irresolute, precarious 11. unequivocal 12. questionable 13. indeterminate, problematical, untrustworthy

uncertainty ... 5. doubt 6. wonder 7. dubiety 8. suspense 9. dubiosity 10. fickleness, skepticism 12. irresolution 14. precariousness

unchanging ... 7. eternal, settled, uniform 9. immutable, unvarying 11. invariable, stationary

unchaste ... 4. lewd 5. bawdy 6. impure 7. obscene 8. immodest

unchecked ... 4. free 5. loose 7. rampant 9. permanent, unbridled

unchristian ... 5. pagan 7. heathen, infidel, ungodly 9. barbarous, excessive 11. irreligious, uncivilized

uncivil ... 4. rude 6. savage 7. ill-bred 8. impolite 9. barbarous 10. indecorous, ungracious 11. ill-mannered, uncivilized 12. discourteous 13. disrespectful

uncivilized ... 4. rude, wild 5. feral 6. brutal, ferine, savage 8. barbaric 9. primitive, unrefined

uncle ... 3. eme (yeme), oom

unclean ... 4. foul, tref, vile 5. dirty 6. filthy, immund, impure 8. polluted, unchaste 11. unwholesome

Uncle Tom's Cabin (pert to) ...

U

author .. **5.** Stowe (Harriet Beecher)
character .. **5.** Topsy **6.** Legree **8.** Uncle
Tom **9.** Little Eva
subject .. **7.** slavery
unclose ... **3.** ope **4.** open **6.** reveal
7. expound **8.** disclose
uncolored ... **7.** genuine **9.** colorless
10. achromatic
uncommon ... **3.** odd **4.** nice, rare
5. novel **6.** scarce, unique **7.** special,
strange, unusual **8.** unwonted
10. infrequent, remarkable
11. exceptional **12.** unaccustomed
13. extraordinary
uncommunicative ... **6.** silent
8. reserved, reticent **9.** secretive
10. unsociable
uncomplaining ... **5.** stoic **7.** stoical
uncompromising ... **4.** firm **5.** rigid
6. strict **9.** obstinate, unbending
10. inflexible, unyielding
12. conservative, intransigent
unconcerned ... **4.** cool, free **8.** careless
9. apathetic **10.** insouciant
11. indifferent, not involved
13. disinterested
unconditional ... **4.** free **8.** absolute,
explicit **10.** unreserved
unconfined ... **5.** loose **9.** boundless,
limitless, unlimited **12.** unrestrained
unconscious ... **3.** out **6.** asleep
7. unaware **8.** heedless, ignorant,
mindless **9.** inanimate, senseless,
unfeeling **10.** abstracted, insensible
11. involuntary **12.** subconscious
unconstrained ... **4.** easy, free **6.** candid
7. natural **8.** informal **11.** spontaneous
12. unrestrained
uncontrolled ... **4.** free, wild **5.** loose
7. lawless **9.** impulsive, irregular,
unmanaged **10.** capricious, changeable,
licentious, ungoverned **11.** not
governed, unregulated **12.** unrestrained
unconventional ... **4.** easy **5.** outré
6. casual **7.** devious, offbeat
8. Bohemian, informal **10.** unorthodox
13. unceremonious
uncorrupted ... **8.** pristine
uncouth ... **3.** odd **4.** rude **5.** crude
6. clumsy, rustic **7.** awkward, boorish,
strange **9.** inelegant, unrefined,
untrained **10.** outlandish, uncultured,
unpolished
uncover ... **4.** bare, open **6.** detect,
divest, expose, remove, reveal, unveil
7. divulge, lay bare, take off, undrape
8. disclose, discover
uncovered ... **4.** bald, bare, nude, open
7. exposed **8.** divested, revealed,
stripped, unveiled **9.** décolleté
10. bareheaded **11.** unprotected
unction ... **4.** balm, rite **6.** fervor
7. lanolin, unguent **8.** flattery, function
(divine), ointment **10.** anointment
unctuous ... **4.** oily, smug **5.** bland,
fatty, salvy, suave **6.** fervid, greasy
7. gushing, pinguid, plastic
10. flattering, oleaginous
12. hypocritical **13.** sanctimonious
uncultured ... **7.** artless, boorish, uncouth
8. Bohemian **9.** unlearned, unrefined

10. Philistine **11.** countrified,
undeveloped
undaunted ... **4.** bold **5.** brave **7.** Spartan,
untamed **8.** fearless, intrepid, unafraid
9. confident, dauntless **10.** courageous,
undismayed **11.** persevering,
unconquered
undecided ... **4.** moot **7.** pending
8. doubtful, wavering **9.** uncertain,
unsettled **10.** inconstant, irresolute,
unresolved **13.** problematical
undependable ... **6.** fickle **7.** erratic
9. uncertain **13.** irresponsible,
untrustworthy
under ... **3.** sub **4.** alow **5.** below, least,
neath, sotto **6.** nether **7.** beneath
8. guidance **9.** lower than **10.** subjection,
underneath **11.** subordinate
undercover ... **6.** secret **7.** furtive
11. clandestine, underground
13. surreptitious
underestimate ... **8.** belittle, minimize
9. set too low, underrate **10.** undervalue
underfong ... **6.** entrap **7.** ensnare,
receive, sustain **9.** undertake
10. circumvent
undergo ... **4.** bear, dree, pass **5.** shirt
6. endure, suffer **7.** sustain
9. undermine **10.** experience
underhanded ... **3.** sly **4.** dern, mean
5. shady **6.** covert, crafty, secret,
sneaky **8.** sneaking, unfairly **9.** deceitful,
dishonest **10.** fraudulent **11.** clandestine,
short-handed **13.** unobtrusively
15. surreptitiously
underling ... **6.** menial, minion **7.** servant
8. inferior **11.** subordinate
underlying ... **5.** basic **8.** cardinal
11. fundamental
undermine ... **3.** sap **4.** ruin **5.** drain,
erode **6.** weaken **7.** subvert **8.** enfeeble,
excavate
understand ... **3.** ken, see **4.** know
5. grasp, infer, savvy, sense **6.** follow,
reason **7.** discern, explain, realize,
signify **8.** conceive, perceive
9. apprehend, interpret **10.** comprehend
understandable ... **5.** clear, lucid
12. intelligible
understanding ... **5.** amity, sense
6. accord, reason, treaty **7.** compact,
concept, entente, knowing **8.** sympathy,
Verstand **9.** agreement, intellect,
knowledge, tolerance, unanimity
10. acceptance, accordance, perception
11. discernment, penetration
12. intelligence **13.** comprehension
understatement ... **7.** litotes
understood ... **5.** clear, known, lucid,
tacit **7.** assumed, implied, settled
8. implicit **11.** traditional
undertake ... **3.** try **4.** dare **6.** accept,
assume, pledge **7.** attempt, promise,
reprove **8.** contract, covenant, endeavor,
engage in, set about **9.** guarantee,
underfong
undertaker ... **5.** cerer **6.** surety
7. manager, rebuker, sponsor
8. embalmer **9.** godfather, mortician
12. entrepreneur ·
undertaking ... **3.** act **4.** task **6.** cautio

7. calling, project, promise, venture
8. business 9. adventure, guarantee
10. enterprise
undertone ... 4. tone (low) 5. aside
6. murmur 12. subdued color
undertow ... 7. riptide
underworld ... 3. Dis 4. hell 5. Hades,
limbo, Mafia, Orcus, Sheol 6. Erebus,
Tophet 7. Abaddon, Xibalba 8. Dis
pater, gangland 9. Black Hand,
chthonian, perdition, purgatory
underwrite ... 6. assure, insure 7. finance,
sponsor 8. submit to
underwriter ... 7. insurer 8. endorser
9. financier 10. underclerk 13. Stock
Exchange 14. Lloyd's of London
undesirable condition ... 6. malady
undetermined ... 5. vague 7. dubious
8. not fixed, unproved 9. uncertain,
undecided 10. irresolute
undeveloped ... 5. crude 6. embryo,
latent 8. immature 10. unprepared
11. rudimentary
undignified ... 6. vulgar 8. informal,
infra dig, unworthy 9. inelegant
undine ... 3. nix 5. gnome, sylph 6. vessel
(glass) 9. planetoid 10. salamander
undivided ... 3. one 5. total, whole
6. entire, intact, joined 7. unitary
8. unbroken 9. not shared
10. continuous
undo ... 4. open 5. annul, loose
6. cancel, defeat, foredo, unlash,
unwrap 7. destroy, disjoin, nullify,
release, uncover, unravel 8. unfasten
10. disconnect, invalidate
undoing ... 4. ruin 6. defeat 8. downfall
9. annulment, overthrow
11. destruction, disassembly
undomesticated ... 4. wild 5. feral
6. ferine
undone ... 3. raw 9. neglected
10. defeasible
undue ... 5. wrong 6. unjust 7. extreme
8. improper, not owing 9. excessive
10. exorbitant, immoderate, inordinate,
undeserved, unsuitable 11. unwarranted
13. inappropriate
undulating ... 4. wavy 6. waving
7. aripple, rolling 8. rippling
11. fluctuating 16. rising and falling
undulation ... 4. beat, wave 5. heave,
surge, swell 6. motion, waving
7. tremolo, vibrato 8. waviness
9. pulsation 11. convolution
undying ... 6. eterne 7. ageless, endless,
eternal 8. immortal, unending
9. deathless 11. amaranthine
12. imperishable 14. indestructible
unearth ... 4. find 5. dig up 6. exhume,
expose 7. uncover 8. disclose, discover,
disinter 12. bring to light
unearthly ... 5. eerie (eery), godly, weird
7. awesome, ghostly, strange, uncanny
8. heavenly, terrific 9. appalling,
deathlike 10. mysterious, outlandish
12. preposterous, supernatural
13. preternatural
uneasiness ... 5. worry 6. unrest
7. anxiety, malaise 8. disquiet
10. impatience 11. displeasure,

disquietude, disturbance
12. apprehension
uneasy ... 5. stiff 7. anxious, awkward,
inquiet, restive, worried 8. agitated,
cramping, restless 9. difficult, impatient,
perturbed 10. disquieted, distressed
11. constrained, troublesome
unemotional ... 4. cold 5. stoic 7. stoical
10. phlegmatic
unemployed ... 4. idle, lazy 6. otiose,
unused 7. not used 8. inactive, leisured
11. not invested
unencumbered ... 4. free
unending ... 7. endless, eternal
8. termless, timeless 9. boundless,
perpetual 10. continuous
12. interminable
unequal ... 3. odd 4. odds 5. aniso
(comb form) 6. uneven, unfair, unjust
8. variable 9. disparate, irregular
11. fluctuating, not adequate
12. asymmetrical 16. disproportionate
unequaled ... 7. supreme 8. peerless
9. matchless, nonpareil, unmatched,
unrivaled 10. inimitable, surpassing,
unbeatable, unexcelled 12. unparalleled
unequivocal ... 5. clear, plain 6. candid
7. sincere 8. explicit 9. downright
11. categorical, indubitable
unerring ... 4. sure, true 5. exact 7. certain
8. accurate, virtuous 9. unfailing
10. infallible
unessential ... 8. needless 9. extrinsic
10. irrelevant 11. superfluous,
unimportant 13. insignificant, void of
essence
unethical ... 6. amoral
uneven ... 3. odd 5. erose, rough
6. rugged, unfair, unjust 7. erratic,
unequal, varying 8. not level 10. ill-
matched 11. fluctuating
unexamined ... 7. a priori
unexampled ... 8. peerless 10. unimitated
12. unparalleled 13. extraordinary,
unprecedented
unexpected ... 6. abrupt, sudden
7. unusual 9. inopinate 10. unforeseen
14. not anticipated
unfair ... 4. foul 5. wrong 6. biased,
uneven, unjust 8. unseemly
9. dishonest, unethical 10. not cricket,
unsporting 11. inequitable, unfavorable
12. disingenuous, not equitable
unfaithful ... 6. betray 7. infidel,
traitor 8. apostate, recreant, turncoat
9. faithless 10. inaccurate
12. nonobservant 13. untrustworthy
unfamiliar ... 3. new 7. strange, unknown
8. not known 12. unaccustomed,
unconversant
unfasten ... 4. free, open, undo 5. unbar,
unfix, unpin, untie 6. detach, loosen,
unhook, unlock 7. unloose 8. unbutton
9. disengage
unfavorable ... 3. bad, ill 6. averse
7. adverse, opposed 8. contrary,
untimely 9. repulsive 12. inauspicious
unfeeling ... 4. dull 5. cruel, stoic,
stony 6. brutal, steely, stolid, unkind
7. callous 8. numbness, obdurate
9. apathetic, bloodless, heartless,

inanimate, insensate **10.** insensible
11. hardhearted **13.** unsusceptible
16. unimpressionable
unfeigned . . . **4.** real **7.** genuine, natural,
sincere **11.** undeceptive **14.** not
counterfeit **15.** not hypocritical
unfermented grape juice . . . **4.** stum
unfertile . . . **4.** arid **6.** barren
unfettered . . . **4.** free **5.** broad **9.** liberated,
unchained **10.** unshackled
unfinished . . . **5.** crude, rough **7.** sketchy
9. imperfect **10.** incomplete
11. uncompleted
unfit . . . **5.** inept **6.** faulty, not fit,
unable **8.** disabled **9.** untenable
11. handicapped, incompetent,
unqualified **12.** disqualified
unfledged . . . **4.** eyas **5.** green **6.** callow
8. immature **11.** undeveloped **12.** not
feathered
unflinching . . . **7.** staunch **8.** resolute,
unafraid **9.** steadfast **10.** unwavering,
unyielding **12.** not shrinking
unfold . . . **3.** ope **4.** open **6.** evolve,
expand, flower, reveal, spread, unfurl
7. develop, display, divulge, evolute,
explain, release **8.** disclose
unfortunate . . . **3.** ill **4.** poor **6.** wretch
7. hapless, unlucky **8.** luckless, untimely
10. calamitous **12.** inauspicious,
unsuccessful
unfounded . . . **4.** idle, vain **8.** baseless
9. untenable **10.** chimerical
11. unsupported, unwarranted
unfriendly . . . **3.** icy **4.** cool **7.** asocial,
hostile, not kind, opposed **8.** inimical,
unsocial **10.** unsociable **12.** inhospitable
unfruitful . . . **6.** barren, wasted **7.** sterile,
useless **9.** fruitless, infertile
12. unproductive, unprofitable **13.** not
productive
unfurl . . . **4.** open **6.** expand, spread,
unfold, unroll
ungainly . . . **5.** gawky, lanky **6.** clumsy,
gauche **7.** awkward, uncouth
8. bungling **10.** cumbersome,
ungraceful
ungenteel . . . **6.** vulgar **7.** ill-bred
8. plebeian **9.** inelegant **10.** unmannerly
ungentle . . . **4.** rude **5.** harsh, rough
7. ill-bred **12.** discourteous
ungodly . . . **6.** sinful, wicked **7.** impious
9. atheistic **11.** unbelieving
ungovernable . . . **4.** wild **6.** unruly
9. unbridled **10.** disorderly, licentious,
rebellious, refractory **12.** incorrigible,
obstreperous, recalcitrant
13. irrepressible **14.** uncontrollable
unguent . . . **4.** balm **5.** salve **6.** cerate,
chrism, pomade **7.** unction **8.** ointment
9. lubricant, unguentum
ungula . . . **4.** claw, hoof, nail **6.** unguis
ungulate . . . **3.** pig **4.** deer **5.** horse,
swine, tapir **6.** hoofed **8.** elephant,
Ungulata **10.** rhinoceros **15.** hoofed
quadruped
unhallowed . . . **6.** unholy, wicked
10. desecrated
unhappy . . . **3.** sad **6.** dismal, woeful
8. dejected, ill-fated, wretched
9. miserable, sorrowful **10.** calamitous,

displeased **11.** melancholic, unfortunate
12. discontented, unsuccessful
unhealthy . . . **3.** ill **4.** sick **6.** sickly, unsafe
11. unwholesome
unhesitating . . . **4.** sure **5.** ready
8. implicit, resolute **10.** undoubting
unholy . . . **6.** wicked **7.** impious, profane
8. shocking **10.** scandalous, unhallowed
unicellular organism . . . **6.** amoeba
(ameba)
unicorn . . . **4.** reem (Bib), unie **7.** monster
8. narwhale **9.** monoceros, spike
team **10.** pursuivant (Her), rhinoceros
(one-horned)
uniform . . . **4.** even **5.** equal **6.** livery,
outfit, simple, smooth **7.** equable,
orderly, regular **8.** constant, equiform
9. unvarying **10.** consistent, invariable,
unchanging **11.** symmetrical
uniformity . . . **5.** order **8.** equality,
evenness, sameness, symmetry
10. compliance, conformity,
smoothness **11.** consistency,
homogeneity **13.** invariability
unify . . . **5.** merge, unite **7.** combine,
make one **8.** coalesce **9.** integrate
11. consolidate
unimaginative . . . **4.** dull **7.** literal, prosaic
10. unfanciful
unimpaired . . . **4.** free **6.** entire, intact
8. unmarred **9.** undamaged, unspoiled
unimpressed . . . **6.** unawed **7.** unmoved
9. unstirred **10.** unaffected, uninspired
uninformed . . . **8.** ignorant, nescient
9. unknowing **10.** unapprized
13. unenlightened, unintelligent
uninhabited . . . **5.** empty **6.** vacant
8. deserted, desolate, forsaken
9. abandoned, unpeopled
10. unoccupied, untenanted
uninspired . . . **4.** dull **6.** stodgy
9. uninhaled
unintelligent . . . **4.** dumb **5.** brute
6. stupid, unwise **7.** foolish **8.** ignorant
9. senseless
unintentional . . . **7.** unmeant **9.** unwitting
10. accidental, unintended
11. inadvertent, involuntary,
unmeditated **14.** unpremeditated
uninterested . . . **5.** bored **9.** apathetic,
impartial, incurious **11.** unconcerned
13. disinterested
uninteresting . . . **3.** dry **4.** arid, drab, dull
6. boring, prolix, stupid **7.** humdrum,
insipid, prosaic, tedious **8.** tiresome
9. colorless **10.** unexciting
union . . . **3.** one **4.** bond **5.** joint,
unity **6.** accord, fusion, league,
merger **7.** amalgam, entente, liaison,
oneness **8.** alliance, junction, marriage
9. coalition **10.** federation **11.** affiliation,
association, combination, concurrence,
confederacy, conjunction
13. juxtaposition
Union (pert to) . . .
ensign, British . . **12.** three crosses (St
Andrew, St George, St Patrick)
General . . **7.** Sherman (Civil War)
of States . . **6.** Empire **12.** United States
of workers . . **5.** artel, guild
Union of So Africa . . .

capital.. **8.** Cape Town (Legis), Pretoria
(Admin)
city.. **6.** Durban **9.** Germiston
12. Johannesburg
famed Park.. **6.** Kruger
Union of Soviet Socialist Republics ...
see also *Russia*
anc citadel.. **7.** Kremlin
capital.. **6.** Moscow
city.. **9.** Leningrad
Republics (number).. **7.** fifteen
resort.. **5.** Yalta **6.** Crimea
river.. **2.** Ob **3.** Don **4.** Lena, Neva,
Ural **5.** Volga **7.** Dnieper
sea.. **4.** Aral, Azov **5.** Black, White
6. Baltic **7.** Caspian
strait.. **6.** Bering
unique ... **3.** odd, one **4.** rare, sole
5. alone, novel **6.** single **7.** notable,
special, unusual **8.** original, peculiar,
peerless, singular **9.** matchless
12. single-valued **13.** extraordinary
unison ... **5.** union **6.** accord, assent
7. concord, harmony **9.** agreement,
unanimity **10.** concordant, consonance
unit ... **3.** ace, ane, one **4.** item, word
5. digit, group **6.** entity **7.** measure
8. syllable
unit (pert to) ...
area (land).. **3.** rod **4.** acre **7.** hectare
astronomy.. **6.** parsec
biology.. **5.** idant
electrical.. **3.** amp, mho, ohm, rel **4.** volt,
watt **5.** farad, henry, joule **6.** ampere,
proton **7.** coulomb
energy.. **3.** erg, rad **5.** ergon **6.** kilerg
7. quantum
fluidity.. **3.** rhe
force.. **4.** dyne **5.** tonal **7.** kinetic
heat.. **3.** BTU **5.** therm (therme) **7.** calorie
(calory)
induction.. **5.** henry
light.. **3.** lux, pyr, rad **5.** lumen **6.** Hefner
linear.. **3.** ell, rod **4.** foot, inch, mile,
yard **7.** furlong
magnetic.. **5.** gauss, weber **7.** maxwell,
oersted
matter.. **5.** monad
measure.. **3.** are, rod **4.** pint **5.** maund,
meter, stere
military.. **7.** brigade, platoon **8.** regiment
power.. **2.** HP **3.** bel **5.** dynam, horse
pressure.. **5.** barad, barie
reluctance.. **3.** rel
resistance.. **3.** ohm
speed.. **4.** velo
telegraphic.. **4.** baud
thermal.. **7.** calorie (calory)
velocity.. **4.** velo
volume.. **3.** ton **4.** cord, peck, pint
5. ounce, pound **6.** barrel, bushel,
gallon **8.** hogshead
weight.. **3.** ton **5.** carat (karat), ounce,
pound
wire.. **3.** mil
work.. **3.** erg **5.** ergon, joule **6.** kilerg
yarn.. **6.** denier
unite ... **3.** fay, tie, wed **4.** ally,
bind, fuse, join, knit, link, meld,
weld **5.** annex, graft, marry, merge
6. adhere, cement, concur, mingle,

solder **7.** combine, connect **8.** coalesce,
condense, converge, federate, side with
9. affiliate, associate **10.** amalgamate,
federalize **11.** consolidate, incorporate
unite (pert to) ...
by freezing.. **8.** regelate
by interweaving.. **5.** plash **6.** pleach,
splice
by joints.. **10.** articulate
closely.. **11.** concentrate
in concordance.. **9.** harmonize
timbers.. **6.** rabbet
united ... **3.** one, wed **4.** knit, tied **5.** added
6. allied, banded, joined, linked,
merged, welded **7.** cohered, grafted,
rallied, spliced **8.** cemented, clannish
9. concerted, corporate **10.** concurrent,
corporated
United Provinces ... **11.** (The)
Netherlands **13.** Dutch Republic
United States ... **9.** Etats-Unis
United States ... see also *American*
artist.. **4.** Wood **5.** Flagg, Homer,
Peale, Ryder, Sloan, Wyeth **6.** Benton,
Eakins, Hopper, O'Keefe, Stuart,
Warhol **7.** Bellows, Bingham, Cassatt
8. Rockwell, Whistler **9.** Remington
12. Grandma Moses
author.. **3.** Ade, Poe **5.** Alger, Crane,
Harte, James (Henry), Lewis (Sinclair),
Stowe, Twain (Clemens) **6.** Alcott,
Cather, Chopin, Cooper, Ferber,
Holmes, Irving, Jewett, London,
Lowell, O'Henry (Porter) **7.** Dreiser,
Ellison, Emerson, Hurston, Thoreau,
Whitman **8.** Faulkner, Melville, Whittier
9. Hawthorne, Hemingway
10. Fitzgerald, Longfellow, Tarkington
canal.. **4.** Erie **6.** Panama
capital.. see separate States
composer.. **4.** Ives, Kern **5.** Foote, Nevin
6. Berlin, Foster **7.** Copland, Rodgers
8. Gershwin **9.** Bernstein
emblem.. **5.** eagle
explorer.. **4.** Byrd, Long, Pike **5.** Boone,
Clark, Lewis, Logan, Perry
Falls.. **7.** Niagara **8.** Yosemite
9. Multnomah
Indian.. see under *Indian (Am)*
inventor.. **3.** Hoe **4.** Bell, Howe
5. Fiske, Fitch, Morse **6.** Edison, Fulton
7. Whitney
mountain.. **4.** Hood **6.** Elbert, Helena,
Shasta **7.** Rainier, Whitney **8.** Katahdin,
McKinley
naturalist.. **4.** Muir **5.** Beebe, Seton
7. Thoreau
ornithologist.. **7.** Audubon
philosopher.. **5.** James
pirate.. **4.** Kidd
poet.. **3.** Poe **4.** Nash **5.** Benét, Field,
Moore, Wylie **6.** Bryant, Holmes, Kilmer,
Lanier, Lowell, Millay **7.** Whitman
8. Whittier **10.** Longfellow
unity ... **3.** one **5.** union **6.** accord
7. concord, harmony, oneness
8. alliance **9.** agreement **10.** singleness,
uniformity **11.** conjunction, unification
12. completeness
universal ... **3.** all **5.** local, total,
usual, whole **6.** cosmic, entire, public

7. general 8. catholic 9. prevalent, unlimited, well-known 11. widely known
universal (pert to)...
knowledge.. 9. pantology
language.. 2. Ro 3. Ido 9. Esperanto
language, written.. 10. pasigraphy
remedy.. 7. panacea
solvent.. 8. alkahest
successor, heir.. 5. heres (haeres)
universe... 4. olam 5. world 6. cosmos, system 9. macrocosm 10. Great World
universe, controlling principle... 5. logos
unkempt... 5. messy, rough 6. frowsy, shaggy, untidy 7. ruffled, squalid, tousled, uncouth 9. unrefined 10. disarrayed, disheveled, unpolished
unkind... 3. ill 5. cruel, harsh, stern 6. brutal, severe 8. ungenial 9. inclement 10. ungracious, ungrateful 13. unsympathetic 15. uncompassionate
unknowable... 6. mystic 8. mystical, noumenon 9. enigmatic 13. indiscernible 14. unintelligible 15. absolute reality (Kant), ultimate reality (Spencer)
unknowable object... 3. God 7. the soul 8. noumenon
unknown... 7. inconnu, strange 8. stranger 9. anonymous, hereafter, incognito, unheard of 10. unfamiliar, unrenowned 12. incalculable
unlawful... 7. bastard, illegal, illicit, lawless 9. irregular 10. contraband 11. unwarranted 12. illegitimate, unauthorized
unlearned... 4. lewd 5. gross 8. ignorant, untaught 10. illiterate, uneducated 11. instinctive
unleashed... 4. free 5. loose 6. untied 8. released 10. unfettered, unshackled, untethered
unleavened... 7. azymous
unleavened bread... 4. azym 5. azyme 7. matzoth
unless... 4. nisi, save 6. except 7. without 9. except for, excepting 10. except that
unlettered... 8. ignorant 10. illiterate, uneducated
unlike... 6. sundry, uneven 7. dislike, diverse 9. different, irregular 10. dissimilar, improbable 11. unpromising 12. disagreeable 13. heterogeneous
unlikelihood... 11. small chance 13. improbability
unlikeness... 8. contrast 13. dissimilarity
unlimited... 4. vast 9. boundless, unbounded, universal 10. unconfined 11. illimitable 12. immeasurable, unrestricted 13. indeterminate
unload... 3. rid 4. dump, sell 5. empty 7. discard, lighten 9. disburden, discharge, liquidate
unlucky... 3. bad, fey, ill 7. infaust 8. ill-fated, untimely 9. ill-omened 11. unfortunate 12. inauspicious, not favorable
unmannerly... 4. rude 7. boorish, uncivil 8. impolite 10. mannerless

12. discourteous
unmelodious... 9. dissonant 11. cacophonous
unmerciful... 5. cruel 6. unkind 7. extreme, inhuman 8. pitiless, ruthless 9. heartless, merciless 10. relentless
unmistakable... 4. open 5. clear, plain 6. patent 7. certain, evident, obvious 8. apparent, distinct, manifest 11. unqualified
unmitigated... 4. mere 5. sheer 6. arrant 8. clear-cut, thorough 9. downright 11. not softened, unqualified
unmoved... 4. calm, dead, firm 5. inert 6. serene 8. obdurate, unshaken 9. apathetic
unnatural... 5. eerie (eery) 7. labored, strange, uncanny 8. abnormal, affected 9. eccentric, irregular 10. artificial, factitious
unnecessary... 4. fuss 7. useless 8. needless 11. not required, superfluous, uncalled-for 12. nonessential
unobtrusive... 6. modest 8. retiring 11. clandestine
unoccupied... 4. idle, void 5. empty 7. not busy 8. deserted 10. unemployed, untenanted 11. empty-headed, uninhabited
unorthodox... 9. heretical 10. fallacious, left-handed 14. unconventional
unostentatious... 5. quiet 6. lenten, modest 10. restrained
unparalleled... 5. alone 6. unique 8. peerless 9. matchless, unequaled, unmatched 10. inimitable 13. extraordinary
unpleasant... 8. unsavory 9. offensive 10. not amiable, ungracious 11. displeasing, distasteful 12. disagreeable
unpolished... 5. bruit, crude, rough 6. coarse, rugged 7. uncouth 8. agrestic, unpolite 9. inelegant 10. agrestical 11. countrified
unprecedented... 3. new 5. novel 10. unexampled, unimitated 13. extraordinary
unprejudiced... 4. fair 7. neutral 8. unbiased 9. impartial 10. impersonal 13. dispassionate
unprepared... 3. raw 5. unfit 6. unwary 7. unready 9. premature, unskilled
unprepossessing... 4. grim, ugly 9. grim-faced 10. ill-looking
unpretentious... 6. humble, modest, simple 7. natural 10. unaffected 11. in good taste
unprincipled... 7. corrupt 9. dishonest 10. fraudulent, perfidious 12. dishonorable, unscrupulous
unprofessional... 3. lay 6. laical 7. amateur 9. unskilled 10. amateurish 14. unbusinesslike
unprofitable... 6. barren 7. useless 8. gainless 9. fruitless 10. unfruitful
unpropitious... 7. adverse, ominous, opposed 8. untimely 10. disastrous 12. inauspicious
unqualified... 5. unfit 6. unable

7. genuine, plenary 8. absolute, complete, unfitted 9. incapable 10. ineligible 11. incompetent 12. not qualified 13. unconditional

unquestionable ... 7. certain, decided, evident 8. positive 10. undeniable 11. indubitable, irrefutable 12. indisputable 13. unimpeachable

unravel ... 4. undo 5. feaze, solve 6. unfold, unlace 8. separate 9. disengage 10. disinvolve 11. disentangle

unreal ... 5. false, ideal 7. fancied 8. fanciful, illusory, spurious 9. fantastic, imaginary, visionary 10. artificial, fictitious 11. imaginative 13. unsubstantial

unreasonable ... 3. mad 6. absurd, unwise 9. excessive, fanatical, illogical, senseless 10. capricious, exorbitant, immoderate, irrational 11. extravagant, impractical 13. unjustifiable

unrecognizable ... 3. dim 5. vague 7. blurred, obscure, unclear 9. undefined 10. indistinct 14. unintelligible

unrecognized ... 6. unsung 7. unknown 13. unappreciated

unrefined ... 3. raw 4. loud, rude 5. crass, crude, gross, rough 6. coarse, common, earthy, vulgar 7. uncouth 9. inelegant 11. countrified 12. uncultivated

unrefuted ... 4. true 6. proved 8. undenied 10. unanswered

unrelaxed ... 4. taut 5. rigid, tense 7. nervous

unrelenting ... 4. grim, hard, iron 5. stern 6. severe, strict 8. rigorous 9. merciless 10. inexorable, relentless, unyielding

unreliable ... 6. fickle, unsafe 9. uncertain 10. capricious, changeable 12. undependable 13. irresponsible, untrustworthy 14. tergiversating

unremitting ... 4. busy 8. constant 9. continual, incessant, perpetual 10. continuous, persistent 11. persevering

unrequited ... 6. unpaid 9. forgotten, unthanked 10. ungrateful, unrewarded

unreserved, unreservedly ... 4. free, open 5. frank 6. openly 7. frankly 8. candidly, outright, thorough 9. outspoken 12. unrestricted

unrest ... 6. bustle 8. disquiet 9. commotion 12. restlessness

unrestrained ... 3. lax 4. free, wild 5. loose 6. candid, wanton 7. lawless, riotous 9. unbridled, unlimited 10. capricious

unrestricted ... 4. free, open 9. unlimited 11. extravagant 12. undiminished 13. communicative

unruffled ... 4. calm, cool 5. still 6. placid, poised, sedate, serene, smooth 9. quiescent, unexcited 10. unaffected 11. undisturbed

unruly ... 7. lawless 9. fractious, obstinate, turbulent 10. disorderly, licentious, refractory 11. disobedient 12. recalcitrant, ungovernable, unmanageable

unsafe ... 7. dubious, exposed, unsound 8. insecure, perilous 9. dangerous 10. unreliable 12. undependable

unsatisfactory ... 8. inferior 10. inadequate, unbearable 11. intolerable 12. insufficient, ungratiating 13. disheartening, unsupportable

unsavory ... 7. insipid 9. offensive, tasteless 10. unpleasant 11. unpalatable 12. disagreeable

unscrupulous ... 7. devious 9. dishonest 12. unparticular, unprincipled 13. untrustworthy 16. indiscriminating

unseasonable ... 8. untimely 9. premature 10. inopportune

unseemly ... 5. inapt, wrong 6. vulgar 8. improper, indecent 9. inelegant 10. indecorous, solecistic, unbecoming 11. undignified 13. ungrammatical

unseen ... 6. hidden 8. unheeded, viewless 9. invisible, unnoticed 12. undiscovered

unsettled ... 4. moot 6. fickle, queasy 8. confused, deranged, restless, unplaced, unproved, unstable 9. ambiguous, disturbed, irregular, uncertain, unquieted 10. irresolute, unoccupied, up in the air 11. unpopulated

unshorn ... 5. hairy, whole 6. shaggy

unshorn sheep (2nd year) ... 3. tag, teg

unsightly ... 4. ugly 8. uncomely, unlovely 9. inelegant, not comely 12. unattractive

unskilled ... 5. green 6. puisne 8. ignorant, malapert

unskillful ... 5. inept 7. artless, awkward 9. maladroit 12. unproficient 13. inexperienced

unsophisticated ... 4. naif, pure, soft 5. green, naive 6. simple 7. artless, genuine 8. gullible, innocent 9. ingenuous 11. uncorrupted

unsound ... 4. weak 5. crazy, dotty, risky, shaky 6. addled, fickle 8. impaired, insecure 9. defective, imperfect

unspoken ... 5. tacit 6. silent 7. implied 9. ineffable, unuttered

unstable ... 4. weak 6. fickle, fitful, labile, scanty 7. astatic, erratic, flighty, plastic 8. insecure, not solid, ticklish, unsteady 9. ephemeral, irregular, unsettled 10. inconstant, precarious, unreliable 11. fluctuating, vacillating

unsteady ... 5. dizzy, shaky 6. groggy, wobbly 7. quavery, rickety, unsound 8. titubate, unstable, wavering 9. irregular, uncertain 10. capricious, changeable, flickering, inconstant, precarious 11. fluctuating, ill-balanced, lightheaded, vacillating

unsubstantial ... 4. airy, rare, slim 5. filmy, light 6. aerial, flimsy, papery 8. illusory 9. illogical, visionary 10. immaterial, intangible, unreliable

unsuitable ... 5. inept, undue, unfit 8. untimely 10. unbecoming 11. inexpedient 13. inappropriate 14. unsatisfactory

unsullied ... 4. pure 5. clean 6. chaste

8. innocent, spotless, virginal
10. immaculate
unsure . . . 4. weak 5. timid 6. infirm
8. doubtful 10. precarious 11. vacillating
unsweetened . . . 3. dry, sec 4. sour, tart
10. unpleasant
unsympathetic . . . 6. unkind 7. hostile
8. pitiless 9. heartless 10. intolerant
11. hardhearted 12. unresponsive
untamed . . . 4. wild 5. feral 6. savage
9. unsubdued 11. uncivilized
untangle . . . 4. free 5. loose, solve
6. sleave 9. extricate 11. disentangle
untenable . . . 10. incredible
11. implausible 12. unbelievable,
unreasonable 13. inconceivable
unthinking . . . 4. rash 7. puerile
8. careless, heedless 9. impetuous,
impulsive 11. injudicious, instinctive,
involuntary, thoughtless
13. inconsiderate
untidy . . . 5. dowdy, messy 6. frowzy,
shabby 8. careless, frumpish, slipshod,
slovenly, unsuited, untimely
10. disheveled
untie . . . 4. free 5. loose 6. loosen,
unbind, unknot, unlash 8. unfasten
9. disengage
until now . . . 8. hitherto
untiring . . . 8. sedulous, tireless
9. unwearied 10. unflagging
13. indefatigable
untold . . . 4. vast 8. infinite 9. boundless,
countless 10. uninformed, unrevealed
11. innumerable, unexpressed
12. immeasurable, incalculable,
undetermined
untouched . . . 3. new 4. pure 6. intact,
unused 8. pristine, virginal
10. impenitent, unaffected
untoward . . . 6. unruly 7. unlucky
8. perverse, stubborn, unseemly
10. indecorous, ungraceful
11. unfavorable, unfortunate
12. unpropitious
untrained . . . 4. soft, wild 5. green
8. indocile 9. unskilled, untutored
10. amateurish 11. unpracticed
14. unaccomplished
untrammeled . . . 4. free 5. loose
8. not bound 9. unimpeded, unlimited
10. unfettered, unhampered,
unhindered
untransferable . . . 11. inalienable
untried . . . 3. new 5. fresh, green
8. unproved 9. unhandled
13. inexperienced
untrue . . . 5. false, wrong 8. disloyal
9. dishonest, erroneous, incorrect, not
honest 10. fallacious, unfaithful
untrustworthy . . . 6. tricky, unsafe
8. slippery 9. deceitful, dishonest,
uncertain 10. perfidious
untruth . . . 3. lie 5. error, fable 7. falsity
9. falsehood, treachery 10. disloyalty
11. fabrication 13. faithlessness
unusual . . . 3. odd 4. rare 5. novel, queer
6. exotic, quaint, unique 7. strange
8. terrific, uncommon 9. anomalous
10. infrequent, remarkable
11. exceptional 13. extraordinary

unutterable . . . 6. sacred, secret
9. ineffable, wonderful 11. unspeakable
13. inexpressible
unvarnished . . . 5. plain 6. simple
7. genuine 9. unadorned, unglossed
11. undeceptive 13. unembellished
unvarying . . . 7. uniform 8. constant
9. permanent 10. monotonous
unwarranted . . . 4. idle, vain 5. undue
7. illegal 8. baseless 9. excessive,
unfounded, untenable 10. exorbitant,
unentitled 11. unjustified
unwary . . . 4. rash 7. unaware 8. heedless,
off guard 9. unguarded 10. unwatchful
unwavering . . . 4. firm, sure 5. solid
8. constant 9. steadfast 10. unweakened
11. not yielding, persevering
unwelcome . . . 8. non grata, unwanted
9. intrusive, uninvited
unwholesome . . . 4. evil, sick 6. impure
7. corrupt, immoral, noisome, noxious
9. unhealthy 12. insalubrious
unwieldy . . . 5. bulky 6. clumsy
7. awkward, restive 8. ungainly
9. ponderous 10. cumbersome
12. unmanageable 13. insubordinate
unwilling . . . 5. loath (loth) 6. averse
9. reluctant 11. disinclined, involuntary
unwilling to prosecute . . . 7. nol-pros
13. nolle prosequi
unwise . . . 7. foolish 9. impolitic,
imprudent, senseless 10. irrational
11. inexpedient, injudicious
unwonted . . . 4. rare 6. unused 7. unusual
8. uncommon 9. not wonted
10. infrequent 12. unaccustomed
unworldly . . . 5. eerie (eery), godly, naive,
weird 8. heavenly 9. spiritual, unearthly
10. immaterial 12. supernatural
unyielding . . . 3. set 4. firm, hard, iron
5. rigid, stern, stiff 6. strict 7. adamant
8. obdurate, stubborn 9. immovable,
obstinate 10. adamantine, determined,
inexorable, inflexible
14. uncompromising
up (pert to) . . .
and coming . . 7. go-ahead 8. hustling
and down . . 6. seesaw, uneven 8. vertical
10. undulating 13. perpendicular
in arms . . 6. at odds 8. prepared
9. resistant
ref to . . 10. at the plate (game)
to . . 4. able, till, unto 5. until 9. cognizant,
competent
to date . . 3. new 6. modern 7. stylish
11. fashionable
upas tree, arrow poison . . . 6. antiar
upbraid . . . 4. twit 5. blame, chide, scold,
score 6. rebuke 7. reprove 8. admonish,
reproach 9. reprimand 10. put to shame
upheaval . . . 5. storm 6. revolt 9. agitation,
cataclysm, elevation 10. convulsion
upheld . . . 5. aided 6. backed 7. abetted
8. defended 9. supported, sustained
10. encouraged, maintained
uphill . . . 6. upward 7. upgrade
9. ascending, difficult, laborious
10. slantingly
uphold . . . 3. aid 4. abet, back, buoy
5. favor, raise 6. defend 7. confirm,
support, sustain 8. maintain, preserve

9. encourage 11. corroborate, countenance, lend support

upkeep . . . 4. cost 6. repair 7. support 11. maintenance

upland . . . 4. wold 5. weald 6. coteau, inland 7. country, plateau 8. highland

uplands . . . 7. country 9. highlands 10. the country

uplift . . . 5. elate, erect, raise 7. elevate, ennoble, glorify, improve 8. upheaval 9. elevation 11. inspiration

upon . . . 2. on 3. sur 4. atop, onto 5. about, above 7. against 9. by means of 10. after which

upon (pert to) . . .
law . . 3. sur
prefix . . 3. epi, sur
that . . 7. whereat 9. whereupon
which . . 7. whereat

upper . . . 6. higher 8. superior

upper (pert to) . . .
bed . . 4. bunk
crust . . 7. society 11. aristocracy 13. highest circle
end . . 3. tip 4. apex, head
hand . . 7. mastery 8. dominion 9. advantage, influence 10. preference
House of Congress . . 6. Senate
shoe part . . 4. vamp

uppermost . . . 3. top 6. upmost 7. highest, supreme, topmost 8. farthest, foremost 9. outermost

uppish . . . 5. drunk, proud 6. uppity 7. haughty, peevish, stuck-up 8. arrogant, assuming, snobbish 9. high-flown

upright . . . 4. good, just, true 5. erect, moral, piano 6. honest, square 7. endwise, sincere 8. vertical, virtuous 9. equitable, honorable, righteous 13. perpendicular

upright (pert to) . . .
chair part . . 4. slat
comb form . . 5. ortho
posture . . 8. orthotic 11. orthostatic
slab . . 5. stela
timber . . 4. jamb, stud

uprising . . . 4. riot 6. ascent, mutiny, revolt 7. sloping 9. acclivity, ascending, rebellion 12. insurrection

uproar . . . 3. din 4. riot, rout 5. noise 6. bedlam, bustle, clamor, fracas, hubbub, outcry, tumult 7. turmoil 8. outbreak 9. commotion, confusion 10. donnybrook, hurly-burly, tintamarre, turbulence 11. pandemonium 12. insurrection

upset . . . 3. irk 4. rile, ruin, stir 6. defeat, refute, topple 7. agitate, capsize, confuse, disturb, fluster, startle, subvert, unnerve 8. distress, overturn, startled, unnerved 9. embarrass, overthrow 10. discompose, disconcert, distressed, frustrated, overturned, refutation, revolution 11. frustration, overwrought

upshot . . . 3. end 5. fruit, issue 6. result, sequel 7. outcome 10. conclusion 11. consequence, eventuality, termination 12. consummation

upside down . . . 8. confused, disorder 9. confusion 10. resupinate, topsy-turvy

upsilon (Gr) . . . 5. hyoid, vowel 7. Y-shaped

upstart . . . 4. snob 7. bounder, parvenu 13. social climber

up-to-date . . . 6. modern 7. alamode, topical 8. informed 11. fashionable

upward . . . 2. up 3. ano (comb form) 4. over 5. above, aloft 6. onward 7. skyward 8. upstream 9. ascending

upward movement of vessels . . . 5. scend

uraeus (Egypt Relig) . . . 3. asp 6. symbol 8. symbolic

Ural . . . 5. river 9. mountains

Urania (pert to) . . .
blue . . 12. independence
epithet of . . 9. Aphrodite
genus of . . 5. moths
Gr Myth . . 4. Muse (Astron)

uranology (study of) . . . 7. heavens 15. celestial bodies

Uranus (pert to) . . .
astronomy . . 6. planet
daughter . . 4. Rhea
father of . . 9. The Titans (12)
personification of . . 6. heaven
satellite . . 5. Ariel 6. Oberon 7. Titania, Umbriel
son . . 6. Cronus

urare, urari . . . 6. curare

urban . . . 5. civic 6. ghetto, polite, uptown 7. oppidan, refined 8. downtown, polished 9. courteous, municipal 12. metropolitan 13. sophisticated

urbane . . . 5. civil, suave 6. polish, polite 7. affable 8. gracious 9. courteous 11. deferential

urbanity . . . 7. amenity 8. civility, courtesy 9. deference

urchin . . . 3. boy, elf, imp, tad 4. arab, brat 5. gamin 6. elfish 8. hedgehog 9. dandiprat, sea urchin, youngster

urge . . . 3. dun, egg, hie, ply, yen 4. abet, coax, goad, prod, push, spur 5. drive, egg on, impel, press 6. advise, compel, dehort, desire, exhort, fillip, hasten, incite, induce 7. animate, entreat, solicit 8. persuade 9. constrain, importune, influence, instigate 10. inducement

urgent . . . 3. hot 5. grave 7. clamant, exigent, instant 8. critical, pressing 9. impelling, important, insistent, necessary 11. importunate

urial . . . 3. sha 5. sheep 6. oorial

Uriel . . . 9. archangel 10. flame of God (Bib)

Urim and Thummim (Bib) . . . 11. instruments 12. interpreters (Mormon)

urn . . . 3. jar 4. ewer, urna (anc), vase 5. grave, steen 6. vessel 7. pitcher, samovar, vaselet 10. jardiniere

urn-shaped . . . 8. urceolus 9. urceolate

Ursa . . . 4. bear 9. Ursa Major (Great Bear), Ursa Minor (Little Bear)

ursal . . . 7. fur seal

ursuk . . . 11. bearded seal

Ursula . . . 5. Saint 7. she-bear 9. butterfly 15. British princess (legend)

urubu . . . 7. vulture

Uruguay . . .

capital .. **10.** Montevideo
city .. **4.** Melo **5.** Minar **9.** Maldonado
estuary .. **5.** Plata **12.** Rio de la Plata
lake .. **5.** Merim
river .. **7.** Uruguay
settler .. **5.** Cabot (Sebastian, 1527)
university .. **10.** Montevideo (1849)
windstorm .. **7.** pampero
urus ... **2.** ox **3.** tur **7.** aurochs
usable ... **3.** fit **9.** practical **10.** functional
  11. serviceable, utilitarian
usage ... **3.** use **4.** wont **5.** habit, ritus
  6. custom, method **7.** utility **8.** behavior,
  practice **9.** treatment **10.** convention
use ... **3.** try **5.** apply, avail, exert, spend,
  treat, wield **6.** employ, expend, occupy
  7. consume, exploit, utilize **8.** function
  10. manipulate **11.** consumption,
  utilization
use (pert to) ...
  abusive language .. **4.** rail
  divining rod .. **5.** dowse
  frugally .. **5.** stint
  pert to words .. **7.** neology, verbose
  8. enallage, pleonasm **9.** verbosity
  poetry .. **4.** vail
  refrain from .. **7.** boycott
  subterfuge .. **7.** chicane
  up .. **3.** eat **7.** consume, deplete, exhaust,
  fatigue
useful ... **4.** good **5.** utile **7.** helpful
  9. practical **10.** beneficial, commodious
  11. serviceable, subservient
  12. advantageous, instrumental
usefulness ... **5.** avail, value **6.** profit
  7. utility **13.** conduciveness
useless ... **4.** idle, null, vain **6.** futile,
  otiose **7.** of no use **8.** bootless,
  hopeless **9.** fruitless, worthless **10.** fifth
  wheel **11.** ineffectual, superfluous
  12. unprofitable **13.** unserviceable
  14. good for nothing
uselessness ... **8.** futility **9.** inutility
  10. inefficacy
usher ... **4.** lead, page **5.** guide **6.** escort
  7. chobdar, teacher **9.** attendant,
  harbinger, precursor **10.** doorkeeper,
  forerunner, inaugurate
usquebaugh ... **6.** whisky **7.** cordial
ustion ... **7.** burning **13.** cauterization
ustulate ... **8.** scorched **10.** discolored
usual ... **7.** average, typical, usitate
  8. everyday, frequent **11.** status in
  quo
usuer ... **5.** shark **6.** loaner **7.** Shylock
  11. moneylender
usurp ... **4.** take **5.** seize **6.** assume
  8. arrogate **11.** appropriate
Utah ...
  capital .. **12.** Salt Lake City
  city .. **5.** Logan, Ogden, Provo
  7. Bingham
  dam .. **10.** Glen Canyon **12.** Flaming
  Gorge
  lake .. **6.** Powell **9.** Great Salt
  mountain .. **5.** Uinta **7.** Wasatch **9.** King's
  Peak
  name desired .. **7.** Deseret
  natural wonder .. **4.** Zion **5.** Bryce
  13. Rainbow Bridge
  settled by .. **7.** Mormons **12.** Brigham

Young **15.** Latter-day Saints
State admission .. **10.** Forty-fifth
State motto .. **8.** Industry
State nickname .. **7.** Beehive
utensil ... **3.** mop, pan, pot **4.** tool
  5. broom, brush **6.** device, ramrod
  7. skillet, sweeper **9.** apparatus,
  appliance, implement **10.** instrument
utilitarian ... **5.** plain **6.** useful
  8. economic **9.** practical **10.** functional
  12. matter-of-fact
utility ... **3.** use **4.** tool **5.** avail **6.** profit
  7. benefit, service **9.** appliance,
  happiness, implement **10.** usefulness
utmost ... **4.** best, last **5.** final **7.** extreme,
  maximum, supreme **8.** farthest, greatest
  9. uttermost **11.** most distant
Utopia ... **4.** Eden **6.** heaven, island
  (imaginary) **7.** Erewhon **8.** paradise
  9. fairyland, Shangri-La **10.** millennium
utopian ... **5.** ideal **6.** Edenic **8.** Quixotic,
  romantic **9.** visionary **10.** chimerical,
  idealistic, millennial
utter ... **3.** say **4.** emit, pass, tell,
  vent **5.** issue, sheer, speak, total,
  voice **6.** assert, entire, mumble,
  reveal **7.** deliver, divulge, express,
  extreme, publish, unusual
  8. abnormal, absolute, complete, disclose,
  disperse, intonate **9.** downright,
  enunciate, out-and-out, pronounce
  10. peremptory **11.** unqualified
  13. unconditional
utter (pert to) ...
  harshly .. **3.** rap **4.** bray
  heedlessly .. **4.** blat
  in devotion .. **4.** pray
  in slow tone .. **5.** drawl
  musically .. **5.** warble
  publicly .. **4.** tell **5.** voice **7.** enounce
  softly .. **6.** murmur **7.** whisper
  want .. **9.** indigency **11.** destitution
  with effort .. **5.** heave
  with impulse .. **9.** ejaculate
  without voice .. **4.** surd **7.** spirate
utterance (pert to) ...
  dogmatic .. **6.** dictum
  gushing .. **8.** effusion
  rhythmic .. **7.** cadence
  voice .. **8.** phonesis, speaking
  9. phonation **12.** articulation
  wise .. **6.** oracle
utterer of pithy remarks ... **8.** aphorist
utterly ... **5.** fully, stark **7.** totally
  8. entirely **10.** absolutely, completely
  17. straightforwardly
uttermost ... **5.** finai **6.** utmost **7.** extreme
utu ... **6.** reward **12.** compensation,
  satisfaction
uva ... **5.** fruit, grape
uvate ... **8.** conserve (grape)
uvea ... **4.** iris
uxor ... **4.** wife
uxoricide ... **10.** wife murder
Uz (Bib) ... **8.** Job's home
Uzbekistan (pert to) ...
  capital .. **8.** Tashkent
  city .. **9.** Samarkand
  formerly part of .. **4.** USSR
  people .. **5.** Uzbek **6.** Turkic
Uzziel ... **5.** angel (Paradise Lost)

V

V . . . **5.** notch **6.** letter (22nd), symbol **14.** five-dollar bill

vaagmer . . . **8.** dealfish (mare of the sea)

Vac (Hind) . . . **7.** goddess (of speech)

vacant . . . **4.** free, idle, void **5.** blank, empty, inane **6.** barren, devoid **7.** leisure, vacuous **8.** unfilled **10.** disengaged, untenanted **11.** thoughtless **12.** unencumbered **14.** expressionless

vacate . . . **4.** free, quit, void **5.** annul, empty, leave **6.** depart **7.** abandon **8.** abdicate, abrogate, evacuate, withdraw

vacation . . . **4.** rest **5.** leave **6.** outing, recess, repeal **7.** nonterm, respite **8.** furlough, justitum **10.** recreation **12.** intermission **14.** leave of absence

vacation place . . . **3.** spa **4.** lake, park **5.** beach **6.** forest, resort **9.** mountains

vaccination . . . **11.** inoculation

vaccine (pert to) . . .
 discoverer . . **4.** Salk **6.** Jenner
 protection for . . **5.** virus **6.** cowpox
 term . . **5.** lymph, serum, virus

vacillate . . . **4.** sway **5.** waver **6.** dacker (daiker), seesaw, teeter, totter **7.** flutter, stagger **8.** hesitate, titubate **9.** fluctuate, oscillate **13.** procrastinate

vacillation . . . **5.** doubt **8.** wavering **9.** faltering, hesitancy **10.** fickleness, indecision, titubation **11.** oscillation, uncertainty **12.** irresolution **14.** changeableness **15.** procrastination

vacuate . . . **5.** empty **9.** evacuate

vacuous . . . **4.** dull, void **5.** blank, empty **6.** stupid **8.** unfilled **9.** senseless **11.** empty-headed, thoughtless **13.** unintelligent

vacuum . . . **3.** gap **4.** void **9.** emptiness **11.** rarefaction

vade mecum . . . **6.** manual **8.** handbook

vagabond . . . **3.** bum, vag **4.** hobo **5.** lorel, scamp, tramp **6.** beggar, picaro, rascal, rodney **7.** vagrant, wastrel **8.** Bohemian, brodyaga, wanderer **10.** ne'er-do-well

vagary . . . **4.** whim **5.** caper, fancy, jaunt, prank, trick **6.** notion, ramble **7.** caprice, whimsey (whimsy) **9.** excursion, wandering **10.** digression **13.** manifestation

vagrant . . . **3.** bum **4.** hobo **5.** rogue, tramp **6.** roving, truant **7.** nomadic, prowler, wayward **8.** brodyaga, vagabond, wanderer **9.** desultory, deviative, itinerant **10.** capricious

vague . . . **3.** dim **4.** dark, hazy **5.** loose, misty **6.** dreamy **7.** obscure, shadowy, unfixed **8.** confused, formless, nebulous, not clear **9.** ambiguous, unsettled, wandering **10.** indefinite, indistinct, intangible **13.** indeterminate

vail . . . **3.** tip **4.** doff (a hat), dole **5.** avail, bribe, yield **6.** humble, submit **7.** descend **8.** gratuity **10.** beneficial

12. advantageous

vain . . . **4.** idle **5.** empty, proud **6.** devoid, futile, otiose, snooty **7.** foolish, trivial, useless **8.** arrogant, boastful, nugatory **9.** conceited, fruitless, worthless **10.** unavailing, unrewarded **11.** empty-headed, overweening, unimportant **12.** vainglorious

vain boasting . . . **11.** fanfaronade

vainglorious . . . **4.** vain **7.** heroics **8.** boastful **9.** gasconade

vain person . . . **3.** fop **5.** dandy **7.** coxcomb **8.** popinjay

vair . . . **3.** fur

vajra (Buddh) . . . **7.** diamond, trident (Indra's) **10.** adamantine **11.** thunderbolt

valance . . . **5.** drape **6.** border, pelmet, ruffle **7.** curtain, drapery, hanging

vale . . . **4.** dale, dell, glen **5.** earth, glade, world **6.** valley

valediction . . . **5.** adieu **7.** address **8.** farewell **11.** valedictory

valedictory . . . **7.** address, oration **10.** apopemptic **11.** leave-taking, valediction

Valentine (pert to) . . .
 romance . . **5.** Orson **8.** love song
 Saint . . **6.** martyr (Rom) **7.** holiday
  8. feast day
 State . . **7.** Arizona (adm 2/14/1912)
 sweetheart . . **11.** one's beloved

valerian . . . **4.** drug **5.** plant **7.** panacea

valet . . . **3.** man **7.** Crispin **9.** attendant, cameriere, chamberer **10.** manservant **11.** body servant **14.** valet de chambre

valetudinarian . . . **6.** infirm, shut-in, sickly, weakly **7.** invalid **11.** languishing

Valhalla (Valhall) . . . **8.** Pantheon (Bavaria) **10.** hall of Odin (Norse Myth)

valiant . . . **4.** bold, fine **5.** brave **6.** heroic, strong, sturdy **7.** doughty **8.** intrepid, stalwart, vigorous, virtuous **9.** steadfast **10.** chivalrous, courageous **11.** meritorious **12.** stouthearted

valid . . . **4.** good, just, true **5.** legal, sound **6.** cogent, lawful, proved **7.** binding, weighty **9.** authentic, effective **10.** sufficient **11.** efficacious **12.** well-grounded

validate . . . **6.** affirm, attest **7.** confirm **8.** legalize **12.** substantiate

validity . . . **5.** force **7.** cogency **9.** authority, soundness **14.** substantiality

Valjean (pert to) . . .
 discoverer . . **6.** Javert
 friend . . **6.** Marius
 hero of . . **13.** Les Miserables (Victor Hugo)
 protégé . . **7.** Cosette

valley . . . **4.** dale, dell, dene, glen, vale, wady **5.** glade, gully **6.** coulee, dingle, ravine, trough **10.** depression

valley (pert to) . . .
 anatomy . . **9.** vallecula

circular . . **6.** rincon
deep . . **6.** canyon
geology . . **5.** atrio
India . . **5.** dhoon
Jerusalem (near) . . **6.** Hinnom
 7. Gehenna, Rephaim
moon . . **5.** rille
open . . **6.** canada
where David killed Goliath . . **4.** Elah
 (Bib)
valonia oak . . . **6.** camata (fruit)
 9. evergreen
valor . . . **5.** merit, worth **6.** virtue
 7. bravery, courage, heroism, prowess
 8. boldness, chivalry **9.** gallantry
 11. distinction **12.** fearlessness
valuable . . . **4.** dear **5.** asset **6.** prized,
 useful, worthy **8.** precious **9.** estimable,
 treasured **10.** worthwhile
value . . . **3.** par, use **4.** rate **5.** price,
 prize, worth **6.** assess, esteem,
 parity, status **7.** apprize (apprise),
 cherish, compute, meaning, respect,
 utility **8.** appraise, estimate, evaluate
 9. valuation **10.** estimation, excellence,
 importance
value (pert to) . . .
equal . . **6.** parity
least possible . . **5.** plack
nominal . . **3.** par
reduction . . **12.** depreciation
valueless . . . **4.** baff **9.** worthless
 10. threepenny **14.** good-for-nothing
valve . . . **3.** tap **4.** cock, door, gate
 6. faucet, piston, spigot **7.** petcock
vamoose . . . **2.** go **4.** blow, scat **5.** leave,
 scram **6.** beat it, decamp **7.** skiddoo
 9. skedaddle
vamp . . . **4.** hose, sock **5.** flirt, patch, upper
 6. recoct, repair, seduce **7.** beguile,
 bewitch, concoct, touch up **9.** improvise,
 temptress, transform
vampire . . . **3.** bat **5.** fiend, ghost, lamia,
 witch **6.** Alukah **9.** bewitcher, sorceress,
 temptress **11.** bloodsucker, extortioner
 12. extortionist
van . . . **4.** lead, wing **5.** front, wagon
 6. shovel, summit, winnow **7.** vehicle
 9. forefront **10.** baggage car **12.** advance
 guard
vandal . . . **3.** Hun **7.** wrecker **9.** destroyer,
 mutilator, plunderer **10.** iconoclast
vandalize . . . **3.** mar **5.** wreck **6.** deface
Vandyke . . . **5.** beard, brown **6.** artist,
 collar **7.** picture
vane . . . **4.** cock **11.** weathercock,
 weathervane
vanish . . . **3.** die **4.** fade, flee, melt, pass
 6. perish **8.** evanesce **9.** cease to be,
 disappear
vanity . . . **5.** pride **6.** egoism **7.** conceit,
 egotism, falsity **8.** futility **9.** arrogance,
 emptiness, vainglory **10.** hollowness
 11. fatuousness, self-conceit
 12. boastfulness **13.** dressing table
vanity case . . . **4.** etui **6.** make-up
 7. compact **9.** cosmetics
vanquish . . . **3.** win **4.** beat, best, rout
 5. expel **6.** defeat, subdue **7.** conquer
 8. confound, overcome, suppress,
 surmount **9.** overthrow

vantage . . . **4.** gain **9.** advantage
 10. perquisite **11.** opportunity,
 superiority
vapid . . . **3.** dry **4.** dead, dull, flat
 5. inane, stale **7.** insipid, prosaic
 8. lifeless **9.** pointless, tasteless
 10. spiritless, unanimated **11.** indifferent
 13. uninteresting
vapor . . . **3.** air, fog, gas **4.** fume,
 haze, mist **5.** brume, cloud, fancy,
 humor, smoke, steam **6.** breath,
 bubble **7.** halitus **8.** humidity, illusion,
 phantasm **9.** evaporate **10.** exhalation
vaporous . . . **4.** vain **5.** foggy, misty
 6. cloudy, steamy **7.** gaseous
 8. ethereal, fanciful, fleeting
 13. unsubstantial
variable . . . **6.** fickle, fitful, mobile
 7. protean, unequal **8.** shifting, unstable,
 unsteady **10.** capricious, changeable,
 inconstant
variance . . . **3.** out **7.** dissent **9.** deviation,
 disaccord **10.** contention, difference
 11. discrepancy **12.** disagreement
varied . . . **5.** mixed **6.** daedal, motley
 7. changed, dappled, diverse, mottled,
 piebald, several, various **8.** speckled
 9. different **10.** variegated **11.** diversified
variegated . . . **5.** pinto **6.** daedal, motley,
 varied **7.** dappled, diverse, mottled,
 painted **9.** different **11.** diversified,
 many-colored
variegation . . . **7.** variety **9.** diversity
 10. multicolor
variety . . . **4.** kind, mode, sort **5.** class
 6. change **7.** species **9.** diversity,
 variation **10.** assortment, difference
 13. entertainment
variola . . . **6.** cowpox **8.** smallpox
various . . . **4.** many **6.** divers, sundry
 7. diverse, several **8.** manifold, variable
 9. different, many-sided, uncertain
 10. changeable, inconstant, variegated
 11. diversified
varnish . . . **4.** spar **5.** adorn, gloss, japan,
 paint **7.** distort, falsify, furbish, lacquer,
 pretext **8.** coat over **9.** embellish
Varuna (pert to) . . .
art consorts . . **5.** Jumna **6.** Ganges
deity . . **6.** cosmic (supreme)
god . . **3.** sea
Vedic equiv . . **13.** Avestan Ormazd
Vedic Relig . . **5.** Aditi (fem deity)
vary . . . **5.** alter, range, shift **6.** change,
 differ, modify **7.** deviate, dissent,
 diverge **8.** disagree **9.** alternate,
 diversify, fluctuate, vacillate, variegate
 13. differentiate
vas . . . **4.** duct **6.** pledge, surety, vessel
vascular (pert to) . . . **5.** hemic (haemic)
 6. vessel (blood, lymph) **7.** tubular
 9. vesicular **10.** hot-blooded
vase . . . **3.** jar, urn **4.** bowl **5.** ascus
 6. vessel **8.** ornament **10.** cassolette,
 jardiniere
vase (pert to) . . .
covered . . **7.** potiche
Etruscan . . **7.** canopic
Greek . . **5.** askos, diota **6.** deinos (dinos)
 7. amphora
Roman . . **8.** murrhine

vassal . . . **3.** man **4.** esne, serf **5.** helot, liege, slave **6.** varlet **7.** bondman, servant, servile, subject **9.** dependent, feudatory **11.** subordinate, subservient **12.** feudal tenant

vassalage . . . **5.** valor **6.** fealty **7.** courage, enfeoff, prowess, slavery **8.** dominion **9.** servitude **10.** subjection

vast . . . **4.** huge **5.** broad, great, large **6.** cosmic, mighty, untold **7.** immense, mammoth **8.** colossal, enormous, gigantic, spacious **9.** cyclopean, extensive **11.** far-reaching

vast (pert to) . . .
expanse . . **5.** ocean **6.** desert, empire, region
numbers . . **6.** myriad
period . . **3.** eon, era **5.** cycle
space . . **5.** waste **9.** boundless, immensity, limitless

vastness . . . **6.** extent **7.** expanse **9.** greatness, magnitude

vat . . . **3.** bac, pit, tub, tun **4.** cask, gyle, kier, tank **6.** barrel, vessel **7.** caldron (cauldron), chessel, cistern, measure, salt pit **8.** chessart

Vatican (pert to) . . .
chapel . . **7.** Sistine
church . . **8.** St Peter's
city . . **10.** Papal State (Rome)
palace of . . **4.** Pope
statuary group . . **7.** Laocoon

vaticination . . . **8.** prophecy **10.** prediction **11.** prophesying

vault . . . **3.** sky **4.** arch, dome, leap, over, tomb **5.** bound, crypt, enbow, groin **6.** canopy (of heaven), coffer, curvet, grotto, welkin **10.** depository **11.** testudinate

vaunt . . . **4.** brag **5.** boast

Vauxhall . . . **6.** resort **13.** London Quarter (Thames) **14.** Lambeth Gardens

Veda (pert to) . . .
hymns . . **8.** Sama-Veda
language . . **13.** Vedic Sanskrit
literature . . **6.** sacred (most anc)
oldest . . **7.** Rig-Veda
prose, poetry (popular) . . **11.** Atharva-Veda
ritualistic . . **9.** Yajur-Veda

Vedic (pert to) . . .
cosmic order . . **4.** Rita
dialect . . **4.** Pali
god . . **4.** Agni **5.** Dyaus **6.** Aditya, Varuna **7.** Savitar
goddess . . **5.** Aditi
hymn . . **6.** mantra
language . . **4.** Pali **8.** Sanskrit
sky serpent . . **3.** Ahi
text, treatise . . **6.** shakha (sakha) **9.** Upanishad

veer . . . **3.** shy, yaw **4.** slue, sway, turn **5.** alter, shift, sidle **6.** careen, change, swerve **7.** deviate, digress **9.** fluctuate

veery . . . **6.** thrush **9.** Wilson's thrush

vegetable . . . **3.** pea, yam **4.** bean, beet, corn, leek, okra **5.** onion **6.** carrot, celery, lentil, potato, radish, squash, tomato, turnip **7.** cabbage, lettuce, parsnip, rhubarb, shallot, spinach (spinage) **8.** broccoli, eggplant, rutabaga, scallion **9.** artichoke **11.** cauliflower

vegetable (pert to) . . .
and meat dish . . **4.** stew **6.** ragout
caterpillar . . **5.** aweto
dealer . . **8.** huckster **11.** greengrocer **12.** costermonger
green . . **5.** sabzi
herb . . **7.** salsify
leafy, salad . . **5.** chard **6.** endive **7.** lettuce, romaine, spinach
oil . . **7.** soybean **8.** macassar
poison . . **5.** abrin
stew . . **11.** ratatouille
sugar yielding . . **4.** beet

vegetate . . . **4.** grow, rest **5.** exist

vegetation, goddess of . . . **5.** Ceres

vehemence . . . **3.** ire **4.** fire, fury, rage, zeal **5.** anger, ardor **8.** violence **9.** eloquence **11.** impetuosity

vehement . . . **3.** hot **5.** angry, eager, fiery **6.** ardent, fervid, heated **7.** animose, furious, intense, violent, zealous **8.** forceful, vigorous **9.** impetuous **10.** passionate

vehicle . . . **3.** ark, bus, cab, car, van, wag **4.** auto, cart, dray, hack, jeep, limo (sl), semi, shay, sled, tank **5.** buggy, coach, lorry, moped, sulky, tonga, truck, wagon **6.** go-cart, hansom, hot rod, jalopy, landau, sleigh, travoy, troika, wheels (sl) **7.** caleche, caravan, chariot, clunker (sl), kibitka, minibus, omnibus, phaeton, scooter **8.** brougham, carriage, dragster **9.** buckboard, dune buggy, limousine **10.** automobile, conveyance, jinrikisha (jinriksha), motorcycle **11.** convertible

vehicle for oil colors . . . **6.** megilp (meguilp)

veil . . . **3.** dim **4.** caul, film, mask **5.** cloak, cover, orale, shade, velum, volet **6.** fannel, masque, screen, shroud, soften **7.** conceal, curtain, garment, pretext, secrecy **8.** disguise **9.** incognito **11.** superimpose

veiled . . . **5.** vague **6.** masked, shaded, velate **7.** covered **8.** shrouded **9.** curtained

veiling . . . **5.** tulle, voile **7.** curtain **8.** covering **10.** obvelation

vein . . . **3.** rib **4.** dash, hilo, lode, mood, tang, vena, wave **5.** costa, shade, smack, spice, tinge, touch **6.** cavity, streak **7.** bonanza, channel, crevice, fissure, mineral, stratum

vein (pert to) . . .
arrangement . . **9.** neuration
inflammation . . **9.** phlebitis
leaf . . **3.** rib
ref to . . **5.** veiny **6.** veinal, venous **7.** marbled **8.** venulose
small . . **6.** venule **7.** veinlet
stone . . **6.** gangue, matrix **9.** lodestuff
without a . . **7.** avenous

velar . . . **7.** palatal, throaty **8.** gutteral

veld, veldt . . . **6.** meadow **8.** bushveld **9.** grassland, grassveld

velleity . . . **4.** hope **6.** desire **8.** volition **9.** faint hope **10.** slight wish

vellicate . . . **3.** nip **5.** pinch **6.** tickle, twitch **9.** titillate

vellum ... **9.** parchment **10.** manuscript (on parchment)
velocity ... **4.** pace **5.** speed **8.** celerity, rapidity **9.** quickness, swiftness **10.** speediness
velocity measure ... **4.** velo
velum ... **6.** palate (soft) **8.** membrane
velvet (pert to) ...
 breast .. **9.** merganser
 cotton .. **9.** velveteen
 fabric .. **5.** panne **6.** velure
 Japanese .. **6.** birodo
 knife .. **6.** trevet
 leaf .. **6.** mallow **7.** mullein
 return .. **4.** gain **6.** profit
 texture .. **4.** soft **5.** nappy **6.** smooth
venal ... **5.** hired **6.** venous **7.** corrupt, salable (saleable) **8.** hireling, vendible **9.** mercenary **11.** corruptible
vend ... **4.** hawk, sell **5.** trade **6.** market, peddle **8.** dispense **13.** publish abroad
vender, vendor ... **6.** seller **7.** alienor
vendetta ... **4.** feud **8.** bad blood
vendue ... **4.** sale **7.** auction
venerable ... **3.** old **4.** aged, hoar, sage **5.** hoary, olden, title **6.** august, sacred **7.** ancient, antique, classic, elderly, revered **9.** dignified **11.** reverential
venerate ... **4.** love **5.** adore **6.** revere **7.** worship
veneration ... **3.** awe **4.** fear **5.** dulia, piety **6.** esteem, latria **7.** respect, worship **8.** devotion **9.** adoration, reverence
Venetian (pert to) ...
 barge .. **9.** bucentaur
 beach, resort .. **4.** Lido
 boat .. **4.** topo (toppo) **7.** gondola
 bridge (famed) .. **6.** Rialto
 magistrate .. **4.** doge **7.** podesta
 medal (New Year's) .. **5.** osela (osella)
 painter .. **6.** Titian **7.** Bellini (family), Vecchio **10.** Tintoretto
 school of .. **8.** painting
 song .. **9.** barcarole
 window (Arch) .. **9.** Palladian
Venezuela ...
 anc name .. **12.** Little Venice
 capital .. **7.** Caracas
 city .. **8.** LaGuaira, Valencia **9.** Maracaibo **6.** Ciudad, Guyana **13.** Ciudad Bolivar
 copper center .. **4.** Aroa
 Falls (world's tallest) .. **5.** Angel (found 1937)
 hero, liberator .. **7.** Bolivar
 lake .. **9.** Maracaibo, Tacariqua
 Mt .. **5.** Andes **6.** Concha, Parima, Sierra **9.** Pacaraima
 plains .. **6.** llanos
 river .. **6.** Caroni **7.** Orinoco
 sea .. **9.** Caribbean
 snake .. **4.** lora
vengeance ... **4.** harm **7.** revenge **8.** reprisal, requital **10.** avengement, punishment **11.** retaliation, retribution
Vengeance, goddess of (Gr) ... **3.** Ara, Ate **7.** Nemesis
Vengeance, god of (Gr) ... **6.** Erinys **7.** Alastor
veni, vidi, vici ... **19.** I came, I saw, I conquered (Caesar)
venial ... **7.** trivial **9.** excusable, tolerable

10. pardonable **13.** insignificant
Venice ... see also *Venetian*
 beach .. **4.** Lido
 bridge .. **6.** Rialto
 canal .. **5.** Grand **8.** Merceria, San Marco
 capital of .. **7.** Venetia (province)
 color .. **4.** blue
 island .. **6.** Rialto
 landmark .. **9.** Campanile **12.** Doges' Palaces **13.** Bridge of Sighs
 of the North .. **9.** Stockholm
 river .. **6.** Brenta
venison ... **8.** pemmican (pemican)
vennel ... **4.** lane **5.** alley, sewer **6.** gutter
venom ... **4.** gall **5.** spite, virus **6.** malice, poison **9.** animosity, malignity, virulence
venomous ... **5.** toxic **6.** deadly **7.** baneful, noxious **8.** spiteful, virulent **9.** envenomed, malicious, malignant, poisonous, rancorous
vent ... **3.** say **4.** exit, hole, slit **5.** eject, utter **6.** egress, escape, outlet **7.** air hole, fissure, opening, publish, release, ventage, volcano **8.** aperture, let loose **10.** escapement
venta ... **3.** inn
ventilate ... **3.** air, fan **5.** utter **6.** aerate **7.** discuss, publish, refresh **9.** oxygenate
ventose ... **5.** windy **9.** flatulent **12.** cupping glass
ventral ... **7.** sternal **9.** abdominal
venture ... **3.** hap, try **4.** dare, risk, wage **5.** brave, guess, stake **6.** be bold, chance, danger, gamble, hazard **7.** attempt, presume **8.** run a risk **9.** adventure, haphazard, speculate **10.** enterprise, investment **11.** speculation, undertaking
venturesome ... **4.** bold, rash **5.** brave, risky **6.** daring, heroic **8.** fearless, reckless **9.** dangerous, foolhardy, venturous **11.** adventurous, temerarious **12.** enterprising
venturous ... **4.** bold, rash **5.** hardy, risky **6.** daring **8.** fearless **9.** dangerous, hazardous **11.** temerarious, venturesome
venue ... **4.** bout, site **5.** match, onset **6.** thrust **7.** arrival, assault **9.** encounter
Venus (pert to) ...
 astronomy .. **6.** planet
 church .. **11.** Verticordia
 goddess .. **7.** Victrix **9.** Aphrodite
 goddess of (Rom) .. **6.** Beauty
 son .. **5.** Cupid
 sweetheart .. **6.** Adonis
 zoology .. **7.** mollusk
Venus status (marble) ...
 Florence .. **8.** de Medici
 Louvre .. **7.** of Arles **8.** Genetrix
 Melos .. **6.** de Milo
 Naples .. **7.** of Capua
 Rome .. **8.** Borghese **12.** of the Capitol
veracity ... **5.** truth **7.** honesty **8.** accuracy, trueness **11.** correctness **12.** truthfulness
veranda, verandah ... **4.** pyal, stoa **5.** lanai, porch, stoep **6.** loggia, piazza **7.** gallery, portico
verb (Gram) ... **5.** rhema **6.** action

verbal . . . **4.** oral **5.** wordy **7.** literal, verbose **8.** verbatim **9.** talkative, vocabular
verbal noun . . . **6.** gerund
verbatim . . . **6.** orally **7.** literal **8.** verbally **11.** word for word
verbiage . . . **4.** talk **7.** chatter, diction, fustian, wording **8.** claptrap **9.** prolixity, verbosity, wordiness **10.** redundancy
verbose . . . **5.** wordy **6.** prolix **7.** diffuse **9.** redundant
verbosity . . . **10.** redundancy
verboten . . . **5.** taboo (tabu) **9.** forbidden **10.** prohibited
verdant . . . **3.** raw **5.** color, green **6.** unripe **9.** evergreen **13.** inexperienced **15.** unsophisticated
verdelho . . . **4.** wine (white)
verdict . . . **4.** word **7.** finding, opinion **8.** decision, judgment **13.** consideration
verdigris . . . **4.** drug **5.** green **6.** aerugo **7.** deposit (on copper)
verecund . . . **6.** modest **7.** bashful
verge . . . **3.** lip, rim, top **4.** edge, tend, wand **5.** brink, limit, marge, range, scope **6.** border, emblem, extend, margin **7.** incline **9.** extremity **10.** contiguous **13.** circumference
Vergil (pert to) . . .
  birthplace . . **6.** Mantua (It)
  called . . **10.** Roman Homer
  famed as . . **4.** poet
  friend . . **8.** Maecenas
  name (last) . . **4.** Maro
  poem . . **6.** Aeneid **8.** Eclogues, Georgics
  poetic form . . **4.** epic **15.** heroic hexameter (Aeneid)
verification . . . **4.** oath, test **8.** averment **9.** collation **12.** confirmation **13.** ascertainment
verify . . . **4.** back, test **5.** check, prove **6.** affirm, attest, second **7.** confirm, support **8.** maintain **12.** authenticate, substantiate
verily . . . **3.** yea **4.** amen **5.** truly **6.** certes, indeed, in fact, really **9.** certainly **10.** positively **11.** confidently
verisimilitude . . . **5.** truth **10.** likelihood **11.** probability, verisimilar
veritable . . . **4.** real, true **6.** actual, gospel, honest **7.** genuine **9.** authentic
verity . . . **4.** fact **5.** truth **7.** honesty, reality **8.** veracity
vermilion . . . **3.** dye, red **7.** pigment, vermeil **8.** cinnabar
vermin . . . **4.** lice, mice, rats **5.** filth, fleas, flies, moths, worms **7.** bedbugs, beetles, insects, spiders, weasels, weevils **8.** riffraff, termites **9.** parasites **10.** centipedes, mosquitoes **11.** cockroaches
Vermont . . .
  capital . . **10.** Montpelier
  city . . **5.** Barre **7.** Rutland **10.** Burlington **11.** Brattleboro
  first town . . **10.** Fort Dummer
  hero . . **10.** Ethan Allen
  historic group . . **17.** Green Mountain Boys
  lake . . **9.** Champlain
  mountain . . **5.** Green **7.** Taconic
  9. Mansfield
  museum . . **9.** Shelburne **10.** Bennington
  product . . **6.** marble **10.** maple sugar
  river . . **5.** Otter **11.** Connecticut
  State admission . . **10.** Fourteenth
  State motto . . **15.** Freedom and Unity
  State nickname . . **13.** Green Mountain
vernacular . . . **5.** lingo, local **6.** common, jargon, native, patois, vulgar **7.** dialect **10.** colloquial, indigenous
vernal . . . **4.** mild, warm **5.** fresh **10.** springlike
verse . . . **4.** epic, poem, rime **5.** canto, lyric, rhyme, stave, stich **6.** poetry, rondel, sonnet, stanza **7.** measure, strophe, triolet, trochee **8.** limerick
verse (pert to) . . .
  art . . **10.** orthometry
  book of . . **5.** poesy **9.** anthology
  devotion . . **8.** antiphon
  form . . **7.** virelay **10.** villanelle
  Homeric . . **4.** epic **6.** epopee
  Irish . . **4.** rann
  pause . . **6.** cesura **9.** diaeresis (dieresis)
  romantic . . **7.** sestina
  satiric . . **6.** iambic
  scripture . . **4.** text
  stress . . **5.** ictus
  term . . **5.** ictic, meter **6.** accent, poetic, rhythm, scheme **7.** cadence **8.** eye rhyme, scansion **10.** synaeresis (syneresis) **12.** alliteration
  trivial . . **6.** jingle **8.** doggerel, limerick
verse (pert to feet) . . .
  eight . . **9.** octameter
  four . . **10.** tetrameter
  one . . **9.** monometer
  three . . **7.** tripody
  two . . **7.** dimeter
versed . . . **5.** adept **7.** erudite, learned, skilled **8.** familiar **9.** practiced **10.** acquainted, conversant, proficient
versification . . . **7.** prosody **10.** orthometry
versifier . . . **4.** bard, muse, poet **5.** rimer **6.** rhymer **7.** poetess **8.** ballader, eulogist **9.** poetaster, rhymester
version . . . **7.** edition **9.** rendition **10.** paraphrase **11.** translation
version, Bible . . . **5.** Douay, Greek, Latin **6.** Coptic, Geneva, Gothic, Italic (Itala) **7.** Aramaic, Bishops, Luther's, Revised, Targums, Vulgate **8.** Cranmer's, Georgian, Matthew's, Peshitta, Slavonic **9.** Apocrypha, King James, Serampore **10.** Pentateuch, Septuagint **11.** Alexandrian
vers libra . . . **9.** free verse
verso (opp of recto) . . . **7.** reverse **9.** back cover **12.** left-hand side
versus . . . **3.** con **7.** against **8.** contrast, opposite **11.** alternative
vertebra, vertebrae . . . **4.** axis **8.** backbone **12.** spinal column
vertebrate . . . **6.** linked **8.** well-knit **9.** backboned
vertebrates (pert to) . . .
  division . . **6.** somite **10.** Vertebrata
  feathered . . **5.** birds
  group . . **4.** Aves **7.** Amniota
vertex . . . **3.** top **4.** apex **6.** summit

11. culmination
vertical . . . 5. apeak, erect, plumb, sheer
6. height 7. upright 10. upstanding
13. perpendicular
vertical panel . . . 5. stile
verticil . . . 5. whorl 6. circle
vertigo . . . 5. dinus 6. megrim
9. confusion, dizziness, giddiness
11. disturbance 12. bewilderment
verve . . . 3. pep 4. dash, élan 5. vigor
6. energy, fervor, spirit 8. vivacity
9. animation 10. liveliness
vervet . . . 6. monkey
very . . . 3. eri (comb form) 4. much,
real, très, true 5. truly, utter 6. actual,
in fact, really 7. exactly, genuine
8. absolute, especial, peculiar, truthful
9. extremely, precisely, veracious,
veritable 10. legitimate 11. exceedingly
Very light . . . 5. flare 6. signal (Very
system)
vesica . . . 7. bladder
vesicate . . . 7. blister
vesicle . . . 3. sac 4. cyst 5. bulla 6. bubble,
cavity, vessel 7. bladder, blemish,
blister
Vespa . . . 4. wasp 6. hornet
vespers . . . 6. prayer 7. service
8. ceremony, evensong
vessel . . . 3. ark, can, cup, jar, jug, mug,
pod, pot, tub, urn, vas, vat 4. boat,
bowl, dhow, drum, duct, ewer, junk,
olla, olpe, proa, said, seed, ship,
tank, vase, yawl 5. bocal, craft, crock,
cupel, glass, gourd, jorum, ketch,
stein 6. aftaba, aludel, ampule, barrel,
bottle, bucket, caster, cutter, dipper,
firkin, goblet, kettle, picard, retort,
trader, trough 7. catboat, cistern,
coracle, cruiser, frigate, pitcher, psykter,
steamer, tankard, utensil 8. aiguière,
ciborium, decanter, demijohn,
hogshead, schooner 9. alcarraza,
catamaran, privateer, washbasin
10. receptacle 11. earthenware
vessel (pert to) . . .
anc . . 3. nef 5. yanky 6. bireme 7. caravel,
galleon, trireme
Arab . . 4. dhow
baptismal . . 4. font 7. piscina
chemist . . 4. etna 6. aludel, beaker,
retort
Columbus . . 7. caravel
cooking . . 9. autoclave
druggist . . 4. vial 5. phial 8. gallipot
Dutch . . 4. koff 5. yanky 6. galiot (galliot)
Eccl . . 3. ama, pyx 4. wine 5. amula
7. stamnos
Hebrides . . 7. birlinn (birling)
heraldry . . 7. lymphad
India . . 6. shibar
Mediterranean . . 5. xebec 6. settee
(setee), tartan 7. polacre
merchant . . 6. argosy 7. baggala
Nile houseboat . . 8. dahabeah
oil-burning . . 7. cresset
part . . 4. deck, keel, prow, skeg 5. brail
8. steerage
sacred . . 3. ama
Scottish . . 6. pourie
Thames (fishing) . . 6. bawley

Venice . . 9. bucentaur
war . . 3. sub 5. Maine 6. corvet
7. carrier, cruiser, felucca, flattop,
Monitor 9. submarine 11. dreadnaught
12. Old Ironsides
vessel (sailing) . . . 3. hoy 4. bark, brig,
koff, proa, saic, ship, yawl 5. ketch,
sloop, smack, xebec
vest . . . 4. robe 5. endow, gilet 6. invest,
jerkin, linder, weskit 7. furnish, garment
9. waistcoat
vesta . . . 5. match
Vesta (Rom) . . . 7. goddess (Hearth)
8. asteroid
vestal . . . 4. pure 6. chaste 8. virginal
vestige . . . 4. mark, sign 5. relic, shred,
tinge, trace, track 7. remains 8. footstep
9. vestigium
vestiture . . . 4. garb 5. dress 8. clothing,
covering
vestment . . . 3. alb 4. cope, garb, gown,
hood, robe 5. amice, cotta, dress,
ephod, miter, orale, tunic 6. saccos,
tippet 7. cassock, garment, maniple
8. chasuble, crucifix, dalmatic, scapular,
surplice 10. habiliment, omophorion
vestry . . . 4. room 5. group (Eccl)
8. sacristy, wardrobe 10. repository
Vesuvius (pert to) . . .
Great Eruption (79 AD) . . 6. buried
city . . 7. Pompeii 11. Herculaneum
mountain . . 8. volcanic
site . . 6. Naples
veteran . . . 4. long 7. old hand, soldier
8. seasoned 9. practiced
11. experienced
veterinarian . . . 7. farrier, surgeon
veto . . . 6. forbid 8. negative, prohibit
10. disapprove 12. interdiction
vex . . . 3. irk 4. cark, fret, fuss, gall,
miff, rile, roil 5. anger, annoy, harry,
spite, tease, worry 6. bother, harass,
nettle, plague, pother, ruffle 7. agitate,
chagrin, despite, dispute, disturb,
pervert, provoke, torment 8. disquiet,
irritate 9. displease
vexation . . . 7. anxiety, chagrin, fatigue,
trouble 8. disquiet, irritate
9. annoyance, weariness 10. affliction,
foreboding, harassment, irritation
11. disturbance 13. mortification
vexatious . . . 5. pesky 6. thorny 7. irksome
8. annoying 9. disturbed, pestilent,
provoking, worrisome 10. afflictive
11. troublesome
vexillum . . . 3. web 4. flag 5. cross
6. banner, colors, ensign 7. labarum,
pennant 8. standard 10. Jolly Roger
via . . . 2. by 3. way 4. away, road
6. begone 7. by way of, passage,
through
viaduct . . . 4. span 6. bridge 7. trestle
vial . . . 5. cruet, phial 6. bottle, caster,
castor, vessel 7. ampoule (ampul),
ampulla 9. container
viameter . . . 7. measure 8. odometer
12. perambulator
viander . . . 4. host 6. vendor
viands . . . 4. cate, fare, food 7. viandry
8. victuals 10. provisions
viaticum . . . 5. money 8. supplies

9. allowance, last rites 10. provisions
14. Extreme Unction
viator . . . 8. traveler, wayfarer
vibrant . . . 5. alive 7. pulsing, travale
8. resonant, sonorous, vigorous
9. energetic, thrilling, vibrating
10. resounding
vibrate . . . 4. beat, rock, tirl, whir 5. pulse,
quake, swing, throb, waver 6. dindle,
quaver, quiver, shimmy, shiver, thrill
7. agitate, resound, tremble 8. brandish,
flichter, resonate 9. fluctuate, oscillate
vibration . . . 6. quiver, thrill, tremor
7. flutter, pulsing 9. resonance,
throbbing 11. oscillation
vibration, music . . . 5. trill 7. sonance,
tremolo, vibrato
vibration measure . . . 9. tonometer
vicar . . . 5. proxy 6. curate, deputy, priest
9. churchman, clergyman 10. substitute,
vicegerent
vice . . . 3. sin 4. evil 5. crime, fault,
taint 6. defect 7. blemish, stopper
8. iniquity 9. depravity, in place of,
instead of 10. corruption, substitute,
succeeding, wickedness, wrongdoing
11. viciousness
viceroy . . . 5. nabob 6. satrap 8. governor
9. butterfly
vicinity . . . 6. region 9. proximity
11. propinquity 12. neighborhood
vicious . . . 3. bad, ill 4. evil, foul, lewd,
mean, ugly, vile 6. faulty, impure,
wicked 7. corrupt, immoral, noxious
8. depraved, spiteful 9. dangerous,
malicious, nefarious, obstinate,
perverted 10. iniquitous, profligate
11. ill-tempered
vicissitude . . . 6. change 8. mutation,
shifting 9. variation 10. revolution
11. fluctuation
victim . . . 4. dupe, gull, prey 5. cully
6. sucker 7. patient 8. sufferer
victor . . . 6. captor, master, winner
8. unbeaten 9. conqueror
10. vanquisher
victor fish . . . 3. aku 6. bonito
Victoria, victoria . . . 4. plum 5. cross
(Maltese) 7. goddess 8. asteroid,
carriage 10. automobile
Victorian . . . 3. era 4. prim 6. stuffy
7. antique, archaic, prudish
10. antiquated 11. puritanical, strait-
laced
victorious . . . 7. winning 8. unbeaten
9. defeating 10. conquering, triumphant
victory . . . 7. mastery, success, triumph
8. conquest 9. supremacy
victory (pert to) . . .
at too great cost . . 7. Pyrrhic
Day . . 9. Armistice
goddess . . 4. Nike
hymn . . 9. epinicion (epinikion)
memorial . . 6. trophy
symbol . . 4. palm
Victrola dog (symbol) . . . 6. Nipper
victuals . . . 4. food, grub 6. viands
8. supplies 11. nourishment
videlicet . . . 3. viz 5. to wit 6. namely
8. scilicet
vie . . . 3. bet 4. cope, life 5. bandy,

stake, wager 6. endure, oppose, strive
7. compare, compete, contend, contest,
emulate 8. struggle 9. challenge
Vienna . . .
artist . . 4. Lieb, Pilz 6. Makart, Zauner
7. Kisling
boulevard (famed) . . 11. Ringstrasse
capital of . . 7. Austria
Ger name . . 4. Wien
musician . . 5. Gluck, Haydn 6. Czerny,
Mozart 7. Strauss 8. Schubert,
Schumann 9. Beethoven
palace . . 10. Schönbrunn
park . . 6. Prater
river . . 6. Danube
Vietnam (pert to) . . .
capital . . 5. Hanoi
city . . 13. Ho Chi Minh City (Saigon)
gulf . . 6. Tonkin
holiday (New Year) . . 3. Tet
historic region . . 5. Annam 6. Tonkin
11. Cochin China
river . . 3. Red 6. Mekong
view . . . 3. aim, end, eye, ken, see 4. look,
scan 5. scene, vista 6. apercu, aspect,
object, regard, survey 7. examine,
glimpse, opinion, outlook, picture
8. attitude, judgment, panorama,
prospect 9. intention 10. appearance,
perception, scrutinize 11. contemplate,
expectation 13. contemplation
vigil . . . 3. eve 4. wake 5. guard, watch
6. patrol 8. watchman 9. keep guard
11. wakefulness 13. sleeplessness
vigilant . . . 4. agog, wary 5. alert, awake,
aware 6. awatch 7. wakeful 8. cautious,
open-eyed, watchful 9. attentive,
observant, sleepless 11. circumspect
vigilantes . . . 5. posse 9. committee
(vigilance)
vigor, vigour . . . 3. pep, vim, vir 4. life,
zeal 5. force, power, verve 6. energy,
health 7. potency, stamina, sthenia
8. strength, validity, virility 9. animation,
fraîcheur, vehemence 10. liveliness
vigorous . . . 4. able, hale, racy, spry
5. eager, frank, fresh, hardy, lusty,
tough 6. potent, robust, strong
7. healthy, zealous 8. athletic, forceful,
spirited, vehement 9. effective,
energetic, sprightly, strenuous
11. efficacious, flourishing
Viking . . . 4. Eric 5. rover 6. pirate
8. Norseman, Northman, sea rover
9. plunderer 12. Scandinavian
vile . . . 3. bad 4. base, evil, foul, mean
5. cheap, lowly, nasty 6. coarse, filthy,
impure, odious, sinful, sordid, wicked
7. corrupt, debased, ignoble, obscene,
unclean, vicious 8. depraved, infamous
9. degrading, loathsome, nefarious,
repulsive 10. abominable, disgusting
12. contaminated
vilify . . . 5. abuse, curse, libel 6. debase,
defame, malign, revile 7. asperse,
cheapen, degrade, slander, traduce
8. belittle, disgrace, reproach, vilipend
9. blaspheme, disparage 10. calumniate,
stigmatize
vilipend . . . 6. slight 7. despise 8. belittle
9. disparage 10. depreciate, slanderous

12. calumniatory
villa ... **5.** aldea, dacha **9.** residence, villaette **10.** villanette
village ... **3.** mir **4.** dorp, stad **5.** thorp (thorpe), tract **6.** aldeia, castle, hamlet, pueblo
Village Blacksmith author ...
10. Longfellow
villain ... **4.** boor, lout, ogre, serf **5.** demon, heavy, knave, rogue **6.** rascal **7.** caitiff **9.** miscreant, scoundrel
villainous ... **3.** bad, low **4.** base, evil, mean, vile **6.** vulgar, wicked **7.** boorish, knavish **8.** criminal, rascally, terrible, wretched **9.** dastardly **10.** detestable, iniquitous **11.** scoundrelly **13.** objectionable
villous ... **5.** nappy **6.** napped, shaggy
vim ... **3.** pep, zip **4.** dash, élan, fire, gimp, kick **5.** drive, force, verve, vigor **6.** energy, esprit, spirit **8.** strength
vinaigre ... **7.** vinegar
vindicate ... **4.** free **5.** claim, clear **6.** acquit, assert, avenge, defend, excuse, uphold **7.** absolve, justify, support, sustain **8.** maintain **9.** exculpate, exonerate
vindication ... **7.** defense
vindictive ... **7.** hostile **8.** punitive, spiteful, vengeful **10.** revengeful **11.** retaliatory, retributive
vine ... **3.** hop, ivy **4.** bine, odal **5.** betel, grape, liana (liane), Vitis **7.** cupseed, trailer **8.** clematis, wisteria **9.** grapevine **10.** chilicothe **11.** honeysuckle **12.** morning glory
vinegar ... **4.** acid, sour **6.** acetum, alegar **8.** vinaigre
vinegar (pert to) ...
acid.. **6.** acetic
comb form.. **5.** aceto
dregs.. **6.** mother
eel.. **4.** worm
ester.. **7.** acetate
fly.. **5.** fruit
preserve in.. **6.** pickle **8.** marinate
salt.. **7.** acetate
spice.. **8.** tarragon
tree.. **13.** staghorn sumac
Vinegar Joe (Army) ... **9.** Stillwell (Gen)
vinegarroon ... **8.** scorpion, vinagron
vinegary ... **4.** sour, tart **7.** acetose, crabbed, pungent **9.** unamiable
vineyard ... **3.** cru **7.** Priapus (god of) **10.** plantation
vinology (science of) ... **5.** vines **10.** grapevines
vinous ... **4.** winy **5.** color
vintner ... **8.** merchant (wine)
viol ... **3.** gue **4.** rope **5.** rebec, ruana **6.** vielle **7.** quinton, sarinda **9.** organ stop
viola ... **5.** gamba **7.** sarangi **9.** organ stop **11.** tenor violin
violate ... **5.** abuse, break, wrong **6.** defile, invade, ravage, ravish **7.** debauch, outrage, pollute, profane **8.** deflower, dishonor, mistreat **9.** desecrate **10.** transgress
violation ... **7.** offense **10.** infraction **11.** anacoluthon, disturbance,

profanation **12.** infringement, interruption **13.** nonobservance, transgression
violence ... **5.** anger, force **6.** unjust **7.** assault, cruelty, outrage **8.** coercion **9.** vehemence **10.** roughhouse **11.** profanation **12.** infringement
violent ... **4.** loud **5.** acute, great, rabid, sharp, vivid **6.** fierce, savage, stormy **7.** extreme, furious, intense **8.** coercive, vehement **9.** turbulent **10.** passionate **11.** tempestuous
violent (pert to) ...
Norse folklore.. **8.** warriors **9.** beserkers
outbreak.. **4.** riot **6.** tumult, uproar **8.** eruption
pain.. **4.** pang **5.** throe **6.** fierce
violet (pert to) ...
color.. **5.** mauve **6.** purple **7.** blue-red
dye.. **6.** archil (orchil)
emblem of.. **7.** gravity **8.** chastity
genus.. **9.** Violaceae
perfume.. **5.** irone **6.** ionone **9.** orrisroot
tip.. **9.** butterfly
violin (pert to) ...
ancient.. **5.** rebab, rebec, rocta **12.** viola de gamba
bar.. **4.** fret
bass.. **11.** violoncello
bow.. **5.** arcus
city (famed).. **7.** Cremona (It)
make.. **5.** Amati **7.** Cremona **10.** Guarnerius **12.** Stradivarius
maker.. **5.** Amati **9.** Guarnieri **10.** Stradivari
reference to.. **4.** pins **5.** belly
Scot.. **6.** fiddle
small.. **3.** kit
tenor.. **4.** alto
violinist (famed) ... **5.** Elman, Stern **7.** Heifitz, Menuhin
violinist, first ... **13.** concertmaster
viper ... **3.** asp **5.** adder, Echis, snake **6.** kupper **7.** serpent **8.** cerastes, ophidian **9.** scoundrel **10.** bushmaster
vir ... **5.** vigor
virage ... **5.** scold, shrew, vixen, woman **7.** beldame, rullion **9.** termagant
Virgil ... see *Vergil*
virgin ... **3.** new **4.** maid, pure **6.** chaste, maiden, vestal **8.** spinster **9.** undefiled, unsullied, untouched **13.** unadulterated
virginal ... **3.** new **5.** piano (spinet) **6.** chaste, ritual **7.** natural **8.** maidenly **9.** unmarried, unsullied
Virginia ...
bay.. **10.** Chesapeake
capital.. **8.** Richmond
city.. **7.** Norfolk, Roanoke **9.** Arlington, Lexington, Lynchburg **11.** Newport News **12.** Hampton Roads
famed sites.. **8.** Mt Vernon **10.** Monticello **12.** Williamsburg **13.** Stratford Hall
first white child born.. **12.** Virginia Dare
historic town.. **8.** Yorktown **9.** Jamestown **10.** Appomattox
Indian sachem.. **8.** Powhatan
mountain.. **9.** Blue Ridge **11.** Alleghenies
resort.. **13.** Virginia Beach

river.. **4.** York **5.** James **7.** Potomac, Rapidan **12.** Rappahannock
settlement (first).. **9.** Jamestown
State admission.. **5.** Tenth
State motto.. **17.** Sic Semper Tyrannis **19.** Thus Always to Tyrants
State nickname.. **11.** Old Dominion
Virgin Islands, British...
capital.. **8.** Road Town
crop.. **9.** sugar cane
group.. **7.** Leeward
number islands.. **6.** thirty
Virgin Islands, United States...
capital.. **8.** St Thomas **15.** Charlotte Amalia (former)
discoverer.. **8.** Columbus (1493)
largest.. **6.** St John **7.** St Croix **8.** St Thomas
virginity... **8.** celibacy, chastity **10.** maidenhood **12.** spinsterhood
Virgin Mary... **5.** Pietà (image) **7.** Our Lady **11.** Maris Stella, Mother of God **12.** Star of the Sea **13.** Mother of Jesus
viridity... **5.** youth **7.** verdure **9.** freshness, greenness **10.** grass color
virile... **4.** male **5.** manly **8.** forceful, powerful, vigorous **9.** masculine, masterful
virose... **5.** fetid **8.** virulent **9.** poisonous **10.** malodorous
virtu... **5.** curio **7.** antique **8.** artistry **12.** love of curios **15.** artistic quality, study of fine arts
virtual... **9.** essential, potential **10.** energizing **12.** constructive
virtually... **7.** morally **11.** potentially, practically
virtue... **5.** valor, value, worth **6.** energy, purity **7.** potency, probity **8.** chastity, efficacy, goodness, morality **9.** godliness, innocence, integrity, rectitude **11.** uprightness **13.** righteousness
virtue, logic... **8.** aretaics
virtues, cardinal... **4.** hope **5.** faith **7.** charity
virtuoso... **6.** expert **7.** scholar **11.** connoisseur, philosopher
virtuous... **4.** good, pure **5.** brave, godly, moral **6.** chaste, honest, potent **7.** upright, valiant **8.** valorous **9.** righteous **11.** efficacious
virulent... **5.** acrid, rabid **6.** deadly, potent **7.** noxious **8.** venomous **9.** animosity, malignant, poisonous **10.** infectious, resentment **11.** acrimonious
visa, visé... **7.** endorse **9.** signature **11.** certificate, endorsement (passport)
visage... **4.** face, look **5.** image **11.** countenance **14.** visible surface
vis-à-vis... **4.** seat, sofa **8.** carriage, opposite **9.** encounter **10.** face to face
viscera... **4.** guts **6.** bowels, vitals **7.** insides **8.** entrails **10.** intestines **11.** inside parts
visceral... **3.** gut **7.** enteric **10.** intestinal, splanchnic
viscid... **4.** ropy, waxy **5.** slimy **6.** sticky

7. viscous **8.** adhering, adhesive **9.** glutinous
viscosity... **8.** tenacity **10.** stickiness
viscous... **4.** ropy, sizy **5.** gluey, gummy, tarry **6.** mucous, sticky, viscid **7.** stringy **9.** glutinous **10.** stickiness
vise... **3.** jaw **4.** tool **5.** clamp, winch **6.** device **7.** squeeze
Vishnu (pert to)...
consort.. **3.** Sri **7.** Lakshim
deity (supreme).. **6.** bhakti **9.** preserver
eighth.. **7.** Krishna
epithet.. **8.** bhagavat
seventh.. **4.** Rama
tenth, last incarnation.. **5.** Kalki
vehicle.. **6.** Garuda
visible... **4.** open, seen **5.** clear **6.** extant, in view **7.** evident, in sight, obvious **8.** apparent, manifest **10.** noticeable **11.** discernible, perceivable, perceptible
Visigoth king... **6.** Alaric
vision... **3.** eye **5.** dream, fancy, image, sight **6.** glance, mirage **7.** glimpse, imagine, specter **8.** eyesight **10.** apparition
vision (pert to)...
comb form.. **4.** opto
daylight.. **8.** photopia
defect.. **6.** anopia, myopia
double.. **8.** diplopia
illusory.. **5.** image
lacking.. **8.** purblind
measure.. **9.** optometer
night.. **8.** scotopia
science of.. **9.** optometry
term.. **5.** optic **6.** ocular **9.** binocular, monocular
visionary... **4.** aery, airy, seer, wild **5.** ideal **6.** dreamy, unreal **7.** dreamer, Laputan, utopian **8.** delusive, idealist, quixotic, romantic **9.** fantastic, imaginary **10.** chimerical, rhapsodist **11.** imaginative, impractical
visit... **3.** see, vis **4.** call, chat, go to, slum **5.** haunt **6.** attend, call on **10.** inspection, visitation **12.** conversation
visitor... **5.** guest **6.** caller **7.** company **8.** visitant
visne... **5.** venue **8.** neighbor, vicinage
vison... **4.** mink
visor, vizor... **4.** mask **6.** vizard **8.** disguise **10.** camouflage
vista... **4.** view **5.** scene, visto **7.** outlook **8.** corridor, panorama, prospect
visual... **5.** optic **6.** ocular **11.** perceptible
visualize... **7.** imagine, picture **8.** envisage, envision **9.** objectify
vital... **4.** live **5.** basic **6.** living, mortal, viable **7.** animate, exigent, needful, organic **8.** inherent, vigorous **9.** essential, important, necessary, requisite **10.** imperative **11.** fundamental **13.** indispensable
vital (pert to)...
air.. **6.** oxygen
force.. **6.** energy, spirit **7.** neurism **8.** bathmism, phrenism **9.** theosophy
impulse.. **6.** libido **8.** instinct
organs.. **6.** vitals **7.** viscera
records.. **10.** demography, statistics
strength.. **7.** stamina

vitality ... **3.** sap, vim **4.** life **5.** vigor **8.** strength **9.** animation, lustiness **10.** liveliness

vitals ... **7.** insides, viscera **9.** internals **11.** vital organs (heart, liver, lungs, brain)

vitamin ... **6.** biotin, niacin **7.** carotin, thiamin **10.** riboflavin **11.** lactoflavin **12.** ascorbic acid

vitellus ... **4.** yolk **7.** egg yolk

vitiate ... **5.** spoil, taint **6.** debase, impair, poison, weaken **7.** corrupt, deprave, pervert, pollute **10.** adulterate, demoralize, invalidate **11.** contaminate

vitiated ... **5.** pical **6.** wicked **7.** corrupt, debased, spoiled **9.** defective **11.** ineffective, invalidated

vitiosity ... **4.** vice **6.** defect **9.** depravity **11.** viciousness

vitium ... **5.** fault **6.** defect

vitric ... **9.** glasslike

vitrics ... **9.** glassware, glasswork

vitrify ... **5.** glaze **13.** make into glass

vitriolic ... **4.** acid **5.** sharp **6.** biting, bitter **7.** caustic **8.** scathing, virulent **11.** acrimonious

vituperate ... **5.** abuse, curse, scold **6.** berate, revile **7.** censure

vituperative ... **7.** abusive, railing **8.** reviling, scolding **10.** scurrilous **11.** maledictory, opprobrious

vivacious ... **3.** gay **4.** airy **5.** merry **6.** active, lively **8.** animated, gamesome, spirited, sportive **9.** energetic **12.** lighthearted

vivacity ... **4.** dash, élan, fire, keen, zeal, zest **5.** ardor, verve, vigor **6.** energy, gaiety (gayety) **9.** animation **10.** liveliness

Viverra ... **6.** civets **9.** civet cats

vivers ... **4.** food **8.** victuals

vix ... **8.** scarcely

vixen ... **3.** cat, fox **5.** scold, shrew, witch **6.** virago **9.** termagant **12.** female animal

viz ... **5.** to wit **6.** namely **9.** videlicet

vizard ... **4.** mask **5.** guise, visor **8.** disguise

vlei (vley) ... **5.** creek, marsh, swamp

voar ... **6.** spring (of the year)

vocabulary ... **5.** words **6.** jargon **7.** diction, lexicon **8.** glossary, wordbook **10.** dictionary

vocabulist ... **6.** writer **13.** lexicographer

vocal (pert to) ...
chink .. **7.** glottis
composition .. **4.** aria, song **5.** motet **7.** cantata
expression .. **4.** oral **9.** utterance
flourish .. **7.** roulade
handicap .. **4.** lisp **7.** stutter
sound .. **5.** vowel **6.** sonant
statue .. **6.** Memnon

vocalist ... **4.** alto **5.** basso, tenor **6.** artist, cantor, singer **7.** caroler, crooner, soprano, yodeler **8.** songster **10.** coloratura, prima donna, songstress

vocalization ... **11.** melismatics

vocalize ... **4.** sing **5.** sound, utter **6.** phrase

vocation ... **4.** call **5.** trade **6.** career

7. calling **8.** business **10.** employment, occupation, profession

vociferous ... **4.** loud **5.** noisy **7.** blatant **8.** brawling, strident **9.** clamorous, turbulent **11.** loudmouthed **12.** obstreperous

vogue ... **3.** ton **4.** mode **5.** style **6.** custom **7.** fashion **8.** practice **10.** popularity

voice ... **3.** say, vox **4.** alto, bass, tone, vote, wish **5.** rumor, tenor, utter **7.** divulge, opinion, soprano **8.** announce, falsetto **9.** utterance **10.** expression **12.** articulation

voice (pert to) ...
box .. **6.** larynx
Greek .. **9.** phthongos
handicap .. **4.** lisp **7.** stammer, stutter
loss of .. **7.** anaudia, aphonia
loud .. **12.** megalophonic
phonetics .. **9.** affricate
quality .. **6.** timbre (timber)
quiet .. **5.** sotto
raise .. **6.** insist **10.** supplicate
raise against .. **5.** decry **6.** accuse, object
singing, above natural .. **8.** falsetto
singing, natural .. **7.** dipetto
stress .. **5.** arsis
with one .. **9.** unanimous **12.** concurrently

voiced ... **6.** sonant, spoken **7.** sounded **9.** phthongal **11.** articulated

voiceless ... **4.** dumb, mute, surd **6.** atonic, silent **7.** spirate **9.** not voiced **12.** not expressed

void ... **4.** idle, lack, null, want **5.** abyss, annul, egest, empty **6.** devoid, hollow, vacant, vacuum **7.** abolish, nothing, nullify, useless **8.** evacuate **9.** destitute, emptiness **10.** unoccupied **11.** ineffectual, nonexistent

void of ...
interest .. **6.** jejune **7.** insipid
sense .. **5.** inane, silly
space .. **5.** blank **6.** vacuum

volaille ... **4.** fowl **7.** poultry

volant ... **5.** agile, light, quick **6.** flying, nimble **7.** current **8.** volatile, volitant

volatile ... **4.** airy **5.** light **6.** fickle, flying, lively, volant **7.** alcohol, ammonia, buoyant, flighty, gaseous **8.** fleeting, vaporous **9.** ephemeral, mercurial **10.** capricious, changeable, transitory **11.** vaporizable **12.** lighthearted

volatile (pert to) ...
alkali .. **7.** ammonia
flux .. **5.** smear
liquid .. **5.** ether **7.** alcohol
oil .. **7.** essence, perfume

volcanic (pert to) ...
glass .. **6.** pumice **7.** perlite **8.** obsidian
matter .. **2.** aa **4.** lava, slag, tufa **5.** trass **6.** pumice **8.** lapillus, pahoehoe
mud .. **5.** salse
orifice of gas issue .. **8.** fumarole
ref to .. **9.** excitable, explosive **11.** hot-tempered
rock .. **5.** trass **6.** dacite **8.** tephrite
saucer .. **6.** crater

volcano (pert to) ...
Africa .. **11.** Kilimanjaro
Alaska .. **6.** Katmai **8.** Wrangell

Chile . . **6.** Lascar
Ecuador . . **8.** Cotopaxi
goddess . . **4.** Pele (Hawaii)
Guatemala . . **5.** Fuego **7.** Atitlan
Hawaii . . **8.** Mauna Loa
Iceland . . **5.** Askja, Hekla
Italy . . **4.** Etna **8.** Vesuvius **9.** Stromboli
Japan . . **4.** Fuji **9.** Asamayama
Java . . **4.** Gede
Mexico . . **12.** Popocatepetl
Philippines . . **3.** Apo (Mindanao)
Sumatra . . **6.** Merapi
United States (mainland) . . **6.** Lassen,
  Shasta **7.** Rainier
West Indies . . **5.** Pelée
vole . . . **6.** craber, rodent **8.** water rat
  10. field mouse **11.** meadow mouse
volée . . . **6.** flight, volley
volery (volary) . . . **6.** aviary **8.** bird cage
volition . . . **4.** will **6.** choice **11.** voluntarily
  13. determination
volley . . . **4.** fire **5.** blast, salvo, shots
Voltaire volume . . . **7.** Candide
voluble . . . **4.** glib **6.** fluent **8.** rotating,
  unstable **9.** garrulous, revolving,
  talkative **10.** loquacious
volume . . . **4.** book, bulk, mass, size, tome
  6. amount **7.** compass **8.** capacity,
  fullness (fulness) **9.** aggregate,
  Decameron **10.** crassitude **14.** fullness
  of tone
voluntary . . . **4.** free **7.** prelude, willing
  8. elective, intended, purposed
  9. volunteer, willingly **10.** deliberate,
  volitional **11.** intentional, spontaneous
  13. not accidental
volunteer . . . **5.** offer **6.** enlist **7.** proffer
  9. be willing, voluntary **11.** be of
  service
Volunteer State . . . **9.** Tennessee
volute . . . **4.** turn **5.** whorl **6.** cilery (cillery)
  8. rolled up **10.** scroll-like
voodoo . . . **5.** magic, obeah **6.** fetish
  8. sorcerer
voracious . . . **6.** greedy, hungry
  8. edacious, esurient, ravening,
  ravenous **9.** devouring, rapacious
  10. gluttonous, immoderate, unsatiable
voracity . . . **5.** greed **7.** edacity **8.** gluttony,
  rapacity **9.** esurience
vorago . . . **4.** gulf **5.** abyss
vortex . . . **4.** apex, eddy **5.** whirl **7.** tornado
  8. flatworm **9.** whirlpool, whirlwind
  10. waterspout
votary . . . **6.** zealot **7.** devotee **8.** adherent,
  aesthete, follower **9.** supporter
  10. enthusiast
vote . . . **3.** vow **5.** elect, straw **6.** ballot,
  choice, ticket **7.** declare **8.** suffrage
  9. designate **10.** plebescite, referendum
vote (pert to) . . .
  group . . **4.** bloc
  in . . **5.** elect
  of assent . . **6.** placet
  plump . . **14.** straight ticket
  receptacle . . **6.** situla
voter . . . **6.** poller **7.** elector **8.** balloter
  11. constituent
voters . . . **10.** electorate
votive . . . **7.** devoted **11.** consecrated
vouch . . . **4.** back **6.** affirm, attest,

depose **7.** confirm, declare, promise,
  sponsor, support **8.** accredit **9.** assertion
  11. attestation, bear witness
vouchsafe . . . **4.** give **5.** deign **6.** accept,
  assure, bestow, permit **7.** concede
  9. guarantee **10.** condescend
voussoir . . . **8.** keystone
vow . . . **3.** vum **4.** oath **5.** swear,
  vouch **6.** behest, devote, pledge
  7. declare, promise **8.** dedicate
  9. assertion **10.** consecrate,
  obligation **11.** asservation
  12. supplication
vowel (pert to) . . .
  change of . . **6.** umlaut
  contradiction . . **6.** crasis **7.** digraph
    9. diphthong
  loss of . . **7.** aphesis
  mark . . **6.** macron
  point (Heb) . . **4.** sere (tsere)
  separate syllables . . **9.** diaeresis (dieresis)
  short . . **5.** breve
  two, contracted . . **6.** crasis
  two, group . . **6.** digram **7.** digraph
    9. diphthong (dipthong)
  unaspirated . . **4.** lene
vowels, none . . . **6.** syzygy
vowels in sequence . . . **8.** caesious
vox (pert to) . . .
  clandestina . . **7.** whisper
  Dei . . **10.** Voice of God
  Latin for . . **5.** voice
  populi . . **16.** voice of the people
voyage . . . **4.** trip **6.** cruise, travel
  7. journey, passage, passing (sea)
  9. excursion **10.** expedition, pilgrimage
  11. undertaking
Vulcan (pert to) . . .
  consort . . **4.** Maia
  epithet . . **8.** Mulciber
  feast of . . **10.** Vulcanalia
  god of . . **4.** fire
  Greek . . **10.** Hephaestus
  work site . . **4.** Etna
vulcanite . . . **7.** ebonite
vulcanize . . . **9.** rubberize
vulgar . . . **3.** low **4.** lewd **5.** crude,
  gross **6.** coarse, common, garish,
  public, ribald **7.** boorish, general,
  obscene, profane **8.** indecent, ordinary,
  plebeian **9.** inelegant, offensive,
  unrefined **10.** boisterous, in bad taste,
  rowdydowdy
vulgarian . . . **4.** snob **9.** pretender
Vulgate . . . **10.** Scriptures
vulnerable . . . **6.** liable **7.** exposed
  8. beatable **9.** pregnable, subject
  to **10.** expugnable **11.** conquerable,
  defenseless, susceptible
vulpine . . . **4.** foxy **6.** artful, crafty,
  tricky **7.** cunning, foxlike **9.** alopecoid
  10. vulpecular
vult . . . **4.** mien **6.** aspect **10.** expression
  11. countenance
vulture (pert to) . . .
  African . . **8.** aasvogel
  American . . **4.** aura **5.** urubu **6.** condor
    13. turkey buzzard
  European . . **7.** griffin **11.** lammergeier
    (lammergeir)
  king . . **4.** papa

large.. **6.** condor **11.** lammergeier
Mexican.. **8.** zopilote
raven.. **9.** Corvultur
Spanish.. **9.** gallinazo
term.. **5.** harpy **9.** raptorial **10.** bird of

prey, predacious
vulturous... **6.** lupine **7.** wolfish
8. ravenous **9.** rapacious
vying... **7.** emulous **8.** rivaling
9. competing **11.** competitive

W

W... **6.** letter (23rd) **7.** double U
WAAC... **24.** Women's Auxiliary Army
Corps
waag... **6.** grivet, monkey
waapa... **5.** canoe
wabber... **4.** cony **5.** daman
wabble... see *wobble*
wabby... **4.** loon (red-throated)
wabe, wabi... **5.** shrub **8.** huisache
wachna... **7.** codfish
wad... **3.** pad, ram **4.** cram, lump, mass,
plug, roll, tuft **5.** money, stuff, track
6. bundle, pledge, wealth **7.** stopper
8. bankroll
wadding... **4.** wads **6.** lining **7.** padding
8. compress, stopping, stuffing
waddle... **4.** sway **5.** mince **6.** toddle,
wabble, wamble, wobble **10.** clumsy
gait
waddy, waddie... **3.** peg **4.** beat, club
5. stick **6.** attack, cowboy
wade... **4.** ford, pass **5.** study **6.** attack,
drudge, paddle, plodge **8.** struggle
wader... **4.** coot, ibis, rail **5.** crane, heron,
snipe, stork **6.** jaçana **9.** sandpiper,
shore bird **11.** Grallatores
wadi, wady... **5.** oasis, river **6.** ravine,
valley **7.** channel **11.** watercourse
waeg... **9.** kittiwake
wafer... **4.** cake, disk, ring, seal, snap
5. bread **7.** biscuit, cracker **10.** altar
bread
waff... **3.** wag **4.** flap, wave **5.** ghost
7. lowborn, vagrant **8.** inferior
9. worthless **12.** disreputable
waft... **4.** gust, puff, wave **5.** carry, float,
whiff **6.** beckon, convey, convoy, signal
7. glimpse, pennant **9.** beckoning,
transport
wag... **3.** wit **4.** card, wave **5.** joker,
rogue, shake **6.** signal, waddle, wiggle
7. farceur, vibrate **8.** humorist, jokester
9. oscillate
wagang... **5.** death **9.** departure
11. leave-taking
wage, wages... **3.** bet, fee, pay, utu
4. hire, levy, pawn, risk **5.** fight, incur,
stake, yield **6.** employ, engage, pledge,
reward, salary **7.** attempt, contend, hire
out, stipend, venture **9.** emolument
10. recompense **12.** compensation,
remuneration
wage insurance... **7.** chômage
wager... **3.** bet, bid, vie **4.** risk **5.** sport,
stake **6.** gamble, hazard, parlay, pledge
7. venture
waggish... **5.** droll, merry **7.** jesting,

jocular, parlous, roguish **8.** humorous,
sportive **9.** facetious **10.** frolicsome
11. mischievous
Wagnerian opera... **6.** Rienzi **8.** Parsifal
9. Lohengrin **10.** Tannhauser
15. Gotterdammerung
wagon... **3.** car, van **4.** cart, dray,
tram, wain **5.** araba, coach, lorry,
tonga **6.** telega **7.** caisson, chariot,
vehicle **8.** carryall, schooner (prairie)
12. perambulator
wagon (pert to)...
canvas-covered.. **15.** prairie schooner
lit.. **7.** Pullman **11.** sleeping car
load.. **6.** fother
maker.. **10.** wagonsmith, wainwright
on the (wagon).. **8.** sworn off, teetotal
part.. **4.** neap **5.** blade, thill
police.. **3.** van **10.** Black Maria
sideless.. **6.** rolley
wah... **5.** panda
wahine... **4.** wife **5.** woman **8.** mistress
10. sweetheart
wahoo... **4.** bark, fish, peto **5.** shrub
7. rock elm **8.** nonsense, tommyrot
9. buckthorn, guarapucu **12.** umbrella
tree
waif... **4.** Arab, flag **5.** gamin, stray
7. vagrant, wastrel **8.** castaway,
homeless, wanderer **9.** lost sheep
wail... **3.** cry, sob **4.** howl, moan,
weep **5.** mourn **6.** bemoan, grieve,
lament **7.** deplore, screech, ululate
11. lamentation **14.** mournful outcry
wainscot... **4.** base, ceil, line **5.** panel
6. lining **8.** paneling (panelling)
9. partition
waist... **4.** wasp **5.** shirt **6.** basque,
blouse, bodice, dickey, middle, taille
7. corsage, garment **9.** garibaldi
12. undergarment
waistcoat... **4.** vest **5.** benjy **6.** jacket,
jerkin, weskit
wait... **4.** bide, rest, stay, stop **5.** dally,
defer, delay, hover, serve, tarry,
watch **6.** attend, expect, linger, remain
7. observe **8.** hesitate, postpone
11. expectation **12.** watchfulness
waiter... **4.** tray **6.** garçon, salver,
server **7.** messboy, messman, servant,
steward **8.** servitor **9.** attendant
wait on... **4.** help **5.** await, cater, serve
6. escort **7.** toady to **9.** accompany
waive... **5.** defer, forgo (forego) **6.** desert,
give up, reject, vacate **7.** abandon, cast
off, forsake **8.** postpone **9.** disregard
10. condescend, relinquish

waka ... **5.** canoe
Wakashan Indian ... **6.** Nootka **8.** Kwakiutl
wake ... **4.** call, stir **5.** rouse, track, vigil, waken, watch **6.** arouse, awaken, excite, revive **10.** death watch
wakeful ... **5.** alert **8.** restless, vigilant, watchful **9.** sleepless, wide-awake
Wake Island ... **6.** Ottori (Jap name)
wake-robin ... **4.** Arum **8.** Trillium **9.** Anthurium **10.** cuckoopint **12.** philodendron
wale ... **3.** rib **4.** welt **5.** ridge, wheal **6.** stripe
Wales ... see also *Welsh*
anc .. **7.** Cambria
city .. **7.** Rhondda, Swansea **8.** Hereford, Pembroke **9.** Carnarvon
congress of literati .. **10.** eisteddfod
deity .. **4.** Bran
emblem (floral) .. **4.** leek
language .. **7.** Cymraeg
mountain .. **7.** Snowdon
native .. **5.** Cymry (Kymry)
patron saint .. **5.** David
port .. **7.** Cardiff
river .. **3.** Dee, Wye **6.** Severn
sea .. **5.** Irish
walk ... **3.** mog, pad **4.** foot, gait, hike, hoof, pace, path, plod, ramp, step **5.** allee, amble, scuff, strut, tramp, tread **6.** ramble, sphere, stride, stroll, toddle, travel, trudge **7.** conduct, shuffle, traipse **8.** ambulate, behavior, frescade, province, sidewalk **9.** esplanade, promenade, wandering **10.** passageway **11.** base on balls, perambulate **13.** peregrination
walk (pert to) ...
a beat .. **6.** patrol
about .. **11.** perambulate
clumsily .. **5.** mince **6.** lumber, totter
health .. **14.** constitutional
lime-bordered .. **9.** tilicetum
proudly .. **5.** strut **6.** prance
public .. **4.** mall **6.** arcade **7.** alameda **9.** esplanade, promenade
wearily .. **4.** limp, plod **5.** tramp **6.** hobble, trudge
with speed .. **10.** heel and toe
walking (pert to) ...
about .. **7.** passant (Her) **11.** peripatetic
bearlike .. **11.** plantigrade
meter .. **9.** pedometer
papers .. **7.** deposal, the sack **8.** mittimus, pink slip **9.** discharge, dismissal **10.** retirement
wall ... **4.** dado, dike, ha-ha, mure, pier **5.** fence, levee, panel, redan **6.** escarp, hinder, immure, paries, podium, septum, shut in **7.** barrier, defense, enclose, fortify, parapet, rampart **8.** espalier, palisade, restrain, stockade **9.** barricade, enclosure, encompass, partition, precipice, revetment **13.** fortification
wall (pert to) ...
bracket .. **6.** corbel, sconce
creeper .. **4.** bird
go to the (wall) .. **4.** fail **10.** go bankrupt
lining .. **8.** wainscot

lizard .. **4.** newt **5.** gecko
masonry .. **9.** revetment
pert to .. **5.** mural **8.** parietal
recess .. **5.** niche **6.** alcove
Street .. **9.** Manhattan **11.** money market, stock market
up .. **6.** immure
wallaby ... **8.** kangaroo, Macropus, wallaroo **10.** paddymelon
wallah, walla ... **5.** agent **6.** master, person **7.** servant
waller ... **4.** wels **9.** saltmaker, sheatfish
wallet ... **3.** bag **4.** pack, poke, sack **5.** purse **8.** billfold, knapsack **10.** pocketbook **12.** porte-monnaie
walleye ... **9.** exotropia **10.** strabismus
wallow ... **4.** fade, sail **5.** surge **6.** grovel, welter, wither **7.** debauch, founder, insipid **8.** flounder, kommetje, nauseous **9.** tasteless
Wall Street org ... **3.** SEC **4.** NYSE **6.** NASDAQ
walnut ... **6.** bannut
walrus ... **3.** pod (group) **5.** morse **6.** mammal, sea cat **8.** pinniped **9.** rosmarine (fable) **10.** pinnipedia
Waltonian ... **6.** angler **16.** disciple of Walton (Izaak)
wamble ... **5.** twist **6.** quiver, ramble, rumble, totter, writhe **7.** revolve, stagger, wriggle
wame ... **4.** room, womb **5.** belly **7.** stomach
wampum ... **4.** peag **5.** beads, money, uhllo **6.** shells **7.** jewelry, roanoke **8.** ornament **10.** wampumpeag
wan ... **3.** dim, sad **4.** ashy, dark, pale, sick **5.** ashen, black, dusky, faint, lurid **6.** dismal, gloomy, pallid, sickly **7.** ghastly, languid **9.** deathlike, sorrowful **10.** lusterless **11.** lead-colored
wand ... **3.** rod **4.** mace, pole **5.** baton, osier, staff, stick (magic) **6.** switch, wattle **7.** pointer, rhabdos (magic), scepter (sceptre) **8.** caduceus **9.** horsewhip
wander ... **3.** err, gad **4.** moon, rave, roam, rove **5.** drift, prowl, range, stray **6.** cruise, depart, ramble, stroll, travel **7.** digress, meander, saunter, traipse **8.** divagate, traverse **9.** circulate, itinerate, scamander **11.** peregrinate
wanderer ... **4.** Arab, waif **5.** gypsy, nomad, rover **6.** ranger, roamer, truant **7.** migrant, pilgrim, vagrant **9.** butterfly, itinerant, straggler **10.** covenanter **12.** peregrinator
wandering ... **5.** vague **6.** astray, errant, roving, vagary **8.** aberrant, delirium, straying **9.** delirious, deviating, deviation, itinerant **10.** circuitous, discursive, journeying **11.** noctivigant, perambulant **13.** peregrination
wandering (pert to) ...
bird .. **9.** albatross
long .. **7.** odyssey
minstrel .. **4.** bard **10.** troubadour
stars .. **12.** seven planets
tattler .. **9.** shore bird
votary .. **6.** palmer
wanderoo ... **6.** langur, monkey

W

7. macaque
wand-shaped ... **7.** virgate
wane ... **3.** age, ebb **4.** fail, sink, want
5. abate, peter **6.** defect, lessen, recede,
repine **7.** decline, grow dim, subside
8. decrease, diminish **10.** defervesce
13. deterioration
wanga ... **5.** charm, spell **6.** voodoo
7. philter, sorcery
wangle ... **4.** fake, plot **6.** adjust,
juggle, obtain, totter, wiggle **7.** finagle
(finaigue), wriggle **8.** contrive,
maneuver (manoeuvre) **9.** extricate
10. manipulate
want ... **4.** lack, miss, need, wish **5.** crave
6. dearth, desire, hunger, penury
7. absence, craving, lacking, poverty
8. scarcity, shortage **9.** deficient,
indigence, privation **10.** inadequacy
11. destitution, requirement
want (of) ...
appetite .. **6.** asitia
desire .. **11.** inappetence
lacking .. **4.** sans **5.** out of **7.** empty
of, scant of, short of **8.** bereft of
10. deprived of
power .. **5.** atony
sense (good) .. **5.** folly
wanting ... **4.** void **5.** minus, needy
6. absent, bereft, devoid **7.** lacking,
missing, short of, without **9.** deficient,
destitute, imperfect
wanting (pert to) ...
be found .. **9.** fall short **10.** be inferior
confidence .. **11.** distrustful
in energy .. **6.** atonic
in firmness .. **7.** flaccid
in intelligence .. **12.** feebleminded
wanton ... **3.** gay **4.** lewd **5.** merry
6. frisky, harlot, unruly **7.** immoral,
lustful, wayward **8.** flagrant, insolent,
sportive, unchaste **9.** dissolute,
merciless **10.** capricious, frolicsome,
licentious **11.** extravagant
13. undisciplined
wapiti ... **3.** elk **4.** deer, stag
war ... **5.** fight **6.** attack, battle **8.** conflict
war (pert to) ...
agreement .. **6.** cartel
cause of .. **10.** casus belli
club .. **4.** mace
fleet .. **6.** armada
gas .. **8.** adamsite
German .. **5.** krieg **10.** blitzkrieg
god .. **3.** Ira, Tyr **4.** Ares
goddess .. **5.** Bella **6.** Ishtar
hating .. **13.** misopolemical
hawk .. **5.** jingo **7.** bailiff
horse .. **5.** steed **7.** charger **8.** partisan
10. campaigner, politician
of words .. **9.** logomachy
religious .. **5.** jihad (jehad)
vessel, ship .. **3.** sub **7.** cruiser, frigate
8. corvette (corvet) **9.** destroyer,
submarine **11.** dreadnought
(dreadnaught)
war bird ... **7.** aviator, tanager (scarlet)
warble ... **4.** sing **5.** carol, trill, yodel
6. quaver **7.** twitter, vibrate
warbler ... **4.** wren **6.** singer **8.** blackcap,
grosbeak, redstart, songster **9.** beccafico

10. bluethroat **11.** whitethroat
ward ... **4.** jail, part, rule **5.** watch
6. govern, prison **7.** custody, keeping
8. district, garrison, guardian,
watchman **9.** dependent **10.** stronghold
12. guardianship
ward (pert to) ...
division .. **4.** army, jail **6.** forest
8. hospital
French .. **14.** arrondissement
heeler .. **8.** henchman **10.** politician
off .. **4.** fend **5.** fence, parry, repel, stave
7. expiate, forfend, prevent
warden ... **5.** guard, nazir **6.** dizdar
(disdar), jailer, keeper, ranger, sexton
7. alcaide (alcaid), turnkey **8.** director,
guardian, official, watchman
9. concierge, custodian **10.** gatekeeper
warder ... **6.** warden **7.** turnkey
wardrobe ... **4.** room **6.** closet **7.** almirah,
apparel, cabinet, clothes **8.** costumes
12. clothespress
ware ... **4.** sage, wary, wise **5.** aware,
china, goods, spend **6.** shrewd
7. careful, heedful, pottery, prudent,
seaweed **8.** cautious, vigilant
9. cognizant, commodity, conscious,
porcelain **11.** commodities,
earthenware, merchandise
warehouse ... **4.** silo **5.** depot, étape
6. fonduk (fondouk), godown **7.** storage
8. entrepôt
warfare ... **7.** contest **8.** conflict, struggle
11. hostilities **12.** armed contest
wariness ... **7.** stealth **8.** distrust
9. chariness, suspicion
warlock ... **6.** wizard **7.** monster (Myth)
8. conjuror, magician, sorcerer
warm ... **3.** red **4.** heat, keen, mild
5. angry, calid, eager, humid, muggy,
tepid, toast **6.** ardent, excite, genial,
hearty, heated, torrid **7.** clement,
cordial, fervent **8.** friendly, generous
10. responsive **11.** sympathetic
12. affectionate, enthusiastic **13.** near
discovery, near the object (see also
hot)
warm (pert to) ...
bath .. **5.** therm
growing .. **8.** calescent
hearted .. **4.** kind **6.** hearty, kindly,
tender **7.** cordial **8.** friendly, generous
11. sympathetic **12.** affectionate
pert to .. **7.** thermal
praise .. **8.** encomium
room .. **10.** tepidarium
springs (Rom) .. **7.** thermae
warmblooded ... **6.** ardent **9.** irascible
13. homoiothermic, quick-tempered
14. haematothermal (hematothermal)
warmed over ... **5.** stale, trite
8. rehashed, reheated **9.** rechauffé,
twice-told
warmonger ... **4.** hawk
warmth ... **4.** élan, glow, heat, zeal
5. ardor **7.** ardency, thermal **8.** fervency
9. animation, eloquency, geniality,
vehemence **10.** enthusiasm, excitement
11. calefaction, earnestness
warn ... **4.** flag **5.** alarm, alert **6.** advise,
exhort, inform, notify, remind, signal

7. apprise (apprize), caution, counsel, previse 8. admonish, forebode, threaten 9. reprehend

warning . . . 4. bell, omen 5. alarm, alert, radar, siren 6. alarum, beacon, beware, caveat, signal, threat, tocsin 7. blinker, sematic, summons 10. admonition, admonitive 12. caveat emptor

warp . . . 4. bend, bias, hurl, sway, turn, woof 5. fling, throw, twist, weave 6. buckle, swerve 7. contort, deflect, distort, pervert 9. fabricate 10. aberration, distortion 12. misinterpret

warp (pert to) . . .
cross threads . . 4. woof
threads . . 5. lease 6. stamen
yarn . . 3. abb

warragal, warrigal . . . 5. dingo, horse, myall

warrant . . . 4. earn, writ 5. order 6. attest, ensure, permit, secure 7. defense, justify, precept, promise, voucher 8. document, guaranty, sanction, security 9. authorize, guarantee, safeguard 10. credential, instrument, protection 11. acknowledge, certificate 13. authorization

warranty . . . 4. writ 5. proof 7. promise, warrant 8. guaranty, sanction, security 13. authorization

warrior . . . 4. hero, impi 5. brave 6. Amazon 7. fighter, martial, soldier 10. halberdier

warrior (pert to) . . .
Bib . . 4. Ehud
female . . 6. Amazon
Indian . . 6. sannup
Roman . . 9. gladiator
Trojan . . 6. Agenor, Hector

Warsaw (pert to) . . .
capital . . 6. Poland
river . . 7. Vistula
suburb . . 5. Praga

wary . . . 3. shy 5. alert, canny, chary, leery 7. careful, guarded, prudent 8. cautious, discreet, watchful 10. economical 11. circumspect

wash . . . 3. lap, pan 4. lave 5. bathe, clean, elute, flush, leach, marsh, paint, purge, rinse, slosh, swash 6. debris, drench, dry bed (river), purify, splash 7. cleanse, immerse, launder, overlay, shampoo 8. ablution 9. lixiviate

wash (pert to) . . .
basin . . 4. bowl 6. lavabo
bear . . 7. raccoon
dish . . 11. pied wagtail
for gold . . 3. pan
one's hands of . . 6. give up, refuse 10. relinquish
out . . 4. fade 5. elute, flunk 7. failure, freshet
sale (finance) . . 10. fictitious

washing . . . 7. coating 8. ablution 9. drenching

Washington, DC (famed sites) . . .
7. Capitol (Bldg), The Mall 8. Pentagon, Treasury 10. Blair House, White House 11. Mount Vernon 12. Ford's Theater (Lincoln Museum), Supreme

Court 14. cherry blossoms 15. Iwo Jima Monument, Lincoln Memorial 16. National Archives, Naval Observatory 17. Jefferson Memorial, Library of Congress 18. Walter Reed Hospital, Washington Monument 19. Unknown Soldier's Tomb 22. Smithsonian Institution 25. Arlington National Cemetery

Washington (State of) . . .
capital . . 7. Olympia
city . . 6. Tacoma, Yakima 7. Everett, Seattle, Spokane 10. Bellingham, Walla Walla
dam . . 10. Bonneville 11. Grand Coulee
discoverer . . 4. Gray 9. Vancouver
explorer . . 5. Clark, Lewis 6. Wilkes 7. Fremont
Falls . . 10. Snoqualmie
Fort . . 5. Lewis
lake . . 5. Union 6. Chelan 8. Crescent
mountain . . 7. Rainier 8. Cascades, Olympics
river . . 5. Snake, White 7. Spokane 8. Columbia
Sound . . 5. Puget 7. Rosario
State admission . . 11. Forty-second
State motto . . 4. Al-Ki (By and By)
State nickname . . 9. Evergreen
wind (SW) . . 7. chinook

wasp . . . 5. Sphex, vespa, whamp 6. dauber, hornet, Tiphia, vespid 8. Vespidae 12. Hymenopteron, yellow jacket

waspish . . . 4. mean 5. cross, testy 6. cranky 7. bearish, peevish, slender 8. choleric, churlish, petulant, snappish, spiteful 9. fractious, irascible, irritable 12. cantankerous

wasp's nest . . . 8. vespiary

wassail . . . 4. lark, orgy, romp 5. toast 6. frolic, shindy 7. carouse 8. beverage, carousal 9. festivity 10. salutation 11. celebration 12. drinking bout

waste . . . 3. eat 4. idle, junk, loss, rind, ross, sack, slag, vain, wear, wild 5. chaff, chips, dross, havoc, spill, trash 6. barren, desert, expend, lavish, ravage, refuse 7. atrophy, exhaust, fritter, rubbish 8. clinkers, demolish, desolate, squander 9. dissipate 10. desolation, diminution 11. destruction, devastation, dissipation, prodigality, uninhabited 12. uncultivated, unproductive 13. unserviceable

waste (pert to) . . .
allowance . . 4. tret
away . . 3. age 6. shrink, sicken 7. decline 8. marasmus 11. deteriorate
lay waste . . 4. sack 6. ravage 7. destroy 8. decimate
matter . . 3. ort 4. slag 5. dross 7. clinker
mine . . 3. gob
silk . . 4. knob, noil 6. frison
time . . 4. idle, lazy 5. dally 6. daddle, footle, loiter 10. dillydally

wasted . . . 7. haggard 8. phthisic

wasteful . . . 6. lavish 10. thriftless 11. extravagant, improvident

wasteland . . . 5. heath, marsh, swamp

6. desert, morass **8.** badlands **10.** barren land, everglades
wasting ... **5.** aging **6.** awaste **8.** marasmic **10.** enfeebling **11.** consumption, devastating **13.** deteriorating
wastrel ... **4.** waif **5.** idler **8.** vagabond **10.** profligate **11.** spendthrift
watch ... **3.** eye, spy **4.** espy, heed, mark, mind, tend, time, wake (funeral) **5.** guard, vigil **6.** ambush, patrol, police, sentry **7.** bivouac, lookout, observe **8.** horologe, sentinel **9.** ambuscade, timepiece, vigilance **11.** chronometer, observation, wakefulness
watch (pert to) ...
  chain .. **3.** fob **6.** Albert
  face .. **5.** bezel
  maker .. **10.** horologist
  military .. **5.** perdu (perdue) **6.** sentry **7.** vedette
  stop .. **5.** timer
  tower .. **6.** beacon **7.** atalaya, mirador **10.** lighthouse
  word .. **6.** signal **10.** shibboleth (Bib) **11.** countersign
  works .. **10.** escapement
watchful ... **3.** Ira (Heb) **4.** wary **5.** alert, aware **7.** careful, heedful **8.** cautious, open-eyed, vigilant **9.** observant, regardful **11.** circumspect
watchman ... **5.** guard **6.** sentry, warder **8.** sentinel, watchdog **10.** gatekeeper
watchword ... **4.** hint, word **6.** signal **8.** party cry **10.** intimation, shibboleth (Bib) **11.** countersign
watchworks ... **10.** escapement
water ... **3.** eau, ice, wet **4.** aqua, rain **5.** fluid, flume, spray **6.** dilute, lagoon, liquid **7.** moisten **8.** beverage, calendar, irrigate, sprinkle **10.** adulterate
water (pert to) ...
  baptismal .. **5.** laver
  bath .. **7.** balneum
  bird .. **4.** coot, loon **5.** diver, ouzel **6.** dipper **7.** pintail, swimmer **9.** merganser
  bottle .. **4.** olla **6.** carafe
  buffalo .. **2.** ox **7.** carabao
  channel .. **5.** canal, flume **6.** strait **8.** tailrace
  chart .. **10.** hydrograph
  color (art) .. **9.** aquarelle
  comb form .. **5.** hydro **6.** hydato
  congealed .. **3.** ice **4.** snow **5.** glacé **6.** icicle
  course .. **4.** clow **5.** bayou, gorge, gully **6.** nullah, ravine, sluice **9.** watergate
  cow .. **6.** sea cow **7.** buffalo, manatee
  cure .. **10.** hydropathy **12.** hydrotherapy
  deer .. **10.** chevrotain
  destitute of .. **9.** anhydrous
  divination by .. **10.** hydromancy
  eagle .. **6.** osprey
  element .. **6.** oxygen **8.** hydrogen
  elephant .. **12.** hippopotamus
  exhibition .. **8.** aquacade
  fowl .. **7.** pelican
  gauge (rain) .. **8.** udometer
  goddess .. **4.** Nina **7.** Anahita, Anaitis
  hare .. **11.** swamp rabbit

  heater .. **4.** etna
  history .. **10.** hydrognosy
  hog .. **8.** capybara
  hole .. **5.** oasis **6.** tinaja **7.** alberca
  jug .. **4.** lota (lotah), olla **5.** banga **6.** hydria, kalpis
  lava .. **12.** hellgrammite
  lily .. **5.** lotus **6.** Nuphar **7.** Nelumbo **8.** Nymphaea, Victoria **11.** spatterdock
  measure .. **10.** hydrometer
  meter .. **7.** Venturi
  mineral .. **5.** Vichy **6.** Shasta **7.** Seltzer
  monster .. **6.** nicker (fabled)
  nymph .. **5.** naiad **6.** undine **7.** Oceanid
  of oblivion .. **5.** Lethe **12.** river of Hades
  opossum .. **5.** yapok (yapock)
  pert to .. **7.** aqueous **8.** hydatoid
  plug .. **3.** tap **4.** cock, cork **6.** faucet, spigot **7.** hydrant
  pocket .. **6.** tinaja
  rat .. **4.** vole **8.** vagabond
  reddish (with iron) .. **6.** riddam
  reservoir (underground) .. **6.** cenote
  rough .. **4.** eddy **5.** ocean **6.** rapids **7.** riptide **8.** undertow
  sapphire .. **6.** iolite **10.** saphir d'eau
  scorpion .. **4.** Nepa **7.** Ranatra
  search for .. **5.** dowse
  sheet of .. **5.** nappe
  spirit .. **3.** Nix **5.** Ariel, Nixie **6.** kelpie, nicker, sprite
  spout .. **5.** spate **8.** gargoyle
  sprite .. **3.** Nix **5.** Nixie
  stratum .. **7.** aquifer
  study, science of .. **9.** hydrology **11.** hydrography
  surface .. **4.** ryme
  swelling .. **5.** edema
  turkey .. **9.** snakebird
  vessel .. **3.** jug **4.** ewer, lota (lotah), pail **5.** cruse, flask **6.** bottle, bucket, tinaja **7.** pitcher, stamnos **8.** decanter
  wheel .. **5.** noria **6.** sakieh (sakiyeh) **7.** turbine **8.** tympanum
  without .. **9.** anhydrous
watery ... **8.** ichorous
Watling Street (London) ... **6.** Galaxy **8.** Milky Way **9.** Roman road
wattle ... **3.** rod **4.** beat, flog, plat, wand **5.** fence, twist, weave, withe **6.** barbel, dewlap, hurdle, lappet **8.** caruncle **9.** boobyalla, loose flap **10.** intertwine, interweave **11.** skin process **12.** native willow
wattlebird ... **4.** crow **10.** honey eater **11.** brush turkey
Wattle Day ... **7.** holiday
wave ... **3.** ola, sea, wag **4.** flap, tide **5.** crest, eagre, flood, ridge, surge, swell, tilde **6.** beckon, billow, comber, flaunt, hairdo, marcel, ripple, roller, signal **7.** breaker, decuman, flutter, tsunami, vibrate **8.** brandish, coiffure, flourish, greeting, undulate **9.** fluctuate, vibration **10.** undulation
waver ... **4.** reel, sway, veer **5.** demur, quake **6.** falter, quiver, totter **7.** flicker, flutter, stagger, tremble, vibrate **8.** hesitate **9.** fluctuate, oscillate, vacillate **12.** be indecisive
wavering ... **6.** fickle **8.** doubtful,

unsteady 9. desultory 10. irresolute
wavy . . . 4. onde, undé (undee) 5. curly,
snaky 6. repand, undate 7. billowy,
rolling, sinuous 8. undulant
9. undulated 10. undulatory
wax . . . 4. cere, grow 6. candle, cerate,
polish 7. beeswax, cerumen 8. increase,
paraffin 9. lubricant, lubricate
12. zietrisikite (mineral)
wax (pert to) . . .
beeswax cells . . 9. honeycomb
beeswax substitute . . 7. ceresin
candle . . 6. cierge
chemical . . 9. adipocere
Chinese . . 4. pela
molded in . . 7. fictile 9. ceroplast
ref to . . 5. ceral
substance . . 5. cerin
way . . . 3. via 4. lane, mode, path, plan,
ramp, road 5. alley, habit, means, Milky,
route, track 6. avenue, course, manner,
method, street 7. highway, passage
8. causeway, distance, sidewalk
9. banquette, direction, procedure
way (pert to) . . .
astronomy . . 6. Galaxy 8. Milky Way
give . . 5. break, yield 6. weaken
7. despair 10. depreciate
god of . . 6. Hermes
in . . 7. ingress 8. entrance
in a way . . 8. as it were, somewhat
13. theoretically
inclined . . 4. ramp
out . . 4. exit 6. egress, escape
roundabout . . 6. detour
waylay . . . 3. rob 5. await, seize
6. ambush, lay for 8. surprise
9. ambuscade
wayward . . . 6. unruly 7. erratic, willful
8. perverse, stubborn, untoward
10. capricious, headstrong, refractory
11. disobedient, intractable
weak . . . 3. dim, lax, wan 4. pale,
puny, thin, worn 5. faint, frail,
washy 6. dotish, feeble, infirm, sickly,
simple, unwise, watery 7. flaccid,
foolish, fragile, insipid 8. cowardly,
decrepit, fatigued, impotent, wavering
9. enfeebled, exhausted, nerveless,
powerless 10. effeminate 11. debilitated,
ineffective 12. unconvincing
weak (pert to) . . .
fish . . 7. totuava 9. gray trout
10. squeteague
hearted . . 6. afraid 7. fearful
12. fainthearted
kneed . . 8. cowardly, yielding
10. irresolute
sister . . 6. coward 8. weakling
11. mollycoddle
weaken . . . 3. sap 4. tire 5. break 6. dilute,
impair, lessen, reduce 7. cripple,
disable, exhaust, unnerve 8. enervate
9. undermine 10. debilitate
weakness . . . 4. flaw 5. atony, fault
6. defect, foible, liking 7. failing, fatigue,
frailty 8. asthenia, debility 9. cowardice,
impotence, infirmity 10. feebleness,
infirmness 11. decrepitude
12. imperfection 13. powerlessness
weal . . . 4. mark, wale, welt 5. ridge,

wheal 6. riches, wealth 7. welfare
9. happiness, well-being
10. commonweal
wealth . . . 4. good, weal 5. money
6. assets, mammon, riches 7. capital,
fortune, welfare 8. opulence, property,
treasure 9. abundance, affluence, well-
being 10. prosperity 11. possessions
wealth (pert to) . . .
god of . . 6. Plutus
person of . . 6. monied 7. magnate,
opulent 9. plutocrat
pursuit of . . 10. plutomania
study of . . 9. economics, plutology
worship of . . 10. plutolatry
wealthy . . . 4. rich 5. ample 8. abundant,
affluent
wealthy (pert to) . . .
English slang . . 4. oofy
man . . 5. nabob 10. capitalist
rule by . . 10. plutocracy
wean . . . 6. detach 8. alienate, estrange
9. reconcile
weapon . . . 3. arm, gat, gun 4. bola, bolo,
celt, club, dart, epee, snee 5. arrow,
knife, lance, rifle, saber (sabre), spear,
sword 6. dagger, musket, pistol, poleax
(poleaxe), rapier 7. bayonet, bazooka,
carbine, gisarme, halberd, machete,
trident 8. battle-ax (battle-axe), catapult,
crossbow, revolver, stiletto, tomahawk
9. derringer, Excalibur 11. blunderbuss
wear . . . 3. use 4. bear, fray, fret,
show 5. chafe, weary 7. fatigue
12. disintegrate
wear (pert to) . . .
away . . 3. eat, end 5. erode 6. abrade
7. corrode, decline
down . . 4. tire 8. persuade 9. influence
out . . 4. tire 5. waste 7. fatigue
weariness . . . 5. ennui 6. tedium
7. boredom, fatigue 9. lassitude
wearisome . . . 4. hard 6. boring, dismal,
dreary, tiring 7. irksome, tedious
8. tiresome, toilsome 9. fatiguing,
laborious, vexatious 10. monotonous
weary . . . 3. fag, irk, sad 4. bore, jade,
pall, tire, weak 5. bored, spent, tired
6. plague 7. fatigue, languid 9. forjesket
weasel . . . 4. stot, vare 5. ratel, stoat
6. ermine, ferret
weasellike . . . 4. mink 5. otter, tayra
9. musteline, musteloid
weather (pert to) . . .
cock . . 4. vane
glass . . 9. barometer, baroscope
man . . 13. meteorologist
map . . 6. isobar
weave . . . 3. mat 4. knit, lace, reel,
spin, sway 5. plait, unite 6. devise,
wattle 7. canelle, entwine, fashion
8. contrive 9. fabricate, interlace,
interwind 10. intertwine, intertwist
11. push one's way
weaver bird . . . 4. baya, maya, taha
5. Munia
weaving (pert to) . . .
art of . . 4. loom
fabric (rich) . . 3. web 7. brocade, webbing
French . . 5. lisse 8. Jacquard
material . . 5. reeds, twigs 6. raffia

term . . **4.** beam, dent, loom, sley **7.** shuttle
together . . **7.** plexure
weazen (wizen) . . . **6.** shrink, wither **7.** shrivel
web . . . **3.** net, ply **4.** caul, tela, trap, veil, warp **5.** snare **6.** tissue **7.** network, texture **8.** filament, gossamer, membrane, vexillum **12.** entanglement
web (pert to) . . .
footed . . **7.** palmate
like . . **4.** lacy **5.** telar **7.** spidery
spinning . . **6.** telary **7.** retiary
term . . **5.** telar
toed . . **11.** totipalmate
winged . . **3.** bat
work . . **4.** maze, mesh **6.** tangle **11.** Gordian knot
wed . . . **4.** join, mate **5.** marry, mated, unite **6.** joined **7.** espouse, pledged, spliced **13.** give in wedlock
wedding . . . **8.** ceremony, espousal, marriage, nuptials
wedding (anniversary) . . .
1st . . **5.** paper
2nd . . **5.** straw
3rd . . **5.** candy
4th . . **7.** leather
5th . . **6.** wooden
7th . . **6.** floral
10th . . **3.** tin
12th . . **5.** linen
13th . . **4.** lace
15th . . **7.** crystal
20th . . **5.** china
25th . . **6.** silver
30th . . **5.** pearl
35th . . **5.** coral
40th . . **5.** emerald
45th . . **4.** ruby
50th . . **6.** golden
75th . . **7.** diamond
wedding (pert to) . . .
flower . . **13.** orange blossom
proclamation . . **5.** banns (bans)
snow . . **4.** rice
term . . **7.** marital, wedlock **8.** marriage, nuptials **9.** matrimony **11.** espousement
wedge . . . **3.** jam **4.** club, shoe **5.** cleat, ingot, split **6.** sector, wedgie **7.** niblick **8.** triangle, voussoir **9.** machinery
wedge-shaped . . . **7.** cuneate **9.** cuneiform (cuniform)
Wednesday . . . **5.** Woden (wise god) **9.** fourth day, Woden's Day
wee . . . **3.** bit **4.** dock, fine, tiny **5.** small, teeny **6.** little, minute **10.** diminutive, teeny-weeny
weed . . . **3.** bur (burr), hoe, rag **4.** loco, milk, sida, tare **5.** cigar, flesh, vetch **6.** darnel, excise, Jimson, knawel, spurge, tumble **7.** allseed, mallows, mustard, ragweed, tobacco **8.** plantain, purslane, toadflax **9.** cultivate, dandelion **11.** undergrowth
weeds . . . **8.** garments (mourning)
week . . . **8.** hebdomad **9.** seven days
week (pert to) . . .
day . . **6.** ferial
Eccl . . **4.** Holy **7.** Passion

of Sundays . . **5.** seven **8.** hebdomad
of years . . **5.** seven
past . . **10.** yesterweek
weekly . . . **5.** aweek **10.** hebdomadal, periodical **11.** publication
weeks, two . . . **9.** fortnight
weel . . . **4.** pool, trap **6.** basket **8.** fish trap
ween . . . **5.** think **6.** expect **7.** believe, imagine, suppose **8.** conceive
weep . . . **3.** cry, orp, sob **4.** drip, rain, wail **5.** exude, mourn **7.** blubber, lapwing **9.** percolate, shed tears
weeping . . . **6.** crying **7.** sobbing **9.** festering
weeping (pert to) . . .
monkey . . **8.** capuchin
queen . . **5.** Niobe
tree . . **5.** cedar **6.** spruce, willow
Weeping Philosopher (anc) . . . **10.** Heraclitus
weevil (pert to) . . .
cotton . . **4.** boll
malt . . **4.** boud
snout . . **8.** curculio
type (other) . . **3.** pea **4.** palm, pine, rice, seed **5.** flour
weigh . . . **4.** tare, test **5.** hoist, poise, scale **6.** ponder, regard **7.** balance, be heavy, compare, measure **8.** consider, encumber, estimate, ruminate **9.** apportion, press hard
weigh down . . . **4.** lade, load **6.** burden, hamper **7.** ballast, depress, oppress **11.** overbalance
weight . . . **4.** load, mass **5.** force, power **6.** burden, import, moment **7.** gravity, tonnage **8.** encumber, pressure **9.** authority, heaviness, influence **10.** importance **11.** consequence **12.** significance
weight (pert to) . . .
allowance . . **4.** tare, tret **7.** scalage
comb form . . **4.** baro
gem . . **4.** carat (karat)
light . . **6.** suttle
system . . **3.** net **4.** troy **6.** metric **10.** apothecary **11.** avoirdupois
total . . **5.** gross
weighty . . . **3.** fat **5.** bulky, heavy, hefty, large, obese **6.** solemn **7.** massive, onerous, serious **8.** forcible, powerful **9.** corpulent, important, momentous, ponderous **10.** burdensome, cumbersome, impressive, oppressive **11.** influential **13.** authoritative
weir . . . **3.** dam, net **4.** bank **5.** fence, levee, seine **7.** barrier, milldam **9.** floodgate
weird . . . **3.** odd **4.** omen, wild **5.** eerie (eery), queer, scary **6.** creepy, spooky **7.** awesome, curious, ghostly, macabre, strange, uncanny **8.** eldritch **9.** deathlike, frightful **10.** mysterious, prediction
Weird Sisters (Scot) . . . **5.** Fates
welcome . . . **4.** hail **5.** adopt, greet **7.** acclaim, accueil **8.** grateful, greeting, pleasing **9.** agreeable, bienvenue, desirable **10.** acceptable, salutation
weld . . . **5.** unite **11.** consolidate
welfare . . . **4.** good, weal **5.** Salus

(goddess) **9.** good cheer **10.** prosperity
14. material plenty
welkin . . . **3.** air, sky **6.** heaven
10. atmosphere
well . . . **3.** fit, gay, pit **4.** gush, hale, pool
5. aweel, fount, fully **6.** easily, gusher,
hearty, justly, kindly, source **7.** cistern,
closely **8.** artesian, expertly, fountain,
friendly **10.** full degree, intimately
11. excellently **12.** satisfactory
well (pert to) . . .
being . . **4.** weal **7.** comfort **8.** eucrasia
9. happiness
Bib . . **4.** Esek
born . . **5.** noble **7.** eugenic
bred . . **6.** polite **7.** genteel, refined
8. cultured, wellborn **9.** pedigreed
10. cultivated **11.** gentlemanly
12. thoroughbred
comb form . . **4.** mene
defined . . **8.** distinct **11.** distinctive
groomed . . **4.** neat **5.** sleek **6.** soigné
(soignée)
grounded . . **5.** valid **7.** logical **9.** plausible
11. established, substantial **12.** well-
informed
gushing . . **8.** artesian
heeled . . **4.** rich **5.** armed **7.** moneyed,
wealthy, well-off **8.** well-to-do
known . . **6.** famous **7.** eminent
12. acknowledged
land drain . . **4.** sump
lining . . **5.** steen
off . . **5.** lucky **10.** prosperous
oil . . **6.** gusher
pole . . **5.** sweep
prefix . . **2.** eu
timed . . **6.** timely **9.** opportune
versed . . **7.** erudite
watered . . **9.** irrigated, irriguous
welsh (welch) . . . **5.** cheat **6.** not pay,
renege **7.** swindle **10.** shirk out of
Welsh (pert to) . . . see also *Wales*
boat . . **7.** coracle
congress of literati . . **10.** eisteddfod
fine, for murder . . **7.** galanas
god, underworld . . **4.** Bran
instrument (reed) . . **7.** pibcorn
man . . **5.** Taffy **8.** Cambrian
onion . . **5.** cibal
population . . **6.** Cymric
rabbit . . **7.** ramekin (ramequin), rarebit
romance collection . . **10.** Mabinogion
(Mabinogi)
welt . . . **4.** mark, wale **5.** ridge **6.** stripe,
thrash
welter . . . **4.** reel, roll, sail, toss **6.** grovel,
tumble, wallow **7.** stagger **8.** flounder,
overturn **9.** confusion
wen . . . **4.** cyst, rune **5.** tumor **7.** blemish
11. excrescence **12.** protuberance
wench . . . **4.** doxy, gill, girl **5.** child,
squaw, trull, woman **6.** damsel,
maiden **7.** consort, servant **8.** strumpet
11. maidservant
wend . . . **2.** go **4.** fare, pass **6.** depart,
direct, travel **7.** circuit, proceed
8. progress
went (pert to) . . . see also *go*
astray . . **6.** failed **10.** miscarried
away . . **4.** left **8.** departed

before . . **3.** led **8.** preceded **9.** anteceded
swiftly . . **3.** ran **4.** sped **6.** darted
7. scooted, scudded **8.** decamped
wenzel . . . **4.** jack (card game) **5.** knave
werewolf . . . **6.** jaguar **8.** uturuncu,
werefolk **11.** lycanthrope
wergild . . . **3.** cro **4.** eric **7.** galanas
9. Brehon Law
Wesleyan . . . **9.** Methodist **14.** Wesley
follower
West African (pert to) . . .
baboon . . **5.** drill **8.** mandrill
city . . **5.** Accra, Dakar
gazelle . . **4.** kudu, mohr (mhorr), oryx
lemur . . **5.** potto **8.** kinkajou
monkey . . **4.** mona **6.** guenon
native . . **7.** Ashanti (Ashantee)
people . . **5.** Igara
pepper . . **5.** cubeb
tree . . **5.** iroko, odoom
West End, London . . . **7.** Mayfair
9. Belgravia **11.** fashionable
12. aristocratic
Western . . . **9.** Hesperian **10.** Occidental
Westernmost US . . . **9.** Aleutians **11.** Attu
Islands **12.** Cape Wrangell
West Indies . . .
bird . . **4.** tody **6.** mucaro
boat . . **7.** drogher (droger)
chief . . **7.** cacique
clingfish . . **6.** testar
crop . . **5.** sugar **7.** bananas
ebony . . **9.** cocuswood
fish . . **4.** cero, paru, sesi **6.** testar
flea . . **6.** chigoe
fruit . . **5.** papaw (pawpaw)
islands . . **4.** Cuba **5.** Haiti **6.** Cayman,
Virgin **7.** Antigua, Bahamas, Leeward
8. Antilles, Windward
liquor . . **5.** mobby (mobbie), tafia (taffia)
lizard . . **6.** arbalo
magic . . **5.** obeah
music . . **7.** calypso
owl . . **6.** mucaro
resident . . **9.** Antillean
rodent . . **6.** agouti (agouty)
snuff . . **8.** Maccaboy
tea . . **8.** goatweed
tortoise . . **7.** hicatee
tree . . **4.** ausu **5.** ebony, papaw **6.** bonduc
8. bayberry **9.** sapodilla, satinwood
volcano . . **5.** Pelée
wood . . **9.** cocuswood, sapodilla
10. granadilla
Westminster clock (London) . . . **6.** Big
Ben
West Pointer . . . **5.** cadet, plebe
8. yearling
West Point motto . . . **16.** Duty, Honor,
Country
West Virginia . . .
capital . . **10.** Charleston
city . . **5.** Logan **8.** Wheeling
11. Parkersburg
crop . . **4.** coal
mountain . . **10.** Spruce Knob
11. Alleghenies
park (famed) . . **12.** Harpers Ferry
river . . **4.** Ohio **7.** Kanawha
11. Monongahela
Springs (resort) . . **8.** Berkeley **12.** White

Sulphur
State admission . . **11.** Thirty-fifth
State motto . . **19.** Montani Semper Liberi
22. Mountaineers Always Free
State nickname . . **8.** Mountain
West wind . . . **8.** Favonius, Zephyrus
wet . . . **4.** asop, damp, dank, dewy,
rain **5.** foggy, humid, leach, misty,
moist, mushy, rainy, soggy, soppy
6. dampen, drench, soaked, sodden,
watery **7.** moisten **8.** sprinkle
wet blanket . . . **7.** kill-joy **8.** deadhead
10. discourage, spoilsport
whale . . . **3.** orc **4.** cete, lash, whip
5. whack **6.** beluga, blower, thrash
7. grampus, ripsack **8.** hardhead
9. zeuglodon **13.** sulphur-bottom
whale (pert to) . . .
Arctic . . **7.** narwhal
bird . . **4.** gull **6.** petrel **9.** phalarope
blubber pot . . **6.** try-pot
blue . . **9.** Sibbaldus
bone . . **6.** baleen
carcass . . **5.** kreng
constellation . . **5.** Cetus
fat . . **7.** blubber
food . . **4.** brit
gray . . **7.** ripsack **8.** hardhead
killer . . **4.** orca
killer of . . **8.** ceticide
legendary . . **9.** Mysticeti
monster . . **4.** Cete
mustache (legend) . . **9.** Mysticeti
Order . . **7.** Cetacea
ref to . . **5.** cetic, sperm **6.** baleen
7. blubber **8.** cetacean
school of . . **3.** gam, pod
secretion (perfume) . . **9.** ambergris
small . . **7.** grampus
sperm type . . **8.** cachalot
study of . . **8.** cetology
toothed . . **10.** odontocete, zeuglodont
type . . **3.** orc **4.** blue, orca **5.** right, sperm
6. killer **7.** dolphin, rorqual **8.** cachalot,
humpback, porpoise **9.** whalebone
wax . . **10.** spermaceti
whalebone . . **6.** baleen **10.** stiffening
young . . **4.** calf **9.** shorthead
wharf . . . **4.** dock, pier, quay **5.** jetty
6. staith **7.** landing
wharf (pert to) . . .
fish . . **6.** cunner
master . . **10.** wharfinger
worker . . **9.** stevedore
whatnot . . . **5.** thing **6.** object
(nondescript) **7.** étagère **10.** miscellany
what's what . . . **4.** fact **5.** truth **7.** reality
10. what's right
what wonders has God wrought (Arabic
exclamation) . . . **9.** mashallah
whaup . . . **6.** curlew, outcry **9.** scoundrel
wheal . . . **4.** wale, weal, welt **5.** whelk
6. stripe **7.** pustule
wheat (pert to) . . .
beard . . **3.** awn
beverage . . **6.** zythem
bird . . **4.** lark **8.** wheatear **9.** chaffinch
chaff . . **4.** bran
duck . . **7.** widgeon **8.** baldpate
Europe . . **5.** emmer, spelt (speltz)
flour . . **4.** atta **5.** Hovis

hard . . **5.** durum
India . . **4.** suji **8.** semolina
storage bin . . **4.** silo **8.** elevator
wheedle . . . **4.** coax, gain **5.** tease
6. banter, cajole, entice **7.** blarney,
flatter **8.** blandish, inveigle, persuade
9. influence
wheel . . . **3.** cam, cog **4.** bike, disc, helm,
ride, roll, rota **5.** drive, pivot, rotor,
rowel, whirl **6.** caster, roller, rotate
7. bicycle, revolve, rotator, torture,
vehicle **8.** tricycle **10.** water wheel
wheel (pert to) . . .
gem-grinding . . **5.** skive
hub . . **4.** nave
man . . **5.** pilot **7.** cyclist **8.** helmsman,
pedalist **9.** bicyclist
monkey . . **3.** gin
part . . **3.** rim **5.** felly (felloe), spoke
6. hubcap
pulley . . **6.** sheave
shaped . . **8.** circular, rotiform
spoke . . **6.** radius
spur . . **5.** rowel
stopper . . **4.** grig **5.** sprag
swiveled . . **6.** caster
toothed . . **3.** cog **4.** gear **6.** pinion
turbine . . **5.** rotor
type . . **3.** cog, fly, pin **4.** cart, mill, spur
5. wagon **6.** Ferris, paddle **7.** balance,
potter's **9.** of fortune
water . . **5.** noria **6.** sakieh (sakiyeh)
wheels, logging . . . **7.** katydid
wheen . . . **3.** few **5.** group **7.** several
8. division, quantity
wheerikins . . . **10.** posteriors
wheetle . . . **5.** chirp **7.** whistle
wheeze . . . **3.** gag **4.** joke **5.** hoose (hooze)
6. cliché, saying **7.** breathe **8.** sibilate
9. witticism **10.** sibilation
whelk . . . **4.** acne **5.** snail **6.** papule,
pimple **7.** pustule
whelp . . . **3.** boy, cub, pup **5.** child, puppy,
tiger, youth **9.** give birth, youngling
when . . . **2.** as **3.** tho **5.** until **6.** though
7. how soon, whereas **8.** although,
whenever **10.** how long ago **11.** at
which time
where . . . **4.** here, spot **5.** place, there
7. whither **10.** inasmuch as **11.** at what
place, whereabouts
whereas . . . **5.** since
whereby . . . **7.** perquod
whereness . . . **6.** ubiety
whereupon . . . **4.** when **7.** on which
9. upon which **10.** after which
wherewithal . . . **5.** means, money
9. resources
whet . . . **4.** hone **5.** grind, point,
rouse **6.** excite **7.** quicken, sharpen
9. intensify, stimulate
whether . . . **2.** if **6.** either
whey . . . **4.** curd **5.** serum
whiff . . . **4.** blow, fish, gust, odor, puff,
waft **6.** breath, exhale, stanch **7.** puff
out **8.** blow away **10.** inhalation
while . . . **2.** as **3.** yet **4.** time **5.** until
7. beguile, interim, whereas **11.** space
of time
whilom . . . **4.** erst, once **5.** of old **6.** former
8. sometime **9.** erstwhile

whim ... 3. fad, pun, toy 4. idea
5. fancy, freak 6. megrim, notion,
vagary 7. boutade, caprice, whimsey
(whimsy), widgeon 8. migraine
whimper ... 3. cry, sob 4. mewl, moan,
pule, weep 5. whine 7. sniffle
whimsey, whimsy ... 3. wit 4. whim
5. craze, fancy, freak 7. caprice
whimsical ... 3. fad, odd 4. dish 5. droll,
queer, witty 7. amusing 8. fanciful,
freakish, notional 9. crotchety, eccentric,
fantastic, grotesque 10. capricious
whine ... 4. moan, pule, wail 6. snivel
7. screech, ululate, whimper 8. complain
12. moaning sound
whinny ... 4. bray 5. neigh, whine
whip ... 3. cat, tan 4. beat, crop,
flag, flog, goad, lace, lash, wale
5. birch, froth, quirt, seize, spank,
strap 6. defeat, incite, punish, strike,
swinge, thrash 7. agitate, chabouk
(chabuk), conquer, scourge 8. emulsify,
lambaste 9. bullwhack 10. discipline
11. congressman
whip (pert to) ...
hand .. 8. dominion 9. advantage,
influence
mark .. 4. wale, weal, welt
political .. 5. party 11. floor leader
riding .. 4. crop 5. quirt
Russian .. 4. plet (plete) 5. knout
sewing .. 8. overcast
socket .. 5. snead
whir ... 3. fly 4. burr, buzz, whiz 5. hurry,
swirl, whizz 6. hurtle 7. revolve, vibrate
9. commotion
whirl ... 4. eddy, reel, spin, tirl, turn
5. twirl 6. circle, gyrate, rotate 7. revelry,
revolve 9. commotion, pirouette, turn
about 10. excitement
whirlpool ... 4. eddy 6. gurges (Her),
vortex 7. sea puss (sea purse)
9. maelstrom
whirlwind ... 2. oe (Faroes) 7. cyclone,
tornado, twister, typhoon 9. hurricane,
maelstrom 10. willy-willy
whisk ... 4. tuft, whip, wist 5. froth,
sweep, swish 6. convey 7. agitate
whiskers ... 4. chin 5. beard 8. vibrissa
9. sideburns
whisky, whiskey ... 3. rye 4. corn
6. poteen, redeye 9. moonshine
10. usquebaugh
whisky (pert to) ...
base .. 3. rye 5. wheat 6. barley
drink .. 4. soda, sour 5. punch, smash
7. stinger
Insurrection .. 12. Pennsylvania (1794)
Ring .. 10. Conspiracy (1875)
term .. 6. lively 7. flighty
whisper ... 3. tip 4. blow, buzz 5. rumor
6. breeze, murmur 7. divulge 14. vox
clandestina
whist, game ... 9. Cavendish
10. Yarborough
whistle ... 4. hiss, pipe, sing, toot
5. alarm 6. rustle, warble, wheeze
12. interference
whistle (pert to) ...
duck .. 9. goldeneye
fish .. 8. rockling

pig .. 9. woodchuck
stop .. 12. one-horse town
tree (for boys' whistles) .. 5. maple
6. willow
whistling (pert to) ...
coot .. 6. scoter
dick .. 6. thrush
duck .. 6. scoter 9. goldeneye
hawk .. 5. eagle
snipe .. 8. woodcock
sound .. 7. stridor
teal .. 6. scoter 8. tree duck
whit ... 3. bit, jot 4. atom, iota 5. bodle,
speck 8. particle
white ... 3. wan 4. milk, pale, snow
5. ashen, chalk, color, happy, ivory,
snowy 6. albino, chalky, chaste, honest,
pallid 7. ivorine, silvery 8. innocent,
platinum 9. alabaster, albescent,
Caucasian, favorable, fortunate,
honorable 11. snow-covered
white (pert to) ...
admiral .. 9. butterfly
ant .. 4. anay (anai) 7. termite
belly .. 6. pigeon 7. widgeon 14. prairie
chicken
cat .. 7. catfish
cell .. 9. leucocyte
chub .. 10. spawneater
cloud .. 6. cirrus 7. tendril
coal .. 10. water power
crow .. 7. vulture
curlew .. 4. ibis
devil .. 7. nailrod
elephant .. 6. burden 8. Oriental
ensign .. 12. British naval
fish .. 5. cisco 6. atinga, beluga
8. menhaden 9. Coregonus 10. white
whale
grouse .. 9. ptarmigan
growing (hoary) .. 9. canescent
head .. 6. pigeon 9. blue goose 10. surf
scoter
heat .. 5. anger 13. incandescence
livered .. 6. feeble 8. cowardly
13. pusillanimous
matter (nerve) .. 4. alba
merganser .. 4. smew
miller .. 11. clothes moth
monk .. 10. Cistercian
mule .. 3. gin 6. whisky (illicit)
9. moonshine
oak .. 5. roble
of egg .. 5. glair
partridge .. 9. ptarmigan
person .. 9. Caucasian
plague .. 7. disease 8. phthisis
11. consumption 12. tuberculosis
plantain .. 8. pussytoe
poplar .. 5. aspen
pot .. 7. pudding
pudding .. 7. sausage 9. whitehass
pyrite .. 9. marcasite
shark .. 8. man-eater
throat .. 6. muffet (Eng) 7. warbler
whale .. 6. beluga
White (pert to) ...
Chapel (Jewish) .. 13. London Quarter
Holland .. 6. turkey
Horse .. 6. emblem (Saxons) 7. carving
House designer .. 5. Hoban

Relig . . **6.** Friars **7.** Fathers, Sisters
8. Brethren
Rose (Eng) . . **6.** emblem (House of York)
Sands (N Mex) . . **13.** proving ground
Squadron . . **4.** Navy (US Navy 1883)
Tower . . **13.** Tower of London
whiten . . . **6.** blanch, bleach **8.** etiolate
9. whitewash
whitewash . . . **5.** paint **6.** defeat, whiten
7. conceal **9.** disinfect, exculpate, gloss
over
whither . . . **5.** where **7.** whereto **11.** to
what place, whereabouts
whiting . . . **4.** fish **5.** chalk **6.** tomcod
10. butterfish
whitish . . . **4.** pale **5.** white **9.** albescent
whitlow . . . **4.** herb, sore **5.** felon
6. agnail, fetlow **8.** hangnail **9.** saxifrage
10. paronychia **12.** inflammation
Whitsunday . . . **9.** Pentacost
Whittington, Dick . . . **9.** Lord Mayor
(London)
whittle . . . **3.** cut, hew **4.** gash, hack,
pare, trim **5.** knife **6.** reduce **7.** blanket
whiz, whizz . . . **3.** hum **4.** buzz, hiss,
pirr, whir, zizz **5.** whirr **6.** corker, rotate
8. sibilate **10.** speed along **12.** clever
person
who . . . **3.** wer, wha **5.** which **6.** person
7. one that, pronoun
whole . . . **3.** all, sum **4.** pure, sole, unit
5. gross, total, uncut, unity **6.** entire,
intact, mostly, system **7.** healthy, perfect
8. absolute, complete, entirety, totality
9. aggregate, generally, unanimous,
undivided
whole (pert to) . . .
comb form . . **4.** toti, toto
footed . . **5.** frank **8.** intimate **9.** ingenuous
10. flat-footed
hearted . . **7.** devoted, earnest, sincere
8. complete **10.** unreserved
11. unmitigated
hog . . **8.** whole way **12.** all or nothing
note . . **9.** semibreve
number . . **7.** integer
skinned . . **6.** unhurt **9.** unscathed
souled . . **5.** noble **7.** devoted, sincere,
zealous **11.** noble-minded
12. wholehearted
wholesome . . . **4.** sane **5.** sound **6.** hearty,
robust **7.** healthy **8.** salutary, vigorous
9. favorable, healthful **10.** beneficial,
propitious, salubrious
wholly . . . **3.** all **4.** toto (comb form)
5. fully, quite **6.** solely **7.** totally
8. entirely, entirety **9.** perfectly
10. altogether, completely, thoroughly
11. exclusively
whoop . . . **4.** call, hoot, urge, yell **5.** cheer,
shout **6.** halloo, hoopee **10.** enthusiasm
whooping cough . . . **9.** pertussis
whoop it up . . . **7.** be noisy **8.** energize
9. make merry **12.** create gaiety
whop . . . **4.** bang, beat, bump, fall, flop,
whip **5.** knock **6.** strike, stroke
whopper . . . **3.** lie (monstrous) **5.** story
(false)
whorl . . . **4.** curl **5.** helix, spire **8.** flywheel,
verticil, volution (shell) **11.** fingerprint
wicked . . . **3.** bad, ill **4.** evil, vile **6.** guilty,

sinful, unjust **7.** heinous, hellish,
profane, roguish, ungodly, vicious
8. criminal, depraved, devilish, diabolic,
flagrant **9.** abandoned, atrocious,
malicious, nefarious, perverted
10. diabolical, flagitious, iniquitous,
villainous **11.** irreligious, mischievous,
unrighteous
wickedness . . . **3.** sin **4.** evil **6.** Belial
(Bib) **7.** badness **8.** baseness, iniquity
10. sinfulness **13.** maliciousness
wicked one . . . **5.** Demon, Satan **7.** Evil
One **8.** The Devil
wicker (pert to) . . .
basket . . **5.** cesta **6.** hamper, kipsey
7. pannier
cradle . . **8.** bassinet
material . . **5.** twigs **6.** osiers, willow,
withes
ware . . **8.** basketry, plaiting
wicket . . . **4.** arch, door, gate, hoop
6. grille, window **7.** grating, guichet,
lattice **8.** loophole **12.** grated window,
ticket window
wickiup, wikiup . . . **3.** hut **7.** shelter
Widal's, Widal reaction . . . **16.** typhoid
fever test
widbin . . . **7.** dogwood **8.** woodbine
11. honeysuckle
widdy . . . **4.** rope (twig) **5.** noose, widow,
withy **6.** halter **7.** gallows **11.** gallows
bird
wide . . . **5.** ample, broad, large, loose,
roomy **6.** opened **7.** liberal **8.** expanded,
spacious **9.** capacious, distended
13. comprehensive
wide-awake . . . **3.** hat **4.** keen, tern
(sooty) **5.** alert **7.** knowing **8.** watchful
wide-eyed . . . **4.** agog **5.** naive **6.** amazed
9. surprised
widemouthed . . . **4.** loud **5.** noisy
6. greedy **7.** barking **9.** devouring
widen . . . **4.** ream **5.** dilate, expand,
extend, spread **7.** amplify, broaden,
enlarge
widespread . . . **4.** rife **5.** broad **7.** diffuse,
general **8.** not local, sweeping
9. dispersed, extensive, prevalent,
scattered, universal **13.** comprehensive
widgeon . . . **4.** duck, smee **5.** goose
6. Mareca, zuisin **7.** poacher **8.** baldpate
9. simpleton
widow . . . **6.** relict **7.** bereave, dowager,
viduate
widow (pert to) . . .
bird . . **5.** finch, Vidua **6.** whidah
cremated . . **6.** suttee
fish . . **5.** viuva
monkey . . **4.** titi
suicide . . **6.** suttee
widower . . . **6.** relict
widow's (pert to) . . .
lock . . **8.** hairline **10.** widow's peak
mite . . **4.** coin **6.** lepton
portion . . **5.** dower
right . . **5.** terce
weeds . . **8.** mourning **9.** black veil,
widowhood
width . . . **5.** girth **7.** breadth **8.** diameter,
latitude, wideness
wield . . . **3.** ply, use **4.** cope, deal, rule

5. power, swing 6. direct, employ, handle, manage 7. control 8. brandish 10. manipulate

wife . . . 4. frau, mate, rani, uxor 5. bride, mujer 6. matron, spouse 7. consort 8. gudewife (guidwife), helpmate, helpmeet 10. better half 12. married woman

wife (pert to) . . .
French . . 5. femme
killing . . 9. uxoricide
of a rajah . . 4. Rani (Ranee)
one . . 8. monogamy
pert to . . 7. uxorial
slave's . . 9. broadwife

wig . . . 4. tête 5. jasey 6. peruke, toupee 7. censure, periwig 8. seal hood 9. dignitary

wight . . . 3. man 4. loud 5. brave, fairy, swift, witch 6. active, nimble 7. valiant 8. creature, powerful 11. living being

wigwag . . . 6. signal 8. to and fro 11. oscillation

wigwam . . . 4. tent 5. hogan, tepee 6. teepee

wild . . . 3. mad 5. feral, myall, waste, weird 6. ferine, savage, stormy, unruly 7. bestial, howling, riotous 8. aberrant, desolate, dramatic, frenetic, reckless, untilled, wildwood 9. barbarian, barbarous, ferocious, imprudent, primitive, unbridled, uncertain 10. boisterous, chimerical, irrational, profligate, tumultuous, unexplored, wilderness 11. harum-scarum, uncivilized, uninhabited 12. obstreperous, uncontrolled, uncultivated 14. uncontrollable

wild (pert to) . . .
alder . . 8. goutweed
animal . . 3. gnu 4. bear, deer, lion, lynx 5. kiang, moose, tiger 6. dragon, onager 7. polecat 8. antelope 10. wildebeest
banana . . 5. papaw (pawpaw)
beasts . . 4. ziim
buffalo . . 4. arna 5. arnee
carrot . . 8. hilltrot
cat . . 4. balm, eyra 6. ocelot 7. panther
coffee . . 9. feverroot
crocus . . 12. pasqueflower
fancy . . 6. vagary
fowl . . 4. duck 5. goose, quail 8. pheasant 9. partridge
garlic . . 4. moly
goat . . 3. tur 4. tahr 7. markhor (markhoor)
gourd . . 7. pumpkin 11. calabazilla
growing . . 8. agrarian
hog . . 4. boar 9. razorback 10. babiroussa
hop . . 6. bryony
horse . . 6. tarpan
ibex . . 5. Capra
Irishman (shrub) . . 10. tumatakuru
jalap . . 8. mayapple
mustard . . 8. charlock
ox . . 3. yak 4. anoa
pieplant . . 7. rhubarb
pineapple . . 7. pinguin
plum . . 4. sloe 5. islay
sheep . . 3. sha 5. urial (oorial) 6. argali
sweet potato . . 7. manroot

West show . . 5. rodeo

wildebeest . . . 3. gnu

wilderness . . . 5. waste, wilds 6. forest 8. wildwood 9. confusion 12. complication

wile . . . 3. art, toy 4. lure, ruse 5. fraud, guile, trick 6. deceit 7. cunning 8. artifice, trickery 9. stratagem

will . . . 4. wish 6. behest, choice, decree, demise, desire 7. bequest, command 8. volition 9. intention, testament 10. resolution 11. disposition, inclination 13. determination

will (pert to) . . .
appendix . . 7. codicil
convey . . 6. demise 7. bequest
having made . . 7. testate
maker of . . 8. testator
power . . 7. purpose 10. resolution 13. determination 14. strength of mind
proof of . . 7. probate
to live (Buddh) . . 5. tanha

willful, wilful . . . 3. mad 4. rash 5. heady 7. wayward 8. perverse, stubborn 9. impetuous, obstinate, voluntary 11. intentional 14. self-determined

willing . . . 4. free 5. prone, ready 6. minded 8. desirous, disposed, unforced 9. agreeable, voluntary 10. consenting, deliberate, ready to act, volitional 11. intentional 12. well-disposed

willingly . . . 4. fain, lief 6. freely, gladly 7. happily, readily 10. cheerfully 12. with pleasure

willow . . . 3. iva 4. Itea 5. osier, salix 6. sallow, teaser

willow (pert to) . . .
basket . . 7. prickle
genus . . 5. Salix
green . . 6. reseda
lark . . 12. sedge warbler
pattern . . 7. Nanking 11. earthenware
twig . . 5. withe 6. sallow
wren . . 10. chiffchaff

willowy . . . 5. lithe 6. pliant, supple, svelte 7. slender 8. flexible, graceful 15. tall and graceful

Will Rogers' plane . . . 9. Winnie May

wilsome . . . 4. wild 6. astray, dreary 7. violent, willful (wilful) 8. desolate 9. bewildered

wilt . . . 3. sag 4. flag, tire 5. droop, quail 6. sicken, wither 8. languish 11. deteriorate, lose courage, make flaccid

Wilton . . . 3. rug 6. carpet

wily . . . 3. sly 4. foxy 5. canny, smart 6. artful, astute, crafty, shrews, subtle 7. cunning 9. cautelous

wimble . . . 3. awl 4. bore 5. auger, brace, scoop, twist 6. gimlet, pierce 9. sprightly, whimsical

wimick . . . 3. cry 7. whimper

wimple . . . 4. fold, veil 7. meander 8. covering (head)

win . . . 3. get 4. earn, gain 5. to get 6. attain, defeat, obtain, secure 7. achieve, acquire, succeed, triumph 8. be victor, endeavor, vanquish 9. captivate 10. accomplish

win (pert to) . . .
all tricks (game) . . **4.** slam
by guile . . **8.** inveigle
one's spurs . . **10.** knighthood
over . . **7.** convert **8.** convince
persuade . . **10.** conciliate
wince . . . **4.** reel **5.** start **6.** cringe, flinch,
   recoil, shrink **8.** draw back, windlass
   10. shrink from
wind . . . **2.** oe **3.** air **4.** bora, coil, gale,
   gust, talk, turn, wrap **5.** blast, buran,
   crank, trade **6.** boreal, breath, breeze,
   simoom, zephyr **7.** chinook, conceit,
   cyclone, deviate, etesian, meander,
   monsoon, sinuate, sirocco, tempest,
   tornado, typhoon **8.** convolve, williwaw
   9. hurricane, idle words, windstorm
   10. instrument
wind (pert to) . . .
action on land . . **8.** eolation
around . . **6.** master **8.** dominate
   9. influence **13.** lead by the nose
cloud . . **4.** scud
comb form . . **5.** anemo
fall . . **7.** godsend **8.** buckshee, gratuity
flower . . **7.** anemone
gauge . . **4.** vane **10.** anemometer
god . . **4.** Adad **6.** Aeolus
god of north wind . . **6.** Boreas
god of SE wind . . **5.** Eurus
instrument . . **3.** sax **4.** fife, horn
   5. flute, organ **6.** cornet **7.** bassoon,
   hautboy, helicon, ocarina **8.** clarinet
   9. harmonica, saxophone
in the (wind) . . **5.** drunk **7.** sailing
   8. imminent **9.** happening
into a ball . . **11.** agglomerate
personified . . **6.** Caurus **7.** Caecias
   8. Favonius, Zephyrus
ref to . . **7.** Aeolian (Eolian)
rose . . **5.** poppy
science . . **9.** anemology
storm . . **4.** gale **7.** cyclone, typhoon
   9. hurricane
up . . **3.** end **7.** prepare **8.** complete,
   conclude
yarn . . **6.** windle
wind (type) . . .
Adriatic (cold) . . **4.** bora
cold . . **4.** bise, bora, puna **7.** mistral
   8. williwaw
desert . . **6.** simoom **7.** sirocco
dry . . **9.** harmattan
East . . **8.** levanter
Egypt . . **7.** khamsin (kamsin)
equator . . **5.** trade
fierce . . **4.** gale **6.** buster, squall
   7. monsoon **8.** blizzard **9.** hurricane
gentle . . **4.** aura **6.** zephyr
Malta (cold) . . **7.** gregale
Mediterranean . . **6.** solano **7.** etesian
   8. levanter
North . . **6.** Boreas
Northwest . . **6.** Caurus **7.** etesian
Oriental . . **7.** monsoon
Peru . . **4.** puna
S America . . **4.** puna **7.** pampero
South . . **6.** Auster
Southeast . . **5.** Eurus
Southwest . . **7.** chinook
Spain . . **6.** solano

West (personified) . . **8.** Favonius
whirl . . **2.** oe
windiness . . . **7.** conceit **12.** boastfulness
winding . . . **5.** curve, snaky **6.** spiral
   7. sinuous, twining **8.** rambling,
   tortuous **9.** deviative, meandrous
   10. circuitous
windjammer . . . **6.** bugler, talker, vessel
   (sailing) **8.** bandsman **9.** trumpeter
windlass . . . **4.** reel **5.** winch **6.** windle
   7. capstan, machine (hoisting)
windle . . . **4.** reel **5.** winch **6.** basket
   7. measure, redwing
window (pert to) . . .
arrangement . . **8.** fanlight **12.** fenestration
bay . . **5.** oriel
dormer, roof . . **5.** gable **7.** lucarne
   8. skylight
frame . . **4.** sash
Latin . . **8.** fenestra
leading . . **4.** came
nautical . . **8.** porthole
oval . . **5.** oxeye
part . . **4.** pane, sash, sill **5.** glass
   7. shutter
recess . . **6.** exedra **9.** embrasure
ship's . . **4.** port **8.** porthole
ticket . . **6.** wicket **7.** guichet
type . . **4.** port **5.** gable, oriel **7.** eucarne
   8. casement, skylight
windpipe . . . **6.** gullet, throat **7.** trachea,
   weasand
windrow . . . **5.** swath (swathe) **6.** furrow
Winds, Father of (Gr) . . . **8.** Astraeus
windward . . . **5.** aloof **8.** aweather
   9. weatherly
Windy City . . . **7.** Chicago
wine (pert to) . . .
and honey . . **5.** clary, mulse **7.** oenomel
Baden . . **8.** Ruländer
bag . . **8.** wineskin
bibber . . **3.** sot **5.** toper **7.** tippler
   8. drunkard
Bordeaux . . **6.** claret
bottle . . **6.** magnum **8.** decanter
cask . . **3.** tun
cellar . . **6.** bodega
comb form . . **4.** oeno
cruet . . **7.** burette
cup . . **3.** ama **6.** goblet **7.** chalice
divination by . . **9.** oenomancy
dry . . **3.** sec
film . . **8.** beeswing
French . . **6.** Masden, Pontac (Pontacq)
   8. muscatel **9.** Hermitage
   10. Montrachet **12.** Saint-Emilion,
   Saint-Estèphe
glass . . **6.** rummer (Rom)
grower . . **8.** vigneron
hater of . . **11.** oenophobist
Italian . . **7.** Orvieto **8.** muscatel
kind . . **4.** port **5.** Medoc, Rhine, tinta,
   Tokay **6.** canary, claret, Malaga, sherry
   7. Chablis, Madeira **8.** Burgundy,
   muscatel, sauterne, vermouth
   9. champagne
lover of . . **11.** oenophilist
maker . . **6.** abkari (abkary)
making . . **10.** oenopoetic
merchant . . **5.** abkar
miracle scene . . **4.** Cana (Bib)

palm .. **5.** taree
Persian .. **6.** Shiraz
pitcher .. **4.** olpe **8.** oenochoe
reference to .. **5.** vinic
residue .. **4.** marc
sherry .. **5.** Xeres **7.** Catawba, Moselle, oloroso
shop .. **3.** bar **6.** bistro, bodega
Spain .. **6.** Malaga
sparkling .. **8.** mousseux
study of .. **8.** oenology
sweet .. **5.** lunel
taster .. **10.** oenologist
Tuscan .. **7.** Chianti
white .. **6.** Malaga **8.** Riesling, sauterne, verdelho **12.** Marcobrunner
year .. **7.** vintage
wing .. **3.** ala, arm, fly **6.** convey, flight, member, pinion **7.** faction **8.** addition, dispatch
wing (pert to) . . .
anterior .. **7.** elytron
comb form .. **7.** pterygo
false .. **5.** alula
fish .. **8.** sea robin
footed .. **6.** aliped
Greek .. **6.** pteryx
quill .. **7.** remiges
shaped .. **7.** aliform
tip .. **7.** aileron
winglike .. **4.** alar **7.** pteroid **9.** pterygoid
winged . . . **4.** aile (Her), fast **5.** alate, lofty, rapid, swift **7.** pennate, sublime **9.** aliferous, aligerous
winged (pert to) . . .
boots (of Hermes) .. **7.** talaria
child .. **6.** cherub
fruit .. **6.** samara
monster .. **5.** harpy
Winged Horse (Gr Myth) . . . **7.** Pegasus
Winged Victory . . . **4.** Nike
wingless . . . **7.** apteral, Apteryx, exalate **8.** dealated (dealate)
wink . . . **3.** nap, nod **4.** hint **5.** blink, flash **6.** glance, signal, twitch **7.** flicker, instant, nictate, twinkle **9.** nictation, nictitate, twinkling **10.** palpebrate, periwinkle
winker . . . **3.** eye **7.** blinker, eyelash **8.** blinkard
winking . . . **13.** blepharospasm
winks, forty . . . **3.** nap **6.** catnap **10.** light sleep
winner . . . **3.** ace **6.** earner, reaper, victor **7.** sleeper **8.** bangster **9.** conqueror **11.** breadwinner
winning . . . **7.** gaining, lovable, victory, winsome **8.** alluring, charming **10.** attractive, successful, victorious **11.** acquisition, captivating
winninish, winnonish . . . **6.** salmon (landlocked) **10.** ouananiche
winnock . . . **6.** window
winnow . . . **3.** fan **4.** sift, stir **6.** assort, select, thresh **8.** disperse, separate **9.** eliminate
winsome . . . **3.** gay **5.** bonny, merry **7.** lovable, winning **8.** alluring, charming, cheerful, pleasant **10.** attractive **11.** captivating **12.** lighthearted

winter . . . **4.** bise, snow **5.** hiems **6.** old age, season **8.** coldness
winter (pert to) . . .
beer .. **6.** Schenk
berry .. **4.** Ilex **5.** holly
bloom .. **6.** azalea **10.** witch hazel
bonnet .. **4.** gull
duck .. **7.** pintail **8.** old squaw
fever .. **9.** pneumonia
god .. **5.** Hiems
lettuce .. **6.** endive
mew .. **4.** gull
pert to .. **6.** brumal, hiemal
quarters .. **10.** hibernacle **12.** hibernaculum
sleep .. **11.** hibernation
teal .. **9.** greenwing
Winter Palace (Leningrad) . . . **6.** museum
wipe . . . **3.** dry, mop, rub **5.** cheat, clean, erase **6.** cancel, remove **7.** abolish, defraud **10.** obliterate **11.** exterminate
wire . . . **4.** coil, cord, line, whip **5.** cable, snare **6.** thread **7.** fencing, lametta (gold), netting, reticle **8.** telegram, wirework **9.** cablegram, telegraph **10.** pickpocket **14.** knitting needle
wirepuller . . . **10.** influencer, machinator, politician, strategist
wiry . . . **4.** lean **5.** hardy, stiff, tough **6.** sinewy, strong **7.** stringy **8.** enduring, muscular
wis . . . **5.** think **7.** imagine, suppose
Wisconsin . . .
capital .. **7.** Madison
city .. **6.** Racine **7.** Kenosha, Oshkosh **8.** Green Bay **9.** Fond du Lac, Milwaukee
famed as .. **17.** America's Dairyland
first white man .. **7.** Nicolet (Jean)
lake .. **8.** Michigan, Superior **9.** Winnebago
river .. **7.** St Croix **11.** Mississippi
State admission .. **9.** Thirtieth
State motto .. **7.** Forward
State nickname .. **6.** Badger
wisdom . . . **5.** logos **8.** judgment, learning, sagacity, sapience **9.** erudition, knowledge **10.** discretion, profundity
wisdom god . . . **4.** Nebo (Nabu) **6.** Ganesa (Ganesha)
wisdom goddess . . . **6.** Athena **7.** Minerva (Gr)
wise . . . **3.** hep **4.** sage, sane, wary **5.** aware **6.** shrewd, subtle, versed **7.** erudite, knowing, learned, politic, sapient **8.** discreet, informed, profound **9.** cognizant, expedient, judicious, provident **10.** omniscient **11.** circumspect, enlightened, philosophic **13.** sophisticated
wise (pert to) . . .
councilor .. **6.** mentor, nestor
man .. **4.** sage **5.** solon, witan **6.** nestor, wizard **7.** Solomon
saying .. **4.** rede **5.** adage
Wise Men (three) . . . **6.** Gaspar **8.** Melchior **9.** Balthasar
Wise Men of Greece . . . **5.** Seven
Wise Men of the East . . . **19.** Three Kings of Cologne
wish . . . **4.** care, hope, will, wuss **5.** yearn **6.** aspire, desire, invoke

7. longing, request 8. optative, petition
10. aspiration 11. imprecation
wishbone ... 7. furcula 8. furculum
10. fourchette 12. merry thought
wisp ... 4. floc 5. brush, flock, shred
6. bundle 7. handful 8. fragment
wistful ... 7. longing, pensive 8. desirous,
yearning 9. nostalgic 10. melancholy
wit ... 3. pun, wag 5. humor, sense
6. acumen, esprit, satire, wisdom
7. punster 8. comedian, humorist,
repartee 9. alertness 11. philosopher,
savoir-faire 12. intelligence
13. understanding
wit (to) ... 3. viz 5. truly 6. indeed,
namely, that is 8. scilicet 9. videlicet
witch ... 3. hag, hex 4. baba 5. Circe,
crone, lamia, shrew, vixen 6. cummer,
Hecate (Hekate), Lilith (Lilis), wizard
7. warlock 8. old woman 9. grimalkin,
sorceress 11. witch doctor 12. ugly
old woman
witchcraft ... 5. charm, magic, wanga
7. cunning, hexerei, sorcery 8. brujeria
9. sortilege, voodooism 10. bewitchery,
black magic 11. enchantment
12. invultuation
witch doctor ... 3. hex 6. shaman
9. voodooist, wangateur
witchery ... 5. charm, spell 7. sorcery
8. wizardry 10. allurement, necromancy
11. enchantment, fascination
with (pref) ... 2. co 3. com, con, cum,
mit, syn 4. avec
with ... 5. among 7. jointly 8. together
9. alongside, including 10. hand in
hand 11. association 12. concurrently
13. co-operatively
withal ... 5. still 9. thereupon 10. for all
that
withdraw ... 6. absent, deduct, recall,
recant, recede, remove, repeal, retire,
secede 7. abandon, detract, disavow,
forsake, refrain, regress, retract, retreat,
subside 8. alienate, evacuate, renounce
9. disengage 10. relinquish
withdrawal ... 6. repeal 7. regress,
retiral, retreat 8. escapism 9. departure,
recession, seclusion 10. detachment,
extraction, retraction, separation
11. abandonment, recantation,
resignation
withdrawn ... 7. ingrown 8. detached,
secluded
withe ... 4. band, rope 5. snare 6. halter,
wattle, willow
wither ... 3. age, die, dry 4. fade, sear,
sere, wilt 5. decay, droop, dry up,
wizen 6. blight, shrink 7. shrivel, wrinkle
8. languish 11. deteriorate
withered ... 4. sere 8. shrunken
9. shriveled
withering ... 7. caustic 9. shrinking
10. marcescent 12. contemptuous
13. deteriorating
withhold ... 4. curb, deny 5. check
6. detain, refuse, retain 7. abstain,
prevent, refrain, repress, reserve 8. hold
back, postpone, restrain
within ... 6. at home, during, inside
7. indoors 8. inside of, inwardly 9. inner

side
without ... 4. sans, sine 5. minus
6. beyond, except, lack of, unless
7. lacking, not with 9. absence of,
outwardly 10. externally, out-of-doors
without (pert to) ... see also *absence of*
action .. 8. deedless
animation .. 5. amort
appointment (of day) .. 7. sine die
beginning, or end .. 7. eternal
cause .. 10. unprovoked
connections .. 7. tieless
delay .. 9. summarily
doubt .. 9. sine dubio
ethics .. 6. amoral
exception .. 11. universally
feet .. 4. apod 6. apodal
foliage .. 8. aphylous
friends .. 4. lorn 7. forlorn 8. forsaken
knowledge .. 8. ignorant
mate .. 3. odd
prefix .. 4. ecto
rule .. 8. anarchic
substance .. 5. inane
support .. 7. legless 9. dependent
teeth .. 8. edentate 9. toothless
this .. 7. sine hoc
warning .. 12. out of the blue
wings .. 7. apteral
withstand ... 4. bear, bide, defy, last
5. abide 6. endure, oppose, resist
8. confront 10. contradict
witless ... 3. mad 5. crazy, dazed
6. stupid 7. foolish, unaware 8. heedless
9. brainless, unknowing 10. indiscreet
13. unintelligent
witness ... 3. eye, see 4. know 5. swear,
teste, vouch 6. attend, attest, beheld,
behold, testor 7. observe, testify
8. beholder, deponent, evidence,
observer, onlooker 9. informant,
spectator, subscribe, testimony
11. attestation
witticism ... 3. mot, pun 4. jest,
joke, quip 5. droll, sally, slent
8. repartee 9. wisecrack 10. pleasantry
11. gauloiserie, witty saying
wittingly ... 8. by design 9. knowingly
13. intentionally
witty ... 4. wise 5. comic, droll, sharp
6. clever, facete, jocose, jocund
7. amusing, comical, jocular, knowing
8. humorous 9. facetious, whimsical
wivern, wyvern (Her) ... 6. dragon
(2-legged)
wizard ... 4. mage, sage 6. expert, genius,
Merlin, pellar, shaman 7. magical,
prodigy 8. conjurer, magician, sorcerer
10. Wizard of Oz 11. necromancer,
thaumaturge, witch doctor
13. thaumaturgist
Wizard of the North ... 14. Sir Walter
Scott
wizen ... 3. age, dry 4. thin 6. gullet,
shrink, weazen, wither 7. shrivel
8. windpipe 11. deteriorate
wlo (obs) ... 3. hem 6. fringe
woad ... 3. dye 4. herb 5. tinge 8. dyestuff
10. pastel blue
wobble, wabble ... 4. walk 5. shake,
waver 7. stagger, tremble 8. hobbling

9. fluctuate, oscillate, vacillate
Woden, Wodan (Myth) . . . 3. god (chief)
  4. Odin 9. Wednesday (named for
  Woden)
woe . . . 4. bale, bane 5. grief 6. misery,
  sorrow 7. anguish, trouble 8. anathema,
  calamity 10. affliction, melancholy,
  misfortune
woebegone . . . 3. sad 6. woeful
  7. unhappy 8. dejected, desolate
  10. dispirited, melancholy
woeful . . . 3. sad 6. paltry 7. direful,
  pitiful 8. grievous, mournful, wretched
  9. afflicted, miserable, sorrowful,
  woebegone 10. deplorable
  12. disconsolate
wold . . . 3. lea 4. wood 5. downs, plain,
  weald 6. forest, meadow 7. low hill
wolf . . . 4. lobo 5. lupus 6. coyote,
  mammal 7. Isegrim 8. werewolf
  9. libertine 11. philanderer
wolf fish . . . 6. blenny
wolfhound . . . 6. borzoi
wolflike . . . 6. lupine, thooid
wolverine . . . 4. Gulo 11. Michigander,
  Michiganite
Wolverine State . . . 8. Michigan
woman . . . 4. dame, girl, lady, rani, wife
  5. adult, begum, gemme, madam,
  squaw 6. female 7. distaff 8. feminine,
  paramour, senorita 9. womankind
  10. sweetheart
woman (pert to) . . .
  adviser . . 6. Egeria (Rom Myth)
  apartment of . . 3. oda (harem)
    8. thalamus
  beautiful . . 4. doll 5. filly, pin-up, siren,
    sylph, Venus 7. charmer, Zenobia
    8. Musidora
  bewitching . . 4. peri 5. siren, vixen
    7. charmer
  celibate . . 7. agapeta
  chaser . . 9. libertine 11. philanderer
  club (of women) . . 7. sorosis 8. sorority
  comb form . . 3. gyn
  dignified, elderly . . 7. dowager
  dowdy . . 5. frump 6. untidy 8. slattern
  gossipy . . 3. cat 9. flibbertigibbet
  graceful . . 5. sylph 7. slender
  gypsy . . 5. romni
  hater . . 10. misogynist
  hatred of . . 8. misogyny
  kept . . 8. mistress 9. concubine
    12. demimondaine
  killer . . 8. femicide
  learned . . 12. bluestocking
  loose . . 4. drab 5. whore 6. harlot
    7. trollop 10. prostitute 12. streetwalker
  lover of . . 11. philogynist
  modest (affectedly) . . 5. prude
  mythical (ugly) . . 6. Gorgon
  noisy . . 9. termagant
  of rank . . 4. dame
  old . . 5. crone, frump 6. granny 7. carline,
    dowager 8. grandame 9. cailleach
  ruler . . 9. matriarch
  scolding . . 5. shrew 6. virago
  socialite . . 3. deb 6. subdeb 9. debutante
    13. fashion leader
  stately . . 4. lady 6. matron
  suffragist . . 8. feminist

vixenish . . 5. shrew 6. virago 8. harridan
weeping . . 5. Niobe
will maker . . 9. testatrix
young, unmarried . . 4. lass 6. damsel
  8. spinster 10. demoiselle
womanhood . . . 4. Emer 10. femininity
woman's property (free) . . .
  10. parapherna
wonder . . . 3. awe 6. marvel, rarity
  7. miracle, prodigy 8. surprise
  9. amazement 10. admiration,
  wonderment 12. astonishment
wonderful . . . 6. superb, unique
  7. amazing, corking, mirific, strange
  8. wondrous 9. admirable, marvelous,
  mirifical 10. remarkable, surprising
  11. astonishing 13. extraordinary
wont . . . 3. use 5. habit, usage 6. custom
woo . . . 3. sue 6. invite 7. beseech,
  entreat, solicit
wood . . . 4. tree 5. xylon 6. lignum,
  lumber, timber 8. firewood
wood (pert to) . . .
  aromatic . . 5. aloes, cedar 8. agalloch
  ash . . 6. potash
  black . . 5. ebony
  block . . 3. nog 4. dook
  boring (of insects) . . 8. xylotomy
  bundles . . 6. fagots
  carving . . 10. xyloglyphy
  clearing . . 5. glade
  color . . 7. biscuit
  comb form . . 4. hylo, xylo 5. ligni, ligno,
    xylon
  core . . 3. ame
  curved strip . . 5. stave
  dealer . . 10. xylopolist
  deity . . 3. Pan 4. faun 5. Diana, Satyr
    7. Silenus 8. Silvanus
  eating . . 11. xylophagous
  goddess . . 5. Diana
  growing on . . 6. fungus 11. xylophilous
  growth . . 7. boscage, coppice, thicket
  hard . . 3. ash, elm 4. rate, teak 5. ebony,
    maple 6. walnut 8. mahogany
  inlay . . 9. marquetry
  nymph . . 4. moth 5. dryad
  overlay . . 6. veneer
  resembling . . 6. xyloid
  stork . . 4. ibis
  strip . . 4. lath, slat 5. sprag, stave
    6. batten
  touch . . 4. punk 5. spunk (sponk)
    9. touchwood
  tough, elastic . . 3. ash
  tract . . 5. grove 6. forest
woodchuck . . . 6. marmot 9. ground
  hog
Woodchuck Day . . . 9. Candlemas
woodcock . . . 5. pewee 6. peewee, shrups
  10. woodpecker
wooden (pert to) . . .
  container . . 3. box 4. case 6. barrel
  horse . . 6. Trojan
  Indian . . 15. cigar-store brave
  joint . . 5. tenon
  made of . . 5. treen
  pert to . . 4. dull 6. clumsy, stolid, stupid
    8. lifeless 14. expressionless
  pin . . 3. fid, nog, peg 5. dowel, spile
  pole . . 4. palo

shoe . . **5.** sabot **6.** patten
stand . . **5.** criss
tub . . **3.** soe
woodpecker . . . **4.** chab **5.** Picus **6.** yaffle, yukkel (yuckle) **7.** flicker, wryneck **8.** hickwall **9.** sapsucker **10.** carpintero, pickerwood **11.** woodknacker
woods (pert to) . . .
inhabiting . . **7.** nemoral
lover of . . **11.** nemophilist
pert to . . **6.** sylvan (silvan) **10.** sylvestral
sacred (grove) . . **10.** Nemorensis
woodwind . . . **4.** oboe **5.** flute **7.** bassoon, piccolo **8.** clarinet **9.** saxophone
woody . . . **6.** sylvan, xyloid **8.** ligneous
woof . . . **3.** abb **4.** weft **6.** fabric **7.** filling, texture
wool . . . **3.** fur **4.** down, hair **5.** cloth, llama, sheep **6.** fleece **8.** barragan (barragon)
wool (pert to) . . .
card . . **3.** tum **4.** comb **5.** tease
clean . . **7.** garnett
cloth . . **5.** serge, tweed, yerga **6.** angora, duffel, kersey, satara, tartan, tricot, vicuña **7.** doeskin, flannel, ratteen **8.** cashmere **10.** broadcloth
comb form . . **4.** lani
dead sheep's . . **8.** mortling
dryer . . **5.** fugal
fat . . **7.** lanolin (lanoline)
fatty substance . . **5.** suint
garment . . **6.** alpaca, linder
implement . . **6.** carder, shears, teaser **7.** distaff, spindle
inferior, dirty . . **7.** cleamer
kind . . **6.** alpaca, angora, merino **8.** picklock
leg . . **4.** gare
reclaimed . . **5.** mungo **6.** shoddy
reference to . . **5.** wooly **6.** lanate, lanose **10.** flocculent
spun . . **4.** yarn
tuft . . **8.** floccule **9.** flocculus
undyed, natural . . **5.** beige
waste . . **3.** fud **4.** noil
yarn . . **3.** abb **7.** eis wool
wooly (woolly) . . . **5.** downy, fuzzy **6.** fleecy, lanate **7.** blurred **8.** confused, floccose, peronate
word . . . **4.** news, oath **5.** adage, maxim, parol **6.** avowal, remark, report **7.** command, dispute, message, promise, tidings, vocable **8.** acrostic, password **9.** discourse, statement **11.** declaration, information **13.** communication
word, words (pert to) . . .
action . . **4.** verb
battle of . . **9.** logomachy
blindness . . **6.** alexia
book . . **6.** Gradus **7.** lexicon, speller **8.** glossary **9.** thesaurus **10.** dictionary
contraction . . **9.** haplology
deletion at end . . **7.** apocope
derivation . . **6.** etymon **9.** etymology
distinguishing (Bib) . . **10.** shibboleth
divine . . **5.** Logos
excessive interest . . **10.** verbomania
figurative use . . **5.** trope
figure of speech . . **7.** metonym, paronym

first on walls (Bib) . . **21.** mene, mene, tekel, upharsin
for word . . **8.** verbatim **9.** literally
hard to pronounce . . **10.** jawbreaker
inventor of . . **6.** coiner **9.** neologist
last syllable . . **6.** ultima
last syllable but one . . **6.** penult
last syllable omitted . . **7.** apocope
law . . **7.** by parol **11.** word of mouth
letter . . **8.** logogram **9.** logogriph **11.** grammalogue
longest in dictionary . .
   28. antidisestablishmentarianism
loss from middle . . **7.** syncope
magical . . **6.** presto, sesame
meaning . . **9.** semantics
misuse . . **11.** catachresis, heterophemy, malapropism
mysterious (Bib) . . **5.** selah
new . . **9.** neologism
new usage . . **7.** neology
of different name for same thing . . **9.** heteronym
of honor . . **6.** parole **7.** promise
of opposite meaning . . **7.** antonym
of same derivation . . **7.** paronym
of same meaning . . **7.** synonym
of same sound . . **7.** homonym
of imitation . . **6.** echoic **9.** onomatope **12.** onomatopoeia
play on . . **3.** pun
popular . . **6.** cliché **8.** buzzword
pretentious use . . **10.** lexiphanic
puzzle . . **5.** rebus **7.** anagram **8.** acrostic **9.** crossword
repetition . . **5.** ploce
root . . **6.** etymon
same back to front . . **10.** palindrome
science . . **10.** lexicology
scrambled . . **7.** anagram
song hits . . **6.** lyrics
substitution . . **5.** trope **7.** metonym
theory . . **6.** bowwow **8.** pooh-pooh
The Word (Bib) . . **5.** Logos
with loss of vowel at beginning . . **7.** aphasia
without vowels . . **6.** rhythm, syzygy
with vowels (all) . . **7.** eulogia, miaoued, sequoia **12.** ambidextrous
with vowels in sequence . . **8.** caesious
wordiness . . . **8.** pleonasm, verbiage **9.** prolixity, verbacity **10.** redundance
wording . . . **8.** phrasing **10.** expression
wordless . . . **5.** tacit **6.** silent
wordy . . . **6.** prolix **7.** verbose **9.** garrulous **10.** long-winded **12.** long-drawn-out
work . . . **3.** gig, job, mix **4.** book, deed, duty, make, opus, plan, task, to-do, toil **5.** chore, ergon, labor, solve, trade **6.** action, Arbeit, create, effect, effort **7.** ferment, operate, perform, product, travail **8.** business, drudgery, endeavor, function, industry, struggle **10.** accomplish, employment, engagement, management, occupation, profession **11.** achievement, performance, undertaking
work (pert to) . . .
agreement . . **4.** code, pact **8.** contract
bag . . **7.** tote bag **8.** reticule
carelessly . . **5.** scamp

clothes . . **8.** overalls **9.** blue jeans, coveralls, dungarees
comb form . . **3.** erg **4.** ergo
divine . . **7.** miracle, theurgy **9.** occult art
hard . . **3.** peg, tew **4.** char, moil, plug, toil **5.** labor, sweat **6.** drudge **7.** travail **9.** lucubrate **18.** burn the midnight oil
hate of . . **10.** ergophobia
helper . . **3.** aid (aide) **9.** assistant, paralegal, paramedic
horse . . **4.** mule **5.** burro
hours . . **9.** flexitime (flextime)
household . . **4.** char **5.** chare
incomplete art . . **7.** ébauche
inlay . . **6.** mosaic, niello
lover of . . **9.** ergophile
measure of . . **9.** ergometer
of excellence . . **4.** opus **7.** classic **9.** calculate
out . . **5.** solve **7.** arrange, develop **9.** calculate
over . . **6.** recast, rehash, revamp **9.** brainwash, influence
shift . . **5.** swing **9.** graveyard, moonlight
slowly . . **6.** potter, putter **7.** ca'canny
study of . . **8.** ergology
together . . **4.** team **9.** cooperate **11.** collaborate
unit of . . **3.** erg **5.** ergon, joule
up . . **4.** plan **5.** rouse **6.** excite, incite **7.** advance, agitate, develop **10.** manipulate
workable . . . **6.** pliant **7.** operant **8.** feasible, operable, solvable **9.** practical **11.** practicable
worker . . . **3.** CPA **5.** diver, mason, miner **6.** barman, cooper, slater, smithy, tanner, warper, wright **7.** analyst, cobbler, glazier, plumber, riveter, sandhog, servant, spinner **8.** honeybee, mechanic, strapper **9.** carpenter, clinician, machinist, stevedore **10.** accountant **11.** breadwinner
worker (pert to) . . .
fellow . . **5.** buddy **8.** confrere
group . . **4.** crew, gang, team **5.** corps, staff **9.** personnel
hard . . **6.** beaver, drudge, fagger **10.** workaholic
head . . **4.** boss **7.** foreman **8.** employer, overseer **14.** superintendent
indifferent . . **4.** scab **11.** scissorbill
migrant . . **4.** hobo **6.** boomer **7.** floater, wetback
workhouse . . . **6.** prison **9.** almshouse, poorhouse
workman . . . **4.** peon **6.** coolie, earner **7.** artisan, laborer **8.** operator, opificer **9.** artificer, craftsman, performer
workshop . . . **3.** lab **4.** mill **5.** plant **6.** studio **7.** atelier, factory **10.** laboratory **11.** ergasterion
world . . . **5.** globe, realm **6.** cosmos, domain **7.** kingdom, society **8.** creation, humanity, universe **9.** multitude, the public
world (pert to) . . .
external . . **6.** nonego
great . . **9.** macrocosm
lower . . **5.** Hades, Orcus
miniature . . **9.** microcosm

of fairies . . **6.** faerie (faery)
precreation . . **10.** premundane **11.** antemundane
reference to . . **7.** mundane **11.** terrestrial
worldly . . . **7.** earthly, mundane, secular, terrene **11.** terrestrial **13.** materialistic, sophisticated
world's oldest city, still inhabited . . . **8.** Damascus
world's speech . . . **7.** Volapuk **9.** universal
worm . . . **3.** ess **4.** coil, grub, wind **5.** borer, tinea **6.** blight, insect, maggot, vermin, wretch **8.** helminth **9.** trematode, vermicule **10.** Nemertinea (Nemertina)
worm (pert to) . . .
Africa . . **3.** loa **6.** Guinea
aquatic, marine . . **7.** eunicid, lugworm **8.** flatworm **9.** planarian **13.** platyhelminth
arrow . . **7.** sagitta
bait . . **9.** angleworm, earthworm
bloodsucking . . **5.** leech
caddie . . **5.** cadew
cotton . . **8.** bollworm **10.** boll weevil
edible . . **6.** palolo
eye-infecting . . **3.** loa
genus . . **6.** Virmes **7.** Ascaris, Filaria **8.** Annelida **10.** Nemertinea (Nemertina)
grublike . . **5.** larva
killer . . **9.** vermicide
larva . . **4.** army, slug **5.** cadew **6.** caddis, looper **8.** wireworm **11.** caterpillar
luminous . . **8.** glowworm
marine . . **7.** eunicid
measuring . . **6.** looper **8.** inchworm
parasitic . . **7.** Ascaris, Filaria **8.** trichina, woodworm **9.** trematode **10.** Guinea worm **12.** enthelmintha
ref to . . **8.** anneloid **9.** nemertean, nemertine, nemertoid, trematoid
ring . . **5.** tinea **7.** annelid
round . . **7.** ascarid, Ascaris
segmented . . **8.** Annelida
ship . . **5.** borer **6.** teredo
silk . . **4.** eria
soft . . **4.** grub
study of . . **10.** vermeology **13.** helminthology
tape . . **6.** taenia
track . . **7.** nereite **11.** helminthite
wire . . **4.** lava **9.** millepede
worm (type) . . . **3.** cut, dew, lug, pin **4.** army, boll, eria, flat, glow, inch, ring, ship, silk, slug, tape, wire, wood **5.** angle, earth, larva, leech, round, tinea **6.** marine **9.** measuring, parasitic
wormlike . . . **7.** vermian **11.** helminthoid
wormy . . . **6.** earthy, humble, rotten **8.** crawling **9.** groveling
worn . . . **3.** old **4.** sere, used **5.** stale, trite **7.** abraded, haggard **8.** attrited, tattered, weakened **9.** exhausted, hackneyed **10.** secondhand **11.** commonplace
worn-out . . . **4.** used **5.** jaded, passé, seedy, spent, trite **6.** shabby, used up **7.** haggard **8.** consumed, fatigued, impaired, tired out **9.** enfeebled, exhausted **10.** threadbare
worried . . . **5.** cared, fazed **6.** stewed **7.** annoyed, anxious, fearful, fretted

8. troubled 9. perturbed

worry . . . 3. nag, rux, vex 4. care, cark, faze, fret, stew 5. annoy, brood, harry 6. bother, harass, pester, plague, pother 7. anxiety, bedevil, concern, perturb, torment, trouble 8. distress 9. annoyance 10. harassment, uneasiness

worship . . . 5. adore, honor, serve 6. bhakti, homage, revere 7. idolize, liturgy, respect 8. blessing, devotion, idolatry, venerate 9. adoration, deference, reverence 10. veneration

worship (pert to) . . .
form of . . 6. preces, ritual 7. liturgy
house of . . 6. chapel, church, mosque, shrine 9. cathedral, synagogue 10. tabernacle
object of . . 4. icon, idol 5. totem 6. fetish
place of . . 5. altar
system of . . 4. cult 6. cultus, fetish, ritual 8. doctrine

worshiper . . . 6. adorer, bhakti, votary 8. disciple, idolater 10. ignicolist 12. iconomachist

worshipful . . . 6. devout 7. notable 8. esteemed 9. honorable, venerable 13. distinguished

worship of . . .
a god . . 9. theolatry
angels . . 5. dulia
genii . . 10. geniolatry
god . . 6. latria (RCCh)
idols . . 8. idolatry
images . . 10. iconolatry
nature . . 11. physiolatry
one god . . 9. monolatry
snakes . . 10. ophiolatry
soul . . 7. animism
sun . . 10. heliolatry
the mob . . 9. mobolatry

worst . . . 3. bad 4. beat, evil 6. defeat, wicked 7. harmful 8. inferior 10. calamitous, pernicious, unpleasant 12. disagreeable

worsted . . . 4. yarn 6. crewel 7. genappe

worth . . . 5. merit, price, value 6. desert, repute, riches, stiver, wealth 8. eminence, meriting, property 9. deserving 10. excellence, importance, usefulness

worthless . . . 3. bad, ort 4. base, evil, mean, raca (Bib), vile 6. futile, nought (naught), paltry 7. fustian, useless 8. nugatory, rubbishy, unworthy 9. valueless 11. undeserving 14. good-for-nothing

worthwhile . . . 6. useful 7. gainful 9. expedient, well-spent 10. invaluable, profitable

worthy . . . 3. fit 7. merited 8. eligible, valuable 9. celebrity, competent, deserving, estimable, excellent, honorable, qualified, reputable 11. meritorious

worthy of . . . 8. credible, meriting 9. deserving 10. entitled to

wound . . . 3. cut 4. gore, harm, hurt, pain, rist, scar, sore, stab 5. sting 6. breach, damage, grieve, injury, lesion, offend, trauma 8. distress 9. detriment

wound (pert to) . . .
discharge . . 5. ichor 6. sanies
dressing . . 7. bandage, pledget
mark . . 4. scab, scar, welt 7. blister

woven . . . 4. spun 10. fabricated

wow . . . 4. howl, rave, wail 5. whine

wrack . . . 4. kelp, rack, ruin 5. tease, trash, weeds, wreck 6. refuse 7. seaweed 8. eelgrass, wreckage 9. shipwreck 11. destruction

wraith . . . 4. food 5. ghost, spook 8. illusion 10. apparition 12. Doppelgänger, doubleganger

wrangle . . . 4. herd, spar 5. argue, brawl 6. bicker, debate 7. contend, dispute, quarrel 8. haggling 9. altercate, bickering 11. altercation, controversy 12. disagreement

wrangler . . . 6. cowboy 7. debater, student (Cambridge, Eng) 8. herdsman, opponent 9. combatant, disputant 10. antagonist

wrangling . . . 11. belligerent, contentious

wrap . . . 3. rug 4. cape, cere, furl, roll, wind 5. cloak, gange 6. afghan, encowl, enfold, swathe 7. blanket, conceal, package 8. covering, enshroud, enswathe, envelope 9. encompass

wrapped up . . . 7. bound up, selfish 8. absorbed, included, involved 9. dependent, devoted to, engrossed 11. inseparable

wrapper . . . 4. gown 5. cerer 6. fardel, kimono, tillot 7. garment, pelisse 8. envelope, peignoir

wrapping . . . 6. charta 7. wrapper 8. cerement, covering 9. parchment

wrasse . . . 4. fish 6. ballan, cunner, Labrus 7. seawife 11. peacock fish

wrath . . . 3. ire 4. fury, grim, rage 5. anger 6. choler 7. passion 8. violence 10. turbulence 11. indignation 12. exasperation

wrathful . . . 3. mad 5. angry, irate 6. ireful, raging 7. angered 8. incensed 9. indignant, malignant 10. passionate

wreak . . . 4. do to 6. avenge 7. gratify, indulge, inflict 13. bring down upon

wreath . . . 3. lei 4. band, orle 5. crown, torse (Her), whorl 6. anadem, circle, corona, laurel, trophy 7. coronet, festoon, garland, Iresine 8. encircle

wreathe . . . 4. coil, wind 5. crown, twine, twist 7. entwine 8. decorate, encircle 9. interlace 10. twist about

wreck . . . 4. raze, ruin, undo 5. crash, smash 6. jalopy 7. destroy, disable 8. accident, demolish, derelict 9. shipwreck 10. broken form 11. disassemble, The Hesperus

wreckage . . . 5. ruins 6. jetsam 7. flotsam 8. driftage

wrench . . . 4. jerk, pipe, pull, tear 5. twist, wrest 6. sprain, twinge 7. distort 8. crescent, distress

wrench, type of . . . 3. box, pin 5. wramp 6. monkey 7. spanner 8. carriage, Stillson 9. alligator

wrest . . . 4. rend, turn 5. exact, force, seize, twist, wring 6. elicit, extort, wrench 7. distort, extract, pervert,

wrestle **8.** misapply
wrestle ... **3.** tug **6.** squirm, tussle
7. contend, grapple, scuffle, wriggle
8. struggle **9.** throw down **10.** twist
about **11.** come to grips
wrestling school ... **9.** palaestra
(palestra)
wretch ... **3.** dog **5.** miser, ronin
6. outlaw, pariah **7.** caitiff, cullion,
outcast **8.** derelict, sufferer **9.** miscreant
10. base person **11.** offscouring,
rapscallion **14.** good-for-nothing
16. pitiable creature
wretched ... **3.** sad **4.** base, mean
6. dismal, paltry, woeful **7.** baleful,
forlorn, squalid, unhappy, very bad
8. grievous **9.** execrable, miserable
10. despicable, distressed
12. contemptible, disreputable
wretchedness ... **6.** misery **8.** distress,
meanness, poorness **10.** paltriness
11. unhappiness **13.** penuriousness
wriggle ... **5.** twist **6.** squirm, writhe
7. meander
wriggle out of ... **4.** turn, wind **5.** dodge,
snake, twist **6.** squirm, writhe **8.** slip
away **10.** crawl out of **11.** squirm out
of **13.** find a loophole
wring ... **5.** twist, wrest **6.** extort, wrench
7. extract, torture, wrestle **8.** compress,
convolve **9.** cause pain **10.** contortion,
extraction
wrinkle ... **3.** fad **4.** fold, idea, ruga,
seam **5.** crimp, knack, ridge, rivel
6. crease, furrow, pucker, rimple, ripple,
rumple **7.** crinkle, novelty **8.** contract
9. corrugate **11.** corrugation **12.** clever
notion
wrinkled ... **4.** aged **5.** savoy **6.** rugate,
rugose, rugous **7.** creased **8.** crinkled,
crumpled, furrowed, puckered, rugulose
9. shriveled **10.** contracted, corrugated
wrinkles ... **5.** rugae
wrist ... **5.** joint **6.** carpal, carpus **8.** os
magnum **9.** capitatum
writ ... **5.** breve, tales **6.** capias, elegit,
venire **7.** process **8.** detainer, document,
mittimus, replevin, subpoena
10. certiorari, instrument **11.** fieri facias
writ (pert to) ...
common law .. **11.** fieri facias
court .. **7.** summons **8.** subpoena
execution .. **6.** elegit
jury .. **5.** tales **6.** venire
law .. **4.** capo, pone **5.** breve, error
6. capias, elegit **7.** mandate, process,
warrant **8.** citation **10.** certiorari
write ... **3.** pen **5.** draft, trace **6.** decree,
depict, draw up, enroll, indite, record,
scrive **7.** compose, scriven **8.** inscribe,
scribble **11.** communicate
write (pert to) ...
carelessly .. **6.** scrawl **8.** scrabble,
scribble
in large hand .. **7.** engross
off .. **4.** drop **6.** cancel, deduct, repeal
out .. **6.** record **8.** spill out **12.** put in
writing
poetry .. **7.** versify
up .. **6.** record, report **7.** article
9. publicize **11.** press report

writer ... **4.** hack, poet **6.** author, penman,
penner, scribe **7.** elegist, glosser,
hymnist **8.** annalist, composer, lyricist,
novelist, parodist, scriptor **9.** annotator,
columnist, scrivener **10.** chronicler,
journalist **13.** correspondent
writer's afterthoughts ... **7.** addenda
writhe ... **4.** bend, coil, curl, wind **5.** twist,
wring **6.** squirm **7.** contort, distort,
wriggle
writing ... **4.** book, poem **6.** script
7. article, epistle **8.** covenant, document,
makimono **10.** expression, penmanship,
profession **11.** chirography,
composition, handwriting, inscription,
publication
writing (pert to) ...
alternate .. **13.** boustrophedon
ancient characters .. **9.** cuneiform
ancient manuscript .. **6.** uncial
cipher .. **12.** cryptography
instrument .. **3.** pen **5.** quill **6.** stylus
italic .. **7.** cursive
mania for .. **11.** graphomania
material .. **3.** pad **5.** paper, slate **6.** tablet
9. parchment **10.** stationery
omission of a letter .. **8.** lipogram
10. lipography
pert to .. **7.** scribal
record .. **3.** log **5.** album, diary
script .. **5.** ronde
scroll .. **8.** makimono
scroll hanging .. **8.** kakemono
secret .. **4.** code **10.** cryptogram
12. cryptography
unrhymed .. **5.** prose
writings, sacred ... **5.** Bible, Koran
6. Psalms, Talmud **9.** Testament (Old,
New) **10.** Scriptures
written (pert to) ...
agreement .. **6.** cartel
characters .. **6.** script
it is .. **8.** it must be **10.** in the books,
in the cards **12.** the die is cast
law .. **10.** legislated
law, unwritten .. **6.** common
memo .. **5.** scrip
wrong ... **3.** bad, off, out, sin **4.** awry,
evil, harm, side, tort, vice **5.** amiss,
cheat, crime, false, malum, unfit
6. faulty, injure, injury, seduce, sinful,
unjust, wicked **7.** defraud, immoral,
misdeed, offense **8.** improper, iniquity,
mistaken **9.** erroneous, incorrect,
injustice, violation **10.** inaccurate,
iniquitous **11.** impropriety, inexpedient,
malfeasance, misfeasance
12. illegitimate
wrong (pert to) ...
go (wrong) .. **3.** err **4.** fail **5.** lapse
8. go astray, go to ruin **9.** backslide
10. misbelieve **11.** go to the dogs
in the .. **6.** guilty **7.** at fault, in error
8. mistaken **9.** violation
law .. **4.** tort **5.** crime, malum
name .. **8.** misnomer
nor right (neither) .. **7.** neutral
11. adiaphorous
prefix .. **3.** mis
side of .. **5.** shady
way .. **5.** amiss **6.** astray **10.** out of

place
wrongdoer . . . **6.** sinner **8.** criminal, evildoer, violator **10.** malefactor, trespasser **12.** transgressor
wroth . . . **3.** mad **5.** angry, irate **7.** violent **8.** incensed, wrathful **9.** turbulent, wrought up **11.** exasperated
wrought . . . **4.** made **6.** formed, shaped, worked **9.** decorated, fashioned, processed **10.** elaborated, ornamented **11.** embroidered **12.** manufactured
wrought up . . . **4.** agog **5.** angry, eager **7.** excited **9.** disturbed, stirred up
wry . . . **4.** awry **6.** biased, swerve, turned **7.** crooked, twisted **9.** contorted
wryneck . . . **4.** Jynx, weet **5.** loxia **9.** snakebird **11.** torticollis
Württemberg, Germany . . .
capital . . **9.** Stuttgart
city . . **3.** Ulm **9.** Esslingen, Heilbronn, Hohenheim
lake . . **9.** Constance
river . . **6.** Danube, Neckar

Wyandot . . . **6.** Indian (Iroquois)
Wyandotte . . . **4.** cave, city, fowl
Wycliff (Wyclif), **John** (pert to) . . .
birthplace . . **9.** Yorkshire (Eng)
disciple . . **4.** Huss
remains cast into . . **10.** Swift River
translator of . . **5.** Bible
Wyoming . . .
capital . . **8.** Cheyenne
city . . **4.** Cody **6.** Casper **7.** Big Horn, Laramie **8.** Cheyenne, Sheridan
historic site . . **11.** Fort Laramie **17.** Buffalo Bill Center
mountain . . **6.** Tetons **7.** Rockies **11.** Gannett Peak
park . . **10.** Grand Teton **11.** Yellowstone
river . . **4.** Wind **6.** Platte **7.** Big Horn
river source . . **8.** Colorado, Columbia, Missouri
State admission . . **11.** Forty-fourth
State bird . . **10.** meadowlark
State flower . . **16.** Indian paintbrush
State motto . . **11.** Equal Rights
Woman Suffrage . . **10.** First State

X

X . . . **3.** ten **5.** error **6.** letter (24th), symbol **7.** unknown
xanthic . . . **6.** cyanic, yellow
Xanthippe, wife of . . . **8.** Socrates
xanthoma . . . **9.** xanthosis **11.** skin disease **13.** yellow patches
xanthos . . . **6.** yellow
Xanthus (pert to) . . .
ancient site . . **7.** marbles (Xanthian)
placed now . . **13.** British Museum
xebec . . . **6.** vessel **7.** corsair
xen, xeno (comb form) . . . **7.** foreign **8.** stranger
xenium . . . **4.** gift **7.** present (official)
Xenocrates (Gr) . . . **11.** philosopher
xenogamy . . . **18.** cross-fertilization
xenophobic . . . **9.** strangers (afraid of) **12.** chauvinistic
Xenophon's historic tale . . . **8.** Anabasis
xenophthalmia . . . **11.** foreign body (eye) **14.** conjunctivitis
Xenopus . . . **5.** toads
Xenorhynchus . . . **6.** storks
Xenurus . . . **7.** tatouay **10.** armadillos
Xeres . . . **5.** jerez **6.** sherry
xerophagy . . . **4.** Fast (Lenten)
xerotes . . . **7.** dryness (body)
Xerox (tm) . . . **4.** copy **9.** duplicate, replicate, reproduce
Xerus . . . **9.** squirrels

Xerxes (pert to) . . .
crossing of . . **10.** Hellespont
destroyer of . . **6.** Athens (BC)
king of . . **6.** Persia
xibalba . . . **10.** underworld
Xinca . . . **6.** Indian, Jincan
Xipe, Xipe-totec . . . **11.** god of sowing
Xiphias . . . **5.** comet (sword-shaped) **6.** Dorado (constellation) **9.** swordfish
xiphoid . . . **4.** bone **8.** ensiform **9.** swordlike **12.** xiphisternum
Xiphopagus . . . **7.** monster (twinlike)
Xiphosura . . . **8.** king crab
Xiuhtocutli . . . **7.** fire god (Aztec)
Xmas . . . **9.** Christmas
X ray (pert to) . . .
measure . . **3.** rad **11.** quantimeter
named . . **12.** Roentgen rays
type . . **7.** CAT scan **8.** tomogram **9.** myelogram **11.** arteriogram
xyloglyphy . . . **11.** wood carving (art)
xylography . . . **13.** wood engraving
xyloid . . . **5.** woody **8.** ligneous, woodlike
xylomancy, divination by . . . **4.** wood **10.** wood pieces
xylophone . . . **5.** saron **7.** gambang, marimba **8.** gamelang (gamelan), gigelira, sticcado
xyrid . . . **4.** iris **5.** Xyris
xystus, xyst (Gr) . . . **16.** portico colonnade

X

Y

-y pl ... **3.** -ies
Y ... **4.** tube **5.** curve, track **6.** letter
(25th), prefix, suffix
yabber ... **4.** talk **6.** jabber
yabby, yabbie ... **8.** crayfish
yaboa ... **10.** night heron
yabu, yaboo ... **4.** pony
yacht ... **4.** boat, race, sail, ship
yaffle ... **6.** armful **7.** handful
10. woodpecker
yahoo ... **4.** lout, rube **5.** brute
Yahoo (pert to) ...
represented by .. **10.** Houyhnhnms
(horses of reason)
tale .. **16.** Gulliver's Travels
yakalo, yakattalo ... **8.** creature
10. crossbreed (yak, cattle)
yakka ... **4.** work **5.** labor
yaksha ... **4.** ogre **5.** demon, dryad, fairy,
gnome, jinni **6.** Kubera (Chief), spirit
7. tree-god **13.** guardian angel
Yale (pert to) ...
college .. **8.** New Haven
color .. **4.** blue **7.** Rameses
founded at .. **8.** Saybrook
founder .. **9.** Elihu Yale
graduate .. **9.** Yalensian
Yalta Conference ... **6.** Crimea (1945)
yam (pert to) ...
Fiji .. **6.** uviyam **8.** white yam
Hawaiian .. **3.** hoi
reference to .. **5.** tuber **6.** igname
Scot .. **6.** potato
tropical .. **8.** cush-cush
US .. **11.** sweet potato
yamstchik ... **7.** postboy **8.** coachman
9. postilion
yang ... **4.** good, male **6.** bright (opp of
yin)
yang-kin ... **8.** dulcimer
yank ... **4.** jerk, pull **6.** Yankee
Yankee ... **12.** New Englander
Yannigans ... **9.** scrub team (baseball)
Yao ... **6.** Indian **9.** aborigine
yap ... **3.** cur, dog, gab **4.** bark, talk, yell,
yelp **6.** jabber **7.** bumpkin, hoodlum
8. easy mark **9.** greenhorn
yapok, yapock ... **6.** monkey **7.** opossum
yapp ... **11.** bookbinding
yapster ... **3.** dog
Yaqui ... **6.** Indian
yard ... **3.** rae (sail) **4.** lawn, spar,
wand **5.** garth, stick, verge **6.** campus
7. confine, enclose, measure
9. courtyard, curtilage, enclosure,
yardstick **10.** playground
yarn ... **3.** abb, cop **4.** hank, joke, tale
5. fiber, skein, story **6.** caddis, crewel,
spinel, thread **7.** genappe **9.** falsehood
yarn (pert to) ...
clew .. **4.** ball
holder .. **3.** cop
measure .. **4.** hank, hasp **5.** skein
7. spangle
size .. **6.** denier

winder .. **10.** yarnwindle
yashiro ... **3.** sha **6.** temple (Shinto)
yashmak ... **4.** veil (double)
yati ... **7.** ascetic, devotee
yaw ... **4.** sail, tack **5.** steer, tumor
7. deviate **9.** deviation
yawl ... **4.** boat, howl, wail, yell, yowl
5. ketch **9.** jolly boat
yawn ... **3.** gap **4.** gape **5.** chasm, mouth
7. opening, stretch **8.** open wide,
oscitate **12.** seek greedily
yaws ... **9.** frambesia
yawweed ... **5.** shrub **7.** rhubarb **12.** wild
mulberry
Yazoo (pert to) ...
Fraud .. **9.** land grant (1795)
Indian .. **11.** Mississippi
river .. **11.** Mississippi
yclept, ycleped ... **5.** named **6.** called,
styled
year (pert to) ...
after year .. **10.** constantly, repeatedly
11. over and over
book .. **7.** almanac
division of .. **6.** season **8.** semester
9. trimester
Latin .. **5.** annus
of mourning .. **11.** annus luctus
of our Lord .. **10.** Anno Domini **11.** annus
Domini, year of grace
of thirteen months (384 days) ..
10. embolismic
of travel .. **10.** sabbatical, Wanderjahr
14. leave of absence
old (Zool) .. **10.** annotinous
pert to .. **5.** epact
quarter .. **5.** raith
record .. **5.** annal **8.** calendar
yearly (pert to) ...
church income .. **7.** annates
payment .. **4.** cens
recurring .. **6.** annual **7.** etesian
8. annually
yearn for ... **3.** yen **4.** ache, hope, itch,
long, pine, sigh, wish **6.** desire, hanker
yearning ... **3.** yen **4.** wish **5.** eager
7. anxious, longing **9.** hankering,
nostalgia **10.** tenderness **11.** languishing
12. homesickness
years (pert to) ...
adolescent .. **4.** teen
ago .. **4.** ages **9.** long since **10.** days
of yore, yesteryear
eight .. **9.** octennial
fifteen .. **9.** indiction
five .. **6.** pentad **7.** lustrum
hundred .. **9.** centenary **10.** centennial
ten .. **6.** decade **9.** decennary
thousand .. **7.** chiliad **10.** millennium
two .. **8.** biennial, biennium
yeast ... **4.** barm, foam, koji **5.** froth
6. leaven **7.** anamite, ferment
9. agitation
yeasty ... **5.** foamy, light, spumy **6.** frothy
8. restless **9.** frivolous, leavening

yegg . . . **5.** thief, tramp **6.** robber
7. burglar, yeggman **8.** criminal
10. safeblower **11.** safebreaker,
safecracker
yell . . . **3.** cry **4.** howl, roar, wail, yowl
5. cheer, shout **6.** outcry, scream, shriek
yelling . . . **7.** bawling **8.** shouting, strident
9. clamorous **11.** full of yells
yellow . . . **3.** dun, sil **4.** buff, cuir, deer,
ecru, flax, gull, mean, nude, yolk
5. amber, beige, color, cream, grège,
jaune, lemon, maize, ocher (ochre),
straw, taupe, topaz, twine **6.** bisque,
butter, canary, Cassel, chrome, citron,
creamy, flaxen, golden, mimosa,
sallow, Seasan **7.** anamite, annatto,
aureate, egg yolk, envious, etiolin,
jealous, jonquil, saffron, sulphur,
xanthic, xanthin **8.** cowardly, ocherous,
primrose, recreant **9.** champagne,
dandelion, flavicant, goldenrod,
jaundiced, lutescent, sunflower
10. flavescent, melancholy
11. treacherous
yellow (pert to) . . .
brown . . **3.** dun **5.** straw **6.** manila
coloring . . **7.** xanthic **8.** xanthine
comb form . . **5.** luteo
dyestuff . . **5.** morin **7.** annatto **8.** luteolin
golden . . **2.** or (Her) **4.** gild, gilt
green . . **5.** olive **8.** tarragon
10. chartreuse, serpentine
herb . . **3.** iva
jacket . . **4.** wasp
medical . . **7.** icterus **8.** jaundice
11. xanthoderma
mustard . . **8.** charlock
ocher, ochre . . **3.** sil
pert to . . **7.** xanthic
pigment . . **7.** etiolin **8.** orpiment
race . . **9.** Mongolian
red . . **4.** roan **5.** aloma, sandy **6.** bisque,
dorado, orange **7.** annatto, nacarat
sensational . . **5.** press **7.** journal
yellow fever mosquito . . . **12.** Aëdes
aegypti
yellowhammer . . . **4.** yite **5.** ammer, finch,
skite **6.** gladdy **7.** flicker **10.** woodpecker
13. yellow bunting
Yellowhammer State . . . **7.** Alabama
yellow jacket . . . **4.** wasp **8.** eucalypt
Yellowstone Park geyser . . . **11.** Old
Faithful
yelp . . . **3.** cry, yip **4.** bark, yell **5.** shout
6. outcry, shriek, squeal **7.** ululate
8. complain **9.** criticize
yelper . . . **8.** redshank **10.** yellowlegs
11. hunting call
yeme . . . **4.** heed **5.** guard **6.** govern,
regard
Yemen (pert to) . . .
archeology site . . **4.** Sana **5.** Marib
Bib kingdom . . **5.** Sheba (Saba)
capital . . **4.** Sana
citadel . . **5.** Damar
division of . . **6.** Arabia
plateau . . **7.** El Jebel
port . . **5.** Mocha **7.** Hodeida, Loheiya
ruler . . **4.** Imam
sea . . **3.** Red
yemochik . . . see *yamstchik*

yen . . . **4.** coin, urge **5.** yearn **6.** desire,
hanker **7.** longing
yeoman . . . **4.** exon **5.** clerk **6.** butler,
seaman **8.** retainer **9.** assistant,
attendant **10.** freeholder **11.** subordinate
12. petty officer
yep . . . **3.** yes **4.** bold **5.** alert, smart
6. active **8.** vigorous
yerba . . . **4.** herb, maté **5.** plant
11. Paraguay tea
yes . . .
English . . **3.** aye, yea, yep **5.** uh-huh
6. assent **11.** affirmation
French . . **3.** oui
German . . **2.** ja
Italian, Spanish . . **2.** si
Russian . . **2.** da
yes man . . . **5.** toady
yesterday . . . **6.** yester **7.** the past
10. days gone by, heretofore, yesteryear
11. bygone times
yet . . . **3.** but **5.** still **6.** algate **7.** besides,
however **10.** eventually **11.** nonetheless
15. notwithstanding
yeti . . . **17.** Abominable Snowman
yew . . . **5.** green, Taxus **7.** conifer, hemlock
9. evergreen
Yiddish . . . **6.** Jewish **12.** Judaeo-German
(Judeo-German)
yield . . . **3.** bow, net **4.** bear, bend,
cede, crop, give, lose, obey, vail
5. admit, allow, defer, grant, stoop,
waive **6.** accede, afford, comply, give
up, relent, render, reward, soften,
submit **7.** concede, consent, produce,
provide, requite, revenue, succumb
9. acquiesce, surrender
10. capitulate, relinquish
11. acknowledge
yielding . . . **4.** meek, soft **6.** pliant, supple
7. bearing **8.** flexible **9.** compliant,
deference, producing, tractable
10. compliance, manageable,
submissive
Yigdal . . . **4.** poem (Jew Relig)
yill-caup . . . **6.** ale cup
yin . . . **4.** dark, evil (opp of yang)
Ymir, Ymer (pert to) . . .
blood of . . **3.** sea
bones of . . **9.** mountains
brains of . . **6.** clouds
flesh of . . **5.** earth
killed by . . **2.** Ve **4.** Odin, Vili
Norse Myth . . **3.** God **13.** rime-cold
giant (body-shaped world)
yodel, yodle . . . **4.** call, sing (falsetto)
5. carol, shout **6.** warble
yoga (pert to) . . .
follower of . . **4.** yogi (yogin) **5.** fakir
7. ascetic **9.** occultist
objective . . **16.** mental discipline
stages . . **5.** jnana, karma **6.** bhakti
trance . . **6.** dhyana **7.** dharana, samadhi
yoke . . . **3.** two **4.** join, link, pair, span,
team **5.** frame, marry **6.** cangue,
couple, inspan **7.** bondage, enclave,
harness, oppress, pillory, shackle,
slavery **9.** associate, servitude
yoked . . . **6.** united **7.** coupled **9.** conjugate
yokel . . . **3.** oaf **4.** boor, clod, hick,
lout, rube **6.** rustic **7.** bumpkin,

hayseed, plowboy **8.** abderite (anc),
gullible **9.** simpleton **10.** countryman,
slow-witted
yokemate . . . **4.** mate **6.** fellow, spouse
7. partner **9.** companion
yolked (egg) . . . **6.** yellow **8.** lecithal,
vitellus
Yom Kippur (Jew) . . . **7.** fast day **14.** Day
of Atonement
Yom Teruah (Jew) . . . **15.** Feast of
Trumpets
Yom Tob, or Tov (Jew) . . . **8.** festival
yon, yonder . . . **4.** away **6.** beyond
7. distant, thither **11.** at a distance
yore . . . **5.** of old, olden **6.** before **9.** in
old time, long since
young . . . **3.** fry, new **4.** tyro **5.** brood,
fresh, green **6.** litter, novice, tender
7. pliable **8.** childish, immature,
juvenile, youthful **9.** offspring, succulent
13. inexperienced
young (pert to) . . .
bear, fox . . **3.** cub
birds . . **5.** brood
calf (motherless) . . **5.** dogie
hare . . **7.** leveret
herring . . **4.** brit
horse . . **4.** colt, foal
oyster . . **4.** spat
pigeon . . **5.** piper
youngling . . . **5.** youth **6.** novice
8. beginner, neophyte
youngster . . . **3.** boy, kid, lad, pup, tad
4. baby, lass, tike **5.** child, youth
6. filius, shaver, urchin **7.** Aladdin
(Arab Nights) **8.** teenager **9.** fledgling,
stripling
younker . . . **5.** child, youth **6.** knight
7. gallant **8.** nobleman **9.** stripling
youth goddess . . . **4.** Hebe
yo-yo . . . **3.** top, toy
Ypres, Belgium . . .
famed for . . **7.** Battles (WWI)

lace . . **12.** Valenciennes
province of . . **8.** Flanders
ruins rebuilt . . **9.** Cloth Hall **15.** Gothic
Cathedral (St Martin)
ypsiliform, shape of . . . **7.** letter T (Gr)
yu (Chin) . . . **4.** jade
Yucatan, Cent America . . .
anc domain of . . **5.** Mayas
capital . . **6.** Mérida
city . . **5.** Sisal
peninsula of . . **6.** Mexico
yucca (pert to) . . .
called . . **11.** Adam's needle
family . . **9.** Liliaceae
native of . . **7.** America
species . . **9.** bear grass
State flower of . . **9.** New Mexico
Yugoslavia . . .
capital . . **8.** Belgrade
former leader . . **4.** Tito (Communist)
river . . **5.** Drava, Drina **6.** Danube
sea . . **8.** Adriatic
yukkel . . . **7.** flicker **10.** woodpecker
Yukon . . .
famed for . . **4.** gold (mining)
ocean . . **6.** Arctic
river . . **5.** Lewes, Yukon
territory of . . **6.** Canada
town . . **10.** Whitehorse
Yule . . . **4.** Noel **8.** Nativity (Feast of the),
yuletide **9.** Christmas **13.** Christmastide
Yule (pert to) . . .
plant . . **5.** holly **9.** mistletoe
good cheer . . **11.** wassail bowl
Yuma (Ariz) . . . **4.** city **9.** Talkepaia (Indian)
yun . . . **10.** Laos people (tattooed)
Yunca . . . **6.** Indian (Peru)
Yurma . . . **6.** Indian (Brazil)
Yurok . . . **6.** Indian (Calif)
yurt, yurta . . . **4.** tent (Siberia)
Yuruk . . . **10.** Turkish rug
yutu . . . **7.** tinamou
Yuzen birodo . . . **6.** velvet (designed)

Z

Z . . . **3.** end, zed, zee **5.** omega **6.** izzard,
letter (26th)
zac . . . **4.** ibex
zacate . . . **7.** herbage **9.** rice grass
Zacchaeus, Zaccheus . . . **4.** pure
8. innocent, publican (Bib)
Zachariah, Zacharias (Bib) . . .
father . . **9.** Barachias
father of . . **14.** John the Baptist
literally . . **21.** Jehovah hath remembered
Zadkiel (Jew) . . . **5.** angel (of planet
Jupiter)
zaftig . . . **5.** buxom **7.** shapely
Zagreus . . . **3.** god **8.** Dionysus (identified
with)
Zaire, Africa . . .
capital . . **8.** Kinshasa
formerly . . **12.** Belgian Congo
river . . **4.** Uele **5.** Kasai, Zaire (Congo)

zaman, zamang . . . **8.** rain tree
Zambia, Africa . . .
capital . . **6.** Lusaka
formerly . . **16.** Northern Rhodesia
wealth . . **6.** copper (3rd largest)
Zamenhof, inventor of . . . **9.** Esperanto
zampogna . . . **7.** bagpipe, panpipe
zanja . . . **5.** canal, gully **6.** arroyo
zany . . . **3.** wag, wit **4.** dolt, fool **5.** clown,
crazy, goofy, kooky, nutty **6.** madcap,
sawney **7.** acrobat, bonkers, buffoon,
idiotic **8.** clownish **9.** simpleton
10. lieutenant, mountebank **11.** merry-
andrew
Zanzibar, Africa . . . see *Tanzania*
zap . . . **4.** slay, stun **5.** smite **6.** strike
zapatero . . . **7.** boxwood, cobbler,
dogwood
zarf . . . **9.** cup holder (Levant)

Z

zati ... **6.** monkey (bonnet)
zeal ... **5.** ardor, piety **6.** desire, fervor
7. passion **8.** devotion **9.** eagerness
10. enthusiasm, fanaticism
zealot ... **4.** sect **5.** bigot, freak (sl)
6. votary **7.** devotee, faddist, fanatic,
pietist **8.** partisan **10.** enthusiast
zealous ... **5.** eager, pious **6.** ardent,
fervid **7.** devoted, fervent **9.** phrenetic
11. industrious
zebra (pert to) ...
ally .. **6.** quagga
Burchell's .. **4.** dauw (nonstriped legs)
hybrid .. **8.** zebrinny
insect .. **9.** butterfly
ref to .. **7.** zebrine, zebroid
zebrawood ... **5.** shrub **7.** araroba
10. marblewood
zebu ... **2.** ox **5.** zebus (group) **6.** cattle
12. Brahmany bull (sacred)
zecchino ... **6.** sequin (chequeen)
Zechariah (Bib) ... **7.** prophet **12.** King
of Israel
zed ... **7.** letter Z (Brit)
zeekoe ... **12.** hippopotamus
zeism ... **8.** pellagra **11.** morbid state
zemi ... **4.** holy (Peru) **5.** huaca (huaco)
6. fetish, sacred, spirit (magic)
Zemzem ... **10.** sacred well (Mecca)
Zen ... **12.** Buddhist sect
zenana ... **5.** harem, serai **7.** mission
8. seraglio
Zenda, Prisoner of ... **9.** Ruritania
Zend-Avesta ... **10.** sacred text
(Zoroastrian)
zenith ... **3.** top **4.** acme, apex, blue,
peak **6.** apogee, climax, summit, vertex
11. culmination **14.** greatest height
(opp of nadir)
Zeno ... **5.** Stoic **11.** philosopher (Gr)
zenography, study of ... **7.** Jupiter
(planet)
zenu ... **5.** sheep
zephyr ... **5.** shawl **6.** breath, breeze
zero ... **3.** nil **4.** hour **5.** zilch **6.** cipher,
nought (naught) **7.** nothing, nullity
11. temperature
zest ... **4.** tang **5.** gusto, savor **6.** flavor,
relish **8.** membrane (fruit), piquancy,
pungency **9.** eagerness **10.** enthusiasm
Zeus (pert to) ...
attendant .. **4.** Nike
consort .. **6.** Europa
brother of .. **5.** Hades **8.** Poseidon
deity .. **7.** supreme **12.** father of gods
father .. **6.** Cronus
games in his honor .. **6.** Nemean
8. Olympian
messenger .. **4.** Iris **6.** Hermes
mother .. **4.** Rhea
oracle .. **6.** Dodona
Roman .. **7.** Jupiter
sister .. **4.** Hera
son .. **4.** Ares **5.** Argus **6.** Apollo, Hermes
7. Perseus **8.** Dionysus, Hercules,
Tantalus
temple (Athens) .. **8.** Olympium
ziara, ziarat ... **4.** tomb (Muslim saint)
6. shrine
zibet, zibeth ... **5.** civet
ziganka ... **5.** dance (rustic)

zigeuner ... **5.** gypsy **7.** czigany, Zincalo,
zingaro
ziggurat ... **11.** temple tower **12.** Tower
of Babel (Bib)
zigzag ... **5.** turns **6.** angles **7.** stagger
8. flexuous, wavering **9.** alternate
zillion ... **4.** many **9.** countless
Zimbabwe ...
capital .. **6.** Harare
Falls .. **8.** Victoria
Falls discoverer .. **11.** Livingstone (1855)
formerly .. **8.** Rhodesia
people .. **5.** Bantu
zinc (pert to) ...
alloy .. **5.** bidri **7.** paktong
alloy with copper .. **6.** oroide
crude .. **7.** tutenag (tutenague)
slabs .. **6.** solder **7.** spelter
symbol .. **2.** Zn
zing ... **3.** pep, vim, zip **5.** vigor **6.** energy,
spirit, thrill **10.** enthusiasm
zingaresca (gypsy) ... **4.** song **5.** dance
zingaro ... **5.** gypsy
Zion (pert to) ... **4.** hill (Jerusalem)
10. Israelites **12.** chosen people
zip ... **4.** zing **5.** close, speed **6.** energy
8. pungency **10.** sibilation
zizith ... **7.** fringes (Bib), tassels
zoanthropy ... **9.** monomania
15. changed to animal (belief)
zobo ... **6.** hybrid **10.** zebu and yak
zodiac ... **4.** belt, zone **5.** stars **7.** circuit
zodiac signs (twelve) ... **3.** Leo **5.** Aries,
Libra, Virgo **6.** Cancer, Gemini,
Pisces, Taurus **7.** Scorpio **8.** Aquarius
9. Capricorn **11.** Capricornus, Sagittarius
zoetic ... **5.** vital **6.** living **7.** organic
zombie, zombi ... **6.** corpse, voodoo
zone ... **4.** area, band, belt, isle,
path **5.** Canal, clime, girth, tract
6. assise, circle, course, Frigid, region,
Torrid **7.** stratum **8.** cincture, latitude
9. Temperate
zoo ... **9.** menagerie **10.** collection
12. animal garden
zoo, zo (comb form) ... **6.** animal
zoologist ... **9.** biologist, scientist
zoology, science of ... **7.** animals
zoology branches ... **8.** taxonomy
9. bionomics, phylogeny
10. embryology, entomology
11. herpetology, ornithology
zoom ... **4.** lens, rise **5.** climb
zoopathology, science of ... **8.** diseases
(animal) **11.** zoonosology
zoophilist ... **11.** animal lover
zoophobia ... **13.** fear of animals
zoophyte ... **5.** coral **6.** sponge **10.** sea
anemone
zootomy ... **13.** animal anatomy
16. animal dissection
zootrophy ... **13.** animal rearing
zoril, zorillo ... **5.** skunk **7.** polecat
Zoroaster, Zarathustra ... **7.** Persian
8. reformer (Relig)
Zoroastrianism (pert to) ...
adherence to .. **5.** Parse (Parsee)
doctrine .. **7.** dualism **11.** good and evil
evil spirit .. **4.** deva **7.** Ahriman
fire worshiper .. **6.** Gheber
founder .. **9.** Zoroaster

literature.. **6.** Avesta
lord of creation.. **6.** Ormazo
religion of.. **6.** Persia (anc)
zoster ... **4.** zona **6.** girdle **8.** shingles
(Med) **12.** herpes zoster
Zouave ... **4.** Zu-Zu **8.** chasseur
11. infantryman
Zu (Bab Myth) ... **8.** storm god (evil)
9. blackbird (symbol)
Zuider Zee (pert to) ...
gulf.. **8.** North Sea
Netherlands.. **4.** dike **7.** highway
present name.. **9.** Ijsel Lake, Ijselmeer
zuisin ... **7.** widgeon
Zulu (pert to) ...
army.. **4.** impi
boy.. **6.** umfaan
conference.. **6.** indaba
marauders.. **4.** Viti
people.. **6.** Santus **7.** Kaffirs

spear.. **7.** assagai (assegai)
Zululand capital ... **6.** Eshowe
Zuñi (pert to) ...
famed for.. **19.** Seven Cities of Cibola
(Myth)
Indian.. **4.** Hopi **6.** Ashivi
kingdom of Cibola.. **16.** gold-paved
streets (Myth)
zwieback ... **4.** rusk **7.** biscuit (toasted)
Zwinger ... **6.** palace (Dresden)
zygal ... **7.** H-shaped
zygodactyl (zygodactyle) ... **8.** yoke-toed
10. paired toes
zygon ... **5.** bench **6.** thwart **9.** brain
part
zygous ... **5.** yoked **6.** paired
zymology (science of) ...
12. fermentation
zymosis ... **12.** fermentation
zythum ... **4.** beer (anc Egypt)

TABLES

BOOKS OF THE BIBLE

Old Testament Books and Abbreviations

Book, Letter Count	Abbreviation
Genesis 7	Gen
Exodus 6	Exod
Leviticus 9	Lev
Numbers 7	Num
Deuteronomy 11	Deut
Joshua 6	Josh
Judges 6	Judg
Ruth 4	Ruth
1 Samuel 6	1 Sam
2 Samuel 6	2 Sam
1 Kings 5	1 Kings
2 Kings 5	2 Kings
1 Chronicles 10	1 Chron
2 Chronicles 10	2 Chron
Ezra 4	Ezra
Nehemiah 8	Neh
Esther 6	Esther
Job 3	Job
Psalms 6	Psalms
Proverbs 8	Proverbs
Ecclesiastes 12	Eccles
Song of Solomon 13	Song of Sol
Isaiah 6	Isa
Jeremiah 8	Jer
Lamentations 12	Lam
Ezekiel 7	Ezek
Daniel 6	Dan
Hosea 5 (Osee)	Hos
Joel 4	Joel
Amos 4	Amos
Obadiah 7	Obad
Jonah 5	Joh
Micah 4	Mic
Nahum 5	Nah
Habakkuk 8	Hab
Zephaniah 9	Zeph
Haggai 6	Hag
Zechariah 9	Zech
Malachi 7	Mal

New Testament Books and Abbreviations

Book, Letter Count	Abbreviation
Matthew 7	Matt
Mark 4	Mark
Luke 4	Luke
John 4	John
Acts of the Apostles 17	Acts
Romans 6	Rom
1 Corinthians 11	1 Cor
2 Corinthians 11	2 Cor
Galatians 9	Gal
Ephesians 9	Eph
Philippians 11	Phil
Colossians 10	Col
1 Thessalonians 13	1 Thess
2 Thessalonians 13	2 Thess
1 Timothy 7	1 Tim
2 Timothy 7	2 Tim
Titus 5	Titus
Philemon 8	Philem
Hebrews 7	Heb
James 5	James
1 Peter 5	1 Pet
2 Peter 5	2 Pet
1 John 4	1 John
2 John 4	2 John
3 John 4	3 John
Jude 4	Jude
Revelation 10	(Apocalypse) Rev

Books of the Apocrypha and Abbreviations

Book, Letter Count	Abbreviation
1 Esdras 6	1 Esd
2 Esdras 6	2 Esd
Tobit 5	Tob
Judith 6	Jth
Rest of Esther 12	Rest of Esther
Wisdom of Solomon 15	Wisd of Sol
Ecclesiasticus 14	Ecclus
Baruch 6	Bar
Song of the Three Holy Children 26	Song of Three Children
Susanna 7	Sus
Bel and the Dragon 15	Bel and Dragon
Manasseh 8	Man
1 Maccabees 9	1 Macc
2 Maccabees 9	2 Macc

Books of the Bible by Letter Count

3. Job 4. Acts (of the Apostles), Amos, Ezra, Joel, John, Jude, Luke, Mark, Osee, Ruth 5. Hosea, James, Jonah, Kings, Micah, Nahum, Peter, Titus, Tobit 6. Baruch, Daniel, Esdras, Esther, Exodus, Haggai, Isaiah, Joshua, Judges, Judith, Psalms, Romans, Samuel 7. Ezekiel, Genesis, Hebrews, Malachi, Matthew, Numbers, Obadiah, Susanna, Timothy 8. Habakkuk, Jeremiah, Manasseh, Nehemiah, Philemon, Proverbs 9. Ephesians, Galatians, Leviticus, Maccabees, Zechariah, Zephaniah 10. Apocalypse, Chronicles, Colossians, Revelation 11. Corinthians, Deuteronomy, Philippians 12. Ecclesiastes, Lamentations, Rest of Esther 13. Song of Solomon, Thessalonians 14. Ecclesiasticus 15. Bel and the Dragon, Wisdom of Solomon 17. Acts of the Apostles 26. Song of the Three Holy Children

CHEMICAL ELEMENTS

Listed by atomic number, name, letter count, and symbol.

Atomic Number	Element, Letter Count	Symbol	Atomic Number	Element, Letter Count	Symbol
1	hydrogen 8	H	58	cerium 6	Ce
2	helium 6	He	59	praseodymium 12	Pr
3	lithium 7	Li	60	neodymium 9	Nd
4	beryllium 9	Be	61	promethium 10	Pm
5	boron 5	B	62	samarium 8	Sm
6	carbon 6	C	63	europium 8	Eu
7	nitrogen 8	N	64	gadolinium 10	Gd
8	oxygen 6	O	65	terbium 7	Tb
9	fluorine 8	F	66	dysprosium 10	Dy
10	neon 4	Ne	67	holmium 7	Ho
11	sodium 6	Na	68	erbium 6	Er
12	magnesium 9	Mg	69	thulium 7	Tm
13	aluminum 8	Al	70	ytterbium 9	Yb
14	silicon 7	Si	71	lutetium 8	Lu
15	phosphorus 10	P	72	hafnium 7	Hf
16	sulfur 6	S	73	tantalum 8	Ta
17	chlorine 8	Cl	74	tungsten 8	W
18	argon 5	Ar	75	rhenium 7	Re
19	potassium 9	K	76	osmium 6	Os
20	calcium 7	Ca	77	iridium 7	Ir
21	scandium 8	Sc	78	platinum 8	Pt
22	titanium 8	Ti	79	gold 4	Au
23	vanadium 8	V	80	mercury 7	Hg
24	chromium 8	Cr	81	thallium 8	Tl
25	manganese 9	Mn	82	lead 4	Pb
26	iron 4	Fe	83	bismuth 7	Bi
27	cobalt 6	Co	84	polonium 8	Po
28	nickel 6	Ni	85	astatine 8	At
29	copper 6	Cu	86	radon 5	Rn
30	zinc 4	Zn	87	francium 8	Fr
31	gallium 7	Ga	88	radium 6	Ra
32	germanium 9	Ge	89	actinium 8	Ac
33	arsenic 7	As	90	thorium 7	Th
34	selenium 8	Se	91	protactinium 12	Pa
35	bromine 7	Br	92	uranium 7	U
36	krypton 7	Kr	93	neptunium 9	Np
37	rubidium 8	Rb	94	plutonium 9	Pu
38	strontium 9	Sr	95	americium 9	Am
39	yttrium 7	Y	96	curium 6	Cm
40	zirconium 9	Zr	97	berkelium 9	Bk
41	niobium 7	Nb	98	californium 11	Cf
42	molybdenum 10	Mo	99	einsteinium 11	Es
43	technetium 10	Tc	100	fermium 7	Fm
44	ruthenium 9	Ru	101	mendelevium 11	Md
45	rhodium 7	Rh	102	nobelium 8	No
46	palladium 9	Pd	103	lawrencium 10	Lr
47	silver 6	Ag	104	rutherfordium 13	Rf
48	cadmium 7	Cd	105	hahnium 7	Ha
49	indium 6	In			
50	tin 3	Sn			
51	antimony 8	Sb			
52	tellurium 9	Te			
53	iodine 6	I			
54	xenon 5	Xe			
55	cesium 6	Cs			
56	barium 6	Ba			
57	lanthanum 9	La			

Chemical Elements by Letter Count

3. tin 4. gold, iron, lead, neon, zinc 5. argon, boron, radon, xenon 6. barium, carbon, cerium, cesium, cobalt, copper, curium, erbium, helium, indium, iodine, nickel, osmium, oxygen, radium, silver, sodium, sulfur 7. arsenic, bismuth, bromine, cadmium, calcium, fermium, gallium, hafnium, hahnium, holmium, iridium, krypton, lithium, mercury, niobium, rhenium, rhodium, silicon, terbium, thorium, thulium, uranium, yttrium 8. actinium, aluminum, antimony, astatine, chlorine, chromium, europium, fluorine, francium, hydrogen, lutetium. nitrogen, nobelium, platinum, polonium, rubidium, samarium, scandium, selenium, tantalum, thallium, titanium, tungsten, vanadium 9. americium, berkelium, beryllium, germanium, lanthanum, magnesium, manganese, neodymium, neptunium, palladium, plutonium, potassium, ruthenium, strontium, tellurium, ytterbium, zirconium 10. dysprosium, gadolinium, lawrencium, molybdenum, phosphorus, promethium, technetium 11. californium, einsteinium, mendelevium 12. praseodymium, protactinium 13. rutherfordium

CHIEF JUSTICES OF THE U.S. SUPREME COURT IN CHRONOLOGICAL ORDER

Name, Letter Count	Term	Name, Letter Count	Term
Jay, John 3	1789-95	White, Edward 5	1910-21
Rutledge, John 8	1795	Taft, William 4	1921-30
Ellsworth, Oliver 9	1796-1800	Hughes, Charles 6	1930-41
Marshall, John 8	1801-35	Stone, Harlan 5	1941-46
Taney, Roger 5	1836-64	Vinson, Frederick 6	1946-53
Chase, Salmon 5	1864-73	Warren, Earl 6	1953-69
Waite, Morrison 5	1874-88	Burger, Warren 6	1969-86
Fuller, Melville 6	1888-1910	Rehnquist, William 9	1986-

Chief Justices by Letter Count

3. Jay 4. Taft 5. Chase, Stone, Taney, Waite, White 6. Burger, Fuller, Hughes, Vinson, Warren 8. Marshall, Rutledge 9. Ellsworth, Rehnquist

FAMOUS NAMES IN CROSSWORD PUZZLES

Listed alphabetically, with letter count and identification.

Aalto, Alvar 5 (Finnish architect)
Adams, John Quincy 5 (U.S. president)
Alcott, Louisa May 6 (U.S. writer)
Alexander, Grover Cleveland 9 (U.S. baseball player)
Amin, Idi 4 (Ugandan leader)
Angelico, Fra 8 (Italian painter)
Angelou, Maya 7 (U.S. poet)
Antony, Marc 6 (Roman general)
Arnaz, Desi 5 (U.S. actor & producer)
Astor, John Jacob 5 (U.S. fur trader & financier)
Attucks, Crispus 7 (American Revolution figure)
Auden, W(ystan) H(ugh) 5 (English poet)
Baer, Max 4 (U.S. boxer)
Barnes, Djuna 6 (novelist)
Beiderbecke, Bix 11(U.S. jazz musician)
Belloc, Hilaire 6 (English writer)
Ben-Gurion, David 9 (Israeli leader)
Benton, Thomas Hart 6 (U.S. painter)
Berg, Alban 4 (Austrian composer)
Bierce, Ambrose 6 (U.S. satirical writer)
Bombeck, Erma 7 (U.S. humorist)
Borges, Jorge Luis 6 (Argentine writer)
Borglum, Gutzon 7 (U. S. sculptor)
Bourke-White, Margaret 11(U.S. photographer)
Boutros-Ghali, Boutros 12 (Egyptian diplomat)
Bragg, Braxton 5 (U.S. Confederate general)
Brecht, Bertolt 6 (German dramatist)
Bryan, William Jennings 5 (U.S. politician)
Bryant, William Cullen 6 (U.S. writer)
Burne-Jones, Edward 10 (English painter)
Burroughs, Edgar Rice 9 (U.S. writer)
Cabell, James Branch 6 (U.S. novelist)
Cannon, Dyan 6 (U.S. actress)
Capote, Truman 6 (U.S. writer)
Carey, Mariah 5 (U.S. popular singer)
Caruso, Enrico 6 (Italian operatic singer)
Carver, George Washington 6 (U.S. inventor)
Casals, Pablo 6 (Spanish cellist)
Castro, Fidel 6 (Cuban leader)
Chanel, Coco 6 (French fashion designer)
Chaplin, Oona 7 (daughter of Charlie Chaplin)
Charles, Ezzard 7 (U.S. boxer)
Clemens, Samuel Langhorne 7 (U.S. writer)
Coca, Imogene 4 (U.S. comedienne)
Cooper, James Fenimore 6 (U.S. writer)
Copland, Aaron 7 (U.S. composer)
Crane, Hart 5 (U.S. poet)
Cronyn, Hume 6 (actor)
Cummings, E(dward) E(stlin) 8 (U.S. poet)

Cunningham, Merce 10 (U.S. choreographer)
Dahl, Arlene 4 (U.S. actress)
Dali, Salvador 4 (Spanish artist)
Dare, Virginia 4 (first English person born in America)
Davis, Jefferson 5 (U.S. Confederate leader)
Davis, Miles 5 (U.S. jazz musician)
de la Renta, Oscar 9 (fashion designer)
Derek, Bo 5 (U.S. actress)
Dinesen, Isak 7 (Danish writer)
Dior, Christian 4 (French fashion designer)
Doyle, Arthur Conan 5 (English writer)
Du Bois, W(illiam) E(dward) B(urghardt) 6 (U.S. writer & civil rights leader)
Dulles, John Foster 6 (U.S. diplomat)
Dunbar, Paul Laurence 6 (U.S. poet)
Duns Scotus, John 10 (Scottish theologian)
Eban, Abba 4 (Israeli leader)
Edison, Thomas Alva 6 (U.S. inventor)
Fawkes, Guy 6 (English conspirator)
Ferrari, Enzo 7 (Italian car designer & manufacturer)
Gandhi, Indira 6 (Indian leader)
Gandhi, Rajiv 6 (Indian leader)
Gardner, Erle Stanley 7 (U.S. writer)
Gerry, Elbridge 5 (U.S. jurist)
Gilman, Charlotte Perkins 6 (U.S. writer)
Hammer, Armand 6 (U.S. businessman)
Havel, Vaclav 5 (Czech writer & politician)
Helmsley, Leona 8 (U.S. businesswoman)
Hendrix, Jimi 7 (U.S. musician)
Henie, Sonja 5 (skater)
Hilton, Conrad 6 (U.S. businessman)
Holmes, Oliver Wendell 6 (U.S. jurist)
Howells, William Dean 7 (U.S. writer)
Hubbard, L. Ron 7 (U.S. writer)
Huie, William Bradford 4 (U.S. writer)
Kemal Atatürk 5 (Turkish leader)
Kent, Rockwell 4 (U.S. artist)
Keynes, John Maynard 6 (English economist)
Khrushchev, Nikita 10 (Soviet leader)
Kierkegaard, Søren 11 (Danish philosopher)
Lajoie, Nap(oleon) 6 (U.S. baseball player)
Lévi-Strauss, Claude 11 (French anthropologist)
Lewis, C(live) S(taples) 5 (English writer)
Lewis, Meade Lux 5 (U.S. jazz musician)
Lewis, Meriwether 5 (U.S. explorer)
Limbaugh, Rush 8 (U.S. radio/TV personality)
Lincoln, Elmo 7 (actor)
Mather, Cotton 6 (American clergyman & writer)

Mather, Increase 6 (American clergyman & writer)
Maupassant, Guy de 10 (French writer)
Meir, Golda 4 (Israeli leader)
Midler, Bette 6 (U.S. singer & actress)
Mies van der Rohe, Ludwig 14 (U.S. architect)
Miró, Joan 4 (Spanish artist)
Monk, Thelonious 4 (U.S. jazz musician)
Morton, Jelly Roll 6 (U.S. jazz musician)
Murphy, Audie 6 (U.S. war hero & actor)
Nasby, Petroleum V. 5 (U.S. humorist)
Negri, Pola 5 (actress)
Nin, Anaïs 3 (diarist)
O'Connor, Sandra Day 7 (U.S. jurist)
O'Neal, Shaquille 5 (U.S. basketball player)
Oates, Joyce Carol 5 (U.S. writer)
Odets, Clifford 5 (U.S. dramatist)
Olds, Ransom 4 (U.S. inventor)
Omar Khayyam 11(Persian poet)
Oswald, Lee Harvey 6 (U.S. assassin)
Ozawa, Seiji 5 (conductor)
Parrish, Maxfield 7 (U.S. artist)
Parsons, Talcott 7 (U.S. sociologist)
Pascal, Blaise 6 (French philosopher)
Peacock, Thomas Love 7 (English writer)
Pei, I. M. 3 (U.S. architect)
Piaf, Edith 4 (French singer)
Picasso, Pablo 7 (Spanish artist)
Pike, Zebulon 4 (U.S. explorer)
Plath, Sylvia 5 (U.S. poet)
Poe, Edgar Allan 3 (U.S. writer)
Pollock, Jackson 7 (U.S. artist)
Pol Pot 6 (Cambodian leader)
Pound, Ezra 5 (U.S. poet & critic)
Powell, Adam Clayton 6 (U.S. politician)
Powys, John Cowper 5 (English writer)
Presley, Elvis Aron 7 (U.S. singer & actor)
Rand, Ayn 4 (U.S. writer)
Rembrandt van Rijn 16 (Dutch artist)

Ride, Sally 4 (U.S. astronaut)
Roberts, Oral 7 (U.S. evangelist)
Rockne, Knute 6 (U.S. football coach)
Rose, Axl 4 (U.S. singer)
Rushdie, Salman 7 (writer)
Saarinen, Eero 8 (Finnish architect)
Sackville-West, Vita 13 (English writer)
Sartre, Jean-Paul 6 (French writer & philosopher)
Savalas, Telly 7 (U.S. actor)
Shelley, Percy Bysshe 7 (English poet)
Sherman, William Tecumseh 7 (U.S. Union general)
Sommer, Elke 6 (actress)
Sousa, John Philip 5 (U.S. composer)
Speaker, Tris 7 (U.S. baseball player)
Spenser, Edmund 7 (English poet)
Stanton, Elizabeth Cady 7 (U.S. reformer)
Stevenson, Robert Louis 9 (Scottish writer)
Stowe, Harriet Beecher 5 (U.S. writer)
Strachey, Lytton 8 (English writer)
Stravinsky, Igor 10 (Russian composer)
Synge, John Millington 5 (Irish dramatist)
Tharp, Twyla 5 (U.S. choreographer)
Toklas, Alice B. 6 (U.S. writer)
Torme, Mel 5 (U.S. singer)
Vaughan Williams, Ralph 15 (English composer)
Washington, Booker T. 10 (U.S. educator & reformer)
Washington, Denzel 10 (U.S. actor)
Weaver, Sigourney 6 (U.S. actress)
Webber, Andrew Lloyd 6 (English composer)
Williams, William Carlos 8 (U.S. poet)
Winfrey, Oprah 7 (U.S. TV personality)
Wodehouse, P(elham) G(renville) 9 (English writer)
Wright, Frank Lloyd 6 (U.S. architect)
Yeats, William Butler 5 (Irish writer)

NATIONS OF THE WORLD

Listed alphabetically by nation, with letter counts.

Nation	Capital	Currency
Afghanistan 11	Kabul 5	afghani 7
Albania 7	Tirana 6	lek 3
Algeria 7	Algiers 7	dinar 5
Andorra 7	Andorra la Vella 14	franc 5, peseta 6
Angola 6	Luanda 6	kwanza 6
Antigua and Barbuda 17	St. John's 7	dollar 6
Argentina 9	Buenos Aires 11	peso 4
Armenia 7	Yerevan 7	dram 4
Australia 9	Canberra 8	dollar 6
Austria 7	Vienna 6	schilling 9
Azerbaijan 10	Baku 4	manat 5
Bahamas 7	Nassau 6	dollar 6
Bahrain 7	Manama 6	dinar 5
Bangladesh 10	Dhaka 5 (Dacca)	taka 4
Barbados 8	Bridgetown 10	dollar 6
Belarus 7	Minsk 5	ruble 5
Belgium 7	Brussels 8	franc 5
Belize 6	Belmopan 8	dollar 6
Benin 5	Porto Novo 9	franc 5
Bhutan 6	Thimphu 7	ngultrum 8
Bolivia 7	La Paz 5, Sucre 5	boliviano 9
Bosnia and Herzegovina 20 (Hercegovina)	Sarajevo 8	dinar 5
Botswana 8	Gaborone 8	pula 4
Brazil 6	Brasília 8	real 4
Brunei 6	Bandar Seri Begawan 17	dollar 6
Bulgaria 8	Sofia 5	lev 3
Burkina Faso 11	Ouagadougou 11	franc 5
Burundi 7	Bujumbura 9	franc 5
Cambodia 8	Phnom Penh 9	riel 4
Cameroon 8	Yaoundé 7	franc 5
Canada 6	Ottawa 6	dollar 6
Cape Verde 9	Praia 5	escudo 6
Central African Republic 22	Bangui 6	franc 5
Chad 4	N'Djamena 8	franc 5
Chile 5	Santiago 8	peso 4
China 5	Beijing 7 (Peking, Peiping)	yuan 4
Colombia 8	Bogotá 6	peso 4
Comoros 7	Moroni 6	franc 5
Congo 5	Brazzaville 11	franc 5
Costa Rica 9	San José 7	colón 5
Croatia 7	Zagreb 6	kuna 4
Cuba 4	Havana 6	peso 4
Cyprus 6	Nicosia 7	pound 5
Czech Republic 13	Prague 6	koruna 6
Denmark 7	Copenhagen 10	krone 5
Djibouti 8	Djibouti 8	franc 5
Dominica 8	Roseau 6	dollar 6
Dominican Republic 17	Santo Domingo 12	peso 4
Ecuador 7	Quito 5	sucre 5
Egypt 5	Cairo 5	pound 5
El Salvador 10	San Salvador 11	colón 5
Equatorial Guinea 16	Malabo 6	franc 5
Eritrea 7	Asmara 6	birr 4
Estonia 7	Tallinn 7	kroon 5
Ethiopia 8	Addis Ababa 10	birr 4
Fiji 4	Suva 4	dollar 6

Nation	Capital	Currency
Finland 7	Helsinki 8	markka 6
France 6	Paris 5	franc 5
Gabon 5	Libreville 10	franc 5
Gambia 6	Banjul 6	dalasi 6
Georgia 7	Tbilisi 7	lari 4
Germany 7	Berlin 6	deutsche mark 12
Ghana 5	Accra 5	cedi 4
Greece 6	Athens 6	drachma 7
Grenada 7	St. George's 9	dollar 6
Guatemala 9	Guatemala City 13	quetzal 7
Guinea 6	Conakry 7	franc 5
Guinea-Bissau 12	Bissau 6	peso 4
Guyana 6	Georgetown 10	dollar 6
Haiti 5	Port-au-Prince 12	gourde 6
Honduras 8	Tegucigalpa 11	lempira 7
Hungary 7	Budapest 8	forint 6
Iceland 7	Reykjavik 9	króna 5
India 5	New Delhi 8	rupee 5
Indonesia 9	Jakarta 7	rupiah 6
Iran 4	Tehran 6 (Teheran)	rial 4
Iraq 4	Baghdad 7 (Bagdad)	dinar 5
Ireland 7	Dublin 6	pound 5 (punt)
Israel 6	Jerusalem 9	shekel 6
Italy 5	Rome 4	lira 4
Ivory Coast 10	Yamoussoukro 12	franc 5
Jamaica 7	Kingston 8	dollar 6
Japan 5	Tokyo 5	yen 3
Jordan 6	Amman 5	dinar 5
Kazakhstan 10	Alma-Ata 7 (Almaty)	tenge 5
Kenya 5	Nairobi 7	shilling 8
Kiribati 8	Tarawa 6	dollar 6
Korea, North 10	Pyongyang 9	won 3
Korea, South 10	Seoul 5	won 3
Kuwait 6	Kuwait 6 (Kuwait City)	dinar 5
Kyrgyzstan 10 (Kirghizstan)	Bishkek 7	som 3
Laos 4	Vientiane 9	kip 3
Latvia 6	Riga 4	lats 4
Lebanon 7	Beirut 6	pound 5
Lesotho 7	Maseru 6	loti 4
Liberia 7	Monrovia 8	dollar 6
Libya 5	Tripoli 7	dinar 5
Liechtenstein 13	Vaduz 5	franc 5
Lithuania 9	Vilnius 7	litas 5
Luxembourg 10	Luxembourg 10	franc 5
Macedonia 9	Skopje 6	denar 5
Madagascar 10	Antananarivo 12	franc 5
Malawi 6	Lilongwe 8	kwacha 6
Malaysia 8	Kuala Lumpur 11	ringgit 7
Maldives 8	Malé 4	rufiyaa 7
Mali 4	Bamako 6	franc 5
Malta 5	Valletta 8	lira 4
Marshall Islands 15	Dalap-Uliga-Darrit 16	dollar 6
Mauritania 10	Nouakchott 10	ouguiya 7
Mauritius 9	Port Louis 9	rupee 5
Mexico 6	Mexico City 10	peso 4
Micronesia 10	Palikir 7	dollar 6
Moldova 7	Kishinev 8	leu 3
Monaco 6	Monaco 6	franc 5
Mongolia 8	Ulan Bator 9	tugrik 6

Nation	Capital	Currency
Morocco 7	Rabat 5	dirham 6
Mozambique 10	Maputo 6	metical 7
Myanmar 7	Yangon 6 (Rangoon)	kyat 4
Namibia 7	Windhoek 8	dollar 6
Nauru 5	—	dollar 6
Nepal 5	Katmandu 8 (Kathmandu)	rupee 5
Netherlands 11	Amsterdam 9	guilder 7
New Zealand 10	Wellington 10	dollar 6
Nicaragua 9	Managua 7	córdoba 7
Niger 5	Niamey 6	franc 5
Nigeria 7	Abuja 5	naira 5
Norway 6	Oslo 4	krone 5
Oman 4	Muscat 6	rial 4
Pakistan 8	Islamabad 9	rupee 5
Palau 5	Koror 5	dollar 6
Panama 6	Panama City 10	balboa 6
Papua New Guinea 14	Port Moresby 11	kina 4
Paraguay 8	Asunción 8	guaraní 7
Peru 4	Lima 4	sol 3
Philippines 11	Manila 6	peso 4
Poland 6	Warsaw 6	zloty 5
Portugal 8	Lisbon 6	escudo 6
Qatar 5	Doha 4	riyal 5
Romania 7	Bucharest 9	leu 3
Russia 6	Moscow 6	ruble 5
Rwanda 6	Kigali 6	franc 5
San Marino 9	San Marino 9	lira 4
São Tomé and Príncipe 18	São Tomé 7	dobra 5
Saudi Arabia 11	Riyadh 6	riyal 5
Senegal 7	Dakar 5	franc 5
Seychelles 10	Victoria 8	rupee 5
Sierra Leone 11	Freetown 8	leone 5
Singapore 9	Singapore 9	dollar 6
Slovakia 8·	Bratislava 10	koruna 6
Slovenia 8	Ljubljana 9	tolar 5
Solomon Islands 14	Honiara 7	dollar 6
Somalia 7	Mogadishu 9	shilling 8
South Africa 11	Pretoria (administrative) 8	rand 4
Spain 5	Madrid 6	peseta 6
Sri Lanka 8	Colombo 7	rupee 5
St. Kitts and Nevis 15	Basseterre 10	dollar 6
St. Lucia 7	Castries 8	dollar 6
St. Vincent and the Grenadines 25	Kingstown 9	dollar 6
Sudan 5	Khartoum 8	pound 5
Suriname 8	Paramaribo 10	guilder 7
Swaziland 9	Mbabane 7	lilangeni 8
Sweden 6	Stockholm 9	krona 5
Switzerland 11	Bern 4	franc 5
Syria 5	Damascus 8	pound 5
Taiwan 6	Taipei 6	dollar 6
Tajikistan 10 (Tadzhikistan)	Dushanbe 8	ruble 5
Tanzania 8	Dodoma 6	shilling 8
Thailand 8	Bangkok 7	baht 4
Togo 4	Lomé 4	franc 5
Tonga 5	Nukualofa 9	pa'anga 6
Trinidad and Tobago 17	Port-of-Spain 11	dollar 6
Tunisia 7	Tunis 5	dinar 5
Turkey 6	Ankara 6	lira 4
Turkmenistan 12	Ashkhabad 9	manat 5

Nation	Capital	Currency
Tuvalu 6	Fongafale 9	dollar 6
Uganda 6	Kampala 7	shilling 8
Ukraine 7	Kiev 4	hryvnia 7
United Arab Emirates 18	Abu Dhabi 8	dirham 6
United Kingdom 13	London 6	pound 5
United States 12	Washington (DC) 10	dollar 6
Uruguay 7	Montevideo 10	peso 4
Uzbekistan 10	Tashkent 8	som 3
Vanuatu 7	Vila 4	vatu 4
Vatican City 11	—	lira 4
Venezuela 9	Caracas 7	bolívar 7
Vietnam 7	Hanoi 5	dong 4
Western Samoa 12	Apia 4	tala 4
Yemen 5	Sana 4 (Sanaa)	rial 4
Yugoslavia 10	Belgrade 8	dinar 5
Zaire 5	Kinshasa 8	zaire 5
Zambia 6	Lusaka 6	kwacha 6
Zimbabwe 8	Harare 6	dollar 6

SELECTED NOBEL PRIZE WINNERS

Listed alphabetically with letter count, prize category, and year.

Addams, Jane 6 (Peace) 1931
Agnon, Samuel 5 (Literature) 1966
Aleixandre, Vicente 10 (Literature) 1977
Alfven, Hannes 6 (Physics) 1970
Alvarez, Luis 7 (Physics) 1968
Andric, Ivo 6 (Literature) 1961
Angell, Sir Norman 6 (Peace) 1933
Appleton, Sir Edward 8 (Physics) 1947
Arafat, Yasir 6 (Peace) 1994
Arias Sánchez, Oscar 12 (Peace) 1987
Arrhenius, Svante 9 (Chemistry) 1903
Asturias, Miguel 8 (Literature) 1967
Aung San Suu Kyi 13 (Peace) 1991
Banting, Sir Frederick 7 (Physiology or Medicine) 1923
Bardeen, John 7 (Physics) 1956
Becker, Gary 6 (Economics) 1992
Beckett, Samuel 7 (Literature) 1969
Becquerel, Antoine Henri 9 (Physics) 1903
Begin, Menachem 5 (Peace) 1978
Bellow, Saul 6 (Literature) 1976
Benavente, Jacinto 9 (Literature) 1922
Bergson, Henri 7 (Literature) 1927
Bethe, Hans 5 (Physics) 1967
Bjornson, Bjornsterne 8 (Literature) 1903
Bloch, Felix 5 (Physics) 1952
Bohr, Niels 4 (Physics) 1922
Böll, Heinrich 4 (Literature) 1972
Borlaug, Norman 7 (Peace) 1970
Born, Max 4 (Physics) 1954
Brandt, Willy 6 (Peace) 1971
Brattain, Walter 8 (Physics) 1956
Braun, Karl (Carl) 5 (Physics) 1909
Briand, Aristide 6 (Peace) 1926
Brodsky, Joseph 7 (Literature) 1987
Buchanan, James 8 (Economics) 1986
Buchner, Eduard 7 (Chemistry) 1907
Buck, Pearl 4 (Literature) 1938
Bunche, Ralph 6 (Peace) 1950
Bunin, Ivan 5 (Literature) 1933
Butenandt, Adolf 9 (Chemistry) 1939
Butler, Nicholas Murray 6 (Peace) 1931
Camus, Albert 5 (Literature) 1957
Canetti, Elias 7 (Literature) 1981
Carducci, Giosue 8 (Literature) 1906
Carrel, Alexis 6 (Physiology or Medicine) 1912
Cassin, René 6 (Peace) 1968
Cela, Camilo José 4 (Literature) 1989
Chadwick, Sir James 8 (Physics) 1935
Chain, Ernst 5 (Physiology or Medicine) 1945
Chamberlain, Sir J. Austen 11 (Peace) 1925
Chandrasekhar, Subrahmanyan 13 (Physics) 1983
Cherenkov, Pavel 9 (Physics) 1958
Churchill, Sir Winston 9 (Literature) 1953

Compton, Arthur 7 (Physics) 1927
Corrigan, Mairead 8 (Peace) 1976
Crick, Francis 5 (Physiology or Medicine) 1962
Cronin, James 6 (Physics) 1980
Curie, Marie 5 (Chemistry) 1911
Curie, Marie 5 (Physics) 1903
Curie, Pierre 5 (Physics) 1903
Dalai Lama 9 (Peace) 1989
Dawes, Charles 5 (Peace) 1925
de Broglie, Prince Louis-Victor 9 (Physics) 1929
de Klerk, F.W. 7 (Peace) 1993
Delbrück, Max 8 (Physiology or Medicine) 1969
Deledda, Grazia 7 (Literature) 1926
Dirac, Paul 5 (Physics) 1933
Eccles, Sir John 6 (Physiology or Medicine) 1963
Echegaray, Jose 9 (Literature) 1904
Ehrlich, Paul 7 (Physiology or Medicine) 1908
Einstein, Albert 8 (Physics) 1921
Eliot, T.S. 5 (Literature) 1948
Elytis, Odysseus 6 (Literature) 1979
Enders, John 6 (Physiology or Medicine) 1954
Erlanger, Joseph 8 (Physiology or Medicine) 1944
Esquivel, Adolfo Pérez 8 (Peace) 1980
Eucken, Rudolf 6 (Literature) 1908
Faulkner, William 8 (Literature) 1949
Fermi, Enrico 5 (Physics) 1938
Feynman, Richard 7 (Physics) 1965
Fischer, Emil 7 (Chemistry) 1902
Fischer, Ernst 7 (Chemistry) 1973
Fleming, Sir Alexander 7 (Physiology or Medicine) 1945
Florey, Sir Howard 6 (Physiology or Medicine) 1945
France, Anatole 6 (Literature) 1921
Franck, James 6 (Physics) 1925
Friedman, Milton 8 (Economics) 1976
Galsworthy, John 10 (Literature) 1932
García Márquez, Gabriel 13 (Literature) 1982
Gell-Mann, Murray 8 (Physics) 1969
Gide, André 4 (Literature) 1947
Gjellerup, Karl 9 (Literature) 1917
Glashow, Sheldon 7 (Physics) 1979
Golding, William 7 (Literature) 1983
Golgi, Camillo 5 (Physiology or Medicine) 1906
Gorbachev, Mikhail 9 (Peace) 1990
Gordimer, Nadine 8 (Literature) 1991
Grignard, Victor 8 (Chemistry) 1912
Haber, Fritz 5 (Chemistry) 1918
Hahn, Otto 4 (Chemistry) 1944

Hammarskjöld, Dag 12 (Peace) 1961
Hamsun, Knut 6 (Literature) 1920
Hauptmann, Gerhart 9 (Literature) 1912
Heaney, Seamus 6 (Literature) 1995
Heisenberg, Werner 10 (Physics) 1932
Hemingway, Ernest 9 (Literature) 1954
Hertz, Gustav 5 (Physics) 1925
Hesse, Hermann 5 (Literature) 1946
Heyse, Paul 5 (Literature) 1910
Hull, Cordell 4 (Peace) 1945
Jensen, Johannes 6 (Literature) 1944
Jiménez, Juan 7 (Literature) 1956
Johnson, Eyvind 7 (Literature) 1974
Joliot-Curie, Frederic 11 (Chemistry) 1935
Joliot-Curie, Irene 11 (Chemistry) 1935
Josephson, Brian 9 (Physics) 1973
Kapitsa, Pyotr 7 (Physics) 1978
Karlfeldt, Erik 9 (Literature) 1931
Kawabata, Yasunari 8 (Literature) 1968
Kellogg, Frank 7 (Peace) 1929
King, Martin Luther, Jr. 4 (Peace) 1964
Kipling, Rudyard 7 (Literature) 1907
Kissinger, Henry 9 (Peace) 1973
Koch, Robert 4 (Physiology or Medicine) 1905
Krebs, Sir Hans 5 (Physiology or Medicine) 1953
Lagerkvist, Pär 10 (Literature) 1951
Lagerlöf, Selma 8 (Literature) 1909
Landsteiner, Karl 11 (Physiology or Medicine) 1930
Lawrence, Ernest 8 (Physics) 1939
Laxness, Halldor 7 (Literature) 1955
Le Duc Tho 8 (Peace) 1973
Leontief, Wassily 8 (Economics) 1973
Lewis, Sinclair 5 (Literature) 1930
Lorentz, Hendrik 7 (Physics) 1902
Lorenz, Konrad 6 (Physiology or Medicine) 1973
Luthuli, Albert 7 (Peace) 1960
MacBride, Sean 8 (Peace) 1974
Maeterlinck, Maurice 11 (Literature) 1911
Mahfouz, Naguib 7 (Literature) 1988
Mandela, Nelson 7 (Peace) 1993
Mann, Thomas 4 (Literature) 1929
Marconi, Guglielmo 7 (Physics) 1909
Marshall, George 8 (Peace) 1953
Martin du Gard, Roger 12 (Literature) 1937
Martinson, Harry 9 (Literature) 1974
Mauriac, François 7 (Literature) 1952
McClintock, Barbara 10 (Physiology or Medicine) 1983
McMillan, Edwin 8 (Chemistry) 1951
Medawar, Peter 7 (Physiology or Medicine) 1960
Menchú, Rigoberta 6 (Peace) 1992
Michelson, Albert 9 (Physics) 1907
Millikan, Robert 8 (Physics) 1923
Milosz, Czeslaw 6 (Literature) 1980
Mistral, Frederic 7 (Literature) 1904

Mistral, Gabriela 7 (Literature) 1945
Mommsen, Theodor 7 (Literature) 1902
Monod, Jacques 5 (Physiology or Medicine) 1965
Montale, Eugenio 7 (Literature) 1975
Morrison, Toni 8 (Literature) 1993
Mössbauer, Rudolf 9 (Physics) 1961
Mother Teresa 12 (Peace) 1979
Myrdal, Alva 6 (Peace) 1982
Myrdal, Gunnar 6 (Economics) 1974
Nansen, Fridtjof 6 (Peace) 1922
Neruda, Pablo 6 (Literature) 1971
Noel-Baker, Philip 9 (Peace) 1959
O'Neill, Eugene 6 (Literature) 1936
Oe, Kenzaburo 2 (Literature) 1994
Ostwald, Wilhelm 7 (Chemistry) 1909
Pasternak, Boris 9 (Literature) 1958
Pauli, Wolfgang 5 (Physics) 1945
Pauling, Linus 7 (Chemistry) 1954
Pauling, Linus 7 (Peace) 1962
Pavlov, Ivan 6 (Physiology or Medicine) 1904
Paz, Octavio 3 (Literature) 1990
Pearson, Lester 7 (Peace) 1957
Penzias, Arno 7 (Physics) 1978
Peres, Shimon 5 (Peace) 1994
Perse, Saint-John 5 (Literature) 1960
Pirandello, Luigi 10 (Literature) 1934
Pire, Dominique Georges 4 (Peace) 1958
Planck, Max 6 (Physics) 1918
Pontoppidan, Henrik 11 (Literature) 1917
Prudhomme, René 9 (Literature) 1901
Quasimodo, Salvatore 9 (Literature) 1959
Rabi, Isidor 4 (Physics) 1944
Rabin, Yitzhak 5 (Peace) 1994
Ramsay, Sir William 6 (Chemistry) 1904
Reymont, Wladyslaw 7 (Literature) 1924
Robles, Alfonso Garcia 6 (Peace) 1982
Roentgen (Röntgen), Wilhelm 8 (Physics) 1901
Rolland, Romain 7 (Literature) 1915
Roosevelt, Theodore 9 (Peace) 1906
Root, Elihu 4 (Peace) 1912
Ross, Sir Ronald 4 (Physiology or Medicine) 1902
Rotblat, Joseph 7 (Peace) 1995
Rubbia, Carlo 6 (Physics) 1984
Russell, Bertrand 7 (Literature) 1950
Rutherford, Ernest 10 (Chemistry) 1908
Sachs, Nelly 5 (Literature) 1966
Sadat, Anwar 5 (Peace) 1978
Sakharov, Andrei 8 (Peace) 1975
Salam, Abdus 5 (Physics) 1979
Samuelson, Paul 9 (Economics) 1970
Sanger, Frederick 6 (Chemistry) 1980
Sartre, Jean-Paul 6 (Literature) 1964
Sato, Eisaku 4 (Peace) 1974
Schrödinger, Erwin 11 (Physics) 1933
Schweitzer, Albert 10 (Peace) 1952
Seaborg, Glenn 7 (Chemistry) 1951

Seferis, George 7 (Literature) 1963
Seifert, Jaroslav 7 (Literature) 1984
Shaw, George Bernard 4 (Literature) 1925
Sherrington, Sir Charles 11 (Physiology or Medicine) 1932
Shockley, William 8 (Physics) 1956
Sholokhov, Mikhail 9 (Literature) 1965
Sienkiewicz, Henryk 11 (Literature) 1905
Sillanpää, Frans 9 (Literature) 1939
Simon, Claude 5 (Literature) 1985
Singer, Isaac Bashevis 6 (Literature) 1978
Söderblom, Nathan 9 (Peace) 1930
Solzhenitsyn, Aleksandr 12 (Literature) 1970
Soyinka, Wole 7 (Literature) 1986
Spitteler, Carl 9 (Literature) 1919
Steinbeck, John 9 (Literature) 1962
Stigler, George 7 (Economics) 1982
Stresemann, Gustav 10 (Peace) 1926
Tagore, Sir Rabindranath 6 (Literature) 1913
Thomson, Sir Joseph 7 (Physics) 1906
Tinbergen, Nikolaas 9 (Physiology or Medicine) 1973
Tobin, James 5 (Economics) 1981
Tutu, Bishop Desmond 4 (Peace) 1984

Undset, Sigrid 6 (Literature) 1928
van der Waals, Johannes 11 (Physics) 1910
von Behring, Emil 10 (Physiology or Medicine) 1901
von Frisch, Karl 9 (Physiology or Medicine) 1973
von Hayek, Friedrich 8 (Economics) 1974
von Heidenstam, Verner 13 (Literature) 1916
Waksman, Selman 7 (Physiology or Medicine) 1952
Walcott, Derek 7 (Literature) 1992
Walesa, Lech 6 (Peace) 1983
Watson, James 6 (Physiology or Medicine) 1962
Weinberg, Steven 8 (Physics) 1979
White, Patrick 5 (Literature) 1973
Wiesel, Elie 6 (Peace) 1986
Wilkins, Maurice 7 (Physiology or Medicine) 1962
Williams, Betty 8 (Peace) 1976
Wilson, Robert 6 (Physics) 1978
Wilson, Woodrow 6 (Peace) 1919
Yeats, William Butler 5 (Literature) 1923
Zeeman, Pieter 6 (Physics) 1902

PULITZER PRIZE WINNERS FOR FICTION

Listed alphabetically, with letter count, year, and title of work.

Agee, James 4 (1958) *A Death in the Family*

Barnes, Margaret 6 (1931) *Years of Grace*

Bellow, Saul 6 (1976) *Humboldt's Gift*

Bromfield, Louis 9 (1927) *Early Autumn*

Buck, Pearl 4 (1932) *The Good Earth*

Butler, Robert Olen 6 (1993) *A Good Scent from a Strange Mountain*

Cather, Willa 6 (1923) *One of Ours*

Cheever, John 7 (1979) *The Stories of John Cheever*

Cozzens, James 7 (1949) *Guard of Honor*

Davis, Harold 5 (1936) *Honey in the Horn*

Drury, Allen 5 (1960) *Advise and Consent*

Faulkner, William 8 (1955) *A Fable*

Faulkner, William 8 (1963) *The Reivers*

Ferber, Edna 6 (1925) *So Big*

Flavin, Martin 6 (1944) *Journey in the Dark*

Glasgow, Ellen 7 (1942) *In This Our Life*

Grau, Shirley Ann 4 (1965) *The Keepers of the House*

Guthrie, A.B., Jr. 7 (1950) *The Way West*

Hemingway, Ernest 9 (1953) *The Old Man and the Sea*

Hersey, John 6 (1945) *A Bell for Adano*

Hijuelos, Oscar 8 (1990) *The Mambo Kings Play Songs of Love*

Johnson, Josephine 7 (1935) *Now in November*

Kantor, MacKinlay 6 (1956) *Andersonville*

Kennedy, William 7 (1984) *Ironweed*

La Farge, Oliver 7 (1930) *Laughing Boy*

Lee, Harper 3 (1961) *To Kill a Mockingbird*

Lewis, Sinclair 5 (1926) *Arrowsmith*

Lurie, Alison 5 (1985) *Foreign Affairs*

Mailer, Norman 6 (1980) *The Executioner's Song*

Malamud, Bernard 7 (1967) *The Fixer*

Marquand, John 8 (1938) *The Late George Apley*

McMurtry, Larry 8 (1986) *Lonesome Dove*

McPherson, James Alan 9 (1978) *Elbow Room*

Michener, James 8 (1948) *Tales of the South Pacific*

Miller, Caroline 6 (1934) *Lamb in His Bosom*

Mitchell, Margaret 8 (1937) *Gone with the Wind*

Momaday, N. Scott 7 (1969) *House Made of Dawn*

Morrison, Toni 8 (1988) *Beloved*

O'Connor, Edwin 7 (1962) *The Edge of Sadness*

Peterkin, Julia 8 (1929) *Scarlet Sister Mary*

Poole, Ernest 5 (1918) *His Family*

Porter, Katherine Anne 6 (1966) *The Collected Stories of Katherine Anne Porter*

Proulx, E. Annie 6 (1994) *The Shipping News*

Rawlings, Marjorie Kinnan 8 (1939) *The Yearling*

Richter, Conrad 7 (1951) *The Town*

Shaara, Michael 6 (1975) *The Killer Angels*

Shields, Carol 7 (1995) *The Stone Diaries*

Sinclair, Upton 8 (1943) *Dragon's Teeth*

Smiley, Jane 6 (1992) *A Thousand Acres*

Stafford, Jean 7 (1970) *Collected Stories*

Stegner, Wallace 7 (1972) *Angle of Repose*

Steinbeck, John 9 (1940) *The Grapes of Wrath*

Stribling, T.S. 9 (1933) *The Store*

Styron, William 6 (1968) *The Confessions of Nat Turner*

Tarkington, Booth 10 (1919) *The Magnificent Ambersons*

Tarkington, Booth 10 (1922) *Alice Adams*

Taylor, Peter 6 (1987) *A Summons to Memphis*

Taylor, Robert 6 (1959) *The Travels of Jaimie McPheeters*

Toole, John Kennedy 5 (1981) *A Confederacy of Dunces*

Tyler, Anne 5 (1989) *Breathing Lessons*

Updike, John 6 (1982) *Rabbit is Rich*

Updike, John 6 (1991) *Rabbit at Rest*

Walker, Alice 6 (1983) *The Color Purple*

Warren, Robert Penn 6 (1947) *All the King's Men*

Welty, Eudora 5 (1973) *The Optimist's Daughter*

Wharton, Edith 7 (1921) *The Age of Innocence*

Wilder, Thornton 6 (1928) *The Bridge of San Luis Rey*

Wilson, Margaret 6 (1924) *The Able McLaughlins*

Wouk, Herman 4 (1952) *The Caine Mutiny*

SHAKESPEARE'S PLAYS AND CHARACTERS

Listed by play, with characters by letter count.

Comedies

All's Well That Ends Well . . . 8. Parolles (Paroles)
As You Like It . . . 5. Arden (forest), Celia 6. Jaques 7. Orlando 8. Rosalind 10. Touchstone (fool)
The Comedy of Errors . . . 7. Ephesus (setting)
Cymbeline . . . 6. Imogen 9. Cymbeline
Love's Labour's Lost . . . 7. Navarre (setting) 10. Holofernes
Measure for Measure . . . 6. Angelo, Vienna (setting) 7. Claudio 8. Isabella
The Merchant of Venice . . . 5. Tubal 6. Portia 7. Antonio (the merchant), Jessica, Shylock (villain)
The Merry Wives of Windsor . . . 6. Pistol 7. Quickly (Mistress), Windsor (setting) 8. Falstaff (Sir John)
A Midsummer Night's Dream . . . 4. Puck (Robin Goodfellow) 6. Athens (setting), Bottom (Nick), Helena, Hermia, Oberon (Fairy King) 7. Titania (Fairy Queen) 8. Lysander 9. Demetrius
Much Ado About Nothing . . . 7. Messina (setting) 8. Beatrice, Benedick
Pericles, Prince of Tyre
The Taming of the Shrew . . . 5. Padua (setting) 9. Katherina (Kate), Petruchio
The Tempest . . . 5. Ariel (fairy) 7. Caliban (ogre), Miranda 8. Prospero
Troilus and Cressida . . . 4. Troy (setting) 7. Troilus 8. Cressida, Pandarus
Twelfth Night . . . 5. Belch (Sir Toby), Feste (fool), Viola 6. Olivia, Orsino (duke) 7. Illyria (setting) 8. Malvolio 9. Aguecheek (Sir Andrew)
The Two Gentlemen of Verona . . . 5. Julia 7. Proteus 9. Valentine
The Two Noble Kinsmen
The Winter's Tale . . . 7. Leontes, Perdita 8. Hermione 9. Autolycus (thief)

Tragedies

Antony and Cleopatra . . . 6. Antony (Mark) 7. Octavia 8. Charmian, Octavius (Caesar) 9. Cleopatra, Enobarbus 10. Mark Antony
Coriolanus . . . 8. Volumnia 10. Coriolanus
Hamlet . . . 6. Hamlet (prince) 7. Denmark (setting), Horatio, Laertes, Ophelia 8. Claudius (uncle), Elsinore (castle), Gertrude (queen), Polonius 11. Rosencrantz 12. Guildenstern
Julius Caesar . . . 6. Antony (Mark), Brutus, Portia 7. Cassius 9. Calpurnia 10. Mark Antony 12. Julius Caesar
King Lear . . . 4. Lear 5. Edgar, Regan 6. Edmund 7. Goneril 8. Cordelia
Macbeth . . . 6. Banquo, Duncan (king) 7. Macbeth, Macduff 9. Inverness (castle) 11. Lady Macbeth
Othello . . . 4. Iago (villain) 6. Cassio, Cyprus (setting), Emilia, Venice (setting) 7. Othello (the Moor) 9. Desdemona
Romeo and Juliet . . . 5. Romeo 6. Juliet, Mantua (setting), Tybalt (Juliet's cousin), Verona (setting) 7. Capulet (Juliet's family) 8. Laurence (Friar), Mercutio, Montague (Romeo's family)
Timon of Athens
Titus Andronicus

Histories

Henry IV, Parts 1, 2 . . . 3. Hal (Prince) 6. Pistol 7. Hotspur, Quickly (Mistress) 8. Falstaff (Sir John)
Henry V
Henry VI, Parts 1, 2, 3
Henry VIII
King John
Richard II
Richard III

PRESIDENTS AND FIRST LADIES OF THE UNITED STATES

Listed chronologically by term, with letter count and first names of first ladies.

Name	Term	First Lady
Washington, George 10	1789-97	Martha
Adams, John 5	1797-1801	Abigail
Jefferson, Thomas 9	1801-09	Martha
Madison, James 7	1809-17	Dorothea (Dorothy, Dolley)
Monroe, James 6	1817-25	Elizabeth (Eliza)
Adams, John Quincy 5	1825-29	Louisa
Jackson, Andrew 7	1829-37	Rachel
Van Buren, Martin 8	1837-41	Hannah
Harrison, William Henry 8	1841	Anna
Tyler, John 5	1841-45	Letitia; Julia
Polk, James Knox 4	1845-49	Sarah
Taylor, Zachary 6	1849-50	Margaret
Fillmore, Millard 8	1850-53	Abigail
Pierce, Franklin 6	1853-57	Jane
Buchanan, James 8	1857-61	—
Lincoln, Abraham 7	1861-65	Mary Todd
Johnson, Andrew 7	1865-69	Eliza
Grant, Ulysses S. 5	1869-77	Julia
Hayes, Rutherford B. 5	1877-81	Lucy
Garfield, James A. 8	1881	Lucretia
Arthur, Chester A. 6	1881-85	Ellen
Cleveland, Grover 9	1885-89	Frances
Harrison, Benjamin 8	1889-93	Caroline
Cleveland, Grover 9	1893-97	Frances
McKinley, William 8	1897-1901	Ida
Roosevelt, Theodore (Teddy) 9	1901-09	Edith
Taft, William Howard 4	1909-13	Helen
Wilson, Woodrow 6	1913-21	Ellen; Edith
Harding, Warren G. 7	1921-23	Florence
Coolidge, Calvin 8	1923-29	Grace
Hoover, Herbert 6	1929-33	Lou
Roosevelt, Franklin Delano 9	1933-45	Anna Eleanor
Truman, Harry S 6	1945-53	Bess
Eisenhower, Dwight D. 10	1953-61	Mamie
Kennedy, John Fitzgerald 7	1961-63	Jacqueline
Johnson, Lyndon Baines 7	1963-69	Claudia (Lady Bird)
Nixon, Richard Milhous 5	1969-74	Thelma (Pat)
Ford, Gerald R. 4	1974-77	Elizabeth (Betty)
Carter, Jimmy (James Earl, Jr.) 6	1977-81	Rosalynn
Reagan, Ronald 6	1981-89	Anne (Nancy)
Bush, George 4	1989-93	Barbara
Clinton, Bill (William Jefferson) 7	1993-	Hillary Rodham

Presidents of the United States by Letter Count

4. Bush, Ford, Polk, Taft 5. Adams (John and John Quincy), Grant, Hayes, Nixon, Tyler 6. Arthur, Carter, Hoover, Monroe, Pierce, Reagan, Taylor, Truman, Wilson 7. Clinton, Harding, Jackson, Johnson (Andrew and Lyndon Baines), Kennedy, Lincoln, Madison 8. Buchanan, Coolidge, Fillmore, Garfield, Harrison (Benjamin and William Henry), McKinley, Van Buren 9. Cleveland, Jefferson, Roosevelt (Franklin Delano and Theodore) 10. Eisenhower, Washington

STATES OF THE UNITED STATES

Listed alphabetically, with number counts for states and capitals.

State	Capital
Alabama 7	Montgomery 10
Alaska 6	Juneau 6
Arizona 7	Phoenix 7
Arkansas 8	Little Rock 10
California 10	Sacramento 10
Colorado 8	Denver 6
Connecticut 11	Hartford 8
Delaware 8	Dover 5
Florida 7	Tallahassee 11
Georgia 7	Atlanta 7
Hawaii 6	Honolulu 8
Idaho 5	Boise 5
Illinois 8	Springfield 11
Indiana 7	Indianapolis 12
Iowa 4	Des Moines 9
Kansas 6	Topeka 6
Kentucky 8	Frankfort 9
Louisiana 9	Baton Rouge 10
Maine 5	Augusta 7
Maryland 8	Annapolis 9
Massachusetts 13	Boston 6
Michigan 8	Lansing 7
Minnesota 9	St. Paul 6
Mississippi 11	Jackson 7
Missouri 8	Jefferson City 13
Montana 7	Helena 6
Nebraska 8	Lincoln 7
Nevada 6	Carson City 10
New Hampshire 12	Concord 7
New Jersey 9	Trenton 7
New Mexico 9	Santa Fe 7
New York 7	Albany 6
North Carolina 13	Raleigh 7
North Dakota 11	Bismarck 8
Ohio 4	Columbus 8
Oklahoma 8	Oklahoma City 12
Oregon 6	Salem 5
Pennsylvania 12	Harrisburg 10
Rhode Island 11	Providence 10
South Carolina 13	Columbia 8
South Dakota 11	Pierre 6
Tennessee 9	Nashville 9
Texas 5	Austin 6
Utah 4	Salt Lake City 12
Vermont 7	Montpelier 10
Virginia 8	Richmond 8
Washington 10	Olympia 7
West Virginia 12	Charleston 10
Wisconsin 9	Madison 7
Wyoming 7	Cheyenne 8

NOTES

NOTES

NOTES